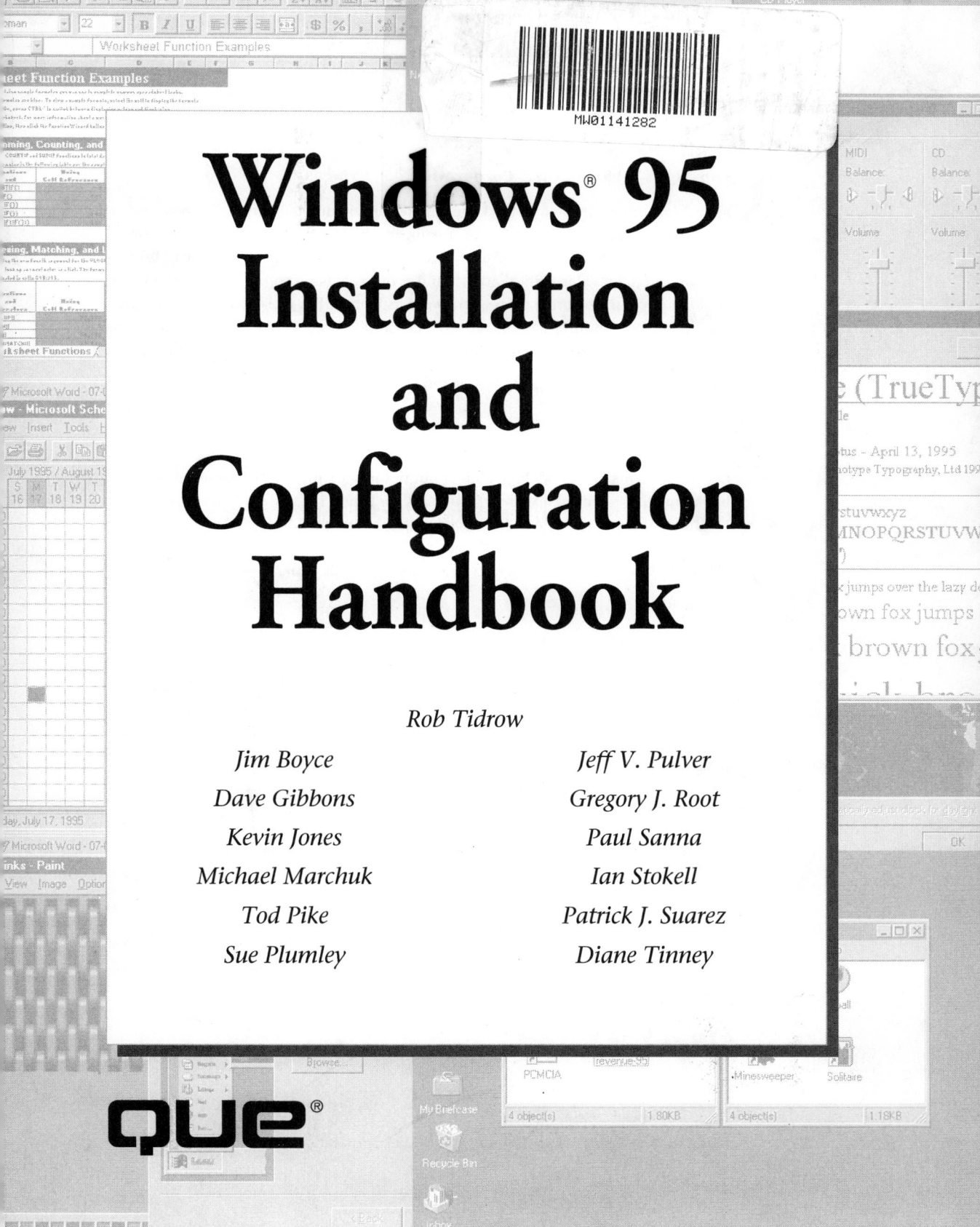

Windows® 95 Installation and Configuration Handbook

Rob Tidrow

Jim Boyce
Dave Gibbons
Kevin Jones
Michael Marchuk
Tod Pike
Sue Plumley
Jeff V. Pulver
Gregory J. Root
Paul Sanna
Ian Stokell
Patrick J. Suarez
Diane Tinney

QUE®

Windows 95 Installation and Configuration Handbook

Library of Congress Catalog No.: 95-71470

ISBN: 0-7897-0580-x

97 96 95 6 5 4 3 2 1

Interpretation of the printing code: the rightmost double-digit number is the year of the book's printing; the rightmost single-digit number, the number of the book's printing. For example, a printing code of 95-1 shows that the first printing of the book occurred in 1995.

Screen reproductions in this book were created using Collage Plus from Inner Media, Inc., Hollis, NH.

Composed in *Stone Serif* and *MCPdigital* by Que Corporation.

Credits

President
Roland Elgey

Vice President and Publisher
Marie Butler-Knight

Associate Publisher
Don Roche, Jr.

Editorial Services Director
Elizabeth Keaffaber

Managing Editor
Michael Cunningham

Director of Marketing
Lynn E. Zingraf

Senior Series Editor
Chris Nelson

Acquisitions Editor
Deborah F. Abshier

Product Director
Lisa D. Wagner
Steve Rigney

Production Editor
Lisa M. Gebken

Editors
Geneil Breeze
Silvette Pope
Linda Seifert

Assistant Product Marketing Manager
Kim Margolius

Technical Editor and Graphics Specialist
Cari L. Skaggs

Acquisitions Coordinator
Tracy M. Williams

Operations Coordinator
Patty Brooks

Editorial Assistant
Carmen Phelps

Book Designer
Ruth Harvey

Cover Designer
Dan Armstrong

Production Team
Angela D. Bannan
Claudia Bell
Brian Buschkill
Jason Carr
Maxine Dillingham
Joan Evan
Brian Flores
Amy Gornik
Mike Henry
Darren Jackson
Daryl Kessler
Michelle Lee
Bobbi Satterfield
Andy Stone
Colleen Williams
Jody York

Indexer
Mary Jane Frisby

About the Authors

Rob Tidrow has been using computers for the past six years and has used Windows for the past four years. Tidrow is a technical writer and recently was the Manager of Product Development for New Riders Publishing, a division of Macmillan Computer Publishing. Rob is coauthor of the best-selling *Windows for Non-Nerds*, and has coauthored several other books including *Inside the World Wide Web, New Riders' Official CompuServe Yellow Pages, Inside Microsoft Office Professional, Inside WordPerfect 6 for Windows, Riding the Internet Highway,* Deluxe Edition, and the *AutoCAD Student Workbook*. Tidrow has created technical documentation and instructional programs for use in a variety of industrial settings. He has a degree in English from Indiana University. He resides in Indianapolis with his wife, Tammy, and their two boys, Adam and Wesley. You can reach him on the Internet at **rtidrow@iquest.net**.

Jim Boyce is a contributing editor and columnist for *WINDOWS Magazine*, a columnist for *CADENCE Magazine*, and the author and contributing author of over two dozen books on computers and software. You can reach Boyce at **76516,3403@compuserve.com**.

Dave Gibbons is a former technical trainer and writer for DATASTORM TECHNOLOGIES in Columbia, Mo., and LaserMaster Technologies in Eden Prairie, Minn. He began his professional writing career in chilly Cando, N.D., at age 16. Now a freelance writer and consultant, Gibbons spends much of his free time rock climbing on the Internet (**dgibbons@bigcat.missouri.edu**).

Kevin Jones has worked in the computer industry for 15 years, from large corporations such as IBM and Unisys down to very small startups. He has worked on such flagship products as dBASE III and IV, PC Tools for Windows, and Norton Navigator. Currently, he is a principal software engineer with the Peter Norton Division of Symantec Corp. He has been actively working with Windows 95 since October 1993.

Michael Marchuk has worked in the computer industry since 1979 when he started as a part-time BASIC programming instructor. Along with his bachelor's degree in finance from the University of Illinois, Marchuk has received certification as a Netware CNE and a Compaq Advanced Systems Engineer. He has designed and built an international multi-protocol wide area network for a Fortune 500 company and now serves as an integration engineer and network security chairman for a Forbes 400 corporation.

Tod Pike is a graduate of Carnegie Mellon University, where he first became familiar with the Internet. A system administrator for almost 10 years, he works daily with UNIX, UseNet, and Internet mail. He can be reached on the Internet at **tgp@cmu.edu**.

Sue Plumley owns and operates Humble Opinions, a consulting firm that offers training in popular software programs and network installation and maintenance. She is the author of 12 Que books, including *Crystal Clear DOS*, *Crystal Clear Word 6*, and *Microsoft Office Quick Reference*, and coauthor of 16 additional books, including *Using WordPerfect 6 for DOS*, *Using OS/2 2.1*, and *Using Microsoft Office*, for Que and its sister imprints.

Jeff V. Pulver has been involved in data processing for more than 25 years, with the last 15 years spent as the President of Intercomp Design, Inc., a computer consulting firm. Pulver specializes in the planning and migration of software and operating systems for mainframes and PCs. His other areas of specialty include systems programming, applications programming, documentation, re-engineering of application systems, and beta testing mainframe and PC software, including Windows 95.

Gregory J. Root started his work with computers when TRS-80s were in style and 16K of RAM was equivalent to infinity. Root has worked for Northern Trust Bank and Follett Software Company. He also has made part of his living as a computing consultant for lawyers, churches, and government agencies. Throughout his career, Root has administered and installed peer-to-peer and server-based networks, developed applications using Fortran and Visual Basic, and managed software development projects. He lives in Lake in the Hills, Ill., with his beautiful wife and lifelong companion, Tracy.

Paul Sanna is a project manager in the Development department of Hyperion Software, Inc., in Stamford, Conn. He works on the company's line of client-server financial accounting applications. Sanna has taught, tested, and developed software for the past seven years. He has contributed to *Understanding Windows 95* and *Inside Windows 95* (New Riders Publishing). Paul lives in Bethel, Conn., with his wife Andrea and three daughters: Allison, Rachel, and Victoria.

Ian Stokell is a freelance writer and editor living in the Sierra Foothills of northern California with his wife and three young children. He is also Managing Editor of *Newsbytes News Network*, an international daily newswire covering the computer and telecommunications industries. His writing career began with a 1981 article published in the UK's *New Statesman* and has since encompassed over 1,500 articles in a variety of computing and non-computing publications. He wrote the networking chapter of Que's *Using the Macintosh*, Special Edition, and has also written on assignment for such magazines as *PC World* and *MacWeek*. He is currently seeking representation for two completed novels and a screenplay.

Patrick J. Suarez is an Internet author, software developer, and lecturer. He is most noted for his "The Beginner's Guide to the Internet" series of tutorial software, books, and seminars. Suarez has a B.A. in Constitutional Law and a Master of Science in Administration degree. He is a member of the prestigious Dayton Microcomputer Association and writes a monthly column called "Internet.Talk" for the DMA newsletter, *Databus*. Mr. Suarez is an adjunct professor at Wright State University and Urbana University. He is a proponent of First Amendment cyber-rights and can be reached at **pat@bgi.com**.

Diane Tinney is proprietor of The Software Professional, a business that provides education, development support, and consulting on a variety of Windows 3.x , Windows 95, and Windows NT applications. Tinney specializes in the integration of Windows products, and specifically, database design and implementation. She is the author of Que's *Paradox for Windows Programming By Example,* and is a contributing author to Que's *Killer dBASE 5.0 for Windows, Using Microsoft Office for Windows, Using Paradox for Windows,* and *Using Microsoft Office 95*. You can reach Diane via the Internet at **dtinney@warwick.net**.

We'd Like to Hear from You!

As part of our continuing effort to produce books of the highest possible quality, Que would like to hear your comments. To stay competitive, we *really* want you, as a computer book reader and user, to let us know what you like or dislike most about this book or other Que products.

You can mail comments, ideas, or suggestions for improving future editions to the address below, or send us a fax at (317) 581-4663. For the online inclined, Macmillan Computer Publishing has a forum on CompuServe (type **GO MACMILLAN** at any prompt) through which our staff and authors are available for questions and comments. The address of our Internet site is **http://www.mcp.com** (World Wide Web). Our Web site has received critical acclaim from many reviewers—be sure to check it out.

In addition to exploring our forum, please feel free to contact me personally to discuss your opinions of this book:

CompuServe:	**74404,3307**
America Online:	**ldw indy**
Internet:	**lwagner@que.mcp.com**

Thanks in advance—your comments will help us to continue publishing the best books available on computer topics in today's market.

Lisa D. Wagner
Product Development Specialist
Que Corporation
201 W. 103rd Street
Indianapolis, Indiana 46290
USA

Note

Although we cannot provide general technical support, we're happy to help you resolve problems you encounter related to our books, disks, or other products. If you need such assistance, please contact our Tech Support department at 800-545-5914 ext. 3833.

To order other Que or Macmillan Computer Publishing books or products, please call our Customer Service department at 800-835-3202 ext. 666.

Contents at a Glance

Appendixes

Appendixes

Contents

24 Configuring CD-ROM Drives 513

25 Configuring Floppy Disk Drives 525

26 Configuring Hard Disk Drives 537

27 Configuring Backup Systems 565

Introduction

What—you didn't have problems installing Windows 95? You only experienced problems when you restarted your computer to *run* Windows 95? Don't worry. You're not alone. Most Windows 95 installation problems occur after you've installed the software, when you reboot your computer. This is when the Windows Setup program configures your computer to work with Windows 95.

Windows 95 is designed to ease installation and configuration burdens. Setting up your Windows environment has never been easier. If you're new to the world of Windows, you'll find installation very easy and simple.

So why is this book needed? In short, because nothing is perfect...including Windows. It's not that Microsoft doesn't want Windows 95 to be perfect and fit every situation perfectly. The problem is that no two computer systems are alike. In fact, chances are if you have two computers in your office or home, they have two different setups and configurations. Even if the two computers are the same make and model, they are unique and have their own idiosyncrasies. What all this means is that Windows 95 must be flexible enough to work on different configurations, yet offer a simple way to customize each individual PC.

That's where this book comes in. *Windows 95 Installation and Configuration Handbook* guides you through the entire Windows 95 installation process. You are shown how to prepare your computer before you install Windows 95, as well as how to add hardware, memory, software, and other devices after Windows 95 is up and running.

For the most part, you can use Windows 95 straight "out of the box" and get most of your work done. If you need to change a setting (called a *property* in Windows 95), you'll need to dig a little deeper into the operating system and become familiar with some of Windows 95's new configuration features. Some of these include the Add/Remove Software and Add New Hardware utilities, the Device Manager, and property sheets. You find out about all these in this book.

Who This Book Is For

This book is designed for users who need to install Windows 95 and who want to customize and reconfigure the way Windows behaves and looks. For beginning Windows users, this book includes step-by-step procedures that guide them through setting up the Windows environment. The new Help utility available in Windows 95 is a much-welcomed addition to Windows. However, not all procedures are covered in Help, and many assumptions are left up to the user to figure out. This book attempts to fill in many of those gaps.

For experienced Windows 3.x users, this book includes customization procedures and techniques to help them configure the Windows 95 environment the way they want it. In many places in this book, comparisons to how a procedure or step was performed in Windows 3.x are included. This helps the experienced user become comfortable with Windows 95 more quickly.

Who This Book Is Not For

Any user of Windows 95 who wants to install new hardware, add software, or reconfigure the Windows 95 environment should appreciate this book. If you need a tutorial of the way in which Windows 95 works, however, you may find this book not meeting your need. Although some chapters give basic overviews of how a feature works, or some of the benefits of using a configuration setting versus another setting, you will need another book to learn how to use Windows 95.

Fortunately, an outstanding book is available that does just this. Que's *Special Edition Using Windows 95* is packed full of instructions, tutorials, and reference materials to help you understand and master Windows 95. If you need to learn how to use Windows 95, you may want to pick up a copy of that book.

Another audience segment that is not addressed specifically is the network administrator. Although many of the procedures and configuration instructions included help administrators troubleshoot common workstation problems, you will not find comprehensive instructions on setting up and configuring Windows 95 across a network. You can find that material in the *Windows 95 Resource Kit* available from Microsoft, or by referencing Que's *Windows 95 Connectivity*.

How to Use This Book

Use this book as you would a reference book. Unless you find your local library or bookstore lacking entertaining novels, you probably don't want to read this book from cover to cover. The best way to use this book is to look over the table of contents at the front of the book and the index in the back to find the topic you want. Turn to that chapter or section and use the instructions and discussions provided. Then close the book and start working with Windows 95.

If you have specific questions, turn to the troubleshooting sections in the book. Troubleshooting sections are provided in almost all chapters to help you solve many of the common problems associated with installing and configuring Windows 95. Appendix B, *Troubleshooting Windows 95*, is a compendium of all the troubleshooting sections from the book, plus additional troubleshooting tips and techniques that help you get up and running and keep Windows 95 functioning properly.

How This Book Is Organized

The following is a quick look at each of the chapters in this book.

Part I: Installing Windows 95

Chapter 1, "Preparing to Install Windows 95," is the place to start if you have not installed Windows 95. It shows you how to prepare your system for Windows 95, and introduces the new Windows 95 installation features.

Chapter 2, "Installing Windows 95 on a Desktop PC," is intended for readers who have prepped their machines and want to install Windows 95 using the Typical installation option during Setup. The Typical install option is designed for users who do not want to monkey around with selecting specific components to install. They just want Windows 95 to install so they can start using it.

Chapter 3, "Installing Windows 95 on a Laptop PC," is for users who have mobile computers and want to install only those files and programs that are necessary for laptop computers. Windows 95 includes some new components that enable mobile users to transfer files back and forth between the mobile computer and the stationary computer. This chapter shows how to configure these options.

Chapter 4, "Using Custom Installation Options," is an overview of the different components you can select during installation. This chapter is intended for users who are comfortable with their computers and know which components they want to install.

Chapter 5, "Installing Windows 95 over a Network," is a primer for setting up Windows 95 in a networked environment. Windows 95 has built-in networking capabilities that make it a powerful operating system for the workgroup environment. This chapter starts you on the path for understanding how to configure these features.

Part II: Configuring Windows 95

Chapter 6, "Configuring the Windows 95 Desktop and Display," picks up after you have Windows 95 installed and running. Now you are ready to customize your Windows 95 environment.

Chapter 7, "Configuring the Taskbar and Start Menu," helps you modify the way the Windows 95 taskbar behaves and looks. You are shown how to add programs and files to the Start menu, which gives you one-button access to them.

Chapter 8, "Configuring Windows 95 Audio," is your guide to setting event sounds in Windows 95, setting sound volumes, and configuring MIDI sounds.

Chapter 9, "Configuring Microsoft Exchange," shows you how to set up Microsoft's new universal "inbox"—Microsoft Exchange. With Microsoft Exchange, you can send, receive, and store Microsoft Mail messages, Microsoft Fax messages, and other documents in one central place.

Chapter 10, "Configuring Microsoft Fax," shows you step-by-step how to set up Microsoft's built-in fax software—Microsoft Fax. In this chapter, you find all the Microsoft Fax options discussed, including those intended for more advanced audiences.

Chapter 11, "Configuring Windows 95 for Online Connections," shows you how to connect to the Microsoft Network, CompuServe, America Online, Prodigy, and local bulletin board systems (BBSes).

Chapter 12, "Configuring a Windows 95 Internet Connection," leads you step-by-step to setting up Windows 95 built-in support for the Internet, as well as how to use the Microsoft Plus! Companion for Windows 95.

Chapter 13, "Configuring Memory, Disks, and Devices," provides information on using system memory, modifying virtual memory, improving hard disk performance, and how to use the Device Manager.

Chapter 14, "Using Norton Desktop Utilities with Windows 95," shows you how to integrate a third-party package—Norton Utilities—to get the most out of your Windows 95 setup.

Part III: Setting Up Windows 95 for Your Software

Chapter 15, "Using DOS Software," is intended for those still using their favorite (or forced to use their least favorite) DOS software under Windows 95.

Chapter 16, "Using Windows 3.x Software," shows how to optimize Windows 95 for Windows 3.x software. Many users will have to rely on Windows 3.x applications for many months after they start using Windows 95 before Windows 95 specific applications hit the market. This chapter shows how to configure your software to perform its best under Windows 95.

Chapter 17, "Using Windows 95 Software," shows some of the Windows 95 applications available on the market and how to use Windows 95 software on the Windows 95 operating system.

Part IV: Setting Up Windows 95 for Your Hardware

Chapter 18, "Configuring Monitors and Video Cards for Windows 95," shows you how to set resolution settings, configure color palettes, and set font sizes for your monitor.

Chapter 19, "Configuring Speakers and Sound Cards," helps you set up your sound card to work with Windows 95.

Chapter 20, "Configuring MIDI Cards," is intended for those users who are adding and configuring a MIDI device to work with Windows 95.

Chapter 21, "Configuring Joysticks and Game Cards," provides information on maximizing your Windows 95 environment for games by showing how to set up joysticks and game adapters.

Chapter 22, "Configuring Mice and Other Pointing Devices," shows how to set mouse properties, troubleshoot common problems with installing pointing devices, and how to configure your pointing device to work with Windows 95.

Chapter 23, "Configuring Keyboards," is just that: how to configure a keyboard for Windows 95.

Chapter 24, "Configuring CD-ROM Drives," may become dog-eared from use if you upgrade or add a CD-ROM to your system. This chapter shows you how to install and set up a CD-ROM to work with Windows 95.

Chapter 25, "Configuring Floppy Disk Drives," leads you through adding a floppy drive to your system, and includes troubleshooting topics that help you configure your floppy drive for Windows 95.

Chapter 26, "Configuring Hard Disk Drives," is similar to Chapter 25, but is written for hard disk drives. You also learn how to partition and prepare a new hard drive to use with Windows 95.

Chapter 27, "Configuring Backup Systems," shows you how to install a backup system to work with Windows 95. Although you may not use a tape backup system, DAT system, or other backup media, you should seriously consider adding one to your system.

Chapter 28, "Configuring Modems," should be used in conjunction with the earlier chapters on setting up online and Internet connections, configuring Microsoft Exchange, and installing Microsoft Fax. You'll need to configure your modem before you start any of those other configurations.

Chapter 29, "Configuring Printers," helps you install a printer for a single computer as well as for a networked PC. The Add Printer Wizard makes installation a breeze, but you may have some problems that this chapter can help you correct.

Chapter 30, "Configuring Scanners and Digital Cameras," shows how to set up scanners to work with Windows 95.

Chapter 31, "Configuring Network Hardware," shows how to configure network adapters, install network cables, configure Microsoft Fax for a workgroup environment, and how to share CD-ROMs on a network using Windows 95.

Part V: Appendixes

Appendix A, "Installing and Using Microsoft Plus! Companion for Windows 95," leads you through installing the Microsoft Plus! Companion software for Windows 95.

Appendix B, "Troubleshooting Windows 95," gathers all the troubleshooting notes from the book and organizes them into one handy reference. This appendix also includes several additional troubleshooting items not included in the rest of the book. Use this appendix to isolate and correct a specific installation or configuration problem you are having.

Using the Bonus Disk

The CD-ROM included in this book contains a variety of software programs developed for Windows 95. The software includes productivity tools, animated cursors and icons, Windows 95 shell replacements, and a few entertainment packages. Appendix C gives a brief explanation of each application and lists the files you need to install or run the application.

Obtaining Additional Windows 95 Information

This book was written during the beta releases of Windows 95 and checked against the final release of Windows 95. Because of changes that occur each time a piece of software appears on the market, software manufacturers sometimes include small changes in their software without announcement. Some changes that appear in release versions after the initial distribution of Windows 95 may not be reflected in this manuscript. For that reason, you should read any text files or directions that come with your Windows 95 disks or CD-ROM. Files named README.DOC, README.TXT, and similar names may contain late-breaking changes in the software that can help answer some of your problems.

Other valuable sources of information include Microsoft's Internet FTP site (**ftp.microsoft.com**) and World Wide Web site (**http://www.microsoft.com**). You can find some technical support documents and updated drivers for some hardware devices at those sites.

Conventions Found in This Book

You find four visual aids that help you on your Windows 95 installation journey: **Notes**, **Tips**, **Cautions**, and **Troubleshootings**.

Note

This paragraph format indicates additional information that may help you avoid problems or that should be considered in using the described features.

Tip

This paragraph format suggests easier or alternative methods of executing a procedure.

Caution

This paragraph format warns the reader of hazardous procedures (for example, activities that delete files).

Troubleshooting

This paragraph format provides guidance on how to find solutions to common problems. Specific problems you may encounter are shown in italic. Possible solutions appear in the paragraph(s) following the problem.

Windows 95 Installation and Configuration Handbook uses margin cross-references to help you access related information in other parts of the book. Right-facing triangles point you to related information in later chapters. Left-facing triangles point you to information in previous chapters.

Windows 95 enables you to use both the keyboard and the mouse to select menu and dialog box items. You can press a letter, or you can select an item by clicking it with the mouse. Letters you press to activate menus, choose commands in menus, and select options in dialog boxes are underlined: File, Open.

Names of dialog boxes and dialog box options are written with initial capital letters. Messages that appear on-screen are printed in a special font: `Document 1`. New terms are introduced in *italic* type. Text that you are to type appears in **boldface**.

The following example shows typical command sequences:

> Open the File menu and choose Copy, or press Ctrl+Ins.

Chapter 1

Preparing to Install Windows 95

by Rob Tidrow

Installing Windows 95 is not tricky, but it can be frustrating at times. You'll notice two things about Windows 95 when you start installing it. First, you need to decide if you want to keep your previous operating system, such as Microsoft Windows 3.11, installed. Second, you need to be patient. The Windows 95 installation process can take some time to install completely. To begin, you should set aside 30 to 60 minutes to install Windows 95. If you need to prepare your hard disk or decide to customize the setup, don't be surprised if you invest two or more hours to ensure everything is properly set up.

This chapter is your guide to preparing for the Windows 95 installation. You don't actually install Windows 95 in this chapter, but you do gain helpful suggestions and pre-install tips that make the installation process go more smoothly. In this chapter, you learn about the following:

- What's new in Windows 95 setup
- Requirements of Windows 95
- Features of Microsoft Plus!
- Preparations for Windows 95 installation
- Installation options
- Boot configuration options

What's New with Windows 95 Setup

Windows 95 is a new operating system, and with it comes a new installation process. Many of the options and customization procedures that users had to perform with older versions of Windows after they installed Windows are now included during setup. Some of these procedures include configuring hardware devices, networking components, and online connections. The following is a list of improved areas over previous versions of Windows setup:

- Use of installation wizards to guide and interact with users. Novice and beginning users benefit from the easy-to-understand instructions Windows 95 offers them. Advanced users have the capability to select and modify options during setup.
- Automatic detection of hardware during setup provides users the freedom from configuring all their hardware devices after the setup stage.
- Introduction of Plug-and-Play technology to help facilitate hardware setup.
- Use of smart recovery system in case of interrupted setup process. Windows 95 knows when a previous installation has failed and returns to the point of interruption to continue setup.
- Creation of setup log to verify system is set up properly.
- Improved network setup, including use of batch installs across local area networks (LANs).

Two of the most obvious changes with Windows 95 are support of Plug-and-Play devices and the use of wizards during installation. These two areas are discussed in the following sections.

Plug and Play Overview

Before preparing your system to install Windows 95, you should learn about one of the most daunting tasks that users have when making system changes and updates—hardware upgrades. Users who decide to add hardware devices to their systems know how difficult it is to reconfigure their operating system and software to work correctly with the new hardware. Updating to a new operating system also requires a great deal of fiddling to get all your hardware devices working in sync. Technical support calls, visits from MIS staff, and working late nights or weekends usually are the only remedies to hardware problems. Sometimes it seems the operating system and hardware are designed NOT to work with one another.

A new specification called Plug and Play hopes to challenge problems associated with hardware upgrades and installations. As you learn in Part IV, "Setting Up Windows 95 for Your Hardware," Plug-and-Play devices soon will dominate the hardware market. Plug and Play is a hardware and software specification supported by Microsoft, Compaq, Intel, and many other manufacturers that free the user from configuring hardware components. The purpose of Plug and Play is to provide a tight integration between the operating system (Windows 95) and the hardware device, such as a sound card, CD-ROM device, or mouse. System settings, memory access, and other configuration settings are now handled by Windows 95 and the device, not by the user.

If you've upgraded your Windows 3.x system or have added hardware to it, you know the frustrations of configuring device drivers, updating INI settings, figuring out the correct IRQ and DMA channels, and determining other details of setup. Each time you upgrade your system, you have to make sure the newest device drivers are on your system to run with your software. Many times the device driver has to be obtained from the manufacturer through a technical support system or bulletin board system, such as CompuServe.

If you are a mobile user, Plug and Play is designed to solve problems associated with linking laptops to desktop computers. A new breed of computers called *docking stations* enables users to detach part of their computers and carry them as portables. When they return to the office, the portable part of the computer can be reattached to the desktop portion. With Plug-and-Play docking stations, users do not have to reboot the computer after they are reattached.

Docking stations without Plug-and-Play specifications require users to reconfigure hardware and software setups when they arrive back at the office to reattach the units. Settings such as network configurations or modem options need to be changed depending on the location or devices to which users connect. One situation, such as docking a PC at a corporate office, may call for a network to be hooked up to an Ethernet connection. Another situation, such as from a home office, may require a dial-up network connection. Plug-and-Play devices search for components to evaluate the environment in which the PC is working and determine how the hardware and software should interact.

Built in to Windows 95 installation is Plug-and-Play support. As it goes through the setup process, Windows 95 hunts down and configures any Plug-and-Play device you have on your system. You are not required to memorize IRQs and DMA settings just to get a piece of hardware working. Plug and Play takes care of all this when Windows 95 is set up.

What if you don't have a Plug-and-Play computer on which to install Windows 95? In an ideal world, you could run out and buy new hardware when you buy a new operating system. Those of us who can't afford such a luxury must rely on current systems to run Windows 95, including 80386 machines built in the early 1990s. Even if you don't have Plug-and-Play hardware—which many PC users do not—Windows 95 still locates many of your devices already set up on your system using Windows' autodetect feature. Known as *legacy hardware*, the hardware you already have installed is automatically set up when you install Windows 95.

Note

As a clarification, Windows 95 snoops out the hardware on your system and attempts to set it up during Setup. If Windows 95 can't figure out what to do with your hardware device and doesn't set it up during install, you can use the Add New Hardware utility in the Windows Control Panel after you have Windows 95 up and running. This utility is examined in more detail in each of the chapters in Part IV, "Setting Up Windows 95 for Your Hardware."

How Plug and Play Works

How does Plug and Play work? For the most part, you don't need to know. You can just rest comfortably knowing that it does work. Sometimes, though, you may have to troubleshoot an installation or configuration concern. For this reason, a basic understanding of the way in which Plug and Play works is in order.

A major component of Windows 95 is the inclusion of the Registry. The *Registry* is a centralized database of your system settings. The Registry is a hierarchical structure that stores text or binary value information to maintain all of the configuration parameters that were stored in INI files in Windows 3.x (see fig. 1.1).

One role of the Registry is to enable the Plug-and-Play system components to access the hardware-specific information. As new hardware devices are added to your system, Windows 95 checks your Registry settings for hardware resource allocations, such as IRQs, I/O addresses, and DMA channels, and determines the settings for the new hardware device. With Plug-and-Play devices, all of these configuration settings are performed at the software level, not the hardware level as before. This (virtually) eliminates the need to adjust settings on the hardware itself prior to installation. You can install the hardware and let Windows 95 do the rest.

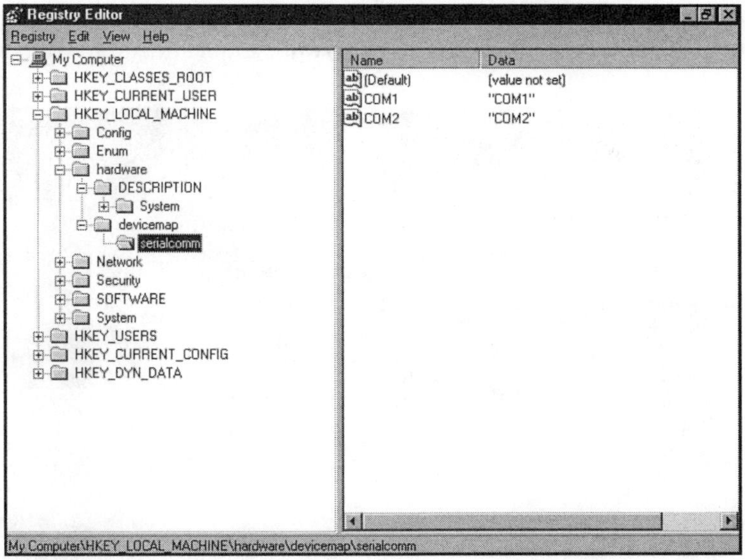

Fig. 1.1
Plug and Play relies on the Windows 95 Registry to determine system information.

> **Note**
>
> After you install Windows 95, you can access the Registry by opening the REGEDIT.EXE application in your Windows 95 main directory.

You activate Plug and Play in one of four ways. The first way is during the Windows 95 installation process. As you learn in Chapter 2, "Installing Windows 95 on a Desktop PC," you are prompted as to whether you want Windows 95 to automatically detect hardware devices during setup, shown in figure 1.2. If you answer Yes, the Plug-and-Play feature sniffs out and attempts to set up your hardware.

The second way in which Plug and Play is activated is when you start the Add New Hardware Wizard in the Windows 95 Control Panel. Again, Windows 95 (see fig. 1.3) asks if you want it to automatically detect your hardware. If you know you have a Plug-and-Play compatible device, your best bet is to answer Yes. Otherwise, you can click No and specify the device type and manufacturer.

▶ See "Analyzing Your Computer," p. 50

The third way is during the normal boot process of Windows 95. As Windows 95 boots, it builds the Registry databases (USER.DAT and SYSTEM.DAT) according to the user information and system information on your computer. If the boot-up process locates a new device—for instance, a sound card—the Plug-and-Play system sets it up. On hardware devices that are not

Plug-and-Play compatible, Windows 95 reports that a new device has been detected and that the Add New Hardware Wizard should be run to configure it.

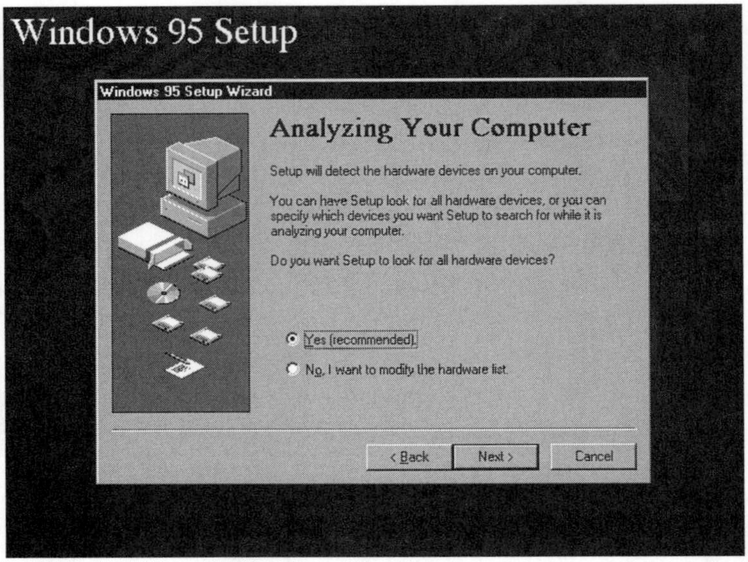

Fig. 1.2
During installation, Windows 95 asks if you want the Plug-and-Play feature to set up your hardware.

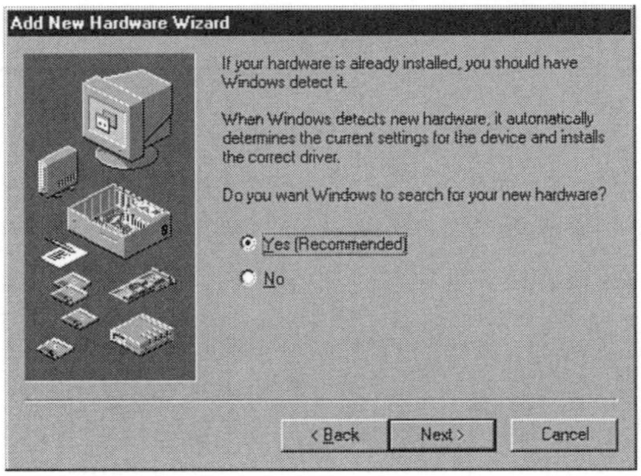

Fig. 1.3
The Add New Hardware Wizard uses Plug-and-Play features to set up hardware.

A fourth way to initiate the Plug-and-Play feature is during a warm or hot docking situation. *Hot docking* refers to inserting a computer in a docking station while the computer is running at full power. (You also can *undock* a computer, or remove a computer from a docking station.) *Warm docking* refers to docking or undocking a computer while it is in *suspended mode*, a state in which the computer is "put to sleep" but not shut off completely. Laptop or portable computers that include a Plug-and-Play BIOS (Basic Input/Output System) and are part of a docking station PC can be hot or warm docked and undocked.

Benefits of Plug and Play

Regardless of your user level, you probably don't like spending large chunks of your time pulling cards out of your system to reset DIP switches or IRQ settings. You probably dread installing SCSI (Small Computer System Interface) devices because of the inevitable software/hardware/operating system incompatibilities that always seem to crop up during hardware installations. In short, you hate adding hardware to your system.

As defined, Plug and Play is intended to let users buy hardware, unwrap it, "plug" it into the system, and begin working. Specifically, Plug and Play addresses the following benefits to users:

- *Compatibility with older hardware.* As Windows 95's Plug-and-Play system detects hardware on your system, it checks the Registry for device information. Non-Plug-and-Play devices normally cannot be reconfigured through software settings, so they take precedence over Plug-and-Play devices when resources such as IRQ lines and DMA channels are allocated. The purpose of this action is to enable your older hardware to coexist with newer, Plug-and-Play-specific hardware.

  Some older hardware devices, including the Microsoft Sound System, are software-configurable, so Windows 95 should not have a difficult time setting them up. Many users have found Windows 95 friendlier than Windows 3.x during the hardware setup stage. Part of this is due to the Registry settings and how it allocates system settings automatically.

- *Easier PC management and support.* MIS support staff, system administrators, power users, and users with above average computer skills can breathe a sigh of relief. Problems typically associated with installing hardware diminish when Plug and Play manages the system setup. Device driver setup, jumper settings, and IRQ conflicts are not an issue with Plug-and-Play devices. Cost savings for large corporations can be realized when upgrading systems is not a support nightmare requiring hundreds of hours of upgrade and maintenance time.

- *Universal device driver development.* The number of new device drivers available weekly is impossible to keep track of. As hardware devices are upgraded and improved (and grow older), device drivers are upgraded, making the older ones obsolete. Sometimes, the device drivers that worked fine with one application do not work well or at all with a maintenance release of the software. You are required to find a new and improved device driver to get your system working normally again.

With Plug and Play, this will begin to be a thing of the past with the support of a new proposed standard known as the *universal driver model*. In Windows 3.1, printer drivers were based on this model, but no other hardware components were. Under Windows 95, however, hardware vendors can write device drivers under the universal driver model for the following devices, making device drive updates obsolete:

Communication devices

Display devices

Input devices, such as mice

Disk devices

Availability of Plug-and-Play Devices

Currently, only a handful of Plug-and-Play devices are available on the market. Many OEMs (Original Equipment Manufacturers) are providing Plug-and-Play BIOSs (Basic Input/Output Systems) on new PCs. Over the course of several months after the release of Windows 95, market pressure and user feedback should help drive the need for more Plug-and-Play hardware components on the market. If you don't have a Plug-and-Play device now, chances are you will by this time next year if you upgrade your system or purchase a new one.

Installation Wizards

Probably the most significant new feature to Windows 95's setup process is the use of wizards. If you are a user of Microsoft Word or Access, you probably encounter wizards on a daily or weekly basis. *Wizards* are on-screen guides that walk users through a particular process, such as installing Windows 95 (see fig. 1.4) or adding a modem to your system.

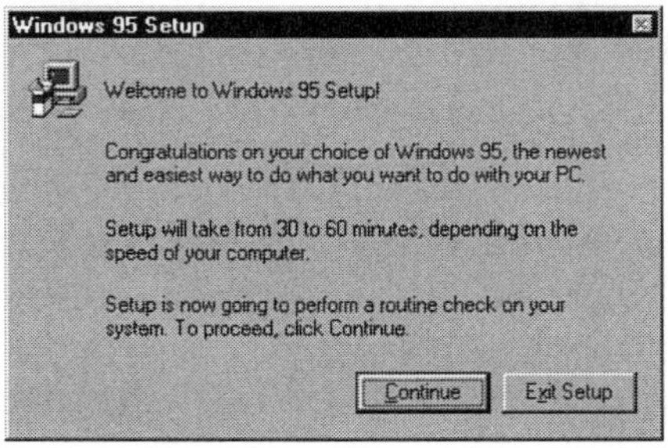

Fig. 1.4
Wizards offer a great deal of help during the installation stage.

Two features of wizards set them apart from normal installation programs:

- They generate questions for the user that are straightforward and intended to be non-intimidating.
- They are designed so that users can press a button and return to the previous screen if necessary. This feature is handy if users are confused or want to change an installation option before Windows 95 installs onto their system.

Wizards are intended to help all users, not just beginners. More advanced users who feel comfortable setting configuration parameters are given opportunities in some wizards to manually set up devices. The Modem Wizard, for instance, enables users to select the modem name and manufacturer from a list (see fig. 1.5). Many users, however, opt for Windows 95 to automatically determine and set up their modem or other hardware device. If Windows 95 cannot detect their modem, then users can manually configure the device by following on-screen instructions that help guide them through the process.

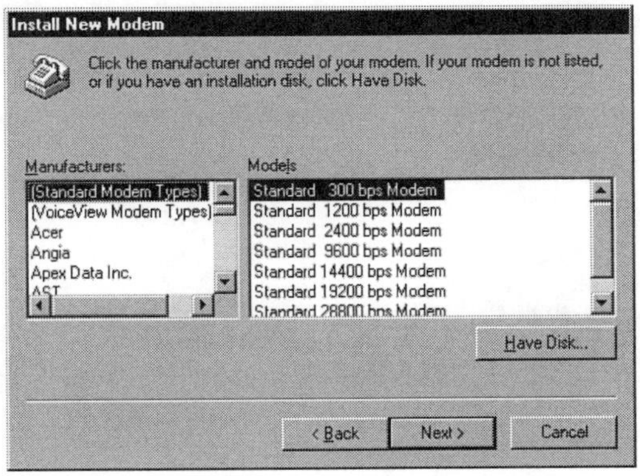

Fig. 1.5
The Modem Wizard enables you to select the name and manufacturer of the modem.

During the Windows 95 installation process, you are presented with numerous wizards that help you get through the installation. Some wizard screens only provide information (see fig. 1.6), while others require you to choose an option or configuration setting (see fig. 1.7).

Wizards have three buttons along the bottom of the screen that provide navigation. They are as follows:

- *Next.* Presents the user with the next step in the wizard. Next is the default button on many wizard screens and can be activated by clicking it or by pressing Enter.

- *Back*. Sends the user back one screen or step. Use this button if you want to change a setting or reread the previous step. Most wizards let you back up as far as you want in the wizard.
- *Cancel*. Exits the wizard without performing any actions or making system changes.

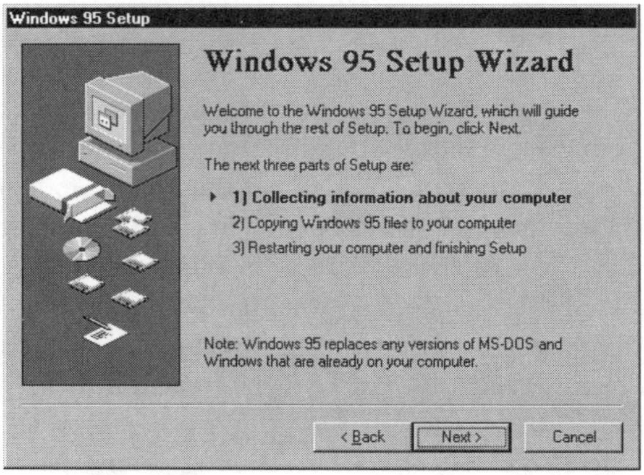

Fig. 1.6
Installation wizards can include information screens that simply inform users or warn them against potential hazards.

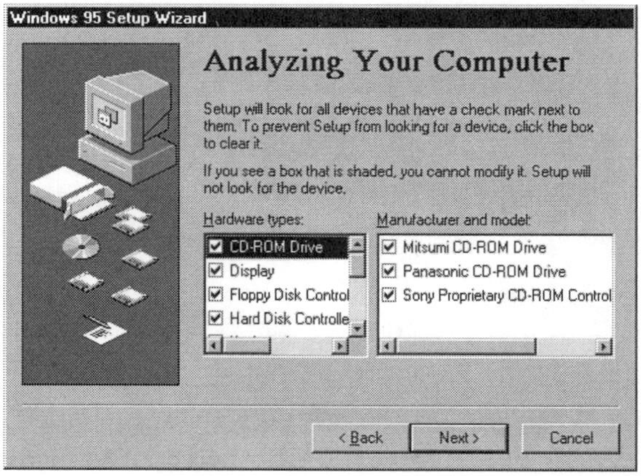

Fig. 1.7
Many wizard screens require users to interact with the wizard and fill in or select specific information as it pertains to their system.

> **Note**
>
> Depending on the wizard and the application you are in, the screen may have a Help button. Use the Help button to obtain online help for that screen or function.

Requirements of Windows 95

One of the primary differences between Windows 95 and previous versions of Windows is its system robustness. Some of the improvements in this area include enhanced resource cleanup after an application has crashed, support of long file names (file names up to 255 characters long), preemptive multitasking for 32-bit applications, and better memory management. With all of these features, plus many more not included here, you need a robust computer that can handle Windows 95.

Specific requirements for installing Windows 95 are addressed in this section. These requirements include the following:

- Operating system
- PC system
- Hard drive setup

Operating System Requirements

First you'll need to make sure your current PC has an operating system to install Windows 95. The recommended choice is to have Windows 3.x or Windows for Workgroups installed. Windows 95 is designed to upgrade these systems.

If you do not have Windows 3.x or Windows for Workgroups, you must have MS-DOS 3.2 or higher installed. If your primary operating system is Windows NT or IBM OS/2, you still are required to have DOS installed in a bootable partition. You cannot install Windows 95 straight from OS/2 or NT.

Note

If your system has a version of DOS but not MS-DOS 3.2 or higher, make sure it can exceed the 32M partition limit, which Windows 95 supports. Some OEM versions of DOS do not meet this standard. Check your system manuals to make sure your version of DOS does. If you do not know what version of DOS you have, type **VER** at the command prompt for this information.

Troubleshooting

Can I set up Windows 95 to dual boot with Windows NT?

Yes, but you must install Windows 95 in a separate directory than Windows NT and have a FAT partition on the hard disk. When you start your PC, select the MS-DOS option from the Windows NT OS Loader menu to boot Windows 95.

System Requirements

A PC that currently runs Windows 3.1 or 3.11 without many performance problems should have few problems running Windows 95. A good way to judge your PC against one that will perform well with Windows 95 is to open three to four applications and check the system resources. You can do this by choosing Help, About Microsoft Windows in the Windows 3.x Program Manager (see fig. 1.8)

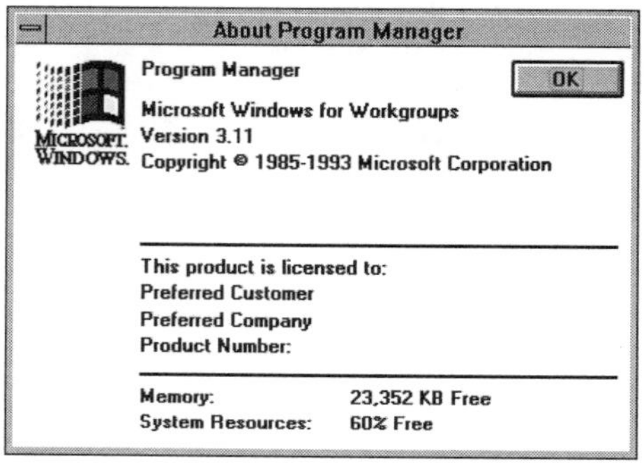

Fig. 1.8
Run a few Windows 3.x applications to test your PC's performance prior to installing Windows 95.

If you can run three to four applications simultaneously and keep the system resources above 50 percent, you should find your system adequate for Windows 95.

Table 1.1 lists the Microsoft minimum system requirements. Table 1.2 lists the recommended requirements.

Table 1.1 Microsoft's Minimum System Requirements

Component	Requirement of Windows 95
Processor	80386 or higher
Hard drive	30M of free disk space for a compact installation; 40M for a typical installation
Memory	4M
Input device	Mouse
Floppy disk	Required for installation from floppy disks
CD-ROM drive	Required for installation from CD
Monitor	VGA
Fax/modem	Required to use Microsoft Network, Remote Access, HyperTerminal (included in Windows 95), Microsoft Fax, and Phone Dialer

Caution

Although Windows 95 is a powerful operating system, it is designed only for Intel x86-based processors. Windows 95 also does not support multiple processors, as does Windows NT.

Another processor limitation you need to be aware of is that Windows 95 cannot install on a 386-based B-step processor. A B-step processor has an ID of 0303, which can be determined from your system documentation or by using a utility such as Microsoft Diagnostics from MD-DOS. Type **MSD** from the DOS command line to start the Microsoft Diagnostics program and check in the CPU settings for the ID of your processor.

Table 1.2 Recommended System Requirements

Component	Recommended for Windows 95
Processor	80486/33 or Pentium
Hard drive	50M of free disk space, particularly if you want to install the Microsoft Plus! pack
Memory	8M minimum; 16M recommended for running four or more applications
Input device	Mouse
CD-ROM drive	Double-speed or quad-speed for multimedia applications
Monitor	Super VGA
Fax/modem	14.4bps; 28.8bps for Internet connectivity

Tip

The recommended hard disk space in table 1.2 does not take into consideration the disk space requirement for installing or reinstalling applications to run under Windows 95. For those requirements, refer to the documentation that comes with the specific application you plan to install.

Also, if you install the Microsoft Exchange client, you need at least 4.6M of hard disk space on top of what Windows uses. If you install Microsoft Fax, The Microsoft Network, and the Microsoft Mail client, you need another 12M of hard disk space. You also need at least 8M of RAM to run Exchange and Microsoft Fax. The Microsoft Network also demands a large amount of memory. You should have at least 8M minimum, and 16M is recommended.

▶ See "The First Step: Adding a Network Configuration," p. 300

If your budget allows for a system upgrade or replacement, try to settle for nothing less than a Pentium processor, 16M of RAM, 500M+ hard disk, and a quad-speed CD-ROM. You also should look for a system that includes Plug-and-Play devices or a Plug-and-Play BIOS.

You must decide if you want to install Windows 95 on top of your existing Windows 3.x installation. If you choose to install a new directory to preserve your old setup, you must reinstall all your applications to work with Windows 95. (Some applications may run under Windows 95 without reinstalling them, so you might want to try them before reinstalling them.) This means that each must occupy space again on your hard disk if you plan to use the same application under Windows 3.x and Windows 95. For this reason, a hard disk with lots of free space is necessary.

Troubleshooting

What happens to my AUTOEXEC.BAT and CONFIG.SYS files when I install Windows 95 on my system?

Windows 95 creates its own AUTOEXEC.BAT and CONFIG.SYS files and renames your existing ones. When Windows 95 loads, it renames the DOS version of the files to `AUTOEXEC.DOS` and `CONFIG.DOS`. When the regular DOS/Windows 3.x loads, the Windows 95 files are renamed `AUTOEXEC.W40` and `CONFIG.W40`.

Hard Drive Requirements

Aside from sheer volume, your hard drive needs to be prepared to handle Windows 95. "Preparing for Installation" later in this chapter shows you how to optimize your hard disk before you install Windows 95. This section discusses partitioned drives and compressed drives.

Partitioned Drives

Many users use partitioned drives to organize files (to get around the 512-file, single-root directory limitation) or to install another operating system on the same hard disk. To install Windows 95, you must have a file allocation table (FAT) partition on your hard disk. Windows 95 includes new 32-bit, protected-mode enhanced FAT system that enables long file names (file names with more than eight plus three characters) and exclusive access to disk devices, such as ScanDisk. Windows 95 does not support HPFS (High Performance Files System) or NTFS (NT File System) partitions. As you install Windows 95, the setup routine writes information to the master boot record and reads most partitioning schemes, such as those set up by FDISK in MS-DOS.

Note

FAT is the 16-bit standard file system used by MS-DOS, OS/2, and Windows NT and allows only eight plus three character file names.

HPFS is a UNIX-style file system that OS/2 and Windows NT can access. HPFS allows file names to be 256 characters long. DOS applications cannot access HPFS files unless DOS is running under OS/2 or Windows NT.

NTFS is the Windows NT file system that allows 256 character file names and is accessible by Windows NT and OS/2.

Windows 95 installs over existing MS-DOS FAT partitions as long as you have enough space in the partition for Windows 95. You also need at least 5M for the Windows 95 swap file. Partitions set up by third-party schemes, including Disk Manager DMDRVR.BIN and Storage Dimensions SpeedStor SSTOR.SYS are also recognized by Windows 95.

Tip

If you use FDISK to partition removable drives, such as Bernoulli Drives, you shouldn't have a problem with Windows 95 accessing them.

If you have IBM OS/2 installed on your system, you must have MS-DOS installed as well to install Windows 95. Windows 95 must run from MS-DOS if OS/2 is in your primary partition, which usually is the case when running OS/2 to take advantage of the OS/2 dual-boot feature.

As indicated earlier, Windows 95 does not recognize the NTFS system that can be set up for Windows NT. If you are running NTFS, you can install Windows 95 on a FAT partition if enough disk space is present and you use NT's multiple-boot feature to boot into Windows 95. If you do not have a FAT partition established, set up one and then perform the Windows 95 installation.

Caution

If you want to delete disk partitions on your hard disk prior to installing Windows 95, do so with caution. You may want to delete a partition to free up disk space or if you no longer need a particular partition. Make sure you have all critical data backed up and secure before deleting the partition. Keep in mind that during the partitioning stage, you will lose all the data on the hard disk and will need to reload MS-DOS on your hard drive before you can run the Windows 95 Setup.

Troubleshooting

Do I have to be an advanced user to run Windows 95 Setup?

If you are comfortable installing Windows 3.x applications, you should be able to run the Setup program without a problem. You should, however, know the kinds of hardware devices that are installed in your computer and make sure you have prepared your computer for installation, as discussed throughout this entire chapter.

What type of performance hit do I get when I run Windows 95 Setup from MS-DOS?

If you run Setup from MS-DOS and it detects Windows 3.x on your system, it recommends that you quit Setup and run it from within Windows 3.x. If you choose to run Setup from DOS, all your devices may not be detected and Setup may run slower, especially if you are installing from floppy disks.

You can use the DOS-based FDISK command to delete partitions before creating a new primary partition. You must delete partitions in the following order:

- Any non-DOS partitions
- Any logical drives in the extended DOS partition
- Any extended DOS partition
- The existing primary DOS partition

To delete a partition or logical drive, follow these steps:

1. In the FDISK Options screen, type **3**, and then press Enter. The Delete DOS Partition Or Logical DOS Drive screen appears.
2. Press the number as shown on the screen for the kind of partition you want to delete, and then press Enter.
3. Follow the directions on the screen, and repeat the steps for deleting any additional logical drives or partitions.

▶ See "Partitioning a Hard Drive," p. 549

Tip

If FDISK cannot delete a non-DOS partition, quit FDISK, delete the non-DOS partition by using the software used to create it, and then restart FDISK.

Compressed Drives

Another hard disk situation you may encounter is the use of compression applications to increase the virtual size of your hard disk. Most compression software, such as Microsoft DriveSpace or DoubleSpace, is supported by Windows 95. One point to keep in mind before you start Windows 95 Setup is to make sure you have enough free space on an uncompressed drive for a swap file. Swap files, which Windows 95 uses, can be set up on compressed drives only if you use the DriveSpace utility provided with Microsoft Plus! for Windows. If you do not have this utility, you must set up your swap file on an uncompressed drive.

> **Note**
>
> A Windows *swap file* is a special file on your hard disk that is used by Windows to store files temporarily as you work. Swap files also are known as *virtual memory* because they "virtually" increase the amount of storage area where information can be stored during a Windows operation. The information stored in swap files is lost when you leave Windows.

As a rule of thumb, you need 14M of memory on your system. To figure this amount, add the amount of physical memory you have to the amount of virtual memory you have (this is your swap file size). This gives you your total system memory. If you have 4M of memory in your system, for example, you need a swap file that is at least 10M. Free up that amount of uncompressed disk space before running Windows 95 Setup. Even if you have more than 14M of RAM on your system, you should set aside at least 5M of uncompressed disk space for a swap file in case you ever need it.

> **Note**
>
> For information on freeing up uncompressed disk space, consult your DOS documentation or the documentation that comes with your compression software. You also can pick up a copy of Que's *Special Edition Using MS-DOS 6.2* for coverage of compressed disks.

Windows 95 includes built-in support for Microsoft DriveSpace and is compatible with DoubleSpace, both of which are provided with MS-DOS 6.x. Windows 95 compression uses a 32-bit virtual device driver to give it better performance over the 16-bit product available in MS-DOS 6.x. The 32-bit driver also frees up conventional memory so MS-DOS-based applications can use it. If you currently use DoubleSpace or DriveSpace with DOS 6.x or with

Windows 3.x, you do not need to make changes to the compressed volume file (CVF) that these applications are currently using. Except for freeing up enough space for a swap file, as pointed out earlier, you do not have to change any settings or instruct Windows 95 to install over the compressed drive. It does it automatically.

Using Microsoft Plus!

Plus!

Microsoft Plus! for Windows 95 is a companion software package for Windows 95. Plus! is designed to enhance the look and performance of Windows 95-based computers and also includes an Internet connection application, the Internet Jumpstart Kit. Plus! is a CD-ROM package that users must buy separately from Windows 95. It is not included with the price of Windows 95.

Plus! includes several utilities to help you optimize and customize the look and feel of your Windows 95 configuration. Plus! consists of System Agent technology and disk utilities that help you keep your computer running at peak performance. It also contains Desktop Themes that incorporate sounds, fonts, color schemes, wallpaper, screen savers, photo-realistic icons, and animated cursors to improve the looks of your computer. The Internet Jumpstart Kit provides easy sign-up and one-button access to the Internet. It also includes a version of NCSA Mosaic by Spyglass, Inc. that enables you to use the World Wide Web (see fig. 1.9).

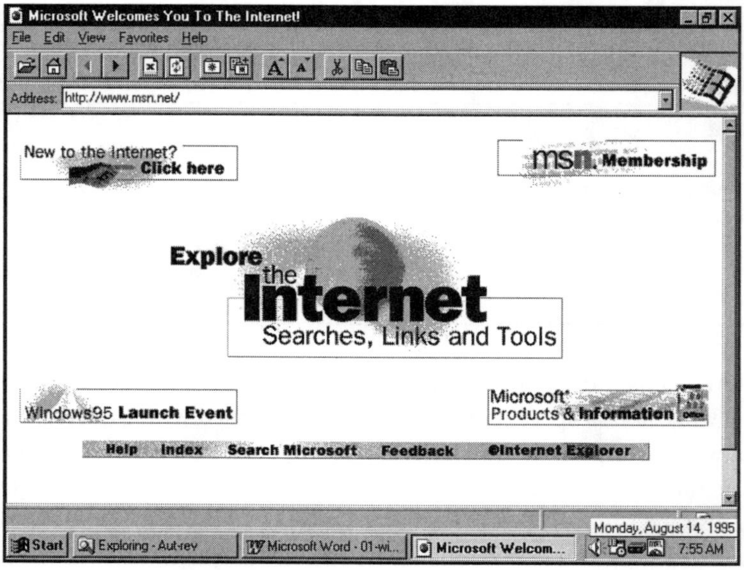

Fig. 1.9
Surf the Web with the Microsoft Plus! Internet Jumpstart Kit.

Plus! System Agent and Disk Utilities

The Microsoft Plus! System Agent and disk tools automate PC maintenance, making it faster and easier to keep a computer optimized for performance. Plus! disk utilities are designed to automatically service your computer so that you don't have to think about it. Included with the Plus! software are the following utilities:

- *DriveSpace 3*. This is an enhanced version of the DriveSpace disk compression that ships with Windows 95. DriveSpace 3 supports large compressed volumes (up to 2G) and greater compression ratios.
- *Compression Agent*. As a companion application to DriveSpace 3, the Compression Agent is an intelligent offline compression utility that automatically chooses the most appropriate compression algorithm for each file on your system. When used with the System Agent, the Compression Agent enables you to automatically compress data when your computer is not in use but still turned on (such as when you attend a meeting or go to lunch).
- *System Agent*. This is a "smart" assistant that works in the background to keep your system optimized for top performance (see fig. 1.10). While the system is idle, the System Agent works with the disk utilities to compress data to free up hard disk space and to clean up the hard disk, correcting any disk errors and defragmenting the hard disk. You also can configure the System Agent to automatically back up your files.

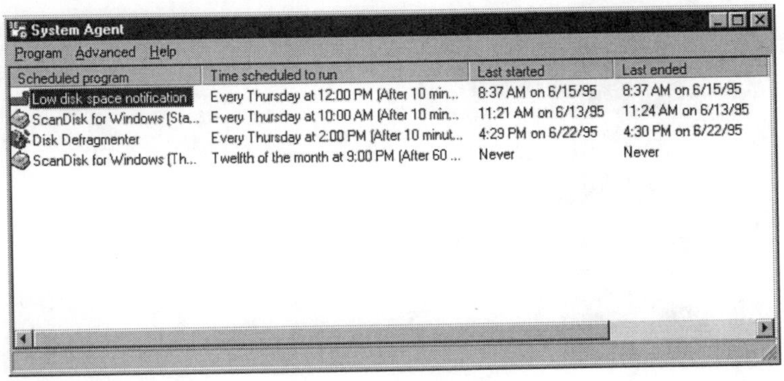

Fig. 1.10
The System Agent in Plus! helps keep your computer running at peak performance.

Microsoft Plus! Desktop Themes

The Desktop Themes bundled with Windows 95 are painfully drab, to say the least. These include themes such as Pumpkin, Eggplant, and Dessert. With the Plus! package, however, you can dress up and animate your desktop with eye-catching and interesting items. The Plus! Desktop Themes provide sounds, fonts, color schemes, wallpaper, screen savers, photo-realistic icons, and animated cursors. To hear the Desktop Theme sounds, you'll need an audio device and speakers in your system.

Each Desktop Theme sets more than 75 different desktop parameters for Windows 95, using a common theme to guide the choice of selections. The following list specifies the Desktop Themes included in Plus!:

Travel	Dangerous Creatures
Nature	Sports
Mystery	The Golden Era
The 60s USA	Inside Your PC
Leonardo da Vinci	More Windows
Science	Windows 95

An example of the background wallpaper for the Mystery Theme is shown in figure 1.11.

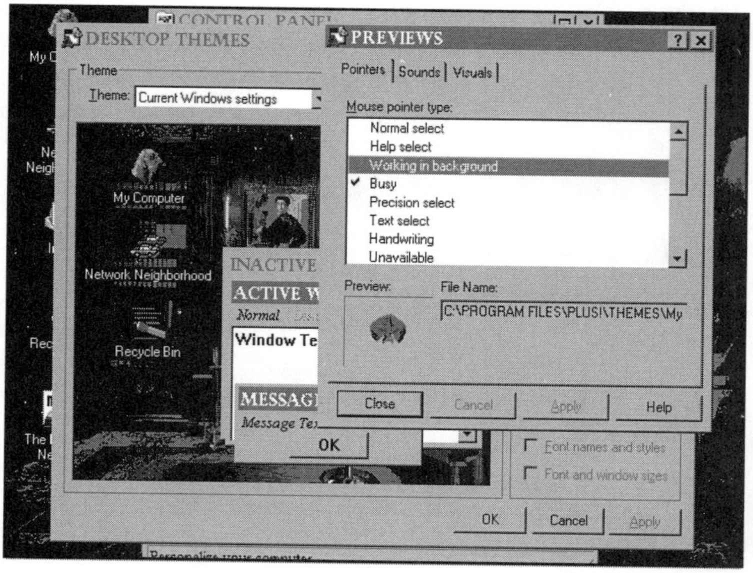

Fig. 1.11 The Mystery Desktop Theme is included with Plus!. Notice the bat icon for the mouse pointer in the Preview box.

Additional Plus! Features

Plus! includes Multimedia Pinball, a game that takes advantage of built-in multimedia support in Windows 95 to look, sound, and play like an authentic pinball game. Another feature of Plus! is a full-window drag and font smoothing utility. With full-window drag, windows are dragged as solid blocks rather than outlines. Font smoothing is performed using anti-aliasing techniques and *hinting* of fonts, making them smoother and easier to read.

▶ See "Working with Desktop Themes," p. 665

Internet Jumpstart Kit

The Plus! Internet Jumpstart Kit provides easy sign-up and one-button access to the Internet through The Microsoft Network. The Internet Jumpstart Kit includes a setup wizard to help you sign up with an Internet service provider. The Internet Explorer is Microsoft's Windows 95-based World Wide Web browser, which is a version of NCSA's popular Mosaic software. You also get an Internet mail reader for the Windows 95 Exchange mail client.

System Requirements for Plus!

Microsoft Plus! requires a Windows 95-based PC with a minimum of a 486 processor and 8M of RAM. Depending on which Desktop Themes you install, hard disk requirements vary from 25M to 40M on top of the disk space requirement for Windows 95. You also need a display that can handle at least 256 colors, such as an 8- or 16-bit video card. A sound card is recommended for Desktop Themes and Multimedia Pinball. A modem or LAN-based connection is required to access the Internet using the Internet Jumpstart Kit.

▶ See "Setting up a Microsoft Network Connection," p. 276

Tip

If you use the DriveSpace 3 compression driver, you need approximately 113K of conventional memory, which may affect DOS programs running in real mode. It should not affect applications you run under Windows 95.

Preparing for Installation

You'll find that the Windows 95 installation process goes much smoother if you do a few pre-setup tasks before you launch Windows 95 Setup. You should keep in mind that installing Windows 95 is a major upgrade to your computer. If you decide to do so, you can use Windows 95 to totally replace your existing operating system, such as DOS or Windows 3.x. This section describes many of the preliminary tasks you should do before installing Windows 95 to your system.

▶ See "Installing Microsoft Plus!," p. 658

Back Up System Files

One of the most overlooked areas of computing is backup procedures. You may be one of those lucky users who are connected to a local area network and the system administrator takes care of all your backup needs. Or, you may have been victim to a system crash in the past, so you now regularly run a system-wide backup every day.

If you are like many other users, you don't take the time to back up your data and only think about it when you lose some critical data. Before you run Windows 95 installation, however, back up all the files that you don't want to lose. It is better to assume that you will lose something as opposed to thinking you won't.

> **Tip**
>
> Besides backing up your system, you should also create a boot disk of your current system. A *boot disk* enables you to boot your system from a floppy disk in case you have a major problem during the Windows 95 installation process.
>
> To create a boot disk in Windows 3.x, place a floppy disk in the floppy drive from which your system boots, which usually is drive A. Next, in Windows File Manager choose Disk, Make System Disk, and select the Make System Disk check box. Click OK. Store this disk in a safe place and don't copy over it.
>
> In DOS you can make a system disk by using the Format command, such as **FORMAT A:/S**.

As a place to start, you should back up the files shown in the following list. Back up these files onto a tape backup system, recordable CD-ROM, network backup system, floppy disks, or other backup media. Do not back them up to your local hard disk if that's where you are installing Windows 95. You may encounter data loss at some point and may not be able to access your local drive.

- *AUTOEXEC.BAT*. As Windows 95 installs, it modifies your current AUTOEXEC.BAT file to include Windows 95-specific instructions. If a problem occurs during the Windows 95 install process, you may need to reboot into your old configuration. Having a backup of AUTOEXEC.BAT will speed up this process. You can find this file in your root directory.

- *CONFIG.SYS*. As with the AUTOEXEC.BAT file, Windows 95 modifies CONFIG.SYS during installation. A backup copy of it will save you time and headaches if you need to restore your original system. This file is found in your root directory.

- *INI Files*. If you currently run Windows 3.x, you need to make sure all your INI files are backed up. Not all INI files are stored in the same directory, so you'll need to look for them. A quick way to locate all your INI files is to run a search for ***.INI** in Windows File Manager.
- *Personal Documents*. Often overlooked during backup procedures, your personal documents, such as memos, spreadsheets, drawings, and so on, should be backed up. Any templates that you have customized should be backed up as well. In short, anything you don't want to spend time re-creating needs to be backed up.
- *Group Files*. Group files tell Windows 3.x what to display in groups in Program Manager. Group files, denoted as GRP, are in the WINDOWS directory. You can use GRP files to populate the Start menu in Windows 95.
- *Network Files*. Although Windows 95 has built-in networking support, many installations will rely on their existing network setups. Check with your system administrator to find out the files associated with the network that you should back up.

Turn Off TSRs and Time-Out Features

During the Windows 95 installation process, your system may appear at times to pause or stop working. During these times, Windows 95 is preparing system files and checking your existing system configuration. For this reason, if you have power-down features, such as those in laptops, turn off these features so that the installation process is not terminated prematurely.

You also should disable *TSR programs* (terminate-and-stay programs) and screen savers that may turn on during the install process. You need to clear out all but the necessary device drivers and batch files from memory. You can do this by remarking out (using the REMlabel) appropriate lines in your AUTOEXEC.BAT and CONFIG.SYS files (after you've backed them up, of course). Do not, however, delete settings for the following drivers: network drivers, CD-ROMs, video cards, and the mouse. You can remark out lines by starting the DOS EDIT utility, opening the appropriate file, such as AUTOEXEC.BAT, and inserting the word **REM** in front of the line you want to disable. Save the file and restart your machine for these settings to take place.

> **Caution**
>
> Do not turn off TSRs that are used for partitions or hard disk control or you may encounter problems booting your computer into the primary disk partition.

Delete the Windows Swap File

In the "Compressed Drives" section earlier in the chapter, you read that Windows 95 uses a swap file. Windows 3.x uses a temporary or permanent swap file, but Windows 95 uses a dynamic swap file. A *dynamic swap file* changes as needed by the system. Your old permanent swap file is no longer needed by Windows 95, so you can remove it for added hard disk space.

> **Caution**
>
> Before removing your permanent swap file, make sure to read the section "Determining Your Boot Configuration" later in this chapter. Here you learn that Windows 95 enables you to boot into Windows 3.x and Windows 95, if you desire. If you choose to have both operating systems on your computer, DO NOT delete the swap file from your system. You'll still need it for Windows 3.x to run.

Defragment and Check Your Hard Disk

After you back up and delete files from your hard disk, you should run a disk defragment utility to clean up your hard drive. When you run a disk defragment utility, the hard disk reorganizes files so that you get optimal performance from the drive. As you use your computer—copying, deleting, and creating files—your hard disk becomes fragmented, increasing the disk-access time. A disk defragment utility cleans up your disk and eliminates fragmented files.

Microsoft DOS 6.0 and higher includes a disk defragment utility called Defrag. To run it, exit Windows 3.x and type **DEFRAG** at the DOS prompt. Follow the instructions on-screen to optimize your hard drive. Other programs, such as Norton Utilities and PC Tools, include defragment programs as well.

During the Windows 95 installation process, Windows 95 automatically runs ScanDisk to check your drive. ScanDisk is another disk defragment utility included with Windows 95 Setup. The problem with Windows 95 running ScanDisk during installation is that if you have a problem that ScanDisk cannot fix (which occurs many times), you may have trouble cleaning up the problem in DOS. The reason is because during the initial part of the Windows 95 install (even before ScanDisk is executed), long file names are created on your hard drive. If ScanDisk reports a hard disk error it cannot fix, the Windows 95 install stops and you are returned to your old Windows 3.x or DOS setup. Then, when you try to run a disk defragment utility such as DEFRAG, to correct the problem ScanDisk found, you get an error when the software encounters the long file names that Windows 95 placed there. You have to delete those files manually if this occurs. The best solution is to defragment your hard disk before starting the Windows 95 installation process.

Another utility you should run is CHKDSK. Run CHKDSK /F from the DOS prompt to analyze and fix any surface-level problems with your hard disk. If CHKDSK encounters errors or bad files, it prompts you if you want CHKDSK to fix them or leave them for you to fix. You should let CHKDSK fix them in most cases.

Installation Options

Windows 95 provides you with several different installation options from which to choose. Depending on the configuration of your system, you have the following setup options:

- Install Windows 95 from DOS
- Upgrade Windows 3.x to Windows 95
- Choose from Custom, Typical, Portable, or Compact install
- Install Windows 95 from across a local area network
- Create a customized and automated installation
- Maintain or update an installation

The following sections briefly describe the installation options.

▶ See "Performing a Server-Based Install," p. 121

Installing from MS-DOS

If you do not have Windows 3.x installed on your system, you can install Windows 95 from DOS. Windows 95 first installs a mini-version of Windows on your system. The Windows 95 Setup program that runs is a 16-bit, Windows-based application, so it needs to use these files to execute. You cannot run install from an MS-DOS prompt from within Windows 3.x.

▶ See "Starting Windows 95 Setup from Windows 3.x," p. 40

Note

Windows 95 comes in two versions: an upgrade version and a full version. The upgrade version is used when you are upgrading from an existing version of Windows 3.x. If you only have DOS installed, you need to purchase the full version.

In cases where you do not have MS-DOS installed, such as upgrading from OS/2 or NT, you need to install DOS on partition and run the Windows 95 Setup program from the DOS partition.

Upgrading Windows 3.x to Windows 95

The preferred installation method is to install Windows 95 from Windows 3.x. When you do this, Windows 95 migrates your SYSTEM.INI, WIN.INI, and PROTOCOL.INI configuration settings and your Windows 3.x Registry associations into the Windows 95 Registry. The Registry entries in your Windows 3.x configuration are file and program associations. You need to preserve these to make your applications work under Windows 95.

Another conversion that takes place during the Windows 95 setup is that of Windows 3.x Program Manager to Windows 95 *folders*. Folders in Windows 95 have replaced program groups. You access program folders from the Start button in Windows 95.

By default, Windows 95 installs over your existing Windows 3.x. When this occurs, applications installed are automatically updated. If, however, you decide to keep your existing Windows 3.x setup, you need to reinstall all your applications under Windows 95. For more information see the section "Determining Your Boot Configuration" later in this chapter.

Choosing the Install Type

As you read Chapters 2 through 5, you can choose from four installation types: Typical, Custom, Portable, or Compact. Each of these gives you the flexibility you need to configure your computer as you like it to be set up.

The Typical Setup is designed for the average computer user who does not want to interact a great deal with the Setup routine. A Typical install performs most installation steps automatically and only asks the user to confirm the folder where Windows 95 files are installed, provide user identification and computer information, and if the user wants a startup disk created.

Caution

Do not select the Typical Setup option if you want to use the dual-boot feature. The Typical option installs the files over the default directory, which is your old Windows 3.x directory. Use the Custom installation to change the directory in which the files are installed.

Custom Setup enables you to choose many of the installation options offered by Windows 95, such as application settings, network settings, and device configurations. You also can specify the directory in which Windows 95 is installed. If you are an experienced user, use this setting to get more control over the type of utilities and applications that Windows 95 installs. In the Custom Setup, for instance, you can choose the type of applets that Windows 95 installs. In the Typical Setup, you do not have this flexibility.

The Portable Setup is designed particularly for mobile users with laptop computers. Windows 95 installs the Briefcase application and the software for direct cable connections to other computers. Briefcase is a Windows 95 application used to synchronize files that you transfer between your mobile computer and your stationary one. The Direct Cable Connections option enables you to link one computer to another through your parallel or serial ports.

If you have limited disk space on your computer, select the Compact Setup option. This Setup option installs only those files necessary to run Windows 95, which ranges from 10M to 30M of hard disk space.

How do you know which is the best Setup option for you? Table 1.3 lists the files that install during different installation procedures.

Note

You can change many of the options included during the Custom Setup. For instance, if you want to install the Windows Calculator but not the Character Map (both classified as Accessories), you can make these changes during the installation stage.

Table 1.3 Files Installed During Windows 95 Setup

File Type	Typical	Custom	Portable	Compact
Accessories	Yes	Yes	No	No
Backup	Yes	Yes	No	No
Bitmaps	Yes	Yes	Yes	No
Briefcase	No	No	Yes	No
Compression Utilities	Yes	Yes	Yes	Yes
Dial-Up Networking	Yes	Yes	Yes	No
Direct Cable Connection	Yes	Yes	Yes	No
Games	Yes	Yes	No	No
HyperTerminal	Yes	Yes	Yes	No
Multimedia Files	Yes	Yes	Yes	No
Maintenance Tools	Yes	Yes	Yes	Yes
Paint	Yes	Yes	No	No
Screen Savers	Yes	Yes	Yes	No
Windows 95 Tour	Yes	Yes	No	No
WordPad	Yes	Yes	No	No

The following items also are available, but must be selected during the installation process or added after setup:

- Internet Mail Service (you must acquire Microsoft Plus! to obtain this service)
- Microsoft Exchange
- Microsoft Fax
- The Microsoft Network
- Network Administration Tools
- Online User's Guide

Maintain or Update an Installation

If you encounter an error during setup, you can use the Safe Recovery option, which runs automatically if the Setup Wizard detects a previously unsuccessful installation. Safe Recovery skips over the problem that was previously encountered and continues with the installation.

Windows 95 gives you several ways in which to update your installation after it is installed. The applications you use to add, remove, or configure Windows 95 are part of the Control Panel options and are usually wizards. This means users of all levels can feel comfortable adding components such as printers, modems, and other options to their configurations.

This list summarizes these applications and enables you to do the following:

- *Add/Remove Programs*. Install options that you didn't install during the Setup procedure. You also can create a startup disk from this wizard.
- *Add New Hardware*. Install new hardware by starting the application. This wizard walks you through installing hardware device drivers.
- *Display*. Install and configure display drivers.
- *Printer*. Install and configure printers.
- *Modem*. Install and configure modems.
- *Fonts*. Add and remove fonts from your system. You also can view a sample of the font.
- *Mouse*. Configure and set up a new mouse.
- *Network*. Install and configure network components on your system.

Determining Your Boot Configuration

The dual-boot feature of Windows 95 enables you to keep Windows 3.x (actually, the previous version of MS-DOS) intact so you can boot into it. You may want to keep Windows 3.x on your system if a particular application is known not to work under Windows 95, such as Ocean Isle's Reachout for Windows 3.1. Another reason to keep Windows 3.x on your machine is in case you have problems with Windows 95 installing properly. In situations where Windows 95 does not work, you can boot into Windows 3.x and fix the problem or totally remove Windows 95 and restart the installation. This is much easier and quicker than rebuilding your computer system from the ground up.

Dual boots work by displaying a message on your screen during the boot process. When you see the message `Starting Windows`, you can press F4 to bypass the Windows 95 boot-up and boot into your old version of DOS. From DOS, you then can start Windows 3.x.❖

Chapter 2

Installing Windows 95 on a Desktop PC

by Rob Tidrow

You learned in Chapter 1, "Preparing to Install Windows 95," that there are steps you take to prepare your machine for Windows 95. After your machine has gone through these preparations, you are ready to start installing Windows 95. This chapter shows you how to install Windows 95 using the Typical install option you read about in Chapter 1. You are not shown how to customize your setup options in this chapter.

In this chapter, you learn how to

- Start Windows 95 Setup
- Specify the Windows 95 folder
- Create a Windows 95 startup disk
- Select online connection options
- Test your Windows 95 installation

Using Windows 95 Setup

After you prepare your computer for Windows 95, you can start the Windows 95 Setup program. Setup is located on the Windows 95 installation disks or CD-ROM. The Windows 95 Setup program uses a Setup Wizard that displays many dialog boxes and useful prompts to help you install Windows 95 on your system.

Note

You'll find valuable information contained in various text files (such as README.TXT and SETUP.TXT) on the Windows 95 CD-ROM or installation disks. Read these files for information that may pertain to your specific system hardware or software.

Taking Your System's Inventory

Before you start Setup, make a note of the following items on your system:

- Video card and monitor type
- Mouse type
- Network configuration, including network operating system (such as NetWare 3.12), protocol supported (such as TCP/IP), and mapped drive specifications (such as H)
- Printer type and port
- Modem type
- CD-ROM
- SCSI adapter, if installed
- Identification number of your Windows 95 disks or CD
- Other devices, including sound cards, scanners, and joystick

Note

The easiest way to determine your network configuration settings is to ask your system administrator for them.

Starting Windows 95 Setup from Windows 3.x

You are ready to start the Windows 95 Setup program and install Windows 95. If you do not have Windows 3.x installed, you need to install Windows 95 from DOS. For details on running Setup from DOS, see the next section, "Starting Windows 95 Setup from DOS." Use these steps to install Windows 95 from Windows 3.x:

1. Start your computer and run Windows 3.x. Make sure all applications are closed before running Setup.

2. For installation from floppy disk, insert the disk labeled `Disk #1` in the floppy drive. If you are installing from CD-ROM, place the CD-ROM in the CD drive.

3. From Program Manager, choose File, Run. In the Run dialog box, type the letter of the drive containing the disk or CD-ROM, a colon, a backslash (\), and the command **SETUP** (see fig. 2.1). The following command, for example, starts Setup from a floppy drive labeled A:

   ```
   A:\SETUP
   ```

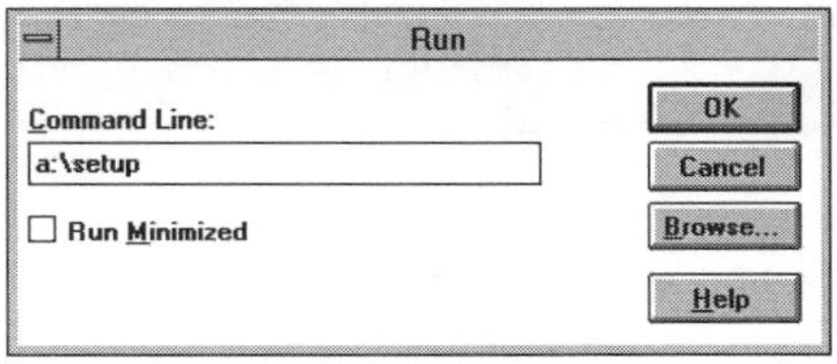

Fig. 2.1
From the Run dialog box in Windows 3.x, you can start the Windows 95 Setup program.

4. Click OK. Setup starts and the Windows 95 Installation Wizard initializes and begins installing Windows 95. See the section "Collecting Setup Information" for the next step in the Windows 95 installation process.

Starting Windows 95 Setup from DOS

To start Windows 95 Setup from DOS, use the following steps:

1. Start your computer.

2. For installation from floppy disk, insert the disk labeled `Disk #1` in the floppy drive. If you are installing from CD-ROM, place the CD-ROM in the CD drive.

3. At the DOS command prompt, type the letter of the drive that contains the setup disks, a backslash (\), and the command **SETUP** (see fig. 2.2). The following command, for instance, starts Windows 95 Setup from a floppy disk labeled A:

   ```
   C:\A:\SETUP
   ```

4. Press Enter. Setup starts and the Windows 95 Installation Wizard initializes and begins installing Windows 95.

Fig. 2.2
You can start Windows 95 Setup from the DOS prompt using the SETUP command.

Using Special Setup Switches

Windows 95 Setup is designed to be used by any level user. No system, however, can satisfy every user's needs and special configurations. Windows 95 includes command-line switches to control the installation process. To use these switches, add them to the end of the SETUP command line, such as the following:

```
A:\SETUP /?
```

The preceding switch tells Windows 95 Setup to display help on using the command-line switches.

The following describes each of the switches you can type to customize the Setup procedure:

- **/?**. Displays help on using Setup switches. Shows syntax of each switch.
- **/ih**. Instructs Setup to run ScanDisk in the foreground so that you can see the results. Use this switch if the system stalls during the ScanDisk check or if an error results.
- **/nostart**. Directs Setup to copy only the required Windows 3.x DLL (Dynamic Link Library) used by Windows 95 Setup. After Setup copies these files, it exits to DOS without installing Windows 95.
- **/iL**. Instructs Setup to load the Logitech mouse driver, if you have a Logitech Series C mouse.
- **/iq**. Directs Setup to bypass the ScanDisk quick check when running Setup from DOS. Use this switch if you use compression software other than DriveSpace or DoubleSpace.

- **/is**. Directs Setup to bypass the ScanDisk quick check when running Setup from Windows 3.x. Use this switch if you use compression software other than DriveSpace or DoubleSpace.
- ***script_file***. Directs Setup to use custom script files you create to automatically install Windows 95.
- **/d**. Directs Setup not to use your existing version of Windows 3.x during the first part of Setup. Use /d when you experience problems with Setup that are due to Windows 3.x files missing or damaged.
- **/C**. Directs Windows 95 Setup not to load the SmartDrive disk cache.
- **/id**. Directs Setup to bypass the checking of required minimum disk space to install Windows 95. Use this switch if a previous install of Windows 95 failed but Setup began copying files to your hard disk. This way, you do not get an "Out of Disk Space" error during your next attempt of running Setup.
- **/t:*tempdir***. Specifies the directory in which Setup is to copy its temporary files. This directory must already exist, but any existing files in the directory are deleted after Setup finishes installing Windows 95.

Collecting Setup Information

After you start Setup, a Welcome screen appears (see fig. 2.3), telling you that Windows 95 is ready to start installing Windows 95 and that the process may take 30 to 60 minutes to complete. Click OK.

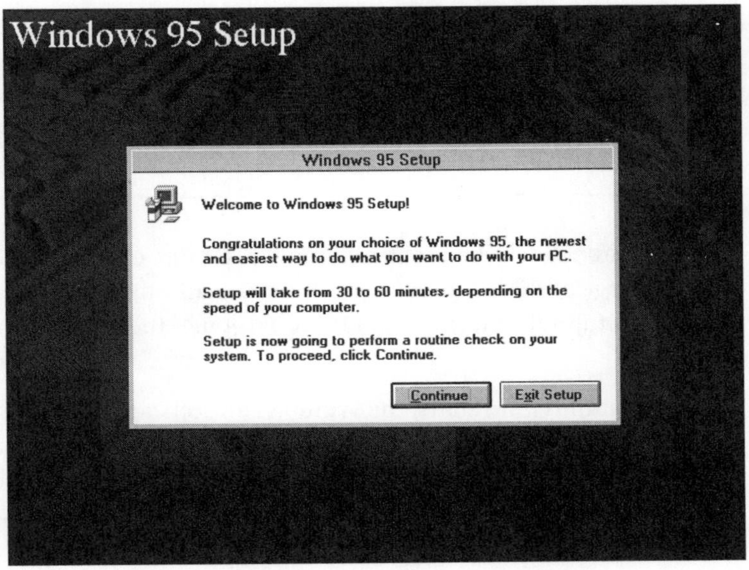

Fig. 2.3
The initial Windows 95 Setup screen tells you how long it typically takes to install Windows 95.

Windows 95 Setup automatically gathers most of the information it needs during the installation process. Some of the items you need to provide manually include the directory name in which to install Windows 95 and the type of Setup you want to perform. Windows 95 by default installs into your current directory of Windows 3.x if it is installed, but you can change this directory if you want to run Windows 95 and your current Windows 3.x installation.

Tip

Press F3 or, if available, the Cancel button to exit Setup anytime.

Use the following steps to continue installing Windows 95:

1. Click Continue on the Setup Welcome screen. Windows 95 checks your system (see fig. 2.4) for available disk space, possible hard disk problems, and other system setting information.

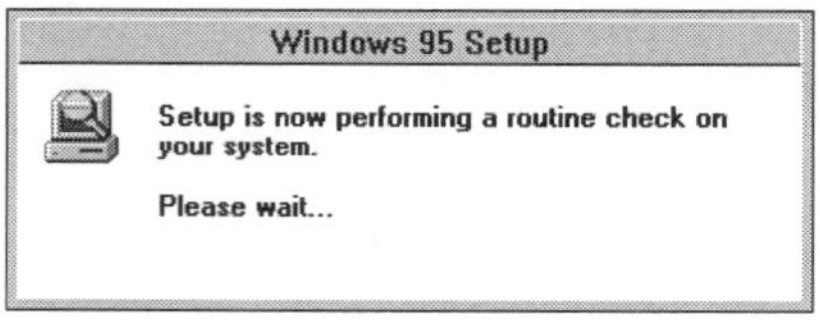

Fig. 2.4
When you first start installing Windows 95, Setup checks your system for hard disk problems and disk space.

Caution

If Setup detects a problem with your system, such as a hard disk problem, an error message appears. Be sure to read the message and perform the recommended actions. Click OK to leave Windows 95 Setup and return to DOS or Windows 3.x. Setup does not let you continue with the installation process if an error is found.

2. If Setup does not detect a problem during its routine check, it begins the next stage of the installation process automatically. This stage prepares the Setup Wizard, which guides you through the rest of the installation.

3. After the Setup Wizard starts, the Windows 95 Software License Agreement appears, as shown in figure 2.5. Read the license agreement and click Yes if you accept the terms of the agreement. If you do not accept the terms, click No and Setup exits, ending the installation process. You must accept the terms of the agreement to install Windows 95.

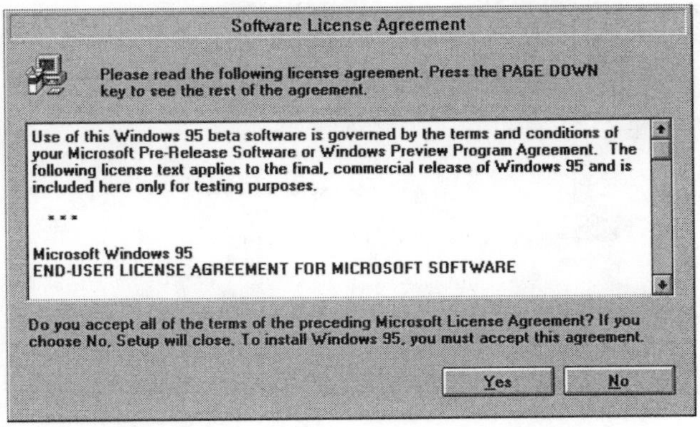

Fig. 2.5
Read and accept the terms of the Software License Agreement to continue installing Windows 95.

As mentioned earlier, you should close all applications before running Setup. If you do not, a warning message appears advising you to do so (see fig. 2.6).

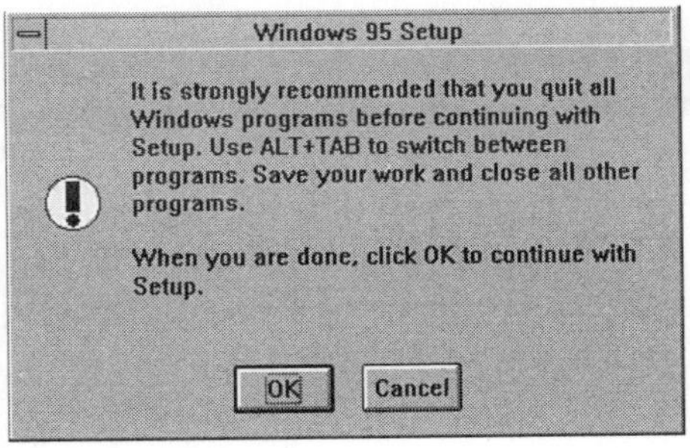

Fig. 2.6
In case you have another Windows application running, Setup displays a message telling you to exit from it before continuing with the installation.

To close any application, follow these steps:

1. Press Alt+Tab to task switch to the open application.
2. Use that application's menu to close it.
3. Continue until all applications are closed. Do not close Program Manager.
4. Click OK when you are ready to continue with Setup.

Starting the Windows 95 Setup Wizard

The Windows 95 Setup Wizard appears on-screen. This is your hands-on guide to installing Windows 95 on your system. The wizard screen (see fig. 2.7) lists the three major parts of the Windows 95 setup procedure:

- Collecting information about your computer
- Copying Windows 95 files to your computer
- Restarting your computer and finishing setup

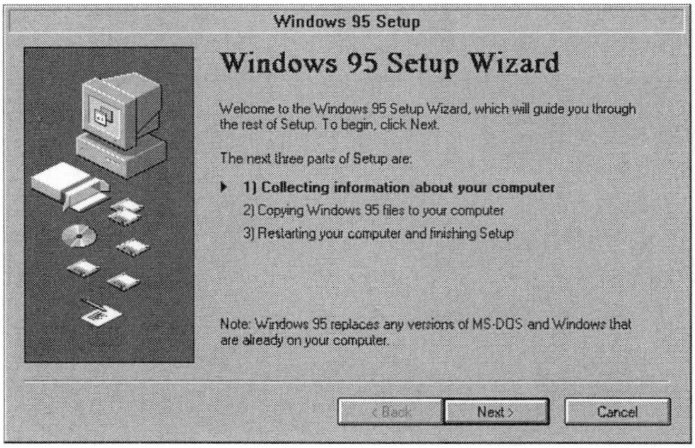

Fig. 2.7
The Setup Wizard helps you navigate through the Windows 95 installation process.

Each of these parts is described in the following sections.

Click Next to advance to the next wizard screen. Click Cancel to exit Setup.

Tip

Click Back any time to return to the previous wizard step.

The Choose Directory screen appears (see fig. 2.8). This is where you must decide to keep or install over a previous version of Windows or DOS. To install over your current version of Windows, select the C:\WINDOWS option and click Next. The directory in which your current version of Windows is installed may differ from the one shown in the figure 2.8.

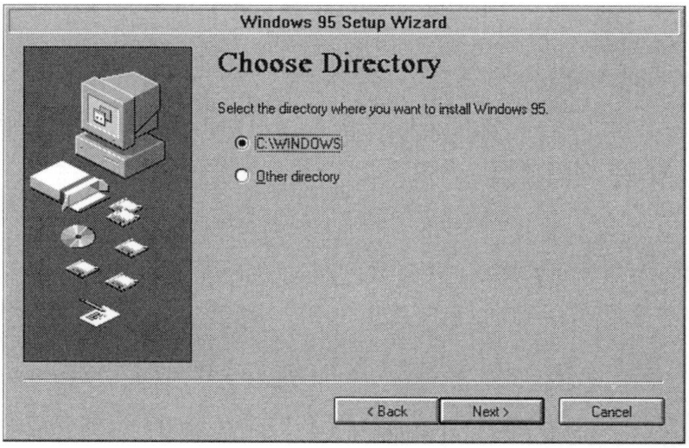

Fig. 2.8
You can tell Windows 95 to install into a new directory, or copy over your previous version.

If you want to install Windows 95 into a separate directory and keep your previous version of Windows 3.x, select the Other Directory radio button; click Next.

> **Note**
>
> You need to decide if you want to install Windows 95 over your existing version of Windows. If you decide to keep both versions of Windows on your machine, then you need to reinstall all your applications under Windows 95. The advantage is that you have a fail-safe mechanism if Windows 95 does not work properly on your machine. You can move back to Windows 3.x immediately. Once you test out your new Windows 95 installation, delete your old Windows 3.x files, including the applications installed under Windows 3.x.
>
> On the other hand, if you install over your previous version of Windows, your applications work as soon as you install Windows 95. Also, you do not need as much free disk space to start Windows 95 Setup when upgrading.

If you choose to install Windows 95 to a separate directory, the Change Directory screen appears (see fig. 2.9). This is where you name the directory for Windows 95. Although Setup advises that only advanced users and system administrators modify this directory, you must change the directory name to retain your previous version of Windows.

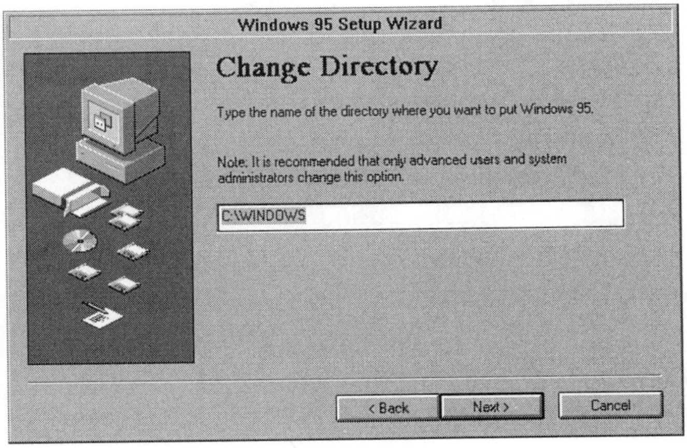

Fig. 2.9
You must give a new directory name in which to install Windows 95 if you want to keep your previous version of Windows.

In the text box, type the new directory name, such as **C:\WIN95**. The new name must be unique and no more than eight characters. Click Next when this box is filled out. At this point, Setup displays a screen warning you that you must reinstall all your applications.

> **Note**
>
> If you do not choose to install to a new Windows directory, Setup bypasses the preceding step and displays the Preparing Directory screen instead.

Click Yes to continue or No to return to the Change Directory screen. The Preparing Directory screen appears. The Preparing Directory screen informs you Windows 95 is creating your new directory or preparing your existing Windows 3.x directory for Windows 95.

After the directory is prepared, the Setup Options screen appears (see fig. 2.10), in which you select the type of installation you want to perform. To setup Windows 95 on a computer that has adequate hard disk space (35M to 50M), select the Typical option. The Typical install assumes that you do not want to customize the components that Windows 95 installs. As you see in the section called "Selecting Windows Components," you can modify the options that install, although it is not necessary to do so with the Typical install type.

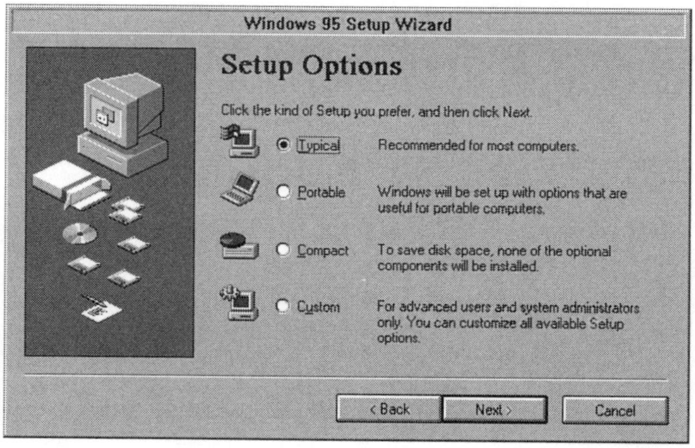

Fig. 2.10
From the Setup Options screen, you can select the type of installation the Windows 95 Setup program performs.

▶ See "Selecting Windows Components," p. 83

▶ See " Selecting Custom Install Options," p. 107

Click Next when you are ready.

When the User Information screen appears (see fig. 2.11), enter your name and company name. Company name is optional, but you must fill in a user name. Click Next.

Caution

As a word of caution, the name and company name you put here are permanent. You cannot change them unless you reinstall Windows 95. Don't use names that you may want to change later. Cute names grow tiresome after awhile.

The next screen, the Product Information screen, is used to input the serial number of your Windows 95 disks (see fig. 2.12). This number is unique to your disks and is used for product support and for registering your software with Microsoft Corporation. You must input this number to successfully install Windows 95.

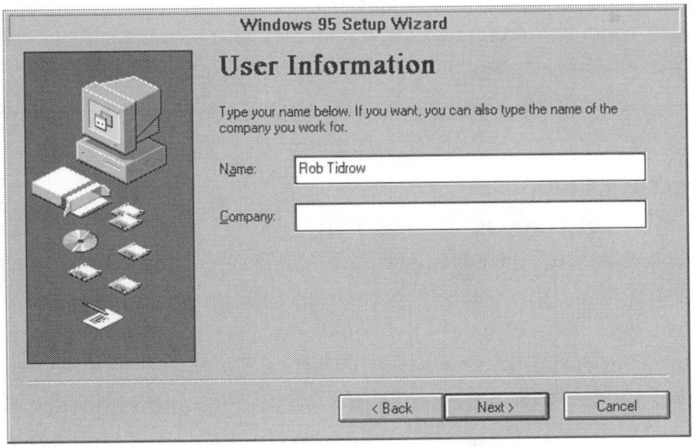

Fig. 2.11
Fill in your name and company name in the User Information screen.

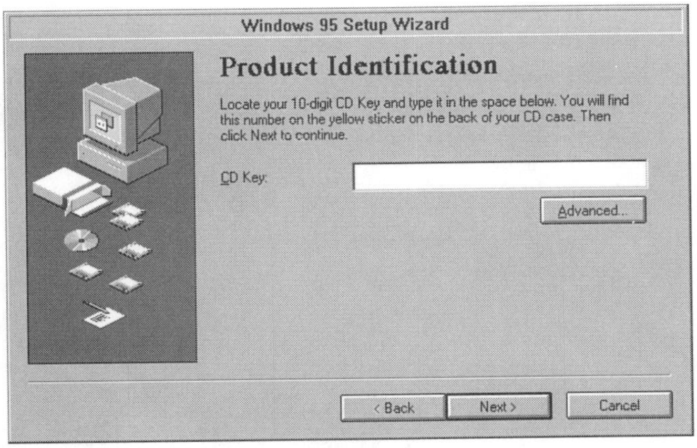

Fig. 2.12
This screen prompts you for the product identification of your Windows 95 disks or CD-ROM discs.

You find this information on your disks or on a yellow sticker on the back of your CD case. It might also be on some paperwork that came with your disks or computer. Click Next after you enter the ID.

> **Note**
>
> Select the Advance button on the Product Information screen if you are installing Windows 95 in a networked environment and have purchased a group license. See Chapter 5, "Installing Windows 95 over a Network," for more information.

Troubleshooting

Do I need to reinstall my programs when I install Windows 95?

Windows 95 picks up program settings when you upgrade an existing version of Windows or Windows for Workgroups. If Windows 95 is installed in a separate directory, all Windows-based programs need to be reinstalled.

Analyzing Your Computer

After you enter your Product ID, the Setup Wizard is ready to check your computer's hardware. In figure 2.13, the Analyzing Your Computer screen appears, displaying the choices from which to select specific hardware devices. Regardless of the choices shown, Windows 95 will autodetect the devices in your computer. In this example, the only choice is Network Adapter. If you have a network interface card in your system and you want Windows 95 to search for and configure it, make sure this option is selected. Depending on your system, other options may appear in this screen. Select the appropriate ones for your system.

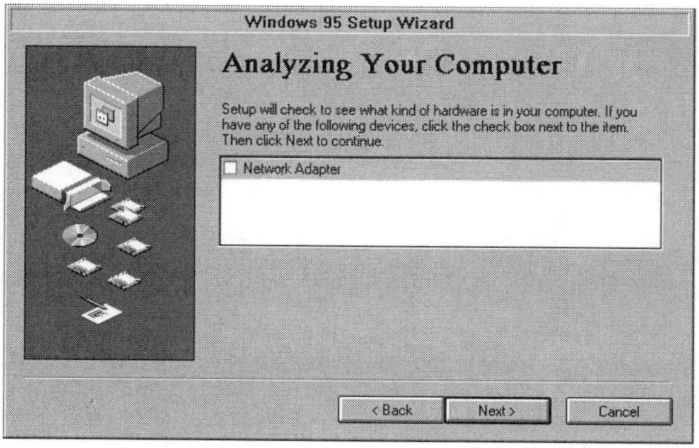

Fig. 2.13 The Analyzing Your Computer screen shows some of the devices Windows will detect during Setup.

Click Next to have Windows 95 analyze your system. This process may take a few minutes to complete. Often, the on-screen progress bar (which appears at the bottom of your screen) moves rapidly through the first 90 percent of the process and then seems to quit. This is normal and you should not reboot your PC at this point. Give Setup some time to complete this part. It's a good practice to let it sit for 20 minutes before you attempt to recover your computer.

If, after a long time of inactivity (watch your hard drive light on the front of the computer for activity), your system seems to have crashed, reboot the system by turning off your computer, waiting 10 seconds, and restarting it. Start Setup again and use the Smart Recovery program, which starts automatically if Setup can salvage anything from the previous installation attempt. If Smart Recovery does not start automatically, you need to restart Setup by running SETUP.EXE from Windows 3.x or MS-DOS.

Troubleshooting

I was running Setup and my machine crashed. Do I have to run Setup from the beginning again?

The best answer for this is yes, you should restart Setup from the beginning and install all the Windows 95 files again. This is because some files may have become corrupted during the system crash. On the other hand, Windows 95 Setup includes a Smart Recovery mechanism that maintains a log file during Setup. If Setup crashes, the last entry in the Setup log identifies where Windows needs to start from to resume installation.

Getting Connected

Windows 95 provides built-in support for many electronic and online services, including e-mail (using Microsoft Mail), The Microsoft Network, and Microsoft Fax services. After the Setup Wizard analyzes your system, you need to select the types of services you would like Setup to automatically configure. You can select any combination of choices, or pick none. If you are not sure if you want to install one of these choices, you can bypass it now and install it manually after Windows 95 is installed by using Add/Remove Programs in Control Panel.

The Get Connected screen (see fig. 2.14) enables you to select the service or connection you want Setup to install automatically.

If you don't read the Setup Wizard screen for this option closely, you may overlook an important point. If you install one or more of the Get Connected options, Windows 95 automatically installs Microsoft Exchange. Exchange is Microsoft's new electronic mail and communications client that acts as a universal inbox and outbox for your e-mail and faxes.

▶ See "The First Step: Adding a Network Configuration," p. 300

Exchange requires 4.6M of hard disk space by itself. If you install all three Get Connected options, the total hard disk space required is over 12M. You also need at least 8M of RAM to run Exchange and Microsoft Fax. The Microsoft

Network also demands a large amount of memory. You should have at least 8M minimum and 16M recommended.

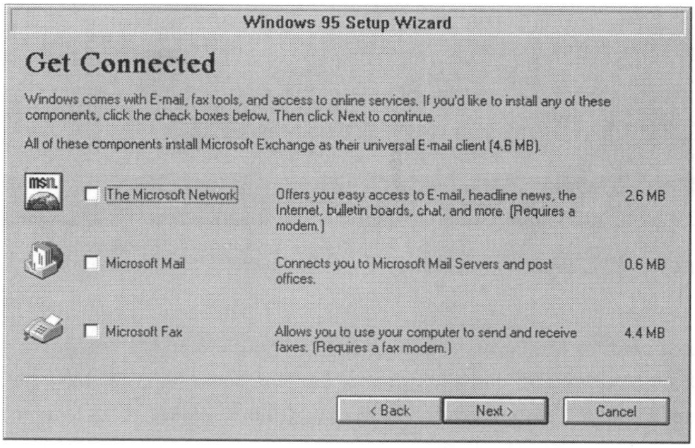

Fig. 2.14
If you want Setup to establish your Microsoft Fax, Microsoft Mail, or The Microsoft Network connections, select those choices here.

After you make your choices, click Next.

Selecting Windows Components

The Setup Wizard gives you a choice to modify the list of components to install on your system. The default setting installs the most common Windows 95 components, but you can change the list by selecting the Show Me the List of Components So I Can Choose option (see fig. 2.15).

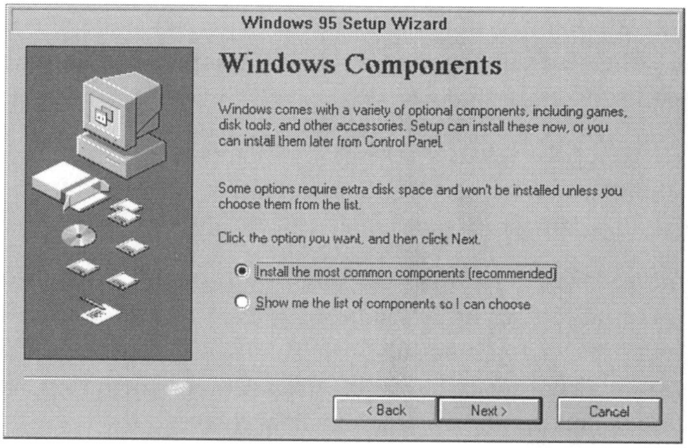

Fig. 2.15
Although you select the Typical install type, Windows 95 Setup gives you the option of selecting components now.

For most users, the default list of components is recommended, especially if you are a new user and are not familiar with Windows 95 components, many of which are available in previous versions of Windows. If you change your mind later about an option, you can add additional components or remove any by using Add/Remove Programs in Control Panel after Windows 95 is installed. Click Next to continue with Setup. The Startup Disk screen appears.

▶ See " Understanding the Custom Install Process," p. 105

> **Note**
>
> If you're more advanced and want to choose the specific components, click the second choice from the list and click Next. The Select Components screen appears (see fig. 2.16). This screen and its options are discussed in Chapter 4, "Using Custom Installation Options."

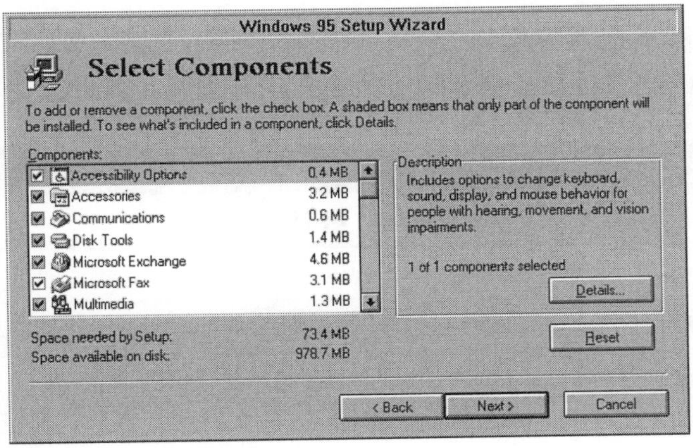

Fig. 2.16
You can select the individual components Setup installs from this screen.

Creating a Startup Disk

Setup lets you create a startup disk. Regardless of how well you think the Windows 95 Setup program is going, *always* choose to make a startup disk. The startup disk is your life preserver in case you experience problems with Windows 95 after it's installed. By taking a few minutes now and using one floppy disk, you insure yourself against potential problems.

You'll need one floppy disk to reformat when the startup disk is created. Because you will lose all the data on this disk, make sure it does not contain anything important. The floppy disk must be one for the floppy drive that your PC can boot from, which is drive A.

> **Note**
>
> Many older PCs have 5 1/4-inch floppy disk drives as drive A. Many users, however, have abandoned the use of 5 1/4-inch floppy disks. If your drive A is the 5 1/4-inch drive, you must use this size floppy disk as your startup disk. You cannot change Setup to create a startup disk on drive B.

The startup disk is a bootable floppy disk that stores several system files (more than 1.2M) on it. In case you need to use the startup disk, place it in your floppy drive and reboot your machine. You are presented with an MS-DOS command line that provides utilities and maintenance instructions to help you recover your installation. Appendix B, "Troubleshooting Windows 95," discusses how to use the startup disk in more detail.

Note

The startup disk has limitations. It cannot, for instance, be used to provide access to a CD-ROM device or to a network connection. You need to fix any problems associated with your installation to recover from these problems.

The files that Setup copies to the startup disk are shown in table 2.1.

Table 2.1 Startup Disk Files

Name	Description of File
ATTRIB.EXE	Sets file attributes, such as hidden and read-only
CHKDSK.EXE	Checks a disk and displays a status report
COMMAND.COM	Starts a new copy of the Windows Command Interpreter, which is the primary operating system file for MS-DOS
DEBUG.EXE	Runs Debug, a testing and editing tool program
DRVSPACE.BIN	DriveSpace disk-compression utility
EBD.SYS	Utility for the startup disk
EDIT.COM	Text editor in MS-DOS
FDISK.EXE	Configures a hard disk for use with MS-DOS
FORMAT.COM	Formats a hard disk or floppy disk for use with MS-DOS
IO.SYS	Core operating system file
MSDOS.SYS	Core operating system file
REGEDIT.EXE	Starts the Registry Editor
SCANDISK.EXE	Starts ScanDisk

Name	Description of File
SCANDISK.INI	Stores system configuration settings for ScanDisk
SYS.COM	Copies MS-DOS system files and command interpreter to a disk you specify
UNINSTAL.EXE	Starts utility for recovering deleted files

A few other files that you may want to copy to the startup disk after Windows 95 is installed include AUTOEXEC.BAT, CONFIG.SYS, WIN.INI, and SYSTEM.INI. Other INI files may also come in handy as well. These files are ones that you should already have backed up in Chapter 1, "Preparing to Install Windows 95."

To instruct Setup to create a startup disk, make sure the Yes, I Want a Startup Disk (Recommended) choice in the Startup Disk screen is selected and click Next.

Troubleshooting

I want to uninstall Windows 95 but I didn't make a startup disk. What do I do now?

You can do one of two things. The suggested choice is to make a startup disk by selecting Start, Control Panel, and double-clicking the Add/Remove Programs icon. Click the Startup Disk tab and click the Create Disk button. You need one floppy disk that works in your A: drive.

The second choice is to use the following steps:

1. Boot from an MS-DOS boot disk.

2. Enter the following at the A: prompt

C:\WINDOWS\COMMAND\UNINSTALL.EXE

In the preceding syntax, C is the drive letter where Windows 95 is installed, and \WINDOWS is the name of your Windows 95 folder.

Copying Files

Setup has gathered enough information to begin copying files to your hard disk. In figure 2.17, Setup displays a message telling you that it is ready to start copying the files. Click Next to continue.

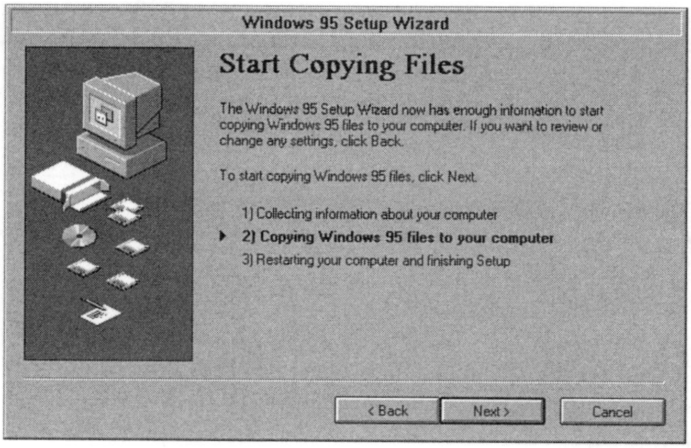

Fig. 2.17
The moment you've been waiting for! Setup starts copying files to your system.

Setup begins copying files to your hard disk and displays a meter showing the progress of the action. If you indicated to create a startup disk, Setup instructs you to insert this disk when the progress meter hits about 20 percent. Insert the floppy disk and click OK. After the startup disk is created, Setup displays a message telling you to remove the floppy disk from the drive. Do this now and store it in a safe place.

Tip

To exit from Setup at any time, click the Exit button or press F3. This returns you to Windows 3.x or DOS, depending on where you started Setup. If you exit Setup while Windows 95 copies files to your system, Windows 95 may or may not delete them from your system. In many cases, Windows 95 leaves the files on your system so that if you decide to restart the Setup program later, it does not have to recopy those files.

Setup continues installing Windows 95. As it's copying files, Windows displays screens describing some key features of Windows 95. Some of these are shown in figures 2.18 and 2.19.

Finishing Setup

When the Setup files finish copying onto your system, Setup begins the third and final phase of installation: Finishing Setup. This part restarts your computer and configures your hardware and software to work with Windows 95.

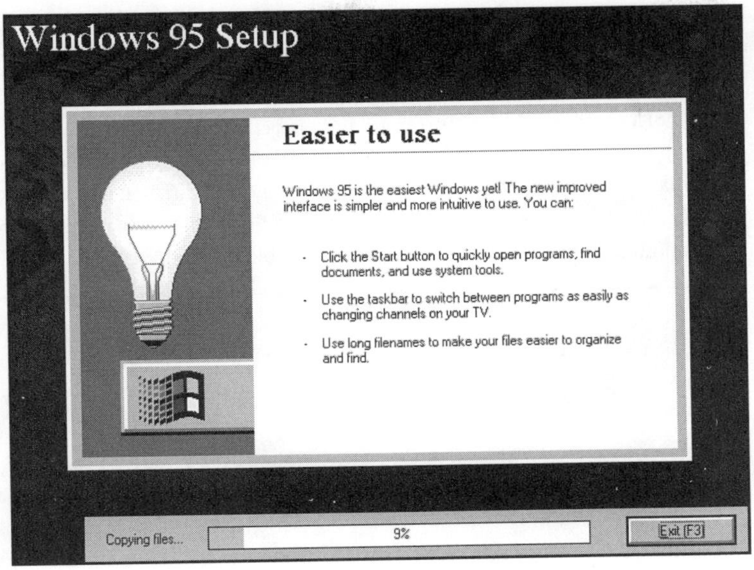

Fig. 2.18
To get a quick idea of what is in store for you with Windows 95, read the messages that flash on-screen during installation.

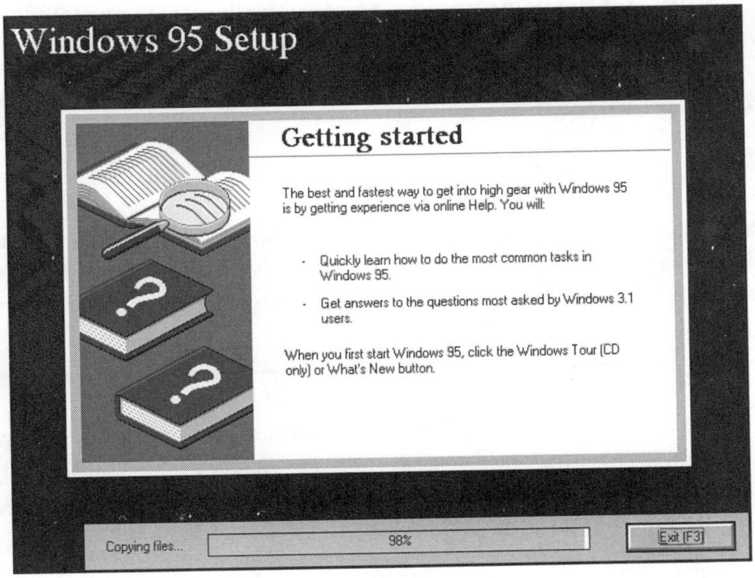

Fig. 2.19
Another helpful screen explains how to get help in Windows.

Some of the tasks that Windows 95 performs during this final stage include the following:

- Adds a new system file (IO.SYS) to replace the old MS-DOS IO.SYS and MSDOS.SYS. These old files are renamed IO.DOS and MSDOS.DOS.

> **Note**
>
> Even though you've made it to this point in the installation process, you still are not "home free." Many installation errors occur after the Windows 95 Setup restarts your computer and starts configuring your system. One of the primary problems occurs when the Plug and Play configuration part of Windows 95 tries to locate incompatible devices. If you experience any problems during this stage, reference Appendix B, "Troubleshooting Windows 95."

- Copies SYSTEM.DAT to SYSTEM.DA0 and SYSTEM.NEW to SYSTEM.DAT. This is the primary system database that the Registry reads.
- Combines all the virtual device drivers (VxDs) to create VMM32.VXD, which is the 32-bit virtual device driver.
- Renames ARIAL.WIN, USER32.TMP, and LOGO.SYS files used by Setup.

Click Finish to finish setting up Windows 95. This last stage typically takes several minutes to complete.

> **Note**
>
> If your PC does not restart after a reasonable time, such as 20 minutes or more, reboot your system manually. You may be able to boot into Windows 95. If not, you may be able to boot into Windows 95 in Safe Mode, which you select from a menu that automatically displays during the boot process if Windows 95 cannot completely load. See Appendix B, "Troubleshooting Windows 95," if you have problems finishing this stage of Setup.

After your computer restarts and everything functions properly, Windows 95 starts and runs your AUTOEXEC.BAT and CONFIG.SYS files. You'll see the Windows 95 opening screen flash for a few seconds, and then the DOS screen appears. You'll see the following message in DOS:

```
Please wait while Setup updates your configuration files.
This may take a few minutes...
```

Configuring Run-Once Options

After the configuration files are updated, Windows 95 reappears and runs through setting Run-Once options. These options include PCMCIA and MIDI devices, printers, Time Zone, Microsoft Exchange, Windows Help, programs on the Start menu, and the Control Panel setting. Other hardware devices also can be configured at this point. A screen display lists these options as they are being set up.

Troubleshooting

I can't boot into Windows. What can I do?

Reboot your computer and press F8 to start the Startup menu in MS-DOS. Select the Safe Mode option to start Windows 95 in Safe Mode. Now you can boot into Windows and diagnose the problem. In many cases, you may have a device driver conflict. To see if you do, select Start, Settings, Control Panel, and double-click on the System icon. Click on the Device Manager tab and review the device settings listed. If you see a big red X next to a device, select it and click on the Remove button. Click OK. You'll need to reboot your machine to see if this fixes your problem. If this doesn't work, review Appendix B, "Troubleshooting Windows 95."

Many of the items on the list configure automatically, such as the Control Panel and programs on the Start menu. Some, however, require user interaction. When Setup runs the Time Zone option, for instance, you must select the time zone in which you live (see fig. 2.20). Click the list on the Time Zone tab and select your time zone. To modify the time and date, click the Date & Time tab. Click Apply to save these settings, then click Close when you are finished.

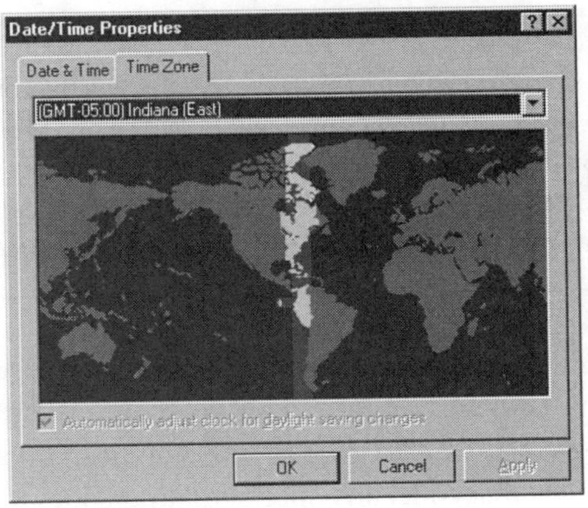

Fig. 2.20
During the Run-Once stage, you can set your time zone and the correct time and date.

Configuring Microsoft Exchange

Next, Setup configures Microsoft Exchange on your system. If you did not select a choice in the Get Connected screen earlier (see "Getting Connected" earlier in this chapter), Setup does not perform this task. You can proceed to the "Starting Windows 95" section.

Setup displays the Inbox Setup Wizard, which guides you through setting up Microsoft Exchange's universal mail inbox. This box is also used to receive e-mail and faxes, and to connect to The Microsoft Network, if you selected this option earlier. Use the following steps to configure Exchange:

1. If you've never used Exchange, choose No when the Setup Wizard asks if you have used Exchange before. Otherwise, click Yes. Click Next.

2. In the next screen, you are prompted to select the services you want to use with Exchange. The services listed include only those you select in the Get Connect screen earlier. These choices include:

    - Microsoft Mail
    - Microsoft Fax
    - Microsoft Online Network

3. By default, the items listed are selected, including the Use the Following Information Services radio button. If you want Setup to automatically configure these services (which is recommended for most users), click Next.

> **Note**
>
> If you are an advanced user, or if you need to modify the configuration of the services, select the Manually Configure Information Services option. This enables you to change, among other settings, the Exchange profile name, which by default is set as MSEXCHANGE. Any configuration setting can be changed later by using the Add/Remove Program option in Control Panel.

▶ See "Adding Exchange After Installing Windows 95," p. 206

4. When you let Setup automatically configure Exchange, the Location Information dialog box appears. This box configures the way in which your phone calls are dialed. In this box, you need to set the country in which you live, area code, any special dialing codes to get an outside number (such as 9), and the type of phone system you use, either tone or pulse. Click OK when you have this dialog box filled out.

5. The next Inbox Setup Wizard screen that appears sets up your Microsoft Fax connection, if this is one of the selections you picked earlier. You are given two choices when installing Microsoft Fax. First, you can set up Fax so that it runs from your local computer. Click the Modem Connected To My Computer option to use Fax only from your computer.

Second, you can set up Microsoft Fax so that others can share it across a network. To do this, you must connect a fax modem to a networked computer and use it as a fax server.

For this chapter, make sure the option that sets up your fax modem on a single computer is selected. Click Next.

▶ See "Setting Up a Fax Server," p. 259

Detecting a New Modem

In the Install New Modem Wizard, you need to configure your modem to work with Windows 95. Before working through the Install New Modem Wizard, make sure your fax modem is attached to your computer and that it is turned on and connected to a phone line. If you need to install an internal modem, skip over this section and finish Setup first. Then install your modem (you'll need to shut down your computer to do this) and start the Add Hardware option in Control Panel to configure the modem. Chapter 28, "Configuring Modems" guides you through setting up and configuring a modem.

If your modem is turned on and ready to be configured now, use the Install New Modem Wizard. Unless you want to select your modem manually, click Next. If you want to specify your modem type, click the Don't Detect My Modem; I Will Select It From a List option and click Next.

Installing Your Printer

After Setup establishes Exchange and other online connections, it configures the printers that are connected to your computer. If you do not want to install a printer now, you can set one up later by selecting the Printers folder after choosing Start, Settings. Double-click the Add Printer icon to start the Add Printer Wizard.

During Setup, you need to specify whether the printer is located locally or on a network. You also need to tell Windows 95 Setup the manufacturer of the printer, such as Hewlett-Packard, and the printer name, such as HP LaserJet IIIP. Click Next to have Setup install the printer drivers on your system. If Setup detects a driver from a previous installation, you can elect to keep it or use an updated one from Windows 95. Select the option and then click Next. Setup next asks if you plan to print from from MS-DOS based programs. Select Yes or No as necessary.

▶ See " Using the Add Printer Wizard," p. 606

The next screen prompts you for the port or connection to which your printer attaches. Select the appropriate connection and click Next. Windows asks you to name the printer, giving you a default name such as HP LaserJet IIIP. Keep or change this name as necessary and click Next.

Note

If you are on a network and will be printing to a network printer, you can instruct Windows 95 to print to a queue name versus a printer port.

Setup then displays a screen that asks if you want to print a test page on your printer. If your printer is set up to your machine or network, it's a good idea to do this. This way Setup can diagnose any problems you may have with your printer now. Click Finish. After your text page prints and you respond that everything is fine, tell Setup that the page printed correctly.

Congratulations! Setup is finished setting up Windows 95.

Starting Windows 95

After Setup installs Windows 95 and configures Exchange, your printer, and other options, Windows 95 starts. Figure 2.21 shows the Windows 95 Welcome screen that includes helpful suggestions for navigating Windows 95.

Tip

If you do not want to see this screen the next time you boot Windows 95, clear the Show This Welcome screen next time you start Windows option on the Welcome dialog box. To show this screen again, double-click the Welcome application in the Windows 95 folder in Windows Explorer.

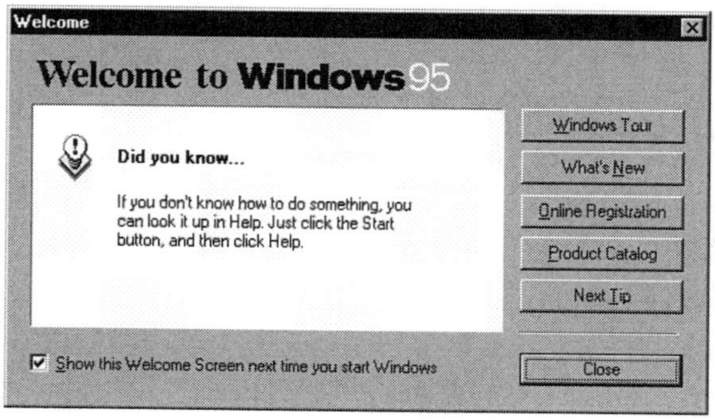

Fig. 2.21
Welcome to Windows 95!

Testing Windows 95 Setup

Before you use Windows 95 for the first item, test to see if it is properly installed. Shut down Windows and restart it by clicking the Start button at the bottom of the screen (this is called the Taskbar) and select Shut Down. The Shut Down Windows dialog box appears (see fig. 2.22). Make sure the Shut Down the Computer? option is selected; click Yes. This begins the Windows 95 shut down procedure, which you must do whenever you want to exit Windows 95.

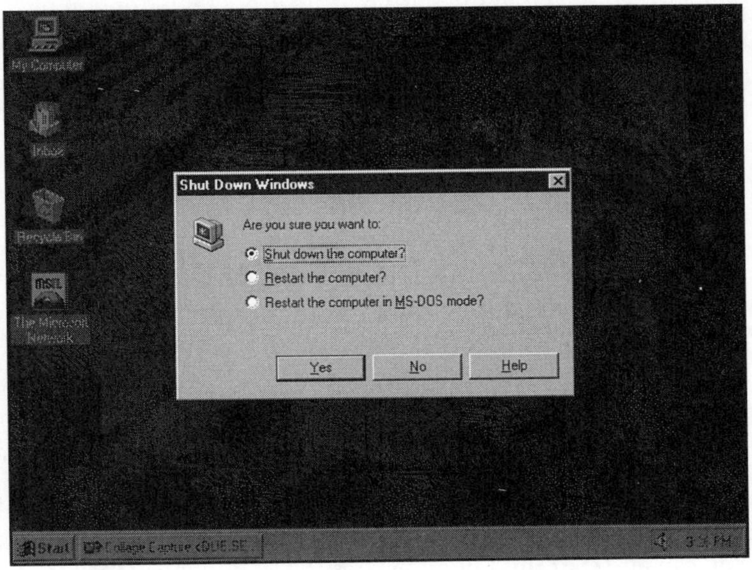

Fig. 2.22
The Shut Down utility is a new feature in Windows 95.

When a message appears on your screen telling you it's OK to turn off your machine, press the reset button on your computer. As your PC reboots, watch the screen to see if you notice any errors. If Windows 95 starts, your system probably works fine and you can start using Windows 95.

If it doesn't start or if you get a DOS screen, your setup has encountered some problems. You can start Windows 95 in Safe Mode and fix the problem.

Using Windows 95 Safe Mode

With luck, your computer starts and you have no problems running your new Windows 95 installation. Many times, however, Windows 95 encounters a problem (such as a Registry setting missing or corrupted) during startup that it cannot fix. When this happens, you need to run Windows in Safe Mode from the Startup menu. You can display the Startup menu by pressing F8 during the boot process. Press F8 when the instructions Starting Windows displays. This usually appears after your system checks the internal RAM on your system. Windows 95 also starts Safe Mode automatically if it detects a problem with the startup files.

The Startup menu has the following options from which to choose. Depending on your specific setup, you may or may not have the same settings.

- *Normal*. Enables you to start Windows 95 in its normal startup manner, loading all device drivers and Registry settings. If Windows 95 automatically displays the Startup menu, choosing this selection will probably just return you to the Startup menu. Choose this option only if you want to watch what happens on-screen during the failed startup.

- *Logged* (\BOOTLOG.TXT). Creates a file called BOOTLOG.TXT in your root directory that contains a record of the current startup process. This file is created during Setup and shows the Windows 95 components and drivers loaded and initialized, and the status of each. You can view this file in Notepad.

- *Safe Mode*. Starts Windows 95 but bypasses startup files and uses only basic system drivers. In Safe Mode, many devices in Windows 95 are not available, such as the Add New Hardware utility in Control Panel. Safe Mode is intended to diagnose and fix problems in the Windows 95 environment. You also can start Safe Mode by pressing F5 during bootup or typing **WIN /D:M** at the command prompt.

- *Safe Mode with Network Support*. Starts Windows 95, but bypasses startup files and uses only basic system drivers, including basic networking. You can also start this option by pressing F6 or typing **WIN /D:N** at the command prompt.

- *Step-By-Step Confirmation*. Enables you to confirm each line in your startup files, including AUTOEXEC.BAT and CONFIG.SYS. Answer **Y** to lines you want to run; answer **N** to lines you want to bypass. You can also start this option by pressing F8 when the Startup menu displays.

- *Command Prompt Only*. Starts MS-DOS (Windows 95 version) with startup files and Registry settings, displaying only the MS-DOS command prompt.

- *Safe Mode Command Prompt Only*. Starts MS-DOS (Windows 95 version) in Safe Mode and displays only the command prompt, bypassing startup files. Same as pressing Shift+F5.

- *Previous Version of MS-DOS*. Starts your previous version of MS-DOS if you have a multi-boot configuration. You must install Windows 95 into a different directory during Setup for this option to be available. You also can start this option by pressing F4 during startup. This option is only available if `BootMulti=1` is in the MSDOS.SYS file.

When Safe Mode is selected from the Startup menu, it bypasses startup files, including the Registry, CONFIG.SYS, AUTOEXEC.BAT, and the `[Boot]` and `[386Enh]` sections of SYSTEM.INI. Table 2.2 shows the files that the three most common Safe Mode options bypass and initiate. As the table shows, Safe Mode does not load all the Windows drivers. In fact, during Safe Mode, only the mouse, keyboard, and standard Windows VGA device drivers are loaded. If you are using other drivers, such as a Super VGA video driver, they are not available in Safe Mode.

Table 2.2 Files Loaded During Startup Menu Options

Action	Safe Mode	Safe Mode, Network Support	Command Prompt Only
Process CONFIG.SYS and AUTOEXEC.BAT	No	No	No
Process Registry information	No	Yes	No
Load COMMAND.COM	No	Yes	Yes
Run Windows 95 WIN.COM	Yes	Yes	No
Load HIMEM.SYS and IFSHLP.SYS	Yes	Yes	No
Load DoubleSpace or DriveSpace if present	Yes	Yes	(Loaded if Safe Mode Command Prompt Only option is selected)
Load all Windows drivers	No	No	No
Load network drivers	No	Yes	No
Run NETSTART.BAT	No	Yes	No

After Windows 95 starts in Safe Mode, you can access the configuration files, modify configuration settings, and then restart Windows 95 normally. If you still encounter problems, see Appendix B, "Troubleshooting Windows 95."

Using the Windows 95 Startup Disk

If you instructed Windows 95 to create a startup disk during Setup (see section "Creating a Startup Disk" earlier in this chapter), you can use it to load your previous operating system and display an MS-DOS command prompt.

The startup disk also contains utilities for troubleshooting your Windows 95 operating system. To use the Startup disk, place the disk in drive A and reboot your computer. A command prompt appears, from which you can diagnose and fix problems associated with your installation.

Note

If you did not create a startup disk during Setup, you can create one using a single floppy disk. In the Add/Remove Programs option in Control Panel, click the Startup Disk tab. Then click the Create Disk button, and follow the instructions on-screen. You should do this even if you are not having problems starting Windows 95 now. In the future, you may experience a problem that only the startup disk can remedy.

Troubleshooting

I've changed my mind. Can I uninstall Windows 95?

Yes. You can uninstall Windows 95 and return to a previously installed version of Windows 3.1 by running the Uninstall program. To uninstall Windows 95, you must select the Save System Files during Windows 95 Setup. If Windows 95 is running, use the following steps:

1. Click the Start menu, point to Settings, and then choose Control Panel.
2. Double-click the Add/Remove Programs.
3. In the Add-Remove Programs properties dialog box, click the Install/Uninstall tab.
4. In the list of software that can be removed by Windows, click Windows 95.
5. Click Add/Remove, and then follow the directions on your screen. The Uninstall program removes all long file name entries from your hard disk, and then runs an MS-DOS-based program to remove Windows 95 and restore your previous MS-DOS and Windows 3.x files.

I can't get Windows 95 to start and I want to remove it from my computer. How can I do this?

You will have to boot your computer into MS-DOS and uninstall Windows 95 from there. To uninstall Windows 95 from MS-DOS, use the following steps:

(continues)

(continued)

1. Boot from startup disk you created during setup.
2. Enter **UNINSTAL** at the A prompt.

After I uninstalled Windows 95, I still have some files left on my machine from Windows 95. Why?

These are long file names that Windows 95 installs. If you uninstall Windows 95 using a method other than uninstalling it from Windows 95, you are left with these long file names. You can remove them by running Windows 3.x File Manager and deleting them one at a time.

Chapter 3

Installing Windows 95 on a Laptop PC

by Rob Tidrow

You learned in Chapter 1, "Preparing to Install Windows 95," that you should take steps to prepare your machine for Windows 95. Chapter 2 showed you how to install Windows 95 using the Typical install option. If you have a notebook or portable PC, however, you can set up special options to take advantage of Windows 95's filesharing capabilities. This chapter walks you through installing Windows 95 on a portable computer and shows you how to configure the Briefcase and Direct Cable Connection applications that ship with Windows 95. If you followed Chapter 2's installation instructions, you do not need to read this chapter.

Windows 95 also supports PCMCIA adapters, which are common on portable computers. The end of this chapter discusses the way in which Windows 95 enables you to set up PCMCIA (Personal Computer Memory Card International Association) support for your hardware.

In this chapter, you learn how to

- Start Windows 95 Setup
- Specify the Windows 95 directory
- Instruct Setup to perform a Portable installation
- Test your Windows 95 installation
- Configure Windows 95's Direct Cable Connection feature
- Understand Windows 95's PCMCIA support

Using Windows 95 Setup

After you prepare your computer for Windows 95, you can start the Windows 95 Setup program. Setup is located on the Windows 95 installation disks or CD-ROM. The Windows 95 Setup program uses a Setup Wizard that displays many dialog boxes and useful prompts to help you install Windows 95 on your system.

Note

You'll find valuable information contained in various text files (such as README.TXT and SETUP.TXT) on the Microsoft Windows 95 CD-ROM or installation disks. Read these files for information that may pertain to your specific system hardware or software.

Taking Your System's Inventory

Before you start Setup, make a note of the following items on your system:

- Video card and monitor type
- Mouse type
- Network configuration, including network operating system (such as NetWare 3.12), protocol supported (such as TCP/IP), and mapped drive specifications (such as H:)
- Printer type and port
- PCMCIA adapters
- Modem type
- CD-ROM
- SCSI adapter, if installed
- Identification number of your Windows 95 disks or CD
- PCMCIA card or external network adapter model and their settings

Note

The easiest way to determine your network configuration settings is to ask your system administrator for them.

Starting Windows 95 Setup from Windows 3.x

You are ready to start the Windows 95 Setup program and install Windows 95. If you do not have Windows 3.x installed, you need to install Windows 95 from DOS. For details on running Setup from DOS, see the next section, "Starting Windows 95 Setup from DOS." Use these steps to install Windows 95 from Windows 3.x:

1. Start your computer and run Windows 3.x. Close all applications before running the Windows 95 Setup.
2. For installation from a floppy disk, insert the disk labeled `Disk #1` in the floppy drive. If you are installing from CD-ROM, place the CD-ROM in the CD drive.
3. From Program Manager, choose File, Run. In the Run dialog box, type the letter of the drive containing the disk or CD-ROM, a colon, a backslash (\), and the command **SETUP** (see fig. 3.1). The following command, for example, starts Setup from a floppy drive labeled A:

```
a:\setup
```

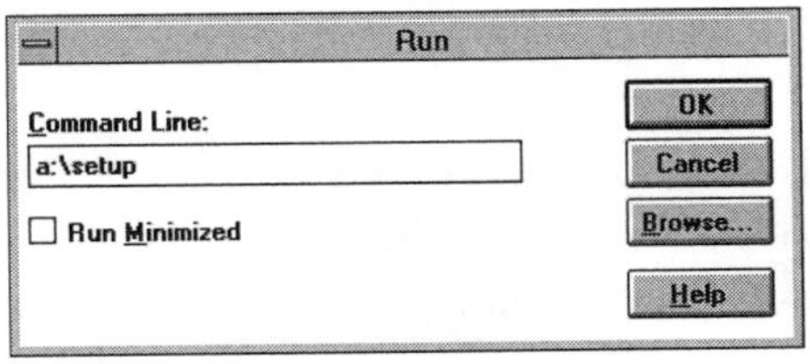

Fig. 3.1
From the Run dialog box in Windows 3.x, you can start the Windows 95 Setup program.

4. Click OK. Setup starts, and the Windows 95 Installation Wizard initializes and begins installing Windows 95. See the section "Collecting Setup Information" for the next step in the Windows 95 installation process.

Starting Windows 95 Setup from DOS

To start Windows 95 Setup from DOS, use the following steps:

1. Start your computer.
2. For installation from a floppy disk, insert the disk labeled `Disk #1` in the floppy drive. If you are installing from CD-ROM, place the CD-ROM in the CD drive.
3. At the DOS command prompt, type the letter of the drive that contains the setup disks, a backslash (\), and the command **SETUP** (see fig. 3.2).

The following command, for instance, starts Windows 95 Setup from a floppy disk labeled A:

```
A:\A:\SETUP
```

Fig. 3.2
You can start Windows 95 Setup from the DOS prompt using the SETUP command.

4. Press Enter. Setup starts, and the Windows 95 Installation Wizard initializes and begins installing Windows 95.

Using Special Setup Switches

Windows 95 Setup is designed to be used by any level user, including novice, intermediate, and advanced. No system, however, can satisfy every user's needs and special configurations. Windows 95 includes command-line switches to control the installation process. To use these switches, add them to the end of the SETUP command line, such as the following:

```
A:\SETUP /?
```

The preceding switch tells Windows 95 Setup to display help on using the command-line switches.

The following describes each of the switches you can type to customize the Setup procedure:

- **/?**. Displays help on using Setup switches. Shows syntax of each switch.
- **/ih**. Instructs Setup to run ScanDisk in the foreground so that you can see the results. Use this switch if the system stalls during the ScanDisk check or if an error results.
- **/nostart**. Directs Setup to copy only the required Windows 3.x DLL (Dynamic Link Library) used by Windows 95 Setup. After Setup copies these files, it exits to DOS without installing Windows 95.

- **/iL**. Instructs Setup to load the Logitech mouse driver, if you have a Logitech Series C mouse.
- **/iq**. Directs Setup to bypass the ScanDisk quick check when running Setup from DOS. Use this switch if you use compression software other than DriveSpace or DoubleSpace.
- **/is**. Directs Setup to bypass the ScanDisk quick check when running Setup from Windows 3.x. Use this switch if you use compression software other than DriveSpace or DoubleSpace.
- ***script_file***. Directs Setup to use custom script files you create to automatically install Windows 95.
- **/d**. Directs Setup not to use your existing version of Windows 3.x during the first part of Setup. You should use /d when you experience problems with Setup that are due to missing or damaged Windows 3.x files.
- **/C**. Directs Windows 95 Setup not to load the SmartDrive disk cache.
- **/id**. Directs Setup to bypass the checking of required minimum disk space to install Windows 95. Use this switch if a previous install of Windows 95 failed but Setup began copying files to your hard disk. This way, you do not get an `Out of disk space` error during your next attempt of running Setup.
- **/t:*tempdir***. Specifies the directory in which Setup is to copy its temporary files. This directory must already exist, but any existing files in the directory are deleted after Setup finishes installing Windows 95.

Collecting Setup Information

After you start Setup, a Welcome screen appears (see fig. 3.3), telling you that Windows 95 Setup is ready to start installing Windows 95 and that the process may take 30 to 60 minutes to complete. Click Continue

Windows 95 Setup gathers most of the information it needs automatically during the installation process. Some of the items you need to provide manually include the directory name where you need to install Windows 95 and the type of Setup you want to perform. Windows 95 by default installs into your current directory of Windows 3.x if it is installed, but you can change this directory if you want to run Windows 95 and your current Windows 3.x installation.

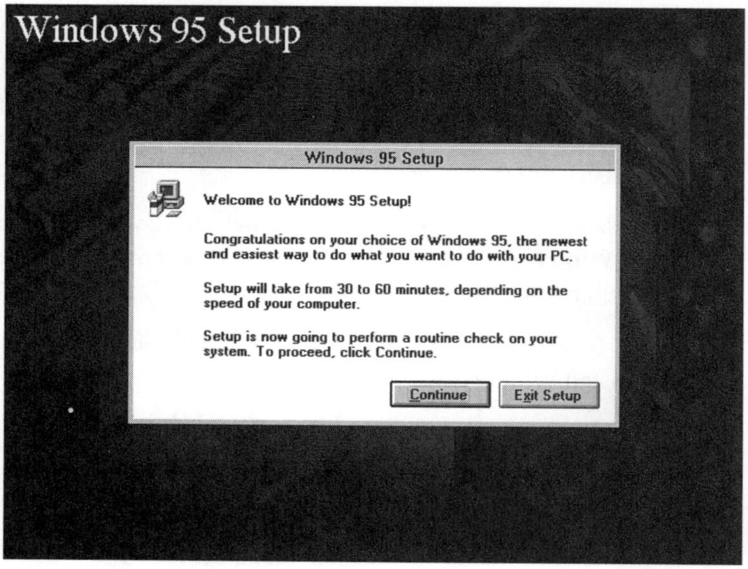

Fig. 3.3 The initial Windows 95 Setup screen tells you how long it typically takes to install Windows 95.

Tip

Press F3 or, if available, the Cancel button to exit Setup anytime.

Use the following steps to continue installing Windows 95:

1. Click Continue on the Setup Welcome screen. Windows 95 checks your system for available disk space, possible hard disk problems, and other system setting information (see fig. 3.4).

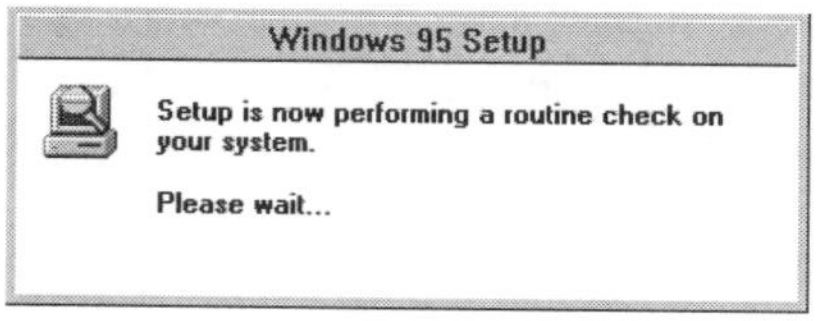

Fig. 3.4 When you first start installing Windows 95, Setup checks your system for hard disk problems and disk space.

Note

If Setup detects a problem with your system, such as a hard disk problem, an error message appears. Be sure to read the message and perform the recommended actions. Click OK to leave Windows 95 Setup and return to DOS or Windows 3.x. Setup does not let you continue with the installation process if an error is found.

2. If Setup does not detect a problem during its routine check, it begins the next stage of the installation process automatically. This stage prepares the Setup Wizard, which guides you through the rest of the installation.

3. After the Setup Wizard starts, the Windows 95 Software License Agreement appears, as shown in figure 3.5. Read the license agreement and click Yes if you accept the terms of the agreement. If you do not accept the terms, click No and Setup exits, ending the installation process. You must accept the terms of the agreement to install Windows 95.

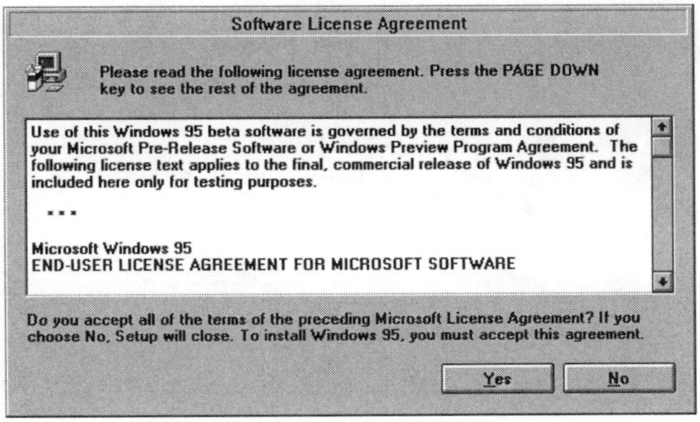

Fig. 3.5
Read and accept the terms of the Software License Agreement to continue installing Windows 95.

As mentioned earlier, you should close all applications before running Setup. If you do not, a warning message appears, advising you to do so (see fig. 3.6).

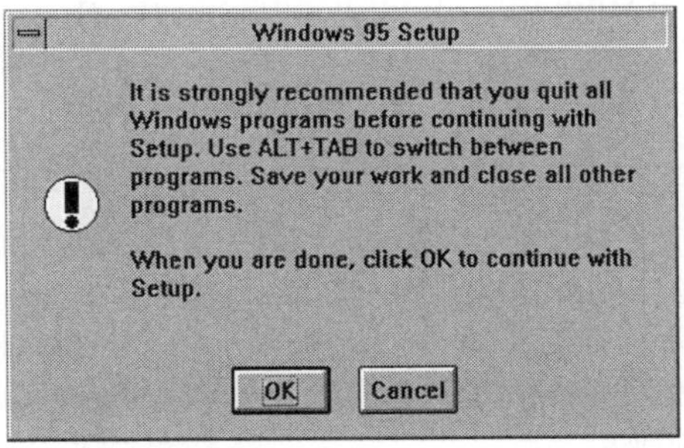

Fig. 3.6
In case you have another Windows application running, Setup displays a message telling you to exit from it before continuing with the installation.

To close any applications you may have running, follow these steps:

1. Press Alt+Tab to task switch to the open application.

2. Use that application's menu to close it.

3. Continue until all applications are closed. Do not close Program Manager.

4. Click OK when you are ready to continue with Setup.

Starting the Windows 95 Setup Wizard

The Windows 95 Setup Wizard appears on-screen (see fig. 3.7). This is your hands-on guide to installing Windows 95 on your system.

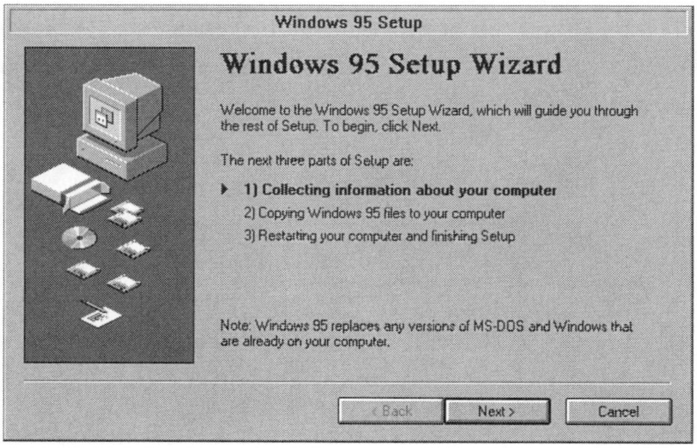

Fig. 3.7
The Setup Wizard helps you navigate through the Windows 95 installation process.

The wizard screen lists the three major parts of the Windows 95 setup procedure:

- Collecting information about your computer
- Copying Windows 95 files to your computer
- Restarting your computer and finishing setup

Each of these parts is described in the following sections.

Note

A note at the bottom of the wizard screen informs you that Windows 95 replaces your existing DOS and Windows versions. You can instruct Setup to install Windows 95 in a separate directory from DOS and Windows 3.x, enabling you to keep your previous version installed.

Tip

Click Back at any time to return to the previous wizard step, or Cancel to exit Setup.

Click Next to advance to the next wizard screen.

The Choose Directory screen appears next (see fig. 3.8). This is where you must decide to keep or install over a previous version of Windows or DOS. Make sure the C:\WINDOWS option is selected and click Next to replace Windows 3.x with Windows 95. The directory in which your current version of Windows is installed may differ from the one shown in figure 3.8.

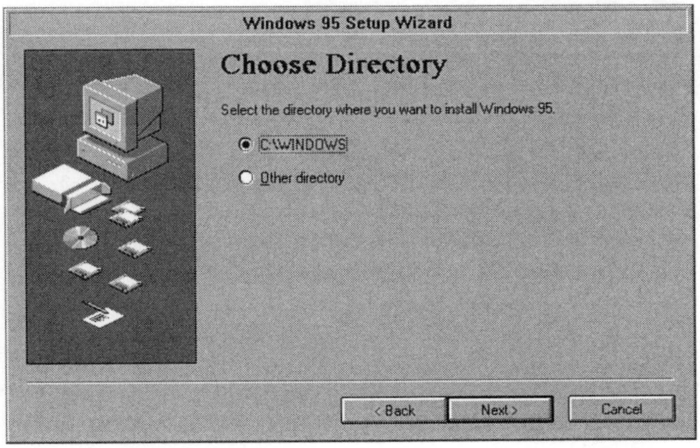

Fig. 3.8
You can tell Windows 95 to install into a new directory or copy over your previous version.

If you want to install Windows 95 into a separate directory and keep your previous version of Windows 3.x, select the Other Directory radio button and click Next.

Should You Replace Windows 3.x?

Should you install Windows 95 over your previous versions of Windows? There are advantages to both sides. If you decide to keep both versions of Windows on your machine, you need to reinstall all your applications under Windows 95. The advantage is that you have a fail-safe mechanism if Windows 95 does not work properly on your machine. You can move back to Windows 3.x immediately. Once you test your new Windows 95 installation, delete your old Windows 3.x files, including the applications installed under Windows 3.x.

On the other hand, if you install over your previous version of Windows, your applications work as soon as you install Windows 95. Also, most laptop PCs have smaller hard disks installed. When you install over your existing Windows 3.x installation, you do not need as much free disk space available to start Windows 95 Setup.

Depending on if you chose to install Windows 95 to a separate directory, the Change Directory screen appears (see fig. 3.9). This is where you name the directory for Windows 95. Although Setup advises that only advanced users and system administrators should modify this directory, you must change the directory name to retain your previous version of Windows.

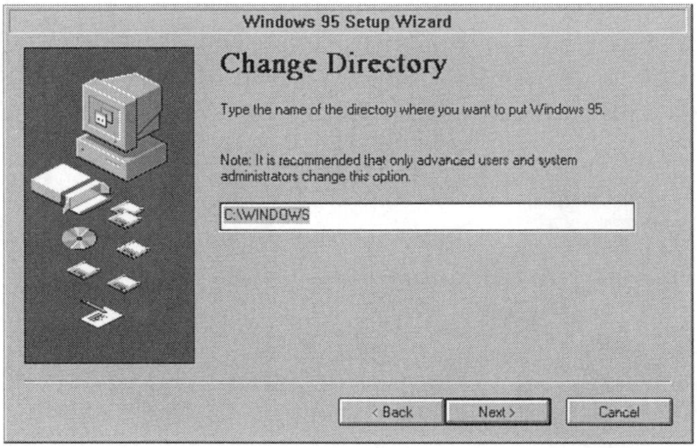

Fig. 3.9
You must give a new directory name in which to install Windows 95 if you want to keep your previous version of Windows.

In the text box, type the new directory name, such as **C:\WIN95**. The new name must be unique and no more than eight characters. Click Next when this box is filled out. At this point, Setup displays a screen warning you that you must reinstall all your applications. Click Yes to continue or No to return to the Change Directory screen.

> **Note**
>
> If you did not choose to install to a new Windows directory, Setup bypasses the preceding step and displays the Preparing Directory screen instead.

The Preparing Directory screen appears next. This screen informs you that Windows 95 is creating your new directory or preparing your existing Windows 3.x directory for Windows 95.

After the directory is prepped and ready, the Setup Options screen appears (see fig. 3.10), in which you select the type of installation you want to perform. For this chapter, choose Portable. You need between 30M and 45M of hard disk space to install the Portable installation. If you decide to install Microsoft Exchange (necessary when you install Microsoft Mail, Microsoft Fax, or Microsoft Network options), you should add another 6M to your estimated disk requirements.

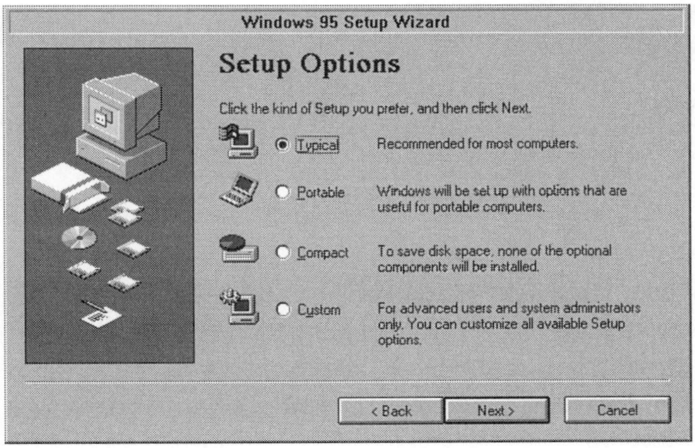

Fig. 3.10
To install components for a laptop or portable computer, select the Portable option from the Setup Options screen.

Note

Two options that install during the Portable installation that are not discussed in Chapter 2 are the Briefcase and Direct Cable Connection options. See "Configuring Briefcase and Direct Cable Connection" at the end of this chapter for instructions on configuring these options.

Click Next when you are ready.

When the User Information screen appears (see fig. 3.11), enter your name and company name. Company name is optional, but you must fill in a user name. Click Next.

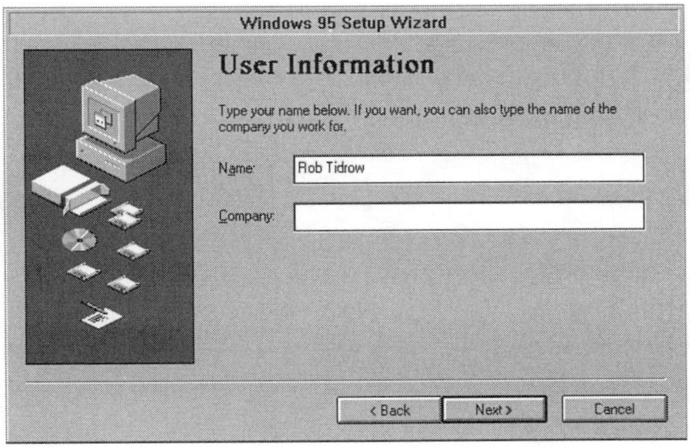

Fig. 3.11
You must enter your name in the User Information screen. Company name is optional.

Caution

As a word of caution, the name and company name you put here are permanent. You cannot change them unless you reinstall Windows 95. Don't use names that you may want to change later. Cute names grow tiresome after awhile.

The next screen, the Product Identification screen, is used to input the serial number of your Windows 95 disks (see fig. 3.12). You input the serial number in the CD Key text box (if you are installing from floppy disks, this line will be named Disk Key). This number is unique to your disks and is used for product support and for registering your software with Microsoft Corporation. You must input this number to successfully install Windows 95.

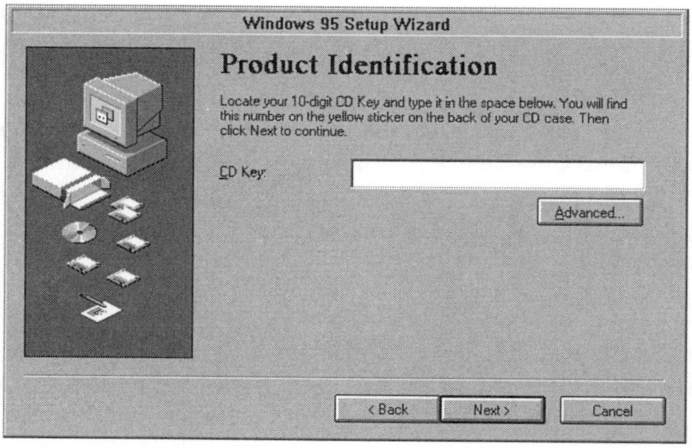

Fig. 3.12 This screen prompts you for the product identification of your Windows 95 disks or CD-ROM discs.

You find this information on your disks or on a yellow sticker on the back of your CD case. It might also be on some paper work that came with your disks or computer. Click Next after you enter the ID.

Note

The Advance button on the Product Identification screen is used if you are installing Windows 95 in a networked environment and have purchased a group license. See Chapter 5, "Installing Windows 95 over a Network," for more information.

Analyzing Your Computer

After you enter your Product ID, the Setup Wizard is ready to check your computer's hardware. In figure 3.13, the Analyzing Your Computer screen appears, showing the choices from which to select specific hardware devices. Regardless of the choices shown, Windows 95 autodetects the devices in your computer. In this example, the only choice is Network Adapter. If you have a network interface card in your system and you want Windows 95 to search for and configure it, make sure this option is selected. Depending on your system, other options may appear in this screen. Select the appropriate ones for your system.

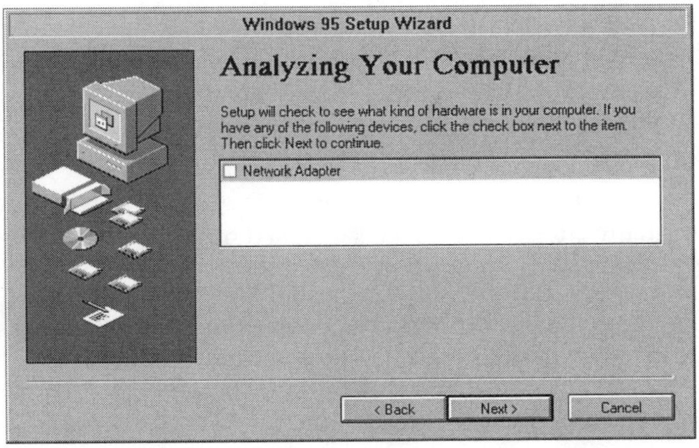

Fig. 3.13
The Analyzing Your Computer screen shows some of the devices Windows detects during Setup.

Click Next to have Windows 95 analyze your system. This process may take a few minutes to complete. You can watch the Progress bar at the bottom of the screen to see Setup's progression through the analyzing stage.

Troubleshooting

I've been watching the Progress bar, but it stopped moving. What happened?

Many times the Progress bar moves rapidly through the first 90 percent of the process and then seems to quit. This is normal, and you should not reboot your PC at this point. Give Setup some time to complete this part. It's a good practice to let it sit for 20 minutes before you attempt to recover your computer.

If, after a long time of inactivity your system seems to have crashed, reboot the system by turning off your computer, waiting 10 seconds, and restarting it. Start Setup again and use the Smart Recovery program, which starts automatically if Setup can salvage anything from the previous installation attempt. If Smart Recovery does not start automatically, you need to restart Setup by running SETUP.EXE from Windows 3.x or MS-DOS.

Tip

You can tell if your hard drive is active or not by watching the hard drive light on your computer. Sometimes this light is labeled HDD and is green or red. You also can put your ear close to the computer to hear whether the hard drive is spinning.

Getting Connected

Windows 95 provides built-in support for many electronic and online services, including e-mail (via Microsoft Mail), The Microsoft Network, and Microsoft Fax services. After the Setup Wizard analyzes your system, you need to select the types of services you would like Setup to automatically configure. You can select any combination of choices or pick none. If you are not sure if you want to install any of these choices, you can bypass it now and install it manually after Windows 95 is installed by using Add/Remove Programs in Control Panel.

The Get Connected screen (see fig. 3.14) enables you to select the service or connection you want Setup to install automatically.

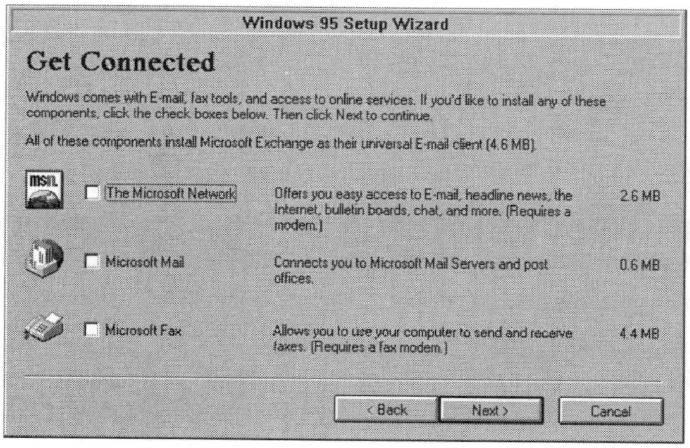

Fig. 3.14
If you want Setup to set up your Microsoft Fax, Microsoft Mail, or The Microsoft Network connections, select those choices here.

▶ See "Installing the Exchange Client," p. 202

If you don't read the Setup Wizard screen for this option closely, you may overlook an important point. If you install one or more of the Get Connected options, Windows 95 automatically installs Microsoft Exchange. Exchange is Microsoft's new electronic mail and communications client that acts as a universal inbox and outbox for your e-mail and faxes.

Exchange requires 4.6M of hard disk space by itself. If you install all three Get Connected options, the total hard disk space required is more than 12M.

You also need at least 8M of RAM to run Exchange and Microsoft Fax. The Microsoft Network also demands a large amount of memory. You should have at least 8M minimum, and 16M is recommended.

After you make your choices, click Next.

Selecting Windows Components

The Setup Wizard now gives you a choice to modify the list of components to install on your system. The default setting installs the most common Windows 95 components, but you can change the list by selecting the Show Me the List of Components So I Can Choose option (see fig. 3.15).

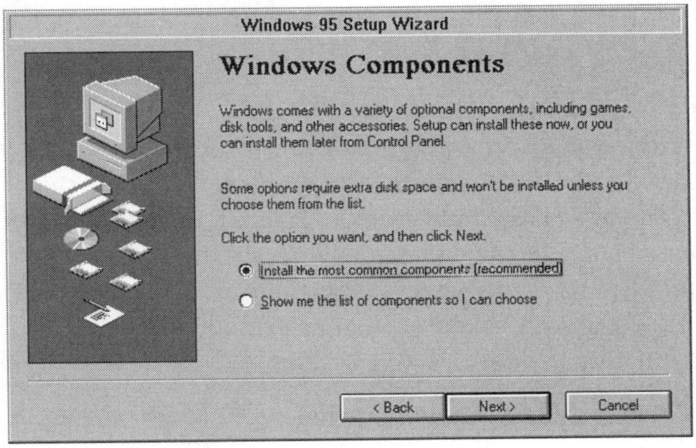

Fig. 3.15
Although you selected the Portable install type earlier, you can modify the list of components Setup installs.

For most users, the default list of components is recommended, especially if you are a new user and are not familiar with Windows 95 components, many of which are available in previous versions of Windows. If you change your mind later about an option, you can add additional components or remove any by using Add/Remove Programs in the Control Panel after Windows 95 is installed. Click Next to continue with Setup. The Startup Disk screen appears.

> **Note**
>
> To select specific Windows components to install, select the Show Me the List of Components So I Can Choose option and click Next. The Select Components screen appears (see fig. 3.16). This screen and its options are discussed in detail in Chapter 4, "Using Custom Installation Options."

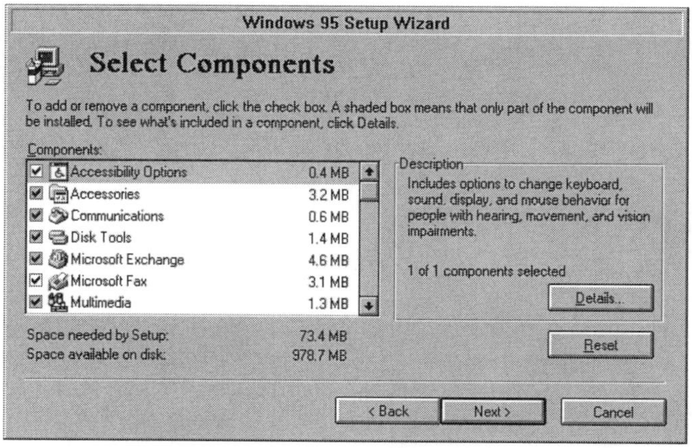

Fig. 3.16
You can modify the list of components Setup installs from this screen.

Creating a Startup Disk

Setup now gives you an opportunity to create a startup disk. The *startup disk* is a bootable floppy disk that stores several system files (more than 1.2M) on it. In case you need to use the startup disk, place it in your floppy drive and reboot your machine. You are presented with an MS-DOS command line that provides utilities and maintenance instructions to help you recover your installation. Appendix B, "Troubleshooting Windows 95," discusses how to use the startup disk in more detail.

Regardless of how well you think the Windows 95 Setup program is going, *always* choose to make a startup disk. The startup disk is your life preserver in case you experience problems with Windows 95 after it's installed. By taking a few minutes now and using one floppy disk, you insure yourself against potential problems down the road if you experience problems.

You'll need one floppy disk that can be reformatted when the startup disk is created. Because you will lose all the data on this disk, make sure it does not contain anything important. The floppy disk must be one for the floppy drive from which your PC can boot.

Tip

Add the startup disk to the collection of disks you carry in your laptop case. You never know when you will need it.

Caution

The startup disk does have some limitations. It cannot, for instance, be used to provide access to a CD-ROM device or to a network connection. You need to clean up any problems associated with your installation to recover from these problems.

The files Setup copies to the startup disk are shown in table 3.1.

Table 3.1 Startup Disk Files

Name	Description of File
ATTRIB.EXE	Sets file attributes, such as hidden and read-only
CHKDSK.EXE	Checks a disk and displays a status report of it
COMMAND.COM	Starts a new copy of the Windows Command Interpreter, which is the primary operating system file for MS-DOS
DEBUG.EXE	Runs Debug, a testing and editing tool program
DRVSPACE.BIN	DriveSpace disk-compression utility
EBD.SYS	Utility for the startup disk
EDIT.COM	Text editor in MS-DOS
FDISK.EXE	Configures a hard disk for use with MS-DOS
FORMAT.COM	Formats a hard disk or floppy disk for use with MS-DOS
IO.SYS	Core operating system file
MSDOS.SYS	Core operating system file
REGEDIT.EXE	Starts the Registry Editor
SCANDISK.EXE	Starts ScanDisk
SCANDISK.INI	Stores system configuration settings for ScanDisk
SYS.COM	Copies MS-DOS system files and command interpreter to a disk you specify
UNINSTAL.EXE	Starts utility for recovering deleted files

A few other files that you may want to copy to the startup disk after Windows 95 is installed include AUTOEXEC.BAT, CONFIG.SYS, WIN.INI, and SYSTEM.INI. Other INI files may also come in handy as well. These files are ones that you should already have backed up in Chapter 1, "Preparing to Install Windows 95."

◀ See "BackUp System Files," p. 30

To instruct Setup to create a startup disk, make sure the Yes, I Want a Startup Disk (Recommended) choice in the Startup Disk screen is selected and click Next.

Copying Files

Setup now has gathered enough information to begin copying files to your hard disk. In figure 3.17, Setup displays a message telling you that it is ready to start copying the files. Click Next to continue.

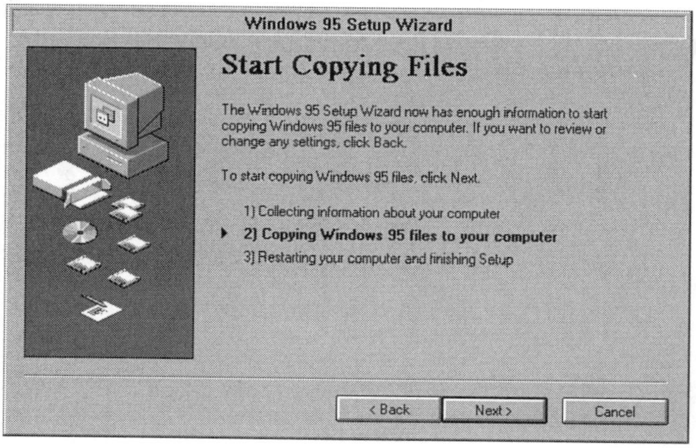

Fig. 3.17
The moment you've been waiting for! Setup starts copying files to your system.

Setup begins copying files to your hard disk and displays a meter showing the progress of the action. If you asked to create a startup disk, Setup instructs you to insert this disk when the progress meter hits about 20 percent. Insert the floppy disk and click OK. After the startup disk is created, Setup displays a message telling you to remove the floppy disk from the drive. Do this now and store it in a safe place.

Tip

To exit from Setup at any time, click the Exit button or press F3. This returns you to Windows 3.x or DOS, depending on where you started Setup. If you exit Setup while Windows 95 copies files to your system, Windows 95 may or may not delete them from your system. In many cases, Windows 95 leaves the files on your system so that if you decide to restart the Setup program later, it does not have to recopy those files.

Setup continues installing Windows 95. As it's copying files, Windows displays screens describing some key features of Windows 95. Two of these are shown in figures 3.18 and 3.19.

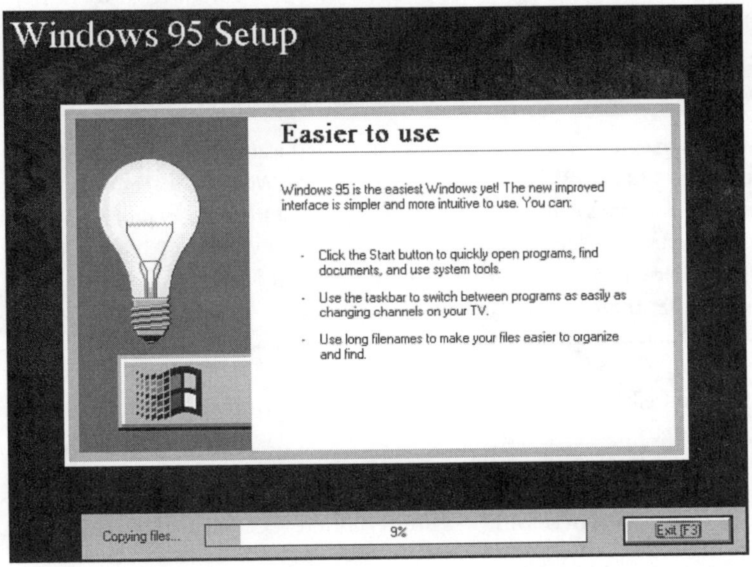

Fig. 3.18
To get a quick idea of what is in store for you with Windows 95, read the messages that flash on-screen during installation.

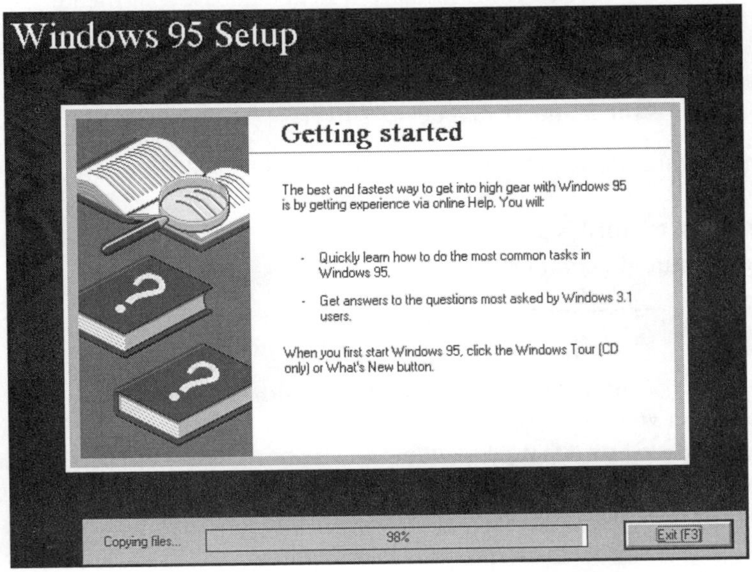

Fig. 3.19
Another helpful screen explains how to get help in Windows.

Finishing Setup

When the Setup files finish copying onto your system, Setup begins the third and final phase of installation: the Finishing Setup phase. This part restarts your computer and configures your hardware and software to work with Windows 95.

> **Note**
>
> Even though you've made it to this point in the installation process, you still are not "home free." Many installation errors occur after the Windows 95 Setup restarts your computer and starts configuring your system. One of the primary problems that occurs is when the Plug and Play configuration part of Windows 95 tries to locate incompatible devices. If you experience any problems during this stage, see Appendix B, "Troubleshooting Windows 95."

Some of the tasks that Windows 95 performs during this final stage include the following:

- Adds a new system file (IO.SYS) to replace the old MS-DOS IO.SYS and MSDOS.SYS. These old files are renamed IO.DOS and MSDOS.DOS.
- Copies SYSTEM.DAT to SYSTEM.DA0 and SYSTEM.NEW to SYSTEM.DAT. This is the primary system database that the Registry reads.
- Combines all the virtual device drivers (VxDs) to create VMM32.VXD, which is the 32-bit virtual device driver.
- Renames ARIAL.WIN, USER32.TMP, and LOGO.SYS files used by Setup.

Click Finish to finish setting up Windows 95. This last stage typically takes several minutes to complete.

> **Note**
>
> If your PC does not restart after a reasonable time, such as 20 minutes or more, reboot your system manually. You may be able to boot into Windows 95. If not, you may be able to boot into Windows 95 in Safe Mode, which you select from a menu that automatically displays during the boot process if Windows 95 cannot completely load. See Appendix B, "Troubleshooting Windows 95," if you have problems finishing this stage of Setup.

After your computer restarts and everything acts as normal, Windows 95 starts and then runs your AUTOEXEC.BAT and CONFIG.SYS files. You'll see the Windows 95 opening screen flash on-screen for a few seconds, and then the DOS screen appears. You'll see the following message in DOS:

```
Please wait while Setup updates your configuration files.
This may take a few minutes...
```

Configuring Run-Once Options

Your PC may appear dormant for several minutes, but be patient. After the configuration files are updated, Windows 95 reappears on-screen and starts to run through setting Run-Once options. These options include PCMCIA and MIDI devices, printers, Time Zone, Microsoft Exchange, Windows Help, programs on the Start menu, and Control Panel setting. Other hardware devices also can be configured at this point. You will see a screen that lists these options as they are being set up.

Many of the items on the list configure automatically, such as the Control Panel and programs on the Start menu. Some, however, require user interaction. When Setup runs the Time Zone option, for instance, you must select the time zone in which you live (see fig. 3.20). Click the list on the Time Zone page and select your time zone. To modify the time and date, click the Date & Time tab. Click Apply to save these settings, and click Close when you are finished.

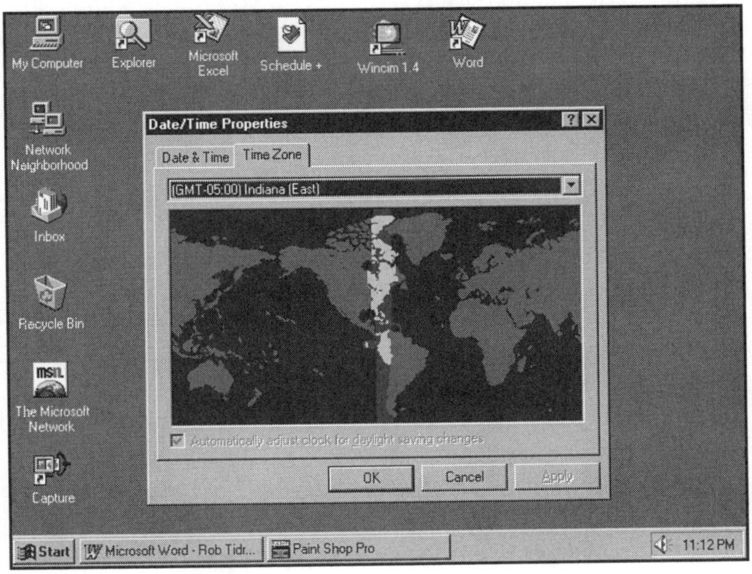

Fig. 3.20
During the Run-Once stage, Setup asks you to select your time zone and set the correct time and date.

Configuring Microsoft Exchange

Next, Setup configures Microsoft Exchange on your system. If you did not select a choice in the Get Connected screen earlier (see "Getting Connected" earlier in this chapter), Setup does not perform this task. You can proceed to the "Starting Windows 95" section.

Setup displays the Inbox Setup Wizard, which guides you through setting up Microsoft Exchange's universal mail inbox. This box is also used to receive e-mail and faxes and to connect to The Microsoft Network, if you selected this option earlier. Use the following steps to configure Exchange:

1. If you've never used Exchange before, make sure No is selected when the Setup wizard asks if you have used Exchange. Otherwise, click Yes. Click Next.

2. In the next screen, you are prompted to select the services you want to use with Exchange. The services listed include only those you selected in the Get Connect screen earlier. These choices include:

   - Microsoft Mail
   - Microsoft Fax
   - Microsoft Online Network

3. By default, the items listed are selected and the Use the Following Information Services radio button is selected. If you want Setup to automatically configure these services (which is recommended for most users), click Next.

> **Note**
>
> If you are an advanced user, or if you need to modify the configuration of the services, select the Manually Configure information Services option. This enables you to change (among other settings) the Exchange profile name, which by default is set as MSEXCHANGE. Any configuration setting can be changed later by using the Add/Remove Program option in the Control Panel.

▶ See "Installing the Exchange Client," p. 202

4. When you choose to let Setup automatically configure Exchange, the Location Information dialog box appears. This box configures the way in which your phone calls are dialed. In this box, you need to set the country in which you live, area code, any special dialing codes to get an outside number (such as 9), and the type of phone system you use, either tone or pulse. Click OK when finished.

5. The next Inbox Setup Wizard screen that appears sets up your Microsoft Fax connection, if this is one of the selections you picked earlier. You are given two choices when installing Microsoft Fax. First, you can set up Fax so that it runs from your local computer. Click the Modem Connected To My Computer option to use Fax only from your computer.

   Second, you can set up Microsoft Fax so that others can share it across a network. To do this, you must connect a fax modem to a networked computer and use it as a fax server.

   ▶ See "Setting Up a Fax Server," p. 259

   For this chapter, make sure the first option is selected and click Next.

Detecting a New Modem

In the Install New Modem Wizard, you need to configure your modem to work with Windows 95. Before working through the Install New Modem Wizard, make sure your fax modem is attached to your computer and that it is turned on and hooked to a phone line. If you need to install an internal modem first, skip over this section and finish Setup first. Then install your modem (you'll need to shut down your computer to do this) and start the Add New Hardware program in Control Panel to configure the modem. Chapter 28, "Configuring Modems," guides you through setting up and configuring a modem.

If your modem is turned on and ready to be configured, use the Install New Modem Wizard. Unless you want to select your modem manually, click Next. If you want to specify your modem type, click the Don't Detect My Modem; I Will Select It from a List option and click Next.

▶ See "Installing Your Modem," p. 588

Installing Your Printer

After Setup establishes Exchange and other online connections, it installs the printers connected to your computer. If you do not want to set up a printer now, you can set one up later by selecting the Printers folder after choosing Start, Settings. Double-click the Add Printer icon to start the Add Printer Wizard.

During Setup, you need to specify whether the printer is located locally or on a network. You also need to tell Windows 95 Setup the manufacturer of the printer, such as Hewlett Packard, and the printer name, such as HP LaserJet IIIP. Click Next to have Setup install the printer drivers on your system. If Setup detects a driver from a previous installation, you can elect to keep it or use an updated one from Windows 95. Select the option and then click Next. Setup next asks if you plan to print from MS-DOS based programs. Select Yes or No as necessary.

▶ See "Using the Add Printer Wizard," p. 606

The next screen prompts you for the port or connection to which your printer is connected. Select the appropriate connection and click Next. Windows asks you to name the printer, and gives you a default name such as HP LaserJet IIIP. Keep or change this name as necessary and click Next.

> **Note**
>
> If you are on a network and will be printing to a network printer, you can instruct Windows 95 to print to a queue name versus a printer port.

Setup then displays a screen that asks if you want to print a test page on your printer. If your printer is set up to your machine or network, it's a good idea to do this. This way Setup can diagnose any problems you may have with your printer now. Click Finish. After your text page prints and you respond that everything is fine, tell Setup that the page printed correctly.

Congratulations! Setup is now finished setting up Windows 95.

Starting Windows 95

After Setup finishes installing Windows 95 and configuring Exchange, your printer, and other options, Windows 95 starts. Figure 2.21 shows the initial Windows 95 screen, with a Welcome screen that includes helpful suggestions for navigating Windows 95.

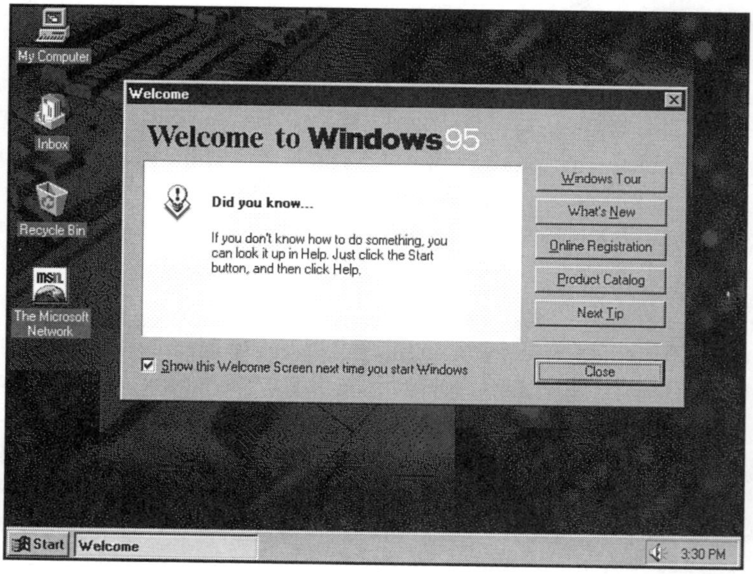

Fig. 3.21
The Welcome to Windows 95 screen displays a different tip each time you start up Windows.

Tip

If you do not want to see this screen the next time you boot Windows 95, clear the Show this Welcome screen next time you start Windows option on the Welcome dialog box. To show this screen again, double-click the Welcome application in the Windows 95 folder in Windows Explorer.

Testing Windows 95 Setup

Before you start using Windows 95 for the first item, you should test to see if it is properly installed. To do this, shut down Windows and restart it by clicking the Start button at the bottom of the screen (this is called the *Taskbar*) and select Shut Down. The Shut Down Windows dialog box appears (see fig. 3.22). Make sure the Shut Down the Computer? option is selected and click Yes. This action begins the Windows 95 shut down procedure, which you must do whenever you want to exit Windows 95.

▶ See "Setting Taskbar Options," p. 173

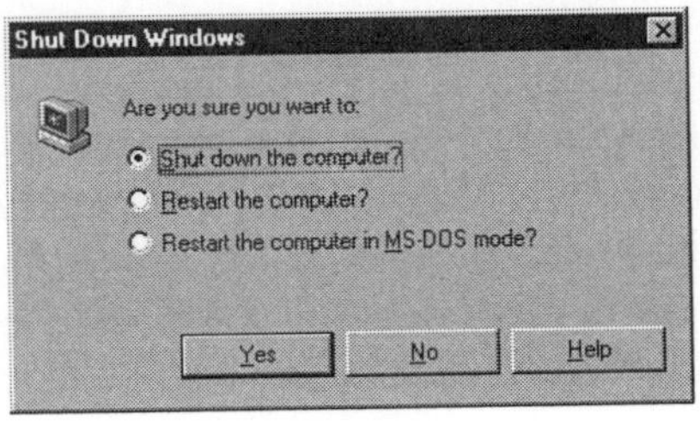

Fig. 3.22
You must use the Shut Down Windows dialog box each time you turn off your computer.

When a message appears on your screen telling you it's OK to turn off your machine, press the Reset button on your computer or flip the power switch off and then on. As your PC reboots, watch the screen to see if you notice any errors. If Windows 95 starts, your system probably is working fine and you can start using Windows 95.

If it doesn't start or if you get a DOS screen, your setup has encountered some problems. You can start Windows 95 in Safe Mode and fix the problem.

Using Windows 95 Safe Mode

With luck, your computer starts and you have no problems running your new Windows 95 installation. Many times, however, Windows 95 encounters a problem during startup that it cannot fix (such as a Registry setting missing or corrupted). When this happens, you need to run Windows in Safe Mode from the Startup menu. You can display the Startup menu by pressing F8 during the boot process. Press F8 when the instructions `Starting Windows` appear on-screen, usually after your system checks the internal RAM on your system. Windows 95 also starts Safe mode automatically if it detects a problem with the startup files.

The Startup menu has the following options from which to choose. Depending on your specific setup, you may or may not have the same settings:

- *Normal*. Enables you to start Windows 95 in its normal startup manner, loading all device drivers and Registry settings. If Windows 95 automatically displays the Startup menu, choosing Normal probably will not do anything except return you to the Startup menu. Choose this option only if you want to watch what happens on-screen during the failed startup.

- *Logged* (\BOOTLOG.TXT). Creates a file called BOOTLOG.TXT in your root directory that contains a record of the current startup process. This file is created during Setup and shows the Windows 95 components and drivers loaded and initialized, and the status of each. You can view this file in Notepad.

- *Safe Mode*. Starts Windows 95 but bypasses startup files and uses only basic system drivers. In Safe mode, many devices in Windows 95 are not available, such as the Add New Hardware utility in the Control Panel. Safe mode is intended to diagnose and fix problems in the Windows 95 environment. You also can start Safe mode by pressing F5 during boot-up or typing **`WIN /D:M`** at the command prompt.

- *Safe Mode with Network Support*. Starts Windows 95 but bypasses startup files and uses only basic system drivers, including basic networking. You can also start this option by pressing F6 or typing **`WIN /D:N`** at the command prompt.

- *Step-By-Step Confirmation*. Enables you to confirm each line in your startup files, including AUTOEXEC.BAT and CONFIG.SYS. Answer Y to lines you want to run; answer N to lines you want to bypass. You can also start this option by pressing F8 when the Startup menu is displayed.

- *Command Prompt Only*. Starts MS-DOS (Windows 95 version) with startup files and Registry settings, displaying only the MS-DOS command prompt.

- *Safe Mode Command Prompt Only*. Starts MS-DOS (Windows 95 version) in Safe mode and displays only the command prompt, bypassing startup files. Same as pressing Shift+F5.

- *Previous Version of MS-DOS.* Starts your previous version of MS-DOS if you have a multi-boot configuration. You must install Windows 95 into a different directory during Setup for this option to be available. You also can start this option by pressing F4 during startup. This option is only available if `BootMulti=1` in the MSDOS.SYS file.

When Safe mode is selected from the Startup menu, it bypasses startup files, including the Registry, CONFIG.SYS, AUTOEXEC.BAT, and the `[Boot]` and `[386Enh]` sections of SYSTEM.INI. Table 3.2 shows files that the three most common Safe mode options bypass and initiate. As you can see in the table, Safe mode does not load all the Windows drivers. In fact, during Safe mode, only the mouse, keyboard, and standard Windows VGA device drivers are loaded. If you are using other drivers, such as a Super VGA video driver, they are not available in Safe mode.

Table 3.2 Files Loaded During Startup Menu Options

Action	Safe Mode	Safe Mode, Network Support	Command Prompt Only
Process CONFIG.SYS and AUTOEXEC.BAT	No	No	No
Process Registry information	No	Yes	No
Load COMMAND.COM	No	Yes	Yes
Run Windows 95 WIN.COM	Yes	Yes	No
Load HIMEM.SYS and IFSHLP.SYS	Yes	Yes	No
Load DoubleSpace or DriveSpace if present	Yes	Yes	(Loaded if Safe Mode Command Prompt Only option is selected)
Load all Windows drivers	No	No	No
Load network drivers	No	Yes	No
Run NETSTART.BAT	No	Yes	No

After Windows 95 starts in Safe mode, you can access the configuration files, modify configuration settings, and then restart Windows 95 normally. If you still encounter problems, see Appendix B, "Troubleshooting Windows 95."

Using the Windows 95 Startup Disk

If you instructed Windows 95 to create a startup disk during Setup (see the section "Creating a Startup Disk" earlier in this chapter), you can use it to load your previous operating system and display an MS-DOS command prompt. The startup disk also contains utilities for troubleshooting your Windows 95 operating system. To use the Startup disk, place the disk in drive A and reboot your computer. A command prompt appears from which you can diagnose and fix problems associated with your installation.

Note

If you did not create a Startup disk during Setup, you can create one using a single floppy disk. In the Add/Remove Programs option in Control Panel, click the Startup Disk tab. Then click the Create Disk button, and follow the instructions on-screen. You should do this even if you are not having problems starting Windows 95 now. In the future, you may experience a problem that only the Startup disk can remedy.

Configuring Briefcase and Direct Cable Connection

After Setup finishes installing Windows 95 and you have tested it, you can configure Briefcase and the Direct Cable Connection applications. The following sections discuss how to do this.

Briefcase

An option installed during the Portable Setup installation is the Windows 95 Briefcase. Mobile computing users who have both a portable and desktop PC spend several hours a week transferring files from one machine to the other. Part of this time is devoted to ensuring that the most current file is copied and being used each time the file is modified. Briefcase enables users to synchronize files and copy them between their PCs if they have a network or use the Direct Cable Connection (see the next section). Briefcase helps eliminate the possibility of errors and overlooked files that users work on.

To use Briefcase, double-click its icon on the Windows 95 desktop to start it. There are no configuration settings for Briefcase, expect for those related to setting up a network connection or the Direct Cable Connection. After you start Briefcase, drag and drop files and directories from Explorer or your desktop to the Briefcase (see fig. 3.23). This is the same paradigm used for carrying a briefcase or attaché to the office: you stuff your papers and folders into your briefcase to carry them home or on a trip, or back to the office. Windows 95's Briefcase extends this concept to the electronic platform.

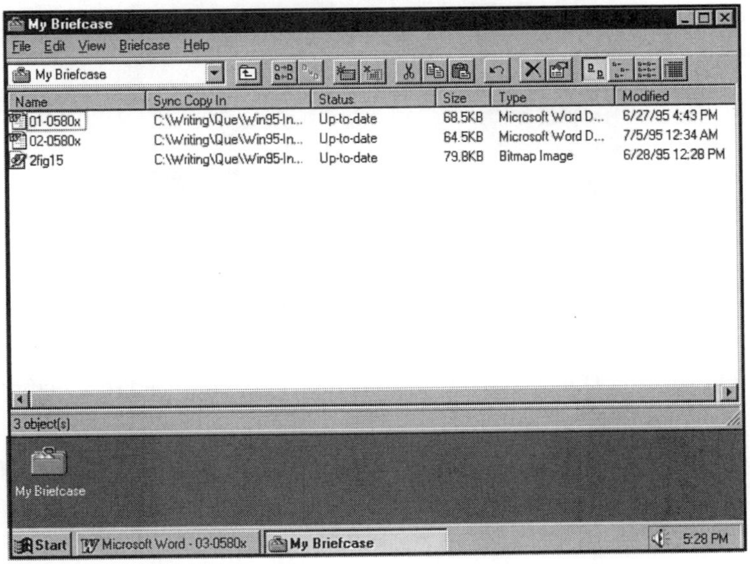

Fig. 3.23
You can use the Windows 95 Briefcase to help you synchronize your files from your portable PC to your desktop PC.

> **Note**
>
> For more information on using Briefcase, see Que's *Special Edition Using Windows 95*.

Direct Cable Connections

Another feature that mobile users can use is Windows 95's Direct Cable Connection. This feature enables users to hook together two PCs using serial or parallel port cables. With Direct Cable Connection, you can share folders, files, or printers with another computer without being on a local area network (LAN). This is handy if you transfer files from a laptop PC to a desktop PC, but your laptop does not have a network adapter. If your other PC is on a network, however, the connected PC (in this case, the laptop PC) can access the network and share files or network printers.

By default, Direct Cable Connection is automatically installed during the Portable Setup (it's also installed by default during Custom and Typical Setups). After Setup installs Windows 95, you need to configure the Direct Cable Connection for each computer you hook together. To do so, use these steps:

1. From Accessories, click Direct Cable Connection. The Direct Cable Connection Wizard starts (see fig. 3.24).

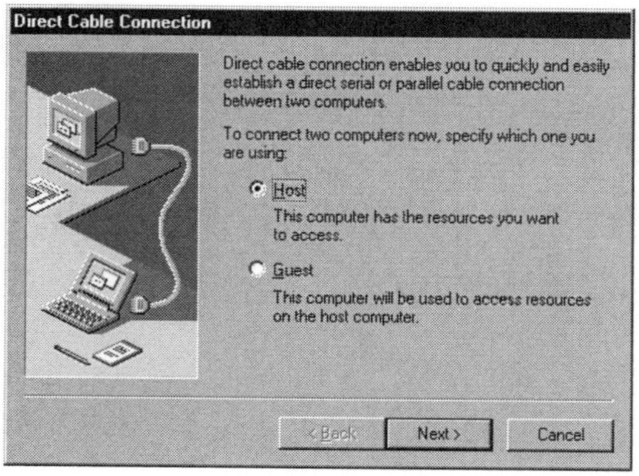

Fig. 3.24
Use the Direct Cable Connection Wizard to let you hook two computers together using a serial or parallel port.

2. On the first Direct Cable Connection screen, you need to specify which computer you are configuring. You have two choices:

   - *Host.* This is the PC that contains the files or printer connection you want to copy or share.
   - *Guest.* This is the PC that accesses files from the host PC.

   Select Host or Guest.

3. Click Next.

> **Tip**
>
> Host and guest PCs must use the same port connections.

4. Specify the port to which you want to connect. You can use serial (usually COM1 or COM2) or parallel (usually LPT1 or LPT2) ports (see fig. 3.25).

> **Note**
>
> If you need to add a port to your computer, click Install New Port. Windows 95 automatically searches your system for the new port and configures it. If Windows cannot find a new port on your system and you recently installed one, shut down Windows 95, reboot your system, and retry this option. You also can run the Add New Hardware Wizard from the Control Panel and add the new port using that wizard.

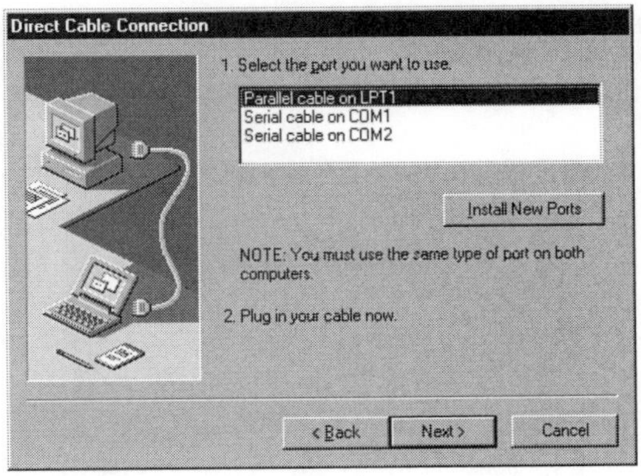

Fig. 3.25
Select the type of port that each computer will use.

5. Plug in the cable to the port you specify in step 4.
6. Click Next. If you set up your PC as the guest computer, skip to step 15. Otherwise continue to step 7.
7. You now must specify if you want to enable the guest PC to share printer and file resources on the host machine (see fig. 3.26). To do this, click the File and Print Sharing button to start the Network Control Panel.

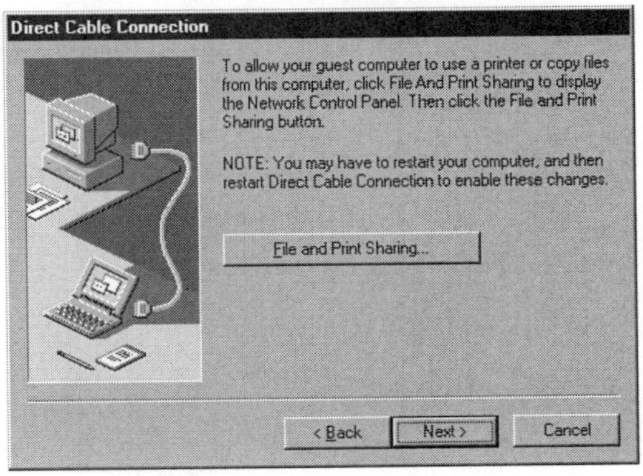

Fig. 3.26
You can configure the host computer to enable the guest computer to use its printer or files.

8. From the Network dialog box (see fig. 3.27), click File and Print Sharing. Select this option so that your PC can share files and a printer with another PC.
9. In the File and Print Sharing dialog box, you can choose to have the guest computer share only the host's printer, the host's files, or both (see fig. 3.28). Click OK.

10. Click OK in the Network dialog box.

11. Click Next in the Direct Cable Connection Wizard.

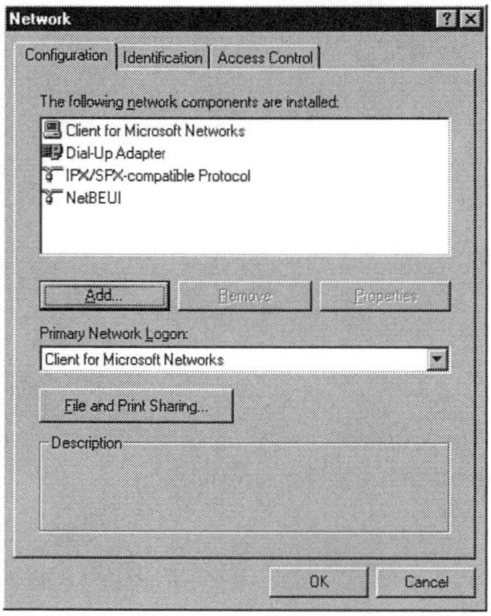

Fig. 3.27
The Network dialog box is used to enable File and Print Sharing from one PC to another.

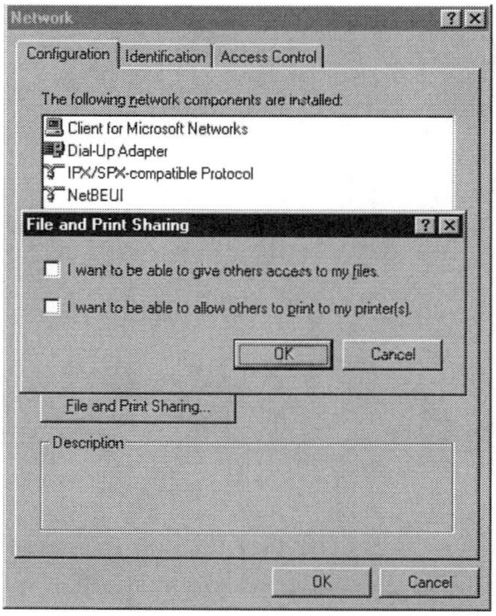

Fig. 3.28
Select the type of file and printer sharing that you want between your connected computers.

If you do not enable file or printer sharing, the warning screen shown in figure 3.29 appears. Click OK and then click Next again to go to the following wizard screen. If file and print sharing is enabled, this screen is bypassed.

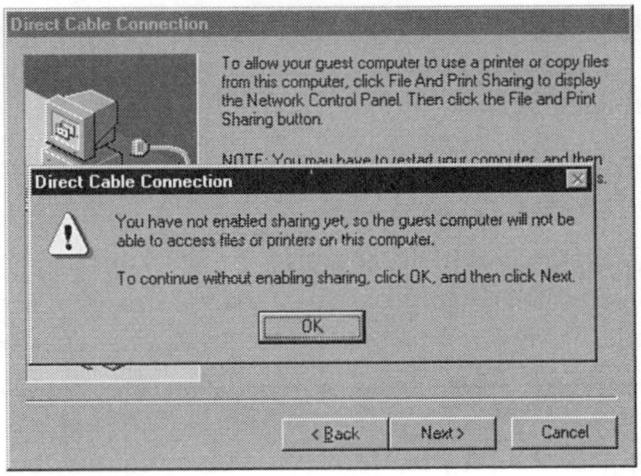

Fig. 3.29
The Direct Cable Connection Wizard tells you that you have not set up file and printer sharing between your two computers.

12. The host computer is now configured. To add a layer of security to the connection, you can require that the guest computer input a password to access the host system. To do this, click Use Password Protection and then click the Set Password button (see fig. 3.30).

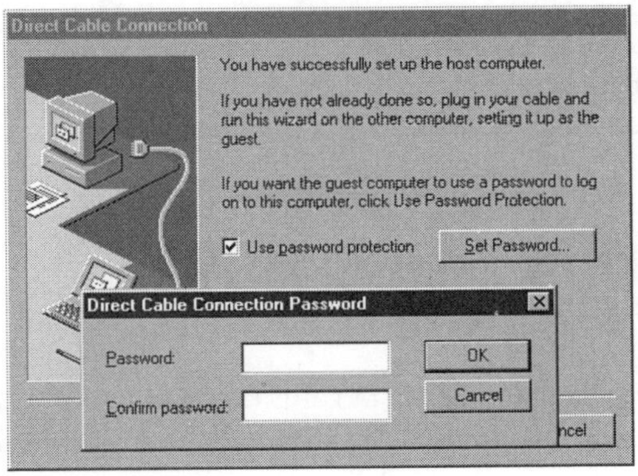

Fig. 3.30
Use a password to help keep intruders from accessing the host computer from the guest computer.

Tip

Be sure to share this password with other users if they are accessing the host computer via Direct Cable Connection.

13. In the Direct Cable Connection Password dialog box, enter the password and reenter it to confirm the spelling of it. Click OK.

14. If you have not done so already, configure the other computer as the guest system. Otherwise, click Finish to initialize the host machine.

15. To configure the guest computer, make sure the Direct Cable Connection Wizard is running (see step 1) on the guest machine and click Guest. Then click Next.

> **Note**
>
> If your PC has previously been configured as a host computer, click Change after the Direct Cable Connection Wizard starts to change the configuration. You also can change from guest to host by clicking the same Change button.

16. Select the port to which you want to connect. Remember, the port on the guest computer must match the port on the host machine.

17. Plug in the cable and click Next.

18. Click Finish to start using the Direct Cable Connection.

> **Note**
>
> See Que's *Special Edition Using Windows 95* for information on using Windows 95's Direct Cable Connection application.

Configuring Windows 95's PCMCIA Support

Windows 95 supports many PCMCIA cards (also known as *PC cards*) including modems, network adapters, SCSI cards, and others. Windows 95 PCMCIA drivers are 32-bit, dynamically loadable virtual device drivers and consume no conventional memory. Windows 95 enables you to plug in your PCMCIA card in your computer and start using the card immediately. You are not required to shut down and restart your PC for it to recognize the PCMCIA card. (You must have Plug-and-Play compliant drivers for this feature to work properly.) If you have a PCMCIA network card, for instance, you can plug it into your computer and Windows 95 does the rest: it detects the network card, loads the drivers, and connects to the network.

PCMCIA card installation is performed automatically by Plug and Play if Windows 95 includes supporting drivers for your PCMCIA card and socket. If your card is not automatically configured by Windows 95, you'll need to start the PCMCIA Wizard and set up the card manually. When you run the

PCMCIA Wizard, Windows 95 modifies your AUTOEXEC.BAT and CONFIG.SYS files by removing the lines that start the real-mode driver and adds a line that enables the PCMCIA socket.

To check if your PCMCIA socket is detected by Windows 95, do the following:

1. In Control Panel, double-click the System icon. In the System Properties dialog box (see fig. 3.31), select the Device Manager tab.

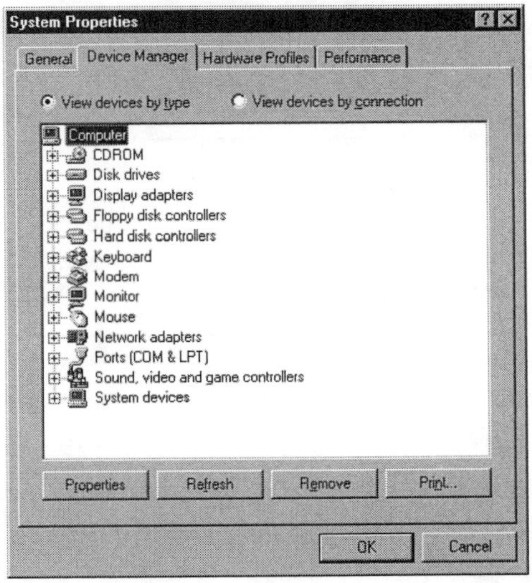

Fig. 3.31
Select the Device Manager tab to check for Windows 95 support of your PCMCIA card.

2. Select View Devices By Type and see if the PCMCIA Socket listing is included with the list of devices. If it's not, you must run the Add New Hardware Wizard from the Control Panel. If it is, you should be able to use your PCMCIA device.

3. In the Control Panel, double-click the Add New Hardware icon.

4. The Add New Hardware Wizard starts. In the first screen, click Next and then click No. This tells Windows 95 that you want to select the PCMCIA socket from a list, instead of Windows 95 searching for it automatically.

5. In the Hardware Types list box, select PCMCIA Socket. Click Next.

6. In the next screen (see fig. 3.32), select the manufacturer and model of your PCMCIA device. Click Next to have Windows 95 install the socket. If you have a setup disk from the manufacturer, click Have Disk instead. This installs the drivers from the floppy disk instead of from the hard disk.

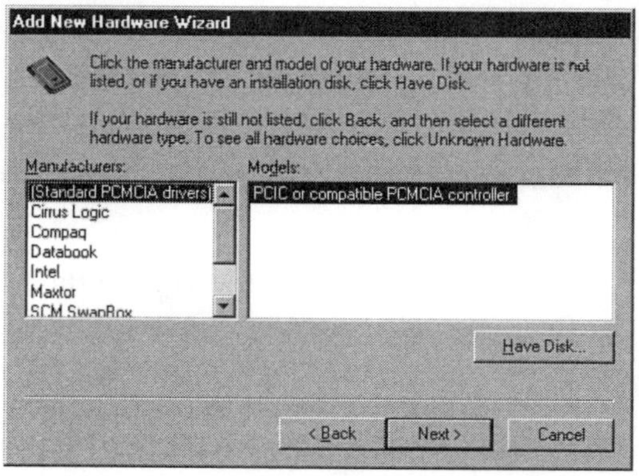

Fig. 3.32
Select the manufacturer and model of your PCMCIA device to set up the PCMCIA socket on your computer.

Note

Some legacy PCMCIA cards are not supported "out of the box" with Windows 95. If your PCMCIA card is not included on the list of supported cards, contact the card's manufacturer for updated installation disks for Windows 95.

If you have problems installing the PCMCIA socket on your computer, see Appendix B, "Troubleshooting Windows 95," or contact your specific PCMCIA manufacturer. They may have updated information and instructions on using your card with Windows 95.

Troubleshooting

When Windows 95 Setup runs ScanDisk, it reports errors on my hard disk. I run ScanDisk from DOS and everything is OK. Can I bypass ScanDisk during Setup?

Yes. Just use the /IS switch when you run SETUP.EXE from Windows 3.x or MS-DOS.

My drive is compressed using Stacker. Will Windows 95 work?

Yes, but all your drivers will run in real mode instead of protected mode. This goes for all third-party disk-compression utilities. If you use DriveSpace this is not the case, however.

My icons in Windows 95 are black. Is this normal?

No, this is not normal and may mean that the SHELLICO file has been corrupted. This file is a hidden file and is in your Windows folder. Delete this file and reboot your computer. As Windows 95 restarts, the SHELLICO file rebuilds automatically and your icons should display correctly. If this doesn't work, reboot the computer and press F8 when your computer boots. At the Startup menu, select Safe Mode and start Windows. Shut down Windows and then reboot your computer again.

Chapter 4

Using Custom Installation Options

by Rob Tidrow

Chapters 2 and 3 walked you through installing Windows 95 using the Typical and Portable installation processes. During both of those installations, you had an opportunity to select the Custom installation type and to choose several options that Windows 95 provides for you to load on your system. This chapter does not walk you through the entire Setup process for the Custom installation type, but it does explain the options from which you can choose to install.

In this chapter, you find out about the following:

- How to start the Custom installation process
- What Windows 95 options are available
- Descriptions of Windows 95 options

Understanding the Custom Install Process

During the Windows 95 Setup Wizard, Windows 95 displays the Setup Options screen, as shown in figure 4.1. (It is assumed that you already have started Setup and have completed the earlier stages of Setup.) The Custom Setup type enables you to pick and choose the way in which Windows 95 is installed on your computer. Custom is designed mainly for those users comfortable setting up their own environment, such as advanced users or system administrators. Even if you don't fall into one of those two categories of users, you still may want to modify the components that Windows 95 installs on your computer.

◀ See "Starting the Windows 95 Setup Wizard," p. 45

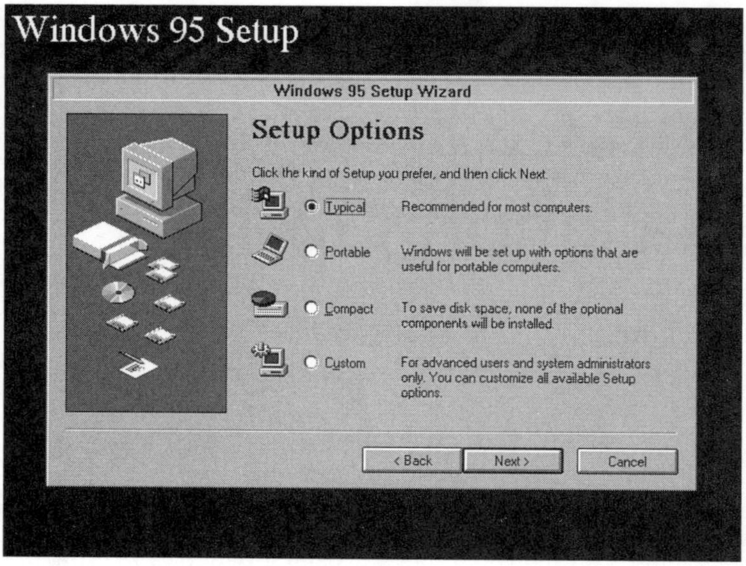

Fig. 4.1
Choose the Custom installation type to select the individual components for Windows 95.

After you click the Custom option and choose Next, you need to fill in your user information and Windows 95 identification data. Next, Windows 95 analyzes your computer and searches for the installed hardware that you may be using. When the Get Connected Wizard screen appears (see fig. 4.2), select those options you want to install, such as The Microsoft Network, Microsoft Mail, and Microsoft Fax. Click Next to continue.

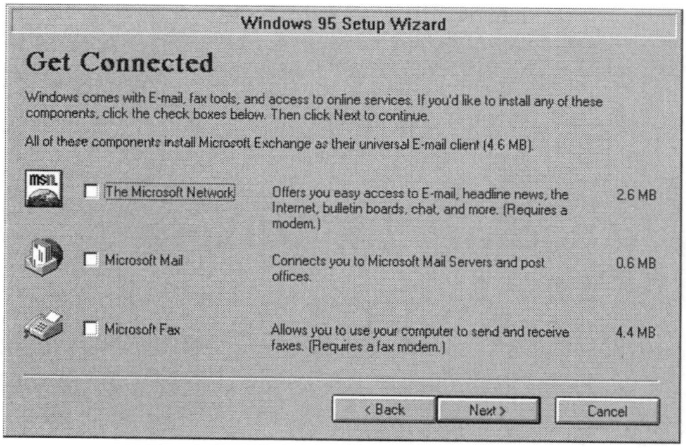

Fig. 4.2
Select the Get Connected options that you want Windows 95 to automatically install. Remember that Microsoft Exchange is installed (4.6M) if any of these options are selected.

◄ See "Getting Connected," p. 51

Setup next displays the Windows Components Wizard screen (see fig. 4.3) from which you can select to have Windows 95 install the most common components or enable you to choose the components. Because you want to modify the list of options to install, click the Show Me the List of Components So I Can Choose option. Click Next.

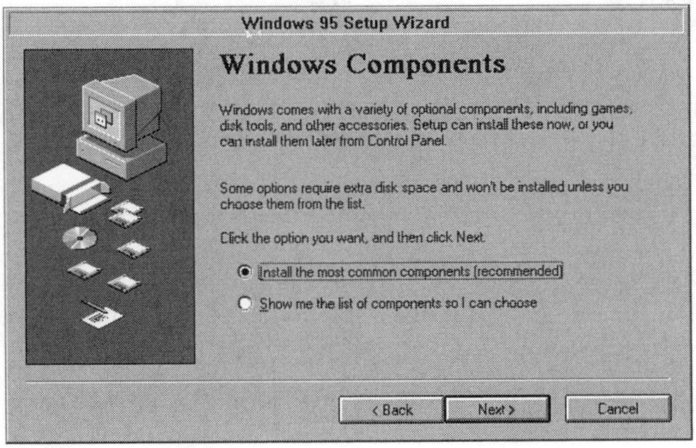

Fig. 4.3
Click the second choice in this screen to display all the options that Windows 95 can install.

The Select Components screen appears, as shown in figure 4.4. You now can pick the options that are installed on your computer. The next section, "Selecting Custom Install Options," describes all the options in detail.

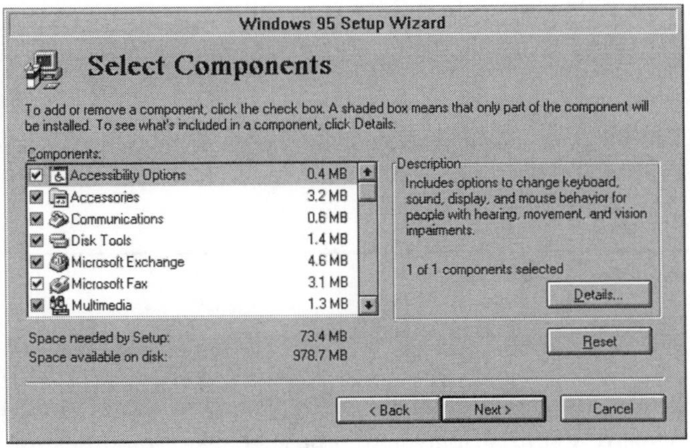

Fig. 4.4
Select the options you want to install on Windows 95 from the Select Components Wizard screen.

Selecting Custom Install Options

In the Select Components screen, you can see that several items are already checked. These are the default settings that Windows 95 installs if you do not change any of the choices manually. Check boxes that are shaded indicate that only part of the options for that component are selected. To see all the options of a component, such as Accessories, highlight that component and click the Details button. A screen appears that enables you to select specific options for the Accessories component.

Note

Depending on the type of hardware and network connections you have, your installation options may differ. If you do not have a sound card installed, for instance, you may not have all the sound schemes available to you in the Multimedia components options.

The component list is broken down into eight categories. The following list also includes the required hard disk space to install the component on your computer:

- Accessibility (0.3M)
- Accessories (space varies)
- Communications (1.5M)
- Disk Tools (space varies)
- Microsoft Exchange (4.3M)
- Microsoft Fax (2.1M)
- Multimedia (0.9M)
- The Microsoft Network (2.1M)

Each of these categories with their hard disk space requirements is explained in detail in the following sections.

Note

You can add any of these options after you install Windows 95 by double-clicking the Add/Remove Programs icon in Control Panel. You must have your Windows 95 Setup disks or CD available when you add these options.

Accessibility Options (0.3M)

Windows 95 includes several utilities that enable users who have hearing, movement, or vision impairments to use Windows 95 easier. These utilities include keyboard, sound, display, and mouse behavior modifications, such as high-contrast color schemes, StickyKeys, and SoundSentry. By default, Windows 95 installs the Accessibility options (see fig. 4.5), which you can access from the Accessibility Options icon in the Control Panel.

Table 4.1 lists and briefly describes the utilities available when you install the Accessibility Options.

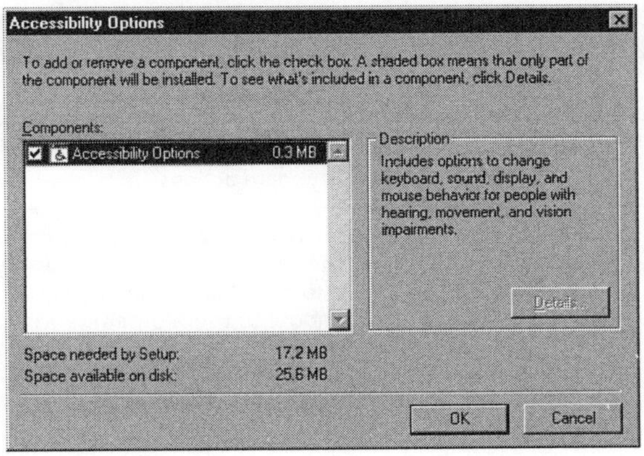

Fig. 4.5
By default, the Accessibility Options item is installed under the Custom Setup type.

Table 4.1 Accessibility Options

Type	Name	Description
Keyboard		Options that control the way in which the keyboard operates
	StickyKeys	Enables you to use the Ctrl, Shift, and Alt keys by pressing one key at a time, instead of holding down both at the same time
	FilterKeys	Instructs Windows 95 to ignore brief or repeated keystrokes. You also can slow down the repeat rate of keystrokes.
	ToggleKeys	Assigns a sound to beep when you press Caps Lock, Num Lock, and Scroll Lock
Sound		Options that display visual cues when your computer generates a sound
	SoundSentry	Instructs Windows 95 to display visual warnings when your system makes a sound. Some of these actions include flashing the active caption bar or desktop when a sound occurs.
	ShowSounds	Configures your applications to display captions for the speech and sound they make
Display		Option that controls how your monitor displays information
	High Contrast	Directs Windows 95 to use colors and fonts that are easy to read, such as white on black, black on white, or a custom combination that you provide

(continues)

Table 4.1 Continued

Type	Name	Description
Mouse		Option that replaces the mouse with keyboard actions
	MouseKeys	Enables you to control the pointer by using the numeric keypad on your keyboard. You also can change the pointer speed and choose to use MouseKeys with Num Lock on or off.
GeneralSettings		Option that Configures Accessibility Options
	Automatic Reset	Turns off Accessibility feature if idle for a specific amount of time. The default is five minutes.
	Notification	Prompts you when an Accessibility feature is turned on or off
	SerialKeys	Enables you to access keyboard and mouse features by using an alternative input device, such as head pointers and eye-gaze systems

If you do not want to install the Accessibility Options, click the check box next to its entry in the Components list to deselect it.

Accessories

If you used Windows 3.x, you are familiar with the Windows Accessories. These include the Calculator, screen savers, and wallpaper. In Windows 95, some of the Accessories are improved and have been replaced by other applications. WordPad, for instance, is a more powerful word processor that replaces Microsoft Write which is available in Windows 3.x. To access these options, click the Define button. The screen in figure 4.6 appears.

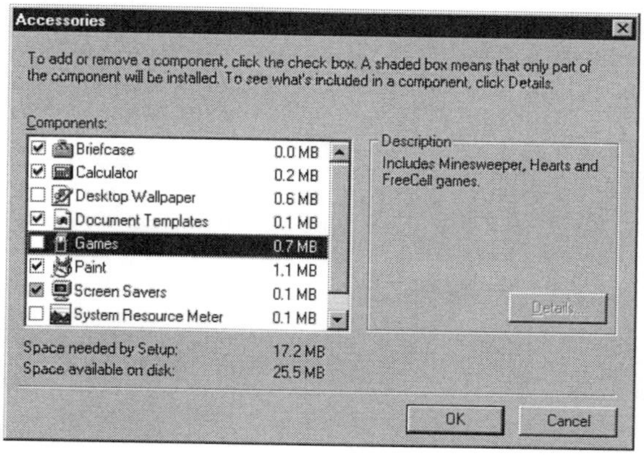

Fig. 4.6
You can select the Accessories options you want from this screen.

As you can see, only five of nine options are installed by default. You can select all the options or modify the list to your tastes. Each option is described in the following list:

- *Briefcase* (0.6M). Synchronizes files between computers. Installed by default.
- *Character Map* (0.1M). Inserts symbols and characters into your documents.
- *Clipboard Viewer* (0.1M). Displays the Clipboard's contents.
- *Calculator* (0.2M). Enables you to perform calculations. Installed by default.
- *Desktop Wallpaper*. Includes background pictures for your Windows Desktop.

> **Note**
>
> Included on the Microsoft Plus! disk are additional wallpaper files called Desktop Themes. Desktop Themes are full-color bitmaps that also include icons, sounds, and mouse pointers. If you have the Plus! disk from Microsoft, you might want to leave the Desktop Wallpaper option unchecked.

Plus!

- *Document Templates* (0.1M). Enables you to easily create new documents for your most common programs. You can see these file types after you install Windows 95 and right-click the Windows desktop. On the context-sensitive menu, choose New and the file type you want to create. Installed by default.
- *Mouse Pointers* (1.4M). Installs easy-to-see pointers for your mouse (see fig. 4.7).
- *Net Watcher* (0.2M). On a network, Net Watcher enables you to monitor your network server and connections. Installed by default.
- *Online User's Guide* (7.8M). Installs the online version of the *Windows 95 User's Guide.*
- *Games* (0.7M). Entertainment for your entire family! Includes Minesweeper, Hearts, and FreeCell games.

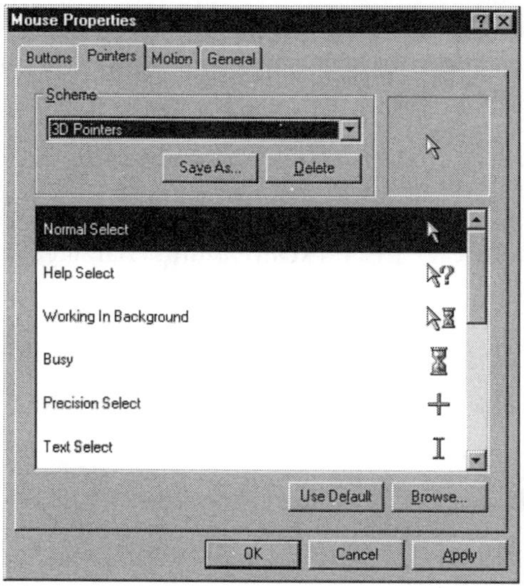

Fig. 4.7
You can select the types of pointers that your mouse uses by choosing different Schemes in the Mouse Properties sheet.

> **Note**
>
> On the Microsoft Plus! CD-ROM you can find a copy of a 3-D multimedia pinball game called 3D Pinball.

- *Quick View* (1.8M). Displays a preview of a document without opening it in its native application.
- *Paint* (1.1M). Replaces Windows 3.x's Paintbrush application. Paint is used to create, modify, or view bitmap graphics (see fig. 4.8). Installed by default.
- *System Monitor* (0.2M). Enables you to monitor your system performance. Not to be confused with the System Resource Meter.
- *Screen Savers* (0.1M). By default, Windows 95 installs one of the two screen saver options—Flying Windows. You can select the Additional Screen Savers option and use the following screen savers:

  Flying Through Space

  Mystify Your Mind

  Curves and Colors

  Scrolling Marquee (you provide the message to display)

  Blank Screen

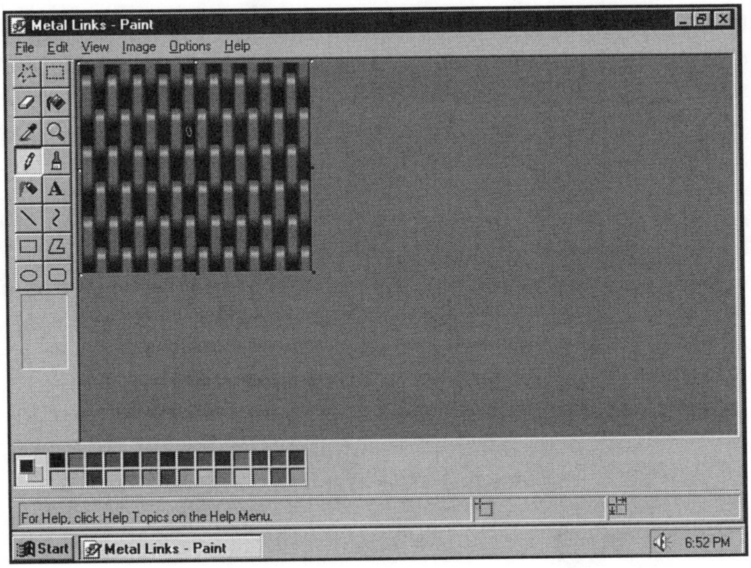

Fig. 4.8
Use Paint if you don't have a drawing package installed on your system.

- *Windows 95 Tour* (2.5M). Quickly teaches you some basic Windows 95 features and tasks. Only available with the CD-ROM version of Windows 95.
- *WinPopup*. On a network, use this utility to send and receive pop-up messages to other users.
- *System Resource Meter* (0.1M). Although this option is not selected by default, you may want to install it. It's a helpful utility that lets you view system resource levels, including GDI (Graphics Device Interface) and user resources. As you work, the Resource Meter appears on the far left side of the Windows Taskbar. To see the system meter in more detail, double-click the meter to display the screen shown in figure 4.9.

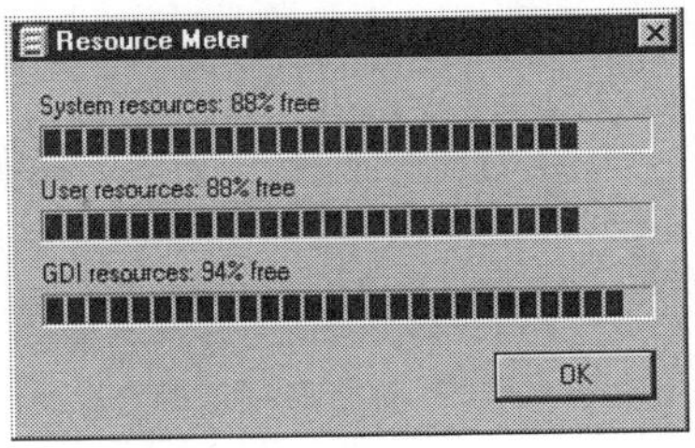

Fig. 4.9
Use the Resource Meter to see how your system resources are being used by Windows 95.

- *WordPad* (1.2M). An accessory in Windows worth using. WordPad replaces Windows Write that came bundled with Windows 3.x and is a full-featured, OLE 2.0-compliant word processor. You can create and edit documents in WordPad. It reads and saves files in the Microsoft Word DOC format by default. It can read Word 6.x DOC files, Windows Write (WRI), Rich-Text Format (RTF), and text files (TXT). Installed by default.

Communications (1.3M)

The Communications components (see fig. 4.10) include options for connecting to other computers or to online services. By default, all four options are selected, but you can modify these selections if you don't want all the options to install.

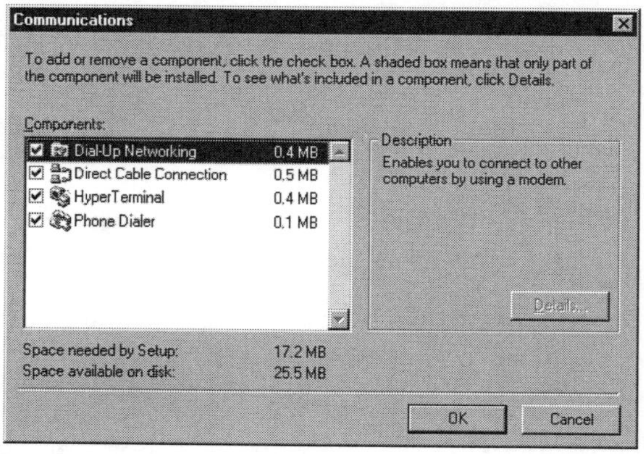

Fig. 4.10
The Communications components are helpful if you have a modem installed on your computer.

The options available are as follows:

- *Dial-Up Networking* (0.4M). Enables you to connect to other computers by using your modem.
- *Direct Cable Connection* (0.5M). Enables you to connect to another computer by using the parallel or serial ports and a cable.
- *HyperTerminal* (0.4M). Replaces Terminal in Windows 3.x and is a full-featured communications package, which enables you to connect to other computers and online services (see fig. 4.11). HyperTerminal is a superior product if you need a general communications package.

◀ See "Configuring Briefcase and Direct Cable Connection," p. 96

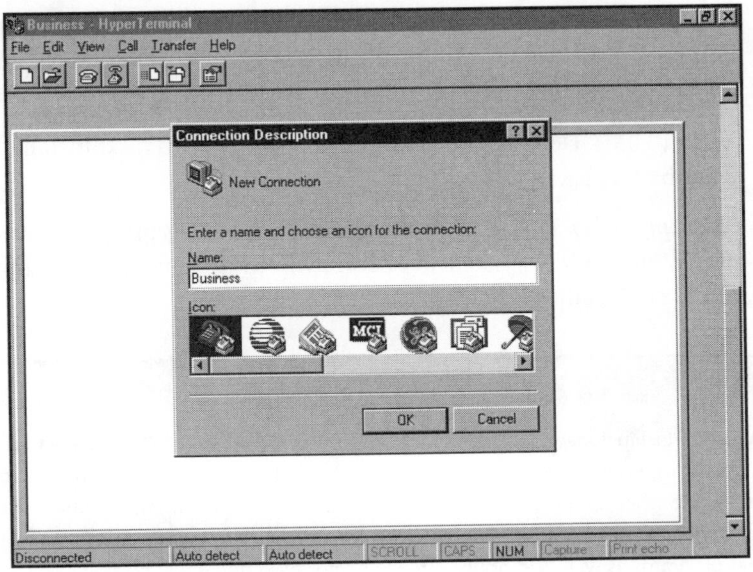

Fig. 4.11
Unless you swear by another communications package, give HyperTerminal a try. It's a very good (and fast) application.

> **Troubleshooting**
>
> *I accidentally installed HyperTerminal during the Windows 95 custom setup. I use another communications package instead. How can I get rid of HyperTerminal?*
>
> To remove HyperTerminal (or any other application for that matter) from Windows 95, click Start, Settings, Control Panel, and double-click the Add/Remove Programs icon. Click the Windows Setup tab, select Communications, and choose Details. Deselect the HyperTerminal check box and click OK. Click OK again, and Windows uninstalls HyperTerminal from your hard drive.

- *Phone Dialer* (0.1M). Enables you to use your computer to dial a phone number by using your modem. Once dialed, you can pick up the receiver and start talking (assuming someone picks up on the other end). Phone Dialer can be used by itself or with other applications, such as Microsoft Exchange. With Exchange, you can access the Phone Dialer and make calls from Exchange's Address Books.

Disk Tools

The Disk Tools that Windows 95 provides help you maintain and compress your disks. By default, only two of the three options are selected to install. The third option—Backup—is not installed but should be if you plan to back up your hard disk to floppy disks or tape units:

▶ See "Installing the Exchange Client," p. 202

- *Backup* (1.0M). Enables you to back up and restore backed up files from your hard disk to tape or floppy disks. Note that Windows 95 doesn't work with all tape drives, including DAT tape drives.
- *Defrag* (0.3M). Defragments and optimizes your hard disk. Installed by default.
- *Disk compression tools* (1.0M). Compresses your disks using DriveSpace after Windows 95 is installed. Enables you to pack more files onto your hard disk. Installed by default.

> **Note**
>
> Microsoft Plus! includes DriveSpace 3, an improved version of the DriveSpace that is included with Windows 95. Plus! also includes the System Agent, which enables you to schedule when to run other programs, including system maintenance utilities like Disk Defragmenter, ScanDisk, and compression utilities. The System Agent can run other programs as well, and notify you when your hard disk is low on space.

Microsoft Exchange (4.3M)

Microsoft Exchange is a new application that includes e-mail and messaging utilities. Exchange is a universal "in-box" for all the e-mail and fax communications you have. Figure 4.12 shows an example of what Exchange looks like on your desktop. Chapter 9, "Configuring Microsoft Exchange," describes how to set up Exchange on your system.

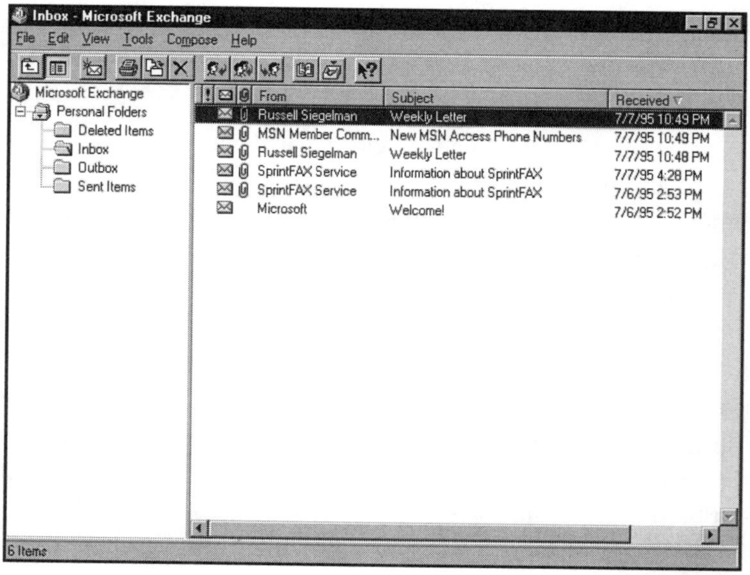

Fig. 4.12
Exchange can be used as your universal in and out box for most of your electronic correspondence.

The options that install by default under the Exchange component are as follows:

- *Microsoft Exchange* (3.7M). Includes integrated mail, MAPI (Message Application Programming Interface), and other messaging applications. You must install Exchange if you choose to install Microsoft Mail, The Microsoft Network, or Microsoft Fax.

> **Note**
>
> The *Messaging Application Programming Interface* (MAPI) is a programming API designed by Microsoft that enables software developers to create message-related applications that use a consistent interface. Some of these applications include electronic mail, voice mail, and fax applications.

- *Microsoft Mail Services* (0.6M). Enables you to access Microsoft Mail post offices to which you are connected. You must have a network connection to use this option.

Microsoft Fax (2.1M)

If you selected the Microsoft Fax option in the Get Connected Wizard screen during Setup, this option is selected by default. Microsoft Fax is built-in fax software that enables you to create, send, and receive faxes through Windows 95. The following options are available:

▶ See "Installing Microsoft Fax," p. 241

- *Microsoft Fax Service* (1.8M). Enables you to send and receive faxes.
- *Microsoft Fax Viewer* (0.4M). Enables you to view Microsoft Fax images.

Multilanguage Support

Windows 95 provides support for multilanguages. To write documents in different languages, select the Multilanguage Support component and select from the following options:

- *Central European language support* (2.3M). Includes support for Czech Republic, Hungarian, Polish, and Slovenian languages.
- *Cyrillic language support* (2.3M). Includes support for Bulgarian, Belarussian, and Russian languages.
- *Greek language support* (2.3M). Includes support for the Greek language.

Troubleshooting

How can I add support for multiple languages on Windows 95?

During Windows 95 Setup, you can select the Multilanguage Support option in the Select Components screen during the custom installation. If you've already installed Windows 95, click Start, Settings, Control Panel, and double-click the Add/Remove Programs icon. Click the Windows Setup tab and select Multilanguage Support. Click OK, and then click OK again. You'll need to have your Windows 95 Setup disks or CD handy.

Multimedia (0.9M)

By default, Windows 95 installs all seven options for the Multimedia component, which includes programs for playing sound, animation, and video. To use these options, you must have a multimedia-compliant computer, such as one with a CD-ROM and sound card installed.

- *Audio Compression* (0.2M). Utility that compresses audio for playback or recording on your computer. Installed by default.
- *CD Player* (0.2M). Enables you to play audio CDs on your computer's CD-ROM drive.
- *Media Player* (0.2M). Utility to play audio and video clips (see fig. 4.13). Media Player plays the following file formats: Video for Windows (AVI), Wave (WAV), MIDI (MID and RMI), and CD Audio. Installed by default.

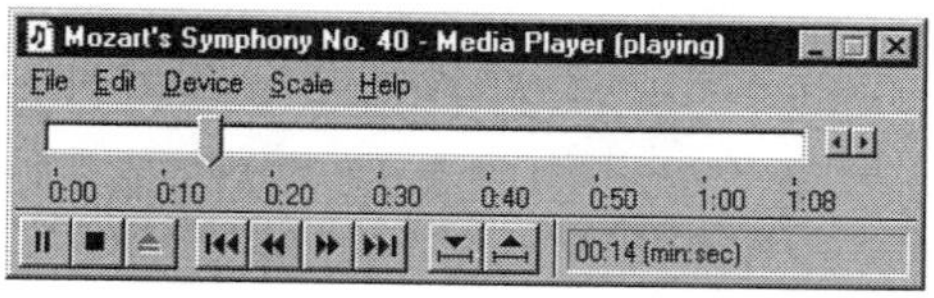

Fig. 4.13
In Media Player, you can play back that cool audio clip that you've been dying to hear.

- *Sound schemes*. You can choose from Jungle (3.4M), Musica (0.7M), Robotz (2.0M), and Utopia (1.0M) sound schemes. Sound schemes are sounds associated with different Windows 95 events, such as starting Windows 95 or maximizing a window.

Plus!

Note

If you have the Microsoft Plus! CD, don't bother installing the sound schemes that come with Windows 95. The ones included on the Plus! CD are much better (plus, if you've paid extra for them, you might as well use them).

- *Sound Recorder* (0.2M). Enables you to record and play sounds on your PC if you have a sound card and microphone. Installed by default.
- *Video Compression* (0.4M). Compresses video for multimedia playback or recording on your computer. Installed by default.
- *Volume Control* (0.1M). Utility to adjust the volume of the sound from your sound card (see fig. 4.14). Installed by default if Windows 95 detects a sound card.

▶ See "Configuring Sound Cards," p. 443

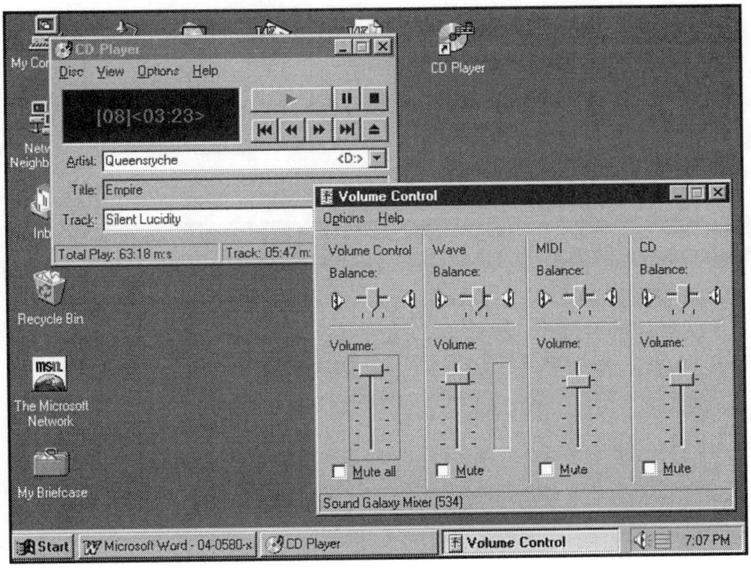

Fig. 4.14
You can adjust the volume of your speakers by using the Volume Control utility.

The Microsoft Network (2.1M)

If you chose to install The Microsoft Network on the Get Connected Wizard screen earlier in the Setup process, this option is automatically selected. The Microsoft Network enables you to connect to Microsoft's new online service. This option requires that you have a modem and that you also install Microsoft Exchange.

Finishing Custom Install

After you select the options that you want to install, click Next to continue the Setup Wizard. As you select components and options, you need to make sure the hard disk requirements do not exceed the space available on your hard disk. Below the Components list, Setup displays the hard disk requirements of your selections, as well as the space you have left on your hard disk.

▶ See "Setting Up a Microsoft Network Connection," p. 276

Keep an eye on this area and make sure the space needed by Setup does not exceed the space available. Even if it does, you will not get a warning until you click Next and want to continue installing Windows 95. Go back over your selections and decrease the number of items you have selected. A good place to do this is in the Accessories or Multimedia area.

Tip

Click Reset to restore the default selections that Custom installs.

Setup continues and starts copying files to your hard disk. Some of the components you install are configured at the end of Setup, such as Microsoft Exchange, Microsoft Fax, and The Microsoft Network. Some options are ready to go once Windows 95 is installed and running correctly.

Troubleshooting

I'm running Setup and I've made a complete mess of things choosing components. I want to go back to what Windows 95 initially had selected when I started the Custom Install option.

If you are still selecting options to install, you can click the Reset button in the Select Components screen.

Chapter 5

Installing Windows 95 over a Network

by Gregory J. Root

Windows 95 offers improved features for installing and running Windows over a network. Windows 95 provides programs and utilities to help you manage the installation of Windows to any number of computers on the network, whether you have 5 or 500 network users. This chapter teaches you how to plan for and take advantage of these new capabilities to successfully deliver Windows 95 to every desktop in your organization.

In this chapter, you learn

- Considerations and requirements for a server-based install
- What to plan for a shared installation
- How to perform the actual installation from a server
- What details remain to finish a server-based install

Performing a Server-Based Install

What is a server-based install? A *server-based install* provides a central storage location of the files necessary to set up Windows 95. Server-based installations provide control over the distribution of Windows 95 to network clients. There are two types of server-based installations you can perform:

- *Shared installation*. Installs the Windows 95 files onto the server. Windows, therefore, is only installed once and then shared with any number of workstations; the Windows 95 files are *not* actually present on the workstation's local drive.

- *Installation from a network to a workstation.* Performed when the Windows 95 files are copied to a network drive and then installed from the network drive to each individual workstation. In this case, the Windows files do reside on each workstation's hard drive. Installing Windows in this manner is much faster than from floppies or a CD because the network transfers the files quickly.

Tip

Installing from a network to a workstation is an excellent method of installation to use when only the server contains a CD-ROM drive.

Overview of Server-Based Install

It's important to review the major tasks that are part of a server-based install so you know what to expect at each turn as you install. The further you progress in installing Windows, the more decisions you need to make. Planning your task now will help save time and energy later.

The four steps to installing Windows are the following:

1. Planning the server-based install
2. Installing the setup files to the server
3. Installing Windows 95 on the network clients
4. Refining the server-based install

Planning the server-based install and shared-installation is the most important part of installing Windows 95. The decisions you make now affect your network situation in the future. You want to plan for your organization's growth and development as well as prepare for new and improved technologies. This chapter can help you plan for and complete your network installation.

Considerations of Server-Based Install

In conjunction with choosing the method of installation—shared or from the server to each workstation—you must decide how you want to start Windows 95 from the workstations. Preferably all workstations on a network will boot using the same method. The three methods of booting the workstations are as follows:

- The workstation boots from a local hard drive and then runs Windows 95 from the shared installation.
- The workstation boots from a floppy disk and then runs Windows 95 from the shared installation.
- The Windows 95 files are installed and run locally on the hard drive (the server was just a source of setup files).

Note

You also can create remote boot workstations using a disk image created on the server. Since this method of booting the workstation is seldom used with any Windows programs, it is not covered in this chapter; however, for more information about remote booting, see WIN95RK help file in the ADMIN, RESKIT, and HELPFILE folders on the Windows 95 CD.

The first two methods of booting to Windows 95 are used with a shared installation; the last method in the list is used only for workstations containing their own Windows 95 installation.

If you intend to have all the network clients run Windows 95 from a server (the first two items in the preceding list), you'll be able to:

- Control how each type of machine is configured to access the network.
- Give users the ability to move from computer to computer while retaining their desktop, Start menu, and network user ID.
- Reduce the amount of local hard drive space used to install the Windows 95 operating system. A major advantage to setting up Windows with the shared installation is that workstations with low resources can run Windows 95 without upgrading memory and space.

But, be aware that using a shared installation also has its disadvantages, including the following:

- More network traffic is created and thus, the entire system becomes slower, including access to the server's resources.
- Windows will run slower on each workstation than it would if installed to the local drives from the server.
- More hard drive space on the server is used than would be using an installation on a local hard drive.

- If the workstation has no hard drive or a very small hard drive, the swap files will be stored on the server instead of on the workstation; thus slowing the system even more.

> **Note**
>
> *Swap files* are temporary files created only when needed and only for the current Windows session. They do not permanently take disk space but they do rely on available disk space temporarily.

One final consideration to your network planning: in past Windows versions, the supervisor control over the program setup was a major reason to perform a shared installation. The supervisor, or network administrator, could control each workstation's files, folders, shared resources, and desktop. With Windows 95, however, a shared installation is no longer necessary for this type of control; a supervisor can easily go into a local setup of Windows and perform these same functions and protect those settings with Windows 95 security features.

Requirements of Server-Based Install

To perform a server-based install, you have to follow some technical requirements. First, the server-based installation programs and scripts are only available on the Windows 95 CD-ROM (in the ADMIN\NETTOOLS\NETSETUP directory). They are not available via online connections or on the Windows 95 floppy disks.

Second, a server-based setup can only be configured from a workstation with Windows 95 already installed. This workstation must also have a compatible network client running. And it must have access to the server on which the setup files are expected to reside and where the shared installation files will be placed.

You need to allocate at least 90M of hard disk space to store the server-based Windows 95 source files. The hard disk space requirements for the server may increase depending on how you have each network workstation start Windows 95. Use table 5.1 to determine how much hard disk space on the server will be used by all the network workstations. First, determine how many of each startup type you'll be using, then multiply the number of configurations of each type by the space required. Total all the startup types to get an estimate for how much space you need.

Table 5.1 Hard Disk Space Requirements for a Server-Based Install by Startup Type

Windows 95 Network Startup Type	Workstation Disk Space Required	Server Disk Space Required
Local hard disk startup, running Windows 95 locally	20M	0M
Local hard disk startup, running Windows 95 from server	2M	1.5M
Floppy disk startup, running Windows 95 from server	1.2M on floppy	2M

For each network workstation, you have to plan the amount of memory in each computer. No matter whether your workstation client is protected-mode or real-mode, 16M of RAM is recommended.

Planning Shared Installation

It's important to plan ahead before you define and create the shared installation so you make the most of your time and resources. Incorporate the following topics into your installation strategy:

- Network client components
- Machine directories
- Network card addresses
- Setup scripts

> **Note**
>
> The Windows 95 Resource Kit contains a Deployment Planning Guide that identifies other planning issues a network administrator would want to consider before installation. The Resource Kit help files are located on the Windows CD in the ADMIN, RESKIT, and HELPFILE folders.

Component Issues

Certain technical limitations exist with respect to network access before each workstation installation can begin. Other technical requirements affect which network clients or protocols are available. By considering these issues now, you can avoid hours of frustration.

To create a shared installation environment, you can install the Windows 95 source files on the following networks:

- Banyan VINES 5.52
- Microsoft Windows NT Server
- Novell NetWare 3.x and 4.x

Other types of networks will support a server-based installation to a local hard drive; however, they don't have the technical capabilities to support machine directories and user profiles. A *machine directory* is a directory on the server containing setup information about each workstation, such as memory, disk space, network card, and so on. A *user profile* is a directory that contains setup information about each user's Windows environment, such as desktop, customizations, files, and folders. The administrator uses each of these directories to identify workstations and users on the network.

To execute the installation process on a network workstation, the computer is required to have network access. It must be able to see the location where the server-based installation files are stored. If the workstation doesn't have network access, it won't be able to read the source files to perform the installation.

After you've confirmed all workstations will have network access, you need to consider which components you'll use. Windows supplies the necessary components for the aforementioned networks, including the client, protocol, and service. You can use Microsoft's supplied components or you can supply your own; however, Microsoft's seem to work more smoothly and efficiently than any third-party components. You choose the components in the Network Properties sheet (access through the Control Panel) on the Configuration page.

Note

Windows 95 supports 32-bit components, such as the protocol, network adapter, and File and Printer Sharing services. The Windows IPX/SPX-compatible protocol and TCP/IP (with a DHCP client) are 32-bit versions; Windows also supports a variety of 16-bit clients.

Troubleshooting

I'm using 32-bit protected-mode networking software components instead of the real-mode equivalents, but I'm having trouble with some of my programs. Could the 32-bit components be the problem?

Yes. Although 32-bit protected-mode components ensure speed and stability across the network, you might find compatibility problems with certain programs. Your only choice, at this time, is to stick with the real-mode networking components if you're having trouble, or you can try using different Windows programs.

Some of the workstations on the network use both 32-bit and 16-bit components. Could this cause a problem when I install Windows 95?

Yes. Each workstation must use all 32-bit protected-mode networking components or all 16-bit real-mode components. A workstation cannot use a combination of 16- and 32-bit components.

Client

Client software enables you to use the shared resources, such as files and printers, of other network computers. Microsoft includes the following network clients:

- Client for Microsoft Networks provides the client for a peer-to-peer network between other Windows 95 computers.
- Client for NetWare Networks provides a client that works well with NetWare 3.x and 4.x.

Caution

If you use Microsoft-supplied clients for a shared installation, each workstation *must* use all 32-bit, protected-mode networking components.

You can install other clients, such as Banyan or Novell, using a disk. You *are* able to install more than one network client, if required. However, for the sake of configuration management, you'll want to create as few variations as possible while still fulfilling the needs of the network users. Additionally, more network clients loaded on a computer and accessing data on the server reduce the amount of memory available to other resources and slow down productivity.

Protocol

The *protocol* is the language the computer uses to communicate over a network; and all computers on a network use the same protocol. Microsoft provides the following protocols:

IPX/SPX-compatible

Microsoft DLC

NetBEUI

TCP/IP

Again, you can install another protocol, such as Banyan or Novell, if you have a disk; however, Microsoft's protocols work well as they are.

Service

One type of service enables you to share your files and printers with others on the network. Other services include an automatic backup, network monitor agent, and so on. Microsoft provides file and printer sharing services for Microsoft Networks. You also can install other services, such as Arcada or Cheyenne Backup software, if you have the software disks.

Machine Directories

The concept of a machine directory is new in Windows 95. The *machine directory* contains configuration information specific to a particular computer, called the *hardware profiles*. This information includes video card, mouse type, memory, and so on. Hardware profiles enable Windows to adjust system capabilities to match the hardware. A machine directory can exist anywhere on the network and is required for computers that start from a floppy disk, but optional for a workstation with Windows 95 installed to the local hard drive.

A machine directory is different than a user directory. The *user directory* is where the preferences for the specific person are stored, such as icons on the desktop or screen savers. In cases where someone may move from computer to computer throughout the day, configuration settings like the video card, network card, and monitor type stay with the computer. User profiles, such as Start menu items, desktop items, and font and color preferences, should follow the user when he/she logs onto any workstation on the network.

Machine directories offer several benefits:

- Each workstation's settings are stored in a central location on the network so that no matter who logs onto that workstation, the correct settings are used.

- The administrator can use a single boot image from the network to start several computers.
- The administrator can easily replicate shared installations for new computers without running Setup again.

If you plan to specify machine directories for multiple computers, you can save time by creating a text file that contains the computer names and locations of the machine directories. You can use this file later to specify the machine directories after installation of Windows 95.

To create the text file, use the following format:

computername,*servername**directory**machinedirectory*

where *computername* is the name of the workstation, *servername* is the name of the server, *directory* is the name of the directory and in some cases the drive or volume, and *machinedirectory* is the name of the directory for the workstation.

An example of an entry for the text file is

director,\\humble_41\vol1\winsetup\ibmpc350

In the text file, use only one entry for each machine directory per line. Save the file in text-only format (ASCII), and store it in a shared directory on the server.

Network Card Addresses

For each computer that uses a shared installation machine directory, you need to identify the address of the network card. The network card address is usually a 12-digit alphanumeric field. If any of the addresses are less than 12 digits, zeros must be added to the left side of the field until it is exactly 12.

Tip

The network card address can be found in NetWare environments by typing the command **USERLIST /A** at a command prompt. Each user ID has a network address after it. The address can be found in Windows for Workgroups networks by typing the command **NET DIAG /S** at a command prompt.

In a text editor, compile a list with three columns. The first column should be the computer name. The second column should be the name of the machine directory you create. The third column is the network card address, such as:

```
I.E.Dell   f:\machine\DellPC        00123a5542d3
```

Save the text under any name you can easily recognize later while setting up machine directories and addresses. You can print the file now, or later when you're ready for it. The file you enter this information to is called the MACHINE.INI. The MACHINE.INI file points the computer to the correct machine directory during Windows 95 Setup and thereafter. See the section "Using Network Card Addresses" later in this chapter.

Setup Scripts

Setup scripts are mini-programs that assist in making choices—such as choosing protocols, services, security, clients, and so on—during the Windows setup and installation. Windows offers default scripts that take care of most installation settings; however, you can edit these scripts or create your own as you work with the server-based installation.

The MSBATCH.INF setup script comes on the Windows 95 CD and installs with the other Windows source files to the server. The MSBATCH.INF file contains instructions Windows needs to set up the workstations.

The MSBATCH.INF file contains the following scripts:

[Setup]	WorkstationSetup=1
CCP=0	DisplayWorkstationSetup=0
ProductID=*xxx-xxxxxxx*	Display=1
ProductType=1	Hdboot=1
Uninstall=0	RPLsetup=1
[Network]	

Each line in the script represents a setting for the workstation. Product ID, for example, lists the product's number that you enter when you're installing Windows 95. Uninstall lists whether you choose to enable uninstall (1) or disable uninstall (0). The Network section contains script that affects your remote, floppy, or local drive install of the workstations.

Caution

Creating setup scripts is beyond the scope of this book. Before you choose to write setup scripts, see the MS Windows 95 Resource Kit Help file for clarification.

Note

The Windows 95 CD includes an additional program you can use to create a setup script. The Batch program is located in the Admin, Nettools, Netsetup folder. The Batch file displays a dialog box in which you enter your name, computer's name, workgroup, and so on. Additionally, you can choose network options (protocol, client, and so forth) and installation options (set prompts, search folders for devices, and so on). After you make your choices in the dialog box, you can save the batch file as an INF file and copy it to the Windows directory on the server. Also in the NETSETUP folder is a BATCH help file that you can use if you have problems.

To find out more about creating setup scripts, see the Windows 95 Resource Kit help on Server-Based Setup, located on the Windows 95 CD-ROM. In the ADMIN folder, choose RESKIT, HELPFILE, and the WIN95RK help file.

Tip

The Windows 95 CD-ROM contains some sample scripts with different levels of security. They can be found in ADMIN\RESKIT\SAMPLES\SCRIPTS.

Installing Windows 95 from a Server

After you plan your installation, you're ready to actually install Windows. Installing Windows 95 is a threefold process:

- Copy the installation source files to a server
- Create machine directories
- Install Windows to the workstations

Copy Files to Server

To make the Windows 95 setup files available to everyone on the network, they must be placed in a common area. If you are only creating a common location for everyone on your network to install Windows 95 to their local hard disk, you'll learn everything in this section. If you're creating a shared installation environment, the rest of this chapter will guide you step by step.

For shared installation, you can install the Windows 95 source files on one of the following networks:

- Banyan VINES 5.52
- Microsoft Windows NT Server
- Novell NetWare 3.x and 4.x

For installing from the server to a workstation, you can install on the following networks:

- Artisoft LANtastic 5.x
- DEC PATHWORKS
- IBM OS/2 LAN Server 1.2 or greater
- Microsoft LAN Manager 2.x
- Microsoft Windows 95 peer server (using Client for Microsoft)
- NetWare using Microsoft's Client for NetWare Networks
- SunSoft PC-NFS 5.0

To create a server directory containing the Windows 95 source files, follow these steps:

1. Log onto the network file server with administrator privileges from a machine running Windows 95. Logging on as administrator also guarantees you have the security rights to create new directories and files on the server.

> **Note**
>
> System administrators may want to protect any directories they create (or directories that Windows 95 creates) from the average user so that no one can delete or modify the directories on the server.

> **Note**
>
> The computer you use to install Windows 95 to the server must have a CD-ROM drive. You need your Windows 95 CD as well.

2. Start Windows 95 and open the Explorer.
3. Open the Windows 95 CDI. In the ADMIN\NETTOOLS\NETSETUP\ folder, double-click NETSETUP.EXE. The Server Based Setup dialog box appears, as shown in figure 5.1.

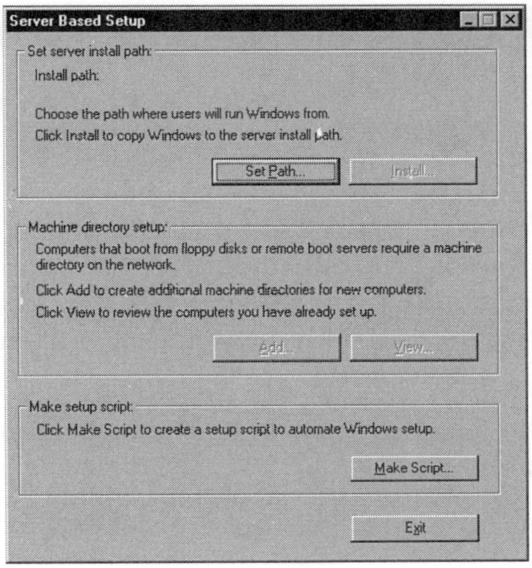

Fig. 5.1
The Server Based Setup dialog box lists the current server where the source files are to be installed.

4. If the path to the server listed in the Set Server Install Path area is not correct or there is no path listed, click the Set Path button (or Change Path if a path has already been set). When you click this button, the Server Path dialog box appears (see fig.5.2). Enter the Universal Naming Convention (UNC) path to hold the source files, and click OK or press Enter.

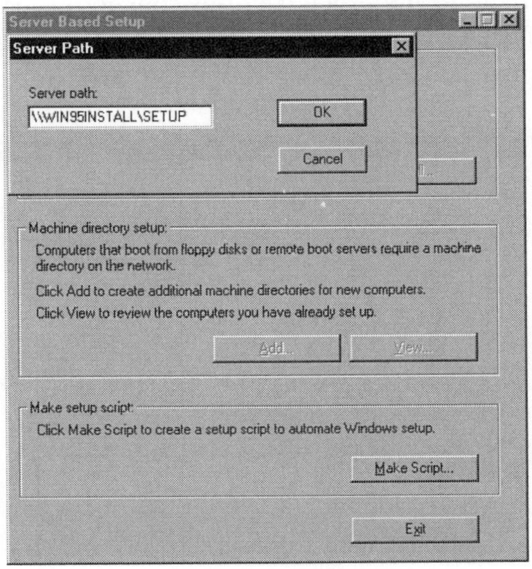

Fig. 5.2
Enter the server and path name in UNC format to specify the destination for the source files.

Tip

The UNC format for a NetWare server directory is
*servername**volumename**directoryname*

If you enter a directory name that doesn't exist, you are prompted to create it. If you don't remember the exact path for the location, use the Network Neighborhood to browse the network. After you've identified the path, you can click the Server Based Setup icon in the taskbar to bring the application forward.

5. After entering the UNC path of the directory, choose Install. The Source Path dialog box appears (see fig. 5.3). From the following options, choose the Server install policy for installing the Windows 95 files to the server:

- *Server*. Select this option to store the files on the server as a shared installation.
- *Local Hard Drive*. Select this option to install all Windows 95 files to the workstation's hard drive.
- *User's Choice*. Select this option to enable the user to choose where to install the Windows files.

The Path to Install From should already contain the location from which you will be copying. If not, enter the correct path to the CD-ROM drive. Enter the Path to Install To path.

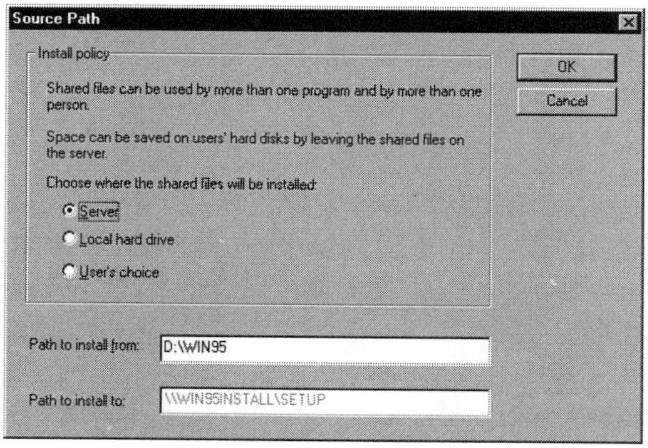

Fig. 5.3
Select the install policy for shared files and enter the directory name from which the Windows 95 source files will be copied.

6. Click OK to confirm your settings. At this point, you are given the option to create a default script. Figure 5.4 shows the Create Default dialog box. You can choose Don't Create Default to begin installing Windows 95 source files to the server; Windows uses the default MSBATCH.INF setup script from the server drive.

   Alternatively, you can click Create Default to choose specific configuration settings by creating your own setup scripts.

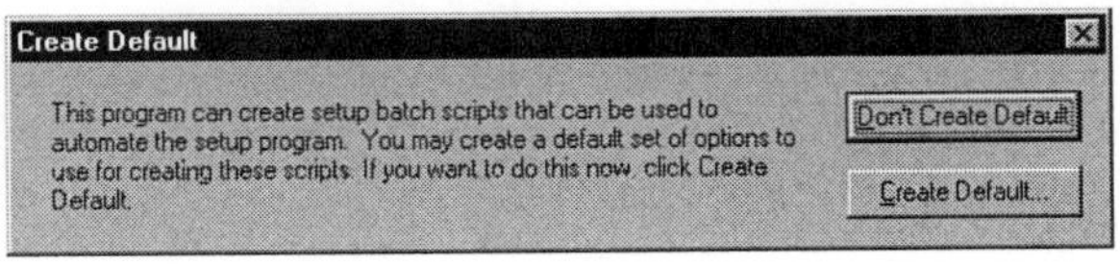

Fig. 5.4
Choose whether you want Setup to create the default script.

7. Next, you are prompted for your CD Key number to identify the product. The 10-digit number is located on the back of the Windows 95 CD case on an orange sticker. Enter the number in the text box, as shown in figure 5.5.

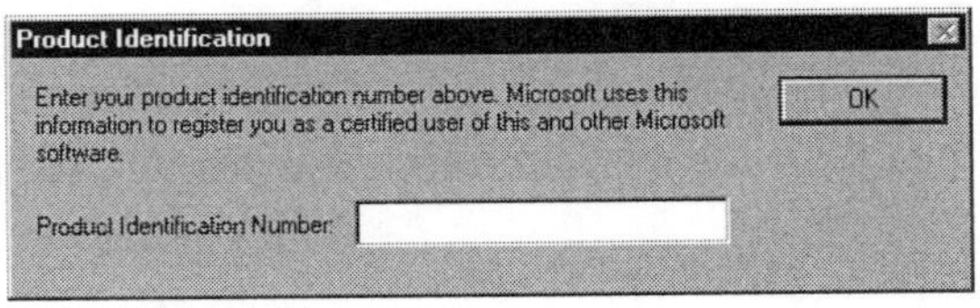

Fig. 5.5
Enter your product identification number from the orange sticker on the back of the Windows 95 CD case.

8. After you confirm your entry in the Product Identification dialog box, Setup copies all the files into the directory you specified earlier. You are able to track the progress in the Copying Files dialog box.

   If you need to stop the process, click the Cancel button in the Copying Files dialog box. Notice during the process that Net Setup has marked all the necessary files and folders as Read Only, just as they would be marked on the CD. When copying is complete, choose OK.

Note

If you use a special virus scanning-application, a company-wide sales application, or other such application, be sure to copy the required DLLs and VxDs into the appropriate subdirectories on the server. You should also add these files to the default MSBATCH.INF file.

Troubleshooting

I get a warning message when I try to enter a UNC path in the Server Path dialog box. Why can't I complete the installation?

You're not logged in as system administrator, or you do not have the access you need to create a directory on this server. You can specify another server, if you have privileges for it, or you can quit Setup and log on using the appropriate account.

Or, perhaps you're not entering the correct path; be sure you include the double backslashes, server name, volume name, and so on.

How do I set sharable attributes in the new Windows 95 folder? Can I use the FLAG command?

You don't need to use the NetWare FLAG or any other command to set sharable attributes; Windows source files are marked read-only automatically so they're ready to be used by the workstations.

If you're creating a shared installation, read the next section to learn how to set up machine directories. If you used Net Setup to copy the files to a central location just for users who will install all of Windows 95 on a local hard drive, you can install those files to the workstation now. Users can double-click the Setup icon in the server's directory to begin the installation.

Create Machine Directories

The machine directories are used by computers that start Windows 95 by booting from a floppy disk. The machine directory is required by the network and contains the WIN.COM, full Registry, and startup configuration files, such as the SYSTEM.INI and WIN.INI, of a workstation on the network. For workstations on which Windows is locally installed, the machine directory is optional.

Tip

For floppy boot disk workstations, the swap files and TEMP directory are also in the machine directory.

Note

If you plan to specify machine directories for multiple computers, you must first create a text file containing the computer names and locations as described in the section, "Machine Directories," earlier in this chapter.

To create the machine directories, follow these steps:

1. In the Server Based Setup dialog box, choose Set Path (or Change Path) and specify the path to the server containing the Windows source files if the path is incorrect or missing. Click OK.

2. In the Machine Directory Setup area, click the Add button. The Set Up Machine dialog box appears.

3. To define a single computer's machine directory, choose the Set Up One Machine option. Enter the computer name and the path to its machine directory (see fig. 5.6).

   To set up multiple machine directories using a batch file, choose the Set Up Mulitiple Machines option. Enter the path and file name of the batch file containing the list of computer names and machine's directories.

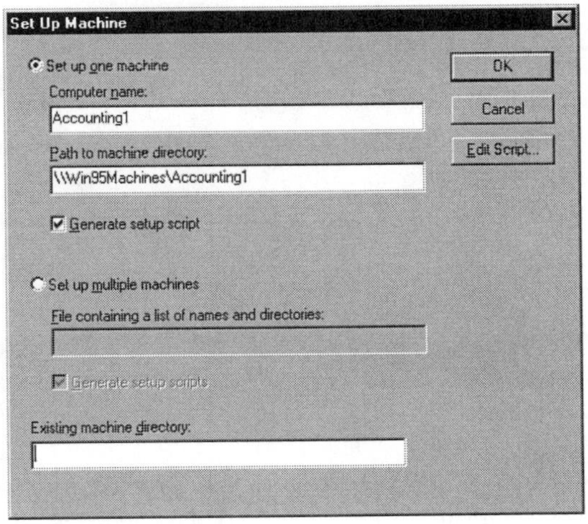

Fig. 5.6
For a single computer, enter its name and the path to the machine directory your creating.

4. To let the Server-based Setup create a default script, select the Generate Setup Script check box.

> **Note**
>
> To edit the default script for the machine directory, click the Edit Script button to display the Default Properties dialog box. This dialog box enables you to create or edit a setup script. For more information about setup scripts, see the Windows 95 Resource Kit help files located on your Windows 95 CD. Click OK when finished editing the script to return to the rest of the steps.

5. If you want to use an existing machine directory instead of creating new machine directories, enter the directory location in the Existing Machine Directory text box.

> **Note**
>
> If you would like to view the list of computers using this shared installation directory, click the View button in the Server Based Setup dialog box. A list of computer names appears. As you highlight each entry in the list, its machine directory is displayed at the bottom of the dialog box.

6. After you've made your choices in the Set Up Machine dialog box, click OK. Setup then creates the machine directories (if you named new directories) and the default installation scripts (if you specified a script should be created). Setup stores the setup script in each machine directory.

> **Note**
>
> You can also click the Make Script button to create a setup script from the Server Based Setup dialog box.

7. Choose Exit to close the Server Based Setup dialog box.

> **Troubleshooting**
>
> *The Registry for one of the workstations is corrupted. What can I do to fix it?*
>
> The SYSTEM.DAT and USER.DAT files are stored in the machine directory along with other configuration information, such as the SYSTEM.INI and WIN.INI. If the Registry becomes corrupted, you may be able to discern the problem by viewing these files in a text editor. If you cannot restore the Registry in any other way, you need to run the Windows 95 Setup again for that workstation.
>
> If you archive your custom setup scripts, you can save time and energy when running Setup again.

Using Network Card Addresses

Every computer starting Windows 95 from a floppy needs an entry in the MACHINES.INI file. If the computer doesn't have an entry, it can't access Windows 95.

Each entry in this file contains a network card address, the machine directory location, and the drive letters to associate with UNC names required for setup. Using the data you collected in the section Network Card Addresses earlier in this chapter, fill in the data. Format each entry in the MACHINES.INI to look like the example in the file:

```
;[node address]
;SYSDATPATH=drive:\path
;drive=\\server\share specified in sysdatpath
```

;[*node address*] is a 12-character address of the network adapter. In ;SYSDATPATH=*drive*:*path*, the *drive*:*path* is the one mapped to a drive letter in the same MACHINES.INI section.

Installing to the Workstations

Now that you've created a server-based installation, performing the installation on each workstation is your next step. Choose the method you want to use for booting the workstations and create or modify the startup scripting to give you the appropriate results.

The choices for starting Windows 95 Setup on the workstation are

- Starting Setup from a local hard drive
- Starting Setup from a local floppy disk
- Starting Setup on the workstation's hard disk

Booting from a Local Floppy Disk

If computers on your network will be booting from a local floppy disk, you'll run Windows 95 Setup once for each unique network card configuration. A *unique configuration* is defined as the make, model, and hardware settings for the card. The unique configuration has nothing to do with the computer type or model. After Setup creates a boot floppy for each configuration, you can duplicate the disks and distribute them to the corresponding users who have network cards in each configuration.

You need to create a startup disk and install the network client to that disk so you can attach to the network if you're starting Setup from a local floppy disk. Next, you need to edit the MSBATCH.INF, or other scripting file you may have created, to include entries for the appropriate boot type.

To create a startup disk in Windows 95, insert a formatted floppy disk into the floppy drive of the computer from which you run Windows 95. Follow these steps:

1. Click the Start button and choose Settings.
2. Choose Control Panel.
3. Double-click the Add/Remove Programs icon.
4. Choose the Startup Disk tab and click Create Disk. Windows creates the disk using the floppy disk.
5. When Windows is finished, choose OK to close the dialog box.
6. From the server or a workstation to which you're logged on as administrator, install the network client to the startup disk to enable you to attach to the network.

To edit the startup script, log on to the network. You can edit the startup script file—whether MSBATCH.INF or another file you created—in a DOS or Windows text editor, such as DOS Edit or Windows Notepad. Edit the [Network] section to include one of the following entries for booting from a floppy drive:

WorkstationSetup=1

Hdboot=0

RPLsetup=0

Save the file under the same name and in the same directory. The name must use an INF extension, and the directory must be the directory to which you copied the Windows source files onto the server.

To install to the workstation, follow these steps:

1. Insert the startup disk into the workstation's floppy drive and reboot the computer. You can press Ctrl+Alt+Delete to warm boot.
2. Attach to the network.
3. You can change to the directory on the server that holds the Windows source files on the server and enter the following command:

   setup msbatch.inf

   SETUP is the Windows setup command, and MSBATCH.INF is the name of the default setup script; you want to substitute another setup script file name if you created the file yourself.

> **Note**
>
> Alternatively, you can enter the UNC paths from the A prompt in this format:
>
> **share_dir_server****directory**\SETUP.EXE **machines_server****directory****computer**\MSBATCH.INF
>
> Press Enter. *Share_dir_server* is replaced with the name of the server holding the server-based Windows 95 source files. *Directory* is the directory name containing the source files. *Machines_server* is the name of the server holding the machine directories. *Computer* is the name of the machine being set up. MSBATCH.INF is the name of the script being used. MSBATCH.INF is the default file name, although you may have created your own installation script.

4. Windows performs the ScanDisk system check. Click Continue to continue with the regular setup program.

5. Windows then copies the setup files it needs to complete the workstation installation you specified. As Windows leads the user through the process, it prompts for a new startup disk. Do not overwrite the existing boot floppy; insert a new formatted disk in the drive.

> **Note**
>
> If you are currently using a real-mode client to access the network, you are asked to insert the existing boot disk. Setup retrieves files from your current configuration, and then places them on your new startup floppy.

6. Repeat this process for each unique network card configuration. Then, duplicate enough copies for the number of users of each type. Don't forget to keep one of each type on file in a safe place!

   Each user will restart his/her computer using the new boot disk. Because the network card address is entered in the MACHINES.INI file, the correct information is placed in each machine directory.

Troubleshooting

Accessing the swap file takes too long on my workstation. Is this a network problem that can be fixed?

Workstations that boot from a floppy disk are set up so the swap file and TEMP directory are stored in the workstation's machine directory on the server. Since the workstation must go across the network to access the swap file, it will take longer to get through network traffic and back again. If you have sufficient space on your hard drive, you can change the location of the swap file to your hard drive. Add a **pagingfile=** path entry to the [386Enh] section of the SYSTEM.INI file stored in the machine directory.

Booting from a Local Hard Drive

If the computers on your network will be booting from a local hard drive to run the shared copy of Windows 95 on the network, you must change the setup script (INF) file to include the following:

WorkstationSetup=1

Hdboot=1

Each workstation must run Windows 95 Setup by following this process:

1. If you're installing from Windows 3.x or Windows for Workgroups, and a drive letter isn't already mapped to the shared installation directory, choose Disk, Select Drive from the File Manager. Then, choose File, Run in the Program Manager.

   Or, from a DOS prompt, change the current working directory to the shared installation directory.

2. You can change to the directory on the server that holds the Windows source files on the server and enter the following command:

   setup msbatch.inf

   SETUP is the Windows setup command, and MSBATCH.INF is the name of the default setup script; you want to substitute another setup script file name if you created the file yourself.

3. The Windows 95 installation process starts and leads the user through the process. When complete, about 2M of files will reside on the local hard drive. The remaining files will be shared from the shared installation directory.

Note

Alternatively, you can enter the UNC paths in this format:

\\share_dir_server\directory\SETUP.EXE

\\machines_server\ directory\computer\MSBATCH.INF

and press Enter. *Share_dir_server* is replaced with the name of the server holding the server based Windows 95 source files. *Directory* is the directory name containing the source files. *Machines_server* is the name of the server holding the machine directories. *Computer* is the name of the machine being set up. MSBATCH.INF is the name of the script being used. MSBATCH.INF is the default file name, although you may have created your own installation script.

Troubleshooting

While installing to the workstation, Setup asked if I wanted to create a local installation or a shared installation of Windows 95. What should I do?

The setup script file you used to start setup contains the line `DisplayWorkstationSetup=1`, which offers the user the choice of how to set up Windows to the workstation. To select a shared installation, you must specify the path for the machine directory. For future installations, remove the `DisplayWorkstationSetup=1` statement from the INF setup script file.

Installing Windows to the Workstation's Hard Disk

To install Windows from the server to the Workstation's hard disk, change directories to the directory containing the Windows setup files on the server. Type **setup**. If you have specified a setup script file, enter the name of the file after setup and press Enter. Setup installs the Windows files to the local hard disk.

Finishing Server-Based Install

Now that you've installed Windows to the server and to the workstations, you'll want to make some adjustments to the network configurations.

Networking Support

If you installed Windows 95 on top of a real-mode network client, all network access will be in 16-bit real-mode unless and until you switch to a protected-mode client. The 32-bit protected-mode clients supported by Windows 95 include the Client for Microsoft Networks and the Client for NetWare Networks.

Some advantages to using the protected-mode in Windows include the following:

- Supports multiple network redirectors that access the network file system simultaneously
- The NetWare network adapter driver is installed automatically and improves performance and reliability
- Supports peer resource sharing
- Supports plug and play, client-side caching, and automatic reconnections
- Enables the use of remote administration of the Registry and the use of the Network Monitor
- Supports long file names, if the server supports long file names
- All configurations are stored in the Registry so you don't have to maintain separate configuration files

If you installed Windows 95 to use a local hard drive with a real-mode client, you must install the protected-mode client using the network icon located in the Control Panel.

If you are still using a real-mode client after creating floppy disk-based installation, Windows 95 Setup was not able to locate a protected-mode client in its source files. You have to obtain the protected-mode client from the network vendor and re-create the floppy boot disk.

Setting Configuration Information

When configuring the workstations for shared installations, you may need to modify the AUTOEXEC.BAT of each workstation. If, for example, the AUTOEXEC.BAT previously contained a statement to start the network, such as `NET START`, Windows Setup places the shared installation commands at the same location. The modification you need to make is to ensure any command lines for DOS-based utilities in the AUTOEXEC.BAT come *after* the comand to start the network:

```
@ECHO OFF
SET PROMPT=$P$G
DOSSHELL
NET START
```

Until the DOSSHELL command is moved after the NET START entry, the DOS utility will never load. The AUTOEXEC.BAT file should be rearranged to look like the following:

```
@ECHO OFF
SET PROMPT=$P$G
NET START
DOSSHELL
```

The following programs reside in the shared installation directory:

CHOICE.COM	FDISK.EXE	SCANDISK.EXE
DISKCOPY.COM	FIND.EXE	SHARE.EXE
DOSKEY.COM	LABEL.EXE	SORT.EXE
EDIT.COM	MEM.EXE	START.EXE
FORMAT.COM	MOVE.EXE	SUBST.EXE
KEYB.COM	MSCDEX.EXE	XCOPY.EXE
FC.EXE	NLSFUNC.EXE	

File and Disk Management

This section offers a few considerations about files and file management when working with shared installations of Windows 95. Windows includes many disk tools you can use to analyze, report, and repair problems with physical disks. Additionally, Windows includes tools you can use to manage and protect the data on the drives.

Consider the following when managing your network workstations:

- *Microsoft Backup or network backup agent.* Back up user data regularly using either MS Backup or one of the two network backup agents included with Windows: Arcada and Cheyenne. Backing up user data safeguards against file loss and corruption.

- *Disk Defragmenter.* Use to organize fragmented files—files stored in noncontiguous sectors on the disk—to improve file access time.

- *DriveSpace.* Use to free space by compressing the drive space and the files on the drive. You can decompress the drive at any time without damaging data on the drive.

- *ScanDisk.* Use periodically to analyze and repair areas on the hard or floppy disks, including file allocation table, long file names, file system structure, directory tree structure, and so on.

You should plan to use the file and disk management utilities at regular intervals. You might, for instance, run ScanDisk every day or two, run Backup every week, and run Disk Defragmenter every third month.❖

Chapter 6

Configuring the Windows 95 Desktop, Display, and Fonts

by Rob Tidrow

By far, the most significant change in the Windows 95 user interface is its Desktop. Instead of limiting the Desktop to open applications or minimized icons, the Windows 95 Desktop can be used to launch applications, store folders, display shortcuts to files or programs, and provide quick access to Windows 95 configuration settings.

You also learn how to install and remove fonts on your system in this chapter. Windows 95 makes it easier than ever to add a font to your system and use that font from any folder on your system or a network folder.

In this chapter, you learn how to

- Create shortcuts
- Set background and wallpaper images
- Change screen savers
- Specify Desktop colors
- Configure the display
- Install and remove fonts

Creating Shortcuts

Windows 95 enables you to create shortcuts. A *shortcut* is a link to an object that enables you to access that object more quickly. Shortcuts are similar to program icons in Windows 3.x, but differ in that shortcuts can be created for any object on your system, including programs, files, documents, or even hardware devices. You might, for instance, provide a shortcut to your word processor application, such as Word for Windows, that you can double-click to start the application. You also might create a shortcut to a specific document, such as an Excel spreadsheet (see fig. 6.1). When you double-click the spreadsheet shortcut, if Excel is not opened, the shortcut opens Excel and loads your linked spreadsheet.

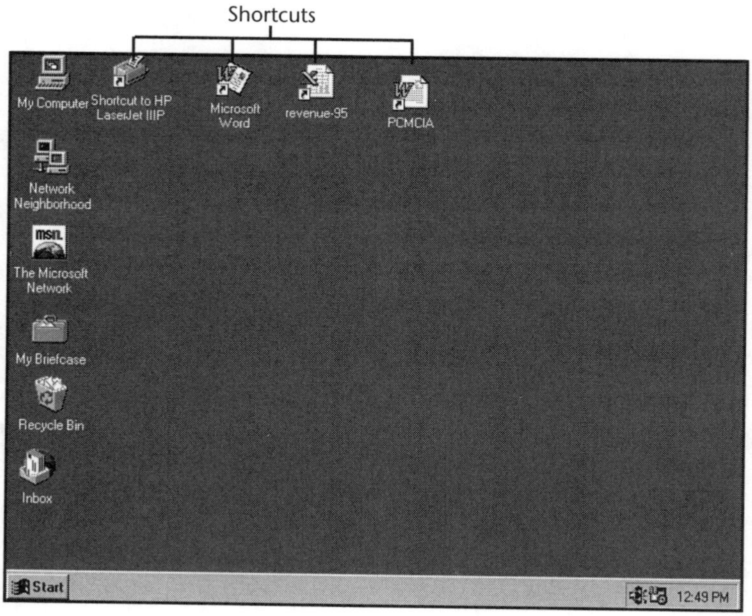

Fig. 6.1
Shortcuts can be created for folders, applications, devices (such as hard drives), files, or other objects.

You can distinguish shortcuts from other items on the Desktop, such as folders, by the small arcing arrow on the icon (see fig. 6.2). This denotes that the icon is linked to an object that you can start or open by double-clicking it.

You can add shortcuts to your desktop or place them in a folder so that you can quickly access them as you work. The next two sections show you how to add and delete shortcuts to your desktop.

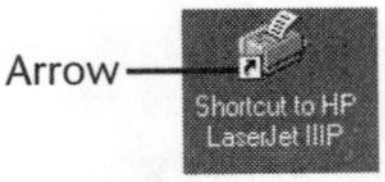

Fig. 6.2
Shortcuts have tiny arrows on them.

> **Troubleshooting**
>
> *One of my shortcuts lost its link. How can I reestablish it?*
>
> For the most part, Windows 95 automatically updates a shortcut when you move the object's file. If, however, Windows cannot find the file name, you can right-click the shortcut and click Properties. Display the Shortcuts page on the Shortcuts Properties sheet. In the Target box, enter the full path of the file name to which the shortcut is linked.

Adding Shortcuts to Your Desktop

Windows 95 provides a few different ways to add shortcuts to your desktop. You can stay on the Desktop to create a shortcut, or use the Explorer to drag and drop objects to the Desktop.

The following steps show you how to create a shortcut using the Desktop context-sensitive menu:

1. Move the mouse pointer to the Desktop and press the right mouse button. The context-sensitive menu appears (see fig. 6.3).

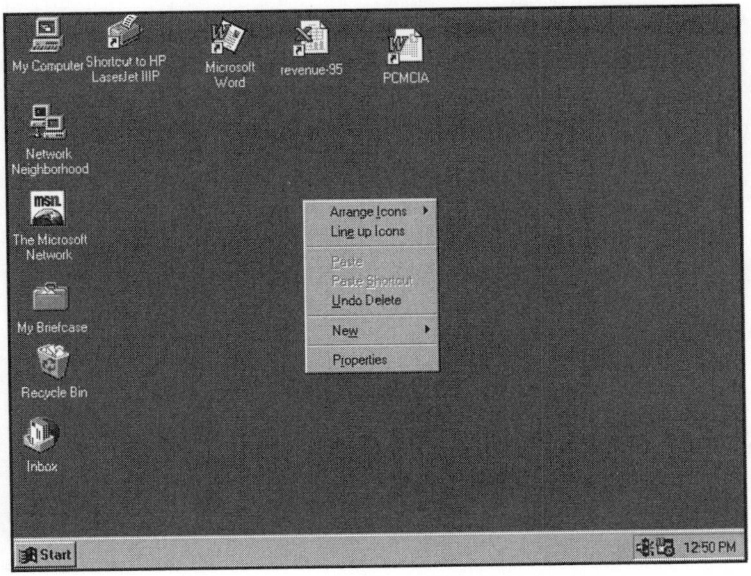

Fig. 6.3
Use the context-sensitive menu on the Desktop to create a shortcut.

2. Choose New, Shortcut. The Create Shortcut dialog box appears, as seen in figure 6.4.

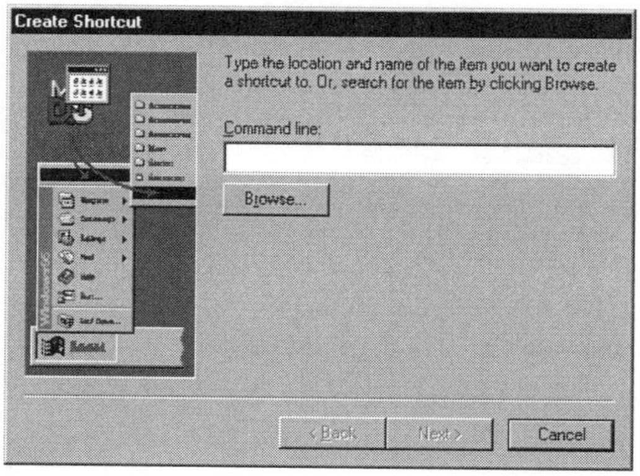

Fig. 6.4
The Create Shortcut dialog box enables you to add shortcuts to your desktop.

3. In the Command Line box, type the path and file name of the object you want to create a shortcut for.

> **Tip**
>
> Click the Browse button to search your system for a specific object name and location. By default, Windows 95 displays only programs. You can locate any file or object by clicking the Files of Type drop-down button and selecting All Files. Select the object you want, and click the Open button.

4. Click Next. The Select a Title for the Program dialog box appears (see fig. 6.5).

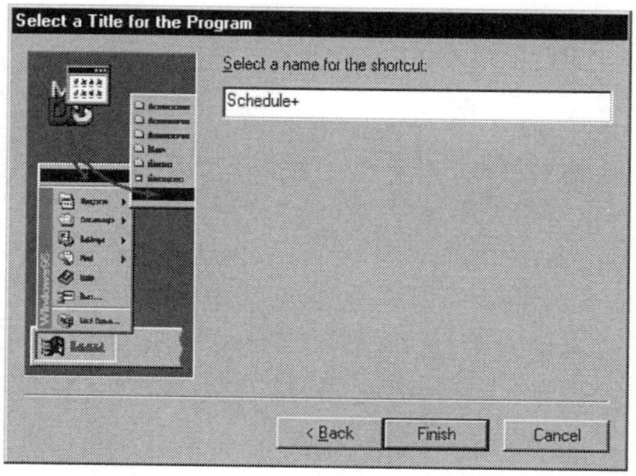

Fig. 6.5
In the Select a Title for the Program dialog box, you need to specify a name for your new shortcut.

5. In the Select a Name for the Shortcut box, enter a name for the new shortcut. Windows 95 provides a default name that is the same as the file name of the object. You can use this name or type over it to create your own.
6. Click Finish.

Tip

Changing the shortcut name does not alter the original file name.

Note

When you create a shortcut name, you can use up to 256 characters in it. This is probably overkill. You should, however, name the shortcut using an easy-to-understand name. If you have shortcuts for several documents that use the same application (such as a word processor or spreadsheet), make sure that your shortcut names are distinguishable so you open the appropriate document (see fig. 6.6).

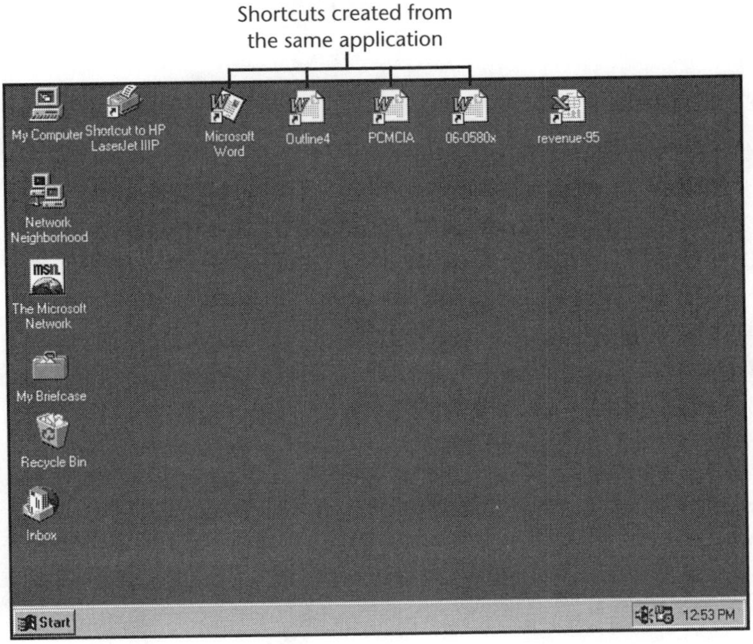

Fig. 6.6
Shortcuts created for different documents within the same application can be difficult to keep straight.

Windows places your new shortcut on the Desktop. You can move it on the Desktop, rename it, or delete it (see "Deleting Shortcuts" later in this chapter).

Another way to create a shortcut is to use the Explorer to drag objects onto the Desktop. This is the quickest way to create several shortcuts at once. Use the following steps to create a shortcut using the Explorer:

1. Open the Explorer to the folder that contains the file or object you want to set up as a shortcut.

2. Press the right mouse button on top of the item you want as a shortcut and drag it to the Desktop. Release the mouse button (see fig. 6.7), and click Create Shortcut Here from the context-sensitive menu.

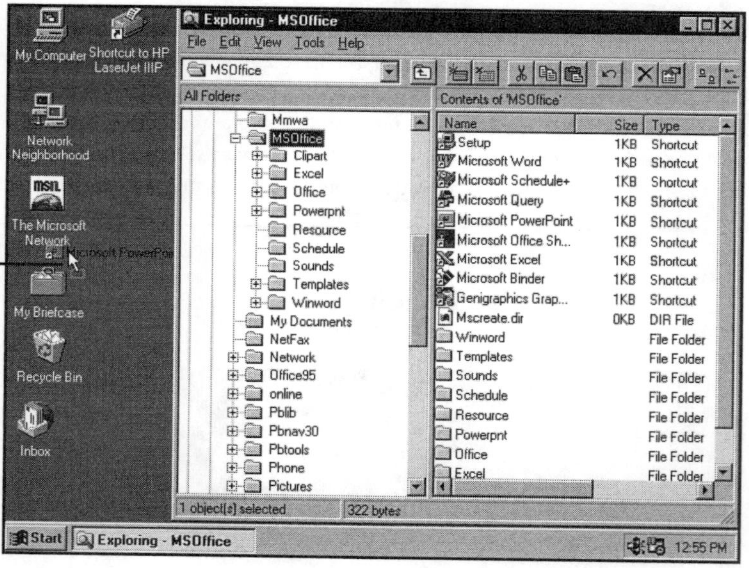

Dragging a shortcut from the Explorer

Fig. 6.7
Click the right mouse button to drag an object to the Desktop so you can create a shortcut for the object.

Caution

If you drag an item from the Explorer to the Desktop using the left mouse button, Windows 95 automatically moves that item to the Desktop folder. This occurs for any object except for applications. If you drag an application using the left mouse button, Windows 95 automatically creates a shortcut to that application, without moving the application file.

Note

After a shortcut is created, you can quickly rename it by clicking the shortcut name and typing a new name. Press Enter. You also can right-click the shortcut and select Rename from the context-sensitive menu. Type the new name and press Enter.

As mentioned earlier, you can quickly create several shortcuts at once by dragging several objects from the Explorer. To do this, press Ctrl when clicking objects in the Explorer (see step 2 in the preceding series of steps), and then release both Ctrl and the right mouse button on the Desktop. You then can rename the shortcuts.

Note

To create a shortcut to a printer, choose Start, Settings, Printers. In the Printers folder, click the printer to which you want to create a shortcut and press the right mouse button. Drag the printer icon onto the Desktop and select Create Shortcut(s) Here. Now you can drag files from the Explorer or Desktop on top of the printer shortcut to print your documents.

Changing Shortcut Properties

You can view or change the properties of a shortcut by right-clicking the shortcut and selecting Properties. Click the Shortcut page. Figure 6.8 shows a typical shortcut property sheet. Here you can change the icon, what kind of window it appears in, or the key combinations used to start it.

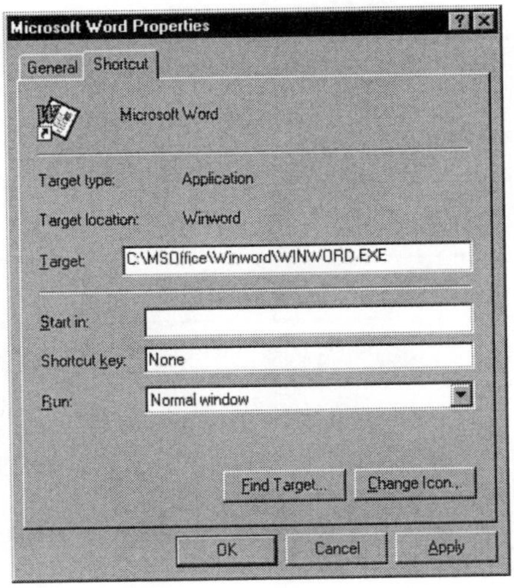

Fig. 6.8
A typical shortcut property sheet enables you to customize your shortcut.

The icon that appears when you create a shortcut may not suit your need. Or, you may have a difficult time seeing it against the Desktop wallpaper. You can change the icon by clicking the Change Icon button and scrolling through the Current Icon list (see fig. 6.9) until you find one you like. Click it and click OK. On the Shortcut Properties sheet, click Apply. The shortcut's icon changes to the one you selected.

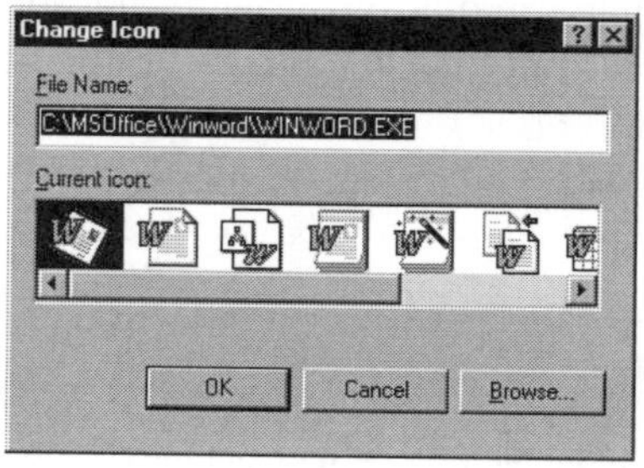

Fig. 6.9
Tired of that drabby icon for your shortcut? Change it by modifying the shortcut's properties.

Tip

Click the Browse button to find other icons on your computer.

Another setting that you can change for your shortcuts is the keyboard combination that activates or switches to the shortcut. In the Shortcut Key box on the Shortcut page (refer to fig. 6.8), enter the keyboard shortcut you want to use. This key combination can be used in any Windows application to start or switch to the shortcut's application. For instance, you might want to assign Ctrl+Shift+W to start Word for Windows.

Caution

Any key combination set up using the preceding instruction cannot be used in any other application or feature in Windows 95. The Windows 95 shortcut key combination overrules all other settings you may already have set.

Note

The shortcut property settings also include an option to set the way in which the shortcut item opens. In the Run drop-down list, you can select Normal, Minimized, or Maximized. Normal displays the window sized as you last used it. Minimized opens the object and places it on the taskbar in a minimized state. Maximized displays the object in a maximized window.

Deleting Shortcuts

Shortcuts placed on the Desktop are a handy way to start items that you frequently use. Through the course of a week, if you add a shortcut for each file, application, or device you use, your desktop may start getting cluttered. Even though the resource requirement of shortcuts is minimal, each one adds up after awhile. If you find yourself being hampered by the number of shortcuts set up, delete a few.

You can delete shortcuts in several ways. The quickest way is to click the shortcut and press Delete. Answer Yes to the confirmation dialog box that appears, such as the one in figure 6.10. Another way to delete a shortcut is to right-click on a shortcut and select Delete. Again, answer Yes to confirm the message.

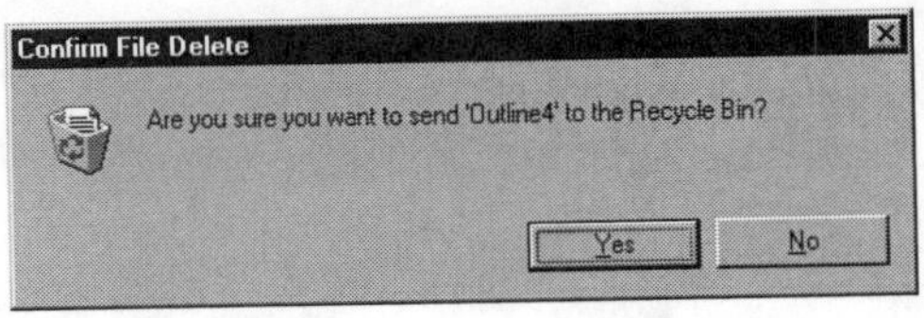

Fig. 6.10
If you are sure that you want to delete a shortcut, answer Yes. Otherwise, select No.

Adding Folders to Your Desktop

Although you can add a shortcut to a folder on the Desktop, you also can create a folder that exists on the Desktop. You might, for instance, want to place a folder on the Desktop that contains all your business-related documents—memos, faxes, spreadsheets, databases—so that you can open one folder to access all of them (see fig. 6.11).

In fact, when you install Windows 95, a few common folders are placed on your desktop automatically (see fig. 6.12), including the following:

- My Computer
- Network Neighborhood, if a network is installed
- Recycle Bin
- Inbox
- The Microsoft Network

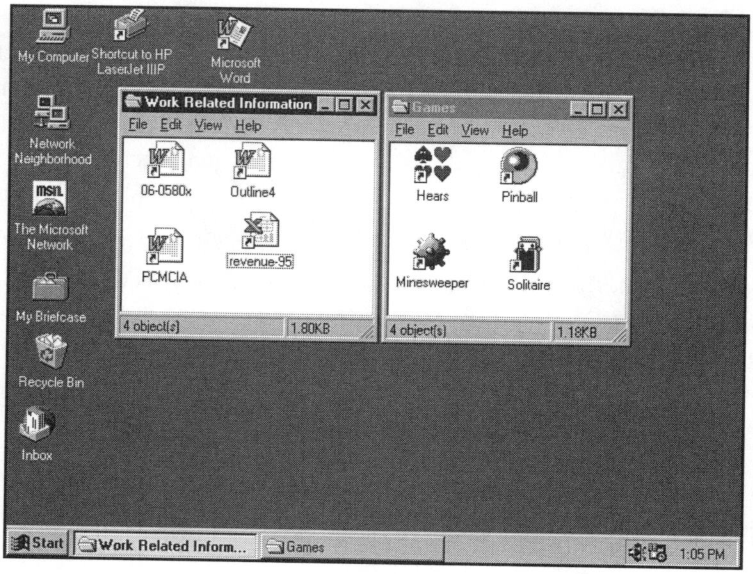

Fig. 6.11
Create folders on your desktop to hold all your important—or not so important—documents.

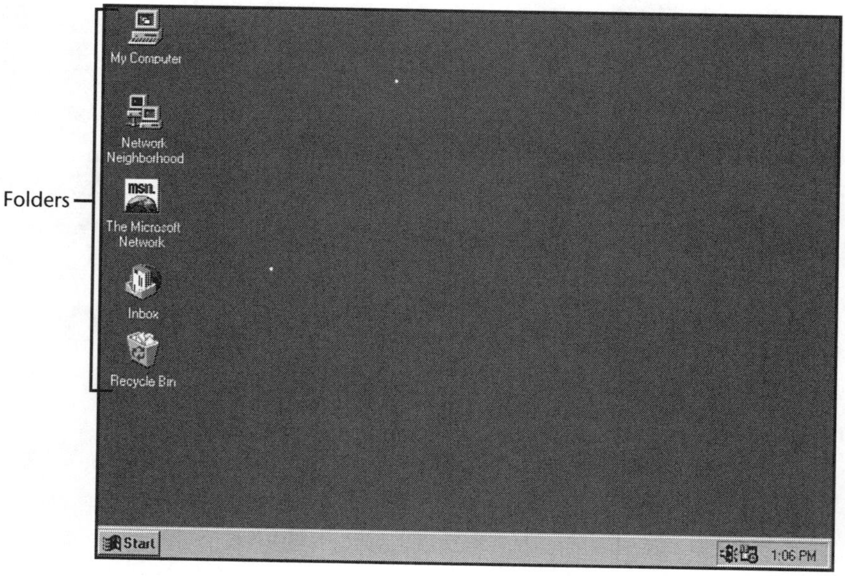

Fig. 6.12
Upon installation, Windows 95 gives you a few folders to start using.

To add a folder to the Desktop, use the following steps:

1. Move the mouse pointer to the Desktop and press the right mouse button.

2. From the context-sensitive menu, choose New, Folder.

3. A new folder appears on the Desktop. Name the folder and double-click it to add items to it.

4. In the new folder, choose File, New, Shortcut to add shortcuts to the folder, or File, New, Folder to add a folder within the folder.

Tip

You also can drag files, folders, and other objects from the Explorer into your new folders to store them. For added convenience, the folder does not have to be open for you to drag an object to it. Just drag and drop the object over the closed folder.

Setting Background and Wallpaper Properties

On your wall or desk in your office, you probably have family pictures, awards, Post-It notes, photographs of the ocean, and other items that help you escape the pressures of the day. Not to be outdone, Windows 95 enables you to jazz up your desktop to add color to it. You can change the background patterns and wallpaper, and even create your own wallpaper. The following sections show you how.

Note

The Microsoft Plus! Companion for Windows 95 gives you more than a dozen different desktop themes to help you dress up your Windows 95 environment.

Plus!

Changing Patterns and Wallpaper

When Windows 95 installs, it loads a standard Windows Desktop theme and wallpaper. You can experiment with the background patterns and wallpaper to suit your taste. To change the desktop settings, you modify the Desktop properties, which you can access by right-clicking anywhere on the Desktop and selecting Properties from the context-sensitive menu. The Display Properties sheet appears (see fig. 6.13).

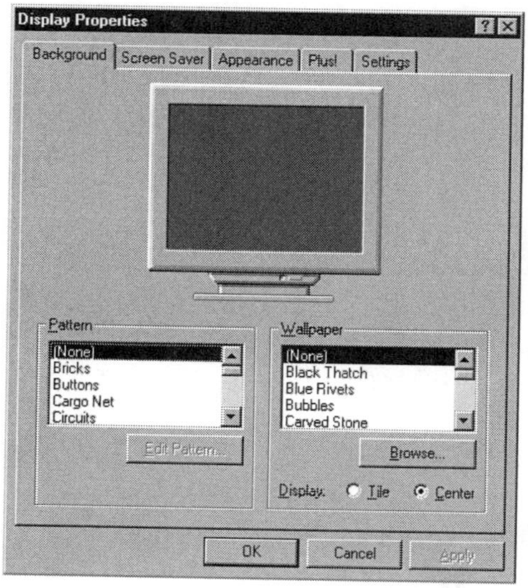

Fig. 6.13
You change the way your desktop looks using the Display Properties sheet.

Tip

You also can display the Display Properties sheet by double-clicking the Display icon in Control Panel.

In the Pattern drop-down list box, you can choose from a number of different patterns to display on your desktop. These range from Bricks and Buttons to Triangles and Waffle's Revenge. You also can choose `(None)`, which places no pattern on the desktop. Scroll through the list of patterns and click one to view an example of how it looks in the "monitor" on the Background page. Click Apply to place the pattern on your desktop.

Note

You can change the way the pattern looks, or create your own by choosing a pattern in the Pattern list and clicking Edit Pattern. In the Pattern Editor (see fig. 6.14), click the Pattern box to edit or create a new pattern. If it is a new pattern, type in a new name in the Name box. Click Done when you finish and then click OK.

You can remove a pattern when you are in the Pattern Editor by selecting its name from the Name list and clicking Remove.

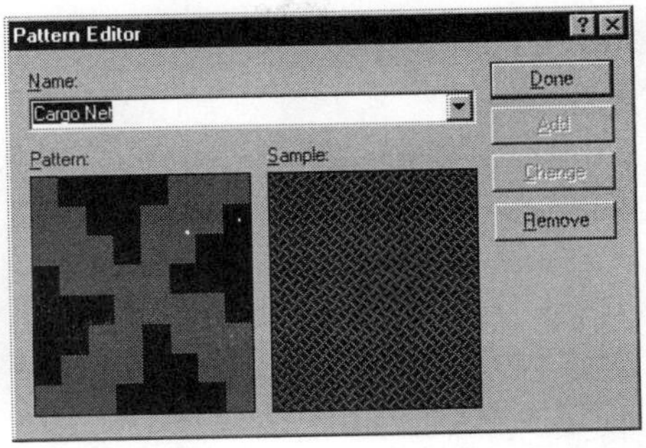

Fig. 6.14
Use the Pattern Editor to modify the way your desktop pattern looks.

When you select a pattern, it fills the entire background. The color of the pattern is determined by the color you have set up for your background, which is set in the Appearance tab of the Display Properties sheet and discussed later in this chapter in "Specifying Desktop Colors."

To change the wallpaper, scroll down the Wallpaper list box. The names of wallpaper from which you can choose include Black Thatch, Blue Rivets, Clouds, Metal Links, Setup, and more.

Note

By default, only a few wallpaper files are installed during Windows Setup. To add additional wallpaper files, double-click the Add/Remove Programs icon in Control Panel. Then select the Windows Setup page and select the Accessories item in the Components list. Click the Details button, select Desktop Wallpaper, and click OK twice. Make sure that you have your Windows 95 installation disks or CD handy when you do this.

After you select the wallpaper, you can preview it in the preview monitor in the Display Properties sheet. Click Apply to place the wallpaper on your desktop. You can display the wallpaper in the center of your screen by clicking the Center radio button, or have it cover the entire screen by clicking the Tile button.

Tip

When you tile wallpaper, it covers any pattern that you may have selected earlier.

Choose OK when you have the pattern and wallpaper you like. Your desktop displays your selections, as shown in the example in figure 6.15.

Fig. 6.15
The Forest wallpaper and Buttons patterns is added to the Windows 95 desktop.

Creating Your Own Wallpaper

If you don't like the ready-made images that Windows gives you for wallpaper, you can do one of three things. First, you can elect not to have wallpaper. Second, you can buy the Microsoft Plus! CD and get about a dozen new desktop themes that include colorful wallpaper images. Or third, you can create your own wallpaper image. To do this, all you need is a bitmap image saved as a BMP file. If you have a graphic that you've installed on your computer, such as from an online service like CompuServe or Prodigy, or from a CD loaded with pretty pictures, you can convert it to BMP format using graphic converters. If the file is already in BMP format, you don't need to worry about converting it.

Note

An excellent graphic utility that enables you to convert graphics formats is Paintshop Pro, a shareware utility from JASC, Inc. You can find it on many bulletin boards and online services. It reads several different file formats, including PCX, JPG, TIF, and GIF and then converts them to BMP.

Place the BMP file in any folder on your system and then open the Display Properties sheet. On the Background page, click the Browse button and locate the file on your system. Click OK when you select the file, and then click OK again to place your custom-made wallpaper on the Desktop. Again, you can tile or center the image to your liking.

Changing Screen Savers

Another way to set up the way your desktop behaves is to use a screen saver that starts when your computer is inactive for a specified time. When you set up a screen saver, you need to specify the screen saver name, the time to wait for it to start, and if it will be password-protected. The following sections discuss these items.

Choosing a New Screen Saver

To choose a screen saver, right-click the Desktop and select Properties from the context-sensitive menu. In the Display Properties sheet, click the Screen Saver page (see fig. 6.16). A list of your installed screen savers appears in the Screen Saver drop-down list. Select a screen saver from this list and look at a preview of it in the preview monitor on the Screen Saver page. Click Apply when you locate the screen saver of your choice.

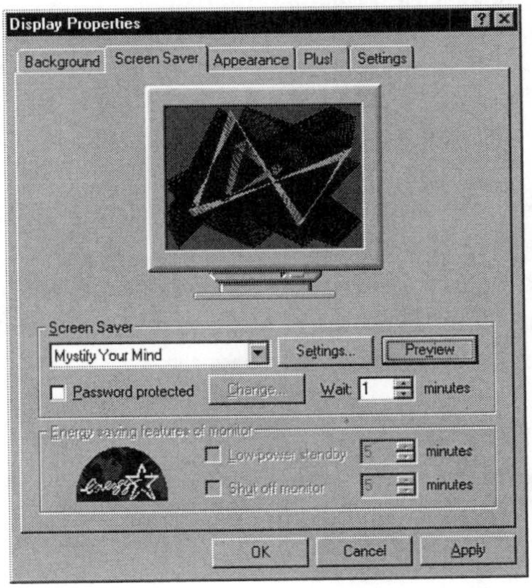

Fig. 6.16 Select a screen saver from the Screen Saver page in the Display Properties sheet.

Tip

Click the Preview button to get a full-screen view of a screen saver. Move the mouse to stop the preview.

You can configure the behavior of the screen saver by clicking the Settings button. This displays a dialog box in which you can adjust specific settings for each screen saver. The name of the dialog box varies depending on the screen saver you select. If you have installed the Microsoft Plus! screen savers, a General Properties sheet appears instead of a dialog box.

Not all screen savers have the same settings in this box. The Marquee screen saver, for instance, has options that enable you to create a message to display on-screen as well as the font, font size, color, and other text characteristics. The Curves and Colors screen saver, for instance, has the following options you can set:

- *Speed and shape*. Set the speed of the screen saver by using the scroll bar. You can set the number of lines that appear in the Lines box, and the number of curves in the Curves box.
- *Density*. Set the thickness of the curves by using the scroll bar. Set the number of colors and the color choices by clicking either the One Color or Multiple Random Colors radio boxes. If you select One Color, you can choose the color by clicking the Choose Color button and selecting the color from the Color dialog box.
- *Clear screen*. Check this option when you want the screen saver to appear against a black background. If this option is not selected, the screen saver runs "on top" of your desktop.

When you set the screen saver's settings, click OK and click Apply in the Display Properties sheet. On the Screen Saver page, you can adjust the time for the screen saver to wait until it starts. Set this time in the Wait box. You can select between 1 and 99 minutes. After your display is inactive for the selected number of minutes, the screen saver starts.

Setting Passwords

You can use your screen saver to ward off sinister snoopers who like to use your computer when you are away from your desk. To do this, set a password that users must type to stop the screen saver. The following steps show you how to set up a password:

1. On the Screen Saver page in the Display Properties sheet, click the Password Protected check box.
2. Click the Change button to set the password. The Change Password dialog box displays.
3. Type in a password in the New Password box. Retype the password in the Confirm New Password box.
4. Click OK to set the password.

To disable the password, deselect the Password Protected check box on the Screen Saver page.

Tip

Remember your password. If you forget your password, you can restart your computer and boot Windows 95. Before your screen saver starts, go in and disable the password option for that screen saver or click the Change button and create a new password. Now at least you can work and not be disrupted by your screen saver!

Specifying Desktop Colors

Earlier you saw how to change the background and wallpaper on your computer. You also can select the colors of your desktop, including the color of the menu bars, dialog boxes, and other elements. Windows 95 provides more than two dozen predefined color schemes that you can choose from, or you can create your own scheme. Another way is to use a predefined scheme and then modify it some to suit your taste.

Using Predefined Color Schemes

In the Display Properties sheet, click the Appearance page (see fig. 6.17) to access the different color schemes available to you. In the Scheme drop-down list, select from the various choices, including Pumpkin, Brick, Storm, and others.

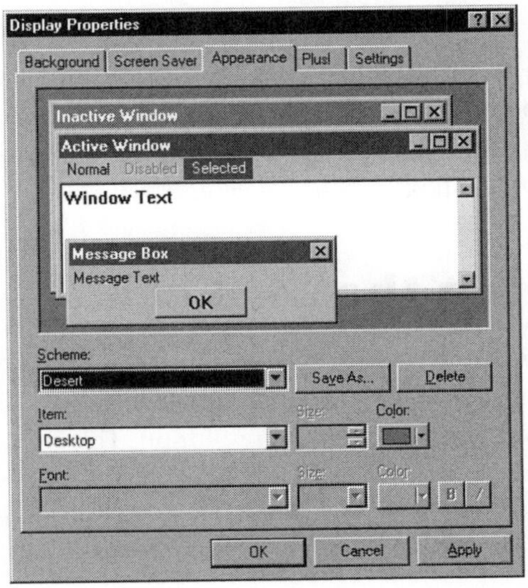

Fig. 6.17
Color schemes are a nice way to add some color to your life.

The best way to decide if you like a scheme is to click it and look at it in the preview window. Some color schemes have interesting names (such as Rainy Day and Marine), but their schemes are somewhat hard on the eyes. Pick the one that's best for you and your display.

After you select one, click OK to change your display to the selected scheme.

Customizing Color Schemes

If you get tired of looking at the built-in schemes that Windows 95 provides, create your own. To do this, return to the Appearance page in the Display Properties sheet. In the Item drop-down box, click the name of an item you want to change, such as Active Title Bar. Depending on the item you choose, you can modify the color, font size, font characteristic (bold or italic), and font.

The following list describes the options you can modify:

- *Size.* Set the size of the selected item. This may be the size of the window and its borders.
- *Color.* Click this button to select the color of the item.
- *Font.* Set the font of the item. You can choose from all the fonts you currently have installed on your system.
- *Size.* Set the font size for the selected item.
- *Color.* Set the color of the font for the selected item.
- *Bold, Italic.* Use these settings to display the selected item's text in bold or italic.

After you create a new color scheme, you can save it and name it. Click the Save As button and type in a name in the Save This Color Scheme As dialog box. Click OK. To delete a color scheme, select the color scheme in the Scheme drop-down list box and click Delete.

Configuring the Display

One of the most-welcomed features of Windows 95 is its capability to change the display resolution on-the-fly. In previous versions of Windows, users had to restart Windows after they reset the resolution. This required that you save your work and shut down all your applications just to get a different resolution. Many users switch between standard VGA resolution (640 × 480) and

Super VGA resolution (1024 × 768) depending on the application and work they are performing.

Windows 95 enables you to change these settings quickly and without restarting Windows. You also can change the font size of elements on your screen as well as the color palette used. The next two sections show you how to modify these settings.

Caution

You can change the resolution of your display without restarting Windows 95 only if the new display uses the same font as the current display. Otherwise, you must restart Windows 95 to change display drivers.

Troubleshooting

When I change the resolution of my display, Windows 95 displays a black screen or has a bunch of wavy lines on it. What happened?

You probably selected a setting that your video adapter and monitor cannot display. To return to your previous setting, reboot your computer and enter Safe Mode by pressing F8 when your system boots and selecting Safe Mode from the Start menu. During Safe Mode, the Windows 95 Standard VGA driver is loaded, enabling you to boot into Windows and change the resolution of your monitor.

Changing the Display Resolution and Palette

In the Display Properties sheet, click the Settings page (see fig. 6.18). From here, you can change how your display looks and behaves. The Color Palette drop-down list shows the number of colors and color palette (high-color or true color) that your monitor supports. For many users, 256 Color is appropriate. For artists or users who work with graphics-intensive software, high color or true color is required to achieve professional results.

The Font Size drop-down list enables you to set the size of the text that appears. You can select either Large Fonts or Small Fonts. If your monitor does not enable you to change the way in which fonts appear, this setting is dimmed.

▶ See "Installing Your New Video Card into Your PC," p. 420

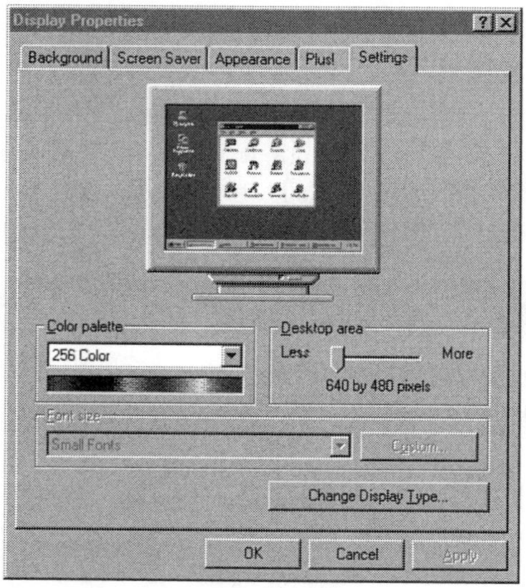

Fig. 6.18
Use the Settings page to configure your monitor type and resolution.

> **Note**
>
> Click the Custom button to create a custom font size for your display. In the Custom Font Size dialog box, set the scale of the font and look at the Sample area for an example of the way the font will look. You also can click on the ruler in the Sample area and drag it to the right or left to increase or decrease its scale. Click OK when you are satisfied with the font size.

Changing the Display Resolution

Now for the *piece d'resistance*. Change the display resolution by clicking the slider in the Desktop Area section. (The slider only appears if your adapter and monitor support higher resolutions.) This changes the amount of information that your monitor displays. A higher setting (such as 1024 × 768), shown in figure 6.19, gives you a lot of room to display windows and icons. A lower setting (such as 640 × 480) yields a much lower area to display information.

> **Tip**
>
> Generally, the higher the resolution, the slower the display refreshes.

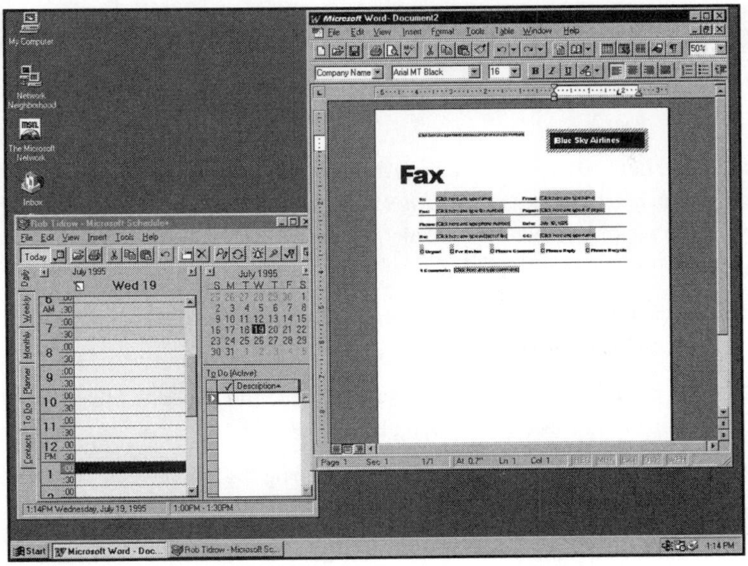

Fig. 6.19
A higher resolution enables you to place more on your desktop, but it may slow down your system too much.

After you set the slider where you want it, click Apply. A warning message appears, telling you that Windows will change your display and that it may take 15 seconds or so. Click OK and then wait a few seconds. Your screen goes black for a moment and then pops, sometimes quite loudly. When it returns, click Yes when Windows 95 prompts you if you would like to keep the setting.

> **Note**
>
> If your display doesn't appear correctly or if you see nothing at all, you need to reboot Windows 95 and start in Safe Mode. In Safe Mode, Windows boots with a standard VGA display driver. After Windows 95 boots, go through the shut-down process and reboot your machine. When it restarts and goes into Windows, it should return to your old display settings.

◀ See "Using Windows 95 Safe Mode," p. 63

If you cannot adjust the slider bar, your monitor and video card do not support other display resolutions from the one you have installed. You'll need to get a new driver or upgrade to another video card and/or monitor.

Troubleshooting

My monitor doesn't work right with the drivers included with Windows 95. Can I use a Windows 3.x driver?

Yes you can, but you should upgrade to Windows 95 drivers to take advantage of the enhanced graphics support in Windows 95. For instance, Windows 3.x drivers do not support changing your monitor resolution on-the-fly. To install Windows 3.1 display drivers, use the following steps:

1. Double-click the Display icon in Control Panel, click the Settings page, and then click Change Display Type.
2. Click the Change button next to Adapter Type, and then click the Have Disk button in the Select Device dialog box.
3. Specify the path to the disk or folder containing the Windows 3.1 drivers you want to use.
4. Select the correct driver to use from the list that appears, and then click OK to install.

Some Windows 3.1 drivers require the screen resolution to be specified in the `[boot.description]` section of SYSTEM.INI, such as in the following example:

```
display.drv=GD5430 v1.22, 800x600x256
```

Adding Fonts to Your System

Windows 95 includes an enhanced way to manage and view fonts on your system. The Windows 95 FONTS folder stores all the fonts on your system. When you open the FONTS folder, a window similar to the one shown in figure 6.20 appears. You can view a sample of the way in which a font looks by double-clicking the font icon. This displays a window that contains sample text of the font and includes details of other font properties, including font name, file size, version number, and the manufacturer of the font. Figure 6.21 shows the font window for a particular font.

To access the FONTS folder, select the Start button and click Settings, Control Panel. Double-click the FONTS folder in Control Panel. You also can access it by locating the \FONTS folder in your Windows 95 folder, such as \WINDOWS\FONTS. Once the folder appears, you can view, delete, print, and install fonts.

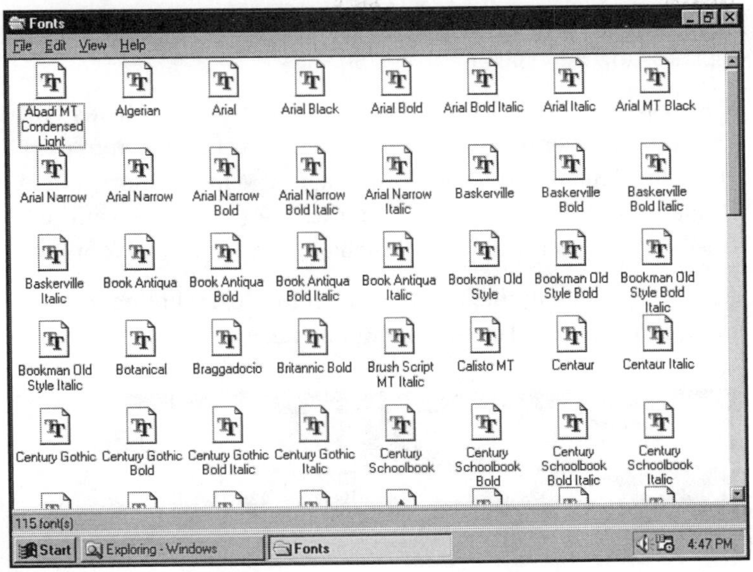

Fig. 6.20
The FONTS folder is used to store and manage all the fonts on your system.

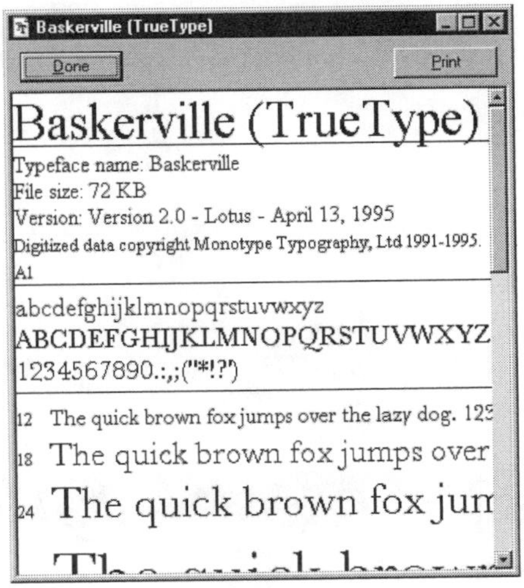

Fig. 6.21
You can see a sample of a font by double-clicking it and viewing the sample in a window.

You can display a toolbar on the FONTS folder by choosing View, Toolbar. On the toolbar, you can reconfigure the way the fonts display in the FONTS folder by clicking the different toolbar buttons. The following list describes how the FONTS folder appears when selecting these buttons:

- *Large icons*. Displays icons of each font. Each icon includes the font name and type of font, such as TrueType (TT), and screen and printer fonts (A).

- *List*. Displays a list of the icons on your system, with small icons representing the type of font installed.
- *Similarity*. Sorts each font to show fonts according to their similarity with one another (see fig. 6.22). You can select a font from the List Fonts By Similarity To drop-down list, and Windows sorts the fonts by similarity to the chosen font. You might, for example, want to know how similar other fonts are to the Baskerville family of fonts.
- *Details*. Displays all the details of the font file, including font name, file name, file size, and last modification date.

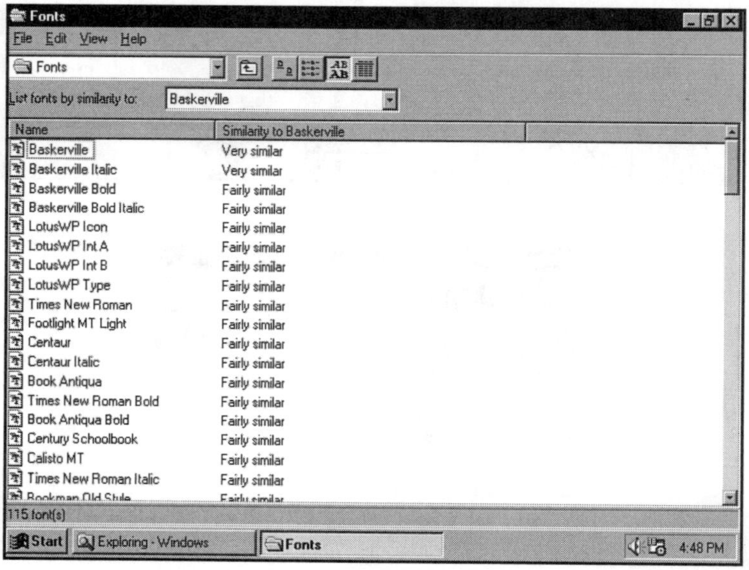

Fig. 6.22
You can find fonts that are similar to each other by clicking the Similarity button on the toolbar.

Tip

Use the Details view to obtain the file name of a font that you want to copy or delete from your system.

Installing New Fonts

Simply copying a font file to the \FONTS folder does not install the font for use with your Windows applications. You must install the font by choosing File, Install New Font in the FONTS folder. When you install a new font, Windows 95 places a setting in the Windows Registry to make it available for your applications.

To install a new font, use the following steps:

1. Select File, Install New Font to display the Add Font dialog box (see fig. 6.23).

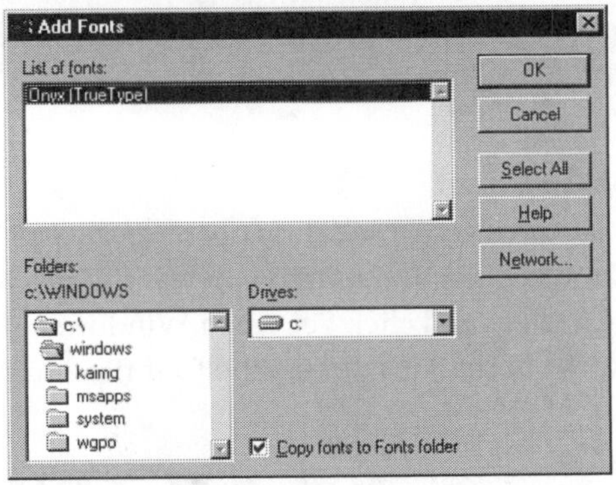

Fig. 6.23
Use the Add Fonts dialog box to install new fonts on your system.

2. Select the font name(s) in the List of Fonts box.

Tip

To select more than one font name in the List of Fonts box, hold the Shift key down as you select contiguous fonts, or hold down the Ctrl key to select non-contiguous fonts. To select all of the listed fonts, click the Select All button in the Add Fonts dialog box.

3. If the font is in another folder, locate the folder in which the font is stored in the Folders list box. You also can change the drive by clicking the Drives drop-down list and selecting the appropriate drive.

4. Click the Copy Fonts to Fonts Folder check box to instruct Windows to copy the selected font(s) to your \WINDOWS\FONTS folder. This places a copy of the font file in the \FONTS folder on your system, effectively duplicating the font file on your system. If you leave this check box clear, the font files remain in the original source location, but the Windows 95 Registry includes references to these locations. This enables you to use those fonts in your applications, even when they are not in your \WINDOWS\FONTS folder.

5. Choose OK to finish the installation steps and to install the fonts on your system.

Tip

When you operate in a network environment, you may want to leave your font files on the network server to conserve space on your local machine. You can install fonts from the network by clicking the Network button and locating the font file names on your server. Make sure the Copy Fonts to Fonts Folder check box is not checked.

Removing Fonts

You can remove a font from your system by opening the FONTS folder in Control Panel and then clicking the font(s) you want to delete. Next, press Delete or choose File, Delete and click Yes when Windows asks if you are sure you want to delete these fonts. This deletes the font file and places the font file in the Recycle Bin.

Tip

Windows 3.x had a problem of using up a lot of memory when you installed numerous fonts on your system. Windows 95 does not have this same problem, even though you may want to reduce the number of font files on your system if you need to clean up some disk space.

Troubleshooting

How do I view only TrueType fonts in my applications?

If you use only TrueType fonts in your applications, such as Word for Windows, you can instruct Windows 95 to display only TrueType fonts when you are working. In the FONTS folder, choose View, Options and click on the TrueType page. Click the Show Only TrueType Fonts in the Programs on My Computer check box. Click OK.

Chapter 7

Configuring the Taskbar and Start Button

by Rob Tidrow

If you are a Windows 3.x user moving to Windows 95, you'll be in for a big surprise the first time you start Windows 95—Program Manager is gone. For some, this is a big relief. Others may feel a little lost. Microsoft has replaced Program Manager with the Start button. When you want to start a program, change system settings, or do whatever, you can find it using the Start button and its menu.

The taskbar is another fundamental change in Windows 95. The taskbar sits at the bottom of the screen (you can move it, as you'll learn later) and enables you to switch between open applications quickly, shows the time, and displays other system features. It's also where the Start button resides.

This chapter contains useful configuration information about the taskbar and Start button. When you install Windows 95, you don't have to do anything for these two items to work. But you might want to spend a few minutes customizing how they look and function.

In this chapter, you learn how to do the following:

- Set taskbar options
- Hide the taskbar
- Set Start button options

Setting Taskbar Options

You'll first examine the taskbar, which usually is the first item users interact with in Windows 95. By default, it sits at the bottom of the screen, as shown in figure 7.1. The taskbar is intended to make 95 percent of what you want to do in Windows 95 easy to accomplish.

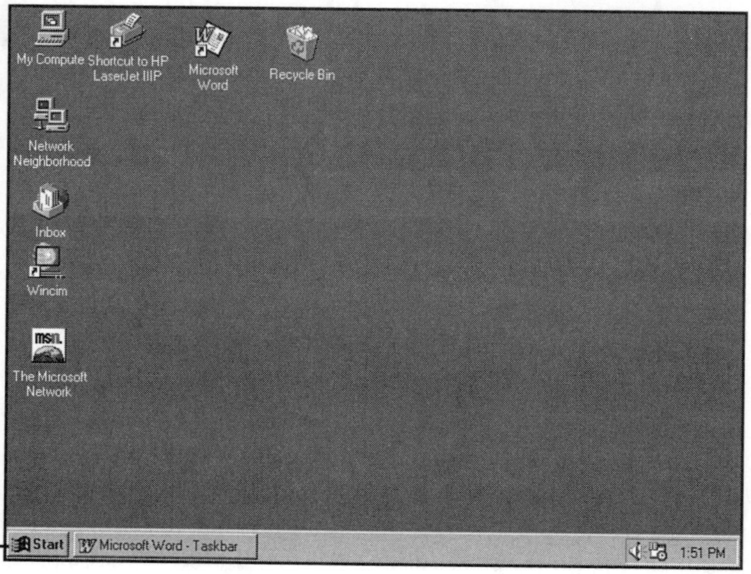

Taskbar

Fig. 7.1
The taskbar is a simple, yet powerful new addition to Windows 95.

> **Note**
>
> The taskbar includes a few items of interest, namely the Start button and task buttons. The Start button is discussed in detail in "Setting Start Button Options" later in this chapter. *Task buttons* (see fig. 7.2) represent all the open applications you are using in Windows 95. Task buttons appear on the taskbar even when an application is not minimized, giving users a quick way to switch between tasks.

Other items that are on the taskbar are shown on the far right side of it. In this area, you can find the clock and applications running in the background, such as the System Agent available in Microsoft Plus!, modems, printers, and sound cards. You can quickly modify the configurations of these items by right-clicking over the tops of their icons. Next, select an item from the context-sensitive menu, such as Adjust Audio Properties if you are want to see the properties for a sound card. This brings up the property sheet of that device, as shown in figure 7.3. After you make adjustments, click OK.

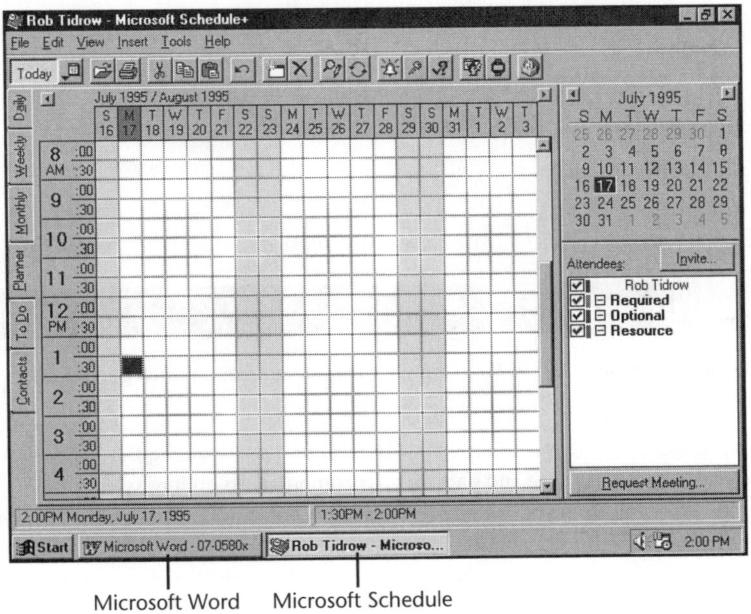

Fig. 7.2
Task buttons make it easy to switch between applications.

Tip

Move the mouse pointer over the time to see the day and the date.

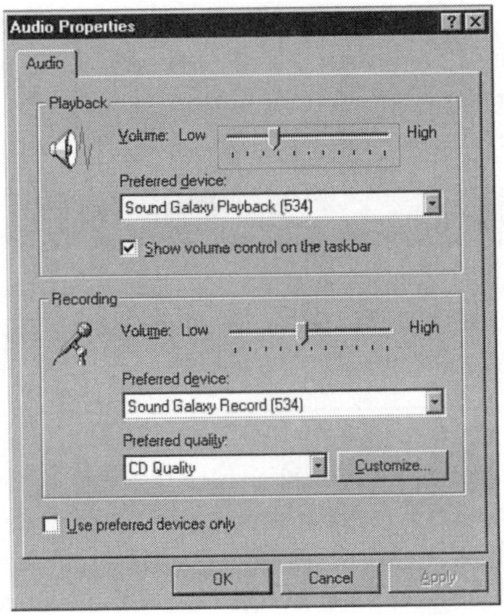

Fig. 7.3
Use the taskbar to access properties of the devices running in the background, such as your sound card.

▶ See "Managing Utilities with the System Agent," p. 670

Some of the ways to customize the taskbar include the following:

- Reposition and resize the taskbar
- Set the way in which the taskbar appears
- Show the clock

These items are discussed in the following sections.

Troubleshooting

I change the time in Windows 95, but my system clock displays a different time. Can you help?

On some systems, you must start your system startup utility during the boot process to change the system time and date on your computer. To do this, refer to the manual that came with your computer to see how you can start the system utility. On some computers, you can press Ctrl+Alt+Esc or press a function key assigned to the utility. Once in the system settings screen, use the navigational commands, such as the arrow keys and Page Up and Page Down, to navigate the screen and to make changes to the system time and date. The way in which you make changes depends on your system.

Repositioning and Resizing the Taskbar

If you don't like the taskbar at the bottom of the screen, grab it with your mouse pointer and drag it to another location on your Desktop. Don't try to put it in the middle of the screen. It only sits on the edges of the Desktop, either on the left or right side, top, or bottom. Figures 7.4 and 7.5 show how the taskbar looks on the top and left sides of the Desktop.

Caution

Depending on the width of the taskbar, you may only see the application icon and its first two letters when the taskbar is moved to the side of the Desktop. This can make it difficult to recognize your open applications.

Another way to customize your taskbar is to resize it. Move your mouse pointer over the taskbar's edge that is exposed. This is the side that is closest to the Desktop, such as the top edge if the taskbar is at the bottom of the screen. When the mouse pointer changes to a double-sided arrow, press and hold your left mouse button and drag the taskbar to the size you want. Figure 7.6 shows a taskbar diagnosed with elephantiasis!

Fig. 7.4
Having the taskbar at the top of the screen is not a bad option.

Fig. 7.5
But, having the taskbar on the side requires you to get familiar with your application icons to understand which application is which, because you can't see the words describing what the icon stands for.

Tip

You can resize the taskbar up to the size of your desktop by dragging it with your mouse.

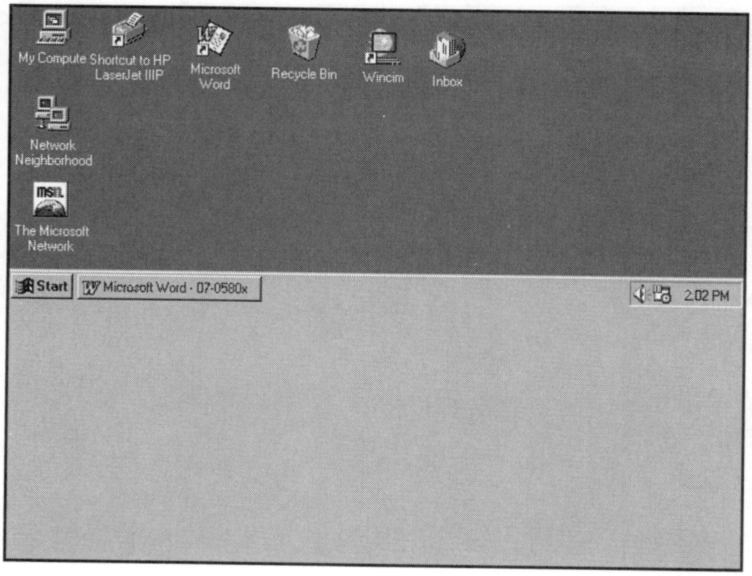

Fig. 7.6
Get frustrated when you can't find the taskbar? Just make it a little bigger.

Troubleshooting

How do I remove the Network Neighborhood icon from my desktop?

The Network Neighborhood icon appears on your desktop automatically when you install network resources under Windows 95. You cannot drag the Network Neighborhood icon to the Recycle Bin, or click on it and select Delete to remove it. You must use the System Policy Editor to delete it. The System Policy Editor should be used only by advanced users who feel comfortable making system changes to their computers. If you are not, you should not try this. Also, before you start the System Policy Editor, be sure your system is backed up in case you encounter problems and lose data. The System Policy Editor is available on the Windows 95 installation CD in the \ADMIN\APPTOOLS\POLEDIT\ folder. Double-click on the Poledit application to start the System Policy. Chose Open Registry from the File menu, open Local User (or your user ID), switch to \User\Shell\Restrictions, and check the Hide Network Neighborhood item. Click OK, close the System Policy Editor, and restart Windows 95.

Setting Display Options

By default, the taskbar always appears. Even when you maximize an application, such as the one shown in figure 7.7, the taskbar is still visible at the bottom of the screen. Microsoft refers to this state as being *Always on Top* and is probably the most efficient way to use the taskbar. When the taskbar is on top, you can quickly see which other applications are open, the time of the day, and the status of your printer or modem, and can readily access any of these items.

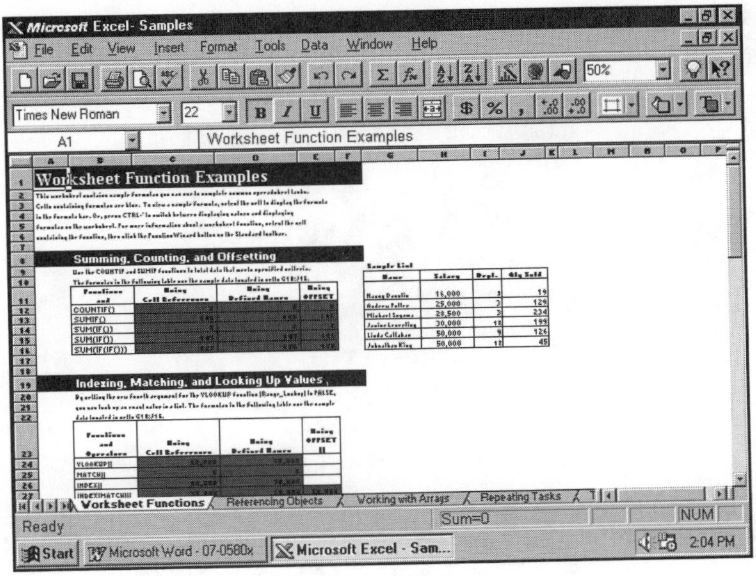

Fig. 7.7
Even though the application is maximized, the taskbar is still visible.

You can make the taskbar disappear when you are not using it. To do so, you need to set the Auto Hide feature, as shown in the following steps:

1. Right-click any exposed part of the taskbar.

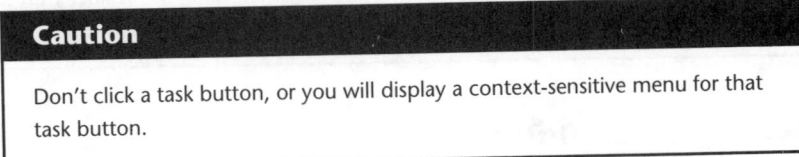

> **Caution**
>
> Don't click a task button, or you will display a context-sensitive menu for that task button.

2. Select Properties to display the Taskbar Properties sheet (see fig. 7.8).
3. On the Taskbar Options page, select Auto Hide and deselect Always on Top.
4. Click OK.

Now when you move the mouse pointer off of the taskbar, the taskbar disappears by sliding below the surface of the screen. To make it reappear, move the mouse down to the bottom of the screen (or wherever you have the taskbar). It automatically "slides" back into view, unless you have an application covering that part of the screen. If you disabled the Always on Top option in the preceding step 3, the taskbar does not appear on top of the open application. You must move or resize the application's window to see the taskbar. Use this option when your screen real estate is limited and you want to use the entire screen for your applications. Otherwise, leave the default as-is.

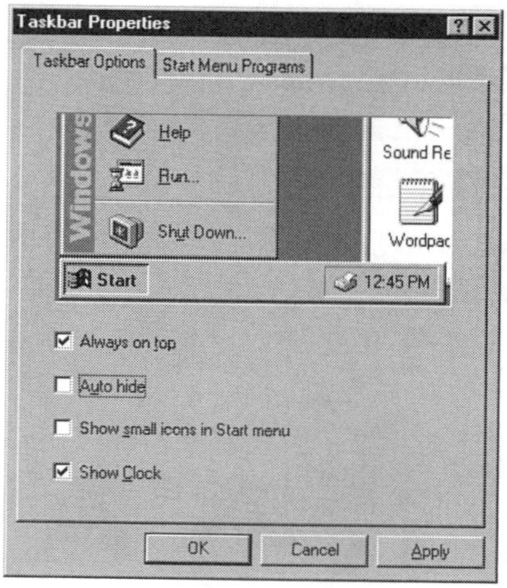

Fig. 7.8
You can choose how the taskbar behaves by changing its properties.

> **Note**
>
> Generally, if you run in 800 × 600 or higher resolution, and you use the taskbar or Start button a great deal, you should have no problem keeping the taskbar visible at all times.

Setting Clock Options

You can change the time that the clock displays by double-clicking it on the taskbar. This displays the Date/Time Properties sheet (see fig. 7.9).

On the Date & Time page, you can adjust the following properties:

- *Date*. Use the drop-down list to select the month, and set the year in the option box next to it. On the calendar, click the correct day of the month. The highlighted day is the current day.
- *Time*. Set the correct time that you want Windows to display in the option box. The large analog clock displays the time. Note that this box does not reset your system clock. You must do this using system utilities that come with your computer.

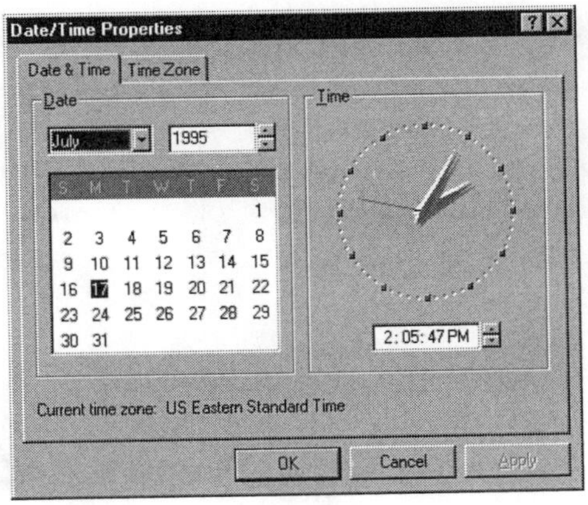

Fig. 7.9
Set the time, date, and time zone by double-clicking the clock on the taskbar.

On the Time Zone page, you can configure the time zone in which you live or work. Use the drop-down list box to choose the time zone. If you live in an area with Daylight Savings Time, click the option at the bottom of the screen to have Windows automatically update your clock during these time changes. Click OK when you have these options configured.

If you don't want the clock to show at all, use the following steps:

1. Right-click on any exposed part of the taskbar.
2. Select Properties, to display the Taskbar Properties sheet.
3. Deselect the Show Clock option, and click OK.

Setting Start Button Options

The Start button resides on the far left of the taskbar by default. The Start button's purpose is to give users a leg up on getting their work done. When you click the Start button, a menu pops up (see fig. 7.10) that contains several items. You can use the Start button to launch programs, start Help, shut down Windows 95, and find files. You also can access Control Panel to configure many of your system settings and devices.

Tip

You can quickly display the Start button on the taskbar by pressing Alt+S.

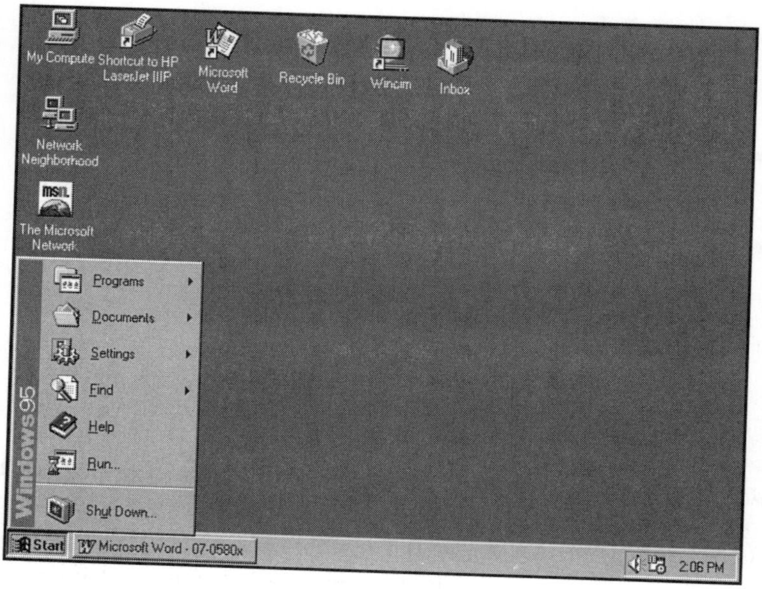

Fig. 7.10
The Start button's menu gives you access to all your files, applications, and settings.

Windows 95 gives you several Start button options to customize according to your tastes. The Start button menu can be set up with the programs or files you use most often to give you one-button access to them. You might, for instance, use WinCIM to dial into the CompuServe Information Service. Place WinCIM on the Start button to quickly start it each time you want to dial CompuServe.

Tip

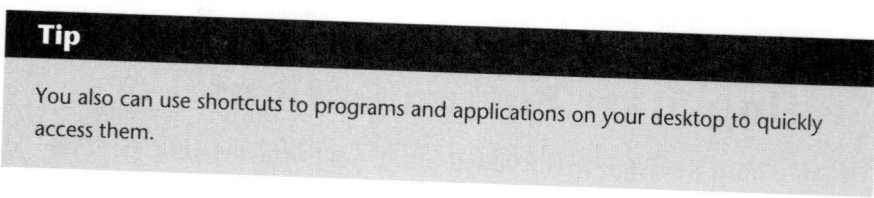

You also can use shortcuts to programs and applications on your desktop to quickly access them.

Another way to take advantage of the Start button is to add documents or specific files that you use all the time. This may be a daily spreadsheet you fill out, or a document template in Word for Windows.

By default, the Start menu shows large icons and a Windows 95 logo. You can reduce the size of the menu (see fig. 7.11) by using the Show Small Icons options on the Taskbar page, as shown in the following steps:

1. Right-click any exposed part of the taskbar.
2. Select Properties to display the Taskbar Properties sheet. Make sure the Taskbar page is selected.
3. Select the Show Small Icons in the Start menu, and click OK.

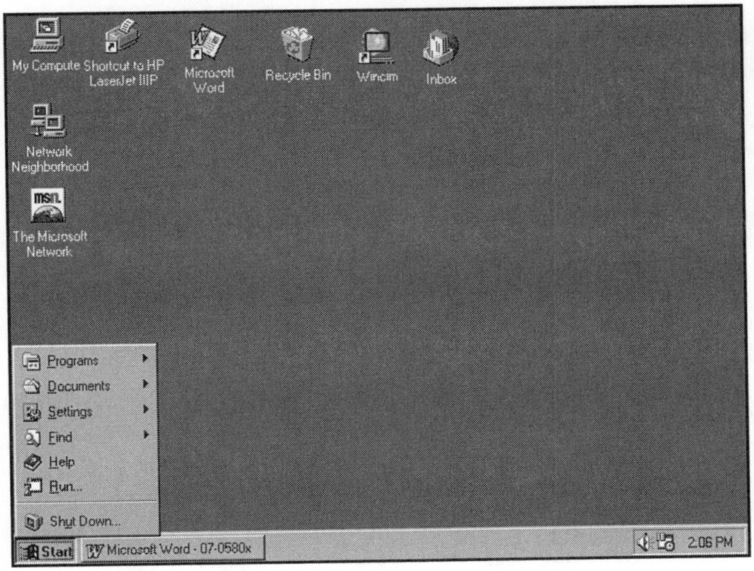

Fig. 7.11
You can configure the Start menu to use small icons to reduce the amount of space the menu takes up.

Add and Remove Items

The Start menu contains programs that are placed there during the Windows 95 installation. If you install Windows 95 over your existing Windows 3.x setup, Windows 95 automatically places all your installed applications on the Start menu. As you use Windows 95 and install new applications, you can add these programs to the Program folder on the Start menu, much as you can add program groups to Program Manager in Windows 3.x.

If you upgrade your system from Windows 3.x to Windows 95, Windows 95 automatically converts your old program groups to folders. You can locate these programs by choosing Start, Programs and looking at the folders that appear, such as those shown in figure 7.12.

Troubleshooting

How can I use my old Windows 3.x Program Manager instead of the new Windows 95 Desktop?

You can use Windows 3.x's version of Program Manager from within Windows 95 if you installed Windows 95 to its own directory (for dual booting). Launch the PROGMAN.EXE file from the Windows 3.x directory to start Program Manager. The only difference you may notice is the groups are not arranged in the same fashion on the desktop as they were when running under your previous Windows 3.x configuration.

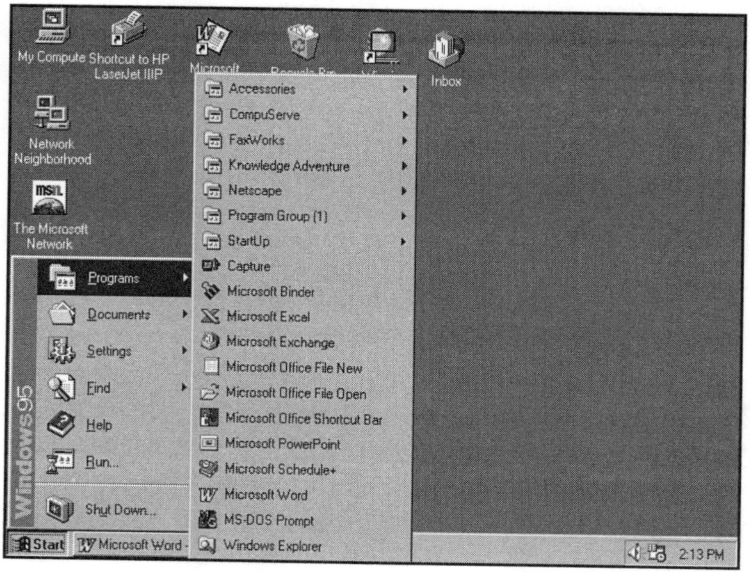

Fig. 7.12
On the Start menu, you can access program folders in much the same way as you can program groups in Windows 3.x.

Tip

Another way to see the contents of the Programs folder is to view it in Windows Explorer. You can view it by opening the folder in which Windows 95 is stored, and then opening the Start menu and the Programs folder. From here, you can view, and delete items, and drag and drop other items to the Programs folder.

You can add items to the Start menu by using the following steps:

1. Right-click any exposed part of the taskbar.
2. Select Properties to display the Taskbar Properties sheet.
3. Click the Start Menu Programs tab (see fig. 7.13).
4. Click the Add button to display the Create Shortcut Wizard.
5. In the Command Line text box in the Create Shortcut Wizard, enter the full path to the program or file shortcut you want to add to the Start menu.

Tip

Use the Browse button to search for the program or file you are looking for.

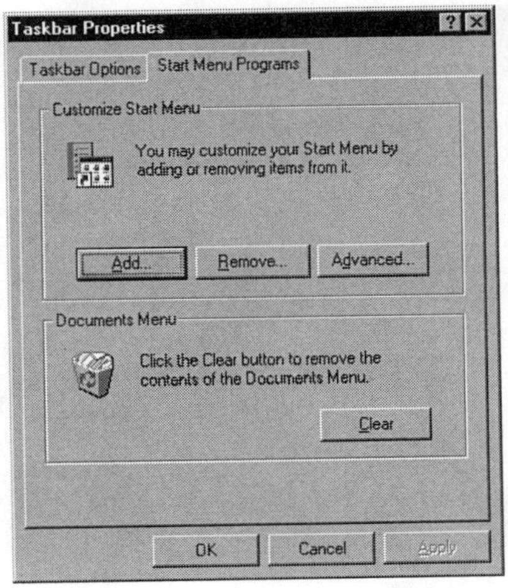

Fig. 7.13
Use the Start Menu Program page to add new programs and program folders to the Start menu.

6. Click Next.
7. In the Select Program Folder dialog box (see fig. 7.14), click the folder where you want to place the program or file shortcut. Generally, you'll add the program to the Programs folder or create a new folder by using the New Folder button and entering a new folder name.

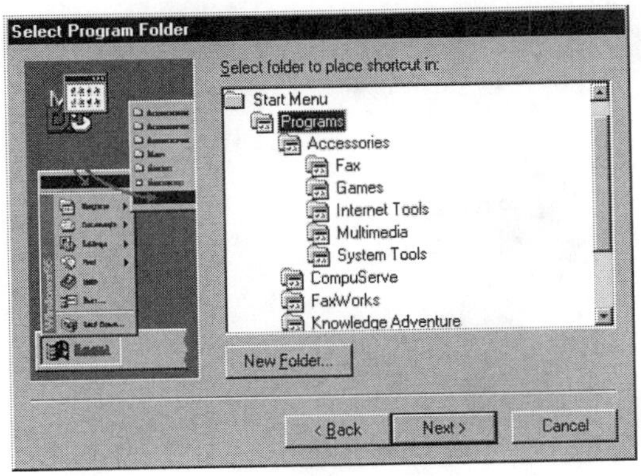

Fig. 7.14
Tell Windows the folder in which to place the program or shortcut.

8. Click Next.

> **Note**
>
> To add a program or shortcut to the Start menu, add the program or shortcut to the Start Menu folder in the Select Folder To Place Shortcut In list box (see fig. 7.15).

Fig. 7.15
By adding shortcuts to the Start menu, you can decrease the time it takes to start a program.

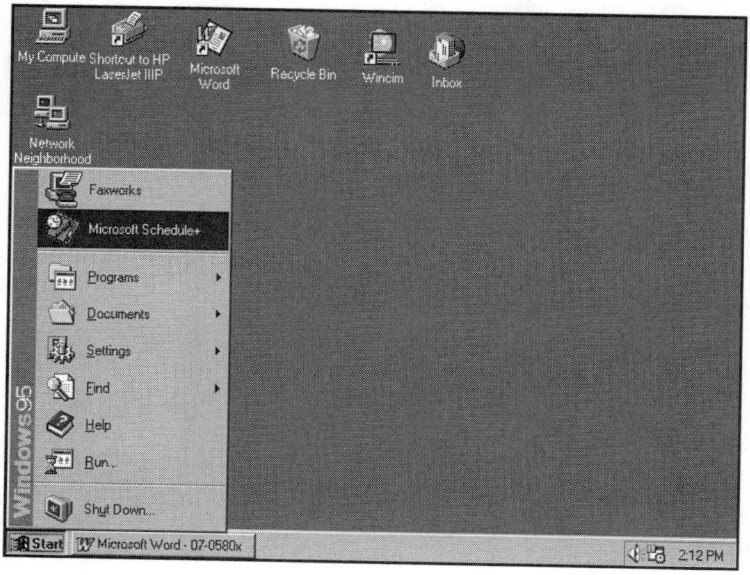

9. In the Select a Title for the Program box, enter a name for the program in the Select a Name for the Shortcut box (see fig. 7.16).
10. Click Finish.

Fig. 7.16
Accept the default name or change it according to your tastes.

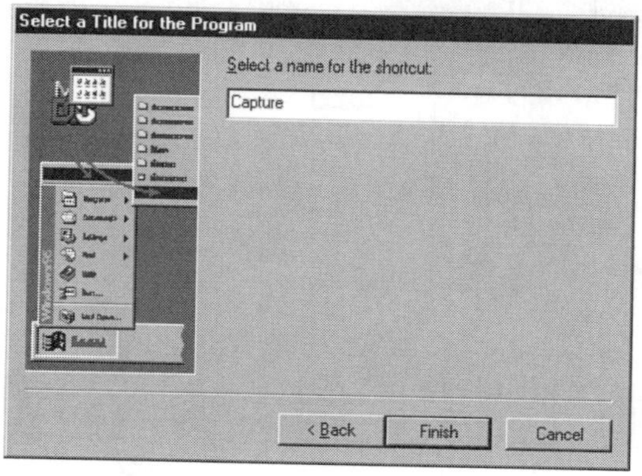

If you want to add more programs or shortcuts, click the Add button on the Start Menu Programs page. If you are finished, click OK to close the Taskbar Properties sheet.

Tip

Click the plus sign (+) next to a folder to expand it.

You can remove a program, file, or folder shortcut by clicking the Remove button on the Taskbar Properties sheet and following these steps:

1. Scroll down the list of items in the Remove Shortcuts/Folders dialog box (see fig. 7.17).

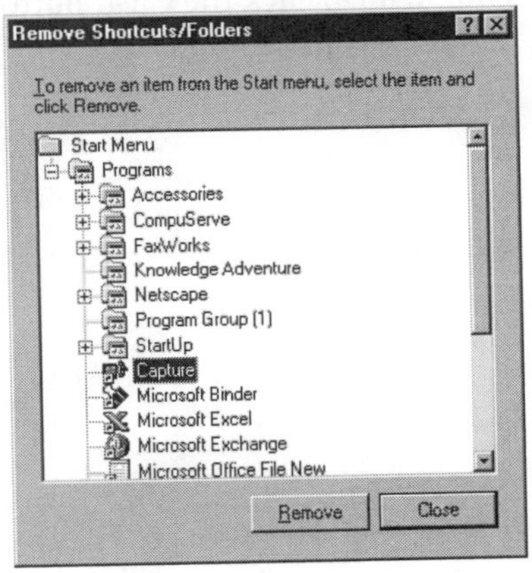

Fig. 7.17
You can remove a program or shortcut from the Start menu as quickly as adding one.

2. Click the item to remove.
3. Click the Remove button.
4. Continue selecting and removing items, as needed. When finished, click Close.
5. Click OK.

Note

You can click the Advanced button on the Taskbar Properties sheet to see your Start menu in Explorer view. You can add items to the Start menu using this view by clicking the Advanced button and then opening another session of the Explorer. Next, drag items from the Explorer view that contains all your directories into the Start Menu Explorer view.

You also can remove items from your Start menu using this view. To do so, click the item you want to remove and press Delete. When the Confirm File Delete dialog box appears, click Yes to send the item to the Recycle Bin.

Clear the Documents Menu

On the Start menu is another new feature—the Documents folder. This folder contains shortcuts to the last 15 files that you worked with in Windows 95, giving you quick access to these files for reviewing or editing.

To remove the items from this folder, use the following steps:

1. Right-click any exposed part of the taskbar.
2. Select Properties to display the Taskbar Properties sheet. Click the Start Menu Programs page.
3. In the Documents Menu area, click the Clear button.

Chapter 8

Configuring Windows 95 Audio

by Gregory J. Root

Configuring audio in Windows 95 can be easy. Knowing how to configure your sound can be valuable when you have to adjust your audio quickly. For example, if you are listening to CD audio when the phone rings, it's important to turn down or mute the volume.

Not only do you have control over every sound source, you can adjust and personalize your audio environment to your exact taste. If you've grown tired of the standard "bings" and "beeps" your computer makes, you can create a personalized audio environment no one else has ever heard before.

In this chapter, you learn how to configure your audio environment by learning how to do the following:

- Specify event sounds
- Work with sound schemes
- Use the taskbar volume control
- Use the Volume Control window
- Configure MIDI sounds

Setting System Sounds

When using Windows, you may want to assign sounds to specific events. Or, you may want to use a predefined set of sounds that were placed on your system when you installed Windows 95. If you've made a personalized group of event sounds, you may want to save the configuration or delete an old set of sounds you don't use anymore. In the next few sections, you learn how to do these tasks confidently.

Specifying Event Sounds

Windows knows when certain events occur while you use your computer. For example, it knows when you open or close a program. You can specify sounds to play when these events occur.

To begin configuring event sounds, do the following:

1. From the Start menu, choose Settings, Control Panel. Windows 95 displays the Control Panel window shown in figure 8.1.

Fig. 8.1
The Control Panel is the central location for customizing your Windows environment.

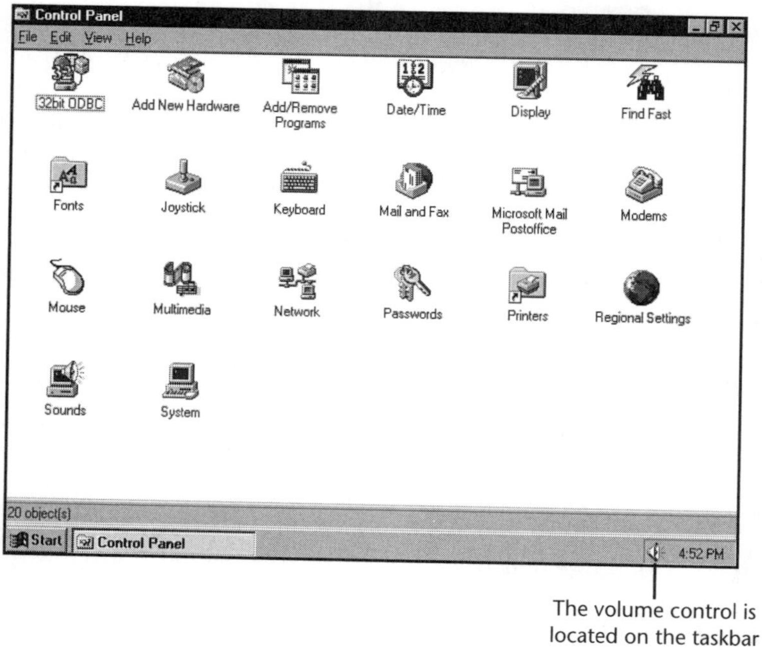

2. Open the Sounds control panel. The Sounds Properties sheet appears, containing the Sounds page, shown in figure 8.2. In the upper-half of the screen, you see the list of events to which you can assign sounds. You can tell that an event has a sound assigned to it because of the speaker icon to the left of the event name.

> **Note**
>
> When you installed Windows, a default set of sounds and events was chosen for you.

3. Choose an event from the list. For example, choose the Asterisk event. You notice several things happen in the middle of the window shown in figure 8.3. Working from left to right, the name of the sound (Chord in our example) is placed in the Name drop-down list box, the Browse and Details buttons are enabled, the Preview window shows the sound's icon, and the Play button is enabled (it looks like the Play button on a VCR remote control).

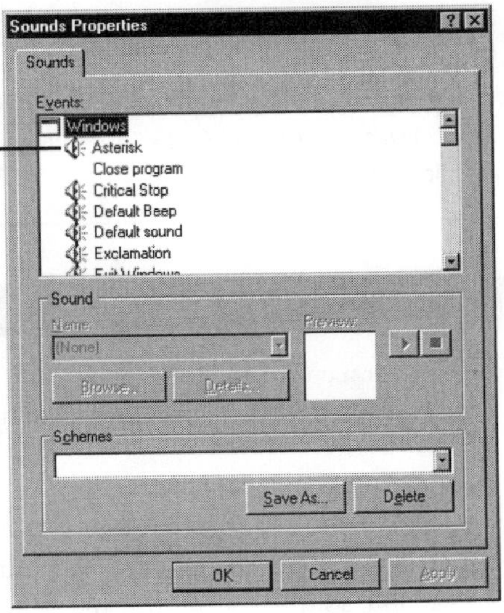

Fig. 8.2
The Sounds Properties sheet allows you to assign sounds to an event.

4. To listen to this sound, press the Play button. If you like the sound, play it again! Then, select other events in the list and listen to their assigned sounds until you find one you want to change.

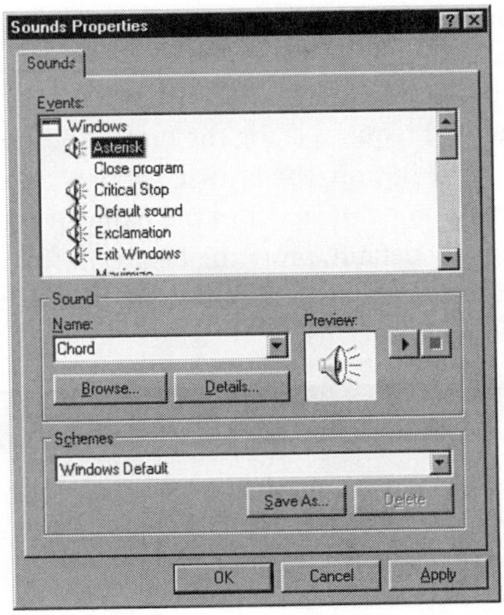

Fig. 8.3
If you've selected an event with a sound, the controls in the middle of the window become enabled.

Note

When you install other programs, more events are listed as those programs make their events known to Windows, giving you an even more personalized audio environment.

▶ See "Configuring Sound Cards," p. 443

Note

If you don't hear sound when you press the Play button, refer to the "Setting Volume" section in this chapter. If you're still having problems, see Chapter 19, "Configuring Speakers and Sound Cards," to verify that your hardware is installed and configured correctly.

Tip

If you know the exact location and file name of the sound you want, you can skip the next step by typing it into the Name drop-down list box.

5. You can assign a WAV file to the selected event in two ways. First, you can click the down arrow at the end of the Name drop-down list box to display a list of available sounds. Scroll through the list and select one of the sounds. To preview what your current selection sounds like, press the Play button again.

Note

The sounds in this drop-down list reside in the WINDOWS/MEDIA folder.

The second method requires using the Browse button to assign a sound. When you click the button, the Browse window appears, as shown in figure 8.4 (the window title matches the name of the event with which you're working). By default, browsing begins in the WINDOWS/MEDIA folder. If you find the name of a sound that piques your interest, highlight it (don't double-click it).

Caution

If you double-click the name of the sound, it is immediately assigned to the event. Since you can't undo this change unless you cancel all the changes you've made so far, just select the name of the sound.

Notice at the bottom edge of the window is another set of preview buttons. These allow you to preview the sounds while you browse. Once you've highlighted the sound you want to use, click the OK button. The name of the sound is placed in the Name drop-down list box of the Sound Properties sheet.

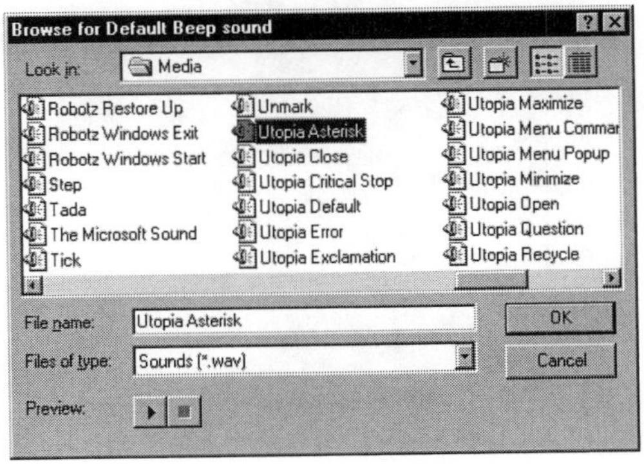

Fig. 8.4
You can preview a sound from the Browse window by using the Preview buttons at the bottom of the window.

6. Sometimes, sounds have extra information which contain useful details. If you like a particular set of sounds and want more, these details sometimes contain the name and address of who to contact to obtain similarly styled sounds. These details can be viewed for the current sound by clicking the Details button.

   Figure 8.5 shows the Copyright, Media Length, and Audio Format data in the properties sheet. If more detailed information is available, the Other Information group box is also seen in at the bottom of the window. Select an item in the left-hand list of the group box to display its details in the right-hand list.

7. To immediately apply the change you made to the event, click the Apply button in the far lower-right corner of the sheet.

> **Note**
>
> You can repeat these six steps to change other events' sounds without clicking Apply between each change. Windows temporarily remembers all your changes until you're ready to save them.

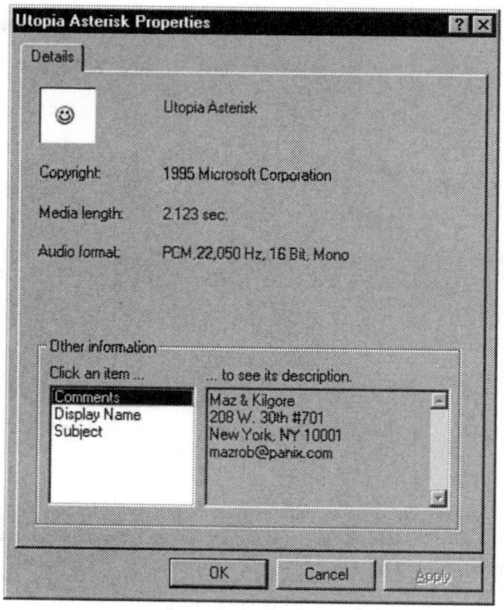

Fig. 8.5
You can view the Copyright, Media Length, Audio Format, and other details of a sound.

8. If you decide you like the new combination of sounds, clicking the OK button in figure 8.3 saves them and closes the Sounds control panel. If you aren't sure what changes you've made or didn't like what you created, clicking the Cancel button restores the event sounds to the state they were the last time Apply was selected, and then closes the Sounds control panel.

Working with Sound Schemes

Sometimes, setting individual sounds for each Windows event can take longer than you have time to spend. Or, you may have taken the time to carefully craft a set of event sounds you want to preserve for special occasions or holidays. But right now, you don't want sounds for a national holiday every day of the year. With Windows 95, you can pick a predefined sound scheme.

◀ See "Selecting Custom Install Options," p. 107

Similarly, you can save that special set of event sounds for the correct time of the year.

To begin working with sound schemes, follow these steps:

1. From the Start menu choose Settings, Control Panel. Windows 95 displays the Control Panel window shown in figure 8.1.

2. Open the Sounds control panel. The Sounds Properties sheet appears containing the Sounds page as seen in figure 8.2. In the upper-half of the screen, you see the list of events to which you can assign sounds

(see the previous section, "Specifying Event Sounds"). At the bottom of the Sounds Properties sheet is the Schemes group box. Here you can select, save, and delete sound schemes.

Selecting a Sound Scheme

Choosing a predefined sound scheme is quick and easy. Many of these schemes were placed when you installed Windows. Other schemes are available to be downloaded from online services.

To select one of these schemes, follow these steps:

1. Click the down arrow next to the Scheme name.
2. Pick an intriguing, favorite, or personal scheme name.

> **Note**
>
> If you see a dialog box pop up, asking if you want to save the previous scheme, you should choose Yes to save your current sound scheme, No to not save your scheme, or Cancel to stop selecting a new sound scheme. If you choose Yes, name the scheme so that it can appear in the Schemes drop-down list box.

3. Choose OK at the bottom of the Sounds Properties sheet.

> **Note**
>
> If you've installed Microsoft Plus!, your initial scheme name is blank. The Desktop Themes control panel takes care of your event sound assignments for you. But, feel free to change individual sounds at any time.

Plus!

Saving a Sound Scheme

If you created your own set of event sound settings or modified an existing one, you should save it for future use. You can do this by following these steps:

1. Click the Save As button in the Schemes group box (refer to fig. 8.2). The Save Scheme As dialog box appears, as shown in figure 8.6.

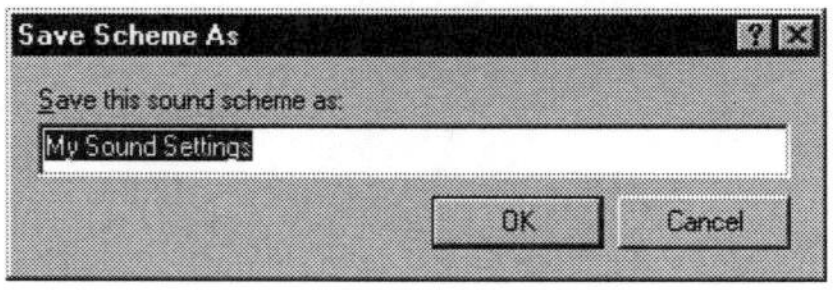

Fig. 8.6
The Save Scheme As dialog box allows you to name your group of event sounds.

2. Enter a name for the scheme of event sounds defined in the Sounds Properties Events list. If you use the same name as an existing scheme, the dialog box shown in figure 8.7 asks you to confirm your decision to replace the existing scheme.

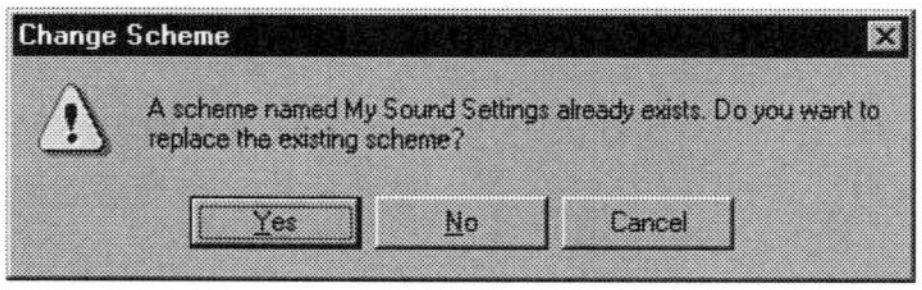

Fig. 8.7
The Change Scheme confirmation dialog box helps prevent you from accidentally changing a sound scheme.

Once you've completed these steps, you can click OK to close the Sounds Properties sheet.

Deleting a Sound Scheme

If you want to delete a configuration of event sounds, you may do so by following these steps:

1. Locate the scheme you want to remove by opening the Schemes drop-down list box (see fig. 8.8).

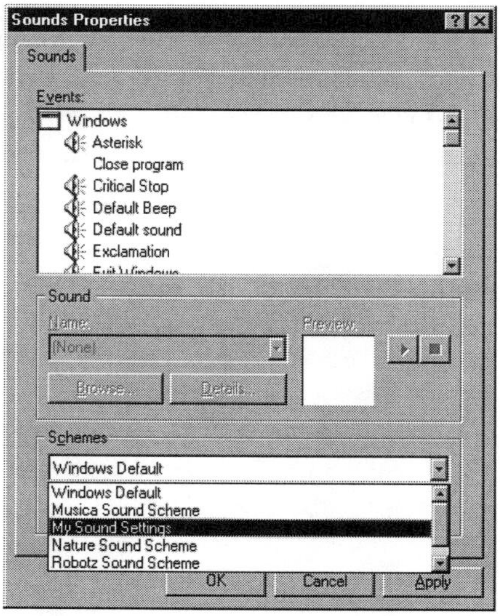

Fig. 8.8
Select a sound scheme to delete from the Schemes drop-down list box.

2. Click the Delete button in the Schemes group box (refer to fig. 8.8). The Sounds Properties sheet in figure 8.9 asks you to confirm your decision to replace the existing scheme.

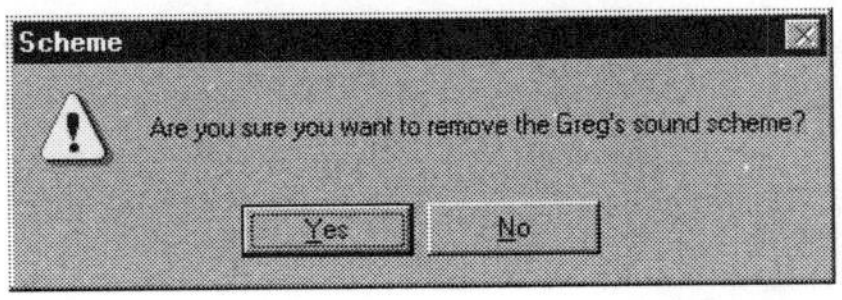

Fig. 8.9
The Delete Scheme confirmation dialog box helps prevent you from accidentally deleting a sound scheme.

> **Note**
>
> Deleting the scheme does not delete the actual WAV file, just the connection between the event and which sound to play.

Once you've completed these steps, you can click OK to close the Sounds Properties sheet.

Setting Volume

While using your computer, you may notice that your volume is too loud or too soft. Your CD-ROM drive, sound card, and MIDI instrument (usually part of your sound card) are all sources of the sounds and music. It's not unlikely that one of them is much louder or softer than the rest. In the next two sections, you learn how to adjust the master volume for Windows audio, and how to adjust each sound source's volume.

Using the Taskbar Volume Control

If you need to adjust the overall volume of sound coming out of your computer, use the taskbar speaker icon for quick and easy volume changes.

If the yellow sound icon does not appear on your taskbar like it does in the lower right-hand corner of figure 8.1, use the following steps to enable the taskbar speaker icon:

1. From the Start menu, choose Settings, Control Panel. Windows 95 displays the Control Panel window.

2. Open the Multimedia control panel. The Multimedia Properties sheet appears containing the Audio page, as seen in figure 8.10. In the upper-half of the screen, you'll see the Playback group box. At the bottom of this group box, place a check mark in the Show Volume Control on the

Taskbar check box. Selecting this option shows the volume control icon in the taskbar.

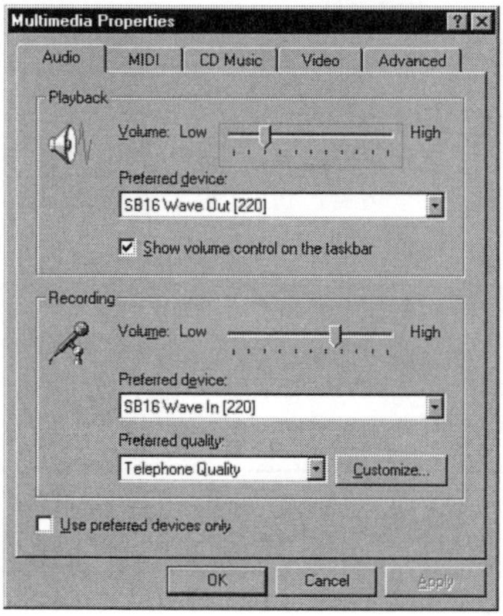

Fig. 8.10
The Multimedia Properties sheet allows you to turn on the taskbar volume control.

▶ See "Using the Add New Hardware Wizard for Sound Board," p. 438

Troubleshooting

I can't seem to find the Multimedia control panel or the Audio page in the Multimedia Properties sheet. What's wrong?

Either you don't have a sound card installed in your computer or Windows 95 did not recognize it.

3. Click OK to save the new setting and close the Multimedia Properties sheet.

Now that the speaker icon is visible, you'll be able to learn how to adjust the volume or quickly mute the audio level.

To adjust or mute the master volume, use these steps:

1. Position your mouse over the speaker icon and click once. A panel appears with a vertical slider and a check box, shown in figure 8.11.

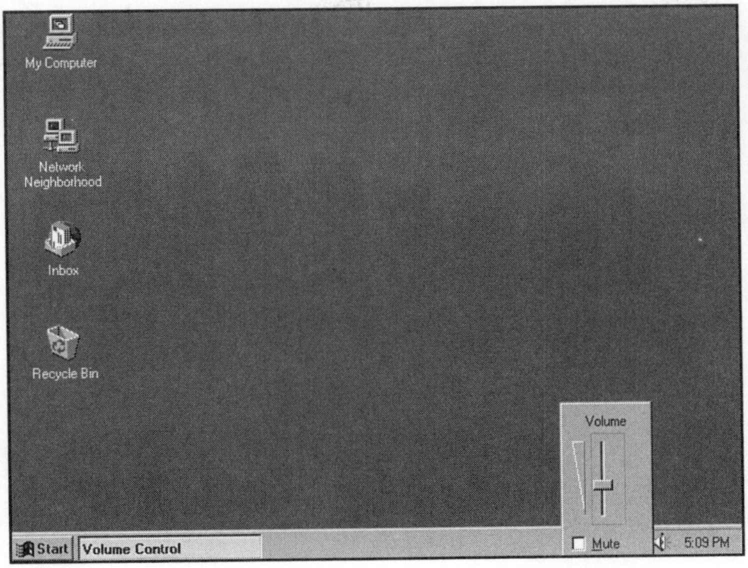

Fig. 8.11
The taskbar's Volume control panel appears when you click the taskbar speaker icon.

2. Drag the slider up or down to adjust the master volume accordingly. If you need to mute the volume, check the Mute check box to instantly mute every source of audio on your computer.

> **Note**
>
> If you mute the volume, notice how the speaker icon changes to a speaker icon covered by a red circle with a line through it.

3. To close the Volume control panel, click anywhere else on the screen except on the volume panel.

Using the Volume Control Window

While using Windows 95, you may have noticed that one source of sound is louder or softer than the rest. Or, a particular sound source may not be producing *any* sound. In this section you learn how to access individual sound source volumes and adjust them by following these steps:

1. Verify that the yellow taskbar speaker icon is visible. If it isn't, see the previous section, "Using the Taskbar Volume Control," to enable it.

2. Position your mouse over the speaker icon and double-click. A Volume Control window appears, similar to that in figure 8.12. You may have more or fewer controls and features depending upon the capabilities of your sound card.

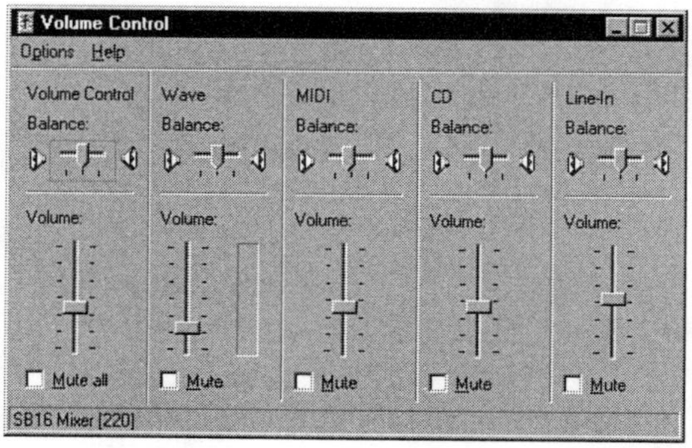

Fig. 8.12
The Volume Control window allows access to each sound source.

3. The leftmost slider and Mute All check box is the same as the Volume Control panel displayed when you single-click the speaker icon in the taskbar. Each column to the right of this, is a control dedicated to an individual sound source. Each one has a vertical slider and Mute check box. If your sound card supports stereo audio, a left-right balance slider appears above each vertical slider that supports stereo. By causing selected pairs of sound sources to play long segments of sound, you can adjust the vertical sliders correspondingly.

4. Once you have made your adjustments, choose Options, Exit to close the Volume Control window and save your settings.

Chapter 9

Configuring Microsoft Exchange

by Jim Boyce

Windows 95 includes an electronic mail (e-mail) application named Exchange that enables you to combine many, if not all, of your e-mail and faxes into a single inbox. With Exchange, you can send and receive e-mail to a Microsoft Mail post office, the Internet, The Microsoft Network, and CompuServe. Exchange's support for Internet and CompuServe e-mail gives you a gateway to send and receive messages to almost anyone in the world who has an e-mail account on the Internet or on an online service such as CompuServe, America Online, Prodigy, or others.

This chapter helps you install and configure Exchange to enable you to send and receive e-mail and faxes, both locally on your network, and through your modem to remote sites and services. In this chapter, you learn how to

- Install Microsoft Exchange
- Configure Exchange and service providers
- Create and edit an Exchange profile
- Set up your personal message store and address books
- Add other e-mail and fax services to Exchange
- Set up Exchange for remote mail access
- Customize Exchange

Naturally, before you can begin using Exchange, you must install the Exchange software. The following section helps you do just that.

Installing the Exchange Client

Microsoft Exchange is a typical Windows 95 application (see fig. 9.1) that works in conjunction with various *service providers* to enable you to send and receive e-mail and faxes to others. You can think of a service provider as an add-on module that enables the Exchange client to work with specific types of mail and online services. For example, Windows 95 includes service providers that enable it to work with Microsoft Mail, Microsoft Fax, and The Microsoft Network. The Windows 95 CD contains a service provider that enables Exchange to send and receive e-mail to and from CompuServe. Microsoft Plus! for Windows 95 includes a service provider that lets you send and receive mail on the Internet through a network or dial-up connection to the Internet.

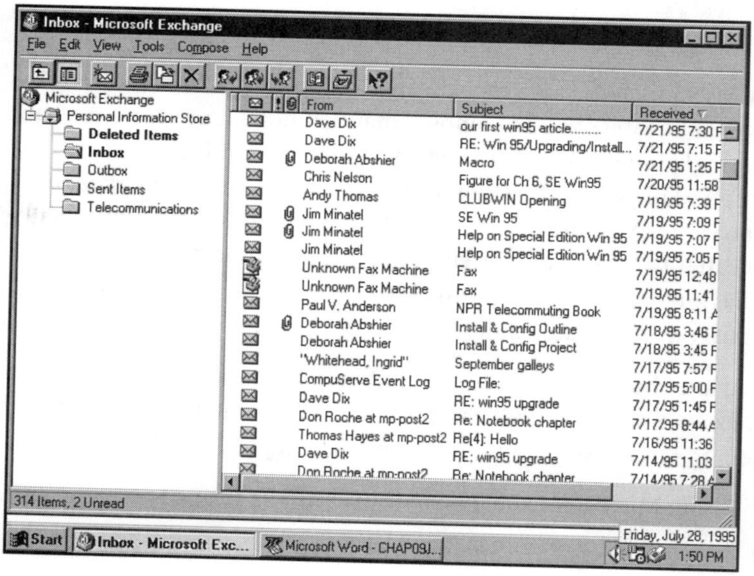

Fig. 9.1
Exchange provides a unified inbox for all of your e-mail and faxes.

> **Tip**
>
> You can expect other e-mail vendors to offer service providers for Microsoft Exchange that support their e-mail applications. Also look for online services such as America Online and Prodigy to provide Exchange service providers that work with their online services.

Installing and configuring Exchange consists of four phases, which are described in the following list:

- *Install Exchange.* You can install Exchange when you install Windows 95, or you can easily add Exchange to your PC at any time after you install Windows 95.
- *Create at least one profile.* Your Exchange settings and service providers are stored in an Exchange profile. Each profile can contain one or more service providers to support different e-mail and fax systems. A *profile* is a collection of settings you can use to specify which service providers and settings you want to use with Exchange.
- *Add a personal information store and address book.* You need somewhere to store your messages, so the third phase in configuring Exchange is to add a personal information store to your profile, along with an address book to store e-mail and fax addresses.
- *Add service providers.* The final phase of installing Exchange is to add to your profile the service providers you want to use. These could include Microsoft Mail, CompuServe Mail, The Microsoft Network, and Internet e-mail.

Setup doesn't automatically install Exchange when you install Windows 95. Instead, you must specifically select Exchange as an option to install when you run Setup. Or, you can add Exchange after installing Windows 95. The following sections explain how to install the Microsoft Exchange client software. Later sections explain how to create and modify Exchange profiles, add service providers, and set other Exchange options.

Installing Exchange During Windows 95 Installation

If you have not yet installed Windows 95, you can install Exchange at the same time you install Windows 95. To install Exchange, use the following steps:

1. Run Setup from the Windows 95 floppy disk 1 or the \WIN95 folder on the Windows 95 CD.
2. Follow the prompts and windows to choose installation options as explained in Part I of this book.
3. When the Setup Options window appears (see fig. 9.2) and prompts you to select the type of installation you want, choose Custom, then click Next.
4. Follow the prompts and windows to enable Setup to detect your PC's hardware.

5. When the Get Connected window shown in figure 9.3 appears, select the service provider(s) you want to use with Exchange. The listed providers include Microsoft Mail, The Microsoft Network, and Microsoft Fax. You can select one, or more than one. If you want to use only the Internet or CompuServe mail providers (included with Plus! and the Windows 95 CD, respectively) and not use any of the three service providers in the Get Connected window, leave all of the check boxes cleared—you have an option to install only Exchange in step 6. When you've made your selections, choose Next.

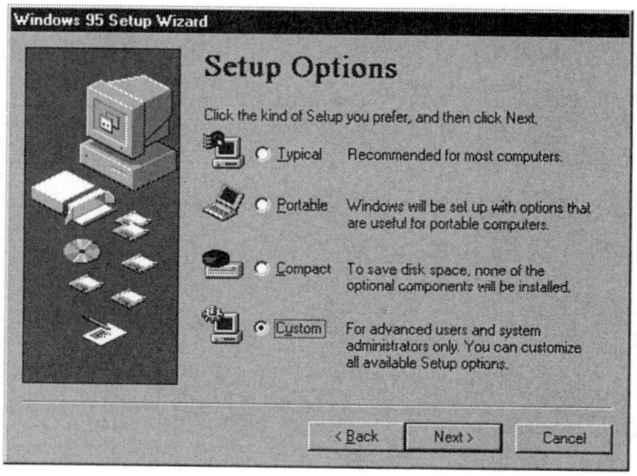

Fig. 9.2
Select the Custom option to install Exchange with the rest of the Windows 95 components.

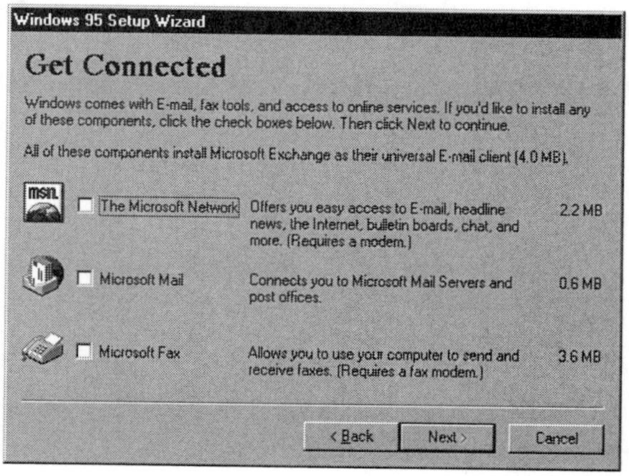

Fig. 9.3
Choose one or more service providers from the Get Connected window.

Note

If you forget to add a service provider when you install Windows 95 or add Exchange to your system, you can add the service provider later. Check the section "Creating and Editing User Profiles" later in this chapter to learn how to add a service provider.

6. In the Select Components window (see fig. 9.4), click Microsoft Exchange, then choose Details to display the Microsoft Exchange dialog box. If the Microsoft Exchange check box does not contain a check mark, enable the check box. If you also want to install the Microsoft Mail provider, enable the Microsoft Mail Services check box. Then, choose OK.

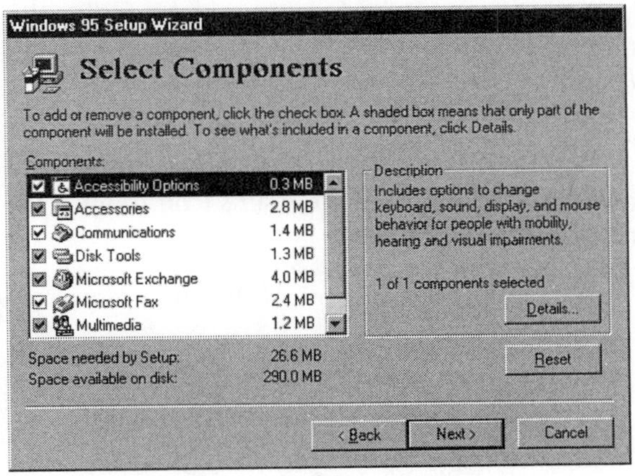

Fig. 9.4
Double-click the Microsoft Exchange item to install Exchange.

7. Choose Next, then follow Setup's remaining prompts to complete the installation process.

After Setup completes the installation process and you start Windows 95, you'll see an Inbox icon on the Desktop. This is the icon you later use to start Exchange. Before using Exchange, however, you need to complete the configuration process. Skip to the section "Creating and Editing User Profiles" later in this chapter to learn how to complete the configuration process for Exchange.

> **Troubleshooting**
>
> Plus!
>
> *When Exchange starts, I receive error messages saying that my Internet Mail server is not available. I don't have an Internet Mail server, and don't use Internet Mail. What's wrong?*
>
> You probably installed Plus! for Windows 95, and ran the Internet Wizard, which installed the Internet Mail service provider. Open Control Panel and click the Mail and Fax icon. From the list of installed services, choose Internet Mail, then choose Remove. Windows 95 prompts you to verify that you want to remove the Internet Mail service provider from your profile. Choose Yes to remove the service from your profile.

Adding Exchange After Installing Windows 95

If you didn't install Exchange when you installed Windows 95, don't worry—it's easy to add Exchange. Use the following steps to add Exchange after installing Windows 95:

1. Choose Start, Settings, then Control Panel to open the Control Panel.
2. Double-click the Add/Remove Programs icon to open the Add/Remove Programs Properties sheet.
3. Click the Windows Setup tab and the Windows Setup page shown in figure 9.5 appears.

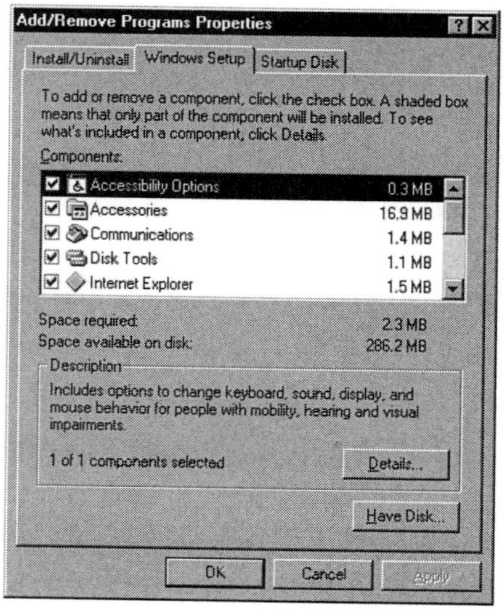

Fig. 9.5
Use the Windows Setup page anytime you need to add some software to Windows 95.

4. Scroll through the Components list to locate and select Microsoft Exchange, then choose Details.

5. In the Microsoft Exchange dialog box, place a check mark beside Microsoft Exchange. If you want to use Exchange to connect to a Microsoft Mail postoffice, place a check mark beside the Microsoft Mail Services item. Then, choose OK.

6. If you want to use Microsoft Fax, place a check mark in the Components list beside the Microsoft Fax item.

7. Choose OK. Windows 95 adds the necessary software to your system, prompting you if necessary to supply one or more of the Windows 95 disks or the Windows 95 CD, if needed.

Tip

If you want to use Microsoft Exchange to send and receive messages on The Microsoft Network, you must first install The Microsoft Network on your system. In the Components dialog box, place a check mark beside The Microsoft Network item. You can add The Microsoft Network to your system at the same time you add Exchange, or you can add it separately.

Creating and Editing User Profiles

Besides installing Exchange, you need to configure at least one user profile. The following section explains user profiles to help you understand how to create and edit them.

Understanding Profiles

A collection of information stores, address books, and service providers is called a *user profile*. For example, you might use a profile that contains your personal information store, one address book, a Microsoft Mail service provider, and a CompuServe service provider. In addition to giving you a means of grouping the service providers and information store you use most often into a named group, Exchange profiles also store the settings for each item in the profile. Figure 9.6 shows items in an Exchange profile.

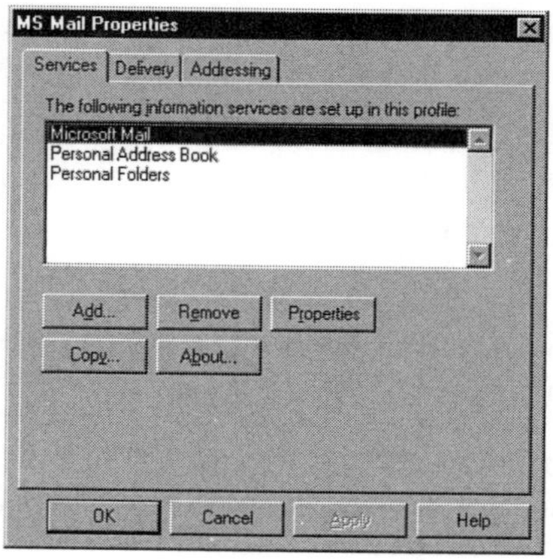

Fig. 9.6
An Exchange profile stores your Exchange settings by name.

If you're like most people, you will use a single profile. But, you can use multiple profiles. For example, if you use Microsoft Fax very seldom but use Microsoft Mail all the time, you might want to place the Microsoft Fax provider in a separate profile. When you have to use Microsoft Fax, you can make the Microsoft Fax profile active (explained in the next section), then start Exchange to use it.

Tip

Information stores and address books are service providers, just like Microsoft Mail, CompuServe, and other service providers. All of these service providers are often referred to as just *services*.

Configuring Profiles

As with most configuration tasks in Windows 95, you create and edit user profiles from the Control Panel. When you install Exchange, Windows 95 creates a default profile for you named MS Exchange Settings. To view or edit your default profile, open the Control Panel, then double-click the Mail and Fax icon to display the MS Exchange Settings Properties sheet shown in figure 9.7.

From the MS Exchange Settings Properties sheet you can add services to a profile, delete services, set properties for services, and create and view other profiles. You also can set the properties of services in a profile. If you are using the CompuServe Mail provider, for example, you can specify your CompuServe user ID, password, and other properties that control how and when the CompuServe provider logs onto CompuServe to send and receive your CompuServe mail.

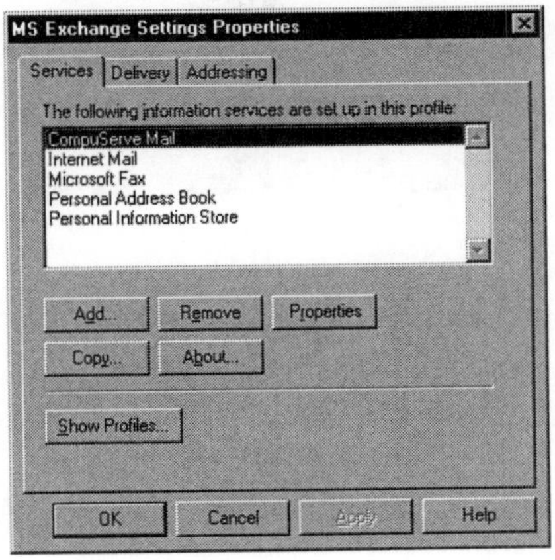

Fig. 9.7
Windows 95 creates a default profile for you named MS Exchange Settings.

Each service is different from another, so the properties that you can set for each service varies from one service to another. Later sections, "Setting Up Personal Information Stores," "Setting Up Address Books," and "Adding Information Services to Exchange," explain how to add services and set their properties. The following section explains how to create and delete profiles.

Creating and Deleting Exchange Profiles

As explained earlier, you might want to use more than one Exchange profile to store different sets of properties and services. You can create a profile in one of two ways—create a completely new profile, or copy an existing profile. Regardless of which method you use, you can edit the profile to add, remove, or edit services after you create the profile.

To copy your existing profile, follow these steps:

1. Open the Control Panel and double-click the Mail and Fax icon to display the MS Exchange Settings Properties sheet.
2. Click the Show Profiles button to display the Microsoft Exchange Profiles property sheet shown in figure 9.8.
3. Select the profile you want to copy, then click the Copy button. A dialog box prompting you to enter a name for your new profile appears (see fig. 9.9).
4. In the New Profile Name text box, enter a unique name for your new Exchange profile, then choose OK. Windows 95 will copy all of the services and settings in the selected profile to your new profile.
5. Use the steps explained in the following sections of this chapter to configure the services in your new profile.

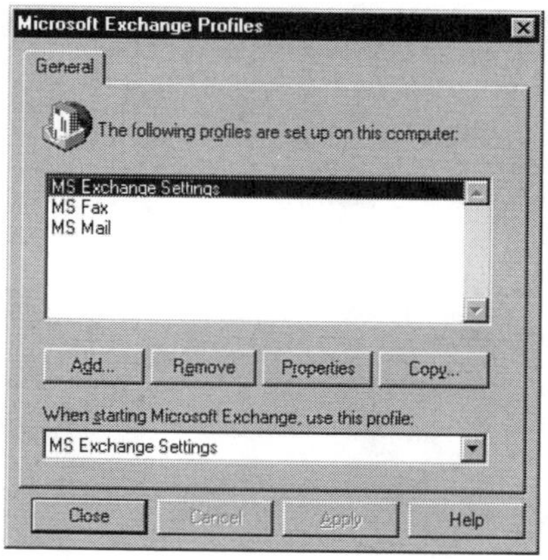

Fig. 9.8
With the Microsoft Exchange Profiles property sheet, you can create a new profile or copy an existing profile.

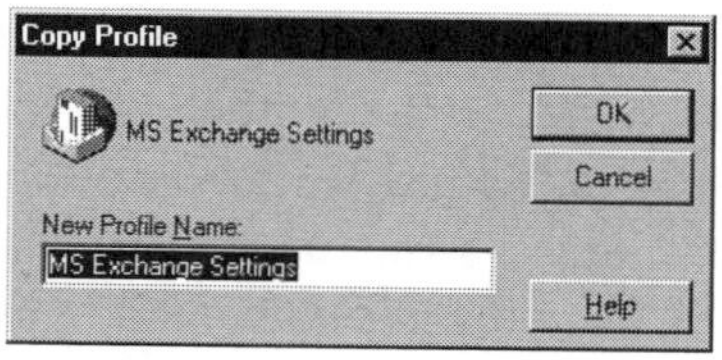

Fig. 9.9
Enter a unique name for your new profile.

Tip

After you create a profile, you need to specify it as your default profile before you can use it with Exchange. Refer to the section "Setting Your Default Profile" to learn how to begin using your new profile.

In addition to copying an existing profile, you also can create an Exchange profile from scratch. Windows 95 provides a wizard to step you through the process. Use the following steps to create a new Exchange profile:

1. Open the Control Panel and double-click the Mail and Fax icon.
2. Click the Show Profiles button to display the Microsoft Exchange Profiles property sheet.
3. Click the Add button and the Inbox Setup Wizard shown in figure 9.10 appears.

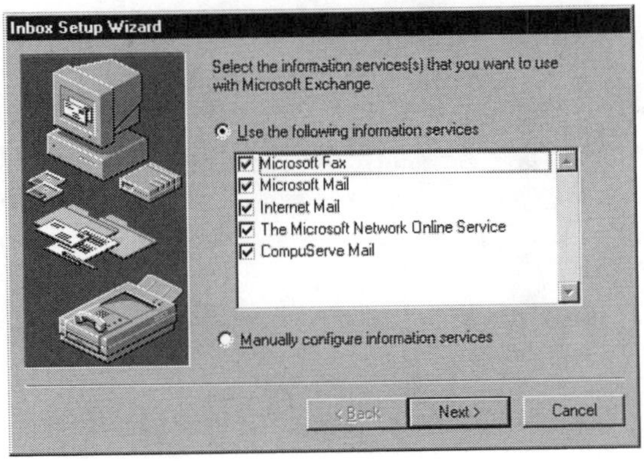

Fig. 9.10
Exchange provides a wizard to help you set up a profile.

4. Click the Use the Following Information Services option button.
5. Place a check mark beside each of the services you want to include in your profile. Deselect any services you don't want included in the profile, then click Next. The wizard displays a new window prompting you for a name for your new profile (see fig. 9.11).
6. Enter a unique name for your profile, then click Next.
7. Depending on which services you selected, the wizard prompts you for information to configure the services. Refer to the sections later in this chapter that describe setup options for services to help you configure the services.

Tip

If you use the previous steps to create a profile and add services to the profile, Windows 95 uses a wizard to step you through the process of configuring the services. If you add services manually as explained later in this chapter, Windows 95 doesn't use a wizard, but instead displays a set of property sheets for the service. Use these sheets to set its properties. If you read through the following sections on configuring services manually, you will have no trouble at all configuring the services using the wizard.

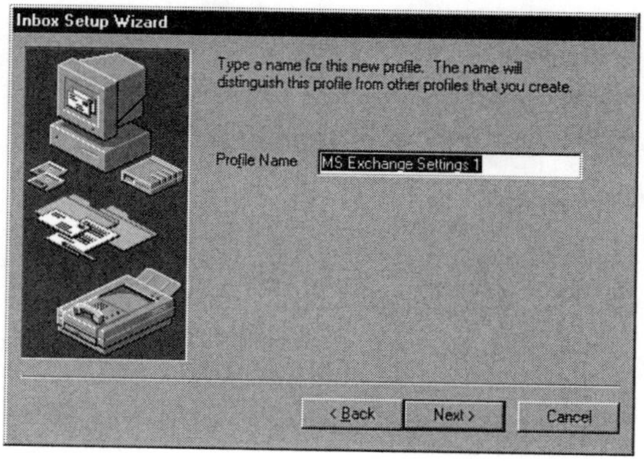

Fig. 9.11
Enter a unique name for your new profile.

Setting Your Default Profile

Although you can create as many Exchange profiles as you want, you can only use one profile at a time. You have two options for specifying which Exchange profile you use. Each time you want to use a different profile, you must exit Exchange, use the Control Panel to specify which profile to use, then restart Exchange. Or, you can configure Exchange to prompt you to specify which profile to use each time Exchange starts.

To specify a default profile, follow these steps:

1. Open the Control Panel and double-click the Mail and Fax icon.
2. Click the Show Profiles button.
3. From the drop-down list labeled When Starting Microsoft Exchange, Use This Profile, choose the profile you want Exchange to use as a default.
4. Choose Close, then start Exchange to verify that it is using the correct profile.

To have Exchange prompt you to select a profile each time Exchange starts, follow these steps:

1. Start Exchange (double-click the Inbox icon on the Desktop).
2. Choose Tools, Options to display the Options property sheet.
3. From the control group named When Starting Microsoft Exchange, choose the option labeled Prompt for a Profile to be Used. Then, choose OK. The next time you start Exchange, you'll be prompted to select which profile you want to use.

To learn about other general Exchange options you can specify, refer to the section "Setting General Exchange Options" later in this chapter.

Setting Up Personal Information Stores

Without a place to store all of your messages, Exchange wouldn't be much use to you. So, each profile should include at least one information store. An *information store* is a special type of file that Exchange uses to store all of your messages. Whether the message is a fax, an e-mail message from your network mail post office, or other service, incoming messages are placed in the Inbox folder of your default information store. A typical information store contains the following folders:

- *Deleted Items*. This folder contains all of the messages you have deleted from other folders. By default, Exchange will not delete items from your information store unless you select them in the Deleted Items folder and delete them. As explained later in the section "Setting General Exchange Options," you can configure Exchange to immediately delete a message instead of moving it to the Deleted Items folder.

- *Inbox*. Exchange places all of your incoming messages—including error and status messages generated by the various service providers, e-mail, and faxes—in the Inbox.

- *Outbox*. Items that you compose are placed in the Outbox until the appropriate service delivers the message automatically or you manually direct the Exchange to deliver the message(s).

- *Sent Items*. By default, Exchange places in the Sent Items folder a copy of all messages you send. You can configure Exchange not to keep a copy of sent messages (see the section "Setting General Exchange Options" later in this chapter).

In addition to the folders listed previously, you can add your own folders to an information store. And, you're not limited to a single information store—you can add as many information stores to a profile as you like. The folders in each information store show up under a separate tree in the Exchange window. Figure 9.12 shows Exchange with two information stores being used: Personal Folders and Personal Information Store.

Adding multiple message stores to a profile is useful mainly for copying messages between message files. If you are using the latest version of the Microsoft Mail service provider that supports shared folders, however, you can add a shared folder message store to your profile. The shared folder enables you to share messages with other users.

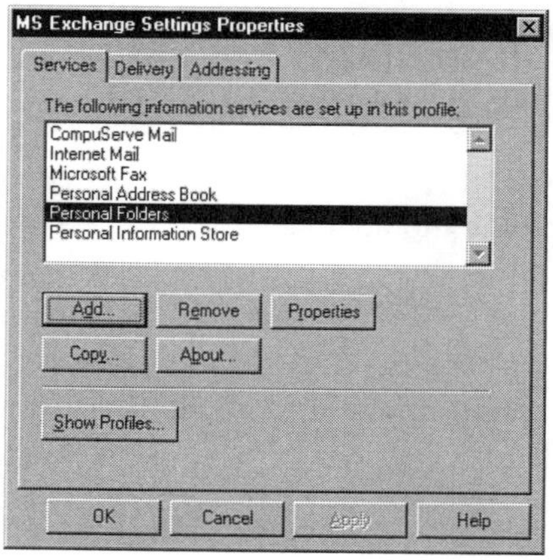

Fig. 9.12
You can use as many information stores in a profile as you like.

There is one other reason to add a set of personal folders to your profile: you can't use encryption on the Personal Information Store, but you can use encryption on a Personal Folder. The two are identical in function, so if you want to use encryption for your message file for extra security, add a Personal Folders item to your profile, copy your messages from the Personal Information Store to the Personal Folders, then remove the Personal Information Store from your profile. Make sure you configure Exchange to use the Personal Folders to store incoming messages, as explained in the next section.

Troubleshooting

I would like to add a second Personal Information Store to my profile, but Exchange tells me I can only have one in a profile. Is it possible to add another?

You can only have one Personal Information Store in a profile, but you can add as many Personal Folders to a profile as you like. Personal Folders are essentially identical to the Personal Information Store. The only difference is that your incoming mail is directed into the Personal Information Store. If you simply want more places to segregate your incoming mail, create new folders in your Personal Information Store instead of adding Personal Folders to your profile. You can create as many additional folders in the Personal Information Store as you like. To create a new folder, open the folder in which you want the new folder created. Then, choose File, New Folder. Exchange displays a dialog box in which you enter the name for the new folder. Then, you can drag messages to the new folder as you desire.

Configuring Your Personal Information Store

You can change a handful of settings for a Personal Information Store. To change properties for a Personal Information Store, use the following steps:

1. Open the Control Panel and double-click the Mail and Fax icon.

2. If you want to set properties for a Personal Information Store in a profile other than the default profile, choose the Show Profiles button, select the profile you want to change, then choose Properties.

3. Select Personal Information Store from the list of services in the profile, then choose Properties. The Personal Folders property sheet shown in figure 9.13 appears.

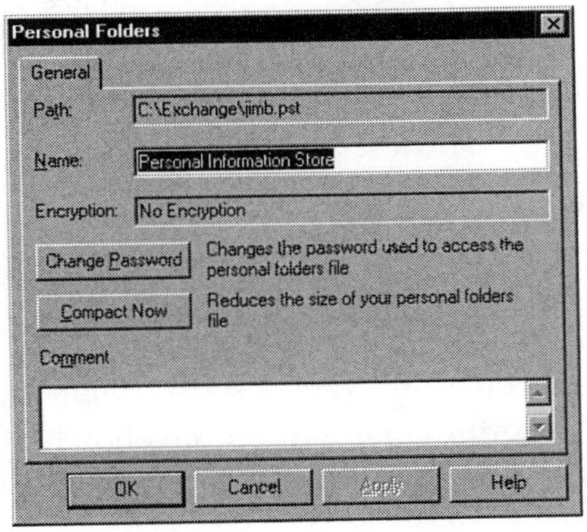

Fig. 9.13
Use the Personal Folders property sheet to set properties for the information store.

4. Set the properties for the Personal Information Store according to the following descriptions and your needs:

   - *Name.* If you like, enter a new name for the Personal Information Store. This name will appear in the profile instead of "Personal Information Store."

   - *Change Password.* Click this button to change the password for your Personal Information Store. The Create Microsoft Personal Folders dialog box appears. The four properties you can set in the password dialog box are described in table 9.1.

Table 9.1 Password Properties for an Information Store

Property	Purpose
Old Password	Enter in this text box the current password, if any, for the Personal Information Store.
New Password	Enter in this text box the new password you want to assign to the Personal Information Store.
Verify Password	Enter in this text box the new password you want to assign to the Personal Information Store to enable Windows 95 to verify that you have entered the password correctly.
Save This Password in Your Password List	If you want the password stored in your password cache so you don't have to enter the password each time you open Exchange, place a check mark in this check box.

- *Compact Now.* Choose this button to compress (compact) your Personal Information Store. Windows 95 compresses the file, reducing its size. Compressing a Personal Information Store has no effect on your ability to use the file to store messages.
- *Comment.* If you want to add a short comment about the Personal Information Store, enter it in this text box.

After you have specified all of the necessary properties, choose OK, then choose OK again to save the changes.

Adding Other Information Stores

As explained earlier, you can add as many information stores to a profile as you like. These additional stores are called Personal Folders, but they have essentially the same structure and function as your Personal Information Store. You can add a new Personal Folders file to a profile or add an existing file. Adding an existing file enables you to easily import messages from other information stores that you or others have created separately.

To add an information store to a profile, use the following steps:

1. Open the Control Panel and double-click the Mail and Fax icon.
2. If you want to add Personal Folders to a profile other than the default profile, choose the Show Profiles button, select the profile you want to change, then choose Properties.
3. Choose Add, then from the Add Service to Profile dialog box, select Personal Folders and choose OK.

4. The Create/Open Personal Folders File dialog box appears. If you are adding an existing file, locate and select the file in the dialog box, then choose Open. If you want to create a new file, enter a name for the file in the File Name text box, then choose Open.

5. If you are creating a new file, Windows 95 displays a dialog box similar to the one shown in figure 9.14. The Name and Password properties are the same as those explained in the previous section. From the Encryption Setting group, choose one of the following options:

   - *No Encryption.* Choose this option if you don't want the file to be encrypted. If the file is not encrypted, other users can open the file and read its contents with another program, such as a word processor.

   - *Compressible Encryption.* Choose this option if you want the file to be encrypted for security, but you also want to be able to compress (compact) the file to save disk space.

   - *Best Encryption.* Choose this option if you want the most secure encryption. You will not be able to compress the file if you choose this option.

   Or, if you are adding an existing Personal Folders file, the dialog box shown in figure 9.13 appears. Adjust settings as explained.

6. Choose OK, then choose OK again to close the MS Exchange Settings Properties sheet.

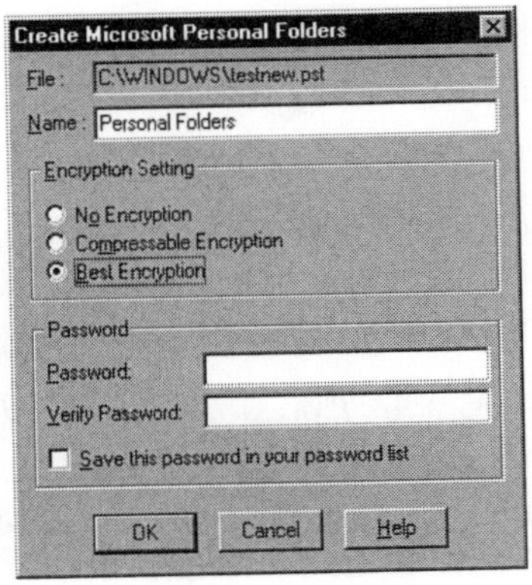

Fig. 9.14
The Create Microsoft Personal Folders dialog box enables you to set various properties for your information store.

Setting Delivery Options

Even though you can add multiple information stores to a profile, only one can be assigned to receive incoming messages. You can, however, assign an alternate information store to be used to store incoming messages if the primary store is unavailable for some reason.

To set these delivery options, follow these steps:

1. Open the Control Panel and double-click the Mail and Fax icon.
2. Click the Delivery tab to display the Delivery page (see fig. 9.15).

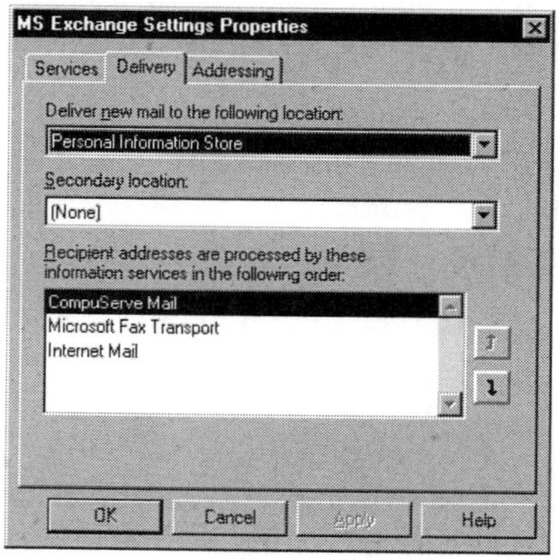

Fig. 9.15 Specify which store will receive incoming messages.

3. Specify settings in the Delivery page based on the following descriptions:

   - *Deliver New Mail to the Following Location.* Select from the drop-down list the information store in which you want incoming mail to be placed.
   - *Secondary Location.* Select from the drop-down list the information store in which incoming mail should be placed if the primary message store is unavailable.
   - *Recipient Addresses Are Processed by These Information Services in the Following Order.* This control lists the order in which mail providers distribute mail when you direct Exchange to deliver mail using all services. To move an item in the list, select it, then click either the up or the down arrow.

4. After specifying the desired settings, choose OK to save the changes.

Setting Up Address Books

Although you can send and receive mail without an address book, adding an address book to your profile makes it possible for you to store addresses and quickly select an address for a message. You can add addresses to the address book yourself, or let Exchange add originating addresses of received mail.

A profile can contain only one Personal Address Book. When you install Exchange, Windows 95 automatically adds a Personal Address Book to your default profile. You can add a new, blank address book, or add an existing address book that already contains address entries.

If you want to add a Personal Address Book to a new profile, or you have accidentally deleted your Personal Address Book from your default profile, follow these steps to add the address book:

1. Open the Control Panel and double-click the Mail and Fax icon.
2. If you want to add a Personal Address Book to a profile other than the default profile, click the Show Profiles button, select the profile you want to change, then click Properties.
3. Click the Add button, then from the Add Service to Profile dialog box, choose Personal Address Book and click OK. The Personal Address Book property sheet shown in figure 9.16 appears.

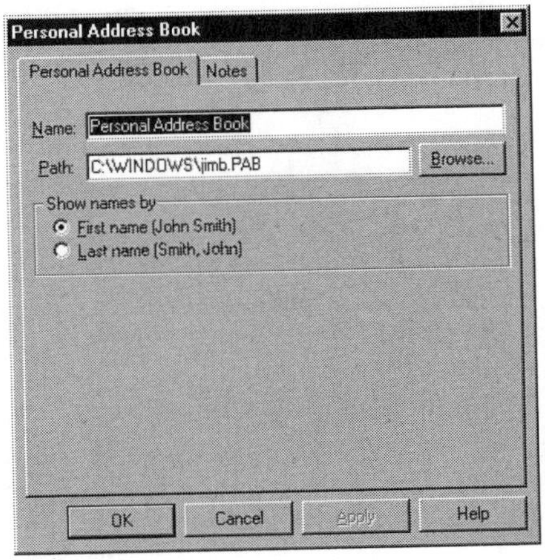

Fig. 9.16
Set properties for your Personal Address Book.

4. In the Name text box, enter a name for the address book (or leave the name as-is, if you prefer).
5. In the Path text box, enter the path and file name for the new address book file, or in the case of an existing address book, enter the path and

file name of the existing file. If you prefer, you can choose the Browse button to browse for the file.

6. From the control group Show Names By, choose how you want names to appear in the address book (sorted by first name or last name).

7. Choose OK, then OK again to save the changes.

Setting Addressing Options

Although you can have only one Personal Address Book in a profile, you can add other types of address books. For example, a CompuServe Address Book is included in the CompuServe Mail provider. Other service providers that you add might also include their own address books. For this reason, you need a way to specify which address book Exchange displays by default, and other addressing options.

To set addressing options, open the Control Panel and double-click the Mail and Fax icon. Then, click the Addressing tab to display the Addressing page shown in figure 9.17.

The properties you can specify on the Addressing page are described in the following list:

- *Show This Address List First.* Select from this drop-down list the address book you want Exchange to display when you click the To button in the compose window, or choose Tools, Address Book. You'll have the option in Exchange of selecting a different address book if more than one is installed.

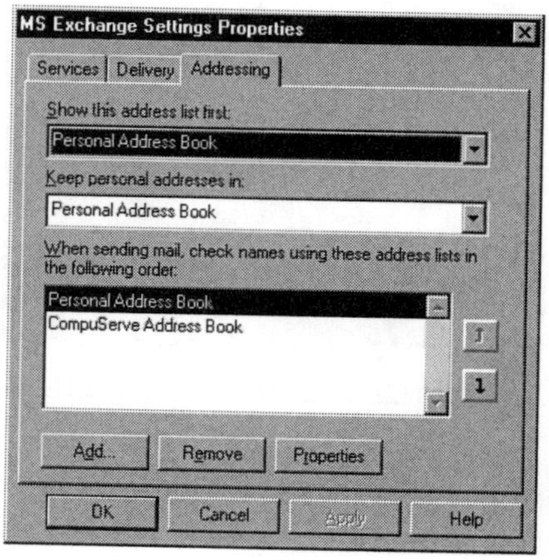

Fig. 9.17
Use the Addressing page to specify your default address book.

- *Keep Personal Addresses In.* Select from this drop-down list the address book in which you want a new address to be added unless you specifically choose a different address book.
- *When Sending Mail, Check Names Using These Address Lists in the Following Order.* Use this list to set the order in which Exchange checks addresses for validity when you send a message or click the Check Names button in the compose window toolbar.

After you specify the Addressing properties you want to use, choose OK to save the changes.

Tip

For help adding and modifying addresses, see Que's *Special Edition Using Windows 95.*

Setting General Exchange Options

It might sometimes seem to you like Exchange offers an overwhelming number of properties and options that you can set. This section helps you understand and set those properties and options. If you've read through the earlier parts of this chapter, you've already set some general Exchange options, including delivery and addressing options. The following sections explain the other options you can set. To reach the property pages referenced in the following sections, open Exchange, then choose Tools, Options.

Setting General Options

The General page specifies a handful of properties that control how Exchange alerts you to new incoming messages and other common actions, such as deleting messages (see fig. 9.18).

The following list explains the properties you can set on the General page:

- *When New Mail Arrives.* This group contains three options you can enable to control how Exchange notifies you of incoming messages.
- *Deleting Items.* Enable the option Warn Before Permanently Deleting Items if you want Exchange to warn you when you permanently delete a message (rather than deleting it to the Deleted Items folder). Enable the option named Empty the 'Deleted Items' Folder Upon Exiting, if you want Exchange to permanently delete messages from the Deleted Items folder when you exit Exchange.

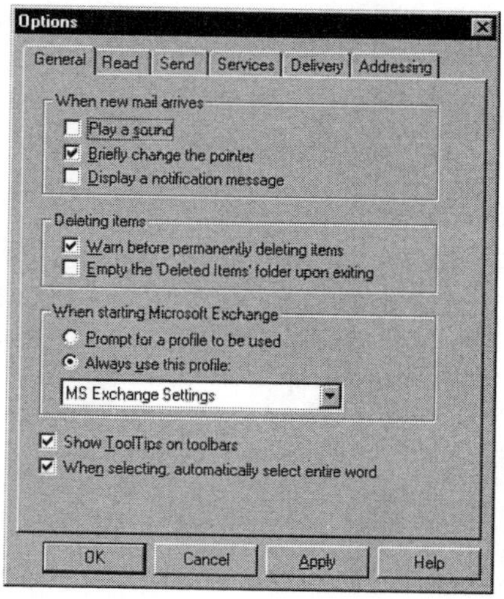

Fig. 9.18
Use the General page to set general Exchange options.

- *When Starting Microsoft Exchange.* Use the options in this group to either specify a default Exchange profile, or to cause Exchange to prompt you to select a profile each time Exchange starts.

- *Show ToolTips on Toolbars.* Enable this option if you want Exchange to display a ToolTip for a toolbar button when you rest the pointer on the button for a second.

- *When Selecting, Automatically Select Entire Word.* Enable this option if you want Exchange to automatically select entire words when you drag over the words with the pointer.

Setting Read Options

The properties on the Read page control the way Exchange handles messages when you read, reply to, or forward the messages (see fig. 9.19).

The properties you can set with the Read page are explained in the following list:

- *After Moving Or Deleting An Open Item.* The three options in this group control Exchange's actions when you read, move, or delete a message. The options are self-explanatory—select whichever option suits your preferences.

- *When Replying To or Forwarding An Item.* These properties control how Exchange handles messages when you reply to or forward a message. Enable the option labeled Include the Original Text When Replying if you want Exchange to include the text of the original message in your reply. If you want the original message text to be indented in the message, with your new text at the left margin, click Indent the Original Text When Replying. Enable the option labeled Close the Original Item if you want Exchange to automatically close the original e-mail message window after you start your reply. Choose the Font button to specify the font used for your reply text.

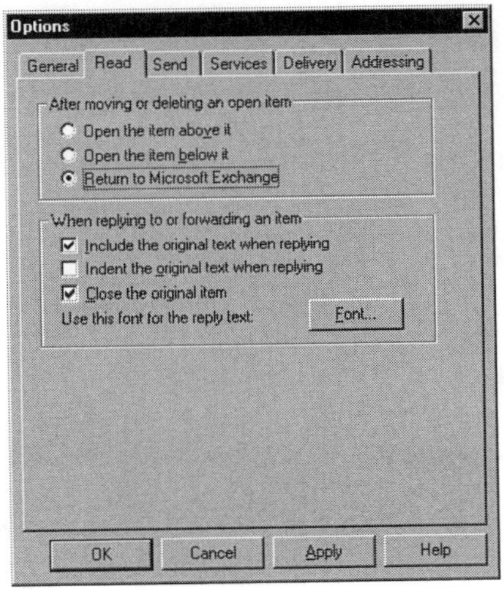

Fig. 9.19
Set options for reading messages using the Read page.

Tip

If you indent original message text or use a special font in a reply or a forwarded message, the recipient will see those message characteristics only if he or she is using Microsoft Exchange and a service provider that is capable of sending and receiving messages in RTF (Rich Text Format). Examples of such providers are the Microsoft Mail and Microsoft Network services.

Setting Send Options

You also can specify a few properties that control the way Exchange handles items you are sending. Click the Send tab to display the Send page shown in figure 9.20.

You can click the Font button to choose the font Exchange will use by default for your outgoing messages. As with indented text, the recipient must also be using Exchange and a service provider that supports message transfer in RTF.

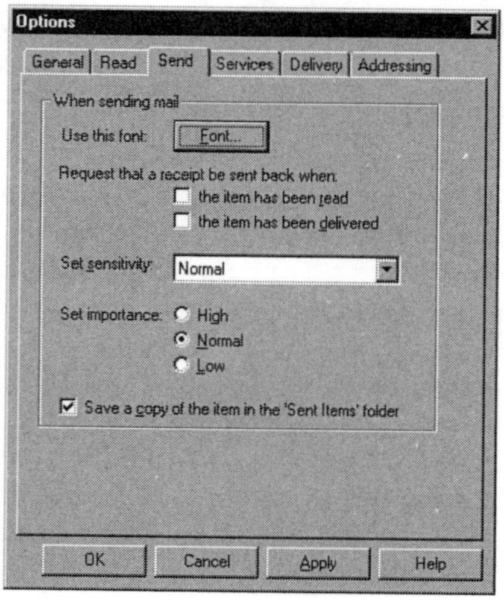

Fig. 9.20
Control outgoing message options with the Send page.

The two options in the group labeled Request That a Receipt Be Sent Back When control whether you receive a return receipt from the recipient's mail system. The available options are

- *The Item Has Been Read.* If you choose this option, you'll receive a return receipt only after the recipient reads the message, which could happen well after he receives the message.
- *The Item Has Been Delivered.* Choose this option to receive a return receipt as soon as the message is delivered, regardless of whether the message has been read.

The Set Sensitivity and Set Importance options are self-explanatory. Choose the options you want to use by default. Note that you can override either of these settings when you create a message.

If you enable the option labeled Save a Copy of the Item in the 'Sent Items' Folder, Exchange automatically places a copy of your outgoing message in the Sent Items folder. This is helpful if you need to review a message you've previously sent. Just remember to periodically clean out the Sent Items folder to avoid having a huge message file filled with old messages.

Configuring Exchange for Microsoft Mail

If you are using Windows 95 on a Microsoft-based network (Windows NT, Windows for Workgroups, or Windows 95), it's a good bet that you want to use the Microsoft Mail service provider—all of these Microsoft operating environments include a workgroup version of Microsoft Mail. Or, you might want to connect through Dial-Up Networking to a remote site, such as your district office, that uses Microsoft Mail. In either case, you need to create and configure a workgroup postoffice (WGPO) if your network does not yet include one. The following sections help you do just that.

Tip

A *workgroup postoffice* is a special set of directories that Microsoft Mail clients and Microsoft Mail Exchange clients can use to send and receive e-mail. Before you can begin sending and receiving mail on your LAN using the Microsoft Mail provider, you must have a WGPO on your LAN. Fortunately, Windows 95 makes it easy to create and manage a WGPO, as you learn in the next section.

Setting Up a Workgroup Postoffice

The Control Panel contains an object specifically for creating and managing a workgroup postoffice. Open the Control Panel and double-click the Microsoft Mail Postoffice icon. Windows 95 starts a wizard as shown in figure 9.21. This wizard lets you either create a new WGPO or administer an existing WGPO.

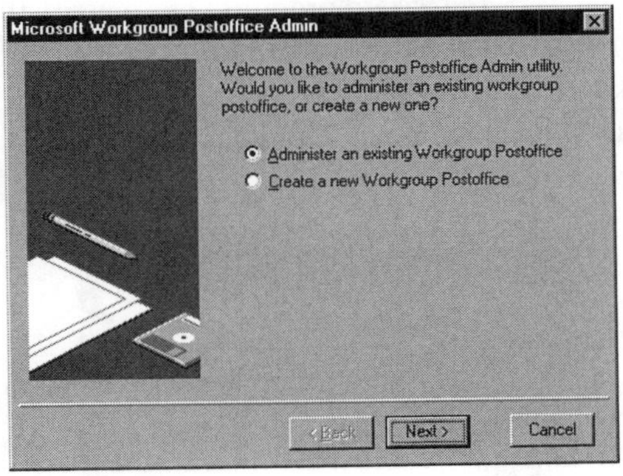

Fig. 9.21
You can create a new WGPO or administer an existing one.

Note

When you create a WGPO, you also create an administrator's account. The administrator is responsible for creating and managing user mail accounts. Before you begin creating the WGPO, decide who will be administering the postoffice. In the following steps, you create an administrator account and should be ready to provide the name of the person who will be administering the postoffice.

To set up a new WGPO, follow these steps:

1. Start the Microsoft Workgroup Postoffice Admin wizard as explained previously.

2. Choose the Create a new Workgroup Postoffice option, then choose Next. Windows 95 then prompts you for the name and location for your new postoffice (see fig. 9.22). Enter the name or choose Browse to browse for a folder for the WGPO.

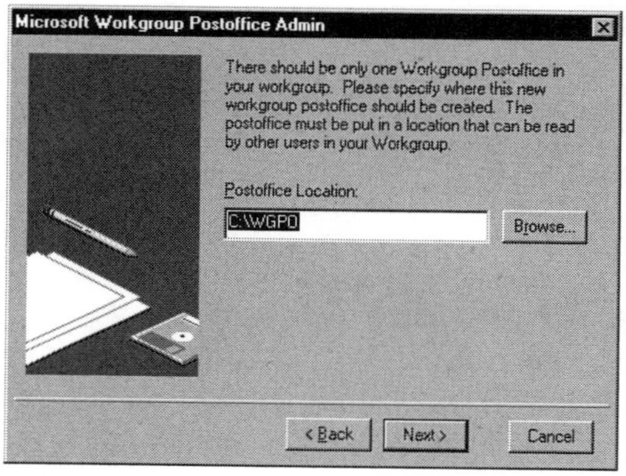

Fig. 9.22
Enter the path and file name for your new postoffice.

3. After you click Next, the wizard prompts you to verify the path and file name you entered. Choose Next if the path and file name are correct, or choose Back to change the path or file name. After you click Next, the wizard displays the Enter Your Administrator Account Details window shown in figure 9.23.

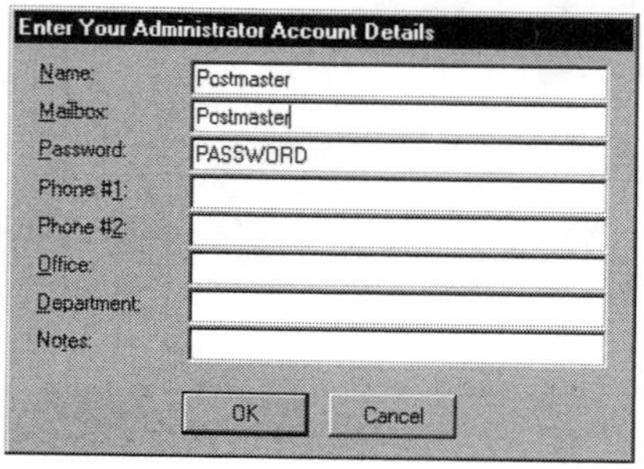

Fig. 9.23
You must specify details for an administrator account for your WGPO.

4. Fill out the fields in the account window. You must provide entries for the following three items:

- *Name.* In this field, enter the first and last name of the person who will be administering the postoffice.

> **Tip**
>
> If you don't want to specify a particular user's name, use Postmaster as the Name and Mailbox entries for the account. When you or anyone else needs to log into the postoffice to administer it, simply log in using the Postmaster account.

- *Mailbox.* Enter in this field the name of the mailbox for the administrator's account. Windows 95 suggests your Windows 95 network name, but you should consider creating a general Postmaster account.

- *Password.* Although you can leave the password blank, it's a bad idea to leave your WGPO administrator's account unprotected. Windows 95 suggests PASSWORD as the account password. You should enter a different password that others won't be able to guess. Just make sure you don't forget the password. If you do, you won't be able to administer the WGPO without re-creating the entire WGPO (and losing all messages contained in it).

The remaining options in the account window are optional, and are self-explanatory. Choose OK after you have specified the information you want included with the account. The general information (not the password) will appear to other users when they browse the postoffice list of accounts.

Administering a Postoffice

After you create the administrator account, you can begin adding, removing, and modifying mail accounts for users. To administer mail accounts, follow these steps:

1. Open the Control Panel and double-click the Microsoft Mail Postoffice icon.

2. Choose Administer an Existing Workgroup Postoffice, then click Next.

3. Enter the path to your WGPO (or click Browse to browse for the WGPO), then click Next.

4. Windows 95 prompts you for the account name and password of the administrator's account. Enter the mailbox name and password, then

choose Next. A Postoffice Manager window similar to the one shown in figure 9.24 appears.

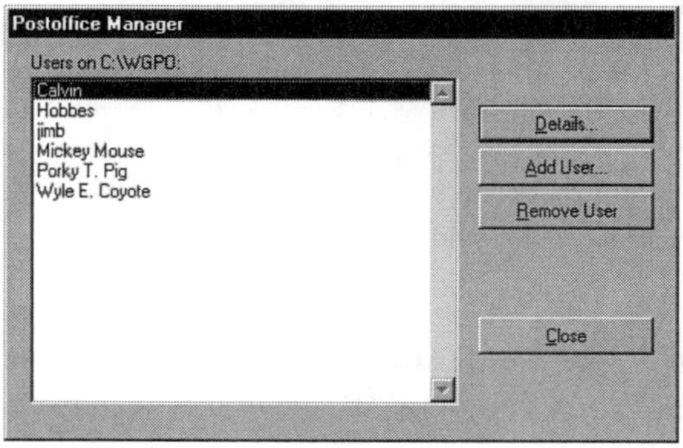

Fig. 9.24
The Postoffice Manager window lets you manage user mail accounts.

5. To view the account details for a user's account, select the account and choose the Details button. A window similar to the one shown in figure 9.25 appears. Modify any of the properties for the user, then choose OK.

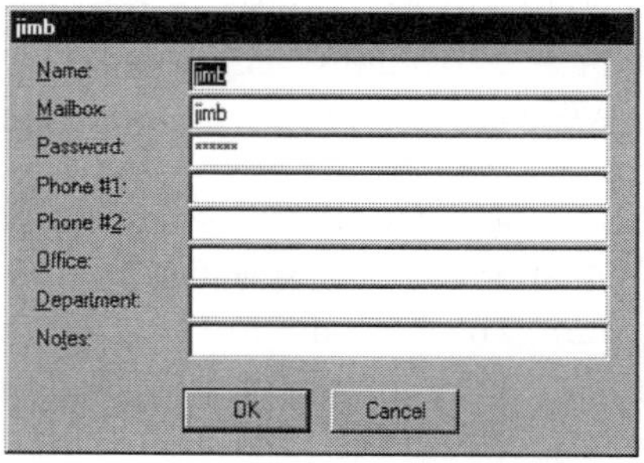

Fig. 9.25
You can modify any mail account property, including the password.

6. To add a user, click the Add User button. Windows 95 displays a dialog box nearly identical to the Details dialog box shown in figure 9.25. Enter the account details for the mail account, then choose OK.
7. To remove a user, select the user and choose Remove User. Windows 95 prompts you to verify that you want to remove the account. Choose Yes to delete the account, or choose No to cancel the deletion.
8. When you are finished administering the WGPO, choose Close.

Troubleshooting

I created an administrator account for the WGPO, but I've forgotten the password. Can I reassign another account as the WGPO administrator account?

Unfortunately, there's no way to change the administrator account. Unless you can recall the password, you have no way of gaining access to the account or administering the WGPO. Fortunately, new users can create their own mail accounts in the WGPO, so new and existing users alike can continue to use the WGPO while you attempt to resolve the problem. First, direct all users to back their message folders. A simple way to do this is to make a backup copy of their PST file. Any users who store their messages in the WGPO instead of locally must copy their messages to a local folder. When all users' messages are backed up, delete the WGPO and re-create it, making sure to create an administrator account with a password you can remember. Re-create all of the user accounts in the WGPO.

Adding Information Services to Exchange

Previous sections of this chapter explained how to install Exchange and set a few general options. If you're like most users, you probably want to take advantage of some of the service providers included with Windows 95 and with Microsoft Plus! for Windows 95. This section helps you install and configure the Internet Mail and CompuServe service providers so you can begin using them.

Installing Internet Mail Service

Microsoft Plus! for Windows 95 includes additional Internet features not included in Windows 95. Among these additional features is an Internet Mail service provider for Exchange that enables you to use Exchange to send and receive mail through an Internet mail server.

To install the Internet Mail service for Exchange, you must use the Plus! Setup program. Appendix A, "Installing and Using Microsoft Plus! Companion for Windows 95," explains how to install Plus!, but you can use the following steps as a guide to help you install the Internet Mail service:

▶ See "Configuring Microsoft Fax," p. 237

▶ See "Installing Microsoft Plus!," p. 658

1. Start Windows 95 and insert the Plus! CD in your CD-ROM drive. The Plus! CD will autoplay, opening a window on the Desktop.
2. Click the Install Plus! button.

3. Follow the prompts to start the installation process, and when Setup prompts you to select which Plus! components to install, make sure you select the Internet Jumpstart Kit, then click Next.

4. Follow the prompts to continue the installation process. Eventually, Setup starts an Internet Setup Wizard. When this wizard appears, click Next.

5. Through the next few dialog boxes, the wizard prompts you to specify information about how you connect to the Internet, DNS servers to use, and default gateway. Provide the settings that apply to your connection.

6. The wizard then displays the dialog box shown in figure 9.26, prompting you to specify your e-mail address and mail server. Place a check mark in the Use Internet Mail check box. In the text box labeled Your Email Address, enter your e-mail account name. In the Internet Mail Server text box, enter the domain name of your Internet e-mail server. If you're not sure what to enter for these properties, check with your system administrator or Internet service provider for help. After you enter the necessary information, click Next.

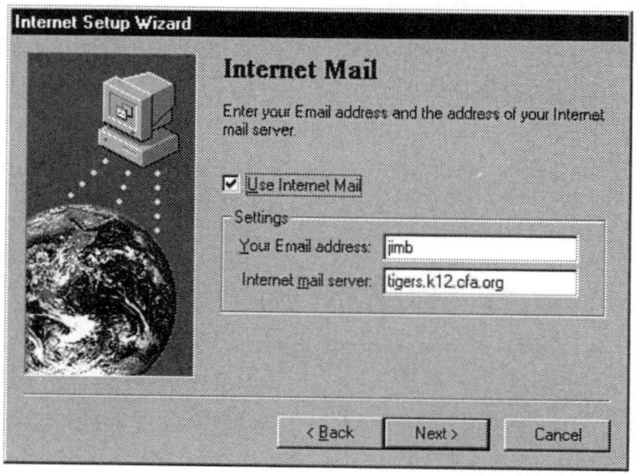

Fig. 9.26
Enter your e-mail address and mail server names.

7. The Internet wizard then displays the window shown in figure 9.27, prompting you to specify in which Exchange profile you want to place the Internet Mail service provider. Select an existing profile from the drop-down list, or choose the New button to create a new profile.

8. After you create or specify a profile to contain your Internet Mail provider, click Next, then follow the prompts and windows to complete the installation process.

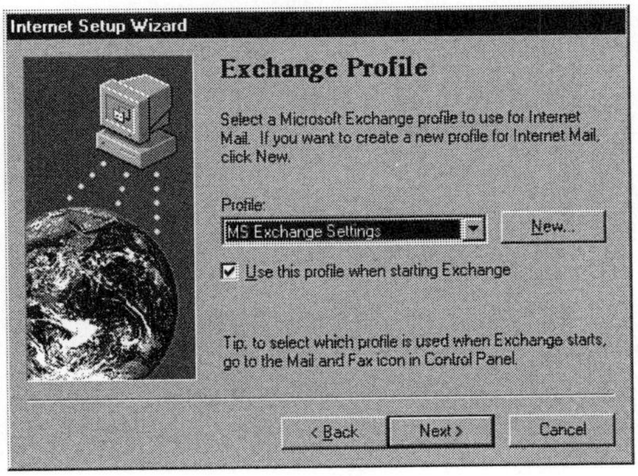

Fig. 9.27
Select or create a profile to contain your Internet Mail service.

After you install the Internet Mail provider, you can use the Control Panel to set other Internet Mail properties. To do so, open the Control Panel and double-click the Mail and Fax icon. Select the Internet Mail provider, then click Properties to display the General page shown in figure 9.28.

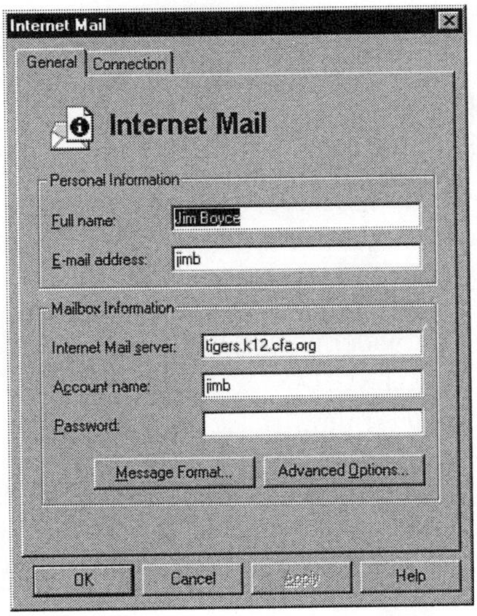

Fig. 9.28
Use the General page to set general Internet Mail properties.

The following list explains the settings on the General page:

- *Full Name.* Enter your first and last names as you want them to appear in message headers.
- *E-mail Address.* Enter your e-mail account name.
- *Internet Mail Server.* Enter the domain name of your Internet mail server.

- *Account Name.* Enter your e-mail account name (generally, the account you use to log onto the Internet server).
- *Password.* Enter the password for your Internet e-mail account.
- *Message Format.* Click this button to specify whether the Internet Mail service uses MIME encoding to send your e-mail messages and attachments.
- *Advanced Options.* Click this button to specify the name of a server to which you want all of your outbound mail forwarded. This is necessary if your default Internet Mail server doesn't process outbound mail.

Tip

Click the Connection tab if you want to change the type of connection you use to connect to the Internet, or to specify a different Dial-Up Networking connection.

Installing the CompuServe Mail Service

If you are a CompuServe member, you'll be happy to know that Windows 95 includes a service provider that enables you to use Exchange to send and receive mail through CompuServe. In addition to exchanging mail with other CompuServe users, the CompuServe Mail provider enables you to exchange e-mail with anyone who has an Internet mail account because CompuServe serves as a mail gateway to the Internet.

The CompuServe Mail provider is included on the Windows 95 CD in the folder \DRIVERS\OTHER\EXCHANGE\COMPUSRV. To install the CompuServe Mail provider, follow these steps:

1. Hold down the Shift key while you insert the Windows 95 CD (this prevents the CD from autoplaying).
2. Open My Computer, right-click the CD icon, then choose Open from the context menu.
3. Open the folder \DRIVERS\OTHER\EXCHANGE\COMPUSRV and double-click the Setup icon. Setup starts and copies the necessary files to your system.
4. Setup asks you if you want to add CompuServe Mail to your default Exchange profile. Choose Yes to add the service to your default profile, or choose No if you want to later add the service to the default profile or a different profile.

Configuring the CompuServe Mail Service

After you add the CompuServe Mail service to your Exchange profile, you need to configure various settings that define how Exchange connects to CompuServe and sends and receives your CompuServe mail. To configure your user account information in the CompuServe Mail service, follow these steps:

1. Open the Control Panel and double-click the Mail and Fax icon.
2. Select CompuServe Mail from the list of installed services, then choose Properties.
3. In the Name text box on the General page (see fig. 9.29), enter the name you want to appear in mail message address headers (not your CompuServe account name).

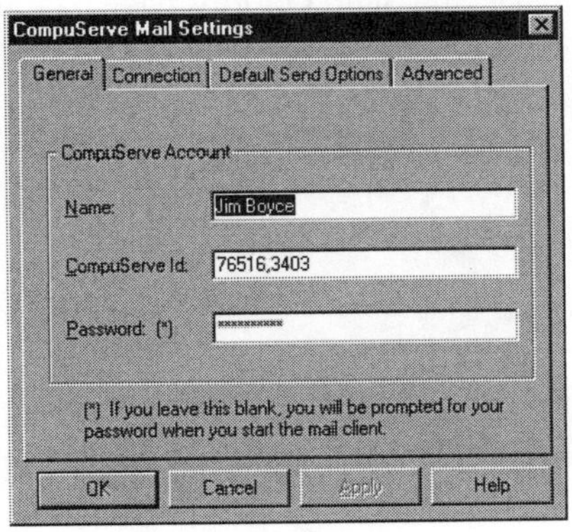

Fig. 9.29
Use the General page to specify your CompuServe account information.

4. In the CompuServe Id text box, enter your CompuServe account ID.
5. In the Password text box, enter your CompuServe account password.

In addition to configuring your account information, you also need to specify how the service will connect to CompuServe. To do so, use the Connection page and the following steps:

1. Click the Connection tab to display the Connection page (see fig. 9.30).
2. In the Phone Number text box, enter your CompuServe access number.
3. From the Preferred Tapi Line drop-down list, choose the modem you'll be using to connect to CompuServe.
4. From the Network drop-down list, choose the type of network connection provided by your CompuServe access number.

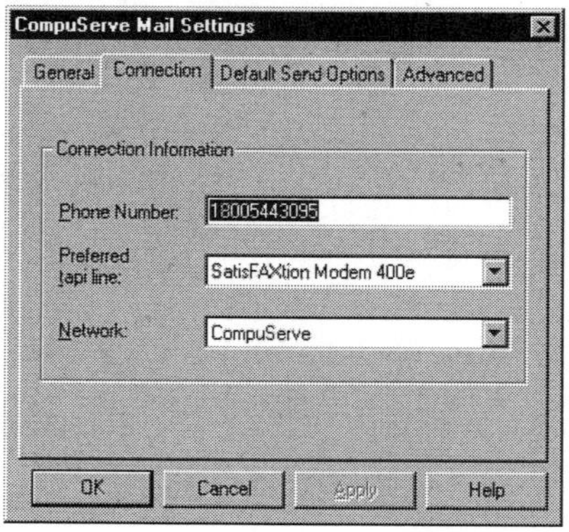

Fig. 9.30
Use the Connection page to specify how the connection to CompuServe is made.

▶ See "Setting Up a CompuServe Connection," p. 278

At this point, you can choose OK, then OK again to begin using your CompuServe Mail service in Exchange. You might, however, want to set a few advanced options. The Default Send Options page contains a selection of properties that define how messages are sent (see fig. 9.31).

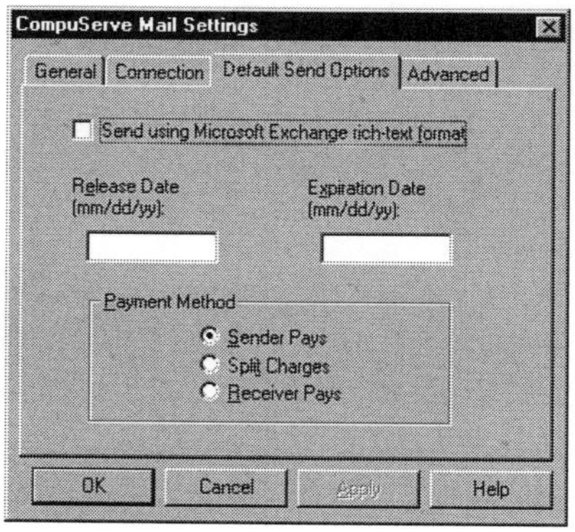

Fig. 9.31
The Default Send Options page controls how messages are sent.

The following list explains the properties on the Default Send Options page:

- *Send Using Microsoft Exchange Rich-Text Format.* Enable this check box if you want Exchange to include character (color, font, etc.) and paragraph formatting in your message. Only recipients who are using Microsoft Exchange will see the special formatting—other recipients receive plain text.

- *Release Date.* If you enter a date in this field, messages will be held in your Inbox until the date specified, then forwarded on that date to the intended recipients. Leave this field blank if you want the messages to be sent as soon as the service connects to CompuServe.

- *Expiration Date.* If you enter a date in this field, the message will be deleted from the recipient's mail box when the date is reached.
- *Payment Method.* Select one of the three option buttons in this group to specify who pays for surcharged messages.

You can use the Advanced page to schedule automatic connection to CompuServe and other advanced connection options (see fig. 9.32).

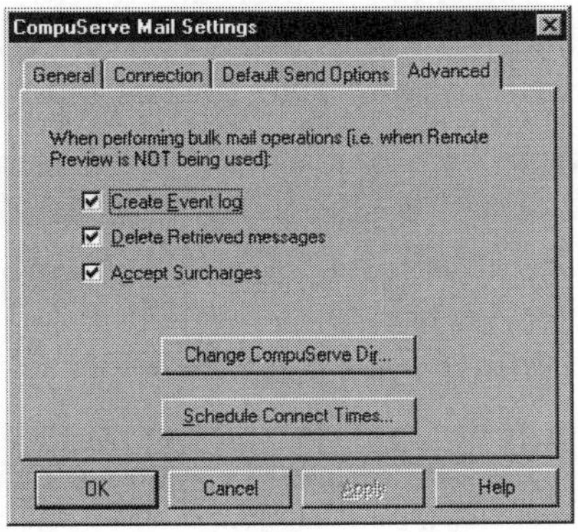

Fig. 9.32
Use the Advanced page to control advanced service options.

The following list describes the controls on the Advanced page:

- *Create Event Log.* Enable this check box if you want the CompuServe Mail provider to place in your Inbox log messages describing the results of each connection attempt.
- *Delete Retrieved Messages.* Enable this check box if you want the CompuServe Mail provider to delete mail from your CompuServe mailbox after the mail is retrieved and stored in your Exchange Inbox.
- *Accept Surcharges.* Enable this check box if you are willing to pay for messages that carry a surcharge. Messages such as those from the Internet generally carry a nominal postage-due fee.
- *Change CompuServe Dir.* Click this button to change the folder in which the CompuServe Mail provider stores configuration and address book settings. If you are using another CompuServe product such as WinCIM, the CompuServe Mail provider can use the same address book and connection settings as your other CompuServe product.
- *Schedule Connect Times.* Click this button to display the Connection Times dialog box (see fig. 9.33) and schedule automatic connections to CompuServe. If you want, you can use a selection of different scheduled connection times.

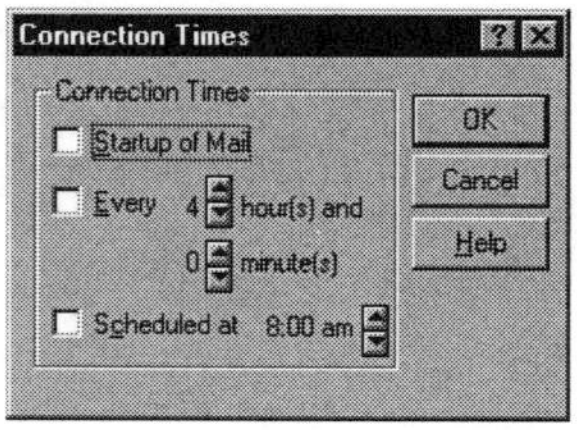

Fig. 9.33
You can schedule the CompuServe Mail provider to connect automatically to CompuServe.

After you have specified all of the settings and properties you want to change for the CompuServe Mail provider, choose OK, then OK again to save the changes. Restart Exchange to begin using the new settings.

Troubleshooting

I configured the CompuServe Mail provider to check for messages at 8 a.m. and every four hours. But, Exchange doesn't check at 8, 12, 4, and so on. It checks for mail at 8 a.m., but the four-hour interval falls at odd times. Why is this?

The CompuServe Mail provider doesn't base its interval connection times on the explicit 8 AM setting you've specified. Instead, the provider checks at four-hour intervals based on the last time it automatically checked for mail. Open Control Panel and click the Mail and Fax icon. Select the CompuServe Mail provider and choose Properties. Choose Advanced, Schedule Connect Times to display the Connection Times dialog box. Clear the Every check box and close the dialog box, then close the Profile property sheets. Shortly before the time when you want one of your hourly interval connections to be made, open the Control Panel, click the Mail and Fax icon, then enable the Every check box in the Connection Times dialog box and specify the interval you want to use. Close the property sheets. Exchange should then connect close to the time you want.

Chapter 10

Configuring Microsoft Fax

by Rob Tidrow

If you run a business today, more than likely you have a dedicated fax machine or you have a fax modem device on your computer. You've come to rely on your fax machine for many of your daily communications needs. In some respects, the fax machine has replaced your phone for the type of critical information that you send and receive with others. Likewise, your computer is a vital piece of equipment in your workplace. By merging the two—the fax and computer—you create a powerful business tool that enables you to communicate by using hard copy faxes or electronic transmissions.

In Chapters 2 and 3, you are shown how to install Microsoft Fax automatically during Windows 95 installation. If you did not install Fax then, this chapter shows you how to set it up manually. This chapter covers the following items:

- Features of Microsoft Fax
- Installing and configuring Microsoft Fax
- Configuring Microsoft Fax for workgroup sharing
- Protecting faxes

Features of Microsoft Fax

Windows 95 includes Microsoft Fax that enables you to send and receive faxes through your fax modem on your computer. You can use Microsoft Fax on a separate computer to service one user, or connect it to a network to use it as a fax server in a workgroup environment. Microsoft Fax has the capability to send a facsimile to another fax modem device or to a dedicated fax machine. If you use Microsoft Fax to send a fax to a fax modem, you can encrypt it with a password to provide a layer of security for the document.

Microsoft Fax is part of Microsoft Exchange and replaces any fax software you may already have installed on your computer. Microsoft Fax enables you to create fax messages, add cover pages, and send the messages to another fax machine or fax modem device. Because Fax is a *MAPI—Messaging Application Programming Interface*—compliant application, you can use other applications, such as Microsoft Word for Windows 95, to send faxes through Windows 95.

Tip

Microsoft Fax includes fax printer drivers so that you can print to a fax modem from within any Windows application.

You also can use Microsoft Fax to receive fax messages. A message can be faxed to you by the sender calling your fax number and delivering the fax. Or, if you use fax-back services to receive technical support information, sales information, or other data, you can dial the service and have it download the document to your fax modem using Microsoft Fax.

Tip

You can store fax messages in the Microsoft Exchange universal inbox.

A Microsoft Fax message can be sent in one of two ways:

- Binary file
- Hard copy fax

The latter option is the traditional way in which fax messages are sent and received via a fax machine, known as a Group 3 fax machine. The limitation of sending faxes this way is that the recipient cannot edit the document or use it as a binary file, unless the document is scanned or keyed into a file. A *binary file* is simply a file created in an application, such as Word for Windows or Lotus 1-2-3 for Windows. Another frustrating aspect of paper faxes is that they may be difficult or impossible to read.

When you use Microsoft Fax to send a binary file to another fax modem, the recipient can view and edit the fax in the application in which it was created and modify it. This feature is handled by Microsoft Fax's *Binary File Transfer* (*BFT*) capability. BFT was originally created for Microsoft's At Work program and is now supported by Microsoft Exchange so that you can create a mail message and attach a binary file to it. Windows for Workgroups 3.11 and other Microsoft At Work enabled platforms also can receive BFT messages.

One way in which you can take advantage of the BFT feature in Microsoft Fax is to use it with other applications, such as Microsoft Word for Windows. You could, for example, create a Word document and send it as a Microsoft Fax message to another user who has Microsoft Fax installed (and Word for Windows). The recipient receives the message and can read it as a Word document.

If the recipient doesn't have a fax modem card and Microsoft Fax, and instead has a Group 3 fax machine, Microsoft Fax automatically prints the Word document as a printed fax image. A problem with sending files this way is the transmission speed and compression feature of the recipient fax machine. Fax machines are much slower than fax modems, so a large binary file (such as a 50-page Word document), may take a long time to transmit and print on the recipient's fax machine. Before you send a large attached document to someone's fax machine, you might want to test this feature first.

Setting Up Microsoft Fax

Microsoft Exchange must be installed on your computer to use Microsoft Fax. If you have not configured Exchange yet, turn to Chapter 9, "Configuring Microsoft Exchange," and install Exchange. You also need to have a fax modem device installed and working on your computer. This topic is covered in Chapter 28, "Configuring Modems." (The type of fax modem required is covered in "Requirements of Microsoft Fax" later in this chapter.)

After you have Exchange set up and a modem working, you need to set up Microsoft Fax to work with Windows 95, Exchange, and your modem. All this is handled by Exchange's profiles.

◀ See "Installing the Exchange Client," p. 202

Fax Modem Requirements of Microsoft Fax

Besides having Windows 95 and Microsoft Exchange installed, your fax modem must meet the following requirements:

- High-speed fax modem, such as a 14.4 kbps fax modem
- Phone line
- Minimum requirements of Windows 95, but an 80486-based computer with 8M of RAM is recommended

◀ See "Requirements of Windows 95," p. 19

When you install Microsoft Fax on a network, your system must meet the following requirements:

- High-speed fax modem, such as a 14.4 kbps fax modem
- Phone line
- At least an 80486-based computer with 8M of RAM
- If the computer will be used as a workstation as well, you'll want to have at least 12M of RAM

Regardless of the way in which you set up Microsoft Fax, either as a stand-alone or networked fax service, you need to make sure that your fax modem is compatible with Microsoft Fax. The technology behind Microsoft Fax is a mature technology that originally was introduced in the Microsoft At Work products and was included as part of Windows for Workgroups 3.11. Because of this, many fax modem manufacturers have ensured that their hardware meets the needs of Microsoft Fax, giving you many choices from which to choose for your hardware.

The following lists and describes the compatible fax modems and fax machines that you can use with Microsoft Fax:

- *Class 1 and Class 2*. You need Class 1 or Class 2 fax modems to send BFT messages with attachments. These classes of fax modems also are required to use security features in Microsoft Fax.
- *ITU T.30 Standard*. This standard is for Group 3 fax machines, which are traditional fax machines common in many business environments. Microsoft Fax converts any BFT fax messages to a T.30 NSF (nonstandard facilities) transmission to enable compatibility with these types of fax machines. (ITU is the International Telecommunications Union.)
- *ITU V.17, V.29, V.27ter standards*. These types are used for high-speed faxes up to 14.4 kpbs.
- *Microsoft At Work platforms*. You need Windows 95, Windows for Workgroups 3.11, or another Microsoft At Work compatible platform to use Microsoft Fax.

Caution

Check the fax modem documentation to ensure that it adheres to the preceding requirements and works with Microsoft Fax. Beware that some fax modems on the market today do not work with Microsoft Fax.

Troubleshooting

My fax modem doesn't work with Windows 95, but I don't know if it is a hardware or software issue.

Many fax modems available on the market today are compatible with Windows 95 and should work fine. For hardware concerns, check with your manufacturer to make sure your fax modem works with Windows 95. It may be one of the few that does not. You also need to make sure your fax modem is a Class 1 or Class 2 fax modem for it to work.

How can I diagnose problems with Microsoft Fax and my modem?

One of the ways is to see if your fax modem is working correctly by selecting Modems from Control Panel. In the Modem Properties sheet, select the Diagnostics page. In the list of ports, select the port to which your fax modem is connected. Click More Info for Windows 95 to run a diagnostics of your fax modem. If everything is okay, you get a report of your modem's properties. If your fax modem is awaiting a call, you receive a message saying that the port is already opened. You need to exit from Microsoft Exchange and rerun the modem diagnostics to get an accurate reading.

If you still experience problems, you need to open the Modem Properties sheet and change some of the advanced settings. It may require you to experiment with these settings before you find one that works for your modem. You also should make sure that you have a Microsoft Fax service set up for Exchange. If not, see the section "Installing Microsoft Fax."

Installing Microsoft Fax

To configure Microsoft Fax, you first need to install the Microsoft Fax software onto your system using the Add/Remove Programs Wizard. You need to have your Windows 95 installation disks or CD-ROM to add these files.

Use the following steps to do this:

1. Double-click the Add/Remove Programs icon in Control Panel.
2. Click the Windows Setup page (see fig. 10.1).
3. Scroll down the Components list box and select Microsoft Fax. Be sure to not click any other component that is already selected, or you will inadvertently remove those programs from your Windows 95 setup.
4. Click OK.

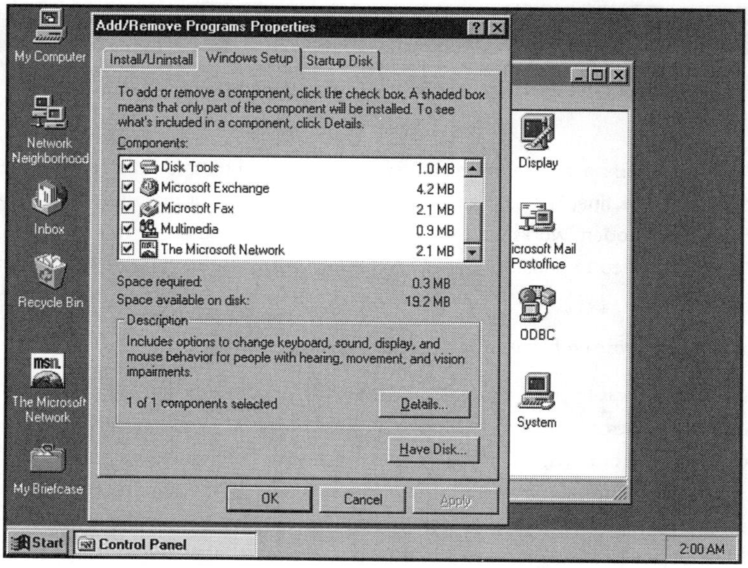

Fig. 10.1
Make sure that the Windows Setup page is active.

5. When Windows 95 prompts you for a specific Windows 95 Setup disk or CD-ROM, place it in the disk drive. Windows 95 copies the files onto your hard disk and returns you to the Desktop when it finishes.

Now that you have Microsoft Fax on your system, you can configure it as a Microsoft Exchange information service and start sending faxes. You can do this in one of two ways: by using the Control Panel or by using Microsoft Exchange. Do the following steps:

1. Double-click the Mail and Fax icon in Control Panel (see fig. 10.2).

   The Microsoft Exchange Profiles sheet appears (see fig. 10.3), to which you can add Fax to a profile.

> **Note**
>
> If you do not see this sheet, click Show Profiles on the General page to reveal the Microsoft Exchange Profiles set up on your system.

2. Choose a profile that you want to add Microsoft Fax to, such as MS Exchange Settings.

3. Click the Properties button to show all the information services set up for the selected profile (see fig. 10.4). Make sure that the Services page is displayed.

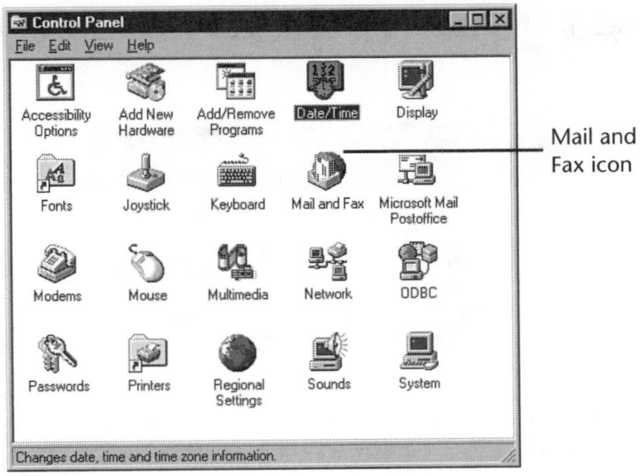

Fig. 10.2
Double-click the Mail and Fax icon to configure Microsoft Fax for your system.

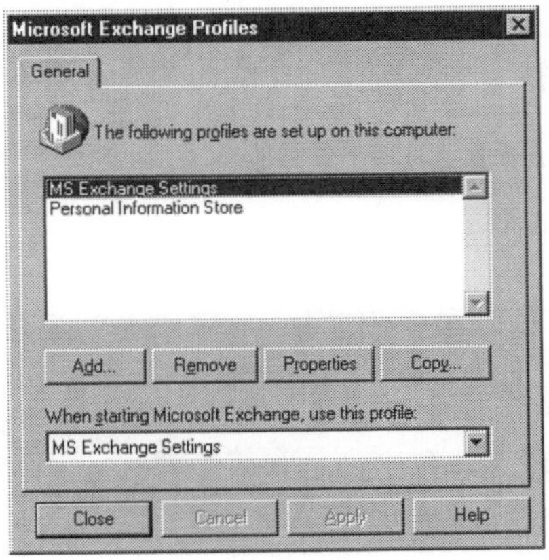

Fig. 10.3
The Microsoft Exchange Profiles sheet contains all the profiles that you configured during Windows 95 setup or when configuring Exchange.

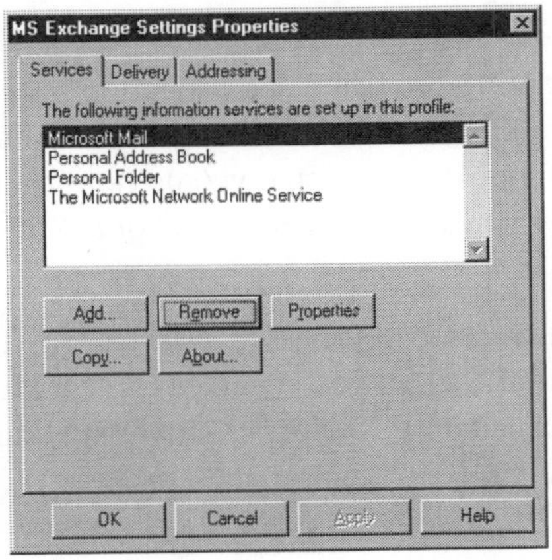

Fig. 10.4
All the information services set up on your system appear on the Services page.

4. Click Add to display the Add Service to Profile dialog box, shown in figure 10.5.

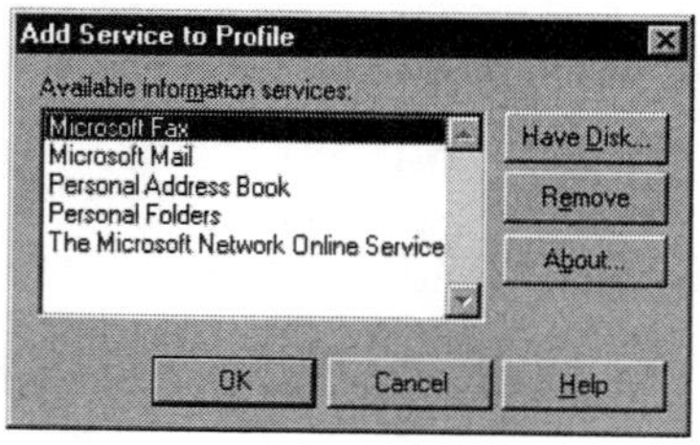

Fig. 10.5
The Add Service to Profile dialog box contains all the available services on your system that you can configure.

5. In the Available Information Services list, select Microsoft Fax. Click OK.

6. A message appears (see fig. 10.6) asking you to provide the following information:

   - Your name
   - Your fax number
   - Your fax modem type

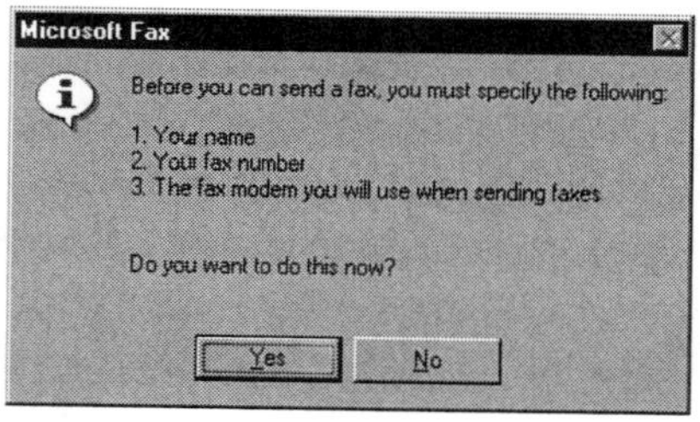

Fig. 10.6
Enter your user information so that Windows 95 can automatically set up Microsoft Fax now.

   If you do not want to provide this information now and let Windows take care of it, you can configure it the first time you use Microsoft Fax. It's best to configure it now so that you do not have to waste time doing it later when you are in a rush to send or receive a fax. Click Yes to continue.

7. The Microsoft Fax Properties sheet appears (see fig. 10.7). Fill out this sheet with the information you are asked for. For the most part, the text boxes are self-explanatory. The only text box that might need some explanation is the Mailbox (optional) item.

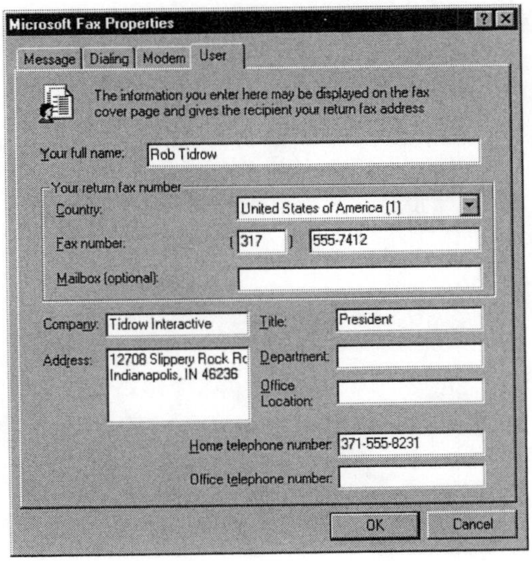

Fig. 10.7
Fill in the information on this sheet so that your fax recipients know who you are.

> **Note**
>
> Believe it or not, according to Federal Communications Commission (FCC) regulation Part 68, Section 68.318(c)(3), you must include the following items on all fax transmissions either on the top or bottom margins of all pages or on a cover page:
>
> - Date and time fax is sent
> - Identification of the business, "other entity," or the name of the sender
> - Telephone number of the sending fax machine

The Mailbox (optional) item in the Your return fax number section pertains to in-house mailboxes you may have set up to receive fax messages. To fill in this box, type the name your administrator has assigned you, which might be your name, e-mail name, or some other identifier. Otherwise, leave this item blank.

8. After you fill out this page, click the Modem page to set up your fax modem to work with Microsoft Fax (see fig. 10.8). If your fax modem already has been configured for Windows 95 (which it should be if you have an online service set up), your modem should already appear in the Available Fax Modems list.

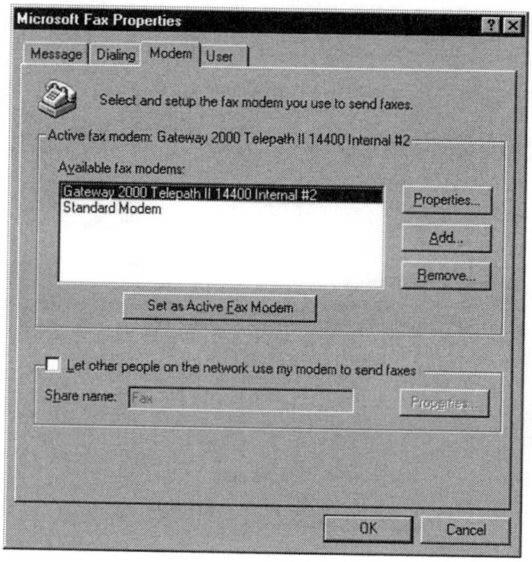

Fig. 10.8
You need to assign a fax modem to work with Microsoft Fax from this page.

▶ See "Installing Your Modem," p. 588

9. If more than one modem appears in this box, click the modem you want to use as the default fax modem and click the Set as Active Fax Modem button.

Configure Fax Modem Options

Microsoft Fax is a sophisticated application that you can set up to answer your phone automatically after so many rings, let you answer it manually, or not answer your phone at all (if you tend to send instead of receive most of your faxes). As part of the configuration process, you need to tell Microsoft Fax how to behave during a call, and whether it's a received or delivered call. As in most other Windows 95 components, you do all this by configuring Microsoft Fax's properties.

Use the following steps:

1. Click Properties to display the Fax Modem Properties sheet, as shown in figure 10.9.
2. Set up each option, as described in the following list:
   - *Answer After*. Set this option to have Microsoft Fax answer a fax call after a certain number of rings. For some reason, you cannot set this value for 1 ring or for more than 10; 2 or 3 are good numbers to set this to.

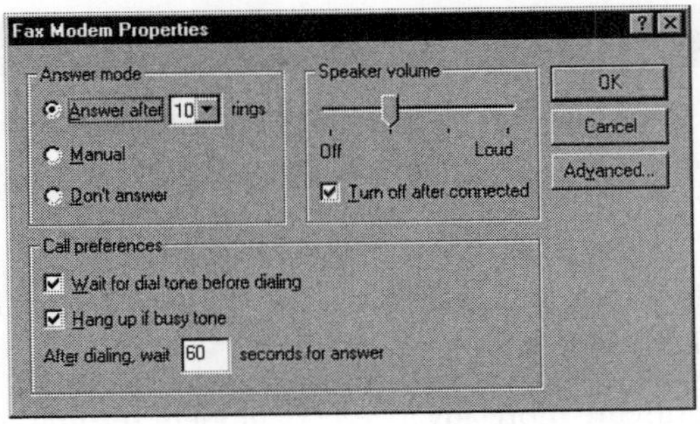

Fig. 10.9
Set the Microsoft Fax properties for your fax modem.

- *Manual*. Use this option if you want Microsoft Fax to display a message on-screen when a call comes in. You then answer the call manually. As a recommendation, use this option only if you have one phone line that you use for both voice and fax. Otherwise, select the Answer After option.
- *Don't Answer*. Why have a fax modem if you don't want it to answer incoming faxes? Because you might have to share COM ports with another device. Activate this option if your fax modem shares a port with another device, such as a mouse.
- *Speaker Volume*. It's not a bad idea to set this value to about the middle of the scroll bar so that you can hear when a fax is being received. If it's set too high (such as Loud), your ears may start bleeding when a fax starts transmitting.
- *Turn Off After Connected*. Make sure that a check mark is in this box, unless you enjoy listening to two fax devices talk to each other.
- *Wait For Dial Tone Before Dialing*. For most phone systems, this option needs to be selected to instruct Microsoft Fax to wait until a dial tone is heard before making an outgoing call.
- *Hang Up if Busy Tone*. Leave this option selected so that your fax modem doesn't stay on the line if the number you're calling is busy.
- *After Dialing, Wait x Seconds for Answer*. Many fax machines and fax modems take a few seconds to synchronize after they've been called. This option sets the number of seconds Microsoft Fax waits for the receiving machine to get "in synch" after it answers the call. The default is 60 seconds, which is a good starting number. Increase this number if you notice Microsoft Fax canceling calls too soon.

Tip

Disable the Turn Off After Connection option if you want to hear if your fax transmission is still connected.

After you fill out this screen, click OK to save these configuration settings and to return to the Fax Modem Properties screen.

If you want to configure more advanced fax modem settings, click the Advanced button and read the next section. If not, skip to the "Setting Dialing Properties" section.

Troubleshooting

How do I turn off the fax modem speaker?

Double-click Mail and Fax in Control Panel. Click Microsoft Fax on the MS Exchange Settings Properties sheet and click the Properties button. Select the Modems page and click the Properties button. In the Speaker Volume area, move the slider bar to the Off position.

Configure Advanced Fax Modem Settings

In the Advanced dialog box (see fig. 10.10), you have the option of configuring more sophisticated fax modem settings.

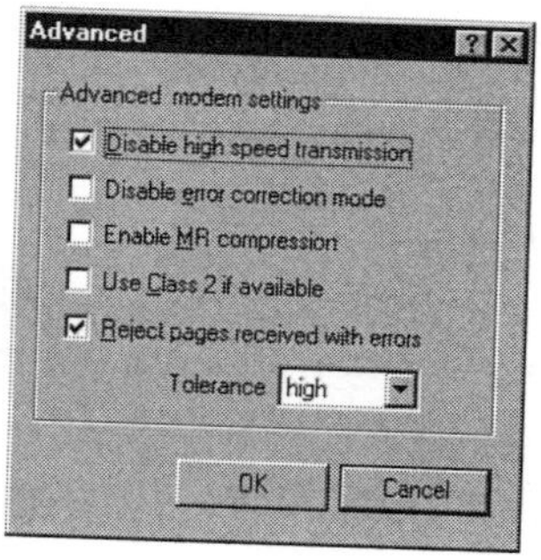

Fig. 10.10
Use the Advanced dialog box to troubleshoot fax modem problems you may be experiencing.

These options are detailed in the following list:

- *Disable High Speed Transmission*. High speed transmissions are anything over 9,600 bps. If your fax modem is rated for higher speeds, such as 14.4 bps, you might experience transmission errors communicating with other devices. Keep this setting disabled (unchecked) unless your outgoing and incoming faxes are not being handled reliably. Select this option to slow down your transmission speeds.

- *Disable Error Correction Mode.* Fax transmissions demand a great deal of cooperation between the sending fax device and the receiving fax device. You need built-in error-correction procedures to make sure that the fax you send is received properly. This option is used to direct Microsoft Fax to send non-editable faxes, either to a fax machine or as bitmap file, without using error correction. Keep this option disabled unless you cannot send or receive faxes reliably.
- *Enable MR Compression.* Select this option to compress faxes you send or receive, decreasing the amount of time you're online. This option is disabled by default and is grayed out if your fax modem does not support MR compression.

Caution

Compressed faxes are more susceptible to line noise and interference. If a transmission experiences too much line noise or interference, your fax may become corrupted, or your fax modem connection may be lost.

- *Use Class 2 if Available.* Select this option if you have problems sending or receiving messages using a fax modem that supports Class 1 and Class 2 fax modems. The default is to leave this option disabled.
- *Reject Pages Received with Errors.* Most fax transmissions have some sort of problem occur during sending or receiving. You can set Microsoft Fax to have a high tolerance (more errors can occur during transmission), medium tolerance, low tolerance, and very low tolerance (fewer errors can occur during transmission) for errors before rejecting the page being received. The default is to have a high tolerance for errors.

Caution

If you select the Use Class 2 if Available option, you cannot use error-correction, or send or receive editable faxes.

Click OK when these settings are ready. Click OK to return to the Fax Modem Properties sheet.

Setting Dialing Properties

Now that you have Microsoft Fax set up to work with your fax modem, you need to start setting user-specific information, such as how Microsoft Fax should dial your phone. Click the Dialing page in the Microsoft Fax Properties sheet. To begin, click the Dialing Properties button to display the My Locations page (see fig. 10.11).

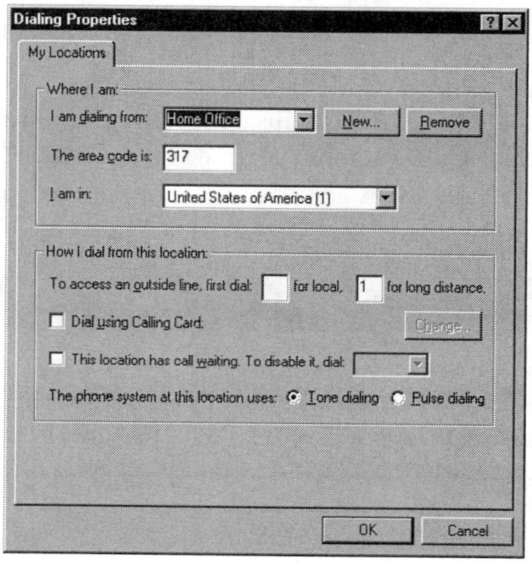

Fig. 10.11
Set your dialing options, such as area code, calling card numbers, and other user-specific options, in the My Locations page.

> **Note**
>
> The My Locations information may already be filled in if you set up your modem to make a call out, or if any of your Exchange services previously dialed online services, such as the Microsoft Network.

Microsoft Fax enables you to use several different configurations depending on where you are when you send a fax. If your computer always stays in one place (such as in your office or home), you generally need only one location configured. If, however, you use a portable PC and travel from work to home, or to other places, you can configure several different locations to dial using different configuration settings.

When you are in your office, for instance, you may not need to use a calling card to make a long distance phone call to send a fax. You can set up Microsoft Fax to use a configuration that doesn't require a calling card to be entered first. On the other hand, your office phone system may require you to dial an initial number to get an outside line (such as 9). You can place this in the Microsoft Fax configuration settings that you use from your office.

Another scenario where you use a different dialing procedure is when you stay in hotels. For these calls, you may always place them on a calling card. Set up Microsoft Fax to use your calling card number to place these calls. All your configurations are saved in Windows 95 and can be retrieved each time you use Microsoft Fax.

The following steps show you how to create a new dialing location in Microsoft Fax:

1. Click New to display the Create New Location dialog box on the My Locations page (see fig. 10.12).

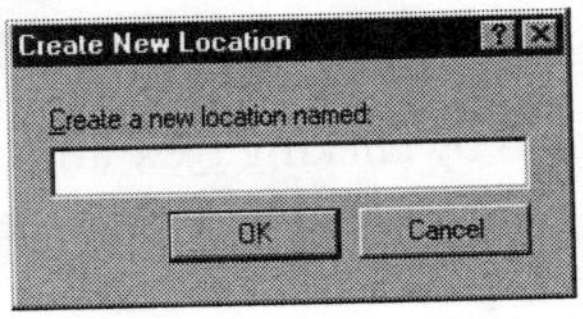

Fig. 10.12
Set up new locations for each dialing scenario you might use to send faxes, such as home, office, travel, and leisure.

2. Enter a new name for the location, such as **Office** or **On the Road**. Click OK.
3. In The Area Code Is text box, enter the area code from which you are calling. You may need to change or update this if you are not sure of the area code in which you are staying, such as when you are traveling.
4. Select the country in which you are calling.
5. Enter the number (if any) you need to dial to get an outside line (such as **9**) and to make a long distance call (usually **1**).

> **Note**
>
> Most hotels use their own phone system to get outside lines, so you need to enter those numbers when you know what they are.

6. Click the Dial Using Calling Card option to enter your calling card information. When you do this, the Change Calling Card dialog box appears (see fig. 10.13).
7. Click the Calling Card to Use drop-down list and select your card name.
8. Enter the card account number in the Calling Card Number text box.

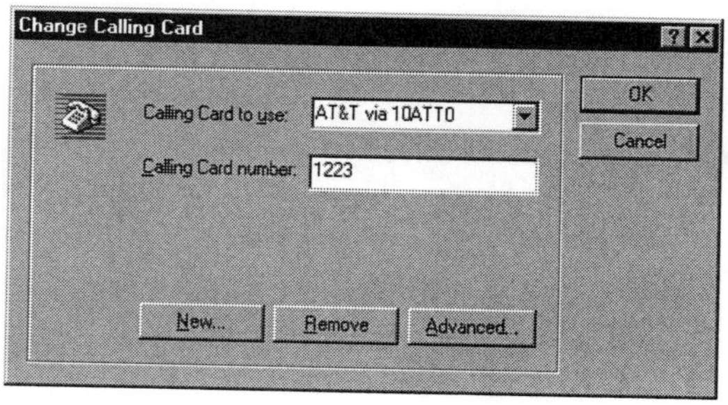

Fig. 10.13
Microsoft Fax can use calling card numbers to place your fax calls.

Another powerful feature of Microsoft Fax is one that enables you to write dialing scripts, or *rules*, for each calling card you use. Actually, each calling card you set up has rules set up for it. Microsoft Fax enables you to create your own rules if there are any special considerations that you need to make for a certain dialing situation. To use this feature, follow these steps:

1. Create a new calling card by clicking New and entering the name in the Create a New Calling Card Named text box (see fig. 10.14)

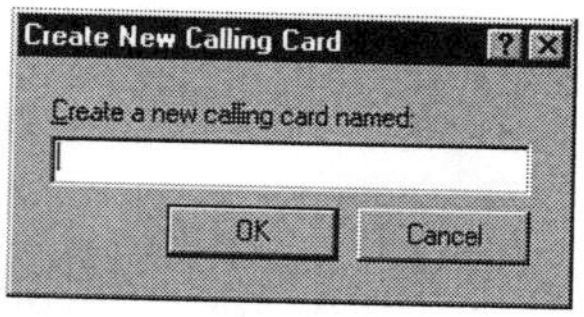

Fig. 10.14
Enter the name of the new calling card in this dialog box.

   Click OK to enter that name in the Calling Card to Use drop-down list.

2. Click Advanced. This is where you write the rules for your new card for these dialing scenarios: Calls Within the Same Area Code; Domestic Long Distance Calls; and International Calls. Table 10.1 shows the characters to use to specify how each dialing rule is processed.

Table 10.1 Dialing Rule Characters

Character	Function
0-9	Specifies number to dial
ABCD	Characters used on some tone dialing units to control certain features
E	Specifies country code
F	Dials area code or city code
G	Dials number as a local number

Character	Function
H	Uses specified calling card number
*, #	Characters used for tone dialing units to control certain features
T	Instructs Microsoft Fax to dial the following numbers using tone dialing
P	Instructs Microsoft Fax to dial the following numbers using pulse dialing
,	Pauses dialing for a fixed time, usually one second per ,
!	Used to send a hookflash (1/2 second on-hook, 1/2 second off-hook), which is like pressing the plunging to hang up the phone
W	Instructs Microsoft Fax to wait for a second dial tone
@	Directs Microsoft Fax to wait for a quiet answer from receiving fax, which is a ringback followed by five seconds of silence
$	Pauses until calling card prompt ("bong") is finished
?	Prompts for user input before continuing dialing

3. Create a rule for a calling card (which is optional) and click Close to save it. Click OK to return to the My Locations page.

Note

To see examples of some rules, or to use a predefined rule, click the Copy From button and select a calling card from which to copy (see fig. 10.15) from the Copy Dialing Rules dialog box. Click OK to enter the rule in the Dialing Rules dialog box.

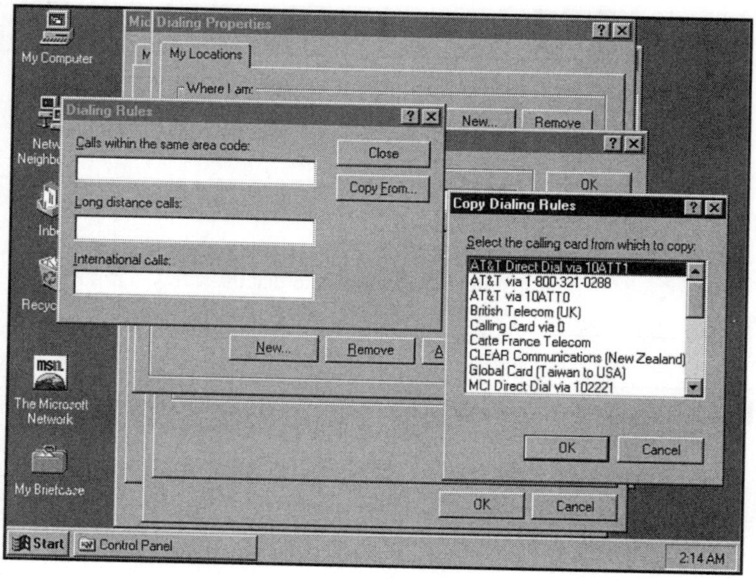

Fig. 10.15 Review other calling card rules or copy a set of rules from a card by clicking the Copy From button.

Finishing Setting Dialing Properties

Have you ever been using your modem or fax modem and it crashed for no apparent reason? Although many things can cause this (line noise, interrupt conflicts, port problems, kids pulling out the phone line), if you have call waiting, you probably can blame it first. Many people who use modems and have call waiting do not think to disable call waiting before making an online connection.

Microsoft Fax enables you to add a switch that automatically disables call waiting each time you send a fax (or use your modem for other purposes). Use the following steps to disable call waiting:

1. Click the This Location Has Call Waiting option.
2. Enter the code that disables call waiting. You need to obtain this code from your local phone company, because each system uses a different code. Microsoft Fax provides three common codes in the drop-down list box next to this option: *70, 70#, and 1170. After you finish faxing and your fax modem hangs up, call waiting is turned back on.
3. Next, tell Microsoft Fax the type of phone system—Tone dialing or Pulse dialing—you have. Click OK when you have this location set up. You can create as many locations as you need to.

Setting Toll Prefixes

Now that you have the locations set up, you need to tell Microsoft Fax which numbers in your local calling area require you to dial as a toll call. To do this, click the Toll Prefixes button. In the Toll Prefixes dialog box (see fig. 10.16), click all the numbers from the Local Phone Numbers list to the Dial 1-*xxx* First list (*xxx* is your area code) that require you to dial your area code first. Click the Add button to place numbers from the list on the left to the list on the right. Click OK when you finish with this dialog box.

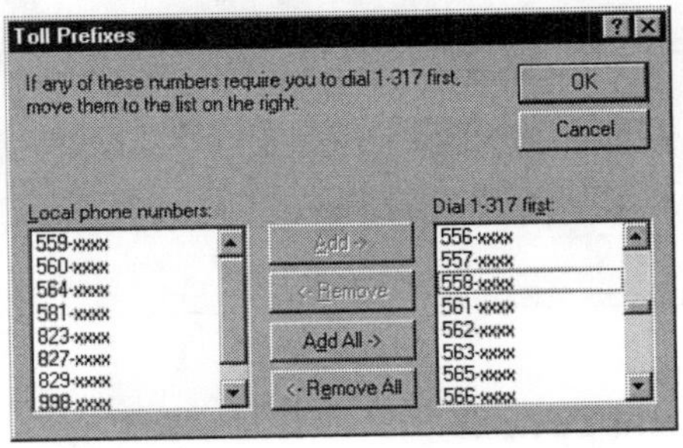

Fig. 10.16
Tell Microsoft Fax which prefixes in your local calling area code are long distance calls.

Every time you call a fax number, you're not going to be lucky enough to get through. You'll hit busy signals. The fax on the other side of the line won't be ready to accept your call. Or, your fax modem and the recipient's fax device won't synchronize properly.

In these cases, you need Microsoft Fax to keep retrying the number you're calling. In the Dialing dialog box, set the Number of Retries option to the number of times you want Microsoft Fax to dial the number before quitting. The default is three times. You also need to tell Microsoft Fax the amount of time you want it to wait before it tries the number again. In the Time Between Retries box, set this time in minutes. The default is two minutes.

Now that you've taken care of the dialing options, you now are ready to configure the default settings for your fax messages. Click the Message page.

Configuring Message Options

The Message page (see fig. 10.17) has three main areas:

- Time to Send
- Message Format
- Default Cover Page

Fig. 10.17
Microsoft Fax lets you customize the way your default fax message looks by using settings in the Message page.

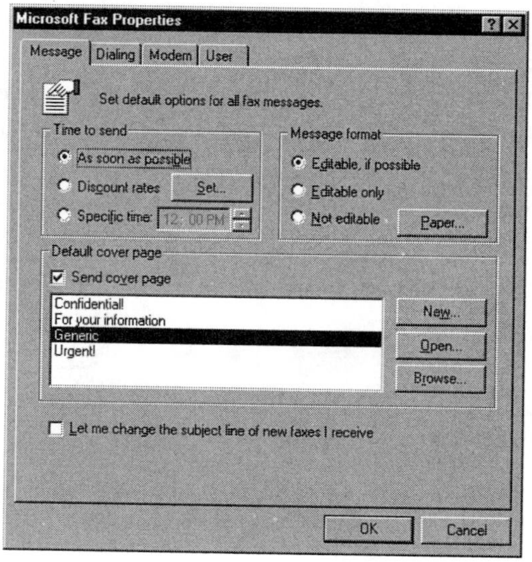

Setting Time to Send Options

You may or may not always want to create a fax message and then zip it off to your recipient. You may want to create a message, or several messages, and then send them at specific times, such as when you are going to lunch or when long distance rates are lower. Microsoft Fax enables you to set the time you send fax messages in one of three ways:

- *As Soon As Possible.* This is the default selection; use this option to send faxes immediately after you create one.
- *Discount Rates.* Use this option to send your fax message(s) during predefined hours when long distance tolls are lower. Click the Set button to set the discount rates start and end times. The Set Discount Rates dialog box opens and shows the default discounted rate hours—between 5 p.m. and 8 a.m. Click OK when you set the appropriate times for your long distance carrier, or keep the default settings.
- *Specific Time.* Set this option to an exact time to send any fax messages you have in the outbox.

Configuring Fax Message Formats

Microsoft Fax can send fax messages in two primary formats: editable formats (as a binary file) and noneditable formats ("hard copy" faxes). Editable fax messages can be manipulated much the same way a word processing document can be changed. A Microsoft Fax editable fax can be received and edited only by a recipient who also has Microsoft Fax installed. A noneditable fax is a fax that you receive from a "regular" facsimile machine.

In the Message format area, you set the default way in which your messages are sent. Select the Editable, If Possible option when you send faxes to both fax modems and regular fax machines. This is the default selection. If your fax messages always must be edited by the recipient, or if you want to encrypt your fax message with a password, enable the Editable Only option. (See "Setting Up Security" later in this chapter for information on using security options in Microsoft Fax.) This sends all your fax messages as binary faxes. When using this option, if the recipient does not have Microsoft Fax installed, the fax is not sent. Microsoft Fax places a message in your Microsoft Exchange Inbox folder telling you that the message was not sent.

When you're sure that your recipient doesn't have Microsoft Fax installed, or you don't want your fax to be edited, send it as Not Editable. Even if the receiving device is a fax modem, the fax message is sent as a bitmap image, so the recipient cannot directly edit the message. If, however, the user has an OCR (optical character recognition) program, he or she can export the faxed image or text as a file to edit in another application.

With the first and third options, you also can specify the type of paper used to print your fax message. Click the Paper button to display the Message Format dialog box and adjust paper settings, such as size, image quality, and orientation. For most faxes, the default settings are fine. Click OK when your paper settings are configured.

Configuring Default Cover Pages

You can opt to send a cover page with your fax message. Click the Send Cover Page option to send a cover page with all your fax messages. Microsoft Fax includes four standard cover pages that you can use:

- Confidential
- For Your Information!
- Generic
- Urgent

Select a cover page that suits your needs. Generic is the default. As Microsoft Fax creates your fax message and prepares it to be sent, it fills in data fields on the cover page with information, such as recipient name and fax number, your name, and so on.

Tip

Select a cover page name and click Open to see what a cover page looks like.

The New button is used to create new cover pages by using Microsoft Fax's Cover Page Editor. Also, the Browse button can be used to locate cover page files (denoted as CPE) on your computer.

Note

This book does not show you how to modify or create cover pages, or how to use the Microsoft Fax Cover Page Editor. See Que's *Special Edition Using Windows 95* for details on using these features.

Finishing Configuring Message Options

One final option on the Message page is the Let Me Change the Subject Line of New Faxes I Receive option. Use this option to change the subject line of any faxes you receive. Because all incoming faxes are stored in the Microsoft Exchange Inbox, the subject (if it contains a subject) appears in the subject field there. This option gives you control over what appears in the subject field, enabling you to organize your messages as they come in. On the other hand, you must perform one more action as each fax message is received. The default is to leave this option disabled.

Click OK to save all the Microsoft Fax properties and to return to the MS Exchange Setting Properties sheet.

Congratulations! You're ready to send a fax using Microsoft Fax.

Configuring a Shared Fax Modem

To reduce the number of fax devices and dedicated phone lines for fax services, many businesses have one centralized fax machine that everyone shares. Because of their convenience and ease of use, most people do not complain too much about walking to a fax machine to send a message or document to another fax machine. Microsoft Fax enables you to extend this sharing of fax devices by letting users in a network environment share a fax modem.

The computer that contains the shared fax modem is called the *fax server* and is not required to be a dedicated PC. A fax server can be anyone's computer that is set up in a workgroup of other Windows 95 users. When a fax is received on the fax server, it then is routed to the recipient in the workgroup via Microsoft Exchange (or by attaching it as an e-mail message using an e-mail application such as cc:Mail).

Tip

The fax server should have at least 12M of memory and be a 486 or Pentium machine.

Caution

Microsoft Fax cannot automatically route fax messages to workgroup recipients. They must be manually delivered.

Setting Up a Fax Server

Again, make sure that Microsoft Exchange is installed and that a fax modem is installed and working on the fax server before completing these steps.

◄ See "Installing the Exchange Client," p. 202

► See "Installing Your Modem," p. 588

Start Microsoft Exchange and then perform the following steps:

1. Choose Tools, Microsoft Fax Tools.
2. Click Options.
3. In the Microsoft Fax Properties sheet (see fig. 10.18), click the Modem page.
4. Click the Let Other People on the Network Use My Modem to Send Faxes option.
5. If the Select Drive dialog box appears, select the drive the network fax will use from the drop-down list and click OK.
6. Enter the name of the shared directory in the Share Name text box.
7. Click the Properties button to configure the shared modem's properties (see fig. 10.19). The NetFax dialog box appears, in which you tell Microsoft Fax the name of the shared fax modem folder. The NetFax dialog box also enables you to set up passwords for users to connect to the fax server.

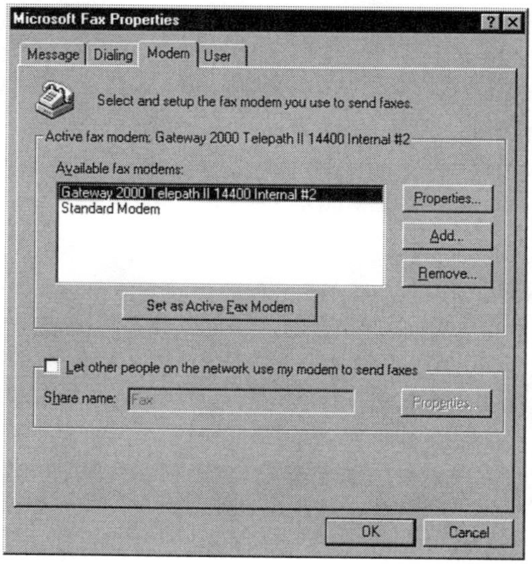

Fig. 10.18
Make sure that the Modem page is active to begin setting up a fax server.

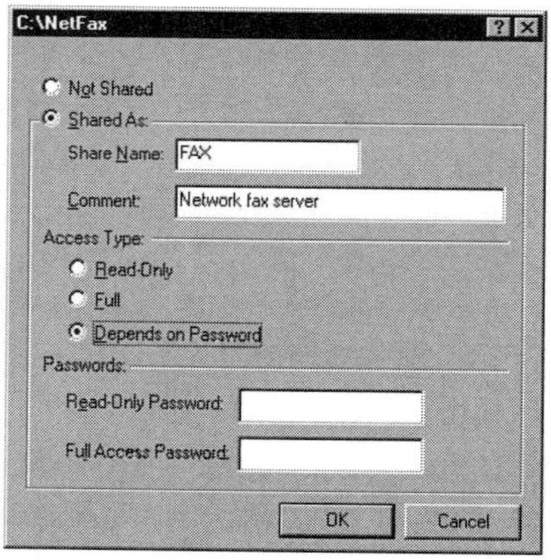

Fig. 10.19
Use the NetFax dialog box to set the shared fax folder and other settings for sharing a fax modem.

Note

If the Properties button does not work, switch to Control Panel and double-click the Network icon. Click the File and Print Sharing File button on the Configuration page of the Network sheet. Next, select both options in the File and Print Sharing dialog box for the Microsoft network service. You then need to restart Windows 95 for these settings to take affect. These settings enable sharing on your system, so you can share the fax modem with other users in your workgroup.

8. In the Share Name field, type the name of the shared folder for the fax server. Microsoft Fax displays the name of the network fax shared directory as the default. When a user in your workgroup wants to use this folder, she searches for this folder on your computer on your network.

9. In the Access Type section, select the type of access you want users to have to the shared folder. The default is Full. Select Read-Only if you want users to read, but not modify, items in the folder. The Depends on Password option is used if you want to give different people different rights to the shared folder. You can give one password—the Read-Only Password—to users who can only have read rights. You then can give another password—the Full Access Password—to users who can have full access to the folder.

10. Fill out the Passwords section as necessary, based on your selections in step 9.

For users in the Windows 95 workgroup to access the fax server, they must know the fax server's full network name. The name is formed by joining the server's computer name (defined in the Network option in Control Panel) with the shared folder name, for example, \\RTIDROW\FAX.

Setting Up a Fax Server Client

Not only must you configure a fax server to share a fax modem, but you also must configure the client's access to the server. The clients are those users who want to share the fax server. Start Microsoft Exchange on the client machine and then use the following steps:

1. Choose Tools, Microsoft Fax Tool.

2. Select Options.

3. In the Microsoft Fax Properties sheet, click the Modem page.

4. In Modem properties, click the Add button to display the Add a Fax Modem dialog box (see fig. 10.20).

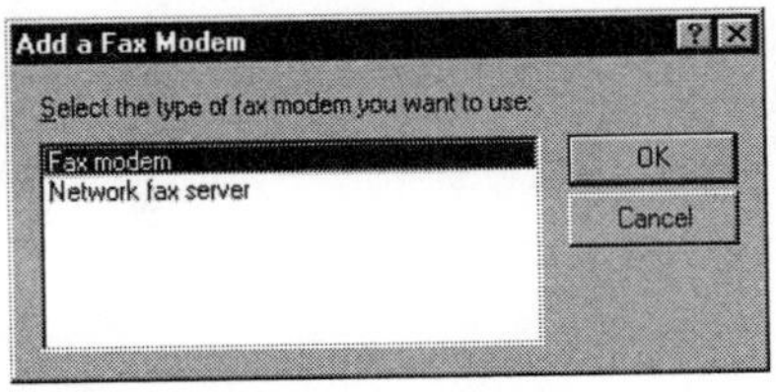

Fig. 10.20 The Add a Fax Modem dialog box includes the types of fax modems to which you can connect.

5. In the Add a Fax Modem dialog box, click Network Fax Server, and then click OK. The Connect To Network Fax Server dialog box appears, as seen in figure 10.21.

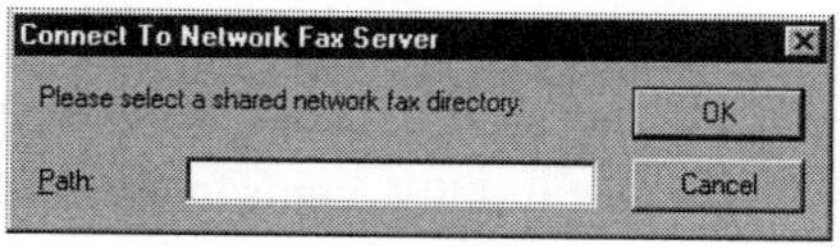

Fig. 10.21
To set up a client to use a shared fax server, enter the path of the shared fax server in this dialog box.

6. In the Connect To Network Fax Server dialog box, type the network name of the fax server, such as **\\RTIDROW\FAX**. If you do not know the network name, ask your network administrator. Click OK.

7. In the Microsoft Fax Properties dialog box, click the server name, and then click the Set as Active Fax Modem button.

You may have to reboot your computer for the settings to take effect.

Setting Up Security

One of the most discussed topics in the computer industry is security. You hear about security and the Internet. You hear about LAN security. You hear about voice mail security. Microsoft Fax enables you to securely send fax messages using public key encryption developed by one of the leaders in security, RSA Inc. Microsoft Fax also enables you to password encrypt and use digital signatures on your messages with confidence. The security features, of course, only extend to sending digital messages and files, not to printed or hard copy faxes. These types of faxes are still subject to anyone's eyes who happens to be walking by the fax machine when your transmission comes through.

Note

A *digital signature* is an electronic version of your signature. For most business transactions, such as purchase requests and employee timesheets, a signature is required to process the request. You can use a secure digital signature to "sign" requests, timesheets, and other sensitive documents.

One way to secure your fax messages is to password-protect them as you send them. As you create a fax message and the Send Options for This Message dialog box appears, set the type of security you want to have for your fax message. Click the Security button to display the Message Security Options dialog box (see fig. 10.22).

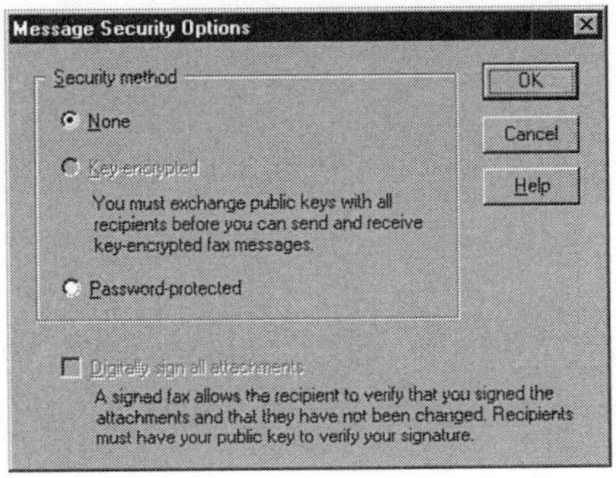

Fig. 10.22
You can set the type of security for your fax message in this dialog box.

Tip

Share your password so that the recipient can open and read your fax message.

If you have not set up public key encryption, you have to before you can use the Key-Encrypted option or use a digital signature on your message. You can, however, secure the fax message with a password by choosing the Password-protected option. Figure 10.23 shows you the Fax Security—Password Protection dialog box that you need to fill out when you want to send a message with a password.

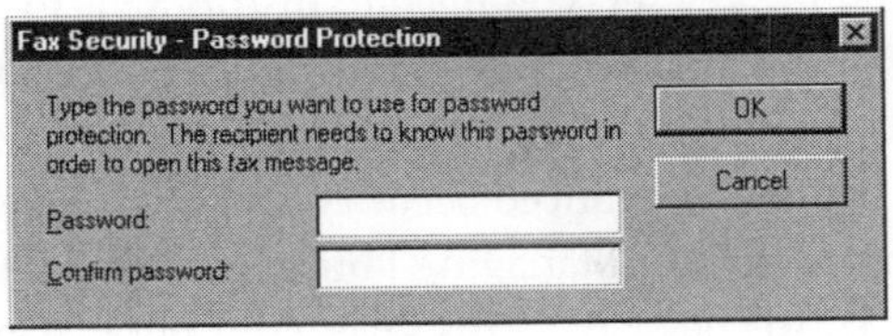

Fig. 10.23
To password-protect your faxes, enter a password in this dialog box.

Setting Up Key Encryption

A *key-encrypted message* uses a public key to unlock the message for viewing. This public key is made available to your fax recipients (who must also have Microsoft Fax installed) so that only they can open your document.

You must create a public key in Exchange. To do this, choose Tools, Microsoft Fax Tools, Advanced Security. The Advanced Fax Security dialog box appears (see fig. 10.24). In this dialog box, if this is first time you have created a public key, the only option you can choose is the last one, New Key Set.

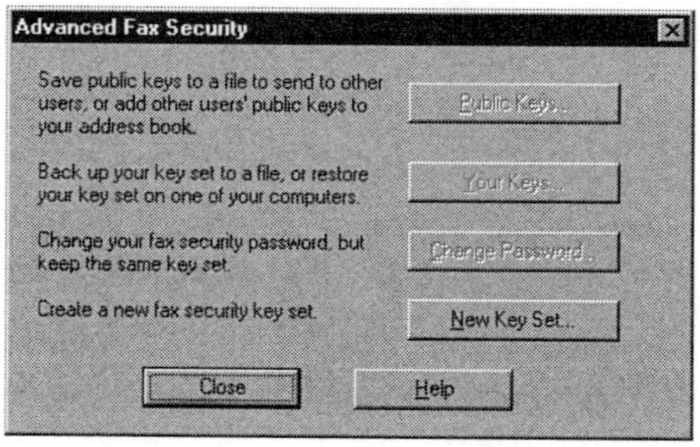

Fig. 10.24
Create a public key.

In the Fax Security—New Key Set dialog box, type in a password in the Password field, and then retype it in the Confirm Password field (see fig. 10.25). As you would expect, the password is not displayed; only a string of ***** denotes your password. Don't forget this password; it is now your public key. Click OK to have Exchange create a new public key set on your system. An information box appears, telling you it may take a few moments to create your key set.

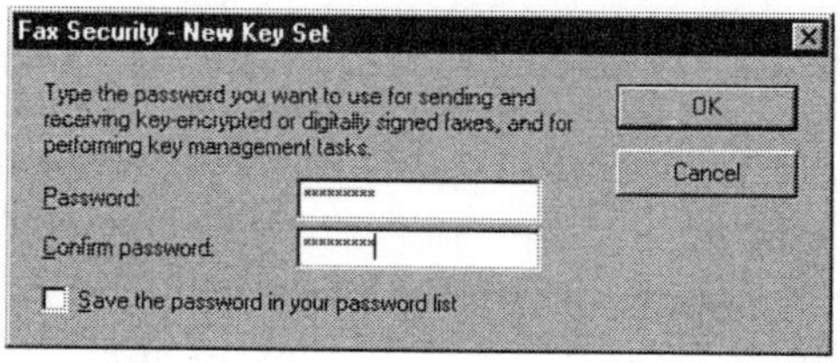

Fig. 10.25
You need to enter a new password to create a new public key.

Sharing Public Keys

After you create a public key set, you need to distribute it to your fax recipients in order for them to read your key-encrypted messages. Do this by clicking the Public Keys button in the Advanced Fax Security dialog box (choose Tools, Microsoft Fax Tools, Advanced Security if you've already closed this dialog box). The Fax Security—Managing Public Keys dialog box appears, from which you need to click Save. This saves your public key to a file so that you can send it to other recipients.

In the Fax Security—Save Public Keys dialog box, click the name or names of the public keys you want to share. As a minimum, you should click your name here. Click OK and in the resulting window, select a name and folder in which to store the keys. This file has an AWP extension. To finish, you need to send this file to your recipients either via an attachment to a Microsoft Exchange message or on a floppy disk.

Receiving Public Keys

When you send your public key to a list of recipients, they will need to import the AWP file into Microsoft Fax. Likewise, when you receive a public key from someone, you need to import it into your Microsoft Fax settings and add it to your address book. This enables you to read key-encrypted messages from those users.

After you receive an AWP file from someone, store it on your system and click the Add button in the Fax Security—Managing Public Keys dialog box. Locate the file name that contains the public keys and click Open. Click the key or keys that you want to add. ❖

Receiving Public Keys

Chapter 11

Configuring Windows 95 for Online Connections

by Dave Gibbons

The online world offers fun, business, information, and interesting people. But we don't want to waste too much time and effort *getting* there—it's *being* there that's important. Windows 95 takes most of the work out of going online and makes being there an easier experience.

Before Windows 95, setting up a modem with Windows entailed its share of guesswork (and luck). Even if your modem operated in DOS, there was no guarantee Windows 3.x would have any idea the modem existed—or that it wouldn't introduce a new conflict that disabled your modem and more (usually your mouse). Data transfer speed was a problem, too, with Windows 3.x acting as an extra layer of overhead between communications programs and the modem.

Now, Microsoft has addressed the speed and setup issues, removing the Windows-on-top-of-DOS overhead and making Windows 95 much smarter about modems. Many users won't face any obstacles getting their modems to work with Windows 95; if you run into any snags, Windows 95 provides the tools to track down almost any problem, making it an operating system that is more than adequate for modem communications. If you haven't installed your modem, turn to Chapter 28 for step-by-step installation and troubleshooting instructions.

In this chapter, you learn how to

- Use HyperTerminal and other terminal software to connect to a BBS
- Install and use The Microsoft Network
- Set up Windows 95 for Prodigy
- Set up Windows 95 for America Online
- Set up Windows 95 for CompuServe

Using HyperTerminal

Windows 95 includes HyperTerminal, an improved version of the Terminal program from the previous Windows versions. HyperTerminal is a basic *terminal emulation program*, which means it enables Windows 95 to interpret terminal commands from a BBS, online service, or mainframe. It lacks the automation and flash of a high-end terminal program (like its big sibling HyperAccess V), but works well for basic functions. You can use any of these emulations:

- *ANSI.* Used for BBSes.
- *Minitel.* French public terminal program.
- *TTY.* Doesn't interpret any incoming data, just displays it. Useful for machine tools and other simple serial devices like computer-connectable watches.
- *VT52.* Commonly used with mainframes.
- *VT100.* Another terminal commonly used with mainframes.
- *Viewdata.*

The other option in the terminals list is Auto-Detect. When you don't know what kind of system you're calling, this is a pretty good choice. It allows HyperTerminal to analyze the incoming data and guess what the correct terminal type is.

Each BBS or online service you call with HyperTerminal gets a separate icon, called a *connection*, in the HyperTerminal folder. When you select a connection, it tells HyperTerminal to use all the settings you've saved for that connection—not just switch to a different phone number. A connection can contain information about the following:

- Terminal type you want to use
- Speed and settings of the modem
- Which modem or serial port to use if you've installed more than one
- Icon you'll see with the connection's name in the HyperTerminal window
- The phone number (if any) of the connection
- Location you're calling from (very handy for use on a laptop)

Any changes you make in a connection affect only that connection.

Starting HyperTerminal

To start HyperTerminal, follow these steps:

1. Select the Start button.
2. Choose Programs.
3. Choose Accessories.
4. Select the HYPERTERMINAL folder.

> **Tip**
>
> If you use one particular connection in HyperTerminal a lot, you may want to put its shortcut directly on the Start menu so you don't have to open HyperTerminal's folder each time you start it.

5. Double-click the Hypertrm icon (see fig. 11.1) or the icon of the connection you want to use. If you start HyperTerminal with the Hypertrm icon, it assumes you want to create a new connection (see "Creating a New Connection in HyperTerminal" later in the chapter). If you haven't yet installed a modem, Windows 95 prompts you to do so.

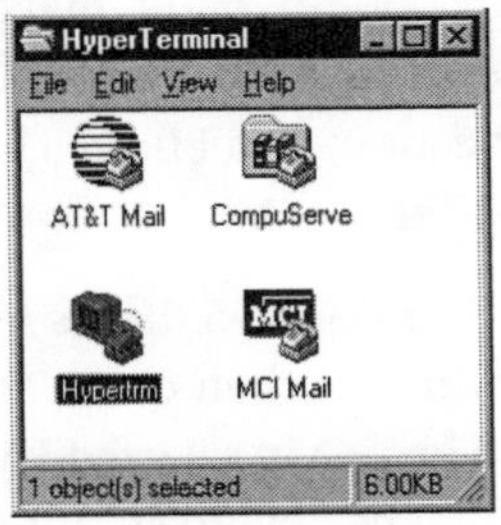

Fig. 11.1 HyperTerminal's folder is somewhat reminiscent of Windows 3.x groups, down to its cryptic eight-letter name.

Caution

Don't use the CompuServe icon in the HyperTerminal window. Get WinCIM instead—it's much more advanced than HyperTerminal, and makes your CompuServe use much easier. See "Setting Up a CompuServe Connection" later in the chapter.

If you don't see HyperTerminal's folder in the Accessories menu, it may not be installed. Try using the Start menu's Search function to find the program (HYPERTRM). If that fails, follow these steps to install it from your disk:

1. Click the My Computer icon.
2. Open the Control Panel.
3. Select Add/Remove Programs.
4. Use the Control Panel's easy Add/Remove Programs option to install a Windows 95 program you forgot originally. Don't be tempted to rerun the Setup program (see fig. 11.2) and select Communications.

Fig. 11.2
Don't rerun the Setup program to install a Windows program you forgot originally. Use the Control Panel's easy Add/Remove Programs option.

5. Click the Details button.
6. In the Communications pop-up menu, make sure to put a check in the box beside HyperTerminal. You can choose to install Dial-up Networking, Direct Cable Connection, and Phone Dialer if you want, but they're not necessary for HyperTerminal.
7. Make sure the original Windows 95 disk is in your drive. Click OK in the Communications window, then click OK in the Add/Remove Program Properties sheet. The newly selected HyperTerminal is installed to your computer, and you'll be able to start it using the previous set of steps.

Creating a New Connection in HyperTerminal

When you start with HyperTerminal, you naturally have to build each new connection from scratch. You should know a few things in order to create each one:

- Phone number, if any
- Terminal type (if you don't know, stick with Auto-Detect)
- Port settings (usually 8-N-1 for BBSes, 7-E-1 for mainframes and online services like CompuServe)

To create a connection, follow these steps:

1. If you've just opened HyperTerminal, you see the Connection Description window (see fig. 11.3). If HyperTerminal is already open to the blank terminal screen, you'll have to choose New Connection from the File menu first, but then you'll see the same screen. Enter the name you want to use for the connection and choose an icon. Click OK.

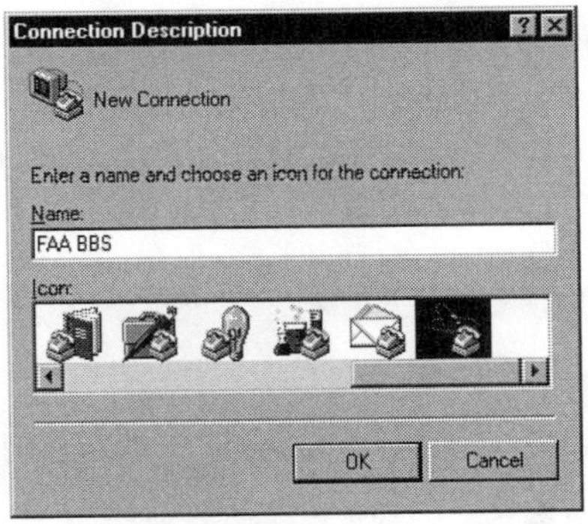

Fig. 11.3
You can choose from 16 different icons for each new HyperTerminal connection.

2. In the Phone Number window (see fig. 11.4), enter the phone number (if any) and choose the connection you want to use. If you're connecting directly to a machine (without a modem), choose the down arrow beside Connect Using. You'll see a `Direct to COMx` for each COM port. Choosing any of those options prevents HyperTerminal from trying to send modem commands through the port. Click OK.

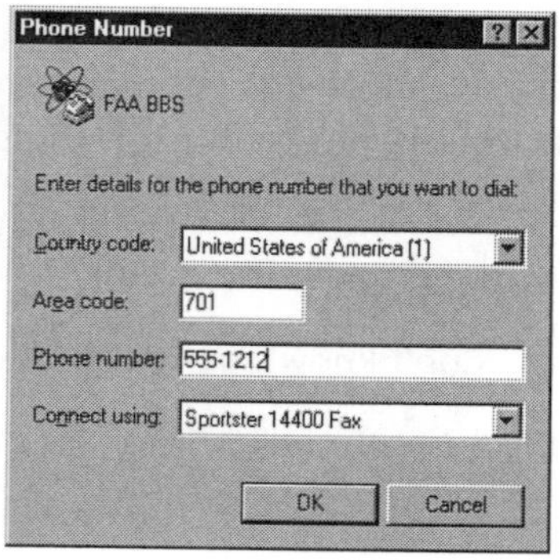

Fig. 11.4
If you put the area code in the Area Code box—not in the Phone Number box—Windows can decide whether or not to dial it based on your current location.

3. The Connect window enables you to make any changes to the phone number or your current location. Most of the time, you'll just click the Dial button and let HyperTerminal complete the connection.

4. When you're finished with the call, choose File, Save to add the connection to the HyperTerminal window.

Viewing the HyperTerminal Screen

While you're online with HyperTerminal, the communication between you and the remote system takes place on the terminal screen, the framed area in the middle of the HyperTerminal window (see fig. 11.5).

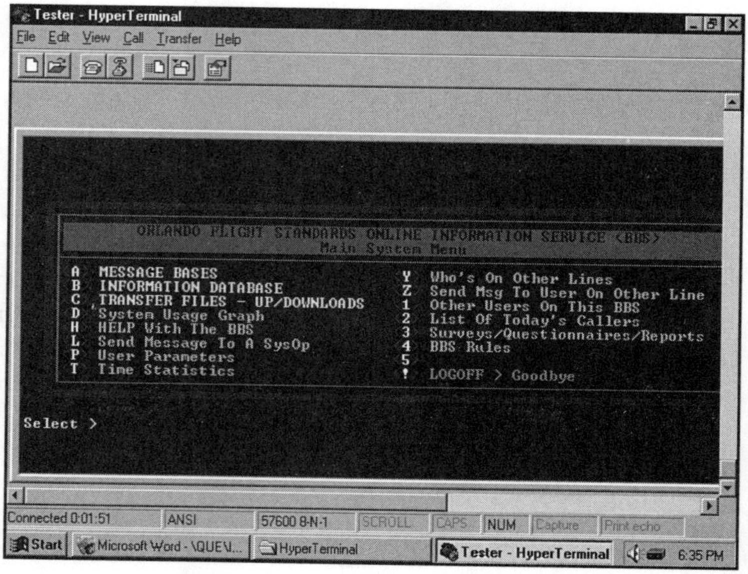

Fig. 11.5
If HyperTerminal's terminal screen is too big or small, choose a different font size in the View menu's Font selection.

HyperTerminal has a functional (if somewhat sparse) button bar. All the basic functions are covered, from left to right. See table 11.1 for a description of each button.

Table 11.1 HyperTerminal's Button Bar

Button	Description
	New Connection
	Open Connection
	Connect (using the currently active connection)
	Disconnect
	Upload (receiving side must be ready to receive before you select the Upload icon)
	Download (sending side must be ready to send before you select the Download icon)
	Properties (used to change any aspect of the current connection's setup)

Along the right side of the terminal window is a scroll bar (the *backscroll* bar—refer to fig. 11.5) which you can use to see any text that has scrolled off the top of the screen.

If you call a BBS with HyperTerminal, you may notice a strange effect in the BBS's graphics. Instead of lines and boxes on the screen, you may see rows of odd letters (see fig. 11.6). This happens because most Windows fonts don't offer the line drawing characters the BBSes expect. To correct the problem, choose View, Font and select the Terminal font. It's not a TrueType font (so it's not scalable on the screen), but it offers the correct characters. You'll probably want to use a video resolution higher than 640 × 480, since the Terminal font makes the terminal screen too big to completely fit on a 640 × 480 screen (refer to fig. 11.5).

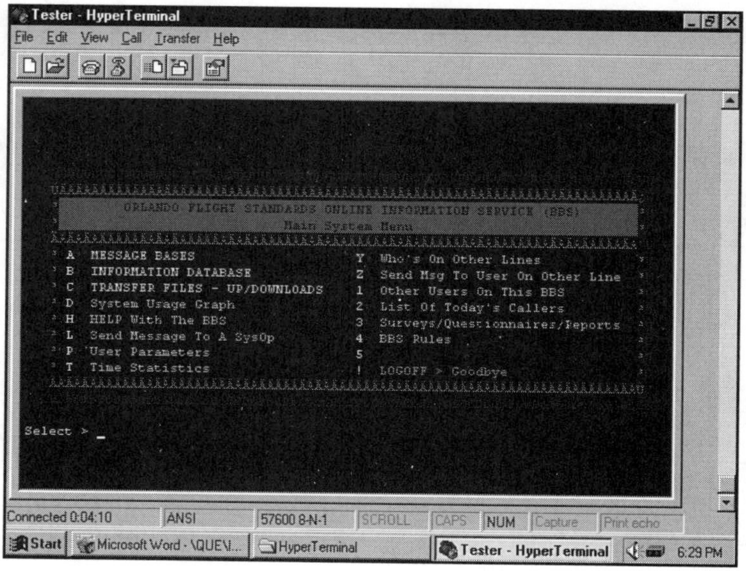

Fig. 11.6
This BBS's menu normally has a line-drawn box around it, but not when Courier New is the active font.

Other Software Options

For more advanced terminal operations, including automating your online sessions, you need something beyond HyperTerminal. Some of the major communications programs on the market are the following:

- PROCOMM PLUS for Windows
- WinCOMM PRO/Delrina Communications Suite
- QModem
- Reflections
- HyperAccess (made by Hilgreave, the company that wrote HyperTerminal)

These programs offer enhanced BBS and mainframe connections, along with their own sets of features to make your online time easier and more productive. You may also decide to get an advanced terminal emulation program for dialing into a UNIX host for an Internet connection. If, however, you only plan to use an online service like Prodigy, America Online, or The Microsoft

Network, an enhanced terminal program won't do you much good—each of these services has its own Windows-based graphical interface. You can use a terminal program with CompuServe, but you'll probably have an easier time with WinCIM, CompuServe's graphical front-end program.

If you decide to get an enhanced terminal emulation program, you shouldn't have much trouble using it with Windows 95. You're able to install it like any other new Windows software (choose Add/Remove Programs in Control Panel and click Install), but you'll need to keep a few things in mind:

- You may have to tell the program what kind of modem you use and what port it's on, because it might not be able to get that information from Windows 95. Most terminal programs are able to automatically sense your modem during the installation (see fig. 11.7), so this may not be a big issue.

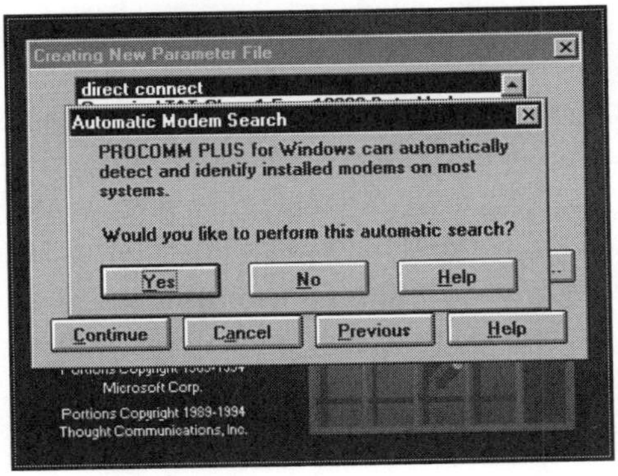

Fig. 11.7
Most big-name terminal programs detect your modem automatically during their installation process.

- The program may try to install a new communications driver. If so, make sure you have a version that is Windows 95-compatible.

- If you're using a DOS-based program, you probably won't have trouble with Windows 95's long file names. Most well-written terminal emulation programs are able to deal with transferring files with long file names. Many non-DOS operating systems allow longer names, so communications programs have to know how to deal with them (see fig. 11.8).

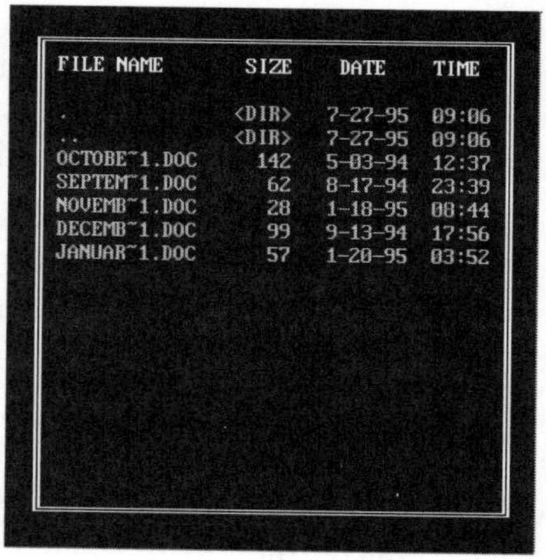

Fig. 11.8
Long file names show up as standard eight-and-three names, with a tilde representing the truncated portion.

Setting Up a Microsoft Network Connection

The Microsoft Network is one of the most fascinating aspects of Windows 95. It's a full-fledged online service that combines most of the best elements from the other services in this chapter and tosses in a few goodies the others don't have yet. It has standard features like e-mail, Internet access, file libraries, support forums, and games, but the real reasons many people will keep their Microsoft Network accounts (along with or instead of other online services) will probably be twofold:

- The interface is extremely well laid-out and easy to use (see fig. 11.9).
- Microsoft's industry (and financial) position will help it draw major celebrities of all types for online conferences.

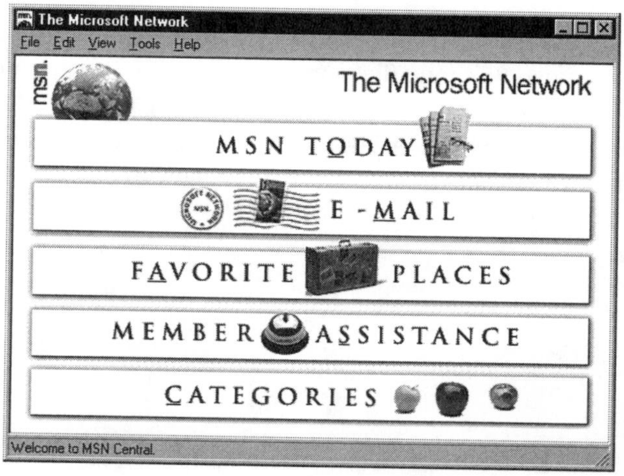

Fig. 11.9
The Microsoft Network's interface is straightforward and elegant—a step up from the standard (and confusing) dozens-of-icons approach.

If you choose the default installation of Windows 95, the Microsoft Network software is installed automatically. Its icon should appear on your desktop near the Recycle Bin. If you don't see the Microsoft Network icon, install it from your original disks by following these steps:

1. Choose the My Computer icon on your desktop.
2. Open the Control Panel.
3. Open the Add/Remove Programs icon.
4. Choose the Windows Setup tab of the Add/Remove Program Properties window and select The Microsoft Network.
5. Make sure the original Windows 95 disk is in your drive. Click OK in the Add/Remove Program Properties window. The Microsoft Network is then installed.

To set up The Microsoft Network for the first time, follow these steps:

1. When you first open the Microsoft Network icon, it asks whether you're already a member or if you're a new member. Select New Member.

> **Note**
>
> To become a member, you need a credit card, even though your early use is free.

2. In the next screen (see fig. 11.10), you see the three steps you need to complete to join. The setup is extremely simple. Enter your address (during which you select a local access number to use during all future calls), your credit card number, and read the licensing and fee information for The Microsoft Network.

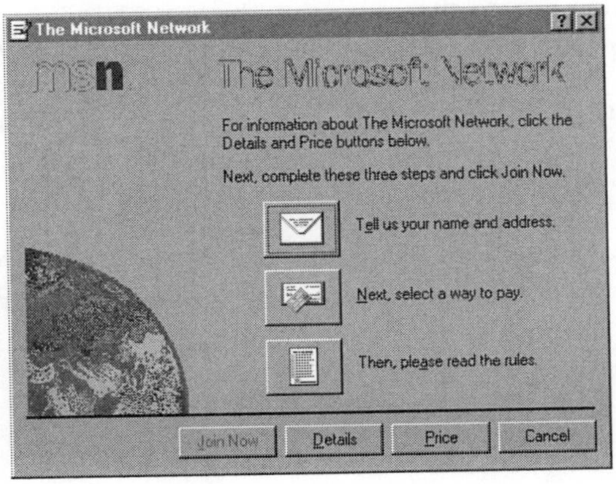

Fig. 11.10
Follow these three simple steps (or at least the first two) to set up your connection.

Signing On

Run The Microsoft Network with its icon, and follow these steps:

1. Enter your name and password (see fig. 11.11).

Fig. 11.11
Select the Remember My Password option if you want the password entered automatically each time. Just make sure no one else has access to your computer.

2. Click Connect.

Signing Off

Click the Close button on the far right of the title bar, just like you'd close any other Windows 95 application. When The Microsoft Network asks if it's all right to hang up, select Yes.

Setting Up a CompuServe Connection

Almost every modem, computer, or software/hardware piece you buy includes a trial offer from CompuServe.

Everyone who joins CompuServe gets a free trial (usually one month of free basic services and a $25 credit for extended services) to try out the service. Even though there are no charges during the trial period, you need one of these to sign up with CompuServe:

- Credit card
- Checking account

To start the free trial period, go through the actual sign-up process. If you decide you don't want to keep CompuServe, remember to cancel your membership within a month of your sign-up—monthly fees are automatically charged to you *even if you don't use the service.*

To get a free copy of CompuServe's WinCIM software (make sure you get version 1.4 or above), call 800-848-8199. You can also find WinCIM at the newsstand bundled with computer-oriented magazines, as well as on many CD-ROMs.

Tip

Make sure you have WinCIM 1.4 or above. Older magazines and CD-ROMs may have version 1.3.1 or earlier.

Installing WinCIM is very straightforward:

1. Choose the My Computer icon on your desktop.
2. Open the Control Panel.
3. Open the Add/Remove Programs icon.
4. Click the Install button.
5. Insert the program disk (or CD-ROM) into your drive.
6. Click Next. Windows 95 searches your drives, starting with A, then goes onto other floppy and CD-ROM drives in sequence until it finds a valid disk. It searches for a SETUP.EXE program (which is correct for WinCIM's installation) or a variation of INSTALL.EXE and displays what it finds (see fig. 11.12). CD-ROMs may have many different SETUP.EXE programs, so you'll probably have to click the Browse button to find the correct one for WinCIM.

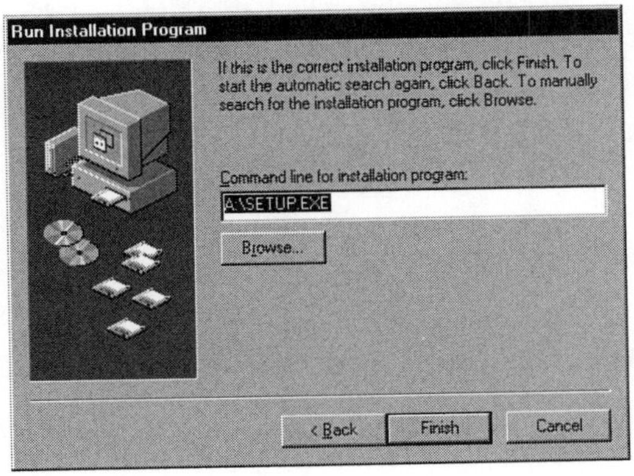

Fig. 11.12
If you're installing from a floppy drive, the default SETUP.EXE is a safe bet, but choose Browse on a CD-ROM to find the correct folder first.

Tip

If you're installing from a CD-ROM (drive D for example), make sure you don't have any disks in drives A or B. This saves you a few steps in the Windows 95 Installation Wizard.

7. The Setup program prompts you for a folder name for your WinCIM installation. The default is CSERVE. Select OK to continue. The program then begins copying files from the disk or CD-ROM onto your hard drive, occasionally prompting you for additional information. Make sure you answer Yes to `Do you want to copy the signon files?` if you don't have a CompuServe membership.

8. After the files are copied, you are prompted to sign up with CompuServe (see fig. 11.13). Choose Sign Me Up to answer all the required questions about your home location, billing method, and so on. When you select OK, the WinCIM installation program dials a toll-free number to set up your account. After you're set up, you can start WinCIM by selecting it in the Start menu's Programs menu under CompuServe.

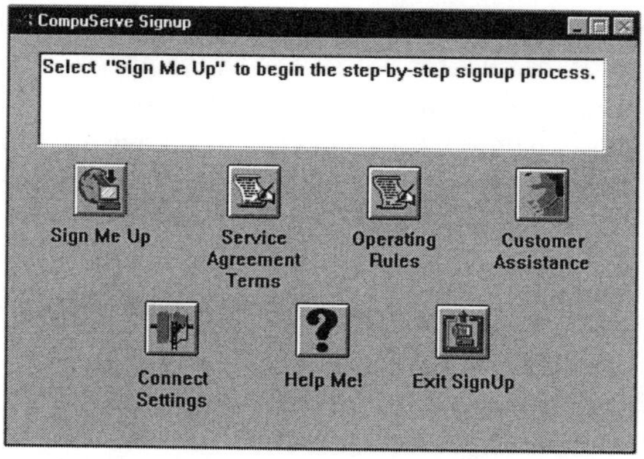

Fig. 11.13
WinCIM's sign-on menu has you answer most of your setup questions before you call the toll-free number.

After you get the kit and install the software, you need to get an access number (the local number you use for all your calls to CompuServe):

1. Call 800-848-8199 with a regular phone—not a modem.

2. Press 1.

3. Follow the prompts (which ask you to enter your area code and phone number, then which modem speed you want to use).

4. Write down the access number(s) and the network (for example, CompuServe, Tymnet, or SprintNet).

Tip

If you're in an area that doesn't have a local number, you'll probably save money if you use the closest high-speed access number in the nearest neighboring state. This allows you to avoid the intrastate telephone tax and additional charges some long distance companies add for longer distances.

To set up WinCIM to use the access number, your user ID, and your password, follow these steps:

1. Install WinCIM with the instructions listed earlier in the section.
2. Run WinCIM.
3. At the Connect screen, choose Continue.

Tip

If you don't want to go through this extra step each time, deselect the Show at Startup box.

4. Choose Special, Session Settings.
5. Enter all the correct information in the Name, User ID, Password, Phone, Connector, Baud Rate, and Network fields. Remember your password is case-sensitive, so you have to enter it exactly as it appears on your membership. If you don't know some of that information, you may find some help in Chapter 28, "Configuring Modems."
6. Choose OK.
7. Click Basic Services or one of the other icons, or you can choose File, Connect, then click the Connect button. WinCIM should sign you onto CompuServe at this point.

Signing On with WinCIM

When you use WinCIM, signing on is as simple as clicking the Connect button in the Connect to CompuServe window that pops up when you start WinCIM. Assuming you've already set WinCIM up with your ID and password, it logs on automatically.

Signing Off

Click the Disconnect button on the far right of the ribbon or just exit the program to sign off.

Note

The buttons on the CIM button bar change around a lot. While you're online, for example, there isn't an Exit button at all—it shows up when you log off, when the Disconnect button disappears.

Setting Up an America Online Connection

America Online (AOL) has made many changes to its interface in recent months, mostly due to its World Wide Web (WWW) integration. The new interface (version 2.5 and above) also takes advantage of Windows 95's multimedia strengths.

Becoming a Member

Everyone who joins America Online gets a free trial—usually 15 hours online. Even though there are no charges during the trial period, you'll need one of these to sign up with America Online:

- Credit card
- Checking account

To start the free trial period, go through the actual sign-up process. If you decide you don't want to keep AOL, remember to cancel your membership within a month of your sign-up—monthly fees are automatically charged to you *even if you don't use the service.*

To get a free copy of AOL's software, call 800-827-3338. You can also find AOL's software at the newsstand bundled with computer-oriented magazines.

Installing AOL is pretty simple:

1. Choose the My Computer icon on your desktop.
2. Open the Control Panel.
3. Open the Add/Remove Programs icon.

4. Select the Install button.
5. Insert the program disk (or CD-ROM) into your drive.
6. Select Next. Windows 95 searches your drives, starting with A, then goes sequentially to other floppy and CD-ROM drives until it finds a valid disk. It searches for a SETUP.EXE program (which is correct for AOL's installation) or a variation of INSTALL.EXE and displays what it finds (refer to fig. 11.12). CD-ROMs may have many different SETUP.EXE programs, so you'll probably have to click the Browse button to find the correct one for AOL. Look for an AOL25 or AOL250 folder.

Tip

If you're installing from a CD-ROM (drive D for example), make sure you don't have any disks in drives A or B. This saves you a few steps in the Windows 95 Installation Wizard.

7. Choose Finish to begin installing AOL.
8. In the America Online-Setup dialog box, choose Install. If you want to change the destination folders for the incoming files (for example, if you have a previous version of AOL which you want to upgrade), select Review.
9. Select Continue to see the folder where files will be copied. You can change this if you like.
10. Click Install to begin copying files. After the files are on your drive, select OK to complete the installation.

After you install the software, you need to get an access number (the local number you use for all your calls to AOL). Run the software (double-click the AOL icon) and choose Sign On. The software dials a toll-free number where it finds a local number—you just enter a little information about your location. Depending on where you live, you may have several choices for local numbers. Always choose the fastest one your modem can handle.

Note

If you are calling from a phone that uses a special prefix to dial long distance (9, for example), click Setup before you try to dial. In the Network Setup dialog box, click the Use The Following Prefix to Reach an Outside Line box and enter the prefix.

Tip

If you're in an area that doesn't have a local number, you'll probably save money if you use the closest high-speed access number in the nearest neighboring state. This allows you to avoid the intrastate telephone tax and additional charges some long distance companies add for longer distances.

When you've got the new local number, choose Sign On again to set up your account. You are prompted for the user ID and password for your trial account (it should be in the documentation that came with the disk). After you click Continue, enter all your acount information: your name and address, credit card number, etc. The service walks you through the process relatively painlessly. After you've set up the account, you are then connected to AOL to start exploring.

Signing On

America Online's interface is very simple to use. To sign on, for example, you need just these four steps:

1. Double-click the AOL icon. If you had already installed AOL before Windows 95, choose the AOL25 icon from the Start menu, Programs, America Online.

2. Select your screen name from the list in the middle of the Welcome window (see fig. 11.14). If you only have one screen name, it automatically appears in the Screen Name box.

Fig. 11.14
AOL allows you to have several screen names for each account.

3. Type your password in the Password box. Don't worry about anyone else seeing it over your shoulder—each letter you type shows up as an asterisk (*) on the screen.

4. Click the Sign On button.

The software then calls the local America Online number, signs you on, and opens two windows: the Main Menu (which has buttons for most major areas) and the Welcome window.

The Welcome window covers up the Main Menu at first, so you can check your mail, read the news, and check out the three featured services (if desired) before diving into AOL's web of other services.

The featured services change at least once a day, giving you a chance to see areas of AOL that you'd probably miss if you had to search through all the menus to get to them. The first few days of each month, one of the featured services is a letter from AOL's CEO Steve Case about new offerings.

When you're done with the Welcome screen, click the Go To Main Menu button at the bottom.

Signing Off

To sign off America Online at any point

1. Select the Go To menu.

2. Select Sign off.

The only time you won't be able to sign off this way is when the AOL software is busy transferring a file or displaying a large amount of text. In both cases, the mouse pointer changes to an hourglass until you're able to sign off normally.

Setting Up a Prodigy Connection

Prodigy is another simple installation, but it is unique because it doesn't matter what version you begin with. Prodigy's network automatically senses which version you're using and gives you the option of upgrading to the current version when you call in.

Becoming a Member

Call 1-800-PRODIGY to get a free trial offer, including Prodigy's software. Though the first 10 hours of online time are free (maybe more or less, depending on the offer you get), you need a credit card to sign up.

To install Prodigy

1. Choose the My Computer icon on your desktop.
2. Open the Control Panel.
3. Open the Add/Remove Programs icon.
4. Select the Install button.
5. Insert the program disk (or CD-ROM) into your drive.
6. Select Next. Windows 95 searches your drives, starting with A, then goes on to other floppy and CD-ROM drives in sequence until it finds a valid disk. It searches for a SETUP.EXE program (which is correct for Prodigy's installation) or a variation of INSTALL.EXE and displays what it finds (refer to fig. 11.12). CD-ROMs may have many different SETUP.EXE programs, so you probably have to click the Browse button to find the correct one for Prodigy. Because version numbers change so often at Prodigy, you probably won't see a folder with a number (like PRODIGY9.99). It's usually just PRODIGY.

> **Tip**
>
> If you're installing from a CD-ROM (drive D, for example), make sure you don't have any disks in drives A or B. This saves you a few steps in the Windows 95 Installation Wizard.

7. Choose Finish to begin installing Prodigy. The program files are copied to your hard drive. Prodigy prompts you occasionally for additional information about your setup, trial offer, and location.

After you install the software, you sign onto Prodigy with the member ID and password supplied with your trial offer. In the first session, you choose your own password and a local number to use for all future calls to Prodigy.

Signing On

Prodigy's Windows software offers two ways to sign on:

- Manually
- Autologon

To sign on manually

1. Choose the PRODIGY® software for Windows icon in the Start menu.
2. At the Prodigy Network—Sign On screen, type your user ID in the User ID box and your password in the Password box (see fig. 11.15).

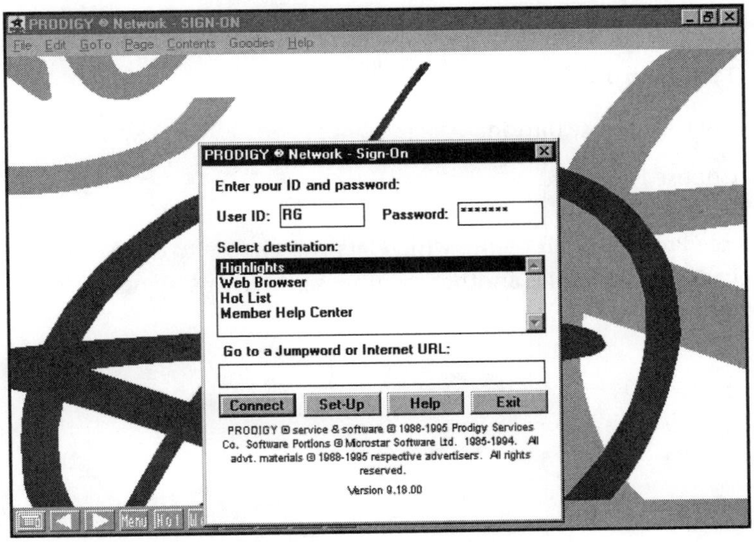

Fig. 11.15
Be careful of typographical errors in the password—you can't see what you're typing.

3. Click one of the buttons in the Select Destination box. For example, if you want to see Prodigy's main screen, select Highlights. If you like to start off in one of Prodigy's other areas, click type one in the Go To a Jumpword or Internet URL box. Whichever option you choose, the software dials the number, logs you on, and shows your selection.

Prodigy's IDs are notoriously tough to remember, so you might want to set up the Autologon feature. Autologon lets you skip typing your ID (and password, if you choose) every time.

To use Autologon

1. Dial Prodigy with the manual procedure, and type **Jump Autologon**.
2. The Autologon screen lets you choose to have your ID *and* password entered automatically (option 1) or just your ID (option 2). Click the option you want.
3. Type your password when asked.
4. Enter a nickname for your account (in case more than one person in your household wants to use Autologon).

Signing Off

When you're done, sign off one of these ways:

- Type **Jump Exit**.
- Click the Close button.
- Choose File, Exit.

You'll see Prodigy's Exit menu, which lets you choose to close Prodigy entirely, hang up and let another member sign on, or stay online.❖

Chapter 12

Configuring a Windows 95 Internet Connection

by Patrick Suarez

The Internet is a global collection consisting of more than 40,000 independent networks and nearly five million computers. These computers, which are sometimes called *hosts*, offer a wealth of information on thousands of subjects and allow millions of people to communicate with one another.

This chapter teaches you how to do the following:

- Obtain a PPP/SLIP account
- Install and configure the Microsoft TCP/IP software stack
- Install and configure the program that dials into your Internet provider
- Troubleshoot your Internet dialup connection

Why You Want an Internet Connection

Tip

Que's *Special Edition Using the Internet*, Second Edition, describes all the Internet tools in detail, and you should acquire a copy of that book as soon as possible if you are new to the Net.

It seems as if the range of resources of Internet hosts is limitless, and more come online every day. With an Internet connection, you can make discoveries well beyond what radio, TV, newspapers, and magazines offer.

▶ See "Setting up the Internet Explorer," p. 662

Tip

If you purchased Microsoft Plus!, you probably discovered Miscrosoft's World Wide Web browser, the Internet Explorer. When you install the Explorer, it will look for the Internet connection configuration data you learn about in this chapter. If it does not find it, Explorer's Installation Wizard prompts you for it. If you are unfamiliar with configuring Internet connections, you should complete this configuration chapter before installing the Internet Explorer. You may save yourself some potential confusion because the Explorer Installation Wizard will take these steps out of the sequence in this chapter!

Note

If you have experience with the Internet and just want to configure Windows 95 for Internet connectivity, skip to "The First Step: Adding a Network Configuration" later in this chapter.

Also, if you have the Microsoft Internet Jumpstart Kit (which is available on the Microsoft Plus! Companion for Windows 95 CD and on some new computers that are pre-installed with Windows 95), see Appendix A, "Installing and Using Microsoft Plus! Companion for Windows 95" for installation and configuration options.

Troubleshooting

What is the Internet Jumpstart Kit and how do I set it up?

The Jumpstart Kit is available in the Microsoft Plus! for Windows 95 CD and from various FTP sites (such as **ftp://ftp.microsoft.com/PerOpSys/Win_News**). If you've purchased a new computer that has Windows 95 pre-installed, the Jumpstart Kit may be installed as well.

Here are the basic tools available to you:

- *Electronic Mail (E-mail).* Electronic messages created with e-mail software and sent over Internet routers to their destinations, where recipients can read, print, send, save, or forward those messages to other users.

- *Mailing Lists*. Discussion areas that employ the electronic mail system as the means of transmitting an endless stream of opinions and information on about 7,000 different topics.
- *Newsgroups*. Electronic versions of cork bulletin boards to which you post and read messages. Newsgroups store the ideas and opinions of millions of users on approximately 12,000 different subjects. You must use a program called a *newsreader*, of which several exist. You can discuss virtually any topic from A to Z within the newsgroup system. Newsgroups are also called *UseNet News*, a reference to the store-and-forward system that carries the postings.
- *Telnet (remote login)*. The ability to log in from your computer to a network across the street or on another continent and use it as if you were there onsite. Thousands of networks allow *guest* logins, and you can find out almost anything from library holdings, to Vatican paintings, to your local weather forecast.
- *FTP (file transfer protocol)*. Almost 1,300 host systems exist as computer file storage sites and allow people to log into those sites and transfer copies of the files held there to the users' own computers. These servers hold more than two million files and do not charge for the transfer.
- *Archie*. A database and search device to locate files stored on FTP host computers.
- *Gopher*. An ingenious information retrieval program that is menu-based. When you log into a Gopher session, a menu appears on your screen. As you select menu items, you see succeeding menus, layer after layer, until you locate what you want. Gopher incorporates other Internet tools such as file transfer and remote login. Gopher is fast, easy to use, and comprehensive.
- *Veronica and Jughead*. Two programs found on Gopher menus that search Gopher menus. You enter a keyword, and either program searches all or a selection of Gopher machines for the text string you entered.
- *WAIS (Wide Area Information Server)*. A database tool that searches the contents of documents, not just the titles of those documents.
- *Internet Relay Chat (IRC)*. Real-time "chatting" via the computer keyboard. IRC resembles CB radio, except that the "talking" is done by entering text from the keyboard while you are logged into an IRC session.

- *World Wide Web*. An information retrieval medium that has taken the online world by storm and appears to be doing nothing less than redefining how we might get information in the future. The Web employs the client-server model, in which a Web "client" program, such as Netscape or Mosaic, requests information from a Web *server*, a computer set up to dispense information to the client program. Upon receipt, the client program processes the information and displays it. The retrieved information can take the form of text, photos, sound, and/or video. The Web uses *hypertext linking*, in which text, an icon, or a photo on a Web screen page can link to another Web page or Web computer elsewhere. The links can be endless. More than 10,000 Web servers provide a phenomenal amount of useful and fun information, and more servers go online every week. World Wide Web users also refer to it as *WWW*, *W3*, or simply as the *Web*.

Relating Windows 95's TCP/IP Software to Internet Application Programs

Take a look at what Windows 95's TCP/IP program is, what it does, and how it relates to Internet application programs that enable you to send e-mail, browse the contents of other Internet host computers, and see the technicolor wonders of the World Wide Web. You will also see that the TCP/IP program is not all that you need to make a connection to the Internet.

First, you need to understand two acronyms:

- *TCP*. Transmission Control Protocol
- *IP*. Internet Protocol

Basically, Transmission Control Protocol breaks your outgoing message or file into "byte-sized" packets called *datagrams*. Internet Protocol routes the datagrams through the system in search of a target router. When the datagrams find the correct router, they navigate onward to the destination computer, where Transmission Control Protocol reassembles the packets into their original form.

Understanding Routers

A *router* is just one of several pieces of special computer hardware that send Internet messages through the Internet system. Understanding router systems takes some getting used to. But, follow the sequence of events below, then read the handy analogy at the end of the sequence, and the concepts should become clear. The chain of hardware looks something like this:

1. Using Windows 95's Internet tools, your computer and modem dial into an Internet service provider's (or ISP) computer system. Your message goes from your computer and modem to your ISP.

2. The provider's computer system is connected to special communications equipment, one item of which is a router. Your message passes through your ISP's system and out of its router to a high-speed telephone line connected to another "major" Internet provider.

3. Most small- to medium-sized providers connect their routers—via special telephone lines or fiber optic cable—to "major" Internet providers. The systems belonging to the major ISPs also have routers, both incoming (to receive your message) and outgoing (to send your message to one of the many backbones, or high speed fiber optic superhighways, that interlink the major providers). Your message now passes from the major ISP to the backbone system.

4. While riding the backbone, your message passes from router to router, in search of the correct destination router and computer. Simply reverse the preceding steps to get your message to its destination.

5. Your message routes to a target major ISP which hands it off to the correct target mid-sized ISP, which then passes it to the correct target computer.

Here's a nifty analogy: think of the computer, router, backbone system in terms of interstate highways. The backbone cable is the interstate highway road; the router is the highway interchange and exit ramp; the computer is the destination town at the bottom of the interchange ramp.

As you just learned, the TCP/IP program manages the datagrams from and to Internet hosts. But by itself, the TCP/IP stack is useless. It needs a connection to other routers. Windows 95 provides that connection with a program that finds your modem, dials into a provider, locates a PPP connection (which you will learn about later) to the Internet, and matches the Internet addressing information that you gave to Windows 95 with the addressing information that the provider's system expects to see from Windows 95's configuration. Later sections in this chapter show you how to configure both the TCP/IP stack and the dialer program.

Once you have installed and configured the TCP/IP stack and the dialer, and Windows 95 has made contact with your Internet service provider, you can finally connect to another Internet host and do something! You will need separate application programs to send and receive e-mail, contact Gopher servers, download files, log onto remote networks, view World Wide Web sites, and so on. But where do you find application programs that will do these wonderful things for you?

You get application programs from a number of sources. One is from the CD that accompanies Que's *Special Edition Using the Internet*, Second Edition. Another source is your local computer store. Yet another source is shareware that you download yourself from the Microsoft Network, a commercial service such as America Online, an electronic bulletin board service, or a file transfer protocol site.

Chief among the shareware programs are PC Eudora for e-mail, Trumpet News Reader for UseNet News, WSGopher for Gopher, WSArchie and WS_FTP for file transfer protocol, and Netscape and Mosaic for World Wide Web browsing. These are all available from the sources mentioned in the preceding paragraph.

Understanding Internet Services

There are several ways to obtain an Internet connection. The first is to use standard communication software such as Procomm Plus for Windows. You can use this program to dial into a network or Internet service provider and use its computer system.

This service does not work with Windows 95's TCP/IP program. Instead, it accesses Internet hosts "indirectly" by dialing into your Internet provider's network and turning your computer into a temporary terminal on your provider's network. This access, called *terminal emulation*—usually accomplished through a *shell account*—is not as comprehensive as the kind of connection that Windows 95 offers, but it does work. I won't go into detail on shell accounts in this chapter, but you can learn about them in Que's *Special Edition Using the Internet*, Second Edition.

A second method is to use an online service such as The Microsoft Network or America Online. You need special software provided by the online service to make a successful connection. The Microsoft Network software is included in Windows 95.

A third and more comprehensive way is to use the special Internet software that is included in Windows 95. As you've learned, the software is called TCP/IP, and is easy to set up. If you use Windows 95's TCP/IP software with a dial-up connection called *PPP* or *SLIP* (about which you will learn soon), your computer will be directly linked with the Internet router system and will be an actual Internet host any time it is online. This setup has several positive implications, including the capability to download files from Internet file servers directly onto your hard drive and to navigate the World Wide Web.

◀ See "Setting Up a Microsoft Network Connection," p. 276

Windows 95 offers several ways to configure Internet connections. This chapter focuses on the steps needed to get a direct Internet session using a modem connected to a personal computer. If you access the Internet through a company or school network, some of the settings you will read about may be different. Your organization's network manager or Information Services department should be able to give you the required configuration settings, if not install them for you.

Before you continue, make sure that you have installed and configured a modem for Windows 95.

PPP and SLIP Connections

If you want to enjoy the full glory of the Internet, your computer must have direct access to the Internet system. Direct access to Internet routers and computers is achieved with expensive hardware and a special "dedicated" line wired right to your computer.

▶ See "Installing Your Modem," p. 588

Most people cannot afford dedicated, leased line access. But most *can* afford the functional equivalents, PPP (Point to Point Protocol) and SLIP (Serial Line Internet Protocol) connections. PPP and SLIP trick the Internet system into thinking that your computer has a dedicated line, even though PPP and SLIP are really dial-up communication protocols that need modems or networks as intermediaries between Internet routers and your computer.

PPP is newer than SLIP. A description of their differences is beyond the scope of this chapter, but most Internet service providers normally issue PPP, not SLIP, accounts. This chapter describes how to establish both PPP and SLIP connections in Windows 95.

PPP and SLIP accounts are associated with the type of Internet addressing that routers understand. This addressing scheme is numeric and has four positions, separated by periods known as "dots." An example of an IP (Internet Protocol) address is

198.6.245.121

This address identifies a specific host machine among millions of Internet hosts.

Since humans remember strings of letters better than strings of numbers, many numeric IP addresses have text equivalents. If a text equivalent, called a *Fully Qualified Domain Name* (*FQDN*), exists, use it in lieu of the IP address.

FQDNs are constructed like this:

host_computer_name.location.domain_type

An example is **kiwi.wright.edu.** Kiwi is the name of the host machine you are addressing; wright is the location (Wright State University); edu is the *domain type*, or the type of facility that operates the host machine.

Table 12.1 lists the six major domain types.

Table 12.1 Domain Types

com	Commercial organization
edu	Educational institution
gov	Government facility
mil	A military organization
net	Internet service provider
org	Miscellaneous, usually nonprofit, organization

Countries outside the United States use two-letter identifiers at the end of their fully qualified domain names. A few examples are CA (Canada), UK (United Kingdom), and ES (Spain).

Two Types of IP Addresses

If your computer has a *static* IP address, that IP address is permanently assigned to your computer. Whenever you go online with a PPP or SLIP connection, your computer uses and is identified with that address throughout the system. An advantage of a static IP address is that you can register a specific domain name to that static IP address; you or your business then can be identified all over the world with either the IP address or domain name.

Your computer might also have a *dynamic* IP address which your provider assigns from a pool of IP addresses available whenever you log into a PPP or SLIP session. This is often a less expensive, but very viable, way of getting connected.

The difference between the two is important because Windows 95's TCP/IP configuration will ask you which IP address type, static or dynamic, you have.

Tip

Work closely with your Internet service provider as you configure your TCP/IP setup.

Troubleshooting

My modem connects to my ISP, but my ISP's system doesn't recognize my IP address.

Ensure that your IP address (if you have a static IP address) and your ISP's IP address and DNS are configured properly in Windows 95's TCP/IP configuration. Even a single wrong number or letter can negate a connection.

Why Do I Need a Direct Connection to the Internet?

Millions of Internet users connect to Internet sessions using traditional UNIX *shell accounts.* These accounts are functional and have existed for over a quarter of a century. But UNIX shell accounts cannot display the popular graphical images provided by such World Wide Web browsers as Netscape and Mosaic. Your computer must have the kind of "direct" access to the Internet router system that dedicated leased lines and PPP or SLIP connections provide.

As more and more businesses and information services create Web home pages, you will find yourself needing this enhanced connectivity. Fortunately, the cost of a PPP or SLIP account has dropped dramatically so that many individuals and small business owners can afford this level of service. You might wish to create your own Web page for you or your business. A PPP or SLIP account would be required to view it.

How to Find an Internet Service Provider

You need an ISP in order to establish a PPP or SLIP link. Most large- and medium-sized cities in the U.S. now have providers who sell accounts at a reasonable rate, usually for $20 to $40 per month, depending on whether your PPP connection is static or dynamic. Dynamic IP accounts cost less than static IP accounts. Both function the same way while online. Again, static IP accounts afford you the advantage of establishing your own global identity.

Some ISPs give you a set number of hours for a set price, such as $20 for 15 hours. After you use up the set number of hours, the ISP charges an hourly rate, usually $1 to $3 per hour.

Caution

Do not sign up to this kind of arrangement unless you know beyond any doubt that you will not use more hours than the set price permits. If you find that you will exceed those hours, as many users do, contact your ISP for a revised arrangement.

Most ISPs offer quarterly, semiannual, and annual rates which permit you to stay online as long as you want and not worry about hourly charges.

If your phone book does not list a local ISP, ask someone at your local computer user group or computer store. If there is no local ISP, national ISPs such as UUNET/AlterNet sell accounts. National providers also might have toll-free 800 numbers or use the Tymnet or Sprintlink system to give you a local number. If you contact a national provider, they will explain the options that suit your needs and pocketbook. The last option, a toll call to the nearest dial-up number, is also available, but it is an expensive option.

Selecting an ISP takes some research because there are good ones and bad ones. If you live in a major metropolitan area such as Chicago or Washington, D.C., there are several ISPs from which to choose. If you live in a medium-sized city such as Dayton or Austin, there is still some flexibility. If you live in a small town away from a city or in a rural area, your choices are limited.

Whatever choice you make, your ISP should charge a monthly, quarterly, or annual flat rate instead of charging by the hour, a practice called *metering*. Technical support should be available during business hours and in the early evening. The ISP's connection from the backbone system to its system should be at least a T1 line, and enough incoming lines should exist so that you do not reach a continuous busy signal when you dial in. The ISP should offer all Internet services and should make all UseNet newsgroups available without "filtering" out any of them.

On the other hand, you must be a good customer. Do your own research on Internet basics. There are dozens of books on the subject, including Que's *Special Edition Using the Internet*, Second Edition, previously mentioned. Do not expect miracles. Providing Internet connectivity is a profoundly complex, expensive, and difficult task. If you are having trouble dialing in, make sure that your computer's hardware or software configuration is not the problem. If you have an older computer and a very slow modem (anything under 14,400 baud is too slow), you will probably be underpowered. Invest in new equipment. Of course, if you are running Windows 95, your hardware is probably acceptable. If there is a problem, work with the ISP instead of yelling at him.

Tip

The most important hardware components for a successful Internet session are those that bring data in and draw it to your screen. Ensure that your modem is fast and that you have a UART 16550 chip in your modem's COM port, at least 16M of system RAM, and a fast graphics card.

Troubleshooting

What type of service does my Internet Service Provider (ISP) need to offer to configure Windows 95 for the Internet?

Ask the ISP the following questions:

- Does the access provider offer full Internet access?
- Does the access provider support PPP? SLIP?
- Does the access provider offer technical support?
- What kind of connection speeds does the access provider support?

What kind of information do I need from my ISP?

You must obtain the following data from your access provider to use during configuration:

- Access phone number, preferably local
- Logon name and password
- Your host and domain name (be sure to repeat the numbers to the provider to ensure you have this written down correctly)
- The Domain Name System (DNS) server and IP address

▶ See "Windows 95 Setup and Bootup," p. 680

The First Step: Adding a Network Configuration

Your first task is to create the network tools under the Network icon located in the Windows 95 Control Panel. After you install the network tools, you will be able to install and configure the rest of the tools that are needed for a PPP dial-up.

To add network configuration tools, follow these steps:

1. Click the My Computer folder.
2. Click the Control Panel folder.
3. Double-click the Network icon.
4. The Network sheet opens, with one page, Configuration. If you have not configured a network connection in Windows 95, the Configuration page has no items installed. Otherwise, you may have a few items already installed. Click the Add button.
5. A new sheet called Select Network Component Type opens with four items. Double-click the first item, Client.
6. The Select Network Client window opens with two lists (see fig. 12.1). In the Manufacturers list box, select Microsoft; in the Network Clients list box, select Client for Microsoft Networks. Click OK.

Tip

If you are running under a network such as Novell Network, you need to use the Microsoft's Client for NetWare Networks. You may want to consult your network administrator for more information.

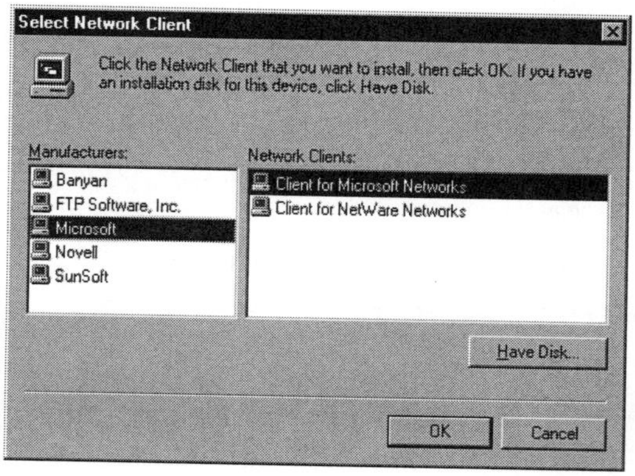

Fig. 12.1
Select the two components highlighted in the Select Network Client window.

Adding the TCP/IP Protocol to Windows 95

You must add the TCP/IP protocol to the new Network Configuration menu you created in the previous section:

1. The four new network menu items appear in the Configuration page, as shown in figure 12.2. Click Add to create the TCP/IP network component.

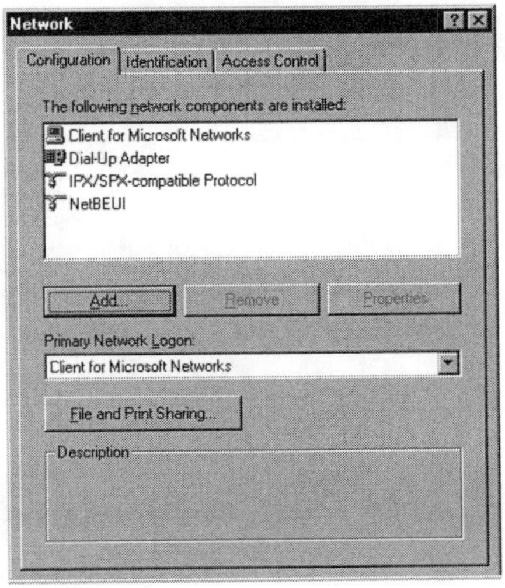

Fig. 12.2
Clicking the Add button will enable you to create the TCP/IP network component.

2. The Select Network Component Type sheet appears. Select Protocol from the list of four items, and then click the Add button.

3. The Select Network Protocol window appears, as shown in figure 12.3. In the Manufacturers list box, select Microsoft; in Network Protocols, select TCP/IP. Click OK.

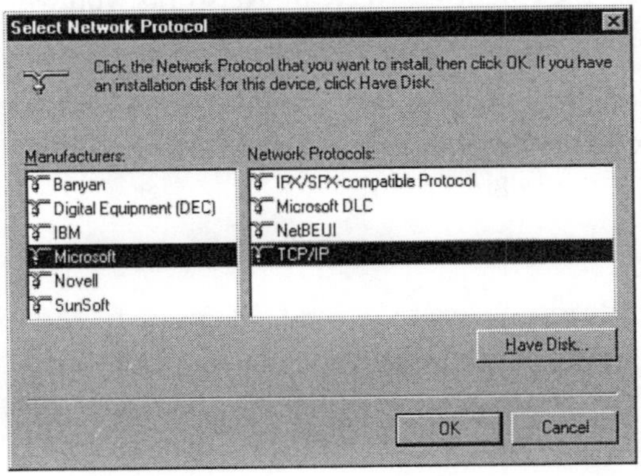

Fig. 12.3
Select Microsoft and TCP/IP as highlighted.

TCP/IP is now added to the list of Network Configuration items, as shown in figure 12.4.

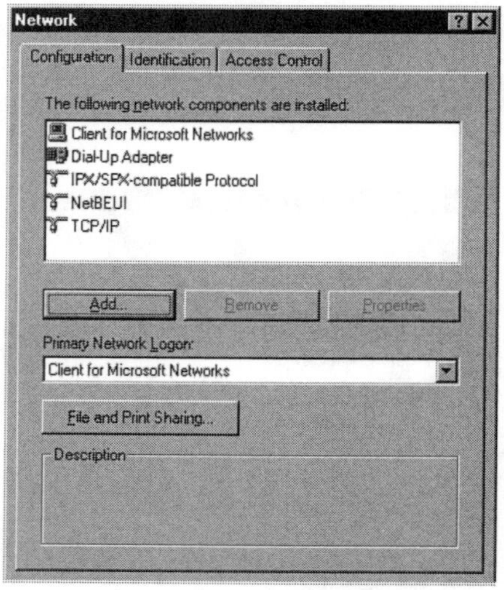

Fig. 12.4
TCP/IP becomes the fifth component in the configuration list.

Tip

The TCP/IP program is sometimes referred to as the TCP/IP *stack* because the various functions of TCP/IP occur in vertical layers from the application programs (at the top of the stack) to the network hardware level (at the bottom).

Setting the Dial-Up Adapter Properties

You must next set the properties for Windows 95's dial-up adapter. The Network sheet should still be on-screen, with the Configuration page still selected. (If you use the Client for NetWare Networks, you will not have to set up the Dial-Up adapter.) Follow these steps:

1. Double-click the Dial-Up Adapter item in the Configuration page. The Dial-Up Adapter Properties sheet appears, with the Driver Type page selected. Click the Bindings page.

2. Click the small check box next to TCP/IP to activate it.

3. Click the Advanced page to select it. There are two to four items in a list. To the right of the list, there is a Value box which can read Yes or No. All of the items in the list should be No except for the third one, Use IP header compression, which should be Yes. Select these now. Click OK when finished.

Configuring Your TCP/IP Host

This section configures Windows 95's TCP/IP stack with your specific Internet protocol numbers, or the numbers the Internet router system you will use to interact with other Internet hosts.

> **Caution**
>
> The IP numbers used in the configuration are examples. Do not use them to configure your TCP/IP host! Your Internet service provider will give you the data you need for this section.

As before, the Network Configuration screen should appear. Follow these steps:

1. Double-click the TCP/IP item in the Configuration page.
2. The TCP/IP Properties sheet loads. Note that it has six pages. You will use four of them, beginning with IP Address. If the IP Address page is not selected, select it.
3. If you use a dynamic IP address to dial into your provider, select the Obtain an IP Address Automatically radio button. If you use your own static IP address, select the Specify an IP Address radio button and enter your four-segment numeric IP address in the IP Address box. Note that this is *not* the provider's Domain Name Server (DNS) address, which you will enter elsewhere. This is *your* specific (static) IP address, if you have one.
4. Next, your IP address is probably a Class C address which is what 99 percent of all single-user PPP dial-ups get. Check with your Internet provider to be sure. If your IP address is a Class C, enter **255.255.255.0** in the Subnet Mask field, as shown in figure 12.5.

You have configured your own IP address. You now must configure your provider's Domain Name Server (DNS) information by following these steps:

1. In the TCP/IP Properties sheet, click the DNS Configuration page.
2. Select the Enable DNS radio button.
3. In the Host field, enter the user ID which your provider assigned to you. Some networks require additional information in the Host field. Your provider or network administrator should give you this data if this is the case.

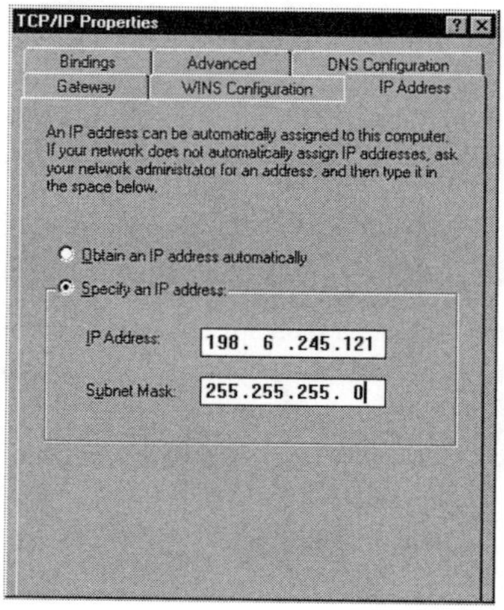

Fig. 12.5
Be sure that the IP address you use is your specific IP address and not your provider's DNS address. Accuracy counts!

4. Next, enter your provider's domain name in the Domain field.
5. Enter your provider's DNS IP address in the four-segment DNS Server Search Order area. After you enter the number, click the Add button next to it. Enter as many numbers as your provider gives you. The example in figure 12.6 shows two IP addresses, a primary and secondary. Some providers will give you a backup IP address in case there is a problem with the primary one.

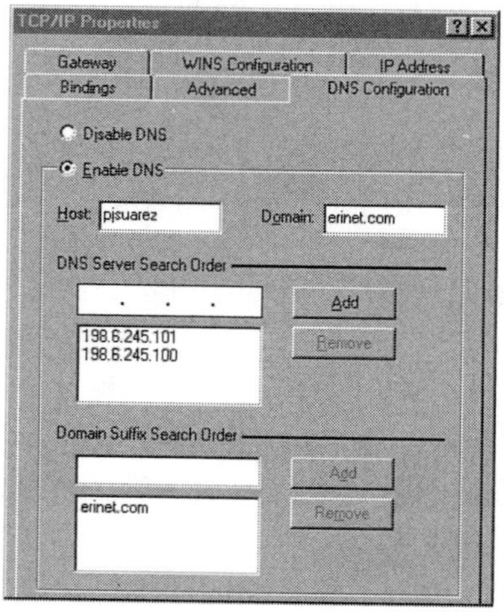

Fig. 12.6
The accuracy of this information is also very important!

6. In the Domain Suffix Search Order area, type your provider's domain name and click the Add button.
7. Select the Advanced page in the TCP/IP Properties sheet. The only item that you must set is at the bottom of the page. Click the Set This Protocol to be the Default Protocol check box.
8. Select the Bindings page in the TCP/IP Properties sheet. Click the Client for Microsoft Networks check box. Click OK to complete the TCP/IP Properties configuration.
9. A System Settings Change dialog box appears. Click Yes to reboot your computer. This will cause the changes you have made to take effect.

Adding a Dial-Up Network Folder

After Windows 95 reboots, your system is now able to process the Internet packet sending and receiving protocols. You must now add communications dial-up capability to the TCP/IP configuration so that your host system (Windows 95) can find your provider's host system:

1. Open the Control Panel folder in the My Computer folder. Double-click Add/Remove Programs.
2. The Add/Remove Programs Properties sheet appears. Select the Windows Setup page to find a list of component programs.
3. Double-click the Communications program. The Communications sheet appears. Select Dial-Up Networking. If Dial-Up Networking is already selected, the Dial-Up Networking capability is already installed on your system. Click Cancel and skip to the next section, "Creating a Dial-Up Icon for Your Provider."
4. Windows 95 then asks you to insert either Windows 95 floppy disks or the CD-ROM. At the end of the disk install procedure, click OK. The Dial-Up Networking folder now appears in the My Computer folder, as shown in figure 12.7.

Note

These steps may have been completed during Windows 95's installation.

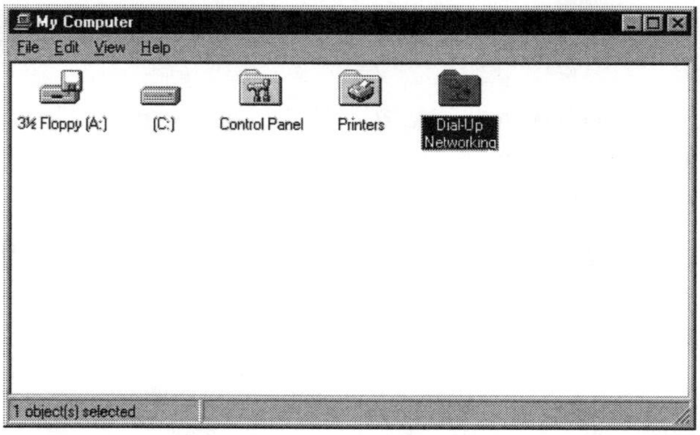

Fig. 12.7
The new Dial-Up Networking folder is installed.

Creating a Dial-Up Icon for Your Provider

Windows 95 allows you to create an icon that launches an Internet session representing a specific source or provider. You can have more than one. Each icon locates information about your Internet account and your provider that you stored earlier into Windows 95. This is handy if you have a single provider or if you must have more than one on-ramp to the Net.

Tip

If you use a third-party TCP/IP stack—such as NetManage's Internet Chameleon—to access the Internet under Windows 95, you still must install the TCP/IP stack using the Control Panel, but you do not have to create a dial-up connection icon. Many third-party TCP/IP programs include their own software for establishing the connection.

You will now create a dial-up icon configured for your Internet service provider's host. Follow these steps:

1. Open the Dial-Up Networking folder you just created. Double-click the Make New Connection icon that appears in the folder.
2. The Make New Connection Wizard opens, into which you enter information about your service provider. In the Type a Name for the Computer You Are Dialing field, enter an identifying name for your provider, such as **Iquest Connection**.
3. Your modem should be identified in the Select a Modem field in the folder. If not, select it from the drop-down list box.
4. Click the Configure button located under the modem name.

5. The Modem Properties sheet appears. Select the Options page.

6. Under Connection control, click the Bring Up Terminal Window After Dialing check box. In the same page, click the Display Modem Status check box under Status Control. Click OK. The Make New Connection dialog box returns to the screen. Click the Next button.

7. In the Make New Connection window, enter your provider's area code and dial-up (not voice) telephone number. Choose `United States of America (1)` or another country in the Country Code drop-down list box. Click the Next button.

8. Windows 95 announces that you have successfully created a new connection for your provider. Click Finish. An icon for your provider is now in the Dial-Up Networking folder, shown in figure 12.8.

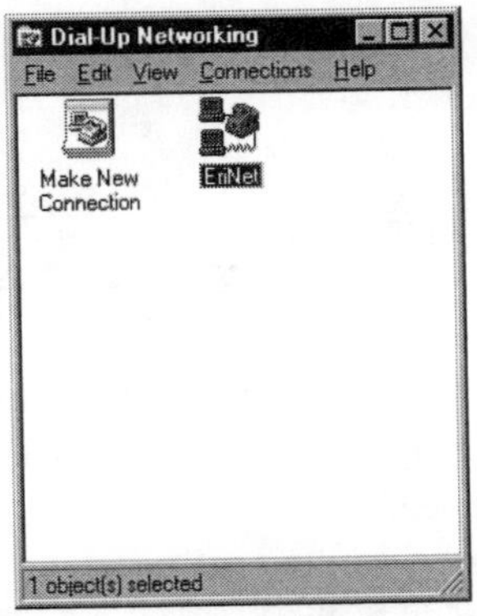

Fig. 12.8
Your new icon for your Internet dial-up appears in the Dial-Up Networking folder.

You're almost ready to dial into your Internet provider and start a PPP or SLIP session! There are a few more configuration steps left to go:

1. The Dial-Up Networking folder should be open, and the icon representing your provider should be highlighted. Using the right mouse button, click *once* on the provider's icon. A small drop-down menu unfolds. Select the last item, Properties.

2. The provider's General configuration screen appears (see fig. 12.9). Enter the Area Code and Telephone Number of your provider's system. If the call to your provider is a local call, you may leave the Area Code blank.

3. If you're calling outside of an internal telephone system, you need to add **8** or **9** in front of the provider's telephone number, as in **9,7654-321**. Add the comma (,) after the 8 or 9 exit code to allow a short pause while Windows 95 gets an outside dial tone.

4. Select the country name you're calling from, such as `United States of America (1)`, in the Country Code drop-down list box.
5. Select the Use Country Code and Area Code check box.
6. Select your modem in the Connect Using area.

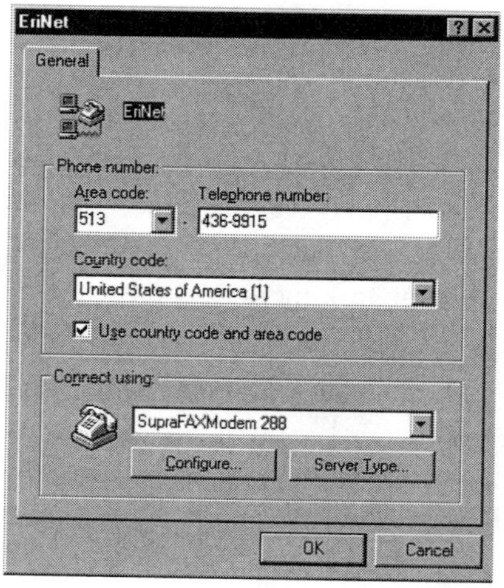

Fig. 12.9 Ensure that your modem is properly identified in the Connect Using area.

7. Click the modem Configure button. You are now in the Modem Properties sheet's General page (see fig. 12.10). Select your modem's COM Port and Maximum Speed.

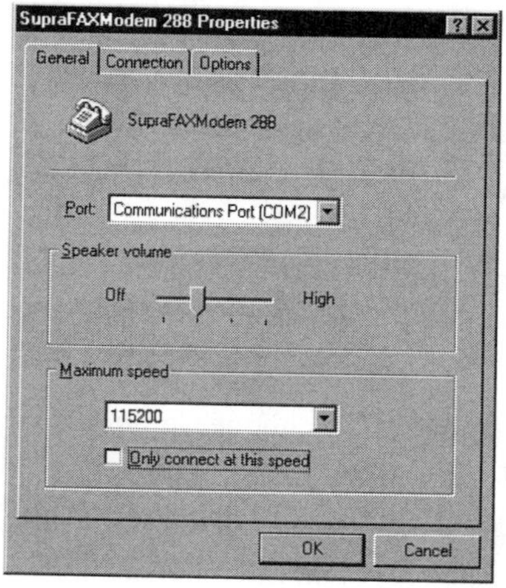

Fig. 12.10 Ensure that you select the correct serial (COM) port.

Caution

Do *not* select the Only Connect At This Speed check box. Although you want the connect rate to be as fast as possible, your dial-up might not always achieve that maximum rate. If you select the Only Connect At This Speed check box, Windows 95's dialer will *only* work at the connect rate selected and not at a lower, and probably viable, speed. If your connect rate does not reach the setting you entered, Windows 95 will hang up the connection even though you could have used the lower line speed you encountered.

8. While still in the Modem Properties sheet, select the Connection page, shown in figure 12.11. Ensure that Data Bits is 8, Parity is None, Stop bits is 1; this term is sometimes referred to as *8N1*.

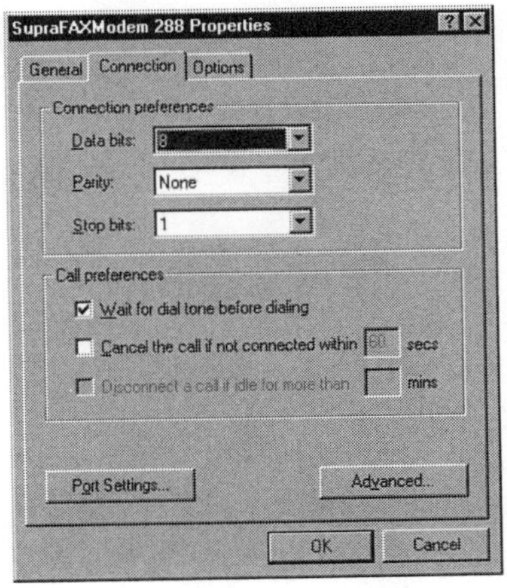

Fig. 12.11
The connection preferences are important. If you set these to anything other than 8N1, your connection will not work.

9. In the Modem Properties sheet, select the Options page (see fig. 12.12). Select the Bring Up Terminal Window After Dialing check box. Select the Display Modem Status check box in the Status Control area. Click OK. The provider's General configuration screen reappears. Click the Server Type button.

10. The Server Types sheet appears (see fig. 12.13). If you have a PPP connection, select `PPP: Windows 95, Windows NT 3.5, Internet` from the Type of Dial-Up Server drop-down list box. If you have a SLIP connection, select `SLIP: Unix Connection`.

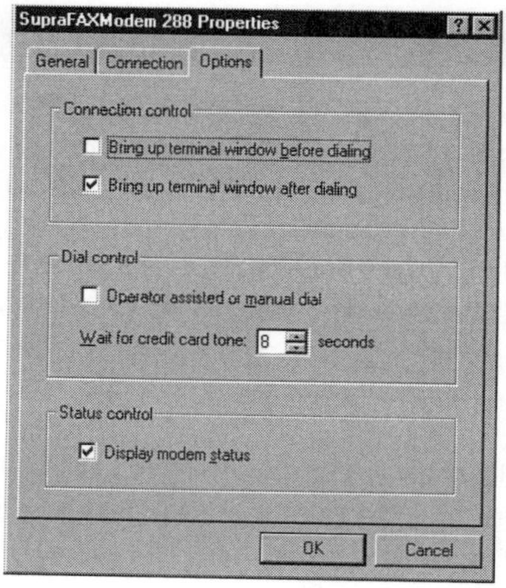

Fig. 12.12
This is the last modem configuration screen. You can see the status of your dial-up as it attempts to connect to your provider.

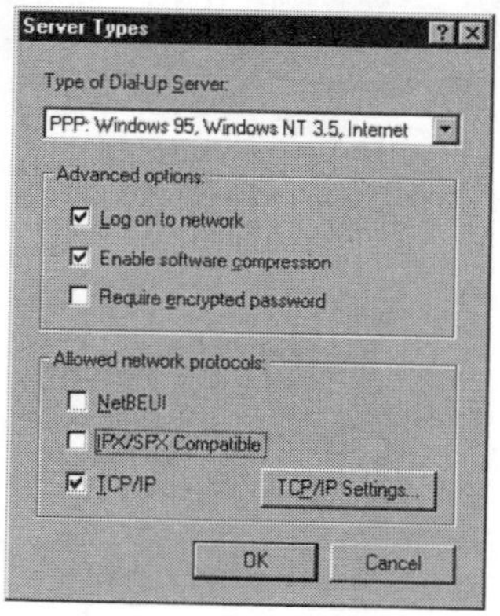

Fig. 12.13
TCP/IP should be selected, not NetBEUI or IPX/SPX Compatible.

> **Note**
>
> Windows 95 does not automatically install SLIP connection software on your system. You must install it using the Add/Remove Programs icon in Control Panel. See the section "Adding SLIP Connectivity to Windows 95" later in this chapter for more information.

11. In the Advanced Options area, select the Log on to Network and Enable Software Compression check boxes.

12. In the Allowed Network Protocols area, select TCP/IP. Deselect the NetBEUI and IPX/SPX Compatible check boxes. Click the TCP/IP Settings button.

13. You move along to the TCP/IP Settings sheet, shown in figure 12.14. If you use a dynamic PPP account, select the Server Assigned IP Address radio button. If you use a static PPP account, select the Specify an IP Address radio button and enter your specific IP address. Check the Specify Name Server Addresses radio button and enter your provider's Primary DNS number and Secondary DNS number—if there is a secondary number—in the fields provided under the radio buttons. Select the Use IP Header Compression and Use Default Gateway on Remote Network check boxes. Click OK.

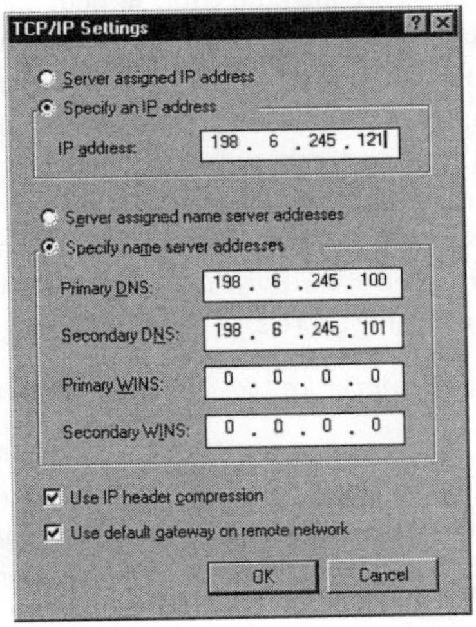

Fig. 12.14
This sheet demonstrates the difference between your specific IP address and your provider's DNS address(es).

14. Click OK in the Server Types dialog box and then click OK in the General connection page.

Tip

If you already have an existing TCP/IP program—for example, Trumpet Winsock or Internet Chameleon—on your hard drive, you can continue to use it if you don't want use Windows 95's TCP/IP stack. If you want to delete your current TCP/IP program, you should install and configure the Windows 95 stack, ensure that it works, then delete the TCP/IP program you want to discard from your hard drive *after* you're sure that the Windows 95 stack functions to your satisfaction.

Troubleshooting

I've connected to my ISP, but each time I use Netscape (or Mosaic), I get the following error message:

```
Netscape is unable to locate the server:
home.netscape.com
The server does not have a DNS entry...
```

What is wrong?

A few things may be wrong. First, double-check the URL that you typed in. Make sure it is exactly right or you will encounter this error. Second, the site may be busy or require specific authorization (such as a password or ID number). Start chopping off the end of the URL and try accessing the site again. Third, the site may have moved locations or shut down. Fourth, you've lost connection to your ISP and you didn't know. Check the Dial-Up Network connection that is opened to see if your connection is still live. If not, reconnect. Fifth, you may not have your IP addresses set up properly in the network connection areas. In the TCP/IP Settings dialog box, make sure the IP addresses are typed in correctly. You may have to call your ISP technical support line to reconfirm your IP address.

How can I increase the speed with which I connect to my ISP using a PPP or SLIP connection?

Right-click the Dial-Up Networking icon for your Internet connection and select Properties. Click the Server Type button. In the Server Type dialog box, make sure the Log On To Network, NetBEUI, and IPX/SPX Compatible options are not checked.

Dialing In

The big moment has arrived! It's time to dial into your PPP session. Follow these steps:

1. Double-click the provider dial-up icon.
2. Enter your the User Name and Password that your provider's system expects to see from you in the Connect To dialog box.
3. Select the Save Password check box. Your provider's data line Phone Number should appear. If it isn't there, type it in the box. `Default Location` is normally selected in the Dialing From drop-down list box.
4. Click the Connect button. Windows 95 begins the dial-up process (see fig. 12.15).

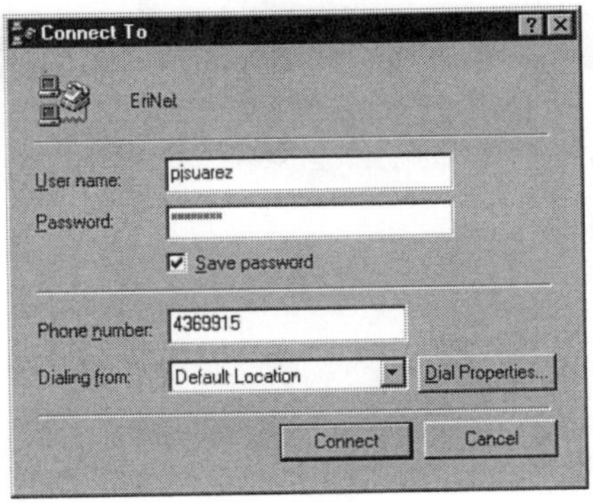

Fig. 12.15
Click the Connect button to begin the dial-up process.

5. Once connected, the Post-Dial Terminal Screen emerges (see fig. 12.16). After entering both user ID and password, a string of ASCII characters will zoom horizontally across the screen. Click the Continue (F7) button or press the F7 function key. A series of status messages during the dial-up process appear.

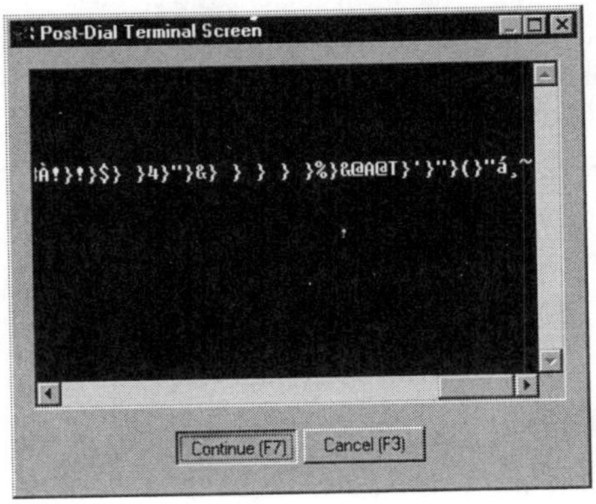

Fig. 12.16
Click the Continue (F7) button to complete the connection process. Do this as quickly as you can so the connection does not drop.

6. Finally, the system will alert you that you are connected. Minimize the Connected sheet by clicking the Minimize icon in the upper right-hand corner of the sheet and open an Internet client program such as Netscape or Mosaic. Once you open a client program, proceed with whatever you want to do online.

Tip

Remember, you can open more than one application at a time while online. That means you can download weather information from a World Wide Web server at the same time you check for new e-mail!

Troubleshooting

I have a 28,800 baud modem, but the fastest connection I get is 19,200. Sometimes the connection is choppy and laden with errors when I download files.

Check for any of the following:

- Line noise
- Incorrect modem settings in your communication software
- Modem incompatibilities between your modem and your ISP's modem
- The presence of a UART 16550 in your modem's COM port

If your phone company uses old switches in its central office, there is nothing you can do except get faster, dedicated service.

My modem connects with my ISP's modem, and then it dumps the carrier (hangs up spontaneously).

This is a potential nightmare with many sources. Did you set your parity to 8 bits, No stop bit, 1 parity bit? Is the initialization string in your communication software appropriate to your modem? Does the modem name and other settings in your communication software match your modem? Is there an incompatibility between your modem and your ISP's modem? Carrier dumping requires sleuthing. Be patient and work with your ISP until the problem is solved.

Windows 95 Dial-Up Networking supports SLIP and can connect to any ISP using the SLIP standard. SLIP is available only on the Windows 95 CD-ROM, and you must manually install it after you install Windows 95.

To install SLIP, use the following steps:

1. In the Add/Remove Programs option in Control Panel, click the Windows Setup tab, and then click the Have Disk button.
2. In the Install From Disk dialog box, enter the pathname **D:\ADMIN\APPTOOLS\DSCRIPT\RNAPLUS.INF** and click OK.
3. In the Have Disk dialog box, click the SLIP and Scripting for Dial-Up Networking option (see fig. 12.17). Click the Install button.

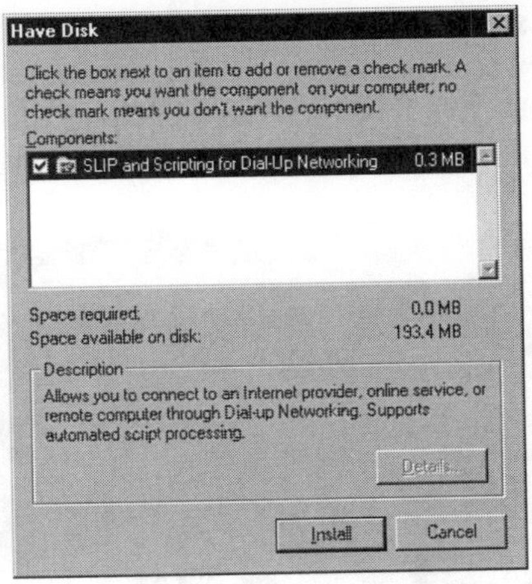

Fig. 12.17
The SLIP connection software is available on the Windows 95 CD and is set up using the Add/Remove Programs icon. It requires only 0.3M hard disk space.

4. Click OK when the Add/Remove Programs Properties sheet appears.

The SLIP software is now available on your system, and you can select it in step 10 in the previous section.

> **Note**
>
> Because SLIP servers cannot negotiate TCP/IP addresses, you must configure the Dial-Up Network connection to display a terminal window after you connect to your ISP. In most cases, your ISP displays the IP host address and your IP address. Write down these addresses and place their values in the SLIP Connection IP Address dialog box that appears. Click OK.

Other Windows 95 Internet Configuration Features

The majority of users who have had Internet access for a number years have become familiar with a few standard tools to help them use the Internet's wealth of information. Two of these tools, Telnet and FTP, are included in Windows 95. Windows also includes a TCP/IP configuration utility. The following sections show you how to set up these utilities to use with Windows 95.

Windows 95 FTP Utility

File Transfer Protocol (FTP) is used to transfer files on the Internet from one site to another. Even if you have World Wide Web access, chances are you'll log into an FTP site sooner or later. Windows 95 includes an FTP utility that you can use after you establish an Internet connection. To start an FTP session, click Start on the Windows 95 taskbar and select Run. In the Open field, type **ftp** and click OK. The Ftp window opens (see fig. 12.18).

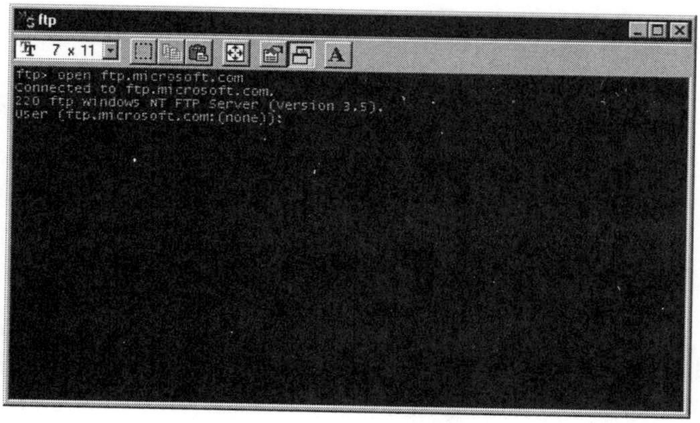

Fig. 12.18
Windows 95 includes its own FTP utility to access FTP sites on the Internet.

Once you start FTP, you can log onto an FTP site by using the OPEN command, such as

open ftp.microsoft.com

Other FTP commands can be found by typing **?** at the `ftp>` prompt and pressing Enter.

Windows 95 Telnet Utility

Like FTP, much of the information on the Internet is still available only if you use Telnet. Telnet enables you to log into another computer and use it as if you were there onsite from your own computer. Windows 95 provides a version of Telnet that you can run from the Start menu, as shown in the following steps:

1. Open the Start menu, click Run, and type **telnet** in the Open field. Click OK. The Telnet window opens.
2. In Telnet, choose Connect, Remote Session.
3. In the Connect dialog box (see fig. 12.19), type the host name of the Telnet site to which you want to connect in the Host Name field.
4. In the Term Type field, select a terminal mode. The default is VT-100, which is a good place to start.
5. In the Port field, select a port. The default is Telnet.
6. To start the Telnet session, click the Connect button in the Connect dialog box.

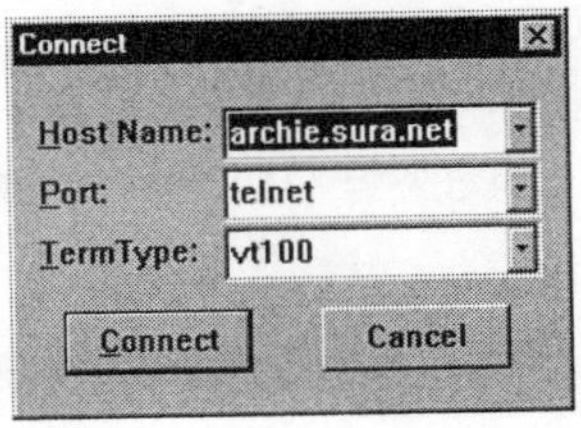

Fig. 12.19
Windows 95's Telnet utility enables you to log onto other computers remotely as if you were sitting in front of them.

Verify Internet Connections with WINIPCFG

Windows 95 includes an IP Configuration utility called WINIPCFG (see fig. 12.20), which you can use to display all the current TCP/IP network configuration values of your computer. Your computer must be running Microsoft TCP/IP to use WINIPCFG. To run WINIPCFG, select the Start button, click Run, and type **WINIPCFG** in the Open field. Click OK.

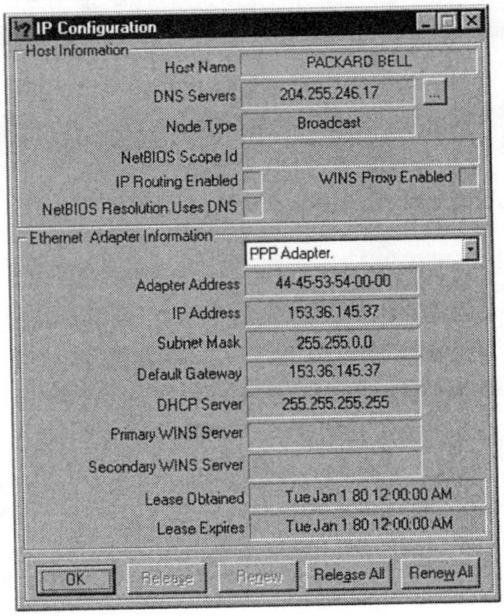

Fig. 12.20
To see current IP settings, use the WINIPCFG utility available with Windows 95.

When you run WINIPCFG, you can see the current IP address allocated to your computer and other useful data about the TCP/IP allocation. The IP Configuration utility does not, however, dynamically update information. If you make any changes, such as disconnecting from your ISP, you must close the IP Configuration utility and restart it.

Microsoft's Internet Explorer

Plus!

Microsoft Plus! includes a powerful World Wide Web browser called the Internet Explorer (see fig. 12.21), which you can use to display Web sites. Your computer must be connected online to use Internet Explorer. To run Explorer, click the Explorer icon which Plus! installed on your Windows 95

Desktop. Explorer processes information from specially programmed Web servers using its proprietary Blackbird software code. Future Web sites that use the Blackbird system will present vivid pages that, for now, only Explorer will decode and display.

Fig. 12.21
Microsoft's Internet Explorer World Wide Web home page connects you to Microsoft information and the rest of the Web world.

Troubleshooting

How do I know if I'm connected to the Internet?

You can use the PING command to quickly get your answer. To use the PING command, open a DOS window in Windows 95 and type the following, which is the address for the Microsoft FTP server:

ping 198.105.232.1

If this works, then TCP/IP is set up correctly.

You also can start the WINIPCFG utility to see if your IP addresses display. To run WINIPCFG, enter **WINIPCFG** in the Open field after choosing Start, Run.

I'm connected to the Internet through my network at work. I have the same error that I received in the previous question. Can you help?

The best answer is to ask your network administrator to help you configure your Internet connection. He or she is the best qualified to set these settings. You might, however, check to make sure the DNS Configuration tab is set up correctly for your network. You can access this by double-clicking the Networking icon in Control Panel, selecting TCP/IP, and clicking Properties. Click the DNS Configuration page on the TCP/IP Properties sheet and ensure these settings are properly configured.

Chapter 13

Configuring Memory, Disks, and Devices

by Kevin Jones

The Windows 95 installation program does a good job of setting up your computer. It analyzes your hardware and prepares your system for optimal performance. However, as you use your computer, two things may happen. First, you may notice that your system's performance goes down. This is very likely due to your hard disk becoming fragmented. Second, you may add new hardware or software. For example, you may use new programs or perform more complex analysis with your existing programs. You might add a faster CD-ROM or a more powerful video display card. When these types of changes occur, you will require more than the original settings to accommodate your growing needs.

In older versions of Windows, changes of this kind were often very difficult. You'd have to run many different programs to make all the changes. Fortunately, Windows 95 makes performing all of these tasks much simpler than it used to be.

In this chapter, you learn how to

- Modify virtual memory
- Improve hard disk performance
- Set device properties

Modifying Virtual Memory Options

As Windows 95 executes programs—especially when executing several programs at once—it performs better when it possesses more memory. To achieve better performance, Windows 95 uses spare room on your hard disk as additional memory. This is called *virtual memory*. The room on your hard disk that is used by Windows 95 as virtual memory is called the *swap file*. This file grows and shrinks as you use your computer. The more programs you run at once, the larger the swap file grows. As you close programs, the swap file shrinks. Normally, you won't need to adjust the default settings for virtual memory. However, if your hard disk doesn't have much spare room on it, you may want to control how Windows 95 grows and shrinks the swap file.

To change the virtual memory settings, use the Virtual Memory dialog box. To open the Virtual memory dialog box, follow these steps:

1. Click the Start Menu.
2. Choose Settings, Control Panel.
3. Open the System icon by double-clicking it.
4. Select the Performance tab in the System Properties Sheet (see fig. 13.1).
5. Click Virtual Memory.

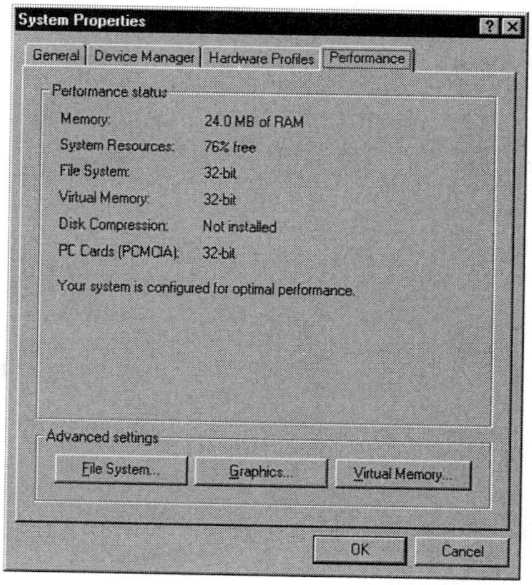

Fig. 13.1
You can change System Properties by using properties sheets.

The Virtual Memory dialog box opens.

You only have two main choices when dealing with virtual memory. You can either let Windows decide how to manage the virtual memory, or you can specify your settings. If you need to specify your settings, there are three parameters to set:

- Where (on what disk) should Windows create the swap file
- What's the smallest size the swap file should shrink to
- What's the largest size the swap file can grow to

Caution

If you have 12 or more megabytes of RAM, you will be given the option of turning off virtual memory. Don't do this. If you do turn off virtual memory, you may not be able to run more than a few, small programs simultaneously, or work with large amounts of data. Microsoft (and I) recommend that you don't disable virtual memory.

Hard Disk

Normally, Windows will create the virtual memory swap file on the same disk that Windows 95 is installed. However, you can have Windows 95 create the swap file on a different disk. You may want to use a different disk because it has more free space (allowing you to have more virtual memory) or you may want to use another disk because it is a faster disk drive (improving performance). All of the available disks are listed in the drop-down list box, as well as the amount of free disk space on each disk.

To change the default location for the swap file, follow these steps:

1. Click the Start Menu.
2. Choose Settings, Control Panel.
3. Open the System icon by double-clicking it.
4. Select the Performance tab.
5. Click Virtual Memory.
6. Select the Let Me Specify My Own Virtual Memory Settings option.
7. Show the list of available drives by clicking the down arrow at the far right of the Hard Disk drop-down text box.
8. Click the disk you want to use for the swap file.
9. Choose OK.

Note

Windows 95 is constantly reading and writing to the swap file. Reading and writing to a compressed drive is slower than reading and writing to a non-compressed drive. This is because you have the overhead of compressing and uncompressing data when you read and write it. So, for the best performance, you shouldn't locate the swap file on a compressed drive.

However, if you need more virtual memory than you can fit on any non-compressed drive, you can use a compressed drive. While it works more slowly, you will be able to run more programs simultaneously. For example, if you run large programs, like Word and Excel, and you are using OLE to share data between them, you will need a lot of memory. If you run out of memory using the default swap file, your only option to get everything to work may be to put the virtual memory swap file on a compressed drive.

Set Minimum

You can specify the smallest swap file that Windows 95 will create. If you know you are going to be needing a lot of memory—because you are running several programs or manipulating a large amount of data—you can have Windows 95 pre-allocate the memory. If you don't, you may notice an additional delay as you load new programs or data and Windows 95 has to grow the swap file to increase the amount of virtual memory.

To specify the minimum size for the swap file, follow these steps:

1. Click the Start Menu.
2. Choose Settings, Control Panel.
3. Open the System icon by double-clicking it.
4. Select the Performance tab.
5. Click Virtual Memory.
6. Select the Let Me Specify My Own Virtual Memory Settings option.
7. In the Minimum edit field, type in the size for the smallest swap file (in megabytes).
8. Choose OK.

Caution

Windows 95 will not let you set the minimum memory less than 12M (the total of your physical RAM and virtual memory). However, if you do set your total memory to 12M, you may have problems trying to run additional programs, work with OLE documents, and so on. If you plan to run any large program or work with OLE objects, keep the minimum memory to at least 16M.

Set Maximum

Windows 95 will grow the swap file for virtual memory as large as it needs, unless you set a maximum size. If you don't need a certain amount of space left over, you don't need to set a maximum. However, if you know you need a certain amount of space available for an application to use, you will need to set the maximum value. For example, if you have 20M of room left on your hard disk and know that you will need 5M free for downloading a file, limit the swap file to 15M.

To set the maximum size of the swap file, follow these steps:

1. Select the Let Me Specify My Own Virtual Memory Settings option.
2. In the Maximum edit field, type in the size for the largest swap file (in megabytes).
3. Choose OK.

Tip

You can also get to the System properties sheet page by right-clicking the My Computer icon on the desktop. This will bring up a context menu. Choose Properties, and the System property sheet will open.

Improving Hard Disk Performance

The performance of your hard disk will affect the performance of your system under Windows 95. This happens for several reasons. First, the time it takes to load programs and data files affects performance. Second, since Windows 95 uses the hard disk as virtual memory, maintaining your hard disk's efficiency affects overall performance. Windows 95 provides three tools to help you maintain your hard disk:

- *ScanDisk*. Error checking and correction
- *Disk Defragmenter*. Organizes files into contiguous files
- *Backup*. Make backup copies of files on your hard disk

Given the "object" oriented nature of Windows 95, you can easily keep your hard disk in top condition by working from the properties sheet of the hard disk itself. The individual property pages provide you with information about the drive and ways to easily access the tools you'll use to maintain the drive.

To access the properties of a drive, follow these steps:

1. Open the My Computer folder by double-clicking the My Computer icon on the desktop.
2. Right-click the drive to bring up its context menu.
3. Choose Properties.

The Properties sheet normally contains three pages. These are

- *General*. Displays drive information such as disk label, disk type, and disk usage
- *Tools*. Provides easy access to ScanDisk, Disk Defragmenter, and Backup, as well as informing you of how many days ago you last ran these tools
- *Sharing*. Allows you to control how, and if, you share this drive with other networked users

By selecting the Tools tab, the page shown in figure 13.2 appears. From this page, you can quickly run any of the three disk maintenance tools. The examples in the remainder of this chapter run the disk maintenance tools from the Start menu. But remember, by selecting the "object"—the disk—and choosing its properties, you can access all of the tools from one location.

Perform Error-Checking

While Windows 95 is a much more robust operating system than the DOS–Windows 3.1x combination, the files on your computer are still vulnerable to application errors. When an application crashes—or worse—crashes your entire system, your files and folders may get a bit scrambled. Left unfixed, these scrambled files and folders can produce a domino effect, causing more crashes and further scrambling your disk. Fortunately, Windows 95 comes with ScanDisk, a tool that unscrambles your files and folders.

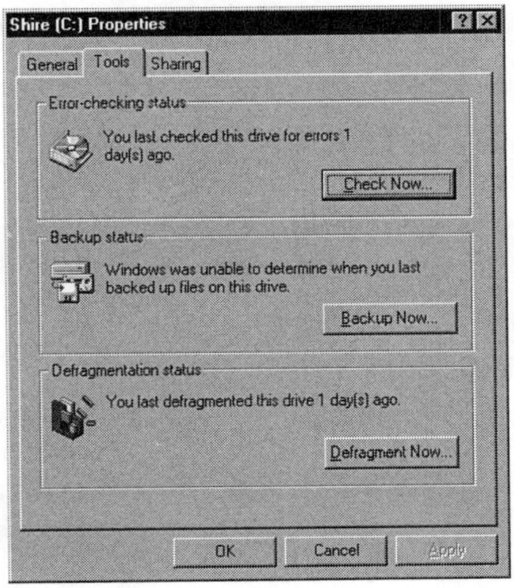

Fig. 13.2
Using the Properties sheet box to configure a drive.

> **Note**
>
> If you did not install ScanDisk, refer to Chapter 4, "Using Custom Installation Options," for information on how to install individual components.

ScanDisk checks your hard drive(s) for any problems. ScanDisk can perform one of two types of tests: *Standard* and *Thorough*. A Standard test checks the file system for errors such as fragments of files or cross-linked files. A Thorough test adds a surface scan test to the Standard test, which helps to detect when a portion of the hard disk is beginning to malfunction.

> **Note**
>
> A Thorough test takes much longer to complete than a Standard test. Depending on the size and speed of your hard disk and your computer's speed, a Thorough test can take a long time to complete. You should either perform a Thorough test on a monthly basis, or if you suspect a problem.

Performing a Standard ScanDisk

To run a Standard ScanDisk on a drive, follow these steps:

1. From the Start Menu, select Programs, Accessories, System Tools, ScanDisk.

2. Select the drive you want ScanDisk to check for errors.

3. Click Standard, or press Alt+D.

4. Choose Start, or press Alt+S.

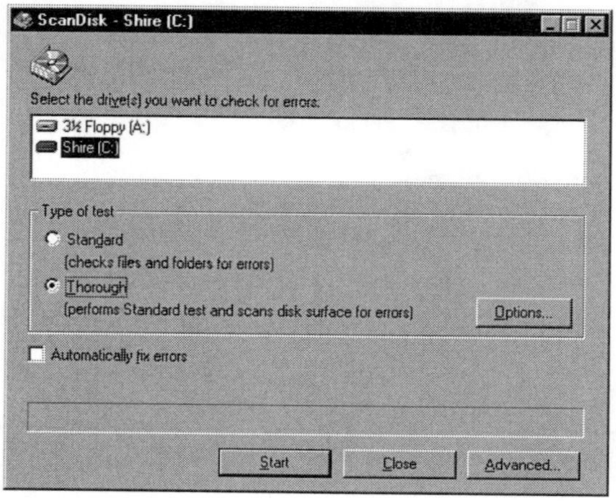

Fig. 13.3
You can perform a Thorough test on drive C.

Setting Advanced ScanDisk Options

You can customize the behavior of ScanDisk by choosing the Advanced button in the ScanDisk main window. The dialog box shown in Figure 13.4 appears.

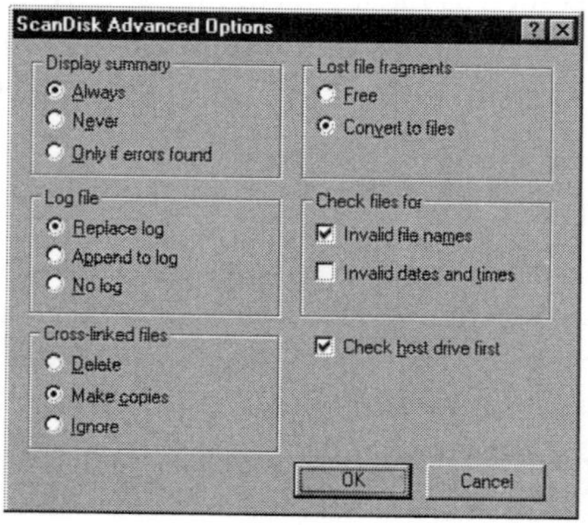

Fig. 13.4
Set advanced options for ScanDisk in the ScanDisk Advanced Options dialog box.

From this dialog box, you can set the following options:

- If and when to display the results of the ScanDisk test
- If and how to create a log file of the test
- How to handle cross-linked files

- How to handle lost file fragments
- What file information to check
- Whether or not to check the host drive of a compressed volume

Select each item by clicking the corresponding radio button or check box. You can also press Alt+the underlined character for each item. For example, to select to always display a summary, you would press Alt+A.

ScanDisk allows you to control six different aspects of its behavior. These are

- *Display Summary*. After ScanDisk finishes testing the drive, it can display a summary of the test. You can choose to always have the results displayed if you wanted to verify any of the hard disk statistics—size, number of files, allocation unit size, and so on. You can choose to never display the results if you automatically run ScanDisk during Start Up. Your third option is to only display the results if an error was detected.
- *Log File*. You can choose to have ScanDisk create a log file. This file contains detailed results of the test. The file is created in the root folder of each drive that is tested and is called, you guessed it—SCANDISK.LOG. You have three choices—always create a new log file (Replace log), add on to the existing log file (Append to log), or never create a log file (No log).
- *Cross-linked Files*. Cross-linked files occur when two (or more) files all use the same part of the disk. When ScanDisk detects a cross-linked file, you can have ScanDisk perform one of three actions. First, ScanDisk can Delete all files containing the cross-link. Second, ScanDisk can Make Copies of the cross-linked information for each file. Third, ScanDisk can simply Ignore the cross-link and continue.
- *Lost File Fragments*. ScanDisk may encounter pieces of data that are no longer contained in any file. You can have ScanDisk either free the data and reclaim that portion of the disk as free space, or you can have ScanDisk convert the data into a file. If you select the latter option, the file will be saved in the root folder of the drive, and given names like `File0000` or `Dir0000` (if the data was part of a folder).
- *Check Files For*. ScanDisk can also check files to make sure that file names, file dates, and file times are all valid. If any invalid information is discovered, ScanDisk will prompt you and ask whether it should fix the problem.

- *Check Host Drive First.* If the drive you want ScanDisk to check is compressed with either DoubleSpace or DriveSpace, you can specify whether or not ScanDisk checks the uncompressed host drive for errors first. Only deselect this option if you have already checked the host drive for errors.

Performing a Thorough ScanDisk

To run a Thorough ScanDisk on a drive, follow these steps:

1. From the Start Menu, select Programs, Accessories, System Tools, ScanDisk.
2. Select the drive you want ScanDisk to check for errors.
3. Select Thorough, or press Alt+T.
4. Choose Start, or press Alt+S.

Setting Thorough ScanDisk Options

If you want ScanDisk to perform a thorough test, you may set several options. These options allow you to customize how ScanDisk will perform the surface scan portion of the test (see fig. 13.5). These options allow you to

- Select the areas of the disk to scan
- Restrict ScanDisk to only reading from the disk
- Restrict the types of files that ScanDisk will repair

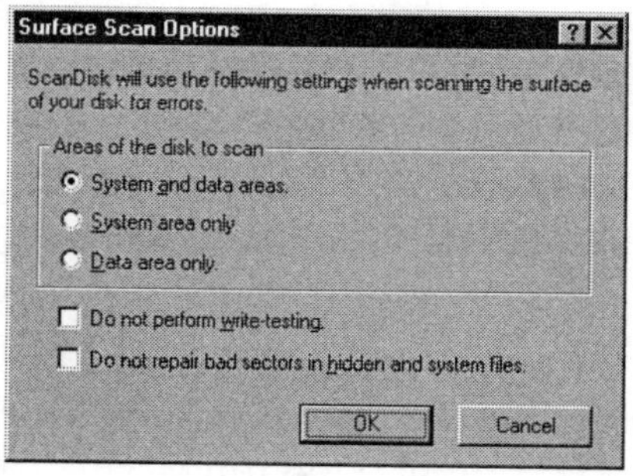

Fig. 13.5
Set ScanDisk to scan both the system and data areas of the disk.

ScanDisk allows you to control three aspects of its Thorough disk test. These are

- *Areas of the Disk to Scan.* You can specify ScanDisk to scan your entire disk, only the system portion of your disk, or only the data portion of your disk.

- *Do Not Perform Write-Testing*. Normally, to perform the surface test on a disk, ScanDisk will read and write to the drive. You may disable the writing to the disk by selecting this option.
- *Do Not Repair Bad Sectors in Hidden and System Files*. If ScanDisk finds errors, it will move the information to another location on the drive. Normally, you should allow ScanDisk to repair these errors. However, a few older programs require that certain hidden files not be moved. If they are moved, the programs may not work properly. If you run older programs that use this technique as a copy protection scheme, then disable this type of repair.

Automatically Fix Errors

You can have ScanDisk automatically repair errors that it discovers. To set this option, follow these steps:

1. From the Start Menu, select Programs, Accessories, System Tools, ScanDisk.
2. Select the drive you want ScanDisk to check for errors.
3. Select Automatically Fix Errors, or press Alt+F.
4. Choose Start, or press Alt+S.

If you choose to have ScanDisk automatically fix errors, set the advanced options so that

- You make copies of cross-linked files.
- You convert lost fragments into files.
- You append new information to your existing log file.

By setting these options, you will prevent ScanDisk from removing information from your disk without your approval. You need to periodically review the log file to see what ScanDisk has done. At that time, you can delete or recover any files ScanDisk created.

Tip

You can run ScanDisk on several drives at once. To do this, when you select the disk on which to run ScanDisk, press Ctrl and click each drive you want to check for errors.

Tip

Plus!

You can automate the running of ScanDisk by installing Plus Pack's System Agent. With System Agent, you can schedule when any program—especially the disk maintenance tools—will run.

Troubleshooting

I've tried to run ScanDisk, but it says it can't fix a problem it found.

ScanDisk may be unable to repair errors for files that are in use while ScanDisk runs. Since Windows 95 itself has many files in use, ScanDisk may not be able to completely repair all the errors it finds. To fix these errors, select Shut Down from the Start menu and choose Restart the Computer in MS-DOS mode. Then, run the DOS version of ScanDisk. This file is located in the WINDOWS\COMMAND folder.

Performing Backup

The Backup tool provided with Windows 95 will copy the files on your computer to either floppy disks or supported tape drives. There are two main ways to use Backup. First, the application can be used in a manual mode. In this mode, the Backup program looks and behaves very much like the Explorer. You manually select the folders and files you want to backup. In the second method, you can use the Backup program by creating backup sets. With backup sets, you can back up files using a simple drag-and-drop operation.

Caution

The Windows 95 Backup tool does not support all tape drives. It supports QIC 40, 80, 3010, and 3020 tapes drives connected to the primary floppy disk controller and QIC 40, 80, and 3010 Colorado tape drives connected to the parallel port. It does not support SCSI tape drives. Existing Windows 3.1 backup programs that support SCSI drives should not be used. Because they do not support long file names, backing up and restoring files using one of these programs makes Windows 95 stop working.

Performing a Manual Backup

To perform a manual backup, follow these steps:

1. From the Start Menu, select Programs, Accessories, System Tools, Backup.

2. Select the folders and files you want to back up by clicking the small rectangle to the right of each folder or file (see fig. 13.6). Drives, folders, or files that are selected for Backup have a check mark in the box. Those files that are not selected for Backup will be empty. If the box for a drive or folder is shaded gray, it means that some items within it are selected for backup, and some are not.

3. Choose Next Step.

4. Select where you back up the folders and files to by clicking the disk drive or tape drive you want. For example, to back up the files to the floppy disks, click one of your floppy drives in the Select a Destination for the Backup window.

5. Start the backup by choosing Start Backup.

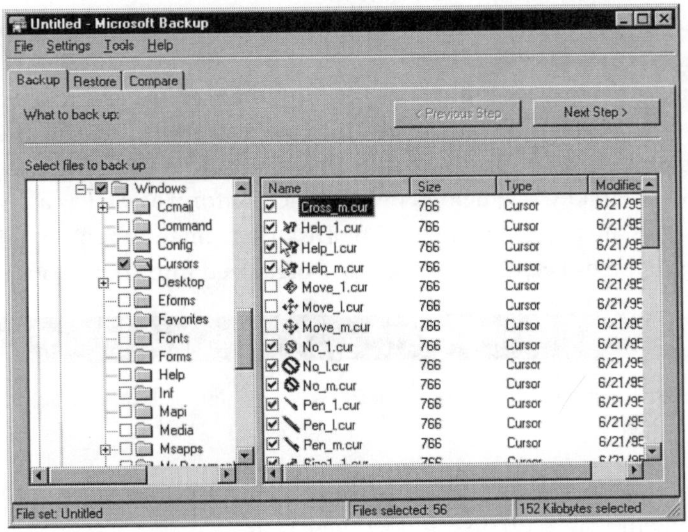

Fig. 13.6
Use Backup to back up the Windows/Cursor folder, except for the "move" cursors.

Using Backup File Sets

Backup file sets make backing up specific sets of files to specific locations easy. After you have created backup sets, you can simply drag-and-drop a set onto the Backup application icon to perform the backup. This icon is located in the Program Files\Accessories folder. To simplify the backup process, you can drag this icon to your desktop so it is always available.

To create a backup set, follow these steps:

1. From the Start Menu, select Programs, Accessories, System Tools, Backup.
2. Select the folders and files you want to back up by clicking the small rectangle to the right of each folder or file.
3. Choose Next Step.
4. Select where you want to back up the folders and files to by clicking the disk drive or tape drive you want to use.
5. Choose File, Save As to save the backup file set definition.

After you have created Backup file sets, you can launch the Backup tool and then choose File, Open File Set to use one of the file sets. Alternately, you can open the folder containing your backup sets and drag-and-drop the Backup file set onto the Backup application icon.

Defragment Hard Disk

Over time, as a hard disk is used—as files are saved, edited and resaved, and deleted—the files become fragmented into pieces scattered on the disk. Then, when a file needs to be loaded, it takes longer to load the file because it is not in one piece. A badly fragmented disk will not perform as well as a disk where all of the files are neatly organized. The Disk Defragmenter tool supplied by Windows 95 helps keep files on your disk organized into contiguous pieces.

Plus!

Tip

The System Agent in Microsoft Plus! will schedule and automatically run Disk Defragmenter for you.

◀ See "Using Microsoft Plus!," p. 26

To defragment your hard disk, follow these steps:

1. From the Start menu, select Programs, Accessories, System Tools, Disk Defragmenter.
2. Select the drive you want defragmented by choosing the drive from the list in the drop-down list box (see fig. 13.7).
3. Choose OK, or press Enter.
4. Choose Start, or press Alt+S.

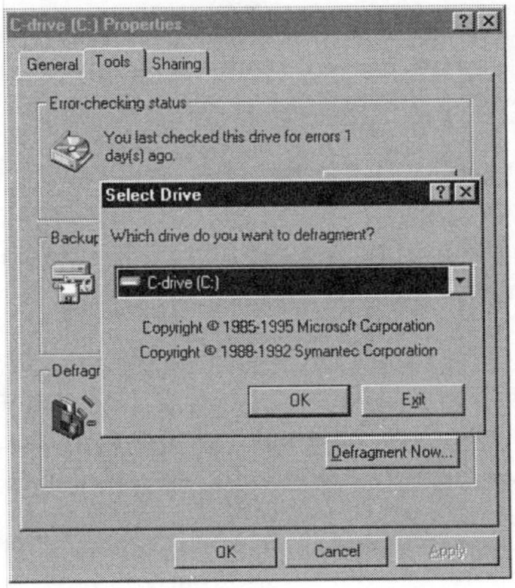

Fig. 13.7
The Disk Defragmenter can defragment a drive you choose, such as the C drive.

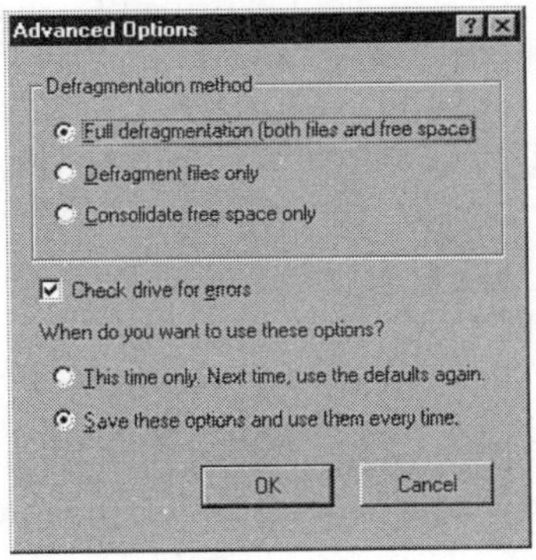

Fig. 13.8
Set the Disk Defragmenter to perform a full defragmentation.

Setting Advanced Disk Defragmenter Options

You can control how Disk Defragmenter works by setting the Advanced options (see fig. 13.8).

To set advanced options, follow these steps:

1. From the Start menu, select Programs, Accessories, System Tools, Disk Defragmenter.
2. Choose the drive you want defragmented by selecting the drive from the list in the drop-down list box.
3. Choose OK, or press Enter.
4. Click Advanced, or press Alt+A.
5. Select the options you want by clicking the corresponding radio button or check box. These are described in the following section.

Advanced Options

You may select the Defragmentation Method. You have three choices:

- *Full Defragmentation (Both Files and Free Space).* You may choose to have Disk Defragmenter perform both operations. It will rearrange your files so each file is contiguous and so you have one large contiguous free space available. This is the best method of defragmenting your disk; it also takes the most time to complete.
- *Defragment Files Only.* First, you may select to only have Disk Defragmenter rearrange your files, making each existing file contiguous. However, when the Disk Defragmenter tool rearranges your files in this manner, any new files you add to your system will likely be fragmented.
- *Consolidate Free Space Only.* You may select to only have Disk Defragmenter rearrange your files so that you have one large, contiguous, free space on your disk. Any new files you add to your system will not defragment. However, your existing files may actually wind up being more fragmented.

Disk Defragmenter will check a drive for errors before it attempts to defragment the drive. However, you can disable this error-checking by deselecting Check Drive For Errors. Only disable this feature if you are positive that the drive doesn't have any errors. For example, if you have just run ScanDisk on the drive, you could disable the error-checking.

After you have set the advanced disk defragmentation options, you can either save these options to be used whenever Disk Defragmenter is run, or you can use these options for the current session only. Make this selection by choosing either Save These Options and Use Them Every Time or This Time Only Next Time Use the Defaults Again.

Using the Device Manager

While Windows 95 supports Plug-and-Play hardware devices, most of the devices in use are not Plug-and-Play devices. Windows 95 consolidates the management of all of these different devices into one central spot—the Device Manager. With the Device Manager, you can quickly see all the devices in your system and change the setting for any device.

Changing Device Properties

To change the properties of a device using the Device Manager, follow these steps:

1. Right-click My Computer.
2. Choose Properties. The System Properties sheet opens.
3. Select the Device Manager tab in the System Properties sheet. The Device Manager page opens (see fig. 13.9).
4. Click the plus sign in the small rectangle to the left of the type of device you want. This expands the item, showing all of the devices of that type in your system. For example, by clicking the DISK DRIVES folder, the tree expands to show all physical drives in the system.
5. Click the device you want to modify or examine.
6. Choose Properties.

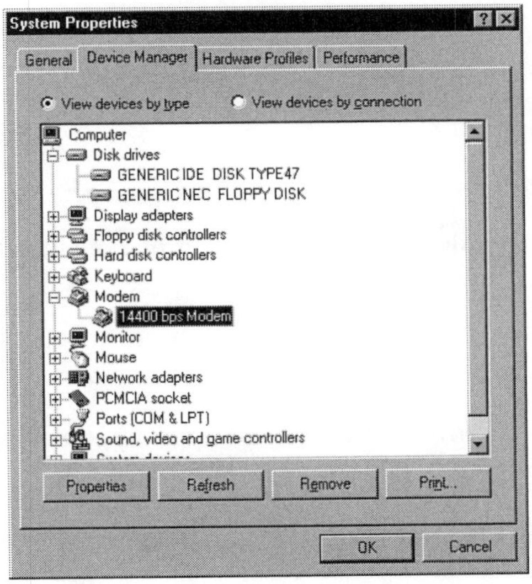

Fig. 13.9
The Device Manager page enables you to change the properties of a device.

While the property sheet for each device is unique, you will see standard pages. All devices have a General page. The General page lists the following information:

- Device name
- Device type
- Manufacturer
- Hardware version
- Device status
- Device usage

Changing Device Resources

Some devices will only have the General page. However, if the device uses system resources, such as IRQ settings, the device will also have a Resources page.

To change the resources for a device, follow these steps:

1. Right-click My Computer.
2. Choose Properties.
3. Select the Device Manager tab in the System Properties dialog box.
4. Click the plus sign in the small rectangle to the left of the type of device you want. This expands the item, showing all of the devices of that type in your system. For example, by selecting the DISK DRIVES folder, the tree expands to show all physical drives in the system.
5. Click the device you want to modify or examine.
6. Choose Properties.
7. Choose the Resources tab. The Resources page opens (see fig. 13.10).
8. If the Use Automatic Settings check box is marked, deselect it; or press Alt+U.
9. Click the resource type you want to change in the Resource Settings list box.
10. Choose Change Settings. A dialog box appears, allowing you to edit the specific resource settings.

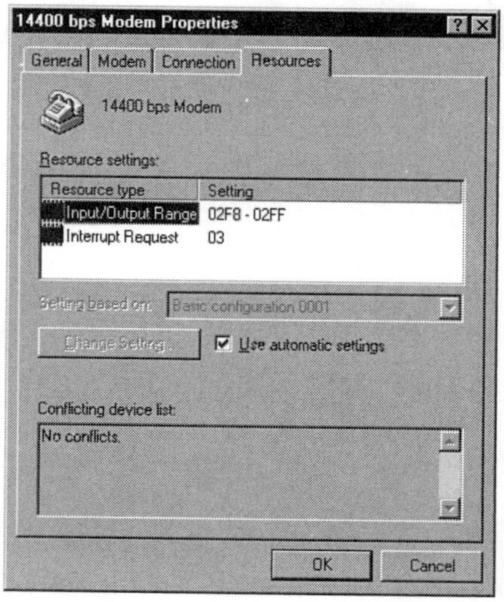

Fig. 13.10
You can change the resources used by a modem in this page.

Troubleshooting

I changed the resource for one of my devices and now Windows 95 won't restart.

If you can't restart Windows 95, restart your computer and when the words `Starting Windows 95...` appear on your monitor, press F8. The Windows 95 Startup menu appears. Select Safe mode to restart Windows in a default configuration. You should be able to go back and undo your changes using Device Manager.

Changing Device Drivers

Some devices will have a driver associated with it. If a device does have a device driver, there will be a Driver page. This page displays the following information:

- Device name
- Driver files—the files that are used by the driver
- File details—information about the driver, such as the company that wrote the driver and version of the driver

To change the driver for a device, follow these steps:

1. Right-click My Computer.
2. Choose Properties.
3. Select the Device Manager tab in the System Properties dialog box.
4. Click the plus sign in the small rectangle to the left of the type of device you want. This expands the item, showing all the devices of that type in your system. For example, by clicking the DISK DRIVES folder, the tree expands to show all physical drives in the system.
5. Click the device you want to modify or examine.
6. Choose Properties.
7. Select the Driver tab. The Driver page opens (see fig. 13.11).
8. Choose Change Driver. The Select Device dialog box appears, allowing you to install a new device driver.

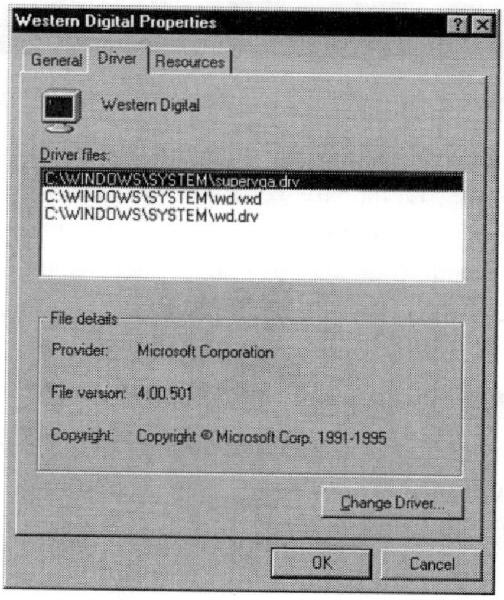

Fig. 13.11
You can change a device driver to a display device.

Chapter 14

Using Norton Desktop Utilities with Windows 95

by Kevin Jones

Norton Utilities for Windows 95 is a package of data protection and recovery utility programs designed specifically for Windows 95. These utility programs can be broadly divided into three categories.

First, there are DOS versions of the utility programs. These are used prior to installing Windows 95 to make sure that your computer is top shape. They are also used in the unfortunate event that your system crashes and cannot run Windows 95.

The second category includes the Windows 95 utility programs. These are 32-bit programs designed to fully exploit the power of Windows 95.

The final category contains a single program—System Doctor. Whereas the other programs recover data or analyze your computer for problems, System Doctor continuously monitors your computer and automatically invokes the necessary utilities to correct any problems.

In this chapter, you learn how to

- Tune-up your system prior to installing Windows 95
- Install Norton Utilities for Windows 95
- Configure the behavior of the individual utilities

- Customize the appearance of the individual utilities
- Uninstall Norton Utilities for Windows 95

Note

Although this is the latest release of Norton Utilities, this is not Norton Utilities 9.0. In other words, this is not an upgrade from Norton Utilities 8.0, but rather is designed specifically for Windows 95. Norton Utilities 8.0 will continue to be sold for the Windows 3.1 platform. While there are some components in Norton Utilities 8.0 that are not included in Norton Utilities for Windows 95, there are some totally new components included in Norton Utilities for Windows 95 (for example, System Doctor).

Performing a Pre-Installation TuneUp

The Norton Utilities for Windows 95 contains a collection of DOS-based utilities specifically designed to be run before you install Windows 95. These utilities make sure that your computer is ready to be upgraded to Windows 95. This is called the *Pre-Installation TuneUp* or P.I.T.

The P.I.T. consists of the following three main steps:

- Using Norton Disk Doctor to make sure that your disk is free of errors.
- Using Norton Diagnostics to make sure that you don't have any hardware problems, such as device conflicts.
- Using SpaceWizard to free up as much room as possible on your disk.

Note

A full installation of Windows 95 requires more than 80M. This is substantially more hard disk space than Windows 3.1 required. Because of this and the fact that new 32-bit Windows 95 applications require even more hard disk space, it is very important to clean up your hard disk before you install Windows 95.

To run the Pre-Installation TuneUp, follow these steps:

1. If you are in Windows, exit Windows. The P.I.T. can only be run from DOS.
2. Insert the Norton Emergency Disk.

3. Change to the floppy drive where you inserted the Emergency Disk (for example, A).
4. Type **TUNEUP** and press Enter.
5. Select the drive you want to install Windows 95 onto.

> **Tip**
>
> You can also run the P.I.T. on other drives. Simply rerun TuneUp and select another drive.

6. Click OK.
7. Follow the step-by-step instructions to complete the tune-up. The exact steps vary depending on any problems that may be found.

> **Note**
>
> After you complete the P.I.T. and install Windows 95, you may still find it useful to run the P.I.T. Some of the extensive diagnostic tests available in Norton Diagnostics can only be fully used when executing in MS-DOS mode. To get into MS-DOS mode, select Shut Down from the Start Menu and choose Restart the Computer in MS-DOS Mode. Then follow the preceding steps.

Checking Your Disk with Norton Disk Doctor (DOS)

The DOS version of Norton Disk Doctor analyzes your hard disk for any problems and repairs any problems that it discovers. Although this is a DOS version, it was written for the Windows 95 file system. This means that it can detect and correct problems with long file names (LFN). This is especially important for dealing with serious disk problems that occur after you've installed Windows 95. If the problem is serious enough to prevent Windows 95 from loading and running, you won't be able to use any of the Windows-based applications to fix the problems.

To run Norton Disk Doctor (DOS), follow these steps:

1. Make sure that you run Norton Disk Doctor from MS-DOS mode. If you are running Windows 3.1, exit Windows. If you are running Windows 95, restart the computer in MS-DOS mode.
2. Insert the Norton Emergency Disk or change to the directory where you installed Norton Utilities.
3. Type **NDD** and press Enter.

4. Select Diagnose Disk, or press Alt+D.
5. Select the Drive you want to diagnose.
6. Choose Diagnose, or press Alt+D.
7. If any errors are found, Norton Disk Doctor prompts you before taking any corrective action. NDD walks you through step-by-step to fix the problem.
8. After the test is complete, choose Skip Test (unless you suspect that your drive has physical damage).
9. Select Done, or press Alt+D.
10. You can now diagnose another disk by choosing Diagnose again, or you can choose Quit Disk Doctor if you are finished.

Checking Your Hardware with Norton Diagnostics (DOS)

Norton Diagnostics analyzes your computer to make sure that no problems exist. Although it can be used to test individual components, it can also be used to run the complete set of tests. After each test, you can automatically run the next test. By using this method, you exhaustively test your entire system prior to upgrading to Windows 95.

To run Norton Diagnostics, follow these steps:

1. Make sure that you run Norton Disk Doctor from MS-DOS mode. If you are running Windows 3.1, exit Windows. If you are running Windows 95, restart the computer in MS-DOS mode.
2. Insert the Norton Emergency Disk or change to the directory where you installed Norton Utilities.
3. Type **NDIAGS** and press Enter.
4. Read the Description dialog box.
5. Disconnect all peripherals connected to your computer—printer, modem, and so on—except for your mouse.
6. Choose OK.
7. Let the testing begin!

As Norton Diagnostics takes you step by step through each test, it provides you with a Description of the test and any options you have. After you choose OK (your only choice), the testing begins. After each test is complete, choose Next Test to continue. Norton Diagnostics performs the following tests:

- System Information
- System Board
- Serial Port(s)
- Parallel Port(s)
- CMOS
- IRQ Status
- Base Memory
- Extended Memory
- Hard disk(s)
- Floppy disk(s)
- Video RAM
- Video Mode (Text modes)
- Video Grid (Graphic modes)
- Video Color
- Video Attributes
- Speaker
- Keyboard Press
- Keyboard Lights

Troubleshooting

I was running Norton Diagnostics and my system just stopped running. What should I do now?

If your system crashes or freezes during a test, reboot your machine and restart NDIAGS. This time, instead of restarting all the tests, use the menus to restart the test that the computer failed on. Norton Diagnostics tracks where it was at in the testing and attempts to further diagnose what caused the failure.

While the actual time it will take to run the complete set of tests will vary depending on how fast your machine is, how much memory you have installed, how large and fast your hard disk is, and so on, you should expect the testing to take around 15 minutes on a fast machine, or 30 minutes on a slow machine.

Cleaning Up Your Disk with SpaceWizard (DOS)

SpaceWizard checks your hard disk for any files that can be deleted or moved to another volume. SpaceWizard looks for files that are normally temporary in nature (for example, TMP files, files in the Windows TEMP folder), commonly discardable files (for example, BAK files), and very large files. After scanning your disk, you have to explicitly choose to delete the files, so don't worry about accidentally deleting important files.

To run SpaceWizard, follow these steps:

1. Make sure that you run SpaceWizard from MS-DOS mode. If you are running Windows 3.1, exit Windows. If you are running Windows 95, restart the computer in MS-DOS mode.
2. Insert the Norton Emergency Disk or change to the directory where you installed Norton Utilities.
3. Type **SPACEWZD** and press Enter.
4. Select the drive you want to analyze and choose Next, or press Alt+N.
5. Deselect any temporary files you don't want to delete or move, and click Next, or press Alt+N.
6. Deselect any discardable files you don't want to delete or move, and choose Next, or press Alt+N.
7. Select the smallest file to include (the default is 10M). Remember, SpaceWizard is looking for a few really large files that will free up a lot of space, so don't set this value too small.
8. Deselect any large files you don't want to delete or move, and choose Next, or press Alt+N.
9. You can either choose to Delete Files, Move Files, or do nothing.

Troubleshooting

I accidentally deleted some important files using SpaceWizard. What now?

Not to worry; you can run the DOS version of UnErase to recover any files you inadvertently deleted. You must run UnErase before you run any other programs. You can run UnErase by typing **UNERASE** at the DOS prompt.

Installing Norton Utilities for Windows 95

After you have successfully completed the Pre-Installation TuneUp and you have upgraded your computer to Windows 95, you are ready to install Norton Utilities. The Symantec installation program is used by all the Symantec utility packages for Windows 95 (Norton Utilities, Norton Anti-Virus, and Norton Navigator) and follows the guidelines outlined by

Microsoft for installation programs. The installation program allows you to either perform a complete installation of Norton Utilities or a custom installation, installing just the components you want. In either case, the installation program uses a Setup Wizard to walk you step-by-step through the installation process (see fig. 14.1).

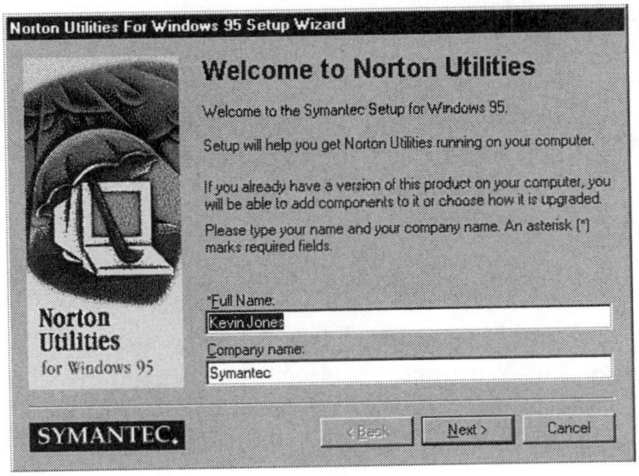

Fig. 14.1
Use the Setup Wizard to install Norton Utilities for Windows 95.

Performing a Complete Installation

A complete installation of Norton Utilities requires about 14M of hard disk space. This installs all the following Windows utilities:

- Image
- Norton Disk Doctor
- Rescue Disk
- Speed Disk
- SpaceWizard
- System Information

And all the DOS utilities:

- Disk Editor
- Norton Diagnostics
- Norton Disk Doctor
- SpaceWizard
- UnErase
- UnFormat

To perform a complete installation of Norton Utilities, follow these steps:

1. Open My Computer by double-clicking the My Computer icon on the Desktop.
2. Open the drive containing the Norton Utilities installation files (floppy, CD, or network drive). If you are on a network drive, you will have to open the folder containing the installation files.

3. Start the installation program by double-clicking SETUP.
4. Type in (or verify) your name and, optionally, your company and choose Next.
5. After reading the License Agreement, choose Next.
6. Select Complete installation and choose Next.
7. After Setup explores your disk for other versions of Norton products, specify where you want to install Norton Utilities.
8. If you want to be able to simply type in the command name when running the DOS versions of the Norton Utilities, you must check Add Program Location to Path.
9. Choose Next.
10. If you want to add Norton file deletion protection to the protection already offered by Windows 95, check Add Norton Protection to the Recycle Bin.
11. Choose Next.
12. If you want to use System Doctor to continuously monitor your computer, check Run Norton System Doctor Every Time Windows Starts.

> **Note**
>
> If you later want to stop System Doctor from automatically running every time you start Windows, open the Windows StartUp folder and delete the shortcut to Norton System Doctor.

13. Choose Next.
14. If you want to create a rescue disk now, check Yes.
15. Choose Next.
16. Review your installation settings and choose Next.
17. Setup now copies the files. If you are installing from floppy disks, you are prompted when you need to switch disks.
18. If you selected to create a rescue disk, Setup runs rescue disk now. Simply insert a floppy disk and choose Save.

19. A series of informative screens appear by the installation program. After reading each one, simply choose Next until you reach the final screen.

20. At this point, choose Finish to complete the installation.

Performing a Custom Installation

If you don't want to install all 14M of Norton Utilities, you can perform a custom installation. You can choose to install only the DOS or only the Windows utilities, or you can select the exact mix of DOS and Windows utilities you want.

To perform a custom installation of Norton Utilities, follow these steps:

1. Open My Computer by double-clicking the My Computer icon on the Desktop.
2. Open the drive containing the Norton Utilities installation files (floppy, CD, or network drive). If you are on a network drive, you have to open the folder containing the installation files.
3. Start the installation program by double-clicking SETUP.
4. Type (or verify) your name and, optionally, your company and choose Next.
5. After reading the License Agreement, choose Next.
6. Select Custom installation, and choose Next.
7. To install all of the Windows utilities, check Norton Windows Utilities (see fig. 14.2). To install only some of the Windows utilities, click Select (across from Norton Windows Utilities). Then select the utilities you want to install.

Tip

While the exact mix of components to install during a custom install depends on many factors, a simple recommendation is to create a rescue disk with all DOS utilities and to install all of the Windows utilities. Since you will almost always be in a Windows environment, and since the Windows utilities help keep your system running smoothly (thereby avoiding problems), these are the best candidates for installing on your computer.

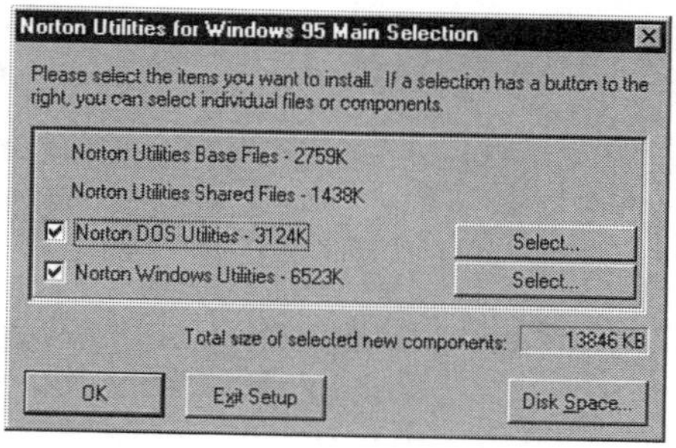

Fig. 14.2
Use the Setup Wizard to select components to install.

8. To install all of the DOS utilities, select Norton DOS Utilities. To install only some of the DOS utilities, click Select (across from Norton DOS Utilities). Then check the utilities you want to install.
9. Click Next.
10. After Install explores your disk for other versions of Norton products, specify where you want to install Norton Utilities.
11. If you want to be able to simply type in the command name when running the DOS versions of the Norton Utilities, you must select Add Program Location to Path.
12. Click Next.
13. If you want to add Norton file deletion protection to the protection already offered by Windows 95, select Add Norton Protection to the Recycle Bin.
14. Click Next.
15. If you want to use System Doctor to continuously monitor your computer, select Run Norton System Doctor Every Time Windows Starts.
16. Click Next.
17. If you want to create a rescue disk now, select Yes.
18. Click Next.
19. Review your Install settings, support policies, and so on, and click Next after each step.
20. Setup now copies the files. If you are installing from floppy disks, you are prompted when you need to switch disks.
21. If you selected to create a rescue disk, Setup will run Rescue Disk now. Simply insert a floppy disk and choose Save.

22. The installation program displays a series of informative screens. After reading each one, simply click Next until you reach the final screen. At this point, click Finish, and the installation is complete.

Configuring Norton Utilities for Windows 95

The programs in Norton Utilities for Windows 95 are highly configurable. You can change the appearance of the programs. This can be anything from changing colors and fonts to changing the amount of information displayed during execution. You can change advanced options. These include controlling exactly which tests are executed and controlling background operation. You can also configure whether each utility should run during Windows startup.

> **Note**
>
> If you are using System Doctor, you won't need to run any utility during Windows startup. System Doctor continuously runs in the background and monitors your system. If any of the parameters Disk Doctor is monitoring exceed their limits—and Disk Doctor can monitor a lot of stuff—it automatically takes action. Disk Doctor either invokes the needed utilities to fix any problems or alerts you so that you can take care of the problem.

Configuring System Doctor

System Doctor (see fig. 14.3) is like an automobile dashboard. It is a collection of gauges and monitors that show the status of various parameters. System Doctor is capable of tracking and measuring more than 80 different system resources. You can configure System Doctor in several ways. You can alter its appearance, screen colors, fonts, gauge size, and so on. You can also change the resources it is monitoring. You can configure specific gauges, both in appearance and functionality.

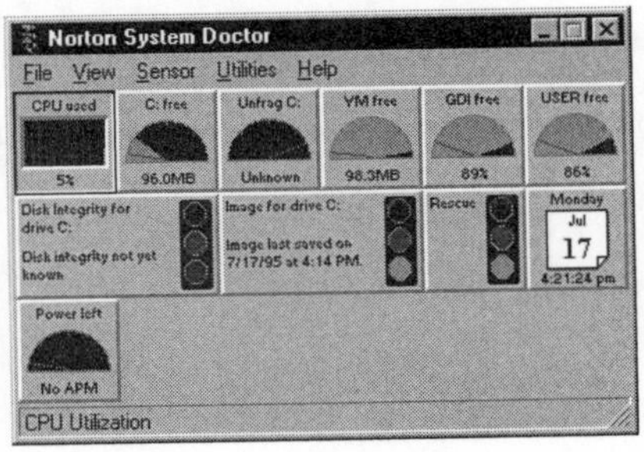

Fig. 14.3
The Norton System Doctor is the program that you will probably interact with the most.

Configuring the System Doctor Window

To change the appearance of the System Doctor, follow these steps:

1. Right-click System Doctor.
2. On the pop-up context menu, choose View, Options.
3. Select the Appearance page.
4. To change the colors of the items of System Doctor, select an Item in the drop-down list box and choose Color.
5. To change the order of the gauges, select a gauge in the Sensor Order list box and then choose Up or Down.
6. Select how you want the window to display.
7. Select if you want System Doctor to automatically load when Windows starts.
8. Choose OK.

To change the size of all the gauges, follow these steps:

1. Right-click System Doctor.
2. On the pop-up context menu, choose File, Options.
3. Select the Dimensions page.
4. To change the size of the gauge, click the horizontal and/or vertical sliders. While holding down your mouse button, drag the sliders to make the gauge larger or smaller.
5. To change the font on the gauge, choose Normal and select the font you want to use.
6. To change the font used in the Date & Time and Up Time sensors, choose Calendar and select the font you want to use.
7. Choose OK.

To change the resources that System Doctor monitors, follow these steps:

1. Right-click System Doctor.
2. On the pop-up context menu, choose View, Options.
3. Select the Active Sensors page.
4. To add more Sensors, click the sensor you want to add in the Available Sensors list box and choose Add.

5. To remove an active sensor, click the sensor you want to remove in the Current Sensors list box and choose Remove.

6. To configure an active sensor, click the sensor you want to configure in the Current Sensors list box and choose Properties.

7. Choose OK.

Configuring a Gauge

To change the appearance of a gauge, follow these steps:

1. Right-click the gauge you want to configure (for example, GDI resource).

2. Choose Properties on the pop-up context menu to bring up the property sheet for the gauge.

3. Select the Style page.

4. To change the type of gauge, select either Bar Gauge, Analog Gauge, or Histogram (see fig. 14.4).

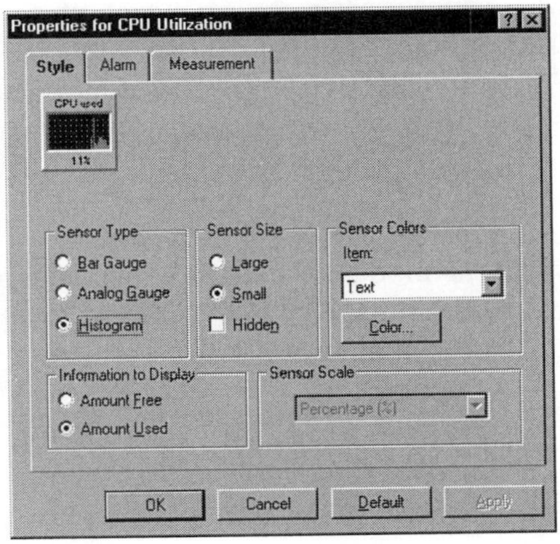

Fig. 14.4
Use the properties sheet to change the style of a gauge in System Doctor.

5. To change the size of the gauge, select either Large or Small.

6. To hide the gauge, select Hidden.

7. To change colors for the gauge, select the colors for each item in the Item drop-down list box and choose Color.

8. To change what type of information to show—how much is free or available, or how much is used or unavailable—select one of the options in the Information to Display group.

9. On some sensors, you can change the scale of the gauge. If you are able to, the drop-down list box in the Sensor Scale group will be active (not grayed out). Select the scale you want. (On some sensors, you can't change the scale. For example, the gauge for the CPU Utilization measures the usage as a percentage. The scale is from 0 to 100 percent and can't be changed.)

10. Choose OK.

To change what happens when a threshold event occurs, follow these steps:

1. Right-click the gauge corresponding to the event (for example, Disk Integrity for drive C:).

2. Choose Properties on the pop-up context menu to bring up the property sheet for the gauge.

3. Select the Alarm page.

4. To turn the alarm on (or off), check (or uncheck) Enabled. If the alarm is enabled, you can set the value at when the alarm will go off.

5. To change what happens when the alarm goes off, select one of the options in the Alarm Action group. You can either decide to do nothing (No Action), have System Doctor make a recommendation to correct the problem (Display Action Recommendation), or have System Doctor automatically try to fix the problem (Take Corrective Action Immediately).

6. To have an audio alarm sound, check Play Sound. To browse for a sound file to use, click the little folder to the right of the edit window. To test the sound, click the little speaker.

7. To change how frequently the alarm goes off after reaching its threshold, type in the number of minutes to wait under Alarm Snooze.

8. Choose OK.

To change how often System Doctor measures each resource, follow these steps:

1. Right-click the gauge corresponding to the resource you want to measure (for example, CPU utilization).

2. Choose Properties on the pop-up context menu to bring up the property sheet for the gauge.

3. Select the Measurement page.
4. To change how often System Doctor checks the resource, change the Time Between Sensor Readings slider.
5. To change the maximum reading to a value you want to specify, click Use Fixed Maximum and type a new maximum. Otherwise, System Doctor sets the maximum to the highest value it has encountered so far.
6. To change the measurement type, click either Actual Value (the number System Doctor has determined) or Decaying Average (an average value that is weighed so that more recent values are more important).
7. Choose OK.

To change the drive that System Doctor is monitoring, follow these steps:

1. Right-click the gauge corresponding to the resource you want to configure (for example, free space on a drive).
2. Choose Properties on the pop-up context menu to bring up the property sheet for the gauge.
3. Select the Drive page.
4. Select the drive in the Drive to Monitor drop-down list box.
5. Choose OK.

Adding a Gauge

To add a gauge to System Doctor, follow these steps:

1. Right-click the background of System Doctor (or on any one of the gauges).
2. Choose Add from the pop-up context menu.
3. Choose the resource or item you want to monitor.
4. You can configure the gauge if you don't like the default settings by following the instructions in the earlier section, "Configuring a Gauge."

Removing a Gauge

To remove a gauge from System Doctor, follow these steps:

1. Right-click the gauge you want to remove.
2. Choose Remove on the pop-up context menu to remove the gauge.

Note

Under most normal conditions, System Doctor will only use 2 to 4 percent of your computer's system resource. You can even use the gauges within System Doctor (GDI Resources and User Resources) to monitor the overhead of using the other gauges.

Configuring Norton Disk Doctor

To make Norton Disk Doctor run each time you start Windows, follow these steps:

1. From the Start menu, choose Programs, Norton Utilities, Norton Disk Doctor.
2. Choose Options.
3. Select the General page.
4. Click Run on Windows Startup.
5. Select the drive(s) you want Disk Doctor to check at startup.
6. Choose OK.

To change what Norton Disk Doctor does when it finds an error, follow these steps:

1. From the Start menu, choose Programs, Norton Utilities, Norton Disk Doctor.
2. Choose Options.
3. Select the General page.
4. Select either to have Disk Doctor ask what you want to do (Ask Me First), to automatically fix the problem (Auto-Repair), or to do nothing (Skip Repairs); or you can customize Disk Doctor to do one of the preceding choices for each different kind of error it finds (Custom and then choose Select).
5. Choose OK.

To change the appearance of Norton Disk Doctor, follow these steps:

1. From the Start menu, choose Programs, Norton Utilities, Norton Disk Doctor.

2. Choose Options.
3. Select the Appearance page (see fig 14.5).
4. To turn on the cartoon animation, choose Enable Animation.
5. To play music while Disk Doctor executes, click Play Music. To browse for a sound file to use, click the little folder to the right of the edit window. To test the sound, click the little speaker.
6. To display a special message if a serious error is encountered, select Show Custom Message. Choose Edit to type the message you want to display.

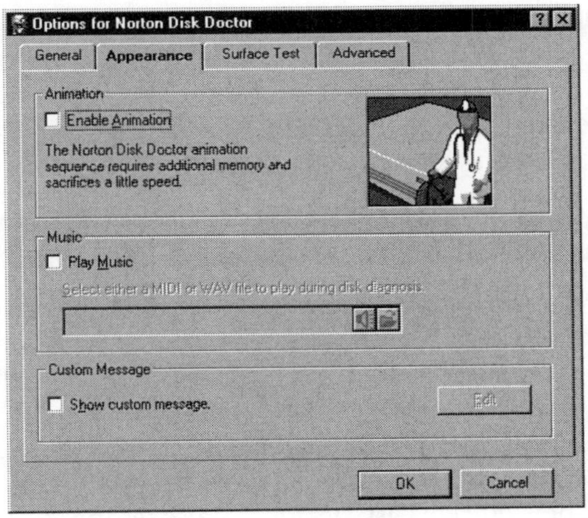

Fig. 14.5
Use the Options sheet to change the appearance of Norton Disk Doctor.

To control how Norton Disk Doctor performs the surface test, follow these steps:

1. From the Start menu, choose Programs, Norton Utilities, Norton Disk Doctor.
2. Choose Options.
3. Select the Surface Test page.
4. To turn on surface testing, choose Enable Surface Testing.
5. To have the test repeat, you can either choose Repetitions and type in the number of times to repeat the test, or you can select Continuous to have the test repeat forever (until you click the Cancel button).
6. To have Disk Doctor perform an in-depth test, check Thorough Test. By default, Disk Doctor performs a quick scan of the disk (Normal Test).

7. To have Disk Doctor only test the area of the disk used by files, select Area Used by Files. By default, Disk Doctor tests the entire disk (Entire Disk Area).

8. To display a map of the disk during the testing, check Show Disk Map During the Surface Test.

9. Choose OK.

To restrict the tests Norton Disk Doctor performs, follow these steps:

1. From the Start menu, choose Programs, Norton Utilities, Norton Disk Doctor.

2. Choose Options.

3. Select the Advanced page.

4. You can restrict the types of tests Disk Doctor performs by checking the items in the Tests to Skip group box.

Caution

You should only need to restrict the types of tests Disk Doctor performs if you have a machine that is not 100 percent compatible and Disk Doctor stops during one of the tests. If this happens, stop Disk Doctor (Ctrl+Alt+Delete) and disable the test that caused the problem.

5. To change how quickly Disk Doctor resumes testing after it has been interrupted, type the number of minutes (Alt+B) and the number of seconds (Alt+D) to wait after Disk Doctor detects idle time.

6. To change what Disk Doctor does when it detects an error, pick one of the four options in the When Errors Are Found drop-down list box—sound a short alarm, flash the taskbar area, sound alarm and flash the taskbar area, or display the report window.

7. Choose OK.

Tip

You can launch all the utilities directly from System Doctor by right-clicking any gauge, choosing Utilities, and then selecting the utility on the pop-up context menu.

Configuring Speed Disk

To configure how Speed Disk optimizes your disk, follow these steps:

1. From the Start menu, choose Programs, Norton Utilities, Speed Disk.
2. Allow Speed Disk to initialize by scanning your drive for errors. If any errors are discovered, Speed Disk exits and suggests you run Norton Disk Doctor.
3. Choose File, Options.
4. Select the Optimization page (see fig. 14.6).

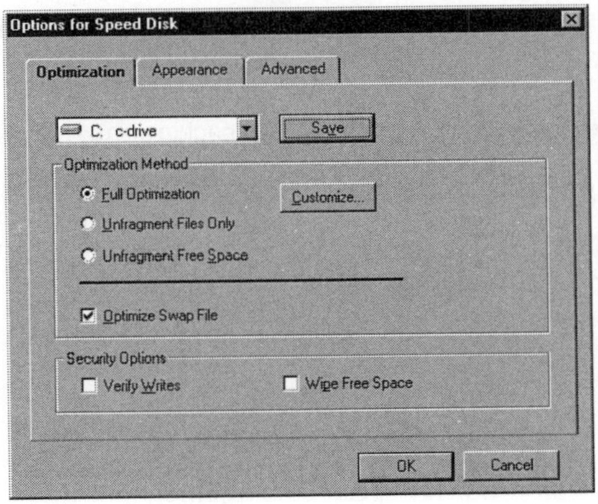

Fig. 14.6
Configure the way Speed Disk optimizes a disk.

5. To change the method used to optimize your disk, select either Full Optimization, Unfragment Files Only, or Unfragment Free Space.
6. To custom a Full Optimization, choose Customize.
7. To have Speed Disk optimize your swap file, check Optimize Swap File.
8. To have Speed Disk erase the data leftover after it moves data around, check Wipe Free Space.
9. To have Speed Disk check to make sure that any data it moves was moved successfully, check Verify Writes.
10. Choose OK.

To configure how Speed Disk looks, follow these steps:

1. From the Start menu, choose Programs, Norton Utilities, Speed Disk.

2. Allow Speed Disk to initialize by scanning your drive for errors. If any errors are discovered, Speed Disk exits and suggests that you run Norton Disk Doctor.
3. Choose File, Options.
4. Select the Appearance page.
5. To change the display Speed Disk uses, select either Block (the default) or Bar.
6. To have Speed Disk play music while it optimizes your disk, select Play Music and enter the name of a sound file. To browse for a sound file to use, click the little folder to the far right of the edit window. To test the sound, click the little speaker to the near right of the edit window.

To configure when Speed Disk runs in the background, follow these steps:

1. From the Start menu, choose Programs, Norton Utilities, Speed Disk.
2. Allow Speed Disk to initialize by scanning your drive for errors. If any errors are discovered, Speed Disk exits and suggests that you run Norton Disk Doctor.
3. Choose File, Options.
4. Select the Advanced page.
5. To change how quickly Speed Disk resumes optimizing your disk after it has been interrupted, type in the number of minutes (Alt+B) and the number of seconds (Alt+D) to wait after Speed Disk detects idle time.
6. To have Speed Disk monitor the communications port for activity, check Watch Communications Port. You should check this if you are using fax software to send and receive faxes. Otherwise, Speed Disk and your communications program may interfere with each other.
7. Choose OK.

Caution

Because Speed Disk was designed for Windows 95, it correctly handles long file names. Also, Speed Disk works with uncompressed drives and drives compressed with DoubleSpace and DriveSpace. However, it does not work with drives compressed with Stacker 4.0, because Stacker 4.0 uses a 16-bit device driver.

Configuring Rescue Disk

To configure Rescue Disk, follow these steps:

1. From the Start menu, choose Programs, Norton Utilities, Rescue Disk.
2. Select whether you want to include the Emergency Programs by checking or unchecking Include Emergency Programs. The Emergency Programs are the DOS versions of the Norton Utilities.
3. Select Options.
4. Select the Rescue Items page (see fig 14.7).

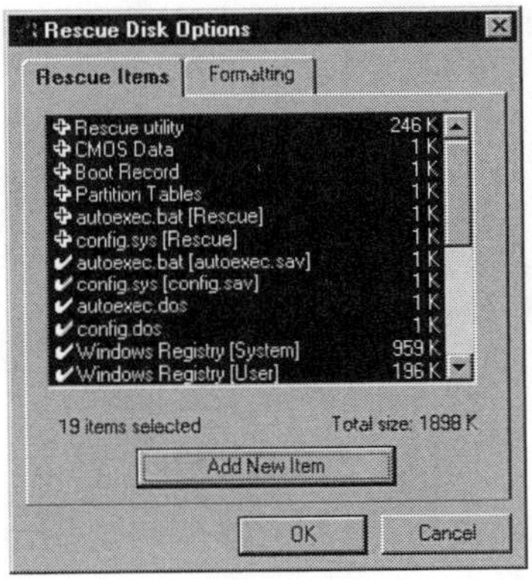

Fig. 14.7
Select items to be placed on the Rescue Disk.

5. Items with a + are automatically included on the rescue disk(s). Selected items (with a check mark) are included, whereas unselected items (without a check mark) are not. You may change any of these by clicking the item you want to change.
6. Select the Formatting page.
7. Choose how you want to use the floppy disks for rescue disks by clicking one of the three options. Your options are to completely format each disk as you use it, perform only a quick format on each disk, or to use only available disk space on the disk. This last option does not destroy any data already on the floppy disk.
8. Choose OK.

Configuring Norton Protected Recycle Bin

To configure Norton Protected Recycle Bin, follow these steps:

1. Right-click the Norton Protected Recycle Bin icon on the Desktop.
2. Choose Properties on the pop-up context menu.

3. Select the Norton Protection page on the Property Sheet dialog box.
4. Select the drive you want to change the settings for.
5. Select Enable Protection to turn on the enhanced protection of the Norton Protected Recycle Bin. Deselect Enable protection to turn off this protection.
6. Click Purge Protected Files if you want to purge files after a certain number of days, even if the space is not needed on your disk. If you do choose to purge the files, set the number of days to retain the files before purging them.
7. Click Exclusions if you want to exclude certain file types or folders from being protected. This is useful so you don't save copies of temporary files.
8. Choose OK.

Setting Norton Image Options

To configure Norton Image, follow these steps:

1. From the Start menu, choose Programs, Norton Utilities, Image.
2. Unless you have just run Norton Disk Doctor and are certain that the disk is free of errors, make sure that the Create Image Backup File option is checked.
3. Choose Options.
4. Check Run on Windows Startup to have Norton Image run automatically each time you start your computer. You don't need to do this if you are using System Doctor to monitor your computer.
5. If you are having Norton Image run each time you start Windows 95, you must select the drives you want to image. Select the tries by clicking each drive in the list box (see fig. 14.8). Image creates an image file for those drives with a check mark.
6. Select Create Image Backup File to make a backup copy of IMAGE.DAT when Image is run during Windows startup.

Caution

If you run Image on a damaged drive, don't rerun Image or you will destroy your backup copy. Instead, delete the IMAGE.DAT file (which won't be any good) and rename IMAGE.BAK to IMAGE.DAT.

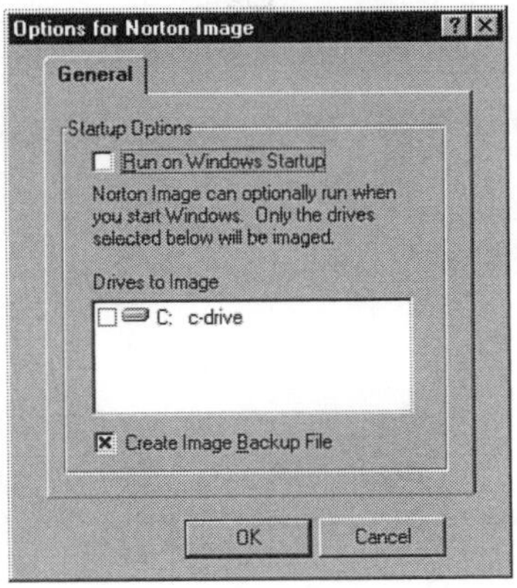

Fig. 14.8
Use the Options property sheet to configure Norton Image.

Customizing Norton Utilities for Windows 95

While the Norton Utilities are highly configurable—that is, you can control their behavior—they are also highly customizable. This means that you can also control the appearance of the applications. This section focuses on customizing the two programs that you most often have visible on your screen—System Doctor and the Norton Protected Recycle Bin.

Customizing System Doctor

You can customize System Doctor to appear in three distinct forms. First, you can have System Doctor appear as a normal window complete with title bar, menus, and a status bar. To save some screen real estate, you can change System Doctor into a tool palette (a window without a title bar, frame, menu, or status bar). Finally, you can turn System Doctor into an application taskbar. This behaves just like the taskbar in Windows 95, and you can "dock" it to any of the four edges of the screen.

To make System Doctor appear as a normal window, follow these steps:

1. Right-click any System Doctor gauge.
2. Select View from the pop-up context menu.
3. Uncheck Dock.
4. Right-click any System Doctor gauge.
5. Select View from the pop-up context menu.
6. Check Title Bar.

To make System Doctor appear as a tool, follow these steps:

1. Right-click any System Doctor gauge.
2. Select View from the pop-up context menu.
3. Uncheck Dock.
4. Right-click any System Doctor gauge.
5. Select View from the pop-up context menu.
6. Uncheck Title Bar.

To make System Doctor appear as a taskbar, follow these steps:

1. Right-click any System Doctor gauge.
2. Select View from the pop-up context menu.
3. Select Dock.

Tip

To keep your desktop uncluttered, you can choose to Auto Hide System Doctor. When you do this, system doctor disappears just off the screen, leaving only a single thin line along the edge of the screen. To make System Doctor appear, simply move your mouse to the edge of the screen where you've docked System Doctor. It "pops" back onto the screen.

Customizing Norton Protected Recycle Bin

To customize Norton Protected Recycle Bin, follow these steps:

1. Right-click the Norton Protected Recycle Bin icon on the Desktop.
2. Choose Properties on the pop-up context menu.
3. Select the Desktop Item page on the Property Sheet dialog box (see fig. 14.9).
4. To change the title, type a new title in the Title edit window.
5. To enable the icon to change to reflect the status of the Norton Protected Recycle Bin, select Show Norton Protection Status.
6. To set the default action that should happen when you double-click the Norton Protected Recycle Bin icon, select one of the four options in the Double-clicking Item Opens box—Norton UnErase Wizard, Recently Deleted Files, All Protected files, Standard Recycle Bin.
7. Choose OK.

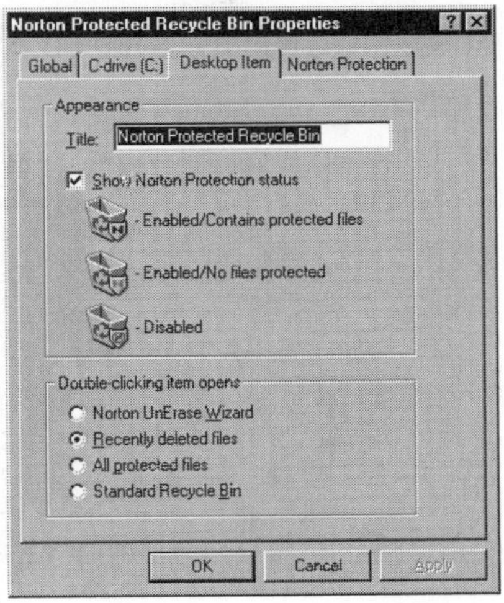

Fig. 14.9
Customize the look of Norton Protected Recycle Bin.

Uninstalling Norton Utilities for Windows 95

To uninstall all the Norton Utilities, follow these steps:

1. From the Start menu, choose Settings, Control Panel.
2. Open the Add/Remove Programs Wizard by double-clicking its icon in the Control Panel folder.
3. Select Norton Utilities and choose Add/Remove.
4. Choose Next.
5. Select Full Uninstall.
6. Answer each question the Uninstall Wizard asks and choose Next.

To uninstall a portion of the Norton Utilities, follow these steps:

1. From the Start menu, choose Settings, Control Panel.
2. Open the Add/Remove Programs Wizard by double-clicking its icon in the Control Panel folder.
3. Select Norton Utilities and choose Add/Remove.
4. Choose Next.
5. Select Partial Uninstall.
6. Check the components you want to remove and choose Next.
7. Answer each question the Uninstall Wizard asks and choose Next.

Chapter 15

Using DOS Software

by Diane Tinney

Operating systems are great, but it's the software that you use every day that makes a difference in your life. Once the operating system is up and running, you should be able to install and use application software without noticing that an operating system is even under the hood. But in reality, we've all wasted hours trying to tweak the operating system to correctly run the application we need, without sacrificing the executability of the other applications we also need.

Windows 95 was designed from the ground up to make the installation, configuration, and execution of application software easier, quicker, and more reliable. DOS software in particular runs better in Windows 95 than in DOS 6.22. In this chapter, we examine how the design of Windows 95 makes this possible and explore the DOS application environment in detail. At the end of the chapter, we explore the most challenging DOS software Windows 95 must run: DOS-based game software.

In this chapter, you learn

- The effect of the Windows 95 architecture on software execution
- How to access and work with the DOS command prompt
- The best way to execute a DOS application
- How to configure and optimize DOS software
- The issues involved in executing DOS game software

Exploring the Windows 95 Architecture

Before you delve into the nitty gritty of how to install and configure software to work with Windows 95, it is important that you understand a few foundation concepts regarding the Windows 95 architecture. First, Windows 95 is an operating system. *Operating systems* provide the link between hardware and software. When a software application needs to write a file to the hard disk, print a document, or display something on-screen, it is the operating system that provides these services. While Windows 95 and Windows NT are operating systems, keep in mind that Windows 3.x is just an application that runs on top of DOS.

◀ See "What's New with Windows 95 Setup," p. 10

Windows 95 executes software differently, depending on the type of software you are running. Software is divided into three basic categories:

- Applications written for DOS
- Applications written for Windows 3.1 (generally referred to as *16-bit applications*)
- Applications written for Windows 95 and Windows NT (generally referred to as *32-bit applications*)

The Windows 95 application execution environment changes depending on the type of software. The key architectural areas which differ include the Virtual Machine (VM), multitasking, and internal messaging.

Understanding Virtual Machines

To meet the various needs of each type of software application, Windows 95 creates a fictional computer called a virtual machine. A *virtual machine* is an environment created by the operating system and processor that simulates a full computer's resources. To the software application, the virtual machine appears to be a real computer.

The operating system keeps track of the application needs and hardware resources. Windows 95 determines which resources each application will have access to and when it can have access.

All software applications in Windows 95 run in virtual machines (VM). Figure 15.1 illustrates the various VMs and what services run in each VM.

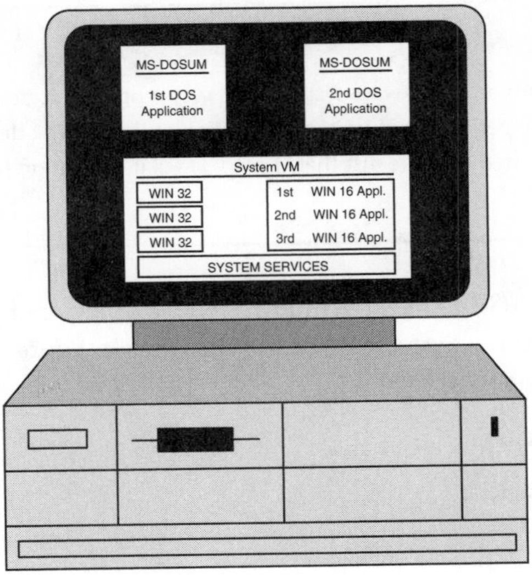

Fig. 15.1 Software applications execute in virtual machines created by Windows 95.

> **Note**
>
> Each DOS application runs in a separate MS-DOS VM. For example, if you ran your DOS-based version of WordPerfect and a DOS-based version of Lotus 1-2-3, Windows 95 would create two separate MS-DOS VMs, one for each DOS-based program.

Providing each DOS application with its own VM is beneficial because most DOS-based programs were created in a single application environment. That is, DOS-based programs usually assume they are the *only* program executing at any particular point in time. This single-mindedness of DOS applications has been known to cause grief (system hang-ups, sudden re-boots and general protection faults) when running DOS applications under Windows 3.x.

Another benefit of the single DOS VM is that each DOS application is shielded from other DOS applications as well as Windows 3.x and Windows 95-type applications. Thus, a misbehaving DOS, Win16, or Win32 application cannot bring down another DOS application. The MS-DOS VM insulates the DOS application from other misbehaving programs.

Note

As we all know from other software systems, the way a product is designed to work and how it actually performs can be two very different things. The design features of Windows 95 presented here are just that. Time will tell if the design holds up in the real world.

In addition to the MS-DOS VM, Windows 95 creates another virtual machine environment called the System VM. As you can see in figure 15.1, the System VM executes the following:

- System services
- 16-bit applications
- 32-bit applications

The system services such as the *kernel* (core program of the operating system), graphics, and Windows management execute in a separate area (memory address). Each Windows 95 32-bit application executes in its own separate memory address. This design prevents 32-bit applications from interfering with other currently executing 32-bit, 16-bit, or DOS applications.

However, the 16-bit Windows applications all run in the same memory address within the System VM. This design aspect of the Windows 95 architecture was done to maintain downward compatibility with the old Windows 3.x 16-bit Windows-based applications. So, although Windows 95 is compatible with the older Windows 3.x applications, it doesn't offer any better protection against misbehaving 16-bit applications. That is, a misbehaving 16-bit application can still bring down all currently executing 16-bit applications.

Note

DOS applications execute in separate virtual machines (VMs). Windows 3.x (16-bit) applications execute in the System VM, in a single address space. Windows 95 (32-bit) applications run in the System VM, but in separate address spaces.

DOS applications can't bring down the system, other DOS applications, or other Windows (16- or 32-bit) applications. Windows 3.x (16-bit) applications can bring down other 16-bit applications. Windows 95 (32-bit) applications can't bring down other 32-bit, 16-bit, or DOS applications.

Multitasking Your Applications

Running multiple programs at the same time is called *multitasking*. Windows 95 provides a multitasking feature that enables multiple applications to run concurrently by sharing processor cycles. A *processor cycle* is a time slice that the operating system gives a program so that the program can use the CPU, or central processing unit. In Windows 95, this enables you to print a document while sending e-mail and editing a spreadsheet at the same time. Under the PC cover, all three applications are sharing CPU time, one slice at a time.

First, you need to familiarize yourself with some terms:

- A *process* is an executing application.
- A *thread* is a unit of execution within a process, such as one task within a process.

> **Note**
>
> Windows 95 supports multitasking on one microprocessor. Windows 95 doesn't support *Symmetric Multiprocessing* (SMP), which allows the use of multiple microprocessors within one PC. Windows NT and OS/2 Warp do support SMP.

In Windows 95, each executing DOS and Windows application is a single process. For example, if you have Word for Windows 95, Paradox for DOS, and Lotus 1-2-3 for Windows 3.x running, the CPU is handling three processes (in addition to the work of the operating system). Within a process, Windows 95 allows 32-bit applications to schedule individual threads of execution. This is called *multi-threaded processing.*

How an application multitasks depends on the type of application (DOS, 16-bit, or 32-bit). For DOS and 32-bit applications, Windows 95 uses *preemptive multitasking*. In preemptive multitasking, each thread is executed for a preset time period, or until another thread with a higher priority is ready to execute. The Windows 95 Task Scheduler manages multitasking and ensures that no one application monopolizes the processor. At any time, the operating system can *preempt* (take control away from) an application and hand the system resources to another application with a higher priority task.

For Windows 3.x (16-bit) applications, Windows 95 uses a *cooperative multitasking* system. In cooperative multitasking, the program (rather than the operating system) is in control of CPU scheduling. Although programs should yield to the operating system after a reasonable amount of time, we have all encountered the Windows 3.x program which fails to return control of the system resources back to the operating system, and eventually locks up the entire system. Windows 95 uses the less reliable cooperative multitasking model to provide compatibility with existing 16-bit Windows 3.x programs.

For Windows 95 (32-bit) applications that choose to schedule their own threads of execution (multi-threaded processing), Windows 95 again uses the cooperative multitasking method. Up to 32 levels of priority can be assigned.

Note

Windows 95 uses cooperative multitasking for multi-threaded processing, whereas Windows NT uses the more reliable preemptive multitasking method. It remains to be seen how many 32-bit Windows 95 applications lock themselves up by failing to return CPU control after a reasonable time to another thread within their process slot.

How Applications Communicate

Applications communicate with the operating system via the Windows 95 messaging system. The messaging system passes information between the hardware, the applications, and the operating system. For example, when a user moves the mouse, Windows 95 converts the hardware interrupt into a message which is sent to the appropriate message queue.

Caution

Although each DOS and 32-bit application has its own message queue, all the 16-bit applications share one common message queue. Thus, if a 16-bit application hangs, all running 16-bit applications must wait until the hung application is cleared. If the hung application is not cleared, all 16-bit applications may lose their messages.

Summarizing the Application Environment

Table 15.1 summarizes the key architectural features in the Windows 95 application execution environment by application type. Review the table, and refer back to previous text as needed to ensure your understanding of these key concepts before proceeding with Chapters 16 and 17. Once you understand these concepts, it will be easier to understand how to best use DOS, Windows 3.x, and Windows 95 software in the Windows 95 operating environment.

Table 15.1 Application Execution Environment

Feature	DOS Application	16-Bit Application	32-Bit Application
Virtual Machine (VM)	One MS-DOS VM per executing DOS application System VM	All run within a single memory address	All run in System VM executing DOS, but each in a separate memory address
Multitasking	Preemptive scheduling	Cooperative scheduling	Preemptive scheduling
Multi-processing	None	None threaded	Yes, uses cooperative scheduling
Messaging	Each has its own message queue	All share a common message queue	Each has its own message queue

Executing DOS Applications

On a Windows 95 computer, DOS is available in two flavors:

- DOS session (multitasking)
- MS-DOS mode (single task, real mode)

The DOS session starts from within Windows 95. You can switch the DOS session between a windowed view and full-screen view. From a DOS session, you can switch back to Windows 95 and to any other currently running applications. Windows 95 is a multitasking environment, and each DOS session runs in a separate MS-DOS VM. In a windowed DOS session, Windows 95 even provides a toolbar for quick access to cut, copy, paste, property sheets, and fonts. The property sheets are similar to the old Windows 3.x PIF files. The property sheets for DOS sessions allow you to control the MS-DOS VM and what the DOS program sees (you can even hide Windows 95 from the DOS program!).

The MS-DOS mode can start from within Windows 95, or can be accessed during bootup. *MS-DOS mode* (also known as real mode) is a single-task environment. No other programs are in memory, so you can't switch over to another program. Windows 95 leaves a small footprint of itself in memory so that when you close your DOS application (or type **exit** at the DOS prompt),

Windows 95 can load automatically. In MS-DOS mode, you cannot cut, copy, or paste to the Clipboard. The DOS application has complete control of the CPU and all resources. For DOS programs that you start from MS-DOS mode, you can specify certain properties. Properties that require Windows 95, such as fonts, memory management, and screen display are not available. You can, however, specify a custom AUTOEXEC.BAT and CONFIG.SYS to be run for each DOS program running in MS-DOS mode (no more creating separate boot disks for finicky DOS programs that require special treatment!).

In the following sections, you learn how to do the following:

- Display and work with the DOS command prompt
- Start a DOS application from within Windows 95

Displaying the DOS Command Prompt

Although most of the time Windows 95 provides tools for your computing needs via a user-friendly graphical interface, there may be times when you need to or (for us old-timers) want to access DOS. You don't need to exit Windows 95 to access the DOS command prompt or issue a DOS command.

Tip

To start a Windows 95 program from the command prompt, type the new DOS command **START** followed by the program name.

To display the DOS command prompt from within Windows 95, follow these steps:

1. Click the Start button, then choose Programs, MS-DOS Prompt. By default, Windows 95 opens a windowed DOS session (see fig. 15.2).

Note

You can also start a DOS session by clicking the Start button, choosing Run, typing the word **command,** and pressing Enter.

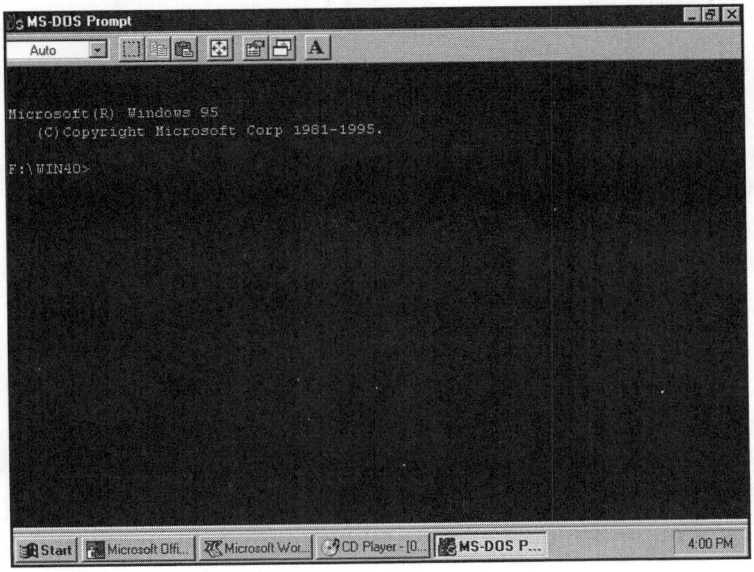

Fig. 15.2
The windowed DOS session provides you with more control over the DOS environment.

2. If you prefer working in a DOS full-screen session, press Alt+Enter (see fig. 15.3).

Fig. 15.3
A full-screen DOS session lets you see more on-screen.

3. If you need to switch between the DOS session and Windows 95, press Alt+Tab.

4. When you finish, type **exit** at the DOS prompt to close the DOS session or, if working in a DOS window, click the (X) close button in the top right-hand corner.

Caution

Be careful when using the X button to close a windowed DOS session. Any open DOS applications with unsaved data or open data files could result in data loss or file corruption. Always close data files and end DOS applications before using the X button.

Tip

Create a shortcut to DOS and place it on the desktop for quick access to DOS.

Note

To display help for a DOS command, type the name of the command you want followed by a space and **/?**. For example, type **md /?** to display help text on the MAKE DIRECTORY (MD) command.

Adding the pipe character | and the word **More** to the end of the statement displays help text one screen at a time. For example:

md /? | more

To start the computer at the DOS prompt in MS-DOS mode, follow these steps:

1. Choose Start.
2. Choose Shut Down.
3. Choose Restart the Computer in MS-DOS Mode. A full-screen, single application DOS prompt appears.
4. When you finish, type **exit** to start Windows 95.

Note

You can also enter MS-DOS mode when your machine boots up. When the message Starting Windows 95 appears, press F8 and select Command Prompt Only to boot up the computer in the real-mode version of DOS. When you finish, type **exit** to start Windows 95.

Working with DOS Commands

The Windows 95 set of DOS commands are functionally the same as in prior versions of DOS. You can view a list of these commands by opening up the \WINDOWS\COMMANDS folder. File manipulation commands such as COPY, DIR, and RENAME have been enhanced to support long file names. To use a long file name in DOS, enclose the long file name in quotes; for example,

◀ See "Preparing for Installation," p. 29

◀ See "Installation Options," p. 33

◀ See "Determining Your Boot Configuration," p. 37

```
RENAME eastsale.wk1 "Eastcoast Sales.wk1"
```

Caution

Be careful when using long file names. Although the Windows 95 DOS commands support long file names, existing DOS and Windows 3.x programs do not. Furthermore, be careful when using a file in Windows 95 with a long file name and then accessing the file in a DOS or Windows 3.x program. Doing so deletes the long file name!

The DIR command has been enhanced to display a seventh column which shows the long file name. DIR also sports a new command line switch called verbose: **/v**. The verbose switch displays additional information such as file attributes and last access date stamp.

Windows 95 DOS also supports the *Universal Naming Convention* (UNC). UNC makes it easier to refer to and use networked resources such as printers and network folders (you no longer need to map folders and remember those cryptic addresses). For example, to copy a file to a shared network folder named "Accounting Sales Data," you would issue the following command line:

```
COPY "Eastcoast Sales.wk1" "\\Accounting Sales Data"
```

Many of the DOS commands included in prior versions of DOS are not included in Windows 95 because they are no longer needed. In these cases, Windows 95 provides the feature elsewhere. Furthermore, if your computer did not have DOS installed prior to installing Windows 95, you will not have some of the older DOS commands that Windows 95 does not need, but leaves in the old DOS folder.

A powerful new command included in Windows 95 is the START command. You can use START to launch DOS and Windows programs from the DOS command prompt (START is not available in MS-DOS mode). Two syntax forms can be used. The first supplies the program name. The second syntax supplies the document name. For the document name to launch the program and display the document, the file name extension must be properly registered:

```
START [options] program [arg...]
START [options] document.ext
```

The options available include

- **/m**. Run the new program minimized (in the background).
- **/max**. Run the new program maximized (in the foreground).
- **/r**. Run the new program restored (in the foreground). [default]
- **/w**. Does not return until the other program exits.

Suppose that files with the extension DOC are registered as Word for Windows files. Then issuing the following command statement automatically loads Word for Windows and the document SALES.DOC:

```
START sales.doc
```

Using START at the command prompt to load a DOS program actually opens a new MS-DOS VM for that program. If instead you type the name of the DOS program without the command START, the DOS program loads in the current MS-DOS VM.

Note

If you type the DOS command VER at the command prompt, the version information that appears is Windows 95. However, DOS programs which ask internally for the DOS version get the number 7. This could cause conflicts with DOS programs that only work for a specific DOS version number.

Some DOS commands should NOT be used in Windows 95. You should avoid using the following commands in Windows 95:

- CHKDSK /F. You can run this command at the DOS prompt, but not in Windows 95.
- FDISK. Avoid running at the DOS prompt. It can't be used when Windows 95 is running.
- RECOVER. This command exists from an older version of DOS, and doesn't work well with Windows 95 or at the command prompt.

Tip

To configure the DOS command line sessions, set file properties for COMMAND.COM, which is located in the Window's COMMAND folder.

Starting a DOS Program

Starting a DOS program takes a few more steps than you may be used to, but it does have the advantage of being less cryptic than navigating the DOS prompt and cryptic command lines.

To start a DOS program, follow these steps:

1. Open the My Computer folder.
2. Locate the program file.
3. Double-click the program file.

You can also start a DOS program by using any of the following options:

- Choose Run from the Start menu
- Type the START command at a DOS command prompt
- Create a shortcut on the desktop or menu

Working in a DOS Window

When you work in a DOS window, Windows 95 provides you with a very helpful toolbar for easy access to the following features:

- Copy, cut, and paste to and from DOS windows
- Change fonts and font sizes

- Switch between exclusive and foreground processing
- Change property sheets without leaving the DOS window

> **Note**
>
> You cannot paste text into a DOS program when it is running in full-screen mode.

> **Tip**
>
> To select text by dragging the cursor over the selection, open the Properties sheet for the DOS program, select the Misc tab, and click QuickEdit.

To view the toolbar, click the MS-DOS icon in the title bar and click Toolbar (refer to fig. 15.2).

Configuring DOS Applications

In Windows 3.x, DOS applications were configured by editing a *Program Information File* (PIF). The PIF file had to be manually created and maintained by the user via the PIF Editor. This was cumbersome at best. Windows 95 automates the PIF file creation and moves the configuration maintenance into a series of property sheets.

When you first start a DOS application, Windows searches for a PIF file with the same name as the executable file. If Windows finds an existing PIF file, Windows uses the PIF file settings. If no PIF file exists yet, Windows uses default settings to control the DOS application. Windows 95 uses a database of known DOS application settings to create the automatic PIF. The PIF files are viewed and maintained via the property sheets.

> **Note**
>
> Windows 95 stores all PIFs in a hidden PIF folder in the Windows 95 directory. This keeps novice users from inadvertently altering the actual PIF files.

Displaying DOS Property Sheets

You set properties for a DOS program the same way you set properties for any object in Windows 95—by right-clicking the object and choosing Properties.

Windows 95 then displays the property sheet for the DOS application (see fig. 15.4). DOS program properties are organized into six property pages. You'll learn more about each of the property pages in the following sections.

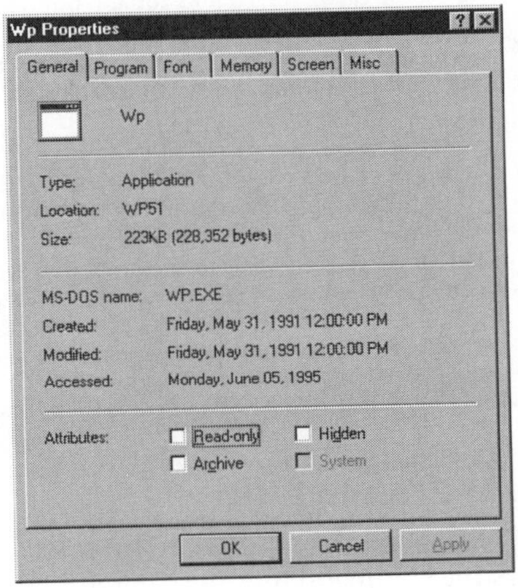

Fig. 15.4
You control how DOS programs execute in Windows 95 by setting program properties.

To display the property sheet, follow these steps:

1. Open the My Computer folder.
2. Locate the DOS file, and right-click it.
3. Choose Properties. Windows 95 displays the property sheet for that DOS file (refer to fig. 15.4).

Tip

To display property sheets while running the DOS program session, press Alt+space bar and choose Properties.

Setting General Properties

The General property page (refer to fig. 15.4) displays the file name, size, location, file type, and other general information. The only configuration settings that you can change are the file attributes. Changing file attributes here is identical to using the DOS ATTRIB command at a DOS prompt. Table 15.2 describes each file attribute setting.

Table 15.2 File Attribute Settings

Attribute	Description
Read-only	File can be read, moved and copied, but not changed or erased.
Archive	Marks a file as having been changed since it was last backed up.
Hidden	File will not display in directory listings. Most DOS commands such as COPY and DEL won't work on hidden files.
System	Marks a file as belonging to the operating system (Windows 95 or DOS). System files are not shown in directory listings. Currently, Windows 95 does not allow you to set the System attribute here. However, if a file has the system attribute set, it will appear checked although dimmed.

Setting Program Properties

The Program properties page (see fig. 15.5) allows you to control many application settings such as the command line, working directory, shortcut key, and icon. From the Program properties page, you can click the Advanced button to configure how Windows 95 emulates the DOS environment for this program. Clicking the Change Icon button allows you to browse through icon files and select a new icon for the program.

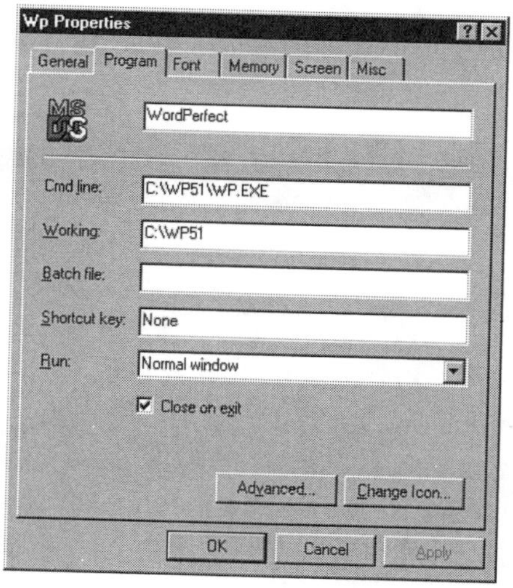

Fig. 15.5
On the Program properties page, you can specify the working folder.

To set Program properties, follow these steps:

1. Open the property folder for the desired DOS program.
2. Edit the name text box as needed.
3. Edit the Cmd Line as needed.
4. Edit the Working folder as needed.
5. If you would like to run a batch file each time this program executes, enter the name of the Batch File.
6. If you would like to assign a Shortcut Key, press Ctrl and/or Alt and the other key.

> **Note**
>
> Assigning a shortcut key to a DOS program gives you quick access to your favorite DOS programs. You can use the shortcut key to start the program or switch back to it once it is running.
>
> Windows 95 contains many shortcut keys (called *access keys*), so you need to be careful when assigning your own shortcut keys. Here is a list of the rules:
>
> - Use Ctrl and/or Alt and another key (for example, Alt+W).
> - The other key cannot be Esc, Enter, Tab, space bar, Print Screen, or Backspace.
> - No other program can use this key combination.
> - If the shortcut key is the same as an access key used by a Windows program, the access key won't work (the shortcut key does work).

7. From the Run drop-down list, select the window size: Normal window, Maximized (full screen window), or Minimized (a button on the taskbar).
8. If you want the MS-DOS window to stay open after you exit the program, deselect the Close On Exit box. Otherwise, Windows 95 will automatically close the MS-DOS window on exit.
9. Click OK to save your changes, or Apply to save the changes without closing the Properties sheet.

Setting Advanced Program Properties

The Advanced Program Settings sheet (see fig. 15.6) allows you to configure the DOS environment in which the DOS program will run. You can hide

Windows 95 from the DOS program, allow Windows 95 to switch to MS-DOS mode as needed, or require that the DOS program always be run in MS-DOS mode. Table 15.3 describes the Advanced Property settings available.

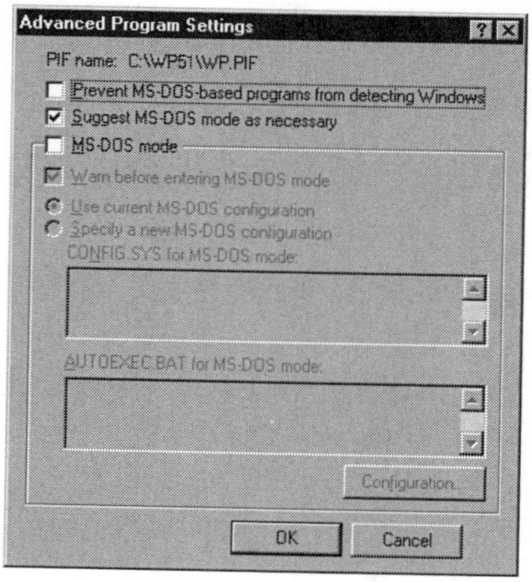

Fig. 15.6
Use the Advanced Program Settings sheet to control the DOS program execution environment.

By default, DOS programs run from Windows 95 in a DOS window. Alternatively, DOS programs can be executed in MS-DOS mode (also called *single application mode* and *real mode*). In MS-DOS mode, the DOS program controls all system resources. Before running a program in MS-DOS mode, Windows 95 closes all active Windows and DOS programs. Only a small portion of Windows 95 remains in memory so that Windows 95 can reload itself into memory when you exit the program. Setting a program up to use MS-DOS mode is the same as shutting down Windows 95, restarting in MS-DOS mode, and then re-booting your machine to Windows 95. MS-DOS mode is usually used for DOS programs such as DOS games that won't run under Windows.

Note

Windows 95 property sheets exist for all DOS programs, whether started in MS-DOS mode, from the command prompt, or as a Windows 95 DOS session. For those applications set up to run in MS-DOS mode, many properties do not apply and are therefore not available. When MS-DOS mode is selected, only the following properties are enabled:

- *General.* File attributes.
- *Program.* Icon text, command line, close on exit, change icon, and the advanced MS-DOS mode options.

Font, Memory, Screen, and Misc sheets are blank.

Table 15.3 Advanced Program Settings

Setting	Description
Prevent MS-DOS-Based Programs From Detecting Windows	Hides Windows 95 from DOS program. Not enabled if MS-DOS mode is selected.
Suggest MS-DOS Mode As Necessary	Windows 95 automatically detects if DOS program runs better in MS-DOS mode. If so, Windows 95 executes a wizard to set up a custom icon to run the program. Not enabled if MS-DOS mode is selected.
MS-DOS Mode	Runs the program in MS-DOS mode.
Warn Before Entering MS-DOS Mode	Windows 95 displays a warning message that it will close all programs before running MS-DOS mode.
Use Current MS-DOS Configuration	By default, Windows 95 uses the existing AUTOEXEC.BAT and CONFIG.SYS files when it enters MS-DOS mode.
Specify a New MS-DOS Mode	Select to create alternative CONFIG.SYS and AUTOEXEC.BAT files. Enables CONFIG.SYS and AUTOEXEC.BAT text boxes and Configuration button.
CONFIG.SYS for MS-DOS mode	Edit as needed to create custom CONFIG.SYS file for MS-DOS mode.
AUTOEXEC.BAT for MS-DOS mode	Edit as needed to create custom AUTOEXEC.BAT file for MS-DOS mode.
Configuration	Instead of typing in commands, click this button to have Windows 95 create custom configuration files for you.

Tip

If a DOS program detects Windows 95 and won't run properly, select Prevent MS-DOS-based Programs From Detecting Windows from the Advanced Program Settings sheet.

To allocate all system resources to a DOS program (run in real mode, single application mode), follow these steps:

1. Open the Properties folder for the DOS program.
2. Select the Program tab.
3. Click the Advanced button.
4. Choose MS-DOS Mode.
5. If you do not want the warning message, deselect Warn Before Entering MS-DOS Mode.
6. If you do not want to use the current MS-DOS configuration, choose Specify a New MS-DOS Configuration.
7. For manual configuration, type or edit configuration commands in the CONFIG.SYS and AUTOEXEC.BAT text boxes.
8. To have Windows 95 generate the configuration commands for you, click the Configuration button. The Select MS-DOS Configuration Options dialog box appears, as shown in figure 15.7. Select the desired options and click OK to return to the Advanced Program Settings dialog box.
9. Click OK to return to the Program properties page.
10. Click OK to save your changes, or click Apply to save the changes without closing the Properties sheet.

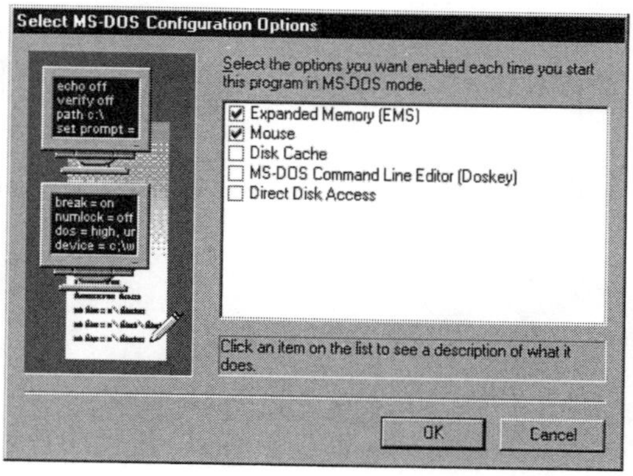

Fig. 15.7
For programs starting in MS-DOS mode, you can create custom AUTOEXEC.BAT and CONFIG.SYS files by selecting options.

Changing Program Icons

As with every object in Windows 95, DOS-based programs have a graphical picture called an *icon* associated with the program file. By default, the icon can appear in the following places:

- Within file lists
- When you press Alt+Tab to switch between running applications
- On the Start menu
- On the taskbar

If the program file doesn't specify an icon, Windows 95 uses the MS-DOS icon. You can change the icon by displaying the DOS Program property page and clicking the Change Icon button. Windows 95 displays the Change Icon dialog box, as shown in figure 15.8. To view the contents of another icon file, type in the file name or use the Browse button to find the file. After selecting the icon, click OK twice to save your changes.

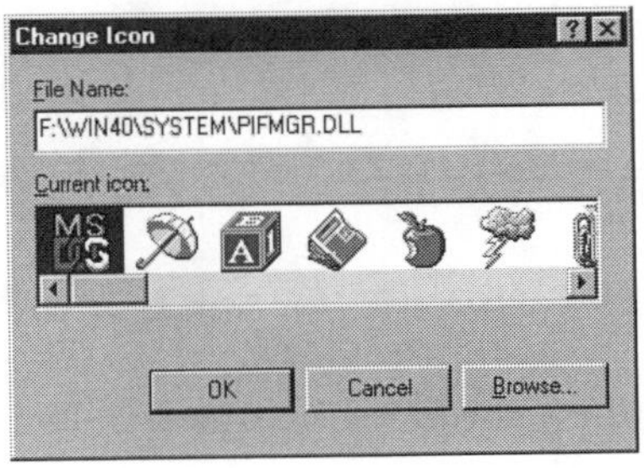

Fig. 15.8
The PIFMGR.DLL file contains many icons to which you can assign a program file.

Note

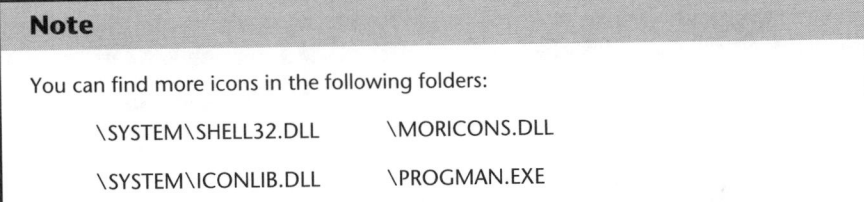

You can find more icons in the following folders:

\SYSTEM\SHELL32.DLL	\MORICONS.DLL
\SYSTEM\ICONLIB.DLL	\PROGMAN.EXE

Setting Font Properties

A new feature in Windows 95 which is not supported in Windows 3.x is the ability to control the font size and appearance. Windows 95 allows you to use any bitmapped or TrueType font installed on your computer. The font settings work in full-screen and windowed DOS sessions. Figure 15.9 shows the Font property page, which you can use to improve the display of your DOS sessions.

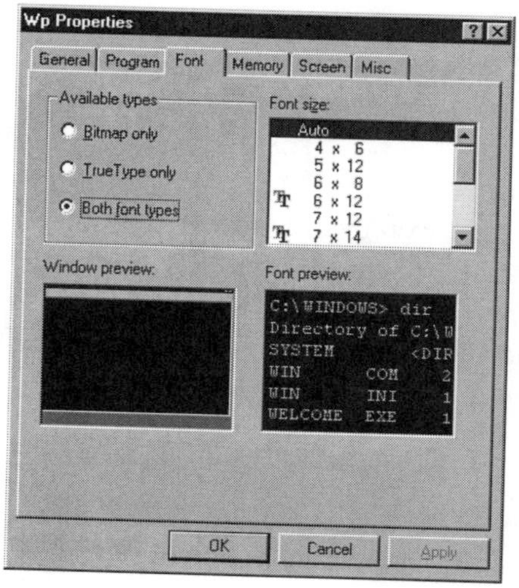

Fig. 15.9
You can reduce eye strain by changing the font type and size.

In addition to giving you control over the font type and size, Windows 95 provides an Auto font size feature (found in the Font Size drop-down list) which automatically adjusts the font size to fit the size of the DOS window. This allows you to see all 80 characters, even when you reduce the size of the DOS window.

Tip

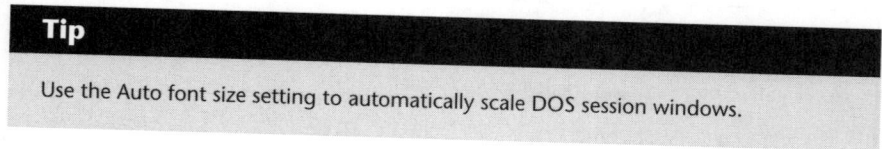

Use the Auto font size setting to automatically scale DOS session windows.

To set font properties for a DOS program, follow these steps:

1. Open the Properties folder for the DOS program.
2. Select the Font page.
3. Select the available types to list in the Font Size scroll box: Bitmap Only, TrueType Only, or Both Font Types.
4. Select the desired font size in the Font Size scroll box. Windows 95 shows you what your selection will look like in the Window Preview and Font Preview boxes.

5. Click OK to save your changes, or click Apply to save the changes without closing the Properties sheet.

Setting Memory Properties

The settings on the Memory page (see fig. 15.10) control the way the DOS application uses the PC's memory. Settings are provided to control conventional, expanded (EMS), and extended (XMS) memory. Note that since each DOS application executes in its own MS-DOS VM, the memory settings apply only to that DOS application. Other executing DOS, Windows 3.x, and Windows 95 applications are unaffected by these memory settings. Table 15.4 describes the Memory property settings.

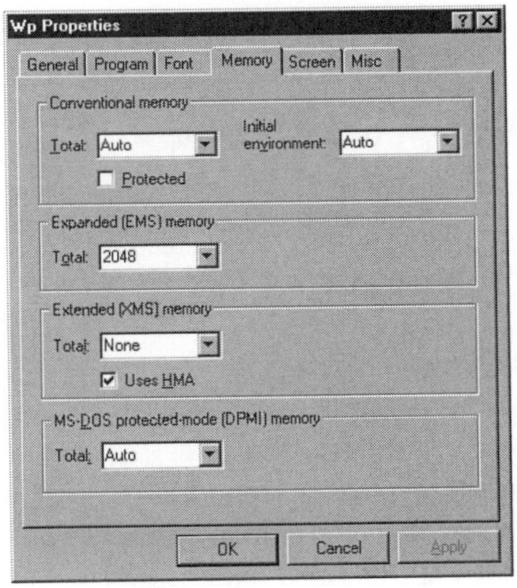

Fig. 15.10
You can customize the memory configuration for each DOS application.

Table 15.4 Memory Settings

Setting	Description
Conventional Memory	
Total	Amount of conventional (lower 640K) memory program requires. If unsure, choose Auto.
Initial Environment	Number of bytes to reserve for COMMAND.COM. If set to Auto, the size is determined by the SHELL= line in CONFIG.SYS.
Protected	If selected, system is protected from any problems caused by the program. The program may run slower when this is selected.

(continues)

Table 15.4 Continued

Setting	Description
Expanded (EMS) Memory	
Total	Maximum amount of expanded memory allotted to program. The Auto setting sets no limit. If you experience problems, try setting to 8192.
Extended (XMS) Memory	
Total	Maximum amount of extended memory allotted to program. The Auto setting sets no limit. If you experience problems, try setting to 8192.
Uses HMA	Indicates whether program can use the High Memory Area (HMA).
MS-DOS Protected Mode (DPMI) Memory	
Total:	Maximum amount of DOS protected mode memory (DPMI) to allocate to the program. The Auto setting lets Windows 95 configure based on your setup.

Setting Screen Properties

The settings on the Screen page (see fig. 15.11) control the way the DOS application appears. You can set up the DOS program to load in a window or full-screen—with or without a toolbar—and determine how many lines of text should appear. In addition, you can set display performance features such as dynamic memory allocation and fast ROM emulation. Table 15.5 describes the screen properties.

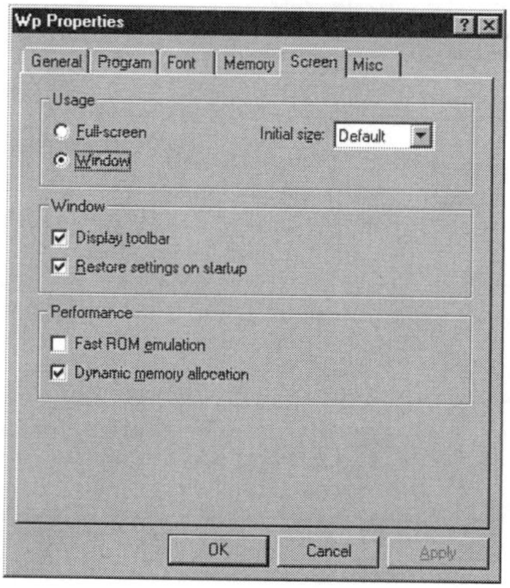

Fig. 15.11
By turning on dynamic memory allocation, you can speed up the display performance of a DOS program.

Table 15.5 Display Settings

Setting	Description
Usage	
Full-Screen	Starts program in a full-screen mode.
Window	Starts program in a window.
Initial Size	Sets the number of screen lines displayed (25, 43, or 50 lines). A setting of `Default` uses the program's number of lines.
Window	
Display Toolbar	If running in a window, checking this box displays the toolbar.
Restore Settings On Startup	If running in a window, restores the font and screen settings when you close the program.
Performance	
Fast ROM Emulation	Controls the read-only video memory usage. Select this to speed up screen display and refresh. If the program has problems writing text to the screen, deselect this setting.
Dynamic Memory Allocation	Controls amount of memory available to switch between text and graphics mode in a DOS program. If you want to maximize the amount of memory available to other programs while this program runs, check this box. If you want to maximize the memory available to this program, clear this setting.

Setting Miscellaneous Properties

The remaining DOS program properties are grouped under the Misc page (see fig. 15.12). On the Misc page, you can control foreground and background settings, the mouse, shortcut keys, and other items. Table 15.6 describes the miscellaneous settings.

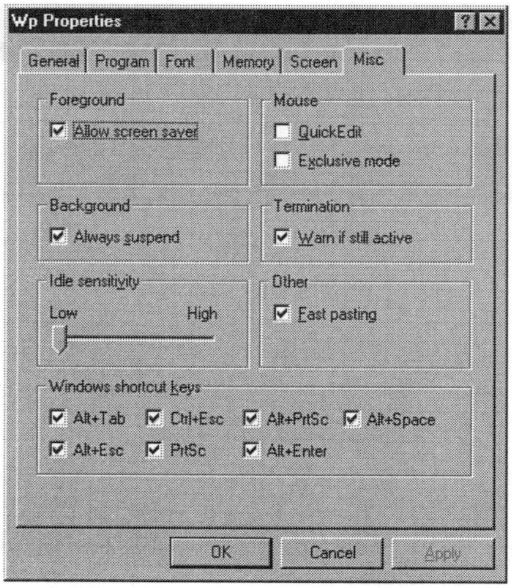

Fig. 15.12
The Misc page allows you to resolve conflicts between Windows shortcut keys and DOS programs.

Table 15.6 Misc Settings

Setting	Description
Foreground	
Allow Screen Saver	Allows screen saver to work even when this program is active.
Background	
Always Suspend	Prevents program from using system resources when not active.
Idle Sensitivity	Specifies how long Windows allows the program to remain idle before redirecting CPU resources to other programs. Slide toward Low to give the DOS program a longer idle time (more resources). Slide toward High to take resources away from the DOS program sooner.
Mouse	
Quick Edit	Enables the Quick Edit feature which allows you to select text for cut and copy functions with the mouse (otherwise, you must mark text first).
Exclusive Mode	When selected, mouse is controlled exclusively by the DOS program. Mouse is no longer available in Windows.
Termination	
Warn If Still Active	When selected, displays warning message if you try to close a running DOS application.

Setting	Description
Other	
Fast Pasting	Enables the fast-paste feature. Could cause problems with older DOS programs.
Windows Shortcut Keys	Deselect the desired Windows shortcut key to disable the shortcut key when this program is running.

Configuring DOS Games for Windows 95

DOS games are by far the greatest challenge of Windows 95. By nature, DOS-based games (especially graphically intense multimedia games) want full control of all your computer resources. And, they like to be in charge of CONFIG.SYS and AUTOEXEC.BAT, too. Running a DOS-based game in older versions of DOS often required creating a separate boot disk to properly configure the game (sometimes you even needed a separate boot disk for each game!). But to die-hard gamers, the trade-offs were worth the end result—a realistic, high-quality video and sound experience.

In fact, software vendors who write game software prefer to work in DOS for this simple fact alone. DOS allows the game software engineer to be in complete control of all hardware and the operating system, which allows the gamers to push the hardware to the edge. Often game software bypasses DOS and works directly with the hardware to achieve a higher-quality game. Windows 3.x could not handle this bypassing. The Windows 3.x services and libraries interfere with game software execution. Consequently, game software engineers avoided developing in Windows 3.x, or developed very basic games for Windows 3.x.

When Microsoft began designing Windows 95, they failed to resolve the issues in DOS and Windows 3.x. The first beta of Windows 95 released to the industry in 1994 did not address the needs of game software and hardware. Hardware designers wanted an operating system that would let game developers take advantage of their sound and video board's special features. Soon after that, The PC Games Consortium formed and Microsoft began working closely with it to develop Windows 95 as a solid gaming platform. Microsoft has since created the Game Software Developer Kit for Windows 95. As a result, many DOS-based game vendors such as Origin will port their DOS games to Windows 95, completely bypassing Windows 3.x development.

▶ See "What Windows 95 Software Offers," p. 405

▶ See "Using the Registry," p. 407

▶ See "Optimizing Windows 95," p. 410

Another vendor, Spectrum HoloByte (makers of STTNG Final Unity), says it will design its long-awaited Falcon 4.0 for Windows 95.

For the existing DOS-based games, Windows 95 offers many benefits. The MS-DOS virtual machine design keeps each DOS game in a separate VM for which you can set properties. If running the DOS game from a Windows 95 session does not work well, you can always run the game in MS-DOS mode. Furthermore, you can create custom AUTOEXEC.BAT and CONFIG.SYS files for each game, rather than shuffling DOS boot disks back and forth. ❖

Chapter 16

Using Windows 3.x Software

by Diane Tinney

Although Windows 95 32-bit software promises to out-perform today's Windows 3.x and DOS software, presently most companies run Windows 3.x software. Its programs are the product of years of performance tuning; businesses and home computer users have invested millions of dollars in Windows 3.x software. In contrast, very few Windows 95 products are available, and when the 32-bit applications are released, they will be brand new and probably need some breaking in.

So, at least for the near future, most of us will be installing, configuring, and using Windows 3.x software in Windows 95. The good news is that Windows 3.x software runs virtually unchanged in Windows 95. With the exception of older Windows 3.0 and perhaps shareware/freeware programs, all third party and custom-developed Windows 3.x software that ran well in Windows 3.x should run well—or better—in Windows 95.

In this chapter, you learn the following:

- How to install Windows 3.x software
- Changes in the user-interface
- How to access the property sheets
- How to view and edit INI files
- Areas that optimize performance
- How to recover from application problems

Setting Up Windows 3.x Software

Windows 3.x applications (also called *Win16 applications*) install and execute in Windows 95 without modification. If you installed Windows 95 to an existing Windows 3.x directory, Windows 95 automatically set up and configured the existing Win16 applications for you. If you installed Windows 95 to a different directory, you need to install (or re-install) the Windows application in Windows 95.

◄ See "Exploring the Windows 95 Architecture," p. 366

◄ See "Multitasking Your Applications," p. 369

◄ See "How Applications Communicate," p. 370

In this section, you learn how to install Windows 95 software and how Windows 95 sets up Windows 3.x software.

Installing Windows 3.x Software

The process for installing Windows 3.x software in Windows 95 is essentially the same as in Windows 3.x. Instead of using the File menu's Run command in Program Manager to install programs, in Windows 95 you use the Start menu's Run command. Alternatively, you could use the Add/Remove Programs feature in the Control Panel. Either way, the installation works the same.

Caution

Be careful when installing or updating Windows 3.x programs that share components (such as MS Graph which is shared by Word and Excel). Setup programs cannot update a component that is being used by a running application. To avoid conflicts, it is best to shut down related programs (and any critical applications/data) before installing or updating software.

To install Windows 3.x software, follow these steps:

1. Start Windows 95.
2. Place the installation disk in the appropriate drive.
3. Choose Start.
4. Choose Run.
5. Enter the full path and name of the installation file (usually SETUP.EXE or INSTALL.EXE), or click Browse to locate the file.
6. Click OK.
7. Follow the Windows 3.x installation instructions and screen prompts.
8. When installation completes, you return to Windows 95.

Figure 16.1 shows a newly installed Windows 3.1 application called Day-Timer Organizer. Notice that instead of a program group, a folder appears with two icons: a shortcut icon that launches the application, and a shortcut icon that uninstalls the application. In addition, Windows 95 added Day-Timer Organizer to the Program group on the Start menu. Within the Day-Timer Organizer menu folder appear the two shortcuts for launching and uninstalling.

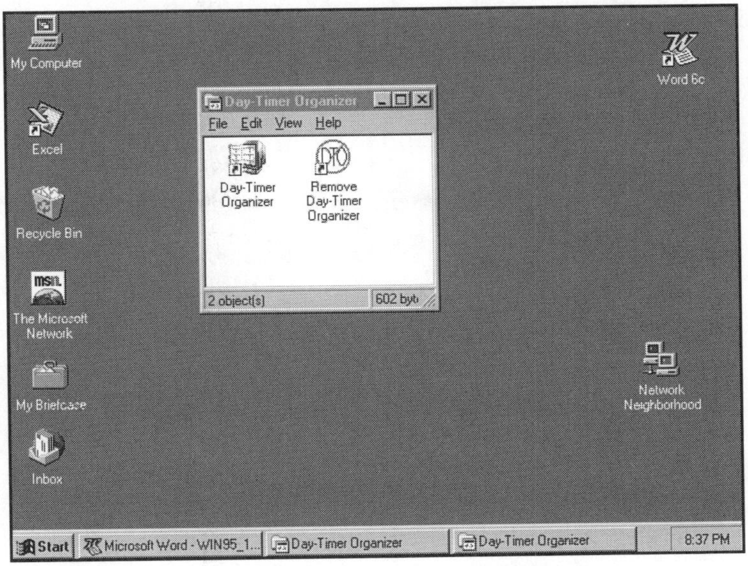

Fig. 16.1
Windows 95 automatically creates shortcut icons for your Windows 3.x programs.

Executing Windows 3.x Programs

When you execute a Windows 3.x program, you notice a few interface changes. First, the window (even in full-screen mode), has the Windows 95 title bar at the top and (by default) the Windows 95 task bar at the bottom (see fig. 16.2). The next interface change that you notice is that menus work like menus in Windows 95—a single mouse click activates the menu. Running the mouse pointer down a menu moves the Select bar. This happens because Windows applications rely on the graphical operating system to display common user interface items such as title bars, drop-down lists, and dialog box controls. As a result, your Windows 3.x programs look and feel like Windows 95 programs.

Although many of the graphical interface features change to a Windows 95 look and feel, the features behave in the same way. For example, the

Windows 3.x control box is replaced by an icon in the top-left corner of the title bar of each window. Clicking this icon displays the familiar menu of window control options (see fig. 16.3).

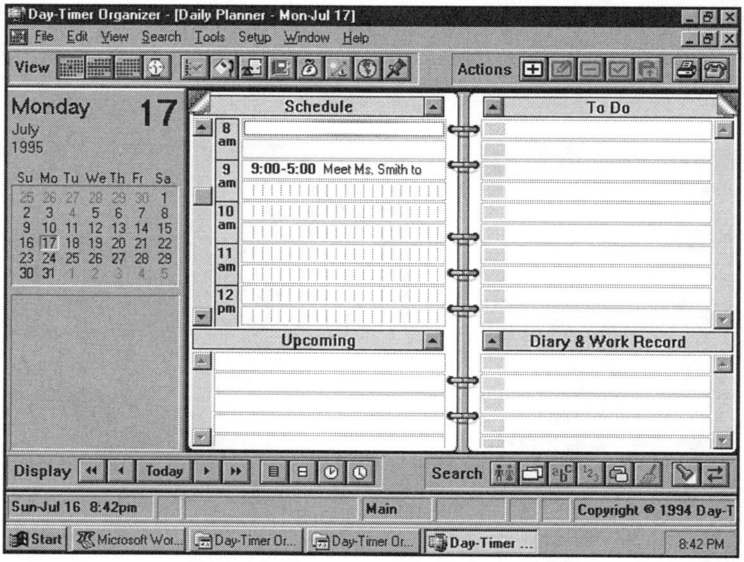

Fig. 16.2
Windows 3.x programs that are set up in Windows 95 automatically incorporate the Windows 95 GUI look and feel.

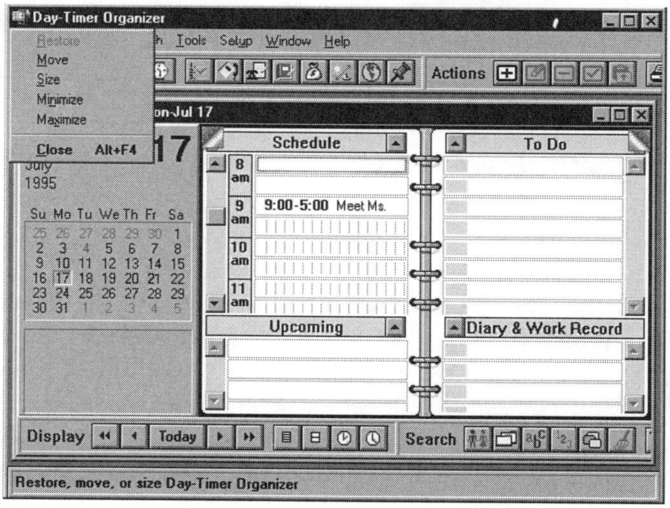

Fig. 16.3
You can still press Alt+F4 to close a program.

Accessing Windows 3.x Property Sheets

Since Window applications share a common configuration, their property sheets consist of only a General Properties sheet, and possibly a Version sheet. All other properties, such as memory, display, and fonts are managed by Windows 95 in other areas.

To display the property sheets for a Windows 3.x program, right-click the file name and choose Properties. Figure 16.4 shows the General Property sheet for the Day-Timer Organizer program file DTORG.EXE. The only settings you can change here are the file attributes.

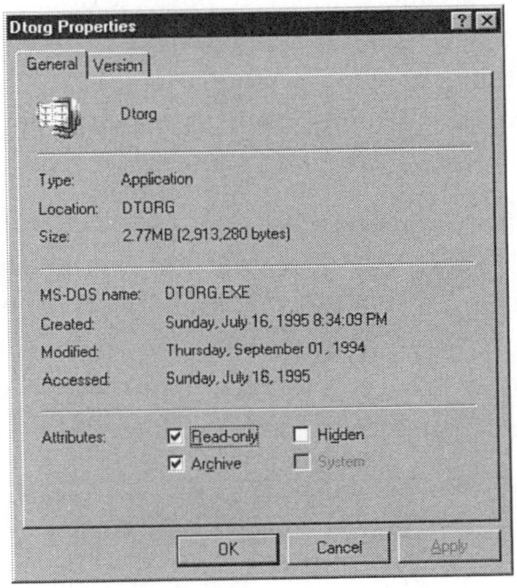

Fig. 16.4
The General Properties sheet for a Windows 3.x program displays the same information as for a DOS program.

Figure 16.5 shows the contents of the Version Properties sheet. Note that you cannot change any settings here; you can only view the program information.

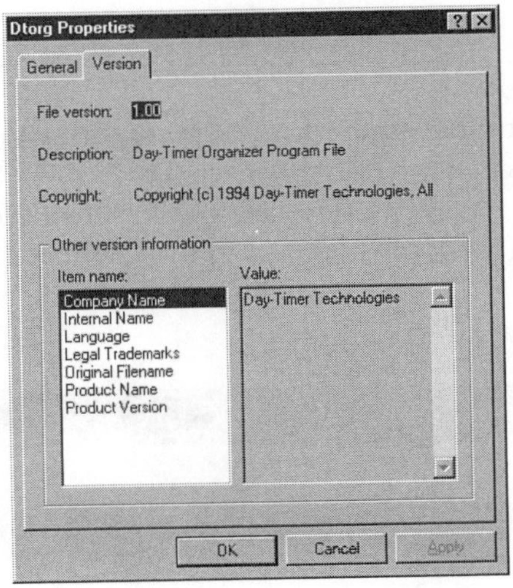

Fig. 16.5
The Version Properties sheet displays information such as the internal Windows 95 program name.

III

Setting Up Software

Uninstalling INI files

Windows 3.x programs relied on *initialization files* (which have the file extension INI) to load real mode and virtual device drivers during the Windows boot process. Windows 3.x applications often created their own initialization files or edited (without backing up or asking for permission) the Windows initialization files (WIN.INI and SYSTEM.INI). Over the years, as you add, update, and delete Windows 3.x applications, the contents and number of INI files increase. Settings and INI files for obsolete or deleted versions of Windows 3.x programs remain unless you invest the time to extract them manually, or spend the money for a Windows uninstall utility. Recently, a few Windows 3.x programs have begun to address this problem by providing their own "uninstall" routines.

In Windows 95, program configuration and initialization data is kept in a database known as the Registry. Ultimately, the Registry will replace not only the INI files but also the AUTOEXEC.BAT and CONFIG.SYS files. Meanwhile, Windows 95 maintains and uses the INI files to provide full compatibility with Windows 3.x programs. For a full description of the Registry and how to edit the Registry, see Chapter 17, "Using Windows 95 Software."

Note

Almost all of the Windows 95 configuration settings can be made interactively through the Control Panel and other settings folders. Although the data is stored in the Registry, you can (and should) view and set these properties via the Windows 95 graphical dialogs. Areas like Control Panel have built-in safeguards that keep you from making critical errors. An incorrect edit to the Registry database could bring your entire system down.

The INI files can be viewed and edited by using any plain ASCII text editor. Windows 95 provides a new version of the Windows 3.x SYSEDIT.EXE program, which allows you to quickly view and edit all of the setup files. You can find SYSEDIT.EXE in the Windows 95 SYSTEM folder. As you can see in figure 16.6, the Day-Timer installation program edited our WIN.INI file and added special initialization settings.

Tip

Before making any changes, you should make a backup copy of the INI files.

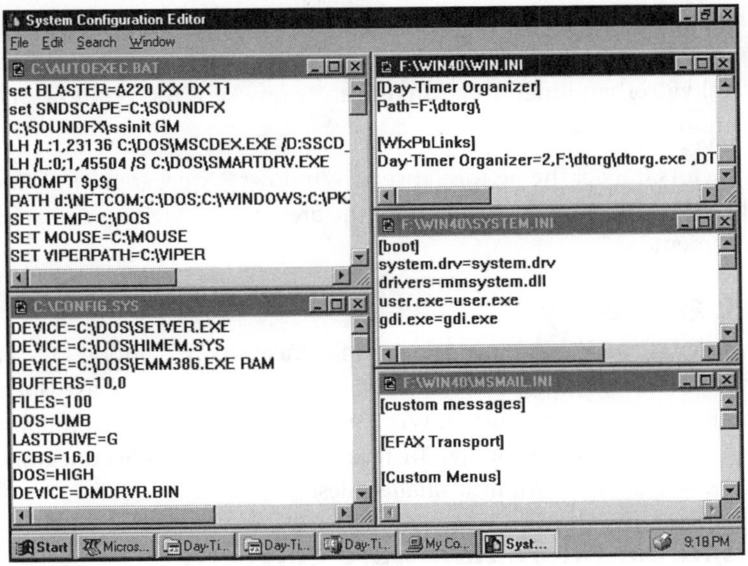

Fig. 16.6
Use the System Configuration Editor to check setup files.

> **Tip**
>
> Create a shortcut icon for SYSEDIT.EXE and place it on your desktop. Use this icon before and after installing Windows 3.x software to review and document changes.

Optimizing for Windows 3.x Software Execution

All of the known tricks on optimizing for Windows 3.x software still apply. Since Windows 95 runs Windows 3.x software in a Windows 3.x environment, the modifications that worked under Windows 3.x should operate under Windows 95. So, for example, if your database program worked best when the INI file contained a special command line, you should continue to use that command line. For optimization techniques which involve memory management, swap files, and other AUTOEXEC.BAT and CONFIG.SYS manipulation, you may find that you don't need them. The architecture of Windows 95 enables smoother multitasking, improved memory management, and better protection for other applications when an application crashes.

You may also find that the Win16 applications perform faster under Windows 95. Although the Win16 applications cannot run at the 32-bit speed, they take advantage of the operating system's 32-bit services, such as 32-bit printing and communications. Windows 95 also sports a much improved graphical video handling, which significantly quickens the Windows 3.x applications.

Many factors impact the performance of Windows 3.x programs in Windows 95. The following sections touch upon the areas which yield the greatest improvement.

Work Efficiently

You can optimize performance by working efficiently in Windows 95. Limit the number of applications that you run concurrently. Don't leave open programs that you are not using. Work in a less graphical environment (such as Draft instead of Layout mode). Instead of working in a huge document, break the document down into smaller files.

Use and Configure Hardware Correctly

Choosing the right hardware can make the difference between getting the job done now, or an hour later. Make sure the hardware meets the minimum requirements to run Windows 95. Whenever possible, buy Plug-and-Play components so you won't need to get involved in managing devices and resolving conflicts. For legacy devices (older, non-Plug-and-Play devices), contact the manufacturer for an up-to-date Windows 95 device driver.

Invest In Powerful Hardware

◀ See "Plug and Play Overview," p. 10

◀ See "Taking Your System's Inventory," p. 40

If possible, upgrade the PC to a faster processor, with more memory and state-of-the-art communication and multimedia features. The more optimized the hardware is, the more optimized Windows 95 and all your software applications will be.

Monitor and Maintain Resources

Windows 95 provides many utilities which you can use to periodically check on and improve system resources. The following utility programs can be found under the System Tools folder (Start, Programs, Accessories, System Tools):

- *Disk Defragmentor.* Improves disk access speed.
- *Scan Disk.* Checks disk surface and files for errors.
- *System Monitor.* Reports on performance of system resources.
- *Resource Meter.* Displays percentages of free system, user, and GDI resources.

> **Note**
>
> If your Systems Tools folder does not include all of these tools, you can install them from your Windows 95 Setup disk. Use Add/Remove Programs and select the custom setup option. Select System Tools and click Details. Select the missing tools to be installed.

Fine-Tune Windows 95

If all else fails, you may need to adjust the Windows 95 system configuration. In the Control Panel folder, the System Properties sheet contains a Performance page. The Performance page allows you to configure file system, graphic, and virtual memory options.

◀ See "Installation Options," p. 33

◀ See "Improving Hard Disk Performance," p. 323

Troubleshooting Application Problems

Typically, the user realizes that an application has a problem when the keyboard or mouse fails to respond, or when Windows 95 displays an error message. Application execution problems are usually caused by one of the following:

▶ See "Optimizing Windows 95," p. 410

▶ See "Fine-Tuning Virtual Memory," p. 416

- General Protection Fault (GPF)
- Hung application

For assistance in troubleshooting application problems, look in the Help index for the topic "Troubleshooting."

Handling a GPF

A *General Protection Fault* (GPF) occurs when an application violates system integrity. The following list provides examples of common GPFs:

- Application tried to use a memory address currently being used by another application.
- Error code returned by a system application programming interface (API).
- A memory fault caused by an invalid reference in memory.

When Windows 95 encounters a GPF, it displays a General Protection Fault message which tells the user which application caused the problem and provides the module name and a reference number. By relaying this information to the application vendor, the problem can be quickly resolved.

The effect of a GPF on the other applications that are executing depends on whether the offending application is a DOS application, a Windows 16-bit application (Win16), or a Windows 32-bit application (Win32).

GPFs in DOS Applications

Because each DOS application executes in a separate VM, a GPF in one DOS application has no effect on the other DOS, Win16, or Win32 applications currently executing. When the GPF message appears, record the error message information and choose OK to terminate the offending DOS application.

GPFs in Win16 Applications

Because all Win16 applications execute in a single VM, all Win16 application execution ceases until the application which caused the GPF is terminated. When the GPF message appears, record the error message information and choose OK to terminate the offending application. Once the offending application is terminated, the other Win16 applications resume execution.

GPFs in Win32 Applications

Because Win32 applications execute at a separate memory address within the System VM, a GPF in one Win32 application should have no effect on the other DOS, Win16, or Win32 applications currently executing. When the GPF message appears, record the error message information and choose OK to terminate the offending application. Any unsaved data in the offending application will be lost.

When an application is terminated by Windows 95, the normal closing routines are not performed, which could cause problems when you restart the program. For this reason, you may consider contacting the vendor before trying to re-execute the program.

Handling Hung Applications

Applications that are still executing, but fail to respond to system messages, are called *hung applications*. When an application hangs up the computer, the screen may look odd, the mouse may not work, or the keyboard may lock up. As with GPFs, the effect on other applications currently executing depends on whether the offending application is a DOS application, a Windows 16-bit application, or a Windows 32-bit application.

Handling Hung DOS Applications

Because DOS applications execute in a separate VM, a hung DOS application has no effect on the other DOS, Win16, or Win32 applications currently executing.

To end a hung DOS application, follow these steps:

1. Switch back to Windows 95.
2. Display the Properties sheet for the application.
3. Select Terminate the Application.

◀ See "Exploring the Windows 95 Architecture," p. 366

◀ See "Understanding Virtual Machines," p. 366

◀ See "Multitasking Your Applications," p. 369

◀ See "How Applications Communicate," p. 370

Handling Hung Win16 Applications

Because all Win16 applications share a common message queue, all running Win16 applications are also hung because they cannot access the message queue. The hung Win16 applications have no effect on any running DOS or Win32 applications.

To end a hung Win16 application, follow these steps:

1. Switch back to the offending Win16 application.
2. Press Ctrl+Alt+Delete. A list of the programs that are not responding to the system appears.
3. Choose End Task to terminate the application. Note that data loss is limited to that in the offending application.

Handling Hung Win32 Applications

Because each Win32 application has its own separate message queue, no other DOS, Win16, or Win32 applications are affected.

To terminate a hung Win32 application, follow these steps:

1. Switch back to the offending Win32 application.
2. Press Ctrl+Alt+Delete. A list of the programs that are not responding to the system appears.
3. Choose End Task to terminate the application. Note that data loss is limited to that in the offending application.

> **Note**
>
> Generally, if an application hangs a critical resource, other applications that need that resource are stopped. By terminating the hung application, you free up the resource and allow the stopped applications to resume execution.

Chapter 17

Using Windows 95 Software

by Diane Tinney

So now you've installed Windows 95. There are many features, particularly the Registry and preemptive multitasking, that you can work with to best optimize the Windows 95 environment for your new 32-bit applications. This chapter starts you down the 32-bit highway.

In this chapter, you learn

- The advantages of using 32-bit Windows 95 software
- How to access and edit the Registry
- How to fine-tune system performance

What Windows 95 Software Offers

The key advantages of Windows 95 software are the following:

- 32-bit processing
- Preemptive multitasking
- Multi-threaded processing
- Easy maintenance

You learn how each feature can save you both time and money.

Fast Processing

The easiest way to understand the difference between 16-bit processing and 32-bit processing is to imagine each as a highway with 16 or 32 lanes.

Imagine your data as buses and cars commuting at rush hour. When the traffic is heavy and the heat is on, 32 lanes provide for more throughput, fewer accidents, and less stress on system resources. In your computer, the Windows 95 operating system is already running at 32-bit speed. The more 32-bit applications that you use, the more work that gets done, fewer GPFs and less stress on the computer resources.

As covered at the beginning of Chapter 15, DOS applications execute in separate virtual machines (VMs). Windows 3.x (16-bit) applications execute in the System VM in a single address space. Windows 95 (32-bit) applications also run in the System VM, but in separate address spaces.

◀ See "Understanding Virtual Machines," p. 366

◀ See "How Applications Communicate," p. 370

DOS applications can't bring down the system, other DOS applications, or other Windows (16- or 32-bit) applications. Windows 3.x (16-bit) applications can bring down other 16-bit applications. Windows 95 (32-bit) applications can't bring down other 32-bit, 16-bit, or DOS applications.

The fastest, best protection exists for the 32-bit applications, which execute within the 32-bit Windows 95 operating system.

Preemptive Multitasking

The 32-bit applications use *preemptive multitasking,* where each thread is executed for a preset time period, or until another thread with a higher priority is ready to execute. The Windows 95 Task Scheduler manages multitasking and ensures that no one application monopolizes the processor. At any time, the operating system can *preempt* (take control away from) an application and hand the CPU to another application with a higher priority task.

This is better than the quirky Windows 3.x (16-bit) applications, which use a *cooperative multitasking system.* In cooperative multitasking, the program (rather than the operating system) is in control of CPU scheduling. Although programs should yield to the operating system after a reasonable amount of time, we have all encountered the Windows 3.x program which fails to return control and eventually locks up the entire system.

Multi-Threaded Processing

Windows 95 32-bit applications can take advantage of *multi-threaded processing* (schedule their own threads of execution). Multi-threaded processing is not available for DOS or Win16 applications. The advantage of multithreading is that you get to do your work faster. For example, printing a document in Word for Windows 95 is much faster than in Windows 3.1, and you get control of your document back quicker because Word for Windows 95 takes advantage of multi-threaded processing for print jobs.

Easier Maintenance

Consolidation of the system initialization and setup files into a single database—which is maintained by the operating system—makes the Win32 platform easier to use. Once consumers move to Win32 and no longer need DOS or Win16 applications, the AUTOEXEC.BAT, CONFIG.SYS, WIN.INI, SYSTEM.INI, and other INI files will no longer be needed. This information is kept in the Registry database and automatically modified as software and hardware is installed, removed, and updated. This feature, coupled with the Plug and Play standard, makes Windows 95 a self-configuring system.

Using the Registry

DOS depended on the AUTOEXEC.BAT and CONFIG.SYS configuration files to initialize and set system parameters on what resources were available and how they should be used. Windows 3.x relied on initialization files (which had a file extension of INI) to tell Windows and Windows applications what resources were available and how to work with those resources.

When Microsoft began designing Windows 95, they identified many problems with these resource setting files. These files were difficult to maintain, often contained remnants of old program setups no longer needed, and usually required user intervention to improve performance. To solve these problems, Windows 95 borrowed a good idea from Windows NT: the Registry.

The *Registry* is a single database that contains system and application execution information. Ultimately, the Registry replaces all INI files as well as AUTOEXEC.BAT and CONFIG.SYS. The Windows 95 Registry replaces REG.DAT which was used by Windows 3.1 to store file extension application associations and register OLE applications.

Exploring the Registry

The Windows 95 Registry consists of three data files:

- *USER.DAT*. Stores user preferences such as the Desktop.
- *SYSTEM.DAT*. Stores the computer's hardware configurations such as drives, printers, and sound card settings.
- *POLICY.POL*. Stores administrative policies set up on a network server.

Precautions are taken to protect these data files. First, the Registry data is kept in binary format, so the files cannot be read by a regular text editor. Second, the file attributes are set to read-only, hidden, system files. This prevents accidental deletion.

When you first install Windows 95, the setup program creates the SYSTEM.DAT file and enters the data regarding installed hardware. If you installed to the Windows 3.x directory, Setup copies the data from REG.DAT into the new SYSTEM.DAT file. From then on, whenever you install new hardware or change a configuration, Windows 95 automatically updates the SYSTEM.DAT data file.

You can view the hardware data stored in SYSTEM.DAT by opening the Control Panel folder and selecting System. Figure 17.1 shows the installed devices, as reported by SYSTEM.DAT.

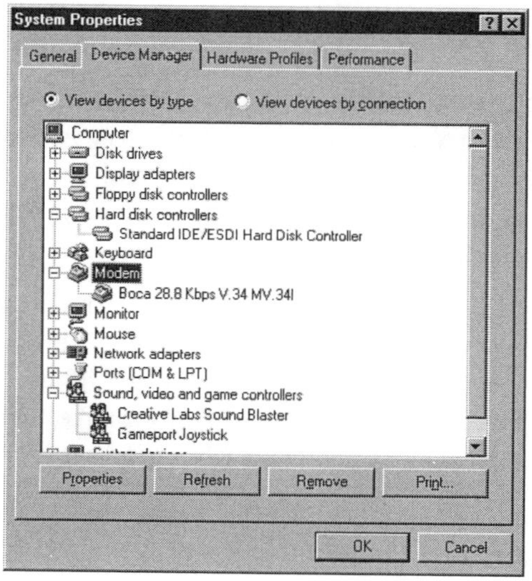

Fig. 17.1
The Device Manager page displays installed devices by type.

Using REGEDIT

The Registry Editor (REGEDIT) is located in the Windows 95 folder. To run REGEDIT, choose Run from the Start menu, type **REGEDIT**, and press Enter. Figure 17.2 shows the Registry Editor and data for My Computer.

Tip

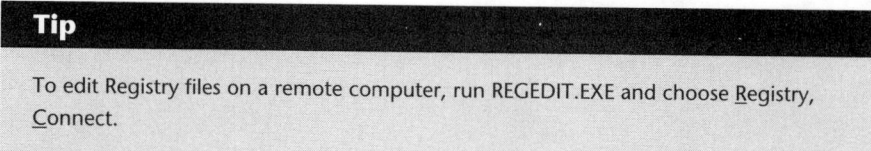

To edit Registry files on a remote computer, run REGEDIT.EXE and choose Registry, Connect.

Caution

Before you open the Registry Editor and start modifying the settings, be sure you understand what you are changing and why. If the modification desired can be effected by using Control Panel or by setting some other property, make the change there. Avoid using Registry Editor unless it is absolutely necessary.

Microsoft advises that you don't use the REGEDIT utility unless you are on the phone with one of their technicians. That's why they didn't include an icon for it by default—you have to manually create one.

Incorrect edits to the Registry could prevent Windows from working properly and result in a loss of critical data.

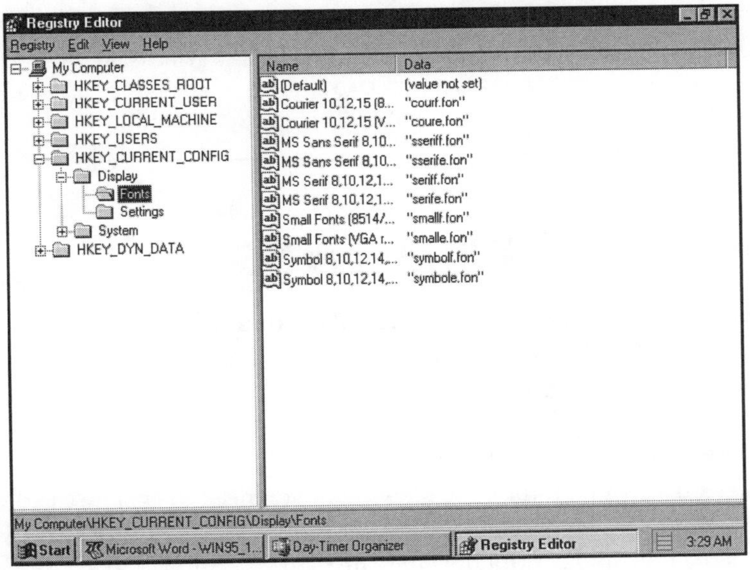

Fig. 17.2
The Registry Editor lists the installed fonts on My Computer.

The Registry is organized into matched keys and values. The keys are listed on the left pane (refer to fig. 17.2) as a hierarchical tree. As you double-click items and drill-down within branches, the values appear in the right pane. To change a key's value, right-click on the value in the right pane. The Registry Editor then displays an object menu: Modify, Delete and Rename. Figure 17.3 shows the Edit String dialog box for a Registry value.

As you change entries, the Registry Editor automatically changes the applicable database file (DAT). However, the changes don't take effect until you restart Windows 95.

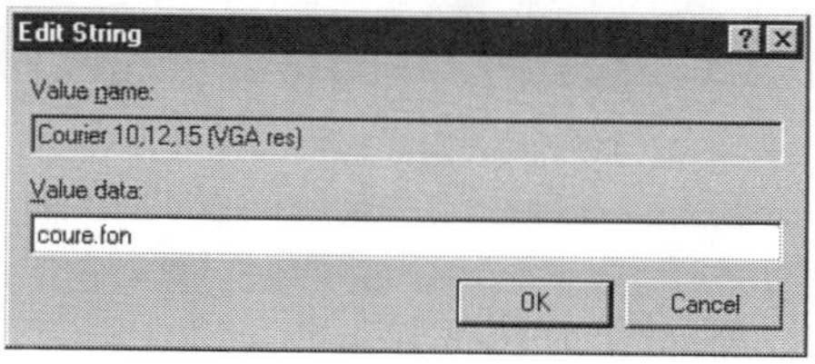

Fig. 17.3
Enter or edit the Value data in the Edit String dialog box.

Tip

Double-click a Registry value to modify the value.

Note

Windows 95 maintains backup copies of the Registry data in the Windows 95 folder. The backup files SYSTEM.DA0 and USER.DA0 are used by Windows 95 in the event that the actual DAT files become corrupt.

Optimizing Windows 95

In the Control Panel folder, the System Properties sheet contains a Performance page. The Performance page allows you to configure the file system, graphic, and virtual memory settings.

Exploring File Systems

Before you start fine-tuning the file system, you need to explore the design of the Windows 95 file system. Operating systems use a file system to organize files, store files, and control how files are named. Windows 95 continues to use the DOS File Allocation Table (FAT) file system as its default file system. However, Windows 95 implements a new approach to file system management, called the *Installable File System* (IFS). IFS is a program that provides an interface between the application file requests and various supported file systems.

Windows 95 ships with the following installable file systems:

- Virtual File Allocation Table (VFAT)
- CD-ROM File System (CDFS)
- Network Redirector

In addition to these supported file systems, vendors may create and add their own installable file systems. For example, a vendor may create an installable file system to allow users to access and work with UNIX or Apple files.

The IFS Manager can work with application programming interface (API) calls from Win32 applications and interrupt 21 (INT 21H) calls generated by Win16 or DOS applications. The file system design in Windows 95 supports up to 32 layers from the input/output subsystem (IOS) down to the hardware level. Each layer has defined interfaces with the layers above and below. This enables each component to cooperate with its neighbors.

VFAT

The FAT file system was developed to work with DOS. A clear advantage of FAT is that a disk formatted for FAT can be read by DOS, Windows NT, Windows 95, and OS/2. However, the DOS FAT file system has the following limitations:

- File names are limited to eight characters with a three-character extension.
- Every file access from a Windows-based application requires the system to switch to 8086 mode to execute DOS code, which slows down performance.
- The use of the INT 21H interrupt as the sole interface to every file system function causes conflicts between TSRs, disk caching, disk compression, and network systems.

VFAT is a 32-bit virtualized FAT file system. The VFAT.VXD file system driver (FSD) controls this file system and uses 32-bit code for all file access. VFAT is a protected mode implementation of the FAT file system. The VFAT system supports long file names (up to 255 characters), eliminates the over-reliance on INT 21H, uses 32-bit processing, and allows multiple, concurrent threads to execute file system code.

CDFS

The CDFS file system replaces MSCDEX TRS, which is used to support most CD-ROM devices. CDFS is a 32-bit protected mode ISO 9660 compliant CD-ROM file system. Applications send file requests to the CDFS, which handles the request and passes it to the IOS. The IOS routes the request to the type specific driver (TSD), which converts the logical request to a physical request. From there, a special SCSI translator sends the request to the SCSI port driver and then to the Miniport driver.

Network Redirector

The Network Redirector installable file system is a 32-bit protected mode VXD responsible for implementing the structure of a remote file system. When an application sends or receives data from a remote device, it sends a call to the Redirector. The Redirector communicates with the network via the protocol driver. Windows 95 supports two kinds of redirectors:

- Windows Networking (SMB over NetBEUI protocol)
- Microsoft Client for NetWare (NCP protocol)

Working with Long File Names

◀ See "Networking Support," p. 143

◀ See "Setting Configuration Information," p. 144

▶ See "Installing Network Interface Cards," p. 637

Whereas DOS limited users to file names that were up to eight characters plus a three-character extension (8.3), Windows 95 supports the use of long file names (also known as *LFN*). The long file names follow these filenaming rules:

- File names can be up to 255 characters long, including extensions.
- Uppercase and lowercase are preserved, but are not case-sensitive.
- Filename characters can be any characters (including spaces) except for the following:

  ? / \ " : < > | *

- File size of up to 16 exabytes (16E).

> **Note**
>
> An exabyte is a billion gigabytes. A stack of 3.5-inch disks to equal the capacity of 16E would be 2,300 times the distance from the earth to the moon.

Preserving FAT 8.3 File Names

Windows 95 maintains FAT 8.3 file names for each long file name. For example, the file named "East Coast Sales.EXCEL" would have a FAT name of EASTCOAS.EXC. By doing so, Windows 95 ensures that a program designed for FAT file names can access and work with files created under Windows 95. LFNs also provide additional information about a file, such as the date of the last file modification.

The following rules are used by the Windows 95 file system to convert long file names into the DOS 8.3 format:

- Remove special characters (such as spaces).
- If unique, use the first eight characters of LFN.
- If not unique, use the first six characters, a tilde (~), and a number (for example, EASTCO~2.EXC).
- For the extension, use the first three characters following the last period.

For example, if you have three files in Windows 95 called East coast budget.xls, East coast expenses.xls, and East coast sales.xls, their 8.3 DOS file names become EASTCO~1.XLS, EASTCO~2.XLS, and EASTCO~3.XLS consecutively.

Note that 8.3 file names do not preserve the case of characters (all uppercase).

Several problems arise when using a file in a Windows 95 application and in a non-LFN aware application:

- Changing the LFN file name or copying the LFN to a new name, while in a non-LFN application, deletes the long file name.
- Files created according to the 8.3 file naming rules have an LFN, which is the same as the 8.3 file name.
- Files created according to the LFN file naming rules have a different 8.3 file name (as outlined in the prior rules).
- LFNs use a previously reserved area of the File Allocation Table (FAT). DOS utilities that also use this area of FAT may damage this section of FAT.

Note

The Windows NT and Windows 95 long file name schemes are *not* compatible. Also, Windows NT version 3.5 and earlier does not support LFNs in the FAT file system. Windows 95 supports LFNs in FAT.

The OS/2 LFN naming scheme is not compatible with Windows 95 LFNs.

Caution

Do not use disk or backup utilities that are not aware of long file names. If you need to use a backup/restore utility that does not support LFNs, Microsoft supplies a utility called Long File Name Backup (LFNBK) that preserves the LFNs (it comes on the Win95 CD or you can contact Microsoft for this utility).

Modifying File System Properties

Windows 95 automatically sets file system properties to optimize the performance based on the current configuration. However, there may be times when you need to set a certain property or become aware of a unique need to boost performance. The System object in the Control Panel enables you to view and set disk and CD-ROM file system properties.

To set file system properties, follow these steps:

1. Open the Control Panel folder.
2. Open the System icon.
3. Select the Performance page (see fig. 17.4).
4. Click File System. The File System Properties sheet appears (see fig. 17.5).

Fig. 17.4
The System Performance property page reports on the status of key resources.

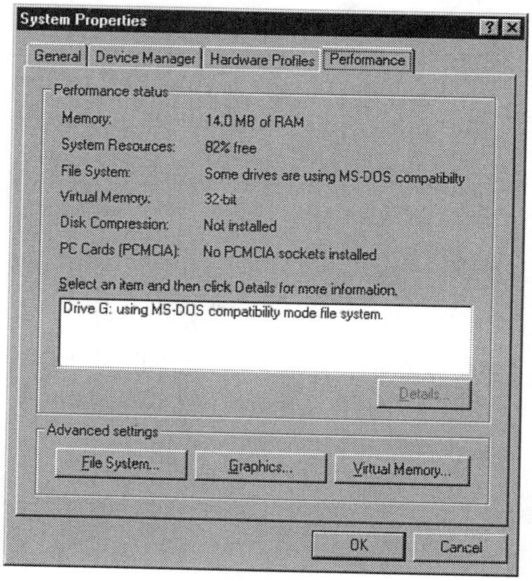

Fig. 17.5
Increase the Read-Ahead Optimization to speed up performance.

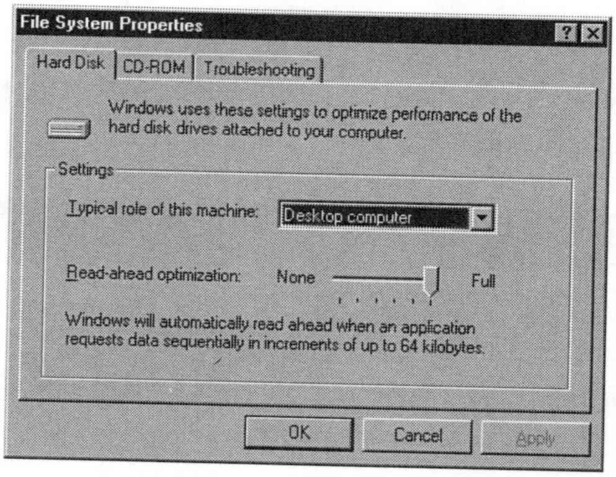

5. Set the desired options.

6. Select the CD-ROM page (see fig. 17.6).

7. Choose OK twice to implement the changes the next time Windows 95 loads.

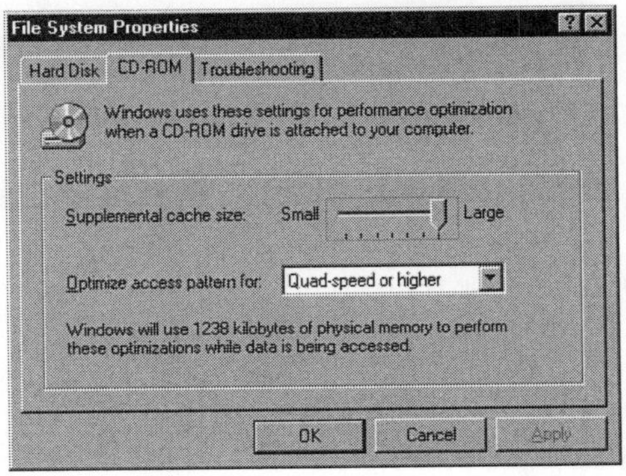

Fig. 17.6
To optimize the CD-ROM performance, select the correct access pattern.

Troubleshooting the File System

If an application does not respond properly to the Windows 95 file system, you can use the File System Troubleshooter to detect the cause of the problem. Using the troubleshooter, you can disable the following Windows 95 file system features:

- File sharing and locking
- Preservation of long file names in non-LFN programs
- Protect-mode hard disk interrupt handler
- 32-bit protect-mode disk drivers
- Write-behind caching for all drives

To start the File System Troubleshooter, follow these steps:

1. Open the Control Panel.

2. Open the System icon.

3. Select the Performance page.

4. Choose File System.

5. Select the Troubleshooting page (see fig. 17.7).

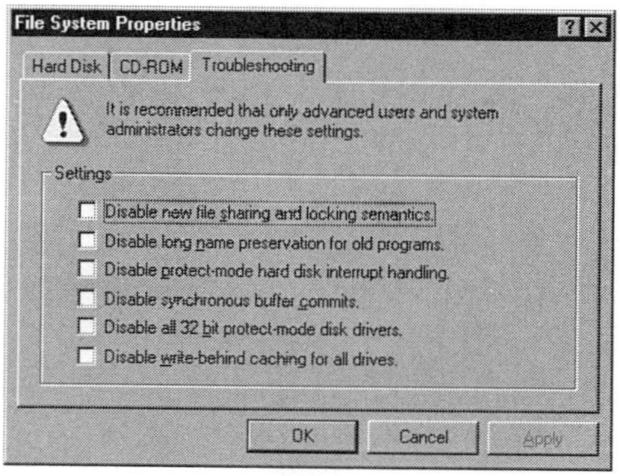

Fig. 17.7
Use the Troubleshooting page to disable file system properties when trying to locate a problem.

6. Select the setting to be tested.
7. Choose OK to test the setting.

Fine-Tuning Graphics

You can control the graphics accelerator used to control how Windows uses your graphics hardware. To adjust the acceleration rate, open the System Properties Performance page, choose Graphics, and adjust the Hardware Acceleration slide (see fig. 17.8). Click OK twice to save your changes.

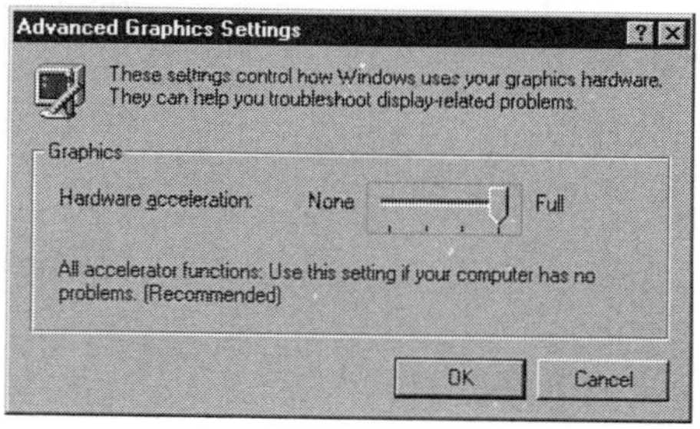

Fig. 17.8
The Advanced Graphics Settings dialog box allows you to control the graphics acceleration rate.

Fine-Tuning Virtual Memory

It is highly recommended that you let Windows manage your virtual memory settings. However, if needed, you can specify your own VM settings and even completely disable virtual memory. To modify Virtual Memory performance, open the System Properties Performance tab, choose Virtual Memory, and select Let Me Specify My Own Virtual Memory Settings. Set the Hard Disk location, and Minimum and Maximum values (see fig. 17.9). Select Yes to continue. Then click OK to save your changes.

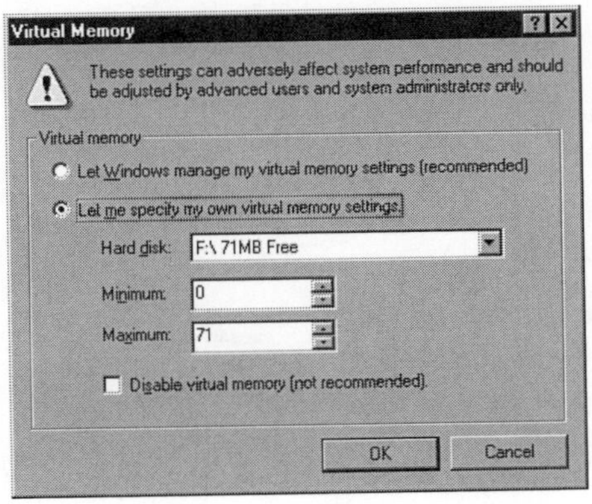

Fig. 17.9
If necessary, you can manually set Virtual Memory options.

Chapter 18

Configuring Monitors and Video Cards for Windows 95

by Paul Sanna

The components of your PC that require the least amount of care and feeding most likely are the monitor and video card. With most PCs, when you change your monitor or video card, or when you start your PC for the first time, the correct image usually appears on-screen immediately.

Making changes to your machine's video hardware sometimes spells TROUBLE if you are a Windows 3.x user, however. If you make an inadvertent change to your video configuration from within Windows, there is a chance you won't be able to start Windows again without manually editing an initialization file. Fortunately, Windows 95 makes it easy and safe to configure your video adapter and monitor.

In this chapter, you learn how to

- Install your new video card and tell whether your new device is a Plug and Play device
- Start the Add New Hardware Wizard
- Specify what video card is installed in your PC
- Let Windows 95 detect what video card is installed in your PC
- Configure your screen's resolution, color palette, and font settings

Installing Your New Video Card into Your PC

Before learning how to configure Windows 95 to work with a new video card, you should first know how to get the new piece of equipment installed into your PC, as well as how to run Windows 95 the first time with that new equipment. In fact, after you have installed the card or monitor, you may have very little (or no) work to do to configure Windows 95. For example, if you have a Plug and Play system, Windows 95 will do all the work necessary to configure your new video adapter or monitor.

Tip

What's the most important rule when you are setting up a new appliance? *Have the user's manual or documentation handy.* This rule also applies to setting up new hardware equipment. Before you start to configure a new video card or monitor, be sure you have on hand relevant documentation. You may need to supply information included in the user's manual.

Also, be sure you have any disks (floppy or CD-ROM) supplied with the device; Windows 95 may need software supplied on the disk.

In this section, you learn what happens when you install a new video card or monitor into a PC running Windows 95, including if your system is ready for Plug and Play.

Note

Windows 95 supports PCs with Plug and Play devices. This means that when you install a Plug and Play device such as video adapter, into your PC, or simply plug one in, such as a monitor, Windows 95 automatically detects the presence of the new device and configures it for use in Windows 95. For more information about Plug and Play, refer to Chapter 1, "Preparing to Install Windows 95."

To install a new video adapter into your PC, follow these steps:

1. Shut down Windows 95, turn off the power on your PC, and follow the instructions enclosed with the adapter to install the card into the PC.

2. Turn on your PC. If your PC does not boot Windows 95 automatically, start Windows 95.

3. If the video adapter you installed in step 1 is Plug-and-Play compatible, Windows 95 notifies you that it has detected it. Windows still might ask you for the driver for the video card to complete the setup of the card. If so, enter the location on the hard drive or network where the driver is located. If the driver is on a floppy disk supplied by the manufacturer of the card, insert the disk into the disk drive and then specify the name of the drive (for example, **A**). Refer to the section "Configuring Video Cards and Monitors" for instructions on how to fine-tune your new hardware with Windows 95.

Note

Drivers for video cards are needed so that Windows 95 can properly display images on the screen based on the specifications and capabilities of the video adapter.

4. If the device is not Plug-and-Play compatible, Windows 95 does not prompt you for any information. You should start the Add New Hardware Wizard to configure your new video card and monitor .

Starting the Add New Hardware Wizard

Like all other hardware, new video cards are identified and configured for use in Windows 95 through the Add New Hardware Wizard. The Add New Hardware Wizard automates most of the work you had to complete in Windows 3.1 and DOS to set up a new monitor or video card. The Add New Hardware Wizard can be found in the Control Panel folder, where Windows 95 installs it by default (see fig. 18.1).

Tip

Though the Add New Hardware Wizard is located in the Control Panel folder, you can create a shortcut so you can launch the wizard from wherever you choose. If you plan to do a lot of work with the hardware in Windows 95, you could save some time by creating a shortcut to the wizard right on the Desktop. For instructions on creating a shortcut, refer to Chapter 6, "Configuring the Windows 95 Desktop, Display, and Fonts."

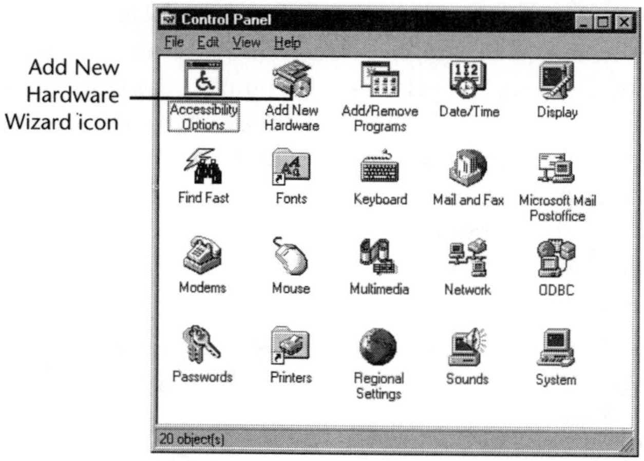

Fig. 18.1
The Add New Hardware Wizard can be found in the Control Panel folder.

Follow these steps to launch the Add New Hardware Wizard:

1. Start the Add New Hardware Wizard. It is located in the Control Panel folder. The dialog box shown in figure 18.2 appears.

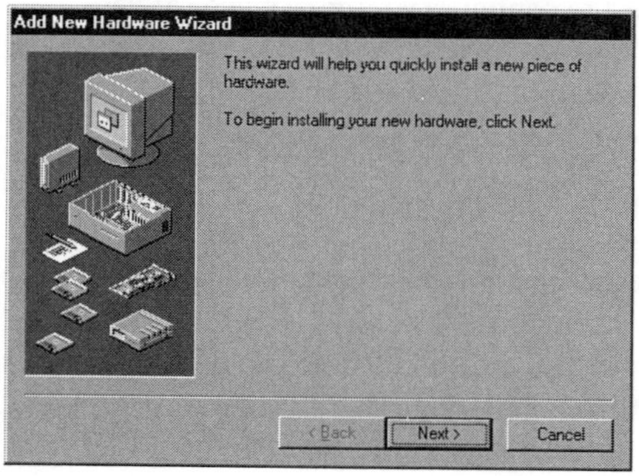

Fig. 18.2
The first dialog box that appears when you start the Add New Hardware Wizard tells you what the wizard does and gives you the opportunity to cancel.

2. The dialog box that appears is part of many wizards in Windows 95. It is used simply to tell you which wizard you started and to give you the opportunity to cancel. To clear this dialog box and continue, click the Next button. To cancel the wizard, click Cancel.

The next step in using the Add New Hardware Wizard to configure a video card or monitor is to decide who will identify which hardware is installed: you or Windows 95.

Deciding Who Specifies the Hardware

There are two different approaches you can use to specify the video adapter and monitor you will use with Windows 95. You can let Windows 95 try to identify your video adapter and monitor automatically, or you can tell Windows 95 explicitly which video adapter and monitor is installed on your PC. The Add New Hardware Wizard gives you the option of choosing which approach to take.

If Windows 95 detects the hardware, the clear advantage is that Windows 95 does all the work. All you do is confirm that Windows 95 properly identified the components on your PC. But, you can also encounter some disadvantages:

- Windows 95 may make a mistake. It is possible Windows 95 will misidentify your adapter or not be able to identify it at all.
- It can take up too much time. Windows 95 attempts to identify all of the hardware on your PC, which sometimes can take 30 minutes. You cannot instruct Windows 95 to detect just your new video card or monitor.

You could also tell Windows 95 what hardware you have. One clear advantage is that there is less chance of error. Provided you know what hardware is installed on your PC, you can be sure Windows 95 installs the correct driver by explicitly telling Windows 95 what hardware to configure.

However, this option involves more work for you. You need to know exact manufacturer and model information in order to supply that information to Windows 95.

Lots of work went into the development of Windows 95's ability to recognize your hardware—why not take advantage of it?

Letting Windows 95 Detect the Video Card

The process for letting Windows 95 detect your video card is simple. First, you start the Add New Hardware Wizard. Windows 95 inspects your system and identifies any hardware devices it doesn't recognize since the last time it inspected your system. If Windows 95 finds a video card that it does not recognize, it informs you what model video card it thinks it found. Next, you confirm that information, and then Windows 95 configures itself so it always loads the correct drivers for use with the adapter. Most likely, you won't have to reboot your machine.

To let Windows 95 detect your video card, follow these steps:

1. Follow the instructions to start the Add New Hardware Wizard shown in the earlier section, "Starting the Add New Hardware Wizard."

2. Click the Next button in the first dialog that appears (see fig. 18.3).

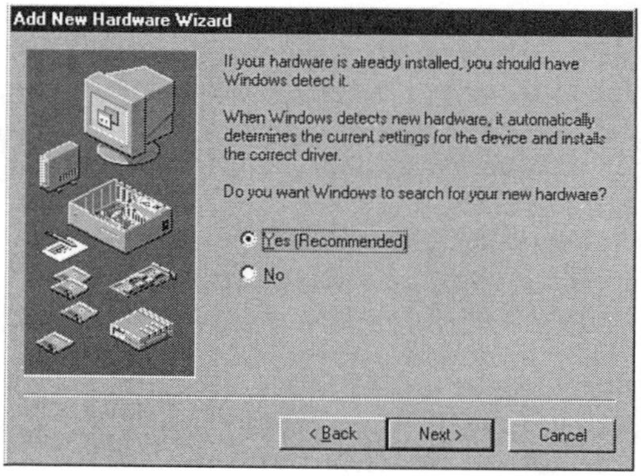

Fig. 18.3
Windows 95 lets you specify whether it should detect all new hardware on your PC.

3. Click the Yes (Recommended) option button and then click Next.

4. The dialog box shown in figure 18.4 appears. This dialog box asks you to confirm that you want Windows 95 to detect the hardware on your PC. Click Next. Windows 95 now starts the detection phase when it inspects your PC for installed hardware.

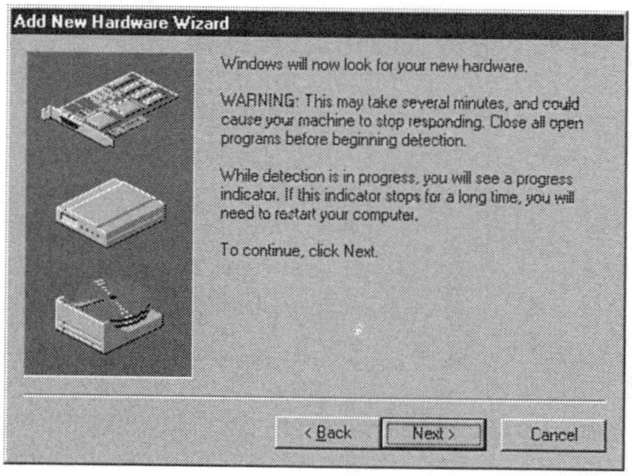

Fig. 18.4
Just before it begins to inspect your system for installed hardware, Windows 95 asks you to verify that you want to continue.

Caution

Windows 95 warns you that your system might freeze while it tries to automatically detect the hardware installed on your system. Don't worry (too much). Be sure you close down any applications you might have running before starting the automatic detection phase. Should your system freeze, reboot the computer and use the manual detection method for configuring your hardware. See "Manually Specifying Your Video Card" later in this chapter.

5. After Windows 95 completes the detection phase, it displays the dialog box shown in figure 18.5. Click the Details button to view the list of new hardware found by the Add New Hardware Wizard.

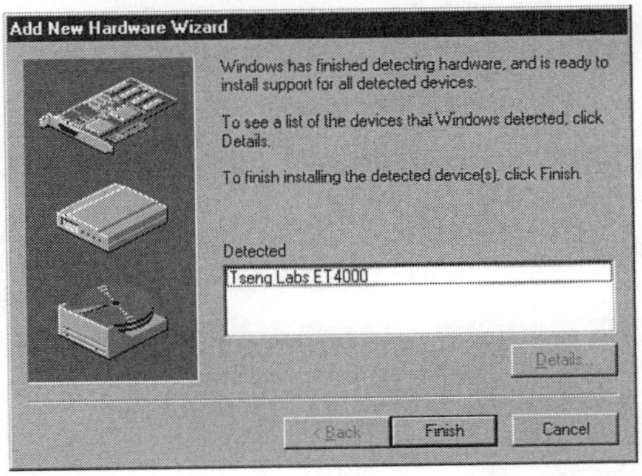

Fig. 18.5
Windows 95 permits you to see the new hardware devices it detected.

6. To configure Windows 95 with the new video adapter, click Finish. Depending upon the capabilities of your video card and monitor, Windows 95 may ask if it can reboot the system for the changes to take effect. If asked, choose Yes to complete installation of the new video card immediately.

Manually Specifying Your Video Card

The process to manually specify your video card has a number of steps, but the process is straightforward and each step is easy to complete: start the Add New Hardware wizard, tell Windows 95 you want to install a display adapter, and pick the adapter from a list provided by Windows 95. Windows 95 configures itself so it always loads the correct driver for use with the card. Most likely, you will not have to reboot your machine.

To manually specify that the video card is installed on your PC, follow these steps:

1. Follow the instructions to start the Add New Hardware wizard shown earlier in the section "Starting the Add New Hardware Wizard."

2. Click the Next button in the first dialog that appears (see fig. 18.6).

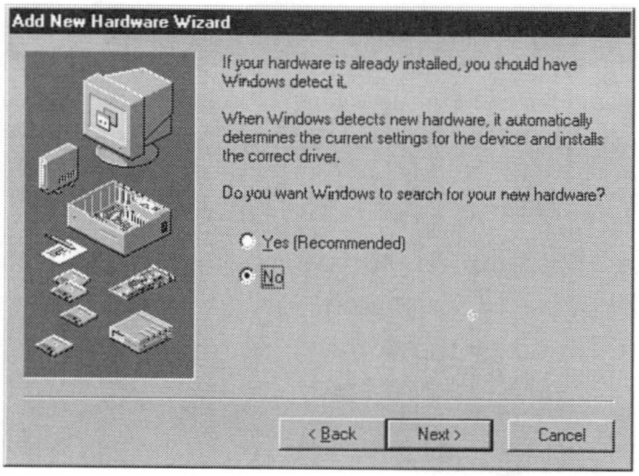

Fig. 18.6
You can override the Windows default of inspecting your system for new devices by selecting the No button.

3. Click No to instruct Windows 95 not to automatically detect new hardware, and then choose the Next button. The dialog box shown in figure 18.7 appears.

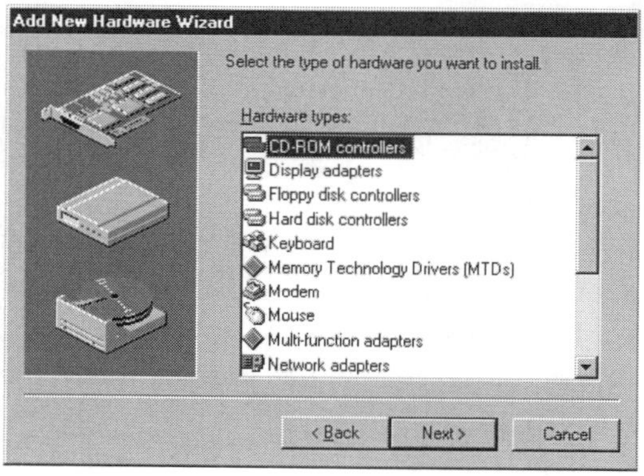

Fig. 18.7
Windows 95 lets you specify what type of hardware you want to install.

4. Choose Display Adapters in the Hardware Types list box, and then click Next. The dialog box in figure 18.8 appears.

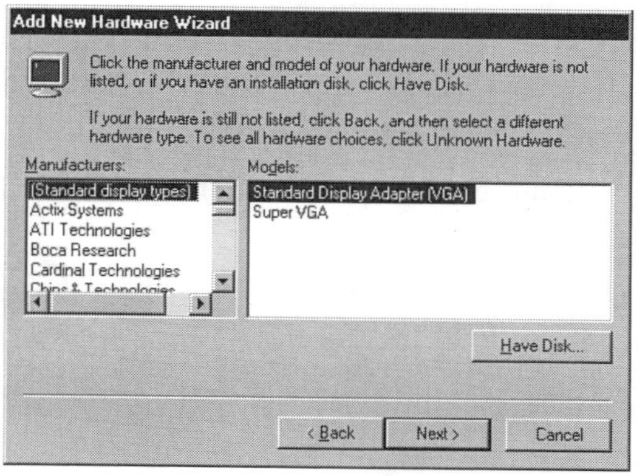

Fig. 18.8
Windows 95 provides a list of supported video card models (and their manufacturers) for you to choose from.

5. Click the manufacturer of your video card in the Manufacturers list box. The list of supported video cards for the manufacturer you chose appears in the Models list box.

6. Click the model of your video adapter in the Models list box.

Tip

You can avoid having to pick the manufacturer and model of your video card from the lists provided with Windows 95 if you have the software installation disk that was shipped with the video card. Insert the disk into a floppy drive and then click the Have Disk button in the dialog box shown in figure 18.8. Follow the prompts to specify the location of OEMSETUP.INF, which should appear on the disk. This file contains all the information needed to configure the video card. This technique also can be useful if you have a late model adapter that is not yet supported by Windows 95. If no software is supplied with the video card, or if you cannot locate the OEMSETUP.INF file, contact the manufacturer of the card.

6. Click the Next button. Windows 95 informs you that it has completed the installation of the video card.

7. Click the Finish button.

Troubleshooting

I don't recognize (or I don't know) either the manufacturer or the model of my video card in the lists that appear in the Add New Hardware Wizard. Also, I can't find any disks that might be associated with my video card.

Windows 95 lets you choose a generic driver for use with your adapter if you are not sure what video adapter is installed in your PC. Choose Standard Display Types from the Manufacturers list box and either Standard Display Adapter (VGA) or Super VGA from the Models list box. If you are not sure whether your monitor is Super VGA capable, choose the VGA option.

Configuring Your Monitor and Video Card

Once your video card has been configured for Windows 95, there are a few options you can use to configure your display. For example, you can change the resolution for your display, or you can choose the color palette Windows 95 uses to display image on your screen. Depending on the capabilities of your video card, you may have more or fewer choices to select from for each option. For example, if you have a capable video card, you may have a number of resolution settings to choose from.

You can configure your monitor and video card from the Settings page of the Display Properties sheet (see fig 18.9).

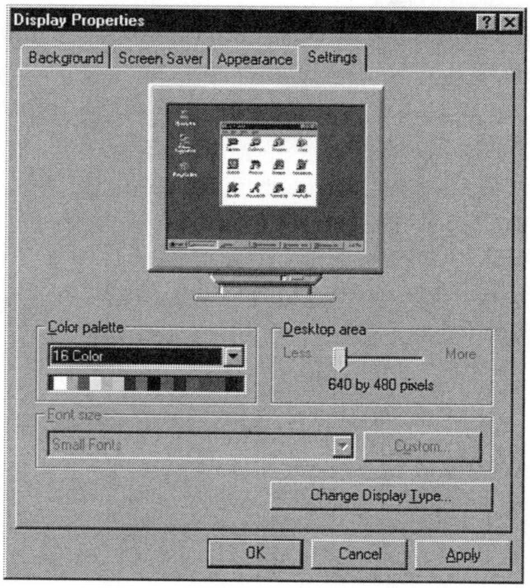

Fig. 18.9
The Display Properties sheet is used to modify the behavior of your monitor and video card.

There are a few different methods you can use to view the Display Properties sheet:

- Right-click the Desktop to display the Desktop context menu. The Display Properties sheet appears. Choose the Settings page.
- Open the Control Panel and then click the Display icon. The Display Properties sheet appears. Choose the Settings page.

Specifying Resolution Settings

The Desktop Area slider on the Settings tab in the Display Properties sheet enables you to specify the resolution setting for your monitor and video adapter. This setting determines how much information you see on-screen. By dragging the slider to the right, you are able to see more images on your screen, though the images appear smaller. For comparison purposes, figures 18.10 and 18.11 show the Windows 95 desktop at 640 × 480 resolution and 800 × 600 pixels, respectively.

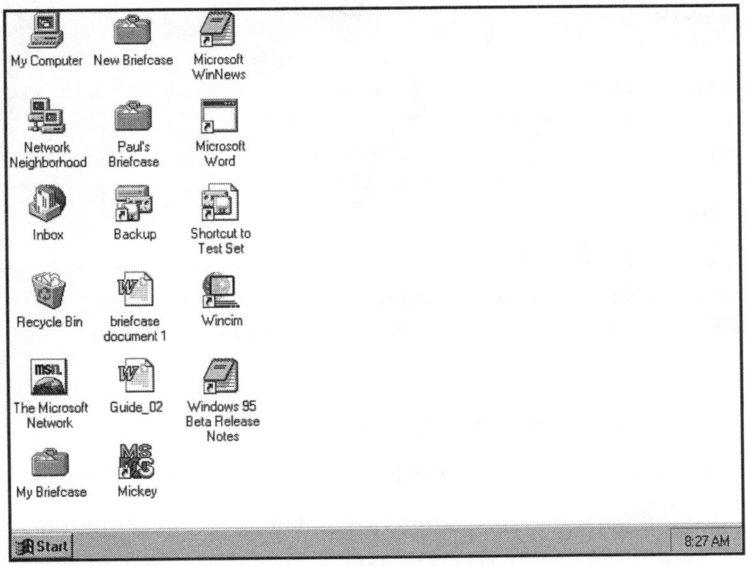

Fig. 18.10
The resolutions setting for the system shown in this picture is 640 × 480 pixels.

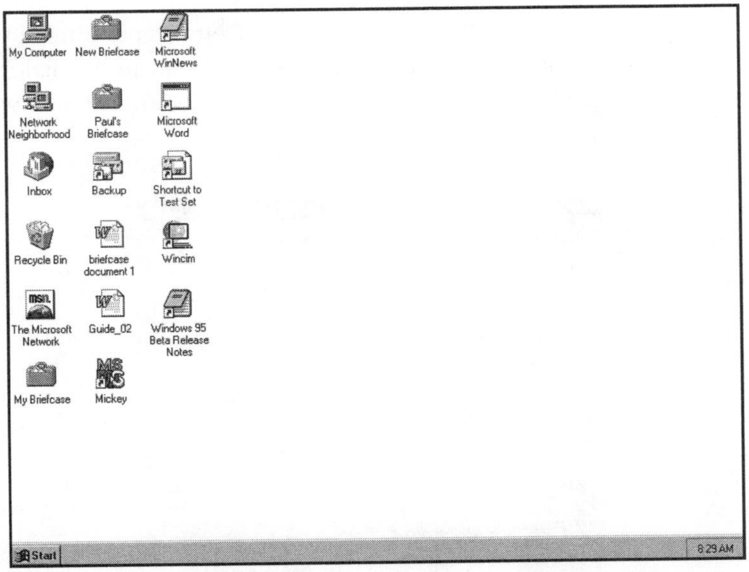

Fig. 18.11
The resolutions setting for the system shown in this picture is 800 × 600 pixels.

Pixels and the Desktop Area Setting

By changing the Desktop Area setting, you change the number of pixels used to create the images that appear on your screen. Pixels (*pic*ture *el*ements) are the small units of color that make up the images you see on-screen. The setting that appears

(continues)

(continued)

beneath the slider tells how many pixels will be used to make up the images on the screen. The first number refers to the number of pixels in each row; the second number refers to the number of pixels used in each column. For example, a setting of 640 × 480 pixels means that the images on your screen will be made up of 640 rows of 480 pixels each.

The greater the number of pixels used to create the images on your screen, the more clear the resolution. The smaller the size of the pixels, the greater number of pixels can be used, hence the sharper the resolution is while you see more images on-screen.

To change the resolution, follow these steps:

1. Select the Settings page of the Display Properties sheet.
2. Click the slider in the Desktop Area and drag it to the resolution setting you want; or press Alt+D and then use the left or right cursor keys to move the arrow icon (see fig. 18.12).

   As the slider stops at the different resolution settings permitted by your video adapter, the image of the Desktop that appears in the dialog box changes to show you the relative effect of the resolution setting you have stopped at.

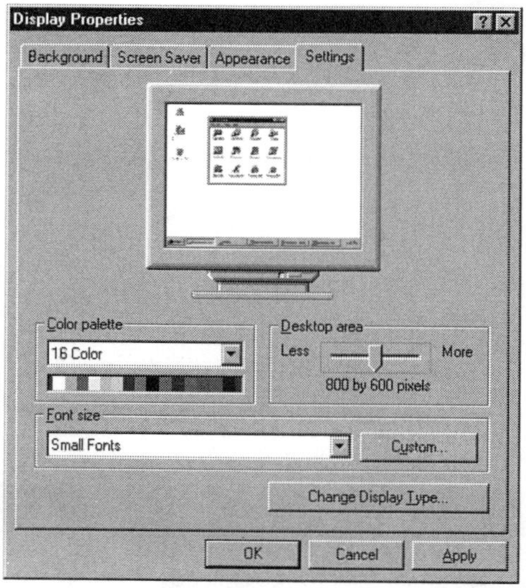

Fig. 18.12
The Desktop Area slider lets you specify the resolution setting for your monitor.

3. Click the Apply button for the resolution setting to take effect immediately and to continue working in the Display Properties dialog box, or choose OK for your changes to take effect and for the Display Properties sheet to close.

Caution

Depending upon the capabilities of your video adapter, Windows 95 might need to shut itself down and then restart in order for the resolution changes to take effect. This is normal and no reason for worry. You will always be warned first, and you have the option of not letting Windows 95 restart itself. If you choose this option, Windows 95 will continue to operate normally, but the changes you've made to your configuration will not take effect until the next time you start Windows 95.

Troubleshooting

I can't seem to move the slider in the Desktop Area in any direction. The `Less` *and* `More` *labels appear to be dimmed.*

The points along the slider at which you can stop the slider are determined by the capabilities of your video card and monitor. If your video card and monitor are only capable of one setting, you cannot move the slider in the Desktop Area at all. The labels `Less` and `More` at each end of the slider appear dimmed if your video adapter and monitor are not capable of multiple resolution settings.

Setting the Color Palette

You can specify the color palette that Windows 95 uses to display colors onscreen. Rather than choose specific colors, you can specify the breadth of the palette Windows uses. For example, you might choose the 16-color palette, or you might choose the 256-color palette.

Caution

While choosing a palette with more colors enhances the images on your screen, more memory is used to display these colors, so overall system performance may suffer.

You choose the color palette from the Color Palette drop-down list box that appears on the Settings page on the Display Properties sheet (see fig. 18.13). The capabilities of your video adapter determines how many choices are shown in the Color Palatte drop-down list box.

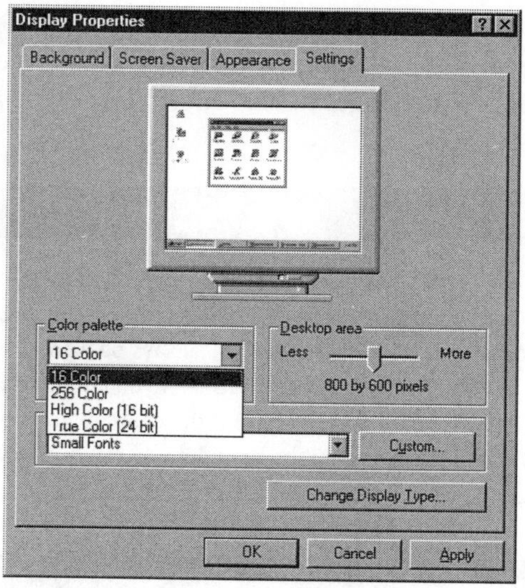

Fig. 18.13
You can choose how many colors are used to paint the images you see on your screen.

To change the color palette, follow these steps:

1. Display the Settings page of the Display Properties sheet.

2. Choose the palette from the Color Palette drop-down list box. After you make a selection, the rectangular area beneath the drop-down list containing all the colors in the current palette you are using changes to show the palette you chose.

Caution

Depending on your video adapter, Windows 95 might need to shut itself down and then restart in order for the resolution changes to take effect. Windows 95 will always ask for your permission first. Also, you have the option of not letting Windows 95 restart itself. If you choose this option, Windows 95 will continue to operate normally, but the changes you've made to your configuration will not take effect until the next time you start Windows 95.

Setting Font Size

Many users are concerned with screen real estate, that is, having more of it. Users like to see more information on-screen at the expense of the clarity of the on-screen image. You can display more information on your screen by changing the resolution setting, as demonstrated in the Specifying Resolution Settings section. Now, you'll learn how to squeeze more information on the screen by changing the font size of the text used in Windows 95. You could also use the change font size functionality to enlarge the font size in order for text to appear larger in Windows 95.

As an example of changing the font size, figure 18.14 shows the Control Panel with font size enlarged to the Large fonts setting. Notice how the space between the icons has increased and how you can see fewer icons in the folder at one time. Figure 18.15 shows the Control Panel folder with font size decreased to the Small fonts setting. Notice how the space between icons has been decreased so you can see many more at the same time in the folder.

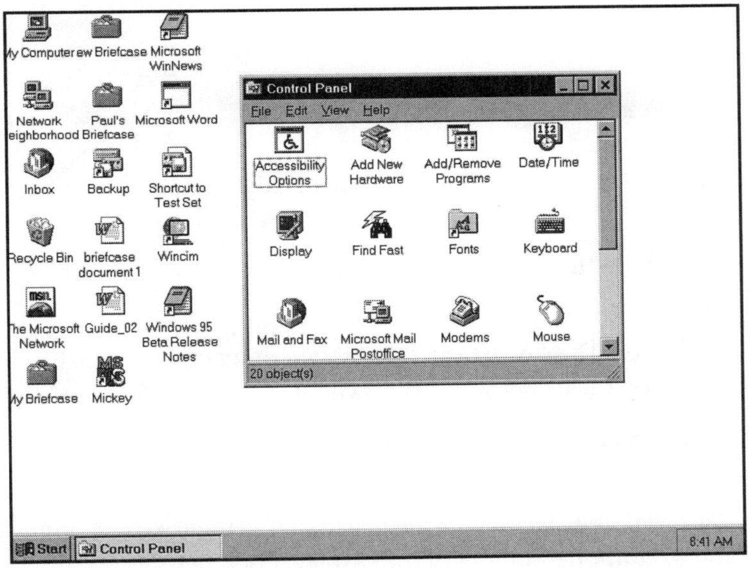

Fig. 18.14
The font size in this figure has been increased to the Large Fonts setting.

Changing the font size in Windows 95 is easy. You can choose from two predefined sizes, small fonts or large fonts, or you can specify a custom size by supplying a percentage size based on the normal size. You may also increase and decrease the size of the font by maneuvering a graphical ruler.

Tip

Your monitor and video card must be capable of multiple resolution settings in order to change the font size. Windows 95 forces users to choose a resolution setting other than 640 × 480 pixels in order to change the font size.

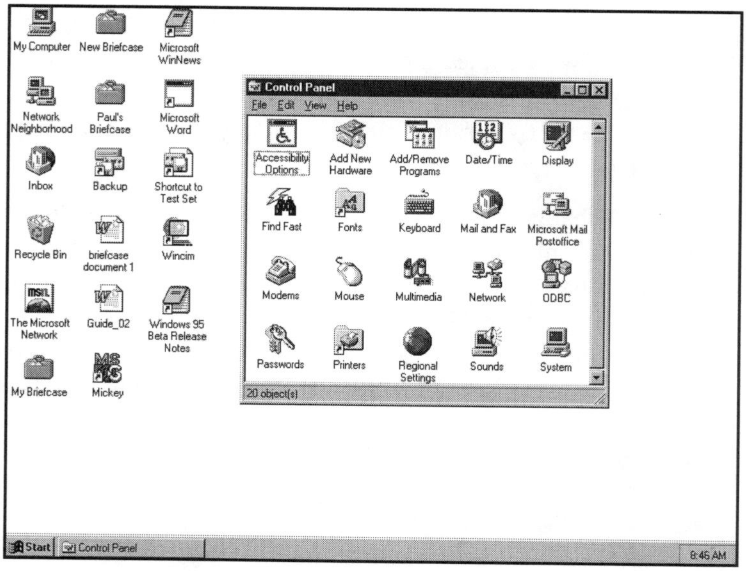

Fig. 18.15
The font size in this figure has been decreased to 80 percent of its normal size.

To change the font size by using one of the predefined settings, follow these steps:

1. Select the Settings page of the Display Properties sheet (refer to fig. 18.12).
2. Change the Display Area setting to something other than 640 × 480 pixels (see the earlier section "Specifying Resolution Settings" for help).
3. Choose either Small Fonts or Large Fonts from the Font Size drop-down list.
4. Click the Apply button for the new font size to take effect immediately and to continue working in the Display Properties sheet.

   Or, choose OK for your changes to take effect and for the Display Properties sheet to close. Depending upon the capabilities of your video adapter, Windows 95 might shut itself down and then restart in order for the font size changes to take effect.

To change the font size by specifying a custom size, follow these steps:

1. Display the Settings page of the Display Properties sheet.
2. Change the Display Area setting to something other than 640 × 480 pixels (see the earlier section "Specifying Resolution Settings" for help).
3. Click the Custom button in the Font Size area. The Custom Font Size dialog box shown in figure 18.16 appears.

4. Enter the new percentage size in the Scale Fonts To Be edit box. You can also choose from a predefined percentage by clicking the down arrow icon; or click anywhere on the ruler and drag to the left to decrease the size or to the right to increase the size.

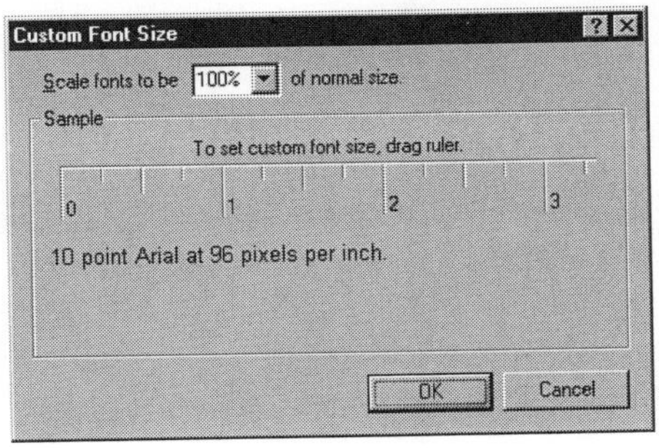

Fig. 18.16
You can specify a custom size for the font used in Windows 95, expressing the size as a percentage of the normal size.

5. Choose OK.

6. Click the Apply button for the new font size to take effect immediately and to continue working in the Display Properties sheet, or choose OK for your changes to take effect and for the Display Properties sheet to close. Depending upon the capabilities of your video adapter, Windows 95 might shut itself down and then restart in order for the font size changes to take effect.❖

Chapter 19

Configuring Speakers and Sound Cards

by Ian Stokell

Historically, IBM-compatible PCs, unlike the competing Macintosh platform, came with no sound capabilities to speak of, aside from a pathetic beep here and there. Now, most PCs that are shipped into the consumer retail market include built-in multimedia components, such as a CD-ROM drive and sound capabilities in the form of a sound card and speakers. But if you didn't include such multimedia components when you bought your PC, apart from kicking yourself now, you probably realize that a basic PC is severely lacking in terms of entertainment value without a CD-ROM and sound.

This chapter covers how to install and configure a sound board. It also briefly mentions speakers, although there really isn't much to say about them—after you've installed a sound board, you plug them into the card or a suitable port on the PC and *voilà*, they either work or they don't! More about that later. First though, there is the subject of the sound board.

In this chapter you learn how to do the following:

- Use the Add New Hardware Wizard to install a sound board
- Install and configure software drivers for your sound board
- Change multimedia and volume control settings
- Move MIDI instruments between sound cards

Using the Add New Hardware Wizard for Sound Board

Before you can configure sound capabilities under Windows 95, you need to install a suitable audio board in an available expansion slot within your PC. If you are thinking of getting into multimedia when you buy your PC, it's worth paying extra to get one with a sound board and other multimedia components already built-in. This will save you the trouble of configuring the various components when you are ready to start using them.

Under the old DOS/Windows combination, it was quite a hassle to add multimedia components such as a sound board. When adding a new hardware component, you needed to assign it available system resources for it to work properly, such as *input/output* (I/O) and *interrupt request* (IRQ) parameters. Keeping track of such resource allocations was problematic to say the least. However, the good news is that Windows 95 eases the installation pain by providing a central registry where such information is kept and graphically displayed; this place is referred to as the *Device Manager*.

◄ See "Using the Device Manager," p. 334

In addition, the new Plug and Play standard, supported in Windows 95, allows for hardware components manufacturers to ensure their products are instantly compatible with the new operating system. They do this by adhering to the new Plug and Play standard. Then, when you add the new hardware device, Windows 95 can take over installing the necessary software drivers and allocating available system resources. More about that in a moment.

◄ See "Plug and Play Overview," p. 10

The other way Windows 95 helps in the installation of new hardware components—whether they're Plug and Play or not—is through the very useful Add New Hardware Wizard Control Panel. The wizard takes the user through the installation of a hardware device step-by-step. It can take anywhere from 10 to 20 minutes for the manual Add New Hardware Wizard installation procedure to complete.

To show how the Add New Hardware Wizard works in relation to sound cards, you should go through the motions of installing a Sound Blaster 16 AWE-32. Alternatively, if you are installing a new sound card, go ahead and use the manufacturer and model you want to install instead of the Sound Blaster 16 AWE-32.

First, you need to access the Add New Hardware Wizard, which can be accomplished either through the Control Panel or by choosing Sound Cards, Setting Up from the Help Topics option. Follow these steps after selecting the Control Panel option:

1. Click the Start menu.
2. Select Settings, Control Panel.
3. Open the Add New Hardware Control Panel. An introductory screen appears, from which you click the Next button. The real Add New Hardware Wizard appears (see fig. 19.1).

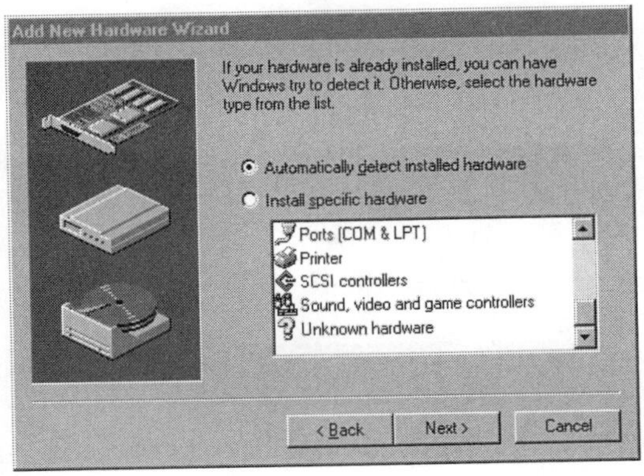

Fig. 19.1
The wizard can automatically detect newly installed hardware, or you can go through the process manually.

4. Select the Automatically Detect Installed Hardware button to let Windows 95 automatically find any new devices that you have added recently. Or, select the Install Specific Hardware option to allow you to select the new hardware to be installed.
5. Choose the type of hardware device you want to add from the wizard list. Select Sound, Video and Game Controllers and then click Next. The hardware manufacturer and model list appears for the device you selected (see fig. 19.2).

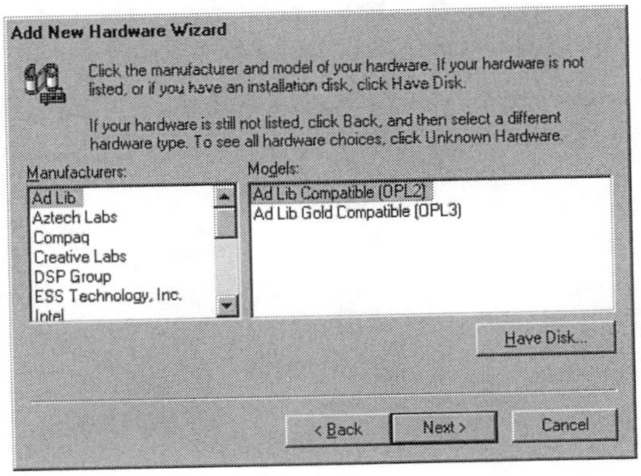

Fig. 19.2
You select the type of device that you want to install.

6. In the left window, click the sound board manufacturer's name. A list of the company's products that Windows 95 supports appears in the right-hand window.

7. Select the board you want to add: Creative Labs Sound Blaster 16/AWE-32. Click the Next button.

Note

At this point you may need to install a software driver from an installation disk if Windows 95 does not support the device. If you do need to install a software driver from a suitable installation disk, just continue along with these steps. If, on the other hand, you do not need to install a driver from a floppy, skip steps 8 through 10 and continue with step 11.

Caution

You might want to use the sound board's own installation program instead, because the wizard can sometimes run into problems identifying the correct interrupts for some components.

8. Click the Have Disk button from the Add New Hardware Wizard panel. The Install From Disk window appears (see fig. 19.3).

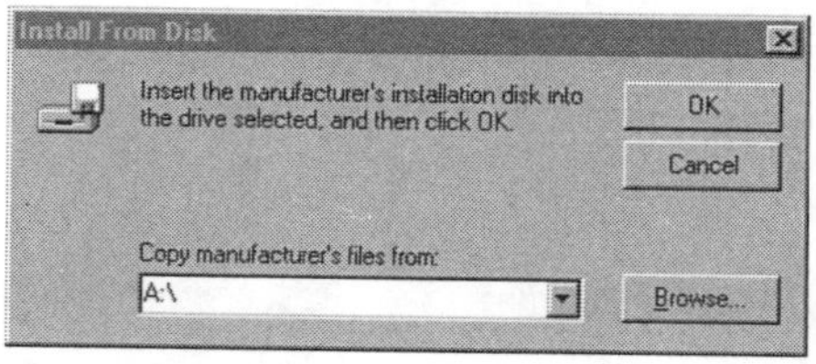

Fig. 19.3
Insert the installation disk into the selected drive to install a new device driver from a floppy disk.

9. Specify the folder and disk that contains the manufacturer's installation files.

10. Click OK. The Install From Disk window disappears, and you are back to the Add New Hardware Wizard. Now you can click the Next button. The wizard window changes to display the settings you should use for the new board (see fig. 19.4).

Tip

Not all vendors have the correct setup information for Windows 95 on their disks. If this is the case, the disk may not work with Windows 95; call the company and ask them if they have an update.

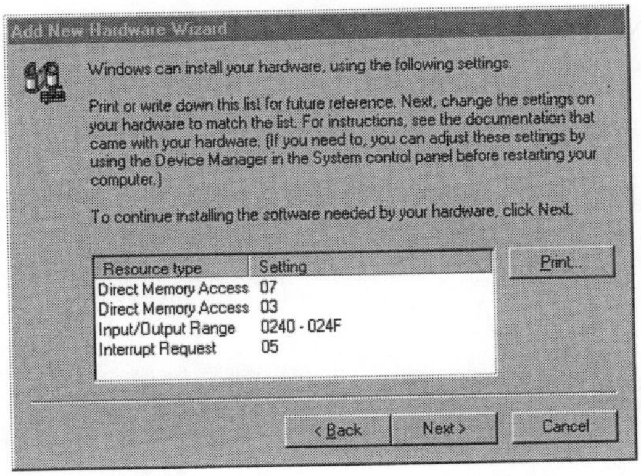

Fig. 19.4
The Add New Hardware Wizard gives you the settings you can use for your new board.

Note

This list of settings is important, and is based on what settings are available as defined in the Windows 95 Device Manager registry.

11. Write down these settings or print them out. These are the settings that the new board should have before you install it.

12. If the wizard asks you for a manufacturer's installation disk, go ahead and install the software direct from the floppy.

13. Shut down your PC.

14. You now need to configure the new sound card according to the settings given by Device Manager during the wizard installation process. However, changing card settings can be a little tricky, so it's important to refer to the documentation that comes with your sound board for how to make changes to I/O, IRQ, and DMA settings.

15. Install the sound card.

A feature in Windows 95 allows for the automatic detection of newly installed hardware devices, such as a sound board. To automatically detect a newly installed sound board, open the Add New Hardware Wizard, as described in the previous section, and do the following:

1. Check the Automatically Detect Installed Hardware button on the Add New Hardware Wizard (refer to fig. 19.1).

2. Click the Next button. The screen that appears will tell you that Windows 95 will now look for new hardware and that this may take some time (see fig. 19.5).

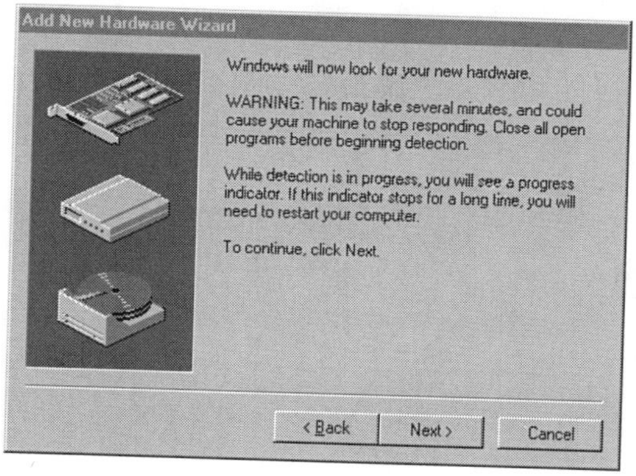

Fig. 19.5
The first Add New Hardware Wizard screen tells you that the search for new hardware may take some time.

3. Click the Next button. The next thing that appears on the bottom of the screen is a progress bar that tells you how the search is going (see fig. 19.6).

> **Tip**
>
> It is normal for the progress bar to quickly complete about 90 percent of the search and then slow down. The last 10 percent often takes longer than the previous 90 percent altogether!

4. When the search is complete, click the Next button.

The wizard then tells you if it has found any new hardware components. If none are found, it asks if you want to install a new device manually. If so, it will bring you back to the Add New Hardware Wizard screen, from where you can manually install the sound board.

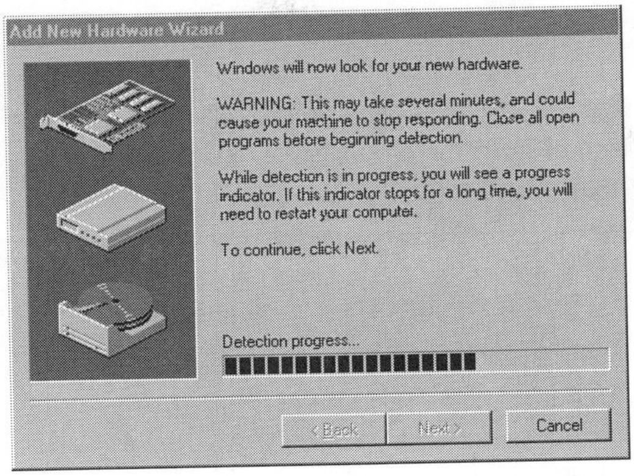

Fig. 19.6
The progress bar gives you continuous updates regarding the hardware search.

Troubleshooting

I hear hissing during the playback of a sound file.

The file may be recording in 8 bits and playing back in 16 bits. The 16-bit board doesn't realize that the 8-bit file isn't the same high quality as a 16-bit file, so playing the file with expectations of higher sound quality emphasizes the lower detail.

Configuring Sound Cards

Once you have installed the sound board, there are a number of ways to configure the board. You also may need to change the software driver for a specific board, or add a driver from a floppy disk. This section covers a number of configuration and driver installation issues.

Adding or Changing Sound Card Drivers

A sound board, as with all hardware devices attached to a PC, requires special software that communicates with the computer's operating system. This specialized software, called a *driver*, acts as a sort of intermediary between the hardware device and the operating system on the PC. Without this special driver, the two would not be able to communicate properly and the PC would likely grind to a halt until they are reconciled.

But adding software drivers and communicating their location on the PC to the operating system has historically been a tedious and—for many nontechnical users—a somewhat challenging operation. However, with Windows 95, much of the complexity revolving around the task has been removed. This is because you can add or change device drivers using the Device Manager.

> **Note**
>
> Windows 95 doesn't work with all the different sound cards on the market. If you have drivers that come from the component manufacturer, the Device Manager may not properly recognize the board.

As an example, check out the drivers available for MS Windows Sound System Compatible sound:

1. Click the Start menu.
2. Choose Settings, Control Panel.
3. Double-click the System Control Panel. The System Properties sheet appears.
4. Click the Device Manager page (see fig. 19.7).

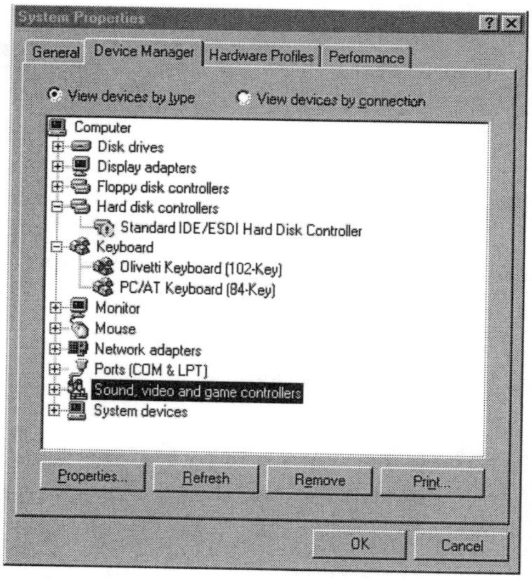

Fig. 19.7 Device Manager allows you to change the software driver for a sound board.

5. Click the plus sign that corresponds to the hardware device you want to change—for example, "Sound, Video and Game Controllers." A list of devices appears under Sound, Video and Game Controllers.
6. Double-click the specific hardware device you are interested in—MS Windows Sound System Compatible, in this case.
7. In the resulting panel, click the Driver page (see fig. 19.8).
8. Click the Change Driver button. The Select Device window appears (see fig. 19.9).

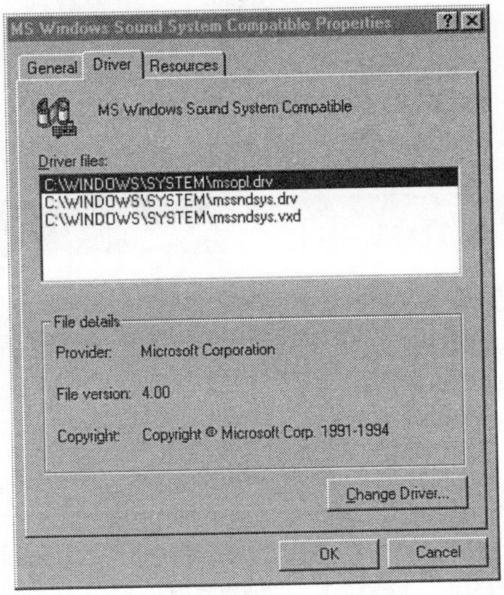

Fig. 19.8
Available software drivers are listed in the Driver page.

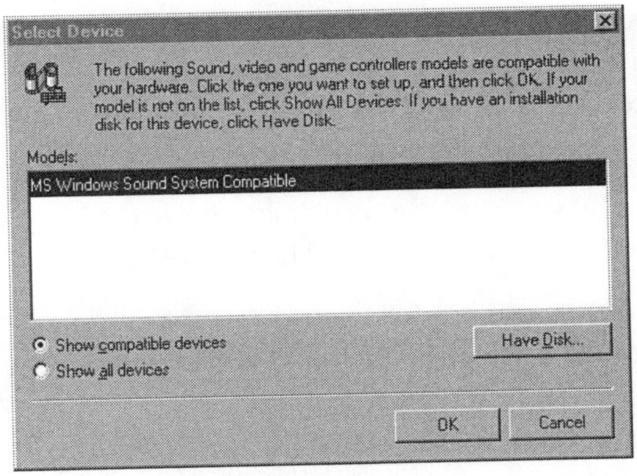

Fig. 19.9
A list of compatible devices allows you to select a suitable software driver.

> **Note**
>
> The Models list shows all compatible sound models available for your PC. The Show Compatible Devices option needs to be selected. If you are changing the driver on a sound board and it is not listed, select the Show All Devices option. The list will change to show all such boards. However, if your board requires a software driver to be installed from a floppy disk, click the Have Disk button and refer to the next section, "Installing a Driver from a Floppy Disk." If no installation disk is required, continue with step 9.

9. Select the device you want to set up and click OK. The Driver tab showing the driver files and their correct folder path reappears.

10. Select your new driver and click OK. You are now back to the Device Manager hardware type list.

11. Click Close.

Troubleshooting

I try to play video with sound and it isn't synchronized.

You may have a computer that isn't fast enough. You can try improving performance and adding RAM, but if you have an older, slower processor and a relatively slow hard drive, you may need to think about upgrading to a new PC with fast video capabilities built in.

Installing a Driver from a Floppy Disk

At some point you may be required to install a driver from a floppy disk, such as when a newer version is distributed by the manufacturer, for example. To install a software driver from a floppy disk, you need to be in the Select Driver sheet accessed from the Driver page. Here's how:

1. From Driver page in your designated hardware properties sheet, which is accessed by selecting the specific hardware device in Device Manager, click the Change Driver button. The Select Driver window appears (refer to fig 19.9).

2. Click Have Disk. The Install From Disk box appears (see fig. 19.10).

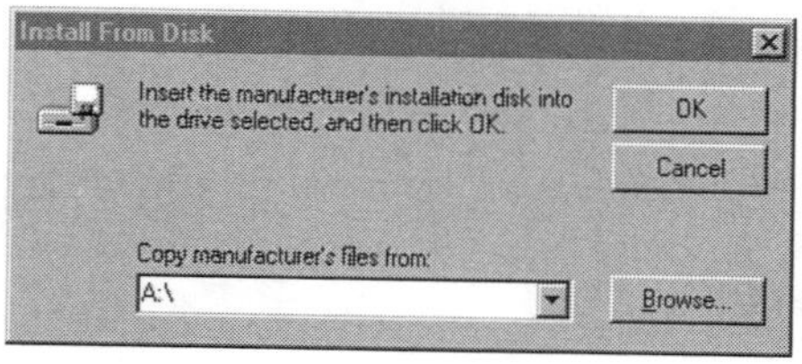

Fig. 19.10
Specify the actual drive and directory where the software drivers can be found.

3. Specify the disk and directory where the drivers can be found.

4. Click OK.

5. You return to the Select Device window. Click OK. You are back to the Driver page of System Properties.

6. Click OK. You are now back to the Device Manager sheet.

Volume Setting

You can adjust the volume level of a sound card by using the Volume Control feature. This feature also allows you to adjust speaker balance when playing audio files.

To adjust the volume level, follow these steps:

1. Click the Start menu.
2. Choose Programs, Accessories, Multimedia.
3. Select CD Player (see fig. 19.11).

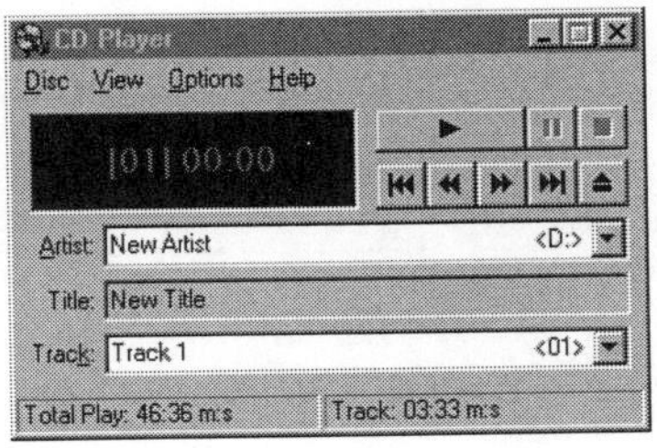

Fig. 19.11
CD Player allows you to control the audio volume via the View menu.

4. Choose View, Volume Control. The Volume Control dialog box appears (see fig. 19.12).

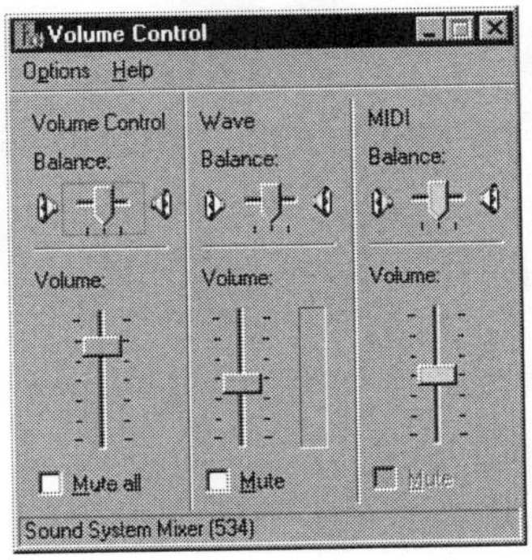

Fig. 19.12
Volume Control allows for the adjusting of both volume and speaker balance.

5. Select the desired volume by dragging the Volume Control slider.
6. Adjust the balance between speakers by dragging the Balance slider.
7. When the volume and balance are set, exit Volume Control by clicking the close box at the top right of the window.

Changing Multimedia Settings

There may be occasion for you to change the settings assigned to a multimedia device, such as a sound board. You can change such device settings via the Multimedia Control Panel. Follow these steps:

1. Open the Start menu.
2. Choose Settings, Control Panel.
3. Open the Multimedia Control Panel.
4. In the Multimedia Properties sheet, select the Advanced page (see fig. 19.13).

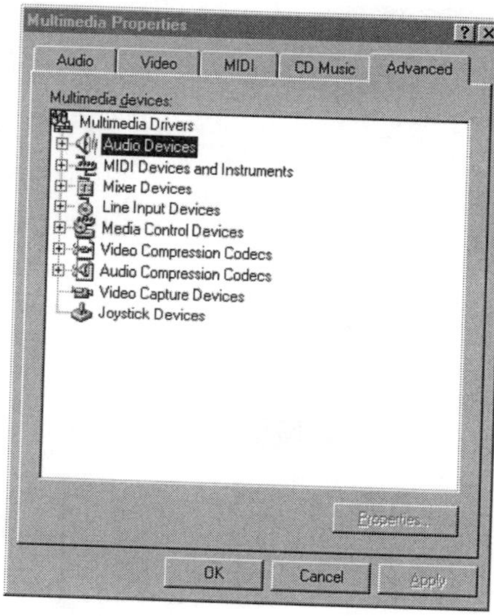

Fig. 19.13
You can change multimedia device settings by selecting the component from the Multimedia Devices list.

5. Click the plus sign next to the multimedia device category you are interested in.
6. Click the device you want from the resulting list.
7. Click the Properties button at the bottom of the window.
8. Make whatever changes you want using the different pages, and click OK when you are done.

Changing Sound Quality When Recording

You can change the sound quality of your recording reproduction depending on your needs. A presentation will probably require a better quality sound reproduction than something like a short voice file you would attach to an in-house e-mail message to distribute to coworkers. To change the recording sound quality, do the following:

1. Open the Start menu.
2. Choose Settings, Control Panel.
3. Open the Multimedia Control Panel.
4. In the Multimedia Properties sheet click the Audio page (see fig. 19.14).

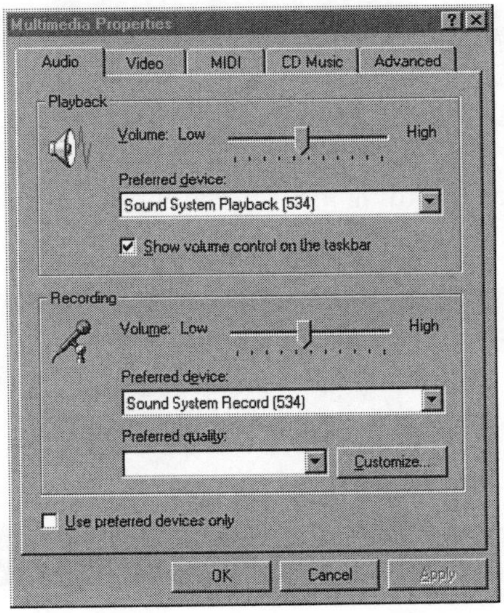

Fig. 19.14
Recording sound quality can be changed according to your needs via the Audio page in Multimedia Properties.

5. Select the quality you want from the Preferred Quality drop-down list box.
6. Click OK.

You may want to create custom recording formats yourself to add to your Preferred Quality list. To do so requires an extra step in addition to those in the previous section. From the Audio tab in Multimedia Properties, do the following:

1. Click the Customize button. The Customize window appears (see fig. 19.15).
2. Name the file in the Name drop-down list box.
3. Select the desired format from the Format drop-down list box.

4. Select the reproduction attributes for the new customized format from the Attributes drop-down list box.

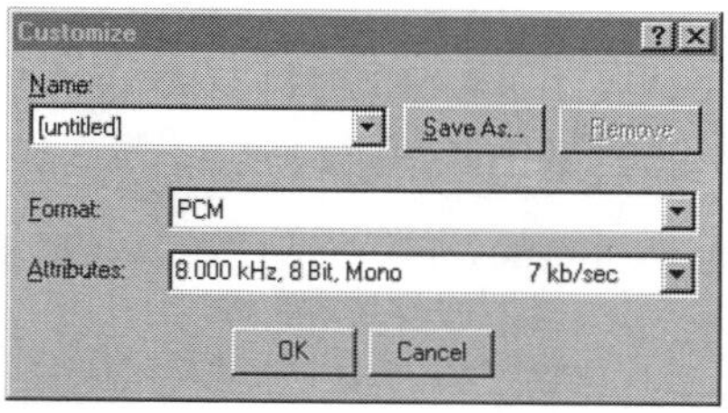

Fig. 19.15
Create your own quality formats using the Customize button on the Audio page in Multimedia Properties.

5. Click OK.

Your newly customized recording format now appears in the Preferred Quality list box in the Audio page.

Tip

The higher the quality sound file, the more disk space is required. If you have limited disk storage space, don't select the highest sound quality unless you really need it.

Troubleshooting

My system hangs during a 16-bit digitized sound test, but an 8-bit test works fine.

You may need to switch to a low DMA setting. This result means your system cannot handle high DMA at full speed.

Moving MIDI Instruments Between Sound Cards

There may be an occasion when you want to move a MIDI instrument between sound boards, perhaps if you have both a high-quality 16-bit board and a lower-quality 8-bit board installed at the same time. It's a pretty straightforward operation. Here's how you do it:

1. Open the Start menu.
2. Choose Settings, Control Panel.
3. Open the Multimedia Control Panel.

4. In the Multimedia Properties sheet, click the Advanced page (refer to fig. 19.13).
5. Click the plus sign next to MIDI Devices and Instruments.
6. Click the plus sign next to the sound board your MIDI instrument was connected to from the resulting list.
7. Select the instrument you want to move, and then click the Properties button at the bottom of the window.
8. Click the Details page.
9. From the MIDI Port list box, select the name of the sound board you want to connect the instrument to.
10. Connect your MIDI instrument to the new sound board you just specified using the designated port, according to the instructions that come with your sound board.

Troubleshooting Sound Cards

Because of the complexities involved in getting sound to reproduce properly on PCs, it will be a lucky person indeed who can go through their entire multimedia-use life without running into audio problems. And while Windows 95's Plug and Play and easy-to-use Device Manager Registry help track available IRQs and I/O addresses, things can still go wrong.

Under the old DOS/Windows combination, one of the most intimidating aspects of getting a sound board to work effectively on a PC was figuring out what IRQ, DMA, and I/O settings to use. Getting one of them wrong often meant assigning already-allocated resources to the new sound board, which inevitably resulted in an infamous "hardware conflict." In other words, your sound board wouldn't work.

The Device Manager registry in Windows 95 is designed to track available system resources, such as IRQ and I/O settings. Then, when a new hardware component is added, such as a sound board, you can use the Add New Hardware Wizard to take you step-by-step through the installation process. Part of that process is to check the registry for available settings and graphically present them to you so you can configure your board before you install it. The result should be that the new component will work when it is installed, although that isn't always the case.

Hardware conflicts can occur, often at the most inappropriate moments. Fortunately, not only does Windows 95 include a very thorough Help option from the Start menu, but it also features an especially useful step-by-step Hardware Conflict Troubleshooter, which you access by choosing the Hardware, Troubleshooting Conflicts option from the Help Topics Index.

The Troubleshooting Wizard will take you on a step-by-step investigation that should solve the problem.

Getting Speakers to Work

There's not really much to be said about the subject of speakers. Having installed your sound board, you simply take the cable from the speakers and plug it in, either to the card's Speaker Out port or an external speaker socket in the main chassis of a suitably configured PC. Speakers being what they are, they will either work or not work.

Invariably, if they don't work, you need to check a few basic elements to get them working. This may sound pretty obvious to some people, but you'd be surprised at how often the basic things are overlooked in the hysteria of non-working multimedia sound devices.

In the first place, are the speakers switched on? Do they run from a power source such as the mains, and if so, are they plugged in via a mains adapter? If they are battery-driven, are there any batteries installed, and if so, are they fully charged? You might also check to see if the volume on the speakers is turned up! Also, are the speakers plugged into the sound board? If they are plugged into the card and they still don't work, it may not be the speakers at all. In fact, it may be that the board has been misconfigured and the IRQ and DMA settings are wrong. Of course, it may also be a defective set of speakers, but that is extremely rare, especially if they are new.❖

Chapter 20

Configuring MIDI Cards

by Ian Stokell

The MIDI interface card acts as a connection between the MIDI controller, such as a keyboard or guitar, and your PC. Also in that equation is a synthesizer, which actually generates the MIDI sounds. The MIDI interface can be part of a sound card, which is how most users will come to know about MIDI, or as a separate interface card. Either way, without a MIDI interface you can make use of an external controller for your MIDI recordings. If you have a sound board with a MIDI interface in the form of the MIDI/joystick port, you won't need a separate MIDI interface card.

This chapter covers installing and configuring a separate MIDI interface card. The MPU-401 interface protocol is mentioned throughout this chapter. It is actually the MIDI "language" originally invented by Roland and is now virtually the *de facto* standard when it comes to MIDI use on the PC.

In this chapter you learn to do the following:

- Add a MIDI board using the Add New Hardware Wizard
- Install and change MIDI board software drivers
- Set up your MIDI instrument
- Configure your MIDI board—for example, the volume setting

Starting the Add New Hardware Wizard for a MIDI Card

Before you can configure a MIDI card for use with Windows 95, you have to install it. Fortunately, Windows 95 makes it a lot easier to install expansion cards than under the old DOS/Windows combination.

You will see how to install a MIDI board from a hardware vendor such as Music Quest.

The Add New Hardware Wizard can be accessed either through the Control Panel feature or by choosing Sound Cards, Setting Up from the Help Topics option. In this example, we'll go through the control panel option.

1. Click the Start menu.
2. Choose Settings, Control Panel.
3. Open the Add New Hardware Control Panel. The Add New Hardware Wizard appears (see fig. 20.1).

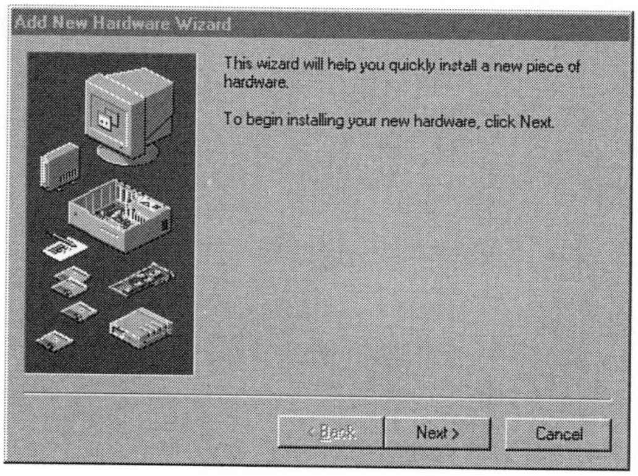

Fig. 20.1
The initial Add New Hardware Wizard screen explains what the wizard does.

4. Click the Next button. The first screen where the user has to make a choice appears, giving you an automatic detection option (see fig. 20.2).

   You are then asked to answer the question, "Do you want Windows to search for your new hardware?" Answering Yes (Recommended) will let Windows 95 automatically detect new hardware that you have recently installed. Answering No will allow you to manually add the new hardware using the wizard.

5. To learn how to manually add new hardware, click No. The Hardware Types list box appears (see fig. 20.3).

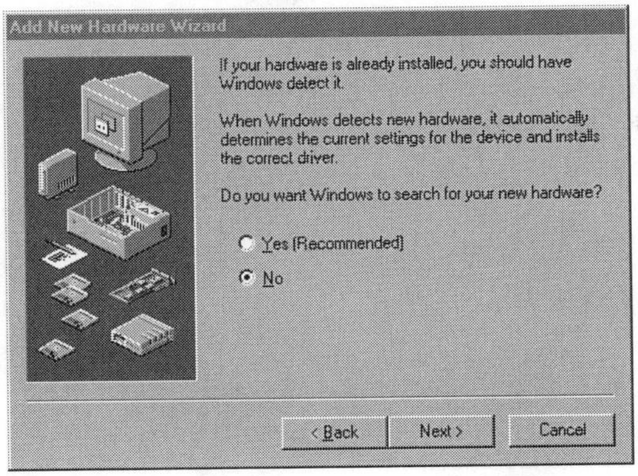

Fig. 20.2
You have the choice to automatically detect new hardware or manually add it.

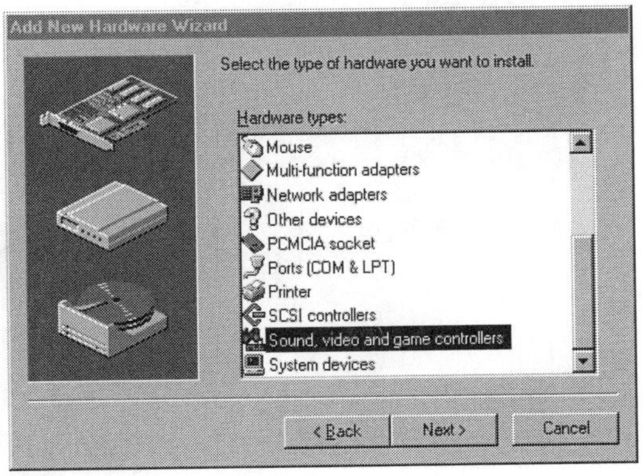

Fig. 20.3
The wizard offers a variety of hardware types from which to choose.

6. Select the type of hardware device you want to add from the wizard list—Sound, Video, and Game Controllers.

7. Click the Next button. A hardware manufacturer and model list appears for the type of device you selected (see fig. 20.4).

8. Click the MIDI board manufacturer's name in the left window. A list of their products that Windows 95 is familiar with appears in the right window. Select the MIDI board you want to add. In this case, it is Music Quest MPU-401 Compatible.

9. Click Next. The window changes to reveal the recommended settings you should use for your new MIDI board (see fig. 20.5).

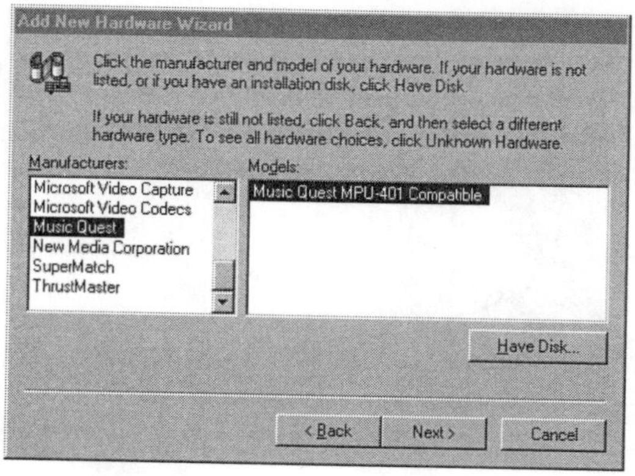

Fig. 20.4
Choose the manufacturer and hardware model you want to install.

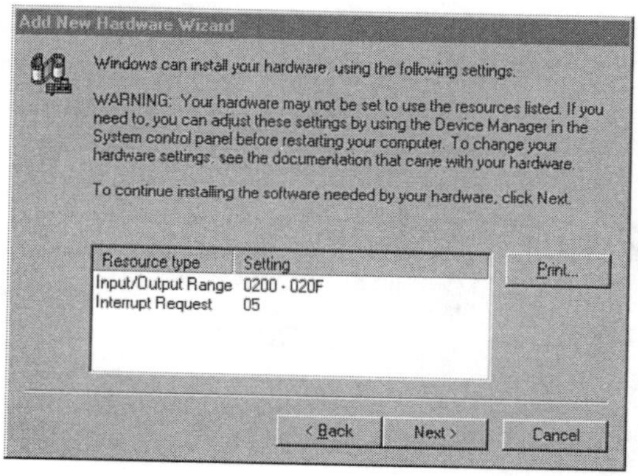

Fig. 20.5
You are provided with the recommended settings for your new MIDI board.

If you need to install a device driver from a manufacturer's floppy disk, refer to the next section, "Installing a Driver from a Floppy Disk."

Note

These settings are very important. They are automatically figured out by Windows 95 based on what resources are available according to the Device Manager registry.

Tip

Because these settings are so important, write them down or print them out. You should configure your new MIDI board according to these settings before you install it.

10. Click the Next button.

11. The wizard screen tells you that the installation of the necessary software for the new board is complete. Click the Finish button (see fig. 20.6).

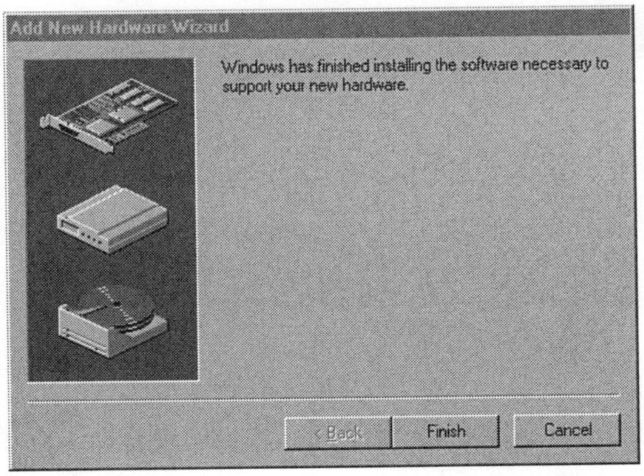

Fig. 20.6
The wizard tells you the software installation is complete.

12. A System Settings Change dialog box appears telling you to shut down your PC and install the necessary hardware (see fig. 20.7).

Answer the question, "Do you want to shut down your computer now?" In this case, click Yes to install the new MIDI card.

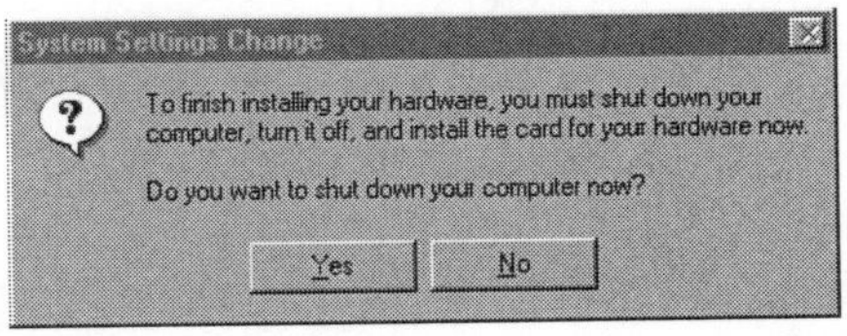

Fig. 20.7
You need to shut down your PC to install the new hardware device.

13. You now need to configure the new MIDI card according to the settings obtained during the wizard process. Read the documentation that accompanies your new MIDI card to learn how to change the interrupt request (IRQ) and input/output (I/O) settings.

14. Install the new MIDI card according to the manufacturer's instructions.

Installing a Driver from a Floppy Disk

You may need to install a driver for a hardware device, such as a MIDI board, from a manufacturer's floppy disk. From the hardware manufacturer and model screen (refer to fig. 20.4), accessed via the steps in the previous section, do the following:

1. Click the Have Disk button. The Install From Disk box appears (see fig. 20.8).

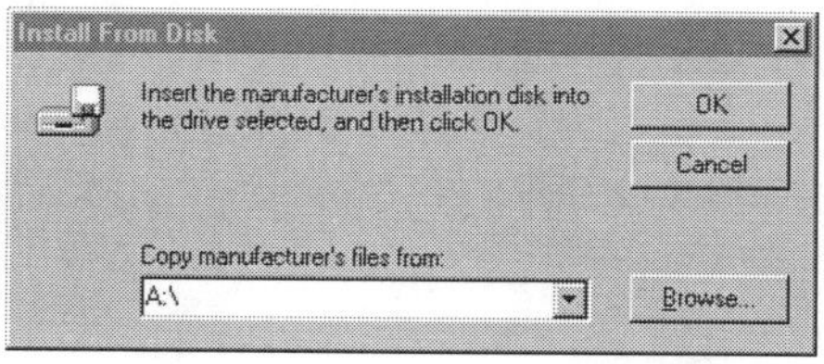

Fig. 20.8
Insert the manufacturer's installation disk into the selected drive if you need to install a device driver not already supported by Windows 95.

2. Specify the disk drive letter and the directory from where the manufacturer's software files should be copied.

3. Click OK.

Letting Windows 95 Autodetect a MIDI Card

Using the Add New Hardware Wizard, you can automatically have Windows 95 detect hardware components that have been newly installed on your PC. To do this, open the Add New Hardware Wizard, as described in an earlier section "Starting Add New Hardware Wizard for a MIDI Card," and follow these steps:

1. In answer to the question "Do you want Windows to search for your new hardware?" choose Yes (refer to fig. 20.2).

2. Click the Next button. The next screen tells you that the wizard will now locate any new hardware (see fig. 20.9).

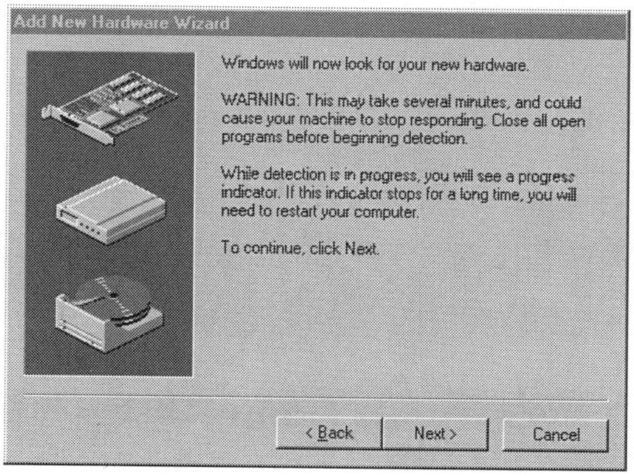

Fig. 20.9
The first screen tells you that the automatic search for new hardware may take a few minutes.

3. Click the Next button. Along the bottom of the screen is a progress indicator informing you of how the search is going (see fig. 20.10).

4. Click the Next button when the search is finished.

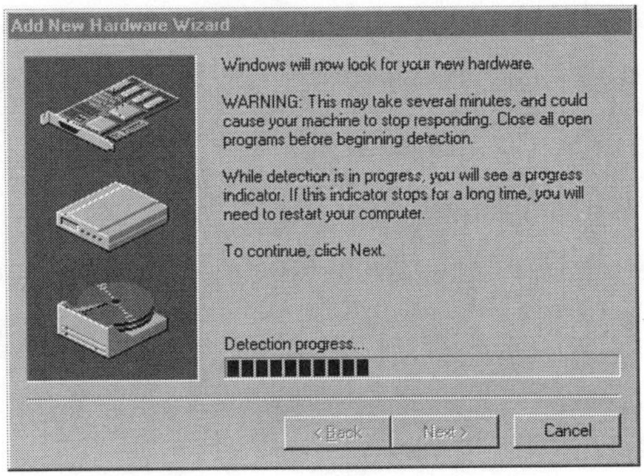

Fig. 20.10
The progress indicator tells you how the automatic search for new hardware is going.

The wizard's final screen tells you of any new hardware devices that it has found. If none are found, you have the choice to install a new device manually using the Add New Hardware Wizard.

Troubleshooting

I can't get MIDI files to play back properly.

To start with, check the card's resource settings, such as IRQ settings, to make sure they are configured correctly for your specific MIDI board. Then make sure the MIDI board is correctly identified in Device Manager.

Configuring Your MIDI Card

Having installed your new MIDI card, you can now adjust the sound and also set up a MIDI instrument to use. You may also want to change software drivers at some point, which is the first subject discussed in this section.

Adding or Changing Hardware Drivers

At some point you may need to add or change a driver for a hardware device, such as a MIDI card. For any peripheral hardware component to work with your PC, there must be a software driver installed. The driver acts as a sort of translator. Without that special software driver, the new device and the computer's operating system will not be able to communicate.

Unlike the old DOS/Windows combination, Windows 95 gives you an easy way to change drivers for specific components—using the Device Manager. If you remember, Device Manager is the centralized registry of system properties and configurations.

◀ See "Using the Device Manager," p. 334

You can change a driver for a hardware device by following these steps:

1. Click the Start menu.
2. Choose Settings, Control Panel.
3. Open the System Control Panel.
4. When the System Properties sheet appears, click the Device Manager page (see fig. 20.11).

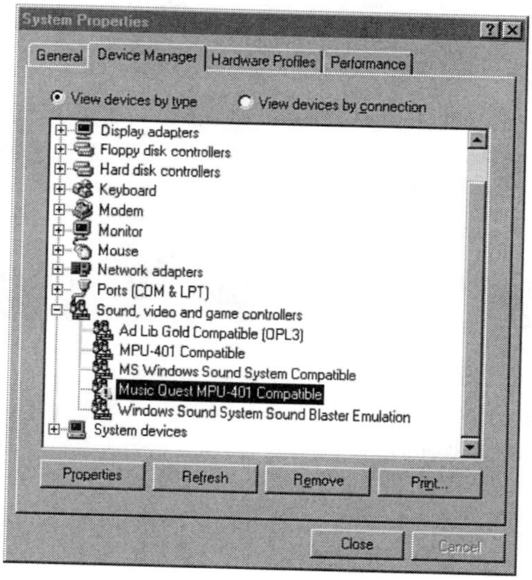

Fig. 20.11
Device Manager is the central registry of hardware component resource settings.

5. Click the plus sign next to Sound, Video and Game Controllers.
6. Double-click the hardware device you are interested in. For this example, choose Music Quest MPU-401 Compatible.
7. The Music Quest MPU-401 Compatible Properties sheet appears. Select the Driver page (see fig. 20.12).
8. Click the Change Driver button. The Select Device window appears (see fig. 20.13).

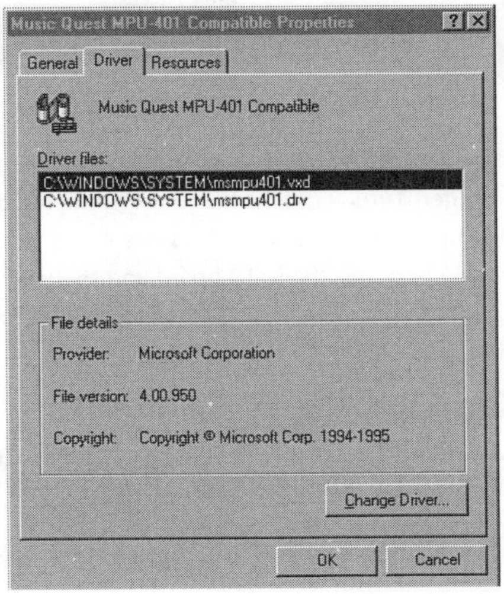

Fig. 20.12
The Driver page shows which drivers are associated with a specific hardware device.

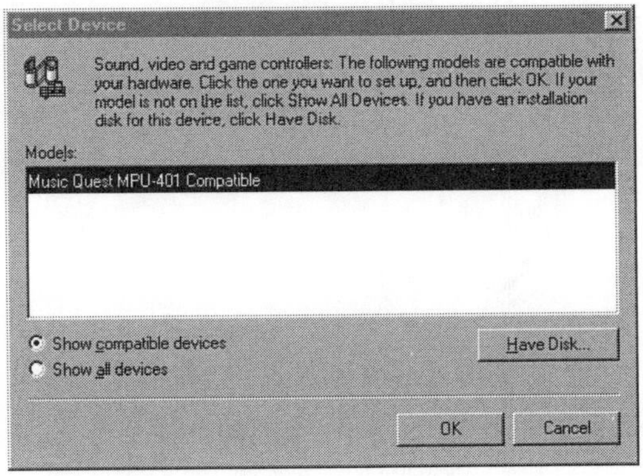

Fig. 20.13
The Select Device window allows you to choose the device that you want to add or change drivers for.

The Models list details the models that are compatible with your PC. Select the Show Compatible Devices option. However, if the hardware model you want is not on the list, you should select the Show All Devices button. The list will then change to show all hardware devices.

9. Click the device for which you want to install the driver and click OK. The Select Device window disappears to reveal the Driver page showing the driver files and their correct directory path.

10. Select the driver you want and click OK. You then return to the Device Manager screen.

11. Click the Close button.

Troubleshooting

There is hissing and distortion when playing MIDI files. How can I get rid of it?

There may be interference coming from either the power source or another card installed in your computer. Turn your PC off and move the MIDI board as far away from both the power supply and other boards as possible. If you can, leave a few empty expansion slots in between the MIDI board and the next card.

Volume Setting

The volume level can be adjusted when using a MIDI card via the Audio page in the Multimedia Properties sheet.

To adjust the playback and recording volume level, do the following:

1. Click the Start menu.
2. Choose Settings, Control Panel.
3. Select the Multimedia Control Panel. The Multimedia Properties sheet appears (see fig. 20.14).

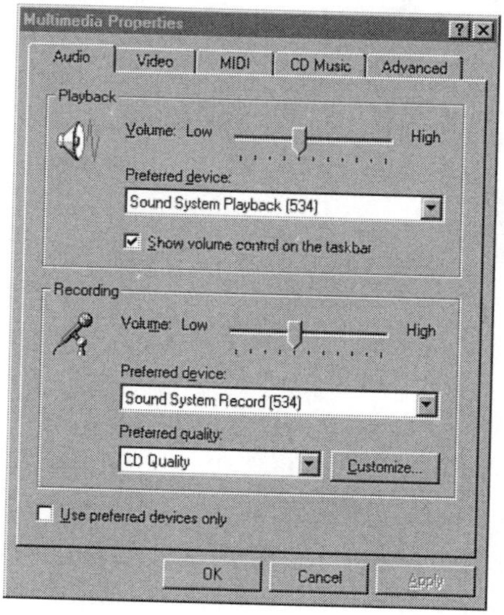

Fig. 20.14 Multimedia Properties sheet's Audio page lets you set the volume for both playback and recording sound.

4. You can change both the playback and recording volume levels by dragging the Playback Volume or Recording Volume slider.
5. When the desired volume level is obtained, click OK.

Setting Up a MIDI Instrument

Setting up a MIDI instrument to work with a MIDI card is a simple process. Here is a quick overview of setting up such an instrument:

1. Plug the instrument into the MIDI card's MIDI port.
2. Click the Start menu.
3. Choose Settings, Control Panel.
4. Open the Multimedia Control Panel.
5. In the Multimedia Properties sheet, click the MIDI page (see fig. 20.15).

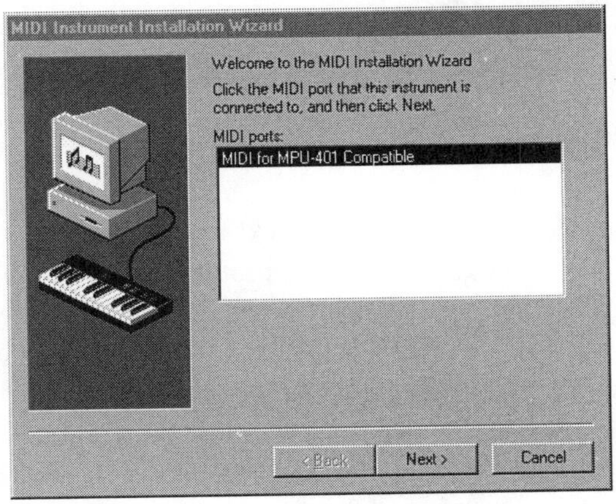

Fig. 20.15
The MIDI page in Multimedia Properties allows you to specify your MIDI output.

6. Click the Add New Instrument button. The MIDI Instrument Installation Wizard appears (see fig. 20.16).

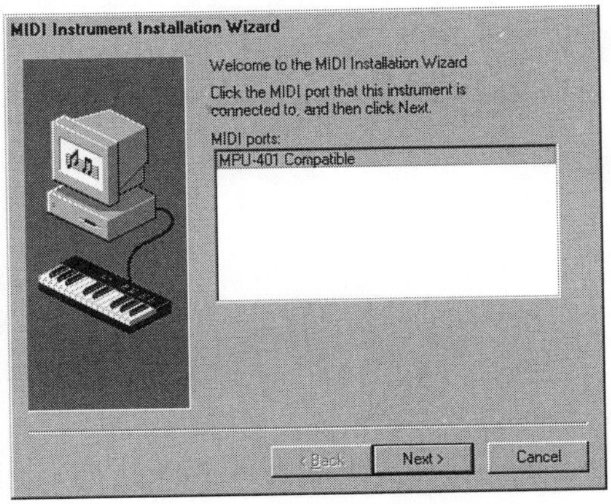

Fig. 20.16
Specify the port that the MIDI instrument is connected to.

7. Click the Next button. The Instrument Definitions screen appears (see fig. 20.17).

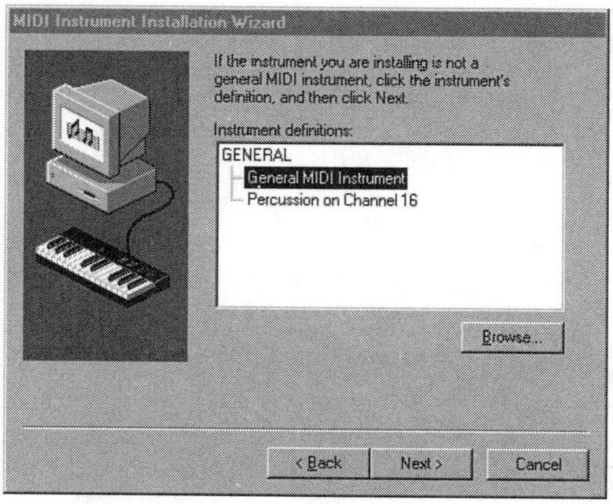

Fig. 20.17
For non-general MIDI instruments, you must select their definitions.

8. Make your selection and click the Next button. The next screen that appears allows you to select a name that identifies the instrument (see fig. 20.18).

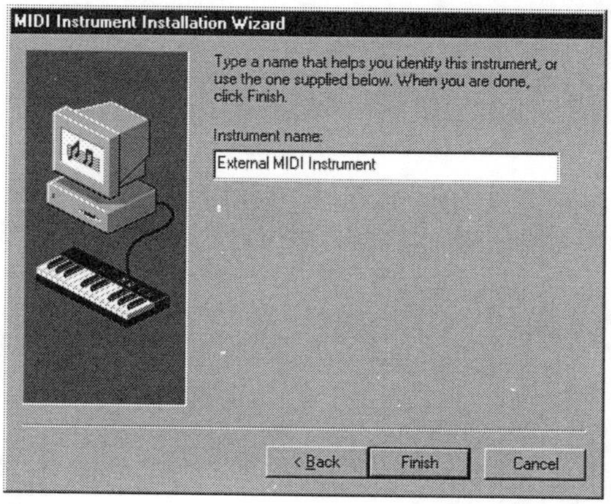

Fig. 20.18
Don't use an elaborate title when you name your new MIDI instrument.

9. Name your new instrument and click the Finish button. You return to the MIDI page, which now contains your new instrument (see fig. 20.19).
10. Select Single Instrument on the MIDI page.
11. Select the instrument you just installed, and click OK.

Your new MIDI instrument is now installed.

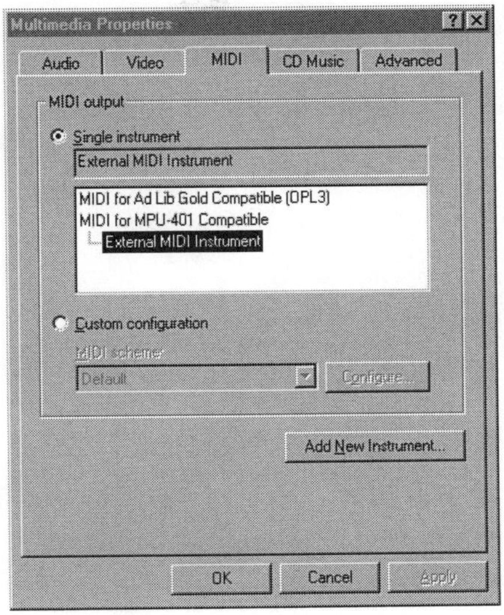

Fig. 20.19
The MIDI page contains the name of your new instrument.

Moving a MIDI Instrument to Another Board

You can move MIDI instruments between boards. There may be an occasion when you have a choice of sound boards for instruments—maybe a high-quality 16-bit board, or a more entry-level 8-bit one. In either case, to move an instrument between boards, follow these steps:

1. Click the Start menu.
2. Choose Settings, Control Panel.
3. Open the Multimedia Control Panel.
4. In the Multimedia Properties sheet, click the Advanced page (see fig. 20.20).
5. Click the plus sign next to MIDI Devices and Instruments.
6. From the ensuing list, click the plus sign next to the board your MIDI instrument was connected to.
7. Click the instrument you want to move, and click the Properties button.
8. From the resulting External MIDI Instrument Properties sheet, select the Detail page (see fig. 20.21).

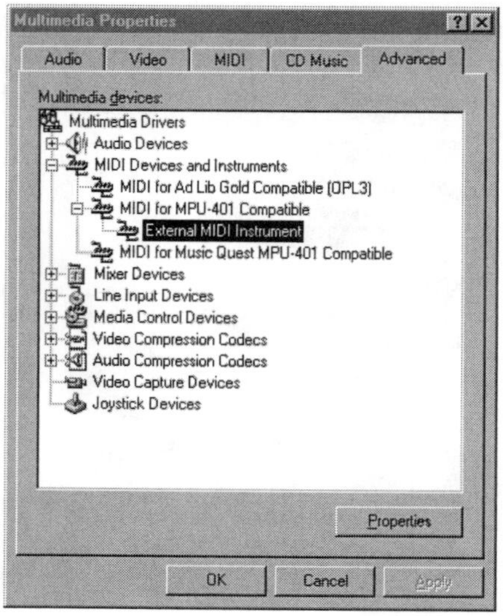

Fig. 20.20
The Advanced page in Multimedia Properties is where you specify the MIDI instrument you want to move.

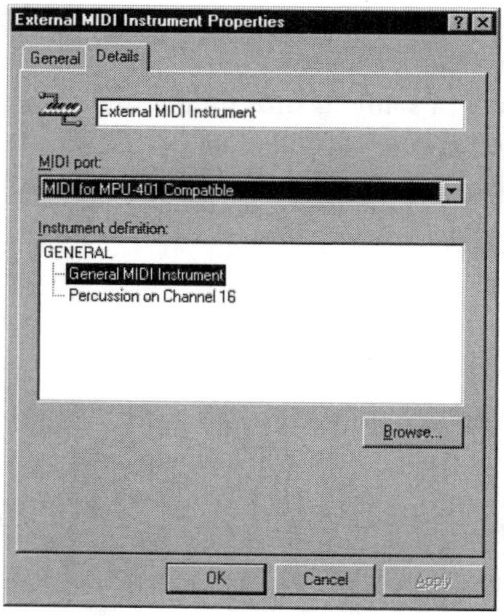

Fig. 20.21
Select the new board from the MIDI port list to where you want to attach the instrument.

9. Choose the name of the board you want to connect the instrument to from the MIDI port list, and click OK.
10. You return to the Advanced page in Multimedia Properties; click OK.
11. Connect your MIDI instrument into the new board you just specified.

Troubleshooting MIDI Cards

Just as with sound cards, getting sound capabilities to run properly using MIDI interface cards can be problematic at times. While the centralized Device Manager registry and system resources and the highly useful Plug and Play standard both help to alleviate problems, problems can still occur.

By far, the most likely source of problems will involve *hardware conflicts*, or two hardware components trying to use the same system resources at the same time. Device Manager will help in this respect as it will suggest available IRQ and I/O settings when you run the Add New Hardware Wizard. But even this is not foolproof.

Fortunately, when hardware conflicts do occur, Windows 95 provides an excellent Help option (accessed from the Start menu), along with an especially useful step-by-step Hardware Conflict Troubleshooter. The latter is accessed via the Hardware, Troubleshooting Conflicts option from the Help Topics Index.

The Troubleshooting Wizard is a step-by-step investigative process that hopefully will identify the offending problem, and provide at least a suggestion for fixing it.

In addition, your MIDI interface card should also include documentation relating to possible hardware compatibility problems, and a toll-free customer or technical support number that users can call for advice. ❖

Chapter 21

Configuring Joysticks and Game Cards

by Paul Sanna

Don't be embarrassed; go ahead and configure your game card to work with Windows 95! Computer games certainly haven't been limited to the domain of younger folks, and recent action/adventure game titles available on CD-ROM clearly have been marketed towards the adult gamer.

Prior to Windows 95, configuring a PC to run a Windows game was as challenging as the game itself. Most games have extremely high memory requirements, but they also require you have a game card driver loaded into memory as well. A *game card* is an adapter you install in your computer that enables game software to work with a joystick plugged into the game card. Windows 95 makes it much easier to run resource-hungry games, as well as to configure the all-important game controller. This chapter helps you get your game card running with Windows 95.

In this chapter, you learn how to

- Install your new game card into your PC
- Specify what model game card is installed in your PC
- Let Windows 95 detect what game card is installed

Tip

What's the most important rule when you are setting up a new appliance, toaster, VCR, new video game, or whatever? Have the user manual or documentation handy. This rule also applies to setting up new hardware for your PC. Before you start to configure a new game card or monitor, be sure you have any relevant

(continues)

(continued)

documentation by your side. You may need to supply information included in the user manual. Also, be sure you have any disks (floppy or CD-ROM) supplied with the device; Windows 95 may need software supplied on the disk.

Installing Your New Game Card into Your PC

The first task in getting a game card to work with Windows 95 is installing the new piece of equipment in your PC. In fact, after you have installed the card, you may have very little (or no) work to do to configure Windows 95. For example, if you have a Plug-and-Play system and the card is Plug-and-Play compatible, Windows 95 does all the work necessary to configure your new game card. In this section, you learn how to install your game card into your PC and how to recognize if your PC and card are both Plug-and-Play compatible.

Note

Windows 95 supports PCs with Plug-and-Play devices. This means that when you install a Plug-and-Play device into your PC, such as a game card, or simply plug one in, such as a monitor, Windows 95 automatically detects the presence of the new device and configures it for use in Windows 95.

This Plug-and-Play functionality also requires the BIOS on your PC to be Plug-and-Play compatible. Even if you do not have Plug-and-Play BIOS or Plug-and-Play devices, Windows 95 can still detect and configure devices using the Add New Hardware Wizard, as you learn in the next few sections of this chapter. Also, certain devices such as joysticks and game cards can be detected immediately when Windows 95 starts.

Here are the steps necessary to install a new game card into your PC; be sure to check the documentation provided with your game card for specific installation instructions:

1. Shut down Windows 95, turn off the power on your PC, unplug the power cord, and follow the instructions enclosed with the card to install the card into the PC.
2. Turn on your PC and boot Windows 95.

3. If the game card is a Plug-and-Play model, Windows 95 notifies you that it has detected and identified the new card. Windows may prompt you in a dialog box for the location, probably a floppy disk, of the driver of the game card. If so, enter the location of the driver in the dialog box. For example, if the driver is on a floppy disk supplied by the manufacturer of the card, insert the disk into the disk drive and then specify the name of the drive (for example, **A**).

> **Note**
>
> A *driver* is software that helps operating systems and other software communicate and work with hardware and other systems. For example, a driver is required for a printer to work with Windows 3.1. In the case of Windows 95, drivers are required to help different hardware devices work with the Windows 95 operating systems.

4. If the game card is not a Plug-and-Play model, Windows 95 does not prompt you for any information. You should start the Add New Hardware Wizard to configure your new game card (see next section).

Starting the Add New Hardware Wizard

Game cards are identified and configured for use in Windows 95 through the Add New Hardware Wizard. The Add New Hardware Wizard automates in Windows 95 most of the work you had to complete in Windows 3.x and DOS to set up a new game card. The Add New Hardware Wizard can be found in the Control Panel folder (see fig. 21.1).

Follow these steps to start the Add New Hardware Wizard:

1. Double-click the Add New Hardware Wizard icon; or right-click the icon and then choose Open from the menu that appears; or click once on the icon and choose File, Open. The dialog box shown in figure 21.2 appears.
2. Click the Next button. The next step in using the Add New Hardware Wizard to configure a game card is to decide who will identify which hardware is installed: *you* or *Windows 95*.

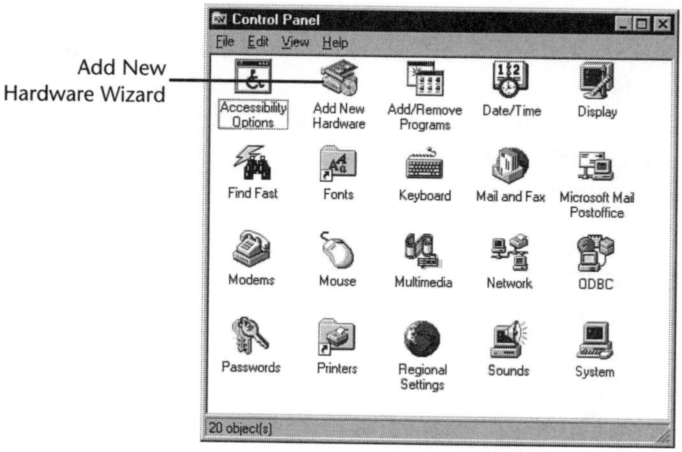

Fig. 21.1
The Add New Hardware Wizard is stored in the Control Panel folder.

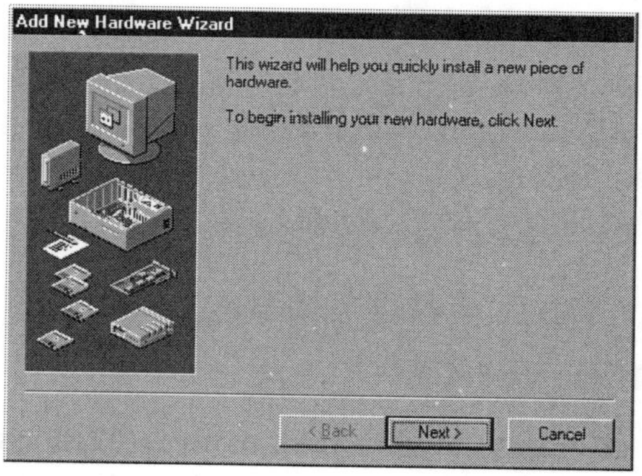

Fig 21.2
The first dialog box that appears when you start most wizards in Windows 95, such as the Add New Hardware Wizard, tells you what the wizard does and gives you the opportunity to cancel.

> **Tip**
>
> Though the Add New Hardware Wizard is located in the Control Panel folder, you can create a shortcut so you can launch the wizard from wherever you choose. If you plan to do a lot of work with the hardware in Windows 95, you could save some time by creating a shortcut to the wizard right on the desktop.

Deciding Who Specifies the Hardware

◀ See "Creating Shortcuts," p. 148

You can use one of two different approaches to specify what game card you have installed in Windows 95. You can let Windows 95 try to identify your game card automatically, or you can tell Windows 95 explicitly what model game card is installed on your PC. There are advantages and disadvantages to both approaches.

Windows Detects the Hardware...

If you let Windows 95 detect the game card, you have little to no work to do. You answer a few prompts, and eventually Windows 95 identifies your game card and configures itself to operate properly with the card. A downside to Windows 95 autodetecting the card, however, is that this is a lengthy process; Windows 95 tries to identify *all* of the hardware in your system. It's impossible to tell Windows 95 to look specifically for a game card. If you are short on time and you know the model of your game card, it may be best for you to tell Windows 95 what hardware you have installed.

I Tell Windows What Hardware I Have...

If you decide to do the legwork and identify for Windows 95 the model of your game card, you have little chance for error. Provided you know what hardware is installed on your PC, you can be sure Windows 95 installs the correct driver by explicitly telling Windows 95 what hardware to configure. However, this approach sidesteps one of the most powerful aspects of Windows 95: its ability to detect hardware. You need to know the exact manufacturer and model information in order to supply that information to Windows 95. Lots of work went into the development of Windows 95's capability to recognize your hardware—why not take advantage of it?

Letting Windows 95 Detect the Game Card

The process for letting Windows 95 detect your game card is simple: start the Add New Hardware Wizard, Windows 95 inspects your system for hardware devices it doesn't recognize, and then you tell Windows 95 you want to configure the game card it found. Next, Windows 95 informs you what model game card it thinks it found, you confirm that information, and then Windows 95 configures itself so it always loads the correct drivers for use with the adapter.

To let Windows 95 detect your game card, follow these steps:

1. Follow the instructions to start the Add New Hardware Wizard shown earlier in the "Starting the Add New Hardware Wizard" section.

2. Click the Next button in the first dialog box that appears. The dialog box shown in figure 21.3 appears.

3. Click the Yes (Recommended) option button and then click Next. The dialog box shown in figure 21.4 appears. This dialog box asks you to confirm that you want Windows 95 to detect the hardware on your PC.

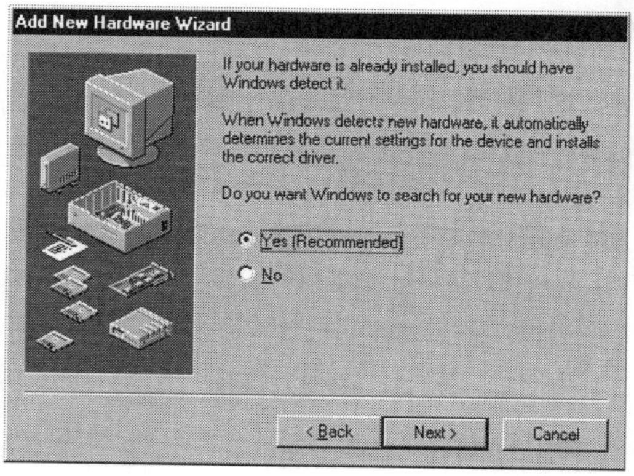

Fig. 21.3
Windows 95 recommends that it detect all of the new hardware installed on your PC.

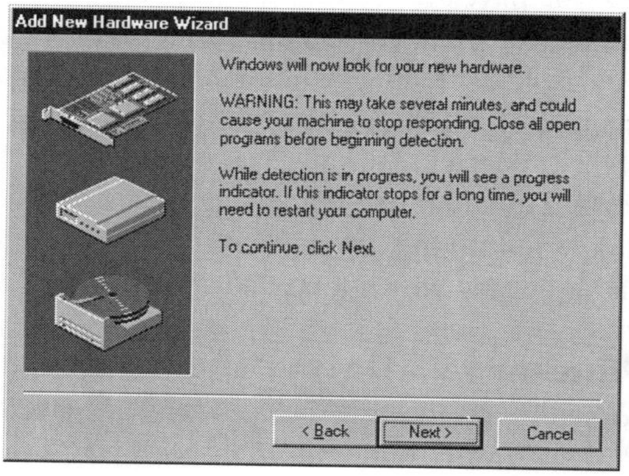

Fig 21.4
Just before Windows 95 begins to inspect your system for installed hardware, Windows 95 verifies that you want to continue.

4. Choose the Next button. Windows 95 now starts the detection phase when it inspects your PC for installed hardware.

5. After Windows 95 completes the detection phase, it displays a dialog box from which you can view the list of new hardware the Add New Hardware Wizard found. To configure Windows 95 with the new game card, click the Finish button. Depending upon the capabilities of your game card and monitor, Windows 95 may ask if it can reboot the system for the changes to take effect.

Manually Specifying Your Game Card

The process to manually specify your game card is simple: start the Add New Hardware Wizard; tell Windows 95 you want to install a sound, video, or game controller; pick the game card from a list provided by Windows 95; and then Windows 95 configures itself so it always loads the correct driver for use with the card. Most likely, you won't have to reboot your machine.

To specify the game card that is installed on your PC, follow these steps:

1. Follow the instructions to start the Add New Hardware wizard shown earlier in the "Starting the Add New Hardware Wizard" section.

2. Click the Next button in the first dialog box that appears. The dialog box shown in figure 21.5 appears.

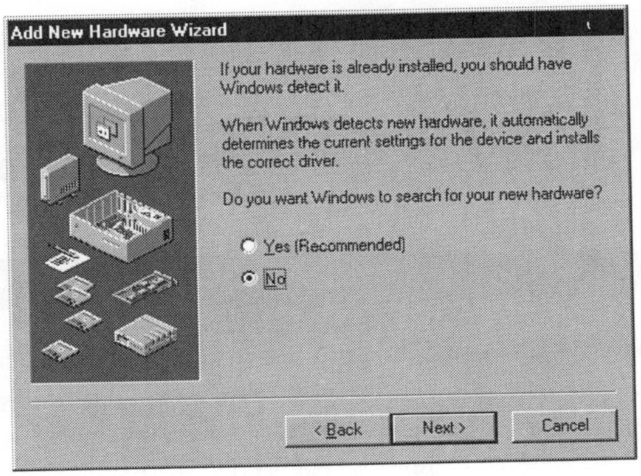

Fig. 21.5
Windows allows you to manually specify what hardware you want to install.

3. Click the No option button and then click Next. The dialog box shown in figure 21.6 appears.

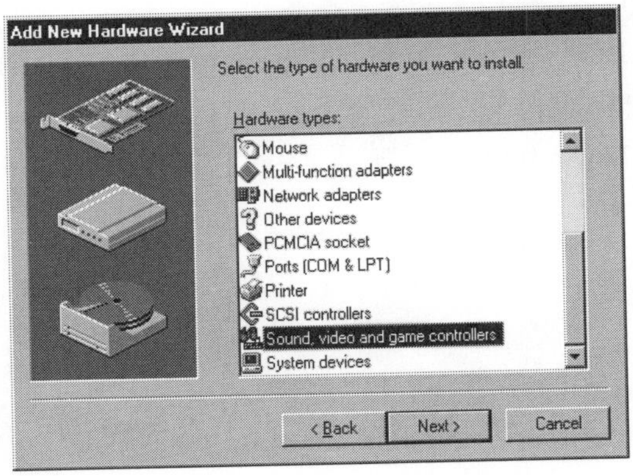

Fig. 21.6
You specify what type of hardware you plan to install.

4. Choose Sound, Video and Game Controllers in the Hardware Types list box and then click Next. The dialog box in figure 21.7 appears.

5. Click the manufacturer of your game card in the Manufacturers list box. The list of supported game cards for the manufacturer you chose appears in the Models list box. Click the model of your game card in the Models list box.

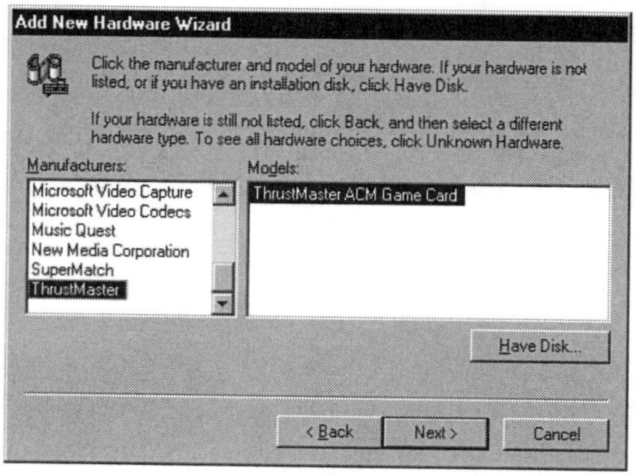

Fig. 21.7
Windows 95 provides a list of supported game card models (and their manufacturers) for you to choose from.

> **Tip**
>
> If you have the software installation disk that was shipped with the game card, you can avoid having to pick the manufacturer and model of your game card from the lists provided with Windows 95. Insert the disk into a floppy drive and click the Have Disk button in the dialog box shown in figure 21.7. Follow the prompts to specify the location of OEMSETUP.INF, which should appear on the disk. This file contains all the information needed to configure the game card.

6. Click the Next button. Windows 95 informs you that it has completed the installation of the game card.
7. Click the Finish button.

Chapter 22

Configuring Mice and Other Pointing Devices

by Gregory J. Root

Most of the time, when you install Windows 95, the installation process will autodetect your pointing device. Windows can autodetect Kensington, Logitech, Microsoft, and other Microsoft-compatible pointing devices. A pointing device is a hardware peripheral controlling the position and movement of the arrow on your screen. Setting up Windows 95 to receive input from your mouse or other pointing device can be a smooth installation process.

Now, Windows 95 has the capability to accept commands from more than one pointing device. Instead of loading special drivers that devour memory resources, Windows 95 provides simultaneous input from accessibility devices like eye-gazers and head-pointers. If you like using a trackball for specific programs but would prefer to use a mouse for everything else, both can control Windows 95 at the same time.

Within this chapter, you learn how to configure your pointing device by

- Adding your mouse or pointing device
- Manually specifying a pointing device
- Setting pointing device properties

Starting Add New Hardware Wizard for Pointing Devices

The Add New Hardware Wizard provides you the ability to let Windows 95 identify your pointing device. The wizard steps you through the process. It can automatically detect your pointing device, or you may manually specify it. After you've told Windows what pointing device you have, you'll want to customize how your buttons react, how sensitive it is to your motions, or other special features of your device.

Letting Windows 95 Autodetect a Pointing Device

Allowing Windows 95 to automatically detect your pointing device is the easiest way to add a new one to your system. Windows 95 comes with many drivers and should know about your new device.

Before you begin the Add New Hardware Wizard, you should connect your new pointing device to the computer. This allows Windows 95 to query it to determine the type, make, and model. If you don't have the device connected when you run the wizard, you have to manually specify it. Because manually specifying a pointing device is a more complex process, it is highly preferable to use the wizard.

Caution

Make sure your computer power is turned off when adding any new hardware. In this case, you don't want to damage your new pointing device.

To begin detecting your pointing device, use the following steps. A Microsoft PS/2 Port Mouse is used in the example. However, these steps work for any device you might want to configure:

Tip

If you aren't sure if Windows 95 supports your pointing device, let Windows 95 try to identify it anyway. Chances are, it will be able to identify the device.

1. Click the Start button (or press Ctrl+Esc if you don't have any pointing devices currently installed), and choose Settings, Control Panel to open the Control Panel. You'll access the Add New Hardware Wizard here.

2. Double-click the Add New Hardware control panel, as shown in figure 22.1, to start the Add New Hardware Wizard. If you're without a pointing device, use the arrow keys on your keyboard to move to the Add New Hardware icon and press Enter.

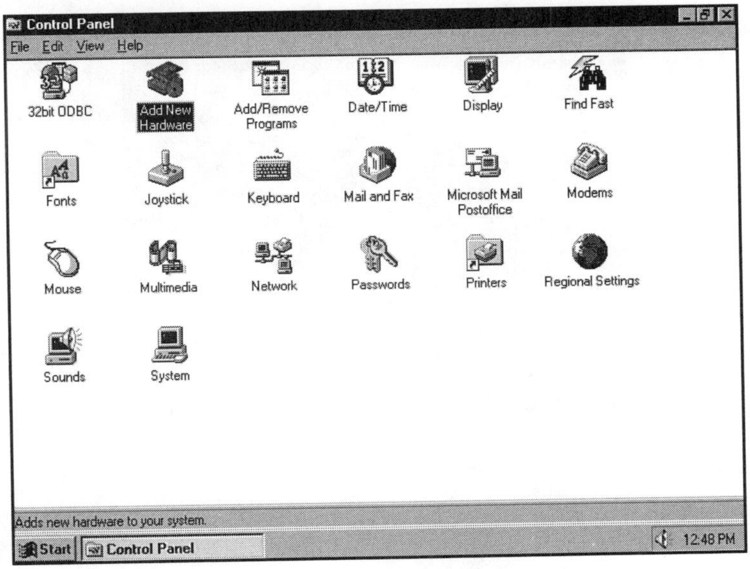

Fig. 22.1
The Add New Hardware control panel is accessed via the Control Panel.

3. As shown in figure 22.2, the Add New Hardware Wizard begins to detect your device when you click the Next button. You can also press Enter to continue. At any time during this process, you can click the Cancel button to stop.

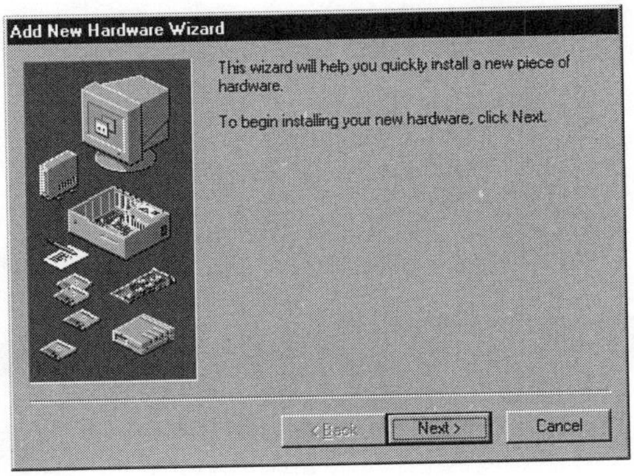

Fig. 22.2
To tell the wizard you're ready for the next step, click the Next button.

4. When the next step of the wizard is shown (see fig. 22.3), make sure the Yes (Recommended) option is chosen when you're asked "Do you want Windows to search for your new hardware?." When using a keyboard to navigate, use the Tab key to select the correct option and press the spacebar. Click the Next button when you're ready to move on.

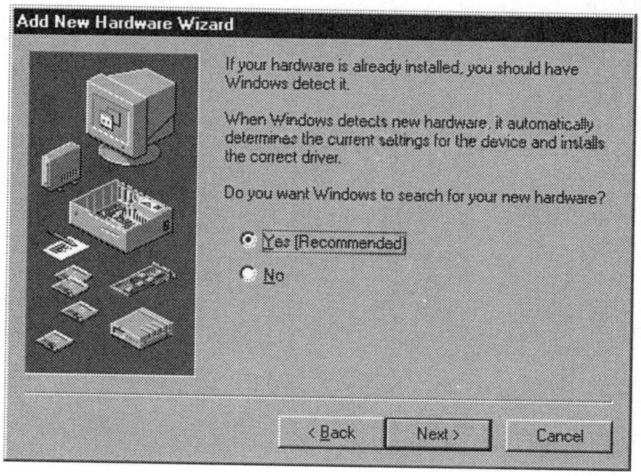

Fig. 22.3
Choose Yes when asked to let Windows search for your pointing device.

5. The next step of the wizard reminds you that detecting your new device may take a long time. As shown in figure 22.4, click Next (or press Enter) to confirm searching for your pointer.

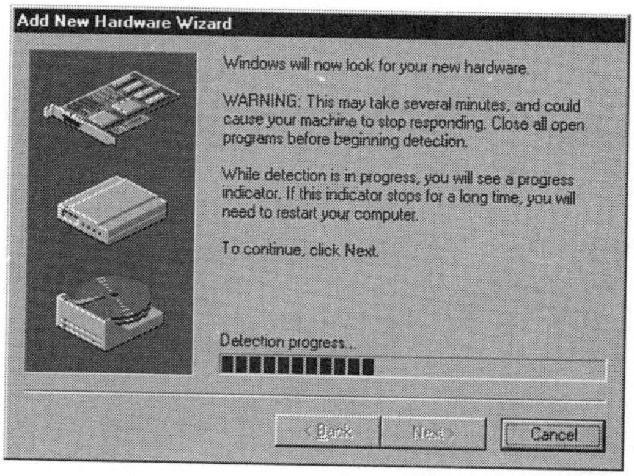

Fig 22.4
Once you make the final confirmation, a progress bar displays the status of finding your new device.

Tip

The progress bar can stop moving for a long time. Before you restart your computer (as instructed on the screen), check to see if the hard drive light is flashing. If you don't have a hard drive activity light, put your ear next to your computer and listen for the clicking of your computer accessing the hard drive. Oftentimes the wizard is still trying to identify a specific device type, even though the progress bar has stopped for a few moments.

Troubleshooting

My computer froze when detecting my new hardware. Shouldn't I just press the Reset button?

If you need to restart your computer because it has stopped responding, don't just use Ctrl+Alt+Delete or press the Reset button on the front of your computer. Turn off the power to your computer, wait three seconds, and then turn it back on. One of the reasons your computer stopped responding was that a piece of hardware became confused. Using Ctrl+Alt+Delete or the Reset button won't initialize your computer hardware to a clean state. Turning the power off and then on is the only way to accomplish this. Once Windows 95 has finished restarting, you need to go back to step 1 in this section.

6. The wizard notifies you that it successfully detected your device (see fig. 22.5). If the wizard was not able to detect your pointing device, you have to manually specify it. See "Manually Specifying a Pointing Device" later in this chapter.

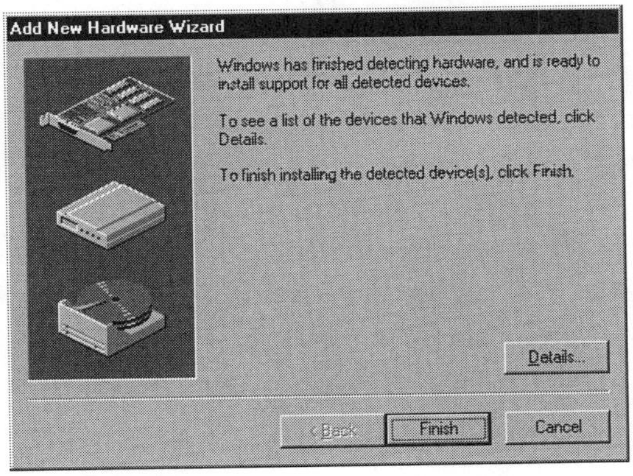

Fig. 22.5
Windows 95 has successfully detected your new pointing device.

7. If you want to see the details of what the wizard found, click the Details button. You see a list of your new hardware.

As shown in figure 22.6, the wizard successfully detected the new Microsoft PS/2 Port Mouse installed in the computer before the power was turned on. If you don't care to see the details or have finished viewing the list of details, click the Finish button to install the drivers that support your device. Your computer is now configured to accept commands from your new pointing device. Congratulations!

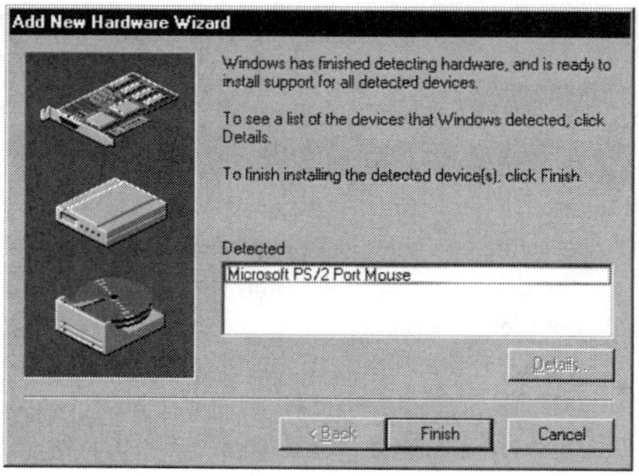

Fig. 22.6
You can view the details of what the wizard found by clicking the Details button.

> **Note**
>
> If the device doesn't work at this time or the name of the device in the Detected list doesn't seem quite right, choose Cancel instead. Follow the procedures in the next section.

Manually Specifying a Pointing Device

You may need to manually specify your pointing device if the Add New Hardware Wizard wasn't able to automatically detect it. Or, you may be installing the driver for the device before you've physically connected it to your computer. Or, you may have a new "designed-for-Windows 95" pointing device that has a setup disk with the correct driver from the manufacturer. You use the Add New Hardware Wizard in any of these cases. Use these steps to let Windows 95 know what type of pointing device you will be using:

1. Click the Start button (or press Ctrl+Esc if you don't have any pointing devices currently installed), and choose Settings, Control Panel to open the Control Panel. You access the Add New Hardware Wizard here.

2. Double-click the Add New Hardware control panel, to start the Add New Hardware Wizard (refer to fig. 22.1). If you don't have a pointing device, use the arrow keys on your keyboard to move to the Add New Hardware icon and press Enter.

3. As shown in figure 22.2, the Add New Hardware Wizard allows you to specify your device when you click the Next button. You can also press Enter to continue. At any time during this process, you can select the Cancel button to stop.

4. When the next step of the Wizard is shown (as in fig. 22.7), make sure the No option is chosen when you're asked "Do you want Windows to search for your new hardware?". When using a keyboard to navigate, press the Tab key to move the focus to the correct option and then press the spacebar. Click the Next button when you're ready to move on.

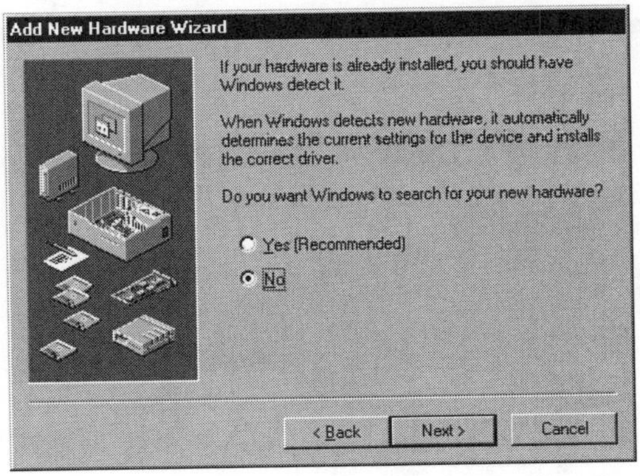

Fig. 22.7
Choose No when asked to let Widows search for your pointing device.

5. From the list of Hardware Types in figure 22.8, choose Mouse if you're adding a mouse, and click the Next button at the bottom of the window.

   If using only a keyboard to navigate, use the arrow keys to select Mouse and then press Enter. Windows now knows you want to manually specify a mouse.

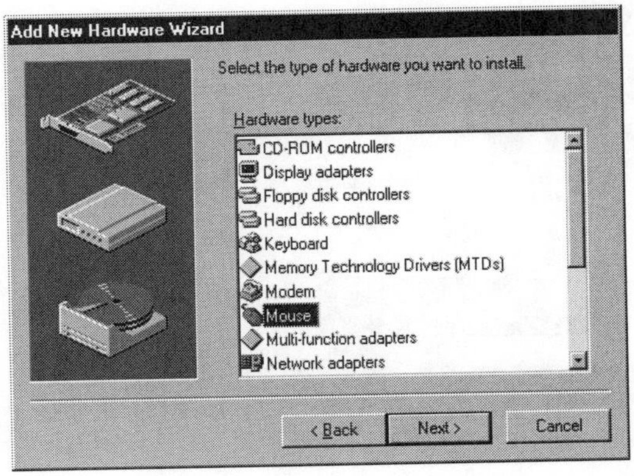

Fig. 22.8
When adding a pointing device, select the Mouse hardware type to manually specify it.

6. From the left-hand side Manufacturers list in figure 22.9, select who made your pointing device. If you don't know who made your pointing device or can't find it in the list, leave the selection on Standard Mouse Types. Then select the specific model you have from the list on the right. If you are using Standard Mouse Types, select the type of input device from the list on the right. In our example, figure 22.9 illustrates a selection of the manufacturer as Microsoft and the model as Microsoft PS/2 Port Mouse.

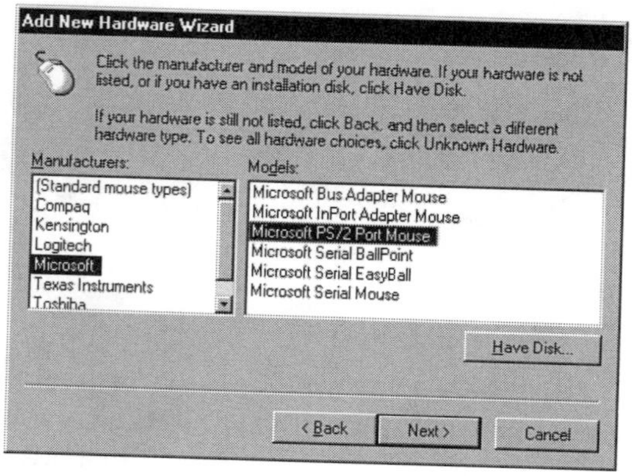

Fig. 22.9
Select a manufacturer's name in the list on the left, and one of the models from the list on the right. Click Have Disk if the manufacturer provided one.

If you have a disk that came with the pointing device from the manufacturer, then click Have Disk instead. Figure 22.10 shows Windows 95 asking for the manufacturer's disk to be inserted in your floppy drive to be processed. Selecting OK begins loading the driver from the floppy disk. Once this is complete, you're ready for the next step.

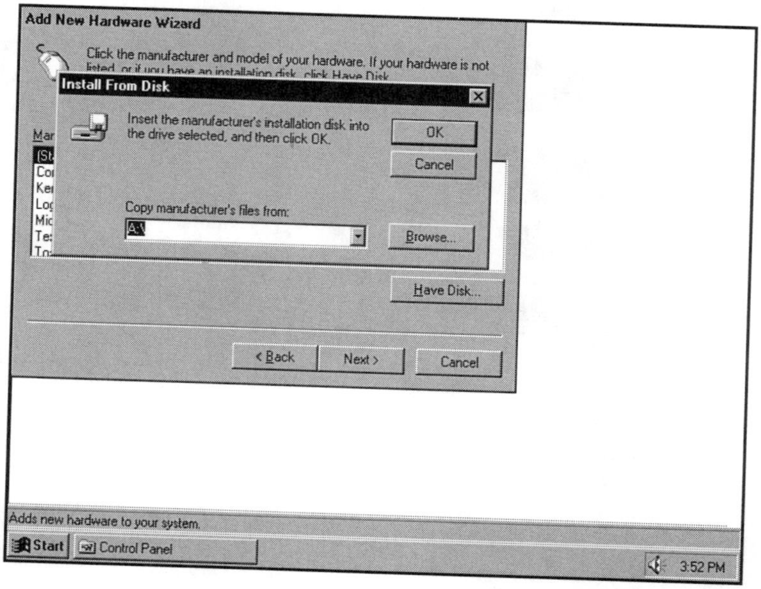

Fig. 22.10
Place the manufacturer's driver disk into the floppy drive to load the new driver.

7. Whether you've selected your manufacturer and model from the list or loaded the driver from the manufacturer's disk, you now need to install the correct drivers by clicking Finish, as illustrated in figure 22.11.

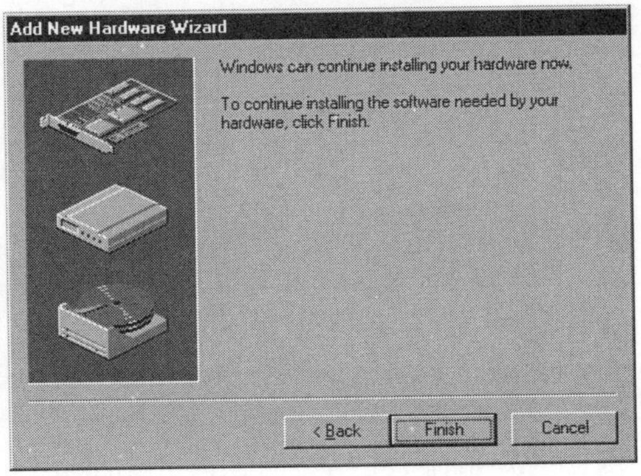

Fig. 22.11
Complete the installation of your pointing device by clicking Finish.

You may need to modify some device properties using the Device Manager. This is the case if the wizard tells you that other hardware is conflicting with the pointing device you are trying to install (see the two examples of fig. 22.12). Or, Windows may have found settings usable by the new pointing device, but wasn't able to change the settings on the actual device. First, click the Next button to complete the installation of the device drivers. Then, use the Device Manager in the System control panel to adjust the pointing device resources before you reboot your computer.

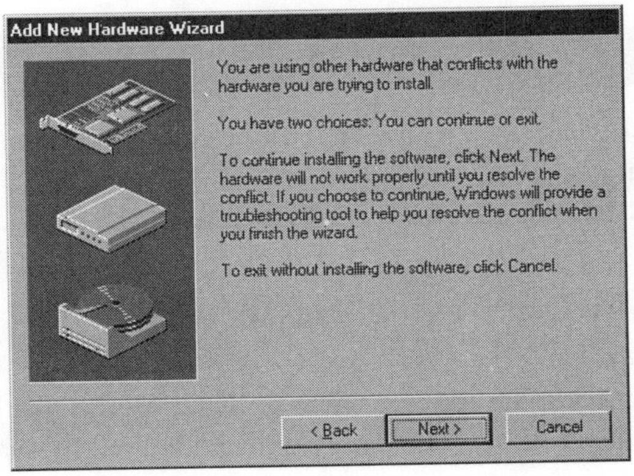

Fig. 22.12
If either of these results appear after you selected your pointing device, you need to modify the device properties using the Device Manager in the System control panel before rebooting your computer.

◀ See "Changing Device Properties," p. 334

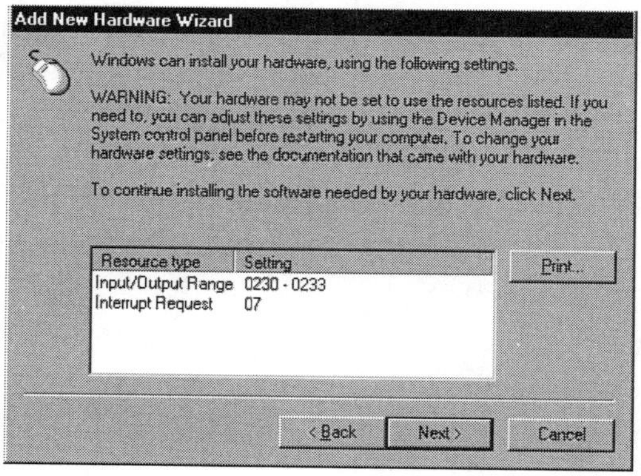

Tip

If Windows was able to allot device settings as shown in the first window shown in fig. 22.12, click the Print button to print a record of what Windows has set aside for your new device. This hard copy comes in handy when you have to use the Device Manager to adjust hardware settings.

8. After completing all these steps, Windows might tell you that the system must be rebooted. You need to reboot the system if your pointing device is not Plug and Play compatible. If you're ready to do so, then go ahead and click Yes to reboot. If you have other devices to set up or need to make modifications to some settings to avoid hardware conflicts, select No.

Caution

Be aware that if Windows is asking to restart the computer, your new pointing device won't work until you do so.

Setting Pointing Device Properties

Your pointing device doesn't have to be a boring little arrow that moves around on the screen. You have a say as to what it looks like. If you're left-handed, you don't have to suffer in a right-handed world—you can reconfigure the buttons. If you don't like to move your pointing device around a lot or think you have to double-click too fast, you can adjust the sensitivity of the device. Also, manufacturers sometimes provide additional features specific to their devices. Read through the next few sections to take advantage of some very nice features.

Every pointing device is adjusted using the Mouse control panel. To get started, access the control panel by following these steps:

1. Click the Start button (or press Ctrl+Esc if you don't have any mice currently installed), and choose Settings, Control Panel to open the Control Panel.

2. Double-click the Mouse control panel, as shown in figure 22.13, to access the properties of your mouse.

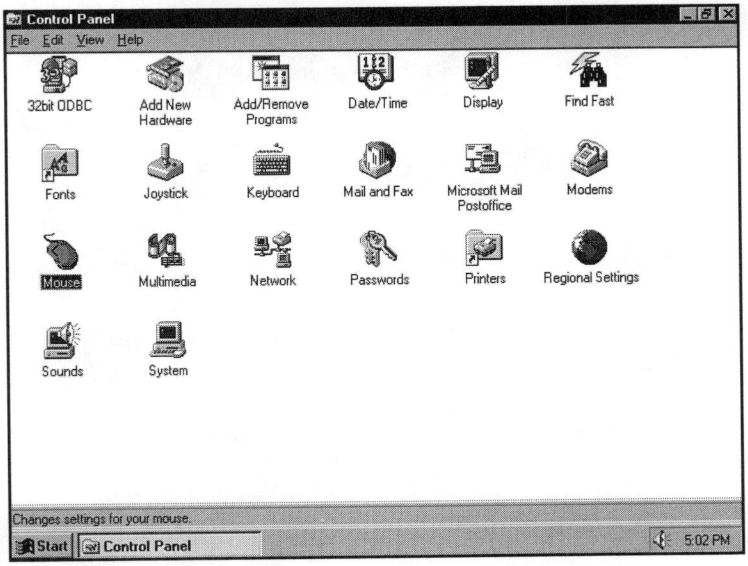

Fig. 22.13
The Mouse control panel is accessed via the Control Panel.

From here, you can set buttons, pointer styles, mouse motions, and general properties. Read on to find out how.

Buttons

The Button tab is the default tab displayed when opening the Mouse Properties control sheet. Here you can adjust how fast or slow you double-click. You can also set which button is the primary button if you're left-handed. To adjust the double-click speed:

1. In the Double-Click Speed group box, drag the slider left or right to adjust the speed as seen in figure 22.14. If you drag it to the right, Windows requires you to shorten the amount of time between the first and

second click. If you drag the slider to the left, Windows allows more time between the first and second click.

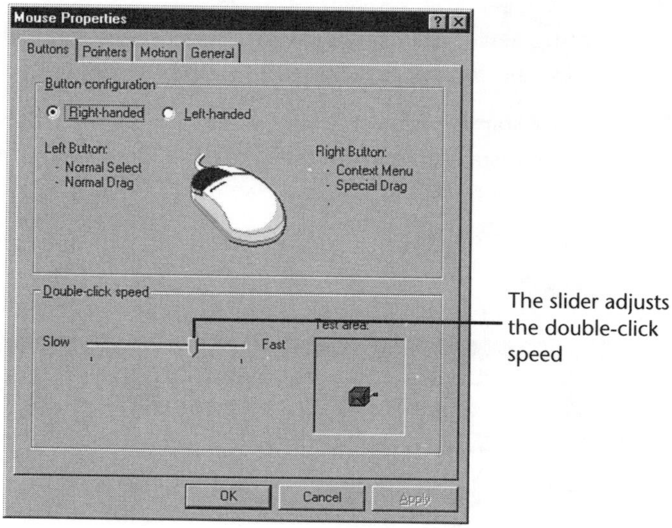

Fig. 22.14
You can adjust the double-click speed by dragging the slider. Adjust the button configuration at the top by selecting a button configuration.

2. To test the amount of time between clicks of a double-click, try out your settings by double-clicking the jack-in-the-box in the lower-right Test Area (see fig. 22.15). You can tell if Windows understood the speed of your double-click when the jack-in-the-box jumps out of its box.

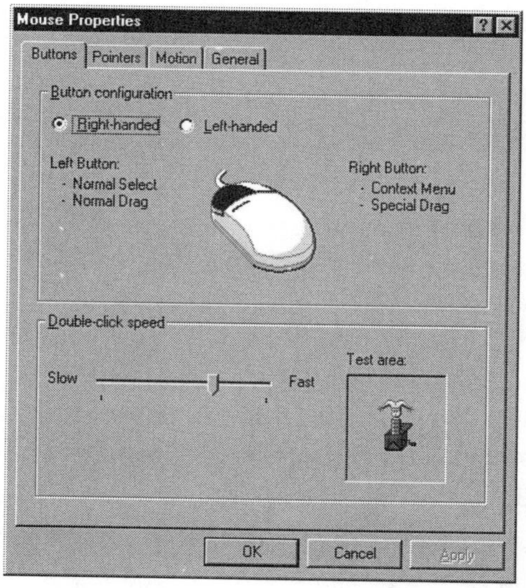

Fig. 22.15
The jack-in-the-box jumps out of its box if Windows understood your double-click in the Test Area.

To set the pointing device as a left-handed device, click the Left-handed radio button in the Button Configuration group box shown in figure 22.15. Conversely, to set it as a right-handed device, click the Right-handed radio button in the group box.

Pointers

As you may have noticed when using Windows, when a program is busy working on something or your pointer is positioned over the edges of a window, the pointer changes to a different shape. Now, with Windows 95, you can choose your own pointers. What's even better is that you can choose animated, color pointers.

You can change your pointers individually or as a scheme. To quickly change the set of pointers from the current scheme to another scheme, select the Pointers page at the top of the Mouse Properties sheet. (see fig. 22.16) Open the Scheme drop-down list and pick a new scheme. If no schemes are listed, you haven't created any yet.

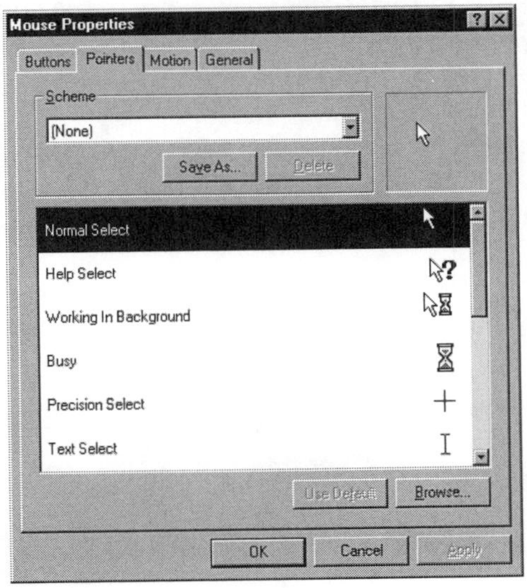

Fig. 22.16
Choose the Pointers page in the Mouse Properties sheet to change the pointers.

> **Note**
>
> If you've installed Microsoft Plus, the Desktop Themes can apply a complete set of mouse pointers appropriate for the theme you've selected. If you want to change a single pointer as part of your current desktop theme, you can do so without permanently changing the desktop theme's regular configuration.

Plus!

Instead of changing all the pointers at the same time, click the Browse button to change a single pointer to something new and interesting. To learn how to do this, select the Pointers page in the Mouse Properties sheet (refer to fig. 22.16). Then perform these additional actions:

1. Highlight the pointer from the list you want to change and click the Browse button.

> **Tip**
>
> You can double-click the pointer for faster access to the Browse window.

2. From the Browse window, select a new pointer from the CURSORS folder. Only pointers with an ANI or CUR extension are listed. When you highlight a pointer name, the Browse window displays a preview of what the pointer will look like, as seen in figure 22.17. Once you've found the pointer you're looking for, click the Open button. This opens the CURSOR file and associates your choice to the pointer in the Pointer properties list. You can do this with as many pointers as you like.

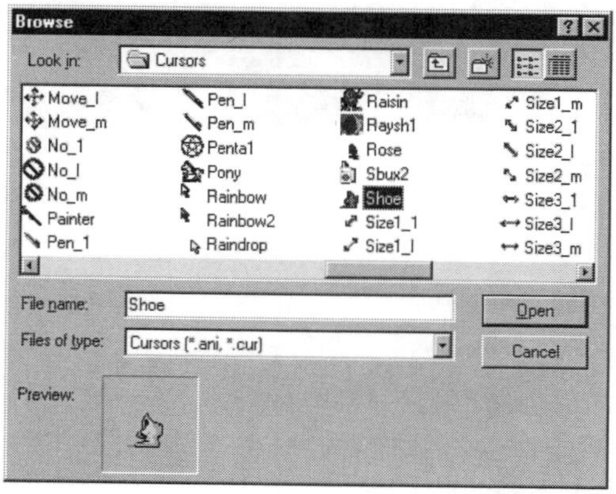

Fig. 22.17
Select a new look for your pointer by selecting a pointer name in the Browse window.

> **Note**
>
> If no pointer names appear in the Browse window, the extra mouse pointers were not installed when Windows 95 was installed. To add them, use the Windows Setup tab of the Add/Remove Software control panel.

◀ See "Selecting Custom Install Options," p. 107

Caution

Even though it's fun to use color-animated cursors in a pointer scheme, consider using ones that have some relationship to the pointer's original appearance. For example, if you change all your pointers to a set of animals, you'll have a hard time remembering which animal means which type of pointer.

3. If you don't like a change you've made to a particular pointer, you can set it back to the default Windows 95 pointer. Select it in the list and click the Use Default button (refer to fig. 22.16).

Tip

If you want to reset all your pointers to their defaults, use the Scheme drop-down list and set the scheme name to `(None)`.

Now that you've made some changes to the pointers on the property sheet, you may want to save the set of pointers as a scheme. You can do so by performing this step:

4. From the Pointers property sheet, click the Save As button.
5. When the Save Scheme dialog box appears as seen in figure 22.18, give your scheme a name and click OK to save it.

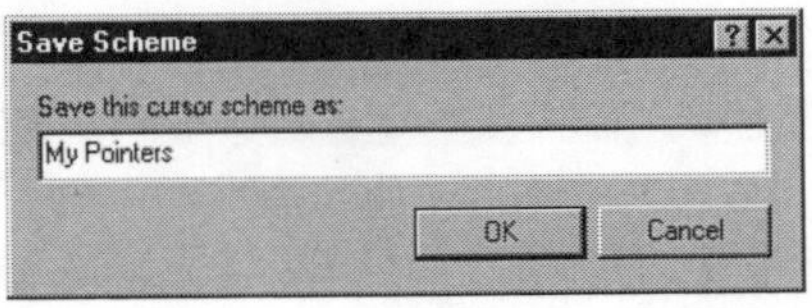

Fig. 22.18
Give your pointer scheme a name in the Save Scheme dialog box.

Caution

Windows does not warn you if you are about to save your new scheme with the same name as an existing scheme. You will replace the existing scheme if it's named the same as the one you use now.

If you would like to delete the current pointer scheme instead, then:

6. Select a pointer scheme name from the list. Then click the Delete button (refer to fig. 22.18). When you delete the pointer scheme, you

won't delete the actual pointers. You're just breaking the association of the pointers from the CURSORS folder to the Pointers list.

Lastly, you want to apply all the changes you've made to your pointer settings. To learn how to do this:

7. Click the Apply button at the bottom of the Mouse Properties dialog box (see fig. 22.19). This saves your changes and leaves the dialog open for you to make other adjustments to your mouse. If you are through making changes, click OK to save all of your changes and close the Mouse Properties dialog box.

Caution

If you've added or deleted schemes, choosing Cancel will not undo those actions. Adding or deleting a scheme is permanent.

Motion

While using your pointing device, you might have come to some conclusions. One of them might be that you're moving it too much or too little when compared to the actual pointer movement on-screen. If you use a portable computer, another conclusion might be that it's hard to follow the pointer around on the small screen. In either of these cases, you want to select the Motion page at the top of the Mouse Properties sheet as shown in figure 22.19.

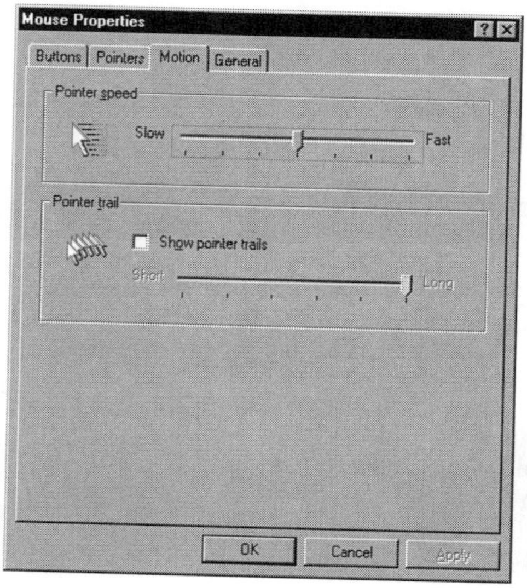

Fig. 22.19 Access the Motion settings in the Mouse Properties sheet by selecting the Motion page.

> **Troubleshooting**
>
> *My pointer moves erratically.*
>
> If, when you shake the cable, it makes the situation better or worse, verify that the connection to your computer is secure. Sometimes, the connector has come loose from the port on your computer.
>
> If that doesn't work, inspect the cable for breaks or cuts. If your cable is broken or pierced, repair or replacement is necessary. If there are no visible breaks, a wire inside the cable may have broken. This may have been caused by severe twisting of the cable, being placed under a heavy object for long periods of time, or a heavy object which dropped on it (for example, a paperweight or stapler).
>
> Also, check the Windows Driver Library (WDL) for an updated driver for your pointing device. The *WDL* is an electronic library of drivers which is updated as new ones become available. You can access the WDL via the Microsoft Network (MSN) in the Windows 95 area; CompuServe via **GO MSL**; the Internet via World Wide Web or Gopher (both at **http://www.microsoft.com**), or FTP (**ftp:/ftp.microsoft.com);** or via the Microsoft Download Service at (206) 936-6735 (you only pay for the phone call).

To learn how to adjust the sensitivity of the pointing device to your taste, follow these steps:

1. Drag the slider left and right to adjust the sensitivity. Dragging the slider towards Slow requires you to move the pointing device more to make the pointer on-screen move in a certain direction. Dragging the slider towards Fast requires less pointing device movement to make the pointer on-screen move in a certain direction.
2. Click the Apply button at the bottom of the Mouse Properties sheet. This saves your changes and leaves the sheet open for you to make other adjustments to your pointing device.
3. If you are through making changes, click OK to save all of your changes and close the Mouse Properties sheet.

> **Troubleshooting**
>
> *My pointer movement around the screen seems slow and jerky. What's wrong?*
>
> It all boils down to this: your computer is very busy performing a task. Or, if you shared a folder on your hard drive, other users may be heavily reading and writing information in it.

If you find it hard to follow the pointer on your portable computer screen, try turning on pointer trails. *Pointer trails* make it easier to locate your pointer on the screen. To learn how to turn on pointer trails and adjust their length, follow these steps:

1. In the Pointer Trail group box, click the Show Pointer Trails check box, as shown in figure 22.20. Then drag the slider left and right to adjust the trail length. Dragging the slider towards `Short` displays less of a trail. Dragging the slider towards `Long` displays a longer trail.

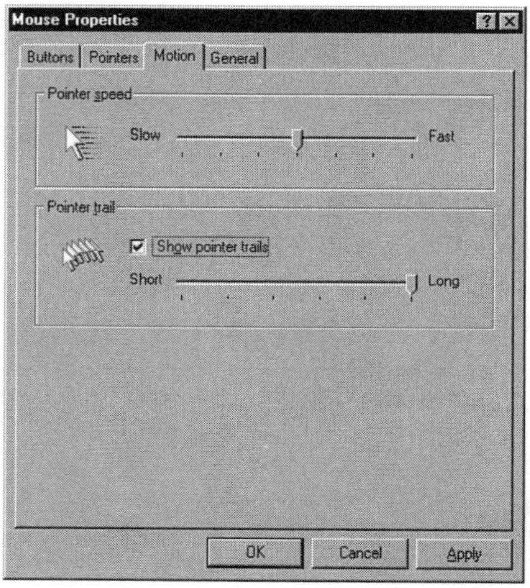

Fig. 22.20
Clicking the Show Pointer Trails check box turns on mouse trails.

2. Click the Apply button at the bottom of the Mouse Properties sheet. This saves your changes and leaves the sheet open for you to make other adjustments to your pointing device.
3. If you are through making changes, click OK to save all of your changes and close the Mouse Properties sheet.

Troubleshooting

My pointer moves in one direction but not another. Help!

Try cleaning your mouse ball, track ball, and/or any internal motion contacts (usually small plastic wheels). If you're using a mouse, clean the glide pads on the bottom (if you have them). If you use a mouse pad, be sure to clean it regularly to prevent a build-up of dirt. Be sure to follow the cleaning and care instructions provided by your manufacturer. If you don't follow them carefully, you could damage the electronics. Pointing devices are designed to be highly sensitive to small motions.

General

The General page of the Mouse Properties sheet allows you to change the driver for your pointer. Additionally, if your pointing device manufacturer has provided additional capabilities with its driver, you're able to access them here. Click the General page at the top of the Mouse Properties sheet to begin learning about it (see fig. 22.21).

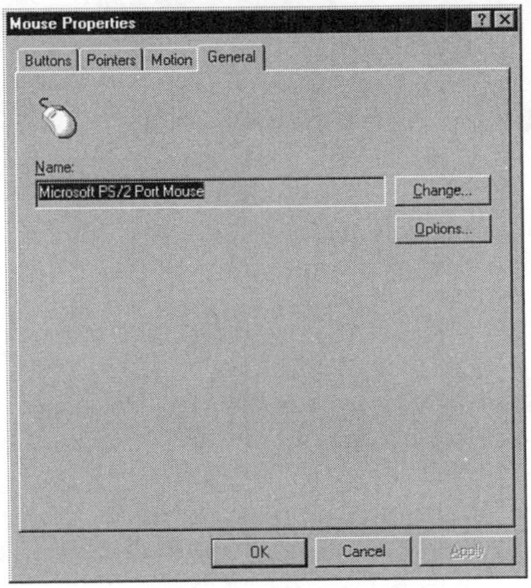

Fig. 22.21
Access the General settings in the Mouse Properties sheet by selecting the General page.

To change the current driver for your pointing device, you can do it via the General properties of the Mouse control panel:

1. Click the Change button on the far right side of the property sheet to display the Select Device window, shown in figure 22.22.

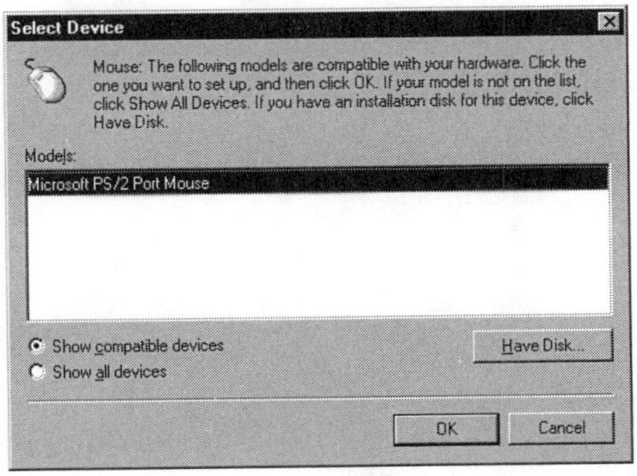

Fig. 22.22
The Select Device window allows you to select a compatible pointing device driver.

2. In most cases, you won't have many choices. Pointing device drivers usually aren't interchangeable. However, if you are presented with other choices, select a compatible driver from the list. You may want to click Show All Devices or Have Disk if you've changed your pointing device since the last time you used your computer.

Tip

If you're configuring a new pointing device, it's best to let Windows 95 try to automatically detect it for you. See "Letting Windows 95 Auto Detect Pointing Device" at the beginning of this chapter.

3. Once you've made your new selection, click the Apply button at the bottom of the Mouse Properties sheet. This saves your changes and leaves the dialog open for you to make other adjustments to your pointing device.

4. If you are through making changes, click OK to save all of your changes and close the Mouse Properties sheet.

If your pointing device manufacturer has provided extra capabilities to control the appearance or actions of your pointer, an Options button appears below the Change button (refer to fig. 22.21). The capabilities vary widely from manufacturer to manufacturer. Some better-known options are to change the size of the pointer or adjust the orientation of the pointing device. To view them, just click the Options button.

Chapter 23

Configuring Keyboards

by Ian Stokell

Despite Windows 95 being a graphical user interface-based operating environment, the keyboard remains a fundamental part of the computer system on which it runs. It does, of course, become essential if you intend to do any word processing or anything that requires more than the point-and-click operation that Windows is known for.

How you set up your keyboard can be a major factor in how efficiently things run. This chapter covers a variety of keyboard-related functions and configurations. In this chapter, you learn how to do the following:

- Install and configure a new keyboard
- Install accompanying keyboard software drivers, which are essential if the hardware device is to communicate properly with the operating system
- Change keyboard properties
- Change resource settings

First, though, you have to install a keyboard before it can be configured, which is the subject of the first section.

Starting the Keyboard Add New Hardware Wizard

Adding a new hardware device, such as a keyboard, is much easier under Windows 95 than under the old DOS/Windows combination because of the new Plug-and-Play standard and the addition of the extremely useful Add

New Hardware Wizard control panel. The wizard is essentially a step-by-step installation guide for any specified hardware device.

You can install a new keyboard by using the Add New Hardware Wizard. The Add New Hardware Wizard can be accessed either through the Control Panel option or by choosing Keyboard, Setting Up from the Help Topics option.

Note

If you turn off your computer and change keyboards, when the computer is switched on again, Windows 95 may be able to automatically detect it if it recognizes the component.

For this exercise you'll go through control panels:

1. Click the Start menu.
2. Choose Settings, Control Panel.
3. Open the Add New Hardware control panel. The Add New Hardware Wizard initial screen appears (see fig. 23.1).

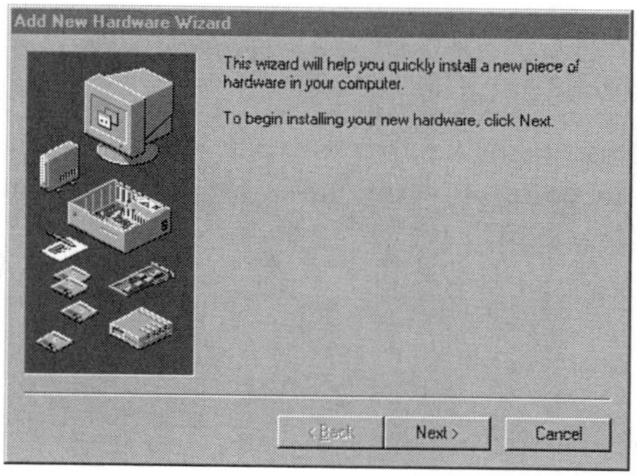

Fig. 23.1
The initial Add New Hardware Wizard screen tells you how it can help you install new hardware.

4. Click the Next button. The new Add New Hardware Wizard screen that appears is the first one that allows you to make a choice as to how you want to proceed (see fig. 23.2).
5. If you want Windows 95 to automatically find any new devices that you have added recently, just click the Automatically Detect Installed Hardware option. Or, if you want to select the new hardware to install, click the Install Specific Hardware option.

   For this example, select the Install Specific Hardware option.

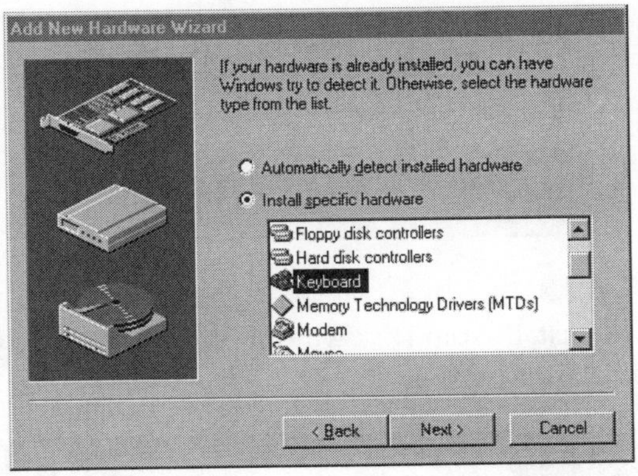

Fig. 23.2
You can use the Add New Hardware Wizard to install a new keyboard.

6. Select the type of hardware device you want to add from the wizard list—for example, select Keyboard.

7. Click the Next button. The hardware models list appears for the type of device you selected—for example, keyboards (see fig. 23.3).

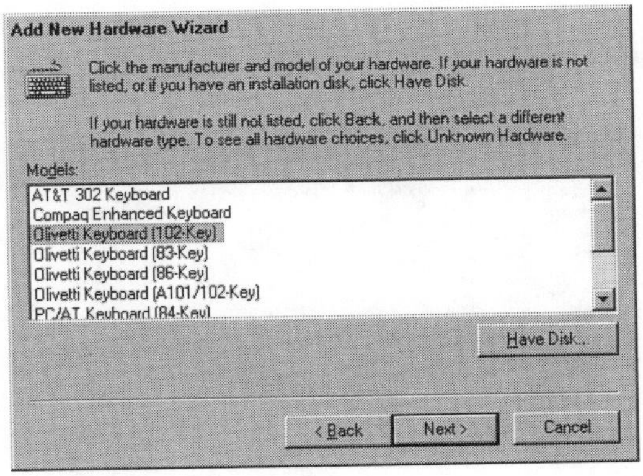

Fig. 23.3
Select the keyboard model you want to add from the wizard's model list.

8. Select the keyboard manufacturer's model type.

9. Click the Next button, or if you have an installation disk for your new keyboard or your keyboard is not listed, follow steps 10 through 12. If you don't need to install from a floppy disk, jump to step 13.

10. From the Add New Hardware Wizard panel, click Have Disk. The Install From Disk dialog box appears (see fig. 23.4).

11. Specify the disk letter and actual folder where the manufacturer's installation files should be copied from.

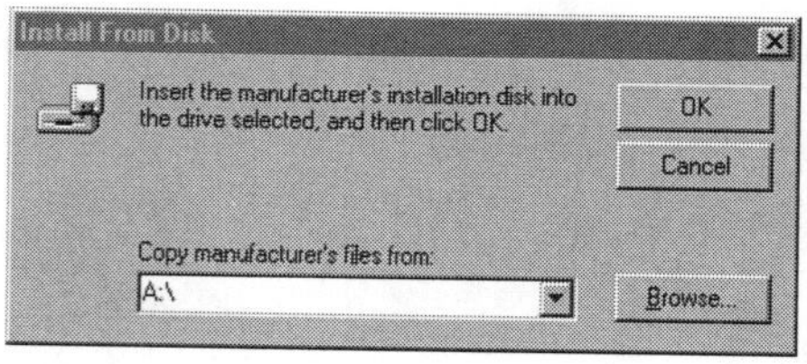

Fig. 23.4
To install a new device driver, you need to specify the file in the Install From Disk window.

12. Click OK. The Install From Disk window disappears, and you are back to the Add New Hardware Wizard.

> **Caution**
>
> Not all hardware vendors support Windows 95. As a result, sometimes software drivers do not work properly with Windows 95. Check this before buying new hardware. If there is a problem with compatibility, contact the component's manufacturer for advice.

13. Click the Next button. The wizard window changes to display the settings it wants you to use for the keyboard (see fig. 23.5).

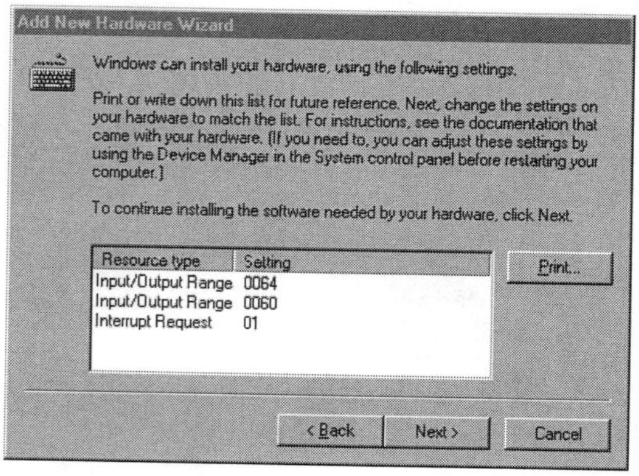

Fig. 23.5
The Add New Hardware Wizard gives you the settings to use for your keyboard.

> **Tip**
>
> This list of resource settings is very important. As a result, you should write down these settings or print them out. These are the settings that the new keyboard should use.

14. Click the Next button. You are then asked to restart your PC.

15. Once you have restarted your PC, go into the System Properties control panel and click the Device Manager page. The Keyboard type listing now shows both your old keyboard type and your new keyboard that you just installed.

    Not only that, but if you click either of those keyboard types listed and then click the Resources page, that page lists the other keyboard as conflicting with the new keyboard's resource settings—not surprising, as you can only have one keyboard working at once. What you then have to do is make the new keyboard's settings current and remove the old keyboard listed, by following steps 16 through 21.

16. Double-click the new keyboard type in Device Manager.

17. Select the General tab if it is not already selected.

18. Select the Original Configuration (Current) box if it is not already checked.

19. Close the General page by clicking OK.

20. You should now remove the old keyboard type. Click the old keyboard model type in Device Manager, and click Remove.

21. A warning box comes up asking if you are sure you want to remove the keyboard (see fig. 23.6). Click OK.

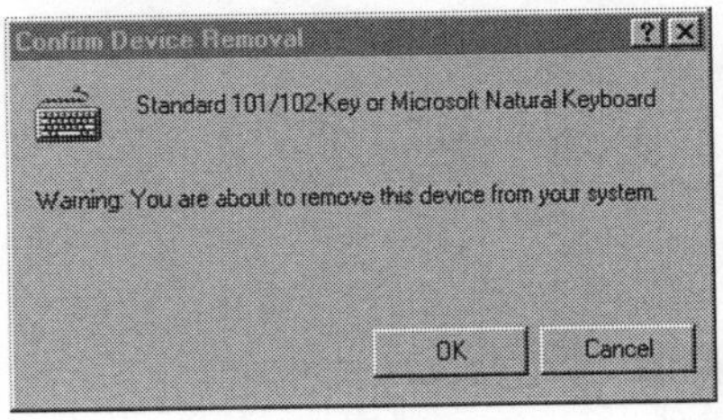

Fig. 23.6
A warning box appears asking you to confirm the keyboard removal.

The box disappears, as does the old keyboard's listing in Device Manager. To make sure, go to the Resources page and you see no conflicts listed for your new keyboard. Conflicts occur when two components, in this case keyboards, are assigned the same system resources.

Windows 95 includes a feature that allows you to automatically detect hardware devices that have been newly attached to the computer on which it is running. To have Windows 95 automatically detect new hardware devices, open the Add New Hardware Wizard and do the following:

1. Select the Automatically Detect Installed Hardware button on the Add New Hardware Wizard in the previous section (refer to fig. 23.2).
2. Click the Next button. A screen appears telling you that Windows 95 will now look for new hardware (see fig. 23.7).

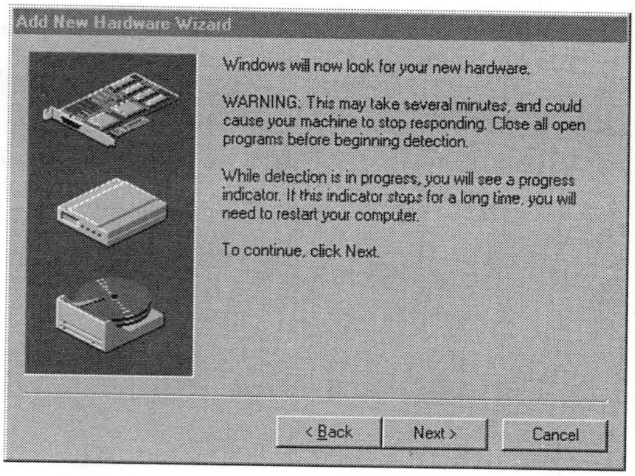

Fig. 23.7
A warning appears telling you the search for new hardware may take some time.

3. Click the Next button. A progress indicator then appears at the bottom of the screen (see fig. 23.8).

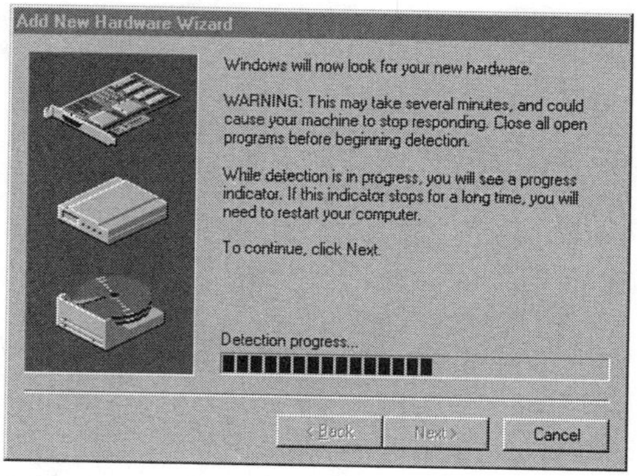

Fig. 23.8
A progress indicator tells you how the search for new hardware is going.

4. When the search is complete, click the Next button.

The screen then notifies you of any new devices it has found. If none are found, it asks if you want to install a new device manually. If you want to manually install a new device, it brings you back to the Add New Hardware Wizard screen in the previous section. You can manually install the keyboard as described.

Adding or Changing Keyboard Drivers

For a hardware device, such as a keyboard, to work with the operating system controlling the computer, you need a sort of intermediary between the two. This is essentially what software drivers do. Every piece of hardware attached to a computer requires some sort of software driver to tell the operating system what the hardware wants to do. Without the correctly installed driver, a hardware device and the operating system will basically be speaking in different languages to each other, not communicating properly, and essentially bringing the system to a standstill.

Adding or changing device drivers has been made substantially easier in Windows 95 than in the previous DOS/Windows combination. With Windows 95, you can add or change device drivers easily using Device Manager, because Device Manager keeps track of assigned system resources.

To change the driver for a standard 101/102-key keyboard, follow these steps:

1. Click the Start menu.
2. Choose Settings, Control Panel.
3. Double-click the System control panel. The System Properties sheet appears.
4. Click the Device Manager page (see fig. 23.9).

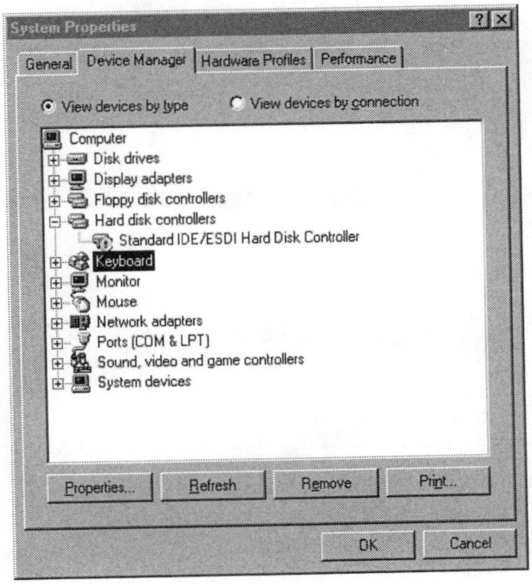

Fig. 23.9
You can change a keyboard driver by using the Device Manager page.

5. Along the left edge are plus signs. Click the plus sign that corresponds to the device you want to change—in this case, Keyboard.

6. Double-click the specific hardware device you are interested in.

7. In the resulting System Properties sheet that appears for the specified keyboard, click the Driver page (see fig. 23.10).

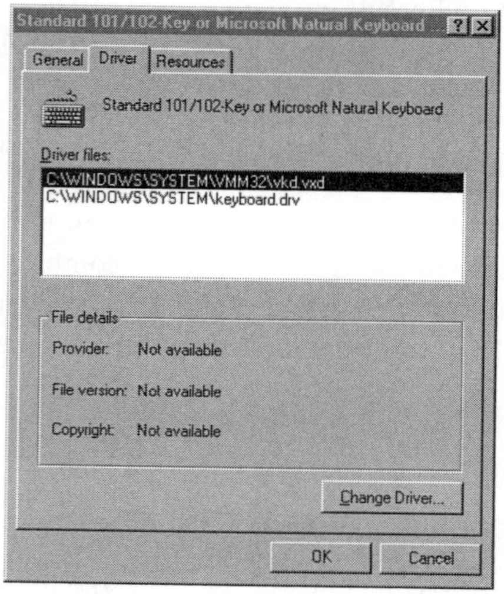

Fig. 23.10
The Driver page for the Standard 101/102-Key or Microsoft Natural Keyboard allows you to change drivers.

8. Click the Change Driver button. The Select Device window appears (see fig. 23.11).

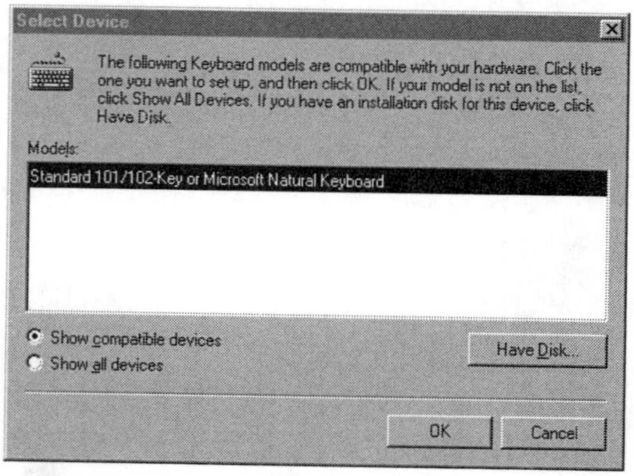

Fig. 23.11
Select the device you want to set up from the Select Device sheet.

Tip

A Models list details the keyboard models compatible with your hardware. Make sure the Show Compatible Devices button is selected. If the keyboard you want to set up is not on the list, you should select the Show All Devices button. The list changes to show all such keyboards.

9. Click the device you want to set up, and then click OK. The Select Device window disappears, leaving the Driver page showing the driver files and their correct folder path.
10. Exit the Control Panel by clicking the OK button.

You may have a separate installation disk for the device—that is, a floppy disk—which contains the software driver. If this is the case, you need to take an extra step. Follow steps 1 through 8 in the previous list and then do the following:

1. From the Select Device sheet, click Have Disk. The Install From Disk dialog box appears (see fig. 23.12).

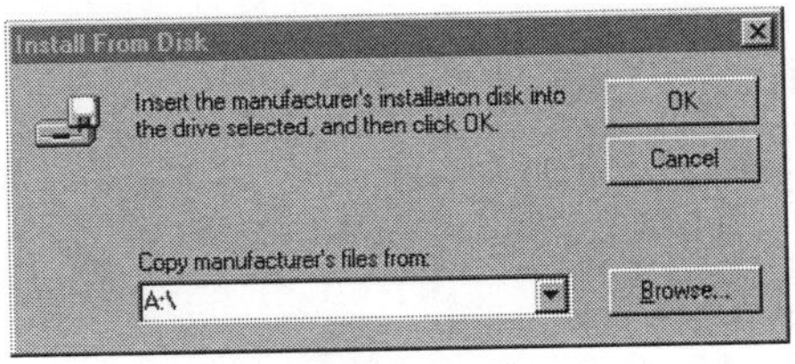

Fig. 23.12
Install manufacturer's software drivers via the Install From Disk dialog box.

2. Specify the directory and disk where the manufacturer's files should be copied from.
3. Click OK.
4. You are now back at the Select Device sheet. Click OK to exit to the Driver page.
5. Click OK on the Driver page to exit.

Changing Your Keyboard Properties

Your keyboard has a variety of properties that dictate how it allows you to interact with the computer. In many cases, they are configurable according to your individual preferences. These include the language used by the keyboard, its layout, and the speed at which keys repeat when pressed. Also, keyboard resource settings can also be viewed and changed, such as I/O and interrupt request settings (IRQs).

You can change the properties associated with a keyboard using the Keyboard Properties control panel. Here's how to open the control panel:

1. Click the Start menu.
2. Choose Settings, Control Panel.
3. Double-click the Keyboard control panel. The Keyboard Properties sheet appears, containing three pages: Speed, Language, and General. Your keyboard layout can be changed using the Language page, detailed in the next section.

Changing a Keyboard Layout

You can change the layout of your keyboard via the Keyboard Properties control panel. After following steps 1 through 3 in the "Changing Your Keyboard Properties" section, do the following:

1. Select the Language page (see fig. 23.13). The top section of the Language page displays the Installed Keyboard Languages and Layout list.
2. Select the language and keyboard layout that you want to change, from the Language and Layout lists.

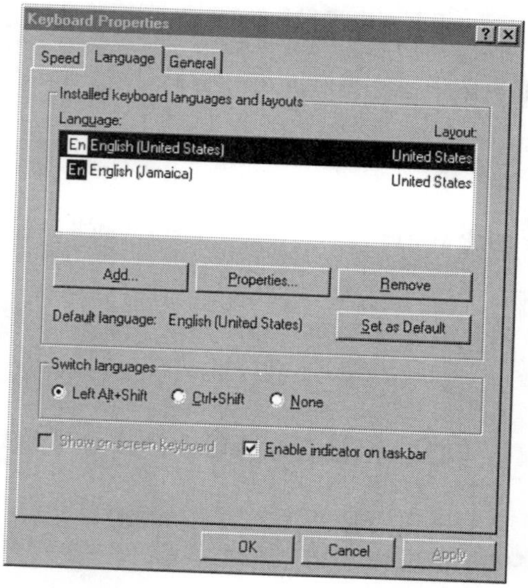

Fig. 23.13
The Language page in Keyboard Properties is where you can change your keyboard layout.

3. Click the Properties button. The Language Properties dialog box appears (see fig. 23.14).

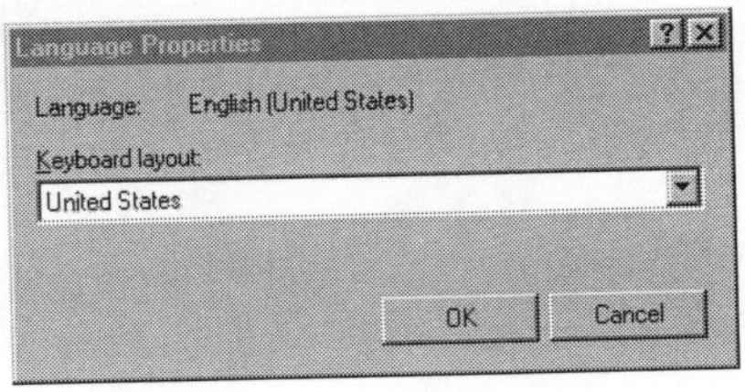

Fig. 23.14
Select the language for your keyboard using Language Properties.

4. Select the new keyboard layout from the Keyboard Layout drop-down list box.
5. Click OK.

Deleting a Language or Layout

You can also delete a language or layout from the Keyboard Properties control panel. Having opened the Language page, do the following:

1. Select the language and layout you want to delete from the Installed Keyboard Languages and Layouts list.
2. Click the Remove button.
3. Click OK.

Adding Another Language or Layout

You can select a different keyboard layout or language using the Keyboard Properties control panel. Having displayed the Language page, do the following:

1. Click the Add button. The Add Language dialog box appears (see fig. 23.15).

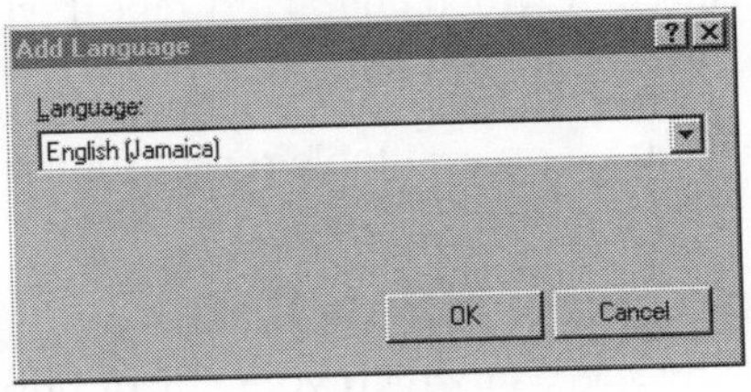

Fig. 23.15
Add another language in Keyboard Properties.

2. Select the language you want from the Language drop-down list box.

3. Click OK. The Add Language dialog box disappears, and the language you just selected now appears on the Installed Keyboard Languages and Layouts area on the Language page.

4. Select the language you want to use as your primary language from the list.

5. Click the Set as Default button.

6. Click OK.

Your new language is now defined as the default language.

Tip

At the bottom of the Language page on the Keyboard Properties sheet is an option box called Enable Indicator On Taskbar. If this is checked, an indicator, called En, appears on the Windows 95 taskbar at the bottom of the main screen. To quickly change between languages, click this indicator and a list of available languages appears. You can instantly switch between available languages by clicking the language you want from that En list.

Changing How the Keys Repeat

You can change the way your keyboard keys repeat using the Keyboard Properties control panel. Follow steps 1 through 3 in the "Changing Your Keyboard Properties" section, then do the following:

1. Click the Speed page (see fig. 23.16).

2. To change the time that elapses before a pressed-down key begins to repeat, drag the Repeat Delay slider to the right for a shorter time, or the left for longer.

3. To change the speed at which characters repeat when you hold down a specific key, adjust the Repeat Rate slider.

4. When you have settled on a suitable repeat setting, click OK.

Changing Your Cursor Blink Rate

You can also change the speed at which your cursor blinks. After accessing the Keyboard Properties control panel, do the following:

1. Click the Speed page (see fig. 23.16).

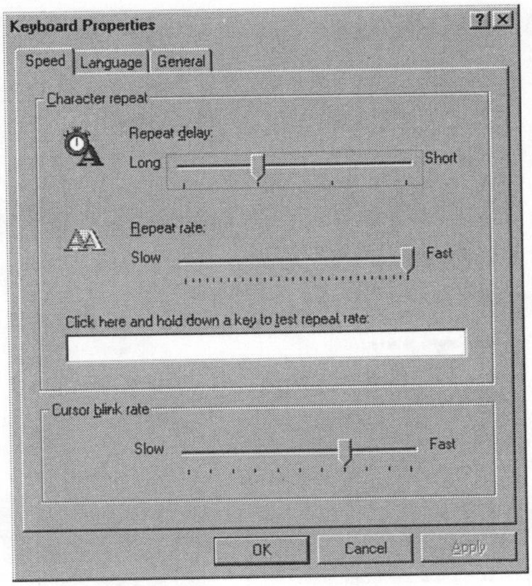

Fig. 23.16
You can change the repeat rate and delay using Keyboard Properties.

2. Adjust the cursor blinking speed by dragging the Cursor Blink Rate slider to the right to make it faster, or to the left to slow it down.

3. When you have it blinking at the speed you want, click OK.

Changing or Viewing Keyboard Resource Settings

You can change resource settings for your keyboard via the Device Manager accessed through the System Properties sheet.

You may need to change the settings if another component you're adding needs to use those same resources, or if you are adding another similar device, such as a keyboard, that wants the same settings.

To make changes to the keyboard resource settings, do the following:

1. Click the Start menu.
2. Choose Settings, Control Panel.
3. Double-click the System control panel. The System Properties sheet appears.
4. Click the Device Manager page (see fig. 23.17).
5. Click the plus sign next to the Keyboard device type.

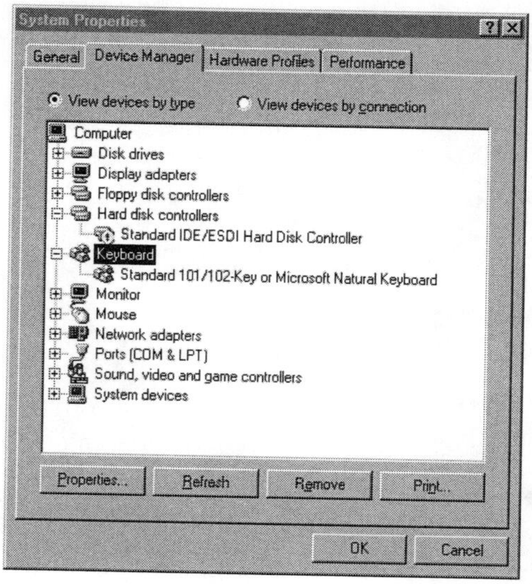

Fig. 23.17
Change keyboard resource settings using the Device Manager page.

6. Double-click the keyboard you are interested in changing the resource settings for.
7. Select the Resources page (see fig. 23.18).
8. Make the changes to the keyboard resource by double-clicking the resource you want to change.

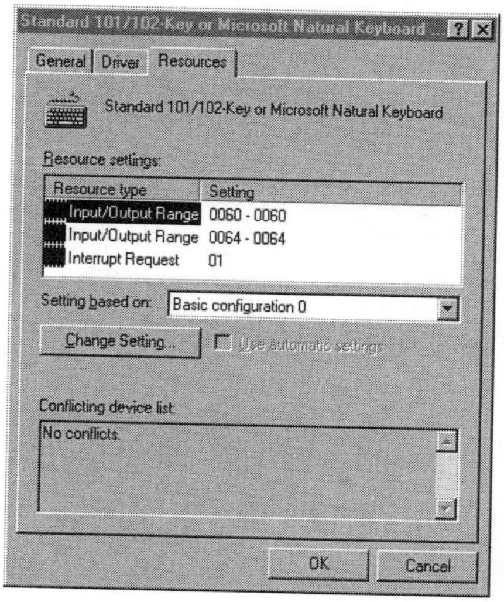

Fig. 23.18
You can identify the specific resources using the Resources page.

Caution

For a component to work properly, it must have the correct resource settings assigned to it. Do not change resource settings unless you know exactly what you are changing. A new component may need certain resources assigned to it, in which case either the product will specify them, or Windows 95 will tell you what to use when you run the Add New Hardware Wizard.

9. Click OK.

Tip

If the Use Automatic Settings option in the Resources tab is checked, you will not be able to change the resource settings, and the Change Setting button will be grayed out.

Troubleshooting Keyboards

Unfortunately, hardware conflicts and problems are virtually inevitable with the complexities of a modern multimedia personal computer, because of the variety of technologies that are required to work together to provide multimedia capabilities—sound, graphics, text, and even video.

When things do go wrong, though, such as with the keyboard, Windows 95 provides a useful feature called the Hardware Conflict Troubleshooter to help you along the path to solving the problem.

The Hardware Conflict Troubleshooter can be accessed through the Keyboard, Troubleshooting Hardware Conflicts option in the Help Topics Index, accessed via the Start menu.

Once selected, the initial Hardware Conflict Troubleshooter screen offers you a choice of starting the troubleshooter or displaying an overview of the process (see fig. 23.19).

The troubleshooter takes you on a step-by-step investigation of the hardware problems you are experiencing and covers such things as whether the device was installed twice, and what to do if it was; and identifies which resource settings could be causing the conflict (if that is the problem) and how to rectify the situation.

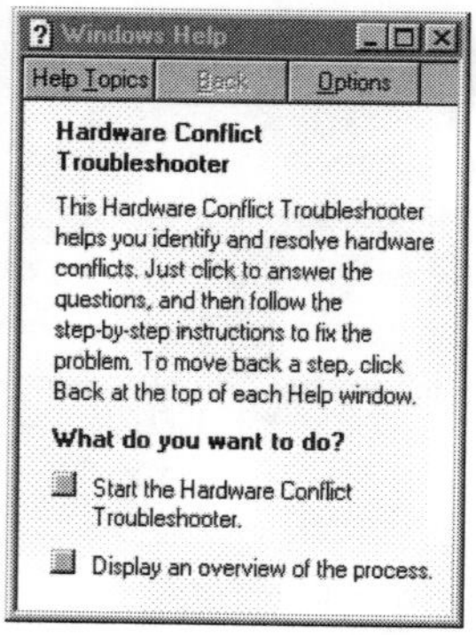

Fig. 23.19
The Hardware Conflict Troubleshooter allows you to investigate the problem.

Hardware problems are very often caused by conflicts between hardware resources, such as I/O settings and interrupt requests. When two hardware devices try to use the same resource setting, you have a hardware conflict. The best place to start solving conflicts is to view the keyboard resources in Device Manager, accessed through the System Properties control panel.❖

Chapter 24

Configuring CD-ROM Drives

by Tod Pike

Most computer systems, whether used at home or at the office, have CD-ROM drives installed in them. Since a large amount of software is distributed in CD-ROM format, and the capability to play audio compact discs is desirable, a CD-ROM drive is a very popular peripheral.

The Windows 95 operating system makes the task of adding and using a CD-ROM drive very easy. This chapter outlines the steps necessary to add a CD-ROM drive to a computer system running Windows 95. In this chapter, you learn how to

- Start the Add New Hardware Wizard for CD-ROM drives
- Set up a CD-ROM drive for network use

Starting Add New Hardware Wizard for CD-ROM Drives

When you install Windows 95 on your computer system for the first time, the Windows 95 installation program automatically runs the Add New Hardware Wizard to detect and install all of the hardware that's in your computer system. After you have installed Windows 95, however, the Add New Hardware Wizard is used if you have added a new device to your computer system, such as a new disk drive, tape drive, CD-ROM, or sound card.

If your computer had a CD-ROM drive installed in it when you installed Windows 95, your system should already support the CD-ROM drive. You can check by opening the Control Panel (from the Start button).

From the Control Panel, you can open the System Properties sheet, which gives you information about the devices connected to your computer system. Figure 24.1 illustrates this sheet.

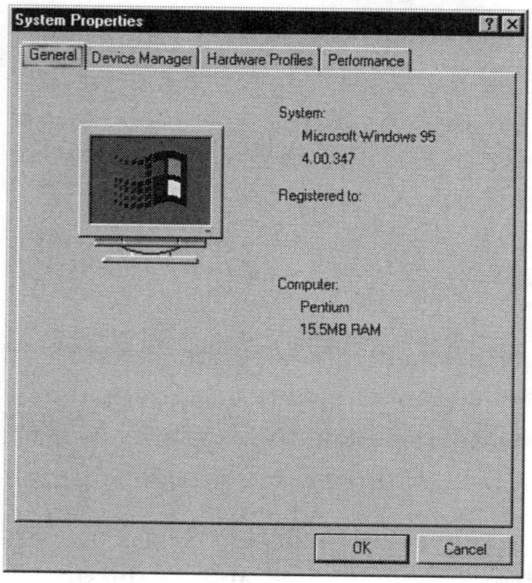

Fig. 24.1
The System Properties sheet describes the devices connected to your system.

From the System Properties sheet, select the Device Manager tab to display the devices on your system. In figure 24.2, the first item in the list is the CD-ROM device.

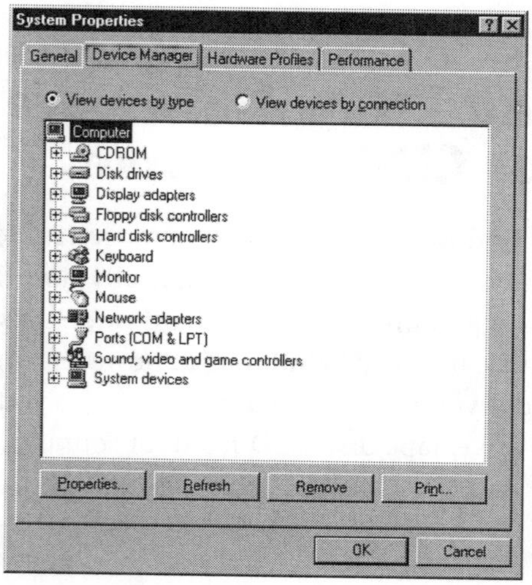

Fig. 24.2
The Device Manager displays a list of the devices on your system.

Using the System control panel, you can see that the system as it is currently configured already shows a CD-ROM device as being available. Clicking the CDROM item in the list shows the individual CD-ROM drives that are configured and available for use. Figure 24.3 shows the CD-ROM device exposed in the list.

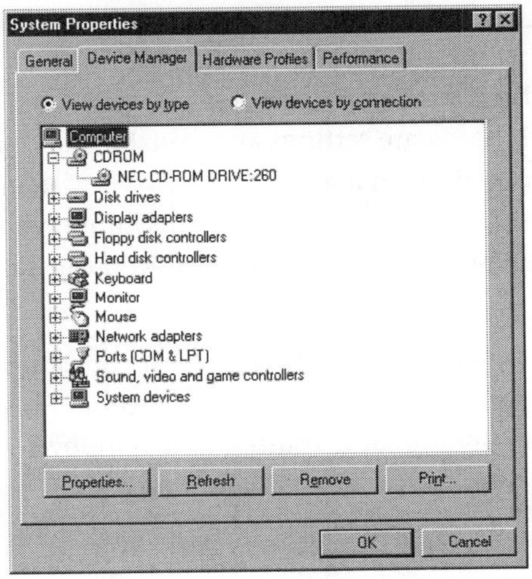

Fig. 24.3
The Device Manager item lists a CD-ROM as being available for use.

If your Device Manager item shows a CD-ROM drive available, but you are unable to use the drive (you cannot access any data on CD-ROM disks, and cannot play audio compact discs), there are several things you can try.

Troubleshooting

I installed the CD-ROM and Windows support, but the CD-ROM still doesn't work.

The most common reason for the CD-ROM not working correctly is a conflict with another device on your system. Open the Control Panel (from the Start menu) and open the System control panel. Select the Device Manager page to display the list of the devices on your system.

Double-click the CDROM entry in the list, and then select your CD-ROM device. Click the Properties button to display the settings for your CD-ROM. The Device Status area tells you if there is a problem with your CD-ROM device. Selecting the Resources page shows you the current settings; this page also tells you if one of the settings for your CD-ROM conflicts with another device in your system.

(continues)

(continued)

If there is a conflict with another device in your system, you have to change one of the hardware settings (such as the Interrupt Request, Input/Output range, or Direct memory access) to another value. You should consult the manual for your CD-ROM drive to determine which values for these settings are legal for your drive.

Once you know which settings you can set your CD-ROM drive to, you have to determine which hardware settings are available on your system. One good way to find out the settings that are in use on your system is to click the Print button on the main Device Manager page. This allows you to print out a summary of all the resources on your system—you can easily find an unused value.

If you have added a new CD-ROM drive to your computer since you installed the Windows 95 operating system, you can run the Add New Hardware Wizard (which is essentially the same routine that Windows 95 runs during installation to detect your hardware configuration).

Before you run the Add New Hardware Wizard, you must install the CD-ROM controller card and any additional hardware that came with your CD-ROM drive. You should follow the manufacturer's instructions to install the drive, including setting any switches or jumpers on the card for the interrupt vector and Input/Output vectors.

Note

If there are default positions for any settings on the CD-ROM device, you should leave the settings at their default. In general, Windows 95 first looks for devices at the default settings for that device. The only time you need to change the settings from their default is if there is a conflict with some other device in your system.

After the CD-ROM hardware has been installed in your computer, you are ready to turn your computer back on and begin the process of telling Windows 95 about the new device.

The Add New Hardware Wizard is run from the Control Panel (choose Start, Settings, Control Panel, Add New Hardware).

When you start the Add New Hardware Wizard, the first screen of the wizard comes up, telling you what the wizard will do. This screen is shown in figure 24.4.

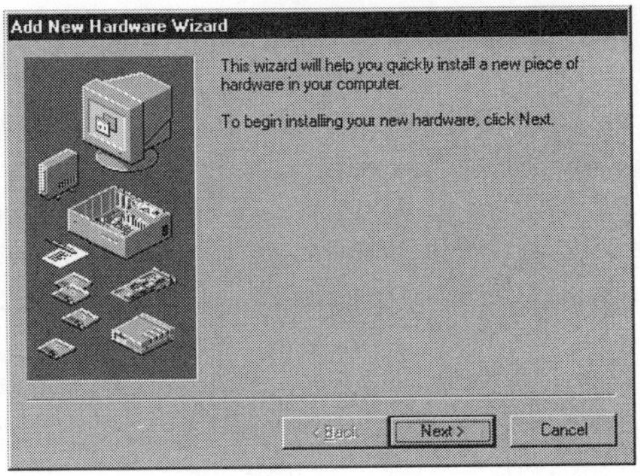

Fig 24.4
The first page of the Add New Hardware Wizard gives general information about the wizard.

Click the Next button to continue to the next page of the Add New Hardware Wizard or click Cancel to stop.

The second page of the wizard (see fig. 24.5) allows you to specify whether the wizard will automatically detect which CD-ROM hardware you have installed.

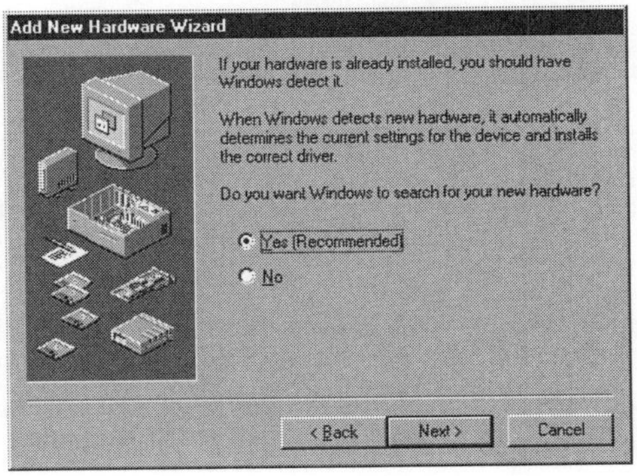

Fig. 24.5
The wizard allows you to specify automatic or manual hardware detection.

Letting Windows 95 Automatically Detect Your CD-ROM

If you are not sure which CD-ROM drive you have installed in your system, or if you just want to let Windows 95 search through your system to detect what hardware you have installed, select Yes (Recommended) on the second page of the Add New Hardware Wizard. This is the first option shown in figure 24.5.

This option is essentially the same process that Windows 95 goes through during the initial installation, and it generally does a good job of locating your installed hardware components. Click Next to proceed to the next page of the wizard.

> **Note**
>
> If you let the wizard automatically detect your installed hardware, it is possible that it may find more than one new hardware component on your system. If all you installed is a CD-ROM drive, you may want to click the Cancel button and restart the wizard, using the option to manually specify the hardware to install.

The next page of the Add New Hardware Wizard is an informational page (see fig. 24.6) telling you what the wizard will do to your system, and how long it will take. It also advises you to close all of your open applications, because the hardware detection process may cause your system to hang. Click Next to proceed to the hardware detection page.

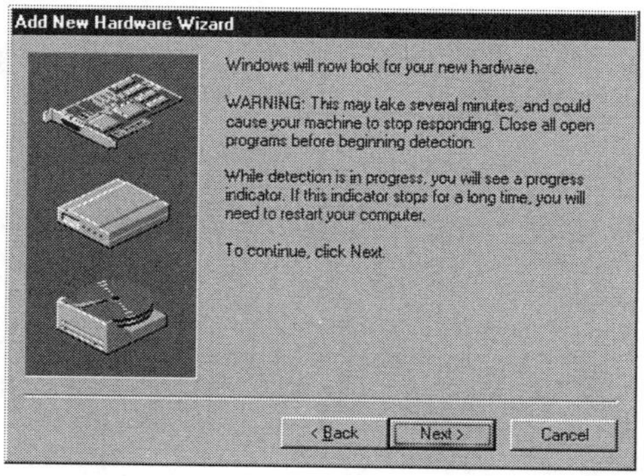

Fig. 24.6
The advisory page in the Add New Hardware Wizard also informs you of the progress indicator.

The next page is the actual hardware detection page. As you can see in figure 24.7, this page has a status bar along the bottom that indicates how far the hardware detection phase has run.

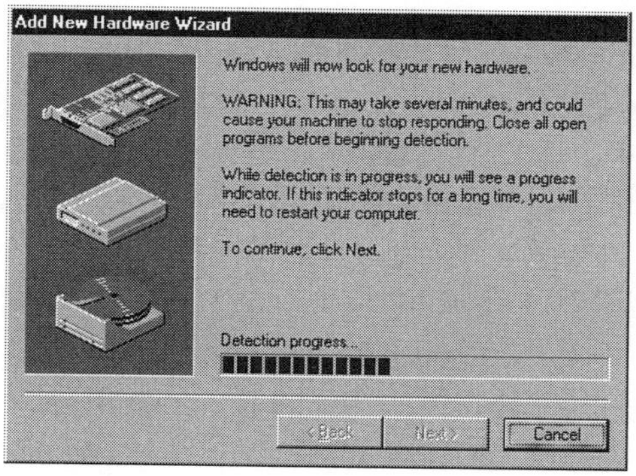

Fig. 24.7
Automatic hardware detection is in progress.

After the Add New Hardware Wizard has completed scanning your system for new hardware, the wizard displays the screen shown in figure 24.8. This screen tells you that the wizard has completed the scan for new hardware and is ready to install support for the new hardware on your system. If you want to see the list of the hardware that was detected, you can click the Details button.

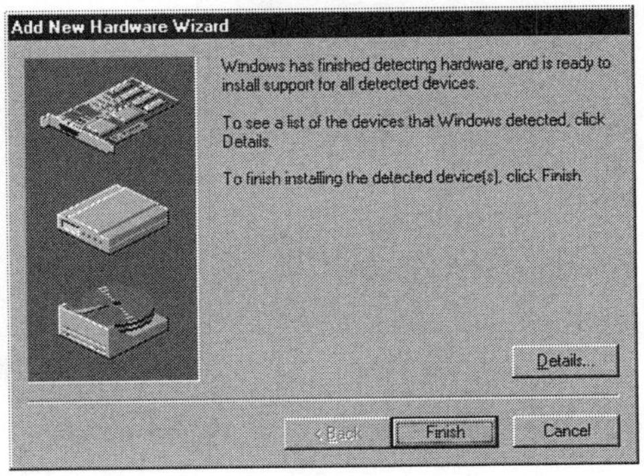

Fig. 24.8
The wizard has finished detecting your new hardware.

When you click the Finish button to install the hardware support, the wizard installs the necessary system drivers and any extra software to support the new CD-ROM drive. Then, the wizard prompts you to restart your system in order for Windows 95 to start supporting your new hardware. If you do not want Windows 95 to restart at this time, just click Cancel.

Note

If the Add New Hardware Wizard couldn't identify your new CD-ROM drive, it tells you that there is no new hardware to install and gives you the option to manually specify the hardware you are installing. This option is discussed in the next section.

Manually Specifying CD-ROM Drives

If you know in advance the type of CD-ROM drive you have installed, or if the Add New Hardware Wizard couldn't identify the type of drive you installed, you can manually tell the wizard the type of drive you have.

After you start the Add New Hardware Wizard, click the Next button to move to the second page. On this page, which asks you whether you want Windows 95 to search for your new hardware, select the No option and click Next. This allows you to manually select the hardware to install.

When you elect to manually install your hardware with the Add New Hardware Wizard, the wizard displays a list of the types of hardware that you can install. This list is shown in figure 24.9.

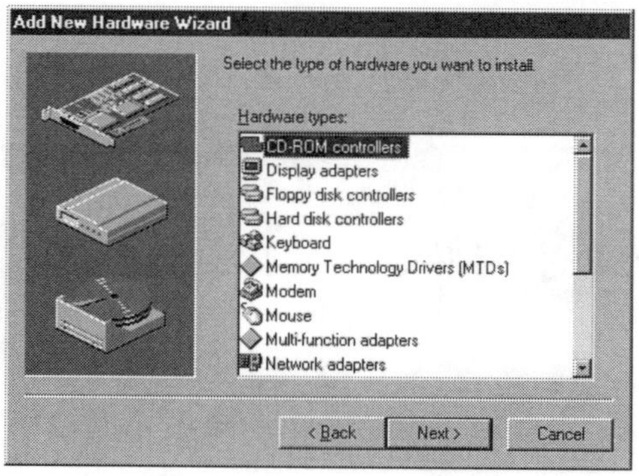

Fig. 24.9
The list of hardware types available to install appear in this wizard box.

From the Hardware Types list, you should select the item `CD-ROM controllers`, since this is the type of hardware you are installing. Click the Next button to continue. The wizard now displays a list of the manufacturers (on the left side of the window) and the types of CD-ROM drives (on the right side of the window) that Windows 95 knows about.

> **Note**
>
> Depending on the version of Windows 95 you are running, this list of manufacturers and drives may be different. As Windows 95 matures, more types of hardware will be recognized by the wizard.

If the manufacturer of your CD-ROM drive is listed on the left side of the window, select it in the Manufacturers list box. The wizard displays all of the CD-ROM drives made by that manufacturer (that the system knows about) in Models list (see fig. 24.10).

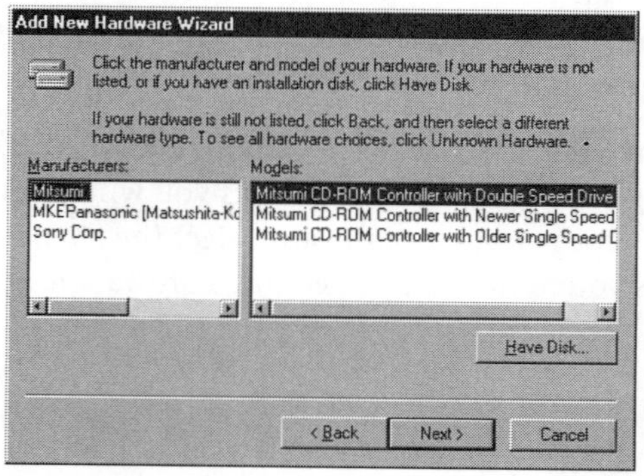

Fig. 24.10
Select a manufacturer and drive type by clicking its entry in the list.

Once you have selected the manufacturer and drive type, click Next to continue with the installation.

> **Note**
>
> If the manufacturer of your CD-ROM drive (or the particular CD-ROM drive you have) is not listed by the wizard, you should check to see if Windows 95 drivers are available for your CD-ROM drive. If so, you can click the Have Disk button instead of specifying the manufacturer and drive type. Windows 95 prompts you for the location of the drivers (generally you load the drivers from your floppy drive) and use those drivers directly to support your CD-ROM drive.
>
> If no Windows 95 drivers are available for your CD-ROM drive, you can use the regular Windows drivers for your drive. See the instructions from your CD-ROM drive and the Windows 95 documentation for help with installing and using Windows/DOS drivers with Windows 95.

On the next page of the wizard (see fig. 24.11), the default settings for the CD-ROM drive are displayed. If these settings do not match the hardware settings on your CD-ROM drive, you either have to change the hardware settings on the drive, or change the Windows 95 configuration using the Device Manager (started from the System control panel). See Chapter 13, "Configuring Memory, Disks, and Devices," for more information about this process.

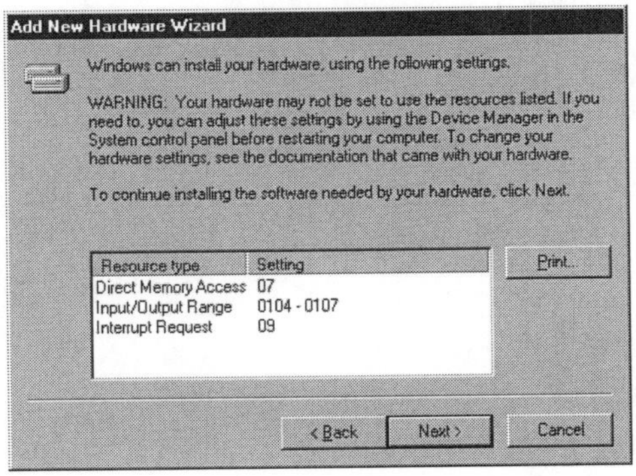

Fig. 24.11
The current hardware settings are displayed for your approval.

Once you have confirmed the current hardware settings, Windows 95 installs the necessary drivers for your CD-ROM drive and prompts you to restart your system (if necessary). After your system has been reset, you are now able to use your CD-ROM drive.

Setting Up Your CD-ROM Drive for Network Use

After you have installed Windows 95 support for your CD-ROM drive, you can easily give people on your network access to the drive. In order to share your CD-ROM drive on the network, you need to make sure that your network hardware is installed and set up and file sharing has been enabled on your system.

To share your CD-ROM on your network, double-click the My Computer icon on your desktop. This brings up the display of all the devices on your local computer disk. Right-click the icon for your CD-ROM drive (generally labeled as D: in the My Computer display) and select Sharing from the options list. This brings up the (currently blank) Sharing page for the CD-ROM drive, as shown in figure 24.12.

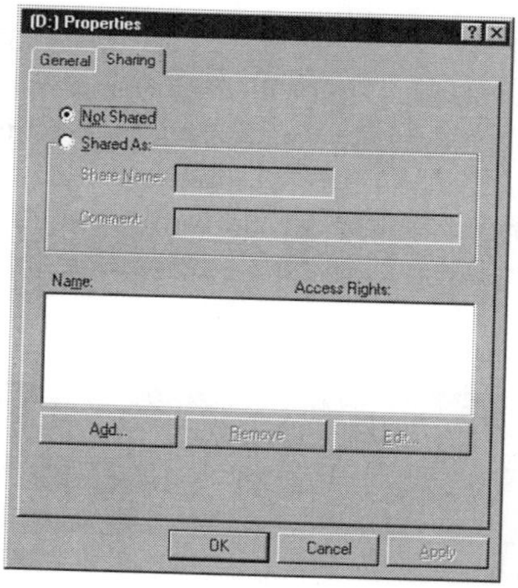

Fig. 24.12
The CD-ROM Properties sheet for the CD-ROM drive appears.

On the Sharing sheet, select the Shared As option. This allows you to fill in the rest of the form. Type a name to share your CD-ROM drive as into the Shared Name box; this is the name that appears when people on your network look at the network resources available on your computer. In the example shown in figure 24.13, the Shared Name is `CD-ROM`. In addition, you should type a descriptive name into the Comment box; this should be something that describes the contents of the CD-ROM you have mounted. In the example, the Comment is `Documentation CD-ROM`.

Next, select a list of people who will have access to your shared CD-ROM. The way you set up the access list depends on how you have your access control set up, but you will either set up a password for the CD-ROM (if you have share access control) or a list of users defined on your network server (if you have user access control). You can find out the type of access control you have set up by looking at the properties sheet for your Network Neighborhood, under the Access control page.

In the example shown in figure 24.13, the system is using User Access control, and I have selected the Everyone group (which means all users registered in the NT or Novell server) and allowed those users to only read the contents of our CD-ROM.

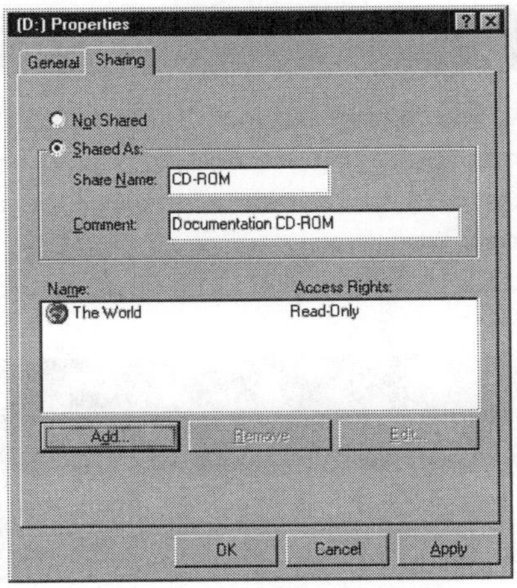

Fig. 24.13
A file sharing window for the CD-ROM is completed.

Once you have filled in the Sharing page, click OK to begin sharing the CD-ROM on your network. The CD-ROM drive appears on the network almost immediately. Other Windows 95 users can access the CD-ROM drive through their Network Neighborhood icon.

New Windows 95 CD-ROM Drive Features

One of the new features of Windows 95 is the capability of the system to automatically recognize and play audio compact disks when they are inserted in the CD-ROM drive. This feature can be controlled from the Properties page for your CD-ROM drive. Double-click the My Computer icon on your desktop and then right-click your CD-ROM drive icon. Select Properties from the list and then click the Settings page from the Properties sheet.

On the Settings page, you see an option called Auto Insert Notification. If this option is checked, the system automatically plays audio compact disks when they are inserted. Deselect this option if you don't want this to happen.

By default, Windows 95 assigns drive letter D to your CD-ROM drive. At times, you may want to change this drive letter assignment, especially if you have more than one CD-ROM drive in your system. You can change this from the Properties sheet for your drive. Bring up the Properties sheet and select the Settings page. You see the setting for Current Drive Letter Assigned; changing this changes the drive letter assigned to your CD-ROM drive.

Caution

If you change the drive letter assigned to your CD-ROM drive, it may force other drives you have mounted (such as network disks) to change to other drive letters, also. This may affect some of your shortcuts or software if they assume that your data was stored on a particular drive letter.

Troubleshooting

My CD-ROM drive seems slow. How can I speed it up?

Windows 95 has several settings for CD-ROM drives, some of which can affect how fast data is transferred from the CD-ROM drive to the system. You can check these settings by opening the System control panel and selecting the Performance tab. Select the File System button and then select the CD-ROM page from the File System Properties sheet.

The two settings on this page affect how much data Windows 95 keeps in memory when reading from your CD-ROM drive. You should keep the Supplemental Cache Size as large as possible (keeping the slider bar as far to the right as possible) unless you are running short of memory.

You should also set the Optimize Access Pattern For option to the type of CD-ROM drive you have (double-speed, for example). When you are finished changing these settings, click OK.

Chapter 25

Configuring Floppy Disk Drives

by Dave Gibbons

One of the most anticipated side effects of Windows 95's introduction was a wave of hardware upgrades. Many people are taking this opportunity to add extra memory, bigger hard drives, and peripherals like sound cards and CD-ROM drives. One of the most basic upgrades is adding a new floppy disk drive. Some upgrade to share disks with others, or convert older 5 1/4-inch archive disks to a more stable format. Others many need a new high-density 3.5-inch drive to install and use new software, much of which is only available in that format. Whatever your reason, installing a new floppy disk drive is an easy process, and Windows 95 doesn't gum up the process too much.

If all the drives in your computer were working before you installed Windows 95, you won't need to do anything to get Windows 95 to recognize them. If you're adding a new drive or having problems, this chapter is for you.

In this chapter, you learn

- What types of floppy disk drives (FDDs) are available
- How to install a new floppy disk drive into your PC
- How to get your PC to recognize the new drive
- How to make sure Windows 95 recognizes the drive
- How to troubleshoot steps if you have problems with the drive

Note

For more in-depth coverage of FDDs, read Que's *Upgrading and Repairing PCs*, 5th Edition.

Types of Floppy Disk Drives

The standard list of FDD types (see table 25.1) has just about doubled with the introduction of Plug and Play (PNP) technology. For most types, you now find a PNP version and a non-PNP (or *legacy*) version. With PNP, new devices announce themselves to the computer at powerup, so (in theory) they don't require any manual setup at all. Installing a PNP drive and controller requires the same steps as installing a legacy drive, minus the procedure in the "Getting the PC to Recognize the New FDD" section later in this chapter.

Table 25.1 Floppy Disk Drive Types

Disk Size	Capacity
5.25-inch	360K
5.25-inch	1.2M
3.5-inch	720K
3.5-inch	1.44M
3.5-inch	2.88M

5.25-inch drives are also sometimes distinguished by their height. Half-height drives (about 1 5/8-inch tall) are the most common, but you still occasionally find full-height drives (about 3 1/4-inch tall) and third-height (about an inch tall) drives—sometimes called *slim line drives*. Though physical size is not a good way to guess a drive's capacity, you won't find too many full-height 1.2M drives—most are 360K or the older 180K capacity.

Tip

Check out F. Robert Falbo's "TheRef," an electronic encyclopedia of floppy, removable, and hard disks. It can help you deduce the capacity or settings for a drive if you have no documentation for it. On CompuServe, search for **TREF43**.

Most PC-compatible floppy drives adhere to a common specification, so you won't have to worry about disks from one brand working with another brand. Exceptions to this rule include *floptical* drives, which can use optical disks of 20M or more, as well as regular-capacity floppy disks.

Setting Up the Hardware

To install a new FDD into your computer, follow these steps:

1. If the FDD is still in its box, check to make sure it has the installation screws (usually four to eight or more) and a cable, if necessary (if you've already got an FDD installed, you can use the existing cable). Also make sure you have the right kind of screwdrivers to open your computer's case and to fit the drive's installation screws. Because you'll be working near very sensitive electronic parts, wear an anti-static wristband (available at most computer and electronics stores).

2. Turn off and unplug the computer.

3. Find the location on the front panel where you'll be installing the drive. Note the direction of the opening (vertical or horizontal).

4. Open the computer's case. This usually involves removing or loosening three to six screws in the back and popping off part of the case. You may also have to remove some exterior cables to get the cover off. On some cases, one flat panel comes off. In most, however, the top and sides can be removed as one piece. Set the cover aside.

5. You should see the space in the front of the chassis where the drive will fit. Slide it into place. Lightly attach the installation screws, tightening them only when you're sure the drive's face will be flush with the front of the PC (if possible, use an existing drive as a guide). Some cases require the addition of plastic or metal rails to the sides of the drive before you can slide it in place.

> **Caution**
>
> Most new cases have what looks like a 3.5 inch-wide metal box beside the drive bays. This looks like a perfect place for a 3.5-inch floppy disk drive, but it's made for a *hard* drive. There is no corresponding opening in the front of the computer's case.

Tip

You'll be attaching two cables to the back of the drive. If it looks like you won't be able to get your fingers behind the drive when it's secured, leave the installation screws off until you've attached the cables.

6. The two cables you need to attach are a ribbon cable and a power cable. If you're adding a second FDD or replacing one, you see the ribbon cable running into the back of the original drive. A few inches from the drive end of the cable you should see another connector, which you use for the second drive (the B drive) in the system. The end of the ribbon cable always goes to the A drive. Slide the connector into place on the back of the FDD.

Note

Even though the cables are set up for your A and your B drive respectively, you have to make sure the CMOS is set up the same way.

Note

You may need an adapter to hook the ribbon cable connector to your FDD. For example, if you want to make a 3.5-inch FDD (with a pin connector), you need to get an edge-to-pin adapter because the A drive and the end of the ribbon cable are for a 5.25-inch drive (edge connector).

7. Find a power lead from the computer's power supply for your drive. You should see leads going to the motherboard and any drives you've already got installed, all from the same location. Find one that's not yet connected to a drive. If there aren't any leads available, get a Y connector from a computer supply store to split one of the existing leads. Connect the power lead to the back of the drive.

Note

You may need an adapter for the power supply lead. If the only available leads are the larger type (about 3/4-inch wide in a D shape) and you're installing a drive with a small, square power socket (like most 3.5-inch drives), you need an adapter. Some drives include this adapter with the mounting kit, but if you don't have one, you should be able to get one at a computer supply store.

You shouldn't put the cover back on your computer until you've tested the new drive. Reconnect the computer's power cable and any other cables you disconnected earlier, then turn it back on to complete the next steps in the process.

Getting the PC to Recognize the New FDD

When you turn your computer on after installing a new FDD, it may squawk, beep, and/or display error messages on the screen. This is perfectly normal (unless the drive is PNP-compliant); the PC doesn't know how to handle the new device until you tell it manually.

The PC's device configuration is stored in the Setup or CMOS section of the computer. The information in this section includes what kinds of drives you have, the time of day, the video controller type, and some more arcane settings. The CMOS has its own battery, which is how it retains these settings (and keeps the clock running) when the computer is turned off or unplugged. When you add a new *basic* device (a floppy drive, hard drive, or video card, as opposed to a nonessential device like a sound card or CD-ROM drive), the CMOS needs to find out about the device's settings before it will work.

If the computer halts during startup after you install the new drive, it may give you a message like

```
Press <Enter> to run setup or Press Ctrl+Alt+Insert now.
```

If it just tells you Incorrect CMOS setup and continues to boot up normally, you'll have to turn the computer off and on to get back to the start of the boot sequence. In the early stages of the boot process, you should see a message on your screen telling you what you have to do to start the CMOS setup program. The message might say `Press <Delete>` to run `Setup` or F2, F12, or almost any other key or key combination. You usually have to press this key sequence *before* you see the `Starting Windows 95` message.

Tip

Some systems don't display any message at all, so you may have to refer to the documentation or manufacturer.

When you've got the Setup program, read its instructions carefully. It may offer you a menu of basic and advanced options. Choosing the floppy drive is usually in the basic section. When you get to the correct screen, you should see a list of drives—usually two FDDs and two hard drives—and some other information about the date, time, and other devices. Instructions on this screen show how to go from section to section. For example, in some Setup programs, you use the arrow keys to move around and the Page Up/Page Down keys to change the settings, while others use Tab or the space bar for these functions. Move to the correct section (usually `Floppy A` or `Floppy B`) and change it until it correctly identifies your drive. It should run through a list of standard drive types (both types of 3.5-inch drives, both 5.25-inch drives, and `None`, which you can use to disable a drive).

After you've selected the correct drive, exit the CMOS Setup program (usually by pressing Esc, Enter, or F10) and make sure you save the settings. You'll probably see a menu with options to ignore the changes or save them, with `Ignore` as the first option. The computer should start up normally after you exit Setup.

How Windows 95 Affects FDD Installation

The only place Windows 95 really has an effect on FDD installation is in diagnosis. It can't change the drive's settings (at least not in legacy drives); it can only tell you if the drive works properly.

To make sure the drive is properly installed and identified in the CMOS setup, follow these steps:

1. Open the Control Panel.
2. Select the System icon.
3. Select the Device Manager page.
4. Click the plus sign next to the Disk Drives icon (see fig. 25.1). The available drives are displayed under it.

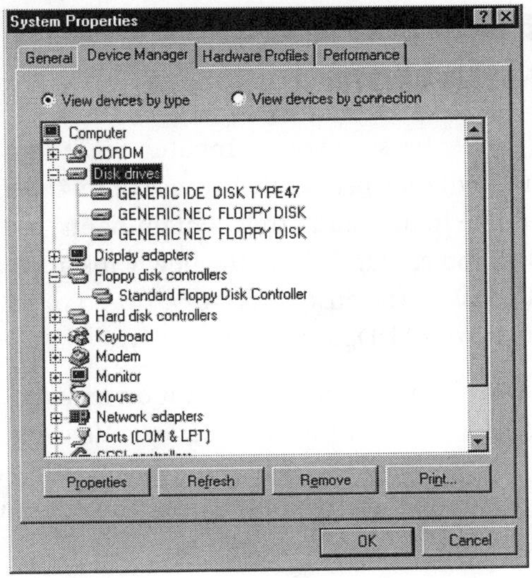

Fig. 25.1
Here you can see the available drives.

Tip

If there is a hardware conflict, Device Manager places an X through the icon meaning that the hardware has been disabled. A circle exclamation point through the icon means the hardware has a problem.

5. Double-click the drive you want to check. The System Properties sheet's General page tells you if the drive is working properly, or if Windows 95 has detected a problem.

Note

If you choose the Settings page and you have a legacy drive, you'll see most of the options grayed out. The current drive letter assignment is one option that looks changeable but isn't. To change the drive assignment, you'd have to switch the cable connections between the floppy drives, then re-run the CMOS setup.

Testing and Troubleshooting FDD Installation

Before you put the cover back on your computer, make sure the FDD works properly. Since the medium (specifically because of its "open air" design) is notoriously susceptible to dust and other contaminants, testing FDDs can be a little taxing. It's all too easy to believe the newly installed drive isn't working when the real problem is a dusty disk—or a strand of hair in the drive. So, before you count out your FDD, test it thoroughly.

The cardinal rule when testing FDDs is to test it on an *entire* disk. Make sure the drive heads can access the entire disk's surface. Viewing a directory of the disk in Windows Explorer, for example, isn't a reliable test because the directory is stored on a very small section of the disk. To verify the drive's operation across the entire disk, try any of these tests:

- Format a blank floppy disk. (Open the My Computer icon, select the drive, and choose Format from the File menu.)
- Run ScanDisk from the Start menu's Accessories/System Tools menu (see fig. 25.2). Make sure you choose Thorough in the Type of Test box before you click the Start button.

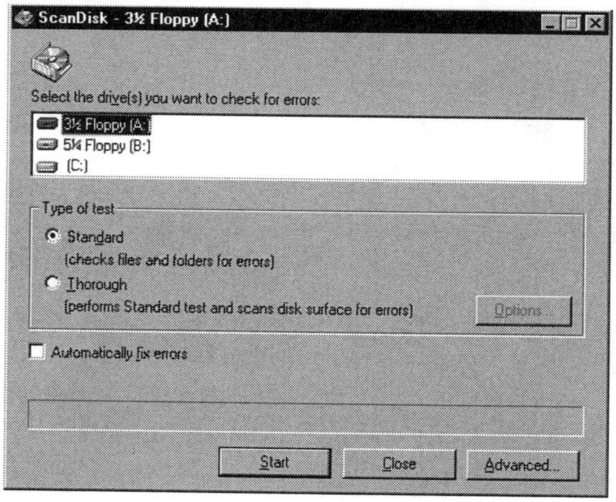

Fig. 25.2
ScanDisk checks the entire surface of a disk for errors.

If your drive can successfully complete one or both of these tests, it's a pretty safe bet that it is installed correctly. If it fails these tests, there are several things you can do to track down the problem.

First, find the *general* location of the problem. It could be any of the following:

- Disk
- Drive
- Ribbon cable
- Power cable
- Drive controller

For example, if the drive doesn't appear in the My Computer or ScanDisk windows, the problem is probably not the disk itself. If the drive shows up in these windows, you know the power cable is connected; Windows wouldn't know the drive was there if it didn't have power. This process is often called the *long-knife approach*, because each question eliminates a large chunk of the problem.

When you have shortened the list of suspects enough, eliminate each one until you find the culprit.

Checking for a Faulty Disk

If the disk itself could be the problem, try to read it in another computer. If the disk works in other computers, it's probably not at fault. Verify this by trying other disks in the problem drive. If other disks work, the first disk may be incompatible with the drive (the wrong size, for example).

> **Tip**
>
> If you have access to CompuServe, the Internet, or another online source, look for the freeware program DRIVTY or DRIVTYPS. When you run it from the MS-DOS command line, it tells you whether your disk drive(s) can accept high-density disks or not.

In rare cases, the alignment of a drive's heads allow it to read and write disks that can't be used on other computers. If you need to share disks with other computers and no one else seems to be able to use disks from your computer, try a different drive.

Checking for a Faulty Drive

If all the cables and disks check out, the problem could be in the drive. If you can, try it in another computer with a working disk drive of the same type. If you don't have a spare computer for testing, see if you can try another drive in its place. You may have to take the computer into a computer repair shop for testing.

Before you give up on the drive, try a commercial drive cleaning kit (about $10 to $15 from any computer store), which can help eliminate dust and other contaminants from the drive heads.

Checking for Faulty Cables

When you turn on the computer, watch the light on the drive. It should light up for about one second, and you should hear the drive's motor spinning or "cranking." If it doesn't light up at all (or if it stays lit all the time), you probably have a problem with your cables.

For a drive that does nothing, check the power cable. Disconnect it and reconnect it to make sure it's seated correctly. If that doesn't work, check another of your power supply's leads (refer back to "Installing the Hardware" for information about leads and adapters).

If the drive light is always on, the culprit is probably the ribbon cable. Though most drives only allow you to put the cable on one way, some can be connected upside-down (especially edge connectors). See if you can flip the ribbon cable's connection, either on the drive end or the card end—but not both. If the connectors will only go one way, check pin connectors for folded (bent) or broken pins.

If all the connectors look alright, the problem may be a short in the ribbon cable itself. Try a different one. If possible, try the ribbon cable on a different computer to see if it works. This could point to a faulty drive or controller.

Checking for a Problem in the Controller

If you've eliminated every other possibility, the controller could be at fault. If possible, try a different controller in its place, or try it on a different machine. Even if your disk controller is on the motherboard, you should be able to disable it and try a different controller—but only after you've disabled the onboard controller. To disable it, you'll probably have to reset a jumper on the motherboard. Some motherboards clearly label the jumper you'll need to switch `FDD` or `FD CNTRL` (Intel motherboards are a good example), but others have cryptic labels that you'll need a manual or technical support person to decode.

Tip

Some jumper settings for drives and motherboards are available online. Check the manufacturer's forum or Internet site. If you use a major online service, try a software search by typing either the name of the company (like Intel or Sony) or the device (Disk Controller or CD-ROM Drive).

If you've installed a new drive controller on a PC that already has one (either on the motherboard or on another card), you may run into a conflict if the earlier controller isn't properly disabled (see fig. 25.3). Check the jumpers and documentation for the card to make sure.

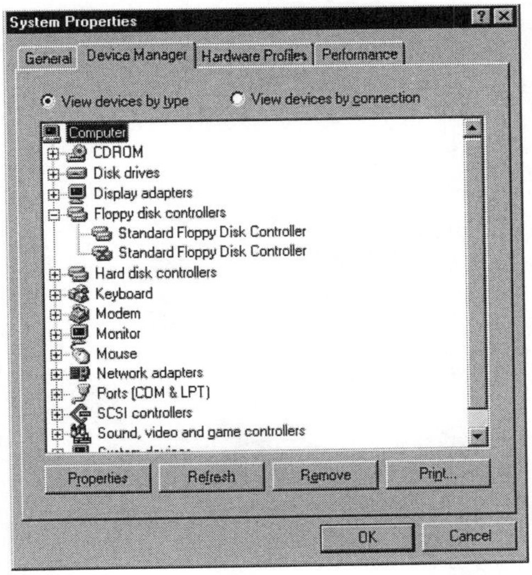

Fig. 25.3
Windows 95 detects most hardware conflicts automatically.

Chapter 26

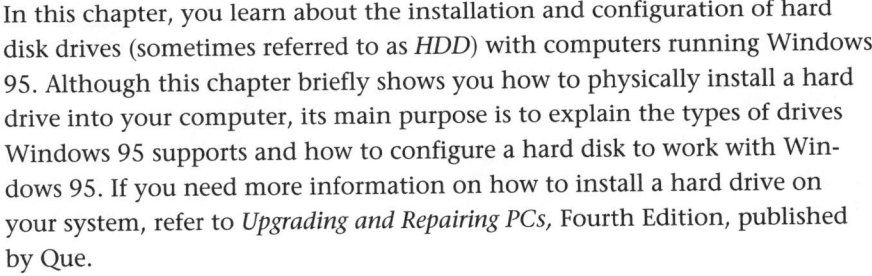

Configuring Hard Disk Drives

by Rob Tidrow and Jeff Pulver

In this chapter, you learn about the installation and configuration of hard disk drives (sometimes referred to as *HDD*) with computers running Windows 95. Although this chapter briefly shows you how to physically install a hard drive into your computer, its main purpose is to explain the types of drives Windows 95 supports and how to configure a hard disk to work with Windows 95. If you need more information on how to install a hard drive on your system, refer to *Upgrading and Repairing PCs,* Fourth Edition, published by Que.

You've learned throughout this book that one of the main features of Windows 95 is its support of Plug-and-Play devices. Unfortunately, most users do not have hard drives that are Plug and Play-compliant, nor are their systems BIOS (Basic Input/Output Systems) Plug and Play ready. Fortunately, Windows 95 makes it easier than ever to install and configure a hard disk to work with your operating system. With Windows 95's autodetect feature, many hard drives are automatically recognized and configured after you get all the hardware-specific issues ironed out.

In this chapter, you learn how to

- Identify the types of hard drives Windows 95 supports
- Install a new hard drive
- Partition a hard drive
- Configure and prepare your hard drive to work with Windows 95
- Format a hard drive
- Test the performance of a new hard drive

Types of Hard Drives Windows 95 Supports

◀ See "Hard Drive Requirements," p. 22

◀ See "Using Windows 95 Setup," p. 62

The majority of users interested in adding a hard drive to their computer already have Windows 95 installed. If you do not have Windows 95 installed and you want to add a new hard drive to your system, you need to install the new hard drive and then install MS-DOS on it to start the Windows 95 Setup routine. Chapters 1 and 2 should be consulted to install Windows 95 on your system.

Note

A valuable resource you need to have handy when you install a new hard drive is your system documentation. This is the booklet or folder that came with your computer when you purchased it. In this manual you find specific information that relates to your system, such as interrupt settings and CMOS settings.

For this chapter, it is assumed that you are adding another hard drive to your PC to use with your current Windows 95 installation. Some users opt for a second hard disk if their first hard disk becomes full or if they need to separate their data and programs from their operating system. This is the case in many situations when you use a removable hard disk that you carry with you or store in a secure place.

Before you rush in and start installing a hard drive, you first should examine the types of hard drives you can install in Windows 95. The following types of hard disk drives are supported under Windows 95:

ESDI	IDE LBA
Hardcards	MFM
IDE	

Windows 95 supports the following types of bus adapters:

EISA	RLL
ISAMCA	SCSI
PCI	SCSI 2
PCMCIA	VL bus

Windows 95 provides better disk device support than Windows 3.1, but it also ensures compatibility with existing MS-DOS-based and Windows-based disk device drivers. In addition, the disk device drivers in Windows 95 are compatible with Windows NT miniport drivers. Windows 95 also provides enhanced support for large media using logical block addressing, including hard disks with more than 1,024 cylinders.

Although Windows 95 supports other types of drives, the following two sections discuss IDE and SCSI devices in more detail. IDE and SCSI devices are the most prevalent devices available on current computers.

IDE Drives

Windows 95 supports *IDE drives* (*Integrated Drive Electronics*), which are the most popular hard disk interfaces used in computers. If you have a computer that was manufactured in the last several years, it more than likely includes an IDE drive.

One of the improvements Windows 95 has with IDE drives is its support for large IDE disk drives. New IDE drives support the *logical block addressing* (*LBA*) scheme, which enables them to exceed the 528M size limitation. These new drives are sometimes referred to as *Enhanced IDE drives*. Windows 95 can support primary partition sizes of 2G, with support of multiple 2G logical drives in extended partitions. Previous versions of Windows supported large hard disks in real mode, but Windows 95 supports large IDE drives using a protected mode disk driver included with Windows 95.

Troubleshooting

I'm on a network using Windows 95, and I cannot access a hard drive. Windows 95 also reports that a hard drive larger than 2G has only 2G of storage space. What is the problem?

The network client in Windows 95 is designed to be compatible with MS-DOS-based applications that can have a 2G limit. When a network drive has more than 2G of free disk space, Windows 95 reports only that 2G are available and 0 bytes are used. Microsoft recommends against using Windows 95 with a FAT volume larger than 2G created in Windows NT. On a dual-boot computer with both Windows 95 and Windows NT installed, you can read from and write to the drive, but you might experience strange results, such as programs reporting 0 bytes free space on the drive.

> **Note**
>
> A term that you see throughout this chapter is *controller.* A hard disk controller acts as a middleman between the hard disk and your computer. A controller is needed because a PC cannot use a hard disk directly. It needs something to communicate instructions to and from the hard drive. In many cases, the BIOS is used to pass hard disk requests from the PC to the hard disk controller. The controller then accesses the hard disk.

Another feature of Windows 95 is its support of a second IDE controller in your computer, if your computer can support it. You need to refer to your computer's documentation to determine how to set up your CMOS configuration to handle this second IDE controller. If you use a laptop, you can use a combination of an IDE controller and a controller in a docking station, if you use a docking station with your laptop.

> **Note**
>
> Windows 95 also supports CD-ROM drives that are IDE-based. This is good news to the millions of users who don't want to configure a proprietary CD-ROM interface or an SCSI controller. Windows 95 supports Mitsumi, Sony, and Panasonic CD-ROM adapters. If your CD-ROM is not supported automatically, you may need to use a vendor's device driver and load MSCDEX in your CONFIG.SYS file.

SCSI Drives

◀ See "Starting the Add New Hardware Wizard for CD-ROM Drives," p. 513

Unlike Windows 3.x, Windows 95 includes 32-bit disk device drivers for several *SCSI* (*Small Computer System Interface*) controllers. Some of these controllers include Adaptec, Future Domain, Trantor, and UltraStor. The SCSI interface is a sub-bus to which you can connect up to seven peripherals. The SCSI interface supports up to eight units, but one of the units is used to connect the adapter card to the PC, leaving seven open units. You can attach hard disks, CD-ROM drives, scanners, and other devices to a SCSI adapter.

> **Troubleshooting**
>
> *I have an Adaptec EZ SCSI for Windows drive, but it doesn't work now. Why?*
>
> The Adaptec EZ SCSI Windows version will not run with Windows 95, but the MS-DOS version does work with Windows 95.

In the past, many DOS- and Windows-based users dreaded installing and configuring an SCSI card because of the seemingly endless installation process of trial-and-error to get the device working properly. With Windows 95, many of these installation headaches have gone away. Also, if you already have a SCSI device installed under MS-DOS and it adheres to the ASPI (Advanced SCSI Programming Interface) or CAM (Common Access Method) specifications, you should not have a problem getting your SCSI device to work properly under Windows 95.

Troubleshooting

My SCSI device worked fine under MS-DOS, but it doesn't work with Windows 95. Can you help?

For many SCSI hardware devices, you can specify command-line parameters when the driver is loaded. By default, the Windows 95 miniport driver runs without parameters (in the same way it does for real-mode drivers). If you want to use a command-line parameter, you can add it to the Settings property for the SCSI controller. For real-mode parameters that the controller supports (and if the device has a Windows 95 MPD file), you can enter parameters in the Adapter Settings box in the controller's properties. For information about the switches that can be used for a particular SCSI device, see the documentation from the device manufacturer. There are no additional parameters added by Microsoft.

For example, if your SCSI adapter has full functionality under MS-DOS, but not under Windows 95, you can add any device parameters previously specified in CONFIG.SYS to the Adapter Settings box. As another example, for Adaptec 7700 SCSI devices, you might specify **removable=off** to disable support for removable media if you want to load another ASPI removable disk.

Installing a Hard Disk

When you install a hard disk, you need to be aware of several factors that help lead you to a successful installation. Because each computer, hard disk, and Windows 95 installation is different, this section shows you some of the general steps to help you physically install your hard disk. You should use this section as an overview and reference another resource for hardware-specific questions you might have.

Before you begin ripping open your computer and stuffing a new hard disk inside it, be sure your computer supports the type of hard disk you are installing. You should be able to find this information on the computer specification that you receive with your PC. If you are the type of user who is not comfortable installing hardware, this chapter probably will not make you more comfortable doing so. It will, however, show you how to configure your hard disk after it's installed. You can find out this information in the later section, "Configuring Your Hard Disk for Windows 95."

Tip

Before you turn off your computer to add the new hard disk, you should back up your system in case you lose any data on your existing hard disk.

Plug and Play, and Legacy Hard Drives

In Chapter 1, "Preparing To Install Windows 95," you learned about Plug and Play and how it helps you set up your devices quickly and easily under Windows 95. Another term that you might hear is legacy. *Legacy* refers to devices that do not support the Plug and Play specification. Many of the troubleshooting problems that you run into under Windows 95 are related to legacy devices because they are older devices.

The Plug and Play feature requires the cooperation between BIOS manufacturers, device manufacturers, and the software developers. Therefore, in order to use this feature, you need a BIOS which supports Plug and Play, a hard disk drive which is Plug and Play-compliant, and Windows 95, which has the support to recognize a new Plug and Play-compliant device and perform an automatic installation of it. This makes the addition of new hardware a simple and painless operation. In some cases, you don't even need to turn off the power to the PC to install a Plug and Play device (although it's recommended that you power down your computer anytime you remove its case).

Disk Drive Addressing

To access a hard disk drive, the address of the disk must be specified. The *address* is a single alphabetic character followed by a colon. If the colon is omitted, Windows 95 thinks you are giving it a file name consisting of a single letter, rather than a disk drive address.

Note

The addressing scheme can become very complicated. If you are connected to a network, each disk you want to have on the network will also have an alphabetic character assigned to it. To further complicate the issue, the DOS command **SUBST** can be used to substitute one disk address for another. Schemes such as these are beyond the scope of this book.

In addition, Windows 95 has specific addresses it uses for the disk devices and CD-ROMs. The addresses of the floppy and hard disks are determined by the cables attached to them. To simplify this discussion, you can use a standard form of addressing. You can safely assume the following:

- An installed CD-ROM has an address of `K:`
- Any network disks have an address starting with `L:`
- The DOS command SUBST is not be used

When Windows 95 is started, the existing disks are assigned an address based upon the following scheme:

- The first floppy disk drive is `A:`
- The second floppy disk drive is `B:`
- The first hard disk drive is `C:`
- The second hard disk drive is `D:`
- The third hard disk drive is `E:`
- The fourth hard disk drive is `F:`
- The CD-ROM address is specified during installation. If it is not specified, its address is the next alphabetic character after the last hard drive.

Tip

Always assign the address for a CD-ROM drive a few letters after your last hard disk drive. If, for instance, your hard drives are C: and D:, make your CD-ROM F: or G:. That way, if you add more hard disk drives, its address does not change and you do not have to change any links to files on a CD-ROM. See Chapter 24, "Configuring CD-ROM Drives," for information on installing a CD-ROM drive.

Referencing the Windows 95 Device Manager

◀ See "Starting Add New Hardware Wizard for CD-ROM Drives," p. 513

The Windows 95 Device Manager is used to display and change the parameters associated with your system's hardware, including hard disk drives. In most instances, the default settings selected by Windows 95 are the correct ones. Sometimes, however, you may encounter a problem after you install your hard drive, and you need to access the Device Manager to fix the problem. For this reason, you should become familiar with the Device Manager, even before you install a new hard drive. To access the Device Manager, use the following procedure:

1. Choose Start, Settings, Control Panel, and double-click the System icon.
2. When the System Properties sheet appears, click the Device Manager tab (see fig. 26.1).

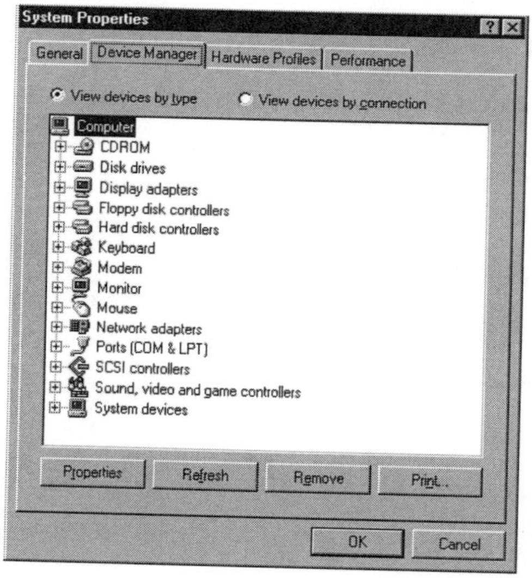

Fig. 26.1
You can view your system's hardware and properties by using the Device Manager.

To view your hard drive properties, you need to look at both the Disk Drives setting and the Hard Disk Controller setting. Click the plus sign (+) next to each of these settings to reveal the type of drives and controllers you have installed (see fig. 26.2).

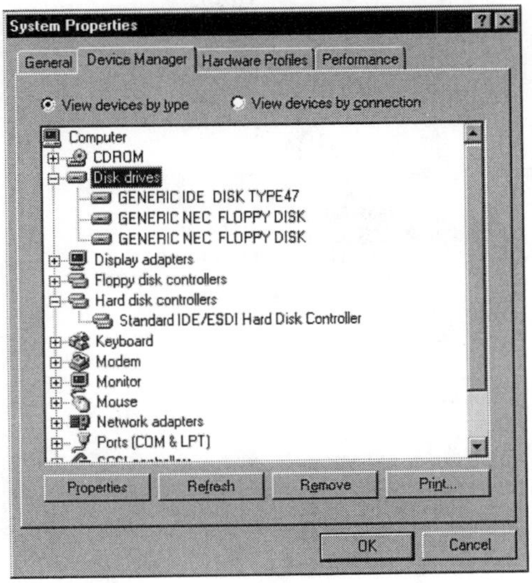

Fig. 26.2
To see the type of hard drive and hard disk controller on your system, click the plus (+) sign next to Disk Drives and Hard Disk Controllers.

In figure 26.2, for instance, three drives are shown under Disk Drives. The drive named `GENERIC IDE DISK TYPE47` is the hard disk on the system. The other drive is the floppy disk drive installed. Under the Hard Disk Controllers, one controller is listed, named `Standard IDE/ESDI Hard Disk Controller`.

> **Note**
>
> If you right-click on any device and select What's This?, Windows 95 explains how you can find out more about that piece of hardware and what the icon looks like when there is a problem with the device.

If there is a hardware conflict on your system, the Device Manager places a circle exclamation point over the icon on the line denoting the conflicting device. Likewise, if a device is disabled but not removed, the Device Manager places a red X over the device. In figure 26.3, for instance, a red X is drawn over the third Standard Hard Disk Controller. In this case, the error occurs because Windows 95 supports only two controllers and the user has attempted to place three on the system.

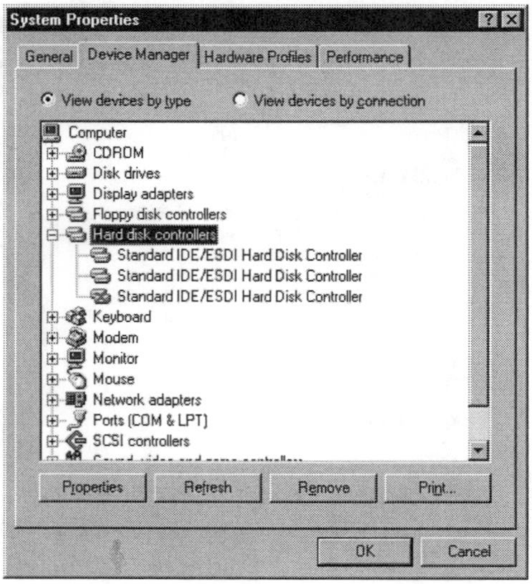

Fig. 26.3
You can readily see which device, if any, is causing a conflict by using the Device Manager.

Installing a Hard Drive

As pointed out earlier, this chapter assumes that you already have one hard drive installed on your system. Unless you piece together your own computer, the first hard disk is always installed when you purchase your computer. Today's computers usually can support at least two hard disk drives.

Before you begin disassembling your computer, you want to find a large, uncluttered area to work in, have adequate light, and have the following tools handy:

- 1/4-inch and 3/16-inch nut drivers
- No. 0 and one Phillips screwdrivers
- 3/16-inch and 1/8-inch slotted screwdrivers
- Pen light
- Antistatic strip to reduce static electricity charges

> **Caution**
>
> Static electricity can be discharged from your body and can cause permanent damage to the chips in the computer. If you do not use an antistatic strip, always touch something metal, such as the case, before touching any components inside the computer.

To install new hardware, including your hard disk, the computer case that protects the internal parts of your PC must be removed. Below are the steps required to open your computer:

1. Turn off the power to the computer and remove the power cord.
2. Disconnect all cables from the computer and note their location with a piece of masking tape.
3. Remove the case by unscrewing the six or eight screws holding it to the frame.

You are now ready to install your second hard disk drive. Because each hard disk and computer is different, this is where you need to read and follow the instructions provided by the hard disk manufacturer to install the hard disk drive. Some generalized guidelines follow:

1. Locate an available bay to install the hard disk. Many hard disks come with a drive kit, usually at an additional charge, with all necessary hardware to mount the drive in the bay. You may need an adapter if your bay is for a 5.25-inch hard disk drive and you are installing a 3.5-inch hard disk drive. In addition, rails, which are attached to the side of the hard disk drive, may also be needed. The drive can now be installed with the appropriate screws (usually four 6/32 × 1/4-inch screws).

Tip

It may be easier to connect the power connector and hard disk drive cable before sliding the hard disk drive into the bay.

2. Next, locate an available power supply connection. If none are available, you have to purchase a Y-cable. The Y-cable allows you to share an existing power connector with two devices. To install it, you would locate a device near the empty bay which has a power connection plugged into it. You would then disconnect that plug, and then plug the female end of the Y-cable into it. Now, one of the male ends is for the device you just unplugged, and the other male end is for your new hard disk drive. Since a hard disk drive uses more electricity than most other devices, you should use a Y-cable of 18 gauge or heavier.

3. You are now ready to attach the hard disk drive cables between the hard disk controller and the hard disk drive. These are two flat wide ribbon cables, with a red or blue stripe along one edge. This colored edge should be next to pin number one when it is connected to the hard disk drive and the hard disk controller. You can locate the pin number by referring to your computer's documentation and looking at the schematic drawing of the motherboard.

   Most disk drives have a single cable that combines the functions of the data cable and the control cable. Also, to help ensure the cable is connected properly, there may a plastic key that is placed between a row of pins in the connector. With this plastic key, the connector can only be attached to the disk drive.

After the hard disk drive is secured to the bay, and the drive cable and power cable are connected, you are ready to close the computer and begin configuring Windows 95 for your new hard disk drive.

Note

Because Windows 95 supports up to two IDE disk controllers, you can install a second controller if you install a third or fourth hard disk in your system. Again, consult your hardware documentation for the placement of the new controller on your PC's motherboard. Some motherboards include a set of golden pins labeled to identify them for the second controller, such as Secondary IDE.

Closing the Computer

With all of the new hardware installed, you can now close the computer to complete the configuration of the new hardware.

Tip

If you're like me, you like to make sure everything is working before you go through all the trouble of refastening all those screws on your computer. You may want to bypass this section for now and go to the "Configuring Your Hard Disk for Windows 95" section to make sure your hard disk works. Of course, you need to attach all the cables and power cords before booting up your computer, but you may save time if the hard disk doesn't work and you need to check loose cables and the like by keeping the case off for now.

These are the general steps to close your computer:

1. Refasten the case by reversing the procedure used to remove it. Namely, place the case back over the frame of the computer and insert the removed screws to refasten the case to the frame. Ensure all cables and wires are neatly placed inside the computer, in a position where they aren't pinched by other components or trapped between the case and the frame of the computer.
2. All cables can now be plugged into their proper ports, according to the labels on each cable.
3. Attach the power cord and plug it into an electrical outlet.

Note

After you install a new hard drive in your computer, you need to configure it to work properly with your specific computer. To do this, reboot your computer and run your computer's setup program to enable you to make changes to your CMOS settings. On some machines, you can start the setup program by pressing F1 during bootup. With Gateway 2000 computers, you can press Ctrl+Alt+Esc to start it. Refer to your computer's documentation at this point to configure your machine to work with the new hard disk. After you make these changes, be sure to save them and then reboot your computer.

You are now ready to begin configuring Windows 95 for your new hard disk drive.

Partitioning a Hard Drive

Before you use your new hard disk with Windows 95, you need to partition it using the FDISK command. When you *partition* a hard disk, you define the areas of the disk for Windows 95 (or any other operating system for that matter) to recognize as a volume. To Windows 95, a *volume* is part of the disk that is specified as the drive letter, such as C or D.

Partitioning Requirements for Installing Windows 95

Windows 95 Setup cannot install Windows 95 unless a FAT partition exists on the hard disk. It cannot install Windows 95 on a computer that has only

HPFS or Windows NT file system (NTFS) partitions. The following list describes how Windows 95 Setup handles different types of disk partitions:

- *MS-DOS Partition.* Windows 95 Setup recognizes and begins installation over existing MS-DOS FAT partitions. Windows 95 supports MS-DOS FDISK partitions on removable media drives such as the Iomega Bernoulli Box drives.
- *Windows NT.* Windows 95 Setup cannot recognize information on an NTFS (NT File System) partition on the local computer. You can install Windows 95 on a Windows NT multiple-boot system if enough disk space is available on a FAT partition. On a Windows NT multiple-boot system, you must install Windows 95 on an existing FAT partition with MS-DOS or MS-DOS and Windows 3.x. Another way to install Windows 95 is to partition and format free space on the hard disk in a FAT partition, then perform a new installation onto this new FAT partition.
- *OS/2.* Again, a DOS partition must be available from which to install Windows 95. You cannot install Windows 95 straight from OS/2.

Tip

To install a new hard disk as your primary hard drive, you need Windows 95 on a floppy disk instead of CD-ROM. Next, place the Windows 95 Startup disk in drive A: and boot your computer. Upon boot, Windows 95 detects the new drive and asks if you want to allocate all of your unallocated space on your new drive. After you answer Yes. Windows runs FDISK and restarts your computer, then automatically formats the new hard disk's partition.

Using FDISK

When you use FDISK, you can partition your hard drive into one or several partitions. You might want to partition your new hard drive into two partitions if you want to install a different operating system, such as OS/2 Warp, on your computer. This way, you can have both Windows 95 and OS/2 residing on the same computer, but occupying different hard drives.

Caution

Running FDISK destroys all data on the partitions you change or create. Do not use FDISK if you are not comfortable making these changes and if you have not backed up all the data on your drive. If you are in a company, consult your MIS or help desk person before continuing.

Another time when you can partition a hard disk is when you have already set up a hard drive and you want to *repartition* it. If you want to repartition a hard disk that has several logical drives into one drive, you must first use FDISK to delete all existing partitions and logical drives, and then create a new primary partition and make it active. The *active partition* is the partition in which your system boots. For this chapter, your active partition is already set up and is not modified. This is the partition on the hard disk that contains Windows 95. You don't need to worry about partitioning that hard drive. In fact, if you repartitioned that drive, you would lose all the data on it, including Windows 95.

Caution

On hard disks that are already installed, you should not repartition the hard disk by using FDISK if the partition was created using Disk Manager, Storage Dimensions SpeedStor, Priam, or Everex partitioning programs. When these programs are used, they replace the existing PC's BIOS in interactions between MS-DOS and the hard disk controller. For these cases, you must use the same disk-partitioning program that was used to partition the disk in the first place. For example, if you use SpeedStor on a computer that has more than 1,024 cylinders, do not use FDISK to partition your hard drive. Use SpeedStor instead.

You can tell the type of program that created the partition by searching for these files on your system: HARDRIVE.SYS for Priam; SSTOR.SYS for SpeedStor; DMDRVR.BIN for Disk Manager; and EVDISK.SYS for Everex. Usually, you find device= entries for these files in CONFIG.SYS. If you need help repartitioning the hard disk or are unsure whether the BIOS is being replaced, contact the manufacturer of the original disk-partitioning program.

As you just read, when you partition a hard drive, you lose all data on it. When repartitioning an existing hard drive, be sure to back up all your data onto another hard drive or tape backup. You cannot recover the data once you've partitioned the drive.

Note

Although Windows 95 replaces MS-DOS as your primary operating system, the partitions that FDISK creates are still called *DOS partitions*.

FDISK is an MS-DOS-based application that you can run from the DOS command prompt. You also can run it in a DOS window in Windows 95. As you use FDISK, each FDISK screen displays a Current Fixed Disk Drive line, followed by a number. This number is the number of the current drive that is selected. Computers with only one hard disk drive use the label 1. Computers with more than one hard disk drive label the drives as follow: the first hard disk drive on the computer is 1, the second is 2, and so on. The Current Fixed Disk Drive line refers only to physical disk drives, not logical drives.

To configure a hard disk by using FDISK, use the following steps:

1. At the DOS command prompt, type **FDISK**. The FDISK Options screen displays the following:

```
1. Create a partition or logical drive
2. Set the active partition
3. Delete a partition or logical drive
4. Display partition information
5. Change current fixed disk drive
   Enter choice [1]
   Press Esc to exit FDISK
```

> **Tip**
>
> You can press Esc anytime to exit FDISK.

2. In the preceding options list, the fifth option is not available when you have only one hard drive installed on your computer. Because we have two hard drives installed now, select 5 to switch to the second hard disk to partition it and press Enter.

3. Now that your new drive is selected, choose option 1 and press Enter. This creates a partition on your drive. When you are prompted to set the size of the partition, the default is to use the entire drive. Select Yes in most cases.

4. Return to the FDISK menu and be sure to select your primary fixed disk (drive C: usually) by selecting option 5 before you exit FDISK. Otherwise, when you reboot your system, your computer will try to boot from your new drive.

Note

If you installed a disk-compression program from Microsoft or another vendor, FDISK displays the uncompressed size of the drives, not the compressed size. Depending on the software, FDISK may not be able to display information about all the drives used by a disk-compression program from another vendor. You should obtain information from the software vendor if you are having difficulties.

Troubleshooting

What do I do when I get an error that Windows 95 Setup can't find a valid boot partition?

This error might be a result of your disk compression software or network components mapping over the boot drive. This can occur if you are mapping a network drive to H, but H is the hidden host drive for your disk compression software. To resolve the invalid partition error, make sure the drive is not mapped over or logically remapped. You should also verify a valid, active partition using the FDISK command. If no active partition exists, use FDISK to mark an appropriate partition as active. Also, make sure the disk compression software's host drive does not conflict with a mapped network drive.

Configuring Your Hard Disk for Windows 95

After your hard drive is installed and the cables reattached to your computer, boot your computer and start Windows 95. During the boot process, Windows 95 looks at your system and, if everything goes as planned, detects your new hard drive. If the hard drive is Plug and Play-compatible, Windows 95 configures it automatically. Windows 95 also automatically configures any Plug-and-Play controller that you may have installed.

One of the problems with Plug and Play is that your computer's BIOS also needs to support Plug-and-Play devices. Most computers being used do not have a BIOS that supports this new specification. For this reason, Windows 95 also includes the auto-detect feature for legacy systems. If Windows 95 finds your new hard drive during bootup, but cannot automatically configure it, you are presented with a screen asking if you want to set up the device now. The best response is to answer Yes to this screen and let Windows 95 try to set it up for you.

Setting Up Plug and Play Controllers

Windows 95 is designed to automatically detect a new Plug and Play-compliant hard disk drive controller. After the physical installation of the hard disk drive controller is complete, and the computer is restarted, the hard disk drive can be configured during the boot process. When that is complete, your new hard disk drive is ready for use.

Follow the procedures for testing your new hard disk drive as outlined later in "Testing the Hard Disk Drive." If the hard disk drive is not operational, you need to install it as a legacy device, as described in the following section.

Configuring a Legacy Hard Disk Drive Controller

Most users need to use the auto-detect or manual detection features of Windows 95 to configure their hard drive for Windows 95. Unless you know that your hard drive will not be detected by Windows 95 during the auto detection phase, you should always try the automatic detection mode first. If that does not work, then use the manual detection mode.

Automatic Detection

To configure a legacy hard disk drive controller, go to the Control Panel and double-click the Add New Hardware icon. The Add New Hardware Wizard displays. Click the Next button to continue. You now are presented with the screen shown in figure 26.4. Make sure the Yes (Recommended) option is marked and click the Next button. The Yes option informs Windows 95 that it should attempt to find the hardware on its own.

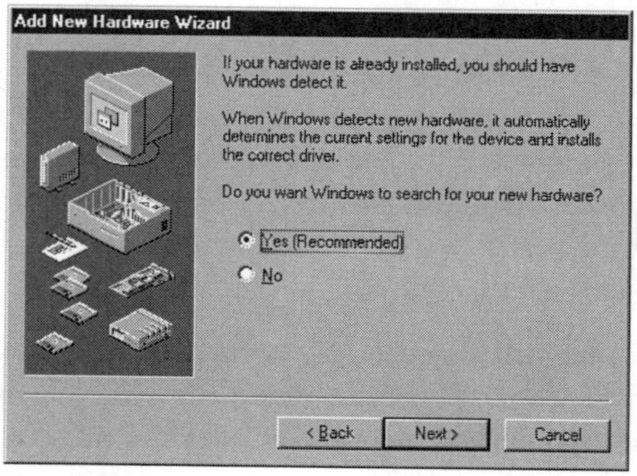

Fig. 26.4
You should consider letting Windows 95 try to automatically detect your new hard disk by choosing Yes when the Add New Hardware Wizard displays.

A warning screen then appears, informing you the detection procedure may take a long time to complete. It may take more than 10 minutes depending on your system. While it is running, you hear a lot of noise from the disk and the HDD light flashes. (The HDD light is an optional red or green light on the front of your computer. When on, it indicates the hard disk drive is being accessed.) When this task is completed, you are informed by another display that your device was detected. Click the Finish button to complete the hard disk drive configuration.

If Windows 95 detects your hard drive and displays the correct model and manufacturer, it usually can install the device without any problems. In some cases, if the device driver and other supporting files are not installed on your machine, you need to provide the installation disk that comes bundled with the hard disk. This disk normally is supplied by the manufacturer of the hardware. Windows copies the drivers onto your system and then informs you that it needs to reboot the computer for the new settings to take effect. Click the Yes button when Windows asks if it can restart the computer. After your computer starts and Windows 95 boots, and your new hard disk device doesn't conflict with your system, you're ready to format it and use it.

Tip

If the installation disks do not include up-to-date drivers for Windows 95, you need to contact the vendor to obtain a driver for your hard disk to work with Windows 95. Another place to look for updated drivers is on CompuServe, the Microsoft Download Service (MSDL), or other bulletin board systems that contain hardware support areas. You can contact the MSDL by calling 206-936-6735 with a modem and following the on-screen instructions.

Manual Detection

If, during the auto-detect stage, Windows 95 cannot detect your new hard drive device, the screen shown in figure 26.5 appears. This display informs you that Windows cannot find the hard disk and that you need to manually detect the new hard drive.

To continue with the configuration, click the Next button. The screen shown in figure 26.6 appears. This is the same display you receive if you selected the No option in the wizard screen shown in figure 26.4. In the Hardware Types list box, select the Hard disk controllers item (see fig. 26.6). Click Next.

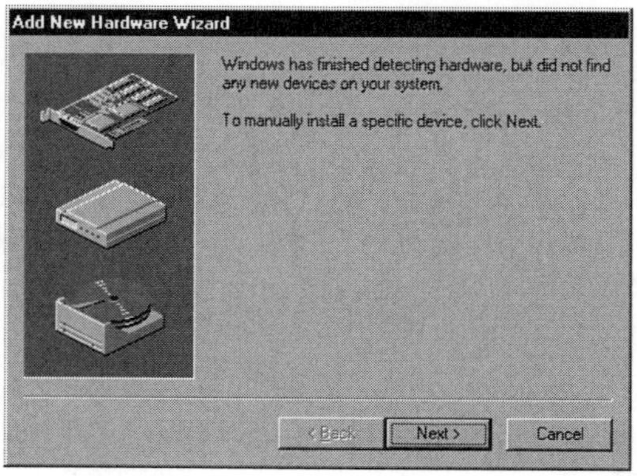

Fig. 26.5
The Add New Hardware Wizard did not find any new devices, namely your new hard disk controller.

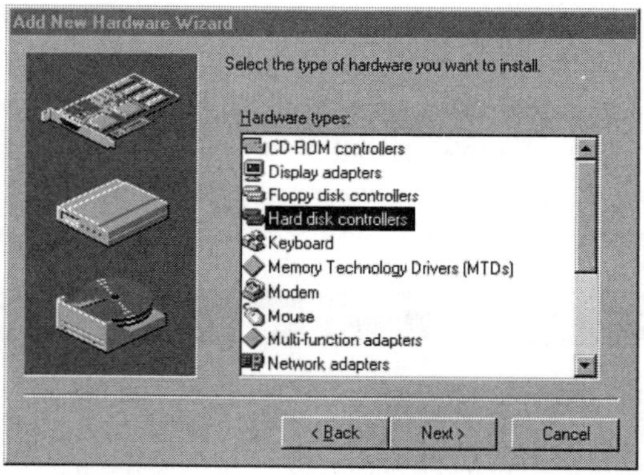

Fig. 26.6
Select the Hard disk controller item to tell Windows to install that type of hardware device.

Windows 95 displays a dialog box letting you know that it is building a driver information database. This database contains the listing of all the hard drive controllers that Windows 95 is currently aware of. After the database is created, you are shown models and manufacturers of hard drive controllers in the Add New Hardware Wizard screen (see fig. 26.7).

If you know the name and manufacturer of your device, select it from the two lists. Click Next for Windows 95 to set up your device with the appropriate files. You may need to insert your Windows 95 Setup disks. Windows 95 copies all the necessary files from the disks to your system.

If your device doesn't appear in the list of manufacturers and models, and you have a disk supplied by the manufacturer, click the Have Disk button and enter the path of where these drivers can be located in the Copy Manufacturer's Files From text box in the Install From Disk dialog box. Click OK. Windows 95 copies all the necessary files from the disks to your system.

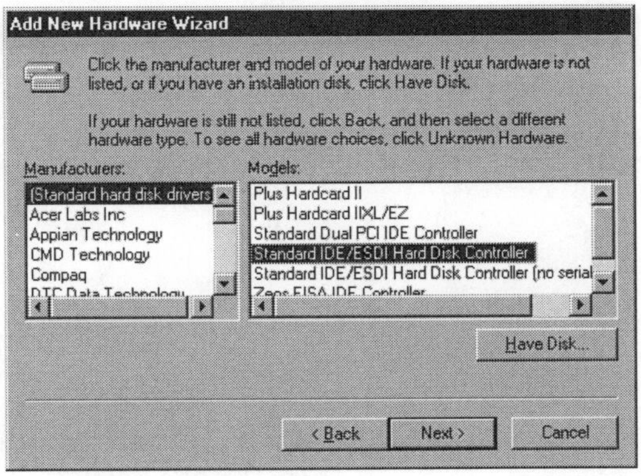

Fig. 26.7 Select the manufacturer and model of the hard disk drive controller installed on your system.

Tip

If you don't have disks from your hard disk vendor and your device doesn't appear in the list of hard disk controllers, select the Standard Hard Disk Drivers selection in the Manufacturer's list. This option uses a generic driver that may work with your device. The problem with this alternative is that the driver may not be optimized for your drive and could limit the performance factors (such as disk access time) of your device.

After all the files are copied to your system, Windows displays the last Add New Hardware Wizard screen. Click the Finish button to complete the hard disk drive controller configuration. Windows 95 prompts you if it can restart your computer so the new device works with Windows 95. Click Yes, sit back and relax, and cross your fingers. When Windows 95 boots up, your hard disk should be ready to be formatted and set up to be used.

If Things Don't Go Right...

If the configuration is unsuccessful, Windows 95 boots with an error message similar to the one in figure 26.8. This message tells you that something is wrong and asks you what to do. In some cases, you may have a conflict with another piece of hardware already installed on your computer. Even though Windows 95 handles the distribution of IRQs and other device settings, your new hard disk drive may not work correctly with the setting Windows is trying to use for it.

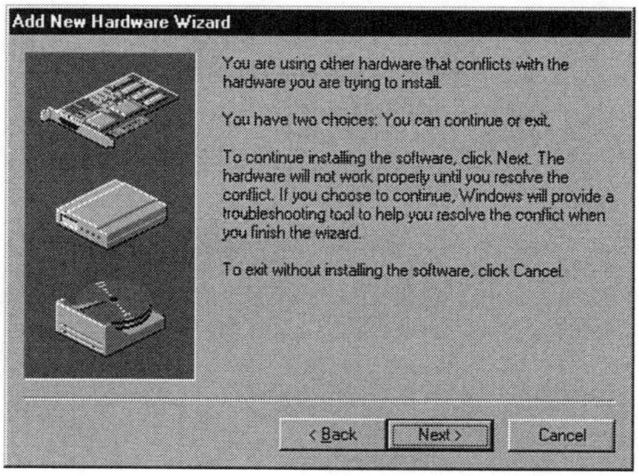

Fig. 26.8
If your new hard drive is not set up properly, you receive a hardware conflict message.

Click the Next button to continue with the hardware configuration, even though something is wrong. This helps you locate the conflict. If you exit at this point, the hardware is not configured and you won't know what is wrong. To continue, follow this procedure:

1. Click Start Conflict Troubleshooter. This displays a Windows Help screen, which you can walk through to troubleshoot and diagnose possible problems with your hard drive.
2. In the Help display, click Start to start the Hardware Conflict Troubleshooter (see fig. 26.9).

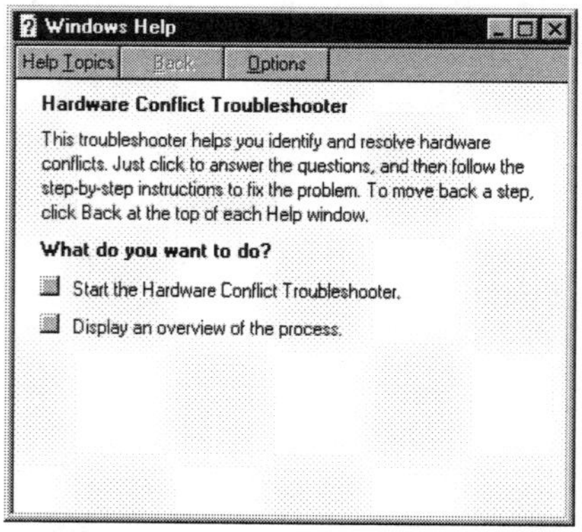

Fig. 26.9
To help you track down possible problems with your hard disk configuration, use the Hardware Conflict Troubleshooter.

3. Another Help screen appears. Click the shortcut arrow to bring you to the Device Manager (you also can start the Device Manager by double-clicking System in the Control Panel).
4. The Device Manager appears, with the Hard Disk Controllers settings displayed (see fig. 26.10). If you do not see the controller settings, click

the plus sign next to Hard Disk Controllers. In the example shown in figure 26.10, a large red X is placed over one of the controllers telling you that it is not set up correctly, or that the system cannot use the second Standard Hard Disk Controller devices.

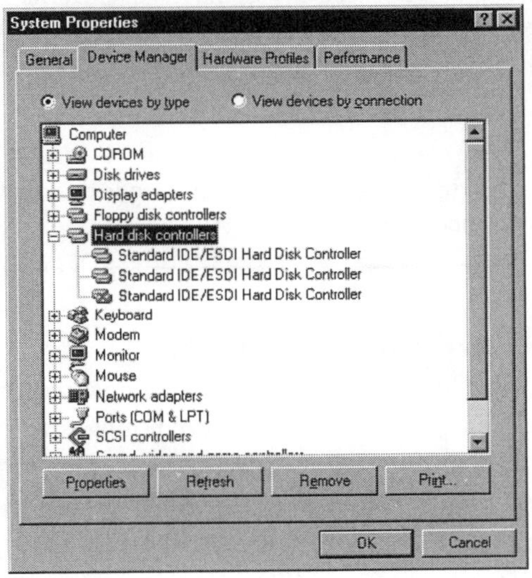

Fig. 26.10
When you troubleshoot a hard drive problem, always check the settings in the Device Manager first.

In this instance, the problem was that a second hard disk controller was defined and only one is allowed. To resolve this problem, highlight the line with the red X in it and click the Remove button. This is one example of how to resolve a hardware conflict. With hard disk drives and hard disk drive controllers, this is usually the only failure.

Troubleshooting

My computer stalls because of hard disk device drivers. What can I do?

The I/O Supervisor requires the hard disk driver files with the extensions PDR, MPD, VXD, and 386 to be located in the SYSTEM\IOSUBSYS subfolder in your Windows 95 folder. The I/O Supervisor is responsible for loading these hard disk device drivers. If your computer locks up during startup or hardware detection, use the following troubleshooting steps to fix the problem:

1. Look for SYS files in the IOSUBSYS folder. These are Windows NT miniport drivers that detect the I/O ports and may cause your computer to stop. Replace the Windows NT driver with either a Windows 95 miniport or a real-mode driver.

(continues)

(continued)

2. Check your IOS.INI file for real mode drivers not replaced by protected-mode drivers.

3. When loading protected mode drivers, the real mode driver generally remains loaded in memory even though the protected mode driver is running. Type **REM** at the beginning of the line in CONFIG.SYS that calls the real mode driver.

4. Some systems may encounter problems with devices that use ASPI drivers, such as tape backup units. Try using only real mode drivers, then try using only protected mode drivers.

Maybe It's a Hardware Problem...

Earlier in the section "Closing the Computer," I suggested that you may not want to replace the computer case just yet. Well, now is when you'll appreciate it. If your device does not work, and it's not because of the preceding failure, the problem might be hardware-related. You need to take a look at the physical connections your new hard disk has inside the computer. Sometimes a loose connection can create huge problems during setup.

Some possible areas to investigate are as follows:

- *Hard disk drive cable is defective.* Replace the cable with another one to see if the problem is resolved.

- *Hard disk drive cable is installed improperly for a single hard disk drive system.* Ensure the hard disk cable has the twist in the center of the cable near the connector to your disk drive. This is how hard disk drive C: is identified. The remaining connector is attached to the hard disk drive controller.

- *Hard disk drive cable is installed improperly for a dual hard disk drive system.* Ensure the hard disk cable has the twist in the center of the cable near the connector to your disk drive. This is how hard disk drive C: is identified. The connector at the center of the cable is for hard disk drive D:. The remaining connector is attached to the hard disk drive controller.

- *Hard disk device is defective.* If the hard disk drive cable is connected properly and the hard disk drive is not working properly, then the fault may be with the hard disk drive itself. Install a different hard disk drive and see if the problem is resolved.

- *Hard disk controller is defective.* If the hard disk drive cable is connected properly and the hard disk drive is working properly (it was tested on another computer), then the fault may be with the hard disk drive controller. Install a different hard disk drive controller and see if the problem is resolved.

Note

In the following list, the term *hard disk drive cable* is used to mean either the controller cable and/or the data cable, depending on which system you have.

After adjusting the cables and/or replacing the hard drive, reboot the computer and walk through the Add New Hardware Wizard again. If none of these solutions help, call the technical support number that is included with your hard drive. New drivers for Windows 95 may be available that they can send to you.

Formatting a Hard Disk Drive

Now that your hard disk is partitioned, and Windows 95 can recognize it, you need a way for it to be accessed. To do this, you need to perform a high-level format on it. Another reason to format a hard drive is if you want to clean up the hard disk by removing all its files and folders. Of course, you cannot do this on hard disks that currently contain data that you are using, including Windows 95.

▶ See "Memory, Disks, and Devices," p. 689

You can format a hard disk in Windows 95 using a graphical approach with Explorer (see fig. 26.11), or using the FORMAT command at the MS-DOS prompt.

Caution

Before using the FORMAT command or utility on a drive that already contains data, make sure your hard disk does not contain valuable data that is not backed up. When you format a hard drive, all data is erased from the disk and you cannot recover it.

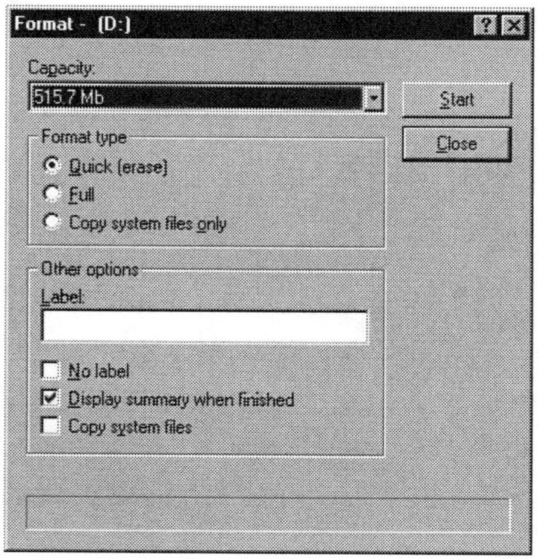

Fig. 26.11
For a more graphical approach to formatting your hard drive, use the Format utility in Explorer.

To format a hard disk drive using Explorer, use the following steps:

1. In Windows Explorer, right-click the drive icon for that disk, and then click Format from the context-sensitive menu.
2. In the Format dialog box, set the appropriate options for the type of format you want to perform. If your hard disk is new, you need to select the Full option in the Format Type section. In the Capacity drop-down list, select the size of your hard disk drive.
3. In the Other options area, type a label for the hard drive in the Label box. The *label* is the name you want to identify this drive with; don't confuse this with drive letter.
4. Click Start. Windows 95 formats the hard drive and, if you selected the Display Summary When Finished option in the Other Options area, a summary sheet appears that shows the amount of space available on the disk and how much space is taken up by system files and bad sectors, if any are found.
5. Click OK when you finish reading the report.
6. Click Close to close the Format dialog box.

Troubleshooting

I've used the Format utility in Explorer and the FORMAT command in MS-DOS, but I still can't format my hard drive.

If the disk was compressed by using DriveSpace, you must use the Format option in DriveSpace to format the compressed drive.

If you need to format a drive at the DOS command line, use the following syntax:

```
FORMAT driveletter
```

The `driveletter` parameter is the letter used to denote the hard drive you are formatting. To include a label for the drive, use the following syntax, with the label name replacing `label`:

```
FORMAT driveletter V:label
```

Your new hard disk is now ready for use.

Troubleshooting

I ran into some major problems with Windows 95 and want to reformat my hard drive. How can I do this?

First, remember that you will lose ALL data on your hard drive, including MS-DOS and Windows 95. If you created a startup disk when you installed Windows 95, you can use that disk to format your hard drive. To do this place the startup disk in drive A and reboot your computer. When the command line appears, type the following:

format driveletter: /s

The driveletter parameter is the letter of the drive you want to format, such as C:. The /s switch copies system files on to the hard disk so that you can reinstall MS-DOS and run the Windows 95 Setup program from DOS. When the warning message appears on-screen, type **Y** to continue with the formatting. Click No to stop. After the hard drive is formatted, you are prompted for a volume label. This is optional. Press Enter, remove the floppy disk, and reboot your computer.

Testing the Hard Disk Drive

Testing the hard disk drive is simple. All you have to do is use it. Before using it, however, you can ask Windows 95 to show you which ones are present. If you have two, they are shown as your C drive and D drives. The third one is the E drive, and the fourth one the F drive. Some possible ways to see it are as follows:

- Double-click My Computer and see which disks are shown.
- From the Explorer, go to the top of the list and see which hard disk drives are listed.

Troubleshooting

My hard disk has become unreadable. How can I repartition it if I can't boot into it?

If you created a startup disk during Windows 95 Setup, a copy of FDISK is on that disk. Place the startup disk in drive A: and reboot your computer. When the A:\ prompt appears on-screen, type **FDISK** and press Enter.

To make sure your new hard drive functions properly, copy a file from your old hard disk to the new hard disk. When finished, compare the two files to see if the file was copied successfully. Likewise, copy the file you just copied to the new hard drive back to the old hard drive and change the name. Now compare the two files on the old hard disk drive to see if they are still identical.

◀ See "Improving Hard Disk Performance," p. 323

Troubleshooting

How do I configure my Sysquest removable IDE drive for Windows 95?

For a Sysquest IDE drive to work properly under Windows 95, be sure to add the entry RemovableIDE=true to the [386enh] section of your SYSTEM.INI file.

Chapter 27

Configuring Backup Systems

by Michael Marchuk

As several-hundred megabyte hard drives become standard on new computers and gigabyte hard drives break the $300 barrier, it is clear that the days of backing up your system to disks are long gone. With that in mind, it is obvious that a tape backup system is needed to perform full system backups.

This chapter discusses tape backup systems and their place as a required peripheral. Additionally, this chapter shows you how to do the following

- Choose a backup system
- Install Microsoft Backup for Windows
- Install tape backup hardware through Windows
- Install unsupported tape backup systems
- Use Microsoft Backup for Windows

Choosing a Backup System

If you already own a tape drive, then you may want to skip this section, since it will cover the basics behind evaluating a tape backup system. If you haven't purchased a tape backup system yet, you'd better read this section quickly and get one soon. Each day you go without a tape backup system you are risking your data against a potential system failure.

When choosing a tape backup system, you have many options to consider. The tape backup market contains several popular tape formats and many new options. You'll look at several of these tape formats and find out the future of tape drives. But first, consider the caveats behind selecting a tape drive that will suit your needs

- Price
- Availability of tape cartridges
- Industry acceptance/standardization
- Capacity
- Support

Price

Pricing affects every decision we make, especially with our computer purchases. When you purchased your computer, you probably shopped around before you spent the couple thousand dollars on the machine you bought. When looking for a tape backup system, the process is similar, but the dollar figures are typically much less.

The average tape backup system will run between $75 and $125. That's not much more than a disk drive or a mouse. Those peripherals are considered "essential" for most every computer, but a tape drive is not. Consider how much time and effort would be lost if your hard drive stopped working today. Wouldn't it be worth $75 to have a backup to be able to restore your system in a few hours?

In addition to the cost of the tape drives, the cost for the tape cartridges cannot be ignored. Most tape cartridges can be purchased for $15 or $20. An average system will need two or three cartridges to complete a full backup. This will be explained more fully in the section "Capacity" later in this chapter.

Availability of Tape Cartridges

When considering a purchase of a tape backup system, flip through a few computer magazines or office supply catalogs. Most tape backup systems will specify a cartridge type that they use. You should be able to find several vendors in the magazines or catalogs who carry tape cartridges for your system. If you cannot find anyone but the manufacturer to sell you tapes, then perhaps you should consider a different tape backup system. The reason for finding alternative sources for tape cartridges is primarily one of standards. If your tape drive manufacturer is the only source for tape cartridges and it goes out of business tomorrow, you may not be able to find secondary sources for your cartridges.

Industry Standards

As with other industries, media formats have certain standards which allow vendors to produce products that consumers can use with their equipment. Audio cassettes, VHS video tapes, and 3 1/2-inch floppy disks all conform to industry standards for each media type. The same holds true for tape backup media.

Several major industry standards exist which are outlined in table 27.1.

Table 27.1 Major Tape Backup Standards

Tape Standard	Native Capacity	Compressed Capacity
QIC-40	60M	120M
QIC-80	120M	250M
QIC-3010	350M	700M
QIC-3020	680M	1.4G
Travan	400M	800M
4mm DAT	2G	4G
8mm DAT	4G	8G

As the technology changes, many standards will be added to this list that will undoubtedly have higher capacities. When looking for a tape backup system, try to buy one that conforms to an industry standard.

Capacity

After seeing the various standards, you may be asking yourself, "Which one should I buy?" Your situation will vary from someone else's because your machine may be used differently. However, a good rule of thumb is to buy a tape backup system that can perform a full backup of your system in two tapes or less. That means that if you have a 500M hard drive with 320M of data, then you should not consider a QIC-40 tape drive unless you cannot spend the extra money for any of the higher capacity systems.

> **Note**
>
> The "Two-Tape" rule is not set in stone. This is a good guideline for most people who want to maintain their backups. Think of it this way: if you need to swap five tapes to back up your system, how often will you back up your system? The time and effort it takes to swap all of those tapes will justify purchasing a tape drive that meets your needs.

When estimating your backup capacity requirements, you may use the estimated compressed tape capacity to determine the tape system that fits your needs. Typically a 2:1 compression ratio is average for most types of data.

Support

When choosing a vendor for a tape backup system, you should buy from a manufacturer who has been around for at least a few years. In the computer industry, many companies who have been established for more than 10 years are considered old-timers. Choose a company that has a reputation for building solid tape backup systems. Some companies that come to mind include

- Colorado Memory Systems
- Conner Peripherals
- Iomega
- Mountain Network Solutions

Internal vs. External Tape Drive

You might have to back up more than one computer; for example, you may need to back up both your laptop and workstation. In this case, you may want to consider an external tape drive system. *External tape drives* usually connect to your computer through the parallel port. The transfer rate is limited to the throughput of your parallel port, so backups would take slightly longer with the external drive when compared to the same drive's internal model. External tape drives are somewhat more expensive than internal units; however, the added flexibility of using an external unit will save you from buying additional tape drives.

The benefits of an internal tape drive include the integration with the system as a whole and the increased backup performance. Also, if you don't have to back up laptops or other stand-alone workstations, you don't need the additional hassles of connecting external cables and finding a place to plug in an external tape drive (which tend to have very large power supplies integrated into the plug).

Installing Microsoft Backup for Windows

Microsoft has included a tape backup application along with Windows 95 which allows excellent integration with the operating system. This backup software works with most of the QIC-40, QIC-80, and QIC-3010 compatible tape drives on the market. However, Microsoft Backup for Windows won't work with the high-end tape backup solutions such as QIC-3020 or 4mm and 8mm DAT tape backup systems. Although Microsoft Backup for Windows doesn't support these drives, manufacturers will provide Windows backup software which works with their drives (usually for an additional cost).

After you have installed your internal tape backup drive by following the manufacturer's instructions or connected the external tape drive to the parallel port, you are ready to load the backup software. Windows default installation will not load the Microsoft Backup for Windows. However, you can easily install this accessory using the following steps:

1. Click the Start button.
2. Click Settings.
3. Select Control Panel.
4. Select Add/Remove Programs. You see a dialog box with several property sheets like the one shown in figure 27.1.

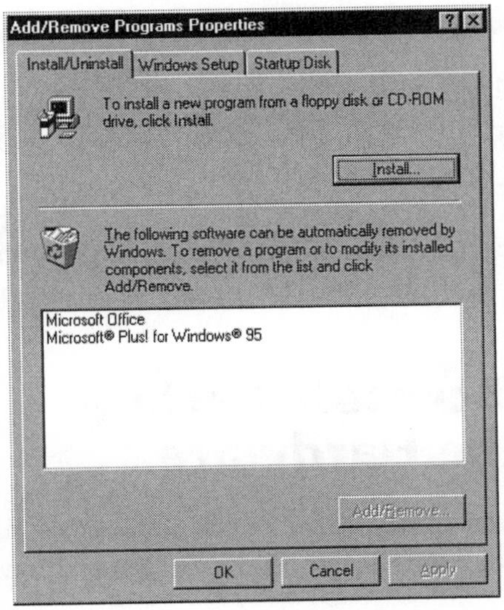

Fig. 27.1
The Add/Remove Programs Wizard enables you to install Microsoft Backup for Windows.

5. Choose the Windows Setup property sheet.
6. Select Disk Tools from the list of components.
7. Click the Details button. This will bring up a list of the default Windows 95 Disk Tools. The tools you have currently installed will be marked with a check, as shown in figure 27.2.

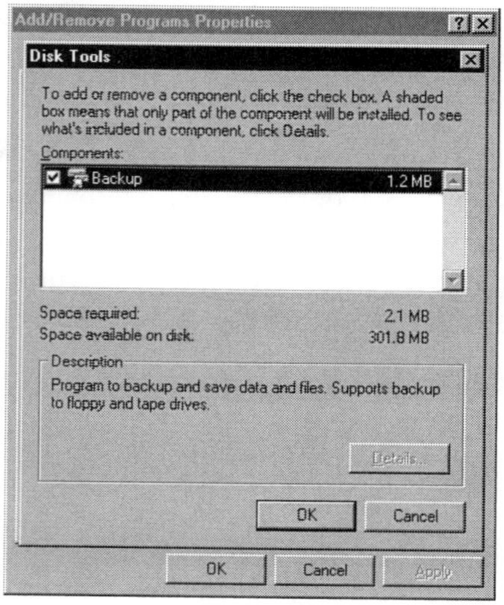

Fig. 27.2
The Disk Tools components currently installed do not include Backup.

8. Check the box next to Backup to mark it for installation.
9. Click the OK button. Windows will prompt you to insert the appropriate diskette or CD-ROM to load the Microsoft Backup for Windows software.

Once the backup software is loaded, you can proceed to the next step by letting Microsoft Backup auto-detect your tape drive system.

Letting Microsoft Backup Detect Tape Hardware

When you run Microsoft Backup for Windows the first time, it will attempt to automatically detect the type of backup system you have. Microsoft

Backup for Windows only supports one of these types of backup systems connected through the floppy disk controller:

- QIC-40
- QIC-80
- QIC-3010
- Colorado Trakker parallel-port backup drives

If your drive type is not listed here, see the next section, "Installing Unsupported Tape Backup Systems."

Once Microsoft Backup for Windows has detected your drive, you may begin backing up your system. You can skip to the section later in this chapter, "Configuring Windows Backup."

Installing Unsupported Tape Backup Systems

Unsupported tape backup systems are only unsupported in terms of Microsoft Backup for Windows. Many vendors have their own backup software which works with their tape backup systems. Some of the systems listed here will not have Windows backup software while others will. Check with your tape drive manufacturer to see if it currently has a Windows 95 backup solution or if its current DOS or Windows backup software will work with Windows 95.

DAT Tape Systems

Many high-capacity systems will use a Digital Audio Tape (DAT) tape backup drive which uses either 4mm or 8mm tape cartridges to store between 2G and 4G of data. While DAT tape systems tend to be more expensive than QIC-based systems, the DAT systems provide significantly more storage capacity per tape.

Most DAT tape backup systems connect to a SCSI interface board in the computer. Windows 95 will be able to detect and install drivers for many SCSI controllers; however, the manufacturer's Windows tape backup software will still be required to perform the backup.

If you are using DOS-based tape backup software, Windows 95 will prompt you with a warning message like the one shown in figure 27.3.

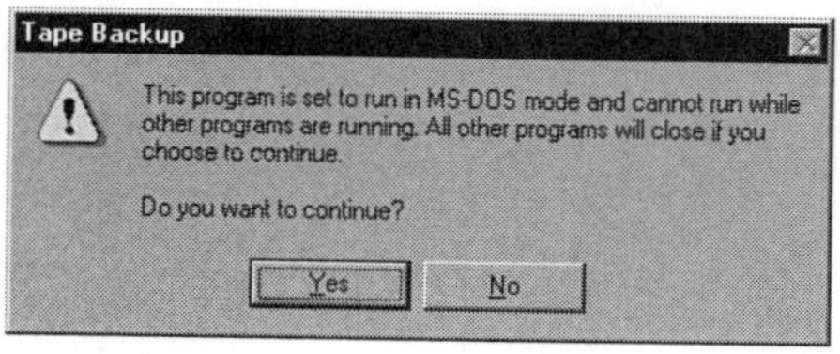

Fig. 27.3
Windows warns you against using older tape backup software within a Command Prompt box in Windows.

In this case, you will need to restart Windows 95 in a command-prompt only mode. This will allow older DOS programs which may communicate directly with the hardware to work properly. After you have completed a backup using DOS backup software, you can reboot your system back to Windows mode.

Additionally, even if your program does run, you will only be able to back up files and directories which match the DOS format FILENAME.EXT naming convention. While Windows 95 does a good job of shortening long directory names like "Data Files" down to `DATAFI[td]1`, you will not be able to restore the original directory to "Data Files" once you have backed it up.

Caution

If you ignore the warnings that Windows presents and run your DOS tape backup software in a Command Prompt box, you may cause Windows to lock up. In the worst case, your software may appear to work properly, but you may actually be losing data as it writes to the tape. If you run your software in this way, you will need to verify every tape you write to ensure that no data has been lost. This is not recommended!

QIC-02 Tape Drives

Many companies have older tape backup hardware which is either in its seventh year of active use or is gathering dust on a shelf in the storage room. In either case, you may want to use such a backup system under Windows 95.

QIC-02 tapes run off of an interface board which is provided with the tape drive unit. These units are typically external, because the drive mechanism is about the size of a lunch box. It's unlikely that Windows 95 will recognize the QIC-02 adapter card in your system, so you should take care to verify that the settings of the tape drive adapter do not interfere with the settings of the other cards installed in your system.

Once you have installed your hardware, you need to run the software which was supplied with the tape drive. Since these units are typically pre-Windows, you will most likely be using DOS backup software. In addition to the fact that the programs were written in DOS, you also want to be aware that the backup programs were written for DOS versions that date back 10 years. The programmers did not have to worry about extended memory management or disk compression software like DriveSpace. Your software may or may not run under the Windows running in command prompt mode.

Additionally, even if your program does run, you will only be able to back up files and directories which match the DOS format FILENAME.EXT naming convention. While Windows 95 does a good job of shortening long directory names like `Data Files` down to `DATAFI[td]1`, you will not be able to restore the original directory to `Data Files` once you have backed it up.

Caution

Using tape backup software built before 1990 may not work, or you may get strange or unexpected results.

Other Tape Drives

Many other tape drives exist which may or may not have Windows backup software available. In all cases, you should contact the manufacturer to see if it has a Windows 95 backup solution for your system. This way, you'll know that your system has been tested with Windows 95. If your manufacturer is not working on a Windows 95 version, ask if it has a Windows 3.1 version which has been tested with Windows 95. Often Windows 3.1 software will work the same under Windows 95.

As the earlier sections on DAT and QIC-02 tape systems mentioned, if you have DOS-based software, run it only in Windows command prompt mode. Also, remember that long file names will be shortened to fit DOS file name structures.

Configuring Windows Backup

Microsoft Backup for Windows can be configured with many options to suit your particular needs. This section will cover the options that correspond with the following:

- Backing up your files to the tape
- Restoring your files from the tape

- Comparing the files on the tape with those on the hard drive
- Backing up your local workstation
- Backing up other workstations on your network

Backup Options

Backing up files to the tape system can be done in several ways. Your backup needs will often determine which option you should choose. Look at the Properties page within Microsoft Backup for Windows to see what these options are. To start Backup, follow these steps:

1. Click the Start button.
2. Choose Programs.
3. Select Accessories.
4. Choose System Tools.
5. Select Backup.

You will see a dialog box which looks like the one shown in figure 27.4.

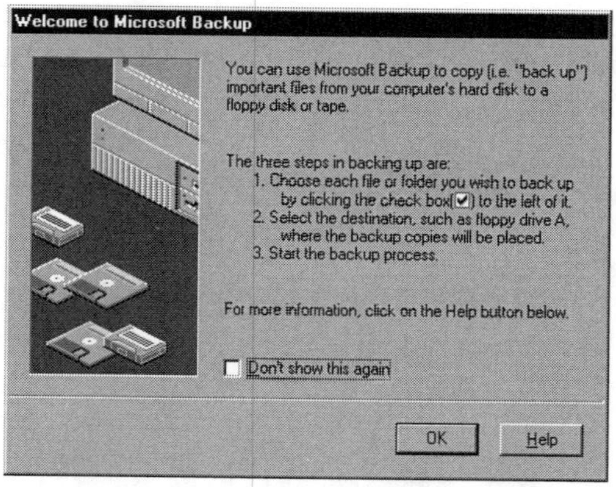

Fig. 27.4
Backup displays a welcome message to instruct you on how to use the program.

This dialog box explains the steps used to select files to be backed up to the tape. Once you read these directions, you may select the Don't Show This Again check box to prevent Windows from displaying the welcome dialog box each time you start Backup.

After you click the OK button to continue running Backup, Windows displays a second dialog box like the one shown in figure 27.5.

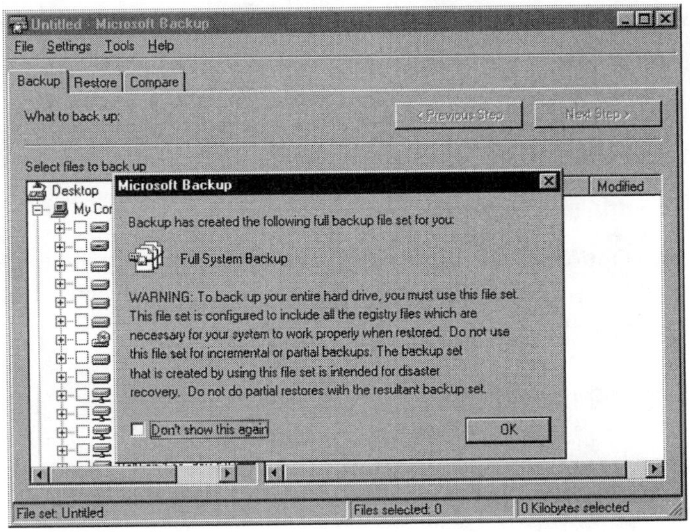

Fig. 27.5
Backup displays a dialog box describing the special backup set which includes Windows registry files.

Registry files include detailed information that holds the configuration data for running Windows. These special files are automatically included in the Full System Backup set which Backup creates for you. You'll find out more about backup sets in "Backup Sets" later in this chapter.

Once Backup has started, you see a screen similar to the one shown in figure 27.6. Notice the three tabs that represent the three operations that Microsoft Backup for Windows can perform.

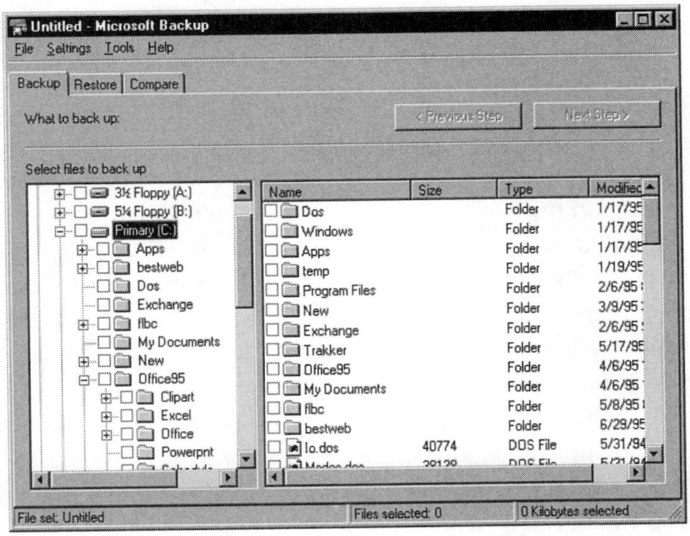

Fig. 27.6
Microsoft Backup for Windows uses the Explorer-style folder display to allow you to choose the files to save to tape.

You'll learn more about the methods for backing up and restoring files later in this chapter in the sections "Backing Up Your Local Workstation," "Backing Up Your Network," and "Restoring Files from Tape." For now, you'll learn about the various options that can affect your backup operations. To view or modify the backup options, follow these steps:

1. Select Settings from the Backup menu bar.
2. Choose Options. You will see a property sheet like the one shown in figure 27.7. The settings on the General property page will not be discussed since these options are straightforward.

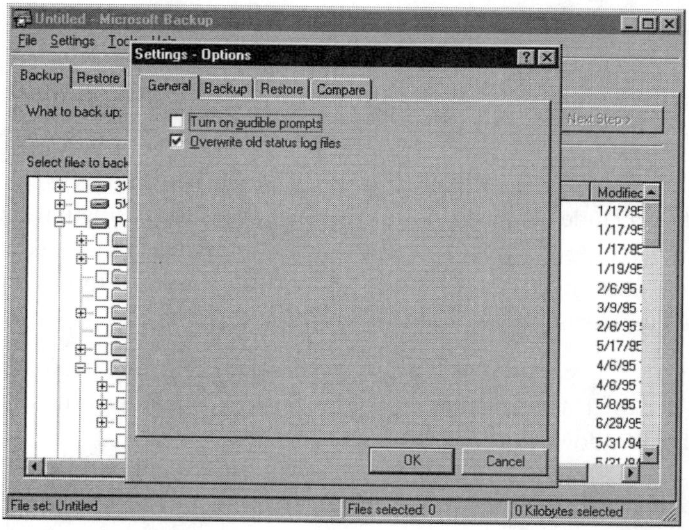

Fig. 27.7
All the settings for Backup can be modified through one of the Options property pages.

3. Select the Backup property page by clicking the Backup tab. This displays the Backup page shown in figure 27.8.

The first setting on the Backup property page describes what you should do after a successful tape backup operation has occurred. Select the Quit Backup After Operation is Finished option if you intend to be running the backup system in an unattended mode. For instance, if your system has 200M to back up, you may want to wait until you are finished using your machine for the day before starting the backup operation. By running Backup with the Quit option selected, Microsoft Backup for Windows will exit after it has finished backing up your system at night. This is also useful if you have a scheduler application like the one found in Microsoft's Plus Pack for Windows 95 which can initiate a backup operation during the evening. After the scheduled backup is finished, the program will exit and allow your computer to continue processing other scheduled jobs.

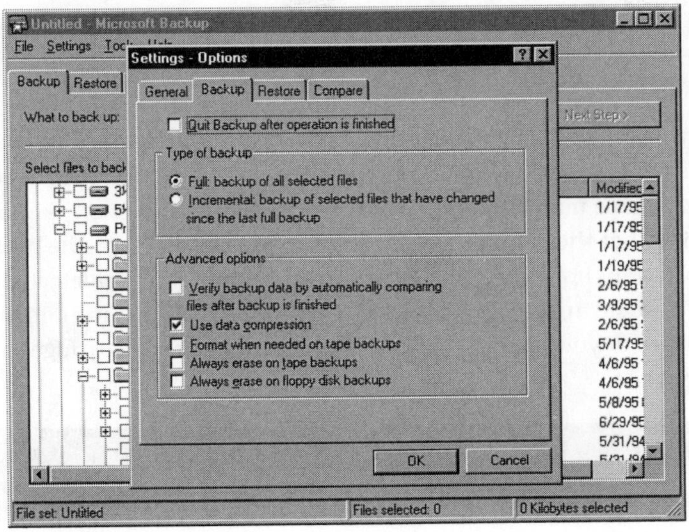

Fig. 27.8
The options listed on the Backup property page can be changed for each backup or left the same for all backups.

The next set of options affect which files will be copied to tape during a backup operation. The two methods are Full and Incremental. A *full backup* is one in which all files are copied to tape regardless if they have changed or not since the last time you backed up your system. This option can take a snapshot of your system as it is right now. An *incremental backup* is one in which only the files that have changed since the last backup operation are copied to tape. This makes the backup go much faster, because few files are changed from week to week under typical circumstances.

Note

Windows keeps track of which files you have modified since the last backup by using the Archive flag on each file. You can see how Windows stores this by right-clicking a file in Explorer and choosing Properties. The Archive check box indicates whether or not the file has been changed since the last backup.

When you perform a full backup, the Archive flag for every file is turned off when it is copied to tape. When you perform an incremental backup, the backup software searches your files for the Archive flag and only copies those files with that flag turned on. After the changed files have been saved on the tape, the Archive flag is turned off.

The last set of Backup options are usually only modified when you have special reason to do so. You can choose from any of the following options in the Advanced Options area:

- *Verify Backup Data by Automatically Comparing Fields After Backup is Finished.* This option is commonly used to make sure that the files copied to the tape match the files on the hard drive. Of course, you would think that they always would, because you just finished the backup operation; however, flaws in the tape media may go undetected when you are saving the files. Select this option if you are uncertain about the quality of your tape media or if you are using a tape cartridge for the first time.

Tip

You should always choose to verify your backups after you have completed a full backup of your system. While it will take twice as long to complete the entire operation, you can rely on the integrity of your system backup.

- *Use Data Compression.* This option enables you to realize the best tape media usage by compressing the files as they are copied to tape. This is how tape manufacturers accomplish the higher storage capacity (usually double the uncompressed capacity) which they advertise for their tape drive systems.

Caution

Data compression can only be estimated over a broad range of file types. For average users, this will approximate the 2:1 compression that most tape system manufacturers advertise. However, you may not get a high compression ratio if you back up these types of files:

- Graphics files with the GIF or JPEG formats
- Compressed archives like ZIP, LZH, PAK, and ARJ files
- Large numbers of EXE files

- *Format When Needed on Tape Backups.* If Microsoft Backup for Windows detects a new or damaged tape to which you are attempting to copy files, Backup will automatically format the tape before it starts the backup operation if you select this option. This option is useful for unattended or scheduled tape backups; however, a tape format operation could take many hours to perform in addition to the backup process.

- *Always Erase on Tape Backups*. The default operation for Backup is to append new backup sets to the end of those already on a tape. If you are going to be using a set of tapes regularly for periodic full backups, you may want to select this option to erase the tape before it starts the backup of the new data.
- *Always Erase on Floppy Disk Backups*. This option is similar to the previous one, but concerns backups to disks rather than to tapes.

Once you have selected the options for your backup, click OK to save your settings.

Restore Options

This section discusses the options that are used for restoring files which have previously been copied to a tape backup set. To access the Restore option settings, follow these steps:

1. Select Settings from the Backup menu bar.
2. Choose Options.
3. Select the Restore page from the Options property sheet by clicking the Restore tab. This will display the Restore property page similar to the one shown in figure 27.9.

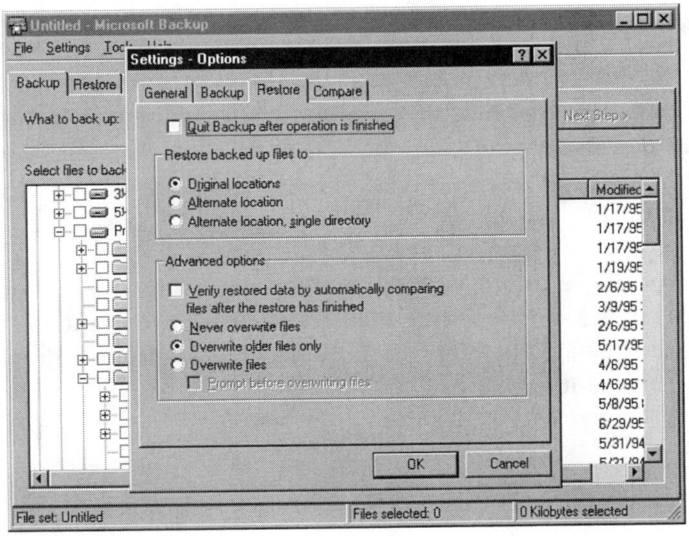

Fig. 27.9
The Restore options affect how your files are copied back to your hard drive from the backup tapes.

The first option is similar to the Quit Backup option explained in the Backup Options section. If you are restoring a large number of files or are running an unattended restore operation, you may want to select the Quit Backup After Operation is Finished option to exit Backup when the files have been restored.

The next set of options configures where restored files will be saved to when they are retrieved from the tape backup. Usually, you will be restoring to the Original Locations because that is where the files came from. However, you may want to choose an Alternate Location if you want to check the differences between a current file on your hard disk and one which was backed up on to tape. Instead of overwriting the current file, you can simply specify that the file be restored somewhere else.

The Alternate Location, Single Directory option will restore all of your files from the backup set into one directory. This will ignore any directory structure that you have saved to tape and only restore the files from those directories. If you have files of the same name in more than one directory, these files will be overwritten as the next file of the same name is restored from tape. Unless you have a specific need to do this, you'll want to stick with the Alternate Location option to avoid overwriting any files that you restore.

The Advanced Options area involves the verification of the restored data. To check that the file which was saved to your hard drive matches the file on the backup tape, select the Verify option. You probably won't need to use this option unless you are uncertain that the hard drive to which you are restoring the files from tape is saving the data properly. The remaining options specify how to handle files that may already exist on the hard drive that the tape backup wants to replace:

- *Never Overwrite Files*. This option allows you to protect any data that you have on your hard drive from being overwritten by the files being restored from tape.

- *Overwrite Older Files Only*. This option overwrites files on your hard drive only if they are older than the files which are being restored from tape.

- *Overwrite Files*. Along with this option, you should also select the Prompt Before Overwriting Files setting. This will prevent you from accidentally losing information if a file on the tape overwrites one you did not want to overwrite.

Compare Options

The options on the Compare property sheet are similar to both the Backup and Restore options previously explained. It's unlikely that you will need to change the Compare options unless you are performing specific tasks, such as unattended tape backup comparisons.

Backup Sets

In most cases, you will perform routine backups on either your entire hard drive or on certain data files. When backing up your data files, it is useful to create a backup set which maintains a list of folders to back up to tape. Instead of choosing several data directories (which may be on multiple drives) every time you want to back them up, you can create a backup set to automate the backup.

Tip

Using backup sets may also help you with your backup routine. By creating a standard backup set for your files, it will be easier to maintain a schedule for saving your files to tape. Running an incremental backup of your files each night could be named "Daily Backup." When you open the Backup application, all you need to do is open your Daily Backup set and let the system do the work.

To create a backup set, follow these steps:

1. Select the folders and files you want to back up.
2. Click the Next Step button.
3. Select the tape drive as the destination for your files.
4. Choose File, Save As.
5. Type a Backup Set name which describes the files which you are backing up.

   Note

   Be descriptive when naming files. For example, if you have a data folder named "Accounting Data," you may want to name your set **Accounting Data - Full Backup** if you are performing a full backup. Try to avoid set names like "Data," "Tape Backup," "Stuff," or "Files" since these are not very descriptive.

6. Click OK to save your backup set.

Any settings you have changed for the Backup or Restore options will be saved with your backup set.

Troubleshooting

I can't see the tape drive from within Microsoft Backup for Windows.

You may not be using a supported tape drive unit. Microsoft Backup for Windows only supports QIC-40, QIC-80, QIC-3010, and Trakker parallel-port backup systems. If you have some other tape drive, you need to use the manufacturer's backup software.

Backing Up Your Local Workstation

The procedure to back up the files and folders on your workstation is easy. Follow these steps:

1. Select the folders and files you want to back up by placing a check in the box next to the folder or file.
2. Click the Next Step button when you have all of the folders and files selected.
3. Choose a backup media from the drives shown in the Select a Destination for a Backup list. Typically, this will be the tape drive system; however, you can back up to floppy disks, other hard drives, or network drives.
4. Click the Start Backup button.
5. You will be prompted for a backup set label that will identify this set of files on the tape. Type a label for the backup and click OK.

Tip

Use a descriptive title for your individual tape backup sets. Don't simply type Files. Type a title such as Full Accounting Data Backup 8/25/95. The more descriptive you are, the easier it will be for you or someone else to find the right files should they need to be restored.

6. If you want to protect your tape backup set from being restored by someone else, click the Password Protect button, which displays a dialog box in which you can type a password. Choose a password you will remember that is not the name of a family member, the name of your

dog, or some other password which could be easily guessed. A password that includes both numbers and letters is more secure than one which has only letters or only numbers.

Microsoft Backup for Windows now begins to store your selected files to the tape. You see a dialog box similar to the one shown in figure 27.10.

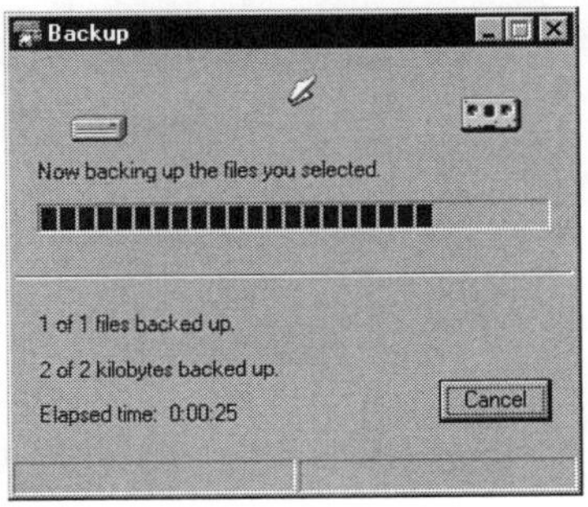

Fig. 27.10
Microsoft Backup for Windows shows the progress of your backup using a graphical display.

When choosing to back up your local workstation, you should set up a rotation of tapes to handle both full system backups as well as incremental file backups. A full system backup might occur only once per month or possibly as frequently as once per week. Incremental file backups can occur either weekly (if you are performing full backups monthly) or daily (if your full backups are performed weekly).

The frequency of your backups will depend on the usage of your machine to store data. If you store most of your data on a network server which is backed up by a computer operations staff, you may find that your backups can occur quarterly. If you store your company's critical data on your computer, you may find that daily backups are essential. In either case, it is important that you actually do the backups when you've planned them.

Tip

You should have at least a full system backup performed twice a year. Even if you don't think your files change much in that time period, you will want to have a backup in case of emergencies.

You don't need to back up applications as frequently as the data files that you use on a day-to-day basis. Because applications can readily be reinstalled from the original disks or CD-ROMs, you should be most concerned about saving your data files which may be difficult to reconstruct if you lose them. Additionally, backing up your applications will take a long time and a lot of room on your tape.

Tip

If you have not already done so, you should create a special folder called DATA in which you create all of your data files. Not only will this make finding your data easier, but it will also make the job of backing it up all that much easier.

Backing Up Your Network

If your computer is used as a server for other Windows workstations, or if you want to centralize the backup operations for all of the workstations in your workgroup, you will want to set up a procedure for backing up your network. Microsoft Backup for Windows can back up other workstations on the network if the computer with the tape backup drive can access the data on the other systems. You may want to set up some policies (either formally or informally) to ensure that network data can be accessed for backup during the specified times. It could even be as simple as keeping the Read-Only share password on everyone's local hard drive the same so that the person performing the backup can access the data to be saved to the tape.

You should decide on a schedule for when the backups occur. Ideally, it should happen after business hours when network traffic is light and the computers are not being used. If you plan on scheduling an after-hours backup, you may want to invest in the Microsoft Plus! Companion for Windows 95 which includes a scheduling application. This way, your backups can be run unattended.

If your network data does not fit on one tape, however, you may need to switch tapes when they fill up. If you suspect that your network backups will fill up more than one tape, you may want to stagger which workstations are backed up each night or consider purchasing a larger tape backup system to handle the larger volume of data.

Troubleshooting

The tape system I use is supposed to hold 250M on a tape, but sometimes I can only get 150M on one tape. Why?

The tape drive manufacturers often inflate their capacity claims to match an estimated 2:1 compression ratio. Your tape probably can only hold 120M of uncompressed data. If you are experiencing less than a 2:1 compression ratio with the particular files you are backing up, your actual tape capacity is less.

I can't schedule a backup to happen at night using Microsoft Backup for Windows. Why not?

Microsoft Backup for Windows does not directly support a scheduled backup. You may want to purchase another tape backup software package which does, or buy the Microsoft Plus! Companion for Windows 95 which contains a scheduling program.

You will also want to create a backup set that includes the data directories of the computers on your network. A backup set is essential if you are performing unattended backups and are extremely helpful even if you manually start the backup operation before you leave work.

Caution

If someone is using a file on the network or the file is left open during a network backup, that file will not be saved to tape, because the contents of that file are not accessible to another user while the file is open.

You will probably not want to make a full system backup of every computer on the network. It would be much wiser to make individual full system backups which you can easily identify should a problem occur. Your schedule should be a weekly backup of all the data files and a daily backup of only the changed data files. You should at least have one tape for each day of the week and two tapes for alternating full backups. Make sure you buy enough tapes to handle this sort of rotation.

Tip

Try to elect (or appoint) someone to maintain the backup rotation for your network. This person may be you, if your computer hosts the tape backup system.

Caution

Do not store all of your backup tapes near your computers. If you have a fire and all the tapes are destroyed, what good is your backup system? Keep at least the alternating weekly data backups offsite. If that means you bring them home with you, then do it. You may save your company by performing this simple procedure.

Restoring Files from Tape

Once you have successfully backed up your files, there may come a time when you need to restore them from your tape. To restore folders or files from a tape, follow these steps from within the Microsoft Backup for Windows application:

1. Click the Restore tab.
2. Insert the tape containing your files to be restored into your tape drive.
3. Choose the tape drive as the source from which you will be restoring.
4. Choose the backup set which contains the data you want to restore.
5. Click the Next Step button.
6. Select the folders or files you want to restore by placing a check next to the item.
7. Click the Start Restore button to begin restoring the data.

Refer to the section earlier in this chapter, "Restore Options," for more information on settings you may want to alter when restoring data. ❖

Chapter 28

Configuring Modems

by Sue Plumley

A modem converts computer signals to telephone signals and back again so that you can use the telephone lines to communicate with other computers. Use a modem to send and receive e-mail, faxes, and files to any other computer with a modem. Also, you can use your modem to connect to online services like America Online and CompuServe, even the Internet. Windows 95 includes various programs you can use with a modem, including HyperTerminal, Microsoft Fax, Phone Dialer, and The Microsoft Network.

Windows can autodetect and install any of hundreds of modems by use of the Modem Wizard. Alternatively, Windows enables you to install your modem manually by choosing the manufacturer and model from a list.

In this chapter, you learn to do the following:

- Choose a modem
- Use the wizard to configure your modem
- Manually configure your modem
- Modify modem settings
- Troubleshoot modem installation and use

Choosing a Modem

You can choose from numerous modems, and the one you choose governs how fast your computer communicates over the phone lines. You'll really notice the speed of your modem when you're transferring large files to or from another computer. The faster your modem, the more efficiently the data transfers.

Note

A device that converts from digital (computer signals) to analog (telephone signals) is called a *modulator*; a device that converts from analog to digital is called a *demodulator*. *Mo*(dulator)-*dem*(odulator) is how *modem* got its name.

The speed of a modem is measured in bits per second (bps). Make sure that you get the fastest available; today's maximum modem speed is 28,800 bps. Slower modem speeds are 14,400, 9,600, and 2,400 bps. A 14,400 bps modem is also acceptable, but don't use anything slower, or you'll be disappointed with your communications.

The two communicating modems must communicate using the same speeds. If your modem, for example, is 28,800 bps and the modem on the other end of the phone lines is only 14,400 bps, your modem slows down to 14,400 to accommodate the other modem.

Tip

When deciding whether to use an internal or external modem, an internal modem is generally less expensive and takes up less space on the Desktop than the external.

Installing Your Modem

Windows includes a wizard that can detect a modem you've added to your system and identify the port, install the appropriate driver, and identify the modem speed. You can let the wizard configure your modem, or you can manually configure your modem.

Install your modem by first turning off your computer and then attaching the cables to the internal or external modem and attaching the phone line. When you're finished, turn on the modem and restart the computer.

Letting Windows AutoDetect the Modem

When you use the Modem Wizard to identify your modem, Windows queries the attached modem and ascertains the port, speed, and driver needed for the modem. Windows asks you to confirm its findings and then sets up the modem for you.

To use the Windows wizard to set up your modem, follow these steps:

1. Open the Control Panel and double-click the Modems icon. The Install New Modem dialog box appears (see fig. 28.1).

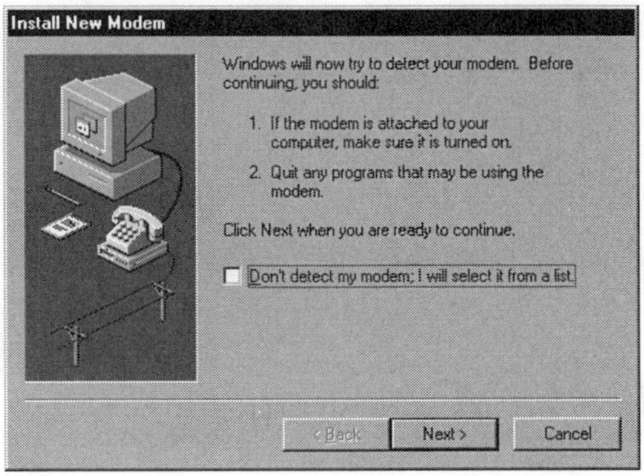

Fig. 28.1
After attaching your modem to your computer, you can use the Modem Wizard to configure the modem for you.

2. Click the Next button to tell Windows to begin checking for your modem. The second wizard dialog box appears (see fig. 28.2).

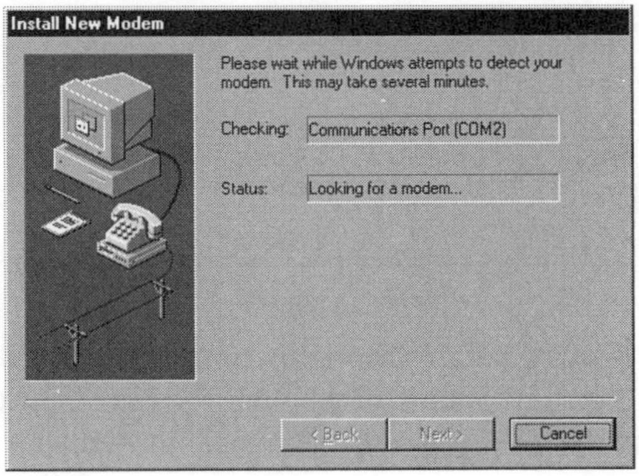

Fig. 28.2
The wizard searches for your modem and identifies the port to which it's connected.

3. When the wizard finishes querying the modem, it displays the Verify Modem dialog box (see fig. 28.3). If the modem is the correct one, choose Next; if you want to change the modem, choose the Change button and then refer to the next section, "Manually Specifying a Modem."

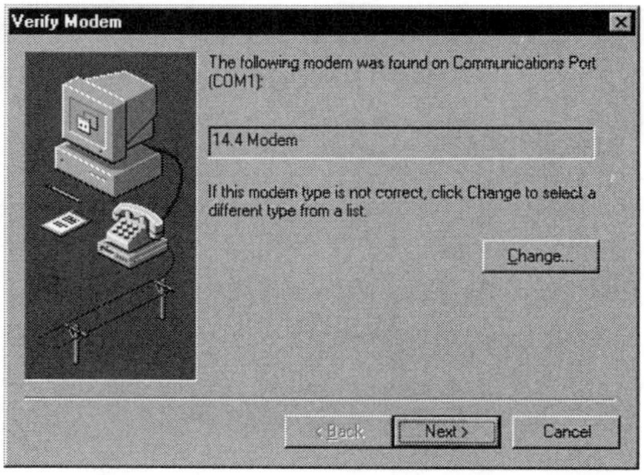

Fig. 28.3
You can accept or change the modem that Windows identifies.

4. Windows sets up your modem and then displays the last wizard dialog box (see fig. 28.4). Choose Finish to close the dialog box.

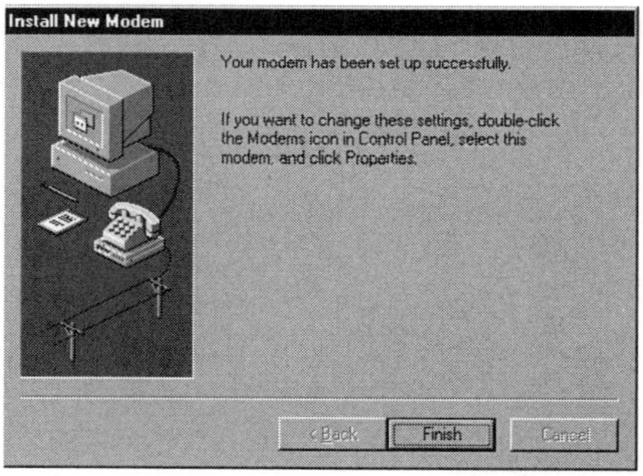

Fig. 28.4
Windows sets up the modem for you automatically.

5. When the Modem Wizard dialog box closes, Windows displays the Modems Properties dialog box in which you can adjust the modem's settings and troubleshoot modem problems. Choose OK to close the dialog box.

Manually Specifying a Modem

If you prefer, you can identify your modem instead of letting Windows detect it. You might for example, want to use the manufacturer's driver with your modem instead of one supplied by Windows. Windows enables you to specify both the manufacturer and the modem type, as well as install the driver from a disk.

To manually specify your modem, follow these steps:

1. Open the Control Panel and double-click the Modems icon. The Install New Modem dialog box appears (refer to fig. 28.1).

2. Choose the option Don't Detect My Modem; I Will Select It from a List and then choose Next. The second wizard dialog box appears (see fig. 28.5).

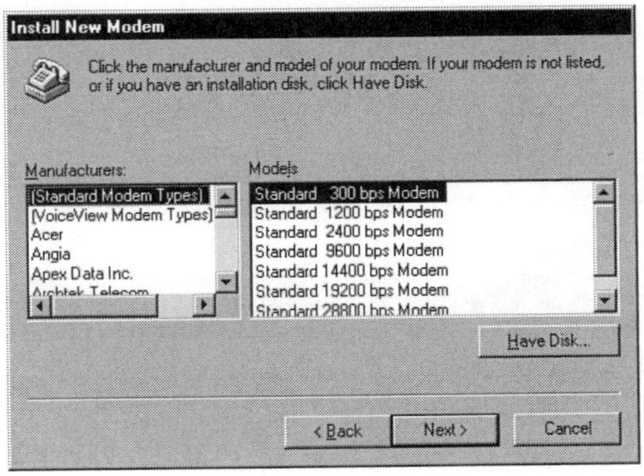

Fig. 28.5
You can choose the manufacturer and model of your modem in this wizard dialog box.

3. In Manufacturers, choose the maker of your modem. In Models, choose the appropriate model of your modem.

   If you do not see the manufacturer or if you want to load the driver from a disk, choose Have Disk. The Install From Disk dialog box appears. Enter the drive letter in the text box and choose OK. Windows installs the driver from the specified disk.

4. Click Next to continue installing the modem. Windows displays the next wizard dialog box (see fig. 28.6).

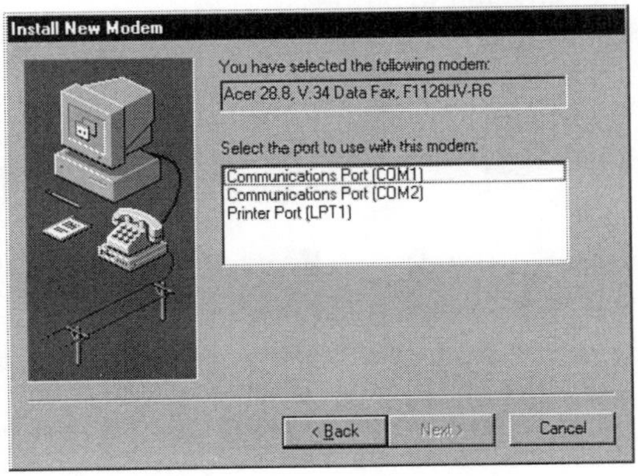

Fig. 28.6
Choose the port the modem is attached to and check to make sure that you've selected the correct modem.

Tip

If you make a mistake in a selection in any wizard dialog box, choose the Back button and try again.

5. Select the port you want to use with the modem. Click the Next button. Windows installs the modem.

6. When it's done, Windows displays the last wizard dialog box telling you that the installation was successful. Choose Finish to close the dialog box. Windows displays the Modems Properties dialog box in which you can adjust the modem's settings and troubleshoot modem problems. Choose OK to close the dialog box.

Caution

Windows lets you set up any type of modem and assign any port to that modem, regardless of whether it's right. If you assign the wrong port or model, the modem does not work when you're ready to use it. If you are unsure of the port or the modem model, let Windows autodetect the modem for you, as described in the preceding section.

Modifying Modem Properties

You can adjust the modem settings at any time after you install your modem. You might want to change ports, adjust the speaker volume, or change the designated speed. Additionally, you can set the modem for specific dialing preferences, change the location from which you're dialing, set up the modem to use a calling card, and so on.

Finally, you can adjust the advanced connections settings, such as flow control, error control, modulation type, and so on.

Note

You can also configure an installed fax modem to share with others on a network, such as The Microsoft Network or a Novell NetWare network.

Modifying Dialing Properties

Use the Dialing Properties sheet to modify how calls are dialed and to set such options as dialing with a calling card, specifying various locations from which to call, and using tone or pulse dialing.

▶ See "Installing Shared Fax Modems," p. 655

To modify dialing properties, follow these steps:

1. Open the Control Panel and double-click the Modems icon. The Modems Properties sheet appears (see fig. 28.7).

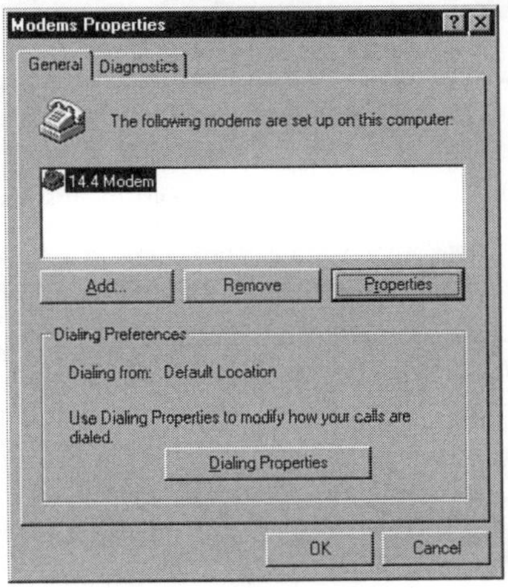

Fig. 28.7
Adjust modem and port settings in the Modems Properties sheet.

2. To set dialing preferences, choose the Dialing Properties button in the General page of the Modems Properties sheet. The Dialing Properties sheet appears (see fig. 28.8).

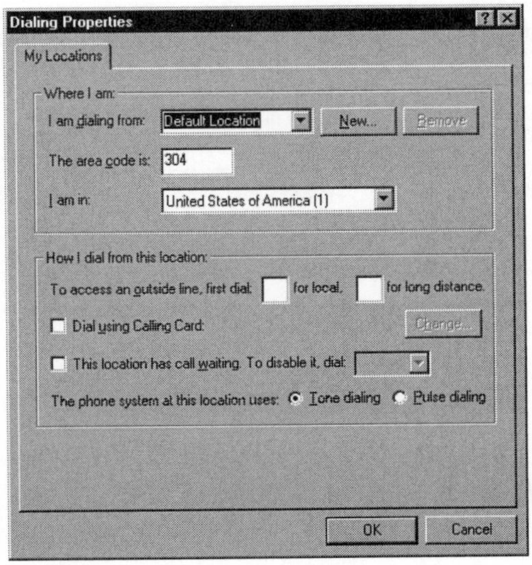

Fig. 28.8
Customize the dialing properties to suit your needs.

3. Enter information and/or choose options as described in table 28.1.

Tip

The dialing properties you define apply to any program from which you dial on the computer.

Table 28.1 Dialing Properties

Option	Description
Where I Am area	
I Am Dialing From	Choose from the list the first location you want to set up. To set up a new location, choose New and enter a location name in the Create New Location dialog box; choose OK. To remove a location, select it from the list and choose Remove.
The Area Code Is	Enter the area code you are dialing from.
I Am In	Choose the country you're in from the drop-down list.
How I Dial From This Location area	
To Access an Outside Line, First Dial	Enter the number for local and/or the number for long distance in the appropriate text boxes; if you do not need to access an outside line, leave these text boxes blank.
Dial Using Calling Card	Select to display the Calling Card dialog box: enter one or more calling card names and numbers. Choose Advanced to enter specific rules for your calling card, such as dialable digits, area code, pauses, second dial tone, and so on.
This Location has Call Waiting	Check if you have call waiting.
To Disable it, Dial	Enter code to disable call waiting.
The Phone System at This Location Uses	Choose either Tone dialing or Pulse dialing.

4. Choose OK to close the Dialing Properties sheet.

Troubleshooting

I can hear the modem sending tones as it dials but nothing happens afterward.

Check the telephone cables to be sure that they're properly connected to the modem and to the wall jack. Verify the modem is dialing with pulses or tone by checking the Dialing Properties sheet.

Modifying Your Modem's Properties

You can have more than one modem attached to your computer, and you can choose each modem and modify its specific properties. Each modem's property sheet may contain slightly different options, but the following example gives you an idea of the options you can modify.

To modify a specific modem's properties, follow these steps:

1. In the Modems Properties sheet, select the specific modem you want to modify and choose the Properties button. The modem's Properties sheet appears (see fig. 28.9).

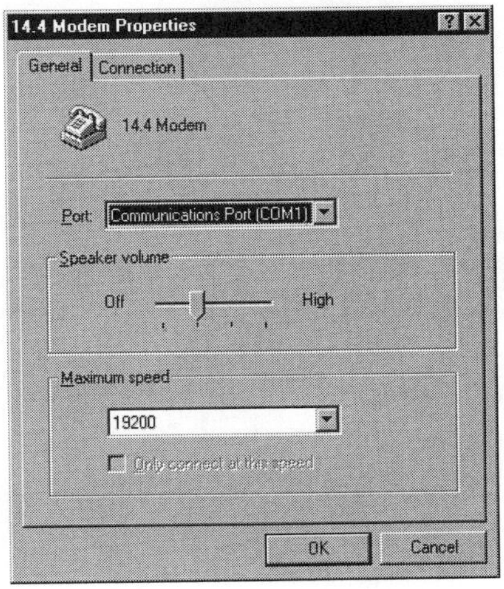

Fig. 28.9
Set the properties of your specific modem in the modem's Properties sheet.

2. On the General page, set your choices for the following options:

   - *Port*. Select the serial port to which your modem is connected.

   - *Speaker Volume*. Adjust the speaker volume for the modem between Off and High.

- *Maximum Speed.* Set the maximum speed your modem can connect with; your modem will connect at that speed and all speeds less than the set speed.

- *Only Connect at This Speed.* Choose this option to limit the modem from connecting at any speed other than the specified one.

3. On the Connection page, choose the options you want to modify (see fig. 28.10). Table 28.2 describes the options on the Connection page.

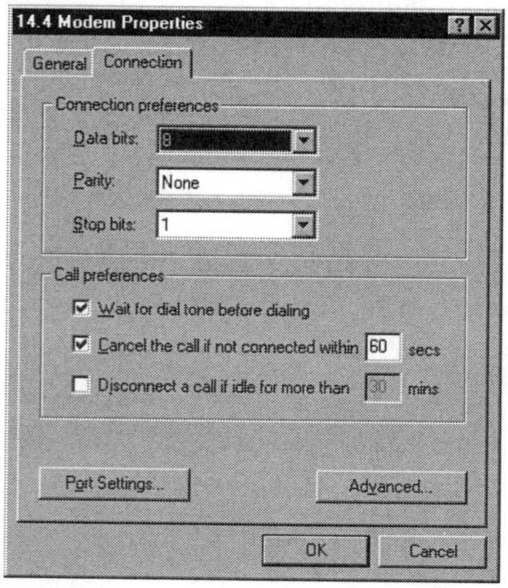

Fig. 28.10
Set preferences for your connection and dialing for your specific modem.

Tip

See the following section for information on port and other advanced settings.

4. Choose OK to close the specific modem's Properties sheet. Choose Close to close the Modem Properties sheet.

Table 28.2 Connection Preferences

Option	Description
Connection Preferences area	
Data Bits	Set the number of data bits—each data character consists of seven or eight bits—specified for your modem.
Parity	Set *parity*—a formula for adding a bit to each byte before sending in data communications—to None, Even, Odd, Mark, or Space.
Stop Bits	Set *stop bits*—the last bit in a set of data—specified for your modem.
Call Preferences area	
Wait for Dial Tone Before Dialing	Choose this option unless you must manually dial the phone for the modem.
Cancel the Call if Not Connected Within _ Secs	Check this option and enter an amount of time for the modem to continue trying to connect before disconnecting.
Disconnect a Call if Idle for More Than _ Mins	Check this option to hang up the phone if there's no activity within the specified amount of time.

Modifying Advanced Settings

Windows enables you to modify specific settings for your modem so that you can control the flow of data between your modem and your computer, and between your modem and the modem with which you're communicating. If you have a question about any advanced settings, refer to your modem's documentation. Not all modems support all the following controls.

Port Settings

If data sent from the computer to the modem is transferred faster than the modem can move it across the line to the other modem, the FIFO data buffers (in conjunction with flow control) keep information from being lost. Adjust buffers in the Advanced Port Settings window.

To change advanced port settings, follow these steps:

1. In the Control Panel, double-click the Modems icon to open the Modems Properties sheet.

2. On the General page, choose the modem from the list and select Properties. The selected modem's Properties sheet appears (refer to fig. 28.9).

3. On the Connection page, select the Port Settings button. The Advanced Port Settings window appears (see fig. 28.11).

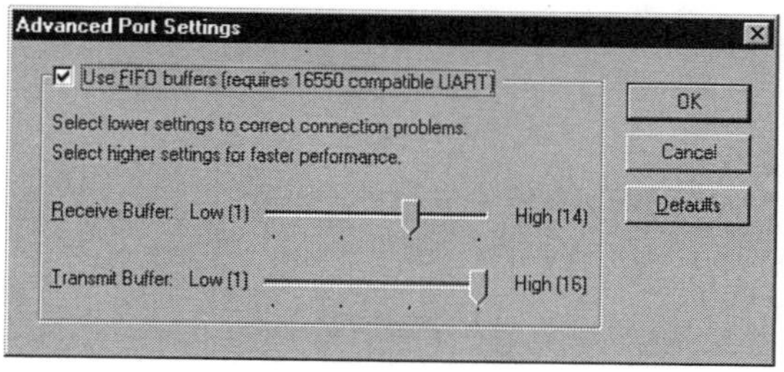

Fig. 28.11
Set the FIFO (First In First Out) buffers for the modem's port.

4. Deselect the Use FIFO Buffers option to disable it.

   If the option is enabled, adjust the settings for Receive and Transmit Buffers.

5. Choose OK to close the window and choose OK again to close the modem's Properties sheet.

Troubleshooting

My modem connects with the remote modem but locks up.

Make sure that you are using the proper modem-to-computer flow control and error control for your modem (click the Advanced button on the Connection page of the specific modem's Properties sheet).

My modem disconnects while online.

Check for loose connections between the modem and the computer, and between the modem and the telephone line. Alternatively, line noise or interference may be the problem; try the connection again with a different phone line or at a different time.

Advanced Connection Settings

The Advanced Connection Settings govern the use of error, flow, and modulation control. *Error controls* ensure accurate data transmission; corrupted data sent across the line is automatically detected and retransmitted. If your modem supports error control, you can also choose to compress the transmitted data, which compacts the data before sending it across the lines. The receiving modem then decompresses the data before sending it to the computer. Compressed data travels faster and more efficiently over telephone lines.

Flow control designates the protocol used between your computer and the modem. The flow defines how fast the data can be transferred between your modem and computer. The protocol you choose must be compatible with your modem, the cable, and your computer. Check your modem documentation for more information.

To change advanced connection settings, follow these steps:

1. In the Control Panel, double-click the Modems icon to open the Modems Properties sheet.

2. On the General page, choose the modem from the list and select Properties. The selected modem's Properties sheet appears (refer to fig. 28.9).

3. On the Connection page, click the Advanced button. The Advanced Connection Settings window appears (see fig. 28.12).

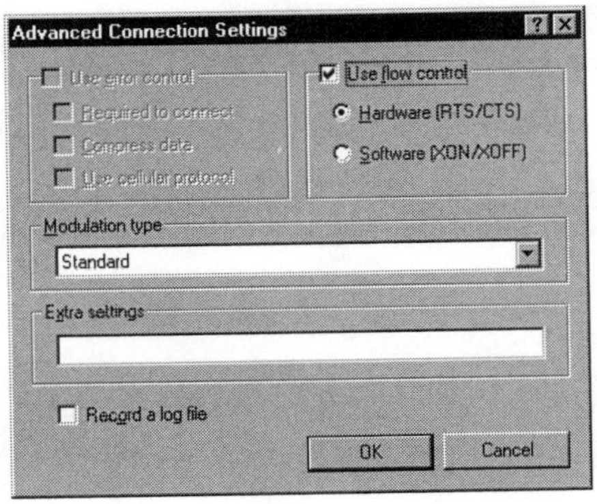

Fig. 28.12 Set advanced settings such as flow control and modulation type.

4. Modify the options as described in the following list:

   ■ *Use Error Control.* Choose to activate or deactivate error control of the transmissions. If you deactivate this option, your data may not be reliably transferred.

- *Use Flow Control.* Specifies the protocol used to control the flow of data between the modem and your computer.
- *Modulation Type.* Specifies the modulation type compatible with both your modem and the modem you're connecting with. Standard works in most cases; however, if you're having trouble connecting, try the nonstandard modulation type.
- *Extra Settings.* Enter additional initialization settings necessary for use of your modem.
- *Record a Log File.* Records your calls, errors, and so on in a file named MODEMLOG.TXT in the Windows folder. Use to monitor calls and problems.

Tip

If you're unsure of any of the settings in the Advanced Connection Settings, refer to your modem's documentation.

5. Choose OK to close the Advanced Connection Settings window; choose OK again to close the modem's Properties sheet. To close the Modems Properties sheet, choose OK.

Troubleshooting

I hear the call being answered at the other end, but there's no tone indicating a connection.

The modem on the other end of the line is not working correctly, or there is no modem there.

After connection, I see many data errors on the screen.

Make sure that no one else is using the telephone line. Try calling the other modem again at another time or from a different phone line to get a better connection.

My modem cannot sign on to the remote modem.

Check the communication parameters of the remote station and make sure that your software is configured for the same number of data bits, stop bits, and parity. (See the Connection page of the specific modem's Properties sheet.)

Troubleshooting Modems

You can fix many common modem and connection problems yourself. Additionally, Windows includes a diagnostic tool that can help you identify your modem's connection, driver, speed, and so on.

The first things you should check when you have a modem problem may sound simple, but can save you a lot of time and energy. Check to make sure that the modem is plugged in and connected to the phone line and that the phone line is connected in the wall jack. If the modem is external, make sure that it's turned on.

Make sure that you're using a modem cable—a straight-through cable that connects the computer's pin 1 to the modem's pin 1. Check the phone number and area code you're dialing. Finally, check the dialing properties, port, data bits, parity, stop bits, and so on to make sure that all settings are correct for your modem.

Using Diagnostics

Windows includes a Diagnostics tab in the Modems Properties sheet that you can use to help you identify your modem's connections and to find errors.

To use Windows' Diagnostics, follow these steps:

1. In the Control Panel, double-click the Modems icon. The Modems Properties sheet appears.
2. Choose the Diagnostics page. Figure 28.13 shows the Diagnostics page.

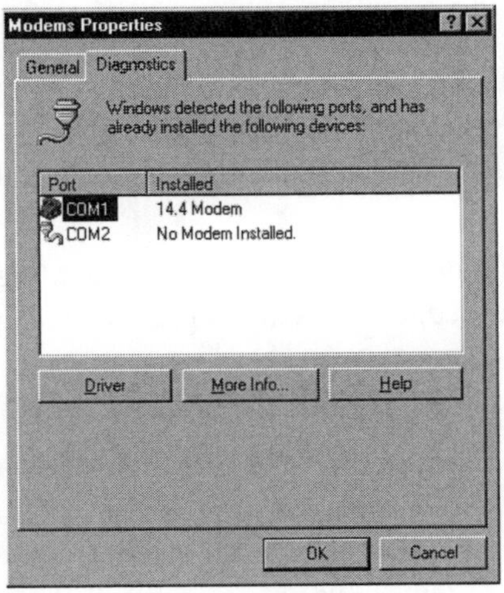

Fig. 28.13
Use Windows' Diagnostics to identify your modem's driver, port, interrupt, address, and so on.

3. Select your modem in the Port list and choose the Driver button. Windows displays a dialog box similar to the one in figure 28.14.

Fig. 28.14 The Current Communications Driver dialog box describes the driver you're using for the modem.

4. Note the size, date, and time the driver was loaded. Installing a more recent or updated driver may solve your problem. Choose OK to close the dialog box.

5. Click the More Info button. Windows displays a Please Wait message box while it checks your modem. Then it displays the More Info dialog box (see fig. 28.15).

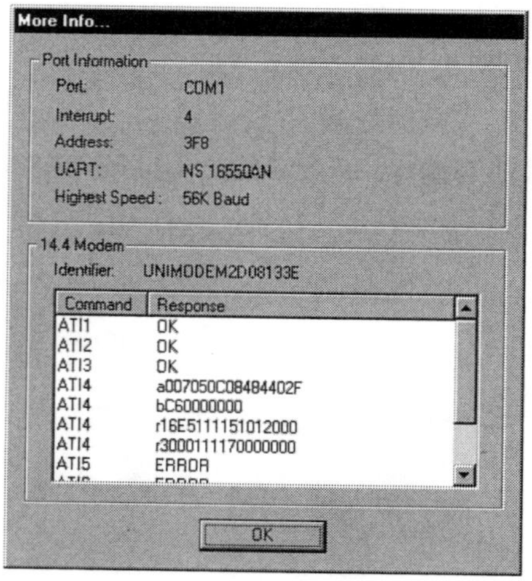

Fig. 28.15 Diagnostics checks your modem and communications port and reports the results in the More Info dialog box.

6. The following text describes the options in the More Info dialog box. When you're finished, choose OK to close the dialog box.

Port Information Area

In the Port Information area of the More Info dialog box, the Port lists the port to which your modem is attached (most always a serial port, such as COM1, COM2, and so on). Although PC architecture allows for as many as four COM ports, most systems have only two installed.

When the serial port is installed to the system, it's configured to use specific interrupts and I/O (Input/Output) addresses. An interrupt, or Interrupt Request (IRQ) line, enables access to the device; the I/O address is the port the modem uses to connect to the computer.

The standard IRQs and I/O addresses for the serial (COM) ports are as follows:

Port	Interrupt	Address
COM1	IRQ4	03F8
COM2	IRQ3	02F8
COM3	IRQ4	03E8
COM4	IRQ3	02E8

Because no two devices can use the same COM port, a conflict may arise if, for example, your mouse and your modem are assigned to the same port. Carefully read the documentation before installing any new hardware. You might even keep a list of addresses and IRQs you've already assigned to keep conflicts to a minimum.

If your modem is not working and you suspect there's an IRQ conflict, remove one of the devices, such as the mouse, and see if the modem works. If the modem does work, the two devices were conflicting in interrupt or address.

Tip

You can use Microsoft Diagnostics (MSD), a program supplied with Windows, or purchase other diagnostic software programs that identify available IRQ lines and create a template detailing your communication channels.

The UART (Universal Asynchronous Receiver/Transmitter) chip controls breaking parallel data in the computer into serial format and then converting the data back again. A 16550A UART serial chip or higher is best suited for high-speed communications. If your UART is 8250, 8250A or B, or 16450, your problems could be coming from the slower chip. Lockups, slow communications, or inaccurate data could be caused by the UART chip. Additionally, the 16550 UART had a few bugs in the buffer area; the 16550A UART corrected these problems.

Highest Speed refers to the baud rate of the modem. *Baud rate* is the rate at which a signal between two devices changes in one second. Most modems transmit several bits per baud so the actual baud rate is much slower than the bits per second rate. Use the highest speed listed in the More Info dialog box when your communication between modems is slow. If your modem speed is 14400, for example, and the highest speed listed in the More Info dialog box is 56K, you know your port is fast enough to handle the modem speed, and the problem is more likely with the line connecting the two modems.

Modem Area

The Modem area of the More Info dialog box contains an area specific to your modem. Diagnostics runs AT (ATtention) commands to test the connection to your modem and then lists the response next to the command.

If you see an ERROR code listed in the Response window, something may be wrong with your modem. The command ATI2, for example, performs a checksum on firmware and as a response either returns OK or ERROR. Alternatively, an ERROR code can be returned for a command that is not applicable to your modem. For information about your modem's response to AT commands, see your modem's documentation.

Tip

Commands beginning with a plus sign (+) and an F designate a fax AT command.

Troubleshooting

My modem won't dial.

Check the hardware for loose cables and the communications software for proper configuration. If your modem is hooked to COM2, make sure that your software is looking for it on COM2.

Note

Windows includes a Modem Troubleshooter you can use to help you diagnose a modem problem. To open the troubleshooter, open the Modems Properties sheet and choose the Diagnostics tab. Choose the Help button, and the Windows Help window appears. Follow the directions on-screen to try to solve your modem problems.

Chapter 29
Configuring Printers

by Sue Plumley

Windows 95 includes several features that enable you to install, configure, share, and use various printers in either a stand-alone computer or a network workstation. A printer wizard helps you install a printer, and Windows supplies the drivers and configuration files for many commonly used printers.

After installing the printer, you can modify printer settings so that you get the most from Windows, your printer, and your applications. You can adjust your printer's properties, such as port, paper size and orientation, fonts, graphics resolution, and so on.

Additionally, Windows makes it easy for you to share printers with others on your network, and you can install someone else's shared printer to your drive. Windows also offers some security features so that you can limit access to shared printers or stop sharing at any time.

In this chapter, you learn to do the following:

- Install a printer to a stand-alone computer
- Configure a printer
- Install a network printer
- Troubleshoot installation and configuration problems

Installing a Printer to a Single PC

Windows makes installing any printer quick and easy with the help of the Add Printer Wizard. The wizard guides you, step-by-step, to configuring the printer and loading the driver. You can use any of Windows' supplied drivers, or you can use your printer manufacturer's disk when installing your printer.

If you have trouble installing your printer, there are a few things you can try to solve the problems. Additionally, Windows supplies a Device Manager that enables you to view printer port settings and see if the problem you're having is with the hardware.

> **Note**
>
> Windows will autodetect your printer when you install the Windows program; use the Add Printer Wizard when you add a printer after Windows is installed.

Using the Add Printer Wizard

Using the Add Printer Wizard, you can quickly and easily add any printer to your system. Before installing the configuration and driver files to your computer, make sure that you attach the printer to your computer and turn on the printer.

To install a printer to your PC, follow these steps:

1. Click the Start button and choose Settings, Printers. The Printers window appears (see fig. 29.1). Alternatively, you can open My Computer and double-click the Printers icon.

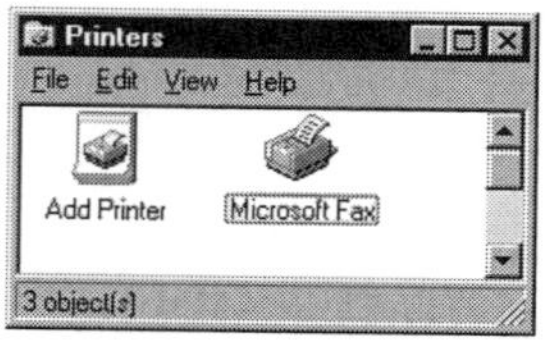

Fig. 29.1
The Printers window lists the current printers and enables you to add new printers.

2. Double-click the Add Printer icon. The Add Printer Wizard dialog box appears (see fig. 29.2).

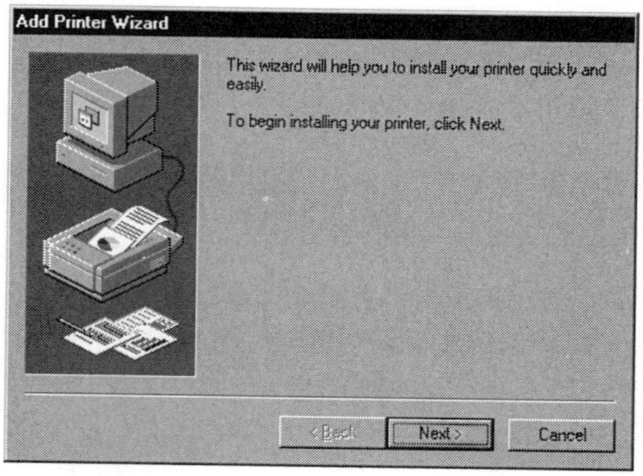

Fig. 29.2
The first Add Printer Wizard dialog box welcomes you; choose Next to continue.

3. Choose the Next button to display the second Add Printer Wizard dialog box (see fig. 29.3).

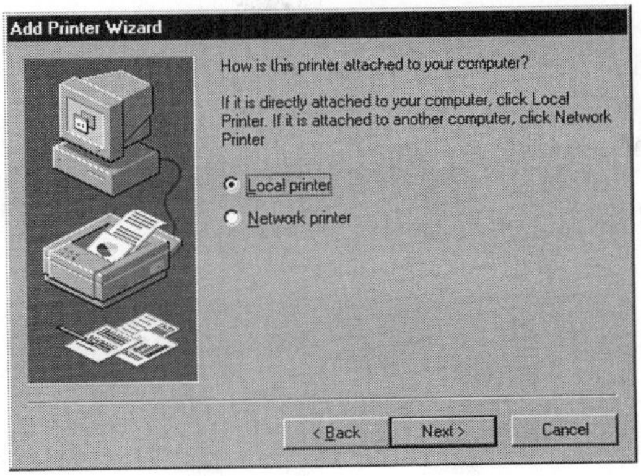

Fig. 29.3
For a stand-alone, or single, computer, choose Local printer.

4. Choose Local printer and choose the Next button. The third wizard dialog box appears (see fig. 29.4).

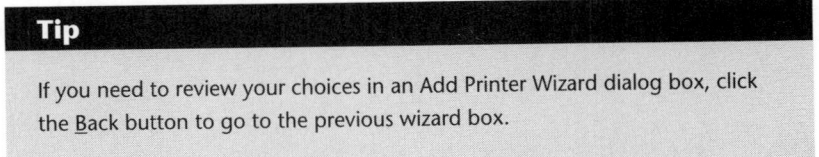

> **Tip**
>
> If you need to review your choices in an Add Printer Wizard dialog box, click the Back button to go to the previous wizard box.

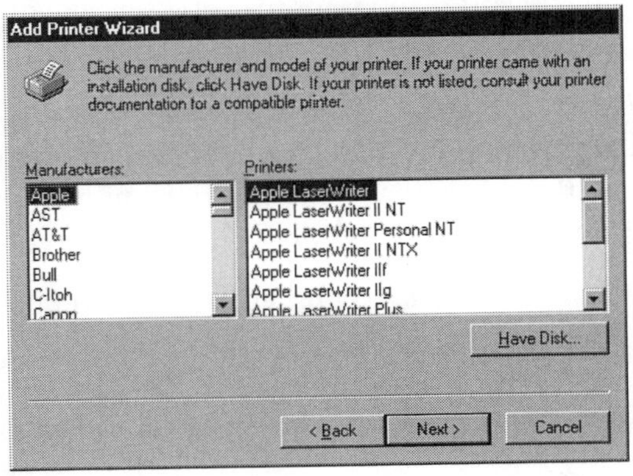

Fig. 29.4
You install the driver and configuration files by choosing the manufacturer and model in this wizard box.

5. In Manufacturer, choose the maker of your printer. The list of Printers changes to reflect those printers made by the selected manufacturer.

6. Select the exact model of your printer in the Printers list.

If your printer is not listed, you can insert the manufacturer's disk that came with your printer and choose the Have Disk button. Windows installs the configuration files and driver from the disk and then returns to this wizard box. Not all printer vendors provide a disk that works with Windows 95; call the printer manufacturer to update the printer drivers.

7. Click the Next button. The fourth Add Printer Wizard box appears, as shown in figure 29.5.

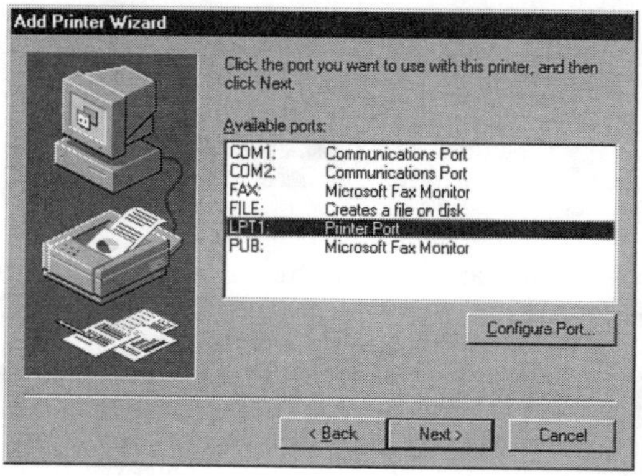

Fig. 29.5
Choose the port your printer is connected to in this wizard box.

8. Choose the port to which the printer is attached.

   Choose Configure Port if you want to change either of the following options:

   - *Spool MS-DOS Print Jobs*. If checked (default setting), spools the documents you print from MS-DOS-based applications. Spooling controls the number of pages sent to the printer at one time so that printing is more efficient.

   - *Check Port State Before Printing*. Runs a check on the connection before sending jobs to the printer.

   Choose OK to close the Configure LPT Port dialog box.

9. Choose Next. The fifth Add Printer Wizard box appears, as shown in figure 29.6.

10. In Printer Name, accept the suggested name or enter a new name for the printer.

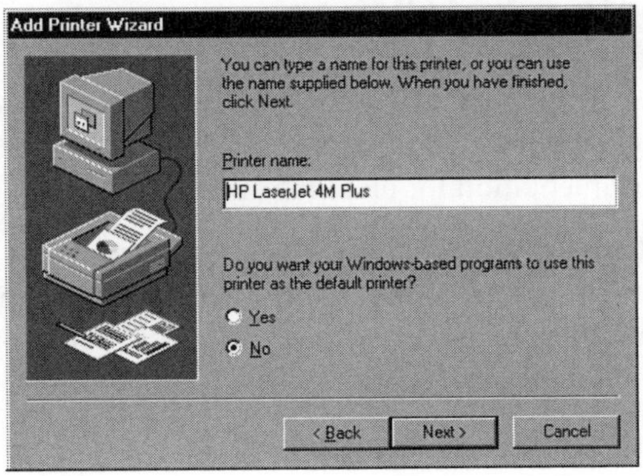

Fig. 29.6
Name the printer so that you'll easily recognize it in your Printers window.

11. If you want this printer to act as the default printer for your Windows applications, choose Yes. If you've already assigned another printer as the default printer, choose No.

12. Click Next. The sixth printer wizard dialog box appears asking if you want to print a test page. Choose Yes to print a test page or No to skip this step. If you choose Yes, Windows displays a dialog box asking if the test page printed OK; if you choose No in this dialog box, Windows tries to diagnose the problem for you.

13. Click the Finish button. Windows may prompt you for the necessary files to set up the printer; insert the Windows CD or disks. The installed printer icon appears in the Printers window.

Troubleshooting

The printer won't print my document; what am I doing wrong?

Check that the printer is plugged in, turned on, and online. Often, turning the printer off and back on clears the memory and makes it start printing again.

Check the cable connections, both to the printer and to the computer, to make sure that the cable is firmly attached. Also, if the cable is old and tattered, borrow a cable from another printer and try it. The cable could be bad.

Check that the paper tray is securely in place and that no broken areas are on the paper tray that would keep it from locking into the printer.

Make sure that all covers on the printer that should be closed are securely closed.

If you're using a print-sharing device or switch box, bypass those devices by cabling the printer directly to the computer and try printing. If the printer prints, something may be wrong with the switch box or print-sharing device.

If you're using a network printer, check to make sure your network cable and connection are good.

Troubleshooting Installation

Following are a few common installation problems you might encounter with your printer. If you need further help with your printer configuration, see the section "Configuring Your Printer" later in this chapter and consult your printer's documentation for more information.

If your printer is not listed in the wizard dialog box, you must use your printer manufacturer's disk to install the configuration files and driver. If you did not receive a disk with your printer, call the dealer who sold you the printer and ask him or her for the disk.

If your selected port is not working with your printer, confirm that you're designating the correct port on your computer. Printer ports are usually the parallel ports LPT1 or LPT2. Next, make sure that your printer cable is appropriate for the port and that the cable is firmly attached to both the computer and the printer.

Confirm that the printer's power cord is plugged into a power outlet and into the printer. Check that the printer is turned on and that the printer's control panel lights are on.

If you're still having trouble with the printer port, follow these steps:

1. Choose the Start, Settings, Control Panel.
2. Double-click the System icon in the Control Panel. The System Properties sheet appears.
3. Choose the Device Manager tab (see fig. 29.7).

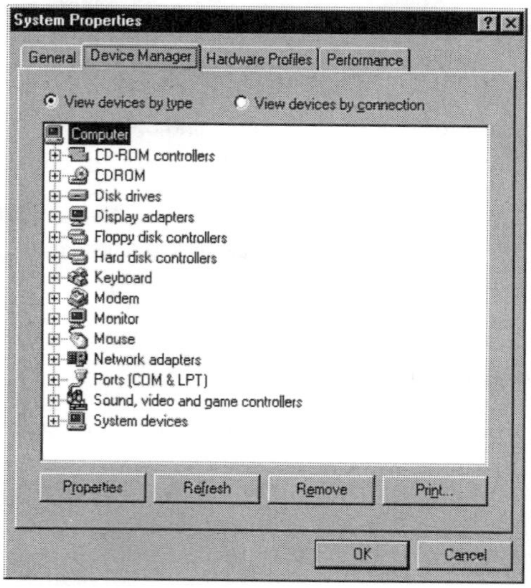

Fig. 29.7
Use the Device Manager page to find information about your printer port.

4. Find the Ports (COM & LPT) icon in the list and double-click it. The available ports display below the icon.

5. Select the Printer Port and then click the Properties button. The Printer Port Properties sheet appears (see fig. 29.8).

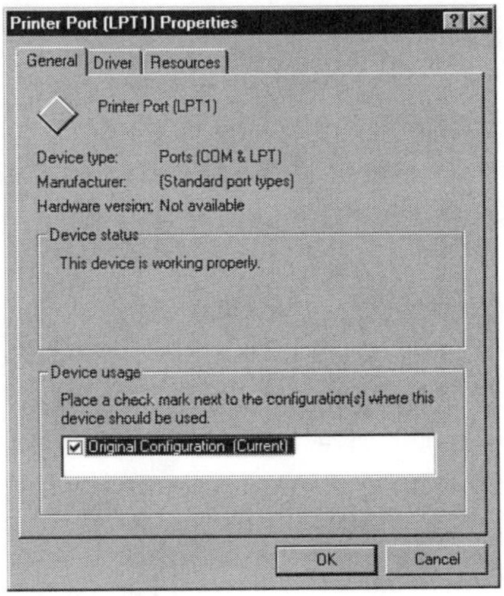

Fig. 29.8
Use the Printer Port Properties sheet to spot problems with the port.

6. On the General page, look in the Device Status area. If the port has a problem, it's listed here with a suggested solution. If there is no problem listed, go on to step 7.

> **Tip**
>
> Note any problem code or number in the Device Status area in case you need to call the printer manufacturer's support line. The number helps identify the problem.

7. In the Device Usage area of the General page, make sure that the Windows-supplied Original Configuration option is checked.

8. To find out about the printer port driver file, choose the Driver tab of the Printer Port Properties sheet (see fig. 29.9).

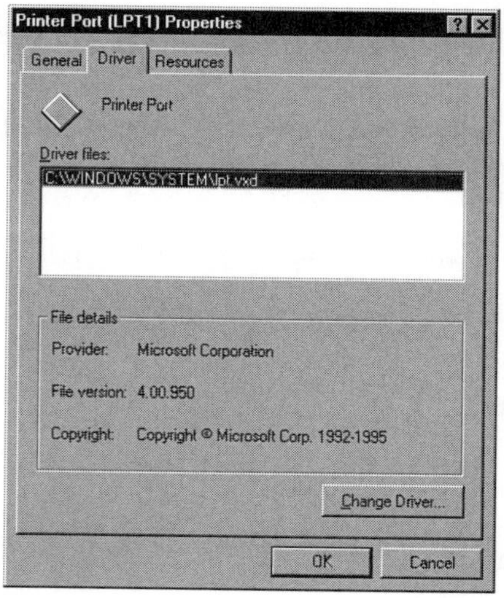

Fig. 29.9
Windows supplies the printer port driver, but you can change to your own driver or an updated driver.

9. The Windows-supplied driver is the C:\WINDOWS\SYSTEM\lpt.vxd driver. If that driver is not selected, select it and try printing to the port again. If the printer port still does not work, go to step 10.
10. Choose the Resources tab on the Printer Port Properties sheet (see fig. 29.10).

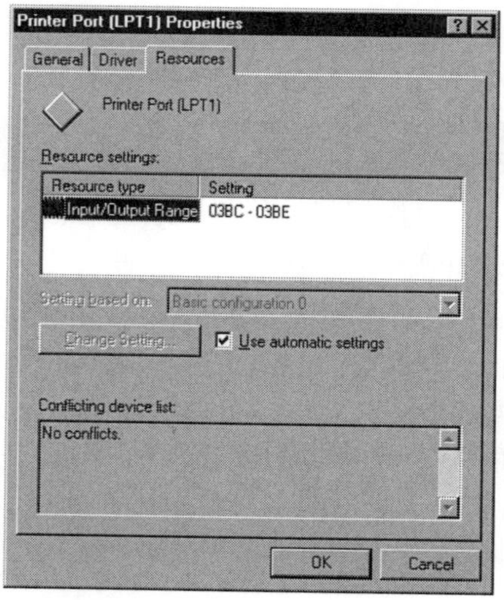

Fig. 29.10
Your safest bet is to use Windows' automatic settings unless there's a device conflict.

11. In the Conflicting Device List box, check to see if there is a conflict.

The Resource Settings list box specifies the resources in use by the hardware. To change settings, double-click the resource type.

> **Caution**
>
> It's best to not change the resources manually because then the resources become fixed, and Windows is limited when configuring other devices.

12. To change the configuration, click the down arrow beside the Setting Based On option. To change settings of the configuration, click the Change Setting button. These options may not be available, which means the settings for the specific hardware cannot be changed.

> **Caution**
>
> If you change a configuration from the default, your port may not work correctly. It could slow considerably and may also lose some functionality.

13. When you're finished, choose OK to close the Printer Port Properties sheet and then choose OK again to close the System Properties sheet.

Configuring Your Printer

After you install a printer to Windows, you can change its configuration to better suit your working practices. Windows makes it easy for you to change the port, paper size and orientation, graphics mode, font options, and more.

When you configure the printer through the printer's Properties sheet, the changes you make apply to all applications in which you use the printer. If, for example, you set the orientation to landscape, landscape becomes the default orientation when you print a page in your applications. You can, of course, change the printer setup in most applications to override the defaults in that application.

To open the printer's Properties sheet, follow these steps:

1. Choose Start, Settings, Printers. The Printers window appears.
2. Select the icon of the printer you want to configure and choose File, Properties. The specific printer's Properties sheet appears.

Tip

You also can display the Properties command from the pop-up menu by pointing to the printer icon and right-clicking the mouse.

See the following sections for information about each page in the printer's Properties sheet. If you want to set options on more than one page, click the Apply button before changing tabs to make sure that the changes are activated. Options and information on individual pages may vary slightly, depending on your printer. The printer in the following examples is the HP LaserJet 4M Plus.

Using the General Page

▶ See "Installing a Shared Printer," p. 652

The General page of the printer's Properties sheet contains options that are handy if you're sharing your printer on a network. Additionally, you can print a test page from this page to make sure that your printer is working correctly. Figure 29.11 shows the General page of the Properties sheet.

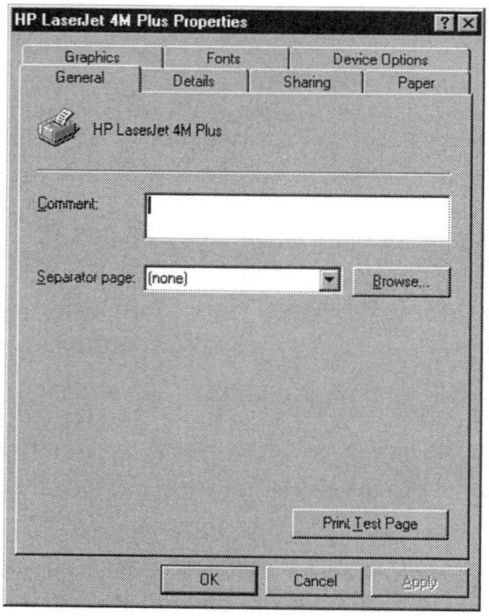

Fig. 29.11
Use the General page to configure the printer for sharing with others on the network.

The options you can choose from include the following:

- *Comment.* The Comment area of the General page enables you to enter a description or comment about your printer, such as what its best use is. When sharing a printer, others on the network who install your printer see the comment.

- *Separator Page*. Select whether to insert a page between each document that's printed from your printer. You may want to use a separator page if several people are printing documents at once; the separator page makes it easy to divide the jobs. You can choose either a Full or Simple page to use as a separator. Full contains a graphic, and Simple contains only text.

> **Note**
>
> You can also click the Browse button beside the Separator Page option to specify a custom separator page, such as a Windows Metafile.

- *Print Test Page*. Click the Print Test Page button to send a page to the printer. The page contains various fonts and graphics, depending on your printer. If the test page prints, your printer is attached and working.

Using the Details Page

The Details page of the printer's Properties sheet enables you to set options such as printer port, capture printer port, spool settings, and so on. Figure 29.12 shows the Details page.

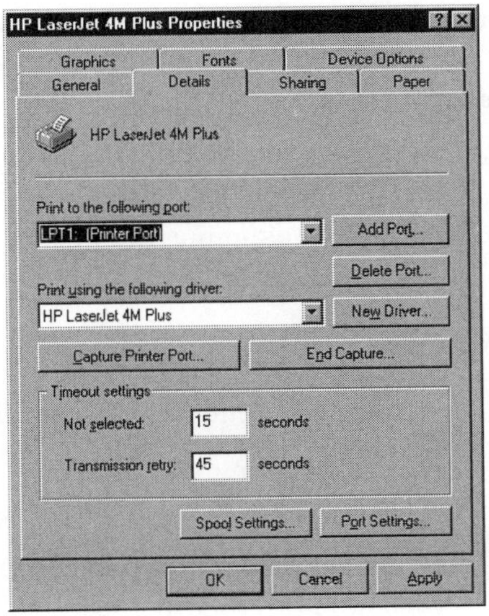

Fig. 29.12
Configure ports and drivers in the Details page of the Properties sheet.

- *Print to the Following Port*. This box displays the port your printer is connected to. If you're using a network printer, the box displays the path to that printer. If you change the connection to your printer, you'll also need to change the port. Click the down arrow beside this option to display available ports and select one. Alternatively, you can add a port by clicking the Add Port button and typing a path in the Specify Path text box.

  When you add a port, the Add Port dialog box appears. Specify whether the port is Network or Other (such as fax modem or local) and enter the path or select the type of port you want to add. Choose OK to close the Add Port dialog box and return to the Properties sheet.

  Select a port and choose Delete Port if you want to delete a port.

- *Print Using the Following Driver*. The driver you're currently using displays in this box, but you can change the driver if your printer supports or emulates the new driver. Click the down arrow for a list of installed drivers or click the New Driver button to change the driver.

▶ See "Installing a Shared Printer," p. 652

- *Capture Printer Port*. Capturing a printer port is the same as mapping to a network printer. Choose the Capture Printer Port button to display the Capture Printer Port dialog box. If the path is not displayed, enter the path to the network printer in the Path text box, choose the Reconnect at Logon option, and choose OK. The next time you start Windows on the network, the network printer is automatically pathed to your drive and ready for you to use. Note you must have rights to the network queue you are capturing to.

- *End Capture*. Click the End Capture button to cancel the mapping to the network printer. If you want to use the network printer after canceling the capture, you must either recapture the printer or work your way through numerous folders to get to the printer.

- *Timeout Settings*. The Not Selected option refers to how many seconds Windows waits for the printer to be online before it reports an error. Enter the amount of time you want Windows to delay.

  Transmission Retry specifies the number of seconds Windows waits for the printer to be ready to print before reporting an error.

- *Spool Settings*. Spool settings govern how your document is sent to the printer. Choose this button to display the Spool Settings dialog box.

The first options specify whether to spool a job or print it directly to the printer. If you spool the job, you can choose to start printing after the first page is sent or after the last page is sent. You spool a print job so that your program can get back to work more quickly while the print queue does all the work. If you choose to print directly to the printer, your computer remains tied up until all the job is sent to the printer.

The Spool Data Format option refers to the way your computer stores the data to be printed. Use EMF (metafile) format to free up your program faster; use RAW format if you have problems with the EMF. RAW format does take longer to print.

Choose the Enable or Disable Bidirectional Support for this Printer to specify whether your printer should communicate with your computer.

Select the Restore Defaults button to change all options in the Spool Settings dialog box back to the default.

- *Port Settings*. Click the Port Settings button to display the Configure LPT Port dialog box, in which you can choose whether to spool DOS application print jobs and whether to check the port before printing.

Using the Sharing Page

The Sharing page refers to how your printer works with a network, such as the peer-to-peer Microsoft Network. If you choose Not Shared, others on the network cannot access your printer. If you choose Shared As, you can specify a password to limit others' access to your printer. Figure 29.13 illustrates the Sharing page with the Shared As option selected.

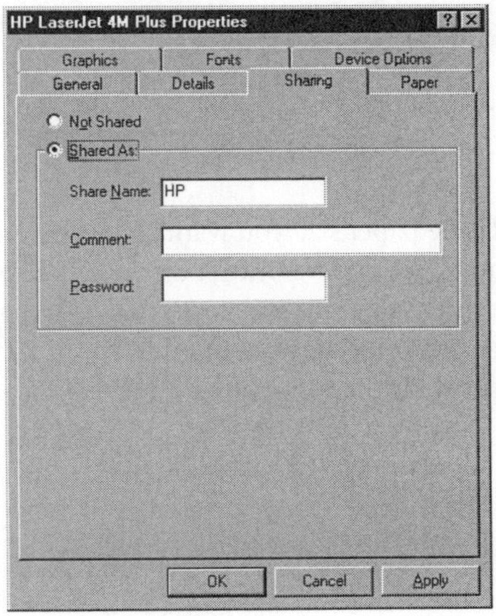

Fig. 29.13
Share your printer with others on the network, but limit access with a password.

▶ See "Installing a Shared Printer," p. 652

In the Shared As area, enter a name to identify your computer on the network in the Share Name text box and enter a Comment if you want. You can also enter a Password to limit those with access to your computer. After you enter the password, Windows displays a confirmation dialog box in which you enter the password again to confirm it.

To stop sharing your printer with the network, click the Not Shared option on the Sharing page.

Using the Paper Page

Use the Paper page of the printer's Properties sheet to set defaults for paper size, orientation, paper source, copies, and so on. The defaults you set on this page are applied to any application using the printer, unless you change printer setup in the specific application. Figure 29.14 illustrates the Paper page.

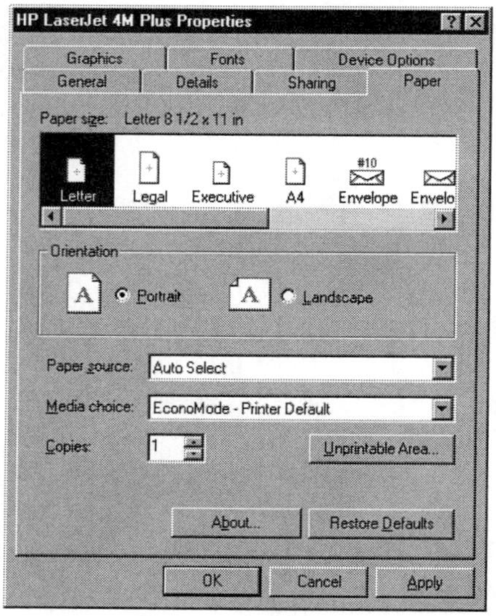

Fig. 29.14
Set defaults for the printer that apply to all applications that use it.

- *Paper Size.* Select the paper size you want to print from as a default. You might, for example, set up one printer on your network to print only number 10 (commercial-sized) envelopes. Choose the envelope size on this page. To choose a size of paper or envelope, click the icon in the scroll box, and its size description appears above the scroll box.
- *Orientation.* Choose either Portrait or Landscape as the default paper orientation for this printer.

- *Paper Source*. Specify the paper source for your printer. You can choose, for example, to use the upper tray or lower tray, or manual feed as with an envelope feeder.
- *Media Choice*. If your printer supports a media choice, you can choose to print to paper or to a transparency for overheads.
- *Copies*. Enter the default number of copies to print.
- *Unprintable Area*. Click this button to display the Unprintable Area dialog box. The unprintable area is the margin around the outside of the page that a laser printer, for example, cannot print to. You can change the area not printed to suit your printer or for special print jobs. Enter the amount of unprintable area for the Left, Right, Top, and Bottom of the page. Choose OK to return to the Paper page of the Properties sheet.
- *About*. Click to display the About dialog box, which displays the printer name and driver version. Choose OK to close the dialog box.
- *Restore Details*. Click the Restore Details button to change all options in the Page page back to their defaults.

Troubleshooting

I'm having problems with the paper in my printer; sometimes it jams and sometimes it curls.

If you have trouble with paper jams, check to make sure that you do not have too much paper in the paper tray; too much paper results in unnecessary pressure on the paper and often causes paper jams.

If your paper curls when printed, the heat is causing one side of the paper to dry and shrink faster than the other side. Try turning the paper over in the tray or try using slightly heavier paper. Also, review your paper storage conditions. If the paper is stored in a humid area, curling often occurs because the paper is damp.

Using the Graphics Page

Use the Graphics page to specify graphics resolution, dithering, intensity, and so on. The settings on this page affect only graphics, not text. Figure 29.15 shows the Graphics page of the Properties sheet.

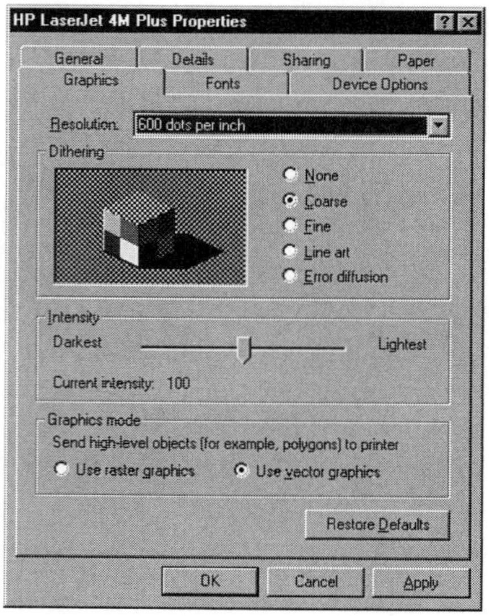

Fig. 29.15
You can speed your print jobs by choosing options in the Graphics page.

- *Resolution*. Listed in the Resolution box are the available choices with which you can print graphics. Higher resolutions (600 dots per inch, for example) produce high-quality graphics but take longer to print. Lower resolutions (75 dpi) produce coarse and grainy graphics but print quickly.
- *Dithering*. Dithering blends grays in black-and-white printing or colors in color printing to produce smoother transitions. Choose None if you do not want dithering. Choose Coarse for a grainy effect or Fine for a higher quality, smooth effect. If your resolution is low, 150 dpi or less, choose Fine dithering to improve the look of the graphics. Choose Line Art if there are no shades of gray in the graphics; contrast between blacks and whites will be sharper. Choose Error Diffusion for sharpening the edges of photographs.
- *Intensity*. Click and drag the lever to Darkest for darker graphics or to Lightest for lighter graphics. The default intensity is 100. The lowest intensity is 0, which would produce black or nearly black graphics; the highest intensity is 200, which would produce white or nearly white graphics.
- *Graphics Mode*. Choose whether to send objects to the printer in raster or vector format. *Vector images* are formed by outline, and *raster images* are formed by pixels or dots. A vector image is sharper, clearer, and probably faster to print. If, however, you have problems printing vector images, try raster.

Using the Fonts Page

Use the Fonts page to specify how TrueType fonts are printed and to indicate any font cartridges you use with your printer. Figure 29.16 illustrates the Fonts page of the Properties sheet.

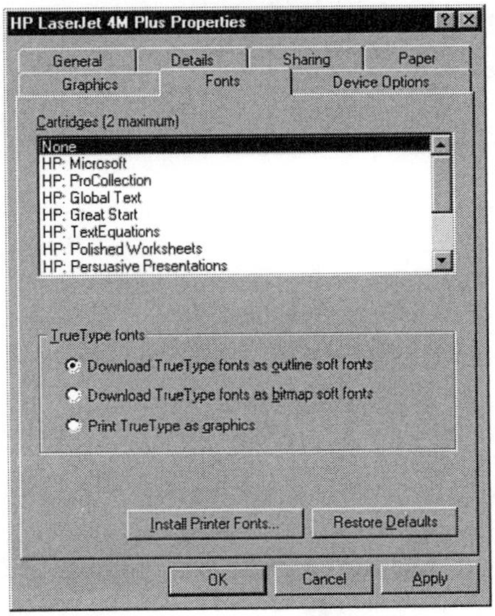

Fig. 29.16
Identify your font cartridges, install printer fonts, and specify TrueType fonts in the Fonts page.

- *Cartridges*. Some printers, mostly Hewlett-Packard printers, enable you to use a font cartridge to add to your list of available fonts. Font cartridges may contain two or twenty fonts and various styles of fonts, such as bold, italic, and so on. If your printer uses a font cartridge, select the cartridge in this list to enable the use of those fonts in your Windows applications.
- *TrueType Fonts*. Choose the Download TrueType Fonts as Outline Soft Fonts option to speed printing and create a high-quality product. Use the Download TrueType Fonts as Bitmap Soft Fonts option for lower-quality output and the Print TrueType as Graphics for artistic effects, such as printing graphics over text so that only part of the character is printed.
- *Install Printer Fonts*. If your font cartridge is not listed in the Cartridges list, choose to install the fonts using the Install Printer Fonts button. From the Font Installer dialog box, click the Add Fonts button. Windows prompts you to insert a disk containing the font files or to enter a directory where the fonts can be found. Choose OK, and the Installer copies the fonts.

- *Restore Defaults*. Click this button to erase any changes you made and to restore the defaults to the Fonts page.

Troubleshooting

The print quality of my graphics is poor. Is there anything I can do?

If the print quality is poor for graphics, make adjustments to the Graphics page of the printer's Properties sheet. If text quality is poor, adjust the print quality settings in the Device Options page of the printer's Properties sheet.

Using Device Options

Use device options to set the print quality of the text and to control printer memory tracking. Figure 29.17 illustrates the Device Options page of the Properties sheet.

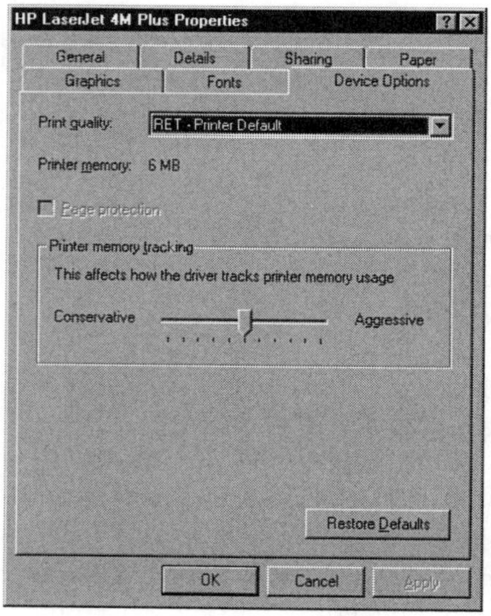

Fig. 29.17
The amount of printer memory, RAM, is listed in the Device Options page of the Properties sheet.

- *PrintQuality*. Select the print quality you want to use for the text in your documents. The selections in this list box depend on the type of printer you're using. In general, use draft quality for proofs and normal or letter quality for finished documents. See your printer's documentation for more information.

- *Printer Memory*. This area lists the amount of RAM in your printer. With some printers, the amount is fixed; with other printers, you can change the amount of memory if you add memory to your printer.
- *Page Protection*. If available with your printer, this option uses some of the printer's memory to apply to complex pages when printing. Although this option makes printing those pages more accurate, it also uses more printer memory.
- *Printer Memory Tracking*. This feature controls printer memory tracking. When printing complex documents, adjust the tracking by dragging the lever to Conservative or Aggressive. The more aggressive the tracking, the more likely the printer driver will attempt to print a complex document; however, the printer's memory may be exceeded, and the print job fails. The more conservative the tracking, the more likely the printer's memory will be available; but the less likely the printer driver will print the complex document.
- *Restore Defaults*. Choose this button to erase any changes you made and to restore the defaults to the Device Options page.

Troubleshooting

I can't get complex pages or graphics to all print on the page; the printer divides it into two pages. What can I do?

Try changing the Printer Memory Tracking in the Device Options page of the printer's Properties sheet. If you still have trouble, consider adding more memory to your printer.

Installing a Network Printer

If you're connected to a peer-to-peer Microsoft Network, you can use other's resources, such as printers, fax modems, files, and so on. If someone else on your network has designated their printer, for example, as a shared resource and designated you as having access to that resource, you can print to that printer from any of your Windows applications.

Note

If you're the one with the network printer connected to your computer, you must first choose to share the printer with the network users through the Network dialog box (File and Printer Sharing) and then through the Sharing page of the printer's Properties sheet.

▶ See "Installing a Shared Printer," p. 652

Installing a network printer is similar to installing a printer connected to your own computer. To install a network printer, follow these steps:

1. In the Printers window, double-click the Add Printer icon.
2. The Add Printer Wizard dialog box appears (refer to fig. 29.2).
3. Choose Next, and the second wizard dialog box appears (see fig. 29.18).

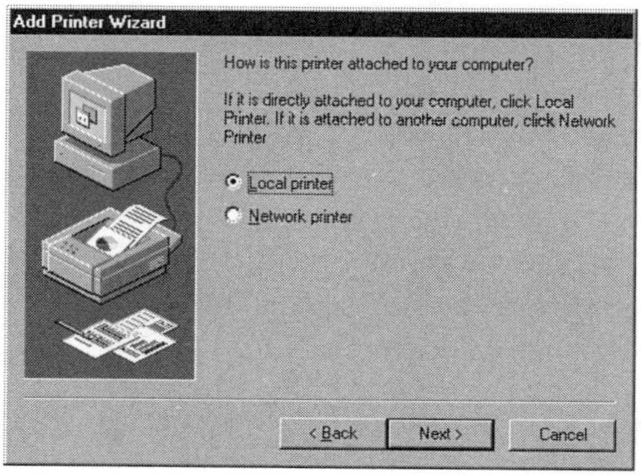

Fig. 29.18 Choose the Network printer if you're attached to a network and have the access rights to share someone else's printer.

4. Choose the Network Printer option and click Next. The third wizard dialog box appears (see fig. 29.19).

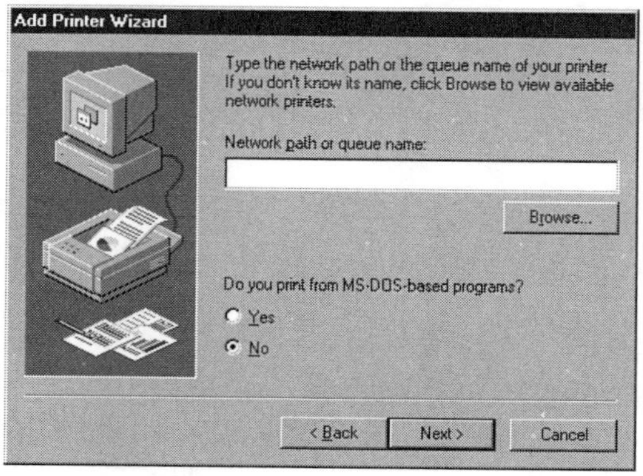

Fig. 29.19 Enter the network path to the printer you want to use.

5. Enter the path to the printer in the Network Path text box. Choose whether to use MS-DOS-based programs with the printer. Click the Next button.

6. The next wizard dialog box appears (refer to fig. 29.6). Enter a name to represent the printer on your computer and click Next.

7. The last wizard appears, asking if you want to print a test page. Choose Yes to print a test page or No to skip this step. If you choose Yes, a dialog box appears confirming the test page printed correctly. If you choose No, Windows will try to diagnose the problem.

8. Choose the Finish button. The installed printer icon appears in the Printers window as a network printer. You can print to this printer as you would a printer attached directly to your computer.

Note

If you have problems with printing from Windows, try the Windows troubleshooter in Help. Choose Start, Help. In the Help Topics dialog box, choose the Index tab. Type **Print Troubleshooting** and press Enter; the Print Troubleshooter appears. Follow the directions on-screen.

Chapter 30

Configuring Scanners and Digital Cameras

by Michael Marchuk

While joysticks, mice, tape backup drives, and modems are relatively commonplace among computers running Windows, scanners and digital cameras are not likely to be found attached to an average Windows workstation. There are many reasons for this trend, including the high price tags that were attached to such peripherals. But now that prices for this hardware are dropping, and demand for faxing and document storage is rising, you may be considering the purchase of a scanner or digital camera.

If you are one of the early adopters of scanner or digital camera technology, you may already have one of these devices connected to your computer. This chapter explains how to install scanners and digital cameras to work within Windows 95.

In this chapter, you learn how to

- Install scanner hardware
- Configure scanner drivers and scanning software
- Install digital camera hardware
- Set up drivers and software to download digital camera images
- View scanned images or digital pictures within Windows 95

Installing Scanner Hardware

Most scanner hardware is connected to your computer through a separate interface board; however, some hand-held scanners can connect to your computer's parallel port. If you have to install a scanner adapter in your computer, turn your computer off and follow these steps:

Tip

If your adapter has dip switches or jumpers that are used to configure the adapter, write down the current settings before you install the adapter into your computer.

1. Install the scanner adapter board into your computer. Follow the manufacturer's installation guidelines closely.
2. Restart your computer.
3. Click the Add New Hardware icon within Control Panel. The Add New Hardware Wizard appears, shown in figure 30.1.

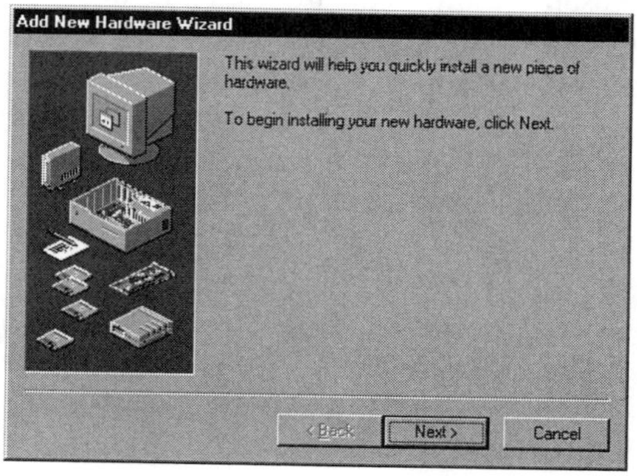

Fig. 30.1
The Add New Hardware Wizard assists you with the installation of the correct drivers for your scanner hardware.

4. Click the Next button to proceed with the installation. The Add New Hardware Wizard displays a dialog box shown in figure 30.2.
5. Select Yes to allow the Add New Hardware Wizard to search for your newly installed adapter. It may take several minutes to detect the hardware that is in your system. If the Add New Hardware Wizard can detect your scanner adapter, you see a list of detected devices that shows which adapter was detected.

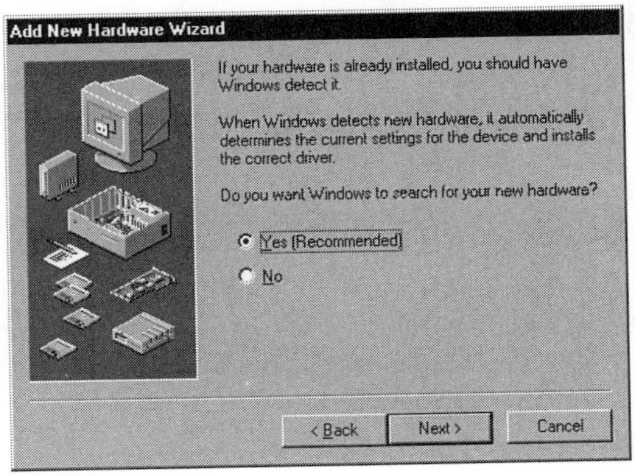

Fig. 30.2
The Add New Hardware Wizard can automatically detect a wide range of hardware.

6. Click the Finish button to complete the installation of the device drivers to your system.
7. Windows displays a dialog box that asks if you want to restart your computer. You should allow Windows to reboot your machine in order to load the new drivers.

If the Add New Hardware Wizard cannot automatically detect your scanner board, you have two options:

- You may run the Add New Hardware Wizard again and select No when the wizard asks to automatically detect your new hardware. You can then manually install the Windows 95 drivers by selecting from a list of manufacturers and their adapter boards. If you cannot find your exact adapter board listed, load the driver disk that was shipped with your scanner adapter. Select Have Disk, which will search the manufacturer's disk for a Windows 95 device driver. If the Add New Hardware Wizard can find a Windows 95 driver for your scanner adapter, the wizard will display the adapter driver in a list, and the installation procedures may continue from step 6 in the preceding installation steps.
- The Add New Hardware Wizard also may not detect your adapter, and the manufacturer disk may not contain a Windows 95 device driver. When the driver disk for your adapter only contains DOS and Windows 3.x device drivers, you need to follow the manufacturer's installation instructions for installing the device drivers on your system. Some manufacturers may offer a Windows 95 installation section within their manuals if their native Windows 95 drivers are not ready yet. Check to

see if the scanner you have or want to purchase will work with Windows 95 or if there are specific installation instructions for Windows 95; otherwise, follow the standard installation procedures outlined in the manuals.

Note

If you are installing a hand-held scanner or a flatbed scanner that connects to your computer's parallel port, you may not need to run any hardware installation procedures. Check your installation manuals regarding this matter.

Troubleshooting

After installing my scanner, I can't seem to scan anything into my word processor. What's wrong?

If you are not using the scanning software, you won't be able to scan anything into your word processor. If you are trying to scan text from a document into the word processor, you will need to use special software that uses Optical Character Recognition (OCR) to actually convert the image into text data. This software may have been shipped with your scanner, so you should review the operation of the OCR software and its usage for scanning into word processing documents.

Installing and Configuring Scanner Software

Scanner software communicates with the hardware through a Windows device driver. The device driver controls the way the scanner works when capturing an image. The scanner software is usually written by the manufacturer of the scanning hardware, because each scanner has various capabilities and resolutions.

Some common controls that the scanner software manages include

- Color resolution (if your scanner supports color)
- Image resolution, usually expressed in dots per inch (dpi)
- Image enhancement
- Image cropping, enlargement, and reduction
- File formatting for the captured image

Proprietary Solutions

Because the scanning software is so closely linked to the scanner hardware, you may not have any choice but to use the software that was provided by the manufacturer to perform your scanning. If you have purchased a brand-name scanner with a good reputation, the delivered software will probably be mature and reliable and may even be a 32-bit Windows 95 program. The features included in this software will probably be much of what you are looking for, plus some additional features that may be new to you. However, if you buy an off-brand scanner to save money, the software which you receive may not be what you expected. Oftentimes, to lower the price of a product, the development costs are cut. This could mean that the software which is provided by the manufacturer may only cover the most basic features, may contain serious omissions of functionality, and may not be a 32-bit Windows 95 program. As with every purchase you make, you should evaluate your product options based on more than just price.

To install your scanning software, follow the instructions provided in your scanner's installation manual. This procedure is typically very quick since there are few options to most scanning software. Once your software is installed, you will be able to start scanning images into your computer.

Scanning Software Example

To give you an idea of some of the functions that are available through scanning software, let's take a look at the Hewlett Packard ScanJet software.

Figure 30.3 shows the Hewlett Packard ScanJet software's main screen. On the left-hand side of the screen are the main controls for configuring the operation of the scanner, while the right-hand side of the screen shows a preview image of the scanner.

Fig. 30.3
Hewlett Packard's ScanJet software lets you preview the images you are scanning.

When scanning an image, it is common for the scanning software to offer a preview mode for cropping an image. The preview mode will perform a fast scan of the entire scanning bed to allow you to see where your image is positioned in the scanner. Once you can see where the entire image is, you can choose the portion you want to scan at a higher quality. Looking back to figure 30.3, notice that the entire scanning area is represented by the box on the right-hand side of the screen.

Once you have completed the preview scan, you can crop the image to the desired size. This will prevent the scanner from scanning in blank space which not only makes your image look poor, but also requires more hard drive space to store and much longer time to scan.

Take the example of a business card. If you walked up to a photocopy machine and placed the card on the machine, you would end up with an 8 1/2- by 11-inch piece of paper with a business card located somewhere on the page. What you really wanted was a copy of the business card, not a copy of the photocopy machine's cover.

If you placed that same business card on a scanner, you could view the preview scan and crop only the business card by drawing a box around that part of the scanning area. When the scanner digitizes that image, it will only include the part of the scanning area that you cropped. Again, this saves time and disk space while giving you the image that you want.

In addition to the cropping features, another important feature includes the scanning mode in which your image is captured. Since images may be used for many different purposes, you may have to change the scanning mode from time to time. Some images you will only view on the computer screen, so these images should match the number of colors that your video mode can support. Other images will be included in word processing or spreadsheet documents, which will be printed in black and white. Still others may be advertising images which are being sent to a high-quality color printer for proofing. Each of these images has different quality needs that your software should handle.

The ScanJet software provides an image quality selection that allows you to use one of several preset image settings or create your own. Figure 30.4 shows some of these image settings.

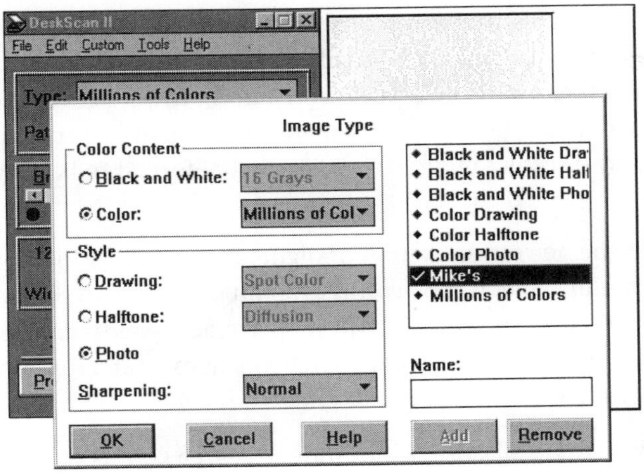

Fig. 30.4 Hewlett Packard's ScanJet software provides preset image quality settings for various image types.

There are many other features that the ScanJet software provides, including automatic contrast and brightness correction, multiple file format support, and image scaling. But this is not a review of the ScanJet software, it is simply a benchmark to which you can measure other scanning software.

Troubleshooting

I bought a scanner to do OCR, but I never thought I'd have to do so much re-typing. Why can't the computer do a better job at reading the documents into my word processor?

It sounds like your expectations were a little too high for this technology. While some OCR software can read text with 99.7 percent accuracy, that still means that you could have between 5 to 10 errors on a "good" page and many more on a page with illegible writing or poor text quality. OCR is wonderful technology, but don't expect it to replace your secretaries anytime soon.

Installing Digital Camera Hardware

Digital cameras were once only used by those who could afford a $50,000 camera that took lower-quality images than a Kodak Instamatic camera. The novelty of digital cameras has begun to give way to the reality of high-technology solutions to digital imaging needs.

Newspapers, magazines, and many other industries have needed the digital camera for a long time. Instead of buying film, paying for quick film development, and then spending time and effort scanning the images into the computer to be used in articles or advertisements, the digital camera bypasses all of these steps by directly saving images in a digital format to be downloaded to a computer.

The quality of the newest generation of digital cameras rivals that of high-quality 35mm film cameras. The cost is dropping, too. For around $300 you can buy an entry-level version that will snap average-quality images for use in a variety of settings, while for around $10,000 you can get a top-of-the-line model to replace your 35mm camera.

The installation of digital camera hardware is often a connection to either a serial port or to an SCSI interface in your machine. The low-end digital cameras will typically use the serial port interfaces, while the high-end cameras may use either type of interface.

Check your installation manual to see what type of connection you have. The SCSI connection will be much faster (700 percent) than the serial port interface, but will require an SCSI adapter in your computer. This section assumes that you will be using a serial port interface for the camera, since the $10,000 you might have spent on a high-end digital camera is still locked up in some lottery ticket that you have yet to buy.

With that in mind, you may have one or more serial ports available to you. Most PCs have two serial ports; however, some use one of these ports for a mouse and the other for a modem. You may want to check the availability of your serial ports to see if you'll need to swap cables with your modem before downloading images from the camera.

Installing Digital Camera Software

Like scanners, digital cameras provide their own software that can download the images from your camera. This software is probably in its first or second release because this technology is relatively new. That means that your feature set may be limited when using the digital camera's software. But for most people, the only thing you'll really need the software for is to get the images out of the camera.

The Logitech FotoMan camera is an example of an affordable digital camera. The FotoMan is a black and white camera (actually it uses 256 levels of gray), while the FotoMan II is a color camera. The software that is used has several functions beyond the simple download of images to your computer.

The FotoMan software makes contact with the camera when it loads and automatically downloads small thumbnail images of the pictures within the camera. This feature lets you see which images you want to download from the camera in their full form (496 × 360 pixels). Figure 30.5 shows this thumbnail view of the images.

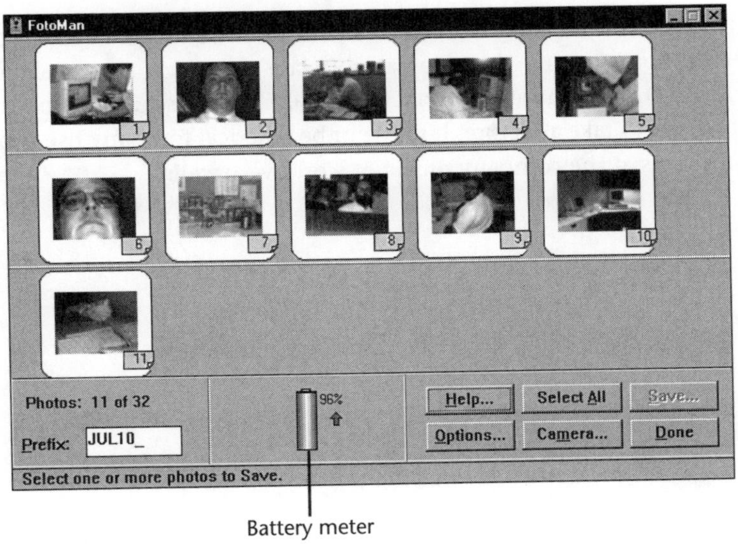

Fig. 30.5 Logitech's FotoMan software lets you preview the images stored in the camera before you download them.

When you have selected the image or images you want to download, you can select one of several popular file formats in which to save them. This allows you to skip a conversion step if you need the images in a particular format.

Another simple feature that makes a lot of sense is the battery strength indicator on the main screen (refer to fig. 30.5). As soon as the FotoMan software makes contact with the camera, the battery meter will read out the current charge level. The FotoMan communication docking base is also the battery charger which lets you see in real-time the charge increasing while you are in the software.

Troubleshooting

I seem to have lost all of my images in my camera that I took only yesterday. What happened? Is my camera or battery bad?

Affordable digital cameras use a flash memory system to store the images. The memory must be refreshed every so often to maintain the images. Logitech estimates that each image consumes 3 percent of the battery life per day. If you have 30 pictures stored in your camera, you may have exhausted the battery just by not retrieving your images sooner.

The last feature shows how the digital camera software can go beyond the simple download feature. The Fotoman software can trigger the camera while it's sitting in the communication docking base. You can set a timer or an instant trigger to take a picture. It may not be practical for many users, but for group shots at the company picnic, it works very well.❖

Chapter 31

Configuring Network Hardware

by Tod Pike

Many computer systems, especially those used at an office, are connected to some kind of computer network. Since Windows 95 has full networking capabilities built in (including the capability to connect to the Internet and use different networking protocols), many users of Windows 95 will be installing networking hardware into their computer systems.

The Windows 95 operating system makes the task of adding and configuring a network interface card (NIC) very easy. This chapter outlines the steps necessary to add an NIC to a computer system running Windows 95 and also how to use resources that may be available on your network. In this chapter, you learn how to do the following:

- Install and configure network interface cards
- Install cables to connect your computer to your network
- Install and configure shared printers from your network
- Install shared fax modems from your network
- Install shared CD-ROM drives from your network

Installing Network Interface Cards (NICs)

When you install Windows 95 on your computer system for the first time, the Windows 95 installation program automatically runs the Add New

Hardware Wizard to detect and install all of the hardware that is in your computer system. After you have installed Windows 95, however, the Add New Hardware Wizard is used if you have added a new device to your computer system, such as a new disk drive, tape drive, NIC, or sound card.

Checking Network Hardware on Your System

If your computer had a network interface card installed when you installed Windows 95, your system should already have support for the card. You can check to see if your system already has support for your NIC by starting the Control Panel (from the Start menu).

From the Control Panel, you can open the System Properties sheet, which gives you information about the devices connected to your computer system.

From the System Properties sheet, select the Device Manager page to display information about the devices on your system (see fig. 31.1).

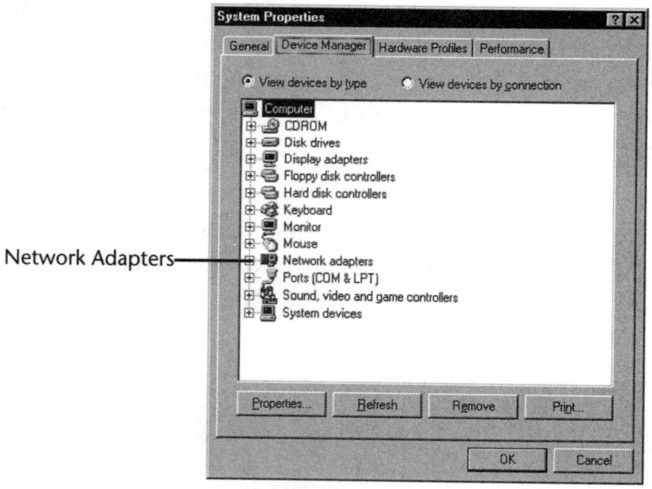

Fig. 31.1
The Device Manager displays a list of the devices on your system.

Using the Device Manager page, you can see that the system as it is currently configured already shows a network device as being available (it is listed as `Network Adapters`). Clicking the Network Adapters item in the list shows the individual NICs that are configured and available for use, as illustrated in figure 31.2.

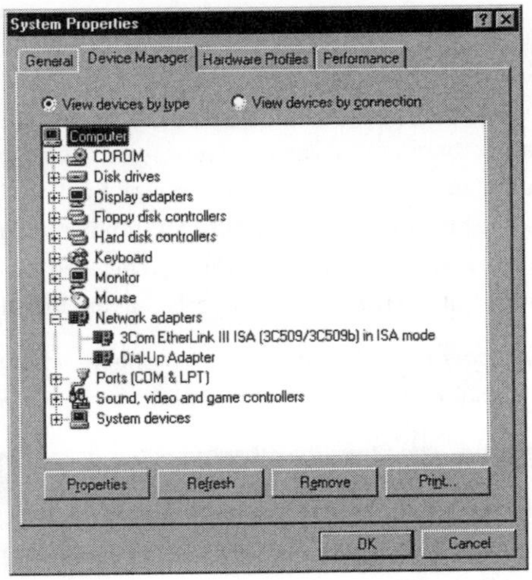

Fig. 31.2
The Device Manager page lists the individual NICs available for use.

If your Device Manager page shows a network interface as being available, but you are unable to use the card (you cannot see any other computers in your Network Neighborhood, for example), there are several things you should check.

Troubleshooting

I installed the NIC and Windows support, but the card still doesn't work

The most common reason for the network card not working correctly is a conflict with another device on your system. Open the Control Panel (from the Start menu) and start the System Properties sheet. Select the Device Manager tab to display the list of the devices on your system.

Double-click the Network Adapters entry in the list on the Device Manager tab, and then select your network device. Click the Properties button to display the settings for your network card. The Device Status area tells you if there is a problem with your network device. Choosing the Resources page shows you the current settings; this page also tells you if one of the settings for your NIC conflicts with another device in your system.

If there is a conflict with another device in your system, you have to change one of the hardware settings (such as the Interrupt Request, Input/Output Range or Direct Memory Access) to another value. You should consult the manual for your network card to determine which values for these settings are legal for your card.

(continues)

(continued)

Once you know which settings you can set your network card to, you have to determine which hardware settings are available on your system. One good way to find out the settings that are in use on your system is to click the Print button on the Device Manager page. This allows you to print out a summary of all the resources on your system—you can easily find an unused value by checking the legal values for your card against the list of interrupts and I/O ports that are used by your system.

If your the Device Manager page does not list any problems with your network card itself, you can look at your network to see if any other computers are shown.

When I browse my network, I don't see the other computers around me.

First, select Entire Network in the Network Neighborhood browser to see if there are any other workgroups available. If there are and computers are in those workgroups, you should make sure that your computer belongs to the correct workgroup.

To set the workgroup for your computer, start the Network control panel and look in the Identification page. Here, you can set your computer's workgroup and computer name. You should check with your network administrator for the workgroups that are available to you.

If you don't see any other workgroups (and you are sure that your network card is working correctly), make sure that you have logged into your network server. If you did not provide a user name and password when you booted your computer system (for example, there was a network login box displayed when your computer booted and you clicked Cancel), you won't see other workgroups in the Network Neighborhood.

Finally, you should check the network cabling that connects your computer to your local network to make sure that you are connected correctly. Your local network administrator can tell you if your connection to the network is active.

Installing a Network Interface Card

If you have added an NIC to your computer since you installed the Windows 95 operating system, you can run the Add New Hardware Wizard (essentially the same routine that Windows 95 runs during installation to detect your hardware configuration) that leads you through the steps necessary for Windows to recognize your new card.

Before you run the Add New Hardware Wizard, you must install the NIC into your computer system. You should follow the manufacturer's instructions for the installation of the card, including setting any switches or jumpers on the card for the interrupt vector and Input/Output vectors.

Note

If there are default positions for any settings on the NIC, you should leave the settings at their default. In general, Windows 95 first looks for devices at the default settings for that card. The only time you need to change the settings from their default is if there is a conflict with some other device in your system.

After the network hardware has been installed on your computer, you are ready to turn your computer back on and begin the process of telling Windows 95 about the new device.

The Add New Hardware Wizard is run from the Control Panel (which can be started through the Start menu).

When you start the Add New Hardware Wizard, the first screen of the wizard comes up (as shown in fig. 31.3), telling you what the wizard will do.

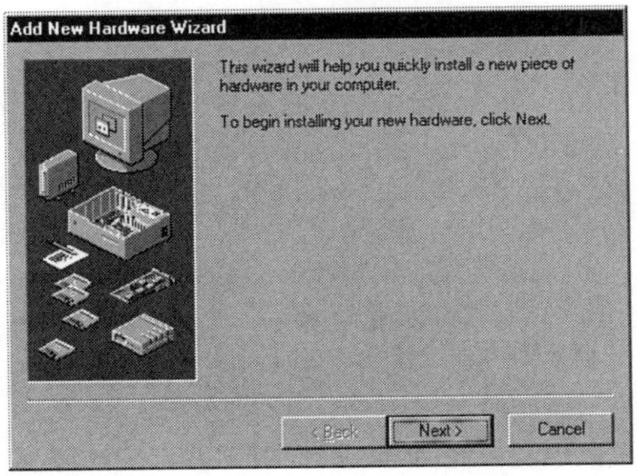

Fig. 31.3
The first page of the Add New Hardware Wizard tells you what this wizard will do.

You should click the Next button to continue to the next page of the Add New Hardware Wizard. If you don't want to continue, click Cancel.

The second page of the wizard (as shown in fig. 31.4) asks you whether you want the wizard to search through your system for new hardware. If you select Yes (the default), the wizard tries to automatically detect the type of network card you have. If you select No, you have to tell Windows 95 what type of card you installed.

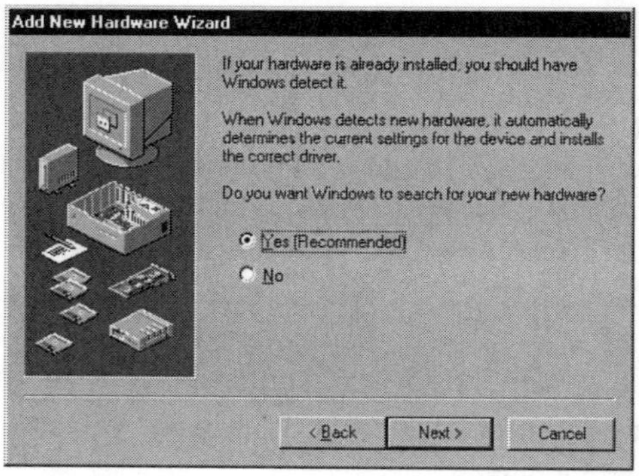

Fig. 31.4
The wizard lets you request automatic detection of your hardware.

Letting Windows 95 Automatically Detect Your NIC

If you are not sure which NIC you have installed in your system, or if you just want to let Windows 95 search through your system to detect what hardware you have installed, select the Yes option on the second page of the Add New Hardware Wizard (refer to fig. 31.4).

This option is essentially the same process that Windows 95 goes through during the initial installation, and it generally does a good job of locating your installed hardware components (although it can fail to detect some cards). Click Next to proceed to the next page of the wizard.

> **Note**
>
> If you let the wizard automatically detect your installed hardware, it is possible that it may find more than one new hardware component on your system. If all you installed is a network card, you may want to click the Cancel button and restart the wizard, selecting No on the second page to manually specify the network card you have.

The next page of the Add New Hardware Wizard (shown in fig. 31.5) is an informational page telling you what the wizard will do to your system and how long it will take. Click Next to proceed.

The next page is the actual hardware detection page. As you can see in figure 31.6, this page has a status bar along the bottom that indicates how far the hardware detection phase has run.

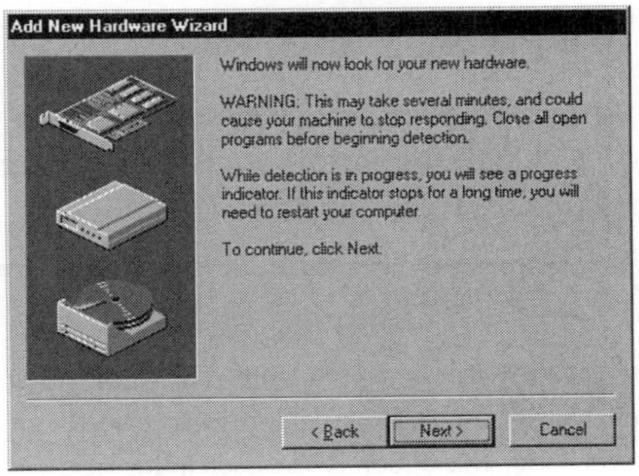

Fig. 31.5
The advisory page in the Add New Hardware Wizard also advises you to close all open applications to prevent your system from hanging.

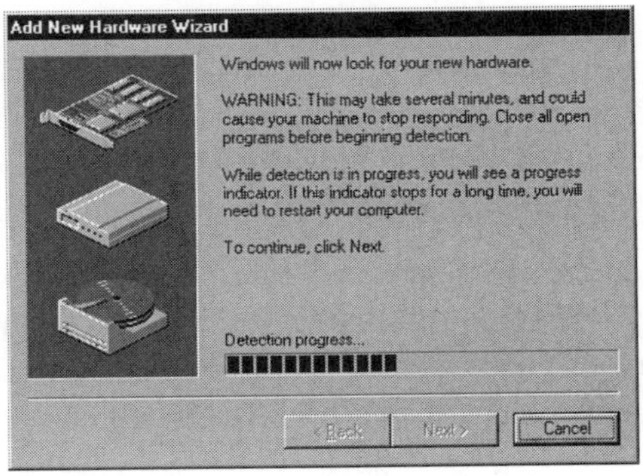

Fig. 31.6
The automatic hardware detection is in progress

After the Add New Hardware Wizard has completed scanning your system for new hardware, the wizard displays the screen shown in figure 31.7. This screen tells you that the wizard has completed the scan for new hardware and is ready to install support for the new hardware on your system. If you want to see the list of the hardware that was detected, you can click the Details button.

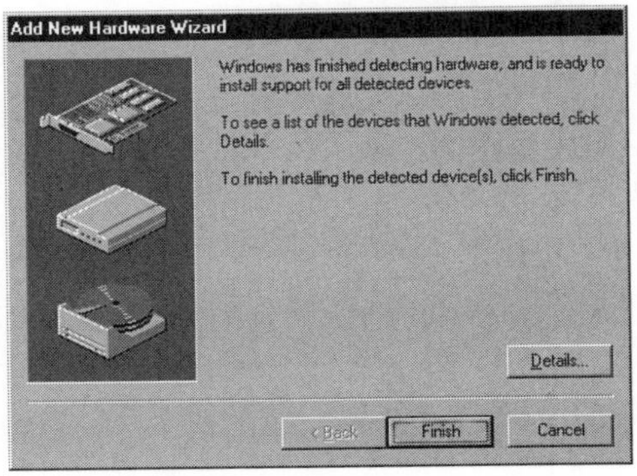

Fig. 31.7
The wizard has finished detecting your new hardware.

When you click the Finish button to install the hardware support, the wizard installs the necessary system drivers and any extra software to support the new network card. Then, the wizard prompts you to restart your system in order for Windows 95 to start supporting your new hardware. If you do not want Windows 95 to restart at this time, just click Cancel.

Note

If the Add New Hardware Wizard couldn't identify your new NIC, it tells you that there is no new hardware to install and gives you the option to manually specify the hardware you are installing. This option is discussed in the next section.

Manually Specifying Your NIC

If you know in advance the type of network card you have installed, or if the Add New Hardware Wizard couldn't identify the type of card you installed, you can manually tell the wizard the type of drive you have.

After you start the Add New Hardware Wizard, click the Next button to move to the second page. Here, the wizard asks you whether you want Windows 95 to search for your new hardware; select the No option and click Next. This allows you to manually select the hardware to install.

When you elect to manually install your hardware with the Add New Hardware Wizard, the wizard displays a list of the types of hardware that you can install.

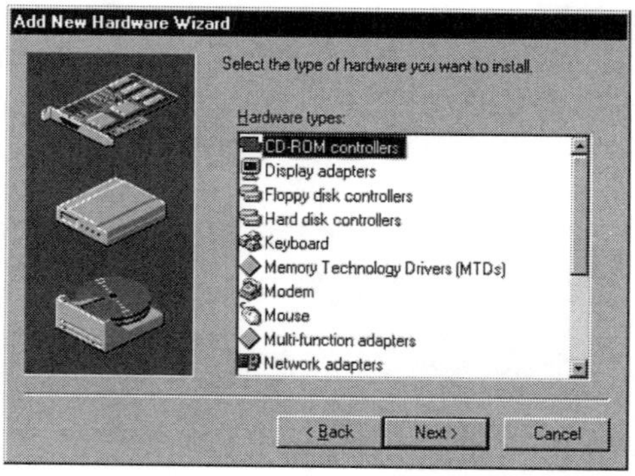

Fig. 31.8 The list of hardware types available to install appear in this wizard box.

From the Hardware Types list, you should select Network Adapters, because this is the type of hardware you are installing. Click Next to continue. The wizard now displays the list of the manufacturers (on the left side of the window) and the types of network adapters (in the right side of the window) that Windows 95 knows about.

Note

Depending on the version of Windows 95 you are running, this list of manufacturers and drives may be different. As Windows 95 matures, more types of hardware will be recognized by the wizard.

If the manufacturer of your NIC is listed on the left side of the window, select that manufacturer. The wizard displays all of the NICs made by that manufacturer (that the system knows about) in the right side of the window.

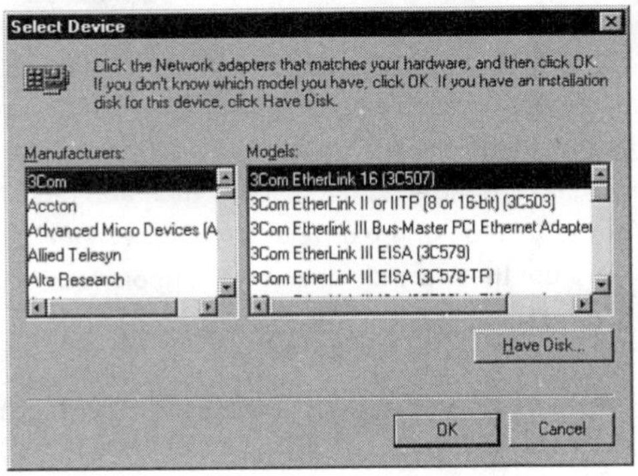

Fig. 31.9
Select a manufacturer and drive type in the Select Device window.

Once you have selected the manufacturer and card type, click Next to continue with the installation.

On the next page of the wizard, the default settings for NIC are displayed. If these settings do not match the hardware settings on your network card, you either have to change the hardware settings on the drive or change the Windows 95 configuration using the Device Manager (started from the System control panel). See the earlier section "Checking Your Network Card" for details on how to do this.

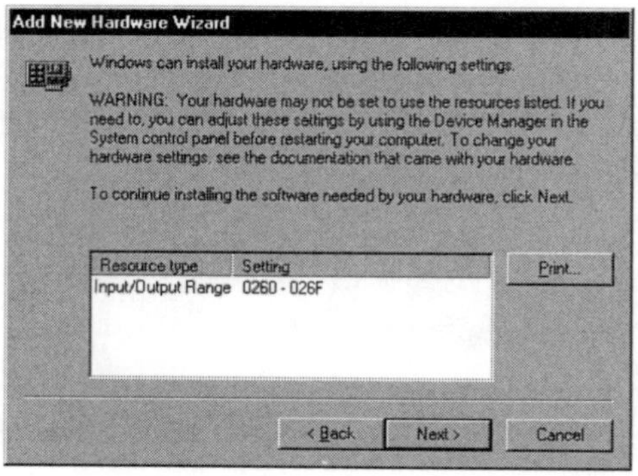

Fig. 31.10
The current hardware settings appear in this wizard box.

Once you have confirmed the current hardware settings, Windows 95 installs the necessary drivers for your network card and prompts you to restart your system (if necessary). After your system has been reset, you are now able to use your new hardware.

> **Note**
>
> If the manufacturer of your network interface is not listed by the wizard, you should check to see if Windows 95 drivers are available for your card. If so, you can click the Have Disk button instead of specifying the manufacturer and drive type. Windows 95 will prompt you for the location of the drivers (generally you load the drivers from your floppy drive) and use those drivers directly to support your NIC.

If no Windows 95 drivers are available for your NIC, you can use the regular Windows drivers for your drive. See the instructions from your card and the Windows 95 documentation for help with installing and using Windows/DOS drivers with Windows 95.

Configuring Your Network Interface Card

Once you have installed Windows 95 support for your network interface card, you may have to configure your card in order for it to work correctly. Configuring your NIC is done through the Network sheet, started from the Control Panel.

> **Note**
>
> If Windows 95 had built-in support for your network card, you may not have to configure your card at all. In many cases, Windows 95 will pick the correct settings for your card to work correctly. Checking the properties for your network card tells you if it's already working.

To change or check the settings for your network card, select your NIC from the list of items on the Network control panel (as shown in fig. 31.11).

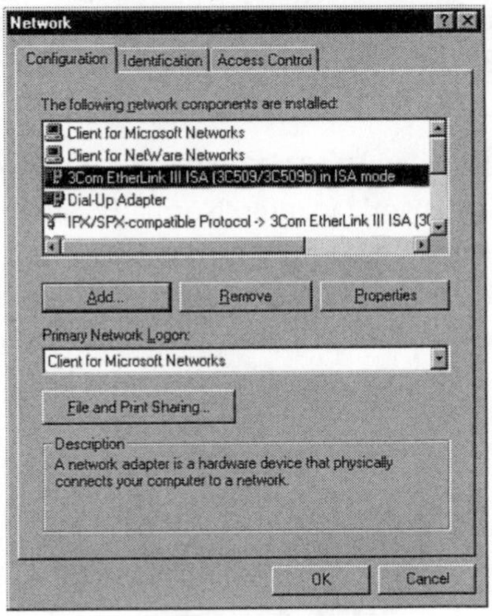

Fig. 31.11
The Network control panel enables you to select your NIC.

Selecting Properties brings up the properties sheet for your network card (as shown in fig. 31.12). The pages on this sheet are the different properties that you can set for your card, and may be slightly different depending on the network card that you have in your system.

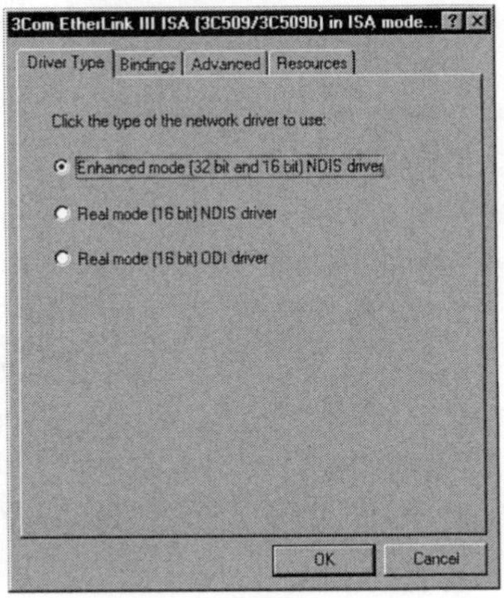

Fig. 31.12
Here's an example properties sheet for a network interface card.

The Driver Type page allows you to select between the different types of drivers that may be available for your card. In general, if there are Windows 95 drivers available, they are listed as Enhanced Mode (32-bit and 16-bit) drivers. You should select this type of driver if possible, as they give the best performance. If Windows 95 drivers are not available, you have to pick one of the DOS drivers listed.

The Bindings page (shown in fig. 31.13) allows you to select which network protocols will use this network adapter. Normally, all of the protocols you have installed are selected on your network adapter, but if you have more than one network adapter (for example, you have an Ethernet card for work and a dial-up adapter for when you are away from work), you may want to have some protocols available only on a particular NIC.

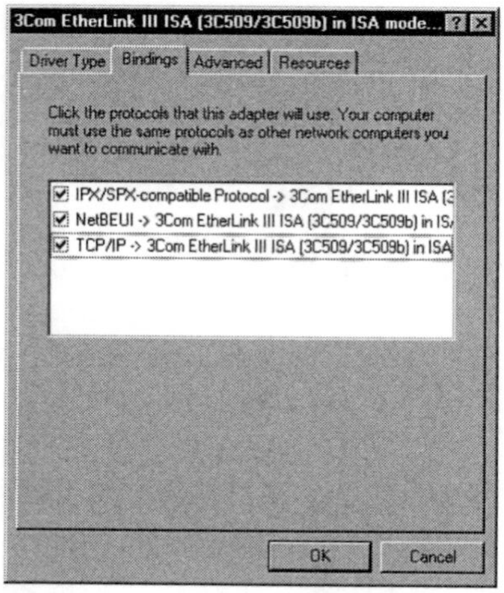

Fig. 31.13
The Bindings page enables you to pick protocols for your adapter.

The features on the Advanced page (shown in fig. 31.14) vary depending on the particular card you have installed. You should consult the hardware manual for your NIC for information on these settings.

Depending on the type of network card you have, the Resources page shows different settings that are available (see fig. 31.15). You should know how your hardware is configured before you change any of the settings on this page, so that you can match the Windows 95 settings with the ones on the card.

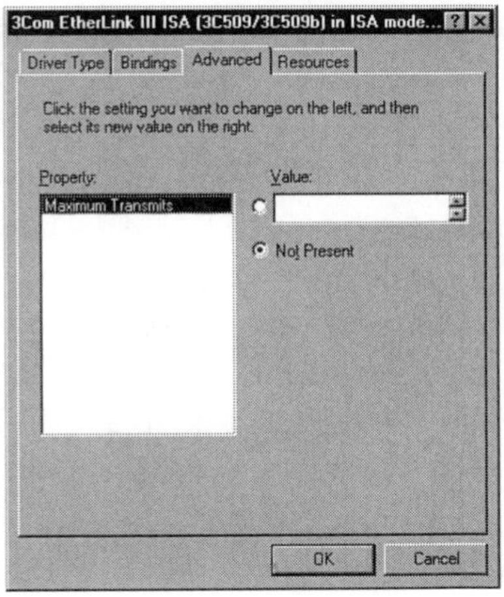

Fig. 31.14
The Advanced page allows you to set certain advanced features of your network interface.

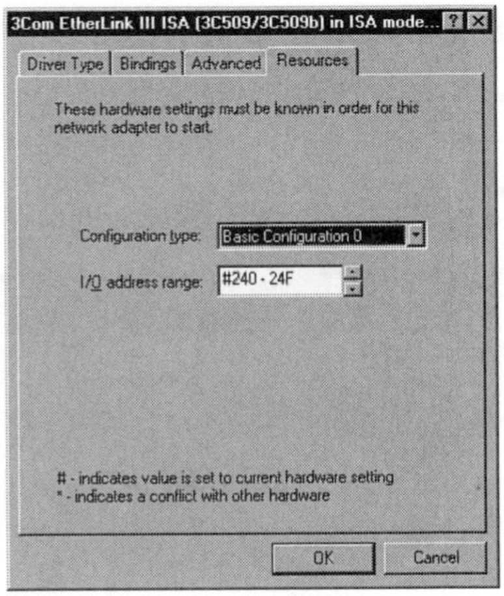

Fig. 31.15
The Resources page allows you to set up the hardware resources such as the I/O address range or Interrupt level.

Caution

Setting one of the resources to a value used by another card can cause the other card to stop working.

In addition to configuring the NIC on your computer system, you may have to change some settings for the network software on your computer. These settings are configured through the Network control panel, on the Identification and Access Control pages.

Configuring the Identification Settings Page

On the Identification page of the Network control panel (as shown in fig. 31.16) are settings which allow you to identify your computer on your local network. The three settings available on this page are:

- *Computer name.* Sets the name that your computer appears under on the network. Often, your computer name is assigned by your local network administrator; it should be unique on your network (no other computer should have the same name as yours).
- *Workgroup.* Sets the default workgroup that your computer belongs to on your network. The workgroup is the group of computers that appear first when you bring up your Network Neighborhood; you should check with either your local network administrator or the people you work with frequently to see which workgroup you should belong to. Also, you can see the workgroups that are available on your network by bringing up Network Neighborhood and selecting Entire Network.
- *Comment.* Sets a comment that appears next to your computer when people browse Network Neighborhood or look up the properties of your computer on the network.

Tip

It is usually a good idea to put the location of the computer and the name of the person who usually uses it in the Comment field so that if there is a problem or question about the computer, it is easy to find.

Configuring the Access Control Settings Page

The Access Control Settings page allows you to select the way that users on your network get access to resources that you make available on your local computer system. The two access control options available are:

- *Share Level Access.* Users on your network must supply a password to connect to a resource on your machine (such as a shared directory or printer). When you make a resource available, you set the password for that resource.

  This type of access is convenient when there is no central control over the resources on your network.

- *User Level Access*. Users on your network must log into a central server (usually running Windows NT) with an account and password. When you make a resource available, you set up a list of users who can access the resource. The list of users is retrieved from the server; you specify the server on the Resource page.

  This type of access is best when everyone on your network logs in through a central server and you want to control exactly who has access to your resources.

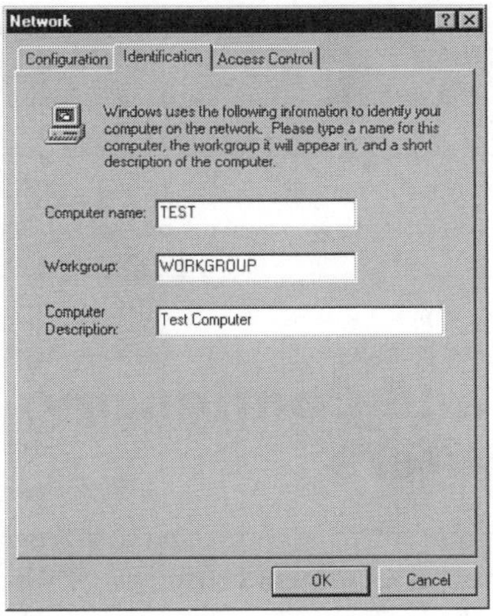

Fig. 31.16
The Identification page shows the name of the computer.

Installing Cables

After your network card is installed on your computer system, you have to attach a cable to connect the network card to your local network. The type of cable you use depends on the type of network hardware that is in use at your site, and also what kind of network card that is installed in your system.

Some network cards support several types of network cabling; the hardware manual included with your card should tell you which cable types are supported. You should also check with your local network administrator to make sure that you are using the right kind of cabling for your site.

Some of the more common types of network cabling include the following:

- *10 Base-T*. Looks like a normal telephone wire with a modular connector at each end. This type of cable plugs into a socket on your NIC.

- *Thin-wire Ethernet.* Looks like cable-television cabling. This type of cable has a round connector (called a *BNC connector*) that attaches to a T connector. The T connector then attaches to the connector on your network card. Normally, if the cabling ends at your machine, you must put an Ethernet terminator on the other side of the T connector.

- *Thick-wire Ethernet.* Looks like large cable-television cabling. This type of cable, which is not used as frequently as the other types, has a connector at the end that has several pins; this connector attaches to the socket on your network card.

Caution

If you are not familiar with the network cabling at your site, check with your network administrator before connecting your computer to your network. An incorrectly connected computer can cause serious network problems!

Installing and Configuring Shared Printers

If you don't have a printer directly connected to your computer, you can use a printer that is connected to another computer on your network, provided that the printer is made available (shared) on the computer it is attached to.

Installing a Shared Printer

The installation process for shared network printers is mostly the same as for installing a printer connected to your computer. The Add Printer Wizard (started from the Printers control panel) leads you through the steps to add a printer to Windows 95.

The first page of the Add Printer Wizard (see fig. 31.17) explains what the wizard will do. Click the Next button to continue.

The second page of the wizard (see fig. 31.18) asks you whether the printer is a local printer (connected directly to your computer) or a printer on the network. Since you are adding a network printer, select the Network Printer option and click Next to continue.

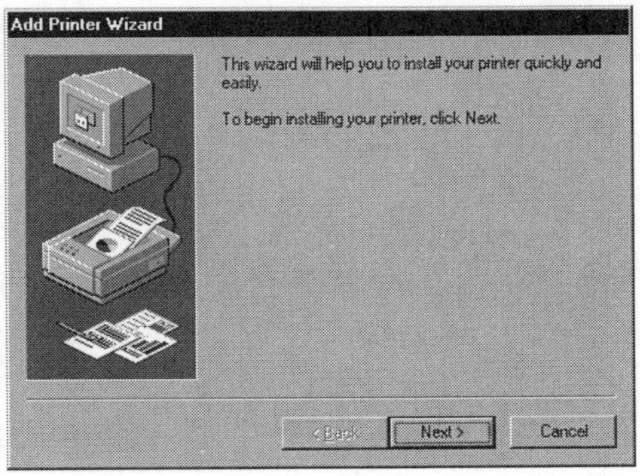

Fig. 31.17
The Add Printer Wizard first page appears.

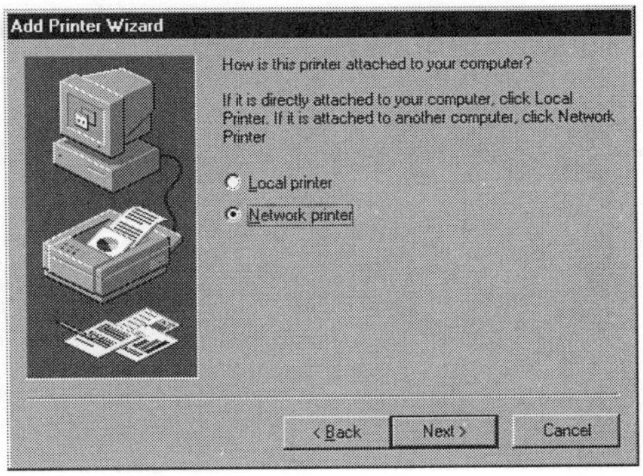

Fig. 31.18
Select a local or network printer in this wizard box.

On the third page of the Add Printer Wizard, you specify the network printer that you are adding. If you are not sure of the exact computer that the printer is connected to (or the name the printer is shared as) you can click the Browse button to bring up a browser similar to the Network Neighborhood; here you can look at the computers on your network to find the printer you want.

Once you have located the printer (or typed in the name of the printer in the standard \\COMPUTER\PRINTER_NAME format), you are ready to continue. If you plan to use the printer to print from a DOS program running under Windows 95, however, you should select Yes to the question `Do you print from MS-DOS based programs?` (see fig. 31.19).

The next page of the wizard (shown in fig. 31.20) asks you to identify the type of printer you are connecting to. Select the manufacturer of the printer from the left hand side of the list and the printer type from the right hand side. If the printer type you want is not listed, you may be able to find a printer in the list that is compatible with the printer you are attaching; you can contact the printer manufacturer or look in the printer manual for a list of compatible printers.

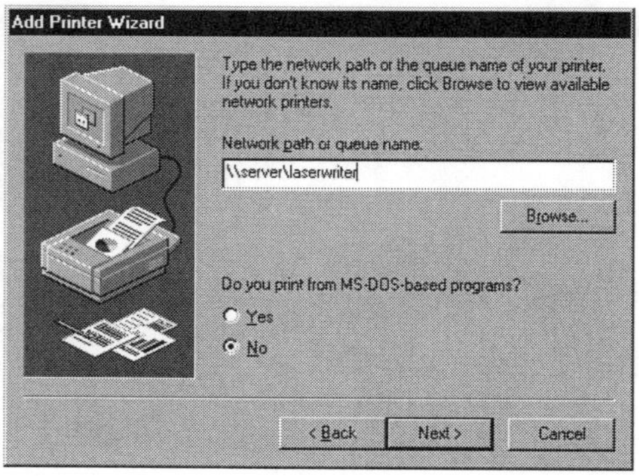

Fig. 31.19
The printer selection form is filled in.

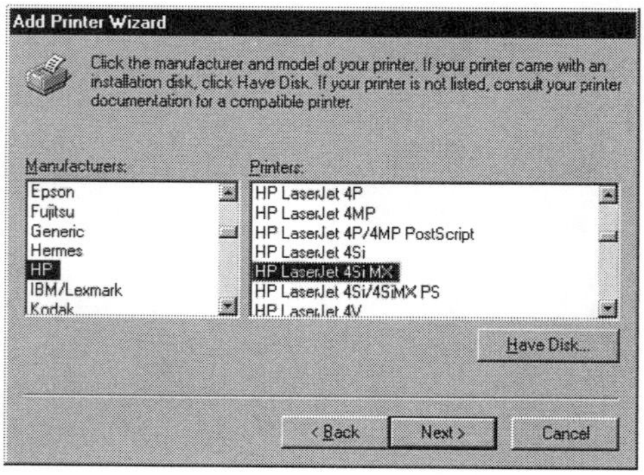

Fig. 31.20
Select a printer type in this wizard box.

Next, the wizard (as shown in fig. 31.21) asks you to type a name for the printer (the name that appears in print dialogs on your local system) and whether you want this printer to be your default printer. If you want to use this printer as your default printer, select the Yes option below the printer name. Clicking the Next button allows you to continue.

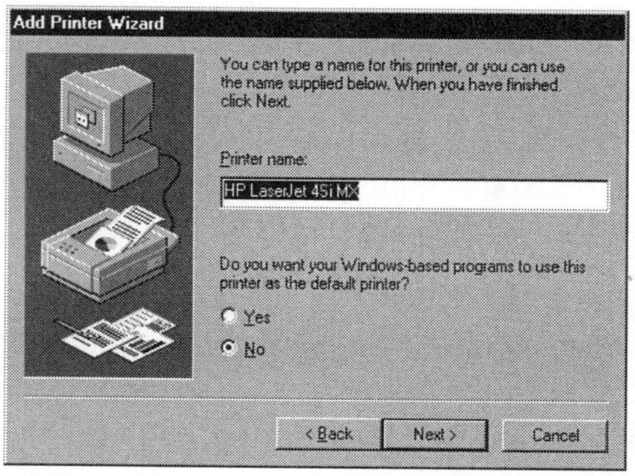

Fig. 31.21
Name the printer on your local system.

The next page asks you whether you want to print a test page after the printer is installed. This is usually a good idea; it allows you to make sure that the printer is connected correctly.

The wizard now installs the drivers for the printer and prints a test page (if you asked for it). During this process, you may be asked to insert several of your Windows 95 installation disks (or the Windows 95 installation CD-ROM if you have a CD-ROM drive); you should have these available.

After the drivers are installed and the wizard prints the test page (if you asked for one), you are asked whether the test page printed correctly. If you answer No, a troubleshooting wizard is started that leads you through several different procedures to try and resolve the problem.

◄ See "Installing a Printer to a Single PC," p. 605

Configuring Network Printers

You can configure the network printer by right-clicking the printer icon from the Printers control panel and selecting Properties. The printer is configured exactly the same as if it were connected to your local machine.

Installing Shared Fax Modems

Adding a shared fax modem from your network is similar to adding a regular modem (one that is connected to your computer system) to the Microsoft Fax server. The Microsoft Fax configuration program is started from the Control panel Mail and Fax sheet. When you start this control panel (as shown in fig. 31.22), you should select the Microsoft Fax profile and click the Properties button to begin configuring this service.

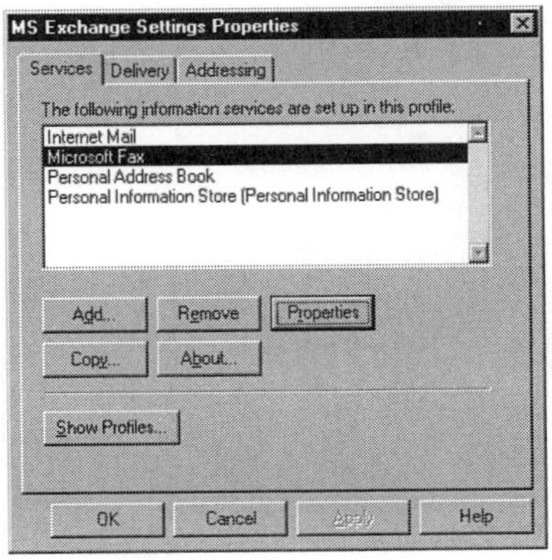

Fig. 31.22
Configure the Microsoft Fax service in this sheet.

On the Microsoft Fax properties sheet, select the Modems page to configure the network modem. Click the Add button to add a new modem to the fax service. This brings up the Add a Fax Modem dialog box, shown in figure 31.23, which asks you to specify the type of modem you are adding. You should select Network Fax Server.

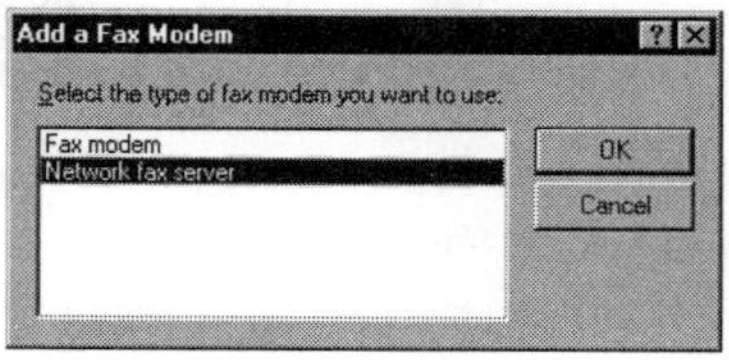

Fig. 31.23
Add a new network modem to the Microsoft Fax service in the Add a Fax Modem dialog box.

You now need to enter the shared fax folder in the usual \\COMPUTER\FOLDER form. If you are not sure of the computer or folder name, you should ask your network administrator.

Once you have specified the network fax folder, you should be able to use the Microsoft Fax service.

Installing Shared CD-ROM'S

CD-ROM drives that are shared on the network are mounted just like any other directory that is shared on your network. You can mount a shared CD-ROM drive by choosing Tools, Map Network Drive in the Explorer. The system prompts you for the machine name and share name; if you don't know these, you should open the Network Neighborhood and look for the machine that has the CD-ROM shared on it.

Once you have found the machine and the share name, you can mount the CD-ROM on your system. It appears as a new drive letter and can be accessed from the Explorer or My Computer icon. You can specify the drive letter on the Map Network Drive sheet.❖

Appendix A

Installing and Using Microsoft Plus! Companion for Windows 95

by Rob Tidrow

When discussing Windows 95, it's appropriate to give some coverage of the Microsoft Plus! Companion for Windows 95. Plus! is an add-on package to Windows 95 that you must purchase separately from Windows 95. Two of the products included with Plus!—System Agent and the Internet Explorer—are worth the price of Plus!. Other tools and features include Desktop Themes, which add zest to your desktop, ScanDisk 3, an expanded version of ScanDisk that comes with Windows 95, Dial-Up Networking Server, and a 3-D pinball game.

This appendix shows how to install Plus! on your system. You learn the following:

- Install all of Plus! or just the components you want
- Set up your system to connect with the Internet through the Internet Explorer
- Customize your desktop with Plus! Desktop Themes
- Schedule system maintenance with the System Agent
- Configure Dial-Up Networking Server to dial into from another computer

Installing Microsoft Plus!

After you install Windows 95 on your system, you can install the Microsoft Plus! Companion separately. Plus! is available in both the 3.5-inch floppy disk and CD-ROM formats. Before you start the Plus! Setup program, make sure you have the required system resources. Because of the enhanced features of Plus!, your computer must meet higher system requirements than the basic Windows 95 requirements. These requirements are as follows:

- At least a 80486 processor. A Pentium processor is recommended.
- CD-ROM or floppy drive and mouse (or similar pointing device)
- Windows 95 operating system installed
- 50M of hard disk space for a complete installation
- 8M or more of RAM. 12 to 16M recommended.
- Monitor and video card that displays 256 colors or more. Some of the Desktop Themes require a 16-bit display.
- Modem/fax modem to use the Internet and dial-up networking features
- Sound card and speakers are recommended, but required to hear the 3-D pinball sounds and music
- Windows 95 installation disks or CD-ROM

Like the Windows 95 Setup program, the Plus! Setup program enables you to install the complete Plus! package using the Typical installation option or only selected components using the Custom installation option.

Starting the Plus! Setup Program

You can use the Typical Setup option to install all components of Microsoft Plus!, which requires up to 16M of hard disk space. If your system is low on hard disk space, or if you don't want to install all of Plus!'s features, perform a Custom Setup. Both of these options are covered in the following procedures.

Start your computer and wait for the Windows 95 desktop to load. Next use these steps to complete the installation:

1. Insert the Plus! CD-ROM in the CD-ROM drive on your system.
2. If the Windows 95 AutoRun feature is activated, the Microsoft Plus! for Windows 95 screen appears. Click the Install Plus! icon. Skip to step 6.
3. If AutoRun is not activated, start the Add/Remove Programs option in Control Panel and choose the Install/Uninstall page.

4. Click the Install button and click Next on the Install From Floppy Disk or CD-ROM Wizard.

5. Windows automatically searches your floppy and CD-ROM drives for setup programs. When it finds the Plus! setup program, click Finish.

6. The Microsoft Plus! for Windows 95 Setup screen appears.

7. Click Continue. The Name and Organization Information dialog box appears, as shown in figure A.1.

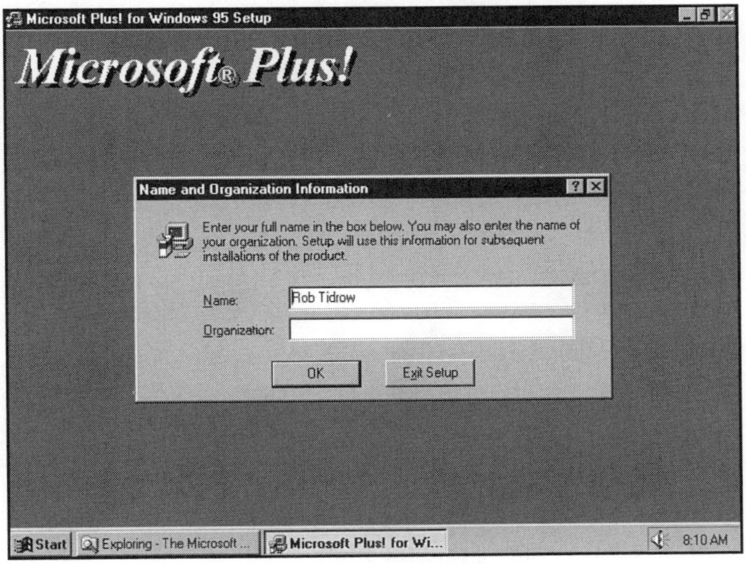

Fig. A.1
Enter your name and business name. Your business name is optional.

8. In the Name and Organization Information dialog box, enter your Name and Organization. Click OK. When the confirmation dialog box appears, click OK to confirm your entries.

9. In the next dialog box, enter the 10-digit CD-key number from your Plus! package in the dialog box that appears. Click OK.

10. The Microsoft Plus! for Windows 95 Setup dialog box appears, which shows you the Plus! product ID number. You should write down this number and store it with your Plus! CD. Click OK to confirm the Product ID number and continue Setup.

11. Next, Setup searches your system and displays a dialog box listing the folder that Setup creates to store the Plus! files (see fig. A.2). In the dialog box asking whether Windows 95 should create the destination

folder, click Yes to continue. Whether you accepted the folder recommended by Setup or specified another one, click OK to accept the Install folder.

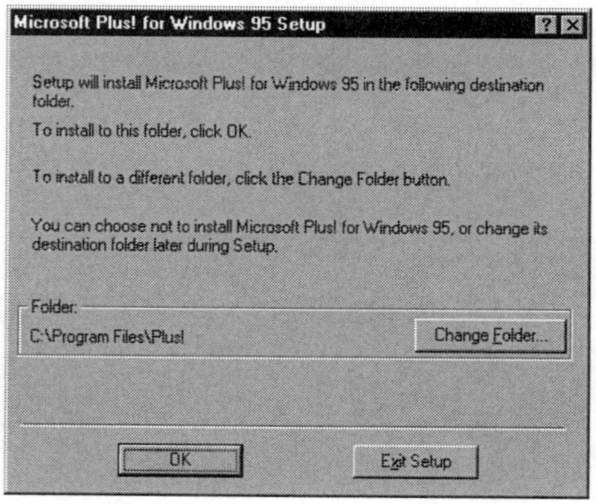

Fig. A.2
You need to confirm if you want Plus! to be installed in the suggested folder.

> **Note**
>
> If you want to install Plus! in a different folder, click the Change Folder button. In the Change Folder dialog box, specify the drive and folder to use by selecting them from the list or typing a path in the Path text box. Click OK.

12. You now need to specify which type of installation to perform (see fig. A.3). Select Typical or Custom option.

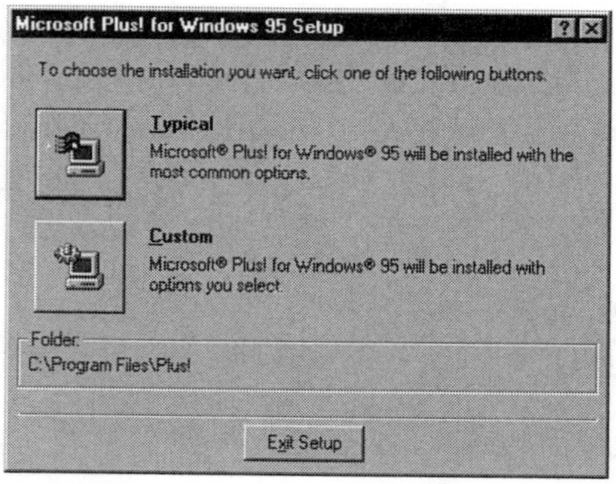

Fig. A.3
If you want to install everything, select Typical. To choose the components that Setup installs, select Custom.

> **Note**
>
> When you select the Custom installation option, you can customize how a particular component installs. To do so, click the component name in the Options list, then click the Change Option button. In the dialog box that appears, click to deselect features you don't want to install in the Options list, then click OK to return to the Custom screen. Repeat this step for each of the components you want to customize.
>
> When you've finished specifying which of the components to install in the Custom screen, click the Continue button. After you click Continue, the Setup process progresses the same as for a Typical Setup.

13. If you selected to install the System Agent, Windows prompts you to choose whether to run system maintenance tasks (such as ScanDisk) at night or during your business day. Click Yes to run these utilities at night, but you must keep your computer on at night. Click No to run these utilities during the day, but during times when you normally don't use your PC, such as during the lunch hour.

14. Setup checks your system's video installation. If your display runs in 256 colors, Setup displays the Video Resolution Check dialog box. This dialog box asks whether you want to install the high-color Desktop Themes, even if your monitor currently displays only 256 colors. If your display is capable of displaying more colors (operating in 16-bit color or higher) and you have ample hard disk space, click Yes. Otherwise, click No.

15. Setup checks your system for necessary disk space, then begins copying files to your computer. Setup displays a message that it's updating your system.

> **Note**
>
> After the preceding step, Plus! Setup displays the initial screen for the Internet Setup Wizard, if you selected to install this option. If you don't want to set up the connection now, click Cancel. You can return to it later. If you do want to set up your Internet connection, click the Next button and see "Setting Up the Internet Explorer" later in this chapter. If you click Cancel, the Internet Setup Wizard asks you to confirm that you want to exit the Internet Setup Wizard. Click Yes to do so.

16. The Set Up a Desktop Theme dialog box appears. Click OK to continue.

◀ See "Setting Background and Wallpaper Properties," p. 157

17. The Desktop Themes dialog box appears, enabling you to select your first Desktop Theme (see fig. A.4). You can select a theme now, or use the Desktop Themes icon in Control Panel after installation to set up a theme. For now, click OK to continue.

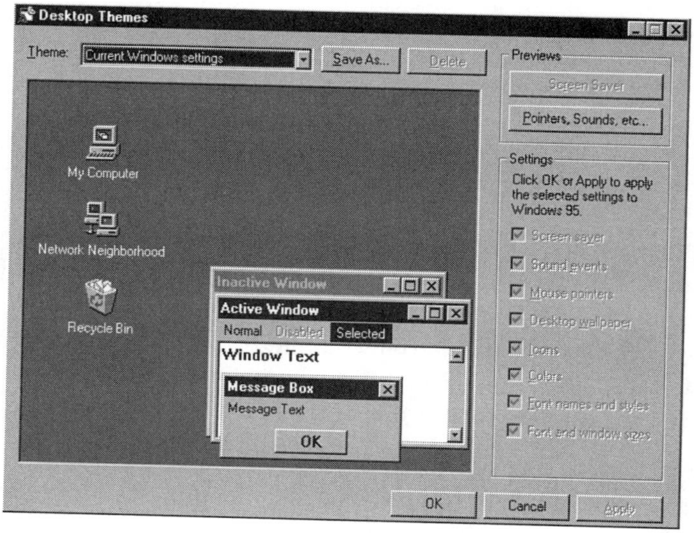

Fig. A.4
You can select a Desktop Theme at this point, or choose one after you have Plus! installed.

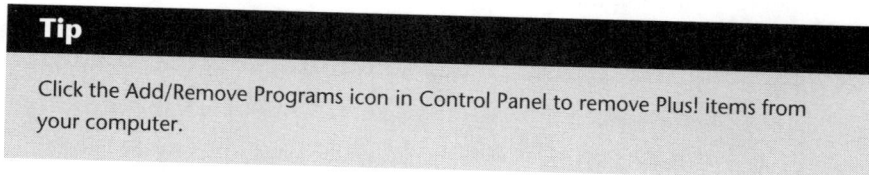

18. Setup displays a dialog box telling you that it needs to restart Windows. To complete the setup, click the Restart Windows button. Your computer and Windows 95 restart. When Windows 95 restarts, you should see the word `Plus!` on the Windows 95 startup screen to indicate that you've successfully installed Microsoft Plus!.

Tip

Click the Add/Remove Programs icon in Control Panel to remove Plus! items from your computer.

Now you can start using the features of Plus!.

Setting Up the Internet Explorer

The Internet Explorer software enables you to connect to The Microsoft Network or the Internet via a direct network connection or a PPP dial-up account from an Internet service provider. Microsoft Plus! provides the Internet Explorer software, plus the Internet Setup Wizard.

You can use the Internet Setup Wizard to install the Internet Explorer while you're installing the rest of Plus!. Or, if you want to use the Internet Setup Wizard later after Plus! is installed, click the Start button on the Taskbar, point to Programs, Accessories, Internet Tools, and Internet Setup Wizard.

To use the Internet Setup Wizard to install the Internet Explorer, follow these steps:

1. Click the Next button from the Internet Setup Wizard Welcome screen to proceed with the setup. The How to Connect screen appears.
2. Specify whether you want to connect via The Microsoft Network or a PPP account you have with an Internet service provider by clicking the appropriate option button. Click Next to continue.

> **Note**
>
> If you choose the I Already Have an Account with a Different Service Provider, you are presented with the Service Provider Information screen. In this screen, you select your provider. See Chapter 12 for information on setting up a provider under Windows 95.

See "PPP and SLIP Connections," p. 295

3. The Installing Files screen appears, reminding you that you may need your Windows 95 setup CD-ROM or disks. Click Next to continue.
4. The Setup Wizard copies files to your hard disk. When it concludes, it may display a dialog box asking you to insert your Windows 95 setup CD-ROM or disk into the appropriate drive. Do so, then click OK.
5. The Setup Wizard copies additional files to your system. Then, The Microsoft Network dialog box appears.

   You can choose to set up a new Microsoft Network account or connect to an existing Microsoft Network account. Depending on which option you choose, the wizard guides you through the process. Simply respond to each wizard screen, providing information such as user name, password, and dial-up options. Click Next after you provide each item of information the wizard requests.
6. The Setup Wizard displays a dialog box telling you that it needs to restart Windows. To complete the setup, click the Restart Windows button. Your computer and Windows 95 restart.

Uninstalling Plus!

If you find that you do not want Plus! on your system any longer, or if you want to remove some Plus! components, you can use the Windows 95 Add/Remove Programs feature. This feature enables you to automatically uninstall a program. To uninstall Plus!:

1. Select Start, Settings, and click Control Panel. The Control Panel window opens.

2. Double-click the Add/Remove Programs icon. The Add/Remove Program Properties sheet appears (see fig. A.5).

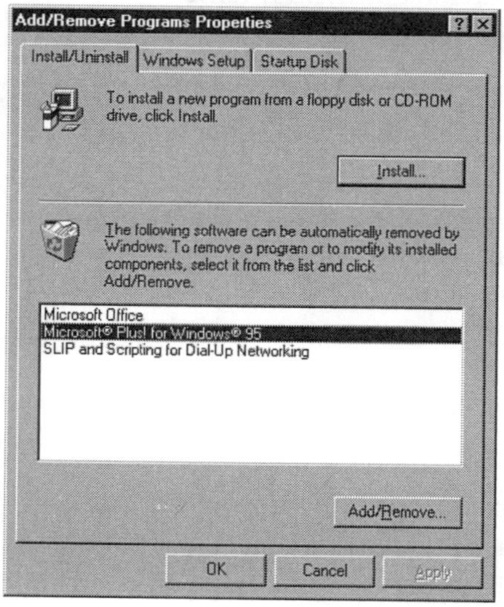

Fig. A.5
Use the Add/Remove Programs feature to uninstall part or all of Plus!.

3. In the Install/Uninstall page, a list shows the programs that can be added or removed from your system. Double-click Microsoft Plus! for Windows 95 in the list.

4. The Microsoft Plus! for Windows 95 Setup installation maintenance screen appears.

5. You can choose to remove part of or all of the Plus! program. To uninstall all of Plus!, click the Remove All button. Or, to choose individual components to remove, click the Add/Remove button to display the Maintenance Install screen (see fig. A.6). In the Options list, click to clear the check mark beside each Plus! component to remove from your system, then click Continue.

6. Whether you're removing all or parts of Plus!, a dialog box appears asking you to confirm the removal. Click Yes to continue the uninstall process.

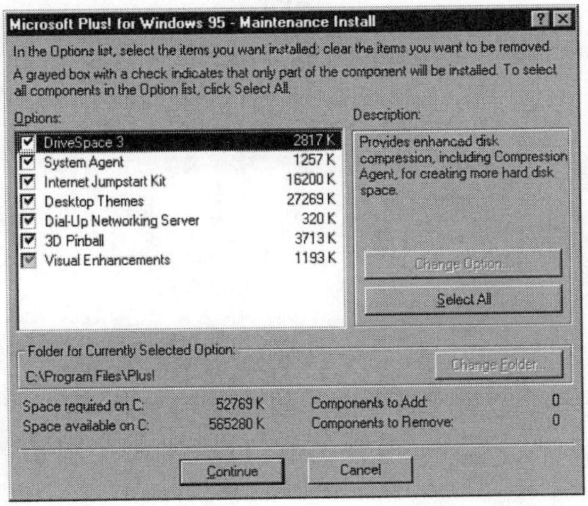

Fig. A.6
You can remove a Plus! component by clearing its check box.

Setup removes the Plus! files from your system.

7. Microsoft Plus! Setup displays a dialog box telling you that it needs to restart Windows. To complete the uninstalling Plus!, click the Restart Windows button. Your computer and Windows 95 restart.

> **Note**
>
> If you uninstall all the Plus! components, the word PLUS! does not appear on the Windows 95 startup screen when Windows 95 reboots.

Working with Desktop Themes

You learned in Chapter 6, "Configuring the Windows 95 Desktop and Display," how to change wallpaper and use different color schemes for your display. With Plus!, you can add even more life to your desktop using Desktop Themes. Desktop Themes combines high-color graphics, sounds, and various icons and mouse pointers to add some zest to your computer.

> **Tip**
>
> Use the Add/Remove Programs icon in Control Panel to add the Desktop Themes if you did not do so during Setup.

Plus! provides Desktop Theme combinations both for computers displaying in 256 colors and computers displaying in 16-bit or higher color. An example of a Desktop Themes screen provided with Plus! is shown in figure A.7.

Fig. A.7
Dangerous Creatures takes you on a walk on the wild side. This is a 256-color image.

When you choose a Desktop Theme, you can specify whether to replace Windows screen elements you specify using the Desktop Theme icon in Control Panel. In the Desktop Themes dialog box (see fig. A.8), you can select from the following elements which to use with your system:

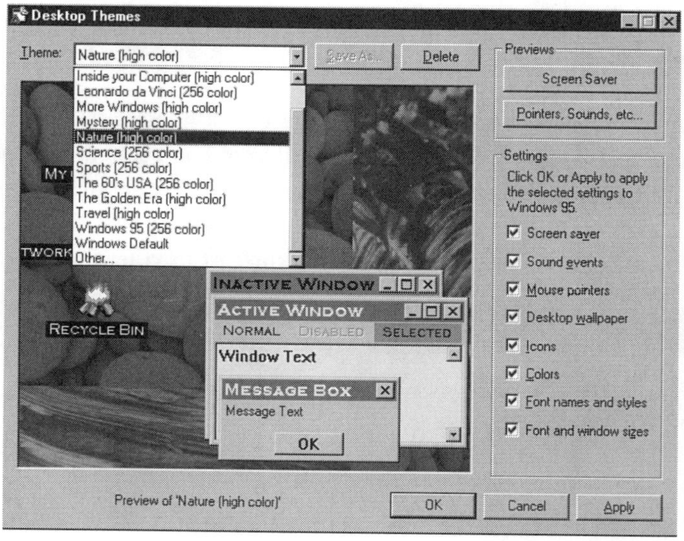

Fig. A.8
Select the theme of your choice from the Themes drop-down list, as well as the elements to use.

- *Screen Saver*. Displays the Theme screen saver when you leave your computer idle.
- *Sound vents*. Assigns Theme sounds to system events such as starting applications and exiting from Windows.
- *Mouse Pointers*. Applies the Theme pointer styles for different types of pointers. Some of these pointers are interesting; others are clunky looking.
- *Desktop Wallpaper*. Covers the desktop with the decorative background provided by the Theme.
- *Icons*. Assigns custom icons to desktop objects, including the Recycle Bin and My Computer.
- *Colors*. Applies the Theme colors to windows and other screen elements. Unfortunately, many of the color schemes are ugly, but you are the final judge of this.
- *Font Names and Styles*. Assigns Theme fonts for screen elements, including window titles and task buttons.
- *Font and Window Sizes*. Uses the Theme font sizes and default window sizes.

Configuring Windows 95 with a Desktop Theme

Plus Setup! creates an object icon for the Desktop Themes in the Windows 95 Control Panel, which contains other objects for controlling Windows' appearance and operation. Use the following steps to use the Desktop Themes object to select a Theme:

1. Click the Start button on the Taskbar. Point to Settings, then click Control Panel.
2. In the Control Panel window, double-click the Desktop Themes icon. The Desktop Themes dialog box appears. Use this dialog box to select and set up a Theme.
3. Click the down arrow beside the Theme drop-down list to display the available Desktop Themes. Click the name of the theme you want to use. A dialog box tells you that the theme files are being imported. When that dialog box closes, the preview area of the Desktop Themes changes to display the appearance of the Theme you selected, as shown in figure A.9.

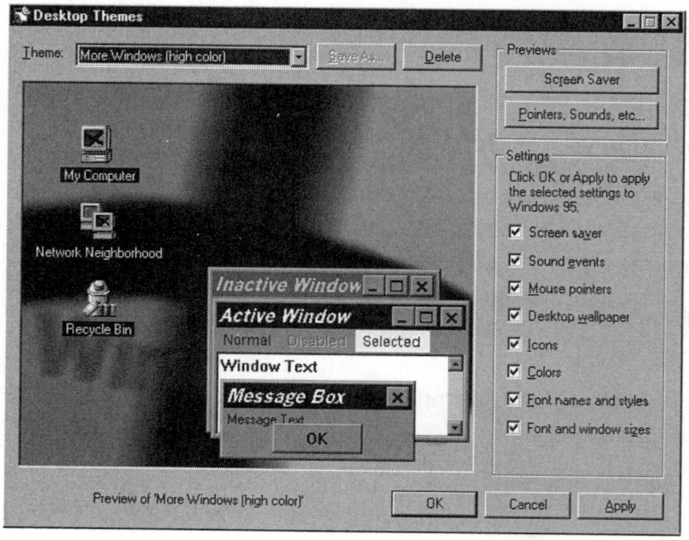

Fig. A.9
You can see a preview of the Desktop Theme before you decide to use it on your system.

4. At the right side of the dialog box, choose the Settings to use for the Theme you selected. To deselect a setting, click to remove the check from the box beside it.

5. To preview the selected Theme's screen saver, click the Screen Saver button in the Previews area in the upper-right corner of the dialog box. The screen saver appears on-screen. Move the mouse or press a key to conclude the preview.

6. To preview several of the selected Theme's other elements, click the Pointers, Sounds, Etc. button in the Previews area. A Preview dialog box for the Theme appears; the dialog box has three tabs for Pointers, Sounds, and Visuals. Click the tab you want to view. Each tab offers a list box with the elements for the theme. For the Pointers and Visuals tabs, simply click an element in the list to see a preview in the Preview or Picture area at the bottom of the dialog box. For the Sounds tab, click an element in the list, then click the right arrow icon near the bottom of the dialog box to hear the sound. Click the Close button to conclude your preview.

7. After you have selected a theme, chosen settings, and previewed elements to your satisfaction, choose OK to close the Desktop Themes window. The selected Desktop Theme appears on your system.

Adjusting Plus! Visual Settings

Plus! adds new features to the Display settings available in the Windows 95 Control Panel. These visual settings are designed primarily to make your desktop more attractive. Plus! enables you to specify new icons for the My Computer, Network Neighborhood, and Recycle Bin Desktop icons. You can choose to show the contents of a window (rather than just an outline when you drag the window). You can choose whether or not you want to smooth the appearance of large fonts on-screen. You also can choose to show icons with all possible colors or expand the wallpaper (when centered using the Background page of the Display Properties sheet from Control Panel) so it stretches to fill the entire screen.

Note

Most of the Plus! visual settings require more system resources than the normal display settings. In particular, showing window contents while dragging and using all colors in icons consumes more RAM. Consider all your computing requirements before you use up RAM by selecting any of these features. If you notice that Windows 95 runs considerably slower with any of these features enabled, turn off the features.

To work with the Plus! visual settings, click the Start button on the Taskbar. Point to Settings, then click Control Panel. In the Control Panel window, double-click the Display icon. The Display Properties sheet appears. Click the Plus! page to display its options, as shown in figure A.10. To assign a new Desktop icon, click the icon you want to change in the Desktop Icons area near the top of the dialog box. Click Change Icon. In the Change Icon page that appears, scroll to display the icon you want, then click OK to accept the change.

To enable any of the other Plus! display features, select the feature in the Visual Settings area of the Plus! page. When a check appears beside the feature, that feature is selected. If you want more information about a particular feature, right-click the feature, then click What's This?. A brief description of the feature appears. Click or press Esc to clear the description. To accept your visual settings and close the Display Properties sheet, click OK. Close the Control Panel window, if you like.

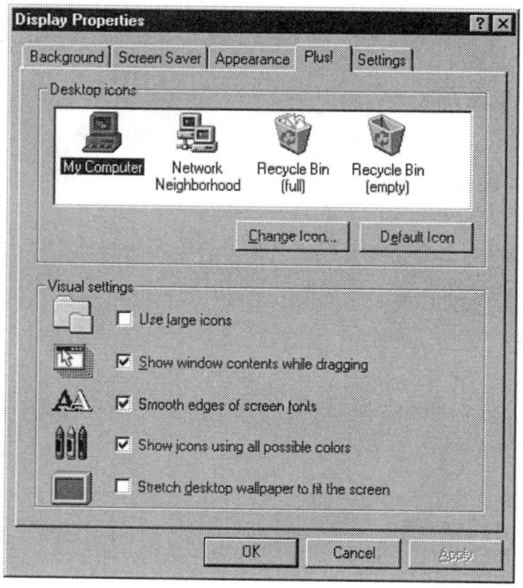

Fig. A.10
You can make adjustments to the Windows display properties using this dialog box.

Managing Utilities with the System Agent

You learned in Chapter 1, "Preparing To Install Windows 95," that you need to run ScanDisk and other hard disk maintenance programs before you run Setup. After you install and configure Windows 95, you should get into the habit of running these same utilities, plus a backup program, weekly or monthly to keep your hard disk optimized. Most users tend not to perform system maintenance operations until after a disaster strikes. Plus! provides the System Agent, a program that enables you to schedule when to run other programs, such as system maintenance utilities like Disk Defragmenter, ScanDisk, and Compression Agent. The System Agent can run other programs as well, and notify you when your hard disk is low on space.

By default, the System Agent is enabled after you install Plus!. This means that each time you start Windows 95, the System Agent starts automatically and runs in the background, only becoming active when it needs to start a scheduled program or notify you of low disk space. Even though System Agent is active by default, it isn't fully set up. After you install System Agent, it automatically places Low Disk Space Notification, ScanDisk for Windows (Standard Test), Disk Defragmenter, and ScanDisk for Windows (Thorough Test) programs in the System Agent. You need to manually tell the System Agent which other programs to run, when to run them, and which program features to use.

To schedule programs with the System Agent, use the following steps:

1. Click the Start button on the Taskbar. Point to Programs, then to Accessories.
2. Choose System Tools, then click System Agent. The System Agent window opens.
3. Choose Schedule a New Program from the Program menu. The Schedule a New Program dialog box appears (see fig. A.11).

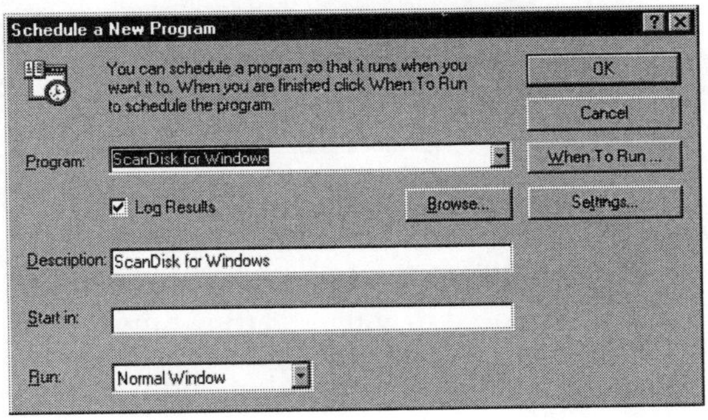

Fig. A.11
The Schedule a New Program dialog box enables you set the schedule for a program to run.

4. Click the drop-down list arrow to open the Program list. Click a program from the list that appears. You can choose ScanDisk for Windows, Disk Defragmenter, Compression Agent, or Low Disk Space Notification. If you want to run a program other than one of these, click the Browse button, select the program to run in the Browse dialog box, then click OK. No matter which method you used, the selected program appears as the Program choice.
5. If needed, you can edit the Description for the program and Start In folder, which specifies the folder containing files to program needs to run.
6. Open the Run drop-down list and specify whether you want the program to run in a Normal Window, Minimized, or Maximized.
7. To specify the schedule for the program, click the When to Run button. The Change Schedule of dialog box appears (see fig. A.12).
8. Click a Run option, such as Weekly or Monthly. Your choice here affects the options available in the Start At area of the dialog box.

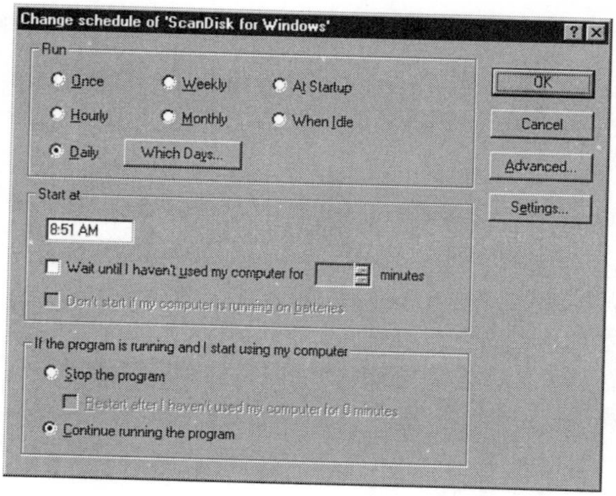

Fig. A.12
Use the Change Schedule dialog box to set up a schedule for the selected program.

9. Specify the options you want in the Start At area of the dialog box. Although there may be other options depending on your choice in step 8, you'll always need to enter a starting time.

   Also, you can turn on the next check box and specify a number of minutes to tell System Agent to wait if you're using your computer when the scheduled program run time occurs.

10. In the bottom area of the dialog box, choose whether System Agent should Stop the Program or Continue Running the Program should you start using your computer when the scheduled program is running. Stopping the program can protect against data loss while running system utilities.

11. Click the Settings button to control which features the selected program uses when the System Agent runs the program. The Scheduled Settings dialog box that appears varies depending on the selected program.

12. Specify the settings you want for the selected program, then click OK to close the Scheduled Settings dialog box.

13. Click OK again to finish scheduling the program. System Agent adds the program to the list of scheduled programs.

Note

Keep in mind that you can schedule the same program to run at different times with different settings. For example, you can schedule a Standard ScanDisk check once a week, plus a thorough check once per month.

Although you can use the Program menu choices to make changes to the schedule and settings for one of the listed programs, it's faster to simply right-click the program you want to make changes to. A shortcut menu appears, from which you can choose the following:

- *Properties*. Changes things like the program startup folder and settings (click the Settings button in the dialog box that appears).
- *Change Schedule*. Adjusts how often System Agent runs the program.
- *Run Now*. Runs the program immediately, using the settings you've specified.
- *Disable*. Prevents the listed program from running at the designated time but leaves the program on the list; choose Disable again to reinstate the program's schedule.
- *Remove*. Deletes the selected program from the System Agent list; confirm the deletion by clicking Yes at the warning that appears.

The Advanced menu in System Agent offers two commands for controlling System Agent itself. Turn on the Suspend System Agent choice whenever you want to stop all your regularly scheduled programs from running; then toggle this choice back on when you need to. The Stop Using System Agent choice completely stops System Agent operation; after you use this option, System Agent no longer loads when you start Windows, and you have to select System Agent from the System Tools Shortcuts to start using it. To close System Agent after setting it up, select Exit from the Program menu.

Configuring DriveSpace 3

Windows 95 offers DriveSpace disk compression, which enables you to pack more data on your hard and floppy disks. DriveSpace 3, included with Plus!, can handle larger disks—up to 2G—than the Windows 95 DriveSpace, which can only handle hard disks up to 512M in size. To be more efficient, DriveSpace 3 works with smaller units of data on the disk—512-byte sectors as opposed to the 32K-byte cluster size regular DriveSpace works with. This ensures that DriveSpace 3 wastes less space on the disk. Finally, DriveSpace 3 offers two new, more dense compression formats, one of which is particularly suited for Pentium systems.

Caution

Although compression provides you with extra disk space, a compressed disk often is slower to use than an uncompressed disk. Also, the greater the compression, the slower your system is likely to perform when working with the compressed disk. Also, compressing your system's primary hard disk can take quite a bit of time, during which you won't be able to work with your system. Some systems may take several hours to compress.

Use the following steps to compress a disk with DriveSpace 3:

1. Click the Start button on the Taskbar. Choose Programs, Accessories.
2. Point to System Tools, then click DriveSpace (after Plus! installation, the icon beside the DriveSpace will include a 3 to indicate DriveSpace 3). The DriveSpace 3 window appears.
3. Click the drive that you want to compress.

Note

You can select a previously compressed disk, then use the Upgrade choice on the Drive menu to convert the disk to DriveSpace 3 format.

4. Open the Advanced menu and choose Settings. The Disk Compression Settings dialog box appears.
5. Click the option button for the compression method you want to use:

   No compression. Does not compress the selected drive.

   No compression unless drive is X% full. Only compresses the disk after it's more full than the percentage you specify.

   Standard compression. Compresses the disk contents by approximately a 1.8:1 ratio.

   HiPack compression. Compresses the disk contents by up to 2.3:1.

6. Click OK to close the Compression Settings dialog box and accept the specified compression method.
7. Open the Drive menu and choose Compress. The Compress a Drive dialog box appears, informing you of the estimated results of the compression operation—that is, how much free space and used space the disk will have after compression.

8. Click the Options button. The Compression Options dialog box appears. Use it to specify a drive letter and free space for the Host drive where DriveSpace 3 will store compressed information about the drive. You should only need to change these first two options if your system is connected to a network that uses drive H for another purpose.

> **Note**
>
> To compress a floppy disk that you use on another computer that doesn't have DriveSpace 3, click to select the Use DoubleSpace-compatible Format check box. Use this option for Windows 95 systems without DriveSpace 3 or for systems using DriveSpace from a DOS 6.x version.

Click OK to accept the compression options you set.

9. Click the Start button in the Compress a Drive dialog box. The Are You Sure? dialog box appears, asking you to confirm the compression operation.

10. Click the Back Up Files button to make a backup copy of the files on the disk before you compress it. Although this is an optional step, you should make a backup of your critical files before compressing your hard disk. If you select the backup option, DriveSpace 3 runs the backup utility installed to work with your system. Follow any on-screen instructions to complete the backup process.

11. When the backup is finished, click Continue to compress the disk. DriveSpace 3 compresses the disk, then redisplays the Compress a Drive dialog box to report on the compression results.

12. Click Close to complete compressing the disk.

Configuring Dial-Up Networking Server

The Dial-Up Networking Server included with Plus! enables you to set up your computer so that others can dial into it from another computer. You can use this option if you travel frequently and use a laptop on the road and want to access files on your stationary PC at your office or home. You also can share files with other people by allowing them to dial into your computer and transfer files back and forth.

To set up the Dial-Up Networking Server, you must have a modem configured and the Dial-Up Networking feature installed. Use the following steps to set up your computer so that you can dial into it:

1. Double-click My Computer, and double-click the Dial-Up Networking icon.
2. In the Dial-Up Networking folder menu, select Connections and then Dial-Up Server. The Dial-Up Server dialog box appears (see fig. A.13).

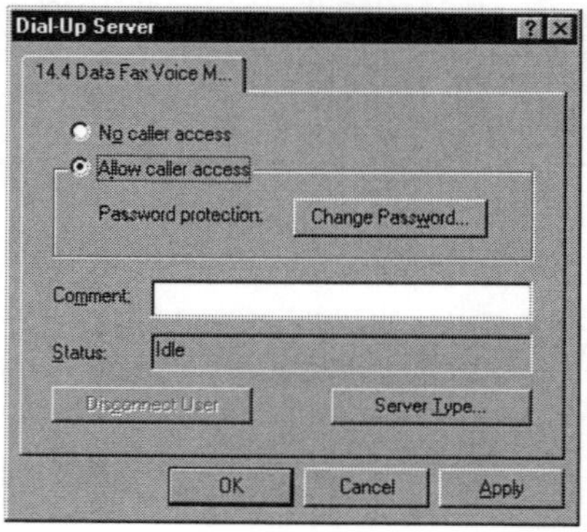

Fig. A.13
You configure the Dial-Up Network Server using the Dial-Up Server sheet.

3. Choose the Allow Caller Access radio button to enable users to dial into your computer.
4. Click the Change Password button to set a password for users to use to gain access to your computer.

> **Caution**
>
> When you use the Dial-Up Network Server feature and do not set a password, you are vulnerable to users hacking into your system. Be sure to set a password and change it periodically.

5. Fill in the Dial-Up Networking Password dialog box and click OK.
6. (Optional) Fill in the Comment field with a description of the connection, such as the phone number needed to access this server.
7. Click the Server Type button to establish the type of server (such as the PPP, Windows 95, Windows NT, Internet server) the Dial-Up Network Server feature uses. The options available are those that are configured for the Dial-Up Adapter for your system.

8. You also can configure the Dial-Up Network Server to use software compression during file transfers and enable the password encryption option. This latter option is used to provide an extra layer of security by encrypting your passwords as you are dialing out. The computer to which you are connected must also support this feature; otherwise, you may encounter problems connecting with it.

Tip

Use the software compression option to speed up the transmission speed between your computer and the connected one.

9. Click OK twice to save your selections and to activate the Dial-Up Network Server.

Caution

When you activate the Dial-Up Network Server feature, your modem port is always open. This means that if you try to use your modem to call out using another communications package (besides those built into Windows 95), you will not be able to initialize the COM port and be unable to dial out. Be sure to deactivate Dial-Up Network Server when you want to use another communications package.

Appendix B

Troubleshooting Windows 95 Installation

by Rob Tidrow

Throughout this book, you've been shown how to install and configure Windows 95 to work with your computer. Many of the chapters include troubleshooting elements to help diagnose and remedy problems you may encounter during setup, whether you're experiencing problems with Windows 95 Setup, installing hardware devices, or configuring your desktop. This appendix gathers all these troubleshooting hints and tips and puts them in one spot for you. In addition, you find many more troubleshooting items that are placed here.

This appendix covers the following topics:

- Windows 95 Setup problems
- Memory, disks, and devices problems
- Windows architecture questions
- Problems associated with applications
- Hardware and printer problems
- Network hardware questions
- Microsoft Fax questions
- Norton Utilities problems

Caution

Windows 95 is a new operating system. With that comes problems supporting every computer and configuration available. The following troubleshooting items are known to work in some situations. We cannot guarantee they work for every computer. Before attempting any of these solutions, make a backup of your entire system. This ensures you against losing critical data if you encounter major problems.

Windows 95 Setup and Bootup

Windows 95 was designed to be easy to install. Although wizards help guide the user through the setup process, the true test comes when you encounter problems during setup or after you boot up Windows 95 for the first time. Use this section to help you troubleshoot some of the most common setup and bootup problems with Windows 95.

Tip

If you are using older hardware device drivers (those not designed for Windows 95), you might encounter problems using some devices. Although this appendix addresses many specific hardware issues, you should contact the device's manufacturer for new Windows 95 device drivers for your component. Another valuable source is to subscribe to the **comp.os.ms-windows.win95.setup** newsgroup on the Internet. You'll find hundreds of messages devoted exclusively to problems with Windows 95.

What are the system requirements for Windows 95?

Windows 95 requires the following components from your system. You may need more or less depending on the installation type you choose:

Component	Requirement of Windows 95
Processor	80386 or higher
Hard Drive	30M of free disk space for a compact installation; 40M for a typical installation
Memory	4M
Input Device	Mouse
Floppy Disk	Required for installation from floppy disks

Component	Requirement of Windows 95
CD-ROM Drive	Required for installation from CD
Monitor	VGA
Fax/Modem	Required to use The Microsoft Network, Remote Access, HyperTerminal (included in Windows 95), Microsoft Fax, and Phone Dialer

I don't have much time. How long does it take to install Windows 95?

Depending on the installation type you choose, Windows 95 requires between 30 minutes and two hours to completely install.

Should I install Windows 95 over my previous versions of Windows?

There are advantages to both options. If you decide to keep both versions of Windows on your machine, then you need to reinstall all your applications under Windows 95. The advantage is that you have a fail-safe mechanism if Windows 95 does not work properly on your machine. You can move back to Windows 3.x immediately. Once you test your new Windows 95 installation, delete your old Windows 3.x files, including the applications installed under Windows 3.x.

On the other hand, if you install over your previous version of Windows, your applications work as soon as you install Windows 95. You also do not need as much free disk space available to start Windows 95 Setup when upgrading a previous version.

What should I do to make this a hassle-free Windows 95 installation?

There are no guarantees for a hassle-free installation, even though most users experience very few installation problems. The best advice is to prepare your system (and yourself) for the installation. Make backup copies of your AUTOEXEC.BAT and CONFIG.SYS files, copy any network files you have, make a DOS boot disk, and back up to floppy or tape *any* file that you cannot live without. These files include documents, graphics, spreadsheets, and the like.

Some other helpful tips include remarking the `load=` and `run=` lines in your WIN.INI files (place a semicolon in front of those lines) and turning off any screen savers or TSRs that you may have running. If you have any unnecessary programs starting from AUTOEXEC.BAT and CONFIG.SYS, you should

REM out those lines as well (keep your network and CD-ROM lines in there, however). You might also want to remove any programs from the Startup program group in Windows 3.x before starting Windows 95 Setup.

I have a CMOS (or system BIOS) anti-virus setting. Will this cause a problem during installation?

Yes, Windows 95 will stop and report an error message. You must remove this setting and turn off the virus scan before proceeding with the Windows 95 installation. Consult your system's hardware documentation for information on this.

During Windows 95 Setup, I get an error message that Disk 2 is corrupted. What can I do?

Many users using the floppy disk version of Windows 95 have encountered this problem. Microsoft is aware of it and offers this explanation:

> We have tracked down a handful of disk sets nationwide from customers that have reported this problem. In every case the second disk turned out to have been corrupted by a virus on the customer's machine that had infected the second disk during install. To be clear, the virus was on the customer's machine prior to installation of Windows 95 and not caused by the Windows 95 disks. This generally happens on disk two because this is the disk where customer registration information is stored during install so setup writes to this disk. The virus, which installs itself undetected on a typical floppy disk, is exposed because of the unique high-density format used for Windows 95 distribution diskettes.
>
> Once the virus has infected the diskette, it is bad. The customer can phone 1-800-207-7766 to receive a new disk one and two. Product Support will also be able to handle this problem.

During Windows 95 Setup, my computer keeps hanging during the information gathering process. What can I do?

First, let it continue working for 20 minutes or so. Sometimes your computer just needs a lot of time to gather the information requested by Windows 95. Second, if you are certain your system has crashed, turn off the computer for 10 seconds and turn it back on. Run Setup again and use the Safe Recovery option if it appears (it may not if your system crashed too soon). Setup bypasses the phase at which it encountered the problem the previous time. If it hangs again, repeat the process a few more times if necessary. If that fails, tell Setup that you want to manually configure the hardware so it doesn't look for it during Setup.

My system hangs on the first boot and I'm installing from a CD-ROM. What happened?

You may have a conflict between real-mode and protected-mode drivers with your CD-ROM. First, remark (REM) out the CD-ROM drivers in your CONFIG.SYS file and reboot. If you still encounter a problem, try to boot into Safe Mode. (Reinstall Windows 95 if you can't boot into Safe Mode.) Also, make sure you have a backup copy of your CD-ROM drivers on a boot disk.

From here, create a BOOTLOG.TXT from the Startup menu to see where Windows failed. Look for a file called DETCRASH.LOG. If you find this, it means that you have a problem with Windows 95 detecting your hardware. In the IOS.INI file, remark out the drivers that are loading in CONFIG.SYS to make sure there isn't a problem with these protected-mode drivers. Also, boot into Windows 95 in Safe Mode and remove any devices from Device Manager that you think may be causing problems. Make a copy of your SYSTEM.INI file (call it SYSTEM.BAK for instance) and copy the SYSTEM.CB file to SYSTEM.INI. Very few drivers load into the SYSTEM.CB file, including the mouse driver. Because of this, you might lose the functionality of your mouse, but that's okay because you are trying to isolate a CD-ROM problem. If this solves your problem, look in your SYSTEM.INI file for any entries made by third-party applications, such as Adobe Type Manager. Remark them out and reboot. After your system reboots, Windows should locate your mouse. If not, add it back to your SYSTEM.INI file and reboot.

Windows 95 has started in Safe Mode. What is this?

In Safe Mode, Windows 95 uses default settings and Windows 95 drivers for your video and mouse, and only the necessary device drivers to run Windows 95. Devices such as network cards and CD-ROMs are not accessible during Safe Mode. Use Safe Mode to diagnose and fix possible problems you may be having with your system.

What can I access during Safe Mode?

When you are at the Setup menu in DOS, you can boot into Windows 95 or boot to a DOS prompt. While in Windows 95, you can open the Settings program in Control Panel to access the Device Manager page. From here, you can disable or remove devices that are causing conflicts with your system.

I'm having too many problems with Windows 95 on my system. Can I uninstall it?

To uninstall Windows 95, you must select the Save System Files option during Setup. This saves a copy of your previous system (such as Windows 3.1) on your computer. Next, while in Windows 95, choose Start, Settings, Control Panel, and double-click the Add/Remove Programs icon. In the Add/Remove Programs Wizard, click the Install/Uninstall page and select the Windows 95 option in the list of software that can be uninstalled by Windows 95. Click the Add/Remove button, and then follow the directions on-screen. The Uninstall program removes all long file names and then runs an MS-DOS program to remove Windows 95 from your computer. Your previous MS-DOS and Windows 3.x files are then restored.

Windows 95 is not running, but I want to uninstall it anyway. How do I do it?

Boot your computer from the startup disk you created during installation (or from a DOS boot disk you created prior to installation) and type **UNINSTAL** at the A:\ prompt. At the A:\ prompt, type the following command:

C:\WINDOWS\COMMAND\UNINSTAL.EXE

The problem with this approach is all long file names are not removed from your system. You may have to delete these manually.

I want to uninstall Windows 95 but I didn't make a startup disk. What do I do now?

You can do one of two things. The suggested choice is to make a startup disk by selecting Start, Control Panel, and double-clicking on the Add/Remove Programs icon. Click the Startup Disk tab and click the Create Disk button. You need one floppy disk that works in your A drive.

The second choice is to use the following steps:

1. Boot from an MS-DOS boot disk you created prior to installation.
2. Enter the following at the A:\ prompt:

   C:\WINDOWS\COMMAND\UNINSTALL.EXE

In the preceding syntax, `C` is the drive letter where Windows 95 is installed, and `\WINDOWS` is the name of your Windows 95 directory.

After I uninstalled Windows 95, I still have some files left on my machine from Windows 95. Why?

These are long file names that Windows 95 installs. If you uninstall Windows 95 using a method other than uninstalling it from Windows 95, you are left with these long file names. You can remove them by running Windows 3.x File Manager and deleting them one at a time.

I had problems removing Windows 95 using the preceding steps. Is there another way?

Yes, but it requires that you are comfortable making changes to system files and deleting several files at the DOS command prompt. The following steps show this method:

1. Make a backup copy of Windows 95's DELTREE command if you don't have it on your previous MS-DOS.
2. Make a copy of Windows 95's ScanDisk.
3. In SCANDISK.INI, make sure the following lines are there:

   ```
   labelcheck=on
   spacecheck=on
   ```

4. Run ScanDisk to remove all long file names.
5. After ScanDisk finishes, use DELTREE to delete the Windows 95 directory.
6. Use DELTREE to delete WINBOOT.*.
7. If you are using the upgrade to Windows 95, use DELTREE to delete *.w40.
8. From your backup disks, copy the following files back to your root directory: CONFIG.DOS, CONFIG.SYS, AUTOEXEC.DOS, AUTOEXEC.BAT, MSDOS.DOS, MSDOS.SYS, IO.DOS, and IO.SYS.
9. Next use DELTREE to delete the following files: SETUPLOG.*, BOOTLOG.*, and DETLOG.*.
10. You may want to reinstall your old version of MS-DOS to be safe.

During Windows 95 Setup, should I make a startup disk?

Yes, the startup disk is fail-safe in case you run into problems after installation. The startup disk contains utilities that help you diagnose problems with your setup. The startup disk does have some limitations. It cannot, for instance, be used to provide access to a CD-ROM device or to a network connection. You need to clean up any problems associated with your installation to recover from these problems. After you create the startup disk, make copies of other important system files, such as CD-ROM device drivers, password files (PWL files), and any network configuration files on your system.

How do I start my computer without booting into Windows 95?

As your computer boots, watch the screen and when the message `Starting Windows 95` appears, press F8. This boots into the Setup menu. You can choose the Step-by-Step Confirmation choice to load the AUTOEXEC.BAT and CONFIG.SYS files one line at a time. This is handy when you want to bypass a configuration instruction that is called during one of these files.

Can I skip my AUTOEXEC.BAT and CONFIG.SYS files during bootup?

Yes. Press F8 during bootup (see previous solution) and choose the Command Prompt Only option. If you want to skip your AUTOEXEC.BAT and CONFIG.SYS files and go to the command prompt without network support, choose Safe Mode Command Prompt Only.

Why do I need an AUTOEXEC.BAT or CONFIG.SYS file? I read that Windows 95 doesn't use them.

In theory, Windows 95 doesn't need to have these files to run. In practice, however, many users still use older devices that need to have drivers loaded (such as CD-ROMs not supported automatically by Windows 95) during bootup. You should, however, look through your AUTOEXEC.BAT and CONFIG.SYS files and remove any lines that you don't need. This will make Windows boot faster and possibly free up additional memory. One way to test whether you need these system files at all is to give them a different name and re-boot your computer. If you notice any problems with certain devices, you need to add these lines back in. If you don't notice any problems, you are probably safe without AUTOEXEC.BAT or CONFIG.SYS.

How do I boot to my previous version of MS-DOS?

If you have MS-DOS version 5.0 or higher, you can boot to it after you install Windows 95. You must modify the MSDOS.SYS file by starting a DOS session in Windows 95 and changing to the root directory of DOS. Next, type the following command:

ATTRIB -R -S -H MSDOS.SYS

Press Enter. Type **EDIT MSDOS.SYS** to start the DOS Editor with MSDOS.SYS loaded.

Place the following line after the `[Options]` section and save the file:

BOOTMULTI=1

Exit from the DOS window and shut down Windows 95. Reboot your computer and press F8. On the Start menu, select the Previous Version of MS-DOS option.

Desktop and Display

Many of the items in this section discuss problems you may encounter with the Windows 95 Desktop and display options. Overall, Windows 95's Desktop is an environment, but you may run into quirks here and there. If you have problems with your graphics display adapter, consult your manufacturer to obtain any available new device drivers.

How do I create a shortcut to a printer?

To create a shortcut to a printer, select Start, Settings, Printers. In the Printers folder, click the printer to which you want to create a shortcut and click the right mouse button. Drag the printer icon on to the Desktop and select Create Shortcut(s) Here. Now you can drag files from the Explorer or Desktop on top of the printer shortcut to print your documents.

I want to change the name of a shortcut, but I can't change the file name. Will this happen?

No. The shortcut name does not alter the original file name.

Every time I double-click a shortcut, the application starts in a maximized window. How can I start it minimized?

The shortcut property settings also includes an option to set the way the shortcut item opens. In the Run drop-down list, you can select Normal, Minimized, or Maximized. Normal displays the window sized as you last used it.

I've changed my screen resolution, but now Windows 95 hangs. What can I do?

If your display doesn't appear correctly or if you see nothing at all, you need to reboot Windows 95 and start in Safe Mode. In Safe Mode, Windows boots with a standard VGA display driver. After Windows 95 boots, go through the shut-down process and reboot your machine. When it restarts and goes into Windows, it should return to your old display settings.

How can I find out which display driver is loading?

You can check the `[boot]` section of SYSTEM.INI for an entry as follows:

```
display.drv=pnpdrvr.drv
```

If you see this setting, any display entries you have in SYSTEM.INI are bypassed and the display drivers are loaded from the Registry; otherwise, your drivers are loaded from SYSTEM.INI.

My display driver worked fine in Windows 3.1, but now it won't support the Windows 95 features for changing resolution on-the-fly. Why not?

If your display driver requires the screen resolution to be written in the `[boot.description]` section SYSTEM.INI, you cannot use the resolution on-the-fly feature.

When I run a multimedia video, my screen is jerky. Can you help?

First, make sure you have the correct display driver loaded by looking in the Device Manager. Next, check your CONFIG.SYS file to determine if the MSCDEX file is installed. If it is, remove it (REM it out temporarily) and use the new Windows 95 built-in CD-ROM file system drivers (if your CD-ROM supports it). When you encounter this problem with DOS applications, increase the amount of XMS memory.

I have a Paradise VLBus3000 accelerator video card. Where can I get Windows 95 video drivers for it?

On the Windows 95 CD-ROM, look in the DRIVERS\DISPLAY\TRIDENT folder for a file called TRID94XX.INF. With this file, you should have no problem using the true color capabilities of the card. You also can receive the drivers from the Microsoft Web server at **http://www.microsoft.com/Windows**.

I'm using the latest ATI graphics driver (machxw4) but I'm receiving GPFs in various applications, particularly when I'm exiting the program. If I switch to the Windows 95 provided driving, I don't experience this problem.

To correct this problem, you might want to switch from 256 colors to 16 million or high color.

Taskbar and Start Button

The taskbar and Start button features of Windows 95 introduce new ways for users to locate and switch between applications. You probably won't run into too many problems with these items, but you might have some questions about how certain things work with them. This section touches on a few of those concerns.

I moved the taskbar to the left side of my screen, but I can't read the task buttons now. Why?

Depending on the width of the taskbar, you may only see the application icon and its first two letters when the taskbar is moved to the side of the Desktop. This can make it difficult to recognize your open applications. Move the mouse pointer over the right edge of the taskbar until it changes to a two-sided arrow. Hold down the left mouse button and drag the taskbar to the right until it is resized to a point that you can read the task buttons.

I've set Auto Hide in the Taskbar Properties sheet but I can't get the taskbar to reappear when I have maximized windows. Why?

When you set the properties for the taskbar, be sure to click Always on Top to ensure that the taskbar appears on the bottom edge of your application window. You also can press Ctrl+Esc to display the taskbar and open the Start menu.

I had Windows 3.x set up with program groups that I still want to use. How can I quickly add these to the Start menu?

You must have Windows 95 installed in a different folder than your previous version of Windows to do this. Using Explorer, locate all the GRP files for your program groups in the old Windows directory, and double-click them. (They are called Microsoft Program Groups in the Explorer.) This places the old program groups as folders in the Programs folder on the Start menu. (If you haven't re-installed your Windows 3.x applications, you still need to do so to have them work in Windows 95.)

Memory, Disks, and Devices

One of the most significant advances in Windows 95 over the previous DOS and Windows 3.x is the way Windows provides a 32-bit multitasking environment. This section describes some of the changes in this area and offers some troubleshooting advice on running ScanDisk.

In Windows 3.x, I used up a lot of disk space just for virtual memory. Do I need to use virtual memory at all with Windows 95?

You may be able to completely disable virtual memory. Windows won't let you do this if you have less than 12M of physical RAM. This is the minimum amount of memory (RAM plus virtual memory) required by Windows 95. But, if you do have 12M or more of physical RAM, you can completely turn off virtual memory. If you do turn virtual memory off, you may not be able to run more than a few small programs simultaneously or work with large amounts of data. Microsoft (and I) recommend that you don't disable virtual memory.

The Windows 95 box says all I need is 8M of memory. Why won't some of the Object Linking and Embedding (OLE) tasks work?

Windows 95 does not let you set the minimum memory below 12M (the total or your physical RAM and virtual memory). However, if you do set your total memory to 12M, you may have problems trying to run additional programs, working with OLE documents, and so on. If you are planning on running any large program or working with OLE objects, you should keep the minimum memory to at least 16M.

I'm out of disk space (or almost out) and want to compress my entire drive, including the swap file. Can I do this?

For the best performance, you shouldn't locate the swap file on a compressed drive. However, if you need more virtual memory than you can fit on any non-compressed drive, you can use a compressed drive. While performance is not as good, you are able to run more programs simultaneously. For example, if you are running several large programs, like Microsoft Word and Microsoft Excel, and you are using OLE to share data between them, you need a lot of memory. If you run out of memory, use the default swap file. Your only option to get everything to work, however, may be to put the virtual memory swap file on a compressed drive. It works, just slower.

The Recycle Bin eats up a lot of my hard disk space. How can I reduce the percentage of disk space that the Recycle Bin uses?

By default, the Recycle Bin uses 10 percent of drive C's total capacity. That's a lot when you have a large hard drive. For a 1.85G hard disk, for example, you're reserving 121M just for an undelete buffer! To reduce it, right-click the Recycle Bin icon on the Desktop and select Properties. On the Global page, click the Configure Drives Separately option. Click on the C page and move the slider until you are satisfied with the undelete buffer size.

I have several disks that I want to run ScanDisk on, but I don't want to select one at a time. What can I do?

You can run ScanDisk on several drives at once. To do this, when you are selecting the disk to run ScanDisk on, hold down the Ctrl key and click each drive you want to check for errors.

How do I automate disk utilities, such as ScanDisk, to run at specific times?

You can automate the running of ScanDisk by installing the Microsoft Plus! for Windows 95 System Agent. With System Agent, you can schedule when any program, especially the disk maintenance tools, will run.

Plus!

ScanDisk ran, but it didn't correct all the errors it found. What do I do?

ScanDisk may be unable to repair errors for files that are in use while ScanDisk is running. Since Windows 95 itself has many files in use, ScanDisk may not be able to completely repair all errors it finds. To fix these errors, shut down Windows 95 and choose Restart the Computer in MS-DOS mode and run the DOS version of ScanDisk. This file can be found in the \WINDOWS\COMMAND folder.

Windows 95 does not recognize my tape drive, so I have to run it in DOS mode. Does this affect long file names when I restore the files?

Yes. If you use a DOS tape software to back up long file names and try to restore them later, they all end up truncated to 8.3 convention of DOS. Use the LFNBK utility supplied on the Windows 95 CD-ROM in the \ADMIN\APPTOOLS\LFNBACK folder.

I'm using the Do_cache utility on a Texas Instruments 486. I'm experiencing some performance problems. What can I do?

Most likely, you need to disable this utility and not load it at bootup. One of the symptoms of this problem is crashing while running Explorer or a DOS prompt.

I'm trying to diagnose some memory problems, but I don't know how Windows uses virtual machines.

DOS applications execute in separate virtual machines (VMs). Windows 3.x (16-bit) applications execute in the System VM, in a single address space. Windows 95 (32-bit) applications run in the System VM, but in separate address spaces. DOS applications can't bring down the system, other DOS applications, or other Windows (16 or 32-bit) applications. Windows 3.x (16-bit) applications can bring down other 16-bit applications. Windows 95 (32-bit) applications can't bring down other 32-bit, 16-bit, or DOS applications.

Can Windows 95 handle multitasking on multiple processors?

Windows 95 supports multitasking on one microprocessor. Windows 95 doesn't support Symmetric Multiprocessing (SMP), which allows the use of multiple microprocessors within one PC. Windows NT and OS/2 Warp do support SMP.

Whereas Windows 95 uses cooperative multitasking for multi-threaded processing, Windows NT uses the more reliable preemptive multitasking method. It remains to be seen how many 32-bit Windows 95 applications lock themselves up by failing to return CPU control after a reasonable time to another thread within their process slot.

I still have a lot of DOS- and Windows 3.x-based software. At the architectural level, how does Windows 95 handle these types of applications?

Table B.1 summarizes the key architectural features in the Windows 95 application execution environment by application type. Once you understand these concepts, it will be easier to understand how to best use DOS, Windows 3.x, and Windows 95 software in the Windows 95 operating environment.

Table B.1 Application Execution Environment

Feature	DOS App.	16-Bit App.	32-Bit App.
Virtual Machine (VM)	One MS-DOS VM per executing DOS application	All run in within a single memory address	All run in System VM executing DOS, but each in a separate memory address
Multi-tasking	Preemptive scheduling	Cooperative scheduling	Preemptive scheduling
Multi-threaded scheduling	None	None	Yes, uses cooperative processing
Messaging	Each has its own message queue	All share a common message queue	Each has its own message queue

DOS Programs

You might have switched to Windows 95 to escape the limitations of MS-DOS, but you still may have plenty of DOS-based applications you want to run. This section provides some troubleshooting items to help you run DOS programs under Windows 95.

I still use the DOS command prompt a great deal, but hate going through the Start menu to start it. What can I do?

Create a shortcut to DOS and place it on the Desktop for quick access to DOS. You can also start a DOS session by choosing Start, Run, typing the word **COMMAND**, and pressing Enter.

I don't want to boot into Windows 95. Can I boot into DOS?

When the message `Starting Windows 95` appears, press F8 and select Command Prompt Only to boot up the computer in the real mode version of DOS. When you finish, type **Exit** to start Windows 95.

How do I get help for a DOS command?

To display help for a DOS command, type the name of the command you want followed by **/?** (make sure you include a space between the command and slash). For example, type **md /?** to display help text on the MAKE DIRECTORY (md) command. Adding the pipe character (|) and the word **more** to the end of the statement displays help text one screen at a time; for example:

```
md /? | more
```

I know Windows 95 supports long file names, but I'm a little hesitant to use them in DOS. Should I be?

A bit of caution is required when it comes to using long file names. Although the Windows 95 DOS commands support long file names, existing DOS and Windows 3.x programs do not support long file names. Furthermore, be careful when using a file in Windows 95 with a long file name and then accessing the file in a DOS or Windows 3.x program. Doing so deletes the long file name!

How do I view long file names in DOS?

The DIR command has been enhanced to display a seventh column which shows the long file name. DIR also sports a new command line switch called verbose: **/v**. The verbose switch displays additional information such as file attributes and last access date stamp.

What version of MS-DOS comes with Windows 95?

If you type the DOS command **VER** at the command prompt, the version information that displays is `Windows 95`. However, DOS programs that ask internally for the DOS version get the number `7`. This could cause conflicts with DOS programs that will only work for a specific DOS version number.

How do I access DOS properties in Windows 95?

To configure the DOS command line sessions, set properties for COMMAND.COM which is located in Windows 95's COMMAND folder.

I used to use PIFs (Program Information Files) all the time in Windows 3.x. I can't find them in Windows 95. Where are they?

Windows 95 stores all PIFs in a hidden PIF folder in the Windows 95 folder. This keeps novice users from inadvertently altering the actual PIF files.

How do I view DOS property sheets?

You set properties for a DOS program the same way you set properties for any object in Windows 95—by right-clicking the object and choosing Properties. Windows 95 then displays the properties folder for the DOS application. DOS program properties are organized into six property sheets.

Windows 95 property sheets exist for all DOS programs, whether started in MS-DOS mode, from the command prompt, or as a Windows 95 DOS session. For those applications set up to run in MS-DOS mode, many properties do not apply and are therefore not available. When MS-DOS mode is selected, only the following properties are enabled:

- *General.* File attributes.
- *Program.* Icon text, command line, close on exit, change icon, and the advanced MS-DOS mode options.
- Font, Memory, Screen, and Misc sheets are blank.

DOS programs that ran fine under Windows 3.x are not working properly under Windows 95. In general, what can I do to fix this?

If a DOS program detects Windows 95 and won't run properly, select Prevent from the Advanced Program Settings sheet for that DOS program.

How can I change the way my DOS program uses memory?

The settings on the Memory property sheet control the way the DOS application uses the PC's memory. Settings are provided to control conventional, expanded (EMS), and extended (XMS) memory. Because each DOS application executes in its own MS-DOS virtual machine (VM), the memory settings apply only to that DOS application. Other applications executing DOS, Windows 3.x, and Windows 95 are unaffected by these memory settings.

What can I do when I get a DOS GPF (General Protection Fault)?

Since each DOS application executes in a separate VM, a GPF (General Protection Fault) in one DOS application has no effect on the other DOS, Win16, or Win32 applications currently executing. When the GPF message appears, record the error message information and choose OK to terminate the offending DOS application.

Windows 3.x Software

When Windows 95 hit the market, very few Windows 95-compliant applications were available. Most users had to stay with Windows 3.x-compliant applications until an upgrade became available. If you have general concerns or questions about Windows 3.x software running in Windows 95, you can find some information here.

Tip

Many Windows 3.x applications have quirks when running in Windows 95. You should look through the README.TXT files available on the Windows 95 setup disks to read about any specific problem that you might encounter with your applications.

I want to set up a dual-boot environment with Windows 95, but I need to reinstall all my Windows 3.x software. Will this be a problem?

The process for installing Windows 3.x software in Windows 95 is essentially the same as in Windows 3.x. Instead of choosing File, Run in Program Manager to install programs, in Windows 95 you choose Start, Run. Alternatively, you could use the Add/Remove Programs feature in the Control Panel. Either way, the installation works the same.

Some of my older 3.x programs share components. What should I do to ensure they are all installed properly?

Be careful when installing or updating Windows 3.x programs that share components (such as MS Graph which is shared by Word and Excel). Setup programs cannot update a component which is currently being used by a running application. To avoid conflicts, it is best to shut down related programs (and any critical applications/data) before installing or updating software.

Can I configure Windows applications property sheets, and if so, how?

Since Windows applications share a common configuration, their property sheets consist of only a General Properties sheet and possibly a Version sheet. All other properties such as memory, display, and fonts are managed by Windows 95 in other areas. To display the property sheets for a Windows 3.x program, right-click the file name and choose Properties.

My Windows 3.x programs use INI files for configuration settings. Where are they in Windows 95?

Windows 3.x programs relied on initialization files (which have the file extension INI) to load real mode and virtual device drivers during the Windows boot process. Windows 3.x applications often created their own initialization files or edited (without backing up or asking for permission) the Windows initialization files (WIN.INI and SYSTEM.INI). Over the years as you add, update, and delete Windows 3.x applications, the contents and number of INI files increase. Settings and INI files for obsolete or deleted versions of Windows 3.x programs remain unless you invest the time to extract them manually, or the money for a Windows uninstall utility. Recently, a few Windows 3.x programs have begun to address this problem by providing their own uninstall routines.

How do I modify an INI file for different configuration and setup settings?

The INI files can be viewed and edited by using any plain ASCII text editor. Before making any changes, you should make a backup copy of the INI files. Windows 95 provides a new version of the Windows 3.x SYSEDIT.EXE program which allows you to quickly view and edit all of the setup files. You can find SYSEDIT.EXE in the Windows 95 SYSTEM folder.

What happens when I get a GPF in a Windows 3.x application?

Since all Win16 applications execute in a single VM, all Win16 application execution ceases until the application that caused the GPF is terminated. When the GPF message appears, record the error message information and choose OK to terminate the offending application. Once the offending application is terminated, the other Win16 applications resume execution. Note that a GPF in a Win16 application has no effect on any currently running DOS or Win32 applications.

Problems with Windows 95 Applications

Each week several new Windows 95-compliant applications hit the market. Many of your favorite Windows 3.x programs are being upgraded to take advantage of Windows 95's 32-bit architecture. This section offers some answers to questions you may have about Windows 95 applications.

I just got a GPF in Windows 95. I thought I wouldn't have these when I upgraded to Windows 95.

A General Protection Fault (GPF) occurs when an application violates system integrity. The following list provides examples of common GPFs:

- Application tried to use a memory address currently being used by another application
- Error code returned by a system API (application programming interface)
- A memory fault caused by an invalid pointer

I had a GPF in Windows 95. What is the dialog box that appears?

When Windows 95 encounters a GPF, it displays a General Protection Fault message that tells the user which application caused the problem, the module name, and a reference number. By relaying this information to the application vendor, often the problem can be quickly resolved.

Do GPFs affect other applications in Windows 95?

The effect of a GPF on the other applications currently executing depends on whether the offending application is a DOS application, a Windows 16-bit application (Win16), or a Windows 32-bit application (Win32).

What can I do when I get a GPF in a Windows 95 application?

Since Win32 applications execute at a separate memory address within the System VM, a GPF in one Win32 application has no effect on the other DOS, Win16, or Win32 applications currently executing. When the GPF message appears, record the error message information and choose OK to terminate the offending application. Any unsaved data in the offending application will be lost.

What are some of the ways to configure the Windows 95 environment after a GPF occurs?

First, look for any unattended timed backups or termination safety features built into the application.

When an application is terminated by Windows 95, the normal closing routines are not performed. This could cause problems when you restart the program. For this reason, you may consider contacting the vendor before trying to re-execute the program.

To terminate a hung Win32 application, right-click the application's Taskbar button and choose Close.

Registry Questions

The Windows 95 Registry is the central information database for all the hardware and software you install on your computer. The Registry simplifies the operating system and makes it more adaptable, and in some cases, the Registry can eliminate the need for AUTOEXEC.BAT, CONFIG.SYS, and INI files. This section includes some tips on troubleshooting Registry problems you may have with Windows 95.

Does the Windows 95 Registry replace all my INI files? Can I delete all of them?

No, don't erase these files. If you are using older Windows 3.x applications that require an INI file, keep it on your system. In general, the Windows 95 Registry consists of three data files that manage the way your applications and environment behave:

- USER.DAT. Stores user preferences such as the Desktop.
- SYSTEM.DAT. Stores the computer's hardware configurations such as drives, printers and sound card settings.
- POLICY.POL. Stores administrative policies set up on a network server.

How can I protect the Registry files from becoming erased or tampered with to conserve my configuration settings?

Several precautions are taken to protect these data files. First, the Registry data is kept in binary format, so the files cannot be read by a regular text editor. Second, the file attributes are set to read-only, hidden system files. This prevents accidental deletion.

Also, Windows 95 maintains backup copies of the Registry data in the Windows 95 folder. The backup files SYSTEM.DA0 and USER.DA0 are used by Windows 95 in the event that the actual DAT files become corrupt.

How do I edit the Registry files to change some settings?

Unless you are an experienced Windows user or system administrator, you should not tamper with the Registry file. However, you can locate the

Registry Editor by running REGEDIT.EXE from your Windows 95 folder. To edit Registry files on a remote computer, run REGEDIT.EXE and choose Registry, Connect.

Help! My Registry has become corrupted. How do I restore it?

Reboot your computer. During the Windows 95 boot process, press F8 to display the startup menu. Select the Command Prompt Only option and then change to the Windows 95 folder. Type each of the following commands and press Enter after each one:

```
ATTRIB -H -R -S SYSTEM.DAT
ATTRIB -H -R -S SYSTEM.DA0
ATTRIB -H -R -S USER.DAT
ATTRIB -H -R -S USER.DA0
```

Make a copy of these files (give them an extension of BAK for instance) and then enter the following commands:

```
COPY SYSTEM.DA0 SYSTEM.DAT
COPY USER.DA0 USER.DAT
```

Reboot your system to restore the Registry.

Windows 95 File System

The Windows 95 file system is designed to handle long file names of up to 256 characters, including spaces. Because Windows 95 users still have to communicate with many DOS-based users (such as Windows 3.x users), you may encounter some problems when handling these files between users. This section includes some ways to isolate and determine problems with the Windows 95 file system.

I have an error with the VFAT.VXD file. What does it do?

VFAT is a 32-bit virtualized FAT file system. The VFAT.VXD file system driver (FSD) controls this file system and uses 32-bit code for all file access. VFAT is a protected mode implementation of the FAT file system. The VFAT system supports long file names (up to 255 characters), eliminates the over-reliance on INT 21H, uses 32-bit processing, and allows multiple concurrent threads to execute file system code.

What happens if my system uses long file names, but my disk utilities do not recognize long file names?

Do not use disk or backup utilities that are not aware of long file names. If you do need to use a backup/restore utility that does not support LFNs, Microsoft supplies a utility called LFNBK that preserves the LFNs. You can obtain this utility on the Windows 95 installation CD in the \ADMIN\APPTOOLS\LFNBACK folder.

I'm having problems with the Windows 95 file system. How can I troubleshoot it?

If an application does not respond properly to the Windows 95 file system, you can use the File System Troubleshooter to detect the cause of the problem. Using the Troubleshooter, you can disable the following Windows 95 file system features:

- File sharing and locking
- Preservation of long file names in non-LFN programs
- Protect-mode hard disk interrupt handler
- 32-bit protect-mode disk drivers
- Write-behind caching for all drives

How do I start the file system troubleshooter in Windows 95?

Follow these steps:

1. Open the Control Panel.
2. Open the System icon.
3. Select the Performance page.
4. Choose File System.
5. Select the Troubleshooting page.
6. Select the setting to be tested.
7. Choose OK to test the setting.

Online Communications

Windows 95 promises to make it easier than ever to get online. In some cases, this is true. In others, you may have problems establishing connections or initializing COM ports. One of the biggest concerns is the way Windows 95 enables you to connect to the Internet. This section includes some problems you might have with Windows 95 and its communications support.

The modem won't dial.

Check the hardware for loose cables and the communications software for proper configuration. If your modem is hooked to COM2, be sure that your software is looking for it on COM2.

My modem connects with my ISP's (Internet Service Provider) modem, then it dumps the carrier (hangs up spontaneously).

This is a potential nightmare with many sources. Did you set your parity to 8N1? Is the "initialization string" in your communication software appropriate to your modem? Does the modem name and other settings in your communication software match your modem? Is there an incompatibility between your modem and your ISP's modem? Carrier dumping requires sleuthing. Be patient and work with your ISP until the problem is solved.

I have a 28,800 baud modem, but the fastest connection I get is 19,200. Sometimes the connection is choppy and laden with errors when I download files.

Check for line noise. Check for any incorrect modem settings in your communication software. Check for modem incompatibilities between your modem and your ISP's modem. Check for the presence of a UART 16550 in your modem's COM port. If your phone company uses old switches in its central office, there is nothing you can do except get faster, dedicated service.

My modem connects to my ISP, but my ISP's system doesn't recognize my IP address.

Ensure that your IP address (if you have a static IP address) and your ISP's IP address and DNS are configured properly in Windows 95's TCP/IP configuration. Even a single wrong number or letter here can negate a connection.

I've tried the Windows Dial-Up Networking software to dial into my Internet provider, but I have problems after I connect with it. None of my applications, such as WinVN, Netscaper, and e-mail readers will work. I get a `Can't resolve host name` or a `Sockets error` message.

This indicates a problem with your Host Name Resolution. You need to set appropriate information regarding your Domain Name Server. Right-click the Your Dial Up Network's Icon that you created, and choose Properties. Click Server Type. Select the TCP/IP settings, and enter the DNS host address. You can obtain this from your Internet provider.

I've filled in all the DNS addresses and have confirmed them with my ISP. I still cannot connect to the ISP with a SLIP or PPP connection. What can I do?

If you had no problems connecting with your ISP under Windows 3.x, you should contact them for up-to-date information about new scripts they may have available. Another solution is to ask your provider if it requires two passwords when you connect to it. Sometimes if your ISP creates logon scripts for you, they will create an encrypted password that you may not know about. Ask them for this password, or ask them to change it to match your regular password.

I use CompuServe's WinCIM software to dial into that service. Because I've installed Exchange and the Plus! Companion, my modem won't initialize. Why?

Windows 95 includes built-in TAPI (Telephony Application Programming Interface) support for Exchange clients (such as MS Fax) and the Dial-Up Networking feature. If your port initializes with these clients (test it by running the modem diagnostics explained in the next section), you need to make sure you are not running any of these features in the background. If you have enabled your modem to accept faxes automatically, you see a fax machine icon on the taskbar. Turn this feature off by changing the setting in the Modems properties sheet, or close Exchange.

If you close Exchange and still can't initialize the COM port in WinCIM, you may have set the Dial-Up Networking Server to accept call-ins. You can change this setting by opening My Computer and double-clicking the Dial-Up Networking folder. Choose Connections, Dial-Up Server. Make sure the No Caller Access option is selected.

How do I run the modem diagnostics utility?

One way to test your modem's working condition is to double-click Modems in Control Panel and click the Diagnostics page. In the Port list, click one of the ports and select More Info. If your modem is not in use, you are returned with Information about the COM port and modem. Note that you cannot get information on your mouse because it is being used at the time.

How do I get access to commercial online services' software?

To get a free copy of AOL's software, call 800-827-3338. For a free copy of CompuServe's WinCIM software (make sure you get version 1.4 or above), call 800-848-8199. Call 1-800-PRODIGY to get a free trial offer, including Prodigy's software.

You can also frequently find AOL's software at the newsstand, bundled with computer-oriented magazines.

HyperTerminal has an icon for CompuServe. Should I set it up with my user ID and password?

If you already have a CompuServe account and you use CompuServe's WinCIM software, your best bet is to continue with WinCIM. If you haven't set up an account yet, use HyperTerminal to establish an account with CompuServe and then order a copy of WinCIM to use.

I went to configure my CompuServe (or Prodigy or AOL) software to use a local access phone number, but there isn't one for my city. Am I stuck using a long distance number?

Yes, but you'll probably save money if you use a high-speed access number in a neighboring state—but not too far away. This allows you to avoid the intrastate telephone tax and additional charges some long distance companies add for longer distances.

Hardware Problems

One of the most difficult issues to address in Windows 95 is hardware problems. Many users are finding that their older legacy hardware devices do not work properly—or at all—under Windows 95. To cover every known (and unknown) problem with hardware would involve thousands of pages of text. If you experience problems, you should try the procedures listed in this section. You should also contact your hardware manufacturer to get updated drivers for your hardware. Regardless of how many different ways you configure Windows 95, if you have an outdated driver, you will only waste your time.

What does the Windows 95 Device Manager do?

The Device Manager Registry in Windows 95 is designed to track available system resources, such as IRQ and I/O settings. Then, when a new hardware component is added, such as a sound board, you can use the Add New Hardware Wizard, which takes you step-by-step through the installation process.

The start of that process is to check the Registry for available settings and graphically present them to you so you can configure your board before you install it. The result should be that the new component will work when it is installed, although that isn't always the case.

What is the quickest way to resolve hardware problems in Windows 95?

Hardware conflicts can occur, often at the most inappropriate moments. Fortunately, not only does Windows 95 include a very thorough Help option from the Start menu, but it also features an especially useful step-by-step Hardware Conflict Troubleshooter, which you access by choosing the Hardware, Troubleshooting Conflicts option from the Help Topics Index.

The Troubleshooting Wizard takes you on a step-by-step investigation that should result in solving the problem. If it doesn't actually solve it, the wizard suggests possible solutions.

What are some common Plug and Play configuration problems in Windows 95?

Windows 95 supports PCs with Plug and Play devices. This means that when you install a Plug and Play device into your PC, such as a video adapter, or simply plug one in, such as a monitor, Windows 95 automatically detects the presence of the new device and configures it for use in Windows 95. This Plug and Play functionality also requires the BIOS on your PC to be Plug and Play compatible. Even if you do not have Plug and Play BIOS or Plug and Play devices, Windows 95 can still detect and configure devices using the Add New Hardware Wizard. Also, certain devices, such as monitors and video cards, can be detected immediately when Windows 95 starts.

When I add a new video card to my system, how do I configure it for Windows 95?

You can avoid having to pick the manufacturer and model of your video card from the lists provided with Windows 95 if you have the software installation disk that was shipped with the video card. Insert the disk into a floppy drive and click the Have Disk button in the dialog box. Follow the prompts to specify the location of the OEMSETUP.INF, which should appear on the disk. This file contains all the information needed to configure the video card. This technique also can be useful if you have a late model adapter that is not yet supported by Windows 95.

I don't recognize (or I don't know) either the manufacturer or the model of my video card in the lists that appear in the Add New Hardware Wizard. Also, I can't find any disks that might be associated with my video card.

Windows 95 lets you choose a generic driver for use with your adapter if you are not sure what video adapter is installed in your PC. Choose Standard Display Types from the Manufacturers list and either Standard Display Adapter (VGA) or Super VGA from the Models list. If you are not sure whether your monitor is Super VGA capable, choose the VGA option.

Video cards can pose real problems with Windows 95 if you do not have a driver that works with Windows 95. If you have problems with your video card, try using Windows 95's built-in VGA driver. You can change to this by pressing F8 at bootup and selecting the Safe Mode option.

I can't seem to move the slider in the Desktop area frame in any direction. The `Less` and `More` labels appear to be dimmed.

The points along the slider at which you can stop it are determined by the capabilities of your video card and monitor. If your video card and monitor are only capable of one setting, you cannot move the slider in the Desktop area frame at all. The labels `Less` and `More` at each end of the slider appear dimmed if your video adapter and monitor are not capable of multiple resolution settings.

When I installed my sound card in Windows 95, it automatically configured the interrupts (IRQs) for it, but the wrong settings were established.

You might want to use the sound board's own installation program instead, because the wizard can sometimes run into problems identifying the correct interrupts for some components.

Sound-related problems can be varied and frustrating, as the following random sample of conflicts illustrate:

- Common settings problems, such as an IRQ conflict or a wrong DMA channel selected, can result in no sound coming out at all. A wrong DMA driver setting may also result in distorted WAV file playback.
- If WAV file sounds repeat when you are using a sound card, you may have a defective parallel port card.
- If you hear a hissing during the playback of a sound file, the file may be recording in 8 bits and playing back in 16 bits. The 16-bit board doesn't realize that the 8-bit file isn't the same high quality as a 16-bit file, so playing the file with expectations of higher sound quality emphasizes the lower detail.
- You may need to switch to using a low DMA setting if your system hangs during a 16-bit digitized sound test, but an 8-bit test works fine. This result means your system cannot handle high DMA at full speed.
- Playing sound files on a slow PC can often lead to problems. For example, playing compressed WAV files results in less performance because of the amount of processor-power required to decompress them.
- If you are trying to play video with sound and it isn't synchronized, you may have a computer that isn't fast enough. You can try improving performance and adding RAM. But if you have an older, slower processor and a relatively slow hard drive, you may need to think about upgrading to a new PC with fast video capabilities built in.

How can I change my keyboard's layout in Windows 95?

You can change the layout of your keyboard via the Keyboard Properties sheet from the Control Panel.

Use the following steps:

1. Click the Language page.
2. Select the language and keyboard layout that you want to change.
3. Click the Properties button. The Language Properties sheet appears.
4. Select the new keyboard layout from the Keyboard layout list.
5. Click OK.

How do I delete a keyboard language or layout from Windows 95?

You can also delete a language or layout from the Keyboard Properties sheet from Control Panel. Having displayed the Language page, do the following:

1. Select the language and layout you want to delete from the Installed Keyboard Languages and Layouts list.
2. Click the Remove button.
3. Click OK.

How do I add a new keyboard language or layout to Windows 95?

You can select a different keyboard layout or language using the Keyboard Properties sheet in Control Panel. After you display the Language page, do the following:

1. Click the Add button. The Add Language panel appears.
2. Select the language you want from the drop-down Language list.
3. Click OK.
4. Select the language you want to use as your primary language from the list.
5. Click the Set as Default button.
6. Click OK.

I switch between keyboard languages a great deal. Do I have to go through all these steps each time?

At the bottom of the Language page on the Keyboard Properties sheet is an option box called Enable Indicator on Taskbar. If this is checked, an indicator called En appears on the Windows 95 taskbar at the bottom of the main screen. To quickly change between languages, click this indicator and a list of available languages appears. You can instantly switch between available languages by clicking the language you want from that En list.

How do I change the cursor blink rate?

After accessing the Keyboard Properties sheet, click the Speed page. Adjust the cursor blinking speed by dragging the Cursor Blink Rate Slider to the right to make it faster, or to the left to slow it down. Click OK.

I'm left-handed, but my mouse is set up to cater to the right-handed user. Can I change this?

To set the pointing device as a left-handed device, click the Left-Handed radio button in the Button Configuration group box. Conversely, to set it as a right-handed device, click the Right-Handed radio button in the group box.

I set up a pointer scheme but I want to return to my original. How do I do this?

If you want to reset all your pointers to their defaults, use the Scheme drop-down list and set the scheme name to `(None)`.

My pointer seems to move slow or jerky around the screen. What's wrong?

It all boils down to your computer being very busy performing a task. Or, if you have shared a folder on your hard drive using file sharing, they may be heavily reading and writing information in it. Use the Net Watcher application to see who is connected to your computer. You can install the Net Watcher by using the Add/Remove Programs option in Control Panel and clicking the Windows Setup page. Select Accessories and click Details. In the list of components, select Net Watcher. You may need your Windows 95 installation disks or CD-ROM.

My pointer moves in one direction but not another. Help!

Try cleaning your mouse ball, track ball, and/or any internal motion contacts (usually small plastic wheels). If you're using a mouse, clean the glide pads on the bottom (if you have them). If you use a mouse pad, be sure to clean it regularly to prevent a build-up of dirt.

My pointer moves erratically. Why?

If, when you shake the cable, it makes the situation better or worse, verify that the connection to your computer is secure. Sometimes, the connector has come loose from the port on your computer.

Inspect the cable for breaks or cuts. If your cable is broken or pierced, repair or replacement is necessary. If there are no visible breaks, a wire inside the cable may have broken. This may have been caused by severe twisting of the cable, being placed under a heavy object for long periods of time, or a heavy object may have been dropped on it (for example, a paperweight or stapler).

It's not the cable or connection. What else can cause it to move erratically?

Check the Windows Driver Library (WDL) for an updated driver for your pointing device. The WDL is an electronic library of drivers which is updated as new ones become available. You can access the WDL via the Microsoft Network (MSN) in the Windows 95 area; CompuServe via **GO MSL**; the Internet via World Wide Web or Gopher (both at **http://www.microsoft.com**), or FTP (**ftp://ftp.microsoft.com**); or via the Microsoft Download Service at (206) 936-6735 (you only pay for the phone call).

I installed the CD-ROM and Windows support, but the CD-ROM still doesn't work.

The most common reason for the CD-ROM not working correctly is a conflict with another device on your system. Open Control Panel (from the Start menu) and start the System option. Select the Device Manager page to display the list of the devices on your system.

Double-click the CD-ROM entry in the list, and then select your CD-ROM device. Click the Properties button to display the settings for your CD-ROM. The Device Status area generally tells you if there is a problem with your CD-ROM device. Clicking the Resources page shows you the current settings; this page also tells you if one of the settings for your CD-ROM conflicts with another device in your system.

If there is a conflict with another device in your system, you have to change one of the hardware settings (such as the Interrupt Request, Input/Output range, or Direct memory access) to another value. Consult the manual for your CD-ROM drive to determine which values for these settings are legal for your drive.

Once you know which settings you can set your CD-ROM drive to, you have to determine which hardware settings are available on your system. One good way to find out the settings that are in use on your system is to click the Print button on the main Device Manager page. This allows you to print out a summary of all the resources on your system—you can easily find an unused value.

How do I control automatic playing of audio compact discs?

One of the new features of Windows 95 is the capability of the system to automatically recognize and play audio compact discs when they are inserted in the CD-ROM drive. This feature can be controlled from the Properties sheet for your CD-ROM drive. Double-click the My Computer icon on your desktop and then right-click your CD-ROM drive icon. Select Properties from the list and then click the Settings page from the Properties sheet.

On the Settings page, you see an option called Auto Insert Notification. If this option is checked, the system automatically plays audio compact discs when they are inserted. Deselect this option if you don't want this to happen.

How do I change the drive letter that is assigned to my CD-ROM drive?

By default, Windows 95 assigns drive letter D to your CD-ROM drive, unless you have another hard drive installed. You can change this from the Properties sheet for your drive. Bring up the Properties sheet and select the Settings page. You see the setting for Current Drive Letter Assigned; changing this changes the drive letter assigned to your CD-ROM drive.

I've changed the drive letter for my CD-ROM. What problems can occur now?

Note that if you change the drive letter assigned to your CD-ROM drive, it may force other drives you have mounted (such as network disks) to change to other drive letters, also. This may affect some of your shortcuts or software if they assume that your data was stored on a particular drive letter.

My CD-ROM drive seems slow. How can I speed it up?

Windows 95 has several settings that affect how it deals with CD-ROM drives, some of which can affect how fast data is transferred from the CD-ROM drive to the system. You can check these settings by starting the System control panel and selecting the Performance page. Click the File System button and then select the CD-ROM tab from this page.

The two settings on this page affect how much data Windows 95 stores in memory when reading from your CD-ROM drive. You should keep the supplemental cache size as large as possible (keeping the slider bar as far to the right as possible) unless you are running short of memory.

You should also set the Optimize Access Pattern For option to the type of CD-ROM drive you have (double-speed, for example). When you are finished changing these settings, click OK.

I've installed a new hard disk but Windows 95 does not recognize it. Why?

Your hard disk drive cable may be defective. Replace the cable with another one to see if the problem is resolved.

Another problem may be that the hard disk drive cable is installed improperly for a single hard disk drive system. Ensure the hard disk cable has the twist in the center of the cable near the connector to your disk drive. This is how hard disk drive C is identified. The remaining connector is attached to the hard disk drive controller.

If the hard disk drive cable is connected properly and the hard disk drive is not working properly, the fault may be with the hard disk drive. Install a different hard disk drive and see if the problem is resolved. On the other hand, if the hard disk drive cable is connected properly and the hard disk drive is working properly (it was tested on another computer), the fault may be with the hard disk drive controller. Install a different hard disk drive controller and see if the problem is resolved.

I'm looking at the Device Manager and it shows I have two floppy disk drives, but I have only one on my computer. What should I do?

As you set up Windows 95 or when you added a new floppy disk drive, a second floppy disk controller was added but only one is installed. To resolve this problem, highlight the line with the red X in it and click the Remove button on the bottom of the display.

I can't see the tape drive from within Microsoft Backup for Windows. Why not?

You may not be using a supported tape drive unit. Microsoft Backup for Windows only supports QIC-40, QIC-80, QIC-3010, and Trakker parallel-port backup systems. If you have some other tape drive, you need to use the manufacturer's backup software.

The tape system I use is supposed to hold 250M on a tape, but sometimes I can only get 150M on one tape. Why?

The tape drive manufacturers often inflate their capacity claims to match an estimated 2:1 compression ratio. Your tape probably can only hold 120M of uncompressed data. If you are experiencing less than a 2:1 compression ratio with the particular files you are backing up, your actual tape capacity will be less.

I can't schedule a backup to happen at night using Microsoft Backup for Windows. Why not?

Microsoft Backup for Windows does not directly support a scheduled backup. You may want to purchase another tape backup software package which does, or purchase Microsoft Plus! Companion for Windows 95 which contains a scheduling program, System Agent.

After I installed my scanner, I can't seem to scan anything into my word processor. What's wrong?

If you are not using the scanning software, you won't be able to scan anything into your word processor. If you are trying to scan text from a document into the word processor, you need to use special software which uses Optical Character Recognition (OCR) to actually convert the image into text data. This software may have been shipped with your scanner, so you should review the operation of the OCR software and its usage for scanning into word processing documents.

I bought a scanner to do OCR, but I never thought I'd have to do so much re-typing. Why can't the computer do a better job at reading the documents into my word processor?

It sounds like your expectations were a little too high for this technology. While some OCR software can read text with 99.7 percent accuracy, that still means that you could have between 5 to 10 errors on a "good" page and many more on a page with illegible writing or poor text quality. OCR is wonderful technology, but don't expect it to replace your secretary any time soon.

I seem to have lost all of my images in my digital camera that I took only yesterday. What happened? Is my camera or battery bad?

Affordable digital cameras use a flash memory system to store the images. The memory must be refreshed every so often to maintain the images. Logitech estimates that each image consumes 3 percent of the battery life per day. If you have 30 pictures stored in your camera, you may have exhausted the battery just by not retrieving your images sooner.

I can hear the modem sending tones as it dials, but nothing happens afterwards.

Check the telephone cables to be sure they're properly connected to the modem and to the wall jack. Verify the modem is dialing with pulses or tone by checking the Dialing Properties sheet.

I can hear my call being answered at the other end, but there's no tone indicating a connection.

The modem on the other end of the line is not working correctly or there is no modem there. You need to contact the person on the other end of the line to see if there is a problem, or try calling later.

Why do I see data errors on-screen after I've made a connection to another modem?

Make certain no one else is using the telephone line. Try calling the other modem again at another time or from a different phone line to get a better connection.

I can't get my modem to sign on to the remote modem. Why not?

Check the communication parameters of the remote station and make sure your software is configured for the same number of data bits, stop bits, and parity. You can access these settings by using the properties sheet of your modem, selecting the Connection page, and filling in the Connection Preferences area.

My modem connects with the remote modem but locks up.

Make sure you are using the proper modem-to-computer flow control and error control for your modem (click the Advanced button in the Connection page of the specific modem's properties sheet).

My modem disconnects while online. Why?

Check for loose connections between the modem and the computer, and between the modem and the telephone line. Alternatively, line noise or interference may be the problem; try the connection again with a different phone line or at a different time.

How do I start the Windows 95 Modem Troubleshooter?

Windows includes a Modem Troubleshooter you can use to help you diagnose a modem problem. To open the troubleshooter, open the Modems Properties sheet and choose the Diagnostics page. Choose the Help button and the Windows Help window appears. Follow the directions on-screen to try to solve your modem problems.

Why do I hear sounds when I use Windows 95?

When you installed Windows, a default set of sounds and events was chosen for you. You can change these by selecting the Sounds program in the Windows 95 Control Panel. On the Sounds Properties sheet, click on a sound and assign it to a Windows 95 event. Click OK.

I can't hear sounds when I'm using Windows 95.

Check the volume of your speakers. If you see a speaker icon on the Windows 95 taskbar, double-click it and set the volume controls. Make sure the Mute All check box is cleared. If a speaker icon does not appear, double-click the Multimedia icon in the Control Panel. On the Volume page, adjust the volume controls.

I have the Microsoft Plus! Companion for Windows 95 software. Can I reassign some of the event sounds for Desktop Themes?

If you've installed Microsoft Plus!, your initial scheme name is blank. The Desktop Themes control panel takes care of your event sound assignments for you. But, feel free to change individual sounds at any time.

Plus!

I've deleted a sound scheme. Is the sound file deleted as well?

No, deleting the scheme does not delete the actual sound file, just the connection between the event and which sound to play. You must use the Explorer or DOS to delete the actual sound file.

I can't get MIDI files to play back properly.

There can be a number of reasons. To start with, check the card's resource settings, such as IRQ settings, to make sure they are configured correctly for your specific MIDI board. Then make sure the MIDI board is correctly identified in Device Manager.

There is hissing and distortion when playing MIDI files. How can I get rid of it?

There may be interference coming from either the power source or another card installed in your computer. Turn your PC off and move the MIDI board as far away from both the power supply and other boards as possible. If you can, leave a few empty expansion slots in between the MIDI board and the next card.

When I print, the quality is low. How can I change this in Windows 95?

If the print quality is poor for graphics, make adjustments to the Graphics page of the printer's properties sheet. If text quality is poor, adjust the print quality settings in the Device Options page of the printer's properties sheet.

My printer does not support complex printing. What can I do?

If your printer does not print a complex page or divides graphics onto two or more pages, try changing the Printer Memory Tracking in the Device Options page of the printer's properties sheet. If you still have trouble, consider adding more memory to your printer.

Why does it take my application so long to print?

You may have the printer spooler turned off. Turn it on by opening the Printers folder in Control Panel. Click the icon for the printer you are using, click the File menu, and then click Properties. Click the Details page, and then click Spool Settings. Try printing your document again.

Why does it take a long time for my document to come out of the printer?

You may need to turn spooling off. If spooling is turned on and Spool Data Format is set to EMF, try changing the setting to RAW. You also can try turning spooling off by clicking Print Directly to the Printer. You might also need to lower the printing resolution of your printer. Open the property sheet for the printer you are using and click on the Graphics page. Select a lower resolution in the Resolution drop-down list.

Should I change the setting on my network card before I try setting up?

If there are default positions for any settings on the NIC, you should leave the settings at their default. In general, Windows 95 will first look for devices at their default settings. The only time you need to change the settings from their default is if there is a conflict with some other device in your system.

Should I let Windows 95 detect my network hardware?

If you let the Windows 95 wizard automatically detect your installed hardware, it is possible that it may find more than one new hardware component on your system. If all you installed is a network card, you may want to click the Cancel button and restart the wizard, using the Install Specific Hardware option.

My network card is not listed in the Network Hardware Wizard. Why not?

Depending on the version of Windows 95 you are running, this list of manufacturers and drives may be different. As Windows 95 matures, more types of hardware will be recognized by the wizard. If no Windows 95 drivers are available for your NIC, you can use the regular Windows drivers for your drive. See the instructions from your card and the Windows 95 documentation for help with installing and using Windows/DOS drivers with Windows 95.

I installed the NIC and Windows support, but the card still doesn't work.

The most common reason for the network card not working correctly is a conflict with another device on your system. Open the Control Panel (from the Start button) and start the System control panel. Select the Device Manager page to display the list of the devices on your system.

Double-click the Network Adapters entry in the list, and then select your network device. Click the Properties button to display the settings for your network card. The Device Status area generally tells you if there is a problem with your network device. Clicking the Resources page shows you the current settings; this page also tells you if one of the settings for your NIC conflicts with another device in your system.

Also, if you are using the Microsoft Network as your network operating system, you can use only 32-bit NICs. If you have a 16-bit card, you need to obtain a new card or install a new network operating system, such as NetWare, to your workgroup.

How can I find out the hardware settings for my network card?

If there is a conflict with another device in your system, you have to change one of the hardware settings (such as the Interrupt Request, Input/Output range or Direct Memory Access) to another value. You should consult the manual for your network card to determine which values for these settings are legal for your card. Once you know which settings you can set your network card to, you have to determine which hardware settings are available on your system. One good way to find out the settings that are in use on your system is to click the Print button on the main Device Manager page. This enables you to print out a summary of all the resources on your system. From this printout, you should be able to find an unused value.

When I browse my network, I don't see the other computers around me.

First, look at the entire network item in the Network Neighborhood browser to see if there are any other workgroups available. If there are, and there are computers in those workgroups, then you should make sure that your computer belongs to the correct workgroup.

Start the Network application in the Windows 95 control panel, and look under the Identification page. On this page, you can set your computer's workgroup and computer name. You should check with your network administrator for the workgroups that are available to you.

If you don't see any other workgroups (and you are sure that your network card is working correctly), you should make sure that you are logged into your network correctly. If you did not log into your computer (for example, there was a network login box displayed when your computer booted and you clicked Cancel), then you don't see other workgroups in the Network Neighborhood.

I use the network, but TCP/IP doesn't work. Why not?

◀ See "Configuring an Internet Connection," p. 289

The TCP/IP support in Windows 95 must be installed separately. The following instructions briefly describe how to set up TCP/IP support.

You need to find out if your network is using a DHCP server to allocate IP addresses automatically. If not, you need to obtain your specific IP address. You can find out this information from your network administrator. Next, in Control Panel, double-click the Network icon and click the Configuration page. Click Add, double-click Protocol, and click Microsoft. Click TCP/IP. After TCP/IP installs, you need to configure it using the settings from your system administrator. Afterwards, you need to reboot your system for these settings to take effect.

Microsoft Exchange and Fax

Microsoft Exchange is destined to revolutionize the way Windows users communicate with each other. Windows 95 includes the Exchange server that consolidates all your e-mail and fax messages. This section describes some of the common problems with Exchange and Windows 95's built-in fax software, Microsoft Fax.

When Exchange starts, I receive error messages saying that my Internet Mail server is not available. I don't have an Internet Mail server, and don't use Internet Mail. What's wrong?

You probably have installed Microsoft Plus! Companion for Windows 95 and ran the Internet Wizard, which installed the Internet Mail service provider. Open Control Panel and click the Mail and Fax icon. From the list of installed services, choose Internet Mail, then choose Remove. Windows 95 prompts you to verify that you want to remove the Internet Mail service provider from your profile. Choose Yes to remove the service from your profile.

Plus!

I would like to add a second Personal Information Store to my profile, but Exchange tells me I can only have one in a profile. Is it possible to add another?

You can only have one Personal Information Store in a profile, but you can add as many Personal Folders to a profile as you like. Personal Folders are essentially identical to the Personal Information Store. The only difference is that your incoming mail is directed into the Personal Information Store. If you simply want more places to segregate your incoming mail, create new folders in your Personal Information Store instead of adding Personal Folders to your profile. You can create as many additional folders in the PST as you like. To create a new folder, open the folder in which you want the new folder created. Then, choose File, New Folder. Exchange displays a dialog box in which you enter the name for the new folder. Then, you can drag messages to the new folder as you desire.

I created an administrator account for the WGPO, but I've forgotten the password. Can I reassign another account as the WGPO administrator account?

Unfortunately, there's no way to change the administrator account. Unless you can recall the password, you have no way of gaining access to the account or administering the WGPO. Fortunately, new users can create their own mail accounts in the WGPO, so new and existing users alike can continue to use the WGPO while you attempt to resolve the problem. First, direct all users to back up their message folders. A simple way to do this is to make a backup copy of their PST file. Any users who store their messages in the WGPO instead of locally must copy their messages to a local folder. When all users' messages are backed up, delete the WGPO and recreate it, making sure to create an administrator account with a password you can remember. Recreate all of the user accounts in the WGPO.

I configured the CompuServe Mail provider to check for messages at 8 a.m. and every four hours. But, Exchange doesn't check at 8, 12, 4, and so on. It checks for mail at 8 a.m., but the four-hour interval falls at odd times. Why is this?

The CompuServe Mail provider doesn't base its interval connection times on the explicit 8 AM setting you've specified. Instead, the provider checks at four-hour intervals based on the last time it automatically checked for mail. Open Control Panel and click the Mail and Fax icon. Select the CompuServe Mail provider and choose Properties. Choose Advanced, Schedule Connect Times to display the Connection Times dialog box. Clear the Every check box and close the dialog box, then close the Profile property sheets. Shortly before the time when you want one of your hourly-interval connections to be made, open the Control Panel, click the Mail and Fax icon, then enable the Every check box in the Connection Times dialog box and specify the interval you want to use. Close the property sheets. Exchange should then connect close to the time you want.

I can't get Microsoft Fax to install properly. What should I do?

First, make sure you have Microsoft Exchange installed. If you do not, read Chapter 9, "Configuring Microsoft Exchange." If you do, you need to make sure that your fax modem is installed and working. Also, send a test fax to a fax machine that you know is working properly. If it faxes fine, your original phone number may be wrong. Make sure that your phone number is set up to call outside lines, if your phone requires this. Another thing you should do is disable call waiting before you make a call or before you receive an incoming fax.

I want to configure Exchange, but I'm not sure what information stores are.

Information stores and address books are service providers, just like the Microsoft Mail, CompuServe, and other service providers. All of these service providers are often referred to as just *services*.

I'm not near a printer but I need to print out a document. How can I do this?

Microsoft Fax includes fax printer drivers so that you can print to a fax machine from within any Windows application. If you are in a hotel or traveling and have access to a fax machine, send a document to the fax machine to get a hard copy of it.

I received a fax with Microsoft Fax, but I don't know where it is.

The Microsoft Exchange universal Inbox is where fax messages are stored. Double-click the Inbox icon on your desktop to start Exchange.

Norton Utilities

Norton Utilities for Windows 95 is a package of data protection and recovery utility programs designed specifically for Windows 95. Use this section to troubleshoot some of the common problems associated with Norton Utilities.

What if the system hangs while running Norton Diagnostics? Do I have to start all over again?

If your system crashes or freezes during a test, reboot your machine and restart NDIAGS. This time, instead of restarting all the tests, use the menus to restart the test that the computer failed on. Norton Diagnostics tracks where it was at in the testing and attempts to further diagnose what caused the failure.

I accidentally deleted some important files using SpaceWizard. What now?

Not to worry—you can run the DOS version of UNERASE to recover any files you inadvertently deleted.

Can I re-run Image on a damaged drive?

If you run Image on a damaged drive, don't re-run it or you will destroy your backup copy. Instead, delete the IMAGE.DAT file (which won't be any good) and rename IMAGE.BAK to **IMAGE.DAT**.

Tip

If you need a break from troubleshooting, start the Windows 95 Easter egg by using the following steps:

1. Right-click the Desktop, choose New, Folder, and name it **And now, the moment you've been waiting for**.
2. Next, right-click the folder, choose Rename, and enter **We proudly present for your viewing pleasure**.
3. Right-click the folder again and rename it **The Microsoft Windows 95 Product Team!**.
4. Open the folder and watch the credits of the Windows 95 developers. You'll need a sound card to hear the music.

Appendix C

What's on the CD

by Rob Tidrow

The CD-ROM included with this book contains a variety of software programs developed for Windows 95. The software includes productivity tools, animated cursors and icons, Windows 95 shell replacements, and a few entertainment packages. This appendix gives a brief explanation of each application and lists the file you need to install or run the application.

Accessing the Software

Each of the software programs is set up in its own folder on the CD-ROM. To install a package, copy its folder onto your hard drive and then double-click the setup or application executable file listed in this appendix. As an example, to install the Barry Press Utilities, copy the BPUTIL folder to your hard drive and double-click the SETUP.EXE file. Follow the setup instructions on the screen.

Tip

Many of these utilities require the file VBRUN300.DLL to run. Before you install anything from this disk, copy this file from the CD-ROM's root directory to your Windows system folder, then reboot your computer. You only need to install this file once.

What's Included?

The software on the CD is organized alphabetically to help you locate each item quickly. To install all the programs on your system, you will need approximately 40-45M of free disk space, depending on the options you can install for some of the utilities. For additional information for each application, read the README.TXT or similar files included with many of the programs.

The following sections briefly describe each of the programs on the CD.

Accent 3.0

Accent enables you to input special characters that are not normally found on a regular keyboard. These characters include accented characters, called *diacritics*, and other special symbols such as the copyright sign © or the trademark sign ™.

File name: ACCENT\ACCENT.EXE

pro++ Software
Gilles Gervais
8045 Place Saguenay
Brossard, Quebec
Canada, J4X 1N2
CompuServe: **72571,724**
Phone: (514) 465-9306

Add Applications v3.1

This is a 32-bit application for Windows 95, Windows NT, and Win32s to help you migrate groups and program icons to new users, move groups from Windows 3.1 to Windows 95 or NT, and more. You can search disks and CD-ROMs to migration applications, icons, and bitmaps to Program Manager or the Windows 95 Desktop.

File name: ADDAPP\ADDAPP.EXE

Timothy D.A. Cox
TDAC Software, Inc.
12 Miner Circle
Markham Ontario
Canada, L3R 1Y2
CompuServe: **70353,3403**
Internet: **cox@io.org**
Phone: (905) 940-1529

Background Noise v1.52

Background Noise is a robust Win32 MCI media player that runs under Windows 95 or Windows NT. Version 1.52 supports Microsoft Video, CD Audio, WAV, and MIDI files. You can create Sound Object Lists of any length and combination, and from more than one device. Hot Keys let you control Background Noise to instantly play predefined selections, skip the current song, or start/stop the playing Sound Object List.

File name: BN\SETUP.EXE

P&J's Software
14150 NE 20th
Box 277
Bellevue, WA 98007
CompuServe: **71303,2375**

The Barry Press Utilities

This is the public release of the shareware Barry Press Utilities for Windows 95 that includes a monthly calendar (CalPop), drag-and-drop ASCII file printer (CodeList), printer-orientation utility (Flipper), ASCII file comparison program (Match), shell extension to add a command line option to Explorer (Runner), digital clock (Time), and multimedia file player (Waver).

File name: BPUTILS\SETUP.EXE

Barry Press
2494 East Cheshire Drive
Sandy, UT 84093-1849
CompuServe: **72467,2353**

BmpView 1.0

BmpView 1.0 is a fast 32-bit viewing program that helps you locate BMP files on your system. When you find a BMP file you want to edit, click on it to activate a BMP editor, such as MS Paint. You also can scroll through an entire directory of BMPs to locate the one you need.

File name: BMPVIEW\BMPVIEW.EXE

Daniel Brum
3219 Yonge St., Office 226
Toronto, Ontario,
Canada M4N-2L3
CompuServe: **74762,315**

Capture Professional 2.0

Capture Professional 2.0 is a demo of an advanced screen capture tool for Windows 95 and Windows 3.1. Capture Professional 2.0 features seven capture modes (Window, Client Area, Region, Oval, Rectangle, Desktop, and Icon). You can set up hot keys for each mode to activate them from any Windows application. Capture Professional enables you to save screen captures with 2, 16, 256, and 16.7M colors in the following file formats: BMP, EPS, GIF, ICO, JPG, PCX, RLE, TGA, and TIF. It can import six file formats for viewing, touch-up (more than 20 effects), or conversions to other file formats.

File name: CAPPRO\SETUP.EXE

Creative Software
2003 Lake Park Drive, Suite G
Smyrna, GA 30080
CompuServe: **74011,206**
Phone: (800) 680-9679
Fax: (800) 430-9679

CD Wizzard CD Player

CD Wizzard is a shareware CD player for Windows 95 that includes a flexible database system and customizable interface. The Disc Database enables you to search for artist, composer, track name, and other search criteria for a particular CD.

File name: CDWIZZRD\CDW.EXE

BFM Software
Brett McDonald
38602 Lancaster Drive
Farmington Hills, MI 48331
CompuServe: **73770,1254**
America Online: **BrettMc**
Phone: (810) 661-1797

Collection of 154 Animated Icons

Enhance the look of your Windows desktop with this collection of 154 public domain animated icons collected from various Windows 95 and Windows NT CompuServe forums.

Folder name: 154ICONS

Drag and File

Drag and File v1 For Windows 95 provides powerful Windows File Manager support—it can list files for an entire drive or for multiple drives and directories. It includes a configurable toolbar, built-in DOS command line, and file descriptions in DOS format. You can use context menus and create shortcuts. It even supports network connections.

File name: DRAGFILE\DFSETUP.EXE

Canyon Software
1537 Fourth St., Suite 131
San Rafael, CA 94901
CompuServe: **74774,554**
Phone: (415) 382-7999
Fax: (415) 382-7998

Drag and Zip

Drag and Zip appears when you run File Manager. You can drag a set of files to the icon on the desktop, specify the ZIP file name, and create a ZIP file or a self-extracting ZIP file that includes all the specified files. You can also drag a ZIP file to the icon or double-click on a ZIP file to display the contents. From the contents window, you can selectively extract (decompress) files, or extract them all. Provided by author, member ASP.

File name: DRAGZIP\DZSETUP.EXE

Canyon Software
1537 Fourth St., Suite 131
San Rafael, CA 94901
CompuServe: **74774,554**
Phone: (415) 382-7999
Fax: (415) 382-7998

Easy Icons 95

Easy Icons 95 is an Icon Management program that enables you to create icon library files and drag-and-drop files between libraries. With Easy Icons 95, you can open many files at once, as well as extract or view any icon(s) from any file and save it as a separate ICO) or BMP) file. Requires the file VBRUN300.DLL.

File name: EASYICON\EASYICON.EXE

Paul Traver
P.O. Box 998
Bishop, CA 93514
CompuServe: **72144,422**
Phone: (619) 873-8754

FaxMail v4.17

FaxMail for Windows enables you to fax from Windows applications (such as Word for Windows) as easily as printing. It does this by adding a Fax button to Windows programs, giving you access to all fax modems or fax machines connected to your computer. Among other features, FaxMail enables you to import up to 1,000 names and phone numbers into each FaxBook phone book using any xBase database. To install FaxMail, you must run INSTALL.EXE from the CD-ROM.

File name: FAXMAIL\INSTALL.EXE

Jon Krahmer
Electrasoft
3207 Carmel Valley Drive
Missouri City, TX 77459-3068
CompuServe: **74464,763**

First Aid 95

First Aid 95 helps you maintain the health of your PC by automatically identifying and fixing more than 10,000 known problems. Exclusive AutoFix technology automatically alerts you when it senses trouble, explains the problem in plain English, and fixes the problem. First Aid fixes GPFs, crashes, multimedia conflicts, Internet access problems, and other performance problems. You also can use First Aid 95 to safely remove features of applications that you never use (or compress them until needed) and help you tweak setup parameters to boost overall system performance. This is a utility that you should install right away.

File name: FIRSTAID\SETUP.EXE

CyberMedia
1800 Century Park East, Suite 1145
Los Angeles, CA 90067
Phone: (310) 843-0800
Fax: (310) 843-0120

FracView 2

FracView 2 v2.01 for Windows 95 plots the Mandelbrot set and enables you to zoom in on a region for closer examination. You can copy the content to the Clipboard to paste into other applications.

File name: FRACVIEW\SETUP.EXE

Pocket-Sized Software
8547 E. Arapahoe Road, Suite J-147
Greenwood Village, CO 80112
CompuServe: **73667,3517**

GrabIt Pro 5.0

GrabIt Pro is a Windows 95 application that enables you to capture a screen, a window, a portion of a window, and a menu. You can select user-defined areas, include child windows and mouse cursors, and select the number of colors in which to save the screen capture. You can use the preview feature to view a file before opening it.

File name: GRABIT\GPSETUP.EXE

Software Excellence by Design, Inc.
14801 North 12th Street
Phoenix, AZ 85022-2515
CompuServe: **7220,576**

Gravity Well 3.4

Gravity Well is a fast-paced action/strategy game. You must pilot a space ship between planets, leading your empire to expand. Planets orbit stars and exert gravity upon your ship. Three computer opponents compete for the same region of space.

File name: GRAVWELL\GWELL32.EXE

David Hoeft
Software Engineering, Inc.
8352 S. Sunnyside Place
Highlands Ranch, CO 80126
CompuServe: **102330,474**
Internet: **DaveH@FreeHome.com**
Phone: (303) 470-7142

Hyper CD

HyperCD is one of the smallest CD audio players for Windows 95 and NT. It's also one of the easiest to use, letting you play, pause, eject, and stop your audio CDs. HyperCD features buttons and controls, and sits on the Windows 95 taskbar when executed.

File name: HYPERCD\HYPERC.EXE

Lou Schillaci (courtesy of HyperDyne 2000)
26/25 Devonshire Street
Chatswood, Sydney
N.S.W. 2067
Australia
CompuServe: **76702,1774**

IFA v4.00.2

Instant File Access adds many time-saving features to the File dialogs of all Windows applications, such as Previous File History, a Toolbar, File Find, and Floating file lists. Give LONG NAMES to your Windows 3.1 files with Instant File Access. Great for Word and Excel. Now works with 16-bit applications under Windows 95.

File name: IFA400\SETUP.EXE

Michael Mondry
Alexoft
507 de la Metaire
Nun's Island, Quebec
Canada, H3E 1S4
CompuServe: **72154,15**

Launchpad 95 v1.0

Shift into high gear with Windows 95 by using Launchpad 95. Easily associate folders with the launchpad and use Launchpad 95 to quickly launch applications from the Windows 95 Desktop. You can use this utility to execute the programs of your choice (such as the programs you use most) much faster than the usual process of navigating through nested menus or nested folders.

File name: LAUNCH\SETUP.EXE

Prasad Thammineni
CompuServe: **102706,3167**

Microangelo

Windows 95 unleashes the power of icon graphics—Microangelo helps you keep pace. In Windows 95, an icon is a "container" of multiple image formats from 16 × 16 to 48 × 48 in size, and up to 256 colors. Microangelo puts them all in your hand, supporting images from 8 × 8 to 64 × 64 pixels in depths to 256 colors. Microangelo finds them, copies them, creates them, and edits them.

File name: MICROANG\SETUP.EXE

Len Gray
Impact Software
P.O. Box 457
Chino, CA 91708
CompuServe: **71630,1703**
Phone: (909) 590-8522
Fax: (909) 590-2202

MIDI Jukebox 2

MIDI Jukebox 2 plays multiple MIDI and WAV files either once or in a continuous loop. You can pause, play, or skip to the next or previous track.

File name: MIDIJB\SETUP.EXE

Pocket-Sized Software
8547 E. Arapahoe Road, Suite J-147
Greenwood Village, CO 80112
CompuServe: **73667,3517**

Milestones, Etc. 4.5 (trial version)

There's only one way to keep a project on track: put it on a schedule. But who wants to struggle with complicated project management software? Milestones, Etc. is an easy and flexible project scheduling tool for Windows 95. Just type in each schedule step, drop a starting symbol into place with your mouse, and "click and drag" to the right to add the time span. Create anything from simple Gantt charts and Line-of-Balance charts to milestone schedules and detailed master schedules in minutes with presentation-quality output. Compatible with MS Project (reads and writes Project MPX files). Supports OLE 2.0 as a server, enabling you to link or embed your Milestones, Etc. schedules in other Windows applications.

File name: MILSTONES\DISK1\INSTALL.EXE

KIDASA Software
1114 Lost Creek Blvd, Suite 300
Austin, TX 78746
CompuServe: **76702,1305**
Phone: 800-765-0167/512-328-0167
Fax: 512-328-0247

Plug-In for Windows v2.60

Plug-In for Windows is an enhancement utility that seamlessly integrates with Windows and works with any Windows Desktop. Major features include Control Center, where you can coordinate all of Plug-In's functions; title bar displays to show date, time, and resource usage; and Power Button, which gives instant access to Plug-In's QuickRun menu. This version works with Windows 95, but does not take full advantage of all of Windows 95's features. A new update is to be released in early 1996.

File name: PLUG_IN\PLUGIN.EXE

Plannet Crafters
P.O. Box 450
Alpharetta, GA 30239-0450
CompuServe: **73040,334**
America Online: **DMandell**
Prodigy: **VSFB48A**
Microsoft Network: **PlanCraft**

PSA Cards 2.5

PSA Cards is an easy-to-use address program. It looks like a card file and it works like a card file. Just click a divider tab or card to open or close it. PSA Cards is also an OLE 2.0 container application, enabling you to link and embed pictures, maps, documents, sounds, and other objects. You can print Rolodex cards, envelopes, mailing labels, shipping labels, and address booklets from within PSA Cards 2.5. Be sure to read the README.TXT file to see all the features of PSA Cards.

File name: PSACARDS\SETUP.EXE

William L. Rogers
PSA Software
1319 Silk Oak Drive
Fort Collins, CO 80525
CompuServe: **72064,1437**

PolyView 1.8

PolyView is a very fast JPEG, GIF, BMP, and Photo-CD (PCD) viewer, with full 32-bit multithreading and supports of long file names. You can drag and drop graphic files from Explorer, File Manager, and other sources into PolyView. Features include the capability to zoom in and out through a chain of image magnifications, use the entire display screen to view an image, use the entire screen to automatically cycle through all the loaded images, resize an image to better utilize the available display, and more.

File name: POLYVIEW\POLYVIEW.EXE

Polybytes
3427 Bever Avenue S.E.
Cedar Rapids, IA 52403
CompuServe: **70222,300**
America Online: **PolyView**

Programmer's File Editor 6.01

PFE version 6.01 is a freeware programming editor and a replacement for Windows Notepad as a text editor. This version is for Windows 95 and the Intel version of Windows NT 3.5. PFE supports multiple files open at one time, drag and drop (for files and text), multilevel undos, most-recently-used file list, and much more. You also can use PFE to send files as e-mail using MAPI-compliant e-mail programs (such as Microsoft Mail).

File name: PROGEDIT\PFE32.EXE

Alan Phillips
Internet: **A.Phillips@lancaster.ac.uk**

Psychedelic Screen Saver Collection

The Psychedelic Screen Saver Collection v 1.0 is a collection of screen savers that generate hypnotic patterns on your Windows 95 Desktop. Included are 16- and 32-bit versions for Microsoft Windows 3.1, Windows 95, and Windows NT, as well as versions for Berkeley Systems' After Dark v2.0c.

Folder name: PSYCHSAV

Mike Irvine
Northstar Solutions
P.O. Box 25262
Columbia, SC 29224

CompuServe: **73323,2322** or **71561,2751**
Phone: 800-699-6395
Fax: 803-699-5465

QuickTutors 95

QuickTutors 95 consists of 40 minitutorials (five in this demo version) that cover important migration topics ranging from how to use the Windows 95 Explorer to how to activate a new modem. Once installed, QuickTutors 95 is immediately available on the Windows 95 Desktop to assist the user. The program leads you through certain tasks in Windows 95 and actually performs them for the user if desired. You can obtain the full version of QuickTutors 95 at local computer software retail stores via the Internet Shopping Network (**http://www.internet.net**), or via e-mail (**esales@ eticket.com**).

File name: QUICKTUT\SETUP.EXE

E-Ticket, Inc.
Attention: Mail Order Sales
2118 Wilshire Blvd., Suite 1118
Santa Monica, CA 90403-5784
Internet: **rgibson@eticket.com** or **esales@eticket.com**
Phone: (520) 577-2221
Fax: (520) 577-2896

SnapShot/32 Screen Capture

Capture entire desktop, individual window or client area, or draw rectangle to select using SnapShot/32. Print with optional reverse black and white, save to BMP or GIF, or copy to Clipboard. If you want to capture a menu pulled down, you can use the SnapShot/32 hot key support without causing the menu to close. When the capture is finished, you can view the image in the SnapShot/32 window. You then can copy the image to the Clipboard to be pasted into a Windows Device Independent Bitmap-compatible application for processing.

File name: SNAPSHOT\SNAP32.EXE

Greg Kochaniak
3146 Chestnut Street
Murrysville, PA 15668
CompuServe: **71461,631**
Internet: **gregko@kagi.com** (preferred)
Phone: (412) 325-4001 (evenings)

Somar ACTS V1.7

Somar ACTS v1.7 is a Windows 95 and Windows NT program that dials the NIST or USNO time source using a modem, obtains the current time, and uses this time to set the system time on your computer. You should note that similar programs designed for MS-DOS will not work under NT because of security issues.

File name: ACTSNT\ACTSNT.EXE

Somar Software
1 Scott Circle, NW Suite 816
Washington, DC 20036
CompuServe: 72202,2574
Internet: **framos@somar.com**
Phone: (202) 232-3748

Stereograms 2

Stereograms 2 converts monochrome bitmap files into random-dot stereograms, which can be viewed on-screen or printed. A *stereogram* is a two-dimensional graphic that appears three-dimensional when viewed properly. Stereograms have been recently popularized by *The Magic Eye* and other books. Many newspapers include stereograms in their comics sections.

File name: ST_GRAMS\SETUP.EXE

Pocket-Sized Software
8547 E. Arapahoe Road, Suite J-147
Greenwood Village, CO 80112
CompuServe: **73667,3517**

Talking Clock 2

Talking Clock 2 displays the time on your computer and optionally announces the time every 15 minutes, if you have a sound card installed.

File name: TCLOCK\SETUP.EXE

Pocket-Sized Software
8547 E. Arapahoe Road, Suite J-147
Greenwood Village, CO 80112
CompuServe: **73667,3517**

TaskView V4.0

TaskView is a utility program for Windows 95 and Windows NT 3.51 that provides the capability to view and manage the active tasks currently operating on the computer. It is particularly useful for terminating programs that are no longer cooperative, as well as setting the priorities of operating tasks. If you use the new Windows 95 shell and miss the old Task Manager, this is the utility for you.

File name: TASKVIEW\SETUP.EXE

Thomas Reed
Reed Consulting
2312 Belvedere
Toledo, OH 43614
CompuServe: **76237,516**

TextPad 1.29

TextPad 1.29 is a 32-bit text editor to use with Windows 95. Some of its features include large file support, Universal Naming Convention (UNC) style name support, multiple file edits, automatic word-wrapping, and much more. You also can drag and drop text and files into TextPad.

File name: TEXTPAD\SETUP.EXE

Helios Software Solutions
Carr Brook House, Chorley Old Road
Brindle, Chorley, Lancaster
England PR6 7Q2
CompuServe: **100041,235**
Internet: **textpad@heliosof.demon.co.uk**
Phone: +44-(0)1772-324353

TILER Image Viewer

TILER is a Windows NT and Windows 95 application that views and manages GIF, JPEG, and Windows BMP image files. Both the "87a" and "89a" versions of GIF are supported. If a GIF file contains more than one image, TILER loads only the first image. TILER can read 1-, 4-, 8-, and 24-bit Windows BMP files; both 4-bit and 8-bit compression is supported.

File name: TILER\TILER.EXE

David Bowman
12050-H Little Patuxent Pkwy.

Columbia, MD 21044
CompuServe: **72057,3253**
Internet: **dbowman@access.digex.net**
America Online: **BowmanDave**

Tessler's Nifty Tools (TNT) v5.0

Tessler's Nifty Tools is a collection of more than 35 high-quality, low-cost Windows 95, NT, 3.1, and DOS programs for both the casual and power user who desires to increase their PC productivity and enjoyment. Some of the utilities available include Cfgcntrl, Grp2ini, Ifwait, Capstat, and others. Review the lengthy PAMPHLET.DOC file included in the TNT folder for more information on all the other utilities included.

Folder names: TNT\PACKAGE1, TNT\PACKAGE2, TNT\PACKAGE3

Gary Tessler
430 Canyon Woods Place, Suite A
San Ramon, CA 94583
CompuServe: **71044,542**

ToolPAL 2.1

ToolPAL 2.1 is a replacement for the Task Manager in Windows 95 and Windows 3.1. With ToolPALs, you can switch between Windows applications, create a launch list of frequently used programs, lock the selected window on the top of the Windows Desktop, set up multiple virtual desktops, move windows between them, and customize the way you use Windows using ToolPAL palettes, file folders, and buttons.

File name: TOOLPAL\SETUP.EXE

Art English
Digital Artistry
3509 Gary Drive
Plano, TX 75023-1266
CompuServe: **74777,1142**
Phone/Fax: (214) 232-3310

Voice Clock 2.02

Voice Clock is a speech clock that can announce the time every 1, 15, 30, or 60 minutes. It has high-quality sound, and includes a title bar clock, desktop clock, and resource clock. The clocks can be set instantly, and feature both male and female voices. Only the male voice is included with the version on the CD-ROM. When you register the product, you are given support for a female voice, too.

File name: VCLOCK\SETUP.EXE

Erwin Koonce
P.O. Box 308
Jacksonville, AR 72078
CompuServe: **72610,1375**

Win Bar Clock 4.1A

Win Bar Clock 4.1A is a utility for the Windows environment that displays information such as the time, date, system resources, or any text message in the title bar of the active window. You also can set it up as a floating bar clock on your system. Win Bar Clock can display date, time, memory, and system resources, display month calendar, and start programs from within any application using the Quick Execute command when you right-click on the clock.

File name: WBCLOCK\WCSETUP.EXE

G.L. Liadis & Associates
5167 1/2 Saling Court
Columbus, OH 43229
CompuServe: **72274,3252**
America Online: **GL Liadis**
BBS: **614-888-4749**

G.L. Liadis Software Inc.
Agali Beach Resort
Kardamyla
83100 Chios, Greece

Win Calculate v4.1+

Win Calculate is a programmer's RPN, a scientific calculator that lets you work with integers ranging from -1 to +2 billion, and includes support of decimal, hexadecimal, octal, and binary modes. You can calculate angles and degrees, logarithmic, trigometric, and hyperbolic values, and determine the cube root, square, and pi of numbers.

File name: WCALC.\WCALC.EXE

G.L. Liadis & Associates
5167 1/2 Saling Court
Columbus, OH 43229
CompuServe: **72274,3252**
America Online: **GL Liadis**
BBS: **614-888-4749**

G.L. Liadis Software Inc.
Agali Beach Resort
Kardamyla
83100 Chios, Greece

Win Calendar v4.1

Win Calendar is a freeware 3-D Windows calendar for Windows 3.11 and Windows 95. Win Calendar displays in monthly format and lets you view any month with one mouse click, or click Today to display the current day and month.

File name: WINCAL\WCALENDR.EXE

G.L. Liadis & Associates
5167 1/2 Saling Court
Columbus, OH 43229
CompuServe: **72274,3252**
America Online: **GL Liadis**
BBS: **614-888-4749**

G.L. Liadis Software Inc.
Agali Beach Resort
Kardamyla
83100 Chios, Greece

Windows 95 and NT Screen Saver Pack

The Windows 95 and NT Screen Saver Pack extends the life of your computer monitor with the following colorful screen savers: Clock, Dancing Lines, HyperCycloids, Life, Snakes, Spheres, and Zoom. In addition, a demo of the Photo Album screen saver is included. See the USERS_GD.WRI file in the SCRNSAVS folder for more information.

Folder name: SCRNSAVS

Pocket-Sized Software
8547 E. Arapahoe Road, Suite J-147
Greenwood Village, CO 80112
CompuServe: **73667,3517**

Windows 95 Motion Cursors

This is a collection of 43 Motion Cursors to use with Windows 95.

Folder name: MOTION

James Snyder
Shattered Rose Studio
CompuServe: **75141,3544**

Wil DLL Extender Library

This is the latest version of the extender DLL library to add network and other support to the Windows Interface Language (WIL) for WinBatch 5.x.

File name: WILDLL\WSETUP.EXE

Wilson WindowWare
2701 California Ave S.W., #212
Seattle, WA 98116
CompuServe: **76702,1072**

WinBatch 32 5.1c

WinBatch 32 is a 32-bit batch language to create batch files for Windows and replaces dozens of single-purpose utilities. WinBatch has more than 350 functions and includes structured programming features, improved network support, time functions, floating-point calculations, binary file access, registration database functions, child window support, and the capability to access third-party DLLs through DllCall.

File name: WINBATCH\WSETUP.EXE

Wilson WindowWare
2701 California Ave S.W., #212
Seattle, WA 98116
CompuServe: **76702,1072**

Windows Commander 2.0 Preview

Windows Commander is a file manager for Windows 95 similar to the Windows file manager WINFILE.EXE. The main difference between File Manager and Windows Commander is that Windows Commander uses two fixed windows. Windows Commander supports drag-and-drop file and print management; copying, moving, renaming, and deleting of entire trees; and a built-in file viewer to view files of any size in hex, binary, or text format. It also has an internal unzip utility by Info-Zip to quickly unzip files. To install Windows Commander, run the INSTALL.EXE file from the CD-ROM, not your hard disk.

File name: WINCMND\INSTALL.EXE

Christian Ghisler
Lindenmattstr. 60
CH-3065 Bolligen
Switzerland
CompuServe: **100332,1175**

WinImage 2.10a

WinImage 2.10a enables you to make disk images from floppy disks to blank floppy disks. It features a toolbar, status bar, and supports drag-and-drop. WinImage reads the images created by several third-party disk copy utilities, including Wimage (in FdFormat utility) from C.H. Hochstätter, CopyVit from Sébastien Chatard, DrDos 6 and OS/2 2.x diskimage utilities, DCF (Disk Copy Fast) from Chang Ping Lee, DF (Disk Image File Utility) from Mark Vitt, Super-DiskCopy from Super Software, SabDu from S.A. Berman, Disk-RW from K. Hartnegg, DiskDupe from Micro System Design, internal disk Microsoft and Lotus image utilities, and the MFMT sample Windows NT application that comes with Windows NT SDK.

File name: WINIMAGE\WINIMANT.EXE

Gilles Vollant
13, rue Francios Mansart
91540 Mennecy
France
CompuServe: **100144,2636**

WinPack32 Deluxe v8.0

WinPack 32 is a file compression utility that supports ZIP, GZIP, TAR, ARJ, UUEncode and UUDecode, and BinHex files. WinPack 32 has a Windows 95 Explorer-type interface with Toolhelp bubbles, support for long file names, and a dockable toolbar.

File name: WINPACK\WPACK32D.EXE

Randy Snow
Retrospect
2115 Industrial Drive
Altus, OK 73521
CompuServe: **71540,1240**
America Online: **RSNOW1**
Microsoft Network: **RETROSPECT**
Internet: **snow@retrospect.com**
Phone: (405) 482-0672
Fax: (405) 482-0284

WinZip 6.0

Have you ever used the Internet, a BBS, or CompuServe? If so, you've probably encountered ZIP files. Are you a Windows user? If so, WinZip is a great way to handle these archived files. WinZip brings the convenience of Windows to the use of ZIP files without requiring PKZIP and PKUNZIP. It features built-in support for popular Internet file formats, including TAR, GZIP, and UNIX compress. ARJ, LZH, and ARC files are supported by using external programs.WinZip 6.0 for Windows 95 features long file name support and tight integration with the Windows 95 shell, including the capability to zip and unzip without leaving the Explorer.

File name: WINZIP95\SETUP.EXE

Niko Mak Computing
P.O. Box 919
Bristol, CT 06011
CompuServe: **70056,241**

Zip Tip Demo

Zip Tip provides a tool to add "Tip of the Day" items to any Windows program. To use Zip Tip, software developers create a text file containing a list of tips (up to 2,000 characters long) pertaining to their application. The file can be created using any word processor. Zip Tip is then launched from within the developer's application, similar to the way in which WinHelp is executed when the user requests Help. A dialog box appears with the Tip of the Day showing. Each time the application is started, a new Tip of the Day appears.

File name: ZIPTIP\ZTDEMO.EXE

Responsive Software
1901 Tunnel Road
Berkeley, CA 94705
CompuServe: **76367,3673**
Phone: (510) 843-1034
Fax: (510) 644-1013

Index

Symbols

A

B

C

D

E

F

G

H

I-J

K

N

Q-R

S

T

U

V

W-X-Y-Z

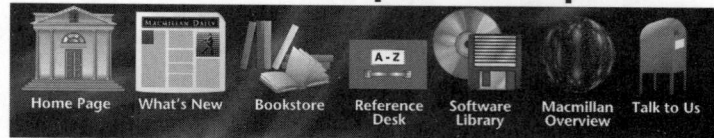

Complete and Return this Card for a *FREE* Computer Book Catalog

Thank you for purchasing this book! You have purchased a superior computer book written expressly for your needs. To continue to provide the kind of up-to-date, pertinent coverage you've come to expect from us, we need to hear from you. Please take a minute to complete and return this self-addressed, postage-paid form. In return, we'll send you a free catalog of all our computer books on topics ranging from word processing to programming and the internet.

Mr. ☐ Mrs. ☐ Ms. ☐ Dr. ☐

Name (first) ____ (M.I.) ____ (last) ____

Address ____

City ____ State ____ Zip ____

Phone ____ Fax ____

Company Name ____

E-mail address ____

1. Please check at least (3) influencing factors for purchasing this book.

- Front or back cover information on book ☐
- Special approach to the content ☐
- Completeness of content ☐
- Author's reputation ☐
- Publisher's reputation ☐
- Book cover design or layout ☐
- Index or table of contents of book ☐
- Price of book ☐
- Special effects, graphics, illustrations ☐
- Other (Please specify): ____ ☐

2. How did you first learn about this book?

- Saw in Macmillan Computer Publishing catalog ☐
- Recommended by store personnel ☐
- Saw the book on bookshelf at store ☐
- Recommended by a friend ☐
- Received advertisement in the mail ☐
- Saw an advertisement in: ____ ☐
- Read book review in: ____ ☐
- Other (Please specify): ____ ☐

3. How many computer books have you purchased in the last six months?

- This book only ☐
- 2 books ☐
- 3 to 5 books ☐
- More than 5 ☐

4. Where did you purchase this book?

- Bookstore ☐
- Computer Store ☐
- Consumer Electronics Store ☐
- Department Store ☐
- Office Club ☐
- Warehouse Club ☐
- Mail Order ☐
- Direct from Publisher ☐
- Internet site ☐
- Other (Please specify): ____ ☐

5. How long have you been using a computer?

- ☐ Less than 6 months
- ☐ 6 months to a year
- ☐ 1 to 3 years
- ☐ More than 3 years

6. What is your level of experience with personal computers and with the subject of this book?

	With PCs	With subject of book
New	☐	☐
Casual	☐	☐
Accomplished	☐	☐
Expert	☐	☐

Source Code ISBN: 1-7897-0580-X

7. Which of the following best describes your job title?

- Administrative Assistant ☐
- Coordinator ☐
- Manager/Supervisor ☐
- Director ☐
- Vice President ☐
- President/CEO/COO ☐
- Lawyer/Doctor/Medical Professional ☐
- Teacher/Educator/Trainer ☐
- Engineer/Technician ☐
- Consultant ☐
- Not employed/Student/Retired ☐
- Other (Please specify): ______________ ☐

8. Which of the following best describes the area of the company your job title falls under?

- Accounting ☐
- Engineering ☐
- Manufacturing ☐
- Operations ☐
- Marketing ☐
- Sales ☐
- Other (Please specify): ______________ ☐

9. What is your age?

- Under 20 ☐
- 21-29 ☐
- 30-39 ☐
- 40-49 ☐
- 50-59 ☐
- 60-over ☐

10. Are you:

- Male ☐
- Female ☐

11. Which computer publications do you read regularly? (Please list)

____

____

____

____

____

____

____

____

Comments: ______________________________

____

____

Fold here and scotch-tape to mail.

NO POSTAGE
NECESSARY
IF MAILED
IN THE
UNITED STATES

BUSINESS REPLY MAIL

FIRST-CLASS MAIL PERMIT NO. 9918 INDIANAPOLIS IN

POSTAGE WILL BE PAID BY THE ADDRESSEE

ATTN MARKETING
MACMILLAN COMPUTER PUBLISHING
MACMILLAN PUBLISHING USA
201 W 103RD ST
INDIANAPOLIS IN 46209-9042

This package contains one CD-ROM that contains software described in this book. See applicable chapters for a description of this program and instructions for its use.

By opening this package you are agreeing to be bound by the following:

Special Edition

USING Windows® 95

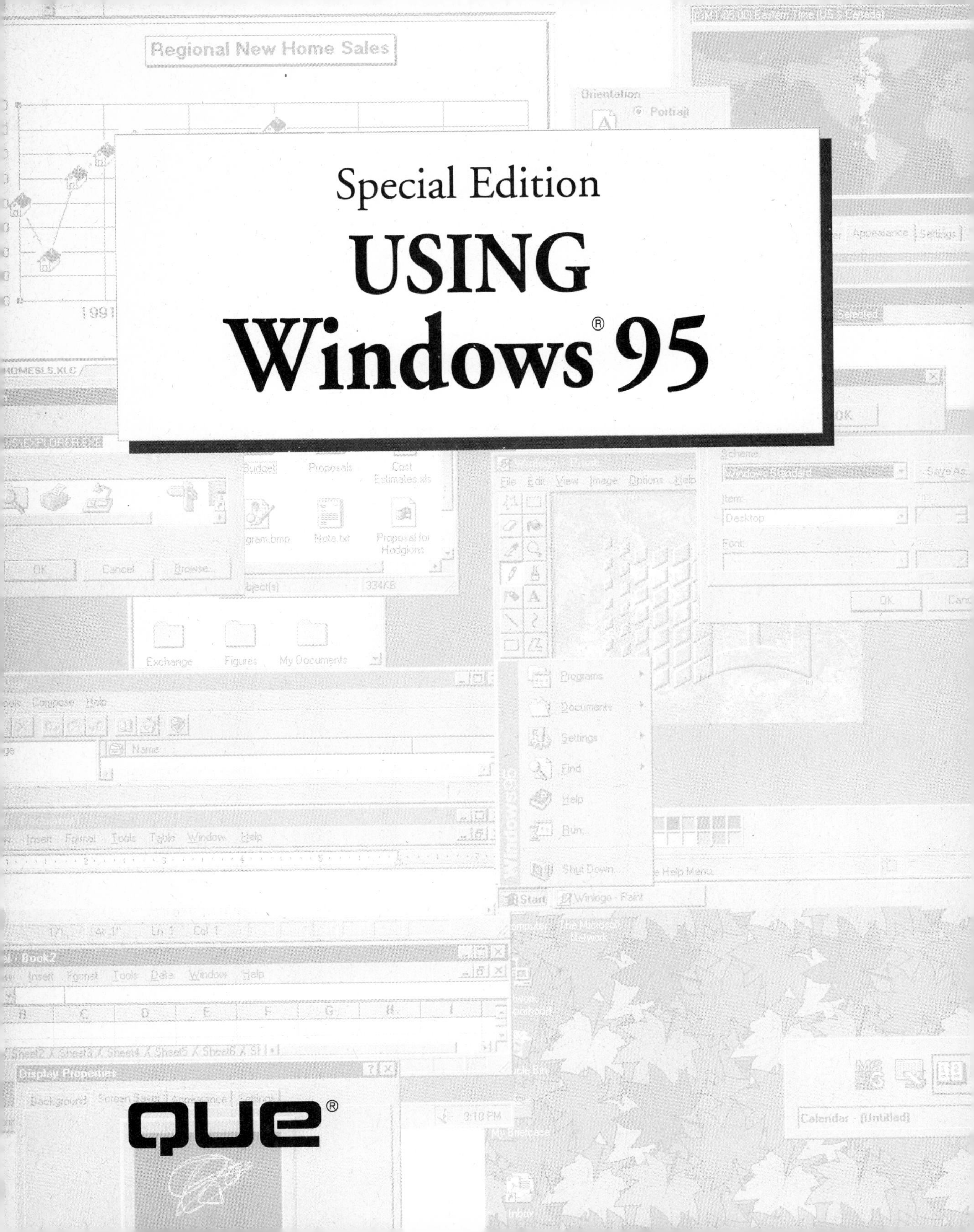

que®

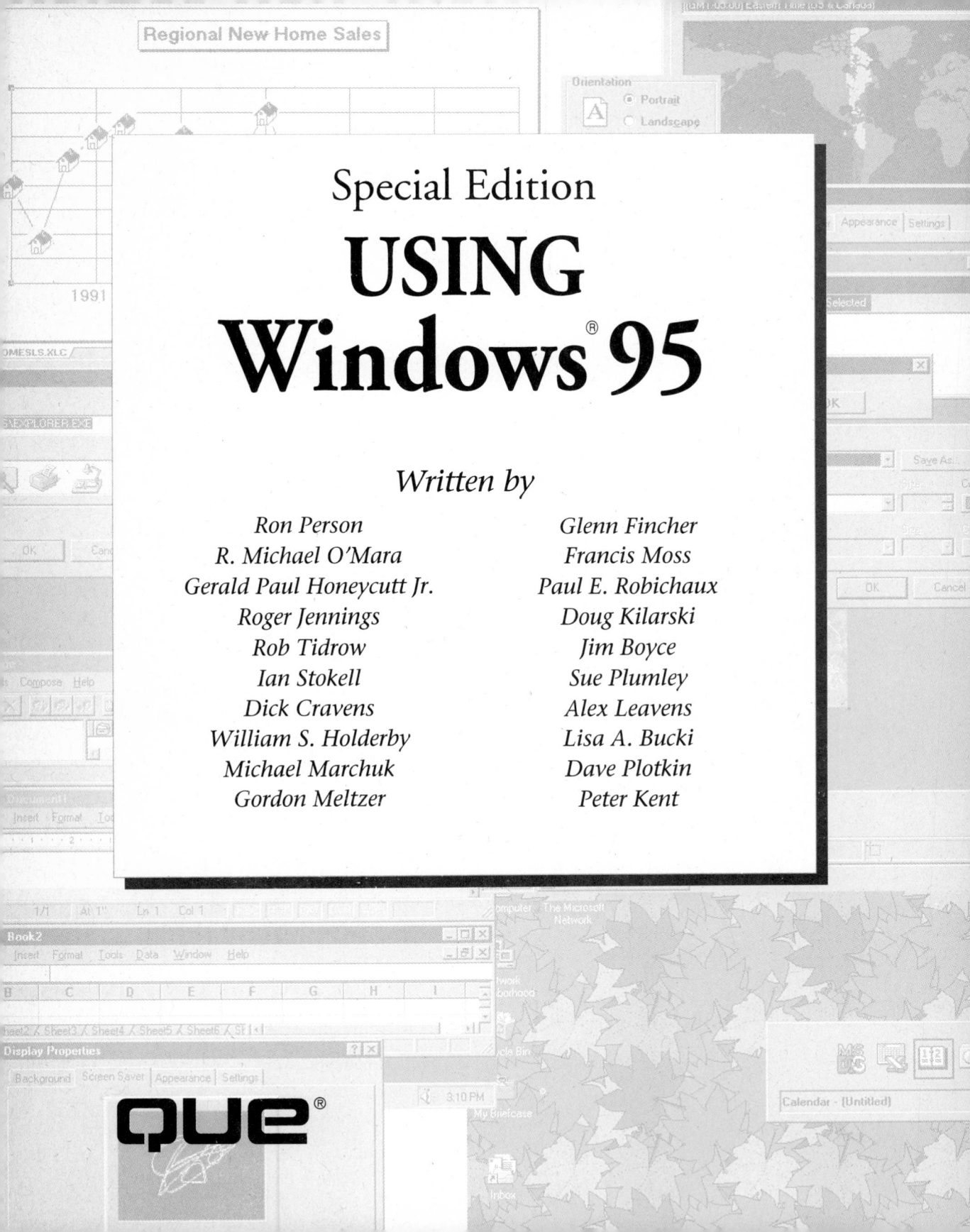

Special Edition

USING Windows® 95

Written by

Ron Person
R. Michael O'Mara
Gerald Paul Honeycutt Jr.
Roger Jennings
Rob Tidrow
Ian Stokell
Dick Cravens
William S. Holderby
Michael Marchuk
Gordon Meltzer
Glenn Fincher
Francis Moss
Paul E. Robichaux
Doug Kilarski
Jim Boyce
Sue Plumley
Alex Leavens
Lisa A. Bucki
Dave Plotkin
Peter Kent

QUE®

Special Edition Using Windows 95

Library of Congress Catalog No.: 95-70648

ISBN: 1-56529-921-3

97 96 95 6 5 4 3 2

Interpretation of the printing code: the rightmost double-digit number is the year of the book's printing; the rightmost single-digit number, the number of the book's printing. For example, a printing code of 95-1 shows that the first printing of the book occurred in 1995.

Screen reproductions in this book were created using Collage Plus from Inner Media, Inc., Hollis, NH.

Composed in *Stone Serif* and *MCPdigital* by Que Corporation.

Credits

President
Roland Elgey

Vice President and Publisher
Marie Butler-Knight

Associate Publisher
Don Roche Jr.

Director of Marketing
Lynn E. Zingraf

Editorial Services Director
Elizabeth Keaffaber

Managing Editor
Michael Cunningham

Senior Series Editor
Chris Nelson

Publishing Manager
Jim Minatel

Acquisitions Editors
Jenny L. Watson, Fred Slone

Product Directors
Lisa D. Wagner, Kathie-Jo Arnoff
Mark Cierzniak, Steve Miller
Steven M. Schafer

Production Editor
Thomas F. Hayes

Editors
Danielle Bird, Geneil Breeze,
Lori L. Cates, Susan Shaw Dunn,
Theresa Mathias, Ginny Noble
Lynn Northrup, Nanci Sears Perry,
San Dee Phillips, Silvette D. Pope,
Christine Prakel, Andy Saff,
Linda Seifert, Kathy Simpson,
Alice Martina Smith, Paige Widder

Assistant Product Marketing Manager
Kim Margolius

Technical Editors
Don Funk, Kurt Barthelmess,
Robert Bogue, Kyle Bryant,
Discovery Computing Inc., Mark Hudy,
James W. Rang, Kevin A. Rang,
Bob Reselman, Tony Wasson

Reviewer
Ned Flaherty

Acquisitions Coordinator
Tracy M. Williams

Operations Coordinator
Patty Brooks

Editorial Assistants
Carmen Phelps, Jill Byus

Book Designer
Ruth Harvey

Cover Designer
Jay Corpus

Production Team
Stephen Adams, Becky Beheler,
Carol Bowers, Amy Cornwell,
Anne Dickerson, Maxine Dillingham,
Chad Dressler, Terri Edwards,
Amy Gornik, Jason Hand, John Hulse,
Damon Jordan, Barry Jorden, Clint Lahnen,
Bob LaRoche, Julie Quinn, Laura Robbins,
Clair Schweinler, Brenda Sims, Craig Small,
Tim Taylor, Mike Thomas, Todd Wente

Indexers
Mary Jane Frisby
Kathy Venable

About the Authors

Ron Person has written more than 12 books for Que Corporation, including *Using Excel 5 for Windows*, Special Edition, and *Using Word 6 for Windows*, Special Edition. Ron is the principal consultant for Ron Person & Co. He has an M.S. in physics from Ohio State University and an M.B.A. from Hardin-Simmons University.

Ron Person & Co., based in San Francisco, has attained Microsoft's highest rating for Microsoft Excel and Word for Windows consultants—Microsoft Solutions Partner. Ron was one of Microsoft's 12 original Consulting Partners. The firm trains Excel and Visual Basic for Applications developers and support staff for corporations nationally and internationally. If your company plans to develop applications using Microsoft Excel or integrating multiple Microsoft applications, you will gain significantly from the courses taught by Ron Person & Co. For information on course content, on-site corporate classes, or consulting, contact Ron Person & Co. at the following address:

> Ron Person & Co.
> P.O. Box 5647
> Santa Rosa, CA 95402

R. Michael O'Mara is a freelance author and technical writer. Previously, he was a staff author with The Cobb Group where he wrote innumerable articles about leading computer software programs and served as Editor-in-Chief of several monthly software journals. He coauthored a best-selling book about Microsoft Windows and has recently contributed to other Que books, including *Using DOS*, *Using Windows 3.11*, and *Special Edition Using CompuServe.* He's been a member of the online community for about 10 years, participating on CompuServe, local BBSs, and the Internet. Mr. O'Mara can be reached on CompuServe at **76376,3441**.

Gerald "Jerry" Paul Honeycutt Jr. is a business-oriented technical manager, with experience developing large-scale applications for Windows using C, C++, and Visual Basic. He is experienced with all aspects of software development, including conception, specification, coding, testing, and delivery. Jerry has provided leadership and technical skills to The Travelers, IBM, Nielsen North America, and, most recently, Information Retrieval Methods, Inc.

When he is not busily delivering products, he is an author and frequent speaker at Comdex and Windows World. You can reach Jerry on the Internet at **jerry@dfw.net**, on CompuServe at **76477,2751**, or on The Microsoft Network at **Honeycutt**.

Roger Jennings is a principal of OakLeaf Systems, a northern California consulting firm specializing in Windows multimedia and database applications. He has more than 25 years of computer-related experience, was a radio-TV broadcast engineer, and is an amateur musician, arranger, and composer. Roger is the author of Que's *Unveiling Windows 95; Using Windows Desktop Video,* Special Edition; *Using Access 2 for Windows,* Special Edition; *Access Hot Tips;* and *Discover Windows 3.1 Multimedia.* He's also a contributing editor for Fawcette Technical Publication, Inc.'s *Visual Basic Programmer's Journal.* Roger's CompuServe address is **70233,2161**, and you can reach him as **Roger_Jennings** on The Microsoft Network.

Rob Tidrow has been using computers for the past six years and has used Windows for the past four years. Mr. Tidrow is a technical writer and recently was the Manager of Product Development for New Riders Publishing, a division of Macmillan Computer Publishing. Rob is coauthor of the best-selling *Windows for Non-Nerds* and has coauthored several other books, including *Inside the World Wide Web*; *New Riders' Official CompuServe Yellow Pages*; *Inside Microsoft Office Professional*; *Inside WordPerfect 6 for Windows*; *Riding the Internet Highway, Deluxe Edition*; and the *AutoCAD Student Workbook*. In the past, Mr. Tidrow created technical documentation and instructional programs for use in a variety of industrial settings. He has a degree in English from Indiana University. He resides in Indianapolis with his wife, Tammy, and two boys, Adam and Wesley. You can reach him on the Internet at **rtidrow@iquest.net**.

Ian Stokell is a freelance writer and editor living in the Sierra Foothills of northern California with his wife and three young children. He is also Managing Editor of Newsbytes News Network, an international daily newswire covering the computer and telecommunications industries. His writing career began with a 1981 article published in the UK's *New Statesman* and has since encompassed over 1,500 articles in a variety of computing and noncomputing publications. He wrote the "Networking" chapter of Que's *Using the Macintosh*, Special Edition, and has also written on assignment for such magazines as *PC World* and *MacWeek*. He is currently seeking representation for two completed novels and a screenplay.

Dick Cravens lives and works in Columbia, MO, where he is a product manager at Datastorm Technologies, Inc., a publisher of PC communications software. Dick and his 10-year-old son, Jesse, are both members of the University of Missouri Internet User's Group, and are active on America Online, CIS, many local BBS systems, the World Wide Web, and the Columbia Online Information System (the local gateway to the Internet).

William S. Holderby is a computer engineering graduate from the University of Central Florida. He has 20 years of experience in systems design and applications development for the federal government and commercial markets. Mr. Holderby frequently contributes magazine articles covering computer systems technology. He is a network systems developer and integrator and is currently working with the Naval Computer Telecommunications Station based in New Orleans, LA.

Michael Marchuk has been working in the computer industry since 1979 when he started as a part-time BASIC programming instructor. Along with his bachelor's degree in finance from the University of Illinois, he has received certification as a NetWare CNE and a Compaq Advanced Systems Engineer. He has designed and built an international, multi-protocol, wide area network for a Fortune 500 company and now serves as an Integration Engineer and the Network Security Chairman for a Forbes 400 corporation.

Gordon Meltzer has been teaching himself about computers since they were made with vacuum tubes. Recently, Gordon had designed and built workgroup networks for a music marketing division of Time-Warner and several New York City law firms. He is a consultant on computing issues to NBC Post Production, also in Manhattan. Gordon has produced a number of jazz records for people like Miles Davis, Michel LeGrand, Al Di Meola, and Wallace Roney, and has a special interest in using computers in the business side of the music industry.

Glenn Fincher has worked in the computer industry for the last 12 years. Working in the fast-moving electronic manufacturing industry, he spent the early years in Test Engineering at SCI Systems, Inc., the world's largest computer contract manufacturer. Spending the bulk of the SCI years in component, board, and unit testing, he became intimately familiar with the building blocks of today's computer technology. He joined Intergraph Corporation in 1991 as a Customer Support Analyst and has applied his wealth of computer knowledge to providing Intergraph's customers with quality, timely, and accurate support for the MicroStation CAD product. Leading the software certification efforts for the successful release of MicroStation 5.0,

Glenn continues to be involved in the day-to-day world of Intergraph's partner Bentley Systems' MicroStation product. Sharing the knowledge gained in the experience of these years in the industry has always been a priority, so it is no surprise that he is in demand as a speaker, writer, and presenter throughout Intergraph. With his present involvement in Intergraph's WWW effort as Webmaster for Intergraphs Software Solutions, Glenn remains at the leading edge of this industry. Continually seeking to stay on this edge has required both the support and understanding of wife Jan and their three children—Ashley, Will, and Aimee—without whom this and all his other endeavors would have been a lonely journey indeed. Glenn can be reached by electronic mail at **gtfinche@ingr.com**.

Francis Moss has been involved with computers for 12 years, a Microsoft beta tester for 5 years, and a writer—primarily in television but more recently books—for 15 years. With his writing partner, he is coauthor of *Internet for Kids*. He likes computers because he enjoys cursing at unarmed inanimate objects. With his wife and two children, he lives in North Hollywood, CA. He can be reached at **fcmoss@directnet.com**.

Paul Robichaux is a software developer and author with a wide range of experience developing, and writing about, desktop operating systems, applications software, and the Internet. He lives in Huntsville, AL with his family.

Doug Kilarski is a freelance writer and an accomplished computer industry analyst. Doug is a former technical editor for *Computer Shopper* magazine and former Editor-in-Chief for *Computer Monthly* and *Reseller World* magazines. He is currently developing global marketing and distribution strategies for the internetworking and telephony industries. Doug can be reached on the Internet at **dkilarski@mcimail.com**.

Jim Boyce is a contributing editor and columnist for *Windows Magazine*, a columnist for *Cadence* magazine, and the author and contributing author of over two dozen books on computers and software. You can reach Jim at **76516.3403@compuserve.com.**

Sue Plumley owns and operates Humble Opinions, a consulting firm that offers training in popular software programs and network installation and maintenance. Sue's husband, Carlos, joined her company two years ago as a CNE. Sue is the author of 12 Que books, including *Crystal Clear DOS*, *Crystal Clear Word 6*, and *Microsoft Office Quick Reference*, and coauthor of 16 additional books, including *Using WordPerfect 6 for DOS*, Special Edition; *Using*

OS/2 2.1, Special Edition, and *Special Edition Using Microsoft Office* for Que and its sister imprints.

Alex Leavens is a software developer with more than 15 years experience. He has developed products that have sold more than a million copies and is one of the few software designers whose work can be found in the permanent collection of the National Museum of American History at the Smithsonian. He develops Windows products and books and can be reached on CompuServe at **70444,43.** In Addition to writing Appendix E, Alex acquired and assembled the materials on the CD-ROM.

Lisa Bucki has been involved in the computer book business for more than five years. She has written Que's *Guide to WordPerfect Presentations 3.0 for Windows, 10 Minute Guide to Harvard Graphics, 10 Minute Guide to Harvard Graphics for Windows, One Minute Reference to Windows 3.1*, and other titles. She has contributed chapters dealing with presentation graphics and multimedia for other books, as well as assisting with the product development for such titles as *Upgrading Your PC to Multimedia*, also from Que. Bucki resides in Fishers, Indiana.

Dave Plotkin is a Business Area Analyst with Integral Systems in Walnut Creek, California. He has extensive experience in designing and implementing databases, both at the desktop and on client-server systems. He writes extensively for various computer periodicals, and his favorite editor is his wife, Marisa.

Peter Kent lives in Lakewood, Colorado. He's spent the last 14 years training users, documenting software, and designing user interfaces. Working as an independent consultant for the last 9 years, Peter has worked for companies such as MasterCard, Amgen, Data General, and Dvorak Development and Publishing. Much of his consulting work has been in the telecommunications business.

Peter is the author of the best-selling Internet book *The Complete Idiot's Guide to the Internet* (QUE). He's also written another six Internet-related books—including *The Complete Idiot's Guide to the World Wide Web*—and a variety of other works, such as *The Technical Writer's Freelancing Guide* and books on Windows NT and Windows 3.1. His articles have appeared in many periodicals, including *Internet World, Windows Magazine, Windows User*, the *Dallas Times Herald*, and *Computerworld*. Peter can be reached electronically at **PeterKent** (Microsoft Network), **71601,1266** (CompuServe), or **pkent@lab-press.com** (Internet).

We'd Like to Hear from You!

As part of our continuing effort to produce books of the highest possible quality, Que would like to hear your comments. To stay competitive, we *really* want you, as a computer book reader and user, to let us know what you like or dislike most about this book or other Que products.

You can mail comments, ideas, or suggestions for improving future editions to the address below, or send us a fax at (317) 581-4663. For the online inclined, Macmillan Computer Publishing has a forum on CompuServe (type **GO QUEBOOKS** at any prompt) through which our staff and authors are available for questions and comments. The address of our Internet site is **http://www.mcp.com** (World Wide Web).

In addition to exploring our forum, please feel free to contact me personally to discuss your opinions of this book: I'm **lwagner@que.mcp.com** on the Internet.

Thanks in advance—your comments will help us to continue publishing the best books available on computer topics in today's market.

Lisa D. Wagner
Product Development Specialist
Que Corporation
201 W. 103rd Street
Indianapolis, Indiana 46290
USA

Contents at a Glance

Contents

Preface

Windows 95 will significantly change the way computers are used at home and in offices around the world. And *Special Edition Using Windows 95* is your reference guide to learning and understanding what Microsoft's newest operating system is all about.

Years of research went into creating this new operating system known as Windows 95 and here at Que we have spent over a year studying and researching what Windows 95 is all about and how it will affect computer users of every level. We gathered the best authoring team in the business and put our top-notch developers and editors in place to produce the most comprehensive book about Windows 95. *Special Edition Using Windows 95* is the result of all this hard work.

Que has established itself over the course of the past decade as the premier publisher of high-quality computer books. While we are proud of our reputation for excellence, we are not content to rest on our laurels. A tradition of excellence is only useful as long as a continuing commitment to quality exists.

When we started planning this book, we knew from the start how important it would be to you. As you make the switch from Windows 3.1 to Windows 95 (or use Windows for the first time), nothing is more important to your computing needs than understanding how to use your new operating system. Without a grasp of how to use Windows 95, you will never get the most out of your computing time.

With this in mind, Que looked at what you would need from a book about Windows 95. It was clear to us that any attempt to rewrite or augment an existing Windows 3.1 book would not do proper service to our readers. Consequently, this book is built new from the ground up and designed especially to fit the way you will use Windows 95.

The other essential ingredient in our plan was an extensive commitment to technical accuracy. Windows 95 has been in beta testing for over a year and we have been there every step of the way. There have been many beta test versions but every technical detail, task, and procedure in each chapter of this book has been carefully checked against the final version of Windows 95. This is the only way to ensure that what you see in this book matches what you find when you start using Windows 95.

With these efforts, we hope you find this book to be valuable as you learn and use Windows 95. I believe it to be the best available book of its type. I sincerely hope it meets or exceeds your expectations.

Roland Elgey
President
Que Corporation

Introduction

With Windows 3.0 and 3.1, Microsoft altered forever the face of PC computing. Microsoft brought an easy-to-use graphical interface to tens of millions of personal computers. At one time regarded as a plaything and not for serious users, Windows became the standard for hardware and software compatibility. Now with Windows 95, Microsoft has added a new look to computers and the look and feel of graphical PC computing has taken another major turn.

Microsoft has devoted years of extensive research to making Windows 95 easier to learn and use than its predecessors. New users will be able to start programs, create documents, and become productive much more quickly with Windows 95.

However, despite its ease of use and graphical interface, Windows 95 is not entirely intuitive. In fact, many experienced users will find that the number and scope of changes to the interface will take them some time to get accustomed to. But, after a short period of transition and learning, you should become more productive and efficient with Windows 95 than you were with Windows 3.1.

And that's where *Special Edition Using Windows 95* steps in to help. This book is the single source you need to get quickly up to speed and greatly enhance your productivity with Windows 95.

How to Use This Book

This book was designed and written from the ground up with two important purposes in mind:

- First, *Special Edition Using Windows 95* makes it easy for you to find any task you need to accomplish and see how to do it most effectively.

- Second, this book covers Windows 95 in a breadth and depth that you won't find anywhere else. So not only does the book show you how to do things quickly and efficiently, you also find out how to accomplish tasks that simply aren't covered by online help, documentation, or other books.

With those goals in mind, how do you use this book?

If you have used Windows 3.1, you may just want to skim through the first few chapters of this book to see what changes there are in Windows 95. After all, you may have read magazine articles and heard from colleagues about all of the new features. The first two chapters help you get a grip on what changes to expect. After that, keep *Special Edition Using Windows 95* handy by your computer as a reference. When you have a question or need to see how to accomplish something, look it up in the table of contents or index and read how to do it. We don't waste your time with anecdotes, witty banter, or cartoons. We do give you the most comprehensive and detailed coverage of Windows 95 of any book on the market and clearly focus that coverage to satisfy the needs of all types of Windows users.

If you are using Windows for the first time, you should find that *Special Edition Using Windows 95* is a clear presentation of the fundamentals of Windows computing. This is a book that can help you understand Windows and use it well. And, if you need to learn more about Windows than just the basics, *Special Edition Using Windows 95* will be there when you need it. To get started with Windows 95, read the first two chapters to get a feel for what Windows does, and then go through Chapters 3 and 4 while sitting at your computer. Once you're comfortable with Windows, move on to the chapters that cover the additional topics you want to learn about.

How this Book is Organized

Special Edition Using Windows 95 is a comprehensive book on Windows 95. The book is divided into nine parts, 35 chapters, and six appendixes to help you quickly find the coverage you need. The parts begin with the most common and basic topics and move forward into more specialized or advanced subjects. This rest of this section describes the content more specifically, chapter by chapter.

Part I: Introducing Windows 95

Chapter 1, "What's New in Windows 95?," shows you an overview of the new features in Windows 95. After reading this chapter, you should be aware of why you moved or need to begin the move from Windows 3.1 to Windows 95.

Chapter 2, "Understanding Windows 95," presents the big picture to understanding Windows 95. If you're a new user, you'll want to get a feel for the important concepts and see where you are going. If you're an experienced user, you'll want to know what's different from previous versions of Windows and what's remained the same.

Part II: Working with Windows 95

Chapter 3, "Getting Started with Windows 95," gives you an explanation of the parts of the Windows screen, how to use the keyboard and mouse, and how to start Windows and applications.

Chapter 4, "Starting and Working with Applications," teaches you information that carries over to all Windows applications. The skills gained from this chapter help you operate control features, such as menus and dialog boxes, and control parts of the display, such as the size and position of the windows in which different documents or applications display. This chapter also covers IRQs, hardware profiles, and I/Os.

Chapter 5, "Customizing Windows 95," shows you how to customize Windows 95 to fit the way you work. You learn to customize the taskbar, the Start menu, the Program menu, the desktop pattern or graphic, as well as all the colors used by Windows elements.

Chapter 6, "Controlling Printers," explains how to use Windows 95 printing. It also introduces each of the new printing features, describes the options, and explains how to create a quality print job.

Chapter 7, "Working with Fonts," explains fonts and how Windows 95 uses them. It also shows you how to install and manage fonts in Windows 95.

Chapter 8, "Plug and Play and Legacy Device Installation." The objective of Plug and Play is to make new device installation a "hands-off" process. Thus, much of this chapter is devoted to explaining what happens "behind-the-scenes" to make Plug and Play work. This chapter also describes how to install the many devices that do not take advantage of Plug and Play.

Chapter 9, "Special Features for Notebook Users," describes how to take advantage of Windows 95 support for PC Cards (formerly called PMCIA adapter cards), advanced power management, docking stations, file synchronization with My Briefcase, and all of the other new features that are of particular use to laptop users.

Part III: Working with Applications

Chapter 10, "Installing, Running, and Uninstalling Windows Applications." With all its power, most users will find Windows to be of little value without installing application software. After all, Windows 95 is just the operating system—to do something, you need applications. This chapter shows you how to install Windows applications (both Windows 95 and older applications are covered), how to run applications, and how to remove applications, including coverage of uninstalling software with Windows 95's new Remove feature.

Chapter 11, "Working with DOS Applications in Windows 95," shows you how to use DOS programs in Windows. This version of Windows makes more memory available to DOS applications and runs DOS games faster and better than previous versions.

Chapter 12, "Using WordPad to Create Documents," shows how to use WordPad, a simple but powerful word processor for Windows. This simple accessory is ideal for many day-to-day word processing tasks. You learn to create and edit a document in WordPad, format and print documents, and save and open documents.

Chapter 13, "Using Paint, Calculator, and other Accessories," shows you how to use Paint to create and edit pictures that you can insert in documents created with other applications, use Calculator to perform calculations, set the clock that displays on the taskbar, and insert special characters into any Windows document with Character Map.

Chapter 14, "Simple Ways of Sharing Data between Applications." Generally, all Windows applications provide some means for sharing data with another application. This chapter shows how to use the most basic and commonly used of these means, including cutting, copying, and pasting within and between documents in Windows and DOS applications, as well as how to link data from one document to another.

Chapter 15, "Building Compound Documents with OLE," shows how to create and modify documents based on the concept of *compound documents*—documents you create by using multiple types of data. You see how to build documents that incorporate different types of data, such as text from a word processor, a spreadsheet, and graphics. You also learn how to use this data within a single application without having to switch between applications to edit the different data types.

Part IV: Working with Disks and Files

Chapter 16, "Working with Disks and Disk Drives," shows you how to work with and maintain your floppy and hard disks. Before you put data on a disk, you usually have to format it to get it ready to receive data. Floppy and hard disks are susceptible to damage, which is very trying when you're dealing with irreplaceable data. Windows 95 comes with a tool to help you check for and repair some kinds of damage. You can monitor the performance of your system using the System Monitor. You can improve the performance of your hard disks by using Disk Defragmenter and enable your system to act as if has more memory (RAM) than is actually installed by using *virtual memory*. This chapter covers all these topics and more.

Chapter 17, "Managing Your Files with Explorer." The first part of this chapter explains how Windows 95 organizes files. The remainder of the chapter is devoted to showing you how to use Windows Explorer to work with and manage the files on your computer. You also learn how to carry out many file management tasks using My Computer.

Chapter 18, "Backing Up and Protecting Your Data," explains how to copy one or more files from your hard disk to another location (usually a floppy disk, a tape drive, or another computer on your network), restore your backed up files to any location you choose (including their original locations), and compare files on your backup disks with the original files to ensure their validity.

Part V: Networking with Windows 95

Chapter 19, "Understanding Networks," introduces one of the most improved features in Windows 95—networking capabilities. This chapter covers the basic concepts of networking and Windows 95. You see what types of networks are supported in Windows 95, how to install hardware and Windows 95 drivers for them, and how to use tools such as Windows Explorer and Network Neighborhood to make use of network resources.

Chapter 20, "Setting Up a Windows 95 Peer-to-Peer Network," presents Windows 95 built-in peer-to-peer networking. Windows 95 peer-to-peer networking brings all the resources of the network to your desktop. You can share any of your PC's resources with other PCs on the network. You can easily make use of the printer down the hall or the CD on your associate's new high-speed desktop. This chapter presents the basics of setting up the network software and hardware to work with Windows 95 and your computer.

Chapter 21, "Sharing Windows 95 Peer-to-Peer Resources," shows how to make resources on your computer available to others on the Windows 95 peer-to-peer network. You see how to share hard drives, CD-ROMs, printers, and fax-modems, and how to manage these shared resources.

Chapter 22, "Connecting Windows 95 to a Novell Network," shows you how to take advantage of Windows 95 and Novell NetWare compatibility. It presents the basics of setting up the network software and hardware to work with Windows 95 and your computer. If your primary network is currently Novell NetWare, Windows 95 seamlessly integrates with your current network.

Chapter 23, "Using Novell Network Resources in Windows 95," shows how to take advantage of some of the advanced networking features available with NetWare and Windows 95. You see how to use network monitoring and maintenance tools, as well as make backups on network tape drives.

Chapter 24, "Using Microsoft Exchange," shows how to use Microsoft Exchange, a central communications client that organizes "received" electronic mail and faxes in one convenient location. You learn how to use Exchange as your universal in-box and how to compose, store, organize, and send messages via e-mail and fax.

Chapter 25, "Working with Network Printers," takes printing a step farther and discusses printing issues from a network perspective. Specifically, you learn to print using network printers, optimize print resources, manage print files, solve common network printing problems, and use custom print managers and utilities.

Chapter 26, "Network Management and Security," presents valuable information for anyone tasked with setting up and maintaining a network in conjunction with Windows 95. You learn how to control the installation and configuration of your network. This chapter exposes weaknesses in network design and tells you how to work around them. It provides tips for keeping your network up and running and for simplifying it without losing functionality. This chapter also provides a guide to help you understand the philosophy behind the Windows 95 network and shows you how to make it work in your individual situation.

Part VI: Online Communications with Windows 95

Chapter 27, "Installing and Configuring Your Modem," explains how Windows' communications system works for you, how to install your Plug and Play modem or legacy modem, how to configure your modem after it's installed, and what TAPI means and does.

Chapter 28, "Communicating with HyperTerminal," discusses using HyperTerminal, the Windows accessory which allows you to connect your computer to another PC or online service. HyperTerminal is a full-featured communications tool that greatly simplifies getting online. With HyperTerminal, you can connect to a friend's computer, a university network, an Internet service provider, or even CompuServe. In this chapter, you learn how to use HyperTerminal by using it for some common tasks, such as creating a connection or downloading a file, and how to configure HyperTerminal and customize your connections.

Chapter 29, "Getting Connected to the Internet," introduces you to the Internet and World Wide Web, two of the fastest growing and most talked about topics in computing. You learn what TCP/IP is, how to choose an Internet service provider, how to connect to the Internet with Windows 95 built-in connectivity tools, and how to use other Internet apps with Windows 95.

Chapter 30, "Using FTP, the World Wide Web, and other Internet Services," covers what to do once you get connected to the Internet. You see how to use Microsoft's FTP program to connect to large archives of shareware and freeware to find and download software, how to log in to remote computers on the Internet with Telnet, how to cruise the Web with Microsoft's Internet Explorer (part of Microsoft Plus!), and how to create Web pages with Microsoft's Internet Assistant.

Part VII: Windows 95 Multimedia

Chapter 31, "Understanding Windows 95 Multimedia," introduces the basic concepts of multimedia and Windows 95. Windows' multimedia features are greatly improved in Windows 95. In this chapter, you see what improvements have been made for multimedia hardware and software and how to install hardware and configure Windows 95 drivers for multimedia.

Chapter 32, "Installing and Using a CD-ROM Drive," shows how to install drivers for Plug and Play and legacy CD-ROM drives, how to use CD-ROM applications, and how to optimize your CD-ROM.

Chapter 33, "Working with Windows 95 Sound Capabilities," shows how to install drivers for Plug and Play and legacy sound cards. You see how to use Windows accessories for recording, playing, and editing sound files and how to play audio CDs on your computer.

Chapter 34, "Using Windows 95 Full-Motion Video Options," describes video enhancements in Windows 95 and shows how the video enhancements have also improved graphics-intensive DOS games. You see the procedure for installing video drivers, adding to your video capabilities with QuickTime for Windows, and how to play videos with Media Player.

Chapter 35, "Desktop Video Production under Windows 95," highlights the improvements to Windows video by showing how to use several applications for video capture and production.

Part VIII: Appendixes

Appendix A, "Installing and Uninstalling Windows 95," presents the steps for preparing your computer for Windows 95 and then for installing Windows 95. Standard and custom installation options are discussed, including a multiple-boot configuration. The appendix also explains how to remove Windows 95 from your system.

Appendix B, "Using Microsoft Network," describes how to get started using Microsoft Network (MSN). MSN is fully integrated into Windows and offers you online access to the world by giving you access to a variety of people and resources. With MSN, you can exchange electronic mail (e-mail) with other people, exchange ideas on bulletin boards, participate in live discussions in chat rooms, access the resources of the Internet, and more. This appendix also describes some of the interesting forum areas and services currently available.

Appendix C, "Exploring the Windows 95 Resource Kit," describes the components of this set of additional documentation and utilities designed primarily for system administrators and other power users.

Appendix D, "Using Microsoft Plus!," shows you how to install and use DriveSpace 3, Internet Explorer, Desktop Themes, and the other special utilities and tools in this add-in from Microsoft.

Appendix E, "What's on the CD," describes the software and utilities you find on the CD that accompanies this book.

Appendix F, "Glossary," provides a great reference for Windows 95 terms and computer terminology in general.

Part IX: Indexes

"Index of Common Problems." This feature goes hand in hand with the Troubleshooting elements. If you are having a problem with Windows 95 and don't know where to look in the book for an answer, look to the Index of Common Problems, located near the back of the book, immediately preceding the index. Use the Index of Common Problems to find all the Troubleshooting sections in the book and other discussions of common problems and fixes.

The Indexes part also contains a standard topic index that lets you quickly find information you need throughout the book.

Other Books of Interest

You may wonder how you could ever need to know anything else about Windows than what we've presented in this book. But with the enormous potential of Windows 95, you'll soon see that depending on your area of special interest, there is much more you can do with Windows. So, here is a short list of other Que books that may be of interest, depending on your computing needs:

- *Killer Windows 95*. If you consider yourself a "power-user," you'll find the advanced techniques and tools presented in this book to be invaluable additions to your Windows 95 tools.
- *Surviving the Move to Windows 95*. This is a good book for users that need a short reference detailing the features that have changed in this version of Windows.
- *Windows 95 Connectivity*. Network and online connectivity are key improved features in Windows 95. This book examines these features in detail.
- *Special Edition Using Microsoft Office*. This book covers everything you need to know about Microsoft's new Windows 95 release of the popular Microsoft Office suite. It includes detailed coverage of Word, Excel, and PowerPoint and how to use those applications together. Other books of interest if you need more detailed coverage of one of the individual Office applications include *Special Edition Using Word for Windows 95*, *Special Edition Using Excel for Windows 95*, and *Special Edition Using PowerPoint for Windows 95*.

- *Special Edition Using the Internet,* 2nd Edition. Windows 95 is the first version of Windows that makes connecting to the Internet a snap. If you want detailed coverage of the many aspects of the Internet such as the World Wide Web, FTP, HTML, e-mail and more, this book is for you.

Special Features in the Book

Que has over a decade of experience writing and developing the most successful computer books available. With that experience, we've learned what special features help readers the most. Look for these special features throughout the book to enhance your learning experience.

Chapter Roadmaps

Near the beginning of each chapter is a list of topics to be covered in the chapter. This list serves as a roadmap to the chapter so you can tell at a glance what is covered. It also provides a useful outline of the key topics you'll be reading about.

Notes

Notes present interesting or useful information that isn't necessarily essential to the discussion. This secondary track of information enhances your understanding of Windows, but you can safely skip notes and not be in danger of missing crucial information. Notes look like this:

Note

If you have many applications open, you may not be able to read the application and document name on the taskbar button. If the application and document name are truncated, pause the pointer over the button. A button tip appears showing the full names.

Tip
Any open application appears as a button on the taskbar. Click the button to activate the application.

Tips

Tips present short advice on quick or often overlooked procedures. These include shortcuts that save you time. A tip is shown in the margin as an example.

Cautions

Cautions serve to warn you about potential problems that a procedure may cause, unexpected results, and mistakes to avoid. Cautions look like this:

Caution

If you have a wallpaper selected with the Display Tile option selected, you will not be able to see your pattern. A full-screen wallpaper shows over the top of the pattern. To see the pattern, select (None) from the Wallpaper list.

Troubleshooting

No matter how carefully you follow the steps in the book, you eventually come across something that just doesn't work the way you think it should. Troubleshooting sections anticipate these common errors or hidden pitfalls and present solutions. A troubleshooting section looks like this:

Troubleshooting

When I double-click a linked or embedded object, a `cannot edit` *error message occurs.*

This means that the source file cannot be opened. Make sure the application you need to edit the file is on your machine. Also make sure that you have enough system memory to run both the container and source applications. Keep in mind that compound documents demand more memory than simple documents.

Cross References

Throughout the book in the margins, you see references to other sections and pages in the book, like the one next to this paragraph. These cross references point you to related topics and discussions in other parts of the book.

► See "Using Drag-and-Drop to Copy Information between Documents," p. 421

In addition to these special features, there are several conventions used in this book to make it easier to read and understand. These conventions include the following.

Underlined Hot Keys, or Mnemonics

Hot keys in this book appear underlined, like they appear on-screen. For example, the F in File is a hot key, or shortcut for opening the File menu. In Windows, many menus, commands, buttons, and other options have these hot keys. To use a hot-key shortcut, press Alt and the key for the underlined character. For instance, to choose the Properties button, press Alt and then R.

Shortcut Key Combinations

In this book, shortcut key combinations are joined with plus signs (+). For example, Ctrl+V means hold down the Ctrl key, press the V key, and then release both keys (Ctrl+V is a shortcut for the Paste command).

Menu Commands

Instructions for choosing menu commands have this form:

Choose File, New.

This example means open the File menu and select New, which in this case opens a new file.

Instructions involving the new Windows 95 Start menu are an exception. When you are to choose something through this menu, the form is

Open the Start menu and choose Programs, Accessories, WordPad.

In this case, you open the WordPad word processing accessory. Notice that in the Start menu you simply drag the mouse pointer and point at the option or command you want to choose (even through a whole series of submenus); you don't need to click anything.

This book also has the following typeface enhancements to indicate special text, as indicated in the following table.

Typeface	Description
Italic	Italics are used to indicate new terms and variables in commands or addresses.
Boldface	Bold is used to indicate text you type, and Internet addresses and other locators in the online world.
`Computer type`	This command is used for on-screen messages and commands (such as DOS copy or UNIX commands).
MYFILE.DOC	File names and directories are set in all caps to distinguish them from regular text, as in MYFILE.DOC.

What's on the CD

The CD-ROM included with this book provides you with a variety of software to use with Windows 95. This software includes programs and data files for everyone, no matter what your interests and level of computer use.

Among the programs on the CD-ROM are Windows utilities, communications programs, editors, graphics programs, and games. There are even video utilities included. The disc also provides popular online service and Internet software that will help get you up and running online.

For those interested in multimedia, the disc offers many great files to use with Windows 95 enhanced multimedia capabilities. In fact, you'll find more than 150M of graphics files, wallpaper, bitmap patterns for your desktop, sound files, and digital video files.

Appendix E, "What's on the CD," discusses the contents of the disc in detail.

Part I

Introducing Windows 95

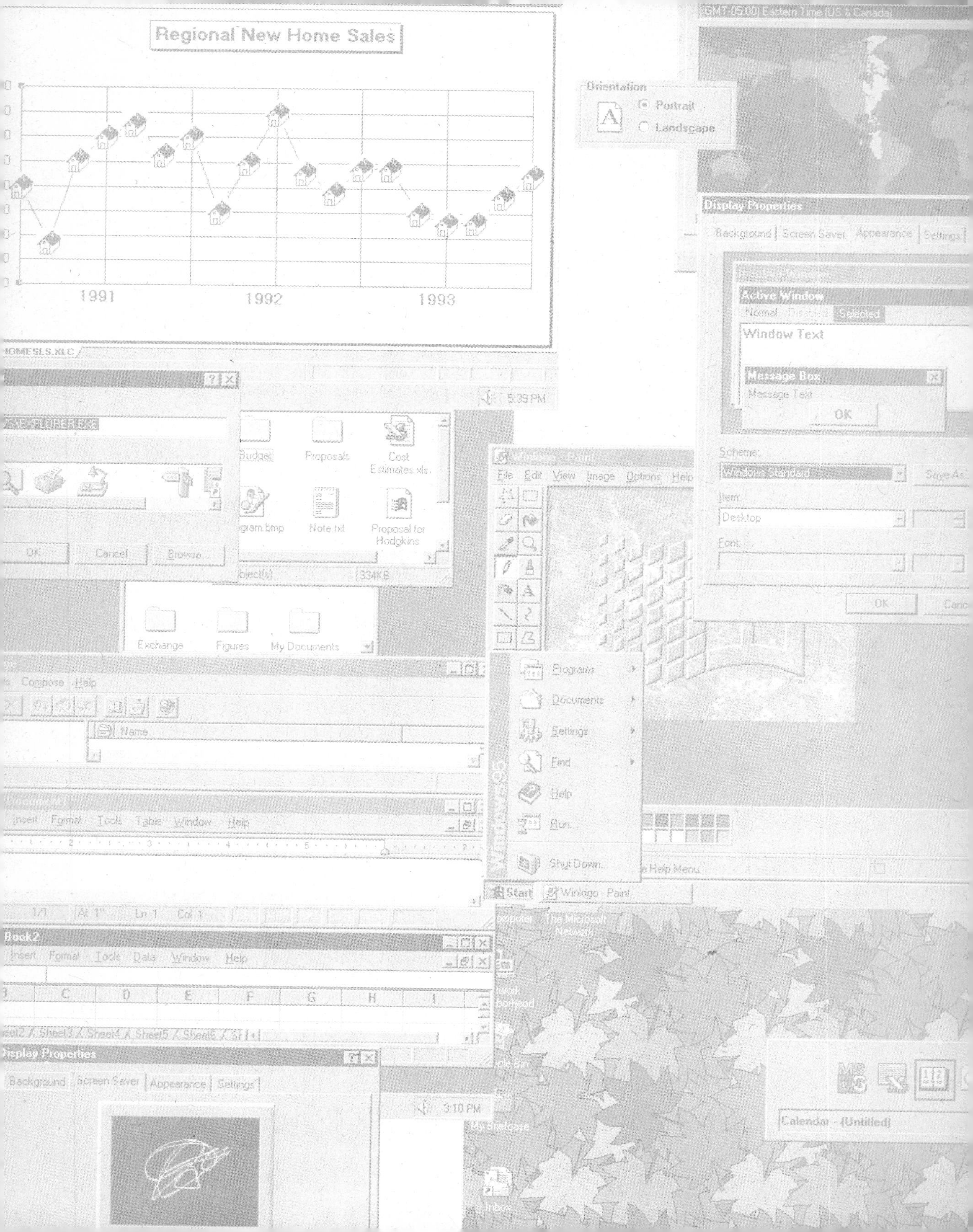

Regional New Home Sales
1991
1992
1993
HOMESLS.XLC
Orientation
Portrait
Landscape
(GMT-05:00) Eastern Time (US & Canada)
Display Properties
Background
Screen Saver
Appearance
Settings
Inactive Window
Active Window
Normal
Disabled
Selected
Window Text
Message Box
Message Text
OK
Scheme:
Windows Standard
Save As...
Item:
Desktop
Font:
Cancel
5:39 PM
Budget
Proposals
Cost Estimates.xls
Note.txt
Proposal for Hodgkins
334KB
Cancel
Browse...
Exchange
Figures
My Documents
Winlogo - Paint
File
Edit
View
Image
Options
Help
Compose
Name
Programs
Documents
Settings
Find
Help
Run...
Shut Down...
Windows95
Start
Insert
Format
Tools
Table
Window
1/1
At 1"
Ln 1
Col 1
Book2
Data
Sheet2
Sheet3
Sheet4
Sheet5
Sheet6
The Microsoft Network
My Briefcase
Inbox
3:10 PM
Calendar - (Untitled)

Chapter 1

What's New in Windows 95?

by Ron Person

Windows 95 will change the way you work with computers. Microsoft's new operating system is more than just a better interface or an easier way of working with the computer. It incorporates more features, better performance, and greater compatibility than any previous operating system. This chapter will give you an overview of the new features in Windows 95. After reading this chapter, you should be aware of why you need to begin the move from Windows to Windows 95.

Windows 95 is an improvement over Windows 3.11 and Windows for Workgroups 3.11. Both of these programs, although significantly easier to use than DOS, needed enhancements to accommodate both first-time users and experienced "power" users.

Some of the problems faced by computer novices when using Windows were:

- Overlapping windows caused confusion due to visual clutter. Windows that filled the screen hid other programs that were open
- Windows seemed to disappear when minimized
- The hierarchical display of directory structures in the File Manager was intimidating and not intuitive to non-technical users
- The File Manager and Program Manager shared some functionality, such as starting applications, but they used different metaphors and appearance
- Switching between running applications and knowing which applications were running was not obvious. Many users started multiple

instances of the same application, thereby using up system resources and increasing the potential for an application failure

- Double-clicking and many keystrokes, such as Alt+Tab, while very important, were hidden in manuals and were inaccessible
- File names were limited to eight characters with a three-letter extension

Windows 95 was created to make work easier for novice and beginning computer users. Yet at the same time it contains many extensions and features that add value for advanced or power users. Some of the areas where power users faced problems with previous versions of Windows were:

- Resources and utilities needed for customizing and fine-tuning were scattered all over the Windows system in different groups, such as Control Panel, Print Manager, Setup, File Manager, and Program Manager
- Information such as IRQ and I/O address settings were difficult to find
- Many graphical elements could not be customized
- Networking with non-Microsoft networks required a lot of study, work, and workarounds
- Power users always want faster performance
- Hardware was difficult to install and could easily cause conflicts with existing hardware. The conflicts were difficult to resolve

This chapter introduces

- Windows 95 compatibility with DOS and previous Windows programs and data
- The ease with which Windows 95 is installed
- Windows 95's improved performance in many areas including file handling, memory management, and application speed
- A graphical interface using the Start menu, taskbar, and desktop that make Windows much easier for first-time users
- Property sheets about items in Windows 95 that show you information about the item and enable you to customize the item
- Program startup and file management, both of which can be handled from within the same My Computer windows

- Shortcut icons that start programs and documents and give you quick access to frequently used folders
- Long names for files and folders that make file management easier than previously
- Networking and communication that is much easier to install. The networking works with adapters and protocols from more vendors than before
- Easier hardware installation where Windows 95 recognizes the hardware and installs the appropriate drivers and settings automatically
- Features for road warriors who travel with a portable computer, but must occasionally work with a desktop computer

Note

Windows 95 addresses all of these issues. Look through this chapter to get a quick overview of how Windows 95 has improved. From here, you will want to go to Chapter 2, "Understanding Windows 95," for a quick understanding of the basic concepts in Windows 95 and then go on to chapters about specific topics in which you are interested.

Compatibility with Windows 3.1 and DOS Programs

With more than 60 million people using Windows 3.1, Microsoft had to include a high degree of compatibility in Windows 95 so that data and applications from previous versions of Windows would still work. Windows 95 also handles DOS programs better. DOS programs can now run in a window that includes a toolbar for commonly used features.

File Manager and Program Manager Are Available

A company with thousands or tens of thousands of Windows users may not want to think about having to train them on how to use Windows 95. One way to make this transition and upgrade smoother is to continue to use the File Manager and Program Manager that are familiar to users of previous versions of Windows. This allows your users to keep what they are familiar with and lets you gain the customizability, performance, and enhancements of Windows 95. You can then help your users migrate over time to the File

► See "Using Windows 3.1 File Manager or Program Manager," p. 77

Manager and Program Manager replacement—either My Desktop or Windows Explorer.

Windows 3.1 and DOS Data Files Are Compatible

The effective use of data seems to be what differentiates winners from losers in the information age. With that in mind, files created in Windows 95 are compatible with files from earlier versions of DOS and Windows.

► See "Using Long File Names," p. 334

Windows 95 is capable of handling file names up to 255 characters long. The long file names can include spaces. For example, what used to be BUDGET96.DOC can now be RON'S VACATION BUDGET FOR 1996.DOC. When you move a file with a long name to a system that uses the older eight-character name with a three-letter extension, the older system sees only an abbreviated version of the long name.

Caution

Don't use file utility software designed for DOS and older versions of Windows in Windows 95 or on files from Windows 95. Windows 95 stores name and file tracking information in different locations. Although this makes no difference to applications, some file-manipulation utilities can scramble this data. The types of utilities to beware of do such things as recover lost files.

Tip

To see the device drivers you have and information about them, open the Start menu and choose Settings, Control Panel. Double-click the System icon and select the Device Manager tab. Double-click any device to see its Properties sheet.

Compatible Drivers

Device drivers act as translators between hardware and software. They make sure the two work together efficiently. Windows 95 comes with 32-bit device drivers for major hardware such as disk drives, display adapters, and CD-ROM drives. This means that when you install Windows 95, it will install new device drivers that give you the hardware's advanced features as well as any speed that comes from a 32-bit driver. Unfortunately, there are thousands of different hardware devices. This makes it almost impossible for Microsoft to ensure that every device driver has been included in the set that initially installs with Windows. Because of that, if Windows 95 cannot find a new device driver during installation, it continues to use any 16-bit device driver that you have already installed from a previous version of Windows or from MS-DOS.

► See "Getting Help," p. 79

If you want to ensure you have the latest device driver, contact the manufacturer of your hardware device. Microsoft has made device drivers much easier to create for Windows 95, and your hardware manufacturer should have a new version available.

Installing Windows 95 Is Easy

You don't have to be a hardware guru to install Windows 95. In previous versions of Windows you were often forced into making choices about hardware configurations. It was up to you to select the appropriate options and settings so that hardware and software were compatible. Windows 95 takes care of many of those decisions and options for you. If you have newer Plug and Play hardware, Windows 95 can detect exactly what is installed and how Windows 95 should be configured to work. If you have hardware, such as modems that aren't Plug and Play, Windows 95 will prompt you for the information necessary for setup.

▶ See "Installing Plug and Play Hardware," p. 246

▶ See "Installing a Plug and Play Modem," p. 833

▶ See "Using Windows 95 Setup," p. 1084

Improved Performance

One of the design goals for Windows 95 is that its speed should be the same or better than Windows 3.11. As memory is added, the performance should improve. At the low end, Windows 95 should be able to run with the same or better speed as Windows 3.11 running on low-end 386DX computers with only 4M of RAM.

Everyone expects new software to run faster, and Windows 95 does. As you add more memory, you find that Windows' performance improves proportionally. You should see a significant performance improvement for new 32-bit applications designed for Windows 95, too. Microsoft Excel for Windows 95 and Microsoft Word for Windows 95 are up to 50 percent faster in many of their operations.

Even 16-bit applications will have improved performance in Windows 95 in areas that involve the 32-bit system, such as printing and file handling. That Windows terror, the `out of memory` error, is less likely to occur. Although Windows 95 still uses a 64K heap to store systems information for 16-bit applications, a lot of the information that was stored in this area by older versions of Windows is now stored elsewhere. As a result, there is less chance of your application failing.

Windows 95 uses a new 32-bit VCACHE, which replaces the older SmartDrive that ran under DOS and previous versions of Windows. VCACHE uses more intelligent caching algorithms to improve the apparent speed of your hard drive as well as your CD-ROM and 32-bit network redirectors. Unlike SmartDrive, VCACHE dynamically allocates itself. Based on the amount of free system memory, VCACHE allocates or reallocates memory used by the cache.

▶ See "Improving Performance with Disk Defragmenter," p. 486

An Easier but More Powerful Interface

To most personal computer users, the interface they see on-screen *is* the computer. Because of that, the world of DOS computers was too difficult for many people. There was a lot of learning involved just to get started with simple tasks. And there was no way to learn as you worked. You had to devote part of your time to learning DOS and the applications, and use the remaining time trying to get productive work done. The advent of Windows improved this quite a bit. With a few hours of instruction on Windows, you could learn on your own by exploring. The work-to-learning ratio improved significantly.

Research by Microsoft found that Windows was still difficult to learn for many people and some people were still too timid to explore and learn on their own. For that reason they had two primary design goals for Windows 95:

- To make Windows more accessible to novice users so that they can quickly get what they need.
- To make Windows more customizable and productive for advanced users by including accessible shortcuts and power techniques.

Windows 95 does a good job on both of these goals. Tests in Microsoft's usability laboratory show that inexperienced computer users are able to find and start applications significantly faster with Windows 95 than with previous versions of Windows. For example, the Start menu enables anyone familiar with a mouse to open a menu and search for the application he or she wants. In earlier versions of Windows, users had to learn about the Program Manager, group windows, and program item icons before they could start their first application.

Tip
Without an overview of Windows 95, your previous experience with Windows may get in the way of how easy it is to use Windows 95.

Experienced and novice computer users will want to review the basics of Windows 95 in order to get a good idea as to how much easier Windows 95 is to operate than previous operating systems. The Windows 95 desktop interface is shown in figure 1.1.

Fig. 1.1
When Windows 95 first loads, your desktop will look similar to this. Depending on the type of setup you used, you may have additional icons or some of these icons may not be present.

The Start Button Makes Starting Applications Easier

The Start button is one of the most important changes to Windows 95. It makes Windows 95 more accessible. Research from Microsoft's usability labs shows that people start applications three to nine times faster when using the Start button than they do when using the old Program Manager. By clicking the Start button, you open the Start menu, which is your avenue to Windows 95.

The Start button not only makes Windows easier to use for beginners, it's an excellent improvement for power users. When you click the Start button, or press Ctrl+Esc, you see a menu that includes not only applications, but also lists of frequently used documents, customizable settings, and frequently used features such as Find, Help, and Run (see fig. 1.2).

Note

Ctrl+Esc is a shortcut key combination used to access the Start menu. Throughout this book, when you see a key+key combination, that signifies a shortcut to accessing an application or opening a menu.

Fig. 1.2
Tests show that Windows 95 is easier to use for beginners and more customizable for experts.

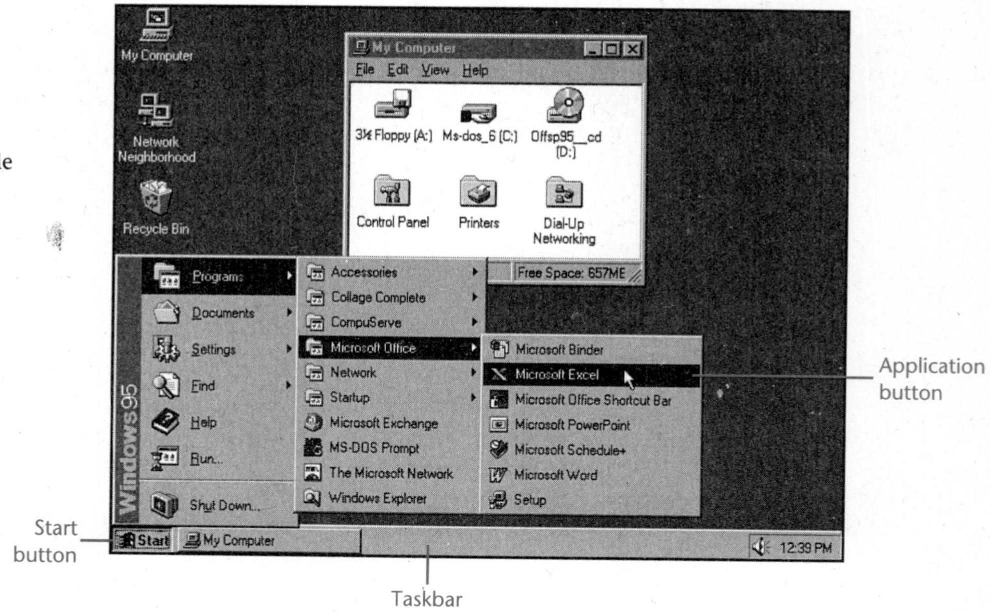

The Taskbar Makes It Easy to Switch between Applications

▶ See "Customizing the Taskbar," p. 122

One of the problems both novice and advanced users face is keeping track of which applications are currently running, and then switching to an already running application. In previous versions of Windows, switching between applications was difficult to figure out. Microsoft estimates that nearly 70 percent of users didn't know they could press Alt+Tab to switch between applications (the Alt+Tab combination still works in Windows 95). With the new taskbar, all the applications that are running appear as buttons on the taskbar (refer to fig. 1.2). Clicking a button opens that running application into its own window.

Tip
Nearly every item in Windows 95 contains a property sheet you can customize. Right-click on an item and choose Properties to see its properties.

Right Mouse Button Information

Windows 95 has many customizable features and the key to unlocking them is clicking the right mouse button. Nearly every item you see on the Windows 95 screen contains a shortcut menu. To see that shortcut menu, right-click on the item. For example, if you want to customize the taskbar, put the tip of the mouse pointer on a gray area of the taskbar and click the right mouse button, then choose Properties. The Taskbar Properties sheet displays (see fig. 1.3). In it, you can change how the taskbar appears and what it contains.

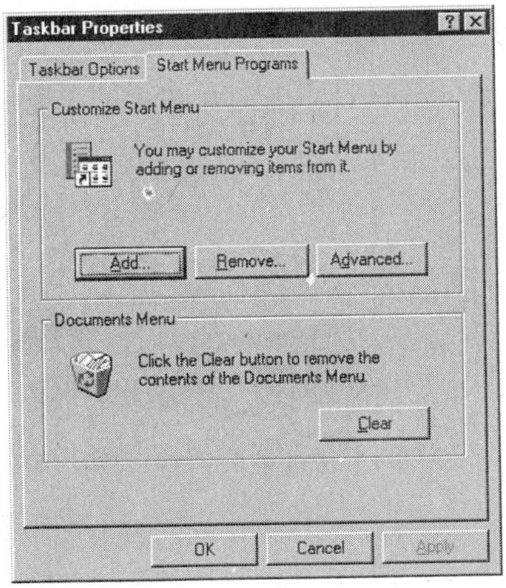

Fig. 1.3
Clicking the right mouse button on the taskbar brings up the Taskbar Properties sheet.

Note

Properties dialogs in Windows 95 are referred to as sheets. When you click a tab within the sheets, the open dialogs are referred to as pages. Figure 1.3 displays the Start Menu Programs page of the Taskbar Properties sheet.

My Computer for Easy Understanding of What's in Your Computer

Hierarchical displays of directories and files confused many new computer users. Microsoft developed My Computer and Network Neighborhood to resolve that problem. Double-click the My Computer icon to see a window that displays the resources available on your computer (see fig. 1.4). Doing the same on the Network Neighborhood icon displays all the resources available on any network to which you are connected. The Network Neighborhood icon does not display unless Windows has been installed for a network.

Tip
If you find it confusing to have too many windows open, you can specify that all the views of My Computer or Network Neighborhood appear in the same window.

Notice in the My Computer Window that the drives and resources available within your computer are displayed. In the example in figure 1.4, the computer has an A, C, and D drive. My Computer will always display a Control Panel icon and in this case a Printers and Dial-Up Networking icon.

Note

The name of the C drive in this example depends on the hard drive having a volume name prior to Windows 95 installation. Most My Computer windows will just show a (C:) drive.

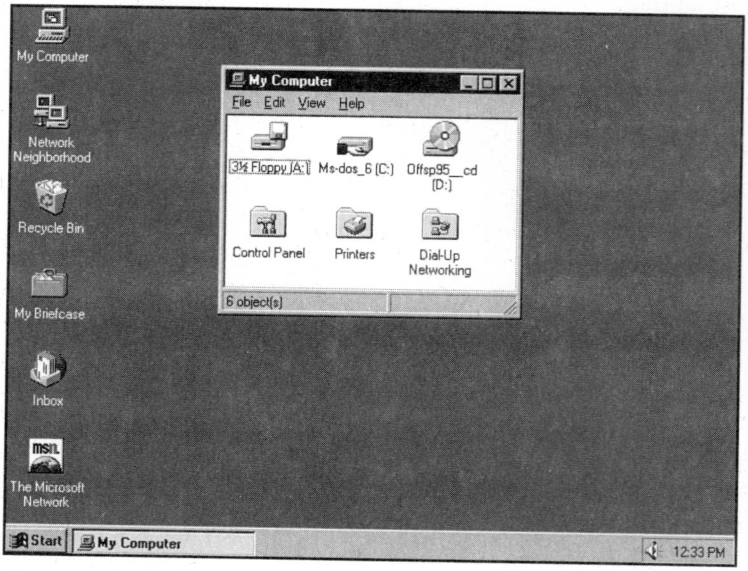

Fig. 1.4
Use the My Computer window to access the drives on your computer. Double-clicking a drive will display the folders and files within that drive.

Folders Make File Management More Intuitive

Directories and files are not a familiar concept to people who are new to computers. But everyone who has worked in an office is familiar with folders and documents. The metaphor of folders and documents in Windows 95 makes file management easier to understand. Double-clicking the My Computer icon on the desktop displays the My Computer window shown in figure 1.4. This window shows the drives on your computer and other peripherals. You can get to files and directories by double-clicking any of the drives.

Double-clicking on the Ms-dos 6 (C:) icon that represents a hard drive in the computer opens the window C:\. Within this window, double-clicking on the My Documents folder opens the window titled C:\My Documents. This window contains document icons. Notice that each icon represents a type of file.

► See "Using My Computer to Manage Files," p. 551

You can perform work on documents by dragging their icon into other folders, onto the desktop (the background), or dropping them onto other icons that represent resources such as printers or applications. Use a right mouse click on a document icon to see frequently used tasks that control documents or to see the properties of the document.

In figure 1.5, the My Computer icon has been opened to show selected contents of the computer. The first window open is the My Computer window. This was opened by double-clicking on the My Computer icon at the top left of the desktop. The name My Computer shows in the title bar. The next window, with the title bar Ms-dos_6 (C:), was opened by double-clicking on the C: drive icon in the My Computer window. Notice that the Ms-dos_6 (C:) window overlaps the My Computer window. Finally, the My Documents window was opened by double-clicking on the My Documents folder visible in the Ms-dos_6 (C:) window. Notice that as each window opens it overlaps the window from which it came.

Each of these windows shows a different view of the computer resources available to you. As the windows open, they layer over the previous window.

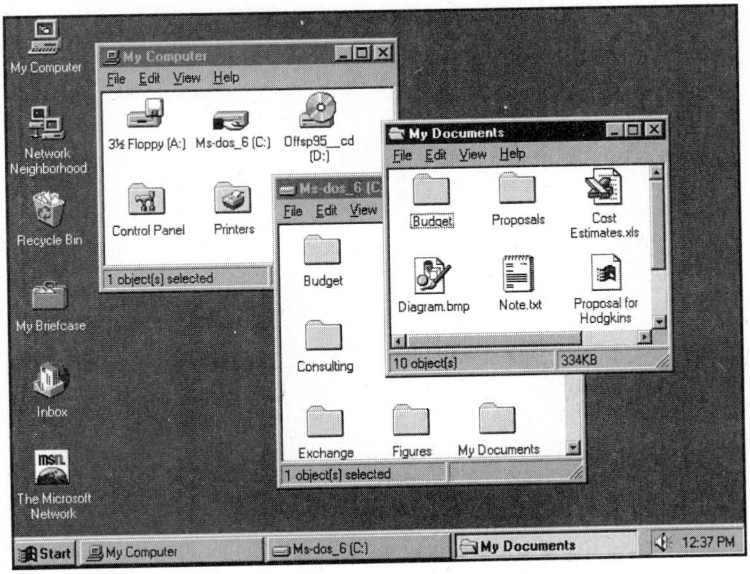

Fig. 1.5
Double-clicking on items in My Computer windows either opens the item to show its contents or opens the document or program.

Windows Explorer for Powerful File Management

Expert users may find My Computer and Network Neighborhood limiting when they need to do a lot of file management and examine different types of computer resources. Windows provides the Windows Explorer (see fig. 1.6) for more advanced users. It uses a single window composed of two panes. The left side shows a hierarchical structure of all the computer resources from hard drives and CD-ROMs to Control Panels and printers. Once you understand how to use the Windows Explorer, you will be able to do more than you could with the old File Manager. For example, you can drag files and folders from the right panel in the Explorer to a subfolder at any level in the right panel. You also can right-click on files to display a shortcut menu that enables you to view the file, print, create a shortcut, and see the file's properties.

▶ See "Using the Windows Explorer to View Files and Folders," p. 499

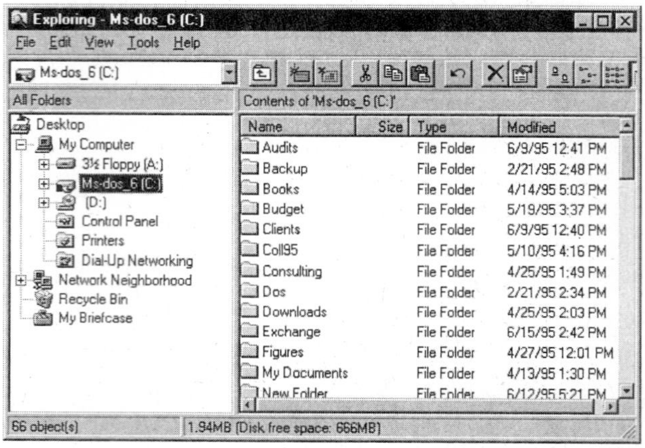

Fig. 1.6
Windows Explorer is a powerful file management tool.

Displaying Properties of Programs, Documents, and Resources

► See "Changing Settings and Properties with the Right Mouse Button," p. 107

Almost everything in Windows can be customized. If you can't customize it, you can at least see what its current settings or properties are. To change or view properties of an object such as the desktop background, the taskbar, the Recycle Bin, a file, a folder, and so on, click the right mouse button on the item. When a shortcut menu displays, choose Properties. A properties sheet displays. Figure 1.7 shows the property sheet for the desktop. It appears when you right-click the desktop, choose Properties, and then select one of the tabs. You can use it to change the colors, background, and screen savers in Windows.

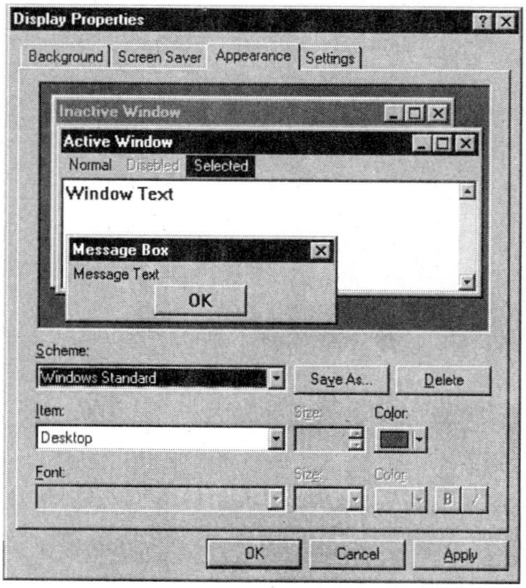

Fig. 1.7
Right-click almost any item and choose Properties to display a property sheet like this Display Properties sheet.

Shortcuts Add Power

Shortcuts are a powerful way of customizing your desktop. You can use a shortcut to start applications, load a document, act as a drop-box into a folder located elsewhere, and so on. You can even put a printer shortcut on your desktop. Dragging a file onto a printer shortcut will then print the file. You can put shortcuts anywhere on the desktop or in any folder.

► See "Creating Shortcut Icons on the Desktop to Start Programs," p. 68

Quick View Displays File Previews

Quick View enables you to see a preview of a file without starting the application that created the file and opening the file. It's a handy browser that can save you time. Quick View works with the files from most major applications. Figure 1.8 shows a Quick View of an Excel sheet.

► See "Previewing a Document with Quick View," p. 527

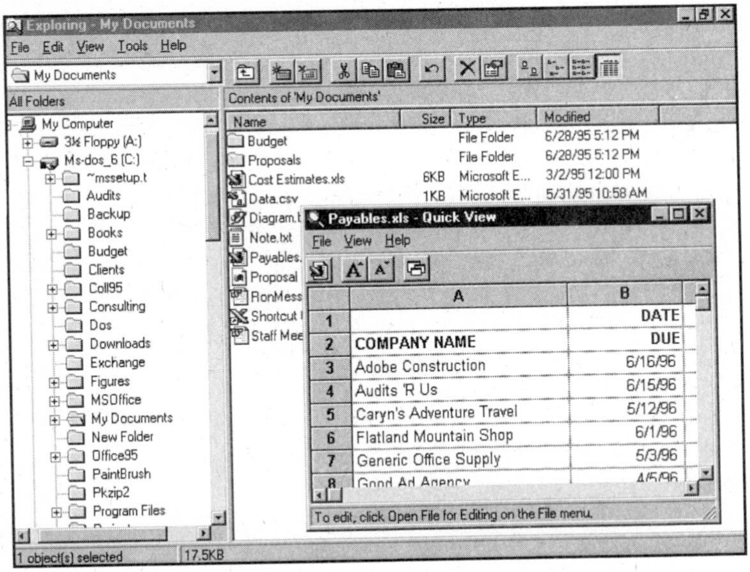

Fig. 1.8
Use Quick View to preview a file without opening it.

Long File Names Make File Names Easier to Read

One of the most aggravating things faced by everyone who used DOS or previous versions of Windows was the 8.3 file-naming restriction. File names were a maximum of eight characters and file extensions were a maximum of three characters. This limit lead to very inventive, but pretty undecipherable, file names. In Windows 95, you can use file names that are up to 255 characters long—they can even include space characters. When a file with a long name is brought back to an 8.3 file system, the long file name is truncated, so that files are still compatible.

Help Is Easy to Use

Help has been simplified, while at the same time it contains more information. Help now enables you to type in phrases and get back a list of related items. Help also includes graphical displays that are designed to help you understand the big picture of how a function or feature works.

More Useful Accessories

Windows includes accessories that are helpful in routine work and doing work such as file and disk management. The simple word processor, WordPad, is more than adequate for most school work or personal letter writing. And it uses a file format that is compatible with Word for Windows, the powerful and most widely sold word processor. Windows also includes accessories such as a new paint program, a calculator, and a clock.

A valuable set of disk management accessories comes with Windows. These accessories improve the performance, integrity, and safety of data on your hard drives. DriveSpace compresses data on your disk so that you can fit almost twice as much data on a drive. The ScanDisk utility checks your hard disk for errors. Disk Defragmenter collects file segments that are stored all over the disk and relocates them so that files are stored in contiguous segments. As a result, your disk runs faster and wastes less storage space. Finally, Windows includes Backup. You can use the Backup utility to make magnetic tape or disk backups of all or parts of your hard disk.

Windows 95 has been improved for use with multimedia equipment. As such, it includes the CD Player that enables you to play music CDs on computers equipped with a CD-ROM and sound board.

Improved Printing

Windows has had a number of improvements in the area of printing. Printing speed is something that everyone will appreciate. Windows now uses a 32-bit print subsystem that enables you to print in the background without causing the application you are using to show significant delays. The apparent print time has been improved because it takes less time for Windows to return to your control after you give a print command.

If you need high-quality print output, you will be able to take advantage of Windows' support for PostScript Level II printers as well as better color matching between the display and output devices.

Mobile computer users will be able to take advantage of *deferred printing*. This enables people with laptop computers to print even though their laptop is not in a docking station. Once it is connected in a docking station, it will automatically print.

Windows also supports more than 800 different models. With newer models that support the Plug and Play standard, installation is very simple. Network administrators will enjoy the automatic printer driver installation from Windows 95, Windows NT, or Novell NetWare servers.

Networking and Communication in Windows 95

Windows 95 is designed to meet the requirements of a corporate networking environment. At the same time, it is easier to use for people on the network and for mobile computer users who connect to the network. Windows 95 includes HyperTerminal, an improved 32-bit version of the basic communications program Terminal that came with previous versions of Windows.

Windows uses a high-performance 32-bit network architecture that includes 32-bit versions of network client software, file and print sharing software, network protocols, and network card drivers. It supports multiple redirectors, protocols, and network card device drivers. It also supports the industry standards TCP/IP, IPX, SNMP, and DMI.

You can build your own network using the integrated networking capability of Windows. Windows 95 is capable of supporting up to ten 32-bit, Protected-mode network clients. With today's heterogeneous networking environments, it's important that Windows be able to run as a client for many different networks. Windows runs client support for Windows NT Server, NetWare, Banyan, DEC PathWorks, and Sun NFS.

► See "Windows 95 Peer to Peer Networking Features," p. 617

► See "Automatic Installation of Windows 95 NetWare Support," p. 678

In addition to supporting corporate networking, Windows 95 has access to Microsoft Network and the Internet. Windows includes TCP/IP support, Windows Socket services, and widely used protocols such as Point to Point Protocol (PPP) and SLIP, so you can connect to the Internet through your corporate network or directly via your own modem or ISDN connection.

Microsoft Network promises to be a collection of resources that will greatly expand the services and information available online. In addition, you will be able to get online help for your Windows software from Microsoft and other companies. If you have a modem in your system, you will be able to subscribe to Microsoft Network during installation. You can install at a later time by double-clicking the MSN icon.

Windows 95 also includes a feature for organizing all your e-mail in one place. This is called the *Inbox*. With this properly set up and configured, you can read all your incoming mail from the Microsoft Network, your LAN's Microsoft mail, CompuServe mail, and even Internet mail in the same place rather than having to use all of these different applications to read mail.

Better Features for the Road Warrior

More and more people are taking advantage of the benefits of mobile computing: being able to work where you want, taking your computer home, taking it to clients, or taking it into the field. However, mobile computing comes with a plethora of difficulties. Windows now addresses many of those difficulties.

Moving your mobile computer usually requires some changes in your hardware configuration. If you are using a desktop monitor, the desktop monitor and your laptop screen may use different colors and resolutions. Some laptops come with pointer devices integrated into the keyboard, yet at your desk you might prefer to use a mouse. And then there is the problem of connecting and disconnecting from a network. When you return from a trip, there is the problem of synchronizing files—integrating the most up-to-date files between laptop and network. Prior to Windows 95, these changes required separate configuration files.

With Windows 95, mobile computer users can easily switch between different named setup configurations. If the mobile computer uses a docking station, the software transition can be completely automatic. Putting the laptop in the docking station causes the laptop to reboot in the correct configuration and connect to the appropriate network, printers, and so on.

The use of PCMCIA cards also has been improved (in Windows 95, however, PCMCIA cards are now referred to as PC Cards). You can install newer PC Cards while the computer is on. Windows will recognize the new card through Plug and Play, and immediately will make its features available.

▶ See "Synchronizing Files," p. 533

One of the advances that Windows 95 includes is the Briefcase to store files shared between desktop and mobile computers. The Briefcase will automatically update files between the systems and ask you to judge files that may be in conflict.

Any mobile computer user will tell you how important power management is. You can't have a battery go dead at the wrong time. In laptop computers that support the new Power Management APIs, Windows can monitor system power, reduce power wastage, and warn you when power gets low.

► See "Special Features for Notebook Users," p. 265

Easier Plug and Play Hardware Installation

One of the most aggravating situations you can face with a computer is installing a sound board, disk drive, or network adapter card with which you are unfamiliar. In fact, many hardware devices used with computers require some arcane knowledge and a few tricks that aren't in the book before they finally work. Plug and Play is designed to do away with the trickery and make the hardware side of computers as easy as installing refrigerators and toasters.

The Plug and Play specification is an industry-wide specification designed to make adding hardware easy. Plug and Play enables you to install or connect Plug-and-Play-compatible devices and let Windows figure out the technical details such as IRQs, I/O addresses, DMA channels, and memory addresses. Where there is conflict, Windows resolves the problem rather than you having to spend hours trying different settings. The information about all installed hardware and software is stored in the Registry, a database of system information. Plug and Play even makes it easier to install hardware that does not meet Plug and Play specifications, so-called "legacy hardware." Windows detects that the legacy hardware may cause a conflict with current system settings and then gives you information from the Registry that makes it easier for you to decide how to install the hardware. You don't have to keep notecards containing all the settings from previous hardware you installed. Nor do you have to pull out hardware manuals that you have probably misplaced.

Plug and Play's ease of use is apparent with, for example, the use of Plug and Play printers or PC cards. With a Plug and Play printer, as soon as you connect the printer, your computer recognizes the new printer, installs a new device driver for it, and sets up your printer configuration to print with that printer. With PC cards used in portable computers, you can slide in a modem card and immediately send a message. Plug and Play configures the modem card for you.

► See "Installing Plug and Play Hardware," p. 246

Improved Multimedia and Games

Windows 95 not only has improved multimedia capability. Windows includes Video for Windows so that you don't have to install video drivers. It also includes drivers for the most commonly used CD-ROM drives and sound cards. And to make it easy for anyone at home to use games or edutainment software, Windows automatically installs and runs newer CD-ROMs when you put them in the computer. Its improvements aren't limited to multimedia, however; Windows now includes Win-G, a programming interface used by game programmers, so they can write faster games that run on Windows. ❖

Chapter 2

Understanding Windows 95

by Ron Person

This chapter gives you "the big picture" to help you understand Windows 95. If you're a new user, you'll want to get a feel for the important concepts and see where you are going. If you're an experienced Windows user, you'll want to know what is different and what is the same in this new version of Windows compared to previous versions. And if you are a power user or consultant, you'll want a quick introduction to ways you can customize and troubleshoot Windows 95.

Tip
People who have used previous versions of Windows should read this chapter so that they can quickly grasp what has changed.

After reading this chapter, you should have a good idea what sections to read to get started learning about Windows 95. Throughout this chapter, you'll find recommendations for three different approaches to learning more. These three approaches are based on whether you are an inexperienced Windows user, an experienced Windows user, or a power user.

Tip
Throughout this chapter, important concepts are broken up by experience level. Rather than repeating basic concepts for each experience level, you should read the concepts from the inexperienced user level up to your level.

This chapter gives you an overview of the most important concepts for controlling Windows 95. It also tells you which book sections are probably appropriate to your experience level. In this chapter, you get an overview of the following concepts:

- The important screen elements in Windows
- The most frequently used ways of starting programs and documents
- How to customize by changing property sheets
- Whether you should use My Computer or the Windows Explorer for file management

- How to learn more about Windows through online Help
- Important differences from previous versions of Windows
- Which control methods are best suited for your work style and experience level

Understanding the Most Important Screen Elements in Windows 95

The appearance of the Windows 95 screen, shown in figure 2.1, is completely different from MS-DOS or previous versions of Windows. The backdrop of the screen is called the *desktop*. On the desktop, you'll find icons that represent programs or documents, a taskbar containing a Start button and minimized application buttons, and windows that contain programs. If your Windows 95 has been used previously and customized, it may appear slightly different from the figure.

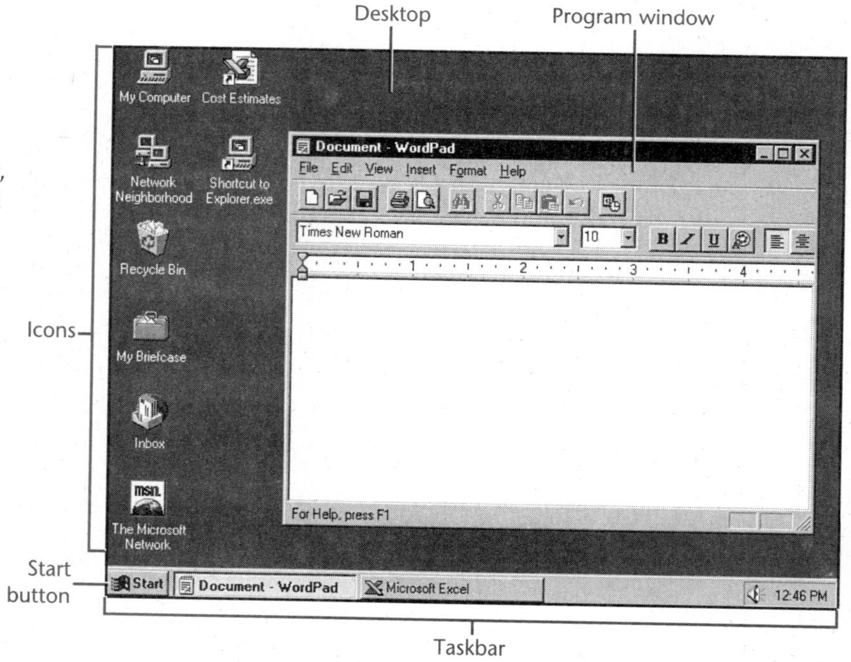

Fig. 2.1
The Windows 95 screen is designed to be easier to use for first-time users, yet more powerful and customizable for power users.

Beginning Users of Windows 95

If you are unfamiliar with previous versions of Windows, the important things to notice are:

- Each graphical item on the screen responds in a particular way when you put the tip of the mouse pointer on the item and click or double-click the left or right mouse button.
- Icons represent programs, documents, or shortcuts. *Shortcuts* are pointers to a program or document.
- You use the taskbar and Start button shown at the bottom of figure 2.1 to start and switch between programs.
- Running programs appear in three ways: as a button on the taskbar, in a window on the screen, or filling the entire screen.

► See "Learning the Parts of the Windows Display," p. 58

► See "Starting Applications from the Start Menu and Taskbar," p. 62

► See "Customizing the Mouse," p. 147

► See "Making Windows Accessible for the Hearing, Sight, and Movement Impaired," p. 150

► See "Creating Shortcut Icons on the Desktop to Start Programs," p. 68

Experienced and Power Users of Previous Windows Versions

If you are familiar with previous versions of Windows or even consider yourself a power user, the important things to notice are:

- Much more of Windows can be customized. Customize by clicking an item with the right mouse button, clicking Properties, and then changing options on the Properties sheet for the item.
- The Program Manager is gone. In its place are icons that appear on the desktop and a taskbar with Start button shown at the bottom of figure 2.1.
- You can drag icons on the desktop to any location and they will stay there. You can even place folders on the desktop. (*Folders* are the new name for directories.)
- *Shortcut* icons on the desktop act as pointers to programs or documents that you don't want to put directly on the desktop. Shortcuts display a small curved arrow at their lower-left corner. Double-clicking a shortcut icon opens the document or program. Deleting a shortcut icon does not delete the file to which it points.

The main purpose for the shortcut is to have access to a program or document from multiple places without having to have it physically stored in both places. If it's a shortcut to a document, you don't have to worry about which icon (the original or the shortcut) was used to open it because, either way, there is only one file that is being modified.

How to Start Programs and Documents

Microsoft has found that starting programs with Windows 95 is much easier than it was in previous versions of Windows. Depending on your experience level and the task, you can start programs or documents in different ways.

Starting from the Start Button

The Start button is a significant enhancement to Windows. Clicking the Start button displays a menu like the one directly above the Start button in figure 2.2. As you move the pointer over an item on the menu, a submenu appears. When you see the program or document you want to open, click it.

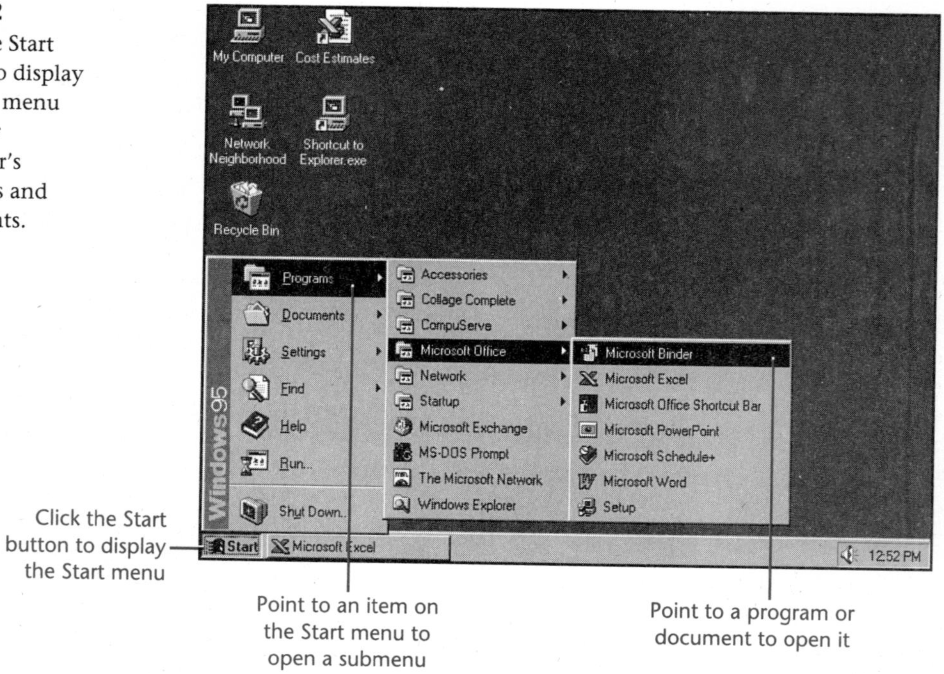

Fig. 2.2
Click the Start button to display the Start menu and your computer's programs and documents.

Beginning Users of Windows 95

If you are unfamiliar with previous versions of Windows, the important things to notice are:

- Starting a program or document is easy. Move the mouse pointer over the Start button and click the left mouse button.
- Windows 95 lists your programs on the Start menu.
- Start a recently used document by pointing to the Documents menu item and then clicking the document. The program opens automatically.
- Find documents or programs by pointing to the Find button and clicking Files or Folders. Enter information about the document or program file you want to find.
- Get Help or demonstrations by pointing to the Help button and clicking.
- Shut down Windows by opening the Start menu and choosing Shut Down.

► See "Starting a Program from the Start Menu," p. 65

► See "Quitting Windows Applications," p. 77

Experienced Users of Previous Windows Versions

If you are familiar with previous versions of Windows, the important things to notice are:

- You no longer need to open and close Group windows in the Program Manager to find program or document icons.
- Your existing Group windows from the Program Manager in previous versions of Windows now appear as submenus off the Programs item of the Start menu.
- Click the Start button to see your programs and most frequently used documents. Click the item you want to open.
- Go directly to the Control Panel or printer settings from the Settings item on the Start menu.
- Make frequently used programs more accessible on the Start menu by dragging their file icon from the Explorer or My Computer and dropping it on the Start button.

► See "Running Programs on Startup," p. 52

► See "Specifying Documents to Open at Startup," p. 54

► See "Customizing the Start Menu," p. 128

Power Users Very Experienced with Windows

▶ See "Controlling How Startup Programs Appear," p. 54

If you consider yourself a power user and are very experienced with Windows, the important things to notice are:

- At first the Start menu may seem to slow you down compared to quickly clicking your way through the Program Manager. It will be faster, however, if you customize by adding your own submenus and repositioning programs and documents on the menu.

▶ See "Customizing the Taskbar," p. 122

- Customize the Start menu to include your own submenus by adding a folder to the Start menu.

▶ See "Managing Windows after an Application Failure," p. 78

- Change the properties of programs so that they open as a button on the taskbar, as a window, or maximized to fill the screen.

Starting from Shortcuts

Shortcuts are icons that point to files. When you double-click a shortcut, it starts the program or opens the document. You can put folder shortcuts on your desktop so that when you drag a file onto the folder shortcut, the file is stored in the folder.

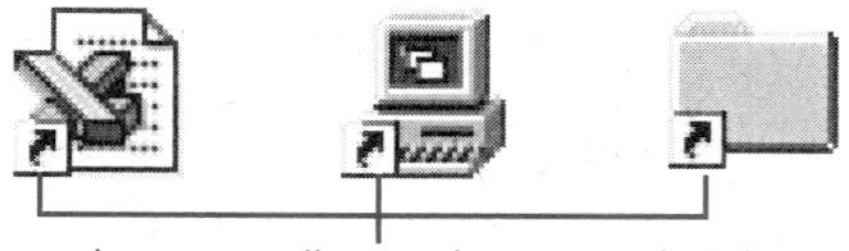
Shortcut icons have a small curved arrow at their lower-left corner

Fig. 2.3
Double-click a shortcut icon to open the program or document.

Beginning Users of Windows 95

If you are unfamiliar with previous versions of Windows, the important things to notice are:

▶ See "Starting Programs from a Shortcut Icon on the Desktop," p. 68

- Shortcuts represent documents, programs, or folders.
- Double-clicking a shortcut opens the document or program.
- You can delete a shortcut icon without deleting the file or folder it represents.

Experienced Users of Previous Windows Versions

If you are familiar with previous versions of Windows, the important thing to notice is:

▶ See "Creating Shortcut Icons on the Desktop to Start Programs," p. 68

- You can create a shortcut for any program, document, or folder by dragging the file or folder from the Explorer or My Computer with the right mouse button and dropping it on the desktop.

Power Users Very Experienced with Windows

If you consider yourself a power user and are very experienced with Windows, the important things to notice are:

- You can create shortcuts that automatically run procedures or programs. For example, in Word or Excel you can create a shortcut to a document or spreadsheet that contains a macro that runs when opened. Another example is the Windows 95 Backup program. It enables you to create shortcuts that automatically backup selected files.
- Customize shortcuts by right-clicking the Shortcut icon, clicking Properties and then clicking the Shortcut tab in the shortcut's Properties sheet. You can add shortcut keys, change the file to which the shortcut points, specify how a program runs, and change the icon.

► See "Modifying and Deleting Shortcuts," p. 72

Starting from My Computer or the Explorer

My Computer and the Explorer are windows used to manage the program and document files on your computer. Figures 2.4 and 2.5 show My Computer and the Explorer windows.

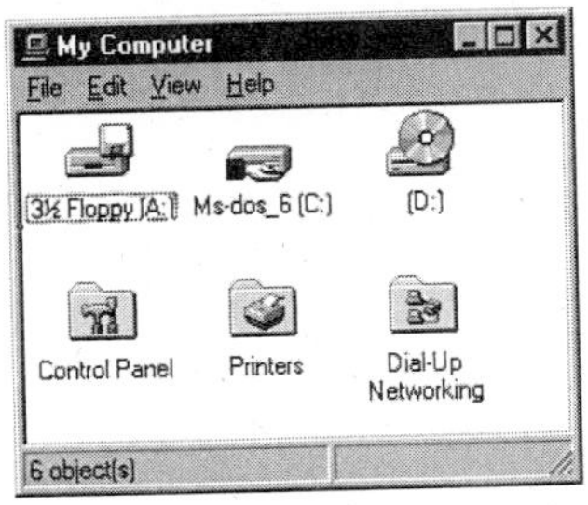

Fig. 2.4
The My Computer window.

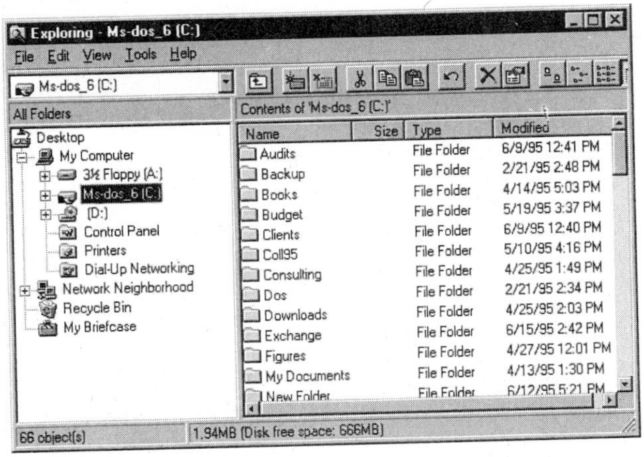

Fig. 2.5
The Explorer window.

Beginning Users of Windows 95

If you are unfamiliar with previous versions of Windows, the important things to notice are:

- You should use the Start menu to open programs whenever possible. Open documents from within the program. If it is a frequently used document, you may find it on the Documents submenu off of the Start menu.

▶ See "Using My Computer to Open Documents," p. 76

- If there is a program that you can't find on the Start menu, use a window from My Computer to display program files. When you find the program you want, double-click the program's icon.

▶ See "Opening a Document or Application from the Explorer," p. 73

▶ See "Using the Windows Explorer to View Files and Folders," p. 499

▶ See "Managing Your Files and Folders," p. 513

Experienced Users of Previous Windows Versions

If you are familiar with previous versions of Windows, the important things to notice are:

- If you are familiar with opening program or document files in the File Manager, you'll know how to open programs or documents from within My Computer or the Explorer. Find the file and double-click it.
- You can register a file type with an application so that double-clicking on a file of that type opens a specific application and loads the file. Most file types are automatically registered, but you can manually register a file or change a file type's registration by choosing View, Options, and then selecting the File Types tab and either adding a new type or editing an existing type.

▶ See "Registering Files to Automatically Open an Application," p. 539

Power Users Very Experienced with Windows

If you consider yourself a power user and are very experienced with Windows, the important thing to notice is:

- Open multiple files at the same time from My Computer or Explorer by selecting the files with Shift+Click or Ctrl+Click, and then right-click one of the selected files. From the shortcut menu, click Open.

How to Customize and See Property Sheets

Property sheets are an important part of Windows 95. Nearly all items you see on-screen have a property sheet that describes the item. To display a properties sheet, click an item with the right mouse button and then click Properties from the shortcut menu. Figure 2.6 shows the Taskbar Properties sheet.

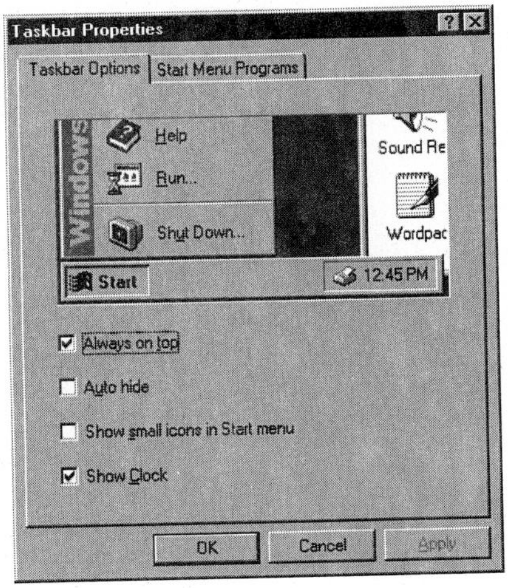

Fig. 2.6
Use properties sheets to get information about an item and change how the item behaves.

Beginning Users of Windows 95

If you are unfamiliar with previous versions of Windows, the important things to notice are:

- You can get a description and change the behavior of many items by displaying the Properties sheets.
- Even within some applications, you can see the properties of a document by displaying the file's Properties sheet from within the Open dialog box.

▶ See "Changing Settings and Properties with the Right Mouse Button," p. 107

▶ See "Customizing the Desktop Colors and Background," p. 131

▶ See "Changing the Screen Resolution, Font Size, and Color Palette," p. 142

▶ See "Changing Custom Settings for Each User," p. 156

Experienced Users of Previous Windows Versions

If you are familiar with previous versions of Windows, the important things to notice are:

- You don't have to go through the Control Panel to customize items anymore. Start clicking with the right mouse button and notice what items have a properties sheet.
- You can customize Windows by right-clicking items you want to change, such as the desktop, and then clicking Properties.

Power Users Very Experienced with Windows

If you consider yourself a power user and are very experienced with Windows, the important things to notice are:

- You can create logon profiles that change Windows hardware configuration depending on a selection at startup. This is useful for laptops that also serve as desktop computers.

- You can use log on IDs to identify different users on a network or isolated computer. Windows will start up with the customized settings which that user has created.

How to Manage Files

Windows 95 has two different approaches to managing files. If you're a new or inexperienced user, you may want to use My Computer. It uses a folder metaphor where files appear as program or document icons (see fig. 2.7). These icons can be moved or copied between folder icons. If you're on a network, examine Network Neighborhood. It shows network files in the same way.

The second way of managing files in Windows 95 is through the Explorer (see fig. 2.8). The Explorer displays folders and files using two panes in a window. The left pane shows the hierarchical relationship between folders—which folder is inside another. The right pane displays the contents of the folder that has been selected in the left pane.

Fig. 2.7
My Computer displays the contents of your computer in windows that contain folders and program/document icons.

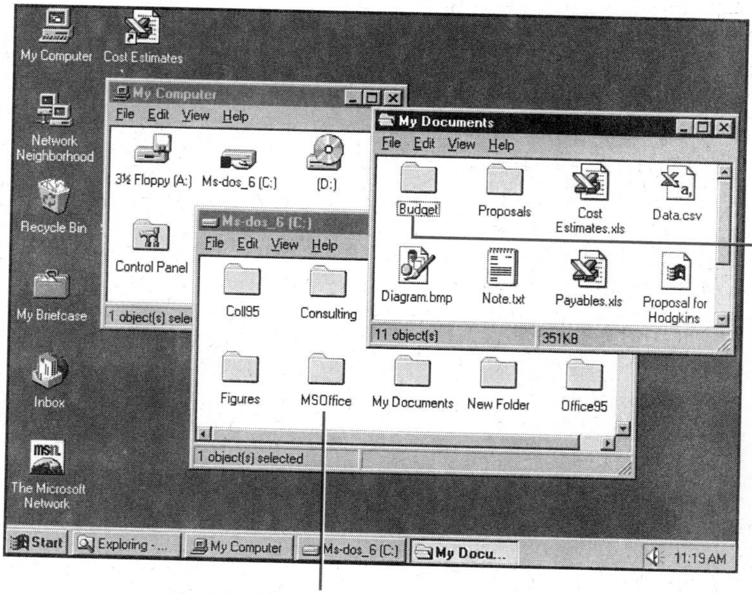

Double-click an icon to open it

Double-click a folder to open it

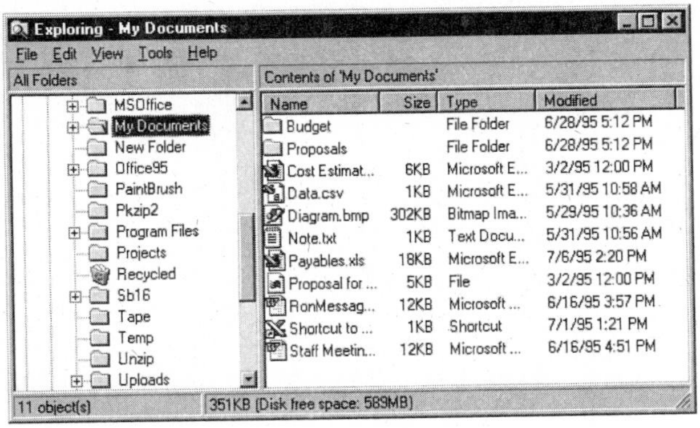

Fig. 2.8
The hierarchical relationship of folders shows in the left pane of the Explorer window.

Beginning Users of Windows 95

If you are unfamiliar with previous versions of Windows, the important things to notice are:

- You should use My Computer to see the contents of your computer. Open disk drives and folders by double-clicking the icon.
- Use My Computer to copy and delete files.
- Create your own folders in a window by clicking File, New, Folder.

► See "Using My Computer to Manage Files," p. 551

Experienced Users of Previous Windows Versions

If you are familiar with previous versions of Windows, the important things to notice are:

- Use either the folder metaphor in My Computer or the hierarchical panes in Explorer to manage your computer's files.
- If you need to see the relationships of folders—how folders are grouped inside other folders—use the Explorer.
- Right-click files in My Computer or Explorer to see the numerous shortcut commands for copying, deleting, printing, and so on.
- At first, you may get frustrated using the Explorer because it doesn't allow multiple windows. You can actually do more in the Explorer than you did in File Manager, but it may take time to figure out how.
- You can change the displays in either My Computer or Explorer to show lists of names with details, and small or large icons.

► See "Managing Your Files and Folders," p. 513

► See "Working with Long File Names," p. 509

► See "Improving Performance with Disk Defragmenter," p. 486

- My Computer and Explorer also give you access to features such as the Control Panel and Printers. Double-click these folders to change computer and printer settings.

Power Users Very Experienced with Windows

► See "Synchronizing Files," p. 533

► See "Using Explorer with Shared Resources on a Network," p. 544

► See "Monitoring Your System," p. 483

If you consider yourself a power user and are very experienced with Windows, the important things to notice are:

- You'll probably prefer to use the Explorer because you can see more file and folder information at a glance.
- If you are used to side-by-side windows from the File Manager, you can recreate them in the Explorer. Open two instances of the Explorer, right-click in a gray area of the taskbar, and then click Tile Vertically.
- All system resources are visible and most are changeable by opening the Control Panel and then System. Click the Device Manager tab. To see properties of any hardware device, click the device and then click Properties. (Select the Computer item to see IRQ and I/O settings for all devices.) ❖

Part II

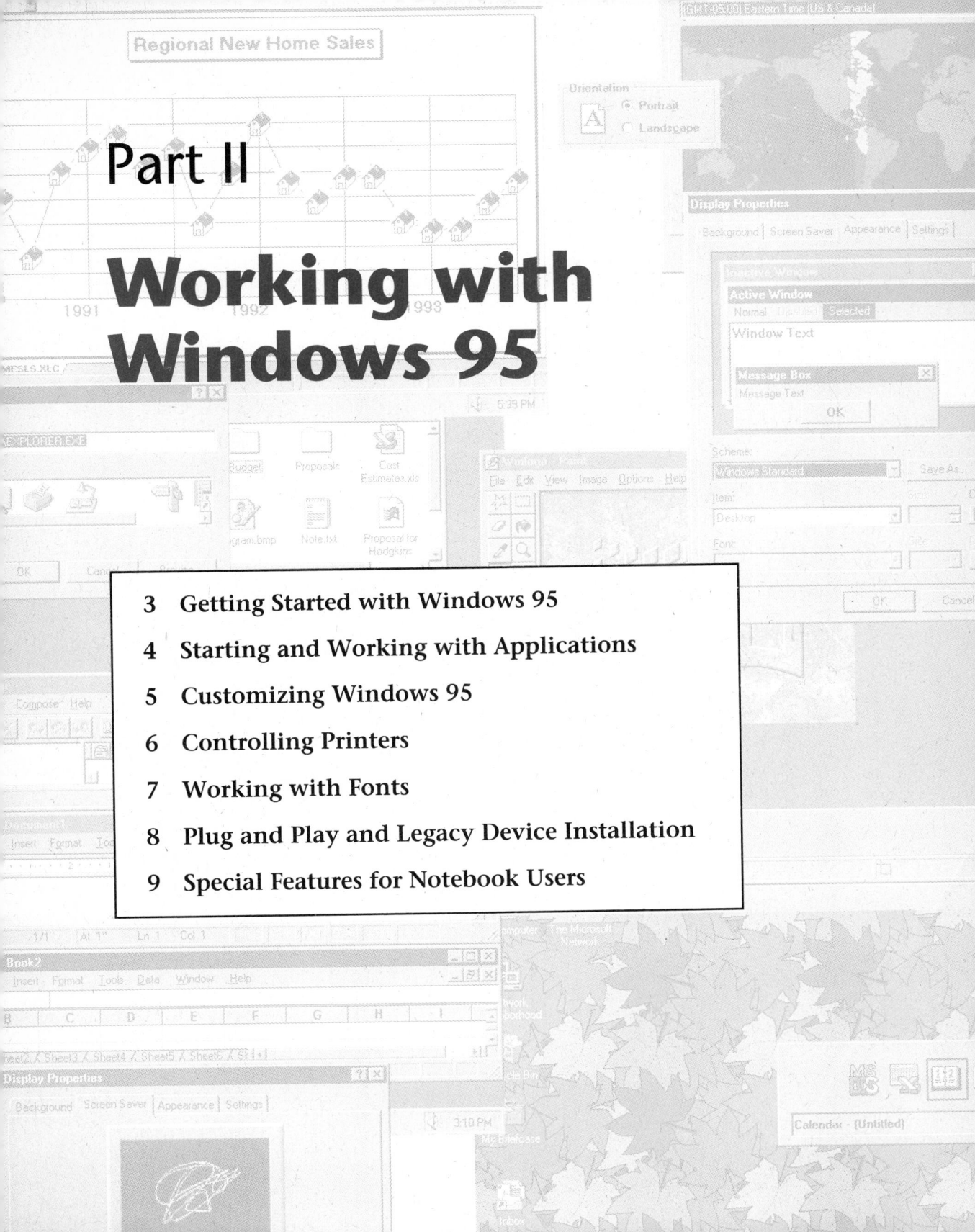

Working with Windows 95

Regional New Home Sales
1991
1992
1993
HOMESLS.XLC
Orientation
Portrait
Landscape
Display Properties
Background
Screen Saver
Appearance
Settings
Inactive Window
Active Window
Normal
Disabled
Selected
Window Text
Message Box
Message Text
OK
Scheme:
Windows Standard
Item:
Desktop
Font:
Winlogo - Paint
File
Edit
View
Image
Options
Help
Budget
Proposals
Cost Estimates.xls
Note.txt
Proposal for Hodgkins
OK
Cancel
Browse...
334KB
Exchange
Figures
My Documents
Compose
Name
Programs
Documents
Settings
Find
Help
Run...
Shut Down...
Windows95
Start
Winlogo - Paint
Document1
Insert
Format
Tools
Table
Window
Help
At 1"
Ln 1
Col 1
Book2
Data
Display Properties
Background
Screen Saver
Appearance
Settings
5:39 PM
3:10 PM
The Microsoft Network
My Briefcase
Inbox
Calendar - [Untitled]

Chapter 3

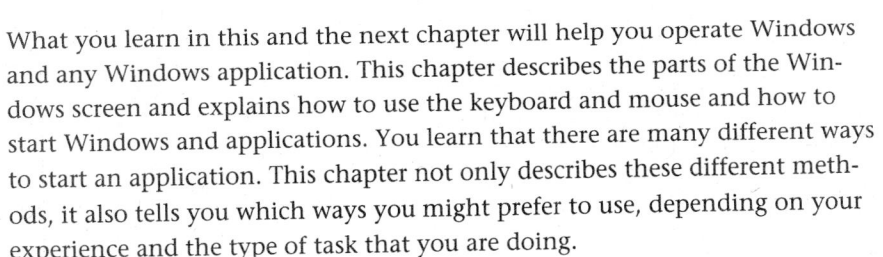

Getting Started with Windows 95

by Ron Person

What you learn in this and the next chapter will help you operate Windows and any Windows application. This chapter describes the parts of the Windows screen and explains how to use the keyboard and mouse and how to start Windows and applications. You learn that there are many different ways to start an application. This chapter not only describes these different methods, it also tells you which ways you might prefer to use, depending on your experience and the type of task that you are doing.

This chapter also briefly introduces the Windows Explorer and My Computer (which Chapter 17, "Managing Your Files with Explorer," covers in more detail) and teaches you some tricks for getting out of trouble when Windows or one of your programs misbehaves.

In this chapter, you learn

- How to start and quit Windows
- How to start Windows after computer problems occur
- The terms for and parts of Windows and Windows applications
- How to use the mouse or keyboard to operate Windows
- How to run programs automatically at startup
- How to start applications from the Start menu
- How to add programs to the Start menu
- How to create shortcuts for starting programs

- How to use the Explorer and My Computer to start applications
- How to manage Windows when a program fails

Starting and Quitting Windows

If you have not yet installed Windows, turn to Appendix A, "Installing and Uninstalling Windows 95," to learn how. After you install Windows, you can start and display Windows simply by turning on your computer. If you are familiar with previous versions of Windows, you might expect Windows 95 to go directly into DOS as it starts, but in most cases Windows 95 starts as soon as you turn on your computer. If your computer requires DOS drivers, you may see a DOS-like text screen as the drivers load. Also, if your Windows has multiple configurations installed—as a laptop or desktop version, for example—a text screen will display asking you to choose between the configurations. Once you make your choice, Windows starts.

Tip
The first time you start Windows, you will see a Welcome to Windows 95 dialog box. You can turn this dialog box off by clicking the Show this Welcome Screen check box.

When Windows appears, you will see a login sheet in which you should type your password. Windows uses the password from the login sheet for two purposes. If the computer is connected to a network, it logs you into the network using your network password. Windows can also use the password from the login sheet to detect which person is using the computer. Because different people may have customized Windows in different ways, the login sheet enables Windows to customize itself to the way you prefer to work with Windows.

Once login sheets are completed, Windows starts and displays the desktop with My Computer, Recycle Bin, and Network Neighborhood icons. You might also see a My Briefcase icon and shortcut icons created by prior users. The *taskbar* usually appears at the bottom of the screen, although it might appear in another location or not at all.

Caution

Incorrectly exiting Windows can result in the loss of data. Be sure you see a display message saying it is safe to turn off your computer before you turn it off.

When you finish running Windows applications and Windows, you must not turn off the computer until you correctly exit Windows. Windows stores some data in memory and does not write it to your hard disk until you choose the Shut Down command. If you turn off the computer without correctly exiting, you might lose this data. To exit Windows correctly, follow these steps:

1. Save the data in the applications in which you are working. If you forget to do so, most applications ask whether you want to save open documents when you exit the application.

2. Exit any DOS applications that you are running.

3. Open the Start menu and choose Shut Down. The dialog box shown in figure 3.1 displays. (Your options may vary depending on your configuration.)

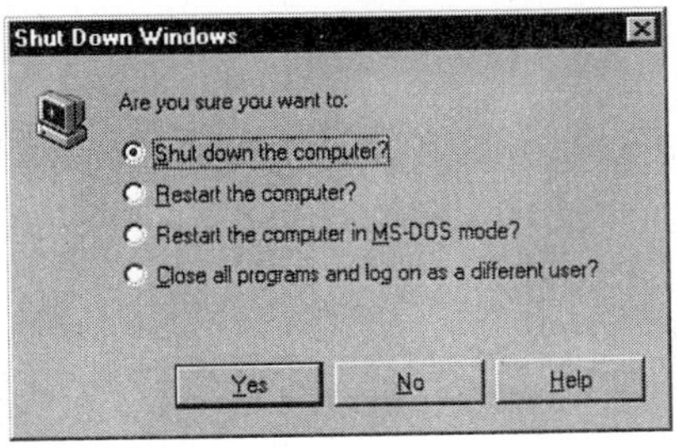

Fig. 3.1
Windows enables you to shut down the computer, restart Windows, restart the computer in DOS mode, or close all applications and log on with another user ID.

4. Choose the Shut Down the Computer? option.

5. Click Yes.

6. Turn off your computer when you see the message that says that it is safe to do so.

If your computer and Windows are set up to work on a network, you see the Close All Programs and Log On as a Different User? option when you choose the Shut Down command from the Start menu.

Tip
If you share a computer with others, you must restart to use your customized features. Shut down with the Close All Programs and Log On as a Different User? option.

Do not turn off the computer hardware until you see a message saying that you can safely do so. This message might take as long as two or three minutes to appear. Turning off the computer before you see this message might result in your losing the data for applications you were working in or not updating the Registry if you made changes to applications.

Starting Applications at Startup

If you work with certain programs each time that you use your computer, you can tell Windows to start these programs automatically when you turn on your computer. You can even tell Windows how you want the program to appear at startup—either in a window, maximized, or minimized—so that it appears as a button in the taskbar.

You can also specify that Windows open certain documents at startup. In this case, Windows starts the program associated with the document in addition to opening the document.

Running Programs on Startup

► See "Customizing the Start Menu," p. 128

To specify the programs that you want to run at startup, you add them to the Startup folder. The easiest way to do this is with the Taskbar Properties sheet, which has a Wizard that guides you through the process step by step. Any programs that you add to the Startup folder appear in the Startup menu, which is a submenu of the Programs menu (see fig. 3.2).

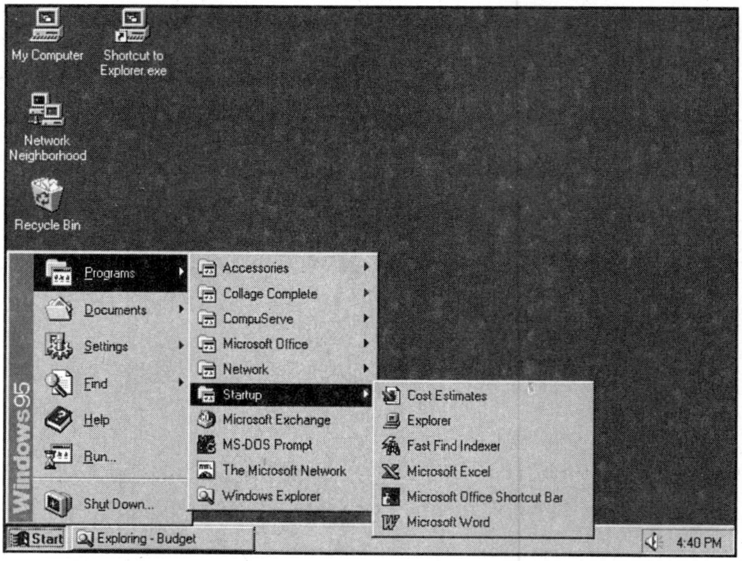

Fig. 3.2
Programs that you add to the Startup folder appear in the Startup menu and run automatically when you start Windows.

To specify programs that you want Windows to run at startup, follow these steps:

1. Open the Start menu and choose Settings, Taskbar.
2. Select the Start Menu Programs tab, as shown in figure 3.3.
3. Choose Add and then Browse.
4. Select the program that you want to add to the Startup folder by double-clicking the folder in which the program is located and then double-clicking the program.
5. Click Next.

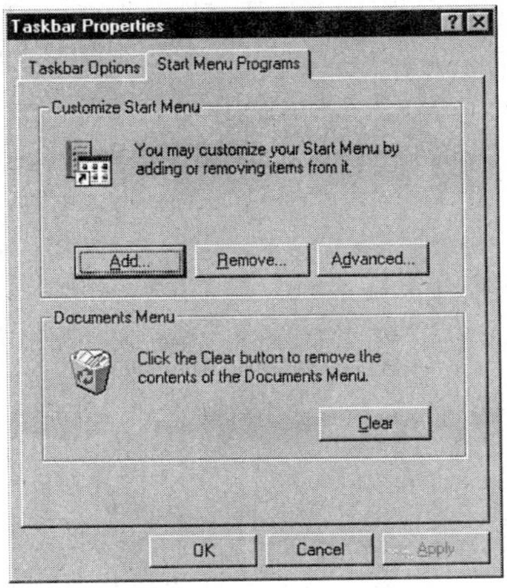

Fig. 3.3
Use the Start Menu Programs page to specify programs to run at startup.

6. Double-click the Startup folder.
7. Accept the default title for the program or type a new title in the Select a Name for the Shortcut text box. The name that you enter appears in the Startup menu.
8. Click Finish.
9. Repeat steps 3 through 8 to add more programs to the Startup folder, or choose OK if you are finished adding programs.

Note

If you frequently change the programs or documents that you want to run on startup, make the Startup folder accessible on the desktop so you can drag program or document files in and out of it. First, create a shortcut icon on the desktop for the Startup folder. Use a right mouse drag-and-drop to drag program or document files from Windows Explorer or My Computer into the Startup folder. Creating shortcuts is described in the section "Creating Shortcut Icons on the Desktop to Start Programs" later in this chapter.

To remove a program from the Startup folder, follow these steps:

1. Choose Remove on the Start Menu Programs page.
2. Double-click the Startup folder.

3. Select the program that you want to remove and choose Remove.

4. Choose Close.

Specifying Documents to Open at Startup

► See "Registering Files to Automatically Open an Application," p. 539

If you regularly work with particular documents each time that you use your computer—for example, if you have a budget worksheet that you work on every day—you can tell Windows to open such documents automatically at startup. For Windows to open a document automatically, the document must be associated with a program. For many programs, Windows automatically associates the documents it creates with the program. This association enables you to open a document and the program that created it simultaneously.

To specify a document to open at startup, you follow the same procedure outlined in the preceding section, "Running Programs on Startup," except that in step 4, you select a document rather than a program. After you do so, the program associated with the document automatically runs at startup and the specified document opens.

Controlling How Startup Programs Appear

Tip
Alternatively, you can double-click the shortcut icon you just created.

After specifying that a program run at startup, you can tell Windows how you want the program to display when it starts. By default, Windows runs the program in a normal window. However, you can also choose to have the program run *maximized*, so that it fills the screen, or *minimized*, so that it appears as a button on the taskbar.

To control how a program appears on startup, follow these steps:

1. Add the program to the Startup folder, as described earlier in the section "Running Programs on Startup."

► See "Using the Windows Explorer to View Files and Folders," p. 499

2. Open the Startup folder in either My Computer or Explorer. The Startup folder is located as a subfolder in WINDOWS\START MENU\PROGRAMS\STARTUP.

3. On the program that you want to appear on startup, click the right mouse button; then choose Properties.

4. Select the Shortcut tab.

5. Select one of the three options from the Run drop-down list, as shown in figure 3.4.

6. Choose OK.

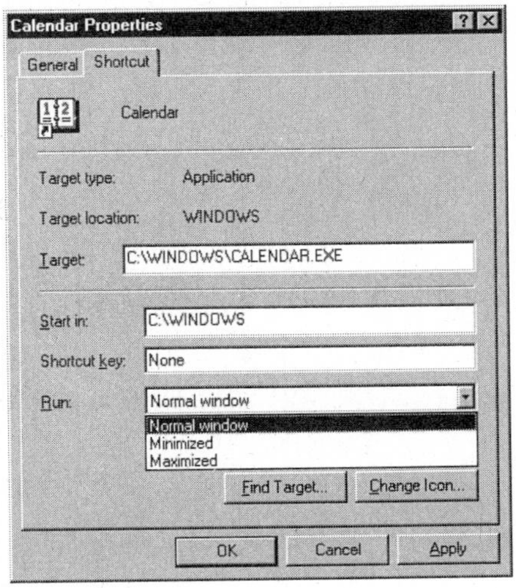

Fig. 3.4
The Properties sheet is being used to configure how the application Calendar will run on startup.

Starting Windows after Technical Problems Occur

If you have any trouble starting Windows after you install it, it's good to know some of the avenues that you can take to get out of trouble. In this section, you learn how to create a startup disk, which enables you to start Windows if it doesn't start normally. You also learn how to start Windows in *safe mode*, which can be helpful if you are having certain kinds of problems.

Creating a Startup Disk

If you have trouble starting Windows, you might need to use a startup disk to start your computer. For example, if you inadvertently delete a file that Windows needs for startup, you must start Windows with the startup disk in your disk drive and then remedy the problem so that you can start Windows normally.

When you install Windows, you have an opportunity to create a startup disk, which you should label and always keep on hand. If you didn't create the startup disk during installation or have misplaced the disk, you can create one after Windows is installed. Be sure to do so now, before you need the disk. Otherwise, if you have problems starting Windows, you won't be able to get into Windows to create the startup disk. (You might, however, be able to use another computer to create a startup disk.)

To create a startup disk, follow these steps:

1. Open the Start menu and choose Settings, Control Panel.

2. Double-click the Add/Remove Programs button.

3. Click the Startup Disk tab, as shown in figure 3.5.

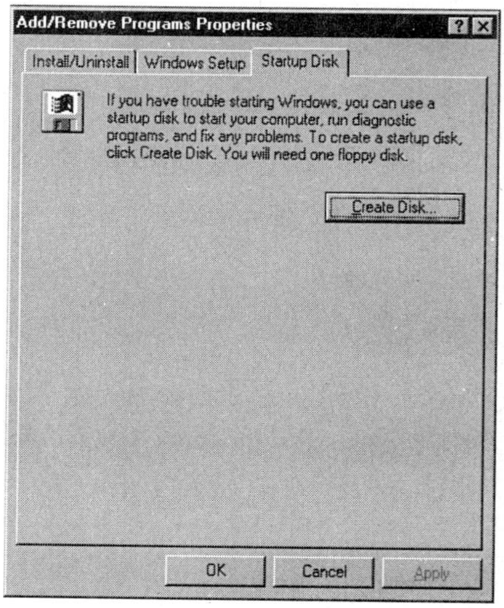

Fig. 3.5
To create a startup disk, click the Startup Disk tab in the Add/Remove Programs Properties sheet.

4. Insert a disk in your disk drive. The contents of this disk will be deleted.

   If you have both a 5 1/4-inch and 3 1/2-inch drive, use the A drive (usually the 3 1/2-inch drive on newer computers). This is the drive from which your computer attempts to boot if a disk is in the drive.

5. Choose Create Disk and follow the instructions as they appear on-screen.

   To create the startup disk, you must have your original Windows program disks (or CD-ROM) handy.

6. Click OK.

Store your startup disk somewhere safe and easy to remember. If you have a laptop, you should store your startup disk in your laptop case.

To use the startup disk, insert it in the disk drive and reboot the computer. You can now diagnose and correct the problem so that you can start

Windows normally. If you are having problems getting Windows started, or it starts but the video or some other piece of hardware does not operate correctly, read the next section for instructions on diagnosing and correcting problems.

Starting Windows in Safe Mode

Sometimes when you have trouble starting Windows, starting Windows in *safe mode* is helpful. When you do so, Windows uses basic default settings that at least get you back into the Windows environment, where you can fix the problem. For example, if you install the wrong driver for a new monitor, you might not be able to see the Windows display when you restart Windows. In this case, restarting Windows with the default settings helps because you can see the screen, enter the Control Panel, and set up a different display.

The default settings use a generic VGA monitor driver, no network settings, the standard Microsoft mouse driver, and the minimum device drivers necessary to start Windows. (*Device drivers* are software that enables hardware to work with Windows.) When you start Windows with the default settings, you cannot access any CD-ROM drives, printers, or other extra hardware devices. But you can at least access Windows and then diagnose and correct the problem.

► See "Getting Help," p. 79

To start Windows in a different mode, follow these steps:

1. Turn on the computer. Make sure that you also turn on the display monitor so that you can see the screen as Windows attempts to start. Be ready to press the F8 key.

2. When the message `Starting Windows` appears on-screen, press F8 to display the Windows 95 Startup Menu. This displays a menu of choices for starting Windows in different modes. Safe Mode is choice 3; Safe Mode with Network Support is choice 4. Or select one of the other startup modes.

3. Type the selection number for the Safe Mode or Safe Mode with Network Support. Press Enter.

To skip the Startup Menu and start directly in a mode, start your computer and press one of the key combinations in the following table when the message `Starting Windows` appears.

Key Combination	Operating Mode
F5	Loads HIMEM.SYS and IFSHLP.SYS, loads DoubleSpace or DriveSpace if present, then runs Windows 95 WIN.COM. Starts in safe mode.
Shift+F5	Loads COMMAND.COM and loads DoubleSpace or DriveSpace if present.
Ctrl+F5	Loads COMMAND.COM.
F6	Loads HIMEM.SYS and IFSHLP.SYS. Processes the Registry, loads COMMAND.COM, loads DoubleSpace or DriveSpace if present, runs Windows 95 WIN.COM, loads network drivers, and runs NETSTART.BAT.

▶ See "Checking Performance Settings," p. 164

A message informs you that Windows is running in safe mode and that some of your devices might not be available. The words `Safe mode` appear at each corner of the screen.

Learning the Parts of the Windows Display

Windows screens display many graphical elements. Learning the names of these graphic elements or icons is important because you'll see these terms throughout this book. Likewise, you need to be familiar with these elements and icons because you can invoke a command for Windows or a Windows program by clicking the mouse pointer on many of them.

Figure 3.6 shows a Windows desktop that contains multiple applications, each in its own window. The figure also identifies the parts of a typical Windows screen.

In the desktop shown in figure 3.6, the Start button appears in the lower-left corner. This button provides one of the easiest ways to start programs or to open documents that you have recently used. (The Start button and taskbar may appear along different edges of the screen if a previous user has moved them.) With the mouse, you can click the Start button to open the Start menu. With the keyboard, you press Ctrl+Esc.

▶ See "Customizing the Taskbar," p. 122

Across the bottom of the screen is the taskbar. The taskbar displays all programs currently open and running. You can switch between different programs by clicking the mouse pointer on the program that you want in the taskbar. To use the keyboard, press Alt+Tab to select the program and then release the keys.

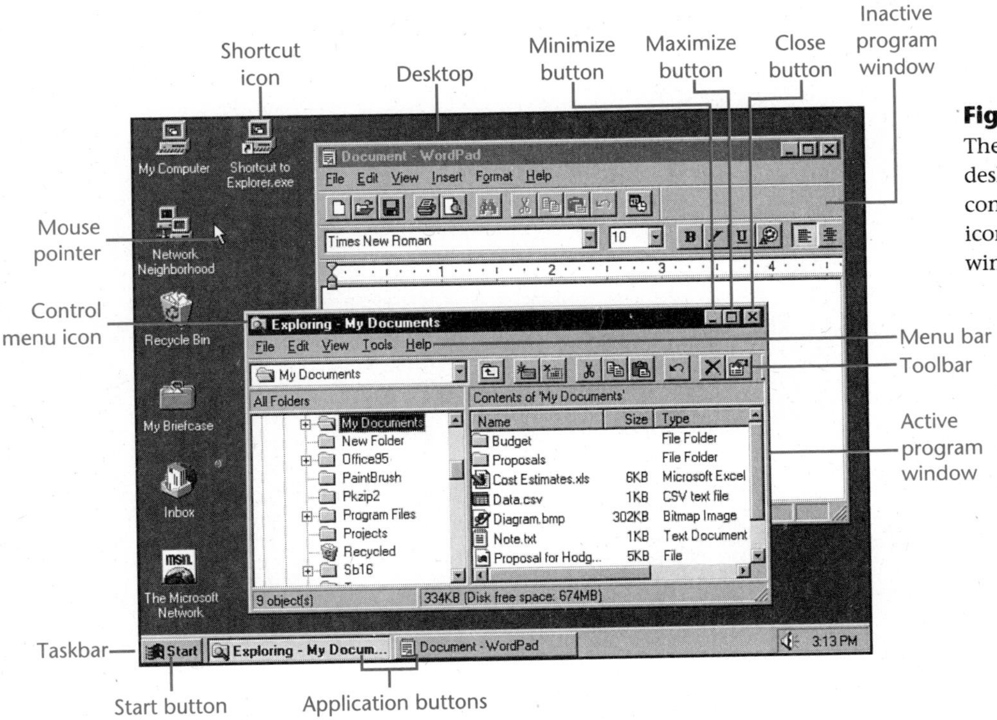

Fig. 3.6
The Windows desktop can contain multiple icons and program windows.

► See "Moving the Taskbar," p. 124

The taskbar might appear in a different location on your screen. You can move the taskbar by dragging it to another location. You can also remove the taskbar from the screen by customizing your screen as described in Chapter 5, "Customizing Windows 95."

With the mouse pointer, you can control Windows applications quickly and intuitively. The mouse pointer enables you to choose commands, select options, and move on-screen items. When you move the mouse, the mouse pointer moves synchronously. At different locations on the screen, the mouse pointer changes shape to indicate that it has capabilities specific to its current location. To select an item on the screen, you position the pointer on the item and then press or hold down the mouse button. You use four actions to affect on-screen items that are under the tip of the pointer: clicking, double-clicking, right-clicking, and dragging.

Windows enables you to run more than one program at the same time. Each program appears in its own window or as an item on the taskbar at the bottom of the screen. When programs are in windows, the program in the topmost window is the *active* program in the *active* window. Usually, the color of the active windows title bar differs from that of inactive windows. The active window receives your keyboard commands. One of the advantages of Windows is that even while you are working with the active program in the active window, other programs can be working.

The title bar at the top of each window displays the name of the application in the window. After you save a file, the title bar also shows the file name. (The active window is the one on top; it contains the currently running application.)

Tip
Throughout this book, the letter that you press in combination with Alt to open a menu command is underlined, as in File.

The menu bar, which is directly under the title bar, displays the menu names. Windows applications use the same menu headings for common functions (such as File, Edit, Window, and Help), which makes it easier for you to learn new applications. To open a menu, click on its name with the left mouse button, or press Alt and then the underlined letter in the menu name.

Icons are small, graphic representations. To reduce the clutter of a filled desktop, you can minimize windows so that they appear as icons on the taskbar. Even if not currently displayed in a window, an application is still running if the taskbar displays its icon. The taskbar appears at the bottom of figure 3.6.

Troubleshooting

Pressing Alt+Tab just seems to alternate between two applications.

Hold down the Alt key as you press Tab and you will see a bar displaying icons of all the running applications. As you continue to hold down the Alt key, each press of the Tab key selects the next application icon on the bar. When the application you want is selected, release both the Alt and the Tab keys.

Using the Mouse and Keyboard on the Desktop

With the dominance of the *graphical user interface* (GUI) on today's personal computers, using a mouse has become second nature to most computer users. In Windows 95, you use the mouse even more than in earlier versions of Windows. Although you can still perform most tasks in the Windows environment with the keyboard, you can accomplish them much more quickly with the mouse. Also, many shortcuts are accessible only with the mouse. For example, in Windows 95 you use the right mouse button extensively to access shortcut menus that can significantly reduce the number of steps that it takes to invoke a command. Even if you are a diehard keyboard addict, you should explore the Windows environment with your mouse. You might be surprised by the things that you can now do with the mouse.

This section explains the basic steps that you need to know to perform tasks with the mouse. If you already know how to use the mouse, you might want to skip this section.

► See "Customizing the Mouse," p. 147

► See "Customizing the Keyboard," p. 148

Windows users routinely use the mouse to select text, objects, menus and their commands, toolbar buttons, and dialog box options, and to scroll through documents. To perform such tasks, you need to know how to point and click with the mouse.

To click items using the mouse, follow these steps:

1. Move the mouse so that the tip of the mouse pointer, usually an arrow, is on the menu, command, dialog box item, graphics object, or a position within the text. (When moved over editable text, the pointer changes to the shape of the letter I, also called the *I-beam*.)

2. With a single, quick motion, press and release the left mouse button.

Throughout this book, this two-step process is called *clicking*. Clicking the mouse button twice in rapid succession while pointing is called *double-clicking*. Double-clicking produces an action different than clicking. In a word processing application, for example, you often click to position the insertion point but double-click to select a word.

You also can use the mouse for *dragging*. Dragging selects multiple text characters or moves graphic objects such as windows.

To drag with the mouse, follow these steps:

1. Move the mouse so that the tip of the pointer is on the object or at the beginning of the text that you want to select. (When over text, the pointer appears as an I-beam.)

2. Press and hold down the left mouse button.

3. Move the mouse while holding down the mouse button. If you are dragging a graphical object, the object moves when you move the mouse. If you are selecting text, the highlighted text area expands as you move the mouse.

4. Release the mouse button.

An important enhancement to Windows 95 is the extensive use of the right mouse button. Putting the tip of the pointer on many objects on-screen and clicking the right mouse button displays a shortcut menu with commands specific to that object. For example, right-clicking a file name produces a shortcut menu containing commands such as Copy, Delete, and Rename. In some situations, such as dragging a file name onto the desktop, you will want to drag using the right mouse button. In this case, you would drag as you would using the left mouse button, but hold down the right mouse key. When you release the item, a shortcut menu will appear, from which you can quickly choose your next action.

The mouse is a useful tool, but you can use the keyboard to do nearly everything that you can do with the mouse. The mouse and the keyboard work as a team for controlling Windows applications. You can perform some tasks more easily with the mouse and some more easily with the keyboard. With most Windows applications, you can perform all functions with either. Experiment with the mouse and the keyboard, and use each where it works best for you. The next section gives you detailed information on how to use the mouse and keyboard to accomplish various tasks in the Windows environment.

Starting Applications from the Start Menu and Taskbar

Most of the work that you do on your computer consists of opening a program, using the program to create or modify a document, saving the document as a file, and then closing the program. Windows is designed to make these routine tasks as simple as possible.

One of the most important tasks that you must know how to do is to open or start programs in Windows. This task is very simple to do in Windows. You can open a program in several ways, so you can choose which works best for you. This section describes the different methods for starting programs and for using the Start menu, shortcuts, the Windows Explorer, and My Computer. You also learn what to do if a program fails or locks up when you are using it.

Using the Start Menu

The simplest way for a new Windows user to open a program is to use the Start menu. When you install Windows, the installation program usually places each of your programs on a submenu that appears off the Start menu. You can open the program simply by selecting it from a menu (see fig. 3.7).

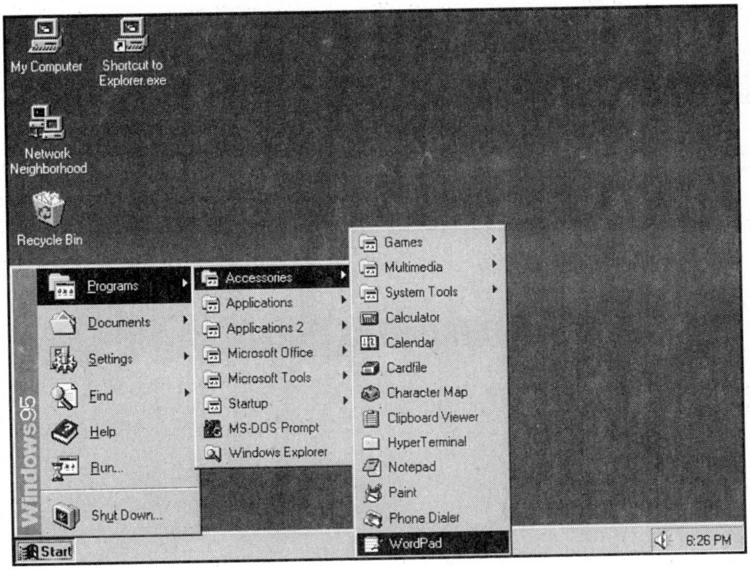

Fig. 3.7
You can select the program that you want to start from one of the menus that cascades from the Start menu. Here, the user is choosing to start WordPad.

Note

If you are upgrading from an older version of Windows to Windows 95, the Group windows that appeared within the Program Manager will become submenus that appear off Programs in the Start menu.

If you are familiar with Windows and want to make your programs more accessible, you can add the programs that you use most frequently to the Start menu. Then you don't have to move through a series of menus to start these programs. In this chapter, you also learn how to create a shortcut icon on the desktop that starts an application. These powerful features of Windows give you immediate access to your programs. You learn these techniques later in this section.

When to Work from the Start Menu

If you are just getting started with Windows 95, you will probably want to use the Start menu to start your programs. Then all you have to learn is how to open the Start menu and select the programs that you want.

After you become more comfortable or familiar with Windows, you might still want to use the Start menu. However, you first will want to add your frequently used programs to the first level of the Start menu. This gives you immediate access to your programs and saves you from having to work your way through a series of submenus.

▶ See "Customizing the Start Menu," p. 128

Understanding the Start Menu

The Start menu is the starting place for many of the tasks you want to accomplish in Windows. You can open the Start menu at any time, from within any program, with one mouse click. From the Start menu, you can open your programs, customize the look and feel of Windows, find files and folders, get help, and shut down your computer (see fig. 3.8). While providing all the power of immediate access, the Start menu also is integral to the clean look of the Windows desktop, enabling you to minimize the clutter on your desktop.

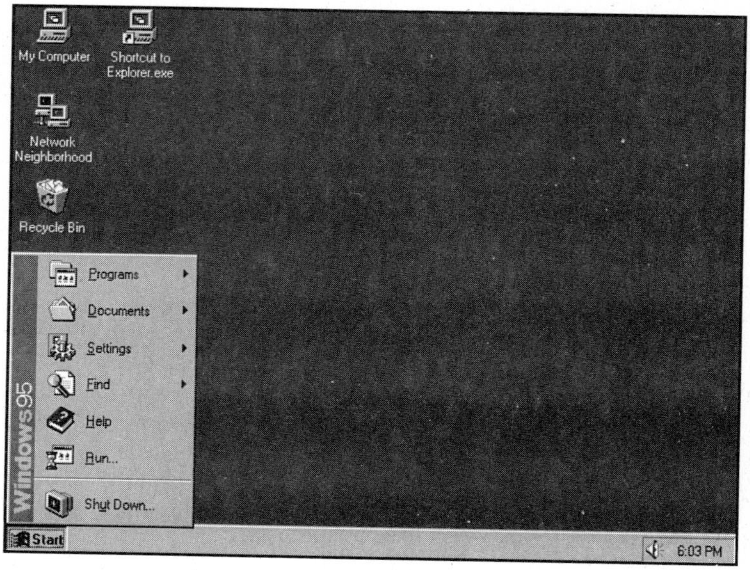

Fig. 3.8
The Start menu is just a mouse click away and gives you instant access to all your programs and many other Windows features.

Tip
If you are an experienced Windows user, do not be put off by the Start menu. Windows 95 can be customized to be much faster to use than previous versions of Windows.

Use the Start menu whenever you need to open a program or access other features of Windows. You can open the Start menu at any time, even when you are working in another application such as Paint, as shown in figure 3.9. This is much simpler than in earlier versions of Windows, where you had to switch back to Program Manager to open other programs.

Troubleshooting

The windows of some programs written for older versions of Windows cover the taskbar, so it is difficult to switch between applications or click the Start button.

Even when you can't see the taskbar, you can switch between applications by holding down the Alt key and pressing Tab. A bar appears with icons for each application. Press Tab until the application you want is selected, then release both keys.

To simultaneously display the taskbar and open the Start menu, press Ctrl+Esc.

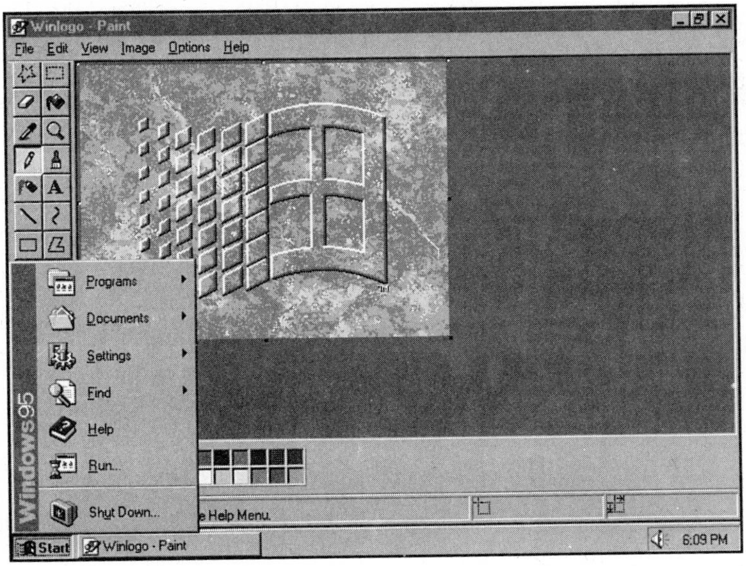

Fig. 3.9
You can open the Start menu without having to leave the program in which you are working. Here, the Start menu appears at the bottom of the Paint program.

Starting a Program from the Start Menu

To start a program from the Start menu, use the mouse to select the program from a menu and then click. It's that easy. You can also use the keyboard, although Windows is definitely designed to work most efficiently with a mouse.

To start a program using the Start menu, follow these steps:

1. Click the Start button in the taskbar to open the Start menu.

   If you have customized your computer, you might not see the taskbar and Start button at the bottom of your screen. If you see a gray line at one edge of the screen, move the pointer to that edge to display the taskbar. With the keyboard you can press Ctrl+Esc to display the taskbar and open the Start menu.

2. Point to Programs on the Start menu. The Program menu then appears to the right. Then point to the program that you want to start and click.

   If the Programs menu doesn't list the program you want to start, click the folder that contains the program. In figure 3.10, the user has selected WordPad from the Accessories submenu; when the user clicks the mouse, Windows opens that program. To find the program that you want, you might have to move through a series of submenus.

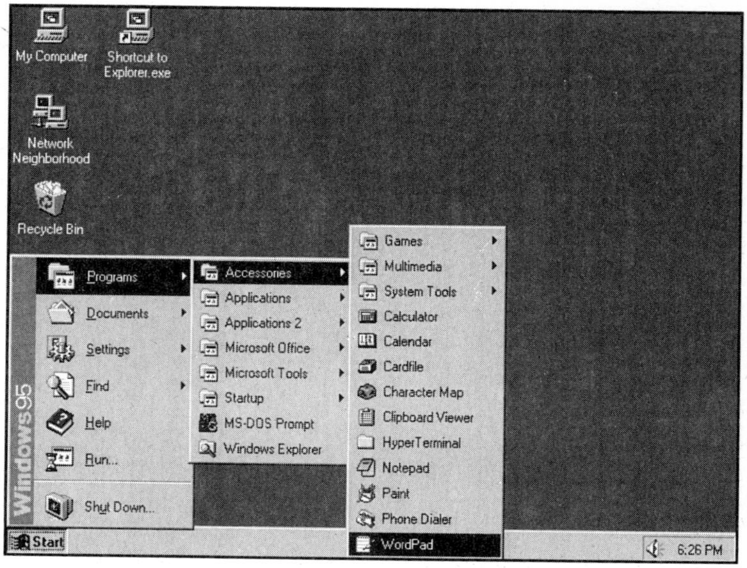

Fig. 3.10
Open the menu that contains the program you want to start and then click the program.

If you are using a keyboard and do not have a mouse available, open the Start menu by pressing Ctrl+Esc, and then use arrow keys to move up and down the menu. Press Enter to select the currently highlighted menu or program.

▶ See "Switching between Applications," p. 118

When you open a program, a button for the program appears in the taskbar. These buttons tell you which programs are open and enable you to move quickly from one open program to another.

▶ See "Customizing the Start Menu," p. 128

Note

Usually you should find the program that you want to open in one of the Start menu's submenus. When you install Windows, the installation program looks for all your applications and puts each in one of the menus. If, however, you can't find your program in the Start menus, you can add a program or folder to the Start menu by following the procedures described in Chapter 5.

Starting a Document from the Start Menu

After you click the Start button, notice a Documents command in the Start menu. When you choose this command, the Documents submenu appears with a listing of the files that you have worked on recently (see fig. 3.11). To open a document in this list, simply click on it. Windows then automatically starts the associated application, if it is not already running, and opens the document.

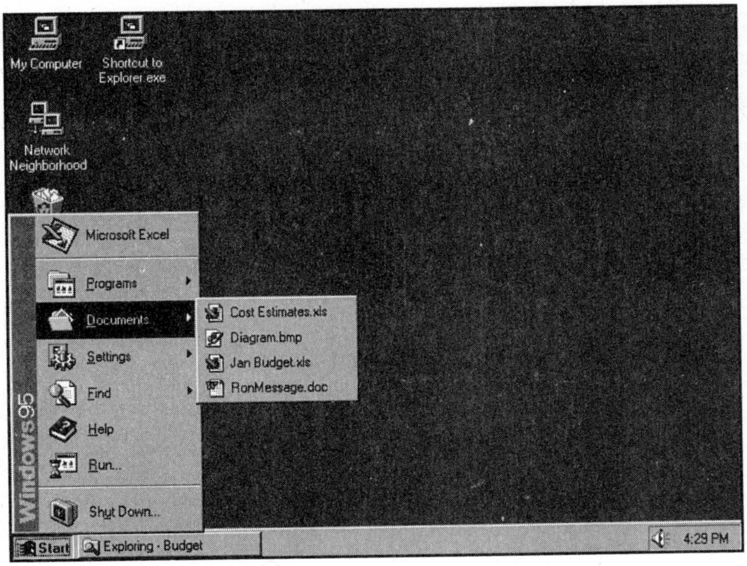

Fig. 3.11
The Start menu maintains a list of the documents that you have worked with most recently. Click on one to load it into its application.

After a while, the listing in the Documents menu can become quite long and contain documents that you no longer are working with. To clear the list, click the Start button, choose Settings, and then choose Taskbar. Select the Start Menu Programs tab on the Taskbar Properties sheet and choose the Clear button (see fig. 3.12). Click OK to close the Properties sheet.

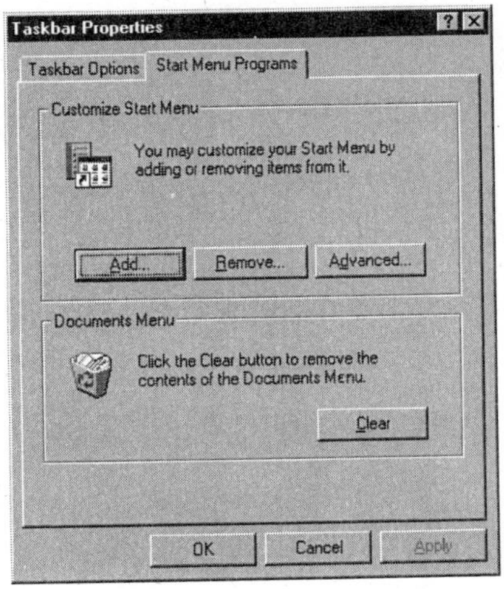

Fig. 3.12
You can clear the Documents list from the Start Menu Programs page.

Starting Programs from a Shortcut Icon on the Desktop

Another method for starting programs is to create shortcuts for the programs that you use most frequently. These shortcuts can appear as icons on your desktop. To start a program, you simply double-click its icon. If you don't like using menus to start your programs, you might prefer using shortcuts. A drawback to this method, however, is that to access the shortcut icons, your desktop must be visible. If a program is maximized, you cannot see the shortcuts.

You can always tell whether an icon represents a shortcut, because a little arrow appears beneath the icon (see fig. 3.13).

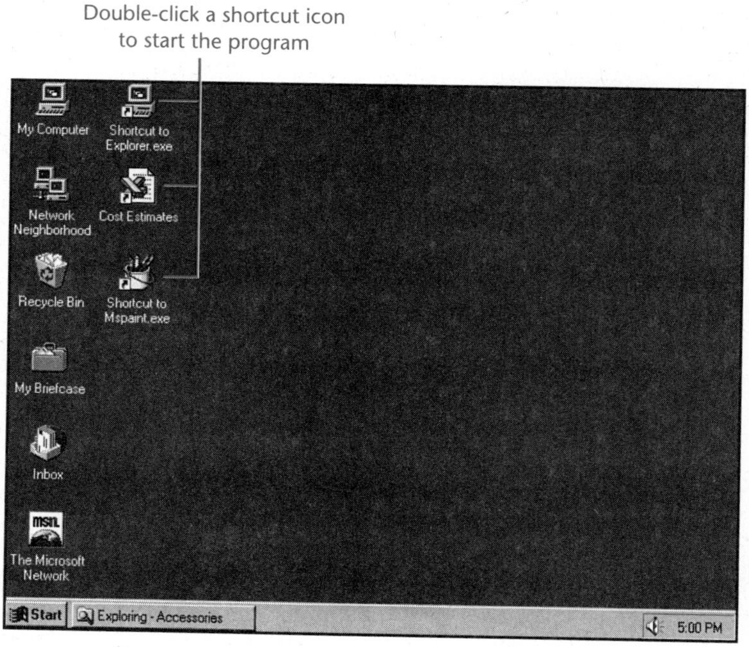

Fig. 3.13
This desktop has three shortcuts, as indicated by the arrows. To start an application, you double-click its icon.

Creating Shortcut Icons on the Desktop to Start Programs

To create a shortcut for a program on your desktop, follow these steps:

1. Using the Explorer or My Computer, locate the program for which you want to create a shortcut.

See Chapter 17, "Managing Your Files with Explorer," to learn how to use the Explorer and My Computer for browsing files and folders.

2. Select the program in the Explorer or My Computer window.
3. Click the program with the right mouse button and choose Copy.
4. Click the desktop with the right mouse button and choose Paste Shortcut.

The icon now appears on your desktop. You can drag the icon to any location. Refer to figure 3.13 earlier, which shows the desktop with three shortcuts.

You also can create a shortcut for a document. Find the document in the Explorer or My Computer, and create a shortcut for the document as described in the preceding steps. If the document is associated (or registered) with a program, you can start the program and open the document by double-clicking its shortcut.

Tip

Drag a file from My Computer or Explorer onto the desktop with the right mouse button. Drop the file and select Create Shortcut(s) Here to create a shortcut icon on the desktop.

Troubleshooting

Double-clicking a shortcut icon no longer opens the document or program.

What may have happened is that the file to which the shortcut pointed was moved or deleted. To correct this problem, you can either delete and then re-create the shortcut, or you can correct its Properties sheet. To delete the shortcut icon, right-click the icon, and then choose Delete. Choose Yes when asked to confirm the deletion. Re-create the shortcut with the methods described in this section. To fix a shortcut to a file that has moved, right-click on the icon, and then choose Properties. Click on the Shortcut tab. Check the file and path name in the Target box. They may be wrong. To find the file, click on the Find Target button. This opens a window in My Computer to the file if it is found. If it cannot be found, you can search in My Computer for the correct file and path name.

Setting the Properties for a Shortcut Icon

You can change how a shortcut icon acts and how it appears by opening its Properties sheet and changing its properties. On the Properties sheet, you can find information such as when a shortcut was created. You also can make a variety of changes, such as the following:

- Change the file that the shortcut opens.
- Make an application start in a folder you specify.

- Add a shortcut key that activates the shortcut.
- Indicate whether you want the document or application to run minimized, maximized, or in a window.
- Change the icon used for a shortcut.

To display the Properties sheet and set the properties for a shortcut icon, follow these steps:

1. Right-click on the shortcut icon.
2. Click the Properties command to display the General page of the Shortcut Properties sheet, shown in figure 3.14.

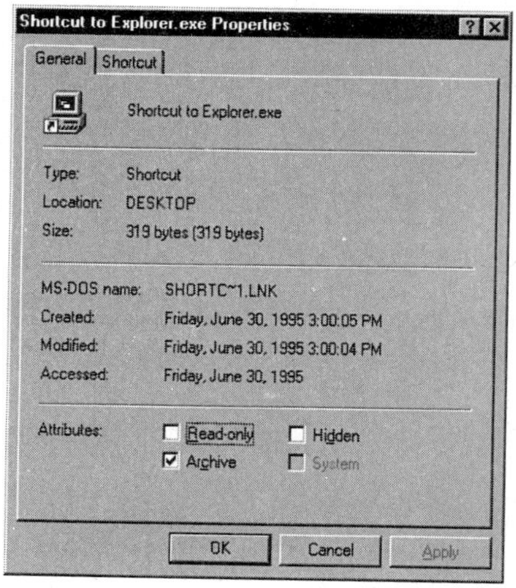

Fig. 3.14
The General page shows you file information about the shortcut icon.

Tip
If your data files for a program are not in the same directory as the program, use the Start In edit box to enter the path to your data files.

On the General page, you can read where the LNK file for the shortcut is stored, as well as when it was created, modified, and last used. You also can change its file attributes.

3. Click the Shortcut tab to see the Shortcut page, shown in figure 3.15.

   At the top of the page, you can read the type of shortcut it is and the folder in which it is located. In the figure, the shortcut is to the Explorer application in the WINDOWS folder.

4. If you want a different file to start from the shortcut, click in the Target edit box and type the folder and file name.

If you are unsure of the location, click Find Target to open a My Computer window in which you can look for the file and folder you want. Once you find the folder and file, close the My Computer window and type the name in the Target text box.

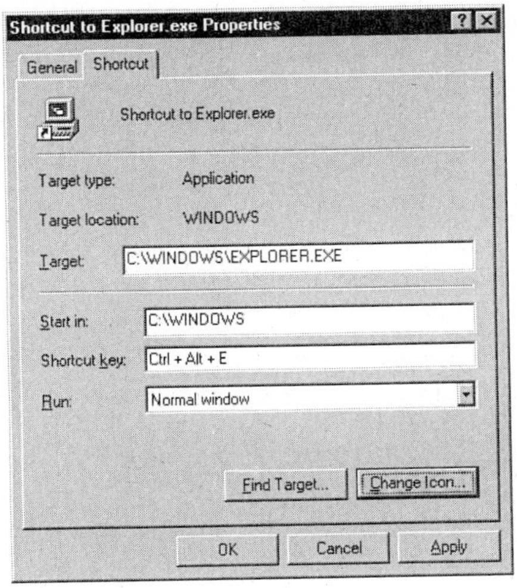

Fig. 3.15
The Shortcut page enables you to specify the file, startup folder, shortcut key, and icon used by a shortcut.

5. To specify a folder that contains the file or files necessary for operation, click in the Start In text box and enter the drive and folders.

6. To specify a shortcut key that will activate this shortcut icon, click in the Shortcut Key text box and then press the key you want as the shortcut key. The key must be a letter or a number. You cannot use Esc, Enter, Tab, the space bar, Print Screen, or Backspace. To clear the Shortcut Key text box, select the box and press the space bar.

   To use this shortcut key, you press Ctrl+Alt and the key you indicated. Shortcut keys you enter take precedence over other access keys in Windows.

Tip
You can press a shortcut's key combination to run the shortcuts program or document even when another program is active.

7. To specify the type of window in which the application or document will run, click on the Run drop-down list. Select from Normal Window, Minimized, or Maximized.

8. To change the icon displayed for the shortcut, click Change Icon to display the Change Icon dialog box, shown in figure 3.16.

   The Change Icon dialog box displays a scrolling horizontal list of icons stored in files with the extensions EXE, DLL, and ICO.

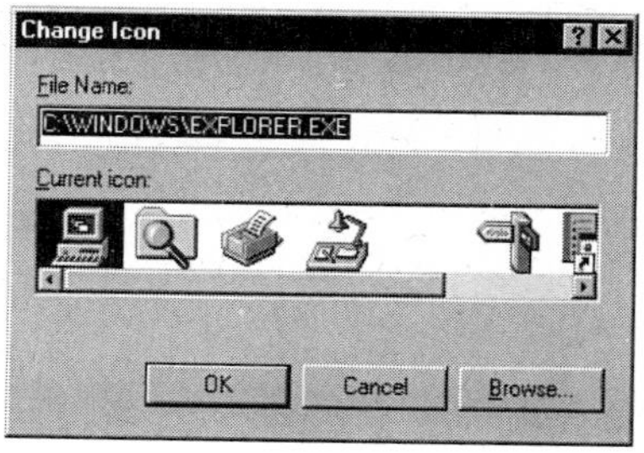

Fig. 3.16
You can select the icon you want for your shortcut.

9. Select the icon you want and then choose OK.

10. Click the OK button to make your changes and close the Shortcut Properties sheet. Click Apply to make your changes and keep the Shortcut Properties sheet open for more changes.

Note

When selecting icons for a shortcut, you don't have to restrict yourself to the icons in the file the shortcut points to. You can select an icon from any other DLL, EXE, or ICO file. To see other icon files from the Change Icon dialog box, click the Browse button.

Tip
Online computer services and computer clubs maintain large collections of icon files that are available for free.

Modifying and Deleting Shortcuts

If you want to modify the name that appears under the icon, click once on the icon to select it. Then click once on the name to select the text in the name. At this point, the pointer changes to an I-beam. You can press Delete to delete the name or click the pointer where you want the insertion point. After you edit the name, press Enter.

To delete a shortcut, click on it with the right mouse button and choose Delete. Choose Yes when the confirmation dialog box appears.

Tip
You can arrange icons on the desktop by right-clicking on the desktop, and then choosing the Arrange Icons command. You are given alternative ways of arranging them.

Caution

Be careful when deleting shortcuts from the desktop. When you delete a shortcut for a file, you delete only the shortcut, not the file. However, when you delete an icon that represents a file, you delete the file. You can always tell whether an icon represents a shortcut because an arrow appears beneath the icon.

If, for example, you drag a document from My Computer to the desktop with the left mouse button, the icon actually represents the file; if you then delete the icon, you also delete the file. Make sure that you know what you are doing before you delete an icon on your desktop.

Starting Programs and Documents from the Explorer or My Computer

The Windows Explorer is an application that comes with Windows 95. The Explorer is similar to the earlier Windows version's File Manager but is much more powerful. You can use the Explorer to view the files and folders on your computer; move, copy, rename, and delete files and folders; and perform other file-management tasks. You can also start programs and open documents from the Explorer. The time that you spend learning how to work with this very useful and powerful tool is well invested.

My Computer is similar to the Explorer. The main difference between them is that, unlike the Explorer window, the My Computer window does not enable you to view the overall structure of or relationships among all your computer's resources. Typically, when you use My Computer, you view the contents of one folder at a time. For some users, this window is less confusing than the Explorer window, which presents a lot of information at once.

This section focuses on starting programs and opening documents. For detailed instructions on using the Explorer and My Computer to manage your files, see Chapter 17, "Managing Your Files with Explorer."

Opening a Document or Application from the Explorer

You can use the Explorer to find any file on your computer. After you find the file, you can also use the Explorer to start the program or document. If the file is a program file, you can start the program by double-clicking on its file in the Explorer. If the file is a document, you can start its associated application and open the document simultaneously. If the application is already running, Windows opens the document in that application.

To open an application or document in the Explorer, follow these steps:

1. Open the Start menu and choose Programs, Windows Explorer. The Explorer window appears, as shown in figure 3.17.

2. In the Explorer's left pane, locate and select the folder that contains the program or document that you want to start or open. Click on the + sign to open a folder or the – sign to close a folder.

   In figure 3.18, the user has selected a folder called Sales Department, and the Explorer's right pane displays the files in that folder.

Tip
Access the Explorer quickly by right-clicking the Start button and then choosing Explore.

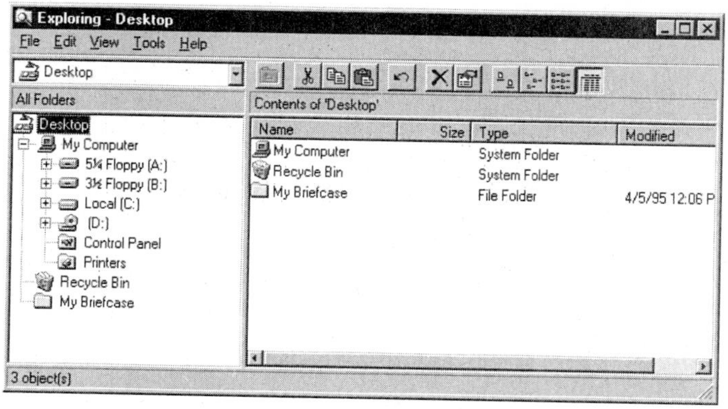

Fig. 3.17
The Explorer window displays all your computer's resources, including folders and files.

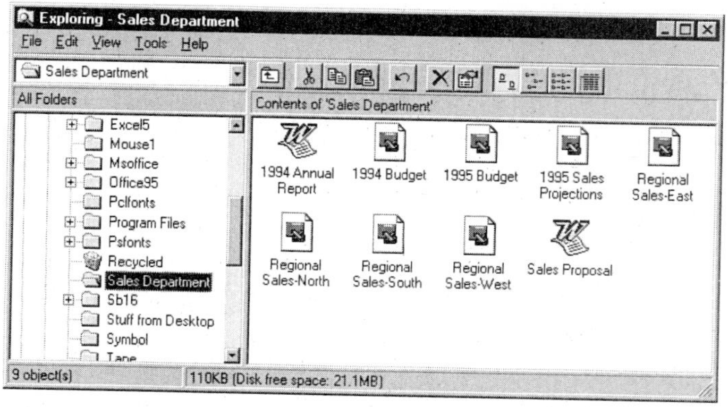

Fig. 3.18
The user has selected the Sales Department folder in the Explorer's left pane, so the right pane displays that folder's contents.

Each document in the folder is represented by an icon that indicates the application that was used to create the document. The name of the document appears beneath the icon. For more detailed information on each file, choose View, Details. The Explorer's right pane then lists the files along with information on the size, type, and the date and time that each file was last modified, as shown in figure 3.19.

3. Double-click the document that you want to open.

   If a document is associated with an application such as a word processor or spreadsheet program, Windows starts the application and opens the document. If the associated application is already running, Windows simply opens the document.

4. To open another document in the same folder, click the Exploring button in the taskbar to redisplay the Explorer, and double-click the document you want to open.

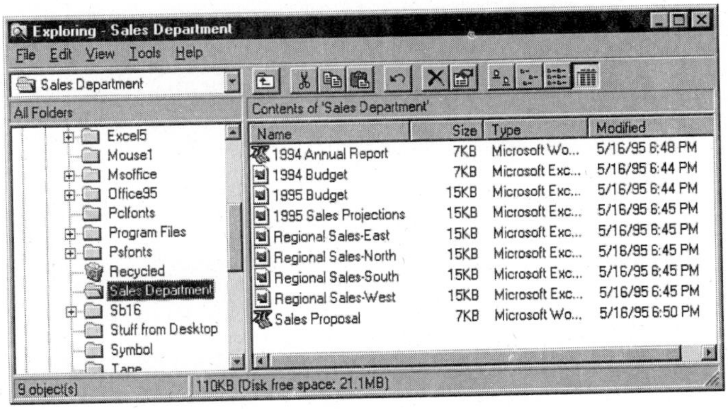

Fig. 3.19
Choose View, Details to display more information for each file in a folder.

5. To open a document in another folder, click the Exploring button in the taskbar to redisplay the Explorer, locate and select the folder containing the document in the left pane, and double-click the document in the right pane.

Troubleshooting

Double-clicking a file in the Explorer doesn't open the file. An Open With dialog box displays, asking which program should be used to open the file.

Windows does not recognize the application to use when opening the document you double-clicked. Windows displays the Open With dialog box so you can select the application to open. Windows records this application so that it can open the same application the next time you double-click on this type of document.

▶ See "Registering Files to Automatically Open an Application," p. 539

If you decide to use the Explorer routinely to open your documents, you can leave it open on your desktop. When you exit and restart Windows, it automatically opens the Explorer window in the same position as you left it.

Figure 3.20 shows how the Explorer window might look if a financial consultant organized her documents by client, creating one folder for each client. Within each folder she would keep all the documents associated with that client and could easily move from client to client, opening documents simply by double-clicking on them. With this approach to document management, the Explorer, rather than the Start menu, becomes the starting point for your work. You can still use the Start menu to access other Windows applications that you use less frequently or that are not associated with documents. Such applications include the Control Panel, which you use to customize Windows.

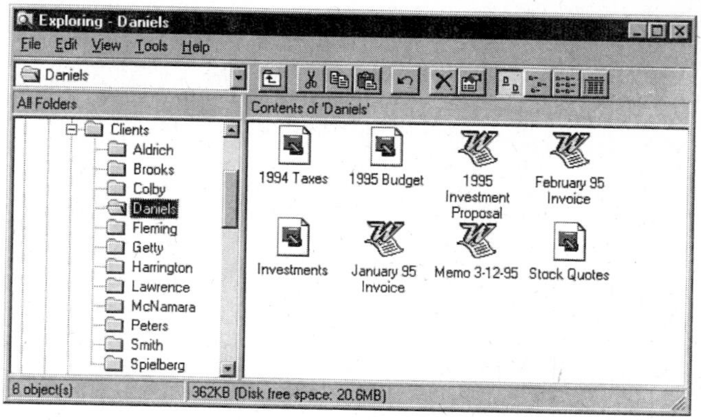

Fig. 3.20
In this desktop, the user has created a folder for each client, and each folder contains all the documents for that client.

Using My Computer to Open Documents

The first time that you start Windows, you will notice an icon called My Computer on your desktop. If you double-click on this icon, the My Computer window appears, as shown in figure 3.21. You can use My Computer to view your computer's resources, including folders and files. Figure 3.22 shows a window of folders that displays after double-clicking on the C: drive icon. My Computer is a different way of viewing folders, files and computer resources than that used by the Explorer.

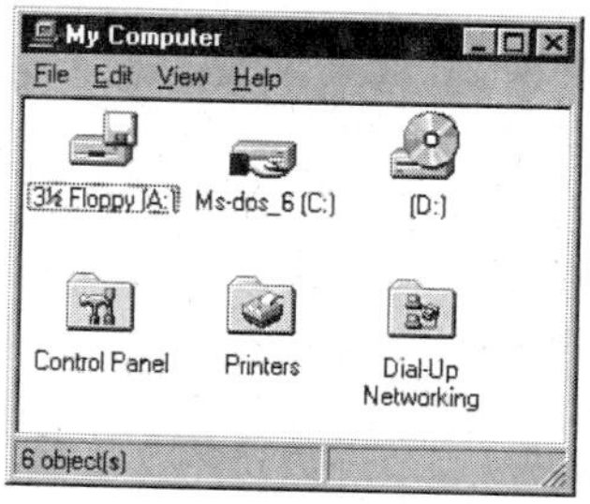

Fig. 3.21
Use the My Computer window to view your computer's resources.

After you open a window for a folder so that you can view its contents, you can open a document (or application) by double-clicking its icon, just as you did in the Explorer earlier in this chapter. Figure 3.22 shows the folders within a C: drive. Some users find this window simpler and less confusing than the Explorer window shown in figure 3.20.

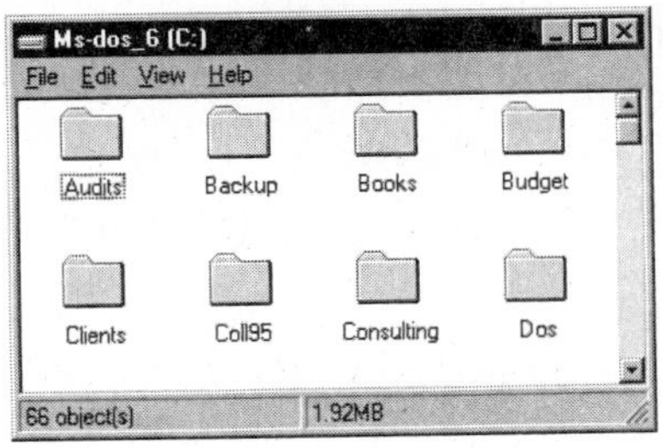

Fig. 3.22
Double-click on a folder to display its contents.

Using Windows 3.1 File Manager or Program Manager

If you upgraded your Windows 3.1 or Windows 3.11 to Windows 95, you still have copies of File Manager and Program Manager available. Although My Computer and Explorer are more flexible, you may prefer to make the transition slowly and take your time learning the new features of Windows 95.

If you prefer to use File Manager and Program Manager, you can easily do so. Their files, WINFILE.EXE and PROGMAN.EXE, are located in the WINDOWS folder. You can use the procedures described in this chapter to add these programs to your Start menu, create shortcut icons for the desktop, or run them when Windows starts.

Quitting Windows Applications

Most Windows applications operate the same way. To quit a Windows application, follow these steps:

1. Activate the application by clicking on the application's window or by pressing Alt+Tab until you have selected the application.
2. Click the Close button, or choose File, Exit.

Note

Throughout this book, instuctions such as "Choose File, Exit" mean that you click the File menu (or press Alt+F) and then click the Exit command (or press Alt+X).

If the application contains documents that you have modified since the last time that you saved them, the application prompts you to save your changes before the application quits.

Managing Windows after an Application Failure

Under Windows 3.0, if an application quit working, the user had two options: prayer and prayer. A hung program meant lost data. Windows 3.1 improved on this by allowing *local reboot,* the ability to trap errant application behavior, thus protecting other applications and data. Under Windows 3.1's local reboot, pressing Ctrl+Alt+Del didn't restart your computer; it closed the misbehaving application and was supposed to leave Windows and other applications running correctly.

Local reboot had two main problems, however:

- People didn't always know which application was misbehaving, so pressing Ctrl+Alt+Del often closed the wrong appplication.
- Windows 3.1 didn't always respond quickly to the Ctrl+Alt+Del command. Users would continue to press Ctrl+Alt+Del until the computer restarted. (A single Ctrl+Alt+Del would bring up a blue screen warning that a second Ctrl+Alt+Del would reset the system.)

Windows 95 significantly improves on how failed or misbehaving applications are handled. Windows 95 continuously polls the applications to see if they are running and responding. When an application fails to respond, Windows 95 displays the Not Responding dialog box, like the one shown in figure 3.23. In this dialog box, you can click the End Task button to close down the application. You lose all changes to data in the application since the last time you saved. Click Cancel to return to the application.

If the application misuses memory or has a fatal error that causes the application to crash, other applications in Windows will not usually be involved. When an application fails to respond—for example, clicks or keystrokes get no response—press Ctrl+Alt+Del to display the Close Program dialog box shown in figure 3.24.

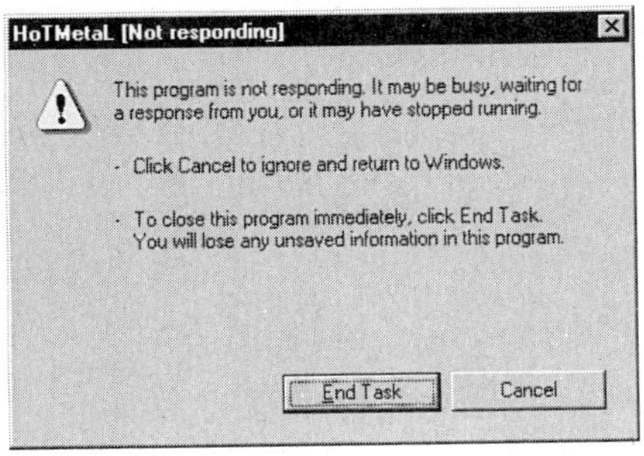

Fig. 3.23
Windows displays the Not Responding dialog box when an application fails to respond.

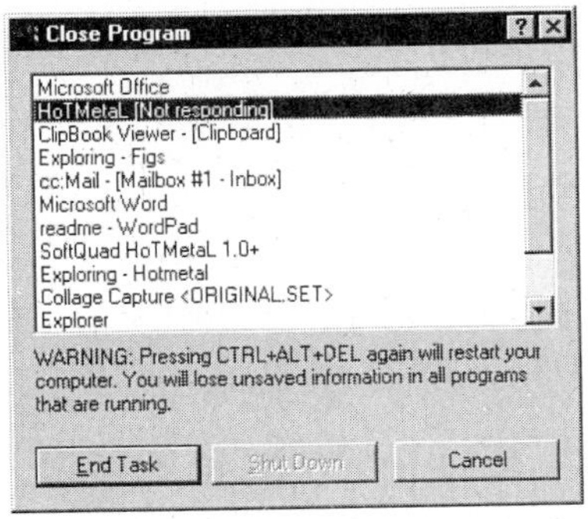

Fig. 3.24
You can check which programs may have failed and shut them down by pressing Ctrl+Alt+Del to display the Close Program dialog box.

The application that has trouble will show the phrase `[Not responding]`. To continue working in Windows on your other applications, you must shut down this application. Select the application and click End Task. If you click Shut Down or press Ctrl+Alt+Delete again, all applications and Windows 95 will shut down. You may be able to click Cancel and return to the application with no problems. However, you should probably be safe and save any work in that application to a new file and close it then restart.

Getting Help

Windows applications and accessories have extensive Help screens to help you find information on procedures, commands, techniques, and terms. Many applications even include numbered lists of steps in Help to guide you through complex procedures. The tools in Windows Help enable you to search for topics, print Help information, annotate the Help screens with your own notes, and copy to the Clipboard information from the Help screens for use in other applications.

Many Windows accessories and applications use similar kinds of commands and procedures. Each application's Help screens differs, however. You can learn how to use the application's Help system by opening the Help menu (from the application's menu bar) and choosing a command such as How to Use Help.

Understanding Windows Help

You start Windows Help by opening the Start menu and choosing Help. Figure 3.25 shows the Contents tab of the Help dialog box. This is the Help dialog box for Windows 95; other Windows applications provide Help dialog boxes that look different, perhaps offering more or fewer Help topics.

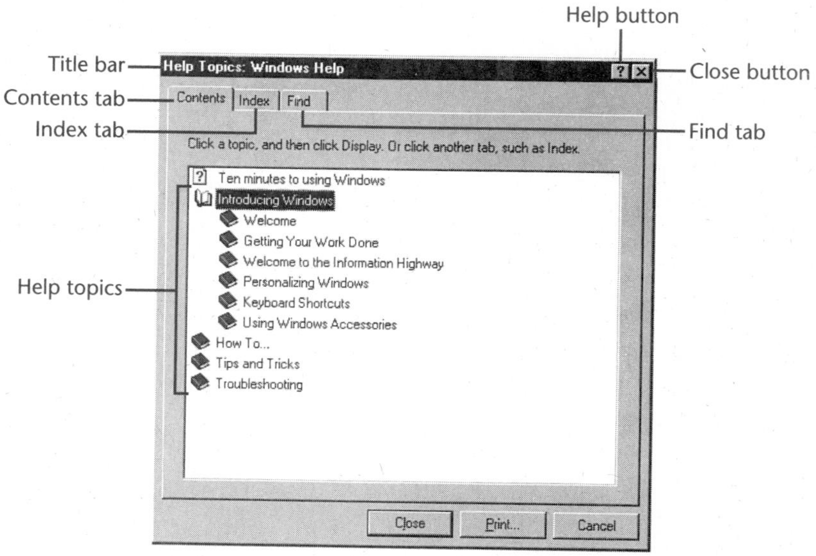

Fig. 3.25
The Windows Help screens offer help regarding all aspects of Windows.

The following table describes the parts of the Help Topics dialog box:

Part	Description
Title bar	Includes the Help button (use it to display pop-up help, discussed later in the chapter), and the Close button.
Contents tab	Displays the available Help topics.
Index tab	Enables you to search through the available Help topics.

Part	Description
Close	Closes the selected book icon on the Contents page.
Open button	Opens the selected book icon on the Contents page.
Display button	Displays the selected Help item from the Index or Contents page.
Cancel button	Closes Help.
Print button	Displays the Print dialog box, from which you can print the selected topic.

The Help Topics dialog box uses the standard Windows controls: scroll bars (as needed), and the Close button.

Note

To start Help from within a Windows application, you can press the F1 key. Help then appears for the active application or window.

Using Pop-Up Help

In most Windows applications, a question mark button (?) appears at the top-right corner of many dialog boxes and windows. You can use this button to find out information about items on the screen. This information can help you learn how to use the dialog box or window. If you see a data-entry box and are unfamiliar with how it works or what it does, click on the Help (?) button and then click on the data-entry box. A pop-up window then displays Help information about the item you clicked.

For example, you might be interested in learning how to check your hardware devices. To get to the Device Manager, you must open the System application from the Control Panel, and then click on the Device Manager tab. Once on the Device Manager page, you can learn how the list of hardware devices works by clicking on the Help (?) button and then clicking on the list. Figure 3.26 shows the pop-up window that tells you about the list in the Device Manager.

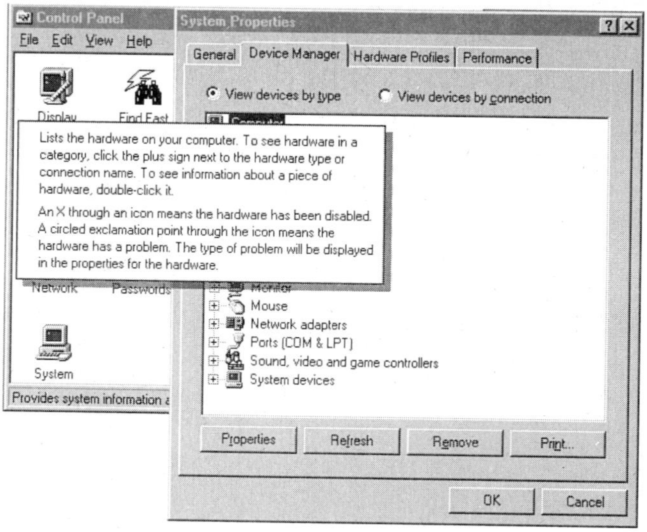

Fig. 3.26
To view a pop-up Help window describing a control on a Properties sheet or dialog box, click on the Help (?) button and then on any control.

The Help (?) button on the title bar of many Properties sheets and dialog boxes enables you to get help on how to use the sheet or dialog box. To use the Help (?) button, follow these steps:

1. Click the Help (?) button. A large question mark attaches to the pointer.
2. Click the control that you have a question about—for example, a list or check box. A description box displays adjacent to the control.
3. Click the left mouse button to close the description box.

Using the Contents Page

The Contents page of the Help Topics window lists Help topics that are available in the Windows application in which you chose Help (refer to fig. 3.25). Topics are categorized into books. Each Help topic icon first appears as a closed book. When you open a book, you see page icons. Displaying a page icon reveals the Help contents for that topic.

Figure 3.27 shows a Help window's contents. In addition to a list of steps, the window also contains a shortcut button. Clicking on that button immediately displays the Password Properties sheet that the Help screen discusses. You can keep the Help window open as you work in the Password Properties sheet. Many of the topics include tips and tricks that offer shortcuts and other timesaving techniques.

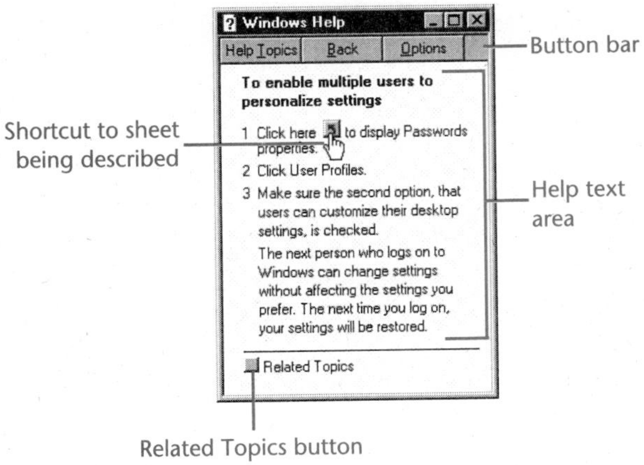

Fig. 3.27
The Windows Help windows display procedural steps and buttons to open dialog boxes described in the procedure.

To display a Help window about one of the topics on the Contents page, follow these steps:

1. Open the Start menu and choose Help.
2. Click the Contents tab.
3. Scroll through the list of topics to locate the topic that you want.
4. Double-click a book to display its contents. The contents of the topic display as page icons.
5. Double-click a page icon to display its contents, or select the topic and choose Display. The Help topic displays in a window sized to fit its contents. You can resize the window to make it easier to work in your application.

Using the Help Window

After you select a Help topic from either the Contents or Index tab, the Windows Help window appears (refer to fig. 3.27). The following table describes the toolbar in the Windows Help window:

Button	Description
Help Topics	Displays the Help Topics window.
Back	Moves the Help window back to the previous topic.
Options	Displays a menu of commands that enables you to use the contents of the Help window in different ways. Following sections in this chapter describe these commands. Options include: Annotate, Copy, Print Topic, Font, Keep Help on Top.

Button	Description
Related Topics button	Displays a list of related Help topics.

Using the Index Page

The Index Help page provides a search feature that finds the topic you want (see fig. 3.28). For example, if you want to learn about adding shortcuts to the desktop, you can type **sho**. The selection bar then moves through the list of index entries to *shortcuts (links), putting on the desktop*. The more letters you type, the closer you get to the topic name.

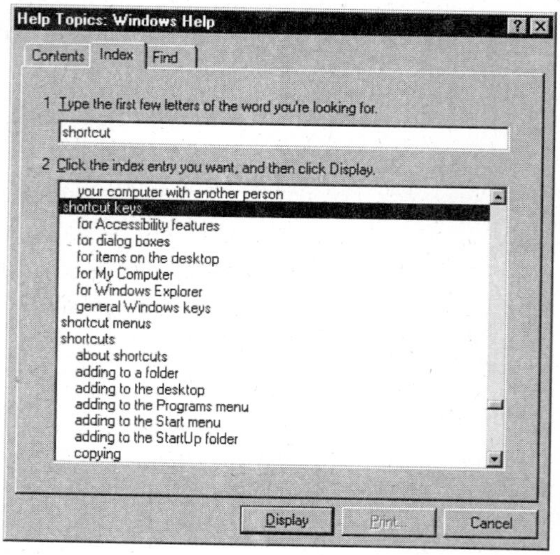

Fig. 3.28
Find a Help topic with the Windows Help Index.

To use the Help Index, follow these steps:

1. Open the Start menu and choose Help.

2. Click the Index tab.

3. Click in the text box and type the name of the subject that you want help on. As you type, the selection bar moves through the list of topics.

4. When you have selected your topic, double-click it, or click it and choose Display. The Help screen displays.

Jumping between Topics

You can easily jump between Help topics by returning to either the Contents or Index page. Simply click the Contents or Index tab in the Help window. For example, if you finish reading a Help window and want to read about another topic, click the Contents tab and the Contents page redisplays. Then select a new topic from the Contents page. The Index tab redisplays the Index page.

When more information related to the topic that you're viewing is available, the Help window includes a Related Topics button. Click the Related Topics button to see a list of related topics. The Topics Found window displays and lists the additional related topics. Click the topic that you want and then click Display to view the topics Help.

Printing a Help Topic

Often, having a printed copy of the Help topic in which you are interested can help you understand the topic more clearly. When the topic for which you want information is in the Help window, choose the Options button and then Print Topic to display the Print dialog box. Click OK to print.

> **Note**
>
> Some of the handiest information that you can print or copy from Help is an application's shortcut keys. If you didn't get a shortcut keystroke template for your application, look in the application's Help contents for a topic similar to Keyboard Shortcuts. Copy these topics (by pressing Ctrl+C) to a word processor, reorganize them, and print them. Alternatively, you can print the topics directly from Help. You can then copy the contents at a reduced size and paste them onto 3-by-5 cards.

Customizing Help

Help is more than just a list of procedures or word definitions. You can print Help screens, copy screens into word processors, and even add notes to help windows so that Help becomes customized to the kind of work that you do.

Adding Custom Notes to Help Topics

You can customize Help information in a Windows application to make Help information more useful to you or to coworkers. You might want to include information about your company's default settings, for example, in a Help window on document formatting, or attach a note that names the templates for mailing labels to a built-in Help window that describes how to create mailing labels. To add such information, you use *annotations*.

To create an annotation, follow these steps:

1. Display the topic that you want to annotate.

2. Click the Options button and then choose Annotate. The Annotate dialog box, a small notepad, appears.

3. Type the notes that you want to save regarding this Help topic.

4. Choose the Save button.

A paper clip icon appears to the left of the topic title in the Help window. Whenever you want to read an annotation, just click the paper clip icon.

To remove an annotation, click on the paper clip icon. When the Annotate dialog box appears, choose the Delete button.

Copying Help Information to Another Application

▶ See "Using the Windows Clipboard," p. 411

You can create a collection of Help topics by copying Help information and pasting this data into a word processor document file. You can copy and paste into another application any information that you see in a Help window. The information transfers as editable text.

To copy the contents of a Help window, choose the Options button and then the Copy command. To paste this information into another Windows application, such as a word processor, open the other application, position the insertion point wherever you want to paste the information, and choose Edit, Paste, or press Ctrl+V.

Finding Help, Support, and Resources

Windows is one of the most popular software applications ever written. Therefore, much support is available for Windows. The following sections describe resources that can help you get the most from Windows.

Getting Telephone Support

Use the following telephone numbers to get technical support or product sales information about Windows or Windows applications.

For questions specific to Windows installation, Explorer, or Windows accessories, call Microsoft Corporation's Windows support line at (206) 637-7098. For customer service and product upgrade information, call (800) 426-9400.

If Windows or applications came preinstalled on your computer, your technical support for the preinstalled software will probably be through the hardware vendor who supplied your equipment.

Getting Online Help

You can also find support online, through the Microsoft Network and various computer bulletin board forums.

The Microsoft Network. Microsoft Network is available to users of Windows 95 who have a modem correctly installed. Once you sign on to Microsoft Network, you have access to forums, libraries of software, and technical support forums.

► See "Connecting to the Microsoft Network," p. 1110

To start Microsoft Network, double-click on The Microsoft Network icon on the desktop. Once you are connected, the Welcome to MSN Central window appears. MSN Central contains the main menu to various parts of MSN. The Member Assistance icon is the one you want to access for help.

After you click Member Assistance, several items appear. For online support, double-click the MSN Center folder. Here you will find the MSN Support Bulletin Board. The Bulletin Board contains support folders for Internet access, e-mail, file transfer, and billing, to name just a few.

Computer Bulletin Board Forums. Computer bulletin boards are computer services that enable you to retrieve information over the telephone line. Some bulletin boards contain a wealth of information about Windows and Windows applications. One of the largest public bulletin boards is CompuServe.

CompuServe contains *forums* where Windows and Windows applications are discussed. You can submit questions electronically to Microsoft operators, who will answer questions usually within a day. CompuServe also contains libraries of sample files and new printer and device drivers. The Knowledgebase available in Microsoft's region of CompuServe has much of the same troubleshooting information that Microsoft's telephone support representatives use. You can search through the Knowledgebase by using key words. The Microsoft region of CompuServe is divided into many different areas, such as Windows users, Windows software developers, Microsoft, Excel, and Microsoft languages, and sections for each of the major Microsoft and non-Microsoft applications that run under Windows.

After you become a CompuServe member, you can access the Microsoft user forums, library files, and Knowledgebase. (You must join CompuServe and get a passcode before you can use the bulletin board.) When you join

CompuServe, make sure that you get a copy of WinCIM, the Windows CompuServe Information Manager. It enables you to avoid typing so many commands, and thus makes using CompuServe significantly easier.

For more information, contact CompuServe at the following address:

CompuServe
5000 Arlington Centre Blvd.
P.O. Box 20212
Columbus, OH 43220
(800) 848-8990

► See "Using FTP," p. 912

► See "Surfing the Web with Internet Explorer," p. 920

Internet Support. Microsoft provides two Internet sites that provide access to free software, updates, technical papers, and device drivers. From within your Internet browser, you can access the Microsoft FTP site with this URL:

FTP:\\ftp.microsoft.com

You can access the same information by using your browser on the World Wide Web with this URL:

HTTP:\\http.microsoft.com

Consultants and Training

Microsoft Solution Providers develop and support applications written for the Windows environment with Microsoft products. They are independent consultants who have met the strict qualifying requirements imposed by Microsoft.

Microsoft also certifies training centers. A certified training center has instructors who have passed a competency exam and use Microsoft-produced training material.

You can find the Microsoft Solution Providers and training centers in your area by calling the following number:

(800) SOL-PROV

Chapter 4

Starting and Working with Applications

by Ron Person

The information that you learn in this chapter carries over to all Windows applications. This "learning carry-over" is important: after you learn how to use one Windows application, you understand most of the concepts necessary to operate other applications. The skills that you acquire in this chapter will help you operate such control features as menus and dialog boxes and learn how to control such display aspects as the size and position of the windows in which different documents or applications display.

In this chapter, you learn how to do the following:

- Open menus and choose commands
- Change the location and size of windows
- Display the properties of the desktop, file, or taskbar
- Work in applications
- Drag-and-drop objects as a shortcut for such actions as opening files or printing documents

Working in the Windows Environment

► See "Making Windows Accessible for the Hearing, Sight, and Movement Impaired," p. 150

Windows uses concepts that, for many people, make computers easier to use. The basic organizational concept is that all applications run on a desktop and that each application runs in its own window. Windows can run multiple applications, just as you might have stacks of papers on your desk from more than one project. You can move the windows and change their size just as you can move and rearrange the stacks of papers on your desk.

► See "Using the Windows Clipboard," p. 411

Just as you can cut, copy, and paste parts between papers on your real desktop, Windows enables you to cut or copy information from one application and paste the information into another. Some Windows applications even share live information; when you change data in one application, Windows automatically updates linked data in other applications.

► See "Using Embedding to Link Information," p. 440

The process for making entries, edits, and changes to text, numbers, or graphics is similar in all Windows applications. The basic procedure is as follows:

1. Activate the window that contains the desired application.

2. Select the text, number, or graphics object that you want to change. You can select items with the mouse or the keyboard.

3. Choose a command from the menu bar at the top of the application.

4. If a dialog box appears, select options to modify how the command works. Then execute the command by choosing the OK button.

An *application window* is the window that contains an application. *Document windows* appear inside application windows and contain documents. In many (but not all) applications, you can have several document windows open at a time; you switch between them by pressing Ctrl+F6 or by selecting from the Window menu the document that you want.

The Control menu contains commands to control a window's location, size, and status (open or closed). Each application and each document window within the application window has its own Control menu. The application Control menu appears at the left edge of the application's title bar. The document Control menu appears at the left edge of the document's title bar (if the document window is smaller than a full screen) or at the left edge of the menu bar (if the document window is a full screen). To open an application Control menu, click once on the application Control Menu icon (the icon at the top-left corner of the program window), or press Alt+space bar. To open a document Control menu, click once on the document Control Menu icon (the icon at the top-left corner of a document window), or press Alt+hyphen (-).

Tip

To minimize all windows with one command, click on a clear area in the taskbar with the right mouse button and choose Minimize All Windows.

To maximize a window so it fills the screen, click on the Maximize button, a square window icon in the window's top-right corner (see fig. 4.1) or double-click the title bar. You can also minimize a window and place it on the taskbar. To do so, you click on another icon in the window's top-right corner, the Minimize button, which looks like an underline representing the taskbar (see fig. 4.1).

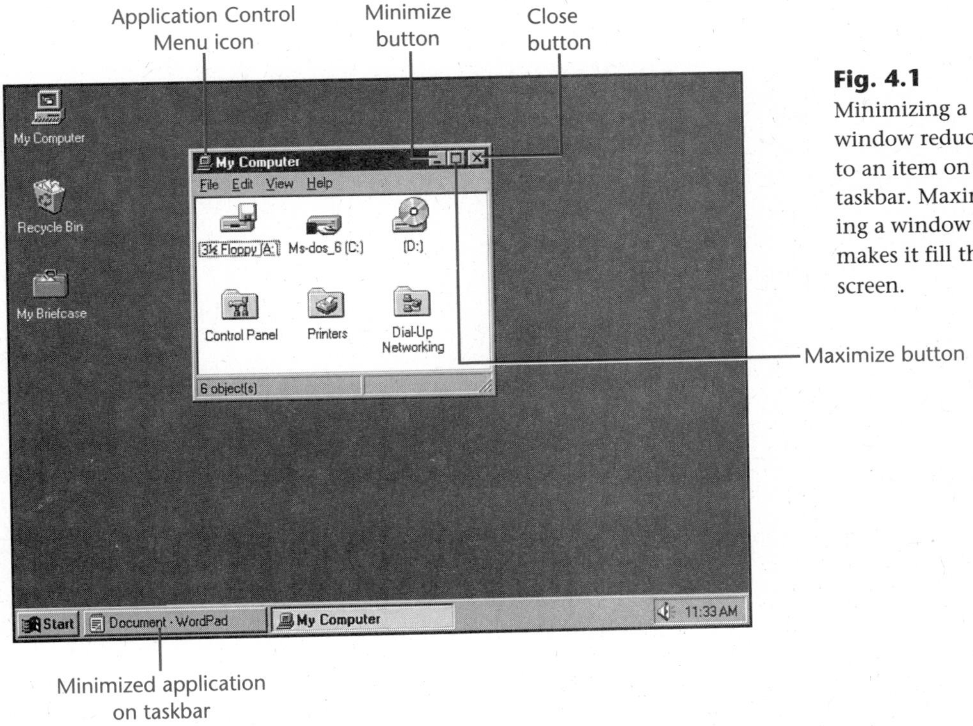

Fig. 4.1
Minimizing a window reduces it to an item on the taskbar. Maximizing a window makes it fill the screen.

When you minimize a program, its window shrinks to become an icon and name on the taskbar. The program still runs even though it is not in a window. To make a program on the taskbar appear in a window, click on the program in the taskbar. (To use the keyboard to activate a program, press Alt+Tab repeatedly until you have selected the appropriate program, and then release the keys.)

Tip
To restore all minimized windows with one command, right-click a clear area in the taskbar and choose Undo Minimize All.

You can resize a window by dragging its window border with the mouse, or by choosing the Size command from the Control menu. You can move a window without resizing it by dragging its title bar with the mouse, or by choosing the Move command from the Control menu.

▶ See "Customizing the Mouse," p. 147

▶ See "Customizing the Keyboard," p. 148

Table 4.1 introduces keystrokes that perform certain actions. You may want to refer back to this table as you read through the book or begin working with Windows 95.

Table 4.1 Keystrokes to Control Windows

Keystroke	Action
Alt+Esc	Activates the next application window.
Alt+Tab	Displays a program bar showing open programs as icons. Each press of Alt+Tab selects the next icon. Releasing Alt+Tab activates the program selected in the program bar.
Alt+Shift+Tab	Moves the selection through the program bar in the opposite direction of Alt+Tab. Releasing Alt+Shift+Tab activates the selected program.
Ctrl+F6	Activates the next document window (if an application has multiple document windows open).
Ctrl+Esc	Displays the Start menu. Press the up- or down-arrow keys to select from the menu.
Alt+space bar	Displays the Control menu for the active program icon or window. Use the Control menu to change the location, size, and status of the program window.
Alt+hyphen (-)	Displays the Control menu for the active document window within the program. Use this Control menu to change the location, size, and status of the document window.

Using Menus and Dialog Boxes

▶ See "Making Windows Accessible for the Hearing, Sight, and Movement Impaired," p. 150

Every properly designed Windows application operates in a similar way. As you will learn, you can move and resize all windows the same way in every Windows application. You also execute commands the same way in all Windows applications.

You can choose a command from a menu by using the mouse or the keyboard (also, many time-saving shortcuts exist for choosing commands). If a command requires information from you before executing, a dialog box appears when you choose the command. In the dialog box, you use the mouse or the keyboard to choose options or enter values that control the command.

Choosing Menus and Commands

When you click on a menu, a list of commands drops down under the menu, as shown in figures 4.2 and 4.3. If you're not sure where to find a command, try browsing through the menus by clicking on them until you find the command that you want. Many applications use similar commands for similar actions—a practice that makes learning multiple Windows applications easier.

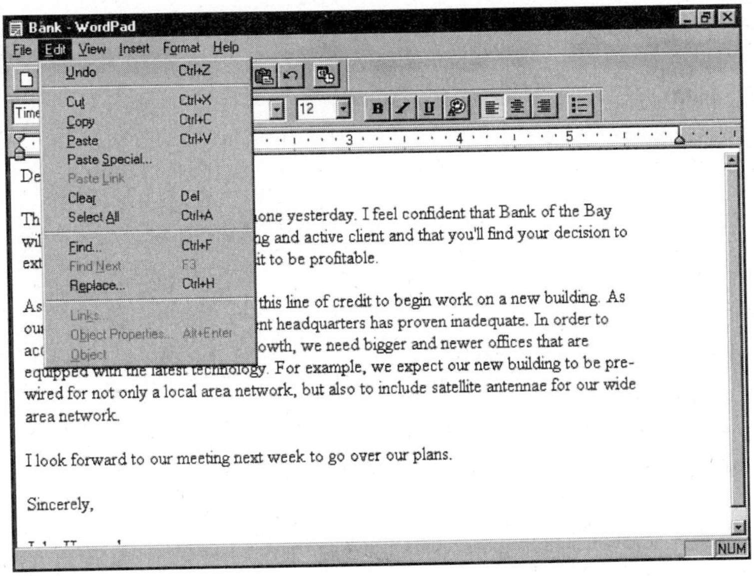

Fig. 4.2
WordPad's Edit menu displays shortcut keys.

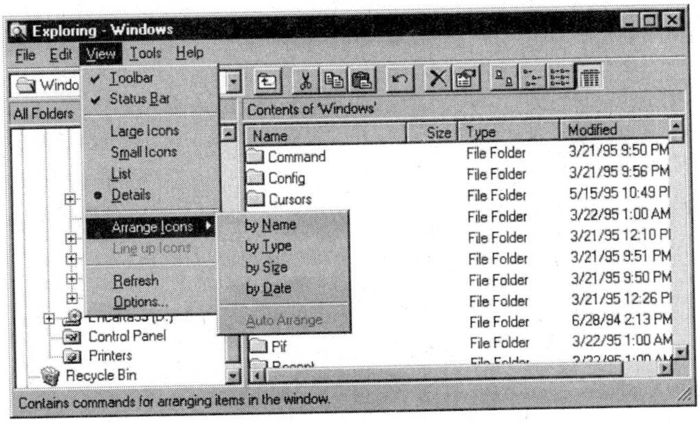

Fig. 4.3
In the Explorer, when you choose View, Arrange Icons, you see a submenu that displays additional commands.

Tip
To change the colors of the text in menu commands, see "Creating Custom Color and Text Schemes" in Chapter 5.

To choose a menu or command with the mouse, move the tip of the pointer over the menu or command name and click the left mouse button. To choose a menu or command with the keyboard, press Alt+*letter* where *letter* is the underlined letter in the menu. When the menu displays, press the key for the underlined letter in the command. For example, to choose the File menu's Open command, you press Alt, then F, and then O.

You can choose commands that appear in a menu in solid black (bold) type. You *cannot* choose commands that appear in gray in a menu, even though you can see them. Gray commands or options are *disabled*. Commands or options appear in bold only when they are available, or *enabled*. For example, the Edit menu's Copy command appears in bold type only when you have selected something to copy.

Command names followed by an ellipsis (...) display an additional dialog box or window from which you can choose options or enter data. If you choose Edit, Find... from a Windows application, for example, a dialog box appears in which you type the word that you want to find.

Commands with a check mark to the left are commands that toggle on and off. A check mark indicates that the command is on; no check mark indicates that the command is off.

Commands with key combinations listed to the right have shortcuts. In Windows Explorer, for example, the Edit menu lists a shortcut for the Copy command, Ctrl+C. Therefore, to copy text, you can choose Edit, Copy, or press Ctrl+C.

Commands with an arrowhead next to them, as in figure 4.3, have submenus that list additional commands. In the Explorer, the Arrange Icons command in the View menu has an arrowhead to its right, indicating that a submenu will show the ways in which you can arrange icons.

If you don't want to make a choice after displaying a menu, click the pointer a second time on the menu name or click outside the menu. If you are using the keyboard, press Esc to exit a menu without making a choice. Continue to press Esc until no commands or menus are selected.

Note

If a dialog box appears on-screen and you aren't sure what to do, you can escape without making any changes. Click the Cancel button or press the Esc key to cancel the current dialog box and ignore any changes to options.

Most Windows applications have an Undo command. If you complete a command and then decide that you want to undo it, check whether the Edit menu includes an Undo command.

Selecting Options from Dialog Boxes

Commands that require more information before they work display a *dialog box*—a window similar to those shown in figures 4.4 and 4.5. Dialog boxes like the one in figure 4.4 have areas in which you enter text (such as the File Name text box) or select from a scrolling list of choices (see the Name list box of file names). Many applications also include drop-down list boxes with lists that appear only when you select the box and press the down-arrow key, or click on the down arrow on the right side of the text box.

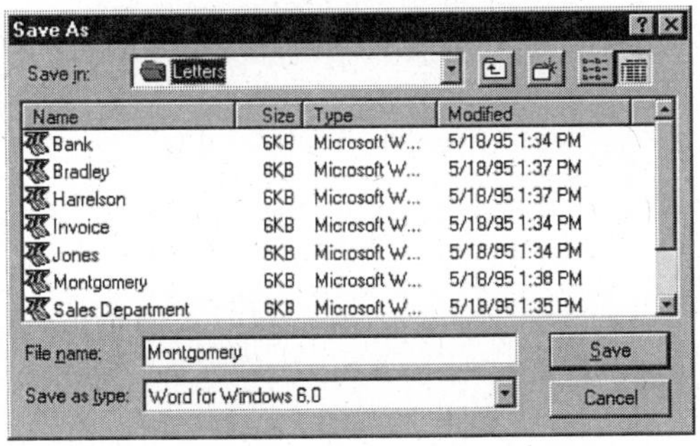

Fig. 4.4
The Save As dialog box is similar among Windows programs.

Figure 4.5 shows that dialog boxes can have round *option* buttons and square *check boxes*. The option buttons are clustered in a group labeled Hidden Files. When options are in such groups, you can choose only one of them. Check boxes act independently of other check boxes so you can select as many of them as you want. After you select options or make text entries, you accept the contents of the dialog box by choosing the OK button or cancel them by choosing the Cancel button.

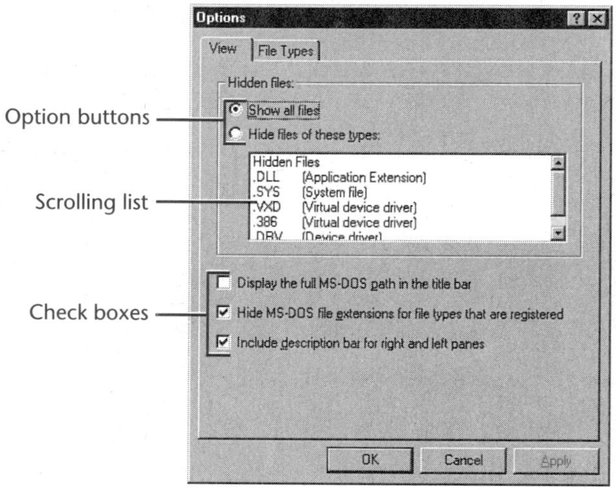

Fig. 4.5
Option buttons, check boxes, and scrolling lists appear in the View tab of the Explorer's Options dialog box.

If a dialog box hides something that you want to see on-screen, you can move the dialog box with the mouse by dragging the dialog box by its title bar to a new position. With the keyboard, press Alt+space bar to open the dialog Control menu and then choose Move. A four-headed arrow appears. Press any arrow key to move an outline of the dialog box. Press Enter when the outline of the dialog box is where you want to place the dialog box. (Before you press Enter, you can cancel the move by pressing Esc instead.)

Figure 4.6 shows the five types of controls used in dialog boxes, and table 4.2 summarizes them.

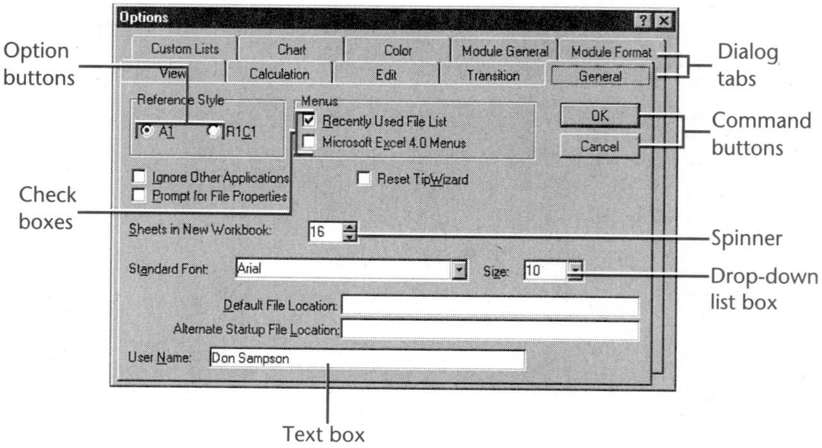

Fig. 4.6
Some of the types of controls presented in dialog boxes.

Table 4.2 Types of Dialog Box Controls

Control	Use
Text box	Move the pointer over the text box until it changes to an I-beam shape, then click. Type text entries manually. If you make a mistake, press the Backspace or Delete key to erase characters.
List box	You will see two types of lists. *Scrolling lists* show a columnar list of choices (refer to fig. 4.5). Click on the up or down arrow on the right side of the list to scroll through the list, and then click on the item that you want. The selected item appears in highlighted text (and might also appear in the text box above the list). The second type of list, a *drop-down list*, like the one shown in figure 4.6, displays its scrolling list after you click the down arrow.
Option button	Click on one option from within a group of option buttons. (You can select only one option button in each group.) The selected option button has a darkened center. To remove a selection, select a different option in the same group.
Check box	Click on a check box to turn it on or off. Check boxes are square and contain an X when selected. You can select more than one check box at a time.
Spinner	Click the up or down arrow on the right side of a spinner to make the number change in increments of one.
Command button	Click on a command button to complete the command, cancel the command, or open an additional dialog box for more alternatives.
Dialog tab	Click on a dialog tab to see another grouping of options.

► See "Editing Text in Text Boxes," p. 102

Using the Mouse in Dialog Boxes

To select an option button or check box, click on it. Clicking on a blank check box selects it by putting an X in it. Clicking on a check box that already has an X removes the X. To turn off an option button, click on one of the other option buttons in the group.

To choose command buttons such as OK, Cancel, Yes, or No, click on them.

To select from a scrolling list box, click in the list box and then scroll through the list by clicking on the up or down arrow in the scroll bar at the right side of the list box. To jump through large sections of the list, click in the scroll bar's shaded area. For long moves, drag the scroll bar's square to the new location. When the desired selection appears in the list box, click once on that selection.

Some Windows applications use drop-down list boxes. When closed, these list boxes look like the Printer list box shown in figure 4.7; when open, they look like the same list box as shown in figure 4.8. To select from a drop-down list box, click on the down arrow on the text box's right side. When the scrolling list appears, select from it the same way that you select from any scrolling list box: click on the item that you want.

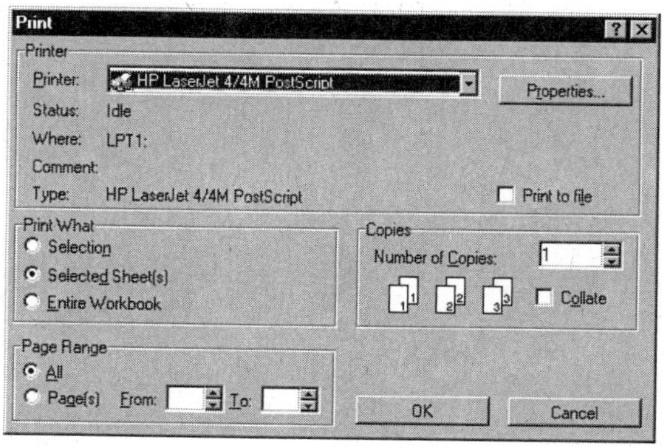

Fig. 4.7
The Printer pull-down list box when closed.

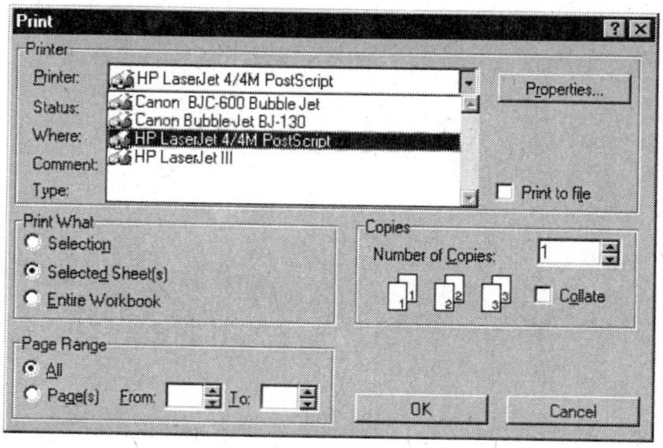

Fig. 4.8
The Printer pull-down list box when open.

Note

In some dialog boxes, double-clicking on an option button or an item in a list selects that option and simultaneously chooses the OK command button. In the Open dialog box, for example, you can double-click on a file name to select and open the file. Experiment with the dialog boxes in your applications to determine whether double-clicking is a viable shortcut.

Using the Keyboard in Dialog Boxes

Some drawing or graphics applications require that you use the mouse. In most Windows applications, however, you have the same functionality available from either the keyboard or the mouse. You might find that in some situations using the keyboard to control Windows is faster or more convenient.

To access a group of option buttons with the keyboard, you press Alt+*letter*, where *letter* is the underlined character that appears in an option's label. If the individual options do not have an underlined letter, press Alt+*letter*, where the underlined *letter* is in the title of the option group; then use the arrow keys to select an option.

To select a check box, press Alt+*letter*, where *letter* is the underlined character in the check box's label. Each time that you press Alt+*letter*, you toggle the check box between selected and deselected. An X appears in the check box when the box is selected. You also can toggle the active check box between selected and deselected by pressing the space bar.

To make an entry in a text box, select the text box by pressing Alt+*letter*, where *letter* is the underlined character in the name of the text box. Press Alt+N, for example, to select the File Name text box in the Save As dialog box shown in figure 4.9. Type a text entry or edit the existing entry by using the editing techniques described in the upcoming section "Editing Text in Text Boxes."

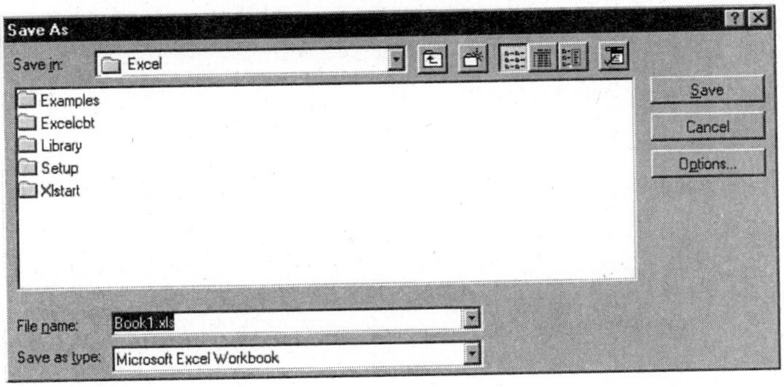

Fig. 4.9
The Save As dialog box's File Name text box when selected.

To select from a list of alternatives in a scrolling list box, select the list box by pressing Alt+*letter*, where *letter* is the underlined character in the name of the list box. When the list box is active, use the up- or down-arrow key or Page Up or Page Down to move through the list. The text is selected and displayed in reversed type. (To use the keyboard to display a drop-down scrolling list, press Alt+*letter* to activate the list and then press Alt+down-arrow to drop the list. Then select items by pressing the up- or down-arrow keys.)

To select a command button, press Alt+*letter*, or if no letter is underlined, press Tab or Shift+Tab until a dashed line encloses the name of the button that you want. Press the space bar to select the active button indicated by the dashed enclosure. At any time, you can select the command button that appears in bold type, usually the OK button, by pressing Enter. Press Esc to choose the Cancel button and escape from a dialog box without making any changes.

Changing Folders in Save As and Open Dialog Boxes

When you save a file on your hard disk, Windows places the file in a folder in your hard disk. Folders are analogous to the file drawers and file folders that you use in your office to help you organize and locate your papers. You can locate files more easily if you store related files together in a folder. For example, you can store all the business letters that you create with your word processor in a folder named LETTERS and all your proposals in a folder named PROPOSALS.

▶ See "Using the Windows Explorer to View Files and Folders," p. 499

Don't store the files that you create in the folders that store your program files. If you ever have to reinstall or upgrade a program, you might lose files that you store in the program folders. Also, these folders are already full of files, and it will be difficult to find yours. Create your own folders, and folders within folders, to store your files.

▶ See "Working with Long File Names," p. 509

The first time that you use the File, Open or File, Save As command in a program session, the application usually assumes that you want to open or save a document in that program's default folder. Usually, however, you want to open or save a file in one of your own folders. You must tell the program where the file that you want to open is located or where you want to save a file—whether that location is a different folder or a different drive on your hard disk. To switch folders or drives, use the appropriate list boxes in the Open and Save As dialog boxes, as discussed in the following paragraphs.

Note

Most applications have a place where you can set the default folder for data files. If any of yours don't, you can get the same result with these steps:

1. Create a shortcut to the application.
2. Right-click on the new icon.
3. Click the Shortcut tab.
4. In the Start In box, type the path for the folder where you want to store data files.

The selected folder appears in the Look In drop-down list (see fig. 4.10). You can display this list to select another drive.

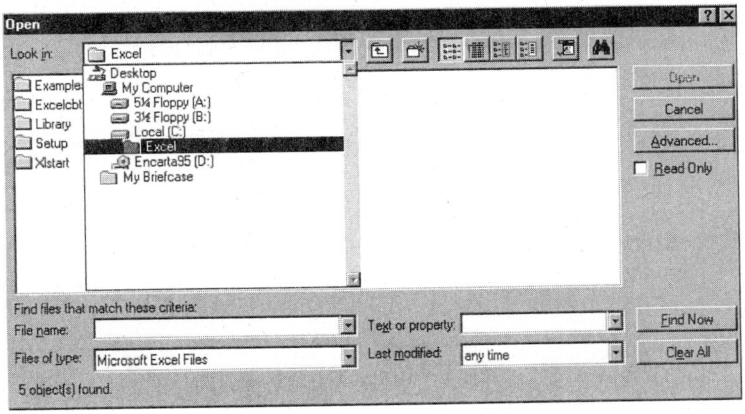

Fig. 4.10
Open the Look In drop-down list to select a different drive in the Open and Save As dialog boxes.

The list box includes all the folders in the current folder. An icon that resembles a file folder represents each folder. If you want to open a file in a folder contained within another folder, you first must open that folder. You can do so by double-clicking on the folder icon.

To change disk drives or folders in the Open or Save As dialog boxes, follow these steps:

1. Display the Look In drop-down list and select the drive that you want.
2. To select a folder, double-click on the folder icon. You can also click the Up One Level button to move up one level in the folder structure.

3. Select the file from the list, or type the file name in the File Name text box.

4. Choose Open or Save.

Editing Text in Text Boxes

You can use the text-editing techniques that you learn in this section in all Windows applications. Although the editing techniques described are specifically for the text boxes that appear in dialog boxes, they also apply to editing text in other locations in Windows applications.

To use a mouse when editing text in a text box, you position the pointer over the text where you want to place the insertion point, and then click. When moving over editable text, the pointer changes from an arrowhead to an I-beam shape. To select multiple characters, drag across the characters.

While positioned in a text box, you can press left- or right-arrow keys to move left or right, End to move to the end of the text, and Home to move to the beginning of the text.

To delete a character to the right of the flashing insertion point, press Delete. Press Backspace to delete a character to the left of the insertion point.

Replace existing text with new text by selecting the text that you want to replace and then typing the new text. Select text with the mouse by dragging the I-beam across the text as you hold down the mouse button. To select text with the keyboard, move the insertion point to the left of the first character that you want to select, press and hold down Shift, and press the right-arrow key.

Note

When editing text in an application, you usually can use Edit menu commands such as Undo, Copy, and Paste. Although these commands often do not work in dialog boxes, the keystroke equivalents Ctrl+C (to copy), Ctrl+X (to cut), and Ctrl+V (to paste) frequently do work.

Controlling the Size and Position of Windows

Just as you move papers on your desktop, you can move and reorder windows on-screen. In fact, you can resize windows, expand them to full size, shrink them to a small icon to save space, and restore them to their original size.

The easiest way to resize and reposition application or document windows is with the mouse. As you will see, you can simply drag title bars or edges to move windows or change their size.

As you move the mouse pointer over edges of application or document windows, the pointer changes shape. Each shape, shown in table 4.3, indicates the type of window change that you can make by dragging that edge or corner. Before you can move a window, it must be active—that is, the window must be on top. To activate a window, you can click on it or press Alt+Tab until you select the application.

Table 4.3 Pointer Shapes When Moving or Resizing Windows

Shape	Pointer	Mouse Action
↔	Left/right	Drag the edge left or right
↕	Up/down	Drag the edge up or down
⤡	Corner	Drag the corner in any direction

Using Taskbar Shortcuts to Arrange Windows

There are times when you want to quickly arrange a few applications on your desktop so that you can compare documents, drag-and-drop between documents, and so forth. Manually moving and resizing each Window is a tedious job, so Windows 95 has a few shortcuts that can make this type of work easier.

Tip
When the taskbar has a lot of application buttons, the titles may be too truncated to read. Pause the pointer over a button to see a pop-up title.

First, you can make your desktop easier to work on by minimizing all applications so they appear as buttons on the taskbar. To do this quickly, right-click on a gray area of the taskbar. When the shortcut menu appears, click on Minimize All Windows.

If you want to compare documents in two or three applications, minimize all applications except the two or three you want to work with and then right-click on a gray area of the taskbar. When the shortcut menu appears, click on either Tile Horizontally or Tile Vertically. Your applications will appear in adjacent windows that fill the screen as shown in figure 4.11.

If you want to be able to quickly see all the application title bars so that you can click title bars to switch between many application windows, right-click in the gray area of the taskbar. When the shortcut menu appears, click on Cascade. The windows will arrange as shown in figure 4.12.

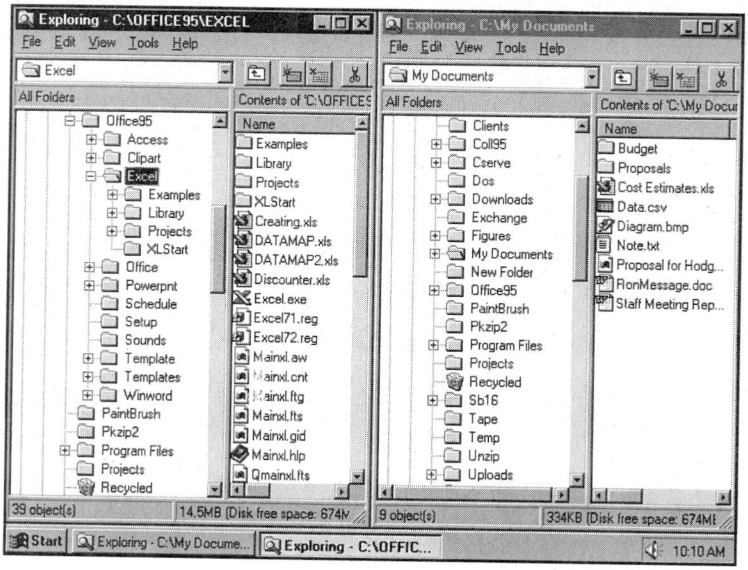

Fig. 4.11
Tiling application windows horizontally or vertically makes it easy to compare documents or to drag-and-drop contents.

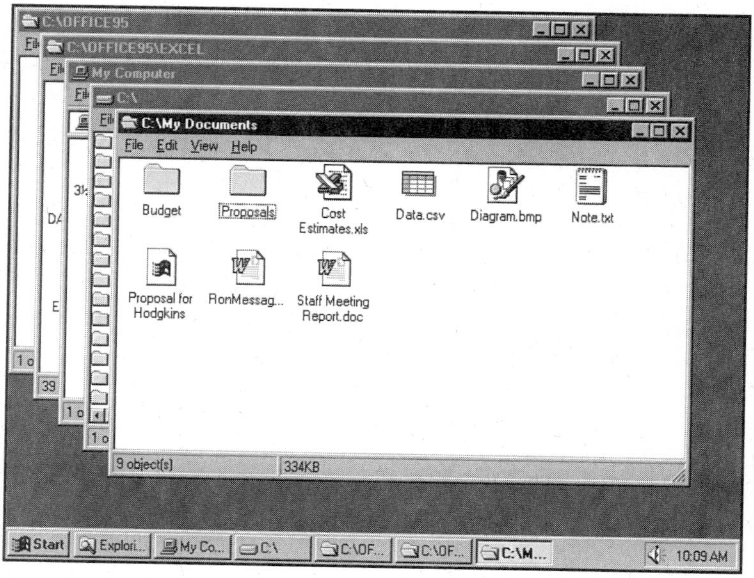

Fig. 4.12
Cascading application windows overlays them so that you can see each title bar. It is then easy to move among windows by clicking the title bars.

Tip
You cannot size a maximized window—a window that fills the screen—because you cannot make it any larger.

Moving a Window or a Desktop Icon

If an application window is not maximized (does not fill the screen), you can move the application's window. Move the pointer over the application's title at the top of its window, hold down the left mouse button, and drag the window to its new location. Windows displays an outline that indicates the application's position. When you release the mouse button, the window moves.

To drag document windows within the application, you use the same technique. As long as the document is within a window, you can drag its title bar. You can more easily arrange some documents within the application by choosing Window, Arrange All. This command puts document windows in predefined layouts.

Changing the Size of a Window

To change the size of a window with the mouse, you first activate the window by clicking on it. Move the pointer to one edge or corner of the window until the pointer changes to a two-headed arrow (refer to table 4.3). Press and hold down the mouse button, and then drag the double-headed arrow to move the edge or corner of the window to resize it. The moving edge appears as an outline until you release the mouse button.

To move two edges at once with the mouse, move the pointer to the corner of a window so that the pointer becomes a two-headed arrow tilted at a 45-degree angle. Drag the corner to its new location and release the mouse button.

Learning about Drag-and-Drop

After becoming proficient at operating Windows and its programs with commands, you will want to learn some of the faster but less obvious methods of controlling Windows and its programs. One of the most powerful methods is *drag-and-drop*.

▶ See "Drag-and-Drop Printing from the Desktop," p. 178

The term *drag-and-drop* specifies exactly the action that the method uses. You click on an object, such as a folder, and then hold down the mouse button as you drag the object to a new location. You drop the object by releasing the mouse button.

▶ See "Embedding an Excel Object by Dragging and Dropping," p. 448

For drag-and-drop methods to work, each Windows object has to know how to behave when dropped on other Windows objects. For example, if in the Explorer you drag the icon of a file and drop it on the icon for a program, the program starts and loads that file.

▶ See "Backing Up with a Simple Drag-and-Drop," p. 572

Figure 4.13 illustrates how you can use drag-and-drop to make frequently used folders more accessible. Instead of tediously having to find the folder each time in the Explorer, you can put on the desktop a shortcut icon that enables you to open the folder directly. To create a shortcut icon with drag-and-drop, follow these steps:

1. Double-click the My Computer icon to open its window. Make sure that the window does not fill the screen.

2. Double-click the local drive icon for your computer.

3. Click on a folder that you frequently use, then hold down the right mouse button and drag the folder out of the window and over the desktop.

   In figure 4.13, the user has dragged the Budgets folder to the desktop.

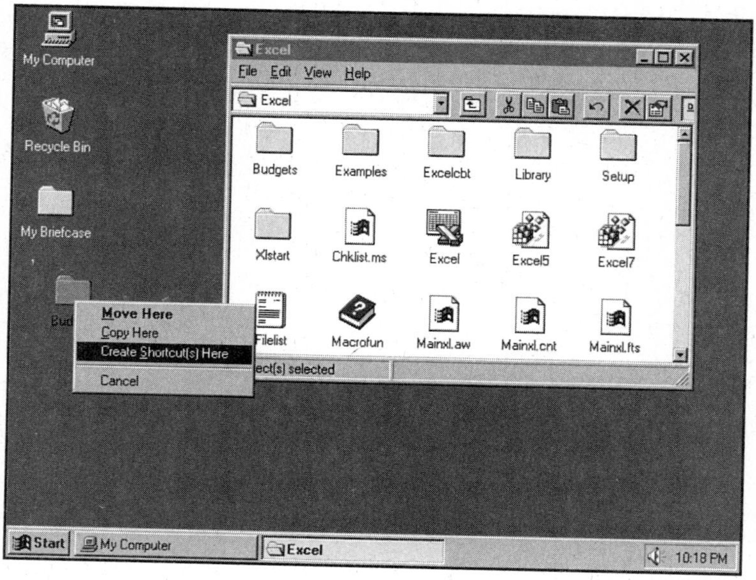

Fig. 4.13 The user has dragged the reverse-colored Budgets folder (by holding down the right mouse button) and dropped the folder to the desktop. When you release the mouse button, a shortcut menu appears.

Tip
You can tell at a glance that an icon is a shortcut by the small arrow at the lower left corner.

4. Release the right mouse button. A menu appears over the folder on the desktop as shown in figure 4.13.

5. Choose the Create Shortcut(s) Here command.

The Shortcut to Budgets icon, shown in figure 4.14, remains on the desktop even after you close the My Computer windows. You can open the folder at any time by double-clicking on the shortcut icon.

Caution

When dragging and dropping a file or folder, make sure that you use the right mouse button and choose Create Shortcut(s) Here from the shortcut menu. This creates a shortcut icon while leaving the original file or folder in its original location. If you delete the shortcut icon, the original file or folder remains intact. If you delete an original icon (which you create by dragging with the left mouse button) from your desktop, Windows deletes the original file or folder along with the icon. If the file is important, this causes a disaster and a lot of intra-office panic.

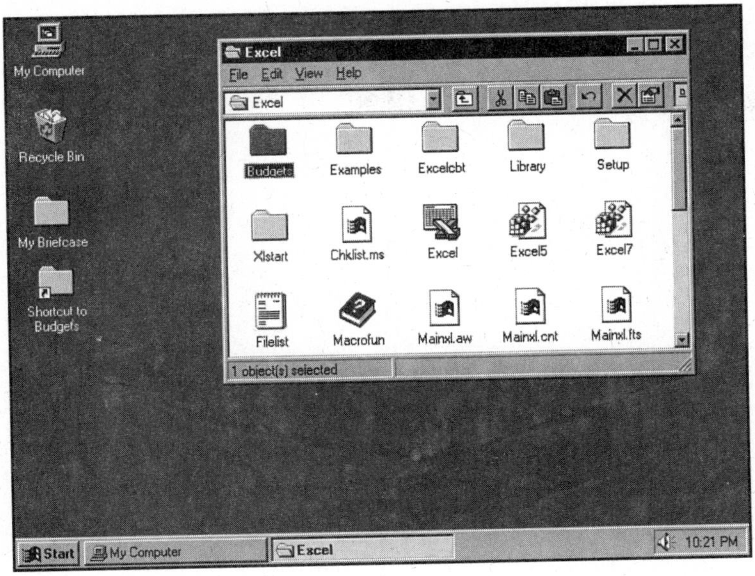

Fig. 4.14
Choosing the Create Shortcut(s) Here command produces on the desktop a shortcut icon that you can click to start the application.

> **Note**
>
> Drag-and-drop features are available only with Windows applications that are compatible with Object Linking and Embedding (OLE).

There are many ways that you can use the drag-and-drop method to save time. You can move and copy files and folders, which makes reorganizing the contents on your computer easy. You can drag a shortcut for your printer onto your desktop, drag documents from My Computer or the Explorer, and then drop them onto the printer icon, which prints the documents. With applications compatible with the OLE 2 specifications, you can even drag and drop objects from one application to another. For example, you can drag a table from a spreadsheet into a word processing document.

▶ See "Using Embedding to Link Information," p. 440

▶ See "Creating an Example Compound Document," p. 446

Throughout this book, you accomplish your computer tasks by using drag-and-drop methods. Always look for ways to use these methods for saving time and trouble.

Changing Settings and Properties with the Right Mouse Button

One important Windows concept is that most objects that you see on-screen have *properties* related to them. Properties can include such characteristics as an object's appearance and behavior.

You can change some properties, but others are *read-only*—you can view them, but cannot change them. For example, changeable properties of the Windows desktop include the types of patterns and wallpapers used as backgrounds and the color of different screen elements. Read-only properties that you can see but not change include a file's size or a program's version number.

You can experiment to find properties in Windows, the Explorer, and most Windows 95 applications. To see an object's properties, point to the object and click the right mouse button (that is, you *right-click* the object). A Properties sheet displays, or a menu displays a Properties command. For example, you can place the pointer's tip on most objects, such as the desktop or a file, and then click the right mouse button. From the menu that appears, select the Properties command.

Note

Don't be afraid to experiment when you look for properties. To discover how you can customize Windows, right-click on files, taskbars, and so on. If you do not want to change the object's properties, press the Esc key or click the Cancel button in the Properties sheet that appears.

To see the properties that you can change on the desktop, right-click on the desktop and then choose the Properties command. The Display Properties sheet shown in figure 4.15 appears. In this dialog box, you can change the display's background, color, and screen saver, and display adapter settings. To learn how to change these settings, see Chapter 5, "Customizing Windows 95." Click the Cancel button to remove the dialog box without making changes.

If you want to change how the taskbar operates, right-click on a blank area of the taskbar and then choose the Properties command. The Taskbar Properties sheet displays. On this sheet, you can add or remove applications from the Start menu, or change when and how the taskbar displays. Chapter 5, "Customizing Windows 95," describes this Properties sheet and how to customize the taskbar. Click the Cancel button to remove the dialog box without making changes.

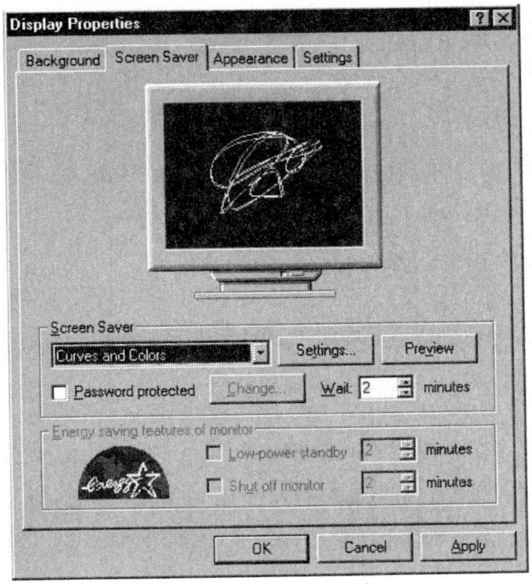

Fig. 4.15
Right-click on the desktop and then choose Properties to see the desktop properties. The Screen Saver page, shown here, enables you to choose a screen saver.

Working with Applications

Many operations are similar among Windows applications. Nearly all Windows applications, for example, start with the File and Edit menus. The File menu includes commands for opening, closing, saving, and printing files. The Edit menu includes commands for cutting, copying, pasting, and other editing actions specific to the application. The procedures you use to control menus and select items in dialog boxes is the same in nearly all Windows applications.

Opening, Saving, and Closing Documents

When you create or edit a document and then save the document, you create a *file* that Windows stores in a magnetic recording on disk. The file contains all the information necessary to recreate the document in your program. When this book uses the term *file*, it usually refers to the information stored on the computer's hard disk or on a removable disk.

When first started, many applications present a new, empty document—a blank page if the application is a word processing, graphics, or desktop publishing application, an empty worksheet if the application is a spreadsheet application. If you finish working on one file, you can start a new file by choosing File, New. Your application might ask you for information about the type of new file to start.

Tip
Double-click on a file name in the Open dialog box to open that file.

To open an existing file, choose File, Open. An Open dialog box similar to the one shown in figure 4.16 appears. In the Look In drop-down list, select the drive that contains your file. The Look In drop-down list displays your computer's drives as icons. Click on the drive you want to look in. In the Look In box, select the folder that contains your file and then choose OK to display the list of files in that folder. From the files presented, select the one that you want to open and then choose OK or press Enter.

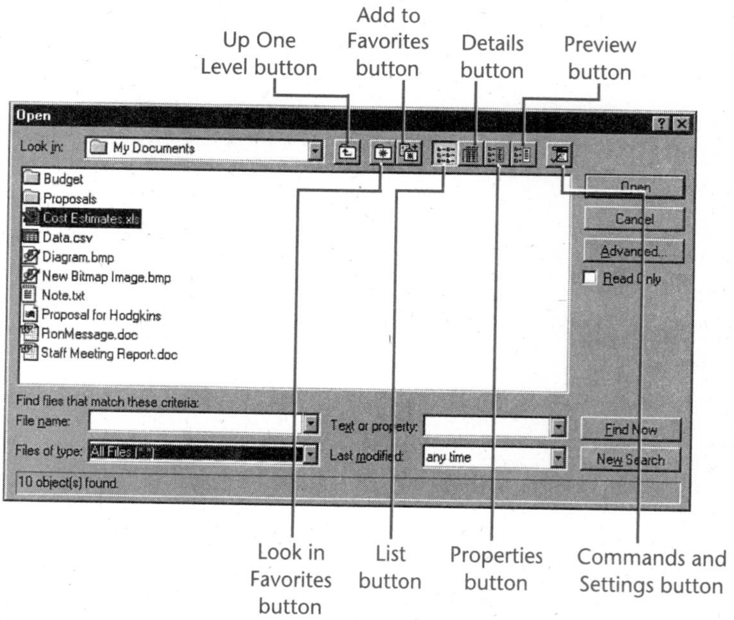

Fig. 4.16
The Open dialog box is common to many Windows applications.

You can do far more in a Windows 95 Open dialog box than meets the eye. Click on a button at the top of the dialog box to get the result you want. Table 4.4 lists the buttons and their results.

Table 4.4 Open Dialog Box Buttons

Button	Result
Up One Level button	Move up to the next higher folder
Look in Favorites button	Look at a list of favorite or frequently used files
Add to Favorites button	Add the selected file to the Favorites list
List button	Display files in a list view

Button	Result
Details button	Display files with all file details shown
Properties button	Display a file or folder properties
Preview button	Display the contents of a file using QuickView
Commands and Settings button	Select from a shortcut menu to print, sort, or search for files and map to a network drive

Explore with your right mouse button by clicking on files or folders to see some of the things you can do to files and folders. When you right-click on a file or folder, a shortcut menu appears with various commands you can choose from. The specific commands on the menu can vary, depending on the file type. Table 4.5 lists the basic options that are available for most file types.

Table 4.5 Shortcut Commands for Files and Folders

Command	Result
Open	Opens the file.
Open Read Only	Open as a read-only document that must be saved to a different file name.
Print	Print the file.
Quick View	Display a preview of the file.
Send To	Copy the file to a shortcut folder, floppy disk, mail or Fax address.
Cut	Remove the file or folder from its location in preparation to paste elsewhere.
Copy	Copy the file or folder in preparation to copy the file elsewhere.
Paste	Paste a file or folder that has been cut or copied. This command appears only when it is appropriate.
Create Shortcut	Create a shortcut to the file or folder.
Delete	Delete the selection(s).
Properties	Display the file or folder properties.

Tip
In some applications, you can open multiple documents by selecting the files with Ctrl+click and then clicking the Open button.

The File menu contains two commands for saving files: Save As and Save. Choose one of these commands the first time that you save a file. They tell Windows where to save the file and enable you to name your file. If you choose File, Save As, you can create a new version of an existing file by specifying a new name for the file. The Save As dialog box is often similar to the Open dialog box shown in figure 4.16. In the Save As dialog box, you must specify the drive and folder to which you want to save your file and name the file.

After you type the file name in the File name text box, choose Save or press Enter to save the file. After you name your file, you can choose File, Save to save the file without changing its name or location. The File, Save command replaces the original file.

To close a document, you often can choose File, Close. If you choose File, Exit, you exit the application. When you close or exit a Windows application, most prompt you to save any changes that you made since you last saved your document.

Scrolling in a Document

Most applications include scroll bars at the right and bottom edges of the screen, as shown in figure 4.17. You can use the vertical scroll bar at the right to scroll up and down in your document. You can use the horizontal scroll bar to scroll left and right. To scroll a short distance, click on the arrow at either end of a scroll bar; you scroll in the direction that the arrow points. To scroll a longer distance, click in the gray area next to the arrow or drag the scroll bar box to a new location. In many applications, the scroll bars are optional; if you want more working space, you can turn them off.

To scroll with the keyboard, you can press the arrow keys to move a character or line at a time, or press the Page Up or Page Down keys to move a screen at a time. The Home key usually scrolls you to the left margin, and the End key takes you to the end of the line or the right side. Holding down the Ctrl key while pressing any other scrolling key extends the scroll: Ctrl+Home, for example, takes you to the beginning of your file; Ctrl+End takes you to the end of the file; Ctrl+left-arrow or Ctrl+right-arrow moves you a word at a time rather than a character at a time. Most applications have many shortcuts for scrolling.

If you use the scroll bars to scroll, the insertion point does not move; it remains where it was before you scrolled. If you use the keyboard to scroll, the insertion point moves as you scroll.

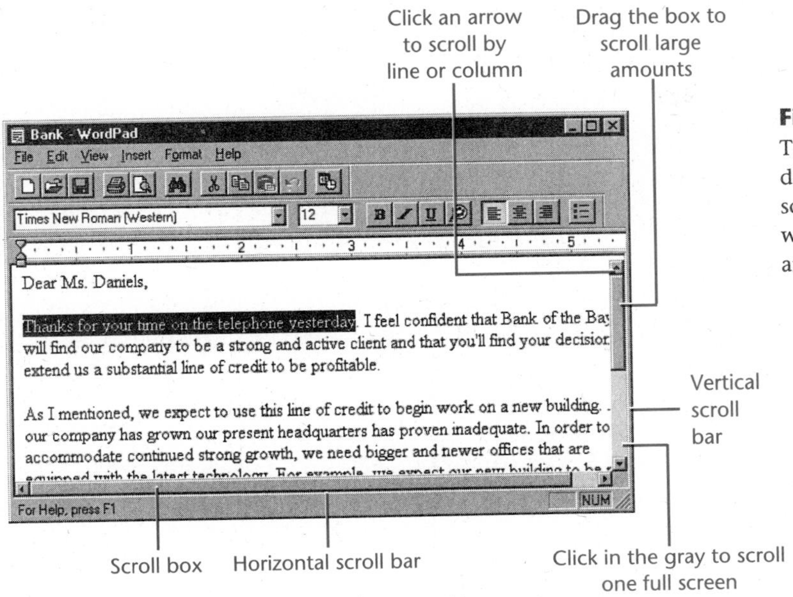

Fig. 4.17
To scroll through a document, use the scroll bars on the window's right and bottom sides.

Using Simple Editing Techniques

Editing text and objects is similar in all Windows applications. When you work with text, in your document or in a dialog box, the mouse pointer turns into an I-beam when you move it over editable text. You can use the I-beam to move the insertion point and select text. The flashing vertical insertion point is where the text that you type appears. (The insertion point is equivalent to the cursor in DOS applications.)

You can use the mouse or the keyboard to move the insertion point. To use the mouse, position the I-beam where you want the insertion point in the text and click the left mouse button. (If you cannot see the insertion point, it might be under the I-beam. Move the mouse a little to move the I-beam.) To use the keyboard to move the insertion point, press the arrow keys.

Tip
Although the pointer changes to an I-beam over editable text, you cannot edit at the location until you click the mouse button.

To insert text at the insertion point, you simply type. Most applications push existing text to the right to make room for the new text (although some applications enable you to select an overtype mode, which replaces existing text as you type). To delete text to the left of the insertion point, press the Backspace key. To delete text to the right of the insertion point, press the Delete key.

> **Caution**
>
> If you accidentally press the Insert key, you turn on Overtype mode, which types new text over existing text. If this happens, press the Insert key again. Some applications display OVR or a similar indicator in the status bar to show when they are in Overtype mode.

Selecting Text and Objects

Tip
Most applications contain an "oops" function: the Edit, Undo command. This command undoes your most recent edit (or more, depending on the program). Use this command when you make an edit that you instantly regret.

You can sum up one of the most important editing rules in all Windows applications with three simple words: select, then do. You must select text or an object before you can do anything to it (if you don't select first, the application doesn't know where to apply your command).

To select text and objects, you can use the mouse or the keyboard. To select text with the mouse, position the I-beam at the beginning of the text that you want to select, click and hold down the left mouse button, drag to the end of the text that you want to select, and release the mouse button. To select text with the keyboard, position the insertion point at the beginning of the text that you want to select, press and hold down the Shift key, use arrow keys to move to the end of the text that you want to select, and then release the Shift and arrow keys. The selected text appears in reverse type, as shown in figure 4.17.

Many shortcuts exist for selecting. Some of the following shortcuts apply to text in many Windows documents and dialog boxes:

- To select a word with the mouse, double-click on the word.
- To select a word using the keyboard, hold down Ctrl+Shift while pressing the left- or right-arrow key.
- To select a length of text with the mouse, you can drag until you touch the end of the screen, which causes the screen to scroll.
- To select a length of text with the keyboard, position the I-beam where you want to start the selection, hold down the Shift key, and scroll to the end of the selection by using any keyboard scrolling technique.

After you select a word, you can change its appearance. For example, you might make the word bold or change its font. In most applications, typing replaces the selection, which enables you to replace text by selecting it and typing the new text. If you select a graphic, you can resize it or apply formatting.

To use the mouse to select an object such as a picture, click on the object. (To select multiple objects, hold down Shift while you click on each one in turn.) To select objects with the keyboard, position the insertion point beside the object, hold down Shift, and press an arrow key to move the object in the direction indicated by the arrow key. Selected objects, such as graphics, usually appear with *selection handles* (small black boxes) on each side and corner.

Copying and Moving

After selecting text or an object, you can use the Edit menu to copy or move the selection. The Edit menu commands that all Windows applications use to copy and move are Cut, Copy, and Paste. The Edit, Cut command removes the selection from your document, and Edit, Copy duplicates it. Both commands transfer the selection to the Clipboard, a temporary holding area. The Edit, Paste command copies the selection from the Clipboard and into your document at the insertion point's location. Your selection remains in the Clipboard until you replace it with another selection.

Tip
To copy and paste between documents and dialog boxes, try using the shortcut keys described in this section.

To copy a selection, choose Edit, Copy; then move the insertion point to where you want to duplicate the selection, and choose Edit, Paste. To move a selection, choose Edit, Cut; then move the insertion point to where you want to move it, and choose Edit, Paste. Many shortcuts exist for copying and moving. Ctrl+X usually cuts a selection, Ctrl+C copies a selection, and Ctrl+V usually pastes the Clipboard's contents. Many Windows applications also take advantage of the Windows drag-and-drop feature, which enables you to use the mouse to drag a selection to its new location and drop it into place.

▶ See "Using the Windows Clipboard," p. 411

▶ See "Using Drag-and-Drop to Copy Information between Documents," p. 421

Because all applications running under Windows share the Clipboard, you can move or copy a selection between documents and between applications as easily as you can move and copy within a file. The next two sections explain how to switch between documents and applications.

Switching between Document Windows

In many (but not all) Windows applications, you can easily open more than one document and switch between the documents in the same application. Use these techniques when you want to copy or move information from one document to another. To open multiple documents, choose File, Open multiple times, each time opening a different document. If your application doesn't support multiple documents, it closes the current file, asking whether you want to save any changes that you made since you last saved.

If your application supports multiple documents, each document opens in its own document window as shown in figure 4.18. Multiple document windows have a document Control menu to control the active document window's size and position.

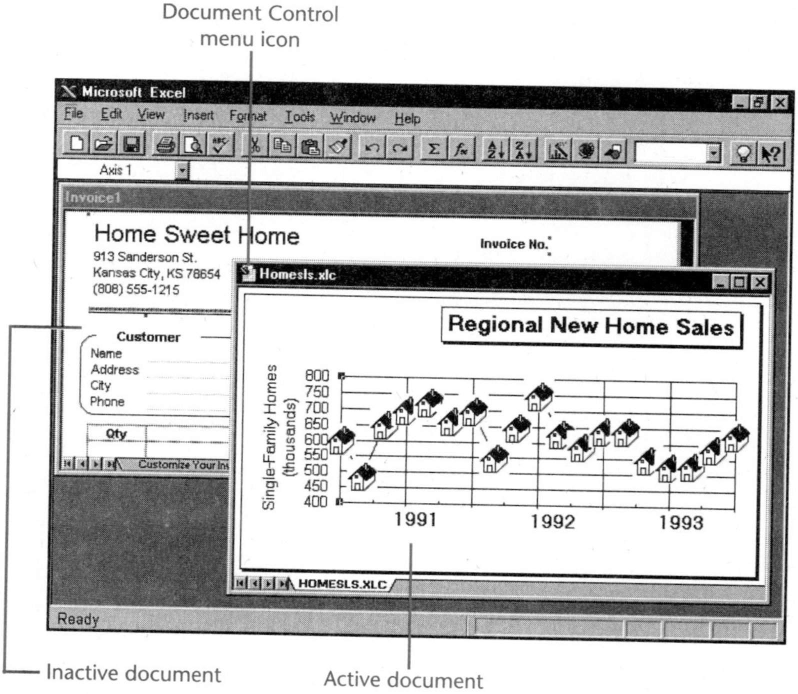

Fig. 4.18
Control document windows with these buttons.

The document Control menu appears to the left of the document title bar, or if the document is displayed as a full screen, to the left of the menu bar. You can click on the document Control menu icon to display the Control menu. This menu enables you to change the window's size or close the document. If you are using the keyboard, press Alt+hyphen (-). There is, however, an easier way to control document windows than through the document Control menu.

A faster way to control documents in Windows is to use the buttons that appear at the top-right corner of each document, as shown in figures 4.19 and 4.20. If the document fills the application window, the Restore Document button appears to the right of the menu bar as shown in figure 4.19.

If a document is in its own window, three buttons appear at the top-right corner of the document's title bar, as shown in figure 4.20. Click on one of these buttons to reduce the document to an icon, enlarge the document to fill the application window, or close the document.

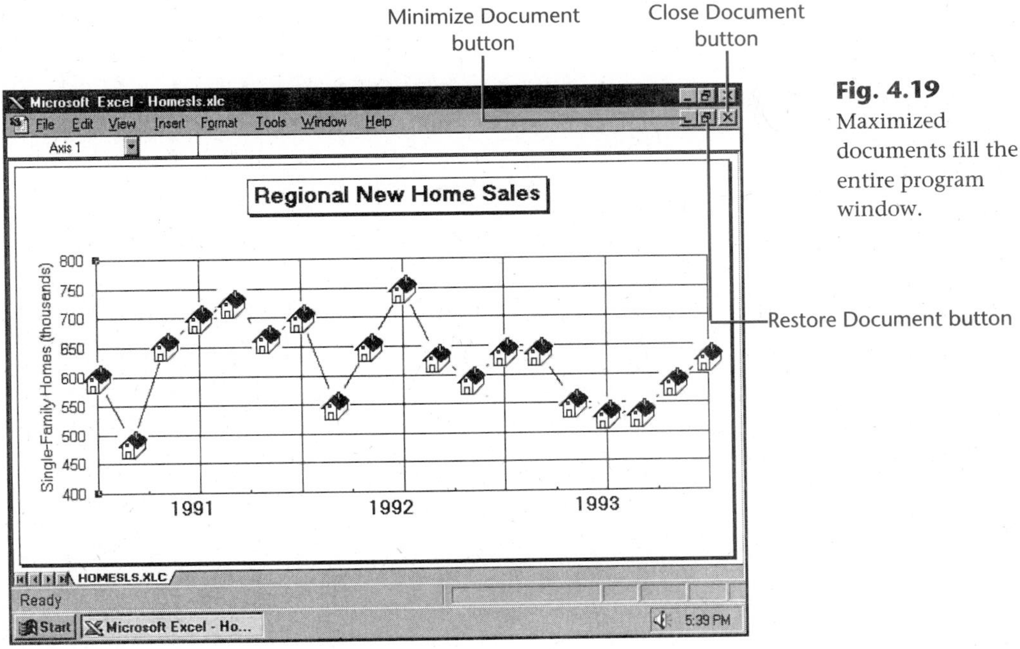

Fig. 4.19
Maximized documents fill the entire program window.

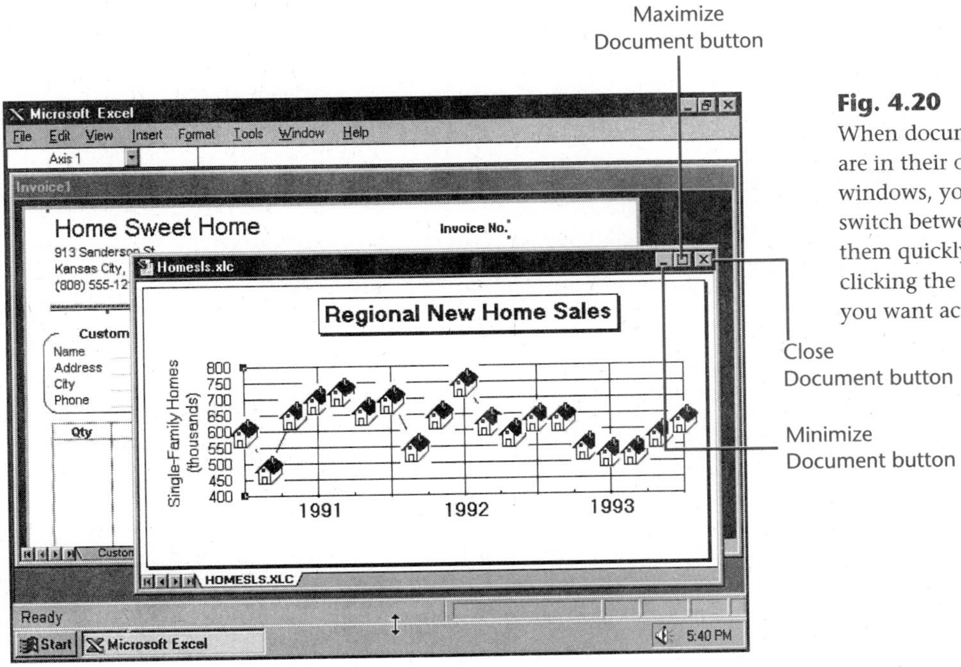

Fig. 4.20
When documents are in their own windows, you can switch between them quickly by clicking the one you want active.

Reducing a document window creates an icon in the application window such as that shown in figure 4.21. Notice that this icon has three buttons that you can click to restore the document to a window, enlarge it to full screen, or close it.

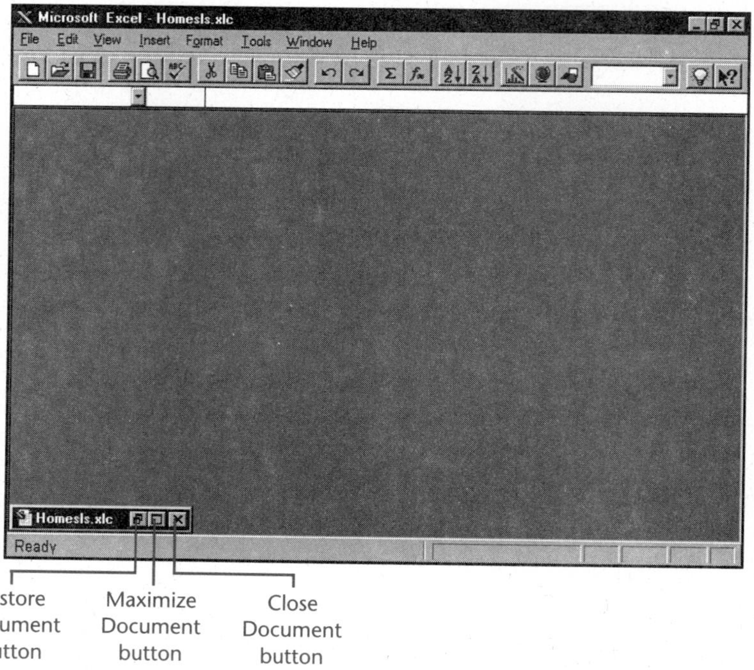

Fig. 4.21 Documents reduced to icons require less space in the program's window.

Switching between Applications

◀ See "Using Taskbar Shortcuts to Arrange Windows," p. 103

When you run several applications, you need an easy way to switch between them. If the taskbar is visible, you can switch to another application by clicking on the application's button in the taskbar. If you cannot see the taskbar, press Ctrl+Esc to display it and open the Start menu.

Another way to switch between applications is to hold down the Alt key and press Tab. When you first press Alt+Tab, a bar with open applications appears as shown in figure 4.22. Continue holding the Alt key to keep the bar onscreen. Each time you press Alt+Tab the next application on the bar is selected. A box encloses the icon of the active application. Press Shift+Alt+Tab to move the selection to the application to the left. Release Alt+Tab when you have selected the application that you want to activate.

Fig. 4.22
Press Alt+Tab to switch to another open application.

To switch between document windows with the mouse, click on the window that you want to activate. If the window that you want to activate is not visible, you might have to move or size the active window on top. (To move a window, drag its title bar; to size a window, drag its border.) To use the keyboard to switch between document windows, open the Window menu and select from the list of open windows the document that you want.❖

Chapter 5

Customizing Windows 95

by Ron Person

The more you use Windows, the more you'll appreciate its customization options. You can save time by setting features so that they normally appear or act in the way you prefer. You can change date and time formats, languages, keyboards, mouse settings, and more. And you can set colors, fonts, and desktop backgrounds so that they are personal to you.

Many Windows users feel more comfortable with their computers after they customize the Windows screen. Applying a personally selected color, pattern, and background makes their computer seem more like a personal belonging. Another way you can customize the screen, and even add protection from prying eyes, is to enable the screen saver that comes with Windows.

There are a number of simple things you can do to make working in Windows easier. For example, you can customize your taskbar to appear only when you want it to. That gives your applications more room on-screen. You can also position the taskbar in locations other than at the bottom of the screen. If you frequently use the same applications, you can add them to the Start menu so they are easy to find.

If you work with different types of Windows software and have a more up-to-date video adapter and monitor, you will want to take advantage of Windows' capability to switch between different display resolutions. This can be useful when you're running different types of applications or when switching a mobile computer between mobile and desktop operation.

In this chapter, you learn to:

- Customize the taskbar and add programs to the Start menu and Program menu
- Customize the desktop pattern or graphic as well as all the colors used by elements in Windows
- Control how your mouse works
- Control how your keyboard works
- Change your computer's date and time
- Change international settings
- Add a password to protect the settings you customize

Customizing the Taskbar

The taskbar is one of the most important and innovative features in Windows 95. It accounts for a lot of the reasons why Windows 95 is easier to use than previous versions of Windows. While the basic taskbar makes Windows easier to use for novices, once you have some experience you can customize the taskbar to fit the way you work. That makes it both easier and more efficient.

When you begin working in Windows 95, the taskbar appears as a simple gray bar at the bottom of the screen, displaying only the Start menu and the clock. As you begin working with applications, you notice that each open application adds a button to the taskbar. These buttons show you what applications are running. Clicking these buttons switches you from application to application.

Tip
Any open application appears as a button on the taskbar. Click the button to activate the application.

If you work with a lot of open applications, your screen can become cluttered with many open windows. Rather than clutter the screen with several open windows, you can reduce the applications you're not using currently to buttons on the taskbar. As more buttons appear on the taskbar, the other buttons shrink to make room. To activate an application, you simply click its button on the taskbar. Figure 5.1 shows a taskbar with several buttons.

Fig. 5.1
Use the taskbar to temporarily store applications while you're not using them.

Note

If you have many applications open, you may not be able to read the application and document name on the taskbar button. If the application and document name are truncated, pause the pointer over the button. A button tip will appear showing the full names.

To reduce an application to a button on the taskbar, click the Minimize button. To reactivate an application, click its button in the taskbar.

Troubleshooting

Right-clicking on the taskbar displays a shortcut menu that appears to control the applications that are minimized as buttons. The taskbar shortcut menu doesn't appear.

Right-click in the gray area between buttons to see the taskbar shortcut menu.

After clicking on Auto Hide in the Taskbar Properties sheet, the taskbar "hides" when an application opens, but when a window is maximized the taskbar won't come back, even dragging the mouse pointer to the bottom of the screen doesn't display it.

Usually you should set two properties when you want the taskbar to automatically hide. But first you must get the taskbar displayed again. When you get stuck without a taskbar, press Ctrl+Esc to display the taskbar and Start menu. Press Esc once to remove the menu so just the taskbar shows. Click with the right mouse in a gray area of the taskbar, then click Properties. Select both the Auto Hide and the Always on Top check boxes. Without the Always on Top option the mouse pointer can't touch the thin gray line at the screen edge that reactivates the taskbar.

Resizing the Taskbar

You can change the size of the taskbar to accommodate a large number of buttons or to make it easier to read the full description written on a button. To resize the taskbar, follow these steps:

1. Point to the edge of the taskbar. The pointer becomes a double-pointing arrow.
2. Hold down the left mouse button, drag to the size you want, and then release the button.

The taskbar resizes in full button widths. If the taskbar is horizontal against the top or bottom of the screen, you can change its height. If the taskbar is positioned vertically against a side, you can change its width.

Moving the Taskbar

The taskbar can be positioned horizontally (the default) along the top or bottom of the desktop or vertically along the side of the desktop (see fig. 5.2). To reposition the taskbar, follow these steps:

1. Point to a position on the taskbar where no button appears, either below or between buttons.

2. Hold down the left mouse button and drag to the edge of the screen where you want to position the taskbar. A shaded line indicates the new position of the taskbar.

3. Release the mouse button.

When the taskbar is positioned at the side of the desktop, it may be so wide that you don't have enough space to work. If so, you can drag the edge of the taskbar to give it a new width. When the taskbar is against a side, you can change its width in pixel increments, not just in full button widths.

Using the Taskbar Menu

As in other Windows screen areas, you can click the right mouse button in a gray area of the taskbar to display a menu (see fig. 5.3). Use the taskbar menu to rearrange windows on the desktop, to reduce applications to buttons, and to change the properties of the taskbar.

Fig. 5.2
Reposition the taskbar for your convenience.

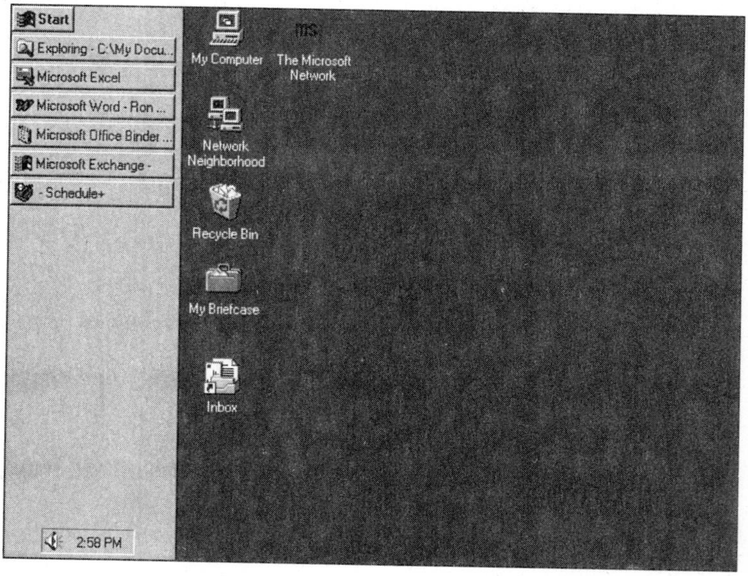

The following table describes each of the commands on the taskbar menu.

Command	Description
Cascade	Display windows one over the other from left to right, top to bottom (see fig. 5.4).
Undo Cascade	(Available only after using Cascade.) Returns windows to their previous sizes and positions after using Cascade.
Tile Horizontally	Display windows top to bottom without overlapping (see fig. 5.5).
Tile Vertically	Display windows left to right without overlapping (see fig. 5.6).
Undo Tile	(Available only after using Tile Horizontally or Tile Vertically.) Returns windows to their previous sizes and positions after using one of the Tile commands.
Minimize All Windows	Reduces all open windows to buttons on the taskbar.
Properties	Displays the Taskbar Properties sheet where you can change the Start menu or taskbar options.

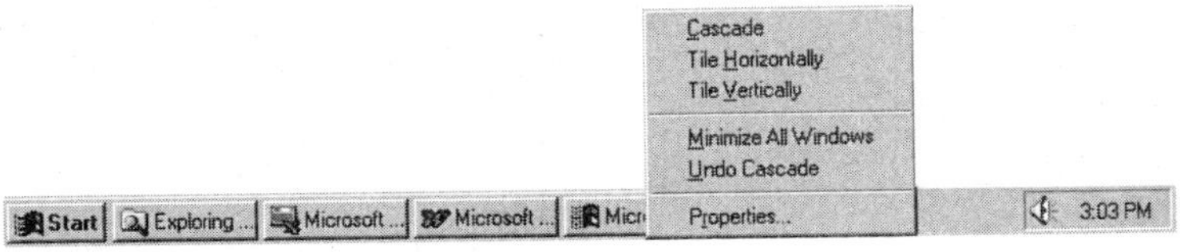

Fig. 5.3
Right-click in the gray area of the taskbar to display the shortcut menu.

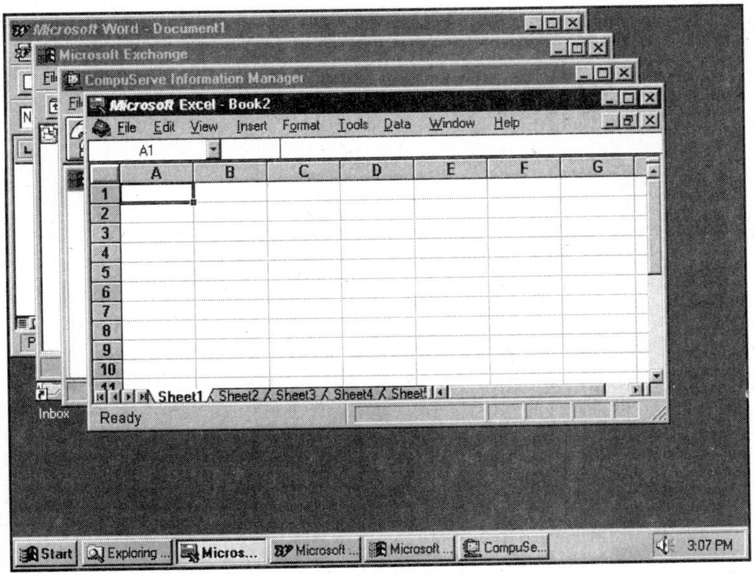

Fig. 5.4
Cascading windows.

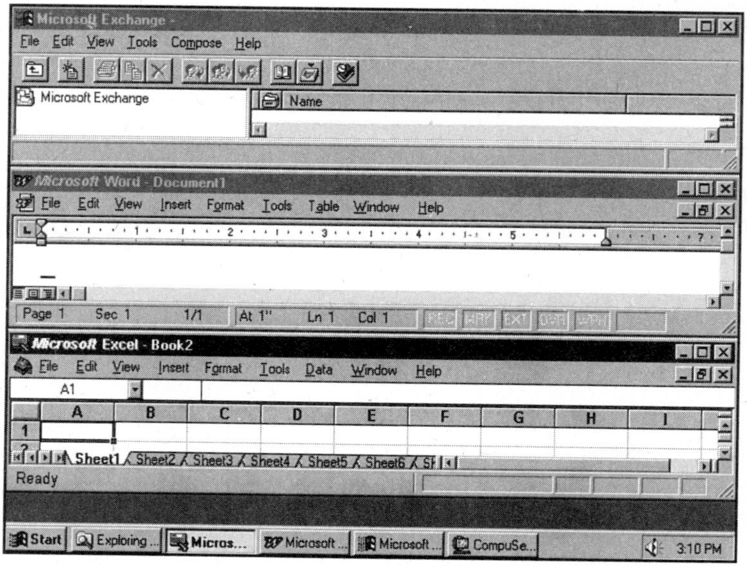

Fig. 5.5
Windows tiled horizontally.

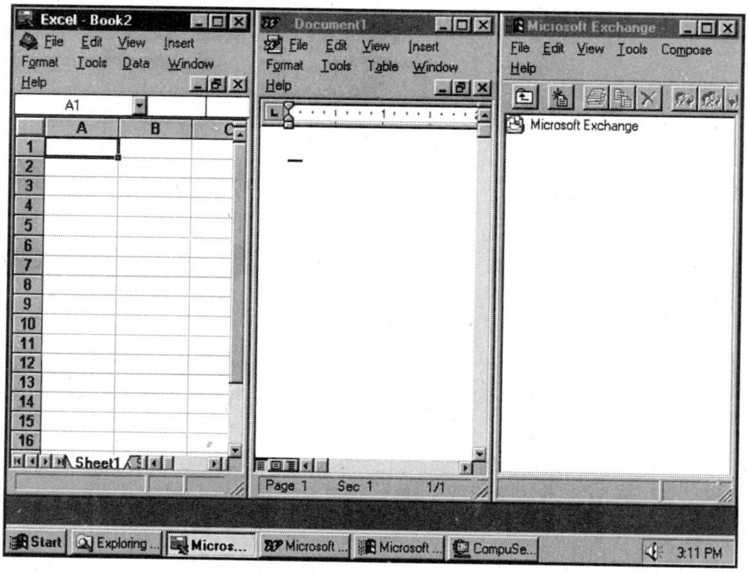

Fig. 5.6
Windows tiled vertically.

Changing the Taskbar Options

You can hide or display the taskbar using the Taskbar Properties sheet. Figure 5.7 shows the commands available from the Taskbar Options tab. You also can turn the clock area of the taskbar on and off.

To change taskbar properties, follow these steps:

1. Point to a position on the taskbar where no button appears, either below or between buttons, and right-click. Choose Properties.

   or

   Open the Start menu and choose Settings, Taskbar.

2. Click the Taskbar Options tab.

3. Click a check box to turn an item on or off. The options are explained in the following table.

4. Click OK.

Option	Description
Always On Top	The taskbar displays over all open windows.
Auto Hide	Hides the taskbar to make more space available on your desktop and in application windows. To see the taskbar, move your mouse pointer to the bottom of the screen (or wherever the taskbar is if you have moved it) and the taskbar reappears. When you move the pointer away, the taskbar disappears again.
Show Small Icons In Start Menu	Displays the Start menu with small icons and without the Windows banner. This enables you to see more of what's on-screen while in the Start menu.
Show Clock	Hides or displays the clock in one corner of the taskbar.

► See "Using the Taskbar Clock," p. 406

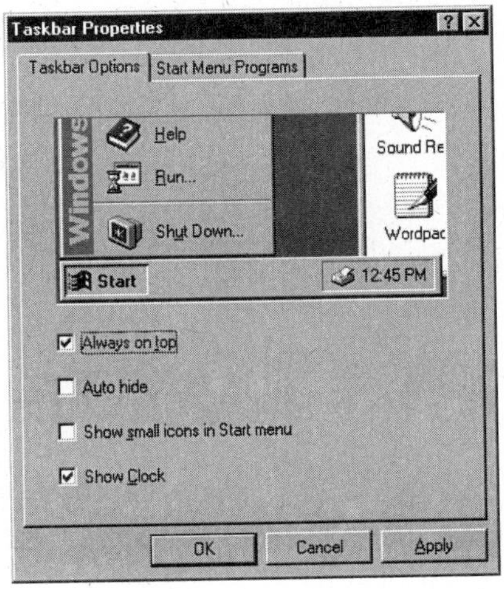

Fig. 5.7
Right-click in the gray area of the taskbar and then choose Properties when you want to change how your taskbar operates.

Customizing the Start Menu

Tip
To quickly add a program to the highest level of the Start menu, drag the program's file from the Explorer or My Computer window and drop it on the Start button.

The contents of the Start menu can be customized. You can add a list of applications you use frequently, and then start those applications directly from the menu. By adding programs to the Start menu, you avoid having to display additional menus.

To add a program to the Start menu, follow these steps:

1. Right-click on a gray area between buttons on the taskbar. Choose Properties.

   or

   Open the Start menu and choose Settings, Taskbar.

2. Click the Start Menu Programs tab.

Fig. 5.8
The Start Menu Programs page enables you to add programs to the Start menu.

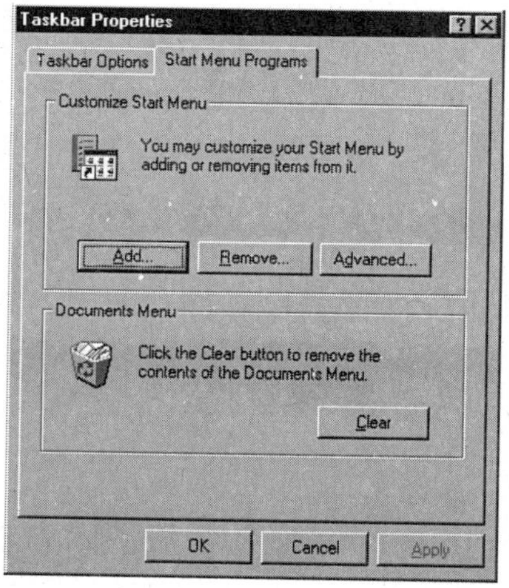

3. Click Add to display the Create Shortcut dialog box shown in figure 5.9.

◄ See "Opening, Saving, and Closing Documents," p. 109

4. Click Browse to display the Browse dialog box. This dialog box looks very similar to an Open File dialog box.

5. Find and click the file that starts the program or document file you want to add to the Start menu. Choose the Open button once you have selected the file.

   You can limit the displayed files to program files by selecting Programs from the Files of Type list at the bottom of the dialog box. For example, if you wanted to start Excel, you would open the Office95 folder, open the Excel folder, and then click on EXCEL.EXE. Most program files use an EXE extension.

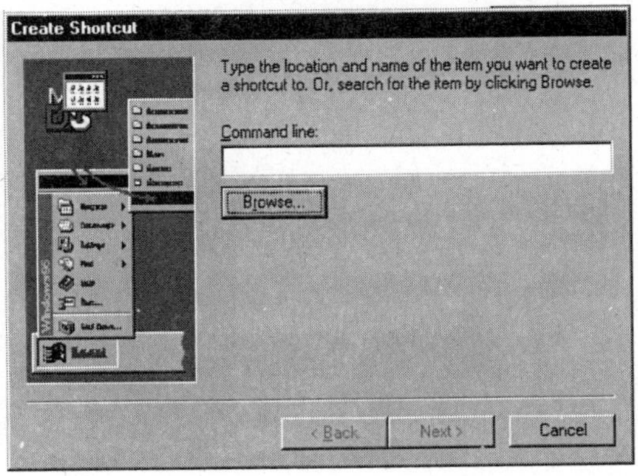

Fig. 5.9
In the Create Shortcut dialog box, you want to type or select the file of the program you want to add to the Start menu.

6. Click Next> to display the Select Program Folder dialog box shown in figure 5.10.

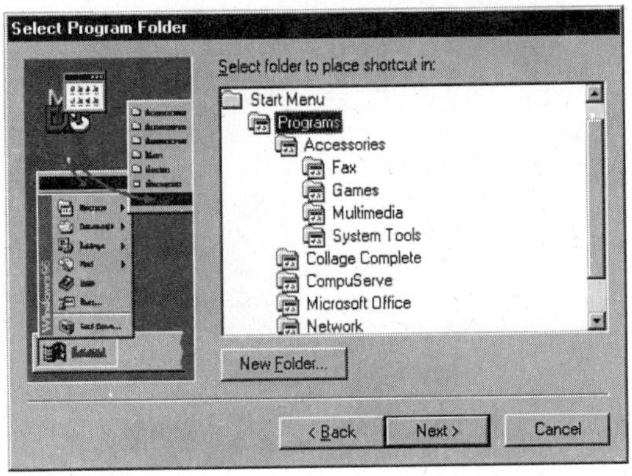

Fig. 5.10
You can position your document or application anywhere on the Start menu.

7. Select the folder that corresponds to the location on the Start menu where you want the program to appear. Choose Next>.

   For example, if you wanted the program you selected to appear at the top of the Start menu, you would select the Start Menu folder. If you wanted the program to appear as an item on the Programs menu, then you would select the Programs folder.

8. Type the name or words you want to appear on the Start menu in the edit box. Choose Finish.

Tip
Adding a document's file to the Start menu enables you to open the document in its related application.

Note

If you frequently copy files to the same folders, put Shortcuts to those folders in the WINDOWS\SENDTO folder. The shortcuts to the folders will then show up on the Send To menu that appears when you right-click on a file.

◄ See "Starting Programs from a Shortcut Icon on the Desktop," p. 68

To remove a program from the Start menu, you follow a similar process:

1. Display the Taskbar Properties sheet as described earlier in this chapter.
2. Click the Start Menu Programs tab.
3. Click the Remove button to display the Remove Shortcuts/Folders dialog box shown in figure 5.11.

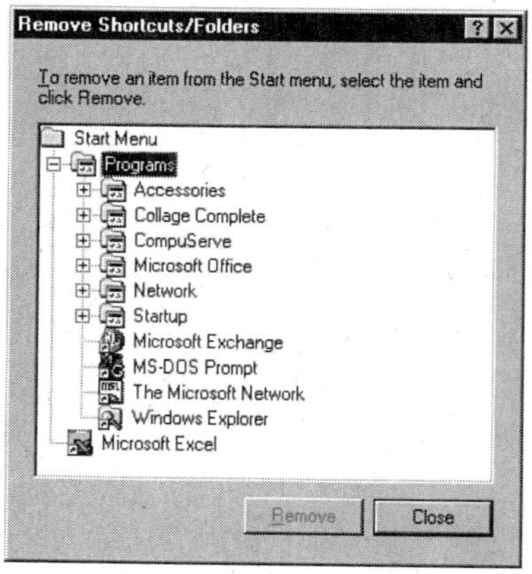

Fig. 5.11
In the Remove Shortcuts/Folders dialog box, select the file or folder you want to remove from the Start menu.

4. Select the shortcut or folder you want to remove from the Start menu.
5. Click the Remove button to remove the file or folder.
6. Remove additional items or choose Close. Choose OK when you return to the Taskbar Properties sheet.

The Start menu contains a Documents item that shows a list of recently used documents. At times this list may become too long, or you may want to clear the list so that documents are easier to find. To clear the documents from the Documents menu, follow these steps:

1. Display the Taskbar Properties sheet.

2. Click the Start Menu Programs tab.
3. Click Clear in the Documents Menu portion of the page.
4. Choose OK.

Customizing the Desktop Colors and Background

Changing colors is just one way you can customize the windows you see on-screen. You also can change the pattern used in the desktop background, add a graphical wallpaper as a background, change the border width of windows, and more.

Wallpaper options you select for the desktop background can include graphics that come with Windows—including some wild and colorful ones—and designs you create or modify with Windows Paint. The graphic images you use as wallpaper are nothing more than computer drawings saved in a bitmap (BMP) format. You also can use the Windows Paint program to create your own bitmap drawings to use as screen backgrounds.

► See "Saving Paint Files," p. 395

► See "Changing the Windows Desktop with Paint," p. 393

You can put wallpaper over just the center portion of the desktop, or you can tile the desktop with wallpaper. When tiling, the wallpaper reproduces itself to fill the screen.

Changing Windows Colors

After working in the drab and dreary DOS or mainframe computer world, one of the first changes many people want to make is to add color to their Windows screens. You can pick colors for window titles, backgrounds, bars—in fact, all parts of the window. Predesigned color schemes range from the brilliant to the cool and dark. You also can design and save your own color schemes and blend your own colors.

Tip
Large, complex bitmap drawings consume a lot of memory. If Windows' performance slows when a large wallpaper is used, you may want to return to a small bitmap that is tiled over the screen, or use no bitmap at all.

Using Existing Color Schemes

Windows comes with a list of predefined color schemes. Each color scheme maps a different color and text to a different part of the screen.

You can select from existing schemes, or you can devise your own (described in the next section). Figure 5.12 shows the Appearance page. To select one of the predefined schemes, follow these steps:

1. Right-click the desktop, choose Properties, and then select the Appearance tab.

You can also open the Start menu and choose Settings, Control Panel; then double-click the Display icon and select the Appearance tab.

The Appearance page of the Display Properties sheet displays, as shown in figure 5.12.

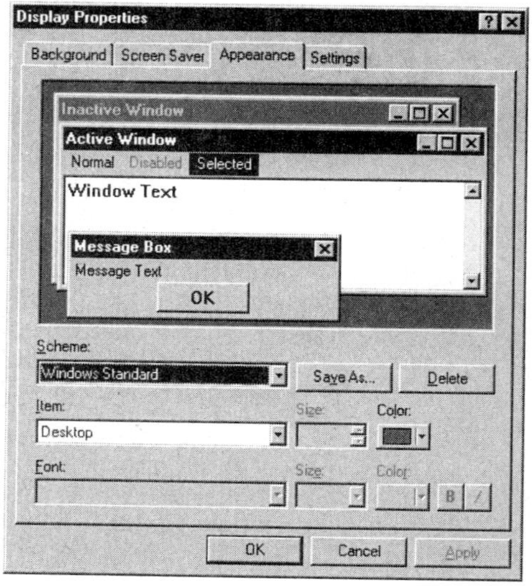

Fig. 5.12
Select from existing color and text schemes on the Appearance page to customize Windows' appearance.

Tip
If you have trouble reading the menus and seeing icons, choose Windows Standard (Large) or Windows Standard (Extra Large) from the Scheme list.

2. Select the Scheme list and select a predefined color and text scheme from the list. The sample screen at the top of the sheet illustrates what this color scheme looks like.

3. Choose OK to use the displayed color scheme or return to step 2 for other predefined schemes.

Creating Custom Color and Text Schemes

If you don't like the predesigned color and text schemes, you can create your own or modify one of the existing schemes. You can change all or some of the colors in a scheme, the text, and even the color and width of borders. To create new color schemes while the Appearance page is open, follow these steps:

1. If you want to use an existing scheme as a base (as opposed to using Windows Standard as a base), select the scheme from the Scheme list.

2. Select from the Item list the screen element you want to modify. Or click on a screen element in the sample window at the top of the sheet. You can select elements such as the Menu Bar, Button, Active Border, and so on.

3. Select from the Size, Font, and Color lists how you want to change the selected element. Some options are only available for certain elements.

4. Choose one of these alternatives for the colors you have selected:

   - If you want to color another window element, return to step 2.
   - If you want to use these colors now but not save them for the next time you run Windows, choose OK or press Enter.
   - If you want to save these colors so that you can use them now or return to them at any time, choose the Save As button. Then type a name in the Save Scheme dialog box and choose OK.
   - If you want to cancel these colors and return to the original scheme, select that scheme from the Scheme list if it was saved, or choose Cancel.

To remove a scheme from the list, select the scheme you want to remove from the Scheme list and click Delete.

Wallpapering Your Desktop with a Graphic

Using a graphic or picture as the Windows desktop is a nice personal touch. For special business situations or for custom applications, you may want to use a color company logo or pictorial theme as the wallpaper.

Windows comes with a collection of graphics for the desktop. You can modify these images or draw new images for the desktop with the Windows Paint accessory. For high-quality pictorials, use a scanner to create a digitized black-and-white or color image.

▶ See "Changing the Windows Desktop with Paint," p. 393

Figure 5.13 shows one of the many wallpaper patterns that come with Windows. Figure 5.14 shows a logo used as a backdrop. Many companies scan and then enhance their corporate logo as a BMP file, then use it as the desktop background. Most of the patterns must be tiled to fill the entire screen, which you learn how to do in the following steps.

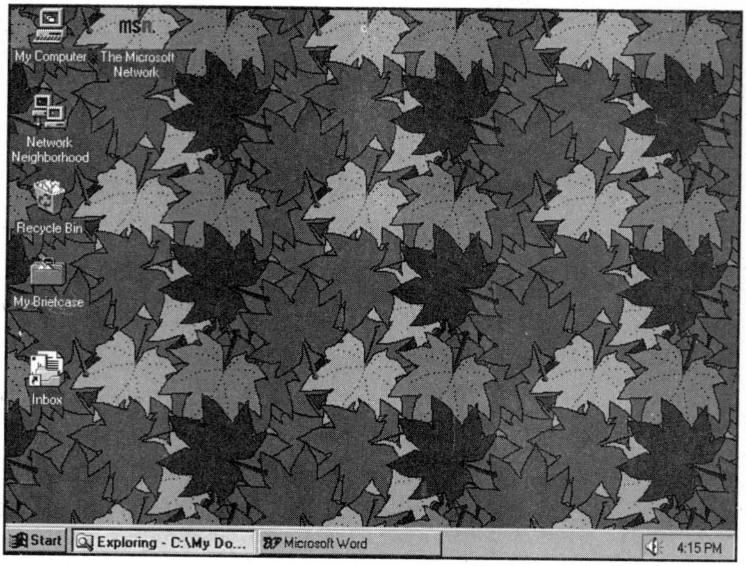

Fig. 5.13
One of the many Windows images you can use to wallpaper your desktop.

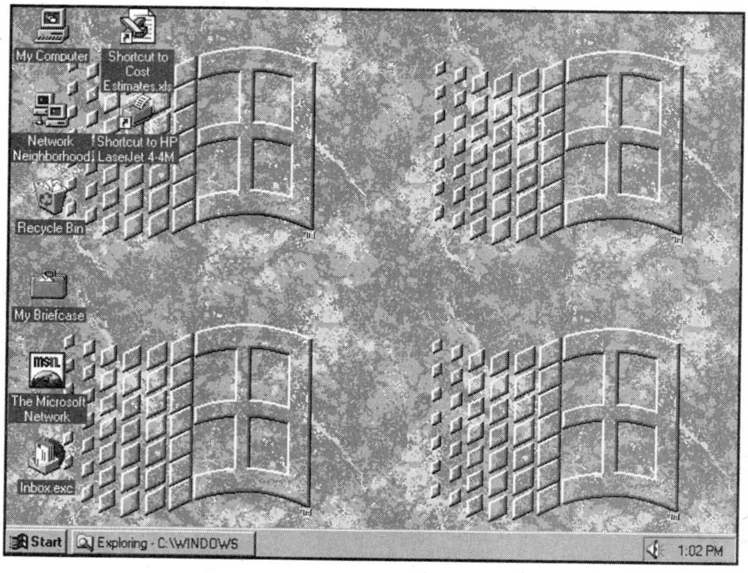

Fig. 5.14
Edit existing wallpaper files or create your own with Paint.

Tip
Using a complex or detailed background or pattern on your desktop may make icons on the desktop difficult to read.

To select wallpaper, follow these steps:

1. Right-click the desktop, choose Properties, and then select the Background tab.

   or

Open the Start menu and choose Settings, Control Panel; then double-click the Display icon, and select the Background tab.

The Background page of the Display Properties sheet will display as shown in figure 5.15.

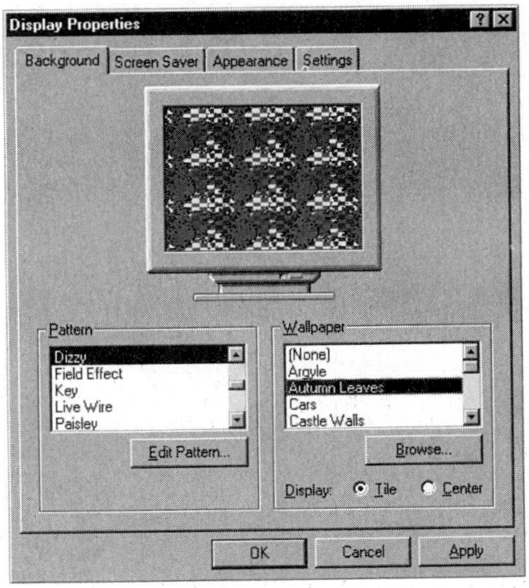

Fig. 5.15
Use the Background tab in Display Properties to select new wallpapers and patterns.

2. Choose a wallpaper in the Wallpaper list box. If the graphic file (with a BMP extension) is located in a folder other than Windows, select the Browse button to find and select the graphic file.
3. If the graphic is large enough to fill the screen, select Display, Center to center the wallpaper in the desktop. If the graphic is small and must be repeated to fill the screen, select Display, Tile.
4. Choose OK if you are finished or make other display property changes.

When you choose a wallpaper from the Wallpaper list, you see a miniature rendition of it in the display shown in the upper portion of the Display Properties sheet. This allows you to preview wallpapers before settling on the one to use.

Tip
Bitmap images displayed as the desktop wallpaper use more memory than a colored or patterned desktop. If you run low on memory, remove the wallpaper.

Wallpaper is created from files stored in a bitmap format. They are located in the Windows folder. These files end with the BMP extension and must be stored in the Windows folder. You can edit BMP formats with the Windows Paint accessory. You also can read and edit files with PCX format in Paint and then save them in BMP format to use as a desktop wallpaper.

You can create your own desktop wallpapers in one of three ways:

- Buy clip art from a software vendor. If the clip art is not in PCX or BMP format, use a graphics-conversion application to convert the image to one of these formats. Use Windows Paint to read PCX format and resave the figure in BMP format. Computer bulletin boards, online services, and the Internet have thousands of BMP graphics files.
- Scan a black-and-white or color picture using a digital scanner. Save the scanned file as BMP format or convert it to BMP format.
- Modify an existing desktop wallpaper, or create a new one with Windows Paint or a higher-end graphics program. Save the files with the BMP format.

Store your new BMP (bitmap) graphics files in the Windows folder so that they appear in the Wallpaper Files drop-down list of the Display Properties sheet.

To remove a wallpaper file from the Wallpaper list, delete or remove its BMP file from the Windows folder. To remove the wallpaper from the desktop, repeat the previous steps but select None as the type of wallpaper.

Troubleshooting

After adding a beautiful and very intricate Chinese dragon to my wallpaper, my computer seems to run slower. I'm running with minimally acceptable memory so Windows is already slow.

Wallpapers consume memory. If you have a very complex wallpaper it's large size could consume enough memory to make Windows slower. You need to install more memory or use less ambitious artwork.

Changing the Background Pattern

Wallpapers, while pretty and often amusing, can consume a lot of memory. If you want a simpler background or want to conserve memory, you can use a background pattern. The pattern is a small grid of dots that repeats to fill the screen. The Sample area of figure 5.16 shows how one background pattern appears. Windows comes with predefined patterns you can select; you also can create your own. The color of the pattern is the same as the color selected for Window Text in the Color dialog box.

Caution

If you have a wallpaper selected with the Display, Tile option selected, then you will not be able to see your pattern. A full-screen wallpaper shows over the top of the pattern. To see the pattern, select None from the Wallpaper list.

To select a pattern, follow these steps:

1. Right-click the desktop, choose Properties, and then select the Background tab.

   or

   Open the Start menu and choose Settings, Control Panel; then double-click the Display icon and select the Background tab. The Background page of the Display Properties sheet displays as shown in figure 5.16.

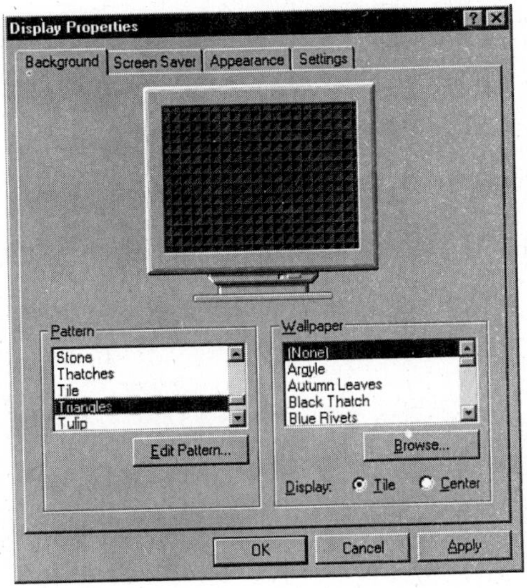

Fig. 5.16 Background patterns are simpler and conserve memory.

2. Select a pattern from the Pattern list. Some of the built-in repetitive patterns you can select are 50% Gray, Boxes, Diamonds, Weave, and Scottie.

3. Choose OK to add the pattern to the desktop. Alternatively, use the following procedure to edit the pattern just selected.

You can edit or create new patterns only if you have a mouse. To edit an existing pattern or create a new pattern while the Background page is displayed, follow these steps:

1. Select a pattern from the Pattern list.
2. Click the Edit Pattern button to display the Pattern Editor dialog box shown in figure 5.17.
3. Click in the editing grid in the location where you want to reverse a dot in the pattern. Watch the Sample area to see the overall effect.
4. Continue to click in the grid until the pattern is what you want.

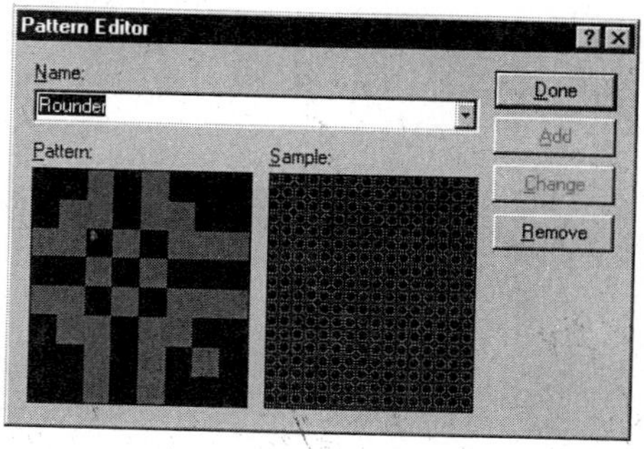

Fig. 5.17 Editing your pattern using an existing pattern as a base may be easier than working from the None pattern.

5. When you are finished creating or editing, continue with one of the following options:
   - If you want to change an existing pattern, click Change.
   - If you want to add a new pattern, type a new name in the Name list box and choose the Add button.
6. When you are finished editing, click Done. Choose OK in the Display Properties sheet.

To remove an unwanted pattern from the list, select the pattern and click Remove. Confirm the deletion by choosing Yes. The Remove button is available only after you select a new pattern name.

Having Fun with the Screen Saver

Screen savers display a changing pattern on-screen when you haven't typed or moved the mouse for a predetermined amount of time. Screen savers were designed to prevent an image from burning onto your screen if the document on-screen did not change frequently. With new display screens this is rarely a problem, but screen savers remain. They are fun and afford a degree of protection against others seeing your work. You can specify the delay before the screen saver activates, and you can set up various attributes—including a password—for most of the screen savers.

To select and set up a screen saver, follow these steps:

1. Right-click the desktop and choose Properties; then select the Screen Saver tab.

   or

   Open the Start menu and choose Settings, Control Panel; then double-click the Display icon and select the Screen Saver tab.

   The Screen Saver page of the Display Properties sheet displays (see fig. 5.18).

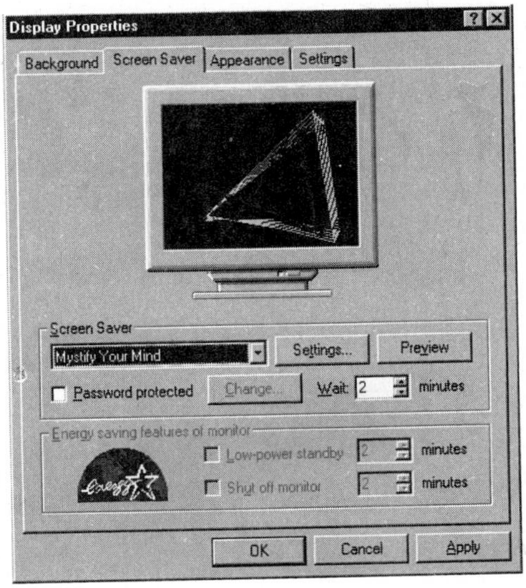

Fig. 5.18
Screen savers display when your computer sits idle for a predetermined amount of time.

2. Select a screen saver from the Screen Saver list.
3. The miniature display shows you a preview of the screen saver. To see a full-screen view, click Preview. Click anywhere on-screen to return to the sheet from the preview.
4. To test other screen savers, return to step 2.

5. To customize the appearance and properties of your screen saver, click Settings. The options and settings for each screen saver are different. Figure 5.19 shows the options to customize the Flying Through Space screen saver. Click OK when you're finished.

6. In the Wait box, type or select the number of minutes you want the screen to be idle before the screen saver displays. A range from 5 to 15 minutes is usually a good time.

7. Choose Apply to apply the Display Property changes you have selected so far. You will see the changes take effect, but the Display Properties sheet stays open. Choose OK to accept the changes and close the sheet.

Fig. 5.19
You can customize screen savers so that they act differently.

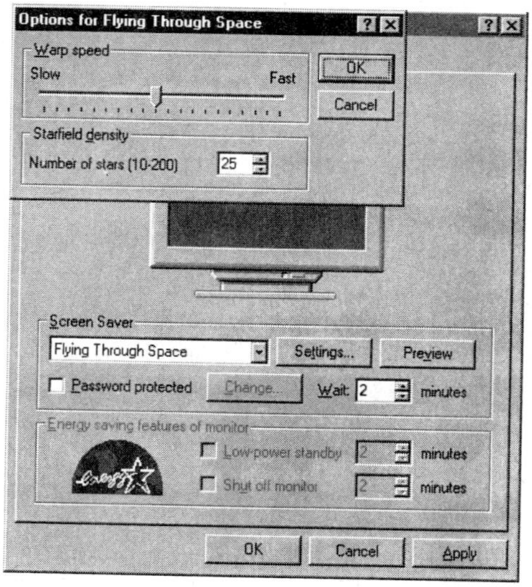

Tip
When your screen saver is on, you need to be careful about pressing keys that might affect the active program. Either move the mouse or press Shift to go back to the normal display.

Protecting Your Computer with a Screen Saver Password

◄ See "Starting and Quitting Windows," p. 50

Although each screen saver has unique settings, all except Blank Screen have an area where you can specify password protection. If you don't want uninvited users to use your computer, you can specify a password that is associated with a screen saver, so that only those who know the password can clear the screen saver and use your computer.

To protect your computer using a password, follow these steps:

1. Click with the right mouse button anywhere on the desktop then choose Properties to open the Display Properties sheet.

2. Click the Screen Saver tab.

3. Select a screen saver from the Screen Saver drop-down list and set its options.

4. Select the Password Protected option and then choose Change.

5. Type your password in the New Password text box, and then confirm your password by typing it again in the Confirm New Password text box.

   Asterisks will appear in the text boxes as you type your password to prevent others from seeing it (see fig. 5.20).

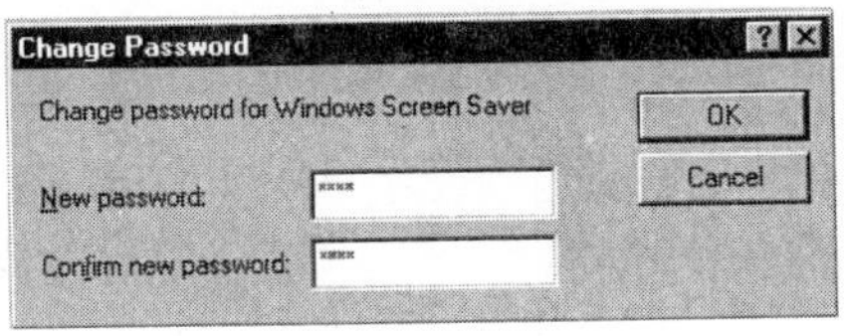

Fig. 5.20
Enter a password for the screen saver in the Change Password dialog box.

6. Choose OK, and when the confirmation message appears, choose OK again.

Now when the screen saver appears and you press a key on the keyboard or move the mouse, a dialog box appears in which you have to type your password to clear the screen saver.

Using Your Display's Energy-Saving Feature

If you leave your computer on continuously, or if you leave your desk for long periods of time while your computer continues to run, you will want to conserve energy by using the energy-saving features that are built in to many newer monitors. Although the energy used by one monitor may seem small, when multiplied by the millions of computers in use across the nation, it is easy to see that selecting this option one time can save a lot of energy and reduce pollution. When you multiply the cost of running the tens of thousands of monitors in a single large corporation, the dollar savings can be significant.

Monitors that satisfy EPA requirements usually display an "Energy Star" sticker on the monitor or in the manual. Older monitors do not have the energy-saving feature.

▶ See "Understanding Plug and Play Architecture," p. 230

If you have a monitor that is an Energy Star but the Energy Saving Features of Monitor options are not available in the Screen Saver page, you should install the correct display drivers for your monitor. To check which display driver is installed, open the Display Properties sheet, choose the Settings tab, and then

▶ See "Creating and Modifying Hardware Profiles," p. 273

choose the Change Display Type button. From the dialog box that appears, you can install the display driver for your manufacturer and model. Once you have the correct driver, select the Monitor Is Energy Star Compliant checkbox. Selecting this checkbox does no good if the monitor is not compliant.

To set Windows so that it takes advantage of the energy-saving features of Energy Star compliant monitors, follow these steps:

1. Click the right mouse button on the desktop and choose Properties.
2. Choose the Settings tab (refer to fig. 5.18).
3. Choose the Low-Power Standby check box, and then select the number of minutes the computer should be idle before the monitor goes into low-power standby. This mode reduces power requirements but keeps the monitor ready to be instantly used.
4. Choose the Shut Off Monitor check box, and then select the number of minutes the computer should be idle before the monitor shuts down. This mode completely turns off your monitor.
5. Choose OK.

When you return to your workstation, you can press any key or move the mouse to return to normal monitor use from low-power standby. The Shut Off Monitor mode shuts off the monitor rather than putting it in standby mode. This saves the most energy. The manual for your monitor will describe the best way to turn the monitor on again.

Changing the Screen Resolution, Font Size, and Color Palette

With Windows, you have the ability to change how your application displays even while you work. This can help you if you run applications that operate with different screen resolutions, or use programs that look better in different font sizes. Some applications, such as graphics programs or multimedia, work better when they use 256 colors and higher resolution.

The resolution is the number of dots shown on-screen. The more dots on-screen, the more detail you can work with. However, with a high-resolution screen, icons or fonts that appeared an adequate size on a VGA screen may now appear small.

Changing the resolution while Windows is running enables you to switch between VGA mode (640 × 480 pixels on-screen) to the more detailed and wider view of SVGA mode (1024 × 768 pixels). This can come in handy when you work on different types of tasks. You may, for example, have a laptop computer that displays on its LCD screen in VGA mode. When you work at your desk and have a high-resolution monitor connected to the laptop, you want to work in SVGA mode.

Changing the Screen Resolution

You can change the screen resolution—the number of dots on the screen—if your display is capable of running Super VGA 800 × 600 resolution or better and Super VGA or better is currently set as the monitor type.

You can change or examine your monitor type by following these steps:

1. Open the Display Properties sheet and click on the Settings tab.
2. Choose the Change Display Type button to display the Change Display Type dialog box.
3. Choose the Change button next to the Monitor Type box.
4. Select the resolution you want to use for your monitor from the Select Device dialog box. Choose the Show All Devices option if you do not see your monitor. If you are unsure, choose the (Standard Monitor Types) option from the Manufacturers list.
5. Choose OK, then choose Close.
6. When you return to the Display Properties sheet, you can change other display properties. Choose OK.

When you exit the Display Properties sheet, you may need to restart Windows in order to implement the new monitor type. You will be asked whether you want to restart at that time.

Caution

Changing to an incorrect monitor type that cannot be implemented may cause your screen to be unreadable. If that happens, shut off your computer. Restart the computer and watch the screen carefully. When the phrase, `Starting Windows 95` appears, press F8. This displays a text menu that enables you to start Windows in *safe mode.* Safe mode displays Windows on any screen, but many resources will not be available such as networking and CD-ROMs. While in safe mode, repeat the steps described in the section, "Changing the Screen Resolution," and select either a monitor type you are sure of or a resolution that will work from the (Standard Monitor Types) list.

Once your monitor is in Super VGA mode or better, you can change between different screen resolutions by dragging the slider in the Desktop area portion of the Settings tab.

Changing the Number of Colors Available to Your Monitor

Depending on your display adapter and the monitor, you can have the same resolution screen, but with a different palette of colors available. For example, you may have some business applications that use only 16 colors, while most games and multimedia use 256 or more colors. Depending on the amount of video memory your video card has, not all color choices will be available at all monitor resolutions.

To change the size of your color palette, click on the down arrow next to Color Palette in the Settings page, then click on the number of colors you need.

Changing Font Sizes

Need glasses to read the screen? You can enlarge (or reduce) the size of the font Windows uses on-screen. All text on-screen will change size. You have to restart Windows, however, to see the change.

You can select from any of the following font size options:

- Small Fonts scales fonts to 100 percent of normal size.
- Large Fonts scales fonts to 125 percent of normal size.
- Custom displays the Custom Font Size dialog box where you can specify your own size.

To change the size of screen fonts, follow these steps:

1. Click the right mouse button on the Desktop and choose Properties.
2. Click the Settings tab to display the page shown in figure 5.21.
3. Click the down arrow next to the Font size box and choose Large Fonts or Small Fonts.

   or

   Click Custom to display the Custom Font Size dialog box (see fig. 5.22). Type or select a percentage of normal size in the Scale box, or drag across the ruler then release the mouse button to resize. Notice the sample font and its size below the ruler. Choose OK.
4. Click OK to accept the change and close the Display Properties sheet.

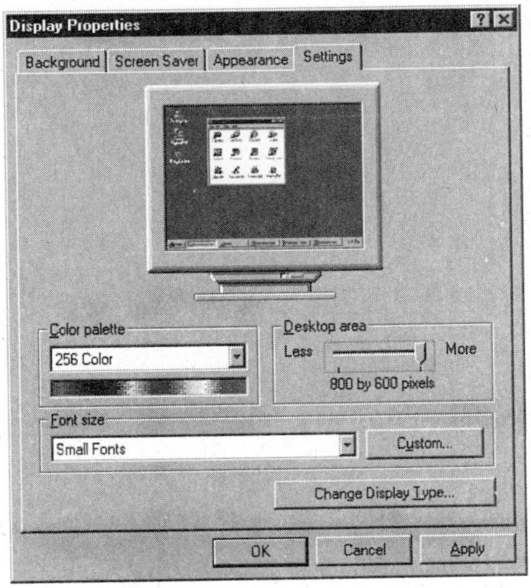

Fig. 5.21
Change your display's appearance in the Settings page.

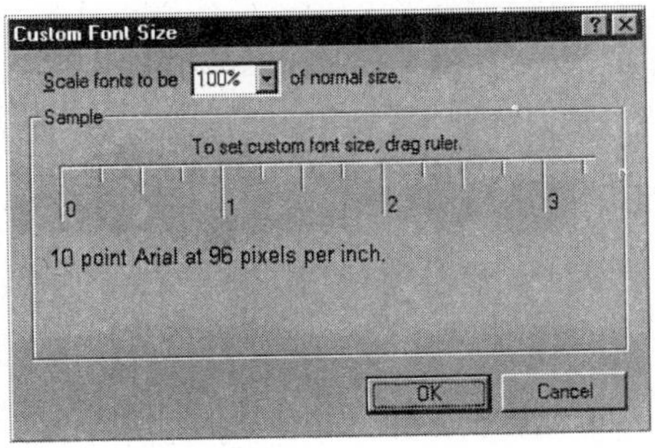

Fig. 5.22
You can create your own custom font size.

Changing the Sounds Related to Windows Events

Windows has sounds related to different events such as errors, closing programs, exiting windows, emptying the Recycle Bin, and so on. You can change the sounds used for each of these events. You can even use your own sound files. (Of course, you need a sound card to hear these sounds.)

To change the sounds related to an event, follow these steps:

1. Open the Start menu and choose Settings, Control Panel.

2. Double-click on Sounds to display the Sounds Properties sheet shown in figure 5.23.

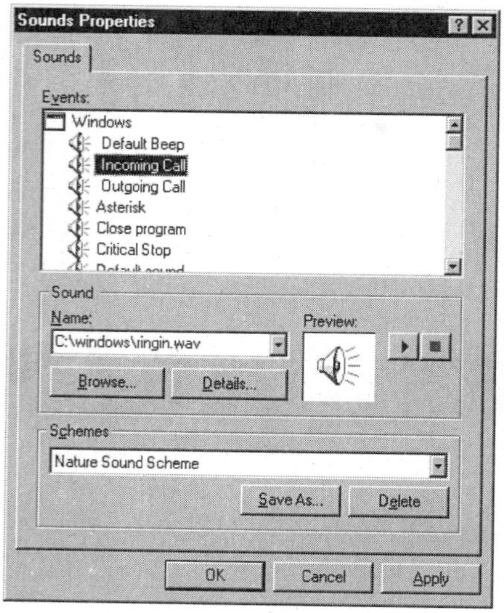

Fig. 5.23
You can assign your own sound files to different Windows or application events.

3. Scroll through the Events list until you see the event whose sound you want to change, then click on that event.

4. Select the WAV file that contains the sound for that event by clicking on the Browse button and selecting a WAV file. Click OK.

   The Browse dialog box opens in the WINDOWS\MEDIA folder, but you can change to any folder.

5. Preview the sound by clicking on the Go button to the right of the Preview icon.

6. Click OK.

Note

You can create your own collection of WAV files by following the procedures described in Chapter 33, "Working with Windows Sound Capabilities." You also may want to look on public bulletin boards, online services, and the Internet. They contain thousands of free WAV files.

Entire collections of sounds have been grouped already for you as sound schemes. To change all the sounds involved in a sound scheme, select the scheme you want by choosing it from the Schemes list.

If you create your own scheme of sounds/events, you can save it with a name so you can return to it by clicking the Save As button, entering a name, and clicking OK.

Customizing the Mouse

If you are left-handed, or if you like a fast or slow mouse, you need to know how to modify your mouse's behavior. Mouse options can be changed at the Mouse Properties sheet, shown in figure 5.24.

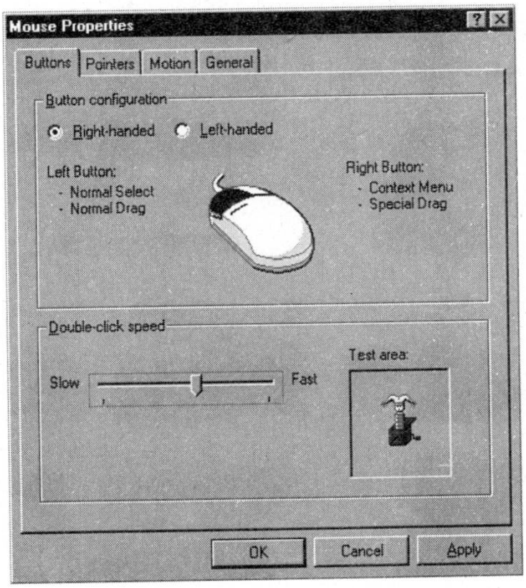

Fig. 5.24
You can change the speed of your mouse and more in the Mouse Properties sheet.

To change how your mouse behaves and appears, follow these steps:

1. Open the Start menu and choose Settings, Control Panel; then double-click Mouse. The Mouse Properties sheet appears.
2. Click a tab and make the changes you want.
3. Click Apply to accept the changes and to continue making changes, or click OK to accept the changes and close the Mouse Properties sheet.

Tip
Double-click on a pointer shape while in the Pointers page to replace one shape within a scheme.

Mouse options are grouped on three tabs—Buttons, Pointers, Motion, and General. Each tab is described in the following table. (Depending on the brand of your mouse, you may have different, though similar, options.)

Tab	Description
Buttons	Select either a Right-Handed mouse or Left-Handed mouse. Set the Double-Click Speed, and then double-click in the Test Area to determine whether you have set a speed you're comfortable with. When you double-click at the right speed in the Test Area, you'll be surprised by what appears.
Pointers	Change the size and shape of the pointer. You can select schemes of pointer shapes so that all pointer shapes for different activities take on a new appearance.
Motion	You can set the Pointer Speed to make the mouse move more slowly or quickly across the screen. You can add a Pointer Trail to the mouse to leave a trail of mouse pointers on-screen. This feature is especially useful if you have a LCD screen where the mouse pointer can sometimes get lost. This option cannot be shown for video display drivers that don't support it.
General	To add a new mouse to your system, click Change and the Select Device dialog box displays. Make your selection from there. You also can add a new mouse with the Add New Hardware wizard, available from the Control Panel.

► See "Installing Legacy Cards after Setting Up Drivers," p. 255

► See "LCD Screen Mouse Trails," p. 298

Customizing the Keyboard

Although changing the keyboard speed doesn't result in a miracle that makes you type faster, it does speed up the rate at which characters are repeated. You also can change the delay before the character repeats.

To change keyboard properties, follow these steps.

1. Open the Start menu and choose Settings, Control Panel; then double-click Keyboard. The Keyboard Properties sheet appears (see fig. 5.25).
2. Click a tab and make the changes you want.
3. Click Apply to accept the changes and to continue making changes, or click OK to accept the changes and close the Keyboard Properties sheet.

Keyboard options are grouped on three tabs—Speed, Language, and General. They are described in the following table. (These tabs will vary for other keyboard and language drivers.)

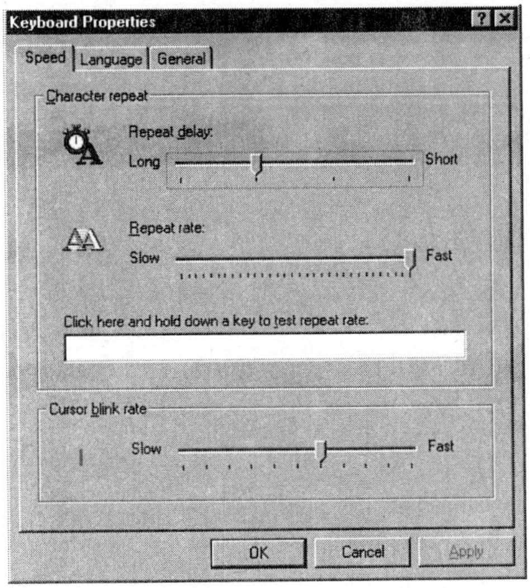

Fig. 5.25
You can change the keyboard repeat and more in the Keyboard Properties sheet.

Tab	Description
Speed	Change the keyboard repeat speed. Drag the Long/Short pointer to change the Repeat Delay speed (how long before the first repeat) or drag the Slow/Fast pointer to change the Repeat Rate. Click in the Click Here box to test the results. Drag the Slow/Fast pointer for Cursor Blink Rate to change the speed the cursor blinks.
Language	Use the Language page to select the language you use. Click Add to display the Add Language dialog box and select a language from the drop-down list. Click Properties to select an appropriate keyboard layout. Click Remove to remove a language from the list. Click the up and down arrows to change the order of the languages you have selected. Changing this option enables your applications to accurately sort words that may contain non-English characters, such as accent marks. However, changing the language setting does not change the language used by Windows. You need to purchase a different language version of Windows to accomplish this.
General	To change keyboards, click the Change button and the Select Device dialog box displays. Make your selection from there. You can also add a new keyboard with the Add New Hardware wizard, available from the Control Panel.

Making Windows Accessible for the Hearing, Sight, and Movement Impaired

In an effort to make computers more available to the more than 30 million people with some form of disability, Microsoft has added accessibility properties that you can use to adjust the computer's sound, display, and physical interface.

To make accessibility adjustments, follow these steps:

1. Click the Start button and choose Settings, Control Panel.
2. Double-click the Accessibility Options icon. The Accessibility Properties sheet appears (see fig. 5.26).
3. Make your selections and click OK.

Troubleshooting

The Accessibility Options icon does not appear in my Control Panel.

Reinstall Windows using a custom installation and select Accessibility Options. Appendix A describes how to reinstall options in Windows.

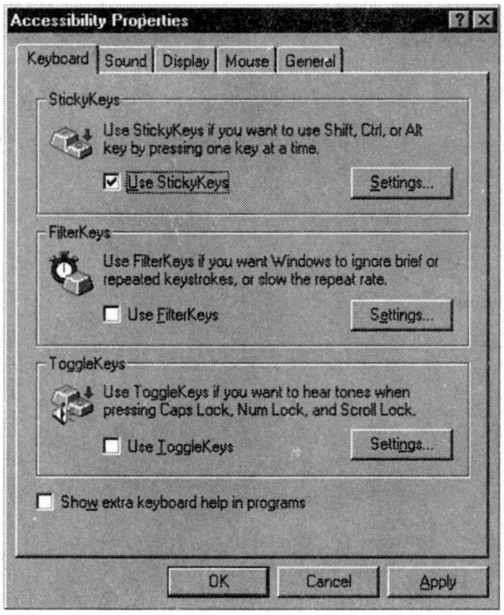

Fig. 5.26
Use the Accessibility Properties sheet to make Windows easier to use for a person with a disability.

The accessibility properties include the following tabs:

Tab	Description
Keyboard	Make the keyboard more tolerant and patient. Select Use StickyKeys if you need to press multiple keys simultaneously but are able to press keys only one at a time. Select Use FilterKeys to ignore short or repeated keystrokes. Select Use ToggleKeys to make a sound when you press Caps Lock, Num Lock, and Scroll Lock.
Sound	Provide visual warnings and captions for speech and sounds. Select Use SoundSentry to make Windows use a visual warning when a sound alert occurs. Select Use ShowSounds to display captions instead of speech or sounds.
Display	Select colors and fonts for easy reading. Select Use High Contrast to use color and font combinations that produce greater screen contrast.
Mouse	Control the pointer with the numeric keypad. Select Use MouseKeys to use the numeric keypad and other keys in place of the mouse. The relationship of keys to mouse controls appears in the table that follows.
General	Turn off accessibility features, give notification, and add an alternative input device. Use Automatic Reset to set Windows so accessibility features remain on at all times, are turned off when Windows restarts, or are turned off after a period of inactivity. Notification tells users when a feature is turned on or off. The SerialKey device enables Windows to receive keyboard or mouse input from alternative input devices through a serial port.

Some of these accessibility features could be difficult for a person with disabilities to turn on or off through normal Windows procedures. To alleviate this problem, Windows includes special *hotkeys*. Pressing the keys or key combinations for the designated hotkey turns an accessibility feature on or off, or changes its settings. The following table gives the hotkeys for different features.

Feature	Hotkey	Result
High-contrast mode	Left-Alt+left-Shift+ Print Screen pressed simultaneously	Alternates the screen through different text/ background combinations
StickyKeys	Press the Shift key five consecutive times	Turned on or off

(continues)

Feature	Hotkey	Result
FilterKeys	Hold down right Shift key for eight seconds	Turned on or off
ToggleKeys	Hold down NumLock key for five seconds	Turned on or off
MouseKeys	Press left-Alt+ left-Shift+NumLock simultaneously	Turned on or off

MouseKeys can be very useful for portable or laptop computer users and graphic artists as well as for people unable to use a mouse. Graphic artists will find MouseKeys useful because it enables them to produce finer movements than those done with a mouse. Once MouseKeys is turned on, you can produce the same effects as a mouse by using these keys:

Action	Press This Key(s)
Movement	Any number key except 5
Large moves	Hold down Ctrl as you press number keys
Single pixel moves	Hold down Shift as you press number keys
Single-click	5
Double-click	+
Begin drag	Insert (Ins)
Drop after drag	Delete (Del)
Select left mouse button	/
Select right mouse button	-
Select both mouse buttons	*

Caution

Use the numeric keypad with MouseKeys, not the numbered keys across the top of the keypad. Make sure the NumLock key is set so that the keypad is in numeric mode rather than cursor mode.

Setting the Date and Time

Use the Date/Time Properties sheet to change the date or time in your system (see fig. 5.27). You also can change the format of the date and time to match another country's standard.

▶ See "Using the Taskbar Clock," p. 406

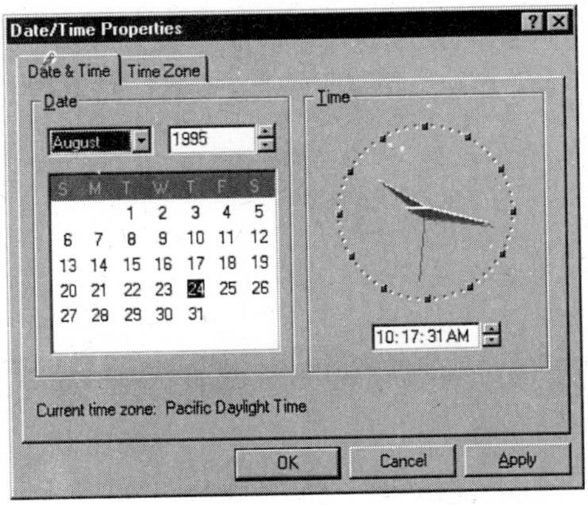

Fig. 5.27
You can change the system date and time at the Date/Time Properties sheet.

To change date and time properties, follow these steps.

1. Double-click the clock on the taskbar.

   or

   Open the Start menu and choose Settings, Control Panel; then double-click Date/Time.

   The Date/Time Properties sheet appears.

2. Click a tab and make the changes you want. See the following table for a description of things you can change.

3. Click Apply to accept the change and to continue making changes, or click OK to accept the change and close the Properties for Date/Time sheet.

Tip
To display the current date, point to the clock on the taskbar and the date will pop up.

Date and time options are grouped on two tabs—Date & Time and Time Zone. They are described in the following table.

Tab	Description
Date & Time	To change the Date, click the down arrow and select a month, or the up and down arrows to select a year. Click on the day of the month in the calendar to change the date. To change the time, click on the element you want to change in the digital time display. For example, to change hours, click on the first two numbers. Click the up and down arrows next to the time display.
Time Zone	Click the down arrow to select a new time zone (see fig. 5.28). Click the Automatically Adjust Clock for Daylight Savings Changes box to have the time automatically adjust for daylight savings time (a check indicates that it is on).

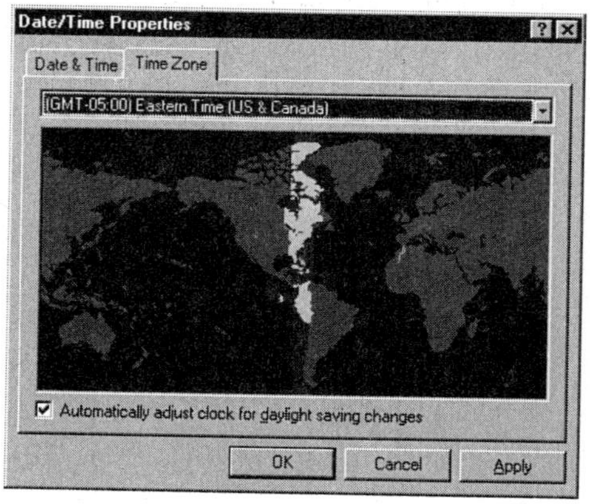

Fig. 5.28
You can change the time zone to reflect the time in any area of the world.

Customizing for Your Country and Language

Windows has the capacity to switch between different international character sets, time and date displays, and numeric formats. The international settings you choose in Control Panel affect applications, such as Microsoft Excel, that take advantage of these Windows features.

Note

Although you can change the language and country formats, doing so does not change the language used in menus or Help information. To obtain versions of Windows and Microsoft applications for countries other than the United States, check with your local Microsoft representative. Check with the corporate offices of other software vendors for international versions of their applications.

The Regional Settings Properties sheet (see fig. 5.29) provides five tabs. The region you select on the Regional Settings page will automatically affect the settings in the other pages.

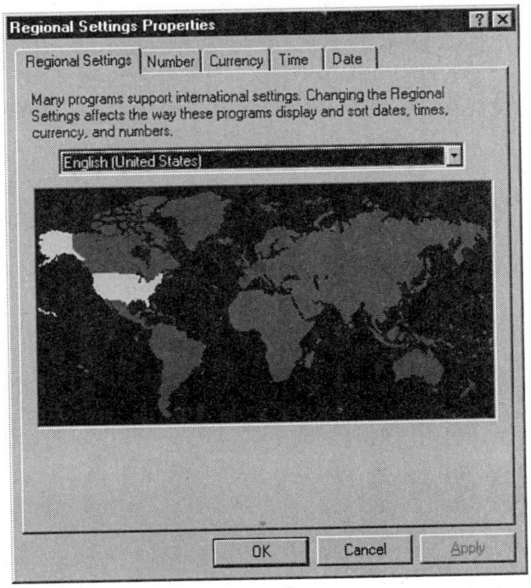

Fig. 5.29
You can change settings, such as number formats on the Number tab, to reflect any region of the world.

To change Regional Settings properties, follow these steps:

1. Open the Start menu and choose Settings, Control Panel; then double-click on Regional Settings. The Regional Settings Properties sheet appears (refer to fig. 5.29).
2. Click a tab and make the changes you want.
3. Click Apply to accept the changes and to continue making changes, or click OK to accept the change and close the Regional Settings Properties sheet.

Each Regional Setting page is described in the following table.

Tab	Description
Regional Settings	Click the down arrow and select your geographic region, or click your region on the global map. This selection automatically changes other settings in the sheet.
Number	To make a change to the format, click the down arrow next to the box you want to change and choose what you want, or click in the box and type what you want.

(continues)

Tab	Description
Currency	To make a change to the format, click the down arrow next to the box you want to change and choose what you want, or click in the box and type what you want. To select some currency symbols, you may have to select a different keyboard first. The No. of Digits After Decimal setting can be overridden by some applications, such as spreadsheets.
Time	Change the symbols, separator, and style of the time display. To make a change to the format, click the down arrow next to the box you want to change and choose what you want, or click in the box and type what you want.
Date	To make a change to the format, click the down arrow next to the box you want to change and choose what you want, or click in the box and type what you want.

Changing Custom Settings for Each User

Windows accomodates situations where people share a computer or move between computers. Windows enables you to store your custom settings for colors, accessibility features, and so on with your logon name. When you log on to the computer, Windows resets the computer with your settings.

User profiles are stored with your user logon ID. But you must tell Windows that you want to store user profiles for each different logon ID.

To create or remove a custom user profile for each logon ID, follow these steps:

1. Open the Start menu and choose Settings, Control Panel; then double-click Passwords.
2. Click the User Profiles tab to display the page shown in figure 5.30.
3. Select one of the following:
   - Select All Users of This PC if you want all users to use the same settings. Go to step 5.
   - Select Users Can Customize Their Preferences if you want Windows to use the customization setup during the last use of that logon ID.

4. If you make the second selection in step 3, you can choose from the following:

   - Select Include Desktop Icons and Network Neighborhood Contents in User Settings if the user profile should remember changes to these items.

   - Select Include Start Menu and Program Groups in User Settings if the user profile should remember changes to these items.

5. Click OK.

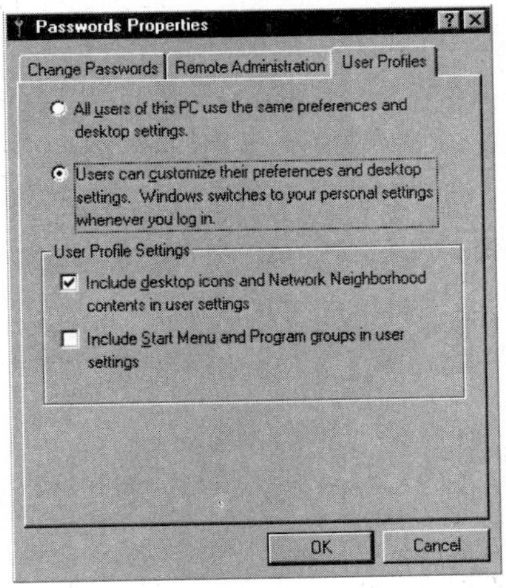

Fig. 5.30
You can customize the size of screen fonts.

When you are done with a Windows computer shared by multiple users, log off the computer so that others can log on and use their custom user profiles. To log off, click the Start button, click Shut Down, then click the option Close All Programs and Log On as a Different User. Choose OK.

If you made the selection Users Can Customize Their Preferences, then whenever a person logs on to Windows and customizes settings, those settings are saved with that logon ID. The next time someone logs on with that logon ID, Windows changes to the settings for that ID.

Preventing Others from Using Windows

You may work in an area where you need to keep your computer secure. For example, your work may involve financial, market, or personnel data that is confidential. One way you can help to protect this information is to require a password before Windows will start.

► See "Securing Your Network Resources," p. 640

To change or create your Windows password, follow these steps:

1. Open the Passwords Properties sheet as described in the previous section.
2. Click the Change Passwords tab, then click the Change Windows Password button to display the Change Windows Password dialog box.

   If you have network passwords, they will be listed so that you can change them to match your Windows password.
3. Type your old password in the Old Password box.
4. Type your new password in the New Password and Confirm Password boxes.
5. Choose OK, then OK again.

Windows provides security for the network environment from the other pages on the Password Properties.

Reviewing Your Computer's System Information

One of the more gruesome aspects of using DOS or earlier versions of Windows was working with configuration files whenever you wanted to customize or optimize your computer. People who wanted to install sound cards or network adapters, change memory usage, or specify I/O (Input/Output) or IRQ (interrupt request) settings faced immersion in the arcane world of configuration files. Configuration files gave you no help; yet if you made an error, part of your hardware might not be recognized, your system might run slower, or it might not run at all.

Windows 95 makes specifying configurations easier. Now you can select only allowable options from straightforward dialog boxes, and you can see settings from other hardware devices that might cause conflicts.

Reading Your Registration and Version Number

You can see your registration number, the version number of Windows, and the type of processor on which Windows is running on the General page of the System Properties sheet. To see this page, follow these steps:

1. Open the Start menu; then choose Settings, Control Panel to display the Control Panel window.

2. Double-click on the System icon.

3. Click the General tab of the System Properties sheet as shown in figure 5.31.

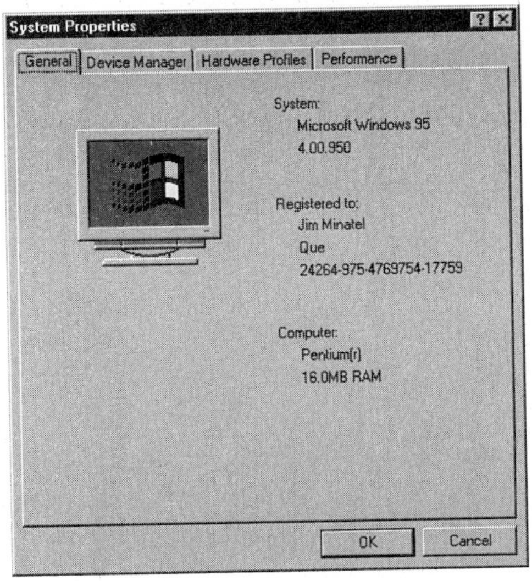

Fig. 5.31
View your registration number and Windows' version number on the System Properties General page.

Examine the Hardware on Your Computer

You may need to examine the configuration settings and drivers for hardware connected to your computer. You also can use the System Properties sheet to help you troubleshoot hardware. If you need to see a list of IRQ and I/O settings, you need to use the Device Manager.

► See "Installing Plug and Play Hardware," p. 246

► See "Installing Legacy Cards after Setting Up Drivers," p. 255

► See "Installing Plug and Play CD-ROM Drives," p. 975

► See "Installation of Full-Motion Video Device Drivers," p. 1012

To display the Device Manager page, follow these steps:

1. Open the Start menu; then choose Settings, Control Panel to display the Control Panel window.

2. Double-click on the System icon.

3. Click the Device Manager tab of the System Properties sheet (see fig. 5.32).

4. To see the drivers installed for a device, click on the + sign to the left of the device. To see information about a device or to remove the device, select one of the following buttons:

Button	Action
Properties	Displays a listing of properties appropriate to the device. Select the Computer item to see IRQ and I/O settings.
Refresh	Windows reexamines the installed hardware and attempts to update the list.
Remove	Removes the selected device or driver.
Print	Prints a report of configuration settings.

5. Choose OK.

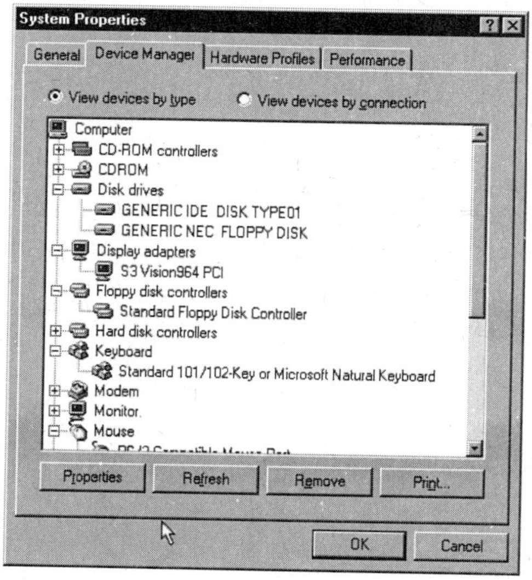

Fig. 5.32 View the hardware devices and their drivers on the System Properties Device Manager page.

Checking IRQ, I/O, DMA, and Memory Settings

► See "Installing a Plug and Play Modem," p. 833

► See "Configuring Your Modem," p. 843

Hardware devices each require a unique section of memory (I/O address). Some hardware devices also require an interrupt request (IRQ) or direct memory access (DMA) to operate. If any of these settings conflicts with the settings for another device, either or both of the devices may not work.

You can see a list of these settings in your computer by selecting the Computer icon on the Device Manager page of the System Properties sheet and then clicking Properties. Select from the option buttons to display the list of settings you want to see. Figure 5.33 shows the list of IRQ settings.

In MS-DOS and in prior versions of Windows, it was difficult to tell the cause of conflicts between hardware devices. In many cases, all that you knew was that something didn't work. The exact cause was often a mystery to the novice. Even for an experienced hardware specialist, resolving such problems often took considerable trial and error and required a lot of time reading manuals. Now the Device Manager shows you lists of IRQ and I/O settings. You can scan through the lists and see where you have accidentally installed two device drivers for the same device or you have set two different devices to the same or overlapping IRQ or I/O settings.

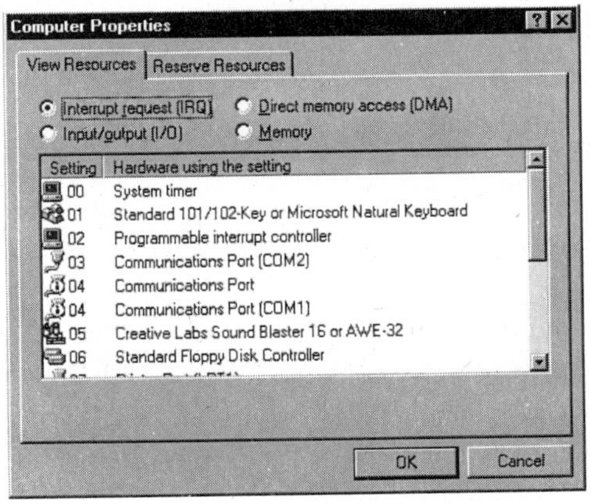

Fig. 5.33
Use the View Resources page to track down conflicts in IRQ and I/O settings.

If you find you have installed two drivers for the same device, you can delete one of them. If you find a conflict because two hardware devices are using the same memory or IRQ settings, you can resolve the conflict easily through the Device Manager. The approach you might take to resolve a conflict is to look through the lists in the Device Manager to find an open IRQ or I/O setting, check the two manuals for the particular devices to determine what other IRQ or I/O settings they will work with, and then change the settings for one of the devices so that it doesn't conflict.

Troubleshooting

One of the hardware devices on a computer is not working.

Click the Device Manager tab on the System Properties sheet and check for an X through a device. This means the hardware has been disabled. Double-click on that device to check its settings. If a device icon has a circled exclamation point, the hardware has problem. Double-click the icon to inspect the type of problem.

It took a couple different attempts with different driver selections before some of the hardware would work. Now some of the devices on the system work slowly, intermittently, or incorrectly.

(continues)

(continued)

Check the Device Manager page of the System Properties sheet to see if you have multiple drivers installed for the same hardware device. Delete all the drivers except the driver for your specific manufacturer and model. If there are multiple drivers, but not one specific to your hardware device, keep the generic driver.

The computer works with either a sound card or a network adapter card, but not both.

The usual cause of this problem is a conflict between IRQ ports and I/O addresses. Each hardware device must have its own IRQ port and its own I/O address. Sound cards and network adapters are notorious for conflicting with each other over these. To see the IRQ port and I/O address used by each device, display the Device Manager page, select the Computer icon, and choose Properties. On the View Resources page that appears, you can select the Interrupt Request (IRQ) or Input/Output (I/O) option to view a list of settings for each device on your computer. Write down the current settings and watch for conflicts. Then change the settings for devices that conflict with others.

Creating, Naming, and Copying Hardware Profiles

► See "Using Your Laptop with a Docking System," p. 273

Hardware profiles are collections of hardware settings. Hardware profiles are useful if you use different collections of hardware on your computer. For example, you might have a laptop computer that uses a VGA LCD monitor on the road, but uses an SVGA large-screen monitor on the desktop. If you have an older laptop that cannot detect when PC Cards are inserted or removed or cards that cannot be "hot-swapped" (inserted or removed while the machine is on), you also may find a need to set up hardware profiles.

By saving a collection of hardware settings as a profile, you only need to choose the profile you want rather than manually change hardware settings whenever you want to run a different combination of hardware.

When you start a Windows 95 computer that has multiple hardware configurations, you have the option of choosing the named hardware profile you want to use. From a text screen in Startup, you see something similar to this:

```
Windows cannot determine what configuration your computer is in.
Select one of the following:

1. Original Configuration
2. Multimedia
3. Desktop
4. None of the above

Enter your choice:
```

Type the number of the profile you want to use and press Enter. Windows 95 then starts with that configuration of hardware, only loading the hardware drivers required.

In order to make use of the distinct hardware profiles, you must first copy the existing default profile. The default profile is named Original Configuration. After you have copied a profile, you can then edit the devices included in it and rename it to help you recognize it. To copy or rename a hardware profile, follow these steps:

1. Open the Start menu; then choose Settings, Control Panel to display the Control Panel window.

2. Double-click on the System icon.

3. Click the Hardware Profile tab of the System Properties sheet (see fig. 5.34).

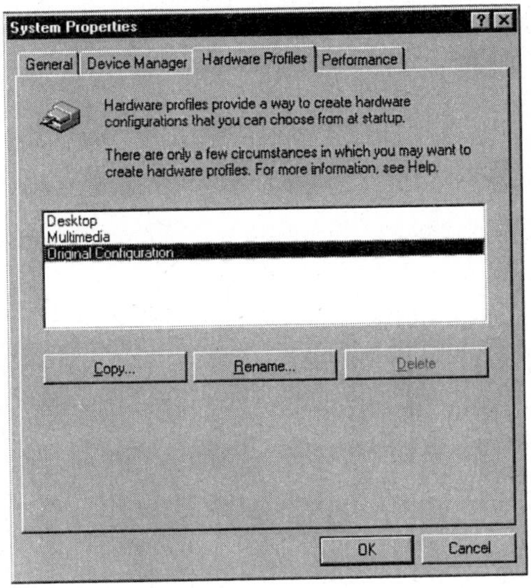

Fig. 5.34
Keep different combinations of hardware devices stored as a named hardware profile.

4. Select the hardware profile you want to work with and then click one of the following buttons:

Button	Action
Copy	Displays a Copy Profile dialog box in which you can enter a new name. Copies the hardware configuration from the selected profile to this new profile.
Rename	Changes the name of a profile.
Delete	Deletes a profile.

5. Choose OK.

To create a new profile or change an existing profile, follow these steps:

1. If you want to create a new profile, copy an existing profile as described in the preceding series of steps. Use a unique, descriptive name for the profile.
2. Click the Device Manager tab on the System Properties sheet.
3. Click the plus sign next to the hardware type you want to change for the configuration; then double-click the specific hardware you want to change. This displays the device's Properties sheet.
4. In the Device Usage area of the Properties sheet, deselect any hardware profile that you don't want to use this device with. By default, all of your devices will be used with all of your profiles until you make changes.
5. Choose OK.
6. Repeat steps 3–5 until you have configured all the hardware for this profile.
7. Choose OK.

Depending on the changes you made, you may be prompted to restart your computer.

Checking Performance Settings

▶ See "Improving Performance with Disk Defragmenter," p. 486

You can check the performance parameters of your computer on the Performance page of the System Properties. To see this page, follow these steps:

1. Open the Start menu; then choose Settings, Control Panel to display the Control Panel window.
2. Double-click on the System icon.
3. Click the Performance tab of the System Properties sheet as shown in figure 5.35.
4. View the performance status parameters on the Performance page, or choose File System, Graphics, or Virtual Memory for advanced performance tuning options.
5. Choose OK.

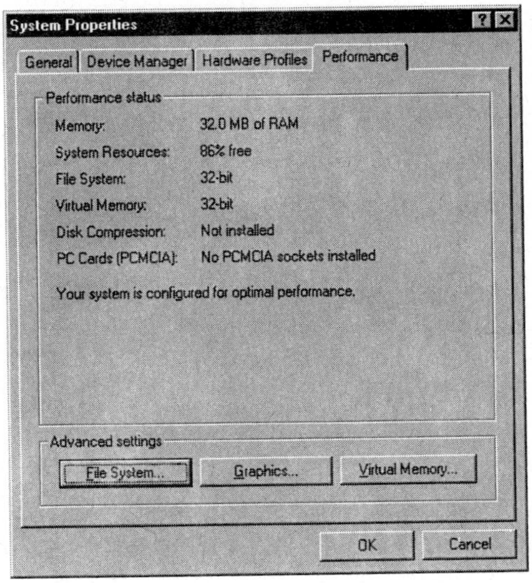

Fig. 5.35
The System Properties Performance page provides information on your computer's performance parameters.

Caution

In general, do not change the settings available on the Performance page. Windows 95 usually sets these parameters optimally.

Chapter 6

Controlling Printers

by William S. Holderby

Microsoft has packed a great deal of its past experience into the features of the Windows 95 printing system.

To appreciate Windows 95 printing, you should take a brief look at the new feature changes Microsoft has made to create faster printing while producing a higher quality output. Although some changes, at first glance, appear to be ho-hum, don't be fooled. Windows 95's new print model is both faster than its predecessors and designed with the user in mind.

In this chapter, we discuss each of the new printing features and how they work in concert to produce a quality print job.

Windows 95 new printing features:

- *Rapid return from printing* is enabled by the 32-bit printer drivers, preemptive spooler, and enhanced meta file spooling.
- *Deferred Printing* enables you to configure your PC to conveniently print to a file when you are on the road or away from your printer. Once the printer has been reattached, simply release the print files to the appropriate printer.
- *Bi-directional printer communications* sends print files to your printer and listens for a response. Windows can quickly identify a printer that cannot accept a print file.
- *Plug and Play* supports the addition of new printers by quickly identifying the brand and model of a printer and assisting you in configuring the appropriate drivers for that printer.
- *Extended capability port support* enables Windows 95 to use the latest in high-speed parallel-port technology to connect your printer.

You learn, in this chapter, how to use Windows 95 printing. This chapter introduces you to each of the new printing features, describes the options, and explains how to create a quality print job. Specifically, you learn how to

- Print from Windows applications
- Print a document from the desktop
- Install, delete, and configure printers
- Understand special printing issues related to printing from MS-DOS applications
- Work with special printing features for laptop and docking station users
- Solve common printing problems

Printing from Applications

When you print from an application under Windows 95, you use the same commands and techniques available under previous versions of Windows; however, there have been changes. You find that application printing now takes less time, the operating system releases your resources quicker, and the color/gray scale found in the printer output is substantially more consistent and accurate. However, many details of the printing architecture are transparent to application users.

Basic Windows 95 Printing Procedure

► See "Printing a Document," p. 371

► See "Printing a Painting," p. 400

Depending on the application from which you are printing, you may have some slightly different printing options. In this section, we look at the printing options available to all applications written for the Windows 95 operating system. The two most common Windows 95 applications are WordPad and Paint, included with Windows 95. The options you see in these applications are the same as the options in many Windows 95 applications.

To print from an application, perform the following steps:

1. Load the file to be printed.
2. Initiate the printing command. In most Windows applications, do this by choosing File, Print. Figure 6.1 shows a typical Print dialog box. The controls in this dialog box let you specify the portion of the file to be printed and the printer designated to complete the job.

Note

Most Windows applications that have toolbars also have a button for printing (similar to the one shown here). In some applications (such as Word, Excel, and other MS Office applications), clicking the Print button immediately prints the document using the current print settings—there are no dialog boxes to go through. Other applications open the Print dialog box shown in figure 6.1 after you click the Print button.

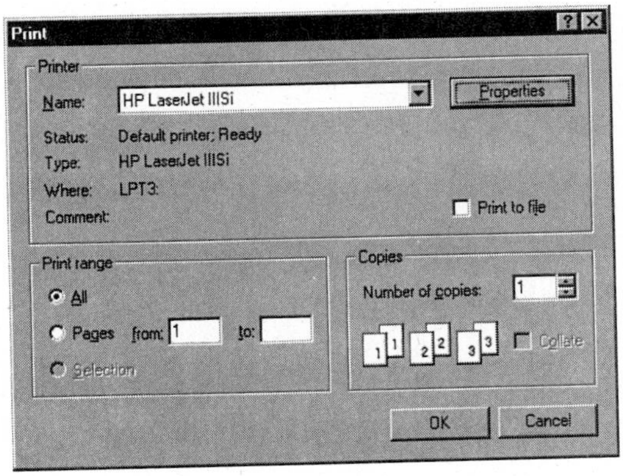

Fig. 6.1
A typical application's Print dialog box lets you send a print job to a specific printer.

3. Determine whether the printer shown in the Name box is the printer you want to use for this document. If it is not the desired printer, click the drop-down arrow for this box and select the desired printer.

4. Specify the number of copies you want to print by clicking the up and down arrows on the Number of Copies control. You may also select the default setting and type a number to replace the default number 1.

5. By default, most applications choose All as the print range. If you want to print something other than the entire document, you must define the print range. To do this, choose one of the three radio buttons in the Print Range box:

   - *All*. Prints all pages contained within the document.
   - *Selection*. Prints only those portions of the document you have selected using the selection features of the application.

► See "Selecting and Editing Text," p. 363

Tip
Some applications allow more complicated ranges to be specified. See "Applications with Special Print Options," later in this chapter.

Tip
The sheets-of-paper icon next to the collate option show whether or not the print job will be collated.

► See "The Print Manager," p. 173

Note

The Selection option is not available in all applications. In applications that do have this option, it is available only when part of the document has been selected.

- *Pages*. Prints the page range you specify in the boxes located to the right of the radio button. Specify a beginning page in the From box and an ending page in the To box.

6. If you are printing more than one copy of the document, you can have the copies collated (each copy of the multipage document is printed completely before the next copy of the document). To collate copies, select the Collate check box. If you don't select this option, all the copies of each page are printed together (for example, four copies of page 1 are printed and then four copies of page 2). The Collate option is not available in all applications.

7. To output the printer information to a print file, select the Print to File check box. Windows 95 prompts you for a file name and directs the print output to the specified file, rather than to a printer. Print files also are used for transferring data between applications with dissimilar file formats.

8. To initiate the links between your application and the Windows print drivers, click OK. Your application should now begin printing the specified document.

   If you change your mind and don't want to print, click Cancel to return to the document without making any changes or starting the print job.

Note

If you plan to print to a file frequently, set up a bogus printer. Use the Add Printer Wizard in the Printers folder to install a new printer; accept the current driver if you already have a printer installed or add the driver if you don't have one installed. Follow the preceding procedures to direct this printer's output to a file. When you're ready to print from the application, choose File, Print Setup (Windows 3.x applications) or use Name drop-down list in the Print dialog box (Windows 95 applications) to select the bogus printer and print.

This basic printing procedure applies to most applications, even if their Print dialog boxes are slightly different than the one shown in figure 6.1. Some applications have additional options, as discussed in the next two sections.

Applications with Special Print Options

Some applications take the basic printing features in Windows 95 and add a few features of their own. This section looks at some of the additional features you may find in other programs, with Word 95 as an example. Although these features vary from application to application, this section should give you an idea of what to look for.

Figure 6.2 shows the Word 95 Print dialog box.

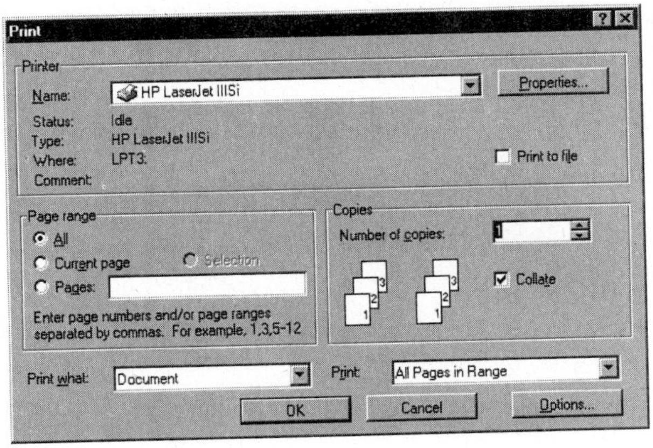

Fig. 6.2
The Print dialog box in Word 95 includes several enhancements not found in the standard Windows 95 Print dialog box.

Here is a quick summary of some of the additional (and different) options provided by this application compared to the standard Windows 95 printing options:

- The Current Page option in the Page Range section. When this option is selected, Word prints the page in which the insertion point is currently located.
- An enhanced Pages option. This enhanced option allows you to specify a page range in the variable box located to the right of the Pages label. The range can be individual pages separated by a comma, a page range separated by a hyphen, or both: for example, 1,2,4-8,10. In this example, pages 1, 2, 4, 5, 6, 7, 8, and 10 are printed.

- The Print What drop-down list. In Word, you can select to print the document itself or other information such as summary information, annotations, and styles.
- The Print option. From this drop-down list, you select to print odd, even, or all pages in the range.
- The Options button. When you click this button, Word displays the Options dialog box, opened to the Print tab. Use this dialog box to set printing options specific to Word.

Note

For a more complete discussion of Word's printing features, see Que's *Special Edition Using Word for Windows 95.*

Keep in mind that the options described here are not the same in all applications.

Windows 3.1 Applications with Special Print Options

The other common type of Print dialog box you may encounter is from a Windows 3.1 application that has a customized dialog box, such as the one for Word 6 shown in figure 6.3.

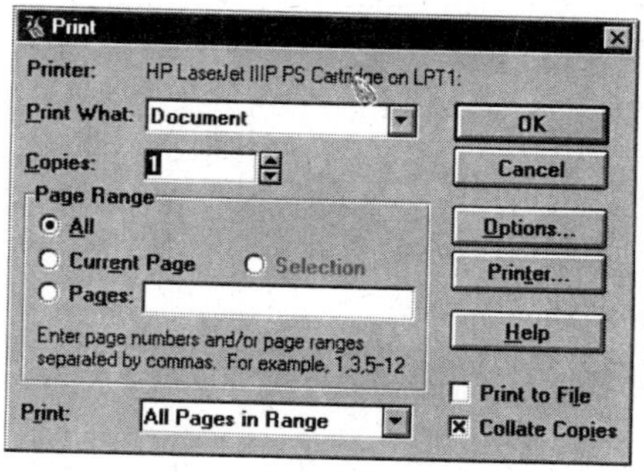

Fig. 6.3
The Word 6 dialog box is still styled like a Windows 3.1 dialog box.

Most options in this dialog box are the same as those shown in figures 6.1 and 6.2. However, there are some differences:

- There is no status entry or comment field that describes the printer's current activity.
- You select a different printer by clicking the Printer button and selecting from a dialog box instead of choosing a printer from a drop-down list.
- There is no Properties button.

► See "Options for Your Printer," p. 187

As with the other printing options discussed in this chapter, the options displayed in the Print dialog box vary from application to application.

Tip
If you have a shortcut to your printer on your desktop, you can open its window by double-clicking the shortcut icon. To create a shortcut for your printer, see " Create a Desktop Printer Icon," later in this chapter.

Managing Print Jobs

Like Windows 3.1, Windows 95 offers the option of printing directly to the configured port or using its 32-bit Print Manager. For most applications, the Print Manager provides facilities to better manage the printing of documents.

The Print Manager

To start the Print Manager, open the Start menu and choose Settings, Printers; then double-click the icon for the printer you want to manage in the Printers window (see fig. 6.4). Depending on the printers you have installed, your window will differ from the one shown in the figure.

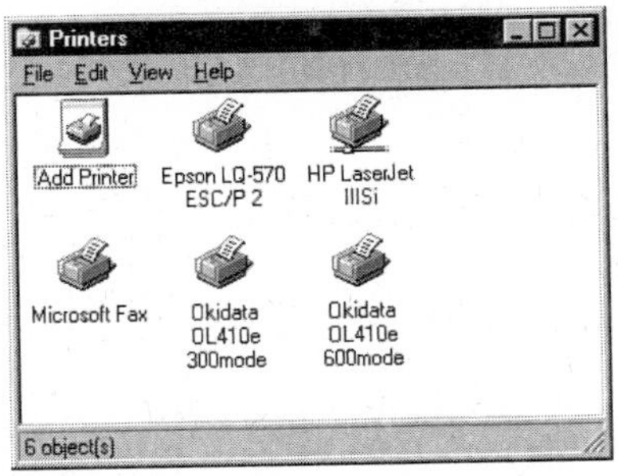

Fig. 6.4
The Printer control panel has icons for each of your installed printers as well as the icon to add a new printer.

Unlike Windows 3.1, Windows 95 uses a separate Print Manager for each printer. Therefore, make certain that you choose the correct Print Manager to view the status of your print jobs.

The Print Manager shown in figure 6.5 displays the current printer status for each print job.

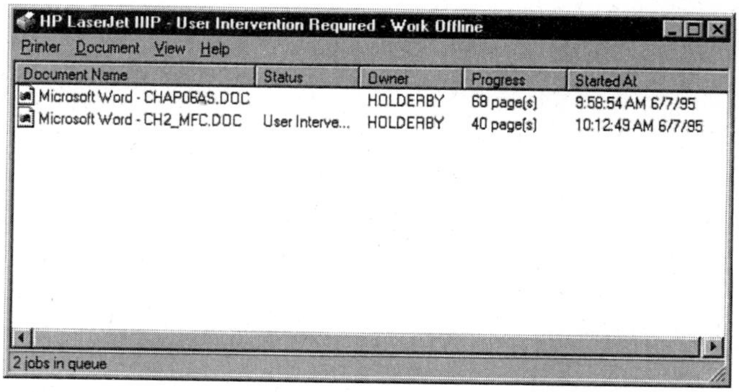

Fig. 6.5
Each printer has its own Print Manager; make sure that you select from the Printer control panel the correct printer for the print jobs you want to check.

The printer status includes the following information:

- The Document Name section shows the name of each application that has submitted a print job as well as the name of each document job in the print queue.
- The Status column describes the current condition of each print job, such as paused or spooling.
- The user's name associated with each document. A print job on your printer may belong to someone else when you share your printer.
- The relative progress of each job in the print queue. The progress of each job monitors the printing of each document and provides information concerning the number of pages printed and the number of pages left to print.
- The time and date when each print job was submitted to the print queue. This is important for those users with deferred print jobs.

► See "Managing Print Files and Sharing," p. 784

Tip
By default, print jobs are listed in the order they entered the queue. You can sort them according to name, status, owner, progress, or start time by clicking the appropriate column heading.

Controlling Printing

The Print Manager coordinates and schedules the printing of files received from your applications. These applications may be Windows based or MS-DOS based.

The Print Manager pull-down menus provide you with the following capabilities, all of which are described in the next several sections:

- Pause Printing
- Purge Printing

- Work Off-Line
- Set Printer as Default
- Change a Printer's Properties
- Pause a Selected Document's Printing
- Cancel a Selected Document's Printing
- View the Status Bar
- Access Windows Help

Note

If you are using a network printer, you can cancel only your own print jobs. You cannot pause printing, even of your own documents. Canceling someone else's print jobs or pausing printing requires network supervisor rights.

► See "Managing Print Files and Sharing," p. 784

Pausing Printing

Pausing a printer temporarily stops print jobs from being sent to that printer. Once a paused printer is restarted all pending print jobs are started and sequentially sent to the printer. This feature is useful when changing toner or performing printer maintenance.

To pause printing, choose Printer, Pause Printing. The Print jobs are paused and the Print Manager's title bar displays `Paused`.

To restart printing, choose Printer, Pause Printing again, which is now prefaced by a check mark. The Pause Printing check mark disappears and printing resumes.

Purging Print Jobs

The Purge Print Jobs command permanently removes all queued print jobs. Choose Printer, Purge Print Jobs. The documents listed by the Print Manager disappear.

Troubleshooting

The printer has started my print job and the Purge Print Jobs command won't stop it.

Purging print jobs stops Windows 95 from sending print jobs to the printer. However, it does not purge the print jobs currently being processed by the printer. You may have to reset the printer to terminate unwanted printing.

Working Off-Line

▶ See "Using Your Laptop with a Docking System," p. 273

▶ See "Understanding Network Printing," p. 772

▶ See "Configuration of the EMF Print Spooler," p. 194

Windows 95 enables you to initiate a print job without being physically attached to a printer. This feature is known as Deferred Printing, or Working Offline. Deferred Printing is available for network printers and laptop users with docking stations. Deferred Printing tracks deferred print jobs and releases them under configuration control when the computer is connected to the printer locally, networked or attached through a docking station.

> **Note**
>
> The spooler must be turned on for you to use Deferred Printing.

To configure a printer to work offline, choose Printer, Work Off-Line. A check mark appears in front of the Work Off-Line command. The Printer is now configured to work offline and defer printouts. The Print Manager changes its title to read `<printer name> User Intervention Required`. This information is then placed in the status line of each print job being sent to this printer. The Print manager defers printouts until you change the status of the Work Off-Line flag.

To change the status of the Work Off-Line flag, choose Work Off-Line a second time. The check mark disappears and the deferred printouts are sent to the printer.

The taskbar normally displays a clock at the lower right of the screen. This box also displays a printer when a document is being printed. If deferred documents are pending, the icon changes to include a question mark circled in red as shown in figure 6.6.

Fig. 6.6
When deferred printouts are stored, the taskbar displays the Printer icon with a question mark to remind you to release the jobs to the printer.

To print documents that have been deferred, follow these steps:

1. Physically connect the target printer to the system by putting the laptop in the docking station or connecting to the network printer.
2. From the Print Manager window, choose Printer. Then choose the Work Off-Line option to remove its check mark.
3. Verify that printing begins immediately to the target printer and that the deferred print jobs are no longer displayed by the Print Manager.

Setting a Default Printer

If you have more than one printer available (either locally or on a network), you should choose which printer you want to use as the default. The default printer is used by all applications unless you choose another printer from within the application.

To set a printer as the default, start that printer's Print Manager and then choose Printer, Set as Default. A check mark appears next to the Set as Default command on the pull-down menu, signifying that this printer is now the Windows default printer.

To remove the printer as the system default, select the Printer, Set as Default command from the Print Manager of another printer. Windows allows only one default printer.

Pausing a Document

You can pause a document if the Print Manager has not started sending it to the printer, or if the printer is local. You cannot pause a document that Print Manager has already started sending to a network printer. Pausing a document that has already been sent to a local printer prevents any other documents from being printed. If Print Manager has not yet started sending a document, pausing that document places it "on hold," while other documents continue to print.

To pause a document, choose one or more documents from the list of documents in the print queue. (Choosing a document highlights the document's entry in the Print Manager.) Choose Document, Pause. The selected documents now display a `Paused` status.

To release a paused document, choose the paused documents from the list of documents in the print queue. Choose Document, Pause. The selected documents no longer display a `Paused` status.

Canceling a Document from Printing

You also can permanently remove selected documents from the list of documents being printed. To cancel documents, choose one or more documents from the documents in the print queue; then choose Document, Cancel.

> **Caution**
>
> Once you cancel a document, Windows immediately removes that document from the print queue. You do not receive a confirmation prompt. You might try Pause first and make certain that you want this document's printout terminated.

Turning the Status Bar Off and On

The status bar lists the status of the print queue and contains the number of print jobs remaining to be printed. To turn off the display of the status bar, choose View, Status Bar. Repeat this action to turn the status bar display back on. The Status Bar option is a standard Windows toggle control: if the option is not preceded by a check mark, the status bar is not visible.

Closing Print Manager

To close the Print Manager, choose Printer, Close; or click the Close button.

> **Note**
>
> Closing the Print Manager in Windows 95 does not purge the associated print jobs (unlike Windows 3.1). Printing continues based on the print Manager's settings.

To rearrange the print queue, select a document, drag it to the correct queue position, and drop it. Dragging-and-dropping a document in the print queue works only with documents that are not currently being printed.

Drag-and-Drop Printing from the Desktop

Tip
Make sure that the document is associated with an application that is available to Windows, or your printing will terminate.

A new feature of the Windows 95 operating system is the ability to print a document without first initiating the associated application or the File Manager. Using desktop icons, you can quickly launch print jobs from the desktop.

In earlier versions of Windows, printing used a four-step operation: open an application, load a file, initiate printing, and finally shut down the application after printing. Windows 95 uses a two-step printing procedure that is quick and convenient. However, before you can print from the desktop, you must take certain steps to set up your system.

Create a Desktop Printer Icon

◄ See "Starting Programs from a Shortcut Icon on the Desktop," p. 68

Before you can drag-and-drop documents to desktop icons, you must first create the icons. Although some icons are automatically created during Windows setup, printer icons are not.

To create a shortcut icon for a printer, follow these steps:

1. Open the Start menu, choose Settings, and then choose Printers. You also can open the Printers folder by double-clicking the Printers icon in the Control Panel window. The Printer's folder is now open.

2. Select the desired printer, drag it onto the desktop, and release it.

3. Windows displays a question window that asks permission to create a shortcut (see fig. 6.7). Answer Yes; the shortcut icon is created.

After you have created the shortcut to the printer, you can modify it by creating a shortcut key or changing the icon. Modifying shortcuts is discussed in Chapter 3, "Getting Started with Windows 95."

◄ See "Modifying and Deleting Shortcuts," p. 72

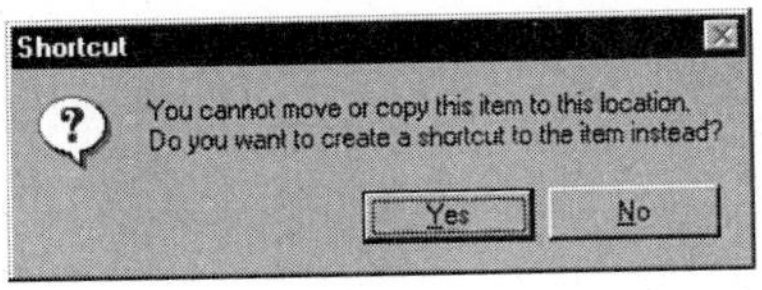

Fig. 6.7
A Windows question window asks your permission to create a shortcut.

Print from the Desktop

Once you have created a shortcut icon on the desktop for your printer, you can print any document from the desktop. To print from the desktop, follow these steps:

1. Open any folder (either in My Computer or Windows Explorer) that contains a printable document.

2. Select that document using the left mouse button.

3. While holding down the left mouse button, drag the document's icon from its folder to a printer desktop icon. Don't worry: this action makes no changes to the file.

4. When the document icon is on top of the printer desktop icon, release the mouse button.

► See "Selecting Files and Folders," p. 513

► See "Using My Computer to Manage Files," p. 551

Windows starts the associated application configured to handle that file type. Windows executes that application's print command. Once the printing has been committed to the background print spooler, Windows releases the associated application, closes it, and background prints the spooled files.

Why all the fuss about such a simple control function? Consider the time it saves you: If you have to print documents quickly, simply point, click, and drag the document to the printer; then you can go back to your other applications. Windows delivers hard copy with minimum effort.

Desktop Printing of Multiple Documents

Using Windows, you can print several files at once by dragging them to the shortcut icon on the desktop. Follow these steps to print several files at once:

Tip
You can select and print multiple documents created using different applications.

1. Select several documents to print by dragging around them or by holding down the Ctrl key and clicking the documents.
2. Drag the selected documents to the desktop printer icon.
3. Drop the documents on the icon.
4. The message window shown in figure 6.8 appears. Select Yes to print. Select No only if you want to stop all documents from printing.

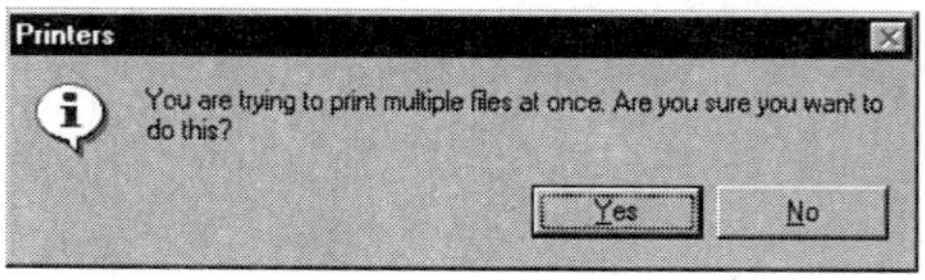

Fig. 6.8
A message window asks permission to print the multiple documents.

Windows starts each of the applications associated with the selected documents and begins printing.

Installing and Deleting Printers

Before you can take advantage of Windows' newest printing features, you must first install a printer. The printer installation process depends largely on the make and model of the printer you have. The next sections describe how to fully install a printer—with an emphasis on the specific areas in which you can expect to find printer differences. The following sections use as an example printer the HP LaserJet 4.

Installing a New Printer

Before you install a printer, you should know the following information:

- Review your printer to find the make and model (for example, Hewlett-Packard IIIP).
- Refer to the printer manual or print a test page using the printer's test feature to find the amount of RAM contained in your printer (for example, 2M).
- Identify the type of communications interface required to connect your printer to the computer (for example, serial, parallel, or a special interface).
- Identify any special features or functions supported by your printer, such as PostScript compatibility. Some printers are multimode and may require installation as two separate printers (for example, the HP LaserJet IV with PostScript option).

- Find the location of a suitable port on your PC to connect your printer. The selected port must correspond to the same port type as required by your printer (that is, serial to serial, parallel to parallel).

This information is required by the Windows printer installation wizard later in the installation process.

Installing a Printer with the Printer Wizard

Microsoft Office's suite of desktop applications pioneered the use of wizards to step a user through an often complex series of operations. The Windows 95 print architecture incorporates a printer installation wizard to step you through the labor-intensive chore of installing a printer.

A quick explanation of the use of the Wizard buttons is in order. The Back button steps you back one Wizard screen every time you click it. The Next button steps you forward one Wizard screen. The Cancel button halts the entire Wizard process and discards all inputs made during this Wizard session. Use these buttons to back up and make changes if later configurations prove to be incorrect.

1. Open the Windows 95 Start menu and choose Settings, Printers. If the control panel is open, double-click the Printer folder. The Printers window appears (see fig. 6.9), showing each installed printer as an icon. Don't worry if you have no installed printers yet: the window also includes the Add New Printer icon. The program associated with the Add New Printer icon is the Add Printer Wizard. You use the Printers window often because it is useful in managing your printers.

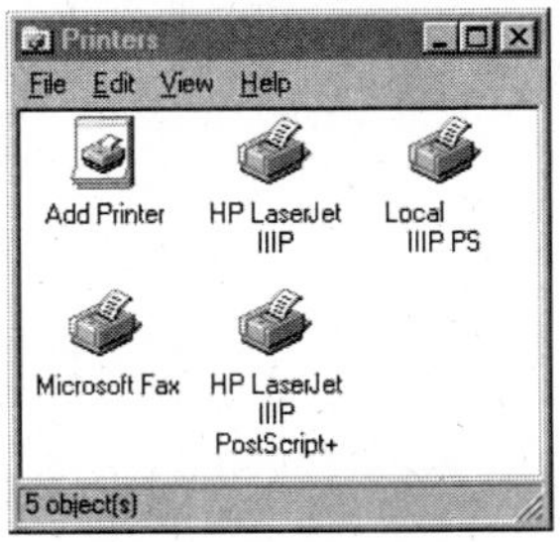

Fig. 6.9
Starting a printer installation by opening the Printers window.

2. Double-click the Add New Printer icon to start the Add Printer Wizard. Windows displays the initial Wizard screen.

3. Choose Next. Windows displays the Add Printer Wizard screen shown in figure 6.10.

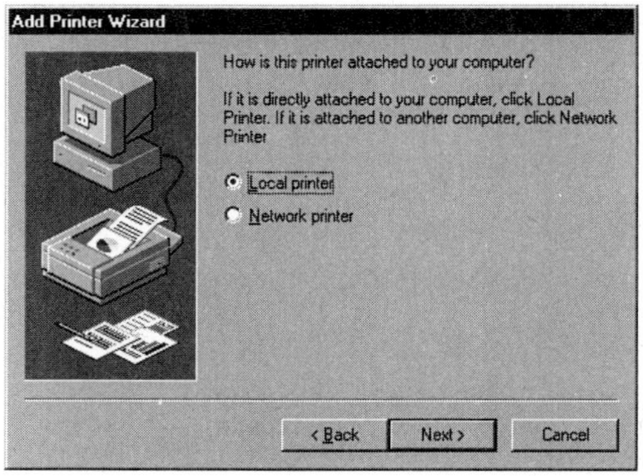

Fig. 6.10
The Add Printer Wizard steps you through the printer installation procedure by first asking whether you are installing a local or network printer.

► See "Installing a Network Printer," p. 774

4. Choose the Local Printer option to install a printer attached directly to your PC. Choose Next. The screen shown in figure 6.11 appears.

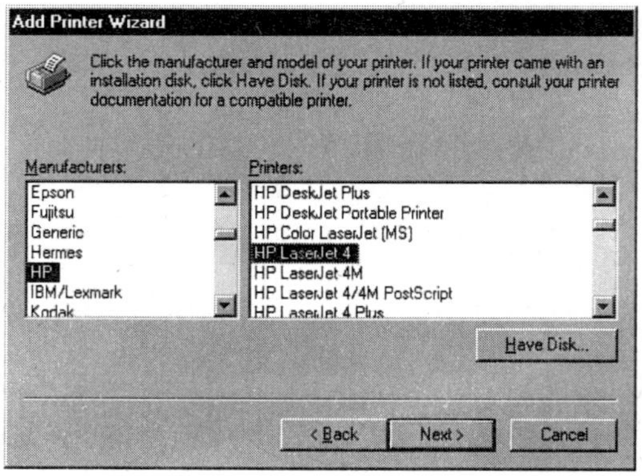

Fig. 6.11
Select the make and model of the printer you are installing from the lists provided.

5. Locate the make and model of your printer by scrolling through the Wizard's screen lists. Windows 95 has drivers that support over 300 printers. When you have selected the appropriate options, choose Next to display the screen shown in figure 6.12.

Tip
Many laser printers are Hewlett-Packard compatible and dot-matrix printers are Epson compatible. If you can't get a driver or the generic driver doesn't work well, try one of the commonly emulated printers.

If you're adding a printer after initial installation, you need the Windows 95 installation disks or CD available. Windows will ask for these if it does not have an existing driver available. You may also use a manufacturer's disk to install custom printer drivers.

Scroll the screen on the far left to identify your printer's manufacturer. Then select the appropriate printer model. If your printer is not on the list, you can install your printer by choosing either the generic printer or the Have Disk button. If your printer came with its own software driver, insert the floppy disk from your printer manufacturer into either drive A or B and choose the Have Disk button to complete the requirements of this screen.

Note

If your printer is not listed, you should contact your printer manufacturer for an updated driver. Choose a generic printer until you can obtain an updated driver version.

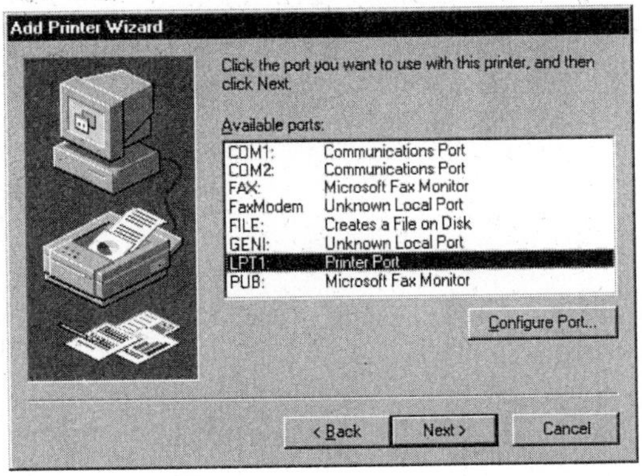

Fig. 6.12
Selecting the printer port to which you want to attach the printer.

6. Provide the printer port information. The Wizard screen shown in figure 6.12 displays ports based on the survey Windows did of your PC hardware. You may have several COM and LPT ports. Refer to the list of information you compiled before you started the installation and choose the port to which you want to attach the printer. The port selected in figure 6.12 is LPT1, a very typical selection.

7. Choose the Configure Port button. The Wizard displays the Configure Port window (see fig. 6.13). The window contains a check box that enables Windows 95 to spool your MS-DOS print jobs. This box should always be checked to enable MS-DOS printing, unless your MS-DOS applications prove to be incompatible with Windows 95 printing. Enable the Check Port State before Printing check box if you want Windows 95 to determine if the printer port is available prior to starting the print job.

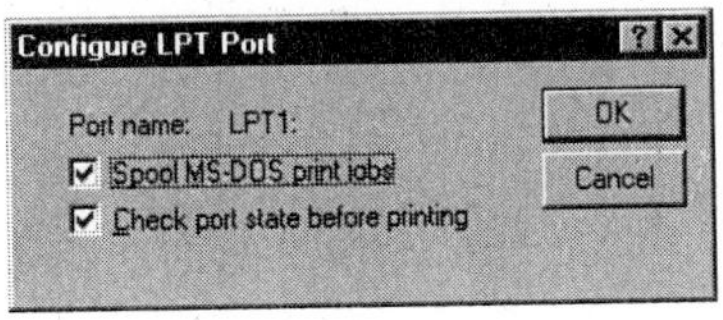

Fig. 6.13
Configuring your parallel printer port enables MS-DOS applications to use the same driver.

8. After you configure the port, choose OK and then Next to display the dialog box shown in figure 6.14. Use this dialog box to name the new printer and define it as your default printer if desired. In the Printer Name field, type the name of the printer. The name can be up to 128 characters long and can contain spaces and nonalphanumeric symbols. The printer's name should include location or ownership.

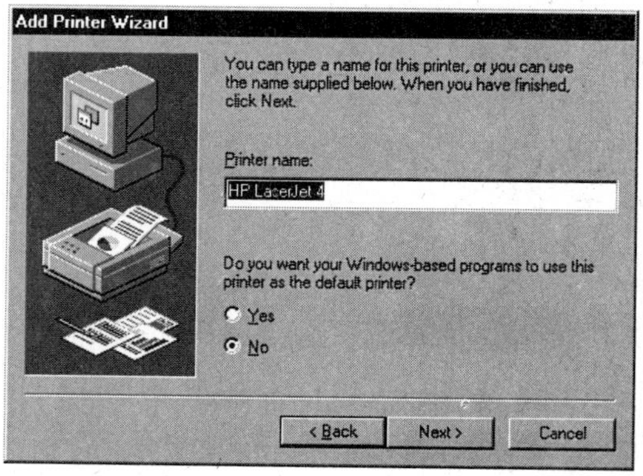

Fig. 6.14
The printer name and default status are specified using this Wizard screen.

> **Note**
>
> If you have access to two printers of the same type, appropriate names would be to name the first one "HP Laserjet Series II Room 5, Building 10" and the second one "HP LaserJet Series II Room 25, Building 15."

9. Choose Yes to set this printer as the system default. By setting this printer as your default, you instruct all applications to use this printer, unless you tell the application to use a different printer. (You can set the default to any other installed printer at any time.) Click Next to continue. The final Wizard screen, shown in figure 6.15, appears.

10. Specify whether you want to print a test page. Printing a test page tests the overall operation of the printer based on the settings you've just entered. Choose Yes and click Finish to print the test page. The Wizard then copies the necessary driver files to your system, prompting you to insert one of the Windows 95 source disks if necessary.

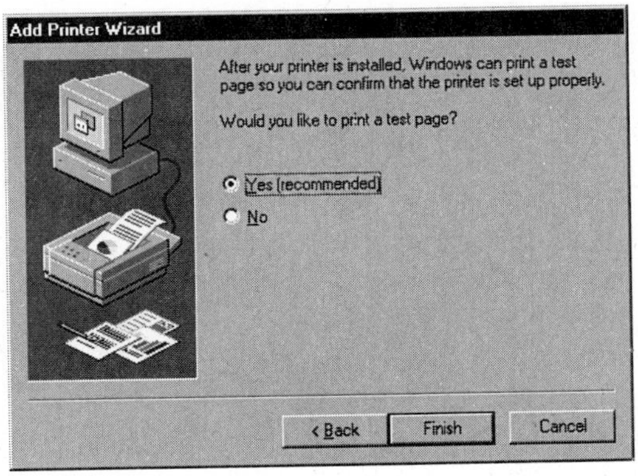

Fig. 6.15
Printing a test page is the final step in configuring and testing your printer installation.

Note

The test page contains information specific to your printer, its configuration, and the drivers Windows uses to interface with it. Once this page is printed, save it for future reference. If your PC is used by others, you may some day have to return to a known installation configuration.

Installing a Plug-and-Play Printer

In addition to the Add Printer Wizard, Windows 95 supports the Plug and Play standards that assist the user in configuring the printer software. Plug and Play technology automatically provides answers to configuration questions you've scratched your head over in the past. Remember the list of information you compiled before you began installing your printer? Plug and Play printers interact with Windows to automatically configure printers by using a dialog transparent to the user. Many printer manufacturers have cooperated with Microsoft to not only make configuration easier, but to automatically update the software when you make changes to the printer hardware configuration.

If your printer is Plug and Play compatible, see Chapter 8, "Plug and Play and Legacy Device Installation," for an explanation of how Plug and Play devices are installed.

Renaming an Existing Printer

Printers named during installation can be quickly renamed using the Printers folder. The Printers folder displays all installed printers, with their individual names located immediately below the printer's icon (refer to fig. 6.9).

To rename a printer after it is installed, follow these steps:

1. Open the Printers folder by opening the Start menu, choosing Settings, and then choosing Printers. If Control Panel is open, double-click the Printers folder.

◀ See "Changing Settings and Properties with the Right Mouse Button," p. 107

2. Select the desired printer and choose File, Rename. Alternatively, right-click the printer icon to open the shortcut menu and choose Rename.

   Windows creates a text box around the printer name and highlights that name.

3. Change the name by typing a new name or deleting portions of the existing name.

4. When finished, press the Enter key. The new printer name is used throughout the Windows operating system.

Deleting an Existing Printer

You can delete an installed printer from the Printers window, which displays all installed printers as icons. To delete a printer from the Printers window, follow these steps:

1. Select the printer you want to delete. Choose File, Delete; alternatively, right-click the printer icon to open the shortcut menu and choose Delete.

   Windows opens a dialog box and asks whether you're sure that you want to delete the printer. The dialog box provides two control buttons: OK and Cancel.

2. Choose OK; the printer is now deleted. Windows then asks whether it can remove the associated software from your hard disk and presents the same OK and Cancel buttons.

   Caution

   If you have a similar printer that could use the same drivers, do not remove the software. Deleting the associated software may remove that driver from use by other printers.

3. Choose OK to remove the deleted printer's software driver.

The printer and its driver are now removed. Windows signifies this event by removing that printer icon from the Printers window.

Note

If you plan to reattach this printer in the future, do not remove the software drivers. This can save you time when reattaching the printer. If you do not plan to reattach this printer or are upgrading the software drivers, remove the software to free up disk space and avoid confusion.

Configuring Your Printer

By now, you have installed one or more printers for use by Windows 95 applications. Both Windows and MS-DOS applications can use these resources without further effort. The initial installation of the printer created a default configuration. You may want to make changes to that configuration. Because few default configurations satisfy all printing requirements, you may want to change the printer's configuration frequently.

Tip
If you change printer settings frequently, you can install duplicate printers and configure each printer with its own set of properties. This eliminates repeated property changes.

Note

Windows 3.1 provided a setting to change the priority of background printing. This feature does not appear in Windows 95.

Options for Your Printer

Printer properties are preset during installation of the printer. The preset values for the many variables may not meet your current printing needs. You may also have to make changes to meet special printing needs or to solve any performance problems that arise.

Like many other printing issues discussed in this chapter, the exact options available depend on the capabilities of your printer. The following discussion focuses on the basic procedures; you must adapt these to fit your specific printer.

To change printer options, open the printer's Properties sheet using one of these two methods:

- If the Print Manager for the printer whose options you want to change is open, choose Printer, Properties.
- Open the Printer window and select the printer whose options you want to change. Choose File, Properties or right-click the printer icon and choose Properties from the shortcut menu.

Both methods open the printer's Properties sheet (see fig. 6.16). This dialog box has several tabs. The settings on each page depend on the manufacturer, printer model, and printer options.

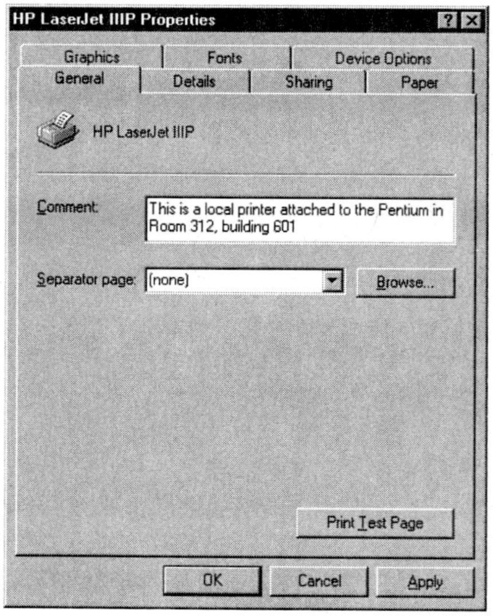

Fig. 6.16
Use the General page of the printer's Properties sheet to get and specify basic information about the printer.

The Properties sheet typically contains the following information. (The details of these pages will change with different printers.)

- *The General page.* Enables you to identify your printer, print a test page, and choose a separator page. A separator page is used to separate print jobs from different users. Each page includes a user name and job specific information such as date, time, and file name. The General page enables you to perform the following actions:
    - Fill in a comment field to identify a printer whose properties are being changed.
    - Specify that Windows will print a separator page between each print job.
    - Print a test page using the Print Test Page control.
- *The Details page.* Contains controls to attach or change ports, add or delete ports, change timeout periods, and specify how Windows will process print files. Use the Details page to configure enhanced meta file printing and the spooler. Typical controls include

- Print to the Following Port specifies the printer port that Windows 95 will use to access the printer.
- Add Port permits the user to add another port.
- Delete Port deletes a port.
- Print Using the Following Driver displays which driver the operating system will use to print to this printer.
- New Driver adds another printer driver for possible use with this printer.
- Capture Printer Port captures a network printer port.
- Release Printer Port releases a network printer port.
- Time-Out Settings enables you to set the time out and not selected periods for printing.
- Spool Settings enables you to configure the print spooler.
- Port Settings enables MS-DOS printing.

■ *The Sharing page.* Enables a printer to be shared or not be shared with other workstations attached to your PC over a network.

■ *The Paper page.* Provides several controls that set the printer's default paper handling, orientation, and the number of pages to be printed. Commonly included controls are

- Paper Size specifies paper or envelope size.
- The Layout block specifies from one to four reduced pages per printed page.
- The Orientation block specifies Portrait or Landscape printing.
- Paper Source specifies which paper tray is the default.
- Copies specifies single or multiple copies.

■ *The Graphics page.* Sets the resolution and other options that define how the printer treats graphic files. Typical settings include

- Default printing resolution.
- The way Windows employs halftoning to create grayscale images from color graphics.

- For PostScript printers, controls that allow you to create negative images and print mirror images.
- Scaling that reduces the size occupied by a printout on the printed page.

- *The Fonts page.* Enables you to adjust how fonts are treated by Windows for this printer. Configurable fonts include printer, cartridge, and software fonts. Typical controls include
  - Sending TrueType fonts to a printer according to the Font Substitution Table.
  - Always Use Built-In Printer Fonts instead of TrueType fonts.
  - Always Use TrueType Fonts instead of any other fonts.

Tip
Be certain to accurately configure the available printer memory. An incorrect value in this variable can change the speed of your printouts or cause your printer to time out or fail during printing sessions.

- *The Device Options page.* Configures the options associated with the printer's hardware. The number and type of controls are specific to the printer's make, model, and hardware. Typical controls include
  - Set printer memory capacity to change the amount of memory in your printer.
  - Specify device-specific options such as Page Protection.

Printing with Color

Microsoft uses licensed Image Color Matching (ICM) technology from Kodak to create an image environment that treats color consistently from the screen to the printed page. The Windows ICM goal is to be able to repeatedly and consistently reproduce color-matched images from source to destination.

In earlier versions of Windows, printout and display quality were application- and vendor-dependent. Using ICM technology, Windows 95 provides a higher quality color rendering. ICM provides more consistent, repeatable quality among various brands of printers and scanners. The term *color* includes grayscale rendering.

The most important feature is consistency between the video screen and the printed page. Now both software applications and hardware devices adapt to improve output quality. The phrase "What You See Is What You Get" (WYSIWYG) takes on much deeper meaning. Not only are black-and-white printouts consistent from screen to printer, but the color, texture, and tone are no longer solely dependent on price.

Many newer printers are capable of printing color in addition to grayscale. Choose a printer that is color aware and compliant with Kodak's ICM specification. For color printers, printouts more closely match the colors and shades seen on your display. Grayscale printers also reproduce outputs with much higher correspondence to the screen using grayscale and shading.

Setting Color Printing Properties

The Graphics page in the printer's Properties sheet for a color printer is shown in figure 6.17. It provides several controls for setting color consistency in the printed output. The controls in this page allow you to configure your printer to produce the best color possible.

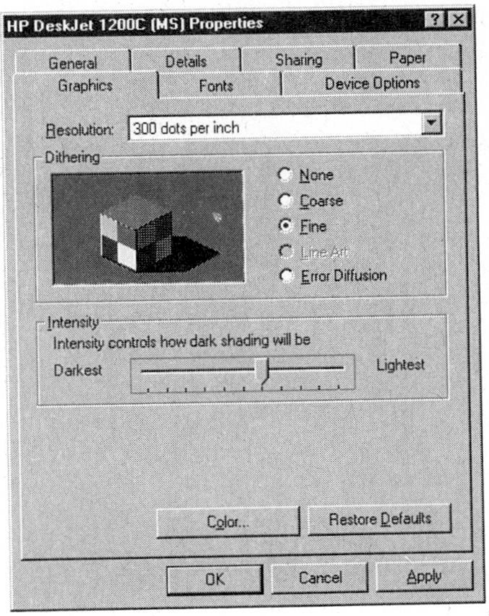

Fig. 6.17
The Graphics page of the printer's Properties sheet for a color printer lets you adjust color and output quality.

- *Resolution*. This drop-down list box specifies the number of dots per inch (dpi) that the printer can produce. The higher the dpi, the clearer the graphics.
- *Dithering*. Dithering is an error-correcting tool used by Windows 95 to more accurately represent an object's color and grayscale.
- *Intensity*. Intensity is a brightness control to lighten or darken a printout to more accurately reflect its screen appearance and to compensate for deficiencies in toner or paper quality.

To access the color settings for a color printer, click the Color button. This dialog box shown in figure 6.18 appears; use this dialog box to set ICM compliance alternatives.

The color settings are used to adjust the level of compliance of your printer with the ICM standards. The dialog box is also useful for trial-and-error adjustment of color printer output quality. Following is a list of the settings:

- *Color Control.* A macro command that enables you to direct the printer to print only black and white or to specify whether or not you want ICM technology.

- *Color Rendering Intent.* Provides the best ICM settings for three of the major uses of color printing: presentations, photographs, and true color screen display printing. Select the choice that works best for your purpose.

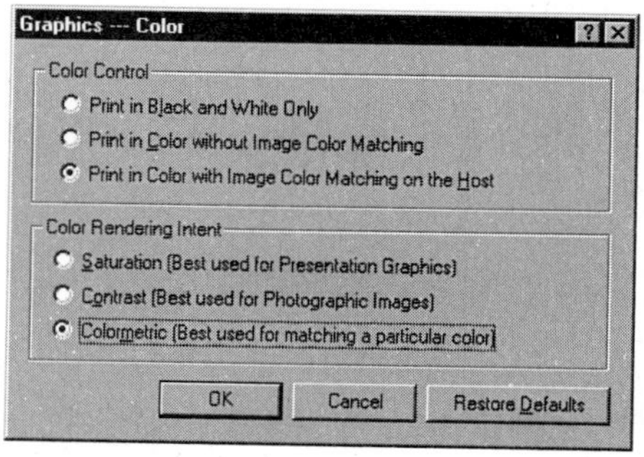

Fig. 6.18 Display the Graphics—Color dialog box by selecting the Color button on the Graphics page of the printer's Properties sheet.

Using the 32-Bit Subsystem

◄ See "Improved Performance," p. 21

Naturally, a 32-bit application is faster than its 16-bit equivalent. However, in Windows 95, 32-bit performance means more than speed. It also means safety. 32-bit applications run in their own address space so that a failure in one application doesn't propagate to others. Because printing is a resource-dependent function, 32-bit performance results in better use of your resources. It permits Windows 95 designers to provide a more robust, feature-rich user interface.

When using the 32-bit printing subsystem, you will find the following differences in Windows 95 versus Windows 3.1 performance.

- *Return from Printing.* When an application prints, it shares memory and resources with the print system. In the Windows 32-bit architecture, 32-bit applications do not share the same memory—each has its own virtual memory resources. Virtual memory, combined with the faster performance of 32-bit drivers, results in the printing subsystem quickly releasing resources. Thirty-two-bit printer drivers share existing resources more equitably, resulting in smoother background printing.

- *System Stalls*. Because the printing subsystem runs in its own 32-bit virtual processor, a printing failure no longer locks out other applications. Another benefit from this design is that Windows can clean up resources after a print failure.

- *Printing Independence*. 32-bit virtual drivers enables Windows to support each printer with an individual, dedicated Print Manager. Multiple Print Managers result in the independent configuration of each printer and maximize the use of all printers without the need for frequent reconfiguration.

To verify that all Windows 95 printing components are 32-bit, perform the following checks:

- Using the Port Configuration dialog box, verify that all port drivers are VxD files. The VxD extension designates a virtual device driver.

- Using the Print Manager Properties sheet, print a test page from the General page. The test page displays the name and version of the current printer driver. Verify that the version of the driver is the latest available for Windows 95. As a general rule, this driver should also have a VxD (virtual device driver) extension. If your drivers are not VxD, check with your printer manufacturer to obtain the latest releases of these drivers. Then perform the Add a Printer installation procedure using the new drivers.

Using Enhanced Meta File Spooling (EMF)

The new Enhanced Meta File (EMF) feature appears to fall in the "so-what" category—or does it? Historically, PostScript printing has employed meta files to produce excellent hardcopy results. A printer meta file contains specific printer instructions to produce a hardcopy printout. Many printer manufacturers use proprietary meta file formats, such as PostScript, to produce their best results. Now meta files can be created within the operating system and be standardized for most printers.

The EMF Process

An application submits a print stream to Windows. If the printer is configured to support Enhanced Meta Files, the print stream is converted into a series of high level printer instructions.

The process of changing a print stream to a meta file converts each page into a series of printer-recognizable macro instructions. Printing EMF files transfers much of the processing overhead from the PC to the printer. Windows uses its 32-bit Graphics Device Interface (GDI) and its Device Independent Bitmap (DIB) engine to create the image to print.

Print Spooling

Print spooling creates a temporary disk file that stores print files. It is temporary because Windows only stores these files until it has finished printing. The spooler is an integral part of the Windows 32-bit print architecture. The spooler itself is a 32-bit virtual device driver.

An application sends a print stream to Windows for printing. The printer driver reviews the printer configuration and verifies that the spooler is required.

The spooler creates a memory-mapped file on the system's hard disk to store the application's print stream. Although this process takes time, it uses fewer system resources for a shorter period of time than does sending the print stream directly to the printer.

Using the spooler enables Windows to smooth out background printing and more quickly return resources to the application.

Configuration of the EMF Print Spooler

The Enhanced Meta File (EMF) Print Spooler is responsible for converting your documents into a printable format prior to sending them to the printer. The spooler is important because it affects both printing speed and how quickly Windows returns control to you after printing.

Note

You cannot configure PostScript printers using the EMF Print Spooler. PostScript is itself a substitute for EMF, and Windows will only configure RAW for PostScript printers.

To use the spooler, follow these steps:

1. Open the Start menu and choose Settings, Printers.
2. Right-click on a non-PostScript printer to open its context menu, and then choose Properties to open the printer's Properties sheet.
3. Click the Details tab to display the Details page.
4. Select Spool Settings. Windows displays the Spool Settings dialog box, shown in figure 6.19. The Spool Settings dialog box has four basic controls: spooler printing, bypassing the spooler, spooler formats, and printer communications.

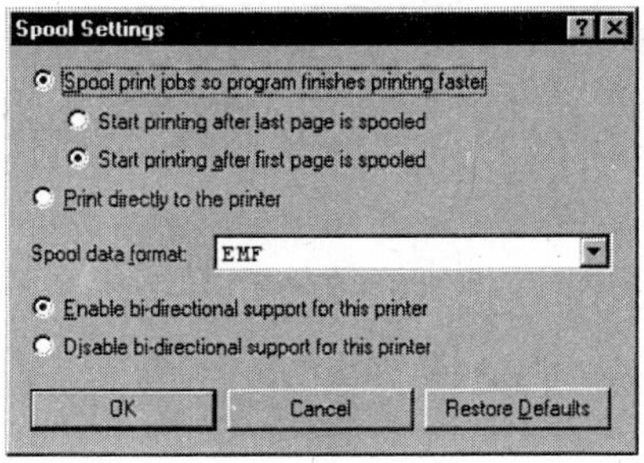

Fig. 6.19
The Spool Settings dialog box provides controls to modify the operation of the Windows printer spooler.

5. Select the Spool Print Jobs So Program Finishes Printing Faster radio button. Selecting this option enables the spooler.

   Alternatively, select Print Directly to the Printer; this option disables the spooler.

6. If you selected the Select the Spool Print Jobs So Program Finishes Printing Faster radio button, you can then choose when you want Windows to start printing during the spooling process. Because this is a radio button list, you can only select one of the following two options:

   - *Start Printing after First Page Is Spooled.* This option tells the Print Manager to print after the first page is spooled.

   - *Start Printing after Last Page Is Spooled.* Printing after the last page is spooled provides the smoothest background printing, even though you wait longer for the printout.

7. Specify EMF in the Spool Data Format drop-down list box. The list has two options: RAW or EMF. RAW saves the print stream to a spooler, but does not convert the print stream to Enhanced Meta File format. Select RAW when printing to a PostScript printer or to a printer with a proprietary meta file print driver. The EMF setting should produce superior results on most printers. However, if your printing slows down or produces poor-quality graphics, try the RAW setting for possible improvement.

8. Select the Enable Bi-Directional Support or Disable Bi-Directional Support radio button to specify whether or not Windows can communicate in both directions with the attached printer. If a printer cannot support any level of bi-directional communications or is not attached, the correct choice is Disable Bi-Directional Support. In all other cases, the appropriate choice is Enable Bi-Directional Support, which allows the Print Manager to monitor the printer status during the printing process.

> **Note**
>
> If your printer or port does not support these options, the options will be dimmed in the dialog box.

Configuring the Printer Port

In addition to configuring settings that affect the printer itself, you can make a few configuration changes to the port to which the printer is attached. These options vary depending on which port you use to print. The most common printing port is an LPT port, usually LPT1 (or LPT2 if you have a second LPT port). Changing the printer port may be required if you attach a printer to a serial port or add a printer switch.

Follow these steps to change the configuration options for port LPT1:

1. Open the Start menu and choose Settings, Control Panel.

2. Double-click the System icon.
3. Windows displays the System Properties sheet; choose the Device Manager tab to configure printer ports (see fig. 6.20).

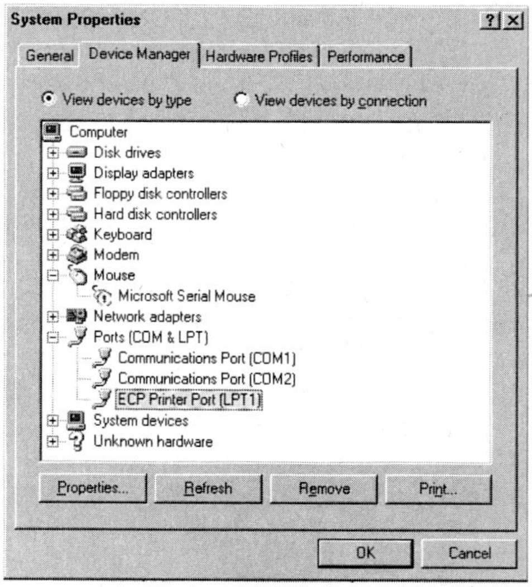

Fig. 6.20 The Device Manager tab of the System Properties sheet identifies the port, its present state of operation, and the hardware configuration being used.

4. Double-click the Ports icon to show the attached ports. Choose the printer port whose configuration you want to change, such as LPT1 or COM1. For this example, choose LPT1. If your printer is attached to another parallel port or a COM (serial) port, choose that port instead.

5. Click Properties. The Printer Port Properties sheet shown in figure 6.21 appears. Note that Printer Port Properties are divided among three pages: General, Driver, and Resources.

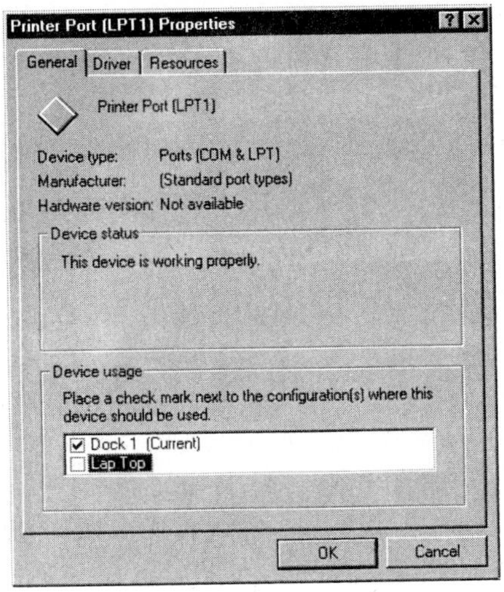

Fig. 6.21
The General page of the Printer Port Properties sheet provides current status and information about the port's hardware.

6. Choose the Driver tab.

7. Verify that the driver file selected on the Driver page is the most current printer driver available (see fig. 6.22). Note that the VxD extension signifies a 32-bit virtual driver that can be expected to provide the best performance. If you have a driver with a .DRV extension, you are not using a 32-bit driver. Check with your printer manufacturer for the latest version.

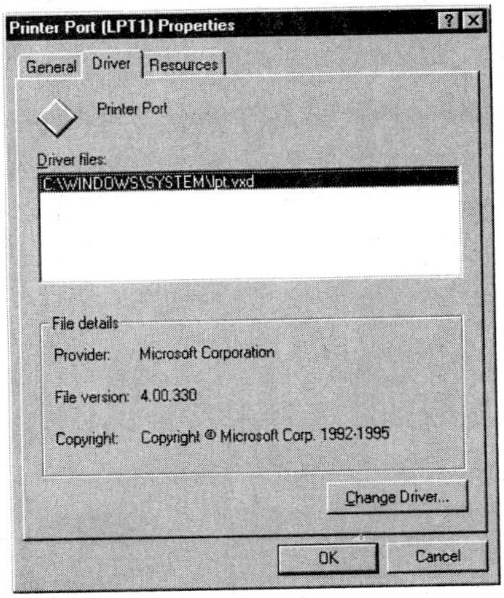

Fig. 6.22
The Driver page of the Printer Port Properties sheet provides the name and version of the currently installed port driver.

8. To install a different driver, click Change Driver. Windows displays the Select Device dialog box shown in figure 6.23. Use this dialog box to load a new driver from either a vendor-supplied disk or choose a previously installed driver. If you have a vendor-supplied disk that contains the new port driver, choose Have Disk.

Fig. 6.23
Select a new or existing printer port driver.

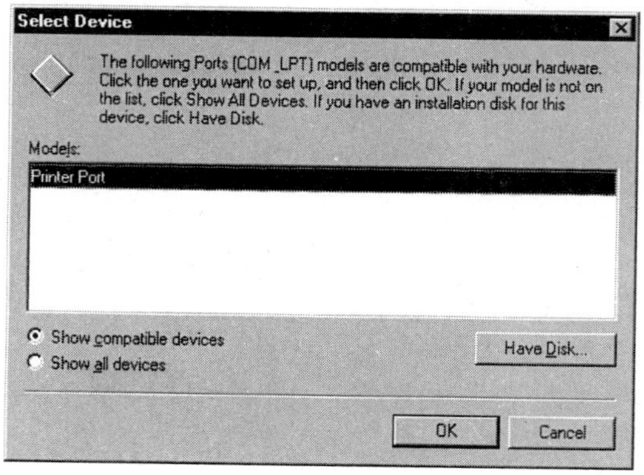

9. Windows displays an instruction window that directs you to insert the manufacturer's disk in drive A. Change the drive by typing the appropriate drive letter over the letter *A*. The window also allows you to browse and select a driver from another location. Windows requests a vendor disk. Insert the appropriate disk and select the OK control button. Otherwise, select the Cancel control button to stop the installation process. Windows installs the vendor software and links it to the selected printer port.

The Resources page contains detailed information about the printer port's addresses and any configuration conflicts. Reviewing this information is a convenient way to verify that Windows has properly installed the driver. In the background, Windows cross-checked the ports configuration with the system startup settings. Windows can and does spot configuration problems but doesn't necessarily notify the user that there's a problem. The resources contain the Input/Output Range of addresses. The addresses of the LPT1 port are shown under the Setting column. If a device uses an interrupt, that interrupt is also shown. If Windows spots a problem, it will designate that a conflict exists and list the information in this window. You can then choose alternative configurations to test other configurations.

To configure the printer port, click the Resources tab. The critical information is the Conflicting Device List (see fig. 6.24). This list contains all items that conflict with your printer port. When installing new hardware, always verify that its address and interrupts do not conflict with existing hardware properties.

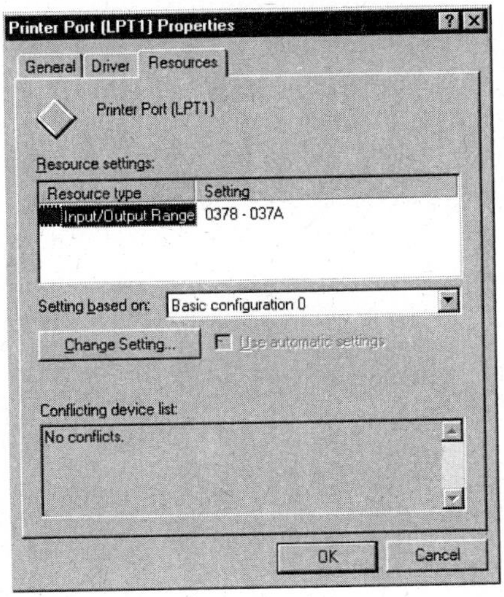

Fig. 6.24
The Resources page of the Printer Port Properties sheet displays detailed hardware information vital to port operation and the diagnosis of communications problems.

You should normally choose Use Automatic Settings. If you have any conflict problems, the Settings Based On list box shown in figure 6.24 provides several optional configurations that Windows can use to configure the printer port.

To use this control, first uncheck the Use Automatic Settings box. You then can use the Settings Based On control to select from a list of Windows configurations. Each configuration shows the port configured to different devices and interrupts. As each configuration is considered, problems associated with the new configuration are shown in the Conflicting Device List information box at the bottom of the tab.

Note

Carefully review the hardware properties for all devices to identify potential conflicts. Windows cannot discover and display all problems in normal operation. Use the Device Manager to check for conflicting devices; doing so may prevent problems later.

Most printer installations do not require changes to the printer port settings. However, unusual address conflicts from older equipment or Enhanced

Capability Ports (ECP) technology provide more configuration options. The number of possible decisions and potential conflicts between pieces of hardware increase as the number of options increase. Select OK to complete the port configuration.

Printing from MS-DOS Applications

Windows provides support for printing from MS-DOS applications in much the same way it does for printing from Windows applications. Although EMF support for MS-DOS applications is not supported, the print stream is spooled using the RAW setting for the print spooler. The result is faster return to MS-DOS applications and the ability to mix Windows and MS-DOS print streams (avoiding contention problems that occurred under Windows 3.1).

Under Windows 3.1, MS-DOS applications could not access the Windows printing facilities. In the past, printing from a DOS application was neither robust nor fail-safe. When printing simultaneously from both Windows and MS-DOS applications, you often received notice of a printer conflict. In most cases, this caused either the MS-DOS application or the Windows application to stall, and you had to reboot.

The major change Windows 95 brings to MS-DOS applications is direct access to the Windows print spooler. MS-DOS applications no longer compete for a share of the printer; you can actually use the Print Manager to queue your MS-DOS printouts with those of Windows applications.

When you print from an MS-DOS application in the Windows environment, the DOS application spools print jobs to the 32-bit print spooler, which takes the output destined for the printer port and spools it before printing. Windows automatically installs the print spooler for MS-DOS applications; the spooler is transparent to users. Although your MS-DOS printouts automatically use the 32-bit spooler, they cannot be processed into Enhanced Meta Files.

Printing from a Docking Station

▶ See "Using Your Laptop with a Docking System," p. 273

Every time you start Windows, it performs an inventory check of all attached hardware. Windows also provides a choice of configurations during startup (that is, it lists the configurations it recognizes). You must choose one of the selections from this list.

You can configure Windows to work offline when the PC is undocked and online when the PC is docked. You can set the system configurations for the printer port to be configured only when the laptop is attached to the docking station. You also can configure the port to be automatically unavailable when the system is being used as a laptop.

Configuring a Hardware Profile

A hardware profile specifies whether Windows will use or not use a specific peripheral. Hardware profiles provide a tool that you can use to specify the hardware configurations to operate your system. Hardware configurations are created and changed through the Control Panel's System icon.

Because the printer is not a system resource, it is not part of the hardware configuration. However, the printer is attached to the system through the LPT1 port. This port *is* a system resource and can be configured to be available when the computer is in a docking station. The port can also be configured as unavailable when the system is used as a laptop.

Use the following steps to create the hardware profile:

1. Open the Start menu and choose Settings, Control Panel.
2. Double-click the System icon. The System Properties sheet appears.

3. Choose the Hardware Profiles tab. The page contains a text window with a single item: Dock 1. When Windows is first installed at a docking station, it creates the Dock 1 setting in the text window.
4. Select the Dock 1 setting and click Copy.

> **Note**
>
> Windows will automatically detect most docking stations and create a Dock 1 profile. Even if you initially install Windows on a laptop, Windows checks the system components each time it starts and will create profiles automatically when it finds changes.

5. Change the name of the newly created configuration from Dock 1 to Lap Top or some other name that indicates that the laptop is not in its docking station. Click OK.
6. Choose the Device Manager tab from the System Properties sheet.
7. Select the port (COM or LPT) from the Device Manager page.

8. Choose the printer's port (LPT1).

   The Printer Port (LPT1) Properties sheet that appears contains a Device Usage block with a hardware configuration window (see fig. 6.25). The Device Usage block now contains two hardware configurations: the initial Dock 1 and the new Lap Top. The two items are check box controls. A check in the Dock 1 box directs Windows to include port LPT1 in its hardware configuration whenever a docking station has been detected.

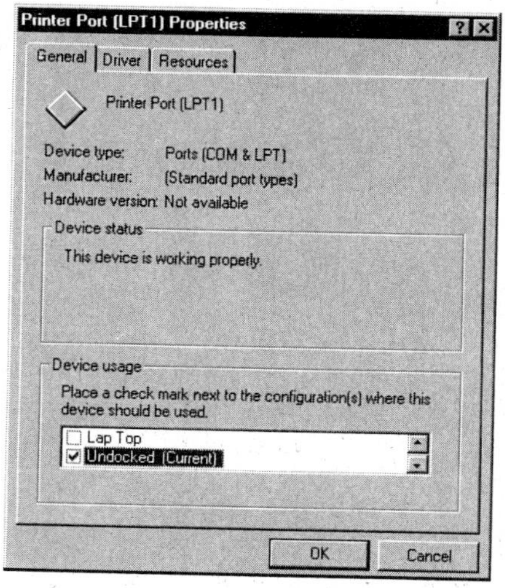

Fig. 6.25
The Printer Port Properties sheet showing which hardware profile is currently configured.

9. Check the Dock 1 box. Leave the Lap Top box unchecked.
10. Reboot your Windows system. During initial boot-up, Windows asks for a configuration. Choose Lap Top.

To verify that you have configured the hardware profile correctly, do not change the hardware and follow these steps:

1. After Windows has started, open the Start menu and choose Settings, Control Panel.
2. Double-click Device Manager.
3. Select the port (COM or LPT) from the Device Manager page.
4. Note that the printer port is now offline, signified by a red X through the port's icon. Printing now results in a diagnostic message that the printer is not attached. The Print Manager deletes all print files.

Therefore, you must set the printer to Work Off-Line so that the system will save all print files.

Repeat the process first by rebooting Windows, this time selecting the Dock 1 configuration setting. The printer port returns. The saved print files can then be released for printing.

Common Printer Problems

You install a printer only on occasion. But you troubleshoot printer problems frequently. The most useful tool in identifying and correcting printer problems is a thorough knowledge of your printer's installation and properties. During installation, test your printer and the wide range of properties available to better identify a starting point for dissecting most problems.

Windows provides fundamental troubleshooting aid with Bi-Directional Printer Communication. If a printer can talk to its drivers, many potential causes for problems can be routinely identified.

Advance preparation is always an excellent safeguard against any PC problem. The following checklists can be useful when you are diagnosing a local printer problem.

Before the Problem: Initial Preparation

Following initial installation of the printer, perform these steps:

1. Make a test-page printout and save the resulting printout for future use. The test page can contain important configuration information including the current printer driver, memory size, and port information. On PostScript printers, it will contain version level and settings.

◄ See "Options for Your Printer," p. 187

2. If your printer can perform a self test, make a printer self-test printout. For most printers, this test page contains the printer's internal configuration. This information may contain the number of pages printed, memory size, a list of configured options, and internal software revision level. Save the printout for future use. This information may be useful in describing your printer to its manufacturer at a later date for upgrading or troubleshooting.

3. Note the proper configuration of your printer's indicators: the Ready or Online light and the display status.

4. Make a record of your printer's internal menu settings for paper size, orientation, interface, and so on.

5. Record the installation results and the information from the Printer Properties screens.

Diagnosing the Problem: Basic Troubleshooting

For a local printer, perform the following steps to start diagnosing a problem:

1. Verify that all cabling is free of nicks, tears, or separations.
2. Verify that all cabling is fully inserted and locked at both the PC and the printer ends.
3. Verify that the printer is online and that all proper indicators are lit (for example, that the Online or Ready indicators are lit).
4. Verify that the printer is properly loaded with paper and that there are no paper jams.
5. Verify that the printer has toner (laser), ink (inkjet), or a good ribbon (dot-matrix).
6. Verify that cabinet doors and interlocks are closed and locked.
7. Verify that the printer's display, if available, shows a normal status.
8. Verify that the Windows printer driver can communicate with the printer using the Printer Properties screens. You should be able to print a test page to verify communication. If you cannot print a test page, Windows generates a diagnostic message providing you with a starting point to diagnose the problem.
9. Verify that the Windows Printer Properties screens display the same information that was contained in the Properties screens when you installed the printer.
10. Attempt to print to the errant printer using another application and a different type of print file (for example, print a text file or a graphics file).

Troubleshooting Tools

If the basic troubleshooting steps listed in the preceding section fail, Windows comes with three important tools you can use to further investigate printer problems. The first tool is Windows 95's new Help file. Initiate the Help file from the Print Manager's Help menu. Then select the Troubleshooting icon.

The Troubleshooter steps you through several of the most probable causes of printing problems (see fig. 6.26). Primarily, this tool verifies that the printer can communicate with the PC. If basic communication is lost, none of the software tools can provide any real assistance. You must resort to hardware exchange until you resolve which component or components are defective. However, with the exception of toner and paper problems, most printing problems are not hardware failures; the problems are primarily software settings or corrupted printer drivers.

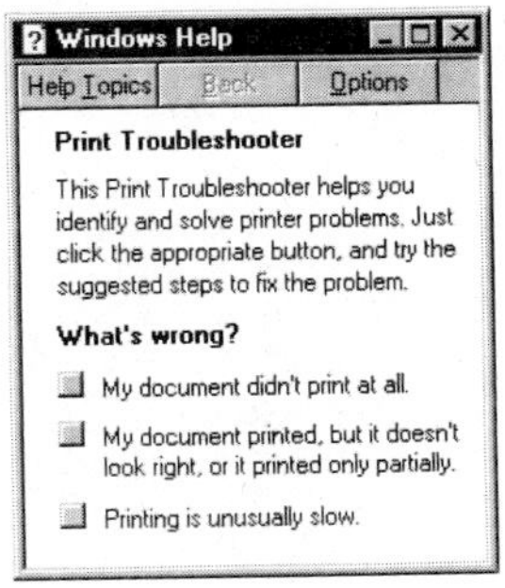

Fig. 6.26
The Windows Print Troubleshooter assists you in isolating problems using logical fault-isolation techniques.

The Windows 95 Print Manager provides a diagnostic tool that can aid you during the process of equipment interchange. The diagnostic screen shown in figure 6.27 is usually the first indication you receive that a printer fault has occurred. The information on this screen varies (Windows provides as much detail as possible about the problem). The increased amount of information is a result of the Bi-Directional Communications between the PC and the printer. For those printers without bi-directional capability, you will receive a standard "Unable to print" diagnostic.

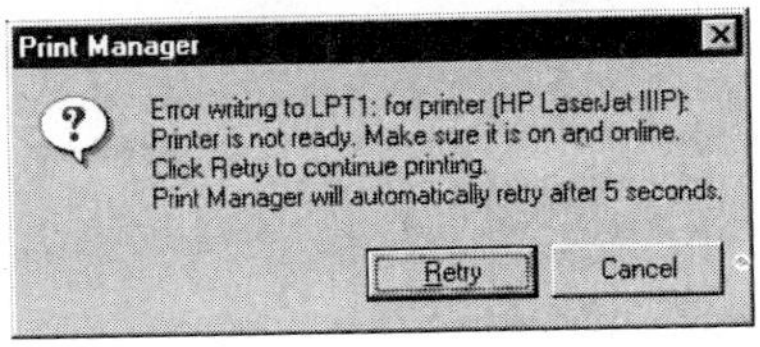

Fig. 6.27
The Print Manager diagnostic reports problems as they are found and continues until either the problem is fixed or the print job is canceled.

If you click the diagnostic's Retry button, Windows continues to monitor the printer's status at approximately five-second intervals. If you click the Cancel button, the diagnostic discontinues and the Print Manager pauses the print file.

The third troubleshooting tool is the Enhanced Print Troubleshooter, shown in figure 6.28. This software application steps you through your problem by asking you questions concerning the problem. As you answer each question, you are provided with a range of possible alternatives to help you narrow in on the potential source of the problem. Clicking the hot buttons next to the most accurate answer brings up another screen with additional insight and questions. This tool is a Windows 95 executable file named EPTS.EXE.

Fig. 6.28
The Enhanced Print Trouble-shooter steps you through a printer problem using plain English-language questions.

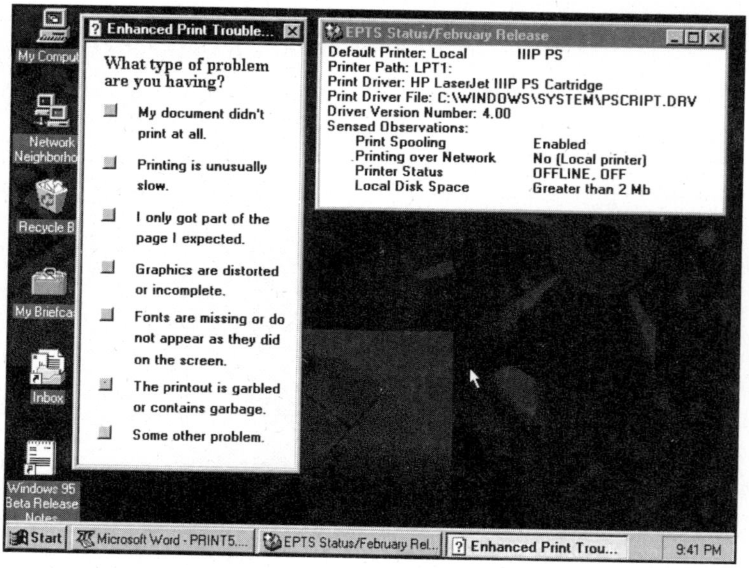

Most Common Printer Problems

The most common printing problems are printing supplies running out or a change that has recently taken place in either the printer or the operating system. In any event, a check list is an excellent place to start because it lets you consider each possible problem. The most common problems, in order of probability, are listed here:

- **The printer is either not selected or is not the default.**

  Make the printer the system default using the Print Manager's Printer menu.

- **The printer doesn't appear to be turned on.**

  Verify that the printer has been plugged in and that the power is in the on position.

- **The printer does not begin printing even though my PC says that I am printing a document.**

  If your system is attached to more than one printer, make sure the appropriate printer is being printed to by checking the Print Manager of each attached printer to find the current print job.

- **The printer is offline.**

  Set the printer online.

- **The printer is out of paper.**

  Reload the printer's paper supply.

- **The printer is out of toner.**

  Reload the printer's supply of toner.

- **The printer is out of ink.**

  Reload the printer's ink cartridge.

- **The printer's ribbon is no longer functional.**

  Remove and replace the printer's ribbon with a new one.

- **The printer's door is open or has a failed interlock.**

  Check for open doors or covers.

- **The printer cable is not properly connected to either the printer or PC.**

  Replace or reseat the cable.

- **The Printer is not connected to the correct port.**

  Remove the cable and connect it to the appropriate port.

- **The printer's software configuration has changed or the drivers have been corrupted.**

  Delete and reinstall the printer.

- **New hardware has been added to either the printer or the PC and a conflict has resulted in addressing or interrupts.**

  Review the installation records of the printer and reconfigure it if required.

- **Additional software has been added to Windows that changed the printer's configuration files.**

  Check the printer's configuration for driver files that have changed using the printed test page created during installation.

- **An application has indicated that it can no longer print to a corrupted print driver and to the selected printer.**

  Delete and reinstall the printer.

- **The operating system has been stalled during a print operation.**

  Reboot Windows 95 and verify printer operation, by printing a test document.

- **A printout stops halfway through printing a large detailed graphic.**

  Using your application, set the print quality to draft. If the graphic printout completes, check your printer's documentation to possibly increase the amount of memory in your printer. If it doesn't complete, run a printer self-test to print a test page.

- **A printer with a cartridge option does not report that the cartridge is installed.**

  Turn the printer off and then check to verify that the cartridge is properly seated. Turn the printer on and retest.

- **A hardware problem may have occurred in either the PC or printer that stops during the printing of a document.**

  Reinitiate printing the document. If it fails again, review the installation records of the printer and note any changes.

Chapter 7

Working with Fonts

by William S. Holderby

Fonts are specifications that tell Windows how to display and print text. Font technology has evolved so much over the last few years that the number of font types now available has grown tremendously. Font types exist for the basic text characters of many of the world's languages, and some special font types display pictures rather than text. These fonts are useful for lines, universal sign language, and many other specialized applications. Fonts are more than just specifications, you must be able to change them to meet your needs. Changing fonts may mean resizing them, changing character spacing, or rotating them to better fit your document. Fonts have names like Courier, Times Roman, Arial; each font creates its own impression on the printed page.

This chapter deals with the standard font offerings that Windows uses to print text. Although Windows comes equipped with several font technologies, the Windows preference is the TrueType font technology. TrueType technology was developed by Microsoft to provide standard fonts, capable of being both displayed and printed with minimal changes in appearance. TrueType fonts were included with previous versions of Windows. Microsoft has included new architectural features that improve their display speed for both the operating system and applications, such as the 32-bit Rasterizer.

► See "TrueType Fonts," p. 216

This chapter discusses the following issues:

- How Windows uses fonts
- How to install and delete TrueType fonts
- How to manage fonts in Windows 95
- How to work with other font types

Understanding Fonts

Individual fonts belong to a family of similar fonts that share various characteristics such as style, size, and special effects. For example, a Times Roman font is really more than a single entity because a character set is associated with the font. To review fonts, you should first understand a few terms:

- *Font size* is the definition of how large, or small, a font character is displayed or printed. Sizes are normally described in points. Each point is approximately 1/72 of an inch.

- *Font style* consists of bold, normal, italic, or bold italic. The style determines how the characters belonging to a font are displayed.

- *Font effects* defines color, special instructions (such as an underline or strikethrough), and in some cases, gradient grayscale fill for outlined fonts.

- *Serif fonts* have projections (serifs) that extend the upper and lower strokes of the set's characters beyond their normal boundaries. The Courier font is an example of a serif font. San-Serif fonts, such as Arial, do not have these projections.

- *Font spacing* refers to the space between characters on the screen or printed page. Fixed-spaced fonts have the same space between each character. Courier is a fixed-spaced font. Proportional-spaced fonts, such as Arial, adjust the inter-character space based on the shape of the individual characters.

- *Font width* describes the width of individual characters. These widths can be fixed, normal, condensed, or expanded. In Windows, certain fonts are fixed, such as the OEM font. Other fonts use variable width to display characters that are out of proportion.

Font technology can seem complex and confusing because of the large number of fonts in use, the somewhat obscure constraints, and the advantages touted by various vendors. Windows and your applications provide standard font choices that eliminate much of the confusion, while allowing you to customize their selection. Windows 95 supports numerous font technologies from many vendors. New fonts are available from Adobe, Bitstream, and other software suppliers.

32-Bit TrueType Font Rasterizer

► See "Reviewing Types of Fonts," p. 213

Microsoft has included a new *rasterizer* that improves the time it takes to create TrueType fonts. A rasterizer prepares a TrueType font for either display, or printing, from a file that contains a mathematical model of the fonts characters. The Microsoft 32-bit TrueType Font Rasterizer was developed as part of Windows new 32-bit printing architecture. A scalable font such as TrueType can be made larger or smaller without losing its distinctive shape and appearance; for example, the appearance of a character shown in size 6 is identical to the same font character at size 18. The Rasterizer creates new sizes and parameters to use in displaying font characters of different sizes, orientations, and effects (such as Arial 12 Bold, Italic).

In Windows 95, a single file—the TTF file—replaces the FOT and TTF TrueType font families. The TTF file contains all the information needed to create fonts of different sizes and complexity.

The FOT file was called a display hint file, because it provided hints to the Windows 3.1 Rasterizer as to where it should begin to create a displayable font. In other words, the FOT file speeded up the Rasterizer by providing initial conditions. Windows 95's new rasterizer eliminates the need for hint files by using an entirely new algorithm to create fonts from the TTF file in less time.

Registry-Based Font Support

In Windows 3.1, fonts were identified and loaded using INI files. Windows 3.1 dutifully loaded each font during startup. The time Windows 3.1 took to start increased as more and more fonts were loaded into the system. In addition, the number of fonts available was restricted under Windows 3.1.

Windows 95 attaches fonts through the Registry. Because Windows has immediate access to these fonts, as needed, it no longer has to load all of them, thereby reducing time and overhead. The Registry also provides better management and enables access to many more fonts. Windows uses the Registry instead of the INI files to configure software options for Windows access. The Registry provides a systematic structure and interface that is available to all software regardless of manufacturer.

Changing to Registry-based fonts provides the following benefits:

- The number of fonts that Windows can configure is limited only by available disk space. The number of fonts you can simultaneously use and print in the same document is approximately 1,000.

- Registry-based fonts create an environment where more than one person can use your PC hardware. Each user can individually configure a unique environment, which can include individual font selection.
- Improved font handling through the universal Registry enables an efficient standard access for both Windows and applications.

Windows 3.1 used initialization files to identify which font files were available for use. Some 16-bit Windows applications use the WIN.INI file to identify which fonts are installed. Under Windows 95, 32-bit applications use the system Registry to access installed fonts. Windows still maintains the WIN.INI file to stay compatible with some 16-bit applications.

Required Fonts for Windows

The number of fonts that Windows 95 requires is defined by the applications that you plan to run under the operating system. If you are primarily interested in word processing, then 10 to 12 scalable fonts is more than adequate. A page of text may require only one or two fonts for emphasis. If you plan to use CAD (computer-aided design), desktop publishing, or imaging applications, consult these packages for their special requirements. Because fonts provide an additional dimension you can use to create special effects or to distinguish a particular area of a document, CAD or desktop publishing documents may require a large number of fonts.

Standard Windows fonts or fonts shipped with the product include:

- *System fonts,* which are used by Windows to draw menus and controls, and to create specialized control text. System fonts are proportional fonts that Windows can size and manipulate quickly. Therefore, Windows uses these fonts to save time when it creates your screen environment.
- *Fixed-width fonts,* which are included with Windows 95 to maintain compatibility with earlier versions of Windows 2.0 and 3.0.
- *OEM fonts,* which are provided to support older installed products. The term *OEM* refers to Original Equipment Manufacturers. This font family includes a character set designed to be compatible with older equipment and software applications.

Fonts You Should Keep

Unlike Windows 3.1, Windows 95 does not slow down when loaded with additional fonts. However, these extra fonts do take up valuable disk real estate. You should carefully weigh the value of these fonts before you load them on your system. Microsoft has optimized the font-handling drivers for the TrueType font family, but you still may use other fonts. The decision about which fonts to keep depends on which applications you use.

The only way to make this determination is to experiment by adding, changing, displaying, printing, and eventually deleting unneeded fonts. Experiment with all the fonts on both the display and printed page before you make this decision.

Note

Experimenting with other font families from various manufacturers provides you with a wide range of optional selections. Other font families can be added to Windows, such as fonts from Adobe. However, Adobe fonts require more Windows resources because they require the Adobe Type Manager to be running. You may want to look for TrueType fonts that will serve your needs if your applications don't specifically require ATM.

Reviewing Types of Fonts

Some fonts are designed to be compatible with special printing devices. These fonts use mathematical outline descriptions to create their character set. The resulting characters can be scaled and rotated. However, fonts designed for special printers are often difficult to display. To solve this problem, Adobe has created the Adobe Type Manager (ATM), a Windows application that converts Adobe PostScript printer fonts into displayable characters for use by Windows 95 applications.

Note

Many printer vendors have designed custom software drivers to support their printers. Your printer manufacturer may have special Windows 95 handler software.

These output devices involve different font handling technology and drivers:

- PostScript printers use PostScript meta file printing which is similar to, but not compatible with Windows Enhanced Meta Files (EMF).

◄ See "Using Enhanced Meta File Spooling (EMF)," p. 193

- Dot-matrix printers range from older, very simple models to newer Near Letter Quality (NLQ) printers. Many of the older dot matrix printers did not support downloading of soft fonts and some of the newer printers may provide better results using proprietary drivers.

- Hewlett-Packard PCL printers use various levels of HP's Printer Control Language (PCL)—for example, the Laserjet II supported level 4 and Laserjet III supports level 5 PCL. Both Windows and HP provide up-to-date drivers that provide the best font settings.
- Plotters primarily use vector fonts as plotter software converts plotter outputs into a series of straight lines.
- Specialized OEM printers may use proprietary fonts to create unique symbols or increase the speed of graphic character creation. Most of the specialized printers provide optimum performance when they are interfaced with their manufacturer's proprietary drivers.

Note

If your printer came with special drivers, check with the manufacturer for the latest updated Windows 95 driver.

We speak of fonts as belonging to *technologies,* or families, that include many styles and variations. A technology determines how a font is created, stored, and what device limitations it has. We use the term *technologies* and *families* interchangeably to refer to a group of fonts with similar attributes.

Standard Windows provides support for three font technologies:

- *Raster fonts.* Fonts that are bit-mapped for fast display. These fonts are created in specific sizes and rotation angles.
- *Vector fonts.* Fonts that are created from mathematical line models, each character consisting of a series of lines (vectors). Vector fonts are an outgrowth of plotter technology. Pen Plotters are used extensively in computer-aided design (CAD) to create line drawings.
- *TrueType fonts.* Scalable, rotatable fonts created from mathematical models. These fonts are a compromise between displayable and printable fonts.

The following sections discuss these and some other font technologies.

Raster Fonts

The name *raster fonts* describes a font set that was designed primarily for the raster display. You cannot scale raster fonts in odd multiples or rotate them effectively. Raster fonts consist of arrays of dots and are stored in bit-map files with the extension FON. Raster fonts need separate files for each point size, resolution, and display device. Therefore, each raster font file has a letter designating its targeted device:

- D = printer
- E = VGA display
- F = 8514 display

The Courier raster font has three files associated with it: COURD.FON for the printer font, COURE.FON for the VGA font, and COURF.FON for the fonts optimized for the 8514 display. Each raster file is optimized for its intended display device and contains attribute-specific information:

- Font type
- Font character set
- Font sizes
- Font optimized resolution

You can scale raster fonts in even multiples up to the point where they no longer appear smooth. By their nature, bit maps that are expanded too far lose their orderly appearance and smoothness. However, these fonts are quickly displayed and reduce the Windows screen refresh time.

Raster fonts are printable only if the chosen font set is compatible with your printer's horizontal and vertical resolution.

Note

Not all printers can print raster fonts acceptably. Before you combine any font type with your printer, you should first test the compatibility. You can test the appearance of printed fonts by creating a page of text using that font type and then printing that page. Another way to test printed fonts is to print the font family from the Control Panel's font folder, shown later in this chapter.

Five raster fonts are supplied with Windows 95, and several other vendors supply additional font sizes. The supplied raster fonts are MS Serif, MS Sans Serif, Courier, System, and Terminal.

Vector Fonts

Vector fonts are derived from lines or vectors that describe each character's shape. You can scale vector fonts to any size or aspect ratio. The characters are stored as a set of points and interconnecting lines that Windows 95 can use to scale the font to any required size. These fonts are very applicable for plotting and CAD. As with the raster fonts, vector fonts are stored in FON files. The way Windows 95 treats this font type is to rasterize the various characters by using function calls to the Graphics Device Interface (GDI). The number of calls required for each font increases the display time required to create the characters and to refresh the display. The fonts are useful for CAD and desktop publishing because they are readily extensible. Large vector font sizes maintain the same aspect ratio as smaller sizes. Windows 95 supplies three vector fonts: ROMAN, SCRIPT, and MODERN. Additional fonts are available from several sources including CAD and desktop publishing software vendors.

TrueType Fonts

In Windows 95, TrueType fonts are each stored in a single TTF file. This file contains both the outline information and the ratios necessary to scale the font. FOT files were used in previous versions of Windows to provide the operating system with a hint to use in creating a displayable font character. Using hints increased creation speed and enabled Windows to display new fonts more quickly. With the new Windows Rasterizer, hints are no longer needed because the speed of creating fonts has increased significantly. Removing the FOT file frees disk real estate.

The Windows 95 print architecture includes a new 32-bit TrueType font Rasterizer for rendering and displaying these fonts faster and with greater accuracy. The Rasterizer uses a technique that Microsoft calls *anti-aliasing* to smooth display mode curves and reduce the jagged effects of the font enlargement. Windows 95 supplies many TrueType fonts including ARIAL.TTF, COUR.TTF (New Courier), and TIMES.TTF (Times New Roman).

Other Fonts

In addition to raster, vector, and TrueType fonts, other fonts exist that perform specialized services. Your printer may have an entire set of fonts or may be capable of being configured with font sets through the use of font cartridges or additional cards. The following list describes additional Windows fonts:

- *System fonts*. The system font files included with Windows 95 are 8514SYS.FON and VGASYS.FON.
- *OEM fonts*. The OEM font files included with Windows 95 are 8514OEM.FON and VGAOEM.FON.
- *Fixed fonts*. The fixed font files included with Windows 95 are 8514FIX.FON and VGASYS.FON.
- *MS-DOS legacy fonts*. Windows 95 includes several MS-DOS compatible font files for DOS applications to use while running in the Windows 95 environment. These files provide backward compatibility to the real-mode DOS environment. Files included are CGA40WOA.FON, CGA80WOA.FON, DOSAPP.FON, EGA40WOA.FON, and EGA80WOA.FON. Although these fonts are primarily used for application display, the DOSAPP.FON is a good choice for printing.
- *Printer soft fonts*. Depending on your printing hardware, you may download soft fonts to your printer. Downloading fonts reduces the time taken by the printer to process printouts. You download soft fonts once to speed up subsequent print jobs.

Installing and Deleting Fonts

During the Windows installation process, Windows loads its standard suite of font files onto the system disk. Windows and your applications use these files as default fonts. You have the option of installing and deleting fonts from your system to change the look of your desktop environment, word-processing, spreadsheet applications, or for use by special application needs, such as CAD.

Caution

Be careful when deleting seemingly useless font sets. Deleting certain sets like fixed, OEM, or system fonts may drastically alter the look and proportion of your Windows desktop and applications. When fonts are deleted, you may see applications and even Windows dialog boxes change appearance. Even though Windows substitutes existing fonts to replace deleted ones, you may not like the substitution. Make sure you have a backup copy of all fonts you delete, as you may want to replace them for aesthetic reasons.

Installing New Fonts

Windows enables you to quickly install new fonts using the Control Panel. Fonts may be installed from the Windows disks or from vendor-supplied disks. This procedure installs new fonts into the Windows Registry for use by both Windows and applications.

1. Open the Start menu and choose Settings; then choose Control Panel. Double-click the Fonts folder in the Control Panel.

2. Windows displays the Fonts window that contains a list of all the fonts currently registered by the system (see fig. 7.1).

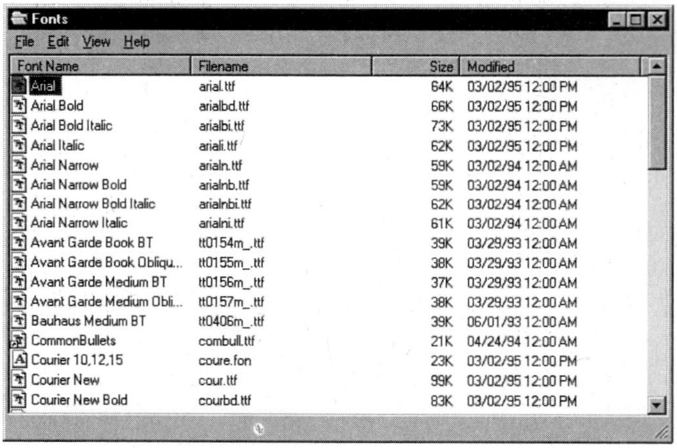

Fig. 7.1
The Fonts window shows which fonts are loaded along with their file name, size, and configuration date.

You can display the list as individual icons with the name of each font below the icons. Or you can display a detailed list that contains the name of the font, the name and extension of the font file, the size of the file, and the date of its creation.

3. To change the look of this list, choose View and then choose Large Icons, List, or Details. Refer to figure 7.1 for an example of Details view.

> **Note**
>
> On occasion, you may want to look at the list of font types displayed without their many variations (such as Bold). You may choose this option in conjunction with other View menu selections by choosing View, Hide Variations (Bold, Italic, and so on).

4. Choose Files, Install. Windows displays the Add Fonts dialog box, shown in figure 7.2.

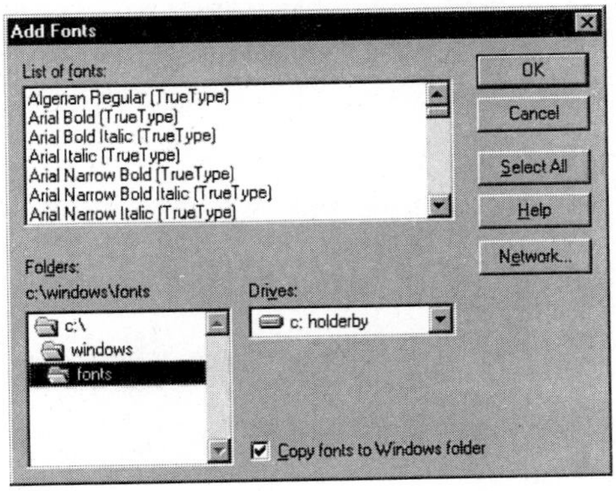

Fig. 7.2
The Add Fonts dialog box provides the controls needed to add a new font to Windows 95.

5. Using the Drives and Folders controls, choose the location of the font you want to install. This location may be a directory on the hard drive or a manufacturer's floppy disk.

6. Windows displays a roster in the List of Fonts window. Select the font or fonts to add.

   If these fonts are located in a location other than the Windows font directory, you may have the files automatically copied to this directory by checking the Copy Fonts to Windows Folder box at the bottom of the Add Fonts dialog box.

7. Choose OK to add the selected font(s). Windows installs the new fonts and enters them in its Registry.

Note

You can also install fonts by dragging and dropping them from a disk into the Fonts Folder, using the Windows Explorer. However, this procedure doesn't always register the font correctly. After you install a font this way, print a test copy to verify installation.

Deleting Fonts from the Hard Disk

Windows also enables you to quickly delete installed fonts from the Control Panel. The following procedure deletes unwanted fonts and removes them from the Windows Registry.

1. Open the Start menu and choose Settings; then choose Control Panel. Double-click the Fonts folder in the Control Panel. In the Fonts window, Windows displays the fonts currently registered by the system (refer to fig. 7.1).

2. Highlight the font or fonts to delete.

3. Choose File, Delete.

4. Windows displays a warning asking you if you really want to delete these fonts. Choose Yes. Windows shows the font being sent to the Recycle bin as it removes the deleted fonts from the Registry.

Tip
If you mistakenly delete fonts, you may recover them from the Recycle Bin.

► See "Restoring Deleted Files," p. 520

Note

For faster deletion, you can also delete fonts by dragging and dropping them from the Fonts Folder into the Recycle bin, using the Windows Explorer.

Using TrueType Fonts

TrueType fonts are created by Microsoft and are integrated as part of the operating system. While all font technologies are optimized for specific applications or hardware, TrueType font design is a compromise between printed text and displayed text. The TrueType text, either displayed or printed, shows virtually no variation, which enables you to create documents that most closely resemble the on-screen representation of your work.

Understanding the Pros and Cons of TrueType

Because TrueType fonts are an integral part of Windows 95, many font styles come bundled with the operating system. The new Windows Rasterizer provides greater speed and accuracy for displaying and printing TrueType fonts.

Windows uses an anti-aliasing, character-generation algorithm that increases font smoothness. However, this technology needs a 256-color mode or higher, requiring more complex and higher priced hardware. For specific printing applications and CAD applications, PostScript fonts repeatedly provide better printing results. In addition, not every printer is compatible with TrueType fonts, causing some printers to treat TrueType fonts as graphics and thus reducing printer efficiency.

Determining Which Fonts Are TrueType

Through the use of icons in the Fonts folder, Windows makes it easy to identify your TrueType fonts. If you work with many MS-DOS applications, you should note that TrueType and other fonts are also distinguishable by their file extensions:

1. Open the Start menu and choose Settings; then choose Control Panel. Double-click the Fonts folder in the Control Panel. Windows displays the Fonts window containing the list of registered fonts.

2. Display the fonts as individual icons with the name of the font below the icon by choosing View, Large Icon. TrueType fonts are shown by an icon containing the letters T_T.

   In the List and Details view, TrueType fonts are shown prefaced by a smaller icon showing T_T. In the Details view, TrueType fonts also are denoted by their file type TTF. Other font types are shown as file type FON.

Adding or Removing TrueType Fonts

You add or delete TrueType fonts the same way you add or delete other font types. To add or remove TrueType fonts, use the previously described Add a Font or Delete a Font procedures, selecting only fonts with TTF file extensions.

Using Windows 3.1 TrueType Fonts

In Windows 3.1, each TrueType font was maintained by two files, TTF and FOT. Windows 95 eliminates the need for an FOT by implementing faster font creation. You can add your existing TrueType fonts to Windows 95 by specifying the TTF file when adding a font. Windows will not ask for a separate FOT file and accepts Windows 3.1 TrueType fonts as well as fonts created from most existing applications.

Using Only TrueType Fonts

To select only TrueType fonts in your applications, you can set the appropriate font option. Microsoft has integrated TrueType fonts into the Windows operating system. If you want to only use TrueType fonts in your applications follow this procedure:

1. Choose the Fonts folder from the Control Panel. Windows displays the Fonts folder containing a list of the registered fonts.

2. Choose View, Options.

3. Choose the TrueType tab in the Options dialog box (see fig. 7.3).

4. Check the box that reads Show Only TrueType Fonts in the Programs on my Computer. Now, only TrueType fonts are shown as available to applications.

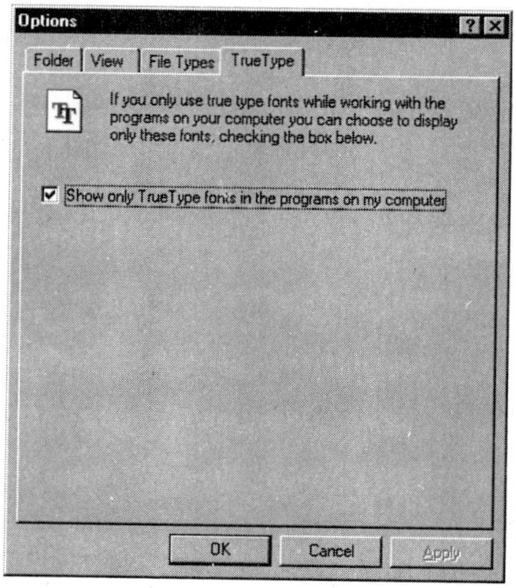

Fig. 7.3
To configure only TrueType fonts for applications, check the box in the Options dialog box that reads Show Only TrueType Fonts in the Programs on My Computer.

Other Font Configurations

◀ See "Displaying Properties of Programs, Documents, and Resources," p. 28

Each printer is configurable through its Printer Properties sheets. The printer property options vary from printer to printer. Many of the printers support downloaded soft fonts. Many printers support TrueType fonts as downloaded soft fonts or printing them as graphics. These options can be readily set on the appropriate Printer Properties Fonts page.

Printing TrueType fonts as graphics increases your printing time, but on some printers it substantially improves the look and quality of the printed font. Downloading TrueType fonts as soft fonts stores the fonts in your printer. If your printer has adequate memory to store fonts, downloading speeds up the printing operation. If the printer is unable to store these fonts, you'll usually receive a "memory overflow" error on the printer following the download.

Note

Assuming that your printer has adequate memory, the look and quality of using graphics mode versus download mode is identical. But if your printer is short on memory and your document is heavy on graphics, using graphics mode may help because the entire font may not have to be downloaded into memory.

PostScript printers provide an option to substitute PostScript fonts for TrueType fonts by use of a Font Substitution Table. The Printer Properties Fonts page for those printers enables you to change which fonts are substituted by changing the table.

Managing Fonts in Windows 95

In Windows 95, fonts are a managed resource. Applications can quickly access fonts through standardized registration, making your fonts quickly available for viewing, printing, comparing, sorting, adding, and deleting.

Previewing and Printing Font Samples

Before you use a font, you may want to preview it or print a sample before committing it to a document. Windows provides quick access to this information by performing the following steps:

1. Open the Start menu and choose Settings; then choose Control Panel. Double-click the Fonts folder in the Control Panel. Windows displays the Fonts window containing the list of registered fonts.

   You have the option to display the font list as either a Details list or as Large icons through the View menu.

2. Select the font you want to view and choose File, Open; or double-click the font to view it. Windows displays the font in various sizes (see fig. 7.4).

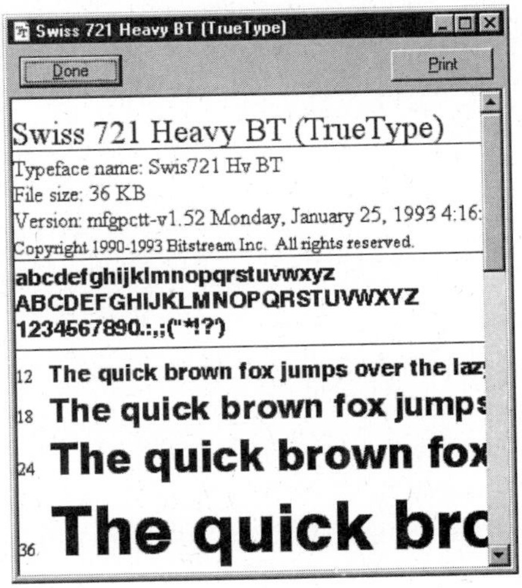

Fig. 7.4
A sample of a font type showing sizes and font detail information.

3. To print the sample page, choose Print.

4. When you are done previewing and printing the font, choose Done.

Tip
You also can print a sample from the Fonts folder by selecting the font and choosing File, Print.

Showing Font Properties

Fonts, like most other Windows objects, have properties. The properties include version information that may contain important information for purposes of upgrading your fonts. Although at present there is no way to change these font properties, you can view the information contained in these screens through the following procedure.

1. Open the Start menu and choose Settings; then choose Control Panel. Double-click the Fonts folder in the Control Panel. Windows displays the Fonts window containing the list of registered fonts.

2. Select the font you want to view.

3. Choose File, Properties. Windows displays a Properties sheet like the one shown in figure 7.5. The Properties sheet contains version and management information for each font type registered by Windows.

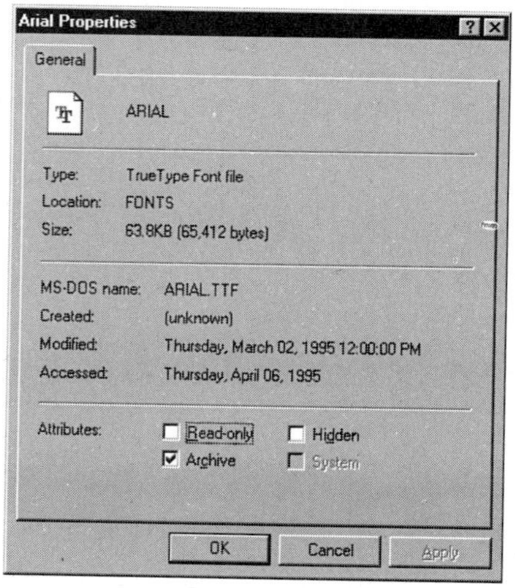

Fig. 7.5
A Properties sheet for the Arial TrueType font provides file and configuration information.

Viewing Fonts by Similarity

Fonts are distinguished by their differences, but they also can be grouped by similar features. Grouping fonts by similarity may be important to you when showing subtly different text in a document or when your printed document doesn't match the display. Substituting a similar font may correct this problem. You will find fonts listed by similarity, except where Windows has insufficient Panose information to make a comparison. *Panose* refers to a Windows internal description that assigns each font a PANOSE ID number. Windows uses several internal descriptions to categorize fonts. The PANOSE information is used to register a font class and is a means to compare similar font features. You can group similar fonts by following this procedure.

1. Open the Start menu and choose Settings; then choose Control Panel. Double-click the Fonts folder in the Control Panel. Windows displays the Fonts window containing the list of registered fonts.

2. Open the View menu and choose Details, List, or Large icons.

3. Select the font to use as a master against which you want to test other fonts for similarity.

4. Choose View, List files by Similarity. Windows redisplays the Font list as shown in figure 7.6. The list now shows all fonts with an assessment of their similarity to the master font. In the case shown in figure 7.6, the Arial font is the master font. The Swiss 721, shown, is listed as being fairly similar to Arial. Compare the similarity between the Swiss 721 and the Arial font.

   Fonts are shown as being very similar, fairly similar, not similar, or insufficient Panose information available.

Tip

You can test the similarity of other fonts by selecting the List Fonts by Similarity To control and choosing another font type.

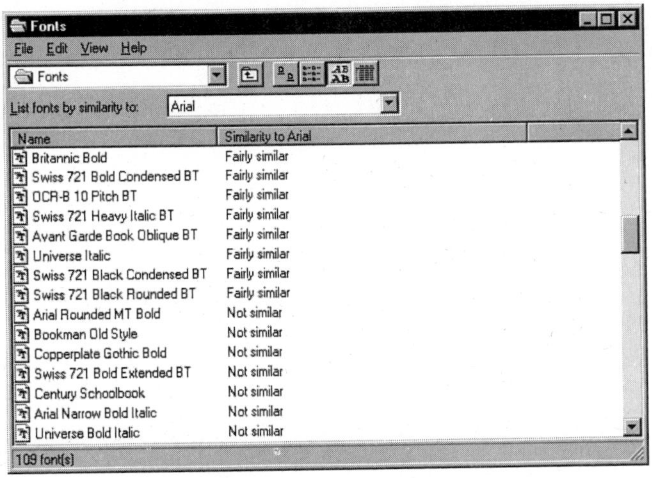

Fig. 7.6
This list shows how closely other font types match the Arial font.

Installing Printer Fonts

Printer fonts reside in the printer as a cartridge or within the printer's memory. You can install printer fonts through Windows or through installation applications that usually accompany your printer. Follow these steps to install printer fonts using Windows:

1. Open the Print Manager for the selected printer.

◄ See "The Print Manager," p. 173

2. Choose Printer, Properties.

3. Choose the Fonts tab on the Properties sheet. See the Printer Properties Fonts page shown in figure 7.7. Note that each printer type is supported by a different set of Properties pages, which depend on the make, model, and hardware configuration of the printer.

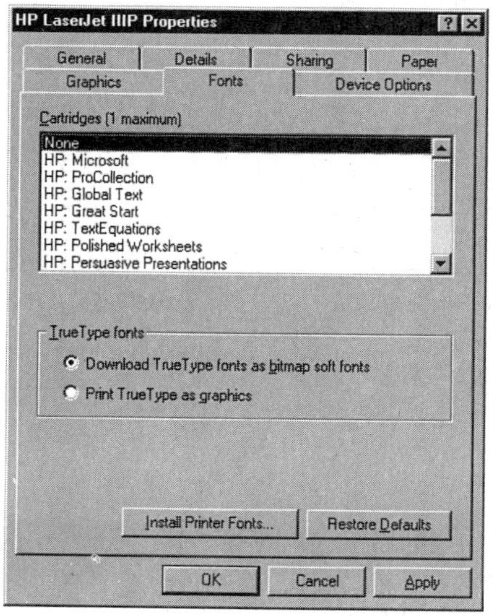

Fig. 7.7
A typical Printer Properties Fonts page.

4. Choose Install Printer Fonts. A dialog box similar to the one in figure 7.8 appears. The printer fonts installer for your printer may look different from the one shown in the figure, but all installers perform similar functions.

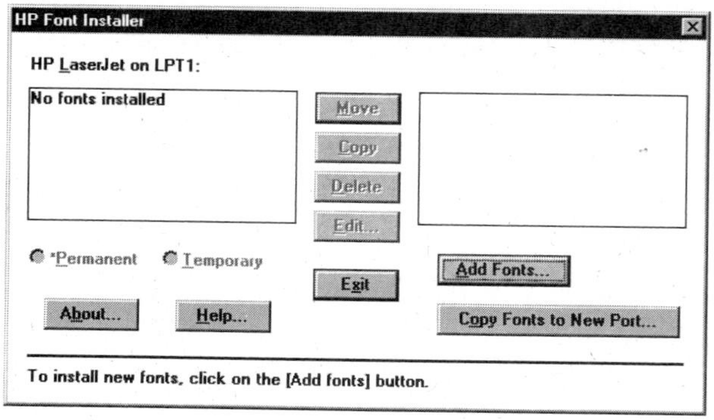

Fig. 7.8
The HP Font Installer dialog box.

Note

The HP Fonts Installer shown in figure 7.8 cannot be used to download TrueType fonts to HP printers. PCL printers can download only PCL-com-patible fonts. Be certain that your printer and the fonts being specified for download are compatible. Refer to the installer's help file for more information on compatible fonts.

5. Select the fonts to be installed in the list on the right side of the Font Installer dialog box.

6. Choose Copy to move the selected fonts to the left window.

7. Choose Add Fonts to register the printer's fonts. A dialog box is then displayed asking for the location of the fonts. This box provides a Browse button to enable you to find the disk location of the fonts to be installed.

8. Identify where the font files are located and select OK to enable Windows to install the selected fonts.

Downloading Fonts as Permanent or Temporary

Most Printer Properties Fonts pages include a set of radio button controls that enable you to select whether a font is to be temporarily or permanently downloaded.

Download frequently used fonts as permanent. This allows you to print faster. However, permanent downloaded fonts limit the amount of printer memory available for printing. Therefore, to stay within normal printer memory limits, keep the number of fonts you specify as permanent to three of four.

Downloading fonts as temporary does not store the font in the printer's memory until it is needed. The font is loaded only temporarily in the printer before a document is printer and removed after the document is complete. This increases printing time, but it increases the amount of available printer memory and reduces print overrun errors. Downloading fonts as temporary is the default setting and works well with most applications.❖

Chapter 8

Plug and Play and Legacy Device Installation

8

by Roger Jennings

Adding a new hardware device, such as a multimedia upgrade kit, to a pre-Windows 95 PC is best described as a daunting experience. The new device—and possibly even your PC—may not work the first time you test the installation, especially if you have a few other special-purpose adapter cards installed in your PC. So you pull out the card, change some miniature jumpers on the upgrade kit's sound card or one of the other adapter cards in your PC (assuming that you didn't lose the jumper under your desk), and then test the device again. The most common refrain during this cut-and-try process is "Let's see—what IRQ and DMA and device addresses did I try last time?"

Windows 95's new Plug and Play (PnP) features, combined with a PnP-compliant PC, take the mystery and the frustration out of installing new hardware devices. Plug and Play abolishes jumpers and software configuration programs; plug in a PnP adapter card, and your PnP-compatible computer makes the card play the first time around. Plug and Play is the most important distinguishing feature of the Windows 95 operating system; no other operating system for Intel-architecture PCs currently offers Plug and Play support.

The hitch in the PnP scenario is that relatively few PnP-compliant adapter cards were available when Windows 95 hit the retail shelves, and most users of Windows 95 don't have new PCs with PnP system BIOS on the motherboard. Microsoft calls hardware that's not PnP-compliant a *legacy* device—a rather derisive term for the vast majority of the PC motherboards and adapter cards in use today. Fortunately, Windows 95 includes new features that help you install legacy devices, too.

Most of the chapters in this book are devoted to hands-on advice for getting the most out of Windows 95. The objective of Plug and Play is to make new-device installation a "hands-off" process. Therefore, much of this chapter is devoted to explaining what happens behind the scenes to make Plug and Play work. This chapter covers the following topics:

- The PnP architecture
- What PC hardware you need to take advantage of new PnP devices
- How Windows 95 handles installation of legacy devices
- Troubleshooting device installation

Understanding Plug and Play Architecture

► See "Using PC Card Devices," p. 266

Plug and Play is a computer-industry standard that automates the process of adding new capabilities to your PC or changing PCMCIA adapters in your notebook PC. (*PCMCIA* stands for Personal Computer Memory Card Interface Association.) The PnP standard is a joint development of Intel Corporation and Microsoft Corporation. Other industry leaders—such as Phoenix Technologies Ltd., Compaq Computer Corporation, NEC Technologies Inc., and Toshiba Computer Systems Division—contributed their expertise to the development of the set of eight specifications that make up the PnP standard.

Microsoft defines a Plug and Play computer system, qualifying for the "Designed for Windows 95" logo, as having the following components:

- *Plug and Play BIOS version 1.0a.* The PnP BIOS (basic input/output system) provides the basic instructions for identifying the devices necessary to boot the computer during the POST (power-on self-test) process. The standard minimum set of devices is a display, keyboard, and disk drive to load the operating system—in this case, a fixed-disk drive to load Windows 95. Computers that sport the "Designed for Windows 95" logo are required to have PnP BIOS version 1.0a or later.

- *Plug and Play operating system.* Windows 95 is the first PnP operating system, but limited support for Plug and Play features is available in MS-DOS 5, Windows 3.1, and later versions of both programs. Microsoft is likely to add Plug and Play features to a future version of Windows NT.

- *Plug and Play hardware.* Plug and Play hardware is a set of PC devices that are autoconfigurable by the PnP operating system. PnP hardware primarily consists of adapter cards (or their equivalent circuitry) on the PC's motherboard; but printers, external modems, and other devices connected to the PC's COM (serial) and LPT (parallel) ports also may support PnP. PCI adapters qualify as Plug and Play hardware. ISA and most EISA adapter cards require modification for PnP autoconfiguration. Microsoft requires PnP compliance for hardware devices to carry the "Designed for Windows 95" logo.

- *Plug and Play device drivers*. Microsoft includes 32-bit device drivers (*VxDs*, which are virtual *anything* drivers) for basic PnP devices, such as IDE and SCSI-2 fixed-disk and CD-ROM drives. Hardware manufacturers are responsible for providing VxDs to support specialty adapters, such as sound and video capture cards. When you install a PnP-compliant device that requires a driver that's not included in the retail version of Windows 95, you're asked to insert the setup disk for the PnP device that has the required device driver.

Virtually every PC manufacturer and assembler offers products claiming PnP compliance and displaying the "Designed for Windows 95" logo. Simply replacing the motherboard's BIOS chip with one that meets the Plug and Play BIOS Specification 1.0a (described in the following section) doesn't make an assembled computer PnP-compliant. The adapter cards, fixed-disk and CD-ROM drives, and other components of the system also must comply with the appropriate PnP specification.

Following are the eight specifications that comprised the Plug and Play standard when Windows 95 was released:

- *Plug and Play BIOS Specification 1.0a*, developed by Compaq, Phoenix Technologies, and Intel. This basic document defines the way that PnP works. (The PnP BIOS specification is described in additional detail in the following section.)

- *Plug and Play ISA Specification 1.0a*, developed by Microsoft and Intel. The purpose of the PnP ISA specification is to define how non-PnP and PnP-compliant cards can coexist on the ISA bus without getting in each other's way.

- *Plug and Play SCSI Specification 1.0*, developed by Adaptec, AT&T Global Information Solutions, Digital Equipment Corporation, Future Domain, Maxtor, and Microsoft. The SCSI 1.0 spec defines the SCSI host adapter card. An additional specification—SCAM (SCSI Configured AutoMagically)—defines the means by which individual SCSI devices (such as fixed-disk drives) support autoconfiguration features similar to

PnP. The SCSI standard is maintained by Committee X3T9.2 of the American National Standards Institute (ANSI).

- *Plug and Play IDE Specification*, developed by Microsoft in conjunction with the ANSI X3T10 Committee and Phoenix Technologies, Ltd. The IDE (Integrated Device Electronics) specification defines the requirements for PnP-compliant adapters on PC motherboards and plug-in ISA and PCI cards for IDE fixed-disk and CD-ROM drives.

- *Plug and Play LPT Specification 1.0*, developed by Microsoft, defines the method by which devices connected to the parallel port identify themselves to the PnP BIOS. Printers, modems, network adapters, and parallel-port SCSI adapters are among the devices defined by the PnP LPT specification. If you plug a Hewlett-Packard LaserJet 4M into your computer's parallel port, Windows 95 finds the driver for the printer and loads the driver automatically.

- *Plug and Play COM Specification 0.94*, developed by Microsoft and Hayes Microcomputer Products, defines the way that serial devices (such as mice, modems, printers, and uninterruptible power supplies) identify themselves. Windows 95 usually is quite capable of identifying the type of mouse and modem installed, even without PnP identification. The PnP COM spec was a draft version when this book was written.

- *Plug and Play APM Specification 1.1*, developed by Microsoft and Intel, handles advanced power management for laptop and energy-efficient desktop PCs.

- *Plug and Play Device Driver Interface Specification for Microsoft Windows and MS-DOS 1.0c*, developed by Microsoft, provides limited support for PnP assignment of I/O, IRQs, DMA, and memory ranges under MS-DOS and Windows 3.1 and later.

Note

In addition to the specifications in the preceding list, the ATAPI specification defines the identification process for PnP-compatible CD-ROM drives that attach to the enhanced, PnP-compliant IDE interface. The Extended System Configuration Data specification (ESCD 1.0) is designed to provide additional information about ISA and EISA adapter cards to the PnP BIOS.

The primary reason for boring you with the preceding list of specifications is this: you may need to inquire whether a computer, motherboard, or device that you are planning to purchase truly is PnP-compatible. The ability to name the applicable specification precisely is more likely to elicit a forthright response than "Is *whatever* Plug and Play?"

A second reason for the list is that it enables you to download current copies of each of the preceding specifications from the libraries of the Plug and Play Forum (GO PLUGPLAY) on CompuServe. Copies of these specifications are not readily available elsewhere. A white paper titled *Microsoft Windows and the Plug and Play Framework Architecture* is available in WINPNP.ZIP (which contains WINPNP.DOC) from Library 1 of the PLUGPLAY forum and (as PNP.ZIP) from the WINNEWS forum. (PNP.ZIP includes Word 6.0, ASCII text, and PostScript versions of the backgrounder.) Library 1 of the Plug and Play Forum also includes the *Plug and Play Catalog,* a Microsoft Word document that contains the latest list of PnP devices and the names, addresses, and telephone numbers of the device manufacturers.

Plug and Play BIOS Specification 1.0a

Clearly, the most important element of a PnP computer system is the PnP system BIOS. *Plug and Play BIOS Specification 1.0a* adds the following major components to the conventional PC's system BIOS:

- *Resource management* handles the basic system resources: direct memory access (DMA), interrupt requests (IRQs), input/output (I/O), and shared memory address ranges. A variety of devices need these system resources, and this situation often leads to the conflicts discussed at the beginning of this chapter. The Plug and Play BIOS resource manager is responsible for configuring boot devices on the motherboard, as well as any PnP devices.

- *Runtime management* of configuration is new to PCs. PnP BIOS includes the capability to reconfigure devices after the operating system loads. This feature is particularly important for notebook PCs that have PCMCIA devices that you can change at will. Previously, the operating system considered all devices detected by the BIOS to be static; static detection requires that you restart the notebook after swapping a PCMCIA device.

- *Event management* detects when devices have been removed or added to the system while the computer is running. PnP BIOS 1.0a provides event management, such as detecting when your laptop or notebook PC is connected to a docking adapter (only for portable PCs, because hot swapping adapter devices of desktop PCs is not a safe practice). Event management relies on runtime management to reconfigure the system.

▶ See "Using Your Laptop with a Docking System," p. 273

If your PC doesn't have a BIOS ROM chip that meets the requirements of PnP BIOS Specification 1.0a, you're likely to be out of luck in the PnP department. The only exceptions are the following situations:

- Your computer has flash BIOS that you can upgrade with a floppy disk from the computer or motherboard supplier. Flash BIOS is a nonvolatile memory chip (NVRAM) that retains the BIOS instructions when the power is turned off.
- The supplier of your computer or motherboard offers a PnP BIOS 1.0a upgrade kit. In this case, you simply remove the existing BIOS chip(s) and plug in the replacement(s).

If the manufacturer or assembler of your computer doesn't offer one of the two preceding options, you need to replace the motherboard to gain the benefits of PnP. Of course, you need PnP-compliant PC adapter cards, such as PCI-bus components, or PCMCIA devices to gain the *full* benefit of Plug and Play.

Determining Whether Your Computer Supports Plug and Play

Some computers' BIOS display a line indicating Plug and Play compliance during the boot process. If you have a PC with an 80486DX2/66 or faster motherboard manufactured in 1995 or later, and you don't know whether the PC supports Plug and Play, follow these steps to check its capabilities:

1. Double-click Control Panel's System icon to open the System Properties sheet.
2. Click the Device Manager tab to display Devices by Type. (Click the Devices by Type option button, if necessary.)
3. Double-click the System Devices icon in the device list to expand the System Devices list.
4. If your PC supports Plug and Play, you see a Plug and Play BIOS entry (see fig. 8.1). The I/O Read Data Port for ISA Plug and Play Enumerator item appears regardless of whether your PC supports Plug and Play.
5. Double-click the Plug and Play BIOS icon to open the Properties sheet for the Plug and Play BIOS.
6. Click the Driver tab to display the device driver (BIOS.VXD) that Windows 95 uses to connect to the PnP feature of your system BIOS (see fig. 8.2).

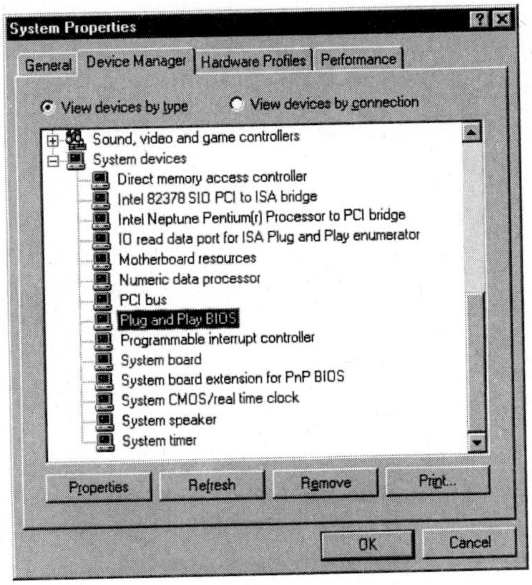

Fig. 8.1
Check the System Devices list to determine whether your PC has Plug and Play BIOS.

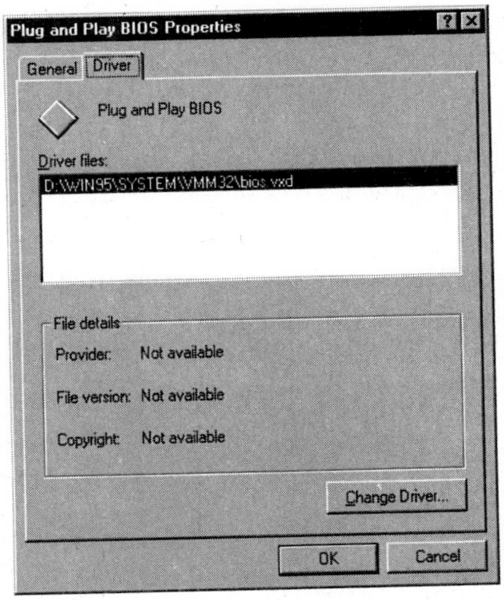

Fig. 8.2
Click the Driver tab to check the properties of Windows 95's Plug and Play BIOS device driver.

PC hardware suppliers have used the term "plug and play" for several years as a generic description of devices that are purported to be easy to install. If you're purchasing a new PC or upgrading your PC's motherboard, make sure that you use the preceding method to verify that the system BIOS supports Plug and Play before you take delivery of your new or upgraded PC.

Caution

Some brands of computers whose motherboards were produced in 1994 display messages during the boot process, indicating that the motherboard supports Plug and Play. Many of these motherboards, however, have early versions of the PnP BIOS, which does not conform to the 1.0a specification. Even if your computer displays a PnP message during the boot process, check Device Manager for the Plug and Play BIOS entry to verify that you have PnP BIOS 1.0a.

Plug and Play Support for Fixed-Disk Drives

► See "Understanding What Your Disk Drive Does," p. 460

Windows 95 supports virtually every type of fixed-disk drive, even including ancient MFM (modified frequency modulation) and RLL (run-length limited MFM) drives. Windows 95 provides Plug and Play support only for IDE and SCSI-2 fixed-disk and CD-ROM drives. The following sections describe how Plug and Play simplifies the installation and configuration of your PC's fixed-disk and CD-ROMs.

Integrated Device Electronics (IDE) Drives

Fixed-disk drives in early IBM PC-ATs and clones required an adapter card that held most of the electronics that the drive needed to communicate with the ISA bus. Subsequently, PC and fixed-disk drive manufacturers determined that there were technical and economic advantages to moving the circuitry from the adapter card to the drive itself. The result was the Integrated Device Electronics (IDE) interface standard for fixed-disk drives. The IDE interface is very simple to implement with a few chips on an adapter card or the PC motherboard.

In mid-1994, the IDE specification was upgraded to provide a higher data rate (11M per second), accommodate up to four fixed-disk drives, support larger disk drives, and provide for PnP support. Today, the majority of drives that have 512M or lesser capacity use IDE. Newer PCs support 1G and larger IDE drives through Logical Block Addressing (LBA) or compatible Cylinder/Head/Sector (CHS) addressing for IDE drives up to 8.4G (1,024 cylinders, 255 heads, and 63 sectors maximum). Windows 95 supports both the LBA and CHS drive geometries.

> **Note**
>
> Limitations in the size of the DOS file allocation table (FAT) require that the fixed-disk cluster size increase as the capacity of the drive increases. 512M drives use 16K clusters, and 1G drives require 32K clusters. Each directory and every file, no matter how small, occupies a single cluster. The empty space in the cluster is called *slack*. A common practice is to partition, with FDISK.EXE, large disks into two or more logical volumes to reduce the cluster size and slack. An alternative is to use Windows 95's DriveSpace disk data compression utility on large drives. DriveSpace creates its own file allocation system, which minimizes slack.

► See "Compressing a Disk," p. 469

Standard IDE adapter cards connect two floppy-disk drives and two fixed-disk drives. Most of these cards now include the functions of the I/O card, providing two serial ports and one or two parallel ports. Most PC manufacturers now incorporate the floppy-disk and one or two IDE drive connectors, plus two serial ports and one parallel port on the motherboard. You can attach one or two IDE devices to each IDE connector (primary and secondary), for a maximum four devices supported by today's system BIOS. (New modem/audio adapter cards with on-board IDE connectors, such as Creative Lab's ViBRA product line, let you add additional IDE devices that the system BIOS doesn't recognize during the boot process.) The primary master IDE device is your boot drive (C); the second primary drive (D) is a slave. The secondary IDE connector, if you have one, also accommodates a master (E) and slave (F) drive.

Detection of the drive and drive geometry, as well as the assignment of drive letters, ordinarily is the responsibility of the PC's system BIOS. Windows 95 has its own automatic drive-geometry-detection system in its Installable File System (IFS) VxD for IDE drives. If Windows 95 can't resolve the drive geometry from BIOS data, IDE fixed-disk access falls back to the system BIOS.

Most manufacturers of CD-ROM drives now offer IDE versions, and IDE (ATAPI) CD-ROM drives that support PnP are likely to be the standard for moderately priced, multimedia-ready PCs. This situation means that manufacturers of audio adapter cards can eliminate the CD-ROM drive interface or substitute a simple IDE interface. (Creative Labs took the latter route for the firm's new Sound Blaster 32.)

Windows 95's built-in drivers support IDE devices that comply with the new ATA-2 (AT Attachment, version 2) standard and ATAPI devices that comply with the SFF8020 2.0 specification. Almost all IDE drives manufactured after mid-1994 are ATA-2 compliant, and every IDE CD-ROM drive conforms to ATAPI requirements. Fortunately, you don't need Plug and Play BIOS to take advantage of Windows 95's automatic configuration features for IDE drives.

> **Troubleshooting**
>
> *I just installed an additional IDE drive, but it doesn't appear in My Computer or Explorer.*
>
> Most PCs with recent system BIOS automatically detect an additional drive connected to the primary IDE controller as a primary slave drive. If you have an older BIOS, you need to use the PC's BIOS setup application to specify the type of drive installed (number of cylinders, number of heads, landing zone, and other drive parameters). If you connect a third drive to a PC with a recent BIOS, you need to enable the secondary IDE controller in the BIOS setup program so BIOS can recognize the drive. IDE CD-ROM drives connected to sound cards usually can be installed as secondary, tertiary, or quaternary IDE drives. Use the default (secondary) setting for an IDE CD-ROM if you don't have a secondary IDE controller in your PC; if your PC has a secondary IDE controller, use the tertiary I/O base address and interrupt for the CD-ROM.

Small Computer Systems Interface (SCSI-2) and SCAM Drives

The Small Computer Systems Interface (SCSI, pronounced "scuzzy") bus is not a PC architecture, but a means of connecting multiple peripheral devices—such as fixed-disk drives, CD-ROM drives, tape backup drives, and graphic scanners—to the PC. You can connect up to seven internal or external SCSI devices to a single SCSI-2 adapter card or a SCSI-2 port on your PC's motherboard, if it has one.

Figure 8.3 is a block diagram of a typical SCSI-2 setup, with an internal SCSI fixed-disk drive, external CD-ROM and tape backup drives, and a page scanner.

Apple Computer was the first major manufacturer to support the SCSI bus; SCSI has been the primary means of attaching most external devices to the Macintosh. The majority of CD-ROM drives use SCSI-2, which is the second iteration of the SCSI bus, and many sound cards include a simple SCSI-2 adapter to connect CD-ROM drives. The advantage of the SCSI-2 bus is that the devices connected to the bus have built-in "intelligence": circuitry that takes some of the processing load off the PC. SCSI devices can "talk" to one another as well as to the PC. The extra circuitry for this intelligence causes SCSI-2 devices, such as disk and CD-ROM drives, to be somewhat more expensive than devices that have IDE or proprietary interfaces.

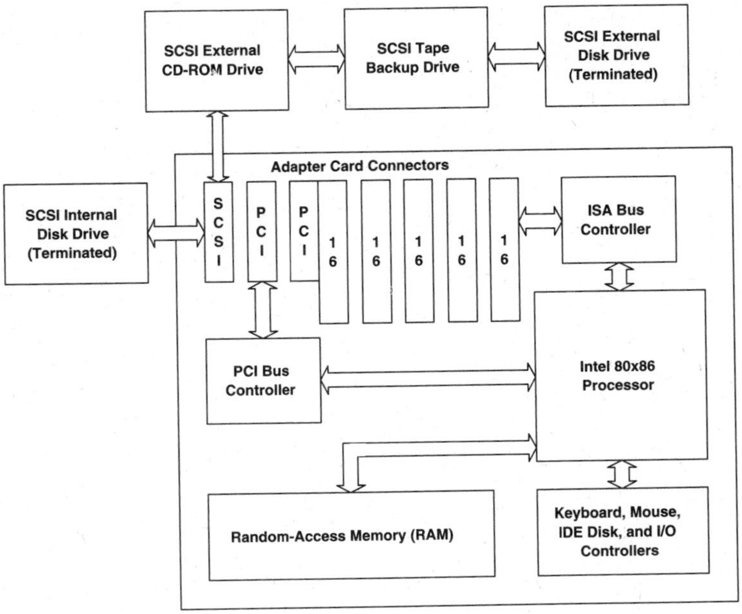

Fig. 8.3
A typical SCSI installation uses a PCI SCSI-2 host adapter to connect up to seven internal and external SCSI devices.

The original SCSI specification was a rather loosely worded document, and the SCSI devices sold by one manufacturer often didn't work with another manufacturer's products. The SCSI-2 specification tightened the requirements and provided a substantial increase in bus operating speed. Today, almost all SCSI-2 devices are fully compatible with one another. SCSI-2 has become the standard architecture for the high-capacity disk drives that are used in network file servers and client–server computing.

Note

SCSI-2 adapter cards have a 50-pin internal SCSI connector that connects to SCSI devices, such as fixed-disk and CD-ROM drives, mounted in your PC's housing. The SCSI-2 connector for external devices is much smaller than the original SCSI-1 connector. You need a special SCSI-2-to-SCSI-1 cable to mate the external connector of the new SCSI-2 adapter cards with conventional 50-pin "Micro Blue Ribbon" connectors used by the majority of today's external SCSI devices, such as scanners.

A recent improvement to the SCSI-2 bus, called fast-SCSI, increases bus speed from about 5M per second to 10M per second. Wide-SCSI uses a 16-bit or 32-bit bus structure to provide a theoretical 40M-per-second (40-M/s) data rate. Wide-SCSI is the basis for the new SCSI-3 specification. PCI multichannel wide-SCSI adapter cards, such as the Adaptec AHA-3940, provide up to a 133-M/s burst rate and 20-M/s synchronous data transfer across two channels.

► See "Video," p. 964

The performance of the basic SCSI-2 bus is adequate for all but the most demanding network file server, client–server, and nonlinear digital-video-editing duties.

Note

SCSI-2 currently is the preferred bus for new 3.5-inch removable media disk drives, such as Iomega's external 100M Zip and forthcoming 1G Jaz drives. The Jaz drive is expected to have a data rate of 6 M/s or faster, making it suitable for recording digital-video data. Iomega plans an internal IDE version of the Zip drive, but Windows 95's support for removable-media IDE read-write devices is "rudimentary," according to a Microsoft white paper.

Even if your computer doesn't have Plug and Play BIOS, Windows 95 automatically detects all popular SCSI-2 host adapters, including SCSI-2 ports on sound cards, and installs the required SCSI *mini-port* driver (MPD file) for the device. Mini-port drivers adapt Windows 95's built-in SCSI-2 device driver for specific SCSI-2 host adapters or SCSI-2 interface chipsets.

Figure 8.4 shows the Device Manager item for the Adaptec AIC-6X60 ISA Single-Chip SCSI Controller used to connect SCSI-2 CD-ROM drives to Creative Labs' Sound Blaster 16 SCSI adapter card. Double-clicking the Adaptec AID-6X60 item displays the Properties sheet for the SCSI controller.

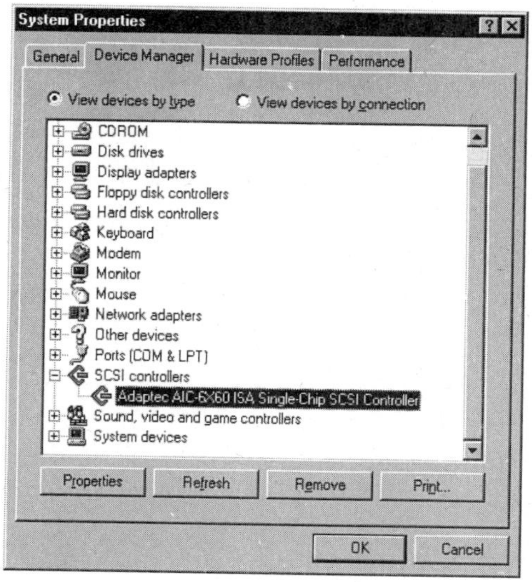

Fig. 8.4
The SCSI-2 controller of the Sound Blaster 16 SCSI adapter card appears in the Device Manager's list of SCSI controllers.

The Resources page of the controller's Properties sheet, shown in figure 8.5, enumerates the Input/Output Range, Interrupt Request, and Direct Memory Address (DMA) channel used by the controller. Device resources are one of the subjects covered in "Dealing with Legacy Hardware" later in this chapter.

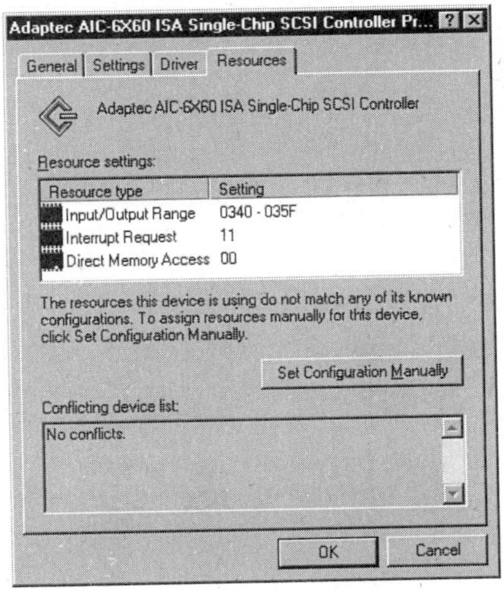

Fig. 8.5
Clicking the Resources tab of the Properties sheet displays the Input/Output Range and Interrupt Request settings for the Adaptec AIC-6X60 ISA Single-Chip SCSI Controller.

SCSI Configured AutoMagically (SCAM) is Plug and Play for the SCSI-2 bus, not just for PCs running Windows 95. The conventional SCSI bus has two basic problems: SCSI buses must be terminated by a set of resistors to prevent reflected signals, and each SCSI device on the bus must have a unique ID number (1 to 7 for SCSI-2; 0 is reserved for the SCSI adapter card). You set the "hard" ID number of SCSI devices with a small rotary switch or jumpers. SCAM-compliant SCSI-2 devices negotiate their own "soft" ID numbers, eliminating the need to set hard ID numbers.

SCSI-2 devices must comply with SCAM Level 1 (one SCSI master with a hard ID) or Level 2 (all soft ID devices) to carry the "Designed for Windows 95" logo. In addition, the internal SCSI-2 cabling, rather than the last SCSI device in the chain, must provide the termination resistors. (External SCSI-2 devices use a plug-in terminator.) Quantum's Lightning series drives were the first commercial SCAM-compliant fixed-disk drives. Make sure that any new SCSI-2 device you buy carries the "Designed for Windows 95" or SCAM logo.

Note

New SCSI-2 devices are quite reliable, but a variety of mishaps can kill the SCSI-2 bus. Therefore, many users of SCSI-2 devices install an IDE drive as the boot device (C) that stores Windows 95 and connect their SCSI-2 drives (D and higher) to a high-speed SCSI host adapter card. Booting from the IDE primary master device allows you to start Windows 95 even if a problem exists with your SCSI controller, device(s), or cabling.

IDE, SCSI, and the PCI Bus

Intel Corporation designed the Peripheral Control Interconnect (PCI) bus in conjunction with the development of the Pentium processor. The PCI bus, like the EISA and MCA (IBM Microchannel Architecture) buses, incorporates the hardware necessary to implement Plug and Play. Most PC motherboards that implement the PCI bus have seven active slots. Four slots are 16-bit ISA; two slots are 32-bit PCI; and one slot has a shared set of ISA/PCI connectors, into one of which you can plug either type of adapter card. You need a mouse that has an IBM PS/2 round (DIN) connector or a PS/2 mouse adapter for most PCI motherboards, because the system also provides mouse support. (If you elect to use a standard serial mouse, you lose one of the two serial COM ports.)

Although the PCI bus got off to a slow start in 1994, the fact that Intel designed the PCI bus carries a great deal of weight in the PC industry. Based on the number of references to PCI in Microsoft's PnP-related documents, PCI is the preferred bus structure for Windows 95. By mid-1995, the PCI bus had displaced the VESA (Video Electronic Standards Association) Local Bus (VLB) as the most popular high-speed bus for Windows graphics accelerator cards and fixed-disk controllers. PCI adapter cards are sure to dominate the digital-video capture and playback market in 1996 and beyond.

The PCI bus and the system BIOS's PCI features comprise a subset of the Plug and Play specification. Windows 95 supports the PCI bus with the following system devices:

- *PCI Bus,* to specify the Windows 95 device driver for the bus (PCI.VXD).
- *Processor to PCI Bridge,* to make the high-speed connection between an 80486DX or Pentium processor and the PCI bus.
- *PCI to ISA Bridge,* to allow legacy ISA adapter cards for IDE drives to use PCI features.

- *PCI-to-PCI Bridge,* to provide the capability for a single PCI adapter card (such as the Adaptec AHA-3940, described earlier in this chapter) to use two PCI data channels. If the system BIOS doesn't include PCI-to-PCI-Bridge support, which usually is implemented only in high-end Pentium motherboards, you can't use multichannel PCI devices.

Even if your PCI-bus PC doesn't have Plug and Play BIOS, Windows 95 takes advantage of the PCI bus and the system BIOS's PCI features to provide basic Plug and Play installation and operation of PCI devices.

How the Windows 95 Operating System Orchestrates Plug and Play

When you boot a PnP computer, the following five steps occur:

1. The system BIOS identifies the devices on the motherboard (including the type of bus), as well as external devices such as disk drives, keyboard, video display, and other adapter cards that are required for the boot process.

2. The system BIOS determines the resource (IRQ, DMA, I/O, and memory address) requirements of each device. Some devices don't require all four of these resources. At this step, the system BIOS determines which devices are legacy devices that have fixed resource requirements and which are PnP devices for which resource requirements can be reconfigured.

3. The operating system (Windows 95) allocates the resources remaining after allowing for legacy resource assignments to each PnP device. If many legacy and PnP devices are in use, Windows 95 may require many iterations of the allocation process to eliminate all resource conflicts by changing the resource assignments of the PnP devices.

4. Windows 95 creates a final system configuration and stores the resource allocation data for this configuration in the registration database (Registry).

5. Windows 95 searches the \WINDOWS 95\SYSTEM directory to find the required driver for the device. If the device driver is missing, a dialog box appears, asking you to insert into drive A the manufacturer's floppy disk that contains the driver software. Windows 95 loads the driver in memory and then completes its startup operations.

Figure 8.6 illustrates the preceding steps in the form of a simple flow diagram. Although the process appears simple on the surface, a substantial amount of low-level BIOS and high-level programming code is required to implement the PnP feature set. Compaq, Intel, Microsoft, and Phoenix Technologies deserve congratulations for making the Plug and Play magic work.

Fig. 8.6
A flow diagram best describes the PnP system configuration process.

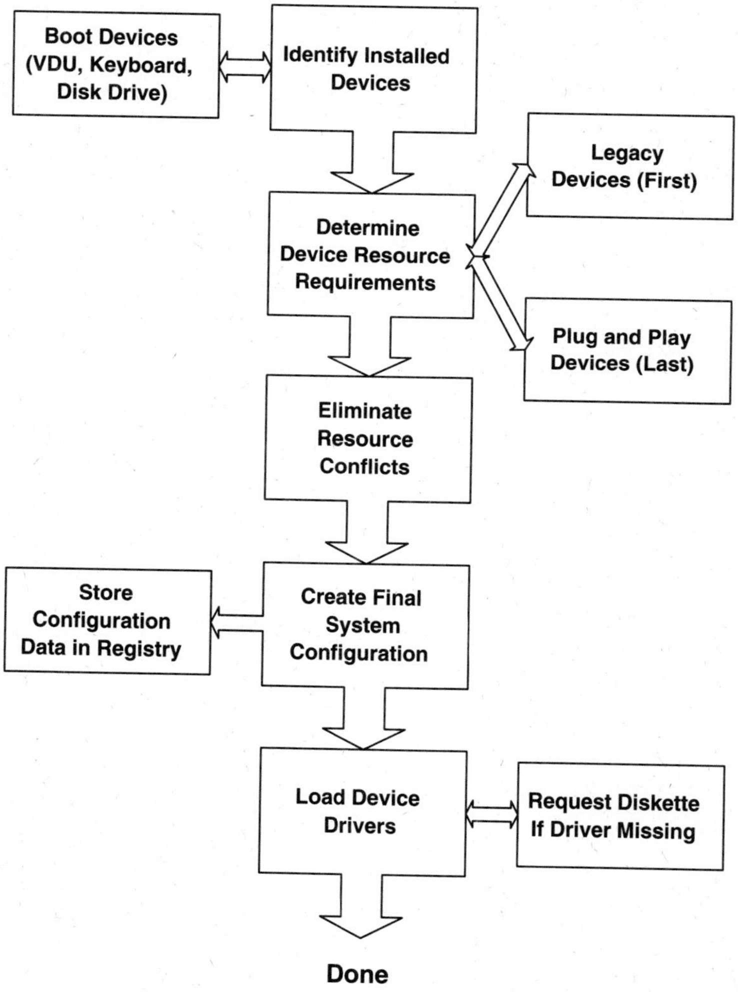

Buying a Windows 95-Ready Plug and Play PC

At this point, you may have learned more than you ever wanted to know about PC architecture. Familiarity with acronyms such as PCI, VLB, IDE, and SCSI is necessary to distinguish between the offerings of suppliers that sell PCs carrying the "Designed for Windows 95" logo. However, your local clone dealer isn't likely to have taken all the necessary steps to be able to apply the Microsoft logo. If you plan to purchase a new PC or upgrade your current PC for Windows 95, the guidelines in the following list ensure that you'll get a "Designed for Windows 95" PC (even if the PC doesn't bear the logo):

- Pentium will be the standard processor for running Windows 95, especially if you're interested in multimedia applications. Pentium PCs now dominate the home-computer market. If you're on a budget, you can save some money by purchasing an 80486-architecture PC. You don't need a clock-tripled, 100-MHz 80486DX4, however, because Windows 95 runs like a champ on the standard 66-MHz 80486DX2 processor used to write this chapter and even on plain-vanilla 80486DX33s. For almost all users of Windows 95, 256K of cache RAM is adequate; discerning the performance improvement offered by a 512K cache is difficult.

- Don't even think about buying a PC or a new motherboard that doesn't have PnP BIOS 1.0a or later and a PCI bus. Plain-vanilla ISA PCs are obsolete, and the VLB is obsolescent; Plug and Play with PCI is where today's action is. Even if you don't plan to experiment with digital video or with playing and recording hi-fi sound today, you likely will be tempted to upgrade to PCI when you discover the 32-bit multimedia features of Windows 95. The cost differential between plain ISA or ISA/VLB and ISA/PCI bus motherboards is inconsequential.

- Buy as much RAM as you can afford. Like money, you never can have too much RAM (or fixed-disk space). The practical minimum for running today's Windows 3.1 and later applications is 8M, and Windows 95 requires about the same amount of RAM as Windows 3.1 and later. The good news is that Windows 95 makes better use of added RAM than Windows 3.1 and later does. For most users who don't run more than one Microsoft Office application at a time, 12M is optimum, but 16M gives a noticeable performance boost to the programs of Microsoft Office 95, especially Access 7.

▶ See "Codec Implementation in Windows 95," p. 1009

- If you're interested in graphics and/or multimedia, make sure that you include a DCI-compliant PCI graphics accelerator card with digital video acceleration in your purchase specification. If you're seriously interested in digital video, buy at least a 90-MHz Pentium so that you can play MPEG-encoded CD-ROMs (video CDs), using the software MPEG codec that Microsoft licensed in mid-1995 from Mediamatics, Inc. The $200 that you save because you don't need a hardware-assisted MPEG-1 playback card more than covers the extra charge for a fast Pentium.

- Make sure that you purchase a fixed-disk drive with 600M or larger capacity. Remember that each full installation of a productivity application (such as Microsoft Excel, Word, PowerPoint, or Access) occupies about the same amount of disk space as Windows 95 itself—or even more. IDE drives with 1G capacity have a street price of less than $400.

- Verify that the adapter cards or the equivalent circuitry on the motherboard is PnP-compliant and that the fixed-disk and CD-ROM drives support PnP. This guideline is especially important for SCSI-2 controllers and fixed-disk drives. Also make sure that the internal modem and sound card (if your purchase includes them) support PnP.

▶ See "Using Your Laptop with a Docking System," p. 273

- If you're buying a laptop or notebook PC, make sure that the PCMCIA cards and the docking station that you purchase are PnP-compliant and come with PnP drivers for Windows 95. Otherwise, you won't gain the advantages of hot swapping and hot docking.

Installing Plug and Play Hardware

Installing a PnP adapter card in your desktop PnP-compliant PC is a simple and straightforward process, at least in most instances. You follow these steps to install both the card and the 32-bit driver (VxD) required for use with Windows 95:

1. Turn off the power to your PC.
2. Open the case and install the adapter card.
3. Close the case and repower your PC.
4. Insert the driver floppy disk in your A or B drive, if requested.
5. Restart Windows 95, if requested.

If the driver for your adapter card is included with Windows 95, you might not need the card's driver floppy disk; Windows 95 automatically sets up the driver for your device. Compare the dates of the driver files, and use whichever is most recent. If Windows applications come with the adapter card, you install the applications by running SETUP.EXE or INSTALL.EXE from the floppy disk after installing the card.

Installing in PCs that have PnP-compliant serial and parallel ports PnP-compliant peripheral devices, such as printers, scanners, and external modems, follows a procedure similar to the one in the preceding list. When you add or change a peripheral device, you don't need to open the PC and, in some cases (modems, for example), a new driver isn't required. If you plug in a Hewlett-Packard LaserJet 4 Plus to your PC's parallel port, as an example, Windows 95 identifies the printer and automatically loads the required printer driver that's included with Windows 95. (You may be instructed to insert the CD-ROM or a specified distribution floppy disk that holds the printer driver.)

Troubleshooting

When I try to install a Plug and Play adapter card, I get a "resource conflict" message and the installation fails.

Most PC adapter cards require at least one I/O base address and one or more interrupts. (The "Setting Resource Values for Legacy Adapter Cards" section that follows shortly describes I/O base addresses and interrupts.) Most adapter cards support only a few of the available I/O base addresses and interrupts. If you already have several legacy adapter cards in your PC, you may have a situation where the I/O base addresses or, more likely, the interrupts supported by the new card are occupied by existing legacy cards. In this case, you need to change the settings of one or more of your legacy cards to free the required resource(s) for use by your new card. The worst-case condition occurs in PCI-bus PCs where all of the available interrupts are assigned before you install the new card. (In many PCI-bus PCs, PCI slots consume one interrupt each, whether or not the slot is in use.) The only solution in the worst case is to free an interrupt by reconfiguring your PC's system BIOS to reassign an interrupt from an unused PCI slot. If your system BIOS doesn't permit reconfiguration, you must remove an existing adapter card to free an interrupt.

Dealing with Legacy Hardware

Almost all PC adapter cards require at least one interrupt request (IRQ) level and a set of I/O base memory addresses for communication with your PC's processor. Some cards require one or more DMA (Direct Memory Access) channels for high-speed communication with your PC's RAM. IRQs, I/O memory, and DMA channels collectively are called *device resources*. Legacy adapter cards use the following two methods for setting their device resource values:

- *Mechanical jumpers* that create a short circuit between two pins of a multipin header. Jumpers commonly are used to designate resource values for sound cards.

- *Nonvolatile memory* (NVM) for storing resource assignments. Nonvolatile memory—such as electrically erasable, programmable read-only memory (EEPROM)—retains data when you turn off your PC's power. Network adapter cards (Intel's EtherExpress products) and sound cards (the Media Vision product line) commonly use NVM.

Note

PCI adapter cards don't have jumpers or nonvolatile memory to designate resource values. Instead, the system BIOS and Windows 95 automatically allocate resources needed by PCI adapter cards during the boot process.

► See "Understanding the Unimodem Driver," p. 841

► See "Using Your CD-ROM Drive," p. 970

► See "Adding a Sound Board," p. 984

The following sections describe how Windows 95 deals with a variety of legacy adapter cards. Later chapters of this book describe in detail the installation process for specific device types, such as modems, CD-ROM drives, and sound cards.

Legacy-Device Detection during Windows 95 Setup

When you run Windows 95's Setup program, Windows 95 attempts to detect all the hardware devices in your PC, including legacy devices such as ISA sound cards and network adapters. If you install Windows 95 over an existing installation of DOS and Windows 3.1 or later, Windows uses the real-mode (16-bit) device drivers that it finds in your current CONFIG.SYS file. In addition, Windows 95 follows any instructions in your AUTOEXEC.BAT file to set up the device to use the drivers and to specify the IRQs, I/O base addresses, and DMA channels used by the device. To use the 32-bit protected-mode device drivers provided with Windows 95, you must disable these instructions manually from CONFIG.SYS and/or AUTOEXEC.BAT (by typing **REM** before entries).

When you install Windows 95 on a new computer or elect to use dual-boot mode, Setup performs a device-detection process similar to the one described in the preceding paragraph. In this case, however, Windows 95 installs its own protected-mode drivers for popular legacy adapter cards, such as sound cards, modems, and network cards. Using Windows 95's drivers eliminates the need to use the real-mode drivers supplied on floppy disk with the legacy card. If Windows 95 detects the device but doesn't have the appropriate built-in driver, a message box asks you to insert the driver disk for the device.

If Windows can't identify the legacy device, you need to install the device manually. "Installing Legacy Cards after Setting Up Drivers," later in this chapter, explains the manual installation method.

Setting Resource Values for Legacy Adapter Cards

You must set the IRQ, I/O base address, and DMA channel of a new adapter card to values that do not conflict with the resource values that already are assigned to system devices, PCI slots, or other legacy adapter cards. One of the problems with the basic design of IBM-compatible PCs is that only 16 interrupts are available, and the majority of these interrupts are likely to be in use. Therefore, your choice of IRQs is limited.

Note

The word *base* in *I/O base address* refers to the location at which the block of I/O addresses for the adapter card begins. The actual number of address bytes occupied by the I/O system of the adapter card varies with the type of card. I/O addresses are separated by 16 bytes, and most adapter cards require fewer than 16 bytes of I/O address space.

Table 8.1 lists the PCs' IRQs and the most common use of each interrupt level.

Table 8.1 Interrupt Assignments and Options for ISA Cards Installed in 80x86-Based PCs

IRQ	Function	Comment
0	Internal timer	Dedicated; not accessible
1	Keyboard	Dedicated; not accessible
2	Tied to IRQ9	Dedicated; see IRQ9
3	Second serial port	COM2 and COM4; usually assigned to a modem
4	First serial port	COM1 and COM3; usually for a serial mouse

(continues)

Table 8.1 Continued

IRQ	Function	Comment
5	Second parallel printer	Often used for bus mouse, network, and scanner cards
6	Floppy disk drives	Dedicated; do not use
7	First parallel printer	Used by some scanner cards; otherwise available
8	Time-of-day clock	Dedicated; not accessible
9	IRQ2 on 80x86 computers	IRQ2 is rerouted to IRQ9; often shown as IRQ2/9
10	Unassigned	Good choice for a sound card, if offered
11	Unassigned	Not a common option; use if 12 is assigned
12	Usually unassigned	Sometimes dedicated to an IBM-style mouse port
13	80x87 coprocessor	Dedicated; do not use even if an 80x87 is not installed
14	Fixed-disk drive	Dedicated; do not use
15	Usually unassigned	Used for secondary IDE controller, if installed

Virtually all PCs come with two serial port devices (COM1 and COM2) and one parallel port (LPT1) device. Unless your PC has a separate IBM PS/2-compatible mouse port, which requires an assignable interrupt, COM1 ordinarily is occupied by the serial mouse. The default interrupt for the Sound Blaster and most MPC-compatible audio adapter cards is IRQ5. Although IRQ7 is assigned to the second parallel printer (LPT2), few users have two printers, and printers seldom require an interrupt; therefore, IRQ7 usually is free. Network cards often use IRQ5.

The upshot of the preceding paragraph is this: use the highest IRQ that your legacy adapter card supports, leaving the lower IRQs for cards that don't support interrupts above IRQ9 or IRQ10. The Sound Blaster 16 audio adapter card, for example, supports only IRQ2/9, IRQ5 (the default), IRQ7, and IRQ10. The Intel Smart Video Recorder Pro video capture card allows you to choose IRQ9, IRQ10, IRQ11, or IRQ15; the best choice for the video capture card is IRQ15 (if you aren't using the secondary IDE connector) or IRQ11.

Note

If your computer has a PCI bus, the BIOS autoconfiguration feature usually assigns one interrupt to each PCI adapter-card slot. You may need to use the BIOS setup feature to assign a specific set of interrupts to the ISA adapter-card slots. In addition, some video overlay and capture cards require sharing upper-memory blocks with the ISA bus, which usually is accomplished by making an entry in one of the pages that appear during the BIOS setup process. See your PC's instruction manual for details on assigning interrupts and shared-memory locations to the ISA bus. Make a note of the IRQs that already are used by adapter cards in your PC.

Many more options exist for I/O base addresses than for IRQ levels, so you seldom encounter an I/O address conflict between adapter cards. The default I/O base address for the Sound Blaster 16 card and most other sound cards is 220H for the digital audio functions and 330H for the MIDI IN and OUT signals (MPU-401 UART). The H or h suffix indicates that the hexadecimal system is used to specify the I/O address. You occasionally see hexadecimal addresses specified in the syntax of the C language (0x220 or 0x240).

Note

Most legacy PC adapter cards use jumpers to set resource values. Cards that store resource settings in nonvolatile RAM require that you run their setup application to set IRQ, I/O base address, and (if applicable, DMA channel). If the setup program unavoidably installs real-mode drivers for the device, don't forget to disable the real-mode drivers by adding temporary REM prefixes before restarting Windows 95.

Installing Adapter Cards with Automatic Detection

The easiest way to install a new legacy card in a Windows 95 PC is to use the Add New Hardware Wizard's automatic-detection feature to identify your added card. The Wizard also is capable of determining whether you have removed a card. Auto-detection is best suited for PCs that have few or no specialty adapter cards, such as sound and video capture cards, already installed. (If you have many specialty adapter cards installed, the manual process described in the next section is a more foolproof approach.) The following steps describe the automatic-detection process in replacing a Sound Blaster 16 SCSI card with a Media Vision Premium 3D sound card:

1. Set nonconflicting resource values for your new adapter card, using jumpers or the card's setup program.

2. Shut down Windows 95, and turn off the power to your PC.

3. Install the new adapter card in an empty ISA slot (remove the existing adapter card, if applicable), and make any required external connections, such as audio inputs and speaker outputs for sound cards.

4. Turn the PC power on, and restart Windows 95.

5. Launch Control Panel, and double-click the Add New Hardware icon to start the Add New Hardware Wizard (see fig. 8.7).

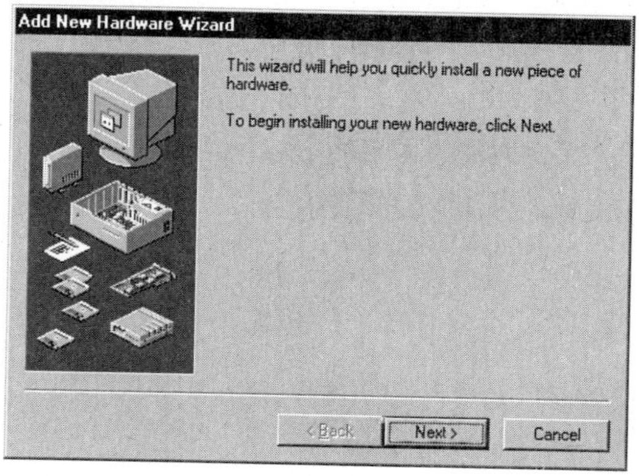

Fig. 8.7
This figure shows the opening dialog box of the Add New Hardware Wizard.

6. Click the Next button. You go to the Wizard dialog box that allows you to choose between manual and automatic hardware detection and installation. Accept the default Yes (Recommended) option (see fig. 8.8).

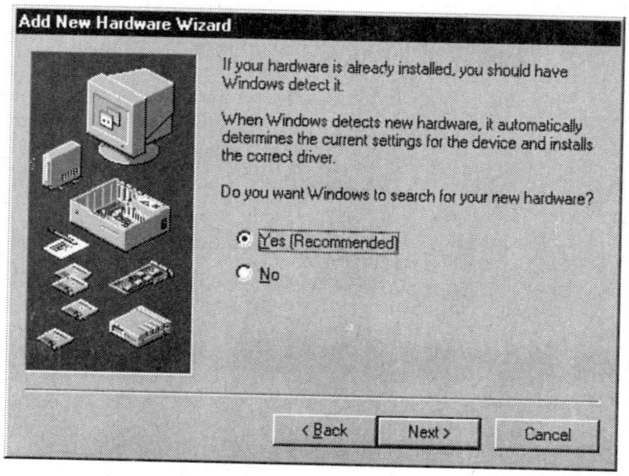

Fig. 8.8
You choose automatic or manual hardware detection in the Wizard's second dialog box.

7. Click the Next button to display the Wizard's boilerplate (see fig. 8.9).

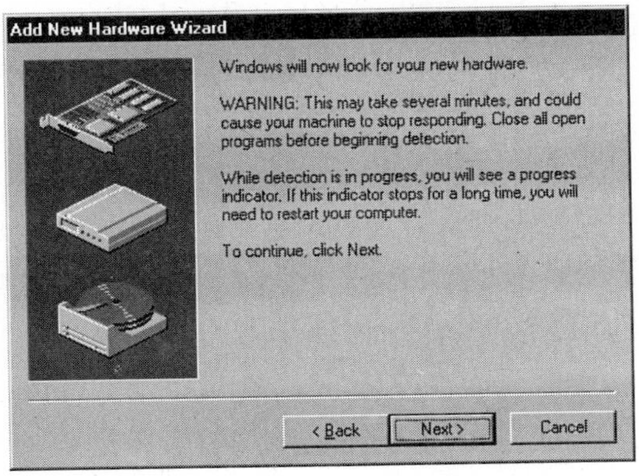

Fig. 8.9
The Wizard warns that detection may take a long time or may lock up Windows.

8. Click the Next button to start the detection process (see fig. 8.10).

After a few minutes of intense disk activity, often interspersed with periods of seeming inactivity, the wizard advises that detection is complete (see fig. 8.11).

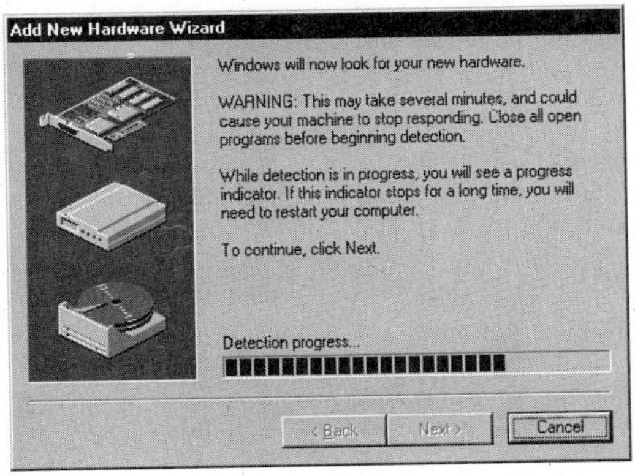

Fig. 8.10
The Wizard detection-progress dialog box tells you when detection is complete.

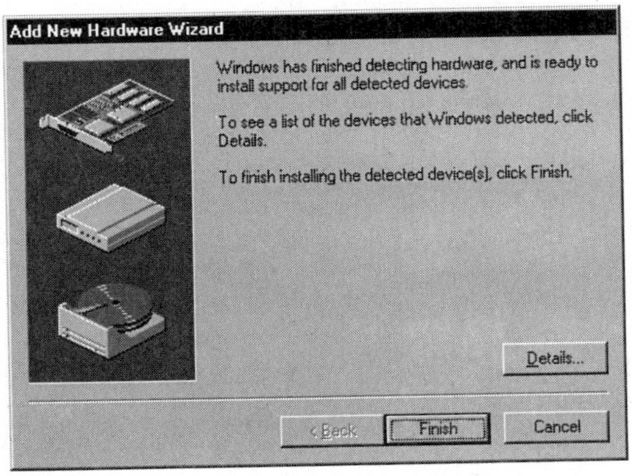

Fig. 8.11
Good news: the Wizard has finally finished the detection process.

9. Click the Details button to display what the Wizard detected. Figure 8.12 indicates that drivers for the Sound Blaster 16 SCSI card are to be removed and drivers for the Media Vision Pro/Premium 3D card are to be installed.

   If the Wizard doesn't detect your newly installed card, you must install the card manually; click Cancel to terminate the automatic-detection process.

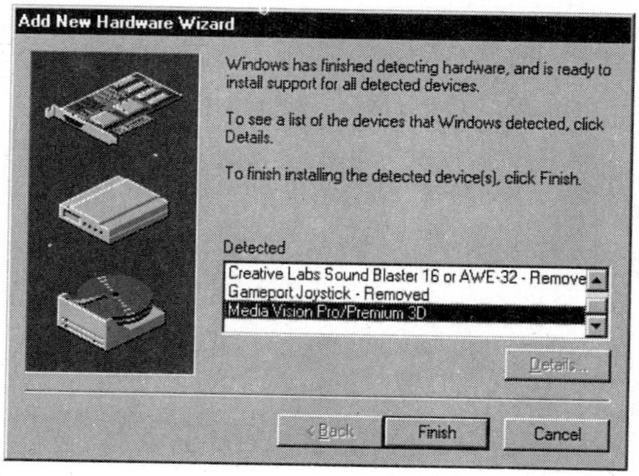

Fig. 8.12 Success: the Wizard detected that the Sound Blaster 16 SCSI card has been replaced by a Media Vision Pro/ Premium 3D card.

10. Click the Finish button to install the required drivers from the Windows 95 CD-ROM or floppy disks. The message box shown in figure 8.13 indicates the expected medium—in this case, the Windows 95 CD-ROM.

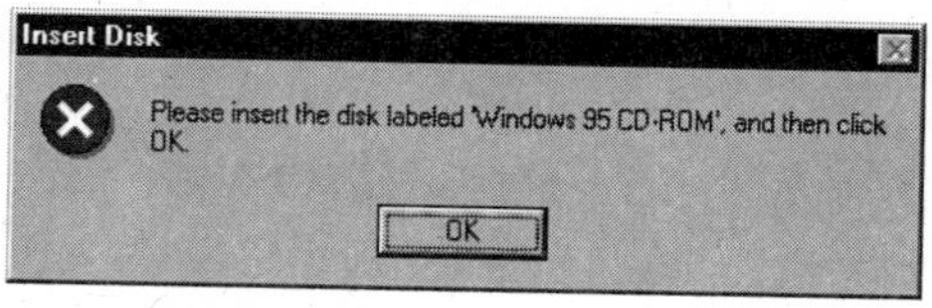

Fig. 8.13 The message box tells you the medium on which Windows 95 expects to find the required drivers.

11. Insert the Windows 95 CD-ROM into the drive, and click OK to install the drivers.

12. If Windows 95 can't find the required device-driver file in the expected location, you see the series of dialog boxes shown in figure 8.14.

    In this example, if your CD-ROM drive previously was connected to the Sound Blaster 16 SCSI card and now is connected to the Media Vision card, Windows 95 cannot read the CD-ROM. You must use the Windows 95 distribution floppy disks to install the drivers. The required setup cabinet file, WIN95_08.CAB, is located on disk 8. Insert the proper disk, click OK to close the Open dialog box, and then click OK again to close the Copying Files dialog box and continue the installation process.

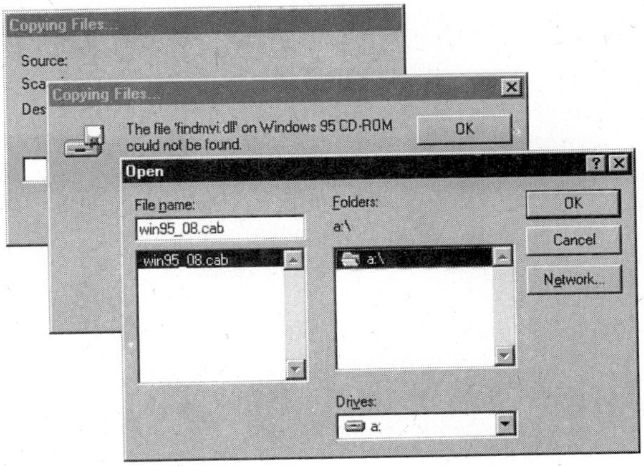

Fig. 8.14
This cascade of dialog boxes is required to change the location or type of the distribution medium for Windows 95.

13. When driver installation is complete, a message box advises you that system settings have changed and asks whether you want to restart Windows 95. Click Restart Now so that your driver changes take effect.

Tests with a variety of modems, sound cards, Windows graphics accelerator cards, and digital video capture cards indicate that the Wizard detects all but very specialized (and, therefore, uncommon) devices.

Installing Legacy Cards after Setting Up Drivers

The alternative to automatic device detection, described in the preceding section, is installing the new adapter card manually after you install its drivers. The advantage to this method is that you can determine in advance resource settings that don't conflict with existing devices. (You also eliminate the CD-ROM driver dilemma described in the preceding section if you install the driver for the new CD-ROM drive before installing the adapter card for the drive.) The following steps describe the process of reinstalling the drivers for the Sound Blaster 16 SCSI card:

1. Launch the Add New Hardware Wizard from Control Panel, and click the Next button in the opening dialog box to display the Wizard dialog box that allows you to choose between manual and automatic hardware detection and installation (refer to fig. 8.8).

2. Choose the No option to select manual installation; then click the Next button to display the Wizard's Hardware Types dialog box (see fig. 8.15).

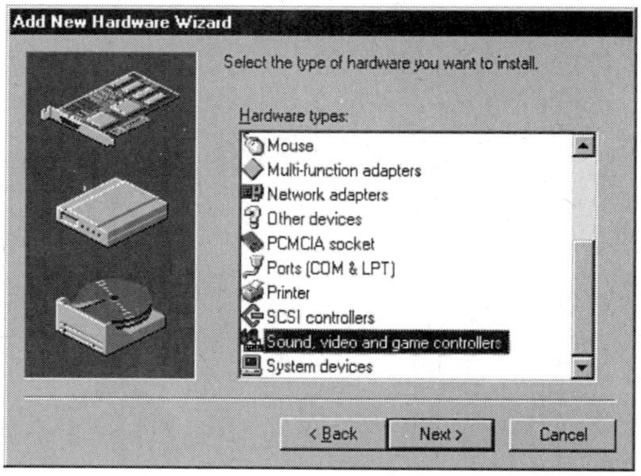

Fig. 8.15
The Add New Hardware Wizard's Hardware Types dialog box lists a variety of adapter card categories.

3. Select the card type in the Hardware Types list; then click the Next button to display the Manufacturers and Models dialog box (see fig. 8.16).

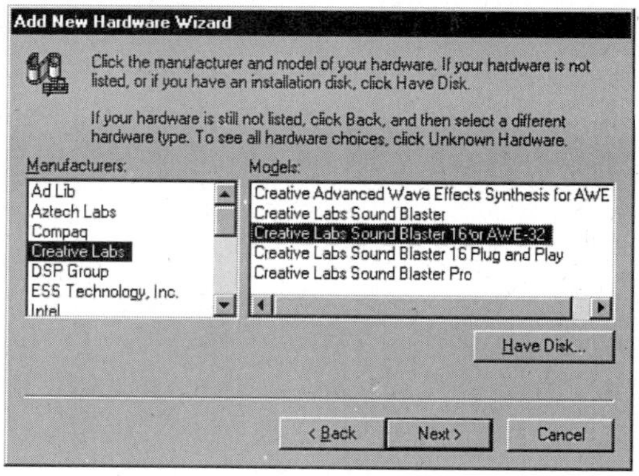

Fig. 8.16
The Wizard dialog box lists manufacturers and models of devices for which drivers are included on the Windows 95 distribution media.

4. Make the appropriate selections in the Manufacturers and Models list boxes; then click the Next button to display the default settings for the new device.

   If you don't see the manufacturer or model in the list boxes, you need a floppy disk or CD-ROM that contains Windows 95 drivers for your device (Windows 3.1 or later drivers won't work). If you have the required Windows 95 drivers, click the Have Disk button to install the drivers from floppy disk or CD-ROM. If you don't have Windows 95 drivers, click the Cancel button to terminate the installation.

5. Windows 95 can't tell what resource value settings you made for your new or replacement adapter card, so the manufacturer's default settings for the device appear in the Wizard's Resource Settings dialog box (see fig. 8.17). Write down or print these default settings.

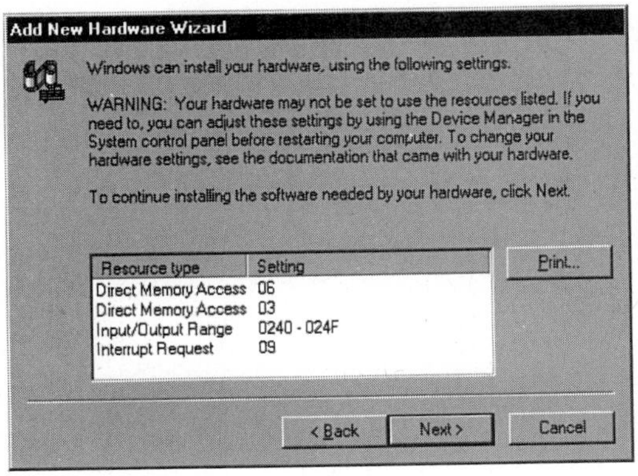

Fig. 8.17
Default values for the Sound Blaster 16 SCSI card appear when opening the Resource Setting dialog box.

6. Click the Next button to display the System Settings Change message box (see fig. 8.18).

   If the default settings in the preceding step correspond to the resource settings of your card, click the Yes button to shut down Windows 95. If you haven't installed the card (which is the normal situation for manual device detection), turn off the power to your PC, install the card, turn the power back on, and restart Windows 95 with the new card activated.

   If any of the resource values in the preceding step are incorrect or you receive a "resource conflict" message, click the No button in the System Settings Change message box so that you can alter the resource values as necessary.

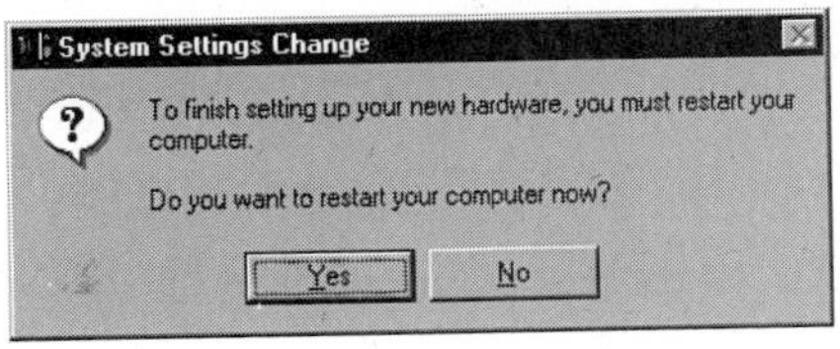

Fig. 8.18
The System Settings Change message box gives you the option to restart Windows 95.

7. Open Control Panel's System Properties sheet, click the Device Manager tab, and expand the entries for the type of device that you're installing.

Exclamation points superimposed on the device's icon(s) indicate that the device is not yet fully installed or has been removed from your PC.

8. If you're replacing a card, entries for both cards appear in the Device Manager list. To remove the old entry, select the entry and click the Remove button. A message box requests that you confirm the removal process (see fig. 8.19).

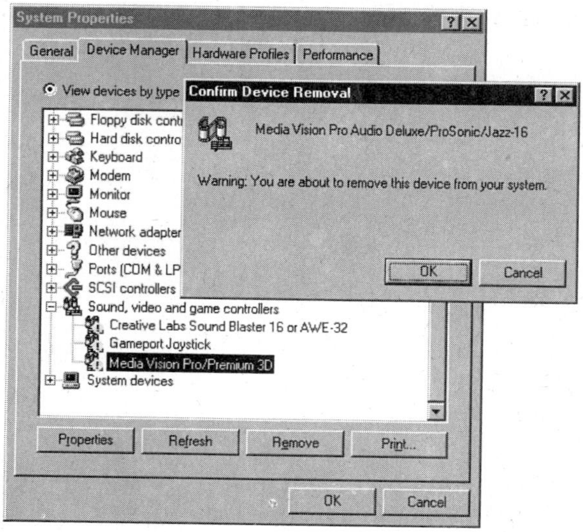

Fig. 8.19
You're asked to confirm removal of an unneeded device with the Device Manager.

9. Double-click the entry for the new adapter card to display the Properties sheet for the device.

10. In the Resource Settings list box, select the resource whose value you want to change; then click the Change Setting button to display the Edit Interrupt Request dialog box for the resource.

11. Use the spin buttons of the Value text box to select the value that corresponds to the preset value for your adapter card. If a conflict with an existing card occurs, the card that has the conflicting value is identified in the Conflict Information text box (see fig. 8.20).

12. Change the Value setting to a value that displays `No devices are conflicting` in the Conflict Information box; then make the corresponding change in the card, using the jumpers or nonvolatile RAM. (Turn off power to your PC before making jumper changes.) Figure 8.21 shows an I/O base address setting changed to remove a conflict at Input/Output Range 0260 - 026F.

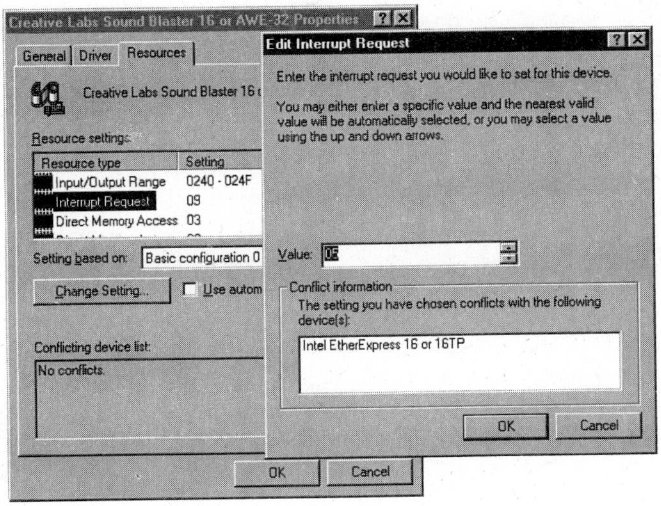

Fig. 8.20
Change the IRQ setting for the new adapter card to avoid a conflict; IRQ5 conflicts with the network card's IRQ in this example.

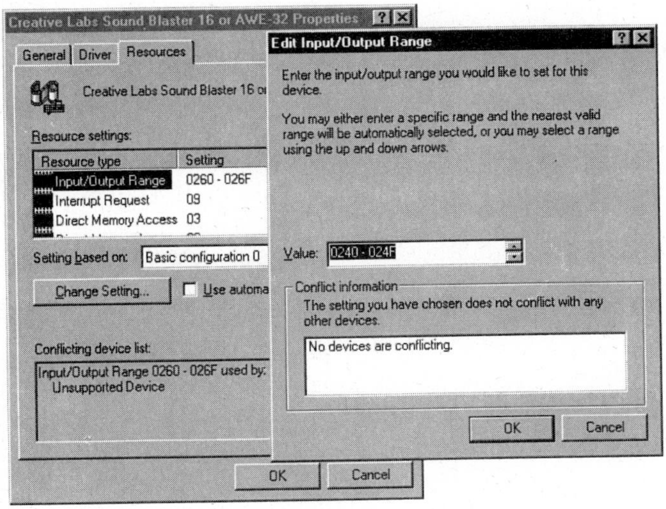

Fig. 8.21
Change the I/O base address (Input/Output Range) to a nonconflicting value.

13. After making all the changes necessary to remove resource conflicts, click OK to close the resource's Edit Input/Output Range dialog box, and then click OK to close the Properties sheet for the device.

14. Click OK to close the System Properties sheet.

15. Shut down and restart Windows 95 so that your new settings take effect.

The process of manually installing a legacy device, described in the preceding steps appears to be complex, but it's a more foolproof process than the one used by Windows 3.1 and later. In particular, the capability to detect resource conflicts with proposed resource value settings for legacy adapter cards eliminates many of the problems associated with installing new devices under Windows 3.1 and later.

> **Note**
>
> Windows 95 includes drivers for an extraordinary number of popular devices but not for low-volume products, such as digital video capture and MPEG-1 playback cards. Reputable manufacturers of specialty legacy devices likely will provide 32-bit protected-mode drivers for Windows 95 in late 1995 and early 1996. You can expect updated Windows 95 drivers to be posted in manufacturers' technical-support forums on CompuServe, in BBSs on the Microsoft Network, and at vendors' World Wide Web sites.

Removing Unneeded Drivers for Legacy Devices

If you remove a legacy device from your PC and don't intend to reinstall it, it's good Windows 95 housekeeping to remove the driver for the device from Device Manager's list. Follow these steps to remove the Device Manager entry for permanently removed adapter cards:

1. Double-click Control Panel's System icon to open the System Properties sheet.

2. Click the Device Manager tab and double-click the icon for the hardware type of the device removed to display the list of installed devices. An exclamation point superimposed on a device icon indicates a removed or inoperable device.

3. Click the list item to select the device you want to remove and then click the Remove button.

4. Confirm that you want to remove the device by clicking OK in the Confirm Device Removal message box (refer to fig. 8.19).

   If you have more than one hardware configuration, a modified version of the Confirm Device Removal message box appears. Make sure the default Remove from All Configurations option button is selected; then click OK to remove the device and close the message box.

Using Windows 95's Registry Editor to Troubleshoot Hardware-Compatibility Problems

In most cases, you can solve hardware-resource-conflict problems by changing jumper positions or using the card's setup program to alter nonvolatile RAM values and then making corresponding changes in resource values in the device's Properties sheet. If you have a problem that changing resource settings doesn't solve, the card supplier's product-support staff probably will need additional information about your system. The primary source of system information is Windows 95's Registry; all device information that appears in Device Manager is obtained from entries in the Registry.

To examine the Registry, you need to set up and use the Registry Editor (RegEdit) application, REGEDIT.EXE. Windows 95 doesn't add a Start menu choice for RegEdit automatically, because Windows 95 neophytes and the faint of heart should not attempt to change Registry values.

If you need to check the Registry values for an adapter card, follow these steps:

1. Open the Start menu, and choose Run.
2. Type **regedit** to open the Registry Editor.
3. Choose Find, Edit to open the Find dialog box.
4. In the Find What text box, type the key word for the card in question; then click the Find Next button to locate the first instance of the key word.

   The support person usually gives you the key word on which to search. The phrase *sound blaster*, for example, finds all references to Sound Blaster hardware in the Registry.
5. The first or second instance of the key word is likely to display the Plug and Play device assignment data for the card. Press F3 to find the successive instances of the key word.

   Figure 8.22 shows the PnP device data for the Sound Blaster 16 card.
6. Pressing F3 might continue finding additional instances of Registry entries for the device in question. Figure 8.23 shows the Registry entry that defines the driver for the Line Input device of the Sound Blaster 16, SB16SND.DRV.

Tip
If you use RegEdit often, create a shortcut for it. The REGEDIT.EXE file is in the \WINDOWS directory.

Fig. 8.22
The Windows 95 Registry Editor displays Plug and Play device assignment values for a Sound Blaster 16 card.

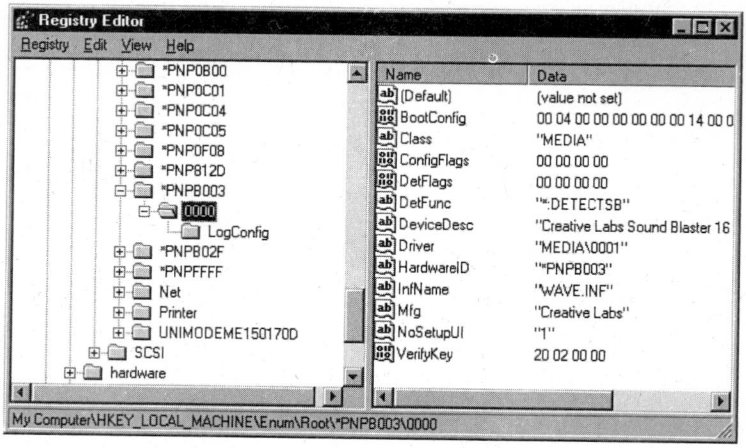

Fig. 8.23
Continued searching in RegEdit displays the settings of the driver for the Line Input device of the Sound Blaster 16 card.

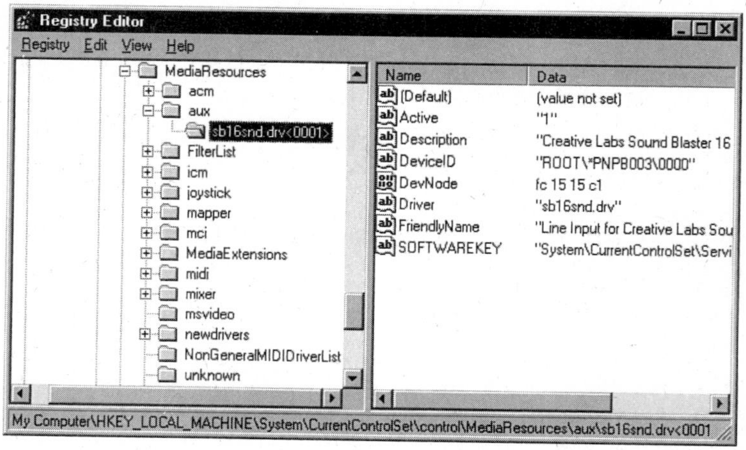

Caution

Do not make any changes in Registry data unless you are instructed to do so by a competent technician who is fully conversant with Windows 95. Improper values of Registry entries can prevent proper operation of Windows 95 and may prevent you from booting Windows 95.

Using Multiple Hardware Configurations

Windows 95 allows you to create multiple hardware configurations for your PC. (Multiple hardware configurations aren't necessary, however, if you have a PC that has PnP BIOS and if all your devices also are PnP-compliant.) The most common use of a multiple hardware configuration is to reflect the docking or undocking of a laptop or notebook PC in a non-PnP docking station. You also can use multiple hardware configurations if you repeatedly change legacy adapter cards in your PC.

To set up one or more alternative hardware profiles, follow these steps:

1. Open the System Properties sheet (by double-clicking Control Panel's System icon), and click the Hardware Profiles tab.
2. In the Hardware Profiles list box, select the Original Configuration profile; then click the Copy button to open the Copy Profile dialog box.
3. In the To text box, type the name of the new profile (see fig. 8.24); then click the OK button to create the new hardware profile.

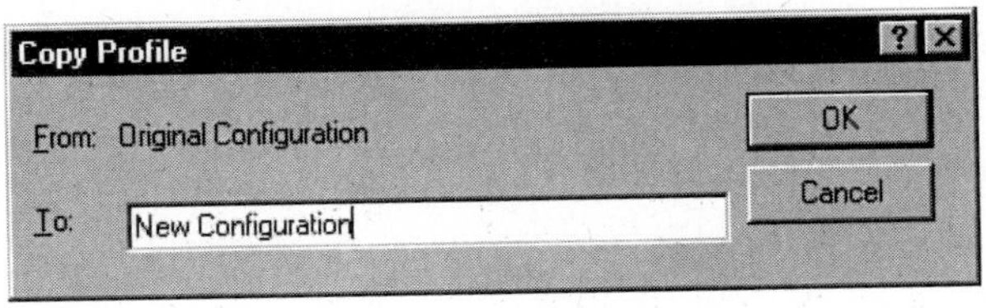

Fig. 8.24
Create a copy of the Original Profile to serve as an alternative hardware profile.

4. Click the Device Manager tab, and select a device that you don't want to use in the new alternative profile.

   By default, all devices in the Original Profile are enabled in the new alternative profile, as indicated by a check in the check box to the left of the hardware-profile name (see fig. 8.25).

5. To prevent a device from being used in the alternative profile, clear the check box for the device.

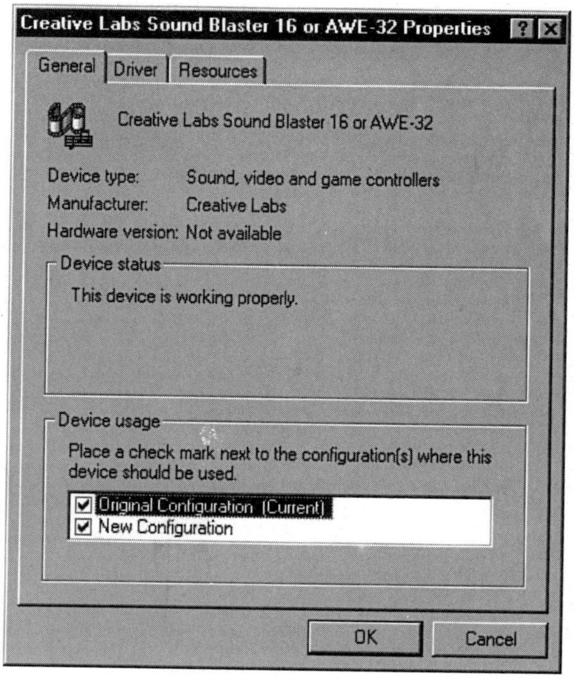

Fig. 8.25
Device Manager shows a device enabled in both the Original Profile and the new profile.

6. To set the default hardware profile for startup, select the profile on the Hardware Profiles page; then click OK to close the System Properties sheet.

7. Shut down and restart Windows to activate the selected hardware profile.

The use of alternative hardware profiles in Windows 95 is uncommon, but it is an example of Microsoft developers' attention to detail, which enables Windows 95 to accommodate almost any set of hardware-related changes.❖

Chapter 9

Special Features for Notebook Users

by Jim Boyce with Doug Kilarski

As computing moved beyond the desktop, Microsoft recognized the need for system services and end-user functionality to improve the mobile-computing experience. With portable PCs forecasted to comprise 33 percent or more of the entire computer system production in 1995, mobile computer support couldn't be an afterthought. Portable support had to be foremost in the minds of Windows 95 developers.

Many business professionals want to be able to take their office with them. Portable technology and Windows 95 make a hard-to-beat combination. Portable PCs enable you to work nearly anywhere, and Windows 95's features for portable computing—which include 32-bit support for PC Card (PCMCIA) devices, file synchronization, Dial-Up Networking, remote mail, and more—make Windows 95 a perfect operating system for your portable PC. Not only does Windows 95 make it easy for you to take your work with you, but features such as Dial-Up Networking and remote mail enable you to keep in touch with coworkers and access disk and printer resources in your main office from anywhere in the world.

Note

What were formerly called "PCMCIA" devices are now referred to as "PC Card" devices.

Simply put, Windows 95 enables users to better utilize their portable PCs. Mobile users have universally asked for three areas of portable-specific features:

- Get the most out of their portable PC hardware
- Maintain access to office LAN resources
- Keep organized

Windows 95 delivers on all three points. PC Card, Plug and Play, disk compression, power management, and support for port replicators and docking stations all complement portable PC hardware. Windows 95 architectural enhancements conserve battery power and manage configuration changes, which helps extend the life of older portables. Dial-Up Networking enables you to access your office file server(s) using your modem and send and receive e-mail to coworkers. Windows 95 keeps users organized as well. Using an advanced file synchronization system called Briefcase and a deferred printing option, roaming users remain "in sync" with their desktop environments (and vice versa).

To help you understand how to get the most from Windows 95's features for portable computing, this chapter explores the following:

- Using PC Card (PCMCIA) devices
- Using a docking system
- Using a direct cable connection to share resources
- Using power management
- Using Dial-Up Networking
- Synchronizing files with Briefcase
- Using mouse trails

Using PC Card Devices

Many notebook PCs contain one or two special bus slots called *PC Card slots* (formerly PCMCIA slots) that accommodate credit card-sized adapters for various functions. Although initially only flash memory cards were available in PCMCIA format, today many types of devices—including modems, hard disks, network cards, sound cards, and other devices—are available in PC Card/PCMCIA format. In addition, PC Card docking stations enable you to use PC Card devices in desktop PCs, making it possible, for example, to use the same PC Card modem in a notebook PC and a desktop PC.

Note

There are three official types of PC Card slots, referred to as Type I, Type II, and Type III. The specification for a fourth type of slot—Type IV—is being finalized by the PCMCIA organization (Personal Computer Memory Card International Association). One of the primary differences between the types of PC Card slots is that each higher-numbered slot accommodates a thicker PC Card than the previous slot. PC Card hard disks, for example, generally require a Type III slot, but modems can be installed in a Type I or Type II slot. Most of today's newer notebook PCs can accommodate one Type III device, or two Type II devices (or any combination of two Type I and Type II devices).

◀ See "Installing Plug and Play Hardware," p. 246

The primary advantage of PC Card devices for portable PC users is that these devices make it possible to expand the capabilities of portable PCs in the same way you can expand desktop systems, enabling you to add optional hardware to the portable PC. Windows 95 improves on the PCMCIA support in DOS and Windows 3.x by providing 32-bit device drivers to support the PC Card controllers in most PCs. This makes it possible for Windows 95 to support a wide variety of PC Card devices without requiring 16-bit, real mode drivers that slow down the system and use conventional memory.

Another improvement for PC Card devices in Windows 95 is expanded support for *hot swapping*, which is the ability to remove and insert PC Card devices in the PC without powering down the computer. If you need to temporarily remove your network card to use a modem, for example, you first use the PC Card object in the Control Panel to turn off the network card (see fig. 9.1). Then, you simply remove the network card from its slot and insert the modem. Windows 95 disables the network driver(s) temporarily and enables the modem drivers.

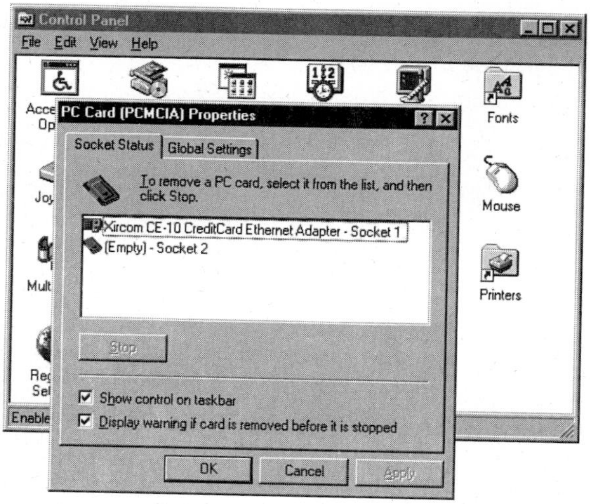

Fig. 9.1
Use the PC Card (PCMCIA) Properties sheet to enable and disable PC Card devices.

Installing PC Card Support

Each computer with PC Card slots or a PC Card docking station includes a PC Card controller that enables the CPU to communicate with the PC Card bus. This controller requires a set of drivers that enable the operating system (in this case, Windows 95) to communicate using the PC Card bus. In addition, each PC Card device requires a device-specific driver that enables the device to function and communicate with the operating system. If you are using a PC Card network card, for example, Windows 95 requires a set of drivers for the PC Card slot itself and a separate driver for the network card.

When you install Windows 95, Setup automatically detects your PC's PC Card controller and installs support for it. Setup does not, however, enable the 32-bit PC Card controller drivers. Setup takes this approach because some portable PCs require that you continue to use 16-bit drivers (which come with the portable PC) to control the PC Card slots.

Note

Windows 95 supports 32-bit drivers for systems based on either an Intel PCIC-compatible PC Card controller or Databook PC Card controller.

In addition to enabling 32-bit PC Card support (if your PC supports it), you must install the drivers for the PC Card devices you'll be using. In many cases, Windows 95 can install these devices automatically using Plug and

Play, even on systems without a Plug and Play BIOS. To install a PC Card modem, for example, simply insert the modem in its slot. Windows 95 detects the new device and starts the Add New Modem Wizard to install the modem driver.

Enabling 32-Bit PC Card Support

After you install Windows 95, you must use the PC Card object in the Control Panel to enable 32-bit support for your PC Card controller. Enabling 32-bit support provides better overall system performance and more effective memory use. In addition, enabling 32-bit PC Card support is required to support Plug and Play installation of PC Card devices and hot-swapping.

Note

When Windows 95 enables 32-bit PC Card support, your existing 16-bit real mode PC Card drivers are disabled. If you are installing Windows 95 from a network server, you must have local access to the Windows 95 source files. Therefore, you must have a set of Windows 95 floppy disks or have a CD-ROM connected to your portable PC to enable Windows 95 to read the 32-bit driver files for the PC Card controller. Optionally, you can copy the Windows 95 cabinet files from the network server to your portable PC's hard disk prior to enabling 32-bit support.

To enable 32-bit PC Card support for your PC, use the following steps:

1. Verify that you have local access to the Windows 95 cabinet files as explained in the previous note.
2. Open the Start menu and choose Settings, Control Panel.
3. Choose the PC Card (PCMCIA) object. The first time you open this object, the PC Card (PCMCIA) Wizard appears (see fig. 9.2).

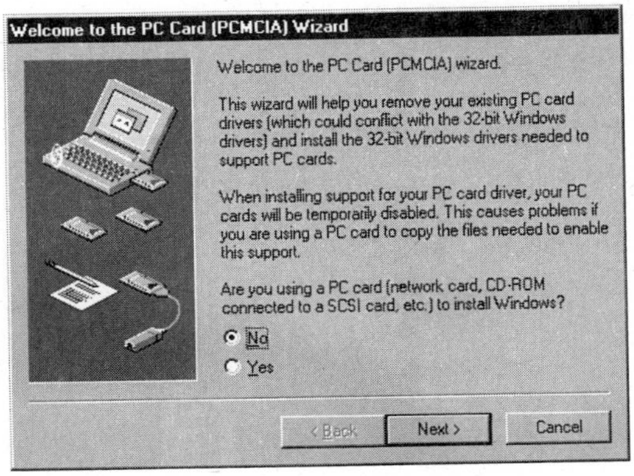

Fig. 9.2
The opening dialog box of the PC Card (PCMCIA) Wizard.

4. Choose No and then Next to inform the Wizard that you are not setting up Windows 95 from a network server. (If your Windows 95 setup disk is on a network server or another device such as a CD-ROM drive connected through a PC Card adapter, choose Yes.)

5. If the PC Card Wizard detects existing real-mode PC Card drivers, it displays the dialog box shown in figure 9.3, enabling you to view the drivers and control the way the Wizard handles the existing drivers. If you want the Wizard to automatically remove the drivers, choose No and then choose Next. If you want to view and verify the deletion of the existing real-mode PC Card drivers, choose Yes and then choose Next.

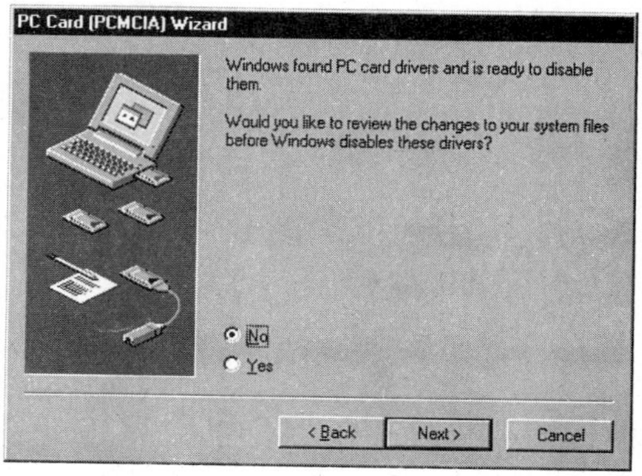

Fig. 9.3
To verify your drivers, choose Yes.

6. If you select Yes, the Wizard displays a set of dialog boxes that show the device entries in CONFIG.SYS, AUTOEXEC.BAT, and SYSTEM.INI that it will delete (see fig. 9.4). If you do not want the wizard to delete a specific driver from one of these files, deselect the line in the appropriate dialog box, and then choose Next.

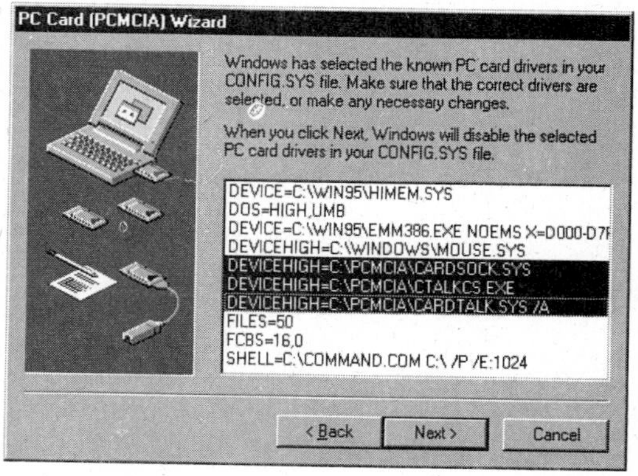

Fig. 9.4
The PC Card (PCMCIA) Wizard enables you to verify real-mode driver deletion.

7. After the PC Card Wizard removes the real-mode drivers (if any) as directed by you, it displays a final dialog box that prompts you to choose Finish to complete the PC Card setup process and enable 32-bit PC Card support. Choose the Finish button to complete the process. Windows 95 shuts down so the change takes effect.

Installing PC Card Devices

After you enable 32-bit PC Card support, Windows 95 can typically install PC Card devices automatically. If you insert a network card in the PC, for example, Windows 95 detects the new card and automatically installs the necessary drivers for the card. If, for some reason, Windows 95 does not automatically recognize your PC Card device, you must manually install support for it.

► See "Installing and Configuring the Network Adapter Cards," p. 624

► See "Installing and Configuring Your Modem," p. 831

To manually install a PC Card device other than a modem or network adapter, use the following procedure:

1. Insert the new PC Card device in the appropriate slot. (Check the PC Card device's manual to determine if the device must be installed in a specific slot.)

2. Open the Control Panel and choose the Add New Hardware object to start the Add New Hardware Wizard. Then choose Next.

3. Choose Yes and then Next to enable the Wizard to automatically detect your new PC Card device.

4. If the Wizard is unable to detect the new device, the Wizard displays a hardware selection dialog box similar to the one shown in figure 9.5. Choose the type of device you are installing and then choose Next.

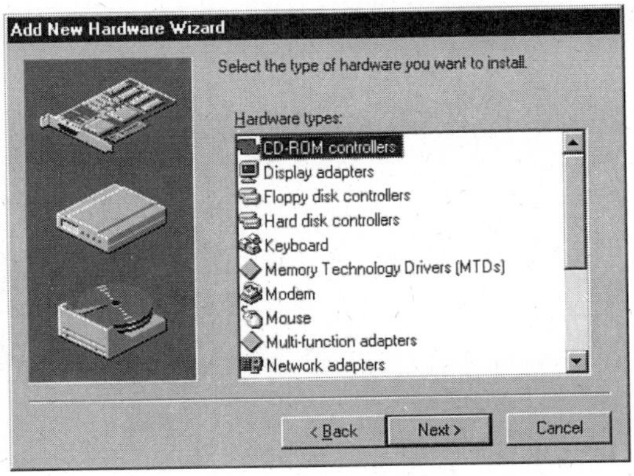

Fig. 9.5
Choose the type of device you are installing and then choose Next.

Tip
If you are installing a PC Card network adapter, use the Network object in the Control Panel to install it. If you are installing a PC Card modem, use the Modems object in the Control Panel.

5. From the Manufacturers list, choose the manufacturer of the device you are installing. Then from the Models list, choose the device model. If your manufacturer or model is not listed and you have a driver disk for the device, choose Have Disk and then follow the prompts to direct the Wizard to the directory on the floppy disk where the necessary files are located.

6. After you have selected the correct manufacturer and model, choose OK to complete the setup process.

Hot-Swapping PC Cards

Windows 95 enables you to remove a PC Card device and replace it with another without powering down the system. This capability enables you to quickly swap PC Card devices. Before you remove a device, however, you should first shut down the device. To do so, choose the PC Card object in the Control Panel. Windows 95 displays a PC Card (PCMCIA) Properties sheet similar to the one shown in figure 9.6, which displays information about the PC's PC Card slots and any currently inserted devices.

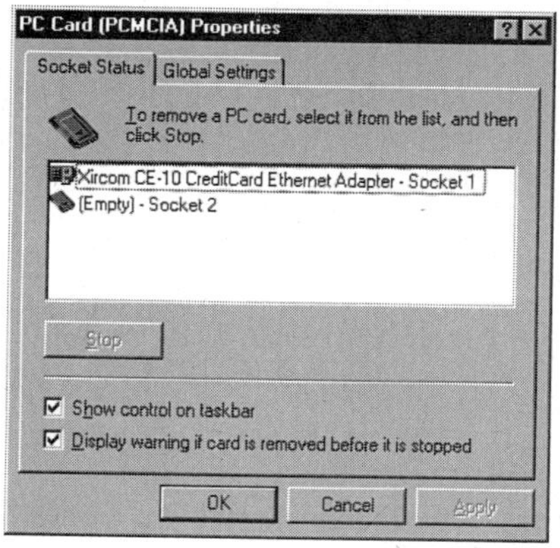

Fig. 9.6
You can view information about slots and installed devices.

To remove a PC Card device from the system, first select the device from the list on the Socket Status page and then choose Stop. Windows 95 shuts down the device and temporarily disables its drivers. After Windows 95 disables the device, the socket is listed as empty. You then can remove the PC Card device.

To insert a new device, simply insert the device in the proper slot. If you have previously installed support for the device, Windows 95 detects the device and automatically enables its drivers. If you have not used the device in the

PC previously, Windows 95 detects the new hardware and automatically installs support for the device.

Using Your Laptop with a Docking System

Before docking stations (see fig. 9.7) and port replicators, portable PC users were often trading mobility for compromises in storage, video quality, and display size. Beyond the lack of accessible resources, the general incompatibility and undynamic docking posed even greater problems. Much time was spent reconfiguring and rebooting systems during docking and undocking.

Fig. 9.7
A docked notebook.

With Windows 95, *hot-docking support* integrates hardware and software for quick and easy docking. Docking and undocking can occur when the power is on or off. Windows 95 automatically detects any configuration changes and manages any conflicts or file disruptions. It also loads and unloads hardware drivers as required. To undock your PC when Windows 95 is running, open the Start menu and choose Eject PC. Windows 95 reconfigures the system automatically for the undocked configuration and then prompts you to remove the PC from the docking station.

Creating and Modifying Hardware Profiles

Windows 95 enables you to create multiple hardware profiles to accommodate different hardware configurations, such as when your PC is docked and when it is undocked. Windows 95 automatically creates two hardware profiles for you—one for the docked configuration and a second profile for the undocked configuration. Windows 95 detects which profile is required at startup and automatically uses the correct one.

> **Note**
>
> If your portable PC contains a Plug and Play BIOS, Windows 95 does not have to use multiple hardware profiles to accommodate hot docking. Instead, the Plug and Play BIOS can detect which devices are available and Windows 95 can configure the system accordingly.

If you want to change an existing profile or create a new one, you can do so through the Control Panel. Use the following procedure to create a new hardware profile:

1. Open the Start menu and choose Settings, Control Panel.
2. Double-click the System icon to display the System Properties sheet.
3. Click the Hardware Profiles tab to display the Hardware Profiles page (see fig. 9.8).

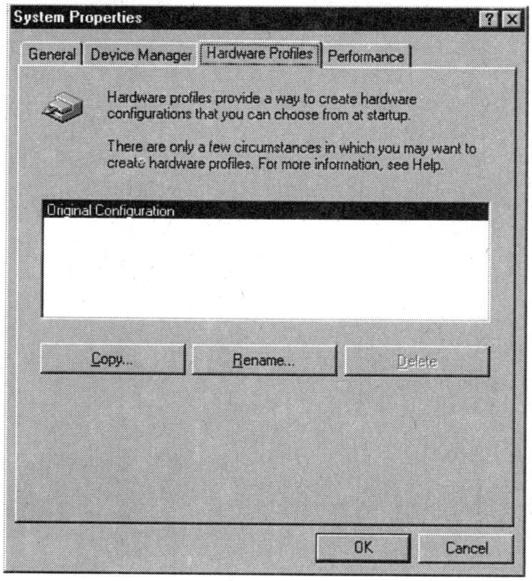

Fig. 9.8
The Hardware Profiles page enables you to modify and create hardware profiles.

4. Select the hardware profile you want to use as a basis for the new profile, and then choose Copy. Windows 95 displays a Copy Profile dialog box in which you specify the name for the new hardware profile (see fig. 9.9).

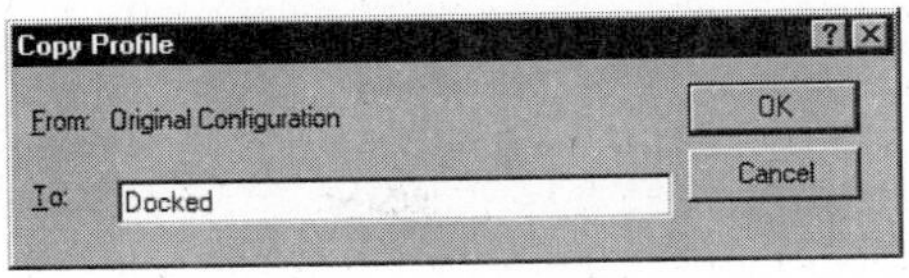

Fig. 9.9
Specify a name for the hardware profile.

5. Enter a name for the new profile and choose OK. The new hardware profile appears in the Hardware Profiles list.

In some cases, you might want to modify a hardware profile. If Windows 95 is unable to properly detect the hardware in a particular configuration, for example, you can modify the profile to add and remove hardware from the profile.

To modify a hardware profile, use the following procedure:

1. Open the Control Panel and double-click the System icon; then click the Device Manager tab to display the Device Manager property page (see fig. 9.10).

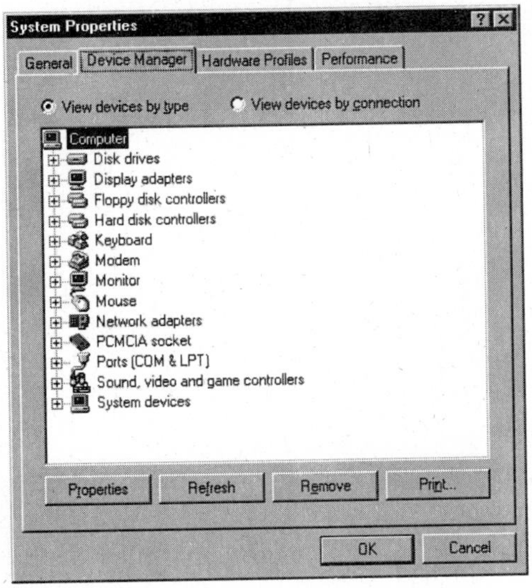

Fig. 9.10
Use the Device Manager page to modify a hardware profile.

2. Select the hardware device that you want to add or remove from a particular profile, and then choose Properties to display the General page of its Properties sheet (see fig. 9.11).

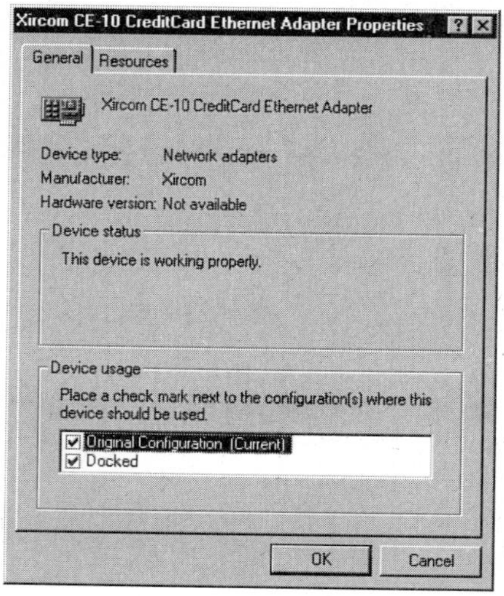

Fig. 9.11
Use the Device Usage list to add and remove hardware from a profile.

3. At the bottom of the device's General page is a Device Usage list that defines which profiles use the device. Place a check in the check box beside a hardware profile to enable the device for that profile. Clear the check box to disable the device for that profile.

4. Choose OK to apply the changes.

When you start the system, Windows 95 detects the hardware configuration you are using and automatically applies the appropriate hardware profile. If the hardware profiles are so similar that Windows 95 cannot determine which profile should be used, Windows 95 displays a menu containing a list of the available profiles and prompts you to select the profile to be used.

Working with Different Configurations

Most hardware settings in Windows 95 are stored relative to the current hardware profile. Changes that you make to a device's settings are applied to the current profile, but not to other hardware profiles. It therefore is possible to maintain different settings for the same device in two or more different hardware profiles. For example, you might use a display resolution of 640 X 480 in one profile, but use 800 X 600 in a different profile. Such is probably the case when you are using an external monitor with your PC. You probably use 640 X 480 with the portable's LCD display and a higher resolution with the external monitor.

To configure unique settings for a device, first start Windows 95 using the hardware profile in which you want the changes to be made. If you want to use a high-resolution mode with an external monitor, for example, select the hardware profile you normally use with the external monitor (or create a profile for use with the external monitor as explained in the previous section). After you've started Windows 95 with the appropriate hardware profile, change the settings for the device. The changes are applied to the current hardware profile and do not affect other profiles you have created.

Troubleshooting

Windows 95 did not automatically select the LCD monitor for my laptop's LCD when I ran setup.

Check the monitor type in the hardware profile that is used when you are working with the internal display. To set the monitor type, right-click on the desktop and choose Properties. Click the Settings tab to display the Settings page. Choose Change Display Type to display the Change Display Type dialog box. Choose the Change button to display the Select Device dialog box. Choose the Show All Devices option button, choose Standard Monitor Types from the Manufacturers list, and then choose the appropriate Laptop Display Panel selection from the Models list.

Using Deferred Printing

When your portable PC is docked, you probably have access to a printer connected to the docking station or that is available across the network. When your PC is not docked, however, it is unlikely that you'll have access to a printer. Even though you might not have access to a printer, however, Windows 95 still makes it possible for you to print documents through *deferred printing*. When you print a document, Windows 95 places the document in the printer's queue, even if the printer is not available. The document remains in the printers's queue even when you turn off your computer.

◄ See "Controlling Printing," p. 174

When you dock your computer and the printer once again becomes available, Windows 95 senses that the printer is available and begins spooling the document to the printer. Deferred printing is handled automatically by Windows 95. You simply print the document, and when the printer becomes available, Windows 95 begins sending the document to the printer.

Sharing Local Resources via Parallel or Serial Connection

A growing number of portable users also have a desktop system. They regularly transfer files between systems by using either a floppy disk and/or a direct parallel or serial cable, and a third-party application to handle the transfer. Windows 95 includes a feature called Direct Cable Connection that integrates the same capability within Windows 95—essentially, you can use a serial or parallel cable to network together your portable and desktop PCs, creating a small peer-to-peer network. The two computers then can access each other's files and other resources (such as a fax modem) as if they were joined by a traditional network interface.

In a direct cable connection, one computer acts as the host (server) and the other computer acts as a guest (client). The host PC also can act as a gateway, enabling the client to access the network to which the host is connected. The host can serve as a gateway for NetBEUI and/or IPX/SPX protocols, but cannot serve as a gateway for TCP/IP.

Setting Up Direct Cable Connection

If you select the Portable option when you install Windows 95, Setup installs Direct Cable Connection on your PC. If you use a different option or deselected the Direct Cable Connection option during Setup, you must install it. To add Direct Cable Connection, use the following procedure:

1. Open the Start menu and choose Settings, Control Panel.
2. Double-click the Add/Remove Programs icon.
3. Click the Windows Setup tab to display the Windows Setup page.
4. Select Communications from the Components list, and then choose Details.
5. Place a check beside Direct Cable Connection, and then choose OK.
6. Choose OK again to cause Windows 95 to add Direct Cable Connection to your PC.

Note

If Direct Cable Connection is already checked in the Components list, the software is already installed on your PC.

After installing the Direct Cable Connection software, you must connect the two computers with an appropriate cable. You can use either a parallel or null-modem serial cable to connect your two PCs. The types of cables you can use for the connection are described in the following list:

- Standard 4-bit null-modem cable, and LapLink and InterLink cables made prior to 1992.
- Extended Capabilities Port (ECP) cable. To use this type of cable, your parallel port must be configured as an ECP port in your system BIOS.
- Universal Cable Module (UCM) cable, which supports connecting together different types of parallel ports. You can use a UCM cable to connect together two ECP ports for fastest performance.

As indicated above, configuring your parallel ports as ECP ports provides the best performance. To use ECP, however, your PC's ports must be ECP-capable, and the ports must be configured as ECP ports in the system BIOS. Older PCs do not contain ECP-capable parallel ports.

► See "Client/Server Networks," p. 582

The final step in setting up the Direct Cable Connection is to ensure that both the guest and host computers are using the same network protocol. You can use the NetBEUI, IPX/SPX, or TCP/IP protocols. In addition, you must use an appropriate network client, such as Client for NetWare Networks or Client for Microsoft Networks. The host computer must be running either the File and Printer Sharing for Microsoft Networks service or the File and Printer Sharing for NetWare Networks service.

Setting Up the Host

In a Direct Cable Connection between two PCs, one PC acts as the host and the other PC acts as the guest. The first step in enabling the connection is to configure the host. To do so, use the following procedure:

1. Open the Start menu and choose Programs, Accessories, Direct Cable Connection. Windows 95 displays the dialog box shown in figure 9.12.
2. Select Host option and then choose Next. Windows 95 displays the dialog box shown in figure 9.13.

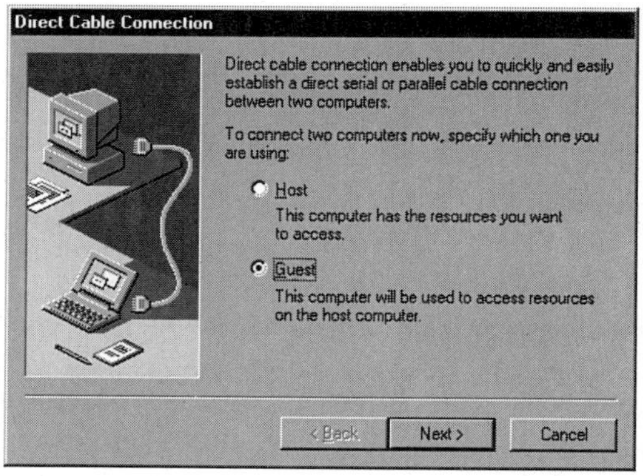

Fig. 9.12
Choose whether the PC will act as host or guest.

3. Choose the port you want to use on the host for the connection. You can choose one of the host's parallel or serial ports. After selecting the port, choose Next.

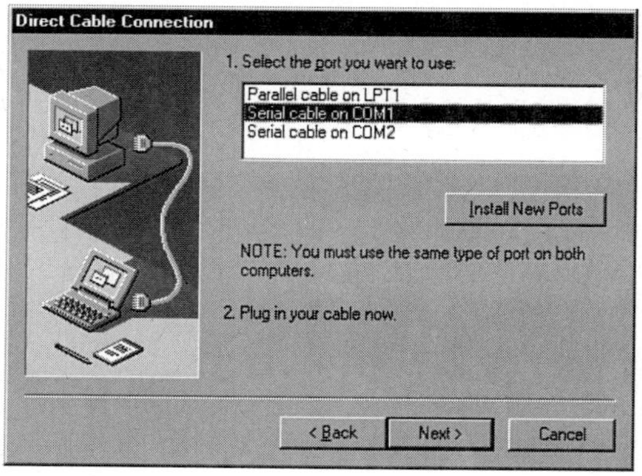

Fig. 9.13
Select the port to be used by the connection.

4. Specify whether you want to use password protection to prevent unauthorized access to the host. To use password protection, enable the Use Password Protection check box. Then choose Set Password, which displays a simple dialog box in which you enter the password that must be provided by the guest computer to access the host. When you've specified the desired password settings, choose Finish to complete host setup.

Setting Up the Guest

After configuring the host, you're ready to configure the guest computer. To do so, use the following procedure:

1. On the guest computer, open the Start menu and choose Programs, Accessories, Direct Computer Connection.

2. From the Direct Cable Connection dialog box, choose Guest and then Next.

3. Choose the port on the guest PC through which the connection will be made and then choose Next.

4. Choose Finish to complete the setup.

Before you begin sharing files using the Direct Cable Connection, you must share a directory in which the files will be transferred. To set up sharing, see Chapter 21, "Sharing Windows 95 Peer-to-Peer Resources."

Using the Direct Cable Connection

When you want to begin using your mini-network connection, you need to start the Direct Cable Connection software on both the host and the guest computers. On the host, open the Start menu and choose Programs, Accessories, Direct Cable Connection. Windows 95 displays a dialog box similar to the one shown in figure 9.14.

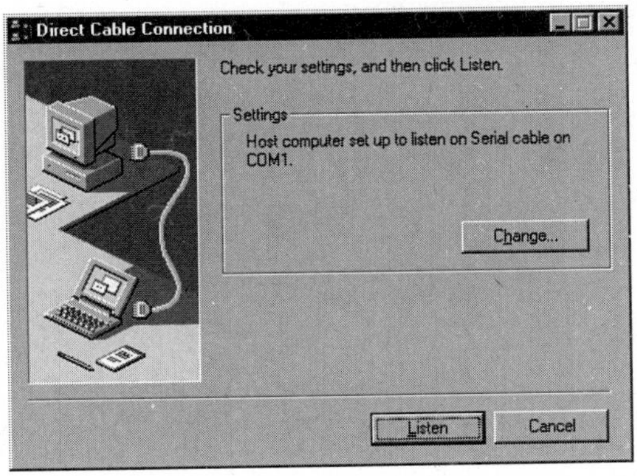

Fig. 9.14
Choose Listen to set up the host for the connection.

▶ See "Windows 95 Peer-to-Peer Networking Features," p. 618

▶ See "Understanding File Sharing," p. 643

If the settings you specified previously are correct, choose Listen to place the host computer in listen mode to listen for a connection by the guest. If you need to change the password or port settings, choose Change.

After placing the host computer in listen mode, start the Direct Cable Connection software on the guest computer. Open the Start menu and choose Programs, Accessories, Direct Cable Connection. Windows 95 displays a dialog box similar to the one shown figure 9.14, except the Listen button is replaced by a Connect button. Choose Connect to connect to the host and begin using the connection.

Using Power Management

Tip
In order for your PC to use power management, the PC's BIOS must include support for power management, and power management must be enabled in the PC's BIOS.

Most portable PCs (and an increasing number of desktop PCs) support some form of power management that allows the PC's devices to be shut down to conserve power while the computer remains on. Power management, for example, can power down the hard disk when the disk is not being used, conserving battery power. When the system is idle, power management can shut down the display and even the CPU to further conserve power. Windows 95 integrates power management into the operating system and adds features to the interface that enable you to easily take advantage of power management.

If your portable PC supports power management, and power management software (such as MS-DOS's POWER.EXE) is enabled when you install Windows 95, Setup adds support for power management automatically. If power management software was not enabled during Setup, you must enable power management yourself through the Control Panel. The following steps explain how to enable power management:

1. Open the Start menu and choose Settings, Control Panel.
2. Double-click the System icon.
3. Click the Device Manager tab and then double-click the System devices item to expand the System devices tree.
4. Select the Advanced Power Management support item and then choose Properties.
5. Click the Settings tab to display the Settings page shown in figure 9.15.

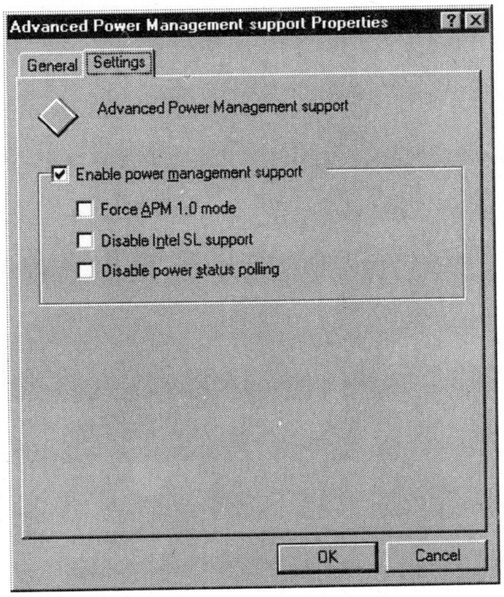

Fig. 9.15
Use the Settings page to control power management.

6. Place a check in the Enable Power Management Support check box and then choose OK.
7. Choose OK to close the System Properties sheet. Windows 95 prompts you to restart the computer for the change to take effect.

The other options on the Settings page control the way power management works. These options are explained in the following list:

- *Force APM 1.0 Mode.* Enable this option if your PC's power management features do not work properly. This option causes Windows 95 to use an APM 1.1 BIOS in 1.0 mode, which overcomes problems with some portable PCs.
- *Disable Intel SL Support.* If your computer uses the SL chipset and stops responding at startup, enable this option.
- *Disable Power Status Polling.* Enable this option if your PC shuts down unexpectedly while you are using it. This option prevents Windows 95 from calling the APM BIOS to check battery status, consequently also disabling the battery meter in the tray.

Setting Power Management Options

► See "Setting SL Options," p. 285

The Power object in the Control Panel enables you to specify options that control power management features. Selecting the Power object in the Control Panel displays the Power Properties sheet shown in figure 9.16. The large SL button appears on the Power page only if your PC uses an SL processor.

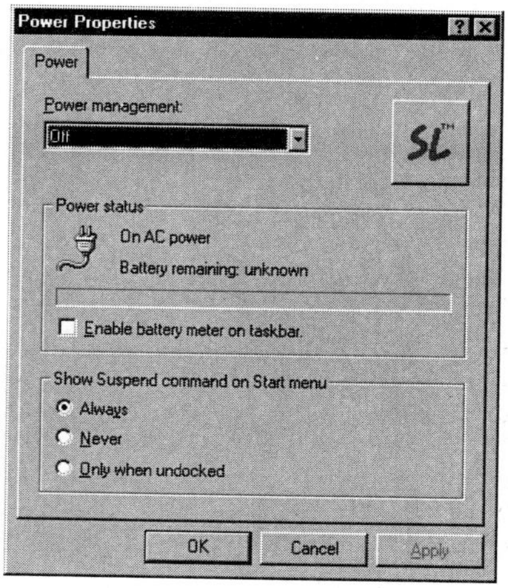

Fig. 9.16
Use the Power page to set power management options.

Tip
When you want to place the PC in suspend mode, open the Start menu and choose Suspend. Windows 95 will immediately place the PC in suspend mode. If you have files open across the network, you should first save or close the files before placing the PC in suspend mode to avoid losing data.

The Power Management list enables you to specify the level of power management your system uses. The options you can select are explained in the following list:

- *Standard.* Choose this setting to use only the power management features supported by your PC's BIOS. Additional features, such as battery status monitoring, are not enabled when you choose this feature.
- *Advanced.* Choose this setting to use full power management support, including features provided by Windows 95 in addition to those provided by your PC's BIOS. These include battery status monitoring and power status display on the tray.
- *Off.* Choose this setting to turn off power management.

Additional options on the Power property page control whether or not the Suspend command is displayed in the Start menu. Choose Always if you want the Suspend command always displayed on the Start menu. Choose Never if you do not want it to appear on the Start menu, even when the system is undocked. Choose Only when Undocked if you want the Suspend command to appear on the Start menu only when the PC is not connected to a docking station.

The Power property page also displays information about battery status and enables you to turn on or off the power status indicator on the taskbar. To view the amount of power remaining in your battery, rest the cursor on the power indicator on the taskbar for a second and Windows 95 will display a Tool Tip listing battery power remaining. Or, double-click the power indicator to display a Battery Meter dialog box similar to the one shown in figure 9.17.

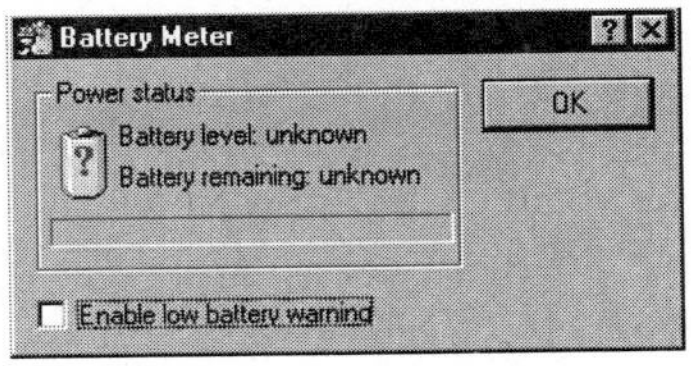

Fig. 9.17
The Battery Meter dialog box shows power remaining.

> **Note**
>
> As you can see in figure 9.17, Windows 95 cannot always detect the amount of power remaining in the battery. This is often due to the way in which the batteries used in portable PCs drain their charges. The voltage remains fairly steady through the battery's cycle, then begins to drop rapidly as the battery nears the end of its useful charge.

Setting SL Options

If your PC uses an Intel SL processor such as the 486SL, you can use SL-specific options to control additional power management features. As previously explained, an SL button appears on the Power property page on systems containing an SL processor. Choosing the SL button displays the SL Enhanced Options dialog box shown in figure 9.18.

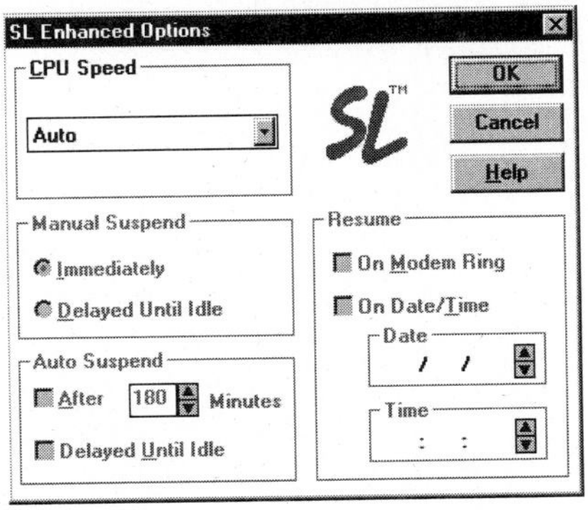

Fig. 9.18
The SL Enhanced Options dialog box controls SL-specific power options.

The following list explains the groups in the SL Enhanced Options dialog box:

- *CPU Speed.* This drop-down list enables you to control how the CPU is managed. Choose Auto to cause the CPU to run at full speed but power down whenever possible to conserve power. Choose 10 percent, 25 percent, or 50 percent to run the CPU at a specific reduced speed. Choose 100 percent to run the CPU at full speed and prevent the CPU from powering down.

- *Manual Suspend.* The two settings in this group control the way the system powers down when you press the Suspend button, close the display (on a notebook PC), or choose Suspend in the Start menu. Choose Immediately in the Manual Suspend group to cause the PC to suspend immediately when you press the PC's Suspend button or close the display. Windows will suspend all applications even if they are currently processing. Choose the Delayed Until Idle option to cause Windows to wait for all applications to finish processing before it powers down the PC. Some applications appear to Windows to be processing when they actually are just waiting for input, so the system might not enter suspend mode if such an application is running and the Delayed Until Idle option is selected.

- *Auto Suspend.* This option controls how the system powers down automatically after a specified period of time with no keyboard or mouse activity. The After option lets you specify an amount of time after which the system powers down automatically. The Delayed Until Idle option causes the system to power down automatically only if there are no active applications. These settings don't affect the screen, hard disk, or other devices individually. Instead, they control shutdown of the entire system, including the CPU.

- *Resume.* These settings control how the system resumes after it has been suspended. The On Modem Ring option, if enabled, causes the system to resume if a call comes in to a line that is connected to the PC's modem. The On Date/Time option enables you to specify a specific date and time at which the system will resume.

Using Dial-Up Networking

▶ See "Creating a Connection," p. 290

Windows for Workgroups includes a remote access client that enables you to dial into remote servers to access files and other network resources such as printers and e-mail. Windows 95 expands and improves on the remote access client in Windows for Workgroups, integrating remote access almost seamlessly within the Windows 95 interface. With the remote access features in Windows 95—collectively called *Dial-Up Networking*—you can connect to a remote computer to access its files and printer(s). If the remote computer is connected to a network and you have the necessary access rights on the remote LAN, dialing into the server is just like connecting locally to the network. You can use the shared resources of any computer on the network, send and receive e-mail, print, and perform essentially any task remotely that you can perform with a workstation connected directly to the network.

Note

A Windows NT server can act as a TCP/IP gateway, routing TCP/IP traffic for your dial-in PC. If your office network is connected to the Internet, for example, you can dial into a server to gain access to the Internet from home. To use this capability, you must install the TCP/IP network protocol and bind it to the dial-up adapter. The Windows NT server's Remote Access Server service must also be configured to allow TCP/IP dial-in and route TCP/IP traffic.

If you did not install Dial-Up Networking when you installed Windows 95, you must do so with the following procedure:

1. Open the Start menu and choose Settings, Control Panel, and then double-click the Add/Remove Programs icon; then choose the Windows Setup tab to display the Windows Setup dialog box.
2. Double-click the Communications item to display the Communications dialog box.
3. Place a check in the Dial-Up Networking check box, then choose OK. Choose OK again and Windows 95 installs Dial-Up Networking on your PC.

Before you can begin using Dial-Up Networking, you must install the dial-up adapter and network protocol required by the remote server. The next section explains how to set up Dial-Up Networking.

Setting Up Dial-Up Networking

Setting up Dial-Up Networking requires four steps: installing the dial-up adapter, installing the network protocol(s) used by the remote server, installing a network client, and installing an appropriate file and printer sharing service.

The dial-up adapter is a special driver supplied with Windows 95 that acts as a virtual network adapter, performing much the same function that a typical hardware network adapter performs. Instead of handling network traffic across a network cable, the dial-up adapter handles network traffic through your PC's modem.

To install the dial-up adapter, follow these steps:

1. Open the Control Panel and double-click the Network icon.
2. In the Configuration page of the Network property sheet, choose Add.
3. Choose Adapter from the Select Network Component Type dialog box, and then choose Add. Windows 95 displays the Select Network Adapters dialog box shown in figure 9.19.

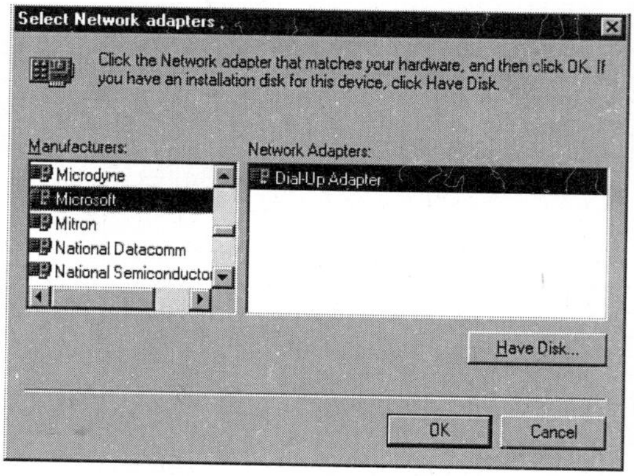

Fig. 9.19 You must install the dial-up adapter before you can use Dial-Up Networking.

4. From the Manufacturers list, choose Microsoft.
5. From the Network Adapters list, choose Dial-Up Adapter, then choose OK. Windows 95 will add the dial-up adapter to your system.

After you install the dial-up adapter, you must install at least one network protocol to be used for the dial-up connection. The protocol you select depends on the protocol used by the remote server. On Microsoft-based networks, the protocol used typically is NetBEUI. On NetWare-based networks, the protocol typically used is IPX/SPX. If you are connecting to a remote network that uses TCP/IP, you should install the TCP/IP protocol.

To install a protocol and bind it to the dial-up adapter, use the following procedure:

1. Open the Control Panel and double-click the Network icon.
2. From the Configuration page, choose the Add button.
3. Choose Protocol from the Select Network Component Type dialog box, then choose Add.
4. From the Manufacturers list, choose Microsoft.
5. From the Network Protocols list, choose the appropriate network protocol, then choose OK.

In addition to a network protocol, you also might need to install a network client. The network client enables your PC to access files and printers on the remote server and network. If you are connecting to a Microsoft network-based computer or network, you should install the Client for Microsoft Networks client. If you are connecting to a NetWare system, you should install the Client for NetWare Networks client.

Tip

If you are using TCP/IP to gain access to the Internet through a dial-up server, and do not want to have access to the remote server's files or shared resources on the LAN to which the server is connected, you do not need to install a network client.

To install a network client and bind it to the dial-up adapter, use the following procedure:

1. Open the Control Panel, double-click the Network icon, and then choose Add from the Configuration page.
2. From the Select Network Component Type dialog box, choose Client, then choose Add.
3. From the Manufacturer's list, choose Microsoft, choose the appropriate client from the Network Clients list, then choose OK.
4. In the Configuration property page, select Dial-Up Adapter from the list of installed network components, and then choose Properties. This displays the Dial-Up Adapter Properties sheet.
5. Choose the Bindings tab to display the Bindings property page shown in figure 9.20.

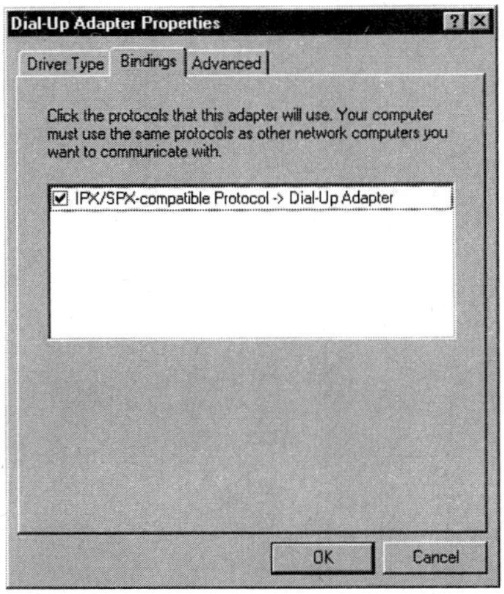

Fig. 9.20
Use the Bindings page to bind a network protocol to the dial-up adapter.

6. Place a check beside the network protocols you want to use with the dial-up adapter, then choose OK. Choose OK again to close the Network dialog box.

► See "Installing and Configuring Your Modem," p. 831

Your PC is now configured to act as a Dial-Up Networking client. Making a connection is explained in the next section.

Note

If you have not already installed your modem, do so before continuing. Your modem must be installed in order to use Dial-Up Networking.

Creating a Connection

To create a new Dial-Up Networking connection, first open My Computer, then choose the Dial-Up Networking folder. The Dial-Up Networking folder contains an object named Make New Connection that starts a wizard to help you create Dial-Up Networking connections. The following steps help you start the wizard and create a Dial-Up Networking connection:

1. Open the Dial-Up Networking folder and double-click the Make New Connection object. Windows 95 displays the Make New Connection wizard box shown in figure 9.21.

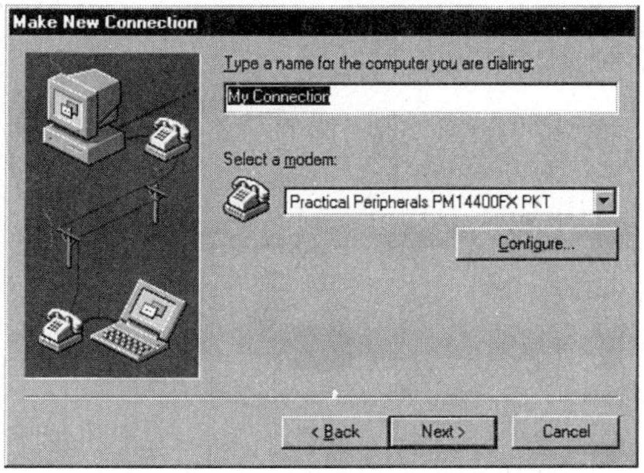

Fig. 9.21
The Make New Connection wizard helps you create Dial-Up Networking connections.

2. By default, the wizard names the connection "My Connection." Highlight the name and enter a name that describes the remote system to which you are connecting. This is the name that will appear under the connection's icon in the Dial-Up Networking folder.

3. Use the Select a Modem drop-down list to choose the modem you want to use for the Dial-Up Networking connection, and then choose Next. The dialog box changes as shown in figure 9.22.

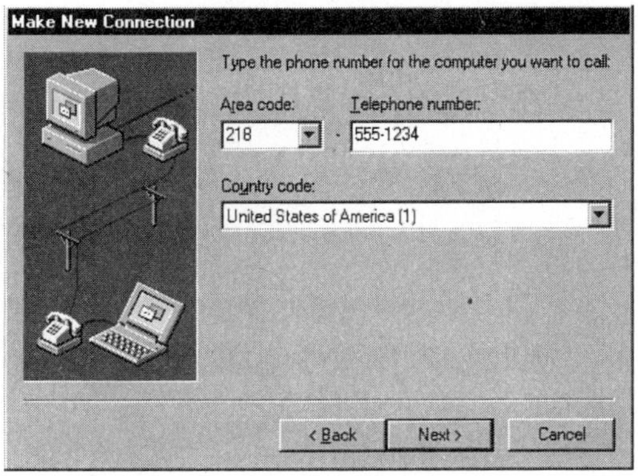

Fig. 9.22
Specify the phone number for the remote connection.

4. Enter the area code and telephone number in the appropriate text boxes.

5. Use the Country Code drop-down list to choose the country in which the remote system is located, and then choose Next.

6. Choose Finish to create the connection and add its icon to the Dial-Up Networking folder.

Connecting to a Remote System

Connecting to a remote system through a Dial-Up Networking connection is simple. Open the Dial-Up Networking folder, and then double-click the icon of the server to which you want to connect. Windows 95 displays a dialog box for the Dial-Up Networking connection similar to the one shown in figure 9.23.

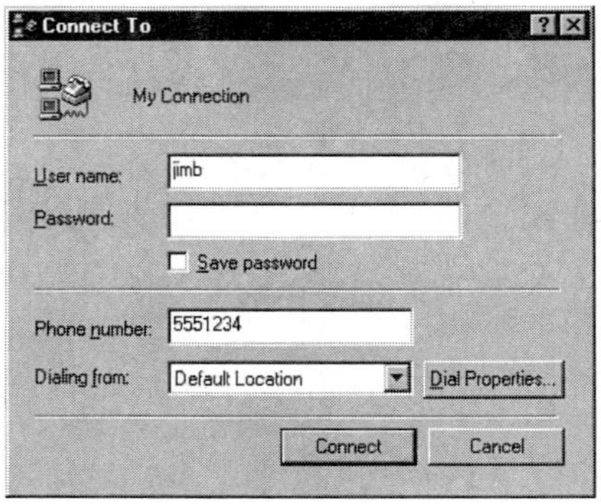

Fig. 9.23
You can verify and change settings prior to making the connection.

► See "Using Network Neighborhood to View Network Resources," p. 550

In the User Name and Password text boxes, enter the account name and password required by the remote server. If you want Windows 95 to save the password so you don't have to enter it each time you use the Dial-Up Networking connection, enable the Save password check box.

Next, verify that the phone number and dialing location specified in the connection are correct; then choose Connect. Dial-Up Networking dials the remote server and attempts to connect and log on using the name and password you have provided. After the connection is established, you can begin using the shared resources of the remote server and the shared resources of other computers on the remote network as if your PC were connected locally to the network.

Maintaining Laptop and Desktop Files with Briefcase

Many users of portable PCs also use a desktop system and often need to juggle files between the two systems. You might, for example, have a set of reports you are preparing with your desktop system and you need to move those files to your portable to work on them while you are out of town.

Windows 95 includes a feature called Briefcase that simplifies the task of synchronizing the files on your desktop and portable PCs, helping you keep track of which copy of the file(s) is most current.

The following is a simplified example of how you might use the Briefcase:

- You create a Briefcase (which appears as a typical folder) on your portable PC.
- You copy one or more files to the Briefcase using a direct cable connection to your desktop PC or through your docking station's network connection.
- You work on the documents contained in the Briefcase while you are away from the office, modifying and updating the files.
- While you are away from the office, a co-worker modifies one of the files on your desktop system that you copied to your Briefcase.
- When you return to the office, you reconnect your portable to your desktop PC, and then open the Briefcase on your portable.
- You use the Briefcase to update the files. The Briefcase informs you which files have been modified and enables you to easily copy the files from the Briefcase to their original locations on the desktop PC. The Briefcase also informs you that a file on your desktop PC (the file modified by your coworker), has changed, and gives you the option of updating your copy in the Briefcase.

The Briefcase also can detect when the original and Briefcase copies of a file have been changed. The Briefcase then prompts you to specify which copy of the file should be retained. The Briefcase also supports *reconciliation* of the two copies of the file. This means that if the document's source application supports reconciliation, the Briefcase uses OLE to communicate with the source application and merge the two files together, retaining the changes made in each copy of the file.

Note

Because the Briefcase is a new feature, few applications currently support reconciliation, but the number of applications that support it should grow as developers take advantage of this new feature.

► See "Synchronizing Files with a Floppy Disk," p. 296

You are not limited to creating a Briefcase on your portable PC. In fact, you can create a Briefcase on a floppy disk or your desktop PC. You might find a Briefcase useful for synchronizing files on which multiple users on the network collaborate. And, you are not limited to creating a single Briefcase—you can create as many as you like. For example, you might create a separate Briefcase for each project on which you are currently working.

> **Note**
>
> Placing a Briefcase on a floppy disk is useful if you do not have the necessary cable to connect your desktop and portable PCs using Direct Cable Connection, or your docking station is not connected to the network. Simply create the Briefcase, then move it to a floppy disk. Drag files from your desktop PC to the Briefcase, then move the Briefcase disk to your portable and begin working on the files.

Creating a Briefcase

If your PC does not already include a Briefcase on your desktop, you can easily create a new Briefcase. To create a Briefcase, follow these steps:

1. Decide where you want the Briefcase to be created (on the desktop, in a floppy disk folder, in a folder on the hard disk, etc.).

2. Right-click in the location in which you want the Briefcase created. If you want the Briefcase created on the desktop, for example, right-click the desktop.

3. From the pop-up menu, choose New, Briefcase. Windows 95 will create a Briefcase and add an icon for it in the location you have selected.

4. If you want to rename the Briefcase, click the Briefcase icon to select it, then click the Briefcase's description. Type a new description and press Enter.

As previously explained, you can create as many Briefcases as you like. By default, Windows 95 creates a Briefcase called My Briefcase on your desktop. You can rename the default Briefcase to suit your preferences.

Placing Files in the Briefcase

Although the Briefcase is a special type of folder, it behaves almost identically to a standard directory folder. You can move or copy files to a Briefcase in the same way you move or copy files to any folder. Simply open the folder in which the files are located, then drag them to the Briefcase. Hold down the Ctrl key while dragging to copy the files, or hold down the Shift key to move the files. If you prefer, you can open Explorer (open the Start menu and choose Programs, Windows Explorer) and drag the files from Explorer into the Briefcase.

In addition to using standard file copying and moving techniques to place files in the Briefcase, you also can use Send To. Locate the file(s) you want to place in the Briefcase, then right-click one of the files. From the pop-up menu, choose Send To, and then choose the Briefcase to which you want to send the selected file(s). Windows 95 will copy the file(s) in the Briefcase.

Tip

If you right-drag a document to the Briefcase, the pop-up menu includes an item labeled Make Sync Copy. Choose this option to create a copy of the object in the Briefcase.

Synchronizing Files

If you travel or work at home on your portable with files copied to your Briefcase from your desktop PC, Briefcase can keep your files updated. When your PC is undocked or you are working remotely, use your files as you normally would, opening and saving them in the Briefcase. When you return to the office desktop or remote network, first reconnect your portable to your desktop system or network, or insert the Briefcase floppy disk in your desktop PC. Then, simply open the Briefcase and choose Briefcase, Update All. Briefcase displays a dialog box similar to the one shown in figure 9.24.

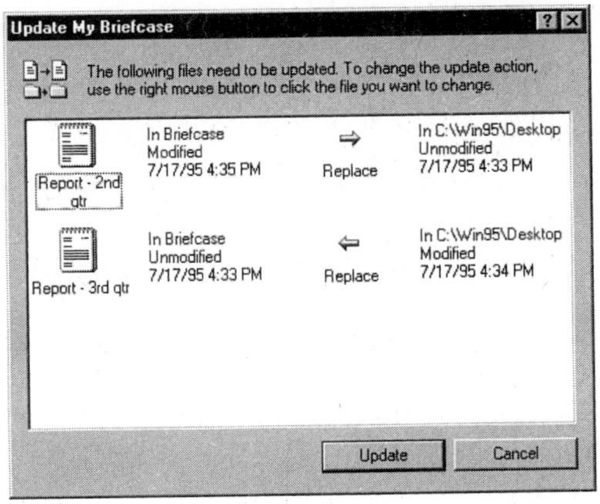

Fig. 9.24
Briefcase prompts you to specify how modified files should be handled.

The left column lists the name of the file, and the second column lists the status of the file in the Briefcase. The third column specifies the update action that occurs if you do not choose a different action. The fourth column indicates the status of the original copy of the file.

If the update actions listed for each file are appropriate, click Update to update the files. To change the update action for a file, right-click the file. Briefcase opens a dialog box as shown in figure 9.24. Choose the appropriate update action, and Briefcase changes the action for the file. When all of the files are set the way you want them, click Update.

Tip
To select a group of files in the Briefcase, hold down the Ctrl key and click on each file you want to update.

Note

If you update a file on a network server, you have no guarantee that another user won't modify the file after you have updated it, placing it once again out of sync with your Briefcase copy. If you again update the files in the Briefcase, however, the Briefcase will indicate that the original copy of the file located on the network server has changed.

If you prefer to only update a few of the files in the Briefcase, simply select the files you want to update, then choose Briefcase, Update Selection. Briefcase lists in the Update My Briefcase dialog box only those files you have selected.

After your selection of files is complete, choose Briefcase, Update Selection to update the selected files. You also can right-click a file in the Briefcase to open a dialog box, and then choose Update from the shortcut menu to update the selected file(s).

Synchronizing Files with a Floppy Disk

You can move a Briefcase to a floppy disk to simplify transferring files between your portable and desktop PCs. To move your Briefcase to a floppy disk, follow these steps:

1. If you do not yet have a Briefcase on the desktop PC, create one; right-click the Windows 95 desktop, and then choose New, Briefcase.

2. Open the My Computer folder and position the folder so you can see the Briefcase icon.

3. Open the folder containing the files you want to place in the Briefcase, then right-drag the files from their folder to the Briefcase icon. From the shortcut menu, choose Make Sync Copy.

4. Place a formatted disk in the desktop PC's floppy disk drive.

5. Right-drag the Briefcase from the desktop to the floppy drive icon in My Computer, and then choose Move Here.

6. Remove the floppy disk containing the Briefcase and insert it in the portable's floppy disk drive.

7. On the portable, work on the files in the Briefcase, opening and saving them in the Briefcase.

8. When you're ready to synchronize the files, place the floppy disk containing the Briefcase in the desktop PC's floppy disk drive. Open My Computer; then open the floppy disk folder. Right-drag the Briefcase from the disk folder to the desktop, then choose Move Here.

9. Open the Briefcase, and then synchronize the files as explained in the previous section.

Synchronizing Files with a Network

You can use a Briefcase to help you synchronize files on a network server on which you collaborate with other users. The process for working with the Briefcase and synchronizing files is the same as for a desktop PC/portable PC scenario. Create the Briefcase on your desktop, and then copy the files from the network server to the Briefcase. Edit the files in the Briefcase. When you're ready to synchronize them again with the original files on the server, open the Briefcase, and synchronize the files as previously explained.

Tip

If you want to check the status of all your Briefcase files, choose Briefcase, Update All. A status window pops up, enabling you to view the status of all files in the Briefcase. Choose Update to update the files, or Cancel to close the dialog box without making any changes.

Checking the Status of Briefcase Files

The update status of each file is listed in the Briefcase folder if you use Details to display the contents of the Briefcase as a detailed list. To configure the Briefcase to display a detailed list, choose View, Details.

You also can view the status of files in the Briefcase by selecting the files, then choosing Briefcase, Update Selection. You also can view the status of individual files in the same way. In addition, you can use a file's pop-up menu to view its status. With the Briefcase open, right-click the file or folder that you want to check. Choose Properties to display the file's property sheet, then choose the Update Status tab to display the Update Status page shown in figure 9.25.

Fig. 9.25
A file's property sheet shows its update status.

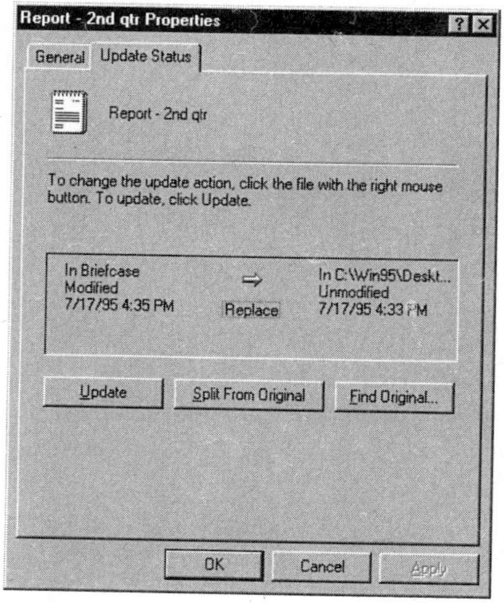

Splitting the Briefcase File from the Original Files

Occasionally, you might want to disassociate (called *splitting*) a file in the Briefcase from its original. Splitting a file removes the link between the two files. To split a file, first open the Briefcase and select the file you want to split. After selecting the file, choose Briefcase, Split From Original. After a file is split from an original, it is labeled an orphan and can no longer be updated.

LCD Screen Mouse Trails

Pointing device features are also enhanced with the mobile user in mind. Switching between integrated pointing devices—track ball or clip-on mouse—to a desktop mouse (Plug and Play-compatible) is now automatically detected and enabled by Windows 95. Installing a serial, Plug and Play mouse amounts to plugging it in, and the system enables its use.

Like Windows for Workgroups, Windows 95 also adds a few special features that make it easier to see the cursor on a passive-matrix LCD panel, which many portable PCs use for their displays (active-matrix panels have much better image quality, and consequently it is much easier to see the cursor on an active matrix LCD). The following sections explain these features.

Using Mouse Trails

When you move the cursor on a passive LCD display, the display typically cannot update fast enough to adequately display the pointer as it moves across the display. This makes it difficult to see the cursor. To alleviate the problem, you can turn on *mouse trails*. When mouse trails is enabled, a set of "ghost" pointers trail the pointer as it moves across the display. This makes it much easier to locate the cursor.

To enable mouse trails, open the Start menu and choose Settings, Control Panel. From the Control Panel, double-click the Mouse icon, and then click the Motion tab to display the Motion property page shown in figure 9.26.

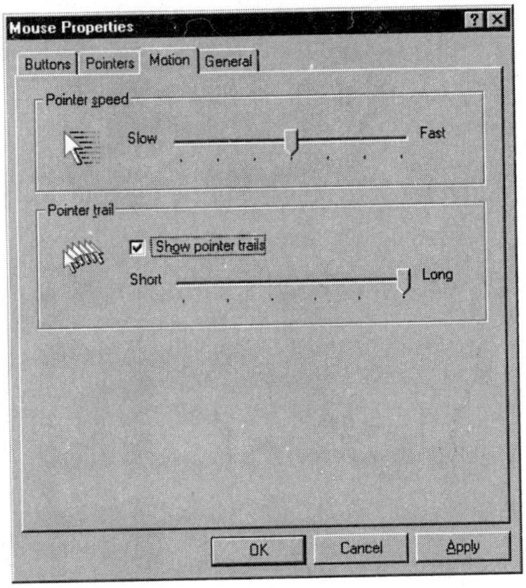

Fig. 9.26
Use the Show Pointer Trails check box to turn on mouse trails.

Place a check in the Show Pointer Trails check box to enable mouse trails. Use the accompanying slider control to specify the length of the mouse trail; then choose OK to apply the changes.

Using Large Pointers

In addition to using mouse trails, you also might want to increase the size of pointer you use on your portable to make it easier to see the pointer. Windows 95 enables you to create pointer schemes much like you create desktop color schemes, saving the pointer schemes by name. Windows 95 includes a small selection of predefined schemes, two of which use large pointers that are much easier to see on a passive LCD panel than the standard Windows 95 mouse pointers.

Note

If you did not install the optional pointers when you installed Windows 95, you must install them before you can use the large pointer schemes. To do so, open the Control Panel, then choose the Add/Remove Programs icon. Double-click Accessories, then scroll through the Accessories list to find the Mouse Pointers item. Place a check beside Mouse Pointers, then choose OK, and OK a second time to add the pointers to your system.

To use a large-pointer scheme, open the Control Panel and choose the Mouse icon, then choose the Pointers tab to display the Pointers property page (see fig. 9.27). From the Schemes drop-down list, choose either the Windows Standard (Large) or Windows Standard (Extra Large) scheme, then choose OK. Windows 95 immediately begins using the new pointers.

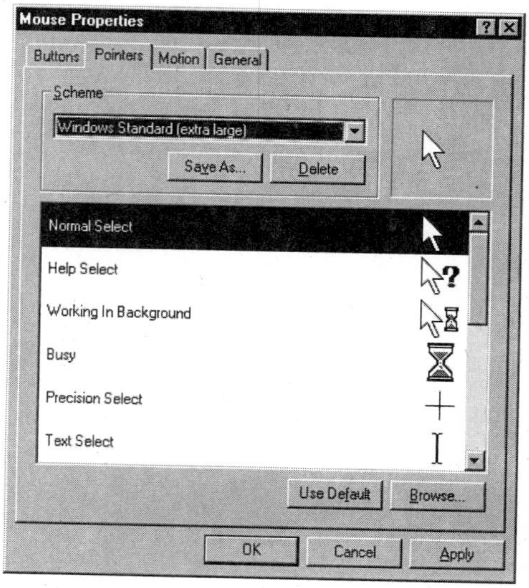

Fig. 9.27
Use the Pointers page to specify a pointer scheme.

Tip
To add a new scheme, customize as many pointers as you want; then click Save As on the Pointers property page to identify the new scheme.

In addition to using a predefined scheme, you also can create your own custom schemes. Display the Pointers property page as described earlier, then select the pointer you wish to change. Choose Browse, and Windows 95 displays a dialog box from which you can select a pointer file. When you select a pointer file, a sample of the pointer appears in the Preview box. When you have selected the pointer you want to use, choose Open to select the pointer and return to the Pointers page. Choose Save As to specify a name for your new pointer scheme.❖

Part III

Working with Applications

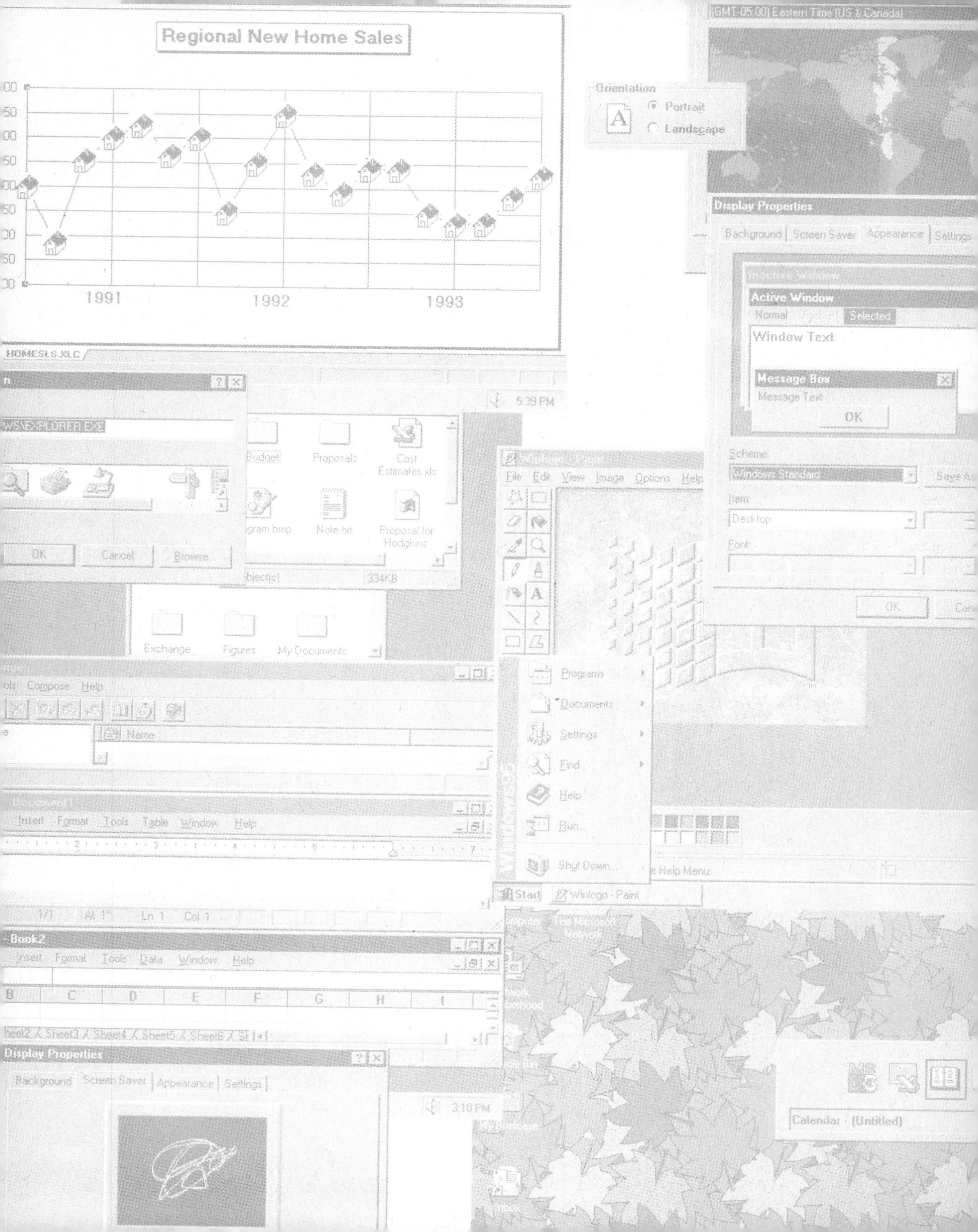

Regional New Home Sales
1991
1992
1993
HOMESLS.XLC
(GMT-05:00) Eastern Time (US & Canada)
Orientation
Portrait
Landscape
Display Properties
Background
Screen Saver
Appearance
Settings
Inactive Window
Active Window
Normal
Disabled
Selected
Window Text
Message Box
Message Text
OK
Scheme:
Windows Standard
Save As
Item:
Desktop
Font:
Cancel
5:39 PM
Budget
Proposals
Cost Estimates.xls
Note.txt
Proposal for Hodgkins
334KB
Browse...
Winlogo - Paint
File
Edit
View
Image
Options
Help
Exchange
Figures
My Documents
Compose
Name
Programs
Documents
Settings
Find
Run...
Shut Down...
Windows95
Start
Document1
Insert
Format
Tools
Table
Window
1/1
At 1"
Ln 1
Col 1
Book2
Data
The Microsoft Network
Sheet3
Sheet4
Sheet5
Sheet6
3:10 PM
My Briefcase
Inbox
Calendar - (Untitled)

Chapter 10

Installing, Running, and Uninstalling Windows Applications

by Michael O'Mara

An operating system provides the foundation for applications such as word processors, spreadsheets, and graphics programs. The applications don't come with the operating system; you must purchase and install your applications separately.

In the old days of DOS-based applications, installing a new program was fairly simple. Usually you just copied files into a directory on your hard disk. Efforts to integrate the application into your system seldom went beyond adding a couple of lines to your AUTOEXEC.BAT or CONFIG.SYS file. Each application stood alone with minimal interaction with the operating system and no interaction with other applications.

Now things have changed. Applications are bigger, more powerful, and much more complex. They've become so intertwined with the operating system that it's hard to tell where the dividing line is between Windows and an application. And nearly every Windows application has the potential to interact with any other Windows application on your system.

Not surprisingly, the process of installing and removing applications has grown more complex as well. Fortunately, as application installation grew more complicated, application developers turned to automated setup programs to handle most installation chores. And Windows 95 adds new features to further automate adding and removing applications.

In this chapter, you learn how to

- Install older 16-bit applications in Windows 95
- Install Windows 95 applications
- Add and remove Windows' component applications
- Uninstall applications

Not long ago, the typical PC user worked with only a couple of applications, and never used more than one program at a time. Now, multitasking is a way of life. The average Windows user probably works with a dozen applications regularly, several of which are likely to be open and running simultaneously. To juggle all those concurrent tasks effectively, you need to understand how Windows manages tasks behind the scenes.

Installing Applications in Windows 95

► See "Installing MS-DOS Applications," p. 345

To install any Windows application, you usually use a setup program or install utility. Installing DOS-based applications is a different matter (and the subject of Chapter 11, "Working with DOS Applications in Windows 95"). These setup programs for Windows applications take care of all the details of installing the application. You don't have to concern yourself with creating directories, copying files, and integrating the application into Windows. That's good, because installing sophisticated applications can be complex. A manual installation of a major software suite is beyond the capabilities of the average user, and a dreaded chore for even the most advanced user.

What Does Setup Do?

A typical setup or installation program begins by prompting you for some information and then installs the application automatically. The better setup programs provide feedback during installation to keep you informed of what it's doing to your system and the progress of the installation. Depending on the complexity of the application you are installing, the setup program might give you an opportunity to select various options and customize the installation. The program might limit your input to accepting or changing the path where you install the application, selecting whether to install various optional components, or specifying configuration settings for the new application.

After receiving your input, the setup program proceeds to perform some or all of the following steps automatically:

- Search for an existing copy of the application it's about to install and switch to upgrade mode if appropriate.
- Scan your system to determine whether your hard disk has enough room for the necessary files and perhaps check for the existence of special hardware or other system requirements.
- Create directories and copy files. Often, the setup program must expand files that are stored in a compressed form on the distribution disks.
- Create a shortcut that you can use to launch the application.
- Add a folder and/or shortcuts to your Start menu.
- Update Windows' configuration files.
- Update the Windows Registry.
- Register the application as an OLE server.
- Register the application's file types so Windows can recognize the file name extensions for the application's document and data files.
- Install fonts, support utilities, and so on.
- Configure or personalize the application.

What If There's No Setup Program?

A few Windows programs don't include a setup utility to install the application—the developer just didn't supply one. Such an application is probably a small utility program for which installation consists of copying a couple of files to your hard disk and perhaps adding a shortcut to your Start menu to launch the application. You'll probably find instructions for installing the application in an accompanying manual or README file.

The installation instructions may assume that you're installing the program in Windows 3.1, not Windows 95. (At least that's likely to be the case for a while after Microsoft releases Windows 95.) Fortunately, this isn't a serious problem. Most of the procedures for installing an application in Windows 3.1 work equally well in Windows 95. For instance, although Windows 95 supplies new tools for managing files, the underlying process of creating directories (folders) and copying files is the same in both versions of Windows. Also, for backward compatibility, Windows 95 includes full support for WIN.INI and SYSTEM.INI files, so any additions that you're instructed to make to those files should work as expected.

◀ See "Customizing the Start Menu," p. 128

▶ See "Registering Files to Automatically Open an Application," p. 539

There are two common manual installation procedures that you must adapt for Windows 95. First, if the Windows 3.1 installation instructions require that you create a file association in File Manager, you must substitute the Windows 95 equivalent of registering a file type. Second, instead of creating a program item in Program Manager, you add a program to the Start menu.

Using Windows 3.1 Applications in Windows 95

According to Microsoft, Windows 95 features full backward compatibility with 16-bit Windows 3.1 applications, and thus you can install and use your Windows 3.1 applications in Windows 95 without modification. And in fact, with only rare exceptions, Windows 3.1 applications do indeed run successfully in Windows 95.

Tip

After the release of Windows 95, technical support facilities will undoubtedly be swamped—especially for applications with compatibility problems. Avoid the logjam by checking online services such as CompuServe and America Online for program patches and information on workarounds.

If you encounter a compatibility problem with a *legacy application*—an older application designed for a previous version of DOS or Windows—running in Windows 95, check with the application's developer for a patch or workaround for the problem. In some cases, perhaps the only solution is an upgrade to a new, Windows 95 version of the application.

Installing Windows 3.1 Applications

You install Windows 3.1 applications in Windows 95 the same way that you do in Windows 3.1. You simply insert the first disk of the program's installation disks in your floppy disk or CD-ROM drives, run the Setup program, and follow the prompts and instructions.

The installation instructions for most Windows 3.1 applications direct you to use the Run command to start the setup program and begin installing the application. The instructions might mention that you can find the Run command on the File menu in either Program Manager or File Manager. However, in Windows 95, you find the Run command on the Start menu.

Note

You might prefer a different technique for launching the Setup program. Open the My Computer window and double-click the drive icon for the drive that contains the installation disk. Then locate the Setup program's icon and launch the program by double-clicking it.

When you use this technique, you need not type the command in the Run dialog box to start the Setup program. The technique also lets you scan the disk for README files before installing the application.

Tip
For a current list of programs with known incompatibility problems with Windows 95 and suggested fixes or work-arounds, read the file PROGRAMS.TXT in the Windows folder.

Of course, the Setup program for a legacy application will be tailored to Windows 3.1 instead of Windows 95. For example, the installation program will probably offer to create Program Manager groups (see fig. 10.1) and update INI files. Fortunately, you can just accept those options when the program offers them. Windows 95 will intercept Program Manager updates and automatically convert them to Start menu shortcuts. Windows 95 also transfers WIN.INI and SYSTEM.INI entries into the Registry.

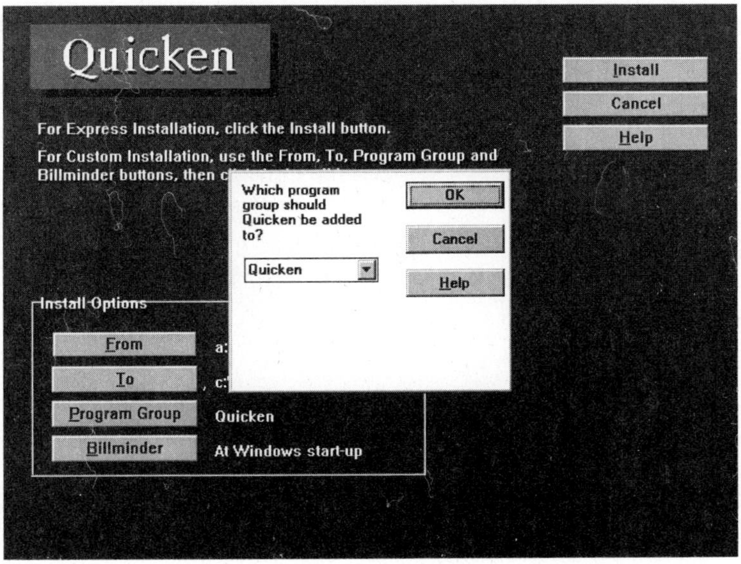

Fig. 10.1
Windows 95 translates some actions of a Windows 3.1 application's Setup program into their Windows 95 equivalent.

If you install Windows 95 as an upgrade to Windows 3.1, the Setup program should take care of such issues. The Windows 95 Setup program automatically transfers information about your existing applications to the Registry when you install Windows 95 onto your existing Windows 3.1 directory. As a result, you shouldn't have to reinstall applications.

Setting Up Existing Applications in a Dual Boot Configuration

If, however, you choose to create a dual-boot system by installing Windows 95 in a directory separate from Windows 3.1, Windows 95 won't know about

► See "Setting Up a Dual Boot System," p. 1105

any Windows 3.1 applications already on your disk. Just adding those applications to your Start menu isn't enough to let you run them successfully in Windows 95.

Caution

Before reinstalling a Windows 3.1 application in Windows 95, be sure to note the directory in which the application is currently installed. You must specify *exactly* the same directory when you reinstall the application. Otherwise, you might waste valuable disk space by having two copies of the same application on your system.

It isn't necessary to have a separate copy of an application on your hard disk in order to use it in Windows 95 as well as Windows 3.1. You can use the same application in both versions of Windows. However, most applications expect to find certain initialization and support files in the Windows directory. If you attempt to run the application from Windows 95, it expects to find those files in the Windows 95 directory. But if you installed the program under Windows 3.1, those files are in the Windows 3.1 directory, not in the Windows 95 directory. In some cases, if you copy the Windows 3.1 applications' initialization and support files to the Windows 95 directory, you can run the applications. But usually, you have to reinstall your Windows 3.1 applications in Windows 95 before you can use them. You'll certainly need to reinstall an application if it uses features such as OLE.

Troubleshooting

When I try to use the same application under both Windows 3.1 and Windows 95 on a dual-boot system, why does the application keep "forgetting" changes I make in the application's user preference settings?

If you change user settings in an application when running it under Windows 3.1, they may not be there when you run the application under Windows 95—and vice versa. Even though there's only one copy of the application on your hard disk, you may have two sets of the initialization files where user preference settings are stored; one each in the Windows 3.1 and Windows 95 directories. The application uses the settings from (and stores revised settings in) the initialization files it finds in the default Windows directory for the version of Windows you're running at the time. Unfortunately, there's no way to keep two sets of initialization files in sync automatically.

Running Windows 3.1 Applications

After installing a Windows 3.1 application in Windows 95, you can launch and run the application just like any other Windows application. Windows 95 changes the application's appearance automatically, giving it the new Windows look (see fig. 10.2). The application window's title bar will have the new format, complete with new style of Minimize, Maximize, and Close buttons, and most buttons and other window elements will take on the new three-dimensional look.

See "Starting and Quitting Windows," p. 50

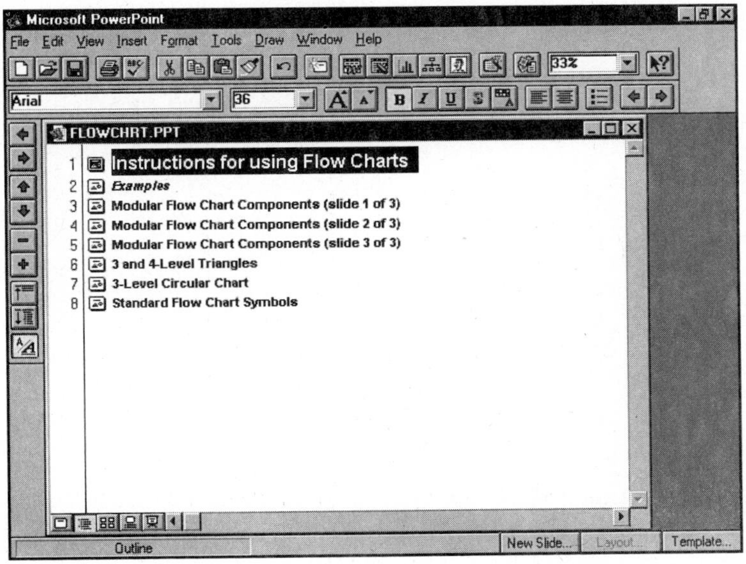

Fig. 10.2
Running a Windows 3.1 application in Windows 95 gives the program an automatic facelift. However, despite the change of appearance, the application performs the same as in Windows 3.1.

Beneath the superficial appearance changes, the application works the same as it did under Windows 3.1. The application might benefit from some Windows 95 performance improvements such as more efficient printing. However, to take maximum advantage of the features and capabilities of Windows 95's 32-bit operating system, you must upgrade to a new version of the application. In the meantime, you should be able to continue using your 16-bit Windows 3.1 applications effectively and efficiently.

Installing Windows 95 Applications in Windows 95

The basic technique for installing Windows 95 applications is essentially the same as installing other Windows applications. You just run Setup (or Install) and follow the prompts. The Setup program takes care of all the details of installing the application. However, the Run feature is located in the Start menu in Windows 95.

One new feature of Windows 95 is an optional way to start an application's Setup program: a new Install Programs Wizard accessible via the Add/Remove Programs icon in the Control Panel. The Add/Remove Programs dialog box provides a common starting point for adding and removing Windows applications and Windows system components and accessories.

When you're ready to run the Install Programs Wizard and use it to install a Windows application, follow these steps:

1. Open the Start menu and choose Settings, Control Panel. This opens the Control Panel window shown in figure 10.3.

> **Note**
>
> Depending on the applications you already have installed, your Control Panel folder may contain different icons.

Fig. 10.3
The Windows 95 Control Panel contains a new Wizard to make installing applications easier.

2. In the Control Panel window, double-click Add/Remove Programs to open the Add/Remove Programs Properties sheet shown in figure 10.4. By default, the Install/Uninstall tab should be active.
3. To start the Install Program Wizard, choose Install.
4. When the Install Program from Floppy Disk or CD-ROM dialog box appears (see fig. 10.5), insert the application's distribution disk (the first floppy disk or compact disk) in the appropriate drive and click Next.

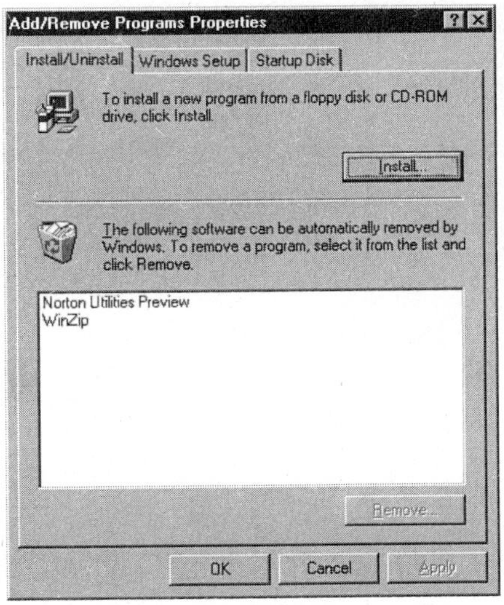

Fig. 10.4
The Add/Remove Programs Properties sheet is master control for adding and removing applications.

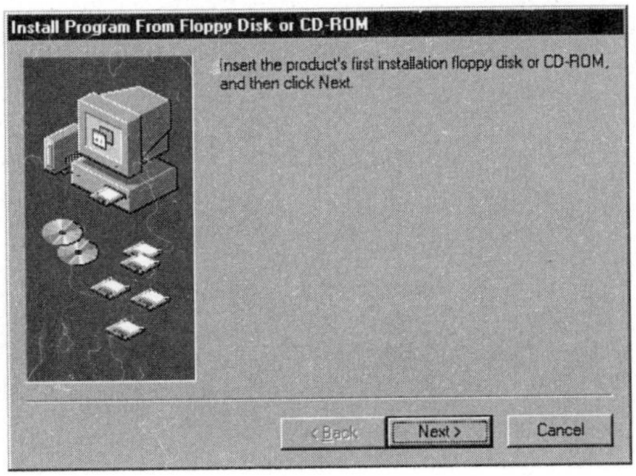

Fig. 10.5
The Install Program Wizard takes you through each installation step.

5. The Wizard searches the disk's root directory for an installation program (usually named SETUP.EXE or INSTALL.EXE) and displays the command line in the Run Installation Program dialog box (see fig. 10.6).

6. If the Wizard fails to find the setup program (perhaps because it is in a subdirectory or has a non-standard file name) or you want to run a different setup program (perhaps from a network drive), you can use Browse and select a different file in the Browse dialog box (see fig. 10.7). Choose Open to insert the selected file name in the Wizard.

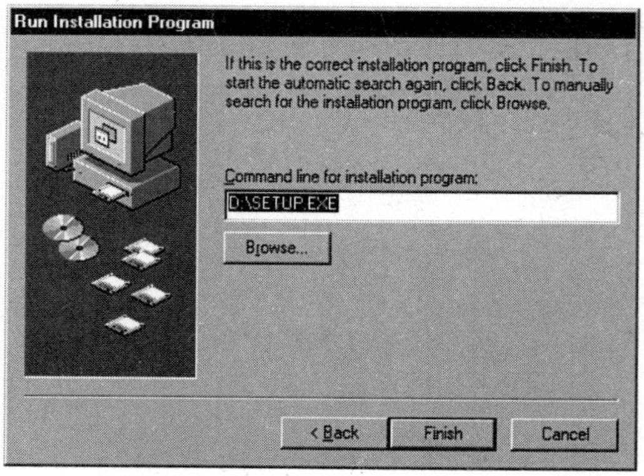

Fig. 10.6
Usually the Wizard finds the application's setup program on the disk.

7. After the correct command line for the Setup program appears in the Run Installation Program dialog box, click Finish to start the Setup program and begin the application installation.

The application's Setup program then proceeds to install the application. You'll probably need to respond to several prompts during the installation process. If the Setup program includes a Windows 95-compatible uninstall feature, the Wizard notes this and adds the new application to a list of programs that you can remove automatically. (The section "Removing Windows Applications," later in this chapter, discusses this new feature in more detail.)

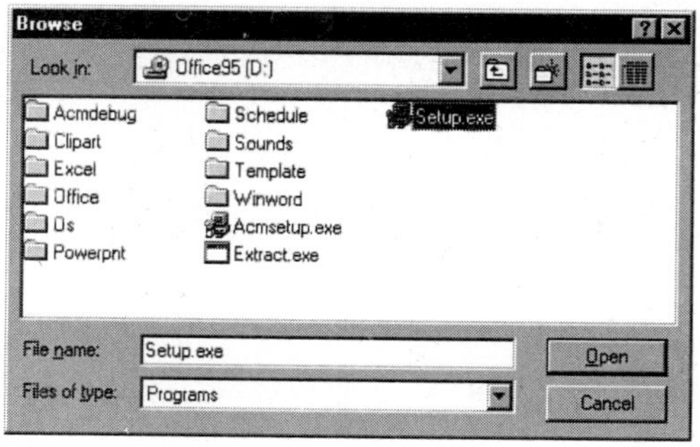

Fig. 10.7
If the Wizard needs help locating the Setup program, you can browse for the correct file.

Note

You also can use the Install Programs Wizard to install Windows 3.1 applications. However, using the Wizard for this purpose yields no significant advantage. Windows 3.1 Setup programs lack the special features that let you use the Add/Remove Programs control panel to remove the applications later.

Adding Windows Component Applications

The Add/Remove Programs icon in Control Panel lets you install and remove Windows components and accessories as well as applications. Therefore, you can reconfigure your copy of Windows 95 without reinstalling it. The feature is a more powerful version of the Windows 3.1 Setup utility.

Adding and Removing Windows Components

To use the Windows Setup feature to add or remove a Windows component, follow these steps:

1. Open the Start menu and choose Settings, Control Panel.
2. Open the Add/Remove Programs Properties sheet by double-clicking the Add/Remove Programs icon.
3. Click the Windows Setup tab to display a list of Windows components as shown in figure 10.8.

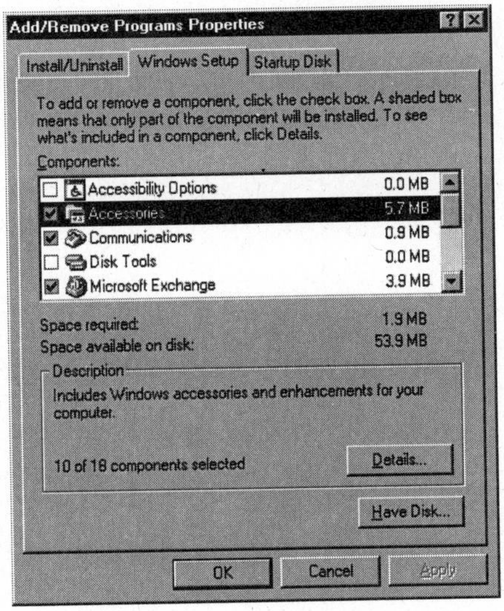

Fig. 10.8 The Windows Setup page of the Add/Remove Program Properties sheet lets you add and remove parts of Windows.

In the Components list box, a check mark next to an item indicates that the component is already installed on your system. If the check box is gray, the Windows component is composed of more than one sub-component and some (but not all) sub-components are currently installed. For instance, in figure 10.8, only some of the sub-components (accessories such as Calculator, Paint, and WordPad) of the Accessories component are installed. To see what's included in a component, choose Details.

4. Select a component in the Components list box. When you do, the Description box in the lower portion of the dialog box displays a description of that component.

5. If the component you selected consists of more than one sub-component, choose Details to open a dialog box listing the sub-components. (For example, figure 10.9 shows the Accessories dialog box listing the sub-components of the main Accessories component.) Sometimes in this dialog box, you can choose Details to narrow your selection further.

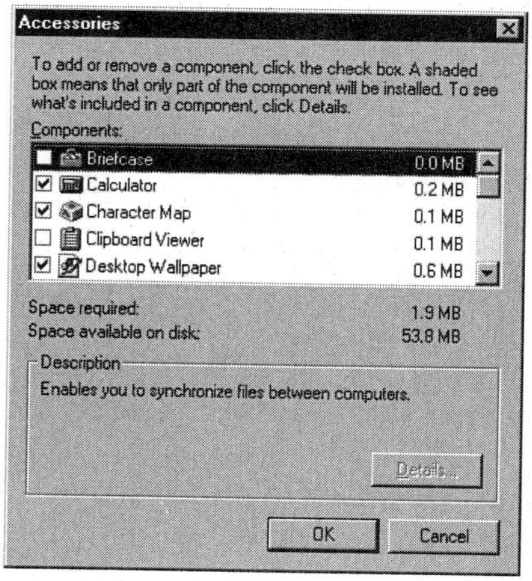

Fig. 10.9
The Accessories dialog box lists a component's parts. By choosing Details, you can narrow your selections.

6. Mark components for installation or removal by clicking the check box beside that item in the Components list. Adding a check mark to a previously blank check box marks that item for installation. Conversely, clearing a previously checked box instructs Windows to uninstall that component.

7. If you're selecting sub-components in a dialog box you opened by choosing Details, click OK to close that dialog box and return to the Add/Remove Programs Properties sheet.

8. When the check marks in the Components list specifies the components that you want composing your Windows system, choose Apply in the Add/Remove Programs Properties sheet. You'll need to supply the Windows Setup disks or CD when prompted.

Troubleshooting

When I use the Windows Setup feature to add new components, it adds those components, but it also removes other components. Why?

Windows Setup adds or removes components as necessary to make the list of components installed on your system match the list of components you checked in the Add/Remove Programs Properties sheet.

Contrary to what you might think, when you mark components in the list, you're not telling Windows Setup what items you want to *add* to your system. You're telling it you want to make sure the item is included in your Windows installation. Windows Setup will check your hard disk and add the component if it isn't already there. Similarly, clearing a checkbox doesn't mean you want to leave the item alone, it means you don't want that component installed on your system. If you clear a previously checked checkbox, Windows Setup will dutifully remove the component from your Windows system.

Installing Unlisted Components

Eventually, you might want to install a Windows component that doesn't appear on the Components list in the Windows Setup tab of the Add/Remove Program Properties sheet. For example, you might want to install one of the system-management utilities from the Windows 95 Resource Kit.

Tip
Alternatively, you can right-click the INF file in a folder window and choose Install from the shortcut menu.

To install a Windows component not listed in the Components list box, open the Add/Remove Program Properties sheet, click the Windows Setup tab, and choose the Have Disk button at bottom of the dialog box. This opens the Install From Disk dialog box (see fig. 10.10).

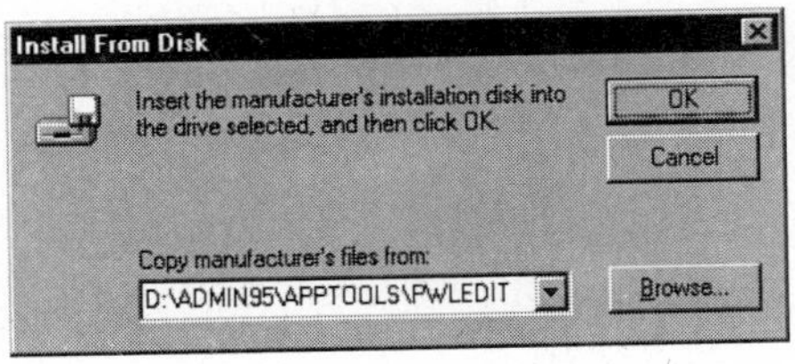

Fig. 10.10
When adding Windows components from a supplemental disk, you must supply the full path to the correct INF file.

In the Copy Manufacturer's Files From field, specify the path to the setup information file (INF) for the Windows component that you want to install. (The setup information file tells Windows Setup what is available to install and how to do it.) You can either type the path and file name or choose Browse and select the file in the Browse dialog box. After specifying the correct path, click OK. Windows opens the Have Disk dialog box (see fig. 10.11), which lists the components available for installation. Check the ones that you want to install, then choose Install. You might have to supply disks and browse for needed files when prompted.

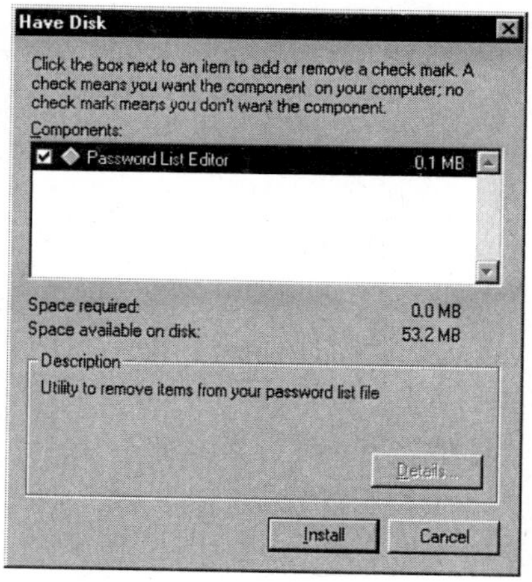

Fig. 10.11 The Have Disk dialog box lists the Windows components available on the supplemental disk, or at least the components described in the INF file that you selected.

Windows not only installs the component, but also adds the component to the Components list in the Windows Setup tab. Later, you can remove the component just like any other in the list.

► See "Installing MS-DOS Applications," p. 345

Installing components for DOS applications is different than the procedure used with Windows. In most cases, installing many of the major DOS applications requires suspending Windows 95 and switching to the "exclusive" DOS mode. This procedure is described in detail in Chapter 11, "Working with DOS Applications in Windows 95."

Running Applications

◄ See "Starting Applications from the Start Menu and Taskbar," p. 62

After you install your application's and Windows' accessories, Windows 95 gives you many options for launching them. You can use any of the methods to run any application. The technique that you choose depends on your personal preferences, working style, and what you're doing at the time.

◄ See "Starting Programs from a Shortcut Icon on the Desktop," p. 68

The various methods for launching applications are discussed in more detail in Chapter 3, "Getting Started with Windows 95," and Chapter 17, "Managing Your Files with Explorer." The following is a summary of the techniques:

- Choose the application's shortcut from the Start menu.
- Create and use a shortcut on the desktop.

- Right-click the application's icon in Windows Explorer or the My Computer window, then click Open in the context menu.

See "Compatibility with Windows 3.1 and DOS Programs," p. 19

- Double-click the application's icon in the My Computer window or Windows Explorer.
- Choose the Run command from the Start menu and then type the path and file name of the application's executable file.
- Choose the Run command from the Start menu, then drag an EXE file from My Computer or Network Neighborhood and drop the file into the Run dialog box.
- Use the Windows 3.1 Program Manager and run the application by double-clicking its program item.

Note

Windows 95 includes updated versions of both Program Manager and File Manager. The optional 3.1 interface will add applications to the Program Manager during installation. If you opt for the Windows 3.1 interface, you also can add program items to the Program Manager manually.

- Open a document or data file associated with the application. When you open a file, Windows launches the application automatically and then opens the file in that application. There are as many ways to open files as there are ways to launch applications. For instance, you can open files in Explorer, by choosing a recently used file from the Documents submenu on the Start menu, or by double-clicking a shortcut on your desktop.
- Finally, for a bizarre twist, try this method of launching a Windows application: you can open a MS-DOS window and type the command to start the application at the DOS prompt (or type **start** followed by the command). You would expect to get an error message saying the program requires Windows to run. But, instead, Windows 95 launches the Windows application for you.

Understanding How Windows Runs Applications

Windows 95 can run applications designed specifically for Windows 95. It also can run most older Windows 3.1 applications, DOS-based applications, and applications designed for Windows NT. Windows 95 no longer requires the traditional CONFIG.SYS, AUTOEXEC.BAT, and INI files for configuration information. However, for backward compatibility, Windows 95 can use settings from INI files and can maintain its own versions of CONFIG.SYS and AUTOEXEC.BAT in order to support loading real-mode device drivers.

Although Windows 95 can run various kinds of applications successfully, it provides different kinds of support for each category of application. Windows applications fall into one of two general categories: 32-bit applications (designed for Windows NT and Windows 95) and 16-bit applications (designed for Windows 3.1 and lower versions). This section describes how Windows 95 runs these programs. Chapter 11, "Working with DOS Applications in Windows 95," discusses DOS-based applications.

Support for Win32 applications

Windows 95 offers several significant advantages over Windows 3.1. Some advantages, such as preemptive multitasking and multithreading support, are available only to 32-bit applications.

► See "Working with Long File Names," p. 509

Support for long file names is one feature of Windows 95's 32-bit operating system that is available to any application designed to make use of it. Of course, all Windows 95 applications will let you create file names containing up to 255 characters, allowing you to assign files names such as "First Quarter Sales Results" instead of "1QSALES." Theoretically, program developers can adapt 16-bit applications to use long file names as well. However, don't expect many older Windows applications to add long file name support; the programmers are likely to concentrate on converting the application to full-fledged 32-bit status instead of spending time on minor upgrades.

◄ See "Managing Windows after an Application Failure," p. 78

Most applications benefit from Windows 95's 32-bit architecture, which makes memory addressing more efficient. In addition, Windows 95 runs each 32-bit application in its own memory space. Ordinarily, such details are of interest only to programmers. However, these advantages have a side-effect that all users will appreciate. If a 32-bit application hangs or crashes, the problem is isolated, confined to the application's own address space, and thus unlikely to affect other running applications. You can simply exit the problem application and, without even rebooting, have Windows 95 clean up the affected memory.

Advantages of Preemptive Multitasking and Multithreading

Despite appearances, our computers can't really perform multiple tasks from several different applications all at the same instant. Generally, computers perform only one or two tasks at a time, but they can do so very fast. Therefore, if the applications are designed to break operations into small tasks, the operating system can switch between tasks from several applications so quickly that it seems that all the applications and their processes are running simultaneously.

Programmers had to design Windows 3.1 applications to surrender control of the CPU voluntarily at various points of execution, enabling Windows to switch to another task. This scheme is called *cooperative multitasking*. However, some applications were more cooperative than others. If an application was reluctant to share CPU capacity with other applications, Windows 3.1 couldn't do much about it.

Preemptive multitasking, on the other hand, enables the Windows 95 operating system to take control away from one running task and pass it to another task, depending on the system's needs. The system doesn't have to wait for an application or process to surrender control of the CPU before another application can take its turn.

With preemptive multitasking, Windows 95 doesn't depend on the foresight of application programmers to ensure that an application performs multitasking successfully. Windows 95 has more power to arbitrate the demands of various running applications.

Multithreading enables an application to create and run separate concurrent *threads* or processes and thus handle different internal operations. Each process gets its own share of Windows 95's multitasking resources. For example, a word processing application might use one thread to handle keyboard input and display it on-screen. At the same time, a separate thread can run in the background to check spelling while another thread prints a document.

Some Windows 3.1 applications implement their own internal multithreading, with varying degrees of success. Now, Windows 95 makes multithreading an integral feature of the operating system, available to all 32-bit applications.

Increased System Resources

One of the most troubling limitations of Windows 3.1 is the restricted size of a special chunk of memory called System Resources. System Resources is where Windows stores things such as menus and other vital parts of the user interface for Windows and Windows applications.

Running a couple of elaborate applications in Windows 3.1 can nearly exhaust the available System Resources memory. You can't run another application if the System Resources doesn't have enough room for the application to load its user interface and other components. Consequently, the size of the System Resources became the principal factor limiting the number of applications that you can run simultaneously in Windows 3.1. Under Windows 3.1, you often run out of System Resources long before you begin to tax the limits of RAM or CPU power.

Note

In Windows 3.1, attempting to launch an application when there was insufficient system resources often resulted in `Not Enough Memory` errors even though there was ample RAM and disk memory available. In Windows 3.1, things like having lots of installed fonts, running in high resolution, and high color display modes would tax system resources. With 32-bit applications, you won't have this problem in Windows 95.

Windows 95 doesn't remove the limitation on System Resources completely, but the improvement is dramatic. The system limits on some kinds of programming information that Windows 3.1 severely restricted are now unlimited. Windows 95 still limits other kinds of programming information, but those limits are significantly higher than in Windows 3.1. As a result, you can run more applications, create more windows, use more fonts, and so on—all without running out of system resources. For instance, as I write this I have two very large, resource-hungry applications running, plus a communications program, a personal organizer, the Explorer, and CD Player. That's more than enough to exhaust system resources in Windows 3.1 and precipitate a flurry of error messages. But in Windows 95, I still have more than 80 percent of the available system resources free.

Support for Windows 3.1 Applications

Most Windows 3.1 applications run in Windows 95 without modification or special settings. Microsoft claims that 16-bit Windows applications run at least as well in Windows 95 as in Windows 3.1.

Windows 3.1 applications continue to use cooperative multitasking; they cannot use Windows 95's preemptive multitasking and multithreading. However, 16-bit applications can benefit from the advantages Windows 95 derives from 32-bit device drivers and improved printing throughput due to multitasking at the operating system level.

Windows 3.1 applications running in Windows 95 all run in the same virtual machine and share the same address space—just as they do when running in

Windows 3.1. As a result, they don't share the same crash protection as Windows 95 applications. If one 16-bit application hangs or crashes, it's likely to affect other 16-bit applications that are running at the same time. In other words, any application failure that would have required rebooting or restarting Windows 3.1 will require you to shut down all the 16-bit applications you're running. However, a failure of a 16-bit application should not affect 32-bit applications, and Windows 95 probably can clean up after an errant 16-bit application without requiring a reboot to recover System Resources and clear memory.

◄ See "Managing Windows after an Application Failure," p. 78

Note

Many times, you can avoid losing data in other open 16-bit applications by pressing the familiar Ctrl+Alt+Del and choosing the offending application from the Close Program dialog box. Quite often, Windows shuts down the errant program and leaves your other 16-bit applications running as normal.

Removing Windows Applications

Installing a Windows application can be a complicated venture. Windows applications are often tightly integrated with the operating system. Installing such applications not only requires copying the application's files into the application's own directory, but also adds numerous support files to your Windows directory and changes Windows' settings. Fortunately, nearly all applications provide Setup programs to automate the installation process.

Removing an application can be similarly complicated. Finding all the support files and settings added or changed during the application's installation can be nearly impossible. Fortunately, many application Setup programs now offer an uninstall option to automate the process when you need to remove the application from your system.

Windows 95 takes this welcome trend a step further by adding a facility to remove applications. That facility is in the same Control Panel dialog box that you use to install applications and Windows components.

Removing Applications Automatically

Windows 95's Add/Remove Programs Wizard adds to the capability of individual setup programs by tracking an application's components in the Registry. This lets Windows delete an application's files and settings but still identify and retain any files that another application might share and use.

Note

Only applications that provide uninstall programs specifically designed to work with Windows 95 appear in the list of applications that Windows 95 can remove automatically.

To uninstall an application automatically, start by opening the Control Panel and double-clicking the Add/Remove Programs icon. This opens the Add/Remove Programs Properties sheet—the same sheet you used to install the application (see fig. 10.12).

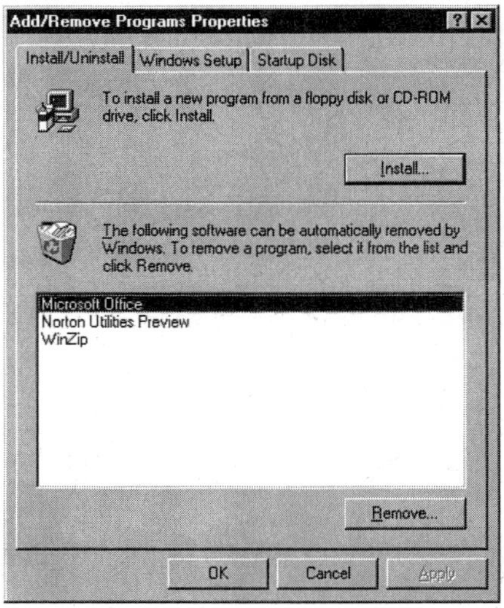

Fig. 10.12 In the Add/Remove Programs Properties sheet, you can remove applications as well as install them.

The lower portion of the sheet lists applications that you can remove. To remove an application, select it from the list and choose Remove. After you confirm that you want to remove the program, Windows runs the selected application's uninstall program.

Tip
If you find support files in your Windows directory that you think are unnecessary, copy them to a separate folder before you remove them. If you don't encounter any problems after a few months, you can delete that folder.

Removing Applications Manually

If you want to remove an application from your system, just hope that it's one that Windows can remove automatically. Removing an application manually can be difficult, and possibly dangerous.

Remove Files from the Application Directory

Getting rid of the files in an application's own directory is fairly straightforward. In fact, that should probably be the first step in removing an application manually.

Many applications install support files in the Windows directories. It's nearly impossible to tell what application added which files, and to make matters worse, several applications can share the same files. If you ignore the files in the Windows directories when you remove an application, you can leave numerous orphaned files on your system needlessly consuming hard disk space. However, if you make a mistake and delete the wrong file or one that another application also uses, you might render the other application unusable.

Remove Shortcuts and Folders from the Start Menu

After you remove an application's files from your hard disk, you want to get rid of any shortcuts that pointed to the application. To delete a shortcut icon from your desktop, simply drag and drop the shortcut onto the Recycle Bin icon on your desktop. The Recycle Bin is like a trash can that stores deleted files until the Bin reaches a certain capacity.

◀ See "Understanding the Most Important Screen Elements in Windows 95," p. 36

To remove the application from the Start menu, open the Start menu and choose Settings, Taskbar. Then, in the Taskbar Properties sheet, click the Start Menu Programs page. Next, choose Remove to open the Remove Shortcuts/Folders dialog box (see fig. 10.13). You also can right-click the Start button and choose Explore from the shortcut menu.

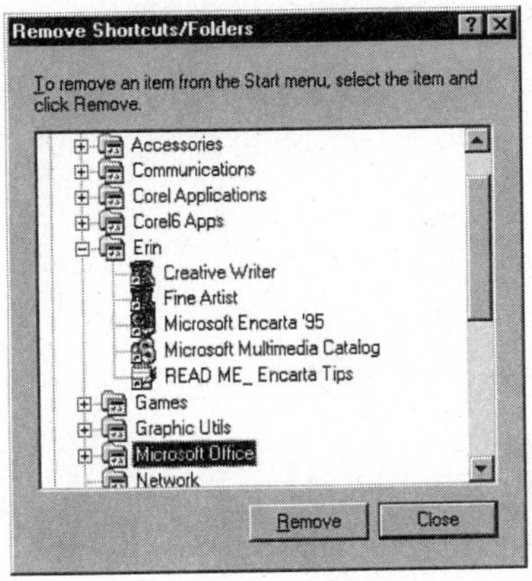

Fig. 10.13
After removing an application, you open the Remove Shortcuts/Folders dialog box to remove the application's folder and shortcuts from your Start menu.

The Remove Shortcuts/Folders dialog box, like the Explorer, displays a hierarchical list of folders and files. To expand the display and show a folder's contents, you can click the plus sign beside the folder. Select the folder or shortcut that you want to delete, then choose Remove. To remove other items, repeat the process as necessary. When you finish removing items, click Close.

▶ See "Managing Your Files and Folders," p. 513

Remove File Associations

After you remove an application, you can remove any associations that might have existed between file extensions and the defunct application. After all, you don't want Windows to try to launch the nonexistent application when you double-click a document file.

To remove the link between a file extension and an application, start by opening the My Computer window. Next, choose View, Options to open the Options dialog box, then click the File Types tab. You then see the screen shown in figure 10.14. Scroll down the Registered File Types list and select the file type that you want to delete, then choose Remove. Windows asks you to confirm your choice. If you answer Yes, Windows abolishes the registration of that file type.

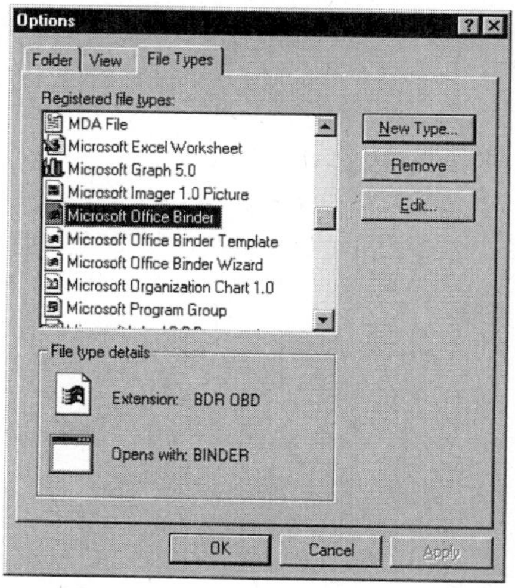

Fig. 10.14
Using the Options dialog box to remove a file type registration is easier and safer than editing the Registry directly.

> **Caution**
>
> Third-party utility programs designed to remove applications from Windows 3.1 probably won't work in Windows 95 because they won't be able to cope with the Registry and other changes. You should check with the company's support staff before using third-party utility programs to see if they work in Windows 95.

Chapter 11

Working with DOS Applications in Windows 95

by Dick Cravens

Although Windows 95 is designed from the ground up to shield the user from the often-confusing world of the command line, AUTOEXEC.BAT, CONFIG.SYS, and the arcane voodoo of memory-management practices, it offers surprisingly rich support for those users who still desire or need to work in the MS-DOS environment. If you have a favorite MS-DOS application, utility, or game, there's absolutely no need to give it up or suffer performance loss. In fact, Windows 95 offers greatly enhanced MS-DOS support compared to earlier versions.

None of this comes without a small price: you must learn a few new concepts and controls to master Windows 95 MS-DOS operations. If you're used to adjusting PIF files, you'll be applying some of that knowledge to Windows 95 Properties management, and learning some new tricks as well. The reward is far greater control over MS-DOS application environments under Windows 95 than under previous versions.

If you're currently using another brand of DOS other than Microsoft MS-DOS, have no fear—Windows 95 MS-DOS support is so compatible and configurable, you can easily adjust for any minor variations between DOS versions from other vendors such as IBM's PC-DOS, or Novell/Digital Research DR-DOS.

In this chapter, you learn:

- What's new in MS-DOS for Windows 95
- How Windows 95 works with MS-DOS applications
- Optimizing Windows 95 MS-DOS Graphics mode support
- Installing, configuring, and uninstalling MS-DOS applications
- Starting and running MS-DOS programs

Understanding How Windows 95 Works with MS-DOS Applications

Just as Windows 3.1 improved drastically on version 3.0 support for MS-DOS applications, Windows 95 improves on its predecessor. Applications that simply would not run under earlier versions of the Windows MS-DOS prompt now perform admirably. For applications that still won't run under the new Windows, a special mode helps you run them quickly and easily from within Windows, and then automatically return to your Windows session when you're finished.

The following are some of the improvements in MS-DOS support Windows now offers to users:

- Better local reboot support
- Zero conventional memory usage for Protected-mode components
- Consolidated setup for MS-DOS-based applications
- Toolbar support for windowed MS-DOS applications
- Graceful shutdown for windowed MS-DOS sessions
- Long file name support, with full backwards compatibility for "8.3" format file names
- Execution of Windows programs from the MS-DOS session
- The capability to open documents from the command line

- Better control over MS-DOS window fonts
- User-scalable MS-DOS session windows
- Improved Cut/Paste/Copy commands for integrating MS-DOS and Windows application information
- Universal Naming Convention (UNC) path name support
- Spooling of MS-DOS-based print jobs

Windows 95 makes dealing with MS-DOS/Windows integration quicker and easier than ever, and makes working with MS-DOS applications very close to working on a machine running only MS-DOS. In addition, MS-DOS emulation under Windows 95 gives the user many of the other benefits of Windows 95: the graphical user interface, multitasking, and networking support.

Gone are the confusing variations and limitations of Real, Standard, and Enhanced-mode MS-DOS. Chances are, you'll never have to make an adjustment to Windows MS-DOS support; but if you do, you'll find the controls vastly simplified, well consolidated, and more reliable than ever.

Note

An added bonus of the overall design of Windows 95 is the greater conservation of conventional memory (that below the 640K mark). By loading eligible device drivers and TSR (terminate-and-stay-resident) programs in Protected mode, above the first-megabyte mark in memory, Windows frees more working memory for MS-DOS applications than any previous version.

Some MS-DOS applications simply couldn't run under Windows 3.1. By the time mouse, network, SCSI, and other necessary drivers were loaded, there simply wasn't enough RAM below 640K. Windows 95 alleviates this situation by checking each driver specified in your installation against a "safe list" of known drivers, and loading approved ones in extended memory, or substituting equivalent drivers.

For example, if your PC is on a NetWare network, uses a SCSI CD-ROM drive, the SMARTDrive disk cache, DriveSpace disk compression, and an MS-DOS mouse driver, you can save more than 250K in conventional memory using the MS-DOS system in Windows 95.

Caution

Just as with earlier versions of Windows, don't run anything in a Windows MS-DOS session that alters the File Allocation Table, or other system-critical files. Examples of this type of software are MS-DOS disk defragmentors and unerase or undelete utilities. Windows now comes with many of these utilities, so use the Windows versions instead (don't just boot to MS-DOS to use your older utilities; some of them will corrupt the Windows 95 long file name system).

Starting the MS-DOS Prompt Session

Getting started with MS-DOS under Windows is as simple as selecting a menu item. To begin a session, follow these steps:

1. Open the Start menu and choose Programs. Windows displays a continuation menu, as shown in figure 11.1.

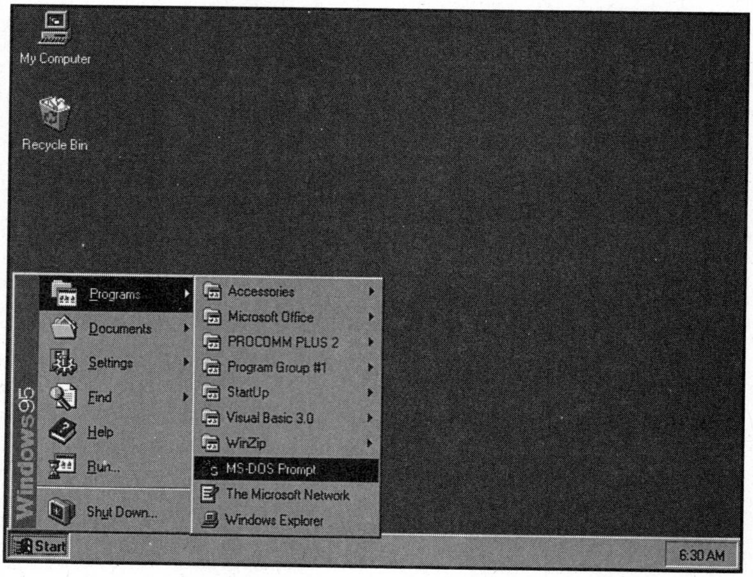

Fig. 11.1
It's simply a matter of two mouse clicks to start MS-DOS.

2. Choose the MS-DOS Prompt menu item. Windows opens the MS-DOS Prompt window, as shown in figure 11.2.

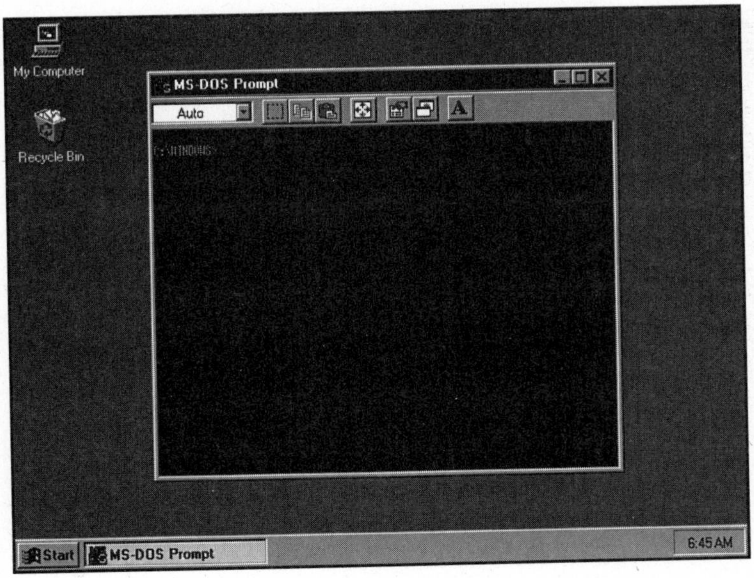

Fig. 11.2
The MS-DOS Prompt window awaits your every command.

Ending MS-DOS Prompt Sessions

Now that you've started an MS-DOS Prompt session, practice closing it before you move on to the finer points of operation. To close the MS-DOS Prompt window, follow these steps:

1. Click in the MS-DOS Prompt window to bring it to the foreground.
2. Find the flashing cursor near the MS-DOS command prompt. At the flashing cursor near the MS-DOS command prompt, type **exit**.
3. Press Enter, and Windows closes the MS-DOS Prompt session window.

Tip
Don't leave MS-DOS Prompt sessions open any longer than you need to. Every session takes a big chunk out of available CPU time, slowing down your entire Windows performance in all applications.

Note

As with most other procedures under Windows, several other ways to close an MS-DOS Prompt session are available. As alternatives, try each of the following:

- Double-click the MS-DOS icon in the upper-left corner of the MS-DOS Prompt session window.
- Click the MS-DOS icon; then choose Close from the menu.
- Click the Close icon in the upper-right corner of the MS-DOS Prompt window.
- Right-click anywhere in the MS-DOS Prompt window title bar. Windows displays a menu, from which you can choose Close.

Ending Sessions with Running Applications

Windows also allows you to close sessions that have applications open; but by default, it warns you if the application is running or has open files.

Besides giving you options for more gracefully ending a session, Windows 95 improves on previous versions by performing better session "cleanup," releasing memory and deallocating system resources much more consistently.

To close an active session, simply follow the same procedures that you tried earlier to close a session with just an MS-DOS prompt. This time, however, Windows displays the warning dialog box shown in figure 11.3.

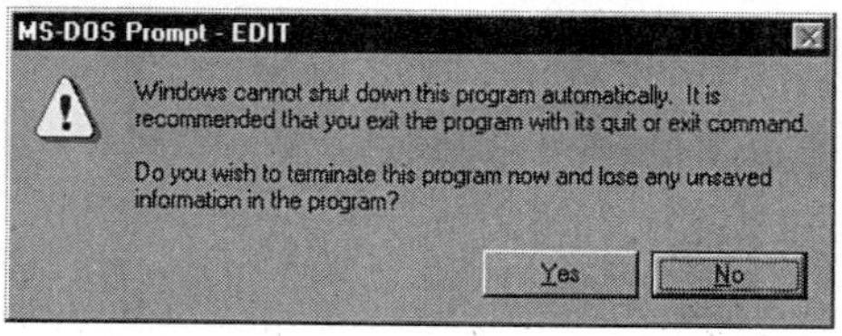

Fig. 11.3
Windows warns you if you try to exit an MS-DOS session while an application is active.

If you choose No, Windows returns you to the MS-DOS Prompt session, and you can exit the program before you close the MS-DOS session.

Otherwise, choose Yes and Windows shuts down the MS-DOS session and terminates the running application. It's not recommended that you close sessions this way, but you can do it in an emergency (for example, if the application is hung and simply won't *let* you exit gracefully).

Troubleshooting

My MS-DOS application simply won't respond, and none of the close procedures you list are working. What can I do to shut down this bad apple and get back to work? Will I lose all my data in other applications?

One great addition to Windows 3.1 was the capability to *local reboot,* or close crashed applications without closing all of Windows. Windows 95 extends this capability with even greater control over shutting down errant applications.

The method used is the same as under Windows 3.1: use the classic "three-fingered salute," Ctrl+Alt+Del, after which Windows 95 displays the Close Program dialog box, instead of the classic Windows 3.1 "Blue Screen of Impending Doom." Windows 95, however, does a much better job of recovering from application failure, because it gives you a choice of which task to shut down, instead of assuming the one in the foreground is the culprit. After you select the application task to deal with, you have the choice of ending the errant task, shutting down the entire computer, rebooting using Ctrl+Alt+Del again, or canceling.

You learn a way to override the Windows warnings about closing an active MS-DOS Prompt session later in this chapter—see the section "Miscellaneous Properties."

► See "Miscellaneous Properties," p. 353

Controlling the MS-DOS Prompt Session

Now that you know how to get in and out of the car, start the engine, and shut it down, you're ready to get behind the wheel and take her for a spin! Windows 95 offers many great options to dress up the classic MS-DOS session.

Using the MS-DOS Prompt Toolbar

Windows MS-DOS sessions now have a variety of interface controls. The toolbar will be familiar to you if you've been using the Windows Explorer.

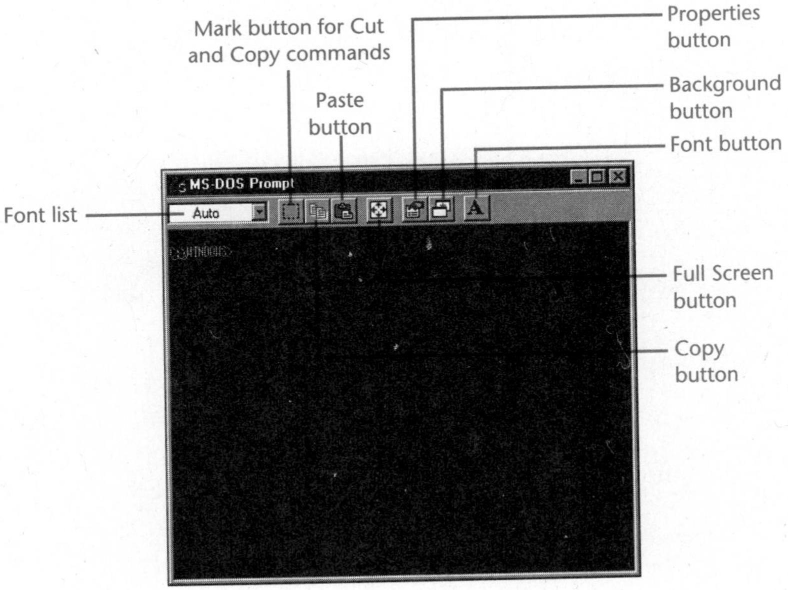

Fig. 11.4
The MS-DOS Prompt toolbar offers tools for quickly controlling the session interface.

Figure 11.4 shows the MS-DOS Prompt toolbar and its controls.

Controlling the MS-DOS Prompt Interface

Although Windows 3.1 offered a choice of fonts for windowed MS-DOS sessions, that choice was limited to bitmapped fonts that restricted the sizing options for the window. It was workable, but it offered nothing like the flexibility available in Windows 95 MS-DOS support.

Windows now offers TrueType scalable fonts in addition to the familiar system fonts, allowing on-the-fly resizing of the entire session window. To try the new font features, open an MS-DOS session and perform the following steps:

1. Click on the toolbar's Font list; then choose TT7 X 14 (the TrueType font for TT7 X 14 resolution). The window should now appear as shown in figure 11.5 (assuming that you're using 640 X 480 standard VGA display resolution).

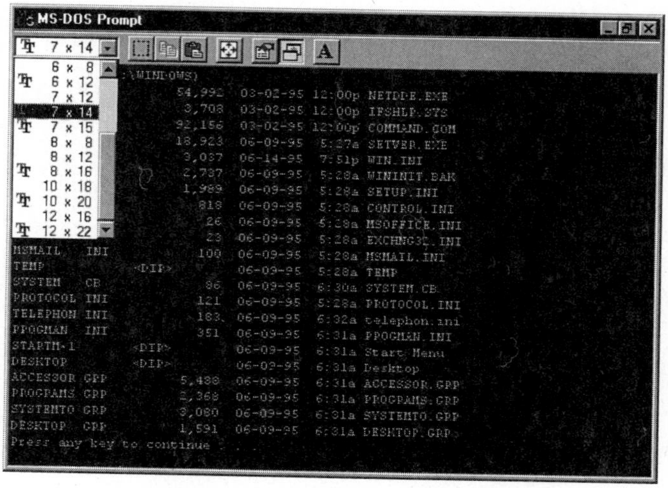

Fig. 11.5
You can use the toolbar to control TrueType fonts in your MS-DOS Prompt session.

2. Grab the window borders in the bottom-right corner and resize the window. Note that the vertical and horizontal window scroll bar controls appear on the window, but the text in the window remains the same, as shown in figure 11.6.

3. Repeat the procedure in the preceding step 1 to select the 4 X 6 font mode. Notice that the text in the window is much smaller, and the window has shrunk to match (see fig. 11.7). Grab the window borders again and try to enlarge the window; note how it is limited to a maximum size.

4. Repeat the procedure in the preceding step 1 to select Auto mode. The window does not change.

Tip
Windows 3.*x* veterans know one of the most basic and useful control tools for MS-DOS sessions: the Alt+Enter key sequence. This great shortcut changes the MS-DOS session from full-screen to windowed and back again, in a flash.

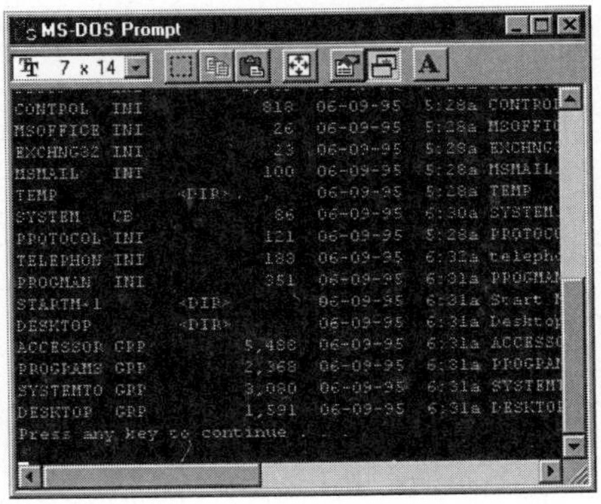

Fig. 11.6
Windows now supports dynamic resizing of the MS-DOS Prompt window. You can access any hidden areas of the session using standard scroll bar controls.

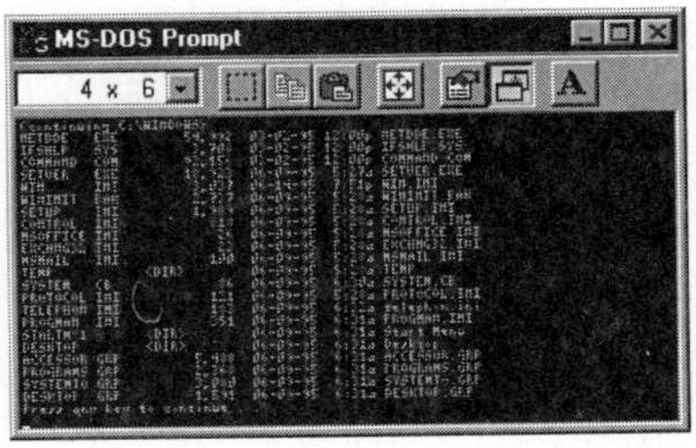

Fig. 11.7
If you choose a font that allows full viewing of the MS-DOS Prompt session, Windows won't let you resize the window larger than the session.

5. Grab the window borders and pull the window to a larger size. Note how Windows alters the font on the fly. When you change the window size again (try a square, or a vertical rectangle), the font adjusts automatically to the nearest available size.

Using the Windows Clipboard with the MS-DOS Prompt

Windows now offers even easier access to the data in your MS-DOS session, via the toolbar. Copying information from your session into a Windows application is quick and easy. Follow these steps to try it out:

1. Using the mouse, click on the Mark tool and highlight text in your MS-DOS application.
2. Click the Copy tool on the MS-DOS Prompt toolbar. Windows places a copy of the text in the Clipboard.
3. Using the mouse, click on your Windows application (for example, NotePad) to make it active. Position the cursor where you want to insert the text; then choose Edit, Paste from the NotePad menu. NotePad displays the text copied from your MS-DOS session window.

Troubleshooting

I used to be able to use the mouse to highlight text in an MS-DOS session, and then press Enter to copy the text to the Clipboard, but now it doesn't work.

This still works under Windows 95; it simply isn't enabled by default. You can use the mouse to highlight and copy text if the application you're running supports it (for example, EDIT); but the MS-DOS prompt itself won't (for example, you can't mark and copy the results of the `dir` command that MS-DOS writes to your window). If you use the toolbar on your MS-DOS sessions, just click on the Mark tool on the toolbar before you select the text. If you've set up your MS-DOS sessions so the toolbar doesn't show, then you can tell Windows 95 to enable the QuickEdit feature.

To enable this feature, simply click the window system icon (the MS-DOS icon in the upper-left corner) and choose Properties; then choose the Misc tab when the Properties sheet appears. Check the QuickEdit box under the Mouse section; then click OK, and you're ready to go.

Using Long File Names

One of the most bothersome limitations of the MS-DOS environment has been the 8.3 file name format. Windows now supports longer file names, and the MS-DOS Prompt offers support for them, too. To see how this works, follow these steps:

1. Using the Windows Desktop, create a new folder called Incredibly Long Folder Name on the root of drive C:, as shown in figure 11.8.

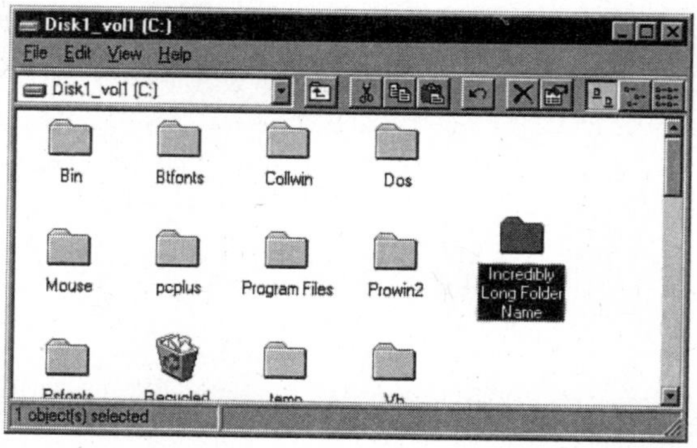

Fig. 11.8
You can use up to 255 characters in a file or folder name.

2. Using the Start menu, open an MS-DOS Prompt. At the prompt, type **dir c:***. The MS-DOS window displays the directory listing for the root of drive C: (an example is shown in fig. 11.9).

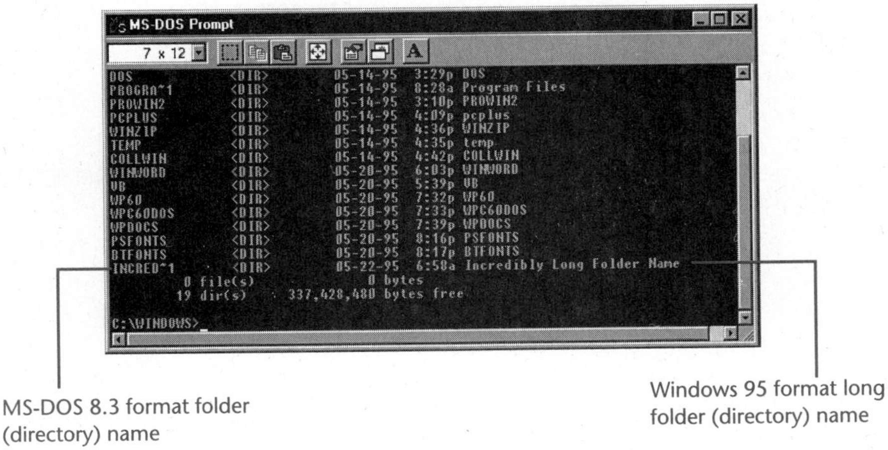

Fig. 11.9
The MS-DOS Prompt session supports and displays both long and short file and folder (directory) names.

Note the dual display of both the 8.3-format and long-format folder names. Windows and MS-DOS coordinate both naming systems, but not without a price; the 8.3 format name uses the tilde character (~) to show the inevitable truncation. Even under Windows, some long names may be shortened using the ellipsis characters (...) when space is at a premium.

► See "Registering Files to Automatically Open an Application," p. 539

To ensure complete backwards compatibility, file extensions are still used, even though they are not displayed in the Windows Explorer or on the Desktop. If you rename a file from the Windows environment, it does not change the hidden file name extension. Windows still uses the extension for file associations with applications and viewers.

Note

Not all applications support long file names just because Windows does. It's doubtful that any MS-DOS applications will support long file names because most were written prior to this version of Windows. Most 16-bit Windows applications won't support longer file names until their first release after Windows 95, if then (some software companies will probably wait for the first release of their application as a true 32-bit program to include this feature).

Many of the native MS-DOS commands in Windows 95 have been enhanced to provide support for long file names. For example, the `dir` and `copy` commands both support long file names.

Using Universal Naming Convention Path Names

More and more PCs are on *local area networks* (*LANs*). Most shared resources on a LAN are stored on *servers*, or PCs dedicated for a particular network task, such as printing, file storage, or database storage.

Gaining access to other PCs on the network, whether server or workstation, can be a tiresome process of mapping the other machine to a virtual drive letter on your system. The Windows 95 MS-DOS Prompt offers a way around this with *Universal Naming Convention (UNC)* support. This is a fancy way of saying that you can view, copy, or run files on another machine without having to assign it a drive letter on your computer. It also means that if you are running short of logical drive letters, you can get to servers that you use only intermittently with a simple command from the MS-DOS Prompt.

For example, if you want to run an application called SHARED.EXE in the directory STUFF on server FRED1, you can enter the following at the command prompt:

\\fred1\stuff\shared.exe

You also can use this feature with any legal MS-DOS command. For example, to see the contents of the directory STUFF, use the familiar `dir` command as follows:

dir \\fred1\stuff

This yields a standard directory listing of the contents of that area of the server.

Printing from the MS-DOS Prompt

The biggest change in printing support for MS-DOS applications comes in the form of better conflict resolution and print job queuing. Windows now handles printer port contention between MS-DOS and Windows applications by shuttling all MS-DOS print tasks to the same printer management utility used by Windows applications.

Understanding MS-DOS Mode

◄ See "Printing from MS-DOS Applications," p. 200

Even the most perfect host can't entertain someone who really doesn't want to be at the party. Windows has the same problem with some poorly designed MS-DOS applications—some MS-DOS applications demand total control over system resources and access hardware in the most direct way, bypassing "standard" Windows methods.

Windows 95 accommodates a poorly behaved guest to the best of its ability, via *MS-DOS mode*. This mode is the equivalent to the Real mode present in older versions of Windows, with some "real" improvements.

MS-DOS mode works by giving the errant MS-DOS application the entire system for the duration of the session. Windows removes itself from memory, leaving only a small "stub" loader in preparation for its return to power.

To use this mode, the user sets a property in the Advanced Program Settings dialog box. When the MS-DOS application runs, Windows literally shuts down, loads the application, and then returns automatically when the application is finished. This process can be slow and cumbersome, but it is faster and more convenient than exiting Windows manually, using the dual boot option, and reloading Windows.

Knowing When to Use MS-DOS Mode

Before you decide to enable MS-DOS mode for an application, try these other options:

- Confirm that you've optimized the MS-DOS session settings for that application. Check the program's documentation for special memory requirements or other unusual needs. You may be able to adjust Windows' MS-DOS support to make the application work in a standard MS-DOS session.

► See "Configuring Your MS-DOS Application," p. 347

- Try running the application in full-screen mode, using the Alt+Enter key sequence.

If either of the preceding methods works, you will have a faster, more convenient alternative, allowing you the full benefit of Windows' multitasking and other features, all of which disappear during the MS-DOS mode session.

Customizing MS-DOS Mode

Just as you can customize the MS-DOS Prompt session properties, you can alter MS-DOS mode properties as well. If your problem application has special needs beyond those addressed by the default MS-DOS session settings, you can override the Windows defaults via the settings in the Advanced Program Settings dialog box, as shown in figure 11.10.

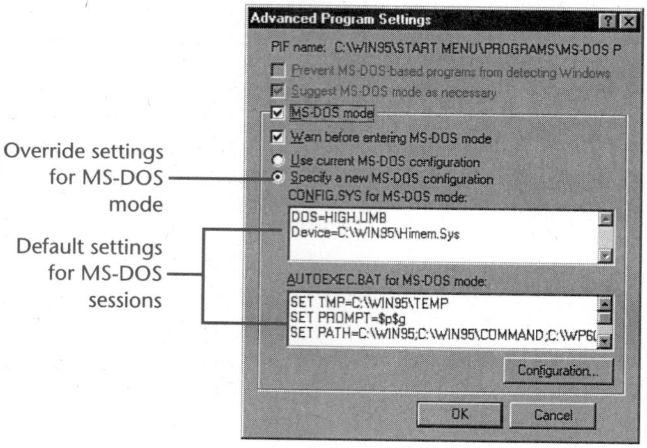

Fig. 11.10
Windows allows you to override the default settings for MS-DOS mode support. You can even run a special CONFIG.SYS and AUTOEXEC.BAT file for each application.

Troubleshooting

I set my main MS-DOS Prompt to run in MS-DOS mode, and now whenever I start it, Windows shuts down completely! How can I set it back if I can't get to the properties? Will I have to reinstall Windows? I just want my windowed MS-DOS back.

Have no fear! You can access the properties of any program or file from the Windows Desktop without running the program or opening the file. When Windows restarts after the MS-DOS Mode session, locate the icon for the MS-DOS prompt program (in the WINDOWS\START MENU\PROGRAMS directory) with the Windows Explorer and right-click the icon to get the menu that offers the Properties function.

When the Properties sheet opens, go to the Program page and choose the Advanced button, which opens the Advanced Program Settings dialog box, as shown earlier in figure 11.10. Simply uncheck the MS-DOS Mode box, and choose OK twice to close the Properties sheet and return to the desktop. See "Configuring Your MS-DOS Application" later in this chapter.

Using PIF Files

Windows 3.1 offered a straightforward, if awkward, means of controlling the session settings for an MS-DOS application through the use of *Program Information Files* (commonly referred to by their extension, *PIF*). Although PIFs offered a high degree of control over the virtualized MS-DOS environment, the user had to understand the relationship between Windows, MS-DOS, the

PIF, the Program Manager icon assigned to the PIF, and the application itself. Advanced training in MS-DOS memory management didn't hurt either. If you add an MS-DOS batch file to the equation, it could be really confusing.

Windows 95 solves this whole mess by using the same mechanism for MS-DOS applications and data that's now used for Windows files: the Properties sheet. With a simple right-click of the mouse, you can directly view and alter the entire gamut of controls for your MS-DOS application. No separate editor, no hunting for the PIF and confirming that it's the correct one. Although Windows 95 still uses PIF files, there's a unified means of viewing the PIF properties for a given application, via the Properties sheet.

One of the more confusing issues under Windows 3.1 was the need to create a PIF file for each MS-DOS application that required custom settings. Windows 95 takes care of that chore automatically—all you need to do is view the properties for your MS-DOS application.

To view an example Properties sheet for an MS-DOS application, follow these steps:

1. Using the Windows Explorer, find the Windows folder. Then open the Command folder.

2. Right-click to open the shortcut menu, and choose Properties. Windows displays the Edit Properties sheet, as shown in figure 11.11.

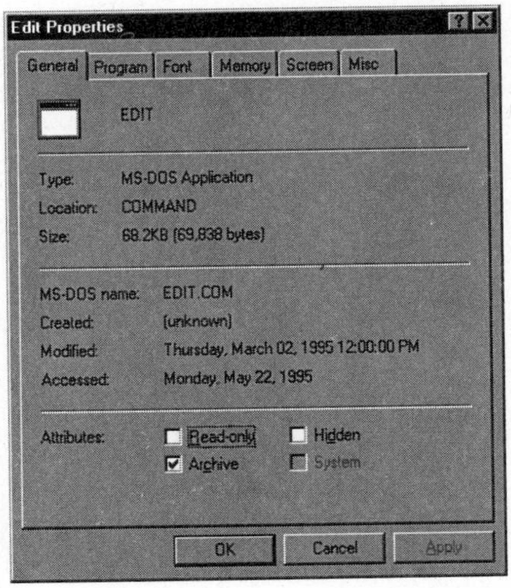

Fig. 11.11
The Windows Properties sheet for MS-DOS applications has several tabs unique to the MS-DOS environment.

If you're mystified by some of the terms and control types you see here, don't worry. The "Configuring Your MS-DOS Application" section, later in this chapter, shows examples of how these controls can help you maximize Windows' performance when you run MS-DOS applications.

Graphic-Intensive Applications

One great example of the enhanced MS-DOS support available under Windows 95 is the capability to run some applications in graphics mode, in a window. Although this doesn't sound like a big trick, remember that earlier versions of Windows don't support this at all; you are forced to run MS-DOS Graphics-mode applications full screen.

Why would you want to take advantage of running MS-DOS applications in a window? For some of the same reasons you like Windows applications: the capability to quickly and easily move back and forth between applications and the capability to easily cut and paste information between programs.

Also, in earlier versions of Windows, moving from a full-screen MS-DOS application in Graphics mode back to Windows involves a time lag during which the display has to reset for a completely different video mode and resolution; some monitors handle this gracefully, but most don't. Running your MS-DOS program in a window avoids this altogether.

Note

Windows 95 contains the capability to self-configure for many popular MS-DOS programs. These configurations are derived from research with the most-used applications and are stored in a file called APPS.INF. When you install an MS-DOS application, Windows checks to see if it's registered in the APPS.INF database; if the application is listed in the APPS.INF file but no PIF file exists, Windows uses the information to create a PIF for future use.

Although this new capability is wonderful, be aware that not all MS-DOS applications are supported. Not all applications follow the "official" guidelines for MS-DOS hardware access (some programmers break or bend the rules to gain faster performance—for example, writing directly to the video hardware versus using the MS-DOS service calls for video); hence, Windows 95 can't support them in a windowed, virtualized MS-DOS environment. The same application may run perfectly full-screen, because there are fewer layers of virtualization for Windows to provide. A great example of this scenario is a game program, which constantly attempts to use the system timer, video, and sound resources as directly as possible.

How do you know if your application will run in Graphics mode in a Windows 95 window? The best test is to try it. Follow these steps to test your program:

1. Locate the icon for the MS-DOS graphics program you want to test and double-click it to start the program. Windows starts the program in full-screen mode, unless you've configured it otherwise or the program was installed with a windowed default. If the program opens in a window, press Alt+Enter to return to full-screen mode.

2. If the program supports both Character and Graphics modes, activate the program feature that requires Graphics mode (such as Page or Print Preview).

3. When the screen has reformatted for graphics display, press Alt+Enter to return to windowed display mode. Windows displays the application as shown in the example in figure 11.12.

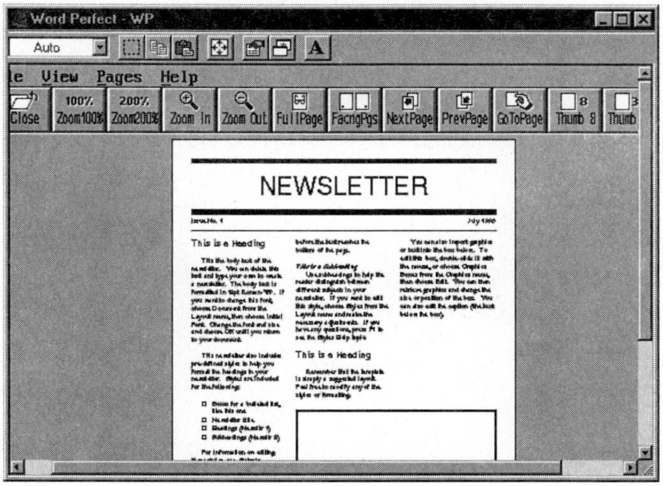

Fig. 11.12
Windows can display MS-DOS graphics mode for many applications, such as the WordPerfect Print Preview feature.

4. If Windows can't support the application in this mode, you see the warning box displayed in figure 11.13.

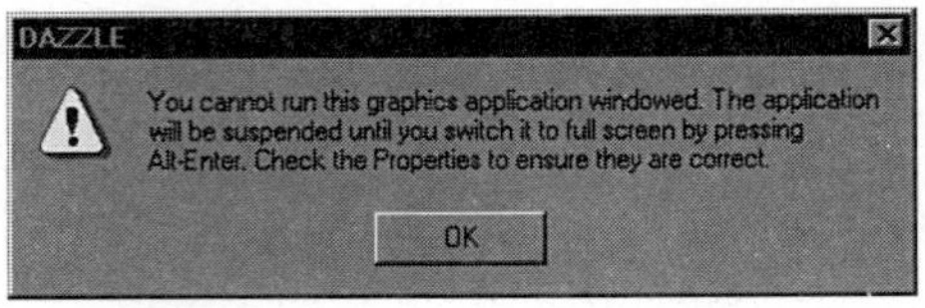

Fig. 11.13 Although Windows now offers improved support for MS-DOS graphics mode, some applications still don't work in a window.

Improved Memory Protection

A bitter lesson learned from running MS-DOS applications under Windows 3.1 was that those applications often inadvertently corrupted the operating system memory areas. MS-DOS programs, not written for a multitasking environment, believe that they have the right to alter the memory for the entire system. This can have catastrophic results in a multitasking environment such as Windows and has been the cause of many a lockup.

Windows 95 offers a much higher level of memory protection for the entire system and specifically for MS-DOS applications. You can specify special protection for conventional system memory by checking the Protected check box on the Memory property page, as shown in figure 11.14.

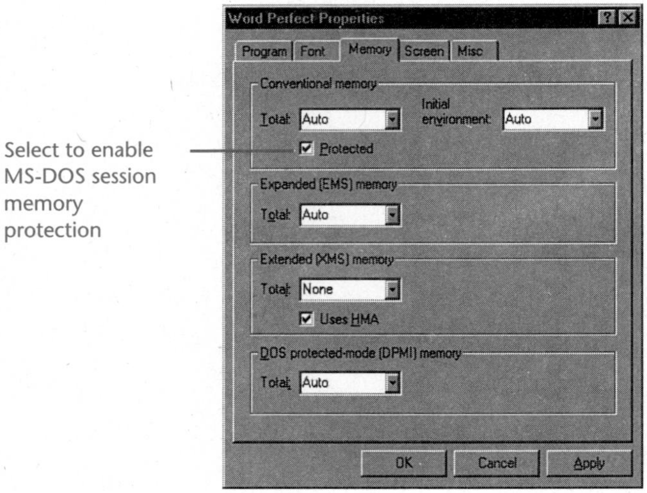

Fig. 11.14 Windows 95 allows you to protect conventional memory from errant applications via the Protected setting on the Memory property page.

Although it might seem logical to enable this option by default for all MS-DOS applications, enough overhead is involved in tracking this for each session that it's really best to turn it on only for those applications that have proven they require it.

Enhanced Virtual Machine Support

MS-DOS application support requires the presence of a virtual MS-DOS environment, or *virtual machine.* This concept and technique, originally from the mainframe environment, is the primary reason for the success and popularity of the Microsoft Windows product. A virtual machine is basically an effective "clone" of the same operating system that MS-DOS applications are written for. Windows provides this environment within Windows so that you can run multiple MS-DOS sessions simultaneously with both Windows and MS-DOS applications.

◀ See "Managing Windows after an Application Failure," p. 78

One problem with Windows 3.1 virtual machine support was that version's particular technique of implementing multiple virtual machines. Because it ran on top of MS-DOS, Windows 3.1 took a "snapshot" of the first megabyte of MS-DOS memory and stored it for later use. When the user asked for an MS-DOS session, Windows re-created this virtual one-megabyte environment, complete with all the original running programs, device drivers, terminate-and-stay-resident programs, and so on, regardless of whether the MS-DOS application running in the virtual environment needed them.

This approach, although workable, had two major problems: it wasted system memory and restricted the customization of individual virtual MS-DOS sessions. Program Information Files (PIFs) allowed the user to alter some parameters of the memory model for each successive virtual machine session, but the overall settings could not be altered once Windows 3.1 was started.

Windows 95 offers many improvements over this model. Because Windows 95 doesn't require a complete, preexisting Real-mode MS-DOS environment before it runs, you can control almost every aspect of the virtual MS-DOS environment because it is more "truly" virtual. You can even run batch files within the session to customize the environment for your application's needs.

Windows 95 also offers better management of MS-DOS session closings. Under Windows 3.1, not all system memory and resources were released when a virtual machine session ended. This resulted in a slow erosion of performance with the eventual inability to open additional applications, requiring the user to restart Windows.

Enhanced Local Reboot Support

Under Windows 3.0, if an application quit working, the user had two options: prayer and prayer. A hung program meant lost data. Windows 3.1 improved on this scenario by allowing *local reboot*, the capability to trap errant application behavior, thus protecting other applications and data. Under Windows 3.1's local reboot, the Ctrl+Alt+Del key sequence didn't restart the machine; it closed the misbehaving application and theoretically left Windows and all other applications fat and happy.

Local reboot had two main problems:

- Users didn't always know which application was hung, so when they used Ctrl+Alt+Del, Windows often closed the wrong one (sometimes offering to shut itself down!).
- Windows 3.1 didn't always respond quickly to the Ctrl+Alt+Del command, and the user "sat" on the keys, resulting in a complete machine reset. (A single Ctrl+Alt+Del would bring up a blue screen warning that a second Ctrl+Alt+Del would reset the system; often this screen was a blue blip as the world came crashing down, and the annual report went to the Great Bit Bucket Beyond.)

Windows 95 improves on this bad scenario by putting a menu between you and data loss. A single Ctrl+Alt+Del displays the Close Program dialog box.

If an application creates a problem or freezes, Windows now indicates that it is "not responding," and you have the choice of ending that task or completing an orderly shutdown of the entire system. Although this doesn't totally insulate your computer from errant applications, it does drastically improve your ability to control otherwise disastrous circumstances.

Troubleshooting

I'm really pleased with how my new computer works with Windows 95 and Windows applications, but it's really slow when I use MS-DOS programs. It also keeps losing my MS-DOS programs, and I have to restart them!

You're probably running too many MS-DOS sessions at once. If you switch back to the Windows Desktop or a Windows application, the MS-DOS application "disappears" (actually it's still open, just hidden by Windows, because it can't display a full-screen MS-DOS session and Windows at the same time). In full-screen MS-DOS mode, Windows can't display the taskbar to show all running applications. If you're running MS-DOS in a window, it's even easier to "lose" it behind another running program's window.

If you restart your MS-DOS application from the same icon, you're really creating a second instance of the program, not moving back to the first one. This only serves to slow down the entire system because every MS-DOS session divides your computing resources by the same amount as all running Windows applications together.

If you can't see your running MS-DOS application, use the old Alt+Tab key trick. Hold down the Alt key and press the Tab key once; this brings up a small window in center screen with icons for all running programs. Another press of the Tab key moves the icon cursor to the next running program, allowing you to move through all open applications "carousel" style. Windows 3.1 didn't show all of the running programs at once in the Alt+Tab window, so many users don't realize they have more than one MS-DOS session open (the icons all look the same, you just have more of them!). Windows 95 Alt+Tab lets you see all running programs' icons at once.

Use the Windows taskbar to help you view and return to running applications. It's really one of the most useful additions to the new Windows, especially for MS-DOS users.

Installing MS-DOS Applications

Now that you have explored the basic concepts, tools, and techniques behind MS-DOS Prompt session support under Windows 95, look at the steps required to install and configure an MS-DOS application.

◄ See "Installing, Running, and Uninstalling Windows Applications," p. 303

You can install any application in the following two basic ways:

- Locate and run the installation program for the application.
- Create a directory for the application and copy the files to that directory.

Note

Although Windows can handle complete installations of true Windows applications, it relies on structures and capabilities that are simply not present in most MS-DOS applications. Thus, you need to set up application shortcuts and Start button menu items manually.

Using MS-DOS Application Installation Programs

Most professionally written MS-DOS applications have an installation or setup program that handles the details of installation for you. Besides simply creating a storage area for the application and moving the files to it, these installation programs perform the additional operating system configuration chores that may be necessary for successful operation.

> **Note**
>
> MS-DOS installation programs that are Windows-aware may handle some of the preceding tasks for you, but most won't—you'll have to handle some of the tasks yourself. How do you know what alterations to make? Look for the documentation for the manual program installation instructions in the program directory. Often this is a simple text file, labeled README.TXT or INSTALL.TXT.

Installing MS-DOS Applications from the MS-DOS Prompt

While it's just as easy to find and run your MS-DOS application installation program from the Windows Explorer or the Start button Run command, you may want to go directly to the MS-DOS Prompt session and install your application directly, or your application may not have a structured installation program. In either case, Windows certainly allows you this level of control.

Using an Installation Program from the MS-DOS Prompt

Running the installation program from an MS-DOS prompt is just like doing it on a machine that's running only MS-DOS. Follow these steps to begin:

1. Open a new MS-DOS session from the Start menu.
2. At the MS-DOS prompt, enter the command to start the installation program (for example, **a:\install.exe**) and press Enter.
3. When the installation program is finished, close the MS-DOS session manually or run the application if you want.

◄ See "Ending MS-DOS Prompt Sessions," p. 329

Installing MS-DOS Programs Manually from the MS-DOS Prompt

Some MS-DOS applications don't have installation programs at all. This is most common with shareware applications or small utility programs.

To install your application manually, follow these simple steps:

1. Open a new MS-DOS session from the Start menu.
2. At the MS-DOS prompt, enter the command to create a directory for your program (for example, **md c:\myprog**) and press Enter.
3. Enter the command to copy the program to the new directory, such as **xcopy a:*.* c:\myprog**. MS-DOS copies the files to the new directory.

> **Note**
>
> You may need to alter the preceding routine slightly if your application comes as a compressed archive (such as a ZIP or an ARJ file). Usually all this means is an additional step for decompression once the files are copied.

Configuring Your MS-DOS Application

Before you explore the myriad options for customizing the MS-DOS environment for your application, there's one point that needs to be stressed: the odds are very good that your program will run perfectly without any reconfiguration at all. Microsoft has done a truly admirable job in observing the reality of how people use MS-DOS applications under Windows, and the design of Windows 95 MS-DOS defaults reflects that. Preset configurations for the most popular MS-DOS applications are stored in Windows, awaiting your installation of the program. So before you begin messing around with all the options, be smart and run the program a few times. The old adage truly applies: if it isn't broke, don't fix it.

Understanding and Configuring MS-DOS Application Properties

You've already been introduced to the Windows Properties sheet and seen how Windows now uses it in place of the PIF Editor. Now you take a closer look at specific property options and how they relate to your application.

◄ See "Displaying Properties of Programs, Documents, and Resources," p. 28

General Properties

The General properties page is primarily informational, with minimal controls other than file attributes (see fig. 11.15).

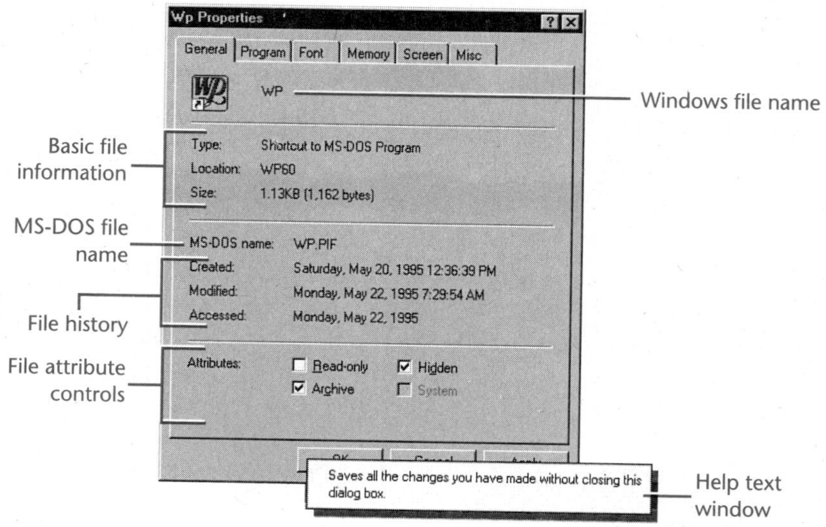

Fig. 11.15 The General properties page gives you most of the basic information about the file and easy access to control of the file attributes. Context-sensitive help is available at any time by using the "?" tool.

The only real controls exposed in the General properties page are the file attribute settings. These are used mainly to protect documents (by setting the read-only attribute), and you shouldn't alter them unless you have a specific reason.

> **Note**
>
> A running MS-DOS application displays only five Properties tabs. (The General tab is not shown when the program is in use.)

Program Properties

The Program properties page gives you control over the basic environment your application starts with (see fig. 11.16).

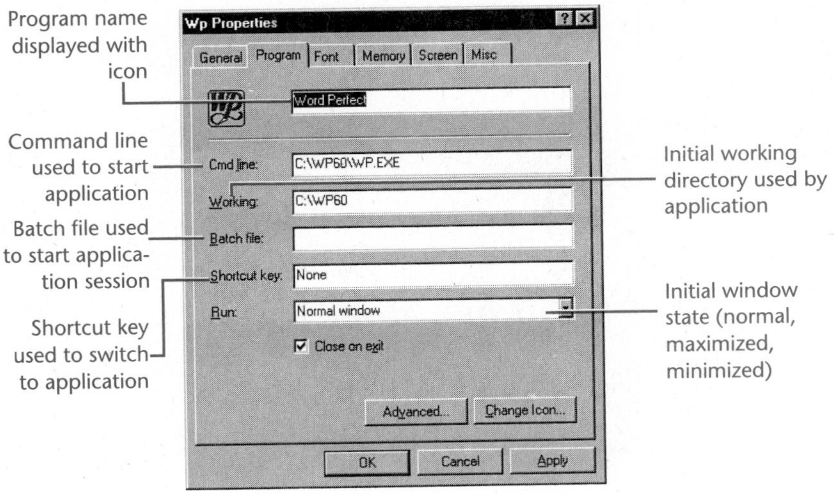

Fig. 11.16
The Program properties page allows you to alter the variables used to name and start the application.

Advanced Program Settings. Clicking the Advanced button in the Program properties page produces the Advanced Program Settings dialog box, shown in figure 11.17.

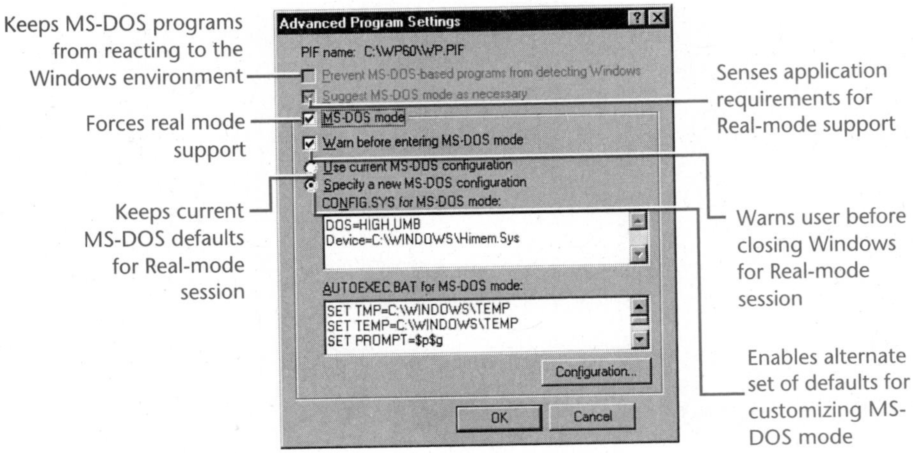

Fig. 11.17
The Advanced Program Settings dialog box enables you to define the precise mode and environment for your MS-DOS session.

If you need to run your application in MS-DOS mode, here's where you can enable it. You can even set up custom CONFIG.SYS and AUTOEXEC.BAT values for your session. If you click the Specify a New MS-DOS Configuration radio button, you can edit the special CONFIG.SYS and AUTOEXEC.BAT values right in this dialog box.

If you click the Configuration button, you see the dialog box displayed in figure 11.18.

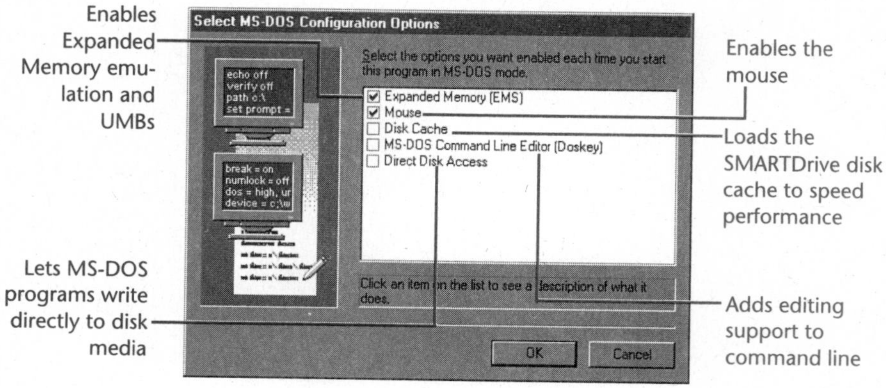

Fig. 11.18 The Select MS-DOS Mode Configuration Options dialog box lets you control expanded memory, disk caching, disk access, and command-line editing.

◀ See "Knowing When to Use MS-DOS Mode," p. 337

All the settings under the Advanced dialog box should be altered only if your MS-DOS application simply won't run in a standard session with the default settings. For that matter, don't even enable MS-DOS mode unless your application demands it.

Changing MS-DOS Application Icons. If you click the Change Icon button shown in figure 11.16, the Change Icon dialog box displays (see fig. 11.19).

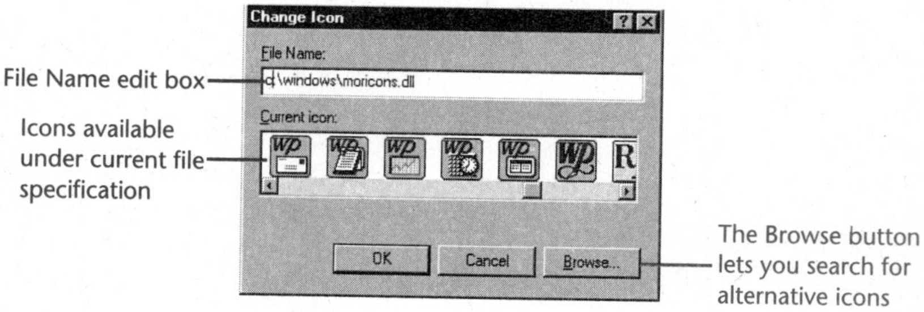

Fig. 11.19 The Change Icon dialog box lets you customize the icon for your MS-DOS application.

It's likely that your MS-DOS application won't come with any icons. Windows 95 will show you the icons in the file PIFMGR.DLL when you choose Change Icon. You can choose icons from other applications simply by specifying them in this dialog box. Or you may want to look in an icon archive that comes with Windows 3.1, MORICONS.DLL. Microsoft threw in icons for a few of the most popular programs so that you can have a choice. If you didn't upgrade from Windows 3.1, MORICONS.DLL probably won't be on your system.

Font Properties

The Font properties page is primarily informational, with minimal controls other than file attributes (see fig. 11.20). It works just like the Font list control on the MS-DOS session toolbar.

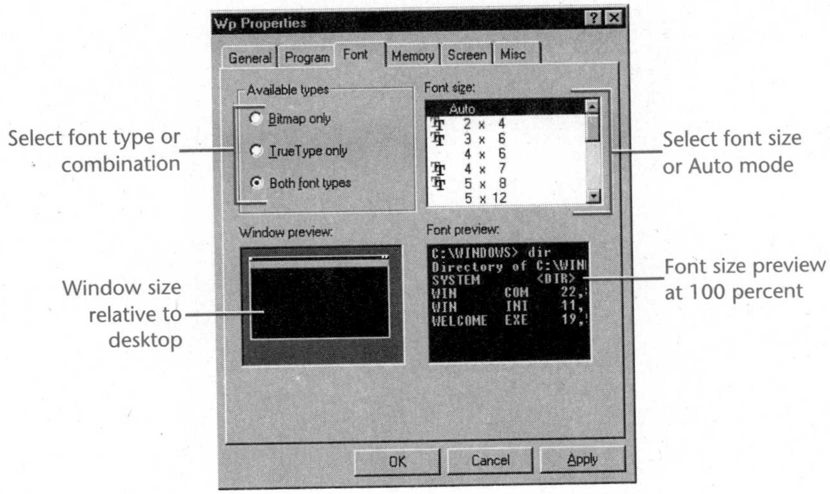

Fig. 11.20
The Font properties page lets you choose the font type and size, and gives you both a window and font preview.

Memory Properties

The Memory properties page makes simple work of the traditional maze of MS-DOS memory management (see fig. 11.21). With a few mouse clicks, you can configure your application memory precisely as needed.

◄ See "Controlling the MS-DOS Prompt Interface," p. 331

◄ See "Improved Memory Protection," p. 342

Several dozen entire books have been written on the subject of MS-DOS memory management. Let's keep it simple: if your application works without altering these values, *do not change them.* If your application doesn't work with the default settings, *consult the documentation* to determine what the appropriate settings are. *Then* you can alter the values in this dialog box. Proceeding in any other way, unless you have considerable experience with the techniques involved, can severely inhibit the performance of your system.

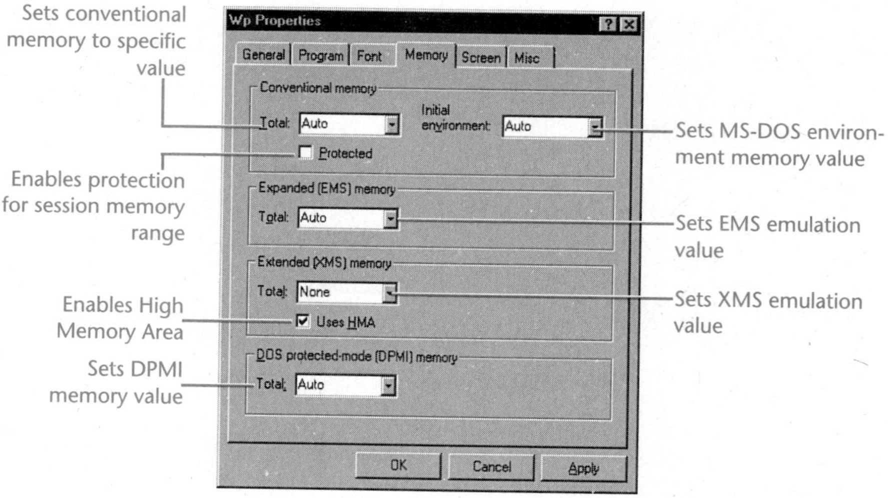

Fig. 11.21 The Memory properties page vastly simplifies this formerly arcane management issue.

Screen Properties

The Screen properties page lets you control the appearance of the MS-DOS session (see fig. 11.22).

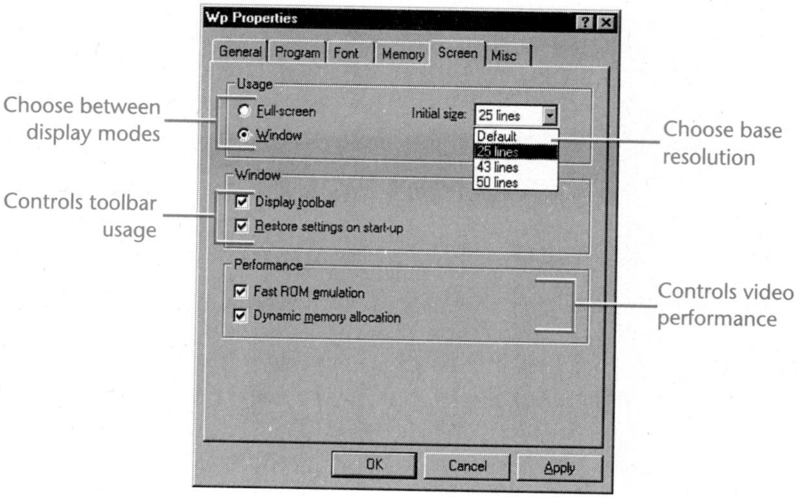

Fig. 11.22 The Screen properties page gives you control of the size, type, and performance of the MS-DOS interface.

You may find that certain MS-DOS programs (especially those running in Graphics mode) respond poorly to the video emulation used in windowed mode. If so, try defeating the performance defaults by unchecking the Fast ROM Emulation and Dynamic Memory Allocation items. Fast ROM Emulation tells the Windows 95 display driver to mimic the video hardware to help display MS-DOS programs faster. Dynamic Memory Allocation releases display memory to other programs when the MS-DOS session isn't using it. If you experience strange display problems with your MS-DOS programs, try changing these settings.

Miscellaneous Properties

The Misc properties page covers the remaining configuration items that don't fit under the other categories (see fig. 11.23).

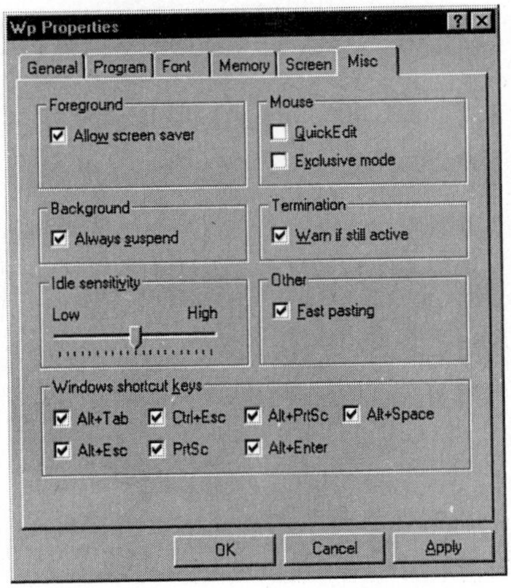

Fig. 11.23
The Misc properties page controls screen saver, mouse, background operation, program termination, shortcut key, and editing options.

- The Allow Screen Saver control lets your default Windows screen saver operate even if your MS-DOS session has the foreground.
- Always Suspend freezes your MS-DOS application when you bring another application (either MS-DOS or Windows) to the foreground. If you have an application that must perform time-sensitive operations (such as a communications program), make sure to disable this option.

- Idle Sensitivity tells your MS-DOS program to yield the system to other applications if it really isn't doing anything important. A word processor, for example, won't have a problem letting go of the system clock when you're not using it. A communications program, however, may need to respond quickly, so you want to set its idle sensitivity to Low.
- The Mouse controls enable QuickEdit mode (letting you mark text using just the mouse) and Exclusive Mode (the MS-DOS application has control of the mouse cursor when the application is in the foreground, even if you try to move the mouse out of the MS-DOS window).
- The Warn If Still Active Item in the Termination box tells Windows to notify you before the MS-DOS session is closed. It's really best to leave this enabled, unless you are absolutely certain that the MS-DOS program will never, ever have open data files when you close it.
- The Fast Pasting setting simply tells Windows that your MS-DOS program can handle a raw data stream dump from the Windows Clipboard. Some MS-DOS programs clog at full speed, so if you paste to your MS-DOS application and you consistently lose characters, turn this one off.
- Windows Shortcut Keys allows you to override the standard quick navigation aids built into the Windows environment, just for your MS-DOS session (some MS-DOS programs think they can get away with using the same keys, and something has to give—Windows!). By default, Windows "owns" these shortcuts, but you can lend them to your MS-DOS application by unchecking them here.

Running Installed MS-DOS Applications

Windows comes set up with a default MS-DOS Prompt configuration designed to run the vast majority of applications. Although your application may have special needs, odds are it will work fine if you start it from within a running MS-DOS Prompt session.

To start your application from an MS-DOS Prompt session, follow these steps:

1. Open a new MS-DOS Prompt session from the Start menu.

2. At the MS-DOS prompt, enter the command to move to the directory of the program you want to start (for example, **cd \wp60**) and press Enter. The MS-DOS prompt now shows the current directory, as shown in figure 11.24.

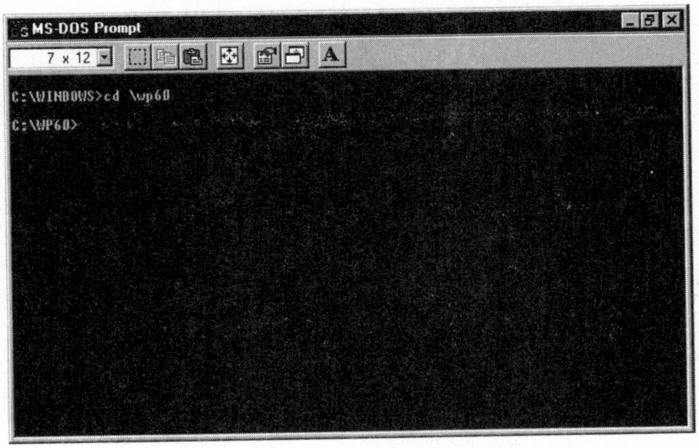

Fig. 11.24
Once you're in the MS-DOS Prompt session, all the basic MS-DOS commands can be used to start your application

3. At the MS-DOS prompt, enter the command to start your application (for example, **wp**) and press Enter. The MS-DOS Prompt window now displays the application you've started, as shown in figure 11.25.

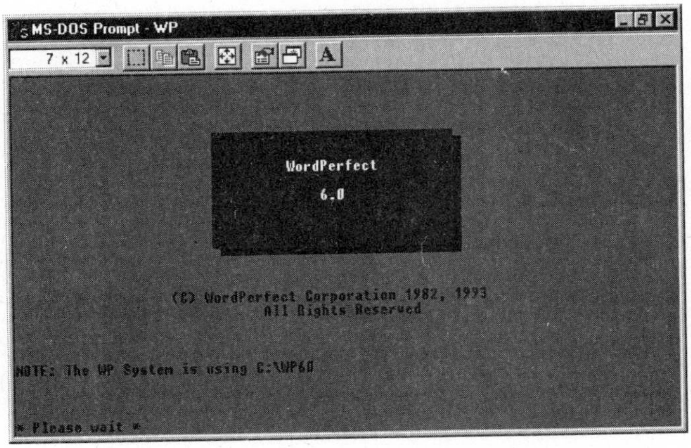

Fig. 11.25
Once your application starts, Windows displays it in the MS-DOS Prompt window space. Note that the window title reflects the command name of the program running.

◄ See "How to Start Programs and Documents," p. 38

Although running an application from within the MS-DOS Prompt window works well and seems familiar to the veteran command-line user, it's not really the most convenient method under Windows.

In addition to the default Windows MS-DOS Prompt, Windows 95 offers four other ways to start an application:

- The Windows Explorer
- The Start button Run option
- The Start button Programs menu
- The Application shortcut

These startup methods work just like they do for their Windows counterparts.

Removing MS-DOS Applications

If you decide to remove your MS-DOS application from your computer, there are two easy ways to do it:

- Use the MS-DOS Prompt `dir` and `deltree` commands
- Use the Windows Explorer and Recycle Bin

Caution

Regardless of which technique you use, make sure that you don't have any data stored with the application you're removing. Some applications allow you to store your documents or data files in the same directory as the application code itself. Although this is inherently poor design, it still happens; and if you don't tell the application to save your files to another folder or directory, you may be very sorry after you've deleted the program itself.

Using MS-DOS Commands to Remove an MS-DOS Application

Perhaps the most straightforward way to remove an MS-DOS application is to use the MS-DOS tools themselves. To do this, follow these steps:

1. Open MS-DOS Prompt session from the Start menu.

2. At the MS-DOS prompt, type the command **dir c:\appdir /p** (where *appdir* is the directory in which your doomed application awaits its final moments). In this example, you'll use **c:\wp60 /p**. The MS-DOS Prompt session displays a directory listing similar to that shown in figure 11.26.

► See "Moving and Copying Files and Folders," p. 515

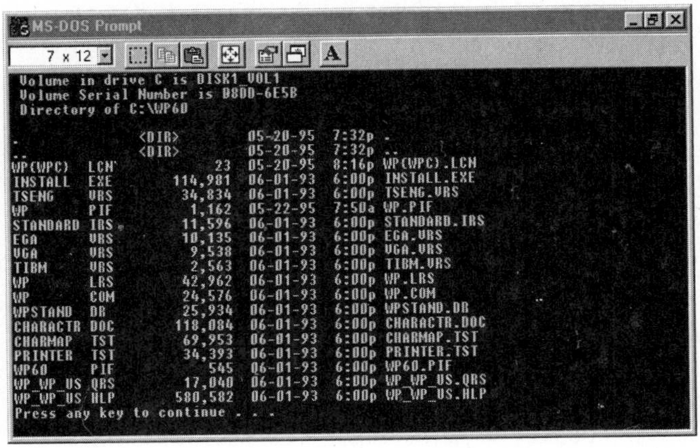

Fig. 11.26
The `dir` command shows the contents of the directory you want to delete. The /p switch displays the listing in a page at a time. Simply press any key to continue through the listing.

3. Look for any files that contain your personal data (be sure to check in any subdirectories). If necessary, copy or move these files to another location.

4. After you've saved any personal data, proceed to delete the application. At the MS-DOS prompt, type **deltree c:\appdir** (where *appdir* is the directory containing the application to be deleted) and press Enter. MS-DOS displays a message asking you to confirm the deletion. If you're absolutely sure, type **y** and press Enter. MS-DOS deletes the application directory and all subdirectories.

Tip
If you need help with an MS-DOS command, try the built-in MS-DOS help system. Simply add **/?** after the MS-DOS command at the prompt (that is, **move /?**) and you'll get help text for that command.

Using the Explorer to Remove an MS-DOS Application

An even simpler way to remove an MS-DOS application is to use the Explorer and the Recycle Bin. It's really as simple as locating the application folder, checking it for your personal data, and then dragging it to the "trash."

For complete instructions on using the Explorer to remove an application, see Chapter 17, "Managing Your Files with Explorer."

► See "Deleting Files and Folders," p. 518

◄ See "Removing Windows Applications," p. 321

Cleaning Up Shortcuts and the Start Menu

Be sure to remove shortcuts to applications after you've removed the application itself. If you don't, Windows will still try to load the application, and ask you to help find it when it can't—a real hassle. If you've placed the shortcut on your Desktop, simply drag it to the Recycle Bin.

If you used the Control Panel Add/Remove Programs feature discussed in Chapter 10 to add the shortcut to the Start menu, just follow the removal steps outlined in that chapter.❖

Chapter 12

Using WordPad to Create Documents

by Ron Person

WordPad is a simple but powerful word processor that comes with Windows 95. This accessory is ideal for many day-to-day word processing needs. WordPad offers many of the editing and formatting capabilities commonly found in more advanced applications, along with the ability to share information with other applications and files. You can cut, copy, and paste text and graphics between WordPad documents and between WordPad and other applications. WordPad uses the same structure of menus, commands, icons, and dialog boxes that all Windows 95 applications use. What you learn about managing text in WordPad applies to most of the Windows 95 applications involving text.

In this chapter, you learn to

- Create and edit a document
- Format text or an entire document
- Print a document
- Open and save a document
- Customize WordPad's Settings

Creating Documents in WordPad

WordPad is easy to use. The features you've learned in other word processors—like how to select commands, enter text, and format text—also work here. Creating a WordPad document is as simple as starting the application and typing the text. Because the margins, a font, and tabs are already set, you can actually begin a new WordPad document as soon as you start the application.

Starting WordPad

Tip
If you want quick access to WordPad, add a shortcut icon to the desktop. Then just double-click the icon to start WordPad.

To start WordPad from the desktop, follow these steps:

1. Open the Start menu and choose Programs; then choose Accessories.

2. Choose WordPad. WordPad starts up and displays the WordPad window (see fig. 12.1).

Note

If your WordPad screen doesn't include the same elements as the one shown in figure 12.1, see the "Changing the Screen Display" section later in this chapter for information on how to add and remove screen elements from the display.

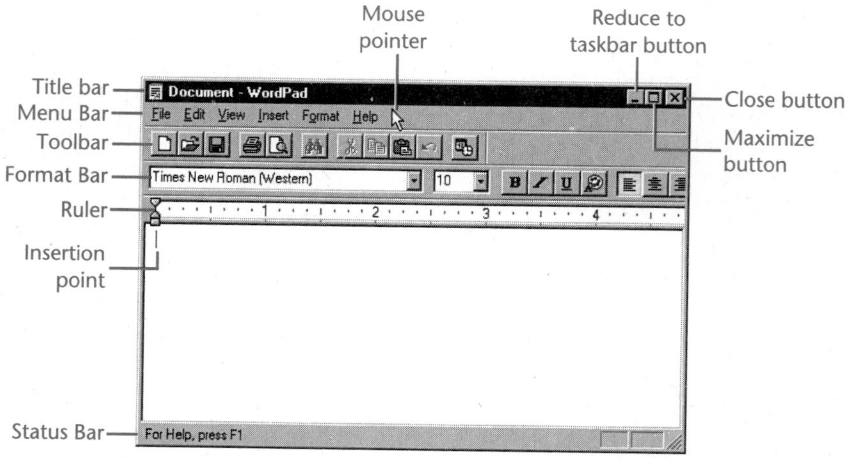

Fig. 12.1
WordPad starts with a new blank document ready for you to being typing.

Creating a New WordPad Document

Unlike more robust Windows applications, WordPad can contain only one document at a time. When you open a new blank document you will be asked if you want to save the current document.

◄ See "Starting Programs from a Shortcut Icon on the Desktop," p. 68

To create a new document once you have started WordPad, follow these steps:

1. Choose File, New, or click the New button in the toolbar. The New dialog box appears (see fig. 12.2).

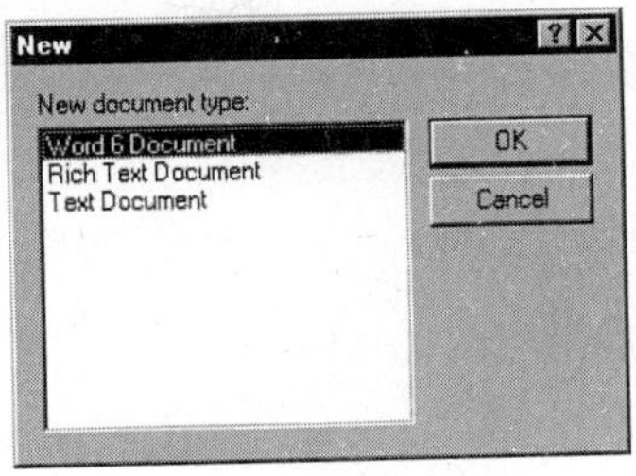

Fig. 12.2
You can create new documents in any one of three formats.

2. Select one of the following document types:

   - *Word 6 Document.* This format can be opened and edited in Microsoft Word 6.0 or Word 95.
   - *Rich Text Document.* This format is compatible with several word processors and includes fonts, tabs, and character formatting.
   - *Text Document.* This format includes no text formatting and can be used in any word processor.

3. Click OK.

Opening WordPad Documents

To open a file that has already been created and saved, follow these steps:

1. Choose File, Open, or click the Open button in the toolbar. The Open dialog box appears (see fig. 12.3).

◄ See "Changing Folders in Save As and Open Dialog Boxes," p. 100

> **Caution**
>
> If you open a file that was created in another word processor such as Word for Windows, same of the formatting can be lost or converted incorrectly.

2. If the file is on a different disk, click the down arrow to the right of the Look In box and select the drive that contains the file you want.

3. Double-click the folder that contains the file you want to open.

4. Click the down arrow to the right of the Files of Type box and select the type of files you want to list.

5. Double-click the file you want open.

   or

   Type in the File Name box the name of the file you want to open and click Open.

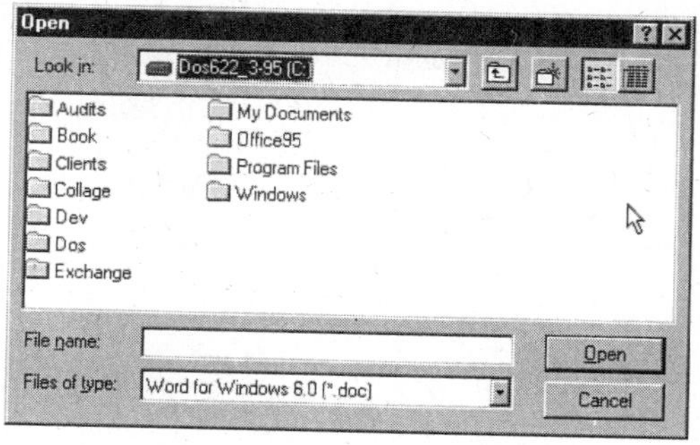

Fig. 12.3 You can open documents from the Open dialog box.

Tip Try using WordPad on older, less powerful laptop computers. It is a small application using less memory and hard disk space, yet it gives you basic word processing features.

Tip To work with multiple WordPad documents, open the WordPad application multiple times.

Note

If a Word for Windows file will not open, try opening it in WordPad. If it opens you may see symbols and characters you do not recognize. Start a new instance of Word for Windows and open a blank document in it. Base this new document on the same template as the document that would not open. Now return to WordPad and copy the entire document. Switch to the blank document in Word for Windows and paste. Reapply paragraph styles as necessary. WordPad seems to be able to open documents that contain file errors that make Word balk.

In WordPad, you can work on only one document at a time. You can start a new document (or open a different document), but the existing document closes. If you haven't saved changes to the existing document, the program asks whether you want to save the changes.

◀ See "Changing Folders in Save As and Open Dialog Boxes," p. 100

▶ See "Working with Long File Names," p. 509

Typing, Saving, and Naming the Document

In the WordPad text area is a flashing insertion point (also known as the cursor). This is where your typing or edits will appear. You can begin typing as soon as you open a file. Use the same word processing techniques you would use in any Windows word processor. As you type, notice that *word-wrap* makes lines of text break and wrap to the next lower line. As you fill the page, the screen scrolls down (or left and right), keeping the insertion point in view.

As you work on your WordPad document, you should save it periodically to avoid losing your work in case of a power failure or equipment malfunction. To save and name a file, follow these steps:

1. Choose File, Save As, or click the Save button in the toolbar. The Save As dialog box appears (see fig. 12.4).

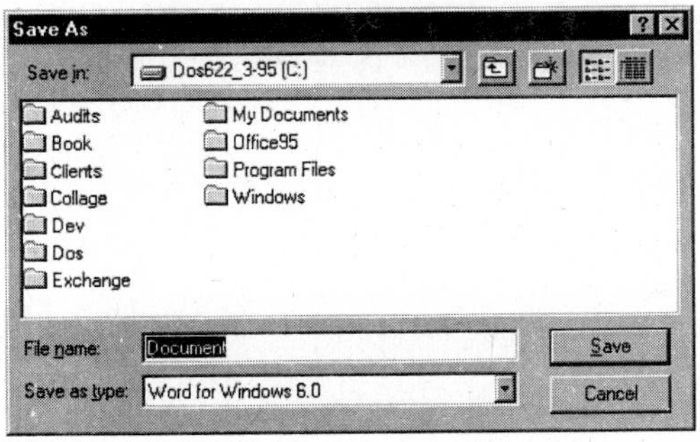

Fig. 12.4
Give a file a name and also indicate where you want it saved in the Save As dialog box.

2. Select the drive where you want to save the file in the Save In box.

3. Double-click the folder in which you want to save the file.

4. Type the file name in the File Name text box.

5. If you want to save the file in a format other than WordPad, select a format from the Save as Type list.

6. Click Save or press Enter.

To resave a file with its current name, choose File, Save; or click the Save button.

Selecting and Editing Text

You can make simple edits in your WordPad documents by moving the insertion point and deleting or inserting text. To make simple insertions, place the insertion point where you want to add text and type. To erase one character at a time, position the insertion point next to the character and press Backspace (to delete characters to the left), or Delete (to delete characters to the right).

However, many edits you need to make are more complex than simply entering or deleting one character at a time. You may want to change a word, delete a sentence, or move a whole paragraph. To do these things, you must identify the text you want to edit or format by selecting it. Selected text appears highlighted (or in reverse video) on-screen, as shown in figure 12.5.

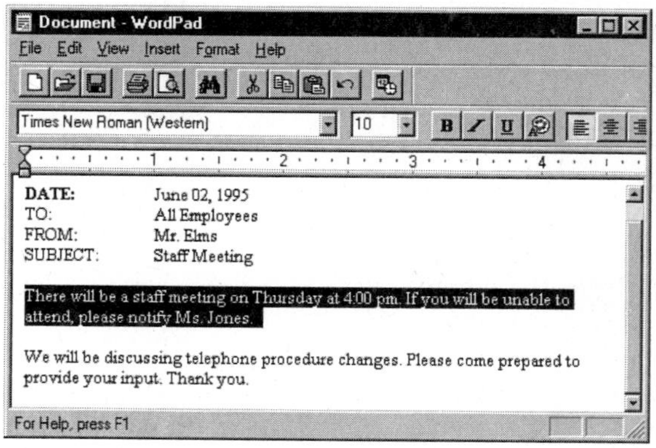

Fig. 12.5
Two sentences selected for editing.

Note

WordPad lets you change your mind about an edit you just made or a sentence you just typed. To undo, choose Edit, Undo; press Alt+Backspace or Ctrl+Z; or click the Undo button in the toolbar. You can restore text you just deleted, delete text you just added, or remove formatting. You can even undo the undo. If you find that Edit Undo removes too much typing, choose Edit, Undo a second time to undo the undo.

Tip
Many of the selection shortcuts you learn in WordPad work in Microsoft Word for Windows.

To select text with the mouse, position the I-beam at the beginning of the text, hold down the mouse button, drag to the end of the text, and release the mouse button. WordPad also offers time-saving selection shortcuts, such as double-clicking to select a word. Techniques for selecting with the mouse are shown in table 12.1.

Table 12.1 Mouse Techniques for Selecting Text

Selection	Action
One word	Double-click the word
Several words	Double-click the first word and drag to the end of the last word
Any amount of text	Press the mouse button and drag from the beginning to the end of the text
Between two points	Move the insertion point to the beginning, click, move to the second point, press and hold down Shift, and click at the second point
One line	Click the selection bar (white space) to the left of the line

Selection	Action
Several lines	Press the mouse button and drag up or down in the selection bar
Paragraph	Double-click in the selection bar (blank area) to the left of the paragraph
Entire document	Press Ctrl and click in the selection bar

To select text with the keyboard, press and hold down the Shift key while moving the insertion point with the arrow keys. You can extend the selection by pressing Shift+Ctrl+an arrow key to select a word at a time. Or, press Shift+End to select text to the end of the line.

◄ See "Selecting Text and Objects," p. 114

To deselect text with the mouse, click once anywhere in the text portion of the window. To deselect text with the keyboard, press any arrow key. Deselected text returns to its normal appearance.

To delete a block of text, select it and press Delete or Backspace or choose Edit, Cut. You also can replace text by selecting it and then typing; WordPad deletes the selected block and inserts the new words.

Moving and Copying Text

Any amount of text—a letter, a word, part of a sentence, or several pages—can be moved from one place in a document to another. You also can copy text from one place in a document to another or to many other places.

To move or copy text, follow these steps:

1. Select the text you want to move or copy.
2. Choose Edit, Cut, or press Shift+Del or Ctrl+X, or click the Cut button (to move text).

   Or choose Edit, Copy, or press F2, Ctrl+Ins, or Ctrl+C, or click the Copy button (to copy text).
3. Move the insertion point to where you want to move or copy the text.
4. Choose Edit, Paste, press Shift+Ins or Ctrl+V, or click the Paste button.

◄ See "Copying and Moving," p. 115

◄ See "Learning About Drag-and-Drop," p. 105

To quickly move selected text, you can use the drag-and-drop technique. Select the text, point to it with the mouse, hold down the left mouse button, and drag to a new location. Release the mouse and the text is dropped. Hold down the Control key while you perform the process to copy the selection.

> **Note**
>
> To make it easier to copy text between applications, minimize applications that are not involved so they are on the taskbar. Right-click in a gray area of the taskbar and choose Tile Horizontal or Tile Vertical. This will put the two application windows side-by-side and make it easy to work.

Finding and Replacing Text

You can use WordPad to search a document and find or change text—for example, to change a misspelled name or correct an old date. The Edit menu includes three commands that help you find text and make changes quickly: Find (you also can click the Find button), Find Next (repeats the previous search), and Replace.

The Find and Replace commands operate through dialog boxes (see fig. 12.6). After you enter the text you want to find or change, WordPad starts at the insertion point and searches forward through the document, locating and selecting the first occurrence of the text.

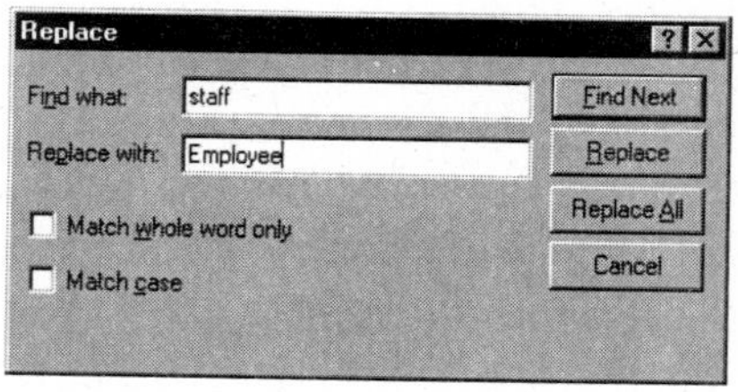

Fig. 12.6
Use the Edit, Replace command to quickly change text.

Formatting the Document

WordPad offers a number of ways to customize the look of your documents. You can add emphasis to individual characters or words with bold or italic, specify the font and point size of the text, and so on. These formats are called *character formatting* and apply to individual characters within words.

You can format paragraphs individually or as a group. For example, you can set up tables with special column alignment, center headings and quotations, and so on. This type of formatting is called *paragraph formatting.*

When the text of your document is finished, it's time to think about the *document formatting.* Do you plan to print the document on letterhead or other special paper that requires certain margins to fit correctly? Document formatting controls the look of the document as a whole.

The following sections describe the three types of WordPad formatting in detail.

Character Formatting

You can control, or enhance, the appearance of characters with the Format, Font command or from the Format bar. You can select, for example, a new font or font size, or select bold to emphasize an important point. If you already have typed the characters, you can change their appearance by selecting the text and choosing options from the Format bar or by choosing Format, Font. If you have not yet typed the text, position the insertion point where you want the enhanced text to begin, choose the enhancement, and type the text.

Many of the character enhancement options, shown in the Font dialog box in figure 12.7, "toggle" on and off like a light switch. You turn them on the same way you turn them off, by simply choosing the command. To make plain text bold, for example, select the text and click the Bold button. To make bold text plain, do the same thing.

To change character formatting, select the text you want to change and select character formatting options from the Format bar or with the Format, Font command.

Tip

To add bold from the keyboard, select the text you want bold and press Ctrl+B. Press Ctrl+I for italic, and Ctrl+U for underline.

Note

You can quickly make up a font chart for reference purposes by using the right click feature in the Font dialog box or the Format bar. When you display the Font dialog box, you can right-click in the Font, Font style, or Size boxes and select Cut, Copy, Paste, or Delete from the menu that displays. (Right-click in the Font or Size boxes in the Format bar for the same menu.) If you select a font, for example, right-click, and choose Copy, you can return to your document, right-click and choose Paste to insert the font name (style or size) into the document. Do that with the entire list of fonts and you will have a sample of each font displayed with its name.

Note

Add special symbols from the ANSI code (check your printer manual for the codes) by pressing and holding Alt as you type the sequence of four digits that describe the letter. The numbers must be typed on the numeric pad. There must be four digits so fill in unused digits with zeros. For example, press Alt+0169, then release Alt to insert the copyright symbol.

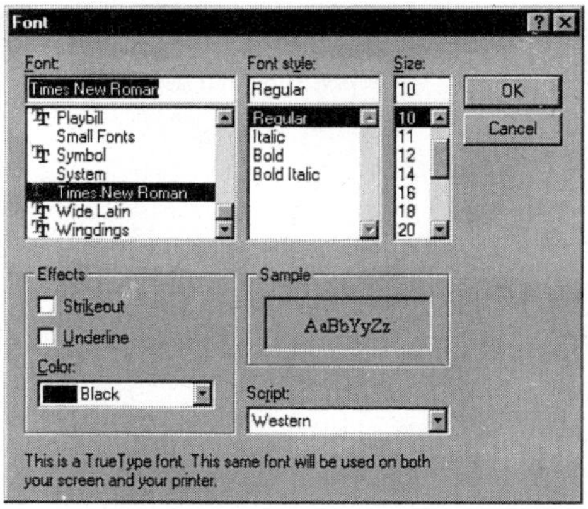

Fig. 12.7
Change the character formatting at the Font dialog box.

Paragraph Formatting

Paragraph formatting describes the appearance of a paragraph (or of a single line that stands by itself as a paragraph). This level of formatting includes text alignment and indentation. Some formatting choices were made for you already: by default, text is left-aligned, and no paragraphs are indented, as you can see in the Paragraph dialog box in figure 12.8.

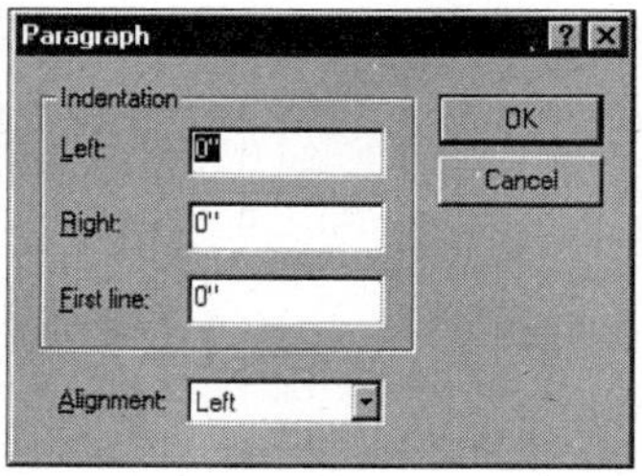

Fig. 12.8
Change the paragraph formatting at the Format Paragraph dialog box.

In WordPad, paragraphs can be aligned with the left or right margin, or in the center between the margins. You can set alignment with either the Format, Paragraph command or with the alignment buttons in the Format bar.

Paragraphs can be indented to set them off from the main body of text—for example, for long quotations. Also, the first lines of paragraphs can be indented so that you do not have to press Tab at the beginning of each paragraph.

Indentations, like all measurements in WordPad, are measured in inches rather than characters, because WordPad supports different font sizes and proportional spacing. (Measurement units can be changed. See the "Changing WordPad Settings" section later in this chapter for more information.)

The indentation options are available in the Paragraph dialog box (refer to fig. 12.8), and also on the Ruler.

▶ See "Changing the Screen Display," p. 373

Note

In *proportional* spacing, the widths of letters are proportional; for example, the letter *i* is narrower than the letter *m*. If margins and indentations were measured in characters, WordPad would not know how large to make an indentation: an inch might contain 16 *i*'s but only 12 *m*'s. Similarly, varying font sizes means that WordPad cannot measure the length of a page by lines.

To indent a paragraph with the ruler, follow these steps:

1. Choose View, Ruler to display the ruler, if it is not currently displayed.
2. Position the insertion point inside the paragraph or select those paragraphs you want to change.
3. Drag the indent markers to the left or right (see fig. 12.9).

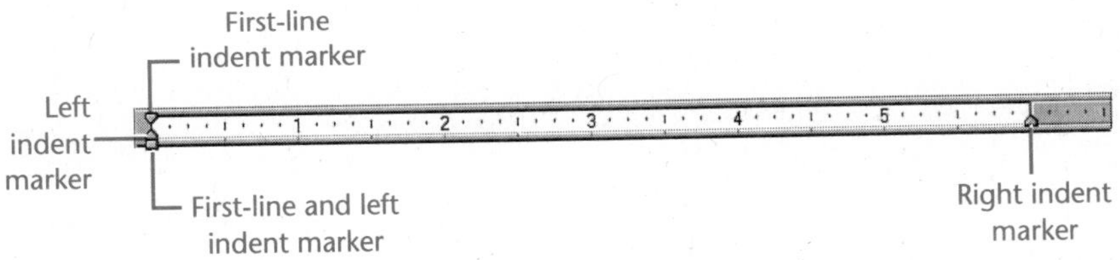

Fig. 12.9
It's easy to change the paragraph indentation with the Ruler.

Document Formatting

Document formatting affects an entire document and its appearance. In a new WordPad document, many document formatting choices are made for you already. Margins, for example, are set to 1.25 inches on the left and right, and 1 inch on the top and bottom. Default tab settings are set every .5 inch. The paper is portrait-oriented.

You can change tabs with the Format, Tabs command or on the ruler. All tabs are left-aligned. Set tabs in inches from the left margin (as shown in figure 12.10), not from another tab setting. The ruler may be the easiest way to set tabs. Click on the ruler where you want a tab set. Move tab settings by dragging the tab arrows left or right. Remove tabs by dragging them down off the ruler.

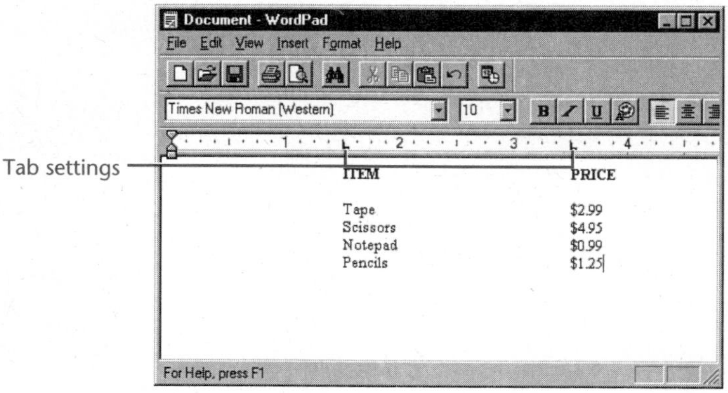

Fig. 12.10 Set tabs on the Tab ruler by clicking the position where you want the new tab set.

Margins and paper instructions, as well as printer selection, are set at the Page Setup dialog box (see fig. 12.11). Follow these steps:

1. Choose File, Page Setup. The Page Setup dialog box displays.
2. Select the Top, Bottom, Left, and Right boxes in turn and type a decimal measurement for each margin.
3. Select a paper Size, Source, or Orientation.
4. Click Printer to select a printer.
5. Click OK or press Enter.

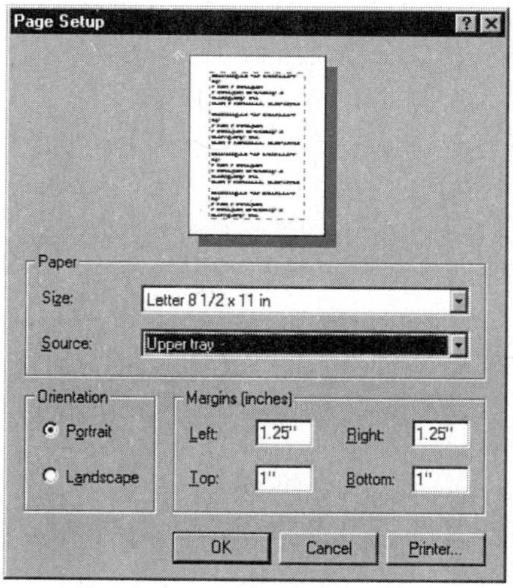

Fig. 12.11 Change the margins in the Page Setup dialog box.

Printing a Document

Printing with WordPad involves two steps—selecting the printer, and specifying what you want to print.

◄ See "Printing from Applications," p. 168

The Print Preview screen displays your document as it will appear in print (see fig. 12.12). Use it to ensure that what you're about to print is what you expect. You'll save printing time and paper.

The pointer at the Print Preview screen becomes a magnifying glass and works like the Zoom In and Zoom Out buttons. To preview your document, choose File, Print Preview, or click the Print Preview button.

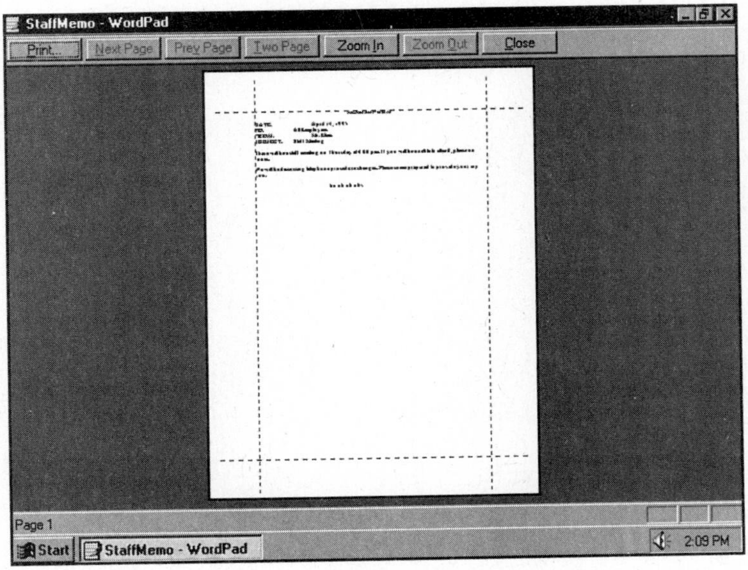

Fig. 12.12 WordPad provides a preview screen where you can examine your document before you print.

Selecting a Printer

Before you can print, you must select a printer. Once a printer is selected, it remains selected for all documents—you won't have to select a printer again unless you want to change to a different printer. To identify and set up the default printer, follow these steps:

1. Choose File, Page Setup (the Page Setup dialog box appears) and click Printer; or choose File, Print (the Print dialog box appears).

2. Select a printer from the Name box.

3. Click OK.

Tip
You can add a shortcut printer icon to the desktop and then drag a saved file onto it. The file will print.

◀ See "Print from the Desktop," p. 179

The printer list includes all the printers installed on the computer for Windows. Click the Properties button to select additional information, such as paper size and graphics resolution.

Printing a File

To print a document, follow these steps:

1. Choose File, Print. The Print dialog box appears (see fig. 12.13).
2. Select Print range All to print all the pages; select Selection to print only the selected text; or type a range of pages to print in the Pages from and Pages to text boxes.
3. Mark the Print to File check box to print to a file rather than to the printer. You are prompted to provide a filename and a location.

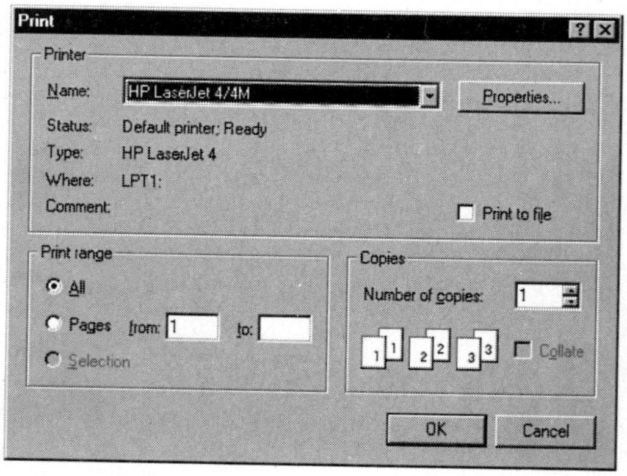

Fig. 12.13
In the Print dialog box you can vary the number of copies you print and select exactly which pages you print.

Tip
To print the whole document without selecting any special options, simply click the Print button.

Note

If the printer you want to use is not connected to your computer, you can create a file that is ready for printing by selecting Print to File. All the printing information is saved in the file you name. Then, when you're ready to print, you can send that file directly to the printer, whether or not the printer's computer has WordPad. If, for example, the printer's computer is running DOS, at the DOS prompt, type **copy *filename* /B PRN**, where filename includes the path and filename.

4. Type the number of copies you want to print in the Number of copies box.

5. Select Collate to collate multiple copies of the document (available if your printer supports collating).

6. Click OK or press Enter.

Changing the Screen Display

WordPad provides options from the View menu that let you add or remove elements from the screen display. Each of these elements, including Toolbar, Format Bar, Ruler, and Status Bar, can be toggled on and off. A check mark in the menu indicates that an item is turned on. To toggle screen elements on or off, click the View menu and choose the command you want. The View menu also includes the Options command for customizing some of the WordPad settings.

◄ See "Changing WordPad Settings," p. 373

Changing WordPad Settings

You can change several of the WordPad default settings in the Options dialog box (see fig. 12.14). Your choices, available on each of the six tabs, include setting the measurement units, determining how word wrap operates, and presetting the toolbars that will display. Choose View, Options, click the tab you want, make your selections, and click OK.

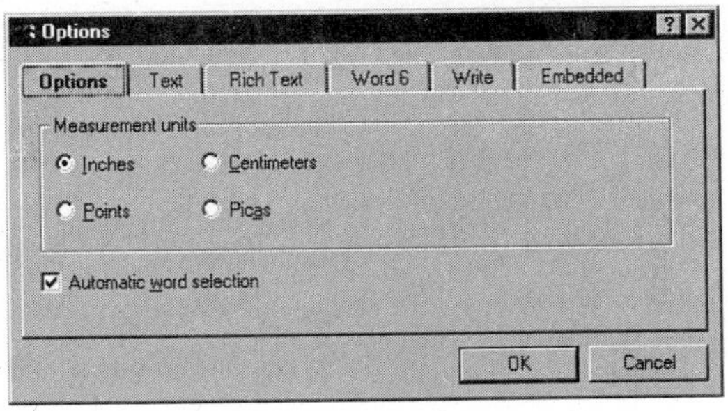

Fig. 12.14
You can customize some of the WordPad defaults in the Options dialog box.

Exiting WordPad

After you finish writing or are ready to stop for the day, exit WordPad and return to the Windows desktop by choosing File, Exit or by clicking the Close button in the upper-right corner of the application window.

Using Notepad

Notepad is a miniature text editor. Just as you use a notepad on the desk, you can use Notepad to take notes on-screen while working in other Windows applications. Notepad uses little memory and is useful for editing text that you want to copy in a Windows or DOS application that lacks editing capability.

Notepad retrieves and saves files in text format. This feature makes Notepad a convenient editor for creating and altering text-based files. Because Notepad stores files in text format, almost all word processors can retrieve Notepad's files.

Use Notepad to hold text you want to move to another application. Clipboard can hold only one selection at a time, but the Notepad can serve as a text scrapbook when you are moving several items as a group.

Starting Notepad

To start Notepad, follow these steps:

1. Open the Start menu and choose Programs; then choose Accessories.
2. Choose Notepad. Notepad starts up and displays a blank document in the Notepad window (see fig. 12.15). You can begin typing.

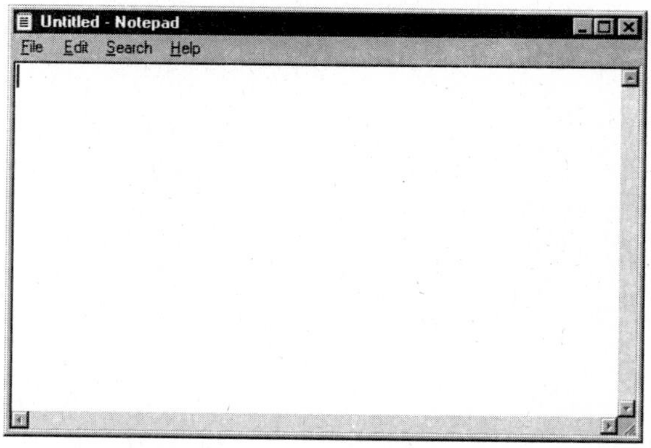

Fig. 12.15
The initial blank Notepad file is ready for text.

> **Caution**
>
> Be careful when you edit with Notepad. Because Notepad creates text files, you can open and edit important system, application, and data files. To avoid loss of data or applications, make sure that you open only files with which you are familiar.

Working with Documents in Notepad

Unlike most word processing applications, Notepad doesn't by default wrap text to the following line. You must either choose Edit, Word Wrap, or press Enter at the end of each line.

You can move the insertion point by using either the mouse or the keyboard. You select and edit text in Notepad the same way you select and edit text in WordPad.

◄ See "Selecting and Editing Text," p. 363

Limited formatting is available from the File, Page Setup command. You can change margins and add a header or footer. You cannot format characters or paragraphs in any way, although you can use Tab, the space bar, and Backspace to align text. Tab stops are preset at every eight characters.

◄ See "Copying and Moving," p. 115

With Notepad's Edit commands, you can cut, copy, and move text from one place in a file to another. Text you cut or copy is stored in the Clipboard. When you paste text, this text is copied from the Clipboard to the document at the insertion point.

Creating a Time-Log File with Notepad

By typing a simple command at the top of a Notepad document, **.LOG**, you can have Notepad enter the current time and date at the end of a document each time you open the file. This feature is convenient for taking phone messages or for calculating the time spent on a project. As an alternative, you can choose Edit, Time/Date or press F5 to insert the current time and date at the insertion point.❖

Chapter 13

Using Paint, Calculator, and other Accessories

by Ron Person

The desktop accessories that come with Windows can help you perform special tasks related to a current project without leaving the application. You may be working in Word for Windows, for example, and need to make a quick calculation; the Windows Calculator can do the job. You can create computer "paintings" in Paint to illustrate a story, to emphasize an important point in a report, or to clarify instructions.

The desktop accessories take advantage of one of Windows' most powerful features: the capability of running several applications simultaneously. As you work in the main application, you can keep the Windows desktop applications running at the same time. Because so little of the computer's memory is used, the desktop accessories don't slow you down.

In this chapter, you learn to

- Use Paint to create and edit pictures that can be inserted into other applications
- Use Calculator to perform calculations
- Set the clock that displays on the taskbar
- Insert special characters into any Windows document with Character Map

Using Windows Paint

Even though Paint is a simple, easy-to-use graphics application, it may be as powerful a graphics application as you will ever need. Paint is fun, but it also is a serious business tool. With Paint, you can create everything from free-flowing drawings to precise mathematical charts, and you can use your creations in other Windows applications, such as WordPad or Word for Windows.

The following are some of the graphic effects you can create with Paint:

- Lines in many widths, shades, and colors
- Brush strokes in a variety of styles, widths, shades, and colors
- Unfilled or filled shapes with shades or colors
- Text in many sizes, styles, and colors
- Special effects such as rotating, tilting, and inverting

Because Paint is a bitmap graphics application, the shapes you create are painted on-screen in one layer. You cannot reshape a box or move an object behind another object, but you can cut out a box and move it somewhere else, cut out a picture of a house and tilt it, cut out a pattern and flip it, or change the colors of your painting. You can also erase your painting (or part of it) and paint something new.

Starting Windows Paint

To start Paint, follow these steps:

1. Open the Start menu; then choose Programs, Accessories.
2. Choose Paint.

Paint starts up and opens a new, empty Paint file (see fig. 13.1).

To open a previously saved Paint file, choose File, Open. Select the file from the Open dialog box.

Selecting Tools and Colors

To paint, draw, fill, color or shade, write, and edit in Paint, you first must select the appropriate tool and shade or color. Figure 13.2 shows the individual tools in the toolbox on the left side of the screen.

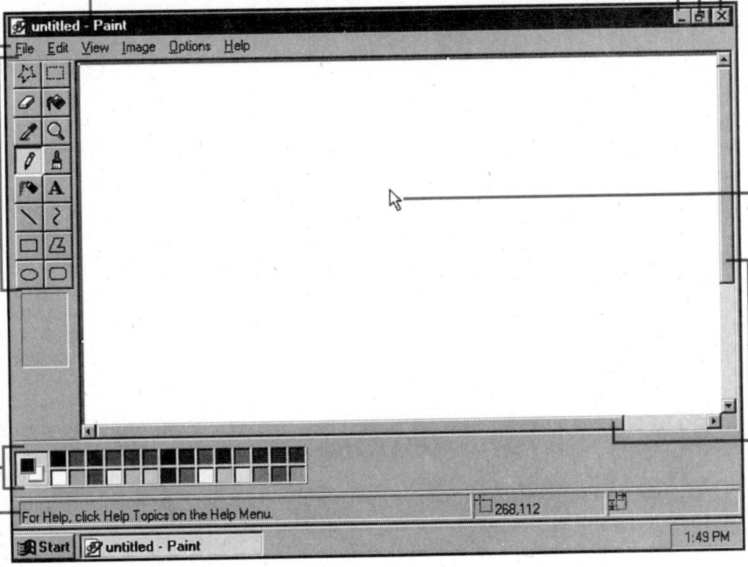

Fig. 13.1
When you start Paint, a new file opens.

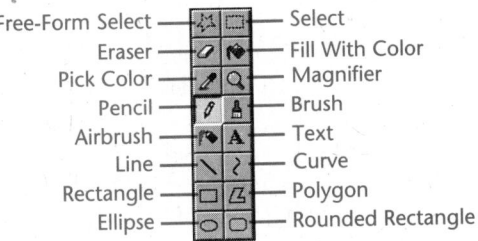

Fig. 13.2
The Paint toolbox provides the tools you need to create and modify a picture.

The palette offers two choices: foreground and background shade or color. At the left end of the palette is a box overlaying a box (see fig. 13.3). The top box is the foreground color; the bottom box is the background color. The color you use depends on which mouse button you use to draw lines, brush strokes, and shapes. The left mouse button selects the foreground color; the right mouse button selects the background color. For example, when you draw a shaded box with the left mouse button, the foreground color borders the box and the background color fills the box. The opposite is true when you draw the box with the right mouse button. (Drawing is discussed in the next section, "Using the Paint Toolbox.")

Tip
If you draw with the right mouse button, the foreground and background colors will be reversed.

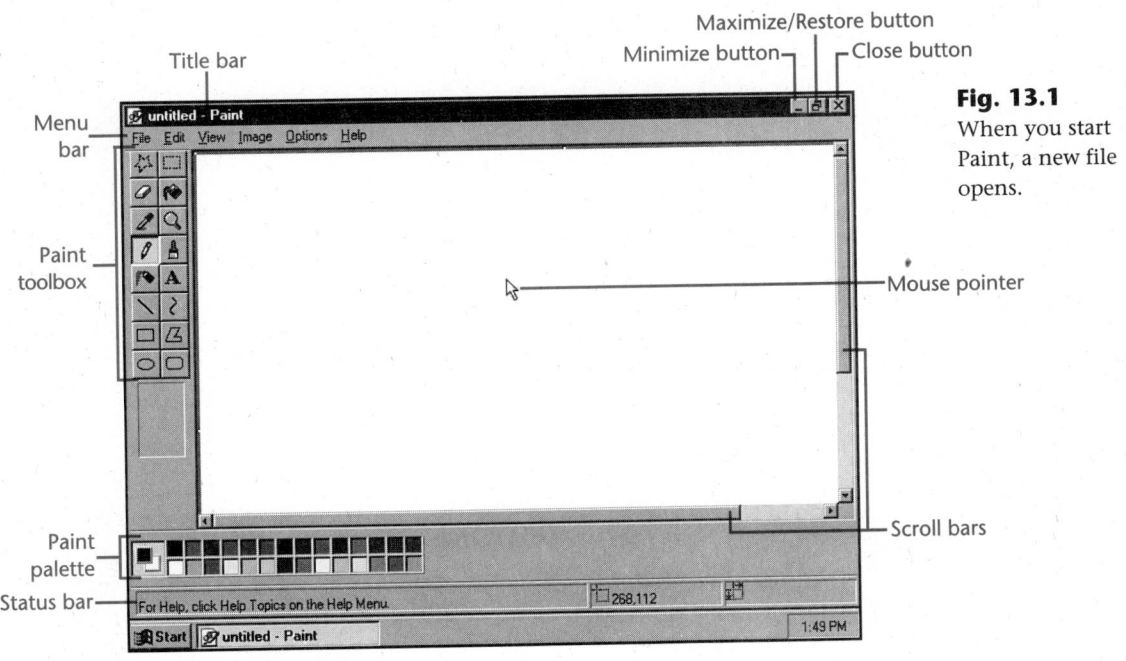

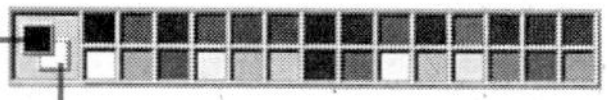

Fig. 13.3 Choose foreground and background colors from the Paint palette.

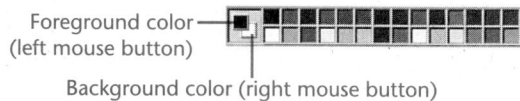

To select a tool or color, position the pointer on the tool or foreground color that you want and click the left mouse button. To select a background color, point to the color you want and click the right mouse button.

Using the Paint Toolbox

The Paint toolbox includes tools for selecting areas, airbrushing, typing text, erasing, filling, brushing, drawing curves or straight lines, and drawing filled or unfilled shapes. Most of the tools operate using a similar process.

To draw with the tools in the Paint toolbox, follow these steps:

1. Click to select the tool you want to use.
2. Move the pointer to where you want to begin drawing.
3. Press and hold down the mouse button as you drag the mouse.
4. Release the mouse button to stop drawing.

Three exceptions to this process are

- The Text tool, which works by clicking and typing.
- The Paint Fill tool, which works by pointing and clicking.
- The Curve tool, which works by clicking, dragging, and clicking.

Aligning Drawn Objects

When you want lines or shapes to line up accurately on-screen, refer to the cursor position indicators in the status bar at the bottom of Paint's window. The two numbers that display tell you the position of the insertion point or drawing tool on-screen. The position is given in X, Y coordinates, measured in pixels, from the top left corner of the painting. The left number is the X-coordinate (the position relative to the left edge of the painting); the right number is the Y-coordinate (the position relative to the top of the painting). If the numbers in the Cursor Position window read *42, 100*, for example, the cursor is 42 pixels from the left edge of the painting and 100 pixels down from the top of the painting.

Whichever tool you use, Edit, Undo is a useful ally. Use it to undo your most recent action. Undo will undo up to the last three actions. Just continue to select Undo to undo the number of actions you desire.

Note

Several tools, including the Selection and Shape tools, use the right mouse button to undo. To cancel the shape you're currently drawing, click the right mouse button *before* you release the left mouse button.

Troubleshooting

What if I choose the wrong option or change my mind?

You can choose Edit, Undo to undo your last choice. If you undo something by mistake, you can choose Edit, Repeat to redo it. Because Undo can only undo the last three changes you've made it is a good idea to save your work with a different file name every ten or fifteen minutes. When you finish working delete the unneeded files.

The following sections describe how to use each of the toolbox tools.

Selecting a Free-Form Area

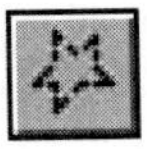

The Free-Form Select tool selects areas inside the line you draw. Click the Free-Form Select tool and select either Transparent (doesn't include the background) or Opaque (does include the background) at the bottom of the toolbox. Draw in any shape to enclose an area of the drawing. If you make a mistake while using the Free-Form Select tool, click the left mouse button outside the cutout area to cancel the cutout and try again. Once enclosed, an area can be moved, cut or copied (and then pasted), resized, tilted, flipped, or inverted with the Edit menu commands. If you cut an area, the selected background color shows the color the cleared area will be. With an area selected, press Delete to delete it from the picture.

Selecting a Rectangular Area

The Select tool selects areas inside the rectangle you drag. Click the Select tool and select either Transparent or Opaque at the bottom of the toolbox. Drag to size a rectangular area. If you make a mistake while using the Select tool, click the left mouse button outside the cutout area to cancel the cutout and try again. Once enclosed, the area can be moved, cut or copied (and then pasted), resized, tilted, flipped, or inverted with the Edit menu commands. If you cut an area, the selected background color shows the color the cleared area will be. With an area selected, press Delete to delete it from the picture.

Erasing Parts of Your Picture

The Eraser tool erases as you drag it over your picture, just like an eraser on a blackboard. Click the Eraser tool and then select the eraser size from the bottom of the toolbox. Drag across the picture with the left mouse button pressed to erase. The selected background color shows the color the erased area will be. Choose Edit, Undo if you want to restore what you have erased.

Filling an Area with Color

The Fill With Color tool fills inside a shape. Click the Fill With Color tool and select foreground and background colors from the palette. Position the pointed tip of the Fill With Color tool inside the shape that you want to fill. Click the left mouse button to fill with the foreground color, or the right mouse button to fill with the background color.

Picking Up a Color from the Drawing

The Pick Color tool picks up the color on which you click for use in the current tool. To pick up the color of the spot where you click, click the Pick Color tool and then click anywhere in the painting. You can resume using the previous tool or select another tool and paint with the new color.

Magnifying the View of the Drawing

The Magnifier tool magnifies the view of the drawing. Click the Magnifier tool and then select a magnification at the bottom of the toolbox (1x, 2x, 6x, or 8x). Position the rectangle over the area you want to enlarge and click the left mouse button. You can work with the individual pixels that make up the painting. You can use any of the tools in the magnified view. To reset the drawing size with the Magnifier tool, choose 1x.

Figure 13.4 shows the original 1x magnification (top) and the area magnified 6x (bottom).

Drawing a Free-Form Line

The Pencil tool draws a one-pixel-wide free-form line in the currently selected color. Draw with the left mouse button pressed to use the foreground color; draw with the right mouse button pressed to draw with the background color.

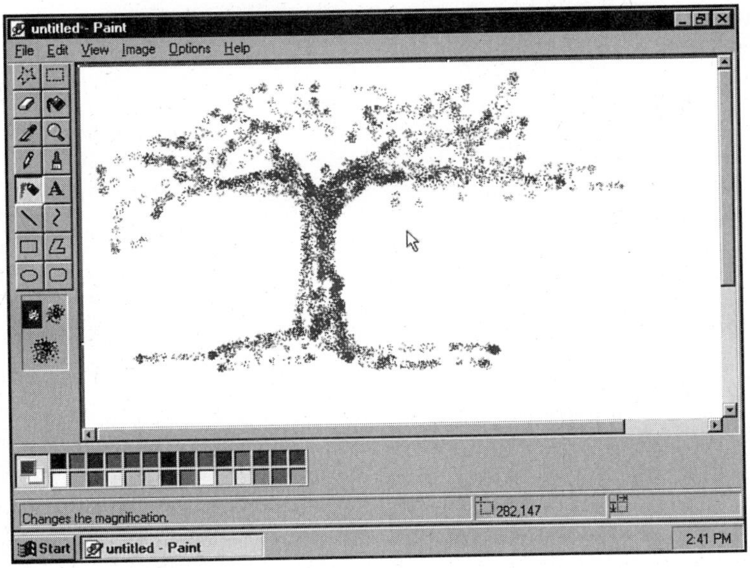

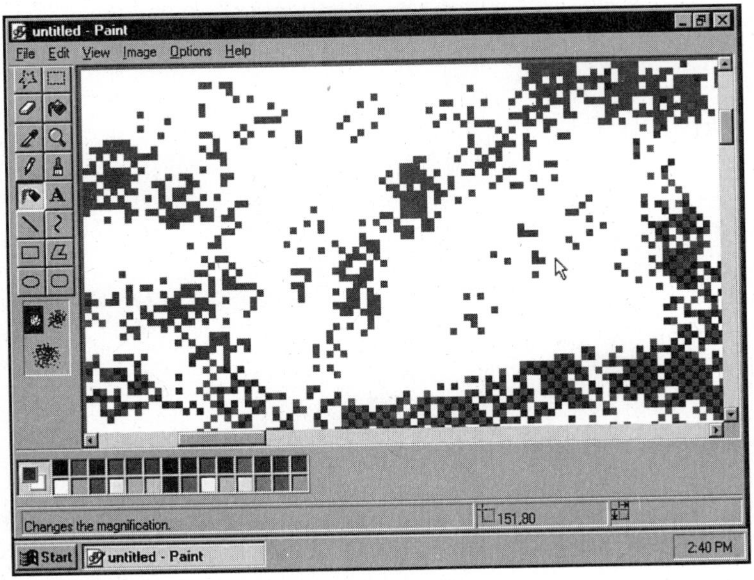

Fig. 13.4
Use the Magnifier tool to enlarge a portion of the picture so you can easily modify it. In this example, the picture has been magnified six times to enable pixel-by-pixel modifications.

Painting with a Brush

The Brush tool paints with a brush. Click the brush and select from the brush shapes that display at the bottom of the toolbox. Paint with the left mouse button pressed to use the foreground color; paint with the right mouse button pressed to use the background color.

Painting with an Airbrush

The Airbrush tool paints with an airbrush effect. Click the Airbrush tool and select from the sprayer sizes that display at the bottom of the toolbox. Select a color from the Color palette: the left mouse button sprays with the foreground color; the right mouse button sprays with the background color. The Airbrush sprays a transparent mist of color; the more densely you spray, the heavier your coverage.

Adding Text to a Picture

Use the Text tool to add text to your painting. Click the Text tool and select Opaque (the background color fills the text box behind the text) or Transparent (the picture appears behind the text) in the area below the toolbox. Next, in the picture area, drag to determine the size of the text box. Choose View, Text Toolbar to display the Paint Fonts toolbar. Select a font, point size, and bold, italic, or underline options. Click in the text box and type. Use the limited set of editing tools, including word-wrap and Backspace. Text appears in the foreground color. Figure 13.5 shows text added to a painting and the Paint Fonts toolbar.

Tip
If your painting will include a lot of text, type the text in Word or WordPad, select and copy it, and then paste it into Paint.

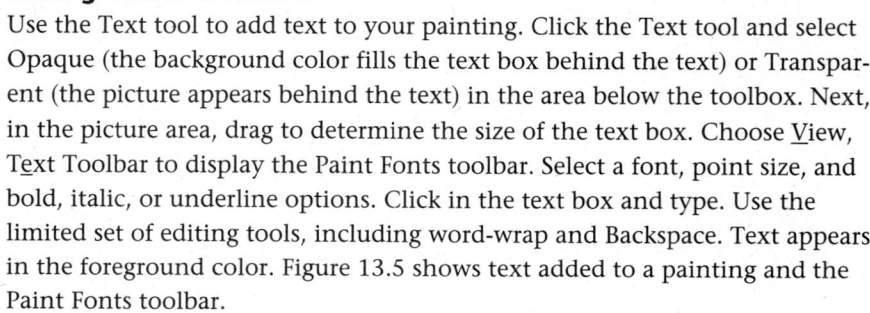

Troubleshooting

Text Toolbar is not available from the View menu.

You must click the Text tool and drag a text area before Text Toolbar is available from the View menu.

An error message appears saying that I need to resize the text box.

The text box isn't large enough to hold the text you are pasting into it. Enlarge the box and try again.

Tip
If your document will have more text than graphics, create the graphic in Paint and copy it; then paste it into your Word or WordPad document.

Drawing a Straight Line

The Line tool draws a straight line. Click the Line tool and select a line width from the display at the bottom of the toolbox. Drag the mouse to draw a straight line. The left mouse button draws with the foreground color; the right mouse button draws with the background color. To undo the line that you're drawing, click the right mouse button before you release the left mouse button. To draw a line that is perfectly vertical, horizontal, or at a 45-degree angle, press and hold down the Shift key as you draw.

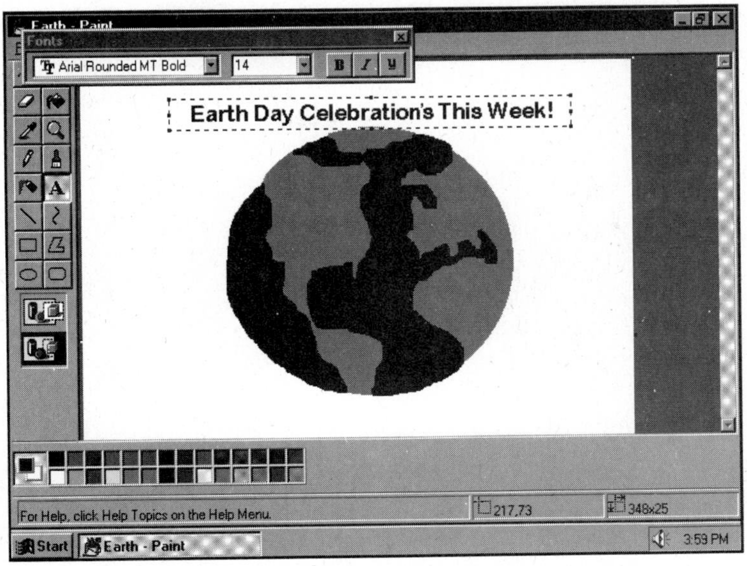

Fig. 13.5
Add text to your picture with the Text tool.

Drawing Curves

The Curve tool draws a curve. To draw a curve, follow these steps:

1. Click the Curve tool.
2. Select a line width from the display at the bottom of the toolbox.
3. Draw a straight line and release the mouse button.
4. Click the left mouse button and drag away from the line to pull the line into a curve.
5. When you've achieved the shape you want, release the mouse button to complete the line. Repeat the process on the other side of the line to create an *s*-shaped curve (see fig. 13.6).

Tip
The left mouse button draws with the foreground color; the right mouse button draws with the background color.

Drawing Rectangles and Squares

The Rectangle tool draws a rectangle or square with different borders or fill color. Click the Rectangle tool and select Border Only, Border and Fill, or Fill Only from the bottom of the toolbox. To create the size box you want, press and hold down the mouse button and drag to that size. Release the mouse button when you have the size you want. Use the left mouse button to border with the foreground color and fill with the background color; use the right mouse button to border with the background color and fill with the foreground color. The size of the border is determined by the last line size you selected.

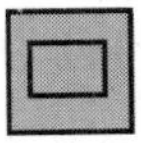

Tip
To draw a square, select the rectangle tool, and then press and hold down the Shift key as you draw.

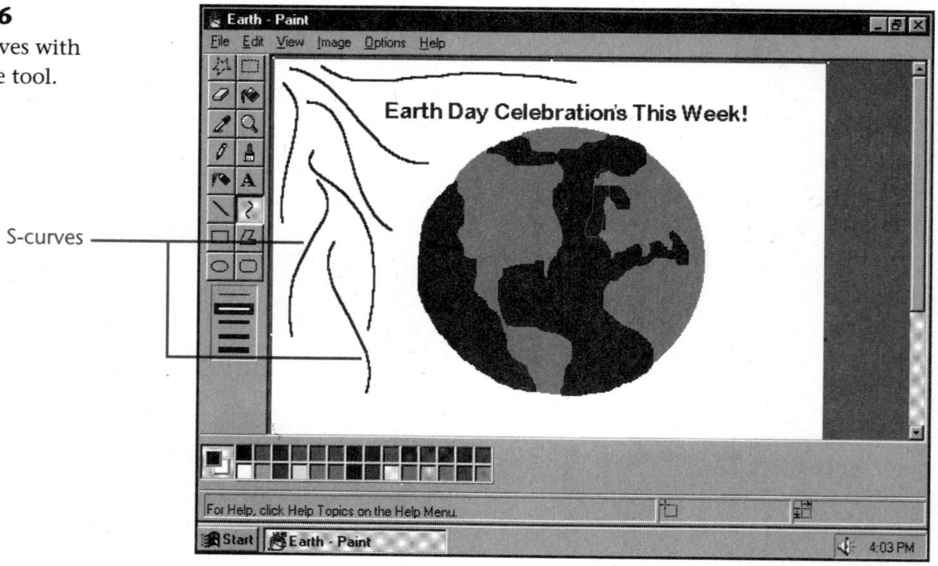

Fig. 13.6
Draw curves with the Curve tool.

Drawing Objects with Many Sides (Polygons)

The Polygon tool draws a multisided shape. Each side on the shape is a straight line. To draw a polygon, follow these steps:

1. Click the Polygon tool and select Border Only, Border and Fill, or Fill Only from the bottom of the toolbox.
2. Click and drag to draw the first side of the polygon.
3. Release the mouse button and click to draw each of the other sides.
4. Double-click to finish.

Use the left mouse button to border with the foreground color and fill with the background color; use the right mouse button to border with the background color and fill with the foreground color. The size of the border is determined by the last line size you selected.

Drawing Ellipses and Circles

The Ellipse tool draws an *ellipse* (an oval) or circle. Click the Ellipse tool and select Border Only, Border and Fill, or Fill Only from the bottom of the toolbox. To draw a circle, press and hold down the Shift key as you draw.

Use the left mouse button to border with the foreground color and fill with the background color; use the right mouse button to border with the background color and fill with the foreground color. The size of the border is determined by the last line size you selected.

Drawing Rectangles with Rounded Corners

Use the Rounded Rectangle tool to draw a rectangle with rounded edges. Click the Rounded Rectangle tool and select Border Only, Border and Fill, or Fill Only from the bottom of the toolbox. Press and hold down the mouse button and drag to create the size box you want. Release the mouse button when you have the size you want.

Tip
To draw a square with rounded corners, press and hold down the Shift key as you draw.

Use the left mouse button to border with the foreground color and fill with the background color; use the right mouse button to border with the background color and fill with the foreground color. The size of the border is determined by the last line size you selected.

Editing a Painting

With Paint, you can edit a painting. As you edit, however, be aware that completed objects cannot be edited, only erased or painted over and replaced. The method that you use to complete an object depends on the object. To complete a straight line, for example, you *release* the mouse button; to complete text, you *click* the mouse button. Any object that has not been completed is subject to edits. You can cancel a line or curve before you complete it, for example, by clicking the right mouse button; you can change the appearance of text *before* you complete it by making a selection from the Text toolbar.

The following sections describe how to use each of the Edit menu commands.

Undoing Changes

To undo changes, choose Edit, Undo (or press Ctrl+Z). Choose Edit, Undo again to continue undoing up to three previous changes.

Repeating a Change

Choose Edit, Repeat (or press F4) to redo the last change you made with the Edit, Undo command.

▶ See "Using the Clipboard to Exchange Data," p. 424

Cutting to the Clipboard

Use Edit, Cut to remove a part of your painting and place it into the Clipboard. Select the area you want to cut or copy, and then choose Edit, Cut (Ctrl+X).

Copying to the Clipboard

Use Edit, Copy to copy a part of your painting and place it into the Clipboard. Select the area you want to cut or copy, and then choose Edit, Copy (Ctrl+C).

Pasting from the Clipboard

Use Edit, Paste to place a copy of the contents of the Clipboard into your painting. Display the area of the painting where you want to paste the contents of the Clipboard and choose Edit, Paste (Ctrl+V). The pasted object appears at the top left of the screen and is enclosed by a dotted line to show that the object still is selected. Drag the selection to the location you want and click outside it.

Removing a Selected Object or Area

Select the area you want to remove. Choose Edit, Clear Selection, or press the Delete key; it is deleted from the painting. This option does not place the selected object into the Clipboard.

Copying Part of Your Painting to a File

Use Edit, Copy To to save a portion of your painting in a file. Select the portion of the painting you want to save to a file. Open the Edit menu and choose Copy To. Give the file a name (use the file extension that is appropriate for the type of graphic file you want to create, such as PCX), select a directory or another drive, and click OK.

Pasting a File into Your Painting

Use the Edit, Paste From command to insert a file into your painting. Use the Rectangular Select tool to select the area of the painting into which you want to paste the file. Choose the Edit, Paste From command. Type the file name, select a directory or another drive, and click OK. The file is pasted in the top left corner of the screen. Drag it to a new location.

Many of the commands described in the preceding sections are also available from a shortcut menu. When you select a portion of your painting with either of the Pick tools and click the right mouse button, a menu appears (see fig. 13.7). Additional commands in the shortcut menu are described in the later section, "Creating Special Effects."

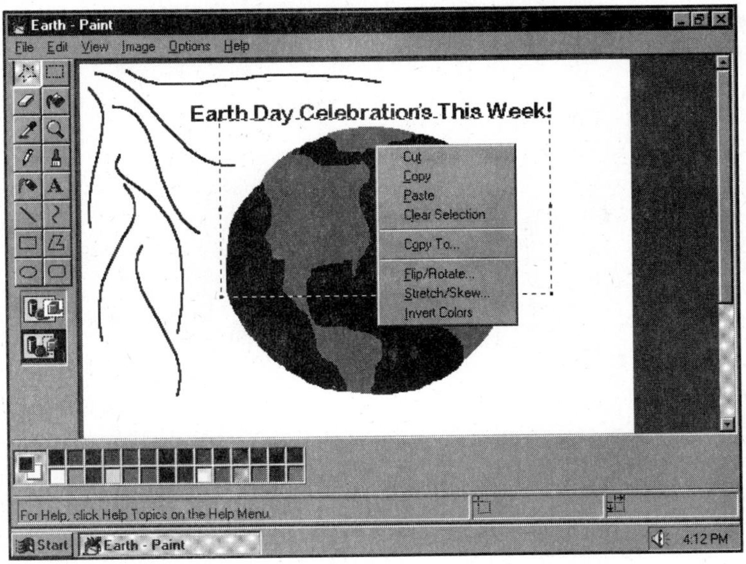

Fig. 13.7
A shortcut menu appears when you click the right mouse button over a selected area of your painting.

Moving a Selection

You can move an object or area on-screen after you select it. (The object is still selected if you just pasted it.) To move a selection, follow these steps:

1. Use one of the Select tools to select an object or area of the drawing. Select either Transparent (to leave the background showing) or Opaque (to hide the background). A dashed line encloses the selection.
2. Move the crosshair over the selection. The crosshair becomes an arrow.
3. Press and hold down the left mouse button to drag the selection to its new location. To copy the selection to a new location rather than moving it, hold down the Ctrl key as you drag the object to its new location.
4. Release the mouse button, and click outside the selection to fix it in its new location.

Getting Different Views of the Painting

You can zoom in to get a closer look at your painting or zoom out to see the whole page. Use either the View, Zoom command or the Magnifier tool.

◄ See "Magnifying the View of the Drawing," p. 382

The larger magnifications of the picture display the *pixels*, or tiny squares of color, that make up your painting. You can paint pixels in the selected foreground color by clicking the dots with the left mouse button, and in the background color by clicking the right mouse button.

To zoom in for a close-up view of your painting, follow these steps:

1. Choose View, Zoom.
2. Select Normal Size (Ctrl+Page Up), Large Size (Ctrl+Page Down), or Custom. If you select Custom, the View Zoom dialog box appears. Select 100%, 200%, 400%, 600%, or 800%.
3. Use the scroll bars to display the part of the painting you want.

To zoom back out to regular editing view, choose View, Zoom again and select Normal Size. Or, click the Magnifier tool and then click in the picture.

You can choose View, View Bitmap (Ctrl+F) when you are in the regular view to display a reduced picture of the entire page. When you choose View, View Bitmap, all toolboxes, menus, and scroll bars disappear, and your picture expands to fill the window. You can only view in this mode; you cannot edit your painting in Picture mode. Click anywhere in the display to return to normal size.

With an enlarged view of your picture, you can choose to add a grid for more exact drawing. Choose View, Zoom, Show Grid (Ctrl+G). You can also add a thumbnail, a small display of the portion of the drawing that has been enlarged. Choose View, Zoom, Show Thumbnail (see fig. 13.8).

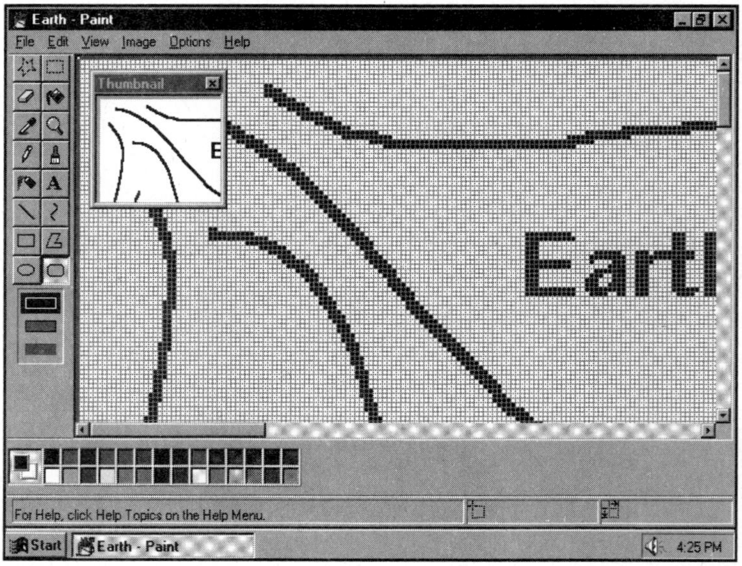

Fig. 13.8
Turn on the Grid and the Thumbnail displays to give you more information about your painting as you work.

You also can switch the Tool Box, Color Box, and Status Bar on or off at the View menu.

Creating Special Effects

Using the Image menu, you can flip, stretch, invert, shrink, enlarge, or tilt objects you select. These special effects can help you refine your painting by altering selected objects in subtle or not-so-subtle ways. The following sections describe each of the Image menu commands.

Flipping or Rotating a Selection

With the Flip/Rotate command, you can flip a selection in two ways: horizontally (left to right) or vertically (top to bottom). Flipping horizontally reverses an image from left to right; you can use this technique to create mirror images by copying the selection and then flipping the pasted copy. Flipping vertically flips an image from top to bottom, making it upside-down.

Alternatively, you can rotate the selection by 90 degrees, 180 degrees, or 270 degrees.

Tip
Select the area you want to flip, rotate, stretch, or skew. Place the pointer over it, and click the right mouse button to display a shortcut menu.

Stretching or Skewing a Selection

With the Stretch/Skew command, you can stretch or skew a selection horizontally or vertically the number of degrees you enter. Figure 13.9 shows a selection that has been skewed horizontally 45 degrees. Use this command to tilt objects precisely.

Fig. 13.9
Stretch or skew selections with the Image Stretch/Skew command.

Inverting the Colors in a Selection

Use the Invert Colors command to invert the colors in your painting, changing them to their opposites on the red/green/blue color wheel. In an inverted black-and-white painting, for example, black becomes white, and white becomes black; in an inverted green-and-yellow painting, green becomes purple, and yellow becomes blue (any white border area turns black). Use this technique to *reverse* a selected object.

Inverting the Colors in a Selection

With the Attributes command, you can override the *default* image area by resizing the image area to make it smaller or larger. Change the following attributes of the picture: Width, Height, the Units of measurement (Inches, Cm, Pels), and Colors (Black and White or Colors). If your picture was originally in black and white, for example, you can switch to Colors and add color to the painting. To return to the default image area size, click Default. Figure 13.10 shows colors converted to black and white.

Fig. 13.10
Colors have been switched to black and white with Image, Attributes.

Clearing the Painting

The Clear Image command is used to clear the screen of all painting you've done without saving or exiting.

> **Troubleshooting**
>
> *There's one drawn object in the picture, a circle, that needs to be resized. But there doesn't seem to be a way to change that circle once other objects are drawn.*
>
> Paint is a bitmap drawing program. When you draw, you change the dots of color on the screen. Once you complete the object you are drawing, it becomes part of the screen's pattern—you can't resize or recolor it. Drawing programs that are object-based enable you to select the individual items that have been drawn and edit them. Items can also be grouped together to act as a single object. There are many standalone object-based drawing programs. Some applications, such as Microsoft Excel and Microsoft Word, include object-based drawing tools so you can draw within their documents.

Changing the Windows Desktop with Paint

You can change the appearance of the desktop directly from Paint with File, Set as Wallpaper (Tiled) or Set as Wallpaper (Centered). Select Tiled to repeat the painting over the entire desktop, or Centered to display it once in the center of the desktop.

◄ See "Wallpapering Your Desktop with a Graphic," p. 133

To use your painting or part of your painting as wallpaper, follow these steps:

1. Display the painting you want to use as wallpaper.
2. If you want to use only part of the painting on the Desktop, select that part.
3. Choose File, Set as Wallpaper (Tiled) to repeat the painting as a pattern over the desktop, or Set as Wallpaper (Centered) to display the painting in the center of the desktop.

Working with Color

Color is a tremendously important component in daily life; it gives meaning to what you see. If you have a color monitor, you can use color in your paintings, and you can use your colorful paintings in applications such as WordPad, Word for Windows, and Aldus PageMaker. If you are lucky enough to have a color printer, you can print your painting in color.

Paint has 48 colors in its palette, including black and white. You can customize the Paint palette and add up to 16 custom colors.

Defining Hue, Saturation, Luminosity, and Dithering

In order to create custom colors, you should be familiar with a few color terms. Although you can create colors by just pointing and clicking without any knowledge of these terms, they will come in handy if you ever need to create a specific color.

Term	Meaning
Hue	Amount of red/green/blue components in the color.
Saturation	Purity of the color; lower saturation colors have more gray.
Luminosity	How bright or dull the color is.
Dithering	Dot pattern of colors that can be displayed to approximate colors that cannot be displayed. In the Custom Color selector, these are the blended colors.

Defining Custom Colors

To create a custom color, follow these steps:

1. Choose Options, Edit Colors. The Edit Colors dialog box appears.

2. Click Define Custom Colors. The Edit Colors dialog box expands to display the following items (see fig. 13.11):

   - Color matrix box
   - Color/Solid box
   - Luminosity bar
   - Color matrix cursor

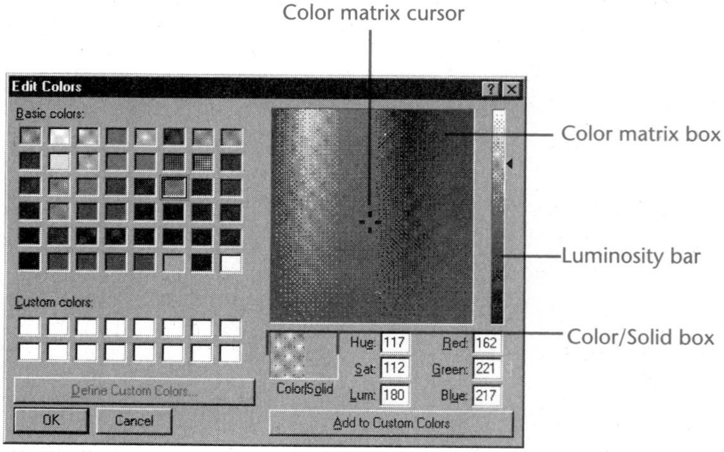

Fig. 13.11 Customize your colors in the Edit Colors dialog box.

3. Click the approximate color you want in the color matrix box. The color matrix cursor moves to the spot where you clicked, and the color you selected appears in the Color/Solid box.

   You can also drag the mouse pointer around in the color matrix box while holding down the mouse button; the color matrix cursor appears when you release the mouse button. This step selects the color's hue and saturation.

   Next, drag the arrowhead up or down along the side of the luminosity bar to adjust the luminosity of the color.

   To specify a particular color whose numbers you know, click the box you want to adjust (Hue, Sat, Lum, Red, Green, or Blue), and type new numbers.

Continue adjusting until the color looks correct in the Color/Solid box.

If you want a solid color (rather than blended), double-click the solid (right) side of the Color/Solid box when the color displayed there is correct.

4. Click the Add to Custom Colors button to add this color to the custom palette.

5. Return to step 3 if you want to add more colors to the custom palette, or click OK to close the Edit Colors dialog box.

The colors you customize don't change the current painting, but they make different colors available on the palette. Your custom palette remains in effect when you start a new Paint painting. Unless you save the custom palette, however, the colors are gone when you close the Paint application. If you save a custom palette, you can retrieve it into any Paint file.

To save a custom palette, choose Options, Save Colors, type a name, and click OK. Paint assigns the extension PAL, but you can specify a different extension if you want.

To retrieve a custom palette, choose Options, Get Colors. Select a palette file or type its name; then choose Open.

Setting Up the Page

Page setup choices affect your printed paintings. Margins, for example, determine where your painting is positioned on the page. You can choose either portrait or landscape paper orientation, select the size and location of the paper, and select a new printer. To set up your page for printing, choose File, Page Setup, make your selections, and click OK.

◀ See "Configuring Your Printers," p. 187

Saving Paint Files

When you save a Paint file, Paint assigns the extension BMP to the file name and saves the file in Windows bitmap format.

◀ See "Using Menus and Dialog Boxes," p. 92

To save a Paint file, follow these steps:

1. Choose File, Save As.

2. Type a name in the File Name text box and select from the Directories box the directory where you want to save the file.

◀ See "Opening, Saving, and Closing Documents," p. 109

3. Click the Save as Type box to select one of the following file formats:

Format	File Extension Assigned
Monochrome Bitmap	BMP
16 Color Bitmap	BMP
256 Color Bitmap	BMP
24-bit Bitmap	BMP

4. Choose Save or press Enter.

To resave your file later without changing its name, choose File, Save.

Troubleshooting

Many graphics files seem to use PCX format, but Paint won't save this format.

Paint saves only with the BMP format. You can open PCX files but if you want to make any changes and resave the file, you will have to save it as a BMP file.

Working with Other Applications

The paintings you create in Paint make wonderful illustrations that you can use with many other applications. If the other application does not support object linking and embedding, you can include a Paint painting by copying the painting and pasting it. You also can link or embed a painting in an application that supports object linking and embedding. You can edit linked and embedded paintings from within the other application.

▶ See "Using the Clipboard to Exchange Data," p. 424

To copy a Paint painting into another application, follow these steps:

1. Select the painting, or portion of the painting, that you want to copy to another application.
2. Choose Edit, Copy (Ctrl+C).
3. Start the other application, open the document into which you want to copy the painting, and position the insertion point where you want the painting to appear.
4. Choose Edit, Paste (Ctrl+V).

Embedding a Paint Object

Besides being a stand-alone painting application, Paint is also an *OLE server* application. OLE stands for *object linking and embedding*. A server is an application that can create objects that can be embedded in or linked to documents created by another application. Paint can create objects that can be embedded in or linked to documents created by applications such as WordPad and Word for Windows. (See Chapter 14, "Simple Ways of Sharing Data between Applications," for more information.)

Embedding a painting is useful when you need to have a painting within another application's document and you want to be able to edit the painting from within the other document. You can use two different methods to embed a Paint painting in a document created by an application that supports OLE. You can either copy the painting and paste it into the client application's document using the Paste or Paste Special command, or you can use a command in the client program to insert the object.

To create a new embedded painting in WordPad, follow these steps:

1. Start WordPad. (WordPad is the word processor that comes with Windows. See Chapter 12, "Using WordPad to Create Documents," for more information.)

2. Type text at the top of the document so that you can see how the embedded painting will appear in relation to existing text. Move the insertion point to a new line after the text.

3. Choose Insert, New Object.

4. Select the Create New option, select Bitmap Image from the Object Type list, and then choose OK. The menus and tools change to reflect the server application, Paint, that is being used to create the object.

5. Draw a new painting within the dashed boundaries. Use the Paint menus and tools as though you were in Paint.

6. Return to the WordPad document by clicking outside the painting and in the text of the document.

You—or anyone receiving this WordPad document—can edit this embedded painting if you have a copy of Paint on your computer. Just double-click on the painting in the document and the Paint menu and tools will appear.

Linking a Paint Object

Linking is most often used when you have many documents that use the same painting—for example, a proposal, an engineering specification, and a marketing sheet that all contain the same Paint painting. If you link the painting to all the documents, changing the original painting's file will automatically update all the word processing documents that depend on it. Because each document contains only a description of where the painting is located on disk, the documents do not increase significantly in size. (For more information on linking, see Chapter 15, "Building Compound Documents with OLE.")

Caution

When you send via electronic mail a client document that contains links, make sure you also send the original files to which the client document is linked.

Some client applications use a command such as Paste Link or Paste Special to paste and link a painting that has been copied. Other applications use an option from within an Insert Object command to create a link to a saved Paint file.

To link a WordPad document to a Paint painting, follow these steps:

1. In Paint, create and save the file you want to link to other documents.
2. Open the WordPad application and create a document.
3. Choose Insert, New Object.
4. Select the Create from File option. This will change the contents of the Insert Object dialog box.
5. Click Browse, and find and select the file containing the painting you want to link.
6. Click OK.
7. Click the Link check box.
8. Click OK.

As with an embedded object, you can edit a linked object from within the client document. The technique for starting the server application is the same as for embedding: double-click on the linked picture, or select the picture and choose an editing command. The application starts, and you edit and save the picture.

Previewing, Mailing, and Printing Paint Files

Paint provides a preview screen where you can see your painting as it will appear in print. You can send your painting via e-mail. And Paint gives you great flexibility in printing paintings.

Previewing Your Paintings

When a painting seems complete, you can check its appearance on the page. To preview a painting, follow these steps:

1. Choose File, Print Preview. The preview screen appears (see fig. 13.12).

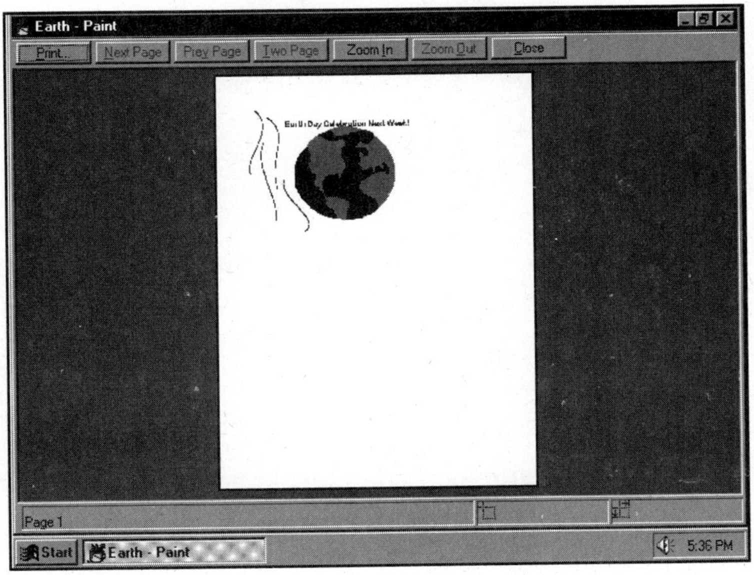

Fig. 13.12
You can examine your painting at the Print Preview screen.

2. Click the buttons to display the view you want.

3. Click Close to return to the painting, or click Print to display the Print dialog box.

You can print all or part of a painting, in draft or final quality, scaled smaller or larger. Before you print, be sure that you have the correct printer selected and set up.

Mailing a Painting

► See "Printing from Applications," p. 773

You can transmit a picture directly via e-mail or fax. To send a picture, display the picture you want to send and choose File, Send.

Printing a Painting

Before you print, be sure that you have the correct printer selected and set up. To select and set up a printer and print your document, follow these steps:

1. Choose File, Print. The Print dialog box appears (see fig. 13.13).

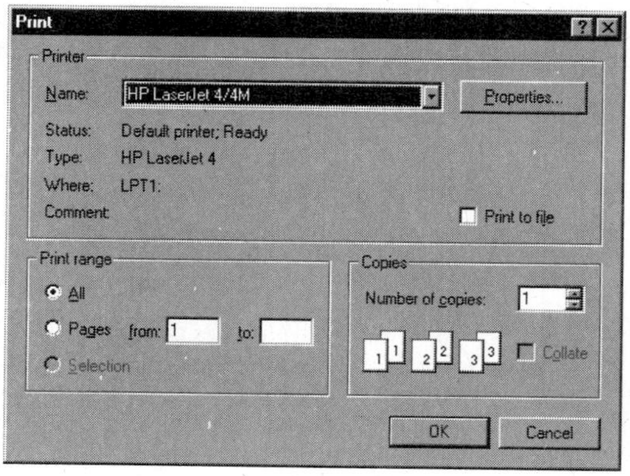

Fig. 13.13
The Print dialog box.

2. Select a printer from the Name list.

   Once a printer is selected, it remains selected for all documents—you won't have to select a printer again unless you want to change to a different printer.

3. Click the Properties button to make additional choices such as paper type and graphics quality. Click OK.

4. Select the Print Range All to print all the pages; select Print Range Selection to print only the selected text, or select the Pages, From, and To text boxes and type a range of pages to print.

5. Type the number of copies you want to print in the Number of Copies box.

6. Select the Collate check box to collate multiple copies of the document (this option is available if your printer supports collating).

7. Click OK.

To learn more about setting up your printer, refer to Chapter 6, "Controlling Printers."

Inserting Symbols with Character Map

The Character Map accessory gives you access to symbol fonts and ANSI characters. *ANSI characters* are the regular character set that you see on the keyboard and more than a hundred other characters, including a copyright symbol, a registered trademark symbol, and many foreign-language characters. One symbol font, Symbol, is included with most Windows applications. Other symbol fonts may be built into the printer. When you set up and indicate the model of the printer, font cartridges, and so on, the printer tells Windows what symbol fonts are available. (Printer fonts appear in Character Map only when they include a matching screen font.)

◀ See "Installing and Deleting Fonts," p. 217

To start Character Map, open the Start menu, click Programs, and then click Accessories. Finally, click Character Map. You are presented with the Character Map window shown in figure 13.14.

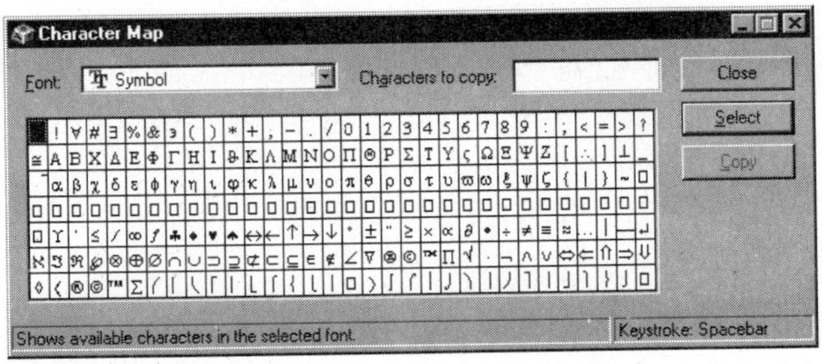

Fig. 13.14
Use Character Map to insert any of hundreds of special characters and symbols into a document.

The Character Map window includes a drop-down Font list box, from which you can select any of the available fonts on the system. After you select a font, the characters and symbols for this font appear in the Character Map table. Each set of fonts may have different symbols. Some fonts, such as Symbol and Zapf Dingbats, contain nothing but symbols and special characters.

Tip
If you plan to use Character Map frequently, you may want to create a shortcut for this application so that you can start Character Map directly from the desktop.

To insert a character in a Windows application from the Character Map, follow these steps:

1. Start the Character Map accessory.
2. Select the font you want to use from the Font list.
3. View an enlarged character by clicking and holding down the mouse button on a character or by moving the selection box over a character by pressing arrow keys.

4. Double-click on the character you want to insert or click the Select button to place the current character in the Characters to Copy text box.
5. Repeat steps 2 through 4 to select as many characters as you want.
6. Click the Copy button to copy to the Clipboard the characters you've selected.
7. Open or switch to the application to which you want to copy the character(s).
8. Place the insertion point where you want to insert the character(s) and choose Edit, Paste (Ctrl+V).

◀ See "Creating Shortcut Icons on the Desktop to Start Programs," p. 68

If the characters don't appear as they did in Character Map, you may need to reselect the characters and change the font to the same font in which the character originally appeared in the Character Map.

Calculating with Calculator

Like a calculator you keep in a desk drawer, the Windows Calculator is small but saves you time (and mistakes) by performing all the calculations common to a standard calculator. The Windows Calculator, however, has added advantages: you can keep this calculator on-screen alongside other applications, and you can copy numbers between the Calculator and other applications.

The Standard Windows Calculator, shown in figure 13.15, works so much like a pocket calculator that you need little help getting started. The Calculator's *keypad*, the on-screen representation, contains familiar number *keys*, along with memory and simple math keys. A display window just above the keypad shows the numbers you enter and the results of calculations. If your computational needs are more advanced, you can choose a different view of the calculator, the Scientific view (see fig. 13.16).

To display the Calculator, open the Start menu and click on Programs. Then click on Accessories. Finally, click on Calculator. The Calculator opens in the same view (Standard or Scientific) as was displayed the last time the Calculator was used.

To close the Calculator, click the Close button in the title bar. If you use the Calculator frequently, however, don't close it; click the Minimize button to minimize the Calculator to a button on the taskbar.

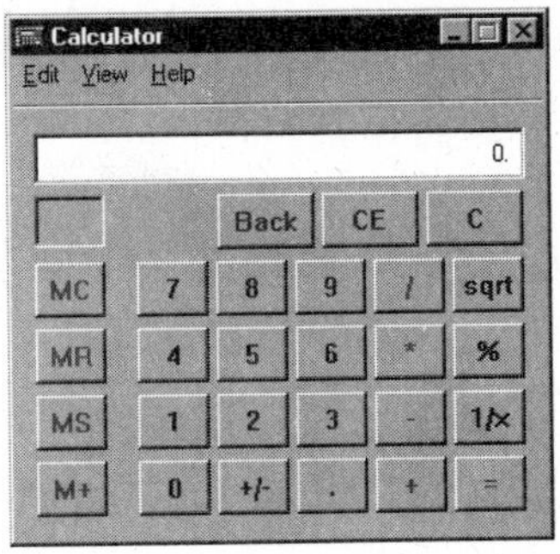

Fig. 13.15
The Standard Calculator.

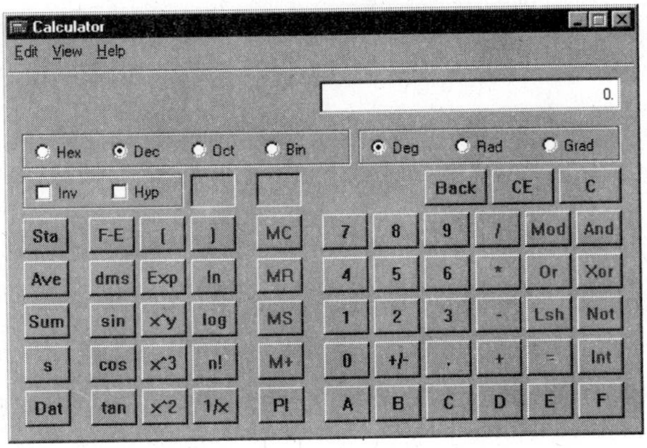

Fig. 13.16
The Scientific Calculator.

The Calculator has only three menus: Edit, View, and Help. The Edit menu contains two simple commands for copying and pasting; the View menu switches between the Standard and Scientific views; and the Help menu is the same as in all Windows accessories.

Operating the Calculator

To use the Calculator with the mouse, just click on the appropriate numbers and sign keys, like you press buttons on a desk calculator. Numbers appear in the display window as you select them, and the results appear after the calculations are performed.

To enter numbers from the keyboard, use either the numbers across the top of the keyboard, or those on the numeric keypad (you first must press the NumLock key). To calculate, press the keys on the keyboard that match the Calculator keys. The following table shows the Calculator keys for the keyboard.

Calculator Key	Function	Keyboard Key
MC	Clear memory	Ctrl+L
MR	Display memory	Ctrl+R
M+	Add to memory	Ctrl+P
MS	Store value in memory	Ctrl+M
CE	Delete displayed value	Del
Back	Delete last digit in displayed value	Backspace
+/–	Change sign	F9
/	Divide	/
*	Multiply	*
–	Subtract	–
+	Add	+
sqrt	Square root	@
%	Percent	%
1/x	Calculate reciprocal	R
C	Clear	Esc
=	Equals	= or Enter

Note

To calculate a percentage, treat the % key like an equal sign. For example, to calculate 15 percent of 80, type **80*15%**. After you press the % key, the Calculator displays the result: 12.

You can use the Calculator's memory to total the results of several calculations. The memory holds a single number, which starts as zero; you can add to, display, or clear this number, or you can store another number in memory.

Copying Numbers between the Calculator and Other Applications

When working with many numbers or complex numbers, you make fewer mistakes if you copy the Calculator results into other applications rather than retyping the result. To copy a number from the Calculator into another application, follow these steps:

1. In the Calculator display window, perform the math calculations required to display the number.
2. Choose Edit, Copy.
3. Activate the application you want to receive the calculated number.
4. Position the insertion point in the newly opened application where you want the number copied.
5. From the newly opened application, choose Edit, Paste.

You can also copy and paste a number from another application into the Calculator, perform calculations with the number, and then copy the result back into the application. A number pasted in the calculator erases the number currently shown in the display window.

To copy a number from another application into the Calculator, select the number in the application and choose Edit, Copy. Next, activate the Calculator and choose Edit, Paste.

If you paste a formula in the Calculator, you can click the equal (=) button to see the result. If you copy 5+5 from WordPad, for example, paste the calculation in the Calculator, and click the = key, the resulting number 10 appears. If you paste a function, such as @ for square root, the Calculator performs the function on the number displayed. If, for example, you copy @ from a letter in WordPad and paste it into Calculator while it is displaying the number 25, the result 5 appears.

Numbers and most operators (such as + and –) work fine when pasted in the Calculator display, but the Calculator interprets some characters as commands. The following chart lists the characters that the Calculator interprets as commands:

Character	Interpreted As
:c	Clears memory.
:e	Lets you enter scientific notation in decimal mode; also the number E in hexadecimal mode.
:m	Stores the current value in memory.
:p	Adds the displayed value to the number in memory.
:q	Clears the current calculation.
:r	Displays the value in memory.
\	Works like the Dat button (in the Scientific calculator).

Using the Scientific Calculator

If you have ever written an equation wider than a sheet of paper, you're a good candidate for using the Scientific Calculator. The Scientific Calculator is a special view of the Calculator.

To display the Scientific Calculator, activate the Calculator and choose View, Scientific.

◀ See "Getting Help," p. 79

The Scientific Calculator works the same as the Standard Calculator, but adds many advanced functions. You can work in one of four number systems: hexadecimal, decimal, octal, or binary. You can perform statistical calculations, such as averages and statistical deviations. You can calculate sines, cosines, tangents, powers, logarithms, squares, and cubes. These specialized functions aren't described here, but are well documented in the Calculator's Help command.

Using the Taskbar Clock

◀ See "Changing the Taskbar Options," p. 126

It's convenient to have a clock always on the screen, and Windows includes one in the taskbar. If yours isn't displayed, you can turn on the clock, adjust the time, and even select a time zone. You'll be surprised at how much control you have over that little clock (see fig. 13.17).

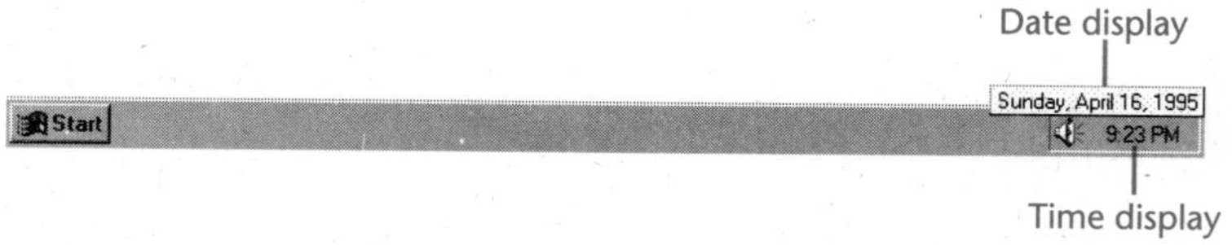

Fig. 13.17
The taskbar clock.

The following table describes the taskbar clock options:

Do This...	To Do This
Point to time	Display date.
Double-click time	Display Date/Time Properties where you can set the date and time, and also select a time zone.
Right-click time, click Properties	Display Taskbar Properties, where you can turn Show Clock on or off.

◄ See "Changing the Taskbar Options," p. 126

Note

If the taskbar Auto Hide option is enabled, the clock will only be visible when the mouse pointer is moved over the hidden taskbar.

Chapter 14

Simple Ways of Sharing Data between Applications

by Rob Tidrow

When Windows 1.0 was introduced in 1985, Microsoft gave users the capability to use more than one software application at a time. With this capability came the need and desire to use data from one document in another document—sometimes in a document that was created by a different application. You may, for example, create a memorandum as a Microsoft Word for Windows document and then reuse all or part of that document in another Word for Windows document. You also can use the data from the Word document in a Microsoft Excel worksheet or a Lotus cc:Mail message.

You can share data from one document or application to another because Windows has *data-exchange* capabilities (also called *data sharing*). These capabilities are as simple as cutting or copying a piece of text from one program to another, and as complex as editing a piece of data in one application that you created in another application. The latter operation, known as *in-place editing,* is a component of OLE 2.0, which is discussed in Chapter 15, "Building Compound Documents with OLE." Cutting, copying, and pasting are relatively simple operations that make you more efficient in Windows.

In this chapter, you learn how to:

- Use the Windows Clipboard and Clipboard Viewer
- Copy text, data, and graphics between documents

- Copy text, data, and graphics between applications
- Copy text from the Clipboard to wizards and dialog boxes
- Transfer data, using file converters

Understanding Windows 95's Data-Sharing Capabilities

Windows 95 supports three types of data exchange: the Clipboard, dynamic data exchange (DDE), and object linking and embedding (OLE). Generally, all Windows applications provide some means of sharing data with another application. All applications, for example, have access to the Windows Clipboard, to which you can copy or cut data. Not all Windows applications, however, have DDE or OLE 2.0 capability.

Benefits of Sharing Data

By sharing data from one source to another, you tap into the strength of a computer in helping automate redundant tasks. How many times do you use the same word, data, or other element in a document? Do you ever write a letter and wish that you could reuse all or part of it in a different letter? Without the capability to share data, you must retype these repeated parts of your document. With the copy and paste features available in Windows 95, however, you just need to highlight the word, phrase, or element that you want to repeat; copy it to your computer's memory; and paste it in the document where you want it. In the section "Using the Windows Clipboard," you learn exactly how to copy and paste.

Take Advantage of Other Applications' Strengths

Another reason why data-sharing capabilities are popular is because they allow you to create more powerful, more informative, and more advanced documents. Many applications that adhere to Windows 95 standards let you copy an element from one type of application and use it in another application. You can, for example, create a picture from Paint and use it in a WordPad document, as shown in figure 14.1.

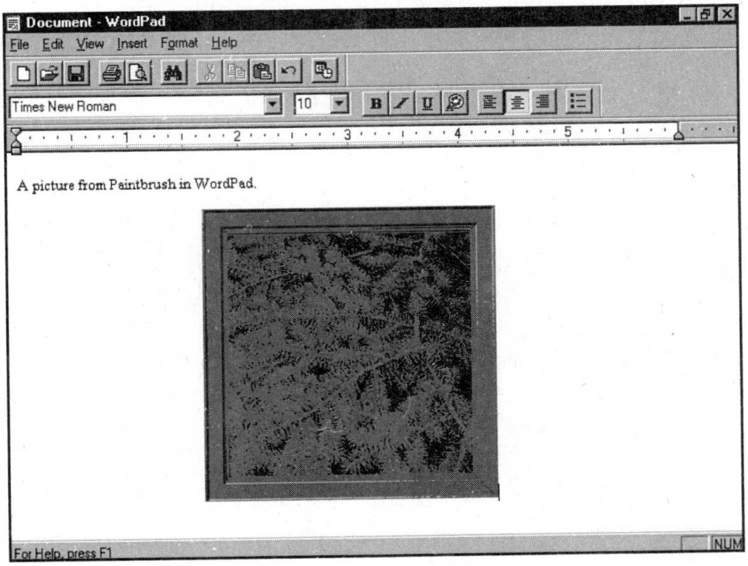

Fig. 14.1
This picture was copied from Paint into WordPad.

Using the Windows Clipboard

The most basic way to exchange data from one source to another is to use the Windows 95 *Clipboard*, an area in memory that applications can access to share data. When you use the Clipboard, you send data to the Clipboard and then place that data in your document. This procedure is known as *copy and paste* or *cut and paste.*

Copy means that you place a replica of the material that you selected in the Clipboard. *Cut* means that you remove the data from your document and place that data in the Clipboard. *Paste* is the process in which you take the data from the Clipboard and place that data in your document.

Note

When you paste data from the Clipboard, you don't remove it from the Clipboard. You can paste the data from the Clipboard into your document as many times as you like. The Clipboard retains your cut or copied data until you clear the contents manually, or until you cut or copy something else to the Clipboard.

Cutting, Copying, and Pasting Data

Applications that let you access the Clipboard generally use standard menu commands or keyboard shortcuts. In many Windows 95 applications, you can transfer data to and from the Clipboard by choosing commands from the Edit menu (see fig. 14.2). Most Edit menus contain the Cut, Copy, and Paste commands.

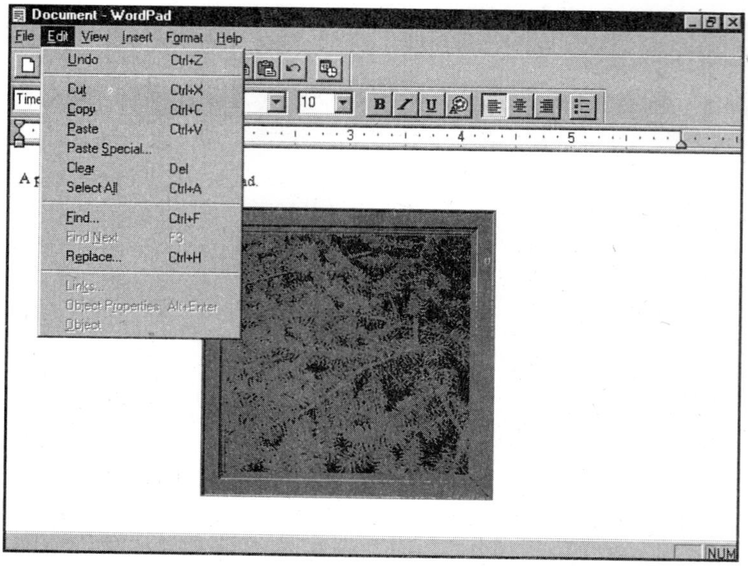

Fig. 14.2
Use WordPad's Edit menu to transfer data through the Clipboard.

Tip
To copy information from a document to the Clipboard, use the same procedure but choose Edit, Copy instead of Edit, Cut in step 3. A copy of the data is placed in the Clipboard, but the original data remains intact.

To cut something from a WordPad document, follow these steps:

1. Start WordPad, and then open a document or start a new document and enter some text.

2. Highlight some of the text in the document, as shown in figure 14.3.

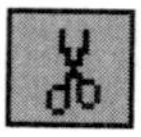

3. Choose Edit, Cut to cut the text to the Clipboard. Notice that the text disappears from your WordPad document.

Now that you have something in the Clipboard, you can paste that element into another document, such as a Paint drawing. To paste, follow these steps:

1. Open Windows Paint (it's usually in the Accessories item in the Programs folder), and open a drawing or create a new one.

2. Pull down the Edit menu. Notice that the Cut and Copy commands are grayed out (see fig. 14.4). This display tells you that you have not selected an item to be cut or copied.

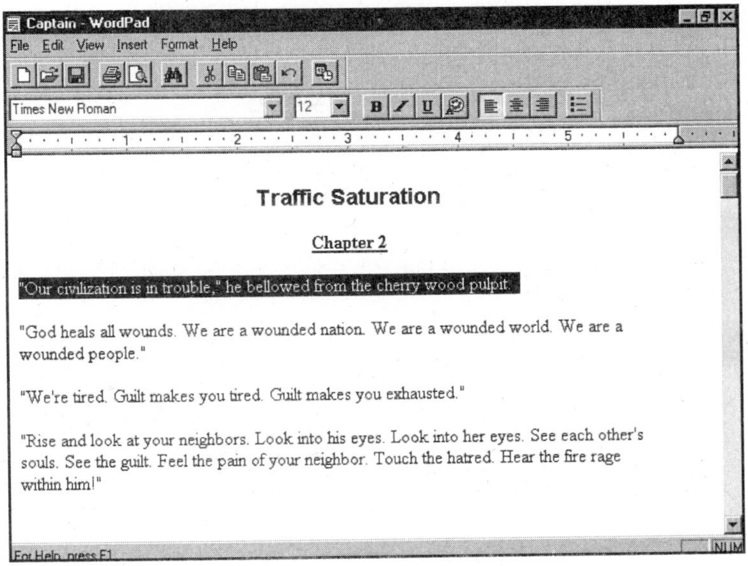

Fig. 14.3
Use the mouse to highlight the text you want to cut.

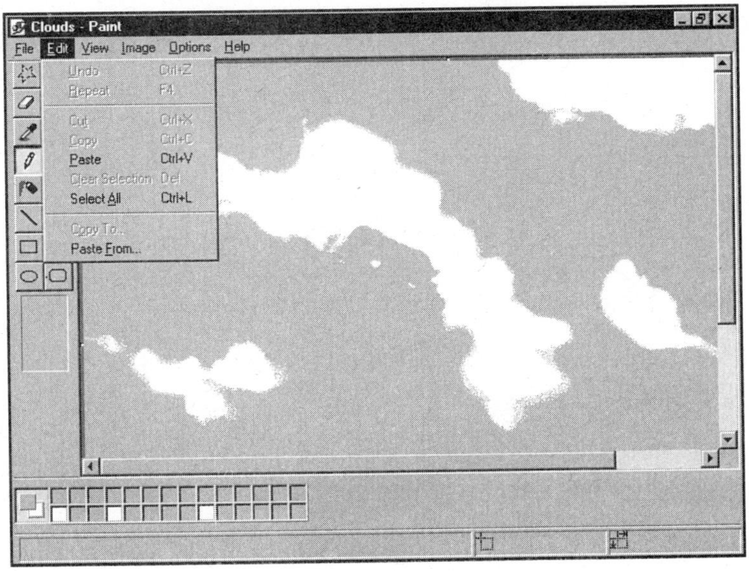

Fig. 14.4
The Cut and Copy commands are grayed out, indicating that you have not selected an item to be cut or copied.

3. Choose Paste to paste the contents of the Clipboard (in this case, the text from the WordPad document) into the Paint drawing. Figure 14.5 shows what this text looks like when it's pasted into a drawing.

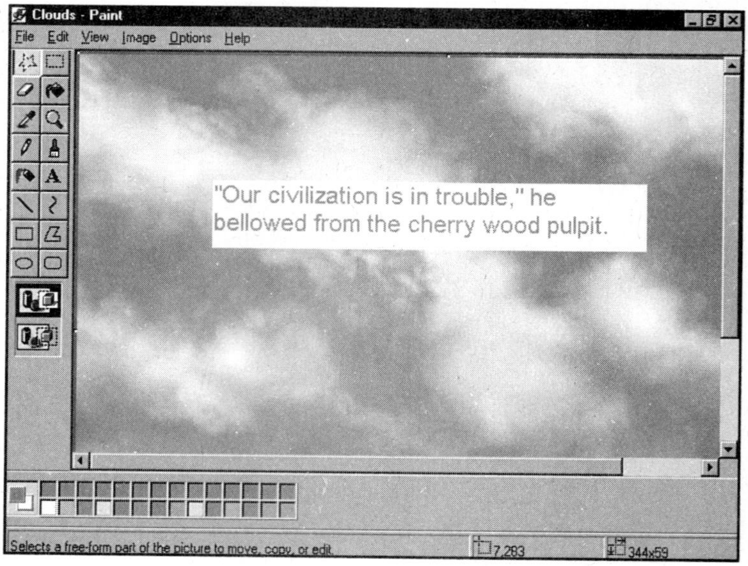

Fig. 14.5
Pasting text from a WordPad document into a Paint drawing.

Another standard way to use the Clipboard is to use the buttons in an application's toolbar. Many Windows 95 applications provide toolbar buttons that let you perform routine tasks quickly and easily—for example, cutting, copying, and pasting data to and from the Clipboard. Figure 14.6 shows an example of these buttons.

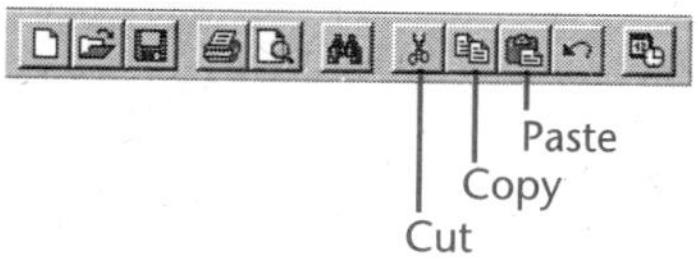

Fig. 14.6
Cut, Copy, and Paste buttons provided in the WordPad toolbar.

Using Keyboard Shortcuts

Tip
By learning these keyboard shortcuts, you can speed data exchange within and between applications.

Many times when you use Windows 95, you don't have access to menus or toolbars. Dialog boxes, wizards, and simple text boxes (such as ones in which you type data to open a file) don't have menus or toolbars that allow you to cut, copy, and paste data from the Clipboard. Fortunately, the Cut, Copy, and Paste commands have keyboard shortcuts.

Windows 95 supports a common set of keyboard shortcuts that, unless the shortcut has been reassigned, you can use in any application that supports data sharing. Table 14.1 shows these shortcuts.

Table 14.1 Cut, Copy, and Paste Keyboard Shortcuts

Action	Windows 95 Shortcut Keys
Cut	Ctrl+X or Shift+Delete
Copy	Ctrl+C or Ctrl+Insert
Paste	Ctrl+V or Shift+Insert

Copying Information to a Dialog Box

You can use a keyboard shortcut to help you fill in a dialog box. The dialog box shown in figure 14.7, the Letter Wizard from Windows 95, is requesting your name and address and the recipient's name and address. You can type the information or copy it from somewhere else, if the information is available. For this example, assume that you have the recipient's name and address stored in a Notepad document and that you want to copy and paste that information into the dialog box.

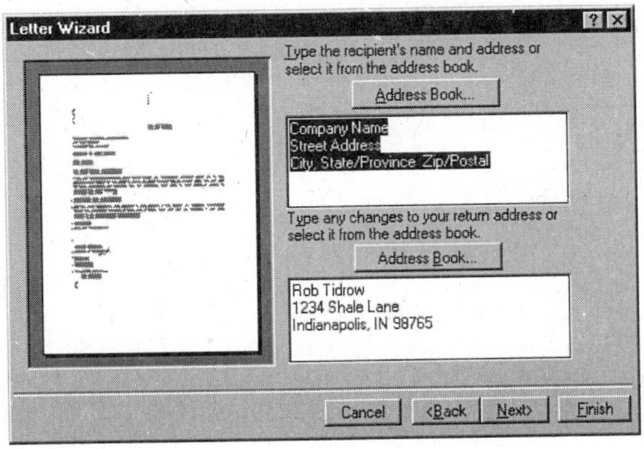

Fig. 14.7
You can cut or copy information to Windows 95 dialog boxes and wizards.

To copy information from the Notepad document to the Word Letter Wizard dialog box, follow these steps:

1. Select the information that you'll replace.
2. Switch to the open Notepad document by clicking the button in the taskbar at the bottom of the screen.
3. In the Notepad window, select the information that you want to copy, as shown in figure 14.8.

Tip
If the document isn't open, you can click the Start button in the taskbar to open programs or documents.

Fig. 14.8
Highlight text in the Notepad document to copy to the Clipboard.

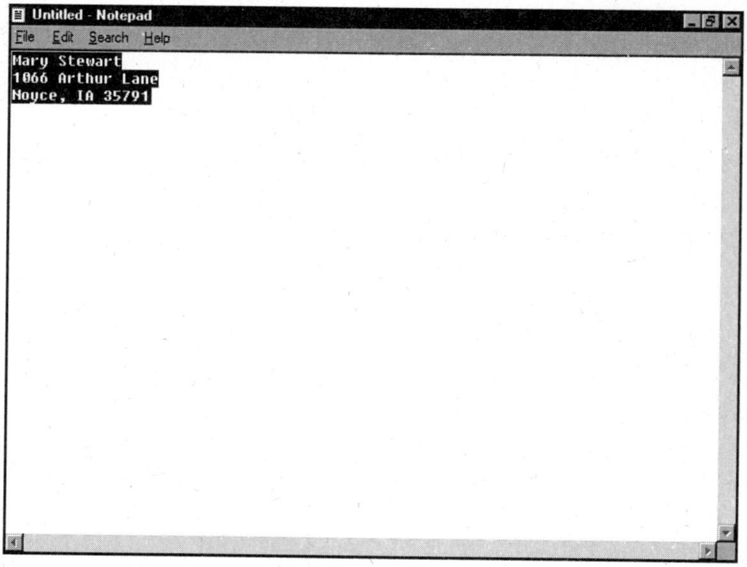

4. To copy the highlighted text, choose Edit, Copy, or press Ctrl+C.
5. Click the Word button on the taskbar to return to the Letter Wizard dialog box in Word. The old entry in the recipient's text box should still be highlighted.
6. Press Ctrl+V to copy the information from the Clipboard to the text box. Figure 14.9 shows the completed text box.

Fig. 14.9
The information from the Clipboard is pasted into the text box.

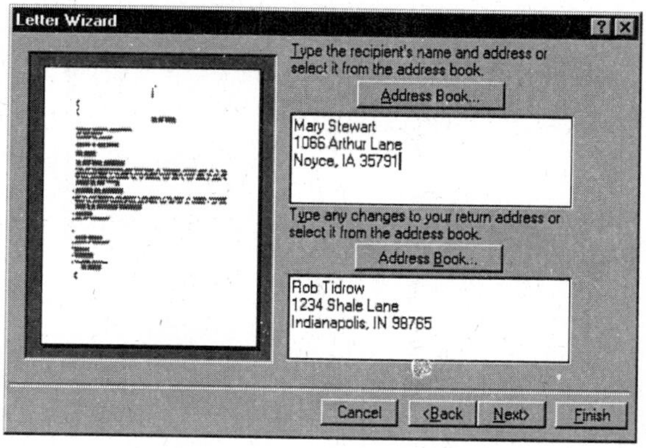

Note

You can't use the Edit menu or any button on a toolbar while you're in a dialog box. The only way to copy from the Clipboard is to press Ctrl+V or Shift+Insert. The same holds true when you're trying to cut or copy from a dialog box. Press Ctrl+X or Shift+Delete to cut, or press Ctrl+C or Ctrl+Insert to copy highlighted text in a text box.

Capturing Screens with the Clipboard

Many Windows screen-capturing programs are available, but you also can use the Clipboard to capture the contents of the screen. When the screen image is captured, it's held in the Clipboard in bitmap format.

To capture the entire screen and paste it into a WordPad document, follow these steps:

1. Press the Print Screen key to capture the entire screen and place it in the Clipboard.

2. Open or switch to WordPad.

3. In a new or existing document, choose Edit, Paste. The screen image, in bitmap format, is pasted into the WordPad document.

Tip

You also can capture the contents of the active window on-screen by pressing Alt+Print Screen or Shift+Print Screen, depending on your keyboard.

◄ See "Using Windows Paint," p. 378

Using the Clipboard Viewer

Windows 95 includes a utility called the *Clipboard Viewer*, which allows you to view and save the contents of the Clipboard. You can start the Clipboard Viewer by choosing Start, Programs, Accessories, Clipboard Viewer. If you recently cut or copied an item to the Clipboard, you see it in the Clipboard Viewer (see fig. 14.10).

◄ See "Adding and Removing Windows Components," p. 313

Note

The Clipboard Viewer isn't installed during the Typical installation of Windows 95. You need to specify this option during installation, using Custom setup. If Windows 95 is already installed on your computer, start the Add/Remove Programs utility in Control Panel, and install the Clipboard Viewer.

◄ See "Installing Windows 95 Applications in Windows 95," p. 309

Fig. 14.10
The Clipboard Viewer with copied text.

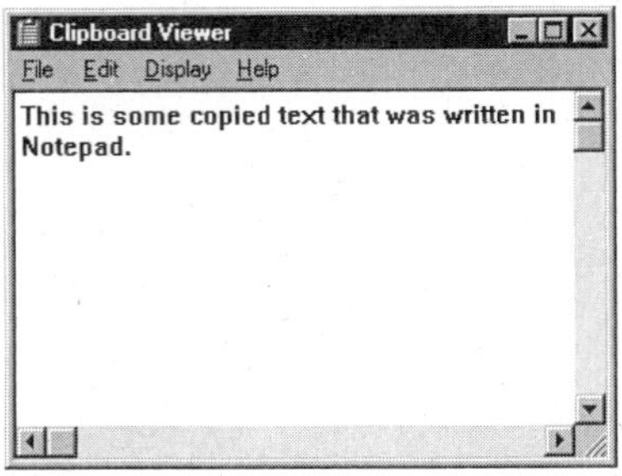

Saving the Contents of the Clipboard Viewer

You can save the information that you cut or copied to the Clipboard to reuse later. You may want to save information if you copy a large amount of data that you can use over and over. To save information that's in the Clipboard Viewer, follow these steps:

1. Choose File, Save As in the Clipboard Viewer. The Save As dialog box appears (see fig. 14.11).

Fig. 14.11
You can save the contents of the Clipboard Viewer.

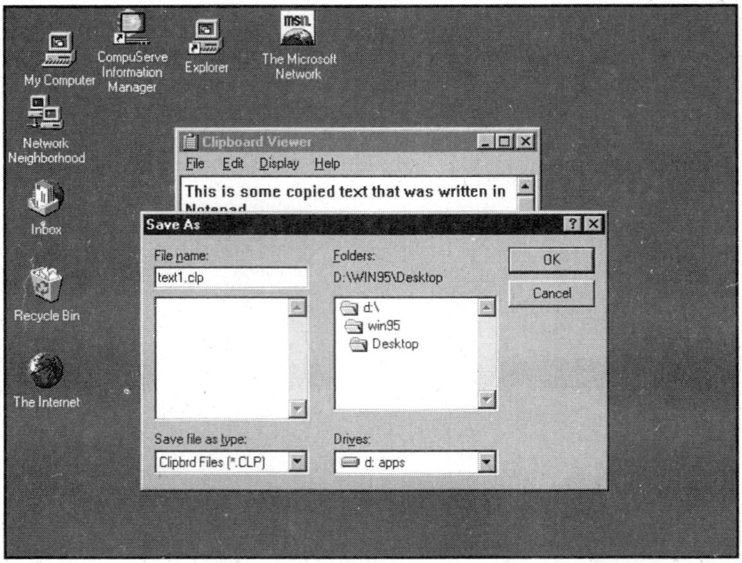

2. In the File Name text box, type a file name (the Clipboard Viewer automatically uses the extension CLP).

3. Click OK.

If you want to open a saved Clipboard file, follow these steps:

1. Choose File, Open in the Clipboard Viewer. The Open dialog box appears.

2. In the File Name list box, select the file you want to open. If necessary, select the file location in the Folders list box.

> **Note**
>
> Every once in a while, Windows displays a warning message, asking whether you want to clear the Clipboard's contents. You usually see this message when you've cut or copied a large item (such as an entire spreadsheet or large picture) to the Clipboard. If you answer yes, Windows keeps the item in the Clipboard. If you answer no, Windows erases that item from the Clipboard to free system memory and resources while you work.

3. Click OK. The Clear Clipboard message appears (see fig. 14.12).

   If you already have something in the Clipboard, this message asks whether you want to clear the contents of the Clipboard so that you can open the CLP file that you selected. (Remember that the Clipboard can hold only one cut or copied item at a time.)

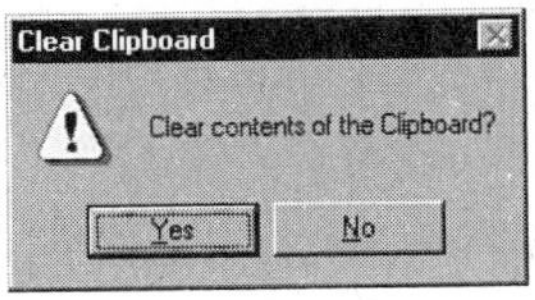

Fig. 14.12
The Clear Clipboard message asks whether you want to clear the contents of the Clipboard.

4. If you want to clear the contents and open the selected file, click Yes.

   If you don't want to clear the contents of the Clipboard, click No. You return to the Clipboard Viewer.

Viewing Text in the Clipboard Viewer

The Clipboard Viewer lets you view the Clipboard contents in different file formats. The Clipboard stores information in multiple formats so that you can transfer information between programs that use different formats.

Tip
The Display menu shows only the formats that are available for the current data that's in the Clipboard. All other formats are grayed out.

◄ See "Reviewing Types of Fonts," p. 213

On the Display menu, you have several options for viewing the contents. Following are the most common of these options:

- *Text* displays the contents in unformatted text, using the current Windows system font.
- *Rich Text Format* displays the contents in RTF (Rich Text Format). RTF retains any character formatting, such as font and font style.
- *OEM Text* displays the contents in the unformatted OEM character set. You usually use this option when you copy text from the Clipboard to DOS applications.

To view the contents in another format, follow these steps:

1. In the Clipboard Viewer, pull down the Display menu and choose a format. The Clipboard Viewer changes to reflect your choice. In figure 14.13, the content shown in figure 14.10 has changed from text to OEM text.

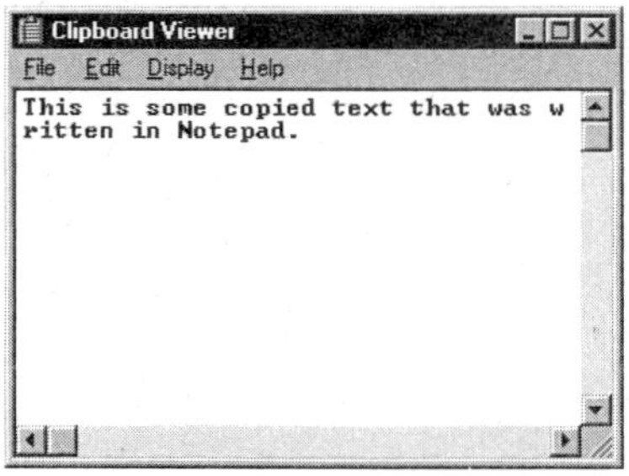

Fig. 14.13
Viewing the Clipboard contents with the OEM text option.

2. To return to the original format, choose Display, Auto.

Viewing a Picture in the Clipboard Viewer

Tip
Use the Picture option to view cut or copied formatted text before you paste it into a document.

The Display menu's Picture option lets you view a picture or formatted text that you cut or copy to the Clipboard. The formatted text shows all the characterizations you add to the text, such as color, fonts, and other formatting. To use the Picture option in the Clipboard Viewer, follow these steps:

1. Cut or copy a picture to the Clipboard, such as from Paint. If you want to view formatted text, open a document in WordPad or a similar application and cut or copy formatted text to the Clipboard.
2. Open the Clipboard Viewer.
3. Choose Display, Picture to display the item that you copied or cut to the Clipboard (see fig. 14.14).

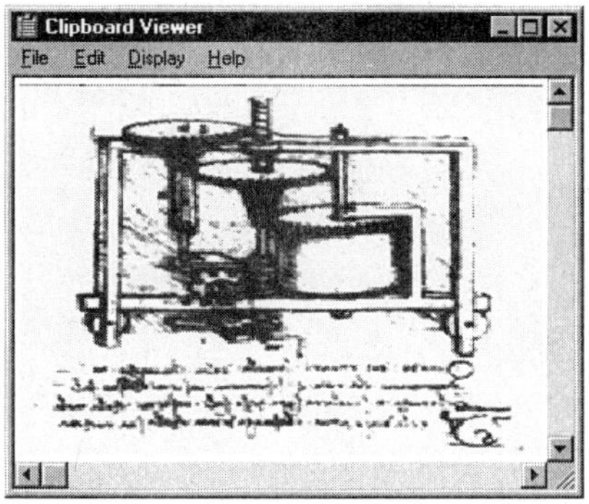

Fig. 14.14
Use the Picture option in the Clipboard Viewer to view graphics or formatted text you cut or copy to the Clipboard.

> **Note**
>
> The picture option stretches the Clipboard image to fit the current size of the Clipboard Viewer window. For a more accurate view of the image, try viewing the image in Bitmap or DIB Bitmap mode.

Using Drag-and-Drop to Copy Information between Documents

With Windows 95, you can drag and drop items to copy or move them. You learned in Chapter 2 how to use drag and drop to perform file management in the Explorer. In this section, you learn how to use drag-and-drop to copy information between documents.

Using drag-and-drop to copy between separate applications creates an embedded object. For more information on object linking and embedding (OLE), see Chapter 15, "Building Compound Documents with OLE."

> **Note**
>
> To use drag-and-drop, you must be working in an application that supports it. Most applications in the Microsoft Office suite, for example, support drag-and-drop, including Word, Excel, PowerPoint, and Access. Check the manual that comes with your application for information on using drag-and-drop.

◄ See "Learning about Drag-and-Drop," p. 105

One way to learn how to copy text by dragging and dropping it is to use WordPad. To copy information with drag-and-drop in WordPad, follow these steps:

1. Open WordPad, and then open a document or create a new document that contains some text.

Tip
When you hold down the Ctrl key, a plus sign appears with the insertion point.

2. Select the text that you want to copy.
3. Position the mouse pointer over the selected area and drag the text.

   In some applications, you must hold down the Ctrl key and then drag the mouse pointer to copy text. If you simply drag the item, the information is moved to another spot in the document. WordPad allows you to copy text without holding down the Ctrl key first.

   The mouse pointer changes as you drag, as shown in figure 14.15.

Fig. 14.15
The gray dashed line indicates where the text will be placed.

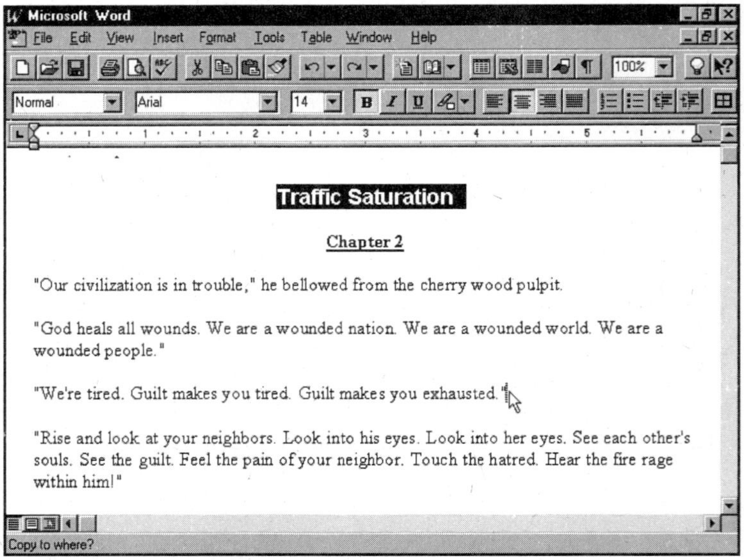

4. Drag the text to the position in the document where you want to place it. The gray vertical bar indicates the position of the new text.
5. Release the mouse button to complete the copy procedure.

Note

Some applications, such as Word for Windows, allow you to drag text between two documents. To do so, make sure that you can see both documents on-screen at the same time, and then drag the item from one document to another.

Troubleshooting

When I copy information with drag-and-drop, the original document loses its information.

You used the move feature instead. Make sure that you hold down the Ctrl key throughout the process. Release the mouse button first and then release the Ctrl key.

My copied text appears in the middle of existing text.

Don't forget to watch the gray dashed line that's part of the mouse pointer. This line shows exactly where the copied text will be inserted.

I get a black circle with a slash through it when I try to copy.

The black circle with the slash indicates that you can't drop the item in the area where the mouse is, such as the title bar or status bar. Make sure that you go all the way into the other document before you release the mouse button.

Copying and Pasting Data with DOS Applications

Although most Windows 95 users use Windows-based applications, millions of copies of DOS applications are used on Windows systems. Applications such as Lotus 1-2-3 for DOS, WordPerfect 5.1, and the MS-DOS prompt remain very popular. Windows 95 lets you copy information from a DOS application or from a DOS command prompt to a Windows application.

Windows 95 supports the following ways to transfer information from DOS applications to Windows documents:

- You can transfer text from DOS to Windows, from Windows to DOS, and between DOS applications by means of the Clipboard.
- You can transfer graphics from DOS to Windows applications by means of the Clipboard.
- You can copy text from the MS-DOS command prompt to the Clipboard.

Using the Clipboard to Exchange Data

Some DOS applications use their own Clipboard equivalent, but none provide an area that lets you transfer text and graphics between applications. When you want to transfer text between applications, you usually have to use text converters or file-conversion utilities that transform the text into a format that the application can read. In many cases, you have to convert the text to an ASCII text file; this process strips out your formatting and special character enhancements.

When you want to share data from a DOS application to a Windows application, you use a process known as *mark, copy, and paste*. The Mark, Copy, and Paste commands are located in the control menu of a DOS window. You also can find the Mark button on the MS-DOS Prompt toolbar.

◄ See "Understanding and Configuring MS-DOS Application Properties," p. 347

To copy a list of your files at the DOS command prompt to a WordPad document, follow these steps:

1. Open the MS-DOS Prompt into a window (see fig. 14.16). You can change the way your DOS window looks by going into its properties and then changing the font or screen options.

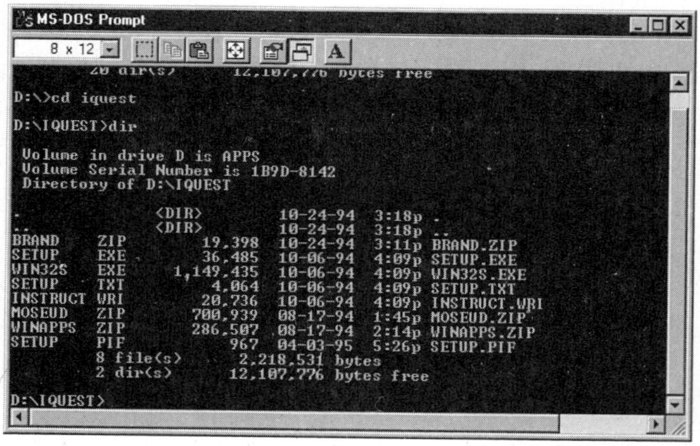

Fig. 14.16 You can copy a directory listing from the DOS window to a Windows document.

2. Type **DIR** to generate the directory listing.

3. Click the Mark toolbar button, or choose Edit, Mark from the Control menu. A blinking cursor appears at the top of the DOS window, indicating that you're in marking mode.

4. You now need to mark the area that you want to copy by drawing a box around it with your mouse pointer. To do so, place your mouse pointer where you want to start marking, hold down the left mouse button,

and then drag the box around the text that you want to copy. Your screen should look something like the one shown in figure 14.17.

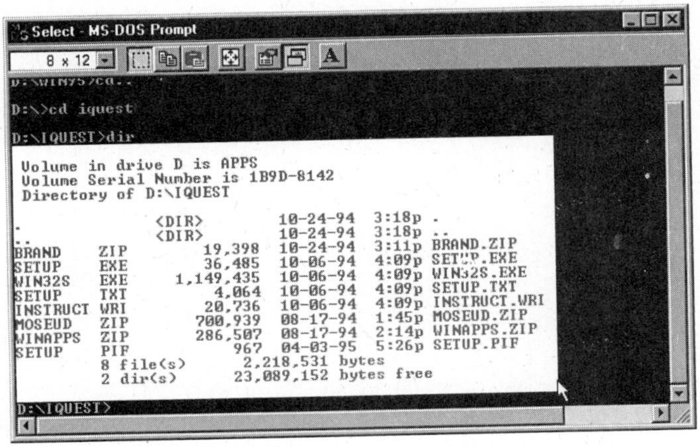

Fig. 14.17
Marking the text that you want to copy.

5. When you're satisfied with the selection, release the mouse button.
6. Click the Copy button in the toolbar; choose Edit, Copy from the Control menu; or press Enter to copy the selection to the Clipboard.
7. Switch to WordPad, and place the cursor where you want the text to be placed.
8. Click the Paste toolbar button, or choose Edit, Paste. The text from the DOS window is placed in your WordPad document (see fig. 14.18).

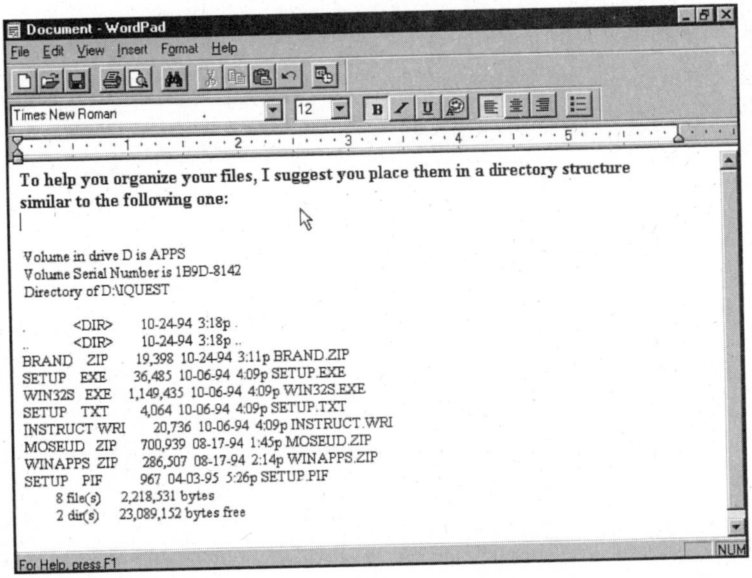

Fig. 14.18
You can place a list of your files in a WordPad document.

Copying Data from Windows to DOS

You also can copy data from a Windows application to a DOS application by cutting or copying the data to the Clipboard and then pasting the data into the DOS application. When you do this, all the formatting that you placed in the Windows document is lost.

To copy data from Windows to DOS, follow these steps:

1. In your Windows application, such as WordPad, select the text that you want to copy.
2. Choose Edit, Copy, or Edit, Cut.
3. Switch to the DOS application, such as WordPerfect 5.2 for DOS. (Make sure that the application is in a window and not full-screen.)
4. Place the text or mouse cursor where you want to paste the text.
5. Choose Edit, Paste from the Control menu of the DOS application. The text now appears in the document.

Transferring Data by Using File Converters

Rather than cut and paste parts of a document into another document, you sometimes need to import an entire file into a different application. You may, for example, want to import a Windows Write file into WordPad. (Write was distributed with Windows 3.x.) Many software companies distribute Write files with their software to announce updates or changes in the software.

To open files that were created in other programs, many Windows applications include built-in file converters. *File converters* take the file format and transform it to a format that the application can read. During a file conversion, text enhancements, font selections, and other elements usually are preserved. Sometimes, however, these elements are converted to ASCII format.

To convert a Write file to WordPad format, follow these steps:

1. Start WordPad and choose File, Open.

2. Open the Files of Type drop-down list and choose Windows Write (*.WRI).

3. Select a file with the extension WRI and open it.

   WordPad starts to convert the file. Look at the lower-left corner of the status bar, which shows the percentage of the file that WordPad has converted. When the display reaches `100%`, WordPad displays the converted file.

You now can edit the file as a WordPad file.

Many other Windows applications include file converters to allow you to read and edit file formats that are created in other applications. Depending on the type of installation you perform, Word for Windows, for example, includes the following set of converters:

Tip
The type of converters you have installed for an application may depend on the installation options you choose at setup. See the application's documentation for specific converters.

- Rich Text Format
- Text File
- Schedule+ Contact List
- Microsoft Excel Worksheets
- Word for DOS 3.x-5.x
- Word for DOS 6.0
- Personal Address Book
- WordStar
- WordPerfect 5.x
- WordPerfect 6.x
- Works for Windows 3.0
- Works for Windows 4.0

Another way to convert files is to save the file in a different format during the Save As process. When you need to import a Word for Windows file into WordPerfect or Word for Macintosh, for example, you can select those formats from the Save As Type drop-down list in the Save As dialog box. This list contains the types of formats in which you can save a Word for Windows document (see fig. 14.19).

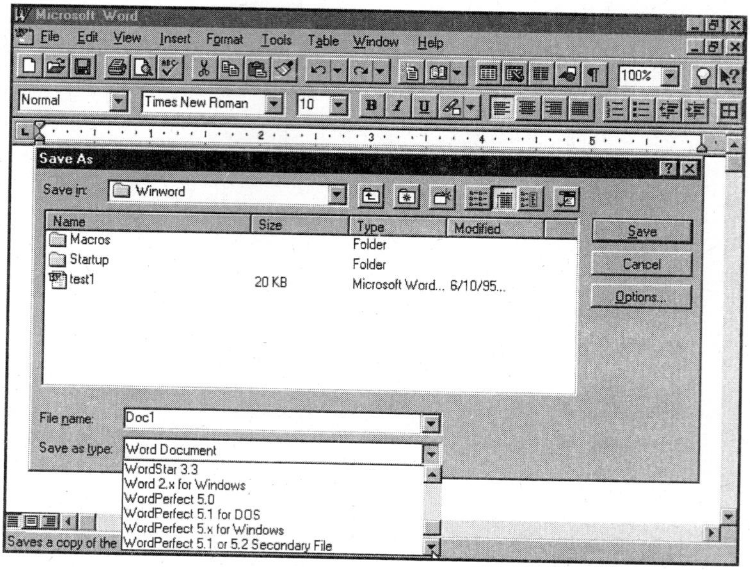

Fig. 14.19
Use the Save As Type list options to transfer files to different applications.

Understanding Dynamic Data Exchange (DDE)

A more sophisticated way to exchange data in Windows 95 is through the use of dynamic data exchange. DDE allows you to create links from one document or file to another document or file. These links can be between documents that are created in the same application (such as Word for Windows) or documents that are created in different applications (such as Word and Excel).

After you establish a link, you can update the information automatically by editing the original source of the information. This procedure lets you use data in various places but update it in only one place. To use DDE, you must set up a *link* between two applications (or two documents) that support DDE or OLE. The application that requests data is called the *client* application. The other application, called the *server* application, responds to the client application's request by supplying the requested data.

► See "Using Embedding to Link Information," p. 440

During a DDE link, you can work in the client application and make changes in data that's linked to the server application. When you change the data in the client application, Windows 95 automatically changes the data in the server application. The advantage to exchanging data by DDE links is that data is kept up-to-date in the client and server applications.

One possible use of DDE is taking data from an Excel worksheet and placing it in a Word document. If you need to change the Excel data, you need to change it only in Excel; the data is updated in Word automatically. In figure 14.20, for example, data for the regional sales of TechTron is shown in an Excel worksheet. Figure 14.21 shows the same numbers in a Word document that can be distributed to the staff in the form of a memorandum.

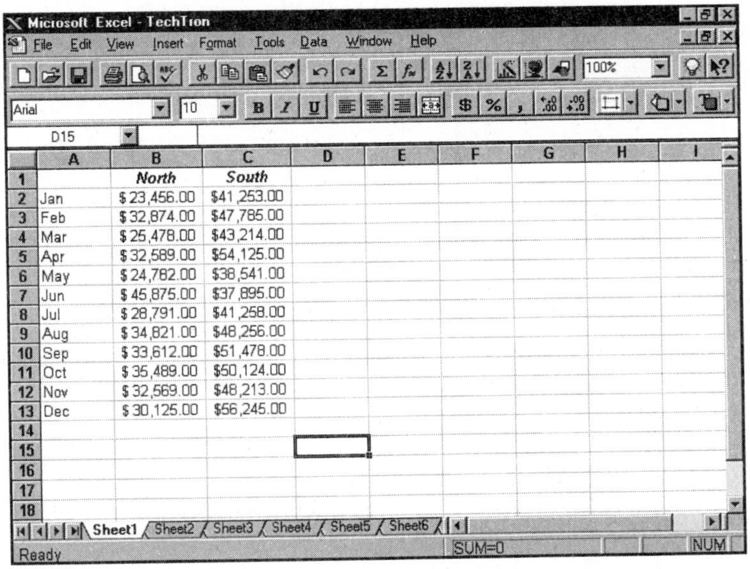

Fig. 14.20
Data from an Excel spreadsheet can be linked to a Word document.

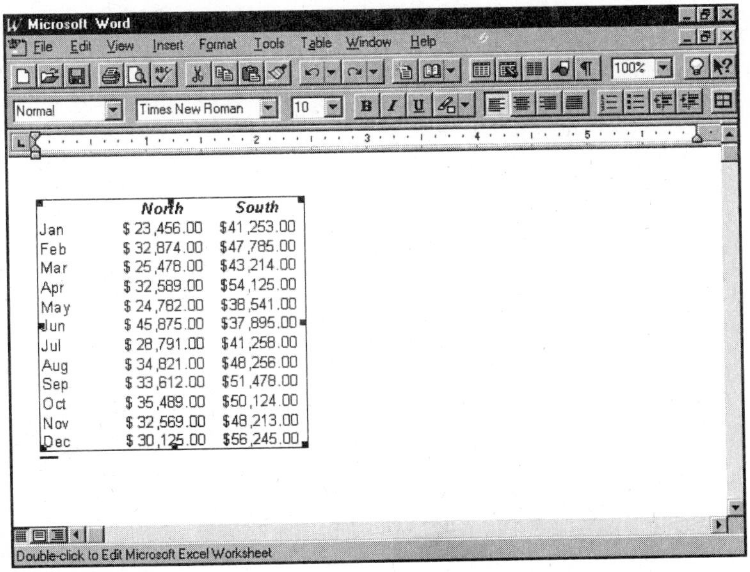

Fig. 14.21
The Word document reflects any changes that you make in the Excel document.

Suppose that you want to put together a new memo each month to detail sales for the entire year, but you want to create the memo document one time and update the sales data in the Word document automatically. You can do this by using a DDE link. In this example, to change the worksheet data in the Word document, you need to change the data while you're working in Excel.

Windows 95 provides two ways to use DDE: interactively and through a macro language. The easiest way to use DDE is the interactive method, which is based on the Clipboard copy-and-paste method that you used earlier in this chapter but has some important differences. The macro method, which involves creating a macro in the application's macro language, isn't discussed in this book.

When you establish a DDE link between applications, you use the Edit menu's Copy and Paste Link or Paste Special commands. Suppose that you have an Excel worksheet that you want to link to a Word for Windows document. Follow these steps:

1. Open Excel and then open a worksheet. You also can create a new worksheet to link data from.

2. Highlight some data in the worksheet, as shown in figure 14.22.

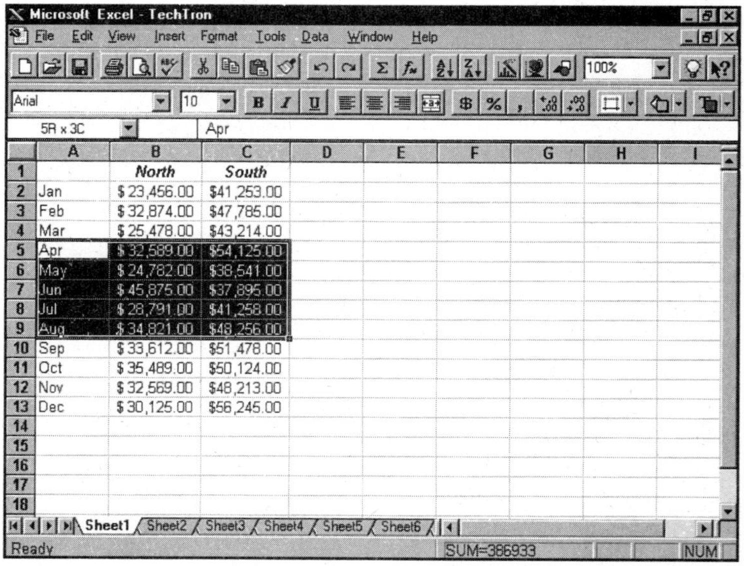

Fig. 14.22
Highlighting data in Excel to link to Word.

3. Choose Edit, Copy to copy the highlighted data to the Clipboard.

4. Open Word for Windows and then open an existing document or start a new document.

5. Choose Edit, Paste Special (see fig. 14.23). The Paste Special dialog box appears.

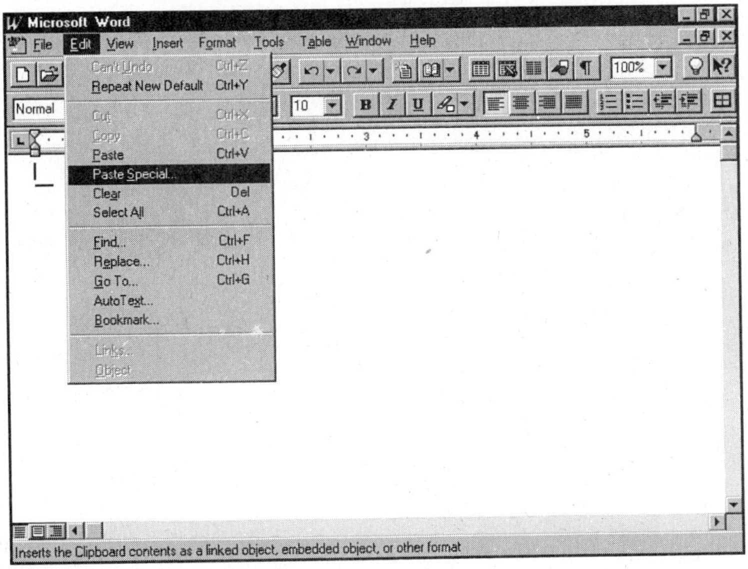

Fig. 14.23
Linking the Excel data to a Word document by using the Paste Special command.

6. In the Paste Special dialog box, click the Paste Link option (see fig. 14.24). If you don't click this button, Word inserts the data from Excel as an OLE 2.0 object rather than set up a DDE link.

► See "Inserting a New Object into Your Document," p. 442

7. In the As list box, select Microsoft Excel Worksheet Object.

8. Choose OK. The Excel data is inserted into the Word document as a picture (see fig. 14.25).

You can't change the data in Word; you can only view it. When changes are made in the data in Excel, those changes are reflected in the Word document.

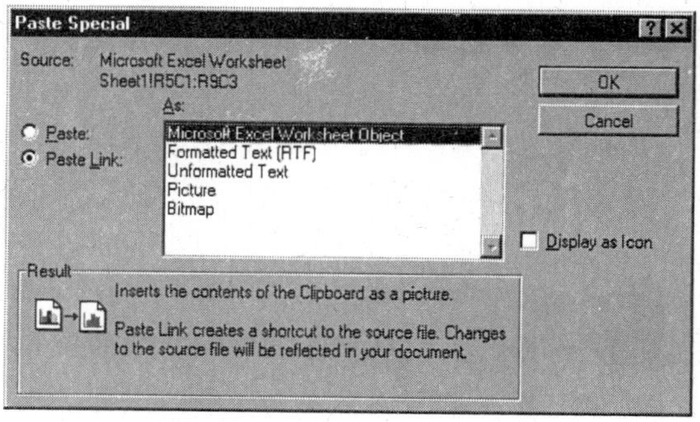

Fig. 14.24
Make sure that you click the Paste Link button to establish a DDE link.

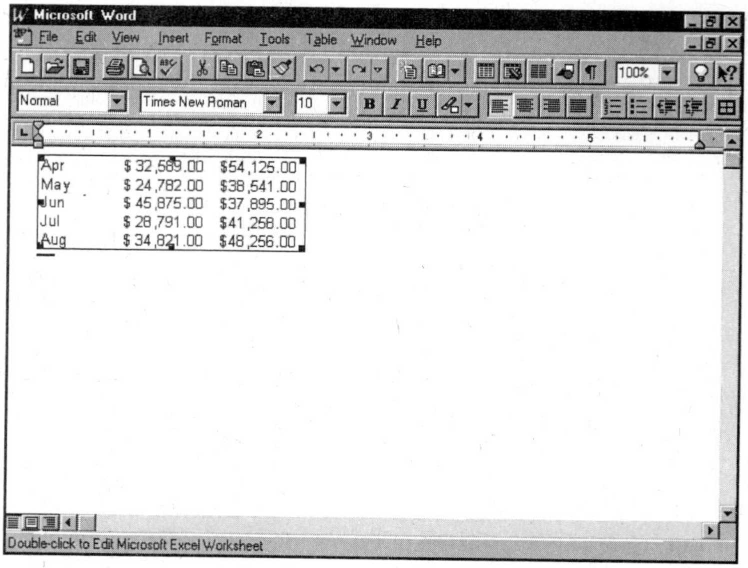

Fig. 14.25
Excel data is now linked to the Word document.

To see changes take place, switch back to the Excel worksheet and then follow these steps:

1. Change some of the data or formatting in the area that you linked to the Word document (see fig. 14.26).
2. Press Enter or click outside the cells that you edited. The data changes in the Word document to reflect your changes.
3. Switch to the Word document to see the updated data (see fig. 14.27).

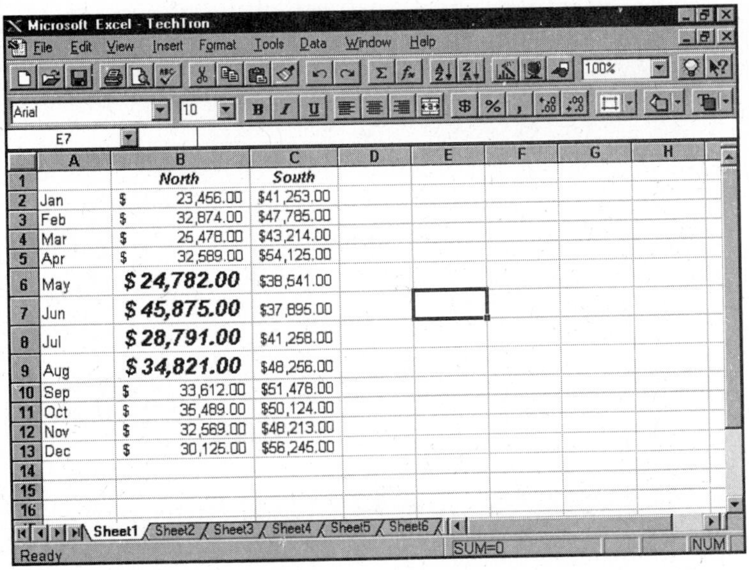

Fig. 14.26
Change some data in the Excel worksheet.

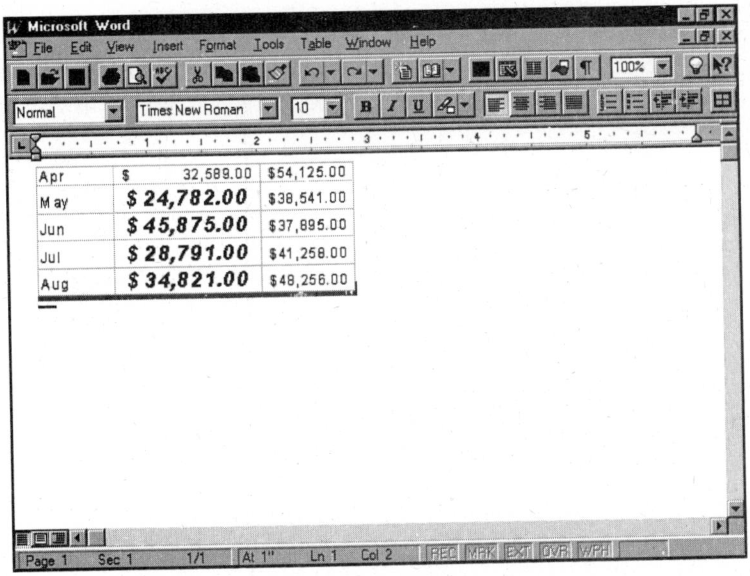

Fig. 14.27
The Word document is updated to reflect your changes.

Note

If you change the name or path of your client or server documents, you must re-establish your DDE links. You should make a habit of changing or creating file names and directories for your documents before you create a DDE link. Otherwise, your data won't update properly, causing you to work with old data.

Chapter 15

Building Compound Documents with OLE

by Rob Tidrow

In Chapter 14, you were introduced to two ways that you can exchange information in Windows 95. The first way was through the Clipboard and the Cut, Copy, and Paste commands. The other way was linking documents by using DDE (dynamic data exchange). Both methods are helpful when you create documents, drawings, spreadsheets, and other Windows files.

As you learned in the preceding chapter, the primary reasons to exchange and share data are to increase efficiency and to keep your information as current as possible. Keeping everyone informed and up-to-date is a difficult task, especially when you have several types of applications that can create and manipulate the information. By using Windows 95's capabilities to exchange information, you streamline the task of providing information to a diverse audience.

Expanding on the topic of data exchange and information sharing, this chapter introduces you to compound documents and object linking and embedding (OLE). *Compound documents* are documents you create by using multiple types of data. *Object linking and embedding* is a technology invented by Microsoft that allows you to build compound documents.

In this chapter, you learn to

- Look at information in a new way
- Understand compound documents and objects
- Embed information within documents

- Edit OLE objects in a document
- Understand OLE automation

Gaining a New View of Information

If you've been around the computer industry for a year or so, you've probably encountered a few obscure terms. Terms such as *compound document, objects, document-centricity*, and *component reuse* probably confuse you, or at least leave you scratching your head a little. For the most part, these terms and phrases are used to describe the way computer users interact with information.

As the personal computer industry matures and more powerful operating systems (such as Windows 95) are developed, users gain the ability to create documents that include almost any type of data, from almost any source. Today, for instance, your children can use sound and video clips from documentaries in their school book reports. You can include charts and graphs from your company spreadsheets in your monthly reports. An architect can include examples of floor plans in a proposal without redrawing a single line.

In the future, you'll be able to access any data on the Internet or online service, link it to your local document, and have it update automatically as the data source updates. You'll no longer be hampered by the boundaries and limitations that your applications and operating system have forced you to work under for years. You don't, for instance, *not* eat if your refrigerator stays empty for days. You find ways to eat. You go to the grocery, you order takeout, or you ask your neighbor for a free meal. The refrigerator doesn't dictate that you eat or how you eat. Why, then, should a word processor or spreadsheet application dictate the way in which you gather and disseminate information?

Introduction to Compound Documents

This section gets you familiar with the concept of compound documents and some of the terms associated with them. When you think about the elements that you place within a document—a sound clip, a picture, a spreadsheet—think about them as objects. An *object* is simply a piece of data that has a characteristic (such as sound) and a behavior (it plays a sound when you click it).

Objects are the basic building blocks of Microsoft's programming interface called object linking and embedding, or OLE (pronounced "oh-lay"). OLE allows you to build *compound documents*, which are documents that you create in one application but with objects from several different applications.

One technical definition of a compound document is that it's a data file maintained by a container application and that it contains one or more embedded objects. If you break this all down, it means that you can, for example, use Word for Windows as your container application and have a Visio drawing be your embedded object. You might be asking yourself, "What's all the fuss about? The Clipboard and DDE did that in Chapter 14."

The major difference between OLE (specifically OLE version 2.0) and simple data exchange (via the Clipboard) or DDE is that OLE lets you edit your Visio drawing (your embedded object) while still in Word for Windows. You can't do that with a simple Clipboard cut-and-paste operation or with a DDE link. With a DDE link, you have to return to the original application (in this case, Visio) to edit or modify the drawing. When you want to edit an OLE object in the compound document (in this case, a Word document), you just double-click the object, and elements common to the Visio interface appear on the Word for Windows interface. Figure 15.1 shows an example of this.

Tip
To edit an object in a compound document, the application that created the object must be installed on your computer.

You're still in Word...

...but these are the Visio menus and tools

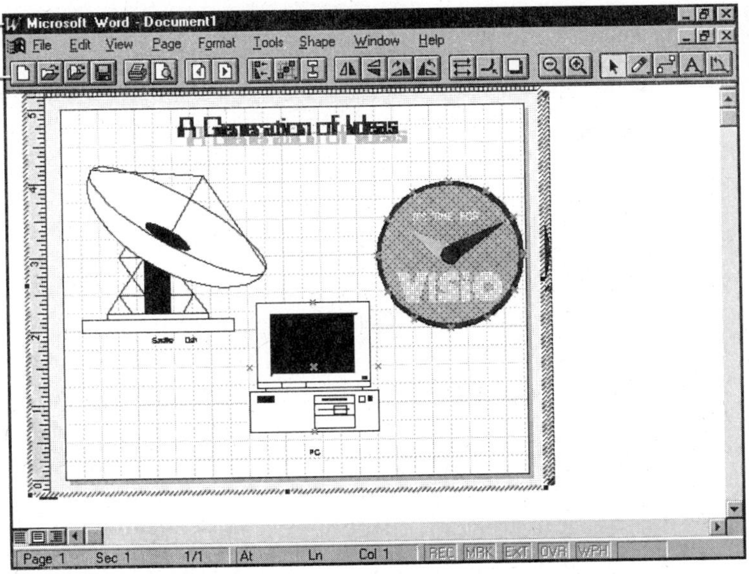

Fig. 15.1
While in Word for Windows, you can edit a Visio drawing using OLE 2.0 capabilities.

The obvious benefit of having the capability to edit an embedded object within a compound document is that you don't have to return to the source application every time you want to change the object. Many times you just need to change the spelling of a word, the position of a graphical element, or one or two entries of data after you place an element in your document. By using OLE 2.0, you double-click the object, wait a few seconds (or minutes, depending on your system) while your application changes, and then make the necessary changes to the object. On the other hand, when you link data using DDE, you must open the application that created the data, open the file that contains the data, change the data, and then update the DDE link.

OLE Technology

Entire books have been written on the topic of OLE technology and the way in which it's implemented in a particular application. Microsoft designed and released OLE 1.0 with the introduction of Windows 3.1 in 1992. In OLE 1.0, users could embed items in a document and then activate the original application by double-clicking the object. When the original application started, the embedded item appeared in the application ready for you to edit it. After editing it, you updated the object in the compound document by using menu commands. You might recall this type of action if you used Microsoft Draw in Word 2 for Windows.

Note

Many applications still support only OLE 1.0 compatibility and haven't upgraded to OLE 2.0. Keep this in mind when you make software upgrades or decide to buy new programs—particularly if you want the capabilities of OLE 2.0 instead of OLE 1.0.

OLE 2.0, released in the last quarter of 1993, coincided with the release of a new suite of Microsoft Office applications, including Excel 5 for Windows, Word 6 for Windows, and Access 2.0. Each application includes OLE 2.0 capabilities. After these applications came others from third-party vendors, including Shapeware's Visio, CorelDRAW!, and Autodesk's AutoCAD for Windows. The benefit to end users is that OLE 2.0 is becoming a standard feature in many applications, increasing the opportunities for creating compound documents.

Some of the advantages of OLE include the following:

- *OLE objects can be updated dynamically.* Like DDE links, OLE objects can be updated dynamically when the source data is edited or changed.

- *OLE enables applications to specialize.* Rather than have one giant application that tries to be everything for everybody, OLE allows applications to do what they do best. A drawing package, for instance, can focus on drawing; spreadsheets can focus on sorting and analyzing data; word processors can focus on creating documents; and so on.
- *OLE lets users get tasks done.* When users use embedded objects, they can focus on getting their task done rather than on the application necessary to get the job completed.

As you become more familiar with OLE and use it in your everyday work, you'll find that it becomes transparent. In fact, many users think OLE is a feature of all applications and are puzzled when they can't perform a task in an application that doesn't support OLE integration when they have done the same task in an OLE-compliant application. They become frustrated, for instance, when they can't drag a piece of text from their word processor to their favorite desktop publishing application. Or they can't share their contact manager information with their database application.

OLE Terminology

Similar to DDE links, OLE uses terms for each part of the embedding and linking stages. Two terms that you need to understand are *client* and *server*. The *client application* uses the services of another application through OLE. The *server application* provides OLE services to a client application.

For example, when you embed a Visio drawing in a Word document, Visio is the OLE server and Word is the OLE client. You can think of this relationship in the same way you think of a relationship with your attorney. The attorney is the *server* because she provides a service to you (legal help). You're the *client* because you're requesting services from the attorney (better known as the server). The services you obtain from the attorney can then be thought of as *objects*. You can use these objects, but if you need to update them or expand them (gain more knowledge of incorporating your business, for instance), you must go back and request help from your attorney. This is the same way you can update your embedded objects by using OLE. The client requests services from the server to help update the object.

Other OLE terms that you need to understand include in-place editing, drag-and-drop, container object, and OLE automation. These terms are defined in the following list:

- *In-place editing.* Refers to the capability to modify an embedded object within the client application without leaving the client application.

- *Drag-and-drop.* Refers to the capability to grab an object, move it across the screen, and place it into a client document. An example of dragging and dropping an object is selecting an Excel chart in Excel, dragging it to Microsoft Word, and dropping it in a document.
- *Container object.* An object that contains another object or several objects. In the preceding example, the Word document is the container object that holds the Excel object.
- *OLE automation.* Refers to the capability of a server application to make available (this is known as *expose*) its own objects for use in another application's macro language. This term is used a great deal among advanced users and software developers. One example of this is Microsoft's Visual Basic for Applications (VBA) programming language. VBA Excel version, for example, can use objects in Microsoft Project's VBA environment, enabling developers to create powerful custom applications.

Using Embedding to Link Information

If you're confused by linking (DDE) and embedding (OLE), keep in mind one major difference between the two—where the information is stored. Linked (DDE) information is stored in the source document. The destination contains only a code that supplies the name of the source application, document, and the portion of the document. Embedded (OLE) information is actually stored in the destination document, and the code associated with OLE points to a source application rather than a file.

In some cases, you can't use the source application by itself; you have to use your destination application to start the application. These applications are called applets and include WordArt, ClipArt, Microsoft Graph, and others. You generally launch the source application by choosing Insert, Object.

Embedding Information in Your Documents

When you embed an object, the information resides in the destination document, but the source application's tools are available for use in editing. You can use any of the following methods to embed information in a document:

◀ See "Understanding Dynamic Data Exchange (DDE)," p. 428

- Copy the information to the Clipboard; choose Edit, Paste Special; and select an object format. (This method was discussed in Chapter 14 when you linked data from one document to another, but you selected the Paste Link To option from the Paste Special dialog box in that chapter.)

- Arrange two windows side by side, and use drag-and-drop to copy information between the applications.
- Choose Insert, Object and open an existing file.
- Choose Insert, Object and create a new object. The following section describes this method.

◄ See "Using Drag-and-Drop to Copy Information between Documents," p. 421

Inserting a File into a Document

You can insert a file into documents by choosing Insert, File, which allows you to insert an entire file as an object. When you use Paste Special to link a file (as you did in Chapter 14), only the text you select before using the Edit, Copy command is part of the target file. If you later go back and insert text before or after the source-document selection, the target document doesn't include the entire text. Choosing Insert, File alleviates this problem.

Tip
The file that you insert can be from the same application or a different application.

To insert a file into a document, follow these steps:

1. Move to the position in the target document where you want to insert the file.
2. Do one of the following, depending on the application you use:
   - In WordPad, choose Insert, Object. Click the Create From File option. The Insert Object dialog box appears (see fig. 15.2).

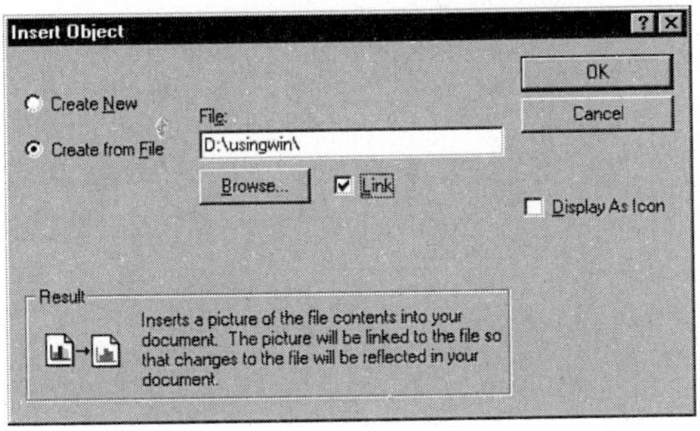

Fig. 15.2
Enter the file name or use the Browse button to indicate the file you want to embed in a WordPad document.

   - In Word for Windows, choose Insert, File. The Insert File dialog box appears (see fig. 15.3).

- In Microsoft Excel, choose Insert, Object. The Object dialog box appears. Click the Create From File tab and choose the application and file.

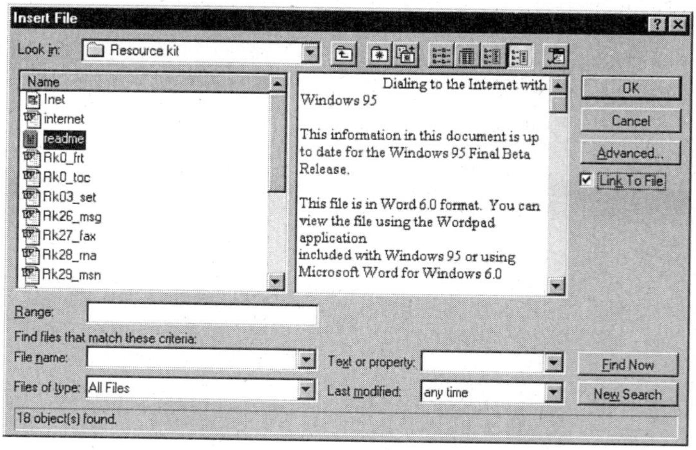

Fig. 15.3
Use the Word for Windows Insert File command to embed a file in a Word document.

3. Identify the file you want to insert, including the drive and directory, if necessary.
4. Select the Link or Link To File option.
5. Click OK.

To see that the file you inserted is a linked object, click anywhere in the document to show a gray highlight or to show the object's field codes.

> **Note**
>
> If you want to insert several word processing documents into a single larger document, give your documents a consistent appearance by using the same formats for each one. You also can use templates and styles to help ensure consistency among documents.

Inserting a New Object into Your Document

If you want to use the features of another application in your compound documents, you can choose Insert, Object and select an application from the provided list. As pointed out at the beginning of this chapter, many applications now support this feature of OLE 2.0, including the standard Microsoft Office applications, the Windows applets, and other Windows applications.

Applets are small applications that can't be run by themselves. When you buy a Windows application, one or more applets may be available.

As examples of the types of applets that support OLE as a server application or client application, the following list of applets come with Microsoft Office. When you install Microsoft Office on your system, these applets are installed in a centralized location, usually in a folder called MSAPPS, which allows many Office applications to access them easily. The WordPad application, which comes with Windows 95, can embed files that have been created in the following list.

Applet	Use
Microsoft ClipArt Gallery	Inserts clip-art pictures
Microsoft Data Map	Inserts a map showing different levels associated with data
Microsoft Equation	Creates mathematical expressions
Microsoft Graph	Inserts charts from data in a Word table
Microsoft Organization Chart	Creates organization charts
Microsoft Word Picture	Inserts a picture and the tools associated with the Word drawing toolbar
Microsoft WordArt	Creates logos and other special text effects

To use the tools from another application or applet within your document to create a new object, follow these steps:

1. Position the insertion point in the destination document.

2. Choose Insert, Object. The Insert Object dialog box appears (see fig. 15.4).

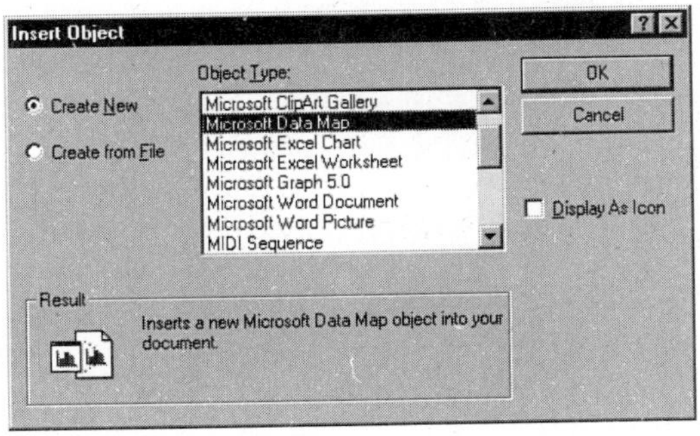

Fig. 15.4
The Insert Object dialog box lists applets as well as Windows applications.

Tip
The title bar identifies the application you are viewing. Applications that support OLE 2.0 display the name of the container application. Applications that support OLE 1.0 display the name of the source application.

3. Select the Create New radio button, and then select an application or applet from the Object Type list.
4. If you want to see only an icon for the object, select the Display as Icon check box.
5. When you finish with the Insert Object dialog box, choose OK.

After you complete these steps, one of two things occurs. You might enter a separate window for the application or the applet (see fig. 15.5). Or you'll remain in your client document window, but the menu bar and toolbar change to reflect the source application (see fig. 15.6).

Create the object by using the application's toolbar and menus. When you finish creating the object, you can exit the object in one of two ways:

- If you launched a separate window for the application or applet, choose File, Exit.
- If you stayed in your destination document, click outside the object.

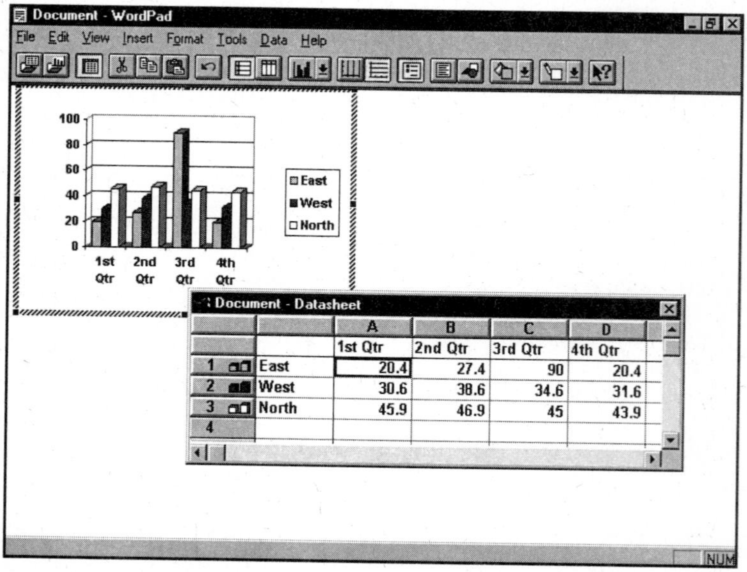

Fig. 15.5
When you choose Microsoft Graph 5.0 Chart, a separate window opens. After you finish with the chart program, click anyplace on the Word document window to return to the Word document.

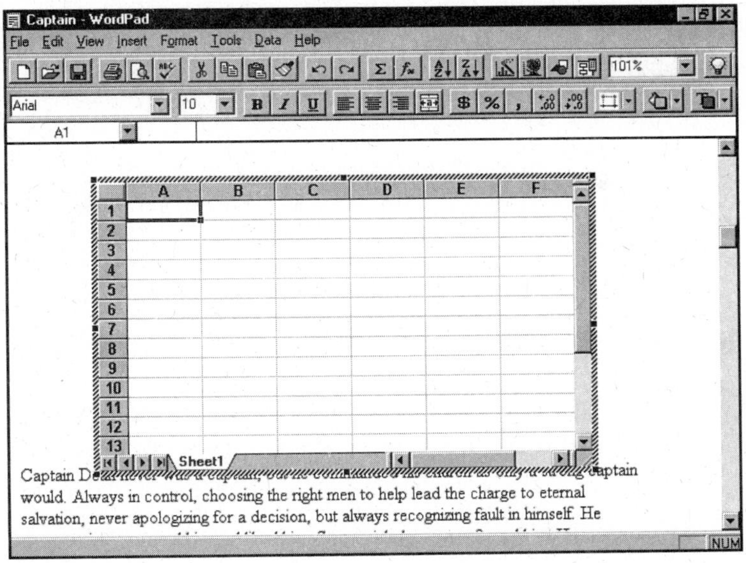

Fig. 15.6
When you choose Microsoft Excel Worksheet, you get in-place editing. The menu bar and toolbar change to Microsoft Excel, enabling you to use Excel features such as the AutoSum button.

Editing an Embedded Object

Regardless of which method you use to embed information into your document, you can edit the embedded object with the tools of the source application. To edit the object, follow these steps:

1. Click the object. Handles appear around the object, and the status bar tells you to double-click the object (see fig. 15.7).

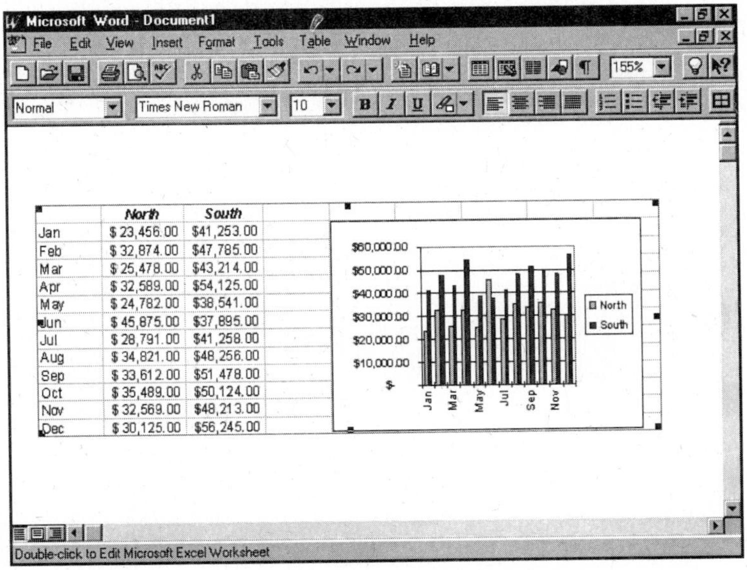

Fig. 15.7
The status bar displays instructions on how to get to the source-application tools.

2. Double-click the object. Depending on the source and destination applications, a separate window for the program appears, or the current window's toolbar and menu bar change to those of the source application.

3. Edit the object, using the application's toolbar and menus.

4. When you finish editing the object, exit the object. If you launched a separate window for the application or applet, choose File, Exit. If you stayed in your destination document, click outside the object.

Creating an Example Compound Document

Much of what you read in this chapter may be brand new information for you. The best way to learn how to use OLE is to actually use it a few times. This section uses Microsoft Excel and some common Windows 95 applications, such as Paint and Sound Recorder, to show you how to build a compound document. If you don't have Excel, you can use another OLE 2.0-compliant application to simulate this exercise.

Embedding a Paint Object in WordPad

To start your document, open WordPad. WordPad will be the container application where you'll embed server objects. In English, this means you'll use WordPad as your main program and embed a Paint bitmap, an Excel chart, and a sound file into your WordPad document.

1. In WordPad, create some text, such as **Let's embed a Paint object first:**.

2. Switch to Paint and open SANDSTONE.BMP, which is provided with Windows 95.

3. Click the Select tool on the Paint tool box. Mark an area on the drawing that you want to embed in your WordPad document. Choose Edit, Copy.

4. Switch to WordPad and place the cursor where you want to insert the drawing object. Choose Edit, Paste Special. The Paste Special dialog box appears (see fig. 15.8).

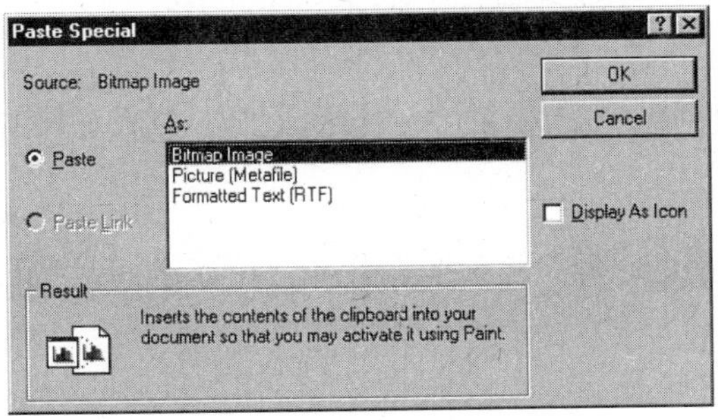

Fig. 15.8 You can imbed objects using the Paste Special dialog box.

5. In the Paste Special dialog box, make sure that the Paste Link check box isn't marked. You don't want to link this object to your document. Also, select Bitmap Image in the As list box. Click OK.

6. After a few seconds, your WordPad document displays an embedded Paint object. How do you know it's embedded? Click the object, and a thin border surrounds it. This is a frame that WordPad puts around the object. Double-click the object, however, and the entire WordPad interface changes to look like Paint (see fig. 15.9).

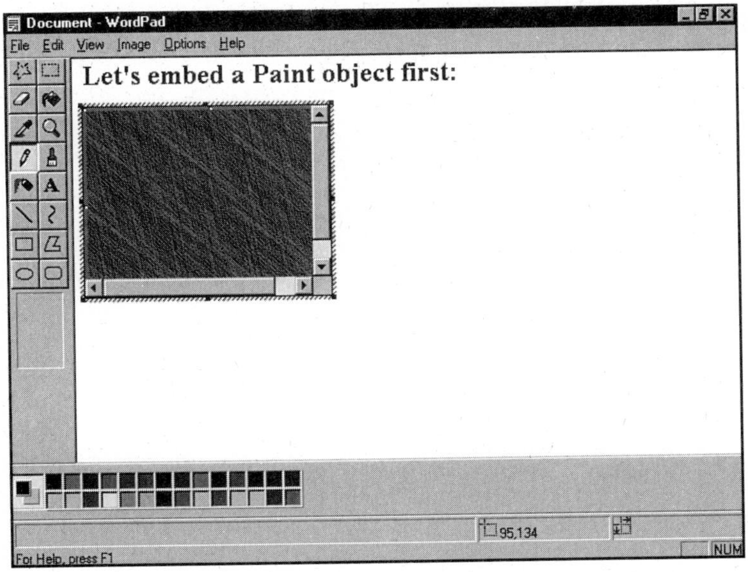

Fig. 15.9 Double-clicking the Paint object changes the WordPad interface to show Paint tools and menus.

Embedding an Excel Object by Dragging and Dropping

Another way to embed an object into your WordPad compound document is by dragging and dropping it from a server application. To drag a chart from Excel into WordPad, use these steps:

1. Open Excel and create a chart. You don't have to load it down with a lot of data, but do a simple one, as shown in figure 15.10.

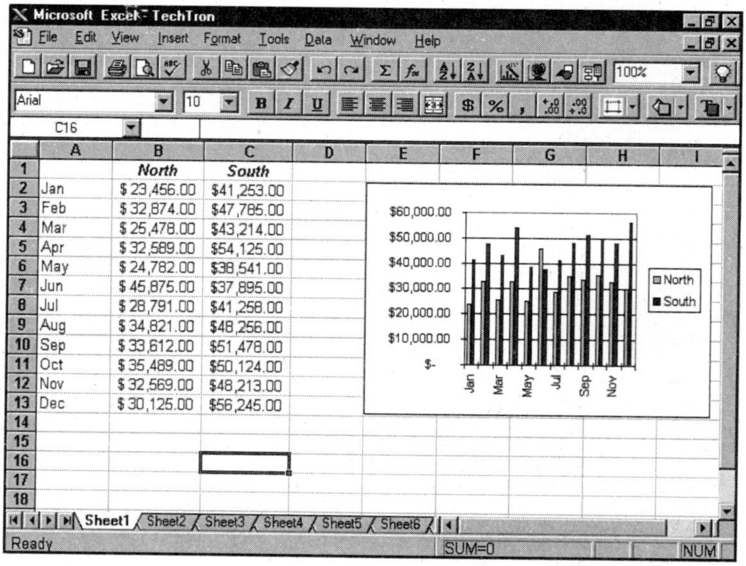

Fig. 15.10
You can drag this chart into your WordPad document.

◀ See "Switching between Document Windows," p. 115

2. Arrange your desktop so that you can see WordPad and Excel at the same time, as shown in figure 15.11.

3. Select and drag the chart into the WordPad window. Place the gray box with a plus sign in it at the spot where you want the chart embedded. If you want it in a special place in the document, you should prepare the document for the object before you start the drag-and-drop process.

4. Release the mouse button. The Excel chart now appears in the WordPad document as an embedded object.

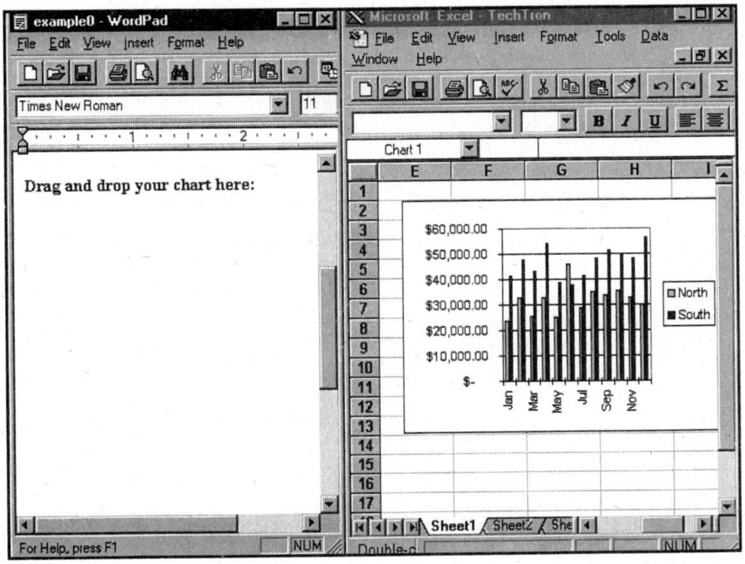

Fig. 15.11
To drag and drop, you should arrange your desktop to see both applications.

Embedding a Sound Clip in WordPad

To add a little flavor to your WordPad compound document, include a sound clip that your readers can click. You need to have a sound card and microphone to create and hear these sounds, but you still can embed the sound clips even if you don't have a sound card installed. To embed a sound clip in your document, follow these steps:

1. In WordPad, choose Insert, Object.
2. In the Insert Object dialog box, select Wave Sound from the Object Type list.

> **Note**
>
> If you have a specific sound clip that you want to embed, click the Create from File option and select the file you want to embed. If you don't click this option, the default setting is to create a new sound clip.

3. Click the Display As Icon check box to embed an icon of the sound clip in your WordPad document. When you use an icon, you reduce the system resources necessary to store the object.
4. Click OK. An icon of the sound object appears in the WordPad document (see fig. 15.12).

5. Double-click the icon to start the Sound Object in Document applet (see fig. 15.13). This applet allows you to record a new sound clip in your document. After you create a message, you can play it back by double-clicking the sound object in your WordPad document.

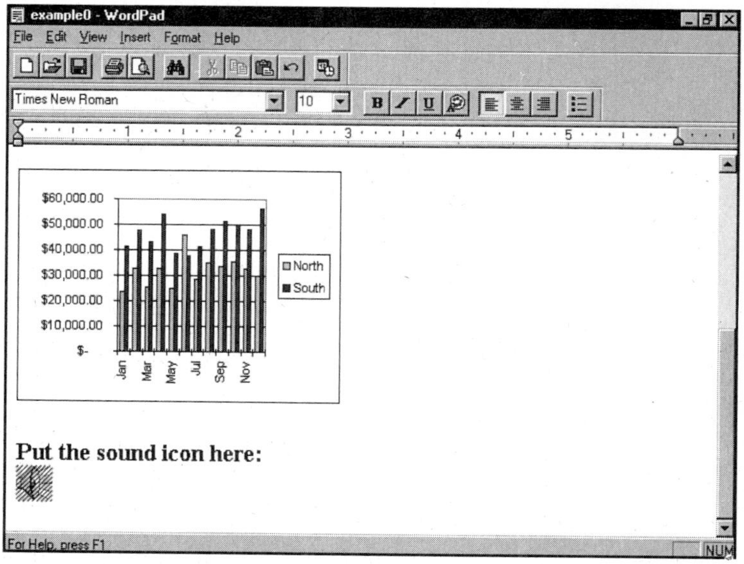

Fig. 15.12
The sound object appears as an icon in your document.

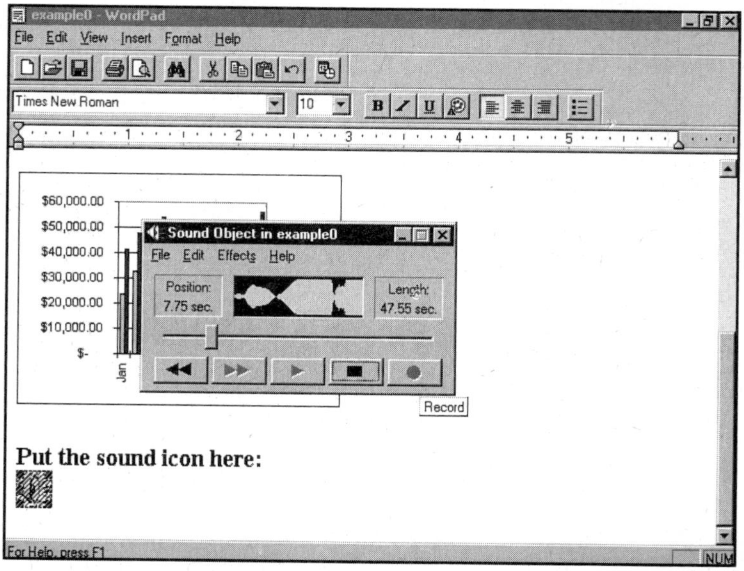

Fig. 15.13
By double-clicking the sound object icon, you activate the sound recorder applet to create a new wave file.

Editing an Embedded Object in Your Compound Document

If your data changes, if your taste in art differs now from what it did when you embedded the graphic object, or if you want to add something to your sound clip, you can edit each object without leaving WordPad. This section shows you how to edit the Excel chart that you embedded earlier, in the section "Embedding an Excel Object by Dragging and Dropping."

To edit the chart, follow these steps:

1. Double-click the Excel chart in your WordPad compound document. The WordPad interface automatically changes to the standard Excel interface (see fig. 15.14).

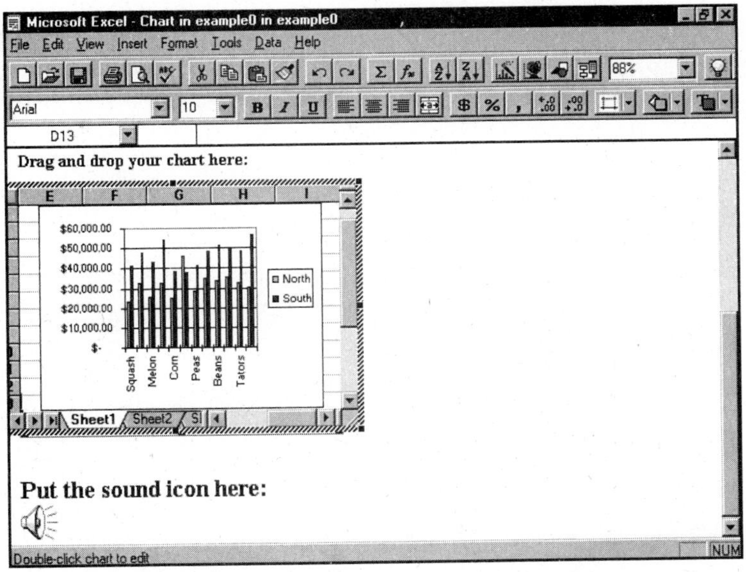

Fig. 15.14
With OLE 2.0, your container application takes on the appearance of the source application.

2. Make changes to the chart by using the toolbars and menu options. When you finish, click outside the chart. This returns the WordPad interface to its original state (see fig. 15.15).

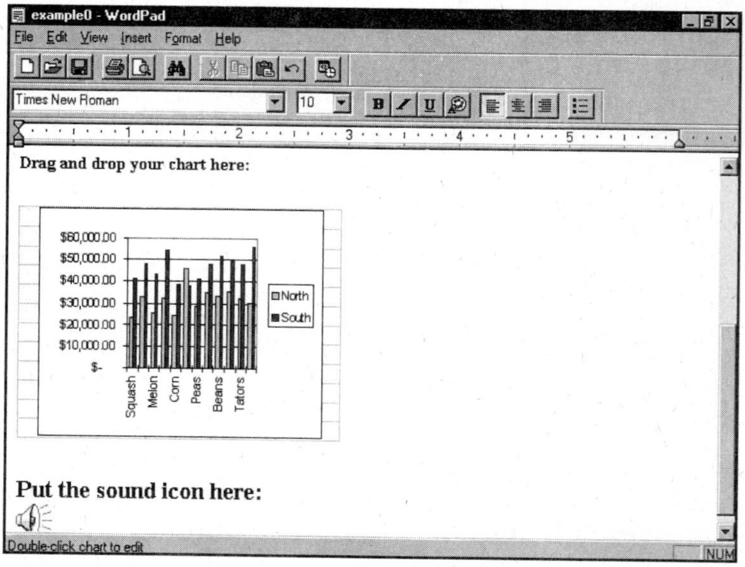

Fig. 15.15
WordPad's interface returns to its original state, but the Excel chart has changed.

Troubleshooting

When I double-click a linked or embedded object, a `Cannot edit` *error message appears.*

This means that the source file can't be opened. Make sure that the application needed to edit the file is on your machine. Also make sure that you have enough system memory to run both the container and source applications. Keep in mind that compound documents demand more memory than simple documents.

The margins are 0 (zero) in all my embedded Microsoft Word objects.

Word sets the margins at 0 (zero) inches in a document object to eliminate excessive white space around the object. To change the margins, double-click the Word document object to open it for editing. Choose File, Page Setup; click the Margins tab; then enter new margin settings.

When I double-click an embedded Microsoft Excel object, Microsoft Excel doesn't open.

You probably have the Ignore Other Applications check box selected, which causes Microsoft Excel to ignore all requests from other applications. In Excel, choose Tools, Options and then click the General tab. Clear the Ignore Other Applications check box.

OLE Automation for Interapplication Programming

As mentioned earlier in the chapter, OLE automation allows developers to use objects from different applications. An Excel program, for instance, can create and edit Microsoft Project objects. The following is a list of some of the applications that you can use to start OLE automation:

- Visual Basic
- Access Basic
- Visual Basic for Application, Excel version

OLE automation is used so that programmers can control and reference objects without worrying about complex and problematic interapplication details during the development cycle. Sophisticated business solutions can be created by using the capabilities of multiple applications with OLE automation. With more and more applications using OLE 2.0 and exposing objects to programmers, businesses can mix and match the applications on their users' desktops and (it's hoped) diversify the vendors who supply the applications. This makes for a much richer computing environment, giving the user more to choose from.

If just one vendor is providing one application to the end user, the end user must devise ways to modify her work to get the desired results. More than likely, these users spend a great deal of time creating workarounds or end up not getting the task done, lowering productivity. With OLE automation, many customized applications can be created to help businesses get done what they need to get done.

Understanding OLE Automation Functions

If you're a developer or power user interested in OLE automation basics, this section briefly describes some of the functions available. By understanding three primary functions in OLE automation, you can begin developing applications that rely on exposed objects or control objects in other applications.

Note

For information on OLE automation, many Que books are available that teach you the fundamentals and expert techniques. A few of these include *Special Edition Using Visual Basic for Applications* and *Special Edition Using Excel for Windows 95*.

The `Set` function is used to set a variable in the application in which you're programming to reference an object in a different OLE 2.0 application. This reference is commonly referred to as *pointing*. If, for example, you're in Microsoft Project and want to reference the active worksheet in Excel, you would use the following syntax:

```
Set ExampleSheet = MSExcel.ActiveSheet
```

When you reference the properties and methods of the `ExampleSheet` object in Project, you affect the worksheet in Excel.

The `CreateObject` function creates the specified object and then returns an object that's linked to the new object. After you get the returned object, you use the `Set` function to link it to an object variable. To use the `CreateObject` function, use the syntax `CreateObject ("`*`ApplicationName.ObjectType`*`")`. The following is an example of using the `CreateObject` function:

```
Set NewObject = CreateObject("Excel.Sheet")
```

In this example, you automatically start Excel, create an object, and create an object variable that can reference the created object. You then use the new object throughout your subroutine.

The last of the primary three OLE automation functions is `GetObject`. This function is similar to the `CreateObject` function, except it accesses its source object from a file. The syntax for `GetObject` is `GetObject("`*`completePathname`*`")`. To reference an object that's on your C:\ drive in the OLE folder, for example, use the following syntax:

```
Set ExampleObject = GetObject("C:\OLE\SAMPLE.OBJ")
```

Creating a Sample OLE Automation Subroutine

This brief introduction to OLE automation isn't intended to teach you how to write OLE automation applications. The intention is to introduce you to what OLE and OLE automation can do if you decide to create a custom application to take full advantage of Windows 95's built-in support of OLE 2.0.

The short sample code, denoted as listing 15.1, creates a Word for Windows object within Excel and then embeds a Word document in an Excel worksheet with the phrase "Sample OLE Automation," as shown in figure 15.16. To create this code, create a new Excel macro and copy this code into the macro window. Try to follow along by reading the lines that start with an apostrophe ('). These *comment lines* are included to *document* (explain) the code. For a subroutine this simple, you can see that OLE automation follows the same basic procedures that you perform when you manually embed objects. On the other hand, more sophisticated OLE automation is very complicated and involves hundreds or thousands of code lines to complete.

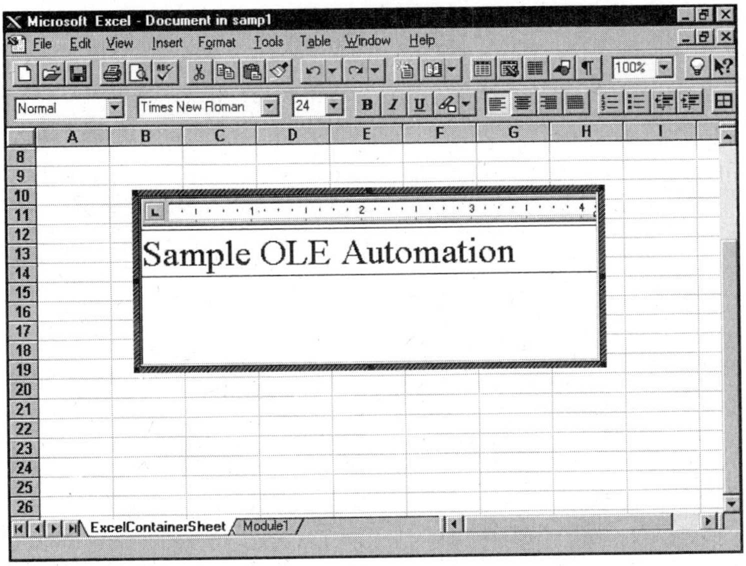

Fig. 15.16 This is an example of OLE automation controlling a Word object from within Excel.

Listing 15.1 <OLE Automation Example>

```
'
' OleAutomationExample Macro
' Macro recorded 6/13/95 by Rob Tidrow
'
'
Sub OLEAutomationExample()
    ' Use DIM to assign two variables as Object data type
    Dim WordObject As Object
    Dim WordBasicObject As Object

    'Displays the Excel worksheet that contains the Word object
    Worksheets("ExcelContainerSheet").Activate

    'Create and assign the Word object to the WordObject variable
    Set WordObject = ActiveSheet.OLEObjects.Add("Word.Document.6")
    Set WordBasicObject = WordObject.Object.Application.WordBasic

    'This line activates the Word object
    WordObject.Activate

    'This line applies a border to the outside of the text
    WordBasicObject.BorderOutside
```

(continues)

Listing 15.1 Continued

```
        'This line sets the typeface
        WordBasicObject.Font Arial$

        'This line sets the font size
        WordBasicObject.FontSize 24

        'This line places the Word text into Excel
        WordBasicObject.Insert "Sample OLE Automation"
End Sub
```

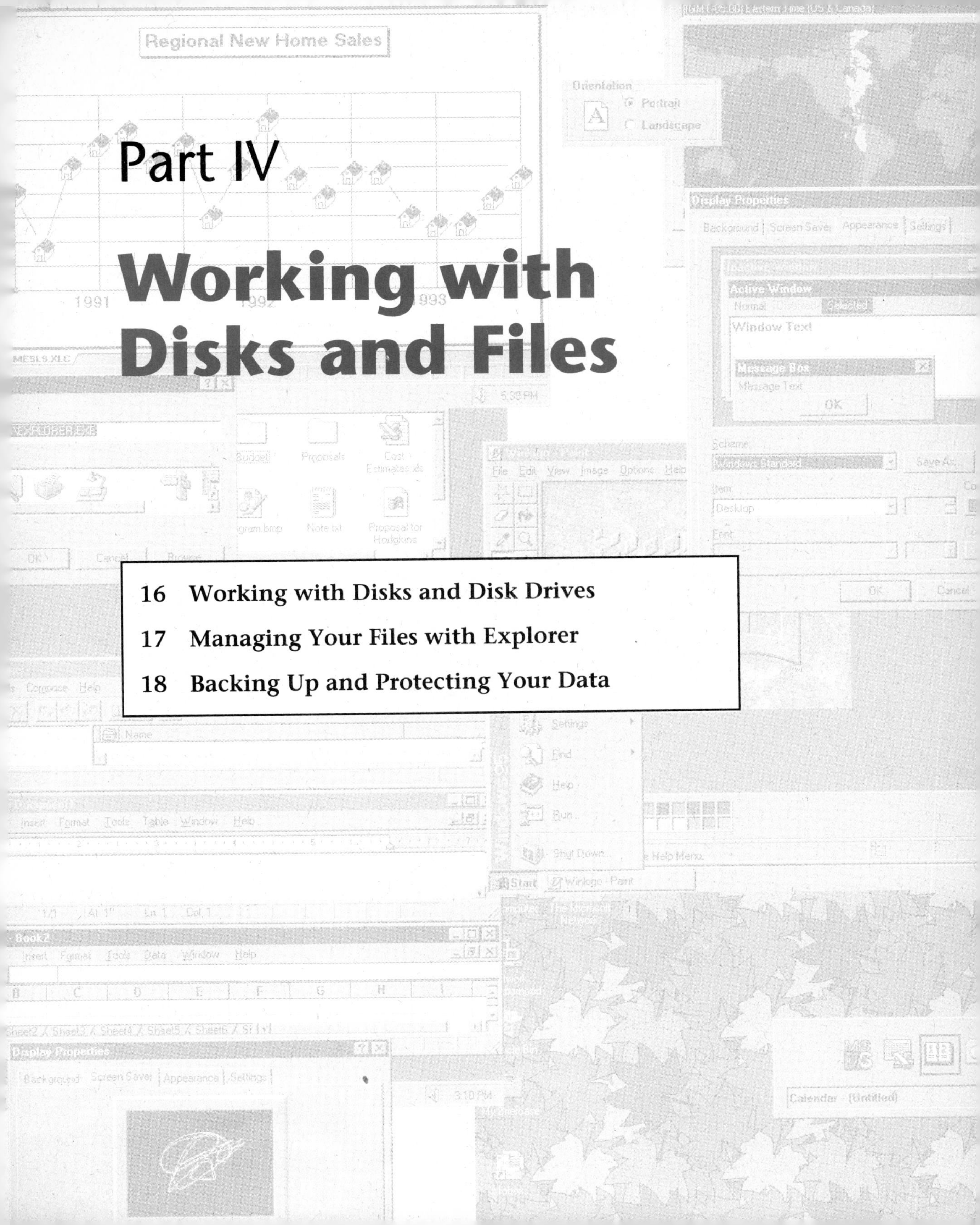

Part IV

Working with Disks and Files

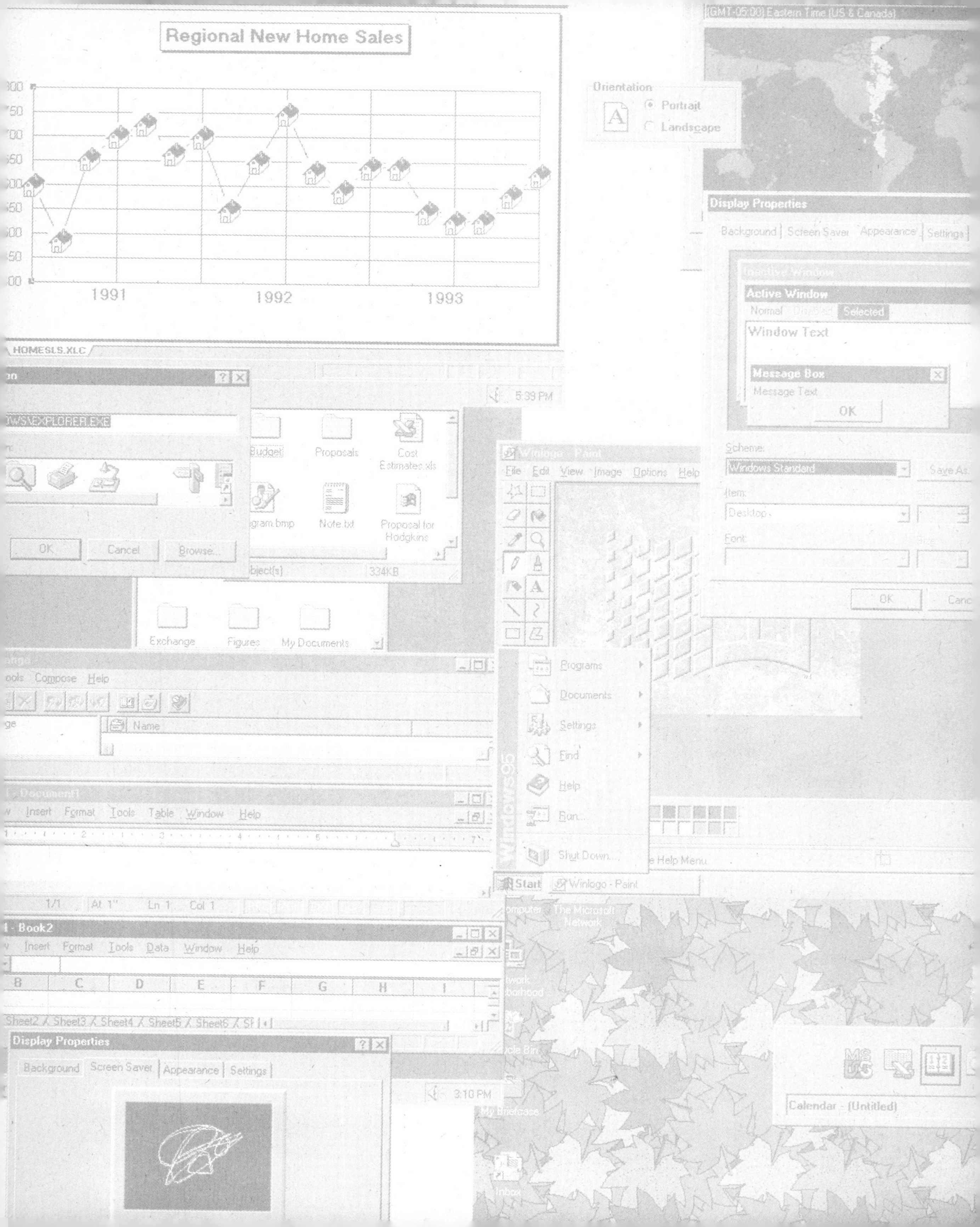
Regional New Home Sales
1991
1992
1993
HOMESLS.XLC
Orientation
Portrait
Landscape
(GMT-05:00) Eastern Time (US & Canada)
Display Properties
Background
Screen Saver
Appearance
Settings
Inactive Window
Active Window
Normal
Disabled
Selected
Window Text
Message Box
Message Text
OK
Scheme:
Windows Standard
Save As...
Item:
Desktop
Font:
OK
Cancel
Browse...
Budget
Proposals
Cost Estimates.xls
Note.txt
Proposal for Hodgkins
334KB
Exchange
Figures
My Documents
5:39 PM
Winlogo - Paint
File
Edit
View
Image
Options
Help
Programs
Documents
Settings
Find
Help
Run...
Shut Down...
Windows95
Start
Winlogo - Paint
Compose
Help
Name
Insert
Format
Tools
Table
Window
Help
1/1
At 1"
Ln 1
Col 1
Book2
Insert
Format
Tools
Data
Window
Help
B
C
D
E
F
G
H
I
Sheet2
Sheet3
Sheet4
Sheet5
Sheet6
Display Properties
Background
Screen Saver
Appearance
Settings
3:10 PM
The Microsoft Network
My Briefcase
Inbox
Calendar - (Untitled)

Chapter 16

Working with Disks and Disk Drives

by Ron Person with Jerry Cox

Before you learn about organizing files on a computer, which is covered in detail in the next chapter, you need to learn how to work with and maintain your floppy disks and hard disks. For example, before you put data on a floppy disk, you usually have to format it to get it ready to receive data. If you want, you can also name your drives to make them easier to identify. Floppy disks and hard disks, not being perfect, are susceptible to damage—which can be very trying if you are dealing with irreplaceable data. Windows 95 comes with a tool to help you check for and repair some kinds of damage.

Everyone likes to get more performance out of their computer. You can monitor the performance of your system using the System Monitor. You can improve the performance of your hard disks using Disk Defragmenter. You can enable your system to act as though it has more memory (RAM) than is actually installed by using virtual memory. You may want to periodically refer back to this chapter when it's time to do maintenance work on your floppy disks and hard disks.

In this chapter, you learn to

- Format your floppy and hard disks
- Name your disks
- Monitor your system's performance
- Increase the effective size of your disks with DriveSpace

- Defragment your hard disk to improve performance
- Use ScanDisk to check for disk damage
- Use virtual memory

Understanding What Your Disk Drive Does

The computer does all calculations and work in electronic *memory*. (Electronic memory is known as *RAM*, or Random Access Memory.) RAM is where Windows and your programs work. The data you work on also resides in RAM. If the computer loses electrical power, the data, program, and Windows are lost from memory. Because electronic memory is limited in size and disappears when electrical power is removed, the computer needs a way to store large amounts of data and applications for long periods of time.

You use *magnetic storage* to store applications and data for long periods of time or when the computer is turned off. Magnetic-storage media include *floppy disks* and *hard disks*. Floppy disks are removable and don't contain much space. Hard disks are internal to the computer and have much larger amounts of space.

Note

There are larger floppies on the market but they are not standard equipment from any of the manufacturers yet. An example is the new 20M and 100M floppies for the Iomega Zip Drives.

► See "Understanding Files and Folders," p. 498

► See "Using the Explorer with Shared Resources on a Network," p. 544

The hard disk you store your data and programs on does not have to reside in the computer at your desk. If you are connected to a network, you can access information stored on the hard disk in the *file server*, the computer that serves the *clients* on the network. When you start an application or open a data file, the computer places a *copy* of the information stored in magnetic storage (on floppy disks or a hard disk) into electronic memory (RAM). If power is lost, the magnetic copy still is available.

You save the work you do in your programs in magnetic *files*, which are stored on a floppy disk or hard disk. Over time, you may have hundreds or even thousands of files. Searching for a specific file among the thousands of files can be very time-consuming.

Large computers and networks have multiple hard disks, each disk with its own drive letter. Figure 16.1 shows two hard disk drives (see the icons for drives C and D), a floppy disk drive (see the icon for drive A), and a CD-ROM drive (drive E). Each disk acts as a separate filing cabinet and can have its own unique folder organization.

Note

Some drives may have more than one letter depending on the controller versus drive size. If the drive is larger than the controller or BIOS can read, it can be partitioned as two drives. It is still only one piece of hardware, but software sees it as two drives. It also is possible for a drive to have more than one letter if it is compressed. In this case, the software doing the compression addresses the drive with one letter, and all other software accesses it using another drive letter, which is controlled by the compression software.

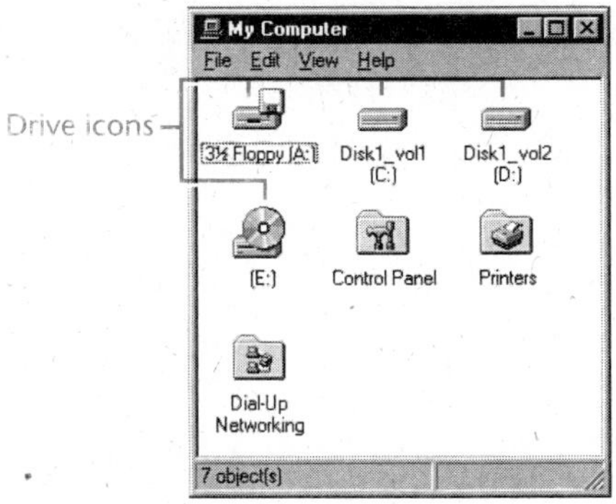

Fig. 16.1
The My Computer window displays all the resources on your computer, including all the floppy disk drives and hard drives.

Formatting Disks

You usually cannot use new disks until you format them (but some disks come already formatted). *Formatting* prepares disks for use on a computer. Formatting is similar to preparing a blank book for use by writing in page numbers and creating a blank table of contents. If a disk contains data, formatting it completely erases all existing data. Part of the process of formatting is checking for bad areas on the disk's magnetic surface. All bad areas found are identified so that data is not recorded in these areas.

Tip
If you attempt to open an unformatted floppy disk in My Computer or Windows Explorer, you will be asked if you want to format the disk. The Format dialog box immediately displays.

Formatting a Floppy Disk

To format a floppy disk, follow these steps:

1. Insert the floppy disk to be formatted in the disk drive.

2. Open the My Computer window by double-clicking its icon.

3. Select the floppy disk drive containing the floppy disk to be formatted.

4. Choose File, Format (or right-click the drive icon and select Format from the shortcut menu). The Format dialog box appears (see fig. 16.2).

Note

If you are working in the Windows Explorer, there is no File, Format command; instead, right-click a floppy disk drive icon in the left pane of the Explorer and select Format from the shortcut menu.

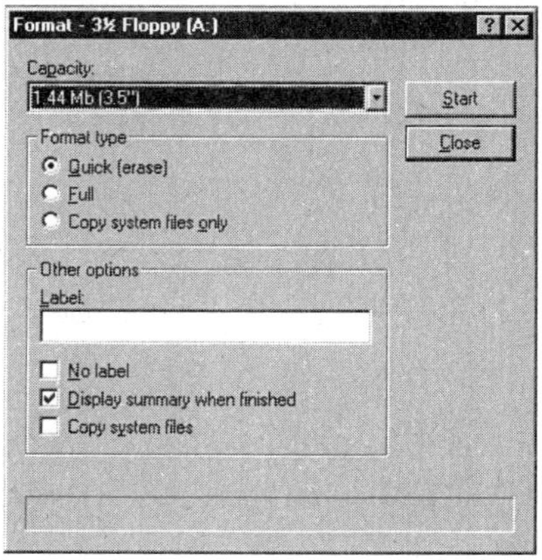

Fig. 16.2
Set up a formatting operation in the Format dialog box.

5. Select the size of the floppy disk from the Capacity drop-down list.

6. Select the type of format you want from the Format Type options:

Option	Function
Quick (Erase)	Formats the disk without scanning it for bad sectors first. Speeds up formatting, but you should be sure that the disk is undamaged. You can use the Quick format option only on disks that have already been formatted.
Full	Checks for bad sectors on the disk before formatting and marks them so that these areas are not used.
Copy System Files Only	Adds the system files to the disk without formatting it so that the disk can be used to start the computer.

7. If you want to assign a label to the disk, type the label in the Label text box. Otherwise, select the No Label option.

8. Select the Display Summary When Finished option if you want to see a screen of information about the disk after it is formatted (see fig. 16.3).

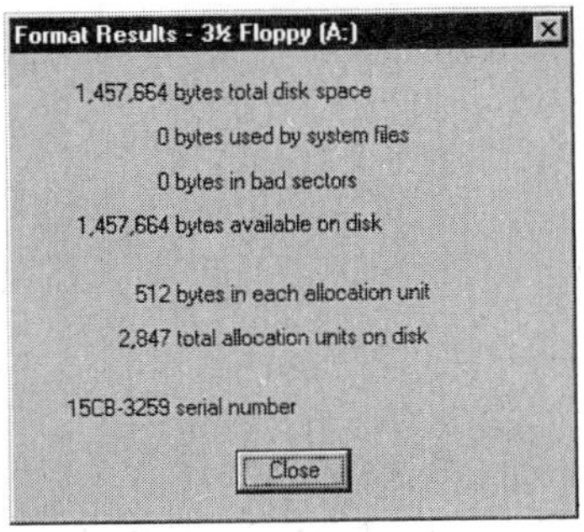

Fig. 16.3
You can get information about a formatted disk in the Format Results message box.

The Format Results message box tells you how much total disk space there is, how many bytes are used by system files and bad sectors, and how many bytes are available.

9. If you want to use the disk to start the computer, select the Copy System Files option. Do not use this option unless you need to, because system files use storage space on the disk that can otherwise be used for data.

10. Choose Start. The progress of the formatting operation is displayed at the bottom of the Format dialog box.

11. To format another disk, insert a new disk and repeat steps 5 through 10.

12. When you are finished formatting disks, choose Close.

> **Caution**
>
> When you format a disk, you remove all the information from the disk. You should check a disk for important files before formatting.

Format an entire box of disks at one time and put a paper label on each disk when it is formatted. This system lets you know that open boxes contain formatted disks; paper labels confirm that the disks are formatted.

Troubleshooting

Windows will not format a disk drive. A dialog says there are files open but all applications and documents on the drive are closed.

Windows 95 prevents you from formatting a disk that has a file open or a disk that is open in My Computer or the Windows Explorer. Close any documents or applications that are open on that disk and close any My Computer or Windows Explorer windows open into the disk.

Caution

Drives that have been compressed with DriveSpace or another compression software must be formatted from DriveSpace or the appropriate compression software.

Formatting Your Hard Disk

Before you can use a new hard drive you need to format it. You also may want to format a hard drive that has been used and is cluttered with data or other operating systems. Formatting does more than just erase old data, it magnetically scrubs the disk so that the files do not exist.

If you have purchased a preassembled computer that contains a hard disk and the computer starts and runs Windows or DOS, then you do not need to format the hard disk. If, however, you install additional hard disks in your computer, you may need to format them before you can use them.

Note

You should format a disk that contains confidential or secret information before giving the computer to someone who should not have access to that data. The erase or delete commands only remove a file's name and location from a disk's table of files. The data still exists on the disk until it is overwritten by another file. Formatting erases the name and location table and magnetically erases the actual data.

Using FDISK to Partition a New Hard Drive

If you are installing a new hard disk as your primary drive, place the Windows 95 Startup disk in the A: drive and turn on your computer. Windows sees the new drive and asks if you want to allocate all of the unallocated space on your drive. Answer "yes" and it will run FDISK behind the scenes and restart your computer. After the restart, it formats the new partition automatically.

Your other alternative is to boot to DOS Mode by pressing F5 during startup and running FDISK from the DOS prompt. When you type FDISK at the DOS prompt it puts a menu on the screen. Be sure to check to see that the drive that you want to partition is the drive that is selected. Option 5 on the menu allows you to select a different drive. After you have confirmed that you have the correct drive selected, choose option 1 from the menu. This option creates a DOS partition on your drive and asks if you want to use the entire drive for your DOS partition. The most common answer is yes. Once the DOS partition is created, your computer will restart and be ready for the formatting of the drive.

As you can see by the two choices of partitioning a hard drive, Windows 95 has made this step much easier.

Formatting an Uncompressed Hard Drive from MS-DOS

To format an uncompressed drive from the MS-DOS prompt, type "Format d:". Where d: is the drive letter of the drive that you want to format.

► See "Compressing a Drive," p. 471

Formatting an Uncompressed Hard Drive from Windows

Before you format an uncompressed hard drive make sure you have backed up or copied any file that may be needed again. Once the formatting process begins you will be unable to retrieve previous data from the drive.

To format a hard drive, follow these steps:

1. Close all documents and applications that are on the drive you want to format. Close any windows from My Computer that look at that drive. Collapse all folders in Windows Explorer for the hard drive you want to format.

2. Open My Computer and select the icon for the drive you want to format. Choose File, Format.

   or

   Open Windows Explorer, and right-click on the hard drive icon you want to format. Choose Format.

   The Format dialog box displays as shown in figure 16.4.

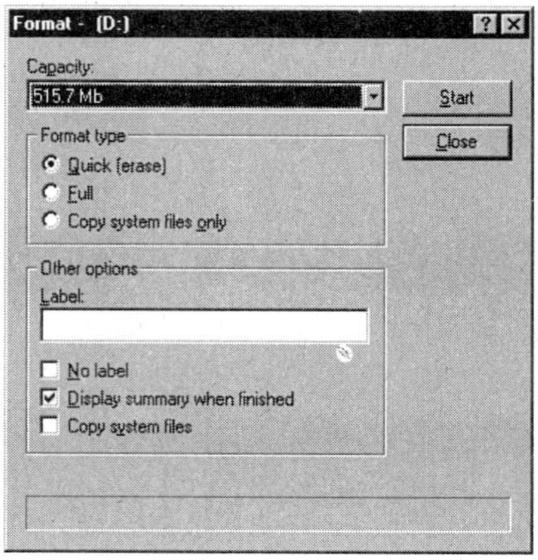

Fig. 16.4
You can use the Format dialog box to do a full format, erase files, and copy system files onto a disk.

3. Select the option you want for formatting your disk:

Option	Function
Capacity	Click the drop-down list arrow to select a different capacity for the drive.
Format Type	
Quick (Erase)	Erases all the files, but does not use ScanDisk to check for bad areas of the disk. The disk must be formatted to use this command. If you think your disk may have bad areas or has shown erratic behavior, be sure to run ScanDisk after the Quick format.
Full	Prepares a disk for use. All files are completely removed. Disks are checked for bad sectors, but hard disks are not. If this is a new hard disk or a disk that has shown erratic behavior, be sure to run ScanDisk after the Full format.
Copy System Files Only	Does not format the disk but it does copy system files to the disk so the floppy or hard disk can be used to start the computer.
Other Options	
Label	Creates a magnetic label on the disk. This label appears in the title bar of My Computer and Windows Explorer.
No Label	Disables the label so the disk will not have a label.
Display Summary When Finished	Displays a report when formatting is complete. The report shows the space available on the disk, the room taken by system files, and the number of bad sectors.
Copy System Files	Copies system files onto the disk after formatting. Select this check box if you need to use this floppy or hard disk to start the computer.

4. Choose Start. A dialog box displays telling you that all files on the disk will be destroyed. Are you sure you want to format this drive? Choose OK to format or Cancel to stop.

5. If you choose OK, you will see the Format dialog box showing you the progression of the file format as shown in figure 16.5.

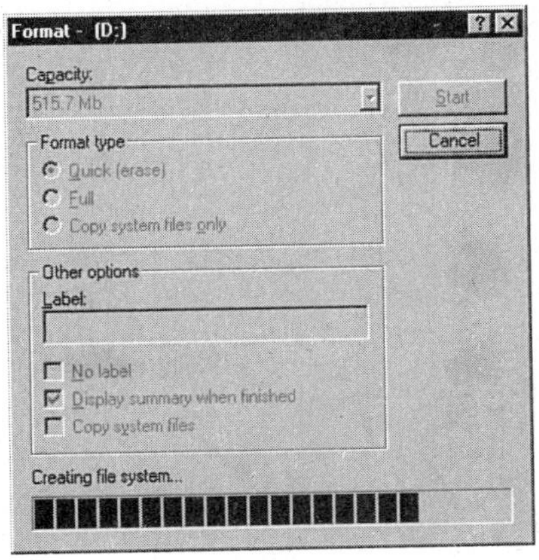

Fig. 16.5
A progression bar at the bottom of the dialog box shows you the progress of disk formatting.

6. When formatting is complete the Format Results dialog box displays the properties of the formatted drive as shown in figure 16.6.

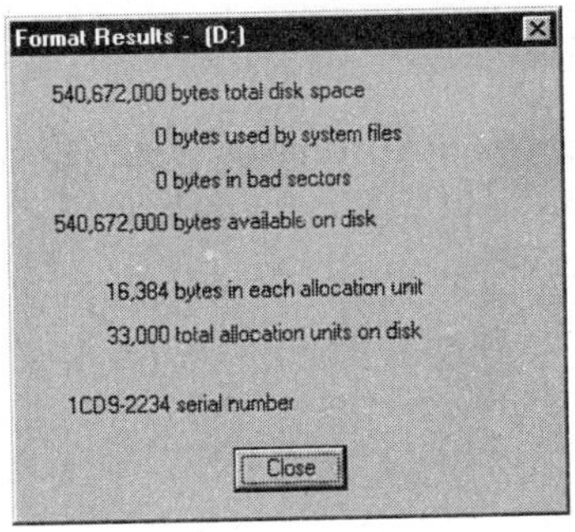

Fig. 16.6
The Format Results dialog box displays a report on disk statistics when formatting is complete.

Note

If you use the Full format option on a hard disk drive, you are reminded to use ScanDisk.

7. Choose Close to close the Format Results dialog box; then choose Close to close the Format dialog box.

◄ See "Using FDISK to Partition a New Hard Drive," p. 464

► See "Using ScanDisk to Check for Disk Damage," p. 489

If My Computer or Windows Explorer does not display the icon for the hard drive you want to format, then you may need to recheck the drive connections to the drive adapter or partition the hard drive using the FDISK command. You also need to check setup to be sure the proper drive type is selected.

Caution

You cannot format the hard disk containing Windows while Windows is running. If you need to format the hard disk containing Windows, you will need either a disk copy of MS-DOS with the FORMAT command or a set of the Windows 95 upgrade disks which contains a disk for formatting hard disks.

The system files, FDISK, and Format are created on the Startup disk that Windows 95 asks if you want to create it during the install. It is *highly* recommended that you create the Startup disk.

Naming Your Drive with a Volume Label

Although you may be accustomed to putting a paper label on disks, both hard disks and floppy disks can have magnetically recorded labels, known as *volume labels*. Volume labels can help you identify disks. You can read the volume label for a disk by looking at the disk's properties.

In the preceding section, you learned how to create a volume label when you format a disk. If you want to create or change a volume label on a previously formatted disk, follow these steps:

1. Open the Explorer or the My Computer window.
2. Select the drive having the volume name you want to change.
3. Choose File, Properties. Alternatively, right-click the drive and choose Properties from the shortcut menu. The Properties sheet appears, as shown in figure 16.7.
4. Type the name you want to give the disk in the Label text box and choose OK.

   If there is already a name in the box, select it first and then type a new name. The Properties sheet also gives you information on the total size of the disk (in bytes), how much space is used, and the amount of remaining space.

Tip
You can view the name of a disk by right-clicking the disk icon in the My Computer or Explorer window and selecting the Properties command.

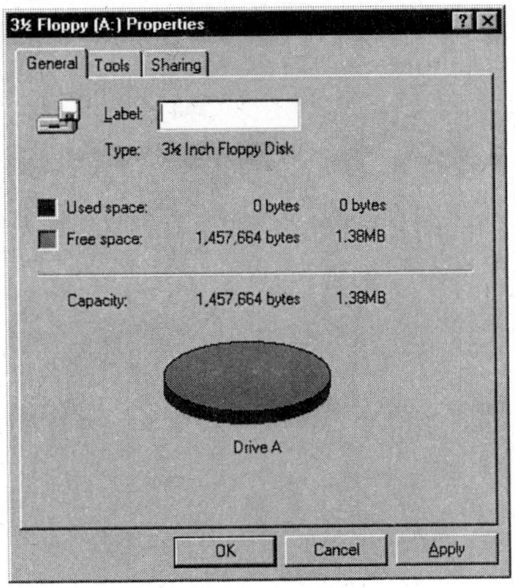

Fig. 16.7
Enter a volume label for a disk in the Properties sheet.

Compressing a Disk

If you are like many computer users, you may find yourself bumping up against the limits of the storage space on your computer as you install new programs and generate more and more data files. You've probably also discovered that new releases of Windows programs seem to take up more and more room on your hard disk. One solution is to install a new hard disk in your computer. But if your finances are limited, or you are working with a laptop in which it is not possible to add another hard disk, you have another option. Windows 95 comes with a program called DriveSpace that enables you to squeeze more storage space from your existing hard drive. DriveSpace is a software solution to your hardware problem. DriveSpace works by compressing the files on your hard disk so that they take up less room. When you need to use a file, DriveSpace automatically decompresses it. The compression and decompression of files happens transparently—you are not even aware that it is happening. You will notice very little delay in file access when you use DriveSpace.

DriveSpace is an optional program that can be installed when you install Windows 95, or you can install it at a later time. To see if you have DriveSpace available, open the Start menu and choose Programs, Accessories, System Tools. If DriveSpace is not listed in the System Tools menu, you will need to install it. For information on how to install DriveSpace after you have installed Windows, see Appendix A, "Installing and Uninstalling Windows 95."

Note

The DriveSpace programs work with disks compressed with DoubleSpace. DoubleSpace was included with MS-DOS 6.0 and 6.2. DriveSpace was initially released in MS-DOS 6.22.

When you run DriveSpace, it creates a compressed drive on your existing hard disk. The compressed drive is actually a file, not a physical hard drive, called a *compressed volume file* (CVF). The CVF is stored on a physical, uncompressed drive, called the *host drive*. The compressed drive is assigned a drive letter, just like a physical drive, and can be accessed like any other drive. From the user's point of view, the only difference after running DriveSpace is that the original drive has a lot more free space and there is a new drive, the host drive.

The file that DriveSpace creates on your hard drive is a hidden, read only, system file; thus, it is not acted upon by most normal DOS commands.

You can run DriveSpace in one of two ways. Typically, you use DriveSpace to compress your entire existing drive to free up more storage space. If you have a C drive, for example, you can run DriveSpace to compress your C drive, which then becomes a compressed volume file on the host drive H. You can also use DriveSpace to compress a specified amount of the free space on your hard drive to create a new, empty compressed drive. The rest of the hard drive is not compressed. If, for example, you have 80M of free space on your C drive, you can use DriveSpace to compress 25M of the free space to create a new drive D with roughly 50M of free space. You then have 55M free on drive C and 50M on drive D for an effective 105M of free space.

DriveSpace only allows the maximum compressed drive size to be 512M or less. If you have a drive of 420M, for example, you could compress the first 256M to 512M compressed and the remaining 163M to 326M compressed. These numbers are based on 100 percent compression.

► See "Changing the Estimated Compression Ratio for Your Compressed Drive," p. 480

As a rule of thumb, DriveSpace will add 50 to 100 percent more capacity to your disk. The amount of actual compression depends upon the types of files stored on the disk. Some files, like text files or certain graphics files, compress significantly, while other files, like an application's EXE file, may barely change.

Troubleshooting

Large files will not copy onto the compressed drive.

The available free space displayed for compressed drives is only an estimate. It is based on the average compression for all files on your disk. If the file you are attempting to save does not compress as much as the average, then it may not fit in the available space.

Compressing a Drive

The DriveSpace that comes with the initial release of Windows 95 does not compress drives larger than 256/512M. If your drive is larger than 256/512M you need to purchase the Microsoft Plus! Pak from Microsoft. This package adds extensions to Windows 95. It will enable you to compress drives up to 2 gigabytes. For information or to order Microsoft Plus! Pak, contact Microsoft at 800-426-9400.

Tip
DriveSpace automatically runs ScanDisk before compressing a drive.

To compress a drive using DriveSpace, follow these steps:

1. Open the Start menu and choose Programs, Accessories, System Tools, and then choose DriveSpace. The DriveSpace window appears, as shown in figure 16.8.

   A drive that has already been compressed will display the phrase "Compressed drive" next to it and will have an associated host drive in the list.

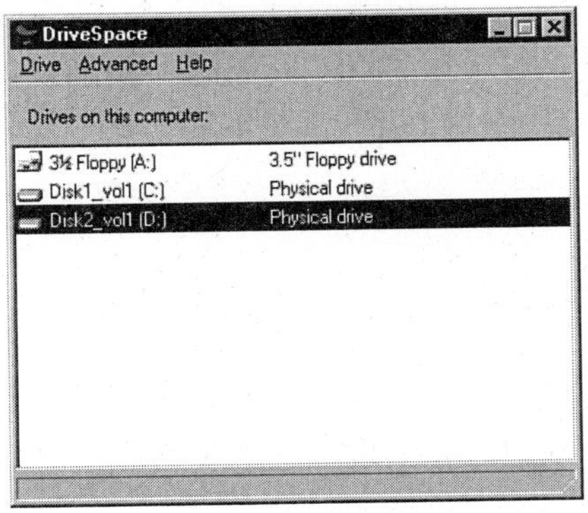

Fig. 16.8
Use DriveSpace to create more free space on your hard drive.

Note

DriveSpace is optional in installation. If it isn't in the System Tools menu, you need to use Add/Remove Programs, Windows Setup to add it.

2. Select the drive you want to compress from the Drives on This Computer list.

Caution

Although you can compress a floppy disk using DriveSpace, you can use compressed floppy disks only in computers that have either DriveSpace for Windows or DoubleSpace for DOS or Windows installed. To use a compressed floppy disk in Windows 95, choose Advance, Options. Select the Automatically Mount Compressed Removable Media option and choose OK.

► See "Returning a Drive to Normal Compression," p. 475

3. Choose Drive, Compress. The Compress a Drive dialog box appears (see fig. 16.9).

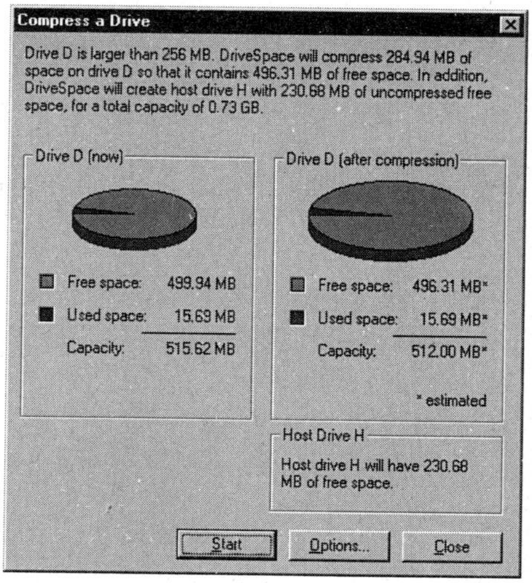

Fig. 16.9
The Compress a Drive dialog box displays information on the size of the selected disk and how much space there will be after running DriveSpace.

4. Choose Options to change the compression options if you want. The Compression Options dialog box displays (see fig. 16.10).

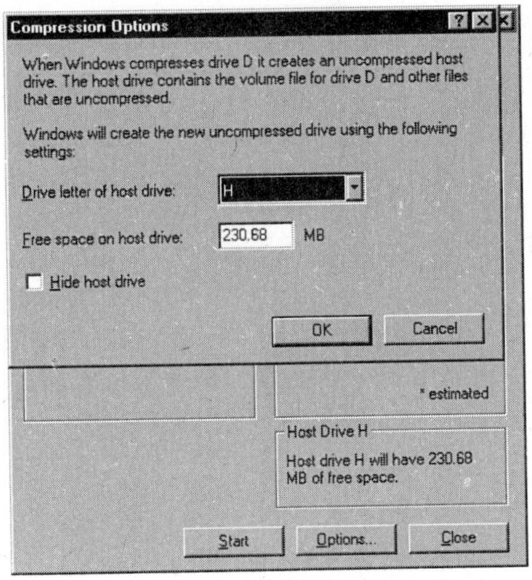

Fig. 16.10
Change the options used for compressing a drive in the Compression Options dialog box.

You can change the following three options:

- To change the drive letter assigned to the host drive, click the down arrow next to the Drive Letter of Host Drive drop-down list and select a new drive letter. You may have to select a new drive letter if you plan on using the default drive letter for another purpose (for example, for a new hard disk).

- To change the amount of free space reserved on the host drive, type a new value in the Free Space on Host Drive text box. Windows will calculate the smallest acceptable size for the Host drive and will not allow you to enter a number that is too small.

- If you don't want the host drive to appear in the Windows Explorer, My Computer, or various dialog boxes such as the Open and Save As dialog boxes, select the Hide Host Drive option. You may want to do this if you are creating a system for novices who may accidentally delete important files from the Host drive.

When you finish making changes, choose OK.

5. Choose Start. A confirmation dialog box appears (see fig. 16.11). (This dialog box does not appear if there are no files on the disk.)

6. If you haven't backed up your files, choose the Back Up Files button to open Backup. See Chapter 18, "Backing Up and Protecting Your Data," for detailed information on how to back up files.

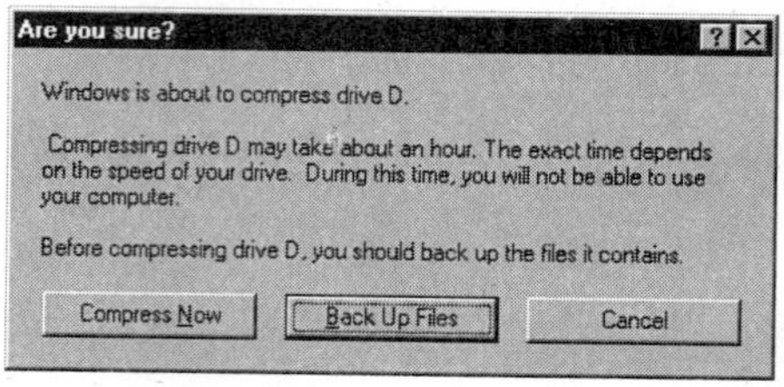

Fig. 16.11
Back up your files before you run DriveSpace by choosing the Back Up Files button.

7. Choose Compress Now to start the compression operation. The progress of the compression operation is displayed in the Compress a Drive message box (see fig. 16.12). Choose Close after examining the results.

   The DriveSpace program will check your hard disk for errors and defragment it as part of the compression operation.

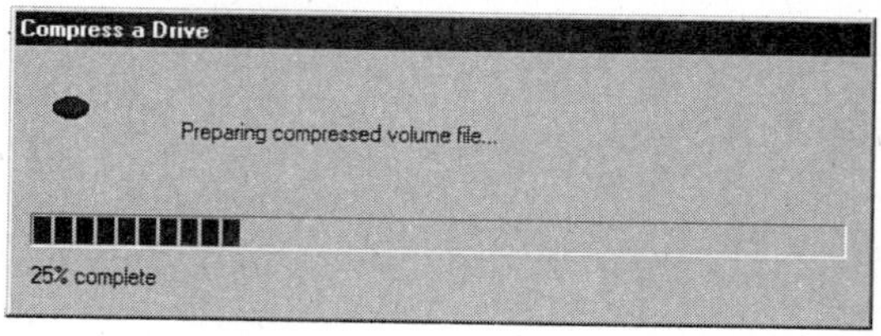

Fig. 16.12
You can monitor the progress of a drive compression operation in the Compress a Drive message box.

8. When the compression operation is completed, the Compress a Drive dialog box informs you that the drive has been compressed and displays how much free space is now on the compressed drive (see fig. 16.13).

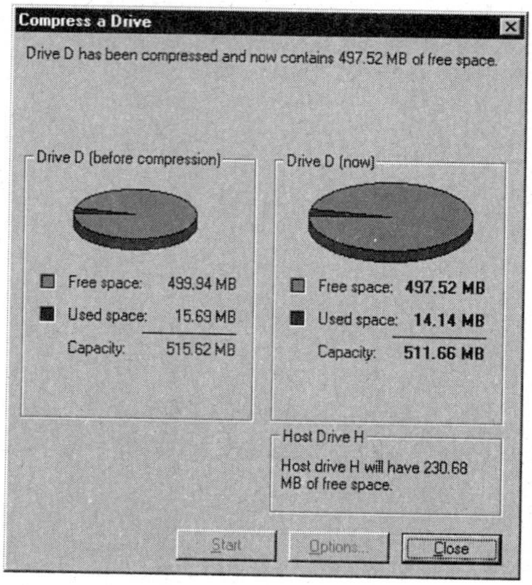

Fig. 16.13
The results of a drive compression operation are displayed in the Compress a Drive dialog box.

9. A Restart Computer dialog box will display asking you if you want to restart your computer. Choose Yes to restart, No to continue working.

   Do not set up new software, change system settings, or run MS-DOS programs until you restart your computer.

> **Note**
>
> Drives compressed with the MS-DOS 6.0 or 6.2 version of DoubleSpace or with the MS-DOS 6.22 version of DriveSpace for MS-DOS are compatible with DriveSpace. You can have drives compressed by both DoubleSpace and DriveSpace on the same computer using Windows 95.

Returning a Drive to Normal Compression

DriveSpace also enables you to decompress a drive. Before you decompress a drive, make sure that there will be enough space on the drive to hold all the files on the drive after it is decompressed.

When you choose to decompress a drive and there is not enough room, you get an error dialog that tells you how much data you have, how much free space is needed, and how much data needs to be deleted or moved off of which drive.

To decompress a drive, follow these steps:

1. Open the Start menu and choose Programs, Accessories, System Tools, and then choose DriveSpace. The DriveSpace window appears.
2. Select the drive you want to decompress from the Drives on This Computer list.
3. Choose Drive, Uncompress.
4. Choose Start. A confirmation dialog box appears. (This dialog box does not appear if there are no files on the disk.)
5. If you haven't backed up your files, choose the Back Up Files button to open Backup. See Chapter 18, "Backing Up and Protecting Your Data," for detailed information on how to back up your files.
6. Choose Uncompress Now to start the uncompression operation. The progress of the uncompression operation is displayed at the bottom of the Uncompress a Drive dialog box.
7. When the message box informing you that the drive has been uncompressed appears, choose OK.

Setting Up Your Floppy or Hard Disk to Read Compressed Files

When you are working with compressed removable storage media (such as floppy disks), you must mount the compressed drive if it wasn't present when the computer was started. Mounting a drive links a drive letter with a compressed volume file (CVF) and enables your computer to access the files on the compressed volume files.

To mount a compressed drive, follow these steps:

1. Open the DriveSpace window and select the drive you want to mount in the Drives on This Computer list.

   For example, if you want to read a floppy disk in drive A and the floppy disk has DriveSpace or DoubleSpace compression, then you would select the A drive.

2. Open the Advanced menu and choose Mount.

3. Select the compressed volume file you want to mount.

   Once you mount a drive, it shows up in the Drives on This Computer list as a compressed drive.

You can select an option so that newly compressed devices are automatically mounted. Choose Advanced, Settings. Select the Automatically Mount New Compressed Devices option and choose OK. Windows now automatically mounts new compressed devices so that you don't have to mount the compressed device each time you insert it in the computer.

To unmount a compressed drive, follow these steps:

1. Open the DriveSpace window and select the compressed drive you want to unmount from the Drives on this Computer list.

2. Choose Advanced, Unmount.

3. When the message box appears informing you that the operation is complete, choose OK.

Compressing Part of a Disk

You don't have to compress your entire hard disk; you can compress some or all of the free space on your hard disk to create a new compressed drive. To create a new compressed drive from part of a hard disk, follow these steps:

1. Open the DriveSpace window and select the drive with the free space you want to use to create a new compressed drive. You cannot select a compressed drive.

2. Choose Advanced, Create Empty. The Create New Compressed Drive dialog box appears, as shown in figure 16.14.

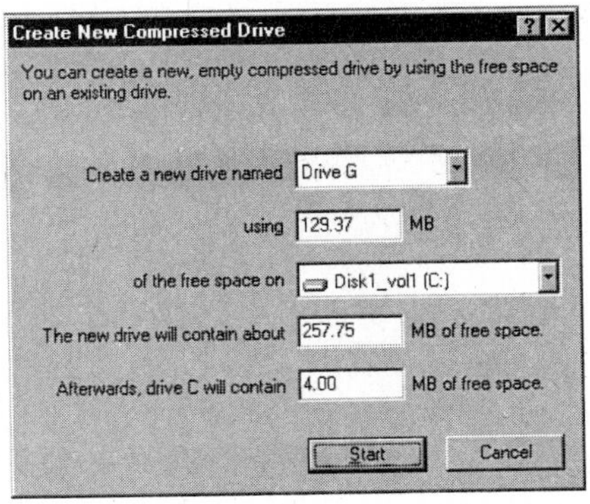

Fig. 16.14
Create a new compressed drive using the free space on your hard disk.

3. Accept the default name for the new drive or select an alternative name from the Create a New Drive Named drop-down list.

4. Enter the amount of free space (in megabytes) you want to use to create the new drive in the Using text box. If you enter a value here, the amount displayed in The New Drive Will Contain about...MB of Free Space text box changes to reflect how much free space will be created in the new drive.

5. Select the drive that has the free space you want to use to create the new drive from the Of the Free Space on drop-down list.

6. If you know how much free space you want the new drive to have, enter that figure in The New Drive Will Contain about...MB of Free Space text box. If you enter a value here, the amount displayed in the Using text box is automatically adjusted to show how much free space on the selected drive will be used for the new drive.

   The amount of free space that will be left on the uncompressed drive is displayed in the Afterwards, Drive *letter* Will Contain...MB of Free Space text box.

7. Choose Start.

8. When the message box appears informing you that the operation is complete, choose OK.

Deleting a Compressed Drive

◄ See "Returning a Drive to Normal Compression," p. 475

Deleting a compressed drive is something you want to think seriously about before doing. Deleting a compressed drive removes all the data from the compressed drive, returning the drive to a blank decompressed state. One reason for deleting a compressed drive is so that you can remove the physical drive from your computer and have it accessible by any MS-DOS computer. If you only want to return the compressed data to its decompressed form and retain the data on the drive, then use the decompress feature.

When you delete a compressed drive, Windows 95 deletes the compressed volume file (CVF) that contains all the compressed data and application files. (The contents of the CVF file are what looks like a compressed disk drive.) The CVF has the name DRVSPACE.000 and is located on the host drive. (The file name extension is different for every file that DriveSpace creates. The first starts at 000, the second at 001, and so forth.) You shouldn't manually delete the DRVSPACE.000 file. Deleting the compressed drive is better.

In addition to deleting the CVF file, deleting a compressed drive also removes from the DRVSPACE.INI file the line `ACTIVATE DRIVE=` for the drive represented by the CVF. If you have only one compressed drive on your hard disk, then you will also be asked whether you want to delete the DriveSpace driver, DRVSPACE.BIN. You can delete this driver if you do not have other compressed drives on this drive.

Caution

When you delete a compressed drive, you lose all the information stored on that drive, so be sure that you have backed up or moved any files you need on this drive before deleting it.

Troubleshooting

An overzealous novice removed the system attribute from the DRVSPACE.000 file and deleted it. Is there a way to recover the data that was on the compressed drive?

If the user has not saved files to that disk after deleting DRVSPACE.000 the drive may be able to be recovered. Use the Recycle Bin to restore the deleted DRVSPACE.000 file; then exit Windows and restart.

To delete a compressed drive, follow these steps:

1. Open the DriveSpace window and select the compressed drive you want to delete from the Drives on This Computer list.

2. Choose Advanced, Delete.

3. When the confirmation message box appears, choose Yes.

4. A message box appears asking if you want to delete the DriveSpace driver. Choose Yes if this is the only compressed drive on your computer and you will not be using compressed floppy disks. Choose No if you have other compressed drives or if you will be using compressed floppy disks.

5. When the message box appears informing you that the operation is complete, choose OK.

6. You will be prompted to restart Windows 95 or continue. (If you are using floppy disks, you won't be prompted to restart Windows.) Switch to any open applications and save the documents, then choose Yes. If you choose No, you will not be able to change system settings, install applications, or use MS-DOS until you restart. (If you are able to, the system may not be stable.)

◄ See "Setting Up Your Floppy or Hard Disk to Read Compressed Files," p. 476

If you are in doubt about whether to delete the driver for DriveSpace, remember that it is much easier to reinstall than it is to deinstall the driver. You can remove it now and add it back at any time using the procedure to mount a compressed drive.

Adjusting the Size of the Free Space on a Compressed Drive

You can adjust the distribution of free space between a compressed drive and its host. When you increase the free space on the compressed drive, you decrease the free space on the host drive and vice versa. To adjust the free space on the compressed and host drives, follow these steps:

1. Open the DriveSpace window and select either the compressed drive or its host from the Drives on This Computer list.

2. Choose Drive, Adjust Free Space; the Adjust Free Space dialog box appears (see fig. 16.15).

3. Drag the slider to change the distribution of free space between the compressed and host drives. The pie charts will reflect the amount of free space and used space.

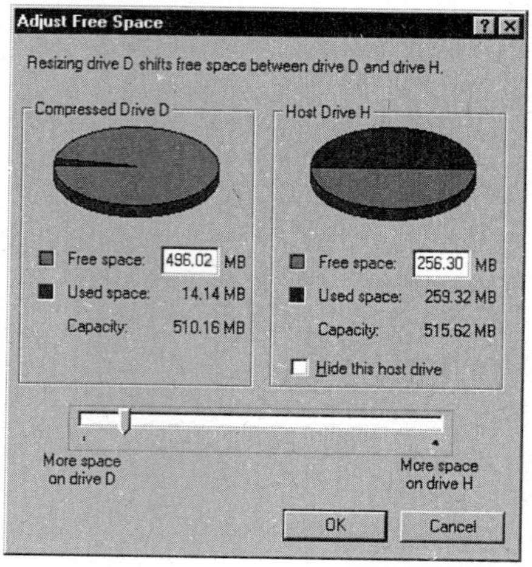

Fig. 16.15 Adjust the distribution of free space between a compressed drive and its host in the Adjust Free Space dialog box.

4. Choose OK.

   A message box shows you the amount of free space on the compressed and host drives when the operation is complete.

5. A Restart Computer dialog box displays asking you if you want to restart your computer. (This dialog box does not appear if you are doing this with floppy disks.) Choose Yes to restart, No to continue working.

   Do not set up new software, change system settings, or run MS-DOS programs until you restart your computer.

Troubleshooting

There seems to be enough space on the hard disk to store some very large video and sound files, but even after resizing the compressed drive there still isn't enough space.

Some files, such as application, video, and music files, may not compress very much. The estimated free space on a compressed drive however, is calculated from the average amount of compression for all files on the drive. As a consequence, files that look like they may fit, may not.

Changing the Estimated Compression Ratio for Your Compressed Drive

DriveSpace contains a command that enables you to change the estimated compression ratio. This does not change how tightly data is compressed on your hard drive. It is just an estimate used by Windows 95 to calculate how much free space remains on your hard drive. The remaining free space as calculated by the estimated compression ratio is then used in Windows 95 dialog boxes to give you an estimate of how much drive space remains. Changing the compression ratio to a larger number would not compress files tighter, but it would give you a very misleading idea of how much free space remains.

Tip
In general, do not change the compression ratio to more than a two to one, 2:1, ratio.

You may want to change the estimated compression ratio in order to see a more accurate calculation of the free space available on your compressed drive. There is a reason that you may be able to calculate this number more accurately than Windows 95. Windows 95 calculates the estimated compression ratio from an average of the actual file size and the compressed file size for all files on the drive. Everytime a file is saved or erased, Windows 95 recalculates the estimated compression ratio and then uses that number to calculate the estimated free space remaining.

The problem with accepting the estimated compression ratio is that Windows 95 has no idea what types of files you will be storing on the hard disk. Since you are familiar with the types of files you store, you may be able to estimate a better compression ratio. This in turn will give you a better idea of the amount of free space available.

To understand the problem, you must know that different files compress by different amounts. Files such as text files and some graphics files contain a lot of repetitive information that can be tightly compressed into a small space. Other files, such as an application's EXE files or a video's JPEG or MPEG files, have little room for compression and may not change significantly in size.

If you have just installed a lot of application files on a compressed drive with few data files, then Windows 95 will calculate a low compression ratio. Conversely, if your compressed drive has few application or multimedia files, then the estimated compression ratio will be higher. As long as you continue saving and removing the same type of files, Windows 95 will report a fairly accurate estimated free space. But if you change the type of files you save, the estimated free space will be wrong because the new files compress to a different amount.

If you will not be adding more application or multimedia files to your compressed drive, but you will be adding a lot more data files, then you may want to increase the estimated compression ratio to get a more accurate reading of free space. Conversely, a drive that has stored word processing files may have much less space available than it appears to have when you begin storing sound, video, and application files on it.

Caution

What you see is not necessarily what you get when dealing with compression ratios. Some files, such as EXE application files or JPEG and MPEG video files compress very little. This means that even though the estimated free space may be 15M, it's doubtful that 12M of JPEG, MPEG, or EXE files would fit because they do not compress as tightly as other files have.

To adjust the compression ratio, follow these steps:

1. Open the DriveSpace window and select the compressed drive whose compression ratio you want to adjust from the Drives on This Computer list.

2. Choose Advanced, Change Ratio; the Compression Ratio dialog box appears (see fig. 16.16).

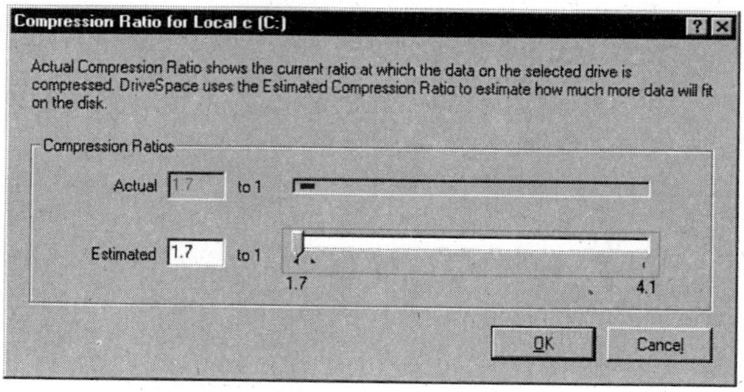

Fig. 16.16 Adjust the compression ratio of a compressed drive in the Compression Ratio dialog box.

3. Drag the Estimated Compression Ratio slider to adjust the compression ratio.

4. Click OK to begin the change. When the message box appears informing you that the operation is complete, choose OK.

Viewing the Properties of a Compressed Drive

You can view the properties of a compressed drive or its host using the Drive Properties command. You can find out the name of the compressed volume file and what drive it is stored on, the amount of free and used space on the drive, and the compression ratio if it is a compressed drive.

To view the properties of a drive, follow these steps:

1. Open the DriveSpace window and select the drive whose properties you want to view from the Drives on This Computer list.

2. Choose Drive, Properties. The Compression Properties sheet appears, as shown in figure 16.17.

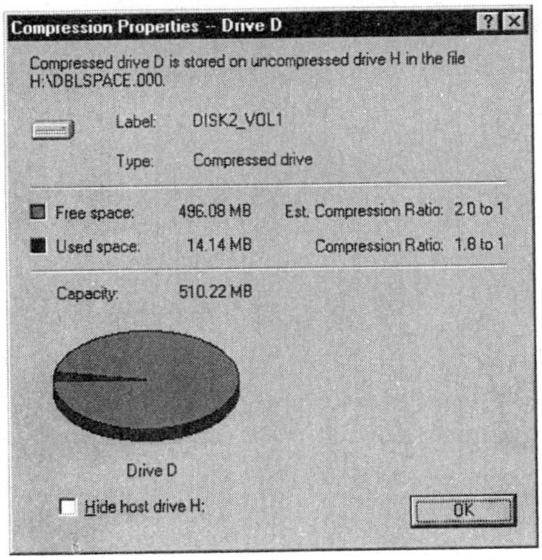

Fig. 16.17
View the properties of a compressed drive or its host in the Compression Properties sheet.

3. You can select the Hide Host Drive option to hide the display of this drive when the drive contents display in the Explorer or My Computer window and in some dialog boxes such as Open and Save As. If you select this option, a message box informs you that you will not be able to use the data or free space on the drive. Choose Yes to confirm that you want to hide the drive.

   You can use the DriveSpace Properties sheet to unhide the host drive if you change your mind at a later time.

4. Choose OK.

Monitoring Your System

Windows 95 comes with an application called System Monitor that enables you to monitor the resources on your computer. You can see if you have the System Monitor installed by opening the Start menu, clicking Programs, Accessories, System Tools, and checking for the System Monitor item. If you do not see it on the menu or if it does not start, then you need to rerun Windows 95 and reinstall the System Monitor. Appendix A describes how to install and reinstall Windows 95.

You can see information about the 32-bit file system, network clients and servers, and the virtual memory manager, among other things. Most of this information is highly technical in nature and useful only to advanced users. You can display the information in either bar or line charts or as numeric values. To open the System Monitor, open the Start menu; choose Programs, Accessories, System Tools, and then System Monitor. The System Monitor window appears, as shown in figure 16.18.

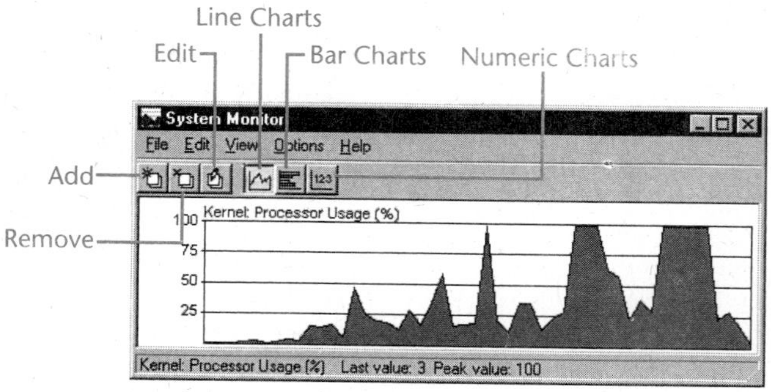

Fig. 16.18
Use the System Monitor to monitor the resources on your computer.

To monitor an item in System Monitor, follow these steps:

1. Select the item you want to monitor by choosing Edit, Add Item; alternatively, click the Add tool. The Add Item dialog box appears (see fig. 16.19).

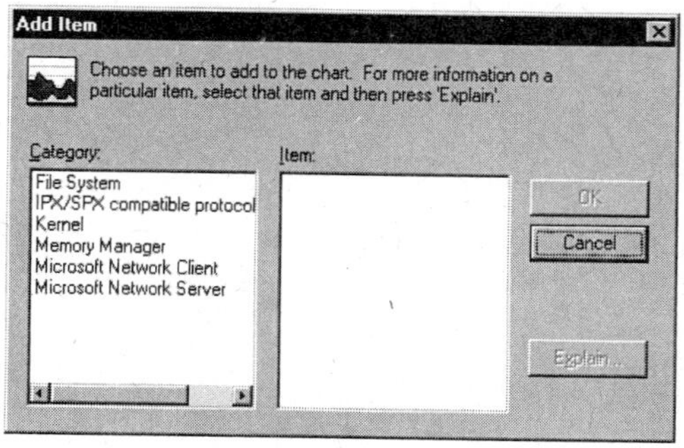

Fig. 16.19
Select the items you want to monitor in the Add Item dialog box.

You can obtain information on what an item is by selecting the item and clicking Explain. When you select an item in the right hand box the explain button becomes an option.

2. Choose OK.

3. Repeat steps 1 and 2 to add additional items to the window.

To remove an item from the window, follow these steps:

1. Choose Edit, Remove Item; alternatively, click the Remove tool.

2. Select the item you want to remove and choose OK.

You can edit an item that is being monitored, changing its display color and the scaling used in its chart. To edit an item, follow these steps:

1. Choose Edit, Edit Item, or click the Edit tool, to display the Edit Item dialog box.

2. Select the item you want to edit and choose OK. The Chart Options dialog box appears, as shown in figure 16.20.

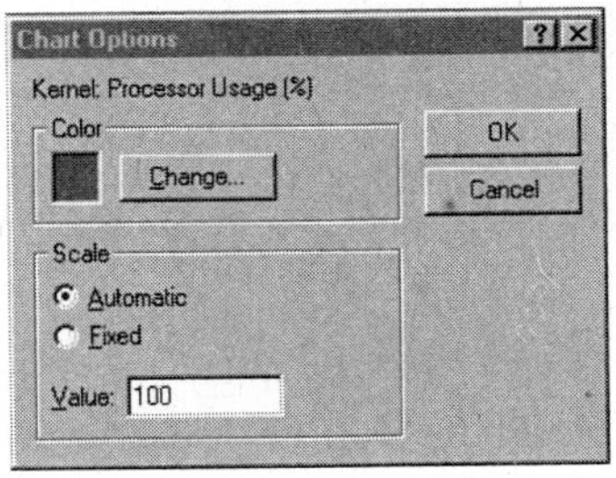

Fig. 16.20
Change the display of an item being monitored in the Chart Options dialog box.

3. Choose Change to change the color of the item.

4. Select Automatic to let System Monitor set the maximum value on the y-axis.

   or

   Select Fixed and type a value in the Value text box to set your own maximum value for the y-axis.

5. Choose OK.

You can display the items being monitored as either a line or bar chart or as a numeric value. To change the display, open the View menu and choose Line Charts, Bar Charts, or Numeric Charts; alternatively, click the appropriate tool on the toolbar.

Tip
Pressing Esc also will hide the title bar if pressed when the title bar is visible.

If you want the System Monitor window to stay on top of other windows, even when you are working in another program, open the View menu and choose Always on Top. This is handy if you want to monitor some resource as you work in a program. You can shrink the window so that it doesn't take up too much room. Choose the View, Always on Top command again when you don't want the System Monitor window to stay on top of other windows. You can also hide the title bar so that all the System Monitor window is devoted to displaying the chart: choose the View, Hide Title Bar command. To redisplay the title bar, double-click the chart or press Esc.

You can adjust the frequency at which the chart is updated by choosing the Options, Chart command and moving the slider to change the update interval. If you are on a network, choose File, Connect to connect to a different computer.

Note

You can quickly find out how much free disk space there is on a hard disk or floppy disk. Select the disk you want to check in either the Explorer or My Computer and choose the File, Properties command (alternatively, right-click the desired disk and choose Properties from the shortcut menu). The amount of free space on the disk is displayed in the Properties dialog box.

Improving Performance with Disk Defragmenter

Tip
To optimize the performance of your hard disk, use Disk Defragmenter on a regular basis to defragment your hard disk.

Information written to a hard disk is not necessarily stored in a *contiguous* (adjacent) block. Rather, fragments of information are more likely spread across the disk wherever the system can find room. The more you use the hard disk, the more fragmented the disk becomes. Obviously, the drive takes more time to hunt for information located in several places than it takes to fetch the same information from a single location. Because of this extra time, disk fragmentation can slow the computer's operation considerably.

The Windows Disk Defragmenter can significantly improve file access time by restructuring files into contiguous blocks and moving free space to the end of the disk.

To defragment a disk, follow these steps:

1. Open the Start menu and choose Programs, Accessories, System Tools, and then choose Disk Defragmenter. The Select Drive dialog box appears (see fig. 16.21).

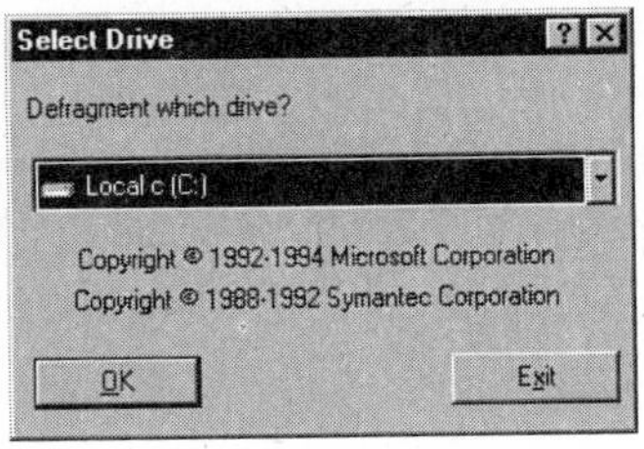

Fig. 16.21
Select the drive you want to defragment in the Select Drive dialog box.

2. Select the drive you want to defragment from the Defragment Which Drive drop-down list and choose OK.

   The Disk Defragmenter dialog box appears, as shown in figure 16.22. The percent fragmentation of the selected drive is displayed in the dialog box. You are also informed whether defragmentation will improve performance.

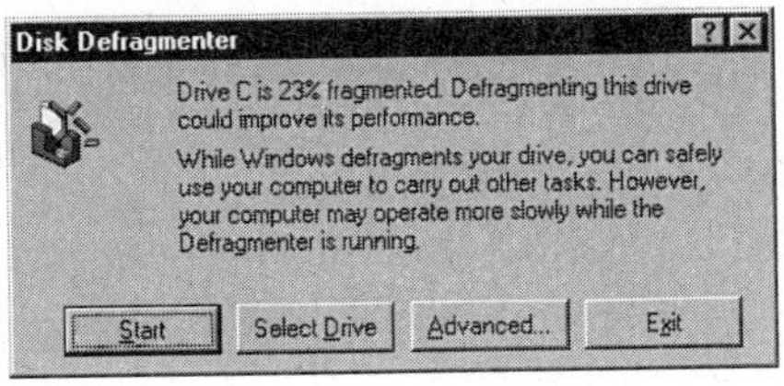

Fig. 16.22
The Disk Defragmenter dialog box tells you how fragmented your drive is and whether defragmenting it will improve its performance.

3. To change the Disk Defragmenter options, choose Advanced. The Advanced Options dialog box appears (see fig. 16.23). Use this dialog box to change the following options:

Option	Function
Full Defragmentation (Both Files and Free Space)	Defragments all the files on the selected disk.
Defragment Files Only	Defragments only the files on your hard disk, without consolidating the free space.
Consolidate Free Space Only	Only consolidates the free space on the selected disk without defragmenting the files.
Check Drive for Errors	Checks the files and folders on the drive for errors before defragmenting.

(continues)

Option	Function
This Time Only. Next Time, Use the Defaults Again	Uses the selected options for this defragment operation only.
Save These Options Use Them Every Time	Saves the selected options and uses them each time you run Disk Defragmenter unless you change them again.

Select the desired options and choose OK. You return to the Disk Defragmenter dialog box.

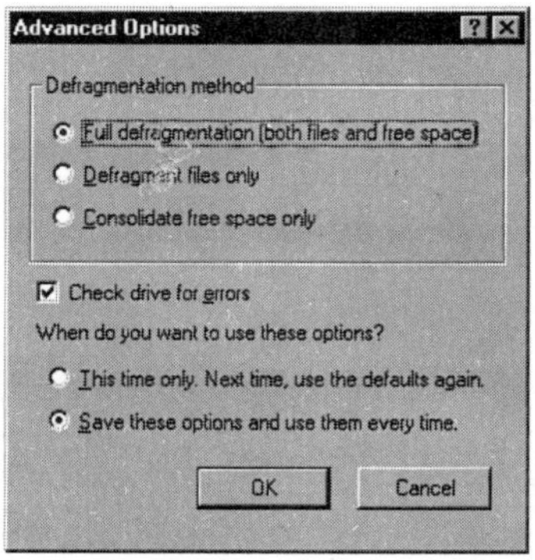

Fig. 16.23
Change the way Disk Defragmenter works in the Advanced Options dialog box.

4. Choose Start. The progress of the defragmentation operation is displayed in the Defragmenting dialog box (see fig. 16.24).

5. When the defragmentation operation is complete, choose Exit to close the Disk Defragmenter, or choose Select Drive to defragment another drive.

Defragmenting a hard disk can take a long time. Although you can continue working on your computer during the defragmentation operation, you will notice a significant slowdown in your computer's operation. For this reason, it is advisable to run the Disk Defragmenter during a time when you do not need to use the computer, for example, after you leave work for the day.

You can pause the defragmentation operation if you need to use your computer before defragmentation is completed and you don't want performance slowed down. Choose Pause from the Defragmenting dialog box to pause Disk Defragmenter. To resume defragmentation, choose Resume. You can also cancel the defragmentation operation by choosing Stop. Choose Show

Details to open a window that displays the details of the defragmentation operation. To close the window, choose Hide Details.

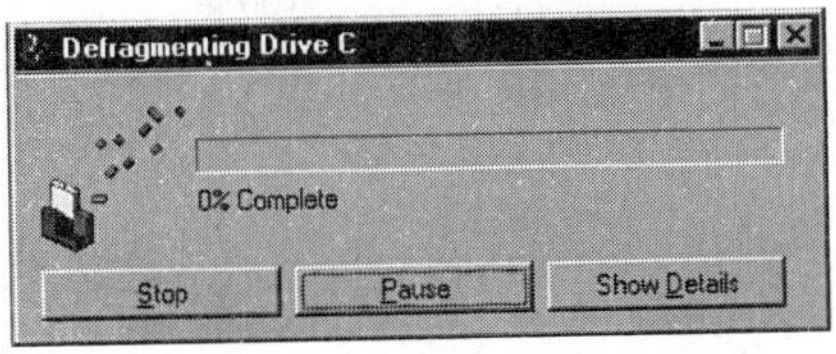

Fig. 16.24
Monitor the progress of the defragmentation operation in the Defragmenting dialog box.

Using ScanDisk to Check for Disk Damage

In an ideal world, you would never have to worry about errors occurring on your hard disk or floppy disks. This not being the case, Windows 95 comes with a program called ScanDisk you can use to check for, diagnose, and repair damage on a hard disk or floppy disk. Part of your routine hard disk maintenance, along with defragmenting your hard disk as described in the previous section, should be to periodically run ScanDisk to keep your hard disk in good repair.

In its standard test, ScanDisk checks the files and folders on a disk for logical *errors*; if you ask it to, ScanDisk also automatically corrects any errors it finds. ScanDisk checks for *cross-linked* files, which occur when two or more files have data stored in the same *cluster* (a storage unit on a disk). The data in the cluster is likely to be correct for only one of the files, and may not be correct for any of them. ScanDisk also checks for *lost file fragments*, which are pieces of data that have become disassociated with their files. Although file fragments may contain useful data, they usually can't be recovered and just take up disk space. You can tell ScanDisk to delete lost file fragments or save them in a file.

You also have the option of having ScanDisk check files for invalid file names and invalid dates and times. When a file has an invalid file name, you may not be able to open it. Invalid dates and times can cause problems when you use a backup program that uses dates and times to determine how current a file is.

You can run a more thorough test in which ScanDisk checks for both logical errors in files and folders and also scans the surface of the disk to check for physical *errors*. Physical errors are areas on your disk that are actually damaged and shouldn't be used for storing data. If ScanDisk finds bad sectors on your hard disk, any data in them can be moved to new sectors, and the bad sectors are marked so that data is not stored in them in the future.

To check a disk for errors, follow these steps:

1. Open the Start menu and choose Programs, Accessories, System Tools, and then choose ScanDisk. The ScanDisk window appears, as shown in figure 16.25.

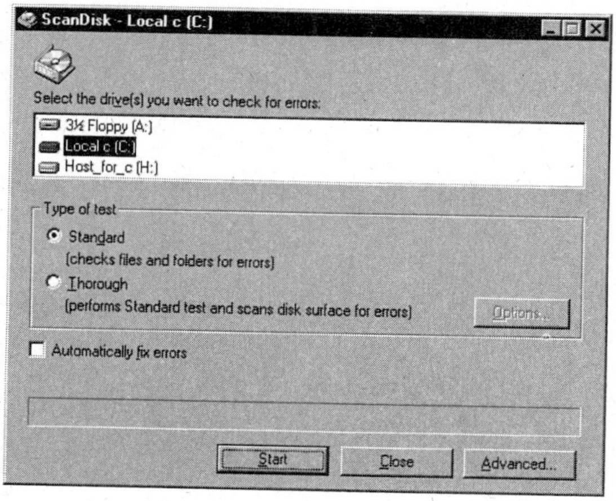

Fig. 16.25 Use ScanDisk to check your hard disk for logical and physical errors and repair any damage.

2. Select the drive you want to check in the Select the Drive(s) You Want To Check for Errors box.

3. To check only for logical errors in the files and folders on the selected disk, make sure that the Standard option is selected.

   To check for logical errors and to scan the disk for physical errors, select the Thorough option.

4. Click the Advanced button to change the settings used for checking files and folders for logical errors. The ScanDisk Advanced Options dialog box appears (see fig. 16.26). Use this dialog box to change the options in table 16.1.

Table 16.1 ScanDisk Advanced Options

Option	Function
Display Summary Options	
Always	A summary with information about your disk and any errors found and corrected is displayed whenever you run ScanDisk.
Never	A summary is never displayed when you run ScanDisk.

Option	Function
Display Summary Options	
Only If Errors Found	A summary is displayed only if errors are detected.
Log File Options	
Replace Log	Saves the details of a ScanDisk session in a log file named SCANDISK.LOG in the top-level folder on drive C. Replaces any existing file with the same name.
Append to Log	Saves the details of a ScanDisk session, appending the information to the end of SCANDISK.LOG.
No Log	The results of the ScanDisk operation are not saved to a log file.
Cross-Linked Files Options	
Delete	Deletes cross-linked files when such files are found.
Make Copies	A copy is made of each cross-linked cluster for each of the cross-linked files.
Ignore	Cross-linked files are not corrected in any way. Using a cross-linked file may lead to further file damage and may cause the program using it to crash.
Lost File Fragments Options	
Free	Deletes lost file fragments, freeing up the space they use.
Convert to Files	Lost file fragments are converted to files, which you can view to see whether they contain data you need. Files are given names beginning with FILE (for example, FILE0001) and are stored in the top-level folder of the disk.
Check Files For Options	
Invalid File Names	Files are checked for invalid file names. Files with invalid file names sometimes cannot be opened.
Invalid Dates and Times	Files are checked for invalid dates and times, which can result in incorrect sorting and can also cause problems with backup programs.
Check Host Drive First	If the drive you are checking has been compressed using DoubleSpace or DriveSpace, ScanDisk checks the host drive for the compressed drive first. Errors on the host drive often cause errors on the compressed drive, so it is best to check it first.

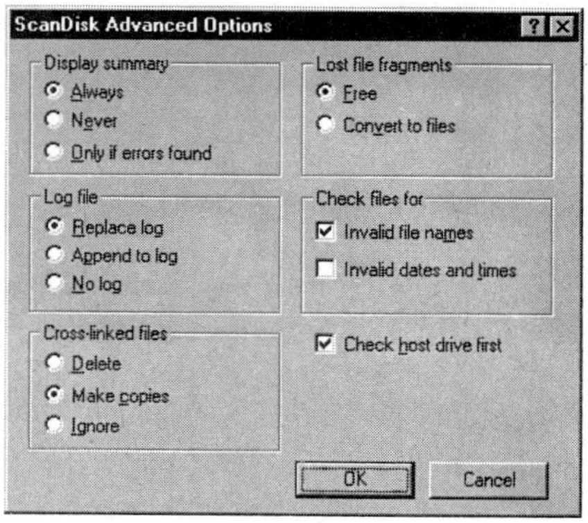

Fig. 16.26
You can change the settings ScanDisk uses to check files and folders for logical errors in the ScanDisk Advanced Options dialog box.

5. If you selected the Thorough option, choose Options to change the settings used to scan the disk for physical errors. The Surface Scan Options dialog box appears (see fig. 16.27). Use this dialog box to change the following options:

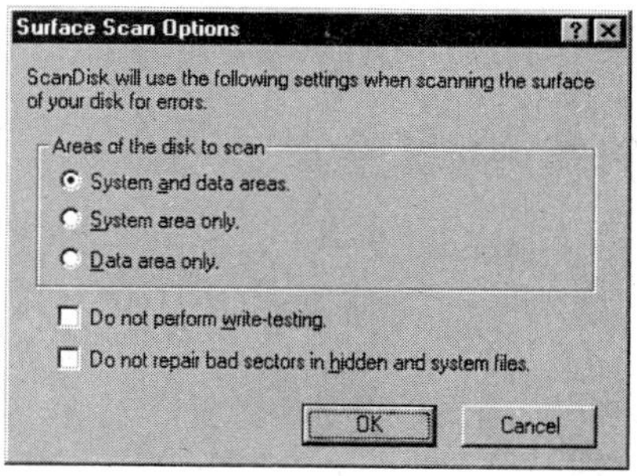

Fig. 16.27
You can change the settings ScanDisk uses to scan the disk for physical errors.

Option	Function
System and Data Areas	Scans the entire disk for physical damage.
System Area Only	Scans only the system area of the disk for physical damage. This is the disk area that contains files used to start the computer and hold the operating system.
Data Area Only	Scans only the data area of the disk for physical damage. The data area contains application and data programs. Use this if Windows behaves erratically even if you have reinstalled it.

Option	Function
Do Not Perform Write-Testing	If this option is not selected (the default), ScanDisk reads and writes every sector to verify both read and write functions. If this option is selected, ScanDisk does not write-verify the sectors.
Do Not Repair Bad Sectors in Hidden and System Files	ScanDisk will not move data from bad sectors in hidden and system files. Some programs look for hidden system files at specific locations and will not work if data in these files is moved.

6. Select the Automatically Fix Errors option if you want ScanDisk to automatically fix any errors it finds without first reporting the errors.

   If you don't select this option, ScanDisk informs you when it finds an error, and you can determine how ScanDisk fixes it.

7. Choose Start to begin the test. The progress of the test is displayed at the bottom of the ScanDisk dialog box. You can halt the test by choosing the Cancel button. If you told ScanDisk to scan your disk for physical errors, the test can take several minutes. When the test is complete, a summary report like the one in figure 16.28 may appear, depending on the options you selected in the ScanDisk Advanced Options dialog box. Click Close to close the Results dialog box.

8. Click Close to exit ScanDisk.

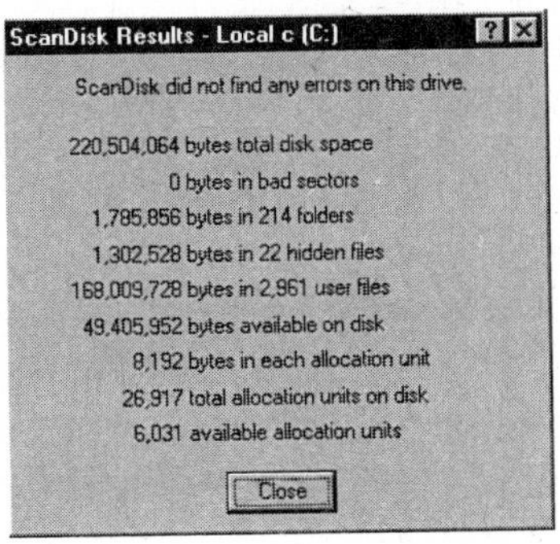

Fig. 16.28
The results of a ScanDisk operation can be displayed in the ScanDisk Results dialog box.

◀ See "Improving Performance with Disk Defragmenter," p. 486

Troubleshooting

Whenever a file is retrieved, the hard disk light seems to come on a lot. It even sounds like the hard disk is chattering. The more we use the computer the worse this problem gets. ScanDisk didn't show any problems with the disk.

The problem is probably not with the physical quality of your hard drive's magnetic surface, which is what ScanDisk checks. The problem is more likely that files on the hard disk are fragmented. Fragmented disks have pieces of files scattered all over the disk. Rather than being able to read a file at one location in one quick continuous movement, the read-head on the drive must skitter around on the disk searching for all the pieces that belong to a file. Once fragmenting is bad it gets worse, which is why your computer seems to be slowing down the more you use it. Windows comes with a defragmenting utility that will reorganize your files on the disk so they are contiguous and can be read quickly.

Improving Memory Use with Virtual Memory

Your computer has a certain amount of physical memory (RAM) installed. Typically, computers running Windows have at least 4M of RAM, and often 8M or more. The more memory you have, the more programs you can run at the same time and the faster your system operates. However, with Windows 95, you can use a special area of the hard disk as an extension of RAM, called *virtual memory*, to increase the amount of memory available to programs. Using virtual memory, you may be able to run more programs at the same time than is normally possible using only the RAM on the system.

When RAM is tight, Windows begins to move *pages* of code and data from RAM to the hard disk to make more room in RAM. Windows uses a *least-recently-used* technique to move pages of memory to the disk, selecting first the pages of code and data not recently accessed by a program. If a program requires a piece of data no longer in physical memory, Windows retrieves the information from disk, paging other information from memory to disk to make room. To programs running in Windows, no difference exists between RAM in the system and virtual memory on the disk.

When you install Windows 95, it automatically determines how much hard disk space to use for virtual memory, depending on the amount of free disk space. Windows 95 also automatically resizes virtual memory as needed. In most cases, you should let Windows determine the settings used for virtual memory on your computer. Unless you know what you are doing, changing the settings manually can adversely affect the performance of your computer. If you do want to specify your own virtual memory settings, follow these steps:

1. Open the Start menu and choose Settings, Control Panel.
2. Double-click the System icon to display the System Properties sheet; select the Performance tab.
3. Click the Virtual Memory tab to display the Virtual Memory dialog box shown in figure 16.29.

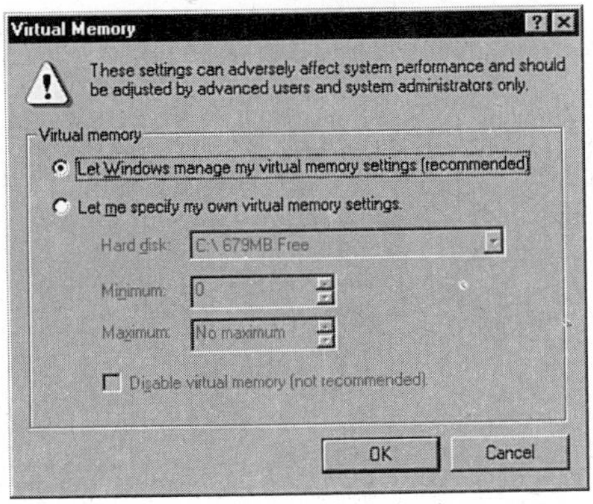

Fig. 16.29
You can let Windows manage your virtual memory settings or specify your own in the Virtual Memory dialog box. Microsoft recommends you let Windows manage virtual memory settings.

4. Select the Let Me Specify My Own Virtual Memory Settings option.
5. If you want to use a different hard disk for virtual memory than is already specified, select a new disk from the Hard Disk drop-down list. The amount of free space on the hard disk is displayed next to the drive letter.
6. Specify the minimum amount (in megabytes) of hard disk space you want Windows to use for virtual memory in the Minimum text box.
7. Specify the maximum amount of memory (in megabytes) you want Windows to use for virtual memory in the Maximum text box.
8. Choose OK.

The Virtual Memory dialog box contains a Disable Virtual Memory (Not Recommended) check box at the bottom. This turns off all use of virtual memory and is not recommended.❖

Chapter 17

Managing Your Files with Explorer

by Ron Person

The information you work with on your computer is stored in files. The programs you use to do your work and the documents you create with these programs are files. For this reason, it is essential that you learn how to work with and manage files. You need to know how to name and save files, as well as how to organize the files on your computer so that you can locate them when you need them. The Windows Explorer is a program that comes with Windows that has all the tools you need for managing your files.

The first part of this chapter explains how Windows organizes files. The remainder of the chapter shows you how to use the Windows Explorer to work with and manage the files on your computer. You also learn how to carry out many file-management tasks using My Computer.

In this chapter, you learn how to

- Use files and folders to store data
- Use the Explorer to view files and folders
- Manage your files and folders
- Protect documents
- Synchronize files by using Briefcase
- Register file types
- Use the Explorer on a network
- Use My Computer to manage files

◄ See "Formatting Disks," p. 461

Note

Before you can store information on a floppy disk, you must format the disk. To learn how to format a floppy disk, see Chapter 16, "Working with Disks and Disk Drives." Chapter 16 also describes how to create a system disk you can use to start your computer.

Understanding Files and Folders

Windows uses the file folder metaphor for organizing the files on your computer. You store the files you create with your programs, as well as the program files themselves, in folders. You store information in folders in the same way you store the paper files in folders in your office. And, just as you can create a filing system in your office to make it easy to locate your files whenever you need them, you can create a filing system on your computer to help you keep track of your files. This system consists of named folders in which you store your files, arranged in a way that makes sense to you.

You may, for example, want to create a folder for each of your clients. In each of your client folders you store any files associated with that client. This is an easy way to quickly locate all the information for a particular client, whether the information is recorded in a word processing document or in a spreadsheet file.

If you're a project manager, you can create a folder for each project in your department and then store any files related to a particular project in its folder. Or perhaps you think in terms of the tasks you perform—for example, completing budgets, writing reports, and sending out memos. In this case, you can create a folder for each type of task you deal with and store your files in the appropriate folders.

Tip
If you installed Windows 95 over Windows 3.1, File Manager is still available. You can continue to use File Manager or use the more powerful Explorer.

There is no limit to how creative you can be in setting up your filing system. With the skills you learn in this chapter, over time you can easily change your system and develop new ways of working. Creating new folders and moving files and folders is easy in Windows.

If you are familiar with the MS-DOS system for organizing files, a folder is analogous to a directory, and a folder within a folder is analogous to a subdirectory of a directory. If you like to think hierarchically, you can continue to visualize the organization of your files in exactly the same way as you did with DOS and earlier versions of Windows. The only difference is that instead of directories and subdirectories, you have folders and folders within folders. And, as you see in the next section, you can view the hierarchical arrangement of your folders by using the Explorer.

Many people don't like to think hierarchically, and they find the directory/subdirectory metaphor confusing. If you're one of these people, simply imagine that your files are stored in folders, and that you can have folders within folders. This capability to have folders within folders enables you to refine your filing system, categorizing your files in a way that makes it easy for you to locate a file even if you haven't used it for a long time.

Using the Windows Explorer to View Files and Folders

Windows 95 comes with a new tool, the *Windows Explorer,* that you can use to see how the files and folders on your computer are organized. With the Explorer, you can view the hierarchical arrangement of the folders on your computer and can look into each folder to see what files are stored there. You can also use the Windows Explorer to reorganize and manage your files and folders. You can create new folders; move and copy files from one folder to another, to a floppy disk, or to another computer (if you are on a network); rename and delete files and folders; and perform other file-management tasks.

To open the Windows Explorer, follow these steps:

1. Open the Start menu and choose Programs.
2. Choose Windows Explorer to open the Windows Explorer (see fig.17.1).

Note

Once you've opened the Windows Explorer, you can minimize it rather than close it. After minimizing the Explorer, you can reopen it instantly by clicking on its button in the taskbar.

Tip

The Explorer is a tool you will use frequently for working with your files and folders, so you may want to add it to the Start menu. "Customizing the Start Menu" in Chapter 5 shows how to add programs to the Start menu.

Tip

To quickly start Windows Explorer, right-click on Start, and then choose Explore.

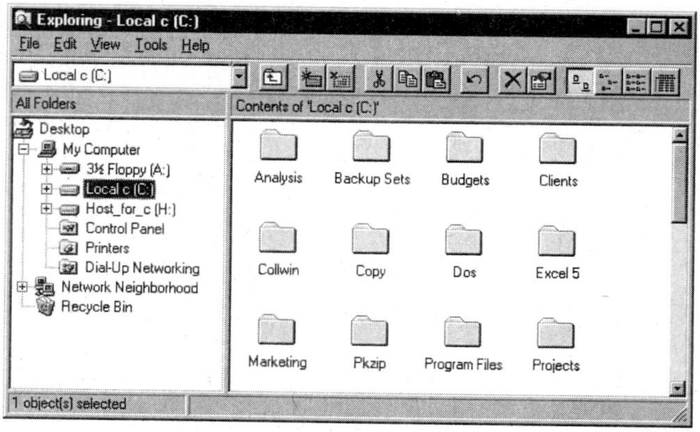

Fig. 17.1
Use the Windows Explorer to view the files and folders on your computer. This view shows the Windows Explorer with large icons and a toolbar.

Viewing Your Computer's Resources

◄ See "Managing Print Jobs," p. 173

◄ See "Managing Fonts in Windows 95," p. 223

One of the first tasks you will use the Windows Explorer for is to view the organization of the folders and files on your computer. The Explorer window is divided into two panes (refer to fig. 17.1). The left pane displays a hierarchical view of the organization of the folders on your computer. At the top of the hierarchy is the Desktop icon. This represents all the hard disks and resources available to your computer. Just beneath Desktop is My Computer, represented by an icon of a computer. Under My Computer are listed all the resources on your computer. These resources include floppy drives (represented by a floppy drive icon) and local hard drives (represented by a hard drive icon). Two special folders—the Control Panel and Printers folders—are used for managing the printers on your computer and for customizing your computer's settings. (You may also have other special folders listed here, depending on what optional components—such as dial-up networking—you have installed.)

► See "Deleting Files and Folders," p. 518

Two other folders that are branches off the Desktop icon are *Network Neighborhood* and the *Recycle Bin.* Network Neighborhood appears on your desktop if you are connected to a network. Open this folder to browse the computers in your workgroup or on your entire network. The Recycle Bin is where files are temporarily held when you delete them from a folder. By holding deleted files, you have the opportunity to recover them if you accidentally delete a file or change your mind.

Tip
If the toolbar is not displayed, choose View, Toolbar to display it.

Depending on the resources on your computer, you may see other folders displayed underneath My Computer. If you have a CD-ROM drive installed on your computer, for example, you will see its icon under My Computer. You may also see an icon for the *Briefcase* folder. The Briefcase is a special folder used for working on the same files at two locations and keeping them synchronized. See "Synchronizing Files" later in this chapter for more information on using the Briefcase.

Just beneath the menu bar is the toolbar. You can use the drop-down list at the left end of the toolbar to open the main folders in the Desktop and My Computer folders. This drop-down list shows all the drives on your computer, including network drives. If you scroll through the list, you'll also find your Control Panel, Briefcase (if installed), printers, Network Neighborhood, and Recycle Bin at the bottom of the list. This list also displays the folder hierarchy of the currently open folder, as shown in figure 17.2. You can, for example, quickly select the Recycle Bin folder without having to scroll to the bottom of the list in the left pane of the Explorer. To select from the list, click the down arrow next to the text box and click the folder you want to open.

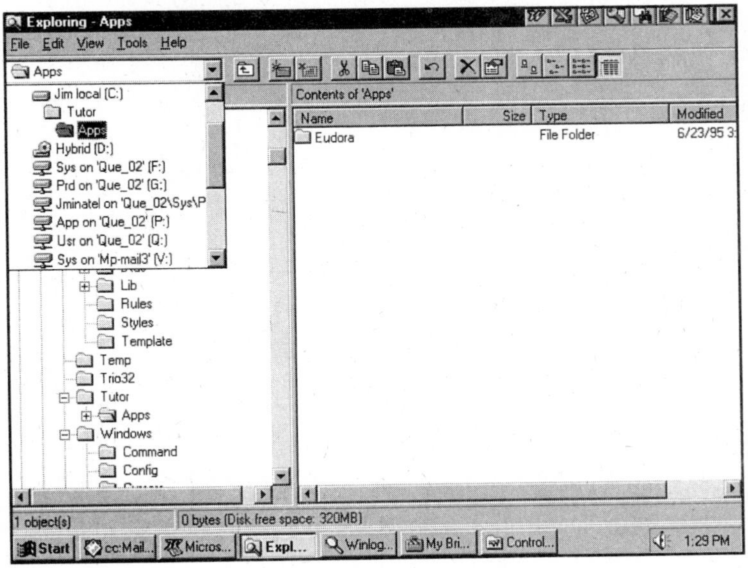

Fig. 17.2
The folders in the hierarchy above the current folder (Apps) are shown in addition to the list of drives and other main resources. The rest of the folder hierarchy is collapsed for quick access.

Browsing the Contents of a Folder

The right pane of the Explorer window displays the contents of whatever folder is selected in the left pane. If you select the Local C: drive under My Computer, for example, you see a list of all the resources on your computer, including the floppy and hard drives (see fig. 17.3). To display the contents of your hard disk, click its icon in the left pane. To see the contents of a folder, select the folder on the left and its contents are listed on the right. You can select a folder by clicking it with the mouse or by using the up and down arrow keys on the keyboard.

Tip
You can jump to a specific folder without wading through the Explorer hierarchy by selecting Tools, Go To. Enter the path of the folder to go to and then click OK.

You can expand and collapse the hierarchical view to display more or less detail. If a plus sign (+) appears next to an icon in the left pane of the Explorer, additional folders are within this folder. To display these folders, click the plus sign (or double-click the folder). All the folders within this folder are displayed. Some of these folders, in turn, may have folders within them, which you can view using the same procedure. To hide the folders within a folder, click the minus sign (–) next to the folder (or double-click the folder). By collapsing and expanding the display of folders, you can view as much or as little detail as you want. Figure 17.3 shows an expanded view of the Local C: drive folder, which is collapsed in figure 17.1. Notice that some of the folders on the C drive have plus signs next to them, indicating that they contain additional folders.

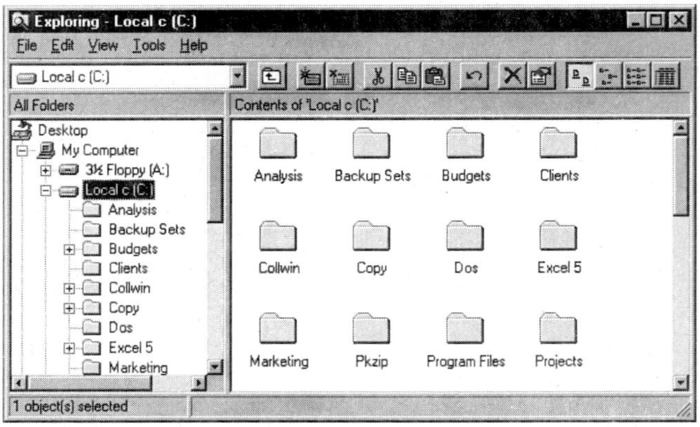

Fig. 17.3
An expanded view of the Local C: drive in the My Computer folder, showing its folders. A plus sign indicates additional folders within a folder.

Understanding the File Icons in Windows

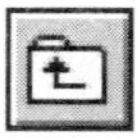

Windows uses various icons to represent folders and different types of files. In figure 17.4, folders within the Windows folder are represented with a folder icon. You can quickly display the contents of a folder within a folder by double-clicking its icon in the right pane of the Explorer. The easiest way to redisplay the original folder is to click the Up One Level button on the toolbar. (If the toolbar isn't displayed, choose View, Toolbar.) The Up One Level button is a picture of a folder with an up arrow in it. You also can redisplay the contents of the original folder by clicking its icon in the left pane of the window.

Note

Icons that have a small curved arrow in the lower left corner are shortcut icons. They are pointers to the actual file and folders that may be located in another folder.

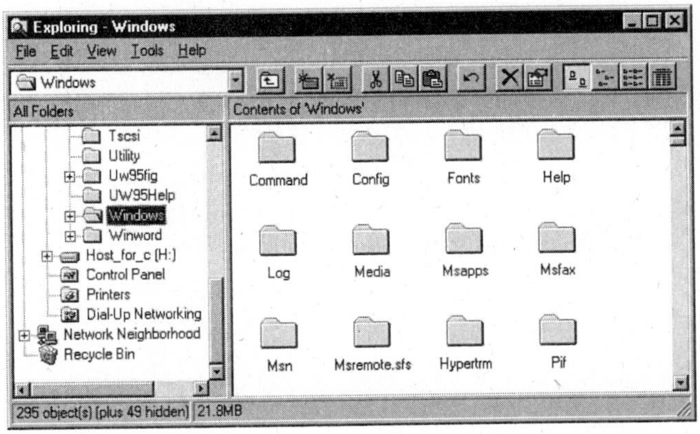

Fig. 17.4
Folder icons in the right pane of the Explorer represent folders within the folder selected in the left pane.

In addition to folders, many types of files can appear in the list of contents. Each type is represented by its own icon. Calendar files, for example, are represented by a calendar icon, and help files have their own special icon, as shown in figure 17.5. These icons are helpful for visually associating a file with its program. You can, for example, readily distinguish a file created in the Calendar program from a file created in Paint (see fig. 17.5).

Tip
You can open a file in its program by double-clicking the file's icon in the Explorer.

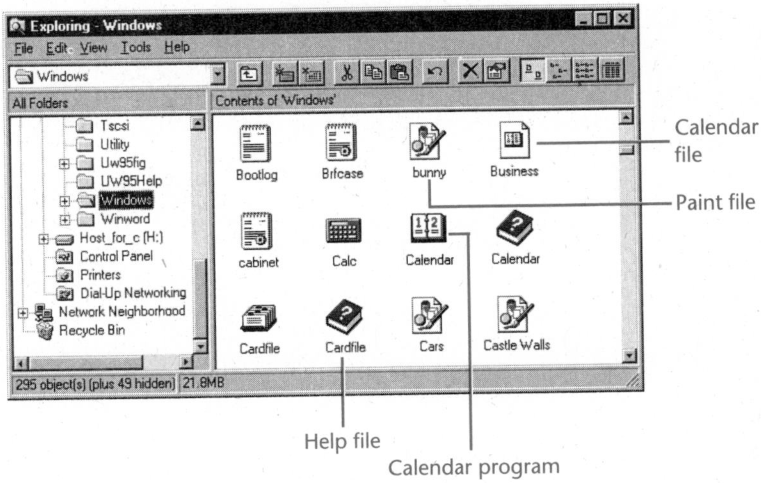

Fig. 17.5
Different icons are used to represent different file types.

You may need to update the display of files and folders in the right pane of the Explorer. If you are viewing the contents of a floppy disk, for example, and you switch disks, you won't see the contents of the new disk unless you *refresh* the window. To refresh the window, click the icon for the folder you want to refresh—in this case, the icon for the floppy drive—in the left pane of the Explorer. You also can refresh by choosing View, Refresh or by pressing the F5 key.

Tip
Unlike in the Windows 3.1 File Manager, you don't need to refresh the Explorer to see changes to the disk contents that were made from the DOS prompt.

Customizing the Windows Explorer

Windows offers many options for changing how the Explorer window looks. You can change how folders and files are listed; hide or display the toolbar and status bar; sort the folder and file icons by name, type, size, or date; hide the display of certain types of files; and make other changes to the Explorer window. Any changes you make remain in effect until you make new changes, even if you close and reopen the Explorer. By customizing the Explorer window, you can make it look and feel the way you want, making it easier for you to view and manage the files on your computer.

Note

If you're used to opening multiple windows in the File Manager, note that you can't do that in the Explorer. You don't need to open multiple windows in the Explorer because you can drag from any file or folder in the right pane into any drive or folder in the left pane. You can display drives or folders in the left pane by clicking on their + sign without disturbing the contents of the right pane. If you ever need to have multiple windows in the Explorer, just open additional copies of the Explorer. You can then copy or move files between them.

Note

If you are wondering where the options for Backup and Drivespace from the Windows for Workgroups 3.11 File Manager are, these are both gone from Explorer. You can still access these features, however, as discussed in chapters 16 and 18. Also gone is the ability to customize the tools on the toolbar.

Changing the Width of Panes

You can use the mouse to change the size of the left and right panes of the Explorer. You can, for example, make the left pane wider if it isn't wide enough to show all the hierarchical levels (folders within folders within folders). To change the width of the two panes of the Explorer window, move the mouse pointer over the bar dividing the two panes (the mouse pointer changes to a double-headed arrow), hold down the left mouse button, and drag the bar left or right to adjust the size of the two panes to your liking. However, you can't hide one pane or the other completely as you could in the Windows 3.1 File Manager.

Changing the Status Bar

The status bar at the bottom of the Explorer window provides information on the item you select. If you select a folder, for example, you see information on the number of items in the folder and the total amount of disk space used by the folder. If you don't use it, you can hide the status bar to make more room for displaying files and folders. To hide the status bar, choose View, Status Bar. Choosing this command again displays the status bar.

Customizing the Toolbar

The tools on the toolbar are shortcuts for commands you otherwise access with menu commands. These tools are discussed in the appropriate sections in this chapter. If you don't use the toolbar, you can hide it by choosing View, Toolbar. To display the toolbar, choose the command again.

Changing How Folders and Files Are Displayed

When you first start using the Windows Explorer, you will notice that folders and files are represented by large icons in the right pane of the window, as in figures 17.4 and 17.5. You also can display files and folders as small icons, as a list, or with file details.

To change the way folders and files are displayed, follow these steps:

1. Open the View menu.
2. Choose one of the following commands:

Command	Result
Large Icons	Large icons
Small Icons	Small icons arranged in multiple columns
List	Small icons in a single list
Details	Size, type, and date modified

The currently selected option appears in the View menu with a dot beside it. Figure 17.6 shows files displayed using small icons.

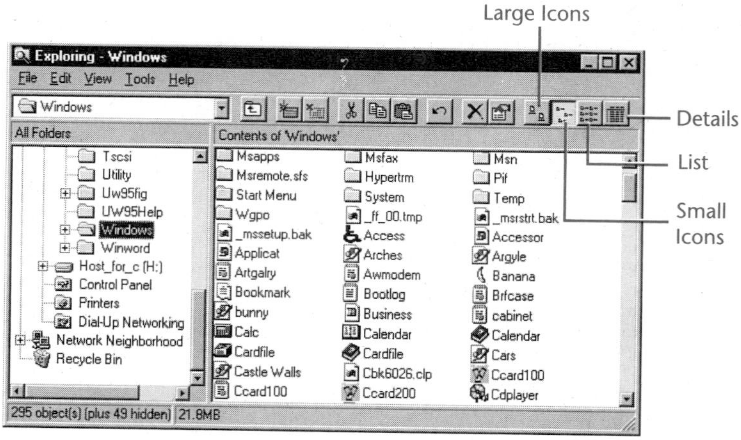

Fig. 17.6
You can view more files and folders in the Explorer when you use small icons.

If the toolbar is displayed, you can also click one of the four tools at the right end of the toolbar to change how items are displayed. From left to right these are Large Icons, Small Icons, List, and Details.

When you select the Details option, information on the size, type, and date the folder or file was last modified appears in columns next to the item in the list, as shown in figure 17.7. You can change the width of these columns by moving the mouse pointer over the line that divides the buttons at the top of each column (the mouse pointer changes to a double-headed arrow), holding down the left mouse button, and dragging the line to change the width.

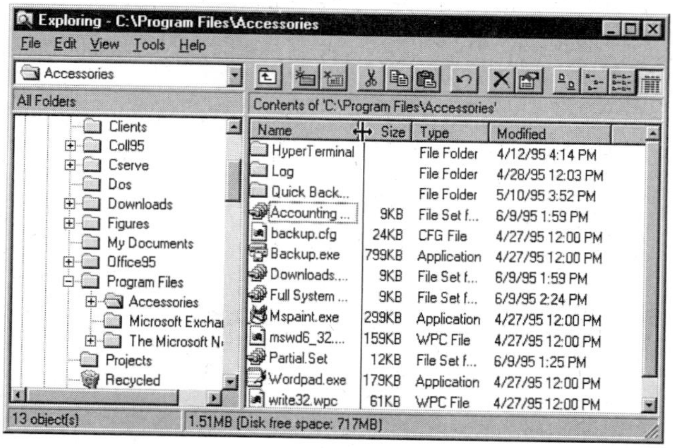

Fig. 17.7
To see information on the folders and files in the Explorer window, choose the Details view. Resize columns by dragging the line between header titles.

Arranging File and Folder Icons

If you select either the Large Icons or Small Icons option for displaying your files and folders, you can choose to let Windows automatically arrange the icons, or you can move the icons around to locate them wherever you want. To arrange the icons automatically, choose View, Arrange Icons. If a check mark appears next to the Auto Arrange command in the submenu, the command is already selected. If not, select Auto Arrange. The icons are now automatically arranged in a grid. If you want to arrange icons at any location in the right screen, deselect Auto Arrange. Some people prefer to have their files and folders arranged in an order of priority, frequency of use, or some other creative arrangement. Figure 17.8 shows PowerPoint files arranged in a circular pattern.

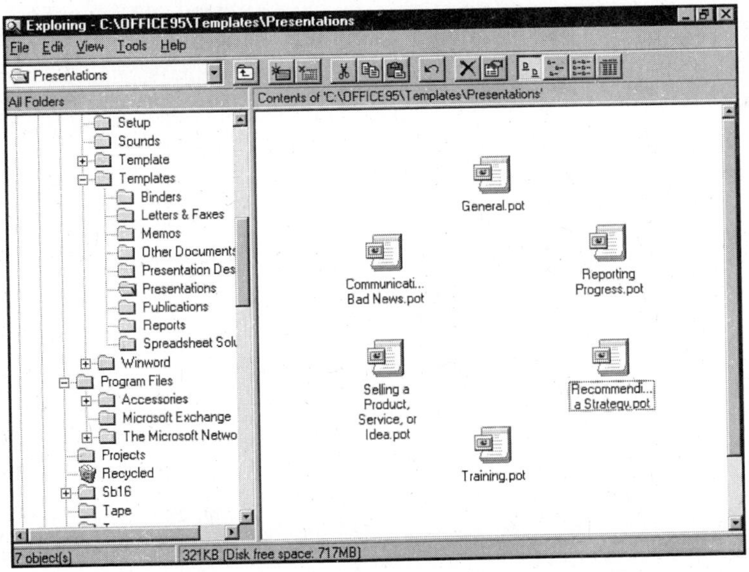

Fig. 17.8
When Auto Arrange is off, you can arrange icons in any way you want.

If the Auto Arrange command is not enabled, you can quickly arrange your icons in a grid by choosing View, Line Up Icons.

Tip
To automatically adjust column widths in the Detail view of the Windows Explorer to show the full content width, double-click the line between the column heads.

Sorting Files and Folders

You can sort the files and folders in the right pane of the Explorer by name, type, size, and date. To sort the items in the Explorer display, follow these steps:

1. Choose View, Arrange Icons.
2. Select one of the four options from the submenu.

Command	Result
by Name	Sort folders and then files by their name
by Type	Sort folders and then files by the type column (this may not be the same as file extension)
by Size	Sort folders and then files by their size
by Date	Sort folders and then files by their date

If you selected the Details option for displaying your folders and files, you can quickly sort the list of items by name, size, type, and date modified by clicking the button at the top of the column you want to sort by. Click Size, for example, to sort the list of items by size.

Changing Other View Options

You can change several other options in the Options dialog box. To change these options, follow these steps:

1. Choose View, Options to display the Options dialog box (see fig. 17.9).

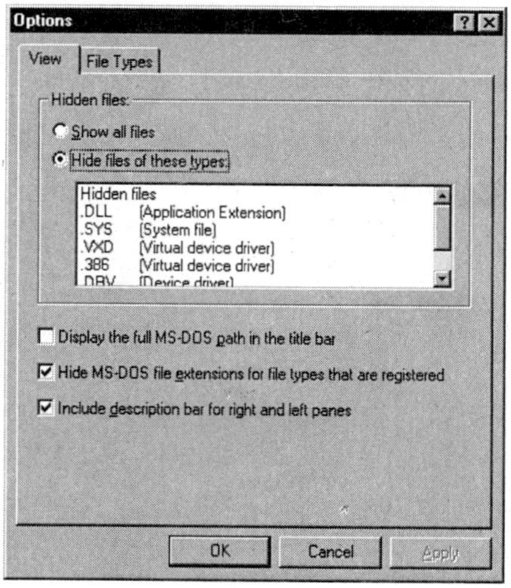

Fig. 17.9
You can change several options on the View page of the Options dialog box.

2. Select Show All Files to list all file types in the Explorer window.

   or

   Select Hide Files of These Types to hide the display of several types of system files.

Hiding these files, which you normally don't have to deal with, shortens the list of items displayed for some folders, and also prevents you and other users from accidentally deleting or moving crucial system files.

3. Select the Display the Full MS-DOS Path in the Title Bar option if you want to see the full DOS path for the folder selected in the left pane.

4. Select the Hide MS-DOS File Extensions for File Types that Are Registered option if you don't want the extensions for files associated with a particular program to be displayed.

   In Windows, a file's icon indicates what program it is associated with, if any. A file created in Calendar, for example, which has the MS-DOS file extension of CAL, is depicted with a Calendar icon. For this reason, you can determine a file's association by its icon and no longer need to see the file's extension. You have the option, therefore, of not displaying the extension in the list of files.

5. Select the Include Description Bar for Right and Left Panes option to display a descriptive bar at the top of the right and left panes of the Explorer window. The Description Bar appears above the panes and shows you such information as the drive letter and path name for the current view.

6. Click OK when you have finished making the selections you want.

Tip
To keep the list of file names in the Explorer manageable and easy to read, limit file names to about 75 characters.

Working with Long File Names

File and folder names help you organize and remember the contents of files and folders. Windows gives you the capability to type file and folder names up to 255 characters long and include spaces. This makes understanding file and folder names much easier than in older versions of Windows or DOS.

Another improvement is that you can now retype a file or folder name without having to display a dialog box—you just click on a name and edit or retype it.

Both of these improvements do not restrict your ability to use Windows files with older Windows or DOS systems that do not use long file names. The file names are compatible.

Renaming Files and Folders

Tip
If you're using a keyboard, you can rename a file or folder by selecting it and then either choosing File, Rename, or pressing F2.

As part of your efforts to keep the files and folders on your computer organized, you may want to rename a file or folder. This is easy to do in the Windows Explorer.

To rename a file or folder, follow these steps:

1. Click the file or folder to select it.
2. Click the name (not the icon) for the file or folder.

   Notice that a box surrounds the name and a blinking insertion point appears.

   > **Caution**
   >
   > If you accidentally double-click the file name, the program for that file opens and loads the file. To return to naming the file, close the program and click once on the file name.

3. Type the new name and press Enter.

If you change your mind while typing a new name, just press Esc to return to the original name. If you have already pressed Enter and the file has been renamed, click the Undo button in the toolbar, choose Edit, Undo, or press Ctrl+Z.

> **Caution**
>
> If you change the three-letter DOS file extension for a name, you will see a Rename alert box with this message: `If you change a file name extension, the file may become unusable. Are you sure you want to change it?` This box warns you that by changing the extension you will not be able to double-click the file and open its program. You can still open the file from within the application by choosing File, Open.

Using Long File Names with Older Windows and DOS Systems

Folders and files with long names can be used on older Windows and DOS systems. The *FAT (File Allocation Table)*, an area on the disk that stores file information, has been especially modified to store both old-style 8.3 file names as well as long file names.

Windows 3.1 used an 8.3 file name convention, where eight characters were used for the first part of a file name, a period was inserted to separate the parts of the file name, and then three letters were used for a file's extension. The file extension usually indicated the type of data in the file and the application that created the file.

> **Caution**
>
> Beware of using MS-DOS based or previous Windows versions of file management software or file utilities with files that have long file names. The software or utilities will probably not correctly recognize long file names and will destroy the long file names. The data in the files may remain usable, however.

In Windows 95, you can have file and folder names up to 255 characters long, and the names can include spaces. This long file name is stored in an extended location in the FAT of the disk. This extended location does not hamper the normal 8.3 name also stored in the FAT.

> **Caution**
>
> Long file names cannot use the following characters:
>
> / \ : * ? " < > |

When you use a long file name, Windows automatically creates a file name fitting the 8.3 convention. This 8.3 file name is saved in its normal location in the FAT so that older Windows and DOS systems can still use the 8.3 file name.

You can see the MS-DOS file name that will be used for a file by right-clicking on the file name and choosing Properties. Figure 17.10 shows the Properties sheet for that file. The long file name is shown at the top of the box; the MS-DOS name appears near the middle.

Some of the rules involved in converting long file names to 8.3 file names are as follows:

- Blank spaces are deleted before truncating long file names.
- File names where the first characters fit in eight characters or less are left unchanged.

- File names involving multiple periods, such as Proposal.Hodgkins.DOC, will use the file name to the left of the first period and the extension to the right of the last period.
- File names longer than eight characters but having a first word that is eight characters long and is followed by a space use the first word as the file name.
- File names that are created by truncating long file names end with ~#, where # is a number.
- No truncated file name will duplicate a file name existing in the same directory. ~# will be placed as the seventh and eighth characters and the # will be a number used to differentiate files with the same names.

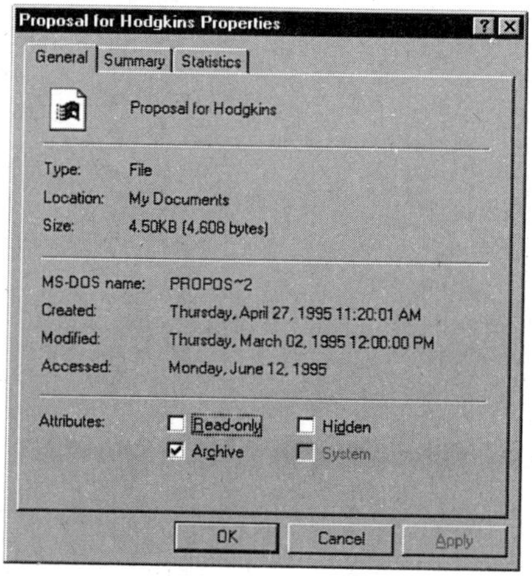

Fig. 17.10
Find out about a file by right-clicking its name and then choosing Properties.

Note

If you often exchange files with someone who uses an older version of DOS or Windows, try to use 8-character file names and the naming conventions you adopted with Windows 3.1 within your long file names. For example, advbgt- Advertising Budget.xls will be easier to identify when it is shortened to an 8.3 file name (advbgt~1.xls) than Advertising Budget.xls (advert~1.xls).

If you use a DOS command from the command prompt, such as `dir` to list a directory containing files with long names, you see the normal file information as well as the long file names. The long file name is displayed in the far right column when using the DOS `dir` command.

Managing Your Files and Folders

You can do much more with the Windows Explorer than display files and folders. The Explorer is an essential tool for managing the files and folders on your computer. You can use the Explorer to create new folders, move folders from one location to another, copy and move files from one folder to another, and even move files from one disk drive to another. You can also use the Explorer to delete and rename files and folders. The Windows Explorer can become your office assistant, helping you keep your files in good order so that you can use your computer more efficiently.

Selecting Files and Folders

Before you learn how to manage files and folders, you need to learn how to select them. Selecting a single file or folder is easy. You simply click on the file or folder with the mouse or use the up- and down-arrow keys on the keyboard. The selected file is highlighted.

You can also select multiple files and folders. This is extremely useful when you want to move or copy more than one file or folder at once. You can, for example, select several files in a list at once, and then copy them to a floppy disk to back them up.

To select more than one file with the mouse, click the first file; hold down the Ctrl key and click on each additional file you want to select. To deselect a file, continue holding down the Ctrl key and click a second time on the file. To quickly select a group of contiguous files, select the first file in the group, hold down the Shift key, and select the last file in the group. All the files between the first and last file will also be selected. Another way to select a group of contiguous files is to drag a box around the group of files with the mouse.

If your files are arranged free form, you may find it convenient to select groups of files by dragging a rectangle around them using the mouse. Figure 17.11 shows how you can click and drag a rectangle around multiple icons. All the icons within the rectangle will be selected. Once they are selected, you can deselect or select additional files by holding down Ctrl and clicking on icons.

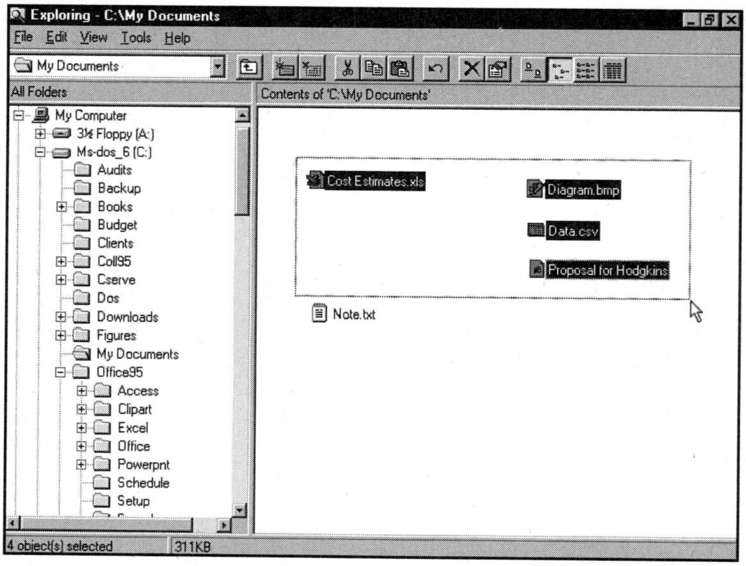

Fig. 17.11
Drag a rectangle around the group of file icons you want to select.

You can also select multiple files with the keyboard. To select multiple adjacent files, press Tab to move to the right pane and then press the down-arrow key to move to the first file. Then hold down the Shift key while pressing the down-arrow key to move to the last file you want to select. To select nonadjacent files, select the first file, hold down the Ctrl key, use the arrow keys to move to the next file to be selected, and press the space bar. While you continue to hold down the Ctrl key, move to each file you want to select and press the space bar. To deselect a file and retain the other selections, hold down the Ctrl key, use the arrow key to move to the file, and press the space bar.

To select all the files and folders displayed in the right pane, choose Edit, Select All (or press Ctrl+A). If you want to select all but a few of the files and folders in the right pane, select the files and folders you don't want to select; then choose Edit, Invert Selection.

To cancel the selections you have made, simply select another file or folder by using either the mouse or the keyboard.

Creating New Folders

You can create as many folders as you want to organize the files on your computer. As you produce more and more files with the programs on your computer, you will probably want to develop a filing system that helps you keep track of those files, just as you do with the paper files in your office. The more files you create, the more you may need to categorize those files to make them easy to locate.

Folders are the key to organizing your files. For example, you may start off with a file where you keep all your business letters. Over time, this folder will fill up with so many files that it becomes difficult to locate a file. At that point, it makes sense to subcategorize those files in some way—for example, by client or by company—and to create a folder for each of those categories. You can use the Windows Explorer to create these new folders. In the next section, "Moving and Copying Files and Folders," you learn how to move files from one folder to another.

To create a new folder, follow these steps:

1. Select the folder in the left pane of the Windows Explorer in which you want to create a new folder.

2. Choose File, New, Folder.

   A new folder appears in the right pane of the Explorer, ready for you to type in a name.

3. Type a name for the folder and press Enter.

Folders can use long names just like files. Folder names can be up to 255 characters long and can include spaces. They can't use these characters:

\ ? : " < > |

Moving and Copying Files and Folders

As essential task when managing the files on your computer is moving and copying files and folders. If you create new folders to break the files in an existing folder into subcategories, you need to move each file from the original folder into its new folder. You may also want to move entire folders from one folder to another. Or you may want to copy files from your hard disk onto a floppy disk to back them up or transfer them to another computer. By using the Explorer and the mouse, you can quickly move and copy files and folders without ever touching the keyboard.

You can use two approaches for moving and copying files and folders. You can either use the Cut or Copy commands or use the mouse to drag-and-drop the files.

To move or copy files by using the menu, follow these steps:

1. Select the files or folders you want to move in the right pane of the Windows Explorer.

2. To move the items, choose Edit, Cut; click the right mouse button on the selected items to display the shortcut menu and click Cut; click the Cut button on the toolbar; or press Ctrl+X.

   or

   To copy the items, choose Edit, Copy; click the right mouse button on the selected items to display the shortcut menu and click Copy; click the Copy button on the toolbar; or press Ctrl+C.

3. In the left pane of the Explorer, select with the right mouse button the folder that will contain the moved or copied items and choose Paste; click the Paste button on the toolbar; or press Ctrl+V.

   You may have to scroll the folders in the left pane to make the new folder visible.

To move or copy files using the drag-and-drop method, follow these steps:

Tip
Drag selected items to the destination folder with the right mouse button. When the shortcut menu appears, click Move Here to move items or Copy Here to copy items to the new location.

1. Select the files or folders you want to move in the right pane of the Windows Explorer.
2. If the folder to which you want to move the selected items is not visible in the left pane of the Explorer, use the scroll bar to scroll it into view. If you need to display a subfolder, click on the + sign next to the folder containing the subfolder.
3. To move the selected items, drag the selected items to the new folder in the left pane of the Explorer.

   or

   To copy the selected items, hold down the Ctrl key and drag the selected items to the new folder in the left pane of the Explorer.

   A plus sign (+) appears beneath the mouse pointer when you hold down the Ctrl key, indicating that you are copying the files.

   Make sure that the correct folder is highlighted before you release the mouse button.

◀ See "Creating Shortcut Icons on the Desktop to Start Programs," p. 68

If you attempt to drag-and-drop a program file to a new folder, Windows creates a shortcut for that program in the new location. This is to prevent you from inadvertently moving a program file from its original folder. When you attempt to drag a program file, an arrow appears beneath the mouse pointer, indicating that you are about to create a shortcut for that program.

Note

If you routinely copy or move files to particular folders or a disk drive, you can create a shortcut for the folder or drive on your desktop. Then you can quickly drag-and-drop files onto the shortcut icon rather than have to scroll to the folder or drive in the Explorer. To create a shortcut for a folder (or drive), select the folder (or drive) in the Explorer, drag it with the right mouse button onto your desktop, and release the mouse button. Choose the Create Shortcut(s) Here command. You can now drag-and-drop files onto this shortcut icon to copy or move files to this folder (or drive).

Tip

To quickly move selected items to a floppy disk, click the selected items with the right mouse button. Click Send To and then click the disk drive to which you want to send the selected files from the submenu.

Copying Disks

At times, you may want to make an exact copy of an entire floppy disk. This is easy to do in either the Explorer or My Computer.

You can copy from one floppy disk to another using the same drive, but both disks must have the same storage capacity. The disk you copy onto will be erased in the process.

Tip

The right mouse button has become invaluable in Windows 95. Try right-clicking on different parts of your screen to learn about tasks you can complete using the shortcut menus.

To copy a disk, follow these steps:

1. Insert the floppy disk you want to copy.
2. Right-click on the disk in My Computer or in the left pane of the Explorer window.
3. Choose Copy Disk from the shortcut menu. This opens the Copy Disk dialog box shown in figure 17.12.

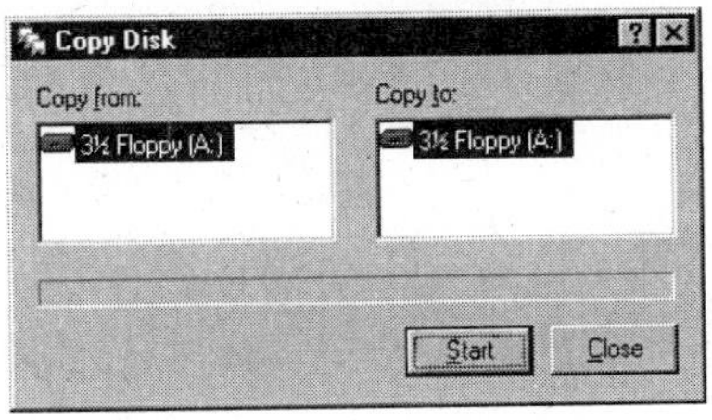

Fig. 17.12
The Copy Disk dialog box shows the selected drives for the copy operation.

If you have only one drive of this size, that drive will be highlighted for both the Copy From and Copy To areas of the dialog. If you have another drive of this same size, it will be listed as well, and you can select it to copy from drive to drive.

4. Choose Start.

5. If you are using the same drive for the master and the copy, you will be prompted to switch floppy disks when necessary.

6. When the disk is duplicated, you can copy another disk by choosing Start, or choose Close if you are done.

Copying disks is much faster in Windows 95 than in prior versions of Windows because of the addition of a high-speed floppy driver. If you frequently copy disks, you will notice the speed improvement.

Deleting Files and Folders

Inevitably, the time will come when you will want to delete a file or folder. This may be because you no longer need the file, or maybe you've created several new folders to subcategorize the files in an existing folder, and you want to delete the original folder after you move the files to their new locations. Deleting files and folders is an essential part of keeping your computer from getting cluttered with excessive and unnecessary files and folders.

Tip
If you realize right away that you have accidentally deleted a file or folder, choose Edit, Undo Delete to restore the files. Press F5 to refresh the file listing and see the restored file or folder.

You must delete files and folders with care so that you don't accidentally delete a file that you still need. Fortunately, Windows now has a folder called the Recycle Bin, where deleted files are temporarily stored until you empty it. You can restore files from the Recycle Bin if you change your mind or accidentally delete a file.

Caution

Files deleted from a floppy disk are not sent to the Recycle Bin. Once you delete them, they cannot be restored.

To delete a file or folder, follow these steps:

1. Select the file or folder you want to delete.

   You can select multiple files or folders by using the techniques described in "Selecting Files and Folders" earlier in this chapter.

2. Click the selection with the right mouse button and click Delete.

   or

   Choose File, Delete (or press the Delete key or click the Delete button on the toolbar).

3. Click Yes when the Confirm File Delete dialog box appears (see fig. 17.13). Or click No if you want to cancel the file deletion.

   If you are deleting multiple files, Explorer displays the Confirm Multiple File Delete dialog box.

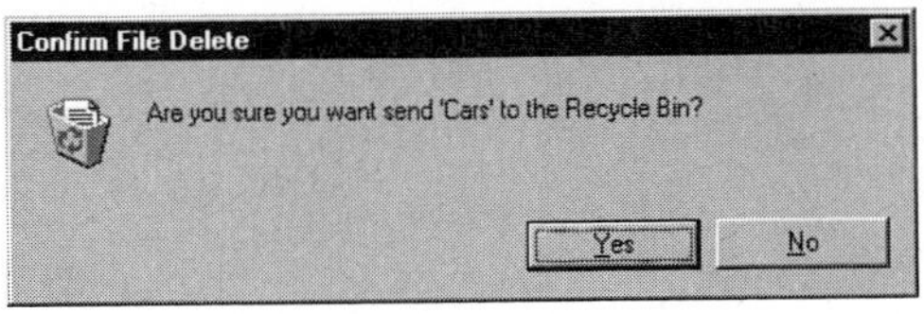

Fig. 17.13 The Confirm File Delete dialog box gives you a chance to check your decision before deleting a file.

Caution

If you delete a folder, you also delete all the files and folders contained in that folder. The Confirm Folder Delete dialog box reminds you of this. Be aware of what you are doing before you delete a folder.

You also should be careful not to accidentally delete a program file. If you attempt to delete a program file, the Confirm File Delete message box warns you that you are about to delete a program. Click No if you don't mean to delete the program, but other selected files will be deleted.

Note

To archive files to a floppy disk before you delete them, select the files, click the selected files with the right mouse button, and click Send To. Click the correct floppy drive to copy the files to the floppy disk. Now click the selected files with the right mouse button and click Delete.

► See "Backing Up Files," p. 559

Note

You can delete files and folders by dragging them onto the Recycle Bin icon on the desktop and dropping them.

When deleting some files, you may see a message warning you that the file is a system, hidden, or read-only file. System files are files needed by Windows 95 to operate correctly and should not be deleted. Hidden and read-only files may be needed for certain programs to work correctly, or they may just be files that you have protected with these attributes to prevent accidental deletion. Before deleting any of these file types, you should be certain that your system does not need them to operate correctly.

► See "Viewing and Changing the Properties of a File or Folder," p. 529

Restoring Deleted Files

Deleted files are moved to a folder called the Recycle Bin. You can open this folder just as you do any other folder and select a file and restore it to its original location. You can also move or copy files from the Recycle Bin to a new location, in the same way you learned how to move and copy files from other folders. The Recycle Bin provides you with the comfort of knowing that you have a second chance if you inadvertently delete a file or folder.

To restore a deleted file or folder, follow these steps:

1. Double-click the Recycle Bin icon on the desktop to open the Recycle Bin window, as shown in figure 17.14.

Fig. 17.14
Select files to restore in the Recycle Bin.

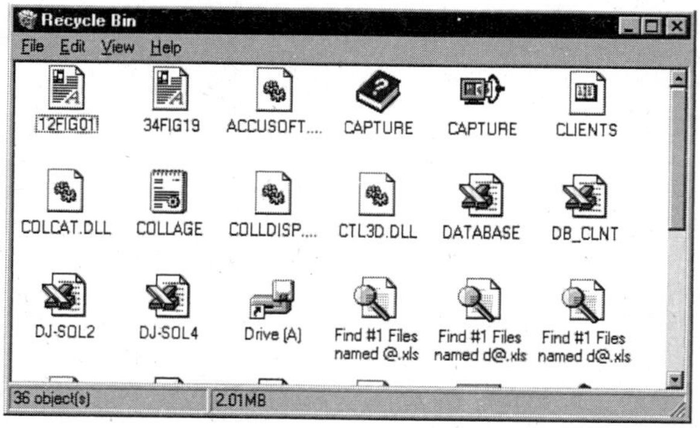

2. Select the file or files you want to restore.

   You can use the techniques described in the "Selecting Files and Folders" section to select multiple files.

3. Click the selected files with the right mouse button and click Restore, or choose File, Restore.

   The files are restored in the folders from which they were deleted. If the folder that a file was originally in has been deleted, the folder also is restored.

◄ See "Moving and Copying Files and Folders," p. 515

You can also restore a file to a different folder than the one it was deleted from. The easiest way to do this is to use the Explorer. Open the Recycle Bin folder in the Explorer, select the files you want to restore, and use one of the techniques discussed earlier in this chapter.

Emptying the Recycle Bin

Periodically, you may want to empty the Recycle Bin to free up space for more files. To empty the Recycle Bin, follow one of these procedures:

- If the Recycle Bin is already open, choose File, Empty Recycle Bin.
- Click the Recycle Bin icon on the desktop with the right mouse button and click Empty Recycle Bin.

Be aware of the fact that once you have emptied the Recycle Bin, you can no longer recover the deleted files and folders that were stored there.

You can also delete selected files from the Recycle Bin. To delete selected files from the Recycle Bin, follow these steps:

1. Open the Recycle Bin and select the files you want to delete.
2. Click the selected files with the right mouse button and click Delete.
3. Choose Yes to confirm the deletion.

> **Caution**
>
> The Recycle Bin can be a lifesaver if you accidentally delete a critical file. But don't forget to delete confidential files from the Recycle Bin so that others can't retrieve them.

Changing the Properties of the Recycle Bin

The Recycle Bin has a couple of properties that you can change. You can change the amount of disk space used for the Recycle Bin, and you can choose to have files permanently purged when deleted rather than be stored in the Recycle Bin.

To change the size of the Recycle Bin, follow these steps:

1. Right-click the Recycle Bin icon on the desktop or in the Explorer and click Properties.

   The Recycle Bin Properties sheet appears, as shown in figure 17.15.

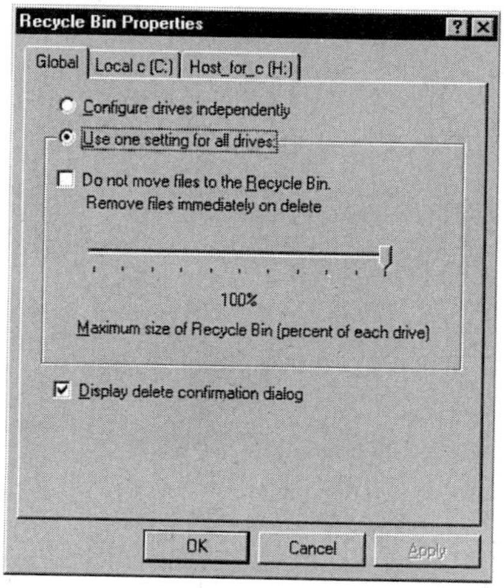

Fig. 17.15
Change the size of the Recycle Bin on the Recycle Bin Properties sheet.

2. Select the Configure Drives Independently option if you want to change the Recycle Bin size separately for each drive.

   or

   Select the Use One Setting for All Drives option if you want to use the same size Recycle Bin for all drives.

3. Drag the slider to change the maximum size of the Recycle Bin, as a percentage of the total disk size.

4. Click OK.

If you don't want to use up disk space storing deleted files, you can tell Windows to purge all files when they are deleted instead of storing them in the Recycle Bin. To purge all files when deleted, follow these steps:

1. Right-click the Recycle Bin icon on the desktop or in the Explorer and click Properties.

2. Select the Purge Files Immediately on Delete option.

3. Click OK.

When you select this option and delete a file, the Confirm File Delete dialog box warns you that the file will not be moved to the Recycle Bin.

Note

You can turn off the confirmation message for the Recycle Bin by deselecting the Display Delete Confirmation Dialog check box on the Recycle Bin Properties sheet.

Finding Files

Despite your best efforts to carefully organize your files, there inevitably comes a time when you can't locate a file you want to use. Windows comes with a tool to help you out when this happens. If you are familiar with the Search command from the Windows 3.1 File Manager, you should be impressed by the new features added for finding files in Windows 95.

The Find tool enables you to look for a specific file or group of related files by name and location. When searching by name, it's no longer necessary to use "wild cards" to specify your search, although you can still use them to fine-tune a search. In addition to this improvement, you can search by date modified, file type, and size. The most powerful new feature allows you to search by the text contained in the file or files. If you ever need to look for a file and can remember a key word or phrase in it but don't know the name of the file, this will be a real time-saver.

To find a file or group of related files, follow these steps:

1. Open the Start menu, choose Find, and then choose Files or Folders.

   or

   In the Explorer, choose Tools, Find, Files or Folders.

   The Find dialog box appears (see fig. 17.16).

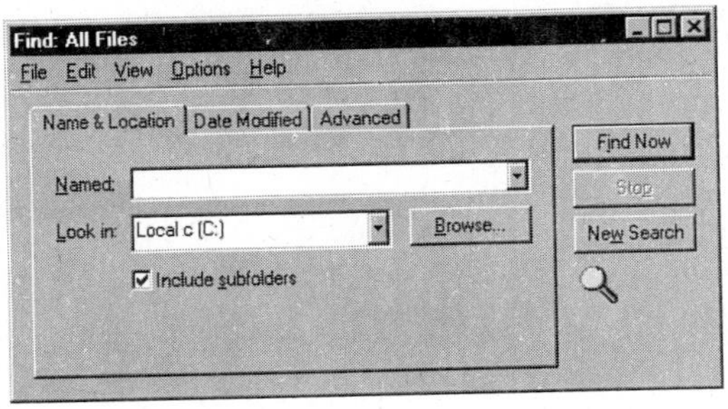

Fig. 17.16 Specify information about files you are searching for in the Find dialog box.

2. If you know the name of the file, type it in the Named text box. If you don't know the complete name of the file, just type whatever portion of file name you do know. Windows 95 will find all files that have these characters anywhere in the name.

   You can also use wild cards to look for all files of a particular type. (You could also use the Type criteria discussed in step 6 to limit files by type.) The following are some examples of how to use wild cards to look for groups of related files:

Entry	What It Finds
*.xls	Files with XLS extension (Excel worksheet files)
d*.xls	Excel worksheet files with file names beginning with the letter d
report??.txt	TXT files beginning with file names starting with *report*, followed by two more characters

   To reuse the same search criteria as one used previously, click the arrow at the right end of the Named text box and select the name search criteria you want to use from the list.

Tip
To search an entire drive, select the drive letter from the drop-down list and select Include Subfolders.

3. Specify where Find should look for the file in the Look In text box. You can type a path name in the text box, select from the entries in the drop-down list, or click the Browse button to select the location to which you want to restrict the search.

   Select the Include Subfolders option if you want to include the subfolders of whatever folders you selected in the search.

4. To limit the search to files created or modified within a specific time period, click the Date Modified tab (see fig. 17.17).

   You can restrict the search to files created or modified between two specified dates, or you can search for files created or modified during a specified number of months or days prior to the current date.

5. Click the Advanced tab to refine your search even more (see fig. 17.18).

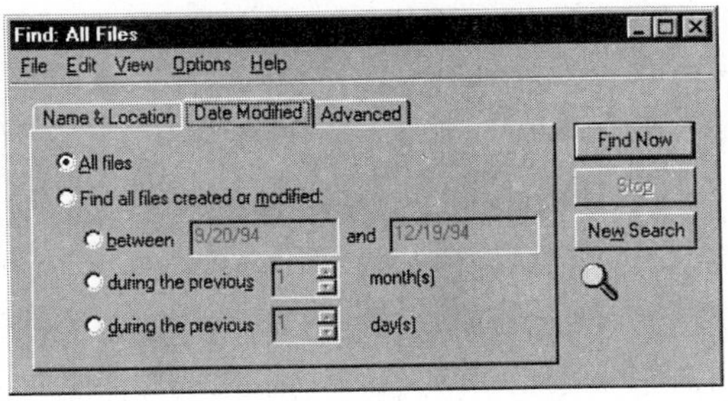

Fig. 17.17
You can narrow your search to a specified time period by using options on the Date Modified page.

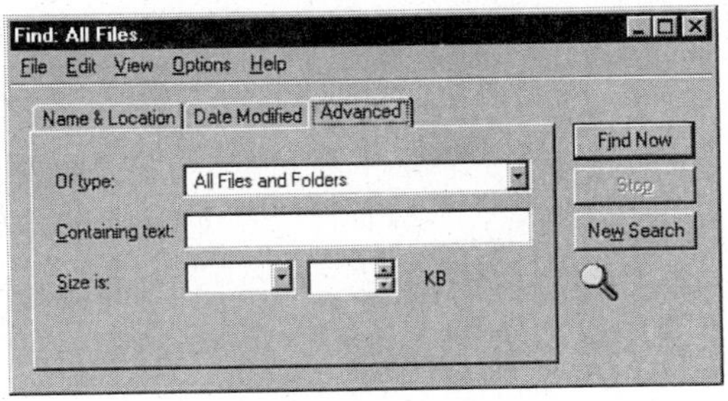

Fig. 17.18
Restrict your file search to files containing specific text or files of a specific size on the Advanced page of the Find dialog box.

6. Select a file type from the Of Type drop-down list to restrict the search to a specific file type. The types listed here are the registered file types discussed in "Registering Files to Automatically Open an Application" later in this chapter. These include document types created by application programs, as well as various types of files needed by Windows such as icons, control panels, and fonts.

7. Enter a text string in the Containing Text text box to search for files containing a specific string of text. If you enter several words separated by spaces, Windows treats the entry as a phrase and finds only documents containing those words in that order.

8. Specify the size of the file in the Size Is box. You can specify that the file be exactly a particular file size, or at least or at most a specified size. Select from the drop-down list the option to use, and then specify a size in the Size Is box.

9. When you have finished setting up your search parameters, click the Find Now button.

The Find dialog box expands at the bottom to show the results of the search (see fig. 17.19). If your search parameters were very specific, the search may take a few moments, especially if you told Find to look for files with a specific text string. All files matching the search specifications are listed, along with their location, size, and file type.

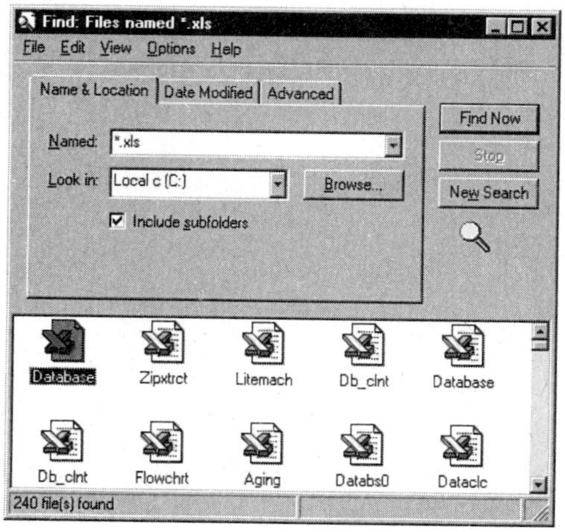

Fig. 17.19
The results of a search are listed at the bottom of the Find dialog box.

At this point, you can perform all the same operations on any of the found files that you can on a file in the Explorer. To work with a file in the Find dialog box, select the file and choose the File menu, or click on the file with the right mouse button to open the shortcut menu. You can open, print, preview, move, copy, delete, rename, or view the properties of the file. You can also drag-and-drop the file to any folder in the Explorer. This is handy if the file you located is in the wrong folder, and you want to quickly move it to the correct folder. The Edit menu contains commands for cutting and copying files.

You can save the search criteria as well as the results in an icon on your desktop. You also can save just the search criteria without saving the results. If you want to save the results with the search criteria, choose Options, Save Results so that Save Results is selected and shows a check mark. To save the criteria (and the results, if you specified that) choose File, Save Search. The saved criteria (and the results, if you specified them) will appear on your desktop as a document icon. You can label the icon by changing its name.

To open the Find dialog box using the saved criteria and result, double-click on the icon. The Find dialog box will show the criteria and results as they were when saved. To redo the search, click Find Now.

The View menu has the same commands as the Explorer for selecting how you want the files to be displayed in the results pane and for sorting the list of files. See "Changing How Folders and Files Are Displayed" earlier in this chapter to learn how to change the display in the results pane.

The Options menu has two commands for fine-tuning your search. Choose the Case Sensitive command if you want Find to distinguish between upper- and lowercase characters in any text you specified in the Containing Text text box.

If you want to set up a new search, click New Search to clear the criteria for the current search. Now you can enter the criteria for the new search.

Previewing a Document with Quick View

As you manage the files on your computer, you may want to look at the contents of a file before you make decisions about moving, copying, deleting, and backing up the file. It can be very tedious and time-consuming to open each file in the program that created the file. Windows has a tool called *Quick View* for previewing many types of files without having to open the original program. You can access Quick View from the Explorer or from any folder window.

To preview a file using Quick View, follow these steps:

1. Select the file you want to preview.

2. Choose File, Quick View. The Quick View item does not appear on the menu if the file type you select does not have a viewer installed.

   or

   Click the selected file with the right mouse button and click Quick View.

   The Quick View window opens, displaying the contents of the file, as shown in figure 17.20.

You can scroll through the document using the scroll bars or keyboard. If you decide you want to open the file, choose File, Open File for Editing (or click the Open File for Editing button at the left end of the toolbar).

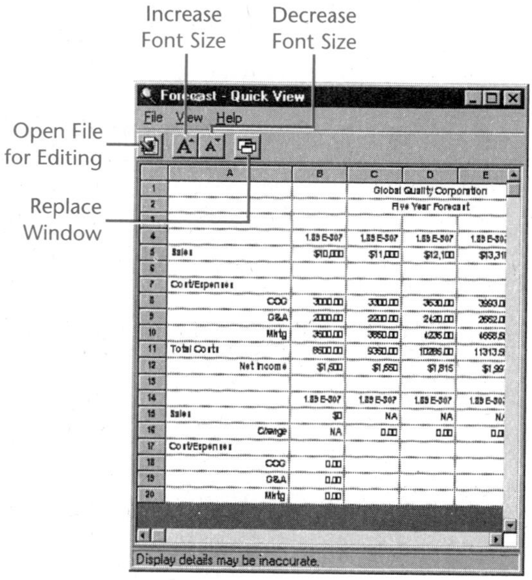

Fig. 17.20
Quickly preview the contents of many types of files using Quick View.

Tip
If you want to compare the contents of two files, you should have a new window opened for each file.

You can choose to have a new Quick View window open each time you select a file to preview, or you can view each new file in the same window. By default, Quick View opens a new window for each file. If this default has been changed, or you need to change it back, choose View and look at the menu. If a check mark appears next to Replace Window in Quick View, choose that option to deselect it and have a new window opened for each file. If you want the contents of the current Quick View window to be replaced when you select a new file for previewing, choose View, Replace Window to select this option. You can use the Replace Window button on the toolbar to activate and deactivate this option.

When you first open Quick View, you see a portion of the page of your document. To view whole pages, choose View, Page View. A check mark appears next to the command when it is activated. When you are in page view, you can click the arrows in the upper-right corner of the page to scroll through the document. To return to viewing portions of a page, choose the command again.

When you are in page view, you can rotate the display to preview the file in landscape orientation by choosing View, Landscape. Choose the command again to return to portrait orientation.

You can also change the font and font size used in the display by choosing View, Font and selecting a new font or size. To quickly increase or decrease the font size, click the Increase Font Size or Decrease Font Size tools on the toolbar. When you change the font and font size, it affects only the display in Quick View and does not alter the original file. It's handy to be able to increase the font size if you can't easily read the contents of the file, especially when you are in Page view.

To exit Quick View, choose File, Exit or double-click the Quick View icon at the left end of the title bar.

Viewing and Changing the Properties of a File or Folder

In Windows, it is easy to check the properties of a selected file or folder. You can find out the type of a file; the location and size of the selected item; the MS-DOS name; and when the file or folder was created, last modified, and last accessed. Each file and folder on a disk also has a set of *attributes,* or descriptive characteristics. Attributes describe whether the file has been backed up, is a Windows system file, is hidden from normal viewing, or can be read but not written over. With the Windows Explorer, you can display these attributes and change them.

To display the properties of a particular file or folder, follow these steps:

1. In the Explorer (or any folder), select the file or folder whose properties you want to check.
2. Right-click and choose Properties, or choose File, Properties. Windows opens a Properties sheet (see fig. 17.21).

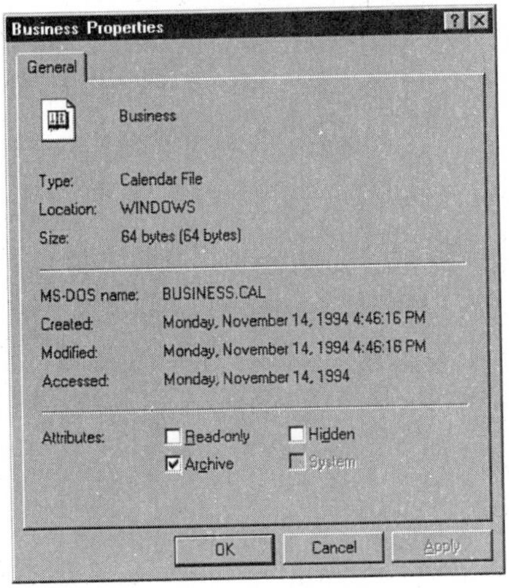

Fig. 17.21
You can check the properties of a file or folder on its Properties sheet.

3. View the file or folder's properties.

4. If you want, change the attributes for the file or folder, as described in the following table:

Attribute	Description
Read Only	Sets the R or Read-Only attribute, which prevents a file or folder from being changed or erased. Set this attribute for a file or folder when you want to prevent someone from accidentally changing a master template or erasing a file that is critical to system operation.
Archive	Sets the A or Archive attribute. Marks with an A any file that has changed since being backed up using certain backup programs, including Backup, which comes with Windows. If no A appears, the file has not changed since you backed it up.
Hidden	Sets the H or Hidden attribute, which prevents files from displaying in the Explorer and My Computer.
System	Sets the S or System attribute, which prevents files from displaying. System files are files that your computer requires to operate. Deleting a system file could prevent your computer from working. Folders cannot have the System attribute set.

Caution

Read-only files can still be deleted from within Explorer. You will see one additional warning dialog box prompting you if you attempt to delete a read-only file. So, setting this attribute does not entirely protect it from deletion.

5. Click OK.

Note

If you want to reduce the odds of accidentally changing or erasing a file, set the attributes to Read Only and Hidden or System. These attributes prevent the file from being accidentally changed and hide the file from standard display. However, hidden files can still be displayed depending on the View options you choose in Explorer, and Read Only and System files require only one additional confirmation to delete. So be careful when confirming the messages prompting you to delete files.

Note

Assigning the Hidden or System attribute to hide files is a good way to prevent tampering or accidental erasure. As an experienced Windows user, however, you may need to see these files to change, erase, or copy them. To display files with the Hidden or System attribute, choose View, Options. Click the View tab and select the Show All Files option. Now hidden and system files are displayed in the list of files. You can carry out these steps in either the Explorer or My Computer window.

Opening a Document from the Explorer

Although you may usually open your documents from within the program that created the document, you can open documents directly from the Explorer. In fact, if you like to think in terms of opening documents instead of opening programs and then opening documents, you can use the Explorer as your primary interface with your computer, doing all your viewing, opening, and printing of files from the Explorer.

To open a document from the Explorer, the file type for that document must be registered with a program. Registering a file type with a program tells Windows what application to use to open and print the document. TXT files, for example, are registered with Windows Notepad, so Windows uses Notepad to open any TXT files. Windows automatically registers certain file types. Microsoft Word for Windows files, for example, are automatically registered with Word.

► See "Registering Files to Automatically Open an Application," p. 539

To open a document in the Explorer, follow these steps:

1. Open the folder containing the file you want to open.
2. Select the file you want to open.
3. Double-click the file or press Enter.

   or

   Right-click the file and choose Open.

The Explorer starts the program for the file and opens the file.

If Windows does not recognize the file type of the file you double-click, it displays the Open With dialog box shown in figure 17.22. This dialog enables you to tell Windows which application should be used to open the file.

Choose the program you want to open the file from the Choose the program list. If you want the program to always be used to open a file of this type, make sure that the Always Use This Program to Open This File check box is selected.

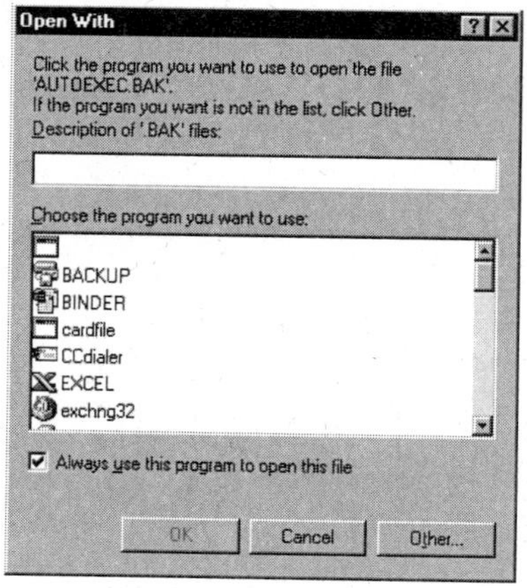

Fig. 17.22 Double-clicking a file that is not recognized produces the Open With dialog box, so you can tell Windows which program to use to open the file.

Printing Files

◄ See "Printing from the Desktop," p. 179

You can send files directly to the printer from the Explorer. For example, many software programs come with last-minute corrections and additional information stored in a text file. The information usually is not in the printed manual. These text files, which usually have the MS-DOS extension TXT, contain information such as helpful tips, corrections to the manual, and hardware configuration settings not covered in the manual. It is often helpful to print these files.

When you print with the Explorer, you send the file to the default printer. To change the default printer, use Control Panel.

To print a file with the Explorer, the file must be registered with a program. TXT files, for example, are registered with Windows Notepad.

To print a file using the Explorer, follow these steps:

1. Open the folder that contains the file or files you want to print.

2. Select the file or files you want to print.

3. Choose File, Print.

   or

   If you have created a shortcut for your printer on your desktop, drag-and-drop the selected file or files onto the Printer icon on the desktop.

Synchronizing Files

With the proliferation of home computers, laptop computers, and networks, you may often find yourself working on the same file on different computers. The inherent difficulty in working with the same file at more than one location is keeping the files synchronized—that is, making sure that the latest version of the file is at both locations. This used to be a daunting and dangerous task. It is not too difficult to accidentally copy the older version of a file on top of the newer version, rather than the other way around. A new feature in Windows, *Briefcase*, makes the task of synchronizing files in different locations much easier.

◄ See "Maintaining Laptop and Desktop Files with Briefcase," p. 292

Briefcase is really a folder with some special extra features. When you want to work on files at a different location—for example, on your laptop while you are away from your office—you first copy the files from your desktop computer into Briefcase. You then transfer Briefcase to your laptop and work on the files in Briefcase. When you return to the office, you transfer Briefcase back to your desktop and issue a command that automatically updates any files on your desktop that were modified while they were in Briefcase. The files on your desktop are then synchronized with the files in Briefcase.

The Briefcase procedure works whether you transfer Briefcase using a floppy disk, keep Briefcase on one of two computers that are physically connected, or use Briefcase to synchronize files across a network.

Creating the Briefcase

If you don't already have a Briefcase folder on your desktop, you need to create one. Unless you chose the Portable option when you were setting up Windows or specified the installation of Briefcase in a custom installation, you will not see the My Briefcase icon on your desktop. To create a Briefcase, follow these steps:

1. Open the Start menu; then choose Settings and Control Panel.
2. Double-click the Add/Remove Programs icon.
3. Click the Windows Setup tab.
4. Select Accessories in the Components list and then click Details.
5. Select Briefcase in the Components list and then click OK.

Note

Briefcase will be listed in these options only if it is not installed. Unlike the other accessories, which are listed here regardless of whether they are currently installed, Briefcase disappears from the list once you install it. If you delete your Briefcase, it will not appear in the list and you won't be able to reinstall it without rerunning the Windows setup.

6. Click OK again and insert the Windows disk specified in the Insert Disk message box that appears. Click OK again.
7. Click OK to close the dialog box.

Synchronizing Files with a Laptop or Another Computer on the Network

You can use Briefcase to keep files synchronized between a laptop and a desktop computer. This is useful because you may update files on the laptop while it is disconnected from the desktop. On reconnecting the two computers, you can ask Windows to synchronize the files between the two computers—comparing and updating files between the two computers. The most up-to-date file replaces the unchanged file. If files on both computers have been changed, you will be asked to choose which file should replace the other.

Caution

Be sure that the times and dates are correctly set on any computer that you use synchronization on. Incorrect dates or times could cause the wrong file to be overwritten.

Tip
The recommended approach is to put Briefcase on the computer you use less often.

Keeping synchronized files between your laptop and desktop computers is most convenient if they can be physically connected by a cable or network. Physically linking two computers is a much faster way to transfer files than by using a floppy disk. Using Briefcase helps you keep synchronized the files you are using on both computers. You can work on either the file on the original computer or the file in Briefcase, and use the Update command to keep the files synchronized.

You may have two computers on which you need to keep synchronized files, but you don't have the computers connected. You can still keep files synchronized by putting Briefcase on a floppy disk and using the disk to move the

Briefcase between computers. You can use this method to synchronize files between your work computer and your home computer or between your desktop and laptop computers. Although it's not as fast as synchronizing files between two connected computers, it works well if you are not working with a large number of files and don't have the means to physically connect the computers.

To synchronize files on two computers that are connected by cable or network or that use a floppy disk to transfer the Briefcase, follow these steps:

1. Copy the files and folders you want to use on both computers into Briefcase.

   The simplest way to copy the files to Briefcase is to drag-and-drop them on the My Briefcase icon on the desktop.

◄ See "Moving and Copying Files and Folders," p. 515

> **Note**
>
> The first time you copy a file to My Briefcase or open My Briefcase, Windows 95 displays a Welcome to the Windows Briefcase Wizard. There's nothing you need to do in this Wizard except read the explanation and click Finish.

2. Move Briefcase to the computer on which you will be working with the Briefcase files. If your computer is not connected to the other computer, move the Briefcase to a floppy disk.

   Once you move the Briefcase, it will not be located on the original desktop. It can be at only one place at a time.

   The idea is to move, not copy, Briefcase onto the other computer, so that it exists in only one location. An easy way to move Briefcase is to select the My Briefcase icon with the mouse, drag it to the new location with the right mouse button, and choose Move Here from the shortcut menu that appears.

Tip

The fastest way to move the Briefcase is to right-click the My Briefcase icon, click Send To, and then click the floppy drive you want to move Briefcase to.

◄ See "Sharing Local Resources via Parallel or Serial Connection," p. 278

3. If you are using a floppy disk, transfer the floppy disk to the other computer you want to work on.

4. Open and edit the files in Briefcase, as you normally would.

   If Briefcase is on a floppy disk and the other computer you are working on has Windows installed on it, you can transfer the files to the hard disk on that computer to speed up editing. Drag the files to the hard disk; after you edit them, drag the files back to Briefcase.

► See "Understanding File Sharing," p. 643

If you are working on computers that are physically connected, open and edit the files from Briefcase. You can work on the files on your portable or laptop even when it is not connected to the desktop.

Caution

If the other computer you are working on does not have Windows, you shouldn't transfer your files to the hard disk. Open and edit them in the Briefcase on the floppy disk. Otherwise, you will defeat the purpose of using Briefcase for keeping the files synchronized.

5. Once you are finished editing the files and you need to synchronize the files between the two computers, reconnect the computers if a cable or network connects them.

   If Briefcase was on a floppy disk, you can open Briefcase from the floppy or move Briefcase back to the desktop of the original computer. Then open Briefcase.

   Double-click the My Briefcase icon to open it (see fig. 17.23).

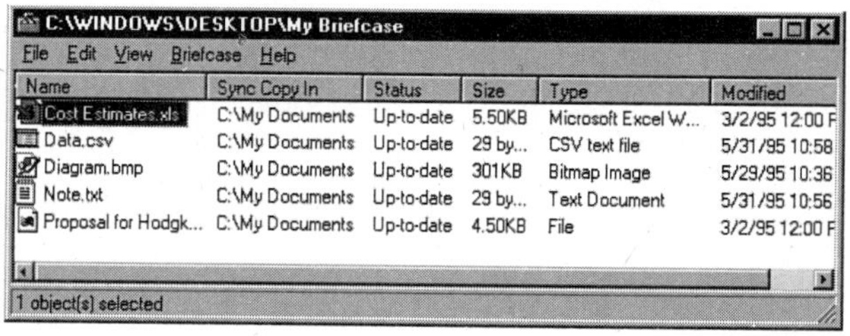

Fig. 17.23
Use Briefcase to keep files in different locations synchronized.

Note

By default, My Briefcase displays files in the Details view. This view is much like the Details view in Explorer with two additional columns. The Sync Copy In column lists the location of the original file. The Status column indicates whether the file is up-to-date, or whether it's older or newer than the original. Like the other columns in the Detail view of a folder, you can sort the list by clicking on the column headings.

6. Choose Briefcase, Update All.

   or

   Select only those files you want to update and choose Briefcase, Update Selection.

   The Update My Briefcase dialog box appears, as shown in figure 17.24.

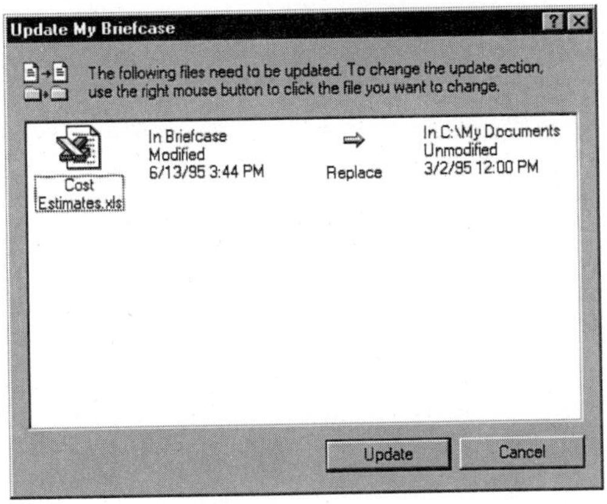

Fig. 17.24
All files that need to be updated are listed in the Update My Briefcase dialog box.

7. Check the proposed update action for each file as it is synchronized with its corresponding file on the other computer.

   The default update action is to replace the older version of the file with the newer version. If you want to change the update action for a file, right-click the file name and change the action using the pop-up menu that appears (see fig. 17.25).

8. Click the Update button to update the files. (The computers must be connected for you to update the files.)

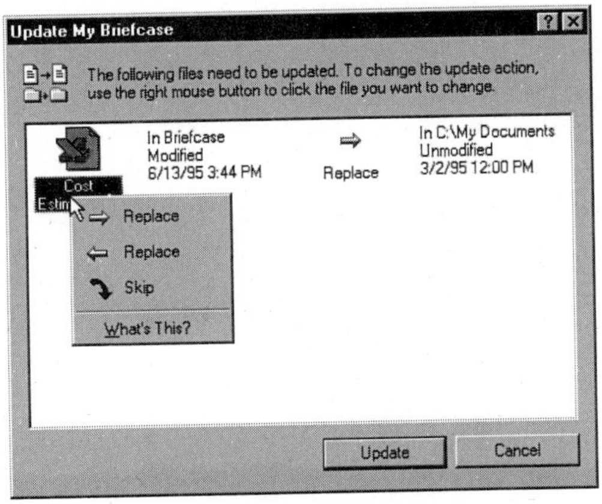

Fig. 17.25
Change the update action that will be applied to a file by clicking it with the right mouse button and then selecting the desired action.

Checking the Status of Briefcase Files

You can check the update status of the files in the Briefcase at any time. To check the status of a file or folder in Briefcase, open My Briefcase by double-clicking on it. Examine the Status column in the window.

If you have the Briefcase files displayed in a view other than Details, you will not see this Status column. To check the status, you can choose View, Details to switch to Details view. Or you can select the file to check and choose File, Properties; then click the Update Status tab (see fig. 17.26). The middle portion of the Update Status page shows the status of the file in the Briefcase on the left and that of the original file on the right. If the files are the same, `Up to Date` is indicated in the center. If the files are not the same, `Replace` is shown in the center along with an arrow. The arrow points to the file that is out-of-date and should be replaced.

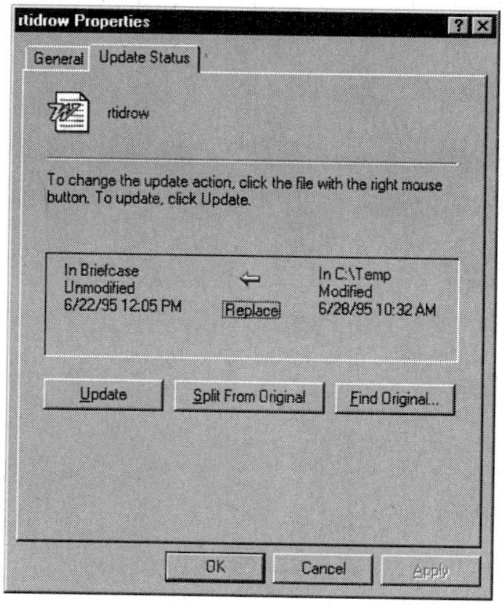

Fig. 17.26
In this figure, the copy of RTIDROW in C:\TEMP is newer than the Briefcase copy, so Windows indicates that the copy in the Briefcase should be replaced.

From within this Properties sheet, you can update the file (as described in the preceding section) by choosing Update. You also can prevent a file from being updated (which is discussed in the next section) by choosing Split from Original.

You can choose Find Original to open the folder with the original file, without having to work your way through the hierarchy of folders in Explorer or My Computer.

Troubleshooting

I modified the original of a file in My Briefcase, but the status still shows `Up to Date`.

If you have Briefcase or the folder with the original open, the status may not be updated immediately. Choose View, Refresh both in My Briefcase and in the folder containing the original file. This ensures that the status indicates any recent changes.

Preventing a File from Synchronizing

You may want to break the connection between a file in Briefcase and its original file, so that when you issue the Update command, the two copies of the file are not synchronized. You may want to do this to preserve the original file or if the portable file is now a file that has changed into a document unrelated to the original.

To split a file from its original, follow these steps:

1. Open Briefcase and select the file you want to split.
2. Choose Briefcase, Split From Original.

   Notice that the file is now referred to as an orphan in the Status field of the Briefcase window.

You can also split a file by clicking the Split from Original button on the Update Status page of the Properties sheet.

Registering Files to Automatically Open an Application

When you register a file type with Windows, you tell Windows that the file type has a certain MS-DOS extension and that a particular program should be used to open the file. The most useful reason for registering a file type is that you can then double-click any file of that type, and the file will be opened using the program you have instructed Windows to use.

Registering a New File Type

Registering a file type is analogous to associating a file in Windows 3.1, although you can now tell Windows even more about the file type; for example, you can now tell Windows which program to use to print a type of file.

To register a new file type, follow these steps:

1. In the Explorer, choose View, Options.

2. Click the File Types tab to display the dialog box shown in figure 17.27.

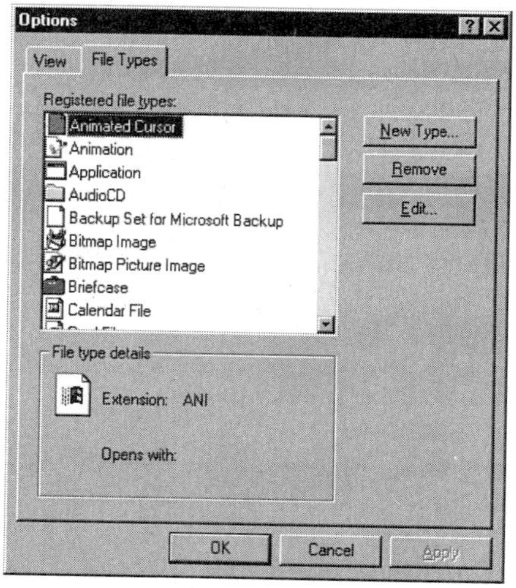

Fig. 17.27 Register and modify file types on the File Types page of the Options dialog box.

3. Choose New Type. The Add New File Type dialog box appears (see fig. 17.28).

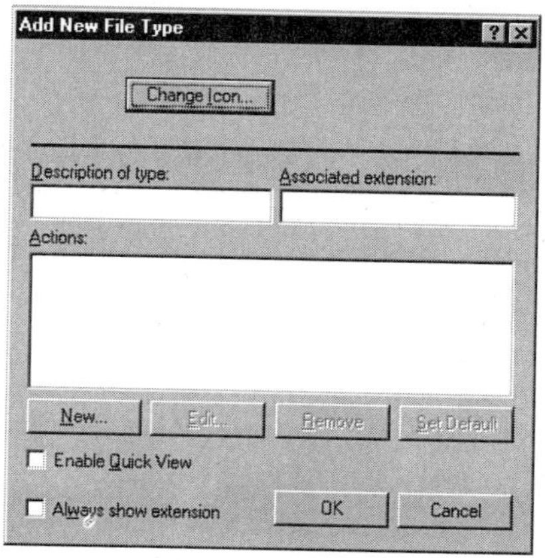

Fig. 17.28 Enter the information for a new file type in the Add New File Type dialog box.

4. Enter a description of the file type in the Description of Type text box.

   This description appears in the Registered File Types list on the File Types page of the Options dialog box. For example, if you want to be able to double-click on mainframe text files that use commas to separate data and have that file load into Excel, you might use a description similar to Comma Separated Values (CSV).

5. Enter the file extension to be associated with this file type in the Associated Extension text box. This is the three-letter file extension associated with DOS-based files. For example, a comma-separated values file uses the extension CSV.

6. Choose New to add a new action to the file type in the New Action dialog box.

   The action is actually a custom command that appears on the shortcut menu when you right-click on the file.

7. Type an action—for example, **Open CSV in Excel**—in the Actions text box.

   What you type will appear as an item on the shortcut menu for this file type. You can type anything, but commands usually start with a verb. If you want the command to have an accelerator key, precede that letter with an ampersand (&).

8. Select the application to be used to perform the action in the Application Used to Perform Action text box.

   In the example used so far, you would enter the path and directory to the EXCEL.EXE file—for example, **C:\OFFICE95\EXCEL\Excel.exe**. You can also use Browse to find and select the application to use.

   The New Action dialog box with information filled in is shown in figure 17.29.

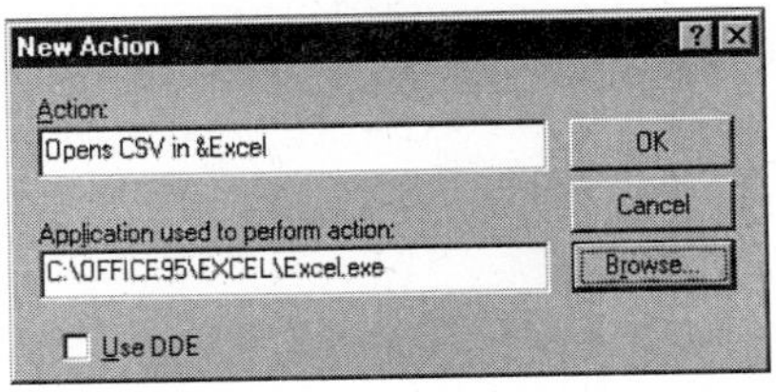

Fig. 17.29 Designate a shortcut menu action and the program used to perform that action in the New Action dialog box.

9. While the New Action dialog box is still displayed, select the Use DDE check box if the program uses DDE (dynamic data exchange).

If you select the Use DDE check box, the dialog box expands (see fig. 17.30), displaying the DDE statements used to communicate with the DDE application. If you know how to write DDE statements, you can customize the action performed with the associated application.

Fig. 17.30
You can enter your own DDE statements to customize the action associated with a registered file type.

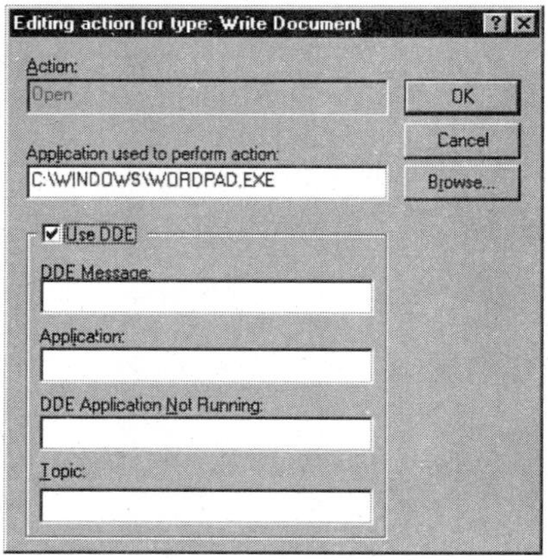

10. Click OK.

11. If you have more than one action listed in the Actions text box, select the one you want to be the default action and choose the Set Default button.

    The default action is the one that is performed when you double-click a file of this type in the Explorer or My Computer.

◀ See "Previewing a Document with Quick View," p. 527

12. Select the Enable Quick View box if the file type supports Quick View. Quick View allows you to view a file without opening it.

13. Select Always Show Extension if you want the MS-DOS file extension for this file type to always be displayed in the Explorer and My Computer windows, even when you have selected the Hide MS-DOS File Extensions option on the View page of the Options dialog box.

14. Choose Close twice.

Editing an Existing File Type

At times, you may want to change existing file-type options. For example, say you wanted to change the action that opens BMP files in Paint so that they would open in a different image editor. You would edit the BMP open action to include the path and file names for that image editor instead of Paint. You also can change the description, icon, and other aspects.

To edit an existing file type, follow these steps:

1. In the Explorer, choose View, Options.
2. Click the File Types tab to display the File Types page of the Options dialog box (refer to fig. 17.27).
3. Select the file type you want to edit in the Registered File Types list.
4. Click the Edit button.
5. Edit the characteristics for the file type using the same procedures outlined earlier for creating a new file type.

   To edit an action, you must first select that action from the list. Actions for a file type depend on parameters or arguments understood by that file type. Some applications may be able to accept macro names as actions, others accept "switches," and still others accept arguments leftover from DOS commands. Check the technical reference manual for the application you are starting to learn more about the actions.
6. Click OK.
7. Repeat steps 3 through 6 for any other file types you want to edit.
8. Click Close.

Removing a File Type

If you no longer want a document to start a specific application, you will want to change or remove its file type description.

To remove a file type, follow these steps:

1. In the Explorer, choose View, Options.
2. Click the File Types tab to display the File Types page of the Options dialog box (refer to fig. 17.27).
3. Select the file type you want to remove in the Registered File Types list.
4. Click Remove.
5. Click OK.

Changing the Icon for a File Type or Other Object

You can also change the icon used to designate a file type, drive, folder, and other objects on your computer. To change the icon used for a particular file type or object, follow these steps:

1. In the Explorer, choose View, Options.
2. Click the File Types tab to display the File Types page of the Options dialog box (refer to fig. 17.27).
3. Select the file type or other object whose icon you want to change in the Registered File Types list.
4. Choose the Edit button.
5. Click the Change Icon button to display the Change Icon dialog box shown in figure 17.31.

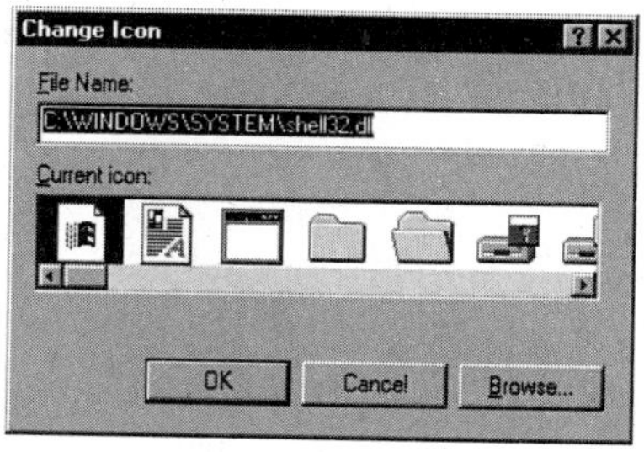

Fig. 17.31
Use the Change Icon dialog box to select a new icon for a file type or other type of object.

6. Select a new icon from the Current Icon scrolling list.

   The name of the file containing the icons currently shown is listed in the File Name text box. You can use the Browse button to search for a new file containing different icons. All Windows programs come with their own icons, and you can also obtain collections of icons on computer bulletin boards and from other sources. Programs are even available that allow you to create your own icons.

7. Click OK three times.

Using the Explorer with Shared Resources on a Network

▶ See "Setting Up File Sharing," p. 643

▶ See "Sharing Your Resources," p. 688

If you are using Windows on a network, you can share resources with other users in your workgroup and use resources that other users have designated as shared. You can open the files in any folder that has been designated as shared by another user, and you can share any of your folders so that the files in that folder can be used by other users. You can use the Explorer to designate resources on your computer as shared and to browse the shared resources in your workgroup or on your entire network.

Browsing Shared Folders

You can open any folder that has been designated as shared by any user on your network. (To learn how to share a folder, see the next section, "Sharing Resources on Your Computer.") You browse a shared folder using the Explorer in the same way you browse a folder on your computer.

► See "Understanding File Sharing," p. 643

To browse a shared folder, follow these steps:

1. Under Network Neighborhood in the left pane of the Explorer, find the computer on Your network where the folder you want to browse is located.

   If a plus sign appears next to the name of the computer, click the plus sign to display the shared resources on that computer (see fig. 17.32).

   Shared resources can include folders, entire drives, CD-ROM drives, and printers, as you can see in figure 17.32.

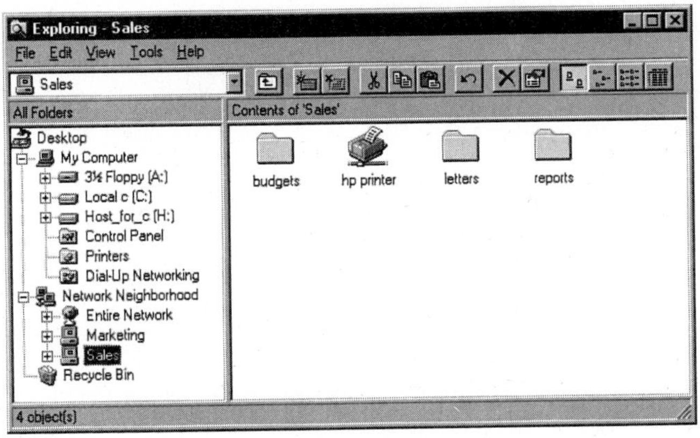

Fig. 17.32 View the shared resources on another user's computer in the Explorer.

2. Select the shared folder to display its contents in the right pane of the Explorer, as shown in figure 17.33.

3. To open a shared file from the Explorer, double-click the file name in the right pane.

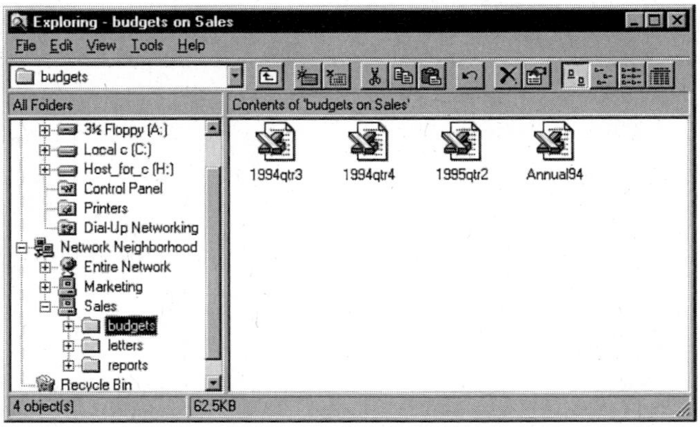

Fig. 17.33 View the contents of a shared folder by selecting it in the Explorer.

Sharing Resources on Your Computer

► See "Setting Up File Sharing," p. 643

► See "Sharing Your Resources," p. 688

You can designate any folder on your computer as shared. When you share a folder, you can assign a *share name* and *password* to that folder. You can also specify what type of access users have to the shared folder. Once you have shared a folder, other users have access to the files in that folder. The computers that have the folders you want to share must be on and logged in to the network.

To share a folder, follow these steps:

1. In the Explorer, select the folder you want to share.
2. Right-click the folder, and then click Sharing to display the Sharing page on the Properties sheet.
3. Select the Shared As option, as shown in figure 17.34.
4. You can accept the default share name for the folder or type a new name in the Share Name text box.
5. Enter a comment in the Comment text box, if you want.

   The comment appears in the Details view of your computer when other users select it in the Explorer or Network Neighborhood. Comments can help users locate shared information.
6. Select one of the Access Type options to specify the access for the shared resource.

   You can grant users two levels of access to a shared folder. If you want users to be able only to read files and run programs in a folder, select the Read-Only option. If you want users to be able to read, modify, rename, move, delete, or create files and run your programs, select the Full option. If you want the level of access to depend on which password the user enters, select the Depends on Password option.

If you want to limit access to the files in the shared folder to certain users, assign a password to the folder and give the password to only those users. If you select the Depends on Password option, you need to enter two passwords—one for users who have read-only access to your files and one for users with full access. If you want all users to have access to your files, don't assign a password.

7. Click OK.

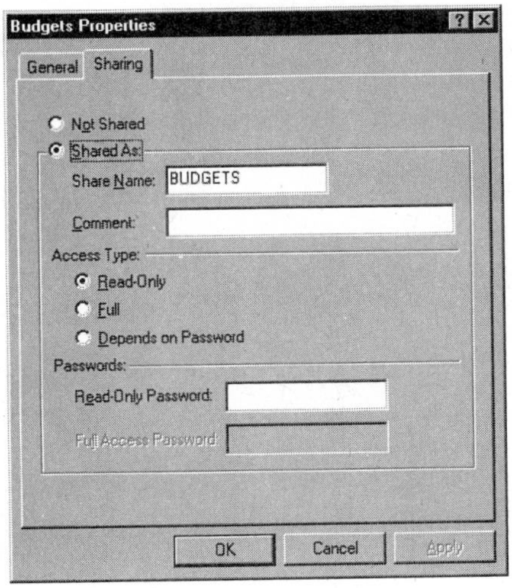

Fig. 17.34
Designate a folder as shared on the Sharing page of the Properties sheet.

You can share an entire disk drive by selecting the drive and following the preceding steps.

You can quickly tell if you have designated a folder as shared by looking for a hand beneath its folder icon in the Explorer or Network Neighborhood, as shown in figure 17.35.

To change the properties of a shared folder, click the folder with the right mouse button and change the share name, comment, access privileges, or password for the shared folder.

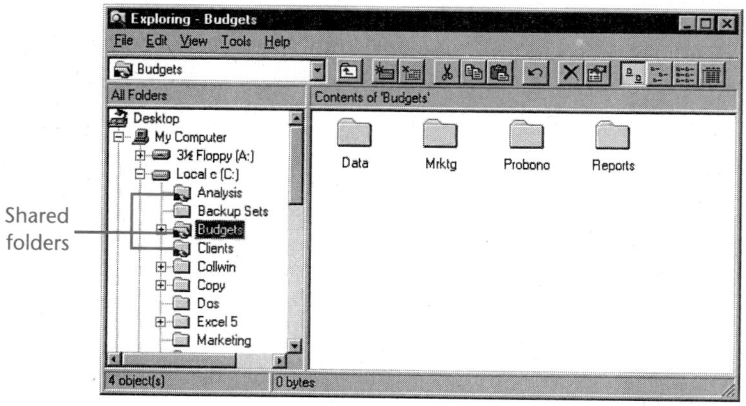

Fig. 17.35
Shared folders are indicated by a hand beneath their folder icons in the Explorer.

> **Caution**
>
> If the Sharing tab is not visible when you open the Properties sheet, you must enable file and printer sharing services.

Stop Sharing a Folder

To stop sharing a folder, follow these steps:

1. Select the folder you want to stop sharing.
2. Right-click on the folder and then click Sharing.
3. Select the Not Shared option and click OK.

Mapping a Network Drive

In earlier versions of Windows, you had to connect to a shared directory to be able to view and use its files. When you connected to a shared directory, Windows created a *network drive* for that directory and assigned a letter to that drive. To view the files in the shared directory, you selected the drive in File Manager. Windows 95 has greatly simplified working with networks by listing all shared resources in the Explorer and Network Neighborhood. You no longer have to map a drive to the shared folder. However, if you prefer to map a drive to a shared resource on another computer, you can still do it. The mapped drive appears under My Computer just like any other drive.

To map a drive to a shared directory, follow these steps:

1. Select the shared folder you want to map in the Explorer or Network Neighborhood.

2. Right-click the folder, and then click Map Network Drive. The Map Network Drive dialog box appears, as shown in figure 17.36.

Fig. 17.36
You can map a shared directory to a drive letter in the Map Network Drive dialog box.

3. By default, Windows assigns the next available drive letter on your computer to the folder you select to map. To assign a different letter, click the drop-down arrow and select a letter from the list.

4. If you want to automatically reconnect to this shared folder at log on, select the Reconnect at Startup option.

5. Click OK.

To remove the mapping for a shared directory, click the Disconnect Network Drive button in the Explorer or Network Neighborhood, select the network drive you want to disconnect, and click OK. Or select the drive in the left pane of the Explorer, click the right mouse button, and then click Disconnect.

Finding a Computer on Your Network

If you know its name, you can quickly find a computer on your network by using the Find Computer command. To find a computer on your network, follow these steps:

► See "Finding a Computer on the Network," p. 614

► See "Identifying Your Workgroup Computer," p. 635

1. Open the Start menu; then choose Find, Computer.

   or

   In the Explorer, choose Tools, Find, Computer.

2. Enter the name of the computer you want to find in the Named text box of the Find: Computer dialog box, as shown in figure 17.37.

3. Click the Find Now button.

   The dialog box expands, listing the location of the specified computer if it is found on the network, as shown in figure 17.38.

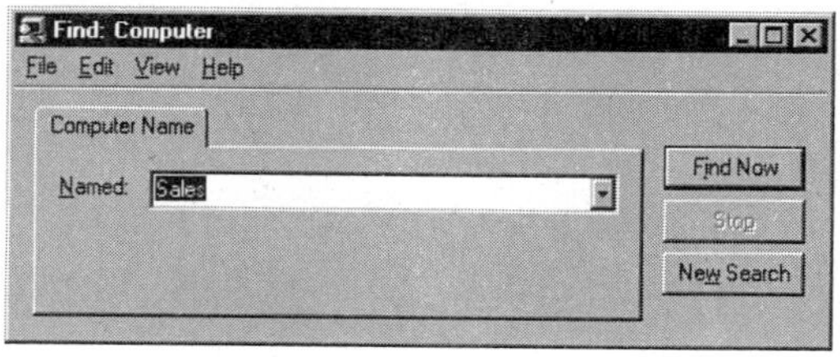

Fig. 17.37
Find a computer on your network by using the Find Computer command.

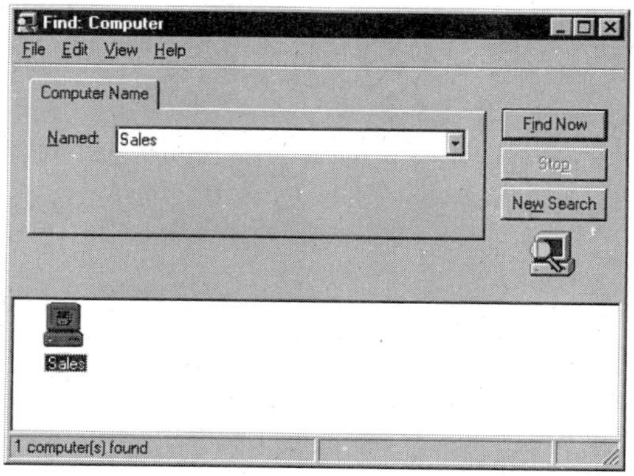

Fig. 17.38
The location of the found computer is listed at the bottom of the Find: Computer dialog box.

4. To open a browse window displaying the shared files and folders on the found computer, double-click on the name of the computer at the bottom of the dialog box, or right-click on the name and click Open.

Using Network Neighborhood to View Network Resources

When you install Windows and are connected to a network, you see an icon for Network Neighborhood on your desktop. You can open Network Neighborhood and use it to work with the shared resources on your network by using the same techniques described in the preceding section. When you first open Network Neighborhood by double-clicking its icon on the desktop, the Network Neighborhood window appears, as shown in figure 17.39.

To view the shared resources on a particular computer on your network, double-click the icon for the computer to open a new window. You can continue this process to open shared folders and view the contents. Many options discussed in the sections on using the Explorer earlier in this chapter are also available in Network Neighborhood. You can, for example, change the way files are displayed; add or remove the toolbar; and move, copy, and delete files.

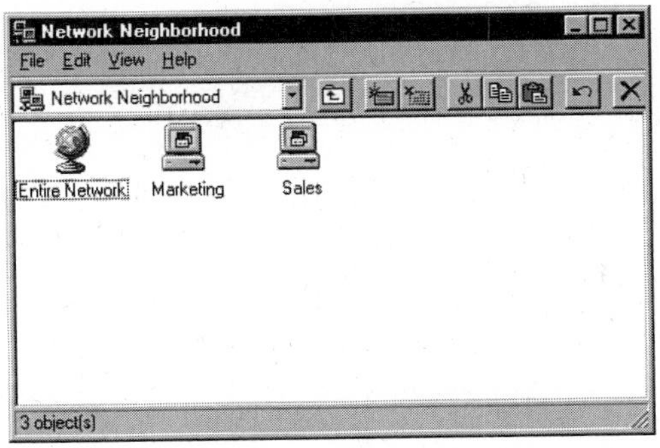

Fig. 17.39 The Network Neighborhood window displays all the resources on your network.

> **Note**
>
> If you have file sharing enabled for your computer, it will appear in Network Neighborhood. However, you can't access your own computer from within the Network Neighborhood. Use Explorer or My Computer to access your computer.

By default, each time you open a folder, a new window appears. This can result in a desktop full of windows and lots of confusion. If you prefer to have a single window open for browsing files, with the contents of that window changing as you open new folders, choose View, Options; and then click the Folder tab, select the Browse Folders by Using a Single Window option, and click OK.

Whether you use the Explorer or Network Neighborhood to work with the files on your network depends on your style of working. Try them both and see which works best for you.

Using My Computer to Manage Files

This chapter has focused on using the Windows Explorer to view and manage your files and folders. For seasoned users of earlier versions of Windows who are used to using File Manager to manage their files, the transition to using the Explorer should be smooth. And these users will appreciate the added power of the Explorer. The many shortcuts available using the right mouse button and Quick View are powerful features that make file management much quicker and easier with the Explorer.

New users of Windows may prefer to use My Computer to work with their files. My Computer is a folder containing folders for all the resources on your computer. When you first open My Computer, by double-clicking its icon on the desktop, the My Computer window displays an icon representing each of the resources on your computer, as shown in figure 17.40.

Fig. 17.40
The My Computer window is another way to view the files and folders on your computer.

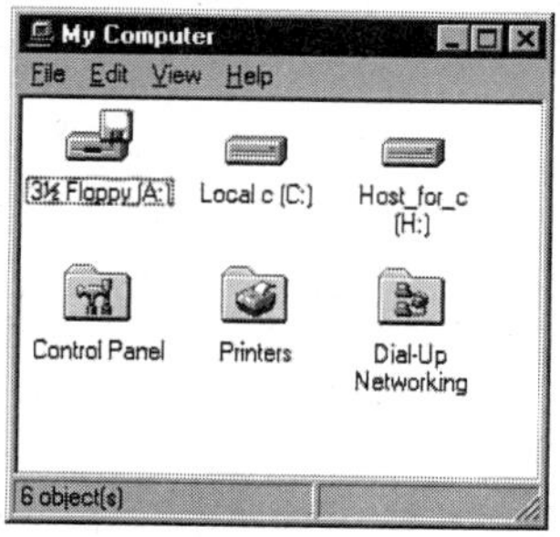

To look at the contents of a resource, double-click its folder. To view the folders on your hard drive, for example, double-click the hard disk icon. A new window opens, displaying the folders on your hard drive (see fig. 17.41). You can continue browsing through the folders on your computer by double-clicking any folder whose contents you want to view.

Fig. 17.41
You can browse through the folders in My Computer by double-clicking the folders whose contents you want to see.

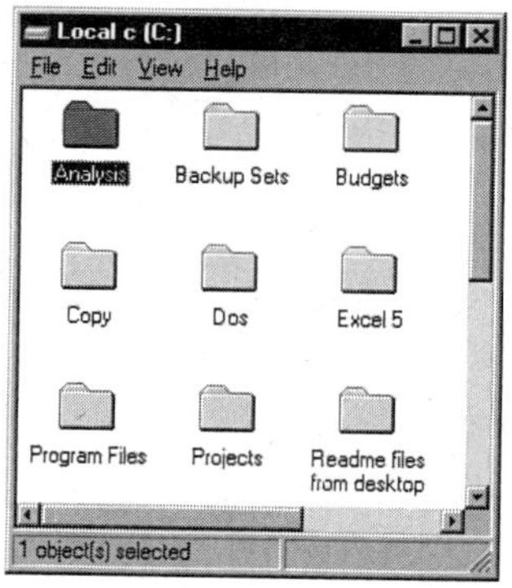

As you open up new windows in My Computer to view the contents of the different folders, you won't really have a sense of the organization of the folders the way you do in the Explorer. In the Explorer, you always have a map of the organization of your folders in the left pane. With My Computer, it is more difficult to visualize the hierarchical structure of your folders. If you don't think hierarchically, this may be a relief, as you may prefer to simply think of folders inside other folders that you open up one by one. You can move back through a series of opened folders by clicking the Up One Level button in the toolbar. This is a handy way to retrace your steps.

If you find it annoying to end up with layer upon layer of folder windows as you open the folders on your computer, you can choose to have the contents of a newly opened folder replace the current contents of the My Computer window, rather than open a new window. Choose View, Options and select the Browse Folders by Using a Single Window option. Now when you open a new folder, the folder's contents replace the contents of the current window. You can still use the Up One Level button to move back through a series of folders that you opened.

You can perform virtually all the file management tasks in My Computer that you learned to carry out in the Explorer. To manage your files in My Computer, use the same techniques described throughout this chapter. You can use either the menus or the mouse to open, move, copy, rename, delete, and preview your files. You can drag-and-drop files from one folder window to another. And all the shortcuts accessible with the right mouse button in the Explorer can also be used in My Computer. The display options described for customizing the Explorer work exactly the same way in My Computer as well.

As you work with Windows, you can decide whether you prefer to use the Explorer or My Computer to manage your files. You may find a combination of the two approaches works best for you. Because the commands are identical in both, you can move back and forth between the two with ease. Whichever approach you take, you will undoubtedly come to appreciate how easy it is to manage your files in Windows.❖

Chapter 18

Backing Up and Protecting Your Data

by Ron Person

Managing your files means more than just your daily work of creating, naming, and deleting files. If you consider your work valuable, part of your file management routine should be to back up your data by creating a duplicate copy.

The backup program that comes with Windows enables you to create backups onto a removable storage device such as floppy disks, a tape, or a removable hard disk. Windows also includes a virus protection program that can prevent viruses from entering your system and can remove them should they get onto the hard disk. In this chapter, you learn how to

- Copy one or more files from your hard disk to another disk (usually a floppy disk, a tape drive, or another computer on your network).
- Restore your backed-up files to any location you choose (including their original locations).
- Compare files on your backup disks with the original files to ensure their validity.

Backing Up Your Files

As you know, there is more information stored on your hard drive than you can possibly fit on a single floppy disk. The Windows Backup program automatically overcomes this problem by creating a duplicate image of your hard disk's data on a magnetic tape or by spreading an image across multiple floppy disks—as many as necessary to back up your data. During the backup operation, each disk in the set is filled to capacity before the next disk is requested. The collection of all these duplicate files and folders is referred to as the *backup set.*

As hard disks grow in capacity, it becomes more and more laborious to use floppy disks to back up your data. A much more convenient method is to use a tape backup system. You can fit much more data on a magnetic tape and may be able to back up your entire hard drive with one tape. With tape backups, you also avoid the inconvenience of having to sit at your computer swapping floppy disks. In fact, you can initiate the backup when you leave for lunch; when you return, it will be done.

Caution

You put the entire concept of having secure data at risk if your backups are not kept in a safe location, physically separate from the original data. For a small company, the physical location for the backup set can be a safe deposit box or the president's house. For a large company, there are services that pick up tapes and store them in disaster-proof vaults. I personally know of two instances in which the backups were lost along with the original system. In one case, a thief stole the backup floppy disks that sat next to the computer. In the other case, the fire that destroyed the legal firm's computers also destroyed their backups, which were in a closet in an adjacent room.

◀ See "Adding Windows' Component Applications," p. 312

Note

Backup does not install as part of a typical or minimum installation. If Backup is not installed and you want it, refer to Chapter 10, "Installing, Running, and Uninstalling Windows Applications," on how to add programs. On the Windows Setup page of the Add/Remove Programs Properties sheet, look for Backup in the Disk Tools items in the Components list.

Tip

Create a Full System Backup occasionally. It has all the configuration and registry files necessary to rebuild your system from a disaster.

To start the backup program, open the Start menu and click Programs, then Accessories, then System Tools, and finally Backup. When you first start Backup, you may see a Welcome to Microsoft Backup dialog box that describes the process of making backups. You can select the Don't Show This Again check box if you do not want to see this dialog box again. You also may see a message box that says `Backup has created a full system backup file set for you.` This means that until you specify otherwise, Backup marks all files and folders to be part of the backup. It is a very good idea to do a Full System Backup at least once a week or once a month, depending on the value of your data and how often program configurations change.

Once you are past these initial dialog boxes, the Backup dialog box appears, as shown in figure 18.1.

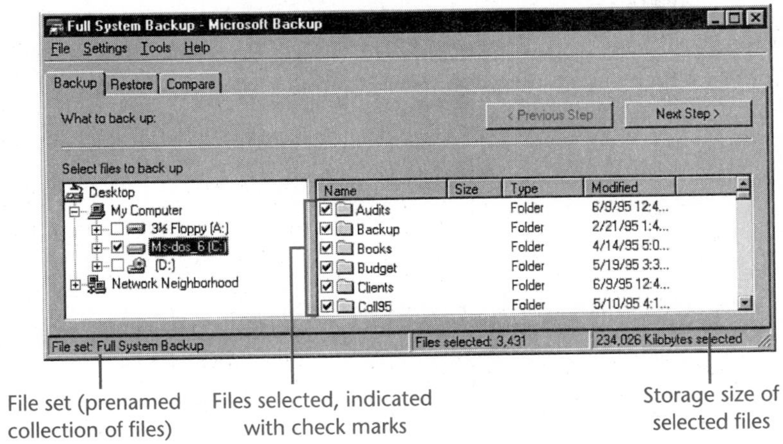

Fig. 18.1
Windows Backup creates duplicate copies of files and folders, compares backups to original files, and restores duplicate files and folders.

The three basic functions of Backup are divided into tabs in the Backup dialog box:

- *Backup*. Copies one or more files and folders from your hard disk.
- *Compare*. Compares the files in a backup set to make sure that they match the source files on the hard disk.
- *Restore*. Copies one or more files from your backup set to the hard disk or to another floppy disk.

In addition to these major functions, several other operations can be accessed from the pull-down menus:

- The File menu enables you to load and save setup files that define settings to be used when backing up and restoring files. The File menu also enables you to print a list of files contained in a backup set.
- The Settings, File Filtering command enables you to filter the folders or file types you want to include in a backup set (this command is discussed in detail later in this chapter). Using the Settings, Options command, you can set various options for each of the major functions, as well as options that affect the program generally.
- The Tools menu contains commands for working with tapes.

An Overview of How to Back Up Your Hard Disk

The Backup program makes it very easy to create backup sets of your data. No longer should you be put off from doing the important chore of backing up. Backup makes it easy to name different sets of backup files so that you don't have to select the files and folders each time. When you aren't using your computer (at lunch time, when you return phone messages, or when you leave work), you can start a backup.

Here is the general procedure for creating a backup:

1. Have enough formatted floppy disks or tapes to store the backup.
2. Start Windows Backup.
3. Select the name of a backup set you previously created. Alternatively, manually select the drives, files, and folders you want to back up.
4. Select the Next Step button, then select the destination to which you want to back up. This could be to a tape, a floppy disk drive, or to another hard disk.
5. Start the backup.

When Backup is finished, you should store the backup media in a safe location physically separate from the computers.

Tip
For an extensive list of tape drives compatible with Backup, choose Help, select the Contents tab, then select the Using Tapes for Backup item.

Windows Backup supports the following tape drives and backup devices:

- Hard disks
- Network drives
- Floppy disks
- QIC 40, 80, 3010, and 3020 tape drives connected to a primary floppy disk controller
- QIC 40, 80, and 3010 tape drives, manufactured by Colorado Memory Systems and connected to a parallel port

Backup supports compression using the industry standard QIC-113 format. It can read tapes from other backup programs that use the same format with or without compression. Full backups can be restored to a hard disk of another type.

Preparing a Backup Schedule

When you back up important or large amounts of data, it's important to have a backup schedule and a rotation plan for the backup tapes.

Tip
Creating a full backup is important to preserving your entire system. Full backups take care of merging Registry settings and the file replacements necessary when restoring a Windows system.

Basically, the backup schedule for most businesses should consist of a full system backup followed by partial or differential backups spread over time. Should your computer ever completely fail, you can rebuild your system using the full backup (which restores Windows, the system Registry, all applications, and their data files as they existed on a specific date). You can then use the partial or differential backups (which store only changed files) to bring the restored system back to its current status. Do a full system backup once a week and a differential backup daily.

Never use one set of tapes for all your backups. If you have only one set of tapes, composed of a full backup and partials, creating another backup means that you overwrite one of the previous backups. Should the tape or computer fail during backup, you might be left with no backups capable of restoring your system.

Some companies create a full system backup every day. At the end of the week, the tapes are taken to an off-site vault and a new set of tapes are started. Multiple sets of backup tapes are used and rotated between the on-site and off-site storage locations.

Backing Up Files

Running a backup operation consists of selecting the files you want to back up, specifying the destination for the backup files, and starting the backup. The files that you select for backup will be stored in a single backup file with the extension QIC. To perform a backup, follow these steps:

Tip
Whenever you frequently work with the same files and settings, save them as a file set.

1. Open the Start menu, click Programs, Accessories, System Tools, and then Backup.
2. Select the drive containing the files you want to back up. To select the drive, click the check box for the drive in the left pane of the Backup window.

   In figure 18.1, local drive C is selected. The files and folders on the drive are displayed in the right pane. You can expand and collapse the hierarchical display in the left pane by clicking the plus (+) and minus (–) signs next to the folders.
3. Select the files and folders you want to back up. If you want to back up using a file set you have previously named, choose File, Open File Set and select the file set you want to back up.

▶ See "Saving File Sets," p. 563

You can select all the files in a folder by clicking the check box next to the folder's name in the left pane of the Backup dialog box.

To view the files and folders inside a folder, in the left pane, open the folder containing the folders or files you want to view. Then in the left pane, click the name of the folder whose contents you want to see; its contents are displayed in the right pane. You can then select individual files or folders inside that folder.

To select the entire drive, click the box next to the drive in the left pane.

If you select a folder with many files, a File Selection dialog box momentarily appears, notifying you that file selection is in progress; the box displays the number of files and their total size as the selection progresses.

The total number of files currently selected and their cumulative size appears in the status bar at the bottom of the window.

4. When you have finished selecting the files and folders you want to back up, click the Next Step button.

5. Select the destination for the backup files (see fig. 18.2).

   If you select a tape drive, the volume name for that tape appears in the Selected Device or Location box. If you select a disk drive, this box shows the drive letter or path, such as A:\.

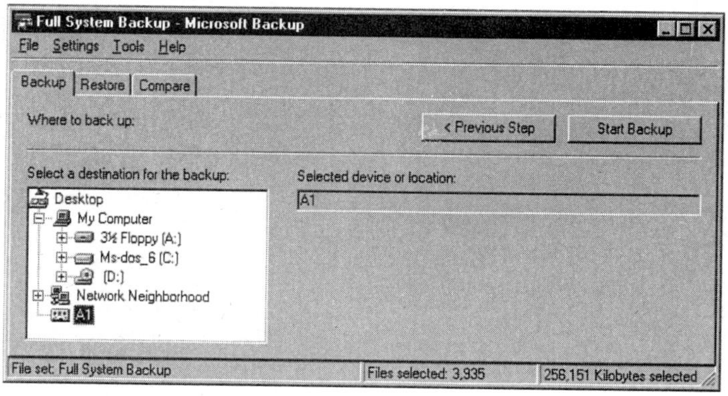

Fig. 18.2
Select the destination for the files you want to back up.

6. Save the file settings for this backup set if you will be doing this backup frequently (see "Saving File Sets," later in this chapter, for more information on saving backup sets).

7. Click the Start Backup button.
8. Type a name for the backup set in the Backup Set Label dialog box that appears (see fig. 18.3). This will be the name of the file containing all the files you have selected for backup.

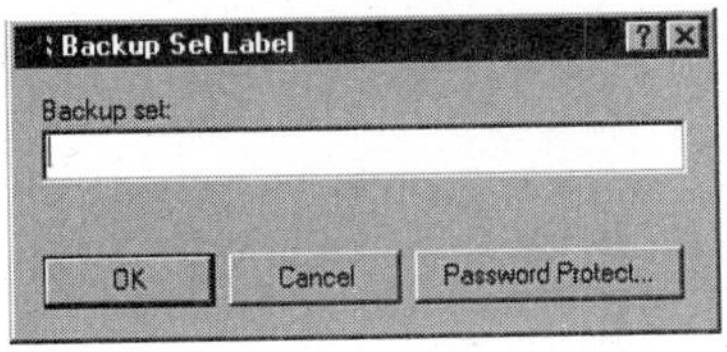

Fig. 18.3
Name the backup set in the Backup Set Label dialog box.

If you want to prevent unauthorized people from restoring the backup and stealing your data, click the Password Protect button in the Backup Set Label dialog box and enter a password.

The name you enter for the backup set is used by you and the computer to identify the data if you ever need to restore or compare it. You can use meaningful names that include spaces, symbols, and numbers. You may want to use a name such as *Accounting, full backup 5/10/95*.

Caution

Do not forget the password you assign to your backup set. Without it, there is no way to use your backup.

When you have specified a backup label and an optional password, choose OK. The Backup message box appears (see fig. 18.4), showing you the progress of the backup operation. You can cancel the operation by choosing the Cancel button.

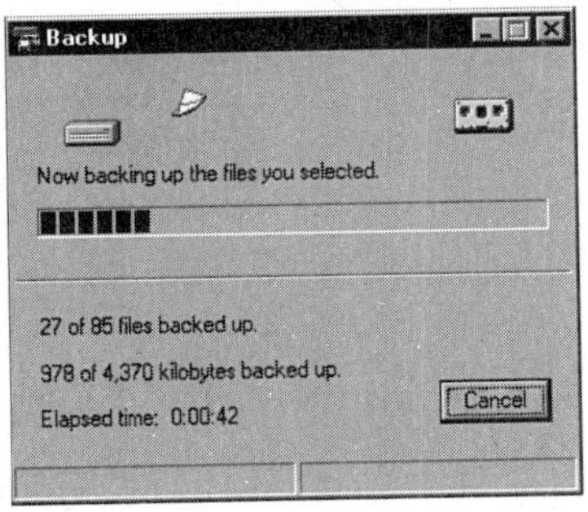

Fig. 18.4
You can monitor the progress of a backup operation in the Backup message box.

If you are backing up to floppy disks, a message box prompts you when you need to insert the next disk, if necessary.

9. When the message box appears informing you that the backup operation is complete, click OK; click OK again to return to the Backup dialog box.

Using Backup to Create an Archive

The Backup program is a handy way to archive files. Suppose that you want to make room on your hard disk by deleting some files you are not currently using but want to use at a later date. Use Backup to archive the files to floppy disks or a tape; then delete the files from the hard disk. If you need the files later, use the restore function to put them back on your hard disk.

Using Backup to Copy Files to Another Computer

▶ See "Restoring Files," p. 566

Another use for Backup is for transferring folders and files to another computer. The benefit of using Backup for this task is that it takes care of spreading the files across multiple floppy disks when necessary, and it preserves the arrangement of folders, so that you can duplicate your folder organization on another computer. If you purchase a laptop, for example, you can use Backup to transfer the information on your desktop computer to the laptop, including the arrangement of your folders.

Changing Backup Settings and Options

You can change several settings and options that affect your backup operations. To change the settings and options for the backup operation, follow these steps:

1. Open the Settings menu and choose Options.
2. Click the Backup tab to display the dialog box shown in figure 18.5.
3. Change or select from the following options and then choose OK:

Option	Function
Quit Backup After Operation Is Finished	Closes Backup when the backup operation is completed.
Full: Backup of All Selected Files	Backs up all selected files, regardless of whether file has changed since the last backup.
Differential: Backup of Selected Files that Have Changed Since the Last Full Backup	Backs up only selected files that have changed since the last full backup.

Option	Function
Verify Backup Data by Automatically Comparing Files After Backup Is Finished	Compares each file that is backed up with the original file to verify accurate backup.
Use Data Compression	Compresses files as they are backed up to allow more files to be backed up on a tape or floppy disk.
Format when Needed on Tape Backups	Automatically formats an unused tape before backup operation. This only works on tapes that have not already been formatted.
Always Erase on Tape Backups	Erases the tape on backup. When this option is not selected, backups are added to the tape if there is room.
Always Erase on Floppy Disk Backups	Automatically erases floppy disks before they are used in a floppy disk backup operation. When this option is not selected, backups are added to the floppy disk if there is room.

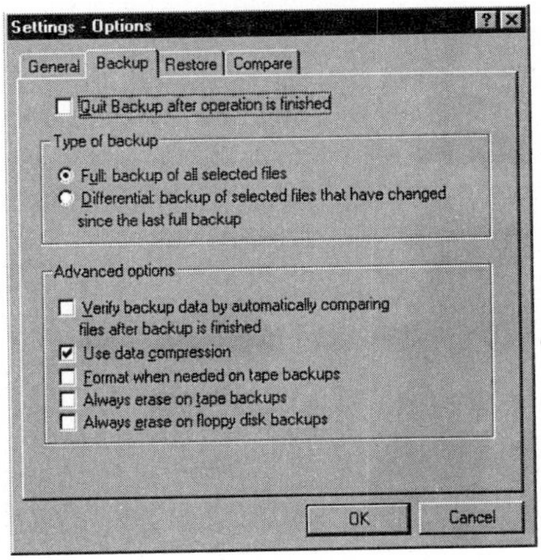

Fig. 18.5
Use the Backup tab in the Settings—Options dialog box to change the settings and options that affect the way backup operations work.

Saving File Sets

If you back up the same set of files regularly, you can save the settings for that file set. Saving backup settings saves you the trouble of reselecting the files and destination each time you want to back up the files.

To save a file set, follow these steps:

1. Open the Backup program. On the Backup page select the files you want to back up, as described earlier in this chapter. Click the Next Step button.

2. Select the destination for the backup files from the Select a Destination list.

3. Choose File, Save As. The Save As dialog box appears (see fig. 18.6).

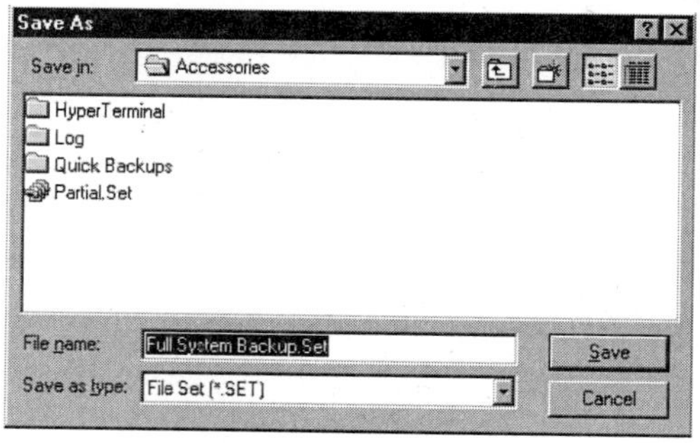

Fig. 18.6
Name your file set with a recognizable name for what it contains and when it was created.

4. Type a name for the backup set in the File Name text box.

5. Choose the Save button.

6. Choose the Start Backup button if you want to continue the backup operation and create a backup using the file set you just specified.

If you make changes to an existing file set, choose the File, Save command to save the file set with the same name without opening the Save As dialog box.

To open a file set for use in a backup operation, follow these steps:

1. Open the Backup program, and then click on the Backup tab. Choose File, Open File Set to display the Open dialog box shown in figure 18.7.

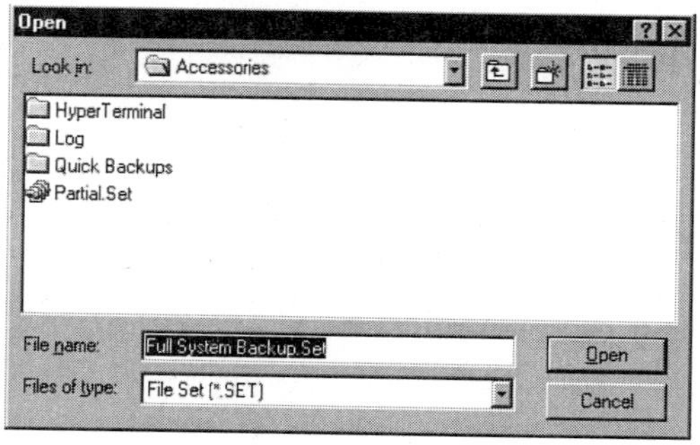

Fig. 18.7
Open a file set to use in a backup or restore operation from the Open dialog box.

2. If you cannot see the file set you want to open, open the folder that contains the file set.

3. Select the file set and choose Open.

The file set is opened, and the files named in this file set are selected in the Backup dialog box.

Filtering Folders and File Types Included in Backup Operations

Backup's file-filtering commands enable you to filter out specific folders and types of files so that they are not included in the backup set. These commands can save you a lot of time when you are creating a file set to be backed up.

You may not want to include all the files on your hard disk in a backup operation. In some cases, you may want to back up all but a few folders; it is easier to specify the folders you *don't* want to include in the backup set than to select all the folders you do want to include. You may not want to include program files in your daily backups because you can always reinstall your programs if your system crashes. You can dramatically reduce the number of disks you use in a backup if you limit the file set to data files only.

To exclude files of a specific type or date from a backup, follow these steps:

1. Choose Settings, File Filtering. The File Filtering—File Types dialog box appears, as shown in figure 18.8.

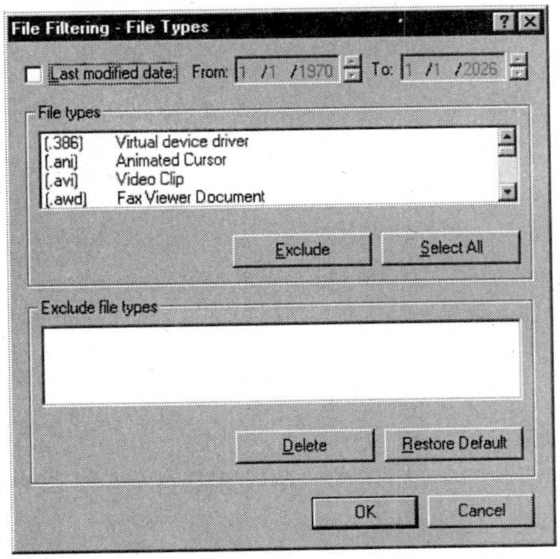

Fig. 18.8
You can exclude files of a specific type or files with specific dates.

2. To exclude files modified between two dates, select the Last Modified Date check box. Enter From and To dates that *exclude* the files you do not want copied. Click the insertion point in the date segment you want to change and then click the up or down spinner arrow to change the date.

Tip
If you want to exclude all but a few of the file types in the File Types list, click Select All, and then click the types of files you don't want to exclude.

For example, if you want to exclude files before November 30, 1995, enter a From date of 1/1/1970 and a To date of 11/30/95.

3. To exclude specific file types from the backup operation, select the types of files you want to exclude from the File Types list and click Exclude. Continue to select file types and click the Exclude button until all the file types you want to exclude appear in the Exclude File Types list at the bottom of the dialog box.

   To select all of the file types in the list, click Select All.

4. To delete a file type from the list in the Exclude File Types box, select the file type and click Delete.
5. To clear the Exclude File Types box, click Restore Default.
6. When you finish making your selections, choose OK.

Restoring Files

If you're lucky, you may never have to use Backup's restore function. When you do need it, however, it's as easy to use as the backup function. You can restore all the files from a backup set or select specific files or folders to restore. You can also choose where you want to restore the files.

To restore files, follow these steps:

1. Open the Backup program and click the Restore tab (see fig. 18.9).

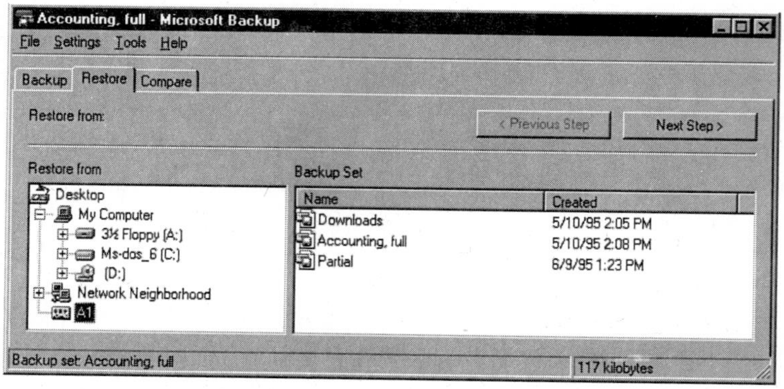

Fig. 18.9
In the Restore tab of the Backup dialog box, select the files you want to restore.

2. Select the drive containing the backup files from the left panel of the window. In figure 18.9, the tape drive has been selected as the backup source.

3. Select the backup set containing the files you want to restore from the right pane. If you have more than one backup file on a floppy disk or tape, select the one containing the files you want to restore. A single backup file, with the extension QIC, contains the files you backed up.

4. Click the Next Step button.

5. Select the folders or files you want to restore as shown in figure 18.10.

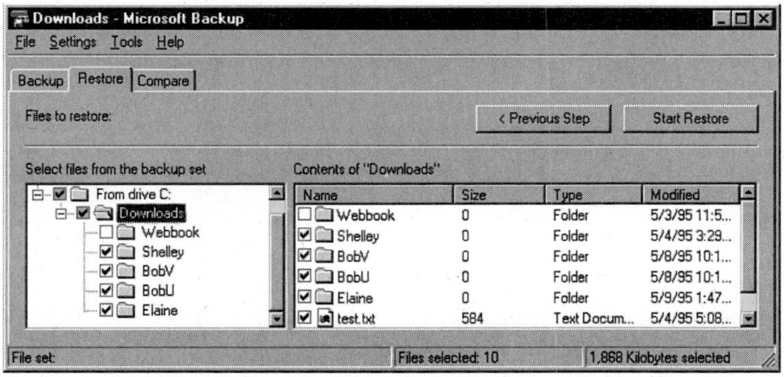

Fig. 18.10
You can select all or part of a backup set when you restore.

6. Click the Start Restore button. The Restore message box appears, showing you the progress of the restore operation (see fig. 18.11).

   By default, the files are restored to their original location. You can choose to restore the files to another location by changing one of the restore options, as described below.

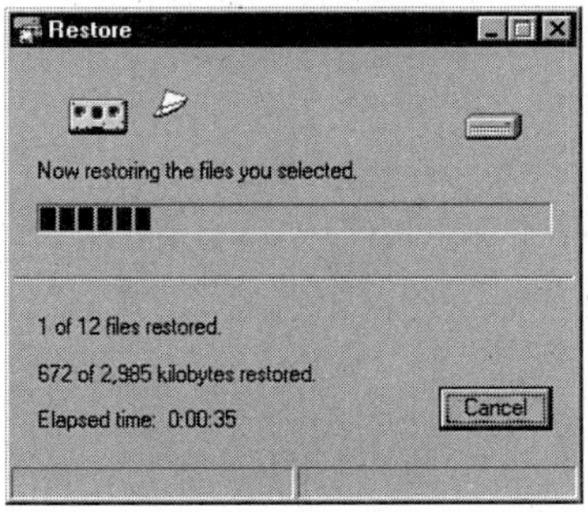

Fig. 18.11
The Restore message box tells you how the restore operation is progressing.

7. When the Operation Complete message box appears, choose OK.

Restoring Files to Other Locations

You can restore files to a location other than their original location (the location from which they were initially backed up). To restore files to an alternate location, follow these steps:

1. Choose Settings, Options.
2. Click the Restore tab.
3. Select the Alternate Location option and choose OK.
4. Perform steps 1 through 6 of the restore procedure described in the preceding section (stop just before you have to click the Start Restore button).
5. Click the Start Restore button. The Browse for Folder dialog box appears (see fig. 18.12).

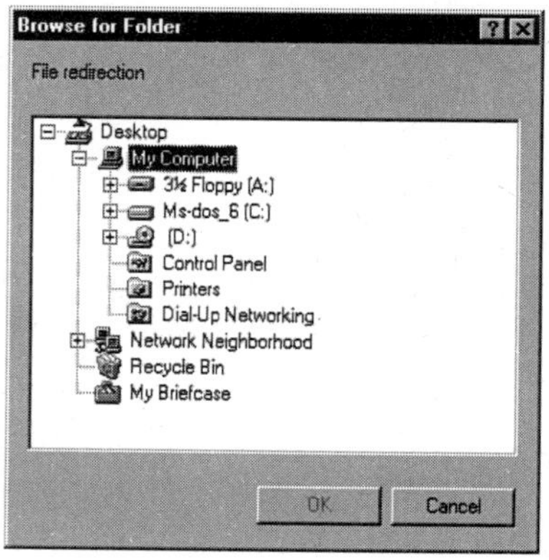

Fig. 18.12
Select the location to which you want to restore files from the File Redirection box.

6. Select the location to which you want to restore the files and choose OK.
7. When the Operation Complete message box appears, choose OK.

Changing Restore Settings and Options

You can change several settings and options that affect your restore operations. To change the settings and options for the restore function, follow these steps:

1. Choose Settings, Options.
2. Click the Restore tab to display the dialog box shown in figure 18.13.

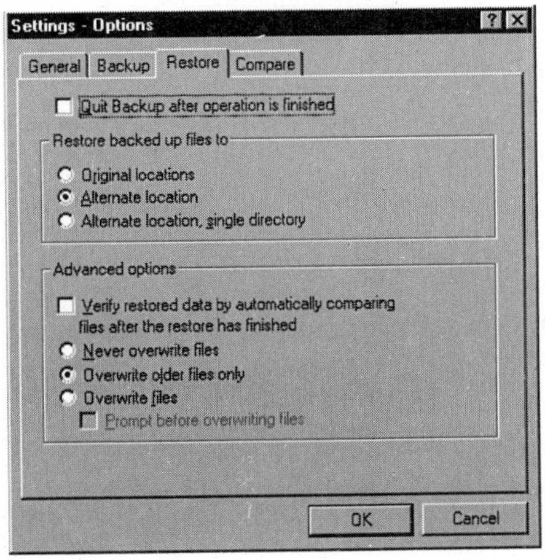

Fig. 18.13
Use the Restore tab in the Settings–Options dialog box to change the settings and options that affect the way restore operations work.

3. Change or select from the following options and then choose OK:

Option	Function
Quit Backup after Operation Is Complete	Closes Backup when the restore operation is completed.
Original Locations	Restores files to their original locations.
Alternate Location	Restores files to an alternate location. (See "Restoring Files to Other Locations," earlier in this chapter.)
Alternate Location, Single Directory	Restores files to a single directory at an alternate location. Doesn't duplicate original folder structure.
Verify Restored Data by Automatically Comparing Files after the Restore Has Finished	Compares each file to file on disk or tape after it is restored to check for accuracy of restore.
Never Overwrite Files	Files that are already on the destination location are not overwritten during a restore operation.
Overwrite Older Files Only	Only files that are older than the files in the backup set are overwritten during a restore operation.
Overwrite Files	All files are overwritten during a restore operation. Use the Prompt Before Overwriting Files check box to specify whether you want to be prompted before a file is overwritten.

Verifying Backup Files

The first time you use a series of disks or a tape for a backup, or any time you want to be absolutely sure of your backup, you should do a comparison. When you compare backups to the original files, you verify that the backup copies are both readable and accurate. To perform a compare, follow these steps:

1. Open the Backup program and click the Compare tab.
2. From the left pane, select the device containing the backup files you want to compare (see fig. 18.14).

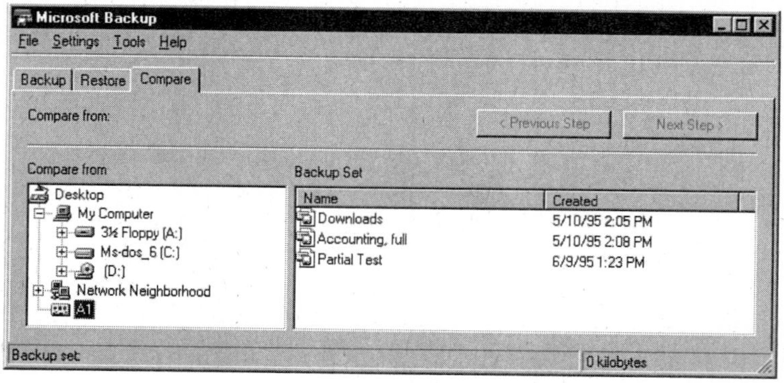

Fig. 18.14
Use the Compare function to verify the accuracy of your backup operations.

3. From the right pane, select the backup set containing the files you want to compare.
4. Click the Next Step button.
5. Select the files or folders you want to compare to the original files.
6. Click the Start Compare button. The Compare message box informs you of the progress of the compare operation.
7. Choose OK when the Operation Complete message box appears; choose OK again to return to the Backup dialog box.

Changing Compare Settings and Options

You can change several settings and options that affect your compare operations. To change the settings and options for the compare function, follow these steps:

1. Choose Settings, Options.
2. Click the Compare tab to display the dialog box shown in figure 18.15.

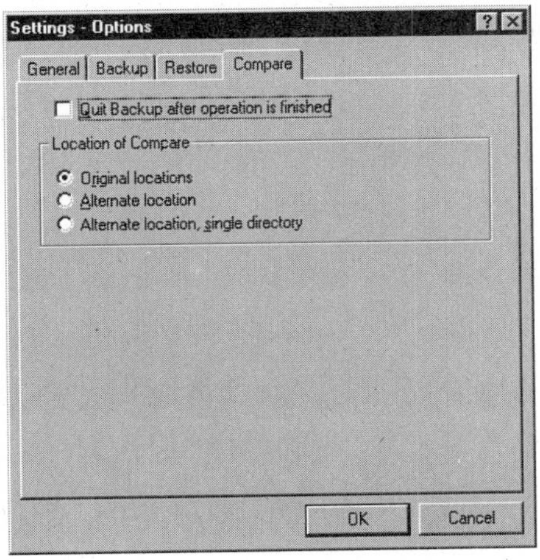

Fig. 18.15
Use the Compare tab in the Settings—Options dialog box to change the settings and options that affect the way compare operations work.

3. Change or select from the following options and then choose OK:

Option	Function
Quit Backup after Operation Is Finished	Closes Backup when the compare operation is completed.
Original Locations	Compare files to files at their original locations.
Alternate Location	Compares files to files at an alternate location.
Alternate Location, Single Directory	Compare files to files in a single directory at an alternate location. Doesn't look for duplicates of the original folder structure.

Changing the General Settings in Backup

You can change two options in Backup that affect the backup, restore, and compare functions. To change these options, choose Settings, Options. Select the General tab to display the dialog box shown in figure 18.16.

- Select the Turn on Audible Prompts option if you want to hear beeps from your computer's speaker during backup, compare, and restore operations.
- Select the Overwrite Old Status Log Files option to replace the old status log with the new one generated by the current backup. The status log records errors and completions of file backups.

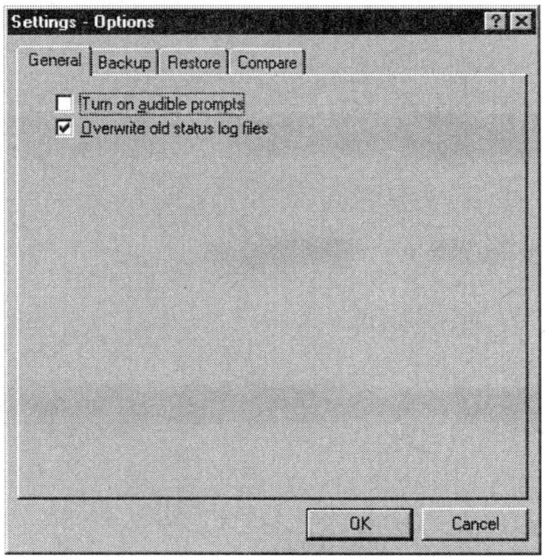

Fig. 18.16
Use the General tab in the Settings—Options dialog box to change the settings and options that affect the way Backup's operations work.

Backing Up with a Simple Drag-and-Drop

Once you understand the importance of backing up files and see how easy it is to do, you will back up frequently. There is an easy way to back up your files if you have created file sets (as described earlier in this chapter). You can drag a file set and drop it onto the Backup icon or you can double-click a file set name. Either of these actions immediately starts the backup. With the appropriate settings, the entire backup operation can go on in the background and you can continue to use the computer for other tasks.

Tip
Experienced Windows users may want to set up other users' computers with drag-and-drop backup so they can easily protect their data.

To prepare Backup for drag-and-drop operation, follow these steps:

1. Choose Settings, Drag and Drop to display the Drag and Drop dialog box shown in figure 18.17.

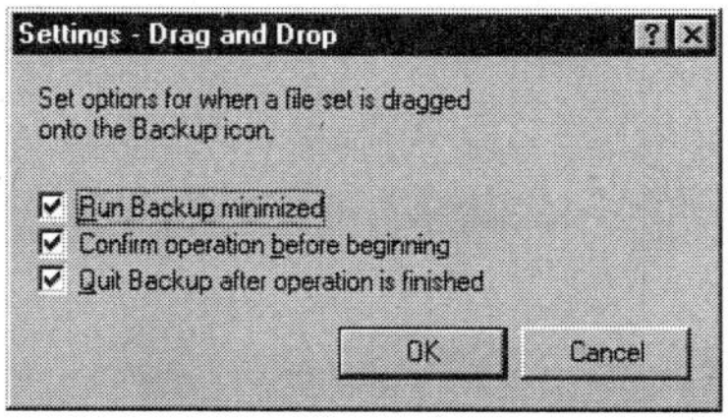

Fig. 18.17
Change the Backup settings to make drag-and-drop backup operate in the background while you work.

2. Change or select from the following options and then choose OK:

Option	Function
Run Backup Minimized	After dragging a file set onto the Backup icon, the Backup window minimizes.

Option	Function
Confirm Operation Before Beginning	Displays a message showing which files will be backed up. Asks you to confirm that you want the files backed up.
Quit Backup after Operation Is Finished	Quits Backup after the file set is backed up.

If Backup is operating in the background, you do not see it as a window on-screen. If you need to stop a backup that is in the background, display the taskbar and click the Backup button. A dialog box displays the current backup status and gives you the opportunity to Cancel the backup.

Note

If you have multiple file sets, but you don't want them all as Shortcuts on your desktop, you can still start them quickly to do a backup. In the Windows Explorer or My Computer window, double-click the name of the file set you want to back up. You are prompted whether you want to make a backup; the backup runs with the settings specified for that file set.

Before you can create backups with a drag-and-drop procedure, you must display the Backup program icon. You can open the Program Files/ Accessories folder in a window in the Windows Explorer or My Computer. A more convenient method is to create a shortcut to BACKUP.EXE and display it on your desktop.

If you also want a quick way to find and display the SET files that specify your file sets, create a shortcut to the directory containing the SET files. You can do this by using the Find command (available on the Start menu) to find all files that end with SET. Create a new folder and drag the SET files into the new folder. Now create a shortcut to this folder and put that shortcut on the desktop (see fig. 18.18). (Creating shortcuts is described in Chapter 3, "Getting Started with Windows 95.")

◀ See "Starting Programs from a Shortcut Icon on the Desktop," p. 68

Note

Normally, the file sets are stored in the Program Files\Accessories folder. If you are unsure where your backup file sets are stored on your hard disk, open the Start menu and choose Find. Search for all files ending with .SET by entering ***.SET** in the Named box.

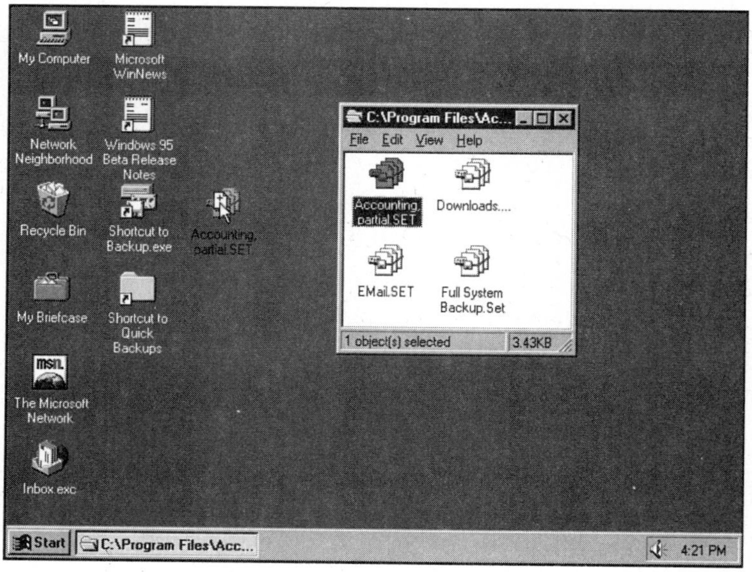

Fig. 18.18
Once drag-and-drop is enabled, backing up is as easy as dropping a file-set icon onto the Backup shortcut.

To back up a file set, you only need to double-click the shortcut to the folder containing the file sets. This opens the folder containing the file sets as a Window on your desktop. Figure 18.18 shows such an open folder. Now drag the file set you want to back up onto the shortcut to BACKUP.EXE and drop it. You are prompted whether you want to continue with the backup operation. Respond by clicking Yes or No.

Formatting and Erasing Tapes

If you use tapes to do your backups, Backup includes two tools for working with tapes. When you purchase a new tape, you must format the tape before you can use it, just as you format a floppy disk. The Format Tape command formats a tape for you. If you want to erase the contents on a tape before you use it for a new backup operation, you can use the Erase Tape command.

To format a tape, follow these steps:

1. Insert the tape in the tape drive.

2. Open the Backup program and choose Tools, Format Tape. If the Format Tape command is grayed out, choose the Redetect Tape command, which enables Backup to detect the tape.

3. When the Format Tape dialog box appears (see fig. 18.19), type a name for the tape and choose OK. You use this name to identify the tape relative to other tapes you use.

Formatting begins. The progress of the formatting operation is displayed in the Format Tape dialog box.

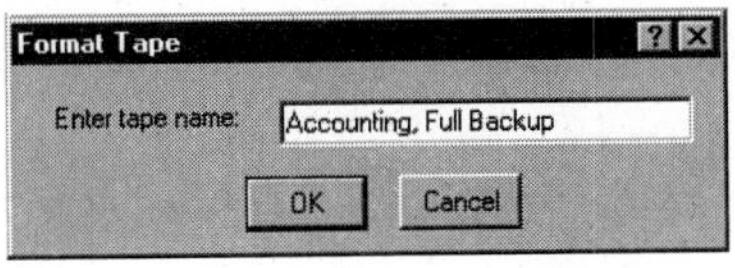

Fig. 18.19
Enter a name for the tape you are formatting in the Format Tape dialog box.

4. When the message box appears telling you the operation is complete, choose OK; choose OK again to return to the Backup dialog box.

To erase a tape, follow these steps:

1. Insert the tape in the tape drive.
2. Open the Backup dialog box and choose Tools, Erase Tape. If the Erase Tape command is grayed out, choose the Redetect Tape command, which enables Backup to detect the tape.
3. Choose Yes when the confirmation message box appears. The progress of the erase operation is displayed in the Erase dialog box.
4. When the message box appears telling you the operation is complete, choose OK; choose OK again to return to the Backup dialog box.

Protecting Your Files from Viruses

You need to take measures for protecting your computer against viruses, a scourge of the modern day computer world. In addition to backing up your system regularly, you should obtain an anti-virus program and make a habit of using it on a regular basis to protect your files against infection, especially if you frequently introduce files onto your hard disk from outside sources.

Understanding How Viruses Hurt Your Computer

A *computer virus* is a program designed to do damage to either your computer or your computer's data. Viruses make copies of themselves and spread from one computer to another, just as they do in people. Just as fitness, good food, and medicine can protect you from sickness, you can use an anti-virus program to protect your computer from a virus.

The best method of protection is prevention. There are only two ways in which viruses can be transmitted between computers:

- Loading and running infected software
- Booting up with an infected floppy disk

If you don't do either of these things, your system won't acquire a virus. But because such an insulated approach to computers is virtually impossible, you should consider using an anti-virus program. Used correctly, a good anti-virus program can protect you against the vast majority of known viruses before they damage your computer.❖

Part V

Networking with Windows 95

Regional New Home Sales
1991
1992
1993
HOMESLS.XLC
(GMT-05:00) Eastern Time (US & Canada)
Orientation
Portrait
Landscape
Display Properties
Background
Screen Saver
Appearance
Settings
Inactive Window
Active Window
Normal
Disabled
Selected
Window Text
Message Box
Message Text
OK
Scheme:
Windows Standard
Save As...
Item:
Desktop
Size:
Font:
Cancel
5:39 PM
Budget
Proposals
Cost Estimates.xls
Note.txt
Proposal for Hodgkins
334KB
Browse...
Exchange
Figures
My Documents
Winlogo - Paint
File
Edit
View
Image
Options
Help
Tools
Compose
Name
Programs
Documents
Settings
Find
Run...
Shut Down...
Windows95
Start
Insert
Format
Table
Window
1/1
At 1"
Ln 1
Col 1
Book2
Data
Sheet2
Sheet3
Sheet4
Sheet5
Sheet6
The Microsoft Network
3:10 PM
My Briefcase
Inbox
Calendar - [Untitled]

Chapter 19

Understanding Networks

by Michael Marchuk

This chapter is dedicated to discussing the basics of networking. Although many people might use computers on a network at work, the concepts behind the system are still unfamiliar. By reviewing the ideas presented in this chapter, you can understand how your computers share information on a basic level. Understanding these basic networking concepts will enable you to participate with other users in your workgroup to design and maintain the best possible network for your situation.

Specifically, this chapter addresses

- The importance of networking in today's businesses
- The basic concepts that make your network run
- The four building blocks of the Windows networking architecture
- Sharing network resources

The Value of Networks in Business Computing

Networking computers together to share information is not a new phenomenon. In fact, universities and the government have been doing it for several decades. Even some large corporations have been involved with networking their computer resources for 20 or more years. But some companies, both large and small, are still relatively new to networking.

Computing without Networks

With the introduction of the PC in the early 1980s, many companies began to realize the benefits of computers within their own businesses. For the first time, computing power was available to companies that didn't have the personnel to staff mainframe operations. Spreadsheet and word processing software became the software of choice in the workplace.

However, as companies bought more computers for their staff, the complications of sharing the information became more difficult. Sharing a data file with someone else in the office meant making a copy of the current file and putting it on a disk. Even this method of file sharing was sufficient when there were few computers. But spreadsheet files began to get larger than one disk could hold and disk-swapping became cumbersome in larger companies. Additionally, since printers were still relatively expensive, they were often either wheeled around on carts, or set up at one computer which was designated as the "print station" for a department.

Businesses needed a way to share information quickly without the need for disks and to share printers without the need for a printer station. In time, the problems and solutions encountered by businesses became common to the PC market.

Business Networking Evolves

The networks of computers that evolved allowed businesses to spend more time working on their data than moving hardware or disks between offices. Networks with central servers could offer hundreds of megabytes of storage that could be shared with others in the office. Expensive printers could be centrally managed by the network server that provided faster printing.

Information sharing within this environment has continued to progress to the point where spreadsheets between departments or divisions can be merged to provide a better picture of their company's health. For example, daily store receipts can be analyzed at the end of each day to provide an up-to-date picture of sales projections, inventory amounts can be managed for many locations using centralized warehouses for distributing products, and customers can be informed about new products and services using fax-back or recorded message systems run by computers.

Inter-Business Networking

Networking continues to expand its importance within the business environment. With Electronic Data Interchange (EDI), businesses can maintain acceptable inventory levels by ordering raw materials from suppliers electronically. Also, many banks are beginning to offer businesses account management software to handle banking transactions through their computer networks.

Another network that is quickly becoming the most important business tool is the world-wide network known as the Internet. Businesses on the Internet can transfer data files with branch offices world-wide as easily as they could exchange data with someone in the local office. Additionally, office workers who once were required to be at an office can now be spread across the globe to handle customer requests for account information.

Future Business Networking

As businesses continue to grow, their physical office space becomes more expensive. Adding workers to handle the workload of increased sales often means moving to larger facilities. But some businesses are beginning to experiment with new networking concepts that will help them maintain a competitive advantage.

Telecommuting

Office workers that handle functions, such as data entry, customer support, accounting, or other tasks, can often do the same work from home as they can from the office. These workers don't physically commute to their offices, rather they use the phone lines to connect into the company's network. These workers are called *telecommuters*. The network saves the business expensive office space as well as providing the worker with the comfort of a home setting in which to work. The jury is still out on this subject, but initial indications show that some workers are more productive at home than at the office.

Video Conferencing

Businesses also are looking into the realm of *video conferencing*, which allows meetings to occur between many people in different parts of the world. Cameras and microphones at each user's workstation transmit their images to the other participants which in turn are seen on the user's workstation. These types of meetings could save businesses a considerable amount of time and travel expenses.

Online Shopping

Shopping from home via catalogs, mail-order, and cable television is a multibillion dollar business. Some companies are beginning to see computer networks as an extension of this market. By promoting and selling through a world-wide network, such as the Internet, companies can lower their costs of doing business while providing the customers with the goods and services they want. This type of networking opportunity is still in its infancy, but a considerable amount of work is being done to make shopping through your computer more convenient.

Approaches to Networks

A network is a way of connecting individual computers so they can share resources. These resources include items such as disk drives, files (databases), printers, and communications equipment. In addition, the network enables greater interaction and communication between the members of the network by using electronic mail, databases, and other data sharing.

The computers connected to a network are called *nodes*. If the nodes are in close proximity (typically within a building) to each other, the network is called a *local area network*, or *LAN*. If the nodes are more widely dispersed (across the state, nation, or world), the network is called a *wide area network*, or *WAN*. If you are using Windows 95, you typically are connected to a LAN, which is the focus of this chapter.

LAN networking uses two general approaches, both of which Windows 95 supports. These approaches are client/server and peer-to-peer networks.

Client/Server Networks

Client/server networks use a dedicated computer (the server) that centrally handles all file and print services for many users. A network may have many servers to handle file and print sharing for specific groups of users or to handle database services for the network.

The clients on the network are *workstations* that connect to the server. Client workstations are typically computers at a worker's desk that they use for spreadsheet or word-processing tasks. Network clients can print to the server's printer or save files to the server's hard drive. Figure 19.1 shows an example of a client/server network.

While clients in a client/server network may be powerful machines used for heavy-duty spreadsheet calculations, they also can be low-powered PC's that are only used for word-processing tasks. Servers, on the other hand, are typically powerful machines that are optimized for providing the fastest response to network clients and the most protection for the network's data. Additionally, since servers must be able to handle the requests of many clients simultaneously and secure the network data from unauthorized users, the server has to run an advanced operating system that is dedicated for this purpose. Some of the client/server operating systems that Windows 95 can connect to include:

- Novell NetWare
- Windows NT Server
- IBM OS/2 LAN Server
- Banyan Vines

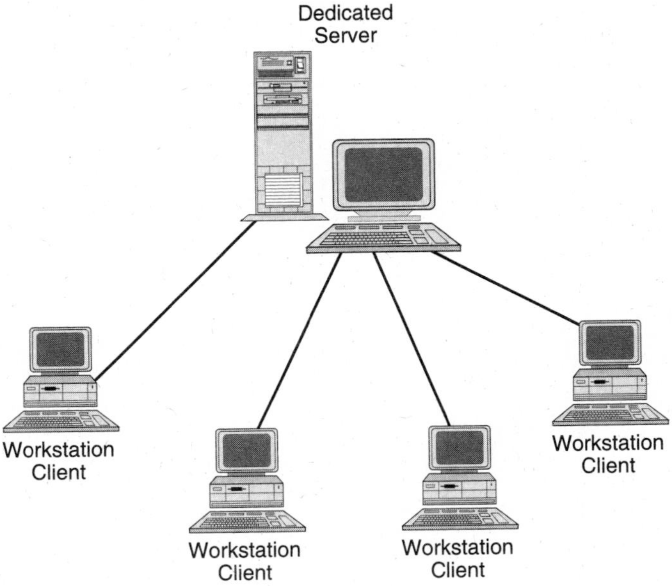

Fig. 19.1
Clients access a dedicated server in a client/server network.

Peer-to-Peer Networks

Peer-to-peer networks do not use a central server to store files or to host printers. In a peer-to-peer network, the workstations share hard drives and printers, acting as part-time servers (see fig. 19.2). In addition to providing computing services to the user at a workstation, the computer must service file and print requests from other computers on the network. Of course, if a workstation is not sharing a printer or any hard drive space, then the workstation acts only as a client to another workstation that provides file and print services on the network. Windows 95 has built-in peer-to-peer networking capabilities.

Caution

While peer-to-peer networks offer great flexibility because any workstation can share printers or hard drive space, low-powered workstations can easily become overloaded with tasks related to both sharing resources and performing work tasks for the local user. If you plan on sharing your printer or hard drive with others on the network, expect to see some performance degradation with your local tasks when others are printing or sharing files on your system. If your computer is sluggish all of the time while sharing resources, you may need to consider moving the shared resources to another workstation with a more powerful CPU, dedicating a workstation as a server, or purchasing a client/server network that can handle the load.

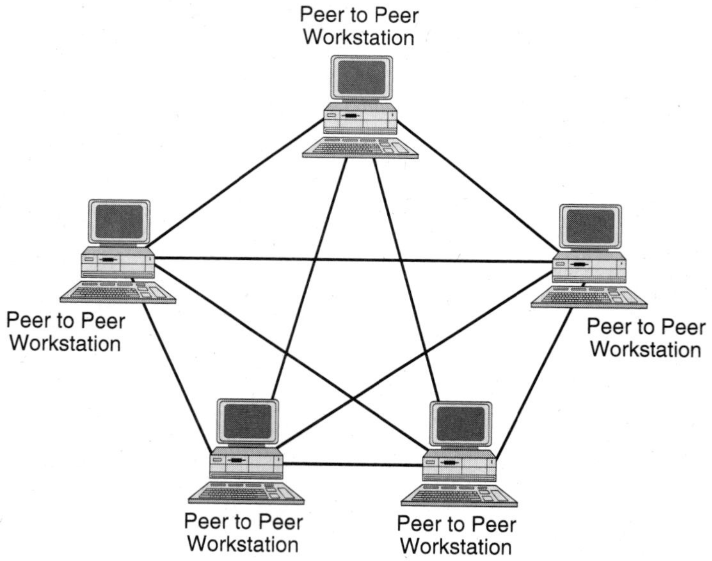

Fig. 19.2
Peer-to-peer networks enable workstations to be both clients and servers on the network.

Although the peer-to-peer networking functions are built into Windows, you may need to connect to one of several other peer-to-peer networks. Other peer-to-peer networks supported by Windows 95 include:

- NetWare Lite
- Artisoft LANtastic

The Different Layers of a Network

In the world of networking, the concept of *one size fits all* does not apply. Each network can be tailored to fit the needs of the company using different technologies to assemble the right network. This section focuses on the various types of networks and the advantages and disadvantages of each.

You can think of networking as many different layers of software that interact with the hardware connecting computers together. The Open Systems Interconnect (OSI) networking model breaks networking into seven layers to illustrate this concept. This discussion is going to present the five layers that most users have the highest need to understand. To begin, try to conceptualize two basic layers on which the communication of the network takes place. These two layers are the *physical layer* and the *logical layer,* as shown in figure 19.3.

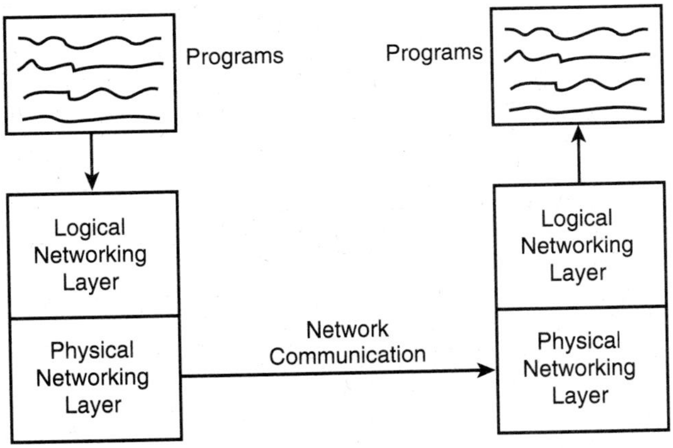

Fig. 19.3 Two networking layers—the physical layer and logical layer—interact to perform the communications between other computers.

Physical Layer

Think of the physical layer as the wire connecting your workstation to others on the network. The physical layer is the tangible piece of the networking system; this layer includes the network interface cards, cabling, connections, and any additional hardware such as concentrators and repeaters.

The logical layer is the layer that interprets the electrical voltage signals and translates them into binary data (0's and 1's) that can be passed to the next layer and interpreted by the computer.

Network Layer

The network layer is responsible for identifying the computers on the network. Each computer on the network uses the addressing mechanism that is run through the network layer to send data to the appropriate workstation.

Transport Layer

The transport layer is responsible for making sure that all of the data sent from one computer is received properly. The transport layer also makes sure that the data that may have been received out-of-order is reassembled into the right order.

Application Layer

The application layer is the software you run on your workstation. When you access a network drive letter or print to a network printer, your program is using the application layer to send the data over the network.

LAN Topologies

Many different methods are used for arranging the computers in a network and connecting them to each other. These various arrangements are called *topologies*. Each topology has certain advantages that make it more desirable in particular situations. By understanding these advantages, you can make sure your network is tailored appropriately.

Bus Networks

In a bus network, all the computers on the network are connected to the main wire of the network (see fig. 19.4). Like a highway with on/off ramps, the bus network funnels all traffic along the main wire that acts as a backbone for the network.

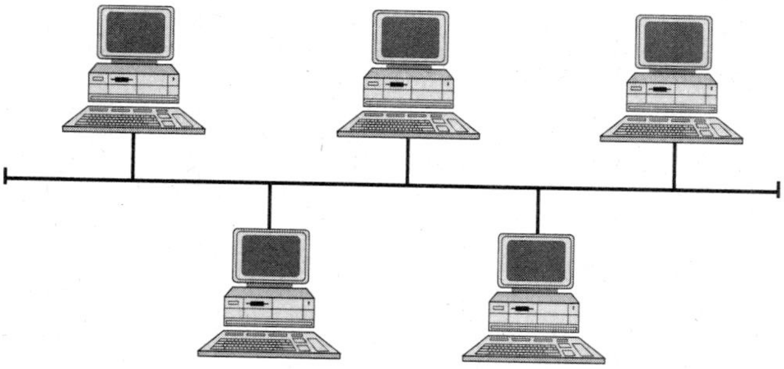

Fig. 19.4
Each computer on a bus network has equal access to the wire for sending data.

Computers connected in a bus network all have equal access to the wire at any point in time. To govern the use of the wire, the logical layer must wait until the wire is free before sending data to another computer on the network. Again, like a highway ramp, the logical layer manages the merging function to prevent collisions.

Bus networks have the advantage of incremental addition. As the network grows, additional workstations can be added to the network one at a time. The disadvantage for bus networks is the dependence on the backbone for all of the traffic. If the network is cut at any point, either by accident or by adding another network node, the entire network is out of service. The bus style network, though, is usually the least expensive to implement since it only requires the cable itself to connect each of the nodes.

An example of a bus network is Ethernet, which is discussed in the "Logical Networks" section later in this chapter.

Star Networks

Star networks connect computers through a central hub (see fig. 19.5). The central hub distributes the signals to all the connecting cables.

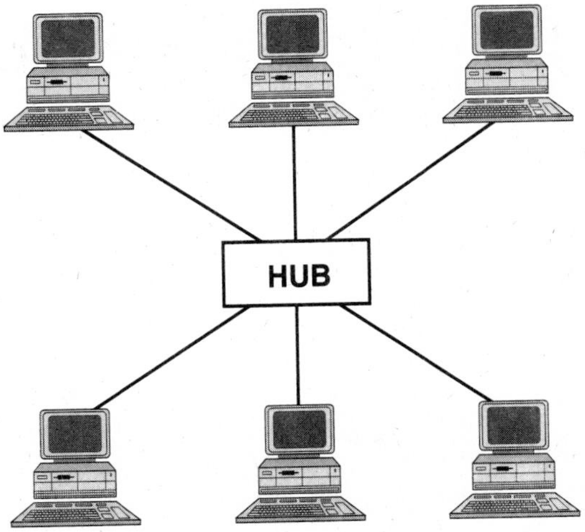

Fig. 19.5
Each node on a star network is linked to the rest of the network through a central hub.

A main advantage of using the star configuration is that each cable connecting the computer with the hub is protected from all the other cables. If one cable connection is broken or the wire is cut, only one of the computers on the network is affected. The other computers can continue to communicate with each other through the central hub. For overall reliability, this type of configuration is best.

The drawback of using a star network configuration affects only very small networks. The central hub equipment can be expensive, up to several thousand dollars depending on the brand of hub and number of connections you purchase. However, some manufacturers have been developing workgroup hubs with four to eight connections that sell for under $200.

Ring Networks

Ring networks connect computers using an In port and an Out port for data. Each computer sends information to the next computer down the wire. Data flows from one computer's Out port to the next computer's In port (see fig. 19.6).

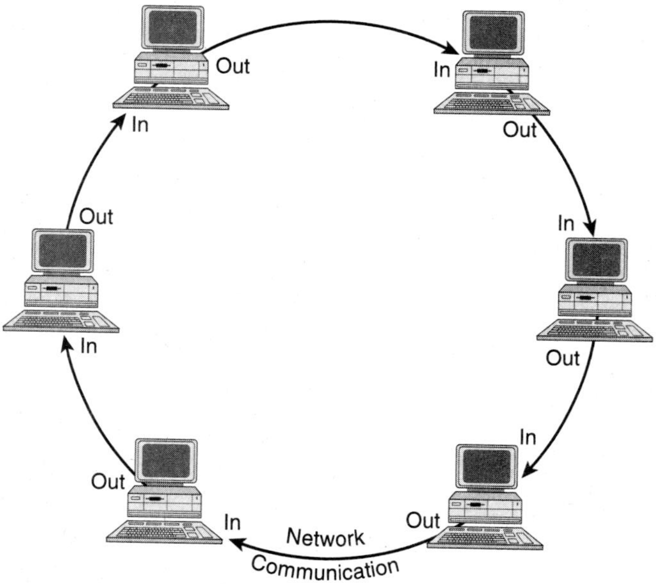

Fig. 19.6
A ring network circulates data between computers on the network.

Most manufacturers do not set up true rings like the one shown in figure 19.6. This setup would make wiring very difficult. Instead, a special central hub is used to complete the ring yet maintain a star network cabling layout. Figure 19.7 shows how this special hub, called a Media Access Unit (MAU), works.

Star-Bus Networks

Like the hybrid star-ring network shown in figure 19.7, the star-bus network makes use of a central hub called a concentrator to connect the nodes of the network. All traffic that is sent by any node on the network is then sent to every other node through the concentrator.

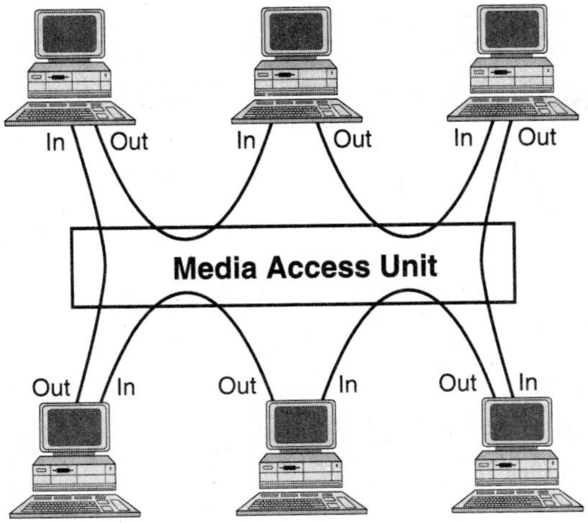

Fig. 19.7
A central Media Access Unit combines the advantages of a star network and a ring network.

This type of network is popular in larger installations and in installations where the physical wiring in a bus network configuration is either undesirable or impractical.

Connecting Network Devices

Once you have decided on a network topology for your network, if you are just adding a Windows workstation to your current network, you need to choose networking equipment to meet your needs. This section covers some of the topics you need to know when connecting network devices.

Network Adapter Cards

Network adapter cards function as the link between the wiring of your network and your workstation. These adapter cards give you connection points to which your network cables connect. The adapter card contains a small amount of memory that is used to buffer some of the incoming network data while your computer is processing it. Some newer network cards even have their own processor that assists in handling network traffic.

Windows 95 probably supports any PC network adapter currently available from any vendor, or any network adapter that has been available for the last five years or more (see table 19.1). Because of the vast range of legacy PC hardware, this statement may have some exceptions, but there are few network adapters that Windows 95 does not support either directly or by using the existing 16-bit drivers for pre-existing hardware. For example, if you are using an adapter to connect to a NetWare network, the same adapter likely works with Windows 95. The specific network topology ultimately determines the type of adapter you must use, but taken as a whole, Windows 95 makes connecting a PC to a NetWare network easier than it has ever been.

Remember these main things when choosing a new network adapter:

- Choose a product that has been designed for Windows 95
- Choose a Plug and Play adapter or modem if available
- Choose the fastest technology available

Table 19.1 lists all of the network cards that are supported by Windows 95 as the product ships out of the box. Any card on this list will work with Windows 95 without any additional drivers. Other cards will work as well, if the manufacturer provides a Windows 95 driver with the card. This list includes all of the model names of cards supported. Some cards have many different submodels supported as well for different interfaces (ISA, VLB, PCI, MCI, PC Card, etc.). In that case, the list includes the main model name to avoid cluttering the table. If you are shopping for cards, keep this list handy (make a photocopy to take to the store with you) to help ensure you get a supported card.

Note

The PCMCIA (Personal Computer Memory Card International Association) designation is now referred to as PC Card.

Note

Windows 95 also supports connecting to networks via a modem rather than a network card. Windows 95 probably supports any Hayes-compatible modem that is currently available or has been available for many years. In the case of dial-up networking, the server you are connecting to might have some requirements that constrain your choice of modem. These requirements can be related to the minimum and maximum speed of the modem connection and also the connection protocol and login methods. Consult the network administrator to confirm specifics that you need to know. Keep in mind that a modem connection is much slower than a network card.

Table 19.1 Network Adapter Cards Supported by Windows 95

Vendor	Models
3COM	Etherlink 16, Etherlink II and IITP, Etherlink III (16 different models of this card are supported), Etherlink Plus, Etherlink/MC, Fast Etherlink 10/100MB TokenLink, TokenLink III (3 models)
ACCTON	EN1660, EN 2216
Allied Telesyn	AT1510
Alta Research	PCMCIA Adapter
AMD	AM2100/AM1500t, PCNET Family (PCI, ISA, ISA+ and VL-Bus)
ArcNet	ARCNET
Artisoft	AE-1, AE-2, AE-3
AST	Token Ring Credit Card Adapter
Boca Research	BOCALANcard, PCMCIA 10BASE-T
Cabletron	E2000, E2100, E2200, E3000, E3100, T2015 4/16 Mbps
Cogent	Cogent Emaster + EM960
Compaq	NetFlex, NetFlex-2 (4 models supported), Elite Ethernet, 16E, Contura Integrated
D-Link	DE220 ISA, DE650 PCMCIA
DCA	IRMATrac (5 models)
DEC	DE100, DE101, DE102, DE200, DE201,DE202, DE210, DE211, DE212, DE425, DE434, DE435, DE500, DEPCA, EE101, Ethernet, Etherworks 3, TokeRing Auto 16/4, 433 WS, Ethernet DECchip 21040, Ethernet DECchip 21041, Fast Ethernet DECchip 21140
Dell	LATITUDE XP
Eagle Technology	NE200T
Everex	SpeedLink
EXOS	Exos 105
Farallon	EtherWave
Fujitsu	MBH10302

(continues)

V

Networking

Table 19.1 Continued

Vendor	Models
HP	Ethertwist, J2573A, J2577A, 16 TL Plus, 16 TP, 16 TP Plus, 8 TL, 8 TP
IBM	Auto 16/4 ISA Token Ring Adaptor, Ethernet Credit Card Adapter, Ethernet Credit Card Adapter II, Token Ring, Token Ring II, Token Ring Credit Card Adapter, Token Ring Credit Card Adapter II
Intel	82595-based, EtherExpress 16, EtherExpress 16TP, EtherExpress 32, EtherExpress PRO/10, EtherExpress PRO/100, TokenExpress
Kingston	Etherx Ethernet PCMCIA Adapter, Token Ring PCMCIA Adapter
Linksys	Combo PCMCIA, Ether 16, EtherFast, EtherPCI
Madge	Smart 16 (13 different models supported)
Microdyne	IRMAtrac (3 models), Novell 4000 PCMCIA Adapter, PCI Ethernet, NE2500, NE2500T
Mitron	LX2100+, PCI Ethernet
National Datacomm	NDC Credit Card Adapter
National Semiconductor	AT/LANTIC EtherNODE, Ethernode 16, NE2000 Plus Informer, NE4100 Infomover
NCR	StarCard, Token Ring 16/4 Mbps, Token Ring 4 Mbps, WaveLAN,
Novell/Anthem	NE/2, NE1000, NE1500T, NE2000, NE2100, NE3200, NE3200T
Olicom	Olicom Token Ring, Olicom Token Ring Server
Ositech	Trumpcard
Piiceon	Piiceon PCMCIA
Proteon	ProNET Token Ring (12 models supported)
Pure Data	PDI508+, PDI516+, PDI9025-32, PDuC9025, Token Ring Credit Card Adapter
Racal	ES3210, NI5210, NI6510
REALTEK	RTL8019
Silicom	Ethernet PCMCIA, Ethernet Pocket

Vendor	Models
SMC	SMC 3000, PC100, PC110, PC120, PC130, PC200, PC210, PC220, PC250, PC260, PC270, PC600W, PC650W, PS110, PS210, ARCNETPC, EtherCard, EtherCard Plus, EtherCard Plus Elite, EtherCard Elite Ultra, EtherElite Ultra, StarCard Plus, TokenCard Plus, TokenCard Elite, ELITE CARD, SMC 9000, Ether EZ, Tiger Card, EtherPower, EtherPower 2
Socket Communications	EA Credit Card Ethernet Adapter
SVEC	FD0421, FD0455
Sys Konnect	Sk-Net
TDK	TDK PCMCIA LAN
Thomas-Conrad	TC5041 PCMCIA, All Arcnet types, TC4035, TC4045, TC4046, TC6042, TC6045, TC6142, TC6145, TC6242, TC6245, TC Card PCMCIA, TC5048, TCTX048 100Base-TX, Token Ring TC4046, Token Ring TC4145Toshiba, Noteworthy PCMCIA, NWETH01 PCMCIA
Tulip	NCC-16
Ungermann-Bass	NIC, NIU, pcNIU
Xircom	CE-10, CE-10/A, CE2, CreditCard Token Ring Adapter, Pocket Ethernet I, Pocket Ethernet II, Pocket Ethernet III, Ethernet+Modem
Zenith	NE2000, Z-Note

Note

If you are buying a network PC Card to use with a laptop for networking, get a card with connectors for both twisted-pair and coaxial cabling. Then you can travel with the laptop and connect to networks with different cabling.

Cabling

The second major physical component of networks is the cabling connecting the nodes. The term *cabling* usually indicates a physical wire of some sort. As networking technology has advanced, other wireless means of connecting nodes have been developed. Therefore, the broader term *media* also applies to cabling. *Bound media* refers to traditional physical cabling, and *unbound media* refers to various wireless forms of connections. This book uses the more generic term *cabling* when referring to both bound and unbound media.

> **Note**
>
> Use a wireless network only in situations where you cannot run a wire or where a long-range connection is too costly via a wired alternative. Wires provide the best security and throughput for almost every application.

Coaxial Cable

The primary reason to use coaxial cable in the bus layout is cost. In most cases, running coaxial cable between your computers is much less expensive than using any of the other types of networks to be discussed. Of course, situations will arise in which coaxial cable will not work. For example, coaxial cabling is quite thick compared to twisted-pair cable. If you have to run cable for several computers through a small hole in a wall or floor, it my be easier to run twisted-pair cable than coaxial cable.

Another aspect of cost savings is very apparent for small networks. You can use coaxial cable to connect several computers in close proximity without the need for costly repeaters, hubs, or MAUs. As you see in the next section, twisted-pair cabling requires additional hardware when connecting more than two devices.

Another advantage that coaxial cable has over some of the other network types is that it is relatively good at shielding the networking signals in the cable from outside electrical "noise," such as the sound fluorescent lights generate.

A disadvantage of coaxial cable is that it is harder to work with and more difficult to install in the walls.

> **Caution**
>
> Because the bus networking architecture requires that computers be connected together sequentially, you are limited on the configurations you can create with coaxial. Also, bus networking relies heavily on all the connections working properly. If a cable has a bad connector, the entire network can stop working. Then finding the bad connector with coaxial cable becomes very difficult because everything might look normal from the outside. It can take hours to find and replace a bad connector, during which time the entire network may be out of service.

Twisted-pair wire has several pairs of wires that are braided within a plastic sheath. By twisting the wires around each other, the electrical signals carried on each individual wire are protected from interference from the other wires in the sheath.

The following list shows several wire types that can be easily confused when installing twisted-pair wiring. We will discuss each one briefly to expose its uses for networking.

Category 3 Twisted Pair

Category 5 Twisted Pair

ATT phone wire

Silver Satin wire

The Category 3 and Category 5 wires are the most common when dealing with twisted-pair networking installations. The Category 3 wire is less expensive than the Category 5 wire due to the less-advanced signaling properties of the Category 3 wire. Category 3 wire is typically used for Ethernet installations that run at 10M. Category 5 wire has much better signaling properties and can be used for high-speed networking up to 100M.

POTS (Plain-Old Telephone Set) phone wire, which looks similar to twisted-pair wiring, is only good for phones and modems. This wire does not have the same advanced data properties as the Category 3 and 5 wires.

Silver Satin wire was used quite extensively for proprietary printer sharing systems before networking was readily available. This wire should not be used for network installations since it too has poor signaling properties.

Fiber Optic Networks

A *fiber optic* network uses light, rather than electrical pulses, to carry the network signal. The fiber optic cable is a thin glass filament that connects to optical equipment on either end.

The main advantage of using fiber optic cabling involves signal strength. Not only is the fiber optic cable immune to electrical interference, which makes it great for factories or other electrical signal jungles, but fiber optic cable can also transmit a signal for two kilometers. A 10BaseT network can transmit for a maximum of 300 feet with a hub in the middle. The capability to transmit a signal over long distances makes fiber optic cable a good choice for underground cabling run between buildings.

Because of the signal characteristics of the fiber optic cabling, network speeds can increase from the 10M (10,000,000 bits per second) to over 1G (1,000,000,000 bits per second). Although personal computer networks are running 100M using FDDI, the capability of the cabling to run much faster can pay for itself over the years as networking technologies continue to increase network speeds.

The disadvantage of using fiber optic cabling is cost. Both the optical equipment that decodes the light signals and the fiber optic cable itself are expensive. For example, a FDDI network adapter may run around $1,000 while the hub to which it connects runs $500 per connection. However, if the conditions require long cable runs through electrically hostile environments, or when potential ground differences exist between buildings, then fiber optic cable may be the only way to go.

Light-Wave Connections

The light-wave transceivers use either infrared light beams to communicate in close proximity to other computers or lasers to communicate between buildings in relatively close proximity. Light-wave connections work well in many conditions but are very susceptible to interference. Because light waves cannot penetrate walls or ceilings, this type of interface is best-suited for communicating between a laptop and a desktop unit or between two computers that are fairly close together. Also, the speed of these units is typically much slower than other network speeds.

Tip
Use light-wave network bridges when distances are short and the view between the two points is unobstructed. Lasers are easily interrupted if any object passes between the two network bridges.

Laser connections can be made between buildings where the cost of running a cable between them may be prohibitive. These units have the capability to transmit a few hundred feet at network speeds, which makes them a good bridge between buildings. Lasers, like the infrared units, are also susceptible to interference and weather conditions.

Radio-Wave Connections

The second camp of wireless networks involves using radio waves. These units have the capability of transmitting between a few hundred feet and several miles. Typically, as the distance increases, the speed of the connections decreases. A big advantage that radio waves have over light waves is their ability to penetrate walls and ceilings.

A network can choose to use internal radio-wave transceivers for two purposes: either the network cannot be wired conventionally or the network includes laptop computers that require mobility.

The other major use for radio-wave networking is to span larger distances between buildings on a network. Whereas the laser-based network bridge requires an unobstructed view with a range of a couple hundred feet, you can use the radio-wave network bridge over several miles with trees in between. The speed is somewhat less than the laser, and radio waves are also susceptible to interference, but the alternative of leasing a network connection from the phone company is much more expensive.

A good application for a radio-wave based network would be a distribution center where fork trucks need computers to identify what location the driver should go to.

Note

Radio-wave network bridges can be affected by weather or nearby sources of radio transmissions. Check your local area for cellular towers or other radio towers before installing radio-wave network bridges.

Direct Cable Networking

Windows 95 supports a direct-cable network between two computers. This is typically used for a laptop to desktop computer connection; however, it also can be used for two desktops.

The cabling that connects the two computers can be either a serial cable with a null-modem adapter that allows the two computers to connect or a special parallel-port cable that connects directly to each computer. The parallel-port cable (also known as a LapLink cable from the software company that created it) is faster than the serial cable, but the parallel-port cable is not as easy to obtain.

These cables are convenient ways to connect two computers, but the distance between the computers is limited to around 50 feet for a parallel-port cable and around 1,000 feet for a serial cable.

Additional Hardware for Connecting Networks

The hubs and MAUs that were mentioned in several of the sections covered earlier are an integral part of all star networks. Many companies use star networks or hybrid-star networks.

Many smaller companies cannot afford to purchase elaborate network hubs for their networks. In these cases, the companies will be purchasing the low-end of the market in terms of price (and probably quality, too). When you are looking for an inexpensive hub, make sure it supports your network type. If you are running a Token-Ring network, you will be looking for a MAU to connect your computers. You cannot use a 10BaseT hub for this type of network, even though the hardware will most likely be much less expensive. Also, when you do purchase a hub, make sure that the number of connections will be able to support your network for a few years. If you fill up your hub when you install it, you will not be able to add any more network nodes unless you buy another hub.

For mid-sized or larger networks, hubs that offer expandability offer the greatest flexibility. Some hubs have stackable units that allow you to add incrementally to the network. Others are chassis-type systems that allow you to plug in add-in cards to grow the network. Which one is right for you depends on your individual needs. In either case, remember that your entire network will be running through these hubs. If they break, the whole network will be down. Buy quality equipment from a reputable vendor or suffer the consequences

Network Layer Protocols

To communicate on the network, your computer must be speaking the protocol of a particular network. The protocols that run on the network allow the computers to exchange information and maintain the integrity of the data transmissions.

Major network operating systems use particular protocols to communicate with their servers. The following list shows the protocol and the network operating system that uses it. Windows 95 supports all of these protocols:

- IPX/SPX—Novell NetWare, Windows NT Server
- NetBIOS—Windows NT Server, OS/2 LAN Server
- TCP/IP—UNIX, Windows NT Server

Logical Networks

The discussion thus far has concentrated on the physical layer of the network. This section covers the logical layer of the network, which determines how the computers communicate with each other over the physical media.

Ethernet

Ethernet is one of the most popular networks because the network adapters, network hubs, and cabling are relatively inexpensive. Also, the 10M network speed in considered acceptable for most networks. If you are considering building a new network, Ethernet is a good choice.

Ethernet uses the bus or star network types to communicate with other computers on the network. Ethernet 10Base2 and 10Base5 use a coaxial cable in a bus network while 10BaseT uses a twisted-pair wire in a star network. Ethernet uses a Carrier-Sense Media-Access Carrier-Detect (CSMA/CD) to determine when the computer can send data. When a computer wants to send data, it must listen on the wire to ensure that no other computer is sending data. If another computer is sending data, your workstation must wait until the line becomes clear before sending.

Token-Ring

Token-Ring was developed by IBM and until recently, you didn't have many alternatives from which to choose. The Token-Ring network tends to be more expensive than the Ethernet network. The adapters are two to three times as expensive as the Ethernet network adapters, and the hubs are also at least twice as expensive. However, for that additional cost, your network can run at 16M. This additional speed is also complemented by the way computers access the wire.

Unlike Ethernet, which requires the computer to listen for a clear line, Token-Ring computers take turns in sending data. A token is passed between computers in a round-robin fashion. When a workstation has the token, it can send data for a certain amount of time. Then that workstation passes the token to the next computer down the line. Token-Ring networks are set up as a ring network to provide this token-passing capability and to increase the throughput of the network.

Unless your network requires Token-Ring for communications to other network nodes or to mainframes, or you will have very heavy traffic loads on a particular network segment, you may want to stick with Ethernet for general purposes to keep the costs down.

FDDI

To get the most speed from the network, some companies are using FDDI, which stands for Fiber Distributed Data Interchange. As the name suggests, this network type requires fiber optic cabling to work, but the throughput is 100M. You might not need to use fiber-optic cabling or FDDI on your network, but now you have a high-speed networking option if you need it.

ATM

This ATM doesn't stand for Automated Teller Machine, but rather Asynchronous Transfer Mode. This networking option is destined to become the high-speed networking option of choice. The ATM network speeds start at 25M and go up to 155M. Future ATM networks may be as fast as 2G. But all this speed comes with a high price tag. Also, because the technology is still evolving, early equipment still has some glitches to work out, such as inoperability between vendors. Look for ATM to be the future network standard for high-speed needs.

Windows 95 Enhancements for Networking

One of the biggest issues with networking prior to Windows 95 was the problem of setting up a workstation to connect to the network. Typically, a workstation would need to have the network software loaded manually, the adapter card configured manually, configuration files edited manually, and start up batch files created manually.

With Windows 95, the process of installing the network has become much easier. The following list describes some of the networking enhancements of Windows 95.

- Automatic installation of networking components when upgrading to Windows 95 from a previous network
- Automatic detection of the network adapter card
- Built-in Novell NetWare support
- Built-in Peer-to-Peer networking
- Multiple network configurations to connect to different network servers simultaneously
- No conventional memory used for network software
- Enhanced network software is twice as fast as older implementations
- Single login for multiple networks
- Graphical setup and configuration for network software
- Automatic reconnection to servers upon login or after a server was down
- Built-in networking support in the Explorer and the Network Neighborhood

The Four Building Blocks of Windows 95 Networking

Now that you have learned the basic building blocks of the networking architecture, you can apply them to Windows 95. Under Windows, networking functions rely on these four building blocks:

- Adapter
- Protocol
- Client
- Services

Figure 19.8 shows how these layers fit together in Windows.

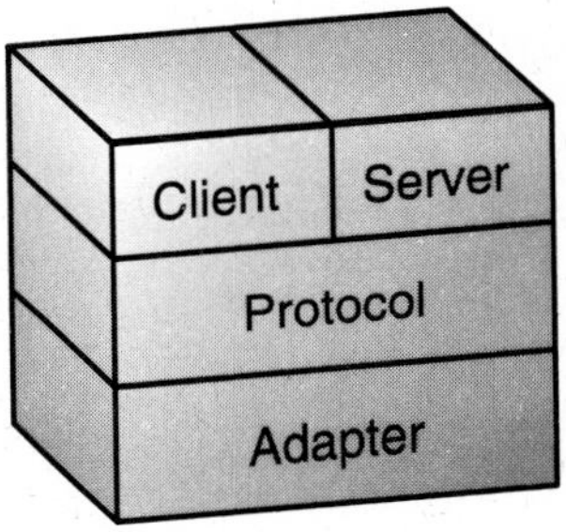

Fig. 19.8
The four building blocks provide the necessary functions for networking in Windows.

The following sections explore how these building blocks work to provide networking services.

Adapter

The adapter is the lowest level of the networking architecture. The adapter provides the interface between the physical wire that connects the computers and the internal networking of Windows. Windows provides a software layer for each network adapter that enables the network adapter card to fit into the structure of the Windows networking environment. Network adapter cards can be Ethernet, Token-Ring, Arcnet, FDDI, or ATM.

Protocol

The protocol is the basic language that computers use to communicate on a network. The protocol defines how computers can find other computers and what rules they use to transfer data. The most popular protocols are IPX/SPX, TCP/IP, and NetBIOS. Windows has built-in support for all of these network protocols.

Client

The network client enables computers to communicate with a specific network operating system. Each network server type from Novell, Microsoft, Banyan, and others requires a client to be loaded to communicate with the server from each of these vendors. Network clients provide the capability to share network drives and printers on the network server.

Services

Services enable your computer to share your hard drive or printer with others on the network. Services also enable central network administrators to manage the software and hardware in your computer. Each service you load enables you to provide value to the network in which you participate.

Fitting Your Workgroup Network into Company Network

Many companies have large mainframe computers that process the volume of core business data. Additionally, these companies might have central network servers that provide large amounts of data storage and high-speed network printers. Unfortunately, even with all of these resources, companies need to provide more personalized services to smaller departments and groups of users.

Tip
Check with your network's system administrator before you set up a peer-to-peer network on the company's network. Often, traffic loads from unknown sources cause system administrators undue troubleshooting time (and stress).

These smaller networks, called *workgroups*, can install their own networking solution that meets their needs. Some of these networks, however, do not fit into the company's network very well because the department did not know how to plan for the connections to the local workgroup server and the connection to the company's main servers.

Windows 95 enables this type of multiple connectivity to occur without the same obstacles that once stood in the way. Your Windows 95 network can use its four building blocks to make connections to almost any type of network in addition to the local workgroup network. Also, your workgroup can load special networking services that enable central computer departments to manage your workgroups as part of the overall company's network.

Finding the Right Networking Solution

As you can see from the earlier sections of this chapter, you have many possible options for networking in Windows 95. No one solution is best for everyone. This section looks at a few benchmark situations and provides some recommendations for each.

Connecting to an Existing Network

This choice is the easiest to make. If you need to connect to an existing network, you should use the same network client, protocol, and cabling as the rest of the network. Ask the system administrator what is right for you in this case.

Networking Two Computers

This situation is common for many home and small business network users. You might have two computers in your home office that you want to network so you can share a printer, transfer files easily from one to the other, or share a CD-ROM drive or other device.

The best solution is to use Windows 95 built-in peer-to-peer network with coaxial cable. The peer-to-peer network with Windows 95 is powerful and enables you to share any drive or device connected to either computer. Because peer-to-peer networking is included with Windows 95, you have no additional software expenses. You can buy two network cards, cabling, and connectors you need for less than $100.

If you need a lower cost solution, you can substitute a serial (null-modem) cable connection for the coaxial cable. However, this solution is much slower. If you plan to use the network frequently, the coaxial cable and network cards will pay for themselves in saved time.

For the protocol, you should use the NetBEUI. This option is the default option when installing Windows 95 peer-to-peer networking.

Tip
If you are setting up a small network in a larger company, you should consider compatibility with other networks in the company—even if you don't have immediate plans to connect to these other networks.

Networking 3 to 20 Computers

This network is common in small businesses or in workgroups in larger businesses. The type of network you choose here depends on how you plan to use it. If your primary use is enabling users to access data on each other's computers, a Windows 95 peer-to-peer network using Ethernet adapters with coaxial cabling is the best bet (as described in the previous section) up to around eight workstations. This solution also is the most economical. However, depending on your office layout it may be impractical to install coaxial cable for this configuration.

If you are planning on having more than eight workstations, invest in a hub and use a star topology. This will allow you more wiring flexibility and will avoid the coaxial cable problems discussed earlier in the chapter.

If you want to use a common printer, share data on a CD-ROM, or store files in a central location, you probably want to consider a client/server network such as Novell. With this many users, a peer-to-peer network might result in unacceptably slow performance if many of the users will be accessing the same computer to print or share a drive when someone else is using it locally. A dedicated server might be the best solution, especially if you have plans for expanding the network in the future. For Novell networks, use the IPX/SPX protocol. For Windows peer-to-peer, use NetBEUI.

The choice of cabling here depends on your plans for the future. If you think your network needs will never grow beyond 30 closely located computers, coaxial is the most economical choice. If you are looking for expandability for the future, go with twisted-pair.

Tip
To add Internet connectivity along with other networking capabilities, add the TCP/IP protocol to the other protocol you use.

Networking More Than 30 Computers

If your networking needs are this large, you should consider only a Novell or other client/server network using twisted-pair cabling. IPX/SPX is the protocol of choice.

Tip
If you haven't bought your network card yet, a Plug and Play card is a good choice. Even if your computer is not Plug and Play compatible, you might buy a computer that is; then you will have a network card ready to use with it.

Installing Network Components in Windows 95

This section examines the basics of installing network components in Windows 95. Regardless of what type of network you install, many of the procedures here are similar or even identical.

Installing a Network Card

The installation of a network card is the same for every type of network. The configuration of the card can depend on your choice of cabling.

If your network card was already installed when you installed Windows 95, the card was probably properly identified and configured by the Windows installation.

Using Plug and Play Configuration

Plug and Play is probably demonstrated no better than in identifying a network adapter. When you have a Plug and Play BIOS and install a Plug and Play adapter, Windows 95 dynamically sets up the adapter with a minimum of user intervention. When Windows 95 starts, it enumerates the hardware resources and sets up each Plug and Play device so no conflict will occur.

Installation of a Plug and Play network adapter results in a similar sequence of events as the preceding dynamic detection. Windows either locates any drivers it needs for the adapter or prompts you for a driver disk if it cannot find a driver specific to the adapter. After Windows installs the correct driver for your Plug and Play adapter, you still need to install the correct protocol driver for your LAN.

Using the Add New Hardware Wizard

Windows 95 has built-in support for hundreds of network cards, most of which are listed in the table 19.1 earlier in this chapter. If your card is on that list, you can use the Add New Hardware Wizard to configure it. After installing your network adapter cards, follow these steps:

1. Open the Start menu and choose Settings, Control Panel.
2. Double-click the Add New Hardware icon.
3. Choose Next in the Add New Hardware dialog box to continue.
4. Choose No when prompted to let Windows detect your hardware. Choose Next.
5. Select Network Adapter and then choose Next to proceed to the Network Adapter choices.
6. Select the card manufacturer in the list on the left side of the dialog box, and then choose the card model on the right side (see fig. 19.9). Click OK.

   If your Windows 95 driver for this card is not included with Windows 95 but came on a disk from the manufacturer, choose Have Disk and provide the drive letter or path for the driver.

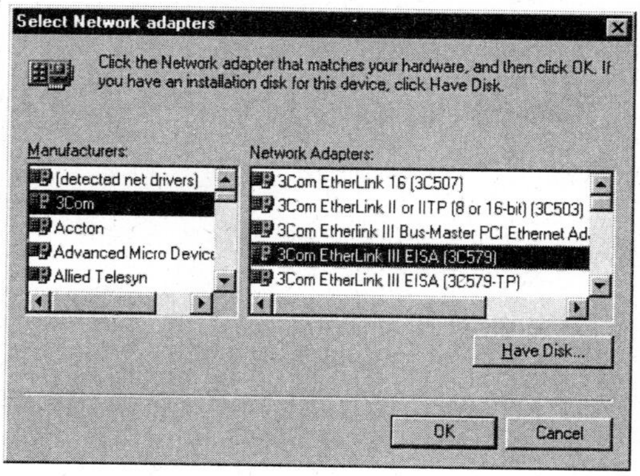

Fig. 19.9
Choose the Manufacturer and the Model of your network adapter board you are installing.

7. Windows displays the hardware settings for this card that will work with your computer (see fig. 19.10).

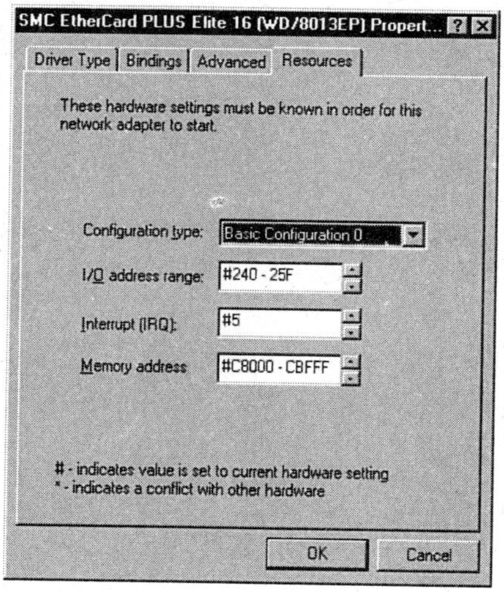

Fig. 19.10
You should review and write down the settings for your installed network adapter to save for future reference.

◀ See "Dealing with Legacy Hardware," p. 247

8. Configure the card to use these settings. Follow the card manufacturer's user manual to change any settings.

9. Click Next.

10. Insert your Windows 95 installation disks or CD-ROM as prompted.

11. Click Finish.

12. When prompted to restart the computer, select Continue.

Troubleshooting

I let Windows 95 detect my network card and it installed the NE2000 Compatible driver. This is isn't the type of card I have and my network connection doesn't work.

Many cards are compatible with the NE2000, which is a popular card. If Windows 95 cannot correctly determine what type of card you have and the card is NE2000 compatible, it will install this driver. Unfortunately, some of these cards are "less compatible" and may not function correctly with this driver. To fix the problem, delete the driver and repeat the installation process. This time, choose the proper card yourself from the list instead of having Windows choose for you. If the card isn't on the list, contact the manufacturer to see if a driver is available.

Installing a Real Mode Driver

Some older network adapters will not have Windows 95 drivers available. In this case, you need to load the Real-Mode drivers for the network card. You probably already have these drivers installed on your machine since they are older cards, so leave your current installation as it is.

You may want to consider replacing your network adapter if Windows 95 does not support it. While this is a strong statement, you must realize that the performance of your computer will be hindered if you are using an old network adapter.

Most new adapter cards from major vendors support Windows 95. But, as always, check before you purchase a network adapter card to see that Windows 95 supports it.

Adding and Changing Network Clients, Protocols, and Services

Now that you have learned about the four major types of network components Windows 95 uses, you need to know how to add, remove, and manage the different components. This information is presented in the following three sections.

▶ See "Setting Up a Windows 95 Peer-to-Peer Network," p. 617

▶ See "Connecting Windows 95 to a Novell Network," p. 673

Adding Network Components

To add a network component, follow these steps:

1. Open the Start menu and choose Settings, Control Panel.

2. Double-click the Network icon to display the Network dialog box (see fig. 19.11).

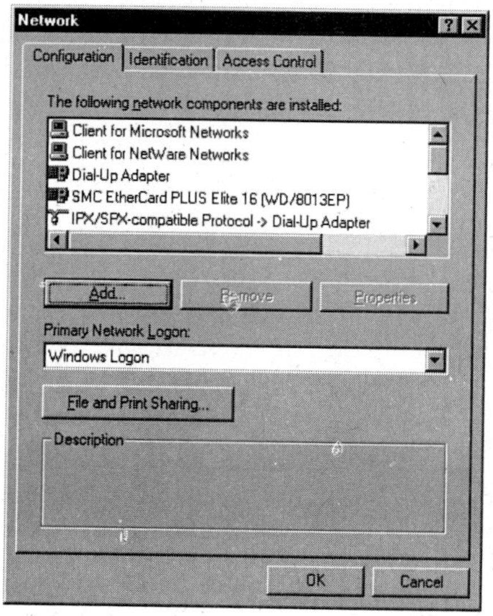

Fig. 19.11
Network settings are configured on the Network dialog box.

3. Click Add, and the Select Network Component Type dialog box appears, as shown in figure 19.12.

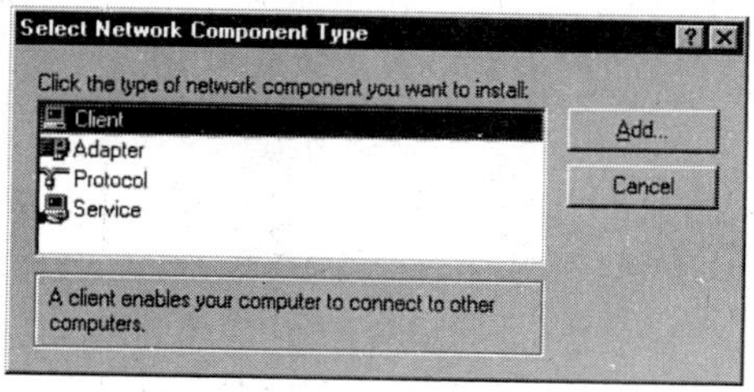

Fig. 19.12
You can add one of four types of networking components to your Windows installation.

4. From the four types of components available, highlight the type you want to add and click Add. A dialog box appears where you can specify exactly what you want to add. Figure 19.13 shows the dialog box you see if you choose to add a network client.

   Regardless of the type of network component you are installing, the dialog box looks essentially the same. The left side lists the various vendors of the component, and the right side lists models supported for that vendor.

5. To add a component, choose a vendor and a model, and click OK.

   If your Windows 95 driver for this component is not included with Windows 95 but came on a disk from the manufacturer, choose Have Disk and provide the drive letter or path for the driver.

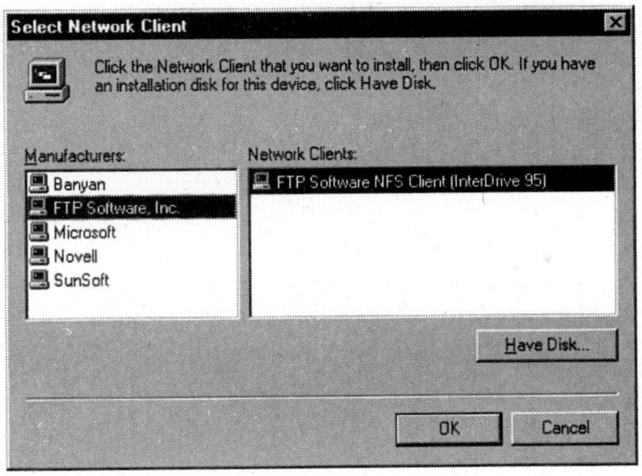

Fig. 19.13
Choose the Client option to add a network client to Windows.

After you have selected a vendor and model for the component and clicked OK, Windows 95 displays the component in the Network dialog box.

When you close the Network dialog box, you might see a message indicating that you need to restart Windows 95. Depending on the components you add, restarting is necessary to reinitialize all components to work together properly. Until you restart the system, you cannot take advantage of the network component changes you have made.

► See "Selecting a Primary Client," p. 612

Note

In addition to using Windows 95 to connect to multiple networks simultaneously, you can use this capability to connect to different networks at different times without making any changes to your system settings. For instance, if your office runs a Novell network and you have a Windows 95 network connecting the computers in your home office, you can have both the Microsoft and Novell clients installed. Windows 95 detects which network is running and presents the proper login dialog box. In previous versions of Windows and DOS, connecting to different networks required having multiple boot configurations or changing your startup settings for each network.

Removing Network Components

As your hardware and network environment changes over time, you might want to delete older networking components you no longer need. Doing so can free up memory and speed up the responsiveness of Windows 95.

Tip
Removing unnecessary network drivers will let Windows focus on providing CPU and memory resources for network components that you are still using. If you won't need a component, remove it.

To delete a network component, follow these steps:

1. Open the Start menu and choose Settings, Control Panel.
2. Double-click Network.
3. In the Network dialog box, click the Configuration tab.
4. At the top of the dialog box, highlight the network component you want to remove.
5. Click Remove. The component is removed from the network component list.
6. Repeat steps 4 and 5 until you have removed all the components you want removed. When you are finished, click OK.

   Windows 95 is then reconfigured to reflect your new selection of components.

Changing Component Properties

You already know that objects in Windows 95 have properties that determine how they or how the operating system treats them. Network components, as objects, are no different—they also possess properties you can control.

> **Note**
>
> In most instances, you will not need to change the properties of a network component—99 percent of the time Windows 95 sets up components to work properly. Change properties only if you keep track of the previous settings and if you have a firm understanding of what the change will accomplish.

To change the properties of a network component, follow these steps:

1. Open the Start menu and choose Settings, Control Panel.
2. Double-click Network.
3. In the Network dialog box, click the Configuration tab.
4. At the top of the dialog box, highlight the network component whose properties you want to change.
5. Click the Properties button. The Properties sheet for the selected network component appears.

The types of properties available depend on the type of component you are configuring. You can see the following Properties sheet pages:

- *Advanced*. Appears for network adapter, protocol, and resource components. Use this page to set the unique advanced settings for the card memory and configuration settings for the protocol, or general options for the resource.
- *Bindings*. Appears for network adapter and protocol components. Bindings define relationships between network components. The settings on this page control which components use this particular adapter card or protocol.
- *Driver Type*. Appears for network adapter components. Use this page to set the access mode used by the driver.
- *General*. Appears for network client and some resource components. Use this page to set miscellaneous properties for the component.
- *NetBIOS*. Appears for IPX/SPX protocol components. This page enables you to control whether NetBIOS applications can be executed through the protocol.
- *Protocol*. Appears for some resource components. In a multi-protocol network environment, use this page to set the protocol that the resource should use.
- *Resources*. Appears for network adapter components. Use this page to set hardware configuration information (such as IRQ and I/O address) for the card.

These pages are the common properties pages; other pages specific to individual network components also may be available. Typically, the use of these pages is very technical and depends on the implementation of your network. Chapters 20 and 22 look at some of the properties in more detail as they apply to Windows 95 networks and Novell networks. If you need more information on properties, refer to the system documentation for your network or contact your network administrator.

After you are finished making changes to the properties, click OK to return to the Network dialog box. You can then make changes in the properties of other network components, if you want. When you are done, close the Network dialog box. Windows 95 then attempts to reconfigure your network system according to your changes. You might receive a message to close Windows and reboot the system so your changes can be implemented with a fresh system.

Selecting a Primary Client

You already know that Windows 95 enables you to have multiple network clients installed in your system. Information is sent over the network one client at a time. Windows 95 enables you to specify which client you want as your primary network client (the client receiving information first).

To select a primary network client, follow these steps:

1. Open the Start menu and choose Settings, Control Panel.
2. Double-click Network.
3. In the Network dialog box, click the Configuration tab.
4. Make sure the network client you want to use is installed. If it is, the client appears in the component list at the top of the dialog box.
5. In the Primary Network Logon list at the bottom of the dialog box, select the name of the network client you want as the primary client.
6. Click OK.

Networking Components of the Windows 95 Interface

Tip
Using the Network Neighborhood is very similar to using My Computer. Both use icons to show the various resources available to you.

Windows 95 is built for networking. In addition to the Network Neighborhood that allows you to browse the servers on your network, you also can access network servers and printers through Explorer. This section describes the components that let you access your network resources easily.

Using Network Neighborhood

If you access a network from Windows 95 or if you manage your network with Windows 95, you should see an icon on your desktop labeled Network Neighborhood. Double-click that icon and you can see how easy it is to travel around your network.

◄ See "Using My Computer to Manage Files," p. 551

The Network Neighborhood depicts the network in a format just like a folder on your own computer (see fig. 19.14). Each device or computer attached is displayed as a computer icon, and depending on the access each computer or device yields, you can access data or explore further with a simple point and click. For example, if want to access a laser printer attached to a computer on the network, you simply double-click the computer icon to reveal the available resources for that computer and then choose the printer you want.

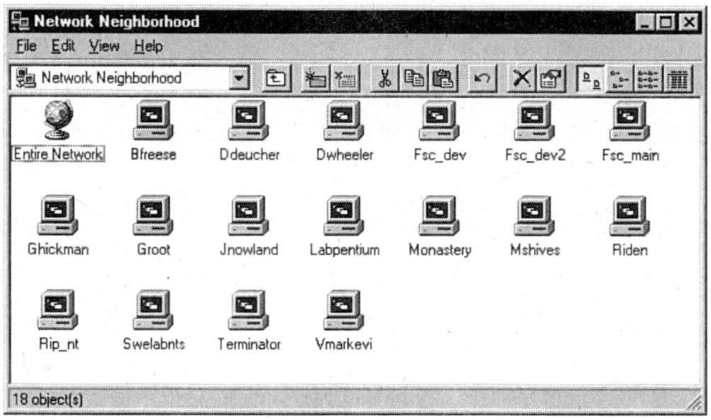

Fig. 19.14
The Network Neighborhood lets you browse your network for servers and printers available to you.

Moving around the Network

Navigating the network is easy from the Network Neighborhood window. Double-click an icon to connect to a computer. When you do, a window shows you the available resources (including shared folders and printers) on that computer. If you find that you consistently use a specific network resource, you can create a shortcut to that resource and place it on your desktop or in any of your folders.

◄ See "Creating Shortcut Icons on the Desktop to Start Programs," p. 68

The Network Neighborhood window displays a toolbar you can use to navigate the network, map network drives, and modify the way network resources appear in the window. If this toolbar is not visible, choose View, Toolbar. On the left side of the toolbar is a drop-down list box. This list box is an aid for navigating and determining your location relative to other network resources.

If you select a different resource from this list, such as your local hard drive, notice how the Network Neighborhood window changes to display that information.

Tip
As you move farther down the directory structure of your network resources, you can return to the previous directory by clicking the Up One Level icon on the toolbar.

Accessing the Entire Network

The network you can access is simply your local network. However, you can also view and access separate networks that are interconnected with yours. Double-click the Entire Network icon in the Network Neighborhood window. After a moment of searching, Windows 95 displays all the networks it can find. From this window, you can select any listed network and navigate as if it were your own local network.

Accessing the Network from Explorer

The Explorer also can be used to browse your network resources. Within Explorer's list of All Folders, (see fig. 19.15) you will notice a section titled Network Neighborhood. Clicking this icon will bring up a list of servers in the same way the Network Neighborhood does.

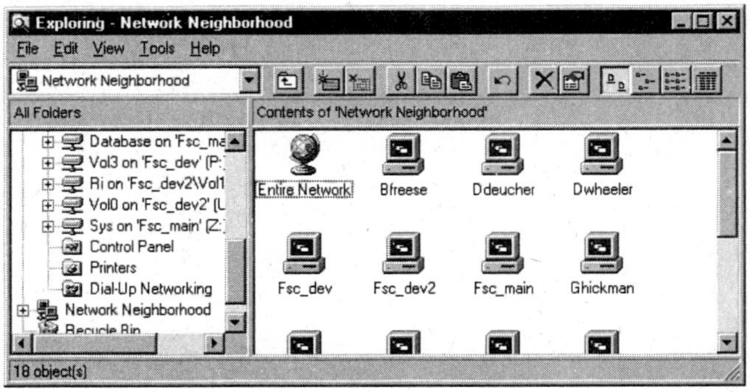

Fig. 19.15
Network Neighborhood browsing also is available through Explorer.

To map a drive letter to a servers folder through Explorer, follow these steps:

◀ See "Using the Explorer with Shared Resources on a Network," p. 544

1. Select the server you want to connect to.
2. Right-click on the shared folder that you want to map to a network drive letter.
3. Select Map Drive Letter from the pop-up menu.
4. Select a drive letter and click OK. If you want to permanently map the drive letter so that it is available the next time you login, mark the Reconnect at Logon check box.

Finding a Computer on the Network

Tip
You can enter any portion of the server name and Windows will find computers that match your selection. This is helpful if you don't know the whole name.

If you have a large network, finding a computer using the Network Neighborhood or Explorer can be difficult. So Windows 95 has a built-in feature for finding computers quickly without scrolling through long lists.

To find a computer, follow these steps:

1. Open the Start menu and choose Find, Computer.
2. The Find Computer dialog box appears. Enter the name of the computer you're searching for in the Named box (see fig. 19.16).
3. Choose Find Now.

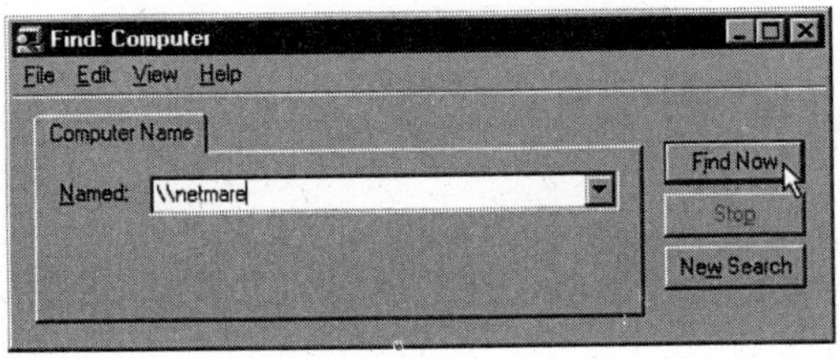

Fig. 19.16
Finding a server on a large network is easy using the Find Computer function in Explorer.

When the computer is located, the dialog box shows the result of the search (see fig. 19.17).

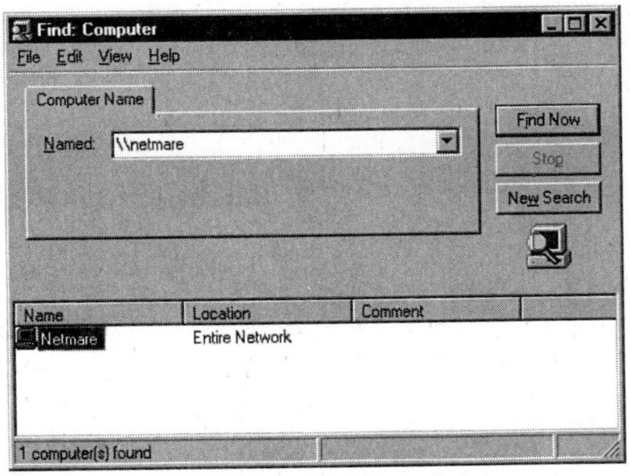

Fig. 19.17
The Find Computer dialog box shows it has located the Netmare server.

This Find Computer dialog box works the same way whether you're looking for a native Windows 95, Windows NT, or NetWare server. The same function, locating a certain computer, uses the same familiar tool.

After you have located the computer you want to explore, use the File, Explore command or double-click the server name to display the contents of the server.

Note

Keep in mind that if the computer you are exploring is a shared computer, some of the physical resources (drives and printers) might not be shared and available to you.

Chapter 20

Setting Up a Windows 95 Peer-to-Peer Network

by Glenn Fincher with Sue Plumley

Windows 95 peer-to-peer networking brings all the resources of the network to your desktop. You can share any of your PC's resources with other PCs on the network. You also can easily use the printer down the hall or the CD on your associate's new high-speed desktop. You accomplish all this through Windows 95's built-in peer-to-peer networking.

The network can be as simple as two PCs set up with Windows 95's Direct Cable Connection or a typical business-network connection where your PC is one of many on a local area network (LAN), wide area network (WAN), or even a city, or metropolitan, area network (MAN). Peer-to-peer networking with Windows 95 can even enable your machine to access the vast shared resources on the Internet. In peer-to-peer networking, each computer can act as both server and client.

In this chapter, you learn about

- System requirements and recommendations
- Installing and configuring your network adapter
- Installing the network drivers and protocol
- Identifying your computer for the network
- Establishing workgroup security
- Setting up and sharing your printer

Windows 95 Peer-to-Peer Networking Features

Windows provides many peer-to-peer networking capabilities, including resource sharing, communication, and compatibility with other networks, including Windows NT, the Microsoft Network, the Internet, and so on. This section explores what you can do with your workstation as part of a peer-to-peer network.

Resource Sharing

Tip
You can set automatic backup if you're using a Novell NetWare or Windows NT server.

The primary networking feature that you use with a Windows 95 peer-to-peer network is resource sharing. Even though each user may need a different type of computer, all users need access to corporate data and resources. In Windows 95, resource sharing enables you to make any of the following computer devices available to the rest of the network:

▶ See "Using Network Tape Drives," p. 714

- *Hard drives.* Sharing hard drives means you can access the other computers on the network and they can access your computer. Each user specifies which folders, files, printers, and so on, to make available; you don't have to share everything on your hard drive. Additionally, hard drive sharing allows for files to be backed up and restored from a central location, saving time, energy, and storage space.

▶ See "Sharing an Entire Drive," p. 643

▶ See "Using Your CD-ROM Drive," p. 970

- *CD-ROMs.* CD-ROM drives, although becoming more prevalent in newer computers, might still be in short supply on your network. You can share CD-ROMs over the network with others in your workgroup; you use CDs to install programs, supply files for copying, view multimedia clips, plus much more. Using CDs saves time in that installation and file access is much faster than with a tape or floppy disks. Sharing a CD-ROM drive saves a workgroup money because you need not purchase a CD-ROM drive for each workstation on the network. Also, by sharing CD-ROMs, you can share information with users who, because they lack CD-ROM drives, may never before have been able to view data distributed on CD-ROM.

Tip
Accounting programs and databases are the most commonly shared programs on peer-to-peer networks.

- *Applications.* Many applications are licensed to run on a network, thus saving installation time and space on individual workstations, and guaranteeing every user has the same version of the application. Additionally, upgrades are faster and easier since you're only upgrading one program instead of many.

Caution

Check your licensing agreements to see if your applications allow network sharing. If your software does not mention network usage and you install it to a network, you could run into problems when running the software. You could even lose valuable data or damage the program; this is especially true for specialized programs, such as those written specifically for churches, real estate offices, clinics, and so on. If there's any question about whether an application is suitable for a network, *always* call the manufacturer before installing.

- *Files*. In addition to sharing applications between workstations, you also can share files. The files are stored in folders on each workstation's hard disk. You can choose to share specific folders and you can limit the access of any folder you choose to share. Only certain files, such as a database file, may be used at the same time.

▶ See "Understanding File Sharing," p. 643

- *Printers*. Although printers are less expensive than they once were, it rarely makes sense to have one for each workstation. By installing one or two shared printers for a workgroup—such as a laser for general output and a color inkjet for special presentations—you can save money and enable all users to print when they need to. Windows makes it easy for you to share your printer with one or more in your network; you also can easily stop sharing the printer, if you need to.

▶ See "Sharing Printers," p. 650

Communicating from the Network

Windows 95 offers several methods of communicating between workstations set up in a peer-to-peer network; you can use one of the built-in applications, such as Microsoft Exchange or MS-Mail; or you can use a third-party e-mail application, such as Lotus Notes. Using the computer to communicate with your co-workers is often more efficient than running over to their office or calling them on the phone. Using e-mail over the network, you can send not only messages or memos, but files as well, thus saving the time you would take to copy the file to a disk and walk it over to the other person's office.

► See "Creating and Sending Mail Messages," p. 738

► See "Introducing HyperTerminal," p. 861

► See "Connecting to The Microsoft Network," p. 1110

► See "Overview of Exchange Features," p. 724

In addition to communicating within the network, Windows offers ways you can communicate outside of the network to remote computers. First, you can use the Fax application to send and receive faxes to other computers; you can even send faxes from within certain programs, such as MS Word. Second, you can use HyperTerminal to connect to bulletin boards, to send or receive files, and to otherwise connect to a remote computer. Third, you can use the Microsoft Network to exchange messages with people around the world and to obtain information about various technical, financial, and entertainment subjects. Use the MS Network to connect to the Internet, as well. Fourth, you can use the Phone Dialer to dial phone numbers from your computer over your modem.

Note

If the Inbox icon is not on your desktop, then Microsoft Exchange is not installed. You must install both Microsoft Exchange and Microsoft Fax to send and receive fax messages. To install these two programs, open the Control Panel and open the Add/Remove Programs dialog box. In the Windows Setup tab, select the Components you want to install; The Microsoft Exchange component includes both the Exchange and Fax applications.

Windows 95 Compatibility with Other Microsoft Networks

► See "Exploring the Windows 95 Resource Kit," p. 1133

If other computers in your office are on networks that run the Windows NT Server, Microsoft LAN Manager 2.x, or Windows for Workgroups networking, Windows 95 peer-to-peer networking is compatible with them. This chapter focuses primarily on the Windows 95 peer-to-peer network by itself. Although the chapter discusses some issues that you might encounter when working with other Microsoft networks, you should refer to the Networking section of the Windows 95 Resource Kit for detailed discussions of using Windows 95 with those networks. Note that Microsoft's other networks work seamlessly with Windows 95 peer-to-peer networking.

System Requirements and Recommendations

The basic system requirements for running Windows are detailed in the *Getting Started with Windows 95* manual that you receive with your copy of Windows 95. There are some additional items you will need for networking and some optional items you may want to add.

To be connected to a network, you must have the following:

- Network adapter card installed to your computer
- Software for the adapter card containing both configuration and driver (if your card is not included in the Windows 95 list, you'll need this software on a manufacturer's disk to install to Windows)
- Cabling (compatible with network topology)

You also may want to include the following hardware when connecting to a network:

◄ See "Connecting Network Devices," p. 589

- Modem (for use with HyperTerminal, Microsoft Exchange, or other e-mail applications)
- Parallel or serial cable (for use when gaining access to a computer on a network when your computer is not connected to the network, such as with a portable computer)

Tip
If you're using 10BaseT (twisted pair) for your network, you'll need a hub; if you're using 10Base2 or Thin Ethernet (coaxial cable), you need no hub.

Note

If you use a parallel cable, it must be a bi-directional cable, also known as a laplink or interlink cable.

Before purchasing additional hardware to set up your peer-to-peer network, make a plan for how you will use the network. If you're sure the network you need is a peer-to-peer network as opposed to a client-server, then you must plan for and purchase the resources you want to share. Consider sharing such items as modems, CD-ROMs, printers, plotters, large disks, optical drives, and, above all, information as you plan for both the present and the future.

If, for example, one workstation will contain most of the software applications to be shared, or a specific application such as accounting software, then supply that workstation with a faster processor, more hard disk space, and more RAM so it can run faster and better provide for the needs of the other workstations. You may also want to include a CD-ROM drive on this more powerful computer for quick and easy installation of programs.

◄ See "Approaches to Networks," p. 582

◄ See "Finding the Right Networking Solution" p. 602

Additionally, if you plan to share a CD-ROM drive, the drive should be the fastest you can afford (4x or 6x) with a quality interface, or controller, card. A slower drive may not be able to serve everyone who needs it and could create a bottleneck on the network.

Similarly, if several users use the network for printing, you may need a higher speed printer than an individual user would use. You may also consider connecting two printers instead of one, or adding a plotter or color printer, as well.

Consider, too, how effectively the resources can be shared among the number of users on the network. If you have only five users, for example, one printer is probably enough; however, if your network has ten users, you may need two or more printers to keep a flood of documents from being released on one printer all at once.

Modems for Dial-Up Networking

Tip
Use dial-up networking for connecting a notebook computer to your network.

This section presents some general guidelines to keep in mind as you start to set up a dial-up network with a modem. In short, get the fastest modem that you can afford. The newest standard, V.34, enables your computer to communicate at 28.8K baud. Because V.34 modems are relatively inexpensive, they are becoming widely available. Even a 14.4K baud modem (the V.32 standard) provides a robust connection for most peer-to-peer resources.

Tip
Dial up the server computer from your home computer to connect to the network and get some extra work done in the evenings and on weekends.

With a modem, a notebook or other computer becomes a *client* by dialing in to another Windows 95 PC. The Windows 95 PC, attached to the network through conventional means, becomes the *server*. The modem connection physically connects the client to the network of the server, or *host,* computer and becomes another computer on the network, enabling connection to and use of any resources for which access has been given. Both the client and server computers must be connected to modems.

Troubleshooting

I can't connect to a remote computer.

Open the Modems Properties sheet by double-clicking the Modems icon in the Control Panel. In the General page, choose the Properties button. Also, in the General page, check to be sure the Maximum speed is the highest that can be used by both your modem and the remote computer's modem. Deselect the Only Connect at This Speed option and choose OK. Choose Close to close the Modem Properties sheet and try the call again.

If you still cannot connect to the remote computer, open the Modems Properties sheet again and choose the Properties button. Choose the Connection page and check the information in Data Bits, Parity, and Stop Bits is correct. If you are not sure about the information, contact your system's administrator or check the modem's documentation. Choose OK and Close and try again.

Network Adapters for Connecting to a LAN

When you install Windows 95, it probably will recognize the network adapter already installed on your computer. Microsoft provides drivers for most manufacturers' hardware. The Network Adapter Wizard takes you step by step through the configuration of your adapter, whether it conforms to the Ethernet, Token Ring, or even the ISDN standard. Adding your network's protocols is equally easy. If Windows does not recognize your adapter, you must use the manufacturer's disk to install the configuration files and driver for your adapter card.

◄ See "Connecting Network Devices," p. 589

◄ See "Network Layer Protocols," p. 598

► See "Installing and Configuring the Network Adapter Cards," p. 624

Note

If you are purchasing a network adapter for the first time or replacing an older adapter, try to select a Plug and Play compatible adapter. Windows 95 can set itself up dynamically for a Plug and Play adapter. Probably more importantly, however, pick a card that is both fast (32-bit) and reliable by evaluating the vendor's reputation, longevity, and technical support services.

If you have a laptop computer with a PC Card (formerly called the PCMCIA) network adapter, Windows 95 can load or unload the network drivers for the card dynamically when you are connected to the network. This important new feature enables you to have separate "connected" and "unconnected" configurations, with Windows 95 maintaining the connection properties.

◄ See "Installing Plug and Play Hardware," p. 246

Finally, if you have a stand-alone PC but periodically must connect it to another PC to avoid doing the "floppy shuffle" (copying to a disk and then walking it to or from another office), you can do so by using the Direct Cable Connection, which is actually another form of peer-to-peer networking. Using either a null-modem cable or a special parallel cable, you can connect to and use the shared resources on another PC as if those resources were actually part of your own PC.

Tip

Even if you don't see an immediate need for the Direct Cable Connection, the cables are relatively inexpensive and come in handy if you eventually buy a laptop or another PC.

Troubleshooting

My PC Card was installed but it isn't working. What can I do?

In the Control Panel, open System Properties by double-clicking the System icon. Select the Device Manager page. Locate the Network adapters in the list and click the plus sign beside it; your network adapter should appear below the heading.

If the device is not listed, locate the PCMCIA Socket in the hardware list and select it. Choose Properties. In the Properties sheet, choose the Global Settings page.

(continues)

(continued)

In the Card Services Shared Memory area, deselect the Automatic Selection option. You can change the memory in the Start and End boxes; check the adapter card documentation for correct settings. Choose OK to close the dialog box, and then choose OK again. Restart the computer.

If the adapter has a red X through it, it's probably disabled. To enable the adapter, double-click the device and the Device Properties sheet appears. In the General page, Device usage area, make sure the current configuration is checked and choose OK.

If the adapter has a red circle and an exclamation point through it, double-click the device and read the Device Status area of the Properties sheet to see what type of problem exists. You can open the Device Manager (from the System icon in the Control Panel) and try disabling the device, identifying a free resource and assigning the device to that resource, or rearranging resources used by other devices to free up those resources needed by the device.

◄ See "Connecting Network Devices," p. 589

◄ See "Installing Network Components in Windows 95," p. 604

Installing and Configuring the Network Adapter Cards

If you already have a network adapter installed in your computer when you install Windows 95, the Install program probably will automatically detect the adapter and install the appropriate driver. If you add a network adapter after installing Windows 95, the Add New Hardware Wizard takes you step by step through the process of installing the hardware.

Tip
You also can connect to the WDL through Compu-Serve in the Microsoft Software Library; type **go msl**.

If Windows 95 does not contain the driver you need to configure the adapter card and you do not have a manufacturer's disk, check the Windows 95 CD Drivers folder for additional drivers added when Windows shipped. If you still cannot find the driver, and you have a modem, you can connect to the Microsoft Network and perhaps find the driver you need in the Windows Driver Library (WDL) in the Windows 95 section. The WDL contains a list of compatible hardware and many device drivers for printers, display, multimedia, network, and other adapters; drivers are updated as they become available.

Installing the Microsoft Network Client

Install the Client software so you can use the shared resources on the network. If you install networking support while installing Windows 95, the Install program installs Client for Microsoft Networks and the appropriate drivers (unless you choose not to install them). If you want to install the network after installing Windows 95, you must install the client as follows:

1. Open the Start menu and choose Settings, Control Panel.

2. Double-click the Network icon in the Control Panel. The Network dialog box appears (see fig. 20.1).

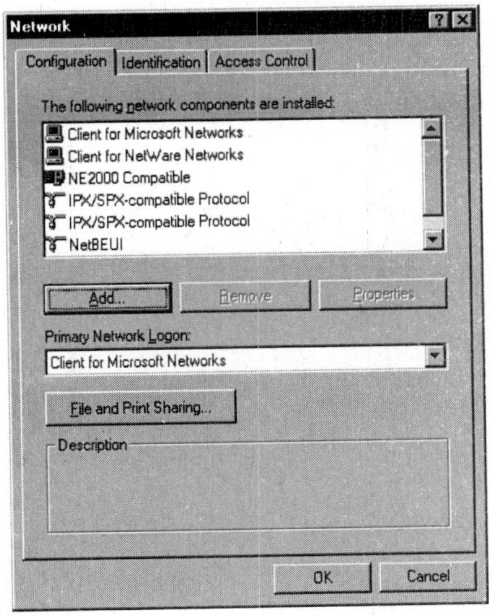

Fig. 20.1
Use the Network dialog box to install the Client software.

3. In the Configuration tab, choose Add. The Select Network Component Type dialog box appears (see fig. 20.2).

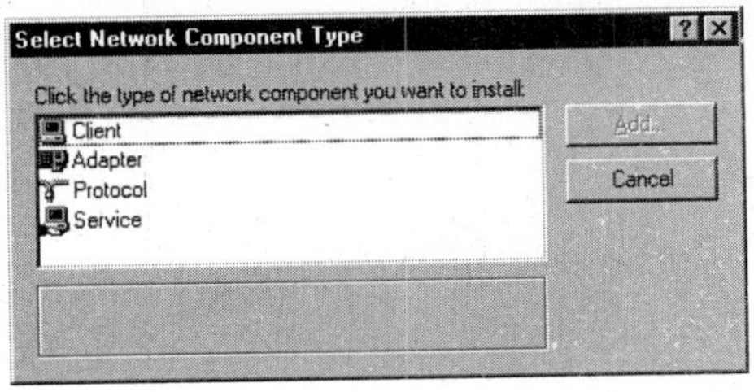

Fig. 20.2
Select the component you want to install from the list.

4. In the Component list, select Client and then choose Add. The Select Network Client dialog box appears (see fig. 20.3).

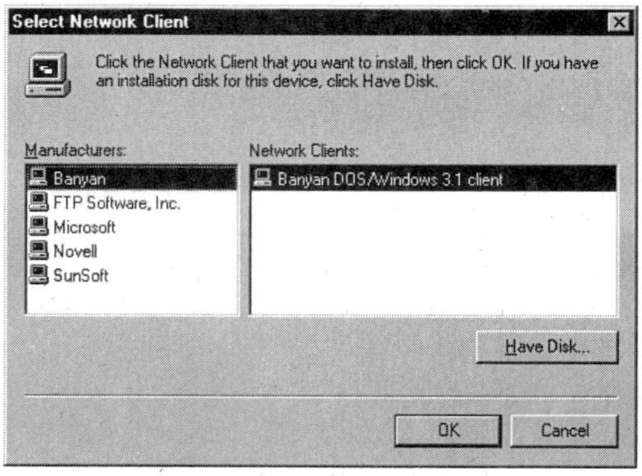

Fig. 20.3
Choose the network client you want to install in the Select Network Client dialog box.

5. In Manufacturers, select Microsoft and then select Client for Microsoft Networks from the Network Clients list on the right (see fig. 20.4).

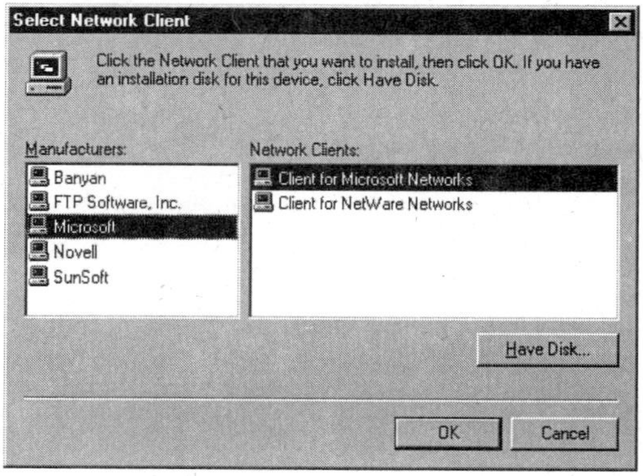

Fig. 20.4
Choose the Client for Microsoft Networks to set up a Windows 95 peer-to-peer network.

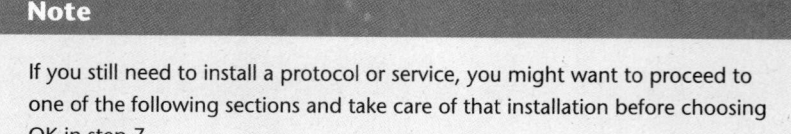

6. Click OK to install the Client. Windows may ask what type of network adapter you are using. Select the adapter from the list or, if you don't know the type of adapter you're using, choose OK and Windows will use the adapter it detected.

Note

If you still need to install a protocol or service, you might want to proceed to one of the following sections and take care of that installation before choosing OK in step 7.

7. When installation is complete, Windows returns to the Network dialog box. Choose OK to close the dialog box. Windows displays a System Changes message prompting you to restart the computer. Choose Yes.

After you restart the computer, Microsoft networking support is added.

◀ See "The Four Building Blocks of Windows 95 Networking," p. 600

You also can change the settings for the network client by opening the Network Properties sheet and selecting the client you want to modify in the Configuration page, Components list. Choose the Properties button and change any of the settings in the Properties sheet. Choose OK to close the sheet and OK again to close the Network Properties sheet.

Installing the Network Protocol

The Protocol is the language, or set of rules, the computer uses to communicate with other computers over the network. Protocols govern format, timing, sequencing, and error control. All of the computers on the network must use the same protocol to communicate with each other.

◀ See "Network Layer Protocols," p. 598

After correctly installing the network adapter, you must install the correct protocol for the network. To do so, follow these steps:

1. Open the Start menu, and choose Settings, Control Panel.

2. Double-click the Network icon in the Control Panel. The Network dialog box appears.
3. In the Configuration page, choose Add without choosing a component from the list. The Select Network Component Type dialog box appears.
4. In the Component list, select Protocol and then choose Add. The Select Network Protocol dialog box appears.
5. Select Microsoft from the Manufacturers list, as shown in figure 20.5. A list of Network Protocols appears in the list on the right.
6. Select a protocol from the Network Protocols list and click OK. (The next several sections explain the best protocol choices for Windows 95 peer-to-peer networking.)

Tip
If you want to connect to the Internet, select TCP/IP from the Network Protocols list.

Note

If you have a protocol that is not listed but is written for Windows 95, you can choose Have Disk in the Select Network Protocol dialog box and follow the instructions on-screen to install the protocol.

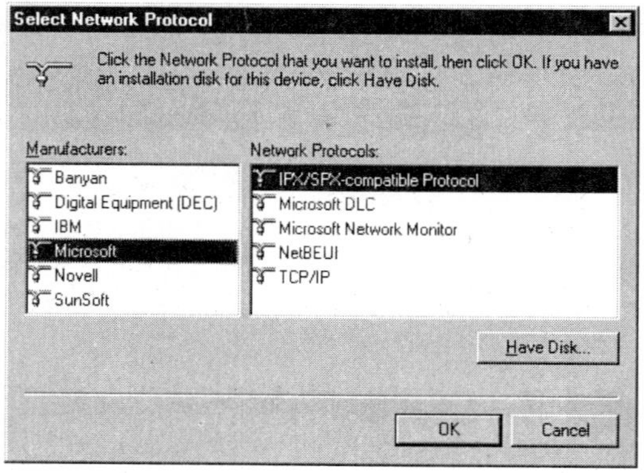

Fig. 20.5
Microsoft supports the most common network protocols.

Microsoft provides drivers for the most common protocols:

- NetBEUI, the protocol for LanMan networks, Windows for Workgroups, and Window NT
- IPX/SPX, the protocol for Novell networks
- TCP/IP, the protocol for UNIX networks and the language of the Internet

Microsoft provides 32-bit, protected-mode drivers for each of these protocols, offering high performance with no conventional memory footprint (drivers are not installed in memory below 640K). These drivers are all also Plug and Play compliant, enabling Windows 95 to load and unload the drivers dynamically as needed.

Using NetBEUI Protocol Drivers

IBM introduced NetBEUI (NetBIOS extended user interface) in 1985. The protocol was primarily designed for small LANs of around 20–200 workstations. Since the mid-1980s, Microsoft has supported the NetBEUI protocol in its networking products. The protocol is well suited for its task because of its powerful flow control, tuning parameters, and robust error detection. The NetBEUI protocol is compatible with Windows for Workgroups peer networks as well as Windows NT Server and LanMan networks. Windows 95 includes both real and protected mode support for NetBEUI. One potential problem with NetBEUI is that it is not *routable*—that is, to cross a router to another LAN, you must also install TCP/IP or IPX/SPX protocols.

You can add, or install, NetBEUI to the list of components in the Network dialog box. See the section "Installing the Network Protocol" earlier in this chapter for information. The default properties for the NetBEUI protocol work fine in most cases; but if you need to change any of the properties, you can. See "Modifying Protocol Properties," later in this chapter.

If you are setting up only a small, localized LAN that doesn't have to cross a router or communicate with mainframes, you need not install any protocol other than NetBEUI; however, Windows automatically installs the IPX/SPX compatible protocol in addition to the NetBEUI. IPX/SPX protocol is used with Novell networks. You can use the IPX/SPX protocol to run programs that normally require NetBEUI and to cross a router to another network.

Using IPX Drivers

Microsoft supplies with Windows 95 both a real and protected mode implementation of the Novell NetWare IPX/SPX (Internetwork Packet Exchange/Sequential Packet Exchange) protocol. The Windows 95 IPX/SPX protected mode protocol (NDIS 3.1-compliant) supports any Novell NetWare-compatible network client. The protocol supports Windows Sockets, NetBIOS, and ECB programming interfaces, and offers a packet-burst mode to improve network performance. With automatic detection of frame type, network addressing, and other configuration settings, Microsoft's IPX protocol is easy to install. Using the IPX/SPX protocol enables you to connect to servers and workstations on NetWare or Windows NT Server 3.5 networks, as well as mixed networks. Also, IPX/SPX is routable for connectivity across all network bridges and routers configured for IPX/SPX routing. With IPX/SPX installed, your computer can share peer resources across the *enterprise*, or to networks that connect to virtually all parts of an organization.

Note

Since IPX/SPX is also applicable to Novell client-server networks, see Chapter 22, "Connecting Windows 95 to a Novell Network," for more information.

▶ See "Windows 95 Support for NetWare," p. 674

Using TCP/IP Drivers

The Internet uses the TCP/IP (Transmission Control Protocol/Internet Protocol) protocol to enable all computers on the Internet to communicate seamlessly. TCP/IP is actually made up of a hundred protocols; two of the most important are TCP, a transport protocol, and IP, which operates on the session layer. The TCP/IP protocol is from the Department of Defense for use over large internetworks, such as the Internet, and uses Unix and other large computer operating systems to connect government, scientific, and academic internetworks.

◄ See "Network Layer Protocols," p. 598

Microsoft's TCP/IP is implemented as a 32-bit protected-mode driver with built-in support for the Point-to-Point Protocol (PPP) used for Dial-Up Networking. TCP/IP enables you to connect across heterogeneous networks of different operating systems and hardware platforms. The following are some of the additional features that make the Microsoft TCP/IP protocol powerful:

- Automatic TCP/IP configuration with Windows NT Dynamic Host Configuration Protocol (DHCP) servers
- Automatic IP-address-to-NetBIOS computer-name resolution with Windows NT's Windows Internet Naming Service (WINS) servers
- Support for the Windows Sockets 1.1 interface, which many client-server applications and public-domain Internet tools use
- Supports an interface between NetBIOS and TCP/IP
- Supports for many commonly used utilities, such as Telnet, ping, and FTP, which the protocol installs

Chapter 29, "Getting Connected to the Internet," explains in detail how to install and configure TCP/IP. You'll particularly want to note the section "Connecting to the Internet via a LAN."

You can connect to the Internet by using a terminal that's connected to an Internet host. Since the terminal is not a computer itself, you use the terminal to access a computer that is on the Internet. If you don't have a terminal to connect to an Internet host, then you can connect to the Internet over the phone lines by use of a modem.

Tip

In using PPP to access the Internet, remember that unless you have a dedicated phone line, your computer is not always connected to the Internet; you must arrange for the connecting computer to save mail messages for you while you are not online.

If you choose to use a dial-up connection over the phone line to the Internet, you need a modem. A modem converts computer signals to telephone signals and back again. The computer signal is "digital" and the telephone signal is "analog." The device that converts from digital to analog is called a *modulator*; the device that converts the signal from analog to digital is called a *demodulator*. A modem is a modulator-demodulator. To use a dial-up connection over the phone line, both computers must have a modem.

When you use your computer and modem to dial-up the Internet, your computer emulates a terminal. You first arrange for some other Internet host to act as your connection point; then you install PPP (Point-to-Point Protocol) programs to your computer. After the connection is made between the two computers, PPP gives your computer TCP/IP capabilities, allowing your computer to be an Internet host with its own official electronic address.

Since your computer is attached to a peer-to-peer network, the Internet becomes available to all computers on the network.

Modifying Protocol Properties

Although the default protocol settings should be sufficient in most cases, Windows enables you to modify protocol properties to suit specific needs, if necessary. Each protocol presents various settings you might change, but the Bindings options are common to all protocols.

Binding is the process of assigning and removing protocols to and from the network adapter. Each network adapter needs at least one protocol bound to the driver, else the driver cannot communicate across the network.

To set binding properties, open the Network dialog box by double-clicking the Network icon in the Control Panel. In the Configuration tab, select the protocol you want to modify from the list of components and choose the Properties button. The protocol Properties sheet appears, as shown in figure 20.6.

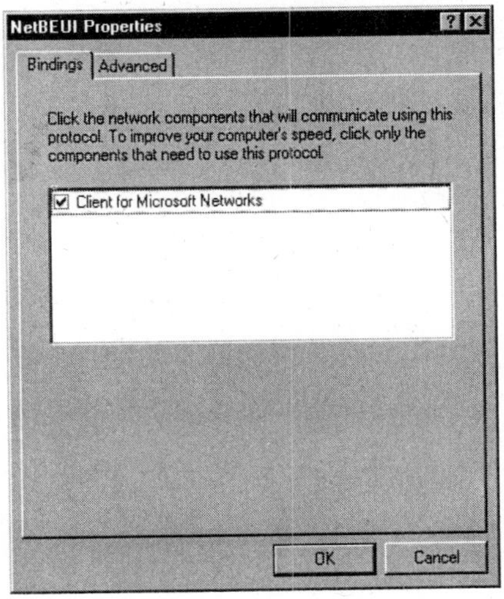

Fig. 20.6
Modify the protocol's settings in the protocol's Properties sheet.

Choose the Bindings page, and in the list select the components that will communicate using that particular protocol. In the Advanced page, you can select any settings you want to change by choosing the setting in the Property list and then entering or choosing the Value. Choose OK when you are finished.

NetBEUI

The Propertites sheet for NetBEUI offers two pages:

- The Bindings page reveals the service to which the protocol is bound.
- The Advanced page enables you to adjust the maximum number of simultaneous connections and the number of network control blocks (NCBs). The default settings are Maximum connections: 10 connections and 12 NCBs.

IPX/SPX

The protocol Properties sheet for IPX/SPX offers three pages:

- The Bindings page reveals the components that use this protocol to communicate.
- The Advanced page enables you to change or adjust several settings.
- The NetBIOS page lets you enable or disable NetBIOS over IPX/SPX.

TCP/IP

Figure 20.7 shows the TCP/IP Properties sheet. The TCP/IP Properties sheet contains six tabs:

- The Bindings page lets you select the components that will use this protocol.
- The Advanced page lets you set properties.
- The DNS Configuration page lets you enable or disable DNS (Domain Name System), a TCP/IP service that translates domain names to and from IP addresses.
- The Gateway page enables you to add and remove gateways, or links to other systems.
- The WINS Configuration page lets you disable or enable WINS (Windows Internet Naming Service) resolution for use with a WINS Server. WINS enables you to use programs that require NetBIOS protocol.
- The IP Address page enables you to assign an IP address to the computer from either a Dynamic Host Configuration Protocol (DHCP) server or a PPP dial-up router.

When you're finished setting changes to the properties for a protocol, choose OK to close the Properties sheet. Choose OK again to close the Network dialog box.

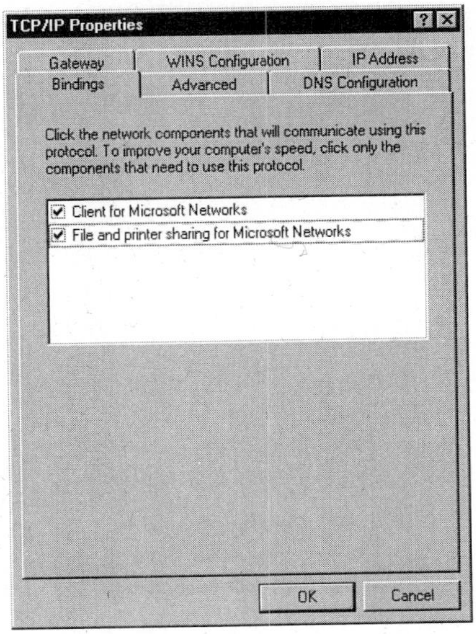

Fig. 20.7
Set the TCP/IP properties for bindings, DNS configuration, gateways, and so on.

Sharing Files and Printers

Many files on your computer are applicable only to you and your work, as are many of the files on other computers in your network. However, some of your files may be useful to your co-workers just as some of their files may be useful to you.

Tip
You also can control who can access your files with a password or with a list of specific users. See "Controlling Access to Shared Files and Printers" later in this chapter.

Peer-to-peer networks also enable printer-sharing, but if the printer is connected to your computer, you govern whether to share that printer with others on your network.

When working on a peer-to-peer network, you can choose to share or stop sharing the files and printer on each computer.

To set file and print sharing, follow these steps:

1. Open the Start menu and choose Settings, Control Panel.

2. Double-click the Network icon in the Control Panel. The Network dialog box appears.
3. In the Configuration page, select Client for Microsoft Networks from the list of installed network components.
4. Choose the File and Print Sharing button. The File and Print Sharing dialog box appears as shown in figure 20.8.

Fig. 20.8
Choose whether to share files and/or your printer with others on the network.

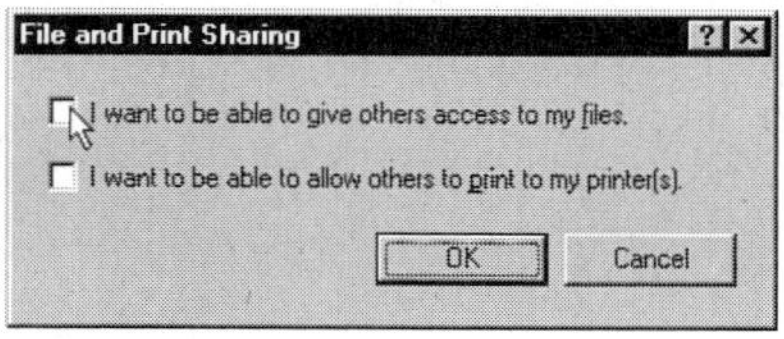

> **Caution**
>
> You cannot have Microsoft and NetWare file-and-print sharing installed at the same time. If you try to do this, you get an error message. If you use both Microsoft and NetWare networks, you have to decide which you want to use for file sharing.

Tip
You can share a specific folder by changing its sharing properties in the Explorer.

5. If you want to give other users on the network access to your files, select the option I Want to Be Able to Give Others Access to My Files. If you want to enable other users to use your printer, select the option I Want to Be Able to Allow Others to Print to My Printer(s). A check in the box means the option is on; no check mark signifies the option is turned off.
6. Choose OK to close the dialog box and Windows returns to the Network dialog box.
7. Choose OK to close the Network dialog box; alternatively, you can modify any of the other settings in the dialog box.

◄ See "Using the Explorer with Shared Resources on a Network," p. 544

This procedure doesn't set up any of your devices (drives, printers, and so on) for sharing. To share your devices, you select each individually and set up the security options for them to determine which users can access the devices. Chapter 21, "Sharing Windows 95 Peer-to-Peer Resources," describes how to set up sharing for specific devices.

Controlling Access to Shared Files and Printers

► See "Securing Your Network Resources," p. 640

After choosing to share your files and printer with others on your network, you can choose who, in particular, will have access to your files. You can choose to specify people or groups who will have access to each shared resource, or you can provide a password for each shared resource and only those with the password will have access.

To set access control, open the Network dialog box and choose the Access Control tab, as shown in figure 20.9. Select either Share-Level Access Control to set a password or User-Level Access Control to provide a list of people. If you choose share-level, you can assign a password to each shared file or printer.

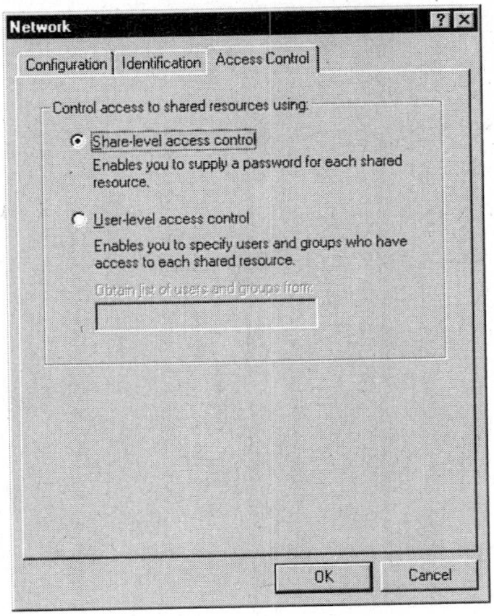

Fig. 20.9
Control the access to shared resources on your computer.

Identifying Your Workgroup Computer

If you did not give your computer and workgroup a name when you first installed Windows, you can name it at any time, or change the names, using the Network dialog box.

You name your computer to identify it to the other people on the network. When naming your computer, you can use up to fifteen characters, with no blank spaces.

The workgroup name identifies the group of computers you are most likely to communicate with—those computers on your network containing most of the resources you'll want to share. You can enter an existing workgroup name in the Workgroup text box or you can enter a new name. The name can contain up to fifteen characters.

> **Caution**
>
> To avoid confusion and erroneous workgroup names on your network, check with your network administrator before creating a new workgroup name.

To identify your computer on the network, follow these steps:

1. Open the Start menu and choose Settings, Control Panel.

2. Double-click the Network icon in the Control Panel. The Network dialog box appears. Click the Identification tab (see fig. 20.10).

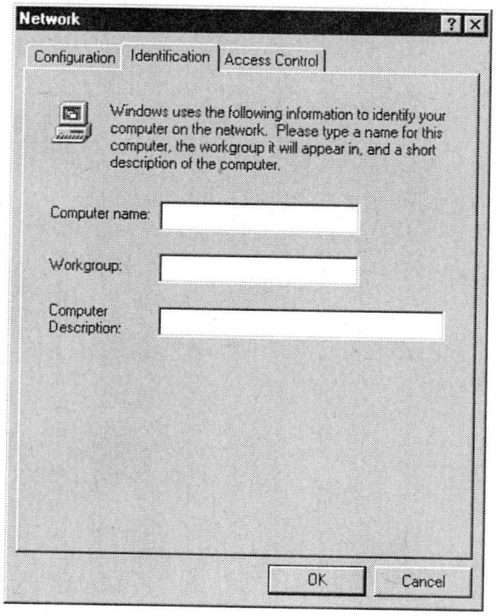

Fig. 20.10
The Identification tab enables you to identify your computer to the rest of the network.

3. In the Computer Name text box, type the name of your computer. The name of your computer must be a unique name on the network but it can be any name, such as Fred, Director, BookEditor12, and so on.

4. In the Workgroup text box, type the name of your computer's workgroup.

5. An optional description of your computer appears in the Computer Description text box. You can enter a different description of your machine, if you want. The text that you enter here is used to identify your machine when users browse the network.

6. Click OK to close the Network dialog box.

Tip
Use the Computer Description to enter your name or department, or perhaps resources connected to your computer.

Identifying the Primary Network Logon

To get onto a network, you usually use a logon, or a password, that initializes your security rights, thus enabling you to access the network and its resources. When you log on, Windows prompts you for a password and perhaps other information, such as a server name.

You can specify the logon option you use most often when logging onto the network or you can choose an option to use when you're not logging onto the network, such as when you're using a portable computer away from the office.

You select the primary logon option in the Network dialog box. Choose the Configuration tab, click the Primary Network Logon down arrow and a list of available network connections appears. Choose the logon option you use most of the time:

- *Client for Microsoft Networks.* Use this option when logging onto the Windows peer-to-peer network.
- *Client for NetWare Networks.* Use this option when logging onto a Novell network.
- *Windows Logon.* Use this option if you don't want to view error messages when you're not logging on to the network.

Logging On to the Network

After you successfully install all the components for Windows 95 networking, the next time that you restart Windows, the Enter Network Password dialog box prompts you to log on to the network. To log in, enter the correct user name and password.

Tip
Use the Passwords Control Panel (as discussed in the section "Restricting Access to Your Computer" in Chapter 4) to add or change the passwords and users that Windows recognizes.

You can set options for the network logon in the Client for Microsoft Networks Properties sheet (see fig. 20.11). To display the sheet, open the Network dialog box and choose the Configuration tab. In the components list, choose the client you want to set logon options for. Choose the Properties button to display the Client for Microsoft Networks Properties sheet.

Following are the options you can choose in the General page of the Client for Microsoft Networks Properties sheet:

- *Logon validation.* Select the Log On to Windows NT Domain option and enter the domain's name in the Windows NT domain text box to connect to the Windows NT domain when you log on to Windows.
- *Network logon options.* Choose Quick Logon to make your previous network connections available but not connected until you use the drive. Choose Logon and Restore Network Connections to restore all network connections when you start windows.

Fig. 20.11
Set logon properties for Windows NT or Windows 95 peer-to-peer networks.

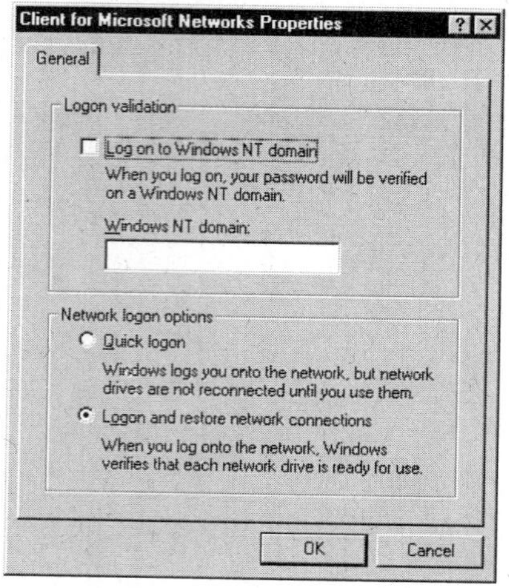

To log off the network, choose the Start button and the Shut Down command. In the Shut Down Windows dialog box, choose Close All Programs and Log On as a Different User? and then choose Yes. When Windows starts again, the Enter Network Password dialog box appears. Choose Cancel and Windows restarts without logging you onto the network.

► See "Network Security," p. 820

Note

To change your Network and/or Windows passwords, open the Passwords icon from the Control Panel. In the Change Passwords tab, choose either Change Windows Password or Change Other Passwords.

Note

If you also have installed the Novell network client and chose it as the primary network logon, you'll see that dialog box first, then the Microsoft client logon. Chapter 23, "Using Novell Network Resources in Windows 95," discusses the Novell logon. If you have installed the Novell client but not the primary logon, you first see the Microsoft logon dialog box, then the Novell logon dialog box.

◄ See "Networking Components of the Windows 95 Interface," p. 612

After connecting your computer to the network, you can browse any of the available resources.❖

Chapter 21

Sharing Windows 95 Peer-to-Peer Resources

by Glenn Fincher with Sue Plumley

As discussed in Chapter 20, "Setting Up a Windows 95 Peer-to-Peer Network," peer-to-peer resource sharing with Windows 95 is much simpler than it has been in previous versions of Windows including Windows NT. This chapter discusses specific steps to sharing certain resources and covers other issues relating to sharing resources.

In this chapter, you can learn about these topics:

- Securing network resources
- File, directory, and drive sharing
- Drive usage policies
- Sharing printers
- Fax modem sharing
- Remote access to your network
- Peer-to-peer network management

Connecting to a Windows 95 peer-to-peer network offers a huge advantage over maintaining a stand-alone computer—resources. Using a network enables your computer to share resources—such as printers, plotters, optical disks, modems, applications, files, and so on—with other computers on the network. In addition, you can share in the resources of the other computers.

Securing Your Network Resources

If your PC is connected to another computer over a LAN, or dial-up network, you probably have given security more than a passing thought. Perhaps you've asked yourself these questions:

- Can others on the network gain unauthorized access to my data files?
- Should others be given *any* access to my data?
- If I do share a resource, can I revoke that access at a later time?
- Can an administrator or other person monitor my computer's resources without my knowledge?

Windows 95 Peer-to-Peer Security Principles

Although security is one of the key features of Windows 95, it is also the main reason that system administrators often do not like peer-to-peer networks. Control of resources resides with each user rather than with a centrally administered server. In other words, if a resource becomes essential for a workgroup, such as a specific directory on a single machine, then that machine becomes a server with expectations that the service or resource will always be available. The administration of these resources becomes a harder task as more power trickles down to the desktop. However, Windows 95 has tools to help track and administer this dilemma.

When you share a resource, you choose to control access to the share in two ways. You can use a password for the resource, called *share-level access control*. Or you can define users with access to the resource, called *user-level access control*. Additionally, you can choose whether to share your files and printer. At any time, you have the control to share or stop sharing your own resources. Of course, everyone else on the network also has those same rights.

Note

User-level access depends on *pass-through validation*—a Windows NT or Novell server authenticates the user from its database of accounts. Windows 95 does not maintain a general user list of its own for this authentication. Windows 95 does maintain the list of users' rights.

◀ See "Controlling Access to Shared Files and Printers," p. 634

◀ See "Sharing Files and Printers," p. 633

As to the questions you may have about the security of shared resources, no one can gain access to data unless you allow it by careful use of Windows 95's built-in access controls. You or the system administrator decide what resources or data, if any, is shareable, and you can revoke the access by simply un-sharing the resource or data at a later time. As long as you assign passwords for share-level access or rely on trusted users from a server with user-level access, only users who *should* have access to the resource can actually access it.

Some points to remember for security:

- If you set up temporary access for a short time, remember to remove the access after the allotted time.
- Always assign passwords for share-level access to a resource; never share a resource with a blank password.
- Consider the cost in performance to a computer set up as a print or fax server. With constant use of these resources, this computer's performance may be affected.
- After a resource is shared and regularly used, the resource might become so necessary that it can be used for little else.

User IDs and Passwords

In Windows 95, each user's unique identification information is stored in separate password USERNAME.PWL files. Each user on the network has a separate PWL file. These password files contain all password information for the respective user, including passwords for these items:

- Resources protected by share-level security
- Password-protected applications specifically written to the Master Password API
- Windows NT computers not in a domain, or the Windows NT logon password if it isn't the Primary Network Logon
- NetWare servers

These PWL files are stored in the Windows directory with each resource having a separate password. The passwords are encrypted in the PWL file, and the encrypted password is sent intact over the network. For any password scheme to work, the passwords must be protected by the user.

◄ See "Identifying the Primary Network Logon," p. 636

An administrator also can enforce certain password policies by implementing system policies using the Policy Editor in the Windows 95 Resource Kit. System policies override local Registry settings, so using system policies allows you to do these things:

► See "Network Security," p. 820

- Restrict a user from changing hardware settings using Control Panel
- Customize parts of the Desktop like the Network Neighborhood or the Programs folder
- Maintain centrally located network settings, such as network client customizations or the capability to install file and printer services
- Set policies for a group of users

► See "What Utilities are Included in the Resource Kit," p. 1138

Virus Protection on Your Network

◄ See "Protecting Your Files from Viruses," p. 575

An argument against allowing peer-to-peer networking is that the increased connectivity gives an easier path for the spread of computer virus infections. A *computer virus* is a program designed to propagate itself throughout the host computer. This propagation can be as simple as attaching its executable code to the beginning or end of an existing file, or as complex as mutating from one form to another to avoid detection and thereby quietly doing its damage.

Well-known viruses like the Michelangelo virus have gotten a lot of press because of their perennial nature. Michelangelo activates on March 6, at which time it formats the system hard disk by overwriting it with random characters from system memory. While it waits for March 6, Michelangelo dutifully copies itself to all disks accessed on the host computer. Then if another computer is booted using the newly infected disk, Michelangelo infects the next computer.

In cases where a documented virus case is discovered, multiple computers and floppy disks are also infected. Virus infections are a real problem, so steps must be taken to prevent their spread.

Regular use of one or more of the popular anti-virus packages decreases the chances of a virus hiding on your computer, and also prevents your own inadvertent propagating of a virus. MSDOS 5.*x* and up shipped with the Microsoft anti-virus MASV.EXE, but Windows 95 does not include an anti-virus product. Several products on the market can both detect and eliminate most virus infections. Because of the relative ease with which a new virus can be created, and the recent spread of so-called *polymorphic* viruses, it is wise to use more than one anti-virus product.

Note

Anti-virus software written for MSDOS or Windows 3.x may not work correctly on Windows 95. Consult your vendor for updated versions of the software.

Understanding File Sharing

Among the many resources you can share in a peer-to-peer Windows 95 network, information is the most crucial. Whether several people on the network share the accounting duties or two people exchange a spreadsheet, you'll be surprised at the amount of information that travels the network during a common workday.

Windows 95 allows workstations on the network to enable drive and directory sharing to help the users complete their work efficiently and effectively. In addition to sharing drives and directories, a user can choose to limit access to certain resources or to stop sharing at any time. This section describes how to share drives and directories and how to access shared drives and directories.

Tip
Drives you can share include the hard drive, floppy drives, CD-ROM drives, and tape drives.

Setting Up File Sharing

When attached to the peer-to-peer Windows 95 network, you can choose to share entire drives or specific folders (directories) on your computer. However, before you choose files or directories to share, you must enable file sharing by choosing that option in the Configuration tab of the Network dialog box.

◄ See "Installing Network Components in Windows 95," p. 604

Note

When choosing to share files or directories with other computers on your network, remember that you also can grant access to those who may share those files or directories.

◄ See "Sharing Files and Printers," p. 633

Sharing an Entire Drive

You can share your entire hard drive with other computers on the network. Additionally, you can choose to share floppy drives, CD drives, optical drives, and so on. When you choose to share a drive with the other computers on the network, those other users can access the files and directories on your computer.

◄ See "Controlling Access to Shared Files and Printers," p. 634

To share an entire drive with the network, follow these steps:

1. Open the My Computer window and select the drive you want to share.

2. Choose File, Sharing. The drive's Properties sheet appears with the Sharing page displayed.
3. To share the drive with the others on the network, choose the Shared As option. The options in the Shared As area are now ready to view and choose from, as shown in figure 21.1.

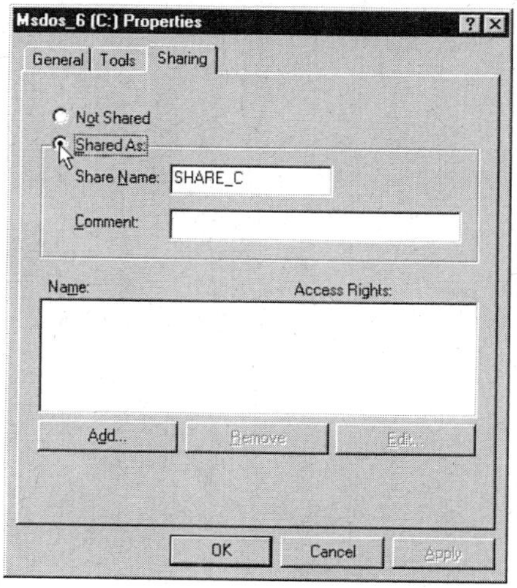

Fig. 21.1
After choosing to share the selected drive, you can choose access types, passwords, and so on in the Sharing page.

4. In the Shared As area, choose the appropriate options as described in table 21.1.

Table 21.1 Sharing Options

Option	Description
Shared As	
Share Name	Enter a new name for the shared drive if you do not want to use the suggested name. This name is the name others will use when accessing the shared drive on your computer.
Comment	Add a comment, if you want, about the shared drive that others can see in Detail view. You can add a comment that will help others locate data on the drive, if you want.
Access Type	
Read-Only	Others can only view the drive and data, even copy files, but they cannot modify or remove data in any way.
Full	Others can change, add, or remove files.
Depends on Password	Enables different people different access, depending on the password they use.

Option	Description
Passwords	
Read-Only Password	Enter a password in this text box that enables those who know the password read-only access to your drive. A confirmation box appears in which you must type the password a second time to confirm.
Full Access Password	Enter a password in this text box that enables those who know the password full access to the drive. A confirmation box appears in which you must type the password a second time to confirm.

Caution

When you grant someone full access to your disk, they can delete files and folders or move items around if they want. Make sure you give full access only to people you trust.

5. Choose Apply and then OK to close the sheet.

Note

You can turn off sharing at any time by selecting the drive and then choosing File, Sharing, Not Shared, and then choose OK.

Tip

Windows adds a hand icon (palm up) in front of the shared drive icon in icon view to indicate it is shared.

Note

If you want to share a *resource* but not make the name of the resource available by browsing, simply use the dollar sign ($) as the last character of the share name. For example, the share name SHARE$ is accessible as you define it, but it will not show up in a list of available resources when someone is browsing the network. You can name that shared device in a batch file, for example, so a user can access it without really seeing it as being available.

Sharing a Directory

Just as you can share a drive, you also can share one or more directories on a drive. You might want to share a document, an application, or another directory with others on your network. Once again, you can limit the access for any directory you share.

To share a directory, open My Computer and locate the directory you want to share. Select the directory; choose File, Sharing. In the Sharing tab, choose the Shared As option and choose any options in the Shared As area as described in table 21.1. A small open hand icon appears in front of the folder's icon to indicate it is shared.

Note

When you share a directory or folder, you share *all* files in that directory. You can, however, make any file in that directory read-only or hidden to keep the file safe. To limit access to a file, open My Computer and then the folder containing the file. Select the file and choose File, Properties. In the General tab of the Properties sheet, choose Read-only or Hidden in the Attributes area. Choose OK to close the sheet.

Troubleshooting

Why can't I use any resources from another computer?

If you cannot see the resources, that computer might not have any resources available. If you can see the resources but cannot access them, you might not have permission to access those resources. Contact the system administrator.

I can't find a computer on the network. What should I do?

Choose Start, Find, Computer. The Find Computer dialog box appears. Enter the computer's name in the Named text box and choose Find Now. Windows should find the computer for you.

If you still cannot find the computer, it might be disconnected from the network. Contact the system administrator.

I tried to access a floppy disk on another computer to which I previously had access, and I received a message saying `\computername\drive is not accessible. The device is not ready`. What can I do?

That error message appears when the drive you're accessing is empty; for example, there is no disk in the floppy drive or CD-ROM drive. Contact the system administrator or send an e-mail to the computer you're trying to connect to and let them know you need the resource.

Some of the files I share are missing.

If you've given full access to someone else on the network, they can delete files from your disk. When someone deletes files from your disk, those files go to their Recycle Bin; you might check with everyone on the network who you've given full access to see if your files are still in their Recycle Bin.

Working with Shared Files

When you assign read-only and full passwords to shared drives and directories, the user must know the password to access those files. Without a read-only password, for example, the user cannot make changes to the file.

The Network Neighborhood window has two workstations: Asst. Director and Director. To open a computer on the network, double-click the icon of that computer; a window appears listing all available resources and/or directories or folders. Finally, to open a directory, double-click that directory. If the directory has read-only or full access, the directory's window opens and displays the contents. If, however, the directory allows only password access, the Enter Network Password dialog box appears (see fig. 21.2). Enter the password and choose OK to open the file. If you choose the Save This Password in Your Password List option, that password saves so you don't have to retype it the next time you open that folder.

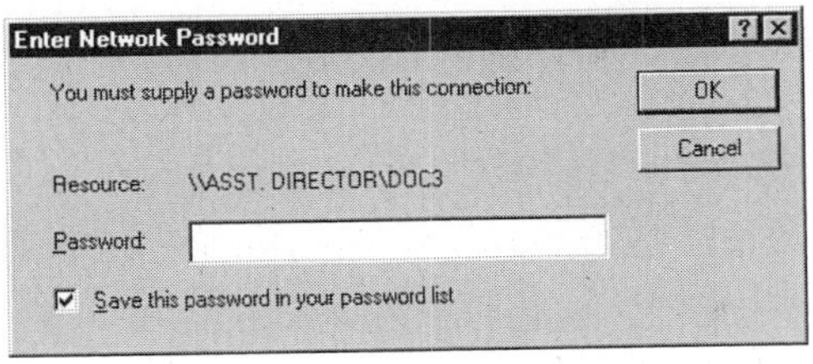

Fig. 21.2
You cannot open password-protected folders without entering the correct password.

Figure 21.3 shows the resulting message box from choosing File, Save while in a read-only shared file in WordPad. You can, however, choose File, Save As and save the document under another name. When saving the file, you can place it on your own drive, on another computer's drive, and in any folder to which you have access.

Fig. 21.3
Read-only password protection keeps you from saving changes to someone else's file.

Mapping Drives

Windows enables you to use drive mapping in peer-to-peer networking. *Drive mapping* is a method of assigning a drive letter to represent a path that includes the volume, directory, and any subdirectories leading to a directory or resource. The drive mapping you create follows the path for you, thereby saving you time; instead of opening folder after folder, you can use the drive map to quickly go to the directory or resource. Mapping is especially handy when you're constantly using a file or resource on another workstation.

To map a drive, follow these steps:

1. Open the window in which you want to place the mapped drive.

2. Choose View, Toolbar to display the Toolbar if it is not already showing.

3. Click the Map Network Drive icon on the toolbar (see fig. 21.4).

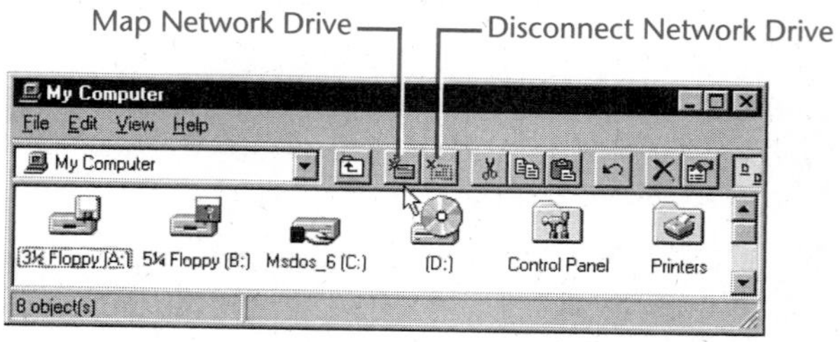

Fig. 21.4
Click the Map Network Drive icon to create a drive mapping shortcut.

4. The Map Network Drive dialog box appears, as shown in figure 21.5. Click the Path down arrow. If you have recently connected to the drive, the path appears in the list box. If the path is not in the list box, enter the path in the following format: *//computername/foldername*.

Fig. 21.5
Enter the Path of the resource or directory you want to map.

Tip
To make the mapping permanent, choose the Reconnect at Logon option.

5. Choose OK to complete the path. Figure 21.6 shows the resulting mapping icon in the My Computer window.

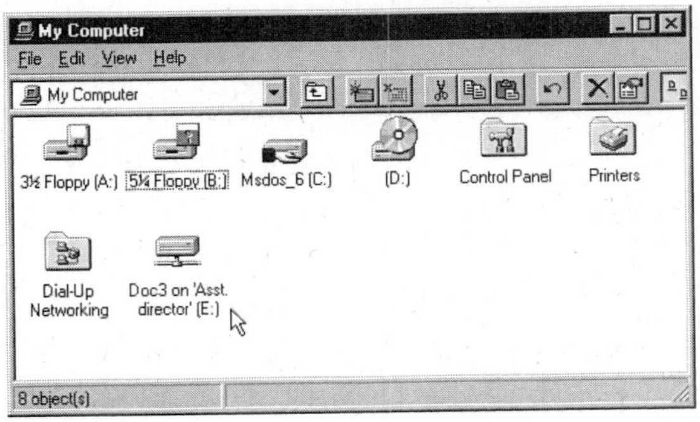

Fig. 21.6
Double-click the mapped drive icon to quickly open the folder.

> **Note**
>
> To break the connection to the mapped drive, select the icon and click the Disconnect Net Drive icon. The Disconnect Network Drive dialog box appears; choose OK to remove the connection and the icon.

Understanding Drive Usage Policies

When working in a peer-to-peer environment, the workstations with the most used resources can easily become burdened and bottlenecks will often form. You must consider some simple resource usage policies to guarantee the most efficient use of those resources.

For example, the computer that contains the accounting or database program that all workstations use is a good candidate for hard drive management. To prevent a bottleneck of activity centered around the workstation containing the application, you might designate that the data files for that application be stored on another computer. Traffic then will be divided between two computers instead of concentrated on just one.

As another example, consider a network that uses MS Office daily. To guarantee the most efficient use of the applications, consider installing Office on each machine instead of sharing the application from one workstation. The applications will run faster, the user's time will not be wasted waiting for access to specific programs, and network traffic will be cut considerably.

Additionally, you might want to assign different workstations for the storage of the shared files used in the Office applications. One workstation can store shared Word files and another can store shared Excel files. Use a different workstation to store PowerPoint files, and so on. In this manner, traffic is disseminated for more efficient use of the network.

Note

Make sure each workstation is assigned only what is necessary for that user to do the work. For example, if a user needs to access only specific folders on the Director's drive, those are the only folders that should be available to that user. Limiting access not only ensures security, but also saves the user time searching for needed files and folders.

An additional shared resource you might want to keep an eye on is the CD-ROM drive. Windows enables each workstation to access a CD in the shared drive and run applications or copy files from that CD. Because workstations might need to access the drive at the same time, traffic can become congested. To alleviate the problem, you could limit specific workstation access to the drive. If all workstations need to use the CD-ROM drive, consider scheduling times for its use; something as simple as having workstations one through eight use the drive in the mornings and the rest using it in the afternoons.

As you become more familiar with how the Windows peer-to-peer network operates, you'll find ways to make sharing resources efficient and effective.

◄ See "Changing the Properties of the Recycle Bin," p. 521

Note

A tool you might overlook when thinking about disk usage is the Recycle Bin. Not emptying the Recycle Bin leaves you with less space than you thought you had. If you use your drive in a networked environment, this extra lost space may be valuable.

Sharing Printers

► See "Understanding Network Printing," p. 772

► See "Managing Print Files and Sharing," p. 784

You can designate a printer attached to your machine as a shared printer. Anyone on the network with access can then print to your printer from their workstation. With a shared printer, users can print from applications or use the drag-and-drop printing method. Users also can cancel, view the print queue, and pause printing.

When sharing your printer with others on the network, you can choose to limit access by assigning a password. Then, only those with the password can use your printer. Additionally, you can stop sharing your printer at any time.

Setting Up Printer Sharing and Security

For others to use your printer, you must designate it as a shared resource. When you choose to share the printer, you also can assign a password to limit access to the printer. Before you can share your printer, you must enable file and printer sharing from the Network dialog box.

◄ See "Sharing Files and Printers," p. 633

To designate a printer for sharing, follow these steps:

1. Choose Start, Settings, and then Printers.

2. In the Printers window, select the printer you want to share and choose File, Sharing. The printer's Properties sheet appears.

3. Choose the Shared As option to activate the shared area of the sheet (see fig. 21.7).

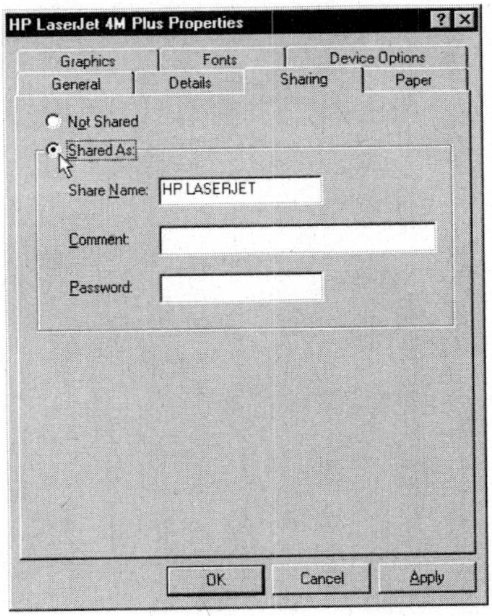

Fig. 21.7
When choosing to share a printer, you can assign a password to limit user access.

4. Accept the default name or type a new name in the Share Name text box.

5. If you want, describe the printer in more detail in the Comment text box.

6. Optionally, give the resource a Password.

7. To implement the changes you have made to the sheet, click the Apply button.

8. Choose OK to close the Properties sheet; the printer icon now displays the shared icon.

Connecting to a Shared Printer

Before you can attach to a shared printer, you must install the network printer to your list of printers. Windows includes a printer wizard to help you install the network printer. After installing it, you can use the printer to print from your applications as you would any printer that's attached to your computer.

To install a shared printer, follow these steps:

1. Open the Network Neighborhood and double-click the computer to which the printer is attached. The computer's window opens and the printer icon appears.

2. Select the printer icon and choose File, Install.

   You also can open the Printers folder and double-click the Add Printer icon.

3. The first Add Printer Wizard dialog box appears. Choose Yes if you plan to print from MS-DOS-based programs to this printer. Otherwise, accept the default selection, No, by choosing the Next button.

4. The second Add Printer Wizard dialog box appears, as shown in figure 21.8. Choose the Network Printer option and choose Next.

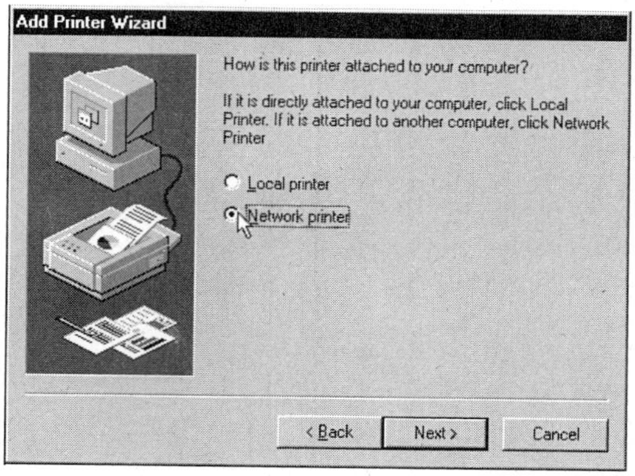

Fig. 21.8
The wizard dialog box specifies Local Printer as a default; use this option only if the printer is physically attached to your computer.

5. The next Add Printer Wizard dialog box appears (see fig. 21.9). In the Network Path or Queue Name text box, enter the path to the printer.

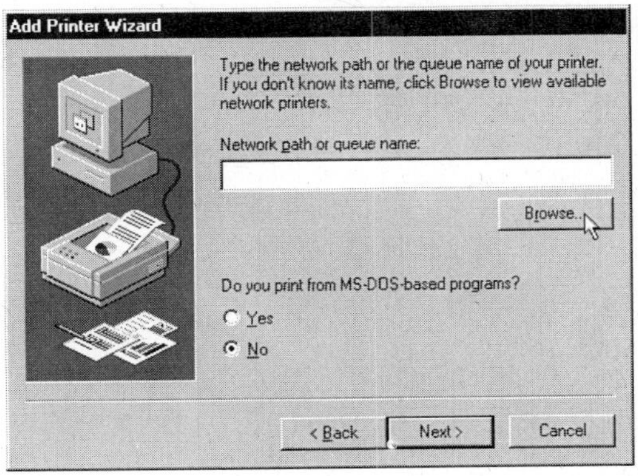

Fig. 21.9
Enter the path to the printer or choose the Browse button to find the correct path.

If you don't know the path, choose the Browse button. The Browse for Printer dialog box opens (see fig. 21.10). Double-click the remote computer and then select the printer. Choose OK to return to the wizard dialog box. The path appears in the Network Path text box.

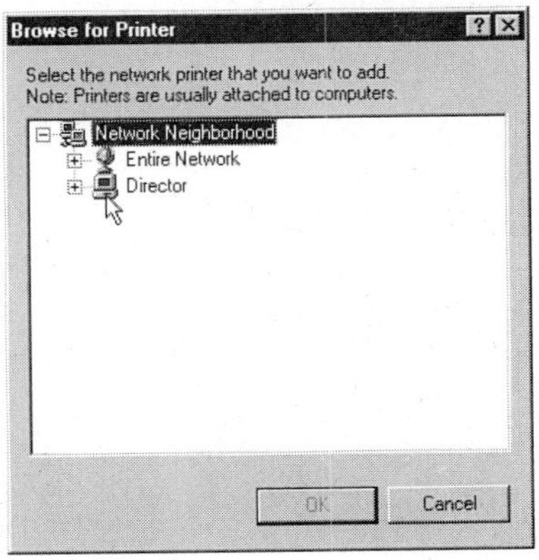

Fig. 21.10
You can select the printer in this dialog box and the path will automatically appear in the Network Path text box.

6. Choose Next. The next wizard box enables you to enter a printer name other than the default, if you want. Choose Next.

7. The final wizard dialog box enables you to print a text page. Choose Yes to print a test page; choose No if you don't want to print a test page. Choose Finish to install the printer.

Windows adds the network printer to your list of printers. Use the printer as you would any printer attached to your computer.

Applying Printer Sharing Policies

When you share a printer in a peer-to-peer network, all jobs sent to the printer are entered into the print queue, where they wait for the printer to become available. Jobs are normally serviced in first-come-first-serve order, although most printers allow users to prioritize print jobs so they can be moved up in line.

While some of the resource users might print jobs with one or two pages of text, there are also those who print 90-page jobs with heavy graphic use. Those large jobs are the ones that can cause frustration for everyone else on the network who needs to print.

The solution? There are a couple of common sense ideas you can apply to the situation. First, you should make available two printers to the network, if at all possible. To justify the expense of two printers, choose one printer (such as a laser) as the workhorse—the most commonly used printer. Choose a second printer (such as a color inkjet or laser) to use for special presentations or reports. Because most color printers also can print black ink, use the second printer for general printing when the first printer is overloaded.

The second idea for controlling printer use is to set forth some common courtesy guidelines for those attached to the network. Anyone having especially large or complex print jobs should contact all concerned and perhaps even schedule a time to print the job. If everyone on the network understands they must cooperate in using all shared resources, almost any problem can be solved.

► See "Understanding Network Printing," p. 772

► See "Managing Print Files and Sharing," p. 784

Troubleshooting

It's taking a long time for my document to print. Can I speed it up?

In the Printers window, double-click the printer icon to see the printer's window. Locate your job and see where you are in line. If there are a lot of jobs in the queue ahead of you, you'll have to wait for the other jobs to print.

If your job is the one printing and progress seems to be slow, graphics added to the document might be causing the problem. You can cancel the print job and then select the printer icon in the Printers window and choose File, Properties. Choose the Graphics tab and choose a lower resolution. Choose OK and try printing the document again.

Sharing a Fax Modem

Windows 95 enables users to easily share a fax modem with other users in the workgroup. Every user can take advantage of the service and send faxes and even editable files using the shared fax modem. Windows 95 makes this capability as easy as printing a file or sending an e-mail message.

Microsoft Fax is compatible with Group 3 faxes worldwide, yet it also offers secure fax transmission as well as binary file transfer to another Microsoft Fax recipient. Microsoft Fax uses MAPI (Mail Application Programming Interface) so you can easily send a fax using an application's File, Send command or File, Print command. The fax printer driver is accessible from any application's Print command, enabling fax in all users' applications. This power makes a shared fax a great addition to a workgroup. This section discusses the features of Microsoft Fax specifically when used as a shared fax server.

Understanding Fax Modem Sharing Policies

For the most part, a peer-to-peer network makes use of each computer's resource while each computer's user continues to work on the computer. When you find the shared resources are so heavily used that one computer becomes overloaded, it is time to consider changing one computer into a server.

Consider these primary issues when determining whether to set up a Windows 95 computer as a fax server:

◄ See "Approaches to Networks," p. 582

- Is the computer on which the fax modem is installed going to be used only as a fax server, or will it also be used as a workstation?
- Which users will need the fax service?
- Is this computer going to host the only fax that the company uses?
- Is this computer also going to serve as a print server?

If the fax server computer is also going to be used as a workstation, you may need to increase the amount of memory installed on the computer. Microsoft makes these recommendations:

- Standalone fax server minimum configuration:

  80486 computer with 8M of memory

- Dual purpose fax server and workstation minimum configuration:

  80486 computer with 12M of memory

If you want to share a fax modem, you must install Microsoft Exchange on each workstation that needs to use the fax service. All faxes are sent to the users through Microsoft Exchange. The Microsoft Exchange InBox of the fax server receives all the incoming faxes for those using the service. The faxes are not automatically routed; this operation is done manually by the administrator of the fax server.

If this fax is the only one the company uses, the fax volume needs to be monitored to assure that the needs of the company are being met. Microsoft states that the preceding recommended configuration typically supports a workgroup of 25 users.

If the computer is also a print server—a common configuration since users can print their faxes from the same computer—additional monitoring may be necessary to assure that the workstation is handling the additional load.

Setting Up Fax Modem Sharing

After you have made the decision to set up a fax server, you take these steps:

► See "Installing a Plug and Play Modem," p. 833

1. Install the modem.
2. Install the Exchange client on the server computer.
3. Install Microsoft Fax on the server.
4. Establish the fax share.

You use similar steps to set up each workstation:

1. Install the Exchange client.
2. Install Microsoft Fax.
3. Connect to the shared fax.

Before configuring the fax modem for sharing, you need to install it on the sharing computer. If the fax modem is not yet set up, see Chapter 27, "Installing and Configuring Your Modem." You also need to have Exchange and Microsoft Fax installed on the server. Both of these topics are explained in Chapter 24, "Using Microsoft Exchange." After that, you are ready to configure Exchange to enable sharing:

1. Open the Start menu and choose Settings, Control Panel.
2. Double-click the Mail and Fax icon. The MS Exchange Settings Properties sheet opens as shown in figure 21.11.

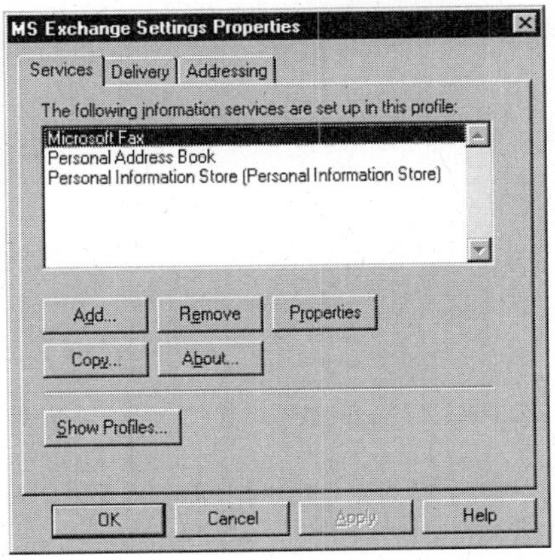

Fig. 21.11
The MS Exchange Settings Properties sheet shows the Microsoft Fax selection.

3. Select Microsoft Fax and click Properties. The Microsoft Fax Properties sheet appears (see fig. 21.12).

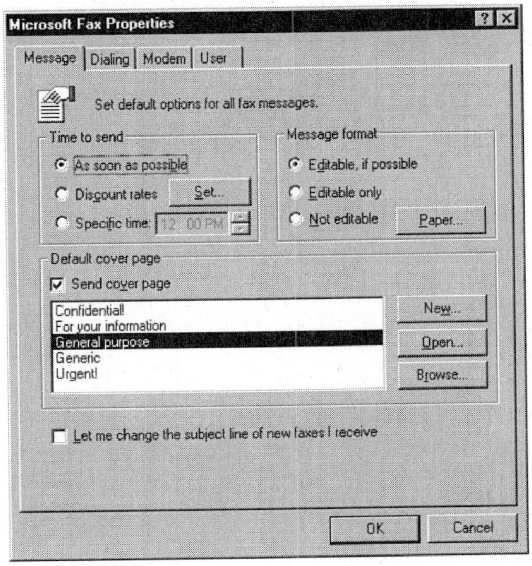

Fig. 21.12
The Message tab appears in the Microsoft Fax Properties sheet.

4. Choose the Modem tab and select the option Let Other People on the Network Use My Modem To Send Faxes, as shown in figure 21.13.

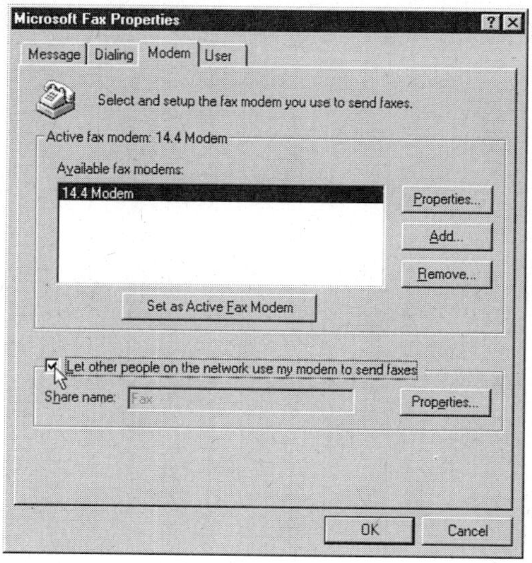

Fig. 21.13
Choose to share the modem in the Modem tab of the Microsoft Fax Properties sheet.

5. Choose the Properties button on the Modem page. The NetFax dialog box appears (see fig. 21.14).

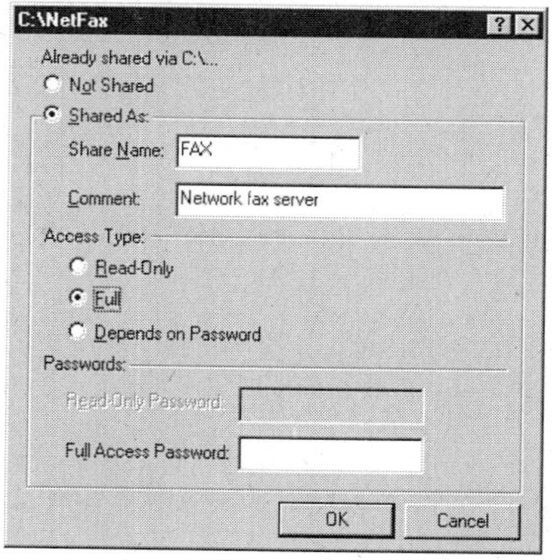

Fig. 21.14
Use the NetFax dialog box to assign a share name, comment, and to limit access to the fax modem.

6. Enter the Share Name, a Comment if you want, and set the Access Type for the fax modem.
7. Enter a password. The Confirmation of Password dialog box appears; enter the password again and choose OK.
8. Click OK in each dialog box to complete the configuration.

Configuring Workstations to Use a Shared Fax Modem

You are now ready to install and configure each workstation to connect to and use the server. Installation is simply a repeat of the steps from Chapter 24 to install Microsoft Exchange and Microsoft Fax software, then you configure Microsoft Fax to use the shared fax modem instead of looking for a local modem. This section doesn't repeat the software installation but just steps through locating and connecting to the shared fax server:

► See "Installing and Configuring Microsoft Exchange," p. 727

1. Open the Start menu, choose Settings, Control Panel.
2. Double-click the Mail and Fax icon. The MS Exchange Settings Properties sheet opens (refer to fig. 21.11).
3. Select Microsoft Fax and click Properties. The Microsoft Fax Properties sheet appears (refer to fig. 21.12).
4. Click the Modem tab and choose Add. The Add a Fax Modem dialog box appears.
5. Click Network Fax Server, as shown in figure 21.15.

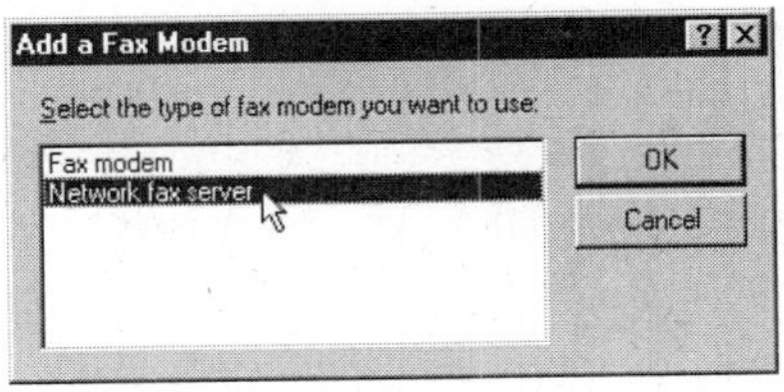

Fig. 21.15
Choose a Network Fax Server to connect to the fax modem on another computer.

6. Choose OK and the Connect To Network Fax Server dialog box appears (see fig. 21.16).

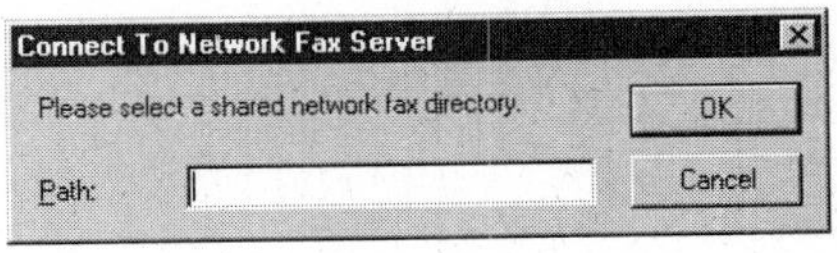

Fig. 21.16
Enter the path to the fax server.

   Type the UNC share name for the fax server (for example, \\SERVER\NETFAX).

7. Click OK to close each dialog box.

You're now ready to use Windows 95's Microsoft Fax.

Using a Shared Fax Modem

You can easily use a shared fax modem from Microsoft Exchange through Microsoft Fax, or from an application such as WordPad or Word.

To use Microsoft Exchange to send a fax, double-click the Inbox to start the application. Compose the fax as you normally would.

▶ See "Faxing a Quick Message or a File," p. 743

To send a fax from an application, compose the fax and then choose File, Send. The Choose Profile dialog box appears. Use the default profile or choose a new one, then choose OK. The New Message dialog box appears. Complete the message as you would in Microsoft Exchange. You can, alternatively, choose File, Print to send a fax. In the Print dialog box choose Microsoft Fax as the name of the printer and choose OK.

▶ See "Working with User Profiles in Exchange," p. 763

To use Microsoft Fax, open the Start menu and select Programs. Choose Accessories, Fax, and Compose New Fax to create a fax to send.

Note

If someone tries to access the fax modem while it is in use, the fax messages are placed in a queue, similar to when jobs are placed in a print queue.

Note

If you send or receive faxes on the network using a shared fax modem, you may want to take advantage of Microsoft Fax's security features to ensure privacy of your fax transmissions. This topic is discussed in Chapter 24, "Using Microsoft Exchange."

Gaining Remote Access to Your Network

▶ See "Connecting to the Internet with a LAN," p. 899

◀ See "System Requirements and Recommendations," p. 620

Remote access with Windows 95 is easier and more robust than in any previous version of Windows. If you are connecting to an Internet service provider, using remote mail from home, or simply connecting to another Windows 95 workstation, Windows 95 Remote Network Access (RNA) and Dial-Up Networking can make the connection for you and enable you to use all the resources on the network as if you were physically connected to the LAN rather than remotely connected through a modem.

Remote access is accomplished with new 32-bit networking components and a dial-up adapter, so you can take advantage of all the interfaces of Windows remote networking. Because remote networking is built-in at the core of Windows 95, programs that require networking invoke the Dial-Up Networking component when they run to automate the connection. A good example is the Internet Explorer that is part of the Plus! Pack for Windows 95. When you attempt to connect to a resource that requires a network connection, the Internet Explorer automatically opens the Dial-Up Networking dialog box to attempt a connection to the network.

◀ See "Modems for Dial-Up Networking," p. 622

Tip
Connecting to an Internet service provider is covered in Chapter 29, "Getting Connected to the Internet."

As indicated in Chapter 20, "Setting Up a Windows 95 Peer-to-Peer Network," Remote Network Access with Windows 95 requires only the addition of a modem, installation of Dial-Up Networking components, and the phone number for the remote connection. This connection can be an Internet service account, a Windows 95 or Windows NT server, a NetWare Connect server, or Shiva's LanRover and NetModem remote-node servers. This section discusses connecting to a Windows 95 server and to a Windows NT server.

◀ See "Installing the Microsoft Network Client," p. 625

◀ See "Identifying Your Workgroup Computer," p. 635

Preparing Your Computer

With Dial-Up Networking, you can connect to a network and access shared information, even if your computer is not a part of the network. You can use a home computer, notebook, or other computer to dial up a server on the network.

1. In the Configuration tab of the Network dialog box, select Client for Microsoft Networks from the Network Components list, as shown in figure 21.17.

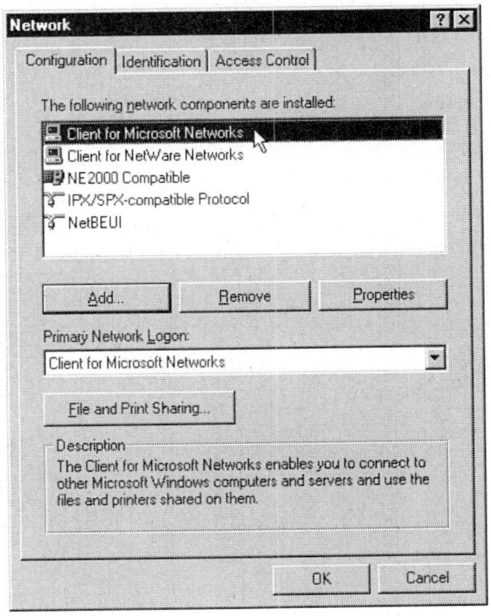

Fig. 21.17
You must first select the client before identifying the host and workgroup.

2. Click the Identification tab of the Network dialog box (see fig. 21.18).

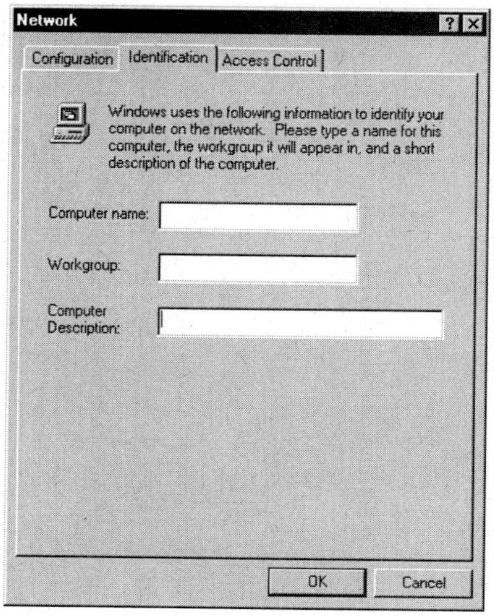

Fig. 21.18
Identify the host and workgroup in the Identification tab.

3. Enter the name of the remote, or host, computer in the Computer Name text box. Enter the Workgroup name; Workgroup refers to a Windows NT, Windows 95, or Windows for Workgroup workgroup, the logical grouping of peer machines in a Windows network.

4. Click the Access Control tab. The Access Control tab appears as shown in figure 21.19.

5. For peer-to-peer networking, choose Share-Level Access Control. A LAN user can choose either option, depending on whether pass-through account validation is needed or desired.

6. Click OK.

7. Window 95 states that you must restart your computer before the new settings will take effect and asks if you want to restart the computer. Choose Yes to restart with the new settings.

Congratulations, you have made it through the hardest part of installation and configuration of your dial-up connection. Now you can proceed to configuring a dial-up connection.

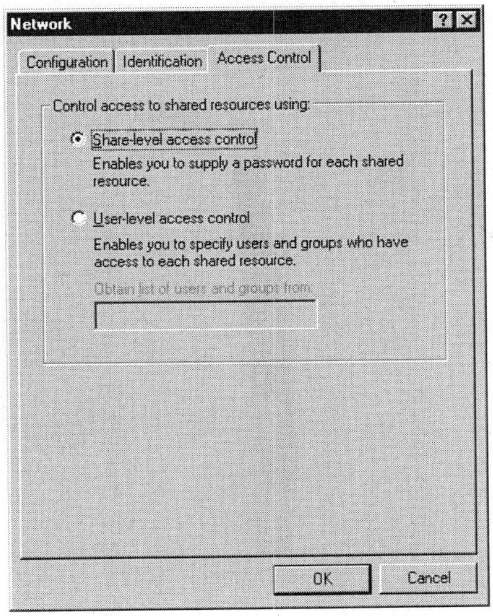

Fig. 21.19
Choose the access control you want for shared resources.

Making the Connection

Windows provides a Dial-Up Connection wizard that makes it easy to create connections for Dial-Up Networking. After the wizard leads you through the process, you're ready to make your call. To run the wizard, follow these steps:

1. Open the Start menu and choose Programs, Select Accessories, and then Dial-Up Networking. The Dial-Up Networking window appears.

2. Double-click Make New Connection. The first box of the Make New Connection wizard appears (see fig. 21.20).

> **Note**
>
> After you have added at least one new connection, opening the Start menu and choosing Programs, Accessories, and then Dial-Up Networking has a different result. Once a connection exists, choosing this as in step 1 opens the Dial-Up Networking Folder instead of the Wizard.

3. Enter the name to identify the computer to which you will attach; for example, use the resource's name such as Laser Printer on Director's.

4. Select your modem.

   Choose the Configure button if you need to set any specific options. The modem's Properties sheet will appear, containing such information as port, speaker volume, baud rate, data bits, parity, and so on. Choose OK to return to the wizard.

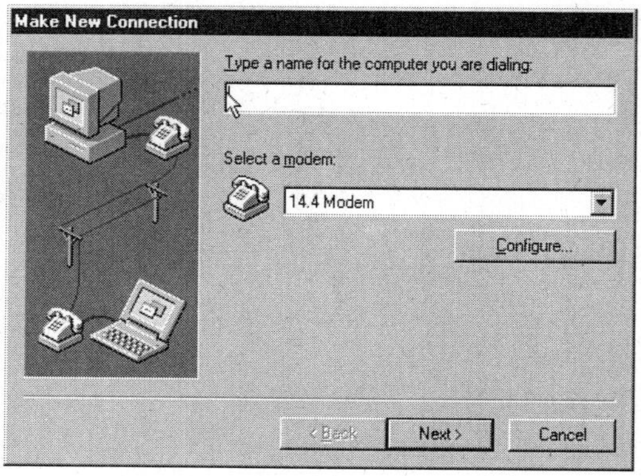

Fig. 21.20
Enter a name for the computer to which you are making the connection.

5. Choose Next. The second wizard dialog box appears (see fig. 21.21).

6. Enter the Telephone Number to the modem of the remote (host) computer and your Country Code.

7. Click Next. The next wizard dialog box appears, telling you the connection was successfully created.

8. Click Finish. The new connection is added to the Dial-Up Networking window.

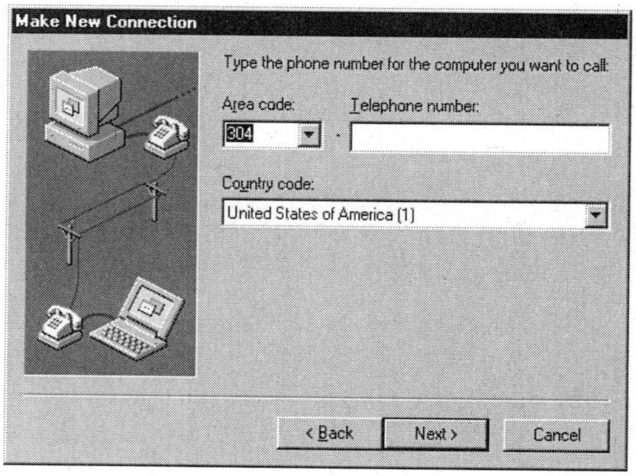

Fig. 21.21
Enter the telephone number and choose a country, if other than the United States.

Modifying a Connection

You can change a phone number, modem configuration, and even the server type for a Dial-Up connection. First, you must open the Dial-Up Networking window and select the connection you want to modify. Then follow these steps:

1. Right-click the Dial-Up Connection icon you want to modify.
2. Select the Properties command. The connection's properties sheet appears, as shown in figure 21.22.
3. To reconfigure the modem, choose the Configure button. The Modem Properties sheet appears and offers options such as port, speaker volume, speed, parity, and so on.

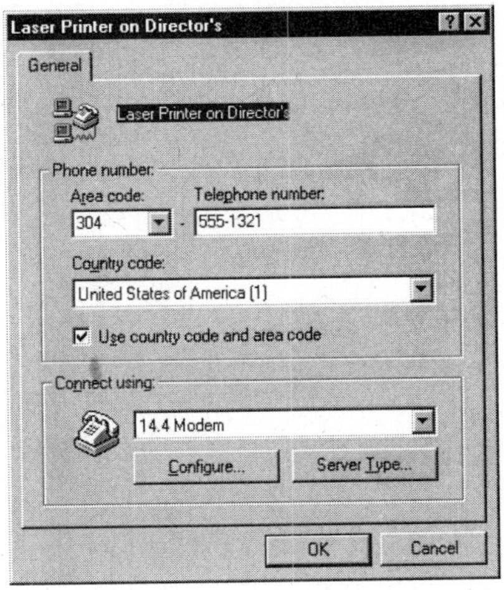

Fig. 21.22 Use the connection's properties sheet to change phone numbers, modem connections, and so on.

4. To set the server, choose the Server Type button. The Server Types dialog box appears (see fig. 21.23).
5. In the Type of Dial-Up Server drop-down list, choose the type of server to which you want to connect from the following:

   PPP; Windows 95, Windows NT 3.5, Internet. Choose to connect to a Windows 95 peer-to-peer network, a Windows NT 3.5 network, or to the Internet.

Windows for Workgroups and Windows NT 3.1. Choose to connect to either of these versions of Windows.

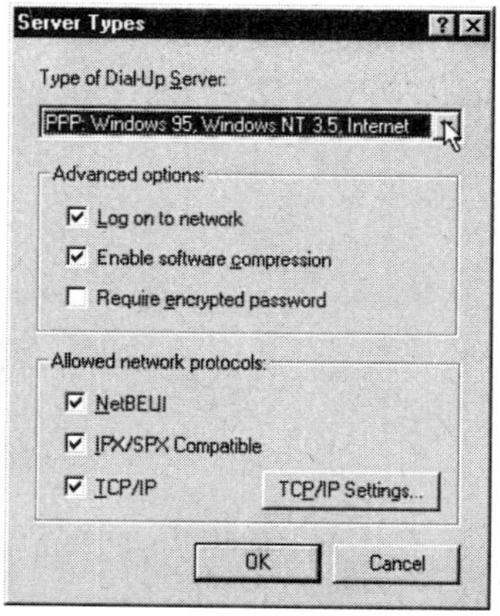

Fig. 21.23
Choose the type of server you want to connect to, such as a Windows NT or Windows 95 server.

6. In the Advanced options area, choose from the following options:

   Log On to Network. Dial-Up Networking logs onto the network using the name and password you use to log into Windows.

   Enable Software Compression. Specifies whether data is compressed before it is sent. Speeds up the transfer but both computers must be using compatible compression.

   Require Encrypted Password. Specifies that only encrypted passwords can be sent to or accepted by your computer.

7. In the Allowed Network Protocols area, choose NetBEUI to connect to the peer-to-peer network.

8. Choose OK to close the dialog box. Choose OK again to close the connection's properties dialog box.

Connecting the Dial-Up Network

You can add more connections to your Dial-Up Networking window at any time. When you're ready to connect to the network, open the Dial-Up Networking window, turn on your modem, and follow these steps:

1. Double-click the connection icon in the Dial-Up Networking window. The Connect To dialog box appears (see fig. 21.24).

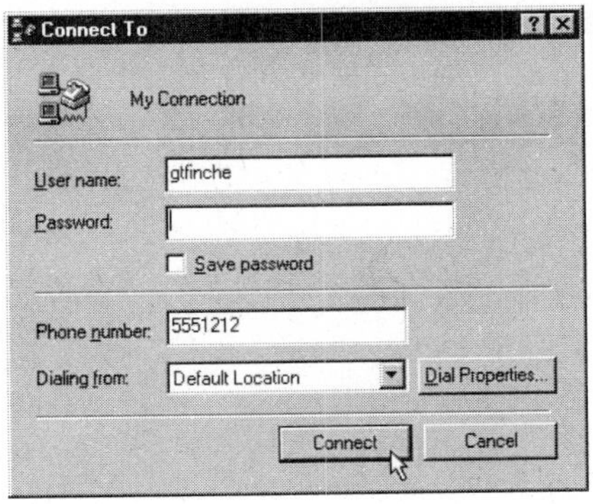

Fig. 21.24
Make any last minute changes in the Connect To dialog box.

2. Enter the Password. You can choose Dial Properties if you have any last minute changes to make to the information.

3. Choose the Connect button. The Connecting To dialog box shows your progress. When the connection is made, Dial-Up verifies your user name and password with the remote computer.

4. When your login is complete, Windows 95 shows the connection status dialog box that monitors the connection. You're connected to the remote network and can access any resources to which you have been given access.

Troubleshooting

The remote computer hangs up on me unexpectedly. What makes it do that?

There might be noise over the phone lines that's interrupting the connection. You could try calling again and hope for a better connection.

If you're still having problems, ask the administrator whether the computer you're trying to connect to is up and running.

Alternatively, you might have gone too long without typing anything. Try again. Also, ask your administrator if there is a time limit on how long you can remain connected to the network. Perhaps the administrator can increase the time.

Managing a Peer-to-Peer Network

With all the useful peer-to-peer features in Windows 95, you may think the network must be a nightmare to administer. But Microsoft has assembled a set of tools to assist in managing this usually unmanageable network topology. The tools range from the fairly simple but powerful Net Watcher to the robust agents that enable remote monitoring in an automated fashion.

▶ See "What Utilities are Included in the Resource Kit," p. 1138

The tools that ship as part of Windows 95 are Net Watcher, System Policy Editor, Registry Editor, and Backup Agents; these tools do not install by default. The System Policy Editor, for example, is an Accessory System tool you can install through Windows Setup, if you did not install it at the same time you installed Windows. Other utilities can be found in the Windows 95 Resource Kit.

Net Watcher

Net Watcher enables you to monitor and manage network connections, as well as create, add, and delete shared resources. To use this powerful tool, you need to configure each workstation to allow remote administration.

To enable remote administration, follow these steps:

1. Double-click the Passwords icon in the Control Panel. The Passwords Properties sheet appears.
2. Click the Remote Administration tab, as shown in figure 21.25.
3. Select Enable Remote Administration of the Server.
4. Enter a Password and then enter it again in the Confirm Password text box. Choose OK.

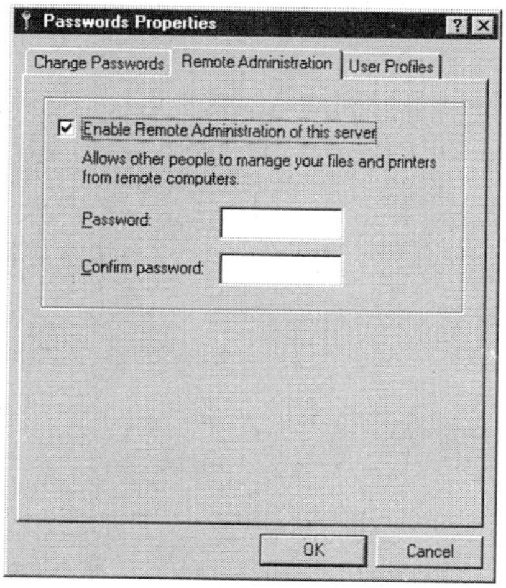

Fig. 21.25
Enable remote administration and enter a password to limit access.

After you have configured the workstations to allow remote configuration, run Net Watcher on the administrator's workstation. To run Net Watcher, click the Start button and then choose Programs, Accessories, System Tools, and then Net Watcher. The Net Watcher window appears as shown in figure 21.26.

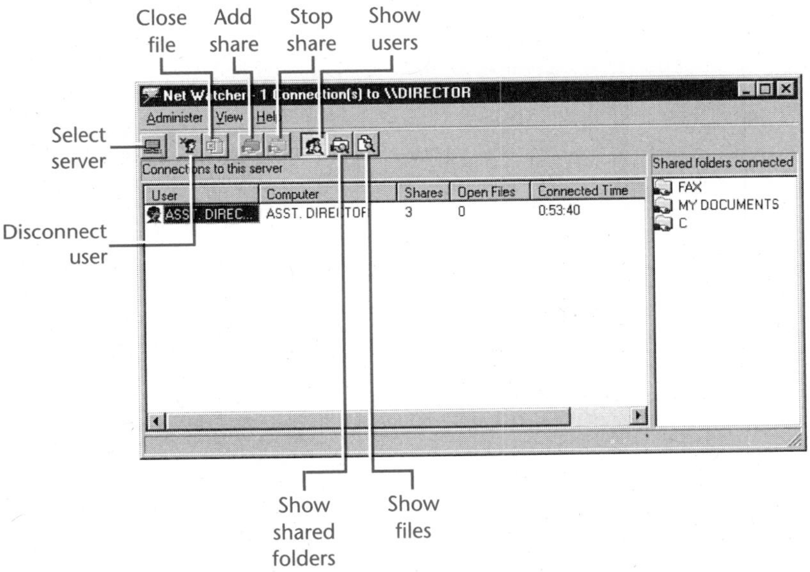

Fig. 21.26
You can view the computers on the network and the folders shared with them.

Note

To install Net Watcher, use the Add/Remove Programs icon in the Control Panel. In the Windows Setup tab, Net Watcher is listed as an Accessory.

This accessory enables a remote administrator to actively monitor and manage shared drives and folders, printers, or even the fax server. Using the icons in the Net Watcher, you can show users, shared folders, and files currently being shared. Additionally, when you show the shared folders, Net Watcher lists access type and comments, as shown in figure 21.27.

◀ See "Adding Windows' Component Applications," p. 312

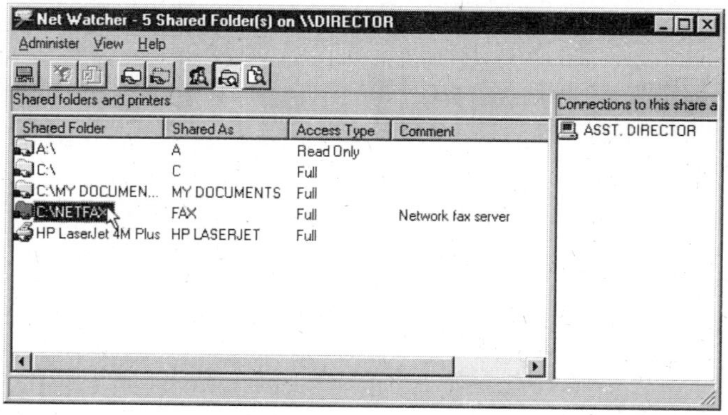

Fig. 21.27 Select a shared folder and view the computer connection to that folder on the right side of the Net Watcher window.

Tip

You can use the Administer menu to add shared folders or to stop sharing a folder; you can even change the sharing properties of any selected folder.

System Monitor

The next tool in the administrator's arsenal is the System Monitor, which gives a graphical picture of network traffic, file system performance, and other settings. Though System Monitor ships with Windows 95, remote monitoring requires the Microsoft Remote Registry service from the Resource Kit. Once this service is installed, you can monitor running processes, memory usage, network traffic, and so on. Figure 21.28 shows the System Monitor on a local machine.

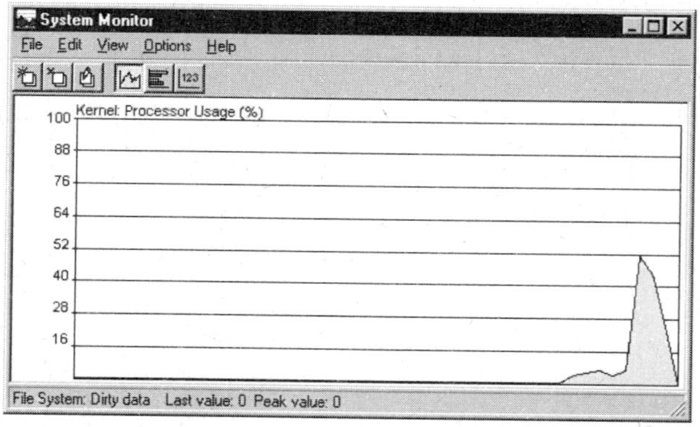

Fig. 21.28 System Monitor dialog box showing processor usage.

► See "What Utilities are Included in the Resource Kit," p. 1138

Note the graphical element showing the current processor usage. This parameter could be useful in determining whether a specific workstation is being overworked.

Install the System Monitor using the Add/Remove Programs icon in the Control Panel. The System Monitor is located in the Accessories component. After installation, open the System Monitor by choosing Accessories, System Tools.

> **Note**
>
> Using both System Monitor and Registry Editor for remote administration requires Microsoft Remote Registry service from the Resource Kit. You also need to configure the workstations for User-Level access control.

Registry Editor

Registry Editor is another powerful but also dangerous tool. With the Registry Editor you can fine-tune Windows 95 performance by adjusting or adding settings to key system information. Because Windows 95 has placed WIN.INI and SYSTEM.INI file settings in the Registry, you can remotely edit these parameters. Often, Microsoft issues "knowledge base" articles with previously undocumented settings in the Registry to fix or work around problems with Windows. But remember, if you edit the Registry directly with Registry Editor, you can cause a running workstation to cease running. The Resource Kit is a required tool when working in the Registry.

Figure 21.29 shows a view of the Registry running on a local workstation. It shows the `HKEY_CURRENT_USER\ControlPanel\desktop` setting for full-window drag operation; `DragFullWindows` is set to "1," which enables this option. If a user has problems with that setting, you can remotely edit the setting to change the operation.

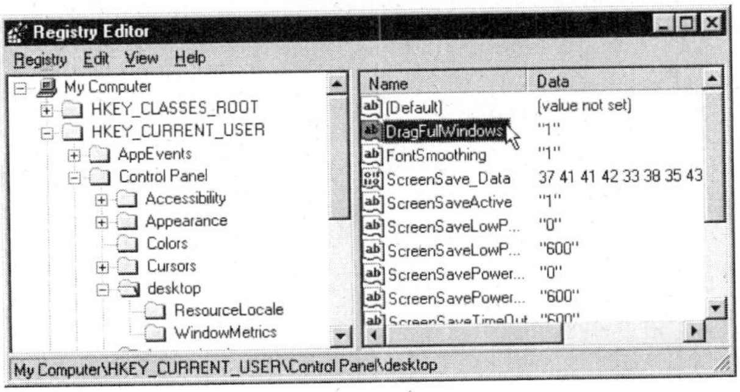

Fig. 21.29
The Registry Editor window.

Network Backups

You can use Windows Backup to back up files from one computer on the network to another. Back up the files to a hard disk or tape drive and then restore the files if the originals are damaged or lost. Start the backup by choosing Start, Programs, Accessories, System Tools, and then Backup.

> **Tip**
>
> You also can choose the Backup program from the Accessories, System Tools menu to restore backed-up files.

If Windows Backup is not installed, you can install Backup by opening the Add/Remove Program Icon and choosing the Windows Setup. The Backup is listed in the Disk Tools.

System Policy Editor

◄ See "Adding Windows' Component Applications," p. 312

The System Policy Editor is another tool from the Resource Kit. As with the tools previously described, the Policy Editor requires the Microsoft Remote Registry service from the Resource Kit. With this tool, an administrator can manage the desktop of a remote workstation by installing system-wide policies that override the local workstation's default parameters. With System Policy Editor, an administrator can force the use of alpha-numeric passwords for resources, as illustrated in figure 21.30.

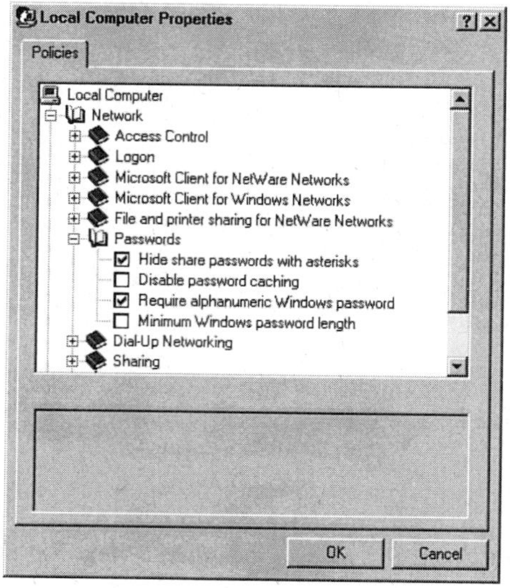

Fig. 21.30
The System Policy Editor dialog box shows your password options.

► See "Who Needs the Windows 95 Resource Kit?" p. 1134

Using the tools described in this section, a system administrator can manage even the unruliest of peer-to-peer resources on the network. Microsoft rounds out the toolkit with two additional remote agents: Microsoft Network Monitor and an SNMP (Simple Network Management Protocol) agent. Both agents enable further monitoring and control using industry-standard, industrial-strength tools such as Microsoft Systems Management Server, Intel® LANDesk™, and HP® Open View for Windows.❖

Chapter 22

Connecting Windows 95 to a Novell Network

by Glenn Fincher with Sue Plumley

This chapter continues the discussion of Windows 95 networking by talking specifically about Windows 95 and Novell NetWare compatibility. If your primary network is currently Novell NetWare, Windows 95 seamlessly integrates with your current network. In most cases, you can accomplish this installation without any additional work besides simply installing Windows 95. If you are running NetWare client software during installation, Windows 95 correctly detects and installs the Microsoft Client for NetWare Networks. With this feature alone, Windows 95 makes installation on an existing NetWare network a breeze.

However, Microsoft has many other reasons for calling Windows 95 "the well-connected client." After reading this chapter, and especially after using Windows 95 with NetWare, you'll undoubtedly agree that Microsoft has really done its homework in designing this piece of the Windows 95 phenomenon.

In this chapter, you learn about the following issues regarding Windows 95 and Novell NetWare:

- System requirements
- Windows support features for NetWare
- Automatic installation of NetWare
- Manually installing a network card
- Manually installing the NetWare client
- Testing and troubleshooting your NetWare installation

System Requirements

As discussed earlier in Chapter 20, "Setting Up a Windows 95 Peer-to-Peer Network," the requirements for networking with Windows 95 are simple. With the addition of either a network adapter for a local area network (LAN) connection or a modem and Microsoft's Dial-Up Networking "adapter," you can connect your computer to virtually any network topology. Because Windows 95 has integrated support for NetWare networks, the only actual requirements to connect Windows 95 to a NetWare network are the following:

- An existing NetWare network
- A PC network adapter for a LAN connection, or a Hayes-compatible modem attached to your computer (the NetWare server must also have a modem attached and modem server software) for a Dial-Up Networking connection
- A method of attaching to the network, such as cabling, infrared interfaces, laser, and so on

Windows 95 Support for NetWare

◀ See "Remote Access to Your Network," p. 660

◀ See "Connecting Network Devices," p. 589

This section looks at some of the specifics of NetWare connectivity as provided in Windows 95, such as built-in drivers and protocols, 32-bit virtual device driver components, and the capability to run the NetWare command-line utilities.

Microsoft provides such excellent support for Novell NetWare because of NetWare's popularity and dominance of the networking market. The opportunity to sell and implement Windows 95 greatly increases if it's easy to use with NetWare—and it is.

Built-In Network Drivers and Protocols

Windows 95 supports simultaneous communication with multiple networks by including clients, protocols, and services that are easy and quick to install. These network components are available for the following networks:

◀ See "Windows 95 Peer-to-Peer Networking Features," p. 618

- *Microsoft Network.* A peer-to-peer network composed of other workstations using Windows 95 with Windows used as the networking software.
- *Novell NetWare 3.x and 4.x.* Client/server software.

The Novell NetWare connectivity components included in Windows 95 are a client, a protocol, and a service. These components enable Windows 95 to connect to any NetWare resource. For example, with Windows 95 you can log in to a NetWare server, use print queues, map NetWare volumes, and share files and printer resources with other NetWare users.

- *Client for NetWare Networks.* The Microsoft Client for NetWare Networks has the built-in connectivity required to connect to any NetWare resources, including NetWare 2.15 and above, NetWare 3.x, and NetWare 4.x. This client also facilitates running all the standard NetWare command-line tools, as Chapter 23, "Using Novell Network Resources in Windows 95," discusses in greater detail. (Netware 4.x commands that require NDS aren't supported.) With the Microsoft Client for NetWare Networks installed, a Windows 95 computer can access NetWare resources, including applications, files, and printers.
- *IPX/SPX-compatible protocol.* Windows supplies a NetWare-compatible protocol—IPX/SPX (Internetwork Packet Exchange/Sequenced Packet Exchange)—that you can install to communicate with a NetWare server.
- *File and printer sharing for NetWare Networks.* Windows also provides file and printer sharing, which enables you to share your files and printers with other computers on the network. When you enable file and printer sharing, you can then choose specific directories and printers to share, limit access to the shared resources, and turn sharing off when you don't want to share.

Note

Windows also provides two versions of the Novell NetWare workstation shell that you can install instead of the Client for NetWare Networks.

Figure 22.1 shows the Network dialog box with the installed client, protocol, and service for use with Netware.

Note

Since Windows 95 makes the three protocols—IPX/SPX, TCP/IP, and NetBEUI—available to you, it's a good idea to install all three as network components if you will be connecting to different networks. IPX/SPX and TCP/IP are routable protocols, meaning they can use other resources across the enterprise. NetBEUI is limited to a single network, such as the Microsoft Network, and is extremely popular; additionally, some vendors have established an interface between NetBEUI and TCP/IP.

Fig. 22.1
The Network dialog box displays the installed features to use with your network.

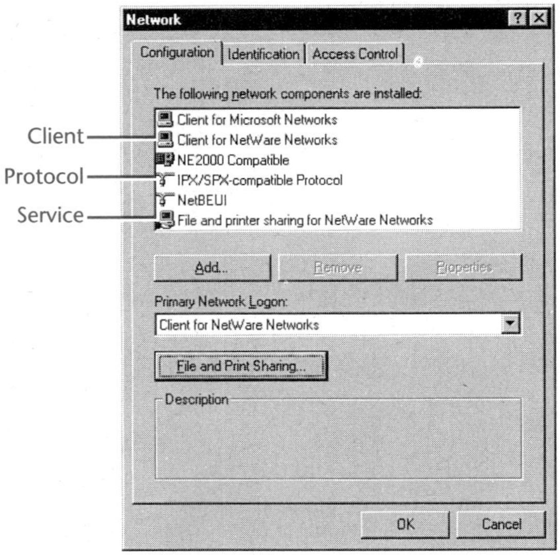

Windows supplies the client, protocol, and service you need to attach to a NetWare server. The installed components include the Client for Microsoft Networks and its primary protocol (NetBEUI). The components necessary for using Windows with NetWare include the Client for NetWare Networks, IPX/SPX-Compatible Protocol, and File and Printer Sharing for NetWare Networks. Naturally the adapter, in this case the NE 2000 Compatible, is necessary to attach to either network.

The 32-Bit Virtual Device Driver Components

The major breakthrough of Windows 95 is the use of the 32-bit virtual device driver. The advantage is that the 32-bit driver is a protected-mode driver, as opposed to real mode. Basically, when running in real mode, only one application or process can be run at a time. Although processors running in real mode operate at a fast clock rate, they are not multitasking. Also, real mode requires 32-bit requests to be translated into 16-bit requests, which slows down the process.

Windows' 32-bit driver runs in protected mode, thus allowing more than one application or process to run at a time. Protected mode allocates memory to the various processes running at one time to allow for multitasking.

Note

An additional benefit derived from using protected-mode components is the increased speed that they inherently achieve. Without the constant overhead of real-mode to protected-mode transitions, the network drivers' performance increases impressively from 50 to 200 percent.

Before Windows 95, communication between a DOS client (operating in real mode) and the Windows client (operating in protected mode) was slow and sometimes caused problems.

Another example of a real-mode versus protected-mode problem occurs when a NetWare server shuts down for some reason. With previous versions of Windows, the real-mode client would often lock up in such situations, and thus caused Windows to lock up. If a lockup didn't occur and the server came back up, the connection was still broken. To restore the connection, you had to exit Windows and then reboot—or at least log out and then log back in. With protected-mode components, the system can handle the error gracefully and actually reconnect the resource automatically, with no lockup or rebooting necessary.

No Conventional Memory Footprint

Another important advantage of the Windows 95 components for NetWare is that their use does not result in conventional memory footprint, meaning these components do not load into the first 640K, thus leaving that memory free for other drivers, programs, and so on. Because all the components were developed to run in protected mode, none of them install in CONFIG.SYS or AUTOEXEC.BAT file. Windows 95 replaces or makes obsolete many of the traditional DOS settings from these files, so in most cases the network components may be the only ones remaining.

Full Interoperability with Novell NetWare 3.x and 4.x Clients and Servers

Windows 95 is particularly the "well-connected client" in regard to interoperability with any Novell NetWare server running NetWare 2.15 and above, including bindery-based NetWare 3.x servers and NetWare 4.x servers that use bindery emulation. Additionally, one advantage of Windows 95 that wasn't possible with Windows for Workgroups is the capability to run all the NetWare command-line utilities, such as LOGIN.EXE, SETPASS.EXE, and SLIST.EXE, to perform network tasks.

► See "Using Windows 95 and Novell Utilities," p. 701

Note

Windows 95 does not, as yet, support Novell's Directory Services (native to version 4.1) if you log in through Windows—only the bindery-based and bindery emulation. The bindery database contains definitions for entities such as users, groups, and workgroups. See the section, "Logging in to the Server," later in this chapter for more information about NDS.

Automatic Installation of Windows 95 NetWare Support

When you install Windows 95 on your PC, the Setup program tries to detect any existing networking components. If you have Plug and Play hardware, this detection proceeds with little or no user intervention. However, even with "legacy" network hardware, the detection program is smart enough to install a working configuration during installation. You might have specific reasons to change things after installation, but such reasons are unlikely to include a completely nonworking configuration.

Windows 95 Setup over Existing NetWare Software

◄ See "Installing Plug and Play Hardware," p. 246

During installation, the Windows 95 Setup program determines whether your computer has NetWare networking components installed. To do so, Setup searches for the following clues:

- An active NetWare connection that uses ODI (Open Data-Link Interface), a standard interface for transport protocols
- A monolithic IPX/SPX driver
- Either NETX or VLM to access NetWare services (executable programs located at a workstation that enable communication with the NetWare server)
- A call to NETSTART.BAT in the AUTOEXEC.BAT file
- At least version 3.26 of NET*.COM or NET*.EXE

When the Windows 95 Setup program detects any of these conditions, it also locates any irreplaceable real-mode terminate-and-stay-running (TSR) programs that may be running. If you are running any TSRs like DOSNP.COM, 3270 emulation software, or TCP/IP software such as Telnet, Windows 95 Setup does not replace them. After detection, Setup installs protected-mode networking components based on Microsoft Client for NetWare Networks unless Setup also discovers incompatible components or the user indicates that the existing network connectivity is to remain unchanged.

Table 22.1 lists some of the conditions that prevent Windows 95 from installing either the Microsoft protected-mode protocol or Microsoft Client for NetWare Networks.

Table 22.1 How Setup Responds after Detecting NetWare-Related Components

Detected Condition	Setup's Response
VLM.EXE with NetWare 4.x using NetWare Directory Services (NDS)	Leaves existing components unchanged
TSRs that require ODI	Installs Microsoft Client for NetWare over ODI
Incompatible TSRs	Installs only the "new" IPX/SPX or leaves existing components unchanged

To complete the configuration, the Windows Setup program makes several adjustments to the existing startup files such as AUTOEXEC.BAT and SYSTEM.INI. Setup comments out unnecessary lines in the SYSTEM.INI file as well as existing lines in AUTOEXEC.BAT that are no longer required when using Microsoft Client for NetWare. Setup also adds to the AUTOEXEC.BAT file lines that invoke the required protected-mode components. The program might move TSRs to the WINSTART.BAT file so that they are executed only when entering Windows 95. Setup also moves settings from NET.CFG to the Registry.

Table 22.2 lists Windows 95's NetWare components.

Table 22.2 Windows 95's NetWare Network Components

Component	Function
NETWARE.DRV	Emulation of the WinNet driver that some applications require
NWLINK.VXD	IPX/SPX-compatible protocol
NWLSPROC.EXE	32-bit login script processor
NWLSCON.EXE	32-bit console
NWNET32.DLL	Common NetWare networking functions for the 32-bit network provider and print provider
NWNP32.DLL	32-bit network provider
NWPP32.DLL	32-bit print provider
NWREDIR.VXD	32-bit file system driver (redirector) to support the NetWare Core Protocol (NCP) file-sharing protocol
NWSERVER.VXD	File and print services

Plug and Play Configuration

With Plug and Play, connecting to NetWare networks couldn't be simpler. If you have Plug and Play-compatible hardware, Windows 95 configures and assigns all the resources dynamically. You then no longer need to worry about network board settings, such as Interrupt Level (IRQ), input/output (I/O) ports, or DMA (Direct Memory Access) channel. Windows 95 therefore resolves problems that sometimes may have taken hours to iron out.

◄ See "Installing Plug and Play Hardware," p. 246

A Plug and Play adapter enables dynamic configuration of network protocols with the capability to load or unload the driver based on detection of resources. Therefore, when you are on the road, your laptop can use Dial-Up Networking; then, when you return to your office, you can install your network adapter or attach to your docking station. In either case, Windows 95 can automatically sense the change and silently reconnect you to the network. This scheme also works in reverse; if you remove your laptop's Ethernet adapter (PC Card, formerly referred to as the PCMCIA card), Windows 95 senses the change and gracefully unloads the network drivers, enabling you to continue working. This capability is another benefit of Windows 95's 32-bit driver architecture.

Windows can easily detect a non-Plug and Play or "legacy" adapter in an otherwise Plug and Play system. The system can correctly detect a vast array of existing hardware types. Windows 95 determines the Plug and Play devices, then offers to detect the legacy adapter, and even suggests the correct settings to choose to ensure that no conflicts exist.

Manually Installing the Network Card

Tip

Access the Add New Hardware Wizard by double-clicking the Add New Hardware icon in the Control Panel; follow the directions on-screen.

◄ See "Installing Network Components in Windows 95," p. 604

If you add a network adapter after installing Windows 95, the Add New Hardware Wizard takes you step-by-step through the process of installing the hardware. Using the Add New Hardware Wizard, you can let Windows find the newly installed hardware and configure it for you or you can configure the hardware yourself.

If you let Windows detect your card, it automatically determines the settings for the card and then installs the correct driver. If you choose, you can select the card from a list provided by Windows. First, choose the manufacturer of the card; second, choose the model. If Windows does not include configuration and driver files for that particular model, you can choose to use the manufacturer's disk to install those files. When you complete the wizard's step-by-step process, the adapter card is successfully installed.

Manually Installing the NetWare Client

Windows 95 enables you to install one of three clients for use with NetWare: one supplied by Microsoft or either of two supplied by Novell. The client you choose depends on your NetWare configuration. Following are a few examples:

- Your site uses NetWare NCP Packet Signature
- Your site uses NetWare IP (Internet Protocol)
- Your site uses 3270 emulators that require a DOS TSR
- Your site uses custom VLM components
- Your site uses NetWare Directory Services (NDS)

In each of the preceding instances, you should not use Microsoft Client for NetWare Networks.

However, if none of the previous examples are true for your network, you can safely and confidently use Microsoft's Client for NetWare Networks. Microsoft's Client for NetWare Networks uses the IPX/SPX-compatible protocol, which works very well with Novell NetWare. Additionally, the Microsoft Client includes file and printer sharing for NetWare networks service, which means you can share your files and resources with other computers on the network.

Of the two clients supplied by Novell, NETX and VLM, you choose the client that best fits the version of the server. NETX works with NetWare versions up to 3.11 and with a 3.12 and 4 server that's configured for 802.3 protocol. VLM requires NetWare DOS Requester software to be installed to complete installation.

Table 22.3 lists the Novell files required for using the Novell-supplied clients with Windows 95.

Table 22.3 Required Novell-Supplied Drivers

File Name	Description
NETWARE.DRV	A Windows-compatible network driver that provides network-redirector functionality from 16-bit applications. Different versions are available for NETX or VLM usage.
NETWARE.HLP	Associated Help file.

(continues)

Table 22.3 Continued

File Name	Description
NWPOPUP.EXE	NetWare messaging utility.
VNETWARE.386	A virtual device driver that provides virtualization services in Windows 95 and in Virtual Machines (VMs).
VIPX.386	Virtual device driver.
NW16.DLL	32-bit to 16-bit interactive link. Required only for use with VLM.

Tip
Before installing the Novell-supplied client to your workstation, copy the required files to a disk from the Novell server and keep the disk handy along with your NetWare disks.

When you install Windows 95 for use with NetWare, Setup looks for these files in the existing Windows directory. If it cannot find these files, Setup requests a location for them. You'll also need the NetWare disks supplied by Novell for setting up the workstation.

Manually Installing the Microsoft Client for NetWare

If you are installing the support for NetWare networks after previously installing Windows 95, you must install the client. The Microsoft Client for NetWare works extremely well with both Windows and the NetWare network. The client provides fast access to the network resources, easy access to your login scripts, and is quite intuitive when it comes to using the network resources.

To install the Microsoft Client for NetWare Networks, follow these steps:

1. Open the Start menu and choose Settings, Control Panel.

2. Double-click the Network icon in the Control Panel.
3. Click the Configuration tab and choose Add. The Select Network Component Type dialog box appears (see fig. 22.2).

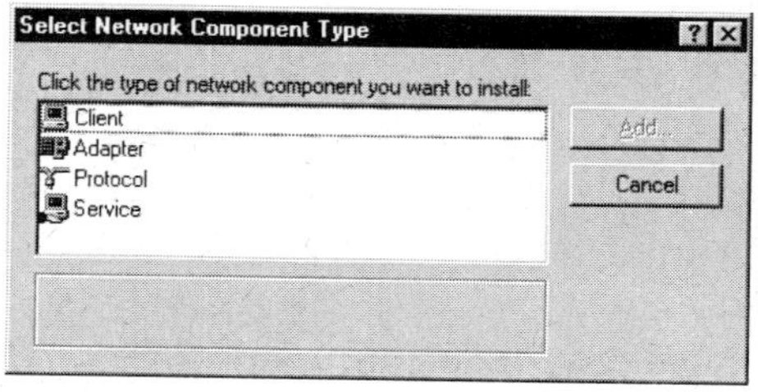

Fig. 22.2
Choose the component type you want to install and then choose Add.

4. Select Client and then choose Add. The Select Network Client dialog box appears (see fig. 22.3).

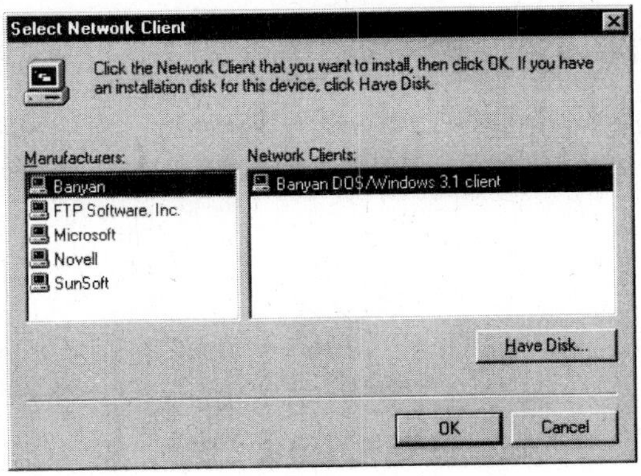

Fig. 22.3
Select a manufacturer and then select a network client.

5. Choose Microsoft from the list of manufacturers on the left and then Client for NetWare Networks from the list on the right.

6. Choose OK. Windows returns to the Network dialog box.

If you still need to install a protocol or service, proceed to the following sections on installation and take care of that before choosing OK. When you do choose OK in the Network dialog box, you will be prompted to restart the computer so the changes can take effect.

After you restart the computer, the NetWare Client is added.

Configuring the NetWare Client

Before you can use the client, you must configure it for your network. To do so, follow these steps:

1. In the Network dialog box, select Client for NetWare Networks and choose Properties. The Client for NetWare Networks Properties sheet appears, as shown in figure 22.4.

2. In the Preferred Server list box, select the server's name or enter it in the text box.

3. In the First Network Drive list box, select the first available drive letter for drive mappings.

4. Select the Enable Logon Script Processing check box.

5. Choose OK to complete the setup for the client; however, leave the Network dialog box open if you want to set protocol or other options.

Tip
Running your logon script automatically sets options for your system when you log on to the network.

Fig. 22.4
Specify the preferred server and the first network drive on the Client for NetWare Networks Properties sheet.

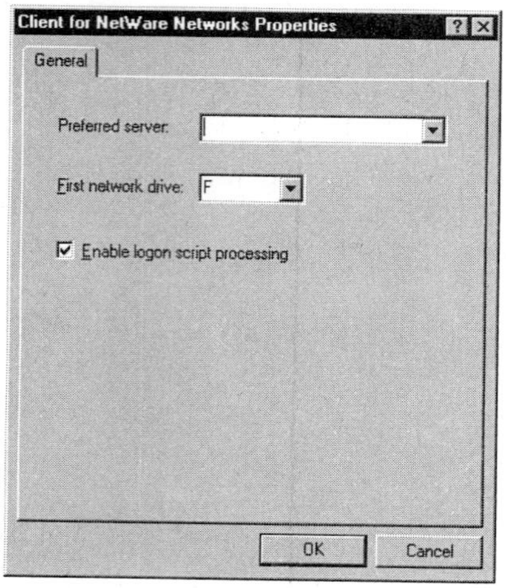

After you set these properties, the next time that you log in, Windows 95 automatically logs in to the NetWare server, runs the login script, and makes any connections, including any drive mappings that the script defines.

> **Troubleshooting**
>
> *I enabled logon script processing, but the mapped drives available in DOS were not available to me in Windows. What did I do wrong?*
>
> You did nothing wrong; the login script did not run, perhaps because of real-mode TSRs included in the login script. Contact your system administrator, who can move the TSRs to either the AUTOEXEC.BAT (which executes before Windows 95 starts) or WINSTART.BAT (which executes when Windows 95 initializes).

Installing the Network Protocol

Your next step is to install the NetWare protocol, IPX/SPX-compatible protocol, using the Configuration page of the Network dialog box. To install the protocol, follow these steps:

1. Open the Network dialog box by double-clicking the Network icon in the Control Panel.
2. Click the Configuration tab and choose Add. The Select Network Component Type dialog box appears (refer to fig. 22.2).
3. Select Protocol in the components list and then choose Add. The Select Network Protocol dialog box appears.
4. In Manufacturers, choose Microsoft. A list of available protocols appears on the right side of the dialog box (see fig. 22.5).

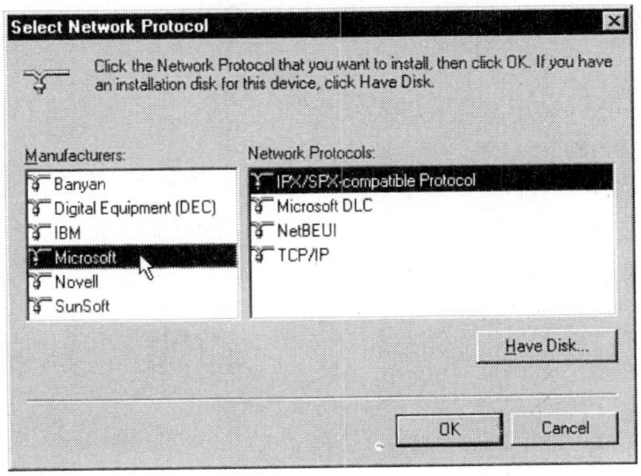

Fig. 22.5
Choose Microsoft as the manufacturer and then select the IPX/SPX-compatible protocol.

5. In Network Protocols, choose IPX/SPX-Compatible Protocol. Windows closes the dialog box and adds the protocol to the list of installed components in the Network dialog box.

6. Leave the Network dialog box open so you can set the primary network logon and install file-sharing support.

Setting the Logon

You must set the logon for NetWare to show which network you will be using. Choose the logon on the Configuration page of the Network dialog box. In the list of components, choose Client for NetWare Networks. In the Primary Network Logon list, choose Client for NetWare Networks.

Note

Windows uses the term "logon" and Novell uses "login," although both terms refer to the same process.

Installing File-Sharing and Printer-Sharing Support

Windows 95 enables you to install file and printer sharing services for NetWare networks. The functional equivalent of Windows 95's file and printer service for Microsoft networks, this service provides peer-to-peer networking connectivity to other NetWare clients using Windows 95.

To use Windows 95's built-in file and printer sharing with Novell NetWare, you must be using Microsoft Client for NetWare Networks. To install file-sharing and printer-sharing support, follow these steps:

◄ See "Understanding File Sharing," p. 643

1. In the Network dialog box, click the Configuration tab.

2. Choose File and Print Sharing. The File and Print Sharing dialog box appears (see fig. 22.6).

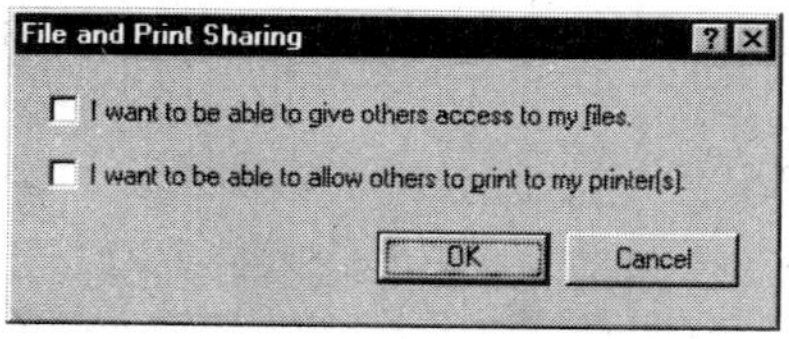

Fig. 22.6
Choose to share your files, printer, or both, with others on the network.

3. You can choose one or both options:

   Choose I Want To Be Able to Give Others Access to My Files if you want to share your files.

   Choose I Want to Be Able To Allow Others To Print to My Printer(s) if you want to share your printer(s) with those on the network.

4. Choose OK to close the dialog box and return to the Network dialog box.

> **Note**
>
> You cannot use file and printer services for both Microsoft and NetWare networks simultaneously. Windows notifies you to remove one service if you try to install the other while one is listed in the component's box. To remove a component, select it and choose Remove.

Setting Access Control

When sharing the files on your local hard drive, and/or your local printer, in a NetWare environment, Windows sets access to your files to user-level access control.

When other computers browse the network, the Windows 95 computer seems as though it has a split personality. To other Windows 95 computers running Client for NetWare Networks, the resources behave like any other Windows resources. To Windows 95 computers running NETX or VLM, shared printers look like NetWare print queues, and shared directories appear to be NetWare volumes. Shared resources, such as a CD-ROM or a printer, are immediately available to any user on the NetWare network with access to the shared resource.

To set access control, follow these steps:

1. In the Network dialog box, click the Access Control tab.
2. Choose the User-Level Access Control option if it is not already selected (see fig. 22.7).

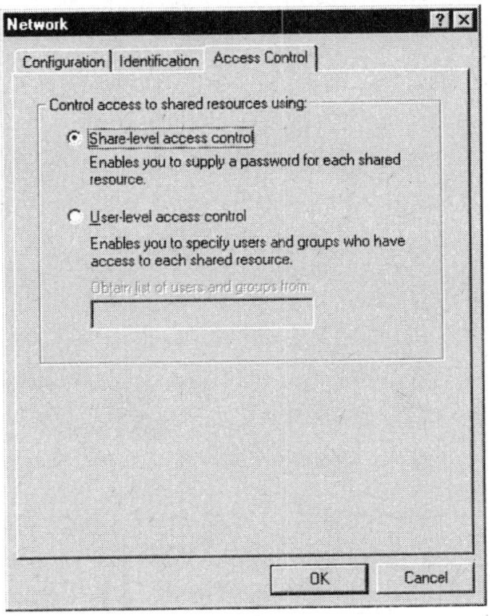

Fig. 22.7
User-level access enables others on the network to use your shared resources.

3. In the Obtain List of Users and Groups From text box, enter the name of the NetWare server.

Completing Installation

When you've completed installing the client, protocol, and service and you've set access control in the Network dialog box, you're ready to complete the installation.

> **Note**
>
> As far as the Identification page of the Network dialog box goes, you do not need to identify your computer or workgroup for NetWare. NetWare identifies your computer by a unique identification number on your network adapter card.

To complete the installation, follow these steps:

1. Choose OK in the Network dialog box.
2. The System Settings Change dialog box appears (see fig. 22.8).

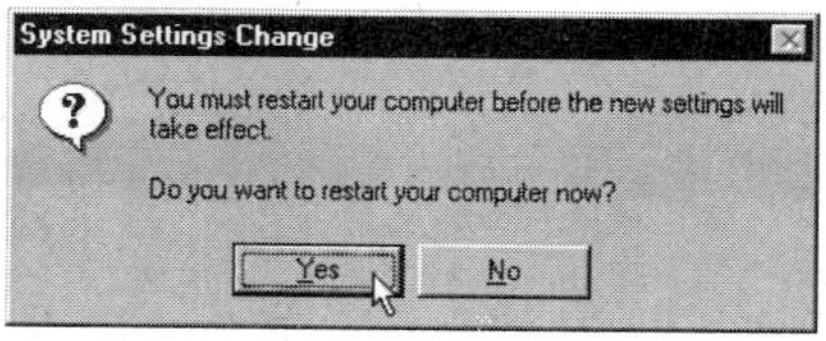

Fig. 22.8
You can choose to reboot the computer later if you do not want to stop work at this time.

3. Choose Yes to reboot the computer.

4. When Windows starts again, the Enter Network Password dialog box appears with your name in the User Name text box, the server's name in the Login Server's text box, and a Password text box in which you enter a password assigned to you by your system or network administrator. Enter your password and choose OK.

5. The Welcome to Windows dialog box appears. Enter your password and choose OK. The Login Script window, if you chose to enable it, flashes by, and then the Windows desktop appears as it normally would.

To view the server's resources, double-click Network Neighborhood.

You also can access the server resources made available to you by your login script in the My Computer window. Figure 22.9 shows the My Computer window with four drives mapped to the NetWare server by the login script.

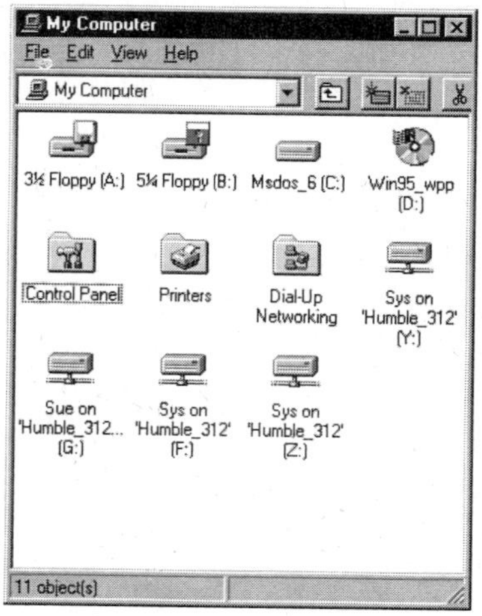

Fig. 22.9
Access mapped drives through the Control Panel after connecting to the network.

Sharing Your Resources

► See "Using Windows 95 and Novell Utilties," p. 701

If you choose to share your files and printer with other users on the network, you must specify the shared resources and indicate who on the network may gain access to your resources. Basically, designating a directory, printer, CD-ROM drive, or any other resource as a shared resource follows the same steps.

To share a resource, follow these steps:

1. Open the window containing the resource to be shared (My Computer to share a drive, Printers to share a printer, and so on).

2. Select the folder or item you want to share and choose File, Sharing. The Properties sheet appears.

3. Click the Sharing tab, and then choose Shared As to activate the Shared As area of the page, as shown in figure 22.10.

► See "Managing Print Files and Sharing," p. 784

► See "Creating Network Resources Wisely," p. 796

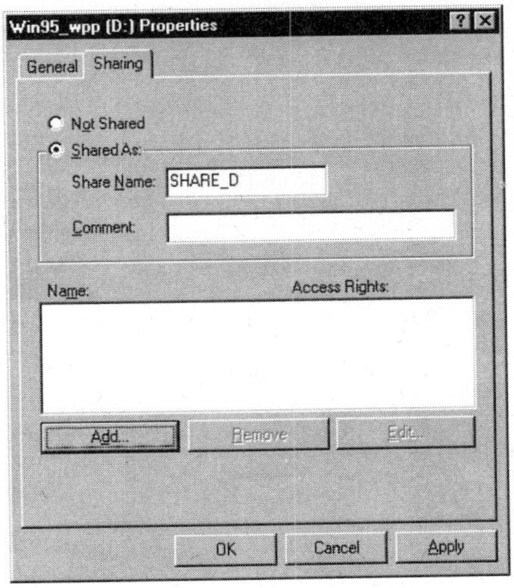

Fig. 22.10 Choose to share the selected resource and then choose Add.

4. Choose Add. The Add Users dialog box appears (see fig. 22.11).

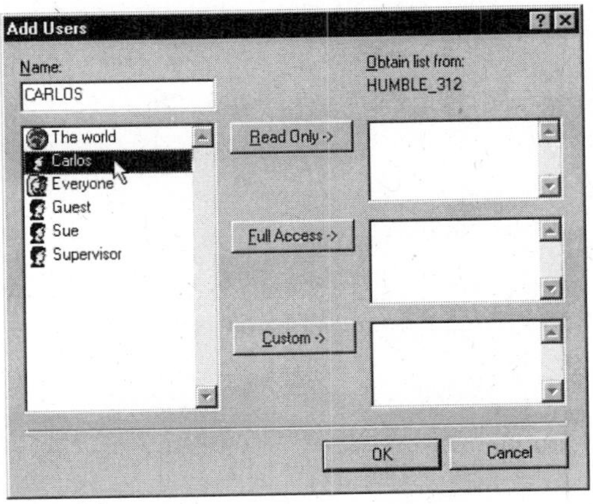

Fig. 22.11 The Add Users dialog box enables you to define a user's access.

5. In Name, enter a name of the user or choose the name from the list. You can choose from the following options:

   - *Read Only.* Selected user can open, read, and copy files but cannot modify the files in any way.
   - *Full Access.* Selected user has full access to your drive, including modification and deletion capability.
   - *Custom.* Enables you to specify specific rights to the selected user. If you choose Custom, the Change Access Rights dialog box appears when you select OK. In this dialog box, you can define whether the user can read, write to, create, list, or delete files or change file attributes or access rights.

6. Choose OK to close the Add Users dialog box. Choose OK again to close the Properties sheet.

Troubleshooting

When I installed the Client for NetWare Networks and chose OK to close the Network dialog box, a message appeared stating I needed to change the Access Control. What do I do?

If you previously installed the Client for Microsoft Networks, your access control was share level; when you install the Client for NetWare Networks, you must change access to the user level and enter the name of the server. Click the Access Control tab of the Network dialog box and choose User-Level Access Control. Enter the server name in the text box and choose OK. You'll have to reboot the computer to change the system settings.

I tried to specify the client for file and print sharing in the Network dialog box as NetWare, but it doesn't appear in the installed components list.

You can only specify one client at a time for file and printer sharing. If you've already specified the Client for Microsoft Networks as available for file sharing, remove it from the components list and then choose the Client for NetWare Networks.

I'm using a notebook computer away from the office and every time I start the computer, I have to verify my network logon and then I get an error message. Is there any way I can skip this when I'm not connected to the network?

Yes. Open the Network dialog box and click the Configuration tab. In the Primary Network Logon list, choose Windows Logon. You will no longer see the error messages; however, don't forget to change the logon back to NetWare when you're ready to connect to the network again.

Manually Installing the Novell Client for NetWare-NETX

You can, as an alternative to the Microsoft NetWare client, install a Novell client supplied with Windows but suited specifically for version 3.11 and below and version 4.0 and above.

The two choices for the NetWare clients in Windows are:

Novell NetWare (Workstation Shell 3.x [NETX])

Novell NetWare (Workstation Shell 4.0 and above [VLM])

The NETX choice applies to the workstation shell up to version 3.11; additionally, you can use this choice for version 3.12 and 4.0 *if* the server is configured for 802.3 protocol.

Note

When you install either Novell-supplied client, Windows automatically installs the IPX ODI protocol needed to communicate with the server. Additionally, you should make sure the access control (Network dialog box, Access Control page) is set to Share-Level Access Control instead of User-Level Access Control.

Installing the NETX Client

To install Novell's NETX client, follow these steps:

1. In the Network dialog box, click the Configuration tab.
2. Choose Add. The Select Network Component Type dialog box appears.
3. Select Client in the component list and choose Add. The Select Network Client dialog box appears.
4. In Manufacturers, choose Novell. The list of Network Clients changes.
5. In Network Clients, choose Novell NetWare (Workstation Shell 3.X[NETX]).
6. Choose OK. Windows installs the client as well as the Novel IPX ODI Protocol.

Note

Before choosing OK in the Network dialog box, make sure that control access is set to Share-Level Access Control on the Access Control page.

Tip

Electronic sources for updated client software are always available from Novell's CompuServe forum, World Wide Web page **http://www.novell.com/**, or FTP server at **ftp.novell.com**.

7. Choose OK to close the Network dialog box. Windows prompts for several Novell NetWare disks, as well as the Windows 95 CD-ROM. Follow the directions on-screen. The following list is of files you will need to complete the installation:

   IPXODI.COM

   NETX.EXE

   LSL.COM

   NWPOPUP.EXE

   NETWARE.DRV

   VIPX.386

   NETWARE.HLP

   VNETWARE.386

   A network adapter driver such as NE2000.COM

   Windows completes the installation. You must restart the computer to attach to the network.

Manually Installing the Novell Client for NetWare-VLM

If your network is using VLMs, you must run at least version 4.0 of NETX.VLM on the workstations and have at least version 1.02 of the VLM client-support files from NetWare.

The VLM choice for NetWare client refers to the workstation shell 4.0 and above. If you choose the VLM option, however, you must also install Novell's NetWare DOS Requester software; Windows cannot complete the installation of the VLM client without the requester.

To install the Novell-supplied VLM client for NetWare, follow these steps:

1. Close all programs in Windows and then open the Start menu and choose Shut Down. The Shut Down dialog box appears.

2. Select the Restart the Computer in MS-DOS Mode option and choose Yes.

3. Install the Novell-supplied NetWare 4 client (NetWare Client for DOS and MS Windows disks). See your system administrator if you need help.

4. Before starting Windows, edit the AUTOEXEC.BAT by adding **REM** before the following statement:

```
@CALL C:\NWCLIENT\STARTNET.BAT
```

5. Save the file and restart your computer.

6. In Windows, open the Network dialog box and click the Configuration tab.

7. Choose Add. The Select Network Component Type dialog box appears.

8. Select Client and then choose Add. The Select Network Client dialog box appears.

9. In the list of Manufacturers, choose Novell.

10. In the list of Network Clients, choose Novell NetWare (Workstation Shell 4.0 and above [VLM]).

11. Choose OK. Windows installs the client and may prompt you to insert the Windows 95 CD-ROM or specific NetWare disks. Insert the disks and follow the directions on-screen.

> **Note**
>
> Windows also installs the Novell IPX ODI protocol when you install the client.

12. Choose OK to close the Network dialog box and Windows prompts for you to restart the computer. Choose Yes.

13. When Windows starts, it will prompt for a Network password. Enter the password and choose OK. Windows starts with your workstation logged on to the server. To view the server and its resources, open Network Neighborhood.

Troubleshooting

I have installed the Novell client 4 and I get a message saying the VLM is not loaded or disabled just as Windows starts and I'm not connected to the network. What can I do?

This is a NetWare message stating Windows is not loading the VLM. Edit the AUTOEXEC.BAT to change the following lines from

```
C:\WINDOWS\LSL.COM
```

(continues)

(continued)

```
C:\WINDOWS\NE2000.COM
C:\WINDOWS\ODIHLP.EXE
C:\WINDOWS\IPXODI.COM
```

to

```
C:\NWCLIENT\LSL.COM
C:\NWCLIENT\NE2000.COM
C:\NWCLIENT\ODIHLP.EXE
C:\NWCLIENT\IPXODI.COM
```

and add the following line:

```
C:\NWCLIENT\VLM.EXE
```

I'm using NetWare 4 but I can't access Network Directory Services. Does Windows support NDS?

Yes. However, to make Network Directory Services (NDS) work with Windows 95, the login must be in the AUTOEXEC.BAT, as discussed in the next section.

Logging In to a NetWare Server

When you restart Windows, Windows attaches to the network and displays a login dialog box for the network and one for Windows. Login is quick and easy. Also, listed in the following section is an alternate method of logging in so that your login scripts run; login scripts contain drive mapping, search drives, and other Login commands.

You also can log out of the network and reattach with very little effort. These procedures are the same whether you're using the client for Microsoft NetWare or either of the two Novell clients.

Logging In to the Network

Windows prompts you to log in to the network when you first start Windows. You are also prompted to log in to Windows. To log in, follow these steps:

1. Turn your computer on to start Windows.
2. The Enter Network Password dialog box appears with your name in the User Name text box, the server's name in the Login Server's text box,

and a Password text box in which you enter a password assigned to you by your system or network administrator. Enter your password and choose OK.

3. The Welcome to Windows dialog box appears. Enter your password and choose OK.

   After logging in to the network, you can view the network server in Network Neighborhood.

The capability to run NetWare login scripts is an important topic for many Novell users. When using Microsoft Client for NetWare, you can set the login scripts to run automatically; however, you cannot run login scripts in the same manner when using the Novell-supplied client.

When using the Novell-supplied client, you can only run the login script if you edit your AUTOEXEC.BAT file to include the `LOGIN.EXE`. When you add the `LOGIN.EXE` to your AUTOEXEC.BAT, you're prompted to log in before Windows starts and so your login script runs. Make sure you also add the first network drive letter (usually F:) before the `LOGIN.EXE` line in the AUTOEXEC.BAT so the login command can be found.

Tip
If you want to use NDS with NetWare 4.0 and above, you must add the `LOGIN.EXE` to your AUTOEXEC.BAT.

If you don't want to execute the login script, you can log in to the network from Windows. If the login script consists of only drive mapping, log in to Windows and then map the drives in the My Computer window. However, if it consists of search paths and other login script commands, add the command to your AUTOEXEC.BAT. See your system administrator for help.

Logging Out of the Network

Logging out of the network means you will no longer have access to the Network resources; your workstation will be a stand-alone computer.

To log out of the network, follow these steps:

1. Open Network Neighborhood and select the network server. Right-click the mouse to display the pop-up menu (see fig. 22.12).

2. Choose Log Out. A confirmation dialog box appears. Choose Yes to log out or No to cancel the procedure.

3. The Logging Out message box appears, as shown in figure 22.13. Choose OK.

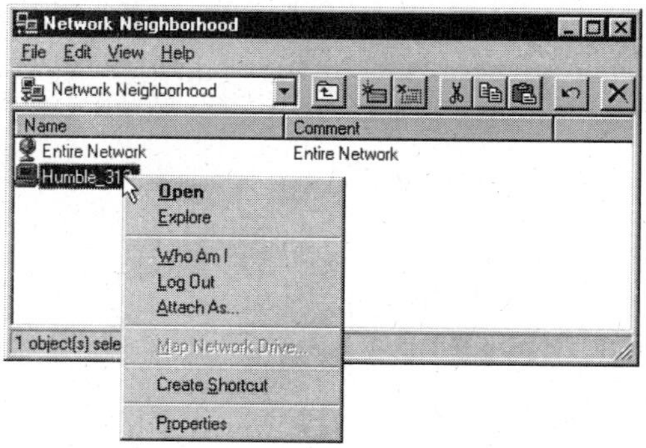

Fig. 22.12
You can quickly log out from the quick menu.

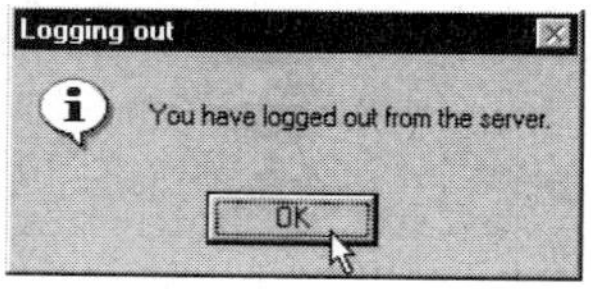

Fig. 22.13
This message informs you that you've logged out from the server.

Attaching to the Network

When you log in to the network, more than one server may appear in the Network Neighborhood. You can attach to any server, as long as you have a password, using the Attach To command.

To attach to a server, follow these steps:

▶ See "Connecting to Other Servers," p. 713

1. Select the network server in the Network Neighborhood dialog box and right-click the icon.

2. Choose File, Attach As. The Enter Network Password dialog box appears (see fig. 22.14).

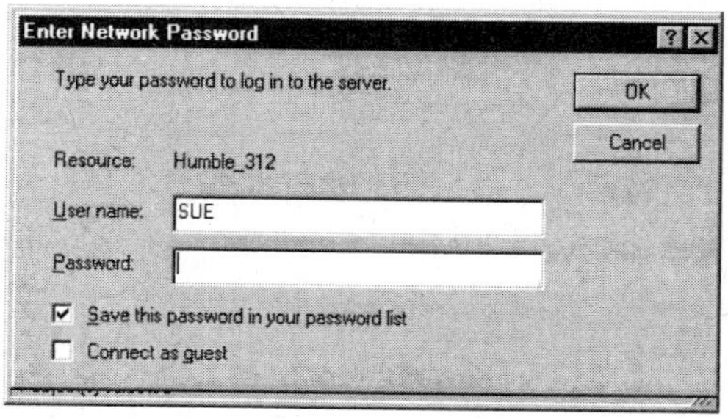

Fig. 22.14
Enter your password to log on to the network.

3. Enter your password and choose OK. Windows attaches you to the network.

Troubleshooting

My search paths before installing Windows are not available to me now.

That problem is occurring because the login script did not run. This problem does not occur when you use Microsoft Client for NetWare or when using the Novell NetWare clients with a login in the AUTOEXEC.BAT.

When I try to access commands or applications from the network, I get a message saying `Cannot find the file... Make sure the path and filename are correct...` *What have I done wrong?*

You may have accessed and modified the search paths without knowing it. When the login script sets search paths, it represents them with drive letters starting at the end of the alphabet: Z, Y, X, and so on. If you are using either the Microsoft Client for NetWare or you added the `LOGIN.EXE` line to your AUTOEXEC.BAT, those search path drives were added to your My Computer window with other mapped drives.

If you opened one of the search drives and moved around in it, you could have altered the search path. When you tried to access the command or application, the search path was wrong so the network couldn't find the file for which you were looking. To alleviate the problem, restart the computer; the login script will run again and set the search paths straight.

From now on, leave the search path drives Z, Y, X, and so on alone and use only those drives represented by letters from the front of the alphabet.

Tip

When you log in using LOGIN.EXE with the Windows Run command, the scripts run.

Testing and Troubleshooting Your NetWare Installation

Although Microsoft has expended extraordinary effort to ensure that you can run and install Windows 95 networking without any problems, every installation differs and sometimes a problem may occur. This section presents a few testing and troubleshooting tips for fixing several problems that you might encounter.

▶ See "Solving Common Network Printing Problems," p. 788

▶ See "Troubleshooting and Network Management Tools," p. 827

Testing your setup is a simple task in Windows 95. To ensure that everything is working, try performing the following actions:

- Start Windows 95 successfully
- Log in to the network
- Access the drives and note whether they are mapped correctly

- Access the printer resources
- Run your Windows applications
- Use all resources from within your Windows applications
- Run your DOS applications
- Use all resources from within your DOS applications
- Access the other tools and resources
- Log off the server, and then access the mapped drives, and so on

Make note of which of the above actions failed and refer to the troubleshooting sections in this and other chapters throughout this book for information on possible problems.

Logon Problems

While processing its startup files, Windows 95 displays the Windows 95 logo screen. To see the output of startup processing, you can press the Esc key, which causes the logo screen to disappear and leaves you with a familiar MS-DOS text screen until Windows 95 actually starts. As the screens flash by, keep an eye out for login and other NetWare information. If you're not logging on to the network, the screen would reveal that.

If you're not logging on to the network, check with the system administrator to make sure the server is on and operating properly. Check the cabling to your computer to see that it is properly attached. Try restarting the computer again.

If you get the message that the `Server name is not valid or the server is not available`, check with the system administrator to see if you have access to that server and that the server is working properly. If you're using Microsoft Client for NetWare Networks, check to see that you have the correct server listed in the client's Properties sheet. (From the Network dialog box, select the client and choose Properties.)

If the login script didn't run and your search drives are not mapped, make sure that if you're using the Microsoft Client for NetWare that you checked the Enable Logon Script Processing option on the client's Properties sheet (Network dialog box). If you're using a Novell-supplied client, you must enter the `LOGIN.EXE` line in the AUTOEXEC.BAT before the login scripts will run.

If the problem persists, check all of the settings in the Network dialog box to make sure you haven't neglected or accidentally changed something.

If you still cannot log in to the network after Windows 95 starts, try the following technique. Turn on your computer. You first see the standard BIOS banner; then, when you see the text string `Starting Windows 95. . .`, press Shift+F5. This starts the computer in safe mode, in which you get a command prompt. Windows 95 provides a real-mode network client in this configuration to assist you in determining problems.

◄ See "Starting and Quitting Windows," p. 50

At the command prompt, enter **NET START** to load this real-mode client. If you can log in with this driver loaded, you might simply have a problem with the NetWare client settings that you specify in the Network dialog box. If you can log in using this real-mode driver, also verify that you can access mapped drives and other expected resources.

> **Note**
>
> Sometimes Windows 95 cannot locate your NetWare server. This typical problem is easy to fix. Check that the frame type in the Advanced Properties sheet for the IPX/SPX-compatible protocol is set for your server. If necessary, change this setting to your server's frame type.

Following are a few more common problems with NetWare networks:

- If you forgot your password, contact the system administrator and ask her to issue you a new password.
- The network denies access to servers. Run SETPASS to synchronize your passwords.
- The network constantly asks you to enter NetWare passwords. Set Windows and NetWare passwords to be the same.
- Can't connect to a server. Ask the system administrator to verify that you have access rights.❖

► See "Using Windows 95 and Novell Utilties," p. 701

Chapter 23

Using Novell Network Resources in Windows 95

by Glenn Fincher with Sue Plumley

You can add a Windows 95 computer to an existing NetWare network by using Microsoft's enhanced NetWare connectivity tools. These tools are the first and best choices in almost every situation to ensure complete compatibility and integration with the very different architectures that Microsoft and NetWare represent. Additionally, Windows 95 has included many utilities and features you can use to communicate and connect to the NetWare network. This chapter discusses those Windows 95 utilities as well as several NetWare utilities and commands you can use from within Windows.

In this chapter, you learn about the following:

- User Maintenance and Novell Utilities
- Drive mapping and changing passwords
- Connecting to other servers
- Using network tape drives

Using Windows 95 and Novell Utilities

Windows' support for Novell's NetWare makes performing general maintenance tasks, as well as requesting information from the server, quick and easy. You can perform many NetWare functions through Windows, such as mapping drives, listing your server connection, managing network print jobs, and so on, without ever using a command line.

Windows enables you to use many of NetWare's commands and utilities directly within Windows. You can check the status of network volumes, change your password, and use several administrative utilities from the MS-DOS prompt or the Run dialog box.

Mapping Drives

Windows provides an easy method of mapping drives from within the Network Neighborhood so you can avoid using Netware's MAP command. When you map a drive, you assign a drive letter to a network resource, such as a drive or folder. Mapping drives makes access to network resources faster and easier than opening several layers of windows to find the resource on the server or network.

Tip
You can make mapping permanent so you don't have to set the mapping each time you login to the server.

◄ See "Logging in to a NetWare Server," p. 694

Additionally, if you're running a login script, mapping drives provides the search and drive maps created by the system administrator. If you choose to not run the login script, you can map the drives yourself within Windows.

You also can choose to connect the map as a root of the drive, which not only helps keep path statements from getting too long but makes your maps a bit more permanent. For example, you can map to a document directory using the path F:\CARLOS\NOTEBOOK\WPDOCS.

Now suppose you go into the F:\CARLOS\NOTEBOOK directory and access another folder, say the REPORTS directory. The next time you want to use the original mapping, to the WPDOCS directory, the map has changed to the F:\CARLOS\NOTEBOOK\REPORTS directory.

Connect the map as a root of the drive to alleviate this problem. In this example, connect F:\CARLOS\NOTEBOOK\WPDOCS as J. Whenever you want to access the WPDOCS folder, you simply type in **J**. Not only is the path shorter and easier to enter, the path remains the same even if you access different folders within the NOTEBOOK directory.

Note

If you have used Windows for Workgroups, mapping a drive in Network Neighborhood should seem familiar because it is similar to mapping a drive from File Manager.

The basic procedure for mapping a network drive is as follows:

1. Open the Network Neighborhood and select the shared folder you want to map to.

2. Choose File, Map Network Drive. The Map Network Drive dialog box appears, as shown in figure 23.1.

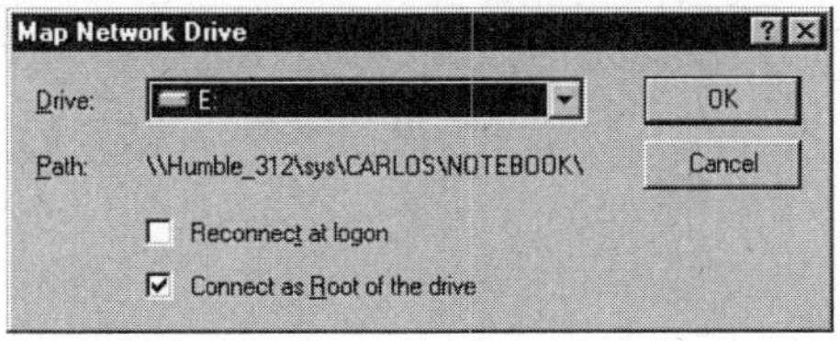

Fig. 23.1
Windows displays the path you've mapped out by selecting each folder.

3. By default, Windows assigns the next available drive letter on your computer to the folder that you select to map. To assign a different letter, select it from the Drive drop-down list.

4. To reconnect to this drive or directory automatically, select the Reconnect at Logon check box. Choosing this option makes the mapping permanent.

5. If you want, choose Connect as Root of the Drive.

6. Choose OK to close the dialog box. View drive mappings in the My Computer window (see fig. 23.2).

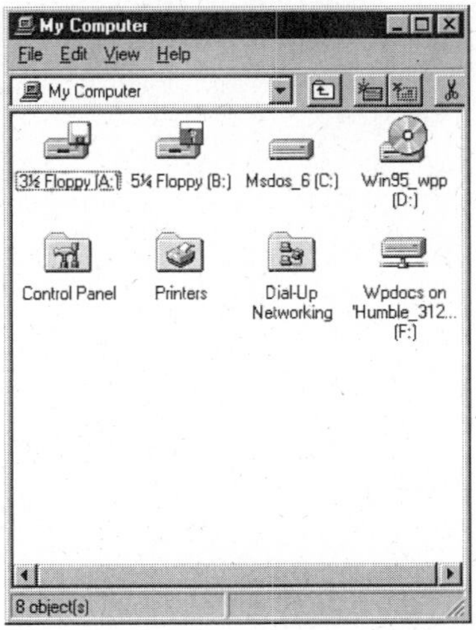

Fig. 23.2
Click on the mapped drive icon to open the folder you want without wading through six, eight, or ten other folders.

Note

Windows supplies the Map Network Drive icon on the toolbar of the Network Neighborhood. However, mapping in this dialog box does not work with NetWare, but it does work with Microsoft peer-to-peer networking.

Tip
If the toolbar is not showing in the Network Neighborhood window, choose View, Toolbar.

To disconnect a mapped drive, open My Computer and select the mapped drive. Right-click the mouse while pointing to the selected drive and choose Disconnect. The drive icon disappears from the window and the drive is disconnected.

If you want a list of the drives and mappings on your system, you might find the NetWare MAP command the best way to do so even though you can view mapped drives in the My Computer window. Enter **MAP** at the DOS prompt or in the Run dialog box, and you should see a screen similar to figure 23.3.

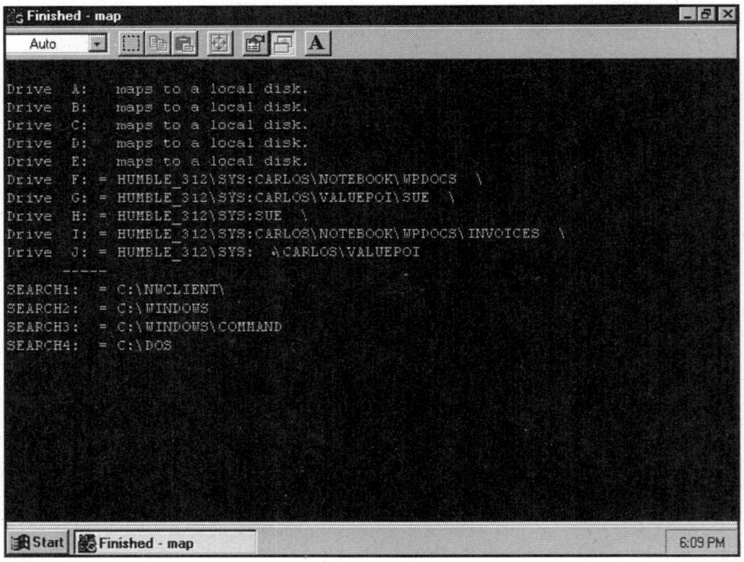

Fig. 23.3
The MAP command lists all the drive letters and the actual resources to which they are connected.

The drive mapping displayed in the figure shows drives F through J are mapped drives you've created in Windows. These drives make it easier for you to access your work on the server. The search section of the drive mapping shows the search paths that the server follows when you try to access a file or folder. The search drives were added by the login script that ran when Windows first logged in to the server.

Troubleshooting

I connected a path as a root of the drive but now I cannot move up one level in the path. What am I doing wrong?

You're not doing anything wrong; the problem is with connecting as a root of the drive. You cannot move up a level within the path. If, for example, you want to move up one level from F:\CARLOS\NOTEBOOK\WPDOCS to F:\CARLOS\NOTEBOOK, you have to create a new mapping or enter the entire path. When connecting as a root of the drive, your only choice is the entire path.

*I typed **MAP** in the Run dialog box, but I got a message that said* `Cannot find the file 'run'....` *What do I do now?*

If you ran the login scripts and the search paths are established, then you can just type **MAP** in the Run dialog box; otherwise, type the path to the MAP command, beginning with the server, public folder, and then the command. A sample path might be \\HUMBLE_312\SYS\PUBLIC\MAP. HUMBLE_312 is the server and SYS is usually the name given to the first drive volume on the server. PUBLIC is the directory normally used to store NetWare commands.

Tip
If you don't want to go through two lonin dialog boxes when Windows starts, change your Windows password to match your Netware password using theh Passwords Control Panel.

Changing Your NetWare Password

The best way you can change your NetWare password, short of asking the system administrator, is to use the SETPASS command. SETPASS enables you to create or change a password on one or more file servers. You must be attached to the server before you can set the password on it.

Tip
If you're attached to more than one server with the *same* password, SETPASS enables you to synchronize passwords (setting all passwords at one time to the same word).

To use SETPASS, follow these steps:

1. Open the Start menu and choose Run. The Run dialog box appears.
2. In the Open text box, enter the path and the SETPASS command. An example of the path might be \\HUMBLE_312\SYS\PUBLIC\SETPASS.
3. Choose OK. Windows opens the MS-DOS prompt with the prompt asking for a new password, as shown in figure 23.4.

Note

As a security measure, some versions of NetWare will prompt you for your old password before asking you to enter a new password.

4. Enter the new password and press Enter.

Tip
If you're unsure of the path, choose the Browse button and look for the PUBLIC folder; then find the command.

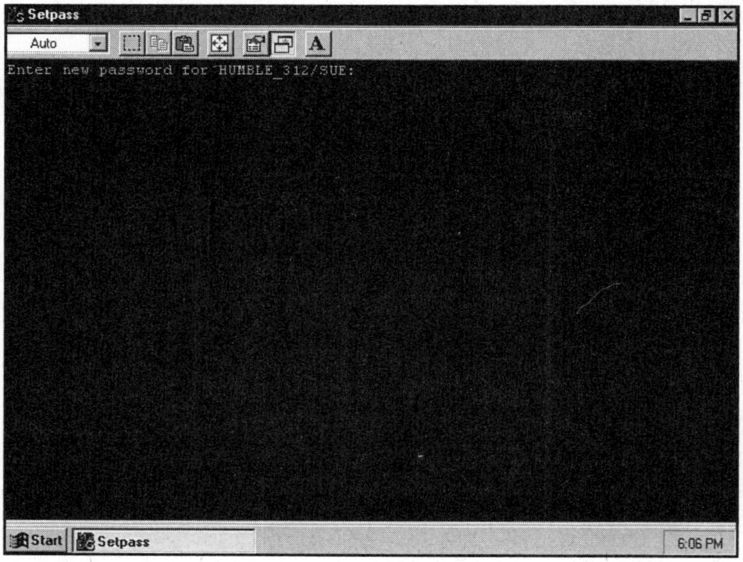

Fig. 23.4
Set a new password using the SETPASS command.

Tip
You also can find the NetWare server version information by running NVER.EXE in a DOS window.

Tip
You also can display the Properties sheet by right-clicking the server icon and choosing the Properties command.

5. Reenter the new password to confirm and press Enter. SETPASS notifies you the password has been changed.

> **Note**
>
> If the new passwords entered in steps 4 and 5 are not identical or if you are prompted for your old password and do not enter it correctly, the password will not be changed.

6. Click the Close button to close the MS-DOS prompt.

Checking the NetWare Version

You can check the version of the NetWare server from within Windows. You'll need to know the NetWare version if a specific application you use is version-specific or version-sensitive.

To find the version of the NetWare used on the server, follow these steps:

1. Open Network Neighborhood and select the server.
2. Choose File, Properties. The Properties sheet appears, as shown in figure 23.5.
3. Once you have the version information, choose OK to close the Properties sheet.

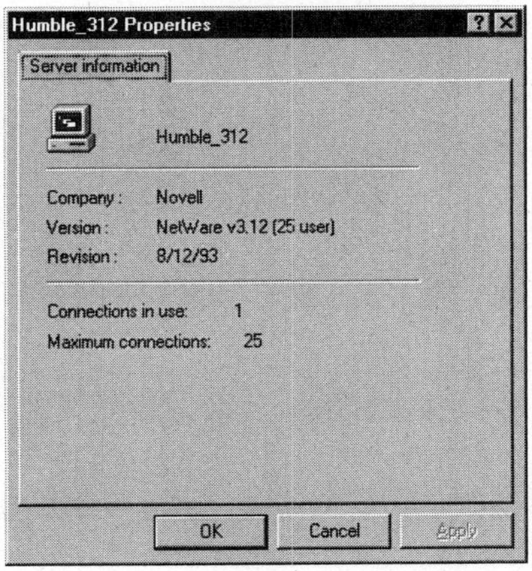

Fig. 23.5
The Properties sheet lists NetWare server version information.

Checking the Status of Network Volumes

A *volume* is a physical portion of the hard disk that stores information on the file server. You can check the space on a volume as well as find out other information about different volumes on the server, using two NetWare utilities: CHKVOL and VOLINFO.

> **Note**
>
> Usually the SYS is the first volume on a server and VOL1 is the second, VOL2 the third, and so on. Although these are the names Novell suggests, they are not always the names used.

To check on the status of the current volume, follow these steps:

1. Open the Start menu and choose Programs, MS-DOS Prompt.
2. At the MS-DOS prompt, change the directory to the primary server drive (usually F:).
3. Type **CHKVOL** and then press Enter. The results appear, as shown in figure 23.6.

> **Note**
>
> You may need to enter a path to the CHKVOL.EXE command; an example path might be \\HUMBLE_312\SYS\PUBLIC\CHKVOL.EXE.

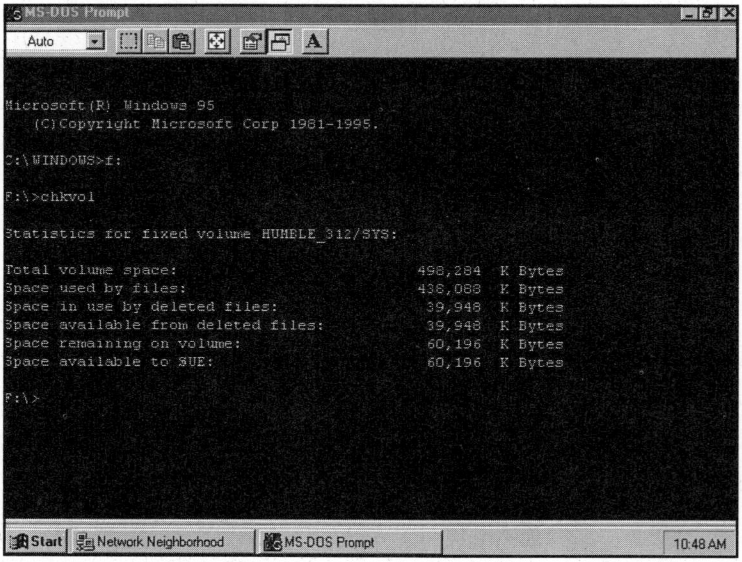

Fig. 23.6
Run CHKVOL at the MS-DOS prompt or from the Run dialog box.

4. Close the DOS window when you finish looking at the CHKVOL statistics.

The CHKVOL statistics list the total amount of space on the volume, the space used by files, the space in use by deleted files and the space available from deleted files, space remaining on the volume, and the space available to you.

Another NetWare information tool that you can use is VOLINFO.EXE, which quickly checks the status of drive usage. To use VOLINFO, follow these steps:

1. Open the MS-DOS Prompt and change to the primary server drive.
2. At the prompt, type **VOLINFO** and press Enter. The Volume Information utility appears (see fig. 23.7).
3. After viewing the volume information, press the Esc key. The Exit VolInfo dialog box appears.
4. Choose Yes and then press Enter.
5. At the MS-DOS prompt, type **exit** and press Enter, or click the Close button in the title bar, to return to the Windows desktop.

VOLINFO reports the name of the volume you are viewing and refers to the storage capacity of that volume in kilobytes, unless the server has more than one gigabyte of storage space, in which case VOLINFO reports space in megabytes.

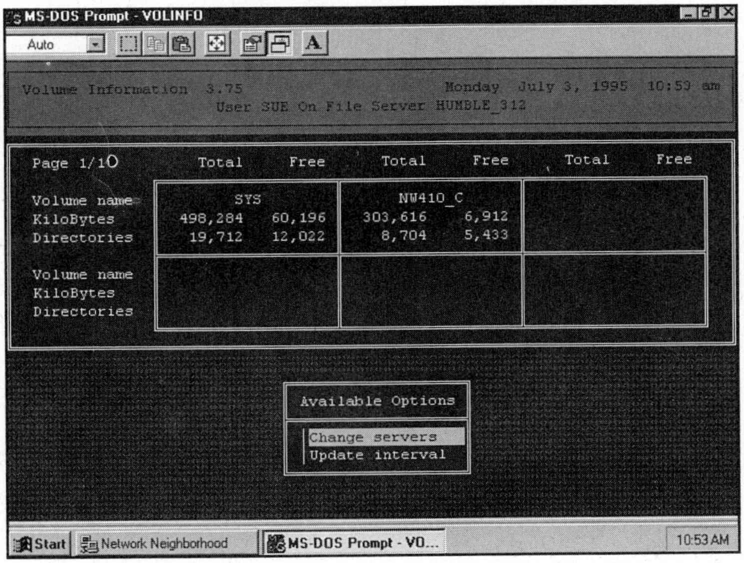

Fig. 23.7
Use Volume Information to view various volumes and their resources.

Listing Your Server Connections

Windows 95 provides a WhoAmI feature that is a graphical user interface (GUI) approach to NetWare's WHOAMI utility. This simplified version of the command shows only the most basic results: your user name and connection number. To see this information, right-click on a server in the Network Neighborhood and choose Who Am I. The results are similar to figure 23.8.

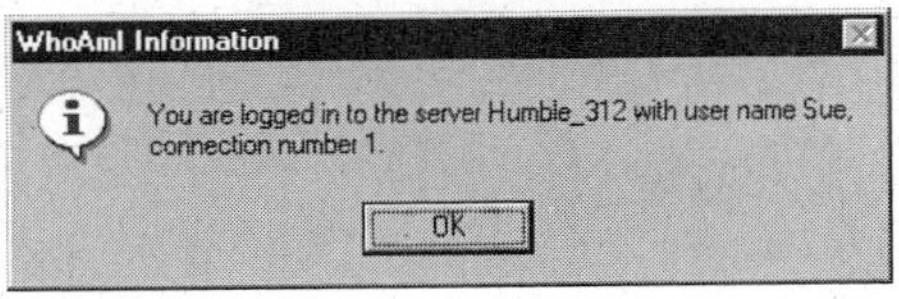

Fig. 23.8
The WhoAmI feature shows your user name, the server to which you're connected, and the connection number.

The NetWare command-line version is much more useful. For instance, if you enter **WHOAMI** at the DOS prompt, you get the same user, server, and connection information. Additionally, WHOAMI lists the NetWare version and allotted user number, date, and time, as shown in figure 23.9.

If you're connected to more than one server, the WHOAMI command also lists those servers and your name on each, the software version on each, your login date and time for each server, and your rights and security equivalencies on each server.

You can enhance the command-line version's output with several parameters. Enter the command as **WHOAMI *[servername] [option]***. The most useful parameters are the following:

Parameter	Description
/s	*Security* lists the security equivalencies on each server you specify.
/g	*Groups* lists your membership in groups on each server specified.
/w	*Workgroup* lists workgroup manager information.
/r	*Rights* lists your rights on each server to which you're attached.
/a	*All* lists all the available information, including your group memberships, your security equivalencies, your rights, object supervisor, workgroup manager, and general system information.

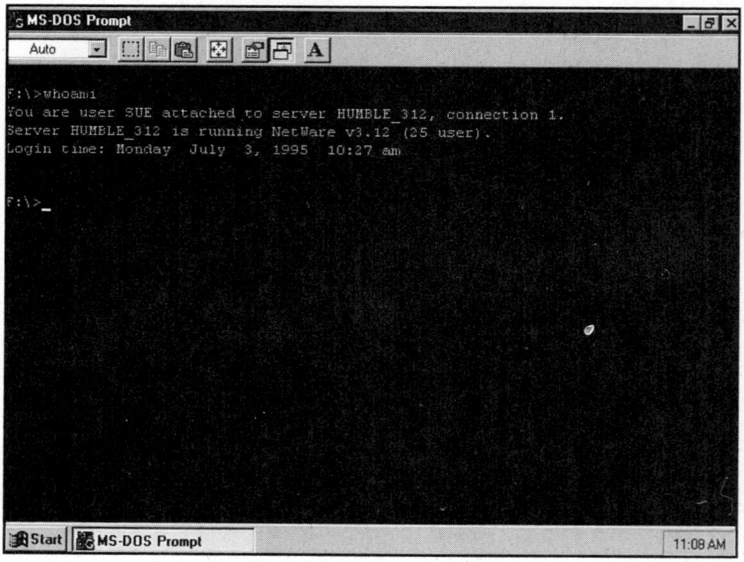

Fig. 23.9
Typical output from NetWare's WHOAMI utility.

Managing NetWare Printers

► See "Understanding Network Printing," p. 772

► See "Solving Common Network Printing Problems," p. 788

If you are comfortable with using NetWare and have done much work printing to a NetWare printer, you have probably seen or used NetWare's PCONSOLE utility for controlling print jobs. Windows 95 improves on PCONSOLE by adding to the printer's control applet in Windows 95 almost all these printer control functions for NetWare printers. Every common task for which you are likely to use PCONSOLE—such as checking the status of a print job and rearranging jobs in the queue (if you have sufficient user rights)—can be done from Windows.

Note

Even though Windows shows nine printer ports you can capture, Novell limits you to capturing on three: LPT1, LPT2, and LPT3. With Novell NetWare, Windows also tells you LPT4 and up are out of range.

PCONSOLE runs just as before, so if you are already familiar with it and want to continue using it, or if you want to access some advanced feature not available in Windows, you can still do so. However, if you only want to see how many print jobs are in front of you in the queue or to delete a print job that you sent accidentally, you can perform all these basic tasks in Windows, as described in Chapter 25, "Working with Network Printers."

Using Administrative Utilities

Most other NetWare utilities that you previously ran from a DOS prompt should now work in Windows 95 as well as from the DOS prompt. You might even find that some network utilities that were difficult to run in DOS 6.X due to memory constraints are easier to run in Windows 95 because more conventional memory is now available.

Table 23.1 lists some common Novell utilities that run in Windows 95. Many other unlisted utilities run as well.

Table 23.1 Some Novell DOS Utilities that You Can Run under Windows 95 Command Prompts

Novell DOS Utility	Function
FCONSOLE	Monitors the file server and lets you perform such functions as broadcast console messages, down the file server, check file server status, and so on
RCONSOLE	Gives you access to the file server console from a workstation (NetWare versions 3.11, 3.12, 4.02, and 4.1)
FILER	Determines file creation date, last access date, size, owner, and so on
SALVAGE	Undeletes files from a NetWare volume
SESSION	Maps network drives with a menu
CAPTURE	Assigns network printers to local LPT ports
SLIST	Displays all NetWare servers on the network (through version 3.x)
SYSCON	Controls accounting, file servers, group, and user information (through version 3.x)

Caution

Deleted files and folders from a network drive do not go to the Windows Recycle Bin; they are deleted permanently. There is no Undo, so be careful. If you do mistakenly delete an item you want, try the SALVAGE command as quickly after deleting the item as possible. When you delete files, the space it occupied remains on the server until the server needs space and is recoverable until that time. Your system administrator may have set NetWare to wait a minimum amount of time before reusing deleted space. You should check with your administrator about this option.

Some utilities cannot run under Windows 95 when you use the Windows Client for NetWare Networks rather than the Novell VLM network drivers. You use these commands in NetWare 4.x networks that employ the NetWare Directory Services (NDS) to manage a multiserver domain. Table 23.2 lists these utilities, which operate under Windows 95 only when the Novell VLM network drivers are used.

Table 23.2 Novell Utilities that Work Only with Novell VLM Network Drivers

Novell Utility	Function
NWADMIN	Administers the NDS directory tree under Windows
CX	Changes contexts within the NDS directory tree
NETADMIN	Administers the NDS directory tree under DOS

◄ See "Using the Explorer with Shared Resources on a Network," p. 544

In addition to the utilities listed in table 23.2 that do not work with the Windows Client for NetWare Networks, the NWUSER Windows 3.x utility is not supported under any configuration in Windows 95. This should not pose a problem because the Explorer application provides all the functionality of the NWUSER utility.

NWPOPUP, a utility that administrators use to broadcast messages across the network, does not work in Windows 95; however, you can install WinPopup to work in its place. WinPopup is a Windows utility in which you can send and receive messages on the NetWare network. Find the WinPopup utility on the migration Planning Kit CD that ships with Windows 95; look in the Admin95 folder, Apptools.

You can add WinPopup to your Startup group (Start menu, Settings, Taskbar, Start Menu Programs tab) so WinPopup automatically starts when you start Windows, so you'll always know when a network message is broadcast.

Tip
In WinPopup, choose Messages, Options and select Pop up Dialog on Message Receipt to be notified immediately of messages from the network.

Troubleshooting

I tried to enter a NetWare command in the Run dialog box but I got the message `Cannot find the file....` *What did I do wrong?*

You may need to specify a path to the server and the folder in which the command or utility resides. If that still doesn't work, close the Run dialog box and use the MS-DOS prompt instead. In the DOS window, change the drives to the primary network drive (usually F:) and then enter the command and the path. Some NetWare commands just do not work from the Run dialog box.

I've forgotten where I placed a file on the server. Is there a NetWare command I can use to find the file?

The easiest way to find a file or a folder in Windows is to use the Windows Find feature. You can use it for network drives as well as for your own drive. Choose Start, Find, and then Files or Folders. In the Find Files dialog box, choose the Browse button. In the Browse for Folder dialog box, double-click the Network Neighborhood. Double-click the server and then choose OK. Enter the file or folder name in the Named text box and choose Find Now. Windows searches the server drive for your file or folder.

Connecting to Other Servers

Connecting to and using the resources on servers within the local network is easy, but how do you connect to servers other than your usual "preferred server"? You accomplish this connection just as you would expect: by using all the standard tools previously discussed.

◄ See "Logging in to a NetWare Server," p. 694

To connect to other servers, follow these steps:

1. Open the Network Neighborhood; all attached servers appear in the list.

2. Select the server name and then choose File, Attach As, or right-click on the server name and choose Attach As. The Enter Network Password dialog box appears.

3. Enter your user name and password. Additionally, you can choose from the following options:

   - Save this Password in Your Password List. Choose this option to save your password in a list so the next time you make this connection, you do not have to retype the password.

   - Connect as Guest. Log on as a guest if you do not have access to that server. Logging on as a guest gives you only limited access to the server.

4. Click on OK to establish the connection. Note that your user name and password may vary from server to server.

◀ See "An Easier but More Powerful Interface," p. 22

If you have logins on multiple servers, this method is probably the easiest. Of course, if you frequently need to connect your computer to the same server, you might create a shortcut on the desktop for this connection.

Using Network Tape Drives

Windows includes a Backup program you can use to back up your files to a network tape drive. Windows 95 works only with 1992 or later versions of certain tape drives (find the list in Backup Help). You might also call the tape drive manufacturer for information about backup software you can use with Windows 95.

Several drives are not compatible with Windows 95, including Archive drives, Irwin AccuTrak tapes and Irwin drives, Mountain drives, QIC Wide tapes, QIC 3020 drives, SCSI tape drives, Summit drives, and Travan drives.

◀ See "Backing Up Your Files," p. 555

In addition, Windows 95 includes an automatic backup feature, a backup agent that efficiently and regularly backs up your system, using industry-standard technology from Arcada (Backup Exec) and Cheyenne (ARCserve). These agents require network connections to a server.

Note

These backup agents require the appropriate software running on the NetWare server. Windows 95 does not include the Arcada or Cheyenne backup software. Additionally, Arcada and Cheyenne are not Novell's native TSA backup agents.

Microsoft considers these agents a service. To install the service to Windows 95, follow these steps:

1. Open the Network dialog box from the Control Panel.
2. On the Configuration page, choose Add. The Select Network Component Type dialog box appears.
3. Select Service and choose Add. The Select Network Service dialog box appears (see fig. 23.10).

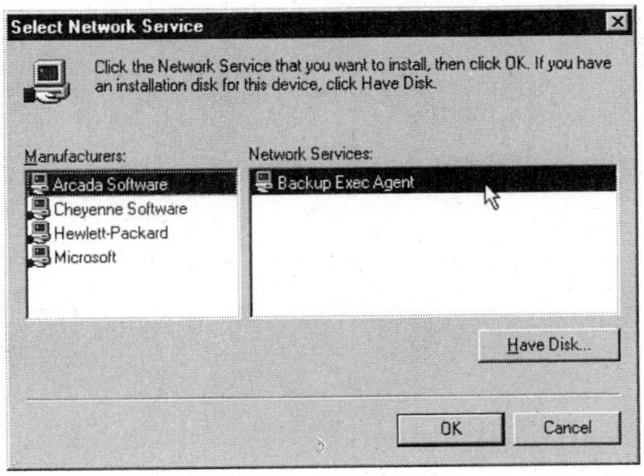

Fig. 23.10
Choose the service from the Select Network Service dialog box.

4. In Manufacturers, choose Arcada Software and in Network Services, Backup Exec Agent becomes selected.

   Alternatively, choose Cheyenne Software in the Manufacturers list and choose ARCserve Agent.
5. Choose OK to select the service. Windows may prompt you to insert the Windows 95 CD. Follow directions on-screen.
6. Windows returns to the Network dialog box. Choose OK to close the dialog box. Windows may copy more files from the Windows 95 CD.
7. Windows prompts you to restart your computer. Choose Yes.

The following sections take you step by step through a typical setup of both of these services. Remember, without one of these backup servers, you cannot use the backup agents.

Note

If your NetWare server uses different backup software, you probably can still use it if you can run it from a DOS command line. Although Windows 95 might not support the software directly, you should still be able to run the software from DOS just as you could with previous releases of Windows.

Backing Up with Arcada

The Arcada Backup Exec agent as delivered with Windows 95 requires Arcada Backup Exec for NetWare, Enterprise Edition or Single Server Edition, version 5.01. If your NetWare server is running either of these Arcada products, you can use the Arcada backup agent to archive important data regularly from your workstation.

Setting Properties

After installing the Arcada service from the Select Network Service dialog box, follow these steps to set up the service:

1. In the Network dialog box, click the Configuration tab.
2. In the components list, double-click on Backup Exec Agent. The Backup Exec Agent Properties sheet appears, as shown in figure 23.11.

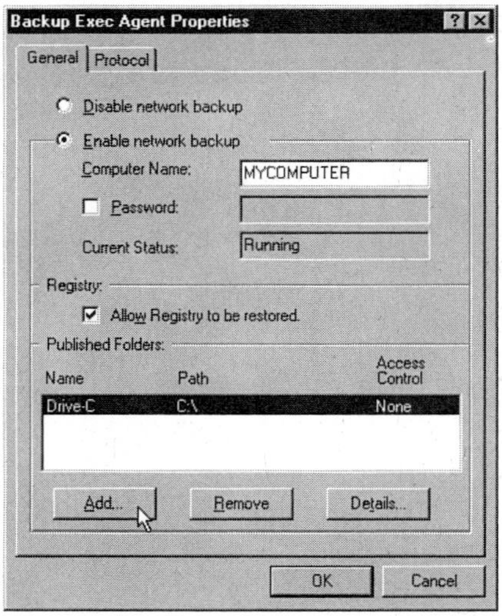

Fig. 23.11
Configure the Backup Exec Agent in the Backup Exec Agent Properties sheet.

3. Click the General tab and choose to Enable Network Backup. The NetWare server software now considers the Windows 95 computer to be a backup source.
4. Enter the name of your computer (as the network knows it) and your password.

Note

Select the Allow Registry to Be Restored check box if you want to enable the software to restore the Registry. If you select the Allow Registry to Be Restored check box, the software overwrites any changes that you made since your last backup.

5. In the Published Folders area, Drive C indicates your entire drive. If you do not want to backup the entire drive, choose Remove.

   To add specific folders, choose Add; the Select Folder To Publish dialog box appears (see fig. 23.12). Choose the folders you want to add to the backup and choose OK. The selected folders are added to the Published Folders list on the Backup Exec Agent Properties sheet.

Tip
You also can choose to backup floppy and CD-ROM drives in the Select Folder To Publish dialog box.

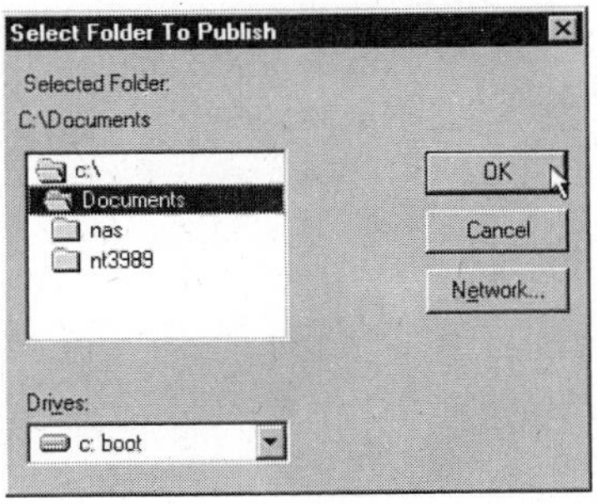

Fig. 23.12
Add drives and/or folders to the Published Folders list (backup list).

6. In the Published Folders area of the Backup Exec Agent Properties sheet, select a folder or drive and choose Details. In the Folder Details dialog box, you can browse the folder's contents and set access limits (see fig. 23.13).

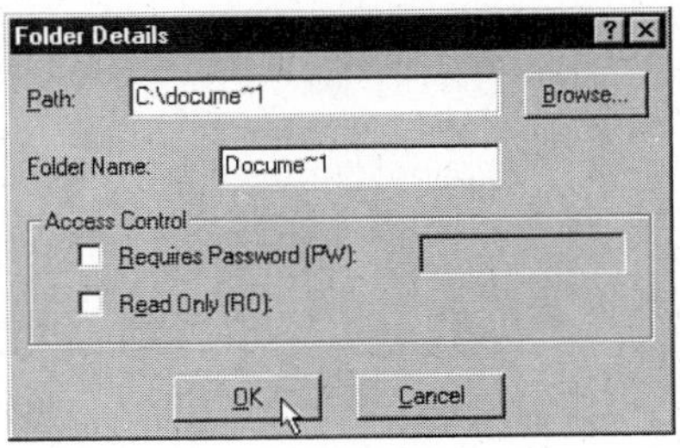

Fig. 23.13
In the Folder Details dialog box, you can assign the required access control.

7. Choose OK to close the Folder Details dialog box. The dialog box closes and the access control limits appear in the Published Folders area of the Backup Exec Agent Properties sheet (see fig. 23.14).

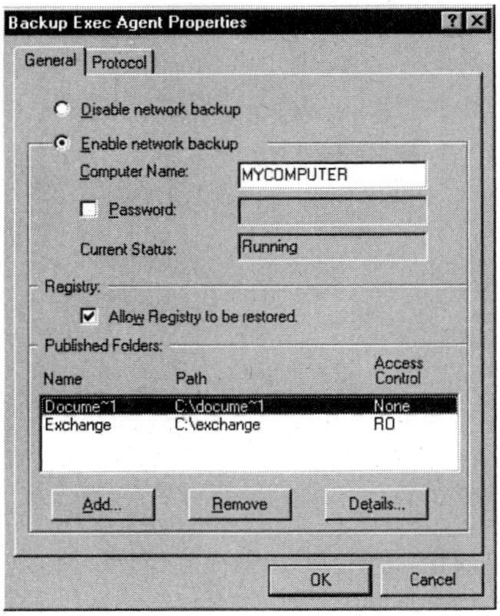

Fig. 23.14
The Published Folders area of the Backup Exec Agent Properties sheet indicates the access control that you have set.

8. Click OK to close the Backup Exec Agent Properties sheet.

> **Note**
>
> When you first install your software, the Properties sheet's Current Status indicates `Not Running`. After you install and configure the agent, this status changes to `Running`.

Setting Protocol

You must set the protocol of the agent to match that of the server. To set the protocol for the Backup Exec Agent, follow these steps:

1. On the Backup Exec Agent Properties sheet, click the Protocol tab (see fig. 23.15).

2. Choose the SPX/IPX protocol for the backup agent.

3. Choose OK to close the sheet.

4. Choose OK in the Network dialog box.

5. When Windows prompts you to restart the computer, choose Yes.

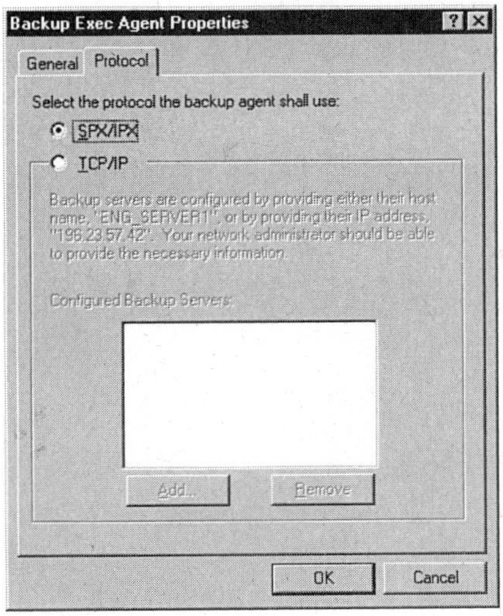

Fig. 23.15
The Protocol page of the Backup Exec Agent Properties sheet.

Note

To use the Arcada Backup Agent, you might have to check whether the system administrator has the latest versions of the Arcada network loadable modules (NLMs) that have been updated for Windows 95. The necessary updated files are NRLTLI.NLM, TNRLAPT3.NLM, TNRLAPT4.NLM, TNRLTCP.NLM, and TNRLSPX.NLM. To get these files, you can contact Arcada directly or call Arcada's BBS at (407) 262-8123.

Backing Up with Cheyenne

If your server is running the Cheyenne backup software, and you've installed the ARCserve backup agent, you can set properties for the agent by following these steps:

1. In the Network dialog box, double-click on ARCserve Agent. The ARCserve Agent Properties sheet appears.

2. Click the General tab and choose Enable Network Backup. The Enable Network Backup area becomes available, as shown in figure 23.16.

3. Specify the settings to configure the Cheyenne software, as follows:

   - *Password*. Enter your password.

   - *Confirm Password*. Enter your password again.

- *Do Not Restore Registry*. Select this option if you do not want your system's registry settings restored when your system is restored.

- *Display Status Information*. Displays information during the backup.

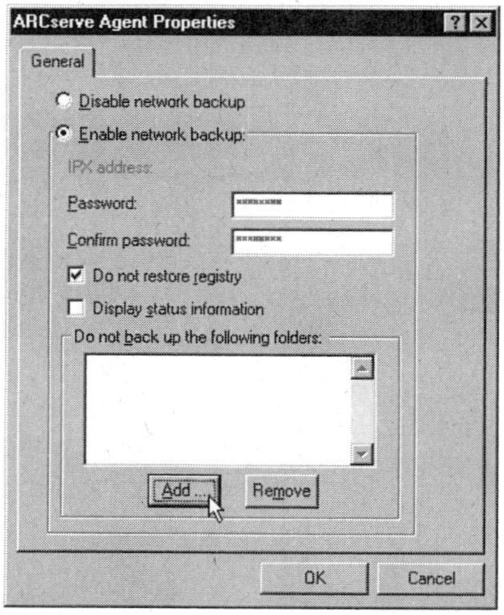

Fig. 23.16
Enable network backup on the ARCserve Agent Properties sheet.

4. Choose Add to enter folders in the Do Not Back Up the Following Folders list. The Add dialog box appears (see fig. 23.17).

   In the Do Not Back Up the Following Folders list, enter only those folders you *do not* want to back up. By default, all folders will be backed up.

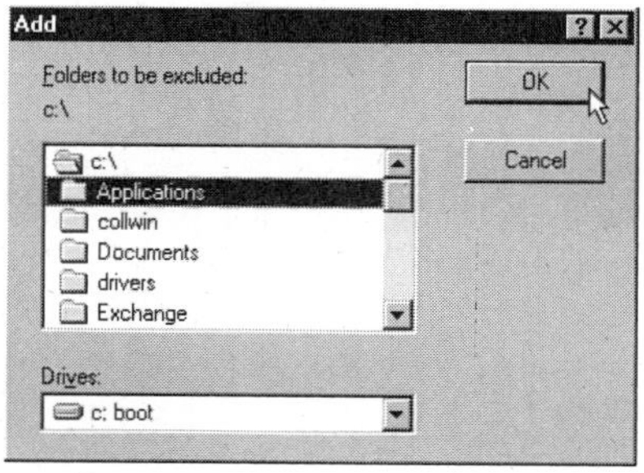

Fig. 23.17
Select the folder you *do not* want to back up in the Add dialog box for Cheyenne ARCserve agent.

Note

If you mistakenly added a folder you do want to back up, select the folder and choose Remove.

5. Choose OK in the Add dialog box to return to the ARCserve Agent Properties sheet. The folders you do not want to back up appear in the Do Not Back Up the Following Folders list box, as shown in figure 23.18.

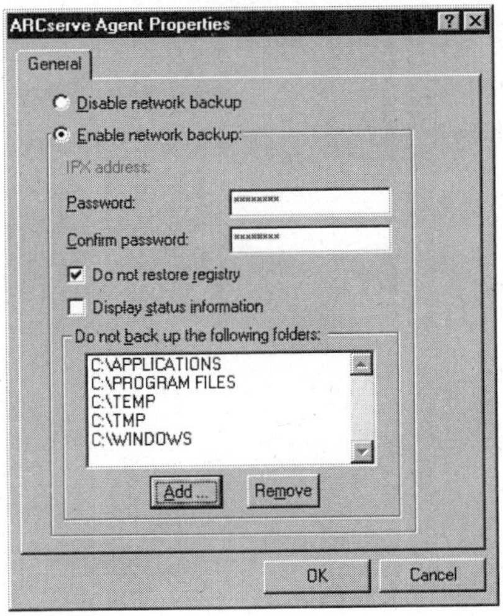

Fig. 23.18
The folders listed in the dialog box are those the agent will *not* back up.

6. Click OK to close the Properties sheet.
7. Choose OK in the Network dialog box.
8. When Windows prompts you to restart the computer, choose Yes.

Note

Cheyenne has updated the network loadable modules (NLMs) specifically for Windows 95. These updated files are APROCESS.NLM, ARCOPY.NLM, and WSTAPE.NLM. To obtain these files, contact Cheyenne directly at (800) 243-9832.

As you have seen in this chapter, Windows 95 and NetWare servers can coexist, and in fact, Windows 95 makes it easier to use NetWare server resources than previous releases of Windows. Microsoft has made Windows 95 truly a "well-connected client."❖

Chapter 24

Using Microsoft Exchange

by Gordon Meltzer with Peter Kent

Microsoft Exchange is a central communications client that organizes the electronic mail and faxes that you receive in one convenient location. Exchange operates not only as your universal in-box, but also as a tool that can compose, store, organize, and send messages via e-mail and fax.

In its basic configuration, Exchange coordinates communication among members of your Local Area Network (LAN) workgroup and handles communications via the Microsoft Network, yet still finds time to send and receive faxes in several formats. In more advanced configurations, Exchange handles communications with other message services, like CompuServe and Internet mail.

In this chapter, you learn to do the following:

- Install Microsoft Exchange
- Configure your Exchange user profile
- Create a Personal Address Book
- Choose and install messaging services
- Create and send messages
- Work with received messages
- Use Exchange remotely from a laptop or other location

Overview of Exchange Features

So that you know how to set up Exchange during the installation process, you should have some detailed information about what Exchange can do. Knowing about Exchange's abilities will help you to make the right installation and setup choices.

You call on Microsoft Exchange when you want to compose a fax. You visit Exchange again when you want to send a message to a workgroup colleague down the hall or to everyone on your workgroup network. When those folks on your workgroup reply to you, your Exchange Inbox is where their missives will land. Faxes sent to your fax card head for the Exchange Inbox, too.

Your messages don't have to be just plain text, either. Because Exchange supports Rich Text Format, messages can be delivered in any font on your system, at any size, in any color. The first time you see a mail message that has been passed around your workgroup and each member has contributed his or her thoughts in a different color, you'll begin to appreciate the power of Exchange.

More important than Rich Text is the ability to work with Object Linking and Embedding (OLE). Your messages can contain OLE documents created in applications that are OLE servers, like Microsoft Word for Windows, Microsoft Excel, or any of the many OLE server applications.

Finally, you can use Exchange to communicate via Microsoft Network, the online service available through Windows 95.

So far, we've looked at Exchange from the point of view of a member of a local area network workgroup. But even if you're on a stand-alone system, Exchange will have value to you, as long as you have a modem and a phone line. In this type of configuration, you can communicate via fax, and your e-mail can reach into the membership of Microsoft Network, and beyond, right out onto the Internet!

Clients and Servers

In the introduction, we said that Exchange was a central communications client. The word *client* is so important in Exchange, and in Windows 95 generally, that we need to explain it and its comrade term, *server*.

For the purposes of programs like Exchange, a server is a program, running on a network, that holds information accessible by users on the network.

These users employ programs called clients to get at the server-based information.

If the server is a mail or fax server, it provides a place to store mail and fax messages for all the clients (users) on the network. This is the kind of server to which the Exchange client connects.

Note

Clients don't have to be permanently connected to the network to get information from or send information to the server. The network connection can be dial-up, the way you access CompuServe.

Inbox

Discussions of Microsoft Exchange have commonly referred to Exchange as the "universal inbox." In fact, one way to start the Exchange program is to double-click the Inbox icon on your Windows desktop. The inbox function is a very important part of Exchange, as this section explains.

You'll be using Exchange to communicate, and a good part of communication is finding out what others have to say. You may receive messages by fax or e-mail. In Windows 95, these received messages are directed to Microsoft Exchange where they can be conveniently read. In this way, Exchange functions as an inbox. We call Exchange a *universal inbox* because all messages, both fax and e-mail, no matter where they come from, go to your Exchange inbox.

In Windows 3.1, incoming messages went to the inboxes of various applications. Faxes would go to WinFax or another fax program, depending on what you had installed. E-mail would go to cc:Mail, Microsoft Mail, or whatever program you were using for e-mail. CompuServe Mail, likewise, would go to the inbox in whatever program you used to access CompuServe.

Windows 95's designers have reasoned that collecting all these messages in one place would be more convenient. That is why the inbox function of Exchange is so important.

Microsoft Workgroup E-Mail

If you're connected to a local area network (LAN), Exchange is the program you'll use to send and receive e-mail with your workgroup colleagues. Windows 95 contains a Microsoft Mail Postoffice so you can set up an e-mail system on your workgroup network.

▶ See "Installing the Workgroup Postoffice," p. 769

Once you have your Postoffice running, Exchange collects all e-mail addressed to you. You then can read, reply to, and forward them, all while using the Exchange program. Other accessory programs, installed on your network, will let Exchange send and receive e-mail over networks wider than your workgroup LAN.

Microsoft Fax

Exchange, working hand in hand with Microsoft Fax, provides a convenient place to compose your fax, attach or embed documents to be included with your fax, and address your fax. Exchange gives you several ways to create faxes. You can use the Compose New Fax Wizard to send a simple typed message or an attached file. (Yes, you can transfer computer files using fax, as you'll find out later.) You can use the same New Message window that you use to compose e-mail, or you can create your fax in another application and send or print it to the fax system. Your faxes can include text, pictures, OLE objects, and files. This richness of function is one of the key features of Microsoft Exchange.

Microsoft Network

The Microsoft Network (MSN) is an online service, similar in concept to CompuServe and America Online. One service Microsoft Network provides to its members is e-mail.

Microsoft Exchange provides a way to dial into MSN and quickly retrieve any e-mail waiting for you. You also can use Exchange to send e-mail to an MSN member.

Rich Text Format

Exchange supports Rich Text Format (RTF). This means you can create messages using any font on your system. You also can change the text's size and use different colors. These text-formatting capabilities let you personalize your messages, and they can be quite useful when messages are routed to various people for comment. Individuals can use different colors and various typefaces and type sizes, which helps set off each set of comments.

OLE Support

OLE allows you to put part of one document into another. This capability has been used by every major Windows applications publisher. You can highlight a section of a document, copy it into Windows Clipboard, and paste-link or paste-embed it into another program. The original program might be a spreadsheet, and the target program might be a word processor. It doesn't matter, as long as the source program is an OLE server, and the target program is an OLE client. Most major programs are both.

Note

The data you copy and paste-link or paste-embed is called an *OLE object*. Often in Windows 95, OLE objects have an associated icon. You can drag the icon into other programs or drop it on the Windows desktop. In other cases, the OLE object simply appears in its original format, such as rows from a spreadsheet.

Exchange extends your powers to work with OLE objects by allowing you to drop them into its universal message form (message window). From the form, you can mail or fax objects as part of your message.

Most modern Windows applications are OLE enabled. Although we mentioned Microsoft Word and Excel objects previously, any OLE object can be embedded in an Exchange message and sent with that message.

Note

Chapter 15, "Building Compound Documents with OLE," explains how to get the most out of OLE.

Installing and Configuring Microsoft Exchange

You can install Microsoft Exchange during your initial Windows 95 installation or afterward. After the first few steps, however, the process is the same. The following sections explain how to install and configure Exchange for your needs.

Note

Microsoft Exchange requires a minimum of 6M of memory in your system to run. For good performance, plan on having at least 8M. Exchange also takes 10M of space on your hard drive for required swap files. The Exchange basic program files take 3.7M of disk space. Due to Exchange's ability to work with all sorts of different data, you should allow a few M for your incoming messages, too. It's easy to end up with 5M or more of faxes and e-mail.

Installing Exchange during Windows Setup

During Windows setup, the Windows 95 Setup Wizard displays the Get Connected dialog box, shown in figure 24.1. In this dialog box, you can choose to install The Microsoft Network online service, Microsoft Mail for use on workgroup networks (LANs), and the Microsoft Fax service.

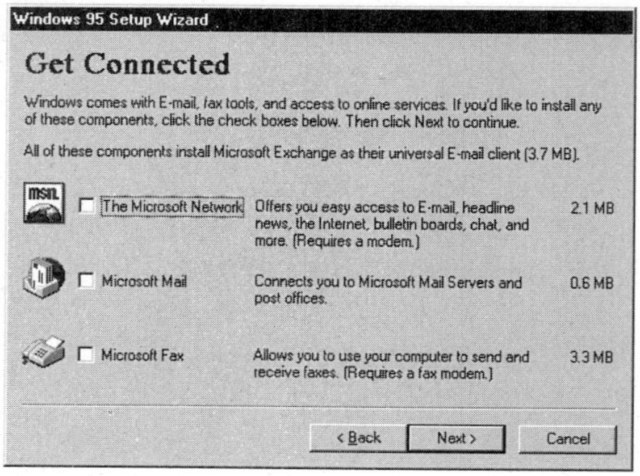

Fig. 24.1
The Get Connected dialog box is the first step to installing Exchange.

You can install any or all of these three connectivity components. (You can always add them later, too.) MSN, Microsoft Mail, and Microsoft Fax all require Microsoft Exchange to work, so when you choose any of them, Microsoft Exchange is installed for you.

Note

For more information on installing and setting up Windows 95, see Appendix A, "Installing and Uninstalling Windows 95."

It's also possible to install Exchange without installing any of these items; for instance, if you want to use Exchange for Internet e-mail. To do so, you must choose a Custom installation—you'll then be able to select Exchange from a list of optional components.

Adding Exchange after Windows Is Installed

If you did not install any of the connectivity components during your Windows 95 installation, you can add Exchange later.

On your Windows desktop, you will see an icon called Inbox. If you right-click the Inbox icon and then choose Properties, Windows confirms that Exchange is not installed (see fig. 24.2).

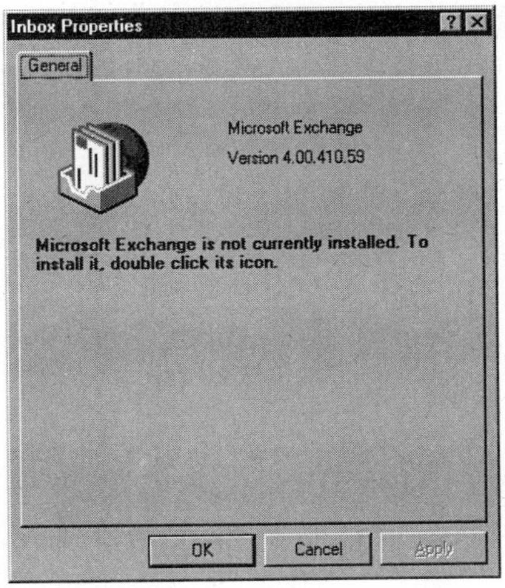

Fig. 24.2
Windows confirms that Exchange is not yet installed.

Follow this procedure to install Microsoft Exchange:

1. Double-click the Inbox icon on your desktop. You'll see a Get Connected dialog box similar to the one shown in figure 24.1 (though it's now called the Inbox Setup Wizard).

> **Note**
>
> If you've installed an Exchange service and now want to install one or more other services, you won't be able to use this procedure; this procedure only works when no Exchange services have been installed. To install Microsoft Fax or Microsoft Network, open the Start menu and choose Settings, Control Panel; then double-click on the Add/Remove Programs icon, click on the Windows Setup tab, and select the item from the list of components. To install Microsoft Mail or Internet Mail, right-click on the Inbox icon, choose Add, and select the service you want to install.

2. Choose one or more of the three information services you are offered. The services are The Microsoft Network, Microsoft Mail, and Microsoft Fax. (To make this example most useful, we'll cover what happens when you choose all three).

3. After selecting the information services you want, choose OK.

4. The Inbox Setup Wizard asks you to insert your Windows 95 CD-ROM or floppy disk. Insert the CD-ROM or disk and choose OK. Windows then installs the needed files.

5. The Inbox Setup Wizard now asks whether you've used Exchange before. Since you're setting up Exchange for the first time, choose No. Then choose Next. Windows displays the dialog box shown in figure 24.3.

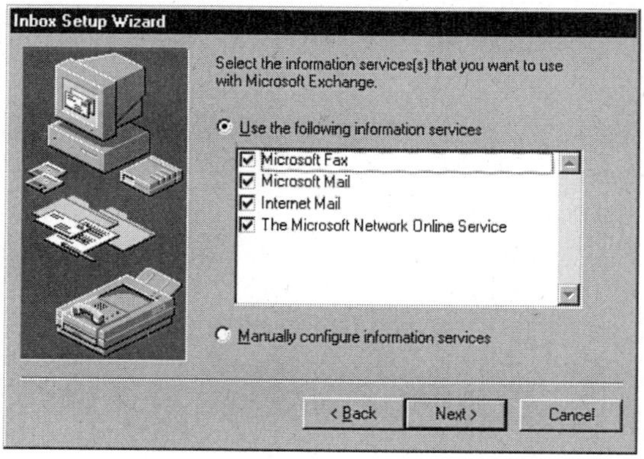

Fig. 24.3
The Inbox Setup Wizard offers you a choice of services.

6. The services you just selected in step 2 are already checked, along with Internet Mail. If you plan to use Exchange for receiving e-mail from an Internet service provider (other than Microsoft Network), leave this check box checked. Otherwise—if you are not going to use Internet e-mail—*clear* the check box.

Note

Microsoft Network has a level of service that provides full Internet access, and it also allows *all* users, at all levels, to send and receive e-mail across the Internet. However, the Internet Mail service referred to by the Inbox Setup Wizard is intended for use with other Internet service providers, not with the Microsoft Network.

7. Choose Next.

The basic setup of Exchange is done, but the Inbox Setup Wizard continues, setting up each of the services you have selected. In the next sections, we work with the Wizard to configure the individual communications services we just chose to use with Exchange.

Troubleshooting

I followed this procedure but couldn't get Exchange to install correctly.

The Inbox Setup Wizard may run into problems—it may even "crash" while setting up your information. For instance, you may get a message telling you that the Wizard was unable to complete something and telling you to click on the Finish button to end the procedure. If this happens to you, double-click on the Inbox icon and the Wizard should start again.

Configuring Microsoft Fax

If you chose to install Microsoft Fax, you see the dialog box shown in figure 24.4. (If you didn't choose to install Microsoft Fax, you can skip this section.) The Wizard asks you to enter information about your telephone number: your area code, the number (if any) that you dial to get an outside line, and whether you are using pulse or tone dialing. Enter all this information, and then choose OK.

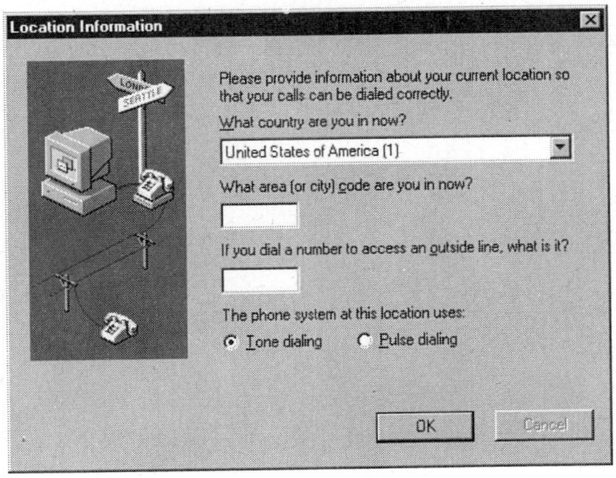

Fig. 24.4
The Wizard's Location Information dialog box.

You are then asked whether you want to use a ems modem or a network-fax service (you can choose only the latter if you have installed network software; if you haven't, the Wizard ignores your selection and assumes that you want to use a modem). Select the appropriate option button and choose Next.

The Wizard now asks for information about the modem or network-fax service. If you have already installed a modem, you see something like the dialog box in figure 24.5. (If you haven't yet installed a modem, the Install New Modem Wizard starts.)

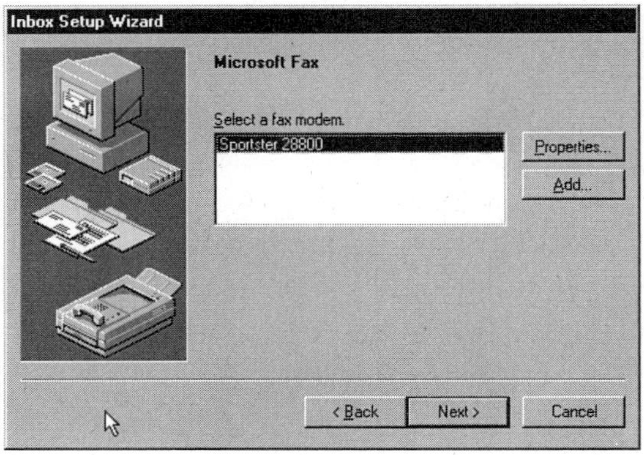

Fig. 24.5
The Microsoft Fax dialog box lets you specify the kind of device you want to use for sending and receiving faxes.

► See "Installing and Configuring Your Modem," p. 831

Select which modem you want to use for your fax messages—in the illustration there is only one choice. You can add another fax modem—or a Network Fax Server—by clicking on the Add button. Or modify the selected fax modem's properties by choosing Properties. When you've selected the fax modem (or added a Network Fax Server), choose Next.

Tip
If you use the modem line to receive phone calls as well as faxes, tell Microsoft Fax not to answer each incoming call. This way, voice calls can be answered by a person, not the modem.

If you select a modem rather than a Network Fax Server, the Wizard asks you whether you want Microsoft Fax to answer each incoming call on the phone line the modem is connected to. Choose Yes or No. (If you choose Yes, you may also want to change the Answer After *n* Rings value—you'll probably want the smallest value, 2 rings. Then choose Next.

Next, the Inbox Setup Wizard asks you for some personal information. This information will be used on any fax cover sheets you send along with your outgoing faxes, so people will know who sent them and how to fax back to you.

Enter your name and other information as requested in the dialog box shown in figure 24.6—you must enter the fax number (the number of the line to which the fax machine is connected) or you will be unable to continue. Then choose Next.

That's all their is to installing the Fax service. If you selected another service, the Wizard now asks for information about that service. If not, skip to "Completing Your Microsoft Exchange Installation," later in this chapter.

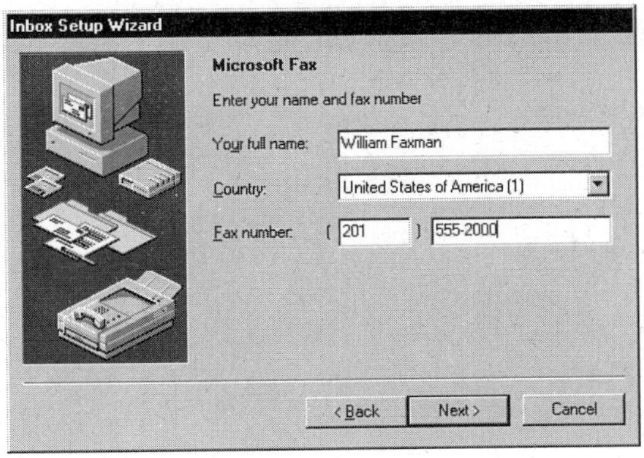

Fig. 24.6
Enter the personal information you want included on your faxes in this dialog box.

Configuring Microsoft Mail

If you chose to install Microsoft Mail, you see the dialog box shown in figure 24.7 now. (If you did not choose to install Microsoft Mail, you can skip this section.)

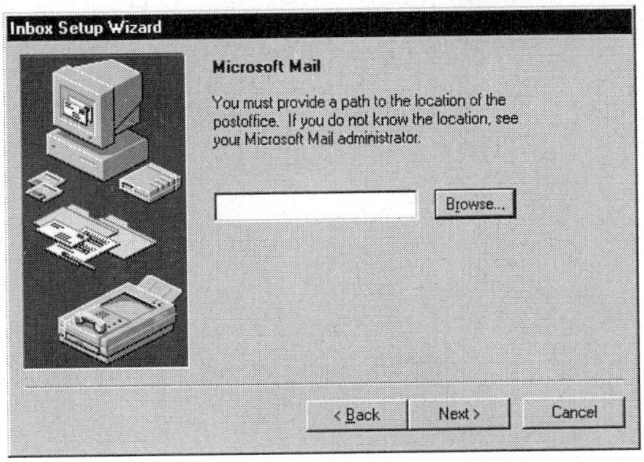

Fig. 24.7
You need to specify a Postoffice location to use Microsoft Mail.

Microsoft Mail requires that one of the computers on the workgroup LAN be set up as a Postoffice. You may have a network administrator who has already done this. If so, ask the administrator for the path to the Postoffice. Then, put the path to the Postoffice in the text box shown in fig. 24.7 (use the Browse button and search for the path if necessary), and choose Next.

> **Note**
>
> When the administrator creates a Postoffice, a folder called WGPO000 is created. For instance, if the administrator creates a folder called Mail and tells the Microsoft Workgroup Postoffice Admin Wizard to place the Postoffice there, the Wizard places the WPGO000 folder inside the Mail folder. You must specify where the WPGO000 folder is. For instance, you would enter C:\MSMAIL\WGPO0000, not C:\MSMAIL.

If you don't have an administrator to set up your Postoffice, go right now to the "Installing the Workgroup Postoffice" section later in this chapter. Then return to this section.

You are shown a list of people who've been given access to the Postoffice. Select your name from this list (if it's not on the list, ask the administrator to add it). The Inbox Setup Wizard then asks for your password. Again, ask your administrator what password he used when creating your account, and carefully type that into the text box. Then choose Next.

The Wizard has finished setting up Microsoft Mail, and you are ready to use it on your workgroup LAN.

Configuring Internet Mail

If you chose to install Internet Mail, you see the dialog box shown in figure 24.8. (If you did not choose to install Internet Mail, skip this section.) The first step is to specify your Internet access method.

> **Note**
>
> In order to use Internet Mail, you must have the TCP/IP protocol installed on your computer. If it isn't, you'll see a message reminding you to install it. To install TCP/IP open the Start menu and choose Settings, Control Panel; double-click on the Network icon and choose Add; select Protocol and choose Add; select Microsoft and TCP/IP, and then choose OK.

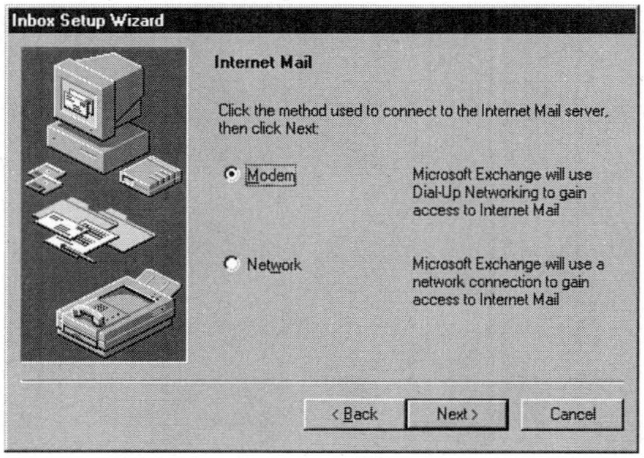

Fig. 24.8 You need to choose an access method to the Internet for Internet Mail.

► See "Installing and Configuring Windows 95 Dial-Up Network Adapter," p. 888

Internet Access Method

The Wizard offers Modem and Network options for Internet access. If you connect to the Internet by modem and Dial-Up Networking, follow these steps:

1. Choose Modem and then choose Next.
2. Now select the connection you created in Dial-Up Networking that dials your Internet Service Provider.

   If you haven't created a connection yet, choose New and create a connection. (Chapter 29, "Getting Connected to the Internet," provides detailed instructions for creating a connection.)

▶ See "Creating a Configuration for Your Access Provider," p. 892

> **Note**
>
> If you haven't yet installed the TCP/IP software, the Wizard skips this step; it doesn't ask you which service provider to use. Later you can specify a service provider by choosing Tools, Services in the Inbox, clicking on Internet Mail, choosing Properties, and clicking on the Connection tab.

3. Choose Next.

If you connect to the Internet via your LAN, choose Network and then choose Next.

Selecting Your Internet Mail Server

Now tell the Wizard about your Internet Mail server. You can tell the Wizard either the Name of the server where your Internet mail is stored, or you can tell the Wizard its IP Address. (Figure 24.9 shows an example, with a mail-server name filled in.) Then choose Next.

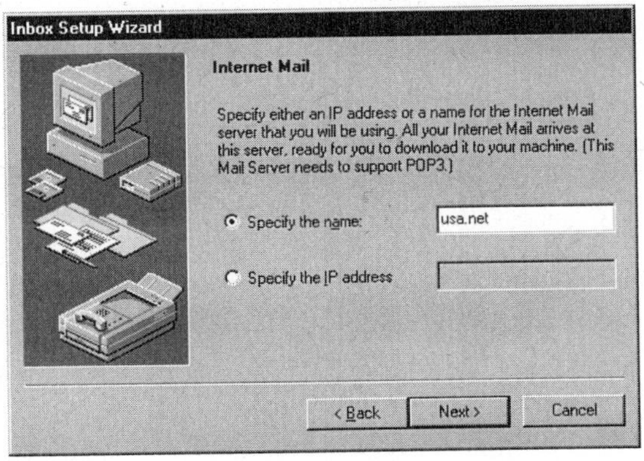

Fig. 24.9
Enter your Internet Mail server information.

Internet Mail Transfer Method

You can choose Off-line or Automatic mail transfers:

- Off-line lets you use Remote Preview to view only incoming mail headers. You selectively decide which messages to download to your Inbox, based on the header contents.
- Automatic instructs Exchange to connect to your Internet Mail server and retrieve all new mail to your Inbox automatically. The Automatic option also automatically sends any outbound Internet mail you've created.

Make your choice, and then choose Next.

Your Internet E-Mail Address

Next, the Wizard wants you to fill in your e-mail address in the form user@domain. Enter this in the text box called E-Mail Address. Also, put your full name in the text box called Your Full Name. When you're finished, choose Next.

Internet Mailbox Information

The Inbox Setup Wizard needs the Mailbox Name and Password you use to access your account in your Internet Mail server. Enter them in the text boxes provided and then choose Next.

Internet Mail is set up and ready to use with Exchange.

Confirming The Microsoft Network Mail System

You cannot set up MSN with the Inbox Setup Wizard. At this point, if you've chosen to install MSN, the Inbox Setup Wizard displays a dialog box confirming you have chosen to install MSN Mail to work with Exchange (see fig. 24.10).

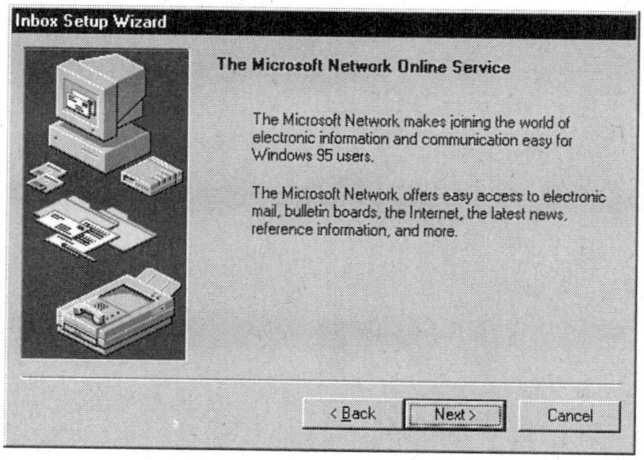

Fig. 24.10
The Wizard confirms that you want to install The Microsoft Network online service mail.

When you choose Next, the Wizard confirms that you've chosen to install MSN Mail to work with Exchange. All setup and configuration of MSN is done by the MSN Setup program—the Setup program begins when you double-click on the MSN icon on your desktop, or open the Start menu and choose Programs, The Microsoft Network. (Appendix B, Using Microsoft Network," covers MSN installation and setup.)

▶ See "Connecting to The Microsoft Network," p. 1110

Completing Your Microsoft Exchange Installation

Now you've set up the various services you selected, the Wizard finishes off the more general Exchange settings. First, it asks you which Personal Address Book it should use.

You probably haven't created a Personal Address Book (as we're assuming that you are installing Exchange for the first time), so simply choose Next.

You then see a similar dialog box, this time asking where your Personal Folder file is. This is the file that stores all your messages. Choose Next to accept the file that the Wizard is suggesting.

Next, the Wizard asks whether you want to run Exchange automatically every time you start Windows. This choice requires some thought; Exchange uses many system resources and can affect performance in low-memory configurations. If you are going to use Exchange only on a dial-up basis, such as with The Microsoft Network or an Internet service provider, choose No.

Tip
If you're connected to a LAN, start Exchange automatically every time you start Windows so that you won't miss any e-mail from workgroup members.

Running Exchange at Windows startup wastes system resources if you don't need to use Exchange's services constantly. If you don't expect much e-mail and will use Exchange and its communications services infrequently, select the Do Not Add Inbox to StartUp Group check box.

If your messaging needs require constant connectivity or periodic automatic logon to an online service to check for new mail, choose To Add Inbox to the StartUp Group.

To complete the installation, choose Next. The Inbox Setup Wizard displays a final dialog box confirming that Exchange is set up to work with all the communications services you selected (see fig. 24.11).

Choose Finish, and after this long setup and configuration process, you are ready to start using Microsoft Exchange. (The Exchange window opens automatically immediately after the Wizard closes.)

Fig. 24.11
Inbox Setup Wizard confirms that the setup of services is complete.

Creating and Sending Mail Messages

After you configure one or more information services, you can create and send a message with the Exchange client. If Exchange were perfect, it would have a universal composition screen in which you could compose any type of message for any type of recipient and for any delivery method. Because of the differences between fax recipients and electronic-mail recipients, however, you have to decide whether to compose a mail message or a fax.

In this section, we explain how to create and send a Microsoft Mail e-mail message to members of your workgroup LAN. Then, in the next section, we describe how to compose and send a fax with Microsoft Fax.

Creating a Mail Message

Tip
You also can get to the New Message window by pressing Ctrl+N in the main Exchange window.

First we'll explain how to send an e-mail message to a member of your workgroup LAN. You'll be working with the message form we discussed earlier in this chapter. Remember that you'll have all the power of Rich Text Formatting and OLE at your fingertips when you create your e-mail message.

If the Exchange window is not open, start the Exchange program by double-clicking the Inbox icon on the desktop. Then choose Compose, New Message. If you prefer to use the toolbar, choose the New Message button. Exchange opens the New Message window.

Figure 24.12 shows the initial blank composition window, which is Exchange's New Message form, or window. You will see this form frequently while you work in Exchange. Now you can work on your message.

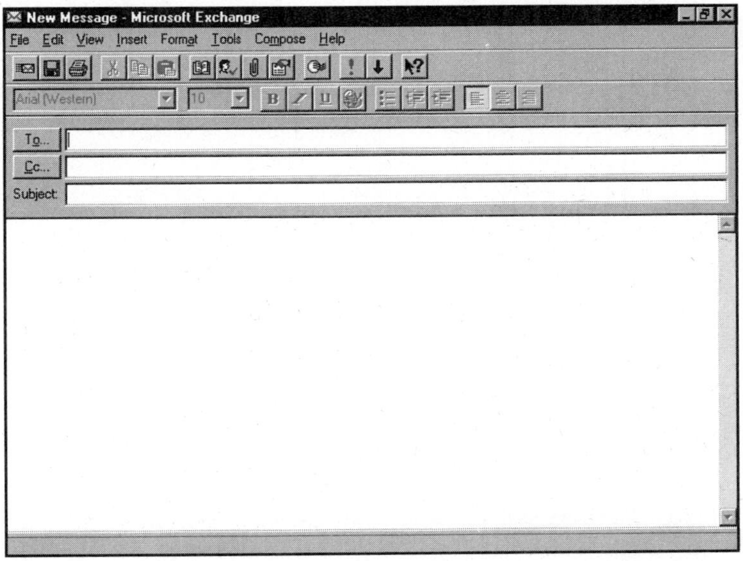

Fig. 24.12
Exchange displays the New Message window in which you compose your message.

Choosing a Recipient

When you click To in the New Message window, your Personal Address Book pops up, showing the list of recipients that you have created. Select the names of the people to whom you want to send your message; you can select names for the To box and names for the Cc box.

► See "Working with Your Address Book," p. 757

You may want to send a blind carbon copy, called a Bcc. The blind copy will be sent to any recipients on the Bcc list. The recipients of the original message and any Cc recipients will not know a copy has gone to the Bcc recipient. The New Message form does not show the Bcc text box by default. You can display this text box by choosing View, Bcc Box.

Entering Text

Start with the Subject box and type the subject of the message.

Tip
Enter your text for the message first and format it later.

Pressing Tab takes you to the main message-entry space, where you can write what you have to say. Start entering text now.

Formatting Message Text

Do you see a remarkable similarity between the menus and toolbars of the New Message form and a good Windows word processor? You do, indeed. The toolbars and menus give you the option of choosing the following formatting options for your message text (the options are listed as they appear on the toolbar, from left to right):

◀ See "Understanding Fonts," p. 210

◀ See "Reviewing Types of Fonts," p. 213

- Font (limited to the fonts on your system)
- Font Size (as small or large as the TrueType font scaler can handle)
- Bold
- Italic
- Underline
- Text Color
- Bullets
- Indents
- Text Alignment (left align, center, and right align)

You combine these options to create messages in Rich Text Format. Whenever you use fonts in varying sizes, colors, and alignments, or other formatting options, you are adding depth to your communications.

Entering OLE Objects in Exchange Messages

You are not limited to text messages, even Rich Text Format messages. One of Exchange's most useful capabilities is that of including objects in messages. When you use objects in your messages, you can add a lot of extra content to those messages with very little work.

You can insert the following types of Windows 95 objects into your messages:

- Audio Recorder
- Bitmap images
- Media clips
- Microsoft Word documents or pictures
- MIDI sequences
- Packages
- Paint pictures
- QuickTime movies
- Video clips
- Wave sounds
- WordPad document

Tip
If the person receiving your message needs a document from you such as a text document, spreadsheet, or a picture, be sure to insert it in the document using the techniques we discuss in this section.

Each application on your system that is an OLE server can create OLE objects that you can place in your messages, so the preceding list is not exhaustive. See Chapter 15, "Building Compound Documents with OLE," to learn how to create OLE objects.

Follow these steps to insert an OLE object in an Exchange mail message:

1. In Exchange, choose Insert, Object. The list of available object types appears (see fig. 24.13).

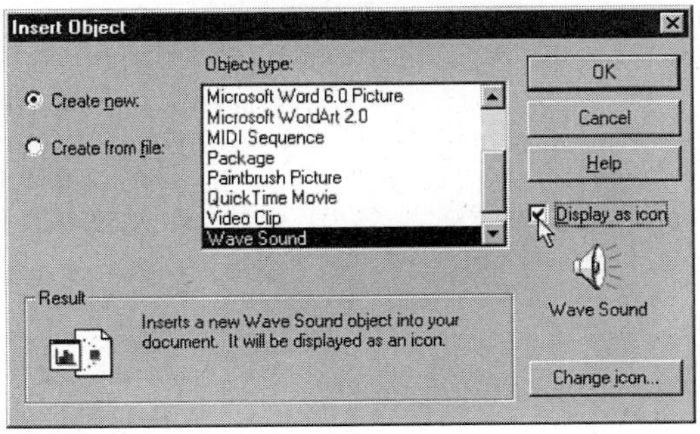

Fig. 24.13
You use the Insert Object dialog box to choose an OLE object type to insert in an Exchange message.

2. Select the type of object that you want to include in your message, and then choose OK. Select Wave Sound, for example, to insert a sound recording in the message. The application used to create the object starts. In the case of a Sound Wave object, the Sound Recorder applet starts.

Tip
If you want your OLE option to appear as an icon, select the Display as Icon option while in the Insert Object dialog box. Leave the check box cleared if you want the data—the spreadsheet rows, word processing text, picture, or whatever—displayed rather than the icon. (Some objects—sounds, for instance—can't be displayed, so their icons will display automatically.)

> **Note**
>
> Notice that the OLE server application that opens will have a special kind of title bar. Instead of saying Sound Recorder, for instance, the title bar says Sound Object in Mail Message. The OLE server applications also have slightly different menus and options from when they run normally. The File menu in Sound Recorder, for example, has a new option: Exit & Return to Mail Message.

3. Use the application to create the object that you want to mail. In this case, record the audio that you want to send with your mail and then choose File, Exit & Return to Mail Message. The application disappears, leaving the Wave Sound icon in your message.

If you are inserting a form of data that can be displayed, and if you didn't choose the Display as Icon check box in the Insert Object dialog box, you see the actual data rather than the icon. You can move this data or the icon around in your message, and you can give the icon a more useful name than the default name (Wave Sound).

When recipients get a message containing an icon, they must double-click the icon. This starts the application that created the OLE object. The object is then played or displayed.

> **Note**
>
> When you insert objects in Exchange messages, rename the icon, including text such as *Click here to play*, to make the icon's intended function obvious to the receiver. Rename the icon by right-clicking it, choosing Rename, and then typing the new name in the text box over the old name. Press Enter when finished.

Embedding an object or file in an Exchange message is an example of OLE at work in Microsoft Exchange.

Rich Text Format and Object Linking and Embedding functions are illustrated in the sample Exchange message shown in figure 24.14.

Fig. 24.14
This Exchange message contains Rich Text Formatting and an OLE object.

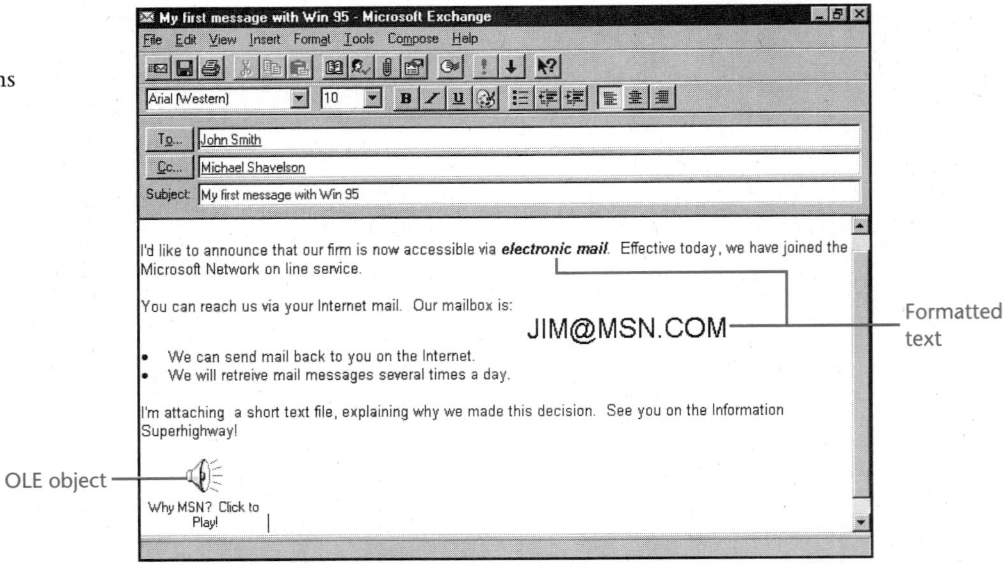

Finishing and Sending Your Mail Message

After you've written your message and added any formatting or OLE objects that you want, there are a few more options you may want to execute.

Choose Tools, Options, and then click the Send tab. This following list describes the items on the Send page:

- *Read Receipt and Delivery Receipt.* Requests that a receipt be sent back when the message has been delivered to or read by the recipient.
- *Sensitivity.* Sets sensitivity rankings to your message such as Normal, Personal, Private, and Confidential.
- *Importance Ranking.* Checks whether you want High, Normal, or Low priority for your message. You can always choose the High/Low icons to perform this task.
- *Save a Copy in 'Sent Items' Folder.* Saves a copy of the message in the Sent Items folder.

Close the Properties sheet. Now you are ready to send your message. Simply choose File, Send, or click the Send toolbar button.

Troubleshooting

I sent a Microsoft Mail message on my workgroup network, but the message wasn't received.

Make sure that only one Postoffice is installed for your workgroup and that the Postoffice is located in a shared folder that everyone in the workgroup can access.

Faxing a Quick Message or a File

There are several ways to send a fax. We'll begin by looking at how to send a very quick text message, or "fax" a file. This method lets you type a quick note (you won't be able to format the note) or transmit a file attached to the fax using the new BFT fax technology. If you want to do more—such as send a nicely formatted fax message, put pictures inside it, or fax from your word processor—see "Sending a More Complete Message," later in this chapter. In the main Exchange window, choose Compose, New Fax. The Compose Fax Wizard appears.

▶ See "Working with Phone Dialer," p. 857

The Wizard first verifies the location from which you are sending the message, as shown in figure 24.15. If you have created other Dialing Locations and moved your portable computer to one of them, choose I'm Dialing From: and specify the new location. (Notice also that you can click on the check box at the bottom of the dialog box to tell the Wizard not to display this next time.) Then choose Next.

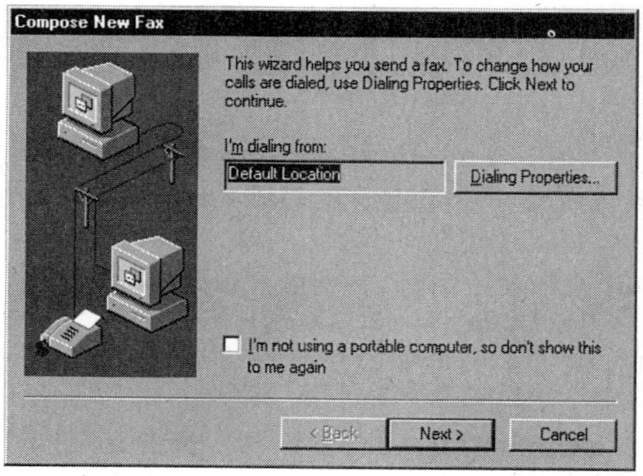

Fig. 24.15 The Compose New Fax Wizard confirms your dialing location.

Addressing a Fax

► See "Working with Your Address Book," p. 757

The Wizard next prompts you for a recipient and offers to show you your Personal Address Book. If you want to choose a name from the Book, choose Address Book to display the Book (see fig. 24.16). Select a recipient and choose OK.

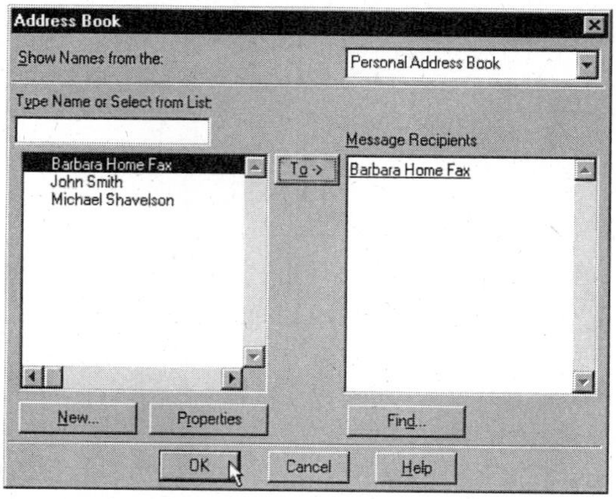

Fig. 24.16 Choose a fax recipient from your Personal Address Book.

You also can just type the recipient information in the text boxes named To and Fax #, without using the Personal Address Book. Use the Add to List button if you want to send the fax to several different numbers. Select the first and choose Add to List; select the second, and choose Add to List; and so on. Choose Next when you are ready to continue.

Selecting a Cover Page

Next, the Wizard asks whether you want to send a cover page with your fax. Windows has the following built-in cover pages:

- Confidential!
- For your information
- Generic
- Urgent!

If you wish to use a cover page, select the page you want from the displayed list. Click on the No button if you don't want to send a cover page.

Tip
If you don't like any of the predesigned cover pages, use the Cover Page Editor to customize one of them or to create your own. See "Fax Cover Page Editor" later in this chapter.

Options for Fax Transmission

There are a variety of fax options that you can set before you move on. Choose Options to display the Compose New Fax Wizard's Send Options dialog box (see fig. 24.17). Use these options to control when your fax is sent, the format you use to send it, the paper size, and the security applied. In this dialog box, you also can choose the Dialing Location or a cover page to send with your fax, as you did in the preceding section.

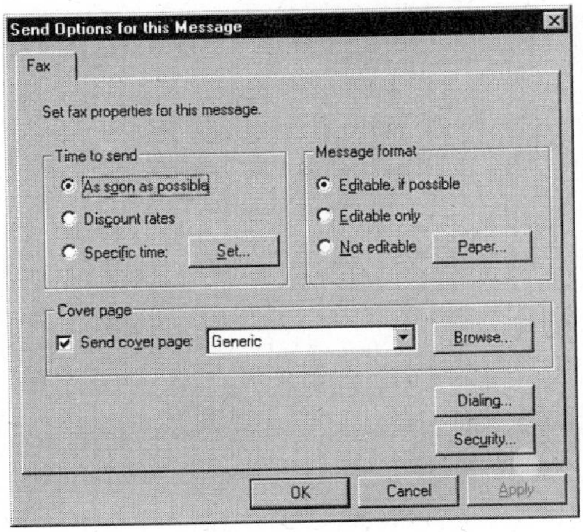

Fig. 24.17
This dialog box lets you specify various fax sending options.

These seven options are available for fax transmissions:

- Message format
- Time to send
- Cover page
- Security
- Dialing
- Paper size and orientation
- Image quality

The following sections explain these options and how to use them.

Message Format

The Message Format option deals with a new technology called *editable faxes.* Editable faxes are something of a misnomer. A traditional fax is a single graphics image. Editable faxes are more like file transfers between computers, with the optional addition of a cover page. In fact, editable faxes are so much like file transfers that the technology behind them is called BFT for *Binary File Transfer.*

An editable fax can be edited by the recipient in the application that created it or in any application that can open its file type. If you send a document created in Microsoft Word for Windows (a DOC file), the recipient can open it in Word, WordPad, AmiPro, or WordPerfect, using import filters if necessary.

Sending editable faxes is very convenient because the receiver's options are increased. The recipient can view or print the fax as you sent it or edit the fax first.

You have three choices with the Message Format option:

- *Editable, If Possible.* Editable faxes can be exchanged only between computers using Microsoft Exchange and Microsoft Fax. This is the optimum way to send a fax.

  If the receiver is using a traditional fax machine, using editable format is not possible, so the fax is sent the old-fashioned way, as a graphic. If the recipient has a fax card in a computer but doesn't have Microsoft Exchange installed, the fax is delivered as a graphic. Exchange automatically determines which way to send the fax when it connects to the receiving machine.

> **Note**
>
> In the near future, other systems may implement BFT in a way that is compatible with the Microsoft system. When that happens, you will be able to exchange editable faxes with those systems, too.

Tip
Editable faxes can be exchanged between Microsoft Exchange systems very quickly because the format used is much more compressed than the format that regular fax machines use.

- *Editable Only*. This option works only for transfers between two Microsoft Exchange systems. If the receiving system is not a Microsoft Exchange system, the fax will not go through.
- *Not Editable*. You use this option when you want all your faxes to be sent as a single graphic image in traditional fax format.

Message Security

Choose the Security button to see the Security options. Security works only with editable faxes. You have two basic choices: None and Password-Protected. If you choose None, your fax can be read immediately upon receipt. Choosing Password-Protected requires the recipient to type the password that you applied to that fax transmission in order to see it.

> **Caution**
>
> If you activate password security on a fax that is sent to a non-Microsoft Exchange recipient or fax machine, your fax will not go through. Do not enable security on such faxes.

Time to Send

You can select a time to send your fax. Your choices are these:

- As Soon as Possible
- Discount Rates (at night and on weekends)
- Specific Time (which you can choose)

Paper Size and Orientation, and Image Quality

Choose Paper to access the Paper Size and Orientation options. These options are usable with noneditable faxes. You can choose letter or legal paper. You also can choose Portrait (horizontal) or Landscape (vertical) page orientation.

You also can change the Image Quality in this dialog box. This determines the resolution at which Exchange prepares the fax. As with a laser printer, the higher the resolution, the crisper and cleaner your fax will be when printed.

Pick one of the following three Image Quality options, based on your need for a high-quality fax balanced against the additional time it takes to send the fax at a higher resolution:

- *Best Available.* This setting is recommended; it makes your fax look as good as possible on the receiving end.
- *Fine* (200 dots per inch, or dpi). Fine mode can result in incompatibilities if the receiving side doesn't support it. If it works with your recipient's hardware, it will look as good as possible.
- *Draft* (200 × 100 dpi). Draft mode looks coarser than Fine or Best Available but transmits faster.

When you've finished selecting all the options you want to use, choose Next, and the Compose New Fax Wizard moves on to let you enter the Subject of the fax and, if you wish, a note to put on the cover page.

Fax Subject and Note

When you've finished working with all the options described in the preceding sections and chosen Next, the Compose New Fax Wizard displays a dialog box where you can enter the subject of the fax and add a note to accompany your fax.

Type the subject in the Subject text box provided for you. Then, if you want to type a note to go along with your fax, type the note in the Note text box. Click in the Start Note on Cover Page check box to start your note on the cover page. If you leave the box unchecked, the note will start on a new page in your fax.

When you've finished with the subject and the note, choose Next.

Adding Files to Your Fax

◄ See "Windows Explorer for Powerful File Management," p. 27

You are able to add a file to be transmitted with your fax. After the Compose New Fax Wizard finishes with the fax subject and note (covered in the preceding section), it offers you a dialog box where you can select files to include with the fax.

If you want to include a file, choose Add File. You can use Explorer to browse and find the file you want to send with your fax.

When you've chosen the file or files to send with your fax, the Wizard shows the files you've selected in the Files to Send text box. When you've finished selecting files to add to your fax, choose Next.

Caution

The files you've chosen to send with the fax can be sent only if the fax is sent in editable format. If you use any other format, Microsoft Fax will not send the fax at all, not even the cover sheet.

For this reason, choose to add files to your fax only if you are certain that the recipient's system can support editable format, and that both your sending system and the recipient's receiving system are configured for editable faxing. (Configuring your fax in editable format was covered in "Options for Fax Transmission," earlier in this chapter.)

After you have added any files you want to send with your fax, it's ready to be sent. Choose Finish, and Microsoft Fax sends your fax.

Troubleshooting

I'm trying to send a fax, but it won't go through.

Do you hear the modem dial the fax? If not, make sure that you have a fax modem selected and that the settings are correct for your modem type. In Exchange, choose Tools, Services, Microsoft Fax, Properties; then click the Modem tab. You should see your fax modem displayed; if not, click Add to configure your modem.

If you can hear the modem dial the phone, but the modem disconnects just after dialing, repeat the preceding procedure. When you see your modem, select it and then click Properties. Make sure that the modem is set to allow enough time to connect after dialing (60 seconds is a good choice). This parameter often is set to one second by Windows for no apparent reason.

▶ See "Configuring Your Modem," p. 843

Sending a More Complete Message

There are a couple of other ways to send fax messages. First, you may want to use the same window you used to create an e-mail message. The only difference between creating a fax message and an e-mail message is in the way you address it. If you address the message to a Fax "address," the message will be a fax message.

▶ See "Adding Names to Your Address Book," p. 759

Tip
Choose File, Send Options to modify fax options we looked at earlier, while working in the New Message window.

How do you address it to a fax address? Start by adding a fax address to your Address Book. Then use the To button in the New Message window to add this address to the To line of your message.

The advantage of sending a fax using this method is that you have all the New Message window's tools available. You can write a message, using all the text-editing capabilities. You can also attach files, and insert pictures into your fax.

The other way to fax is directly from an application. For instance, you could fax from your word processor. Many applications have a Send option on the File menu. If an application you want to use *doesn't* have such an option, you can "print" to the Microsoft Fax on FAX print driver.

Fax Cover Page Editor

The Cover Page Editor is a miniature word processor that allows you to work with graphics as well as Rich Text. Use the Fax Cover Page Editor to create your own custom-made cover pages or to modify one that is supplied with Exchange. You can do the following things with cover sheets that you create or edit:

- Insert data from the Personal Address Book into your cover page
- Paste items from the Clipboard into your cover page
- Import text or graphics (such as a logo) into your cover page

To use the Cover Page Editor, open the Start menu and choose Programs, Accessories, Fax; and then click Cover Page Editor. The Cover Page Editor program starts up.

When you first start the Cover Page Editor program, there is no cover page file loaded. From here, you can design a new cover page. If you start designing a new cover and then decide you want to start over again, choose File, New or click the New File icon on the toolbar.

Tip
Fax Cover Pages have a file name extension of CPE. The ones that come with Exchange are located in the C:\WINDOWS folder.

To edit and customize an existing cover page, choose File, Open on the Cover Page Editor menu. Then select the cover page you want to work with.

The most useful feature of the Cover Page Editor is the ability to insert information from your Personal Address Book into your cover sheets. You do this by choosing Insert from the menu bar and then choosing from the options on that menu and successive submenus. Some of the kinds of information you can insert include:

- Recipient's or Sender's Name
- Recipient's or Sender's Fax Number
- Recipient's or Sender's Company

Figure 24.18 shows a menu of all the different types of information you can insert from your Personal Address Book into your cover sheets.

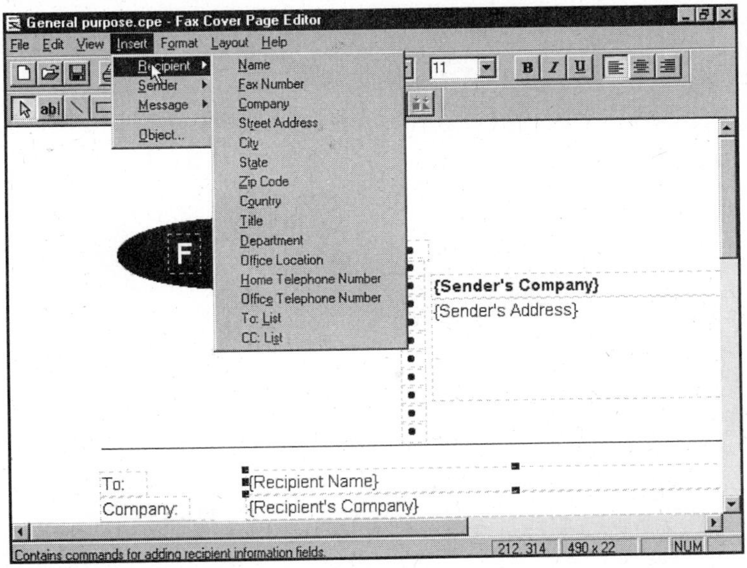

Fig. 24.18
Insert Address Book information into your fax cover sheet.

Viewing Received Mail and Faxes

To view and work with your received mail and faxes, you must have the Microsoft Exchange program running. This section explains how you can see your received mail and faxes and how to keep the Exchange window organized at the same time.

How Things Are Organized in Exchange

First, let's look at the kind of things we'll be organizing. Exchange contains, by default, four Personal Folders, each of which holds a different kind of message. The folder names show the function of the folders:

- *Inbox*. Where messages coming in to you are stored at first.
- *Deleted Items*. Where messages you've deleted from any of the other folders go.

- *Outbox.* Where messages you are sending are stored until you actually send them.
- *Sent Items.* Where messages you have sent are stored after they are successfully sent.

To display all four folders described above, choose View, Folders on the Exchange menu bar. You can also click the Show/Hide Folder List icon on the Exchange toolbar.

Tip
It is very useful to be able to see all four Exchange folders on your screen. If you display all four folders, you can tell what kind of message you're seeing.

When you choose to display the folder list, your Exchange window divides into two parts. On the left side of the window, you see the list of the four folders. When you highlight a folder on the left side of the Exchange window, the contents of that folder are displayed on the right side of the window. For example, if you highlight the Inbox folder, you then see the contents of your Inbox folder on the right side of the window. The contents of the Inbox folder are your received messages and faxes. If a message in the Inbox appears in **boldface**, the message is new and has not yet been read.

The types of messages that you can see in your Inbox depend on the Exchange services that you installed. If you installed Microsoft Fax, for example, you can see faxes. If you installed The Microsoft Network, you can see mail from MSN members and from the Internet. If you have Microsoft Mail installed for your workgroup network, you can see workgroup Mail messages. With Internet Mail installed, you can see mail from your own Internet mailbox. Figure 24.19 shows an Exchange Inbox with several types of messages.

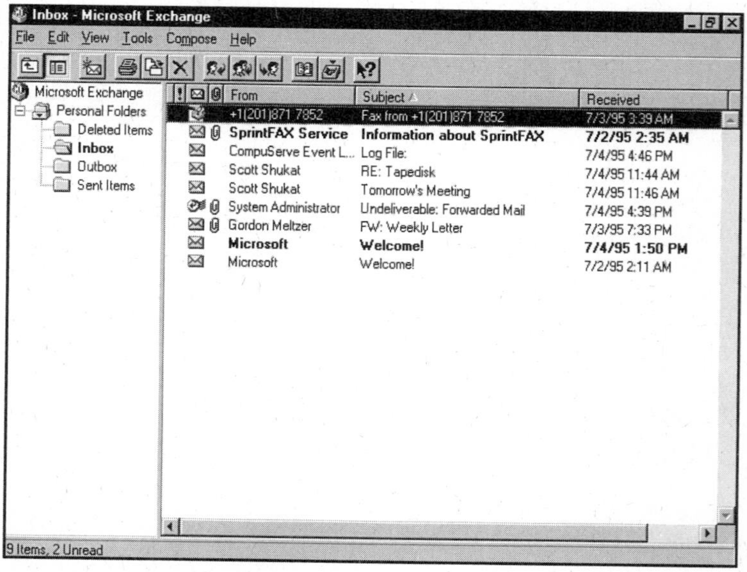

Fig. 24.19
The Exchange Inbox showing received messages.

You can manipulate these messages in several ways. We examine how to manipulate and work with those received messages in the next sections.

Viewing Faxes

When you double-click on a normal, noneditable fax, the Fax Viewer opens and displays the fax. When you double-click a received editable fax, though, or a fax that has attached files, the message window opens. Inside this window, what you see depends on what you received. If you received a fax that the author created in the New Message window, you see exactly what the author saw; the text looks the same, any icons representing attached files look the same, and so on. If, however, you are receiving a fax from another application (sent using the File, Send option), you see an icon representing the fax. Double-click on this icon to open the application associated with that type of file. For instance, if you receive a DOC file, when you double-click on it the program associated with DOC opens: Word for Windows or WordPad.

Note

If you receive a fax that the author "printed" to the Microsoft Fax on FAX driver, it comes through as if it were a normal fax from a fax machine; double-clicking on the fax in the Inbox opens the Fax Viewer, not the Message window.

For instance, figure 24.20 shows a fax received from Notepad. Notice the Notepad icon in the message form to the left of the Notepad window. When the icon was double-clicked, Notepad opened and displayed the fax text. You can edit the text just as though you created the file on your own computer.

Troubleshooting

Someone is trying to send me a fax, but I'm not receiving it.

Make sure that your fax modem is installed. From the Exchange window, choose Tools, Services. Highlight Microsoft Fax and choose Properties. Then click the Modem tab and make sure your modem is shown in the list of Available fax modems. If it is, click the Properties tab and check to see whether the modem is set to answer automatically. If not, select the Answer After check box, and set the number of rings to wait before your fax modem answers calls.

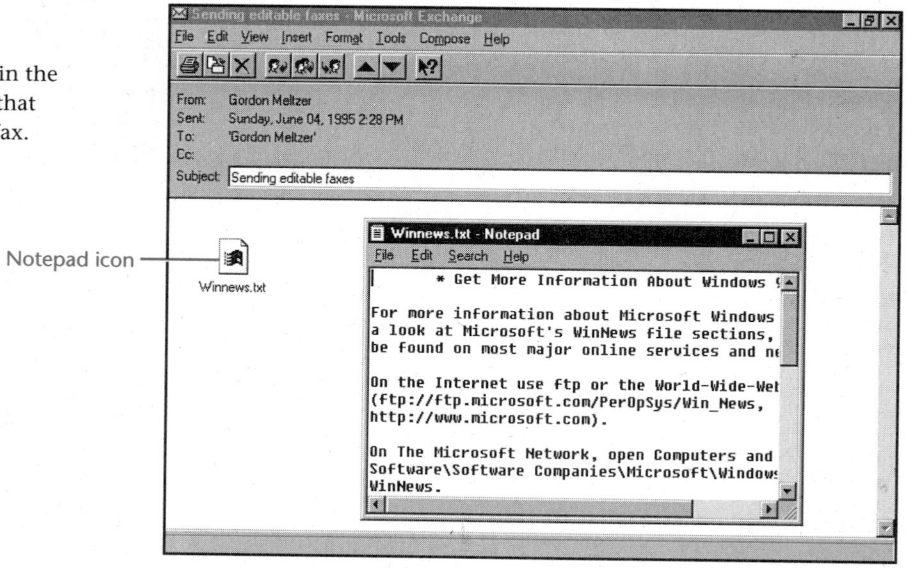

Fig. 24.20
Viewing an editable fax in the application that created the fax.

Reading Mail Messages

To read a mail message, double-click the message in your Inbox. The standard message form opens, displaying the message. The Subject appears in the message form title bar. Figure 24.21 shows a received mail message.

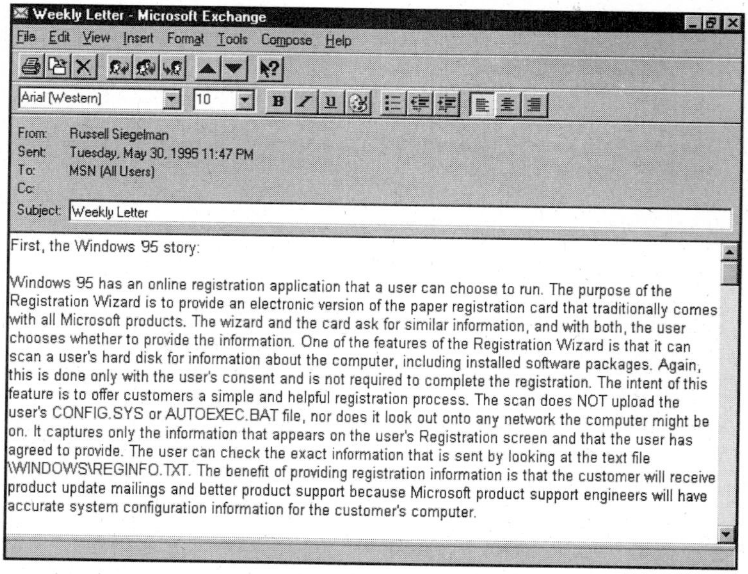

Fig. 24.21
A received mail message.

Editing, Replying to, and Forwarding Messages

The standard message form (refer to fig. 24.21) is an important place where a great deal of messaging action takes place. Notice that the form looks very much like a Windows word processor, complete with formatting toolbar. All the Rich Text tools are available, just as they are when you compose a message. In fact, the standard message form for composing a message is identical to the form for viewing, editing, replying, and forwarding mail messages.

While you're working with a received mail message, you can edit it if you want. Add text, files, or OLE objects. Then use the tools in the Compose menu to whisk your reply on its way (see fig. 24.22).

Tip

As a shortcut to send, reply to, forward, or edit a message without displaying it first, highlight the message in your Inbox and then right-click.

Sorting Messages

Above the messages in any of the Exchange folders are column headings. These headings indicate the following things:

- The importance of the message (according to the sender)
- The item type
- Whether files are attached to the message
- The sender's name
- The subject
- The date and time when the message was received
- The size of the message (in kilobytes)

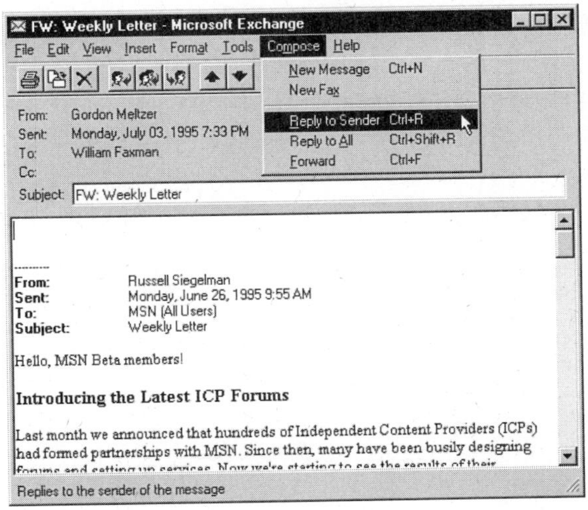

Fig. 24.22
The Compose menu has Reply and Forward options.

You can sort the messages in any of the Exchange folders in the following ways:

- Click the column heading to sort the messages in the folder by the value in that column, in ascending order.
- Right-click the column heading to change the sort from ascending to descending order.
- Choose View, Sort in the main Exchange window to access more elaborate sorting functions. Figure 24.23 shows these functions.

Note

The default From, Subject, Received, and Size columns in Exchange are only the tip of the iceberg. You can display many more columns if the column headings are relevant to your work. You'll find loads of column options, many of which are rather obscure. The options available depend on the message services you have installed, and what works for one service may not work for another.

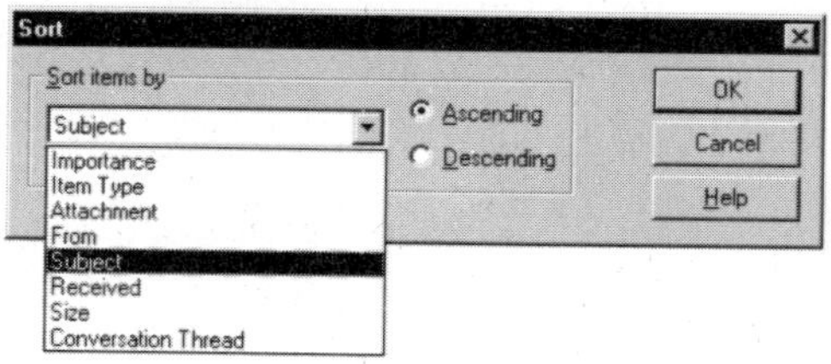

Fig. 24.23 Advanced options you can use to sort your messages.

Deleting Messages

When you finish working with a message in your Inbox and you want to delete it, highlight it and press the Delete key. It's removed from the Inbox, but it's not really deleted. Rather, it's transferred to the Deleted Items folder.

Caution

Deleting a message from the Deleted Items folder removes it completely from your system, not to the Recycle Bin.

Using the Message Finder

You can use Exchange to search through all your Exchange folders, looking for messages that match certain criteria. You can choose among many options, shown in the list below. You can find items matching

- The name of a sender you specify with the From option.
- A message you sent to a certain recipient with the Sent To option
- A message sent Directly to you or Copied (Cc) to you.
- A message with a particular subject by choosing the Subject option.
- Certain text in the message with the Message Body option.

To use Message Finder, choose Tools, Find in the main Exchange window. Then choose the search option you want to use. For example, if you're looking for messages sent to John Jones, enter **John Jones** in the Sent To text box. Exchange then displays a list of messages matching the criteria you have chosen.

Working with Your Address Book

See "Installing and Configuring Microsoft Exchange," p. 727

Microsoft Exchange contains an Address Book feature. The Address Book is, logically enough, the place where you store contact information for the people with whom you correspond. The Address Book can help you keep track of how to contact your correspondents. You enter names into the Book and specify the type of communications to use (fax, Internet mail, Microsoft LAN Mail, and so forth). The Address Book makes sure that your messages are addressed properly.

The entire Address Book in Exchange is built from several different modular, building-block address books. The number of these building-block address books is determined by the communications services you installed when you set up Exchange.

Some of the services you installed come with their own building-block address book modules. For example, if you installed The Microsoft Network online service, a building-block address book for MSN was installed in your Address Book. The MSN Address Book is configured by Microsoft to contain the names and e-mail addresses of all the members of The Microsoft Network.

Microsoft Mail for your workgroup LAN has a building-block address book, built by the network administrator, that is part of your Exchange Address Book. In Exchange, the Microsoft Mail Address Book is called Postoffice Address List.

The final module making up your Address Book is called the Personal Address Book. In it you can store the names and addresses you use most often. You can transfer names into your Personal Address Book from the other address books. For instance, you could copy a name from the MSN address book to the Personal Address Book. Or you can add new names and addresses to your Personal Address Book.

The Address Book also has options that you can use to control how it displays the names you store.

Now, to display and work with the Address Book from the Microsoft Exchange window, choose Tools, Address Book; or press Ctrl+Shift+B.

Setting Display Preferences

How do you like to look for people's names in a list—by first names or by last names? Exchange gives you the flexibility to display names either way. By default, names are displayed with the first name followed by the last name (John Jones). If, however, you have a rather long list or know several men called John, you may find viewing the list sorted by last names to be faster.

You can use the Personal Address Book Properties settings to change the order in which first and last names are displayed. To change the order, follow these steps:

1. From the Exchange main window, choose Tools, Address Book. The Address Book opens.
2. Select Personal Address Book from the Show Names From The drop-down list. The names in your Personal Address Book display.
3. Choose Tools, Options. The Addressing dialog box appears.
4. In the When Sending Mail list, highlight Personal Address Book.
5. Click Properties. The Personal Address Book Properties sheet appears.
6. Now you can choose to show names by first name or last name. Click First Name or Last Name on the Personal Address Book page, as shown in figure 24.24.

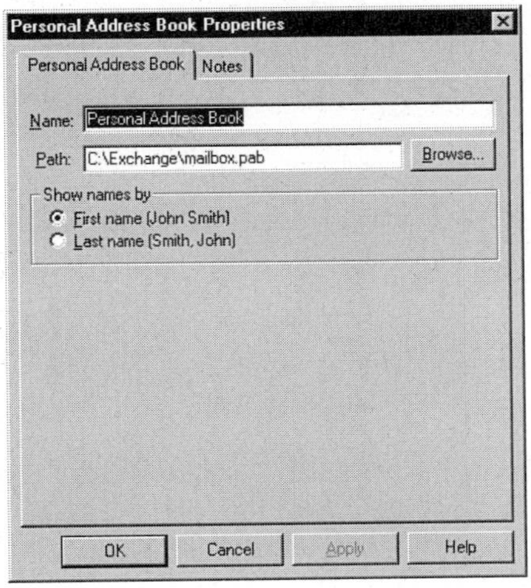

Fig. 24.24
You use this Properties sheet to select how to display names in the Personal Address Book.

7. You also can give the Personal Address Book a more descriptive name. You might want to call it Business Contacts, for example. Type the name you want to use for the Personal Address Book in the Name text box.

8. Click the Notes tab and type, in the text box provided, any information you wish to record about your Personal Address Book.

Adding Names to Your Address Book

You want to use Exchange as the powerful communications tool it can be. Part of harnessing the power of Exchange is as simple as keeping a well-organized Address Book so that you have all the mail addresses and fax numbers you need conveniently at hand. This section focuses on the procedure for putting new names in the address book.

1. Display the Address Book by choosing Tools, Address Book. You also can click the Address Book button on the toolbar.

2. In the Show Names From The drop-down list, select Personal Address Book.

3. Choose File, New Entry. You can also choose the New Entry button on the toolbar. The New Entry dialog box appears (see fig. 24.25).

4. Select the type of address you want to add to your Personal Address Book. In this example, we're adding a Microsoft Fax entry to the Book. Then choose OK. The New Fax Properties sheet appears.

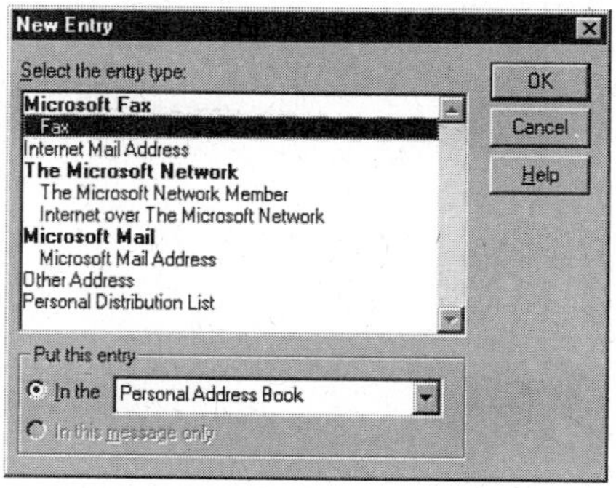

Fig. 24.25 The power of Exchange is evident in the range of address types to which you can send messages.

5. The Properties sheet that you see in figure 24.26 has text boxes for all the names and numbers required to reach your recipient. Type the pertinent information in each page. Then choose OK. The Properties sheet closes, and the new entry appears in your Address Book.

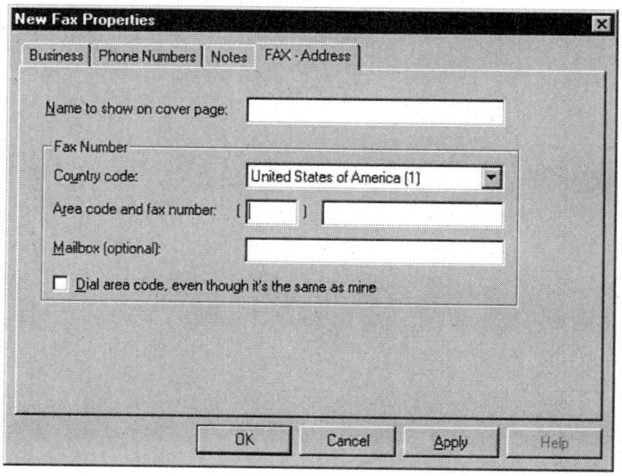

Fig. 24.26 The New Fax Properties sheet is typical of the Properties sheets you fill out when adding entries to your Address Book.

You follow the same steps as those for a Microsoft Fax entry to add different types of addresses, like Microsoft Network addresses or Internet Mail addresses.

The difference between adding the fax address we illustrated and the other possible address types is that after you select the entry type from the New Entry dialog box (step 4 above), the New Properties sheet that appears will be different.

For example, if you choose to add a Microsoft Mail address to your Address Book, the New Mail Properties sheet has a space for the recipient's mailbox, Postoffice, and Workgroup Network name, instead of a space for a fax number. Similarly, a Microsoft Network address needs an MSN Member ID, and an Internet Mail address needs a mailbox name in the form of name@domain.

Adding Groups to Your Address Book

You may want to send a message to a group of recipients. To do this conveniently, create a Personal Distribution List. Once you have a Personal Distribution List, you only have to create a message once, and you can send it to all the members of the list with one click.

Follow these steps to create your Personal Distribution List:

1. Display the Address Book by choosing Tools, Address Book.
2. Choose File, New Entry. The New Entry dialog box appears (refer to fig. 24.25). The New Entry dialog box contains a scrolling list of address types. You can view all the types by scrolling through the list.
3. The last entry in the scrolling list is the Personal Distribution List entry type. Highlight Personal Distribution List at the bottom of the list.
4. In this example, we're putting our Personal Distribution List in our Personal Address Book. At the bottom of the New Entry dialog box is a setting which says Put This Entry In The. Make sure Personal Address Book shows in the text box. If it doesn't, click the down arrow and scroll to select Personal Address Book.
5. Choose OK. The New Personal Distribution List Properties sheet appears.
6. Name your list. Type the name for your list in the Name text box. In this example, we'll name our Personal Distribution List **Staff Members on Project X**.
7. If you want to make some notes about the list, click the Notes tab and type your comments in the text box. You might use this space to document how the group members were chosen. You can enter anything that's useful in this text box.
8. Click the Distribution List tab.

9. Build the Distribution List now. You do this by adding members to the list. Choose Add/Remove Members. A dialog box appears, titled Edit Members of (name of your Distribution List).

10. Perhaps one of the people you want to add to the Personal Distribution List is already in another of your building-block address books. If so, choose the proper address book by selecting it from the scrolling list, which is shown in Show Names From The. When you choose an address book in Show Names From The, all the address entries in that address book become visible. In this example, we'll choose to Show Names from The Microsoft Network. Next, we'll add some addresses from The Microsoft Network online service to our Personal Distribution List.

> **Note**
>
> You can only use The Microsoft Network address book while online. If you select this address book while offline, the Connect dialog box appears so you can log on.

11. Select The Microsoft Network members you want to add to your Personal Distribution List. The best way to do this is to highlight the names, one at a time (hold the Ctrl key and click on each one that you want to add), and then choose Members. The names you've highlighted become members of your Personal Distribution List (see fig. 24.27).

To add other names from existing address books, select Show Names From The, and select the next address book from the scrolling list. Then repeat the steps above from step 10.

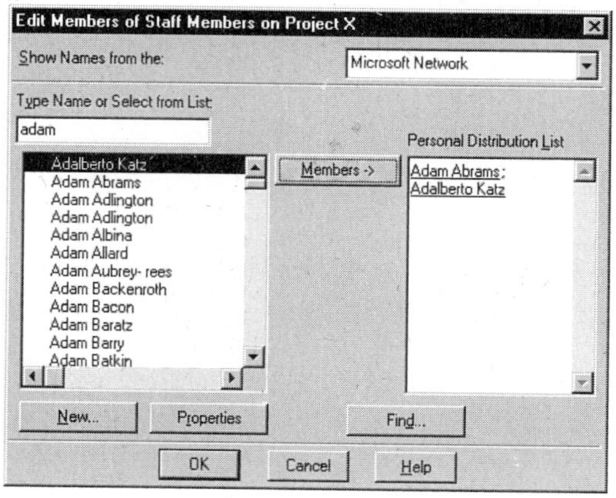

Fig. 24.27
The Edit Members dialog box has two Microsoft Network member names added to the Personal Distribution List.

You also can put people on your Personal Distribution List who are not already in any of your address books. However, you have to put that person into your Personal Address Book first.

See "Adding Names to Your Address Book," p. 759

Choose New. Then follow the steps discussed earlier for adding a name to your Personal Address Book. Once you've made the addition to the book, that name is added to the Personal Distribution List automatically. When you are finished adding members to your Personal Distribution List, choose OK.

Your Personal Distribution List appears in your Personal Address Book, along with any individual addresses you have stored there. By choosing the list as a recipient in a message you create, the message is sent to all members of the Personal Distribution List.

Working with User Profiles in Exchange

When you installed Exchange, you worked with the Inbox Setup Wizard. You gave the Wizard information about yourself, and you installed one or more communications services in Exchange. You also gave the Wizard information about the communications services you chose, such as User ID and Mailbox Name.

When you finished installing Exchange, the Wizard saved all the information you gave it. The Wizard saved your information in something called a *User Profile*.

The User Profile in Exchange is where all your personal information and the information on all your communications services are stored. The name of the User Profile created by the Wizard for you is MS Exchange Settings. MS Exchange Settings becomes the default User Profile for your computer.

Tip
You can add as many User Profiles as you need by following the steps in this section.

This default profile is fine for one user. If your computer has more than one user, however, you may want to create a special User Profile for everyone who uses your machine.

Suppose that you share a computer with a coworker who works the second shift. If you don't use The Microsoft Network but your coworker does, they may want to set up their own User Profile. Then they can configure and personalize Exchange to suit their needs without disturbing the settings that you use during your shift.

Adding Multiple User Profiles in Exchange

To create an additional User Profile, follow these steps:

1. Open the Start menu and choose Settings, Control Panel.
2. In Control Panel, double-click the Mail and Fax icon.
3. Choose Show Profiles. You see the list of existing Exchange profiles.
4. Choose Add to create a new user profile. The Inbox Setup Wizard starts to run.
5. Select the communications services that you want to use with the new User Profile you're creating (see fig. 24.28). Then choose Next.
6. Now give a name to your new User Profile. Type the name in the Profile Name text box (see fig. 24.29). Then choose Next.
7. You then work with the Wizard to set up the communications services you chose in the step above. This works the same way as it did when you first installed Exchange.

◄ See "Installing and Configuring Microsoft Exchange," p. 727

When you've finished with the Inbox Setup Wizard, your new User Profile will be set up for use. Your screen returns to the Microsoft Exchange Profiles dialog box you saw in step 3. You see your new User Profile added to the list of profiles. Figure 24.30 shows Sheila's Exchange Settings, along with the default profile, MS Exchange Settings.

Fig. 24.28
Choose the services to use with your new User Profile

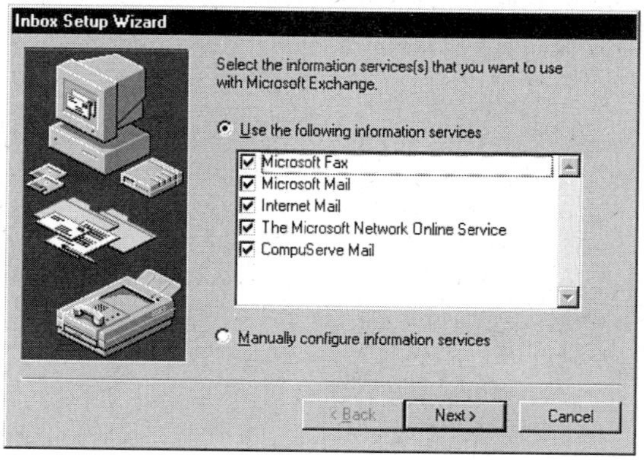

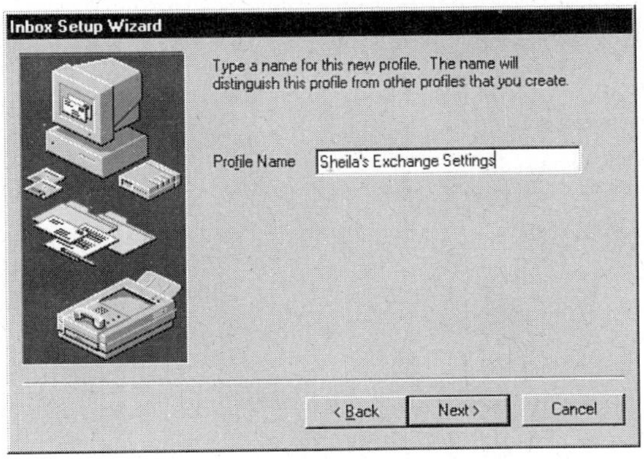

Fig. 24.29
In this example, we called the new User Profile **Sheila's Exchange Settings**.

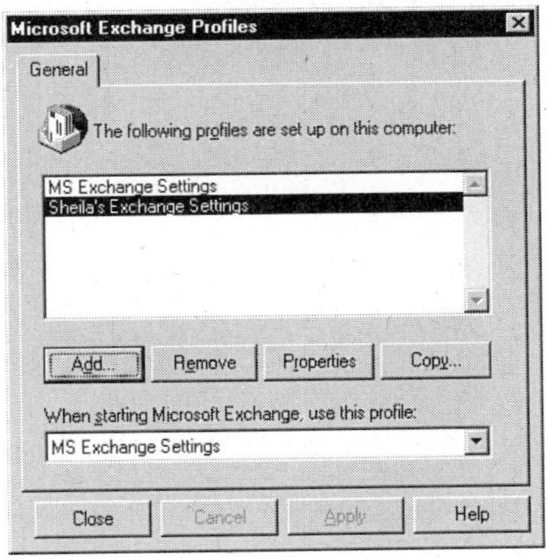

Fig. 24.30
Your new User Profile has been added to Exchange.

Note

Notice that, in the Microsoft Exchange Profiles dialog box shown in figure 24.30, there is a setting called When Starting Microsoft Exchange, Use This Profile. Ignore this setting for now. We'll choose what profile to use when starting Exchange in the next series of steps.

When you have more than one User Profile installed, you'll want to choose which profile to use when you run Exchange. You'll want Exchange to ask you which profile to use each time Exchange starts. Follow these steps to set up Exchange so that it asks which User Profile to use:

1. Start Microsoft Exchange. You can do this by double-clicking the Inbox icon on your desktop.
2. Choose Tools, Options. The Options dialog box appears.
3. In the When Starting Microsoft Exchange area of the General page, check the Prompt for a Profile To Be Used box (see fig. 24.31).
4. Choose OK.

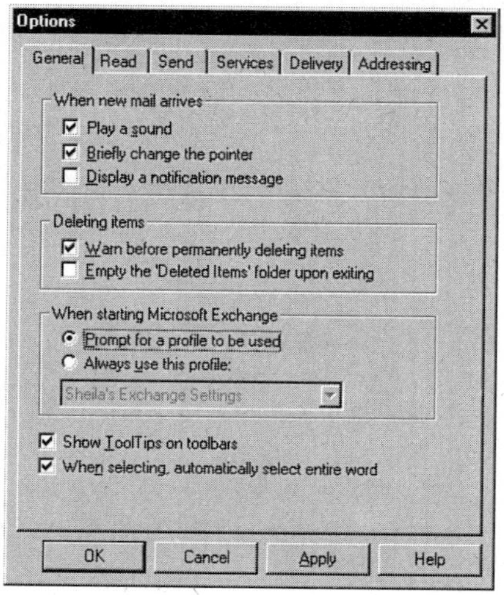

Fig. 24.31
Setting up Exchange so it prompts you for the User Profile to use when you start Exchange.

When you tell Exchange to prompt you for a User Profile, you are ensuring that each user of your computer has the opportunity to pick their own Exchange User Profile.

Troubleshooting

I want to use Microsoft Fax, The Microsoft Network, and Microsoft Mail, but I don't see any references to those services in my Exchange menus.

Install the desired services in Microsoft Exchange. In the main Exchange window, choose Tools, Services, choose Add, and select the desired service from the list. A Wizard guides you in setting up the service, if necessary.

> **Note**
>
> If you have set up your computer with a different session profile for each user—so the user has to log on when Windows starts—you can ensure that each person's profile starts automatically. Each user should log on to Windows; open Exchange; choose Tools, Options; then click on the Always Use This Profile option button and select the appropriate profile.

Enabling Mail and Message Security

Normally, when you run Exchange, your mail folders display immediately in the Exchange window. You can see and work with Inbox, Deleted Items, Outbox, and Sent Items as soon as Exchange is running. This means that anyone who starts Exchange on your computer can access all your mail, in the four folders just listed.

To make your mail secure, you must set a password for access to your mailbox so that nobody else can open your mailbox and read or work with your messages without your permission. Follow these steps to set up password security for your mail folders:

1. With Exchange running, choose Tools, Options. The Options dialog box appears.
2. Click the Services tab, highlight Personal Folders, and choose Properties.
3. When the Personal Folders Properties sheet appears, choose Change Password. The Microsoft Personal Folders dialog box opens (see fig. 24.32).

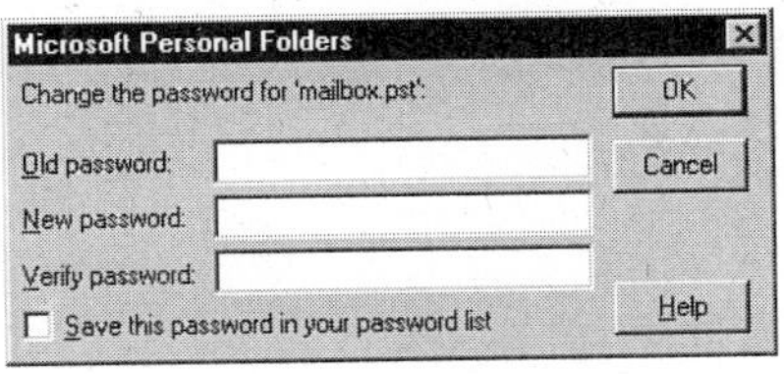

Fig. 24.32
Set a password for your mail folders for security.

4. Enter the password of your choice in the New Password text box. Then repeat the password in the Verify Password text box.
5. Choose OK.

Tip

Don't select Save This Password in Your Password List, unless you've set up Windows for different users and each user has to log on using a password. If you do, you lose password security because Windows enters the password for you whenever you start Exchange.

The next time you run Exchange, you have to enter your password to see the contents of your mail folders.

Caution

If you forget your mailbox password, you cannot access the contents of your mailbox again. You have to delete your Personal Folders and set up Exchange again.

You may want to get rid of your mailbox password. To do this, follow steps 1 and 2. Then in step 3, type your current password in the Old Password text box. Leave New Password and Verify Password blank. This means that you have changed back to having no password security for your mailbox folders. Then choose OK.

Working with the Workgroup Postoffice

Microsoft Mail requires that one of the computers on the workgroup network be set up as a Postoffice. This is usually a job for the network administrator or manager. If this is your function, this section is important for you.

The Postoffice machine is the place where all mail messages are stored for the workgroup. You can choose your machine for Postoffice duties or select another.

The Postoffice must be installed somewhere on the network in a shared folder that all members of the workgroup can access. Windows 95 comes with the Postoffice and a Wizard that helps you install it.

You have to make the following decisions about your Postoffice:

- Which machine to install the Postoffice on (choose a machine that has a shared folder that everyone in the workgroup can access)
- Who will manage and maintain the Postoffice

If you are sure that there is no Postoffice installed on your Workgroup LAN yet, and if you're sure that you are the right person to set it up, the process is simple.

Installing the Workgroup Postoffice

When you are ready to install the Postoffice, follow these steps:

1. Open the Start menu and choose Settings, Control Panel.
2. Double-click the Microsoft Mail Postoffice icon.
3. Select Create a New Workgroup Postoffice, as shown in figure 24.33. Then choose Next.

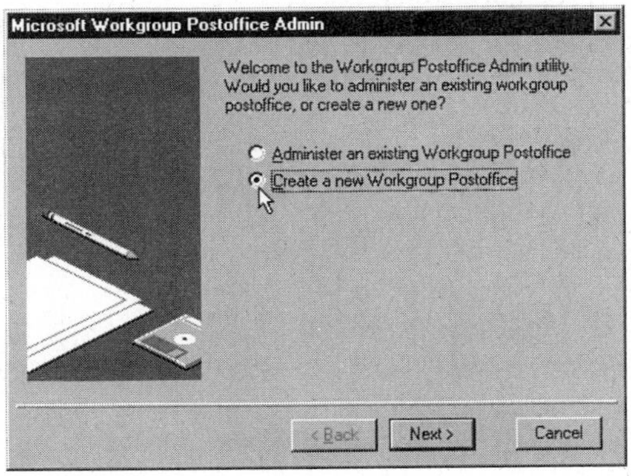

Fig. 24.33 Use the Microsoft Workgroup Postoffice Admin utility to create a new Workgroup Postoffice.

4. Type the full path to the folder you've chosen for the Postoffice in the Postoffice Location text box. Remember, this needs to be a shared folder that everyone on the Workgroup LAN can access. You'll probably want to use the Browse button to find the folder.

► See "Creating Network Resources," p. 796

5. Then choose Next. The folder you've selected for the Postoffice displays for your approval. Choose Next again.
6. The next dialog box that appears requests administration details. Type your name in the Name text box, your mailbox name in the Mailbox text box, and your mail password in the Password text box (see fig. 24.34). Choose OK.
7. You'll see a message box reminding you to allow other users access to the Postoffice—which can be done from Windows Explorer. Choose OK. You have finished creating your Postoffice.

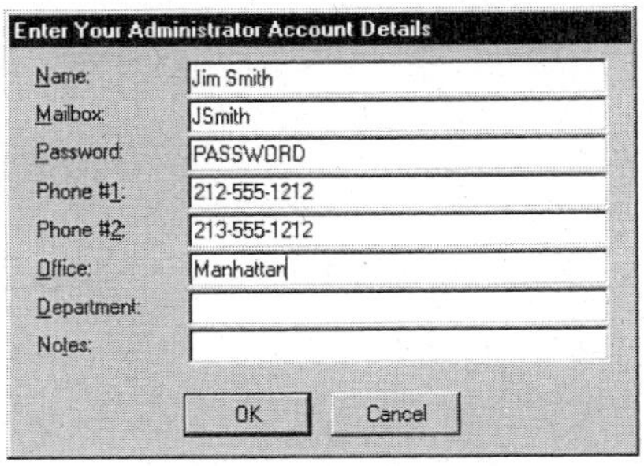

Fig. 24.34
You use this dialog box to fill out Postoffice Administrator information.

Note

The other text boxes shown in the figure may be filled in as you prefer, but are not required to set up the Postoffice.

Caution

Create only one Postoffice on your workgroup network. If you create more than one, the mail system won't work properly.

Chapter 25

Working with Network Printers

by William S. Holderby

In Chapter 6, "Controlling Printers," you learned the basics of installing and working with printers—or at least those attached directly to your computer. Of course, not all printers are connected exclusively to your PC. In many workplaces, a local area network has multiple printer connections. Although Windows 95 makes network printers appear to operate as local printers, network printing may seem more complex. Local printers usually remain attached to the same port and are under your control. Network printers can change location and are controlled by other users or a network administrator. If problems arise when you are using a network printer, troubleshooting is much easier if you understand some of the differences between local and network printing.

This chapter takes printing a step further and discusses printing issues from a network perspective. Specifically, you learn how to:

- Print to network printers
- Optimize print resources
- Manage print files
- Solve common network printing problems
- Use custom Printer Drivers and utilities

Examining Windows 95's New Network Printing Features

Windows 95 incorporates several new features and enhancements that markedly improve network printing. These new features include the following:

- *Network Point and Print* enables users to copy printer drivers automatically from network print servers to their local PC. This reduces the time it takes to set up a new printer and eliminates the need to find and copy vendor driver software. This feature also eliminates the chance of configuring the wrong printer. You can access Network Point and Print from network servers running Windows 95, Windows NT Advanced Server, Windows NT Workstation, Windows for Workgroups 3.11, or Novell NetWare.

- *Windows 95's Network Neighborhood* provides tools to configure print resources quickly on Windows 95, Windows NT, and Novell servers. You can use this feature to find, use, and manage print jobs on printers interfacing any of these devices. Formerly, the user had to memorize locations and complex network commands. Network Neighborhood virtually eliminates this need through its new network user interface.

- *Compatibility with NetWare's PSERVER* enables you to access print jobs from NetWare's print spooler.

- *Deferred printing* provides you with the ability to save printouts until you reattach your printer. Deferred printing automatically stores print jobs after you detach your PC from the network, and automatically restarts them after you reestablish the connection.

- *Printer Driver* provides command resources to remotely stop, hold, cancel, or restart print jobs located on shared printers.

Understanding Network Printing

Before delving too deeply into the nuts and bolts of network printing, you first must become familiar with the terminology you will see frequently in this discussion:

- *LAN Administrators* provide a management function to the local area network by assisting users and directing what resources are available on the network.

- *Systems policies* are software controls that are created by LAN Administrators to define what users can and cannot do on their desktops and the network. For example, you might use a system policy to restrict access to certain network programs.
- A *client* is a workstation that uses the services of any network server that can include server-based software systems, printers, and mass storage devices.
- *Print queues* contain print jobs that are not immediately printed. A queue holds the job until the printer is ready to print.
- *Windows Redirector* is the software module contained in the Windows network architecture that identifies software references to network devices and connects those devices to the workstation through the network.
- *Network resources* are software and hardware features that are available from servers and other workstations on the LAN. Resources such as shared drivers and server-based programs are available for network users.
- *Printing resources* are LAN resources that are dedicated to serving network users for the purpose of printing. These include shared printers, network printers, and print queues.
- *Print servers* service the printing needs of network clients.

Three network printer types are found on most networks:

- Printers attached to the network through a Microsoft Network compatible server.
- Printers connected to a server running a compatible network operating system other than Windows, such as Novell NetWare and Banyan VINES.
- Printers directly attached to a network through a special printer network interface card (NIC).

Printing from Applications

Printing to network printers from within applications requires the same commands and menu items that you use to print locally. Windows handles the network communications and creates a Printer Driver for each attached network printer. As with local printers, you can access network printer configuration information in the Printer Properties sheet. In this sheet, you can change the network printer's properties for default or specific printing tasks.

◀ See "Options for Your Printer," p. 187

Caution

Remember that other users can change a network printer configuration. Before printing, check all important print settings for this printer on your PC, including paper orientation and resolution. Don't assume that they are already set the way that you want them. Printing mistakes on network printers take extra time to recover.

When applications create a print file, they send a print stream to the network server through the Windows 95 Network Redirector. A print file contains spooled printer data and commands that are being temporarily stored prior to printing. The Network Redirector, which is part of Windows 95 network architecture, determines whether the print stream destination is a local printer. A print stream is the data that is being sent to a printer containing both printable and unprintable characters. Unprintable characters are used to control the printer. It also uses Windows network drivers to locate the designated printer.

Drag-and-Drop Printing

◀ See "Drag-and-Drop Printing from the Desktop," p. 178

To perform drag-and-drop printing, you use the same procedure as you do for local printing. Remember, however, that drag-and-drop printing sends the print job to the system's default printer. If the selected printer is not the default printer, Windows will ask you to make it the default printer prior to printing the file. When initially connecting your PC to a network, this printer might not be available. Be sure to log in to the network and verify the printer's network connection before setting it as the default printer (unless you plan to use deferred printing with your default printer in which case anything you print is saved by Windows until the printer becomes available).

Installing a Network Printer

Network printers are usually installed in one of two ways:

- The *Add Printer Wizard* from the Printers folder can be used for any printer connected to the network. The installation of a network printer doesn't change the printer, it simply loads an appropriate printer driver on your PC. Windows 95 uses that driver during printing.

- *Point and Print installation* from the desktop can be used for printers attached to servers that are Microsoft Client compatible.

Using the Add Printer Wizard

Installing a network printer involves the same Add Printer Wizard as the local printer installation described in Chapter 6, "Controlling Printers." However, there are some differences.

When you configure a local printer, the location of your cable to a specific printer port determines the port's selection. The network printer, on the other hand, requires a network resource name. In the example shown in figure 25.1, an HP 1200 CPS print named HP1200CPS is located on the AlphaNT server.

◄ See "Connecting Windows 95 to a Novell Network," p. 673

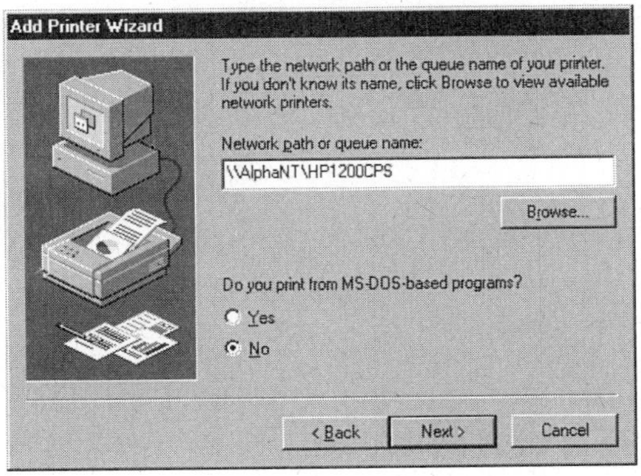

Fig. 25.1
The Add Printer Wizard requires a network address for printer installation.

If you're not sure of the correct address for the network printer, you can choose to browse the network. Browsing enables you to check which network printers are currently available. Some servers require passwords to view what network resources they have available. If you desire access to a server, but do not know the password, contact your LAN Administrator.

◄ See "Setting Up a Windows 95 Peer-to-Peer Network," p. 617

To configure a network printer, you need to know its make and model. You can get this information from your network administrator. Microsoft network servers enable you to install printer drivers quickly.

To set up a network printer with the Add Printer Wizard, follow these steps:

1. Choose Start, Settings, Printers, then double-click on the Add Printer folder.

2. From the first Add Printer Wizard screen, click the Next button. Windows 95 then displays the next Wizard screen, which asks you to decide if you are adding a Network or a Local Printer.

3. Choose the Network Printer option to connect your PC to a network printer. Choose the Next button located at the bottom of the window.

4. Next, you must identify the network path to the printer (refer to fig. 25.1). Select the Browse button to view the Network Neighborhood.

5. The Network Neighborhood displays a list of all servers and workstations connected to your network. Find the appropriate printer and select it. Then choose the Next button.

   The Wizard accesses the selected printer and determines whether its server can download an appropriate printer driver. If a driver is available, the Wizard automatically loads the driver and sets a default configuration for the printer. If a driver is not available, the Wizard asks you to specify the printer's make and model.

Tip
Use the Add Printer Wizard again if you have difficulty connecting to a printer using the Point and Print procedure.

6. Select the manufacturer and printer model by scrolling the Wizard screen lists; then click Next. The screen now offers a default name for your printer. The name should adequately describe the printer for later identification.

7. The Wizard asks whether you want this printer to be your default printer; select Yes or No. Follow this decision by selecting the Next control.

8. The final wizard screen provides the controls to print a test page on the printer you just installed. You can print the test page by selecting Yes; or select No to not print the test page. As a general rule, you should always print a test page to verify the successful completion of the Add a Printer Wizard.

9. Click Finish.

Using Point and Print

Point and Print enables a workstation user to quickly connect to and use a printer shared on another Windows 95 workstation, a Windows NT

Advanced Server, or a Novell NetWare server. When first connecting to the shared printer, Windows 95 automatically copies and installs the correct driver for the shared printer from the server.

1. Choose the Network Neighborhood icon on the Windows desktop.

2. Choose the Entire Network icon. Windows displays all of the servers attached to your network.

3. Choose the Server that supports the printer you want to attach to your workstation. If you don't know which Server that is, ask the LAN Administrator or select each server in sequence until you find the name of the appropriate printer or print queue. Windows displays the server's screen showing its shared resources.

4. Drag a network printer icon from a server's window and drop it on the desktop. You receive a diagnostic message that says `You cannot move or copy this item to this location. Do you want to create a shortcut to the item instead?` Answer Yes. Windows creates a shortcut icon and drops it on the desktop.

5. Drag a document from a local folder and drop it on the New Printer folder icon. Windows displays an information screen such as that shown in figure 25.2. If you select Yes, Windows automatically connects to the printer and downloads the appropriate printer driver from the network printer's server. After loading and configuring the driver, Windows 95 begins printing to the network printer.

Fig. 25.2
If the printer driver is not loaded when you use Point and Print, Windows lets you install the driver on the fly.

Printing on a NetWare Network

To use a NetWare print queue, you must be logged onto a NetWare server. Windows 95 utilizes a PSERVER that can redirect print jobs from NetWare print queues to printers connected to Windows 95 workstations. In addition to the PSERVER capability, your PC must also use the Microsoft Client for NetWare Networks. Windows 95 automatically adapts to NetWare's security for printer and print queue access.

V

Networking

> **Note**
>
> The network administrator can control how NetWare shares printers. If the administrator uses a *policy file* to disable print sharing, the network cannot access the printers. A policy file contains a set of commands that are used by your network administrator to set rules for the operation and configuration of Windows on a network. When entering a new network, check with your network administrator for a sharing policy before attempting to configure shared printing.

NetWare Print Servers

Windows 95 provides printer services for NetWare networks, including a 32-bit PSERVER capability. PSERVER connects NetWare queues to printers shared by Windows 95 PCs. A NetWare print queue contains all the jobs waiting (queued) for a specific printer.

To connect your workstation to a Novell NetWare print server, follow these steps:

1. Choose the Network Neighborhood icon on the desktop. Notice that all servers (Microsoft and NetWare) appear in the Network Neighborhood screen. This screen displays an icon for each network drive currently attached to your system.

2. If you want to attach your workstation to a NetWare printer, choose the appropriate server by double-clicking its icon. The server dialog box opens and displays the shared directories, files, and print queues that are attached to the selected server.

3. Select the appropriate print queue. Choose File, Print and then select the Capture Printer Port control button.

4. The Capture Printer Port dialog box contains the names of currently unattached LPT ports. Select the Reconnect at Logon check box if you want to maintain this connection and have it attached when you restart Windows. Then click OK to attach this print queue to your PC.

   Capturing the printer port attaches the NetWare print queue to the specified port. It does not, however, attach the associated printer to the desktop.

5. To attach the printer associated with that print queue, choose File, Create Shortcut. Windows displays a message warning that you cannot

configure a shortcut printer icon in the Create Shortcut dialog box, but that you can create the icon on the desktop. Click Yes to create the icon.

6. Double-click the printer icon. Windows asks whether you want to set up a printer. Choose Yes.

7. Windows then displays the Add Printer Wizard. Follow the Wizard to finish installing an appropriate printer for the desktop.

Note

You must know the type of printer attached to this print queue. This procedure is different than installing a printer attached to a Microsoft print server.

After configuring the printer, you can print by using the Point and Print procedure on the desktop.

Microsoft Client for NetWare

Windows 95 Microsoft Client for NetWare Networks enables you to connect to new or existing NetWare servers to send files and interact with server-based software. With Microsoft Client for NetWare Networks, you can browse and queue your print jobs using either the Windows 95 network user interface or existing Novell NetWare utilities. The Microsoft Client for NetWare interfaces work equally well with both NetWare 3.x and 4.x servers.

To use Microsoft Client for NetWare Networks, follow these steps:

1. Choose File, Print.

2. Your application might ask you to choose a destination printer. Most applications display a list of attached printers from which you can choose. If so, choose an appropriate network printer. Then choose OK.

   The Windows Redirector accepts the print stream and sends it to the selected printer over the network. Information concerning the status of the printing process automatically returns to you.

3. To monitor the status of your print job on a network printer, open the printer's folder and double-click the appropriate icon. The printer's local Printer Driver opens a status dialog box listing all print jobs in the printer's queue.

Point and Print for NetWare Print Queues

You can enable a Point and Print procedure to use a NetWare-compatible client as a destination. To do so, use the Point and Print procedure discussed earlier.

To print from the desktop to a network printer, follow these steps:

1. Open the folder that contains the document you want to print.
2. Select a document. Hold down the left mouse button and drag the selected document to the network printer's icon on your desktop. The document now appears as an outline.
3. Release the outlined document icon over the printer's icon. Windows 95 interprets the file type, starts the application associated with the file, commands the application to print the document, redirects the print job to the selected printer, and shuts down the application when the print job finishes.

Note

Before Windows can perform the desktop printing operation, you must associate the document with an installed application. If the document is not associated with such an application, Windows displays a message box informing you that it cannot perform the printing task.

Printing on a Microsoft Network

To share files and printers on Microsoft networks, you also can set user rights remotely through the User Manager in a Windows NT Advanced Server.

To connect to a Microsoft print server, follow these steps:

1. Click the Network Neighborhood icon on the desktop. Notice that all servers (Microsoft and NetWare) appear on the Network Neighborhood window. This screen displays an icon for each network drive currently attached to your system.
2. To attach a printer through a Microsoft server, choose the appropriate Microsoft server by double-clicking that server's icon. The server dialog box, named after the appropriate server, appears and displays the shared directories, files, and printers attached to the Microsoft server.

3. Select the appropriate printer queue. Choose File, Print and then select the capture printer port. The Capture Printer Port dialog box is displayed containing the name of a currently unattached LPT port.

4. In the Capture Printer Port dialog box, select the Reconnect at Logon check box if you want to maintain this connection and have it attached when you restart Windows. Then click the OK button to attach this print queue to your PC.

Note

Capturing the printer port attaches the printer to a specified port, but does not attach the associated printer to the desktop.

5. To attach the printer associated with the selected print queue, you must choose File, Create Shortcut. Windows displays a diagnostics message warning that you cannot configure a shortcut printer icon in the Create Shortcut dialog box, although Windows creates the shortcut on the desktop. Click Yes to create the icon.

6. Double-click the printer's shortcut icon. Windows asks whether you want to set up a printer. Choose Yes. Windows then displays the Add Printer Wizard.

7. Follow the Wizard to finish installing an appropriate printer for the desktop. The Add Printer Wizard identifies which printer make and model you are installing and completes the printer connection quickly.

After configuring the printer, you can print by using the Point and Print procedure on the desktop.

Troubleshooting

I can see a network printer using Network Neighborhood, but I can't print to it.

Try the following:

- Check with your network administrator about your access rights to the printer.
- Verify that the printer is properly configured on your PC.
- Check with other users to determine whether they can access the printer.
- Try to print to another printer on the network to check your network connectivity.

(continues)

(continued)

I can't stop, cancel, or delete a print job in a network queue.

Try the following:

- Check whether you have proper authorization from the network administrator to change the print settings. You might be authorized to change only your own print jobs, not others.
- If the print queue is on a shared printer, reload the printer driver or reset the printer properties. The system might not recognize that this printer is attached to your PC.

The network printer doesn't tell me that it is out of paper or toner.

Have the network administrator configure Winpopup to broadcast printer-problem announcements. Winpopup is a utility that comes with Windows. This utility allows the network and network users to send "popup" messages that identify events and get the attention of other network users.

Optimizing Print Resources

Network printing involves many of the same facilities as local printing. Applications create print files that the Network Redirector streams to the destination network printer. When working with network resources, however, you must consider several other issues to ensure that you're getting the most from your system.

Network Printer Configuration and Management

The Printer Properties sheet contains information on each local and network printer attached to your PC. Each printer's properties are specific to its make, model, and hardware configuration.

◄ See "Options for Your Printer," p. 187

You can make several changes to the properties to enhance your printing. The print quality can be enhanced by specific printers, setting device options, graphics, and the procedures for handling TrueType fonts. The following general procedure explores some of these changes:

1. After attaching a network printer, open its Printer Properties sheet by right-clicking the appropriate printer. From the pull-down menu that appears, choose Properties and then click the General tab. The pages in the Properties sheet are specific to your printer and display the options

and selections that match the printer's current hardware and print driver configuration.

2. Click the Device Options tab. Notice the options that the network printer offers.

3. Change the Device Options settings to match your printer's specifications. These options include such pertinent information as printer memory size and page protection. (If you don't see these options, check with your local area network [LAN] administrator.)

4. Click the Details tab. Check the spool settings to determine whether the printer is set to print after the first or last page spools. Usually, waiting until after the last page spools yields better results. Experiment with this setting to gain a better understanding of your configuration.

5. Click the Graphics tab. Change the dithering settings to identify which setting yields the best results for both speed and printout quality.

Troubleshooting

When I print to a printer on the network, my printout quality and settings are not consistent.

Try the following:

- Before printing, check with the printer's Properties sheet. Change the settings if required.
- Check with the system administrator for the printer settings, features, and hardware configuration. The printer might not be capable of handling your print job.
- Relate printout quality to changes in the property settings. Change your printer's properties and make test printouts to see how these changes affect the printouts.

Network Printer Drivers

Windows uses printer drivers to deliver your print files through the network to your printer. How well Windows performs this printing depends on how well the drivers perform. If you use drivers that are several revisions old, you might experience a slowdown. It is a good policy to check your printer drivers and update as revisions become available.

1. In the Control Panel, choose the System icon. Then click the Device Manager tab.
2. Verify that the network interface card driver is a virtual mode driver with a VxD extension. The driver will be listed including its extension. If a real-mode driver with a DRV extension is installed, then contact your LAN administrator or printer manufacturer for an updated revision.
3. Verify that the configured printer driver is a virtual mode driver. The driver should also have a VxD extension. If a real-mode driver with a DRV extension is installed, then contact your LAN administrator or printer manufacturer for an updated revision.
4. Ask your LAN administrator whether your system is configured with the latest driver version for your network printers. If the drivers are not the most current revision, request the latest update from either your LAN manager or the printer's manufacturer.

Managing Print Files and Sharing

After creating print files and sending them to a network printer, you must verify that the print jobs are finished, on hold, or need to be purged. You can check the print job status on both local and remote printers by using the Windows Printer Driver. Print job control is a complex task that involves user security rights on remote printers.

Viewing a Network Print Queue

Although you can view queue information, you cannot change any print job characteristics unless the LAN administrator has authorized you to do so. For some systems, the network administrator is the only user who can control all print jobs, while another user can control only his or her local shared-printing resources. LAN administrator policies determine which users can delete, pause, or purge documents from the queue. Usually, users can change the status of their individual print jobs, but not those of other users.

To view the queue, simply double-click on the printer's icon in the Printers folder or on the desktop. Windows displays the Printer Driver and print queue.

Shared Printing

Shared printing or *peer-to-peer sharing* provides other network workstations access to your local printer. Shared printing access is useful for transferring documents between workstations and for sharing expensive resources with other users. It is also an excellent way to maximize the use of often expensive printing hardware.

To share a printer, follow these steps:

1. Choose Start, Settings, Control Panel. In the Control Panel folder, double-click the Network icon. The Network tabs will appear. These tabs include Configuration, Identification, and Access Control.

2. On the Configuration page, select the Add button. The Select Network Component Type dialog box appears.

3. Choose Service and then click the Add button.

4. Choose Microsoft from the Manufacturers list box.

5. If your primary network logon client is Microsoft Networks, choose File and Printer Sharing for Microsoft Networks. If your primary network logon client is NetWare, choose File and Printer Sharing for NetWare Networks.

6. Choose OK to close the Select Network Service dialog box. For these changes to take effect, you must restart the computer.

Enabling Shared Printing

After configuring the network setup by following the preceding steps, you must enable the sharing feature as follows:

1. From the taskbar, choose Start, Settings, Control Panel. In the Control Panel folder, double-click the Network icon.

2. In the Network dialog box, choose the File and Print Sharing button.

3. In the File and Print Sharing dialog box, select the I Want to Be Able to Allow Others to Print to My Printer(s) check box (see fig. 25.3).

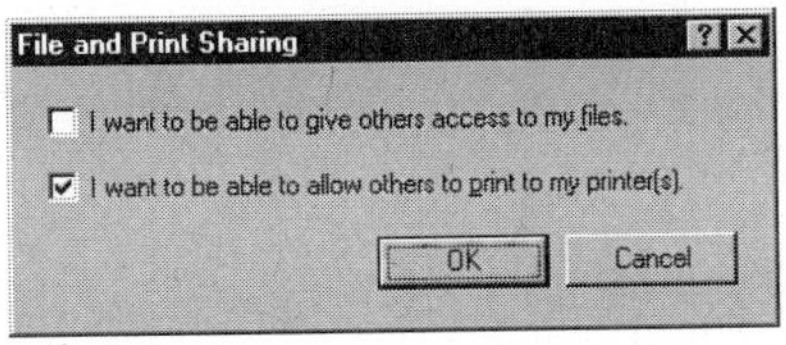

Fig. 25.3
The File and Print Sharing dialog box contains check boxes that enable you to share files and printers with other network users.

4. Choose OK to close the dialog box, and again to close the Network Control Panel. You must restart the computer for these changes to take effect.

Note

If the I Want to Be Able to Allow Others to Print to My Printer(s) check box is grayed (disabled), your system does not support print sharing.

Troubleshooting

My shared printer is unavailable to other workstations on my network.

Try the following:

- In the Control Panel, double-click the Network icon. Choose the File and Print Sharing button. In the File and Print Sharing dialog box, verify that the I Want to Be Able to Allow Others to Print to My Printer(s) check box is selected.
- Verify that all users are running a compatible protocol.
- Verify that your PC shows up in the network browser on other connected PCs.
- Verify that you can print successfully to your attached printer.
- Use the Extended Printer Troubleshooting (EPTS) application available in your Help file.

Disabling Shared Printing

After your workstation printer is shared, you might find that too many users are creating an overload. To disable the share, follow this procedure:

1. From the taskbar, choose Start, Settings, Control Panel. In the Control Panel folder, double-click the Network icon.
2. In the Network dialog box, choose the File and Print Sharing button.
3. Deselect the I Want to Be Able to Allow Others to Print to My Printer(s) check box.
4. Choose OK to close the dialog box, and again to close the Network Control Panel.

Creating Shared-Printer Security

In Windows 95, creating shared-resource security is a multistep procedure. In order to effectively share a resource, you must be able to control who accesses that resource and, to some extent, what they do with it. If you share your printer, you can impose some level of security. Securing your printer requires several steps.

1. Choose the Passwords icon in the Control Panel folder. The Password Properties sheet appears. This Properties sheet has three tabs: Passwords, Remote Administration, and User Profiles. (The Remote Administration tab is not present if file and printer sharing are not installed.)
2. Choose the Enable Remote Administration check box on the Remote Administration page.
3. Type a user-access password in the Passwords text box.
4. In the Confirm Passwords text box, retype the password. Record the password in your system workbook or manual.
5. Select OK.

Network users can now gain access to your system by using the password that you have just created. To access your shared printer, however, users must have the appropriate password information.

Deleting Connections to a Shared Printer

When you delete a shared connection between your workstation and a workstation sharing its local printer, disabling sharing keeps your local printer from being shared by the network.

1. From the taskbar, choose Start, Settings, Printer's Folder. Windows displays a list of all printers, local or network, attached to your workstation.
2. Select the shared printer you want to delete.
3. Choose File, Delete.
4. Windows displays a dialog box warning that it will delete the selected printer. Click Yes.
5. Windows next displays a dialog box asking whether you want to delete this printer's drivers. Click Yes to delete the drivers.

> **Caution**
>
> Before you click Yes and thus delete the printer's drivers, verify that you do not have any other printers attached of the same make and model. If you delete this printer's drivers, you might also disconnect other printers.

Solving Common Network Printing Problems

Windows 95 adds some basic Help tools to aid you in solving network printing problems. These basic tools include the following:

- Windows quickly displays descriptive information in diagnostic messages that appear when Windows encounters printing problems.
- The Help facility includes an interactive Printing Problem Help tool that takes you step by step through the most common solutions to problems.
- An enhanced Help tool incorporates even more detailed steps that can solve quite difficult network printing problems.
- The System Monitor is useful in diagnosing local PC problems caused by network connections.

Diagnostics

The facilities of the Windows Help system can help you diagnose printing problems as follows:

1. Choose Help, Troubleshooting, and Print Troubleshooting from your application or Windows. Windows displays a Windows Help screen with the Print Troubleshooter dialog box.
2. Answer each question by clicking the button next to the appropriate answer. The Help screens provide suggestions for many common troubleshooting problems.

If the troubleshooting Help information is inadequate for solving your problems, Microsoft provides the Enhanced Print Troubleshooter (EPTS) on the Windows 95 CD-ROM:

1. Go to the Windows Explorer. Open the \other\misc\epts folder on the Windows 95 CD-ROM.

2. Choose the EPTS.EXE executable file. EPTS displays a Help screen that contains hypertext buttons. Next to each button is a brief statement describing a printer problem. Start by selecting the statement that best describes your problem.

3. Answer each EPTS question with the choice that best matches your problem. The EPTS helps you identify the most probable cause of your network printing problems.

Diagnosing network printing problems is more complex because the printers are not local and perhaps not readily accessible. After using EPTS, if you are still having difficulty printing to a network printer, call the local Help desk or your LAN network administrator.

Server Overload

A PC that shares a local printer with the network is a *print server*. If your PC is a print server, a percentage of your PC's resources are dedicated to the network. That percentage varies with the number of network connections to your PC. If your system slows down significantly, it might be suffering from *server overload*. This occurs when too many network users are either attached to or overusing your printer.

To test network loading, use the System Monitor to record your PC's server activities. Your Monitor charts might show large changes in network connection activity.

1. Choose Start, Programs, Accessories, System Tools, System Monitor.

2. Choose Edit, Remove to clear all Monitor chart variables.

3. Choose Edit, Add. Windows displays the Add dialog box.

4. Choose the Server Threads option from the Network Server category.

5. Choose the Bytes/sec option from the Network Server category.

6. Choose the NBs (network buffers) option from the Network Server category and then choose the OK button to complete the additions.

7. Choose Options, Chart. Set the update interval to one minute using the slide control in the Chart dialog box.

8. Choose View, Line Charts.

You have now configured the Monitor to show the level of resource loading associated with network clients. If the System Monitor displays large variations in the number of threads or bytes-per-second variables, discontinue printer sharing for a test period. This test period should help you determine whether you can eliminate overload as a cause for system sluggishness.

Using Custom Print Managers and Utilities

Windows 95 provides a standard platform that other vendors use to create software drivers and applications. These custom software packages integrate a specific product with Windows. As a result, many printer vendors work with Microsoft to create new drivers. Some vendors have created printing applications that can substitute for or replace the Windows Printer Driver. Many printer vendors provide custom property configuration utilities for accessing their printers' custom features. Two of these vendors are Hewlett-Packard (HP) and Digital Equipment Corporation (DEC).

- The HP JetAdmin Utility is a substitute for the Windows Printer Driver.
- The DEC utility provides additional property screens that the Windows Printer Driver can call.

Using the HP JetAdmin Utility

You can use the HP JetAdmin Utility to install and configure networked Hewlett-Packard printers that use the HP JetDirect network interface. The HP JetAdmin Utility substitutes for the Windows standard Printer Driver. You also can use JetAdmin to interface printers connected to a NetWare LAN.

Figure 25.4 shows the JetAdmin Utility's main screen. The All Printers tab is displaying a list of printers connected to a Novell NetWare network. The network printers are of diverse makes and models. The utility can identify most of these printers. However, if incapable of identifying a printer's make, model, or network adapter card, JetAdmin displays a large, yellow question mark to designate the unknown printer.

To obtain information about the printer, double-click one of the printers shown listed. The Printer sheet shown in figure 25.5 appears. The sheet identifies the printer's make and model as well as its location, capabilities, and status.

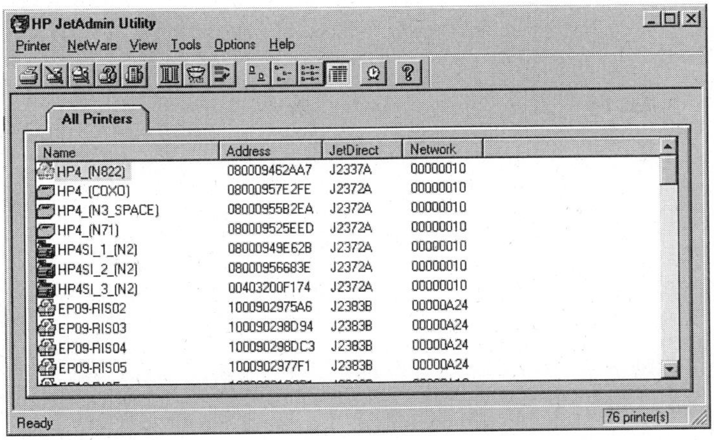

Fig. 25.4
The HP JetAdmin Utility is a vendor-supplied Printer Driver that monitors and controls HP network printers.

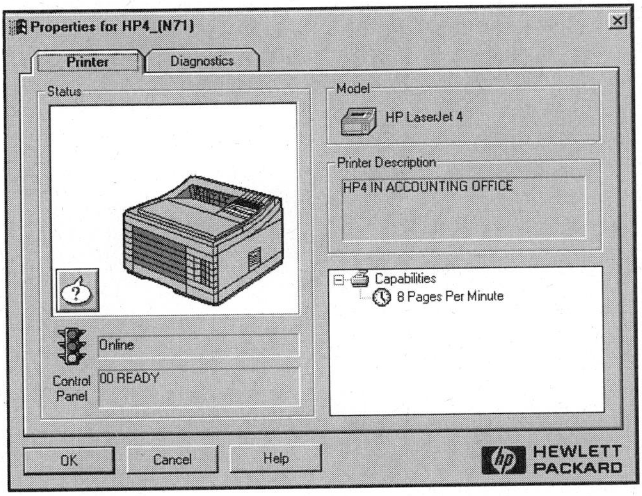

Fig. 25.5
The HP JetAdmin Utility's Printer sheet displays current information about the selected printer.

Notice the traffic light indicator at the screen's bottom-left corner. This indicator is useful for quickly isolating network printing problems. The following are traffic light patterns for diagnosing problem printers:

- A red light indicates that the printer has a critical error that you must correct before printing. Such critical errors include a lack of paper or an open door interlock.
- A yellow light signifies a noncritical error that will soon require service. For example, if the printer's toner is low, the yellow light comes on.

- A green light indicates that the printer is online and functioning normally.

Figure 25.6 shows the Printer sheet for a problem printer. JetAdmin has identified that the printer has a problem, as the question mark in the Status section denotes. The traffic light is now red, indicating a critical error has occurred.

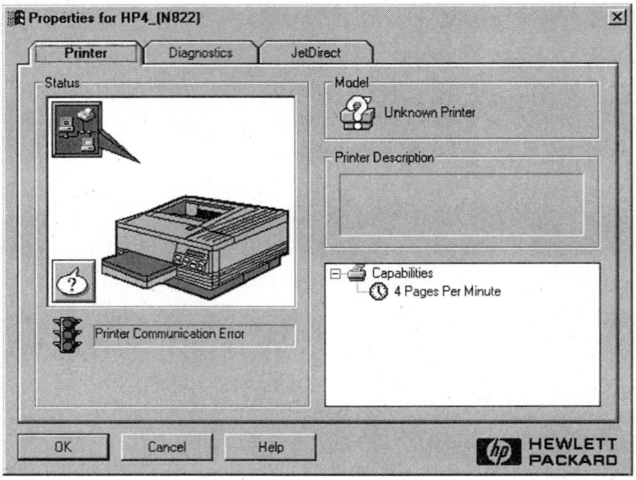

Fig. 25.6
The HP JetAdmin Utility's Printer sheet shows the status of a printer whose current configuration is unknown.

Using the DEC Printer Utility

The DEC printer utility adds features to the standard Windows 95 Printer Driver and updates printer drivers. The utility includes a detailed Help file for configuring both local and network printers. In addition, the utility creates an enhanced set of property menus and screens for configuring DEC printers.

Figure 25.7 shows the Device Options sheet, which presents in detail the current conditions associated with the network printer. This sheet also enables the user to install and quickly set special device options.

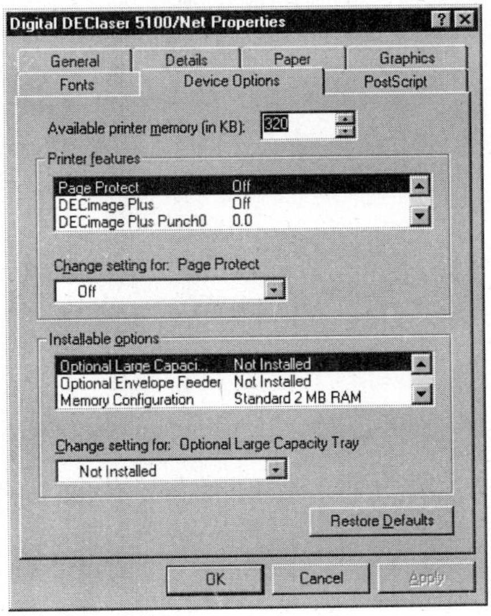

Fig. 25.7
The DEC printer utility's Device Options sheet adds unique features to the standard Windows 95 Printer Driver.

As other printer vendors change their products and software drivers, other highly customized Printer Drivers will be available for use with Windows 95.❖

Chapter 26

Network Management and Security

by Gordon Meltzer

The motive for setting up a Windows 95 network is to share the resources associated with the computers on that network. *Resources* are disks (including CD-ROMs) and their files, printers, and fax modems.

A network, in which resources and information previously available only to people working on their private standalone personal computers now are available for sharing (and possible editing or deletion by the group), raises serious and complex issues. Network issues can best be understood by splitting them into two parts. This chapter examines these two parts: management and security.

In this chapter, you learn how to control the installation and configuration of your network. The chapter tries to expose weaknesses in the network design and tells you how to work around these weaknesses. The chapter provides tips for keeping your network up and running and for simplifying it without losing functionality. This chapter is a guide to help you understand the philosophy behind the Windows 95 network and make it work in your individual situation.

In this chapter, you learn about

- Creating network resources
- Monitoring network resources
- Sharing network resources
- Securing the network

- Managing the network
- Using dial-up networking
- Using Windows 95 with other networks

Creating Network Resources

The basic philosophy of peer-to-peer networks is that every file on every disk on the network is available for sharing by all members of the network. By extension, anyone can print to any printer on the network—and also delete any file, wipe out any directory, and erase any disk anywhere on the network.

That kind of peer-to-peer network, where everybody on the LAN is connected to everybody else's disks and printers, is an unmanageable network. If you draw a diagram of the connections in such a network, you'll see a crazy-quilt of connections. With more than a few machines on the LAN, you'll be unable to follow all the connections. The worst parts of thoughtlessly connecting everybody to everybody are

- *Confusion.* Time is always lost searching for data all over the LAN.
- *Data Loss.* Needed files get erased from one disk because somebody thought somebody else had a copy on another disk.

Don't be tempted to set up your Windows 95 peer network the crazy-quilt way. The problem is that after you set up your network and declare your computer's hard drive to be shared, if you take no steps to manage the network, you've opened the door to network data-loss danger and file-finding confusion. You need to bring safety and sanity to your network environment, and you need to work with the other members of your workgroup to accomplish those tasks.

Data-Storage Tips

Networks are designed to make office life easier. Peer-to-peer networks are supposed to eliminate something called the sneakernet, which is used when all computers in an office are standalone. Following are the steps involved in making a sneakernet connection:

1. You decide that you want to edit a document on which several people have been collaborating.

2. You visit each collaborator's computer, find the file in question, and record the date and time when the file was last modified. You're looking for the most recent version.

3. When you find the computer that has the most up-to-date version of the document, you find a formatted floppy disk, copy the file to the disk, and take the disk back to your computer.

4. Copy the file from the floppy disk to your hard drive.

You think you won't have to go through all that when you set up a network. All the computers will be connected, and you can copy the file to your hard disk over the wire. In fact, however, the default setup for peer-to-peer networks such as Windows 95 leaves each person's version of a collaborative file on his or her own hard disk, where other workgroup members cannot find it easily.

The solution to this problem is setting up your peer-to-peer Windows 95 network in a client/server model. The following sections show how this model enables all members of the network to get their work done but retains the flexibility that is the best feature of peer nets.

Choosing a Storage Area for Your Work

You really don't want to set up each computer on the peer network as a server; you want to make one computer on your network the server, the central storage area for data files. Data files are *work products*—the files created by the programs that you use. If you're not sure about which files are data files, remember that Microsoft Word creates files that have the DOC extension and that Excel creates worksheet files that have the XLS extension. The files with DOC and XLS extensions are the work product (data files) created by Word and Excel.

Files of this nature should be stored on only one computer in your workgroup so that everyone will know where to find them. If you don't do this, you have to search all the computers on your network for a file—not superior to sneakernet at all.

Using a Dedicated Server

You don't have to have a dedicated server in your Windows 95 network, but if you can afford to dedicate one computer on your network to storing everybody's work product, do so. Following are the benefits of storing all the workgroup's data files on one machine:

- The individual workstations can use smaller, slower, less expensive hard drives.
- You don't have to search for the computer that holds the files that you want.
- Complex drive mappings are eliminated.
- In a LAN where all work product is stored on one central file server, File and Printer Sharing will not need to be turned on in Control Panel, Network on most of the computers in the LAN. Memory is used more efficiently on all the machines that do not use file and printer sharing.
- Backing up everyone's work is as simple as backing up one disk because all the work is on that disk.

Setting Up a Data-File Storage Server

Once you've decided that good network management involves setting up a central server, where you and your network neighbors will store their data files, follow these steps:

1. Choose the network machine that you want to use as the data server. This machine will always be turned on.
2. Enable File and Printer Sharing on the data server. Do this by going to the machine that will be your storage server. Use Control Panel, and double-click the Network icon. Then choose File and Print Sharing and put a check in the box that says I Want To Be Able To Give Others Access to My Files.

   Note

   If the server you're working on also has a printer attached, and if you and your workgroup members want to print on that printer, also put a check in the box that says, I Want To Be Able to Allow Others To Print To My Printer(s).

3. Set up a directory structure that will make storing and finding documents easy.

> **Note**
>
> You may create one folder for each user and then create subfolders for the users' projects. You may create a folder for each client and allow the workgroup members to store their work for that client in the client's folder. Setting up folders by project is OK, too, if the projects are long-term. Ideally, the directory structure on the data server should be long-lasting and durable so that everyone in the workgroup can get used to it.

4. Map the server's network drive to each workstation, using the same drive letter (for example, Z:).
5. Set up the applications on each workstation so that the default data directory for each application is the same.
6. Have workgroup members start saving their work not to their local C drives but to the appropriate subfolder on the network drive.

Getting the Best of Peer-to-Peer and Client/Server LAN Features

Although using a central server makes our workgroup look like a big client/server network, the flexibility of a peer-to-peer network still is available. You can call on this flexibility when you want to use a resource on the network that's attached to another computer—a color printer, for example. You can designate the printer as a shared resource, no matter whose computer the printer is attached to; you can't do that in a traditional client/server network.

Drive Mappings

Following a plan like the one shown in the section "Setting Up a Data-File Storage Server" is important because, if you don't, your workgroup ends up with a drive-mapping scheme that looks like a bowl of spaghetti. You don't want everybody in the network to be connected to everybody else's machines and drives. Point everybody in the workgroup to one machine for storage of work-product data files, and you'll always be able to find what you're looking for.

Suppose that you have a 10-user workgroup. If you set up the network in full peer-to-peer fashion so that everyone is looking for files stored on other people's computers, your drive mappings look like figure 26.1.

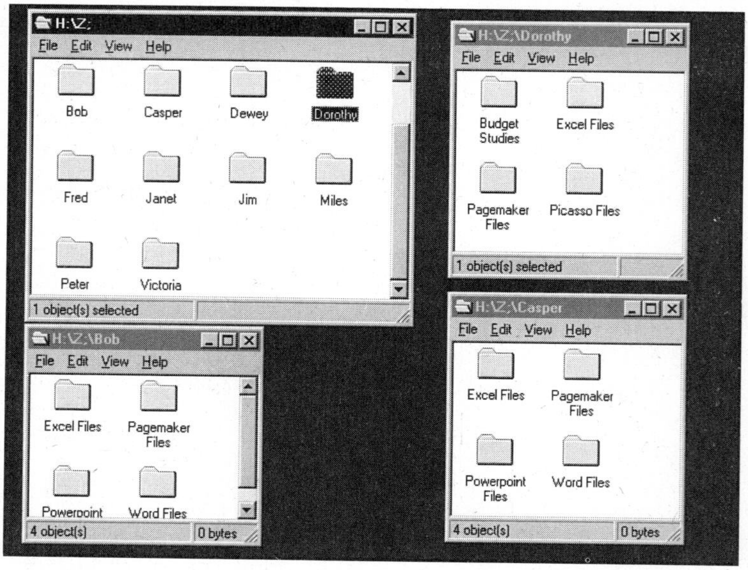

Fig. 26.1
The three smaller windows in this figure show that users have many of the same shared directories—a difficult way to find things on the network.

Since it is a 10-user version, there are 9 other mappings, or drivers, that you must contend with when searching for your data. You need to search for files on all 9 of these other drives/workstations if data files are scattered throughout the network.

Of course, you may be confused by having so many drive mappings and connections in place all the time. You may be dismayed by the drain on your system's performance caused by connecting to so many other workstations and having those workstations connect to yours. You are likely to disconnect from the other members' drives for normal work. Later, when you want to send a file to or retrieve a file from another computer, you must connect to the other computer, map that computer's drive to yours, and do your file-transfer work.

One more reason why all the computers in the workgroup should connect to one central data-storage computer is that you can keep your computer connected to that computer at all times. This persistent connection can be configured to occur automatically when you start your computer or only when you actually try to access the drive. Because you don't have to worry about drive mappings or about connecting and disconnecting network drives, you can consider the network drive to be a permanent part of your computer—the place where you store your work.

Figure 26.2 shows three windows. The parent window shows a mapped network drive called Z:. The first child window shows 10 folders on drive Z—one for each member of the workgroup. The smallest child window shows the folders in user Bob's main folder. The other users have similar folders. More or fewer folders may appear in other users' main folders, depending on the type of work that each user does and the program that he or she uses.

Note

A parent window is the first window displayed by a program. Child windows are subsequent windows the application displays.

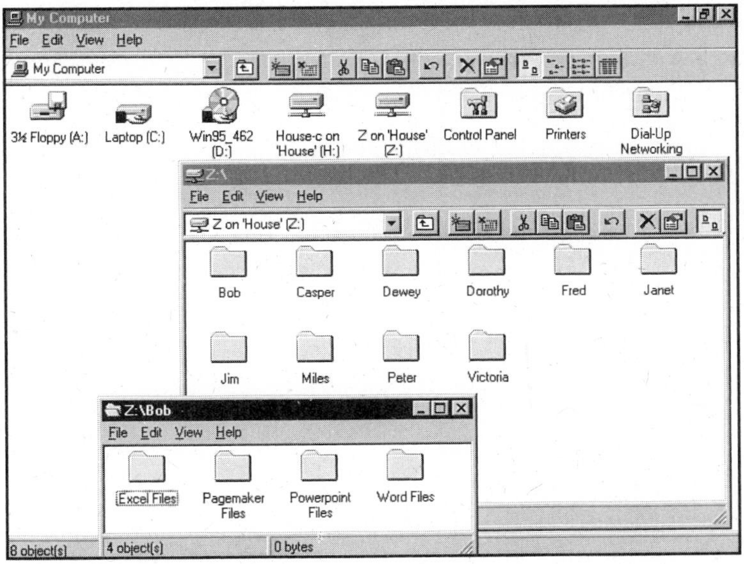

Fig. 26.2
This shows user Bob's folder structure on mapped network drive Z.

You don't have to structure the folder hierarchy on the data-server drive in any particular way. You should, however, have one data-server drive for your workgroup. All the members of the workgroup should connect to that drive permanently and store their work on that drive.

Keeping Applications and Data Separate

The preceding sections discussed only data files—the files that you generate by using your applications. But where should you store application files—your programs? The best method is to store applications locally on each user's C drive, if you have the space on your hard drive, because applications load and run noticeably faster if they run from the local hard drive.

Networks, and application-program vendors, certainly provide the capability for everyone in your workgroup to run programs from a single shared copy, located somewhere on a network file server. This method seems, at first, to be a very interesting way to operate because that huge 15M installation of your favorite word processing program won't have to go on every computer—just on a file server. But the additional network traffic generated by the continual loading of program files over the network wastes bandwidth. Since Windows programs only load part of themselves from the disk into memory at one time, there will be additional network traffic created as various parts of the program are called into memory as needed. If the application was stored on the local hard drive all this unnecessary network traffic could be eliminated.

The users may complain that the program, coming to them from a server over the network, loads and runs too slowly. Finally, if the integrity of the network is interrupted, even momentarily, while a shared copy of an application is running, chances are good that every system running that application at that time will freeze while the application is being loaded, making some users think they need to reboot their machines. This procedure, of course, means that you lose any unsaved data in all applications.

The point here of course is that your workgroup will run much more smoothly if each user has her executable program files stored on her own computer's hard drive.

Being a Good Network Neighbor

If your workgroup is to function effectively, all the members of the workgroup must be good network neighbors. You can implement this simple concept by considering what resources are available on your computer and designating those resources as shared if other members of your workgroup need access to them.

◀ See "Sharing an Entire Drive," p. 643

If yours is the only CD-ROM drive in the workgroup, for example, make it available for other members to use.

You also need to consider the continuity of shared resources. If you have the only CD-ROM drive or the only color printer and other users are connected to those resources, consider the effect on the rest of your workgroup if you turn off your computer without warning. In such a case, your resources disappear from the network and no longer are available to the other workgroup members. Don't discontinue sharing your resources without informing the rest of the workgroup. Use the WinPopup accessory program to send a message to your workgroup saying you are going to take your shared disk or printer offline. In your message, say how long it will be until you shut down. Communicating about a change in status of a shared resource you control is part of being a good network neighbor.

Caution

If a disk resource on your peer-to-peer network is disconnected from the network unexpectedly—if a computer that hosts a shared folder is turned off or if the folder-sharing properties are turned off—network users can lose data.

Network-Management Tools

Windows 95 includes several useful tools that help you learn about and manage your peer-to-peer network. Although *network management* is a very broad term, management tools simply allow you to see how your network is functioning and to change almost everything about the entire network from your own computer. You can use these Network Management tools to enable or disable sharing of resources, add or delete passwords, disconnect users, and so on.

When you look at network management as being a series of toggle switches, with one switch for each possible setting on each possible resource, management tools become less mysterious. The trick is knowing how to set each parameter for optimum network efficiency.

Note

Don't feel that you have to make every connection and map every drive just because you can. Simple is better.

Net Watcher

Net Watcher is installed in the Accessories, System Tools group, which you can find by opening the Start menu and choosing Programs. This utility is useful for examining which resources on which computer are shared. Net Watcher tells you about these resources, as well as who is using the shared resources and which files are open on the shared resources.

◄ See "Understanding File Sharing," p. 643

◀ See "Setting Up Printer Sharing and Security," p. 651

Net Watcher is a "per-server" utility. In order to display meaningful information, Net Watcher shows information about only one server computer at a time. Net Watcher shows information about computers that are sharing their disks or printers. These computers have File and Print Sharing for Microsoft Networks enabled.

Net Watcher provides three main views of the workgroup for each server:

- A view showing the users connected to the server called View by Connections. To see this view, start Net Watcher and choose View, Connections.
- A view showing the shared folders on the server called View by Shared Folders. To see this view from the main Net Watcher window, choose View, Shared Folders.
- A view showing the files that are open on the server called View by Open Files. To see this view, choose View, Open Files.

In the View by Connections, a list of users who are connected to the server appears on the left side of the screen. The right side of the screen displays the folders and printers to which the users are connected, as well as the files that the users have open. If multiple users are connected, you select one user at a time on the left side of the screen. Then you can manage how that user interacts with the network, as you'll see next.

Figure 26.3 represents the View by Connections. In this example, you are looking at a server, called HOUSE (as defined in the caption bar), to which one user, called LAPTOP, is connected.

View by Shared Folders shows detailed information about the disk folders and printers that have been declared sharable on the server. On the left side of the screen is a list of shared folders on the server, the names under which the folders are shared, the type of access available to the folder (full access or read-only), and any comment about the shared resource that was typed in the Comment box when the folder or printer was designated as sharable.

◀ See "Understanding File Sharing," p. 643

Figure 26.4 shows View by Shared Folders. In the figure, LAPTOP is connected to several shared folders and to one printer on the computer known as HOUSE.

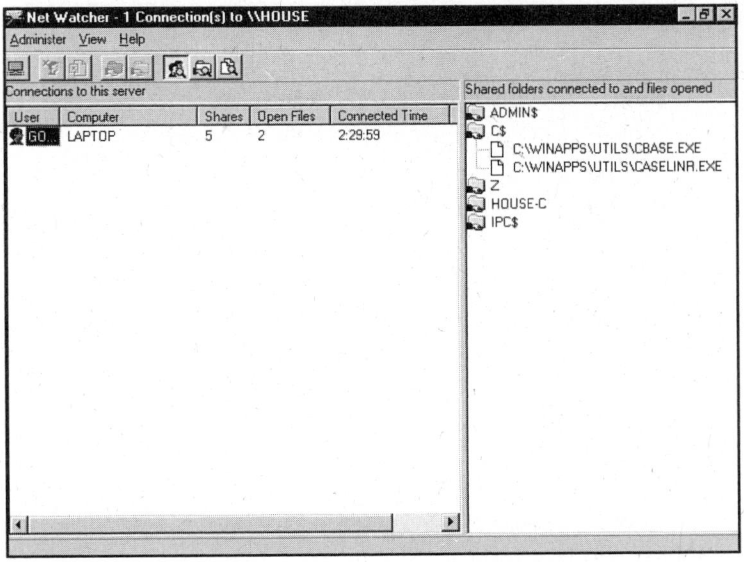

Fig. 26.3
The Net Watcher management program in View by Connections mode, showing user Laptop connected to server House.

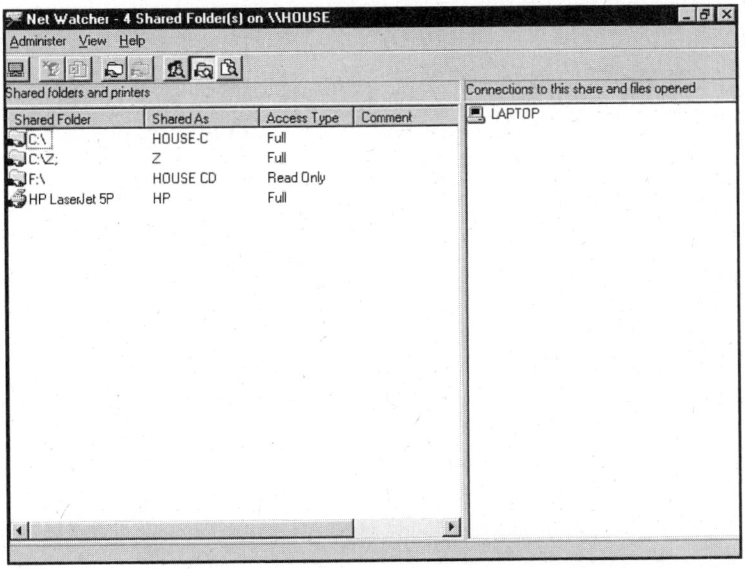

Fig. 26.4
The Net Watcher management program in View by Shared Folders mode, showing four shared folders on the server named House.

View by Open Files is a full-screen display. In figure 26.5, Net Watcher shows the name of two open files on the server, the share name of the server on which the file is located, which computer is accessing the file, and whether the file is open for reading only or for reading and writing.

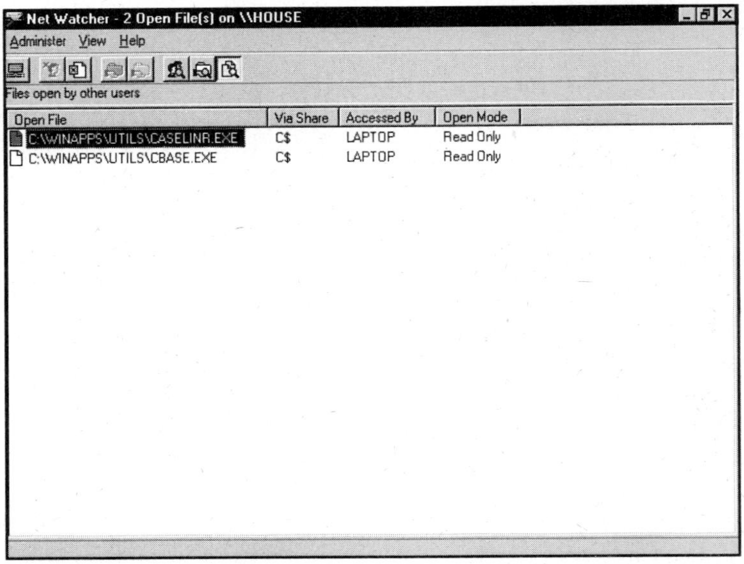

Fig. 26.5
The Net Watcher management program in View by Open Files mode, showing two open files on the server named HOUSE.

Net Watcher can do far more than simply report on network status, however; as a management tool, it can restructure the network. The following sections explain how you can use Net Watcher to accomplish these tasks:

- Disconnect a network user anywhere in the workgroup
- Close an open file anywhere in the workgroup
- Add a shared folder to any server in the workgroup
- Stop sharing folders on any server in the workgroup
- Change the properties of shared folders in the workgroup

Disconnecting a User from a Peer Server

If you want to stop a user from connecting to your computer's shared folders and printers, use Net Watcher's Show Users view. Select the user whom you want to disconnect and then choose Administer, Disconnect User.

Disconnecting a user can have serious consequences for that user; the user can lose data if he or she has unsaved data when the disconnection occurs. In fact, Net Watcher issues a warning when you issue the Disconnect User command, as shown in figure 26.6.

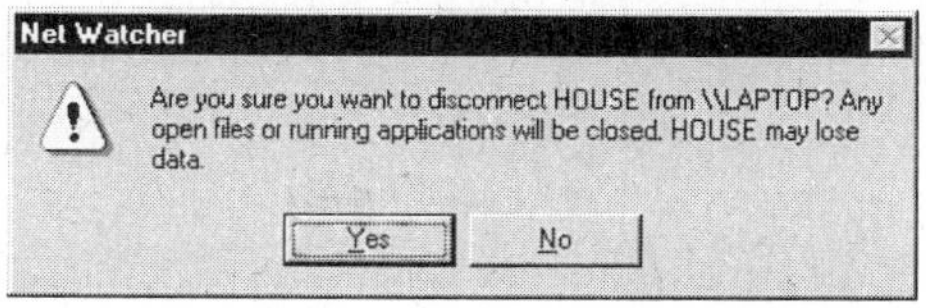

Fig. 26.6 The Net Watcher management program issues a warning when you use it to disconnect a server from a connected user.

Adding a Shared Resource on a Peer Server

Adding a shared resource can be useful when you need access to a resource on another computer in your workgroup. Net Watcher can make the folder that you need sharable. Figure 26.7 shows the shared resources on the peer server called HOUSE—three shared folders and one shared printer. Anyone on a Windows 95 peer network can go and declare a share on any folder for which they have permissions on the workgroup providing the computer they are targeting is a server (has enabled File & Printer Sharing Services).

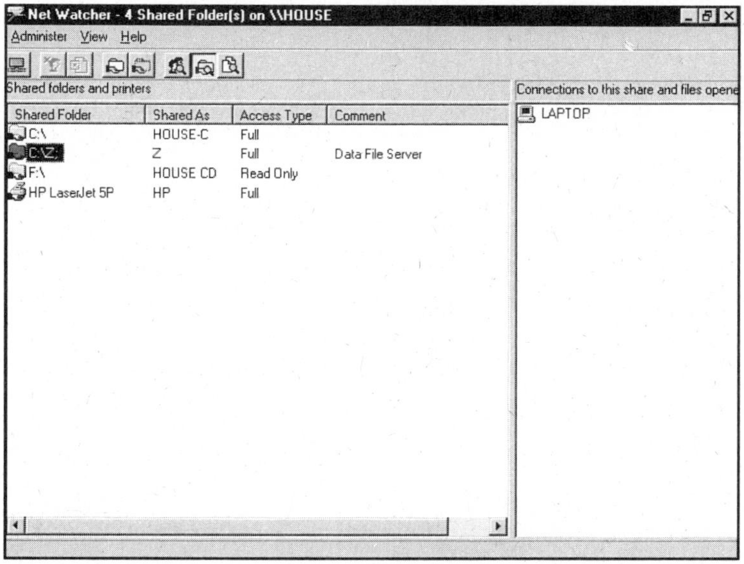

Fig. 26.7 Net Watcher in View by Shared Folders mode, showing three shared folders.

Suppose you want to access programs in the folder named SECURE on the computer named HOUSE. SECURE is not a shared folder, however, so you need to declare it to be sharable. You can do this, from any machine on the workgroup LAN, using Net Watcher. The three requirements are:

- Remote Administration is enabled on the server you are targeting (on which you want to set a resource shared).

- The folder, drive, or printer you want to share is on a server computer. A server computer has File and/or Printer Sharing enabled.
- No password has been established, controlling access to the folder or resource you want to share.

Starting from View by Shared Folders mode on peer server HOUSE, choose Administer, Add Shared Folder, or use the Add Share button on the Net Watcher toolbar. Next, you'll see the Enter Path dialog box asking for the path you wish to share. Then browse for the folder name or type it in the Path box. Figure 26.8 shows the Browse for Folder dialog box where you can find and select the path to the folder you want to share.

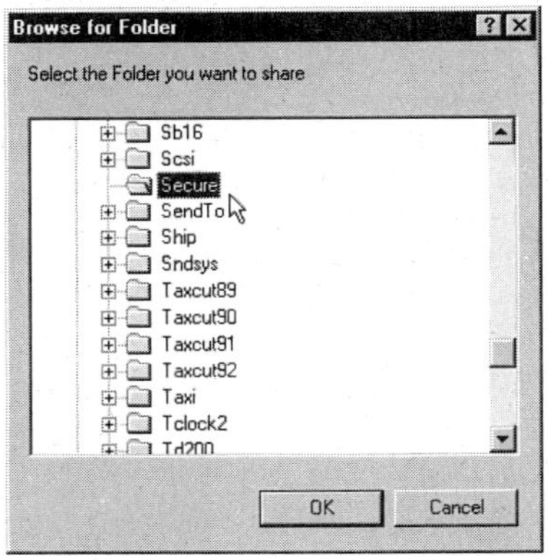

Fig. 26.8
To share a folder on your workgroup LAN using Net Watcher, browse for the folder you want to share and double-click to enter it in the Enter Path dialog box.

After you've chosen the folder you want to add, Net Watcher displays the shared folder's Properties sheet, shown in figure 26.9. In this sheet, you declare the folder to be shared and set its shared properties: Shared As, Share Name, Comment, Access Type, and Passwords.

When you choose OK on the shared folder's Properties sheet, the folder becomes a shared resource on the workgroup and is added to Net Watcher's list of shared folders (see fig. 26.10).

Caution

The process of adding a shared folder just described has deep implications. Any member of the Peer-to-Peer workgroup LAN can add a shared drive or folder on any server computer in the network. The owner of the computer targeted to have a drive or folder shared doesn't need to agree. In fact, the owner of the targeted computer may not even know that a drive or folder has been set as shared, until she happens to examine the drive properties with My Computer or the Windows Explorer and notices the Shared Resource icon attached to one of her drives or folders.

Notice too, that any member of the workgroup, using Net Watcher to add shared drives or folders on server computers on the LAN, can also set passwords for access to the folders he declares as shared, effectively preventing anyone but himself from accessing those drives or folders over the LAN. Again, the owner of the computer containing these shared drives or folders will not know a password has been set without examining the properties for the shared drive or folder.

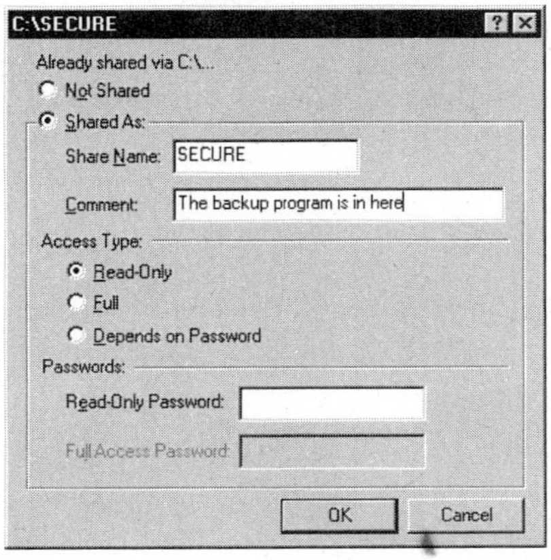

Fig. 26.9
In Net Watcher, you can edit the properties of your newly shared folder.

Troubleshooting

Files on my hard disk drive are changing. Some are being deleted, some are just being modified. I haven't done anything to them. Why is this happening?

The answer may be that another member of your workgroup LAN is causing these changes on your computer. If you have enabled File and Print Sharing in your network setup, another member of your LAN may have declared your hard drive and its folders to be shared. Then, that person can work with your files, modifying them, deleting them, or adding new files to your disk.

There are two ways to prevent having your drives and folders shared by others without your knowledge:

- Turn off File Sharing in Control Panel, Network. Then your computer is not a server, and nobody can access your drives or folders over the LAN.
- Turn off Enable Remote Administration. You do this by using Control Panel, Passwords, and then clicking the Remote Administration tab. There is only one setting on this page. In the sole check box, deselect Enable Remote Administration of this Server.

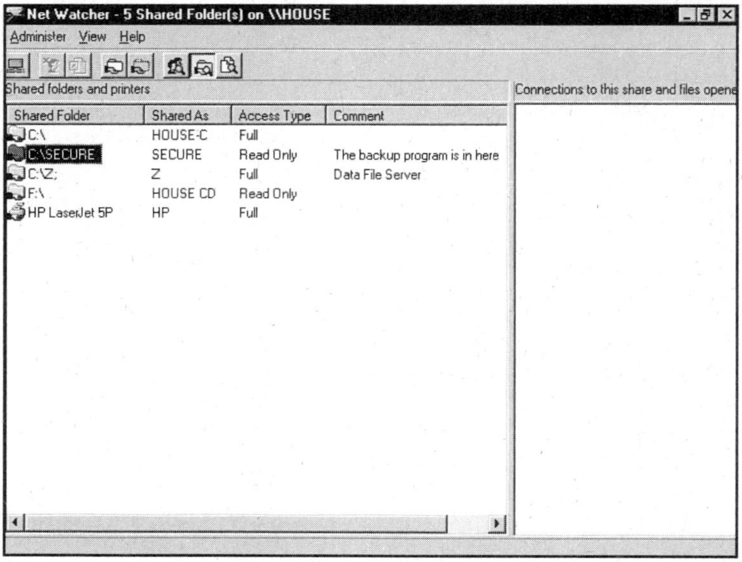

Fig. 26.10
The Net Watcher program has added your newly shared folder, C:\SECURE, to its list of shared folders on the peer server HOUSE.

Stop Sharing a Folder

To stop sharing a folder, start in the View by Shared Folders view of Net Watcher. Select the shared folder that you want to stop sharing on the network and then choose Administer, Stop Sharing Folder. You also can choose the Stop Sharing icon on the Net Watcher toolbar. The warning message shown in figure 26.11 appears. Click Yes to stop sharing the specified folder.

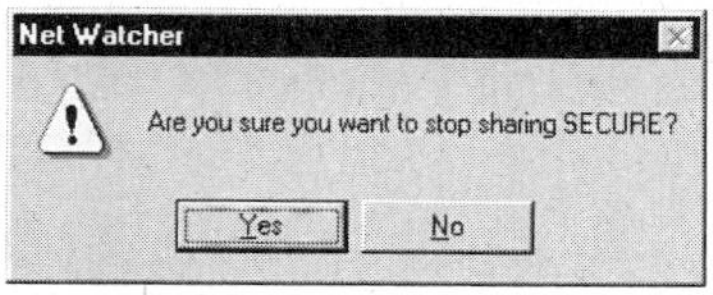

Fig. 26.11
When you use Net Watcher to stop sharing a folder, this confirmation dialog box appears.

Change a Shared Folder's Properties

◄ See "Sharing a Directory," p. 645

This option allows you to stop sharing a shared folder, but it also allows you to change the name of the shared resource on the network, change the access type, and set a password for access. In Net Watcher's View by Shared Folders mode, select the folder that you want to stop sharing on the network and then choose Administer, Shared Folder Properties.

Now, you can perform these kinds of changes on the folder you selected:

- You can set the folder as Not Shared.

- You can set the folder as Shared. If you do this, you must also enter a Share Name. By default, Windows selects the folder name as the Share Name, but you can change it if you have a better description you'd like to use.
- If you've set the folder to be Shared, you can set the access type to Read-Only, or Full, or Depends on Password. You also may enter a password for access to the folder.

Figure 26.9 above shows the dialog box you work with in changing a shared folder's properties.

Stop Sharing a Printer

If you need to stop sharing a printer on the workgroup, start in View by Shared Folder mode of Net Watcher. Select the printer in the list of shared resources, and choose Administer, Shared Folder Properties. The printer-properties dialog box appears (see fig. 26.12), showing the name of the printer you're working with in its title bar. To stop sharing the printer, choose Not Shared in the dialog box.

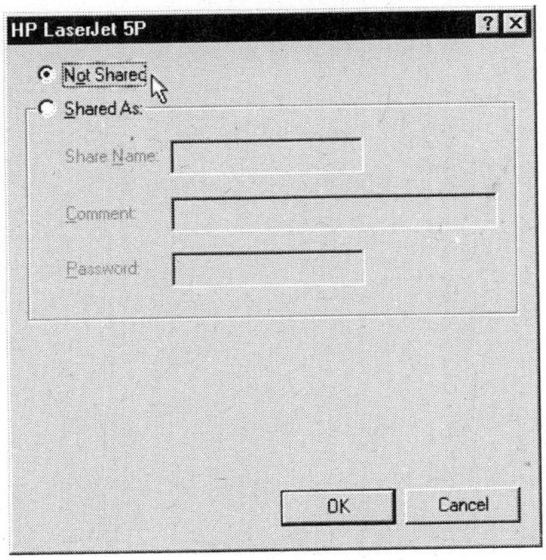

Fig. 26.12 Net Watcher uses this dialog box to allow you to stop sharing a network printer.

Then choose OK. No warning message appears before the printer is made unavailable to the workgroup.

User Profiles as a System-Management Tool

◄ See "Changing Custom Settings for Each User," p. 156

Many workgroups have users who may use more than one computer. Because Windows 95 is very customizable, a user who is sitting at what is not his or her main computer may be unable to work. Network connections may not be the same. Connections to the shared folders that the user needs may not be available. Printer connections may not be what the user expects. Menus may be different. In general, the workstation may be so customized for the primary user that another user may be lost.

Some computers on your workgroup may have no primary user but a group of users, all of whom may have different needs or expectations. You also may have users who are true floaters—who have no primary machine but need to be able to be productive on any computer.

To deal with all these cases, Microsoft introduced User Profiles to Windows 95. With User Profiles, the following settings on any computer can be customized for any user:

- Shortcut lists and their contents
- Items in the Start menu
- Items that can be configured by Control Panel
- (For Windows 95 programs and the applications bundled with Windows 95) Menu configurations, toolbar configurations, status-bar configurations, and font and display settings
- Appearance of the desktop, including shortcuts and icons
- Fonts in use
- Screen saver, screen background, screen colors, color depth, and screen resolution
- Network settings (such as persistent connections and printer connections)
- Network Neighborhood configuration

Enabling User Profiles on the Workgroup

To use User Profiles, you must be sure the proper options are selected on the Passwords Properties sheet. Follow these steps:

1. Open the Start menu and choose Settings, Control Panel, Passwords. The Passwords Properties sheet appears.
2. Click the User Profiles tab.
3. Choose Users Can Customize Their Preferences, as shown in figure 26.13.

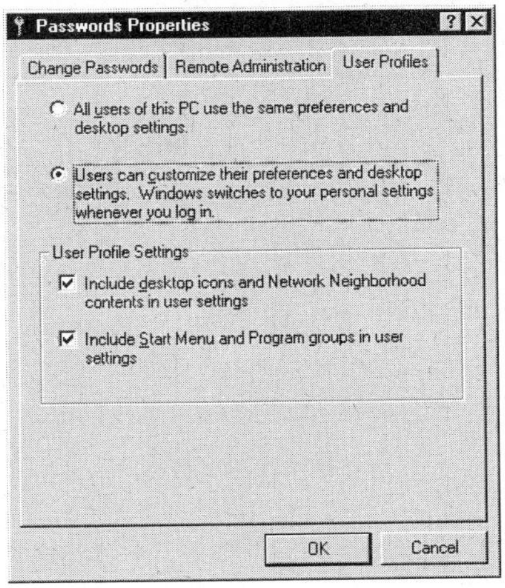

Fig. 26.13
Use the Passwords Properties sheet to enable multiple User Profiles.

4. To make your User Profiles more powerful, choose Include Desktop Icons and Include Start Menu.

5. Click the Change Passwords tab.

6. Make sure that a logon password appears in this tab. You must have a password when you begin to work with User Profiles.

Working with User Profiles

When a user logs on to a Windows 95 computer that has User Profiles enabled, the machine asks for a user name and password. The computer then creates a User Profile, using default settings.

As the user sets up network connections, desktop preferences, and all the other customizable features of the workstation, Windows 95 waits for the user to log off and shut down the machine. Then Windows saves all the settings that User Profiles can track (the settings listed in the preceding sections). Windows writes the User Profile information into the Registry, in the USER.DAT file, and saves the desktop and Start menu in the C:\WINDOWS\PROFILES folder, as shown in figure 26.14 . This figure shows profiles for five users on this computer; the hierarchy of subfolders is expanded for one of the users listed on the left side of the screen.

Tip
When you finish working at a profile-enabled computer, shut down with the Close All Programs and Log On as Different User option. This option prevents anyone from changing your profiled settings and preferences.

User Profiles on the Network

The preceding sections show how one machine can be customized for any number of users. This process is local use of User Profiles. An even more powerful type of User Profiles allows anyone to log in on any machine in the workgroup and have his or her settings restored, even if that user has never set up his or her profile at that machine before. This option requires the use of a Windows NT or NetWare server. On a Windows NT or NetWare network, you can log in from any computer on the LAN and use your customized User Profile. You can do this because your User Profile is stored on the Windows NT or NetWare file server, not on the workstation. Since the profile is stored on the Windows NT or NetWare server, it can be accessed by any workstation on the LAN.

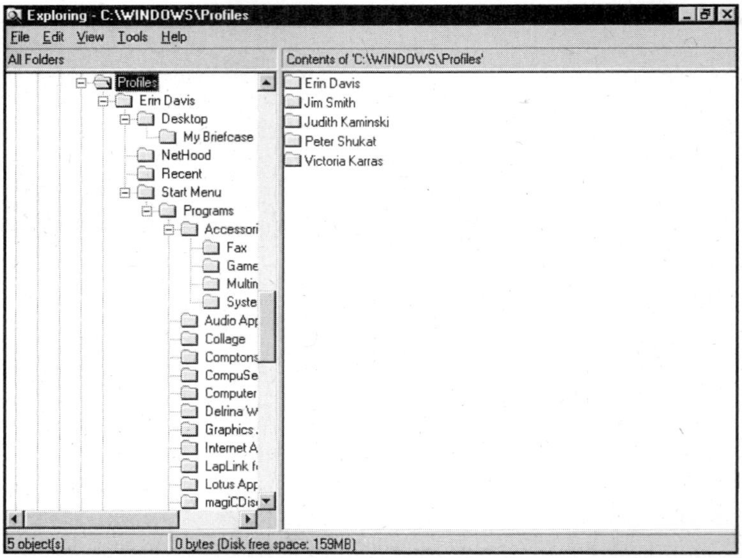

Fig. 26.14
The Windows Explorer shows five User Profiles in the right half of the screen when five users have created Profiles.

On a Windows NT server, use the User Manager tool to create a home directory for each member of the workgroup. When a user logs off his Windows 95 workstation, if User Profiles are enabled, Windows copies the profile information to the Windows NT server. When that user logs on to any other computer on the workgroup, the profile on the Windows NT server is accessed and used to set up the current workstation. (This may not work in cases when you have a shortcut to an application such as Word, and the machine you log in from does not have Word installed.)

The same system works in a NetWare environment.

Note

If the User Profile on the current workstation is newer than the copy on the server, the workstation copy is used, and the server is updated. The procedure also works in reverse, so that the user always has his most recent configuration available.

Note

If you use Microsoft Exchange on a computer that has User Profiles enabled, set Exchange to query for an Exchange profile to use at startup because User Profiles do not control Exchange profiles. (For more on Exchange, see Chapter 24, "Using Microsoft Exchange.")

System Policies and Network Management

System Policies do many of the same things as User Profiles. System Policies are not used along with User Profiles; instead, they are used in place of User Profiles. The members of a workgroup do not set System Policies, as they do their own User Profiles. In this section you will see how the System Policy Editor can change the look and feel of your Windows 95 computer. There may be Windows features that are documented in this book that are not available to you if your network administrator has disabled those features using System Policy Editor. Let's see what can happen using System Policies created by the System Policy Editor program.

Note

The System Policy Editor program, POLEDIT.EXE, is included on the CD-ROM version of Windows 95. It is not included on the floppy-disk version of the operating system.

The simplest way to understand System Policies is to know that these policies, which are created by a system administrator, are used to enforce predetermined User Profiles on a workgroup. The purpose of System Policies is to create a controlled workplace, in which access to certain features of Windows can be restricted or eliminated. System Policies may restrict a user from accessing Control Panel or from getting to a DOS prompt, for example. These policies also may prevent a user from connecting to or disconnecting from shared resources on the network.

Used wisely, System Policies can increase the stability of a Windows workgroup by preventing users who like to experiment from disrupting needed network connections and thereby crashing the system. Used unwisely, System Policies can prevent the natural growth of understanding that is essential if members of a workgroup are to learn how to use their computers to maximum benefit.

System Policies are set through a tool called System Policy Editor, which is the most powerful of the network-management tools included with Windows

95. This tool, which is designed to be used only by the network administrator, is inaccessible to users on the workgroup. The System Policy Editor should be kept in a nonshared folder on the administrator's computer.

With System Policy Editor, the administrator can set two types of policies. The first type of policy applies to individual named computers on the network. The policies created for the named computer determine the default settings that are used when a user logs on to that computer.

The second type of policy applies to individual users, determined by user name at the time of logon. If policies exist for an individual user, they are combined with the System Policies that are in effect for the computer that he or she is using.

System Policies for Individual Computers

The System Policy Editor can control the following settings on a per-computer basis:

Controlling the Network Group of Settings

- Access Control can be set to User Level. This requires the use of authentication on a Windows NT or NetWare server to access shared resources on the network.
- Logon features can display a warning at startup, saying that only authorized users should try to log on. Logon also can require validation by a Windows NT server to access Windows 95.
- Settings for Microsoft Client for NetWare can be controlled.
- Settings for Microsoft Client for Windows Networks can be controlled.
- Password settings can be modified. Use of mixed alphabetical and numeric passwords, for example, can be required, and password caching can be forced off.
- Sharing can be disabled for the computer. In this case, no resources can be declared shared, and all shared information tabs disappear from Properties sheets.
- Remote updating can be enabled.

Controlling the System Group of Settings

- The administrator can enable User Profiles.
- The network path to a shared copy of Windows Setup and Windows Tour can be specified.

- Items to be run at startup can be specified.

System Policies for Individual Users

This area is where System Policy Editor can really show its power. Many options for individual users exist. For users, System Policy Editor works on five groups of settings.

Controlling the Control Panel Group of Settings

- The administrator can restrict the appearance of the Network, Display, Password, Printer, and System icons in the Control Panel.

Controlling the Desktop Group of Settings

- The wallpaper and color scheme can be controlled.

Network Settings

- File and print sharing can be turned off for the user.

Controlling the Shell Group of Settings

- Custom Folder Functions can be disabled.
- Custom Programs Folders can be disallowed.
- Custom Desktop Icons can be disallowed.
- Start Menu Subfolders can be hidden.
- Custom Startup Folders can be disallowed.
- Custom Network Neighborhood can be disallowed.
- Custom Start Menu can be disallowed.
- The Run command can be removed from the Start menu.
- Folders and settings can be hidden so they won't show in the taskbar.
- The Find command can be disabled from the Start menu.
- The display of drives in My Computer can be hidden.
- Network Neighborhood can be hidden.
- Hide All items on the Desktop can be hidden.
- The Shut Down command can be disallowed.

- Windows' automatic saving of settings at shutdown can be disallowed.

Controlling the System Group of Settings

- Registry editing can be disallowed.
- The administrator can set up a list of allowed Windows applications and only the allowed applications can be run.
- The MS-DOS prompt can be disabled.
- MS-DOS mode can be disabled.

Figure 26.15 shows what the user would see if the administrator chose to restrict part of the System icon in Control Panel. The File System and Virtual Memory buttons in the System Properties sheet are missing; the Device Manager and Hardware Profiles tabs are missing, too.

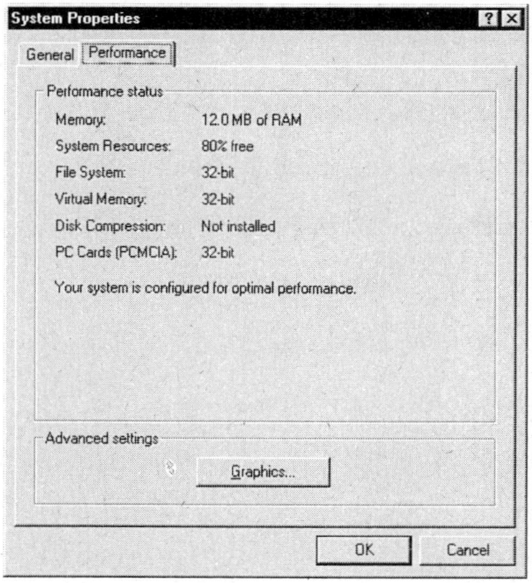

Fig. 26.15
System Policy Editor has removed features from the System Properties sheet in Control Panel.

Figure 26.16 shows the System Properties sheet before restrictions were applied by System Policy Editor.

> **Caution**
>
> System Policy Editor can be unpredictable. If the administrator selects a function and then deselects it, the function may not return to the state that it was in before editing. As a result, user settings can be destroyed without warning. The workaround is to tell your administrator to leave the setting neither selected nor deselected, but dimmed. Dimmed is an option when you edit a policy file.

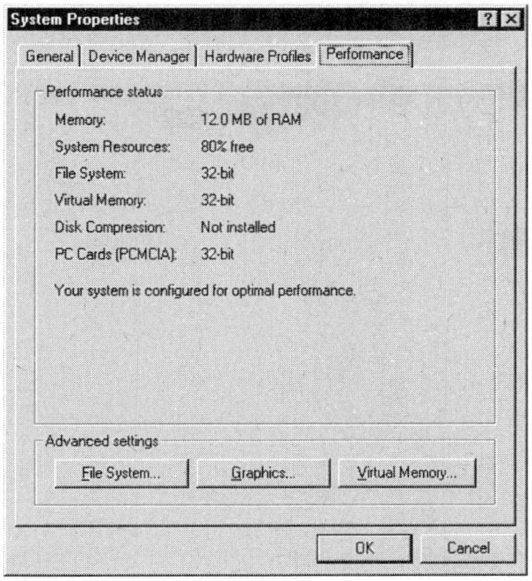

Fig. 26.16
The System Properties sheet in Control Panel looks like this before System Policy Editor removed features.

WinPopup

WinPopup is an applet that is included in the Accessories group when you install the network component of Windows 95. This tool normally is used to send short messages from one computer on the workgroup to another. WinPopup is designed so that when a message is received, the message pops up over anything else on-screen.

The real usefulness of the WinPopup program is that it automatically sends messages from a network printer when a print job finishes. WinPopup sends the message only to the computer that sent the print job for processing.

Figure 26.17 shows the simple network-management function of print-job-finished notification.

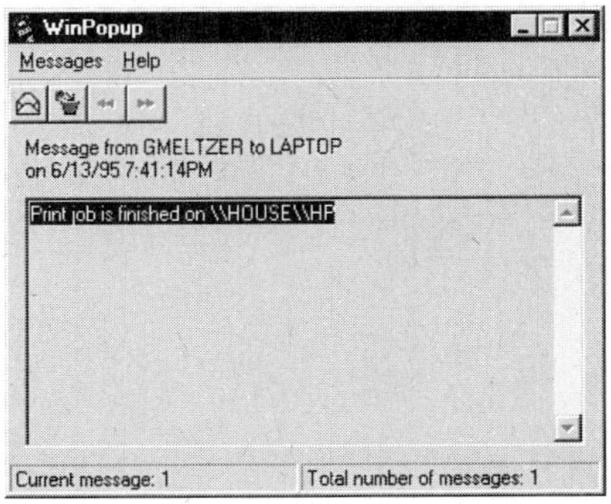

Fig. 26.17
WinPopup has sent a message to a user that her network print job is finished.

Network Security

Security on computer networks is designed to prevent unauthorized or accidental access to the information located on the disk drives on the network. Security can extend to preventing unauthorized users from using any network resource, such as a printer. Security systems also are intended to prevent unauthorized users from using computers on the network.

Windows 95 provides a wide range of network-security options. Some of the most powerful security tools, however, are not available for a workgroup network that consists of computers that run only Windows 95. These functions require that a Windows NT or Novell NetWare server be connected to the network and programmed in a special way to enable Windows 95's advanced security functions.

The following sections examine the security tools that you can use in both environments.

All-Windows 95 Workgroup Network

In an all-Windows 95 workgroup, three types of security are available:

- Logon security
- Share-level password security
- System Policies security

Next, you will learn to use each of these security methods on your workgroup LAN. Whether you use one, two, or all of these techniques, the bottom line is that using security will prevent data loss.

Logon Security

Although Windows 95 requires a logon password, you need to understand that the only things protected by this password are network resources, such as shared folders and shared printers. Windows 95 provides absolutely no password protection at the workstation level; anyone can sit down at your computer and access your local disks and attached resources.

If you need to control access to individual computers, so that only a user with the right password can start the operating system, you should consider using Windows NT, not Windows 95, on individual workstation computers. Windows NT requires a password before any user can work with the computer at all.

When Windows 95 starts, you see a screen that asks for your user ID and password. No matter what you do at this point, including clicking Cancel,

Windows continues to load and to give you access to all the drives and printers on your computer.

Now that you understand that no logon security exists for the workstation in Windows 95, consider logon security for the network.

Windows Logon Password

When Windows 95 starts for the first time, a logon dialog box asks for your user ID and password. Depending on your settings in Control Panel, Network, you will be prompted to log on to Windows 95 or the network. If your Network setting sets your Primary Network Logon as Client for Microsoft Networks, your logon screen looks like the one shown in figure 26.18.

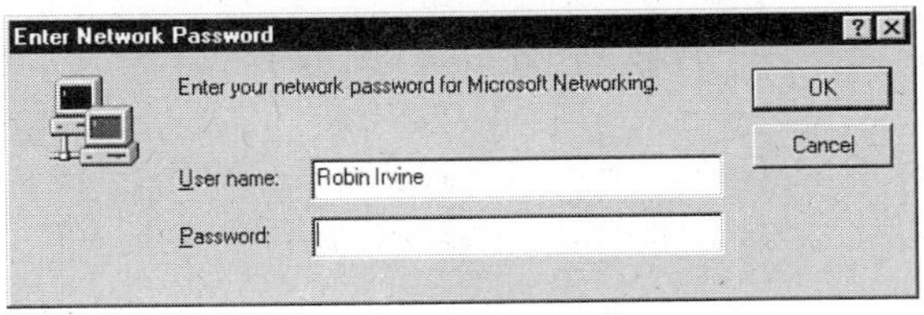

Fig. 26.18
This will be your logon screen, if your Primary Network Logon is set to be Client for Microsoft Networks.

If you set your Primary Network Logon to be Windows Logon, you see a logon prompt like the one shown in figure 26.19.

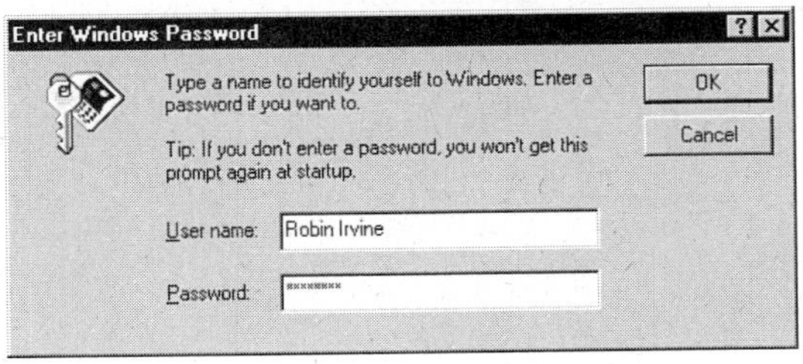

Fig. 26.19
The first time you run Windows 95 on your computer, you'll see this dialog box.

When you type the correct password for network access, you have access to all the shared resources on the network, as long as you know the password required to access them. In fact, you won't have to enter the passwords for network resources more than once; Windows stores the passwords that you enter in a cache so that they are entered for you automatically the next time you log on. Although the cache can be disabled by System Policies and by the Password List Editor program, in a normal installation, the password cache is active.

► See "Removing Cached Passwords," p. 824

This chapter has mentioned passwords in connection with shared resources. The following sections examine the way that passwords work.

Access Control in Workgroups: Share-Level-Access Control

In Chapter 20, you learned how to enable peer-to-peer resource sharing on a Windows 95 workgroup. In this section, you set some passwords for those resources so that only authorized users can find them over the network.

Figure 26.20 shows two types of shared resources.

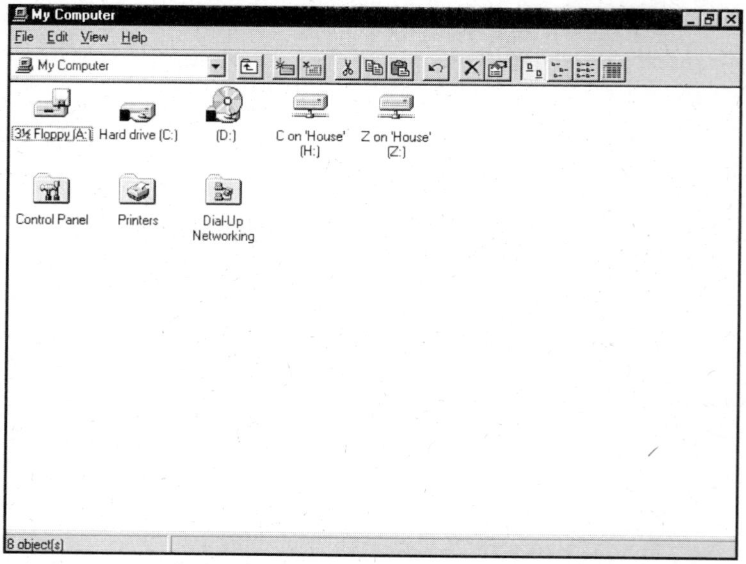

Fig. 26.20
There are two resources shared in this view of My Computer.

Notice that the icon for the local hard drive—drive C—is shared; the icon includes the outstretched hand that signifies sharing. The hand does not mean that the disk is completely open to any user, however. To control how you will share your drive, right-click the icon and choose Sharing from the pop-up menu.

Figure 26.21 shows the sharing properties that are enabled for the local hard drive. Two passwords are set. You want to give full read and write access to users who know the full-access password. Other users will be able only read the disk, not modify it in any way.

This type of security is called *share-level access*, and it is the only kind of access protection available to workgroups in which Windows 95 (or Windows for Workgroups 3.1x) peer server is the only type of server on the network. To see how this access control is enabled, open the Start menu and choose Settings, Control Panel, Network; click the Access Control tab, and select the Share Level access-control option. The other option is not available for peer-to-peer networks.

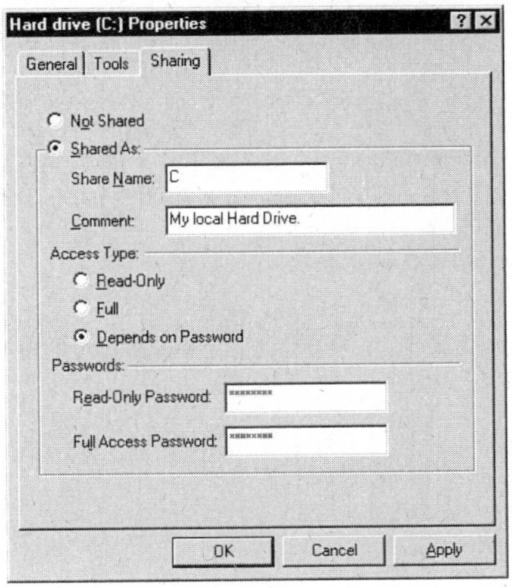

Fig. 26.21
The Hard Drive Properties sheet controls password access to the drive.

Share-Level Access and Network Neighborhood

If you enable sharing on a disk, folder, or printer on your computer, the shared resource appears in Network Neighborhood, from which users may try to connect to your resource or to map a drive letter to it.

At times, you want to share a resource but not broadcast that fact to the workgroup. A mechanism for hiding shared resources exists. To do this, add a dollar-sign character to the end of the share name. The resource still behaves in accordance with its password restrictions, but it does not appear in Network Neighborhood. Another member of the workgroup must know the exact name of the resource to connect to it.

Mapped Drives and Their Security

Figure 26.20, earlier in this chapter, showed two types of shared resources in the My Computer window. This section examines the properties of the resources whose icons look like disks attached to cables. These resources are shared drives and folders on other computers. The owners of those resources may have enabled share-level-security passwords for those resources. That security determines what you can do with the folders—whether you can write to them as well as read from them.

If the owner of a shared folder changes the password required to access that resource, your cached password no longer gives you access to the resource. You see a network drive icon with an X through the connection, like the one shown for the Z on 'House' connection in figure 26.22.

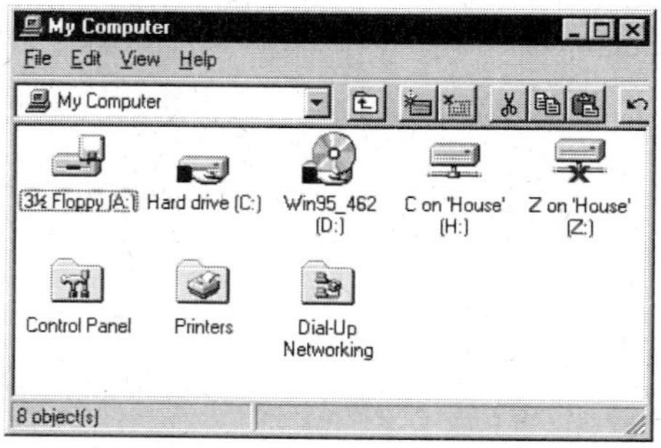

Fig. 26.22
An inaccessible network drive is shown with an X through its icon.

To access the resource again, learn the new access password. Then, when you want to access the shared drive again, you will have to restart Windows.

Removing Cached Passwords

Because password caching is enabled in Windows 95 automatically, the system creates an encrypted file, in which it stores the password entries for all resources used by the computer. By default, the file name is SHARE.PWL. If User Profiles are enabled on the computer, the PWL files are not called SHARE but are created from the user names. When User Profiles are active, each user has a different PWL password-list file, such as TOM.PWL.

If you are having trouble with a cached password, use the Password List Editor program, PWLEDIT.EXE. This program does not show you the actual passwords; it shows you that a password exists and gives you the opportunity to remove the password. This procedure forces you to log in with the correct password the next time you want to connect to the resource that you edited.

Note

The Password List Editor program, PWLEDIT.EXE, is included on the CD-ROM version of Windows 95. It is not included on the floppy disk version of the operating system.

Figure 26.23 shows a Password List Editor screen. Password List Editor shows every password in effect on the computer on which its running. In figure 26.23, there is only one password in effect. Although the display is not very informative, the text "Rna" shown in the Resource column is a hint that the password is for dial-up networking. Rna, in Windows jargon, means Remote node access.

The only option is to remove the password.

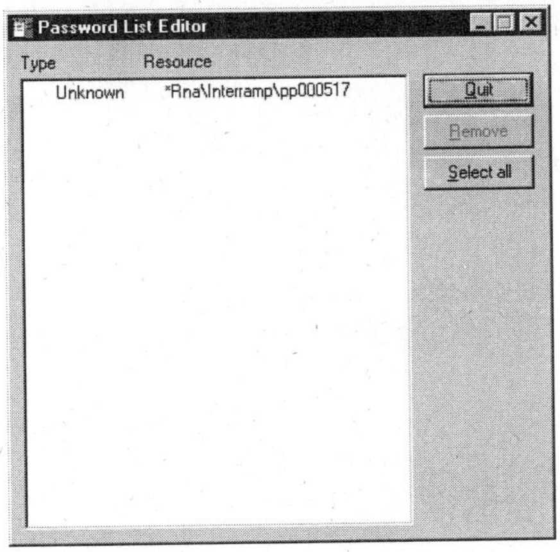

Fig. 26.23
The Password List Editor program can remove passwords from any type of password protected resource on your computer.

Using Windows 95 with a Microsoft Windows NT or Novell NetWare Server

If your network includes a Windows NT or NetWare server, your options for workgroup security are greatly enhanced. You can use the features of those servers to provide and enforce user-level security on the workgroup. In this case, the Windows NT or NetWare server is acting as a security provider and validator. This function works because those two network systems maintain lists of authorized users and those users' network rights and access privileges. This function does not exist in Windows 95 Peer-to-Peer networks.

Table 26.1 compares the features available in user- and share-level-access control.

Table 26.1 Access-Control Comparison

Feature	User-Level	Share-Level
Read Files	×	×
Write to Files	×	×
Create Files and Folders	×	
List Files	×	
Delete Files	×	
Change File Attributes	×	
Change Access Control	×	

You can see that user-level security gives you much finer control of shared resources because you can enable any, all, or none of the preceding sets of rights. If you enable only List Files, for example, users who connect to the folder can execute programs from the folder, but they cannot delete or change anything.

User Lists in User-Level Security

In a Windows NT environment, the administrator uses the User Manager program to set up the security permissions for each user name. Windows 95 uses these permissions to set access rights for the listed resources. A Windows NT administrator also can create groups, simplifying workgroup administration by granting the same rights to several users or perhaps an entire workgroup.

The only thing to remember is that in the case of multiple Windows NT domains, the Windows 95 computer must select one domain server to be the security and list provider.

In NetWare, the same list principles apply. Instead of using User Manager, however, NetWare relies on the Bindery feature. As a result, NetWare 4.x servers must be running Bindery emulation to act as security hosts for Windows 95 computers.

General Network-Security Guidelines

As you've seen by now, network security in a Windows 95 workgroup LAN must be configured, cooperatively, by the network neighbors who are connected to the LAN. To avoid loss of your workgroup's valuable data, accidentally or otherwise, consider the following four guiding principles:

- Although setting up a completely open, password-free network is easy, resist the temptation. Even though you may not have to enter passwords with password caching enabled, require the passwords; they will increase your options later.
- If you can make access to a shared resource read-only, do so. Use full read-write access only when you have to. This practice can prevent accidental deletion of important files and directories.
- Make sure that you and your network neighbors keep their passwords guarded—and not written in plain sight on or near the computer.
- Don't use an obvious item, such as your name, as your Windows password.

Troubleshooting and Network-Management Tools

If you're having problems accessing resources that you can see in Network Neighborhood, check to see whether you have the rights that you need to do your work. Windows provides an easy way to use Net Watcher for this purpose. In Network Neighborhood, right-click the computer that holds the resources that you need, choose Properties, and then click the Tools tab. Figure 26.24 shows the list of management tools that are available.

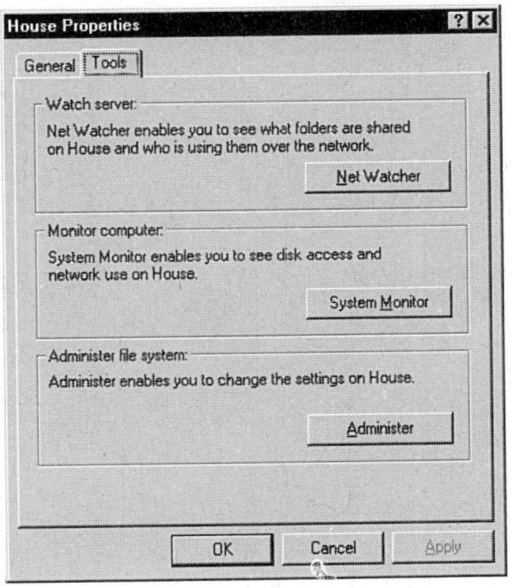

Fig. 26.24
Windows 95 provides Net Watcher, System Monitor, and Administer tools for network management.

From this point, you can select Net Watcher and use it to see whether the folder that you want to use is shared. If not, you can designate the folder as shared. If the problem is that the folder is read-only and you need full access, use Net Watcher to adjust that situation, too.

Using Dial-Up Networking

Just as you can connect to shared resources on a network using a network interface card and network wiring, you can connect to the same kind of resources using a modem and telephone wires. This type of networking is called Dial-Up Networking. Dial-Up Networking is discussed in Chapter 9, "Special Features for Notebook Users," as this feature will be of most interest to laptop and notebook PC users. However, if you want to configure dial-up networking to work on your desktop computer, all of the procedures are the same.❖

Part VI

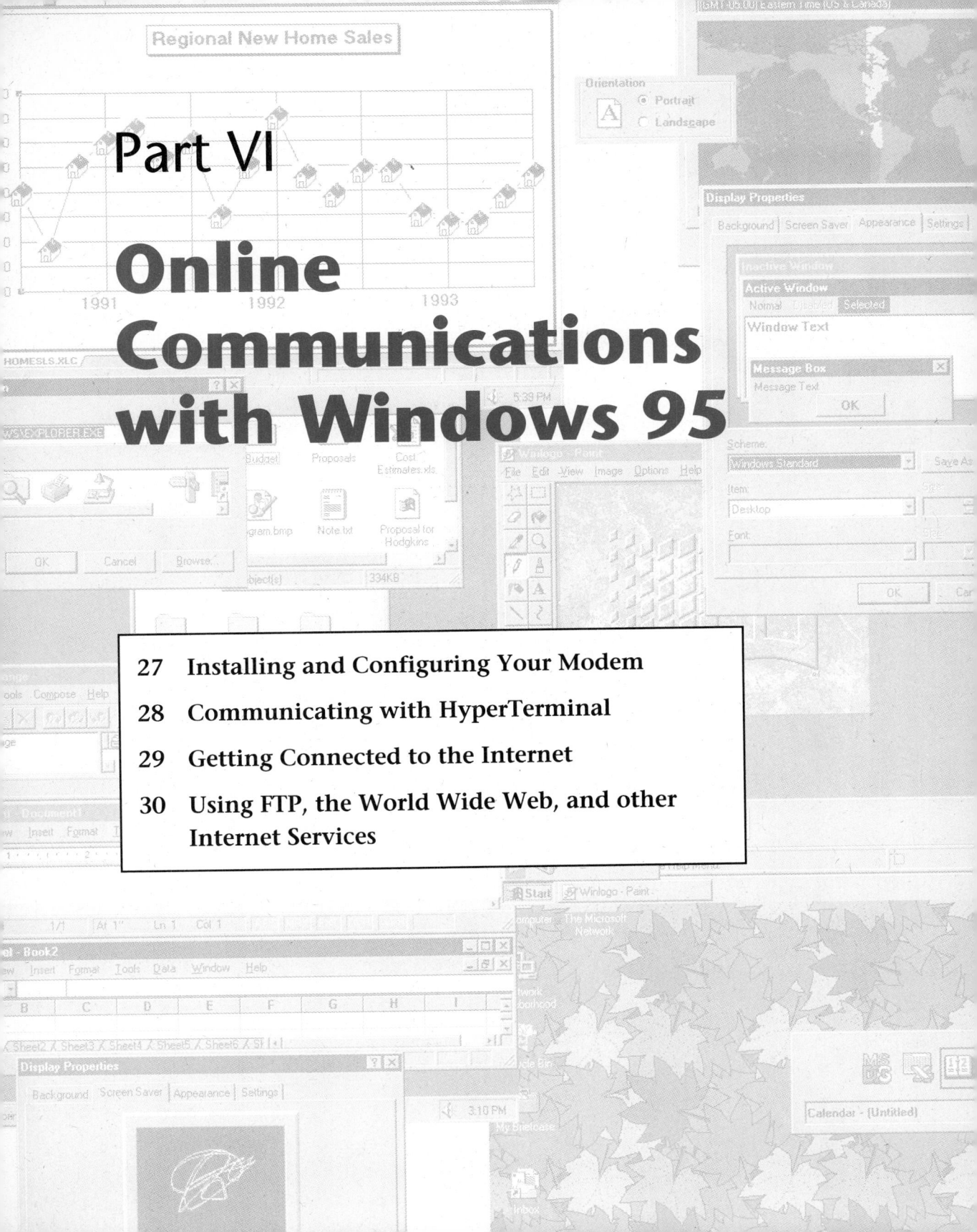

Online Communications with Windows 95

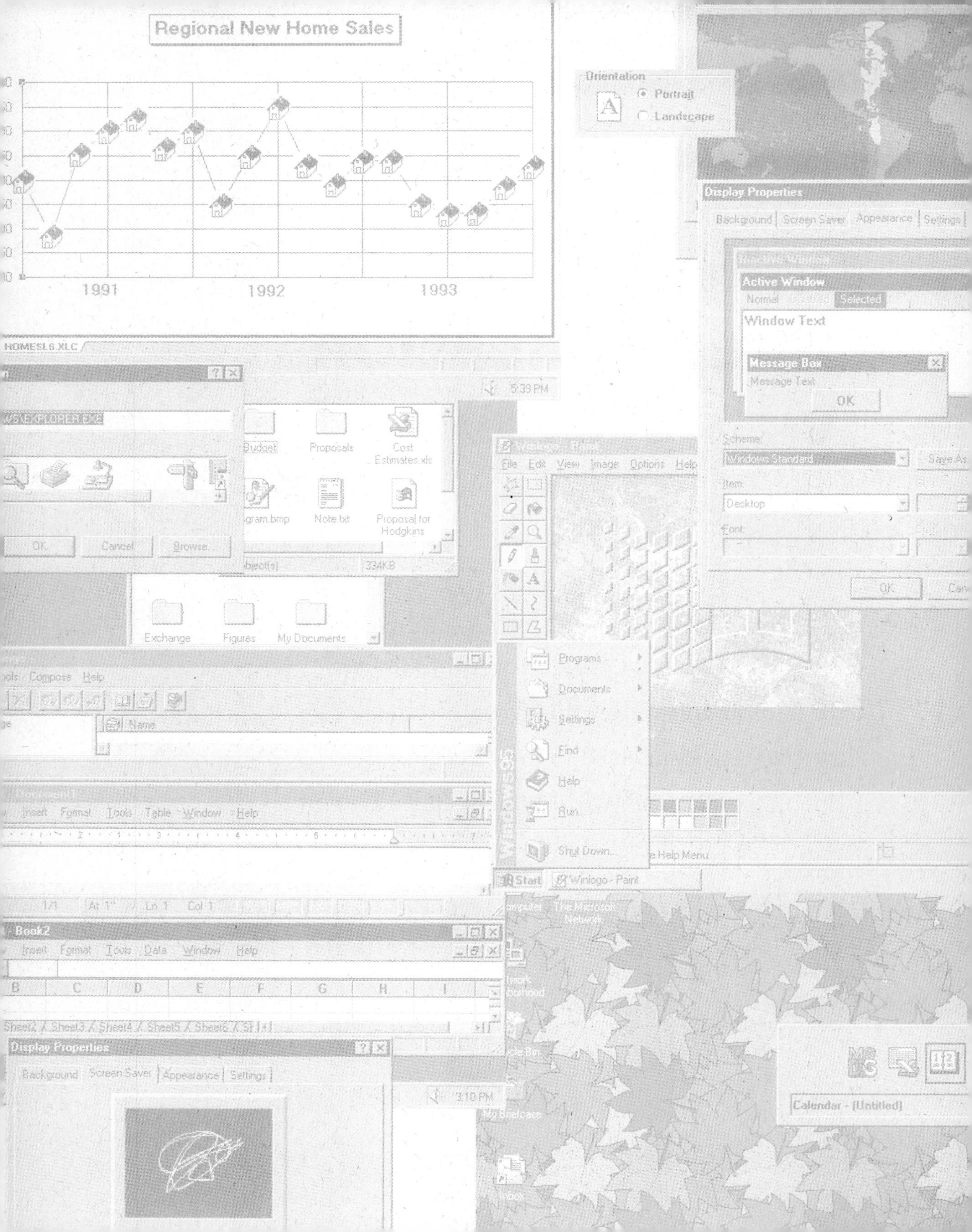
Regional New Home Sales
1991
1992
1993
HOMESLS.XLC
Orientation
Portrait
Landscape
Display Properties
Background
Screen Saver
Appearance
Settings
Inactive Window
Active Window
Normal
Disabled
Selected
Window Text
Message Box
Message Text
OK
Scheme:
Windows Standard
Save As
Item:
Desktop
Font:
OK
5:39 PM
OK
Cancel
Browse...
Budget
Proposals
Cost Estimates.xls
Note.txt
Proposal for Hodgkins
334KB
Exchange
Figures
My Documents
Winlogo - Paint
File
Edit
View
Image
Options
Help
Programs
Documents
Settings
Find
Help
Run...
Shut Down...
Windows95
Start
Winlogo - Paint
Compose
Help
Name
Document1
Insert
Format
Tools
Table
Window
Help
At 1"
Ln 1
Col 1
Book2
Insert
Format
Tools
Data
Window
Help
B
C
D
E
F
G
H
I
Sheet2 / Sheet3 / Sheet4 / Sheet5 / Sheet6
The Microsoft Network
My Briefcase
Inbox
Display Properties
Background
Screen Saver
Appearance
Settings
3:10 PM
Calendar - [Untitled]

Chapter 27

Installing and Configuring Your Modem

by Gordon Meltzer

Modems and the technology that they use—serial communications—have been a problem for Windows since Version 1.0. In Windows 95, however, Microsoft finally got it right—and then some. The operating system now incorporates a rich, reliable, full-featured communications subsystem that is capable of operating today's fastest modems. Even better, Windows 95 is an extensible system that works well with tomorrow's communications devices, such as ISDN adapters, parallel-port modems, and cable modems. These forthcoming devices work at speeds beyond even the fastest of today's modems. Windows 95 can handle all these devices, and more, at the same time.

In this chapter, you learn

- How Windows' communications system works for you
- How to install your Plug and Play modem or legacy modem
- About the Universal Standard Modem Driver and other drivers
- How to configure your modem after it's installed
- Why your modem works smarter with the new 32-bit programs
- More about TAPI

Understanding the Windows 95 Communications System

In the past, getting good performance from modems running with Windows often meant changing the part of Windows that controlled all the serial ports and, therefore, controlled the modems. Various companies supplied these *enhanced communications drivers*, which were sold with high-speed modems, by themselves, or with communications programs. (Often, you couldn't get the modem working without a special driver.) Although literally thousands of enhanced communications drivers were available, all of them took over all the modems and serial communications in Windows.

Windows 95 doesn't need these aftermarket parts to make communications fly. The sophisticated communications subsystem in Windows 95 is designed to automatically recognize, install, and configure modems if they are compatible with the Plug and Play standard.

Tip
When you hear the expression PCMCIA Card, know it is an obsolete way to refer to a PC Card, the credit card size Plug and Play devices we use as modems, network adapters, and more.

Most Plug and Play modems are located on *PC Cards* (formerly known as PCMCIA cards). These cards can support full Plug-and-Play functionality, including hot swapping.

Note

Hot swapping lets PC Cards be removed or inserted while the system is running. The system will load and unload any required software automatically on the fly.

Some Plug and Play modems may be on ISA cards; these cannot benefit from hot swapping, because they are designed to be fixed inside the computer and not removed during operation.

◄ See "Understanding Plug and Play Architecture," p. 230

◄ See "Using PC Card Devices," p. 266

Note

ISA stands for Industry Standard Architecture, and ISA cards are the familiar add-in peripheral cards that have been used in PC's since IBM set the standard.

Windows also has special capabilities for 32-bit communications programs far beyond the capabilities of its predecessor. You learn more about TAPI (Telephony Applications Programming Interface) capabilities in the section "Working Smarter with TAPI and 32-Bit Windows Programs," later in this chapter.

Even if you have a standard modem that does not support Plug and Play, a Windows Wizard can help you install and configure the modem.

Whichever type of modem you choose to install, Windows can use it to communicate more reliably and with better data throughput than ever before. The three reasons for this are:

- New 32-bit TAPI communications system for 32-bit applications
- Improved 16-bit communications driver for older 16-bit programs
- Support for the new 16550-compatible UART (Universal Asynchronous Receiver Transmitter) chips found in new modems and modern serial ports

Windows uses these features to give you more control over communications with your modem, and to make your modem do a better job for you.

Tip

Make sure any internal ISA card modem you buy includes the modern 16550 type of UART chip. All PC Card modems already do. If you're buying a serial port card to put in an ISA slot, check to make sure you're buying one with the 16550 chip, or a compatible chip.

Installing a Plug and Play Modem

Like other devices that support this new technology, Plug and Play modems communicate with Windows to cooperate in setting themselves up. These modems always contain the serial communications port and modulator/demodulator/dialer on the same card, so that Windows can configure them to work together at the same time.

Note

Internal modems consist of three main functional sections. The Serial Communications Port handles communications with your computer. The Modulator/Demodulator handles communications over the phone lines with another modem. The Dialer handles communications with the telephone network and gets your call connected.

External modems don't contain the Serial Communications Port; they attach to one that is built in to your computer.

Plug and Play modems add another section which identifies the modem's capabilities and resource needs to Windows 95 setup.

▶ See "Understanding Windows 95 Setup Requirements," p. 1078

During Windows setup, information is exchanged between your modem and the system. This is what happens, automatically, when Windows comes to the part of setup in which your modem will be configured:

▶ See "How Windows 95 Setup Works," p. 1083

1. Windows searches through all the system's input-output (I/O) ports and finds the Plug and Play circuits on the modem.

2. The system assigns the card an identification number, which Windows stores in its information files.

3. Windows asks the modem about its speeds and specifications. The modem gives the information to Windows setup.

4. Setup then assigns a communications port number (COM1, COM2, and so on) and resources to be used by the port. These resources are an interrupt request and an I/O address. If the Plug and Play modem is on a PC Card, Windows also assigns a memory address to the modem.

Plug and Play—the Play-by-Play

If a Plug and Play modem is installed in your computer before you install Windows, the modem setup occurs automatically and transparently. This section examines what happens if you have a PC Card modem installed in PC Card slot 1 when you install Windows 95.

First, Windows configures the PC Card slots. The PC Card Wizard appears during installation. Figure 27.1 shows the wizard screen.

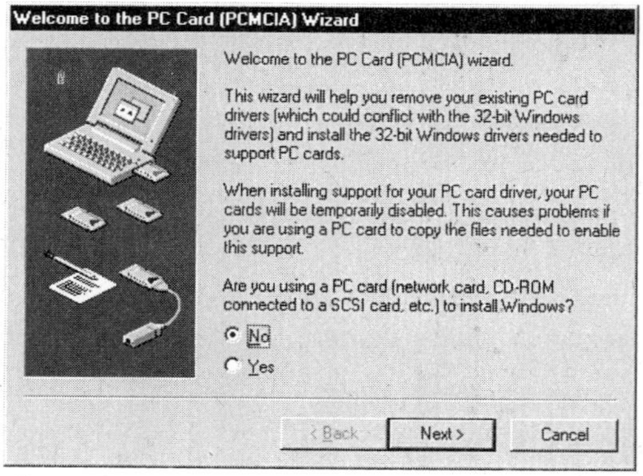

Fig. 27.1
The PC Card Wizard begins installing your PC Card modem.

> **Caution**
>
> Notice in figure 27.1 the wizard warns you that it is about to disable all PC Cards while it works. If you're installing Windows from a CD-ROM connected through a PC Card, setup will fail. For a workaround, use floppy disks for this portion of setup.

Next, Windows proposes removing the old DOS-based 16-bit Card and Socket Services drivers from the CONFIG.SYS, AUTOEXEC.BAT, and SYSTEM.INI files. To review the changes before proceeding, choose Yes and then click Next.

Figure 27.2 shows the real-mode 16-bit drivers in CONFIG.SYS. They are the last five lines in the file. For best results, you should permit the Wizard to remove the old drivers. Click Next to accept the changes. After the Wizard processes CONFIG.SYS, it processes the next two files in the same way.

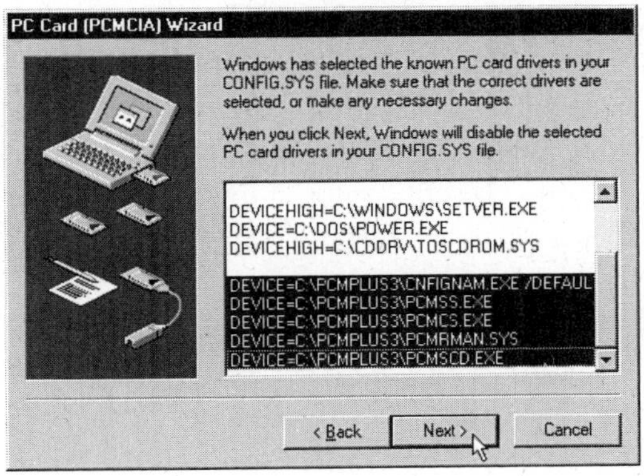

Fig. 27.2
Real mode drivers in CONFIG.SYS that will be removed by Windows 95.

> **Note**
>
> Technically speaking, the statements are not actually removed from the file. Instead, the wizard *comments out* (switches off) the statements by inserting a `REM-Removed By PC Card Wizard` statement at the beginning of each line in which the drivers are referenced.

When the wizard finishes setting up the PC Card slots, it installs the 32-bit protected mode Card and Socket Services driver software for them. These drivers control all the Plug and Play features.

After the drivers are installed, you need to restart Windows to activate the new drivers. Click Finish in the wizard dialog box, close any other applications that you may have running, and click Yes when you're ready to shut down.

Windows loads with the 32-bit drivers enabled for the first time. Now it can "see" (and, therefore, configure) the modem in your PC Card slot. Using the new, protected-mode 32-bit Card and Socket Services, Windows can install any modem in your PC Card slot. In figure 27.3, Windows detected a new modem and installed the software drivers for it automatically.

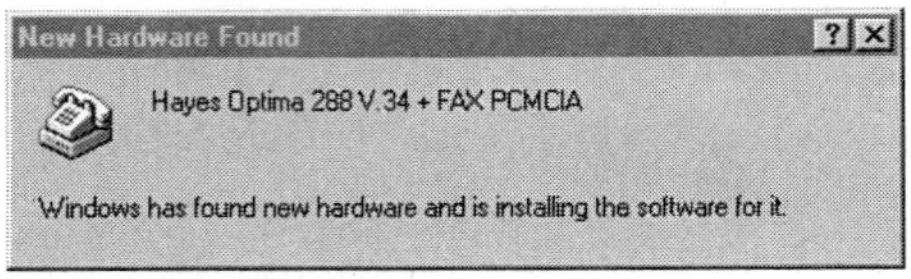

Fig. 27.3
Windows setup finds your modem.

Your Plug and Play modem is now installed. Next, the modem must be configured to allow all Windows advanced features to operate, which is discussed in the "Advanced Settings" section later in this chapter. The following section explains what Windows really did, via the wizard.

Plug and Play—Behind the Scenes

The Windows user interface for the installation of the Plug and Play modem is the Setup Wizard. The wizard does all the setup work, and a lot happens behind the scene.

What has actually happened during the Plug and Play modem installation is this:

1. Windows asks the modem to identify itself , the modem responds, and Windows installs the software to run the modem. Then, the wizard tells you its job is complete and your modem is installed.

2. Windows installs the Unimodem driver for any modems that support AT (Attention) commands. Most modems do. Windows then looks in its database of .INF files. If information is found on the specific modem, it installs the modem mini-driver.

Note

Windows will assign the IBM-compatible standard communications port names to ports and modems. The names will be assigned in order, using the standard resources:

Port Name	I/O Port Resource
Com1	3F8
Com2	2F8
Com3	3E8
Com4	2E8

Caution

If Windows finds a modem configured to a base address that is not listed in the table above, it will assign COM5 to that modem. Programs designed for Windows 3.1 or DOS may not be able to work with a modem on this port. The workaround is to change the non-standard address in Device Manager control panel.

► See "Using Custom Setup Mode," p. 1099

Troubleshooting

I can't get the modem to install.

First, check Device Manager to see whether the hardware Communications Port exists and is working properly. If the Port doesn't exist in Device Manager's list of Ports, follow the steps in the section "Installing a Legacy Modem" later in this chapter to install the Communications Port.

Turn your external modem off and then on again. If you are using an internal modem, shut down Windows, power down the computer, and try again.

Installing a Legacy Modem

Legacy modems don't have the hardware in them to identify themselves to Windows 95 setup—they can't tell Windows about their capabilities, or their resource requirements.

◄ See "Dealing with Legacy Hardware," p. 247

Legacy modems are not Plug and Play devices. They can, however, be either internal or external modems.

An *internal modem* is one that fits into a slot in the computer bus, and contains the serial port on the modem.

An *external modem* does not contain the serial port. The external modem connects via cable to the serial port inside the computer.

Windows considers the serial port to be a separate device from the modem, even if you have an internal modem, in which both the modem and the serial port are on the same add-in card. Windows configures these devices separately. You should be aware of the process that Windows uses to perform the configurations.

If you're trying to install an internal modem, Windows may act differently with different modems. You may be able to install the serial port at the same time you install the modem. If Windows cannot detect and initialize the port, however, you may have to use the Add New Hardware option in the Control Panel to set up the port.

► See "Advanced Installation Techniques," p. 1098

In Windows 95, you can accomplish a task in several ways. You can install a legacy modem in any of the following ways:

- Use the Add New Hardware Wizard.

- Click the Modem icon, in Control Panel.
- Start a 32-bit program that uses a modem. If no modem is installed, Windows suggests you install one.

The following procedure uses the Add New Hardware Wizard to install the modem. Follow these steps:

1. Open the Start menu and choose Settings, Control Panel.

2. Double-click the Add New Hardware icon. The first Add New Hardware Wizard window appears.
3. Click Next.
4. You should allow Windows to try to find your modem by itself, so choose Yes when the wizard asks if you want Windows to detect it automatically. You'll see a progress report during the detection process.

   If Windows can, it sets up the serial port and the modem at the same time. Windows may not find the modem when it finds the port. In that case, run Add New Hardware Wizard again.

   The report from the Add New Hardware Wizard, shown in figure 27.4, shows that Windows has found a new Communications Port.

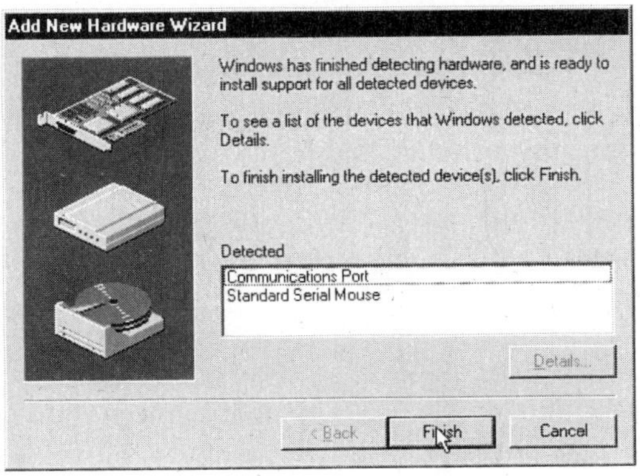

Fig. 27.4
This report from the Add New Hardware Wizard shows two new devices detected.

5. Click Finish.

6. When you are prompted, restart the computer.

After Windows restarts, look in Control Panel's Device Manager (accessed by clicking the System icon in Control Panel). In the Ports section, you'll see a new Communications Port, COM1, has been added, shown in figure 27.5.

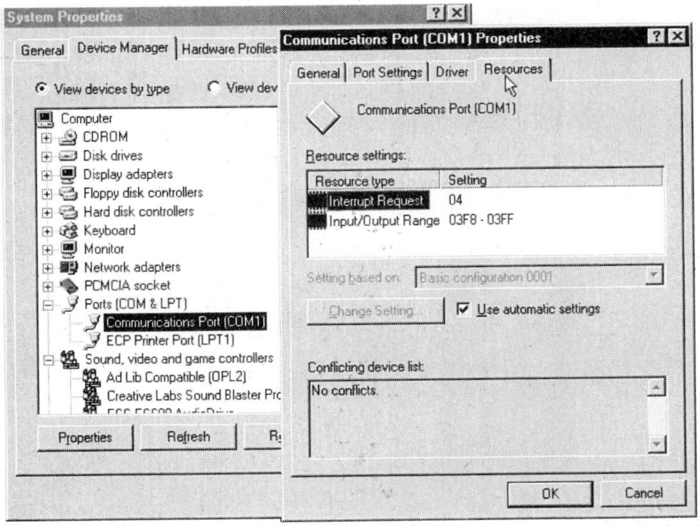

Fig. 27.5
The new Communications Port and its resources.

Note

Many times Windows will not find the port and the modem on the same pass through the installation process. Don't be concerned; follow the next steps.

In this common example, Windows could not detect and install the port and modem in one step. Therefore, you need to visit the Control Panel again. Now that COM1 is working properly, Windows should be able to detect and install the modem connected to that port.

Double-click the Modems icon in the Control Panel. When the Install New Modem Wizard starts, choose Other (see fig. 27.6).

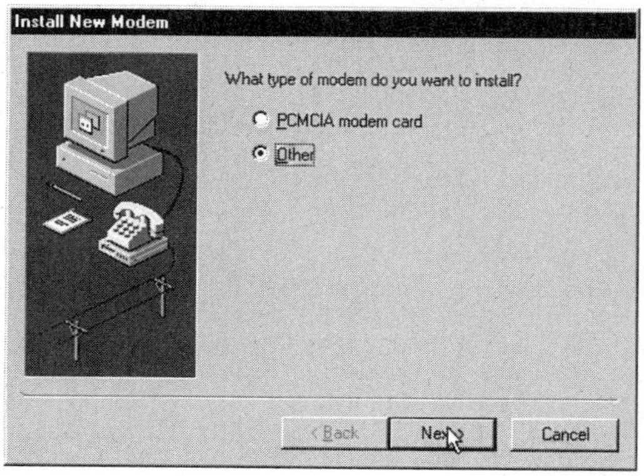

Fig. 27.6
Installing a non Plug and Play modem

In the next dialog box, the wizard asks for another chance to detect the modem. Click Next, and don't tell the wizard what modem you have; you want to see whether Windows can find out now that the port is working. Figure 27.7 shows the window that appears just before automatic modem detection.

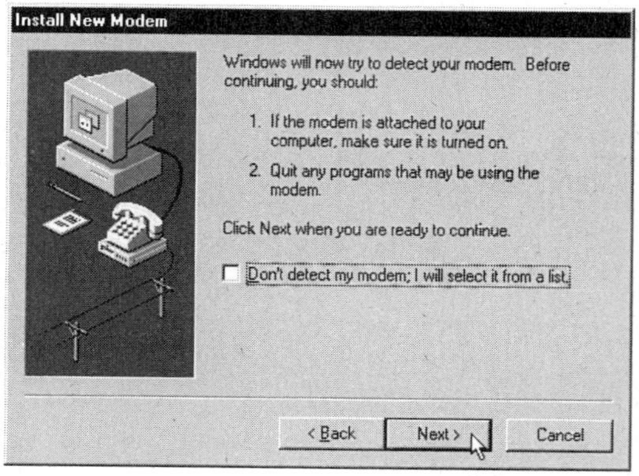

Fig. 27.7
The Modem Installation Wizard set to auto-detect your modem.

At the end of the modem installation process, Windows reports that it found the modem attached to COM1 (see fig. 27.8). Because the reported type matches the type that is installed, you have finished the installation of the standard legacy modem. To close the dialog box, click Next.

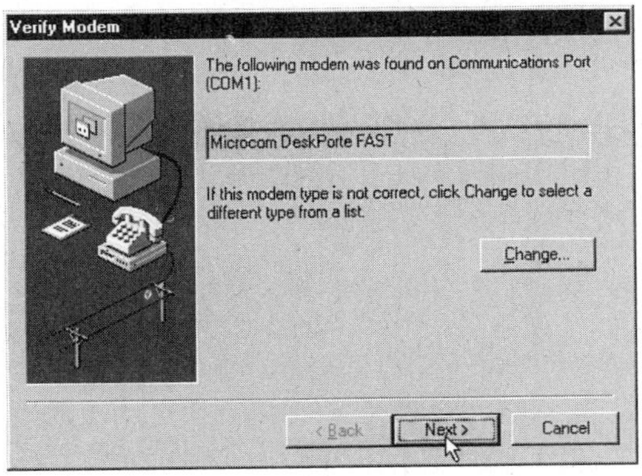

Fig. 27.8
The Modem Wizard has detected the new modem.

Note

Windows chooses slow port speeds by default. If you have a fast computer, change the port speeds in the Modems Properties Control Panel to the modem's maximum speed.

Troubleshooting

When I use the modem, another program—or the entire system—locks up or crashes. How do I fix it?

This problem usually results from an interrupt conflict. Two devices may be trying to use the same interrupt. If you have a serial mouse on COM1, which uses Interrupt 4, and you set up a modem on COM3, which by default also uses Interrupt 4, a conflict will exist.

Use Device Manager on the System Properties sheet (Control Panel, System) to look for a modem or mouse icon that has a yellow exclamation point. Double-click the icon and choose Resources. If a conflict is listed, Windows offers to start the Hardware Conflict Troubleshooter. This program can help you resolve interrupt conflicts by reassigning resources such as interrupts.

Understanding the Unimodem Driver

When Windows 3.1 came on the market, one of its major advances was its capability to use installed printers with any Windows printer. Before Windows, each and every program that wanted to print had to have its own printer driver included. In Windows 3.1, if there was a Windows driver, all programs could print without drivers of their own. The problem—and the burden for programmers—was that for each printer type, a driver had to be written from scratch. Supporting the thousands of printer types on the market was difficult.

During Windows evolution, the idea of a universal driver was developed. In Windows 95, this driver is implemented beautifully.

In Windows 95, the same concept also has been extended to modems.

Most of the modems on the market use a variation of the AT command set, which Dennis Hayes developed for the original Smartmodem in 1980. The command set has evolved over the years, and each manufacturer has its own set of proprietary extensions for advanced features. Still, the most basic commands are the same for all modems that use AT commands. The fact that this lowest common denominator of commands exists for the vast majority of modems allowed Microsoft to write a universal modem driver—the Unimodem driver.

Table 27.1 shows the basic AT commands used by the Unimodem driver.

Table 27.1 Modem Commands for Unimodem Driver

AT Command	Function
AT	Attention
ATZ	Reset modem
ATD	Dial modem
ATI	Identify modem
ATH	Hang up modem
ATO	Go off hook in originate mode

Once the Unimodem driver is talking to the modem, these commands provide enough functionality for the Unidriver to interrogate the modem, find its manufacturer and model number, and try to find a match in its modem database. If a match is found, the Unidriver tells Windows to install the minidriver that matches the modem. This minidriver works with the modem to enable advanced features such as data compression and error correction. These features are likely to be implemented differently by each manufacturer.

Even without a minidriver, the Unimodem driver can make a partially Hayes-compatible modem dial, connect, and disconnect. Modems that are running with only the Unidriver will be shown in Control Panel as a Standard modem.

Using Drivers Provided by Modem Manufacturers

You may encounter a modem that comes with a Windows 95 driver disk. This disk indicates that the modem has features that are not supported by the Unimodem driver and that no proper minidriver comes with Windows 95.

To install the modem with its own driver software, follow these steps:

1. Double-click the Modem icon in Control Panel.
2. Choose Add.
3. Choose Don't Detect My Modem; I will Select It From a List. Then click Next.
4. Now choose Have Disk.
5. Insert the manufacturer's driver disk into the proper disk drive when you are prompted to (or if the disk is in another drive, enter the correct drive and path), as shown in figure 27.9, and then choose OK.

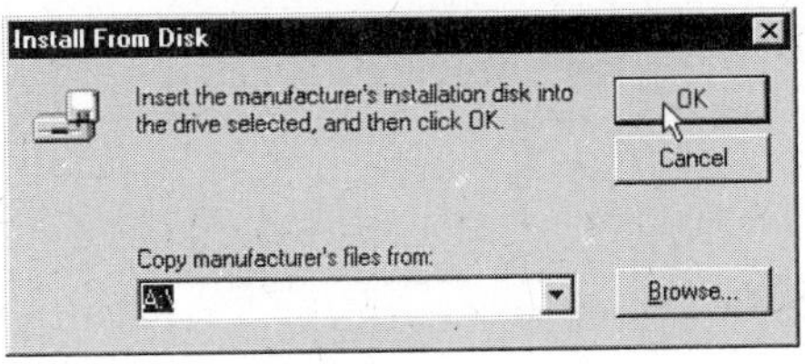

Fig. 27.9
Installing a driver provided by the modem manufacturer.

6. Choose the driver for your modem model from the list that appears (if more than one driver is on the disk), and then choose OK.
7. Choose Finish.

Your modem's drivers are installed in Windows, and the modem's special features are enabled.

Configuring Your Modem

Now that your hardware is installed, you can configure Windows to work cooperatively with it. Windows can take some information from you and supply that information to communications programs to allow them to function more effectively.

To operate your modem with the greatest possible intelligence, Windows automatically collects the following information from you:

- Your location
- Your area code
- Access number(s) needed to get an outside line
- Type of dialing used at this location (tone or pulse)

This information, however, is not enough to make your modem operate at peak efficiency and at maximum data-transfer rates. You should tell Windows other things about your modem, including the following:

- Maximum port speed (computer to modem)
- Default data-formatting properties
- How to handle no-dial-tone situations
- How long the modem should try to connect before stopping
- When to disconnect an idle modem connection
- Your modem's error-control and compression features
- What kind of flow control to use with your modem
- How to handle low-speed connections
- How to record a log file of the modem's interaction with the system, for use in troubleshooting
- How to manually send extra AT commands to the modem during initialization

The following sections explain these items.

General Properties

Use the Modems Control Panel to select the modem that you are working with, and then choose Properties. The Modem Properties sheet, which has two pages, appears. Figure 27.10 shows the General page.

The options in this tab include the following:

- *Port*. This displays which port is in use by your modem.
- *Speaker Volume*. This slider control controls how loud you want your internal speaker.

- *Maximum Speed.* This setting controls the speed you want your modem to work.

- *Only Connect at this Speed.* Checking this box tells your computer to connect at only one speed.

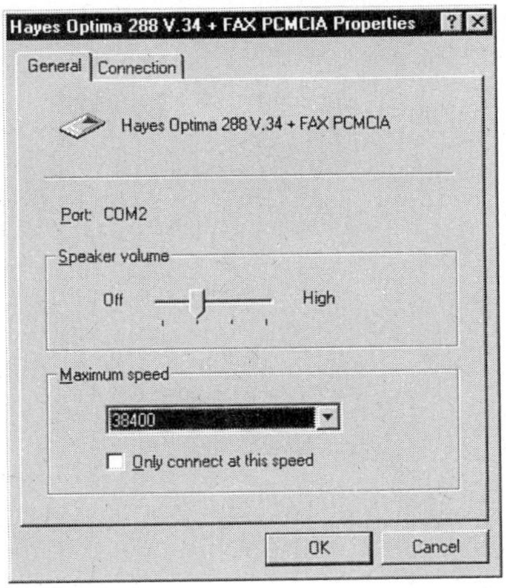

Fig. 27.10
The General page of the Modems Properties sheet displays basic information about your modem.

The General properties page contains settings that can make your modem work better, when the proper values are selected.

Port

The Port option shows the communications port to which Windows assigned the modem. If the modem is an internal Plug and Play type, in which Windows can configure the serial port, you may have a choice in setting which communications port to use with the modem. If other communications ports are used, or if the modem cannot be configured by Windows (you must use jumpers to set its port and address), you will not be able to change the communications port assigned to this modem.

Speaker Volume

The Speaker Volume control is a handy way to tell 32-bit Windows 95 communications programs how loud to set the volume of the modem's speaker.

The volume control slider works with modems that have physical speakers and with modems (such as PC Cards) that rely on the computer's speaker for their sound. If the volume control is grayed out, the modem has no speaker and no way of using the speaker in the computer. (Many ISDN Terminal Adapters will have the Speaker Volume grayed out.)

Note

Sixteen-bit Windows and DOS communications programs ignore the Speaker Volume setting; instead, they set modem volume themselves. These older programs set the volume themselves because when they were written, the operating system had no way to keep track of your preferences.

Maximum Speed

The Maximum Speed parameter is extremely important. This setting has nothing to do with the speed at which your modem connects to another modem; it represents the speed at which your *computer* connects to your modem.

Why is this important? Any modem that operates at 9600 bits per second (formerly referred to as the baud rate) or faster typically supports data compression. The International Telecommunications Union (ITU), the professional society that sets world-wide communications standards, has established four data-compression standards. Your modem may support one or all of these standards.

Table 27.2 shows the standards, the modem speed associated with each standard, and the port speed that you should use with your modem. These general guidelines work for almost all modems.

Table 27.2 Modem Port Speed Settings

Modem Speed	ITU Standard	Port Speed
9,600	v.32	19,200
14,400	v.32bis	57,600
19,200	v.32ter	57,600
28,800	v.34	115,200

Note

You may not be able to set the port speed as high as 115,200 on older, slower computers. These computers may not have the right type of serial-port hardware, which is based on the type 16550A chip. In such a case, use 57,600.

When two modems that are using one of the ITU standards, or one of the older, but still widely used, Microcom MNP compression standards connect, the modems examine the data that they are sending to see whether it can be compressed; if so, the modems compress the data. Sending compressed data raises the effective speed of the modem. Modem speed can approach the speed of the port if the data can be compressed greatly.

Compression works only if the port speed is fast enough to feed the data to the modem as quickly as the modem needs it. If a 14,400 v.32bis modem compresses data into half the space that the data takes up on disk, the port must feed data to the modem at least twice as fast as the 14,400 connect speed. Setting the port to 57,600 allows for the high speed data feed to the modem and also takes care of some overhead for processing.

► See "Advanced Settings," p. 848

Only Connect at this Speed

Check this box if you don't want your modem to adjust its speed to match the speed of the modem on the other end. Checking this box allows only high-speed connections between two modems that are each capable of high speeds.

Sometimes bad conditions on the telephone line can make two high speed modems connect at low speeds. Checking this box prevents the low speed connection from taking place. In that case, you will have to keep trying the call until the modems can connect at their full rated speed.

Connection Properties

Now open the Connection page, shown in figure 27.11.

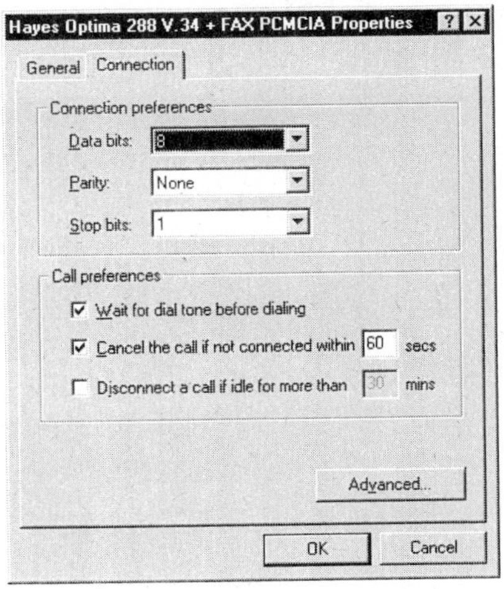

Fig. 27.11
The Connection page allows you to set your preferences.

In this page, you can set the following options:

Tip
In some countries and on some telephone systems, dial tone is so different that American modems may not detect it. If that occurs, deselect the Wait for Dial Tone before Dialing option to allow the modem to dial.

- *Connection Preferences*. The default settings—8 bits, no parity, and 1 stop bit—work for most online services, BBSes, remote-access and remote-control programs, data-transfer services, dial-up networking, and so on. You need to change these settings only if the resource that you are dialing requires changes.

- *Wait for Dial Tone before Dialing*. If you choose this option, you are warned if no dial tone is present when the modem tries to dial. This option allows you to check your phone line and modem cable to make sure that a dial tone is getting to the modem.

- *Cancel the Call if Not Connected Within x Secs*. If the modem that you're calling doesn't answer within 30 or 60 seconds, a problem may exist. When you choose this option, you are notified if your call didn't connect, so that you can check to see whether you have the right phone number.

- *Disconnect a Call if Idle for More Than x Secs*. You may want your communications program to hang up the phone and break the connection if the modems haven't sent any data in either direction after a specified period. This option can save you money if you use commercial online services regularly. If you get interrupted or called away from your computer, Windows disconnects from the service so that you won't continue to rack up expensive online charges.

Advanced Settings

At the bottom of the Connection page is the Advanced button. When you click this button, you see the dialog box shown in figure 27.12.

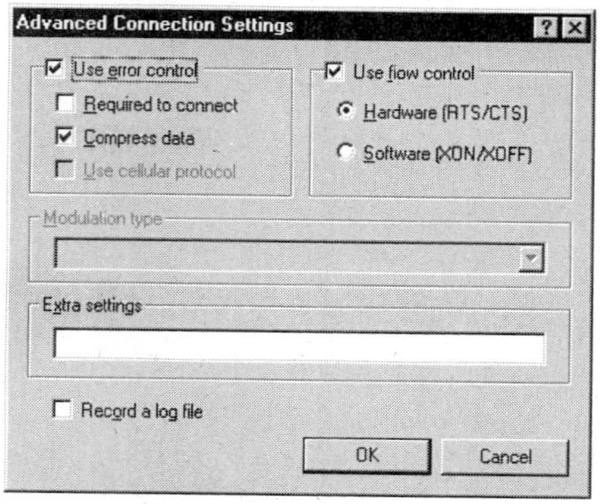

Fig. 27.12
In the Advanced Connection Settings dialog box you can further configure your modem.

The Use Error Control, Compress Data, and Use Flow Control options in the Advanced Connection Settings dialog box work with one another and with the port-speed setting in the General page of the Modem Properties sheet. These options should be selected by default.

Your choices in Advanced Connection Settings will determine if your modem will work as fast, and as reliably, as its manufacturer intended it to.

- For modems with data speeds of 9,600 bps or faster, Windows turns on the Use Error Control option automatically.
- Windows also may turn on the Compress Data option. If it doesn't, but if your modem supports one of the compression standards, you should choose the Compress Data option.
- In the Use Flow Control section of the dialog box, you should choose Hardware on modems rated at 9,600 bps or faster. If you don't choose Hardware, the high port speed that you set in the General tab causes data errors instead of fast throughput, compression, and error correction.

These settings work well for most connections; make sure that they are enabled.

Modulation Type

The Modulation Type setting controls how Windows handles connections at 300 and 1,200 bps. If you connect with an old modem at 300 or 1,200 bps , you have to decide whether to use U.S. or European standards. Bell works with American modems, and CCITT V.21 works with modems in the rest of the world. If you want to connect to a CCITT V.21 or V.22 modem, make sure that your modem can use these standards.

> **Note**
>
> U.S. and European modems used different standards until 9,600-bps modems became popular. At that time, American manufacturers adopted the standards set by the CCITT (in English, the International Telegraph & Telephone Consultative Committee) and its successor, the ITU (International Telecommunications Union). Now modems all over the world can communicate at 9,600 bps and faster.

Extra Settings

If you need to send the modem an AT command that Windows does not include automatically in its initialization procedure, type the command in the Extra Settings box.

Windows hides extra settings away in this obscure location because Windows architects believe the operating system should handle all details of communicating with the modem. The user should be isolated from sending raw AT commands. Because each brand of modem implements the AT command set differently, an AT command that works on one 28.8 kbps modem may not work the same on any other brand of modem.

However, if you are certain about your modem's implementation of the AT command set, Extra Settings is the place to send additional commands at modem initialization time, just before the modem dials out.

For example, if you want to turn off the speaker completely on a Hayes modem, enter ATM0 (that's a zero after the M), in the Extra Settings dialog.

Using Log Files

If you repeatedly have trouble making a connection, tell Windows to keep a record of the commands that it sends to the modem and the replies from the modem. This record can be useful in troubleshooting the problem. You can look for responses from the modem that contain the word ERROR and see what commands caused the errors. To activate this feature, choose the Record a Log File option.

Note

The log file is stored in the Windows directory as MODEMLOG.TXT. You can use Notepad to examine the log file.

When you are done making your choices in the Advanced Connection Settings dialog box, click OK. This returns you to the Modem Properties sheet.

Understanding Your Modem and Your Telephone System

Dialing Properties is a new concept for Windows 95. Dialing Properties gives you a way to control how your calls are dialed. You can create and choose from a list of dialing locations, each of which can be in a different area code, or different country. Windows will still dial the modem properly. Finally, the system knows how to do these things!

Dialing Properties also works with your modem to tell it whether you need to dial an access code to get an outside line. It allows you to make a calling card call with your modem. Dialing Properties can disable call waiting, so your modem calls won't be interrupted by an incoming call. And with Dialing Properties, you can tell your modem whether it can use touch-tones on your phone line, or if the modem must use rotary style pulse dialing.

To control Dialing Properties, choose Dialing Properties from the Modems Properties sheet.

The preceding sections explain how some of the properties settings for your modem control the way that the modem call is made. So far, the only actual dialing parameter that you've given the modem is whether to use tone or pulse dialing.

Many of the things that a modem needs to do to complete a call depend on where you and your computer are located. A modem that's being used at home, for example, usually dials differently than a modem that's being used in a hotel room or at the office. Knowing the phone number of the computer that you want to dial with the modem isn't enough; you also have area codes and outside-line codes to deal with. In addition, you may want to make the call a credit-card call.

These issues used to be problems. Windows 95, however, collects information from you so that communications programs deal with these issues in a seamless, elegant fashion.

Figure 27.13 shows the Dialing Properties sheet, in which you specify location information. This information tells your modem how to work wherever you go with your computer. If you are using your modem at home, where you don't need to dial a code for an outside line but do have the call-waiting feature, your settings may look like the ones in figure 27.13.

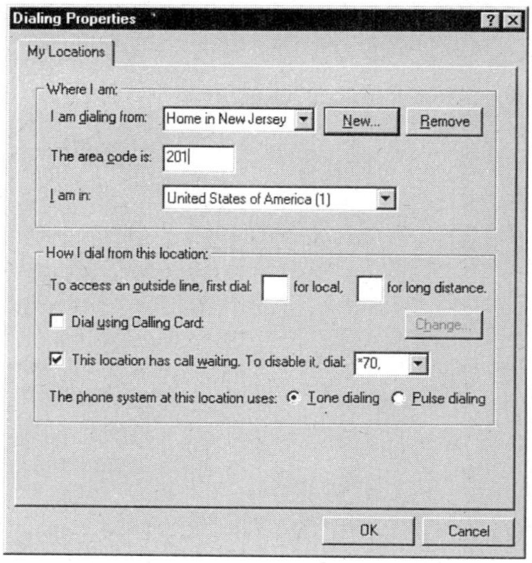

Fig. 27.13
You can set location information in the Dialing Properties sheet.

Suppose, however, that you're working in a hotel room in Washington, D.C., that you need to dial 9 to get an outside line (or 91 to get a long-distance outside line), and that you want to charge the call to a credit card.

Tip
You can create as many locations as you need.

To make a credit card call, you need to check the Dial Using Credit Card box. Your Dialing Properties settings would look like the ones in figure 27.14.

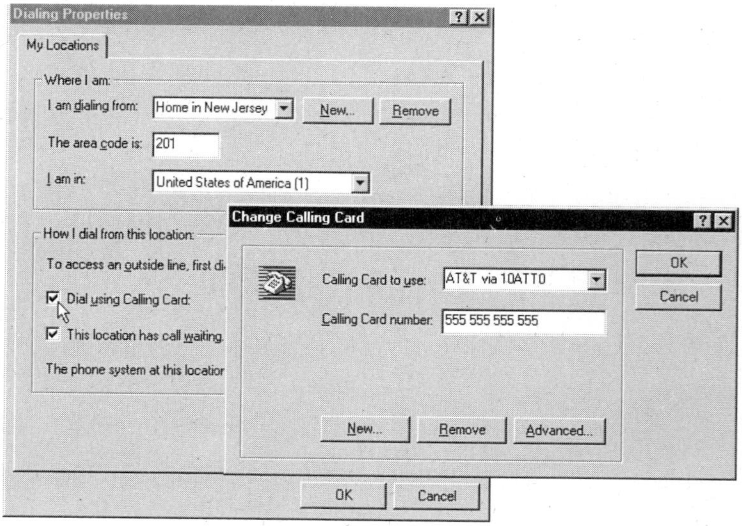

Fig. 27.14
Making a calling card call with your modem is easy.

In the Dialing Properties sheet, Windows has created your first location for you, based on information you gave setup during Windows installation. Windows has named this the Default Location.

► See "Working Smarter with TAPI and 32-Bit Windows Programs," p. 855

Create additional locations by choosing New on the Dialing Properties sheet. Then, name the Location, and fill out the country and area code for the Location. You also can remove a location by choosing Remove.

When you use a communications program that is TAPI-aware and Windows 95-aware, you can specify your location before dialing. Examples of programs that take advantage of Locations are Windows HyperTerminal, Windows Phone Dialer, the Microsoft Network online service, Microsoft Exchange, and any of Exchange's MAPI modules, such as CompuServe Mail and Dial-Up Networking.

To learn more about Microsoft Exchange, and MAPI modules that use modems, see Chapter 24, "Using Microsoft Exchange."

Getting Your Modem to Dial

If your modem is working properly and your settings are correct, then dialing numbers through your modem should be effortless. In most cases, the program will direct-dial the modem. However, if you can't get the modem to dial, try the following procedures:

- In the Modems Control Panel, check to see whether the modem that is displayed matches your model. If not, choose Add New Modem to install your modem. If any modems that are not in your system appear in the Control Panel, delete them.
- In the System Control Panel, choose Device Manager. Choose Modems, select your modem, double-click to display the Properties sheet, and click the General tab. The sheet shown in figure 27.15 indicates that the device is used in the current configuration and that it's working properly.
- Make sure that the communications port is set correctly. Click the Modem tab, shown in figure 27.16, and check the port name and port speed.

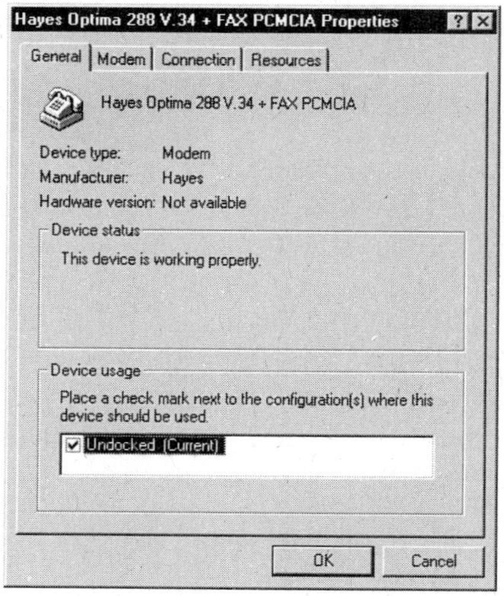

Fig. 27.15
Windows tells you your modem is working properly.

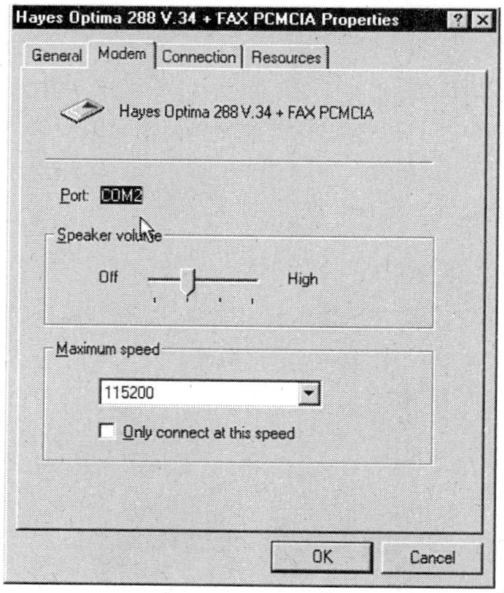

Fig. 27.16
Check the communications Port and Maximum Speed if your modem is not working properly.

- Make sure that the port name matches the port that your application wants to use. If the port is set to COM2, for example, make sure that your application is trying to use the modem on COM2.
- Try lowering the port speed. Perhaps your serial port hardware doesn't support the selected speed. Try a range of speeds between the data speed of your modem and the maximum speed. Use the highest setting that works reliably.

Troubleshooting

My modem connects, but it doesn't stay connected.

If your phone line has call waiting, incoming calls may be throwing you offline. Use Dialing Properties to disable call waiting. You reach the Dialing Properties sheet by choosing Dialing Properties from the Modem Properties sheet.

If that doesn't work, flow control may be set incorrectly. For 9,600-bps and faster modems, make sure that flow control is set to Hardware.

To get to the flow control setting, use Control Panel, double-click the Modem icon, and then choose Properties. Click the Connection tab, and then choose Advanced.

Also, check all cables for quality by swapping them with cables that you know to be good—serial cables for external modems as well as your regular phone cables.

My Windows 95 application keeps dialing the wrong number.

Check to see whether the Dialing Location properties are set correctly. To do this, use Control Panel and double-click the Modem icon. Then click Dialing Properties.

Make sure that the entry in I am Dialing From: matches the location you are in, and that the area code and country shown match where you are, too.

If they don't, Windows 95 programs will be dialing phone numbers incorrectly.

Working Smarter with TAPI and 32-Bit Windows Programs

Telephony Applications Programming Interface, or TAPI, is an API set that lets your modem do more for you than it ever could before Windows 95.

TAPI uses all the information that you gave Windows during the modem-configuration process to set up not only your modem, but also all the 32-bit Windows 95 communications programs. Phone dialer, HyperTerminal, Microsoft Exchange, and Dial Up Networking all share one modem because of TAPI. Communications programs that are written specifically for Windows 95 talk to TAPI, which then issues appropriate commands to the modem. The way Windows uses TAPI for all communications, instead of making each communications program learn to talk to every modem on the market, is called *device independence*. Device independence frees the program developer from having to know everything about your modem.

TAPI provides the following major benefits, which were covered earlier, in the section "Understanding Your Modem and Your Telephone System:"

- The capability to define locations to make dialing effortless
- Support for 16550A UART chips for better throughput

In addition, TAPI provides the following benefits, which are the subject of the following sections:

- Sharing of modems by applications
- Sharing fax modems over a network

Sharing a Modem under TAPI

You know the problem from Windows 3.1—your system has one modem, which is used for data and faxes, and you want to leave the modem under the control of the fax program so that the modem is ready for incoming faxes. When you try to make a data call with the modem, however, an error message appears, telling you that the port is already in use. You have to disable the fax program, use the data program, and re-enable the fax program.

Now suppose that you are using Windows 95. At 3 p.m., Microsoft Fax is waiting for an incoming fax to arrive. At the same time, the CompuServe Mail driver in Microsoft Exchange is scheduled to check CompuServe to see whether any new mail has arrived. Without missing a beat, TAPI allows the mail driver to use the modem; then TAPI hands modem control back to Microsoft Fax. The importance and convenience of this cooperation cannot be overestimated.

Troubleshooting

My Windows 95 communications programs work fine, but I can't access the modem with a DOS or old Windows communications program. How can I make my legacy communications programs work?

You ran into the TAPI gotcha. TAPI only works if all the communications programs you will be using are TAPI aware, 32-bit, Windows 95 programs. If Microsoft Fax is waiting for an incoming fax or Dial-Up Networking is waiting for an incoming call, DOS and old Windows programs cannot access the modem; this capability is reserved for TAPI-enabled Windows 95 applications.

Sharing a Fax Modem Over a Network

TAPI allows any user on a Windows 95 network to send faxes via another network user's fax modem. The user who has the fax modem enables the modem as a shared device; TAPI does the rest.

Note

Data modems cannot be shared over a network.

Working with Phone Dialer

Phone Dialer, an accessory that comes with Windows 95, is a good example of a program that is written to take advantage of the power of TAPI.

To run Phone Dialer, open the Start menu, then choose Programs, Accessories, Phone Dialer. Figure 27.17 shows the main Phone Dialer dialog box.

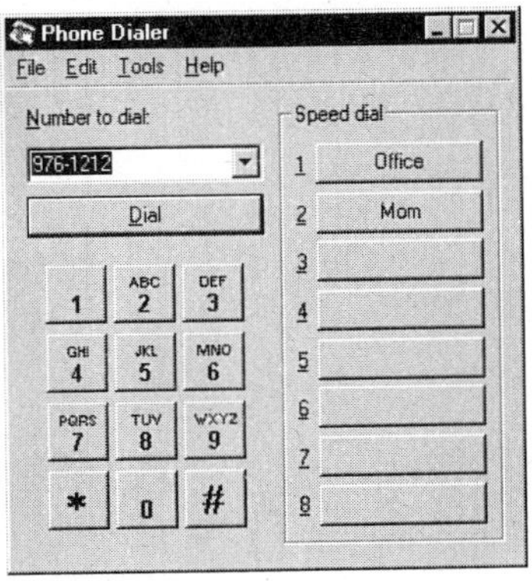

Fig. 27.17
Use Phone Dialer to make calls with your modem.

When you tell Phone Dialer to dial the number shown in the Number to Dial box, it knows how to handle the area code. Because you defined a location earlier in the section "Understanding Your Modem and Your Telephone

System," Phone Dialer knows if you're dialing a number in the same area code as your computer; in that case, it leaves off the area code and dials the call as 976-1212, as shown in figure 27.18. Phone Dialer also knows whether or not to dial 1 before the number, based on what you tell Windows about your Location.

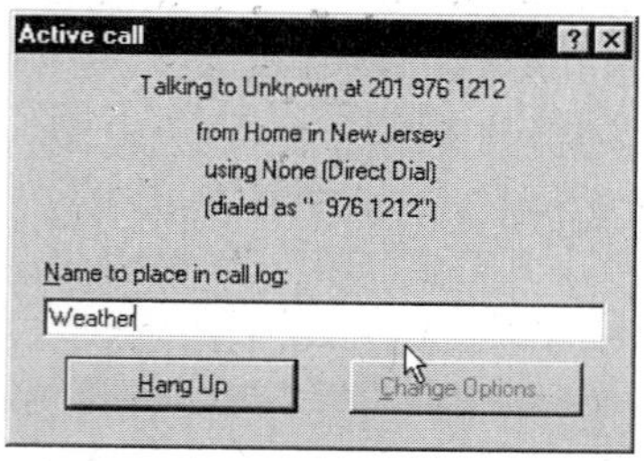

Fig. 27.18
Dialing within the same area code, Windows dials only seven digits.

All the other TAPI features work with Phone Dialer. If Microsoft Fax is waiting for a fax, for example, Phone Dialer can still dial out. When Phone Dialer finishes using the phone line, TAPI gives it back to the fax program.

Note

TAPI features only work with new, 32 bit communications programs that are written to support Windows 95.

If your modem is waiting for a fax under control of the TAPI program Microsoft Fax, and you need to use it to call Compuserve with your Windows 3.1 version of WinCIM, which isn't TAPI aware, you'll first have to turn off Microsoft Fax.

In the same way, if your modem is waiting for a fax under control of your legacy Windows 3.1 version of Delrina Winfax Pro, you'll have to turn Winfax off before you can use the modem with any other program.

For the TAPI features to work, all the applications in the mix must be TAPI aware, 32-bit, and written specifically to support Windows 95.

Using the Diagnostic Tool

Windows has a built-in diagnostic tool that tells you whether your modem can respond to the most basic commands. This tool is useful only to tell you that the modem is alive. Using this tool is as simple as opening the Start menu and choosing, Settings, Control Panel, Modems. When the Modem Properties dialog box appears, click the Diagnostics tab.

Select your modem and then choose More Info. Windows issues a series of interrogatory commands and notes the responses. Figure 27.19 shows sample results.

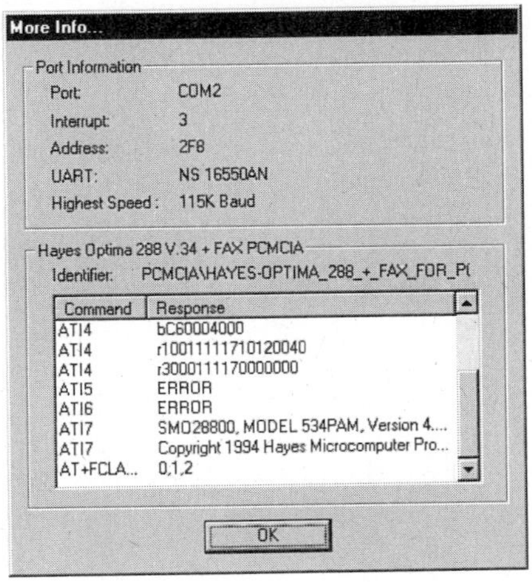

Fig. 27.19
Modem Diagnostics showing the modem responding to AT commands

Understanding File Transfer Errors

Errors occur in file transfers with DOS and old Windows programs. How do I track them down and fix them?

If you're using DOS and Windows 3.1 communications programs, you've probably upgraded from Windows 3.1 to Windows 95. There are settings in the old Windows 3.1 SYSTEM.INI file that can cause problems in your new installation of Windows 95.

To correct these problems, some manual editing of SYSTEM.INI may be necessary. You can use NOTEPAD.EXE to perform these tasks.

In the `[boot]` section of your SYSTEM.INI file, make sure `COMM.DRV=COMM.DRV`. If it doesn't, edit it so it says COMM.DRV=COMM.DRV.

This will make sure Windows 95 is using its own communications driver for older, 16-bit programs.

In the `[386Enh]` section, make sure a line exists that says `DEVICE=*VCD`. If you don't see DEVICE=*VCD, type it on a line by itself anywhere in the [386Enh] section. Use NOTEPAD.EXE to do this.

Next, set the FIFO buffer to 512 bytes. Determine the communications port that you're using with these DOS and old Windows programs. If the port is COM2, for example, add the line `COM2BUFFER=512` in the `[386Enh]` section of your SYSTEM.INI file. Use the same syntax for other ports. You can add COM2BUFFER=512 on a line by itself, anywhere in the [386Enh] section of SYSTEM.INI. You can use NOTEPAD.EXE to do this.❖

Chapter 28

Communicating with HyperTerminal

by Jerry Honeycutt

HyperTerminal is a Windows accessory that enables you to connect your computer to another PC or online service. HyperTerminal replaces the Windows 3.1 Terminal program. HyperTerminal is not just a clone of Terminal, however, but is a full-featured communications tool that greatly simplifies getting online. With HyperTerminal, you can connect to a friend's computer, a university, an Internet service provider, or even CompuServe.

In this chapter, you learn

- What HyperTerminal is and how it compares to the other communications tools provided with Windows
- How to use HyperTerminal for some common tasks such as creating a connection or downloading a file
- How to configure HyperTerminal and customize your connections

Introducing HyperTerminal

Before graphical interfaces to online services such as CompuServe and the Microsoft Network existed, most communications tools were character-oriented. For example, students all over the world used terminal-emulation programs to connect to their schools' computers. They typically used VT-100 terminal emulation, which made their PCs behave like any other display terminal on the system. CompuServe is another example, but instead of emulating a terminal it displays one line of text at a time. Remember the days before WinCIM?

If you can use the graphical communications tools mentioned here, why do you need a character-oriented tool such as HyperTerminal? The reason is that most bulletin boards, Internet shell accounts, and university connections are still character-oriented. Most bulletin boards do not provide a sleek, graphical interface like the Microsoft Network. HyperTerminal does the following:

- Makes the focal point of your activities the connections you create (documents), which allows you to dial or configure a connection without loading HyperTerminal first
- Automatically detects the terminal-emulation mode and communications parameters of the remote computer
- Fully integrates with TAPI and the centralized modem configuration, which provides Windows 95 applications a single interface to your modem for dialing, answering, configuration, and more
- Supports several popular terminal-emulation modes and file transfer protocols such as VT-100, VT-52, and Kermit
- Enables you to greatly customize each of your connections

What You Can Do with HyperTerminal

HyperTerminal is a communications tool with many uses. The following list describes many tasks you can do with HyperTerminal:

- Connect to another computer and exchange files
- Connect to an online service (such as CompuServe) that supports one of HyperTerminal's terminal-emulation modes
- Connect to a school's computer using VT-100
- Connect to an Internet service provider using a shell account and even access the World Wide Web using Lynx

What You Can't Do with HyperTerminal

Although HyperTerminal is a useful communications tool, it is not the only tool you will need for your communications activities. The following list describes some activities you can't do and refers you to other chapters in this book:

◀ See "Gaining Remote Access to Your Network," p. 660

- *Connect to another network.* If you need to connect your computer to another network, use Dial-Up Networking as described in Chapter 21, "Sharing Windows 95 Peer-to-Peer Resources."

- *Connect to the Microsoft Network.* To connect to the Microsoft Network, use the graphical software provided in Windows 95, as described in Appendix B, "Using Microsoft Network."

▶ See "Connecting to The Microsoft Network," p. 1110

- *Graphically connect to the Internet World Wide Web.* While many service providers provide Lynx, a character-oriented Web browsing tool, you'll need a graphical browsing tool to take full advantage of the Web. See Chapter 29, "Getting Connected to the Internet."

▶ See "The World Wide Web," p. 903

Using HyperTerminal

When you installed Windows, you were given the option to install HyperTerminal as one of your accessories. If you did not install HyperTerminal or you removed it from the Start menu, you can install it at any time by selecting Install/Remove Applications from the Control Panel. To open the HyperTerminal folder, click the Start button and choose Programs, Accessories, HyperTerminal.

◀ See "Adding and Removing Windows Components," p. 313

If you have not yet configured your modem, Windows prompts you to set it up the first time you run HyperTerminal.

◀ See "Configuring Your Modem," p. 843

Figure 28.1 shows the HyperTerminal folder. By default, each connection that you create appears in this folder as an icon.

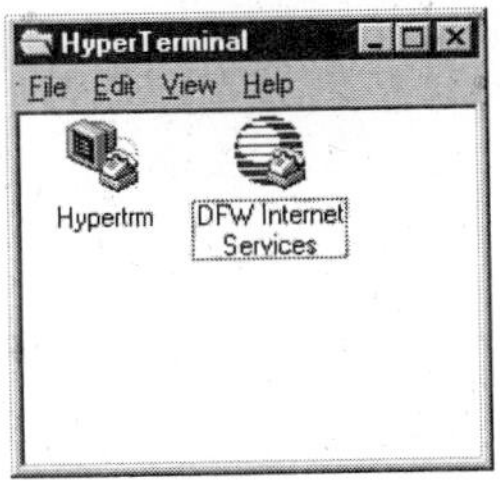

Fig. 28.1 Double-click Hypertrm to create a new HyperTerminal connection, or double-click another icon to open an existing connection.

Creating a New Connection

Before you can connect with HyperTerminal, you need to create a new connection. To do so, follow these steps:

1. Double-click the Hypertrm icon in the HyperTerminal folder. If HyperTerminal is already loaded, choose File, New or click the New button on the toolbar. HyperTerminal prompts you for a new connection description.

2. In the Connection Description dialog box, shown in figure 28.2, type a descriptive name for your new connection, select an icon, and click OK. HyperTerminal then displays the Phone Number dialog box.

Fig. 28.2
Create a new connection and select an icon to help you easily identify it later.

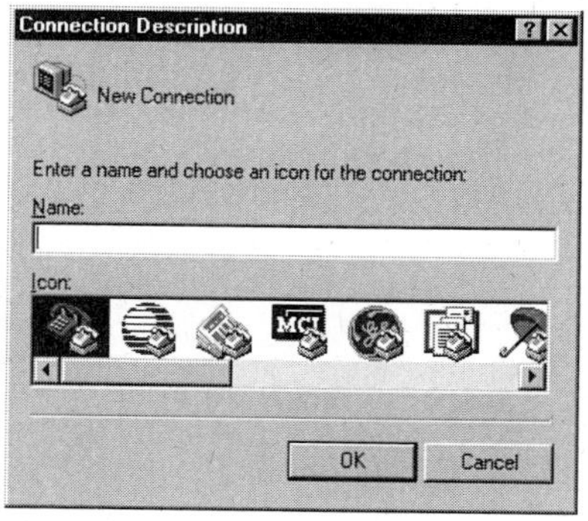

3. Type the phone number for your new connection. Verify the country code, area code, and modem choice. Click OK. HyperTerminal displays the Connect dialog box, as shown in figure 28.3.

4. Select your location (usually Default Location) and click Dial if you want to establish your new connection. You can also click Dialing Properties to change the default location, outside line access, and other dialing properties.

Fig. 28.3
After you have set up the connection, just click Dial to get going.

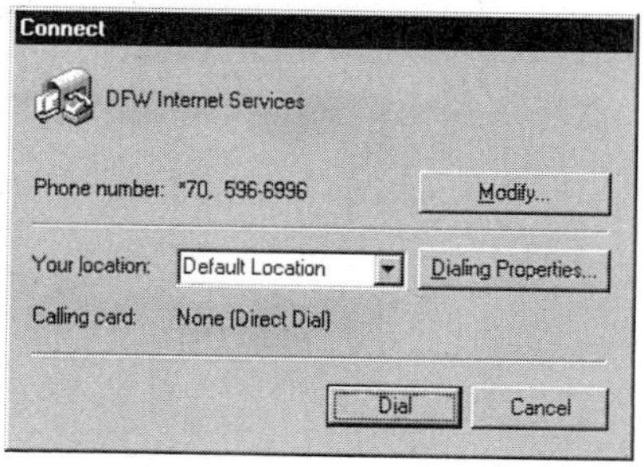

Figure 28.4 shows the entire HyperTerminal window with a session in progress. Most of HyperTerminal's features are available on the toolbar. Table 28.1 describes each toolbar button.

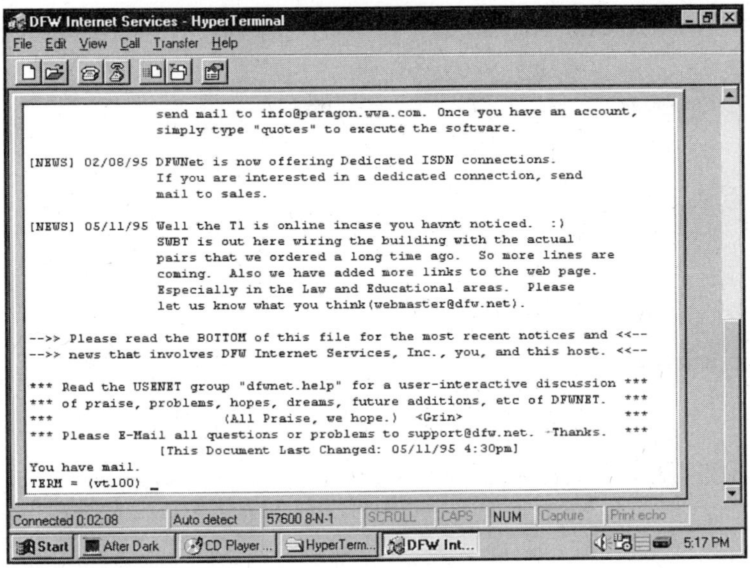

Fig. 28.4
After a connection to the remote computer is established, you interact with it just like a display terminal on the system. Click the scroll bar to review text that was previously displayed.

Table 28.1 The HyperTerminal Toolbar

Button	Name	Description
	New	Creates a new connection
	Open	Opens an existing connection
	Connect	Displays the Connect dialog box
	Disconnect	Disconnects the current connection
	Send	Sends a file to the host
	Receive	Receives a file from the host
	Properties	Displays the Properties sheet for the connection

To save your new connection, choose File, Save As. HyperTerminal prompts you for a file name. If you want your connections to show up in the HyperTerminal folder, accept the default path. If you quit HyperTerminal without saving your new connection, HyperTerminal prompts you for a file name.

To hang up, choose Call, Disconnect or click the Disconnect button on the toolbar.

Troubleshooting

I try to dial a connection, but I get an error that says `Another program is using the selected Telephony device.`

Make sure that you don't have any older Windows communications programs running in the background that might be controlling the modem. Although Windows 95 communications tools can share the modem, older Windows communications programs can't.

I connected to the service fine, but all I see on-screen is garbage—usually at the bottom of the screen.

Choose File, Properties to display the Properties sheet for your connection, click the Settings tab, and set Emulation to Auto Detect. HyperTerminal automatically determines which terminal emulation your service is using.

Using an Existing Connection

◄ See "Shortcuts Add Power," p. 29

The next time you want to use the connection you previously created, it will appear in the HyperTerminal folder. To establish this connection, double-click the icon in the folder and click Dial.

If HyperTerminal is already running, choose File, Open or click the Open button on the toolbar.

Capturing Text from the Screen

Tip
To make access to your connection quicker, copy a shortcut to the connection onto the desktop or the Start menu.

By capturing text, you can save everything that appears in the HyperTerminal window. You may want to save the information displayed by HyperTerminal for the following reasons:

- You want to review or use it later
- The information is scrolling by so quickly that you can't read it

There are two ways to capture text from the remote computer: to a file or to the printer.

Tip
If text is scrolling by faster than you can read it, try pressing Ctrl+S to pause the screen and then press Ctrl+Q to resume.

Capturing Text to a File

To capture text received from the remote computer to a file, follow these steps:

1. Choose Transfer, Capture Text from the menu.
2. Type the name for a file in which you want to put the text, or click Browse to select a file. Your screen should look similar to figure 28.5.
3. Click Start. HyperTerminal stores all text it receives from the remote computer in this file.

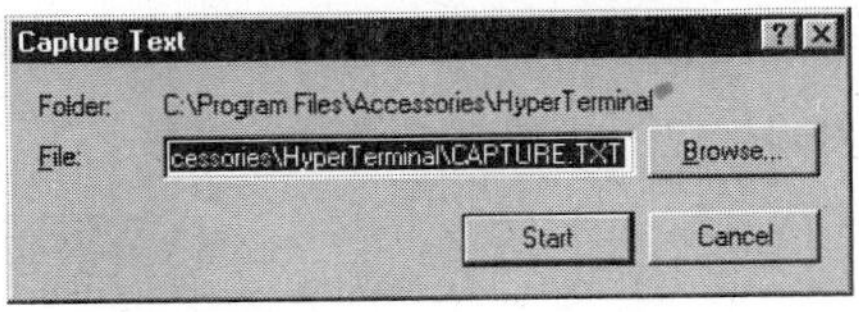

Fig. 28.5
Type the name for a file in which to capture text.

After you start capturing text, you can stop by choosing Transfer, Capture, Stop; pause with Transfer, Capture, Pause; or resume with Transfer, Capture, Resume. Notice that these menu options are available only after you start capturing text to a file. Once you choose Stop, you will be prompted for a file name the next time you choose Capture.

Capturing Text to the Printer

Capturing text to the printer is even easier than capturing to a file. To capture to the printer, choose Transfer, Capture to Printer. All text that HyperTerminal receives will be sent to the default printer. A check mark is displayed next to Capture to Printer, indicating that the option is turned on. To turn it off, choose it again.

Troubleshooting

I captured text to a text file, but when I view the file, I can read some of the lines, but the rest of them are garbled.

If you are using terminal emulation, such as VT-100, this condition is normal. This emulation uses escape codes, which tell HyperTerminal where to put the cursor or how to format text. Escape codes can't be displayed as normal text. However, they are still captured to the file.

Sharing Text with Other Programs

◄ See "Understanding Windows 95's Data-Sharing Capabilities," p. 410

The cut-and-paste process is still one of the most useful features in Windows. With a few keystrokes or mouse clicks, you can transfer data from one program to another. HyperTerminal is no exception. To copy data from HyperTerminal using the mouse, select a block of text in the window and choose Edit, Copy or press Ctrl+C.

Pasting is simple, too. After copying data to the Clipboard from another application such as Notepad, choose Edit, Paste to Host or just press Ctrl+V.

Note

In applications such as Notepad, pasting text from the Clipboard puts the text in the document, which is then displayed in the window. When you paste text into HyperTerminal, it actually transmits the text to the remote computer.

Exchanging Files with the Remote Computer

You can easily exchange files with another computer using HyperTerminal. For example, you may want to download a program update from the bulletin board of your favorite software vendor. You also can download public domain software from a variety of bulletin board systems (BBSes) around the country.

Caution

Before running a program downloaded from a remote computer, run it through a virus scan program to make sure that it's not infected. Otherwise, severe and irreparable damage may occur to your programs and data files if you download a virus.

You also may be asked to upload a data file to a vendor's bulletin board so that the vendor can help you fix a problem. HyperTerminal can do it!

Downloading Files

Before you begin downloading a file, you must make sure that you have a connection with a host computer, as described in the previous section "Using an Existing Connection."

To download a file from a host computer, follow these steps:

1. Start the download process on the bulletin board or host computer. Bulletin boards or other host computers vary in how to start a download—follow the instructions given to you online. Make a note of the file transfer protocol you selected on the host. HyperTerminal supports several popular file transfer protocols. Table 28.2 describes each protocol.

Table 28.2 File Transfer Protocols Supported by HyperTerminal

Protocol	Description
Xmodem	Xmodem is an error-correcting protocol supported by virtually every communications program and online service. It is slower than the other protocols.
1K Xmodem	1K Xmodem is faster than Xmodem, transferring files in 1,024-byte blocks as opposed to the slower 128-byte blocks in regular Xmodem. Otherwise, they are similar.
Ymodem	Many bulletin board systems offer Ymodem, which is another name for 1K Xmodem.
Ymodem-G	Similar to Ymodem, Ymodem-G implements hardware error control. It is more reliable than the first three protocols. However, to use Ymodem-G, your hardware must support hardware error control.
Zmodem	Zmodem is preferred by most bulletin board users because it is the fastest protocol of those listed. Zmodem is reliable, too, because it adjusts its block sizes during the download to accommodate bad telephone lines. Zmodem has two other features that make it stand out from the rest. First, the host can initiate the download—you do nothing beyond this step. Second, you can download multiple files at one time using Zmodem. The host computer initiates a download for each file you selected.
Kermit	Kermit is extremely slow and should not be used if one of the other protocols is available. Kermit is a protocol left over from VAX computers and mainframes.

2. If you selected Zmodem as the protocol, you are done. The host computer initiates the file transfer with HyperTerminal. Otherwise, choose Transfer, Receive File from the menu or click the Receive button. The Receive File dialog box appears.

3. Type a folder name or click Browse to select a folder (see fig. 28.6). Then select a protocol to use for downloading the file. The protocol you use

should match the protocol you chose (or the system chose for you) on the host computer.

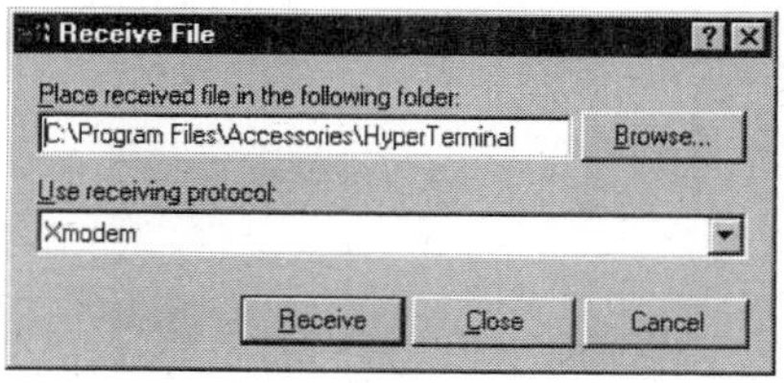

Fig. 28.6 Tell HyperTerminal where you want to store the file; then click Receive to begin the download.

◀ See "Opening, Saving, and Closing Documents," p. 109

4. Click Receive, type a file name, and click OK. HyperTerminal starts your download. Figure 28.7 shows the dialog box that displays the status of your download. (You may see a different dialog box depending on the protocol you chose.)

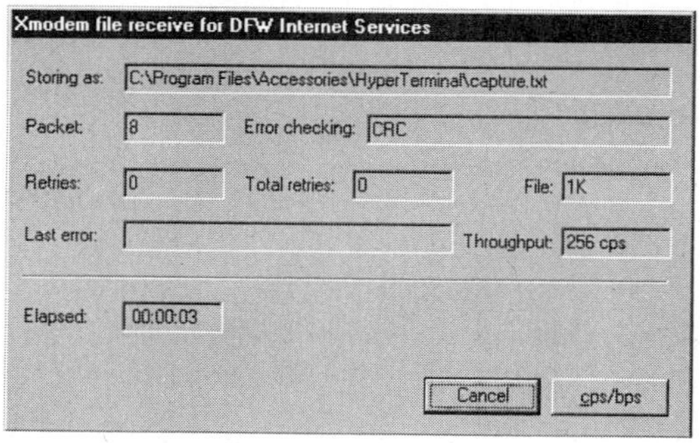

Fig. 28.7 This dialog box shows the status of your download such as the file name and time elapsed. A different dialog box is used depending on which protocol you used for the download.

Uploading Binary Files

You can upload both binary and text files. Binary files include bitmaps, programs, and word processing documents that contain more than just readable text. For example, a program file contains code and program data that is not readable. On the other hand, text files contain characters that are easily read. This section describes how to upload a binary file. To learn how to upload text files, see "Uploading Text Files" later in this chapter.

Before you begin uploading a binary file, you must establish the connection to the host computer, as discussed in "Using an Existing Connection." To upload a binary file to a host computer, follow these steps:

1. Initiate the upload on the bulletin board or host computer by following the on-screen instructions. The host displays a message indicating that it's waiting for you to start uploading.

Note

If you are using Zmodem, you may not need to start the upload on the host computer. Zmodem can initiate the upload on the host for you. To try initiating the upload from your computer, skip step 1. However, if the host computer doesn't understand how to initiate an upload this way, you will have to start over from step 1.

2. Choose Transfer, Send File from the menu or click the Send button on the toolbar. HyperTerminal displays a dialog box similar to the one shown in figure 28.6 in the previous section "Downloading Files."

3. Type a file name or click Browse to select a file.
4. Select a protocol to use for uploading the file. The protocol you use should match the protocol you chose (or the system chose for you) on the host computer.
5. HyperTerminal starts the upload to the host computer. It displays the status of your upload in a dialog box similar to the one shown earlier in figure 28.7.

Troubleshooting

I'm trying to use Ymodem-G as the transfer protocol, but it doesn't work.

Your modem probably doesn't support hardware error control. Try using Ymodem instead.

I initiated a Ymodem upload from my computer, but the host doesn't respond.

The host computer doesn't understand how to initiate an upload this way. You will need to initiate an upload first on the host computer and then on your computer. Alternatively, you may not be at the correct prompt on the host computer.

After reviewing the preceding suggestions, I still can't download or upload a file.

Make sure that you are selecting the exact same transfer protocol the host computer is using. If you continue to have difficulty, contact the sysop (system operator) of the remote computer.

Uploading Text Files

Before you begin uploading a text file, be sure that you're connected to a host computer, as described in the earlier section, "Using an Existing Connection." To upload a text file to a host computer, follow these steps:

1. Start the upload on the bulletin board or host computer. The host displays a message indicating that it's waiting for you to start the upload.
2. Choose Transfer, Send Text File from the menu. HyperTerminal prompts you for a text file name.

> **Caution**
>
> Don't try to upload a binary file using this feature. You may think that the file transferred OK, but the remote computer will receive a file with garbage in it.

3. Type a file name or click Browse to select a file.
4. Click Open. HyperTerminal starts uploading the text file to the host computer. Note that you do not see a dialog box showing the status of the upload.

Configuring HyperTerminal

> **Tip**
> When you change configuration items in HyperTerminal, the changes apply only to the connection you have loaded. Thus, every connection can be customized differently.

HyperTerminal is a flexible communications tool. You can customize all aspects of each of your connections and HyperTerminal automatically saves your settings. For example, you can choose which font a connection uses or which terminal-emulation mode HyperTerminal uses. The next time you use that connection, HyperTerminal uses the settings you previously set. This section shows you how to configure HyperTerminal for each of your connections.

Turning Off the Toolbar and Status Bar

You might want to turn off the toolbar or status bar for a HyperTerminal connection, especially if you do not have enough screen space to display the entire terminal area. To toggle the toolbar, choose View, Toolbar from the menu. A check mark beside Toolbar indicates that the option is turned on.

To toggle the status bar, choose View, Status Bar. Likewise, a check mark beside Status Bar indicates that it is turned on.

Changing Fonts

You can choose a specific font and style for your HyperTerminal connection. For example, if you want HyperTerminal to display a full screen in a smaller window, choose a smaller font size and resize the window.

> **Note**
>
> You can't use a small font size to display 132 columns unless you are using VT-100 terminal emulation. HyperTerminal will always resize the display area to 80 columns.

To choose a different font for this HyperTerminal connection, follow these steps:

◄ See "Understanding Fonts," p. 210

1. Choose View, Font from the menu. HyperTerminal displays the Font dialog box, which is common to most applications.
2. Set the font, style, and size. The Font dialog box shows you a preview of your choice.
3. Click OK when you are satisfied with your choice. HyperTerminal immediately resizes the display area for 80 columns, using the font you have chosen.
4. Optionally, click the right button in the display area and choose Snap. HyperTerminal resizes the window to fit the display area. This technique is useful if you want to use a smaller font to have a smaller HyperTerminal window.

> **Note**
>
> If the display area is larger than the HyperTerminal window, you can use the scroll bars to move the display area up, down, left, or right in the window.

Changing a Connection Setup

It is easy to change the properties for a connection after you create it. You can change the connection's icon, name, country code, area code, phone number, and modem in the connection's Properties sheet, as shown in figure 28.8.

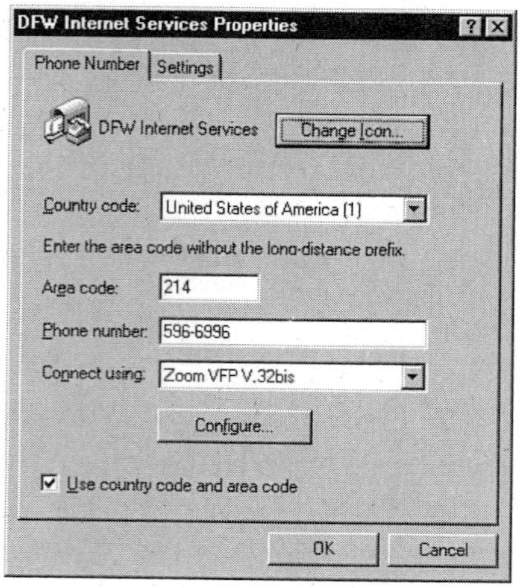

Fig. 28.8
Change the icon, name, phone number, and modem to use for this connection. Click OK to permanently save your settings.

To change the properties of your connection, follow these steps:

1. Choose File, Properties from the menu or click the Properties button on the toolbar.

2. Click Change Icon, select another icon from the list, and change the connection name.

3. Select a country code.

4. Type the area code and phone number. (If you select the default location when you dial, Windows will not dial the area code if it matches your default area code.)

5. Select a modem. Windows displays the modems you currently have installed, or enables you to go directly to the port. If you go directly to the port, you can bypass the Windows 95 modem configuration, controlling the modem directly. For normal usage, select a configured modem so that you can take advantage of centralized modem configuration.

6. Click OK to save your settings.

Tip
To change the HyperTerminal Properties sheet without even running HyperTerminal, right-click the connection you want to change in the HyperTerminal folder; then choose Properties. If you do this, the Properties sheet will have an additional tab, named General, with the file information.

Configuring the Connection Settings

The Settings page of the Properties sheet enables you to change the terminal properties of HyperTerminal. For example, you can change the terminal-emulation mode. Figure 28.9 shows the Settings page of this sheet. Table 28.3 describes each terminal emulation available in HyperTerminal.

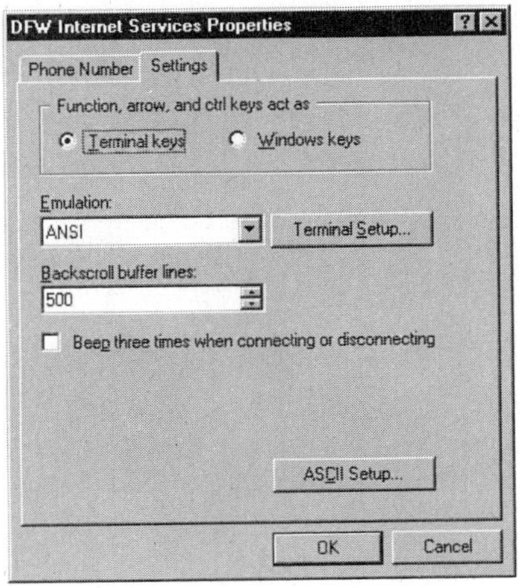

Fig. 28.9
Use the Settings page of the Properties sheet to change the terminal emulation and other useful settings.

Table 28.3 Terminal Emulation Supported by HyperTerminal

Protocol	Description
ANSI	A popular, generic terminal emulation supported by most Unix systems. It provides full-screen emulation.
Auto Detect	Automatically determines which terminal emulation the remote computer is using.
Minitel	An emulation primarily used in France.
TTY	Is actually absent of any terminal emulation. TTY simply displays all the characters it receives on the display.
Viewdata	An emulation primarily used in the United Kingdom.
VT-100	The workhorse of terminal emulations. Many remote systems such as Unix use it.
VT-52	A predecessor to VT 100. It provides full-screen terminal emulation on remote systems that support it.

To change the settings for this connection, follow these steps:

1. Choose File, Properties from the menu or click the Properties button on the toolbar. Alternatively, right-click a connection document in the HyperTerminal folder.

2. On the Settings page, choose Terminal Keys or Windows Keys. Terminal Keys sends function keys F1 through F12 and arrow keys to the remote computer instead of acting on them in Windows; Windows Keys causes Windows to act on them. For example, if you choose Terminal Keys and press F1, the key would be sent to the host, and the host would respond to it. If you choose Windows Keys and press F1, Windows would display help.

3. Set Emulation to the terminal emulation you want. HyperTerminal must be using the same terminal emulation the host computer is using.

Tip

If you set Emulation to Auto Detect, HyperTerminal automatically determines what emulation the host is using and configures itself appropriately. Use this setting for normal situations.

4. Set the number of lines you want in Backscroll Buffer Lines. In the HyperTerminal main window, the current screen is displayed with a white background. If you press Page Up or use the scroll bar to scroll backwards, you see previously displayed text with a gray background. The default value for Backscroll Buffer Lines is 500 lines, which allows you to review about 20 screens and doesn't consume a large amount of memory.

5. Turn on Beep Three Times When Connecting or Disconnecting if you want to be notified when you are making or breaking a connection.

6. Optionally, Click ASCII Setup and set the options for how text files are sent and received. Figure 28.10 shows the ASCII Setup dialog box, and table 28.4 describes what each option does.

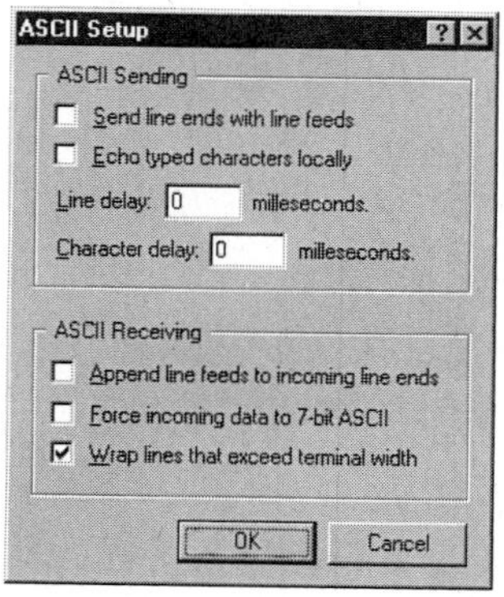

Fig. 28.10
Use the ASCII Setup dialog box to configure how ASCII files will be sent and received. For example, you can choose to send line feeds with line ends.

Table 28.4 ASCII Setup Options

Option	Description
Send Line Ends with Line Feeds	Attaches a line feed to the end of every line that HyperTerminal sends. Turn on this option if the remote computer requires it or you turned on Echo Typed Characters Locally, explained below, and pressing Enter moves you to the beginning of the current line instead of starting a new line.
Echo Typed Characters Locally	Displays each character you type on the keyboard instead of depending on the host to echo each character. Turn on this option only if you can't see the characters you type. If you see each character twice (ssuucchh aass tthhiiss), turn off this option.
Line Delay	Sets how much time to delay between lines. Increasing the amount of time between lines allows the remote computer time to get ready for the next line. Increase this setting in increments of 100 milliseconds if the remote computer frequently loses portions of each line.
Character Delay	Sets how much time to delay between characters. Increasing the amount of time between characters allows the remote computer time to get ready for the next character. Increase this setting in increments of 5 milliseconds if the remote computer randomly loses characters.
Append Line Feeds to Incoming Line Ends	Attaches a line feed to lines received. Turn on this option if the lines you receive from the host computer are displayed one on top of another.
Force Incoming Data to 7-bit ASCII	Changes 8-bit characters to 7-bit. Turn on this option if HyperTerminal displays greek or unrecognizable symbols. This option forces HyperTerminal to stick with readable characters.
Wrap Lines That Exceed Terminal Width	Turns word wrapping on or off. Turn on this option if you want lines that are longer than the terminal width to be continued on the following line.

Note

If you have selected a particular terminal emulation on the Settings tab, you can further refine the configuration by selecting Terminal Setup. HyperTerminal displays a different dialog box depending on which emulation you have chosen. The following table shows the options available for each emulation mode:

Emulation	Options
ANSI	Cursor: Block, Underline, or Blink
Minitel	Cursor: Block, Underline, or Blink
TTY	Cursor: Block, Underline, or Blink Use Destructive Backspace
Viewdata	Hide Cursor Enter Key Sends #
VT-100	Cursor: Block, Underline, or Blink Keypad Application Mode Cursor Keypad Mode 132-Column Mode Character Set
VT-52	Cursor: Block, Underline, or Blink Alternate Keypad Mode

Configuring Your Modem for HyperTerminal

You probably configured your modem after you installed Windows. You set options such as the port, speaker volume, and speed. In HyperTerminal, you can override any of these options. For example, if your modem is configured in the Control Panel to connect at 56,000 bps, you can configure your connection to connect at 2,400 bps. However, changing your connection doesn't change your modem's configuration; it is simply overridden by the connection.

◄ See "Installing and Configuring Your Modem," p. 831

Configuring your modem for a particular connection is the same as configuring it in the Control Panel.

The first two tabs, General and Connection, are the same as those displayed for configuring the modem in Control Panel.

The Options tab is added to the HyperTerminal modem Properties sheet only when you open it from HyperTerminal. This page enables you to set additional properties for HyperTerminal. To set these options for HyperTerminal, follow these steps:

1. Choose File, Properties from the menu or click the Properties button on the toolbar. Alternatively, right-click the appropriate connection icon in the HyperTerminal Connections folder.
2. Click the Options tab. HyperTerminal displays the page shown in figure 28.11.
3. Set options as described in table 28.5 and click OK to save.

Tip
HyperTerminal automatically detects the configuration of the modem you are calling. You don't need to change the data bits, stop bits, or parity settings you might have used in the past.

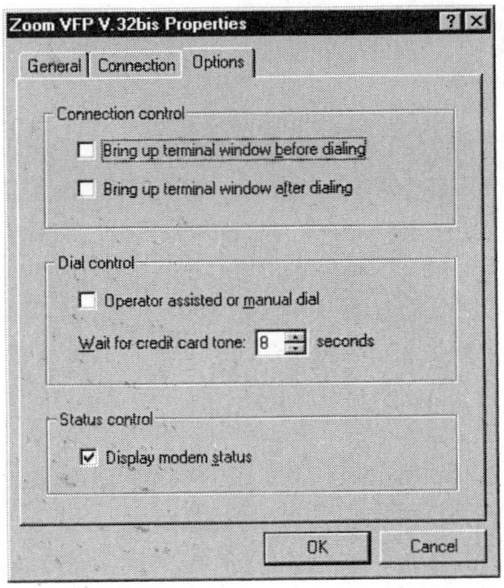

Fig. 28.11
You can refine your modem configuration on the Options page of the Modem Properties sheet by choosing to display a terminal window before and after dialing, which gives you more control over how the phone is dialed and the connection is made.

Table 28.5 Modem Options

Option	Description
Bring Up Terminal Window Before Dialing	Displays a terminal window, shown in figure 28.12, before HyperTerminal starts dialing, enabling you to enter modem commands directly. (See your modem's manual for a list of commands.)
Bring Up Terminal Window After Dialing	Displays a terminal window after HyperTerminal has dialed the phone number, enabling you to enter modem commands directly.
Operator Assisted or Manual Dial	Enables you to dial the telephone number directly. HyperTerminal prompts you to dial the telephone number.

(continues)

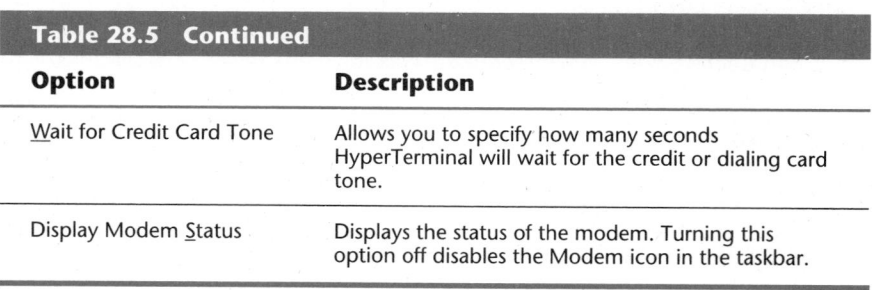

Table 28.5 Continued

Option	Description
Wait for Credit Card Tone	Allows you to specify how many seconds HyperTerminal will wait for the credit or dialing card tone.
Display Modem Status	Displays the status of the modem. Turning this option off disables the Modem icon in the taskbar.

◄ See "Understanding Your Modem and Your Telephone System," p. 850

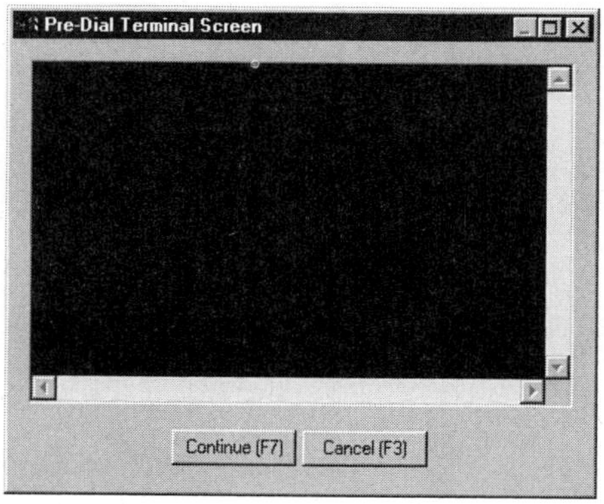

Fig. 28.12
You can use the terminal window to send commands directly to the modem before and after the phone number is dialed.

Note

HyperTerminal doesn't have a menu option or toolbar button to answer an incoming call. However, you can easily answer an incoming call if you have a Hayes-compatible modem by typing **ATA** and pressing Enter in the HyperTerminal window after the phone rings.

Chapter 29

Getting Connected to the Internet

by Francis Moss

Windows 95 provides a flexible and advanced means of connecting to the Internet, whether you are connecting from a stand-alone computer or from a network. Windows 95 has built-in support for TCP/IP dial-up access and PPP or SLIP (all Internet standards), and it supports 16-bit and 32-bit Windows Internet applications through a new Windows Sockets protocol that uses no conventional memory.

In addition, the Microsoft Internet Mail Service and the Microsoft Network provide seamless and universal connectivity.

In this chapter, you learn about the following:

- The Internet and the World Wide Web
- What TCP/IP is
- How to choose an Internet service provider
- How to connect to the Internet
- How to use other Internet applications with Windows 95

The Internet

Unless you've been living in a cave in the Himalayas, you've heard about the Internet. (There are even rumors about gurus with laptops and cellular modems who are surfing the Net!) The Internet is a "network of networks," a global linkage of millions of computers, containing vast amounts of information, much of it available to anyone with a modem and the right software... for free.

The main functions of the Internet are listed here:

- *E-mail* (electronic mail). You can send a message to anyone, anywhere in the world (as long as they have access to the Internet), almost instantaneously and for less than the cost of a regular letter, or "snailmail."
- *The World Wide Web* (the Web, or WWW). The fastest-growing part of the Internet, the Web provides access to files, documents, images, and sounds from thousands of different Web sites using a special programming language called *HyperText Markup Language*, or HTML. This language is used to create "hypertext" documents that include embedded commands.
- *UseNet newsgroups*. These are "many-to-many" discussion groups on topics ranging from science, current events, music, computers, "alternative" issues, and many others. There are currently over 10,000 newsgroups, and the list grows daily.
- *File transfer using File Transfer Protocol* (FTP). FTP is the Internet protocol for file transfer between computers linked to the Internet.

The Internet is an aggregation of high-speed networks, supported by the National Science Foundation (NSF) and almost 6,000 federal, state, and local systems, as well as university and commercial networks. It has links to networks in Canada, South America, Europe, Australia, and Asia, with more than 30,000,000 users. The Internet began with about 200 linked computers; today, there are several million linked computers all over the world. The Internet is growing so fast that no one can say how big it is today, or how large it will grow tomorrow.

The World Wide Web

The World Wide Web, also called the Web or WWW, is the fastest-growing and most exciting part of the Internet. It was developed in 1989 at CERN (which stands for *Centre Européen de Recherche Nucléaire*, but which most people call the Particle Physics Research Laboratory) at the University of Bern in Switzerland. Although the rest of the Internet is text oriented, the World Wide Web is graphics and sound oriented. Clicking a *hypertext* or *hypermedia link* (a specially encoded text or graphic image) takes you to other documents, called *Web pages*, where you can view images from the Hubble telescope, visit an art museum, watch a video clip of skiers (on a ski resort's page), or hear the haunting theme song from the Fox Network's hit show, *The X Files*—all on your computer.

Unlike other Internet file-retrieval systems, which are hierarchical in nature (you wend your way through descending layers of menus or directories to find what you're looking for), the WWW is distributed, offering links to other parts of the same document or other documents, which are not necessarily at the same Web site as the current document. With a program called a *graphical browser* (such as Microsoft's Internet Assistant or the Internet Explorer, a Web browser contained in the Microsoft Plus! Pack for Windows 95, Netscape, or NCSA's Mosaic), when you point and click a phrase on your screen that looks like this

Macmillan Publishing

you jump directly to the Web page of Macmillan Publishing USA, shown in figure 29.1.

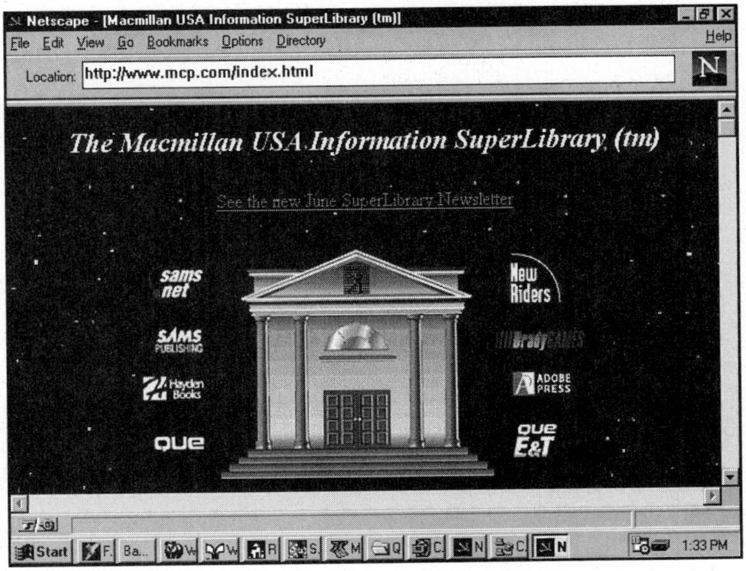

Fig. 29.1
The Macmillan Publishing Company page, as viewed from Netscape. Click elements in the graphic to move to the Web pages for those sites.

New authoring tools, including Microsoft's Internet Assistant (to be used with Word for Windows 6.0a or later), allow anyone with an Internet account to create his or her own *World Wide Web page* (a kind of advertisement for yourself that anyone on the Web can see). You learn more about the World Wide Web later in this chapter and in Chapter 30, "Using FTP, the World Wide Web, and Other Internet Services."

TCP/IP Explained

TCP/IP stands for Transmission Control Protocol/Internet Protocol. TCP/IP is the method used by every computer on the Internet to transfer files. As the name indicates, it's actually two protocols. The earliest model was the Internet Protocol, developed in the days of ARPANET (the Advanced Research Projects NETwork, the original Internet, formed in the 1960s) to send data in packets (self-contained units of information) from one computer network to another. The weakness of IP is its inability to deal with poor transmissions. If a packet gets garbled or interrupted, the receiving IP-based machine just tosses it.

The TCP protocol makes sure that every packet is delivered to the receiving network in the same order it was sent. A kind of numbering system verifies that the packet received is identical to the one sent.

Every network and every computer on the Internet uses TCP/IP to communicate. Until recently, the TCP/IP protocol has caused some problems for DOS-based machines: a version of TCP/IP that you install on your machine may conflict with the version installed on your LAN, or with your Internet service provider's version; certain applications such as FTP or e-mail that employ TCP/IP may call different functions in their own version of the protocol than the functions the network employs. Up to now, the process of connecting to the Internet has been a good candidate for the U.S. Army's advertising slogan: "It's not just a job, it's an adventure."

Versions of Microsoft Windows after version 3.x have encouraged the development of a TCP/IP standard of sorts, called the Windows Sockets Library, or *Winsock*. All manufacturers of Windows-based Internet programs have accepted this standard, which means that, ideally (for example) any Windows mail reader you choose will work with the WINSOCK.DLL in your WINDOWS directory.

But still some problems remain. A version of Winsock bundled with one software manufacturer's Internet application may conflict with another version. Each application may install a version of Winsock in its own directory, causing conflicts with another manufacturer's version. Or an Internet provider may customize its version of Winsock, causing conflicts with Internet applications that cannot recognize the new version. Internet jockeys running Windows must periodically comb their hard drives for mismatched Winsocks.

With Windows 95, such conflicts are less of a problem. Microsoft has created two brand-new Winsocks, one for 16-bit applications and another for 32-bit applications. In addition, a Virtual Device Driver (VxD), called WSOCK.VXD, manages the TCP/IP interface. This driver resides in upper memory—your system performance isn't affected. Most Windows 3.x-based Internet applications work seamlessly with the Windows 95 Winsock. As more Internet software vendors provide Windows 95 versions, Winsock conflicts should disappear.

Note

CompuServe's WinCim Web browser (included with version 1.4) requires a customized Winsock that conflicts with the Windows 95 version. A work-around for this is to put the CompuServe Winsock in the CID folder.

Note

By default, Windows 95 installs the 16-bit WINSOCK.DLL in your Windows folder; it installs a 32-bit version, WSOCK32.DLL, in your \Windows\System folder. If you are using a 32-bit Internet application, Windows 95 knows to use the 32-bit version.

Choosing an Internet Service Provider

As the Internet grows by leaps and bounds, more and more businesses, called *Internet Service Providers* (ISPs), are springing up to provide access. Typically, a local provider offers three or more computers, called *servers*, that are linked directly to the Internet. In turn, they provide a dozen or more high-speed (14.4 Kbps or 28.8 Kbps) modems connected to local telephone lines. In some cities, a new service called *Integrated Services Digital Network* (ISDN) offers modem speeds up to 128 Kbps. Unless you live in a remote part of the world, finding a service provider is not the problem it was as recently as six months ago. The problem is, what kind of service do you need?

Let's examine the ways to access the Internet:

- If you attend a college or university, or are employed at a business of any size, you may already have Internet access. See your supervisor, the computer science department, or an administrator. Make a case for Internet access to your home, or at least for using your organization's access during off-hours.
- Join a commercial online service, such as CompuServe, America Online, Prodigy, or Delphi. These services handle the connectivity problems for you; it's just a matter of "pointing and clicking" your way to the Net. Windows 95 can benefit you because of its improved high-speed serial port support.
- Sign on to the Microsoft Network. Although the version of MSN bundled with Windows 95 provides only limited Internet services, in response to competition from the commercial service providers, MSN is adding increased access. Offerings include: e-mail and read-only access to some UseNet newsgroups, including the following categories: rec (recreation), soc (society, social issues), sci (science), misc (miscellaneous), news (mostly Internet news), talk (online conversation), and comp (computers). Because Microsoft intends to serve young people as well as adults, their UseNet newsreader restricts access to the unmoderated alt.* newsgroups, unless you state you are over 18 years of age. However, the Microsoft Plus! Pack, a separate suite of programs released concurrently with Windows 95, offers complete Internet access through the Microsoft Network.
- Sign up with a national Internet provider, such as NETCOM, PSI Pipeline USA, or PSI Instant InterRamp. If you live in a rural area or travel a lot, this may be your best bet. A national provider has access phone numbers in major cities and often has SprintNet or Tymnet access elsewhere.
- Sign up with a local Internet provider. This is often the most economical way to get on the Net: many services cost as little as $15 to $25 per month. Every major city in the U.S. and around the world has at least one local provider. Look for advertisements in computer magazines, the newspaper, or your classified telephone directory.

What You Need to Connect to the Internet

By now, Windows 95's Hardware Wizard has installed and configured your modem, or you've done it yourself. We hope you're using at least a 14.4 Kbps modem; that's about as slow as you want to go on the Internet. Once you've chosen your Internet provider, you're ready to set up Windows 95 to surf the Net.

◀ See "Installing a Plug and Play Modem," p. 883

◀ See "Using Drivers Provided by Modem Manufacturers," p. 843

Now you have to deal with some more Net jargon: SLIP and PPP. SLIP stands for Serial-Line Internet Protocol; PPP means Point-to-Point Protocol. Both are implementations of the TCP/IP Internet protocol over telephone lines. (Unless you access the Net through a LAN and Ethernet cabling, you'll be using telephone lines and SLIP or PPP.)

There are both technical and practical differences between the two protocols: technically, SLIP is a *network-layer protocol*; PPP is a *link-level protocol*. Practically, this means that PPP is faster and more fail-safe than SLIP. Windows 95 is optimized for PPP, which is the protocol to choose if your provider offers a choice.

If you've chosen an Internet-only service, you need the following information from your Internet provider:

- The kind of connection provided: SLIP or PPP
- Your user name (You can usually choose your own, such as jsmith.)
- A password (Again, you select your own. The most secure passwords have six or more uppercase and lowercase letters and/or numbers.)
- The provider's local access phone number
- Your host and domain name
- Your Domain Name Server's IP address (Briefly, DNS is the method the Internet uses to create unique names for each of the servers on the network.)
- Authentication technique (Some ISPs require users to type in their login name and password in a *terminal window,* which is a DOS window that opens when you connect to the service. Others have automated authentication methods, called PAP or CHAP, discussed later.)

If your service provider gives you a dedicated IP address to use every time you dial in (in other words, you always log on to the same ISP server), you may also need the following:

- *IP address for you.* This is your computer's unique address.
- *IP subnet mask.* A physical world analogy might be the apartment number following a street address as a further way of pinpointing a location.
- *Gateway IP address.* The address of your ISP's server.

Here is an example of the setup requirements for an Internet provider:

IP Address:	1.1.1.1
Subnet Mask:	255.0.0.0
Host Name:	your computer's name
Domain Name:	anynet.com
Dial:	555-0000 (your provider's phone #)
Login:	jsmith
Password:	pAssWoRd (whatever you choose)
Domain Server:	222.222.68.160

Your provider might configure your system for you. At least they will help you over the phone while you enter the information in the correct Windows 95 Dial-Up Adapter dialog boxes (except for your password, which only you and your provider will know).

Installing and Configuring Windows 95 Dial-Up Network Adapter

Now it's time to set up Windows 95 to access the Internet. Here's what to do:

1. Double-click the My Computer icon to see whether Dial-Up Networking is installed. If it is, you see a folder named Dial-Up Networking (see fig. 29.2).
2. If you have Dial-Up Networking already installed, go to the section titled, "Creating a Configuration for Your Access Provider." If you do not have a Dial-Up Networking folder, install it now. Open the Start menu, and choose Settings, Control Panel.

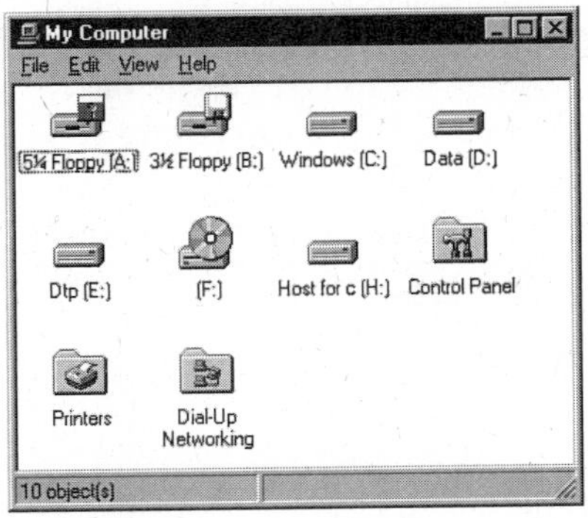

Fig. 29.2
A view of My Computer, showing Dial-Up Networking installed.

3. Select the Add/Remove Programs option. The Add/Remove Programs Properties sheet appears.

4. Click the Windows Setup tab.

5. Select the Communications option and click the Details button. The dialog box in figure 29.3 appears.

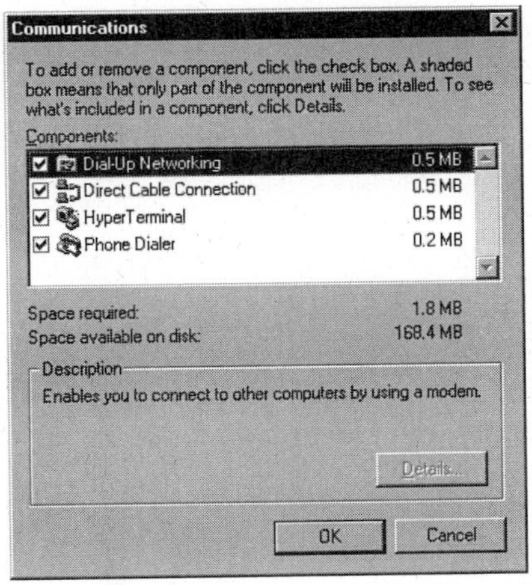

Fig. 29.3
The Communications dialog box, from which you select Dial-Up Networking to install that option.

6. Select the Dial-Up Networking option.

7. Click OK in the Communications dialog box; click OK in the Add/Remove Programs Properties sheet to complete the installation.

Installing TCP/IP

To install and configure TCP/IP, follow these steps:

1. Open the Start menu and choose Settings, Control Panel. Double-click the Network control panel. Click the Add button, select Protocol, and

click the Add button. The Select Network Protocol dialog box appears (see fig. 29.4). Select Microsoft from the Manufacturers list, select TCP/IP from the Network Protocols list, and click OK.

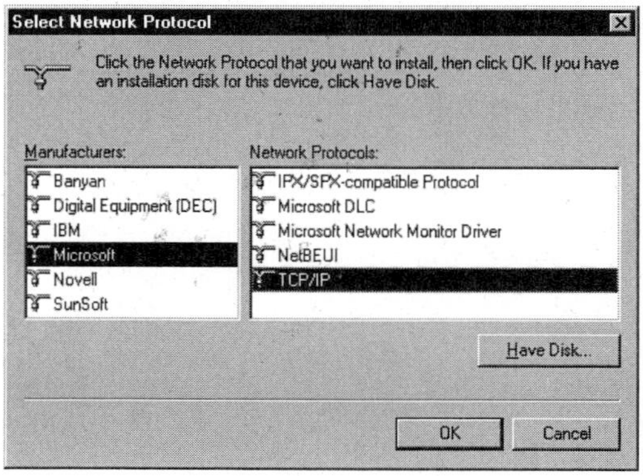

Fig. 29.4
The Select Network Protocol dialog box; select Microsoft from the Manufacturers list and TCP/IP from the Network Protocols list.

◄ See "Installing the Network Protocol," p. 627

2. Now make sure that your dial-up adapter is using (the term is, *is bound to*) the TCP/IP protocol. In the Network dialog box, click the Dial-Up Adapter to highlight it and then click Properties. Click the Bindings tab (see fig. 29.5). Make sure that a check mark is in the box next to the TCP/IP Dial-Up adapter.

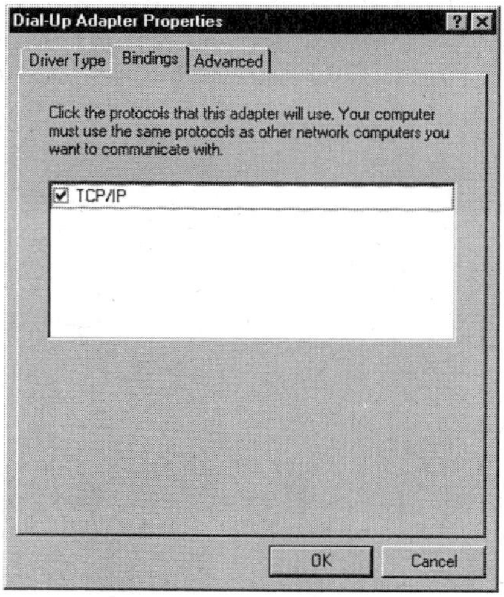

Fig. 29.5
The Bindings tab in the Dial-Up Adapter Properties sheet, showing TCP/IP bound to the adapter.

3. Set the TCP/IP properties. Open the Start menu and choose Settings, Control Panel. Double-click the Network Icon. Highlight TCP/IP -> Dial-Up Adapter in the Network box and click Properties. Select the IP Address tab and make sure that the Obtain an IP Address Automatically

option is checked. This option sets your IP address to 0.0.0.0 (this will not be visible because the box will be grayed-out), which means that your Internet provider will dynamically assign you an IP address when you call in.

Note

If your Internet service provider assigns you a permanent IP address, enter that address manually on the IP Address tab: in the IP Address box, check the Specify an IP Address option and enter the assigned address in the IP Address field. You must also type the subnet mask address for your provider in the Subnet mask field.

When you connect using PPP, the permanent IP address is used instead of the Internet service provider dynamically assigning one to you. When you connect with SLIP, the permanent IP address shows up in the Specify an IP address box to confirm your IP address for your SLIP connection.

Tip
If the address you're typing has less than three numbers before the period, use the Right Arrow key to jump to the next area between the periods in the field. If you type three numbers before the period, the cursor moves to the next area automatically.

4. In the TCP/IP Properties sheet, click the DNS Configuration tab (see fig. 29.6). Select Enable DNS; then set your Host and Domain names. Enter the Host name (this can be "User," unless you are assigned one by your network administrator).

5. Still in the DNS Configuration box, tab to the DNS Server Search Order box and enter the numeric address of the DNS server your provider said to use.

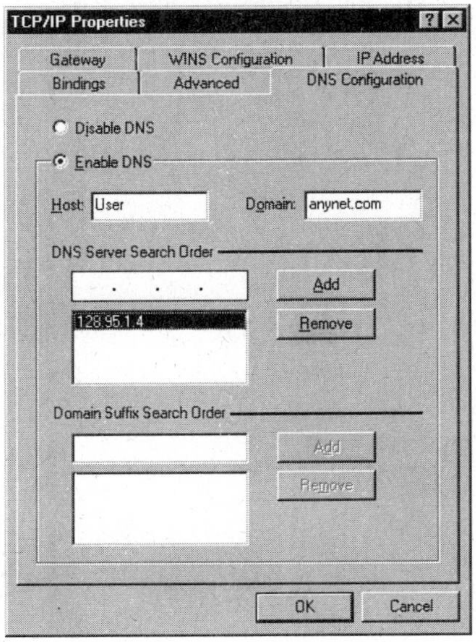

Fig. 29.6
The DNS Configuration tab of the TCP/IP Properties sheet shows the address for Microsoft.

6. Click OK to close the Network control panel. Exit and restart Windows 95.

Creating a Configuration for Your Access Provider

In the preceding sections, you configured Windows 95 for TCP/IP connections. Now you need to tell it about the connection you'll be making to your ISP. To do this, you create and configure a new connection.

◀ See "Starting Programs and Documents from the Explorer or My Computer," p. 73

1. Open the Dial-Up Networking folder from the My Computer window. If this is the first time you've opened it, a Connection Wizard runs to help you enter all the information necessary for a dial-up connection.

2. Double-click the Make New Connection icon (see fig. 29.7). If you have not already configured Windows 95 for your modem, click Configure to do so now.

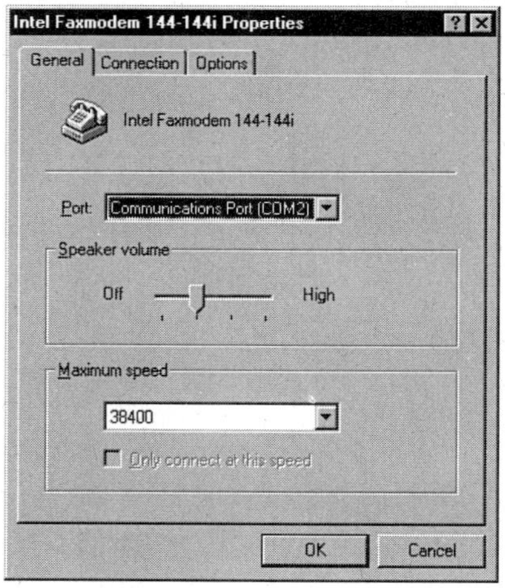

Fig. 29.7
Clicking Configure brings up the Modem Properties sheet.

3. If you have configured your modem, continue by clicking Next; then enter the area code and telephone number for your ISP. Select your country code and area code from the drop-down menus. Click Next, and then click Finish to complete the installation. Now you have a new icon in your Dial-Up Networking Box. For easier access, drag the icon to your desktop to create a shortcut.

4. If your provider requires you to log on by means of a terminal window (it looks like a DOS window where you type in your user name and password), you must enable that function. In the Dial-Up Networking

box, right-click the connection icon you've just created and choose Properties. In the Connect Using area of the dialog box, click Configure. Now choose the Options tab (see fig. 29.8). In the Connection Control section, make sure that the Bring Up Terminal Window after Dialing box is checked. Click OK. This returns you to the first box of the Property sheet.

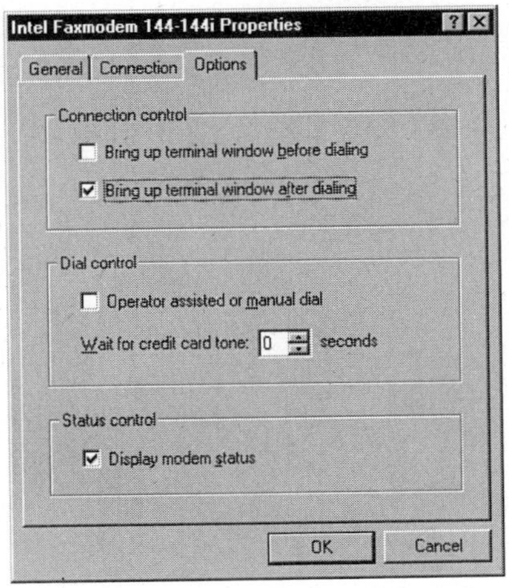

Fig. 29.8
Check the Bring Up Terminal Window After Dialing option to enable this function.

5. In the Property sheet, click Server Type in the Connect Using section. This displays the dialog box in figure 29.9. From the Allowed Network Protocols group, check the TCP/IP option. This option provides quicker connect time after dialing the Internet provider. Uncheck the NetBEUI and IPX/SPX Compatible options because they are not relevant to connecting to the Internet.

   In the Type of Dial-Up Server section of the Property sheet, use the drop-down menu to select the type of connection, PPP, SLIP, or CSLIP (for a Compressed SLIP account). Your Internet provider can tell you which type of account you have. Click OK to close the dialog box for your Dial-Up Connection.

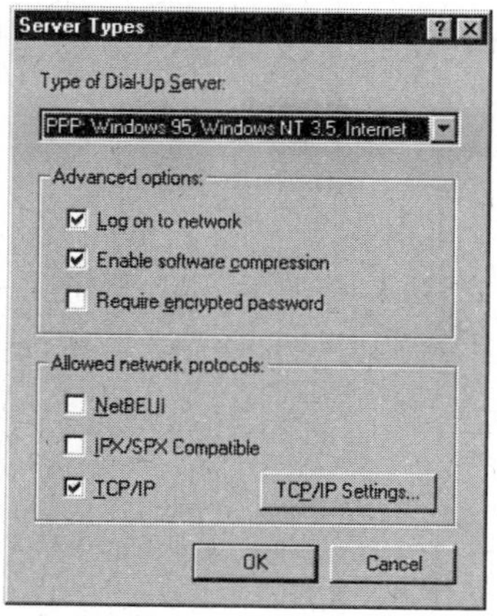

Fig. 29.9
If you are using a PPP connection, your Server Types dialog box should look like this.

Connecting to Your Internet Provider

You are now ready to dial your Internet provider. Follow these steps:

1. To dial, double-click your New Connection icon (either on the desktop, if you've created a shortcut, or in the Dial-Up Networking folder). The Connect To dialog box should display the phone number for your Internet provider. You don't have to enter your user name and password here because you enter that information in the terminal window that appears after you've clicked Connect.

2. After the modem connects and you hear the "hiss," a terminal window appears (see fig. 29.10). Enter your user name and password, and then click Continue (F7); you should be connected within a few seconds.

   Many providers are offering a more modern method of login, like PAP or CHAP. If this is true in your case, you don't have to check the Bring Up Terminal Window after Dialing option (found in the Dial-Up Networking Properties sheet under the Options tab of the Configure dialog box).

   To dial your ISP, just enter your user name and password in the Connect To dialog box that appears after you double-click the Connection icon, as shown in figure 29.11.

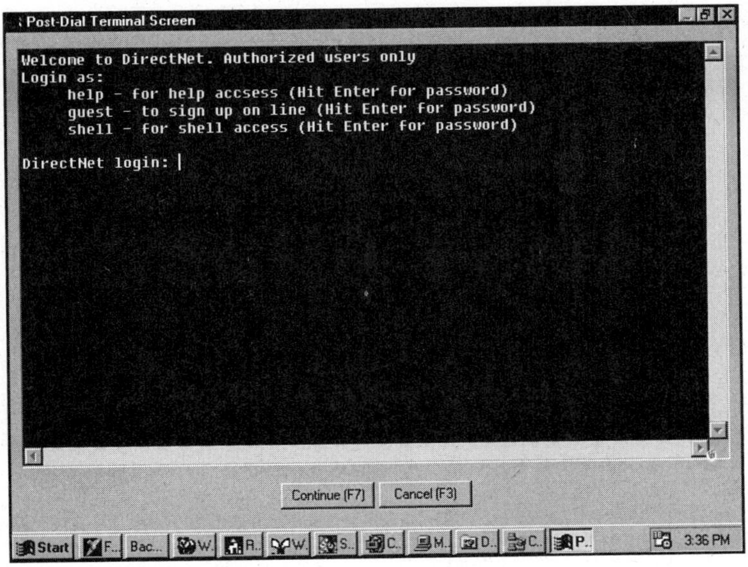

Fig. 29.10
Use the Post-Dial Terminal Screen to enter your user name and password.

Note

PAP stands for Password Authentication Protocol. *CHAP* stands for Challenge-Handshake Authentication Protocol. Both protocols allow you to log in without typing your user name and password in a terminal window.

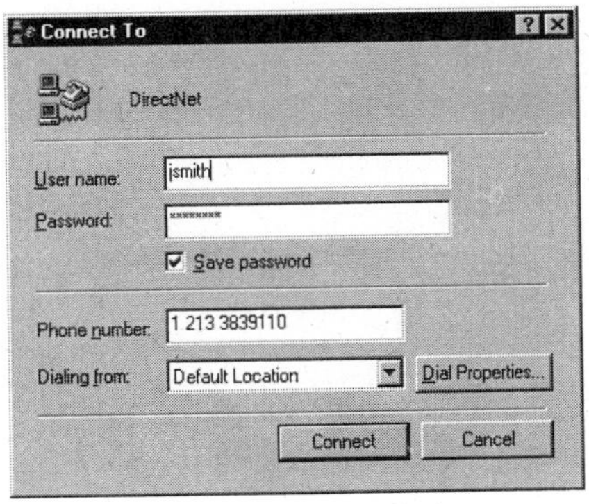

Fig. 29.11
If your provider offers CHAP or PAP, you can check Save Password in the Connect To dialog box to avoid having to retype the password each time you log in.

> **Note**
>
> Unless you configured Windows 95 to require a password at the start of each day's session, you will have to retype your password here the first time each day, or after you reboot.

If you are using a SLIP account, you will need a file called RNAPLUS.INF, available in the ADMIN/APPTOOLS/SLIP directory on the Windows 95 CD-ROM or via download from the Microsoft FTP site. Follow these steps to install it:

1. Open the Start menu and choose Settings, Control Panel. Double-click Add/Remove Programs. Select the Windows Setup tab; then click Have Disk.

2. Click Browse. Select the drive and directory where the file RNAPLUS.INF is located. When you've selected the file, click OK.

3. The Have Disk dialog box appears. Check the box (see fig. 29.12) and then click Install.

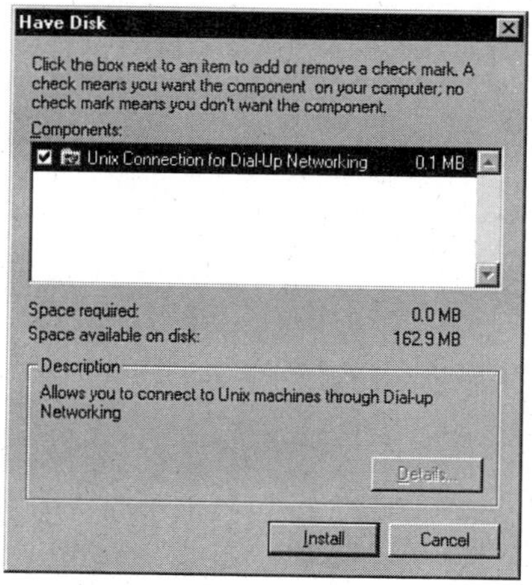

Fig. 29.12
Check the box labeled Unix Connection for Dial-Up Networking.

Now you are ready to add SLIP connectivity to your Dial-Up Networking Folder. Follow these steps to connect:

1. After you enter your user name and password in the terminal window, you should get a message from your provider telling you your IP address for this session. Most providers tell you what your IP address is with a

message like `Your IP address is` or `SLIP session from ###.###.###.### to ###.###.###.###`. The second number is usually your IP address. Write down your IP address and click the Continue button.

2. You should see a dialog box like the one in figure 29.13, asking you to confirm your IP address. Type the IP address you just wrote down and click OK. You should be connected in a few seconds. Make sure that you type the correct IP address when connecting.

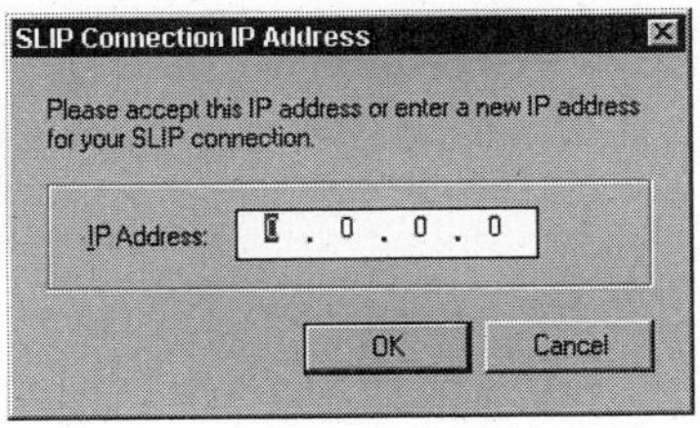

Fig. 29.13
Use this dialog box to enter your IP address. If you are not sure of it, ask your Internet provider what your address is for SLIP.

Note

Most Internet providers can switch your account from SLIP to PPP for no charge. PPP is faster than SLIP and offers error correction. Additionally, PPP accounts may not require you to use the terminal window to log in and do not require you to enter your IP address manually.

Troubleshooting

I've entered all the information in the Property sheet for my connection, and I've configured my modem correctly, but I still can't connect.

If you are having problems connecting with your service, make sure that your server type is correct. In the Dial-Up Networking folder, right-click your Connection icon; then select Properties. Click on Server Type. Make sure that the server type in the connection properties is set to PPP, not SLIP or CSLIP. Uncheck the box labeled Enable Software Compression in the Advanced Options section of the page.

If you have a SLIP account, make sure that you have changed the server type to SLIP or CSLIP (PPP is the default). Make sure that you type the correct IP address when prompted during the login process.

Testing Your Connection

To test whether a connection is working, we'll use a program that comes with Windows 95 called PING. When executed, PING calls the remote computer you designate and sends back a response to let you know you're connected. The program's name comes from submarine sonar, which sends out a *ping* to get an echo of another hull in the water.

1. After you are connected to your ISP, open a DOS window.

2. At the DOS prompt, type **ping ftp.microsoft.com**. If the Microsoft server is busy, it may not answer right away. If so, **ping** your Internet provider's host computer by name—it may be mail, or mach1. Or **ping** 128.95.1.4, a DNS server. After a few milliseconds, the remote host replies:

```
Pinging rftp.microsoft.com [198.105.232.1] with 32 bytes of data:
Reply from 198.105.232.1: bytes=32 time=180ms TTL=18
Reply from 198.105.232.1: bytes=32 time=185ms TTL=18
Reply from 198.105.232.1: bytes=32 time=176ms TTL=18
Reply from 198.105.232.1: bytes=32 time=181ms TTL=18
```

This tells you that your computer is talking to the server. Unless you have ongoing problems connecting, you'll use the `PING` command only once.

Troubleshooting

After connecting with my SLIP account, I can ping the server, but still can't use Winsock applications to connect to a resource.

You may have to switch the server type. From My Computer, open the Dial-Up Networking folder. Right-click on your connection to open the Properties sheet. Select Server Type; then try changing the server type in the connection properties from SLIP to CSLIP or CSLIP to SLIP, depending on what it is currently set for.

I can run my Web browser, but my newsgroup reader and my mail reader won't work. What's wrong?

If you have a Winsock application that is not working properly, check to see whether that application requires a specific WINSOCK.DLL file. Some Winsock applications come with their own WINSOCK.DLL, which may not work with Windows 95. First, try renaming the application-provided WINSOCK.DLL to ensure that you're using the WINSOCK.DLL in your WINDOWS directory. If the application does not work with the Windows 95 WINSOCK.DLL, replace it with the application's WINSOCK.DLL file.

Caution

Renaming your Windows 95 WINSOCK.DLL may cause other Winsock applications not to work and is not recommended. Contact the application vendor to see whether they have an updated version that will work with the Windows 95 WINSOCK.DLL.

Troubleshooting

Everything seems to be configured properly, but I still can't connect to my ISP.

If you are having trouble connecting, open the Network icon in the control panel, select the Dial-Up Adapter, select Properties, select the Advanced tab, and set Record a Log File to Yes. This action writes a file called PPPLOG.TXT to your WINDOWS directory that contains information recorded during the connecting process. You may need this information when you talk to your provider.

I have a PPP connection and sometimes can't connect to my provider.

If you are having problems when connecting with Internet service providers offering PPP accounts, it may help if you turn off IP header compression. To do so, open Control Panel, double-click Networking, click Dial-Up Adapter to select it, and click Properties. In the Properties sheet, select the Advanced tab and uncheck the Use IP Header Compression option.

Connecting to the Internet with a LAN

If your computer is part of a Local Area Network (LAN), connecting to the Internet with Windows 95 is as easy as connecting a single user. The main difference is that instead of getting the information you need from an ISP, you will obtain it from your network administrator. Windows 95 provides seamless integration of Internet and LAN e-mail though a Microsoft API mail driver employing the Microsoft Exchange client. Mail from another computer on the LAN is treated the same as mail from out on the Internet.

Let's get started:

1. Open the Start menu and choose Settings, Control Panel. Double-click the Network icon. If you followed the previous procedures, you will now have both Dial-Up Adapter and TCP/IP installed. Select the TCP/IP protocol and click Properties.

2. Select the IP Address tab. If your LAN has a Dynamic Host Configuration Protocol (DHCP) Server, you will click the button marked Obtain an IP Address automatically.

3. If your LAN does not have a DHCP server, you will have to obtain the IP address from your network administrator. Click the button marked Specify an IP address and fill in the address. Use the arrow key to move between the fields separated by periods. You should also enter the Subnet Mask address at this time.

4. Now click the Gateway tab. This is the address of the connection point between your LAN and the Internet. Enter the address provided by your network administrator.

5. Now select the DNS Configuration tab (refer to fig. 29.6). Select Enable DNS. Obtain your Host and Domain names from your network administrator and enter them in the spaces provided. For example, your computer might be "Zeus," at IBM. The address would be zeus[Host].ibm.com[Domain] (omitting the words in the brackets). If you are part of a smaller organization, you may not have a Domain Name Server of your own, but would be given a domain name by your service provider.

6. Still in the DNS Configuration box, tab to the DNS Server Search Order box and enter the numeric address of the DNS server your network administrator gives you.

7. You are almost done. If your LAN is not using DHCP, or is running Windows NT, you may have to set up the Windows Internet Naming Service, (WINS, pronounced "WIN-S"). Click the WINS Configuration tab and follow your network administrator's instructions.

8. That's it! Click OK to close the Network control panel. Exit and restart Windows 95.

There are a few concerns for networks on the Internet with Windows 95:

◀ See "The Four Building Blocks of Windows 95 Networking," p. 600

- *TCP/IP and System Pauses.* If you are using TCP/IP for your Internet connections and the protocol is bound to both your LAN and dial-up adapter but no DHCP server is present on the LAN, your system may pause for a few seconds every once in a while. To avoid this, unbind TCP/IP from your LAN adapter. Here's how to do it:

Open the Network folder in Control Panel. Select the Network Card (see fig. 29.14); then click on Properties. Click the Bindings tab, and then uncheck the TCP/IP option in the dialog box.

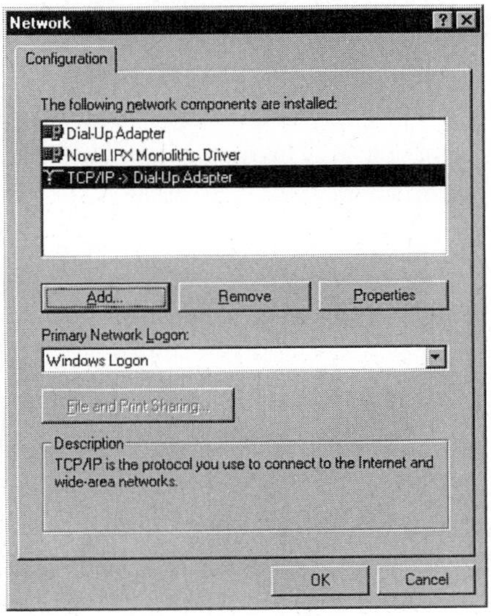

Fig. 29.14
Notice that the TCP/IP protocol is only bound to the Dial-Up Adapter, as it should be.

- If Microsoft's TCP/IP is the only protocol you have loaded on your system, the IP address is not added during setup. If you have a DHCP server, just open the Network control panel applet and then close it; this action updates the IP address. Otherwise, open the Network control panel applet, select Properties on the TCP/IP page, and manually enter your IP address.

Software You Can Use with the Internet

After all the configuration work you went through to get onto the Internet, it may seem that getting connected was the goal. But the real power of the Internet lies not in the connection, but in what you do after you are there. Windows includes the following three Internet applications, but they are of somewhat limited usefulness; you will want to find freeware or commercial software for your Internet applications.

- *Telnet* is a Windows-based program you use to log on to Internet sites as if your computer were a terminal connected to that computer. This version of Telnet is almost identical to the shareware version available at many sites on the Net; it is minimalist but has a good help file. For more information, see the section "Services Available on the Internet," later in this chapter.

- *FTP* is a command-line program, not for the faint of heart, used to download files from remote computers connected to the Internet. FTP is examined further in Chapter 30, "Using FTP, the World Wide Web, and other Internet Services."

With the mushrooming popularity of the Internet, more and more software packages are appearing every day. To make full use of the Internet's potential with Windows 95, you need the following kinds of applications:

- *A World Wide Web browser.* Available browsers include Microsoft's Internet Explorer, Netscape, Mosaic, or Microsoft's Internet Assistant, an add-on to Word for Windows (currently available as freeware from Microsoft's FTP site). You also need programs to view downloaded graphics and play sound files. In some cases, these applications are included with your Web browser.

- *A mail program.* Among the better known Windows programs are Eudora, by Qualcomm, available as both a shareware and a commercial program; OS Mail, from Open Systems; and Z-Mail, from Network Computing Devices, Inc.

- *An FTP program.* A very good freeware Windows-based program is WS_FTP, copyright by John A. Junod, available from your Internet provider or at many FTP sites.

- *A newsreader.* You use newsreaders with UseNet newsgroups. Trumpet News Reader is a freeware version, as is WinVN, by Mark Riordan. Also available are NewsXpress and Free Agent.

- *A file search utility.* There are millions of files on Internet servers all over the world; how do you find the one you're looking for? Three time-tested systems, each performing slightly different functions, are Gopher, Archie, and Veronica. Windows programs to access these Internet tools are available.

See Chapter 30, "Using FTP, the World Wide Web, and other Internet Services," for more information on these and other Internet applications.

Services Available on the Internet

The Internet is a combination communications tool, library, and catalog. Many think it is the most important source of information available today. More realistic Net surfers have found that, although the Internet has more *data* than anyone can ever begin to comprehend, there's not much *information* (defined as *useful* data). The Net-speak phrase that defines this situation is "a high signal to noise ratio."

The best way to decide is to find out for yourself. Windows makes getting connected fairly simple, but you'll have to get other software to do your own Net cruising. The following sections take a detailed look at some of the services on the Net.

The World Wide Web

The most exciting development on the Internet in recent months has been the explosive growth of the World Wide Web. It seems that everyone with access to the Internet has a Web page; you can find pages for groups from Microsoft (see fig. 29.15) to The Whole Internet Catalog (see fig. 29.16).

All Web pages, or World Wide Web sites, are identified by a unique address, called a *Universal Resource Locator* (URL). The Microsoft page's URL address looks like this:

http://www.microsoft.com/

The Whole Internet Catalog page's URL looks like this:

http://www.gnn.com/wic/newrescat.toc.html

All World Wide Web addresses begin the same way: http:// (which stands for *HyperText Transfer Protocol*, the "language" of the Web). With a Web browser, you can also visit FTP sites (described later in this chapter), which have addresses beginning with ftp://.

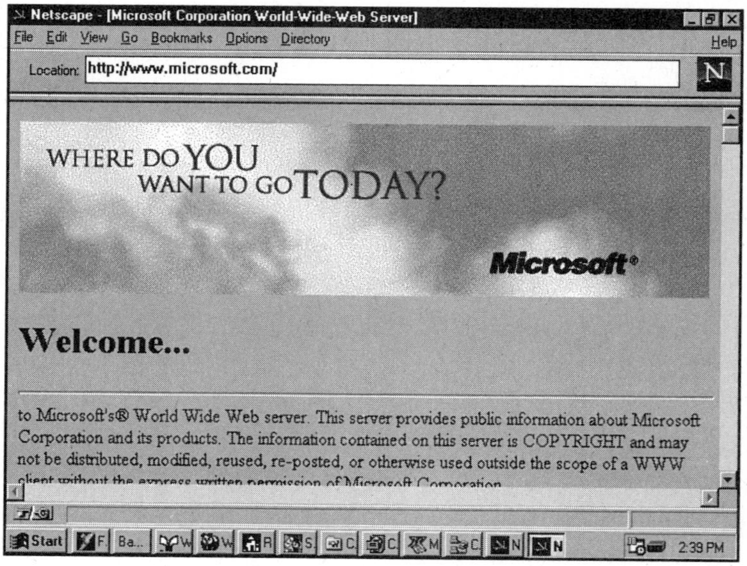

Fig. 29.15
This is the Microsoft Web page.

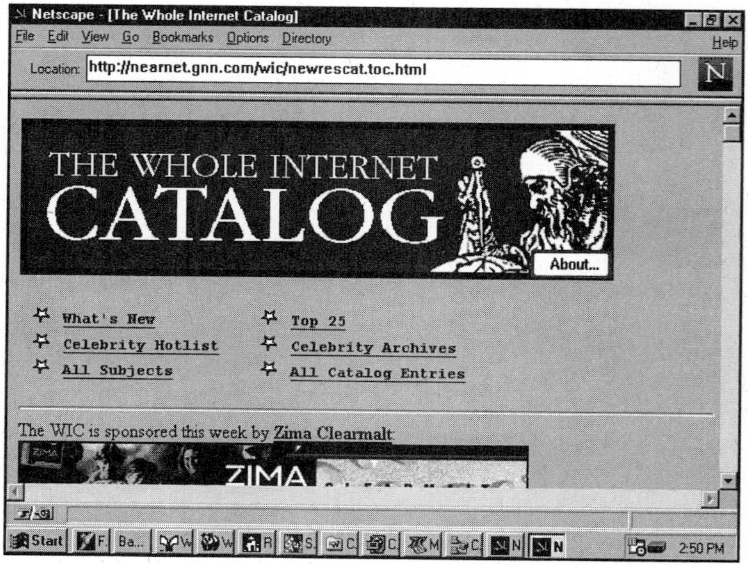

Fig. 29.16
This is The Whole Internet Catalog, a Web search tool you can use to search for any type of document accessible from the Web.

Windows 95 does not currently provide a Web browser, but excellent ones are available as freeware and shareware from NCSA Mosaic, Netscape, Quarterdeck, and many other vendors. The Microsoft Plus! Pack, a CD-ROM with many Windows 95 tools, includes a browser.

After you install your browser, you can configure it to view and download graphical images on many Web sites, listen to music and voice clips, and use hypertext links to jump to other World Wide Web sites around the world.

Time magazine has a Web page (see fig. 29.17). Begin at the Time-Warner Web page at:

http://www.pathfinder.com

The *Time* magazine site has pictures and articles from its recent issues, a database of past issue contents, and even a BBS for chatting with other *Time* aficionados. The Time-Warner page also provides links to other publications like *Sports Illustrated, People*, and *Fortune*.

Fig. 29.17
A Netscape browser view of the *Time* magazine Welcome Web page.

> **Caution**
>
> Like DOS file names, URLs have *no* spaces. Type the URL—or any Internet address you see—without spaces.

Electronic Mail

The most widely used service the Internet provides is electronic mail, or e-mail. With e-mail, you can be in almost instantaneous contact with anyone else on the Internet, no matter where they live or work.

Suppose that you've arranged to meet an associate the next morning in a distant city. It's late at night, your plans have changed, and you need to get in touch with him or her. Send an e-mail message. E-mail users check their mail every day.

How do you send an e-mail message? Just as in the physical world, where addresses include numbers, streets, cities, and states, on the Internet, everyone has a unique e-mail address that looks like this:

username@anynet.com

Businesses, Internet organizations, and services such as Listserv (a program that keeps track of mailing lists) also have addresses. Your address is composed of your user name (such as jsmith) and your provider's domain. If Jane Smith signs on to America Online for her Internet access, she may have an e-mail address like this one:

jsmith@aol.com

If Joe Smith is already using that login name on AOL, Jane has to pick another one.

The Internet also has *mailing lists*, or e-mail discussion groups, on many topics (such as writing, pets, running a small business, and so on), comprised of members who subscribe to that mailing list.

Note

To *subscribe* to a mailing list—in other words, to join the discussion or just read others' postings—you send an e-mail message to the *listserver* who manages that mailing list.

Note

To *send a message* to the members of a mailing list, once you've joined, you post a message to the mailing list itself. You respond to messages in the mailing list in the same way you answer an e-mail message from an individual.

UseNet Newsgroups

Newsgroups are another important service on the Internet. Where e-mail is a one-to-one communication, newsgroups are many-to-many discussions, organized by topics. There are over 10,000 newsgroups currently on the Internet, dealing with every imaginable—and unimaginable—topic. The wildest are the unmoderated alt.* groups (alt is an abbreviation for *alternative*), on topics from **alt.0d** (which seems to be a bunch of test messages) to **alt.zine** (a newsgroup about alternative magazines). You can read messages from a newsgroup to see whether you want to subscribe or not.

Most newsreaders identify *threads* (series of messages on the same topic) by indenting follow-up messages and by allowing the use of Re to indicate the topic of original posting (see fig. 29.18). Some newsreaders allow you to sort messages by thread so that you can follow threads that interest you and avoid those that don't.

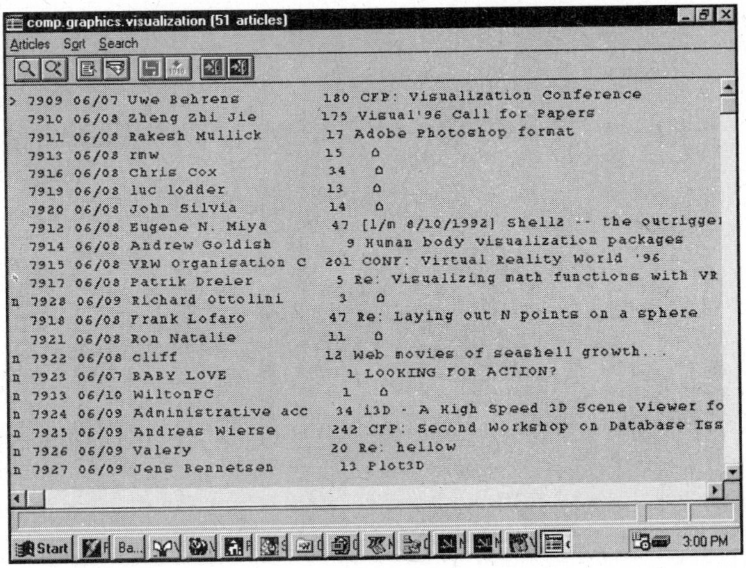

Fig. 29.18
A WinVN newsreader listing of messages in the newsgroup **comp.graphics.visualization**. Notice the indenting for threads.

When you first log on to the Internet and boot up your newsreader program, the newsreader will prompt you to download the current list of newsgroups from the news server. With more than 10,000 newsgroups this might take a few minutes, but you only have to do it once. You can refresh the list from time to time. To read the messages in a newsgroup, you then select it from the list. You can read messages from a newsgroup to see whether you want to subscribe or not. Once you have subscribed, you can just lurk (that's what Net-surfers call it when you read articles but do not post any) or you can enter into a discussion.

FTP

File Transfer Protocol (FTP) is one of the earliest functions of the Internet. FTP enables the movement of files from one computer to another over the Internet. Computers that allow you to dial in to them and download files from them are called *FTP servers*. There are hundreds of FTP servers all over the globe, each with tens of thousands of files. How do you find what you're looking for?

Archie servers are computers that index the files available on FTP sites. Without going to each FTP site and browsing (a project that can take days and tie up Internet resources), you can go to an Archie server and find files by their names. Of course, if the file is about drug use in ancient Egypt, for example, but is named Dr3aeg91.txt, Archie has no clue about what the file contains.

Gopher

That's where Gopher comes in. *Gopher servers* are computers on the Internet that maintain lists of the files residing on their own as well as other computers. With a *Gopher client* (a menu-based Gopher program you run on your computer) you can search many places on the Internet for the files you need. Gopher also allows descriptive comments to be attached to file names. Another advantage is that many Gopher servers have World Wide Web menus: you can use a Web browser, click a file name, and begin downloading a file to your computer.

Another search tool, *Veronica,* allows the user to search menu items on Gopher servers. Veronica servers compile databases of Gopher menus and provide information about the files, in addition to the file names and their locations.

WAIS

Let's say that you're looking for as many documents as you can find about (to continue the previous topic) drug use in ancient Egypt, but you don't know the names of the files. *WAIS* (Wide Area Information Server) is the most useful search tool for this kind of search. WAIS has an index of keywords contained in all the documents on servers all over the world. Using WAIS, you can type **drugs** and **Egypt** to get information on your topic, even if the file names of the documents containing that information are obscure.

Telnet

Telnet, another Internet protocol, allows users to log in to a remote computer and treat that machine as though it were their own computer. In other words, if you want to get a file located on a machine halfway around the world, you can Telnet to a local computer, use that machine to Telnet to still another, and so on, until you reach your destination. Telnet can save you the cost of a long-distance call. All you need is the name of the local host computer. Recently, Telnet has provided a means for participants in *MUD* (Multiple User Dimension) games to play one another on-line.

Tip
Because you use it to connect to several computers, Telnet is slow and uses a lot of system resources. If you have a better way to access a remote site, use it.

Chapter 30, "Using FTP, the World Wide Web, and other Internet Services," discusses all these Internet services in detail.

Sample Fees

The following chart compares what you'll spend logging on to the Internet. Although Windows 95, aside from its modem setup and serial port configuration, plays no part in connecting to the commercial services, the service fees are included as a basis for comparison. "Anynet" is representative of many local access providers.

	AOL	Compu-Serve	Delphi	IBM-Net	NET-COM	Prodigy	Anynet
10 hrs/mo.	$24.90	$24.95	$23	$29.95	$19.95	$29.95	$25
20 hrs/mo.	$54	$24.95	$23	$29.95	$19.95	$29.95	$25
30 hrs/mo.	$83	$44.95	$41	$29.95	$19.95	$29.95	$25
60 hrs/mo.	$122	$102	$95	$89.95	$19.95	$118	$25

It's easy to see, that, for a dedicated Net surfer, a local provider is the least expensive way to go. But those interested in the additional forums and libraries of the commercial services, and who intend to be on the Internet less than 10 or 20 hours a month, may want to investigate CompuServe, Prodigy or America Online. Notice also that, as of this writing, Microsoft has not posted fees for their Internet access.❖

Chapter 30

Using FTP, the World Wide Web, and Other Internet Services

by Francis Moss with Paul Robichaux

Windows 95 provides advanced SLIP and PPP connectivity, but once you're connected to the Internet, you're pretty much on your own. The Internet applications provided with Windows 95 are—to be generous—minimal. While the Microsoft Network provides some Internet (read-only UseNet newsgroups and e-mail), for full access you'll need an Internet service provider and other Net tools.

To fully explore the Internet, you'll need a World Wide Web browser, UseNet newsreader, and an e-mail client in addition to the software that Windows 95 provides. Fortunately, there are servers on the Internet that make these software packages—and hundreds of others—available for free.

In this chapter, you learn the following skills:

- How to use Microsoft's FTP program to connect to large archives of shareware and freeware
- How to find and download software using FTP
- How to log in to remote computers on the Internet with Telnet
- How to use Microsoft's Internet Assistant as a Web browser
- How to use e-mail and UseNet to send private messages or post and read messages that millions of other users can see

- How to explore the World Wide Web (WWW) with Microsoft's Internet Explorer (part of the Microsoft Plus! Pack for Windows 95)
- How to create your own Web pages using the HyperText Markup Language (HTML)

Microsoft is introducing the Microsoft Plus! Pack, which includes the Internet Jumpstart Kit. In the kit are a World Wide Web browser and an e-mail reader for use with the Microsoft Exchange mail client. One feature of the Web browser includes the ability to drag your favorite Internet locations to the desktop to create shortcuts.

Using FTP

The Plus! Pack tools are nice, but Plus! doesn't include all the tools you need. How can you find the software you need to start cruising the Internet now? The best way to get the software (and learn about the Internet at the same time) is to use the command-line version of FTP included with Windows 95.

Before you begin, you need an Internet connection, either through Windows 95's Dial-Up Networking or a direct LAN connection. (To find out more, see Chapter 29, "Getting Connected to the Internet.")

Note

This book is about Windows 95, so we can only scratch the surface of the Internet. For more coverage of the Internet and related software, check out *Special Edition Using the Internet*, Second Edition, *Special Edition Using the World Wide Web with Mosaic, Using FTP, Using Netscape, Easy World Wide Web with Netscape, Using UseNet Newsgroups, Web Publishing with Word for Windows,* or any of the other Que books about the Internet and its parts. Visit the Macmillan Publishing Web page at **http://www.mcp.com** for a complete book list.

◀ See "FTP," p. 908

The File Transfer Protocol, usually called FTP, is the Internet standard for file transfer. A simple, command-line version of FTP is part of Windows 95. You can use it to connect to remote FTP servers and find the files you need.

Most public archive sites allow you to log in as a special user, *anonymous*. All that means is that the FTP server allows you to enter *anonymous* as a user name instead of requiring every individual user to have a unique name and password. Whenever you log in as *anonymous*, provide your e-mail address when the FTP server asks you for a password.

To begin an FTP session, follow these steps:

1. Connect to the Internet. If your connection to the Internet is via a LAN, be sure you are properly connected to your network. If you connect by using a modem and a dial-up Internet service provider, use your Dial-up Connection to log on to your Internet Service Provider (ISP).

◄ See "Installing and Configuring Windows 95 Dial-Up Network Adapter," p. 888

2. When your Internet connection is active, open a DOS window and, at the C:\> prompt, type **FTP**.

3. At the ftp> prompt, type in the **open** command, followed by the name or address of the server you want to connect to (for example, **open ftp.qualcomm.com**).

4. At the login prompt, enter a user name. In most cases, this will be *anonymous*. There may be a brief message from the server along with the login prompt. If there is, read it. Some anonymous servers may ask you to log in as *guest* or some other user name. If so, follow the directions there.

5. At the password prompt, enter a password. If you logged in as *anonymous*, you should enter your e-mail address as a password. Figure 30.1 shows the results of our logon to the QUALCOMM FTP server. (QUALCOMM, Incorporated is the maker of the popular Eudora e-mail client.)

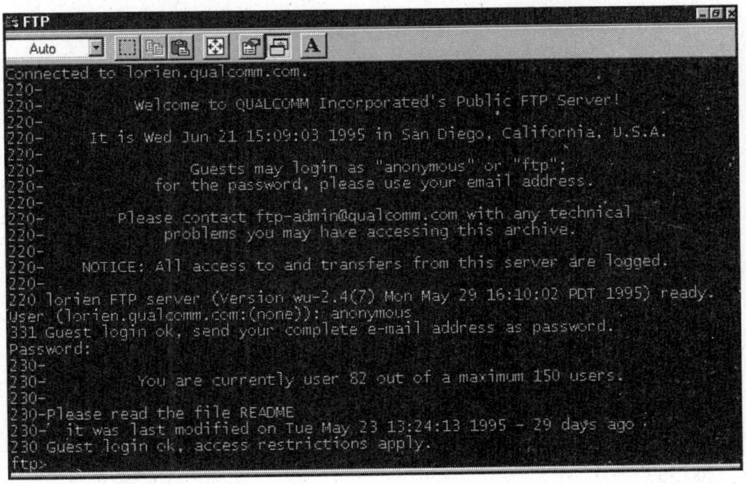

Fig. 30.1
When the QUALCOMM FTP server answers, it asks you to log in. Type **anonymous** as a user name and your e-mail address for a password.

Tip
Every time you log onto a remote server, look for "readme" or "index" files. If you find one, download it, then load it into a word processor to search for names and locations of files to download.

Once you're logged in, you should see the ftp> prompt again. There may be a message from the server, stating the server's policies or giving other information. If there is, read it. At this point, you can use the other FTP commands discussed in the following sections to change directories and find and retrieve files.

Navigating through Directories

Once you've connected to an FTP site, you'll most often need to change to a particular directory to get a specific file. If you're just browsing, you may want to poke around the directory tree. In either case, you need to be able to move around the directory structure. Here's how to do it:

1. The `dir` and `ls` commands list the files in the current directory on the FTP server. `dir` includes more information about each file than `ls` does.

Tip
Some servers display messages when you change into particular directories. Be sure to read them; they can be important.

2. The `cd` command works just like it does in DOS: it changes your current directory *on the server.* If you want to change your current directory on your local computer, use the `lcd` command.

3. At any time, you can change to a directory whose full name you know with the `cd` command. For example, cd/quest/Windows/Eudora will change your current directory from wherever it is to the /quest/Windows/Eudora directory.

Note

Remember that most Internet FTP servers use a forward slash (/) to indicate a directory rather than the back slash (\) used in DOS.

Figure 30.2 shows a sample session with **ftp.ksc.nasa.gov**, a public-access server run by NASA, where you can get the WinVN newsreader.

Caution

Unlike Windows, UNIX (the operating system used by most Internet FTP servers) distinguishes between upper- and lowercase in file and directory names. Be sure to type directory names and file names exactly as they appear, including using the correct capitalization.

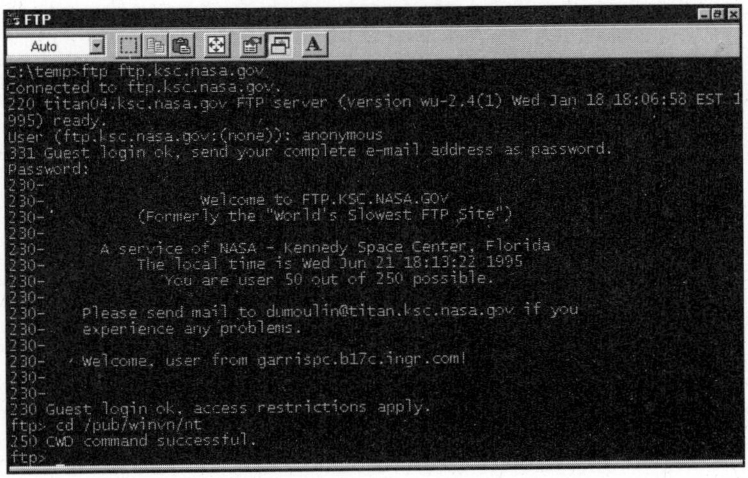
FTP
Auto
C:\temp>ftp ftp.ksc.nasa.gov
Connected to ftp.ksc.nasa.gov.
220 titan04.ksc.nasa.gov FTP server (Version wu-2.4(1) Wed Jan 18 18:06:58 EST 1
995) ready.
User (ftp.ksc.nasa.gov:(none)): anonymous
331 Guest login ok, send your complete e-mail address as password.
Password:
230-
230-   Welcome to FTP.KSC.NASA.GOV
230-   (Formerly the "World's Slowest FTP Site")
230-
230-   A service of NASA - Kennedy Space Center, Florida
230-   The local time is Wed Jun 21 18:13:22 1995
230-   You are user 50 out of 250 possible.
230-
230-   Please send mail to dumoulin@titan.ksc.nasa.gov if you
230-   experience any problems.
230-
230-   Welcome, user from garrispc.b17c.ingr.com!
230-
230-
230 Guest login ok, access restrictions apply.
ftp> cd /pub/winvn/nt
250 CWD command successful.
ftp>

Fig. 30.2
Once you've logged in, you can list files and directories and navigate through the server.

Getting One or More Files

Before you transfer files, you need to know that FTP allows two kinds of transfers: ASCII and binary. On your computer, some files are human-readable text, and others are binary data. Files on FTP servers are the same way, and FTP provides commands for changing the transfer mode. Use them under these circumstances:

- If you're fetching an ASCII file, you can use the `ascii` command before transferring it. The Windows 95 FTP client sets ASCII mode by default.
- If the file you're transferring isn't an ASCII file, you should use the `binary` command to tell FTP to transfer the file in binary mode. If you transfer a binary file, like a ZIP or EXE file, in ASCII mode, it won't be usable after transfer. If you transfer an ASCII file in binary mode, though, it doesn't do any harm.

Tip
To change modes, type **ascii** or **binary** at the ftp prompt.

Now that you can connect to an FTP server and have browsed around until you've found an interesting file and set the right transfer mode, you need a way to copy that file over the Internet onto your computer.

When you copy files with FTP, the FTP client will put them in your current *local* directory. If you start FTP from the C:\WINDOWS directory, that's where your files will end up. To control where your files go:

- Before running FTP, use the DOS `cd` command to change to the directory where you want the downloaded files.

- While running FTP, use the `lcd` command to change FTP's current local work directory. For example, `lcd c:\temp\downloads` changes the current directory on your PC to that directory (assuming that directory exists on your system). Any files downloaded are then downloaded to that directory.

Tip
By default, FTP asks you to confirm each file before it transfers it when you use `mget`. Use the `prompt` command to turn off (or on) interactive prompting.

FTP provides two commands to copy files from the FTP server to your machine. Let's see how they work.

- The `get` command gets a single file that you specify. For example, `get wznt56.zip` fetches the file named "wznt56.zip" to your local disk. You can also specify a name for the local copy; `get wznt56.zip new-file.zip` copies the file, then names it "new-file.zip".

- The `mget` command gets all files that match the pattern you specify. For example, `mget *.zip` copies all files in the current server directory whose names end with ".zip" to your local machine.

Figure 30.3 puts it all together and shows a sample session with **ftp.ksc.nasa.gov**; we connect, get a directory listing with `ls`, and download a file in binary mode.

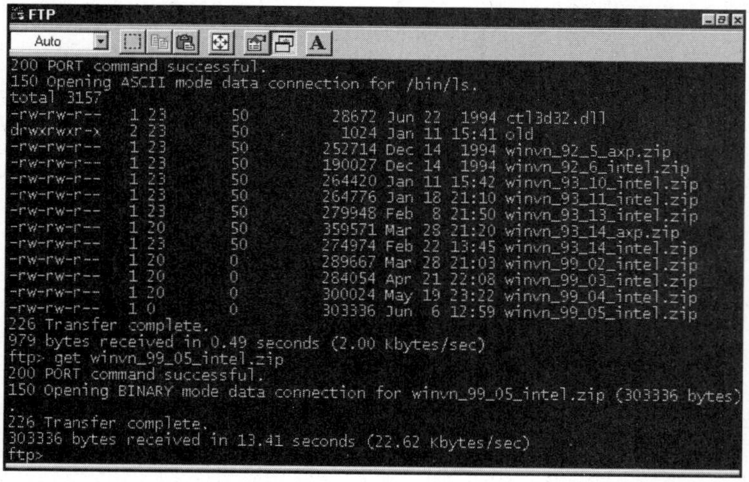

Fig. 30.3
To get files, just connect to the site, then retrieve the files you need. Don't forget to set binary mode when needed.

Leaving the FTP Site and Quitting FTP

When you're done retrieving files, you need to leave the FTP site to make it available to other users. There are several commands for doing so:

- The `disconnect` command closes your connection to the FTP site, but keeps the FTP program active. You can then connect to other sites with the `open` command.

- The `bye` and `quit` commands close your active connection, if any, and exit the FTP program. You'll be returned to the DOS command prompt after using these commands.

Tip
Type the status command to see information about whether various options are on or off. This shows if you are in ASCII or binary mode.

Some Popular FTP Sites

Once you know how to use FTP, you can use the same methods to log in to servers all around the world. There are thousands of servers with thousands of files available. Finding what you need can be impossible if you don't know where to start. Here are the addresses of a few key FTP sites that should be of value.

Tip
CICA is a busy site. There is a mirror that isn't quite as busy at **archive.orst.edu**.

- **ftp.cica.indiana.edu**

  This is the Center for Innovative Computing Applications (CICA) site. Look in the directory /pub/pc/win3 for one of the largest collections of Windows software available. There are many directories, for Windows utilities, applications, add-ins and templates for popular programs such as Word and Excel, and more.

- **ftp.ncsa.uiuc.edu**

  This is the National Center for SuperComputing Applications (NCSA) site. You will find Mosaic software for Windows here in /Web/Mosaic/Windows. Software for writing Web pages in HTML can be found in /Web/html/Windows.

- **ftp.microsoft.com**

  You guessed it, this is the home of Microsoft. Look here for software patches, press releases, technical papers, and more.

- **buckshot.usma.edu**

  This site at the US Military Academy at West Point offers the popular WS_FTP tool. WS_FTP provides a Windows GUI interface for FTP. The file you'll need is /pub/msdos/ws_ftp32.zip.

- **ftp.winzip.com**

  Many programs you get via FTP will be compressed using PKZIP. WinZip provides a slick Windows interface for using zipped files, including drag and drop and long file names. The file you need is /winzip/wznt56.exe. Even though this version is for Windows NT, it works well with Windows 95.

- **ftp.mcp.com**

  The Macmillan Computer Publishing site (Que is a part of MCP). Look here for software related to Que and Macmillan books.

Troubleshooting

I tried to log in anonymously but I got a message that said `Anonymous User Login Denied`. *Why can't I log in?*

Usually, login error messages like this one mean that the server is too busy. FTP servers limit the number of users that can log in at once so that the server doesn't get overloaded. Sometimes the sites will post a message listing the addresses of *mirror sites* (other servers that have the same files), and you can try one of those instead. Educational and business sites often have lower limits on anonymous users during the day so that their students and employees can use the sites without being slowed by anonymous users. You may have better luck logging in to these sites at night. However, more people cruise FTP sites for fun at night, so there may be more anonymous users. Take your chances and keep trying.

I connected to an FTP site, then got up from the computer for a few minutes. When I came back and typed a command, I got a message about the control connection being closed. What happened?

Most FTP sites will log you out automatically if you leave the connection open for several minutes with no activity. This frees up the connection for others to use. Just use the `open` command to reconnect to the site, then transfer the files you want.

Using Telnet

The Internet's Telnet protocol allows you to log in to a remote computer as though you were sitting in front of it. Windows 95 provides a Telnet client, called telnet, that you can use to connect to remote systems where you have accounts. In addition to dial-up access, many Internet service providers allow you to telnet to their hosts for direct UNIX access.

The Windows 95 Telnet client isn't flashy, but since Telnet is based on the idea of emulating a plain ASCII terminal, it doesn't need to be.

Connecting and Disconnecting to Remote Computers

The first step to connecting to remote computers with Windows 95's Telnet client is to start the client from the command prompt (its name is "telnet") or from a shortcut. Once you've done that, you can use the Connect, Remote System option to connect. Figure 30.4 shows Telnet's Connect dialog box.

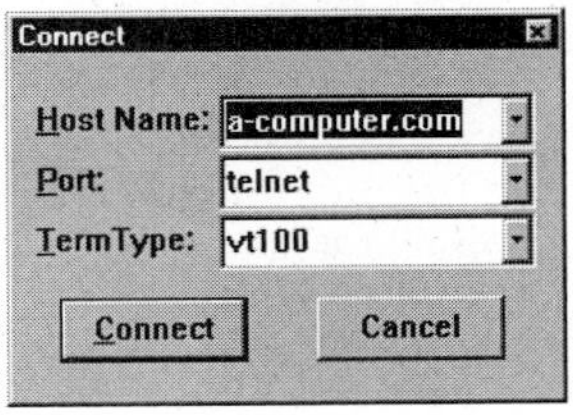

Fig. 30.4
Select a host, port, and terminal type from the Connect dialog box. Don't change the port number unless you know what you're doing.

Once you're connected, you can use all the remote computer's facilities just like you could if you had dialed into that computer via modem, or if you were sitting in front of it.

When you're done, you can choose Connect, Disconnect to close the connection; if you choose Connect, Exit, Telnet will exit. Unfortunately, you can only connect to one computer at a time.

Caution

If you're connected to a remote computer when you choose Connect, Exit, Telnet will exit *without* asking you to confirm.

Keeping a Log of Your Connection

Sometimes it's useful to have a permanent record of a session with a remote computer. Telnet includes a way for you to capture what appears on your screen and save it into a text file for later review.

To turn on logging, select Terminal, Start Logging. Telnet prompts you to choose a location and name for your log file. Once you start logging, your communications with the remote system goes into the log file.

To stop logging, select Terminal, Stop Logging. Telnet closes the log file.

Setting Preferences

Many users like to be able to control the cursor's appearance and behavior in a communications program. Telnet provides a preferences dialog box that allows you to adjust the cursor shape, the text font used in Telnet windows, and other aspects of the program's behavior.

To set Telnet's preferences, choose Terminal, Preferences. Set the options the way you want them, then choose OK to save your changes or Cancel to discard them. If you save changes, Telnet will remember them.

Surfing the Web with Internet Explorer

Internet Explorer is part of Microsoft's Plus! Pack for Windows 95. Internet Explorer offers the same basic tools as other Web browsers, but it was redesigned to take advantage of the full range of Windows 95's features. It supports the full Windows 95 user interface and improves on Windows 3.1-based browsers by supporting shortcuts and long file names. Figure 30.5 shows Internet Explorer's main window and the default page that ships with the software.

Fig. 30.5 Internet Explorer's main window includes a toolbar for quick access to common functions. This is the introductory Internet Explorer start page.

Internet Explorer shares a common look and feel with Microsoft's other applications, and includes Windows 95 features like flyover help and the common file and print dialog boxes. It also has many similarities to other Web browsers; after all, it was based on Mosaic. If you're already accustomed to another browser, you'll find the Internet Explorer both comfortably familiar and excitingly different.

There *is* one difference you need to know about. Microsoft calls hypertext links shortcuts, since clicking them takes you to someplace else. To avoid confusion, I'll refer to hypertext links as "links" or "hyperlinks," and Windows 95 shortcuts as "shortcuts."

Installing the Internet Explorer

The Internet Explorer comes as part of the Plus! Pack for Windows 95. (If your computer came preloaded with Windows 95, you may already have the Plus! Pack installed; check your system documentation.) Like many other Windows 95 products, the Plus! Pack is easy to install. Here's what you should do:

▶ See "Installing Plus!," p. 1142

1. Insert the Plus! Pack disc into your CD-ROM drive.
2. Using the Windows 95 command prompt, the Explorer, or a desktop window, run D:\SETUP.EXE (assuming D is your CD-ROM drive).
3. The Plus! Pack setup installer loads and asks you to choose which modules you want to install. Choose the Internet Jumpstart option.

Navigating the Web

When you start the Internet Explorer, it displays the introductory page shown in figure 30.5 (until you customize it, that is). There are several ways to open a page. The most common way is also the simplest: just click on a hyperlink to jump to it. Hyperlinks are usually shown as underlined and colored text. The next couple let you jump to any Web document, anywhere, by bringing up the Open Internet Address dialog box (see fig. 30.6). When you type in an address, the Internet Explorer opens the Web document you've requested.

Tip

To open an HTML document from a drive on your computer, click the Open File button in the dialog box in step 2.

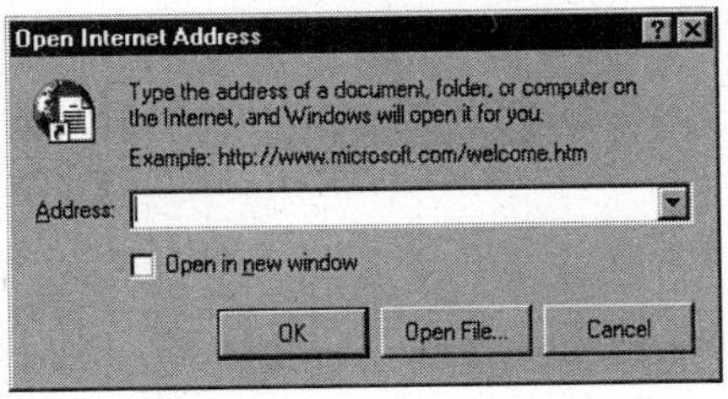

Fig. 30.6
The Open Internet Address dialog box allows you to jump directly to any site on the Internet, or to load Web pages stored on your hard disk.

To go to any page whose URL you know, use the following method:

1. Choose File, Open; or click the Open button on the toolbar.
2. Type in the address or select an address from the pull-down menu. (The pull-down menu contains pages you've previously visited.)

Tip
The Internet Explorer adds pages you've visited to the bottom of the File menu. You can also select File, More History to see a history window of pages you've visited.

3. To open a new window for the page you're opening, select the Open in New Window check box. You can easily work with multiple pages just by switching between their windows.

4. Click OK.

There are several other ways to go to Web pages. You can:

- Type an address into the Address pull-down menu just below the toolbar.

- Select a previously visited site from the Address pull-down menu.

- At any time, you can jump back to your start page (the initial page loaded when you launch the Internet Explorer) by clicking the Open Start Page icon.

- Jump directly to a Favorite site by opening the Favorites folder and then choosing a site. Click the toolbar icon or choose Favorites, Open, then select the site you want to visit.

- Use the left arrow button to go back to a page you've already visited. Once you've gone back to a page, use the right arrow button to go forward again.

Controlling Page Loading and Display

Many popular servers on the Internet are slow. Why? Because they're popular! You may find that some sites impose too long of a wait. To stop waiting for, or loading, a page, click this icon.

Once you've stopped loading a page, you might change your mind and want to reload it. You may also need to reload pages that change over time. To reload a page, click the refresh icon on the toolbar, or select View, Refresh. The Internet Explorer reloads and redisplays the page you're on.

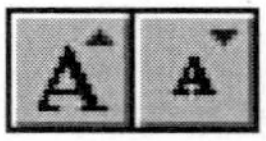

Standard HTML lets page authors set the *relative* font sizes in a document, but you control the actual font sizes. You can enlarge or reduce the font size by using the toolbar buttons or by selecting View, Fonts, then choosing a font size from the pop-up menu.

Keeping Track of Your Favorite Sites

You've probably found that, out of the many sites you've visited on the Web, you have some favorites which you visit frequently. The Internet Explorer supplies two easy ways to keep track of your favorite sites: the Create Shortcut command and the Favorites list.

Create Shortcut creates a shortcut to the currently displayed page and puts it on your desktop. To create a shortcut, follow these steps:

1. If you're not already there, go to the page for which you want a shortcut.
2. Create the shortcut by choosing File, Create Shortcut.
3. You'll be asked to confirm that you want to create a shortcut on the desktop. Choose OK to create the shortcut.

Tip
When you create a shortcut, you can put it on your desktop, mail it to a friend, or use it anywhere else shortcuts work.

To add a page to your Favorites list, follow these steps:

1. If you're not already there, go to the page you want to add.
2. Add the page to your Favorites list by choosing Favorites, Add Favorite, or by clicking the Add to Favorites button.

3. The standard Save File dialog box appears. Choose a location for your entry, then choose OK.

Setting the Internet Explorer's Options

The Internet Explorer lets you control its behavior with the Options dialog box, displayed when you choose View, Options. We'll cover each of the tabs in the Options dialog box in more detail shortly, but feel free to experiment.

Controlling How Pages Appear

You can control settings used for displaying Web pages with the Appearances page of the Options dialog box. To open this dialog box, choose View, Options. You can change how hyperlinks are drawn, whether pictures are displayed, the text and background color for pages, and more. Figure 30.7 shows the Options dialog box when the Appearance page is selected.

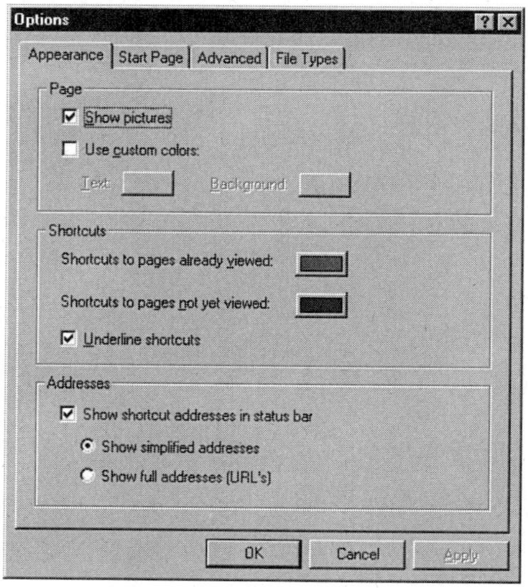

Fig. 30.7
The Appearance page gives you control over how Web pages and links appear on your screen.

Tip
These pictures are usually referred to as *inline graphics* or *inline images*.

Controlling How Graphics Are Displayed. You can ask the Internet Explorer not to download or display pictures on Web pages. This is helpful when using a modem connection, or when trying to reach a busy server. To turn image loading off or on, click the Show Pictures check box until it reflects the setting you want.

Modifying How Hyperlinks Are Displayed. The Internet Explorer lets you control how hyperlinks are displayed. Some users prefer their links underlined, while others like them to appear as plain text. You can set your preference using the Underline Shortcuts check box.

The Internet Explorer also lets you choose what colors to use when drawing links. To change those colors, choose one of these options:

- Click the Shortcuts To Pages Already Viewed button to bring up the Color Selection dialog box. Choose a color from the selected palette, or mix a custom color, then choose OK. The Internet Explorer uses that color to draw links to pages you've already visited.
- Click the Shortcuts To Pages Not Yet Viewed button to bring up the Color Selection dialog box. Choose a color from the selected palette, or mix a custom color, then choose OK. The Internet Explorer uses that color to draw links to pages you haven't yet seen.

Changing How Addresses Are Displayed. Each Web page has its own unique address, or URL. These URLs can be arbitrarily long, and many of them contain confusing query characters or computer-generated indexing markers. If you prefer, you can turn the display of page addresses off altogether, or you can make the Internet Explorer show a shortened, simpler form of the URL for each page.

To control whether the Internet Explorer shows URLs at all, use the Show Shortcut Addresses In Status Bar check box. When unchecked, the Internet Explorer won't show you the URLs. When it *is* checked, addresses appear according to the setting of the two radio buttons below it: Show Simplified Addresses and Show Full Addresses (URLs). Choose Show Simplified Addresses if you want to see a shortened, less complex form of page addresses; choose Show Full Addresses if you want to see the full URL for each link.

Changing Which Page Loads at Startup

The Start Page page of the Options dialog box allows you to specify which Web page loads when you launch the Internet Explorer. You can specify a file on your local hard disk, a shared disk (with a UNC path), or on a Web server.

Here's how to change the start page:

1. Go to the page you want to use as your starting page.
2. Open the Options dialog box (click View, Options) and click the Start Page tab.
3. Click the Use Current button to use the current page, or click Use Default to go back to the previously set start page.

Tip

To minimize waiting when first starting the Internet Explorer, use the Internet Assistant to create your own local start page on your hard drive with links to pages you use often, or to specify a page that you use often that loads quickly.

Adding Helpers and New Document Types

The Internet Explorer comes preconfigured for many common file types, including Microsoft Office documents, JPEG and GIF images, WAV and AU sounds, and various other file types. However, you may need to add new file types for documents whose types Microsoft didn't anticipate, like CAD drawings, files compressed on UNIX machines, or MIDI files. You might also want to change the application launched to handle a certain file type.

Figure 30.8 shows an example of adding a file type; in this case, we've added support for PKZIP files.

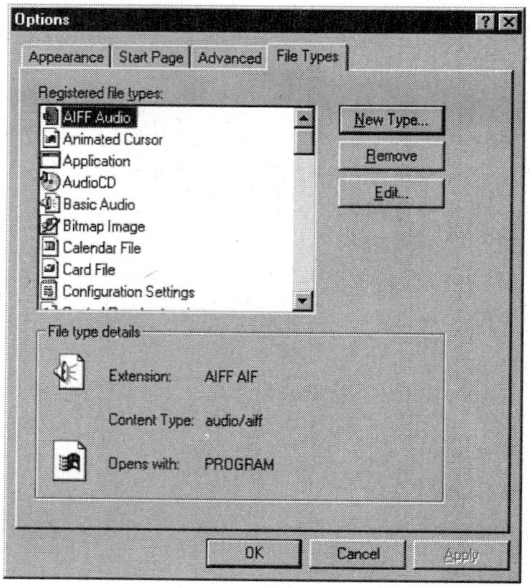

Fig. 30.8
Add new file types through the File Types page in the Options dialog box.

◄ See "Registering Files to Automatically Open an Application," p. 539

To register a new document type so that the Internet Explorer recognizes it, here's what to do:

1. Open the Options dialog box (click View, Options) and select the File Types tab. The File Types page appears.
2. Click the New Type button.
3. The standard Windows 95 file type dialog box appears. Fill in the fields for the file type you want to add and then choose OK.

Dragging and Dropping on the Web

Here are some ideas to get you started on dragging and dropping your way around with the Internet Explorer:

- Drag shortcuts (created with the Create Shortcut command) from your desktop or a folder onto the Internet Explorer window to load them.
- Drag HTML files from the My Computer window or the Explorer into the Internet Explorer window.
- Drag images from a Web page to the My Computer window or the Explorer to copy them onto your disk, or into Exchange to mail them.
- Drag text from a Web page into any application which accepts text, such as WordPad.

Some Popular Sites on the World Wide Web

Once you're comfortable with the Internet Explorer, you can travel to servers all around the world with a few clicks. There are more than 100,000 Web servers available, with millions of files. Finding what you need can be impossible if you don't know where to start. Here are the addresses of a few key Web sites you may find of value:

- **http://www.yahoo.com**

  Yahoo started as a project at Stanford University, but has quickly become such a popular site that it's spun off into a separate server. Yahoo offers a list of Web pages, organized into categories like law, entertainment, and business.

- **http://www.infoseek.com**

  InfoSeek offers a reliable search service that indexes Web pages, articles from computer periodicals, wire-service news articles, and several other sources. Although it's a commercial service, the rates are quite reasonable and it offers free trials.

- **http://www.einet.net**

  EINet, a company that provides electronic commerce consulting and services, operates the Galaxy as a public service. It's organized somewhat like Yahoo, but with a more varied list of topics.

Creating Your Own Pages for the World Wide Web

The World Wide Web, designed by researchers at CERN in Geneva, Switzerland, is a collection of hypertext documents served from computers throughout the world. Web documents, or *pages,* can contain pictures, text, sounds, movies, and links to other documents. Web pages can—and usually do—contain links to documents on other computers. The name "Web" came from the interlinked nature of the pages.

One of the best things about the Web is that it allows anyone with Internet access to *provide* information, not just consume it. If you have access to a Web server and information to share, the Internet lets you do so in a unique way.

Web pages are written in the HyperText Markup Language (HTML). HTML is made up of *elements*; each element contains a *tag* defining what kind of element it is. Most elements also contain text that defines what the element represents. In figure 30.9, the sample HTML page as displayed by the Internet Explorer is shown at the top; the same page shown as HTML form is shown at the bottom.

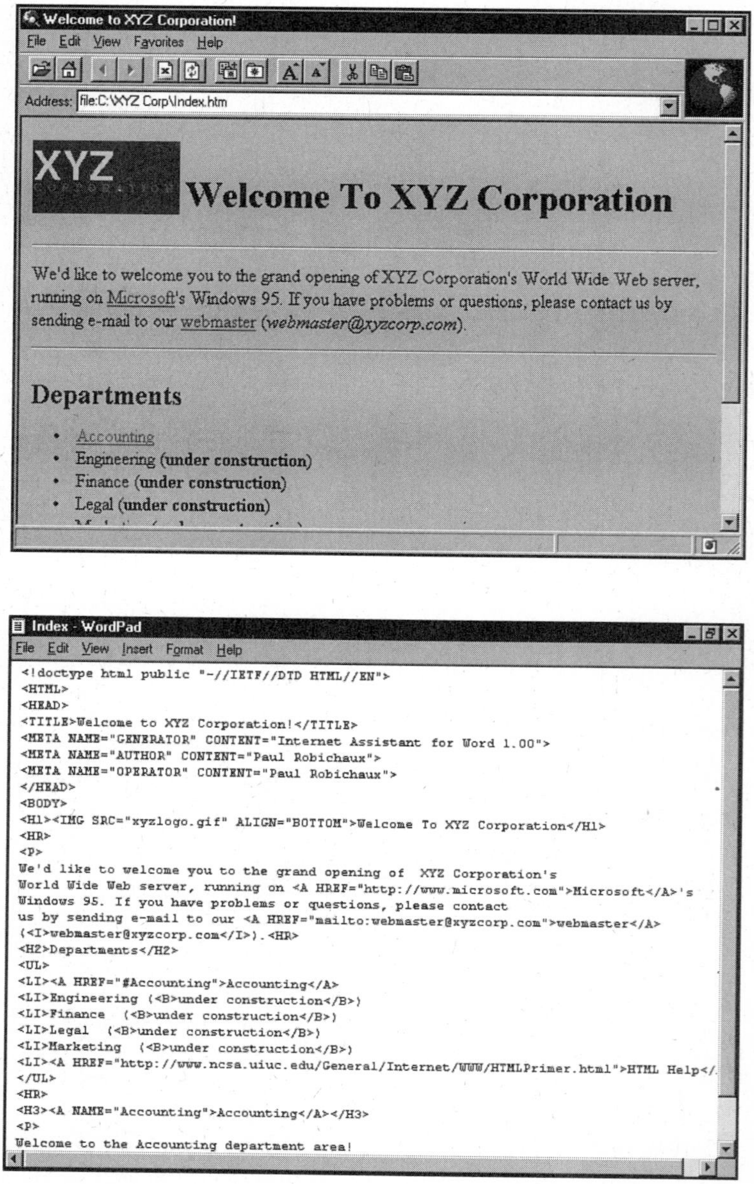


```
<!doctype html public "-//IETF//DTD HTML//EN">
<HTML>
<HEAD>
<TITLE>Welcome to XYZ Corporation!</TITLE>
<META NAME="GENERATOR" CONTENT="Internet Assistant for Word 1.00">
<META NAME="AUTHOR" CONTENT="Paul Robichaux">
<META NAME="OPERATOR" CONTENT="Paul Robichaux">
</HEAD>
<BODY>
<H1><IMG SRC="xyzlogo.gif" ALIGN="BOTTOM">Welcome To XYZ Corporation</H1>
<HR>
<P>
We'd like to welcome you to the grand opening of  XYZ Corporation's
World Wide Web server, running on <A HREF="http://www.microsoft.com">Microsoft</A>'s
Windows 95. If you have problems or questions, please contact
us by sending e-mail to our <A HREF="mailto:webmaster@xyzcorp.com">webmaster</A>
(<I>webmaster@xyzcorp.com</I>).<HR>
<H2>Departments</H2>
<UL>
<LI><A HREF="#Accounting">Accounting</A>
<LI>Engineering (<B>under construction</B>)
<LI>Finance  (<B>under construction</B>)
<LI>Legal  (<B>under construction</B>)
<LI>Marketing  (<B>under construction</B>)
<LI><A HREF="http://www.ncsa.uiuc.edu/General/Internet/WWW/HTMLPrimer.html">HTML Help</
</UL>
<HR>
<H3><A NAME="Accounting">Accounting</A></H3>
<P>
Welcome to the Accounting department area!
```

Fig. 30.9
On-screen and HTML versions of a simple page.

Unlike traditional desktop publishing, the user—not the author—controls how the document is actually displayed. When you create HTML documents, it's important to split the content of your document from its structure and appearance on-screen. The document that looks just right in your 640 × 480 Internet Explorer window may look awful to users of other browsers.

Building Documents with HTML

HTML elements are plain ASCII text, so you can create Web pages with any simple text editor, including WordPad. This section introduces the basic elements of HTML to help familiarize you with the most common elements before we plunge into using Microsoft's Internet Assistant.

> **Note**
>
> HTML offers many features, including on-screen forms. A complete copy of the HTML specification is available from the World Wide Web Organization (W3O)'s Web server at **http://www.w3.org/hypertext/WWW/MarkUp/MarkUp.html**, and the National Center for Supercomputing Applications maintains an excellent HTML tutorial at **http://www.ncsa.uiuc.edu/General/Internet/WWW/HTMLPrimer.html**.

How Documents Are Structured

Like those nesting Russian dolls, elements can contain other elements, and they can be deeply nested. HTML documents usually consist of one element: the HTML element, which contains head and body elements. Each of those elements can, in turn, enclose others.

The head element usually contains a title element, and it may also contain comments, author information, copyright notices, or special tags that help indexers and search engines use the contents of the document more effectively.

The body element holds the actual body and content of the document. For typical documents, most of the body element is text, with tags placed at the end of each paragraph. You can also use tags for displaying numbered or bulleted lists, horizontal rules, embedded images, and hyperlinks to other documents.

Tag Basics

All HTML tags are enclosed in angle brackets (<>). Some elements contain two matching tags, with text or hypertext in between. For example, to define a title as part of your document's <head> element, you'd put this HTML into your document:

```
<title>A Simple WWW Page</title>
```

The first tag signals the start of the title element, while the same tag, prefixed with a slash (/), tells the browser that it's reached the end of the element. Some tags don't require matching tags, like <li>, which denotes an item in a list.

The elements most often used in HTML body elements fall into three basic categories: logical styles, physical styles, and content elements.

Using Logical Styles. Logical styles tell the browser how the document is structured. The HTML system of nesting elements gives the browser some information, but authors can use the logical style elements to break text into paragraphs, lists, block quotes, and so on. Like styles in Microsoft Word, you can use the logical styles in your documents and know that they'll be properly displayed by the browser.

Table 30.1 lists some common logical styles you can use to build your document, along with examples for each one.

Table 30.1 Logical Style Elements

Style Tag	What It Does	Sample
<p>	Ends paragraph	This is a very short paragraph.<p>
 	Inserts line break	First line Second line
<Hx>...</Hx>	Section heading	<H1>HTML Is Easy</H1>
<em>...</em>	Emphasis on text	Use <em>this</em> instead of bold text.
<strong>...</strong>	Stronger emphasis on text really gets the point across!	<strong>THIS</strong>
<code>...</code>	Displays HTML tags without acting on them	The <code><p></code> tag can be handy.

Style Tag	What It Does	Sample
<quote>...</quote>	Displays a block of quoted text	<quote>No man is an island. </quote>
<pre>...</pre>	Displays text and leaves white space intact.	<pre>E x t r a spaces are OK here.</pre>

Using Physical Styles. In ordinary printed documents, **bold**, *italic,* and underlined text all have their special uses. Web pages are the same way; you may want to distinguish the name of a book, a key word, or a foreign-language phrase from your body text. Table 30.2 shows a list of some common physical styles you can use in HTML documents, along with simple examples.

Table 30.2 Physical Style Elements

Style Tag	What It Does	Sample
<b>...</b>	Bold text	<b>Bold</b> text stands out.
<i>...</i>	Italic text	<i>Belle</i> is French for "pretty."
<u>...</u>	Underlined text	<u>Don't</u> confuse underlined text with a hyperlink!
_{...}	Subscript text	Water's chemical formula is H₂O.
^{...}	Superscript text	Writing "x²" is the same as writing "x*x."
<tt>...</tt>	Typewriter text	This tag's <tt>seldom</tt> seen.

Using Content Elements. Many Web documents just contain plain, unadorned text. Content elements enrich your documents by adding embedded graphics, lists, and links to other documents. You can quickly turn a boring, plain-text document into a rich Web page by using content elements.

One of the simplest content elements—and one of the most effective—is the <hr> tag, which inserts a horizontal rule across the page. Use it to separate different sections of material, much as you'd add a page break to a Word document to start a new section.

<ul>...</ul> defines a bulleted or "unordered" list, and <ol>...</ol> defines a numbered or "ordered" list. Both use <li> to define list items. The list items are easy to use; if you've ever used Word or PowerPoint to build a list, you already know how to use these. Here are two quick examples:

```
<ul>
<li>First bullet
<li>Second bullet
</ul>

<ol>
<li>Item 1
<li>Item 2
</ol>
```

Many Web pages contain embedded graphics. These graphics must be in GIF or JPEG format, but they can be as large or small as you like. Embedding the images in your page is easy with the <img> tag. When a browser sees <img>, it fetches the image and displays it in the body of the document.

The simplest form of <img> lets you specify only the name of the graphics file. This instruction causes the browser to download "picture.gif" from the Web server and display it in the text:

```
<img src="picture.gif">
```

Tip
Use the alt= attribute. Users who aren't loading images can see the text tag and decide whether they want the image or not.

You can also add the alt= tag, which specifies a text string to be displayed instead of the image. Why would you want to do this? Some browsers, like Lynx, can't display images. Other browsers can display the alt tag for users who've turned off image loading to boost their connection speed. Adding alt to the above example, we end up with

```
<img src="picture.gif" alt="A pretty picture">
```

Creating Hyperlinks

Now let's talk about the key element that makes the Web different from plain static documents: hyperlinks. Each link points to an *anchor,* or destination for the link. Most anchors are implied; when you specify a page as the target of the link, it's assumed that you want that entire page to be an anchor.

You can also specify named anchors to let you quickly jump to a particular section of a document. Define anchors with <a name>...</a>. The "a" stands for "anchor," and the name attribute names the anchor. Anchors can display text labels, but they don't have to. The anchors below work identically, but the first one displays text in the browser and the other doesn't.

```
<a name="Chapter39">'s anchor</a> is the same as <a
name="Chapter39"></a> this one.
```

The basic element for hyperlinks is <a href>...</a>. The "a" still stands for "anchor," and "href" is a hypertext reference. Let's say you were setting up a Web server containing information about Windows 95. Your start page might link to a page listing new software for Windows 95, like this:

```
New <a href=Software/NewSoftware.htm>software</a> for Windows 95
```

The text in the middle of the link appears as a link on the browser's screen. Notice that the folder "Software" is part of the link. This link points to a file named "NewSoftware.htm" in the directory "Software."

Let's say you also wanted to include a link to Macmillan Publishing Company's Web page so that people visiting your page could find out about Windows 95 books. Notice that this link contains a full URL instead of the name of a local document.

```
The <a href=http://www.mcp.com>Macmillan Publishing</a> home page
has information on Macmillan's books.<p>
```

Both types of link can include anchors. If the target page contains an anchor with that name, then the browser will jump directly to that anchor and display it. For example, you could use a link like:

```
See <a href=http://www.mcp.com/Books/Win95/
UsingWin95.htm#Chapter39>Chapter 39</a>s outline for more
details.<p>
```

to specify a certain position within the link's target document.

Note

If you'd like a tool to check your HTML for correctness, you can use the Weblint tool. Weblint "picks the fluff" off your HTML pages and catches common errors like mismatched tags and bogus attribute names. For more details, see the Weblint page at **http://www.unipress.com/weblint/**.

Using Microsoft's Internet Assistant

If you use Microsoft Word, you can easily create HTML files with Microsoft's Internet Assistant, a Word add-on that already knows all the rules of HTML previously discussed, and then some!

Internet Assistant gives you an HTML document template with styles representing all the major HTML elements, plus converters to let you turn a Word file into HTML with a simple mouse click.

Getting and Installing Microsoft's Internet Assistant

The Internet Assistant is available as a self-extracting executable file called WORDIA.EXE. It can be downloaded at no cost from Microsoft's FTP site at **ftp.microsoft.com** in the directory /Softlib/MSLFILES. Use Windows 95's FTP program to get this file, using the procedure described earlier in this chapter.

> **Caution**
>
> You must have Word 6.0a or later to run the Internet Assistant. If you have an earlier version of Word, you can download the 6.0a patch (WORD60A.EXE) from Microsoft's FTP server by following the instructions for getting the Internet Assistant below.

The Internet Assistant requires the English, French, or German versions of Microsoft Word 6.0a or later. It *does not* work with older versions, other languages, or Word for Windows NT. Once you've downloaded the Internet Assistant, you'll probably be in a hurry to install it and start producing HTML files. Fortunately, installation is easy; just follow these quick steps:

1. Copy WORDIA.EXE to your hard disk and then run it. This executable extracts several files into the directory.

2. Run SETUP.EXE to install the Internet Assistant into your Word directory.

Using Microsoft's Internet Assistant as a Browser

Once you've installed the Internet Assistant, start Word for Windows. You'll discover a new button on the Formatting toolbar and a new command on the File menu.

> **Note**
>
> Before you can browse the Web with Microsoft's Internet Assistant, you need to have your connection to the Internet running. Either dial up to your service provider to log in to your network connection, or use a full-time LAN connection.

To browse the Web, choose File, Browse Web or click the Browse Web button (see fig. 30.10).

Browse Web button

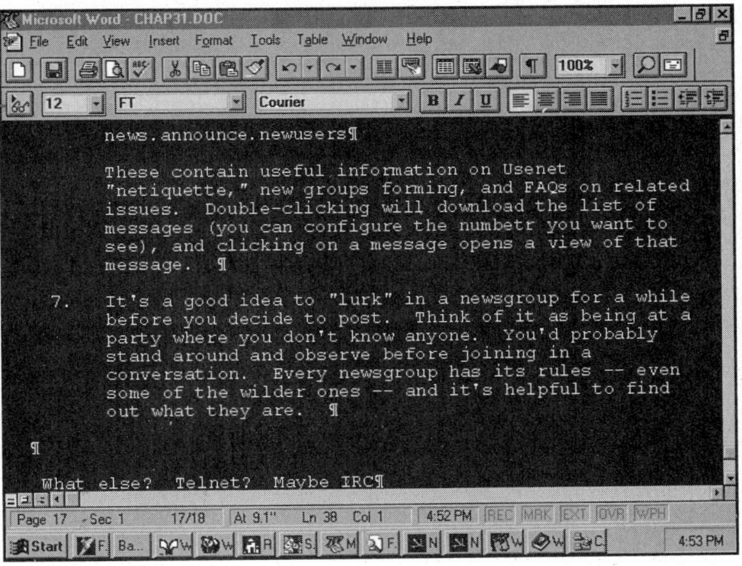

Fig. 30.10
After installing the Internet Assistant, Microsoft Word has a new button on the Formatting toolbar.

Once you start the Browse Web mode, the screen changes to look like the screen shown in figure 30.11.

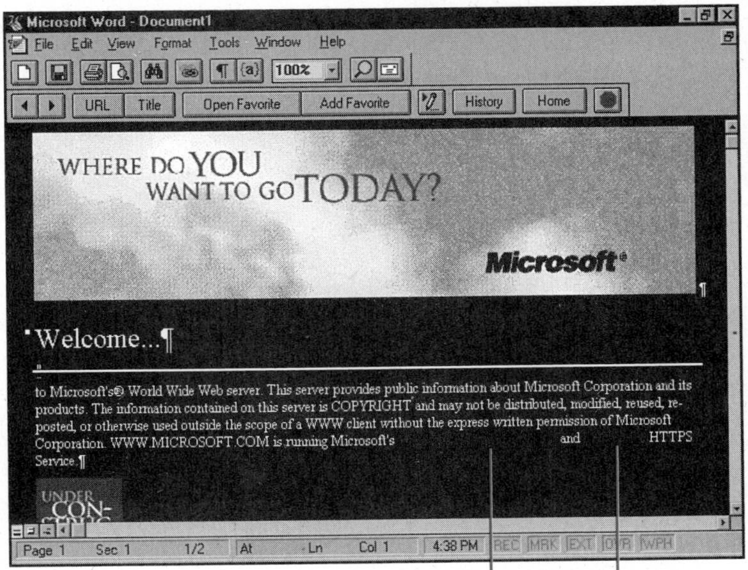

Click hypertext links (they're in color on-screen but barely visible here) to jump to other Web pages.

Fig. 30.11
Microsoft's Internet Assistant Browser, with Microsoft's World Wide Web page on view.

Creating New HTML Documents

When you use Word to create a new HTML document, select the HTML template instead of whatever you normally use. Figure 30.12 shows Word's New dialog box with the HTML template selected.

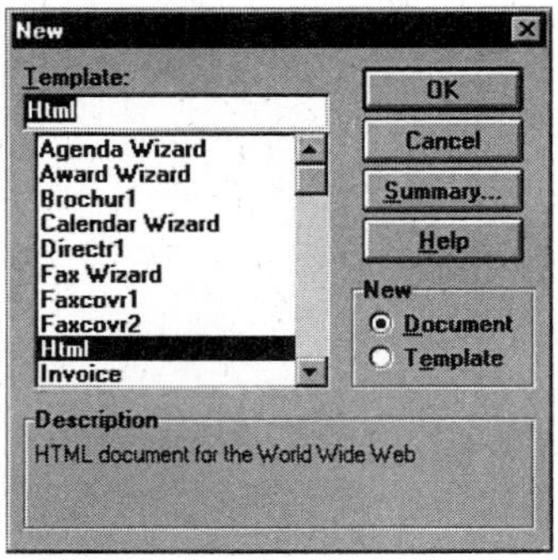

Fig. 30.12
Select the HTML template to create a new Web page with the Internet Assistant.

Tip
Use Netscape, Mosaic, or the Internet Explorer to browse the pages you create with the Internet Assistant—they're faster and use less RAM than Word.

A new document window opens, and you'll notice some new icons on the Formatting toolbar along with the familiar ones. These icons allow you to quickly format your document using HTML elements.

Formatting Your HTML Documents

You've probably noticed some new and unusual icons on the Internet Assistant Formatting toolbar. Here's how to use them to format your documents in HTML:

- The Edit and Browse Web buttons toggle Word between HTML Edit mode (the pencil) and Browse Web mode. You can also toggle with the View menu's Web Browse and HTML Edit options.

- Use the Back and Forward buttons to go backwards or forward among Web pages you've viewed. They don't do anything in normal Word mode.
- Use the Style pull-down menu (just to the right of the Forward button) to select HTML styles for your documents.

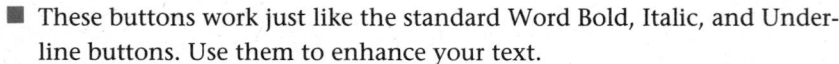

- These buttons work just like the standard Word Bold, Italic, and Underline buttons. Use them to enhance your text.

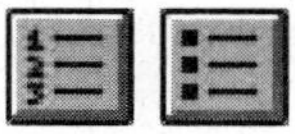

- These buttons let you create numbered and bulleted lists, just like in Word or PowerPoint.

- Use this button to insert a horizontal rule into your document.

- Insert pictures (GIF or JPEG only) into your document with this button. You'll see a dialog box that allows you to select a picture file and enter an alternate text string for the picture. If you have BMP and PCX files that you want to use on your Web pages, convert your images with a tool like the shareware PaintShop Pro or Adobe Photoshop. 
- Use this icon to set the document's title. Clicking it brings up a dialog box that lets you specify a title to be embedded. 

Building Hyperlinks

The Internet Assistant allows you to embed two kinds of links: links to external documents, and links to files and documents on your computer. This is a terrific feature, since you can quickly create links in, and between, several documents at once. Here's how to link your documents together:

Insert *bookmarks* with the Add Bookmark button. Bookmarks are HTML anchors; you can embed bookmarks in your Word documents so that you can build hyperlinks to specific pages or items. When you click this icon, the Bookmark dialog box appears, as shown in figure 30.13.

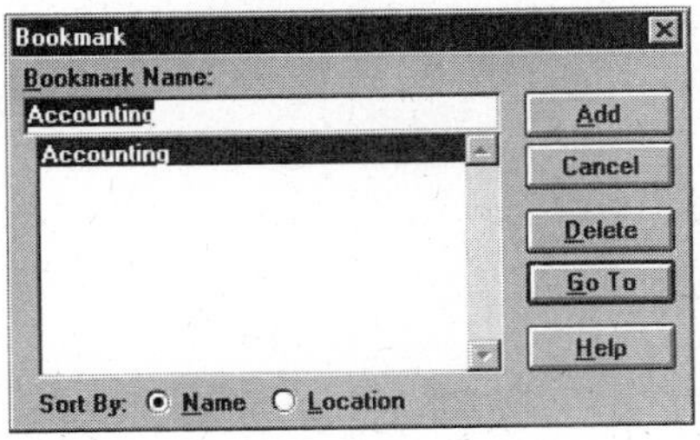

Fig. 30.13
The Add Bookmark dialog box lets you name specific locations in your document so that you can build hyperlinks to them.

Use these steps to work with bookmarks in your documents:

1. Choose Edit, Bookmark; or click the Bookmark button. The Bookmark dialog box appears.
2. To add a bookmark, type a name for the new bookmark in the Bookmark Name field and click Add.
3. To delete an existing bookmark, select it and click Delete. You'll be asked to confirm the deletion.
4. To jump to an existing bookmark, select it and click Go To.

You need to be able to embed hyperlinks in your documents, too. Fortunately, the Internet Assistant has a button for that as well. Clicking the Hyperlink button, or selecting Insert, HyperLink, brings up a dialog box with three tabbed pages: to Local Document, to URL, and to Bookmark. All of these pages have some fields in common. Figure 30.14 shows the Link to Local Document page.

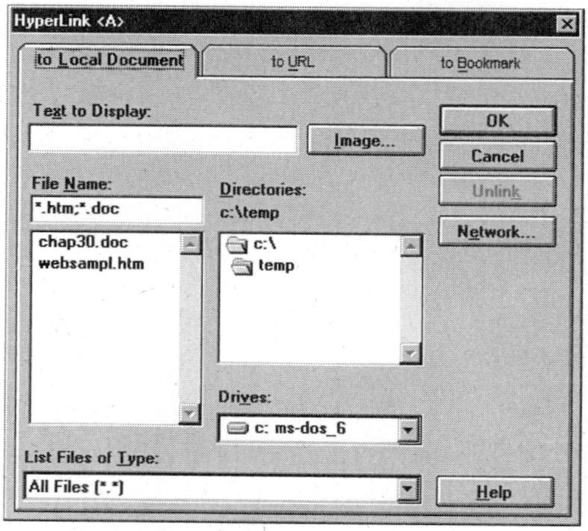

Fig. 30.14
The HyperLink dialog box gives you a quick way to build links to Web pages and Word documents on your computer or on other Web servers.

All three pages have identical upper halves, so we'll talk about the common parts first. Here's how to build hyperlinks:

1. Type the text which you want to appear in the link into the Text to Display field.

2. If you want to have an image as part of the link, click the Image button and select an image file. The Internet Assistant automatically includes it as part of your document.

3. If you're making a link to a local file using the Link to Local Document page, use the file and directory browsers, and click the Network button to find the link's target file.

4. If you're making a link to a URL somewhere on the Internet, type the URL to which you want to link into the text field, or pick a previously used URL from the list.

5. If you're linking to a bookmark you've already defined, select the bookmark to which you want to link from the list displayed.

No matter which of these steps you choose, you must click OK to accept your new link, or click Cancel to dismiss the dialog box.

Saving Your Documents

While you're creating and editing your documents, you'll need to save them to disk. You can save your documents—HTML styles and all—as regular Word documents. When you're ready to save the HTML version, see figure 30.15 for an example and follow these steps:

1. Choose File, Save As.

2. When the Save As dialog box appears, type a file name for your HTML file. You can also choose a directory to put it in from the Directories list.

3. Pull down the Save File as Type combo box and select HyperText Markup Language (HTML) as the file type. Click OK to save the file.

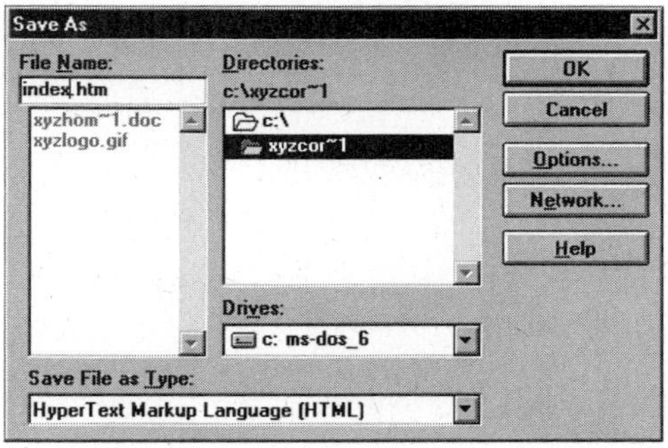

Fig. 30.15
Save your Word documents as HTML with Word's Save As dialog box.

Caution

Many Word elements don't have any equivalent in HTML. If you save a Word document as HTML and then reopen it as a Word document, those element types *will be lost*.

For a complete list of Word elements that can't be translated, use Word's Help facility to view the topic on "What Is Lost When Word Documents Are Converted to HTML."

Note

The Internet Assistant works best with relatively small pages. If you have large Word documents, consider breaking them into several smaller documents. Not only will this improve the performance of the Internet Assistant, but also Web surfers who read your pages will appreciate the reduced download time!

Translating Existing Documents to HTML

You may already have a large stock of Word documents that you want to convert into Web pages. Microsoft anticipated this and has made it easy to convert existing documents. Here's what to do:

1. Open the document you want to translate.

2. Add a title using the Title icon on the Formatting toolbar.

3. Add bookmarks as needed by choosing Edit, Bookmark, or clicking the Add Bookmark button.

4. Add links, as desired, by choosing Insert, HyperLink, or by clicking the HyperLink button.

5. Save the new document as an HTML file.

Note

For more detailed information on converting documents into Web pages, see Que's *Web Publishing with Word for Windows* and *10 Minute Guide to Internet Assistant*.

UseNet Newsgroups

One of the most popular services on the Internet, UseNet groups, covers topics ranging from zero-dimensional geometry ("alt.0.d"), to the "wi.*" hierarchy, consisting of groups with articles about Wisconsin.

Newsgroups are organized into a hierarchy that groups related topics with a mostly logical naming scheme. Each group name starts with a three- or four-letter prefix, followed by a group name. Here are the most common prefixes:

- *alt.* Alternative topics, everything from alien invasions to xenophobia
- *biz.* Covers business affairs, commerce, and commercial products
- *comp.* Computers and computer-related topics
- *news.* News of interest to the Internet community, like announcements of new groups
- *rec.* Recreation, hobbies, and sports
- *sci.* Scientific

- *soc*. Social issues
- *talk*. Discussions and debates
- *misc*. Everything that won't fit elsewhere

Individual regions, countries, and states have hierarchies, too, identified by their two-letter postal ID. For example, the **ca.general** group is for general discussion about Canada, and **tn.general** is for general discussion about the state of Tennessee.

Group names move from the general to the specific as you read them. For example, the **comp.infosystems.www.announce** and **comp.infosystems.www.servers.unix** groups are both about the WWW. The first has announcements about the Web, and the second is about UNIX Web server software.

In most groups, there are no rules except those enforced by the opinion of group members, but there are certain community standards for UseNet newsgroups that are generally agreed upon:

- Don't "spam." This refers to the wholesale posting of advertisements or self-aggrandizing announcements to many groups.
- Don't post sexist, racist, or demeaning messages. Doing so will usually bring down the newsgroup's wrath on the poster, whose later postings will be ignored or flamed.
- Avoid excessive cross-talk, or chatting between two posters. Keep private discussions in e-mail.
- Don't post private e-mail that you receive to a newsgroup without permission of the author.
- Keep articles short, without overly-long quoting of the message to which you're responding. In Net-speak, long, rambling postings are slammed for "wasting bandwidth."

It's a good idea to "lurk" (Net-speak for reading articles but not posting any) in a newsgroup for a while. Think of it as being at a party where you don't know anyone. You might prefer to stand around and observe before joining in a conversation.

Getting and Installing the WinVN Newsreader

Now we'll download a freeware newsreader program called WinVN. WinVN offers an attractive interface, and it's full of useful features. Using the FTP techniques discussed earlier in this chapter, FTP to **ftp.ksc.nasa.gov** and change to the directory /pub/winvn/nt. Get the file winvn_99_05_intel.zip. If there is a file there with a later number in the file name, get it instead.

> **Note**
>
> The name of this directory may change without notice. NASA is close to releasing version 1.0 of WinVN, and they may release future versions customized for Windows 95. The files in /nt were designed for NT, but also run well in Windows 95.

After retrieving WinVN, create a folder for the files on your hard drive. Use WinZip or some other unzipping program to extract the compressed files into the folder. If you want to, set up a shortcut on the desktop or add WinVN to the Start menu.

To configure WinVN, follow these steps:

1. Start the program. WinVN detects that you don't have an INI file or news article ("newsrc") file yet and offers to create them for you by presenting the standard save dialog box for each file. Choose a location for each file, then answer Yes to the Create File confirmation dialog box.

2. WinVN presents a dialog box so you can enter communications settings, as shown in figure 30.16. (You can also bring up this dialog box by choosing Config, Configure Communications.) Enter the name of your news server, your news port, and your mail server. These are available from your ISP or system administrator. Leave the Username and Password information blank unless told otherwise by your service provider or ISP. Then click OK.

3. WinVN presents another dialog box, asking you to enter your real name, your e-mail address, the reply address that people who want to mail you should use, and an organization affiliation. Enter your real name and mail address. If your reply and e-mail address are the same, leave the reply address field blank. If you'd like, you can enter a string in the Organization field.

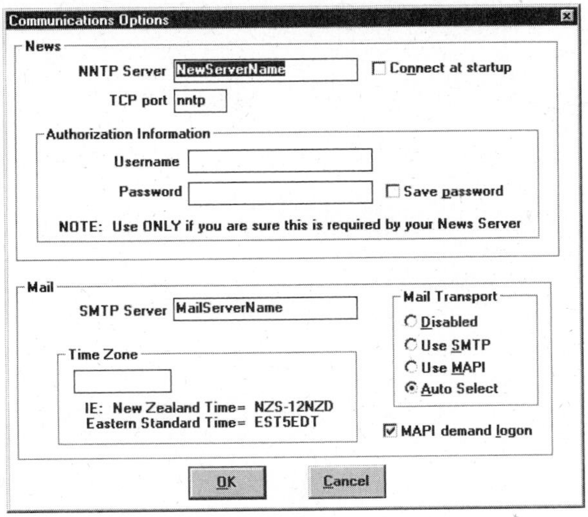

Fig. 30.16
The WinVN Communications Options dialog box. You can leave the optional information blank in most cases.

Reading News with WinVN

To read news, follow these steps:

1. Connect to the Internet. If your connection to the Internet is via a LAN, make sure you are properly connected to your network. If you connect by using a modem and a dial-up Internet service provider, use your Dial-up Connection to log onto your ISP.

◄ See "Installing and Configuring Windows 95 Dial-Up Network Adapter," p. 888

2. If WinVN isn't already running, start it now.

3. Choose Network, Connect To Server. WinVN will connect to the news server. After you connect, WinVN asks if you want to get a list of newsgroups that your server carries.

4. Click Yes, and WinVN fetches the list. Depending on your server, there may be more than 11,000 groups, so it will take some time. You need to do it once at first, then occasionally thereafter, to refresh your list and see new groups as they're created.

Tip
It's best to start with a small number and branch out once you're used to UseNet. You can always subscribe to more groups later.

5. Once WinVN has the list of groups, you'll see the New Newsgroups dialog box. This dialog box allows you to subscribe to newsgroups that interest you. Select a hierarchy from the top-left scrolling list; WinVN shows which groups under that hierarchy you're subscribed to and which you aren't.

6. To subscribe to a group, double-click its name in the Unsubscribed Groups list. The group appears in the Subscribed Group list. You can subscribe to several groups while keeping the dialog box open. When you've finished subscribing, click OK to save your choices. Figure 30.17 shows the dialog box with some groups subscribed.

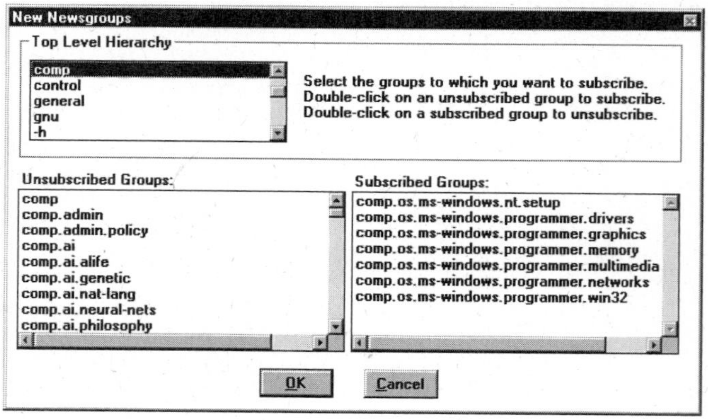

Fig. 30.17 Use the WinVN Subscribe dialog box to choose groups that you want to read frequently. The groups you select will be shown at the top of the WinVN groups window.

By default, WinVN subscribes you to two important UseNet newsgroups: **news.newusers.questions** and **news.announce.newusers**. These contain useful information on UseNet "netiquette," announcements of new groups, and FAQs on related issues.

WinVN's main window lists all the groups from your news server, whether you've subscribed to them or not. Subscribed groups are listed first, so you can easily find them. Double-clicking a group name downloads the list of messages in that group, as shown in figure 30.18, and displays the group's messages in a new window. Clicking a message opens another new window for that message (see fig. 30.19).

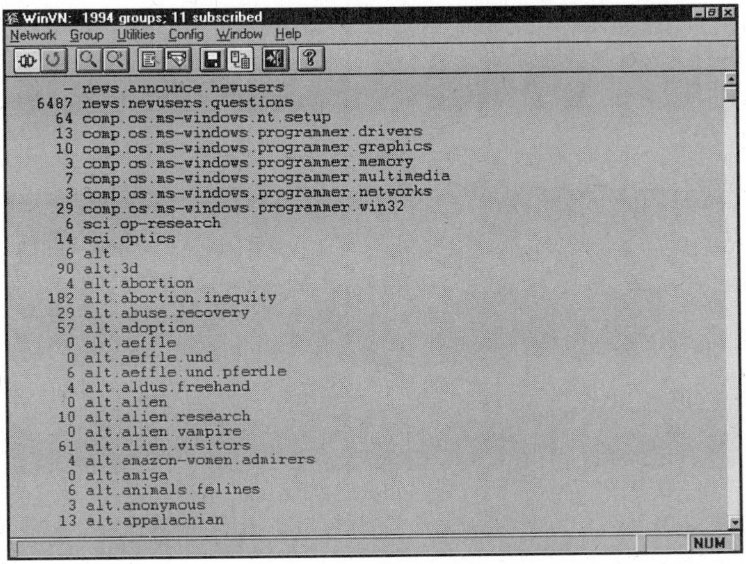

Fig. 30.18
Double-click a group to see what articles are available.

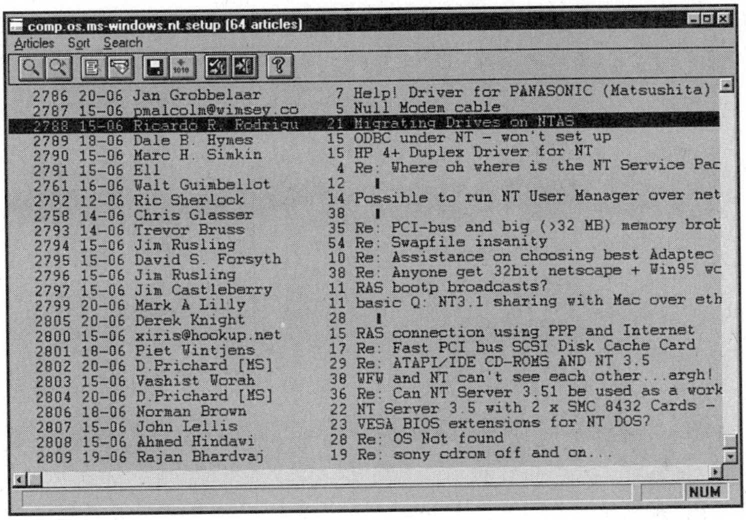

Fig. 30.19
WinVN lists each group's messages in its own window. Double-click an article line to see the article's text.

Part VII

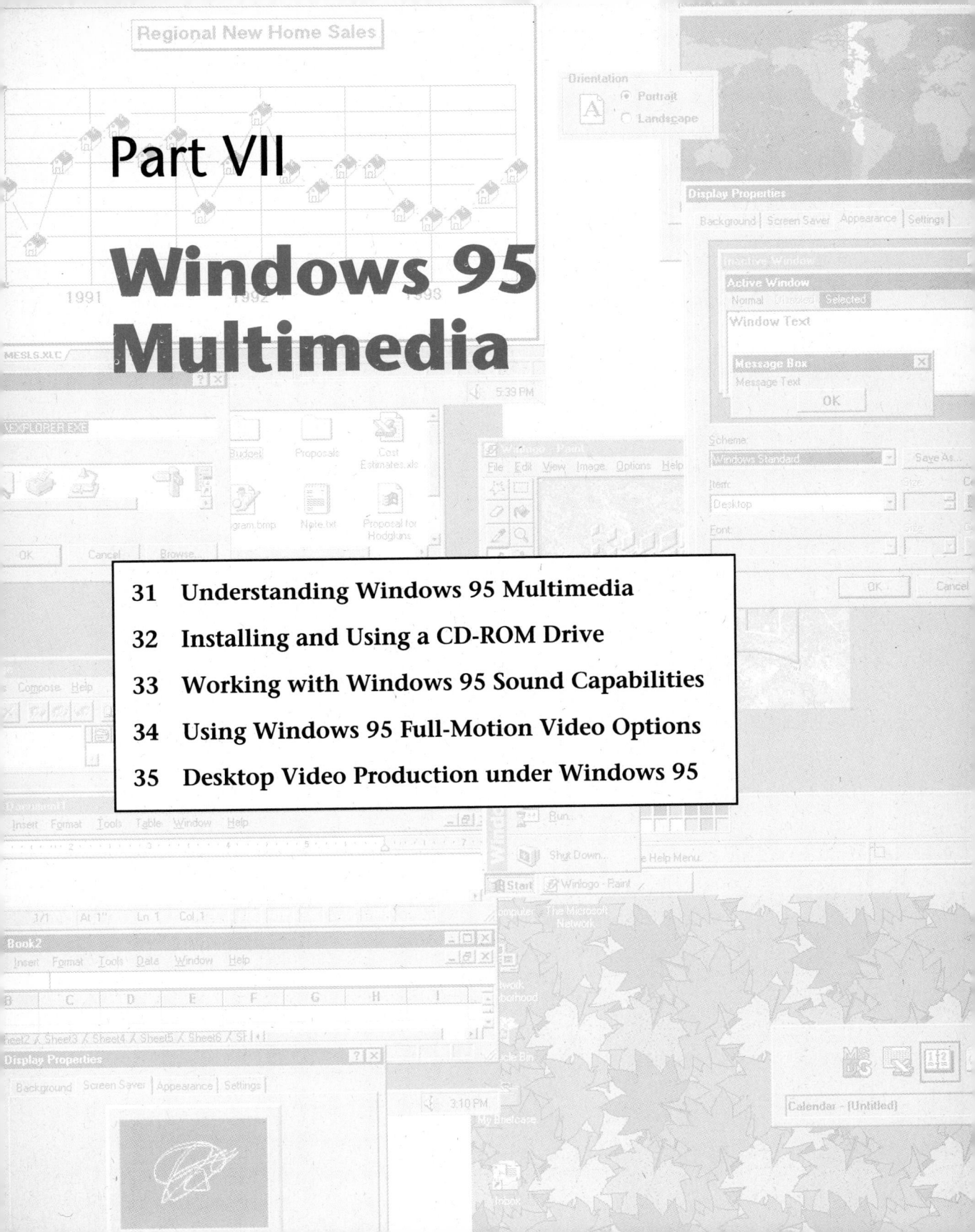

Windows 95 Multimedia

Regional New Home Sales
1991
1992
1993
HOMESLS.XLC
Orientation
Portrait
Landscape
(GMT-05:00) Eastern Time (US & Canada)
Display Properties
Background
Screen Saver
Appearance
Settings
Inactive Window
Active Window
Normal
Disabled
Selected
Window Text
Message Box
Message Text
OK
Scheme:
Windows Standard
Save As...
Item:
Desktop
Font:
OK
5:39 PM
Budget
Proposals
Cost Estimates.xls
Note.txt
Proposal for Hodgkins
334KB
OK
Cancel
Browse...
Exchange
Figures
My Documents
Winlogo - Paint
File
Edit
View
Image
Options
Help
Compose
Help
Name
Programs
Documents
Settings
Find
Help
Run...
Shut Down...
Windows95
Start
Winlogo - Paint
Document1
Insert
Format
Tools
Table
Window
Help
Book2
Insert
Format
Tools
Data
Window
Help
B
C
D
E
F
G
H
I
Display Properties
Background
Screen Saver
Appearance
Settings
3:10 PM
The Microsoft Network
Recycle Bin
My Briefcase
Inbox
Calendar - (Untitled)

Chapter 31

Understanding Windows 95 Multimedia

by Ian Stokell

Unless you have been secluded in a cave for the last few years, you are aware of a major evolution in the computer industry: multimedia technology. Multimedia and the move toward online services and the Internet are two of the most dominant trends in high-technology hardware, software, and telecommunications. Both topics are represented extensively in Windows 95, which includes many advanced multimedia features and the Microsoft Network.

Another major trend is the explosion in the market of home PCs. The existence of more home PCs has resulted in an increased demand for innovative non-business programs, such as multimedia reference CDs and exciting interactive games that feature sound and video. As a result, most PCs are now sold with CD-ROM drives included. In addition, the market for add-in sound boards that support advanced audio capabilities, such as MIDI, has skyrocketed. With this technology movement, it's no surprise that Windows 95 includes extensive multimedia features.

This is good for you, the end user, as it allows you to add multimedia capabilities and take advantage of multimedia features with little extra work on your part. The only thing you will need to ensure is that you either purchase a PC with multimedia hardware built-in, such as a sound board and CD-ROM drive, or add those hardware components before you begin looking toward using multimedia.

Windows 95 features a number of significant multimedia improvements over Windows 3.1, which includes Video for Windows (previously sold only as a separate product). It also includes support for a larger standard video image on-screen, which is important if you plan to view much video on your PC.

Also worth mentioning is the increased ease with which you can add various multimedia hardware components, such as a sound board or CD-ROM drive. Windows 95's Plug and Play standard allows you to add components that adhere to the standard with the minimum of problems. And Windows 95's Device Manager allows you to keep track of the many resources that are used by the multimedia components in order to minimize hardware conflicts.

Windows 95 also includes support for improved game graphics via the use of WinG, an application programming interface that allows for bitmapped graphics held in memory to appear onscreen quickly.

This chapter discusses the multimedia improvements in Windows 95, briefly touching on various multimedia options available to the Windows 95 user, and then discussing the installation of various hardware component drivers.

Specifically, you'll find coverage of the following topics:

- The effects of Multimedia on computer users
- Built-in video, audio, MIDI, and other multimedia features in Windows 95
- Microsoft's Plug and Play feature
- Using Device Manager to configure multimedia features
- Configuring multimedia properties

Multimedia Features in Windows 95

Multimedia is the point where various types of media converge. Historically, computers tended to offer users limited media choices: generally text and low-end graphics. But improved hardware performance in the industry today results in a greater range of processor-intensive products, from high-end graphics features to sound to full-motion video.

With these media choices comes the increased capability for you to interact with the program you are using. Now, many advanced CD games and products enable you to choose the route you want to travel through the program. You are no longer constrained by someone else's linear interpretation of where you should go. Now you can choose different routes each time you use the multimedia product—maybe you want to play a video or sound bite instead of just reading text on the screen or looking at a simple graphic.

Multimedia has its price. Just when you thought PCs were so cheap that anyone could have one, along comes multimedia with its increased hardware requirements. As a result, PCs equipped for multimedia are more expensive than non-multimedia-ready systems. As with all computing technology, however, prices are dropping rapidly.

Taking advantage of multimedia requires additional hardware, more RAM, and probably a larger hard disk drive to store the huge video and sound files you use. If you don't buy a multimedia-equipped PC at the outset, installing multimedia components such as a sound board and CD-ROM drive can be a study in both patience and PC knowledge. Microsoft responded to this dilemma by coming up with Plug and Play, discussed later in this chapter.

So what does Windows 95 offer the new user with regard to multimedia? The following sections provide a brief overview of various multimedia features included in Windows 95:

- Built-in video for Windows
- Larger standard video clip display
- Display Control Interface (DCI)
- MIDI and polymessage MIDI
- Support for digital joysticks
- Audio, including CD player and sound recorder

Built-In Video for Windows

Microsoft has been selling the program Microsoft Video for Windows separately since its introduction in 1992. Now the program is built into Windows 95.

With the inclusion of Video for Windows, you can distribute digital video files to other Windows 95 users using the AVI file format, without purchasing additional video-specific software.

Larger Standard Video Clip Display

Because multimedia is still in its infancy on the desktop, advances made from year to year can be significant. One example is the size of the standard video clip displayed on-screen.

The main problem with digital video is that each frame requires the transfer of a huge amount of data. As a result, the implementation and acceptance of desktop video by consumers is held captive by limited hardware and software technology. However, a number of recent hardware innovations have enabled software companies to develop advanced video applications. One such innovation is the phenomenal increase in CPU processing power and the introduction of local bus video (which increases bandwidth and therefore enables more data to be sent at the same time).

When Microsoft introduced Video for Windows in 1992, the standard video clip display was totally inadequate. The display was just 1/16 the size of a VGA screen, or 160 pixels by 120 pixels. With the inclusion of the updated Video for Windows in Windows 95 and the availability of high-end PCs at relatively low prices, video clips can appear full-screen, or 640 pixels by 480 pixels.

Display Control Interface (DCI)

► See "DCI Standard in Windows 95," p. 1007

Microsoft's Display Control Interface (DCI) is a display driver technology introduced in 1994 that enables Windows 95 to take advantage of a number of advanced features if they are built into display adapters. These features include *double buffering,* which speeds up block transfers; *color-space conversion,* which helps when playing back compressed digital video; *overlay,* which makes partly obstructed objects display faster; and *stretching,* which makes distorted or stretched images render faster. These features may be useful to a variety of graphics-intensive applications, such as computer-aided design, presentation preparation, and high-end desktop publishing.

MIDI

► See "MIDI and WAV Sound Files," p. 981

MIDI, or Musical Instrument Digital Interface, is a common protocol that enables the transfer of music-oriented digital data between electronic devices, be they keyboards or PCs. You cannot obtain sound from MIDI data without the necessary hardware, such as a MIDI-capable sound card in a PC. As such, MIDI data merely contains the instructions that enable the intended musical sound to be reproduced. For this reproduction to happen effectively, both the device that created the instructions from the original sound and the device that intends to reproduce the sound must communicate with each other using the same rules or language—which is where MIDI comes in.

One reason why this may be advantageous compared to a regular WAV file is with regard to file size. WAV files record the entire sound, and as such, can get pretty huge. MIDI files just contain the instructions to reproduce the sound, and are, therefore, much smaller.

As the number of multimedia products and games that include MIDI increases, so does the number of sound cards that are sold with those capabilities, such as a standard MIDI port for plugged-in MIDI instruments. In addition, you can use MIDI to enhance multimedia presentations, for example, where realistic sound can enhance the visual presentation appearing on-screen.

Polymessage MIDI

Windows 95's new polymessage MIDI support technology enables the transfer of multiple MIDI instructions within a single interrupt. The sound card can send and receive batch-processed multiple MIDI messages. In turn, less computing power is required, which frees up more of the CPU for other applications and processes. The CPU no longer needs to deal with each MIDI instruction separately.

This feature also enables highly efficient video playback. Any help that the PC operating system can provide is beneficial, because video playback is notoriously CPU-intensive.

Support for Digital Joysticks

Windows 95 supports the use of joysticks for use with multimedia games and CDs. After you install the joystick and select it, you must calibrate the joystick for it to work properly.

To calibrate your joystick, you need to select the joystick you are using from the Joystick Selection list on the Joystick Properties sheet. Click Custom if your joystick is not selected. Then select Calibrate and follow the instructions on-screen.

Audio

Windows 95 offers a variety of audio features for multimedia use, including the capability to play audio CDs and the customization of sound recording and playback.

► See "Using CD Player," p. 994

Playing audio CDs from a CD-ROM drive installed on your computer is possible using the CD Player feature. Provided you have a sound board installed, just start CD Player after you have the CD in the drive and press Start!

Windows 95 also can automatically recognize audio CDs when they are placed in the CD-ROM drive, without you doing anything. Then when you want to start the audio CD, just click on CD Player. Because CD Player operates in the background, you can listen to audio CDs while you are working in other applications on the PC.

► See "Using Sound Recorder," p. 998

You also can record sounds for personal use with another feature called Sound Recorder. This feature enables the recording of wave files and also their playback. Although Sound Recorder is not as sophisticated as higher-end digital recorders, it does provide a good introduction to the subject of digital recording. The resulting output is suitable for many non-professional presentations and for creating small voice files to send to other users in the form of electronic mail or embedding in documents.

Instead of just sending text e-mail, you can record a short voice message and attach it for distribution across your office network. Alternatively, for example, you can record a short voice annotation and have it run when you play a file in a presentation to a third party.

You will need a PC with enhanced sound capabilities though, such as a sound board and a microphone. Despite the prevalence of multimedia technology today, and the inclusion of multimedia capabilities in most PCs now sold in the consumer channel, you should make sure all necessary sound capabilities are included in your PC when you buy it, or you will have to add them later, which can get quite expensive.

Plug and Play

◄ See "Installing Plug and Play Hardware," p. 246

Most people who have used a PC with Windows can tell you that using the system is fine until it comes to adding a peripheral, such as multimedia components like a MIDI-capable sound card or a CD-ROM drive. Adding hardware components and getting them working often requires endless calls to technical support as you try to figure out where software drivers go and what instructions to put in startup files. Microsoft's new Plug and Play standard is the answer to this problem.

◄ See "Dealing with Legacy Hardware," p. 247

The Plug and Play standard is already supported in Windows 95. As a result, Windows 95 users who want to add a CD-ROM or sound card to their PC just need to look for one that is Plug and Play compatible. After the device is installed, Windows 95 can interact with the device with the minimum of configuration, because it already supports the necessary elements that make a PC a multimedia system (such as MIDI, digital video, and sound).

Windows 95 also includes tools that make recognizing and configuring older, non-Plug and Play devices easier, which should cut down on system conflicts. Windows 95 will automatically recognize resource conflicts for Plug and Play devices because the allocation and settings details are kept in the Registry.

Note

Unlike the old DOS/Windows combination, Windows 95 does not require separate AUTOEXEC.BAT and CONFIG.SYS files. The drivers required by your PC are automatically loaded, and their respective settings are automatically configured by Windows 95.

System Properties Control Panel

Windows 95 enables you to track hardware devices and the resources they are using, such as input/output (I/O) addresses and interrupt requests (IRQs), using the System Properties Registry. It is important to be able to track which multimedia hardware components are assigned which system resources so that, when adding additional peripherals, such as a SoundBlaster board, you do not assign resources that are already in use by another hardware device. Assigning resources already in use will lead to an infamous "hardware conflict," in which your PC will either crash completely or just not function properly.

With reference to multimedia components, SoundBlaster in particular has historically been difficult to configure because of the amount of resources that it uses. While this has been alleviated somewhat by Windows 95, it may be best to use SoundBlaster's own installation software to install the card in an effort to cut down on configuration problems.

Device Manager and Multimedia

Device Manager enables you to easily view the properties and resources allocated to multimedia hardware devices on your PC in a graphical way. Instead of hunting through strangely named files for such things as the IRQ settings, you can click a couple of times in Device Manager to see a familiar Windows window that lists IRQ settings and their corresponding multimedia hardware devices.

To open Device Manager, do the following:

1. Open the Start menu and choose Settings, Control Panel.
2. Double-click the System icon.
3. When the System Properties sheet appears, click the Device Manager tab.

You can view devices by type or connection. With the View Devices by Type option selected, the devices appear according to their type. For example, multimedia devices such as sound cards, full motion video, and game cards are grouped together (see fig. 31.1).

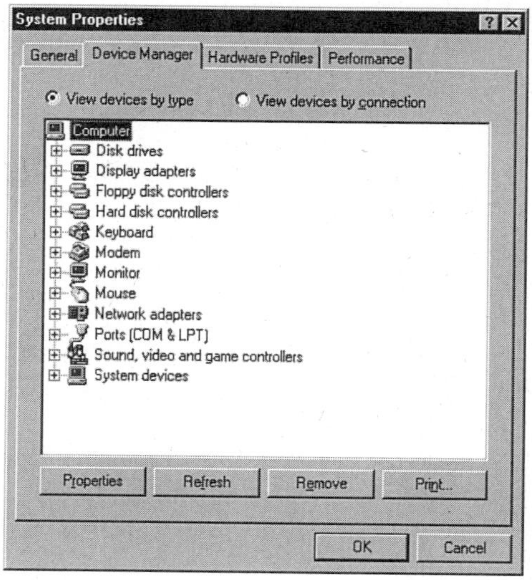

Fig. 31.1
In Device Manager you can view devices by type.

If you select the View Devices by Connection option, the connection type, such as Windows Sound System as shown in figure 31.2 on the popular Sound Blaster type sound card, appears with the corresponding device.

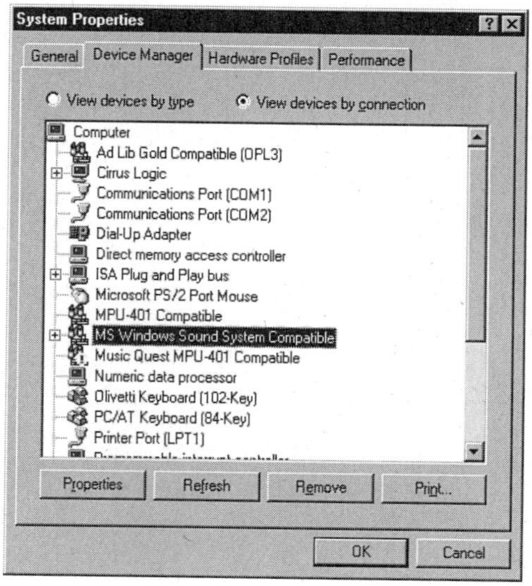

Fig. 31.2
In Device Manager you can view devices by what sort of connection they have, such as a Windows Sound System sound board.

Viewing Computer Properties

Device Manager enables you to view resources and settings allocated to devices attached to your PC by selecting Computer at the top of the device list in Device Manager, which appears when you select the View Devices by Type button.

You then can choose from two tabs: View Resources, which displays the resources being used by which hardware devices; and Reserve Resources, which displays the resources that are reserved system-wide. Each page offers four sets of resources: Interrupt Request (IRQ), Input/Output (I/O), Direct Memory Access (DMA), and Memory.

Interrupt Request (IRQ)

PCs are notorious for interrupt request (IRQ) conflicts when you are adding additional components. Part of the problem revolves around keeping track of which IRQ setting each peripheral or PC component has allocated to it. To make things easier, Windows 95 has the Interrupt Request (IRQ) option within the System Properties sheet's Device Manager.

To find out which IRQ setting is allocated to which component, click the Interrupt Request (IRQ) option. A list of IRQ settings appears, with the hardware using the corresponding setting next to it (see fig. 31.3).

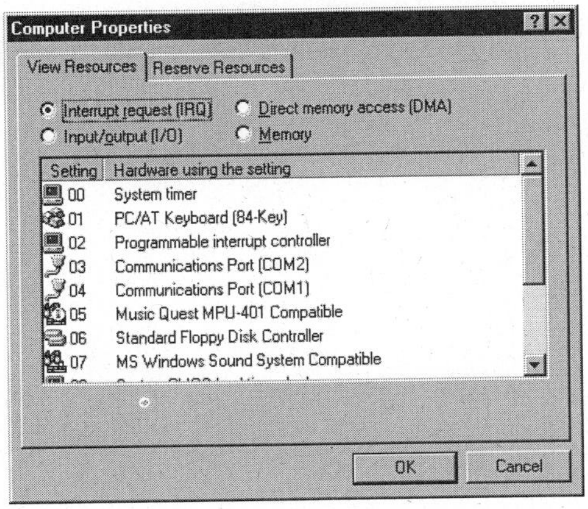

Fig. 31.3 To keep track of multimedia hardware IRQ settings, double-click Computer in Device Manager's View Devices by Type list, and you see the View Resources page.

Input/Output (I/O)

Input/output (I/O) addresses refer to locations in memory that devices use to communicate with software and/or the CPU.

To find out which I/O setting is allocated to which component, click the Input/Output (I/O) option. A list of I/O settings appears, with the hardware using the corresponding setting next to it (see fig. 31.4).

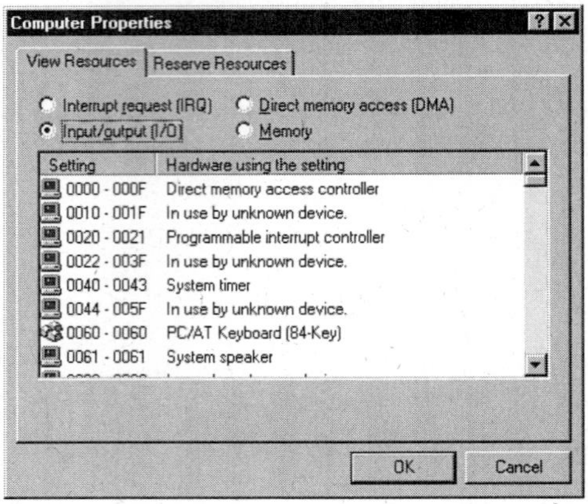

Fig. 31.4
Device Manager enables you to track device I/O settings.

Direct Memory Access (DMA)

Direct memory access (DMA) is a way of improving system performance by accessing memory without using the computer's processor.

To find out which DMA setting is allocated to which component, click the Direct Memory Access (DMA) option. A list of DMA settings appears, with the hardware using the corresponding setting next to it (see fig. 31.5).

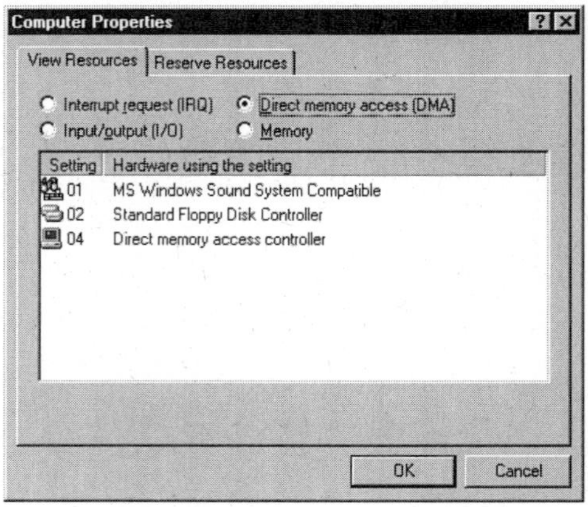

Fig. 31.5
Device Manager enables you to track device DMA settings.

Memory

You can find out what memory is allocated to which component with Device Manager. Click the Memory option. A list of memory settings appears, with the hardware using the corresponding setting next to it (see fig. 31.6).

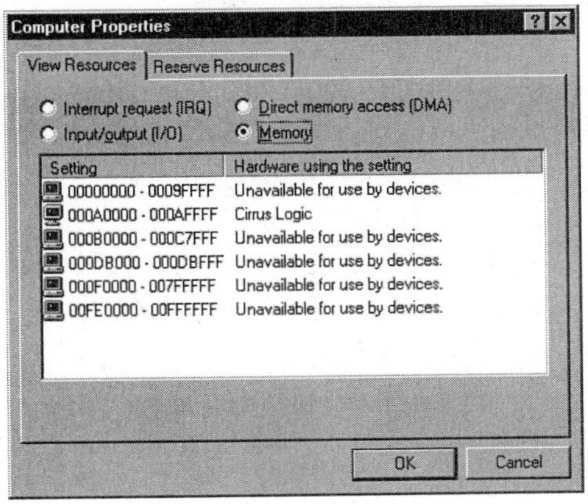

Fig. 31.6
Device Manager enables you to track memory settings.

Viewing and Changing Resource Settings

You can view or change the resource setting of a device using Device Manager. From the Device Manager page of the System Properties sheet, do the following:

1. Click the plus sign along the left edge next to the hardware device type for which you want to change the settings.
2. Double-click the specific hardware device you are interested in.
3. In the dialog box that appears, click the Resources tab (see fig. 31.7).

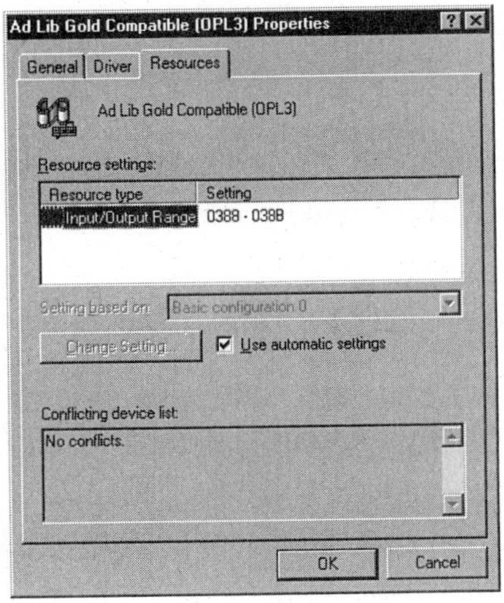

Fig. 31.7
A typical Resources page, from which you can change or view resource settings of a hardware device.

4. Click the resource you want to change. Make the change and click OK.

> **Note**
>
> Sometimes a device doesn't have a Resources tab. In such cases, the device either isn't using any resource settings, or you are not allowed to change its resources. As a result, you are not given the option to change settings.

Adding or Changing Device Drivers

Adding or changing device drivers has historically been a challenge for many people using the DOS/Windows combination. However, Windows 95 enables you to add or change device drivers using Device Manager.

As an example, try changing the driver for MS Windows Sound System Compatible. Start from the Device Manager page on the System Properties sheet, and follow these steps:

1. Click the plus sign along the left edge next to the hardware device type for which you want to change the settings, in this case Sound, Video and Game Controllers.
2. Double-click the specific hardware device you are interested in, in this case MS Windows Sound System Compatible.
3. On the sheet that appears, click the Driver tab (see fig. 31.8).

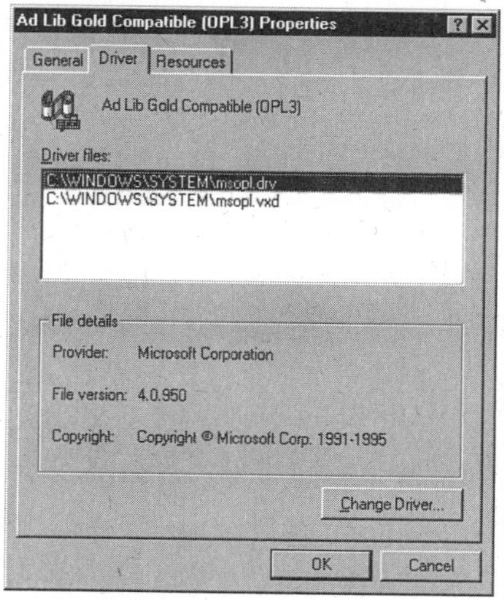

Fig. 31.8
The Driver page enables you to change drivers for a specific multimedia device.

4. Click the Change Driver button. The Select Device dialog box appears (see fig. 31.9).

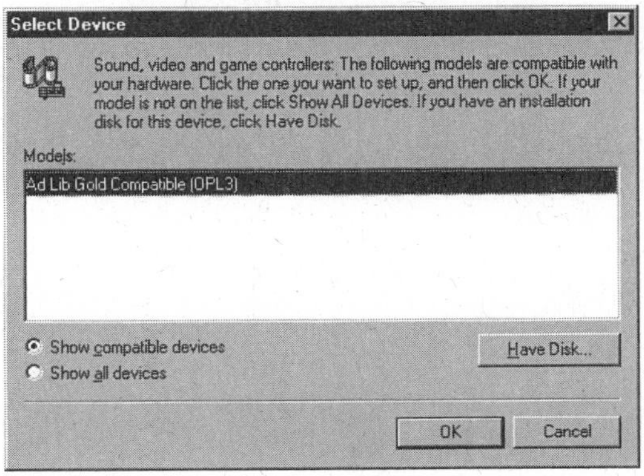

Fig. 31.9
You select the device you want to set up from the Select Device dialog box.

A list details the models compatible with your hardware. Make sure the Show Compatible Devices option is selected (if it is available). If the hardware model you want to set up is not on the list, select the Show All Devices button, if available. The list changes to show all such devices.

5. Click the device you want to set up; then click OK.

   The Select Device dialog box disappears, leaving the Driver page showing the driver files and their correct directory path.

6. Select the driver you want and click OK.

7. The dialog box disappears and you find yourself back at the Device Manager list. Click Close.

If you have a separate installation disk for the device (such as a floppy disk), you need to take these extra steps:

1. From the Select Device dialog box, click Have Disk. The Install From Disk dialog box appears (see fig. 31.10).

2. Specify the directory and disk where the manufacturer's files should be copied from.

3. Click OK.

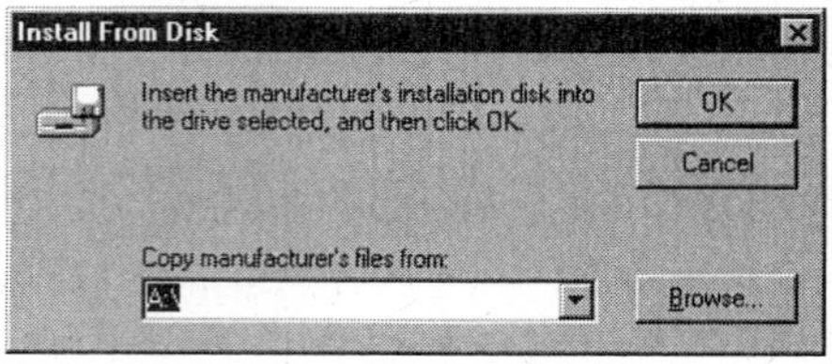

Fig. 31.10
You need to specify the drive and directory where the software drivers can be found.

Resolving Hardware Conflicts Using Device Manager

No matter how much you try to avoid it, you will probably get a hardware conflict sometime—that is, two devices trying to use the same resource at the same time. Device Manager makes resolving these conflicts easier.

If you have a conflict between two devices, open Device Manager and try one of these three things:

- Disable the device that is conflicting, which in turn frees up the device's resources.
- Assign a free resource to the device that is causing the conflict.
- Free up resources that the conflicting device needs by rearranging resources that other devices use.

Note

Windows 95 includes an extremely useful feature as part of Windows Help called Hardware Conflict Troubleshooter, which you can access via the Start button. Select the conflicting hardware and choose the Troubleshooting option from the Help topics index. The Troubleshooter helps you resolve conflicts on a step-by-step basis.

The Multimedia Properties Sheet

Windows 95 offers a Multimedia Properties sheet from which you can change various device properties, such as the following:

- *Audio* changes the volume level on a multimedia device.
- *Video* varies the size of the standard window in which a video clip is displayed.
- *MIDI* sets up a new MIDI instrument.

- *CD Music* adjusts the volume of an installed CD player.
- *Advanced* configures multimedia properties associated with specific attached devices.

To display the Multimedia Properties sheet, follow these steps:

1. Open the Start menu and choose Settings, Control Panel.
2. Double-click the Multimedia icon. The Multimedia Properties sheet appears.

Audio

Adjusting the volume of multimedia devices is possible using the Multimedia Properties sheet. After you display the Multimedia Properties sheet, do the following:

1. Click the Audio tab (see fig. 31.11).

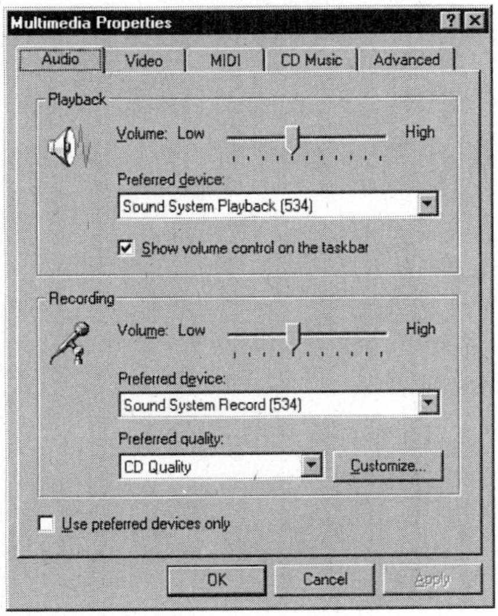

Fig. 31.11
You can adjust the volume of multimedia devices using the Audio page on the Multimedia Properties sheet.

2. Adjust the volume for Playback or Recording by dragging the respective Volume slider; drag to the right for higher, and to the left for lower.
3. Select the device you want used for playback or recording if it is not the default in the Preferred Device list.
4. Check the Show Volume Control on the taskbar if you want the volume control displayed during playback.

5. Select an option from the Preferred Quality list for the quality of the recording (for example, CD Quality).

6. If you want to customize the recording quality, click the Customize button in the Recording area. The Customize dialog box appears (see fig. 31.12).

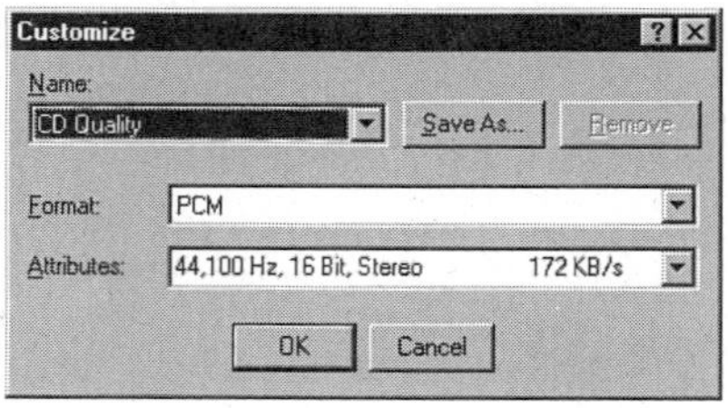

Fig. 31.12 Customize the quality of the recorded sound using the Customize option.

With this option, you can select the sound quality, format, and attributes, and then save the customized format as a special file by clicking the Save As button.

Tip To achieve the smoothest video playback, select the Original Size option from the Window drop-down list.

Video

You can adjust the size of the standard window in which a video clip is displayed using the Multimedia Properties sheet. After the sheet appears, follow these steps:

1. Click the Video tab (see fig. 31.13).

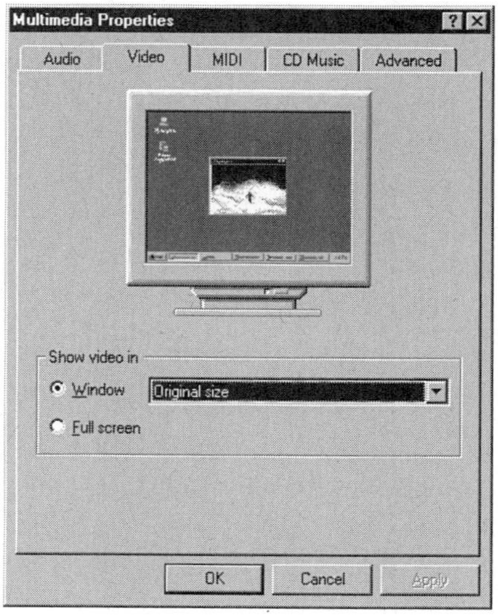

Fig. 31.13 Adjust the size of the video clip window using the Video page of the Multimedia Properties sheet.

2. Click Window or Full Screen in the Show Video In area to either customize the display window or use the entire screen.

3. If Window is checked, select the window size you want from the drop-down list that appears when you click the down arrow.

MIDI

You can use the MIDI page of the Multimedia Properties sheet to set up a new MIDI instrument connected to your PC.

After you display the Multimedia Properties sheet, follow these steps:

1. Connect the MIDI instrument to a MIDI port on your installed sound card.

2. Click the MIDI tab (see fig. 31.14).

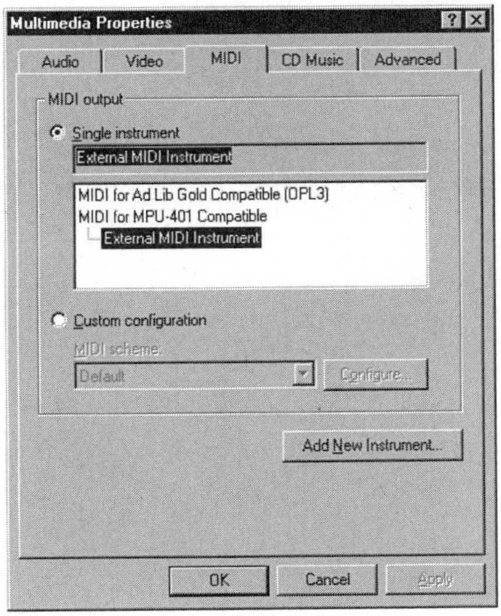

Fig. 31.14
You can set up a MIDI instrument using the MIDI page in the Multimedia Properties sheet.

3. Click the Add New Instrument button near the bottom of the page.

4. Follow the instructions on-screen to install the MIDI device, and then click the Single Instrument button.

5. The device you just installed will be displayed in the list window in the center of the MIDI page. Select the device and click OK.

Moving a MIDI Instrument to Another Sound Card

You can switch MIDI instruments between sound cards using these steps:

1. Click the Advanced tab in the Multimedia Properties sheet (see fig. 31.15).

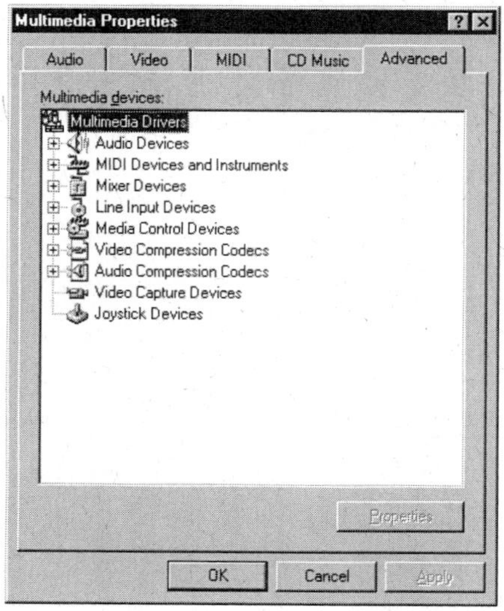

Fig. 31.15
To display multimedia properties related to different devices, click the Advanced tab.

2. Click the plus sign next to MIDI Devices and Instruments.
3. Click the plus sign next to the sound card that is connected to your MIDI instrument.
4. Select the instrument you want to move.
5. Click Properties.
6. On the resulting Properties sheet, click the Details tab (see fig. 31.16).

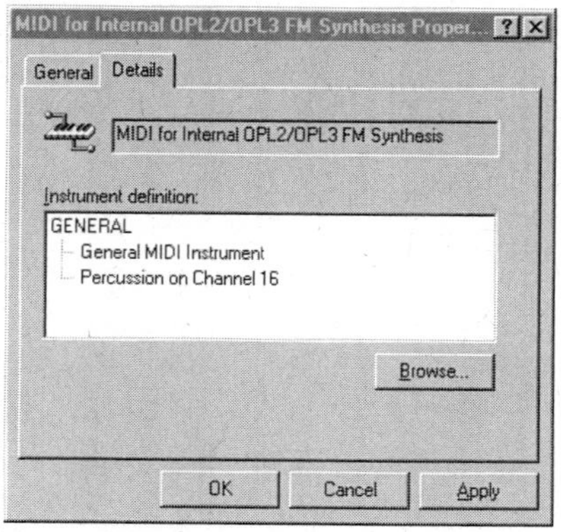

Fig. 31.16
The Details page on the MIDI Properties sheet enables you to move a MIDI instrument to a new sound card.

7. Select the sound card where you want to move the instrument from the MIDI Port list.

8. Plug the instrument into the new sound card.

CD Music

You can adjust the volume of the CD player installed on your PC using the CD Music page on the Multimedia Properties sheet.

Tip
You can set volume levels for different CD drives.

After you display the Multimedia Properties sheet, follow these steps:

1. Click the CD Music tab (see fig. 31.17).

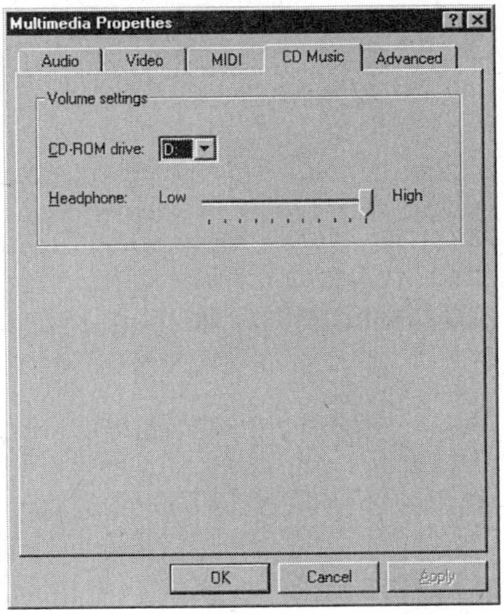

Fig. 31.17
You can change the volume level for a specific CD-ROM drive using the CD Music page on the Multimedia Properties sheet.

2. To adjust the volume, just drag the slider to the right (to increase volume) or the left (to decrease volume).

3. Click OK after you have selected the correct volume level.

If you have more than one CD player installed, you can switch between CD players using the same Multimedia page:

1. Select the CD drive you want to use from the CD-ROM drive list.

2. Click OK.

Advanced

Clicking the Advanced tab of the Multimedia Properties sheet displays multimedia properties associated with different devices attached to your PC (refer to fig. 31.15).

To configure the multimedia device of your choice, follow these steps:

1. Click the plus sign next to the type of multimedia device you are interested in. A sub-list of associated devices appears.
2. Select the device you want to configure.
3. Click the Properties button at the bottom of the window.
4. Make the necessary changes on the Properties sheet and click OK. The Properties sheet is different for each type of device.❖

Chapter 32

Installing and Using a CD-ROM Drive

by Jerry Honeycutt

Do you need a CD-ROM drive in your computer? Of course you do, if you want to use any new software or games in the future. In 1995, most new computers will ship with a CD-ROM drive already installed. A trip to your local computer store reveals aisles of computers with preinstalled CD-ROM drives. In fact, only the most basic machines in current product lines are without one. The large number of CD-ROM drives in desktop computers has escalated the demand for CD-ROM software titles. And you can bet that software vendors are answering the demand.

Vendors are shipping multimedia software and games, reference material, resources, and other applications on CD-ROM. The sheer size of these titles makes the CD-ROM the only practical way for vendors to distribute them. Also, many software vendors will be shipping software on CD-ROM for economical reasons: a single CD-ROM is less expensive to ship than a handful of floppy disks, and many products include documentation on the CD-ROM instead of printed manuals. Most multimedia applications rely on sounds, videos, and images stored on a CD-ROM. For example, Microsoft Bookshelf would not be possible without CD-ROM technology. It ships only on CD-ROM and occupies over 600 megabytes. Shipping Microsoft BookShelf would require almost 500 floppy disks!

In addition to multimedia titles, many popular software packages, such as Microsoft Office, ship on CD-ROM. Installing an application as large as Office is much quicker from CD-ROM: installing Office from disks can take more than 90 minutes, whereas installing it from CD-ROM can take less than 15 minutes. As a bonus, you don't have to swap disks in and out of the drive.

The purpose of this chapter is to help you use the CD-ROM that came with your computer. This chapter also helps you install a CD-ROM drive if you don't already have one. In this chapter, you learn to

- Use your CD-ROM drive with Windows and other applications
- Run applications on the CD-ROM drive without installing them on your hard drive at all
- Install drivers for a Plug and Play CD-ROM drive
- Install drivers for an older CD-ROM drive
- Optimize your CD-ROM drive in Windows

Using Your CD-ROM Drive

◄ See "My Computer for Easy Understanding of What's in Your Computer," p. 25

With a few exceptions, using your CD-ROM drive in Windows is no different than using any other drive. Figure 32.1 shows the E drive icon in My Computer as a CD-ROM. You access it in My Computer or the Explorer just like the other drives in your computer—double-click on the icon to open its folder or right-click to display its context menu.

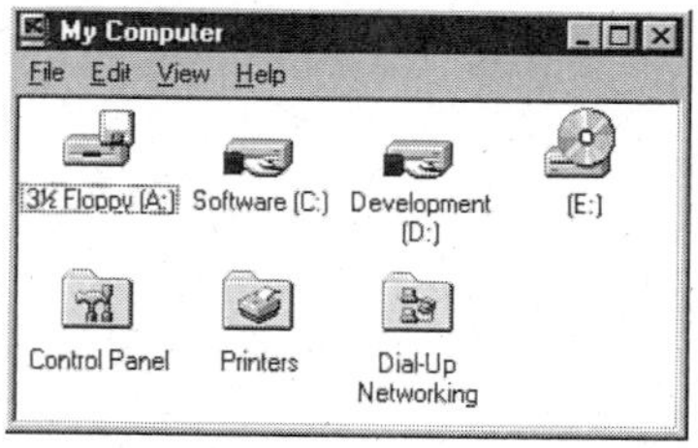

Fig. 32.1 Double-click the CD-ROM icon to open it in a folder. Right-click it and select Properties to see its size or share it.

◄ See "Dealing with Legacy Hardware," p. 247

Troubleshooting

I have a CD-ROM installed in my machine, but it doesn't show up in My Computer or the Explorer.

If you are using an external CD-ROM drive, make sure that it is turned on. At times, Windows may skip detecting your CD-ROM drive when you install Windows for the first time. In this case, use the Add New Hardware Wizard to allow Windows to automatically detect your CD-ROM as described in "Installing Legacy CD-ROM Drives" later in this chapter. If your CD-ROM drive still does not show up in My Computer, right-click My Computer and select Properties. Click the Device Manager tab, select your CD-ROM, and click Properties. A description of the problem and a possible solution is displayed in the Device Status area. If your CD-ROM does not appear in the Device Manager at all, consult the manual that came with your CD-ROM for more troubleshooting information, or call the vendor's support line.

Playing a CD-ROM Automatically

Windows automatically detects when you insert a CD-ROM into the drive. As a result, it displays the label of the CD-ROM next to the drive letter in My Computer. When you remove the CD-ROM, it clears the label.

◀ See "Adding and Removing Windows Components," p. 313

Some CD-ROMs for Windows 95 are set up to automatically run when they are inserted into the CD-ROM drive. If Windows detects an *AutoPlay* CD-ROM, it runs the appropriate program on the disc. The Windows 95 CD-ROM is a good example. After you have installed Windows 95, reinsert the CD-ROM in the drive. Almost immediately, a window opens, which gives you the opportunity to add or remove Windows components by clicking Add/Remove Software, or play a game of Hover! (see fig. 32.2).

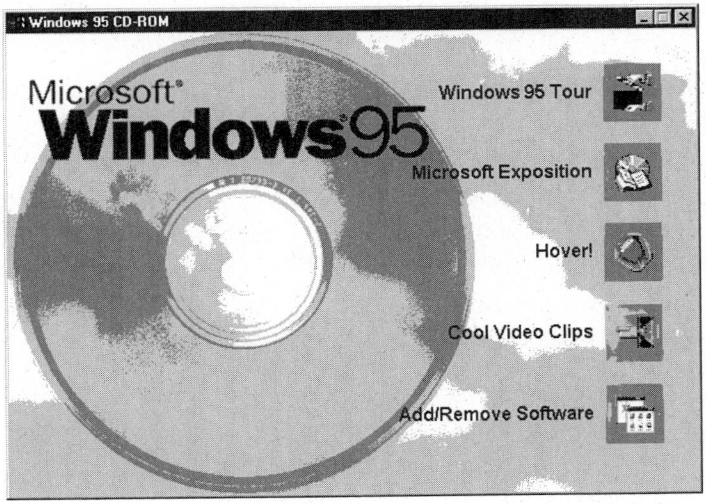

Fig. 32.2
This window opens when you insert the Windows 95 CD-ROM. You don't have to do anything!

In the future, software vendors will use AutoPlay as a significant marketing tool (or "Spin and Grin," as Microsoft calls it). However, AutoPlay is more than a marketing tool. AutoPlay simplifies installation for countless first-time users who would otherwise spend hours figuring out how to install these products. In the future, installation instructions for many programs using Spin and Grin will simply say, "Insert this CD in your drive and follow the on-screen instructions."

Tip
To disable AutoPlay, hold down the Shift key while inserting a CD-ROM in the drive.

Troubleshooting

Windows doesn't automatically recognize a CD-ROM when I insert it. I have to refresh My Computer or the Explorer to see the CD-ROM's contents.

Right-click on My Computer, select Properties, select the CD-ROM in the device list, click the Properties button, and select the Settings tab of the property sheet. Make sure the Auto Insert Notification option is checked.

Sharing Your CD-ROM Drive on a Peer-to-Peer Network

◄ See "Sharing an Entire Drive," p. 643

If other users on your peer-to-peer network don't have a CD-ROM drive, you may want to share yours. Sharing your CD-ROM drive is similar to sharing any other drive on your computer. However, there are two considerations when sharing a CD-ROM drive:

◄ See "Sharing Your Resources," p. 688

- If a user *maps* to your shared CD-ROM drive and no disk is in it, he will receive a message that says `X:\ is not available` when he tries to open it.

- You are sharing a drive, not a particular CD-ROM title. Therefore, if you share the drive with the Windows 95 CD-ROM in it, and then change the disk, you will be sharing the new disk.

Installing a Software Application from a CD-ROM Drive

Tip

With Windows 95 file sharing for Novell Networks, you can share a CD-ROM drive with other Novell clients, even though Novell is a client/server network.

Installing software from a CD-ROM drive is similar to installing from floppy disk, but it's a lot easier. You can double-click the Add/Remove Programs icon in the Control Panel or run the Setup program on the CD-ROM directly. For Windows 95 applications, you should install using the Control Panel. For legacy software (software written for older versions of Windows), either method is appropriate.

In addition to installing an application using the preceding methods, some software is AutoPlay-enabled as described earlier in this chapter. In this case, insert the CD-ROM in the drive and follow the instructions. For information on partial installations, see the section "Partial Installation" later in this chapter.

◄ See "Installing Applications in Windows 95," p. 304

Troubleshooting

When I try to install a program from a CD-ROM using the Control Panel, it complains that Windows was unable to locate the installation program.

Your CD-ROM did not have a SETUP.EXE or INSTALL.EXE file in its root directory. Click Browse to search the CD-ROM for another Setup program such as WINSTALL.EXE or try to run the program directly if there is no Setup program.

I successfully installed a program from a CD-ROM on my hard drive. When I run the program now, I get an error that says `File not found`. *Or, if I try to use Help, the Help window pops up and displays an error that says* `Help file not found`.

First, make sure that you have inserted the CD-ROM you used to install the program in the drive because the program is probably looking for program or data files on the CD. If you still get the error message, make sure that the CD-ROM is still assigned to the same drive letter it was when you installed the program. If it is not, you will need to reassign the drive or reinstall the program. You can change the drive letter the CD-ROM is assigned to by selecting the CD-ROM drive in the Device Manager, clicking the Properties button, and clicking the Settings tab of the property sheet. Select a new drive letter in the Start Drive Letter list box.

Complete Installation

Applications such as Micrografx Picture Publisher do a complete installation. All of the files required to run the program are copied to the hard drive. This is typical of applications that don't require a large amount of space, but are distributed on CD-ROM for convenience. Also, some applications that by default install only partially will give you the opportunity to do a complete installation when performance is important.

Partial Installation

Some applications, such as Automap, shown in figure 32.3, enable you to do a partial installation. In this case, only core components are copied to the hard drive, whereas other files such as data or help files are left on the CD-ROM. The advantage to this method is that you don't lose a significant amount of hard-drive space to store the application. However, the disadvantage is that you must place the CD-ROM in the drive to run the application, and the application will run slower than if you installed it to your hard drive.

Running Applications from the CD-ROM Drive

A very limited number of applications can be run directly from the CD-ROM drive. Many multimedia preview discs exist that contain programs you can run directly on the CD-ROM. However, the performance of applications that are run directly from the CD-ROM is poorer than if you copy the files to your hard drive because a quad-speed CD-ROM transfers data at about 600K per second, whereas a hard drive can transfer data up to 5 megabytes per second.

◄ See "Moving and Copying Files and Folders," p. 515

See the HoverHavoc game on your Windows 95 CD-ROM in \Funstuff\Hover for an example of an application you can run directly from the CD-ROM.

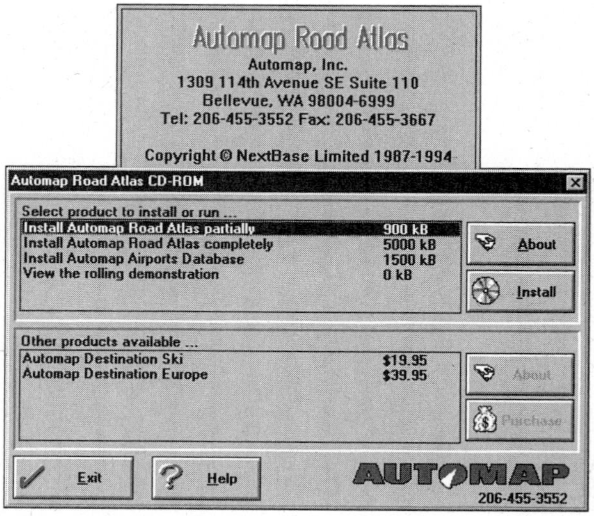

Fig. 32.3
Selecting partial installation will install only the program files, leaving the data files on the CD-ROM. Notice that a partial installation requires 900K versus 5 megabytes for a full installation.

Tip
If the CD-ROM contains a SETUP.EXE file in the root directory, you probably can't run the application from the CD-ROM.

Although programs generally can't be run directly from the CD-ROM, many other types of files can be used directly:

- *Data Files.* Data files include clip art, bitmaps, documents, and other files that you don't use often and would normally occupy a lot of space on your hard drive. You can use these files directly from the CD-ROM or copy them individually to your hard drive.

◀ See "Understanding Fonts," p. 210

- *Font.* A collection of fonts that you install via the Control Panel. Once the font is installed, you don't need the CD-ROM in the drive to use the font.

◀ See "Multimedia Features in Windows 95," p. 950

- *Multimedia.* Some CD-ROMs are packed with sounds and videos you can preview directly from the CD-ROM. For example, see the Funstuff directory on your Windows 95 CD-ROM.

▶ See "Using CD Player," p. 994

- *Audio CD.* Your favorite audio CD. Playing your favorite musical CD can pick up the pace while you are working—but it can distract you, too!

Installing Plug and Play CD-ROM Drives

In Chapter 8, "Plug and Play and Legacy Device Installation," you learned what Plug and Play is and how to install Plug and Play devices. Installing a Plug and Play CD-ROM adapter is similar to installing other Plug and Play devices. They are simpler to install than legacy CD-ROM adapters because you don't have to worry with IRQ, DMA, and I/O port settings. Driver configuration is automatic, too.

Tip
Double-click on \Funstuff\Videos\Goodtime.avi on your Windows 95 CD-ROM to see a great example video!

Windows will take care of the details that previously could take hours: it identifies the hardware, identifies the resource requirements, creates the configuration, programs the device, loads the 32-bit device drivers, and notifies the system of the change. It will appear in My Computer the next time you boot Windows.

Note

For complete Plug and Play installation instructions, see Chapter 8, "Plug and Play and Legacy Device Installation."

Installing Legacy CD-ROM Drives

Installing legacy CD-ROM drives is not as easy as installing Plug and Play drives. However, Windows' Add New Hardware Wizard greatly simplifies the task. This wizard looks for clues in your computer that tell it what hardware is installed. Some clues include the following:

◄ See "Dealing with Legacy Hardware," p. 247

- Signatures or strings in ROM
- I/O ports at specific addresses that would indicate a specifically known hardware class
- Plug and Play devices that will report their own ID
- Drivers loaded in memory before you run Setup
- `device=` lines in the CONFIG.SYS that indicate specific device drivers to the Wizard.

CD-ROM Types Supported

Windows supports three types of CD-ROM drives: SCSI, IDE, and proprietary CD-ROM drives.

- *SCSI*. Often pronounced *skuzzy*, a Small Computer System Interface adapter allows you to connect multiple pieces of hardware to a single adapter: scanners, hard drives, CD-ROM drives, and others. SCSI devices are known for their speed.
- *IDE*. An Interface Device Electronics adapter, commonly integrated into the motherboard, provides an interface for your floppy and hard disks. CD-ROM drives made for IDE adapters are less expensive than drives made for SCSI adapters.
- *Proprietary*. Some CD-ROM manufacturers, such as Sony and Mitsumi, sell drives that require a proprietary adapter. These drives require you to use an open slot for the adapter.

Note

If you haven't purchased your CD-ROM adapter or drive yet, go ahead and buy a Plug and Play adapter. Windows will still be able to take advantage of some Plug and Play features. Also, you will be using the latest technology that you can install in a Plug and Play computer later.

If you will be purchasing a sound card too, consider buying a combination sound/CD-ROM adapter card if you are running out of open slots in your computer. However, if performance is critical and you have the open slots, purchase separate sound and CD-ROM adapters.

Caution

When buying a Plug and Play adapter, be wary of packaging that says "Plug and Play *Ready*" on the box. You may be in for an expensive upgrade when you are ready to use this adapter in a Plug and Play computer. Verify that it is truly a Plug and Play device before you purchase it. See Chapter 8, "Plug and Play and Legacy Device Installation," for a discussion of the Plug and Play standard.

Installing the CD-ROM on an Existing Adapter

If you install your CD-ROM drive to an existing adapter that Windows already recognizes, you do not need to do anything else. All you have to do is complete the physical installation and connect the drive and cables as described in your manufacturer's documentation. Your CD-ROM drive will appear in your device list the next time you boot Windows.

Installing a CD-ROM and Adapter

By installing the driver for your new CD-ROM adapter before actually installing the hardware, you can let Windows suggest a configuration that does not conflict with existing devices in your computer. Therefore, make sure that you have not installed your adapter in your computer before following these steps. To install a legacy CD-ROM adapter and drive in your computer, follow these steps:

▶ See "Adding or Changing Hardware Drivers," p. 989

> **Note**
>
> If you are installing one of the popular combination sound/CD-ROM adapters, install the sound card device drivers as described in Chapter 33, "Working with Windows Sound Capabilities," before continuing installation as described in this chapter.

Tip

If you are absolutely sure that your CD-ROM adapter will not conflict with existing devices in your computer, go ahead and install the adapter and allow Windows to automatically detect it.

1. Open the Control Panel and double-click the Add New Hardware icon. The Add New Hardware Wizard opens.
2. Click Next. The wizard allows you to choose between automatically detecting new hardware and manually installing new hardware. Select No and click Next.
3. Choose your adapter from the dialog box shown in figure 32.4.

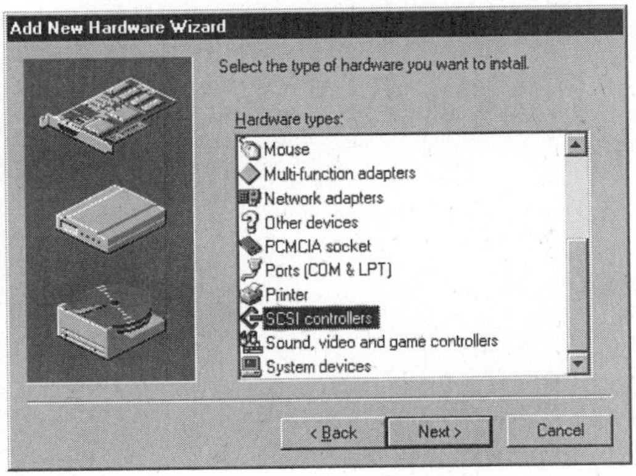

Fig. 32.4
Select either CD-ROM Controllers or SCSI Controllers from the list, depending on which type of adapter you are installing.

4. Select a manufacturer from the Manufacturers list and a specific model from the Models list (see fig. 32.5). Make sure that your selection matches your adapter exactly. Click Next. The wizard displays information about the recommended settings for this device.

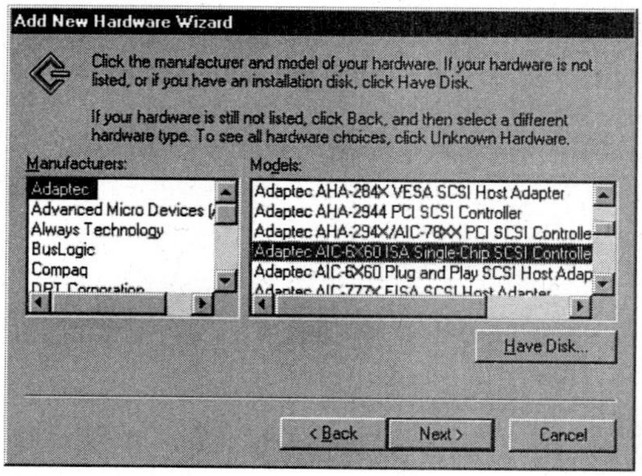

Fig. 32.5
Select a manufacturer and model. If your exact adapter doesn't appear in these lists, you'll need a disk from the manufacturer.

5. Click Print to output the recommended settings to the printer, or write them down on paper. You'll use these settings to configure your hardware before installing it in your computer.

6. Click Next; then click Finish, and Windows installs the necessary drivers on your computer.

7. After Windows has installed the drivers, shut down Windows and turn off your computer.

◀ See "Dealing with Legacy Hardware," p. 247

8. Configure and install the CD-ROM adapter and drive using the instructions provided by the manufacturer and the settings recommended by Windows. For additional information on setting an adapter's I/O address, IRQ line, and DMA address, see Chapter 8, "Plug and Play and Legacy Device Installation."

Note

If you are installing a separate sound card, don't forget to connect the audio output of the CD-ROM drive to the audio input of the sound card. See your manufacturer's instructions for more information.

◀ See "CD Music," p. 967

Congratulations! You have successfully installed your CD-ROM adapter and can start enjoying the benefits right away.

Troubleshooting

I successfully installed my CD-ROM (I can see the files on the CD-ROM using the Explorer), but it won't play audio CDs.

First, check the volume by clicking on the Volume icon in the system tray. Then, run Media Player, select Device, and make sure that there is a menu entry that says CD Audio. If not, install the MCI CD Audio driver as shown in Chapter 31, "Understanding Windows 95 Multimedia." Otherwise, if your CD-ROM plays but you can't hear the music, plug your speakers or headphones into the external audio jack of the CD-ROM. If you hear music using the external audio jack but not through your sound card, your CD-ROM is not properly connected to your sound card. Connect your CD-ROM to your sound card by following the manufacturer's instructions.

I tried to connect my CD-ROM to the sound card, but the cable doesn't fit both cards.

You'll need a new cable that is capable of connecting your CD-ROM drive to your sound card. If you are using commonly available hardware, contact the manufacturer, and they can provide you with a cable.

My computer dies during setup after installing my new CD-ROM adapter.

Restart your computer. Run Windows Setup again and it will ask you if you want to use Safe Recovery to continue the installation. Choose Safe Recovery and click Next. Continue using the steps described in this section. Setup will skip the portions of the hardware detection that caused the failure.

▶ See "Using CD Player," p. 994

Optimizing CD-ROM Drives in Windows 95

Windows 95 incorporates a new file system specifically designed and optimized for CD-ROM drives. CDFS (CD File System) is a 32-bit, protected-mode file system that provides the following benefits:

- Replaces MSCDEX, which loads in conventional memory, with a driver that occupies no conventional memory.
- Improves performance of your applications by providing 32-bit, protected-mode caching. Your multimedia applications run more smoothly.
- Requires no configuration. CDFS is a dynamic cache.

The CD-ROM cache is separate from your disk cache because it is specifically optimized for use with a CD-ROM drive.Windows normally caches the CD-ROM to memory. However, when Windows needs more memory for your applications, it swaps the cache to the hard drive instead of discarding it altogether. The next time Windows needs that particular data, it reads it from the hard drive instead of the CD-ROM. This significantly improves performance as reading data from the hard drive is about ten times faster than reading data from the CD-ROM.

To optimize your CD-ROM, use the following steps:

1. Right-click on My Computer and select Properties.
2. Click the Performance tab of the System Properties property sheet, click File System, and select the CD-ROM tab. Figure 32.6 shows the CD-ROM tab that appears.

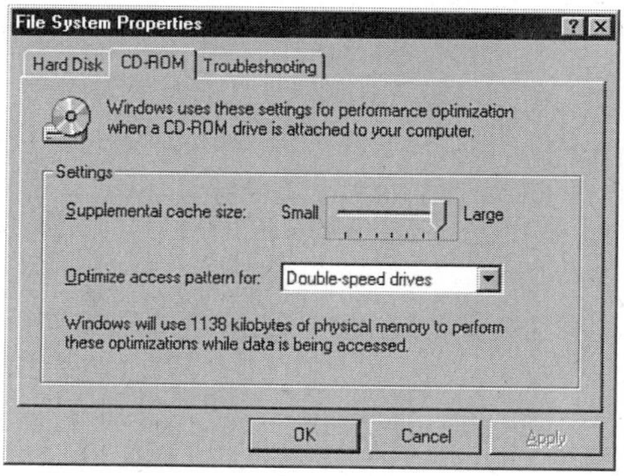

Fig. 32.6
Optimize your CD-ROM in the File System Properties dialog box.

3. Drag the Supplemental Cache Size slider to the setting indicated in table 32.1.

Table 32.1 Recommended Supplemental Cache Sizes

Installed RAM	Cache Size
Up to 8M	114K
8M to 12M	626K
12M and over	1,138K

4. Select the type of CD-ROM in the Optimize Access Pattern For list, and then click OK.❖

Chapter 33

Working with Windows 95 Sound Capabilities

by Ian Stokell

The original IBM PC and resulting compatibles were not built to accommodate extensive sound features. Even today, you usually need to buy an additional audio board and speakers, often pre-installed in a new PC along with a CD-ROM drive. This type of system, advertised as "multimedia-ready," makes your PC capable of playing and recording quality sound files.

This chapter discusses sound-related topics in Windows 95:

- An overview of sound capabilities in Windows 95
- Instructions on playing sound files
- Installation of sound devices and their respective software drivers
- An overview of Windows 95 sound accessories
- Using MIDI capabilities

MIDI and WAV Sound Files

Your system has the capability to utilize two types of audio files:

- Digital audio, or WAV, files
- MIDI, or musical instrument digital interface

Windows 95 includes built-in support for both MIDI and WAV waveform audio. However, you need to install an additional sound device, such as an add-on board, before you can realize these capabilities.

WAV, or sound wave, files take up a great deal of disk storage space compared to MIDI files because WAV files record the entire sound to your hard disk. Although WAV files take up more disk space than MIDI files, the sound is generally better. MIDI doesn't save the entire sound but keeps a record of how the sound is played. The MIDI file then sends the "instructions" when you want to play the sound back and attempts to reproduce that original sound as best it can, sometimes not very successfully if you are using a less expensive 8-bit sound card. These instructions tell the card what instrument to play, the note and volume, when to play it relative to other notes, and how long it lasts.

You can use MIDI files to great effect when integrated into a computer-based presentation, for example. On the other hand, you can attach simple WAV files to electronic mail for distribution to a third party on a network.

MIDI uses either FM synthesis or wave table synthesis to reproduce the required sound. FM synthesis uses artificial sounds that are similar to the required sound, and wave table synthesis uses actual stored samples of sounds from real instruments.

With sampled sound, a small example of the instrument's sound is stored. When sound from that type of instrument needs to be reproduced, the sample is retrieved and it undergoes various changes, such as pitch variation, in order to reproduce a relatively accurate rendition.

Because a MIDI file essentially contains just the instructions on how to play a specific sound, the method of reproducing that sound depends on the quality of the sound board that will be playing it. When it comes to sound boards, what you pay for is what you get. A low-cost 8-bit board is going to give you a low-quality sound reproduction. On the other hand, if you invest in a high-end 16-bit board with extensive wave table synthesis capabilities and a good set of speakers, you are probably going to get great sound reproduction.

Note

Many new PCs are billed as "multimedia-ready" with built-in CD-ROM and sound board capabilities, but these PCs rarely contain high-end sound cards. What you often get is average quality sound, which is adequate for the average user. If you want a new PC capable of playing back recording-quality sound, buy a PC with a built-in CD-ROM drive and then add a high-end sound board of your choice.

Recording sound to your hard drive takes a great deal of disk space. Therefore, Windows 95 offers two groups of sound compression technologies, or *codecs* (coders/decoders). The first technique enables the compression of voice data, such as TrueSpeech. The second method enables you to compress high-quality musical type sound. These capabilities allow for the use of voice compression during recording, which lets the resulting sound file be compressed in real-time—that is, as it is recorded.

► See "Using Sound Recorder," p. 998

Another sound capability, called *polymessage MIDI support*, enables Windows 95 to handle multiple MIDI instructions at the same time. The result is that less processor resources are required, which frees up the CPU for other operations.

Sound Blaster and Windows

Creative Labs' Sound Blaster family of add-on audio boards has become something of an industry standard among multimedia PCs. If you don't have a Sound Blaster board installed, you probably have one that is Sound Blaster-compatible.

Caution

Boards that are advertised as Sound Blaster-compatible are not always true to their claim. The result can be distorted or inadequate sound reproduction. However, most games or CDs that fall under the multimedia label probably support Sound Blaster. Check the packaging thoroughly, and if the retail outlet is unable to verify compatibility, don't be afraid to contact the manufacturer direct.

Because of Sound Blaster's popularity, even Windows 95 comes with a compatible driver for supporting Sound Blaster programs. But if you don't want Sound Blaster, Windows 95 includes a less-popular alternative in the form of the Microsoft Windows Sound System. Windows 95's built-in audio supports capabilities required for Microsoft's own home-grown sound specifications.

Even if you use MS Windows Sound System, you are still going to need an audio board, or at least a "multimedia-ready" PC with enhanced sound capabilities and speakers, for listening to and recording CD-quality sound. The average built-in PC speakers are totally inadequate for the task.

Configuration of Sound Options

Any number of things can lead to sound features' not working properly. Many elements need to be configured properly in relation to one another.

Any time one element doesn't function properly (especially with respect to the next step in the sound playing or recording process), audio problems are likely to result. This section describes how proper configuration can help you avoid sound problems.

Many times the problems are the result of hardware conflicts or wrong settings for specific components, such as IRQs or DMA channels. Hardware conflicts occur when two hardware devices want to use the same system resources. Fortunately, Windows 95 includes a very useful feature called the *Device Manager*, which keeps a centralized graphical registry of all system resources as they relate to the different PC components. As a result, you can more easily locate hardware problems in Windows 95 than you could in the previous DOS/Windows combination.

Sound problems are often the result of an error in installing a new sound device and are likely caused by wrongly assigned resources. The next section discusses the installation of a sound board using Windows 95's extremely useful Add New Hardware Wizard, which reduces the possibility of conflicts.

Troubleshooting

I get no sound at all, and when I do it is distorted.

Common settings problems, such as an IRQ conflict or a wrong DMA channel selected, can result in no sound coming out at all. A wrong DMA driver setting may also result in distorted WAV file playback.

To define the hardware settings, you need to configure groups of pins, called *jumpers*, on the audio board. Jumpers are essential to the smooth running of the audio board, and you must configure them according to available settings as defined by Windows 95 before installing the board. You can configure other necessary settings, such as IRQs and DMAs, using software after the board is installed.

◀ See "Installing Plug and Play Hardware," p. 246

Jumper configuration can vary depending on the board being installed. As a result, a thorough reading of the documentation accompanying your new board is a must.

Adding a Sound Board

The first step in configuring sound is to install a suitable audio board. Windows 95 makes adding sound and MIDI devices much easier than it was under the older DOS/Windows combination.

Windows 95 has made installation easier by implementing the Plug and Play standard and by providing an Add New Hardware Wizard. The wizard takes you through the installation of a hardware device step-by-step.

◀ See "Installing Plug and Play Hardware," p. 246

Microsoft designed its new Plug and Play standard to make it easier to add hardware components to existing PCs. Because Windows 95 supports Plug and Play, a user just has to look for a compatible component in order to ensure that installation will be relatively easy. Windows 95 will then recognize the device being added and notify the user of the necessary resource settings that it must comply to in order to work.

Caution

You might want to use the sound board's own installation program instead, as the Wizard can run into problems identifying the correct interrupts for some components.

As an example of the process as it relates to sound devices, this section reviews the installation of a Sound Blaster board, in this case, the Sound Blaster 16 AWE-32.

You can access the Add New Hardware Wizard through the Control Panel feature or by choosing "sound cards, setting up" from the Help Topics Index page. This example takes you through the Control Panel option.

Caution

With virtually all sound boards, installation problems may occur when you try to install enhanced utilities that come with the board, after you have installed the component using Windows 95's Add New Hardware Wizard. This is because there is rarely an option that allows you to install the utilities separately from the drivers. However, this may be necessary because Windows 95 will have already installed the board without including the separate software utilities.

Caution

Some cards come with CD controllers already built-in. When this happens, you need to install it in Windows 95 and then configure the CD portion at the same time you install the sound card.

◀ See "Installing Legacy CD-ROM Drives," p. 975

1. Open the Start menu and choose Settings, Control Panel.
2. Double-click the Add New Hardware icon. The Add New Hardware Wizard appears (see fig. 33.1).

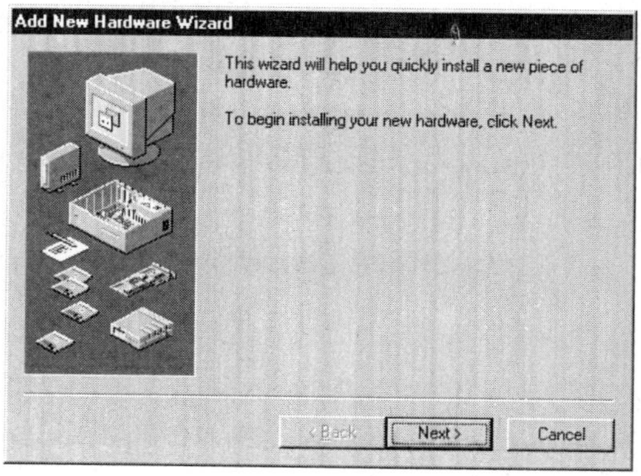

Fig. 33.1
The Add New Hardware Wizard eases the pain of adding hardware components by taking you through the installation step-by-step.

3. Click Next. The Wizard then asks you whether you want Windows 95 to search for new hardware.
4. At this point, select the No radio button as, in this case, we are only going through the steps to install sound devices (see fig. 33.2).

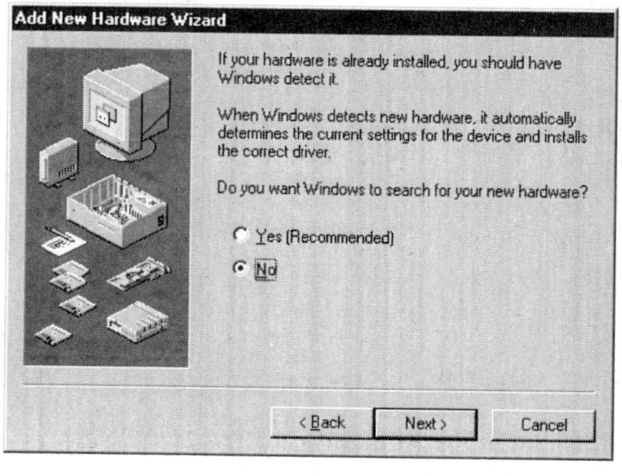

Fig. 33.2
You can choose to have Windows 95 automatically search for new hardware.

5. Click Next. The Hardware Types list appears (see fig. 33.3).
6. Select the type of hardware device you want to add from the Wizard's Hardware Type list box. In this case, select Sound, Video and Game Controllers, and then click Next >. The hardware Manufacturers and Models lists appear for the device you selected (see fig. 33.4).

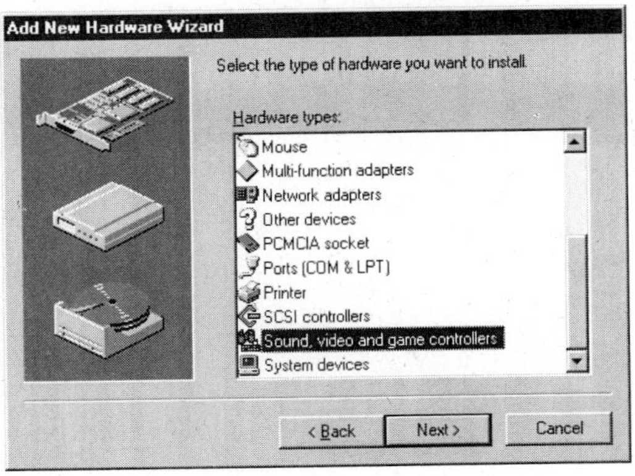

Fig. 33.3
Select the type of hardware you want to install from the Wizard's Hardware Type list.

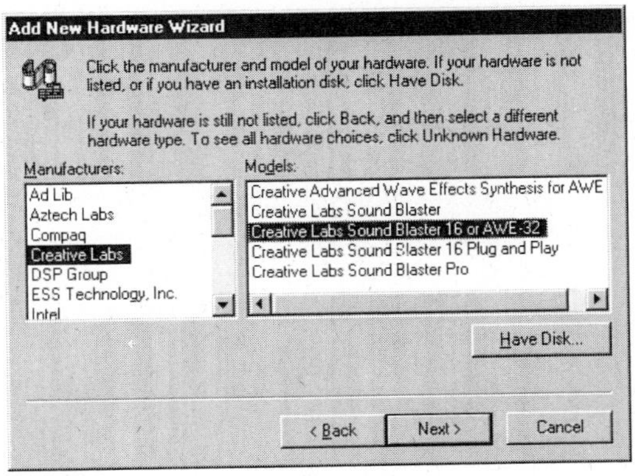

Fig. 33.4
Select the manufacturer and hardware model you want to add from these lists.

7. Click the sound board manufacturer's name in the left window. A list of products that Windows 95 is familiar with appears in the right window.

8. Select the board you want to add—in this case, Creative Labs Sound Blaster 16 or AWE-32. Click Next.

   However, before moving on to the next stage, you may need to install a driver from a floppy disk. If that is the case, you need to take a couple of extra steps. Don't click Next yet, but continue with step 9. If you don't need to install a driver from a floppy disk, go to step 12.

9. From the Add New Hardware Wizard dialog box, click Have Disk. The Install From Disk dialog box appears (see fig. 33.5).

10. Specify the directory and disk where the manufacturer's files should be copied from.

11. Click OK. The Install From Disk dialog box disappears, and you are back to the Add New Hardware Wizard.

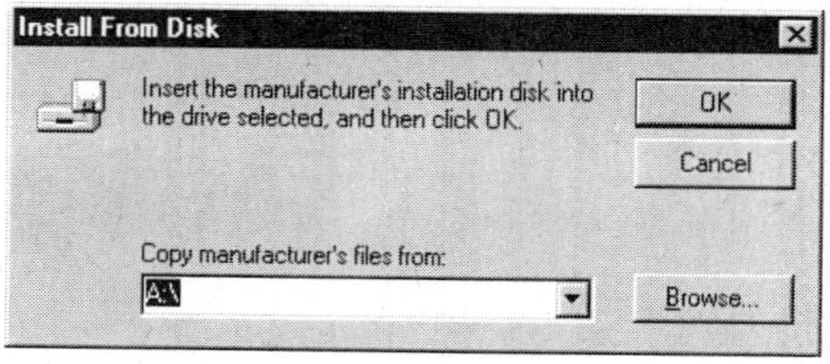

Fig. 33.5
You need to insert the installation disk in the selected drive to install a new device driver from a floppy disk.

> **Note**
>
> If the manufacturer's disk contains drivers for more than one sound card model, you will see a dialog box prompting you to select your card model before you return to the Add New Hardware Wizard in step 11.

12. Now you can click Next. The Wizard window changes to display the settings it wants you to use for the new board (see fig. 33.6).

    This list of settings is important; it is based on available settings as defined in the Windows 95 Registry.

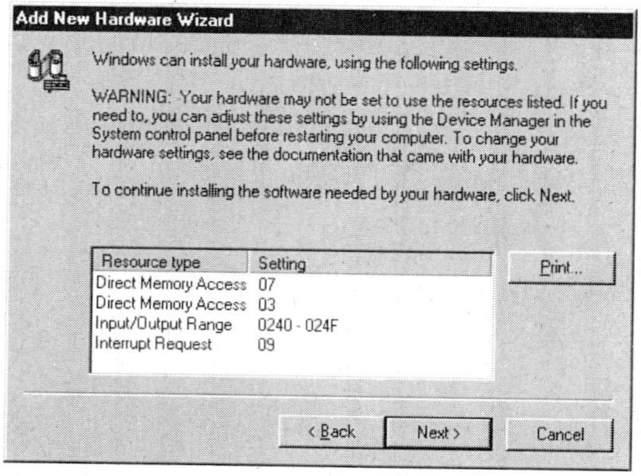

Fig. 33.6
The Add New Hardware Wizard gives you the settings to use for your new board based on what settings are available.

13. Write down these settings or print them out. The new board should have these settings before you install it.
14. Insert the floppy disks containing the drivers that the Wizard requests.
15. Shut down your PC.
16. Configure the new sound card according to the settings given during the Wizard process. See the documentation that comes with your sound board on how to make changes to I/O configuration settings, as well as IRQ and DMA changes.

17. Install the sound card, using instructions that come with the card.

> **Note**
>
> You can also install the sound card prior to running the Add New Hardware Wizard; then choose the Automatically Detect Installed Hardware option in order to let Windows 95 detect new hardware, as previously described.

◀ See "Using Multiple Hardware Configurations," p. 263

Adding or Changing Hardware Drivers

Any time you add a component or peripheral to your PC, you need to make sure a software driver is also installed. The driver acts as a liaison between the computer operating system and the device, so they can communicate.

◀ See "Device Manager and Mutimedia," p. 955

With Windows 95, you can add or change hardware device drivers using Device Manager, which is the centralized registry of system properties and configurations.

As an example, these steps explain what to do to change the driver for Microsoft Windows Sound System:

1. Open the Start menu and choose Settings, Control Panel.
2. Open the System control item in the list box.
3. When the System Properties sheet appears, click the Device Manager tab (see fig. 33.7).

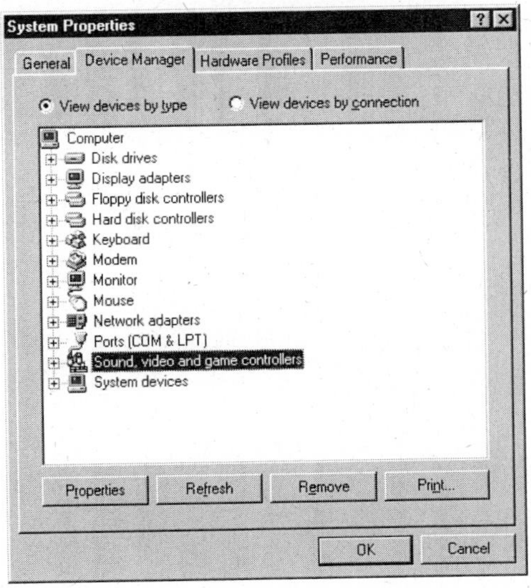

Fig. 33.7
Device Manager enables you to change driver settings.

4. Click the plus sign next to Sound, Video and Game Controllers.

5. Double-click the specific hardware device you are interested in, in this case MS Windows Sound System Compatible.

6. In the Properties sheet that appears, click the Driver tab (see fig. 33.8).

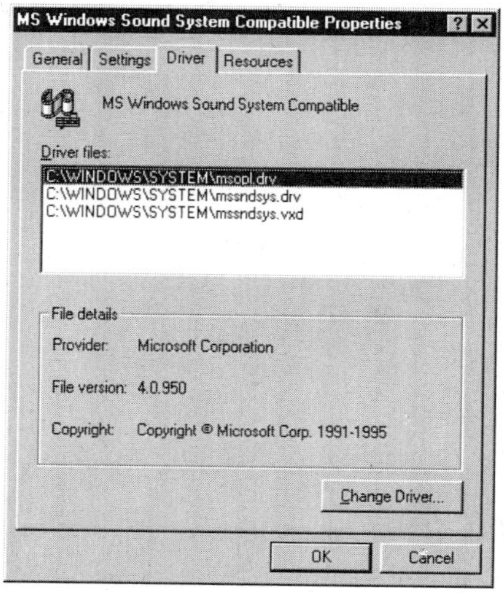

Fig. 33.8
The Driver page for MS Windows Sound System Compatible enables you to change drivers.

7. Click Change Driver. The Select Device dialog box appears (see fig. 33.9).

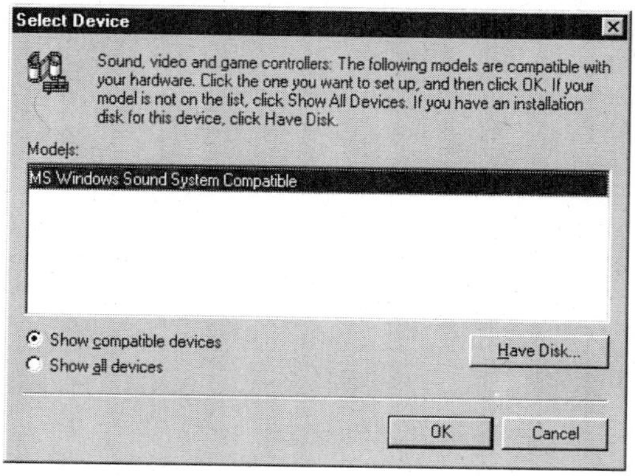

Fig. 33.9
You select the device you want to set up from the Select Device dialog box.

A list details the models compatible with your hardware. Make sure the Show Compatible Devices option is selected. If the hardware model you want to set up is not on the list, you should select the Show All Devices option. The list changes to show all such devices.

8. Click the device you want to set up, and then click OK.

The Select Device dialog box disappears, leaving the Driver page showing the driver files and their correct directory path.

9. Click OK to return to the Device Manager device type list.

10. Click OK to exit System Properties.

> **Troubleshooting**
>
> *I get a hissing sound during playback of sound files.*
>
> If you hear a hissing sound during the playback of a sound file, the file may be recording in 8 bits and playing back in 16 bits. The 16-bit board doesn't realize that the 8-bit file isn't the same high quality as a 16-bit file, so playing the file with expectations of higher sound quality emphasizes the lower detail.

Setting Up a MIDI Instrument

One of the added features of a relatively high-quality sound board is the ability to plug a MIDI instrument into a MIDI port and play sampled sound. Here is a quick overview of setting up a MIDI instrument:

1. Plug the instrument into the sound card's MIDI port.

2. Open the Start menu and choose Settings, Control Panel.

3. Double-click the Multimedia icon.

4. In the Multimedia Properties sheet that appears, click the MIDI tab (see fig. 33.10).

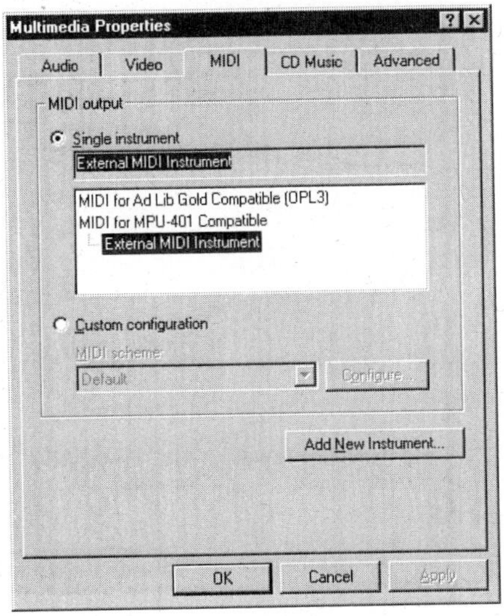

Fig. 33.10
Configure your new MIDI instrument using the Multimedia Properties sheet.

5. Click Add New Instrument.

6. Follow the instructions on-screen to install the instrument.

7. Choose Single Instrument on the MIDI page.

8. Select the instrument you just installed and click OK.

Your new MIDI instrument is now installed.

Moving a MIDI Instrument to Another Sound Board

You can move MIDI instruments between sound boards using these steps:

1. Open the Start menu and choose Settings, Control Panel.

2. Double-click the Multimedia icon.

3. On the Multimedia Properties sheet, click the Advanced tab (see fig. 33.11).

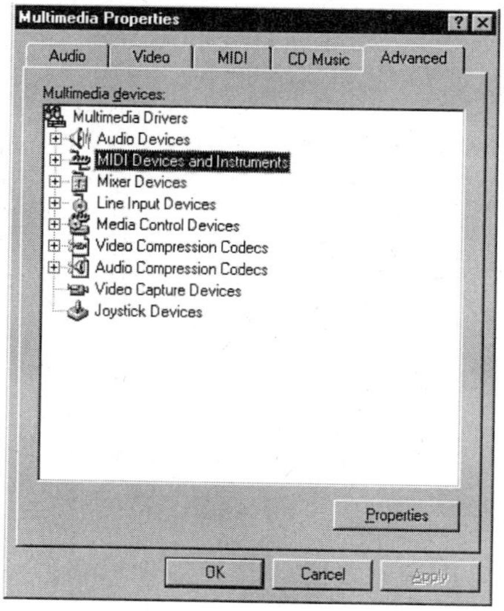

Fig. 33.11
The Advanced page in Multimedia Properties is where you specify the MIDI instrument you want to move.

4. Click the plus sign next to MIDI Devices and Instruments. A sub-list of devices appears under MIDI Devices and Instruments (see fig. 33.12).

5. From the resulting list, click the plus sign next to the sound board your MIDI instrument was connected to.

6. Click the instrument you want to move, and then click Properties.

7. Click the Detail tab.

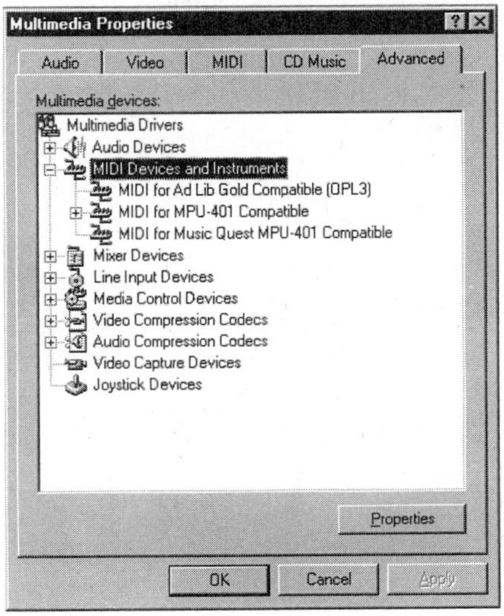

Fig. 33.12 Clicking the plus sign next to MIDI Devices and Instruments brings up a list of devices.

8. Select the name of the sound board you want to connect the instrument to from the MIDI Port list.

9. Connect your MIDI instrument into the new sound board you just specified, using the appropriate port, according to the instructions that come with your sound board.

Changing Multimedia Device Settings

You can change multimedia device settings via the Multimedia Properties sheet:

1. Open the Start menu and choose Settings, Control Panel.

2. Double-click the Multimedia icon.

3. On the Multimedia Properties sheet, click the Advanced tab (refer to fig. 33.11).

4. Click the plus sign next to the multimedia device category you are interested in.

5. Click the device you want from the resulting list.

6. Click Properties.

7. Make whatever changes you want using the different tabs, and click OK when you are done.

Windows 95 Sound Accessories

Windows 95 has some useful sound accessories related to the recording and playing of sound, either from audio CDs or specially recorded files.

CD Player enables you to play audio CDs from your CD drive while you are working in another application. CD Player offers many of the controls found in standalone audio CD players and looks and operates much the same way. In addition, CD Player enables you to edit your playlist that corresponds to the audio CD being played, playing the tracks in the order you want.

Sound Recorder is a good introduction to digital recording using a microphone that plugs into your multimedia PC. This feature enables you to make small recorded files that you can edit and mix into other sound files, although these capabilities are somewhat limited.

Using CD Player

CD Player enables you to play audio CDs in the background while you are working in another application. To access CD Player follow these steps:

1. Open the Start menu and choose Programs, Accessories.

2. Choose Multimedia and then choose CD Player.

If you have used a standalone audio CD player, the controls on CD Player should be quite familiar (see fig. 33.13).

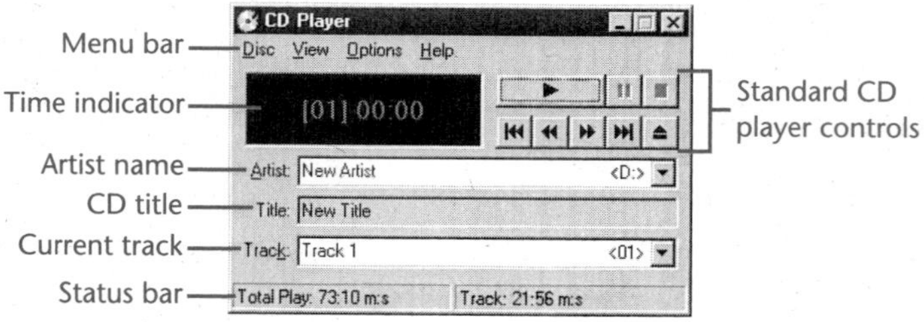

Fig. 33.13
The CD Player allows you to play audio CDs and edit play lists just like a regular high-end CD player.

CD Player includes a number of advanced functions that you access from the menu bar, such as Random Order, Continuous Play, and the ability to edit your play list.

The main CD Player screen offers four menus: Disc, View, Options, and Help. The Disc menu offers two options:

- Edit Play List enables you to edit your personal play list (see fig. 33.14).

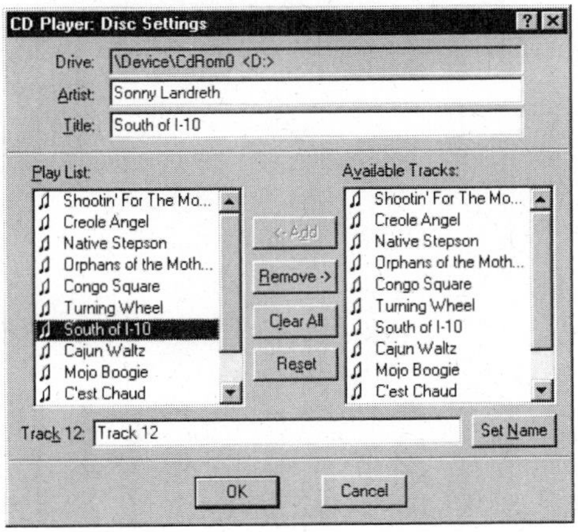

Fig. 33.14
You can customize each CD's play list by choosing the Edit Play List option from the Disc menu.

- Exit closes the CD Player window and turns off the audio CD at the same time.

The View menu offers three sets of options. The first set of options enables you to customize the general CD Player screen:

- Toolbar enables you to display or remove the toolbar. There are seven icons on the toolbar:
  - Edit Play List enables you to edit your play list.
  - Track Time Elapsed tracks the time elapsed since the start of the track.
  - Track Time Remaining lets you know how much time is remaining on the track.
  - Disc Time Remaining shows you how much time is left on the audio CD currently playing.
  - Random Track Order plays the track in random order.
  - Continuous Play starts the CD over again after the last track has played.
  - Intro Play plays the beginning 10 seconds of each track before moving to the next one.
- Disc/Track Info enables you to display or remove the CD disc and track information at the bottom of the general CD Player screen.
- Status Bar enables you to display or remove the status bar at the bottom of the window.

The second set of options on the View menu enable you to change the time displayed in the time indicator window:

- Track Time Elapsed shows how much time has elapsed on the current track.
- Track Time Remaining shows how much time is left on the current track.
- Disc Time Remaining shows how much time is left on the current CD.

The third set on the View menu has a single option:

- Volume Control enables you to set the control levels for volume, wave, and MIDI (see fig. 33.15).

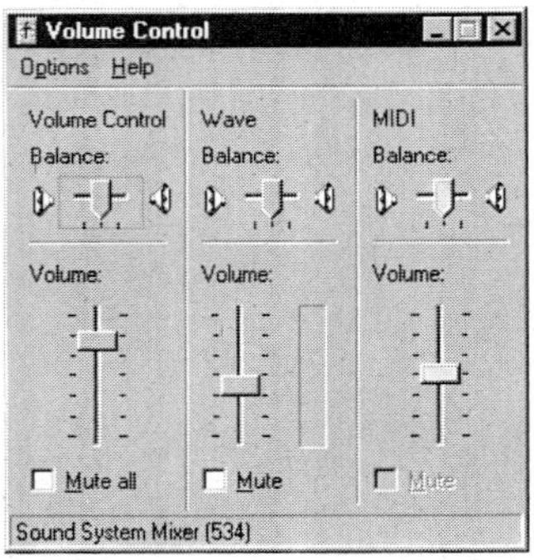

Fig. 33.15
In addition to controlling volume, you can also set WAV and MIDI file balance via the Volume Control option in the View menu.

The Options menu offers four options:

- Random Order enables you to play tracks from different CDs in random order, which can be especially useful if you have more than one CD drive.
- Continuous Play enables you to repeat the track.
- Intro Play plays the first ten seconds of each track.
- Preferences enables you to set preferences for the CD Player (see fig. 33.16).

The Help menu offers two options:

- Help Topics offers help concerning CD Player (see fig. 33.17).
- About CD Player lets you know how much memory is being used.

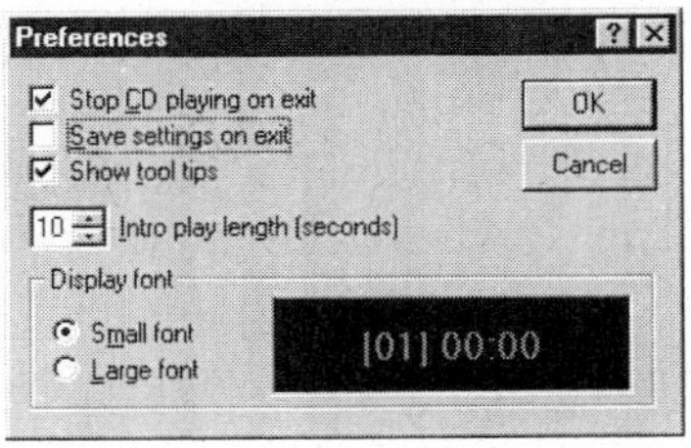

Fig. 33.16
Preferences enables you to set general preferences for CD Player, such as the length of the introduction for each track in seconds for when you choose Intro Play from the Options menu.

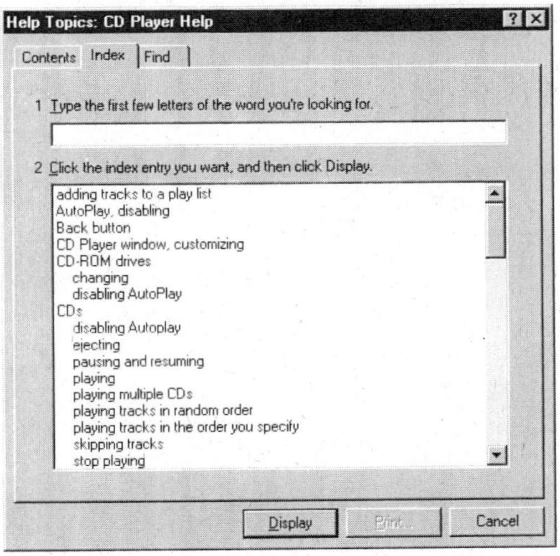

Fig. 33.17
Find help by topic with the Help Topics index option.

Editing a Play List

A play list is a list of tracks from an audio CD that you want to play. With CD Player, you can specify the tracks you want played from a CD and the order in which they should run.

You can change the play list by first choosing the Edit Play List from the Disc menu in CD Player. The CD Player: Disc Settings dialog box appears (refer to fig. 33.14).

The left window shows the desired Play List, and the right window lists all Available Tracks on the audio CD. To remove a track from the Play List, highlight it and choose Remove. To add a track to the Play List from the Available Tracks list, highlight it and click Add.

Using Sound Recorder

The Sound Recorder feature in Windows 95 provides a good introduction to the world of digital recording. Using Sound Recorder you can record small sound files to your hard drive to include in multimedia presentations or attach to documents for distribution among colleagues. You can even e-mail the file across your in-house local area network or the Internet. Sound Recorder does not have the advanced features of high-end digital recorders, but it does provide a feature suitable for most users' needs.

This section provides an overview of the basic features of Sound Recorder. To access Sound Recorder, you do much the same as you do to access CD Player:

1. Open the Start menu and choose Programs, Accessories.
2. Choose Multimedia.
3. Choose Sound Recorder to open the Sound Recorder dialog box (see fig. 33.18).

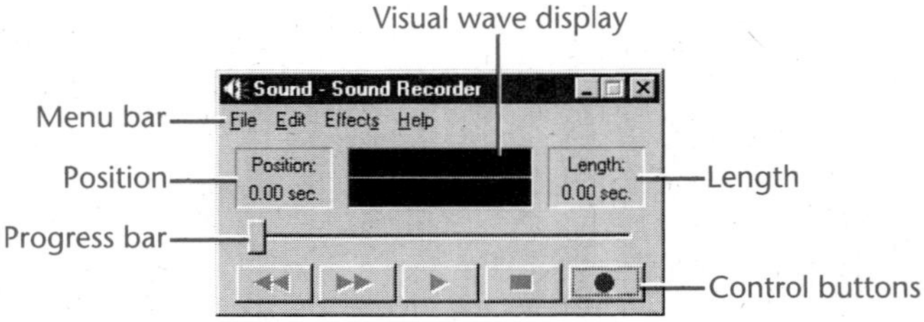

Fig. 33.18 Sound Recorder enables you to record sounds for future playback.

The *menu bar* lists the menus that are discussed briefly here. *Position* represents the current position in the audio file, whereas *Length* tells you the complete length of the file in seconds. The *visual wave display* offers a visual demonstration of the audio file, and the *progress bar* indicates how far along in the file you are. Finally, the *control buttons* control such operations as fast forward and rewind, like a regular tape recorder.

The File menu contains a number of familiar and self-explanatory options, in addition to two not-so-common ones. Revert enables you to undo a deleted section of a sound file, and Properties enables you to change the properties of the file and change the quality of the recording (see fig. 33.19).

Note

The Revert command works only if you have *not* saved the sound file you partially deleted.

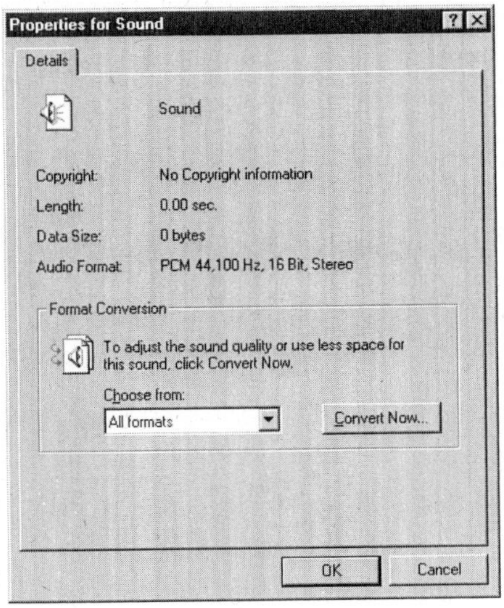

Fig. 33.19
The Properties option from the File menu enables you to change the quality of the recording, by changing the format.

The Edit menu offers a variety of options, some of which may sound familiar but actually accomplish tasks not normally associated with those commands:

- Copy copies a sound (used in conjunction with Paste).
- Paste Insert inserts a sound into a sound file.
- Paste Mix mixes two sound files together. The open file and the pasted clips are mixed and played at the same time.
- Insert File enables you to insert a file into another file at the point where you position the slider.
- Mix with File enables you to mix another file with the file playing at the point where you position the slider.
- Delete Before Current Position deletes everything before a specified point, once you have moved the slider to the point in the sound file where you want to cut.
- Delete After Current Position deletes everything after a specified point, once you have moved the slider to the point in the sound file where you want to cut.
- Audio Properties opens the Audio Properties sheet, from where you can change various properties for both recording and playback, such as volume (see fig. 33.20).

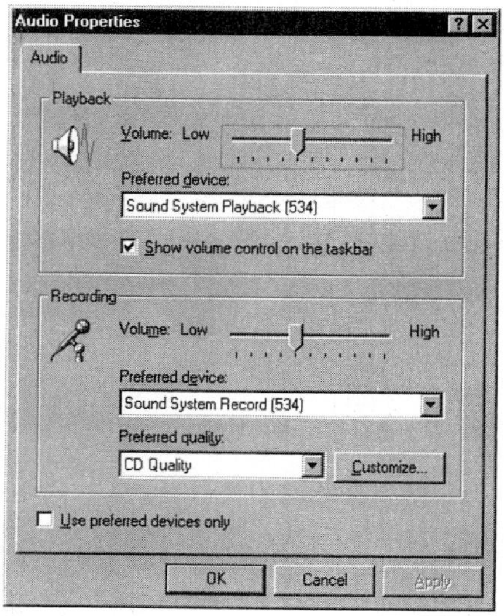

Fig. 33.20
Change recording and playback specifications, such as volume level and designated reproduction device, using the Audio Properties option.

The Effects menu offers options that allow for effects to be added to the sound file:

- Increase Volume [by 25%] increases the volume of a sound file.
- Decrease Volume decreases the volume of a sound file.
- Increase Speed [by 100%] increases the speed of a sound file.
- Decrease Speed decreases the speed of a sound file.
- Add Echo adds an echo to a sound file.
- Reverse plays a sound file in reverse.

Tip
You cannot change the speed of a sound file, or add an echo to a sound file, if it is compressed.

The Help menu offers two options:

- Help Topics accesses the Sound Recorder Help section of the general Windows 95 Help Topics feature.
- About Sound Recorder lets you know who the product is licensed to, how much memory the PC contains, and how much is currently being used.

◄ See "Compressing a Disk," p. 469

Troubleshooting

When I play video and sound files together they appear out of step with each other.

If you are trying to play video that includes a soundtrack and the sound and video aren't synchronized, you again may have a computer that isn't fast enough. You can try improving performance and adding RAM, but if you have an older, slower processor and a relatively slow hard drive, you may need to think about upgrading to a new PC with fast video capabilities built in.

Common Problems with Sound

Many problems can occur when you are trying to get sound capabilities working on a PC because of the complexity of the operation between the system and the components. Windows 95's Plug and Play and easy-to-use Windows Registry help keep track of available IRQs and I/O addresses, but things can still go wrong.

One of the most problematic and intimidating steps required in installing sound devices, or any hardware for that matter, is figuring out available IRQ, DMA, and I/O settings that you can use. If you get the setting wrong and use one that is already assigned to another device, the sound component you are adding will not work properly.

Fortunately, the Windows Registry keeps track of which device is using which resources. This feature is useful because when you want to add a new hardware component you can just start the Add New Hardware Wizard, which takes you step-by-step through installing the device. During the installation process the Wizard gives you suggested free I/O, IRQ, and DMA settings that you should use for the new device, such as a sound board. You then take those settings and configure your board or hardware component to match the settings before you install it. The new device should then work because Windows 95 figured out what free settings to give you in the first place. For more information, refer to the "Adding a Sound Board" section earlier in this chapter.

Should hardware conflicts occur, Windows 95 includes the Help option from the Start menu, plus an especially useful feature: the Hardware Conflict Troubleshooter. You access the step-by-step Troubleshooter by choosing "hardware, troubleshooting conflicts" from the Help Topics Index. If you have a hardware conflict, start the troubleshooting wizard and it will take you through an investigative process that should resolve most hardware conflicts, or at least identify the conflict.❖

Chapter 34

Using Windows 95 Full-Motion Video Options

by Jerry Honeycutt

Before 1991, Windows was silent. The best Windows could muster was a beep when you missed a button. However, in mid-1991 Microsoft introduced the first multimedia extensions for Windows 3.0. These extensions enabled Windows to produce sounds and high-quality images—but not video.

In 1992, Microsoft introduced Video for Windows 1.0, which provided synchronized video and audio. But CD-ROM drives were not as prolific as they are now, sound cards didn't fill the computer store shelves, and video/audio compression technology was just starting to grow. A video was 160 × 120 pixels—barely 1/16 the size of a VGA monitor. While the computer industry held video as a major achievement, the consumer barely noticed. Video hadn't proven to be useful or exciting enough to stimulate demand for multimedia titles.

In 1993, vendors were delivering hardware with stepped-up performance, CD-ROM drives, sound cards, and local bus video. Now that the hardware could handle the increased demands of multimedia, the stage was set for a technological advance. Thus, Microsoft introduced Video for Windows 1.1. Software audio and video compression became a standard part of Windows multimedia. A video was a respectable 320 × 240 pixels, and some users realized a 50 percent improvement in video performance. This time consumers noticed. The demand for multimedia titles skyrocketed. Today, computer stores are lined with shelves full of multimedia games, reference material, and other audio/video applications.

◄ See "Using Your CD-ROM Drive," p. 970

In 1995, Microsoft introduces Windows 95, calling it an immediate multimedia upgrade. Before Windows 95, users had to install Video for Windows separately when they installed their multimedia applications. Video was not a standard part of the Windows architecture—it was more like an afterthought. However, multimedia support such as audio and video are an integral part of the Windows 95 architecture. Windows 95 performance improvements such as *CDFS* (CD File System) and *DCI* (Display Control Interface), coupled with hardware improvements such as PCI (Peripheral Component Interconnect) and local bus video, have made the limiting factor the amount of data you can put on a CD-ROM, not the throughput from a CD-ROM to a display device.

You'll see full-motion video used in many applications designed for Windows 95. For example, you'll find full-motion video used for training, reference materials, and entertainment. Products such as Intuit's Quicken present expert advice in the form of full-motion video. Also, products such as Microsoft Encarta or Automap provide videos so you can visually experience the reference material. And don't forget music videos.

The purpose of this chapter is to discuss the video technology available using Windows and how you can apply it. In this chapter, you can find information on these topics:

- Video enhancements in Windows 95
- The effect DCI has on increasing the performance of video in Windows
- Video compression and decompression drivers available for Windows
- System requirements for using full-motion video in Windows
- Installation and configuration of Plug and Play and legacy video devices
- Using Windows Media Player to play videos
- Multimedia games in Windows
- Apple's QuickTime for Windows

Video for Windows 95

Windows 95 incorporates significant enhancements for the Video for Windows architecture. Windows has made video easier to set up and more exciting with improved video performance. In short, Windows 95 has made multimedia accessible to virtually every desktop with a computer.

This section describes enhancements to full-motion video. For more information about other multimedia capabilities, see Chapter 31, "Understanding Windows 95 Multimedia," and Chapter 33, "Working with Windows 95 Sound Capabilities."

► See "Desktop Video Production under Windows 95," p. 1019

Easy Video Setup

The Video for Windows architecture is built into Windows. When the user installs Windows, the program automatically installs and configures the components necessary to use video, such as device drivers and video compression. Therefore, setting up and configuring video is a much less painful task than in previous versions. Users are more likely to tap into the power of video. An additional benefit of built-in support for video is that you can distribute multimedia files such as AVI to any Windows 95 user without worrying about whether they have Video for Windows installed.

Default Video Devices

Figure 34.1 shows the multimedia devices that Windows installs by default. As you can see, Windows installs device support for media control, video compression, video capture, and others. To see the list of devices installed on your computer, double-click the Multimedia icon in the Control Panel and select the Advanced tab of the property sheet.

◄ See "The Multimedia Properties Sheet," p. 962

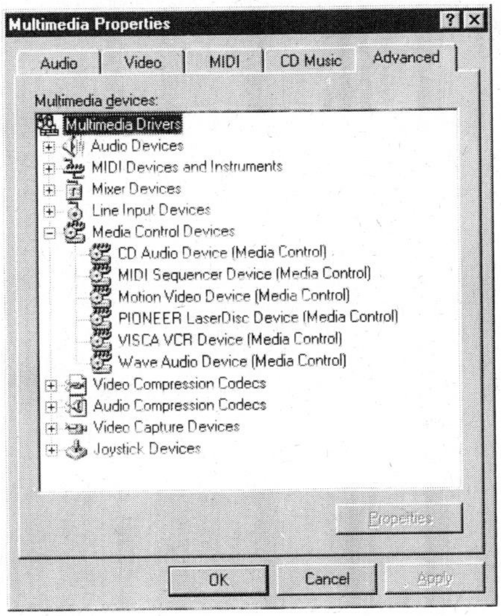

Fig. 34.1
These Multimedia devices were installed by Windows.

Plug and Play Devices

See "Installing Plug and Play Hardware," p. 246

Plug and Play and the Add New Hardware Wizard are new Windows 95 features that enable users to easily install new video hardware such as MPEG (Motion Pictures Experts Group) co-processors. Users can literally insert a Plug and Play video device in their computers, turn their computers on, and Windows automatically recognizes it.

As well, the Add New Hardware Wizard simplifies the task of setting up legacy devices by automatically detecting the hardware and configuring the drivers. Windows comes with drivers for most of the popular video devices available on the market today.

Improved Video Performance

A 60-second video that is 320 × 240 pixels and 15 frames per second requires over 200M of video data—3M per second! Even with video compression, the performance of the CD-ROM and video devices can be a bottleneck to a satisfying video experience because of the sheer amount of information involved. Thus, previous incarnations of Video for Windows were stressed when playing these videos. The perceived symptom was a "jerky" video as opposed to smoothly displaying frame after frame.

The performance improvements incorporated into Windows 95 make it possible to play high-quality videos in a larger window, potentially up to 640 × 480 pixels with the right hardware. Windows 95 includes these performance enhancements:

- *DCI.* The Display Control Interface greatly accelerates the rate at which video memory is updated. DCI enables video software to get closer to the hardware.
- *CDFS.* The CD File System improves throughput from the CD-ROM by providing an optimized, 32-bit, protected-mode file system. The improved performance of CD-ROM drives in Windows means you are not waiting on your system to read data from the drive. Videos look better.
- *Multitasking.* Windows' preemptive multitasking minimizes the pauses and delays during video playback. The video continues to play while other processes, such as decompressing additional video from the CD-ROM drive, are running in the background.

More Exciting Video

Very few multimedia games have been published for Windows and with good reason: performance was too slow for graphically intense games such as DOOM. Many games learned to rely on painting directly to the video device and using device-dependent features. Both traits are a no-no for well-behaved Windows applications. Thus, games were cast to the depths of DOS. In addition, the GDI and windowing environment were just too slow to support gaming software.

Windows 95 provides a significant improvement that opens the door to game developers. WinG (pronounced Win Gee) provides for virtually direct access to the display device while remaining compatible with the GDI. The compatibility with the existing GDI means that programmers can easily port applications to take advantage of WinG's speed. WinG makes it possible for graphics-intensive games such as Doom to run well in Windows.

Developing intense multimedia games for Windows is now practical with WinG. Having a place to play, you can count on vendors to provide the games. The "Gaming in Windows" section later in this chapter has more information on games for Windows 95.

DCI Standard in Windows 95

Display Control Interface (DCI) is the result of a joint effort between Microsoft and Intel to produce a display driver interface that enables fast, direct access to the video frame buffer in Windows. Also, DCI enables games and video to take advantage of special hardware support in video devices that improves the performance and quality of video. For example, a video player can take advantage of color-space conversion that enables color conversion to RGB (Red Green Blue) to occur in hardware rather than software. Although DCI enables direct access to the frame buffer, it remains compatible with the GDI.

DCI is available for the complete spectrum of display devices in Windows. DCI improves access to SVGA display devices and newer devices that include hardware support for stretching, double buffering, and so on. Some of the possible hardware-specific features are described in this list:

- *Stretching.* Stretching enables the hardware to change the size of the image instead of having the software do it. Therefore, the software sends the same number of pixels as before, but the hardware stretches the image to the requested size.

- *Color-space conversion.* Colors are stored in a video using YUV—a representation of color based on how people perceive colors. Before the image can move to the display device, it must be converted to RGB values. Hardware conversion saves a lot of time—potentially up to 30 percent—by freeing the software from this task.

- *Double-buffering.* Double-buffering is the process of displaying the screen currently in the frame buffer while painting the next screen in memory or an additional hardware buffer. Because the new screen is quickly copied to the frame buffer, video playback and animation appear much smoother.

- *Chroma key.* Chroma key enables two streams of video to merge. A particular color in one of the streams is allowed to be transparent before they merge. This process is similar to the "blue screens" that weather forecasters use on your local news broadcast or movies use for special effects.

- *Asynchronous drawing.* In conjunction with double-buffering, asynchronous drawing provides for faster screen painting outside the frame buffer.

Applications using the Video for Windows architecture notice performance improvements automatically. On a 486 DX/2 66 with local bus video, DCI provides reasonable 640 × 480 video at 15 frames per second. This is full-screen video, but you will perceive it as being very jerky video playback.

On the same computer, DCI provides smooth video in a 320-×-240-pixel (quarter-screen) window at 30 frames per second. This playback is much better, but you may have a problem finding videos recorded using 30 frames per second. Figure 34.2 shows a quarter-screen video playing.

Fig. 34.2
A frame from WEEZER.AVI found in the FUNSTUFF\VIDEOS directory of your Windows 95 CD-ROM.

Note

DCI doesn't work with hardware video co-processors such as MPEG. DCI is a software-level interface. MPEG video processors don't use software to draw pixels on-screen and therefore receive little or no benefit from DCI.

Codec Implementation in Windows 95

As noted earlier, a 320-×-240-pixel video playing at 15 frames per second requires the file system to deliver 3M of uncompressed data each second. This demand is not even remotely possible with quad-speed CD-ROMs. Thus, *codecs* have evolved over the last few years to handle *co*mpression and *de*compression of video. Windows 95 comes with software support for four video codecs. Figure 34.3 shows the codecs installed in Windows 95. The four entries for Indeo are really just multiple versions of the same driver.

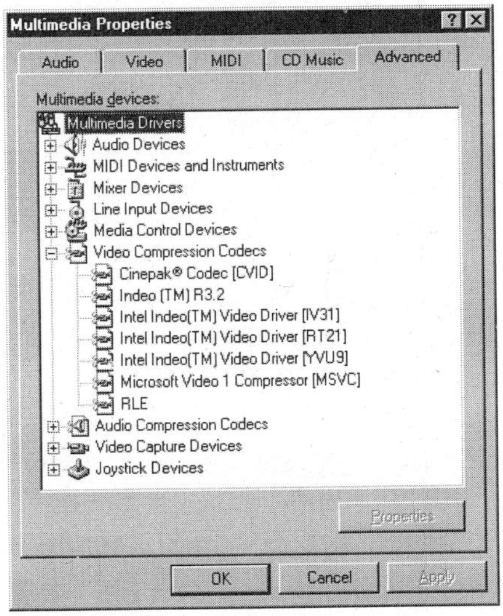

Fig. 34.3
Video codecs installed with Windows 95.

The following list describes the video codecs in Windows 95:

- *Cinepak*. Cinepak is licensed from SuperMac. It provides good quality video playback at 15 frames per second or better and 320 × 240 pixels. Cinepak is a common codec used for both Windows and the Macintosh.

- *Indeo*. Indeo was developed by Intel (*In*tel Vi*deo*). It provides good quality video playback at 15 frames per second or better and 320 × 240 pixels. Indeo is another common codec used for both Windows and the Macintosh.

- *Video 1.* Video is easy on the processor; it has low overhead and is a good, average quality codec. This codec was developed by Microsoft.
- *RLE.* RLE stands for *run length encoding.* RLE is not good for video because it cannot handle the rapidly changing frames. RLE is better-suited to compressing bitmaps.

Note

MPEG (Motion Pictures Experts Group) is a codec, not supplied by Windows, that provides high-quality 640 × 480 video at 30 frames per second. Approximately 75 minutes of VHS-quality video can be compressed and stored on a single CD-ROM. A full-length feature film can be distributed on two CD-ROMs.

MPEG is computationally intensive. It is supported by an MPEG co-processor, usually implemented on a separate interface board. Microsoft has recently licensed a software MPEG codec that will be available for Windows 95. This software codec will play MPEG movies on computers with fast (Pentium) processors.

To see which codec a particular video uses, right-click the AVI file and click the Details tab of the property sheet. Figure 34.4 shows the property sheet for GOODTIME.AVI as found on your Windows 95 CD-ROM.

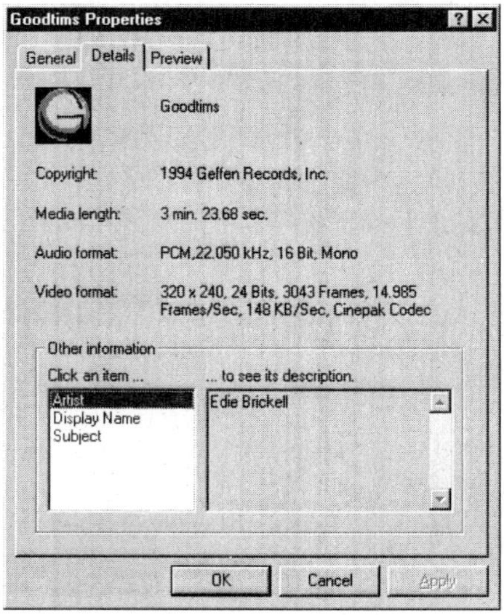

Fig. 34.4
The details of GOODTIME.AVI on your Windows 95 CD-ROM.

Windows System Requirements for Full-Motion Video

Playing full-motion video puts a tremendous burden on the PC. The CDFS must not fall behind or the video will appear to pause in the middle for no reason. In addition, the video data must go through computationally expensive decompression, and the bus must pump megabytes of data to the video device every second to play smoothly. If any one of the components falls down on the job, your video experience will be disappointing.

Modern CPUs are generally not the problem when identifying bottlenecks to video performance. The two primary places to point your finger are the CD-ROM and the video device. The following list shows the minimum hardware requirements for high-quality, 320-×-240-pixel video at 30 frames per second:

- Microsoft recommends a balanced system where each of the components is equally matched. What good does a local bus video device do you if you are using a single-speed CD-ROM? The fastest Pentium processor available doesn't do any good without a fast video device.
- Make sure your computer has at least a super VGA with 16-bit color (65,536 colors), preferably 24-bit true color (16.7 million colors). Eight-bit (256 colors) video just doesn't have enough colors to make a reasonable-looking image. Most new computers have display adapters, such as Cirrus Logic, which support at least 16-bit color.
- A local bus video device is essential for the multimedia experience in 1995, preferably with a DCI provider for improved performance. Local bus video devices are up to 10 times faster than some ISA devices. In addition, an adapter that provides a DCI driver offers substantial improvements by supporting color conversion and other DCI functionality.
- Make sure you purchase a CD-ROM drive with a transfer rate of at least 300K per second (double speed). This rate is required to play 320-×-240-pixel video at 15 frames per second with reasonable quality. As video quality rises, so do file sizes, so you may want to consider a triple- or quad-speed CD-ROM drive to match that local bus video device you bought.
- Use at least 16-bit audio. Before purchasing a sound card for your computer, play samples of WAV (Waveform-audio) and MIDI (Musical Instrument Digital Interface) formats on the demo units at the store. Only the ear can tell.

Installation of Full-Motion Video Device Drivers

◄ See "Installing Plug and Play Hardware," p. 246

If you are installing a Plug and Play video device, install the hardware using the manufacturer's instructions and power up your computer. Windows should literally recognize the device and install its device drivers.

To install device drivers for a legacy video device, follow these steps:

1. Power off your computer.
2. Configure the video device using the manufacturer's instructions.
3. Install the video device in your computer if it isn't already installed. Because installation instructions vary greatly, follow the manufacturer's instructions included with the drive.
4. Power on your computer. Windows may detect the new display device when it starts up. If it doesn't, open the Control Panel and double-click Add New Hardware icon. The Add New Hardware Wizard opens as shown in figure 34.5.

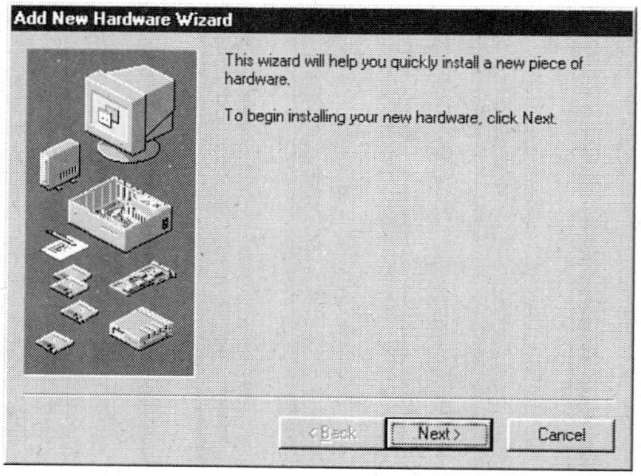

Fig. 34.5
The Add New Hardware Wizard simplifies driver installation.

5. Click Next and select Yes (Recommended) to allow the wizard to automatically detect your new hardware.
6. Click Next. The wizard displays a warning saying the detection process could take a long time. Be patient.
7. Click Next. The wizard displays the dialog box shown in figure 34.6 while it is detecting your new hardware.

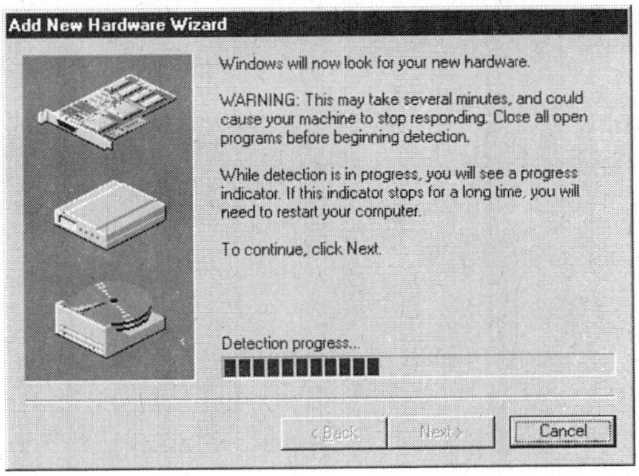

Fig. 34.6
The Add New Hardware Wizard is detecting the display device.

> **Note**
>
> Following the 80/20 rule, the wizard spends 80 percent of its time in the last 20 percent of the progress indicator shown in the dialog box. This slow-down does not indicate a problem.

8. If it found your new display device, the wizard displays the dialog box shown in figure 34.7. Click Finish to install the drivers. If the wizard doesn't prompt you to reboot Windows, shut down using the Start button.

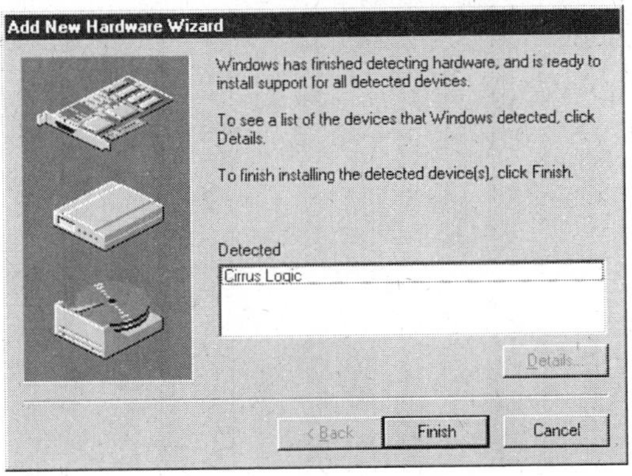

Fig. 34.7
Click Finish to install the drivers for your display device.

9. If the wizard didn't find your display device, click Next. You need to choose your device from the dialog box shown in figure 34.8.

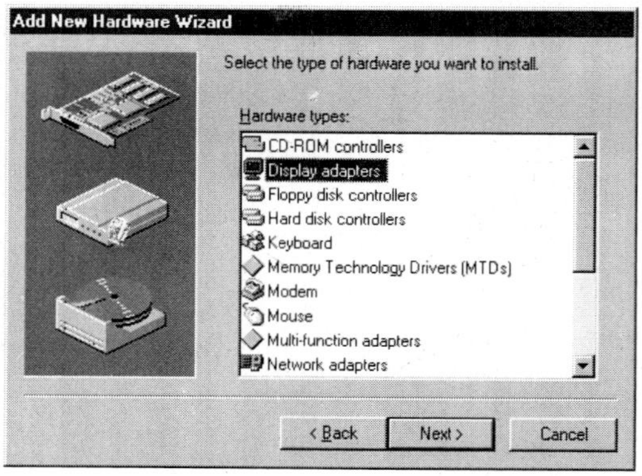

Fig. 34.8
Select your new adapter from the list.

10. Select the type of device you are installing from the list: Display Adapters. Click Next. The wizard displays the dialog box shown in figure 34.9.

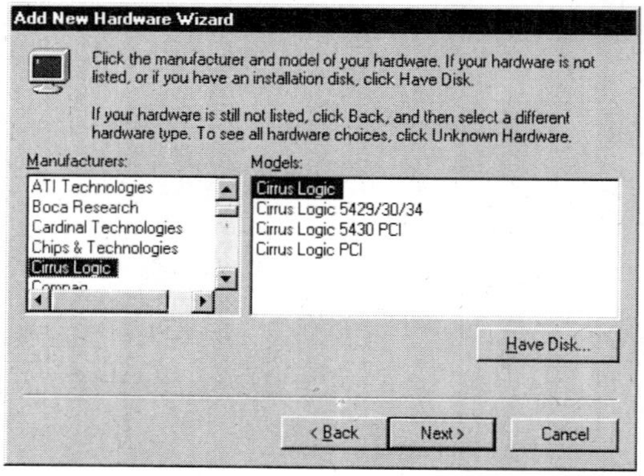

Fig. 34.9
Select an adapter from this list of manufacturers and models.

Tip
If you find that the driver doesn't work properly, contact the vendor or look on the online services for an updated driver.

11. Select a manufacturer from the Manufacturers list and a specific model from the Models list. Make sure your selection matches your display device exactly. Click Next. The wizard displays information about the driver you have chosen and the resources it uses.

12. Click Next to install your drivers. If the wizard doesn't prompt you to reboot Windows, shut down using the Start button.

Using Windows Media Player

Media Player is a Windows accessory that allows you to play multimedia files. It supports Video for Windows (AVI), sound (WAV), MIDI (MID), and CD audio. However, you'll primarily use Media Player to play videos. This section shows you how to play videos, insert portions of a video in your document, and configure Media Player.

Playing Videos in Media Player

Using Media Player to play a video is simple: double-click an AVI file in the explorer. Media Player loads the AVI file and immediately starts playing it. Alternatively, you can load Media Player first and use the following instructions to play a video.

1. Select Device, 1 Video for Windows.
2. Select an AVI file in the Open dialog box and click Open.
3. Click the play button in Media Player (see fig. 34.10).

When a video is playing, the play button changes to a pause button. You can stop the video by clicking the stop button or pause the video by clicking the pause button.

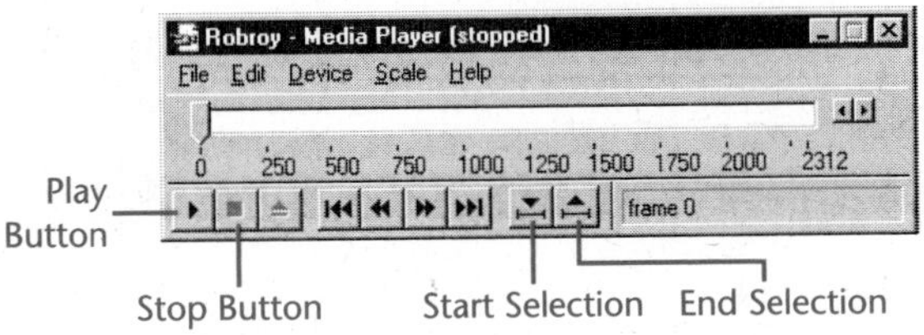

Fig. 34.10
Click the play button to play your video. The play button will change to a pause button while the video is playing.

You also can put a portion of a video in your documents. Then, you can play the video by double-clicking it. To copy a portion of a video to your document, use the following instructions.

1. Position the trackbar thumb on the starting frame of the portion you want to copy.
2. Click Start Selection.
3. Position the trackbar thumb on the last frame of the portion you want to copy.
4. Click End Selection.

5. Select Edit, Copy Object to copy that portion of the video to the Clipboard.

6. Open the document and paste the video clip by choosing Edit, Paste.

If you want to deselect a selection, select Edit, Selection from Media Player's menu, select None, and click OK.

Video Options in Video for Windows

You can change many aspects of how Media Player plays a video. For example, you can have Media Player use time or frames to display its progress by choosing Scale, Time or Scale, Frames respectively.

To choose whether Media Player plays a video full screen or in a window, choose Device, Properties. Then select Window or Full Screen in the Video Properties sheet.

Use the following instructions to set additional options for Media Player.

1. Choose Edit, Options from the Media Player menu.

2. Select Auto Rewind if you want the video clip to automatically rewind after it has finished playing.

3. Select Auto Repeat if you want the video clip to play repeatedly.

4. Select Control Bar On Playback if you want the Media Player controls to be available while a video clip is playing inside another document.

5. Select Border Around Object if you want a border around the video while it is playing.

6. Select Play In Client Document if you want the video to play in the document instead of as a separate window.

7. Select Dither Picture To VGA Colors if the color of your video looks distorted.

Gaming in Windows

All the exciting multimedia PC games, such as DOOM, have typically been targeted at DOS. The reason is performance. Multimedia games are graphically intensive. However, these games are now feasible in Windows 95.

High-quality games for Windows are sprouting up everywhere. A three-dimensional Pinball game is included in the Microsoft Plus! Pack for Windows 95 (see fig. 34.11). Other games you can purchase separately include The Incredible Machine by Sierra, Lode Runner by Sierra, and DOOM by id Software.

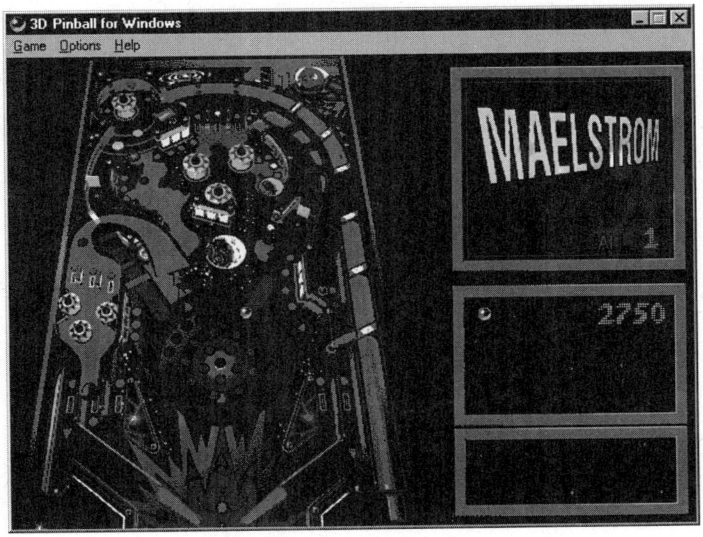

Fig. 34.11
3D Pinball for Windows (with the author getting badly beaten).

Apple's QuickTime for Windows

QuickTime is the standard codec for Apple computers. Why do you care? Because Apple has released a version of QuickTime for Windows that edges out Video 1 for performance. Also, QuickTime enables developers to include MIDI with the video and audio tracks.

Because QuickTime is available for both Windows and Apple, many game developers have used it for their video. By using a single video format for both platforms, developers can significantly reduce their multimedia development time. For example, Cyan uses QuickTime for the video in MYST.

You can expect to see a lot of games developed using QuickTime. However, QuickTime doesn't replace Windows AVI video format. For most Windows applications, AVI is still the format of choice.

Apple has made QuickTime 2.0 for Windows available for download off CompuServe. To download, GO QTIME. Select Download QuickTime 2.0 for Windows from the list and follow the instructions. It is also available on other online services, such as America Online, or directly from Apple.

QuickTime 2.0 for Windows is not a Windows 95 application. Therefore, you do not see the same type of property sheets when you right-click a QuickTime file and choose Properties as you do with AVI files.❖

Chapter 35

Desktop Video Production under Windows 95

by Roger Jennings

Desktop publishing (DTP) with Apple Macintosh computers and Windows-based PCs revolutionized the graphics arts industry in the late 1980s and early 1990s. DTP applications, such as PageMaker, QuarkXPress, and Interleaf, greatly reduced the cost of producing virtually every type of print publication.

A similar revolution is taking place today in the video postproduction industry. (Editing videotape, adding special effects, and creating animated graphics collectively are called *postproduction*. *Production* is the process of shooting the video with studio cameras or portable camcorders.) *Linear* postproduction systems use PCs to control multiple videotape players and recorders, and to add digital special effects, still graphics, and titles during the video editing process. *Nonlinear* editing uses PCs to digitize video and audio content; you assemble the finished production by combining digital video clips stored on large, fast fixed-disk drives. As the television industry moves toward digital video production and distribution in 1996 and beyond, nonlinear digital editing with PCs will dominate the video postproduction business.

Desktop video (DTV) has come of age with the release of Windows 95. DTV hardware and software running under Windows 95 ranges from modest 16-bit home video editing software to 32-bit nonlinear digital video editing applications used for professional video production. Virtually all of the new high-end video editing systems announced in 1995 are 32-bit applications that run only on Windows 95 or Windows NT 3.51+. These new professional-level products, ranging in cost from $5,000 to more than $20,000, are a bit pricey for most Windows 95 users.

Thus, one of the objectives of this chapter is to demonstrate the compatibility of today's low- to moderate-cost 16-bit Windows video editing applications with Windows 95. Windows 95 includes new Media Control Interface (MCI) device drivers for Sony ViSCA (Video System Control Architecture) VCRs and laserdisc players that weren't included with Windows 3.1+. Windows 95 has new features to aid the digital video capture process. This chapter covers the following topics:

- Editing home movies with Video Director 2.0
- Setting up and using Windows 95's new ViSCA and Laserdisc MCI drivers
- Using ViSCA devices for A-B roll editing with Video Magician 1.1
- Capturing digital video under Windows 95 with the Intel Smart Video Recorder Pro
- Nonlinear digital video editing with Adobe Premiere 4.0

Migrating Desktop Video Production to Windows 95

The coming transition from conventional analog to fully digital video production, postproduction, and distribution ensures DTV a major role in cable, satellite, and broadcast TV programming. Windows 95 has an important role in both analog and digital DTV postproduction for the following reasons:

- Traditional postproduction operations require a collection of dedicated video equipment, which typically costs at least $250,000. Windows-based DTV systems reduce this cost by a factor of 10 or more, finally making professional-quality video production affordable to small firms and families.
- DTV needs 32-bit applications with preemptive multitasking and multithreaded execution to provide precise timing of the heavy-duty computations and high-speed disk access required to process digital video and audio.
- Windows 95's Display Control Interface (DCI) makes full-screen, full-motion (30 frames per second) digital video a reality (with the assistance of a DCI-compliant video accelerator card).
- Plug and Play takes the mystery out of installing new DTV adapter cards.

- The new 32-bit CD-ROM file system (CDFS) and 32-bit Video for Windows codecs (*co*mpressor/*dec*ompressors) greatly improve delivery of video and audio from AVI (Audio-Video Interleaved) files on CD-ROMs.

Windows 95 is where the action's at in DTV.

Editing Your Home Videos with VideoDirector

Industry experts estimate that about 75 million North American households own one or more VCRs and that about a third of these households have a camcorder. Most owners use their camcorders infrequently, but several market research studies indicate that between 10 and 15 percent of camcorder owners include amateur video making among their hobbies and also own a home PC. Most home video enthusiasts use traditional linear editing techniques, which presently dominate the video postproduction business, because linear editing lets you use your existing video gear—usually a camcorder and a VCR. Several firms supply dedicated devices, called *edit controllers*, for consumer-level video editing that range in price from about $200 to $500 or more. The combination of a home PC and specialized video editing software is an effective alternative to a dedicated edit controller and provides many useful features that aren't available from low-end dedicated edit controllers.

The sections that follow describe the linear editing process and the use of the most popular PC-based editing software for home video postproduction, Gold Disk, Inc.'s VideoDirector 2.0.

Linear Editing, Control Protocols, and Timecode

Linear editing involves copying selected segments of the video and audio content of one or more source (camcorder) videotapes to a second tape called the *edit master*. The objective of video editing is to add only "good" video content to the edit master, rearranging the sequence of the content to fit a "story line." Linear editing often is called *analog editing* because the audio and video signals remain in the traditional analog formats (VHS, S-VHS, 8mm, and Hi8) used by today's camcorders and VCRs, as well as by broadcast TV. PC-based analog editing systems use the PC only as a control device; no video or audio content is stored on your PC's fixed disk. (You can, however, add still graphics images, such as bitmaps and titles, plus sound stored in WAV files to the video content, if you have the required PC adapter cards.) Storing all motion video and accompanying sound on videotape distinguishes linear analog editing from nonlinear digital editing, which stores digitized video and audio content on very large (multigigabyte) fixed-disk drives.

Analog editing requires the capability to control playback from the source deck and recording to the destination deck. (*Deck* is a term that includes any type of videotape player or recorder.) Virtually all camcorders and VCRs come with infrared remote control devices, and higher-priced decks also offer wired remote control. The following list describes the most common wired remote-control protocols found on consumer camcorders and VCRs:

- *Control-S* (also called *SynchroEdit*) is a simple one-way, start-stop protocol that uses the pause feature of a camcorder or VCR to control playback and recording.

- *Control-L* (also called *LANC*) is a Sony two-way protocol that also is used by several other camcorder manufacturers. Control-L duplicates all of the capabilities of an infrared remote control, including play, record, pause, rewind, and fast-forward functions.

- *Control-M* (also called *Panasonic 5-pin*) is a protocol similar to Control-L that uses a different connector and is found only on camcorders and VCRs manufactured by Panasonic (Matsushita).

Because of Sony's success in the consumer video equipment market, Control-L has become the most popular of the control protocols for advanced consumer camcorders. Control-L has another advantage—the capability to transmit Sony's RC (Rewritable Consumer) *timecode*. Timecode which identifies each frame with the time in *Hours*:*Minutes*:*Seconds*:*Frames* (*HH*:*MM*:*SS*:*FF*) format, makes analog editing much more accurate than other methods of determining tape position, such as reading a tape counter or counting seconds from the beginning of a tape. RC timecode also includes date and time-of-day information and is accurate to within about +/- one frame. Unfortunately, Sony's few high-end consumer camcorders that offer RC timecode, such as the TR-700, record but don't play back timecode data through the Control-L cable. High-end Sony VCRs, such as the EV-S7000, record and play back RC timecode.

VideoDirector 2.0's Editing Features

Gold Disk, Inc.'s VideoDirector 2.0 is a low-cost (about $100), PC-based home video editing application designed for amateur videomakers. The following are some of the highlights of this remarkably economical analog video editing product:

- VideoDirector 2.0 includes a "Smart Cable" that plugs into a COM port of your PC; the cable splits to provide a Control-L (LANC) connector for your camcorder and an infrared remote control (called an I-R wand) for your record VCR. (Control-L is a camcorder control protocol used by high-end Sony, Canon, and a few other brands.) Gold Disk also offers a special Smart Cable capable of controlling Panasonic VHS VCRs and camcorders that use the Control-M (five-pin) protocol.

- VideoDirector 2.0 supports the ViSCA (Video System Control Architecture) protocol described in the "Using Sony ViSCA Devices under Windows 95" section later in this chapter. You can use a Sony CVD-1000 Vdeck as the source or record VCR or use a CI-1000 Vbox to control a Sony EV-S7000 VCR. VideoDirector also reads Sony RC timecode.

- You can add sound effects, narration, and music from digital audio (WAV) and MIDI (MID) files with your MPC2-compliant sound card. You also can mix in music from audio CDs if your CD-ROM drive has an internal analog audio connection to your sound card's CD audio input connector.

- If you have a video overlay card, you can capture still video clips and use thumbnail-images (called *picons*) to represent the in and out points of your source video segments. Picons are small bitmapped images of the first frame of your clip.

- With a video output card or genlock box (NTSC video encoder), you can use VideoDirector 2.0's Title Editor utility to add still images from graphics files and create titles. You record the still images or titles as source video segments, then add the segments during the editing process.

- Gold Disk offers *Coolclips,* an extra-cost, 8mm videotape that includes video segments for calibrating the preroll times of your source VCR and record VCRs. *Coolclips* also has about 20 minutes of animated titles and effects for home movie production.

VideoDirector 2.0 is an entry-level, cuts-only editing system designed to be easy to use. VideoDirector 2.0 runs on any PC that will run Windows 95. If you have compatible video gear, you can't beat VideoDirector's performance-to-cost ratio for editing home movies or creating simple training tapes. You can learn how to use VideoDirector 2.0 and start making trial edits in three or four hours. The sections that follow briefly describe how to set up and use VideoDirector 2.0 under Windows 95.

Note

In 1995, Gold Disk introduced the Video Director Suite, a home video editing product with two infrared remote control wands. Video Director Suite is designed for use with VHS-C and S-VHS-C (compact cassette) camcorders that don't have Control-L or Control-M connectors but do have infrared remote control features.

Setting Up VideoDirector 2.0 and Calibrating Your Decks

After running VideoDirector's Setup application, which adds a VideoDirector 2.0 entry to the Start menu's Programs list, you shut down your PC and make the video, audio, and Control-L connections shown in figure 35.1. This figure illustrates connections for using a camcorder, such as the Sony TR-700, as the video source, and a Panasonic AG-1970P S-VHS VCR for recording.

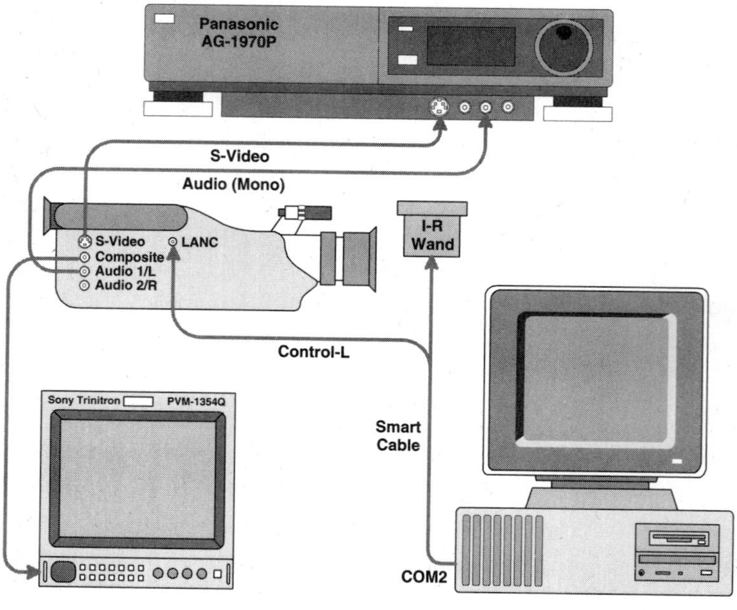

Fig. 35.1
Making video, audio, and control connections for assemble editing with Gold Disk's VideoDirector 2.0.

Note

Using as the source deck a VCR with Control-L capability, such as the Sony EV-S7000, saves wear and tear on the more delicate tape-transport mechanism of your camcorder. The EV-S7000 also reads RC timecode, which makes your editing more accurate. (The example editing process described in the following sections uses an EV-S7000 VCR as the source deck.)

Caution

Make sure you set the Control-L port of your camcorder or source VCR to Slave rather than Master mode. (Most camcorders default to Slave or videotape player/recorder VTR mode, but many VCRs default to Master mode.) Slave mode sets the Control-L port to receive control signals and send tape timecode data, if your VCR supports timecode. Master mode outputs control signals to camcorders and other source VCRs for editing with a built-in edit controller. If you set the source VCR set to Master mode, VideoDirector does not work.

The following steps describe the process of setting up VideoDirector 2.0 for insert editing:

1. After making your video, audio, COM port, and Control-L connections as shown in figure 35.1, position the infrared wand directly in front of your record VCR's remote control window.
2. Launch VideoDirector from the VideoDirector 2.0 entry of the Start menu.
3. In VideoDirector, choose Setup, Source Deck to open the Source Deck Setup dialog box.
4. Select LANC from the Drivers list, choose the NTSC or PAL option, and select the appropriate Options check boxes for your equipment. (The EV-S7000, used as the source deck for this example, has high-speed search, cassette eject, and timecode capability.)
5. Choose the Options button to open the LANC Options - V2.00 dialog box (see fig. 35.2).
6. Choose the Auto Configure button. VideoDirector's LANC driver then tests the control capabilities of your source deck and automatically marks the appropriate check boxes in the Transport Features frame.
7. Choose Setup, Record Deck to open the Record Deck Setup dialog box.
8. Select Infrared from the Drivers list, then choose the Options button to open the Infrared Options - V1.34 dialog box, as shown in figure 35.3. You also can select a ViSCA or Selectra (VuPort) driver if you have compatible equipment.

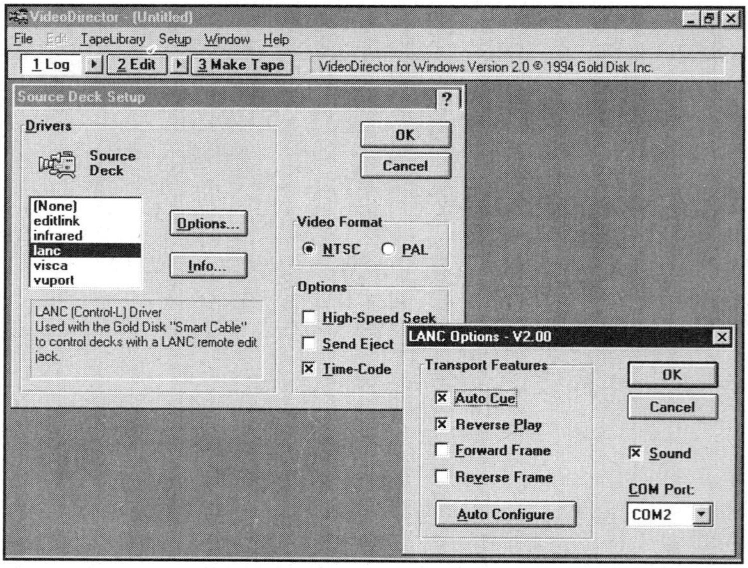

Fig. 35.2 VideoDirector 2.0's dialog boxes for setting up source deck Control-L parameters.

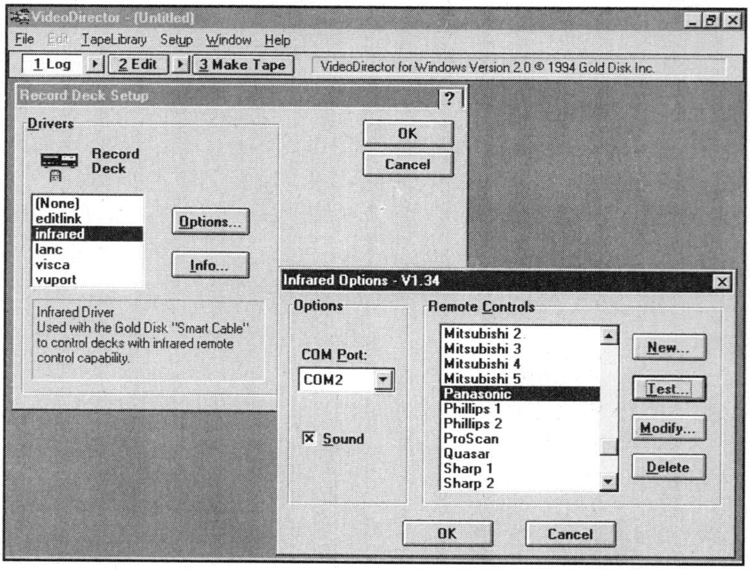

Fig. 35.3 VideoDirector 2.0's dialog boxes for setting up record deck infrared control parameters.

9. When the COM Port drop-down list appears, select the COM port to which the VideoDirector's Smart Cable is connected. Then in the Remote Controls list box, select the name of your record deck's manufacturer. (Some manufacturers use more than one remote control protocol, so you might have to experiment to find the correct selection.) Select

the Sound check box if you intend to add a sound track from your source tapes' audio content.

10. Choose the Test button to have VideoDirector check your selection, and then click OK to accept your settings and close the dialog box.

11. To achieve optimum editing accuracy, you must set record and pause delay parameters (frame-accurate decks use timecode). These settings calibrate your record deck to prevent overdubbing the end of the preceding segment or adding gaps between segments. Click the Record Delay and Pause Delay buttons of the Record Deck Setup dialog box (refer to fig. 35.3) to display the corresponding dialog boxes (see fig. 35.4). The default record delay is 45 frames and the pause delay is 0 frames. If you have a problem calibrating your decks, the Coolclips videotape calibration segments and detailed delay calibration instructions provide welcome assistance.

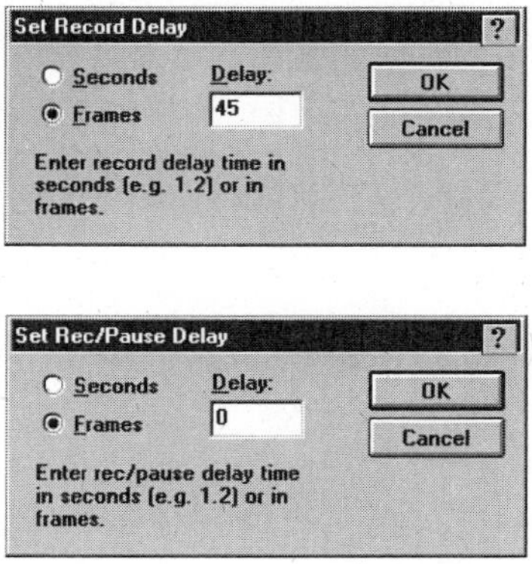

Fig. 35.4
Setting the record and pause delay parameters for the record deck.

12. If you have a video capture or video overlay card, choose Setup, Video Window to add to VideoDirector's Source Deck window a small, onscreen video display. Displaying video in a window enables you to capture picons to identify your segments.

Caution

Before using VideoDirector to log videotapes or edit, make sure that you set the record-protect tab on your source videotapes. There is a very slight chance that a computer malfunction might send a record command to your VCR or camcorder. Making sure that your source tapes are record-protected is cheap insurance against such an accident.

Note

If you have a ViSCA record deck, such as the Sony CVD-1000, or a Selectra VuPort controlling a Panasonic VCR, select the ViSCA or Selectra driver for the record deck. Using VideoDirector's Smart Cable for source deck control and ViSCA or VuPort control of the record deck requires two free COM ports and IRQs. If you're using a serial-port mouse, you probably will have to add a user-definable COM3 or COM4 port for the Smart Cable. Mouse Systems' Serial Bus Card is the simplest and least expensive way to add a COM3 or COM4 port with user-definable IRQ and I/O base address settings.

Troubleshooting

When I open VideoDirector or use the LANC Auto Configure feature, I get a message box indicating that the LANC driver isn't working.

The Control-L mode setting is the most common origin of source VCR problems. Make sure that your VCR's LANC mode is set to Slave, not Master. (Camcorders ordinarily don't offer a Control-L mode setting; most camcorders operate in Slave mode only.) With a camcorder as the source deck, make sure that the camcorder is set to VCR operating mode if the setting is available. Verify that the Control-L stereo miniplug is fully seated in its jack. You must have a tape in the source deck to use VideoDirector's Auto Configure feature.

Logging Tapes with VideoDirector 2.0

The first step in the editing process is to define the video segments that you want to use in the final edits. You use the VCR buttons of the Source Deck window, shown in figure 35.5, to position the source videotape. You can replace the standard VCR buttons with VideoDirector's Smart Buttons to provide two replay options, plus slow advance. The slider below the VCR buttons emulates the jog-shuttle control of high-end VCRs: you use the slider to position the tape to the exact in and out frames of the clip. The slider's behavior depends on your source deck's tape-positioning capabilities.

The following steps describe VideoDirector 2.0's clip-logging process:

1. Place the source tape in the source deck and click the Load Tape button of the Source Deck window to open the Select Source Tape dialog box. (The Load Tape button appears at the top of the Source Deck window prior to entering a tape name in the steps that follow.)

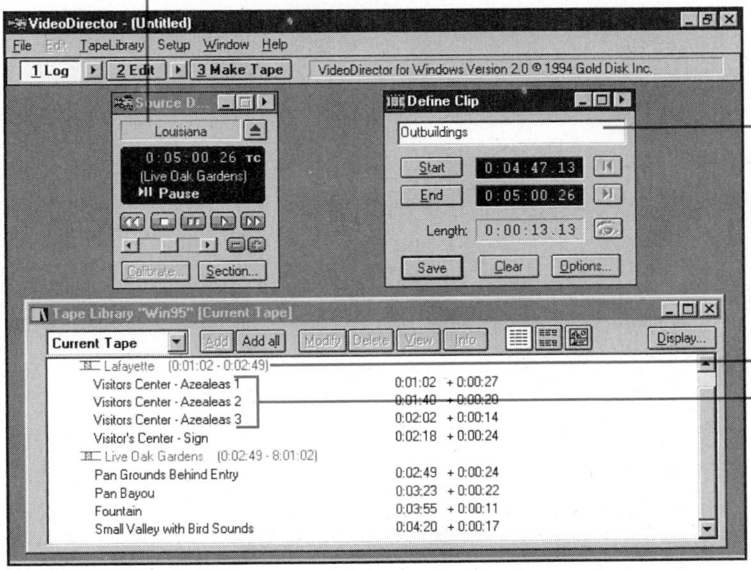

Fig. 35.5
Using VideoDirector 2.0 to log tape segments identified by title.

2. Select [NEW TAPE] in the Tapes list box to open the Create New Source Tape dialog box. Enter the name of the tape and an optional section name in the text boxes. Click the OK button of the Create New Source Tape and Select Source Tape dialog boxes to return to the Source Deck window.

3. Using the VCR buttons and the jog-shuttle slider, position the source tape to the first frame of the segment.

4. Choose the Start button of the Define Clip window to enter the in point (starting frame) in *HH:MM:SS:FF* format. The value derives from the timecode, a frame counter, or tape counter, depending on your source deck's capabilities.

5. In the Define Clip window's text box, enter a descriptive name for the clip.

6. Position the source tape to the out point (ending frame) of your clip, and then choose the End button to enter the clip's out point.

7. Choose the Save button of the Define Clip window to add the segment to the clip list in the Tape Library "Win95" [Current Tape] window (refer to fig. 35.5) and clear the entries in the Define Clip window. Video-Director then adds the segment data and picon as a new record

in its Tape Library database. The Tape Library window and database define the clip by its in point and length, rather than by the in and out points of conventional edit decision lists (EDLs).

8. Repeat steps 3 through 7 for each clip that you want to log.

VideoDirector 2.0 has an intuitive user interface and a variety of searching and editing options for the Tape Library database. The detailed 128-page *User's Guide* that accompanies VideoDirector fully describes the searching and editing options. The two-step process of defining clips enables you to proceed from the beginning to the end of the source tape. This minimizes clip search time and the wear and tear on your precious source tapes. The process also prolongs the life of your camcorder's transport mechanism.

Creating an Edit Decision List and the Edit Master Tape

After logging the tapes that you need for your production, you try a first-cut edit to determine whether your source and record decks are calibrated properly. VideoDirector's Event List is the equivalent of an edit decision list (EDL) used by professional video online-editing systems. The following steps briefly describe the process of creating an EDL and recording your video production on an edit master tape:

1. Choose the 2 Edit button at the top of VideoDirector's window to display the Tape Library window above the Event List window as shown in figure 35.6.

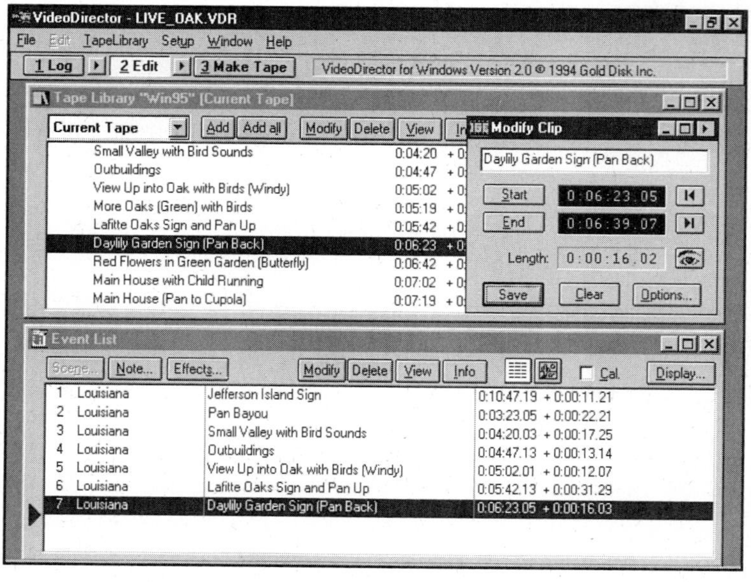

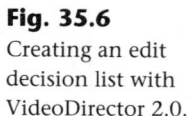

Fig. 35.6
Creating an edit decision list with VideoDirector 2.0.

2. In the Current Tape list of the Tape Library window, select the clip to add to the Event List, drag the clip to the Event List window, and drop it in position. Alternatively, click the Add or Add All button of the Tape Library window to place selected clips at the end of the current Event List.

3. Repeat step 2 for each segment of your production. You can add clips from any tape that you log in the Tape Library. When the Event List encounters clips from another tape, VideoDirector prompts you to insert the new tape.

4. When your Event List is complete, choose File, Save to open the Save File dialog box. Assign a file name to your EDL. The default extension for VideoDirector 2.0 Event List files is VDR.

5. Insert a blank videocassette in your record deck and choose the 3 Make Tape button at the top of VideoDirector's window. The Source Deck, Record Deck, and Make Tape windows replace the Tape Library window, as shown in figure 35.7.

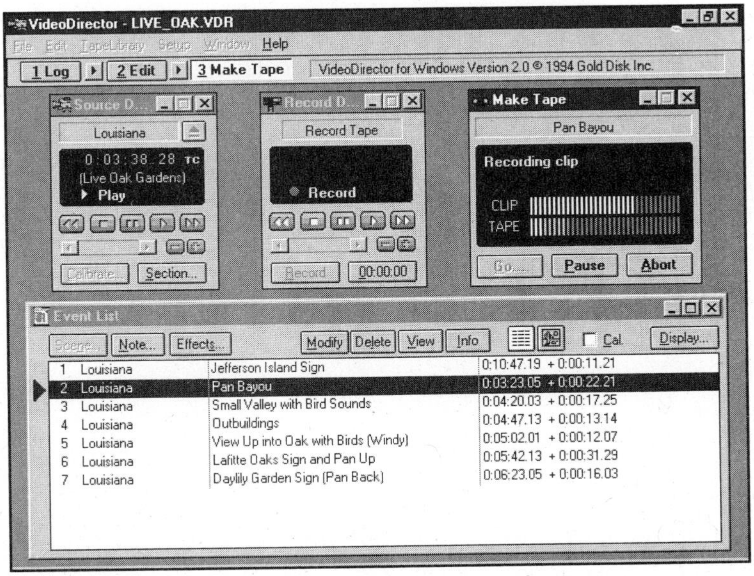

Fig. 35.7 Recording an edit master from the VideoDirector 2.0 Event List.

6. Choose the Record button in the Record Deck window to display the Make Tape dialog box and start recording a 30-second to one-minute black leader (recorded with no audio or video) on the record tape. If you use a ViSCA or VuPort device as the record deck, the Record Deck window includes VCR control for positioning the record tape.

7. As you record the leader, choose in the Make Tape dialog box the Assemble and Calibrate options that you want, then click the OK button to begin the automatic clip assemble process. The Make Tape window displays the progress of recording each clip and the edit master, as shown in figure 35.7.

Note

VideoDirector 2.0 can export edit decision lists from its Event List in the following formats: CMX 216 (CX1), 3400 (CX2), and CMX 3600 (CX3); Grass Valley Group A12V (GG1) and 41 (GG2); and EMME (EME). The equipment in professional video postproduction facilities uses these EDL formats. Thus you can use VideoDirector to define the edits (a process called *offline editing*), then take your tapes to a postproduction facility that can then produce a high-quality edit master.

Troubleshooting

The record deck doesn't go into record mode when I choose the Record button.

The most common cause of record deck control failure is improper positioning of the Smart Cable's IR wand. You should place the wand within six inches of the deck's IR remote control window and at the same level as the window. You might have to experiment to find the IR window on decks that incorporate the IR sensor in the operating display window, such as the Panasonic AG-1970P. You might also have to choose the Record button twice to place the VCR in record mode.

Adding Titles, Graphics, and Special Effects to Your VideoDirector 2.0 Productions

You can add a variety of audio, graphic, and Video Toaster special effects to your production. To do so, select an event and then choose the Event List window's Effects button to display the Add Effect dialog box shown in figure 35.8. Audio effects add waveform audio, audio CD, or MIDI behind one or more segments. If you have a suitable video-output overlay encoder or a genlock card, you also can add graphic special effects, such as animation, still graphics, and titles. For Video Toaster effects, you must have a NewTek Video Toaster connected to your PC. VideoDirector 2.0 also enables you to use the Video Toaster's transition, title, and framestore capabilities.

> **Note**
>
> NewTek, Inc.'s Video Toaster single-handedly brought about the DTV era. The original Video Toaster was an adapter card plus very advanced software (in its time) for the Commodore Amiga computer (which is no longer in production) that let videomakers create special effects, titles, and 3D animation sequences for video postproduction. The Video Toaster has the largest installed base of any linear DTV editing and special effects system. NewTek announced in mid-1995 its new Video Toaster for Windows that runs under Windows 95 and Windows NT.

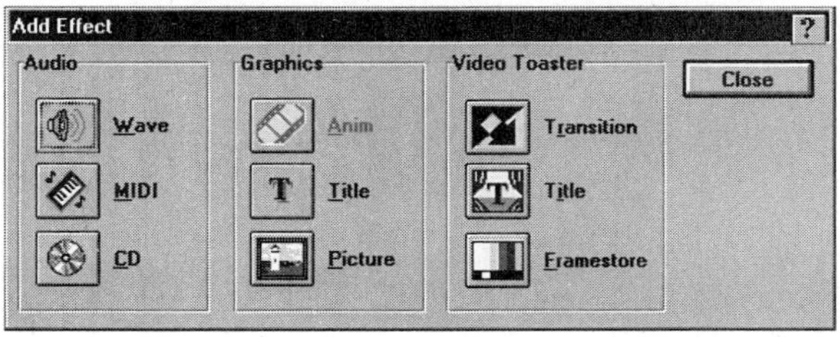

Fig. 35.8 VideoDirector 2.0's Add Effect dialog box.

> **Note**
>
> To mix audio for video with sound from the source tape, plug the source camcorder or VCR's audio outputs into your sound card's line input. Connect the sound card's speaker or line output to the audio inputs of the record deck. Use Windows 95's Volume Control applet to set the levels of your Line, Wave, MIDI, and CD audio sources.

Taking Advantage of Windows 95's New MCI Drivers

Windows' Media Control Interface (MCI) is an intermediary layer that connects hardware devices (such as a sound card) and software devices (such as a video codec) to Windows applications. The purpose of the MCI layer is to make multimedia applications independent of the hardware installed on your PC. MCI defines several generic *device types*, such as *waveaudio* (waveform audio in WAV files), *digitalvideo* (video in AVI files), and *vcr* (videotape player or recorder).

◄ See "Codec Implementation in Windows 95," p. 1009

Manufacturers of adapter cards and other multimedia hardware write MCI-compliant device drivers (usually named MCI*.DRV) that specify the MCI device type and inform MCI of the device's capabilities. Figure 35.9 shows the MCI drivers that come with Windows 95, plus the Apple QuickTime for Windows and Video Blaster SE100 overlay video drivers. MCI devices are identified by the driver name preceded by the prefix [MCI] or followed by a (Media Control) suffix.

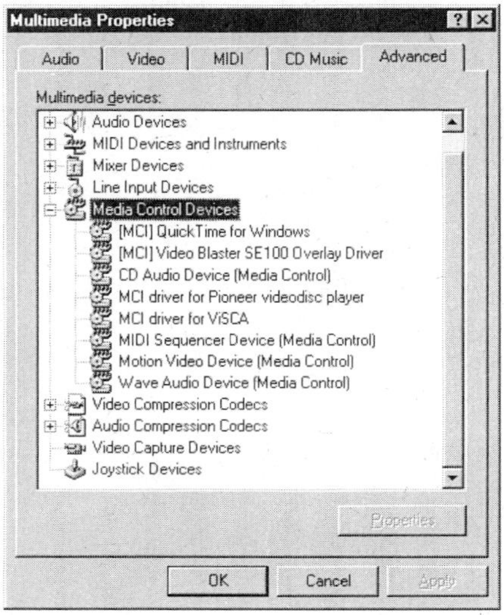

Fig. 35.9 The Advanced page of Control Panel's Multimedia Properties sheet with the Media Control Devices entry expanded.

Windows 95 includes in \WIN95\SYSTEM two MCI device drivers, MCIVISCA.DRV and MCIPIONR.DRV, that Windows 3.1+ did not include. In figure 35.9, these two drivers appear as `MCI driver for ViSCA` and `MCI driver for Pioneer videodisk player`. (You can download from CompuServe's Windows Multimedia Forum, WINMM, the Windows 3.1 versions of these two drivers.) The following sections briefly describe how to set up and use these MCI drivers.

Using Sony ViSCA Devices under Windows 95

MCIVISCA.DRV is a driver for the MCI *vcr* device type that enables you to control Sony video gear that has ViSCA control connections. The following Sony products support the ViSCA control protocol:

- CVD-500 (8mm) and CVD-1000 (Hi8) Vdeck videotape player/recorders (VTRs). The term *VTR* refers to a VCR that doesn't include a built-in tuner and other features designed for off-air TV recording.
- The XV-D1000 digital video mixer and special-effects generator used for A/B roll editing, a process described in the section "Using Multi-Media Computing's Video Magician 1.1 for A/B Roll Editing" later in this chapter.
- CI-1000 Vbox, which translates ViSCA commands to Sony Control-L and Control-S protocols. You can connect a Carlson-Strand GPI-1 interface to the Control-S connector of a Vbox to generate a GPI (general-purpose interface) trigger to control video switchers, mixers, titlers, or special-effects generators. GPI is a pulse-type (on-off) signal that causes the device to execute a predetermined action or a series of actions stored in the device's memory.

Note

Sony's ViSCA products have gained a substantial following among amateur and professional videomakers, but you won't find the Sony products in the preceding list at consumer electronics superstores. ViSCA devices are *prosumer* (a cross between *pro*fessional and con*sumer*) video equipment. Most videomakers purchase prosumer equipment by mail order. B&H Photo-Video (New York City, 800-947-9901, 212-444-6601), for example, stocks the complete line of Sony ViSCA-compliant products.

You can connect as many as seven ViSCA devices in a daisy-chain configuration to a single serial (COM) port of your PC. You need a special cable to connect the COM port to the ViSCA IN connector of the first ViSCA device in the chain. Additional devices connect with standard ViSCA cables from ViSCA OUT to ViSCA IN connectors. Figure 35.10 shows the ViSCA connections for the video device setup used to create this chapter's examples. Each ViSCA device automatically assigns itself a device number (1 through 7) during the device initialization process. Most Windows video editing applications support the ViSCA protocol, and you can write your own Visual Basic programs to control ViSCA VCRs using the MCI custom control (MCI.VBX) or the `mciSendString()` function of Windows 95's MMSYSTEM.DLL.

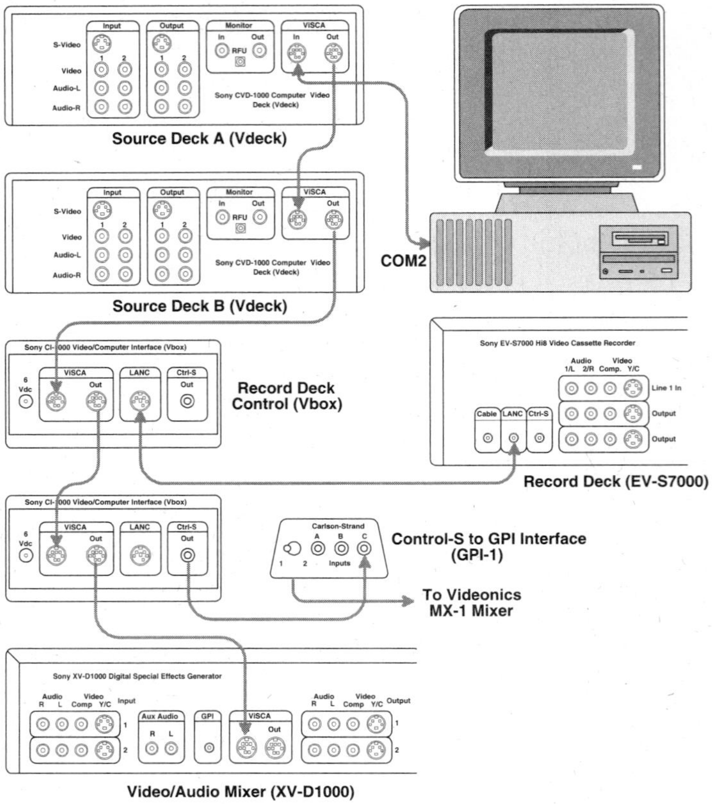

Fig. 35.10
A diagram of a Sony ViSCA setup with two CVD-1000 play decks, a XV-D1000 special-effects generator, an EV-S7000 record deck, and a GPI interface.

To set up the ViSCA driver, double-click the driver's entry in the Multimedia Devices list of the Advanced page of Control Panel's Multimedia Properties sheet. The Properties sheet for the ViSCA driver opens. (Alternatively, select the ViSCA driver item and choose the Properties button.) Choose the Settings button to open the MCI ViSCA Configuration dialog box. The ViSCA driver needs to know the COM port (COM1 through COM4) to which the ViSCA cable is connected and how many ViSCA devices are connected in the daisy-chain. Choose the Detect button to have the ViSCA driver automatically initialize the ViSCA chain and set the number of ViSCA devices. In figure 35.11, the Number of VCR's field indicates the detection of the five ViSCA devices shown in figure 35.10.

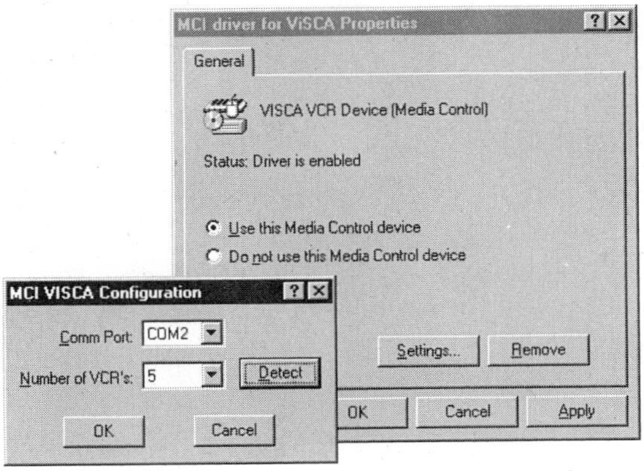

Fig. 35.11
Setting the COM port number and the number of ViSCA devices in the MCI ViSCA Configuration dialog box.

Troubleshooting

The MCI ViSCA Configuration dialog box doesn't report as many devices as in my ViSCA chain.

When you initialize the ViSCA driver, all ViSCA devices in the chain must be turned on. If any ViSCA device is unpowered, your PC terminates the daisy-chain. For example, if the Vbox for the record deck shown in figure 35.10 isn't turned on, the ViSCA driver recognizes only the two source Vdecks "upstream" of the Vbox. If all your ViSCA devices are turned on and you still don't get the correct number of devices, carefully check whether the ViSCA connectors are fully seated in the Vdeck and Vbox connectors.

Note

The version of MCIVISCA.DRV included with Windows 95 has some unfortunate characteristics. The Windows 95 ViSCA driver (developed and maintained by Sony) does not uniquely identify each device with a type, model, or number, and thus treats each device as a VCR—even if the device is a Sony XV-D1000 special-effects generator. If you have more than one ViSCA device, you need to know its device number when using most video-editing applications that support the ViSCA protocol. If you are using the ViSCA driver, opening Media Player might start all your ViSCA VTRs without warning.

Controlling Laserdisc Players

The burgeoning home theater business is breathing new life into an otherwise lackluster market for laserdisc players and videodiscs. Movies and other video content played from 12-inch videodiscs offers *much* better video and audio quality than standard VHS videocassettes offer. The videodisc is the antecedent of audio CDs and CD-ROMs, all of which technically fit in the laserdisc category. Most home theater installations include at least a rear-projection TV set, enhanced audio reproduction system, and a laserdisc player. According to market research data, most home theater enthusiasts also have home PCs. High-end laserdisc players, such as Pioneer's CLD-V2600, include a serial RS-232-C remote-control connector that enables your PC to emulate the player's infrared remote control.

Note

One of the most interesting uses of videodisc players is to calibrate your video equipment. Reference Recordings, Inc. (San Francisco) produces Joe Kane's *A Video Standard,* a CAV (constant angular velocity) videodisc/book combination that serves as an interactive guide to calibrating your TV set or the video and audio settings of your home theater system. Joe Kane, the founder of Imaging Science Foundation, Inc. and a columnist for several home theater periodicals, is an internationally recognized authority on projection TV systems and their calibration.

The Pioneer LaserDisc Device driver is of the MCI *videodisk* device type and has many capabilities (except recording) in common with the MCI *vcr* device. CAV videodiscs offer single-frame accuracy; you can move to any frame on a CAV disc in less than a second or so. Several firms offer recordable CAV videodisc dubbing services at about $350 for 30 minutes of high-quality video and sound. A videodisc played from a CLD-V2600 in conjunction with a digital video capture card, such as the Intel Smart Video Recorder Pro, enables you to step-capture video clips, one frame at a time, to AVI files. The advantage of step-capturing from a videodisk is that you don't need an expensive, frame-accurate VCR or a super-fast PC and fixed-disk drive to capture high-quality video images and sound tracks. Recordable videodiscs are great for archiving valuable video source material that you use repeatedly in your video productions. The laser read head doesn't touch the videodisc, eliminating the tape wear that occurs with repeated playback by VCRs.

Using Multi-Media Computing's Video Magician 1.1 for A/B Roll Editing

A/B roll editing, which enables you to use two video source (player) decks and add a variety of digital special effects during transitions from one player deck to another, is the next step above the cuts-only assemble-editing capability of

VideoDirector 2.0. Multi-Media Computing Solutions, Inc.'s (MMCS's) Video Magician is a Windows A/B roll-editing application designed exclusively for Sony ViSCA devices, as well as VCRs or camcorders with Control-L inputs. (You connect Control-L devices through the Sony Vbox's Control-L output.) Video Magician also enables you to play waveform audio files and control a CD-ROM drive (with an audio CD inserted) to add narration, sound effects, and music to your edit master tape. If you have an MCI-compatible video overlay card, such as the Orchid Videola or Creative Labs Video Blaster SE100, you can view overlay video in Video Magician's Monitor window. (Creative Labs only recently replaced the Sound Blaster FS200 overlay card with the less-expensive SE100.) When you specify the Video Monitor option, another option enables you to capture the beginning and ending frames of each clip that you define as a picon.

Figure 35.10, in the previous section "Using Sony ViSCA Devices under Windows 95," shows the ViSCA control connections that you use to test Video Magician. Figure 35.12 illustrates the video and audio connections between the two Sony CVD-1000 Vdeck source VTRs, the XV-D1000 SEG (special-effects generator), and the EV-S7000 record VCR. The configuration shown in figure 35.12 is not specific to editing with Video Magician; you can use the same setup with other ViSCA-oriented editors, such as Homrich Communication's EzV[2] editor. Video Magician includes a 25-pin serial-to-ViSCA (8-pin mini-DIN) cable, so you don't have to order the special cable for Intel-based PCs with your Vdecks or Vboxes.

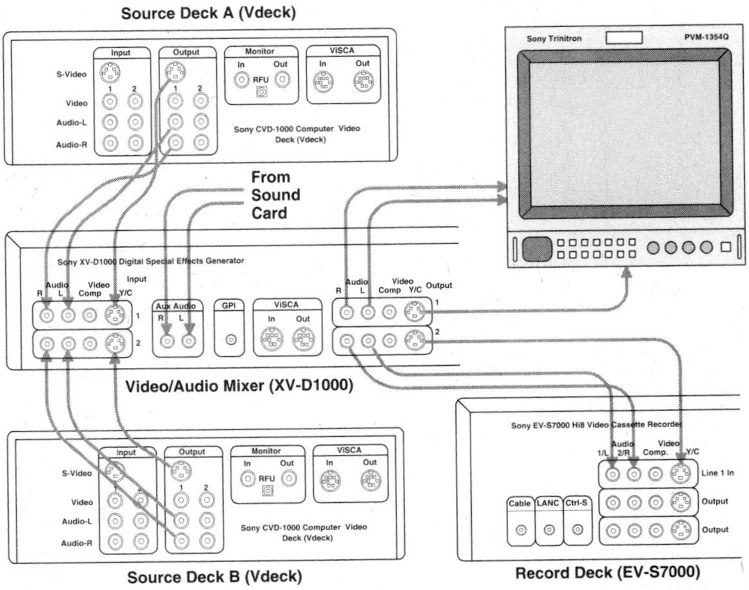

Fig. 35.12
Making video and audio connections for A/B roll editing with Sony ViSCA components.

The sections that follow describe how to set up and use Video Magician for professional-quality video A/B roll editing under Windows 95.

Setting Up Video Magician for A/B Roll Editing

MMCS makes setting up the Video Magician for a typical ViSCA A/B roll-editing suite almost automatic. You follow these steps to set the required parameters:

1. Make sure that your ViSCA cabling is properly connected and that all ViSCA devices are powered on. As was noted earlier in this chapter, any unpowered ViSCA device disables the entire ViSCA chain. The most common chain configuration is source deck A, source deck B, video mixer/special effects generator (if present), record deck, and any other auxiliary devices in the chain.

2. Run the Video Magician's Setup application. During installation, the application asks you to specify the COM port to which the ViSCA cable is connected (usually COM2). Close and relaunch Windows after Setup completes.

3. Launch Video Magician. During startup, Video Magician polls the ViSCA chain for devices and attempts to identify each device. Recognized devices are CVD-1000 or CVD-500 Vdecks, the XV-D1000 special-effects generator, or the Vbox, which is identified as a VCR. During polling, Video Magician exercises each ViSCA device. Figure 35.13 shows Video Magician's five default windows after startup.

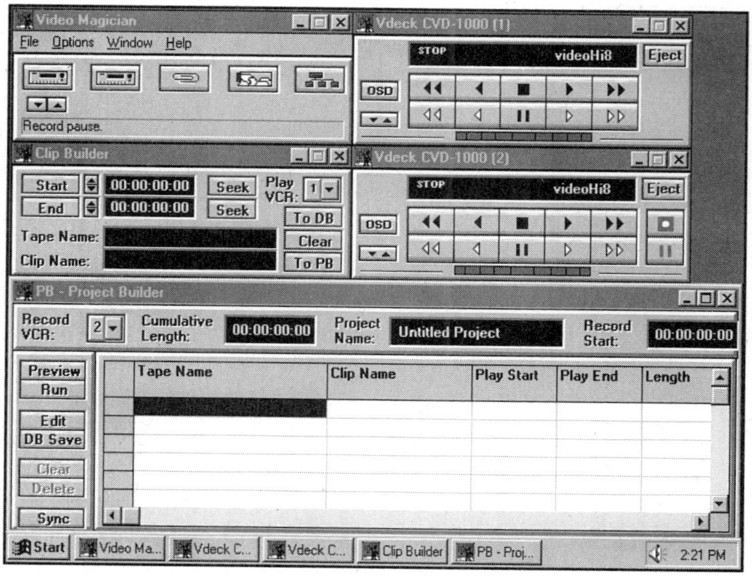

Fig. 35.13
Video Magician's five default windows that appear on startup.

4. Click the button with the up and down arrows (below the OSD button) to expand the window of each of the two playback decks. If you're using CVD-1000 source decks, select the settings shown in figure 35.14 to start.

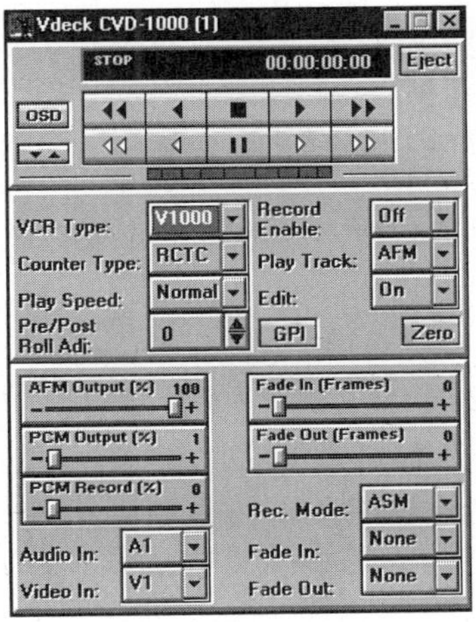

Fig. 35.14
Setting source deck parameters in one of the windows for a Sony CVD-1000 Vdeck.

5. Choose Window, VCRs, then select the submenu's number for the record VCR. The window for the record deck then opens. For the configuration shown in figure 35.10, for example, the record deck is VCR4. Figure 35.15 shows the record deck parameters for a Sony EV-S7000 VCR, which uses the Control-L protocol translated by a Vbox.

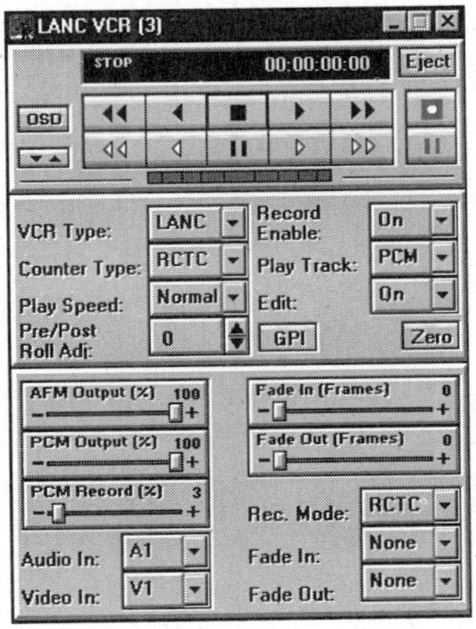

Fig. 35.15
Setting record deck parameters in the window for a Sony EV-S7000 VCR.

6. If you have a Sony XV-D1000 video mixer/SEG, choose Window, XV-D1000 to open the XV-D1000 window, which emulates the appearance of the main Control Panel of the XV-D1000. (Video Magician 1.1 does not implement the additional controls under the Digital SEG region of the window, corresponding to the lift-up panel of the XV-D1000's control unit.)

7. If you have an MCI-compatible video overlay and capture card, choose Options, Video Monitor. To save picons of the beginning and ending frame of each clip that you specify, choose Options, Thumbnails.

8. Most PC users now have a sound card and a CD-ROM drive, so Video Magician enables you to add waveform audio (WAV) and audio CD material to your sound tracks. If you have these devices, choose Options, Compact Disk Player, and Options, Digital Wave Player to open dialog boxes that let you select the track or a file to use for your soundtrack.

Like VideoDirector 2.0, Video Magician requires preroll and postroll calibration of your source and record decks to achieve maximum editing accuracy. The 120-page, spiral-bound instruction manual included with Video Magician provides step-by-step calibration instructions and includes example calibration logs for a pair of CVD-1000 Vdecks or a combination of a CVD-1000 and a Sony SLV-R5UC VCR as playback and record decks.

Editing with Video Magician 1.1

You use Video Magician's Clip Builder to define the videoclips that you want to use in the edit. The process of defining clips is similar to that described for VideoDirector 2.0 earlier in the chapter. The Clip Builder creates a succession of records in the Project Builder that comprise your production's EDL. Figure 35.16 shows how to define a segment in the Clip Builder window. (The clips defined in the Project Builder in fig. 35.16 are imported from a VideoDirector 2.0 Event List saved as a VTX file.)

You click the To PB button in the Clip Builder window to add the clip to the Project Builder. When you complete the list of clips in Project Builder, you save the project to Video Magician's database. Video Magician uses the Microsoft Access 1.1 MDB file format for the MAGICIAN.MDB database, so you can write your own Access 1.1 or Visual Basic 3.0 application to manipulate Video Magician's three database tables. Thumbnail images created with a video capture card are stored as bitmap files in a hierarchical \MAGICIAN*YEAR**MONTH**WEEK* folder structure rather than in a field of the OLE Object data type in the clips table of MAGICIAN.MDB.

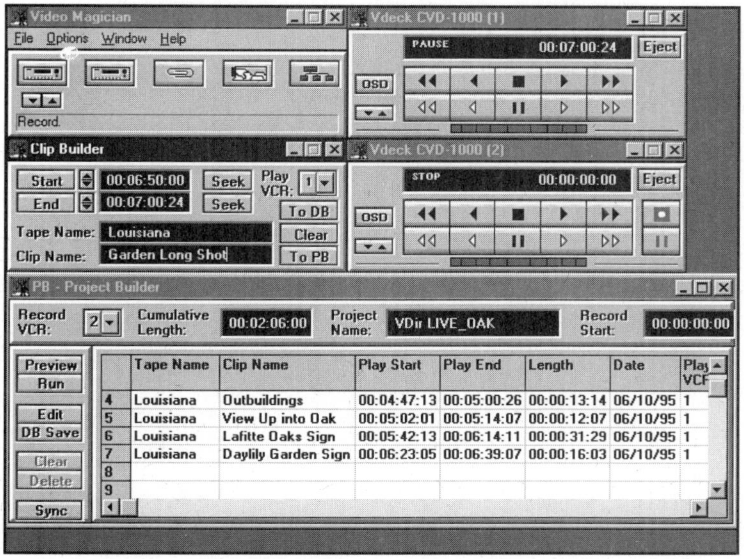

Fig. 35.16 Using Video Magician's Clip Builder window to define a video segment played on VCR1.

Caution

Video Magician 1.1 is a Visual Basic 3.0 application that uses the Access 1.1 file format, so you cannot save changes to the database made with Access 2.0+. Access 2.0+ cannot save MDB files in Access 1.1 format; if you modify and save MAGICIAN.MDB with Access 2.0+, Video Magician 1.1 can no longer read the database.

To edit an entry in the Project Builder, you click the clip number to select the row containing the clip data, then click the Edit button to display the Properties Editor window shown in figure 35.17. The Properties Editor includes controls to change the value of each of the fields of the open database's clip table. Video Magician enables you to apply a property setting to all the records in the Project Builder; the global property feature is especially useful when you import an edit decision list created by Homrich Communications' EZ-V^2 A/B roll-editing application or VideoDirector 1.0 or 2.0.

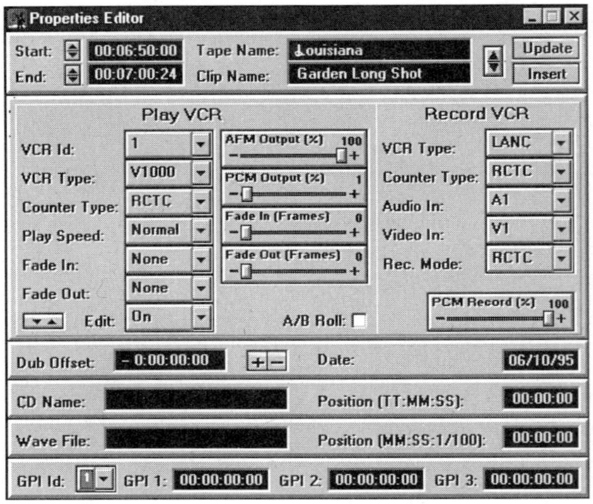

Fig. 35.17
Video Magician 1.1's Properties Editor window for editing clips contained in the Project Builder.

Unlike VideoDirector 2.0, which saves videoclip data in a database separate from the EDL, Video Magician uses a single-step EDL building process. However, you can emulate VideoDirector's two-step process with Video Magician by following these steps:

1. Create a project that consists of a sequential list of all the clips on a particular tape. (If you have VideoDirector 1.0 or 2.0, create an Event List from all the clips in the appropriate tape library, save the Event List in both VDR and VTX formats, then import the VTX file into Video Magician.)

2. Save the project, identified by the tape name or ID, to the default MAGICIAN.MDB database or to a new database with a different file name, such as *CLIENT*.MDB.

3. Repeat steps 1 and 2 for each tape required for your editing session. Make sure to identify in the Clip Builder the playback VCR ID for tapes that you plan to use for A/B roll editing. Also mark the tapes with the VCR ID.

4. After logging each of the tapes required for your editing session, open Video Magician's Database and Project Builder windows.

5. Select the project in the Database window and select Clips in the View drop-down list to display all clips in the database, as shown at the top of figure 35.18.

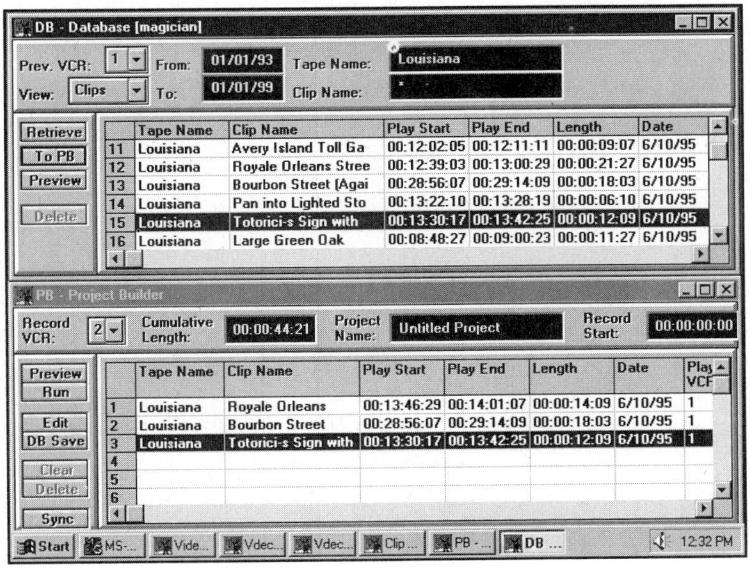

Fig. 35.18
Copying the clips for a new project from a previously saved tape log project.

6. Click the Clear button of the Project Builder window to remove all entries from the grid.

7. Select the first clip for your new project in the Database window and click the To PB button to add the clip to the Project Builder grid.

8. Repeat step 7 to add the other clips that comprise your editing project (see the bottom of fig. 35.18).

9. Use the Properties Editor to alter the properties of each clip as necessary.

10. Give your new project a name and save it in the appropriate database.

A/B Roll Editing with Video Magician 1.1

A/B roll edits involve two source decks playing simultaneously, so their EDL entries are called *roll-edit pairs*. Defining an A/B roll-edit pair with Video Magician 1.1 involves the following steps:

1. Define in the Project Builder two adjacent clips that comprise your A/B roll-edit pair. Each member of the pair must specify a different source VCR. The most common method of creating roll-edit pairs is to define a clip for the A and B elements that is slightly longer than the transition period. You get the best results when the A and B clips are the same length.

2. Define the mixer/SEG transitions for your clips and store the transitions sequentially in the mixer/SEG's memory. (Version 1.1 of Video Magician doesn't support "live" transitions with the XV-D1000; the ViSCA equivalent of a GPI signal triggers stored XV-D1000 transitions.)

3. Select the first member of the roll-edit pair. Click the Project Builder's Edit button to display the Properties Editor window, and select the A/B Roll check box. The source VCR specified in the first entry is defined as the A deck. Video Magician automatically assigns the VCR for the second clip as the B deck.

4. Set the device number for your mixer/SEG in the GPI Id drop-down list, then enter the start points of as many as three transitions in the GPI1, GPI2, and GPI3 text boxes.

5. Click the Update button to store the A/B roll-edit data in the Project Builder grid.

6. Select both members of the A/B roll-edit pair in the Project Builder grid and click the Preview button to verify that you have specified the desired transition.

7. Save the project in the database of your choice.

Creating the Edit Master

After verifying your EDL with Video Magician's Preview feature, you follow these steps to create the edit master on your record VCR:

1. If the EDL for the edit master is not in the Project Builder grid, copy the EDL from the database in which you saved the project.

2. Double-click anywhere in the Project Builder grid to remove any empty rows.

3. Insert the required tapes in the source VCRs.

4. Position the edit master tape in the record VCR.

5. Click the Project Builder window's Run button to start Video Magician's Run Engine to create the edit master. If you have as many source VCRs as tapes for the edit, the process is completely automatic; if not, the Run Engine prompts you to change tapes for the source deck specified for the clip in the EDL.

Video Magician 1.1 is a versatile assemble- and A/B roll-editing application and costs less than $400. Video Magician's imaginative use of the project and clip database and capability to import VideoDirector 1.0 and 2.0 Event List files makes the application the next logical step for videographers who upgrade from consumer-level gear to prosumer-grade ViSCA decks like the CVD-1000. Support for A/B roll editing, Control-L devices (through the Sony Vbox), and dedicated mixer/SEGs (with a Vbox and a Carlson-Strand GPI-1) makes Video Magician 1.1 an ideal editing application for videographers making the transition from dedicated edit controllers to the realm of computer-controlled linear analog editing.

Capturing Digital Video under Windows 95

Just a couple of years ago, PC-based digital video was a curiosity. Early 1/16-screen (160 × 120 pixel) "dancing postage stamps" with telephone-grade audio gave way to 1/4-screen "dancing credit cards" with high-fidelity stereo sound tracks, as Windows users migrated from 80386SX16 to 80486DX2/66 and faster PCs. Windows 95 and Pentium PCs now promise full-screen, full-motion digital video from double-speed CD-ROM drives. Even if you don't have a Pentium PC, new digital video accelerator cards such as the Diamond Viper Pro Video use video interpolation to expand 1/4-screen images to a full 640 × 480 pixels. Windows 95's 32-bit CD-ROM file system (CDFS), Display Control Interface (DCI), and 32-bit video codecs provide the power to make full-screen, full-motion video a reality on high-end home PCs.

Note

Software-only MPEG (Motion Picture Experts Group) decompression for White Book Video CDs is on its way to Windows 95. Microsoft announced in June 1995 a license agreement with Mediamatics, Inc. for a playback-only MPEG-1 codec that will be included "in future releases of Windows 95." Windows 95 currently supports MPEG-1 AVI files, but today you need a $200+ hardware-assisted MPEG-1 decoder card to play video CDs from your CD-ROM drive. You need a 90-MHz Pentium PC to watch 24 frames per second (fps) of full-color video and listen to 11-kHz digital audio with the Mediamatics codec. Motion pictures use 24 fps, so the frame rate is likely to be acceptable; whether 11.025-kHz digital audio will satisfy users remains to be seen.

To create digital movies, you start with a digital video capture process that converts the standard analog NTSC (PAL and SECAM in Europe) video and analog audio signals into a digital format compatible with Windows' Audio-Video Interleaved (AVI) files. A variety of digital video capture cards are available from U.S. and European suppliers, at prices starting at less than $500. The digital version of standard NTSC video that you watch on your TV set today has a data rate of about 135 Mbps (17 megabytes per second, or M/s) and today's highest-quality digital video (D-1, CCIR-601 with 4:2:2 encoding) runs at 270 Mbps (35 M/s), so compression of the video data is vital. Thus all PC digital video capture cards provide some type of built-in video compression circuitry. The sections that follow describe the PC hardware and software required to capture digital video under Windows 95.

A Brief Introduction to Digital Video Technology

Most Windows 95 users gain their introduction to digital video through 1/4-screen video clips that are included with virtually every successful CD-ROM title produced today. The image size and quality, as well as the frame rate of conventional CD-ROM video clips, is determined primarily by the maximum sustained data rate of your CD-ROM drive, which is at least 10 times slower than the data rate of today's fixed-disk drives. If you have a single-speed CD-ROM drive, you must copy most 1/4-screen video clip files to and play them from your fixed disk to view the clips without skipping frames or encountering audio breaks (stuttering). The speed of your PC also influences the playback rate because Windows 95's video codecs, such as Indeo 3.2 and Cinepak, require a substantial percentage of your PC's horsepower to decode the compressed video to the RGB data required by your PC's graphics adapter.

Capturing and playing back professional-quality digital video for nonlinear editing requires hardware assistance for both compression and decompression. The final product is a high-quality videotape rather than an AVI file on a CD-ROM. Video capture and nonlinear editing for industrial and broadcast productions involves the following basic steps:

1. Convert the analog video and audio data of selected segments of the source video tape(s) to uncompressed digital form, a process called *video decoding* or *digitizing*.

   The video-decoding process uses analog-to-digital converters (ADCs) to sample the analog video and audio signals and to create the digital data; video sampling occurs at a much faster rate than audio sampling because the video signal carries much more information (has a greater bandwidth) than the audio signal. Professional-quality ADCs sample

640 or 720 times each line of active video (480 or 486 lines for NTSC). 640 × 480 sampling is called "square pixel format," corresponding to the PC's VGA display. 720 × 486 sampling corresponds to the NTSC version of the CCIR-601 international standard for broadcast-quality digital video.

2. Compress the digital video with a compression ratio that results in a data rate your PC can handle.

   Compression must be done in real time by a very complex digital signal processing (DSP) chip, because there is no way your PC can store uncompressed video data. (It is uncommon to compress audio data; you reduce the audio data rate by reducing the sample rate.) With Motion-JPEG compression, described in the "Moving Up to Motion-JPEG Compression" section later in this chapter, a compression ratio of 4:1 or 5:1 is considered "industrial" quality that's suitable for most broadcast TV purposes.

3. Store the compressed digital video and audio clips in real time on your PC's fixed disk.

   High-quality digital video requires a sustained fixed-disk read/write data rate in the range of 3M/s to 6M/s. As a rule of thumb, it takes 1G of disk space to store *n* minutes of video, where *n* is the compression ratio. As an example, a 1G drive can hold about 5 minutes of 5:1 compressed video, which has a data rate of about 3.3M/s. These values don't include the disk space required to store the digitized sound track.

4. Edit the compressed video and audio data, adding special effects between transitions, plus titles, still graphics, sound effects, and narration.

   Depending on the type of editing system you use, the digital edit master may be an entirely new file or a combination of selected parts of original files, plus new special effects files played in sequence. (Adobe Premiere, as an example, creates a new movie file from your edited digitized clips.)

5. Decompress the video content of the file(s) in real time with the same DSP chip used to compress the data. Decompression also is called *inverse transformation* (the inverse of the compression process).

6. Decompress digital video data to the original analog video format with a digital-to-analog converter (DAC), called *video encoding*. The analog video and audio data is recorded on videotape for playback or distribution.

Note

The terms *video decoding* and *video encoding* commonly refer to the use of video ADCs and DACs, respectively, for uncompressed conversion. When used in conjunction with digital-only compression and decompression, encoding usually refers to compression, and decoding means decompression.

The sections that follow describe the requirements for performing the first two steps of the preceding list, decoding and compression. The "Building Digital Movies with Adobe Premiere 4.0" section later in this chapter describes the remaining four steps. Although the digital video focus of the remainder of this chapter is on CD-ROM-quality video, the techniques described are applicable to industrial- and broadcast-quality digital video productions.

Defining the Video Capture Platform

Successfully capturing and recording live digitized video and audio requires a PC with plenty of horsepower. Fortunately, the cost of Pentium PCs and fast disk drives is decreasing at such a rapid rate that today's "standard" multimedia home PC sports a 75-MHz or 90-MHz Pentium and at least a 500M fixed-disk drive. The following list provides a set of recommended specifications for a Windows 95 PC used to capture digital video:

◀ See "Understanding Plug and Play Architecture," p. 230

- *Processor, chipset, and motherboard.* A 90-MHz or faster Pentium PC is required to obtain optimum performance from low-cost video capture cards and, with a few exceptions, is essential for high-end video capture. The Intel Triton chipset provides somewhat better performance than the Neptune. The PC absolutely must have a PCI (Peripheral Component Interconnect) bus; low-end capture cards plug into ISA slots, but the future of digital video capture and processing is on the high-speed PCI bus. Plug and Play isn't critical for video capture, but almost all high-end 80486DX and Pentium motherboards produced in mid-1995 and afterward include Plug and Play in the system BIOS.

- *Cache and DRAM memory.* For video capture applications, 256K of high-speed cache RAM is adequate. Intel recommends at least 32M of DRAM, but you can get by with 16M if you use the Intel YVU9C video capture codec described in the next section. 32M of DRAM decidedly improves the performance of digital video editing applications.

- *Fixed-disk drives and controllers.* For standard video capture, fast 1G and larger SCSI-2 drives that have an average seek time of 10 milliseconds or less are normally required. However, if you're on a budget, you can get by with high-speed EIDE (Enhanced Integrated Device Electronics) drives connected to a built-in PCI-to-EIDE bridge. The Adaptec AHA-2940 currently is the "standard" PCI SCSI-2 controller card for video capture. Fast, wide SCSI-2 drives connected to an Adaptec AHA-3940W PCI multichannel SCSI controller provide as much as 20 M/s of synchronous data transfer across two drives. If you're buying a new PC, you can minimize the risk of your system's obsolescence by choosing wide SCSI. (You can connect conventional SCSI-2 devices in a wide SCSI chain with special cabling.) For heavy-duty video capture, specify audio-video (AV) drives that don't interrupt data writing with internal thermal recalibration processes.

- *Graphics adapter card and video display unit.* A Windows DCI-compliant graphics accelerator card that provides 24-bit color at 800 × 600 pixel or greater resolution is a necessity; specify at least 2M of VRAM (special Video RAM), not DRAM. If your video capture card decimates the incoming video signal (by capturing alternate video frames) and doesn't include its own interpolated scaling circuitry, you need digital video acceleration to output digital video to tape. A 17-inch multisynchronous monitor with 0.28-mm dot pitch or smaller is the minimum specification for heavy-duty digital video editing.

- *Audio adapter card.* Low-end video capture cards don't include audio digitizing and playback capability, so you need a sound card to handle audio-for-video chores. For reasonable sound quality and optimum Windows 95 compatibility, the Sound Blaster 16 AWE card or the recently announced Sound Blaster 32 is the low-budget choice. Professional-quality audio adapter cards, such as the Turtle Beach Tahiti, deliver full CD-quality audio and better control of audio recording levels.

Windows 95's 32-bit VFAT (virtual file allocation table) file system brings high-speed 32-bit disk access to SCSI drives and supports 32-bit file operations. (Windows 3.1+'s 32-bit disk access doesn't accommodate SCSI drives.) You can mix IDE drives connected to the built-in IDE interface with SCSI-2 drives under Windows 95 without difficulty. The optimum configuration is an IDE drive for your C (boot) drive to hold Windows 95, your applications, and SCSI-2 drives for video capture. By using an IDE drive to boot your PC, you ensure that no problem in the SCSI cabling and termination or a failed SCSI device prevents booting.

Tip

Don't use *any* type of disk data compression system for drives that store digital video data; compression slows disk writes and reads.

Note

Some high-end digital video capture and editing systems, such as the FAST Video Machine with Digital Player/Recorder (DP/R) and Play Incorporated's Trinity system with the Preditor ™ digital video option, provide their own SCSI-2 interfaces to dedicated video disk drives. The Video Machine with DP/R (ISA) and Trinity/Preditor (PCI) both have digital audio recording and playback capability.

Capturing Digital Video for CD-ROM Titles

Tip
Make sure that you install your digital video capture and editing software *before* installing your video capture card under Windows 95.

Windows 95 includes several video codecs, the most important of which are Intel's Indeo 3.2 (IV32) and Supermatch's Cinepak (CVID). Indeo 3.2 predominates on the PC and Cinepak is the preferred codec for Apple QuickTime movies, although Indeo 3.2 is also available for the Macintosh. Both the Indeo and Cinepak codecs use *intraframe* and *interframe* compression. Intraframe compression compresses the video by removing redundancy from individual video images; interframe compression eliminates redundant data between successive compressed frames. Both of these compression methods are called *lossy* compression, because some of the detail or motion is lost during the compression process. By combining lossy intraframe and interframe compression, you can reduce the video and audio data rate for a 1/4-screen, 15-fps movie to about 240 K/s, the limit for reliable playback by double-speed CD-ROM drives. The minimum value required to achieve a semblance of full-motion video is 15 fps. Digital video producers generally consider Cinepak to be the better codec for scenes that contain fast motion, but give Indeo the nod for better overall image quality.

Note

CD-ROM publishers, such as Medio Multimedia, that include substantial amounts of digital video content in their titles are eagerly awaiting the Intel Indeo 4.0 video codec, which is expected to appear in late 1995. Indeo 4.0 is rumored to provide better image quality and to improve rendering of high-motion scenes, rivaling MPEG-1's compression capabilities.

Quality 1/4-screen video capture for subsequent compression with IV32 or CVID uses the Indeo Raw Video capture codec,YVU9, which requires hardware capture assistance from the original Intel Smart Video Recorder (ISVR) or the newer ISVR Pro video capture cards. YVU9 (nine bits per pixel YUV-encoded) video is compressed from the original NTSC signal, but isn't considered a lossy-compressed digital video format.

YUV is a method of determining color by specifying luminance (Y), hue (U), and saturation (V). A lossy compression codec discards video data that isn't needed to provide video of a predetermined image quality. If you use the YVU9 codec for capture, you can choose the final lossy compression codec that best suits your video material. Making this choice often requires trial and error. (If you capture in a lossy-compressed format, subsequent editing is difficult, recompression gives poor quality, and you cannot change codecs.)

The ISVR Pro, which has won several "editor's choice" awards, is the standard of comparison for digital video capture cards designed for creating videos to be distributed on CD-ROM. The ISVR Pro accepts both composite and S-video inputs and comes with Asymetrix Digital Video Producer for video capture and editing.

Note

Creative Labs' Video Blaster RT300 uses the same capture chipset as the ISVR Pro, but comes with its own version of IVU9. The primary advantages of the RT300 over the ISVR Pro are the slightly lower cost and the bundling of Adobe Premiere 1.1 digital video capture and editing software. For only $129, you can upgrade Premiere 1.1 to the $695 Premiere 4.0, described in the "Building Digital Movies with Adobe Premiere 4.0" section later in this chapter.

The data rate for 1/4-screen, 15-fps video capture with the YVU9 codec is about 1.2 M/s, which is within the sustained data-writing capability of Pentium 90s with high-speed SCSI-2 drives. However, most PCs in today's installed base cannot handle this data rate, which results in many dropped frames. Traditionally, Intel's response to this problem was to recommend installing 64M of RAM and then capturing to RAM rather than directly to disk. If you implement Intel's solution, however, you're limited to 60 seconds or less per clip. In Spring 1995, Intel released a "nearly lossless" version of YVU9, YVU9C, that cuts the capture data rate nearly in half. Tests of the YVU9C codec, which works with both the ISVR Pro and Video Blaster RT300 under Windows 95, show no discernible difference between most YVU9 and YVU9C images.

Tip
If you find that you're dropping frames using the YVU9C codec, try immediately repeating the capture. In most cases, you won't drop frames the second time.

Note

The YVU9C codec and example .AVI files captured with the ISVR Pro using the YVU9C codec are included in the YVU9C folder of the accompanying CD-ROM. The video source material for the sample file is from Reference Recording's *A Video Standard* videodisc described earlier in this chapter, and is used with the permission of the copyright holder and publisher.

Before late 1994, almost all PC video capture cards included video capture (VidCap) and editing (VidEdit) applications from the Microsoft Video for Windows (VfW) 1.1 Developer's Kit. Today, commercial digital video editing applications, such as Adobe Premiere and Asymetrix Digital Video Producer, have built-in video capture capability based on the original VidCap design. In late 1994, Microsoft announced the termination of active support for the VfW 1.1 Developer's Kit. The "Capturing Digital Video with Premiere 4.0" section later in this chapter shows you how to use the ISVR Pro and Premiere 4.0's capture features under Windows 95.

Moving Up to Motion-JPEG Compression

The Indeo 3.2 and Cinepak codecs described in the previous section are designed primarily for creating video content for distribution on CD-ROMs. If you want to take advantage of digital editing, titling, and special-effects applications such as Adobe Premiere, and output the movie to videotape, you need a codec that can create high-quality, full-screen video images. Motion-JPEG, a variation on the Joint Photographic Experts Group's compression method for still images, is currently the preferred codec for high-end digital video capture (decoding) and playback to analog video (encoding) for recording. Motion-JPEG, which uses only intraframe lossy compression based on the discrete cosine transform (DCT), has the advantage of precise control of compression ratio and thus of image quality. Digital VTRs use 2:1 DCT compression for broadcast TV. A DCT compression of 5:1 is generally accepted as corresponding to the quality of the Betacam SP component recording format, the most widely used VTR format in the television industry.

Motion-JPEG video capture and playback cards fall into one of the following two categories:

- *Consumer/prosumer.* Relatively inexpensive ($500 to $600) Motion-JPEG adapter cards or daughterboards are limited to 16:1 or higher compression ratios and capture every other pixel of alternate video fields to create a 320 × 240 pixel image. Examples are miro Computer Products' miroVideo DC1 and FAST Multimedia's Movie Line with Motion-JPEG. Usually, the minimum compression ratio that you can achieve is limited by your PC's capture data rate, not by the card's capability. The quality of the 2:1 (line-doubled with interpolation) video output of these cards is about the same as VHS tape: about 200 horizontal lines of TV resolution. With good video gear and a fast PC and disk combination, you can achieve close to Hi8 or S-VHS quality under Windows 95. You capture the audio track with a separate sound card.

- *Industrial/broadcast.* High-end Motion-JPEG cards sample every video field to create a full 720 × 640 pixel (CCIR-601) digitized image and enable you to reduce the compression ratio to as low as 3:1, but require large, high-speed fixed-disk drives to handle the higher data rates. The practical minimum compression ratio is 5:1, but 7:1 or 8:1 is used for most digital video productions. Most suppliers of professional-quality Motion-JPEG cards provide their own 32-bit video capture and editing applications with the cards. For example, D-Vision Systems, Inc.'s OnLINE capture and editing system runs only under Windows 95 and Windows NT 3.5+. By early 1996, probably all suppliers of professional-quality Motion-JPEG capture cards will provide 32-bit versions of their bundled applications. Many high-end Motion-JPEG systems include digital audio capture and playback capabilities; a few, such as Interactive Images' Plum system, use a separate sound card.

Caution

The drivers for many Motion-JPEG adapter cards aren't fully compatible with Windows 95. Check Windows 95 compatibility with the manufacturer's technical service group before purchasing any Motion-JPEG card, except those designed specifically for use under Windows 95 and Windows NT 3.5+.

Note

The forthcoming consumer digital video cassette (DVC) recording format and professional variations on the DVC theme (Panasonic's DVCPRO format) use fixed 5:1 DCT compression. DVCPRO equipment is designed for broadcast field recording, electronic news gathering (ENG), and electronic field production (EFP).

The primary threat to the market for high-end Motion-JPEG video capture systems comes from MPEG-2, the second iteration of the MPEG compression codec. Digital MPEG-2 video compression is used for transmission of DirecTV and USSB programming (as of late 1995) to 18-inch Thomson/RCA and Sony satellite dishes connected to set-top decoder boxes. MPEG-2 is the compression standard for the forthcoming digital videodiscs (DVDs) and U.S. high-definition television broadcasting, or Advanced TV (ATV). MPEG-2 uses DCT intraframe compression, but adds sophisticated motion prediction to improve interframe compression. New, high-powered RISC (reduced instructor set computer) processors provide the capability to capture video with intraframe compression (I-frame) only, so you can edit the MPEG-2 video before applying interframe compression to reduce storage requirements. By the end of 1996 or sooner, MPEG-2 probably will be the preferred format for almost all digital video applications.

Step-Capturing with Frame-Accurate VTRs and Videodisc Players

One way to avoid the issue of high data rates altogether is to use frame-by-frame (step-frame) capture of video content. Step-frame capture requires a single-frame VTR, such as the Sony EVO-9650 Hi8 or Sanyo GVR-S955 S-VHS record deck, or a remotely controlled videodisc player, like the Pioneer CLD-V2600 described earlier in this chapter. Single-frame VTRs are used primarily for recording computer-generated animated graphics onto videotape. (You need a Sony EVBK-66 ViSCA interface board to control the EVO-9650 with most Windows digital video capture and editing applications.)

Most professional-quality videoclips for commercial CD-ROM distribution are step-frame captured. In many cases, the source video content is transferred from Betacam SP or a higher-quality component or digital video format to a recordable CAV videodisc, then step-captured with the YVU9 codec for editing and subsequent compression. Step-capturing enables you to use lower Motion-JPEG compression ratios if your fixed-disk drive has a higher sustained read than write data rate.

Note

You cannot step-capture the sound track of a videotape or videodisc, so the capture applications use an automatic two-step process. The applications first capture the video content (at a rate of about 1 to 2 fps) and then digitize the audio for the range of captured frames in a continuous process. The process is frame-accurate, so it maintains lip-sync.

Building Digital Movies with Adobe Premiere 4.0

Traditional video-editing suites consist of two playback VTRs, a record VTR, an edit controller, and a video switcher/special-effects generator (SEG). Computer-based A/B roll-editing systems, such as FAST Multimedia, Inc.'s Video Machine, replace the edit controller and video switcher/SEG with a PC adapter card and a Windows-based editing application. Videotape-based editing methods, whether traditional or computer-based, are referred to as *linear*, because of the need to position the source videotapes by linear movement past the playback device's read head. Linear video editing remains the prevalent methodology for industrial- and higher-quality video production, despite linear editing's dependence on highly accurate (and thus expensive) source and record VTRs, plus time-consuming tape-positioning operations. Linear editing also takes its toll on the limited-life mechanical components of VTRs because of the need for constant fast-forward and rewind operations; rebuilding VTRs with worn components is extremely expensive.

Digital video technology offers *nonlinear* editing capability, which provides nearly instantaneous random access to digitized video source material. Nonlinear editing eliminates the need for frame-accurate VTRs and minimizes wear and tear on the VTR head and drives, as well as on your valuable source videotapes. Nonlinear editing is ideal for creating short movies for distribution on CD-ROMs. You also can "print to video" to record your digital production on videotape. Even if you don't have the computer horsepower or fixed-disk space to capture Motion-JPEG video at an 8:1 or lower compression ratio, you have another option: offline editing. Capture clips at 15 fps either with Motion-JPEG with a high compression ratio or with the Indeo YVU9C codec, and then create an offline edit decision list (EDL) for later online editing. You don't need to dub your source videotapes to protect them; therefore, you don't encounter generation loss or the timecode offset problems that result from dubbing with lower-cost VCRs that don't have a separate timecode connector. Many professional video editors use offline, nonlinear editing for experimentation because random access to video segments makes trial edits quick and easy.

Adobe Premiere is an inexpensive digital video capture and nonlinear editing and special-effects application that works with most video capture cards. Premiere is available for both Intel-based PCs and Macintosh computers. The 16-bit Premiere 4.0, which works quite well under Windows 95, clearly is the leading contender in the nonlinear editing software market. Most manufacturers of digital video capture boards bundle Premiere 1.1 or Premiere 4.0 LE (Limited Edition) with their products. Premiere 4.0 is compatible with all digital video capture, video overlay, and video output/genlock cards that have drivers adhering to Microsoft's published guidelines for Video for Windows 1.1+ capture and display drivers. Premiere offers many features, including a variety of digital special effects and the capability to overlay bitmapped images and titles on live video. The following sections look briefly at the use of Premiere 4.0 under Windows 95.

Capturing Digital Video with Premiere 4.0

The demise of Microsoft's VidCap and VidEdit applications resulted in a classic video-capture problem: neither the capture card manufacturer nor the capture and editing application's publisher explains how to use the products together. Premiere's *User's Guide* refers you to the capture card documentation, and both the Intel and the Creative Labs hardware manuals suggest referring to your video-editing application's instructions. In case you lack prior VidCap experience, the following sections explain how to set up and capture digital video with the ISVR Pro and Adobe Premiere under Windows 95. Whether you use Digital Video Producer with the ISVR Pro or use Premiere 1.1/4.0 with the Video Blaster RT300, the process is similar; the menu choices and appearance of the capture window and setup dialog boxes vary, but not significantly.

Setting Up to Capture with the Intel IUV9C Codec

Before capturing video with Adobe Premiere 4.0, you must set your capture options. Follow these steps to use the Intel YVU9 or YVU9C codec to capture 320 × 240 pixel images at 15 fps:

1. Install Adobe Premiere 1.1, 4.0, or 4.0 LE under Windows 95.
2. Install the ISVR Pro in an open ISA slot of your PC, following the Intel manual's instructions.
3. Connect a source of live video to either the composite or S-video input of the ISVR Pro, then install the ISVR Pro drivers from the accompanying disk. (You need a live video input to test the video input during the diagnostics process.) Click the Diagnostics button to verify the choices made by the ISVR Pro's Setup program and test the functions of the card. Reboot Windows 95, open Control Panel, double-click the ISVR Pro icon, and rerun the diagnostics to double-check that the card operates properly.
4. Connect the audio output from your live video source to the line input of your sound card. (For mono recording, use the left channel.)
5. Open Windows 95's Volume Control applet and set the Line-In and Volume Control audio levels to the mid-scale position. (You might have to readjust the audio levels after making a test capture.)
6. Install the YVU9C driver from the accompanying CD-ROM if you want to take advantage of YVU9C's lower data rate. (Run Setup from the YVU9C folder of the CD-ROM and restart Windows 95.)

7. Launch Adobe Premiere. In the New Project Presets dialog box, select Presentation - 320 X 240 from the Available Presets list box. Then click OK to close the window.

8. Choose File, Capture, Movie Capture to open the Movie Capture window. If you use the default composite video input of the ISVR Pro, your live video image, updated at about 2 fps, appears in the Movie Capture window's preview area. If your video source is connected to the S-video input of the ISVR Pro, the video image is black.

9. Choose Movie Capture to display the choices for setting your video and audio capture options (see fig. 35.19). Choose the Record Video and Record Audio choices as necessary to toggle the options. The adjacent check marks indicate that Adobe Premiere will capture video and audio.

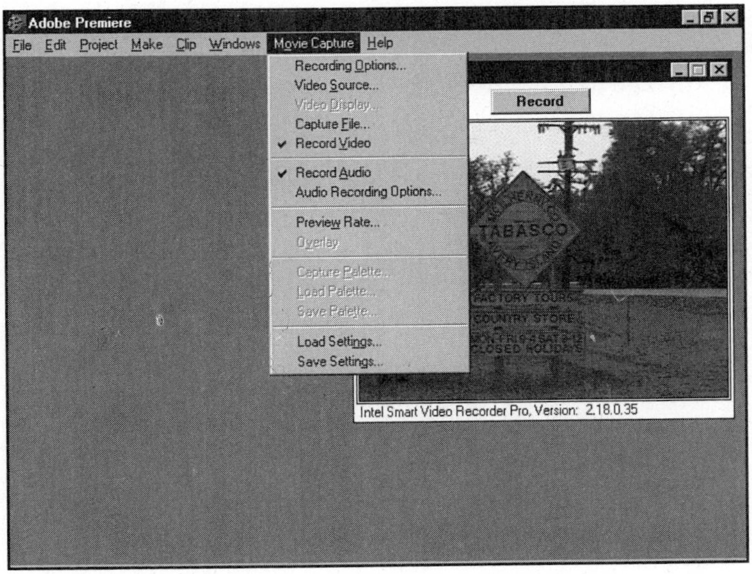

Fig. 35.19
Turning on video and audio capture in the Movie Capture menu. The adjacent check marks indicate that both video and audio capture are enabled.

10. If your live video source is connected to the S-video input, choose Movie Capture, Video Source to open the Video Source dialog box (see fig. 35.20). Select the S-Video (Y/C) option, then choose the Save button to set S-video as the default video input and close the dialog box. Your live S-video image appears in the preview area. (You can also use the Video Source dialog box to adjust the color in your video source material.)

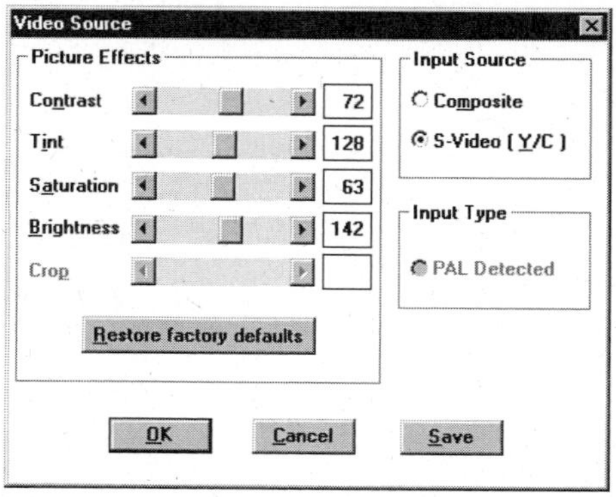

Fig. 35.20
Choosing the input connector of the ISVR Pro capture card. The Video Source dialog box also enables you to correct the color of your video clips.

11. Choose Movie Capture, Recording Options to open the Recording Options dialog box. The defaults—a capture rate of 15 fps and the reporting of dropped frames—are satisfactory for initial capture tests. (If you use the YVU9 codec, select the Capture Directly to Memory check box unless you have a fast fixed-disk drive.)

12. Click the Video Format button to open the Video Format dialog box. Select the video capture codec (YVU9C if you installed the "nearly lossless" codec) from the Video Compression Method drop-down list (see fig. 35.21). Select 320 X 240 from the Size drop-down list (if necessary), choose the Save as Default button, then choose OK to close the Video Format dialog box.

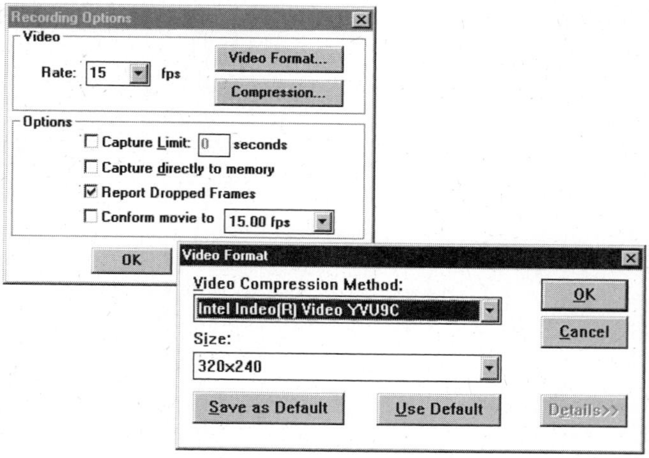

Fig. 35.21
Selecting the video capture codec and the image size.

13. Click the Compression button of the Recording Options dialog box to open the Video Compression dialog box. Verify that No Recompression appears in the Compressor drop-down list (see fig. 35.22). As noted earlier in this chapter, you should capture video clips that you want to edit later in YUV9 or YUV9C uncompressed format. Click OK to close the dialog box.

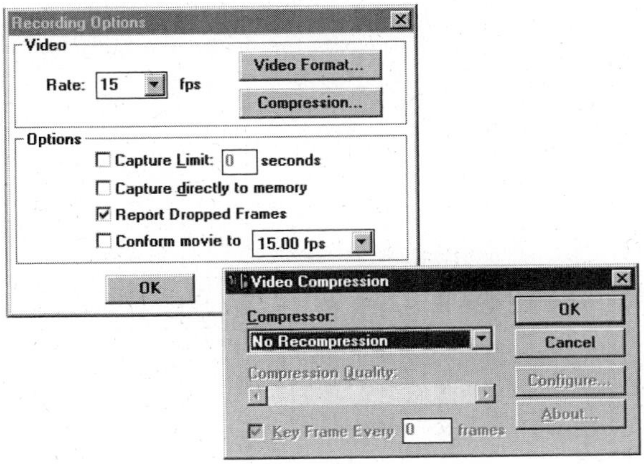

Fig. 35.22
Verifying the use of uncompressed video during the capture process.

14. Choose Movie Capture, Audio Recording Options to open the Audio Options dialog box. Select the audio capture format from the drop-down Format and Rate lists (see fig. 35.23). A format of 22-kHz, 16-bit mono is adequate for most video clips. Click OK to close the dialog box.

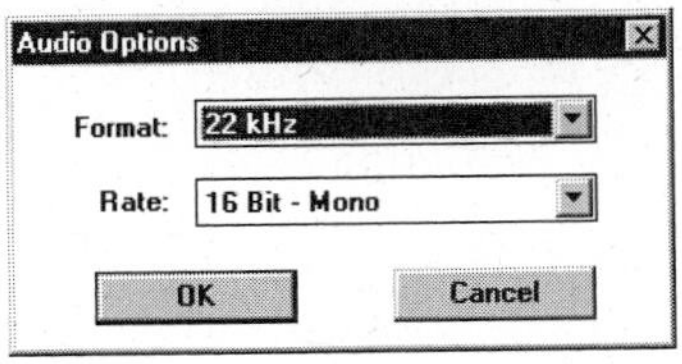

Fig. 35.23
Setting the audio capture format for your sound track.

Note

Motion-JPEG video capture and playback cards use the same capture methodology as the ISVR Pro. The primary differences are in the frame rate, which is 30 fps rather than 15 fps, and the image size settings; high-end (60 fields per second) Motion-JPEG cards capture full 640 (or 720) × 480 pixel images.

Troubleshooting

Windows 95 locks up when I run the ISVR Pro's diagnostics function so that I have to reboot.

The interrupt setting for the ISVR Pro conflicts with another card's interrupt or an interrupt used by a device built in to the motherboard. Choose another interrupt and retry the diagnostics function. (A conflict in an I/O base address results in failure to pass most diagnostic tests, but doesn't lock up Windows 95.)

Using Machine Control for Video Capture

Adobe Premiere 4.0 provides built-in support for several third-party VTR machine control systems, including Arti, VLAN, and MCI VCR (for Sony ViSCA and other MCI drivers that use the MCI *vcr* device type). If you have a VTR that supports timecode, Premiere's device control feature enables you to use timecode to set the in (start) and out (stop) points to capture a series of individual clips. Capturing a separate, trimmed clip for each segment of your movie saves disk space and makes subsequent editing easier.

Tip
Add a couple of seconds to the beginning and end of each clip to provide for transitions, unless you plan to use cuts-only editing.

To use Windows 95's new ViSCA driver with Adobe Premiere, follow these steps:

1. Choose File, Preferences, Device Control to open the Device Control Preferences dialog box.

2. Select MCI VCR from the Device drop-down list, then click the Device Options button to open the ViSCA Device Options dialog box (see fig. 35.24). Premiere polls the ViSCA connection to determine the number and type of devices in the chain. (Premiere 4.0 recognizes the Sony CVD-1000 Vdeck and Sony CI-1000 Vbox as ViSCA devices. The XV-D1000 SEG appears as a CVD-1000.)

3. If you have more than one ViSCA device in the chain, select the source video device for capture from the ViSCA Device drop-down list, and then click the OK button to close the ViSCA Device Options dialog box.

4. Click the OK button of the Device Control Preferences dialog box, and then close the Movie Capture window to return to Premiere's main window.

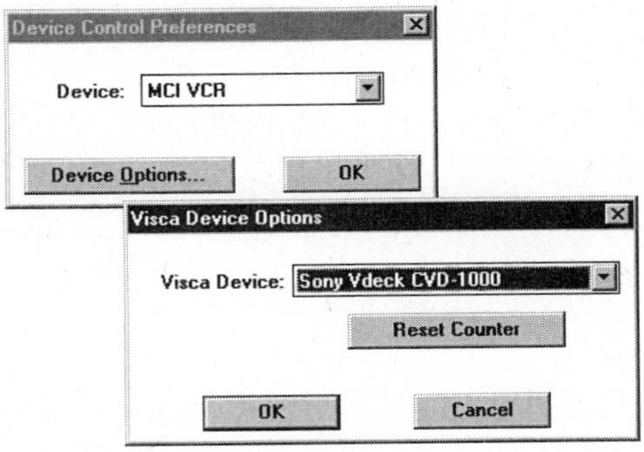

Fig. 35.24
Selecting the ViSCA device to serve as the video and audio source for capture.

Troubleshooting

The ViSCA devices don't appear in the ViSCA Device list in the order of their location in my ViSCA daisy-chain, so I can't tell which device to select for capture.

This is a known problem with the ViSCA driver included with Windows 95, not with the ViSCA device control protocol itself. (The same problem occurs under Windows 3.1+.) The simplest work-around is to connect only the source Vdeck or the Vbox controlling the source deck with the ViSCA serial cable. Click the Reset Counter button in the ViSCA Device Options dialog box to repoll the ViSCA connection so that only one device appears in the ViSCA Device list.

Like Adobe Photoshop, Premiere 4.0 is extensible through the use of Adobe and third-party *addins*. Addins are special Windows applications, stored in the \PREMIERE\ADDINS folder, that take advantage of documented "hooks" into Adobe software. When you launch Premiere, all the addins in the folder automatically are attached to Premiere. Abbate Video, Inc. (Millis, MA) publishes the Video Toolkit (VTK) addin for both the Windows and Macintosh versions of Premiere 4.0. VTK consists of a set of drivers for a remarkable variety of professional (RS-422-A), industrial (RS-232-C), and prosumer (ViSCA, LANC, and Panasonic five-pin) device control protocols. Abbate supplies the appropriate PC serial cable with the VTK for your choice of protocol. (You can order additional cables to support more than one protocol.) Figure 35.25 shows the VTK Setup dialog box for the VTK PlugIn device, displaying in the VCR Family list box just a few of the device control protocols that the VTK addin supports.

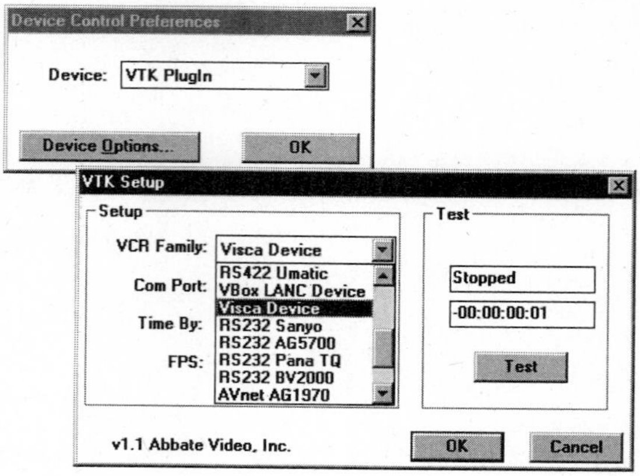

Fig. 35.25
Selecting a device control protocol with Abbate Video's Video Toolkit (VTK) Setup dialog box.

In mid-1995, Abbate Video introduced its new AV/net video device control network. AV/net consists of a connector that plugs into a serial port of your PC and has an RJ-11 (modular telephone) jack at the back. Individual AV/net devices are small, plastic boxes with RJ-11 input and output jacks and a cable that connects to RS-422-A, RS-232-C, Control-L (LANC), Control-M (Panasonic five-pin), and other popular device control interfaces. Abbate even offers an AV/net device with an infrared wand for controlling consumer electronic devices, including low-end VCRs. You interconnect the AV/net boxes with conventional modular telephone cables in a daisy-chain similar to the ViSCA approach. AV/net components are inexpensive and support virtually any collection of VTRs from a single serial port.

Capturing a Test Video Clip

After specifying your capture options and setting up your machine control device, you're ready to capture live video and audio-for-video directly to disk. The following steps describe how to record a video clip with timecode-based machine control:

1. Open the Movie Capture window, which now has expanded to provide additional control objects, as shown in figure 35.26. (Compare fig. 35.26 with the Movie Capture window shown in fig. 35.19.)

2. Click the Reel button to enter in an input box the name of the source videotape. Then click OK to continue.

3. Select the Auto Record check box to use machine control and timecode to automate the capture process.

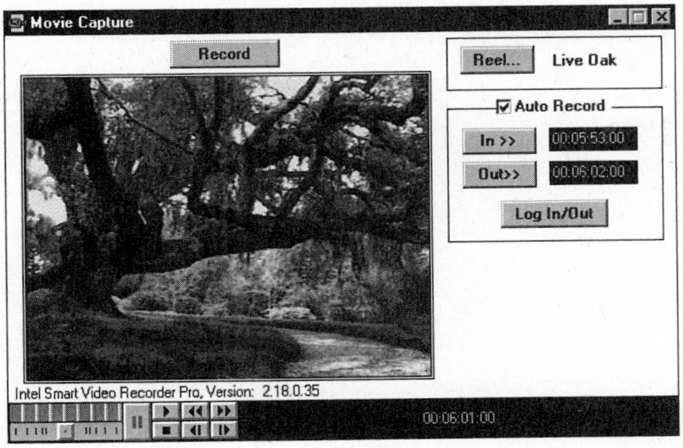

Fig. 35.26 Setting In and Out points to capture a video clip in Premiere 4.0's Auto Record mode.

4. If you know the clip's exact in and out points, you can click the In and Out buttons and then enter the timecode values in the In and Out text boxes using the format *HH*:*MM*:*SS*:*FF*. Otherwise, use the VCR controls at the bottom of the Movie Capture window to position the tape at the In point. Click the In button to transfer the start timecode to the text box, then position the tape to the Out point and click the Out button.

5. Click the Record button to start the Auto Record capture process to a temporary file named TEMP#.AVI, where # is a sequential integer that Premiere automatically assigns. When the capture process completes, a message box appears to indicate the number of frames, if any, dropped during capture. Click OK to close the message box and display the first frame of the clip in the Clip window, as shown in figure 35.27.

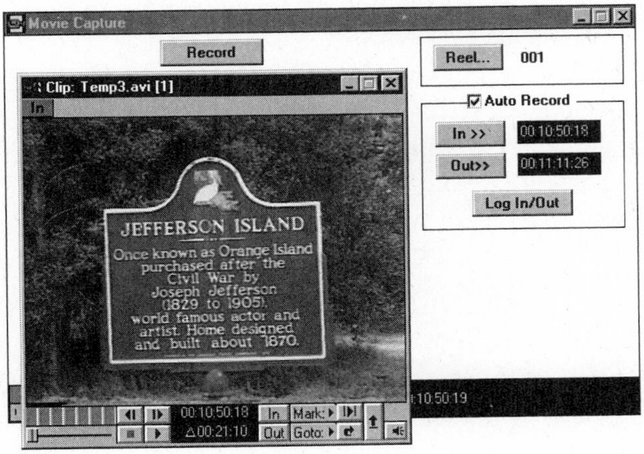

Fig. 35.27 Viewing the captured video file in Premiere's Clip window.

6. Use the VCR controls at the bottom of the Clip window to audition your clip. The sound track plays through the Speaker Out or Line Out of your sound card. Verify that the audio level is correct during playback; if not, use the Volume Control applet to alter the level as necessary.

7. Close the Clip window to open the File Save dialog box. If your clip is what you want and you didn't drop more than one percent of the frames during capture or have problems with the audio level, save your clip with a conventional DOS file name and an AVI extension. Otherwise, don't save the file but instead repeat steps 5 and 6. Recapturing the same clip usually eliminates the dropped frames.

8. Repeat steps 4 through 6 for each clip that makes up your movie.

Troubleshooting

No matter how many times I retry capturing a clip, I get a message indicating more than five percent of the frames were dropped.

Make sure that the disk volume in which your Windows swap file and in which Premiere TEMP#.AVI files are located is not compressed. The most common cause of dropped frames on uncompressed disk volumes is disk fragmentation. Use Windows 95's disk defragmenter regularly to ensure optimum disk-write performance. If defragmentation doesn't solve your dropped-frame problem and you have a network adapter card installed, temporarily remove all network drivers.

Assembling Your Videoclips on the Timeline

Nonlinear editing applications use a timeline rather than an edit decision list to specify the in and out points of each clip used in the movie. Picons identify each clip and its duration on the timeline, with longer clips represented by picons taken from beginning, intermediate, and ending frames. You can expand the timeline's time scale to make your edits more precise or contract the time scale to see an overall view of your movie. To provide A/B roll-editing capability with digital special effects at the transition between clips, Premiere provides A and B timeline tracks, separated by a transition (T) track. Premiere defines a movie by a project (PPJ) file that includes pointers (references) to each of the objects that make up the movie; the default project file is NONAME1.PPJ.

Adobe Premiere 4.0 is a full-featured application for digital video editing that offers a wide variety of editing options. A full explanation of editing with Premiere is beyond the scope of this book, so this chapter provides only a short explanation of the editing process. To assemble your clips into a movie, follow these basic steps:

1. Choose File, Import, File to open the Import File dialog box. Select one of the video clips captured for your movie, then click the OK button to add the clip to the Project window.

2. Repeat step 1 for each of the video clips that comprise your movie.

3. Drag the picon for the first video clip from the Project window to the A timeline of the Construction Window (see fig. 35.28).

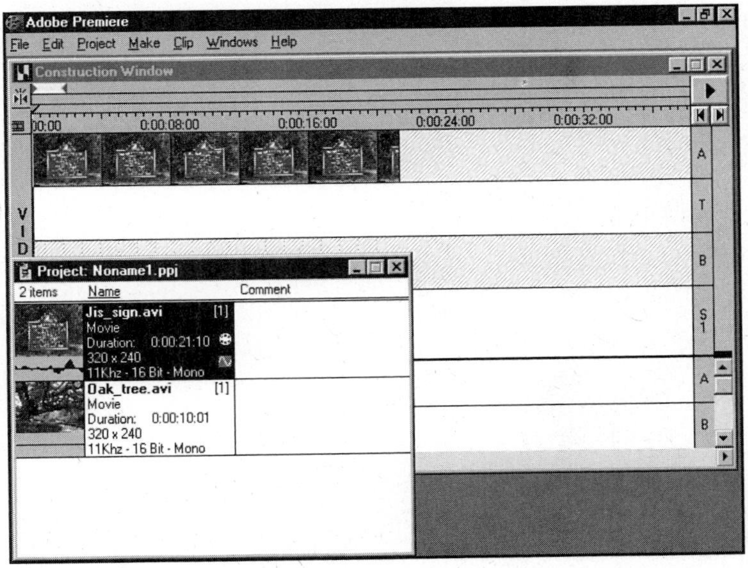

Fig. 35.28
Adding clips from the Project window to the timeline of the Construction Window.

4. Drag the picon for the second video clip from the Project window to the B timeline of the Construction Window.

5. If you want to add effects for the transition between the first and second clip, offset the in point of the second clip to the left of the out point of the first clip.

6. Repeat steps 3 through 5 for each of the clips in sequence, alternating between the A and B timelines.

7. With the focus on the Construction Window, choose Project, Preview and save your project with an appropriate DOS file name and PPJ extension. After you save the file, Premiere assembles the preview and displays your edited movie in the Preview window.

Adding Titles and Digital Special Effects

Tip
Keep the time of superimposed titles and transition effects to a minimum; both take a long time to compile.

Adobe includes a title design and editing feature that takes advantage of all TrueType and Adobe Type 1 fonts installed on your PC. Figure 35.29 shows a simple title with a transparent (white) background to be superimposed on live video at the beginning of the movie. After creating the title, you save it as a file with the PTL extension and add the title file to the Project window. Drag the title to the Superimpose (S1) timeline and adjust the width of the title picon to correspond to the length of time of its appearance (see fig. 35.30).

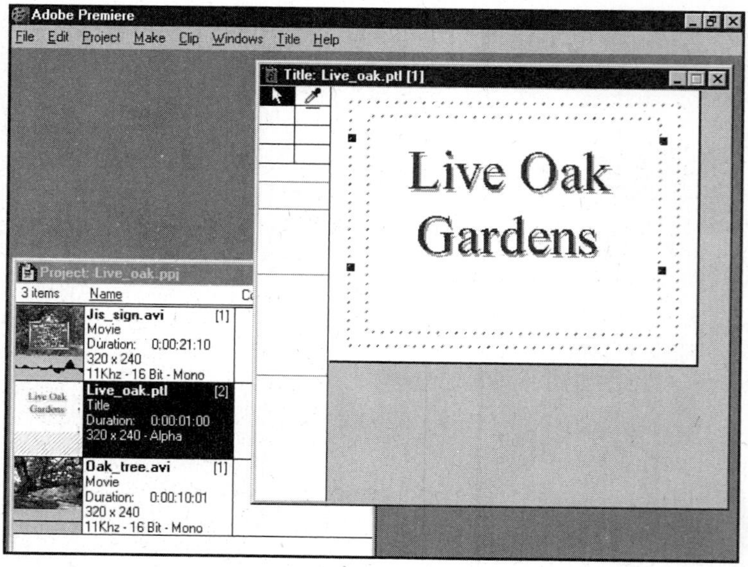

Fig. 35.29
Creating a title with a transparent background for superimposition over live video.

You also can add a variety of digital special effects (DSEs) for transitions between your clips that alternate on the A and B timelines of the Construction Window. You drag the icon for the effect that you want from the Transitions window to the Transitions (T) timeline, as shown in figure 35.30. You can preview the superimposed title and special effects at any time during the editing process. Premiere must compile each of the superimposed titles and special effects before creating a preview or compressing the final movie. Each time that you change any of the timeline's items, expect a substantial wait for the recompilation process to complete.

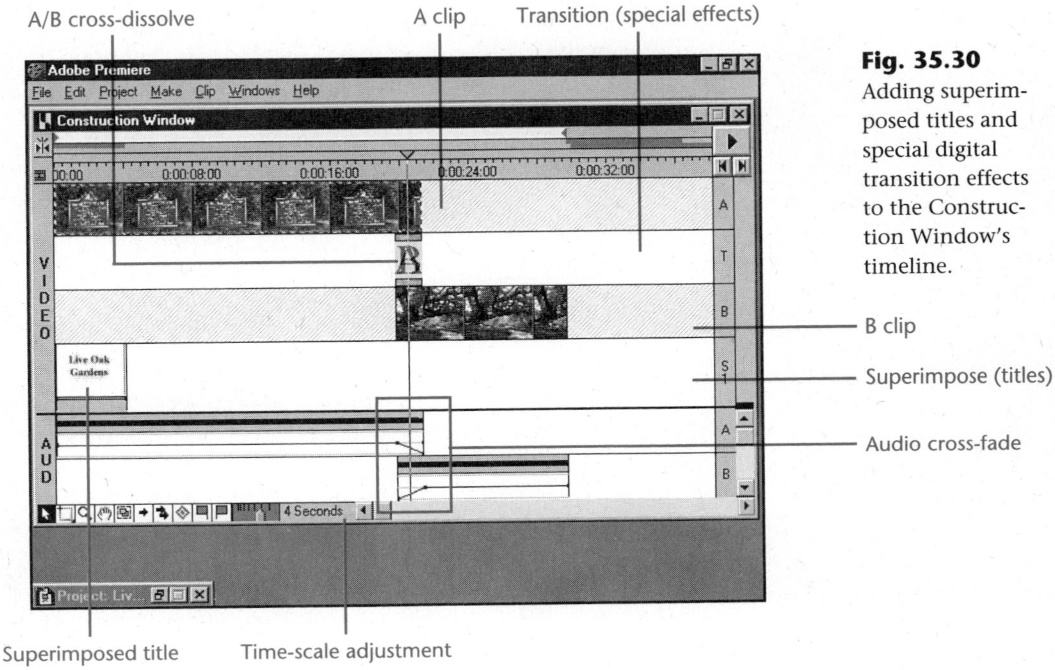

Fig. 35.30 Adding superimposed titles and special digital transition effects to the Construction Window's timeline.

Compressing Your Movie or Printing Digital Video to Tape

After you complete the nonlinear editing process, you have two options for completing your movie:

- Compression to an AVI file with a data rate suitable for distribution on CD-ROM
- Printing a full-screen image to videotape

To compress the movie for CD-ROM distribution, follow these steps:

1. Drag the right arrow of the yellow line at the top of the Construction Window to the end of your last clip or a title that defines the movie work area.
2. Select a clip in the Project window and press Ctrl+C to copy the still image to the Clipboard.
3. Choose Make, Make Movie to open the Make Movie dialog box with Premiere's default compression settings specified (see fig. 35.31). Enter the DOS file name for your compressed movie file with an AVI extension.

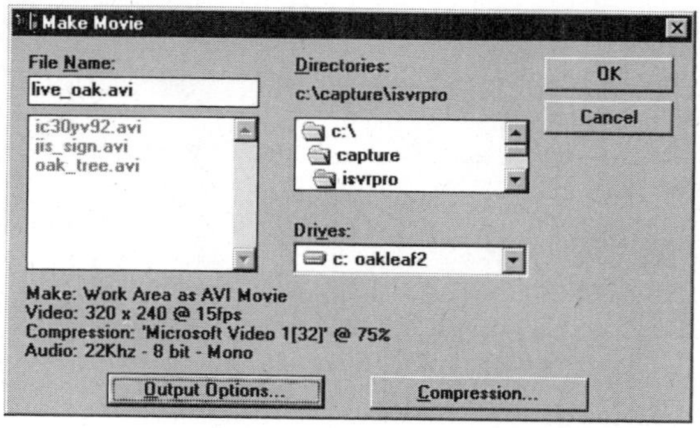

Fig. 35.31 Specifying the file name for the compressed movie.

4. Choose the Output Options button to open the Project Output Options dialog box (see fig. 35.32). In this dialog box, you define the movie's video and audio options. Accept the video options and set the audio options to the sound format that you want. Click OK to close the Project Output Options dialog box.

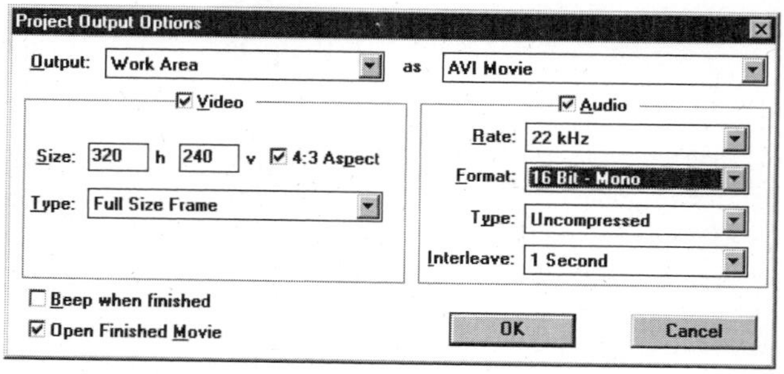

Fig. 35.32 Setting the video and audio output options.

5. Choose the Compression button in the Make Movie dialog box to open the Compression Settings dialog box (see fig. 35.33). Select the compression codec from the Method drop-down list. The video clip that you copied to the Clipboard in step 2 appears in the Sample frame; move the Quality slider to see the effect of varying quality percentages, then set the quality at the High limit.

6. Set the frame rate (usually 15 fps for CD-ROMs) and the key frame ratio. For movies with relatively low motion content, such as talking heads, a key frame every 15 frames is usually adequate. For higher motion videos, use a key frame every four to seven frames. Using fewer key frames allows a lower interframe compression ratio at a constant data rate.

7. Select the Limit Data Rate check box and enter the maximum data rate; 200K/s is a safe starting rate for double-speed CD-ROM drives. Select the

CD-ROM check box to create full 2K blocks (sectors) on the CD-ROM, a process called *data padding*.

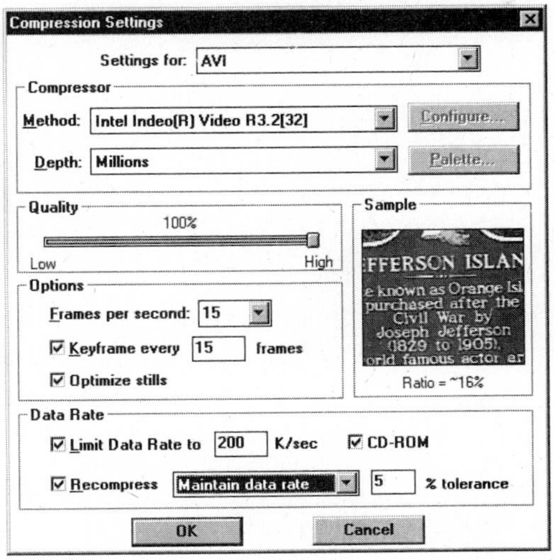

Fig. 35.33
Setting the compression options for a movie to be distributed on CD-ROM.

8. Select the Recompress check box and choose Maintain Data Rate from the drop-down list. Enter the % Tolerance value for the data rate. You can set up to 40-percent tolerance at 200 K/s, which limits the peak data rate to about 280 K/s. The rate is within the range of a double-speed CD-ROM drive's 300 K/s maximum data rate.

9. Click OK to close the Compression Settings dialog box. Click the OK button of the Make Movie dialog box to begin the compression process. Premiere estimates the time required to compress the movie, which depends primarily on the movie's length, your computer's speed, and the compression settings that you choose. A ratio of one minute of compression time for five seconds of work area is common for Pentium PCs with fast fixed-disk drives.

10. When Premiere finishes compiling your compressed movie, the resulting file opens in the Clip window automatically. Use the VCR controls to review the effect of compression on the video quality.

11. To verify that Premiere maintained the data rate and your other compression settings, open the Clip window's Control menu and choose Movie Analysis to open the Analysis dialog box. Click the Data Rate button in the Analysis dialog box to display a graph of the data rate for the entire movie (see fig. 35.34).

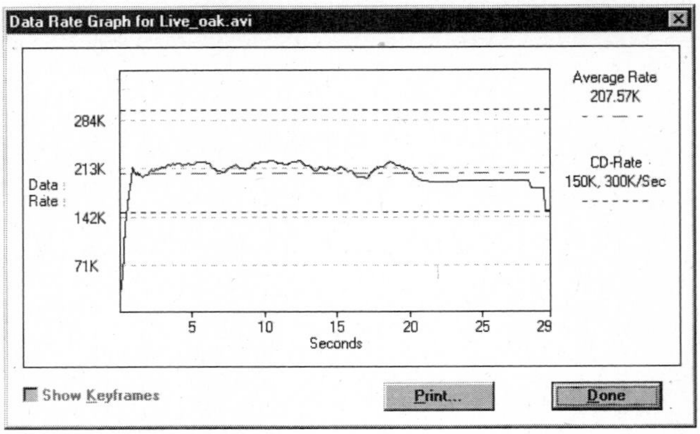

Fig. 35.34
A data rate graph generated by Adobe Premiere.

Troubleshooting

My compressed clips have "fuzzy" areas in them.

Out-of-focus image regions are called *compression artifacts*. All video compression codecs have problems dealing with image regions that contain high-frequency content (small objects in the background, such as leaves on trees). Motion also degrades images compressed at low data rates. You need very high-quality source video to create an acceptable-quality movie at CD-ROM data rates. When shooting video with a camcorder, always use a tripod and turn off both the autofocus and automatic white-balance features. If your camcorder has automatic image stabilization, turn off that feature as well.

To print a movie to videotape, you need a video output card or box (encoder) that converts the RGB (red-green-blue) signals output by your graphics adapter card to the standard NTSC (or PAL in Europe) video signal for recording. You also must connect the Speaker or Line Output of your sound card to the record deck's audio inputs. The following are the basic steps for printing a movie to videotape:

1. After final editing, compile the movie without compression (in the Compression Settings dialog box's Compressor frame, select None from the Method list).

2. With the movie in the Clip window, choose File, Export, Print to Video. The Print to Video dialog box appears.

3. Mark the Full Screen check box to expand the 1/4-screen video image to the full display area. You also can add a specified period of color bars followed by black.

4. Click the OK button and start the record deck.

Printing to video 1/4-screen images captured with the ISVR Pro or Video Blaster RT300 results in sub-VHS quality movie videotapes, but you can have a lot of fun learning the ropes of nonlinear digital video editing with a camcorder, a $400 video capture card, and Adobe Premiere 4.0. If you want to create S-VHS/Hi8 or better-quality edit master tapes, you need a high-end video capture and playback card that uses Motion-JPEG compression and, as noted earlier in this chapter, a fast PC with a large, fast fixed-disk drive.❖

Part VIII

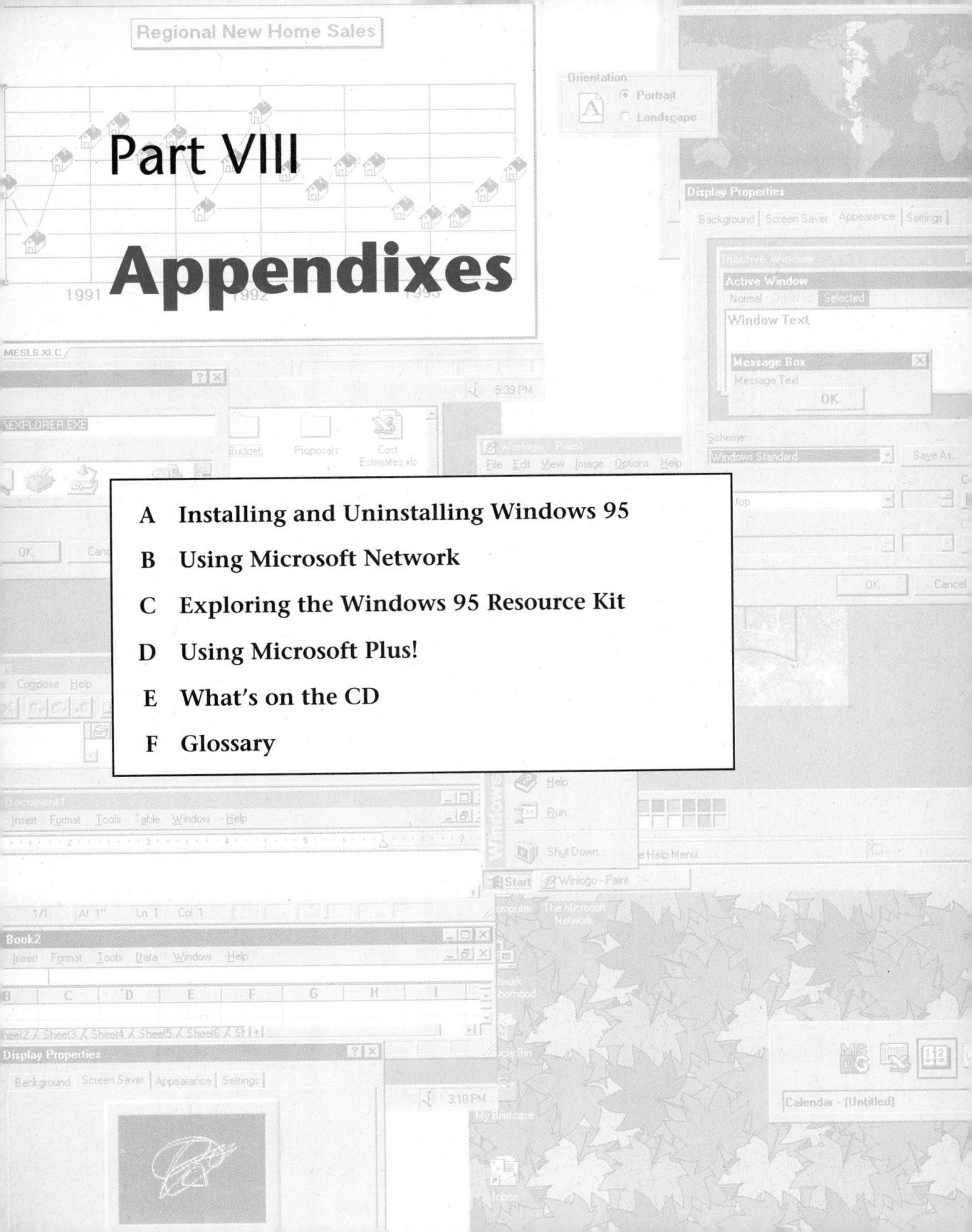

Appendixes

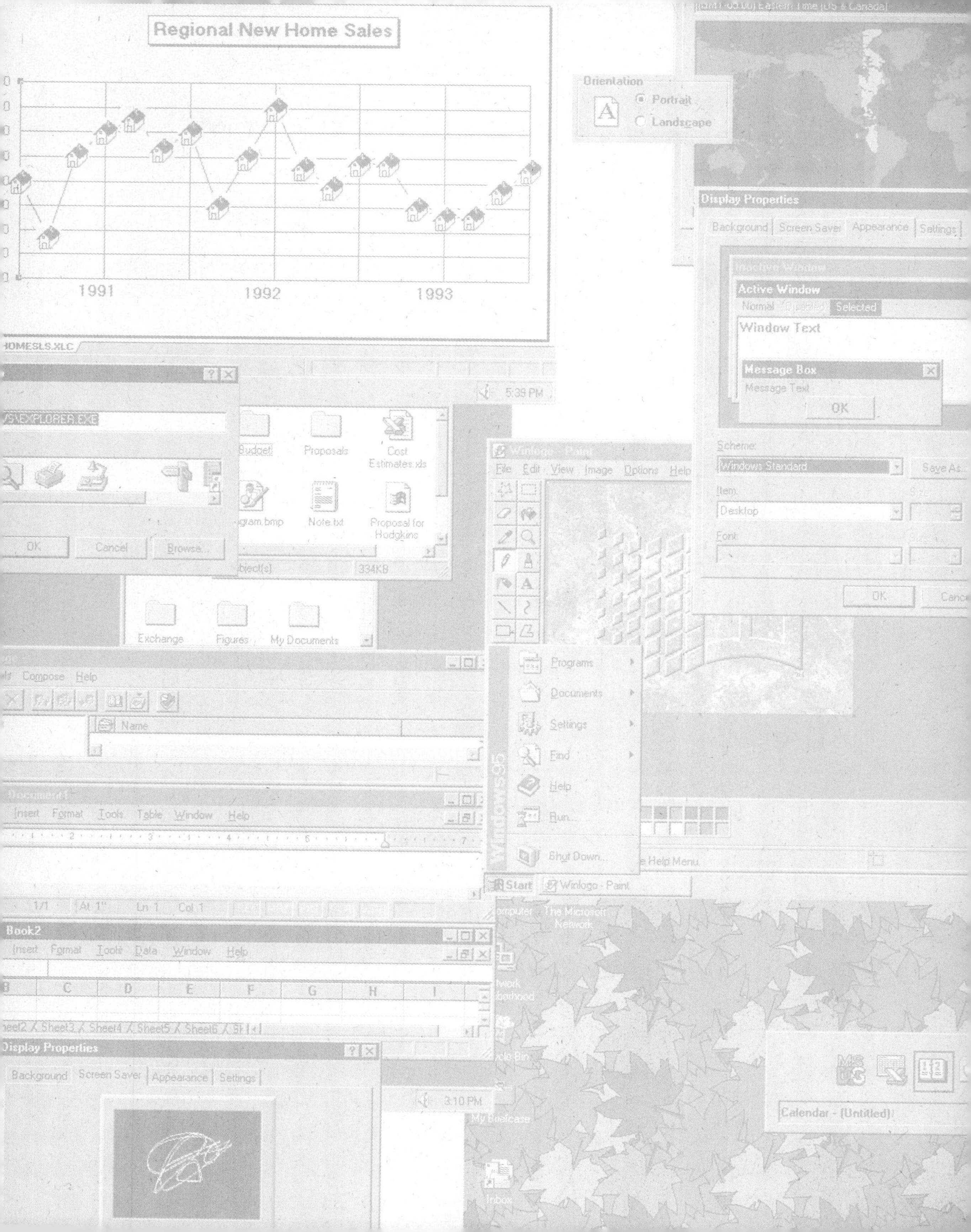
Regional New Home Sales
1991
1992
1993
HOMESLS.XLC
Orientation
Portrait
Landscape
Display Properties
Background
Screen Saver
Appearance
Settings
Inactive Window
Active Window
Normal
Disabled
Selected
Window Text
Message Box
Message Text
OK
Scheme:
Windows Standard
Save As...
Item:
Desktop
Size:
Font:
OK
Cancel
5:39 PM
EXPLORER.EXE
OK
Cancel
Browse...
Budget
Proposals
Cost Estimates.xls
Note.txt
Proposal for Hodgkins
334KB
Exchange
Figures
My Documents
Winlogo - Paint
File
Edit
View
Image
Options
Help
Programs
Documents
Settings
Find
Help
Run...
Shut Down...
Windows 95
Start
Winlogo - Paint
Compose
Help
Name
Document1
Insert
Format
Tools
Table
Window
Help
At 1"
Ln 1
Col 1
Book2
Insert
Format
Tools
Data
Window
Help
B
C
D
E
F
G
H
I
The Microsoft Network
Display Properties
Background
Screen Saver
Appearance
Settings
3:10 PM
My Briefcase
Inbox
Calendar - (Untitled)

Appendix A

Installing and Uninstalling Windows 95

by Dick Cravens

Everyone knows the old saying about first impressions. Setup is the first exposure you'll have to Windows 95, and it will positively affect your opinion of the newest addition to the Windows product family. Microsoft has completely rewritten Setup for Windows 95, adding significant capabilities and stability to the program. You'll be amazed at the depth of Setup's capabilities as it automatically detects and configures hardware and software that literally brought earlier versions of the program to their knees. This appendix explains the basics of installing Windows 95 for the first time. Specifically, you learn about

- Windows 95 system requirements
- Improvements in Windows 95 Setup
- How Windows 95 Setup works: four basic phases
- Using Windows 95 Setup for a typical installation
- Advanced installation techniques
- Configuring for dual-boot operation
- Removing Windows 95

Understanding Windows 95 Setup Requirements

Before you begin to install Windows 95, be sure that your system meets the minimum system requirements. To run Windows 95, you need a system that includes the following:

- A 80386 or later processor (25 MHz or faster) minimum (use at least a 486/33 for serious multitasking)
- A Microsoft- or Logitech-compatible mouse (if you have another type of mouse, be sure to have the drivers for it handy when you begin installation)
- A high-density (1.44M) 3.5-inch floppy drive or CD-ROM drive
- 4M of RAM (8M recommended, 16M preferred)
- VGA graphics video display (Super VGA recommended)
- Microsoft Windows 3.0 or later (including Windows for Workgroups) if you're installing the upgrade version of Windows 95 (the full, non-upgrade version of Windows 95 doesn't require a previous installation of Windows)
- 417K free conventional memory
- 25M to 40M of free hard drive storage space (depending upon your upgrade path and installation options) partitioned with the FAT file system
- Up to 14M of additional free hard drive storage space for the Windows 95 swap file (depending upon the amount of RAM installed on your system)

Windows 95 comes in two versions. The first is an upgrade-only product, which means you must have a previous version of MS-DOS or Windows to install Windows 95. Because Windows 3.x requires MS-DOS, most users will have both. This version is available on CD-ROM and floppy disks.

The other version is a full Windows 95 setup. This doesn't require a previous version of Windows. This is designed mostly for new computers. Most existing PCs that are capable of running Windows 95 have Windows 3.1 installed so they can use the upgrade version of 95. The upgrade version costs about half of what the full version does.

While Windows 95 will certainly install on a 386 computer with 4M of RAM, you won't be able to do a lot with it. To experience the full performance potential of the new Windows, you really need at least 8M of memory. Processor speed is certainly important, but if you have an older 386 system, you may be better off adding additional RAM, or upgrading to a faster hard drive or video system before you splurge on a 486 or Pentium. Processors are usually bottlenecked by one or more of these subsystems. Lack of RAM causes Windows to swap portions of its own code, but mostly application code, to the hard drive. Quick drive access is thus critical to Windows performance, but the fastest hard drive will appear slow if your display takes seconds to paint.

On the other hand, if you're looking at adding significant amounts of memory, plus replacing *both* your drive and video subsystems, it may pay to check out a complete new computer, with the faster CPU. Check with your hardware vendor and review your options.

Note

Windows 95 works with the major drive compression utilities on the market:

- Microsoft DriveSpace and DoubleSpace
- Stacker versions 3.x and 4.x
- Addstor SuperStor

Other compression software may work fine, but it's best to check with the vendor to confirm this prior to installation.

Also, be aware that disk compression may affect the estimate of free drive space available for installation. If you're using compression, be cautious about trusting space estimates. Compression yield depends upon many factors, including data types, so allow extra space if you're installing on a compressed drive.

Improvements in Windows Setup

Microsoft has worked hard to strengthen the Setup program for Windows 95. Among the major improvements:

- New modular architecture for greater customization and flexibility
- Vastly improved hardware detection and configuration accuracy
- Smart recovery modes for problem installations

- Automatic verification of installed components, with correction and replacement of corrupted files or components
- Completely graphical-based installation
- Support for automated installation
- Integrated network installation

Windows 95 is a complete operating system for your PC. As such, it is responsible for installing and integrating the disk operating system, the graphical user interface, and all network support. In addition, it provides support for an incredible number of peripheral devices including monitors, video systems, sound cards, scanners, removable drive media, and modems. While Windows 95 Setup is not perfect, you will be impressed by the simplicity and thoroughness of the new installation approach, the burdens it lifts from the average user, and the backwards-compatibility it provides for older peripheral systems and legacy applications.

Preparing for Windows 95 Setup

While Windows 95 Setup does an amazing job configuring most systems, there are some useful tips and tricks for preparing your machine for installation that will save you time and trouble. Before you begin your installation, be sure to do the following:

- Confirm your system meets the minimum Windows 95 hardware and software requirements
- Confirm the boot drive sequence for your system
- Confirm that you have a working boot floppy disk for your current operating system configuration
- Back up your critical data and system configuration files (a complete system backup is preferred)
- Confirm that your current Windows installation is in the best possible working order
- Defragment your hard drive(s)
- Know the location of all required drivers for any peripherals (including network interface cards)
- Know all user names and passwords you'll need to log in to your network

While this list may seem to suggest a lack of confidence in the Windows 95 Setup program, don't be cynical. You should follow most of these procedures for any major change in your computing system. Anything less is simply flirting with the computing demons well-known to the experienced PC user.

Note

While it's usually wise to make backup copies of the installation disks for a new program before you begin, you can forget about it with Windows 95. Microsoft uses a proprietary disk format for Windows 95 floppies that neither MS-DOS nor Windows 3.x can duplicate. Take care of your original disks!

The first item in this list is obvious. Less clear is the need to have a confirmed boot backup plan for your system. This comes in two parts: having a boot floppy disk and configuring your system to use it. A good boot disk is not just a bootable floppy but one that configures your system as closely as possible to the current boot session configurations you normally use via your hard drive. It's worth the time it takes to create this "boot backup." The few minutes to do this can save you hours of hair-pulling later.

A great boot disk is worthless if your system can't read it. Most systems are configured to search the drives during startup to find a bootable disk, but some are configured to look only at a specific drive, to save time at startup, or for security reasons. If in doubt about your system, *test it.* If you create a boot disk and the system won't read it from a cold start, check the system CMOS settings and correct the boot sequence (see your computer's manual regarding access to the CMOS setup). The ideal is for the system to search drive A and then continue to the next floppy (if present) before looking for startup information on drive C. While you can configure a system for a reverse of this order (C, then A), some systems will fail by looking at C and then staring off into digital space. Check yours to make sure it's set to search A first, before you learn the hard way.

While having a system backup is obvious to experienced users, the new and the brave may blithely go forth without such safety nets. Don't be computing roadkill. If you don't have a backup plan or system, get one before you invest hours of valuable time configuring your system, and before you lose hours of work due to a power failure or drive crash. This is especially true when installing a new operating system, which involves changes to the configuration of almost every component of your computer, including the storage media systems. Much effort has gone into making today's operating systems and hardware as reliable as is affordably possible, but *nothing* can prevent *all* accidents. (Do you have children, pets, or coworkers? Elbows, coffee cups, sleepy fingers?)

Don't expect miracles from the Setup program. If you slapped a sound card in your machine four months ago and never bothered to configure it correctly, how can you expect Windows 95 to do so? If your Windows 3.1x system is working, Windows 95 can use those previous settings to confirm your peripheral configurations. If those settings are incorrect, Windows 95 has no real choice but to try them and fail. Even if your current installation and peripherals are working perfectly, be sure to have your device driver floppy disks handy in case Windows 95 Setup needs to refer to them during installation (especially if you're setting up a dual-boot system).

Defragmenting your hard drive prior to installation insures that Windows 95 will find enough contiguous drive space to create the swap files it needs for virtual memory support. Defragmentation also makes your system run faster (especially during file copy sessions) since the drive system doesn't have to search frantically for free drive clusters.

Backing Up Your Critical Files

A complete system backup is part of the most ideal preparation for any system change. If you don't have the facility for a full backup, then consider backing up your critical operating system data as a minimum preparation. These are the recommended files:

- CONFIG.SYS and AUTOEXEC.BAT (located in the root directory of your boot drive, usually C)
- Any files listed in CONFIG.SYS and AUTOEXEC.BAT
- Any network configuration files (include any login scripts) such as CFG, INI, or DAT files in your network driver or root directory
- Your complete DOS directory
- Any initialization (INI) files for Windows applications
- Any Program Information Files (PIF) for MS-DOS applications
- Registry data files (DAT) in your Windows directory
- Password files (PWL) in your Windows directory

Tip
You can search painlessly by using the recursion function of the MS-DOS `dir` command (**dir c:*.ini /s** will search your entire C drive for initialization files).

While most INI and PIF files reside in the Windows directory, some applications store them in their own directory. Be sure to search all the nooks and crannies of your system. (You can save hours of reconfiguration pain if the worst should occur.)

Or you can skip the search step and copy all the desired files using the recursion switch for the `xcopy` command. For example, the **`xcopy c:\*.pif /s a:`**

command copies all PIF files on drive C to your A drive in one fell swoop, complete with a directory structure if you need to re-create it later.

If you routinely use a backup utility, you may want to simply rely upon your last backup prior to installation, or make a new one for just the file types mentioned here. Consult your backup software documentation for more information on how to accomplish this.

How Windows 95 Setup Works

Before you begin to install Windows 95, it's probably a good idea to know what to expect and when to expect it. Windows 95 Setup has four basic phases:

- Detection
- Question and answer
- File copy
- Startup

Phase One: Setup Detection—Software, then Hardware

Windows 95 Setup starts by detecting what environment it was started from. If you opt to install from within a running Windows 3.1x installation, Setup skips a few steps and gets straight down to the business of analyzing your hardware. If you don't have Windows installed, or choose to start from the MS-DOS prompt, Setup first copies and executes a "mini-window" that runs the remainder of the Setup program and then moves on to hardware detection.

Setup checks your system for the following:

- Installed hardware devices
- Connected peripherals
- IRQs, I/O, and DMA addresses available
- IRQs, I/O, and DMA addresses in use

Don't be surprised if the hardware detection phase takes a few minutes. Windows 95 Setup uses a variety of techniques to perform this hardware query.

Most PCs respond well to this procedure, which results in the creation of a hardware tree in the Registry. Older PCs may represent a problem if the devices are not industry-standard for IRQs or I/O addresses; newer machines with Plug and Play technology report their configurations more quickly, fully, and accurately.

Phase Two: Providing Additional Information

Once Setup has the basic information regarding your hardware, it knows most of what it needs to install Windows on your system. However, there are still a few details to complete, and you also can exercise options regarding exactly which Windows components you want to install. Setup guides you through this process with a few clear dialog boxes. You'll look at these options in more detail when you install Windows later in this chapter.

Phase Three: Copy Chores

Unlike Windows 3.1, Windows 95 Setup asks most questions up front and lets you relax during the actual installation process. Once you tell it what you want, it completes the dreary chores by itself, asking only for disk changes (and if you are installing from a CD-ROM drive, you don't even have to worry about that!).

When all Windows 95 files are copied, Setup upgrades the existing version of MS-DOS on your boot drive with the Windows 95 operating system.

Phase Four: Home Stretch—System Startup

When it has replaced the MS-DOS operating system, Setup then restarts your system and finishes the final cleanup chores required for installation. When this is finished, you're ready to roll with Windows 95.

Using Windows 95 Setup

Now that you have an overview of the basic logic and operation of Windows 95 Setup and some tips for how to prepare your system, you can get down to the nitty-gritty of an actual installation.

This section begins by showing you two primary ways to install Windows 95:

- Installing from a working Windows 3.1x system
- Installing from an MS-DOS-only system (or Windows 3.0, Windows NT, and OS/2)

How do you know which way to install Windows 95? If at all possible, run Setup from within a working installation of Windows 3.1x or later (this includes all versions of Windows for Workgroups). Started this way, Setup can use your existing Windows installation for information on how best to configure your system.

If Windows is not on your computer, Setup installs a "mini-window" to run from. If you're running Windows NT, you need to return your system to MS-DOS (via NT's dual-boot option) before starting Windows 95 Setup. The same is true if you're running OS/2 or Windows 3.0.

If your computer system is completely new and has no operating system installed, or does not have at least Windows 3.0, be sure you have the non-upgrade version of Windows 95. Otherwise, you'll be up the creek, since the standard upgrade version requires a previous version of Windows, or at least earlier Windows disks, to operate.

The question of when to install a dual-boot system is inherently problematic. There are many variables involved, but you can boil it down to a simple question: Am I truly prepared to kiss my current Windows installation good-bye? If you're installing Windows 95 for the first time, you may want to keep your previous installation intact until you've proven Windows 95 is compatible with all of your applications and peripherals. If you do opt for the "dual-Windows" approach, be prepared for some serious impact on your disk space reserves, and be prepared to mentally juggle when you switch from version to version. No matter which approach you choose, *make a backup before you begin.*

► See "Setting Up a Dual-Boot System," p. 1105

Installing Windows 95 from Windows 3.x

You can run Windows 95 Setup from any installation of Windows 3.1 or later. If you don't have at least version 3.1, then skip to the section covering MS-DOS installations, later in this chapter.

► See "Installing Windows 95 from MS-DOS," p. 1097

Starting Windows 95 Setup is just like running any other Windows Setup program. If you haven't already, start your current version of Windows. Once it's running, you have a couple of choices of how to start Setup—from the Program Manager or File Manager.

Before you go further, make sure you have the installation disk set or CD-ROM in the appropriate drive. These examples assume you are using floppies in drive A. If you have a CD-ROM drive, simply substitute the appropriate drive letter for A.

Starting Setup from Program Manager

To start Setup from Program Manager, choose File, Run from the main Program Manager menu. Windows displays the Run dialog box (see fig. A.1). Type **a:\setup** and click OK to begin the installation process.

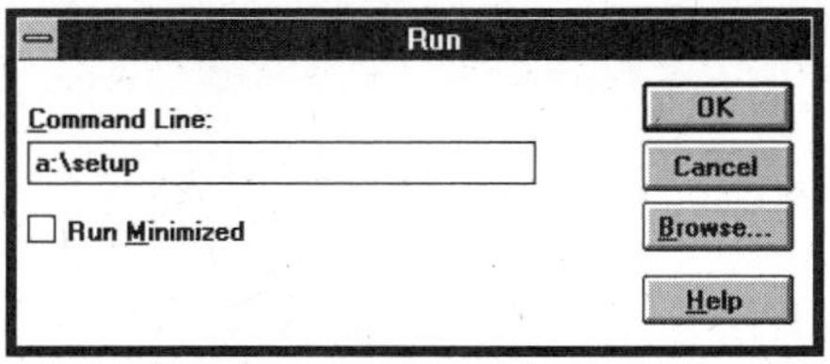

Fig. A.1
Specify the appropriate drive letter, followed by **setup**.

If you're not sure what drive your Windows 95 Setup disk is in, don't despair. You can choose Browse to find it. Windows displays the Browse dialog box to help you (see fig. A.2).

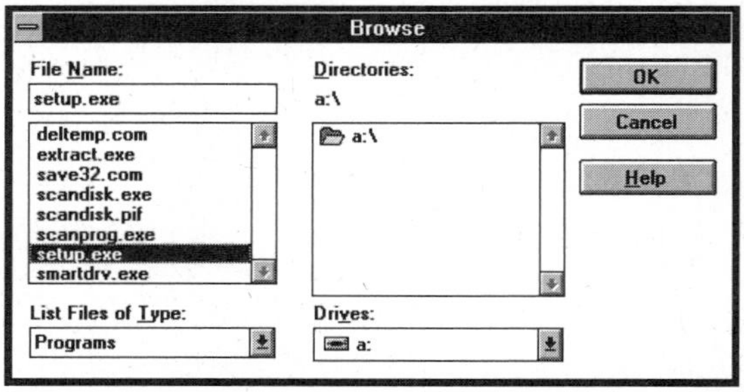

Fig. A.2
You can search for the Setup disk using the Browse dialog box tools.

When you select SETUP.EXE, Windows loads and runs the Windows 95 Setup program. After a few seconds, Setup displays the welcome screen shown in figure A.3.

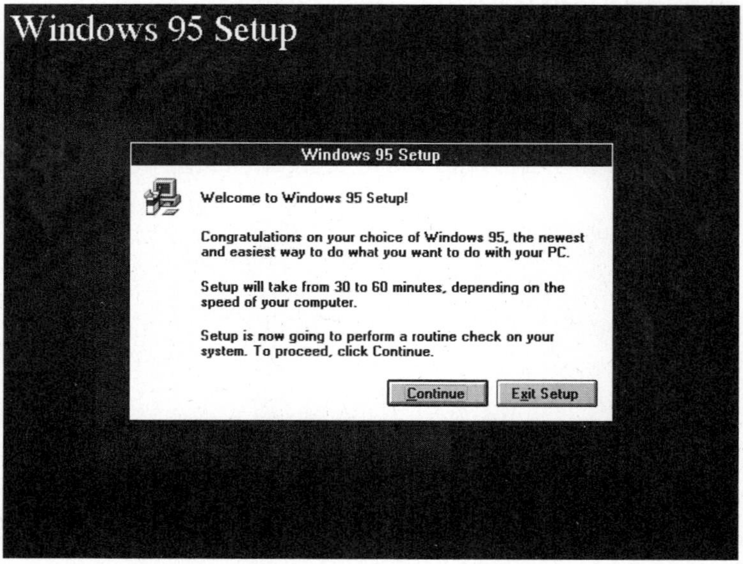

Fig. A.3
You're on your way when you see the big blue screen.

Starting Setup from File Manager

Some users may be more familiar with File Manager. If you prefer to work there instead of Program Manager, feel free. If you haven't already, start File Manager from the Program Manager Main program group by double-clicking the File Manager icon. When the File Manager window appears, click on the icon for the appropriate drive where you've loaded your Windows 95 installation disk or CD-ROM. File Manager then displays the contents of the drive as shown in figure A.4.

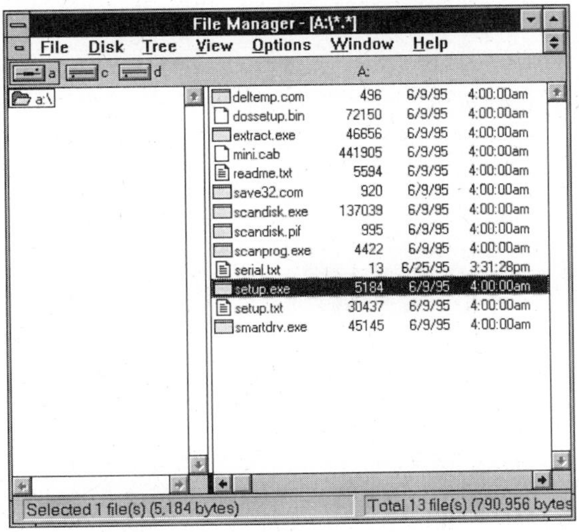

Fig. A.4
You can start Windows 95 Setup from File Manager.

To start Setup, double-click SETUP.EXE. Windows loads the program, and Setup displays the welcome screen.

Getting Down to Business with Setup

To continue Windows 95 Setup, click Continue. Setup displays the message box shown in figure A.5.

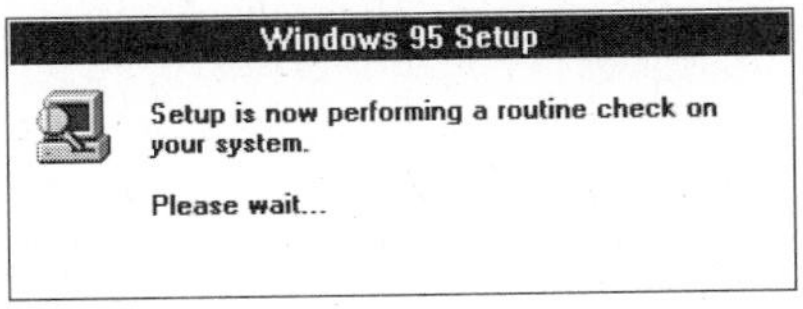

Fig. A.5
Setup keeps you posted during its investigations.

Setup performs a brief check of your hardware, current operating system, and current running programs before proceeding. It then displays the End-User License Agreement. Read it and click Yes to continue.

If you're installing from floppy disks, Setup frequently asks you for new disks via the Insert Disk dialog box (see fig. A.6). You can speed the process by having the disk ready and pressing the Enter key after you switch disks.

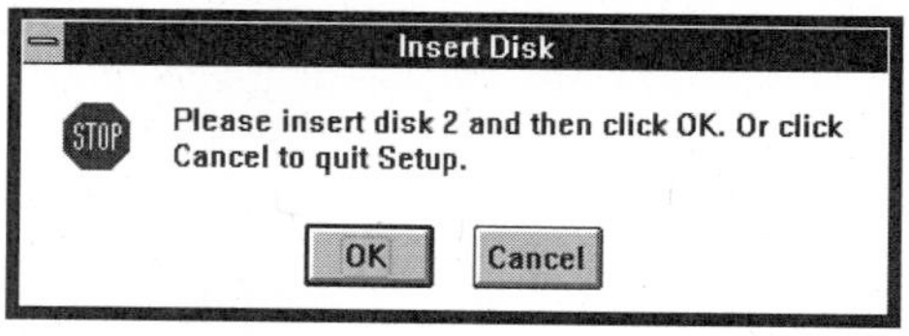

Fig. A.6
Setup asks you most of the important questions upfront, but unless you're installing from a CD-ROM, you'll still have to feed it disks.

When the Setup loader finishes creating the Setup Wizard, Windows may display the dialog box seen in figure A.7. If you have any open programs, it is strongly suggested you close them before proceeding. This is especially wise if you have any unsaved documents in other applications.

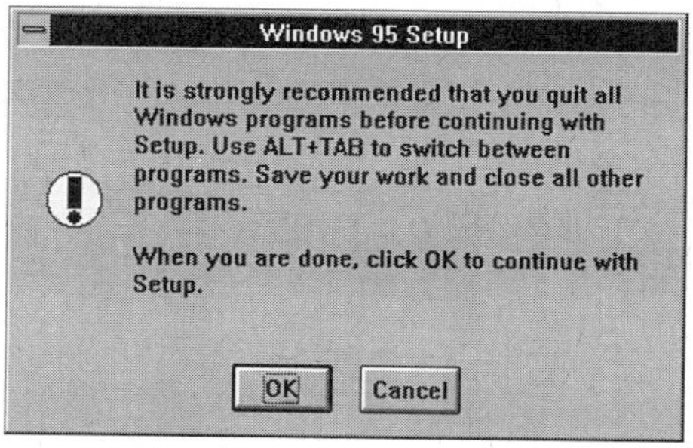

Fig. A.7
While Windows 95 Setup is well-behaved, it's always better to be safe than sorry.

Take the time to use Alt+Tab to close any other open applications or documents. (You won't be able to close Program Manager without exiting Windows.) When you finish, use Alt+Tab to return to Windows 95 Setup, and click OK to proceed. Setup then displays the main Windows 95 Setup Wizard dialog box (see fig. A.8).

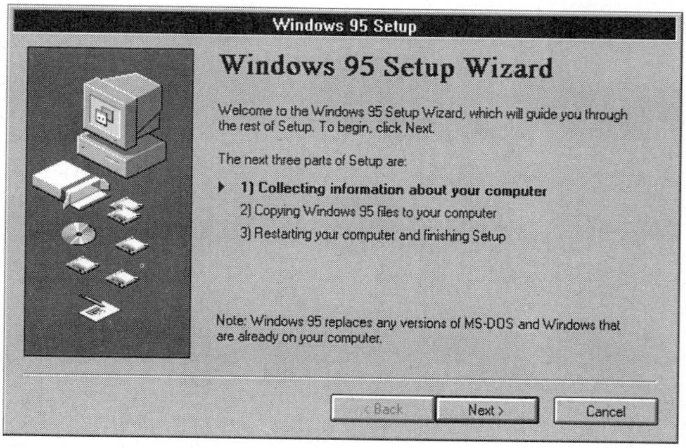

Fig. A.8
We're off to see the Setup Wizard.

Setup begins the first major phase requiring user interaction by collecting information about your system and how you'll use it. Click Next to proceed. Windows displays the Choose Directory dialog box (see fig. A.9).

If you want to install Windows 95 over your current Windows installation, click Next to proceed. If you want to install to another directory, choose Other Directory and Next; then see "Setting Up a Dual-Boot System," later in this appendix.

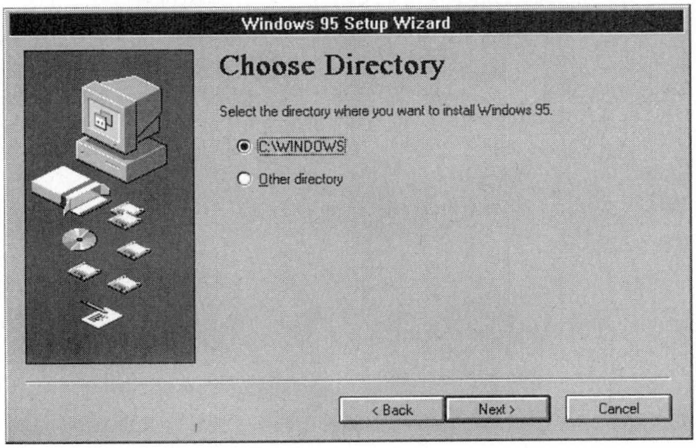

Fig. A.9
Most users will choose to install Windows 95 as an upgrade to their existing Windows 3.x installation (usually in C:\WINDOWS). Choose Next to confirm this option.

The next option is a great idea. Windows 95 setup presents the dialog box shown in figure A.10 and asks if you would like to save your Windows 3.1 and DOS system files. Saving these files takes only about 6M of disk space and it's highly recommended that you do this. Saving these files will allow you to uninstall Windows 95 (as described later in this appendix) at a later time should you ever need to revert to your Windows 3.1 setup. Notice this is *not* a full backup of your system or applications. This just saves files needed to start DOS, Windows, and Windows configuration files. Choose to save these files and then click Next to continue.

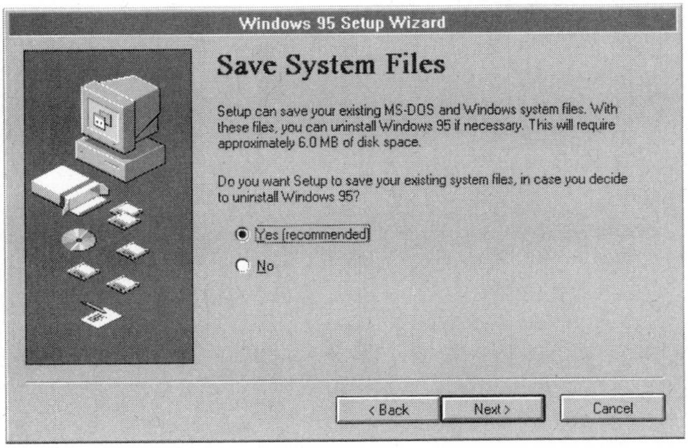

Fig A.10
Save your old Windows 3.1 and DOS system files now and save yourself some grief if you ever need to uninstall Windows 95.

Setup next checks your system for available installed components and disk space. You don't need to take any action for Setup to move to the next stage, Setup Options. As soon as Setup determines your available drive space, it asks you to confirm what type of installation you need (see fig. A.11).

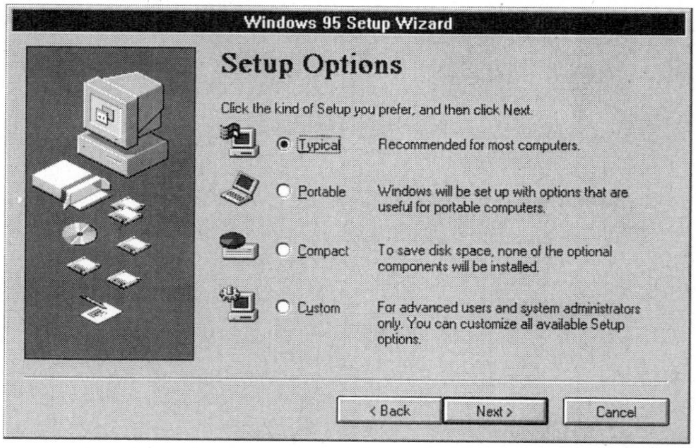

Fig. A.11
You can choose from Typical, Portable, Compact, or Custom installation profiles.

Your choice here depends upon how you use your computer and how you use Windows. The Typical installation option is truly that, fitting most installation types to a "t." With this option, you need only provide some user and computer information, and tell Setup whether you want an emergency startup disk (highly recommended).

Note

The Typical selection won't install all Windows accessories or games that you may expect. To confirm all components, use the Custom option described below.

The Portable setup option is best for laptop or mobile computer users. Setup installs the Windows Briefcase tools for file synchronization and transfer.

The Compact setup option is for systems where you must absolutely minimize the Windows "footprint." This option is for those with truly frugal drive budgets. Windows itself is completely installed, but all extraneous accessories are not (disk compression and maintenance tools are the only accessories installed).

▶ See "Using Custom Setup Mode," p. 1099

The Custom installation option allows the experienced user near-total control over Windows installation. If you are the master of your computing domain, this selection lets you specify network settings, device configurations, and most other variables in your Windows 95 setup. You'll find more information on the Custom option later in this appendix.

The Typical Windows 95 Setup Process

For now, let's look at a typical setup, as that is what most Windows 95 users need. To continue the installation, confirm the default selection (Typical) by clicking Next or pressing Enter. Windows displays the User Information dialog box (see fig. A.12).

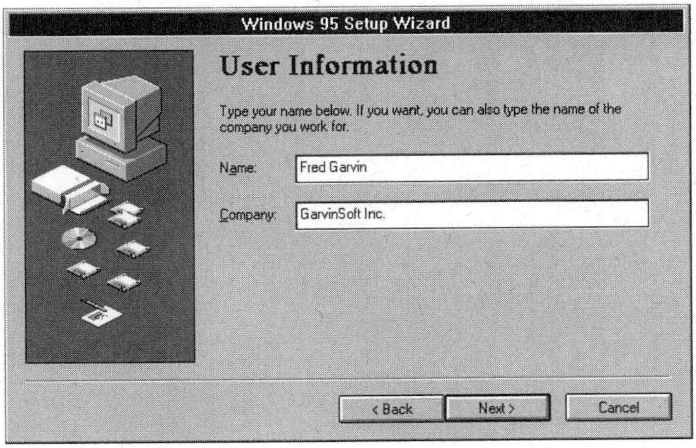

Fig. A.12
Windows Setup wants to get to know you better. Providing your name helps Windows properly identify you in later application installations and helps Windows identify your system on the Windows Network.

Fill in the appropriate information for your installation, and click Next or press Enter. The next stage in Setup is further analysis of your peripheral hardware. Setup displays the Analyzing Your Computer dialog box as shown in figure A.13.

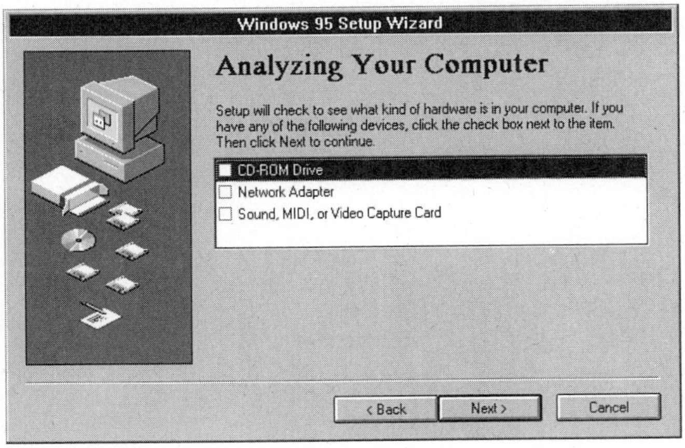

Fig. A.13
Depending upon what hardware is installed on your system, Windows will display several options in this dialog box. Confirm or deny your peripheral stance, and Setup does the rest.

Click Next or press Enter, and Setup then checks your entire system to profile your peripherals (display adapter, sound cards, and so on). When Setup finishes this investigation, Windows Components dialog box appears (see fig. A.14). Be sure to check any items you want Windows to sense, or it will skip them!

Note

If you don't check an item, Setup won't try to detect that class of device. If you do have a network adapter or multimedia card, and you want Setup to find it, you must check these options.

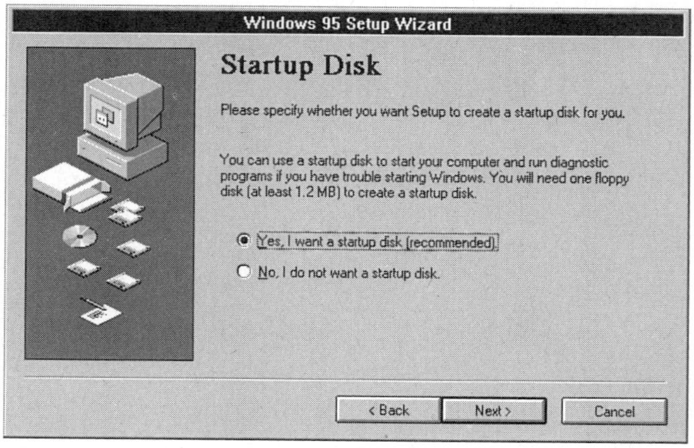

Fig. A.14
In the Typical setup mode, Setup allows you to alter the Windows component defaults.

If you're setting Windows up on a single-user, non-networked machine, odds are the default settings are just fine for you. Click Next or press Enter, and Setup displays the Startup Disk dialog box (see fig. A.15).

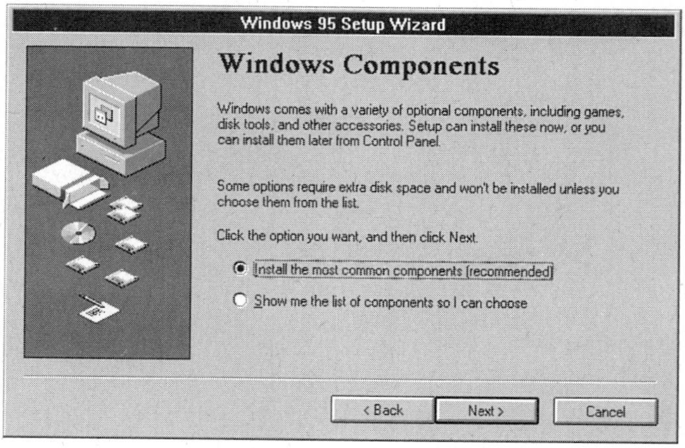

Fig. A.15
Choose wisely. Create a Startup Disk now and avoid regrets later.

Be smart and either click Next or press Enter to tell Setup to create a startup disk. Setup won't prompt you to do it immediately, so you have a few minutes to find a blank floppy disk (see, you really don't have an excuse). The Startup Disk contains all the files your computer needs to run in case the system files on your hard drive should become corrupt.

Click Next or press Enter, and Setup proceeds to the next major section of Windows 95 installation.

The Big Copy Job

Having completed its inquiries, Setup can now get down to the business at hand—moving the Windows 95 program(s) to your hard drive. Setup displays the Start Copying Files dialog box.

Simply click Next or press Enter, and Setup continues. The next displayed screen is the by now familiar Windows 95 Setup background, with a "gas gauge" at the bottom to indicate copy progress (see fig. A.16).

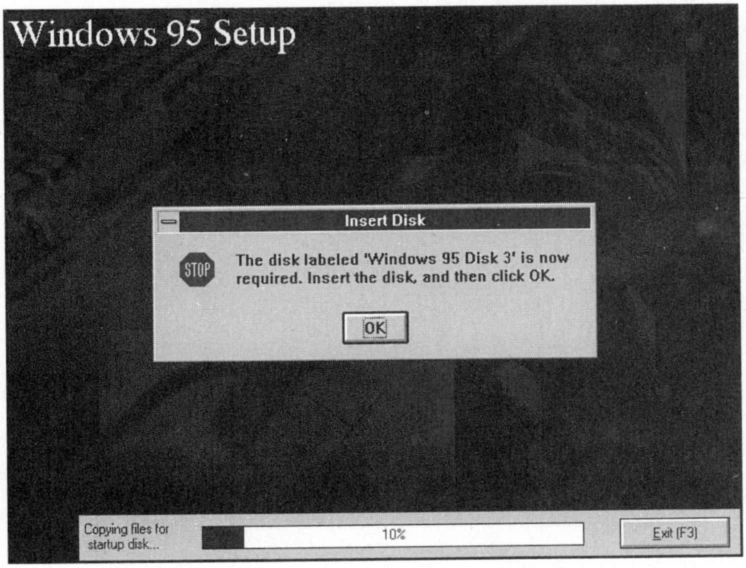

Fig. A.16
Windows 95 Setup won't be bashful about asking for the next floppy disk.

This part of installation can be either a bore or a joy, depending on how your day is going and how close your computer is to your other work. You can actually stray a little as Setup performs its work, but keep an ear or an eye open for disk requests (see fig. A.17).

Right in the middle of installation may seem like a strange time to create a boot disk, but this also is a good way to get you to do it. (You can't really back out this far in, now can you?)

When the gas gauge shows full, your Startup Disk is done, and Setup returns you to the installation.

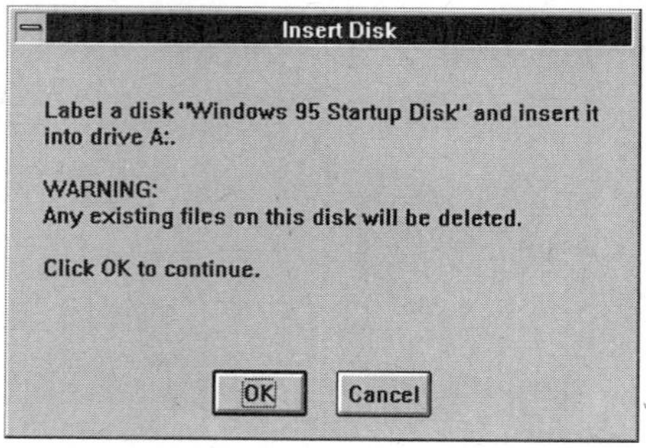

Fig. A.17 Now's the time to invest in some computing insurance by creating your Windows 95 Startup Disk. Be sure you don't need any of the data on the disk, because Windows will overwrite it.

One of the more amusing touches in Windows 95 installation is the little animations used during Setup. A tiny drum signals preparations, calling the installation troops to order (see fig. A.18).

Fig. A.18 Tiny drum rolls call the Setup cadence.

During the remainder of installation, Setup will ease your techno-ennui with informative screens alerting you to the computing delights that await. It actually pays to read these screens, especially if you are new to Windows. Even experienced Windows users can learn from these initial orientation messages (see fig. A.19).

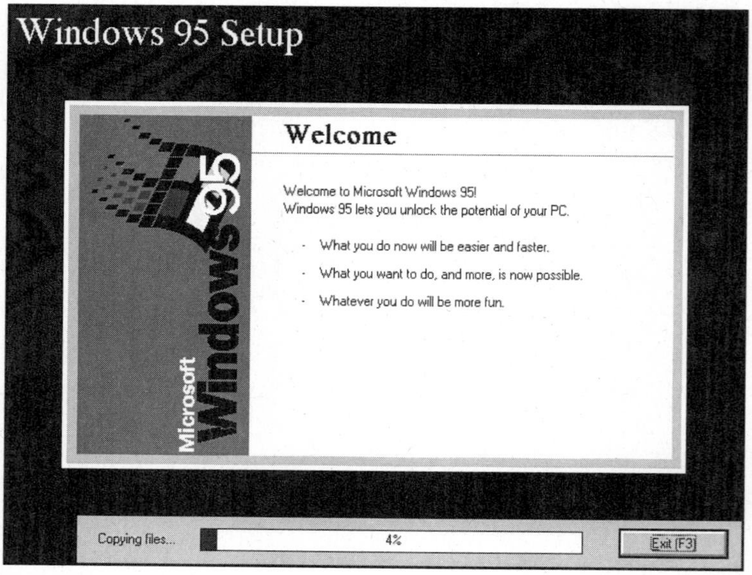

Fig. A.19 Microsoft doesn't waste any real estate using Setup's lag times to inform you of Windows 95 features and benefits. Windows 95 has many new interface components and capabilities.

Completing the Setup Process

After Setup has copied all Windows 95 files to your hard drive, the Finishing Setup dialog box appears, as shown in figure A.20.

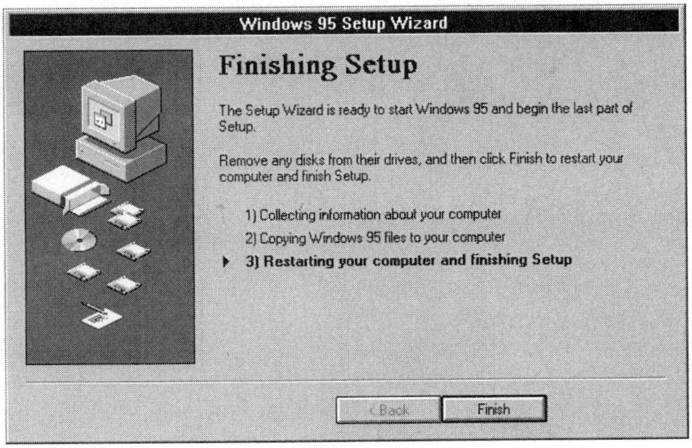

Fig. A.20
Setup needs to restart your system to complete the installation process.

Up to this point, Setup has operated as a 16-bit Windows 3.1 application. When you choose Finish and your system reboots, you'll actually be entering the world of Windows 95 computing for the first time.

Restarting Setup, Starting Windows 95

During the Copy phase of Setup, all primary Windows 95 files were created on your hard drive, and many other components of the operating system were initialized as well. When you restarted Windows 95 Setup, MS-DOS was replaced with the new Windows 95 Real Mode kernel, and your hard drive's boot sector was updated to run the new operating system.

When Setup resumes, it continues the Windows 95 installation by updating remaining configuration files and asking you a few more questions regarding your system peripherals. Most of these tasks are done by a system called the Run-Once Module, which basically fires up the appropriate system wizards to help you complete your installation.

The process begins with a quick scan of the system hardware. After this quick scan, Setup runs several short routines that can only be performed from within Windows 95 (setting up Control Panels for all appropriate devices, setting up program icons in the Start menu, initializing Windows Help, and confirming the local time zone) as shown in figure A.21.

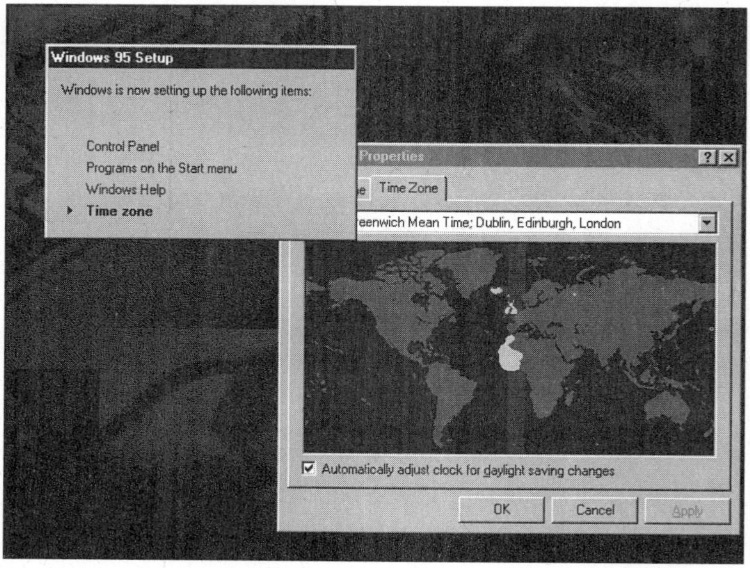

Fig. A.21
Once Windows 95 is running, it can complete Windows 95-specific setup tasks.

A really nice touch is the Time Zone dialog box. Simply click on the map near your part of the planet, and Windows 95 adjusts the system clock accordingly.

When the Run-Once tasks are complete, Setup is complete, and you're in the world of Windows 95 at last (see fig. A.22).

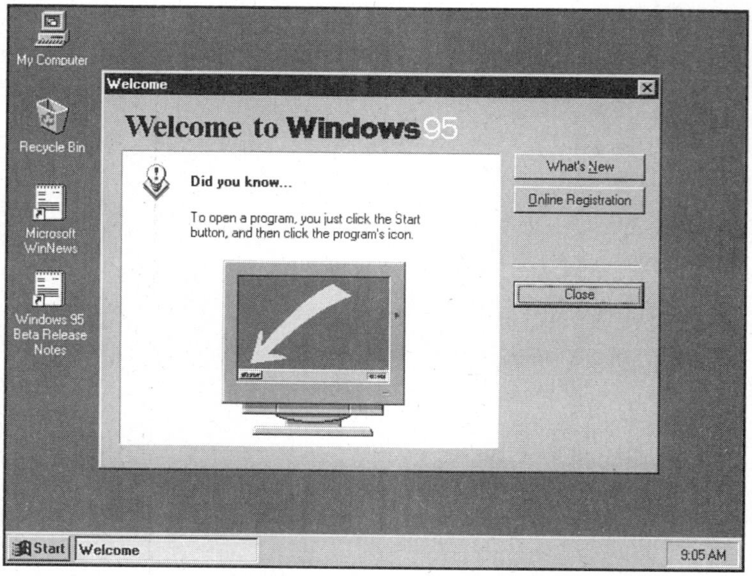

Fig. A.22
The Welcome to Windows 95 dialog box gives you the basic tips for navigation and registration.

The demonstration of a "typical" Windows 95 Setup run is complete. Next, you can learn how to install Windows 95 from MS-DOS; then you can visit some issues regarding Custom Setup and other advanced setup options.

Installing Windows 95 from MS-DOS

If you don't have an installation of Windows version 3.1 or later, or are using Windows NT or OS/2, you need to start Windows 95 Setup from the venerable MS-DOS prompt.

Starting Windows 95 Setup from MS-DOS is just like running any other MS-DOS program. If you're using a plain MS-DOS machine, you need version MS-DOS 3.2 or later. To begin, simply boot the machine just as for any other computing session. If you're using another operating system, you need to use the dual-boot feature or boot from a floppy disk to attain MS-DOS operation.

Again, it is assumed that you are using floppy disks in drive A. If you have a CD-ROM drive, simply substitute the appropriate drive letter for A in the following examples.

The first step in starting Windows 95 Setup from the MS-DOS prompt is to enter the command at the prompt. At the prompt, type **a:\setup** and press Enter.

MS-DOS then runs the Windows 95 Setup program, which starts by running the Windows 95 version of ScanDisk. The first thing you see on-screen is a message saying, `Please wait while Setup initializes. Setup is now going to perform a routine check on your system. To continue, press ENTER. To quit Setup, press ESC.` Press Enter to continue. Setup then starts ScanDisk (as shown in fig. A.23), which runs automatically to check out your drives to make sure they're sound before beginning the Windows 95 installation. Follow the prompts to deal with any drive anomalies.

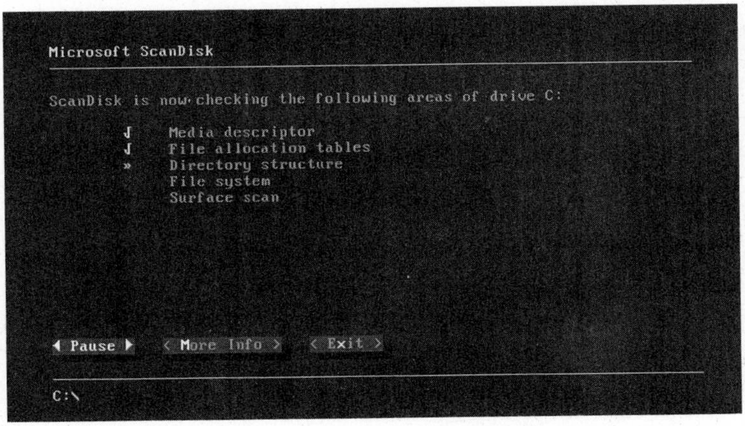

Fig. A.23
Setup needs to check out your disk before it begins.

When ScanDisk finishes, it automatically exits back to MS-DOS, where Setup continues.

Setup copies a small version of Windows 3.1 to your system so the graphical portions of Setup can run. Once that is complete, Setup displays the Welcome screen shown in figure A.24.

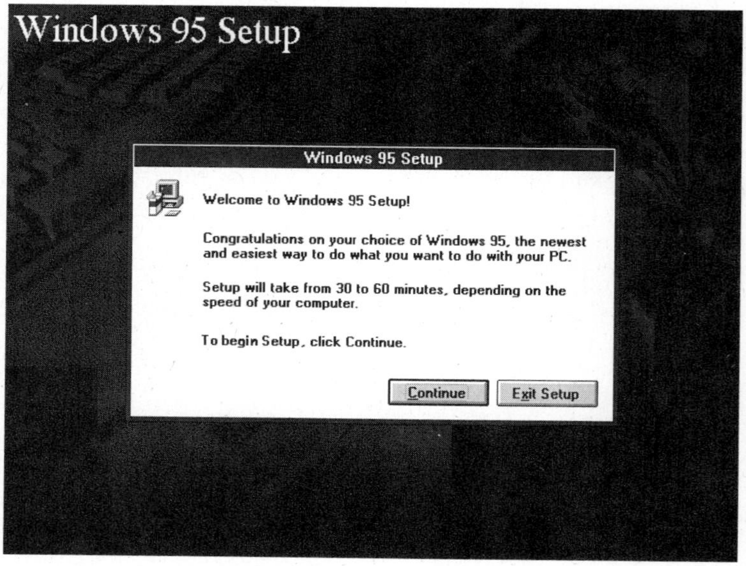

Fig. A.24
From this point on, Setup is the same whether you started from MS-DOS or the latest version of Windows.

◄ See "Installing Windows 95 from Windows 3.x," p. 1085

The remaining Setup procedures are nearly identical to those listed earlier in this chapter for installing from Windows 3.1. If you're installing Windows 95 as your first version of Windows, you have to install all of your Windows applications after Windows 95 Setup is complete. If you installed from MS-DOS but didn't install over your existing Windows subdirectory, you'll have to do the same.

Advanced Installation Techniques

As simple as Windows 95 Setup can be, there are still situations that demand special considerations to meet special needs. There are as many different Windows installations as there are Windows users, and Windows 95 Setup is flexible enough to meet most needs.

In this section, you learn about

- Installing with Custom options
- Using Safe Recovery and Safe Detection

- Installing a dual-boot system (keeping your previous MS-DOS and Windows systems)
- Reconfiguring a single-boot system for dual-boot operation

Using Custom Setup Mode

Microsoft's Windows 95 development team has done an admirable job of establishing compatibility with a wide variety of peripheral components, but no one can perfectly predict all of the equipment variables in the churning world of the PC hardware market.

Installing Windows 95 for special setups is straightforward if you have the appropriate information ready before you begin. The Custom setup option allows you to specify application settings, network configuration options, and device configurations, and gives you more control over the installation of Windows 95 components.

> **Caution**
>
> The Custom installation mode puts a lot of power in your hands. If you don't have the specific experience in network or device configuration, you're better off leaving this to Windows 95 Setup auto-detection, or your MIS department.

Before you begin, know the exact name and model number of the card or device you're installing. Have any special device driver files handy (the original floppy disk is best). Find out the logical memory address defaults for the component, if applicable (see the peripheral documentation).

To use Windows 95 Setup in Custom mode, simply proceed with installation as described earlier in this chapter up to the point of selecting the Setup Options dialog box (shown in fig. A.25).

At this point, select the Custom option and click Next to proceed. Don't expect Setup to change drastically from this point on; you simply see a few more dialog boxes, where Setup asks you the appropriate questions regarding additional options. The next screen you see is the User Information dialog box. When you complete this dialog box, Setup displays the Analyzing Your Computer dialog box shown in figure A.26.

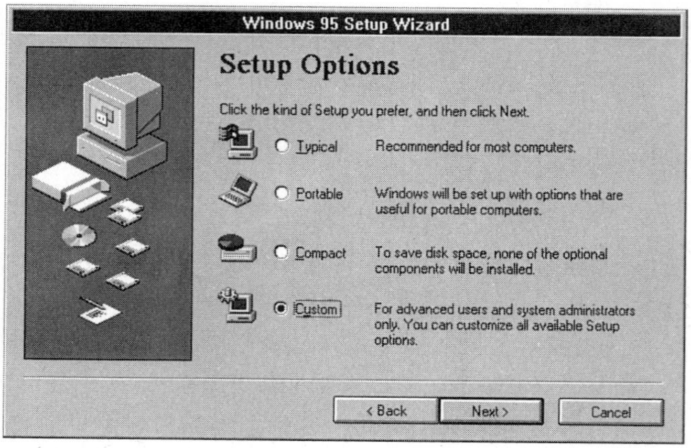

Fig. A.25
Select the Custom option to gain more control over your system configuration.

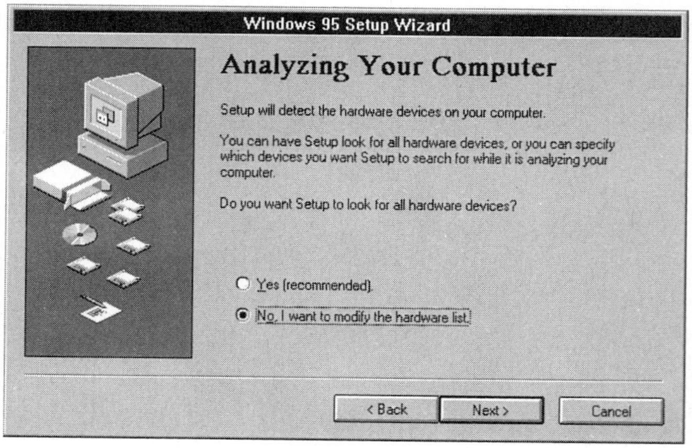

Fig. A.26
If you know you're going to need to alter your device configurations, you can select the option easily in this dialog box.

Customizing Hardware Support

If you know you have nonstandard or unsupported devices in your installation, select the No, I Want to Modify the Hardware List radio button. Then click Next to proceed. Setup displays the screen shown in figure A.27.

Here's where you need the information about your system mentioned earlier. If you *know* that you have an unusual peripheral, look for it here. Setup guides you through installing any special drivers for the device at the appropriate time.

If your device doesn't appear in the lists here, it means one of two things: either Windows 95 has native 32-bit support for the device or no support for it. If Setup didn't detect your device earlier in the installation, you need to tell it to install it now. Or, if it was detected, and the Windows installation didn't work, you can tell Windows to skip it this round. You can manually install the device later using the Add New Hardware control panel.

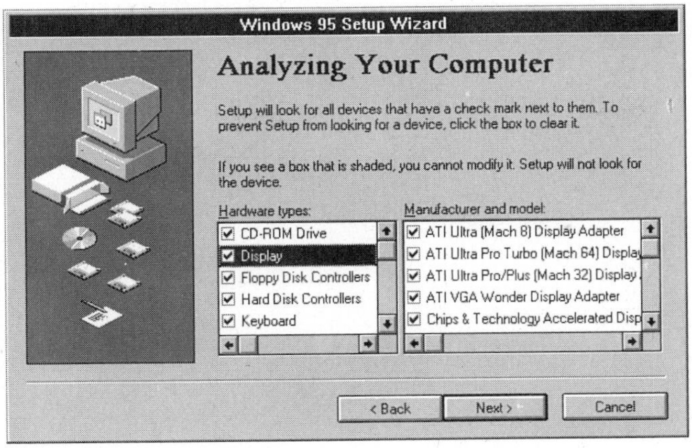

Fig. A.27
Select the device type in the left window and the specific device name in the right. Changing the item on the left changes the list on the right.

When you've selected all the device types you want configured, click Next to proceed. After completing its analysis of your selected equipment, Setup displays the Select Components dialog box, shown in figure A.28.

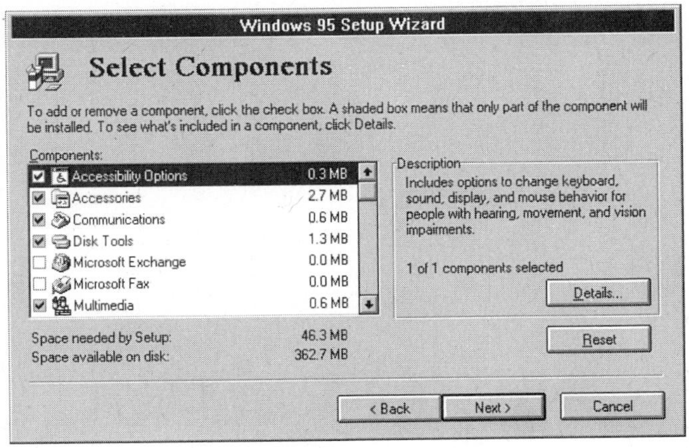

Fig. A.28
Select the Windows 95 components you want Setup to install. Setup can provide additional information about each option when you click Details.

When you've selected all of the Windows 95 components you want installed, click Next to proceed. The remainder of the installation depends on what hardware and software component options you've selected. Setup attempts to locate your devices and prompts you when it needs additional information such as device driver files. In the next section, we look at an example of this, specifically, the basic steps to install network support under Windows 95.

Installing Windows 95 Network Features

If you've selected network support, Setup next displays the Network Configuration dialog box shown in figure A.29.

Fig. A.29
You can install network support for multiple adapters and protocols from this one Setup screen.

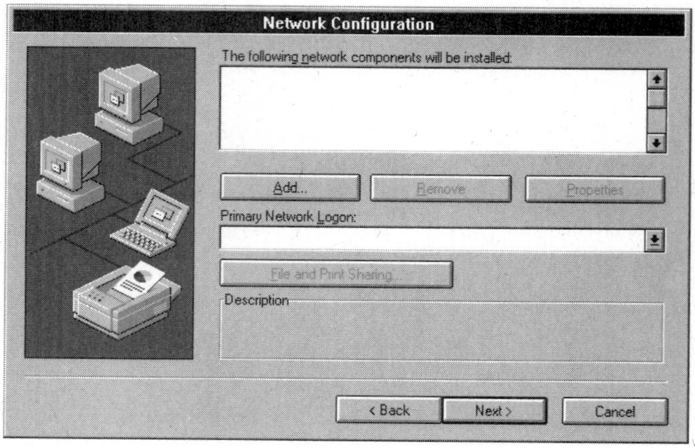

Note

See Part V, "Networking with Windows 95," for additional information on configuring network support in Windows 95.

To begin configuring your network options, click Add. Setup displays the Select Network Component Type dialog box (see fig. A.30).

Fig. A.30
Click on the network component type you want to install.

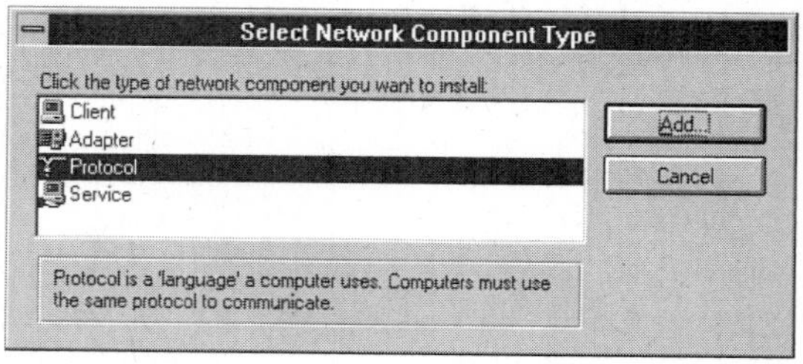

When you select the component type you want to install, Setup displays another selection dialog box for that component classification. For example, if you select Protocol and then click Add, Setup displays the Select Network Protocol dialog box shown in figure A.31.

When you've selected the appropriate protocols network adapter, you can either click OK (to let Setup determine if Windows 95 has native drivers for these types) or click Have Disk to install your own drivers.

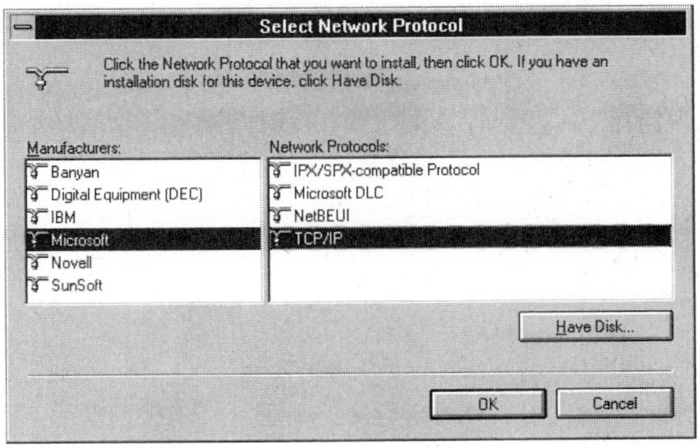

Fig. A.31
Select the protocol publisher in the left list and then the specific protocol type in the right list.

Setup may make assumptions about other network support components based upon the adapter type you select. For example, selecting the Intel EtherExpress 16 or 16TP results in Setup selecting clients and protocols for both NetWare and Microsoft network types, as shown in figure A.32.

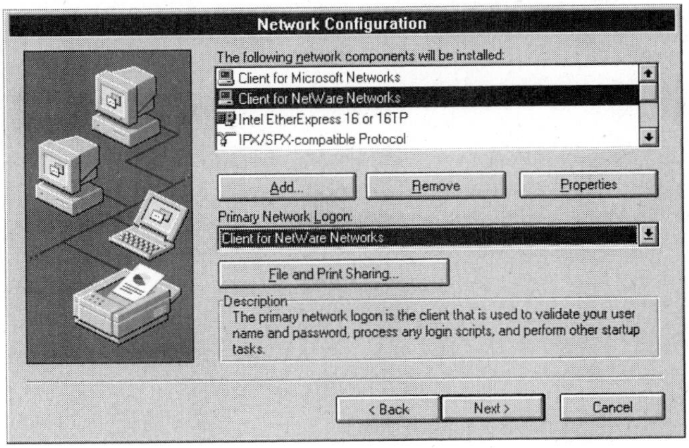

Fig. A.32
Setup may make additional choices based upon your hardware selection. You can override this by using the Remove button, but be sure you don't need the component before you proceed.

Using Safe Recovery

If Setup fails during your installation, it has the capability to recover gracefully. Setup Safe Recovery automatically skips problem configuration items to allow the installation to finish, and then allows you to go back to the problem and correct it.

Safe Recovery also can be used in repairing damaged installations. If you run Setup after a complete Windows 95 installation, it first asks whether you want to confirm or repair your installation, or whether you want to completely reinstall Windows 95 (see fig. A.33).

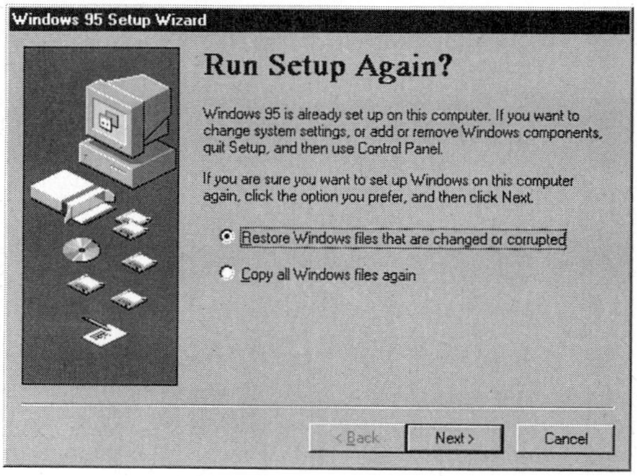

Fig. A.33
You also can use Safe Recovery after a complete installation to repair later damage.

Using Safe Detection

Windows 95 Setup looks for system components in a variety of ways. Setup can detect communication ports, display adapters, processor type, drive controllers, sound cards, and network adapters. Setup also looks for system hardware resources such as IRQs, DMA channels, and I/O addresses to avoid conflicts between devices. Setup can detect both the newer Plug and Play devices and older "legacy" peripherals.

Safe Detection works on four classes of devices:

- Sound cards
- Network adapters
- SCSI controllers
- CD-ROM controllers

One problem with such auto-detection routines is failure during the detection process itself. Plug and Play devices basically identify or announce themselves to the system, but older adapters require interactive tests to locate them and confirm operation. While most devices respond well to this, some don't. In addition, if there's any duplication of IRQ, DMA, or I/O addresses between devices, your system can lock up tighter than a drum during installation.

Windows 95 Setup can recover from such failures. Setup keeps track of the process of testing devices during installation and knows at what point a device failed. When you restart it, Setup knows not to touch that subsystem again until corrections have been applied, such as loading 16-bit device drivers, if the 32-bit native Windows 95 drivers have failed.

Setting Up a Dual-Boot System

A very popular installation option for new Windows 95 users is the *dual-boot setup*. Installing Windows 95 this way allows you to return to your previous operating system as needed or desired.

There are several ways to accomplish a dual-boot installation and several motivations for doing so. The following sections explain the techniques and options available to you under Windows 95.

Setting Up a Dual-Boot System during Installation

The simplest technique for establishing dual-boot is to simply select a new directory for Windows 95 when installing for the first time (see fig. A.34).

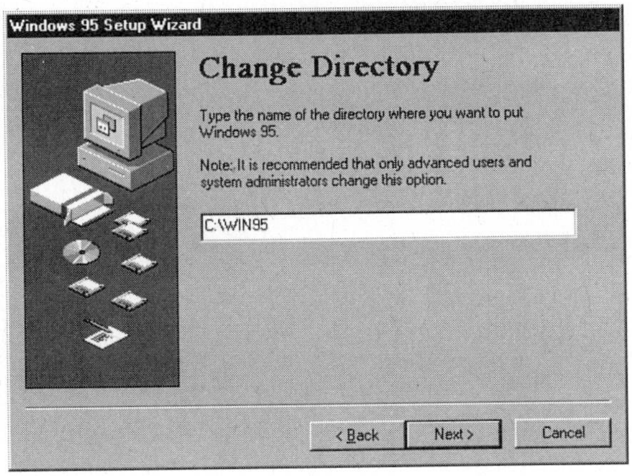

Fig. A.34
Specify a new directory for Windows 95, and Setup takes care of basic dual-boot details. You'll still need to configure Windows 95 for many of the applications in your previous Windows installation.

Setup preserves your current MS-DOS and Windows 3.1x settings if you follow this route, but it can't transfer settings for your current Windows applications to the new Windows 95 installation (see fig. A.35). In addition, Windows 95 will disable, redirect, or outright delete certain files from your DOS directory, so you may want to restore the complete DOS directory from the backup you made before installation.

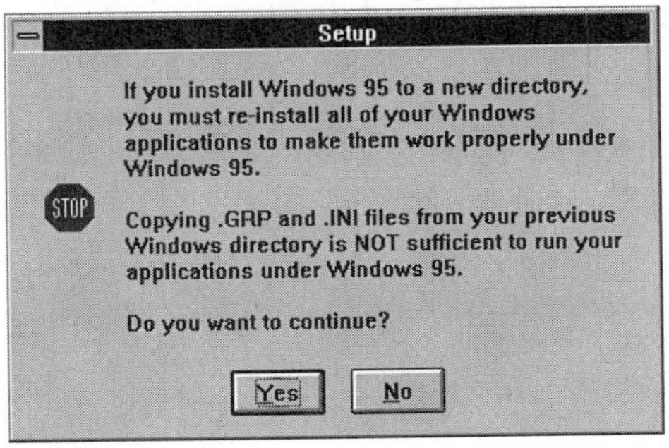

Fig. A.35
Setup warns you of the additional work dual-boot operation installation may entail.

If you're prepared to reinstall your Windows applications after Windows 95 Setup is completed, this is a clean, simple way to proceed. After you install Windows 95 this way, you can return to your previous MS-DOS installation (and from there to your previous Windows installation) with a single F4 keystroke during system startup.

Setting Up a Dual-Boot System after Installation

If you've already installed Windows 95 over your existing Windows 3.1x directory, you can easily set up your system for dual-booting back to MS-DOS. However, since your previous Windows installation was stomped, you can't return to it. In addition, you may notice that some of your favorite MS-DOS commands such as XCOPY are now dust, even when you dual-boot back to MS-DOS (Windows 95 disables some MS-DOS commands, so you'll need to restore your DOS directory from that backup you made prior to installation).

To set up your system for dual-boot to your previous version of MS-DOS, follow these steps:

1. Locate your boot floppy disk for your previous version of MS-DOS (version 5.0 or later). Make a copy of it.

2. On the copy of your boot disk, change the attributes of the IO.SYS, MSDOS.SYS, and COMMAND.COM files to allow you to rename them. (The `attrib -h -r -s` *`filename.ext`* command works for each file.)

3. Rename the IO.SYS, MSDOS.SYS, and COMMAND.COM files on your boot floppy to IO.DOS, MSDOS.DOS, and COMMAND.DOS respectively.

4. Reset the attributes of the IO.DOS, MSDOS.DOS, and COMMAND.DOS files to protect them. (Use the `attrib +r` *`filename.ext`* command for each file.)

5. Rename the AUTOEXEC.BAT and CONFIG.SYS files on your MS-DOS boot disk to AUTOEXEC.DOS and CONFIG.DOS, respectively. You may want to set these files to read-only also. (Use the `attrib +r` *`filename.ext`* command for each file.)

6. Copy IO.DOS, MSDOS.DOS, COMMAND.DOS, AUTOEXEC.DOS, and CONFIG.DOS to the boot directory of the Windows 95 drive.

You can now return to your previous MS-DOS installation with a single F4 keystroke during system startup. You also can use the F8 key during startup (when `Starting Windows 95...` appears on screen) and then select item 7,

"Previous version of MS-DOS." Bear in mind that you may need to restore certain MS-DOS files that Windows 95 has removed from your DOS directory (you can use that DOS directory backup you made prior to Windows 95 installation).

Removing Windows 95

If you decide you need to return to your previous Windows 3.1x installation, want to clean up your system before you trade or sell it, or simply don't want to use Windows 95, you can remove all traces of Windows 95. In order to use this feature to uninstall Windows 95, you had to use the (highly recommended) option to save your old Windows 3.1 and DOS system files during Windows setup.

If you were using drive compression with Windows 95, you need to uncompress your hard drive before uninstalling Windows 95. If you have more files than will fit on your uncompressed drive, you will need to delete files before proceeding.

If you have installed any programs since installing Windows 95, they probably will have to be reconfigured to work with Windows 3.1, or you may have to uninstall them from Windows 95 and reinstall them in Windows 3.1. Of course, any applications written to work with Windows 95 (like Office 95) will not run in Windows 3.1.

Once you are ready to uninstall, open the Start menu and choose Setttings, Control Panel. Double-click the Add/Remove Programs icon. Click the Install/Uninstall tab. This shows the properties sheet shown in figure A.36.

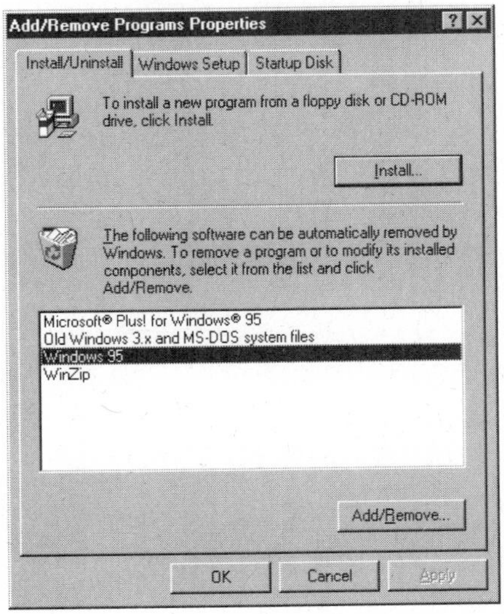

Fig. A.36
The Install/Uninstall Programs page of the Add/Remove Programs Properties sheet includes an option to uninstall Windows 95.

Select Windows 95 and then click Add/Remove. This opens the warning dialog box shown in figure A.37.

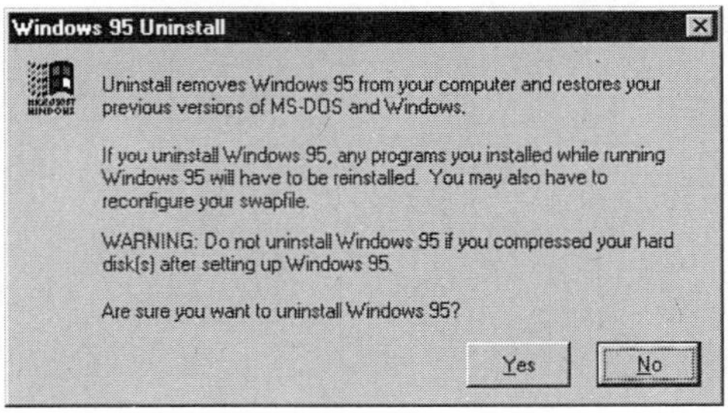

Fig. A.37
If you are sure you want to uninstall Windows 95, click Yes. The uninstaller will remove Windows 95 and restore your old DOS and Windows system files.

Your system should now boot straight to your previous version of MS-DOS. You may need to set up a new Windows 3.1 swap file as your old swap file (if you were using a permanent swap file) no longer exists.❖

Appendix B

Using Microsoft Network

by Jerry Honeycutt

The Microsoft Network (MSN) is an exciting addition to Windows 95. It is fully integrated into Windows and offers online access to the world by giving you access to a variety of people and resources. With MSN, you can exchange electronic mail (e-mail) with other people, exchange ideas on bulletin boards, participate in live discussions in chat rooms, access the resources of the Internet, and do even more! Why should you use this powerful accessory? Here are some important reasons:

- *Getting started is easy.* After installing Windows and MSN, you just double-click the MSN icon on your desktop and then follow the instructions.
- *Using MSN is easy.* MSN is fully integrated into Windows. You have already learned about using folders, shortcuts, drag-and-drop, and the Explorer. MSN uses these same tools to present information to you. Therefore, you can get up to speed more quickly on MSN because you already have the skills necessary to navigate.
- *Multitasking is easy.* You won't get bored in MSN! MSN takes full advantage of Windows' multitasking capabilities. If you are downloading a file from a file area, you can chat with your colleagues in a chat room and read the messages from a bulletin board at the same time.

This appendix explains how to get started using MSN and describes some interesting forum areas and services currently available.

In this appendix, you learn to:

- Create a new account and log on to MSN for the first time
- Use the variety of services available in MSN Central such as MSN Today, E-Mail, Favorite Places, Member Assistance, and Categories
- Use Internet e-mail and UseNet newsgroups in MSN

Connecting to The Microsoft Network

As noted, getting started with MSN is easy. All you need is a modem and MSN software. If you haven't installed MSN yet, take a moment to install it now so that you can follow the examples in this chapter. To install MSN, click the Add/Remove Programs icon in Control Panel and select the Windows Setup page. Select The Microsoft Network, then click OK.

◀ See "Adding and Removing Windows Components," p. 313

◀ See "Understanding Windows 95 Setup Requirements," p. 1078

◀ See "Installing Windows 95 Network Features," p. 1101

MSN automates the process of setting up your online account for the first time. MSN walks you through three major steps: updating a list of access numbers, entering information about yourself, and logging on for the first time to get a user ID and password.

Downloading Local Access Numbers

The list of MSN access phone numbers is dramatically large, covering most of the United States and large portions of the world. Microsoft updates this list periodically. MSN needs to update the list on your computer to find the best connection for you. To get started, follow these steps:

1. Double-click the MSN icon on your desktop. MSN displays a dialog box containing brief information about the services provided. Click OK to continue.
2. In the fields provided, type your area code and the first three digits of your phone number. Based on this information, MSN will find the best matching access number for you to use. Click OK to continue.
3. Click Connect to log on to MSN and update the list of access numbers.

Caution

The desktop icon is created as a registry key, not a file. Therefore, you can't connect to MSN if you remove the icon from your desktop.

Entering Information about Yourself

After MSN updates the list of access numbers, it asks for personal information, such as your address and payment method. This information is required for logging on to MSN. Your screen should now contain the dialog box shown in figure B.1.

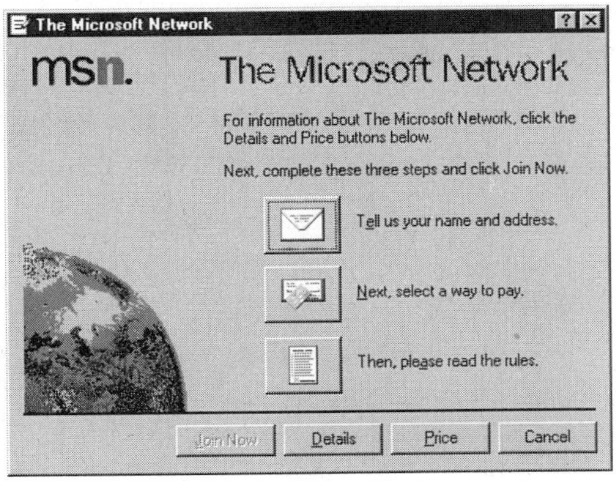

Fig. B.1
Complete each step to join MSN.

Before entering your personal information, take a moment to review the following:

- *Details.* Click Details to see specific information about MSN.
- *Price.* Click Price to see the latest fee structure for time and services on MSN. This price list is updated regularly.

To continue the sign-up process, complete the following steps:

1. Click Tell Us Your Name and Address. MSN displays the dialog box shown in figure B.2. Enter the information requested in each blank field. If you do not want to accept solicitations and other special notices from MSN, click the check box labeled You Are Entitled To... in the bottom-left corner of the dialog box. Click OK to continue, and MSN redisplays the dialog box shown in figure B.1.

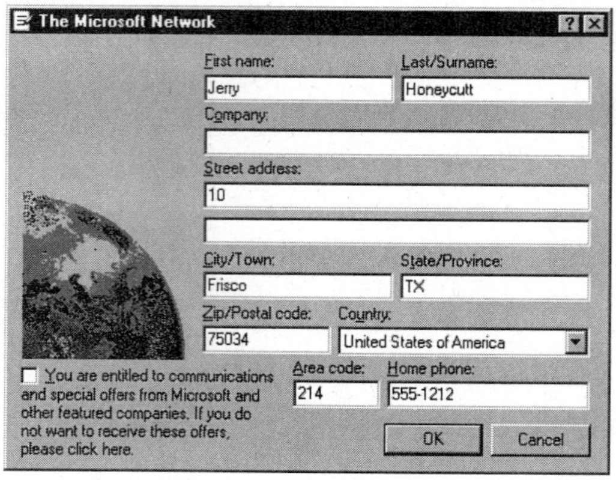

Fig. B.2
Enter information about yourself.

2. Click Next, Select a Way to Pay. Select a payment method from the Choose a Payment Method list. Then enter the card number, expiration date, and cardholder name in the fields provided. You also may be asked to enter the bank's name. Click OK. MSN returns you to the dialog box shown in figure B.1.

3. Click Then, Please Read the Rules. MSN will not let you continue until you view the MSN membership agreement. Click I Agree if you want to continue, or click I Don't Agree if you want to stop. When you click I Agree, MSN redisplays the dialog box shown in figure B.1.

4. Click Join Now to continue the sign-up process.

Logging On for the First Time

MSN provides both primary and backup access numbers. Normally, MSN uses the primary access number. For situations in which the primary number isn't working, MSN uses the backup number. If you can't connect to the phone numbers MSN chose, click Settings, Access Numbers, and then click the Change button beside primary or backup number. Select the country, state, and access number appropriate for your area code in the lists provided.

To log on and get your user ID and password, click Connect to log on to MSN. MSN prompts you for a user ID and password. You will receive an error if the user ID is already used or the password is invalid. If so, try another ID or password.

Troubleshooting

When I dial MSN, I get a message saying that the call was canceled or the modem doesn't connect.

Your hardware may not support high-speed communications. Change your baud rate to 9,600 (or a slower rate) and try again.

See "Configuring Your Modem," p. 843

I entered my new password, and MSN complained that its length was invalid even though I'm positive it was long enough.

MSN tells you that your password length is invalid if your password contains invalid characters such as spaces or other special characters. Passwords can contain only the characters A through Z, a through z, 0 through 9, "-", and ".".

You are now set up on MSN. To log on next time, double-click the MSN icon on your desktop, fill in your ID and password, and click Connect. If you want MSN to remember your password from session to session, click Remember My Password. Figure B.3 shows the logon screen.

Fig. B.3
Click Connect to log on to MSN or click Settings to change your access phone numbers, dialing properties, or modem settings.

Note

From time to time, Microsoft updates the MSN software. If so, you'll be given the opportunity to download the update when you log on to MSN. In some cases, you will not be able to continue logging on to MSN until you download the update because changes to the network may require the new software. Downloading the update is automatic. For example, you don't have to provide paths or file names because the MSN software already has this information.

Using MSN Central

You have already learned about the basic tools required to use Windows 95 folders, shortcuts, drag-and-drop, the Explorer, and many others. MSN is easy to use because it uses these same tools. For example, if you can use the Explorer to browse your hard drive, you can easily browse MSN. The following list explains how some of these tools are used in MSN:

◀ See "Managing Your Files and Folders," p. 513

◀ See "Modifying and Deleting Shortcuts," p. 72

◀ See "Using the Windows Explorer to View Files and Folders," p. 499

◀ See "Viewing and Changing the Properties of a File or Folder," p. 529

◀ See "Overview of Exchange Features," p. 724

◀ See "Moving and Copying Files and Folders," p. 515

- *Folders*. These are used to present categories and forums, enabling you to move easily from area to area within MSN.
- *Shortcuts*. Most documents and folders on MSN can be dragged as shortcuts to your desktop, folders, or documents. Double-clicking an MSN shortcut takes you straight to that MSN area.
- *The Explorer*. This tool gives you a bigger view of MSN and enables you to navigate quickly by showing the entire content of MSN in the left pane.
- *Property sheets*. These are used to display information about an area on MSN. The information may include the type of area, who runs it, and the rating (G, PG, R, and so on).
- *Exchange*. You use this tool to send and receive e-mail from other MSN members or Internet users.
- *Drag-and-drop*. With drag-and-drop, you can download files from a file area.

MSN Central is your home base while logged on. It is the first window you see when you log on (see fig. B.4). You can choose from a number of possible places to go:

- *MSN TODAY*. Gives you current information about news and activities on MSN. For example, it notifies you of service changes or anticipated outages; new and exciting forums on MSN; and upcoming conferences by noted industry leaders.
- *E-MAIL*. Starts Exchange so that you can send and receive e-mail. You can exchange e-mail with other MSN and Internet users. You can also use Exchange to search for other MSN members with interests similar to yours. See "MSN E-Mail" later in this chapter for more information about using Exchange with MSN.

- *FAVORITE PLACES*. Opens a folder containing shortcuts to your favorite places on MSN. Many of the MSN programs allow you to save a shortcut to your current location by clicking a toolbar button or selecting a menu option. You can also save a shortcut by dragging an icon from a forum's folder into the open Favorite Places folder.

- *MEMBER ASSISTANCE*. Opens the Member Assistance forum so that you can get help or find more information on MSN. This is where you'll go when you need help using MSN or want help finding a specific area on the network.

- *CATEGORIES*. Opens the Categories folder, showing all the categories of forums available on MSN. MSN has many different categories of forums such as "Computers & Software" and "Home & Family." The section "MSN Categories," later in this chapter, describes the forums available in each category. Microsoft updates these categories from time to time as forums are added or removed.

Note

MSN displays MSN TODAY each time you log on. If you don't want it displayed each time you log on, choose View, Options from the menu, select the General page, and deselect Show MSN Today Title on Startup.

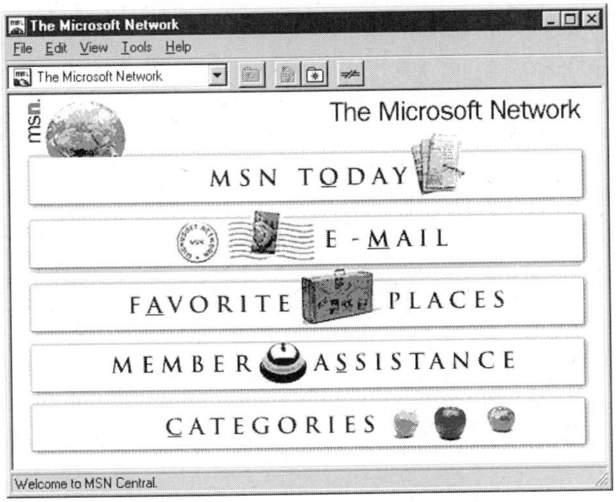

Fig. B.4
From MSN Central, you can launch into a variety of interesting areas such as MSN TODAY or CATEGORIES by clicking on its picture.

As you can see, MSN provides a wealth of tools to make your online experience a positive one. Microsoft undoubtedly will add more tools as they get feedback from users. To keep up-to-date on the latest developments, check MSN Today frequently as described in the following section.

MSN Today

MSN Today is the daily newspaper for MSN. Here, you'll find information about upcoming conferences; new and exciting forums; and service changes or anticipated outages. Figure B.5 shows MSN Today.

Fig. B.5
MSN Today keeps you informed about the latest happenings on MSN. Keep up-to-date by reading MSN Today each day.

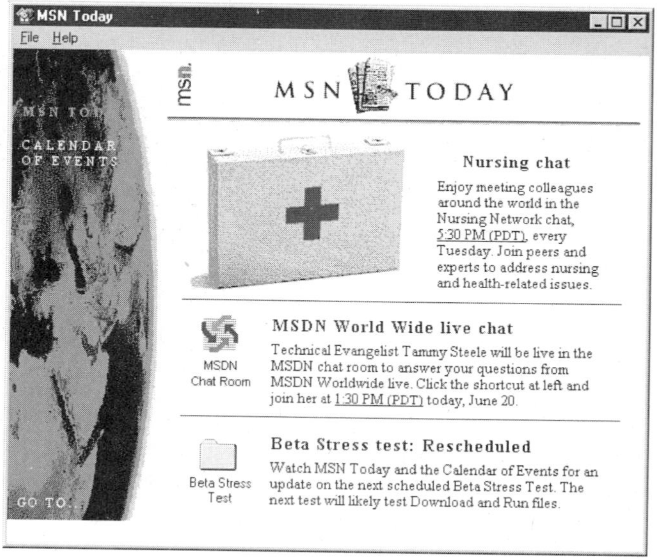

Clicking some pictures or titles in MSN Today opens a document so that you can read more information about that topic. Clicking other pictures or titles takes you to the particular area on MSN relating to that topic. For example, clicking the Nursing Chat picture in MSN Today takes you to the Nursing forum.

MSN Today also gives you a schedule for interesting events occuring during the following week. Clicking Calendar of Events shows you the public events happening each day of the following week.

MSN E-Mail

You already know how to use e-mail on MSN. In Chapter 24, "Using Microsoft Exchange," you learned how to send and receive messages, use the Address Book, use remote mail, and configure Exchange. When you installed MSN, however, it added additional features to Exchange specifically for MSN. For example, MSN added the capability to search for MSN members in the Address Book and make your personal profile available to other MSN members.

◄ See "Overview of Exchange Features," p. 724

This section describes how to use Exchange with MSN. You learn about using the Address Book, updating your personal profile, searching for other members, and setting options for using Exchange with MSN. For information about sending and receiving e-mail see Chapter 24, "Using Microsoft Exchange."

Note

You can share your favorite MSN shortcuts with your friends. For example, if you find an interesting BBS on Golf, you can share a shortcut to that BBS with other MSN members so that they can go to the BBS. Create the shortcut on your desktop by dragging an icon from an MSN folder to the desktop. Create and address your e-mail. Then, right-click your shortcut and choose Copy. Right-click in the body of your message and choose Paste. When the recipient opens the e-mail, she can double-click the shortcut to go directly to that item.

Selecting The Microsoft Network Address Book

Composing a message for MSN is the same as for any message in Exchange. However, you can choose to use MSN addresses when you use the Address Book. To see MSN addresses in the Address Book, select Microsoft Network from the Show Names From The list.

Note

When Exchange checks the address for an e-mail message, it automatically looks up the MSN address in the MSN Address Book. For example, if you are addressing an e-mail to "jb_smith" and type only "jb_s" in the address, Exchange completes the address for you. If more than one address matches the characters you typed, Exchange prompts you for the correct address from a list of possible choices. Clever!

Updating Your Personal Profile

Personal profiles allow other MSN members to see information about you, such as hobbies and profession. Thus, members can search their Address Books to find people with similar interests. Also, personal profiles are useful in chat rooms. If you are chatting with a person in a chat room and want to see more information about that person, such as the company for whom he works, you can right-click his name, and MSN displays his personal profile.

Providing all or part of the personal profile is optional. For example, if you don't feel comfortable broadcasting your company, leave it blank. To make sure that this information is available to other members, you need to fill in your information. To provide your personal profile, follow these steps:

1. Open Exchange by clicking E-MAIL in the MSN Central window.

2. Choose Tools, Address Book or click the Address Book button in the toolbar.

3. Select Microsoft Network from the Show Names From The list. If you are not currently logged on to MSN, Exchange starts MSN, which prompts you to log on. The Address Book displays a list of all the MSN users. This list is updated about every 24 hours.

4. Search for your name by paging down the list. Alternatively, you can start typing your name in the field provided, and MSN displays the entry that matches what you have typed.

5. Right-click your name and choose Properties. The Address Book then displays the property sheet shown in figure B.6.

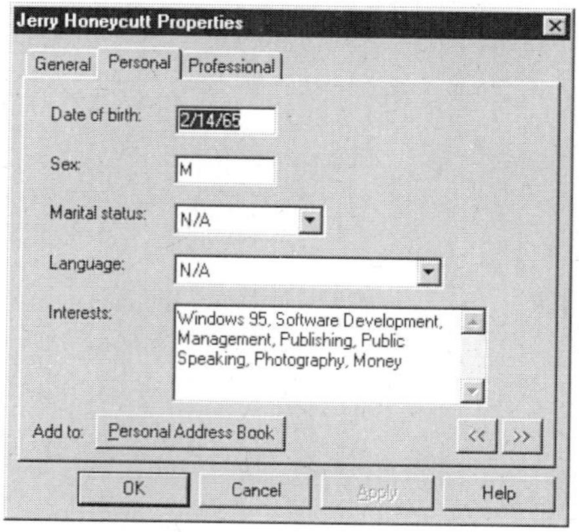

Fig. B.6
Provide useful information in the personal profile so that other users can find you! All the fields in the profile are optional, so you don't have to fill in Sex if you are uncomfortable with people knowing your gender.

6. Fill in the information in the fields provided on the General, Personal, and Professional pages of the property sheet. Click OK, and MSN will update your profile. However, the updating could take as long as 24 hours.

Finding Members in the Address Book

Finding members in the Address Book is a powerful way to find people with similar interests, professions, or even birthdays. To find members in the Address Book, follow these steps:

1. Open the MSN Address Book as described earlier. Click Tools, Find or click the Find button in the toolbar. Exchange displays the property sheet shown in figure B.6, which you used to fill in your own profile.

2. On each page of the property sheet, fill in the information you want to match. Click OK.

3. Exchange redisplays the Address Book with the addresses that match your request. Notice that Exchange sets Show Names From The to Search Results.

4. Select the Microsoft Network in Show Names From The to return to a full list.

> **Troubleshooting**
>
> *After starting a search in the Address Book, Exchange displays this error:* `The search resulted in too many Address Book entries to display.`
>
> Your search criteria were not narrow enough. Provide more information in the property sheet to narrow the search.

Setting Properties for The Microsoft Network in Exchange

Chapter 24, "Using Microsoft Exchange," describes setting up and configuring the various services used in Exchange such as Microsoft Fax, Personal Address Book, and Personal Information Store. When you installed MSN, it added an additional service to this list: The Microsoft Network Online Service. This service provides the capability to exchange e-mail with other MSN members.

To set options for the MSN service in Exchange, follow these steps:

1. Choose Tools, Services from the Exchange main menu.
2. Select The Microsoft Network Online Service from the list of services. Then click Properties. Set the options on the Transport and Address Book pages of the property sheet. Click OK.

MSN Favorite Places

◀ See "Modifying and Deleting Shortcuts," p. 72

While you are exploring MSN, you'll come across many forums, BBSes, and other things you will want to visit again. MSN provides the Favorite Places folder, which allows you to save a shortcut to a place and then go directly to it without starting over from the Categories folder. Any document or folder you visit can be stored in Favorite Places.

Saving a Place in Favorite Places

Most of the MSN programs have the Add to Favorite Places button in the toolbar. If you want to save a shortcut to a particular icon in a folder, select the icon and click the Add to Favorite Places button. Alternatively, you can add an icon to Favorite Places by right-clicking on the icon and selecting Add to Favorite Places in the context menu.

If you want to save a shortcut to the open folder, make sure that no icon is selected in the folder and click the Add to Favorite Places button.

Going to a Place in Favorite Places

After you have saved a place in Favorite Places, you can quickly go there by double-clicking its icon. To display the Favorite Places folder, click the Go to Favorite Places button in the toolbar. Alternatively, right-click the MSN icon in the bottom-right corner of the taskbar and select Go to Favorite Places.

MSN Member Assistance

Member Assistance is the place to go if you need help or have questions about using MSN. Member Assistance is a forum that contains The MSN Member Lobby, Member Assistance Kiosk, Member Guidelines, and other documents containing news flashes about MSN. To go to Member Assistance, click the Member Assistance picture in MSN Central.

If you need help immediately, double-click The MSN Member Lobby; then double-click The MSN Member Lounge. The MSN Member Lounge is a live chat room where you can get immediate feedback to your questions, and it is always packed with interesting people from around the world.

MSN Categories

CATEGORIES, the last major section in MSN Central, represents about 95 percent of the content in MSN. Here you find forums containing BBSes to exchange messages with members, chat rooms to participate in live conversations, file libraries to download files, and more. Double-clicking CATEGORIES opens the Categories folder. This folder contains icons representing the various categories of forums on MSN. For example, under the Computers and Software category, you can expect to find forums and other information relating to computers and software. Figure B.7 shows the current categories available on MSN, and table B.1 shows the forums under each category.

Tip

The Categories folder now contains several language-independent Category subfolders, such as Categories (US), Categories (UK), and Categories (AUS).

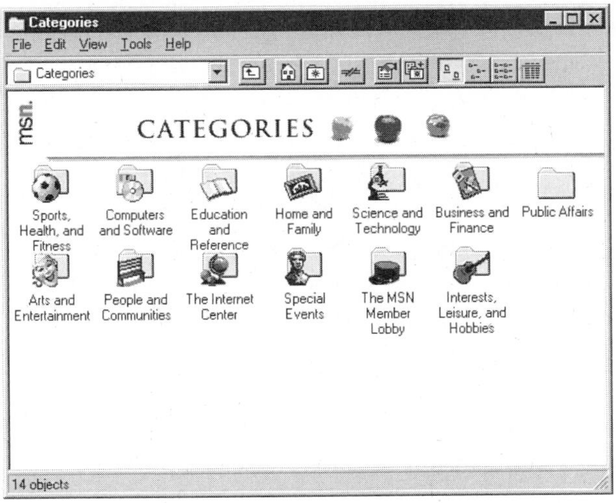

Fig. B.7

You can easily find the area you're interested in by starting in the Categories folder and opening the appropriate category folder.

VIII Appendixes

Note

When you first open a folder, MSN has to send information about it to your computer. This takes time, and you may perceive it as being slow. However, MSN caches (saves the information on your computer so it doesn't have to be transmitted again) the folders on your hard drive. Therefore, the next time you open the folder, it will load significantly faster.

Table B.1 Categories of Forums and Services

Category	Description
Sports, Health, and Fitness	Field and Court Sports, Health and Fitness, Indoor Sports and Recreation, Motorsports, Outdoor Sports and Recreation, Snow and Winter Sports, Sports Psychology and Medicine, Water Sports, Sports Media
Computers and Software	Computer Games, Computer Graphics, Desktop Publishing, Hardware, Multimedia and CD-ROM, Software, The BBS Industry, The MIDI Forum, *PC Magazine,* Computer Telephone
Education and Reference	Colleges and Universities, Computer Education, Educator to Educator, Fields of Study, International Students, Primary and Secondary Education, Student to Student
Home and Family	Genealogy, Home Improvement, KidSpace, Parenting in the 90s, Pets, Teen Forum, Work-At-Home Dads, Working Mothers
Science and Technology	Astronomy and Space, Biology and Life Sciences, Communications Technology, Computer Technology, Earth and Physical Sciences, Electronics, Engineering, Math, Medicine, Social Sciences, and Transportation
Business and Finance	Business Services, Jobs & Careers, News & Reference, Professions & Industries, Small Office/Home Office, UseNet Newsgroups, Wall Street
Arts and Entertainment	Art and Design, Books and Writing, Comedy and Humor, Genres, Movies, Music, Television and Radio, Theater
People and Communities	Advice and Support, Cultures, Menu Online, People to People, Religion, Women Online
The Internet Center	Internet Center BBS, Newgroups
Special Events	List changes daily. Includes special guests, shortcuts to new categories, and lists of special events happening on the network.
The MSN Member Lobby	Members Helping Members BBS, Netiquette Center, The Chat Garden
Interests, Leisure, and Hobbies	Arts and Crafts, Collecting, Games and Gaming, Hobbies and Avocations, Home Interests, Magazine, Mysteries, Outdoor Interests and Activities, Travel
Public Affairs	We the People, Armed Forces, C- SPAN, GoverNet, Inferno, Journalism World, Law Enforcement, Politics, Public Service

Double-clicking any icon in Categories opens a folder containing the forums available under that category. Forums can be nested. For example, the Software forum contains the Microsoft Forum, which is where Microsoft products are supported. Also, forums can contain any of the following six types of folders and documents:

- *Chat room.* A place where you can have a live conversation with other MSN members who see your comments immediately. Many conferences by leaders in various industries are held in chat rooms.
- *BBS.* A message area where you can exchange ideas with other like-minded people. BBSes are not live. Some are set up as file areas, which are read-only, where you can download the files attached to messages. BBSes are organized by areas of interest.
- *Media viewer title.* A file that is downloaded to your computer and viewed in the MSN Online Viewer. You view content in the right side of the viewer, and you can select different pages to view in the left side.
- *Download-and-run.* A file that is downloaded to your computer and executed. On MSN, this file is typically a Microsoft Word document. However, it can be any file type registered with Windows, such as a text file or bitmap file.
- *Kiosk.* A download-and-run document that contains additional information about the forum. Obviously, these documents are typically found in forums.
- *Forum.* A folder with a collection of related documents and subfolders. For example, a forum for cat lovers may have a BBS, chat area, and media viewer title explaining the history of cats.

Tip
The Categories folder now contains several language-independent Category subfolders, such as Categories (US), Categories (UK), and Categories (AUS).

◄ See "Registering Files to Automatically Open an Application," p. 537

Figure B.8, for example, shows the Shareware forum. This forum currently has a BBS, a chat area, a kiosk, and the Association of Shareware Professionals forum.

The path to this forum is \Categories\Computers & Software\Software\Shareware. To get to this forum, you use the following steps:

1. Select CATEGORIES from MSN Central.
2. Double-click the Computers & Software icon representing a category.
3. Double-click the Software Forum icon.
4. Double-click the Shareware icon to go to the Shareware forum shown in figure B.8.

Tip
If it is not obvious what type of folder or document an icon represents, right-click on the icon and select Properties to see its type.

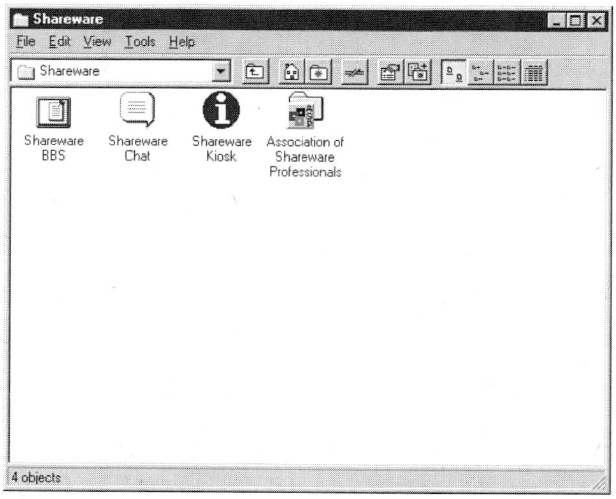

Fig. B.8
The contents of the Shareware forum. To read more information about this forum, double-click the Shareware Kiosk icon.

Note

You can go directly to a folder on MSN. Choose Edit, Goto, Other Location. Then type the *go word* for the folder you want. The go word is a special name given to each folder on MSN. To see a folder's go word, right-click the folder and choose Properties.

Communicating in Chat Rooms

Chat rooms are places on MSN where people gather to have live discussions. Mostly, people do chat in chat rooms. However, you'll frequently hear about conferences, debates, and other events occurring in chat rooms at predetermined times. In addition, MSN Today frequently lists upcoming events.

Tip
You can convey emotion in a chat room. For example, use the smiley *emoticon*—the emotion icon :-)—to indicate that you're grinning. See your MSN online help for more emoticons.

Chat rooms within a forum are dedicated to a particular topic. For example, a Windows 95 chat room will be used to discuss Windows 95. In reality, though, the discussion frequently wanders from the topic at hand to other mysteries of life. That is why chat rooms have *hosts*, or moderators. Hosts are provided to keep the conversation from becoming too brutal or getting off the given topic.

Figure B.9 shows a chat room, the MSN Member Lounge. This chat room is in the MSN Member Lobby forum. As indicated, there are three primary sections in this window:

- *Chat History pane.* Messages are displayed in this area immediately after they are posted. That's why they call it live!

- *Compose pane.* You type a new message in the text box, and then press Enter or click Send. Your message is posted immediately.
- *Member list.* You select a member name to get more information about that member. Then you can contact her or ignore her.

Notice that some members have a gavel beside their names. These members are hosts. They moderate the chat, greet people when they join the chat, and keep things civil.

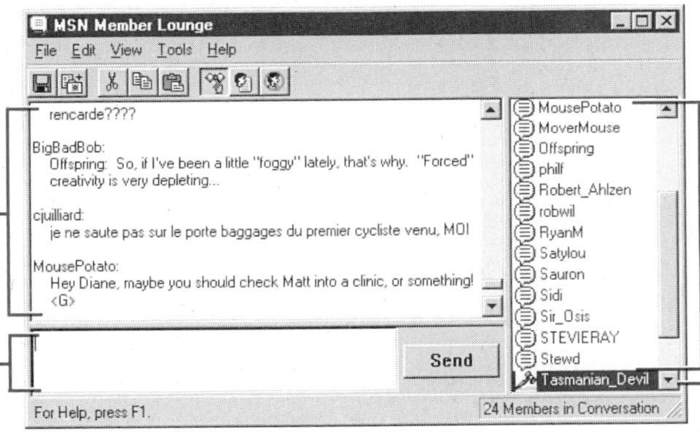

Fig. B.9 Chatting in the MSN Member Lounge.

Table B.2 shows the basic things you can do in a chat room.

Table B.2 Chat Room Tasks

Task	Description
Add the chat room to your Favorite Places folder	Choose File, Add to Favorite Places. Or click the Add to Favorite Places button in the toolbar. 
Ignore a member	Right-click a name in the member list and choose Ignore from the menu. Or select a name from the member list and click the Ignore button in the toolbar. 
Ignore many members	From the member list, select the names of the members you want to ignore. Choose View, Ignore Members from the menu. Then click Ignore Messages from Selected Members. Alternatively, select the names of the members you want to ignore from the member list. Then click the Ignore icon in the toolbar. 

(continues)

Table B.2 Continued

Task	Description
View member information	Right-click a name in the member list and choose Properties. Or select a name from the member list and click the Properties button in the toolbar.
Save the chat history	Choose File, Save History As. Then select or type a file name. The history can be printed with WordPad.
Receive notices when members join or leave	Choose Tools, Options from the menu. Click Join the Chat to receive messages when new members join; click Leave the Chat when members leave.

Exchanging Information in BBSs

A bulletin board is an area in an MSN forum where members exchange messages and files. The messages can be about anything, but typically they are related to the topic of the forum where the BBS is located. BBS messages are great for the following purposes:

- Exchanging ideas and opinions.
- Helping others and getting help with problems related to software, home improvements, pets, and just about any topic you can imagine.
- Reading the latest product information from your favorite vendor.
- Getting product support for hardware, software, and other products supported on the network.
- Posting files for other people to download. A file will not show up in the BBS until the forum manager, the person responsible for the forum's content, has approved it.

Tip
File areas on MSN are really just read-only BBSes. Each message in a file area has one or more file attachments. The message describes the content of the files.

Messages are grouped in a bulletin board by threads. A *thread* is a BBS conversation—a collection of messages related by subject. For example, if you post a message asking for help in a BBS and a kind person replies, both messages appear under the same subject heading as a thread.

Figure B.10 shows the Windows 95 Members To Members BBS. At this level, the BBS has only one message but contains many subfolders. You double-click a subfolder to access it. Many BBSes organize their messages into topics by creating multiple subfolders within the BBS. This approach makes it easier to find the information and the people with which you want to communicate.

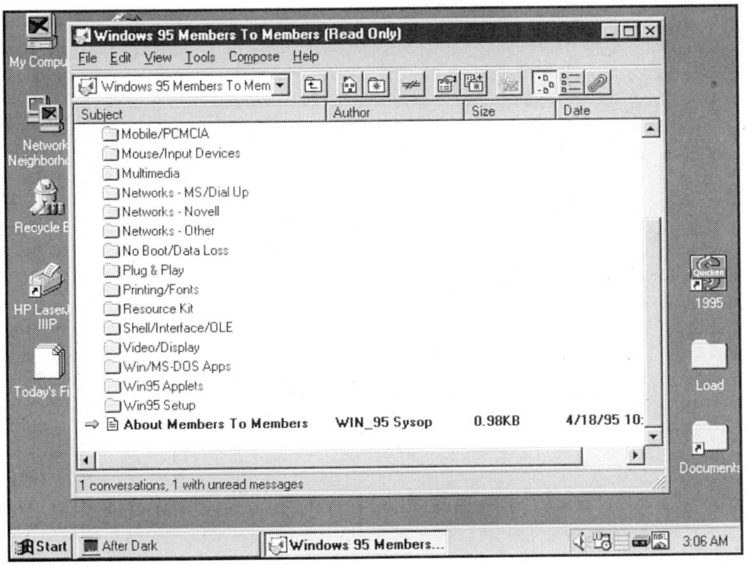

Fig. B.10
The Windows 95 Members To Members BBS.

Figure B.11 shows the General Discussion folder in the Windows 95 Members To Members BBS. As indicated in the figure, MSN provides a lot of feedback about the status of each message and thread. This feedback includes the following:

- Unread messages or threads with unread messages are indicated with the arrow pointing to the message header. When all the messages in the thread have been marked as read, the icon disappears.

- A message that is not a part of a thread or that is the last message in a thread is denoted with the Message icon next to the message header.

- A thread is indicated by the plus sign within a box next to a message header. You click the icon to expand the thread one level. You can expand additional levels of the thread by clicking the icons. The last message header in the thread will not have a plus sign beside it.

Fig. B.11
The General Discussion subfolder.

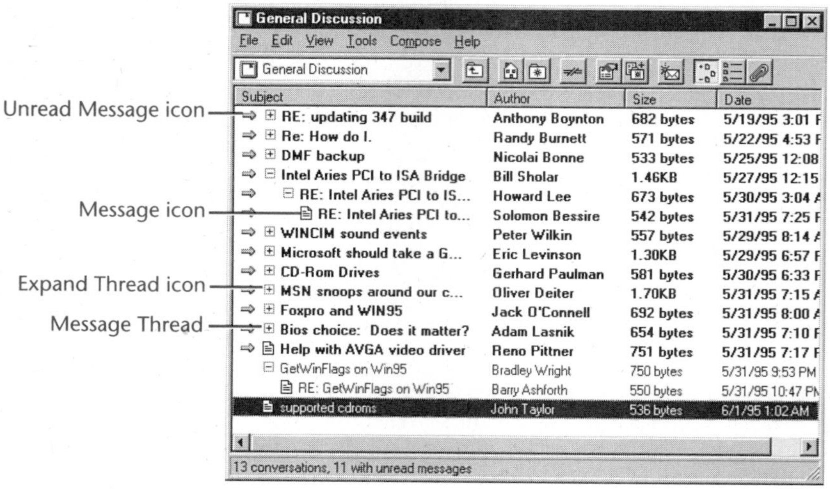

Table B.3 lists the basic tasks you can do in a BBS.

Table B.3 BBS Tasks

	Task	Description
	Add a BBS to your Favorite Places folder	Choose File, Add to Favorite Places. Or click the Add to Favorite Places button in the toolbar.
	Read a message	Double-click the message header.
	Compose a new message	Choose Compose, New Message from the menu or click the New Message button in the toolbar. Then type the message's subject and text. Choose File, Post Message or click the Post Message button on the toolbar.
	Reply to a message	Open the message as described earlier. Choose Compose, Reply to BBS or click the Reply to BBS button in the toolbar. Compose your message as described earlier.
	Reply via E-mail	Open the message as described earlier. Choose Compose, Reply by E-mail. Compose your message as described earlier.
	View a message's properties	Click a message and choose File, Properties. Or click a message and then click the Properties button in the toolbar.
	View attachments	Choose View, Attached Files or click the File View button in the toolbar.

Task	Description
Mark all messages as read	Choose Tools, Mark All Messages as Read.
Download an attached file	Open the message as described earlier. Double-click the attachment and click Download File. Alternatively, right-click the attachment and choose File Object, Download.
View the status of a downloading file	Choose Tools, File Transfer Status.
Send a file as	Begin composing a new message as an attachment, as described earlier. Choose Insert, File and select a file. Alternatively, click the Insert File button in the toolbar and select a file.

Note

MSN automatically decompresses or unzips files when they are downloaded. To disable this feature, choose Tools, Options from the File Transfer Status window. Then deselect Automatically Decompress Files.

Finding Folders and Files on The Microsoft Network

You've already learned how to find files on your computer. Finding folders and files on MSN is not much different. For example, you may want to find a forum about Windows 95, a chat room about golf, or any items relating to a particular company such as Symantec. To find folders and files on MSN, follow these steps:

◀ See "Finding Files," p. 523

1. Choose Tools, Find, On The Microsoft Network. MSN displays the Find dialog box shown in figure B.12.

2. In the Containing field, type the text for which you want to search. Optionally, click Description to include the description of each forum and file in the search.

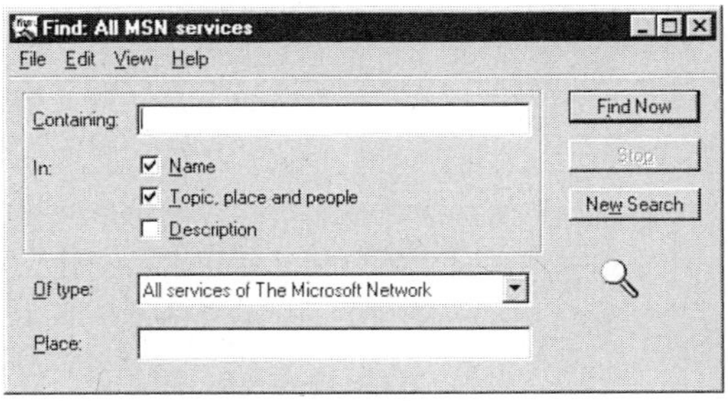

Fig. B.12
Type the text you want to search for; then click Find Now.

3. Select the type of service in the Of Type list and then click Find Now. MSN performs the search and displays the results.

After MSN displays the search results, you can right-click a file or folder to open it or create a shortcut to it.

Note

You can't search files or messages in a particular BBS.

Using the Internet through The Microsoft Network

Eventually, MSN will provide complete support for Internet e-mail, newsgroups, and the World Wide Web. However, MSN is initially supporting basic Internet e-mail and newsgroups. The following list describes the restrictions and plans for each Internet service:

◄ See "UseNet Newsgroups," p. 940

◄ See "Surfing the Web with Internet Explorer," p. 920

- *E-mail*. MSN supports sending and receiving e-mail on the Internet. Currently, you cannot send or receive files using the Internet.
- *Newsgroups*. MSN provides support for viewing Internet newsgroups, but you cannot post messages to newsgroups. Microsoft intends to supply support for posting messages to newsgroups in the near future.
- *World Wide Web*. MSN doesn't support the Web at this time. However, Microsoft is working diligently on such support.

Exchanging E-Mail with Internet Users

◄ See "Electronic Mail," p. 905

Sending e-mail to an Internet address is no different from sending e-mail to an MSN address. Instead of typing an MSN address such as JQ_Doe, you type an Internet address such as john@msn.com. Receiving e-mail from an Internet user is just as easy. Before an Internet user can send you an e-mail message, the sender needs your Internet ID. Your Internet ID is <MSN ID>@MSN.COM, in which <MSN ID> is your MSN log-on ID.

Troubleshooting

I correctly addressed an e-mail message to an Internet user, but when I log on to MSN, it doesn't send the message.

Exchange determines which services will be used for Internet addresses by the order of the services in the Recipient Addresses are Processed in the Following Order list on the Delivery page of Exchange's Option menu. To use MSN to deliver e-mail to Internet users, choose Tools, Options from the Exchange menu. Then click the Delivery page and move The Microsoft Network Online Service to the top of the list.

Using Newsgroups

Internet newsgroups are identical to MSN BBSes. However, the content is not managed by MSN. You can find the Internet newsgroup BBSes at \Categories\The Internet Center\Newsgroups. Additionally, some newsgroups can be found in various forums where the newsgroup complements the forum.

Caution

The content of Internet newsgroups is not managed by MSN. Therefore, you may find some of the postings in newsgroups to be adult-oriented or particularly offensive. It is your responsibility to monitor your children's access to the Internet newsgroups, because MSN makes no provision for locking out offensive messages.

Appendix C

Exploring the Windows 95 Resource Kit

by R. Michael O'Mara

Microsoft split the user documentation for Windows 95 into two parts. The first part contains the User's Guide, help files, tutorial, and so on. This part is aimed at the average Windows 95 user and covers the Windows 95 user interface and features.

The Windows 95 Resource Kit comprises the *rest* of the Windows 95 user documentation. This kit provides more depth and detail about topics that (in Microsoft's estimation) the average user isn't likely to need. You can find information about customized setup and installation, network configuration, and the like. The Windows 95 Resource Kit is a manual, help files, and supplementary utilities aimed at network administrators and others who must support other Windows 95 users.

In this appendix, you learn

- Who needs the Windows 95 Resource Kit?
- How do you get the Resource Kit?
- How is the Resource Kit organized?
- What utilities are included in the Resource Kit?

It's important to understand that the Windows 95 Resource Kit is *not* a programmer's reference or software development kit—that's another area entirely. The Windows 95 Resource Kit is still part of the user-level documentation; it's just aimed at a higher-level user than the rest of the Windows 95 documentation.

Who Needs the Windows 95 Resource Kit?

Are you responsible for installing, configuring, or supporting multiple copies of Windows 95—especially on a network? If so, you need to get a copy of the Windows 95 Resource Kit.

Obviously, MIS managers, network administrators, help desk staff, and other corporate technical support personnel can benefit from the Windows 95 Resource Kit. Consultants and people serving in computer and network support roles in smaller businesses also will need the information in the Windows 95 Resource Kit.

Individual Windows 95 users are much less likely to need the Windows 95 Resource Kit. A high-end user attempting to employ Windows 95's connectivity features without assistance from a corporate network administrator may occasionally use the Windows 95 Resource Kit. However, average networked Windows 95 users are probably better off asking their network administrator for help than trying to look up answers on their own.

How Do You Get the Windows 95 Resource Kit?

The Windows 95 Resource Kit is a technical reference manual that contains information. As such, the manual is mainly text. In addition to the text-based information, the Windows 95 Resource Kit includes a few, small software utilities designed to help system administrators monitor and configure Windows 95 on networks.

If you have the full CD-ROM version of Windows 95, you already have an electronic copy of the Windows 95 Resource Kit. The Resource Kit appears as a Windows Help file in the \ADMIN\RESKIT\HELPFILE folder. The software utilities are available on the Windows 95 CD-ROM in the various subdirectories of the \ADMIN95 directory.

Note

Microsoft does not include the Windows 95 Resource Kit files when distributing Windows 95 on floppy disks. Also, other suppliers who are licensed to sell Windows 95 with their computer systems may not include the Windows 95 Resource Kit files.

If you don't have a copy of the Windows 95 Resource Kit, or you want a printed and bound version, you can order it direct from Microsoft Press or purchase a copy from many bookstores and software outlets. To order, call Microsoft Press at (800) 677-7377. When you purchase a copy of the Windows 95 Resource Kit, you get the Resource Kit in book form plus a CD-ROM containing help files and utility programs.

You may be reluctant to spend money for a paper copy of something you already have on disk—especially if you don't expect to use the Windows 95 Resource Kit much. However, if you expect to refer to the Windows 95 Resource Kit frequently, you will find the paper version much easier to search and use than a series of word processor files on a CD-ROM.

How Is the Windows 95 Resource Kit Organized?

This appendix gives an overview of the contents of the Windows 95 Resource Kit and how it's organized. You can get an idea of the information in the Windows 95 Resource Kit and perhaps get a head start on finding the resources you may need.

The Windows 95 Resource Kit manual is divided into eight sections. The sections of the kit are described following, complete with a list of the chapters in each section.

Part 1: Deployment Planning Guide

The first section presents Microsoft's suggested strategy for MIS managers planning to convert their users from Windows 3.1 to Windows 95. This information is of interest primarily to corporate support staff and has limited appeal for smaller businesses with more informal procedures.

- Chapter 1, "Deployment Planning Basics"
- Chapter 2, "Deployment Strategy and Details"

Part 2: Installation

This section covers installing Windows 95 on network servers and on multiple computers. You can find information on creating custom installations and setup scripts. (Sample setup scripts are included in the Windows 95 Resource Kit files.) You also can find technical details about Windows 95 setup and operating system startup in these chapters:

- Chapter 3, "Introduction to Windows 95 Setup"
- Chapter 4, "Server-Based Setup for Windows 95"
- Chapter 5, "Custom, Automated, and Push Installations"
- Chapter 6, "Setup Technical Discussion"

Part 3: Networking

Network administrators take note—this section makes the Windows 95 Resource Kit a *must have* for you. You can find technical details about configuring peer resource sharing services, configuring network adapters and protocols, and running Windows 95 on Windows NT, Novell NetWare, and other networks.

- Chapter 7, "Introduction to Windows 95 Networking"
- Chapter 8, "Windows 95 on Microsoft Networks"
- Chapter 9, "Windows 95 on NetWare Networks"
- Chapter 10, "Windows 95 on other Networks"
- Chapter 11, "Logon, Browsing, and Resource Sharing"
- Chapter 12, "Network Technical Discussion"

Part 4: System Management

Security and administrative controls are the focus of this section of the Windows 95 Resource Kit. You can gain information you need to implement system policies, user profiles, and management tools such as backup agents. The performance tuning chapter offers instructions for using Windows 95's performance settings.

- Chapter 13, "Introduction to System Management"
- Chapter 14, "Security"
- Chapter 15, "User Profiles and System Policies"
- Chapter 16, "Remote Administration"
- Chapter 17, "Performance Tuning"

Part 5: System Configuration

The system configuration section of the Windows 95 Resource Kit is a valuable reference for anyone installing, configuring, and troubleshooting devices in Windows 95 systems. The printing and fonts chapter is particularly valuable; it addresses printing on networks (both Microsoft and Novell) and using printing management utilities including the Hewlett-Packard JetAdmin utility and DEC PrintServer software.

- Chapter 18, "Introduction to System Configuration"
- Chapter 19, "Devices"
- Chapter 20, "Disks and File Systems"
- Chapter 21, "Multimedia"
- Chapter 22, "Application Support"
- Chapter 23, "Printing and Fonts"

Part 6: Communications

In addition to details on configuring modems, the Communications section includes valuable information on Microsoft Exchange (Microsoft's new universal mailbox) and Microsoft Fax. Road warriors will appreciate the chapter on dial-up networking (also known as remote network access). But the most popular chapter may be the one on Internet access. The information in this chapter provides the keys to unlocking Windows 95's built-in Internet access capabilities.

- Chapter 24, "Introduction to Windows 95 Communications"
- Chapter 25, "Modems and Communications Tools"
- Chapter 26, "Electronic Mail and Microsoft Exchange"
- Chapter 27, "Microsoft Fax"
- Chapter 28, "Dial-Up Networking and Mobile Computing"
- Chapter 29, "The Microsoft Network"
- Chapter 30, "Internet Access"

Part 7: Windows 95 Reference

The chapters on the Windows 95 architecture and international features may come in handy for some readers, as will the troubleshooting guidelines. But the key chapter in this section is the one on the Registry—Windows 95's repository for system configuration, networking, and software settings. This chapter may be the only place you can find information on this critical replacement for INI files.

- Chapter 31, "Windows 95 Architecture"
- Chapter 32, "Windows 95 Network Architecture"
- Chapter 33, "Windows 95 Registry"
- Chapter 34, "International Windows 95"
- Chapter 35, "General Troubleshooting"

Part 8: Appendixes

This requisite section of appendixes contains listings of settings, options, commands, and files. Note the first appendix; it contains a command summary of the Windows 95 replacements for MS-DOS commands.

- Glossary
- Appendix A, "Command-Line Commands Summary"
- Appendix B, "Windows 95 System Files"
- Appendix C, "Windows 95 INF Files"
- Appendix D, "MSBATCH.INF Parameters"
- Appendix E, "Microsoft Systems Management Server"
- Appendix F, "Macintosh and Windows 95"
- Appendix G, "HOSTS and LMHOSTS Files for Windows 95"
- Appendix H, "Shortcuts for Windows 95"
- Appendix I, "Accessibility"
- Appendix J, "Windows 95 Resource Directory"

What Utilities Are Included in the Resource Kit?

The utility programs that come with the Windows 95 Resource Kit provide system administrators with access to some of Windows 95's more powerful network and security features. If you're a system administrator, you should add these utilities to your toolbox—whether you get them as part of the Windows 95 Resource Kit or elsewhere.

You will find all these utilities on the Windows 95 CD-ROM. If you don't have the CD-ROM, you can obtain the utilities by ordering a copy of the Windows 95 Resource Kit from Microsoft. Microsoft also may make the utilities available on The Microsoft Network and other online services.

The following is a list of the utility programs that are included with the Windows 95 Resource Kit.

- *Net Setup*. A Server-Based Setup utility that replaces the `setup /a` command and also lets you automate many Windows 95 installations across a network with installation scripts.
- *Password List Editor*. Enables the system administrator to view a list of resources for which Windows 95 has cached passwords.
- *System Policy Editor*. Use to create system policies that selectively control aspects of a specific Windows 95 environment when a user logs on to the network server.
- *Net Watcher*. Enables you to check the status of all your shared resources in Windows 95.
- *Microsoft Remote Registry Service*. Allows administrators to change Registry entries on other computers over the network.
- *Microsoft RPC Print Provider*. Provides the full set of APIs required for a Windows 95 client to administer printer queues on Windows NT servers.
- *Microsoft Print Agent for NetWare Networks*. Directs print jobs from a NetWare server to a computer running Windows 95 with Client for NetWare Networks and Microsoft Print Agent for NetWare Networks.
- *SNMP Agent*. Use to monitor remote connections to Windows 95 computers with networks using Simple Network Management Protocol (SNMP).

Note

There are additional utilities on the Windows 95 CD-ROM in the \ADMIN\APPTOOLS directory.

Appendix D

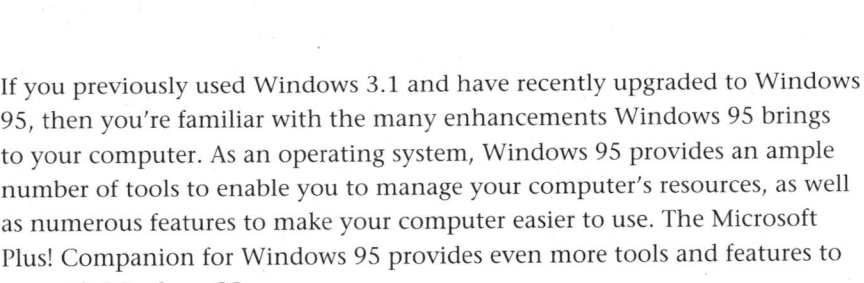

Using Microsoft Plus!

by Lisa A. Bucki

If you previously used Windows 3.1 and have recently upgraded to Windows 95, then you're familiar with the many enhancements Windows 95 brings to your computer. As an operating system, Windows 95 provides an ample number of tools to enable you to manage your computer's resources, as well as numerous features to make your computer easier to use. The Microsoft Plus! Companion for Windows 95 provides even more tools and features to use with Windows 95.

Microsoft Plus! provides Desktop Themes, which enable you to choose new wallpaper, mouse pointers, sounds, and more to customize your Windows 95 desktop. It provides new visual settings to improve the appearance of large fonts, desktop wallpaper, and windows you're dragging. In addition, Plus! provides the System Agent, which enables you to schedule disk maintenance activities like disk backups; and ScanDisk 3, an even better version of the ScanDisk compression technology that comes with Windows 95. Finally, Plus! includes the Internet Explorer, software you can use to connect to the Internet via a local area network, the Microsoft Network, or an account you have with an Internet service provider.

This appendix introduces you to Plus! and the capabilities it adds to your system. In this appendix, you learn to

- Install all of Plus! or just the components you want, or remove Plus! from your computer
- Set up your system to connect with the Internet through the Internet Explorer
- Select and set up a desktop theme to customize Windows' appearance, and choose whether to use other desktop enhancements such as font smoothing

- Play 3D Pinball
- Schedule system maintenance with the System Agent
- Increase the amount of data you can store on a disk with DriveSpace 3

Installing Plus!

You have to install the Microsoft Plus! companion separately, after you install Windows 95 on your system. Plus! is available in both the 3.5 inch floppy disk and CD-ROM formats. For Plus! to run effectively on your system, the system must meet the following minimum requirements:

- 80486 processor or better
- 8M or more of Random Access Memory (RAM)
- Graphics display (monitor and video adapter card) that can display 256 colors or more; a 16-bit display that can handle more colors is recommended, and enables you to use all of the available Desktop Themes
- A sound card is recommended

The Plus! Setup program enables you to install the complete Plus! package (Typical installation) or only selected components of Plus! (Custom installation). Setup also includes the Internet Setup Wizard, which helps you install the Internet Explorer and set up your Internet connection. The next few sections describe how to install Plus! with Windows 95.

Performing a Typical Setup

► See "Performing a Custom Setup," p. 1145

Most users will use the Typical Setup option to install all of the components for Microsoft Plus! The Typical Setup requires up to 12-16M of hard disk space. If your system is low on hard disk space, or if you don't want to install all of Plus!'s features (such as when you're using a laptop computer and don't want to use some desktop features that may require more RAM), perform a Custom Setup.

Note

To install Microsoft Plus! for Windows 95, you need your Windows 95 Setup CD-ROM or floppy disks. Make sure these are available, or you will not be able to complete the Plus! Setup.

To perform a Typical Setup for Plus!, start your computer and wait for the Windows 95 desktop to load. Then follow these steps to complete the installation:

1. Place the first Plus! Setup floppy disk or the Plus! CD-ROM in the appropriate drive on your system.
2. Open the Start menu and choose Run. The Run dialog box appears.
3. Choose F:\SETUP.EXE from the Open drop-down list (F: represents the letter for the drive where you inserted the Setup disk or CD-ROM).
4. Choose OK. The Microsoft Plus! for Windows 95 Setup dialog box appears.
5. Click Continue.
6. At the Name and Organization Information dialog box, enter your Name and Organization. Click OK. Click OK again to confirm the entries.
7. Enter the 10-digit CD-key number or floppy disk key number from your Plus! package in the dialog box that appears. Click OK.
8. Write down the Product ID number shown in the next dialog box and store the number with your Plus! CD or disks. Click OK to confirm the Product ID number and continue Setup.
9. Setup searches your system and displays a dialog box listing the folder Setup will create to hold the Plus! files (see fig. D.1). To install Plus! to a different disk or folder, click Change Folder. In the Change Folder dialog box, specify the drive and folder to use (by choosing them from the list or typing a path in the Path text box), and then click OK. At the dialog box asking whether Windows 95 should create the destination folder, click Yes to continue. Whether you accepted the folder recommended by Setup or specified another one, click OK to accept the Install folder.
10. The next Setup dialog box asks you to specify what kind of install to perform: Typical or Custom. Click Typical. (Skip to the next section to review the Custom setup process.)
11. Setup checks your system's video installation. If your display runs in 256 colors, Setup displays the Video Resolution Check dialog box. This

dialog box asks whether you want to install the high-color Desktop Themes, even if your monitor currently displays only 256 colors. If your display is capable of displaying more colors (operating in 16-bit color or higher) and you have ample hard disk space, click Yes. Otherwise, click No.

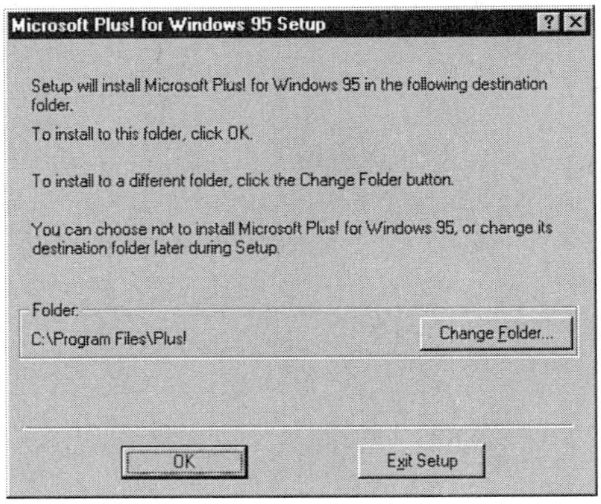

Fig. D.1
The Plus! Setup program tells you which folder the Plus! files will be installed in.

12. Setup checks your system for necessary disk space, then begins copying files to your computer (see fig. D.2). If you're installing Plus! from floppy disks, swap disks into and out of the drive when prompted. Setup displays a message that it's updating your system, then displays the Windows 95 Applet Installation dialog box, reminding you to have your Windows 95 install disks or CD-ROM available. Click OK to continue.

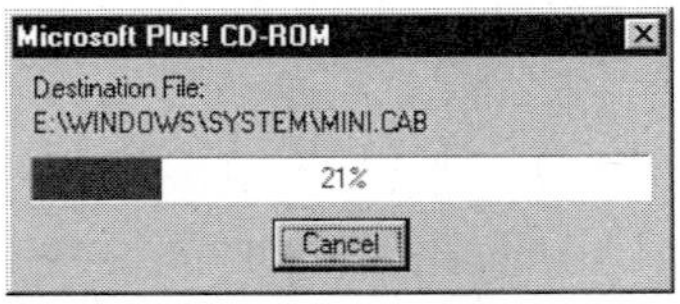

Fig. D.2
Setup shows you its progress in copying files to your hard disk.

13. Setup prompts you to insert the Windows 95 CD-ROM or a particular Setup disk. Insert it into the appropriate drive, then click OK. Windows 95 Setup tells you that it's updating the Shortcuts.

14. Setup next displays the initial dialog box for the Internet Setup Wizard (see fig. D.3). If you don't need to set up to connect with the Internet, click Cancel. If you do want to set up your Internet connection, click Next and proceed to the "Setting Up the Internet Explorer" section later in this appendix.

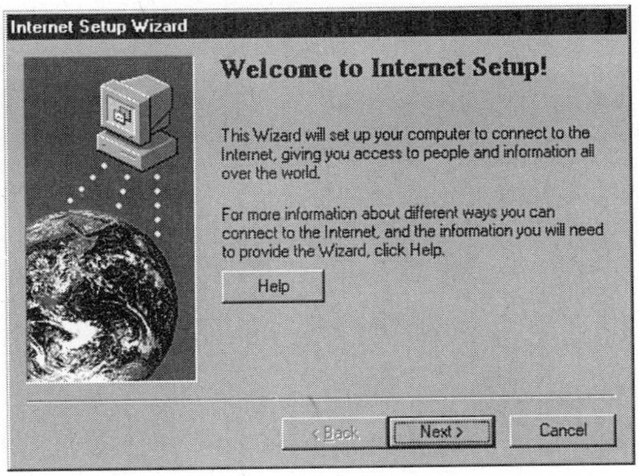

Fig. D.3
The Internet Setup Wizard enables you to set up Windows 95 to connect to the Internet.

15. If you clicked Cancel in step 14, the Internet Setup Wizard asks you to confirm that you want to exit the Wizard. Click Yes to do so.

16. The Set Up a Desktop Theme dialog box appears. Click OK to continue.

▶ See "Working with Desktop Themes," p. 1150

17. The Desktop Themes dialog box appears, allowing you to select your first Desktop Theme. Click OK to continue.

18. Microsoft Plus! Setup displays a dialog box telling you that it needs to restart Windows. To complete the setup, click the Restart Windows button. Your computer and Windows 95 restart. Notice that the Windows 95 startup screen now reads *Microsoft Windows 95 Microsoft Plus!* to indicate that you've successfully installed Microsoft Plus!

Performing a Custom Setup

If you want to install Microsoft Plus! but don't need to install all its features because you're short on hard disk space, you can perform a Custom Setup to pick and choose which features you really want to install. To perform a Custom Setup, use the following steps:

1. Follow steps 1 through 9 of the Typical Setup procedure described in the previous section.

2. When Setup asks whether you want to perform a Typical or Custom Setup, click Custom. The Microsoft Plus! for Windows 95-Custom dialog box appears (see fig. D.4).

3. To customize the installation for a particular component, click the component name in the Options list, then click the Change Option button.

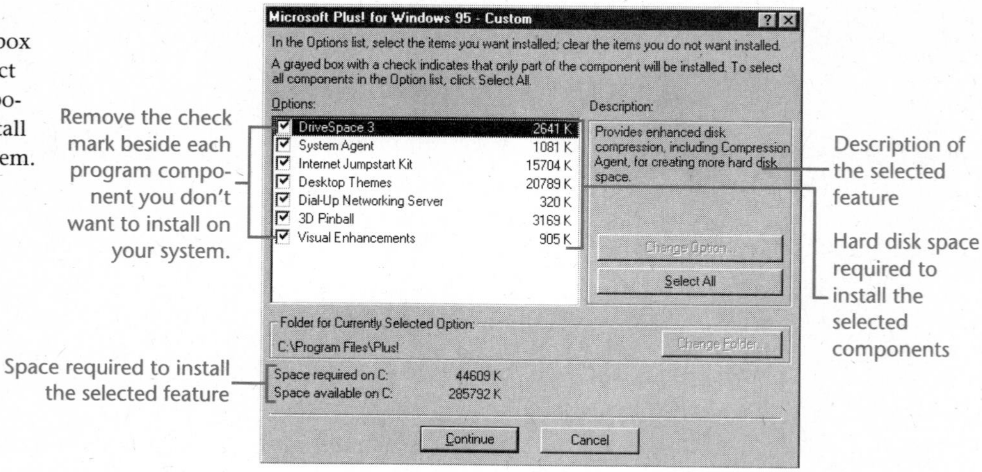

Fig. D.4
This dialog box lets you select which components to install on your system.

4. In the dialog box that appears, click to deselect features you don't want to install in the Options list (a description of each option appears to the right of the list to help you make your selections), then click OK to return to the Custom dialog box. Repeat this step for each of the components you want to customize.

5. When you've finished specifying what components to install in the Custom dialog box, click the Continue button. After you click Continue, the Setup process progresses just like a Typical Setup.

Setting Up the Internet Explorer

The Internet Explorer software enables you to connect to the Microsoft Network or the Internet via a direct network connection or a PPP dial-up account from an Internet service provider. Microsoft Plus! provides the Internet Explorer software, plus the Internet Setup Wizard (refer to fig. D.3). You can use the Internet Setup Wizard to install the Internet Explorer while you're installing the rest of Plus!. Or, if you want to use the Wizard later, after you install Plus!, open the Start menu and choose Programs, Accessories, Internet Tools, and then Internet Setup Wizard.

Note

Chapters 29, 30, and Appendix B explain basic communications and Internet concepts, how to work with the Internet Explorer, and how to work with the Microsoft Network, respectively. See those chapters to learn more about the Internet. In particular, Chapter 30, "Using FTP, the World Wide Web, and other Internet Services," explains how to work with the Internet Explorer after you've installed it.

To use the Internet Setup Wizard to install the Internet Explorer, follow these steps:

1. Click Next from the Internet Setup Wizard Welcome dialog box to proceed with the setup. The How to Connect dialog box appears (see fig. D.5).

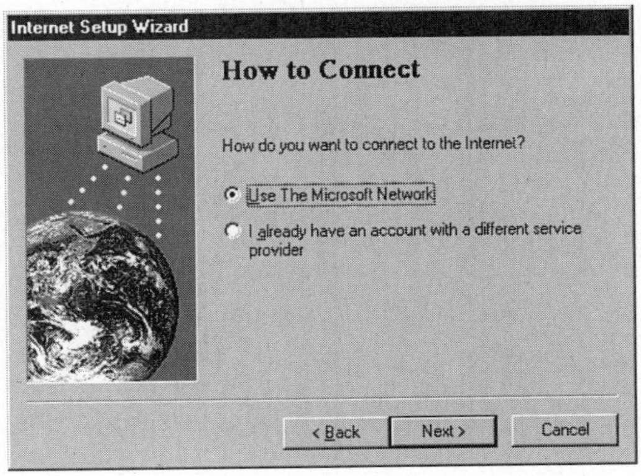

Fig. D.5
The Internet Setup Wizard asks you to specify how you will connect to the Internet—via the Microsoft Network or an existing service provider account.

> **Note**
>
> If you are connected to a LAN,Microsoft Plus! displays a dialog box prompting to see whether you want to connect to the Internet through your LAN or to connect using a modem. Choose the LAN option only if your LAN is using TCP/IP and is connected to the Internet.

2. Specify whether you want to connect via the Microsoft Network or a PPP account you have with an Internet service provider by clicking the appropriate option button. Click Next to continue.

3. The Installing Files dialog box appears, reminding you that you might need your Windows 95 setup CD-ROM or disks. Click Next to continue.

4. The Setup Wizard copies files to your hard disk. When it concludes, it displays a dialog box asking you to insert your Windows 95 Setup CD-ROM or disk into the appropriate drive. Do so, then click OK.

5. The Setup Wizard copies additional files to your system. Then, the process varies, depending on whether you chose to connect via the Microsoft Network or an Internet Service Provider. You can choose to set up a new Microsoft Network account or connect to an existing Microsoft Network or Internet account. Depending on which method you choose, the Wizard will guide you through the process. Simply

respond to each Wizard dialog box, providing information such as your Internet service provider's IP address, and your user name and password. Click Next after you provide each item of information the Wizard requests.

6. A final Setup Wizard dialog box appears, informing you that Setup is complete. Click the Finish button.
7. The Setup Wizard displays a dialog box telling you that it needs to restart Windows. To complete the setup, click Restart Windows. Your computer and Windows 95 restart.

Uninstalling When You Need To

Microsoft Plus! can take advantage of Windows 95's Add/Remove Programs feature, which enables you to automatically uninstall a program. With Plus!, you can remove the whole program or selected components from your hard disk if you no longer use them or want to replace them. To uninstall Plus!, follow these steps:

1. Open the Start menu and choose Settings, Control Panel. The Control Panel window opens.

2. Double-click the Add/Remove Programs icon. The Add/Remove Program Properties sheet appears.
3. The center of the sheet lists programs that can be added or removed from your system. Double-click Microsoft Plus! for Windows 95 in the list.
4. The Microsoft Plus! for Windows 95 Setup installation maintenance dialog box appears (see fig. D.6).
5. You can remove part of or all of the Plus! program. To uninstall all of Plus!, click the Remove All button. Or, to choose which components to remove, click the Add/Remove button to display the Maintenance Install dialog box shown in figure D.7. In the Options list, click to clear the check mark beside each Plus! component to remove from your system, then click Continue.
6. Whether you're removing all or parts of Plus!, a dialog box appears asking you to confirm the removal. Click Yes to continue the uninstall process. Setup removes the Plus! files from your system.

Tip
You also can use this process to reinstall parts of the Plus! package, such as installing the high-color Desktop Themes after you perform the initial Plus! Setup.

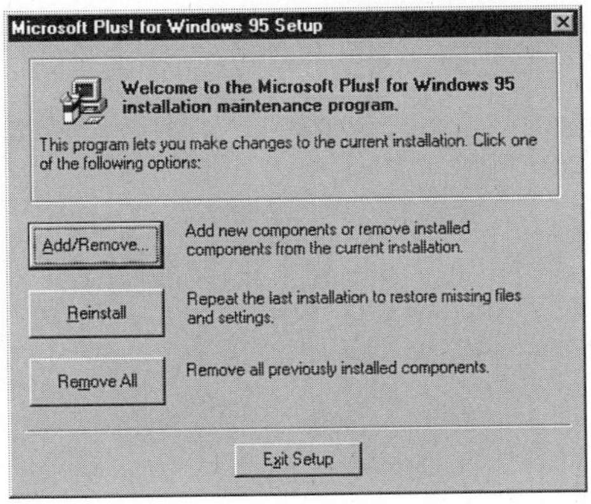

Fig. D.6
This Setup dialog box enables you to uninstall part of or all of Plus!.

Tip
Rerunning the Setup program from the Microsoft Plus! CD-ROM or floppy disks also displays the installation maintenance dialog box.

7. Microsoft Plus! Setup displays a dialog box telling you that it needs to restart Windows. To complete the uninstalling of Plus!, click Restart Windows. Your computer and Windows 95 restart.

Working with Desktop Themes

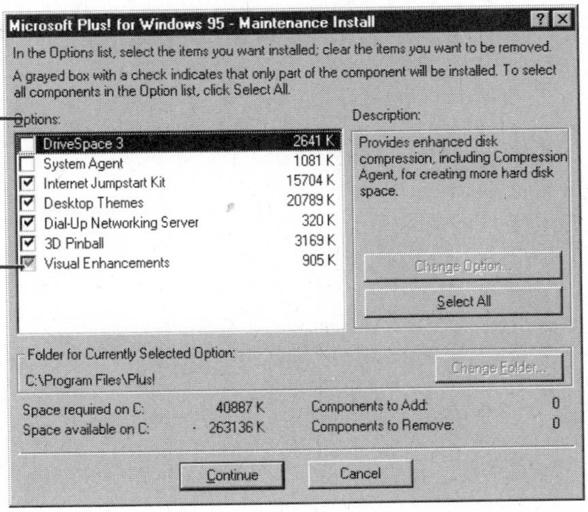

Fig. D.7
To add or remove Plus! components, use the Maintenance Install dialog box.

The Microsoft Plus! Desktop Themes provide you with appealing graphics and sounds to decorate your desktop and highlight system events (see fig. D.8). Each Desktop Theme offers a coordinated set of elements, so you can set the appropriate mood for your computing experience. Plus! provides Desktop

Theme combinations for computers displaying in 256 colors and for computers displaying in 16-bit or higher color. If you did not install the high-color Desktop Themes, you can rerun the Plus! Setup at any time to do so. The following are the Desktop Themes provided with Plus!:

256 Color

Dangerous Creatures (see fig. D.8)

Leonardo da Vinci

Science

The 60's USA

Sports

Windows 95

High Color

Inside Your Computer

Nature

The Golden Era

Mystery

Travel

Fig. D.8
Make every workday a safari by choosing the Dangerous Creatures Desktop Theme.

When you choose a Desktop Theme, you can specify whether to replace Windows screen elements you specify using the Control Panel. (To learn how to change various desktop elements with the Control Panel, refer to Chapter 5, "Customizing Windows 95.") Desktop Themes provides these desktop elements; you can choose which of these you want to use for your system:

- *Screen Saver.* Displays the Theme screen saver when you leave your computer idle.
- *Sound Events.* Assigns the Theme sounds to system events such as Windows startup and exit.
- *Mouse Pointers.* Applies the Theme pointer styles for different types of pointers, such as the pointer used to select text or the one that appears while Windows is busy performing an operation.
- *Desktop Wallpaper.* Covers the desktop with the decorative background provided by the Theme.
- *Icons.* Assigns custom Theme icons to desktop objects like the My Computer object and the Recycle Bin.
- *Icon Size and Spacing.* Makes desktop icons use the icon size and spacing specified by the Theme; keep in mind that larger icons use more computer memory, so if your system is low on memory, don't use this option.
- *Colors.* Applies the Theme colors to windows and other screen elements.
- *Font Names and Styles.* Uses the Theme fonts for screen elements like window titles.
- *Font and Window Sizes.* Uses the Theme font sizes and default window sizes.

Tip

If you need a high degree of accuracy when pointing with the mouse, the Mouse Pointer option for several Themes might make your pointing more difficult because of the pointer shapes assigned by the Theme. If you have trouble with this, deselect the Mouse Pointer option for the current Theme.

As mentioned earlier, the Theme replaces the desktop elements you specify using the Control Panel. You should note, however, that the most recent element you select using either method (Desktop Themes or the Control Panel) becomes active. So, for example, if you apply a Desktop Theme, but aren't quite satisfied with the screen saver, you can use the Control Panel to choose another screen saver to use.

Selecting and Setting Up a Theme

Plus! Setup! creates an object icon for the Desktop Themes in the Windows 95 Control Panel, which contains other objects for controlling Windows' appearance and operation. Use the following steps to use the Desktop Themes object to select a Theme:

1. Open the Start menu and choose Settings, Control Panel.

2. In the Control Panel window, double-click the Desktop Themes icon (see fig. D.9).

Fig. D.9
Select a Desktop Theme using the Control Panel.

3. The Desktop Themes dialog box appears, as shown in figure D.10. Use this dialog box to select and set up a Theme.

Fig. D.10
Plus! provides numerous options for setting up the Desktop Theme of your choice.

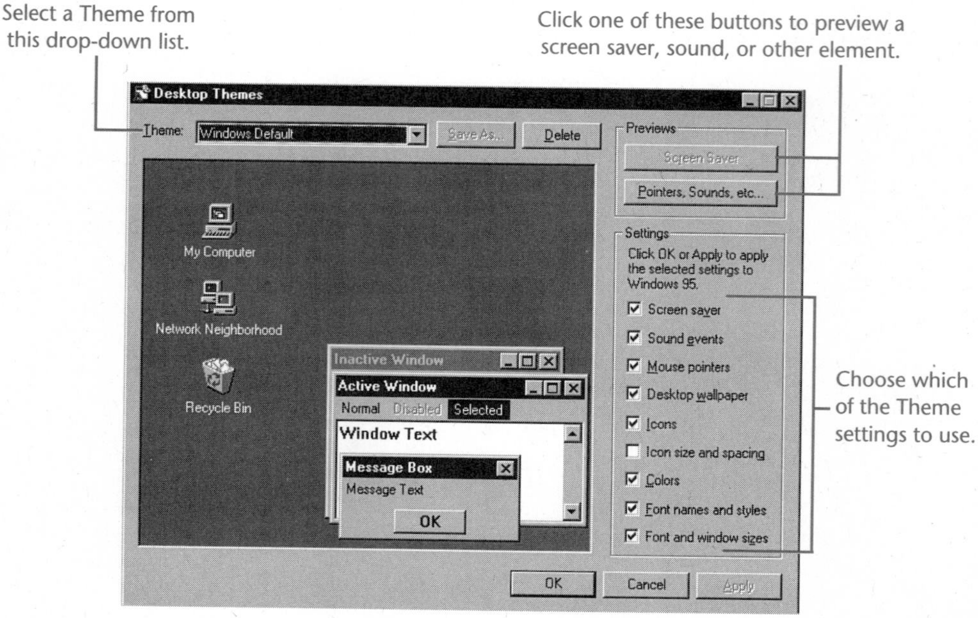

Click the down arrow beside the Theme drop-down list to display the available Desktop Themes. Click the name of the Theme you want to use. A dialog box tells you that the Theme files are being imported. When that dialog box closes, the preview area of the Desktop Themes changes to display the appearance of the Theme you selected, as shown in figure D.11.

This is how the Leonardo da Vinci theme looks.

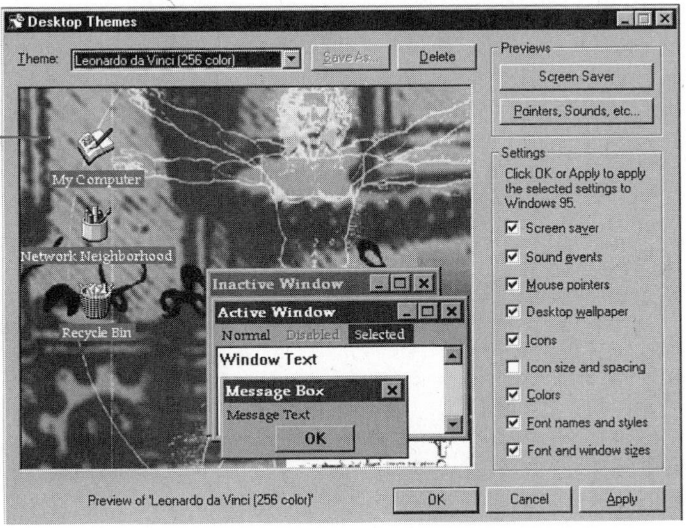

Fig. D.11
After you select a Desktop Theme, you see a preview of your Windows desktop.

4. At the right of the dialog box, choose the Settings to use for the Theme you selected. To deselect a setting, click to remove the check from the box beside it.

5. (Optional) To preview the selected Theme's screen saver, click Screen Saver in the Previews area. The screen saver appears on-screen. Move the mouse or press a key to conclude the preview.

6. (Optional) To preview several of the selected Theme's other elements, click Pointers, Sounds, etc. in the Previews area. A Preview dialog box for the Theme appears; the dialog box has three tabs for Pointers, Sounds, and Visuals. Click the tab you want to view. Each tab offers a list box with the elements for the theme. For the Pointers and Visuals tabs, simply click an element in the list to see a preview in the Preview or Picture area. For the Sounds tab, click an element in the list, then click the right arrow icon near the bottom of the dialog box to hear the sound. Click Close to conclude your preview.

7. After you have selected a theme, chosen settings, and previewed elements to your satisfaction, choose OK to close the Desktop Themes window. The selected Desktop Theme appears on your system.

Saving a Custom Theme

Any Control Panel changes you make after selecting a Theme take precedence over the Theme settings. In fact, you can make desktop setting changes in Control Panel, and then save those settings as a custom Theme. To do so, follow these steps:

Tip
To permanently delete a Desktop Theme, select it in the Theme drop-down list, then click Delete. Click Yes in the dialog box that appears to confirm the deletion.

1. Use Control Panel to change any settings you want, including the wallpaper, screen colors, sounds, and so on. See Chapter 5 to learn how to use Control Panel to customize Windows 95.
2. If the Control Panel window isn't open, open the Start menu and choose Settings, Control Panel.
3. In the Control Panel window, double-click the Desktop Themes icon.
4. Click the Save As button. The Save Theme dialog box appears (see fig. D.12).

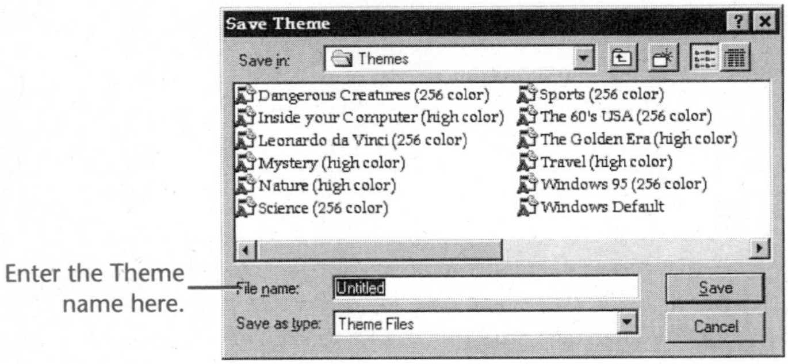

Fig. D.12
You can enter a file name in the File Name text box to save a custom Desktop Theme.

5. (Optional) Choose another folder in which to save the Theme.
6. Enter a unique name for the Theme in the File Name text box.
7. Click Save to save the Theme and return to the Desktop Themes dialog box. The newly saved Theme appears as the Theme selection.
8. Click OK to accept your new Theme and apply it to Windows 95.

Adjusting Plus! Visual Settings

Plus! adds new features to the Display settings available in the Windows 95 Control Panel. These visual settings are designed, primarily, to make your desktop more attractive. Plus! enables you to specify new icons for the My Computer, Network Neighborhood, and Recycle Bin desktop icons. You can choose to show the contents of a window (rather than just an outline) when you drag the window. Choose whether you want to smooth the appearance of large fonts on-screen. You also can choose to show icons with all possible colors or expand the wallpaper (when centered using the Background tab of the Display Properties dialog box from Control Panel) so it stretches to fill the entire screen.

Note

Most of the Plus! visual settings require more system resources than the normal display settings. In particular, showing window contents while dragging and using all colors in icons consumes more RAM. Consider all your computing requirements before you use up RAM by selecting any of these features. If you notice that Windows 95 runs considerably more slowly with any of these features enabled, turn off the features.

To work with the Plus! visual settings, open the Start menu and choose Settings, Control Panel. In the Control Panel window, double-click the Display icon. The Display Properties sheet appears. Click the Plus! tab to display its options, as shown in figure D.13. To assign a new Desktop icon, click the icon you want to change in the Desktop Icons area. Click Change Icon. In the Change Icon dialog box that appears, scroll to display the icon you want, then click OK to accept the change.

To enable any of the other Plus! display features, select the feature in the Visual settings area of the Plus! page. When a check appears beside the feature, that feature is selected. If you want more information about a particular feature, right-click the feature, then click What's This?. A brief description of the feature appears. Click or press Esc to clear the description. To accept your visual settings and close the Display Properties sheet, click OK. Close the Control Panel window, if you want.

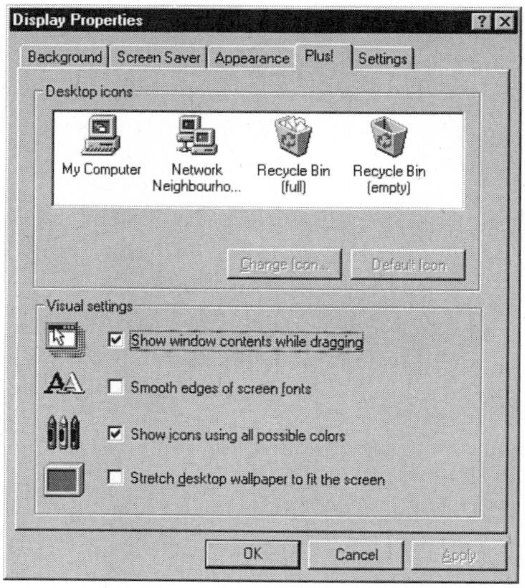

Fig. D.13
Plus! enables you to make additional adjustments to the Windows Display Properties.

Playing 3D Pinball

Most of you already know that playing games is really the best use for your $2,000 computer. Windows 95's smoothly integrated multimedia capabilities promise to make your game-playing experience more satisfying than ever. Plus! gives you an opportunity to take advantage of Windows multimedia via the 3D Pinball game included with Plus!. 3D Pinball offers well-crafted on-screen graphics, fun sounds and music, and a true-to-life pinball game feel—flippers and all.

Starting 3D Pinball and Setting It Up

To start 3D Pinball, open the Start menu and choose Programs, Accessories, Games, Space Cadet Table. After an opening screen briefly displays, the 3D Pinball window appears.

> **Note**
>
> If there is no shortcut to the pinball game in the Start menu, use find file to search for the Pinball program on your hard drive. It should be in the PINBALL folder wherever Plus! was installed which would be \PROGRAM FILES\PLUS!\ PINBALL by default. The file name to run is PINBALL.EXE..

Before you begin playing, you might want to set up a few of the features in 3D Pinball. Here's a review of the key features you can control:

- To toggle between displaying 3D Pinball in a window or as a full screen without the menu bar, choose Options, Full Screen or F4.
- Choose Options, Select Players to set up a game for one to four players.
- Choose Options, Sounds or Options, Music to toggle those features on and off.
- Choose Options, Player Controls, or press F8 to display the Player Controls dialog box. Here, you can change the keys you press to play the game, such as which keys represent the flippers, the plunger, and various table bumps.

Playing and Exiting 3D Pinball

When you initially start the 3D Pinball program it appears ready to begin a new game. At any other time, you can start a new game by choosing Game, New Game or by pressing F2. When you do so, you'll see the `Awaiting Deployment` message in the lower-right corner of the Pinball window.

You use the keyboard to play the game, although there are menu equivalents for several operations. Following are the key commands you'll use:

- Control the plunger with the spacebar. Press the spacebar for a second, then release it to launch the ball. The length of time you depress the spacebar affects the strength of the launch. The Game, Launch Ball command performs a simple launch.
- Press the Z key for the left flipper and the / key for the right flipper. You can press F8 to display the Player Controls dialog box to change these keys.
- You can bump the table with simple keystrokes: X (left table bump), (right table bump), up arrow (bottom table bump).
- Pause or restart the game by choosing Game, Pause/Resume Game or by pressing F3.

Tip
Bumping the table too much will result in a tilt, just like on a real pinball game.

As with other Windows applications, close 3D Pinball by clicking the Window close box. You also can choose Game, Exit.

Managing Utilities with the System Agent

Most users tend not to perform system-maintenance operations until after a disaster strikes. Some of us simply rebel at having to perform any kind of regularly scheduled maintenance; others simply can't keep a schedule. For users in either category, Microsoft Plus! for Windows 95 provides the System Agent, a program that enables you to schedule when to run other programs, especially system-maintenance utilities like Disk Defragmenter, ScanDisk (for more about using these system utilities, see Chapter 16, "Working with Disks and Disk Drives"), and Compression Agent (see the last section in this appendix). The System Agent can run other programs, as well, and notify you when your hard disk is low on space.

By default, the System Agent is enabled after you install Plus! This means that each time you start Windows 95, the System Agent starts automatically and runs in the background, only becoming active when it needs to start a scheduled program or notify you of low disk space. Even though System Agent is active by default, it isn't fully set up. After you install System Agent, it automatically places Low Disk Space Notification, ScanDisk for Windows (Standard Test), Disk Defragmenter, and ScanDisk for Windows (Thorough Test) programs in the System Agent. You need to manually tell the System Agent which other programs to run, when to run them, and which program features to use. To schedule programs with the System Agent, use the following steps:

Tip
Schedule time-consuming programs like Disk Defragmenter for a time you won't normally use your computer. Then, leave your computer on during that time, and System Agent will handle the task for you.

1. Open the Start menu and choose Programs, Accessories, System Tools, and then click System Agent. The System Agent window opens.

2. Choose Program, Schedule a New Program. The Schedule a New Program dialog box appears (see fig. D.14).

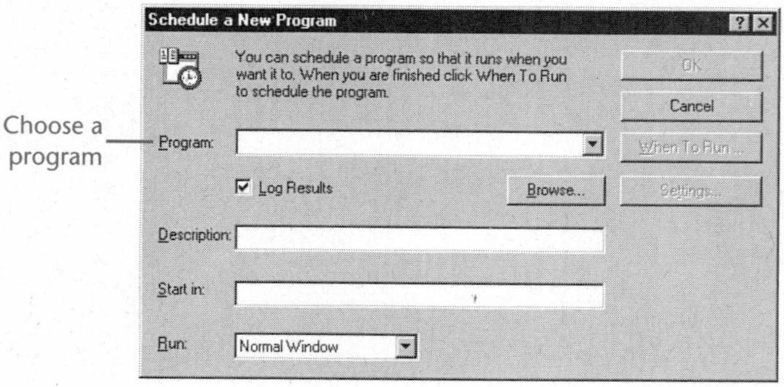

Fig. D.14
Use this dialog box to select programs for System Agent to run according to the schedule you set.

3. Click the drop-down list arrow to open the Program list. Choose a program from the list that appears. You can choose ScanDisk for Windows, Disk Defragmenter, Compression Agent, or Low Disk Space Notification. If you want to run a program other than one of these, click Browse, select the program to run in the Browse dialog box, and click OK. No matter what method you use, the selected program appears as the Program choice.

4. (Optional) If needed, you can edit the Description for the program and the Start In folder, which specifies the folder containing files the program needs to run.

5. (Optional) Open the Run drop-down list and specify whether you want the program to run in a Normal Window, Minimized, or Maximized.

6. To specify the schedule for the program, click the When to Run button. The Change Schedule Of... dialog box appears (see fig. D.15).

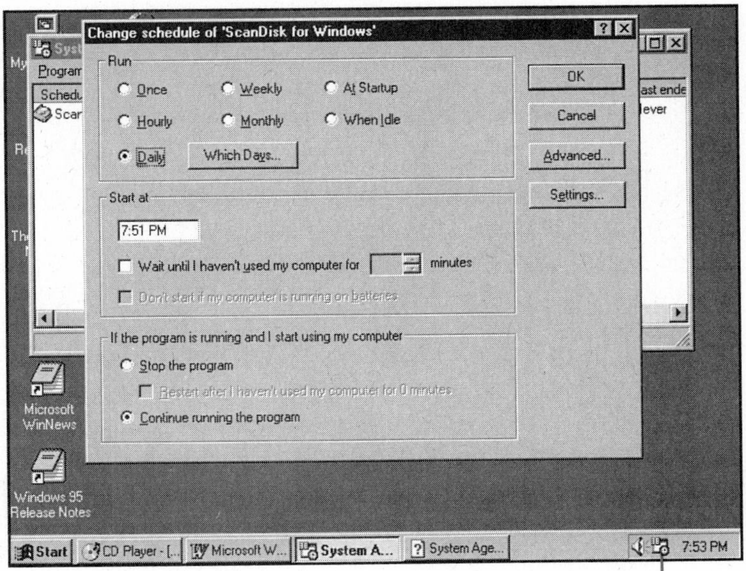

This icon in the status area of the taskbar lets you know that System Agent is loaded.

Fig. D.15
Use the Change Schedule dialog box to set up a schedule for the selected program.

7. Click a Run option, such as Weekly or Monthly. Your choice here affects the options available in the Start At area of the dialog box.

8. Specify the options you want in the Start At area. Although there might be other options, depending on your choice in step 7, you always need to enter a starting time. Also, you can specify a number of minutes to tell System Agent to wait if you're using your computer when the scheduled program runtime occurs.

9. Choose whether System Agent should Stop the Program or Continue Running the Program should you start using your computer when the scheduled program is running. Stopping the program can protect against data loss while running system utilities.

10. Click Settings to accept your changed schedule of options and to control which features the selected program uses when the System Agent runs the program. The Scheduled Settings dialog box that appears varies depending on the selected program. For example, figure D.16 shows the Scheduled Settings dialog box for the Disk Defragmenter program.

Fig. D.16
Choose which settings to use for the selected program when System Agent runs it.

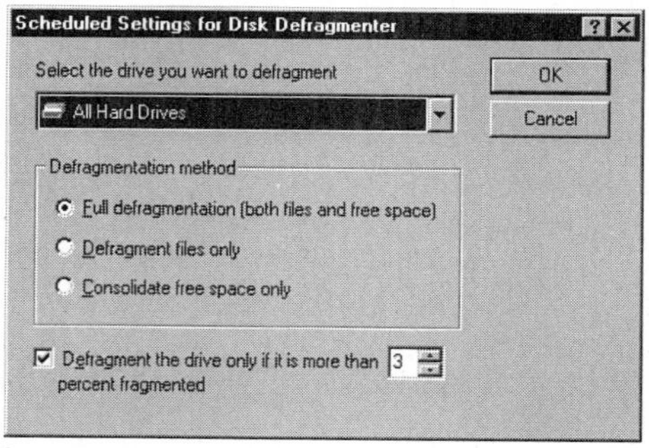

11. Specify the settings you want for the selected program, then click OK to close the Scheduled Settings dialog box.

12. Click OK again to finish scheduling the program. System Agent adds the program to the list of scheduled programs. Figure D.17 shows the System Agent window with two scheduled programs.

Note

Keep in mind that you can schedule the same program to run at different times with different settings. For example, you can schedule a Standard ScanDisk check once a week, plus a thorough check once a month.

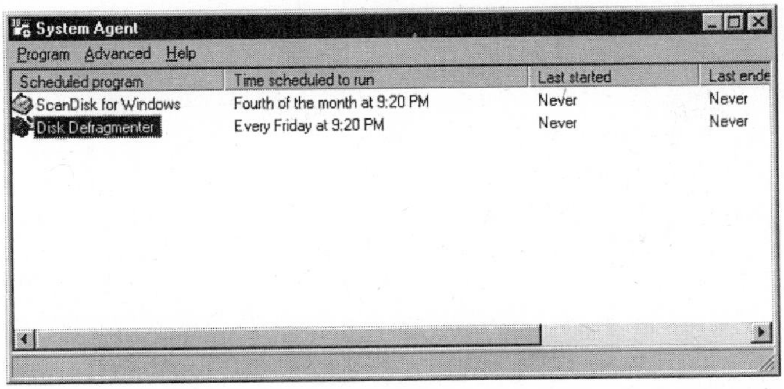

Fig. D.17
Use the System Agent window to view the currently scheduled programs.

Although you can use the Program menu choices to make changes to the schedule and settings for one of the listed programs, it's faster to simply right-click on the program you want to make changes for. A shortcut menu appears, from which you can choose the following:

- Choose Properties to change things like the program startup folder and settings (click the Settings button in the dialog box that appears).
- Use the Change Schedule option to adjust how often System Agent runs the program.
- Choose Run Now to run the program immediately, using the settings you've specified.
- Choose the Disable option to prevent the listed program from running at the designated time, but leave the program on the list; choose Disable again to reinstate the program's schedule.
- Choose Remove to delete the selected program from the System Agent list; confirm the deletion by clicking Yes at the warning that appears.

The Advanced menu in System Agent offers two commands for controlling System Agent itself. Toggle the Suspend System Agent option off whenever you want to stop all your regularly scheduled programs from running; then toggle this choice back on when you need to. The Stop Using System Agent choice completely stops System Agent operation; after you use this option, System Agent no longer loads when you start Windows, and you have to select System Agent from the System Tools Shortcuts to start using it. To close System Agent after setting it up, choose Program, Exit.

Working with DriveSpace 3

Windows 95 offers DriveSpace disk compression, which enables you to pack more data on your hard and floppy disks. Chapter 16, "Working with Disks and Disk Drives," introduces DriveSpace and disk compression; you won't revisit the basic concepts here. Although DriveSpace provides many benefits, it also has its limitations. That's where DriveSpace 3, offered as part of the Microsoft Plus! package, comes in.

For starters, DriveSpace 3 can handle larger disks—up to 2G—than the Windows 95 DriveSpace, which can only handle hard disks up to 512M in size. To be more efficient, DriveSpace 3 works with smaller units of data on the disk—512-byte sectors as opposed to the 32K byte cluster size regular DriveSpace works with. This ensures that DriveSpace 3 wastes less space on the disk. Finally, DriveSpace 3 offers two new, more dense compression formats—one of which is particularly suited for Pentium systems.

Keep in mind that, although compression provides you with extra disk space, it's often slower to used a compressed disk. And, the greater the compression, the slower your system is likely to perform when working with the compressed disk. Also, compressing your system's primary hard disk can take quite a bit of time, during which you won't be able to work with your system. Plan to compress this disk only when you don't have any critical work to perform.

Use the following steps to compress a disk with DriveSpace 3:

1. Open the Start menu and choose Programs, Accessories, System Tools. Click DriveSpace (after Plus! installation, the icon beside the DriveSpace will include a 3 to indicate DriveSpace 3). The DriveSpace 3 window appears (see fig. D.18).

Fig. D.18
The DriveSpace 3 window displays the available drives on your system.

Click the drive to compress.

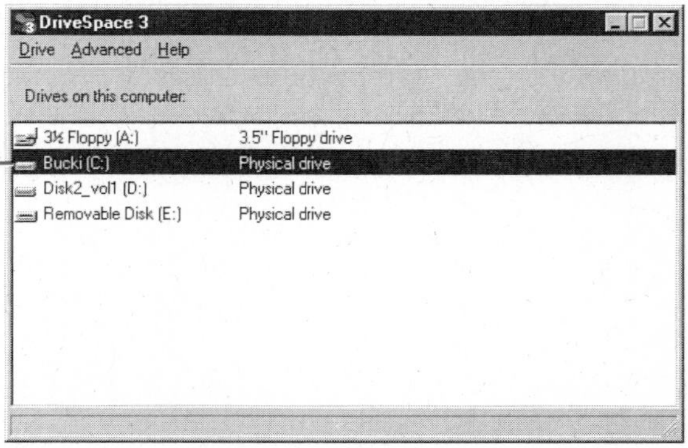

2. Click the drive that you want to compress.

> **Note**
>
> If you've previously compressed a hard disk with DoubleSpace or DriveSpace (for Win 95 or for earlier DOS versions), you can select the disk, then choose Drive, Upgrade to convert the disk to DriveSpace 3 format.

3. Choose Advanced, Settings. The Disk Compression Settings dialog box appears (see fig. D.19).

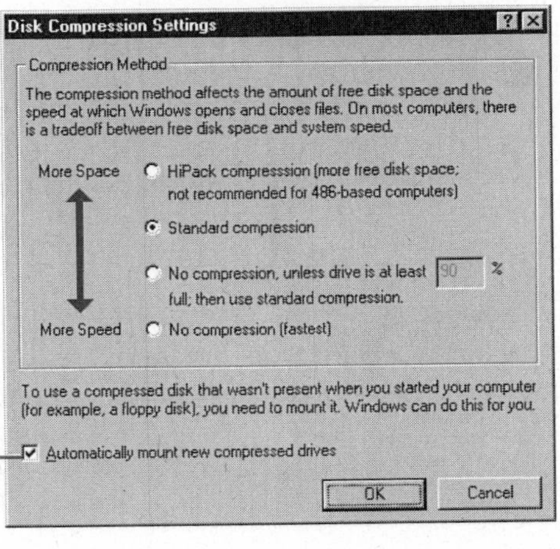

Leave this checkbox enabled when compressing a floppy disk so that Windows will mount it automatically whenever you insert it into your drive.

Fig. D.19
Be sure you understand the trade-offs associated with the different compression methods before choosing one.

4. Click the option button for the compression method you want to use:

   No Compression

   No Compression, Unless Drive Is at least X% Full...only compresses the disk after it's more full than the percentage you specify

   Standard Compression compresses the disk contents by approximately a 1.8:1 ratio

   HiPack Compression compresses the disk contents by up to 2.3:1

> **Note**
>
> As always, the compression ratio on your hard drive will depend on the type of files being compressed.

5. Click OK to close the Compression Settings dialog box and accept the specified compression method.

6. Choose Drive, Compress. The Compress a Drive dialog box appears, informing you of the estimated results of the compression operation—that is, how much free space and used space the disk will have after compression.

7. Click Options. The Compression Options dialog box appears. Use it to specify a drive letter and free space for the Host drive where DriveSpace 3 will store compressed information about the drive. You should only need to change these first two options if your system is connected to a network that uses drive H for another purpose. If you're compressing a floppy disk you might use on another computer that doesn't have DriveSpace 3, click to select the Use DoubleSpace-Compatible Format check box; note that you do need to select this option for Windows 95 systems without DriveSpace 3 or for systems using DriveSpace from a DOS 6.X version. Click OK to accept the Compression Options you set.

8. Click the Start button in the Compress a Drive dialog box. The Are You Sure? dialog box appears, asking you to confirm the compression operation.

◄ See "Backing Up Your Files," p. 555

9. Click the Back Up Files button to make a backup copy of the files on the disk before you compress it. This is an important safety measure; skipping it isn't recommended.

10. DriveSpace 3 runs the backup utility installed to work with your system. Follow any on-screen instructions to complete the backup process.

11. When the backup is finished, click Continue to compress the disk. DriveSpace 3 compresses the disk, then redisplays the Compress a Drive dialog box to report on the compression results.

12. Click Close to complete compressing the disk.

DriveSpace 3 offers numerous other tools for mounting and unmounting compressed disks, uncompressing disks, and more. As you work more frequently with compressed disks, these features will come in handy and help you make your disks much more efficient in the amount of data they handle and the way they perform.

Managing Compression with the Compression Agent

After you compress a disk, you might want to recompress it later to ensure that the compression is optimized and that all files are compressed. Microsoft Plus! for Windows 95 offers the perfect tool to handle this task—the new Compression Agent.

To start the Compression Agent, open the Start menu and choose Programs, Accessories, System Tools. Click Compression Agent. The Compression Agent window appears. Select a drive to work with in this window. Compression Agent will recompress this drive file by file, using the best method for each file. When you click the Settings button in Compression Agent, you can specify whether Compression Agent should use UltraPak compression for some or all of the files on the drive. While UltraPak reduces files to about a third of their normal size, this option isn't generally recommended for 80486 systems; this compression method can be very slow.

After you choose the settings you want in the Compression Agent, use the System Agent (as described earlier in the "Managing Utilities with the System Agent" section) to run the Compression Agent and recompress the specified disk.❖

Appendix E

What's on the CD

by Alex Leavens

The CD-ROM included with this book has a wide variety of software on it that can greatly enhance your productivity (and enjoyment, too) with the new Windows 95 operating system. This appendix describes many of the products on the CD-ROM, as well as how to access them.

Accessing the Software

When you insert the CD-ROM into your CD drive, Windows 95 automatically runs the installer on the CD-ROM. This installer lets you install many of the software products on the CD. You also can manually run the installer by double-clicking the CD-ROM drive icon, and then double-clicking the "Install" icon that is displayed there.

Each of the software packages lives under it's own directory entry; if you are having problems, then simply change to the appropriate directory; run the installer that is there.

What's Included

The CD comes complete with a fabulous list of software packages that will liven up your experiences with Windows 95. The following is a partial list of what packages are included:

- *Icon Safari.* This is a fabulous full-blown icon editor that lets you edit, import, and export icon images from various files (such as ICO (icon) files, and various executable and system driver files), as well as allowing you to edit cursors and small bitmaps. You can attach sounds to different windows events and buttons, which makes your cursor come alive with animation. It even includes a pop-up program launcher that lets you launch programs from anywhere within Windows. It's an even faster way to get to your programs than the taskbar!

- *WinCom Lite.* WinCom Lite gives you a full working terminal on your Windows 95 system so that you can access various information services (such as bulletin boards). You get complete control of your modem settings, your phone dialing settings, and more! WinCom Lite is a powerful terminal product, which can be upgraded to the even more powerful WinCom Pro. WinCom is provided by the folks at Delrina, who also make the popular WinFax utility.

- *WinBatch.* This is a batch file language utility. It allows you to script actions under Windows, such as a series of mouse clicks or menu entries. It can be used to automate a series of repetitive actions that could not otherwise be performed. By using WinBatch, you can create a script for actions that you perform over and over again (such as loading and printing a particular file).

- *WinEdit.* This is a programmer's editor, designed for writing code under Windows. It features many creature comforts needed by programmers, rather than just general text editing usage. If you're writing code for Windows, then this editor is a perfect example of simple power and functionality. If you've balked at paying $300 and more for some of the more expensive Windows editors, then give WinEdit a try—it might be just what you're looking for!

- *Address Manager for Windows.* This is a full-fledged miniature database for Windows, with the purpose of helping you organize your names, addresses, and phone numbers into something approaching a working system. (If you're like me, this product is a real life saver.)

- *TrueSpace2.* If you've ever wondered how they do those great realistic-looking graphics of buildings, ships, and alien scenery, here's your answer! TrueSpace2 lets you create fabulous 3D objects in a matter of minutes. You can add textures, distort images, and much, much more! You can build animations of solid-shaped objects, moving them about in space at your command. TrueSpace2 has been used to create the graphics for some of the most popular CD-ROM games on the market. Now, you too can explore the creation of futuristic worlds, alien artifacts, and anything else you can imagine. TrueSpace2 makes it easy (you'll find some wallpaper that's been created in TrueSpace in the \MEDIA\GRAPHICS subdirectory of your CD).

- *Fauve Matisse in Grey*. If you're looking for something a little more powerful than Paint, then this is the product for you. Fauve Matisse allows you to draw with a variety of different substances, and allows you great control over things like your brush style and type of paint that you use. Even non-artists will have a ball with this one! This version of the software is the full working version! You can load and save all of your artwork to disk, as well as print and edit your documents.

- *Mathematica*. For those of our readers who deal with higher mathematics, Mathematica is a great solution to your problems. This demo of the Mathematica software shows many of its capabilities that you'll need if you do lots of math-related work. (Even if you don't do higher math, it's still a cool demo to show your friends—they'll be impressed at how smart you are!)

- *MapInfo*. If you want information about streets, cities, or other places that have a map, then this demo of MapInfo will show you how your computer can help. Geographic Mapping Software is an area of Windows few people know about, but more people should—you can use your computer to get directions to a specific place, find out more about how streets are organized, and map various kinds of data that you have (such as store sales data) to the positions of people within a geographic location (such as ZIP code areas).

- *CorelDRAW!*. For many years the leading object-oriented drawing package, CorelDRAW!, just keeps getting better and better. The version included on this CD lets you use all of Corel's many drawing features. CorelDRAW! can be used for things like box art, flyers, brochures, business cards, product information sheets, and a hundred more uses (one person I know used it to create classroom materials for her fifth grade science class). See for yourself why CorelDRAW! is the leader in the marketplace.

- *CompuServe, WinCIM 1.4*. Yes, it's true—we've included the *full version* of CompuServe's famous Windows product to access the full power of CompuServe! Not only do we include the entire product, but you'll also find a special 800 number listed in this book that will let you call for a free introductory account! (See the MCP/CompuServe ad at the back of the book.) If you're already a CompuServe member, you can have the latest version of WinCIM without having to spend all that time trying to download it.

- *MorphStudio SE.* If you've been fascinated by those cool looking Morphing effects seen on TV and in the movies, then MorphStudio can help you explore this new world for yourself! Not only can you view several sample "Morphs," but you also can create your own morphs!

Our Internet Section

The Internet is one of the hottest new areas of interest for many people. If you want to get on the Information Superhighway, we're here to help. Here's what we have to help you "surf the Net:"

- *MKS Internet Anywhere.* This software allows you to cruise the net in style—browsing for files, and traversing cyberspace. You'll need an Internet provider to use this software (in English, that means you have to have someone that will give you access to the Internet—this software will do the rest).
- *Netcruiser software from NETCOM.* Not only is NETCOM a leading Internet access provider, but they've got their own Windows-based software to let you browse the Internet, FTP to different sites, surf the World Wide Web, read and post to Internet newsgroups, and more!

In addition, we've gathered the best of the software from several of Que's best-selling Internet books, including

- *WS_FTP.* A GUI FTP client.
- *Microsoft Internet Assistant.* Writes Web pages in Word for Windows.
- *LView.* A graphics file editor recommended for use with Netscape and Mosaic.
- *MPEGWin.* An MPEG movie player.
- *VuePrint.* A graphics editor and utility with a great slideshow mode.
- *Eudora.* The definitive Internet e-mail software.
- *HTML Assistant for Windows.* Another program for writing Web pages.
- *HTML Writer.* Yet another program for writing Web pages.
- *HTMLed.* One more program for writing Web pages.
- *NewsXpress.* A newsreader for reading UseNet newsgroup articles.

- *Windows FTP Daemon*. Be your own FTP site with this!
- *WinCode*. A file decoder for translating encoded mail and news from the Internet into a usable form.

Other Cool Goodies

One of the big new features of Windows 95 is it's multimedia capabilities and we've got lots to help you out here! The CD holds more than 150M of graphics files, wallpaper, bitmap patterns for your desktop, sound files, digital video files, and more!

All of these files are listed in the \MEDIA subdirectory on your disk, with appropriate subdirectories of the different items listed. Since Windows 95 understands many of these formats, you can simply double-click a file that grabs your interest to either view it or hear it.

For those of you doing your own Video for Windows editing, we're including the famous VidCap and VidEdit utilities from the Microsoft Multimedia Jumpstart CD.

You'll also find a ton of Windows Shareware and Freeware utilities on this CD. These include:

- *WinZip*. The famous Windows-hosted Zip/Unzip utility. No longer do you have to shell out to DOS to unzip things! This version supports Windows 95 long file names and several popular Internet file formats, in addition to ZIP files.
- *BmpView*. A program that lets you preview bitmap files in thumbnail (miniaturized) form, and then load them into your favorite editor.
- *PolyView*. A graphics file viewer that handles a wide variety of graphic file formats, including PhotoCD, JPG, GIF, BMP, and more. It also has a slideshow feature!

We've also included the following games:

- *Gravity Well*. A cool game!
- *Insecta*. Design and build your own insects, then bring them to life!

With all that stuff, this CD is sure to make Windows 95 a more enjoyable experience for all levels of computer users. Be sure to check the CD out in detail!❖

Appendix F

Glossary

16-bit In Windows, this refers to the way memory is accessed. 16-bit applications access memory in 16-bit "chunks" (2-bytes). Most pre-Windows 95 applications are 16-bit (*see 32-bit*).

32-bit In Windows, this refers to the way memory is accessed. 32-bit application access memory in 32-bit "chunks" (4-bytes). Large portions of Window 95 and many of its new applications are 32-bit applications, and may run faster because it has become more efficient to access chunks of memory.

16550A UART The name of the most modern chip controlling the serial port. Older chips could not support the data throughput that today's high-speed communications protocols and modems support.

A

accelerator key A keyboard shortcut for a command. For example, Shift+Delete is an accelerator command for the Edit Cut command.

activate To bring a window to the front and make it active.

active printer The printer that will be used by programs.

active window The window that is currently being used. Active windows show the "active window color" in their title bar (settable through the control panel). Other windows are inactive. To activate an inactive window, you must click somewhere in the inactive window or use the taskbar to select the window (*see taskbar*). On the taskbar, the active window looks like a pressed button; inactive windows are represented by unpressed buttons.

address book A list of persons, phone numbers, and other information used by various Windows 95 programs, including Microsoft Fax and HyperTerminal.

Adobe Type Manager (ATM) An Adobe program that enables you to work with Postscript fonts in Windows 95.

Advanced Program-to-Program Communications A communications standard defined by IBM. The APPC standard is intended to allow multiple users to share the processing of programs.

airbrush In "paint" and graphics programs, a tool that "sprays" dots in a randomized pattern around the point indicated by the user. In most programs, the output of the airbrush can be configured to modify the color, pattern, and density of the dot pattern.

alert message A critical warning, confirmational, or informational message appearing in a dialog box.

annotate To add notes. For example, you can add your own notes to Windows Help.

ANSI A standard for ordering characters within a font.

anti-aliasing A graphics technique used to hide the diagonal edges and sharp color changes ("jaggies") in a graphic or font. Because a computer screen possesses limited resolution, such changes highlight the pixels on the screen and don't look smooth. Using anti-aliasing smoothes out the changes and makes them appear more attractive.

Anti Virus A program included with Windows 95 that helps eradicate viruses (*see virus*) from your hard drive or floppy disks.

API *See Application Programming Interface.*

APPC *See Advanced Program-to-Program Communications.*

applet A small application unable to run by itself. When you purchase Windows 95 or another application, it may come with additional applets. For example, Word comes with applets for manipulating fonts (WordArt), drawing graphs (MS Graph), and creating graphics (MS Draw).

application A computer program.

Application Programming Interface (API) A set of interface functions available for applications.

archive bit A single bit stored in a disk directory to indicate if a file has been changed since it was last backed up. Backup programs clear a file's archive bit when they back up the program. Modifying the program resets the bit and a backup program knows to make a backup the next time you do a backup.

ASCII characters A subset of the ANSI character standard.

ASCII file A file consisting of alphanumeric characters only. Although virtually every file can be converted to an ASCII file, all formatting (for example, bold, italics, underline, font size, and so on) will be lost in the ASCII file.

associate Linking a document with the program that created it so that both can be opened with a single command. For example, double-clicking a DOC file opens Word for Windows and loads the selected document.

ATAPI A specification for devices to attach to EIDE buses. This specification is almost identical to the EIDE specification.

AT command set A set of commands, originally developed by Hayes, for modems. Its name originates from the fact that each command starts with "AT" (attention). Today, most modems support the AT command set, enabling Microsoft to supply the Unimodem driver with Windows 95.

ATM Asynchronous Transfer Mode is a high-speed, but expensive, networking solution. ATM networks reach speeds of 155 Mb/s.

attribute A property or characteristic.

attributes (FAT) Settings for each file indicate if the file is used by an operating system, has read-only status, has its archive bit set, or is a hidden file.

auto arrange (Explorer) In Explorer, auto arrange organizes the visible icons into a regular grid pattern.

B

background operation A job performed by a program when another program is in the active window. For example, printing or creating a backup can be done by Windows 95 as a background operation.

Backup A program that comes with Windows 95 and enables the user to back up the files from a hard disk to a floppy disk, tape drive, or another computer on a network.

backup set The set of duplicate files and folders created by a backup program (*see Backup*). This set is stored on tapes, diskettes, or other storage medium that can be removed and stored safely away from your computer. *See Full System Backup.*

Basic Input/Output System (BIOS) A program—usually residing on a ROM-based storage device in your PC—that handles instructions to and from the system bus.

batch program A text file that instructs Window 95 to perform one or more tasks sequentially. Used for automating the loading or execution of programs. Batch files have a .BAT or .CMD extension.

Bezier A mathematically constructed curve, such as the one used in drawing programs.

bi-directional printer port Bi-directional Printer Communications sends print files to your printer and listens for a response. Windows quickly identifies a printer that is unable to accept a print file.

binary A numbering system with only two values: 0 (zero) and 1 (one).

binary file Any file containing characters other than text.

binary file transfer A data transfer in which files aren't converted. Typically used with a modem to send programs or complex documents from computer to computer.

binary transfer protocol When using a communications program to transmit binary files, it is very important to ensure that errors are not introduced into the data stream. Various binary transfer protocols check for matches between the data transmitted and the data received. The most common protocols are Xmodem, Ymodem, and Zmodem.

BIOS *See Basic Input/Output System.*

bit map A screen page in memory. Most bit maps represent some sort of viewable graphics. You can use a "paint" program to edit graphic bit maps and make modifications to them. However, although objects such as rectangles and circles may appear in a graphic bit map, these objects cannot be edited as objects. You must modify these objects one bit at a time using the paint tools in the program.

bits per second (bps) A measurement of data transmission speed, usually over a serial data link. Roughly equivalent to baud rate. A single character requires approximately 10 bits, so a transfer rate of 9600 baud results in about 960 characters per second (cps) being transferred. This speed, however, varies depending on the make of your modem.

boot partition The hard-disk partition that contains the Windows 95 operating system.

bound media In networks, this refers to traditional cabling connecting the nodes of a network together, and to a server, if any. *See unbound media.*

bridge In networks, a device that joins two separate LANs but restricts LAN frame traffic to either side of the bridge (unless forwarding is required). Bridges process LAN frames (not network packets) and are governed by IEEE standards. A bridge should not be confused with a router (*see router*), which uses an entirely different layer of protocol and information for forwarding packets (not frames).

browse To search through or examine a directory tree of files, directories, disks, workstations, workgroups, or domains. Often done via a Browse button in a dialog box.

Bulletin Board System (BBS) An electronic service that can be accessed via a modem. BBS typically includes collections of files, notes from other computer users, and many other services. Examples of commercial BBSs include CompuServe, Prodigy, Delphi, GEnie, and America Online (AOL). Information about Windows 95 and Windows 95 applications can be found on all these BBSs.

burst mode A mode used in MCA and EISA computers and devices to facilitate greater flow of data through the bus. When bus mastering is employed, a bus master and its slave can establish a connection and send large blocks of data without CPU intervention. Without burst mode, each byte requires CPU attention to gain control of the bus, and send a byte of data.

bus The interface between devices in a computer. PC's incorporate bus designs, including ISA, EISA, MCA, PCI, and VLB (VESA Local Bus).

bus mastering A function used to off-load I/O processing to a processor on the interface card. Bus mastering is only truly effective when used with a bus design that can control bus master access to the computer bus, as is the case in EISA, MCA, and PCI computers. Bus mastering alone does not fully utilize the capabilities of this design unless implemented in conjunction with accessing the 32-bit burst mode and streaming data modes of EISA, MCA, and PCI computers.

bus network One of various network topologies. A Bus network is one in which all of the computers on the network are connected to the main wire of the network.

C

cache RAM A small collection of very high speed RAM. In general, modern microprocessors can process information much faster than standard dynamic RAM can even supply the information. Nevertheless, fast dynamic RAM is very expensive. Instead, a very small amount (typically 256K or 512K) of very fast "cache RAM" acts as a buffer between the CPU and the dynamic RAM. If the information needed by the CPU is in the cache, it can be processed without waiting to retrieve it from the dynamic RAM.

Calculator A program that comes with Windows 95 and enables you to perform standard or scientific calculations.

capture text In HyperTerminal, this refers to capturing and saving the text that appears in the terminal window to either a file or the printer. This is handy when reviewing the session at a later time.

Cardfile A program that comes with Windows 95 and enables you to record information cards and sort through them by using their index lines.

cascade (Windows) To arrange all the windows so that they are neatly stacked; only the title bars show behind the active window.

cascading menu A submenu that appears (usually to the left or right of the main menu item) when a menu selection is made.

CD File System (CDFS) An optimized, 32-bit, protected-mode file system that significantly improves the throughput of data from a CD-ROM drive.

CD-ROM Drive A CD-ROM drive uses discs (not "disks") as the storage media. These discs look much like audio CDs but can store about 600M of data on a single disc. They can only be read by a normal CD-ROM drive (hence Read-Only Memory portion of the device's name) and take special equipment to create (write) one of them. CD-ROM drives are rated in multiples of the original (1x) drives that transfer data at the same rate as audio CD Players (150kb/sec). Today, 1x drives no longer exist, and 2x drives (300-330kb/sec) are cheap. 3x (450 kbs), 4x (600 kb/sec), and even 6x (900kb/sec) drives are available. 4x drives fulfill basic requirements needed to achieve decent performance when playing animations from a CD-ROM.

CD Player A program packaged with Windows 95. CD player lets you play audio CDs from your CD drive in the background while you are working in another application. It offers many of the controls found in standalone audio

CD players. As a result, it looks and operates in a similar fashion. In addition, it allows you to edit your playlist that corresponds to the audio CD being played. Thus, the tracks play in the order you want.

character-based Usually used when referring to non-Windows applications. Character-Based applications display information using the ASCII character set, or characters normally found on the keyboard. Also known as "textbased."

character formatting In word processing, this refers to formatting that is applied to individual characters. This type of formatting includes font, effects, size, and color.

chat room A place on Microsoft Network where you can have a live conversation with other MSN members. They see your comments immediately.

check box A square dialog box item that takes an off or on value. Clicking in a check box adds or removes an X in the box, indicating whether the setting is on (checked) or off (unchecked).

checksum A method for creating a calculated number, frequently used as a part of an error-detection protocol. Normally, a checksum is calculated against a copy of a file or other data, and compared to the checksum calculated for the original file/data. If the two numbers match,then it is very likely that the copy matches the original. Checksums are used in some forms of transmission protocols (for example, Xmodem) as well as part of the Antivirus program.

choose A term used in many instructions in this book and in Windows books and manuals. Usually means opening a menu and clicking a command. Also can refer to dialog box items, such as in "Choose LPT1 from the drop-downlist."

clear Typically refers to turning off the X in an option or check box.

clicking Quickly pressing and releasing the mouse button.

client As opposed to *server*, a client is a workstation that connects to another computer's resources. A client also can include the server, and doesn't necessarily have to be another workstation. Basically, a client is just another application or workstation that utilizes resources from another process.

client application In OLE context, a program that uses an object (such as a graphic) supplied by another application (the *server* application).

client/server networking As opposed to *peer to peer* networking, an arrangement in which central computers called *servers* supply data and peripherals for use by *client* computers (workstations). Typically, a server contains a large, hard disk that supplies not only data, but also programs. It even executes programs. A server might also supply printers and modems for clients to use on the network. In other words, client/server refers to an architecture for distributed processing wherein subtasks can be distributed between services, CPUs, or even networked computers for more efficient execution.

clip art A collection of images you can use in your documents. Clip art is often distributed on CD-ROM in large collections (thousands of clip art pieces) organized into categories. Various clip art formats are sold, and the most popular are CGM, WMF, BMP, and GIF format files.

Clipboard A temporary storage area in all versions of Windows used for storing various types of data (for example, text, graphics, sound, and video). The clipboard can hold one piece of information at a time for use in a program or to pass information between programs.

Clipboard Viewer A Windows 95 program enabling you to store and save more than the single item that the clipboard can hold.

clock An area at the far right edge of the taskbar that displays the time (and date if you leave the mouse pointer over the time). You can configure the taskbar to show or hide the clock.

close button A button in the upper right corner of a Window with an "x" in it. When clicked, it closes the program running in the current window.

cluster Segment of space on a hard drive. Each file, no matter how small in actual size, takes up at least one cluster on the hard drive. As drive sizes increase, so does the cluster size. Thus, if you have a large drive and many small files, you may waste a significant amount of space on your drive. To avoid this, physically partition the drive into multiple "logical drives" of a smaller size. These smaller, logical drives also use smaller cluster sizes, wasting less space.

coaxial cable A type of shielded cable used in wiring networks together. Although coaxial cable sufficiently shields network signals from outside electrical noise, "coax" is stiff and difficult to work with, and more difficult to run through walls and ceilings than twisted pair cable (*see twisted pair*).

codec A technique for compressing and decompressing files, typically sound and animation files. Common codecs include Cinepak, Indeo, Video 1, MPEG (*see MPEG)* QuickTime (*see QuickTime*), and RLE.

collapse folders To hide additional directory (folder) levels below the selected directory (folder) levels. In Explorer, you can collapse the view of a folder to hide the folders stored within by double-clicking the folder in the left pane (tree view) of Explorer. When a folder contains no additional folders, a minus sign (-) appears next to the folder.

color pattern A color selection made up of two other colors.

color rendering intent Provides the best ICM settings for three of the major uses of color printing (for example, presentations, photographs, and true color screen display printing).

color scheme A selection of colors that Windows 95 uses for screen display of applications, dialog boxes, and so forth. The color scheme is set from the Control Panel.

COM Refers to the serial port, usually to attach a mouse and/or a modem to the computer. Most computers have two serial ports, labeled COM1 and COM2. The serial port transmits data in a single bit stream. This serial transmission of bits gives the port its name.

command Usually an option from an application's menus. Also refers to commands typed in from a command-prompt session or from the Run dialog box from the Start Menu. In essence, it's a way of telling an application or Windows 95 to perform a major chore, such as running an application or utility program.

command button A dialog box item that causes an action when clicked.

compare files Compares the files in a backup set to make sure they match the source files on the hard disk.

component A portion of Windows 95. When installing Windows 95, you have the option of installing (or not) various components. For example, you might choose to not install HyperTerminal (you might have a better terminal program). Later, you can go back and add/remove components using the original install disks or CD-ROM.

complex document *See compound document.*

compound document A document (created using OLE) that includes multiple types of data. For example, a Word processing document that includes a Paint picture is a compound document.

compressed volume file (CVF) A file, created by DriveSpace (*see DriveSpace*) which is treated like another "volume" (logical disk drive)—it even has a drive letter (for example, "D:") assigned to it. When you save or retrieve files compressed by DriveSpace, they are written or read from the compressed volume file. The compressed volume file exists on a hard drive (called a "host drive"), and looks like a regular file to the FAT (*see File Allocation Table*).

connection (HyperTerminal) In HyperTerminal, a connection sets and saves all the configuration parameters for one party you wish to contact.

connection (Network) A communication session established between a server and a workstation.

container object An object that contains another object or several objects. For example, a Word document might be the container object that holds the Excel object. *See compound document.*

control menu A menu that exists in every window and enables you to modify its parameters or take global actions, such as closing or moving the window.

Control Panel A program that comes with Windows 95 that enables you to make settings for many Windows 95 actions, such as changing network, keyboard, printer, and regional settings. Some programs (including many video card drivers) may add sections to the control panel for you to use to configure that program.

conventional memory Memory located in the first 640K.

cover page The page preceding a fax message. The cover page often includes such information as your name, company, telephone, and return fax number. Windows 95 includes a program (Fax Cover Page Editor) that enables you to create your own fax cover pages.

CPU Central processing unit. Also known as a microprocessor (*see microprocessor*) or processor (*see processor*). The 80386, 80486, and Pentium are examples of CPUs built by Intel.

cross-linked file A disk error (which can be found using ScanDisk) in which at least two files are linked to data in the same cluster.

current directory The directory that activates if you log onto the drive at the command prompt by typing the drive letter and pressing Enter. When you switch drives, the operating system remembers the directory that was current when you switched away. It will still be the active/current directory when you switch back; it becomes the default directory. Applications will store or look for files on that drive if they're not specifically told which directory to use. This concept also works in Explorer: when you switch back to a drive, the last active directory (or *folder*) is still the active one.

current window The windows that you are using. It appears in front of all other open windows (*see active window*).

cursor The representation of the mouse on the screen. It may take many different shapes.

Cylinder/Head/Sector (CHS) An addressing scheme that allows IDE drives to exceed the original 512 megabyte (1/2 gigabyte) size limit. With CHS, an IDE drive can be up to 8.4 gigabytes.

D

database A file or group of related files that are designed to hold recurring data types as if the files were lists.

data bits The number of bits used to transmit a piece of information. Usually 7 or 8.

DCI The Drive Control Interface is a display driver interface which allows fast, direct access to the video frame buffer in Windows. Also, it allows games and video to take advantage of special hardware support in video devices, which improves the performance and quality of video.

DDE *See Dynamic Data Exchange.*

DEC Printer Utility The DEC printer utility adds features to the standard Windows 95 print window and updated printer drivers. The utility includes a very detailed help file for configuring both local and network printers. Additionally, it creates an enhanced set of property menus for configuring DEC printers.

default button The command button in a dialog box that activates when you press the Enter key. This button is indicated by a dark border.

default printer The printer, which is established using the Printer settings, that documents will be sent to if the user doesn't specify another printer.

deferred printing This enables people with laptop computers to print even though their laptop is not in a docking station. Once connected in a docking station, it will automatically print. This also refers to computers whose only printer access is to a network printer, and the computer is temporarily disconnected from the network. When the network connection is reestablished, the print job starts.

density Density is a brightness control to lighten or darken a printout to more closely reflect its screen appearance and to compensate for deficiencies in toner or paper quality.

desktop The screen area on which the windows are displayed.

desktop pattern A bit map decorating your desktop. You can select one of Windows 95's patterns or create one of your own.

destination document The document into which a linked or embedded document is placed.

device driver A program that provides the operating system with the information it needs to work with a specific device, such as a printer.

dialog box An on-screen message box that conveys or requests information from the user.

Dial Up Networking Dialing into a network from a remote sight using a modem.

differential backup A differential backup backs up only those files that have changed since the time a backup was made. Normally, a backup philosophy will involve making a full system backup (which includes all files on the hard drive), and then making periodic differential backups. Windows 95 can determine which files have changed (or been created) since the last backup by the condition of the archive bit (*see archive bit*). To restore a system that has been backed up using this philosophy, first restore using the full system backup, and then successively apply the differential backups *in the same order they were made.*

Disk Defragmenter As you use your hard drive, blocks of information for a file spread across the hard drive, wherever there is room. This "fragmentation" of the information in a file can lead to a significant slow-down in file access times because the disk's read/write head must move all over the disk, looking for the various portions of a file. Disk Defragmenter arranges the blocks of information for a file into adjacent blocks on your hard drive, which may significantly improve file access times.

dither pattern A pattern of dots used to simulate an unavailable color or gray scale in a printout or graphic. Most frequently used when specifying a printout of a color graphic on a monochrome printer or simulating more colors in a graphic than are available in the current graphics mode.

Direct Memory Access (DMA) A PC has eight DMA channels that are used for rapidly transferring data between memory and peripherals such as a hard disks, sound cards, tape backups, scanners, and SCSI controllers. DMA is very fast because it doesn't need the computer's microprocessor to access memory.

docking station For a portable computer, an external device that provides additional resources such as speakers, CD-ROM, keyboard, empty card slots, and so on. A docking station is typically plugged into a portable computer using the port replicator connection.

document A file created using an application. For example, you might create a text document using a word processing application (such as WordPad) or a picture document using a graphic application (such as Paint).

document formatting In word processing, this refers to formatting that is applied to a whole document. Document formatting includes margins, headers and footers, and paper size.

document window The window in which a document appears.

DOS A term used to refer to any variation of the Disk Operating System (for example, MS-DOS and PC-DOS).

double-click To press the mouse button twice in rapid succession while keeping the mouse pointer motionless between clicks.

double buffering The process of displaying the screen currently in the frame buffer while painting the next screen in another portion of RAM. Then the new screen is quickly copied to the frame buffer. This makes video playback and animation appear much smoother.

download Retrieving a file from a remote computer or BBS (*see upload*).

drag To move an object on the screen from one place to another by clicking it with the mouse, holding the mouse button down, and pulling it to where you want it to be.

drag-and-drop "Drag-and-drop" describes a particular action you can make with the mouse. Click an object, such as a folder, then hold down the mouse button as you drag the object to a new location. You drop the object by releasing the mouse button.

DriveSpace DriveSpace is a program included with Windows 95. It enables you to compress your disks and free up more space.

DriveSpace for Windows supports drives that were compressed using DoubleSpace (which was included in MS-DOS versions 6.0 and 6.2) as well as DriveSpace for MS-DOS (which was included in MS-DOS version 6.22). You can use DriveSpace and DoubleSpace drives interchangeably. For example, you can use floppy disks that were compressed using either DoubleSpace or DriveSpace. However, such floppy disks can be used only in computers that have DriveSpace for Windows or DoubleSpace installed.

If you have drives that were compressed using either DoubleSpace or DriveSpace, you can configure them by using DriveSpace for Windows.

drop-down list A dialog box item showing only one entry until its drop down arrow is clicked.

dual boot The ability to reboot and enter either Windows 95 or Windows 3.1 (or whatever version of Windows you had running before installing Windows 95). This option is offered during installation and involves not installing Windows 95 over your previous Windows installation. If you choose dual boot, you will have to reinstall your Windows programs under Windows 95.

Dynamic Data Exchange (DDE) A feature of Windows 95 that allows programs to communicate and actively pass information and commands.

E

echoing keystrokes In a communications program, you may type information at your terminal. If the receiving system doesn't "echo" your keystroke back to your terminal, then you can't see what you type. By setting your own system to echo keystrokes, you can see what you have typed. Systems that echo your keystrokes for you are termed "full duplex"; systems that do not echo your keystrokes are termed "half duplex".

editable fax An editable fax is, essentially, a file transfer between computers, with the addition of a cover page optionally. Once received, the "editable fax" can be edited in the application that created it—or another application capable of reading that file type. For example, if you send a document created in Microsoft Word for Windows, which is a .DOC file, the recipient can open it in Word, WordPad, AmiPro, or WordPerfect, using import filters if necessary.

ellipsis Three dots (...). An ellipsis after a menu item or button text indicates that selecting the menu or clicking the button will display an additional dialog box or window from which you can choose options or enter data.

embedded object Data stored in a document that originated from another application. Differing from a linked object, this type of object doesn't have its own file on the disk. However, it runs its source application for editing when you double-click it. For example, a Paint drawing embedded in a Word document.

encapsulated PostScript (EPS) file A file format for storing PostScript-style images that allow a PostScript printer or program capable of importing such files to print a file in the highest resolution equipped by the printer.

Enhanced Integrated Electronics (EIDE) A design that improves on the Drive limitations of the IDE design. EIDE designs can use up to four devices (split into two pairs). For each pair of devices, one of the devices is the master; the drive electronics on the master control both the master drive and (if applicable) the secondary slave unit attached. Unlike IDE, EIDE supports devices in addition to hard drives, including CD-ROM drives and tape drives. EIDE devices can be up to 8 gigabytes in size, improving on the 524 megabyte limit of IDE devices. As with IDE, this type of drive is interfaced to a computer bus with an EIDE host adapter, not a controller. However, most newer computers include an EIDE host adapter right on the motherboard.

Enhanced Meta File (EMF) The process of converting generic Spooling print instructions to the instruction set "understood" best by a particular printer. This conversion has the capability to create faster printouts of better quality.

Enhanced Small Device Interface (ESDI) A drive controller type that utilizes a hard drive as a slave unit. ESDI controllers generally drive only two disk drives and have an on-board processor to translate drive geometry, manage I/O requests, and provide caching.

escape codes A set of codes that appear in a text string on a terminal (*see terminal emulation*). Although these escape codes (which provide formatting information) aren't visible in terminal emulation, they will show up as non-text characters if you capture the text to the screen or printer. In fact, some escape codes may cause the printed output to skip pages, switch into bold mode, and other undesirable effects because they may coincide with printer command codes.

Ethernet One of the earliest and least expensive network types. Ethernet is capable of speeds of 10Mb/s, and employs Bus and Star network types. When attempting to transmit over an Ethernet network, the transmitting workstation must "listen" to the network line to ensure that it is clear (another workstation is not currently transmitting). If the line is not clear, the workstation must wait until the line clears.

exit When you are finished running Windows applications and Windows, you must not turn off the computer until you correctly exit Windows. Windows stores some data in memory and does not write it to your hard disk until you choose the exit command. If you turn off the computer without correctly exiting, this data may be lost. *See shutdown.*

expanded memory Memory that conforms to the LIM 4.0 standard for memory access. Windows 95 has the capability of converting extended memory (*see extended memory*) to expanded memory (using EMM386.EXE) for programs that require it. However, most modern programs no longer use expanded memory.

expand folders Views the structure of folders that are stored inside other folders. In Explorer, you can expand the view of a folder that has a plus sign (+) next to it to see the folders stored within by double-clicking the folder in the left pane (tree view) of Explorer. When a folder does not contain any additional folders, a minus sign (-) appears next to the folder.

Explorer A program that comes with Windows 95 that helps you view and manage your files.

Extended Industry Standard Architecture (EISA) A computer bus and interface card design based on 32-bit bus mastering. EISA is an extension to ISA (Industry Standard Architecture) bus design and enables EISA and ISA interface cards to be used in a single type of bus interface slot in the computer.

extended memory Memory that can be accessed by Windows 95 beyond the first megabyte of memory in your system.

external command Unlike an internal command, a command that requires a separate file to run.

F

FDDI Fiber Distributed Data Interchange is a network type that requires fiber optic cable (*see fiber optic*). Although expensive, it is immune to electrical interference and can achieve speeds of 100 Mb/s.

fiber optic A type of cable which transmits information via light signals. Although both the cable and the decoders are expensive, such cabling is immune to electrical noise, and capable of much higher transmissions rates than electrical (coaxial or twisted pair) cables.

FIFO buffers First in, first out buffers. In communications programs that use FIFO buffers, the first information added to the buffer is also the first information transmitted when the transmission restarts.

file allocation table (FAT) The native DOS file system that uses a table, called the file allocation table, to store information about the sizes, locations, and properties of files stored on the disk.

file converter File converters take the file format and transform it to a format that the application can read. During a file conversion, text enhancements, font selections, and other elements are usually preserved. Sometimes, however, these elements are converted to a similar format, and then converted to ASCII format.

file name The name that a file system or operating system gives to a file when it's stored on disk. File names in Window 95's file system can be 256 characters long. Additionally, Windows 95 assigns a file name compatible with older DOS (8 characters with a 3 character extension) naming conventions.

file name extension The 3 character extension that you can add to a filename—either the standard 8 characters of DOS and Windows 3.1, or the long filenames of Windows 95. The file name extension is only visible in Explorer if you enable the appropriate option. Otherwise, the extension is hidden. Nevertheless, the extension is still part of the filename, even when you can't see it—it is this extension that Windows 95 (as well as earlier Windows) uses to associate a document with the application that created it.

file set In the Windows 95 Backup program, a collection of files to back up and the destination to back them up to. By saving a file set in Backup, you won't have to reselect the files to back up the next time.

file utility A program that can directly manipulate the information available on the disk that defines where files are found, sized, and other attributes. It is important to NOT use file utilities that were designed for earlier version of Windows, as Windows 95 stores some file information in different places—and earlier file utilities could scramble the file information, destroying the file.

fixed space font Fonts that have a fixed amount of space between the characters in the font.

font A description of how to display a set of characters. The description includes the shape of the characters, spacing between characters, effects (for example, bold, italics, and underline), and the size of the characters.

folder window A window in Explorer that displays the contents of a folder.

folder Folders represent directories on your drives. Folders can contain files, programs, and even other folders.

foreground operation The program in the active window.

forum On Microsoft Network, a folder with a collection of related documents and sub-folders.

frame A unit of data that is exchanged on a LAN. Frame formatting implements an access protocol for the purpose of enabling communications between nodes on a LAN (Ethernet, Token Ring, and so on). A frame should not be confused with a packet, which is encapsulated within a frame for transport across the LAN.

full system backup A backup set (*see backup set*) that contains all the files on your hard drive, including Windows 95 system files, the registry, and all other files necessary to completely restore your system configuration on a new hard drive.

G

grid A background pattern that defines regular intervals—for example, a 1/4" grid displays dots in the background every quarter inch on in a rectangular pattern. Many graphics programs make a grid available. Even when turned on, a grid won't print. When you "snap to grid," your graphic endpoints are constrained to fall on a grid point.

H

handshake A protocol used between two devices to establish communications. For example, a portable computer and a PC Card "handshake" to set up the communications between the devices.

header information Data sent to a printer to define aspects of the printout and prepare the printer prior to printing. PostScript documents include header information.

heap An area of memory (also known as the "System Resources area") that Windows uses to store system information (such as menus) about running applications. If the "heap" fills up, you may get an "out of memory" error, despite the fact that you have plenty of regular memory (RAM) available. In Windows 95, you have a much less chance of getting an "out of memory" error. Although Windows 95 still uses a 64K heap to store systems information for 16-bit applications, a lot of the information that was stored in this area by older versions of Windows is now stored elsewhere. As a result, there is much less chance of your application failing due to this error.

Hearts A card game included with Windows 95 for up to four players. The winner is the player who has the fewest points.

At the end of each round (each player has played all 13 cards), the following points are given:

1 point for each Heart you collected.

13 points for the Queen of Spades.

If one player wins all the Hearts and the Queen of Spades (called Shooting the Moon), then that player gets zero while all other players are penalized 26 points.

Help A program that gives you information about how to run Windows 95 and its programs, including how to use the Help program.

hexadecimal A base-16 numbering scheme with values ranging from 0 to 9, and A to F. Used in many programming languages. Not particularly relevant to users, except that memory address areas are frequently stated in hexadecimal. Hex is used whenever the actual internals of the computer are being revealed as in memory addresses and I/O ports.

hidden file A characteristic of a file that indicates that the file is not visible in Explorer under normal circumstances. However, by selecting the View Option to view all files, hidden files will still be visible.

hierarchical A way of displaying text or graphics in a structure. In a hierarchical structure, items closer to the top of the structure are considered "parents" of items connected to them, but which are lower down in the structure. The tree structure of Windows Explorer is an example of a hierarchical structure.

Home Page A document on the World Wide Web dedicated to a particular subject. From a Home Page, you can use hyperlinks to jump to other Home Pages to gain more information.

host drive The physical hard drive upon which a DriveSpace compressed volume file exists (*see compressed volume file*). You can choose to either show or hide the host drive when working with Explorer.

hot docking For a portable computer, "hot docking" refers to the ability to insert the computer into a docking station (which may provide additional resources such as a CD-ROM, speakers, hard drive, and so on) and have the computer recognize that the new resources of the docking station are now available.

hot swapping For a portable computer, or any other computer that uses PC cards, "hot swapping" refers to the ability to remove a PC card and/or insert a new card, and have the computer recognize the change.

HP JetAdmin The HP JetAdmin Utility is a tool that can be used to install and configure networked Hewlett-Packard printers using the HP JetDirect network interface. The HP JetAdmin utility appears as a substitute for the Windows standard Printer window. This utility can also be used to interface printers connected to a NetWare LAN.

hub A wiring concentrator or multiport repeater (*see repeater and wiring concentrator*). Hubs may be active or passive.

hue The numerical representation of the colors of a color wheel. It is almost always seen with saturation and brightness.

hyperlink A link in a document that, when activated (often by clicking it), links—or jumps to—another document or graphic.

HyperTerminal HyperTerminal is a program included with Windows 95, which enables you to easily connect to a remote computer, a bulletin board, or an online service. It replaces Terminal from Windows version 3.1.

Hypertext Markup Language (HTML) A hypertext language used to create the hypertext documents that make up the World Wide Web.

I

I-beam The shape the cursor takes in the area of a window where text can be entered.

icon A small graphic symbol used to represent a folder, program, shortcut, resource, or document.

image color matching (ICM) Image Color Matching (ICM), a technology developed by Kodak, creates an image environment that treats color from the screen to the printed page. Microsoft licensed ICM from Kodak to be able to repeatedly and consistently reproduce color matched images from source to destination.

import An OLE term. In Object Packager, you can import a file into a package and later embed it into a destination document.

inactive An open window that is not currently in use. On the taskbar, the active window looks like a pressed button, inactive windows are represented by unpressed buttons.

Inbox Inbox holds incoming and outgoing messages and Faxes that are sent or received over Microsoft Exchange.

incremental backup *See differential backup.*

Industry Standard Architecture (ISA) This term describes the design of the 8/16-bit AT bus (sometimes called the "classic bus") developed by IBM in the original IBM PC.

in place editing A feature of OLE 2. With in place editing, you may edit an embedded or linked object WITHOUT that object being placed into an additional window (the way it was in OLE 1.0). Instead of creating an additional window, the tools for the object you want to edit appear in the toolbar for the container object, (*see container object*). Also, the menus for the object you want to edit replace the menus of the container object. In place editing is less disruptive; it is much simpler to ensure that the changes you make to an embedded or linked object are updated to the original complex document.

insertion point A flashing vertical line showing where text will be inserted.

Integrated Drive Electronics (IDE) A later drive design that incorporated an embedded controller on a smaller (3 1/2 inch) disk drive. IDE drives can be connected together, but the second drive must be a slave to the first, using the primary disk controller and not its own embedded controller. This type of drive is interfaced to a computer bus with an IDE host adapter, not a controller.

Integrated Services Digital Network (ISDN) A special phone line that supports modem speeds up to 64Kbps. However, these phone lines can be quite expensive to acquire. Many ISDN adapters support two-channel access.

interface The visible layer enabling a user to communicate with a computer. In DOS, the interface consisted largely of typed commands and character-based feedback. Windows 95 is an entirely graphical interface, using a mouse, menus, windows, and icons to allow the user to communicate his instructions and requirements to the computer.

internal command A command embedded in CMD.EXE, the command interpreter for Windows 95, or in COMMAND.EXE, the MS-DOS equivalent. Internal commands don't require additional support files.

Internet The Internet is a "network of networks," a global linkage of millions of computers, containing vast amounts of information, much of it available to anyone with a modem and the right software...for free. The Internet is an aggregation of high speed networks, supported by the NSF (National Science Foundation) and almost 6,000 federal, state, and local systems, as well as university and commercial networks. There are links to networks in Canada, South America, Europe, Australia, and Asia, and more than 30,000,000 users.

Internet Explorer A web browser bundled with the Windows 95 Plus kit. It takes advantage of features in Windows 95, such as shortcuts and long file names.

Internet Protocol (IP) A network protocol that provides routing services across multiple LANs and WANs that is used in the TCP/IP protocol stack. IP packet format is used to address packets of data from ultimate source and destination nodes (host) located on any LAN or WAN networked with TCP/IP protocol. IP provides routing services in conjunction with IP routers, which are incorporated into many computer systems and most version of UNIX. IP Packet format is supported in NetWare 3.11 and 4.0 operating systems, and is used throughout the Department of Defense Internet—a network of thousands of computers internetworked worldwide.

interoperability Compatibility, or the capability for equipment to work together. Industry standards are agreed upon or used by vendors to make their equipment work with other vendor's equipment.

interrupt request line (IRQ) A line (conductor) on the internal bus of the computer (typically on the motherboard) over which a device such as a port, disk controller, or modem can get the attention of the CPU to process some data.

interframe compression A technique that achieves compression of a video file by eliminating redundant data between successive compressed frames

intraframe compression A technique that compresses the video by removing redundancy from individual video images.

I/O address Input/Output address. Many I/O devices, such as COM ports, network cards, printer ports, and modem cards, are mapped to an I/O address. This address allows the computer and operating system to locate the device, and thus send and receive data. Such I/O addresses don't tie up system memory RAM space. However, there are a limited number of I/O addresses. You can access an I/O port in one of two ways: either map it into the 64K I/O address space, or map it as a memory-mapped device in the system's RAM space.

IPX Internetwork Packet Exchange (IPX) is a network protocol developed by Novell to address packets of data from ultimate source and destination nodes located on any LAN networked with NetWare. IPX also provides routing services in conjunction NetWare and third-party routers. An IPX packet has information fields that identify the network address, node address, and socket address of both the source and destination, and provides the same functionality of the of the OSI Network layer in the OSI model.

J

jumpers Jumpers are small devices that complete a circuit between two pins of a multi-pin header, specifying various aspects about a card—for example, which IRQ, base memory address, or I/O port address to use. Jumpers are not normally used on a card that is compliant with Plug and Play, but were common on "legacy" (pre-Plug and Play) cards.

K

kernel The core of an operating system, usually responsible for basic I/O and process execution.

kernel driver A driver with direct access to hardware. A hardware driver.

keyboard buffer Memory set aside to store keystrokes as they're entered from the keyboard. Once it's stored, the keystroke data waits for the CPU to pick up the data and respond accordingly.

keyboard equivalent *See keyboard shortcut.*

keyboard shortcut A combination of keystrokes that initiates a menu command without dropping the menu down, or activates a button in a dialog box without clicking the button.

kiosk In the Microsoft Network, a download-and-run document that contains additional information about a forum. Kiosks are usually found in forums.

L

legacy Refers to pre-Windows 95 software or hardware. Legacy cards don't support Plug and Play, and legacy software is older software (although you may have just purchased it!) typically designed for Windows 3.1 or Windows for Workgroups 3.11.

license Refers to the agreement you are assumed to have acceded to when you purchase Windows 95. As with much other computer software, you don't own your copy of Windows 95, but instead, just license the use of it. As such, there is a long list of legalese-type things you supposedly agree to when you open the envelope containing your copy of Windows 95. These legal agreements are part of the *license.*

line by line When using terminal emulation (*see terminal emulation*), some primitive terminals only allowed you to edit text on the single line on which you were working. Once you pressed [Enter] to move to the next line, you couldn't go back and change something on the previous line(s)—because those lines had already been sent to the host computer that the PC emulates a terminal of. In line by line editing, there is a line length limit as well, so you can't simply type an entire paragraph before pressing [Enter].

linked object In OLE terminology, data stored in a document that originated from another application. Unlike an embedded object, this type of object has its own file on the disk. The source application is run for editing when you double-click it. For example, a Paint drawing linked to a Word document. Linking saves space over embedding when a particular object must be included in more than one other document, since the data does not have to be stored multiple times. Additionally, you can directly edit a linked file, and all the documents that the link to the file update automatically.

list box A dialog box item that shows all available options.

local area network (LAN) A limited-distance, multipoint physical connectivity medium consisting of network interface cards, media, and repeating devices designed to transport frames of data between host computers at high speeds with low error rates. A LAN is a subsystem that is part of network.

local printer A printer connected directly to your computer.

local reboot The ability of Windows 95 to close down a single misbehaving application. When you use the Alt+Ctrl+Delete key sequence, Windows 95 queries you for the application to shut down. In this way, you can close down only the application you want, without affecting other running applications.

logical block addressing (lba) A type of addressing scheme for IDE disk drives that allows the drive to exceed the original 512 megabyte (1/2 gigabyte) IDE size limit. With logical block addressing, an IDE drive can hold up to 8.4 gigabytes.

logical drive A drive that isn't a physical drive, as in the floppy drive A or B. Instead, a logical drive is a drive created on a subpartition of an extended partition and given an arbitrary letter such as C, D, or E.

long file name A reference to Windows 95's ability to use file names up to 256 characters long.

lossy compression Compression techniques that lose some of the data when compressing the file. Although lossy compression isn't acceptable for compressing application file and certain types of data files (for example, database, word processing), it is often acceptable to have a low degree of loss when compressing video or graphic files, since you likely won't notice the missing data. Also, lossy compression can gain considerably higher compression ratios than "lossless" compression. However, when using lossy compression, you don't want to decompress the file, then use the result to recompress, as the loss of data gets worse with each cycle.

LPT The parallel port (used for printing). Most computers have a single parallel port (labeled LPT1), but some may have two. The parallel port transmits data one byte (8-bits) at a time. This parallel transmission of all 8 bits gives the port its name.

luminosity When working with colors, indicates the brightness of the color.

M

macro A sequence of keyboard strokes and mouse actions that can be recorded so that their playback can be activated by a single keystroke, keystroke combination, or mouse click. Unlike Windows 3.1 and Windows for Workgroups, Windows 95 does not come with a Macro Recorder.

Mailing List (Internet) An e-mail discussion group focused on one or more topics. The Mailing List is made up of members who subscribe that mailing list.

map network drive The act of associating a network drive makes the drive available in My Computer. Windows 95 uses the next available drive letter, and you can access the network drive just like any other hard drive.

maximize button A button in the upper right corner of a Window with a square in it. When clicked, it enlarges the window to its maximum size. When the window is already at its maximum size, the maximize button switches to the restore button, which returns the window to its previous size.

media control interface (MCI) A standard interface for all multimedia devices, devised by the MPC counsel, that allows multimedia applications to control any number of MPC-compliant devices, from sound cards to MIDI-based lighting controllers.

menu A list of available command options.

menu bar Located under the title bar, the menu bar displays the names of all available menu lists.

menu command A word or phrase in a menu that, when selected, enables you to view all the commands.

Micro-Channel Architecture (MCA) A proprietary 32-bit computer and bus architecture designed by IBM to improve bus bandwidth and facilitate bus mastering. MCA is not backward compatible with ISA and requires exclusive use of MCA devices.

microprocessor A miniaturized processor. Previous processors were built in integrated circuit boards with many large components. Most processors today use high-tech, silicon-based technology that improves performance, reduces heat generation, and increases efficiency.

Microsoft Client for Netware Networks Windows 95 Microsoft Client for NetWare Networks allows users to connect to new or existing NetWare servers. It permits you to browse and queue print jobs using either the Windows 95 network user interface or existing Novell NetWare utilities. The Microsoft Client for NetWare interfaces equally well with both NetWare 3.x and 4.x servers.

Microsoft Exchange Microsoft Exchange provides a universal Inbox that you can use to send and receive electronic mail (e-mail). In addition, you can use the Inbox to organize, access, and share all types of information, including faxes and items from online services.

Microsoft Fax Microsoft Fax is a program included with Windows 95 that enables you to send and receive faxes directly within Windows 95.

Microsoft Network (MSN) Access to The Microsoft Network, a new online service, is a feature of Windows 95.

With The Microsoft Network, you can exchange messages with people around the world; read the latest news, sports, weather, and financial information; find answers to your technical questions; download from thousands of useful programs; and connect to the Internet.

MIDI Musical Instrument Digital Interface. Originally a means of connecting electronic instruments (synthesizers) and letting them communicate with one another. Computers then came into the MIDI landscape and were used to control the synthesizers. Windows 95 can play MIDI files.

Minesweeper A game of chance and skill included with Windows 95. When playing Minesweeper, you are presented with a mine field, and your objective is to locate all the mines as quickly as possible. To do this, uncover the squares on the game board that do not contain mines, and mark the squares that contain mines. The trick is determining which squares are which.

If you uncover all the squares without mines, you win; if you uncover a mine instead of marking it, you lose the game. The faster you play, the lower your score. You can use the counters at the top of the playing area to keep track of your progress.

minimize button The button in the upper right corner of the window that has an line in it. When clicked, it reduces the window to display the taskbar only.

mission-critical application An application program considered indispensable to the operation of a business, government, or other operation. Often, these applications are transaction-based, such as for point-of-sale, reservations, or real-time stock, security, or money trading.

modem A device usually attached to a computer through a serial port or present as an internal card. A modem makes it possible to use ordinary phone lines to transfer computer data. In addition to a modem, a communications program is required. "Modem" is short for "modulator/demodulator"—the processes whereby a digital stream of data is converted to sound for transmission through a phone system originally designed only for sound (modulator) and the conversion of received sound signals back into digital data (demodulator).

Motion JPEG Developed by the Joint Photographic Experts Group, motion JPEG is a compression/decompression scheme (Codec) for video files. It is a variation on JPEG, this group's codec for compressing still pictures. It uses only intraframe lossy compression (*see intraframe compression, lossy compression*), but offers a tradeoff between compression ratio and quality.

mounting a compressed drive When you are working with removable storage media—such a diskettes—that are compressed, you must mount the compressed drive if it wasn't present when the computer was started. Mounting a drive links a drive letter with a compressed volume file (CVF). This enables your computer to access the files on the compressed volume files. Mounting a compressed drive is done using DriveSpace.

mouse pointer The symbol that displays where your next mouse click will occur. The mouse pointer symbol changes according to the context of the window or the dialog box in which it appears.

MPEG Created by the Motion Picture Experts Group, MPEG is a specification for compressing and decompressing (*see codec*) animation or "movie" files, which are typically very large. Although extremely efficient at reducing the size of such a file, MPEG is also very processor-intensive.

MS-DOS-based application An application that normally runs on a DOS machine and doesn't require Windows 95. Many MS-DOS-based applications will run in Windows 95's DOS box, but some will not.

multimedia A combination of various types of media, including (but not necessarily limited to) sound, animation, and graphics. Due to the generally large size of "multimedia" files, a CD-ROM is usually necessary to store files. Of course, a sound card and speakers are also necessary.

multitasking The capability of an operating system to handle multiple processing tasks, apparently, at the same time.

multithreading A process allowing a multitasking operating system to, in essence, multitask subportions (threads) of an application smoothly. Applications must be written to take advantage of multithreading. Windows 95 supports multithreading.

My Computer An icon present on the Windows 95 desktop that enables you to view drives, folders, and files.

My Briefcase An icon present on the Windows 95 desktop. My Briefcase is the way that portable computer users can take data with them as they travel. When they return to the office, Windows examines the files in My Briefcase and updates the contents of their desktop computer.

N

NetBIOS An IBM protocol (and packet structure) that provides several networking functions. NetBIOS was developed by IBM and Sytek to supplement and work with BIOS in PC-DOS-based, peer-to-peer networks. NetBIOS protocol provides transport, session, and presentation layer function equivalent to layers 4, 5, and 6 of the OSI model. The NetBIOS software that is used to implement this protocol is the NetBIOS interface.

NetWare A trademarked brand name for the networking operating systems and other networking products developed and sold by Novell.

Netware Core Protocol (NCP) A NetWare protocol that provides transport, session, and presentation layer functions equivalent to layers 4,5, and 6 of the OSI model.

Net Watcher A tool included with the Windows 95. Net Watcher allows you to monitor and manage network connections, as well as create, add, and delete shared resources.

network A group of computers connected by a communications link that enables any device to interact with any other on the network. The "network" is derived from the term "network architecture" to describe an entire system of hosts, workstations, terminals, and other devices.

Network Interface card (NIC) Also called a network adapter, an NIC is an interface card placed in the bus of a computer (or other LAN device) to interface to a LAN. Each NIC represents a node, which is a source and destination for LAN frames, which in turn carry data between the NICs on the LAN.

Network Neighborhood An icon which Windows 95 displays only if you are connected to a network and Windows has been installed for a network. Double-clicking the Network Neighborhood icon displays all the resources available on any network to which you are connected.

non-volatile RAM RAM memory on a card that is not erased when power is cut off. Cards that don't use jumpers often store their resource requirements (IRQ, I/O Base address, I/O port, DMA channel, and so on) in non-volatile RAM. Non-volatile RAM is not normally used on a card that is compliant with Plug and Play but was common on "legacy" (pre-Plug and Play) cards.

non-Windows program A program not designed to be used specifically in Windows. Most non-Windows applications or programs are character-based in nature (for example, DOS programs).

Notepad A program that comes with Windows 95 and enables you to view and edit text files.

null modem cable A serial cable link between computers. Standard modem software is often used to transmit information, but because there are no actual modems in the connection, very high transfer rates with good accuracy are possible. The cable must be different from a regular serial cable, however, because several of the wires in the cable must be cross connected to simulate the modem's role in acknowledging a transmission.

O

object Any item that is or can be linked into another Windows application, such as a sound, graphics, piece of text, or portion of a spreadsheet. Must be from an application that supports Object Linking and Embedding (OLE).

object linking and embedding *See OLE.*

OEM Fonts OEM fonts are provided to support older installed products. The Term OEM refers to Original Equipment Manufacturers. This font family includes a character set designed to be compatible with older equipment and software applications

offline A device that is not ready to accept input. For example, if your printer is offline, it will not accept data from the computer, and attempting to print will generate an error.

OLE A data sharing scheme that allows dissimilar applications to create single, complex documents by cooperating in the creation of the document. The document consists of material that a single application couldn't have created on its own. In OLE, version 1, double-clicking an embedded or linked object (*see embedded object*, and *linked object*) launches the application that created the object in a separate window. In OLE version 2, double-clicking an embedded or linked object makes the menus and tools of the creating application available in the middle of the parent document. The destination document (contains the linked or embedded object) must be created by an application which is an OLE client, and the linked or embedded object must be created in an application that is an OLE server.

OLE automation Refers to the capability of a server application to make available (this is known as expose) its own objects for use in another application's macro language.

online Indicates that a system is working and connected. For example, if your printer is online, it is ready to accept information to turn into a printed output.

Open Data Link Interface (ODI) A Novell specification that separates the implementation of a protocol and the implementation of the NIC hardware driver. Novell's MLID specification enables NIC drivers to interface through Link Support Layer with IPX ODI and multiple ODI-onforming packet drivers.

option button A dialog box item that enables you to choose only one of a group of choices.

orientation For printer paper, indicates whether the document is to be printed normally (for example, in "portrait" mode) or sideways (in "landscape" mode).

OSI Model Opens Systems Interconnect 7-layer Model is a model developed by International Standards Organization to establish a standardized set of protocols for interoperability between networked computer hosts. Each layer of the model consists of specifications and/or protocols that fulfill specific functions in a networking architecture. Novell's UNA was patterned against the OSI model. The OSI model consists of specific protocols that are nonproprietary and offered in the hope of unifying networking protocols used in competing vendor's systems.

P

packet A limited-length unit of data formed by the network, transport, presentation, or application layer (layers 3-7 of the OSI Model) in a networked computer system. Data is transported over the network, and larger amounts of data are broken into shorter units and placed into packets. Higher-layer packets are encapsulated into lower-layer packets for encapsulation into LAN frames for delivery to the ultimate host destination.

Paint A program that comes with Windows 95 and enables you to view and edit various formats of bit maps.

palette A collection of tools. For example, in Paint, there is a color palette that displays the 48 colors available for use in creating a graphic.

pane Some windows, such as the window for Explorer, show two or more distinct "areas" (Explorer's window shows two such areas). These areas are referred to as "panes."

Panose Panose refers to a Windows internal description that represents a font by assigning each font a PANOSE ID number. Windows uses several internal descriptions to categorize fonts. The PANOSE information registers a font class and determines similarity between fonts.

paragraph formatting In a word processing program, this refers to formatting that can be applied to an entire paragraph, including alignment (left, center, right), indentation, and spacing before and after the paragraph.

parallel port A port (usually used for printing) that transmits data 8 bits at a time. This parallel transmission of 8 bits at a time gives the port its name.

parity An additional portion of data added to each byte of stored or transmitted data. Used to ensure that the data isn't lost or corrupted. In HyperTerminal, parity is used to ensure that the data is transmitted and received properly. Parity is also used in RAM chips to determine if RAM errors have occurred.

partial backup *See incremental backup.*

partition A portion of a physical hard drive that behaves as a separate disk (logical drive), even though it isn't.

path The location of a file in the directory tree.

PC Cards Formerly called PCMCIA cards, these are small (usually only slightly larger than a credit card) cards that plug into special slots provided in notebook computers. PC Cards can provide functionality for additional memory, modems, sound, networking, hard drives, and so on. PC Cards normally identify themselves to the computer, making configuring them quite simple.

PCMCIA The old name for PC Cards (*see PC Cards*).

peer-to-peer A type of networking in which no workstation has more control over the network than any other. Each station may share its resources, but no station is the sole resource sharer or file server. Typically less expensive than client/server networks, peer-to-peer networks are also more difficult to administer and less secure because there is no central repository of data.

personal information store The Personal Information Store is Exchange's term for the file that contains the structure of folders that make up your Inbox, Out box, sent files, deleted files, and any other personal folders you may choose to create.

Phone Dialer Phone Dialer is a program that is included with Windows 95 that enables you to place telephone calls from your computer by using a modem or another Windows telephony device. You can store a list of phone numbers you use frequently and dial the number quickly from your computer.

picon Picons are small bitmapped images of the first frame of your video clip. They can be used to represent the in and out source of your video segments.

PIF A file that provides Windows 95 with the information it needs to know in order to run a non-Windows program. Unlike earlier versions of Windows, there is no PIF editor in Windows 95. Instead, you set up a PIF file from the properties for the file. Access the file properties by right-clicking the file from My Computer.

Ping A network utility that determines if TCP/IP is working properly. Simply executing the Ping command (from a DOS prompt) and specifying the IP address should produce a response (the response will depend on how the remote machine has been programmed to respond to a Ping), but virtually any response that references the remote machine's identity indicates that the Ping was successful and TCP/IP is working correctly.

Play List In CD Player, a list of tracks from an audio CD that you want to play.

Plug and Play An industry-wide specification supported by Windows 95 that makes it easy to install new hardware. Plug and Play enables the computer to correctly identify hardware components (including plug-in cards) and ensures that different cards don't conflict in their requirements for IRQs, I/O addresses, DMA channels, and memory addresses. In order to fully implement Plug and Play, you need an operating system that supports it (as stated, Windows 95 does), a BIOS that supports it (most computers manufactured since early 1995 do) and cards that identify themselves to the system (information from these cards stored in the Windows Registry). If you have hardware, such as modems that aren't Plug and Play (so called "legacy hardware"), then Windows 95 will prompt you for the information necessary for setup, and store such information in the Registry.

pointer The on-screen symbol controlled by the mouse. As you move the mouse on the desk, the pointer moves on-screen. The pointer changes shape to indicate the current status and the type of functions and selections available.

polygon A multisided shape, in which each side is a straight line.

port A connection or socket for connecting devices to a computer (*see I/O address*).

port replicator On portable computers, a bus connection that makes all bus lines available externally. The port replicator can be used to plug in devices which, in a desktop computer, would be handled as cards. Port replicators are also the connection used to connect a portable computer to its docking station.

Postoffice This machine that will be the place in which all mail messages are stored for the workgroup.

Postproduction editing The steps of adding special effects, animated overlays, and more to a "production" video.

Postscript A special description language, invented by Adobe. This language is used to accurately describe fonts and graphics. Printers which can directly read this language and print the results are termed "postscript printers."

preemptive processing In a multitasking operating system, multiple tasks (threads) are generally controlled by a scheduler that preempts or interrupts each process, granting processor time in the form of a time slice. This enables multiple tasks to apparently run at the same time. However, each task runs for a time slice and is then preempted by the next process, which in turn is preempted—rotating processor time among active threads. In preemptive multitasking, the operating system is empowered to override (or preempt) an application that is using too much CPU time, as opposed to cooperative multitasking, where the application is responsible for relinquishing the CPU on a regular basis.

primary partition A portion of the hard disk that can be used by the operating system and that can't be subpartitioned like an extended partition can. Only primary partitions are bootable.

printer driver A Windows 95 program that tells programs how to format data for a particular type of printer.

printer fonts Fonts stored in the printer's ROM.

printer settings A window that displays all the printers for which there are drivers present. You can select the default printer from the installed printers, as well as configure each printer using the shortcut menu and the options dialog box.

printer window For each installed printer, you can view the printer window. The printer window displays the status of each print job in the queue, and enables you to pause, restart, and delete the print job.

processor The controlling device in a computer that interprets and executes instructions and performs computations, and otherwise controls the major functions of the computer. This book discusses Intel 80x86-series processors, which are miniaturized single-chip "microprocessors" containing thousands to millions of transistors in a silicon-based, multilayered integrated circuit design.

program file A program that runs an application directly (not via an association) when you click it.

program window A window that contains a program and its documents.

property sheet A dialog box that displays (and sometimes enables you to change) the properties of an object in Windows 95. To access a property sheet, right click the object to view the shortcut menu, and select Properties from the shortcut menu. Property sheets vary considerably between different objects.

proportional-spaced fonts Proportional spaced fonts adjust the inter-character space based on the shape of the individual characters. An example of a proportional spaced font is Arial. The width of a character is varied based on its shape. Adjusting inter-character spacing is really a function of kerning, which is a similar but not exactly the same. For instance, the letter 'A' and the letter 'V' are typically stored in each font as a kerning pair where they will be spaced differently when appearing next to each other. Where in a mono-space font vs. a proportional font you will see a difference in the width of the letter 'i.'

protected mode A memory addressing mode of Intel processors that allows direct "flat memory" addressing (linear addressing) rather than using the awkward "segmented" scheme required by real mode, which was pioneered on the Intel 8088 and 8086 processors. Protected mode derives its name from the fact that sections of memory owned by a particular process can be protected from rogue programs trying to access those addresses.

protocol Rules of communication. In networks, several layers of protocols exist. Each layer of protocol only needs to physically hand-off or receive data from the immediate layer above and beneath it, whereas virtual communications occur with the corresponding layer on another host computer.

Q

QIC A formatting standard for tapes used by various tape backup devices. The amount of information that can be stored on a tape varies by the QIC number. Windows 95's Backup program supports QIC 40, 80, 3010, and 3020 formats. It also supports QIC 113 compression format.

queue Documents lined up and waiting to be printed, or commands lined up and waiting to be serviced. Use the Printer window to view the print queue for a printer.

quick format A quick way to format a floppy disk, quick format doesn't actually wipe the whole disk, nor does it test the media for bad sectors. It just erases the FAT.

QuickTime Developed by Apple, QuickTime is a compression and decompression (codec) scheme for animation files. It is unique in that versions are available for both Windows and Macintosh, enabling software designers to provide their data in a format compatible for both platforms.

Quick View A program included with Windows 95 that enables you to view files stored in 30 different file formats without needing to open the application that created the file. Quick View is available from the File menu of Explorer IF a viewer is available for the selected file type.

R

RAM Random-Access Memory. Physical memory chips located in the computer. Typically, Windows 95 machines have 16 million bytes (16M) of RAM or more. However, Windows 95 will run on machines with 8M of RAM.

raster font A font in which characters are stored as pixels.

read-only Characteristic of a file indicating that the file can be read from, but not written to, by an application. Note however, that a "read-only" file can be deleted in Explorer, although you will get a warning (beyond the normal "are you sure" you normally get when you try to delete a file) if the file is read-only.

real mode As opposed to *protected mode*, real mode is a mode in which Intel x86 processors can run. Memory addressing in real mode is nonlinear, requiring a program to stipulate a segment and memory offset address in order to access a location in memory. Originally appeared on the Intel 8086 CPU and has been the bane of PC programmers ever since. Although subsequent CPU chips supported protected-mode linear addressing, backward compatibility with the thousands of real-mode applications slows the evolution of operating systems. Note that all Intel CPUs boot in real mode and require specific software support to switch into protected mode.

Recycle Bin An icon that appears on the Windows 95 desktop. To discard a file, you drag the file from Explorer, My Computer, or any other file handler to the Recycle Bin. This action hides the file—but doesn't actually erase it from the disk. You can "undelete" the file by dragging it from the recycle bin back to a folder. To actually delete the file, select the recycle bin menu selection to empty the recycle bin.

registering a program The act of linking a document with the program that created it so that both can be opened with a single command. For example, double-clicking a DOC file opens Word for Windows and loads the selected document.

Registry A database of configuration information central to Windows 95 operations. This file contains program settings, associations between file types and the applications that created them, as well as information about the types of OLE objects a program can create and hardware detail information.

Registry Editor The Registry Editor ships with Windows 95. Using this tool you can fine tune Windows 95 performance by adjusting or adding settings to key system information. Since Windows 95 has placed WIN.INI and SYSTEM.INI file settings in the registry, the ability to remotely edit these parameters is an extremely powerful tool. Warning: you can totally destroy a workstation using this tool!

repeater A device that repeats or amplifies bits of data received at one port and sends each bit to another port. A repeater is a simple bus network device that connects two cabling segments and isolates electrical problems to either side. When used in a LAN, most repeaters take a role in reconstituting the digital signal that passes through them to extend distances a signal can travel, and reduce problems that occur over lengths of cable, such as attenuation.

resize button A button located in the lower left corner of a non-maximized window. When the mouse pointer is over this button, it turns into a two-headed arrow. You can click and drag to resize the window horizontally and vertically.

resource (card) When installing a card, certain "resources" are needed: these often include a DMA channel, I/O Base address, and IRQ. Although these are detected and set automatically with Plug and Play compliant cards, you will have to set them using jumpers or the setup program to store the resource values in non-volatile RAM when installing a "legacy" (pre-Plug and Play) card.

restore button A button in the upper right corner of a Window that has two squares in it. When clicked, it returns the window to its previous size. When the window is at its previous size, the restore button switches to the maximize button, which returns the window to its maximum size.

restore files Copies one or more files from your backup set to the hard disk or to another floppy.

Rich Text Format (RTF) Rich Text Format (RTF) is compatible with several word processors and includes fonts, tabs, and character formatting.

ring network One of a variety of network topologies. Ring networks connect computers by using an In and an Out port for data. Each computer sends information to the next computer down the wire. Data flows from one computer's Out port to the next computer's In port.

ROM Read-Only Memory. A type of chip capable of permanently storing data without the aid of an electric current source to maintain it, as in RAM. The data in ROM chips is sometimes called firmware. Without special equipment, it is not possible to alter the contents of read-only memory chips, thus the name. ROMs are found in many types of computer add-in boards, as well as on motherboards. CPUs often have an internal section of ROM as well.

routable protocol A network protocol that can work with non proprietary routers. Traditional routers use the network packet header fields to identify network addresses (network numbers)/node addresses for ultimate source and destination nodes (or hosts) for packets of data. This scheme for routing packets across internetworks is used OSI, NetWare (IPX), TCP/IP, and AppleTalk network protocols.

router In a network, a device that reads network layer packet headers and receives or forwards each packet accordingly. Routers connect LANs and WANs into internetworks, but must be able to process the network packets for specific types of network protocol. Many routers process various packet types and therefore are termed multiprotocol routers.

S

safe mode A special mode for starting Windows 95 that uses simple, default settings so that you can at least get into Windows and fix a problem that makes it impossible to work with Windows otherwise. The default settings use a generic VGA monitor driver, no network settings, the standard Microsoft mouse driver, and the minimum device drivers necessary to start Windows.

safe recovery An installation option provided by Windows 95 to recover from a faulty or damaged installation of Windows 95.

saturation When working with colors, saturation indicates the purity of a color; lower values of saturation have more gray in them.

ScanDisk A program used to check for, diagnose, and repair damage on a hard disk or disk. Part of your routine hard disk maintenance (along with defragmenting your hard disk) should include a periodic run of ScanDisk to keep your hard disk in good repair. In its standard test, ScanDisk checks the files and folders on a disk or disk for *logical* errors, and if you ask it to, automatically corrects any errors it finds. ScanDisk checks for *crosslinked* files, which occur when two or more files have data stored in the same *cluster* (a storage unit on a disk). The data in the cluster is likely to be correct for only one of the files, and may not be correct for any of them. ScanDisk also checks for *lost file fragments*, which are pieces of data that have become disassociated with their files.

screen fonts Font files used to show type styles on the screen. These are different from the files used by Windows to print the fonts. The screen fonts must match the printer fonts in order for Windows to give an accurate screen portrayal of the final printed output.

screen resolution The number of picture elements (or "pixels") that can be displayed on the screen. Screen resolution is a function of the monitor and graphics card. Higher resolutions display more information at a smaller size, and also may slow screen performance. Screen resolution is expressed in the number of pixels across the screen by the number of pixels down the screen. Standard VGA has a resolution of 640 by 480, although most modern monitors can display 1024 by 768, and even higher (larger monitors can usually display a higher resolution than smaller ones).

screen saver A varying pattern or graphic that appears on the screen when the mouse and keyboard have been idle for a user-definable period of time. Originally used to prevent a static background from being "burned into" the screen phosphors, this is rarely a problem with modern monitors. Many screen savers (including those that come with Windows 95) can be used with a password—you must enter the correct password to turn off the screen saver and return to the screen. However, someone could simply reboot the machine, so a screen saver password is not very sophisticated protection.

scroll arrow Located at either end of a scroll bar, it can be clicked to scroll up or down (vertical scroll bar) or left or right (horizontal scroll bar). Clicking the scroll arrow will move your window in that direction.

scroll bar Scroll bars allow you to select a value within a range, such as what part of a document to see, or to what value to set the Red, Green, and Blue components of a color.

scroll box A small box located in the scroll bar that shows where the visible window is located in relation to the entire document, menu, or list. You can click and drag the scroll box to make other portions of the document, menu, or list visible.

select To specify a section of text or graphics for initiating an action. To select also can be to choose an option in a dialog box.

selection handles Small black boxes indicating that a graphic object has been selected. With some Windows applications, you can click and drag a selection handle to resize the selected object.

serial port *See COM.*

Serif Fonts Serif Fonts have projections (serifs) that extend the upper and lower strokes of the set's characters beyond their normal boundaries, for example, Courier. Sans-Serif Fonts do not have these projections, for example, Arial.

server A centrally-administered network computer, which contains resources that are shared with "client" machines on the network.

server application In OLE terminology, an application that supplies an object, (such as a drawing), to a client application, (such as a word processing program), for inclusion in a complex document.

shareware A method of distributing software, often including downloading the software from a BBS or the Microsoft Network. With shareware, you get to use the software before deciding to pay for it. By paying for the software and registering it, you usually receive a manual; perhaps the most up-to-date version (which may include additional functionality). Shareware versions of software often include intrusive reminders to register—the registered versions do not include these reminders.

shortcut A pointer to a file, document or printer in Windows 95. A shortcut is represented by an icon in Explorer, on the desktop, or as an entry in the Start menu. Selecting the program shortcut icon or menu entry runs the program to which the shortcut "points." Selecting a document shortcut runs the application that created the document (provided the document type is associated with a program). Dragging and dropping a document onto a printer shortcut prints the document. Note that a shortcut does NOT create a copy of the program or document itself.

shortcut keys A keystroke or key combination that enables you to activate a command without having to enter a menu or click a button.

shortcut menu A pop-up menu that appears when you right click an object for which a menu is appropriate. The shortcut menu displays only those options which make sense for the object you select and current conditions.

Small Computer System Interface (SCSI) An ANSI standard bus design. SCSI host adapters are used to adapt an ISA, EISA, MCI, PCI, or VLB (VESA Local Bus) bus to a SCSI bus so that SCSI devices (such as disk drives, CD-ROMs, tape backups, and other devices) can be interfaced. A SCSI bus accommodates up to eight devices, however, the bus adapter is considered one device, thereby enabling seven usable devices to be interfaced to each SCSI adapter. SCSI devices are intelligent devices. SCSI disk drives have embedded controllers and interface to a SCSI bus adapter. A SCSI interface card is therefore a "bus adapter," not a "controller."

Small Computer System Interface-2 (SCSI-2) An ANSI standard that improves on SCSI-1 standards for disk and other device interfaces. SCSI-2 bandwidth is 10 Mbytes/sec, whereas SCSI-1 is 5 Mbyte/sec. SCSI-2 also permits command-tag queuing, which enables up to 256 requests to be queued without waiting for the first request. Another SCSI-2 feature is the bus' capability to communicate with more than one type of device at the same time, where a single SCSI-1 host adapter only supported one type of device to communicate on the bus.

SCSI Configured Automagically (SCAM) The specification for Plug and Play or SCSI buses. This specification makes it unnecessary to set a SCSI Id, as the configuration software negotiates and sets the id for each connected SCSI device (that is Plug and Play compliant!).

soft fonts Depending on your printing hardware, soft fonts may be downloaded to your printer. Downloading fonts reduces the time taken by the printer to process printouts. Although downloading soft fonts is done only once (per session), benefits are realized through subsequent printing.

Solitaire A card game included with Windows 95 for a single player. The object of solitaire is to turn all the cards in the seven face-down stacks face-up on top of each of the four aces for each of the four suites.

Soundblaster An extremely popular family of sound boards developed and marketed by Creative Labs. Because of the popularity and large market share of this product family, most sound boards advertise themselves as

"Soundblaster compatible," meaning that drivers provided in Windows, Windows 95, and programs such as games will work with these boards. However, some board's compatibility is not perfect.

source document In OLE, the document that contains the information you want to link into (to appear in) another document (the destination document).

spool A temporary holding area for the data you want to print. When printing a document, it can take some time (depending on the length of the document and the speed of your printer) for the document to come off your printer. By spooling the data, you may continue using your computer while the document is printing, because the computer "feeds" the spool contents to the printer as fast as the printer can handle it. When the print job is completed, the spool file is automatically deleted.

star network One of a variety of network topologies. Star networks connect computers through a central hub. The central hub distributes the signals to all of the cables which are connected.

Start menu A menu located at the left end of the taskbar. Clicking the button marked "Start" opens a popup menu that makes Help, the Run command, settings, find, shutdown, a list of programs (actually, program shortcuts), and a list of recently accessed documents available for you to run with a single click. For some items (such as the Documents item), a submenu opens to the side of the main item to display the list of choices. You can configure the Start menu to specify which programs are available to run from it.

Startup Folder A folder that contains any programs that you want Windows 95 to run whenever you startup. You can drag-and-drop program shortcuts into the StartUp Folder to add them to the list of programs to run.

static object In OLE, where objects have a "hot link" to their original application, static objects are simply pasted into a destination document using the Clipboard. These objects are not updated if the original object is updated. This is the simple "pasting" that most Windows users use on a daily basis.

stroke font A font that can have its size greatly altered without distorting the font.

stop bits In a communications program, the number of bits used to indicate the "break" between pieces of information (*see data bits*). Usually 1 or 2.

submenu A related set of options that appear when you select a menu item (*see cascading menus*).

swap file A file that gives Windows 95 the ability to use a portion of hard drive as memory. With the use of a swap file, you can load and run more programs in Windows 95 than you actually have RAM memory for. A swap file allows Windows 95 to "swap" chunks of memory containing currently unused information to disk, making room in RAM memory for information you need to run the currently selected program. Using a swap file is slower than holding everything in RAM memory, however.

system disk The disk containing the operating system, or at least enough of it to start the system and then look on another disk for the support files.

system fonts System Fonts are used by Windows to draw menus, controls, and utilize specialized control text in Windows. System fonts are proportional fonts that can be sized and manipulated quickly.

System monitor A program that enables you to monitor the resources on your computer. You can see information displayed for the 32-bit file system, network clients and servers, and the virtual memory manager, among other things. Most of this information is highly technical in nature and most useful to advanced users. You can display the information in either bar or line charts, or as a numeric value.

system policies Policies, established by a system administrator, which override Registry settings on individual machines. By setting up policies, a system Administrator can restrict a user from changing hardware settings using Control Panel, customize parts of the Desktop like the Network Neighborhood or the Programs folder, and maintain centrally located network settings, such as network client customizations or the ability to install file & printer services. This program can also control access to a computer, enable user profiles, and maintain password control.

System Resources *See heap.*

T

tab (dialog boxes) In dialog boxes, there may be multiple panels of information. Each panel has an extension at the top that names the panel. This small extension is called a "tab."

TAPI Telephony Applications Programming Interface, or TAPI, provides a method for programs to work with modems, independent of dealing directly with the modem hardware. All the information you give Windows during the modem configuration is used for TAPI to set up its interface. Communications programs that are written specifically for Windows 95 will talk to TAPI, which will then issue appropriate commands to the modem. This is called device independence.

taskbar An area that runs across the bottom of the Windows 95 desktop. The Start button (*see Start menu*) is at the left end of the taskbar, and the clock can be displayed at the right end of the taskbar. Running applications are represented as buttons on the taskbar, the current window is shown as a depressed button, all other applications are displayed as raised buttons. Clicking the button for an inactive application activates that application and displays its window as the current window.

task list A list of currently running applications. You can switch tasks by clicking an item in the task list. The task list is accessed by pressing Alt+Tab on the keyboard.

TCP/IP Transmission Control Protocol/Internet Protocol is a set of networking protocols developed in the 1970s. TCP/IP includes Transport Control Protocol, which is a connection-oriented transport protocol that includes transport, session, and presentation layer protocol functions, which is equivalent to layers 4,5, and 6 of the OSI Model and Internet Protocol, and a widely used routable network protocol that corresponds to layer 3 of the OSI model. User Datagram Protocol (UDP) can be substituted in cases where connectionless datagram service is desired. TCP/IP is an entire protocol stack that includes protocols for file transfers (FTP), termination emulation services (telnet), electronic mail (SMTP), address resolution (ARP and RARP), and error control and notification (ICMP and SNMP). TCP/IP is used extensively in many computer systems because it is nonproprietary—free from royalties. Its use was mandated by Congress for use in computer systems for many government agencies and contract situations. TCP/IP is also used in the Internet, a huge government and research internetwork spanning North America and much of the world. TCP/IP is the most commonly used set of network protocols.

terminal emulation In the "old days" of computing, a "terminal" was an input/output device that was a slave of a CPU, such as a terminal for minicomputer or mainframe. Generally, terminals, had no computing power of their own, but simply provided an interface to a remote host computer.

"Terminal emulation" refers to a mode (character-based) in which a PC emulates one of these terminals to communicate with a remote host—typically a BBS computer or a corporate mainframe that only "knows" how to talk to a terminal.

text-based *See character-based.*

text box A space in the dialog box where text or numbers can be entered so that a command can be carried out.

text file A file containing only text characters .

thumbnail A miniature rendition of a graphic file. A thumbnail gives a idea of what the full-size graphic looks like, and is usually used as a gateway to view the full-size graphic.

thread (program execution) A "thread" is a chunk of a program. In a multi-threading environment such as Windows 95, multiple threads (multiple portions of a program) can execute at the same time—provided the program has been programmed to take advantage of this feature.

thread (BBS/Communications) A set of messages pertaining to one general idea.

tile To reduce and move windows so that they can all be seen at once.

time slice A brief time period in which a process is given access to the processor. Each second is divided into 18.3 time slices; multiple tasks can be scheduled for processing in these slices, yet outwardly appear to be occurring simultaneously.

time-out A time period after which a device or driver might signal the operating system and cease trying to perform its duty. If a printer is turned off, for example, when you try to print, the driver waits for a predetermined period of time, then issues an error message. In computer terminology, the driver has *timed out.*

title bar The bar at the top of a program or document window that shows you what its title is. The control menu, maximize, minimize, restore, and taskbar buttons can be accessed in the title bar.

token ring A network type developed by IBM. It is more expensive than Ethernet to implement, but can run at 16Mb/s. Unlike Ethernet, where the workstations must listen for a clear line before transmitting, workstations on a token ring take turns sending data—passing the "token" from station to station to indicate whose turn it is.

toolbar A collection of buttons that typically make the more common tools for an application easily accessible. Although often grouped in a line under the menus, a toolbar can be located on the left or right side of the working area—or even be relocatable to any area of the screen the user wishes. In some applications (for example, MS Office applications such as Word), the toolbar is user-configurable—the user can display different toolbars, and add or remove tool buttons from the bar.

topology The layout or design of cabling on a network.

TrueType fonts A font technology developed by Microsoft in response to Adobe's success in the scaleable font business with its own Type 1 and Type 3 PostScript fonts. Used as a simple means for all Windows applications to have access to a wide selection of fonts for screen and printer output. TrueType fonts greatly simplify using fonts on a Windows computer. The same fonts can be used on Windows 3.1, Windows NT, Windows 95, and other Windows products, such as Windows for Workgroups. Consisting of two files (one for screen and one for printer), hundreds of TrueType fonts are available from a variety of manufacturers. Depending on your printer, the TrueType font manager internal to Windows, in conjunction with the printer driver, generates either bitmapped or downloadable soft fonts.

twisted pair Cabling that consists of lightly insulated copper wire, twisted into pairs and bundled into sets of pairs. The twists enhance the wire's capability to resist "crosstalk" (bleeding of signal from one wire to the next). This cabling is used extensively in phone systems and LANs, although even moderate distances in a LAN require "repeaters" (*see repeaters*).

U

unbound media In a network, this refers to connections that are not implemented using traditional cabling. Instead, unbound media is wireless—implemented through use of various portions of the radio wave spectrum.

Unimodem driver A universal modem driver supplied by Microsoft as part of Windows 95. The modem driver assumes that the modem supports the Hayes AT command set (most do).

uninstalling applications When you install an application in Windows 95, it places the necessary files in many different places on your hard drive. You can't remove all of a program by simply erasing the contents of its main subdirectory. To uninstall the application—and remove all the files it placed on your hard drive—you must run a special program that should have been included with the application. Many applications do not include the "uninstaller" program. Although, to be certified under Windows 95, the uninstaller program must be included.

Universal Naming Convention (UNC) With UNC, you can view, copy, or run files on another machine without assigning it a drive letter on your own. It also means if you are running short of logical drive letters, you can get to servers that you use only intermittently with a simple command from the MS-DOS prompt.

unprintable area The area, usually around the extreme edges of the paper, in which the printer is incapable of printing. For example, a laser printer cannot print in the 1/4" at the left and right edges of the paper. It is important to know the unprintable area, since graphics or text you place in this area will be cut off when printed.

Upload The act of sending a file to a remote computer (*see download*).

V

VCACHE Windows 95 uses a new 32-bit VCACHE which replaces the older SmartDrive that ran under DOS and previous versions of Windows. VCACHE uses more intelligent caching algorithms to improve the apparent speed of your hard drive as well as your CD-ROM and 32-bit network redirectors. Unlike SmartDrive, VCACHE dynamically allocates itself. Based on the amount of free system memory VCACHE allocates or de-allocates memory used by the cache.

vector fonts A set of lines that connect points to form characters.

video for windows A set of utilities and protocols for implementing full-motion video in Windows 95.

virtual machine A "logical" computer that exists inside a PC. Multiple virtual machines can be running in a PC. Applications that run on one virtual machine are unlikely to affect the applications running on a different virtual machine. 16-bit applications (for example, Windows 3.1 applications) all run on the same virtual machine in Windows 95, thus, if one crashes, it is likely to make the rest of the 16-bit applications unusable as well. However, such an occurrence will likely NOT affect 32-bit applications that are running simultaneously.

virtual memory The use of permanent media (for example, hard drive) to simulate additional RAM (*see swap file*). This allows large applications to run in less physical RAM than they normally would require. When RAM runs low, the operating system uses a virtual memory manager program to temporarily store data on the hard disk like it was in RAM, which makes RAM free for data manipulation. When needed, the data is read back from the disk and reloaded into RAM.

virus A virus is a computer program written to interrupt or destroy your work. A virus may do something as innocuous as display a message, or something as destructive as reformatting your hard drive—or almost anything in between. Your computer can "catch" a virus from a floppy disk, or even from a file downloaded from a remote source, such as a BBS. Once your computer has become "infected," the virus may spread via connections on a network or floppy disks you share with others. A variety of virus-detecting software exists (including one packaged with Windows 95).

ViSCA A protocol for daisy chaining up to seven video devices together and connecting them to a single serial port.

volume Disk partition(s) formatted and available for use by the operating system.

volume label The identifier for a volume (*see volume*) or disk. This is specified when formatting the volume or disk.

W

wallpaper A backdrop for the Windows desktop, made up of a graphics file. The graphics can be either *centered*, appearing only once in the center of the desktop, or *tiled*, repeating as many times as the graphic will fit.

WAV files Named for three-character extension .WAV (for sound wave) these files have, a WAV file is a file containing a digitized sound. Depending on the sampling rate and resolution, the sound recorded in the WAV file seems realistic (provided you have the sound card and speakers to hear it). These files can be quite large, running into the multi-megabyte range for high-quality recordings.

Web browser A software program that enables you to view Home pages and retrieve information from the Internet.

What's This? A new feature of Windows 95 help. In a dialog box, click the small button with a question mark (?) on it. Then, click where you want help. A small description should pop up to explain what the item is and how to use it. Click in the description popup to remove it.

Winpopup Winpopup is an applet that is included in the Accessories group when you install the network component of Windows 95. This tool normally sends short messages from one computer on the workgroup to another (or from a shared printer to a workstation). It is designed so that when a message is received, the program will pop up over anything else on the screen and show the message.

wiring concentrator In a network, a multiple port repeating device used in Ethernet LANs to connect multiple cable segments into one LAN. Sometimes called a "hub" (*see hub*) or "multiport repeater" (*see repeater*), this device isolates cabling problems by separating each workstation connection on an isolated cabling segment.

wizard Microsoft's name for a step-by-step set of instructions that guide you through a particular task. For example, there are many wizards included with Windows 95 for installing new hardware, configuring the Start menu, and changing other aspects of the environment.

World Wide Web (WWW) The fastest growing part of the Internet, the 'Web,' or WWW, is a collection of hypertext documents. It provides access to images and sounds from thousands of different Web sites, via a special programming language called **H**yper**T**ext **M**arkup **L**anguage, or **HTML**. This language is used to create "hypertext" documents, which include embedded commands.

WordPad A program included with Windows 95 that enables you to do basic word processing and save the results in plain text format, Word 6 format, or Rich Text Format.

word wrap In word processing, this refers to words that cannot be completed on one line automatically "wrapping" to the beginning of the next line. Most word processors use word wrap automatically—an exception is Notepad, where you must turn on word wrap.

workgroup A collection of networked PCs grouped to facilitate work that users of the computers tend to do together. The machines are not necessarily in the same room or office.

WYSIWYG Short for "What you see is what you get," this term refers to the ability of an application to display an accurate representation of the printed output on the screen.

X

x coordinate The position of an item relative to the left side of the screen. Values increase as you move to the right.

Xmodem An error-correction protocol (*see binary transfer protocol*) used by the DOS application XMODEM and many other communications programs. Xmodem using CRC (cyclical redundancy check) is a means of detecting errors in transmissions between modems or across wired serial links.

Y

y coordinate The position of an item relative to the bottom of the screen. Values increase as you move down the screen.

Ymodem Another form of Xmodem that allows batch transfers of files and (in Ymodem G) hardware error control.

Z

Zmodem ZModem is a full functional streaming protocol where XModem is a send and acknowledge protocol which causes delays in the transfer equal to twice the modem lag on a connection. ZModem is the preferred way of exchanging data since it is reliable, quick, and relatively easy to implement.❖

Part IX

Indexes

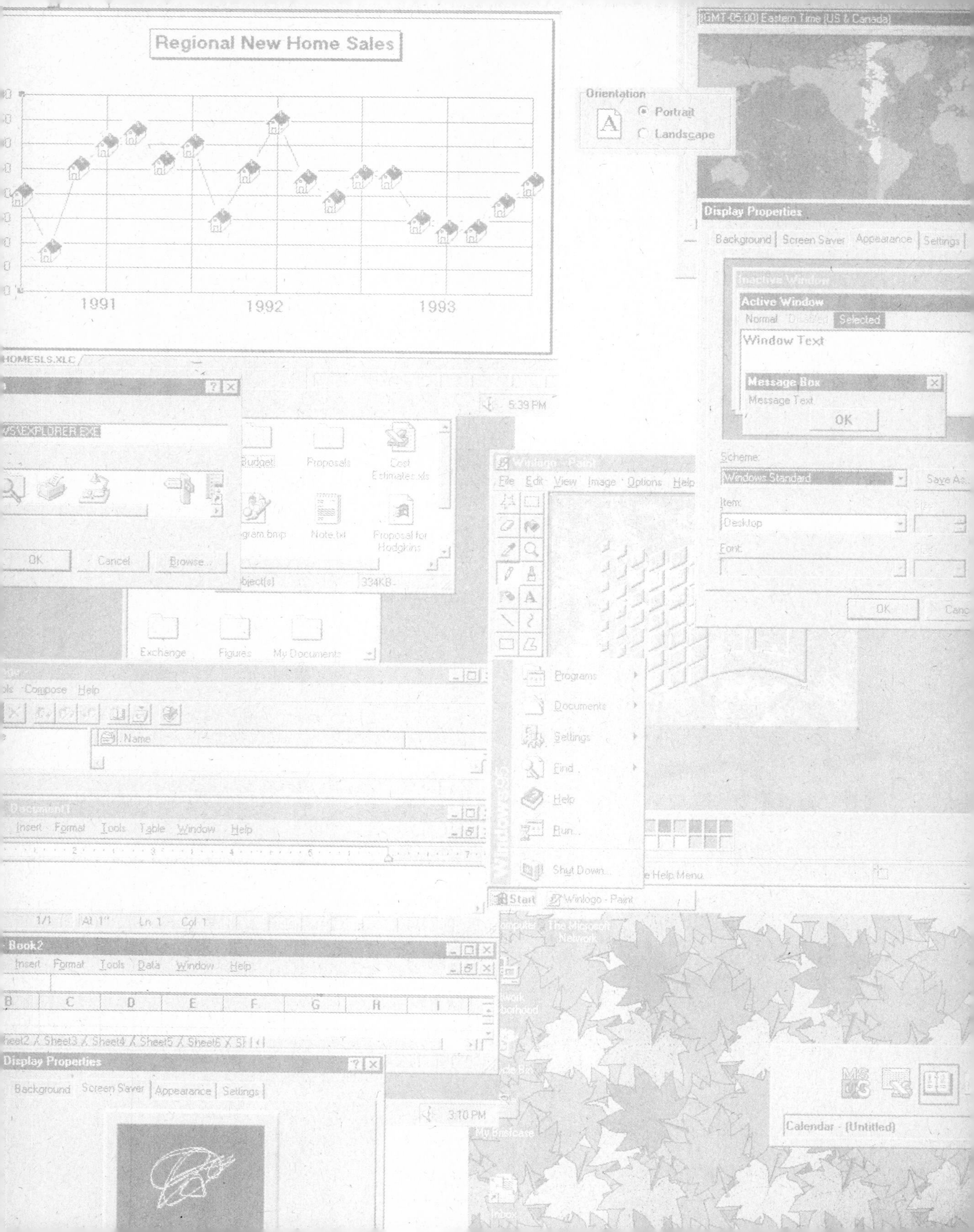
Regional New Home Sales
1991
1992
1993
HOMESLS.XLC
Orientation
Portrait
Landscape
(GMT-05:00) Eastern Time (US & Canada)
Display Properties
Background
Screen Saver
Appearance
Settings
Inactive Window
Active Window
Normal
Disabled
Selected
Window Text
Message Box
Message Text
OK
Scheme:
Windows Standard
Save As...
Item:
Desktop
Font:
5:39 PM
Budget
Proposals
Cost Estimates.xls
Note.txt
Proposal for Hodgkins
334KB
OK
Cancel
Browse...
Exchange
Figures
My Documents
Winlogo - Paint
File
Edit
View
Image
Options
Help
Programs
Documents
Settings
Find
Help
Run...
Shut Down...
Start
Compose
Name
Document1
Insert
Format
Tools
Table
Window
1/1
At 1"
Ln 1
Col 1
Book2
Data
Sheet3
Sheet4
Sheet5
Sheet6
3:10 PM
My Briefcase
Inbox
Calendar - (Untitled)

Index of Common Problems

Windows Setup

If you have this problem...	You'll find help here...
Adding components also removes components	p. 315
Accessibility options aren't available	p. 150
New IDE drive is inaccessible	p. 238
Get a "resource conflict" message while installing a Plug and Play device	p. 247
Network card is not working	p. 623
Can't get the modem to work	p. 837
Modem causes Windows to crash	p. 841
Can't see your CD-ROM drive	p. 970

Windows 3.x and DOS Applications

If you have this problem...	You'll find help here...
Alt+Tab only alternates between two applications	p. 60
Can't see the taskbar when running an older Windows 3.x application	p. 64
Windows 3.x applications seem to forget your settings when you dual boot	p. 308
A DOS application won't respond	p. 330
Mouse doesn't work in DOS applications	p. 334

(continues)

Windows 3.x and DOS Applications (continued)

If you have this problem...	You'll find help here...
Windows shuts down completely when you set the Command prompt for MS-DOS mode	p. 338
DOS programs run very slowly now under Windows 95	p. 344
Can't open very many DOS sessions	p. 344
Can't double-click on a DOS data file to start a DOS program	p. 69
DOS data files don't seem to work from within Explorer	p. 75

Printing

If you have this problem...	You'll find help here...
Printer has started to print, but you can't stop it	p. 173
It takes a long time to print a document	p. 654
Can't see a network printer in Network Neighborhood	p. 781
Network printer doesn't let you know when it is out of paper	p. 782
Network printer gives you inconsistent printout quality	p. 783
Shared printer is unavailable to other workstations on the network	p. 786

Working with Documents

If you have this problem...	You'll find help here...
Need to fix a mistake in a Paint document?	p. 381
Paint gives you an error when you try to add text to the picture	p. 384
Paint won't let you resize an object you've drawn	p. 392

If you have this problem...	You'll find help here...
Can't save a PCX file in Paint	p. 396
Original document loses information when you use drag-and-drop	p. 423
Copied text doesn't go where you want it to	p. 423
Get a black circle with a line through it when you try to copy text	p. 423
Can't edit a linked or embedded object document	p. 452
Excel doesn't start when you click on an embedded spreadsheet	p. 452

Disks and Drives

If you have this problem...	You'll find help here...
Windows won't format a disk	p. 464
Large files won't copy on to a compressed drive	p. 471
Deleted the DRVSPACE.000 to save some space on a compressed drive	p. 478
Resized compressed drive still doesn't seem to have enough space	p. 480
Disk makes a lot of noise and seems kind of slow	p. 494
Modified a file in Briefcase, but it still shows as `Up to Date`	p. 539

Modems

Modem doesn't connect while you're dialing MSN	p. 1113
Dialing MSN tells you your password is invalid	p. 1113
E-mail isn't sent when you dial MSN	p. 1131
Modem connects but doesn't stay connected	p. 855

(continues)

Multimedia and Sound

If you have this problem...	You'll find help here...
Sound is distorted or doesn't play	p. 984
Sound seems to hiss during playback	p. 991
Video and sound files don't play back in sync	p. 1001
VideoDirector says your LANC driver isn't working	p. 1028
Can't record video when you press the Record button	p. 1032
MCI ViSCA doesn't show all of your devices	p. 1037
Windows locks up when you run the ISVR Pro's diagnostics	p. 1062
ViSCA doesn't show your devices in right order	p. 1063
Movies always seem to drop 5% of your frames when captured	p. 1066
Compressed movie clips have fuzzy areas	p. 1073

Networking

If you have this problem...	You'll find help here...
Can't connect to remote computer	p. 622
Can't use shared resources on another networked computer	p. 646
Can't find a computer on the network	p. 646
Remote computer on your dial-up connection hangs up on you unexpectedly	p. 667
Can't access a floppy drive on a network computer	p. 647
Some of the files you share are missing	p. 646

(continues)

Networking (continued)

Index

Symbols

A

IX

Indexes

B

C

D

IX

Indexes

F

G

H

J-K

L

M

N

O

P

Q

R

S

T

U

V

W

X-Y-Z

IX

Indexes

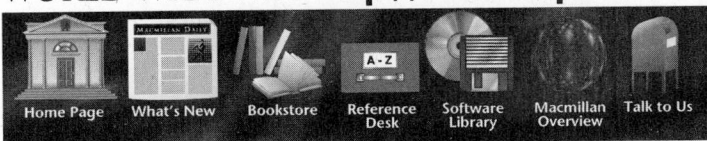

Complete and Return this Card for a *FREE* Computer Book Catalog

Thank you for purchasing this book! You have purchased a superior computer book written expressly for your needs. To continue to provide the kind of up-to-date, pertinent coverage you've come to expect from us, we need to hear from you. Please take a minute to complete and return this self-addressed, postage-paid form. In return, we'll send you a free catalog of all our computer books on topics ranging from word processing to programming and the internet.

Mr. ☐ Mrs. ☐ Ms. ☐ Dr. ☐

Name (first) ______ (M.I.) ☐ (last) ______

Address ______

______

City ______ State ______ Zip ______ ______

Phone ______ ______ ______ Fax ______ ______ ______

Company Name ______

E-mail address ______

1. Please check at least (3) influencing factors for purchasing this book.

- Front or back cover information on book ☐
- Special approach to the content ☐
- Completeness of content ☐
- Author's reputation ☐
- Publisher's reputation ☐
- Book cover design or layout ☐
- Index or table of contents of book ☐
- Price of book ☐
- Special effects, graphics, illustrations ☐
- Other (Please specify): ______ ☐

2. How did you first learn about this book?

- Saw in Macmillan Computer Publishing catalog ☐
- Recommended by store personnel ☐
- Saw the book on bookshelf at store ☐
- Recommended by a friend ☐
- Received advertisement in the mail ☐
- Saw an advertisement in: ______ ☐
- Read book review in: ______ ☐
- Other (Please specify): ______ ☐

3. How many computer books have you purchased in the last six months?

- This book only ☐
- 2 books ☐
- 3 to 5 books ☐
- More than 5 ☐

4. Where did you purchase this book?

- Bookstore ☐
- Computer Store ☐
- Consumer Electronics Store ☐
- Department Store ☐
- Office Club ☐
- Warehouse Club ☐
- Mail Order ☐
- Direct from Publisher ☐
- Internet site ☐
- Other (Please specify): ______ ☐

5. How long have you been using a computer?

- ☐ Less than 6 months
- ☐ 6 months to a year
- ☐ 1 to 3 years
- ☐ More than 3 years

6. What is your level of experience with personal computers and with the subject of this book?

	With PCs	With subject of book
New	☐	☐
Casual	☐	☐
Accomplished	☐	☐
Expert	☐	☐

Source Code ISBN: 1-56529-921-3

7. Which of the following best describes your job title?

- Administrative Assistant ☐
- Coordinator ☐
- Manager/Supervisor ☐
- Director ☐
- Vice President ☐
- President/CEO/COO ☐
- Lawyer/Doctor/Medical Professional ☐
- Teacher/Educator/Trainer ☐
- Engineer/Technician ☐
- Consultant ☐
- Not employed/Student/Retired ☐
- Other (Please specify): ____________ ☐

8. Which of the following best describes the area of the company your job title falls under?

- Accounting ☐
- Engineering ☐
- Manufacturing ☐
- Operations ☐
- Marketing ☐
- Sales ☐
- Other (Please specify): ____________ ☐

9. What is your age?

- Under 20 ☐
- 21-29 ☐
- 30-39 ☐
- 40-49 ☐
- 50-59 ☐
- 60-over ☐

10. Are you:

- Male ☐
- Female ☐

11. Which computer publications do you read regularly? (Please list)

____

Comments: ____________________

Fold here and scotch-tape to mail.

NO POSTAGE
NECESSARY
IF MAILED
IN THE
UNITED STATES

BUSINESS REPLY MAIL

FIRST-CLASS MAIL PERMIT NO. 9918 INDIANAPOLIS IN

POSTAGE WILL BE PAID BY THE ADDRESSEE

ATTN MARKETING
MACMILLAN COMPUTER PUBLISHING
MACMILLAN PUBLISHING USA
201 W 103RD ST
INDIANAPOLIS IN 46209-9042

Broaden Your Mind And Your Business With Que

The *Special Edition Using* series remains the most-often recommended product line for computer users who want detailed reference information. With thorough explanations, troubleshooting advice, and special "Techniques from the Pros" sections, these books are the perfect all-in-one resource.

Special Edition Using Word for Windows 95
0-7897-0084-0
$34.99 USA
Pub Date: 8/95

Special Edition Using Excel for Windows 95
0-7897-0112-X
$34.99 USA
Pub Date: 8/95

Special Edition Using PowerPoint for Windows 95
0-7897-0464-1
$34.99 USA
Pub Date: 9/95

Special Edition Using Microsoft Works for Windows 95
0-7897-0462-5
$29.99 USA
Pub Date: 10/95

For more information on these and other Que products, visit your local book retailer or call 1-800-772-0477.

QUE

Source Code ISBN:0-7897-921-3

Killer Windows® 95

Glenn Fincher
Ewan Grantham
Robin Hohman
Yvonne Johnson
Bill Lawrence
Gordon Meltzer
Benjamin F. Miller
Gregory J. Root
Clayton Walnum
Allen L. Wyatt
Martin R. Wyatt

QUE®

Killer Windows 95

Library of Congress Catalog No.: 95-078885

ISBN: 0-7897-0001-8

97 96 95 6 5 4 3 2

Interpretation of the printing code: the rightmost double-digit number is the year of the book's printing; the rightmost single-digit number, the number of the book's printing. For example, a printing code of 95-1 shows that the first printing of the book occurred in 1995.

Screen reproductions in this book were created by using Collage Plus from Inner Media, Inc., Hollis, NH.

Credits

President and Publisher
Roland Elgey

Associate Publisher
Joseph B. Wikert

Editorial Services Director
Elizabeth Keaffaber

Managing Editor
Sandy Doell

Director of Marketing
Lynn E. Zingraf

Senior Series Editor
Chris Nelson

Title Manager
Bryan Gambrel

Acquisitions Editor
Lori A. Jordan

Product Director
Stephen L. Miller

Production Editor
Mike La Bonne

Editors
Judy Brunetti
Elizabeth Bruns
Tom Cirtin
Susan Shaw Dunn
Patrick Kanouse
Susan Ross Moore
Caroline D. Roop

Assistant Product Marketing Manager
Kim Margolius

Technical Editors
Kyle Bryant, Russell Jacobs

Technical Specialist
Cari Skaggs

Acquisitions Coordinator
Angela C. Kozlowski

Operations Coordinator
Patricia J. Brooks

Editorial Assistant
Michelle R. Newcomb

Book Designer
Barbara Kordesh

Cover Designer
Dan Armstrong

Copywriter
Jennifer Reese

Production Team
Steve Adams, Angela Bannan, Claudia Bell, Lisa Daugherty, Chad Dressler, DiMonique Ford, Amy Gornik, John Hulse, Darren Jackson, Brian-Kent Proffitt, Bobbi Satterfield, Susan Springer, Michael Thomas

Indexers
Kathy Venable, Debra Myers

Composed in *Utopia* and *MCPdigital* by Que Corporation.

About the Authors

Glenn Fincher has worked in the computer industry for the last 12 years. Working in the fast-moving electronic manufacturing industry, Glenn spent the early years of his career in Test Engineering at SCI Systems, Inc., the world's largest computer contract manufacturer. Spending the bulk of the SCI years in component, board, and unit testing, he became intimately familiar with the building blocks of today's computer technology. Joining Intergraph Corporation in 1991 as a Customer Support Analyst, he has applied his wealth of computer knowledge to providing Intergraph's customers with quality, timely, and accurate support for the MicroStation CAD product. Leading the software certification efforts for the successful release of MicroStation 5.0, he continues to be involved in the day-to-day world of Intergraph's partner Bentley Systems MicroStation product. Sharing the knowledge gained in the experience of these years in the industry has always been a priority, so it is no surprise that he is in demand as a speaker, writer, and presenter throughout Intergraph. With his present involvement in Intergraph's WWW effort as Webmaster for Intergraph's Software Solutions, Glenn continues to remain at the leading edge of this industry. Continually seeking to stay on this edge has required both the support and understanding of wife Jan and their three children, Ashely, Will, and Aimee, without whom this and all his other endeavors would have been a lonely journey indeed. Glenn can be reached by electronic mail at gtfinche@ingr.com.

Ewan Grantham's main work is as a consultant specializing in building GUI front-ends for client/server systems, and creating multimedia presentations and training for clients. Equally adept at changing diapers (three kids under the age of 4) and changing jumpers on his IDE controller, he also finds time to work with Visual C++, MS Access, MS Help, and a monthly column on multimedia in *Windows 95 Journal.* Ewan can be reached on CIS at 74123,2232 or through the Internet at 74123.2232@compuserve.com.

Robin Hohman has been writing about computers and other subjects for more than 10 years. Her articles have appeared in newspapers, magazines, and books. She also survived a stint as a writer/producer in television news, and she refuses to be cowed by even the most obstinate computer software.

Yvonne Johnson has been involved in teaching and writing about PCs since they first came into use. For 12 years she owned and operated a successful computer training school. During that time she authored all the training material for the school and wrote several books published by Que and other publishers. She sold the school and now devotes more of her time to writing, consulting, and programming. Her training and writing background has made her exceptionally well-versed in database, word processing, graphics, spreadsheet, presentation, integrated, and publishing software. She holds a BA degree from Centre College of Kentucky with a major in education and English. She did her post-graduate work at the University of South Florida.

Bill Lawrence started using NetWare in 1983, when the software was called ShareNet and was delivered on five low-density diskettes. He is part of the team that manages a 3000-node network for a major western utility, and writes and speaks extensively about networking issues. He is the author of Que's *Using Novell NetWare 4,* which covers NetWare 3.x.

Gordon Meltzer has been teaching himself about computers since they were made with vacuum tubes. Recently, Gordon designed and built workgroup networks for a music marketing division of Time-Warner and several New York City law firms. He is a consultant on computing issues to NBC Post Production in Manhattan. Gordon has produced a number of jazz records for people like Miles Davis, Michel LeGrand, Al Di Meola, and Wallace Roney, and has a special interest in using computers on the business side of the music industry.

Benjamin F. Miller is a features editor at *PC/Computing Magazine*, and has written on Windows 95 and the Internet. He regularly contributes articles on multimedia and application development.

Gregory J. Root started his work with computers when TRS-80s were in style and 16K of RAM was equivalent to infinity. He has worked for Northern Trust Bank and Follett Software Company. He also has made part of his living as a computing consultant for lawyers, churches, and a government contract. Throughout his career he has administered and installed peer-to-peer and server-based networks, developed applications using FORTRAN and Visual Basic, and managed software development projects. He lives in Lake in the Hills, Illinois, with his beautiful wife and lifelong companion, Tracy.

Clayton Walnum has been writing about computers for a decade and has published more than 300 articles in major computer publications. He is the author of several books, covering such diverse topics as programming, computer gaming, and application programs. His most recent book is *Creating Turbo C++ Games,* also published by Que. His earlier titles include *Borland C++ Object-Oriented Programming, Borland C++ Power Programming,* and *QBasic for Rookies* (Que); *PC Picasso: A Child's Computer Drawing Kit,* and *The First Book of Microsoft Works for Windows* (Sams); *PowerMonger: The Official Strategy Guide* (Prima); and *C-manship Complete* (Taylor Ridge Books). Walnum is a full-time freelance writer and lives in Connecticut with his wife and their three children.

Allen L. Wyatt, a recognized expert in small computer systems, has been working in the computer and publishing industries for over 15 years. He has written more than 30 books explaining many different facets of working with computers. These books have covered topics ranging from programming languages to using application software to using operating systems. The books he has written and worked on have helped millions of readers learn how to better use computers.

Allen is the president of Discovery Computing Inc., a computer and publishing services company located in Sundance, Wyoming. Besides writing books, he helps further the computer book industry by providing consulting and distribution services. With his wife and three children, he lives on a 350-acre ranch just outside of town, on the edge of the Black Hills. In his spare time he tends his animals, has fun with his family, and participates in church and community events.

Martin R. Wyatt has been hooked on microcomputers for almost as long as he can remember. In fact, troubleshooting PCs and consulting (and an occasional game or two) have long been a favorite hobby. Only recently, however, has he been able to really earn a living from it. Currently, Marty works at Discovery Computing Inc., in Sundance, Wyoming, where he helps his brother, Allen Wyatt, author books. In his spare time, Marty prepares for those calm Wyoming winters.

We'd Like to Hear from You!

As part of our continuing effort to produce books of the highest possible quality, Que would like to hear your comments. To stay competitive, we *really* want you, as a computer book reader and user, to let us know what you like or dislike most about this book or other Que products.

You can mail comments, ideas, or suggestions for improving future editions to the address below, or send us a fax at (317) 581-4663. For the online inclined, Macmillan Computer Publishing now has a forum on CompuServe (type **GO QUEBOOKS** at any prompt) through which our staff and authors are available for questions and comments. The address of our Internet site is **http://www.mcp.com** (World Wide Web).

In addition to exploring our forum, please feel free to contact me personally to discuss your opinions of this book. You can reach me on CompuServe at 76103,1334, or through the Internet at slmiller@que.mcp.com.

Thanks in advance—your comments will help us to continue publishing the best books available on computer topics in today's market.

Stephen L. Miller
Product Development Specialist
Que Corporation
201 W. 103rd Street
Indianapolis, Indiana 46290
USA

Contents at a Glance

Contents

Introduction

by Allen L. Wyatt

The Windows phenomenon continues, sparked this time by the release of Windows 95. This operating system (and it really is an operating system this time around) has gone through more development and more testing than any other operating system in the history of computers. You are the beneficiary of that Herculean effort—and this book can make all the difference between merely using Windows 95 and making it the most productive partner you've ever had on your computer.

Windows 95 is quite a bit different from the previous versions of Windows. In fact, an entirely new user interface breaks with tradition and provides new ease of use, less learning time, and greater productivity. As you work with Windows 95, don't let the ease with which you are able to perform tasks fool you—this is the most powerful operating system you can place on your desktop.

Who Needs This Book?

So do you need this book? Well, that depends. If you can answer *yes* to any of the following questions, then *Killer Windows 95* is definitely for you:

- Do you need to get a head-start on putting Windows 95 to work on your system?
- Do you want to learn more than just the "bare essentials" about Microsoft's newest operating system?
- Do you want a complete reference that will stay with you for months, if not years?
- Do you want to benefit from the combined expertise of a number of Windows 95 experts?
- Do you want the best Windows value between two covers?
- Are you tired of the marketing hype surrounding Windows 95, and you're ready to "get down to brass tacks"?
- Are you ready to get your hands on powerful Windows 95 software right away?

Killer Windows 95 has been developed over the past 18 months while Windows 95 was developed. It represents a phenomenal amount of work on the part of a lot of people—and you will be impressed with the results.

What Is in This Book?

Killer Windows 95 definitely provides more information about Windows 95 than you can get from any other single volume. If you doubt this statement, take a look at the extensive table of contents, as well as the thorough index. Every topic has been carefully researched, organized, documented, and conveyed in a plain and clear manner.

Part I—Setting Up and Interfacing with Windows 95

Part I, "Setting Up and Interfacing with Windows 95," introduces you to the new world of Windows 95. You learn about the new interface, what has been changed, what new tools are available, how to install Windows 95 on different configurations, and where Windows 95 is heading.

Chapter 1, "The Windows 95 Interface," teaches you how to start Windows 95 and how to use the new interface. You learn about the principles behind the design, how to use the taskbar, and how to get help when you need it.

Chapter 2, "Under-the-Hood Improvements," takes a peek beneath the surface of Windows 95. You learn what makes this operating system so robust. You learn how 32-bit performance can increase your productivity, as well as information about using networks. You also learn exactly what all the excitement is concerning Plug and Play.

Chapter 3, "New Windows 95 Tools," introduces you to the new tools provided with Windows 95. You get a guided tour of the Windows Explorer and the Quick View feature. You also learn how to create shortcuts and search for files on your system or over the network.

Chapter 4, "Installing Windows 95,"explains how to install Windows 95 on three different types of systems: a home computer, an office computer, and a network workstation.

Chapter 5, "Installing Windows 95 on a Laptop," examines the unique features provided by Windows 95 for portable computer users. You learn not only how to install, but also how PCMCIA cards work in Windows 95.

Chapter 6, "Troubleshooting Windows 95 Installation and Startup," discusses the common problems you may face either when installing Windows 95 or when you first power up your system. You get answers that will get you up and running with a minimum of inconvenience.

Part II—Hardware Issues

Part II, "Hardware Issues," takes an in-depth look at the many facets of hardware in your system. You learn what hardware you need for your Windows 95 system. You also examine memory, hard drive space, your video system, and peripherals such as mice and joysticks.

Chapter 7, "How Windows 95 Interacts with Your Hardware," looks at how Windows 95 views hardware. You learn about hardware properties, using the Device Manager, configuring your system with multiple hardware profiles, and how you can easily add new hardware to your system.

Chapter 8, "Examining the Hardware You Need for Windows 95," looks at the stated hardware requirements for Windows 95 and then tells you what you *really* need. Compatibility is addressed, as is the wisdom of looking for Plug-and-Play equipment.

Chapter 9, "Exploiting Memory, Space, and Resources," teaches you how Windows 95 views memory. Gone are the hodgepodge days of multiple types of memory. Instead, you learn about system memory and virtual memory in your system. You also learn how to configure memory use for your various needs.

Chapter 10, "Optimizing Your Disk Drives," unleashes the power of the most important component in your system. You learn about disk caches, RAM disks, compression software, and swap files. You also discover how to use the disk defragmenter and what to look for in a hard drive upgrade.

Chapter 11, "Video Cards, Drivers, and Monitors," teaches you what you need to know to make the most of your video system, including your video card and monitor (as well as the drivers that are used between them). You can greatly affect system performance by applying the information in this chapter.

Chapter 12, "Using Mice and Other Pointing Devices," discusses the various types of pointing devices you can use with Windows 95. You learn not only about mice, but also about other pointing devices such as joysticks, trackballs, and glidepoints.

Part III—Software

Part III, "Software," provides all the information you need to make your software really hum under Windows 95. You learn how Windows 95 interacts with software, how to "tune up" your system, how to manage the startup process, and how to install both Windows and DOS software on your system. You also learn how to fine-tune Windows 95 for your software after it's installed.

Chapter 13, "How Windows 95 Interacts with Software," gives a complete overview of how Windows 95 manages the software in your system. You learn about the Virtual Machines created by Windows, and what type of software you can run in those VMs. You also learn how to remove an application from your system.

Chapter 14, "Tailoring Windows 95 and the Registry," is an in-depth examination of how you can configure Windows 95 to your liking. Not only do you learn how to modify the appearance of your system, but also you learn the power and sensibility of the Registry, Windows' new consolidated configuration database.

Chapter 15, "Taking Control of Windows 95 Startup," discusses the startup process and how you can modify it to fit your needs. You learn how to control which programs run when you start Windows 95, as well as how you can modify the system menus according to your needs.

Chapter 16, "Installing Windows Applications," provides guidance on how to successfully install Windows software. You also learn how Windows 95 interacts with the different types of Windows software (16-bit and 32-bit) you can install.

Chapter 17, "Fine-Tuning Windows 95 for Your Windows Applications," examines what you do after you've installed your Windows software. You learn how to affect the software environment, how to create working folders for your software, and how to improve 16-bit program performance.

Chapter 18, "Installing DOS Applications," discusses the ins and outs of installing DOS-based software in a Windows-based environment.

You also get an in-depth glimpse at how Windows 95 automatically knows the configuration needs of over 400 DOS-based programs.

Chapter 19, "Fine-Tuning Windows 95 for Your DOS Applications," teaches you how to completely control the Virtual Machine that Windows 95 creates for your DOS program. You learn the fine points of fine-tuning program initialization, memory use, your screen display, and a host of other items.

Part IV—Output

Part IV, "Output," takes an in-depth look at getting information out of your system in the form of the printed page. You learn how Windows 95 manages the print process, how to control printing, how fonts are handled, the best way to print graphics, and how you can improve printing performance.

Chapter 20, "Managing Your Printers," provides the information you need to successfully set up printers with Windows 95. You learn what printer drivers are and how to install them. You also learn about configuring your printer and removing it, if necessary.

Chapter 21, "Printing from Windows 95," delves into the internals of the Windows 95 print system. You learn about the spooler and how it works with your printer drivers. You also learn how to use the spooler to your advantage, for both local and network printers.

Chapter 22, "Working with Fonts," examines the improved font management capabilities of Windows 95. You learn the basic differences between all types of fonts—bitmapped, TrueType, and Adobe. Discussions center around successfully installing fonts in your system, controlling how they're handled on a printer, and how to use fonts in your applications.

Chapter 23, "Handling Graphics," looks at how Windows 95 can be optimized for printing graphics. You learn the details you need to successfully print graphics on virtually any type of printer.

Chapter 24, "Getting the Most from Your Printer," examines how you can improve the performance of your printer. You find out what is necessary to both speed it up and troubleshoot problems you may encounter.

Part V—Multimedia

Part V, "Multimedia," jumps into the wild world of multimedia with both feet. You learn how to install multimedia components, how to use multimedia on your system, and how to optimize your system for multimedia. You also learn about full-motion video (new in Windows 95) and how to fine-tune your sound cards for peak performance.

Chapter 25, "Adding Multimedia Capability to Your Computer," looks at what you need to bring the world of multimedia to your desktop. You examine the different components of a multimedia system and discover what is recommended for use with Windows 95.

Chapter 26, "Using Multimedia on Your Computer," teaches you how to put multimedia to work right away. You learn how sounds can be used at both a system and application level. You also learn what MIDI is and how your system can be configured for MIDI.

Chapter 27, "Getting the Most out of Multimedia," covers what you can do to improve the performance of your multimedia system. You learn the tricks that can make the difference between a "run of the mill" system and one that is truly impressive.

Chapter 28, "Understanding Full-Motion Video," provides a full discussion of how you can use full-motion video on your system. The inclusion of Microsoft Video for Windows opens up exciting new possibilities in multimedia.

Chapter 29, "Fine-Tuning Your Windows 95 Sound Card," looks at the special needs and requirements of your sound system. You examine how to get the most out of your 8-bit, 16-bit, or 32-bit sound card.

Part VI—Communications

Part VI, "Communications," provides the information you need to "get connected." You learn how OLE allows applications to communicate with each other, as well as how you can connect your computer to other computers all over the world.

Chapter 30, "Using OLE to Communicate with Other Applications," discusses the expanding world of OLE (object linking and embedding). You learn the details that make it work, as well as how you can put it to work in your system.

Chapter 31, "Serial Communications Basics," introduces you to a sometimes difficult and mystifying area of computing. You learn, in plain English, how serial communications works. You also explore different types of communications software and how you can set up your modem in Windows 95.

Chapter 32, "Communicating with a Modem," provides all the information you need to use your modem to connect with other computers. You learn about dialing properties, the phone dialer, HyperTerminal, and various third-party software packages. You also learn about the world of online services such as CompuServe, Prodigy, and America Online.

Chapter 33, "The Microsoft Network," teaches you what you need to know to take advantage of Microsoft's newest commercial venture. You learn how to set up your Windows 95 system to take full advantage of the network, as well as what you can expect after you're connected.

Chapter 34, "Using Microsoft Exchange," explores the "communications command center" on your desktop. You learn how to use Microsoft Exchange to send and receive both electronic mail and faxes.

Chapter 35, "Internet Communications," looks at the fast-expanding world of the Internet. Windows 95 provides everything you need to get connected, and shows you how to do it. Coverage of dial-up Internet accounts, using both SLIP and PPP, provides you the understanding you need to make the most of your Internet experience.

Part VII—Networking and Remote Computing

Part VII, "Networking and Remote Computing," examines the specifics of networking your system with Windows 95. You learn how Windows 95 views networks, as well as how to put your network to use right away. You also learn what special features are provided for remote computing, and you learn what is needed to stay connected with your office when you're away.

Chapter 36, "Communicating with a Network," covers the specifics of installing a network on your system. You learn about the different Windows 95 network components and how they work together, as well as how you can configure your network for your needs. Both Microsoft and Novell networks are covered.

Chapter 37, "Using Windows 95 on a Network," teaches you how you can put your network to use. You learn how to share information over the network, how to print in a networked environment, and how you should manage your network installation.

Chapter 38, "Setting Up Remote Computing," discusses how you can configure your system for your needs while you're on the road. You learn how to set up both remote e-mail and the Briefcase utility.

Chapter 39, "Seamless Remote Computing," shows you how to put your system to work on the road. Here you learn how to use remote network access to get your e-mail while away from your desk, how to use Briefcase to synchronize your files, and how to manage deferred printing.

Part VIII—Optimizing Performance

Part VIII, "Optimizing Performance," provides the information you need to fully exploit the power of Windows 95. You learn how the DOS command line has changed, how to manage the important files in your Windows 95 system, and how to improve your system security.

Chapter 40, "Operating in Windows 95 DOS," takes an in-depth look at the changes in the DOS command line. Gone are the days when DOS was king; DOS now plays a more subservient role, and the command structure has changed accordingly. You learn what commands have been dropped and which ones have been added. You also learn how to change the properties of a DOS window.

Chapter 41, "Monitoring Your Windows 95 Vital Files," teaches you how to protect the files at the heart of Windows 95. You learn how to both prevent and recover from disasters that may befall your system.

Chapter 42, "Dealing with Viruses and Security," discusses how you can make your system more secure. You learn how to effectively create backups, how to provide security in remote networking, and how user profiles can increase system security.

Part IX—Microsoft Plus!

Part IX, "Microsoft Plus!," looks at this powerful add-on to Windows 95. You examine each part of the product and discover how it can enrich your use of Windows 95.

Chapter 43, "System Agent," discusses how you can use this tool to improve your productivity. The System Agent provides an easy way to run common system management tasks at regular intervals so you can make sure that your system is in top-notch condition.

Chapter 44, "DriveSpace 3 and Compression Agent," examines the more powerful features this element adds to the DriveSpace component of your system. You learn about the newest innovations in disk compression and how they can benefit your system.

Chapter 45, "Desktop Additions," looks at the new customization features provided by Microsoft Plus!. You learn about the Desktop Themes program, the Multimedia Pinball, full-window dragging, and font smoothing.

Chapter 46, "Internet Explorer and Jumpstart Kit," provides the information you need to enrich your Internet experience. Learn about the

tools provided in Microsoft Plus! that open the Internet to your view—tools like the Web browser, mail reader, and a collection of powerful shortcuts.

Appendixes

The two appendixes provided with *Killer Windows 95* provide information on how you can add and remove Windows 95 components, and how you can install the Killer Windows 95 companion CD-ROM.

The Companion CD

Putting Windows 95 to work right away often involves having the proper type of software utilities to take advantage of the new operating system. The companion CD-ROM included at the back of this book provides just that—a wide selection of software that you can put to work right away to enrich your use of Windows 95.

The CD-ROM contains the following utilities, just to name a few:

- **WinZIP** brings the convenience of Windows to the use of ZIP files. TAR, gzip, Unix compress, LZH, ARJ, and ARC files are also supported. WinZip features an intuitive point-and-click interface for viewing, running, extracting, adding, deleting, and testing files in archives. Optional virus scanning support is included. Extract an archive to any directory through drag-and-drop without leaving the Explorer. Use the right mouse button to drag and drop a ZIP from an Explorer window to any directory, then choose "Extract to" from the context menu.
- **InfoSpy** is a Windows utility that interrogates and lists the various items within your Windows environment, including global heap, active windows, Windows tasks, loaded modules, open files, memory information, and DOS information. InfoSpy also acts as a real-time monitoring utility, allowing you to monitor Windows messages and serial communications.

- **PolyView** is a multithreaded 32-bit application that provides viewing and image manipulation support for JPEG, GIF, photo-CD, and Windows and OS/2 8- and 24-bit BMP files.
- **TextPad** is a fast and powerful text editor. Key TextPad features include huge file support (up to the limits of virtual memory), multiple simultaneous edits with up to two views per file, OLE 2 drag-and-drop editing for copying and moving text between documents, unlimited undo/redo capability, and much, much more.
- **Easy Icons** is a complete icon management system. Here are just a few of the features: extract or view all icons from virtually any file, save any icon as a separate ICO or BMP file, and create and maintain icon libraries with simple drag-and-drop operations.

Also included are many more useful and fun utilities that will help you get even more out of Windows 95.

All in all, *Killer Windows 95* provides the information you need to make the most of using Windows 95 on your system. With the information in this book at your disposal, you might not become an expert overnight, but you'll have all the information you need to eventually get there.

Conventions Used in This Book

The conventions used in this book have been established to help you learn quickly and easily how to use Windows 95. Instructions in this book emphasize use of the mouse to do tasks (to accomplish commands, to make choices in dialog boxes and sheets, and so forth).

Windows 95 lets you use the keyboard and the mouse—although the mouse is the preferred method—to select menu and dialog box or sheet items: you can press a letter (or number), or select an item by clicking on it with the mouse. The letter or number you press to select many items is underlined; for example, choose the Print command from the File menu by typing **P**. If you use a mouse with Windows 95, you place the mouse pointer on the relevant menu or dialog box or sheet item and click with the left mouse button to make your selection.

Uppercase letters are used to distinguish file names, such as MYFILE.DOC. In most cases, the keys on the keyboard are represented as they appear on your keyboard (for example, J, Enter, Tab, Ctrl, Insert, and Backspace). For keystrokes separated by plus signs, such as Alt+F4, which closes the active application or window, hold down the first key (in this example, Alt) and press the second key (in this example, F4) to invoke the command. When a series of keys is separated by commas, press and release each key in sequence.

Text you're asked to type appears in **boldface**. On-screen messages from Windows 95 and its applications appear in a special font: `[Left Tab]`. Special words or phrases defined for the first time are introduced in *italic.*

The Windows 95 Interface

by Allen L. Wyatt

At the root of any operating system or any application program lies the user interface—the conventions and methods used to communicate with the software. Windows 95 is no exception; it includes a user interface based on the graphical presentation of information. The user interface provided with Windows 95 is different from that used in previous versions of Windows. Some differences are cosmetic, while others are quite substantial.

In this chapter, you'll learn how you can best use the new Windows 95 interface. Much of the information in this chapter is essential to using Windows 95 effectively. If you're a "dive-in-the-deep-end-of-the-pool" type of person, you may be able to bypass much of this chapter. You'll still need to grapple with and learn the information, however. Even the most die-hard Windows aficionado will benefit by at least scanning through this chapter.

Booting Windows 95

When you first sit in front of a system on which Windows 95 has been installed, you may be tempted to believe there's no difference between the new operating system and your previous DOS- and Windows-based systems. This is both true and false. In reality, there is quite a bit of difference, but you'll also find many similarities between Windows 95 and older Windows systems.

Perhaps the first thing you'll notice is that when you turn on your computer, you no longer see the DOS prompt. This may be disconcerting to some users, while others may notice very little that's odd about this. For instance, if you're used to doing all your work in Windows, you probably configured your computer to automatically start Windows whenever you started your computer. Windows 95 takes this process one step further—you actually boot directly into Windows 95, bypassing DOS altogether. You'll learn more about this in Chapter 2, "Under-the-Hood Improvements."

So what happens when you first start your computer? The booting process has three distinct steps:

1. Initial testing.
2. Windows 95 startup screen.
3. Log-in process, if required.

Step one should look familiar; done on any computer, it involves initial system testing. Copyright notices are displayed, memory is tested and counted, and other components are tested.

After testing is complete, you quickly see the Windows 95 startup screen. While this screen is displayed, Windows 95 is going through a loading and testing process to make sure that everything is in order. The length of time required for this booting step depends on the configuration of your computer. The more resources (memory, disks, and so on) you have and the slower your computer, the longer this startup phase will take.

Finally, you're asked to log in to Windows 95. If you've previously used Windows for Workgroups, this step looks very familiar. Logging in is done so that Windows 95 can identify who is using the system and make sure that you're an authorized user. Generally, all you need to do is type your password. If you have trouble with this, you should talk to your network administrator or whoever installed Windows 95 on your system.

> **Note:** If Windows 95 has already been installed on your system and you aren't connected to a network, you aren't asked to log in to Windows 95.

New Desktop Icons

Once you log in, you see the Windows 95 desktop, as shown in figure 1.1. This desktop looks a bit different from the Windows desktop you're already familiar with. You may have noticed right away that the traditional Program Manager is missing. Instead, everything is done directly from the desktop, without the need for an explicit Program Manager. Rather than have to go through the Program Manager—and program groups—to get to the program you want to start, the program can sit right on the desktop for easy access.

The Windows 95 desktop has six primary parts:

- My Computer icon
- Network Neighborhood icon (optional)
- Recycle Bin icon
- A Microsoft Exchange (InBox) icon
- The Microsoft Network icon (optional)
- The taskbar

These elements are present in a full Windows 95 installation; your system might not have all of them. For instance, you might not see the Network Neighborhood icon if you aren't connected to a network. If your system has been used by someone else, it's also possible that additional elements are on the desktop. This is natural, since Windows 95 allows you to completely customize your working environment right on the desktop.

Fig. 1.1 The Windows 95 desktop appears different from previous Windows desktops.

The next several sections describe each standard element of your desktop.

My Computer

If you double-click on this icon, a window appears with icons that represent the structure of your local computer. Figure 1.2 shows what you typically see if you open this icon.

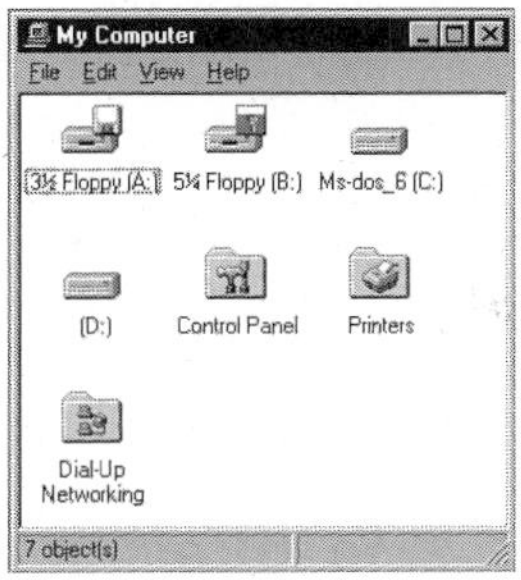

Fig. 1.2 The My Computer window displays information on your local computer.

Notice that this window contains icons for each disk drive on your system (including any CD-ROM drives), as well as the Control Panel, Printers folder, and a Dial-Up Networking folder. (The names of some items, such as the Control Panel, should be familiar if you've used older versions of Windows.) The exact contents of the window will vary, based on the configuration of your local computer. For instance, there is a very good chance you won't have the Dial-Up Networking icon shown on your system. (Dial-Up Networking is an optional feature of Windows 95 that allows you to connect your computer to remote computer networks, including the Internet.)

Primarily, you use the My Computer icon to browse through the contents of your system. For instance, if you double-click a disk drive, the contents of that drive are displayed in another window. You can continue to browse through different folders, or you can double-click a program or document to work with it.

Network Neighborhood

Just as the My Computer icon allows you to browse through your local system, the Network Neighborhood icon allows you to browse around a network. (Remember that this icon is available only if your system is connected to a computer network that Windows 95 can recognize.) Figure 1.3 shows what you might see if you double-click on this icon.

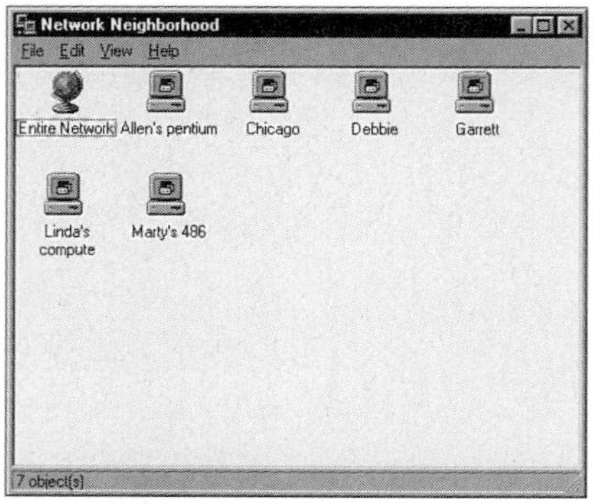

Fig. 1.3 The Network Neighborhood window displays information on networks that you're connected to.

The actual contents of this window vary, depending on the composition of your network. Again, you can browse through the network by choosing different connections or folders.

Recycle Bin

The Recycle Bin icon looks like a wastebasket with an ecological recycling symbol on the front of it. The Recycle Bin is a new addition in Windows 95 and represents a new way to manage the files you've deleted.

As you work with files, sometimes you'll want to delete them. For instance, you could be browsing through My Computer to examine files on a disk drive. If you highlight the icon for a document file and then press the Delete key, the icon is removed. The file hasn't been permanently deleted, however. It has been moved to the Recycle Bin, where it can still be recovered before it's completely deleted.

Look again at the Recycle Bin icon. If the wastebasket looks empty, no files are in the bin. If it looks as though it has paper in it, it contains files. Double-clicking the Recycle Bin displays the files it contains. Figure 1.4 shows an example of how the Recycle Bin window appears.

Fig. 1.4 The Recycle Bin allows you to manage the deletion and recovery of files.

After the Recycle Bin window appears, you can select files and then permanently delete them or recover them (move them back out of the Recycle Bin).

> **Tip:** If you're running low on disk space, you should periodically empty the Recycle Bin. This is done by choosing File, Empty Recycle Bin in the Recycle Bin window.

When you delete a file and it is moved to the Recycle Bin by Windows 95, it stays there until one of three events occur:

1. You recover the file by moving it out of the Recycle Bin and back into another folder on your system.
2. You permanently delete the file by selecting it and pressing the Delete key.
3. You have deleted enough newer files to cause Windows 95 to delete this file automatically.

Once any of these conditions is met, the file no longer is shown in the Recycle Bin. If these conditions are not met, then the file stays there, even from one Windows session to the next.

Microsoft Exchange

If your computer is attached to a network, it's possible that you'll see an icon for Microsoft Exchange. This icon could be named Microsoft Exchange on some systems, but more than likely it's called Inbox. Regardless of the name, this icon allows you to quickly access network-related and communications-related features such as e-mail and faxing. Microsoft Exchange is actually an optional part of Windows 95 and does not appear unless you specifically choose it when you install your system. In many environments where Windows 95 is used, such as a large office, the operating system comes already installed and configured on your machine. In such a case, there is a very good chance that Microsoft Exchange is already installed for you.

Assuming you have Microsoft Exchange installed on your system, when you double-click this icon, its window appears similar to what figure 1.5 shows.

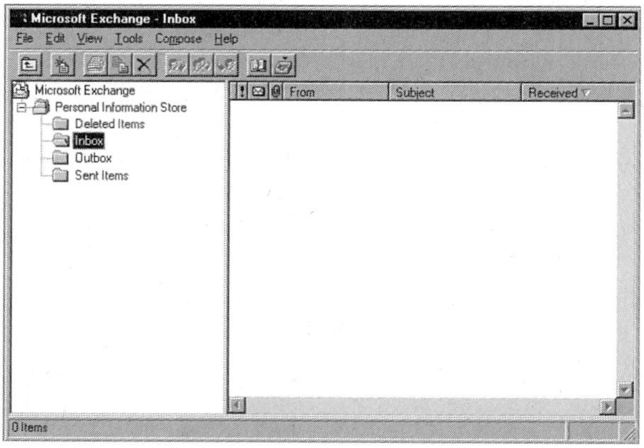

Fig. 1.5 The Microsoft Exchange is an integrated communication center for your computer.

The exact features provided in Microsoft Exchange depend on how your system is configured. It can be used for communication needs as diverse as e-mail on your local network, to faxes, to Internet e-mail, or

to CompuServe. Since the uses of Microsoft Exchange are so diverse, you'll find information about this area in many different chapters of this book.

New Windows Design

By now you've probably already noticed that the actual windows displayed in Windows 95 are different from their predecessors in older versions of Windows. Most of these changes are cosmetic in nature, which can lead to a momentary sense of disorientation as you first use Windows 95. This quickly passes, however, and you're shortly faced with more substantial changes.

Most of the substantive changes are visible in the title bar of any window. Gone are the old-version window-control buttons. In their place are new window-control buttons at the right side of the title bar (see fig. 1.6).

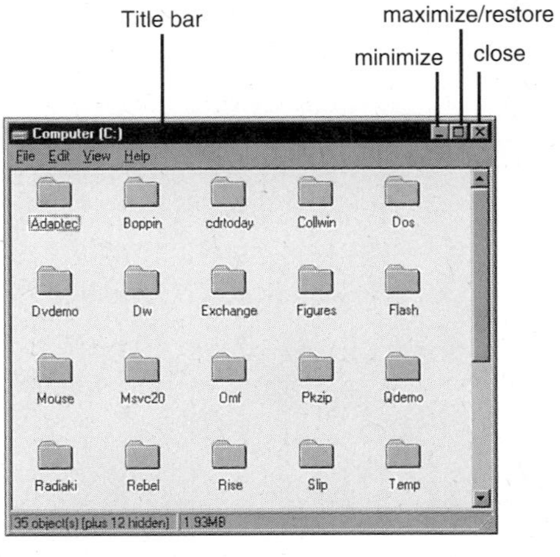

Fig. 1.6 The windows used in Windows 95 appear a bit different from those used in previous versions.

Notice that three window-control buttons are visible on all windows in Windows 95, even for programs you previously used in Windows and DOS. One button has an image that looks like a bar, another has a window image, and the third contains an ×. The button that contains a bar serves the same purpose as the minimize button in older versions of Windows. Rather than minimize the window to an icon, however, it minimizes it to a spot on the taskbar. (The taskbar is discussed fully in the next section.)

The window button serves the same purpose as the maximize and restore buttons in older versions of Windows. If the window doesn't currently occupy the entire screen, clicking this button maximizes it so that it's as large as possible. If the window has already been maximized, clicking the window button restores the window to an open but less-than-full-screen size.

Finally, the button that contains an × is used to close the window. This has the same effect as double-clicking the control menu icon in earlier versions of Windows. If a program was running in the window, the program is ended. If the window contained a data file, the file is closed.

While the new window-control buttons may appear different at first, they do offer greater and more intuitive functionality than what was available in older versions of Windows. You should be able to get used to them within a day of starting to use Windows 95.

> **Tip:** As you're getting used to the new window-control buttons, take a moment to look at them before you click on them. If you go by position alone, you'll easily confuse them with the button that occupied that position in older versions of Windows.

The Taskbar

While the concept behind icons, folders, and other desktop objects is (by this point) intuitive to anyone who has previously used Windows, Windows 95 includes a new desktop feature that's an entirely new departure from previous Windows versions—the taskbar. Depending on how your system is configured, the taskbar can be at the left, right, or

bottom of your desktop. (In most systems it is at the bottom.) You can recognize the taskbar because it has the Start button at the left side, as shown in figure 1.7.

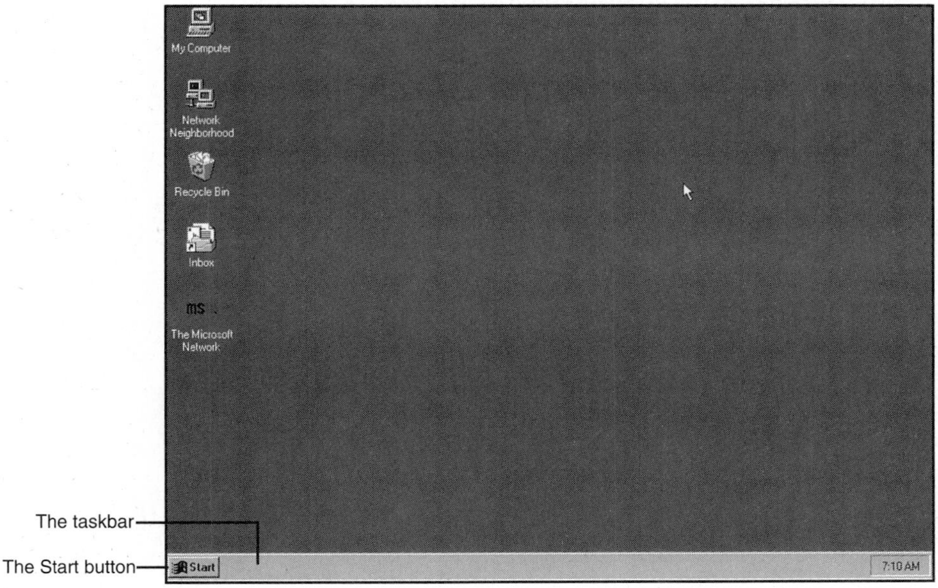

Fig. 1.7 The newest addition to the Windows 95 desktop is the taskbar.

The primary purpose of the taskbar is to quickly and easily allow you to switch between applications on your system. Think of the taskbar as a "command center" for Windows 95. It's analogous to the Task List displayed in older versions of Windows when you pressed Ctrl+Esc. The only difference is that the taskbar can be available all the time. If you prefer not to use the taskbar, you can also turn it off or control how it appears on your screen. (How you do this is covered later in this book.)

The Start Button

At the left side of the taskbar is the Start button. Clicking this button provides a shortcut to access quickly and easily any part of your Windows 95 system. If you click the Start button, you see a series of choices that you can make. These choices are presented in a menu, as shown in figure 1.8.

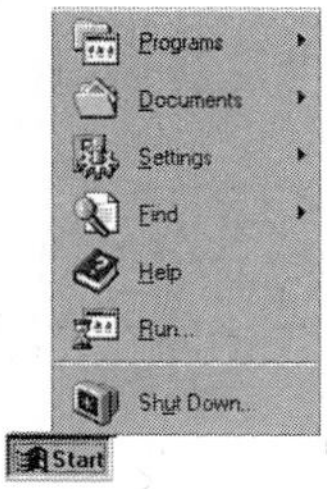

Fig. 1.8 A menu appears when you click the Start button.

Notice that choices can appear on a menu in three ways:

- *Triangles.* Highlighting a menu choice that has a triangle to the right of it displays another menu.
- *Ellipsis.* Selecting a menu choice that's followed by three dots (an ellipsis) displays a dialog box.
- *Regular.* Selecting a menu choice that has no triangles or ellipses opens a folder, starts the indicated program, or loads the document.

To use a menu, all you need to do is use the mouse pointer to highlight a menu choice. As you position the pointer over a menu choice, the choice is automatically highlighted in around half a second. If another menu is associated with the choice (if there's a triangle to the right of the choice), the menu is displayed automatically—you don't even need to click on the choice. For instance, if you use the mouse pointer to highlight the Programs option, you see another menu, as shown in figure 1.9.

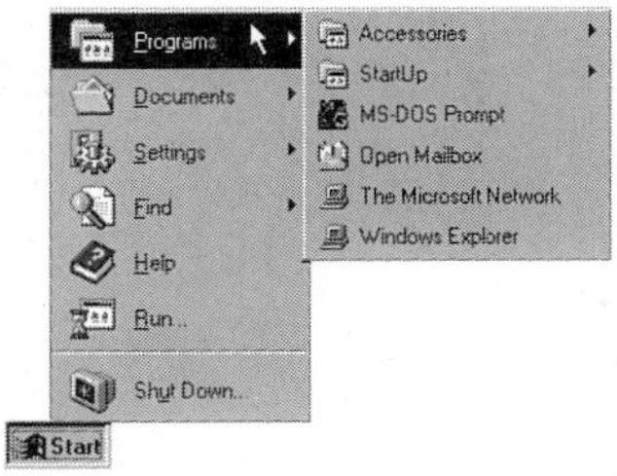

Fig. 1.9 Highlighting the Programs option displays the Programs menu.

To select any other menu choice, all you need to do is highlight it and click the mouse button. The next several sections describe the purpose of each menu option on the Start button menu.

The Programs Menu

If you highlight the Programs option from the Start button menu, you see the Programs menu (refer to fig. 1.9). The Programs menu displays the contents of the Programs folder. Thus, the Programs menu contains an Accessories folder, a Startup folder, the MS-DOS prompt, the Open Mailbox program, the Microsoft Network program, and the Windows Explorer.

Accessories is a menu choice that has another triangle to the right of it. If you highlight it, you see many different accessory programs you can use right away (see fig. 1.10).

The Accessories menu is merely the contents of the Accessories folder, presented in menu format. Many of these accessories should look familiar to you if you've used older versions of Windows.

The StartUp option displays programs that are started whenever Windows 95 is started. Again, this menu lists the contents of a folder (the StartUp folder). If you change the contents of the folder, you automatically change what's displayed in the menu.

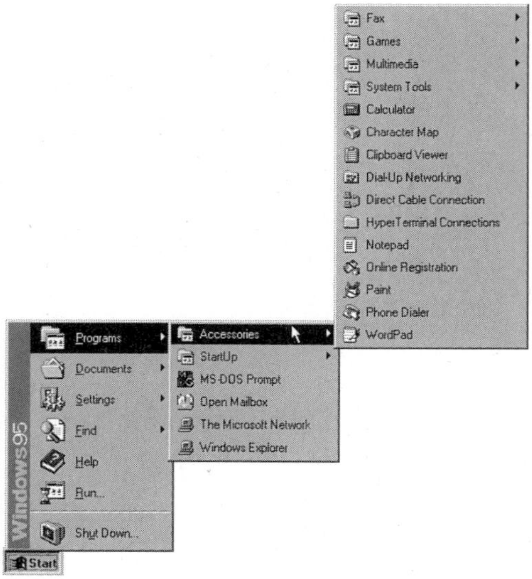

Fig. 1.10 Highlighting the Accessories option displays the Accessories menu.

More information about the other other Programs menu items is discussed later. The Windows Explorer is explained in Chapter 3, "New Windows 95 Tools," and the MS-DOS prompt (probably familiar to anyone who has used an older version of Windows) is covered in Chapter 40, "Operating in Windows 95 DOS."

The Documents Menu

Documents are nothing but data files that are associated with a program. This means that documents are not just things such as memos, reports, or book chapters, but also can be files containing your appointments, a database, or a spreadsheet. Windows 95 keeps track of what program created which document, and then makes those documents accessible through the Documents menu. Figure 1.11 shows an example of how the Documents menu could look.

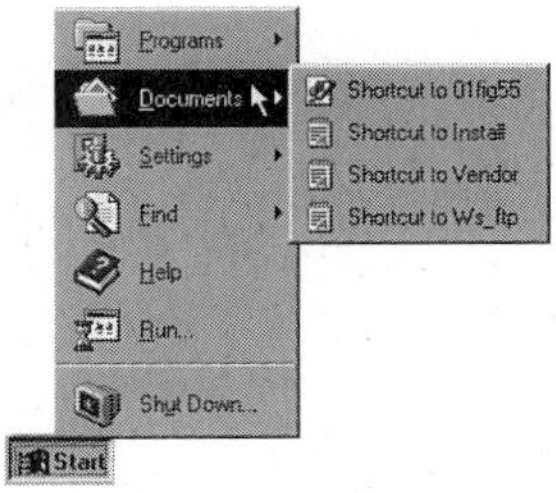

Fig. 1.11 The Documents menu allows quick access to the documents you used most recently.

Exactly how the documents window appears depends on the type and number of documents you've created in your system. To use a document, all you need to do is select it from the menu. Windows 95 starts the program associated with the document and displays it.

The Settings Menu

When you highlight the Settings option on the Start menu, you see three other options (see fig. 1.12). Each option allows you to change settings used to control Windows 95. The Control Panel option displays the Control Panel, a concept that should be familiar to anyone who has used an older version of Windows.

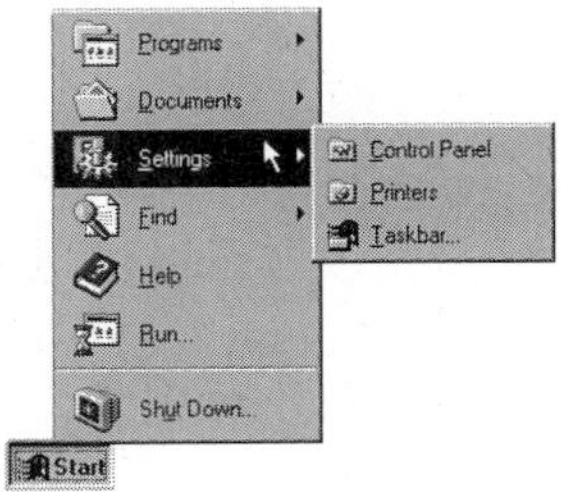

Fig. 1.12 The Settings menu is used to control the appearance of Windows 95.

The Printers option on the Settings menu displays a folder that indicates all the printer drivers you've installed for use with Windows 95 (see fig. 1.13). This folder also contains an option that allows you to add new printer drivers, as desired. Printer drivers are used by Windows 95 to control your printer. You learn how to add printer drivers in Chapter 20, "Managing Your Printers."

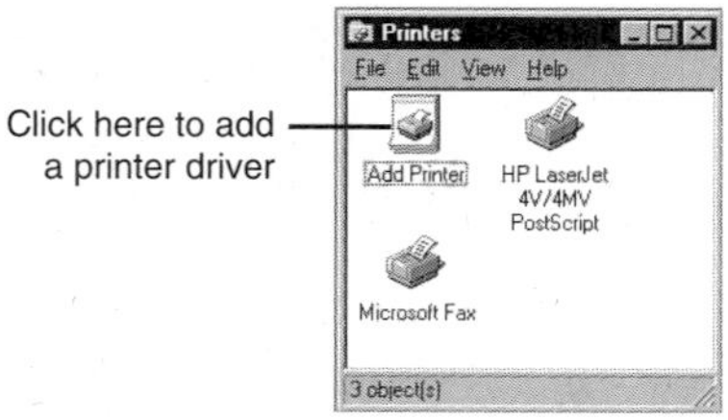

Fig. 1.13 The Printers folder contains icons for the printer drivers you've installed.

The final option on the Settings menu is Taskbar. If you choose this option, you can modify some of the aspects (properties) of the taskbar. Figure 1.14 shows the dialog box displayed when you choose this option.

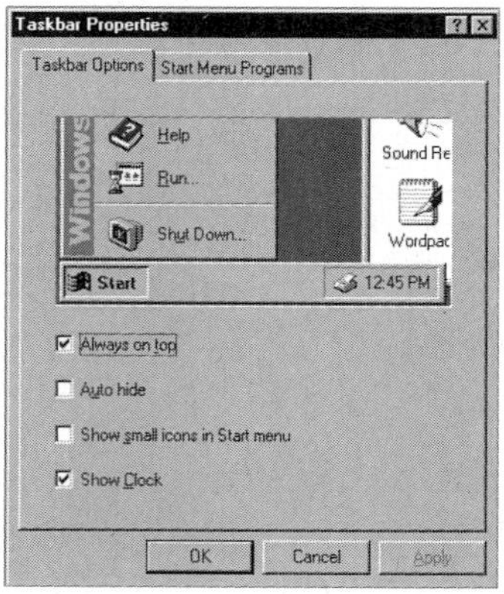

Fig. 1.14 Windows 95 allows you to change the properties of the taskbar.

The Start Menu Programs tab allows you to change the menu options used on the actual Start and Programs menus. The Taskbar Options tab is used to modify what's shown on the taskbar.

Other Start Button Capabilities

The Start menu presents you with several other options as well. The Find option is used to find files, folders, or resources on your computer. (This option is explained in more detail in Chapter 3, "New Windows 95 Tools.") The Help option is covered later in this chapter, in the section titled "The Help System."

If you choose the Run option from the Start menu, you can run a program directly. Users of previous Windows versions will recognize this option as the same as choosing File, Run from Program Manager.

The Shut Down option allows you to end your session with Windows 95. If you choose it, you're given four options (see fig. 1.15). You should choose the option that best describes the type of shutdown you want to perform, and then choose Yes.

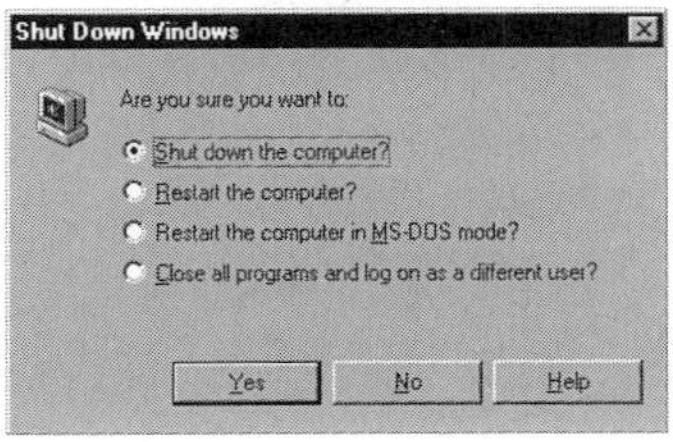

Fig. 1.15 You can select four options when shutting down the computer.

Tip: If you choose Shut Down by mistake, you can stop the shutdown process by choosing No from the Shut Down Windows dialog box.

Using the Shut Down option is the best way to end your computer session. By choosing this option, in effect you give Windows 95 a warning that you're done using it. This allows files to be closed and devices to be shut down in an orderly manner. If you simply turn your machine off, you could loose data that might be important. Shut Down precludes such an event from happening.

Switching to Other Tasks

To the right of the Start button you may see other buttons, each of which represent active tasks you can use. For instance, if you choose a program or option from the Start menu, you see that program or option appear on the taskbar. Figure 1.16 shows an example.

Fig. 1.16 The options on the taskbar represent programs now running.

You can switch to different programs by clicking the taskbar button for that program. For instance, if you choose the Programs button, the Programs folder is displayed. To later minimize a window, use the window-control buttons in the upper-right corner of the window. You've already learned that if you click the button with the bar-shaped image, the window is minimized to the taskbar. Once a window is minimized, the task represented by the window is still running, but it isn't actively displayed.

As you add more and more tasks to your Windows 95 session, these tasks are added to the taskbar. Every time you start a program or open a resource, the taskbar appears. When you close a program or resource, the corresponding task button is removed from the taskbar. If you open more tasks than can be fit across the taskbar, the buttons for all the tasks are made smaller so they can all fit.

The number of task buttons that will fit across your screen depends on the resolution of your screen. For instance, at 640 × 480 resolution, you can fit 19 task buttons, but you can fit 25 at 800×600 resolution. When the maximum number of buttons is passed, Windows still creates a task button for each new task, but these new buttons are not immediately visible. Instead, scroll controls appear at the right side of the task bar, and you can use them to display additional lines of the task bar. If you want to display all the task bar at once, you can increase the size of the task bar by using the mouse to drag the top border of the task bar so it covers a larger area of the screen. For instance, figure 1.17 shows an example of a two-line task bar on the screen.

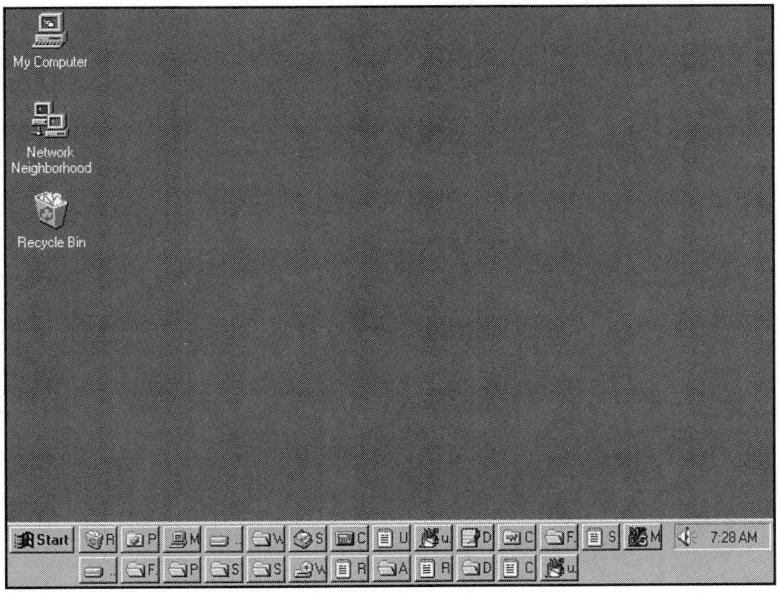

Fig. 1.17 The task bar can use multiple lines on the screen.

Getting Help

Getting help in Windows 95 is easier than in previous versions of Windows. Helpful information is continually presented while you're using Windows 95, and you can quickly and easily get help on a variety of topics. The help available from Windows 95 is presented by using the following features:

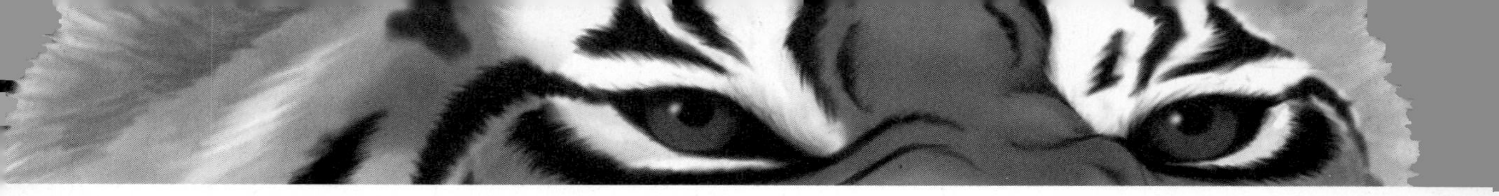

- Tips
- The Help system
- Wizards

Tips

If you move the mouse pointer over an object in Windows 95, you may see a tip about that object appear just below the mouse pointer. This is true whether the object is part of the operating system itself (for instance, a button on the taskbar) or part of a program (see fig. 1.18). This helpful information is designed to jog your memory about what a particular object is for.

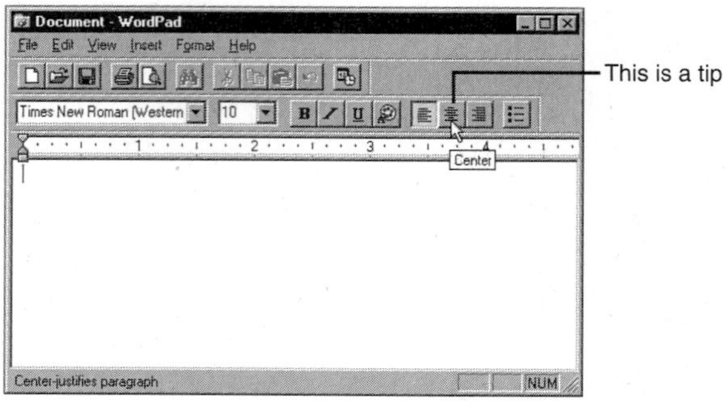

Fig. 1.18 Helpful tips are common in Windows 95.

Tips, as a form of help, are becoming more pervasive in the Windows 95 environment. They're available in many different programs and different parts of Windows 95 itself.

The Help System

Windows 95 features a new and improved Help system that uses an entirely new user interface. The easiest way to access the Help system is to choose Help from the Start menu; you can also start the Help system by pressing F1 at any point while you're using Windows 95. Either way, you then see the dialog box shown in figure 1.19.

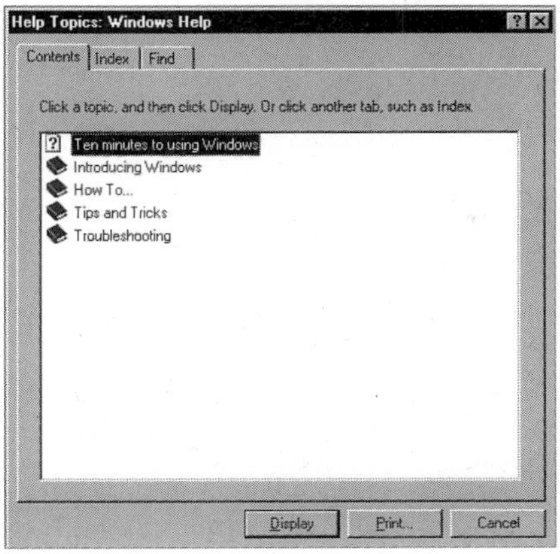

Fig. 1.19 The Windows 95 Help system allows you to quickly gain assistance on a variety of topics.

Notice that the Help Topics dialog box contains three tabs: Contents, Index, and Find. Each of these represent different ways you can find information in the Help system.

The Contents Tab

The Contents tab shows you the major help topics available in the Help system. Three types of icons can be used in the Contents list:

- *Closed Book.* Double-click the book to see more detail on the topic. You can also click the topic and select the Open button.
- *Open Book.* Double-click the open book to show less detail on the topic. You can also click the topic and choose the Close button.
- *Document.* Double-click the document to display the actual help information. You can also select the topic and click the Display button.

The Index Tab

While you can select a general help topic from the Contents screen, it's often more productive to jump directly to the topic you want to view. This is done by selecting the Index tab. When you do, the Help Topics dialog box changes to look like figure 1.20.

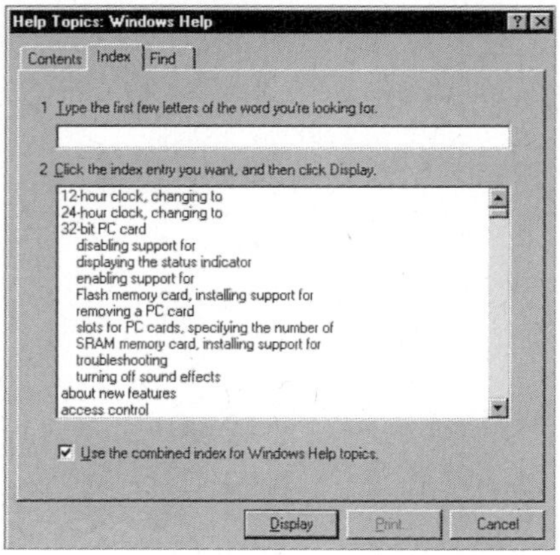

Fig. 1.20 With the Index tab selected, you can use the Help Topics dialog box to search for topics on a particular subject.

With the Index tab selected, the Help Topics dialog box is divided into two sections. In the top section, you can type the name of the subject you want to view. In the bottom section is a list of Help system topics. You can scroll through the list of topics, or you can start typing the name of the topic you want to view. As you type, Windows 95 displays the topics that match what you've typed. When you see a desired topic displayed, highlight it and click the Display button.

The Find Tab

The Contents and Index tabs allow you to quickly find your way through the major headings in the Help system. There are times, however, when the headings just won't do. For instance, you may want to look at documents that contain all occurrences of a particular word or phrase—and that word or phrase isn't included in a major topic heading. The Find tab provides this detailed search capability. When you click this tab, what you see depends on whether you've used the Find tab before.

If you haven't used the Find tab before, Windows 95 needs to make a detailed index of the words in all the topics in the Help system. This can take a while, as indicated in figure 1.21.

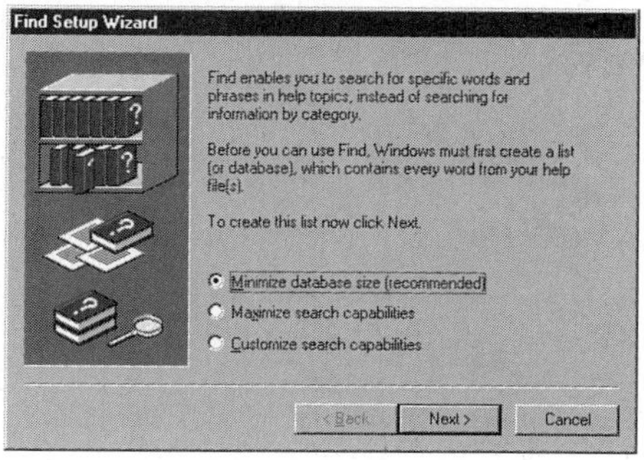

Fig. 1.21 The first time you use the Find tab, Windows 95 needs to create a detailed index you can use.

In most instances, you'll want to use the default choice (Minimize database size). Click on the Next button, and then click on Finish. The Help system files are examined and the necessary index is compiled. Shortly, the Help window changes to a form you can use to actually locate words (see fig. 1.22).

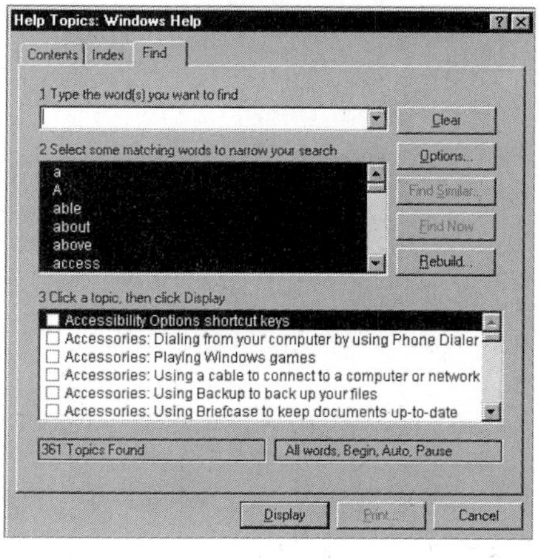

Fig. 1.22 With the Find tab selected you can search by any word in the Help system documents.

The dialog box is divided into three sections. In the top section, you can type the word or words you want to locate. In reality, all you need

to do is type the first couple of letters of the words. You can narrow this search down in the second part of the window by selecting the exact matching words. Finally, the third part of the window (at the bottom) displays a list of Help system topics that contain the selected words. When you see a desired topic displayed, highlight it and click the Display button.

Viewing Help Documents

Regardless of how you locate the topic you want displayed (using the Contents, Index, or Find tabs), when you finally locate the topic on which you want help, Windows 95 displays a document containing the help information. These documents are displayed in a Help window (see fig. 1.23).

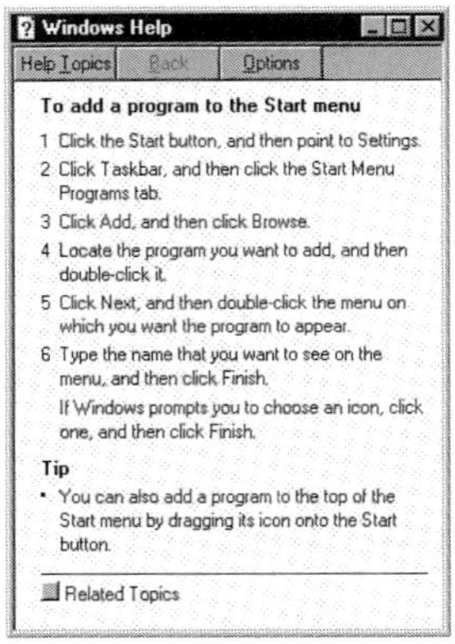

Fig. 1.23 Informational documents are displayed in the Help window.

This window is much simpler in nature than the Help windows used in earlier versions of Windows. It contains only three choices on the button bar: Help Topics, Back, and Options. The first button displays the same Help system dialog box you used to access this topic (the Contents tab, the Index tab, or the Find tab). The second button (when available) allows you to step back through previous help screens you've viewed. The final button is used to change how the help screen is displayed or to print the information in the Help window.

Wizards

A *wizard* is the name used to identify a step-by-step procedure to accomplish a task. Wizards have been used for some time in Windows programs, such as Excel. They lead a user through what might otherwise be a complex set of steps.

Windows 95 provides several wizards for your use. For instance, the process of creating a Find tab index in the Help system (described in the previous section) uses a wizard. You can see another example of a wizard if you open the Control Panel by selecting it from the Settings menu (which is available from the Start menu). The Control Panel should appear as shown in figure 1.24.

Fig. 1.24 The Control Panel contains many familiar icons.

Notice the icon titled Add New Hardware. You can't necessarily tell it by looking at the icon, but when you double-click it, a wizard is started. Go ahead and start it now. You then see the window for the Add New Hardware Wizard (see fig. 1.25).

Wizards always have a series of buttons that control the steps you perform. These buttons, located at the bottom of the window, are fairly standard, regardless of the wizard. They include the following:

- *Hint.* Displays a hint about what can be done at the current time within the wizard.
- *Cancel.* Ends the task without making any changes.

- *Back.* Backtracks to the previous step of the task.
- *Next.* Proceeds to the next step of the task.
- *Finish.* Completes the task by using the information provided so far, along with default information for the steps not yet completed.

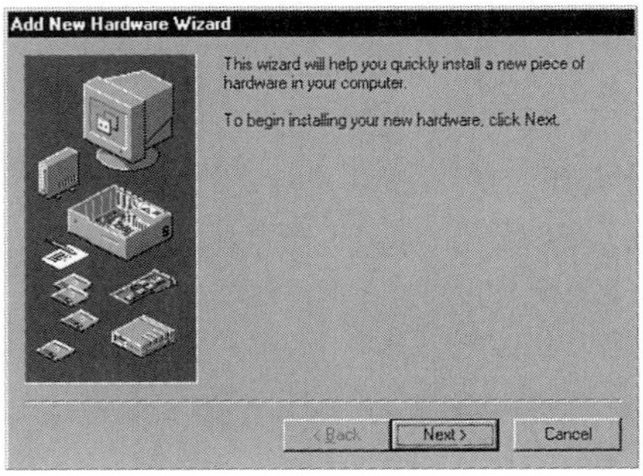

Fig. 1.25 The aim of the Add New Hardware Wizard is to help you configure Windows 95 for new hardware.

To use a wizard effectively, all you need to do is answer the question posed in the present screen, or make a selection when prompted and then click Next. If you make a mistake but don't realize it until you've clicked Next, you can click Back to return to the previous step. The exact steps presented in a wizard depend on the wizard's purpose. Working through concise steps in this manner, however, allows you to complete tasks that otherwise have the potential of being difficult to perform.

Context Menus

A *context menu,* sometimes called a *pop-up menu,* is used to display a series of options applicable to a particular object. You display a context menu by pointing to an object (such as an icon, the desktop, a menu item, a title bar, or a window) and then clicking with the right mouse button. For instance, figure 1.26 shows the context menu displayed when you click the right mouse button while pointing to a disk drive.

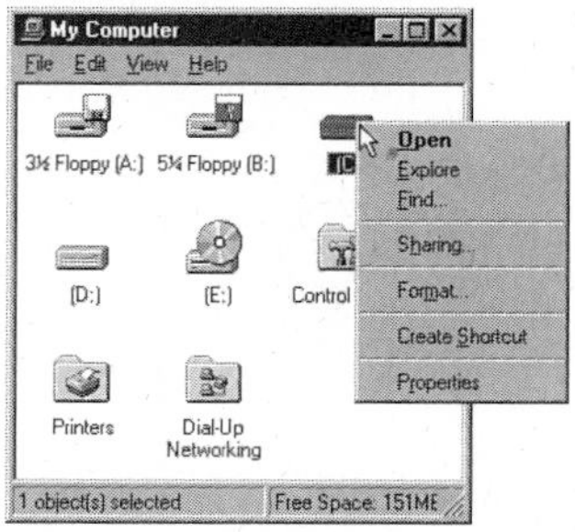

Fig. 1.26 Context menus display options applicable to objects on the desktop.

Once a context menu is displayed, it behaves like any other menu. You can select items and accomplish tasks by selecting options from the menu.

KILLER 2 WINDOWS 95

Under-the-Hood Improvements

by Allen L. Wyatt

In Chapter 1, you learned about the new Windows 95 interface. However, Windows 95 is more than just a pretty face. There are many new improvements to the operating system that you may never see because they function completely behind the scenes or, "under the hood," so to speak. You reap the benefits of the improvements through a more robust and responsive operating system.

In this chapter, you learn about these improvements in Windows 95 and also learn about the following:

- How multitasking has been improved in Windows 95
- How long file names are implemented in the existing file structure

- What benefits are introduced by the new 32-bit architecture
- How improved resource management leads to a more stable environment
- What networking features have been improved
- How the Plug-and-Play specification is supported

A Full-Blown Operating System

Windows 95 is a full-blown operating system, in its own right. Previous versions of Windows have sometimes been referred to as an operating system, but this definition has been a very loose application of the term. This is because previous versions of Windows functioned on top of the DOS platform. Windows 95, however, replaces DOS entirely. Instead, many DOS functions now operate in an environment controlled by Windows. Thus, Windows and DOS have traded places; Windows 95 now provides the base platform on which other services are built.

You already know that Windows takes full advantage of your computer hardware. One of the advantages used fully is called *protected mode operation.* Protected mode is an operational mode that has been available on Intel CPUs since the 286, but has not been used by DOS. In protected mode, a program can address large amounts of memory quickly and easily, and provide protection for different programs running in your system. This protection means that if one program in your system begins acting erratically, that behavior has less effect on the other programs in your system.

Many of the components of Windows have been completely rewritten to take advantage of operating in protected mode. Later in this chapter you will learn what this means in terms of actual use of Windows.

Because Windows now is the controlling force in your computer system, Windows 95 can offer many improvements not available in previous versions. These improvements include preemptive multitasking, better reboot support, and long file names. Some of these features you may have heard of; others may be new to you. Each of these features is explained fully in the following sections.

Preemptive Multitasking

Multitasking is the ability to apparently perform more than one task at a time. This ability has been a feature of Windows for many years, but it has been a feature lacking in many areas. You need to understand these shortcomings to appreciate the improvements in Windows 95.

In previous versions of Windows, users implemented multitasking through a method called *cooperative multitasking*. This method worked fine as long as all the applications behaved well. When an application was functioning under Windows 3.1, for example, it periodically needed to relinquish control of the system so that other programs could run; this voluntary relinquishment is the cooperative part of multitasking. As long as a program gave up control periodically, other programs could use their fair share of time, and everyone was happy.

The problem, however, was that not all programs would give up their fair share of control. If you've used Windows for a while, you're probably familiar with the situation where a program is busy, the mouse cursor changes to an hourglass, and you're stuck waiting for the program to finish before you can do something else. This feature is the downside of cooperative multitasking.

Multitasking in Windows 95 is different and much improved. It uses a method referred to as *preemptive multitasking*. This method means that the operating system itself exercises complete control over what program gets what attention. No longer can a program hog resources, giving them up when it voluntarily decides to. Instead, Windows 95 decides which program gets attention and when. The term *preemptive* means that the operating system can preempt the executing program in favor of another program that may need more attention. This preemption occurs based on internal algorithms that determine when a certain program has had control long enough, although other programs can request control of the CPU earlier by generating system interrupts.

What is the result of this preemptive feature? Basically, you can reliably run historically intensive operations simultaneously. For instance, you can format a floppy disk under Windows 95 at the same time you're downloading a file from the Internet and composing a letter. If you tried that under Windows 3.1, you would never get to second base; you would be stuck waiting for the floppy disk to finish formatting before you could do anything else.

Better Reboot Support

Rebooting your computer has always been an action of last resort. To programmers, it has been a frightening consideration because users could decide to reboot at any time. Rebooting means that critical data might not be saved before the computer wipes the slate clean. (When you reboot, the contents of your computer's memory is erased, thereby wiping out any data contained therein.)

Windows 95 solves this problem completely. Now when you attempt to manually reboot your system (by pressing Ctrl+Alt+Del), Windows grabs control and displays a Close Program dialog box that asks you what you want to do. For instance, you might only want to end the current program, not the three or four programs running in the background. This is a big change from earlier versions of Windows, and a big advantage to using Windows 95.

Stepping in and moderating the reboot process allows Windows to make sure that rebooting is not done at an inopportune time, as far as the operating system is concerned. This moderating capability means there is less chance of corrupting your Windows files by rebooting. However, you can still mess up files maintained by applications running under Windows. For instance, if you choose to terminate a program by pressing Ctrl+Alt+Del, you're asked to confirm your action. If you cancel the reboot, no harm is done. If you end an application, it is terminated immediately—Windows 95 assumes you know the consequences of your actions. If you reboot the entire system, then any unsaved data in all your running programs could be lost. Again, Windows

assumes that you have fully thought through the consequences and want to reboot anyway.

The bottom line is that even though it is possible to reboot your system under Windows 95, the way in which rebooting is handled by the operating system is much more stable than in previous versions of Windows. This stability means you have less chance of inadvertently losing data (you have to *really* want to lose it now) and have one less thing to worry about.

Long File Names

Windows 95 supports long file names. Many people tout this achievement as the single biggest improvement in the operating system. (In fact, as you are learning, it is only one of several major improvements.) It is true that Windows 95 does away with the need to limit files to the "eight dot three" convention of naming files. Now you can provide descriptive names that really mean something. File names can be up to 255 characters long, yet you can still refer to the same file by using a shortened alias that passes as a traditional file name.

The caveat in long file names is that they are based on the historically significant FAT file structure. FAT is an acronym for *file allocation table,* and refers to the file structure used in the DOS operating system. This vestige of DOS is a necessary admission that most people are migrating to the Windows 95 environment from a DOS environment, and those people are happiest when the files they have accumulated over the past 15 years are still accessible.

So how does Windows 95 do it? How does it allow you to create long file names by using the FAT file structure, which is synonymous with short, cryptic file names? The answer is simple, really—it cheats. It exploits quirks in the FAT structure definition to achieve the benefits.

To fully understand how long file names are implemented in Windows 95, you need to understand more about the file structure used. Fair warning—this means you need to understand what may appear to be technical information, but the benefit is that you can wow your friends

and always have something to discuss at cocktail parties. The following sections address the technical aspects of long file names; when you understand this information you will understand exactly how long file names work.

Traditional FAT Directory Entries

At the heart of the FAT file structure is what is referred to as a *directory entry*. Traditionally, directory entries maintain the following information about a file:

- File name and extension
- Type of file
- Time of last update
- Date of last update
- Location on disk
- Size of file

In the FAT file structure, this information is contained in a 32-byte record. Table 2.1 shows the structure of this record, indicating how the directory information is stored.

Table 2.1 Layout of Traditional Directory Entries in the FAT File System

Byte Offset	Length in Bytes	Purpose
0	8	File name
8	3	File extension
11	1	File attribute
12	10	Unused
22	2	Time of last update
24	2	Date of last update
26	2	Beginning disk cluster
28	4	Bytes in file

Everything in the directory entry is fairly straightforward, although there are a few nuances to understanding how the directory entry is actually interpreted. For instance, the first character of the file-name entry has special significance. Normally, the file name is composed of ASCII character values that represent the file name. However, if the ASCII value of the first character is 0, then the directory entry has never been used before. If the first character has an ASCII value of 229 (E5 in hexadecimal notation), then the directory entry represents a file that has been deleted. Finally, if the directory entry begins with the value 46 (2E in hexadecimal), the entry represents a subdirectory. Any other value is interpreted as part of a valid file name.

The file attribute byte at offset 11 may need some explaining, as well. The eight bits that make up this byte have special meaning, and indicate the type of file represented by this directory entry, or possibly the file's status. Table 2.2 shows the meaning of the bits in this attribute byte.

Table 2.2 Meanings for File Attribute Bytes in a Directory Entry

Bit Position	Meaning If Set
0	Read-only file
1	Hidden file
2	System file
3	File name is really a volume label
4	File is really a subdirectory
5	File has been updated since the last backup
6	Unused
7	Unused

Many of the bits in the attribute byte can be combined for a cumulative effect. For instance, a file can be set as read-only and hidden, in which case both bits 0 and 1 would be set.

Windows 95 Directory Entries

To implement long file names, Windows 95 takes advantage of previously unused combinations of information in the directory entry, as well as allows directory entries to be chained together. This chaining of directory entries implies several things. First, there is an initial directory entry which signals Windows that there are additional entries. Second, the initial directory entry is somehow different from subsequent directory entries for the same file.

To understand how this all works, take a look at table 2.3. This table shows the layout for the initial directory entry for a file.

Table 2.3 Layout of an Initial Directory Entry in Windows 95

Byte Offset	Length in Bytes	Purpose
0	8	File name
8	3	File extension
11	1	File attribute
12	6	Unused
18	2	Last access date
20	2	Exclusive access handle
22	2	Creation time
24	2	Creation date
26	2	Beginning disk cluster
28	4	Bytes in file

Notice that the directory entry layout for Windows 95 is essentially the same as the traditional layout, except for three differences. First, four bytes beginning at offset 18 are now used in what was previously unused and reserved space. Now two additional fields are stored in this area. The first is an indication of the date when the file was last accessed, and the other is a handle to be used when the file is being exclusively accessed by a process. Second, the purpose of the time and

date fields at offsets 22 and 24 has changed. Third, now the time and fields are used to indicate the time and date the file was created, not the time and date of last access.

So how does Windows 95 indicate that a file name occupies additional directory entries? This is done through use of the attribute byte. If you refer to table 2.2, you'll recall the traditional meanings of the bits in the attribute byte. You also learned that it's possible for the bits to be treated cumulatively—for instance, to note a file that is both read-only and hidden.

Some attribute combinations are illogical, however, and therefore not allowed in the traditional FAT environment. One of these illogical combinations is used by Windows 95 to signal that the directory entry is the first in a series of directory entries. If the bits 0 through 3 are set (meaning the file is read-only, hidden, system, and a volume label—an impossible combination in normal use), then Windows 95 recognizes the directory entry as the first in the series.

Once the first directory entry is detected, the next directory entry is read and the long file name is concatenated. The structure of these secondary directory entries is shown in table 2.4.

Table 2.4 Layout of Secondary Directory Entries Under Windows 95

Byte Offset	Length in Bytes	Purpose
0	1	Sequence
1	10	File name
11	1	File attribute
12	1	Type
13	1	Checksum
14	12	File name
26	2	Unused (set to 0)
28	4	File name

Notice that there are 26 bytes in each of the secondary directory entries that can be used for a file name, but that these bytes are not contiguous. Instead, they are divided by information used internally by Windows. The sequence number and checksum bytes are used to ensure the long file name (the entire sequence of directory entries) has not somehow been corrupted.

The type byte (at offset 12) is used to indicate exactly what type of information this directory entry contains. Long file names can use secondary directory entries for continuations of the file name, as well as for class information. This information can be used by object-oriented programs to further manipulate the file, as an object. If the type byte indicates the directory entry contains class information, then the information in the entry follows the layout shown in table 2.5.

Table 2.5 Layout of the Class Information Secondary Directory Entry

Byte Offset	Length in Bytes	Purpose
0	1	Sequence
1	10	Class information
11	1	File attribute
12	1	Type
13	1	Checksum
14	6	Class information
20	6	Reserved
26	2	Unused (set to 0)
28	4	Reserved

Notice that the class information can occupy only one directory entry for any given file. This information is included in the sequence of long file name entries, as indicated by the sequence byte at the beginning of the entry.

You probably already know that the PC relies on the ASCII character set to represent information. ASCII uses eight bits (a byte) to define individual characters. Windows 95 uses ASCII as well, but not when storing a long file name. Instead, it uses the Unicode character set, which uses 16 bits (two bytes) to represent a single character. Thus, a file name that is 255 characters long actually occupies 510 bytes of data. Because each secondary directory entry can contain 26 bytes (refer to table 2.4), it takes 20 directory entries to accommodate a full-length file name.

Taken in total then, there is a primary directory entry, up to 20 secondary directory entries, and a single directory entry for class information. Thus, the longest a directory entry chain under Windows 95 can be is 22 entries.

Alias File Names

To maintain compatibility with older programs, every file that has a long file name also has a short file name. In Windows 95, the long file name is called the *primary file name,* and the short file name is called the *secondary file name,* or *alias.* This short file name is automatically created by Windows, based on the long file name you use. It's stored in the primary directory entry for the file, using the older eight-dot-three naming convention. This alias is put together by shortening the primary (long) file name in the following manner:

- Historically illegal characters (except spaces) are replaced with underscores
- Spaces are removed to pack the name together
- The name is truncated at six characters
- The two characters ~1 are appended to the file name
- The file name is converted to uppercase
- If a file already exists with the resulting eight-character name, the number at the end of the name is incremented. The name is checked again; if a conflict still exists, the number is incremented again and repetitive checks are made.

For example, assume you have a spreadsheet file that has the following name:

```
Tests, showing initial data.xls
```

This is the primary file name. The alias for this file would be the following:

```
TESTS_~1.XLS
```

If there were successive files that shared the same initial characters, they would become the following:

```
TESTS_~2.XLS
TESTS_~3.XLS
TESTS_~4.XLS
TESTS_~5.XLS
TESTS_~6.XLS
TESTS_~7.XLS
TESTS_~8.XLS
TESTS_~9.XLS
TESTS~10.XLS
TESTS~11.XLS
```

Improved 32-Bit Architecture

Earlier in this chapter, you learned that Windows 95 fully exploits the protected mode of your computer. One advantage of protected mode operation is that programs can run faster because they can use 32-bit data access techniques. Traditionally, programs have accessed data either 8-bits or 16-bits at a time. The CPUs used in today's computer systems are optimized for 32-bit operations, however. Windows 95 fully exploits this capability, and allows your programs to do the same.

Many parts of Windows 95 have been rewritten in 32-bit code. This means that these components can operate more efficiently and process data more quickly than was previously possible. The following sections describe the major parts of Windows 95 that benefit from 32-bit operations.

The Kernel

The kernel is the heart of Windows. It is the part of the operating system that remains in memory at all times, providing basic functions that form the core of what Windows does. In Windows 95, the kernel provides memory management, file management, and task management functions.

Windows 95 has a new and improved kernel. Earlier in this chapter, you learned about the improved multitasking capabilities of Windows 95; these are part of the kernel. This portion of the operating system has been completely rewritten in 32-bit code that operates entirely in protected mode. Thus, operations occur more quickly and with higher security and stability than in previous versions of Windows.

File Access

You already know how Windows 95 interprets the FAT file structure to implement long file names. Along with rewriting the kernel in 32-bit code, Windows 95 also includes improved 32-bit file management routines that allow enhanced file access. This means that files can be accessed more quickly than was previously possible, even though the file itself has not been changed. Instead, the way in which the files are accessed is modified. This is analogous to using better equipment to dig a hole—the dirt and rock are not changed, you use more powerful equipment. (If the traditional file access routines are a shovel, Windows 95 has replaced them with a back hoe.)

TrueType Font Engine

TrueType fonts were introduced with Windows 3.1. As you'll learn in Chapter 22, "Working with Fonts," these fonts allow precise correlation between what you see on-screen and what you see on your printed output. Windows 95 includes a new TrueType rasterizer (often called a font engine) that provides the following benefits:

- Faster manipulation of fonts
- Faster font loading
- Better output at high resolutions
- Easier handling of complex fonts

The font engine has been written in 32-bit code and was adapted from the engine used in Windows NT. Because manipulating fonts involves heavy use of mathematics, the 32-bit code allows greater precision and accuracy than was previously available. This means crisper output and better support for high-resolution displays and printers.

Printing and Spooling

One of the frustrating parts of dealing with Windows in the past is printing. The output you got was pretty good, but the way in which the printing process was managed many times seemed backward or awkward.

The entire print management system in Windows 95 has been rewritten. No longer do you set up printers under the Control Panel and manage print jobs from the Main program group. Now all printing functions are managed by using the consistent interface of the Printers folder. Combining 32-bit code with preemptive multitasking also means that print jobs are processed smoother and with fewer delays. The result is faster printing to either a local printer or across a network.

Device Drivers

Device drivers control how Windows 95 interacts with equipment you have connected to your system; this basic fact is no different than in previous versions of Windows. The differences in device drivers under Windows 95 are two-fold: quantity and quality.

Windows 95 directly supports many more devices than previous versions of Windows. Most devices are detected either when Windows 95 is installed or when you change the device, and the appropriate driver is loaded from the installation disks or CD-ROM. While you may still need to contact a vendor for device drivers for new or esoteric equipment, the frequency of doing this is diminished greatly.

The quality of the included device drivers is significantly improved. 32-bit device drivers are necessary to work seamlessly with the improved Windows 95 kernel. All of the device drivers distributed with Windows 95 have been rewritten in 32-bit code, which provides faster, more robust throughput.

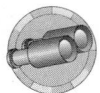

> **Note:** Windows 95 still supports 16-bit device drivers. The disadvantage to using them is that they are inherently slower than 32-bit device drivers. If you have an option, make sure you use a 32-bit device driver designed for use with Windows 95.

Better Resource Management

The other part of the kernel that has been rewritten involves resource management. Resources are components of your computer that can be used by Windows 95 to accomplish a task. For instance, memory is a resource, as is disk space, or a device such as a printer.

In previous versions of Windows, resource management was shaky, at best. This shakiness was due to several factors. First, Windows was built on top of DOS. This meant that many limitations inherent to DOS needed to be compensated for. Because Windows 95 replaces DOS, these limitations are no longer a problem; resources can be directly controlled and accessed by Windows instead of using DOS as an intermediary. Another factor is that Windows did not operate entirely in protected mode. Because some operations were handled outside of protected mode, the resources were open to corruption or compromise during those times.

Windows 95 includes improved resource management routines that have been rewritten from the ground up. These routines affect the operating system in the following areas:

- ***The heap.*** This is a memory area used to hold and manipulate objects in the Windows environment. In the past, the heap was limited to a single 64K area; in Windows 95 the 64K heap still exists but has been supplemented by a 32-bit memory pool used for the more memory-intensive objects. The result is less chance of exhausting system resources (as was common for many users in Windows 3.1).
- ***Memory management.*** When Windows was operating as an add-on to DOS, it still needed to be concerned with (and constrained by) different types of memory. For example, if too much conventional memory was used before Windows even started, then performance could be seriously impaired. Windows 95 removes traditional memory constraints, treating the memory in your system as a single, contiguous linear space. This means that memory operations can occur more quickly, and program throughput can be faster.
- ***The Registry.*** Much of the configuration information previously stored in WIN.INI and SYSTEM.INI files has been moved to the Registry. This is a special database that provides a consistent and secure way to store configuration information.

The result of better resource management is a more stable system that better responds to changing program needs.

Built-In Networking

There is a good chance that you are already familiar with Windows for Workgroups, a networking version of Windows 3.1. Windows 95 does away with the networked and non-networked versions of Windows. Instead, networking is built in, from the ground up. You saw evidences of this in Chapter 1, "The Windows 95 Interface." There you learned about the Network Neighborhood icon and how you can use it to explore a network.

Windows 95 includes the following networking improvements:

- ➤ ***Wider network support.*** Besides the Microsoft peer-to-peer network, Windows 95 also supports third-party networks such as Novell, TCP/IP, and Banyan Vines. Extensions are provided so that other networks can interface with Windows 95, as well.
- ➤ ***Easier network access.*** The result of networking being an integral part of Windows 95 is that you can easily access network resources. You already know about the Network Neighborhood icon, but you can also access the network through virtually any other Windows 95 application program. You can also access dial-up networks quickly and easily.
- ➤ ***More tools.*** Network management is easier than in earlier versions of Windows due to tools included with Windows 95. Tools are provided that allow you to manage connections, resources, and users.

Plug-and-Play Support

One of the major features that Windows 95 boasts is the ability to support the Plug-and-Play standard. Essentially, the Plug-and-Play standard allows you to insert a new device into your computer and the system will automatically recognize the device and go through the configuration process for you, thereby saving you time and headaches.

How many times have you tried to install a modem in your computer only to discover that your mouse stopped working? Or, have you tried installing a CD-ROM and suddenly your system doesn't boot up? Traditional installation of devices such as video or sound cards, network adapters, CD-ROMs, and even additional serial ports requires a major investment of time and frustration. But even this investment doesn't guarantee it will work when you are finished. At the least, the trial-and-error method of changing jumper settings, installing device drivers, and editing the configuration files makes most users anxious.

What Is Plug and Play?

Although Plug and Play is a hardware specification, it is also a concept. This concept is nothing new, either. In the 1980s, IBM introduced the PS/2 with its Micro Channel architecture. Several years later, the EISA bus was also introduced. Both busses included auto-configuration capabilities, but neither bus really took hold; the ISA bus was too firmly entrenched in the market.

As hardware and software have evolved, it seems that the complexity of both has grown exponentially. Because of the drawbacks and problems associated with the traditional ISA bus (including IRQ conflicts, DMA configurations, and manual jumper settings), Plug and Play is an architecture designed to take care of the configuration for you and eliminate the typical bother associated with installing hardware.

Whether you are installing a sound card, a modem, a disk drive, or any other device, Plug and Play will detect and configure your equipment for you automatically. Suppose you want to add a modem to your system. Plug it in, turn on the computer, and after some time for auto-configuration, it works. While this may sound too good to be true, it is possible based on the components you have in your system. Basically, you need three elements to have a true Plug-and-Play system:

- Plug-and-Play hardware devices
- Plug-and-Play BIOS (Basic Input/Output System)
- Plug-and-Play operating system (such as Windows 95)

A true Plug-and-Play system requires all three elements, but you can get similar Plug-and-Play functionality if one of the latter two is missing. Take a quick look at these elements and how each contributes to the overall Plug-and-Play system.

Hardware Devices

The base component of Plug-and-Play architecture is the Plug-and-Play device. A device can be a card, peripheral, or other internal part that interfaces with the computer. Compared to the traditional ISA device, the Plug-and-Play device can "communicate" with the BIOS, the operating system, or both to configure itself automatically. As you can see in figure 2.1, from the moment you power on the system, these devices interact with the BIOS by reporting their presence through a special built-in identifier called *resource data.* If the BIOS is not Plug-and-Play compatible, then the operating system communicates with the devices instead.

Notice the sequence of how Plug-and-Play hardware and the BIOS, and/or the operating system, interact. First, the BIOS and/or the operating system isolate one device. It then reads the card's resource data and configures its resources accordingly. If necessary, the operating system then obtains a driver for the device either by finding it somewhere in the system, or by requesting it through a floppy disk from you.

Don't worry about your current non–Plug-and-Play devices. The Plug-and-Play standard takes into account that you already have existing computer equipment. To maintain compatibility with existing hardware, Plug and Play does not strictly rely on each of these components (although having each would be ideal). In fact, Plug-and-Play components will function alongside regular ISA devices without any problem. The only limitation you might notice when using both together is that the configuration process will not be fully automatic. In such instances, you install the device as-is—that is, plug it into the computer by using its default settings. From that point, either the BIOS or the operating system will configure the other Plug-and-Play devices around the existing components.

The BIOS

The Plug-and-Play BIOS also plays a major role. When you first flip the switch to start your system, the BIOS is the first part of your computer system to obtain control, so this is a natural place to incorporate control for the Plug-and-Play system. The Plug-and-Play BIOS communicates very quickly with each Plug-and-Play device, in turn. It first assigns the device a handle and then reads the resource data. Once this takes place for all components, the BIOS verifies that none of the devices conflict with each other. If there is a conflict, the BIOS quickly communicates with all the devices and alters handles until there are no conflicts.

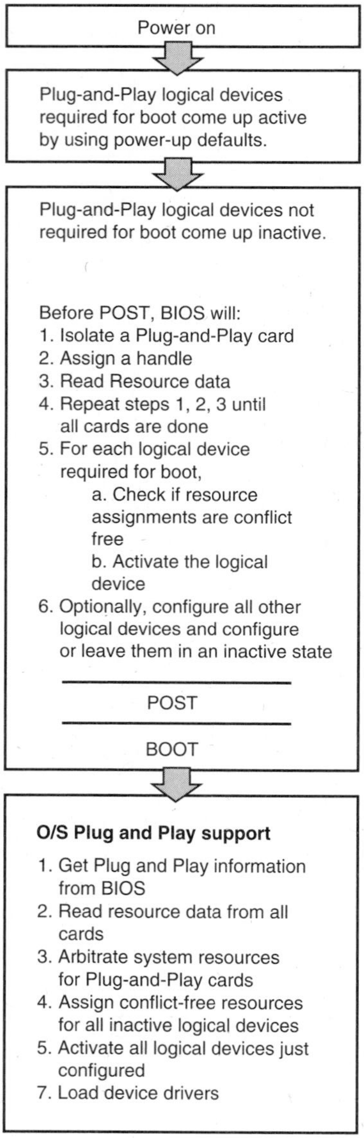

Fig. 2.1 The sequence of events when booting a Plug-and-Play system involves well-defined steps.

If your BIOS does not support Plug and Play, don't worry. You can probably upgrade your BIOS. If not, you can still use a Plug-and-Play operating system (such as Windows 95) and devices that support the Plug-and-Play standard. Of course, you lose some functionality and benefit of Plug and Play, namely the ability to let your computer automatically configure all the devices, but it's still better than nothing.

> **Note:** For a computer system to receive the Windows 95-compatible logo, it must have a Plug-and-Play BIOS version 1.0a (or later) installed on the motherboard.

The unique advantage of incorporating the Plug-and-Play BIOS is that, among other things, it tracks each installed device and allows the operating system to retrieve and update detailed information about each device. It resolves conflicts with hardware that ultimately prevent the system resources from being over-allocated by the operating system.

The Operating System

The operating system, Windows 95 in this case, works in harmony with the Plug-and-Play BIOS and continues the automatic configuration process.

Every time your system boots up, Windows 95 builds and keeps a diagram of the system configuration, called a *hardware tree.* As you make changes, Windows 95 compares the hardware tree with the most recent configuration and, if it finds a change, modifies the configuration files, IRQs, and other related parameters accordingly. Such a system certainly relieves you of the configuration woes that come when you change, add, or remove hardware.

After it reads the BIOS, the operating system mimics the same steps as originally followed by the BIOS. First, it reads the resource data from all the cards and portions out resources accordingly. Then it activates the devices and loads their corresponding device drivers. During the system's up-time, the operating system and BIOS maintain a close connection, watching all device activity.

If you don't have a Plug-and-Play BIOS, as described earlier, you can still obtain most of the benefits of Plug and Play. In such a case, the operating system takes over the responsibility of the BIOS and configures system resources.

Eventually, all PCs will be manufactured with hardware and software that employs the Plug-and-Play standard. Most hardware vendors want to service the needs of their customers and will therefore offer the simplest solution to configuring a system—Plug and Play.

How Does Windows 95 Support Plug and Play?

Windows 95 is the first operating system for the PC to support the Plug-and-Play specification. Because Windows 95 is designed from the ground up to be a Plug-and-Play operating system, it is far more advantageous than other operating systems (such as DOS), which would need to use OS extenders to provide Plug-and-Play compatibility.

When a system is first powered on, the BIOS performs its functions, finally checking all the available devices. That information is retained in the BIOS and is later requested by Windows 95 to continue in the regulation of the system. After the BIOS is finished examining the system, it proceeds with the power-on self test (POST) and boots Windows 95.

During the loading process, Windows 95 performs a series of routine steps, which are supervised by the Configuration Manager. This Windows component communicates with the BIOS and responds to dynamic changes in the system since the last boot. Next, under direction of the Configuration Manager, a new hardware tree is drawn and stored for future reference. Once these steps have been performed, the Configuration Manager works silently in the background, monitoring any changes in the configuration that may occur.

If a device is removed, drivers are instantly removed from memory and resources are freed for use by other system processes.

New Windows 95 Tools

by Allen L. Wyatt

Virtually every tool available in previous versions of Windows has been redesigned for Windows 95. Also, several new tools provide a wider degree of control over your computer system. This chapter describes several of the new tools available within Windows 95, particularly those you'll probably use every day:

- The Explorer
- Quick View
- Shortcuts
- Finding Files

Using the Explorer

Perhaps the most powerful new tool in Windows 95 is the Explorer. This tool is meant to replace the File Manager available in previous versions of Windows, as well as some aspects of Program Manager. The Explorer allows you to view, change, and manage the contents of your disk drives. If you have the proper security permissions, you can perform the same functions on disk drives over the network.

Starting the Explorer

You can start the Explorer in two ways:

- Open the My Computer or Network Neighborhood icons, and then choose a drive. Then choose File, Explore.
- Perhaps the simplest method of starting the Explorer is to click the Start button and then choose Programs, Windows Explorer.

Either way, the Explorer window appears (see fig. 3.1).

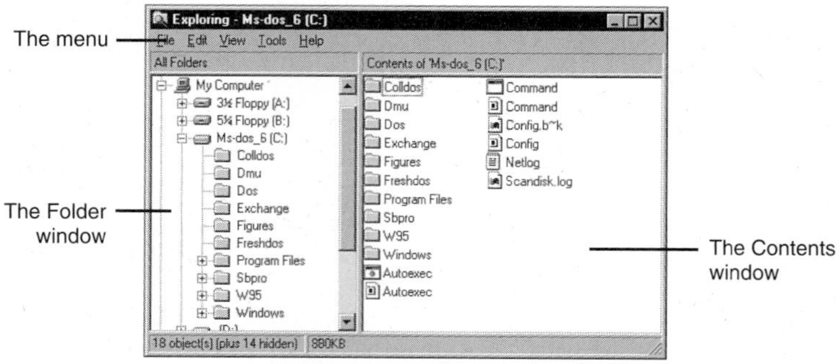

Fig. 3.1 The Explorer window looks different from the previous Windows File Manager.

Understanding the Explorer Window

There are three main parts to the Explorer window: the menu, the Folder window, and the Contents window. The following sections explain each part.

The Menu

Explorer has a menu with five choices. These menus function in the same manner as any other Windows 95 menu; you click the menu desired and then choose an option.

The actual options available on the menus combine the functionality available in Program Manager and File Manager in previous versions of Windows, along with some new features. Many of the menu options are explained later in this chapter.

The Folder Window

The left side of the Explorer window, referred to as the Folder window, is used to show the organization of your system. The format used for this depiction is sometimes called a *tree,* although you can think of it as an outline of your system. For example, if you look at figure 3.2, you can see that the various disk drives (A, B, C, and so on) are directly under the My Computer icon. This is because they're part of your computer, not some other part of your system (such as the network). Under each disk drive, you can also see other subdivisions, such as folders and files.

Take another look at figure 3.2. Notice that many branches in the tree have a small box next to them that contains a plus or a minus sign. This indicates whether more detail is available for a particular branch. If you click a plus sign, the branch is expanded; clicking a minus sign collapses a branch. If there's no plus or minus sign, there's no additional detail for the branch.

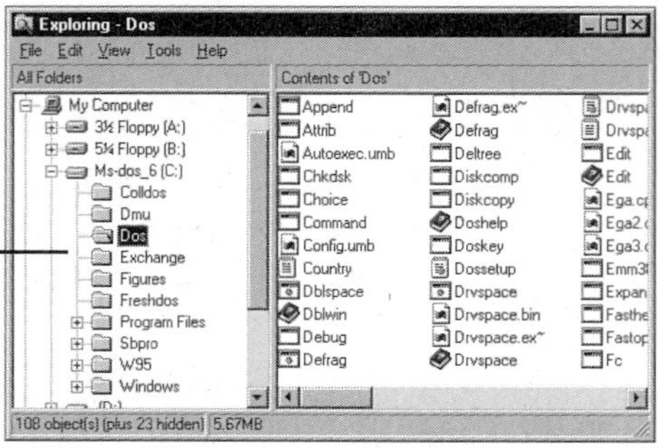

Fig. 3.2 The Folder window shows a logical outline of the information on your system.

> **Note:** When you first start the Explorer, notice that your computer's A and B drives have a plus sign next to them, even if you don't have disks in those drives. This is because there *could* be additional information in those drives. Windows 95 doesn't actually check them unless you choose them; then it removes the plus sign if it detects no disk in the drives.

The Contents Window

The right side of the Explorer window, the Contents window, is used to show the contents of the drive or folder selected in the Folder window. Figure 3.3 shows what a typical Contents window looks like.

To specify how information is displayed in the Contents window, use the View menu. Options on this menu are used to control the display. You can display information displayed in the Contents window in any of four different formats:

- *Large icons.* The files and folders in the Contents window are displayed as large, easy-to-identify icons (see fig. 3.4). Because each icon takes up a larger percentage of the screen, this is a good choice if a lot of objects aren't on disk or in a folder.

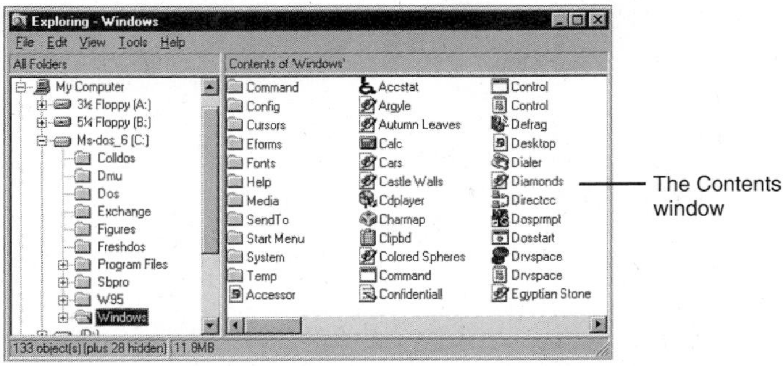

Fig. 3.3 The Contents window shows detailed information about what's in a portion of your system.

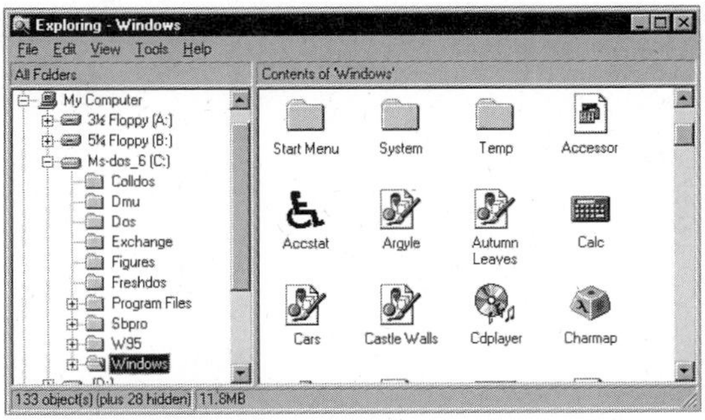

Fig. 3.4 You can display the Contents window with large icons for each file and folder.

- *Small icons.* The files and folders are displayed by using smaller icons and therefore can be closer together (see fig. 3.5). This is a good choice if you still like to see the icons but have quite a few files to display.

- *List.* Information in the Contents window is simply listed in columns with a small icon to the left of each name in the list. This is a good way to pack as much information in the Contents window as possible without having to scroll. Figure 3.3 shows what this type of display looks like.

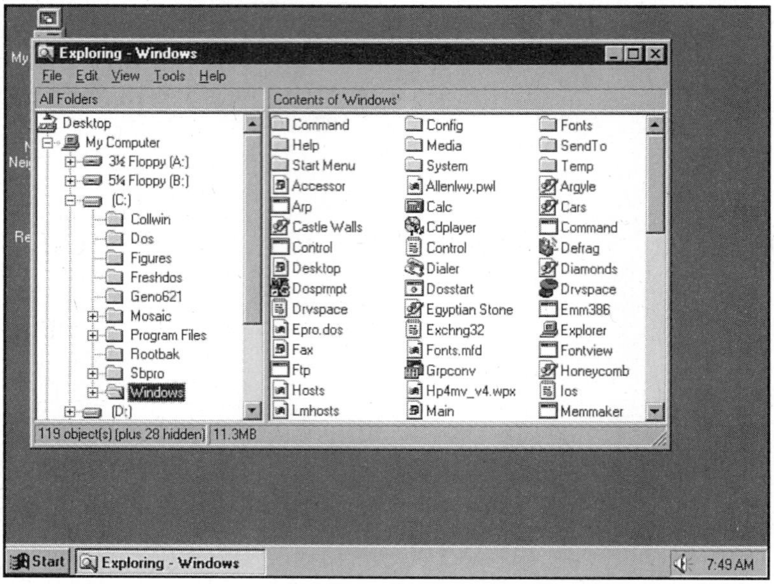

Fig. 3.5 The Contents window can display more information at a time when small icons are used.

➤ *Details.* This view provides the most information about individual files or folders in an object (see fig. 3.6). Each file or folder is shown on a separate line, along with its size, type, and last date and time it was modified.

Other Explorer Features

Besides the menu bar, Folder window, and Contents window, you can use two other features in the Explorer: the toolbar and the status bar. You can turn both of these optional features on or off by using the View menu. A check mark next to the option on the menu means that the feature is displayed. Selecting the menu option again turns the feature off and removes the check mark.

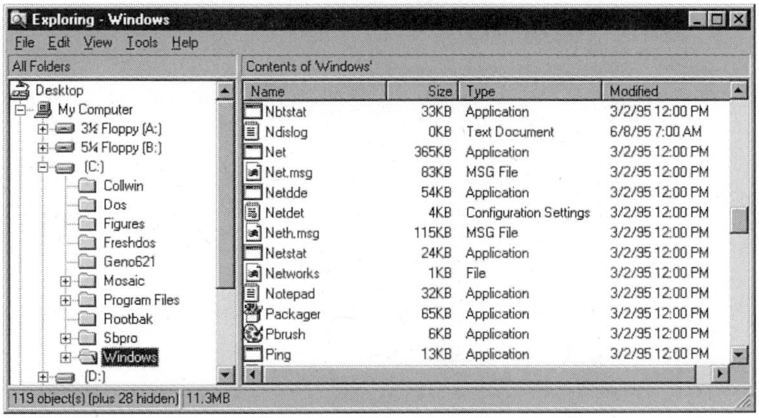

Fig. 3.6 The Contents window can show detailed information about the files on your system.

The Toolbar The Explorer's toolbar is similar to toolbars in most any Windows application. It's displayed just below the menu bar (see fig. 3.7).

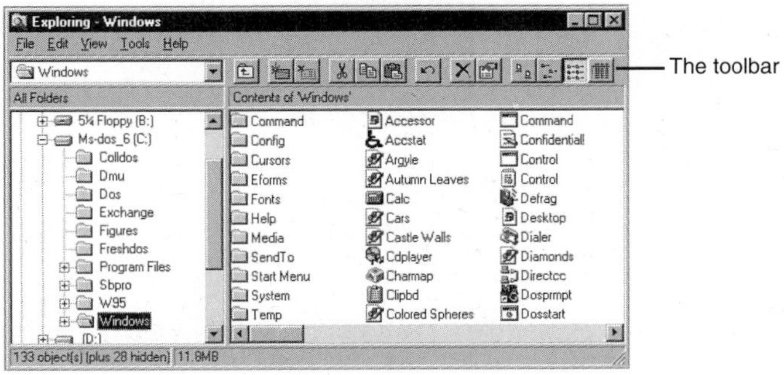

Fig. 3.7 The Explorer toolbar allows easy access to common functions.

The left-most part of the toolbar indicates what object you've selected in the Folders window. If you click the pull-down arrow next to the box, you see a list of drives and folders that looks very similar to what's in the Folders window.

To the right of the current object indicator are the actual tools. To discover the purpose of a tool, move the mouse pointer over it and wait a moment (keep the mouse pointer over the tool); you'll see a tip that indicates what the tool is used for.

Notice that the tools are divided into groups, with a small space between each group of tools. The first group consists of a single tool that has a folder with an upward-pointing arrow on it. You use this tool to move back through the system hierarchy shown in the Folder window. Click it once to move up to the next highest folder level.

The next group to the right consists of two tools, both of which are used to work with objects on the network. If you used Windows for Workgroups, these tools probably look similar to icons you used in File Manager. The first one allows you to connect and map a network drive, and the second allows you to break a connection with a previously mapped drive.

The next group consists of three tools that are standard in many Windows applications. These tools allow you respectively to cut, copy, and paste information or objects (including files). For instance, you could copy a file and then paste multiple copies of it in different places on your hard disk.

To the right of this group is another group that consists of a single tool—Undo. This tool can be used, however, only to undo the previous action, not the last few actions.

Caution: Some actions you accomplish with the Explorer can't be undone. While Undo provides some level of protection, the best rule is to make sure that you really want to perform an action before you do it.

The next group consists of two tools. The left-most tool, with a big × on it, is used to delete a file or folder. The other one is an icon you'll see in many places in Windows 95. It allows you to review or modify the properties of an object. Properties are characteristics of an object and can vary from object to object. For instance, the characteristics of a file

include things such as file size, file type, and creation date, but these are slightly different from the properties associated with another object, such as a folder.

The final group of four tools are used to change how information is viewed in the Contents window. These tools allow you to quickly and easily switch between different program window views, as discussed earlier in this chapter in the section titled "The Contents Window."

> **Tip:** Remember that the toolbar is optional. You can accomplish the same functions provided in the toolbar by using the menu system.

The Status Bar The status bar appears at the bottom of the Explorer window. It's used to display additional information about objects selected in the Explorer, and about menu options. Figure 3.8 shows the position of the status bar in the Explorer window.

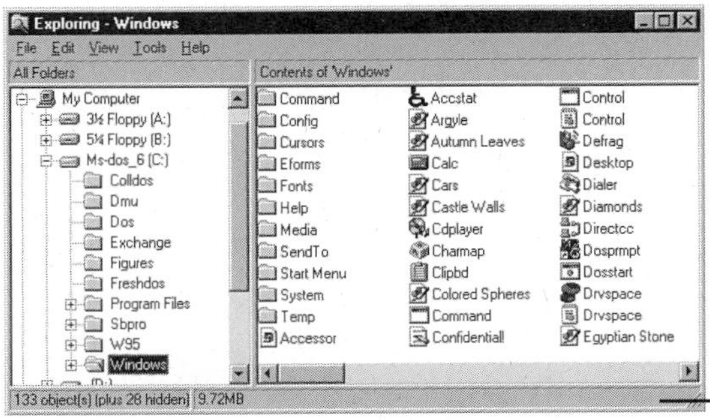

Fig. 3.8 The Explorer's status bar displays helpful information about menu options and objects in the Explorer.

As already mentioned, the Explorer allows you to turn the status bar on or off. Whether you use the status bar or not is strictly personal preference, but you should know that you can display a bit more information on the screen with the status bar turned off.

Putting the Explorer to Use

You've already learned a bit about how you can use the Explorer. If you're familiar with using File Manager in previous versions of Windows, you'll quickly come up to speed with the Explorer.

Managing Files and Folders

The Explorer allows you to perform many different operations on individual files or entire directories. For instance, you can rename, delete, or copy them. You can also set properties for various objects.

The first step in working with a file or folder is selecting it. Then you can do any of the following:

- *Rename.* Choose File, Rename, or right-click and choose Rename from the context menu. The name right under the file or folder becomes active, and you can edit it in any way you want.
- *Delete.* There are four ways to delete an object. You can choose File, Delete; right-click and choose Delete from the context menu; click the Delete tool on the toolbar; simply press the Delete key, or press Shift+Delete (which deletes without moving the object to the Recycle Bin). Regardless of the method chosen, you're asked to confirm the deletion. When you click Yes, the file or folder is removed.
- *Move.* Use the mouse to drag the file or folder to where you want it moved. You can drag from the Contents window to the Folders window, or vice versa.
- *Copy.* Hold down the Ctrl key and use the mouse to drag the file or folder to where you want it copied. You can drag from the Contents window to the Folders window, or vice versa. If you prefer not to use the mouse to do the actual file movement, you can right-click on the file or folder, choose Copy from the context menu, and then enter the name of where you want the object copied.
- *Change properties.* Choose File, Properties; right-click and choose Properties from the context menu; or click the Properties tool on

the toolbar. The type of properties available depend on the type of object you select. For example, figure 3.9 shows the Properties sheet for a program file.

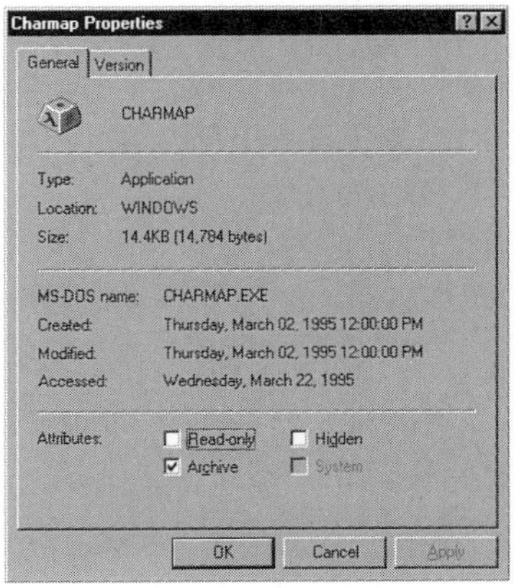

Fig. 3.9 This Properties sheet displays and allows changes to characteristics of a program file.

Sorting the Contents Window

Normally, the Explorer takes care of sorting the files displayed in the Contents window into alphabetical order. Sometimes, however, you may want to change how the information is presented. This is easily done by choosing View, Arrange Icons. This displays a menu with several arrangement choices:

- *Name.* Files are displayed in alphabetic order based on their name.
- *Type.* Files are sorted first by file type (such as DOC, GIF, BMP, and EXE) and then by name. This is handy when you want to view all files of the same type at once.
- *Size.* Files are sorted based on file size, from smallest to largest.
- *Date.* Files are displayed by when they were last modified. The most recently modified files are listed first.

At the bottom of the Arrange Icons menu is a final option, Auto Arrange. This option is available only if you're displaying icons (small or large) in the Contents window. When you select this option, a check mark appears next to it on the menu. You can remove the check mark by selecting the option a second time.

When selected, Auto Arrange ensures that the icons don't run off the right side of the Contents window unless absolutely necessary. Icons are rearranged in the best possible manner to make sure you can see as many of them as possible in the window size. If the window size is too small to display all the icons at once, then Windows adds a scroll bar so that you can easily access the additional icons. If you later change the window size, the icons are again rearranged to fill the window.

It is interesting to note that the Arrange Icons menu does not provide all the sorting options in which you may be interested. For instance, it does not provide a way to sort files in descending order instead of ascending order. You can increase the sorting flexibility by choosing the Details option from the View menu. This displays detailed information about files and folders in the Contents window, as shown earlier in figure 3.6. Notice, as well, that column heads are shown at the top of each column in the Contents window. If you click on a column head, the files are sorted based on that column. Click on the column head a second time, and the sorting order for that column is reversed. For instance, the first time you click on the Size column head, the files are sorted in ascending order by size; click on the Size column head again, and they are sorted in descending order by size.

Creating Associations

As in earlier versions of Windows, Windows 95 allows you to define associations between data files and the programs used to control them. You do this by indicating the type of files created by the application, and then Windows 95 assumes that all files of that type can be manipulated by that application. For instance, you could associate all files with a DOC extension with Word for Windows, and all files with a GIF extension could be associated with a graphics program.

To work with file associations, choose View, Options. In the Options dialog box, click the File Types tab. The dialog box should now appear as shown in figure 3.10.

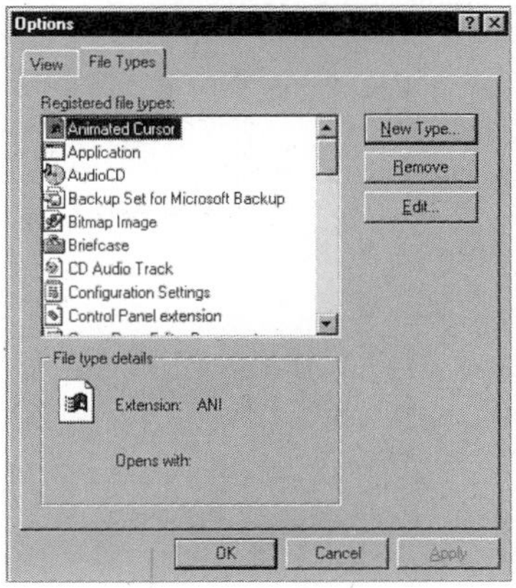

Fig. 3.10 The File Types tab in the Options dialog box shows the associations that exist between files and programs.

This dialog box contains a list of the associations that now exist. The list shows the icon associated with the file type and the name of the file type. If you want to edit an association, you can do so by selecting the existing file type, and then clicking Edit. Figure 3.11 shows an example of the dialog box used when you're editing an association.

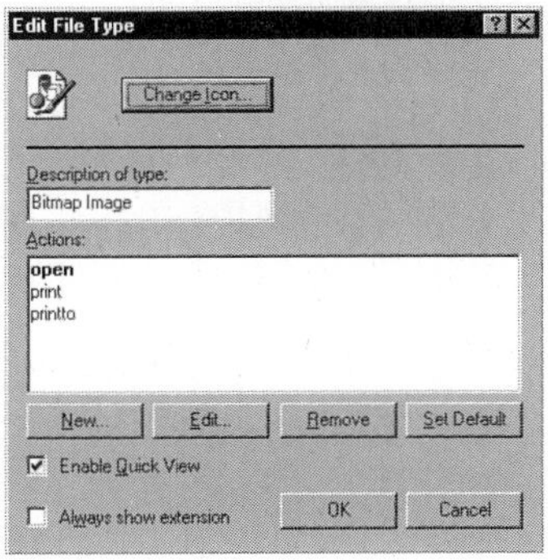

Fig. 3.11 Editing an existing association is done by using the Edit File Type dialog box.

The Edit File Type dialog box has three main parts. At the top of the dialog box, you can specify the icon that's used for this type of file. If you click the Change Icon button, you can select a different icon. Remember that the icon you choose here is used every time this type of file is graphically displayed on your system.

The second part of the dialog box is the field labeled Description of Type. This is simply a name used to describe the association. You can change this to anything; it shows up when you click the File Types tab in the Options dialog box.

The third and most important part of the editing dialog box is the Actions list. By using the four buttons that appear under the Actions list, you can change what appears in the list. *Actions* are nothing more than a definition of what can be done with the file. If you refer to figure 3.11, for example, notice that three actions are listed: open, print, and printto.

Actions are much more versatile than mere file-type associations, which were available in older versions of Windows. Actions allow you to define a wide range of functions that can be performed on a file. Once defined for a file type, actions then appear in the context menu for the file. Thus, you can use actions to define what appears in context menus.

Windows 95 allows you to define what application is used to perform any of a number of actions for a particular type of file. Say that you wanted to add an action for a type of file. All you need to do is click the New button. This displays the New Action dialog box (see fig. 3.12).

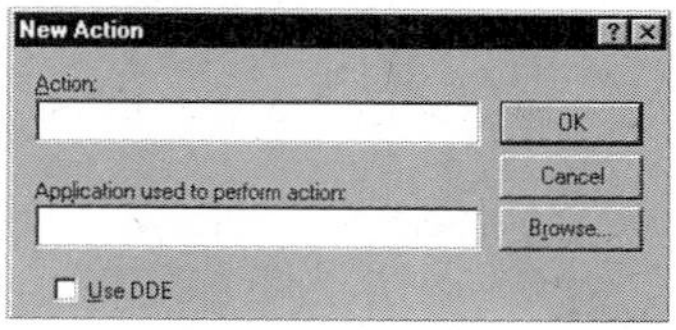

Fig. 3.12 The New Action dialog box is used to define actions for a file type.

All you need to do is to provide a name for the action in the Action field. This can be any name you want, such as *print, delete, process,* or whatever. There are no preset actions, so what you enter as an action is entirely up to you. You could even use multiple words in the Action field, such as Open with Word. Whatever actions you enter are shown in the context menu for the file.

In the next field, Application Used to Perform Action, you provide the complete command line that should be used to achieve the action (when the action is selected from the context menu). When you're satisfied with the action and the command used to carry out the action, click OK. The new action then appears in the Actions list of the Edit File Type dialog box (refer to fig. 3.11).

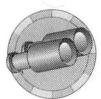

Note: Normally, applications use OLE (object linking and embedding) technology to work with files. This technology is common to many Windows applications, but some older Windows applications don't implement OLE; instead, many of these older applications use DDE (dynamic data exchange). If you choose an application but don't see any actions available for that application, click the Use DDE check box in the New Action dialog box. Actions may be available by using this older technology.

In the Edit File Type dialog box, actions are shown in the Actions list alphabetically. By default, the first action listed is used to control the icon displayed for the file type. You can modify the default action by choosing an action and then clicking the Set Default button. The selected action then appears in boldface in the Action list.

Using Quick View

Windows 95 incorporates a new feature that allows you to quickly view the contents of a file. This feature, known as Quick View, is available from virtually any place you can select files. You can use Quick View, for example, as you're browsing through the My Computer portion of your desktop, or you can use it from within the Explorer. Figure 3.13 shows an example of what you would see if you use the Quick View option to examine the PROTOCOL.INI file, found in the Windows folder.

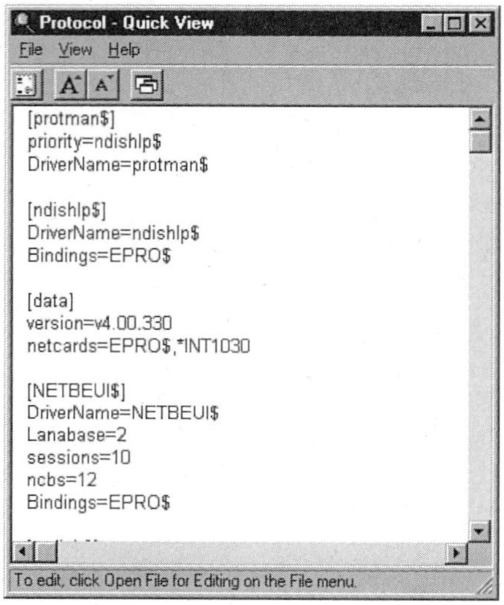

Fig. 3.13 Using Quick View to examine a text-based file is much like viewing it in the Notepad accessory.

Before you can use Quick View, you must select a file. Click the file's icon once to select it; the icon is then highlighted. You can then access the Quick View feature in two ways: from the File menu or from the context menu. Figure 3.14 shows an example of the context menu for a file. Notice that the third option on the menu is Quick View.

Not all files have the Quick View option available. Quick View requires a file type that Windows recognizes and can process. The ability to view a file with Quick View is dependent on the existence of a Quick View filter. Filters are used to define how a particular type of file should be translated and displayed. Table 3.1 lists the file types for which Windows 95 provides Quick View filters.

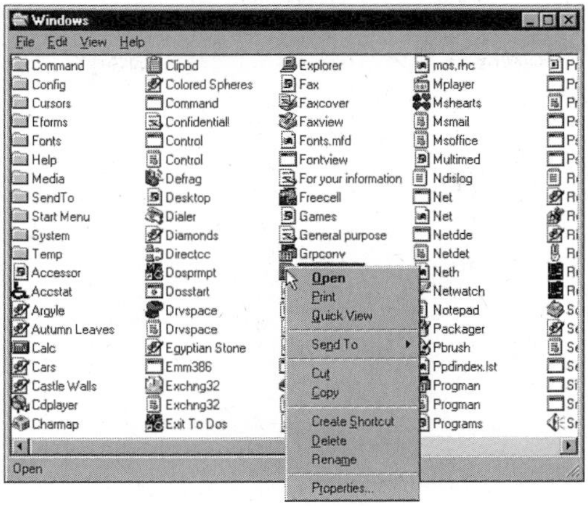

Fig. 3.14 You can access the Quick View feature of Windows 95 from the context menu for an object.

Table 3.1 File Types Supported by Quick View

File Type	Extension
Bit-map image	BMP
Setup information	INF
Configuration settings	INI
Registry files	REG
Rich Text Format file	RTF
Setup information	INF
Text documents	TXT
WordPad documents	DOC
Write documents	WRI

In addition to the file types listed in Table 3.1, the Quick View feature is available for other objects, such as disk drives and folders. It's also possible that Quick View filters are installed with some of your application programs so that their data files can be viewed quickly.

Understanding Shortcuts

Now that the traditional Program Manager has been done away with, Windows 95 provides the capability to create *shortcuts*. These are nothing more than links to documents or programs that you can place on the desktop for quick and easy access.

Why would you use a shortcut to access a program, rather than run the program and minimize it to the taskbar? Because running the program, even if it's minimized, consumes valuable system resources such as memory and a portion of your CPU time. Creating a shortcut, on the other hand, doesn't consume resources, yet your program is still readily available for use at any time.

Creating a Shortcut

The easiest way to create a shortcut is to either browse through My Computer or your Network Neighborhood, or to use the Explorer. When you can see the icon for the program or document for which you want to create a shortcut, drag the icon onto your desktop. But rather than drag by using the left mouse button, you should perform the drag using the right mouse button. When you release the mouse button, a small menu appears with several options (see fig. 3.15). Choose the Create Shortcut(s) Here option.

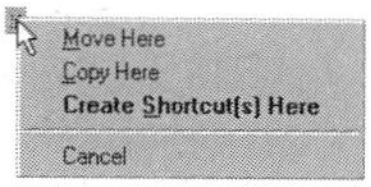

Fig. 3.15 Creating a shortcut is easy when you drag an object by using the right mouse button.

Windows creates a new icon on the desktop. You can tell that the icon is for a shortcut because it has a small diagonal arrow in the lower left corner of the original icon (the one that you dragged to the desktop). Figure 3.16 shows a comparison of the original icon for a program and the shortcut icon to the same program.

Fig. 3.16 A shortcut icon is the same as the original icon, except it has a small diagonal arrow in the lower left corner.

Another way to create a shortcut is to display the context menu for an object. One choice on the context menu is Create Shortcut. If you choose this option, the shortcut is created in whatever folder you're now working. You can then move the shortcut to wherever you want it, such as onto the desktop.

Renaming a Shortcut

Once you create a shortcut, you can treat its icon like any other icon in Windows. To rename the shortcut, simply display its context menu and choose the Rename option; Windows allows you to rename the shortcut to anything you desire.

> **Caution:** To avoid confusion with the original program or document icon, don't give the shortcut the same name as the original program or document.

Deleting a Shortcut

To delete a shortcut, select it and press Delete, or display the context menu for the icon and choose Delete. You're asked to confirm whether you really want to delete the icon; if you click Yes, the shortcut is deleted.

> **Tip:** Deleted shortcuts are moved to the Recycle Bin. If you later decide you want to salvage the shortcut, you may be able to find it in the Recycle Bin.

It's important to remember that shortcuts are nothing more than links to a program or document. When you delete a shortcut, you delete the link—not the original document or program. If you want to delete those, you need to search for the program files or documents and manually delete them.

> **Tip:** If you're deleting an application, the vendor sometimes provides an uninstall feature. Before you spend time searching for application files to delete manually, check the documentation to see whether there's an easier way to uninstall the program.

Searching for Files

As you work with your computer system, one thing you'll notice is that it's rather easy to collect a large number of files. Because it's virtually impossible to keep track of large numbers of files over a period of months, Windows 95 includes a tool that allows you to quickly and easily locate files on your system. You can access this tool by clicking the Start button and then choosing Find. This displays another menu that lists the types of searches you can perform. Since you want to find files on your system, choose the Files or Folders option. You then see the Find dialog box (see fig. 3.17).

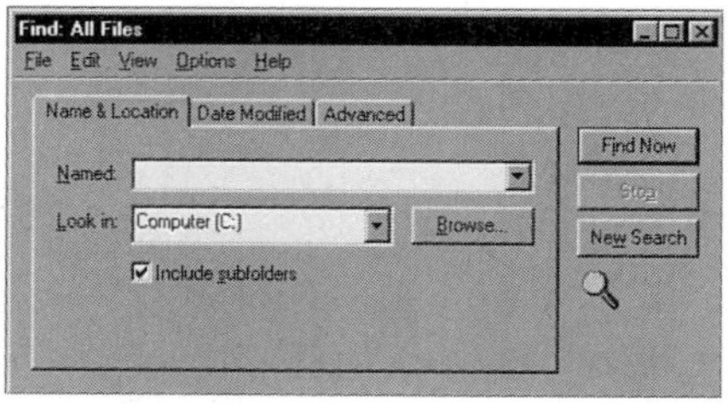

Fig. 3.17 You can quickly and easily search for files by using the Find dialog box.

Entering Your Criteria

Notice that the Find dialog box has three tabs, which allow you to specify the criteria that should be used when searching for a file:

- *Name & Location.* This tab is used to indicate where Find should start looking, how deep the search should go, and any hints on the file name. The Named field is used to specify a file name or partial file name. (You can use the ? and * wild-card characters to provide a partial file name.) The Look In field tells Find where to start looking, and the Include Subfolders check box indicates whether Find should look in any subfolders it encounters.
- *Date Modified.* This tab allows you to specify the age of the file you're looking for. You can specify a date range or a specific age for the files selected. The dates are based on when the files were either created or last modified.
- *Advanced.* Use this tab to specify a file type, text within a file, or a file size. If you're looking for a file that contains specific text, the search can take a while.

Find provides other ways to specify criteria as well. You can use the Options menu to specify this criteria. The choices on this menu are turned on and off every time they're selected. If the option is in effect, a check mark appears to the left of the option. Selecting the option again turns off the check mark and the option.

The first choice on the Options menu allows you to indicate whether the text you specify in your search should be considered Case Sensitive. If this option is selected, how you enter your text (including file names) matters as much as what you enter. For example, the text *Widget* is treated differently from *widget* or *WiDgEt.*

Starting a Search

Once you've specified the criteria for a search, you can start the search by clicking the Find Now button. Your criteria are analyzed, and the appropriate places on your system are searched. During the search, you see information on the status bar about the search's progress. When the search is complete, the files that were located are displayed at the bottom of the Find window (see fig. 3.18).

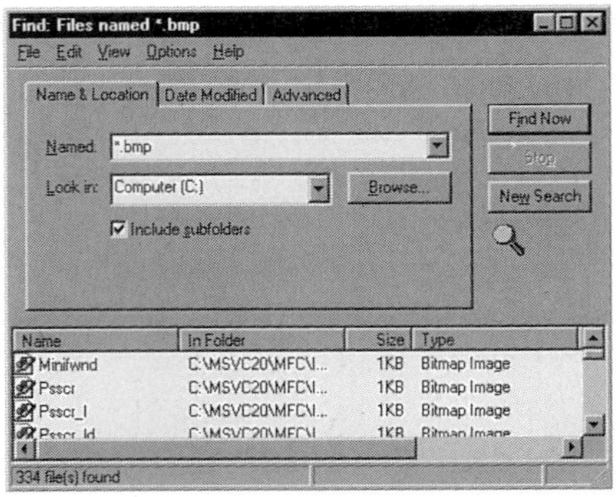

Fig. 3.18 After a search, the Find window lists the files that were located.

You can use the files located in the search in the same way as you would a file list in the Explorer. For instance, you can drag the file icons and drop them into another folder in the Explorer window (if the Explorer is running and open on your desktop), or you can rename or delete the file. What you do with files located by the Find tool is completely up to you.

Saving Your Search Criteria

It's possible to develop searches that are quite complex. In these instances, the Find tool provides a way to save your search criteria. To do so, simply choose Save Search from the File menu. Windows then creates a shortcut to the search, placing it on your desktop. You can then rename the shortcut to reflect a meaningful name.

Installing Windows 95

by Allen L. Wyatt

How you install Windows 95 will vary, to some extent, depending on the primary use for your system. Because of this variance, this chapter provides three different installation sections: installing Windows 95 on a home computer, an office computer, and a network workstation.

In addition to these install instructions, this chapter discusses the following topics:

- What to do before and after installation
- What setup type you should choose
- How to upgrade from a previous version of Windows
- How to configure your system for dual-boot between Windows 3.*x* and Windows 95

The Different Types of Systems

The proliferation of computers in the past few years has enabled many people to set up systems in their homes and offices, including systems attached to networking workstations. In the following sections, you'll learn a little about each of these areas.

What Is a Home Computer?

Depending on who is addressing the issue, a home computer can be many different things. The quick answer would be to say "a home computer is any computer you use at home." The complex and varied uses to which people put their computers makes this answer too simplistic, however.

Obviously, a computer used at home differs from traditional office-oriented systems because of the different workloads placed on it. Although there are exceptions, system components for the home computer typically consist of the following:

- 386- or 486-based computer
- 420M or smaller hard disk
- 4M RAM
- 14-inch SVGA monitor and graphics card
- Dot-matrix or ink-jet printer

In addition, more and more home machines are coming equipped with sound cards and CD-ROM drives. This is in recognition of the rapid growth of multimedia in computer systems in general, as well as the distribution of complex software on CD-ROM. Even Windows 95 is available on CD-ROM, which is definitely the easiest way to install the product.

Just a few years back, that seemingly modest 386 running at 33 MHz was the power user's dream machine. As of this writing, the Pentium has taken a stronghold with processor speeds up to 133 MHz. In

general, home systems stay a step or two behind the "power machines" on the market. As the requirements for home-oriented software continue to increase, so will the specifications for home computer systems. In a couple years, when the Pentium has been superseded by a newer and faster CPU, it will probably become the mainstay of home systems. (Just take a look at Intel's TV advertising, which is focusing on using the Pentium in the home market.)

What Is an Office Computer?

An office computer typically differs from other systems because of the different workloads placed on it. Office systems tend to be used more often than other systems, and their successful use is often more critical to the productivity of the entire office. In addition, office computers may or may not include networking capabilities. Although there are exceptions, system components for the office computer typically (or should) consist of the following:

- 386- 486-, or Pentium-based computer
- 340M or larger hard disk
- CD-ROM drive
- 8M RAM
- 14-inch SVGA monitor and graphics card
- dot-matrix, ink-jet, or laser printer

If you haven't already browsed through Chapter 8, "Examining the Hardware You Need for Windows 95," you may want to do that now. As computer technology advances, so do the minimum system requirements. As mentioned earlier, just a few years ago, a seemingly modest 386/33 was the power user's dream machine. Now, the Pentium/133 has taken the lead. If the trend continues, in two years that Pentium will be yesterday's news.

What Is a Network Workstation?

By definition, a network workstation is any computer connected to a network. Further, the workstation specifically uses resources made available through the network. This means that in a client/server network, the client is synonymous with the workstation. In a peer-to-peer network, each peer on the network is a workstation.

When you look at individual workstations on a network, the capabilities of the machine probably don't differ that much from other stand-alone office systems. However, not all workstations are alike. For instance, some workstations are diskless PCs that provide a trouble-free and secure environment. Portable computers can also be considered workstations, even if they aren't connected to the network at all times. Other workstations may be desktop PCs with their own resources that are not shared over the network.

System Requirements to Install Windows 95

Before you install Windows 95, make sure that your computer system is up to the challenge. Few things are more frustrating than not having adequate hardware to install Windows 95—or your favorite application, for that matter.

According to product information, Windows 95 requires a minimum of a 386 processor with 4M of RAM and a 30M hard disk. This minimum will work, but programs (and Windows) will run very slowly using this configuration. You're better off with 8M or 16M of RAM and as big a hard disk as possible.

Next, do you have the appropriate media? You can install either from floppy disks or CD-ROM. Certainly, installing from CD-ROM requires less effort than swapping more than 20 disks over the course of 45 minutes.

Before You Install

Before you actually begin the installation process, consider what will take place. You're about to make some major changes in your computer system and the software that runs it. Because of this, you'll want to perform a few tasks before you even think of running the Setup program. These tasks are as follows:

- Defragment your hard drive
- Back up your system
- Disable your swap file
- Check your disk compression
- Disable your current programs

The following sections describe the reason for each task in a bit more detail, and some sections describe how to perform the task.

Checking Your Media

Windows 95 is available on either floppy disk or CD-ROM. If you have a CD-ROM drive on your system, it is a nice luxury to be able to install from CD-ROM. By doing so, you eliminate the swapping of about 20 disks over the course of 45 minutes. If you need to install Windows 95 on a number of systems in your office, the CD-ROM version is the only cost-effective method of installing the product.

Defragmenting Your Hard Disk

It is always wise to defragment your hard drive, but this becomes even more of a good idea as you're preparing to upgrade your system. A defragmented disk helps ensure that the installation process goes smoothly. With fragmented files, installation could take longer because it takes longer to read files that are scattered all over the disk. Besides, if the files on your hard disk are highly fragmented, Windows 95 will refuse to install until the disk is defragmented.

If you have MS-DOS (or PC DOS) version 6.0 or later, a defrag utility is included with the operating system. If you prefer, there are a number of third-party defragmenting utilities on the market such as *The Norton Utilities* from Symantec, or *PC Tools* from Central Point Software.

Backing Up Your System

As you install Windows 95, you're making a major upgrade to your system. This means that a new operating system is about to reorganize your existing system and overwrite some previously important files. Some files will be deleted and many new ones added. Consequently, it is in your best interest to perform a backup of your entire system. If you don't, you risk losing some information if something goes wrong with the installation process. It is rare to lose data during a Windows 95 installation, but "better safe than sorry."

If you don't want to back up everything, you should at least copy important files to a floppy disk. At a minimum these files would include the following:

- CONFIG.SYS
- AUTOEXEC.BAT
- Data files, such as word processing or spreadsheet documents

Once the files are copied to a disk, make sure you verify that the copy was accurate and that the disk can be read in another machine.

Disabling Your Swap File

If you're upgrading to Windows 95 (and not using the dual-boot feature), you should disable the permanent swap file used by your current version of Windows. If you're an avid Windows user, you may already be familiar with the term *swap file*. This is a special file, created on your hard disk, that serves as a memory overflow area. When a program needs more memory than is currently available, information is stored in the swap file on hard disk until it is needed later. In many ways, the hard disk serves as an extension of the RAM in your system. (With this understanding, you can envision how less RAM can slow down your system by requiring more swap file activity.)

Windows 95 does not use the same permanent swap file technology as Windows 3.*x*. As you learned in Chapter 2, "Under-the-Hood Improvements," the virtual memory manager within Windows 95 (which manages the swap file) has been rewritten entirely. It now uses more dynamic management, which means that the size of the swap file is adjusted, as necessary, to fit the needs of the operating system. Because a different swap file is used, any previous swap file just sits on your hard disk and wastes space.

To disable your permanent swap file in your current version of Windows, follow these steps:

1. Double-click on the Control Panel icon in the Main program group. The Control Panel appears.
2. Double-click on the Enhanced icon in the Control Panel. The Enhanced dialog box appears.
3. Click on the Virtual Memory button in the Enhanced dialog box. The Virtual Memory dialog box appears.
4. Examine the Swapfile Settings area of the Virtual Memory dialog box. If the Type field shows Permanent, click on the Change button. Otherwise, click on Cancel and exit from all dialog boxes. A permanent swap file is not present.
5. In the New Swapfile Settings area, choose None from the Type list box.
6. Click on OK to close the Virtual Memory dialog box.
7. When asked to confirm your change, click on the Yes button.

At this point, you'll need to restart Windows. When you've done so, your permanent swap file is disabled and deleted.

Checking Your Disk Compression

If you use disk compression, you'll want to make sure that it is compatible with Windows 95. The following disk compression utilities are compatible with Windows 95 and are fully supported:

- Microsoft DriveSpace
- Microsoft DoubleSpace
- Stac Electronics Stacker versions 3.0 and 4.*x*
- SuperStor

Windows 95 uses the DriveSpace utility in preference to the other compression methods that Windows 95 recognizes. Windows 95 includes some built-in utilities specifically designed to work with DriveSpace. For instance, the defragmenting and scanning utilities included with Windows 95 have been tuned specifically to work with DriveSpace. If you use a different compression utility, you may need to use whatever utilities are provided with that utility.

The point at which you upgrade to Windows 95 is a great time to decide if you want to switch over to DriveSpace. If you decide that it makes sense for you, then you'll need to decompress your drives before installing Windows 95. Exactly how you decompress depends on the compression utility you're using; you should consult the documentation for your utility to learn how to best do this.

Once you've installed Windows 95, you can use the DriveSpace utility to compress your hard drives. Full information on how to do this is contained in Chapter 10, "Optimizing Your Disk Drives."

Disabling Programs

Earlier versions of DOS relied heavily on TSR (terminate and stay resident) programs to add features to the operating system. Before installing Windows 95, be sure to disable any TSRs you've installed; these can conflict with the setup process. Examples of common TSR programs

are the bill minder program in Quicken and some device drivers such as MOUSE.COM.

If you plan on installing Windows 95 from within your current version of Windows, be sure you close all open windows except for the Program Manager. Open program windows can slow down the installation process, and may stop necessary files from being copied to the hard disk.

Dual-Booting

Many people who are upgrading to Windows 95 want to set up their systems so they can boot to different operating systems. For instance, a user might want to use both OS/2 and Windows 95 at different times. In most office environments, you'll probably want to stay away from dual booting. Such installations are inherently more complex, and they can open up a technical support can of worms. For this reason, most offices do not implement a dual-boot setup for every Tom, Dick, and Mary in the office.

Instead, it is typically "power users" who choose to use dual-booting. By definition, however, these are the users who should need less technical support because they're more aware of the inner workings of their system.

There is one type of dual-boot situation that should be addressed, however. You may want to still be able to boot to your old version of DOS, as well as to Windows 95. Why? Because you'll need this capability if you want to still use an older version of Windows on your system. As an example, if you are a software developer, you may want both types of Windows systems available so you can test your product on both.

The preferred method of installing Windows 95 is to upgrade your old version of Windows to Windows 95. This upgrade ensures that all your settings, applications, and preferences migrate to Windows 95. However, if you're determined to maintain a previous version of Windows

on your computer *in addition to* Windows 95, you can instruct Setup to install Windows 95 to a separate folder instead of overwriting the previous Windows version.

Ultimately, dual-booting enables you to choose which operating system you use to start your system. (More information is provided in Chapter 15, "Taking Control of Windows 95 Startup.") Some people view dual booting as "the best of both worlds." The drawback to dual-booting is that none of your existing Windows 3.1 settings and applications migrate to Windows 95.

The following questions can help you decide which installation method is best for you:

- **Do you want to be able to run Windows 3.1 and Windows 95 (dual-boot)?** If the answer is yes, then you should install Windows 95 to a folder other than C:\WINDOWS. If the answer is no, then you can allow Setup to install to the default folder and upgrade over the top of Windows 3.1.
- **Do you want Windows 95 to migrate (transfer) your existing Windows settings and applications?** If the answer is yes, then allow Setup to install to the default folder and upgrade over the top of Windows 3.1. If the answer is no, then install Windows 95 to a folder other than C:\WINDOWS.
- **Do you want to be able to load MS-DOS as well as Windows 95?** If the answer is yes, then install Windows 95 to a folder other than C:\WINDOWS. If the answer is no, then allow Setup to install to the default folder and upgrade over the top of Windows 3.1.

Installing Windows 95

More than with any previous version, the setup process for Windows 95 is simple and automatic. You only need to answer a few questions, then sit back and relax. Setup presents a wizard to guide you through the steps of installing Windows 95. When prompted, click on the appropriate buttons, typically either Continue or Next.

As a general rule, if you have Windows 3.1 or Windows for Workgroups 3.11 already installed on your system, you should install from within Windows. If you do not have Windows or if you have Windows 3.0 or earlier, you must install from MS-DOS.

Starting Setup from MS-DOS

If you don't have Windows 3.1*x* on your computer, or if you have an older version of Windows, such as 3.0 or earlier, you can install Windows 95 from the DOS prompt. Follow these steps to install from DOS:

1. If you're installing from a CD-ROM, insert the disc in your CD-ROM drive. If you're installing from a floppy, insert the first disk in your disk drive.
2. At the DOS prompt, type **d:\SETUP** and press Enter. (You should replace the letter *d* with the drive letter that represents the drive you used in step 1.) You'll see the following on your screen:

```
Please wait while Setup initializes.

Setup is now going to perform a routine check on your
system.

To continue, press ENTER. To quit Setup, press ESC.
```

3. Press Enter to continue with the setup. The program then runs ScanDisk to check the integrity of your disk drives.
4. When ScanDisk is complete, press X to exit the program.

At this point, a couple of files are copied to your hard drive in preparation for the rest of the setup procedure. Shortly, you'll see the welcome screen, as shown in figure 4.1. From this point forward, Setup is identical for DOS users as it is for Windows users. Click on the Continue button and proceed to step five in the next section to continue with the Windows 95 installation.

Starting Setup from Windows

During the installation phase, Setup detects whether you already have Windows installed and remembers its location. Setup later informs you

where it was found. To install Windows 95 from Windows 3.1 or Windows for Workgroups 3.1*x*, follow these steps:

1. If you're installing from a CD-ROM, insert the disc in your CD-ROM drive. If you're installing from a floppy, insert the first disk in your disk drive.

2. Choose File, Run from Program Manager (not File Manager). This invokes the Run dialog box.

3. Enter **d:\SETUP** in the Command Line text box and click on OK. (You should replace the letter *d* with the drive letter that represents the drive you used in step 1.) In a moment, you see the Windows 95 Setup welcome screen (see figure 4.1). Click on Continue.

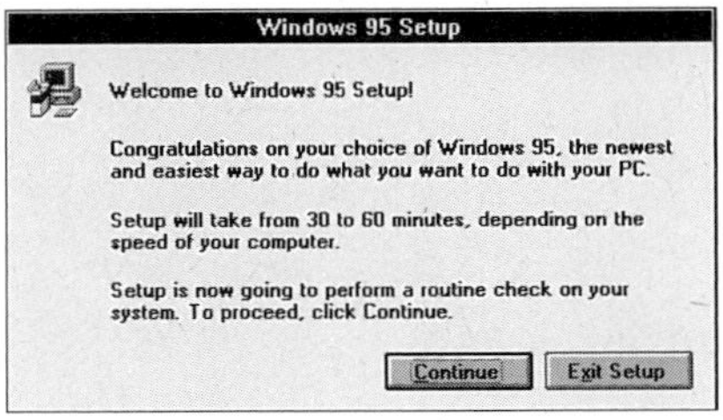

Fig. 4.1 Welcome to Windows 95 Setup.

4. Setup performs a behind-the-scenes ScanDisk. When it is finished, click on Continue. After you do, various files are copied to your hard disk in preparation for the Setup wizard.

5. When you see the software license agreement, read it, then click on Yes.

6. When you see the Setup Wizard shown in figure 4.2, you can see the number of steps required to complete the setup and what will occur. Click on Next.

7. As shown in figure 4.3, you now have the opportunity to specify where Windows 95 will be installed. If you currently have Windows installed and you want to update, you should accept the indicated folder. If you want Windows 95 installed in a different folder for whatever reason (including wanting to dual-boot

instead of upgrade), you should click on Other folder. When you have made your choice, click on the Next button.

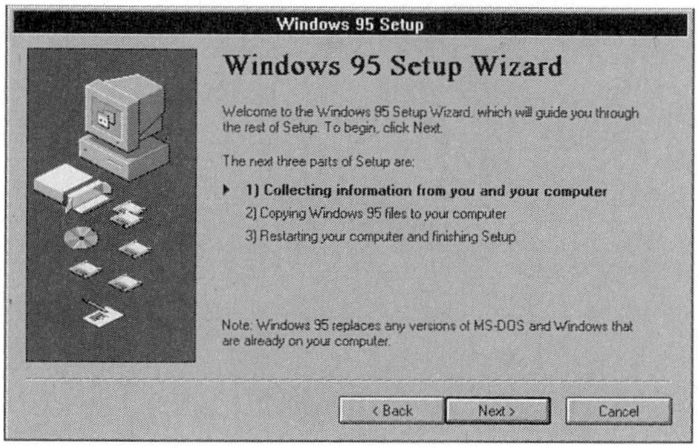

Fig. 4.2 The Setup Wizard outlines what will occur during Setup.

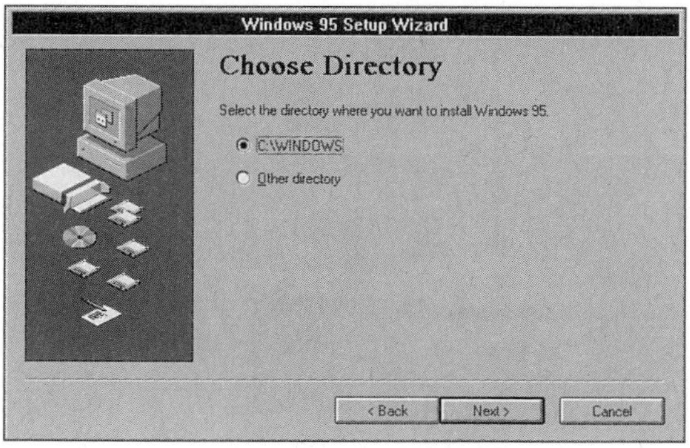

Fig. 4.3 Choose a folder where you want to install Windows 95.

8. If you indicated that you wanted Windows 95 installed in a different folder, you're asked to specify the folder. Pick a folder and click on the Next button.

9. When the Setup Options screen appears (see figure 4.4), choose a setup type. Most home computer users will choose Typical, but if you want to select extra options you can select Custom. (A full discussion of each setup type is found later in this chapter in the section titled, "Choosing a Setup Type.") Make your selection and click on Next.

Fig. 4.4 You can select from four setup types.

10. Enter your name in the User Information screen. You optionally may type the name of your company or organization, too. Click on Next.
11. You'll see the Analyzing Your Computer screen as shown in figure 4.5. If any of the devices are present in your system, and the devices are not Plug-and-Play compatible, choose them and click on Next.

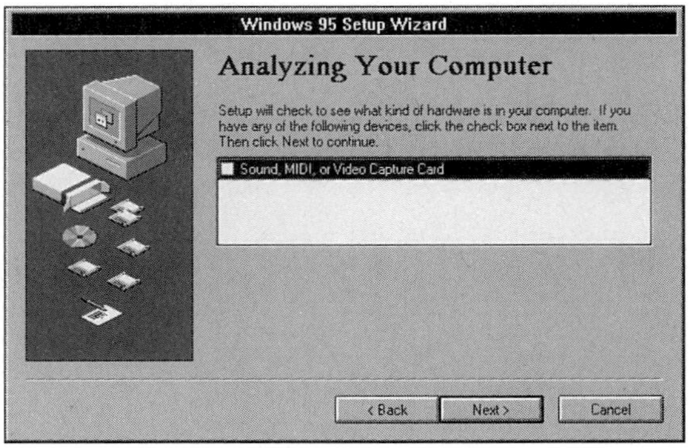

Fig. 4.5 The Analyzing Your Computer screen is used to specify the items present in your computer.

12. Setup now performs a complete hardware analysis, which may take up to five minutes (depending on the speed of your system).

13. After a time you'll see the Windows Components screen. Here you have two choices: you can accept the most common components for your type of installation (this is the recommended default), or you can indicate that you want to modify the components installed. Make your selection and click on Next.

14. If you chose to modify the components installed, you'll see the Select Components screen, as shown in figure 4.6. If you asked Windows to install the most common components, skip to step 16.

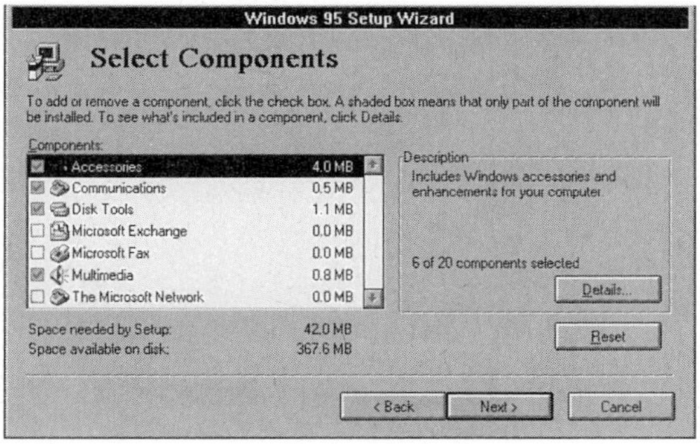

Fig. 4.6 Choose the options you want to install. Grayed entries indicate some components within the group are selected and some are not.

15. Select the options you want installed with Windows 95. If you want more options than are available in the Typical setup, you can pick from this list. Highlight a category and click on Details to choose individual items. To select all items in a component category, highlight it and press the spacebar. Click on Next when you're finished.

16. If your system is not 100 percent Plug-and-Play compatible, Setup may not be able to detect each item by name. If so, you may see the Computer Settings screen that you can safely ignore by clicking on Next. If you want Windows 95 settings to be a little more precise, scroll through the list and change any items marked Unknown to their proper setting. To do so, highlight the item and click on Change. Click on Next when you're finished.

17. Setup next asks if you want a startup disk. Choose Yes (the default) and click on Next. This disk serves as your bootable floppy in case of any future system trouble. Most of the time you'll never need it, but it is a good precaution. For information on how to use this disk, refer to the section titled, "Using the Emergency Startup Disk," later in this chapter.
18. The Setup Wizard displays the second phase of installation—the copying of files. Click on Next.
19. If you chose to create a startup disk, Setup prompts you to insert a disk and click OK. When Windows 95 has completed the disk, remove the floppy, label it clearly, put it in a safe place, and click on OK to continue.
20. Setup then copies the Windows 95 files to your computer; this step takes about 10 minutes. Click on Finish when prompted (see figure 4.7). When you do, the computer restarts and continues to configure Windows 95.

Fig. 4.7 After copying files, Setup is ready to restart your computer.

21. After several minutes of self-configuration, Setup requests your time zone (see figure 4.8). Click on the map to choose the appropriate time zone (or choose from the Time Zone pull-down list) and indicate whether you want to adjust for daylight savings time. Click on Next.

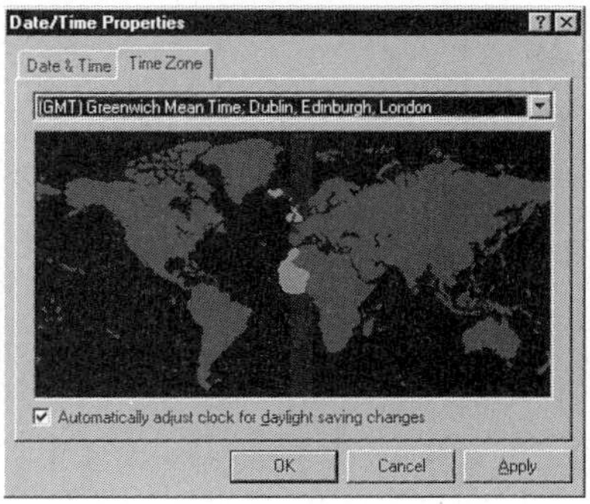

Fig. 4.8 Click on the map to choose your time zone.

22. If you chose to install the communications options, including Microsoft Exchange and Microsoft Fax, the Microsoft Exchange Setup Wizard intervenes, requesting information. For information on setting up Microsoft Exchange and its components, refer to Chapter 32, "Communicating with a Modem."

That's it! You've successfully installed Windows 95. The Welcome dialog box shown in figure 4.9 lets you see what's new in Windows 95. For a quick tour of Windows 95, choose Windows Tour. (The Windows Tour button may not be available if you did not explicitly install the feature.) Click on What's New to find out about the innovations and changes in the Windows interface. Online Registration enables you to dial into Microsoft to register your copy of Windows 95. When you're finished, click on Close. If your installation is unsuccessful, refer to Chapter 6, "Troubleshooting Windows 95 Installation and Startup," for help.

> **Note:** You're not limited to registering Windows 95 with a modem. If you don't have a modem, you can return the registration card provided with your Windows 95 software package.

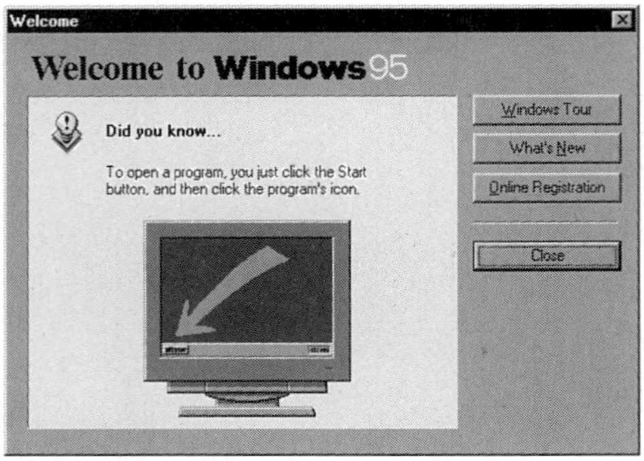

Fig. 4.9 Immediately after you install Windows 95, you see the Welcome dialog box. Choose an option and investigate.

Choosing a Setup Type

In the previous two sections, you learned how to install Windows 95 from start to finish. When performing step nine you learned that the Setup Wizard allows you to indicate what type of installation you want performed. Depending on the type of computer you have and its available resources, including hard disk space (or lack of it), you can select the type of installation you want. Windows 95 offers four distinct setup types—typical, portable, compact, and custom.

Different setup choices require different system resources. The most conservative choice is Compact, then Portable, Typical, and finally Custom. The biggest difference between each option is the number of tools (programs) that the option installs. The following is a quick overview of each installation type:

- **Typical Setup.** This setup type is a common approach for the home computer user, particularly if you have at least 100M of unused hard disk space. The only questions you must answer are to confirm the folder where Windows 95 files are to be installed and to specify whether to create a startup disk.

- **Portable Setup.** If you're a laptop, notebook, or subnotebook owner, this setup type installs the options most appropriate for your type of computer. The options installed with this setup type are geared toward a mobile computer user, basically installing fewer of the "bells and whistles" that accompany a typical setup and adding features that enhance portable computing.
- **Compact Setup.** This setup type installs only the bare essential files necessary to run Windows 95—a minimal installation. This is ideal for users with a small hard disk (less than 80M), and allows users to forego most of the Windows 95 options. Ultimately, this may save about 36M of disk space as opposed to a full Windows 95 installation.
- **Custom Setup.** This setup type lets you choose any or all options available in Windows 95. It is similar to walking through a delicatessen—you pick the pieces and parts you want included in your Windows 95 system. This type of setup is recommended for experienced users who want to control various elements of Windows 95 Setup.

The files installed on your hard drive will vary, depending on the type of setup you choose. Table 4.1 shows the different Windows 95 components that can be installed for each type of limited setup (typical, portable, and compact).

Table 4.1 How Windows 95 Components Are Installed for the Limited Setup Options

Component	Typical	Portable	Compact
Audio Compression	✓	✓	
Blank Screen Saver	✓		
Briefcase		✓	
Calculator	✓		
CD Player	✓	✓	
Disk Defragmenter	✓	✓	✓

continues

Table 4.1 Continued

Component	Typical	Portable	Compact
Document Templates	✓		
DriveSpace	✓	✓	✓
HyperTerminal	✓	✓	
Media Player	✓		
Notepad	✓	✓	✓
Object Packager	✓		
Paint	✓		
Phone Dialer	✓	✓	
Quick View	✓	✓	
ScanDisk	✓	✓	✓
Scrolling Marquee Screen Saver	✓		
Sound Recorder	✓		
Video Compression	✓	✓	
Volume Control	✓		
WordPad	✓		

If you choose the custom setup type, then you can install any or all of the Windows 95 components. Besides those that can be installed with one of the limited setups (as detailed in Table 4.1), there are a wide variety of other components you can choose:

- **Accessibility Options.** A collection of Control Panel tools designed to help people who are physically impaired.
- **Backup.** A disk tool used to back up your hard drive to floppy disks or tapes.
- **Character Map.** An accessory that allows you to access the entire range of Windows 95 characters. You can use Character Map to insert symbols and characters into documents created by other programs.

- **Clipboard Viewer.** An accessory that allows you to view the contents of the Clipboard, and to manage a Clipbook over the network.
- **Curves and Colors Screen Saver.** A screen saver you can use to customize your desktop.
- **Dial-Up Networking.** An accessory that allows you to connect with remote networks, such as the Internet.
- **Direct Cable Connection.** An accessory that allows two computers to be connected through a serial cable.
- **Flying Through Space Screen Saver.** A screen saver you can use to customize your desktop.
- **Games.** Five games that can be used for relaxation. Included are FreeCell, Hearts, Minesweeper, Party Line, and Solitaire.
- **Jungle Sound Scheme.** A collection of related sounds that can be assigned to different system events.
- **Microsoft Exchange.** A communications management accessory that combines e-mail and fax capabilities.
- **Microsoft Fax.** The fax portion of Microsoft Exchange (which is required for this option to be installed).
- **Microsoft Network.** The tools necessary to connect with the new Microsoft Network.
- **Mouse Pointers.** A collection of animated and nonanimated pointers that can be assigned to different mouse activities.
- **Multi-Language Support.** The files necessary to implement the international features of Windows 95.
- **Musica Sound Scheme.** A collection of related sounds that can be assigned to different system events.
- **Mystify Your Mind Screen Saver.** A screen saver you can use to customize your desktop.

- **Nature Sound Scheme.** A collection of related sounds that can be assigned to different system events.
- **NetWatcher.** A system tool that allows you to monitor the performance of the network.
- **Online User's Guide.** Tutorial information on how to use Widows 95.
- **Robotz Sound Scheme.** A collection of related sounds that can be assigned to different system events.
- **Sound and Video Clips.** Sample audio and video multimedia files that can be used with the Media Player accessory.
- **System Monitor.** A system tool used to troubleshoot and refine the performance of Windows 95.
- **System Resource Meter.** A system tool used to monitor the use of your system resources.
- **Utopia Sound Scheme.** A collection of related sounds that can be assigned to different system events.
- **Wallpaper.** Various bitmapped graphics files that can be used to customize your desktop.
- **Windows 95 Tour.** A guided on-screen tour of the newest features of Windows 95. (Available only on the CD-ROM version of Windows 95.)

> **Note:** Windows 95 automatically installs four tools; there is no way to not install them. These tools are the Disk Defragmenter, DriveSpace, ScanDisk, and Notepad.

Remember, you can always add or remove options after Windows 95 is installed on your computer. For information on adding or removing options, refer to Appendix A, "Adding and Removing Windows 95 Components."

Choosing a Network Installation

There are countless network configurations and types that will ultimately challenge an upgrade to Windows 95. But, take heart—it's not as bad as it seems, particularly if you know what to expect and can plan in advance. Windows Setup is very flexible, whether you're installing on a network as small as two PCs or as large as 500 workstations. Each network environment requires a different approach to achieve a (relatively) quick, yet painless, installation.

Generally, there are two ways you can install Windows 95 on your network workstation:

- Connect to the network server and run Setup from a script (automated server-based setup).
- Perform a standard setup on individual workstations and connect manually to the network.

Method number one is the quickest and simplest route to pursue for networks with more than a few workstations, mainly because Setup can be automated with special INF batch (script) files. If you choose to install Windows 95 in this way, proceed to the following section, "Installing on a Client/Server Network."

The second method requires you to specify each setup option just as if you were installing on a stand-alone PC. The section "Performing a Standard Setup," later in this chapter, discusses how to perform a standard setup and afterward connect manually to the network.

Installing on a Client/Server Network

Installing Windows 95 on a client/server network is considerably different than a peer-to-peer network or standard setup. The latter two require you to run Setup from the PC and manually respond to the Setup prompts. In a client/server network, however, files must be copied in a special manner from the CD-ROM to the server's hard disk before installation can take place. This is mainly because, for some

workstations, Windows 95 system files are shared either to save space on the workstation or to protect system integrity. Therefore, running Setup from the CD-ROM will not work.

Installation for a workstation can be handled from either the server or the client PC. Depending on the network configuration, an administrator can set up network workstations in a number of ways:

- Setup requires user response to all questions
- Setup is partially automated (minimal user interaction)
- Setup is completely automated (an unattended or *push* installation)

In any case, the administrator installs Windows 95 files on the server and then initiates the Setup command. This command can be issued from either the client workstation or from a special script created by the administrator. This type of arrangement gives the administrator complete control over how Windows 95 is installed. In addition, the ability to automate the setup procedure through scripts saves a great deal of time over installing Windows 95 on each PC one at a time.

To install Windows 95 on a workstation that is part of a client/server network, you must do the following:

- Run server-based Setup on the server.
- Define home folders for shared files, if necessary.
- Create batch scripts, if necessary.
- Run Setup from the workstation or through a batch script.

The next several sections explain each of these steps.

Running a Server-Based Setup

Before anything else can occur, the Windows 95 files must be copied to the server. Bear in mind that this does not, in itself, install Windows 95. Rather, it creates a location to which Setup (when run from a remote workstation) can look for the necessary installation files.

To give the administrator maximum flexibility and control, server-based Setup copies the files into a folder you specify. Within that folder, several folder hierarchies are constructed to mimic a real Windows 95 installation. This, in essence, serves as the installation files for the workstation. To copy Windows 95 files to the server, follow these steps:

1. Insert the Windows 95 CD-ROM in the CD-ROM drive that can be accessed from the server.
2. From the server, invoke the Run command. Windows NT users do this by choosing Run from the File menu. Windows 95 users select Run from the Start menu.
3. Click on Browse and change to the CD-ROM drive used in step 1. Navigate to the folder admin\nettools\netsetup and type **netsetup.** Click on OK.
4. The Server Based Setup dialog box appears, as shown in figure 4.10. Click on Set Path and provide a path on the server to which the Windows 95 files can be copied. Click on OK.

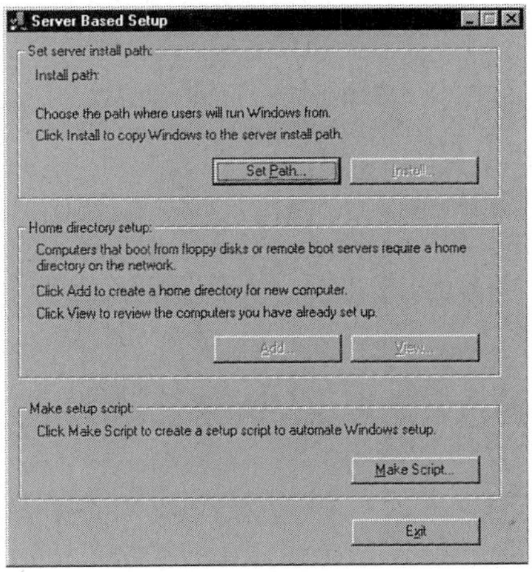

Fig. 4.10 Server-based Setup is the first step in performing a workstation installation.

5. Click on Install. This opens the Source Path dialog box (see figure 4.11) where you define *how* to copy the Windows 95 files to the path defined in step 4.

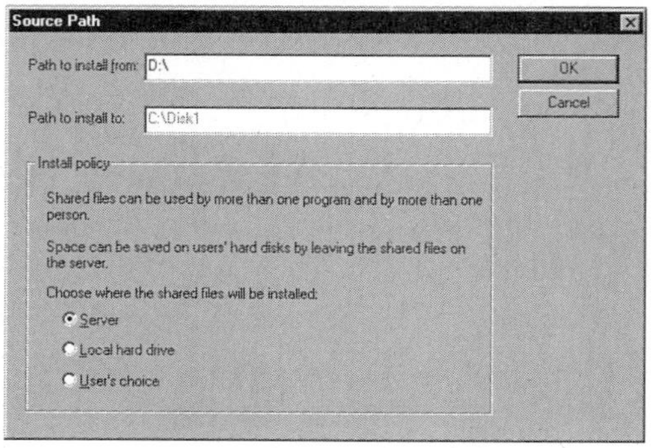

Fig. 4.11 Specify the source and destination of the Windows 95 files in this dialog box.

6. In the field labeled Path to install from, enter the drive letter assigned to the CD-ROM drive you used in step 1. For instance, you might use a location such as D:\ if the CD-ROM drive is drive D.

7. Specify the sharing properties of the files by selecting Server, Local hard drive, or User's choice. This determines how files are installed when a user runs Setup from the workstation. Keeping most files on the server saves space on the workstation, while installing the files on the workstation's local hard disk gives the user more flexibility. Click on OK to continue.

> **Tip:** If you have adequate hard disk resources on your workstations, you might want to always use the Local hard drive option. This cuts down on the amount of information that must be transferred over the network and results in faster response times at the local workstation.

8. To create an MSBATCH.INF batch script for you, click on Create Default to invoke the Policy Editor dialog box. Refer to the section "Creating a Batch Script" (later in this chapter) to learn to use the Policy Editor to create a batch script. If you select Don't Create Default, this dialog box does not appear and a script is not created.

If you choose Don't Create Default, server-based Setup begins copying the Windows 95 files to the folder you specified. Once these are copied, you can then perform the installation process for the workstation. However, if you set up any workstations to use shared files, such as when you keep most Windows 95 system files on the server, you must define the home folders that will be used by Windows after it is set up on the workstation.

Defining Home Directories for Shared Files

Once the Windows 95 files are copied to your computer via server-based Setup, you can define specific folders. As you learned earlier, an administrator can install Windows 95 on a workstation but retain most of the system files on the server in "shared" folders. Ultimately, the user really can't tell, yet the administrator can exercise firm control over the network.

To assign a home folder, click on Add in the Server Based Setup dialog box. In the Set Up Machine dialog box (see figure 4.12), you have a choice between defining a single workstation or many workstations. To set up a single machine, choose Setup one machine and enter the computer's name as you might see it on the network, then insert the UNC (Universal Naming Convention) of the path to be used as the computer's home folder.

To save time, the administrator can define a large number of machines at one time by creating a file that contains a list of machines to be processed. The file is a text file, created with a program such as Notepad. Each line in the file describes a single computer system, with the computer name separated from the UNC path for the computer's home folder, in this manner:

```
Marty's 486, \\OfficeServer\C\Marty
```

To indicate that Setup should use this file, choose Setup multiple machines and provide the name of the text file you just created. When you're finished specifying either a single machine or a text file, click on OK.

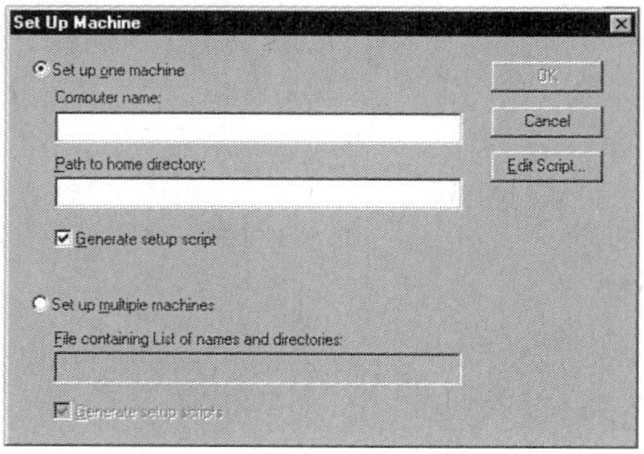

Fig. 4.12 The Home Directory Setup area becomes accessible after you copy Windows files to the server.

Creating a Batch Script

Installing Windows 95 on many computers throughout a network would be a nightmare without the ability to automate the process. A batch script allows you to specify in advance what responses Windows Setup will accept. This way you can invoke Setup on a workstation and effectively walk away from it—a big time-saver.

As Setup begins, it looks for a default batch script called MSBATCH.INF. However, you can specify any batch file you want as a setup parameter. For example, if you create a unique script for three workstations in a particular office, you would type the following at the command line prompt, or in the Run dialog box (accessed from the Start menu):

```
setup msbatch.inf.
```

If a script is differently named, such as station1.inf, provide that in place of MSBATCH.INF. Setup then executes the instructions in the batch script.

What is a batch script? A script is a plain text file consisting of nothing more than predefined responses to the questions asked by Setup. These responses are grouped in sections, similar to what you might find in the old Windows INI files. Individual parameters are followed by a specific value or description depending on the parameter type. For instance, the following are a few lines from a sample batch script:

```
[Setup]
Express=0                                  ; allows user input
InstallType=1                              ; Typical Setup
EBD=1                                      ; create startup disk
InstallDir=C:\WINDOWS
Verify=0
Detection=1
PenWinWarning=1
ProductID=999999999

[NameAndOrg]
Name="Martin R. Wyatt"
Org="Discovery Computing Inc."
Display=1           ; Display User Information dialog box

[OptionalComponents]
"Accessories"=1
"Communications"=1
"Disk Tools"=1
"Multimedia"=1
"Screen Savers"=1
"Disk compression tools"=1
"Paint"=1
```

In step 7 of the section "Running Server-Based Setup," you learned that clicking Create Default invokes the Policy Editor. Although you aren't really editing a policy (POL) file, you use the same interface to make script creation quick and simple. As you can see in figure 4.13, you specify which items you want included in the batch script by double-clicking on a section, such as Setup options, and choosing which parameters should be automated. When you enable a parameter, you must specify a value in the Settings for Automated Install near the bottom of the editing window. When you're finished, click on OK. This saves the batch script as msbatch.inf—the default batch script Setup expects when you run Setup from a workstation. You can later rename and edit this script file by using a program such as Notepad.

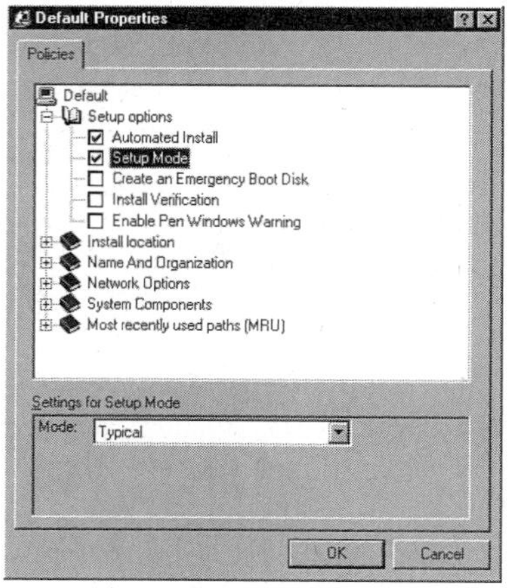

Fig. 4.13 Creating a batch script is as easy as clicking on options.

Granted, this isn't the only way you can create a script, but it's a good way to create your first one. This way, you can choose from all available elements to ensure that the script is complete with correct parameters and corresponding values. Later, you can create scripts with a simple text editor, such as Notepad, or you can modify existing scripts to suit a particular installation. Once the script is completed, you can begin the workstation setup.

Running Setup from a Workstation

Once you've completed the NetSetup installation of Windows 95 files on the server, you're prepared to run Setup. To do so, follow these steps:

1. At the workstation, log on to the network and connect to the server
2. Select the shared folder that contains the Windows 95 setup files.
3. From the command prompt type **setup**. If you're using a batch script you must instead type **setup msbatch.inf**, where msbatch.inf is the name of the script you previously created.

If the setup uses a batch script you created, Windows 95 will install with those parameters. Depending on the script's options, you may be required to respond to various questions Setup throws at you.

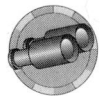

> **Note:** If a script named msbatch.inf exists, Setup will use it by default unless you specify the script to use.

Running Setup from the Server

Instead of formally running Setup from the workstation, the administrator can customize the batch scripts to automatically install Windows 95 on any number of remote workstations. Typically, this is beneficial if you're upgrading a large number of workstations, such as 50 or more. Of course, this can't occur magically during the night when the workstations are turned off or disconnected from the network. In actuality, this automated installation is automatic for the administrator, and depending on the batch script, is mostly automatic for the user.

For instance, the administrator may create a special logon script that triggers the setup script when the user logs on to the network. Therefore, the following circumstances must occur before an automated, or *push,* installation will work:

- The workstation must be on and connected to the network
- A setup script must exist for that workstation
- A logon script must also exist for that workstation

The logon script itself varies according to the network in place and the permissions and resources available to the user. For example, to upgrade Windows for Workgroups, you must create an empty, one-time Startup group with the Setup command as an icon inside it, then copy that STARTUP.GRP to the shared folder that the workstation accesses. Follow these steps to perform this procedure:

1. Modify the MSBATCH.INF file to ensure a one-time upgrade by adding the following sections to the file:

```
[install]
renfiles=replace.startup.grp

[replace.startup.grp]
startup.grp, startup.sav

[destinationdirs]
replace.startup.grp=10
```

2. Create an empty Startup group and place a new icon inside it that runs Setup off the server. In the Command Line field for Setup, enter the SETUP command that is valid for the workstation, followed by the batch script, if any. The following is an example:

```
E:\SETUP E:\msbatch.inf.
```

3. Place the STARTUP.GRP file you just created in the shared folder on the server used by the workstation for the current version of Windows. Thus, if the workstation is running Windows for Workgroups and accesses a shared folder on the server, that is the folder in which the special Startup group file would be placed.

4. Delete the Startup group file from your computer after copying it to the server.

Now, when the user logs in to Windows for Workgroups, the new, special Startup group icon is opened and the Setup program is executed. When Setup is processing the commands in MSBATCH.INF, the sections you added will modify the Startup section of Windows 95 so that the Setup program is not run again.

Using Novell NetWare Servers

You learned in previous sections of this chapter how to place Windows 95's files on a server so that you can in turn install or run Windows 95 from that server. Because the networks in many companies include file servers that run Novell NetWare, you will likely not be placing your Windows 95 files on a file server running Novell NetWare. This section details the steps you follow to prepare to place Windows 95's files on a

Novell NetWare server. You also learn how to enable a Windows 95 workstation to log in to a NetWare server and how to assign drive letters to NetWare disk volumes.

When you prepare to place Windows 95's files on a server, you have to perform several preparatory steps:

- Create the folder or folders that will store the Windows 95 files
- Grant appropriate NetWare rights to the users who need to access those files
- Optionally use NetWare login scripts to automatically assign drive letters to the server-based Windows 95 folders

You learn about these steps in the following sections.

Limitations with a NetWare Server

Earlier in this chapter, you read about the benefits and liabilities of using Windows 95 from a server. When you share Windows 95's program files from a Novell NetWare server, there is another limitation to consider. Running Windows 95 from a server limits your choices for network card drivers and network clients.

What is the reason for this limitation? The situation is not unlike the age-old question: "Which came first, the chicken or the egg?" Because you have to log in to your server before starting Windows 95's graphical interface, you cannot use Windows 95's built-in 32-bit virtual network card drivers or clients. You must instead use DOS-compatible network card drivers and client software. If you're running Windows 95 from a Novell NetWare server, you'd typically need to load NetWare's ODI drivers and requester software in your workstation's AUTOEXEC.BAT file. You learn how to modify this file later in this section.

Creating Directories on a NetWare Server

Creating a folder on a NetWare server is just like creating a folder on a local hard disk, except that you have to log in to the server first and you

also have to have sufficient rights to create the folder. Once you've logged in to the appropriate server and you've located the disk volume on which you wish to create the folder, you can use your favorite method to create the folder. With Windows 95, for example, you can use the Windows Explorer to create a folder by choosing File New Folder from the menu. With Windows 3.1*x*, you can use the File Manager's File Create Directory menu option, or, if you choose to be quaintly traditional, you can use the MD command from the DOS prompt.

Setting the Appropriate Access Levels

Once the required folders are created, you need to grant the appropriate rights, a step that requires a little forethought. If you're setting access levels for a Windows 95 installation folder, you probably want to limit to a chosen few the ability to add, delete, or modify the files in that folder. Users who will be installing Windows 95 from the folder should have the ability to use the files but not change them in any way.

The same sort of access applies for the folder from which users run a shared copy of Windows 95. Most users should have read-only access to the shared Windows 95 files, while the trusted few who are responsible for updating and maintaining the shared files should have the ability to make changes.

In those cases where users share a server-based copy of Windows 95 and also use server-based home folders to store their personal Windows configuration files, you also have to decide what access levels to provide for these home folders. In this situation, each user has a personal home folder, and should have full access to the files in that home folder.

The following table shows the NetWare rights that provide the access levels appropriate for the types of Windows 95 folders that you can create on a server.

Table 4.2 Netware Access Rights Guidelines

Directory Type	NetWare Rights to Grant for Normal Users	NetWare Rights to Grant for Users Who Manage the Folder
Shared installation files	READ, FILE SCAN	READ, WRITE, CREATE DELETE, MODIFY, FILE SCAN
Shared copy of Windows 95	READ, FILE SCAN	READ, WRITE, CREATE DELETE, MODIFY, FILE SCAN
Home folder for personal configuration files	READ, WRITE, CREATE, DELETE, MODIFY, FILE SCAN for personal home folder	READ, WRITE, CREATE DELETE, MODIFY, FILE SCAN for all home folders

Assigning Drive Letters Using Login Scripts

If you're going to provide the Windows 95 installation files on a server so that users can install Windows 95 from the network, you can make the installation process more convenient by automatically assigning a drive letter to the Windows 95 installation folder for users as they log in. You encounter a similar situation when the users on your network use a shared server-based copy of Windows 95. Those users need to have a drive letter assigned to the shared Windows 95 folder before they can run Windows 95. With Novell NetWare, you can use login scripts to create drive letters automatically at login time.

Providing a Drive Letter for the Installation Directory

You can include the following command in the server's system login script to automatically assign drive J to a Windows 95 installation folder called WIN95INS on the SYS disk volume of a server named SERV1:

```
MAP J:=SERV1/SYS:WIN95INS
```

When you place this command in the system login script (if you're using NetWare 3.*x* servers) in each user's container login script (if you're using NetWare 4.*x*), drive J is automatically assigned to the WIN95INS folder for each user at login time.

If you want to add a touch of elegance, you can also display a notice for each user that describes how to start the Windows 95 installation process. If you want to display the following login notice:

```
Windows 95 is now available for installation from the
network. Run the SETUP command from drive J to install
Windows 95 on your PC.
include these additional commands in the system login script:
WRITE "Windows 95 is now available for installation from the"
WRITE "network. Run the SETUP command from drive J to install"
WRITE "Windows 95 on your PC."

PAUSE
```

(see your NetWare reference manuals for information about creating and editing login scripts.)

Providing a Drive Letter for a Shared Copy of Windows 95

You can use similar techniques to create the proper drive letter assignments for users who need to share a copy of Windows 95. Each user who runs Windows 95 from a NetWare server must have a drive letter assigned to the folder that stores the Windows 95 program files. That drive letter also must be a *search drive*, which means that the files in the folder assigned to the drive letter are part of the PC's search path. (You can run an executable file in a search path folder even though the folder is not your current default folder.)

Place the following command in your login script to make the WIN95SH folder the first drive in your PC's search path:

```
MAP INS S1:=SERV1/SYS:WIN95SH
```

Notice that you follow the MAP command by INS (which stands for INSERT and means that the drive letter is added to the current list of

search drives) and S1 (*s* stands for SEARCH and *1* indicates that you want the folder to be placed first in the search order—set this to any number from 1 to 16 to specify the place in the search order).

For complete details about assigning drive letters in login scripts, refer to your NetWare documentation.

Connecting to the Server

If you're running Windows 95 from a NetWare server, you must be sure that your PC's AUTOEXEC.BAT file connects you to the server before you start Windows 95's graphical interface. The following extract from a typical AUTOEXEC.BAT file shows the commands you use to load NetWare's ODI drivers and VLM requester and to then log in to the server:

```
;load ODI drivers
LSL
NE2000
IPXODI
;load VLM requester
VLM
;execute LOGIN command
F:
LOGIN
```

(See your NetWare documentation for complete details about using the ODI network card drivers, the VLM requester, and the LOGIN command.)

After You Install

Once you complete your Windows 95 installation, and if you have the CD-ROM version of Windows 95, be sure to take the Windows Tour. (This assumes, of course, that you selected an installation option in which the Windows Tour was installed.) It takes only a couple of minutes and introduces you to the new concepts you'll encounter by using this operating system.

In addition, you should run the ScanDisk utility to verify that all the files on your hard disk are intact. This also protects against any potential disk problems that might crop up. To start ScanDisk, follow these steps:

1. Select the Programs option from the Start menu.
2. Choose Accessories from the Programs menu.
3. Choose System Tools from the Accessories menu.
4. Choose ScanDisk from the System Tools menu.

When the program starts, choose the hard disk you want to scan and click on Start. For more information on using ScanDisk, refer to Chapter 10, "Optimizing Your Disk Drives."

Installation Problems

A nice feature of the Windows 95 Setup is that if something interrupts the installation, such as the power goes out, the hardware detection phase fails, or you intentionally cancel Setup, you can run Setup again and pick up where you left off. Setup calls it *Safe Recovery.*

In the event that you encounter a problem during installation, the Safe Recovery mode of setup is invoked the next time you attempt installation (see figure 4.14). When this appears, choose Use Safe Recovery and click Next. Setup proceeds as if nothing had happened. This is possible because Setup maintains special files during the setup process to guard against such events.

Additional information on how to overcome installation problems is covered in Chapter 6, "Troubleshooting Windows 95 Installation and Startup."

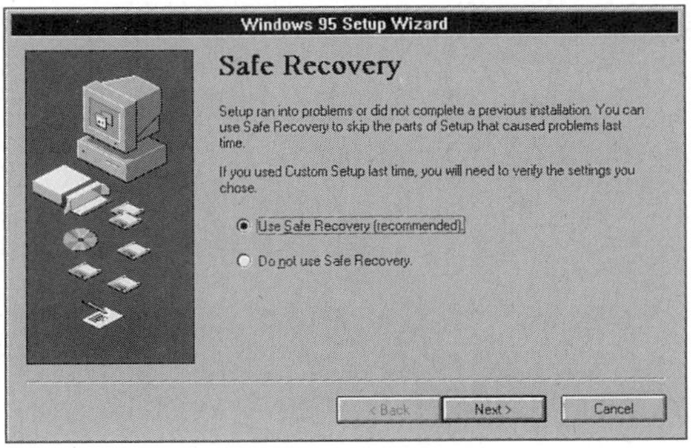

Fig. 4.14 Safe Recovery lets you salvage an aborted installation.

Using the Emergency Startup Disk

When you install Windows 95, you have the option to create a startup disk. This disk is nothing more than a Windows 95 boot disk with the basic system files and other programs such as the Registry Editor, disk utilities, and other useful files. Should your computer ever get corrupted and not boot properly, Windows 95 advises you and starts in a special "safe" mode. It is rare that you would need the startup disk, but it's available just in case of catastrophe.

For more information on the different Windows 95 startup modes and how you can troubleshoot a maligned system, refer to Chapter 6, "Troubleshooting Windows 95 Installation and Startup."

Changing Your Windows Configuration

If you've ever accidentally deleted an important system file in a previous version of Windows, you typically had one solution—reinstall Windows. Of course, if you knew the exact name of the file you deleted, you could copy it from the distribution disks and use the EXPAND command to decompress it, but that required knowing its compressed name and its location on your system.

Fortunately, Windows 95 resolves this dilemma. There is no real need to reinstall Windows 95 (unless you delete a substantial portion of the system files). System components can be reinstalled by doing the following:

1. Double-click on the Add/Remove Programs applet in the Control Panel.
2. Choose the Windows Setup tab.
3. Highlight and select any or all components and options you want to reinstall (or remove).
4. Click on OK.

Once you click on OK, Windows prompts you to shut down the computer. Confirm this action and Windows 95 will shut down and launch as normal. Additional information on adding and removing components is found in Appendix A, "Adding and Removing Windows 95 Components."

KILLER 5 WINDOWS 95

Installing Windows 95 on a Laptop

by Allen L. Wyatt

More and more, people on the road are using portable computers, particularly since they pack the same punch and carry the same load as a desktop computer. However, there are distinct differences between the two, which are mainly due to the compromises in technology made to optimize space.

As Windows 95 has evolved, the needs of the portable computer user have been kept in mind. Similar to its ability to easily adapt to the office computer user, Windows 95 makes portable computing painless. It has built-in features that integrate it with a remote network (if applicable) and accepts common features found on most laptops, notebooks, and subnotebook computers today.

Since networking is integral to the operating system itself, Windows 95 includes features that allow a portable computer user to dial into a remote network. Information can then be transferred to the portable (and vice versa), so that the user can stay in touch. Other

improvements, such as deferred printing, file synchronization, and hot docking support, make Windows 95 a truly productive operating system for anybody on the road.

In addition to learning how to install Windows 95 on a portable computer, this chapter discusses the following topics:

- What to do before and after installation
- What setup type you should choose
- How to upgrade from a previous version of Windows
- Configuring your system for dual-booting between Windows 3.X and Windows 95
- Special Windows 95 features that are unique to portable computers

What Is a Portable Computer?

A portable computer is any unit designed to be easily moved from place to place and is primarily used by people on the go. The size and weight of portable computers vary, and their names are determined by their physical dimensions: subnotebooks are smallest, notebooks a bit larger, laptops larger still, and "luggables" are the largest.

Although it may act like a desktop computer, the portable differs from other systems simply because of size limitations. Manufacturers have incorporated proprietary designs and features into their units and, depending on the model you use, each portable may react differently with Windows 95. The system of a portable computer that is going to run Windows 95 should consist of the following components:

- 386-, 486-, or Pentium-based computer
- 170M or larger hard disk
- 4M RAM

- Dual-scan monochrome or color display
- PCMCIA port or internal modem

If you haven't already browsed through Chapter 8, "Examining the Hardware You Need for Windows 95," you may want to do that now. As computer technology advances, so do the minimum system requirements. The now modest 386 running at 33 MHz was, just a few years ago, the portable user's dream machine. As of this writing, the Pentium has taken a stronghold with CPU speeds of up to 133 MHz in desktop units and up to 90 MHz in portables. If the trend continues, in two years the Pentium will be yesterday's news.

System Requirements to Install Windows 95

According to product information, Windows 95 requires a minimum of a 386 processor with 4M of RAM and a 30M hard disk. This minimum will work, but programs (and Windows) will run very slowly. For a truly productive machine, you are better off with a system that has more resources (disk and memory) and a faster CPU. That is why the definition of a portable system in the previous section reflects higher requirements than the Windows 95 minimum system requirements.

For your system, you're better off with 8M or 16M of RAM and as big a hard disk as possible. (Even an 850M hard drive can be advantageous for the portable computer user.) The cost of disk drives has dropped to the point where you can specify huge drives at previously unheard of prices. In addition, a CD-ROM is a big plus for installing Windows 95—even on a portable.

Windows 95 readily supports PCMCIA cards, which are a feature in most portable computers. However, some older PCMCIA implementations may not be supported and may instantly become obsolete. (The newer, faster 32-bit elements in Windows 95 make this a possibility.) If

you find yourself in this boat, you may want to see if you can either upgrade your system or find Windows 95 PCMCIA support from a third-party source, such as the manufacturer of your system.

Before You Install

Before you install Windows 95 on your portable computer, consider how you will use it to be most productive. Will the computer be networked with one or more Windows 95 computers? Do you want to share information while on the road? How and when will a printer be connected? Whatever your plan, Windows 95 is quite flexible in how it is implemented and is tolerant of any last-minute changes, such as inserting a PCMCIA modem or network card. But it is wise to plan in advance to save yourself from running around later.

In order to make your upgrade to Windows 95 as painless as possible, you will want to perform a few tasks before you even think of running the Setup program. These tasks are:

- Check your media
- Defragment your hard drive
- Back up your system
- Disable your swap file
- Check your disk compression
- Disable your current programs

The following sections describe the reason for each task, and some sections describe how to perform the task.

Checking Your Media

Windows 95 is available either on floppy disk or on CD-ROM. If you have a CD-ROM drive available for your system, it is a nice luxury to be able to install from CD-ROM. By doing so, you eliminate the need to swap about 20 disks during the course of an hour.

Defragmenting Your Hard Disk

It is always wise to periodically defragment your hard drive, but this becomes even more of a good idea as you are preparing to upgrade your system. A defragmented disk helps ensure that the installation process goes smoothly. With fragmented files, installation could take longer simply because it takes longer to read files that are scattered all over the disk. Besides, if the files on your hard disk are highly fragmented, Windows 95 will refuse to install until you remedy the situation.

If you have MS-DOS (or PC DOS) version 6.0 or later, you can use the defrag utility included with your operating system to defragment your hard disk. If you prefer, you can turn to any one of several third-party programs on the market, such as Symantec's The Norton Utilities or PC Tools from Central Point Software.

Backing Up Your System

As you install Windows 95, you are making a major upgrade to operating your system. This means that a new system is reorganizing your existing system and overwriting previously important files. Some files are deleted and many new ones are added. It is in your best interests to perform a backup of your entire system. If you don't, you'll risk losing some information if something goes wrong with the installation process. It is rare to lose data during a Windows 95 installation, but "better safe than sorry."

If you don't want to back up everything, you should at least copy important files to a floppy disk, including:

- CONFIG.SYS
- AUTOEXEC.BAT
- Data files, such as word processing or spreadsheet documents

Once the files are copied to a disk, make sure you verify that the copy was accurate and that the disk can be read by another machine.

Disabling Your Swap File

If you are upgrading to Windows 95 and not using the dual-boot feature, you should disable the permanent swap file used by your current version of Windows. If you're an avid Windows user, you may already be familiar with the term swap file. This is a special file created on your hard disk that serves as a memory overflow area. When a program needs more memory than is currently available, information is stored in the swap file on your hard disk until the information is needed. In many ways, the hard disk serves as an extension of the RAM in your system. (With this understanding, you can envision how less RAM can slow down your system by requiring more swap-file activity.)

Windows 95 does not use the same permanent swap-file technology as Windows 3.x. As you learned in Chapter 2, "Under-the-Hood Improvements," the virtual memory manager within Windows 95 (which manages the swap file) has been rewritten entirely. It now uses more dynamic management, which means the size of the swap file is adjusted, as necessary, to fit the needs of the operating system. Since a new swap file is used, any old swap file just sits on your hard disk and wastes space.

To disable your permanent swap file in your current version of Windows, follow these steps:

1. Double-click on the Control Panel icon in the Main program group. The Control Panel appears.
2. Double-click on the Enhanced icon in the Control Panel. The Enhanced dialog box appears.
3. Click on the Virtual Memory button in the Enhanced dialog box. The Virtual Memory dialog box appears.
4. Examine the Swap File Settings area of the Virtual Memory dialog box. If the Type field shows Permanent, click on the Change button. Otherwise, click Cancel and exit all dialog boxes. A permanent swap file is not present.

5. In the New Swap File Settings area, choose None from the Type list box.
6. Click on OK to close the Virtual Memory dialog box.
7. When asked to confirm your change, click on the Yes button.

At this point, you'll need to restart Windows. When this has been done, your permanent swap file is disabled and deleted.

Checking Your Disk Compression

If you use disk compression software—as many portable owners do—you'll want to make sure it is compatible with Windows 95. The following disk compression utilities are compatible with Windows 95 and are fully supported:

- Microsoft DriveSpace
- Microsoft DoubleSpace
- Stac Electronics Stacker versions 3.0 and 4.x
- SuperStor

Although Windows 95 recognizes several compression utilities, it includes some built-in utilities that are specifically designed to work with Microsoft DriveSpace. For example, the defragmenting and scanning utilities included with Windows 95 have been tuned specifically to work with DriveSpace. If you use a different compression program, you may not be able to take advantage of Windows' built-in utilities.

The best time to consider switching from the compression program you are now using to DriveSpace is when you upgrade to Windows 95. If you decide it makes sense for you to switch, then you will need to decompress your drives prior to installing Windows 95. Consult your utility's documentation to learn how to best decompress your files.

Once you have installed Windows 95, you can use DriveSpace to compress your hard drives. Full information on how to do this is contained in Chapter 10, "Optimizing Your Disk Drives."

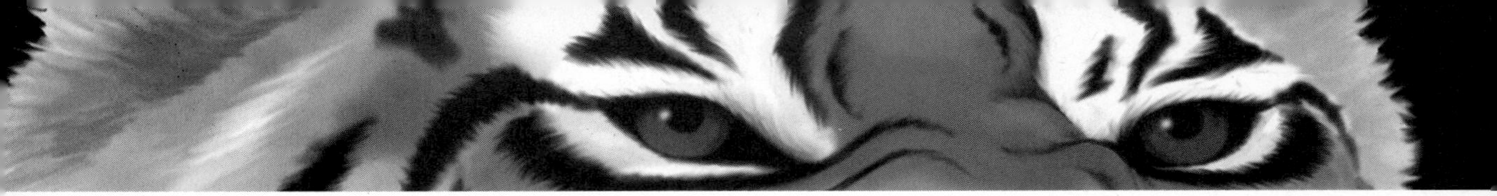

Disabling Programs

Earlier versions of DOS relied quite heavily on TSR (terminate and stay resident) programs to add features to the operating system. Before installing Windows 95, be sure to disable any TSRs you have installed; these can conflict with the setup process. Examples of common TSR programs are those that aid in power management, the bill minder program in Quicken, and some device drivers, such as MOUSE.COM.

If you plan to install Windows 95 from within your current version of Windows, be sure to close all open windows except for the Program Manager. Open program windows can slow down the installation process, and may stop necessary files from being copied to the hard disk.

Dual-Booting

Many people who are upgrading to Windows 95 want to set up their systems so they can boot with different operating systems. For example, a user might want the ability to use both OS/2 and Windows 95 at different times. With most portable systems, you will probably want to stay away from dual-booting. Such installations are inherently more complex, and they can occupy more of your precious disk space (with files for both operating systems).

There is, however, one type of dual-booting that should be addressed. You may still want to be able to boot with your old version of DOS as well as with Windows 95. Why? You will need this capability if you want to use an older version of Windows on your system.

You should understand that the preferred method of installing Windows 95 is simply to upgrade your old version of Windows to Windows 95. This ensures that all of your settings, applications, and preferences are retained by Windows 95. However, if you're determined to maintain a previous version of Windows on your computer in addition to Windows 95, you can instruct Setup to install Windows 95 in a separate folder instead of overwriting the previous version of Windows.

Ultimately, dual-booting enables you to press F4 when you start your computer and choose between booting with Windows 95 and MS-DOS. If you choose DOS, you can use your computer as you always have. Some people view this arrangement as "the best of both worlds." The drawback of dual-booting is that none of your existing Windows 3.1 settings and applications migrate to Windows 95.

The following questions can help you make a decision for your company as to whether dual-booting is to be implemented:

- Do you need the capability to run both Windows 3.1 and Windows 95 (dual-boot)? If the answer is yes, then you should install Windows 95 in a folder other than C:\WINDOWS. If the answer is no, then you can allow Setup to install to the default folder and upgrade Windows 3.1 to Windows 95.
- Do you want Windows 95 to have the same settings and applications used in previous versions of Windows? If the answer is yes, then allow Setup to install to the default folder and upgrade Windows 3.1 to Windows 95. If the answer is no, then install Windows 95 in a folder other than C:\WINDOWS.
- Do you want to be able to load MS-DOS as well as Windows 95? If the answer is yes, then install Windows 95 in a folder other than C:\WINDOWS. If the answer is no, then allow Setup to install to the default folder and upgrade Windows 3.1 to Windows 95.

Installing Windows 95

The setup process for Windows 95 is simpler and more automatic than it was for any previous version of Windows. You only need to answer a few questions, then sit back and relax. Setup presents a wizard to guide you through the steps of installing Windows 95. When prompted, click the appropriate buttons, typically either Continue or Next.

As a general rule, if you have Windows 3.1 or Windows for Workgroups 3.11 already installed on your system, you should install from within Windows. If you do not have Windows or if you have Windows 3.0 or earlier, you must install from MS-DOS.

Starting Setup from MS-DOS

If your computer doesn't have Windows 3.1x installed, you can install Windows 95 from DOS without any problem. Follow these steps to install from DOS:

1. If you are installing from CD-ROM, insert the disc into your CD-ROM drive. If you are installing from floppies, insert the first disk into your disk drive.
2. At the DOS prompt, type **d:\SETUP** and press Enter. (You should replace the letter *d* with the drive letter that represents the drive you used in step 1.) You will see the following on your screen:

   ```
   Please wait while Setup initializes.

   Setup is now going to perform a routine check on your system.

   To continue, press Enter. To quit Setup, press Esc.
   ```

3. Press Enter to continue with the setup. The program then runs ScanDisk to check the integrity of your disk drives.
4. When ScanDisk is complete, press X to exit from the program.

At this point, a couple of files are copied onto your hard drive in preparation for the rest of the setup procedure. Shortly, you will see the welcome screen as shown in figure 5.1. From this point forward, the setup is identical for DOS users as it is for Windows users. Proceed to step five in the next section to continue with the Windows 95 installation.

Starting Setup from Windows

During the installation phase, Setup detects whether you already have Windows installed and, if so, remembers its location. Setup later informs you where it was found. All existing Windows settings will transfer to Windows 95 once the installation is complete. If you have a Windows-based network in place before installation, all the settings will convert without incident.

To install Windows 95 from Windows 3.1 or Windows for Workgroups 3.1x, follow these steps:

1. If you are installing from CD-ROM, insert the disc in your CD-ROM drive. If you are installing from floppies, insert the first disk in your disk drive.

2. Choose File, Run from Program Manager (not File Manager). The Run dialog box appears.

3. Enter **d:\SETUP** in the Command Line text box, and click OK. (You should replace the letter *d* with the drive letter that represents the drive you used in step 1.) In a moment, you see the Windows 95 Setup welcome screen (see figure 5.1). Click Continue.

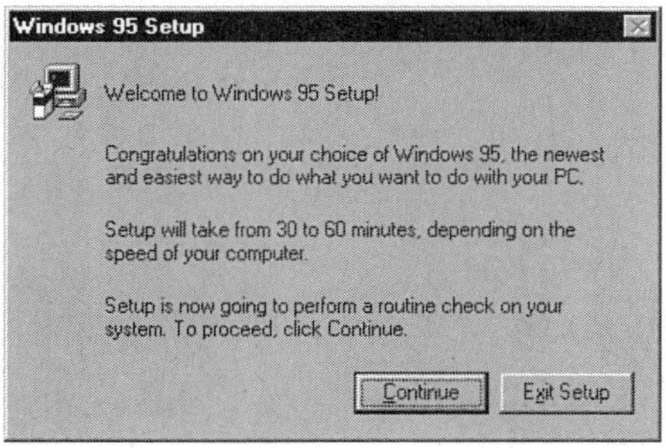

Fig. 5.1 Welcome to Windows 95 Setup.

4. Setup performs a behind-the-scenes ScanDisk procedure. When it is finished, click Continue. After you do, various files are copied to your hard disk in preparation for the Setup Wizard.

5. When you see the software license agreement, read it, then click Yes.

6. When you see the Setup Wizard shown in figure 5.2, you can see the number of steps required to complete the setup and what will occur. Click Next.

7. As shown in figure 5.3, you now have the opportunity to specify where Windows 95 will be installed. If you currently have Windows installed and you want to update, you should accept the indicated folder. If you want Windows 95 installed in a different folder for whatever reason (that is, to have dual-booting capability), you should click on Other folder. When you have made your choice, click on the Next button.

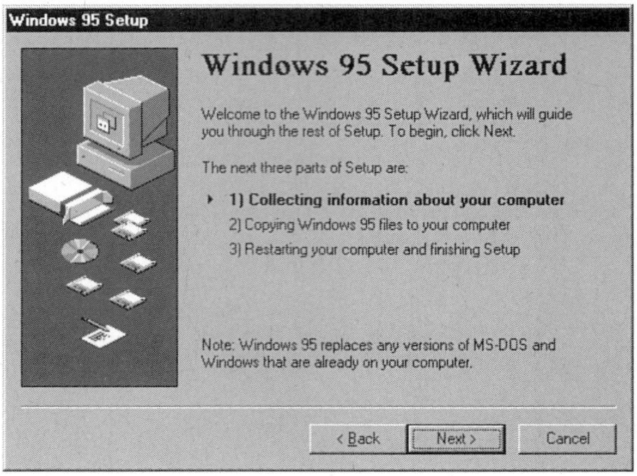

Fig. 5.2 The Setup Wizard outlines what will occur during setup.

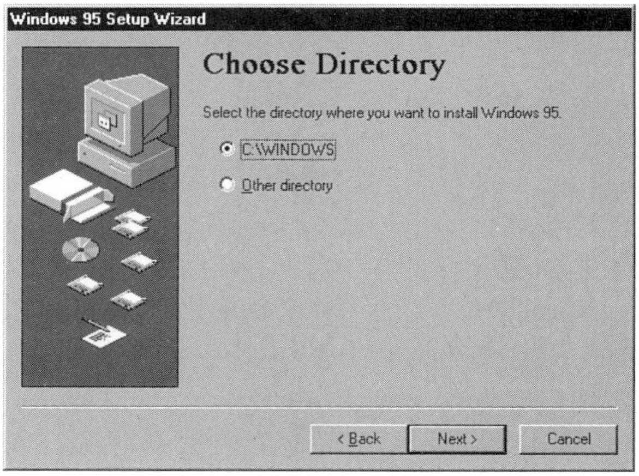

Fig. 5.3 Choose a folder where you want to install Windows 95.

8. If you indicated that you wanted Windows 95 installed in a different folder, you are asked to specify the folder. Pick a folder and click on the Next button.

9. When the Setup Options screen appears (see figure 5.4), choose a setup type. Most portable computer users should choose Portable. For most office installations, you will choose Typical. However, you may want to choose Complete, and tailor the

installation. A full discussion of each setup type (along with system suggestions) is found later in this chapter in the section entitled "Choosing a Setup Type." Make your selection and click on Next.

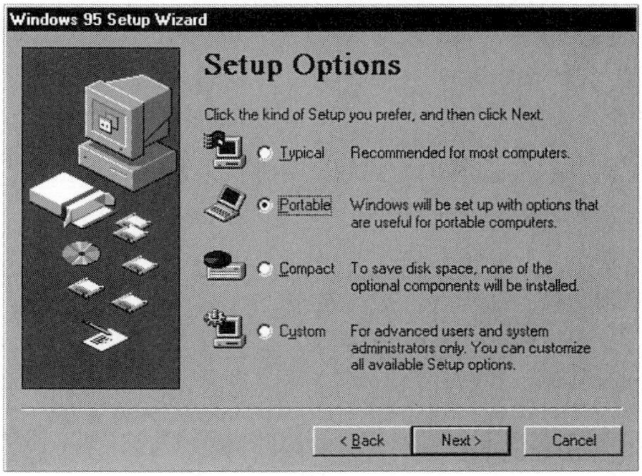

Fig. 5.4 You can select from among four setup types.

10. Enter your name in the User Information screen. Optionally, you may also type the name of your company or organization. Click Next.

11. You will next see the Analyzing Your Computer screen as shown in figure 5.5. If any of the devices listed are present in your system and if the devices are not Plug-and-Play compatible, then choose them and click Next.

12. Setup now performs a complete hardware analysis, which may take up to five minutes (depending on the speed of your system).

13. After a time, you will see the Windows Components screen. Here you have two choices: you can accept the most common components for your type of installation (the recommended default), or you can indicate that you want to modify the components installed. Make your selection and click on Next.

14. If you chose to modify the components installed, you will see the Select Components screen as shown in figure 5.6. If you asked Windows to install the most common components, skip to step 16.

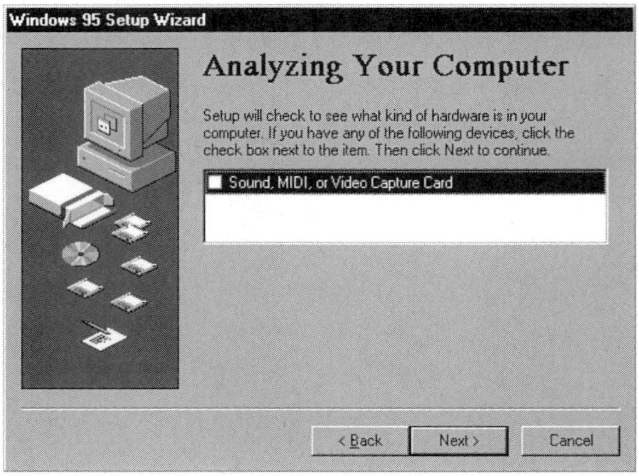

Fig. 5.5 The Analyzing Your Computer screen is used to specify the hardware components that are present in your system.

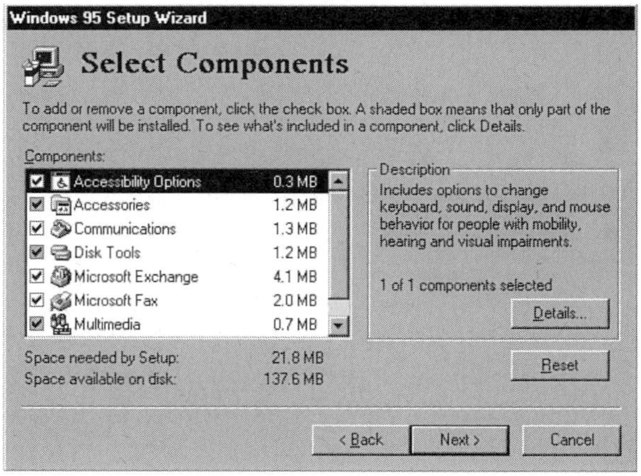

Fig. 5.6 Choose the options you want to install. Grayed entries indicate some components are selected.

15. Select the options you want installed with Windows 95. If you want more options than are normally available in your setup type, you can pick from this list. Highlight a category and click Details to choose individual items. To select all items in a component category, highlight it and press the spacebar. Click Next when you are finished.

16. If your system is not 100 percent Plug-and-Play compatible, Setup may not be able to detect each item by name. Consequently, you may see the Computer Settings screen, which you can safely ignore by clicking Next. If you want Windows 95 settings to be a little more precise, scroll through the list and change any items that are marked Unknown to their proper settings. To do so, highlight the item and click Change. Click Next when you are finished.

17. Setup next asks if you want a startup disk. Choose Yes (the default) and click Next. This disk serves as your bootable floppy in case of future system trouble. You may never need it, but it is a good precaution to create one. For information on how to use this disk, refer to the section "Using the Emergency Startup Disk," later in this chapter.

18. The Setup Wizard displays the second phase of installation—the copying of files. Click Next.

19. If you chose to create a startup disk, Setup prompts you to insert a disk and click OK. When Windows 95 has completed the disk, remove the floppy, label it clearly, put it in a safe place, and click OK to continue.

20. Setup then copies the Windows 95 files to your computer; this step takes about 10 minutes. Click Finish when prompted (see figure 5.7). When you do, the computer restarts and continues to configure Windows 95.

21. After several minutes of self-configuration, Setup requests your time zone (see figure 5.8). Click on the map to choose the appropriate time zone (or choose from the Time Zone pull-down list), and indicate whether or not you want to adjust for daylight savings time. Click Next.

22. If you chose to install the communications options, including Microsoft Exchange and Microsoft Fax, the Microsoft Exchange Setup Wizard intervenes and requests information. For information on setting up Microsoft Exchange and its components, refer to Chapter 32, "Communicating with a Modem."

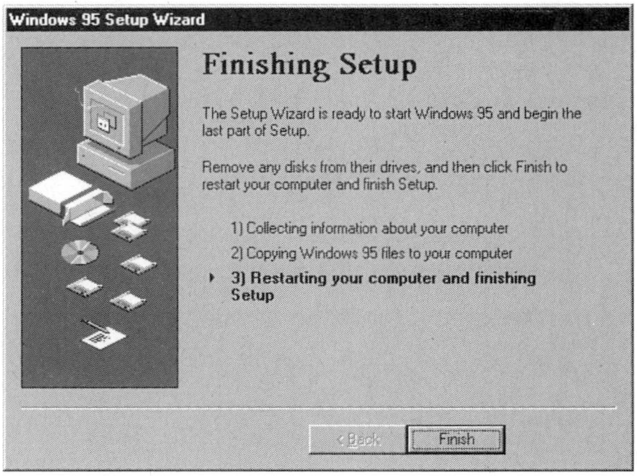

Fig. 5.7 After copying files, Setup is ready to restart your computer.

That's it! You have successfully installed Windows 95. The Welcome to Windows 95 dialog box shown in figure 5.8 lets you see what's new in Windows 95. For a quick tour, choose Windows Tour. (The Windows Tour button is available only if you installed from the CD-ROM and chose to explicitly install the feature.) Click What's New to find out about the innovations and changes in the Windows interface. Online Registration enables you to dial into Microsoft to register your copy of Windows 95. When you are finished, click Close.

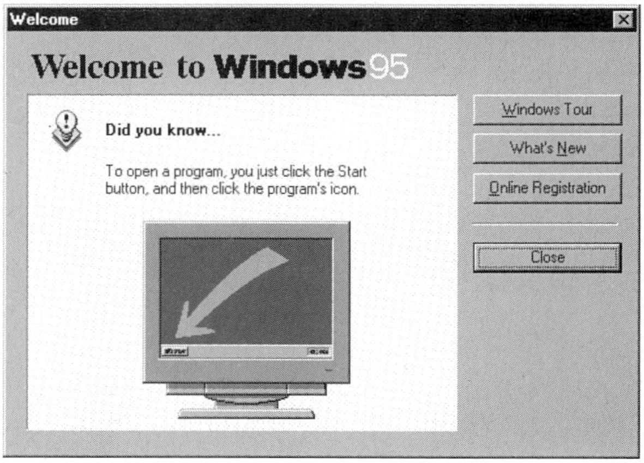

Fig. 5.8 Immediately after you install Windows 95, you see the Welcome dialog box. Choose an option and investigate.

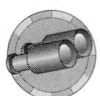

Note: You are not limited to registering Windows 95 with a modem. You can mail the registration card provided with your Windows 95 software package.

Choosing a Setup Type

In the previous two sections, you learned how to install Windows 95 from start to finish. When performing step nine, you learned that the Setup Wizard allows you to indicate what type of installation you want, depending on the type of computer you have and its available resources, including hard disk space (or lack of it). Windows 95 offers four distinct setup types: typical, portable, compact, and custom.

Different setup choices require different system resources. The most conservative choice is compact, then portable, then typical, and finally custom. The biggest difference among the options is the number of tools (programs) that are installed. The following is a quick overview of each installation type:

- Typical Setup. This setup type is the most common installation selection, particularly for users who have at least 100M of unused hard disk space. The only decisions you must make are to confirm the folder where Windows 95 files are to be installed and whether to create a startup disk.
- Portable Setup. The options installed with this setup type are geared toward a mobile computer user. Basically, fewer of the "bells and whistles" that accompany a typical setup are installed, and features that enhance portable computing are added. If you have tons of available disk space and you want all the really cool features that a full Windows 95 installation has to offer, then you can safely choose Typical or Custom setup.
- Compact Setup. This setup type installs the bare essentials—only those files necessary to run Windows 95. A minimal installation that is ideal for those users with small hard disks (less than 80M),

compact setup allows you to forego most of the Windows 95 options and may ultimately save about 36M of disk space.

- Custom Setup. This setup type lets you choose any or all options available in Windows 95, and thus is often appropriate in many office situations. It is similar to walking through a delicatessen: you simply pick the pieces and parts you want included in your Windows 95 system. This type of setup is recommended for experienced users who want to control the various elements of Windows 95 Setup.

The files installed on your hard drive will vary, depending on the type of setup you choose. Table 5.1 shows the different Windows 95 components that can be installed for each type of limited setup (typical, portable, and compact).

Table 5.1 How Windows 95 Components Are Installed for the Limited Setup Options

Component	Typical	Compact	Portable
Audio Compression	✔	✔	
Blank Screen Saver	✔		
Briefcase		✔	
Calculator	✔		
CD Player	✔	✔	
Disk Defragmenter	✔	✔	✔
Document Templates	✔		
DriveSpace	✔	✔	✔
HyperTerminal	✔	✔	
Media Player	✔		
Notepad	✔	✔	✔
Object Packager	✔		
Paint	✔		
Phone Dialer	✔	✔	
Quick View	✔	✔	

Component	Typical	Compact	Portable
ScanDisk	✔	✔	✔
Scrolling Marquee Screen Saver	✔		
Sound Recorder	✔		
Video Compression	✔	✔	
Volume Control	✔		
WordPad	✔		

If you choose the Custom Setup type, then you can install any or all of the Windows 95 components. Besides those which can be installed with one of the limited setups (as detailed in Table 5.1), there is a wide variety of other components you can choose:

- Accessibility Options. A collection of Control Panel tools that are designed to help those who are physically impaired.
- Backup. A disk tool used to backup your hard drive to floppy disks or tapes.
- Character Map. An accessory that allows you to access the entire range of Windows 95 characters. You can use Character Map to insert symbols and characters into documents created by other programs.
- Clipboard Viewer. An accessory that allows you to view the contents of the Clipboard and to manage a Clipbook over the network.
- Curves and Colors Screen Saver. A screen saver you can use to customize your desktop.
- Dial-Up Networking. An accessory that allows you to connect with remote networks, such as the Internet.
- Direct Cable Connection. An accessory that allows two computers to be connected through a serial cable.
- Flying Through Space Screen Saver. A screen saver you can use to customize your desktop.

- Games. Five games which can be used for relaxation. Included are FreeCell, Hearts, Minesweeper, Party Line, and Solitaire.
- Jungle Sound Scheme. A collection of related sounds that can be assigned to different system events.
- Microsoft Exchange. A communications management accessory that combines e-mail and fax capabilities.
- Microsoft Fax. The fax portion of Microsoft Exchange (which is required for this option to be installed).
- Microsoft Network. The tools necessary to connect with the new Microsoft Network.
- Mouse Pointers. A collection of animated and nonanimated pointers which can be assigned to different mouse activities.
- Multi-Language Support. The files necessary to implement the international features of Windows 95.
- Musica Sound Scheme. A collection of related sounds that can be assigned to different system events.
- Mystify Your Mind Screen Saver. A screen saver you can use to customize your desktop.
- Nature Sound Scheme. A collection of related sounds that can be assigned to different system events.
- NetWatcher. A system tool that allows you to monitor the performance of the network.
- Online User's Guide. Tutorial information on how to use Windows 95.
- Robotz Sound Scheme. A collection of related sounds that can be assigned to different system events.
- Sound and Video Clips. Sample audio and video multimedia files that can be used with the Media Player accessory.
- System Monitor. A system tool used to troubleshoot and refine the performance of Windows 95.

- System Resource Meter. A system tool used to monitor the use of your system resources.
- Utopia Sound Scheme. A collection of related sounds that can be assigned to different system events.
- Wallpaper. Various bit-mapped graphics files that can be used to customize your desktop.
- Windows 95 Tour. A guided, on-screen tour of the newest features of Windows 95. (Available only on the CD-ROM version of Windows 95.)

> **Note:** There are four tools that Windows 95 automatically installs: the Disk Defragmenter, DriveSpace, ScanDisk, and Notepad. There is no way to prevent their installation.

Remember, you can always add or remove options after Windows 95 is installed on a system. For information about adding or removing options, refer to Appendix A, "Adding and Removing Windows 95 Components."

After You Install

After you complete your Windows 95 installation, you should run the ScanDisk utility to verify that all the files on your hard disk are intact. This step also protects against any potential disk problems that might crop up. To start ScanDisk, follow these steps:

1. Select the Programs option from the Start menu.
2. Choose Accessories from the Programs menu.
3. Choose System Tools from the Accessories menu.
4. Choose ScanDisk from the System Tools menu.

When the program starts, choose the hard disk you want to scan and click Start. For more information on using ScanDisk, refer to Chapter 10, "Optimizing Your Disk Drives."

Special Portable Features

The characteristics of a portable computer are inherently different than your standard desktop computer, workstation, or server. If you have used a notebook computer for any length of time, you already know such computers are compact. You get most of the features of its desktop PC cousin, except in miniature. It's sort of like an RV with a miniature stove, rest room, and refrigerator. On a notebook you have a hard disk, albeit smaller and a bit slower. The LCD displays, even though they use color, are awkward at best. And forget about expansion unless you plug your notebook into a docking station. Still, even with these limitations, your portable computer gets the job done.

Windows 95 has several built-in features that only appear on specific types of equipment. It's as though the operating system is intelligent in the way it recognizes the needs and demands of your computer. The following sections describe these features and how you can best utilize them.

Power Management

Short battery life is forever the bane of portable computing. (Using a system that has a two-hour battery life on a four-hour plane flight is a real pain.) Someday, someone will develop a portable power source that will last for weeks at time. Until then, you must watch your remaining power until you can get a fresh battery charge or connect your system to AC power.

Windows 95 gives you some control over the battery's power management. It places a battery icon at the right side of the taskbar when you are mobile—that is, when you are using the battery and are disconnected from AC power. This icon notifies you of the remaining battery power in your system. Position the mouse pointer over the icon to see how much power really is left. Most modern portable computers have their own power management features, such as sleep mode and low battery meter. Of course, Windows 95 cooperates with these proprietary features.

You can instruct Windows to manage your precious battery power by shutting down energy-consuming devices, such as the display and the hard disk, until they are accessed. To modify these properties, do the following:

1. Choose Settings from the Start menu.
2. Choose Control Panel from the Settings menu.
3. Double-click on the Power icon in the Control Panel.
4. Choose Advanced, Standard, or Off from the Power Management list box.
5. Click on the OK button.

Standard power management provides sufficient energy conservation for most portables, while the Advanced setting is more beneficial for Pentium notebooks and CPUs with high-voltage consumption. The Advanced setting puts your devices into sleep mode every few seconds to save the most power possible.

If your battery power drops below 20 percent, Windows 95 alerts you with an audible beep and a message box. In addition, an exclamation mark appears next to the battery icon on the taskbar. Simply move your mouse pointer over the icon to see how much power remains.

PC Card (PCMCIA) Properties

PCMCIA, or the PC card, is most commonly used in notebook and subnotebook computers. Special slots accommodate these credit-card-sized devices as virtual hot-swapping mechanisms. This means that you can insert and remove cards while the computer is turned on and functioning without any adverse results. (Try this in a desktop computer with an adapter card, and you'll fry the components!)

As you add devices via the PCMCIA slots, you can view their status in the PC Card Properties sheet. Depending on your computer, you can also modify the card service's shared memory by specifying the exact starting and ending addresses. Normally, Windows 95 handles these addresses automatically, but you can override this by following these steps:

1. Choose Settings from the Start menu.
2. Choose Control Panel from the Settings menu.
3. Double-click on the PC Card (PCMCIA) icon in the Control Panel.
4. Choose the Global Settings tab.
5. Uncheck the Automatic selection check box.
6. Specify the Start address, End address, and Length as shown in figure 5.9.

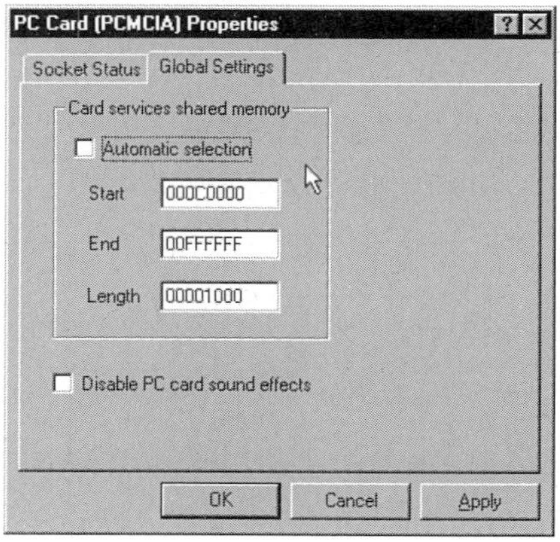

Fig. 5.9 You can change settings in the Global Settings page of this Properties sheet.

7. Click OK. You will be prompted to restart Windows based on your changes.

> **Tip:** To disable the audible beep made by Windows 95 when you insert (or remove) a PC card, check the Disable PC card sound effects in the Global Settings tab (refer to figure 5.9).

Inserting a PCMCIA Card

Inserting a PC card is easy—just slide it into an available PCMCIA slot regardless of whether the computer is on or off. The instant you insert a PC card, Windows 95 recognizes its presence (assuming your computer is on), beeps to alert you, and configures itself accordingly. This action is instantaneous if the card has been previously configured. If the PC card has never been inserted in this computer before, Windows 95 assists you in the setup with the New Hardware Found Wizard, as shown in figure 5.10.

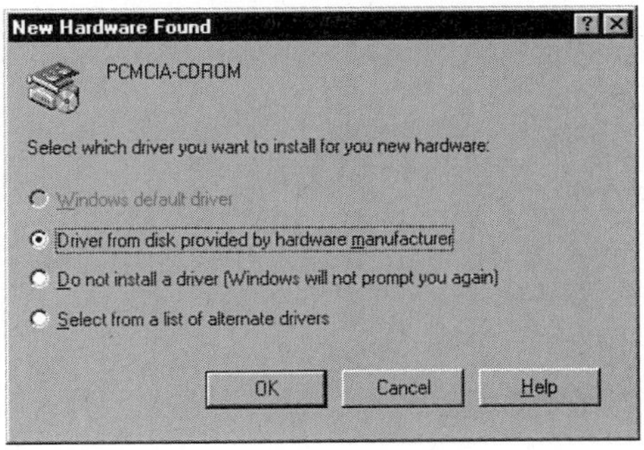

Fig. 5.10 First-time setup of a PCMCIA card is simplicity itself—just choose a driver in the dialog box.

Typically, you must install a driver for a new device, and Windows 95 lets you pick from several options. If this PC card is designed specifically for use with Windows 95, Windows may automatically detect it and install the appropriate driver(s). Otherwise, you have four options:

- Windows default driver. This option is available for only selected devices. In fact, with most PCMCIA devices, this option is not available.
- Driver from disk provided by hardware manufacturer. This is the default option, and should be selected if your vendor provided a disk containing Windows 95 device drivers.

- Do not install a driver. Select this option if you don't want to use the new device you've just added.
- Select from a list of alternate drivers. This option should be used if you don't have a Windows 95 driver disk from the vendor. You can then scroll through a list of vendors and products to select the closest matching driver.

> **Tip:** If your PCMCIA card does not appear in the driver list, you can usually choose a generic substitute. If that doesn't work, call the PC card's manufacturer to obtain a Windows 95 driver disk.

Removing a PCMCIA Card

In previous versions of Windows, inserting and removing a PC card was as simple as sliding it in or out. The same is true for Windows 95, but bear in mind that some PC cards require special treatment. In general, you should disable any PC card via the PC Card Properties sheet before pulling it out of the slot. Granted, this is not mandatory, but for the more finicky devices (such as PCMCIA network cards), it makes the severing of resources a bit cleaner. Consider what would happen if you were connected to the network with your PCMCIA card, and you slid it out without thinking about it. Removing it is no big deal for you, but if someone else is accessing your computer, the removal of the card could be disastrous. Thus, properly disabling a card is desirable.

There are two ways to properly remove a PC card:

- Open the PC Card Properties sheet, highlight the desired card, and click Stop.
- Click (not right-click) on the PCMCIA tray icon on the taskbar and choose the device to stop (remove) from the pop-up menu (see figure 5.11).

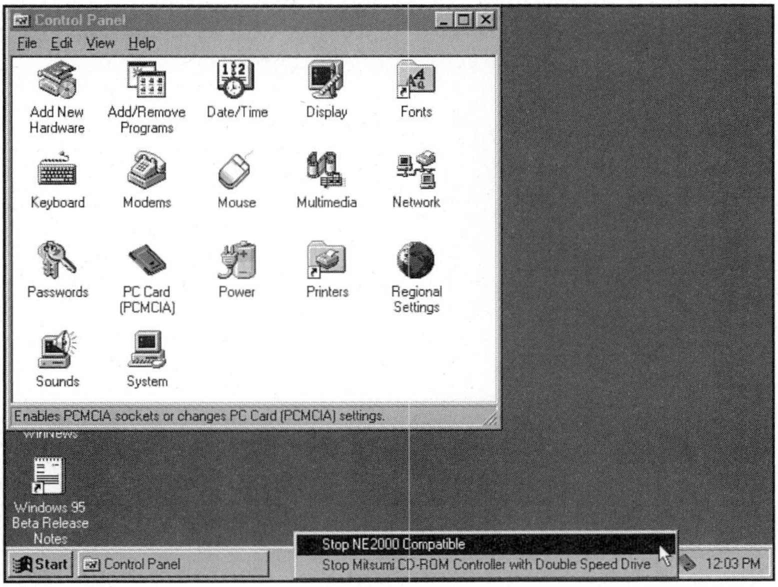

Fig. 5.11 A pop-up menu appears when you single-click the PCMCIA tray icon on the taskbar.

> **Tip:** If your computer has PCMCIA slots, the taskbar should display a PCMCIA tray icon. If the feature is not visible, you can enable it in the PC Card Properties sheet.

If you properly disable a PC card by following these instructions, Windows 95 informs you with a message box stating "You may safely remove this device." Click on OK. Once the card is properly disabled, you can remove it safely. If you don't follow this procedure when removing a PC card, Windows will warn you of your premature removal of the card as shown in figure 5.12.

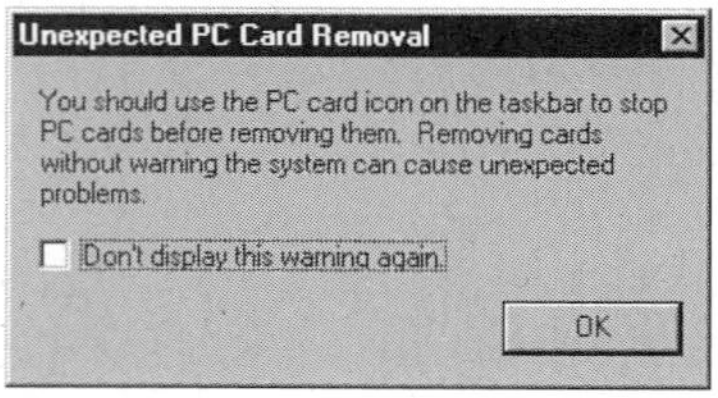

Fig. 5.12 Windows warns you when you remove a PC card without following the proper procedure.

Off-line Printing

Off-line printing, sometimes called deferred printing, is a way for mobile computer users to print documents while they are on the road, away from a printer. These documents are stored in a queue until you can again connect a printer to your computer. Ultimately, it's a time saver simply because you can issue the print command for any number of documents right away while you're thinking about it. The alternative is to wait until you get to a printer, summon the application, try to remember what you wanted to print, and then print.

Although this is not a feature specific to portable computers, it is significant. Desktop and portable computer users alike can use the deferred printing feature. However, off-line printing is automatically engaged when you are using a network printer, and you remove a PCMCIA network card from your system.

To manually enable off-line printing, follow these steps:

1. Choose Settings from the Start menu.
2. Choose Printers from the Settings menu.
3. Right-click on the printer icon you want to use for off-line printing.
4. From the context menu (see figure 5.13), click Work Offline.

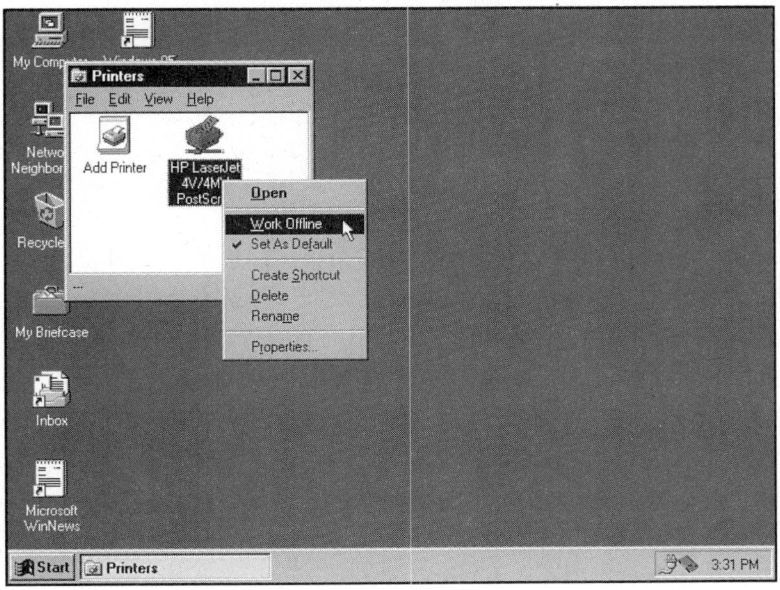

Fig. 5.13 To print without really being connected to a printer, choose Work Offline from the context menu.

Remember, off-line printing is engaged automatically for portable computer users when you remove a network PCMCIA card. A printer set to work off-line is displayed dimly in the Printers folder. Now, whenever you print, Windows creates a queue that holds all print jobs until you reconnect to the network. The instant you plug in the network PCMCIA card and the network printer is available, you get a message similar to figure 5.14. Click OK to print the jobs.

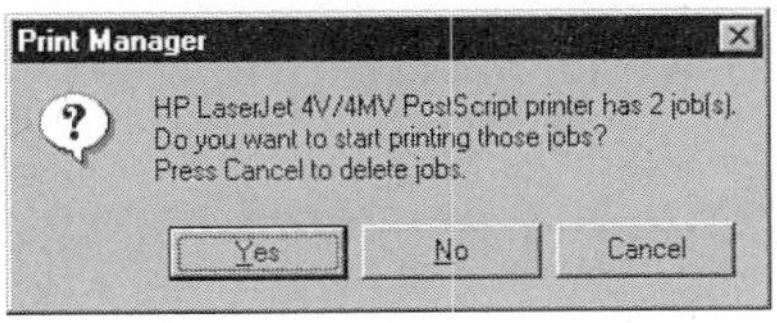

Fig. 5.14 When your printer is set to work off-line, print jobs are queued until you attach to a network or a printer.

Off-line E-mail

Since portable computers are mobile, they aren't always connected to a network or phone line. But you can still prepare e-mail when you're not connected. In fact, off-line e-mail works a lot like off-line printing in that you create your mail off-line via Microsoft Exchange, then when you reconnect your computer to the network (either directly or through Dial-Up Networking), your messages are automatically sent.

As you use Microsoft Exchange off-line, you won't have access to user names on the network (obviously), nor can you send mail into a queue like printer jobs in off-line printing. However, you still have your Personal Address Book from which you can select e-mail addresses. For example, when you attempt to open your Inbox (Microsoft Exchange), you see a screen similar to figure 5.15. When you see this, you can either choose Offline or Remote depending on how you want to work at that moment with Microsoft Exchange. Overall, e-mail functions the same as when you're connected, except you have to wait to connect before you can send e-mail. You can create it; you just can't send it until you connect to a network or the modem.

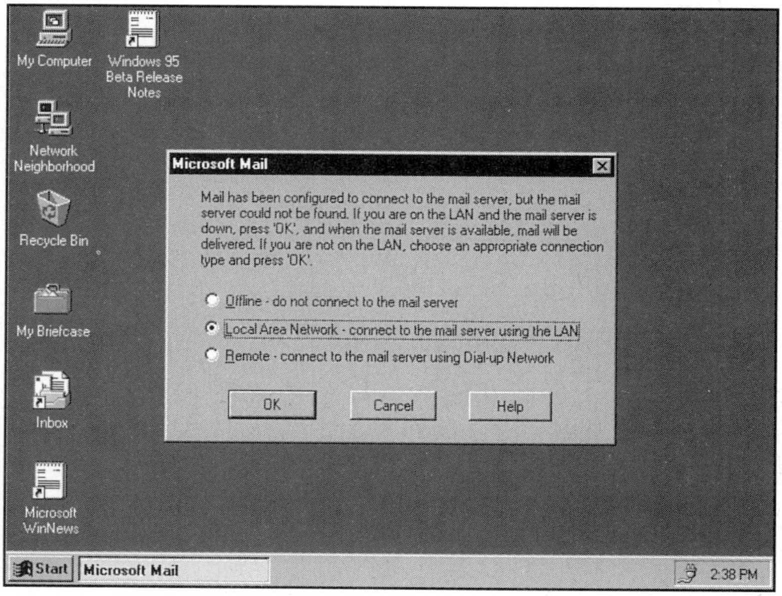

Fig. 5.15 You can work off-line with e-mail, too.

Installation Problems

A nice feature of the Windows 95 Setup is that if something interrupts the installation, such as if the power goes out, the hardware detection phase fails, or you intentionally cancel Setup, you can simply run Setup again and pick up where you left off. Setup calls it Safe Recovery.

If you have problems during installation, the Safe Recovery mode of Setup appears the next time you attempt installation. When this dialog box appears, choose Use Safe Recovery and click on Next. Setup will proceed as if nothing happened. This feature is possible because Setup maintains special files during the setup process to guard against such events.

Additional information on how to overcome installation problems is covered in Chapter 6, "Troubleshooting Windows 95 Installation and Startup."

Using the Emergency Startup Disk

When you install Windows 95, you have the option to create a startup disk. This disk is nothing more than a Windows 95 boot disk with the basic system files and other useful programs, such as the Registry Editor and disk utilities. Should your computer ever get corrupted and fail to boot properly, Windows 95 advises you and starts in a special "safe" mode. It is rare that you would need the startup disk, but it's available just in case of a catastrophe.

For more information on the different Windows 95 startup modes and how you can troubleshoot a damaged system, refer to Chapter 6, "Troubleshooting Windows 95 Installation and Startup."

Changing Your Windows Configuration

If you've ever accidentally deleted an important system file in a previous version of Windows, you typically had one solution—reinstall Windows. Of course, if you knew the exact name of the file you deleted, you could copy it from the distribution disks and use the expand command to decompress it. But that required your knowing its compressed name and its location on your system.

Fortunately, Windows 95 resolves this dilemma. There is no real need to reinstall Windows 95 (unless you delete a substantial portion of the system files). System components can be reinstalled by doing the following:

1. Double-click on the Add/Remove Programs applet in the Control Panel.
2. Choose the Windows Setup tab.
3. Highlight and select any or all components and options you want to reinstall (or remove).
4. Click OK.

Once you click OK, Windows prompts you to shut down the computer. Confirm this action, and Windows 95 will shut down and launch as normal. Additional information on adding and removing components is found in Appendix A, "Adding and Removing Windows 95 Components."

Troubleshooting Windows 95 Installation and Startup

by Allen L. Wyatt

To a degree not seen in any previous version, Windows 95 is a complex, robust operating system. Although well-hidden by the features apparent when you use Windows, the complexity of the operating system can raise problems. Ironing out these problems involves a process called *troubleshooting.*

This chapter attempts to address many of the troubleshooting issues that may arise as you use Windows. As you read through this chapter, pay close attention to the common threads that exist in all troubleshooting attempts. Regardless of the problem, you'll need to:

- **Analyze the symptoms.** Determine whether you can reproduce the problem or if it's random. If you can reproduce it, figure out exactly what steps lead up to the problem.
- **Identify the problem.** Once you know what creates the problem, you can generally figure out what the problem is. Is it due to a driver or a particular piece of hardware?
- **Determine a solution.** Find out what is necessary to correct the issue. Read through this chapter or related chapters. Refer to online help about the problem, if available. You may even need to contact a hardware or software vendor for assistance.
- **Resolve the problem.** Take the steps necessary to implement the solution. This typically involves using Windows to install a driver or make changes to properties. Make the changes.
- **Test the solution.** Once the solution has been implemented, you'll need to try to reproduce the problem again. If you can't after several attempts, and if additional problems don't arise, proceed to use your computer system as you intended.

Troubleshooting the Installation

Windows 95 has undergone extensive testing in order to make it work with virtually all hardware. This helps assure that the setup process for Windows 95 is simple and automatic. However, there is that occasional homemade computer that just isn't quite compatible or that network card that isn't supported (or manufactured) anymore. If you encounter problems during the installation of Windows 95, this section will help you locate and solve many of those problems.

Short of having defective media, it is unlikely that you will have any problem with beginning Windows 95 Setup. Once installation reaches the hardware detection phase, where Setup analyzes your existing hardware, your system may hang and force you to restart your computer. Setup has safeguards for such an event. If this does occur, simply run the Windows 95 Setup program again. This invokes Safe Recovery (see figure 6.1), which will then continue Setup from the point it failed. Safe Recovery consults the DETCRASH.LOG file (a file created during Setup that remains after a failed Setup), skips the conflicting device, and continues on its way. In such an event, you can later manually configure or install the offending device via the Add Hardware Wizard.

Fig. 6.1 Safe Recovery occurs when you run Setup after a failed installation.

Troubleshooting Startup

This section assumes that Windows is installed properly and, up to this point, everything is working as it should. There are times when you might have trouble launching Windows. Some of the more obvious causes might include:

- nonstandard hardware or devices
- corrupted system files (includes the Registry)
- hardware or device failure
- low disk space (not enough room for swap file activity)
- compromised disk integrity (fix with ScanDisk)
- excessive disk fragmentation (fix with Defrag)

A key feature of the Windows 95 startup is the ability to launch it in any of a number of modes. Some of these modes are designed specifically for troubleshooting your startup, while others simply let you access Windows in a different manner. The startup menu provides a menu of these different startup modes (see figure 6.2).

```
Microsoft Windows 95 Startup Menu
==================================

   1. Normal
   2. Logged (\BOOTLOG.TXT)
   3. Safe mode
   4. Safe mode with network support
   5. Step-by-step confirmation
   6. Command prompt only
   7. Safe mode command prompt only
   8. Previous version of MS-DOS

Enter a choice: 1




F5=Safe mode  Shift+F5=Command prompt
Shift+F8=Step-by-step confirmation [N]
```

Fig. 6.2 The Startup menu for Windows 95 lets you control how the startup proceeds.

Isolating a Startup Problem

If you have trouble starting Windows, you can use these modes to help you troubleshoot the problem. But first, you must get an overall picture of how Windows is or isn't starting. To help isolate the problem, look through the following situations. In essence, you will isolate the problem by process of elimination.

Is It a Hardware or Software Conflict?

To find out whether the problem is related to hardware or software, try these steps:

1. Restart your computer. After the POST (power-on self test; the hardware check) is completed, you will see the phrase Starting Windows 95. The moment this displays, press the F8 key.
2. Choose Safe mode command prompt only. This does not load the Windows 95 GUI but takes you to the command prompt. This is equivalent to a bare-bones start without executing the AUTOEXEC.BAT or CONFIG.SYS.

If the computer boots to the command prompt, you can be certain the problem is a device driver or TSR in the startup files, and you can skip to the next situation. If the computer doesn't start properly, you have a hardware conflict or perhaps some defective hardware. Unfortunately, the only solution to this type of problem is discovered by process of elimination. If you've recently added a new piece of hardware, remove it and try to start the computer using the preceding steps.

Is It a Driver Conflict?

To determine which driver is conflicting with startup, you can have Windows launch a step at a time. This lets you see each driver load and discover if one is causing the problem. Refer to the section "Checking for Driver Conflicts" later in this chapter.

Are You Running Low on Hard Disk Space?

Windows needs a minimum of 8M of free disk space during normal use in order to operate correctly. This "extra" space is used for the swap file and should not be curtailed intentionally or otherwise. To display remaining disk space, boot to the command prompt (not a DOS window within Windows) and type **chkdsk**. If you are running low on disk space, remove some unnecessary programs, utilize DriveSpace, or upgrade to a larger hard disk.

Are Files Corrupted?

It is difficult to tell whether files have become corrupted. Your options include using the Emergency Boot Disk (startup disk), restoring from a backup, or reinstalling Windows. You can use the startup disk to help recover the Registry or perform limited diagnostics on a failing system. Refer to the section "Using the Startup Disk" later in this chapter.

Is the Hardware Malfunctioning?

If you have eliminated hardware, software, and driver conflicts, your hardware may be malfunctioning. You can remove some hardware from your computer to see if it starts properly. Other vital hardware, such as the hard disk, must be present in order to start Windows. Hardware diagnostics and repair is a complex, involved topic and is beyond the scope of this book. Discuss the problem with your hardware vendor.

Checking for Driver Conflicts

One of these modes is "Step-by-step confirmation." This mode takes you through each command in the Windows 95 startup and lets you selectively choose which to load. This is similar to the MS-DOS 6.X interactive startup. As you use this mode, pay close attention to the way in which each driver or device initializes. If one fails or loads incorrectly, you have identified the problem. To start Windows in this mode, follow these steps:

1. Restart your computer. Press F8 when you see the phrase Starting Windows 95.
2. Choose Step-by-step confirmation.
3. Just before each line in the startup files is executed, it will be displayed on your screen and you'll be asked whether you want to execute it. Press Enter if you do or Esc if you don't.

The value of starting Windows in this way is that you can see exactly where the startup hangs or where an error occurs. When you process a command, observe the result. If the computer hangs (stalls) after loading a specific driver or running a certain command, you've identified the problem. Reboot using the Safe mode startup, make the proper changes to CONFIG.SYS or AUTOEXEC.BAT (if they exist), and then

restart Windows. You must realize that troubleshooting in this manner can be a time-consuming process—particularly if you are unsure which driver is the culprit. Generally, you can safely ignore the more common drivers in your AUTOEXEC.BAT and CONFIG.SYS, such as HIMEM.SYS or SETVER.EXE.

Don't Remove These Files

While you are working with your CONFIG.SYS or AUTOEXEC.BAT files, you may make changes to correct booting problems. The following files should not be deleted, since the drivers referenced must be present in order for Windows 95 to function properly:

- AH1544.SYS
- ASPI4DOS.SYS
- ATDOSXL.SYS
- DBLSPACE.BIN
- DEVSWAP.COM
- DMDRVR.BIN
- DRVSPACE.BIN
- ENHDISK.SYS
- EVDR.SYS
- FIXT_DRV.SYS
- HARDRIVE.SYS
- ILM386.SYS
- LDRIVE.SYS
- NONSTD.SYS
- SCSIDSK.EXE
- SCSIHA.SYS
- SKYDRVI.SYS
- SQY55.SYS
- SSTBIO.SYS
- SSTDRIVE.SYS
- SSTOR.EXE or SSTOR.SYS
- SSWAP.COM
- STACKER.COM

Using Safe Mode Startup

Choosing this mode forces Windows 95 to start without loading any device drivers or executing your CONFIG.SYS or AUTOEXEC.BAT (if they are on your system). This is useful when you need to determine whether the configuration files are causing problems. To start Windows in this mode, follow these two steps:

1. Restart your machine. After the POST (the hardware check) is completed, you will see the phrase `Starting Windows 95`.... The moment this is displayed, press the F8 key.
2. Choose Safe mode and press Enter.

Windows should start and display a screen similar to figure 6.3. Whenever you start Windows in Safe mode, it displays in the base 640 × 480 resolution, thereby avoiding any possible video conflicts. If Windows starts in this mode, you know that your startup problems lie within the startup files (CONFIG.SYS and AUTOEXEC.BAT). Examine the contents of these files to see if any troublesome commands are evident. You might even try changing the files to disable some statements, which may allow you to boot. If Windows doesn't start, even after bypassing the CONFIG.SYS and AUTOEXEC.BAT files, Safe mode will not do you much good. You must resort to generating a BOOTLOG.TXT file, as described in the section "Using BOOTLOG.TXT."

> **Tip:** Most driver problems occur in the CONFIG.SYS file, so examine that file first.

Of course, if your computer is connected to a network, you will have another option named "Safe mode with network support." When you troubleshoot such a computer, you can choose to let Windows 95 load the appropriate network drivers. This option assumes you have the proper networking hardware in place. To load Windows in this manner, do the following:

1. Restart your machine. After the POST (the hardware check) is completed, you will see the phrase `Starting Windows 95`.... The moment this is displayed, press the F8 key.
2. Choose Safe mode with network support and press Enter.

The screen displays the text `Safe mode with network` in all four corners (see figure 6.4), and it forces Windows to display in 640 × 480 resolution—just like Safe mode. When you start in this mode, check your device settings in the Device Manager to make sure your network settings are correct. If they are, you can rule out a conflicting network card.

Fig. 6.3 Windows 95 displays the phrase "Safe mode" in all four corners of the screen.

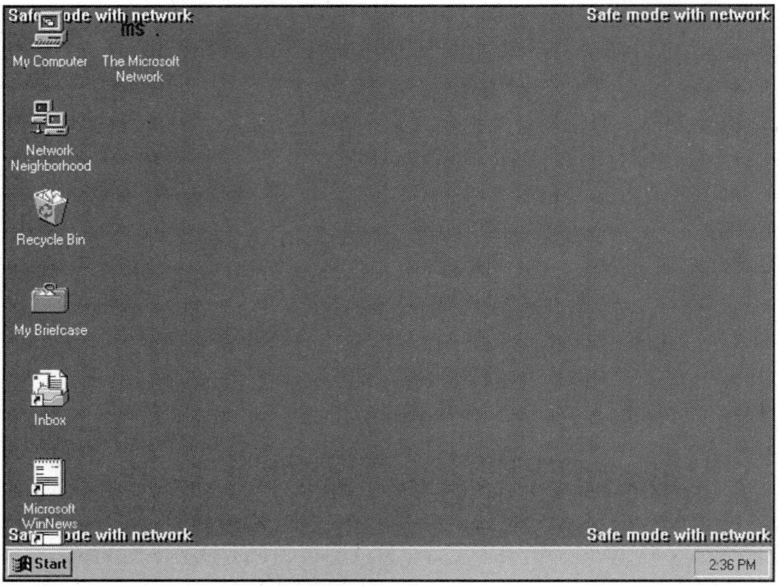

Fig. 6.4 Safe mode with network lets you load just the network drivers in Windows 95.

Using Command Line Switches

Other more technical issues surrounding system settings may cause Windows 95 to not launch properly. Or worse, it may function intermittently. You can force Windows to launch from the Windows 95 command prompt—not to be confused with the MS-DOS command prompt—and troubleshoot from there. Try these options if you can't get Windows 95 to launch properly.

To boot from the Windows 95 command prompt, do the following at startup:

1. Restart your machine. After the POST (the hardware check) is completed, you will see the phrase `Starting Windows 95...`. The moment this is displayed, press the F8 key.

2. From the Startup menu, choose 7, Safe mode command prompt only, and press Enter.
3. At the Windows 95 command prompt, type **win /d:** followed by a switch listed in Table 6.1.

For example, if you have a nonstandard disk controller, you'll want to make certain that 32-bit disk access is turned off. Otherwise, you could get intermittent results or Windows might not work at all. To run this command, type **win /d:f**.

Table 6.1 Command Line Switches

Switch	What It Does
f	Disables 32-bit disk access.
m	Starts Windows in Safe mode (same as Safe mode on the Startup menu).
n	Starts Windows in Safe mode with network support (if you have networking enabled). This is the same as Safe mode with network support on the Startup menu.
s	Instructs Windows not to use a ROM address space between F000:0000 and 1M for a break point.
v	Assigns ROM routines to handle hard disk I/O interrupts.
x	Prohibits Windows from searching for unused memory in the adapter area of memory.

Using the Startup Disk

When you first installed Windows 95, you had the option to create an Emergency Boot Disk (startup disk). You can troubleshoot Windows startup by using the utilities included on this disk. For example, if you get a message informing you of a missing operating system, use the SYS.COM command to restore these important files to the computer.

You can also edit, import, or export the Registry files from the command prompt, invoke ScanDisk on the suspect hard drive, or use various other commands provided on the startup disk. These utilities are placed on the startup disk:

- FORMAT.COM
- SYS.COM
- FDISK.EXE
- ATTRIB.EXE
- EDIT.COM
- REGEDIT.EXE
- SCANDISK.EXE

Using BOOTLOG.TXT

During the booting process, Windows becomes quite active loading drivers and other system files. This is particularly noticeable on slower computers. Most problems occur during this phase of startup. You can force Windows to keep a log of its boot processes, which is named BOOTLOG.TXT. This keeps a chronological account of each driver and system file it loads, and whether its loading was successful. To generate this file at startup, follow these steps:

1. Restart your machine. Press F8 when you see the phrase `Starting Windows 95....`
2. Choose Logged (\BOOTLOG.TXT), which will start Windows and create the BOOTLOG.TXT file in the root directory. Chances are good that the startup will still be unsuccessful, but you now have a record of where the startup failed.
3. Reboot your computer following step 1 again. When you see the Startup menu, choose Safe mode command prompt only to boot to the command prompt. If this option works, proceed to step 5.
4. If step 3 did not work, use your Emergency Boot Disk (startup disk) to boot your system.

Tip: If you don't have an Emergency Boot Disk, you can make a bootable floppy from a friend's or coworker's computer system.

5. Print out the file BOOTLOG.TXT, which is in your root directory.

When you examine the file, check to see what drivers were loaded and whether they were all loaded successfully. You'll notice that there are two entries for each device or driver that Windows 95 attempts to load. In the first entry, it attempts to load or initialize the driver. The second entry shows a message stating whether it succeeded or failed. The following is an excerpt from a BOOTLOG.TXT file:

```
[000F841B] Loading Device = C:\UTIL\ADAPTEC\ASPI4DOS.SYS
[000F8440] LoadSuccess    = C:\ADAPTEC\ASPI4DOS.SYS
[000F8441] Loading Device = C:\WINDOWS\HIMEM.SYS
[000F8445] LoadSuccess    = C:\WINDOWS\HIMEM.SYS
[000F8446] Loading Device = C:\WINDOWS\EMM386.EXE
[000F8452] LoadSuccess    = C:\WINDOWS\EMM386.EXE
[000F8453] Loading Device = C:\WINDOWS\DBLBUFF.SYS
[000F8456] LoadSuccess    = C:\WINDOWS\DBLBUFF.SYS
[000F8457] Loading Device = C:\WINDOWS\SETVER.EXE
[000F845B] LoadSuccess    = C:\WINDOWS\SETVER.EXE
[000F845C] Loading Device = C:\ADAPTEC\ASPICD.SYS
[000F846A] LoadSuccess    = C:\ADAPTEC\ASPICD.SYS
```

If a driver did not load properly, it may not exist (maybe it was deleted or moved elsewhere) or is corrupted. Try replacing the driver, and start Windows again in Logged mode (BOOTLOG.TXT). Then review the file to see if the driver loaded properly.

Hardware Troubleshooting

Although the Windows developers have made great strides in making Windows 95 compatible with almost every imaginable piece of hardware, it is possible that some hardware will not work. In such instances, all you can do is replace it with hardware that is compatible. If you believe that your hardware should work with Windows 95, then you must troubleshoot it.

Depending on the type of computer system you have, this could consume a lot of time. The newer Plug-and-Play-compliant systems allow for easy configuration—they automatically sense when you insert or remove a device. Resources are allocated on demand, and there is (usually) no conflict between devices. However, older devices (referred to as *legacy* devices) don't have Plug-and-Play capability. Many types of devices require resources in the form of IRQ lines (interrupt request lines) and DMA channels (direct memory access channels). The number of such resources is limited in your system. The more devices you install, the more likely you are to run into IRQ and DMA conflicts which arise when two or more devices try to use the same resources. If you have a non-Plug-and-Play computer, you'll want to follow these general guidelines for troubleshooting your system:

- Use the Device Manager to diagnose conflicting IRQ and DMA settings.
- If you have the stamina, use trial and error. (Don't underestimate its value.)
- Some older or nonsupported devices will not work with Windows 95. Generally, any device not detectable by Windows is not compatible.

The Device Manager gives you complete control over each piece of hardware you have installed in your system. All devices are diagrammed according to the information contained in the Registry (see figure 6.5), which is updated every time you restart your computer. From the Device Manager, you get a graphical representation of all devices attached to your computer, the device's complete (real) name, and more.

Consider how hardware configuration used to take place under DOS and previous versions of Windows. You would have to inventory the system to determine which IRQs were being used by existing hardware, then find a free DMA channel and reconfigure some other pieces of hardware (since one device was somewhat inflexible in how it could be set). Then came the trial and error of inserting it in the computer,

slapping the case back on, switching the power on, and fainting as it hung up the system. Back to square one. Double-check dip switches, reconfigure other hardware, slap it back together, try it again.

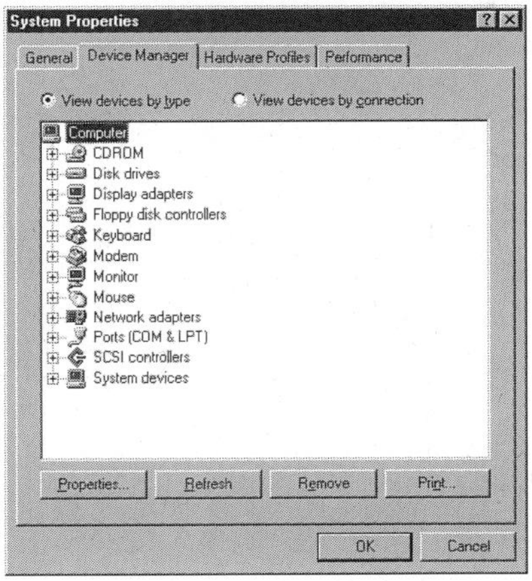

Fig. 6.5 Devices are listed in a diagram, which you can browse by pointing and clicking.

Windows 95 makes things much easier. The Device Manager is the tool which lets you configure the hardware in your system, including the IRQ and DMA channel each uses, and determine whether a device is currently active.

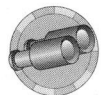

> **Note:** Although Windows 95 makes configuring easier, there still may be times when you must supply a driver on a floppy disk or set a dip switch on a card before inserting it into the computer. But instead of the trial and error method, as I previously described, the Device Manager will assist you.

To access the Device Manager, follow these steps:

1. Open the Control Panel by choosing Settings from the Start menu, and then select Control Panel.

2. Double-click the System applet.
3. Choose the Device Manager tab to reveal a diagram of all the devices in your system.

As you can see, this diagram displays I/O addresses, IRQ settings, and DMA channels for every device. Each item is treated as a category for related items beneath it. Under the category of Mouse, for example, you will only find pointing devices. If you are familiar with the Explorer, you know that this diagram has a similar browse capability. Any icon with a plus (+) beside it indicates items that exist within that category. To view the contents of a category, simply double-click its icon. A closer inspection of an item can be done by highlighting it and choosing Properties.

When you are troubleshooting a device, locate it by its category in the diagram, then double-click on it to reveal its properties. In the properties dialog box, choose the View Resources tab. Figure 6.6 shows the Resources tab for a network card. For any device in question, examine the Interrupt Request (IRQ) and the Input/Output Range (I/O Address). The Device Manager will tell you if a device is conflicting with something else in the system. If you've just installed this device with the Add Hardware Wizard, you may also see suggestions for available jumper and hardware settings. Jot down any pertinent information, and proceed to change the hardware settings accordingly.

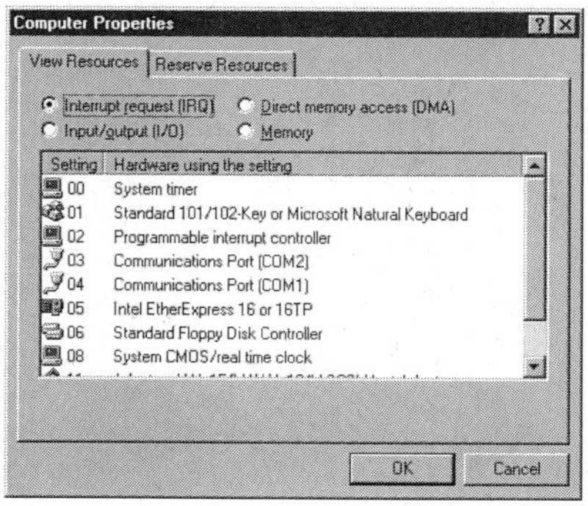

Fig. 6.6 In the View Resources tab, you can see if your device settings are in conflict with other system settings.

KILLER 7 WINDOWS 95

How Windows 95 Interacts with Your Hardware

by Allen L. Wyatt and Bill Lawrence

If you've been using DOS or Windows for some time, you're well aware of how they treated hardware. In most cases, the operating system was separate and distinct from the hardware—sort of an "interested bystander." This detached approach to hardware was fine, as long as everything was working the way it should. However, the operating system never was intelligent enough to recognize the presence or absence of a device, and so it mattered little whether your hardware was there or not. If it wasn't there, the worst case was that your system didn't work, and the best case was that you received an error message stating the obvious. Either way, you needed to resolve the conflict the "old-fashioned way," which of course meant manually.

Windows 95 takes an entirely different approach to the relationship between hardware and the operating system. In Chapter 2, you learned of one aspect of this difference—the Plug-and-Play system. Windows 95 is a Plug-and-Play operating system. The simple act of plugging in a card or other device triggers the reconfiguration process of Windows 95 (once the system is powered on). A database of all pertinent equipment is maintained and updated as changes are made to the system. Resources are reallocated if you remove a compressed drive; a driver is automatically loaded (usually without your knowing it) when you install a network card; and the chore of changing your video card's resolution—a relatively simple task—is taken care of quietly without the fanfare of disk swapping and searching for drivers.

Another aspect of the approach Windows 95 takes to hardware is that it continually attempts to communicate with the hardware. The principle behind Plug and Play dictates that the hardware must communicate with the operating system and BIOS, and vice versa. Of course, most of today's equipment does not comply with the Plug-and-Play standard and, consequently, does not "communicate" with anything—it does its own thing. For the most part, however, Windows 95 recognizes the presence of a great number of hardware items and can accommodate each, often without manual intervention.

In this chapter, you'll learn about the following:

- How device properties reflect the condition of your hardware, as well as help control it.
- How the Device Manager can be used to learn about your system.
- What Device Manager commands can be used to add or remove hardware from your system.
- How you can define hardware profiles to customize your use of Windows 95.
- How to add hardware devices to your system by using a wizard.

Understanding Hardware Properties

You already know that Windows 95 maintains a database of information about the components of your system. Part of this database is configuration information, attributes, or parameters that indicate how the device should be treated by the system. These parameters are referred to as *properties*. Every device in your system has properties you can view, and most devices have properties you can modify as necessary.

As an example, Windows 95 maintains a set of properties related to your entire system. To see your system's properties, right-click the My Computer icon on your desktop. From the context menu, choose Properties. The System Properties sheet appears, as shown in figure 7.1.

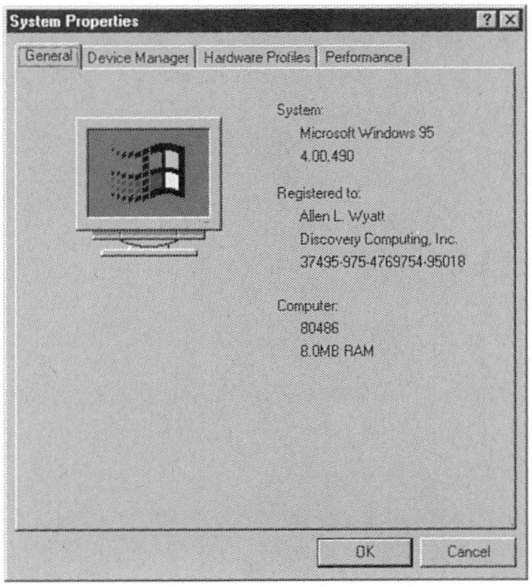

Fig. 7.1 The System Properties sheet is the gateway to the configuration of your entire system.

When you first display the System Properties sheet, the General tab is selected. This tab shows a summarization of several items, including the operating system and version, your registration information, and the computer's CPU type and installed memory.

The System Properties sheet acts as a gateway to several other important areas—areas that allow you to examine, in more depth, exactly how Windows 95 interacts with your hardware. The first of these areas is known as the Device Manager.

Using the Device Manager

The Device Manager is the place where you can monitor and change the properties of each device installed in your system. All devices are diagrammed according to the information contained in the Registry. The Registry is the unified database that contains all the configuration information for your system. The Registry replaces most of the INI files used in older versions of Windows; files such as SYSTEM.INI and WIN.INI. (The Registry is covered in detail in Chapter 17, "Fine-Tuning Windows 95 for Your Windows Applications.") The Registry database is updated every time you restart your computer, and sometimes during your Windows 95 sessions.

To view the Device Manager, start at the System Properties sheet (as described in the previous section), and then click on the Device Manager tab. The System Properties sheet appears, similar to that shown in figure 7.2.

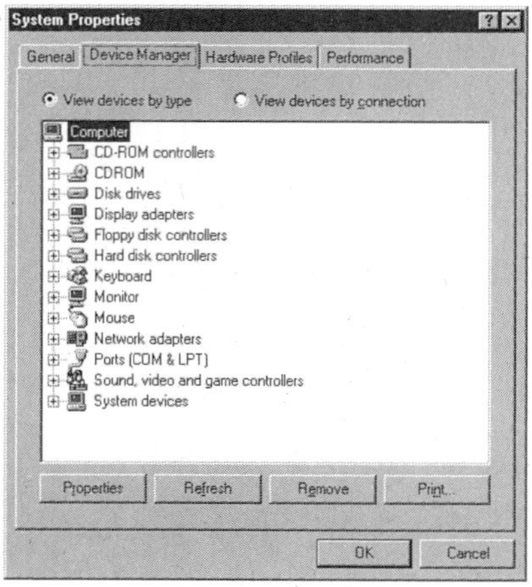

Fig. 7.2 The Device Manager allows you to see "the big picture" regarding your computer's components.

> **Note:** Remember that every system is different. Thus, what you see when you use the Device Manager may be different in some ways from what is shown in figure 7.2.

The Device Manager allows you to see a graphical representation of the devices attached to your computer, the device's complete (real) name, and more. At first, "more" may not sound too exciting, but consider how device configuration used to take place under DOS and previous versions of Windows. Remember how tedious it was to install a network card? Before Windows 95, you would have to inventory the system to determine which IRQs were being used by existing hardware. Then you would find a free DMA channel and reconfigure a few pieces of hardware because the network card was somewhat inflexible in how it could be set. Next came the trial and error of inserting it in the computer, putting on the case, powering on, and fainting as it hung up the system. Back to square one. Double-check dip switches, reconfigure other hardware, put it back together, try it again.

Windows 95 makes things much easier. The Device Manager lets you configure the hardware in your system, including the IRQ and DMA channel each uses, and tells you whether a device is currently active.

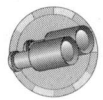

> **Note:** Although Windows 95 makes configuring easier, there still may be times when you must supply a driver on a floppy disk, or set a dip switch on a card before inserting it into the computer. But, instead of the trial and error method previously mentioned, the Device Manager can intelligently assist you in the process.

Inspecting Settings

The Device Manager is useful for configuring because of its accurate Registry list showing I/O addresses, IRQ settings, and DMA channels. It even shows devices that are using certain portions of memory. Each item shown in the Device Manager actually represents a category of related items. For instance, under the Mouse category, you find only pointing devices. If you're already familiar with the Explorer, this method of presenting information uses a similar browsing method. Any icon with a plus sign to the left of it indicates that items exist within that category. To view the contents of a category, click on the plus sign, or double-click on the category icon itself. In figure 7.3, the Ports category has been selected, revealing the available ports on the system.

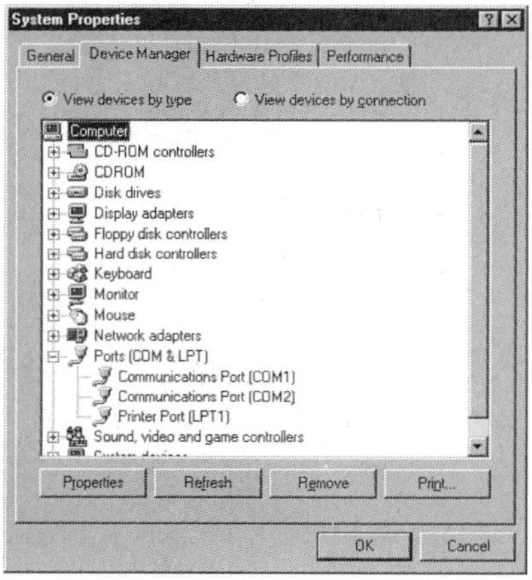

Fig. 7.3 Information in the Device Manager is presented in a hierarchical manner.

For a closer look at an actual device, highlight it and click on Properties. For instance, double-clicking on the first communications port (COM1) displays a properties dialog box for the device. Within the four tabs in the dialog box, you may activate or deactivate the device (discussed later in this chapter), view or change the device driver, or view and change the I/O address or IRQ settings. (The exact attributes and capabilities in the dialog box will depend on the device the dialog box represents.) Figure 7.4 shows the Resources tab for the COM1 port. Notice that the bottom of the dialog box indicates there are no conflicts for the port. Had there been a conflict (such as an internal modem using the same IRQ as the COM port), then this area would have indicated that information. The benefit over previous operating systems is that the Device Manager immediately notifies you if any of your changes conflict with existing devices in the system.

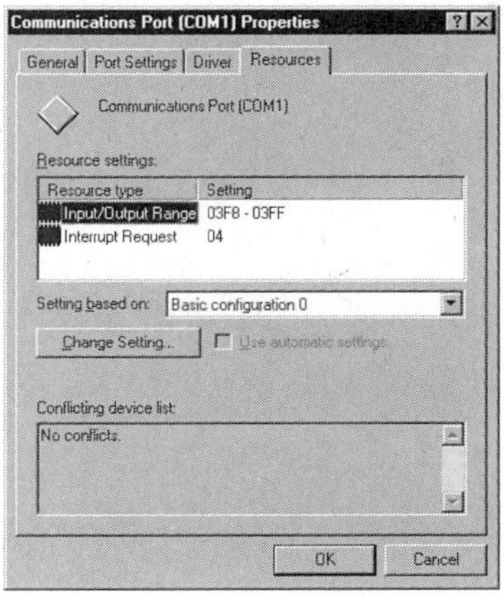

Fig. 7.4 In the Resources tab, you can see if your manual device settings are in conflict with other system settings.

The Device Manager and Adding New Hardware

All Plug-and-Play devices are switchless and jumperless because they're designed to automatically communicate with the operating system and BIOS and receive their configuration information from them. Therefore, there's no need to configure such a device manually. Many newer devices, which are not Plug-and-Play compatible, were designed to be software-configurable and are also switchless and jumperless. Windows 95 will also recognize and configure the majority of these without your intervention.

Older devices neither software configurable nor Plug-and-Play compatible are referred to as *legacy devices.* With these, you may have to manually set jumpers and/or DMA settings, or face potential device conflicts. Even with the inconvenience of having to manually change the jumper settings, Windows 95 helps you every step of the way. When you're ready to figure out which resources are available in your system, grab your device's installation manual and then do the following:

1. In the System Properties sheet, choose the Device Manager tab. (See figure 7.2.)
2. Click on the Computer icon in the device diagram (the one at the top of the diagram).
3. Click on the Properties button. The Computer Properties sheet appears. The Interrupt request (IRQ) radio button should be selected, as shown in figure 7.5.

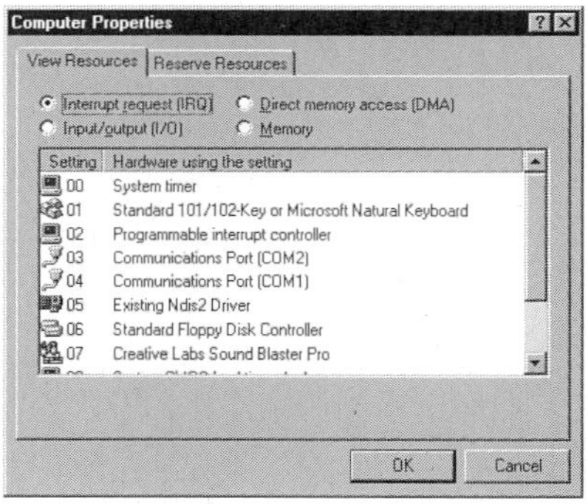

Fig. 7.5 The Computer Properties sheet displays resource information about your system.

4. Scroll through the IRQ list and view the resources allocated within the system. If an IRQ number is skipped (not listed), then it is available for use.
5. In the documentation for your device, find the possible IRQ settings it can use. Then set the jumpers or switches on the device for that IRQ.
6. You can also view the DMA channels currently in use by clicking on the the Direct memory access (DMA) radio button and performing similar setting adjustments as in steps 4 and 5.
7. Shut down your computer, install the device, and restart your system.

> **Note:** After restarting your system, Windows 95 may automatically recognize your addition of a new device and configure itself accordingly. Check the Device Manager and Computer Properties sheets to see whether Windows recognized the addition. If not, perform step 8.

8. Choose Add New Hardware in the Control Panel folder, and the Hardware Installation Wizard leads you through the installation of the device (discussed later in this chapter).

If you don't follow these steps, you risk a device conflict. If a device conflict occurs, Windows 95 will deactivate the device causing the conflict rather than hang the whole system. This action allows you to find out where the conflict resides and what setting(s) not to use. If a device has been deactivated, it will appear in the Device Manager diagram with a "slashed circle" over the device icon. View its properties to see what settings are conflicting and make the appropriate changes—or better yet, follow the preceding steps.

Deactivating a Device

With the Device Manager, you can deactivate some devices to free up system resources, or you simply may not want to use a particular device for a time. Activating and deactivating devices is related to device configurations, which are discussed later in this chapter.

In what circumstances would you want to deactivate a device? One time you might want to do this is when you have two network cards in your system, and you want to use only one at a time. If you deactivate one and activate the other, then Windows uses that configuration to communicate with the network. Another example might be if you suspect there may be a conflict between two devices in your system. You can deactivate one of them, restart your system, and perform your tests.

To deactivate (or later reactivate) a device, start at the Device Manager. Then display the Properties sheet for the device you want to modify. For instance, figure 7.6 shows the properties for a sound card.

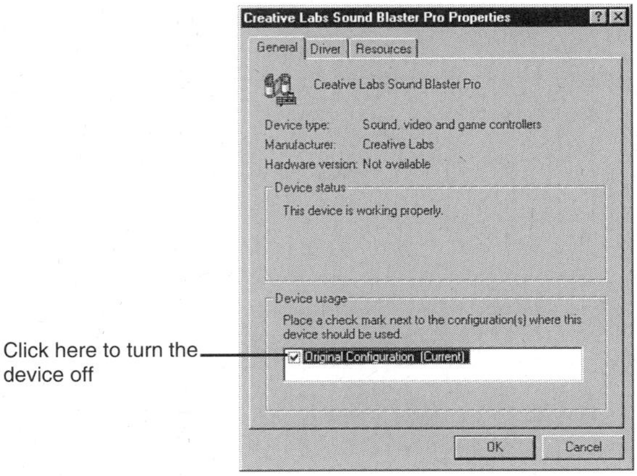

Fig. 7.6 You can turn a device on or off by using its Properties sheet.

To deactivate the device, examine the Device usage area of the sheet. This area lists the hardware configurations (again, discussed later in this chapter) in which this device is used. To turn the device off, clear the check box next to the current configuration. To turn the device back on, turn on the check box. Windows 95 allows you to control most other devices in the same manner, including the following device types:

- network cards
- sound cards
- pointing devices and the keyboard
- communications ports
- hard disk controllers
- monitors
- other system devices

Printing Resource Information

For your convenience, you can make a hard copy printout of your configuration for future reference. This is an excellent tool for troubleshooting and documentation of your system. Besides, if you must call Microsoft for technical support, this information is indispensable.

The first step in printing resource information is to decide exactly what you want to print. If you want to print a summary for your entire system, click on the Computer icon at the top of the device list. If you want to print information about a specific type of device in your system, click on that type of device. For instance, if you wanted to print information about your hard disk controllers, you would click on the hard disk controllers category in the device list.

Once you've selected an item in the device list, click on the Print button at the bottom of the Device Manager. The Print dialog box appears, as shown in figure 7.7.

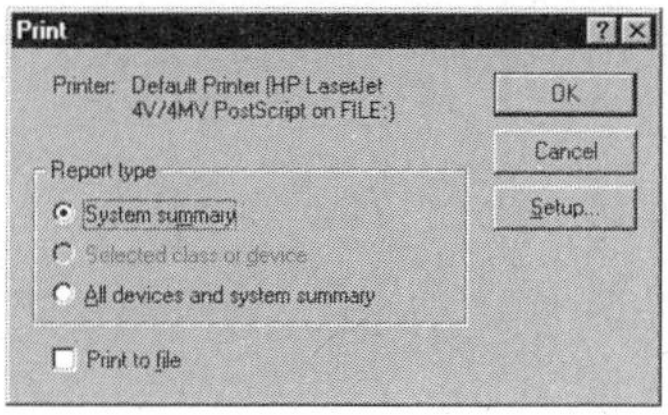

Fig. 7.7 The Device Manager provides an easy way for you to print your resource information.

From the Print dialog box, specify the type of report you want to print. You have three choices—a System summary, Selected class or device, or All devices and system summary. The length of each report depends on the configuration of your system, but the summary generally runs two pages and detailed information up to eight pages.

At the bottom of the dialog box is a check box labeled Print to file. If you click on this check box, then your printed output is sent to a disk file. When you're ready to print (either to a printer or to a disk file), click on the OK button. If you're printing to a printer, your report starts

to appear. If you're printing to a disk file, you are asked to provide the file name that Windows 95 should use for the report. (The file name you pick is up to you.)

Removing Hardware

The time will come when you want to remove hardware from your computer. Or, you might need to replace a device. Perhaps you're upgrading to a 10baseT network card, or you just bought a quad-speed CD-ROM and 16-bit multimedia card to replace an old single-speed CD-ROM/Sound Card combo. Whatever the situation, it's going to involve removing and/or adding hardware as well as the corresponding drivers. One of the nice things about Windows 95 is the ease with which it lets you remove the old hardware, and, if you're replacing it, install the new. Another bonus is how it configures itself appropriately. Again, as mentioned previously in the section on "Adding New Hardware," you may be required to set a jumper setting or two on the device(s); that's not difficult if you follow the steps outlined in that section.

The Microsoft team members have worked hard to incorporate as many device definitions and drivers to automate the installation process as they could. It is likely that any product manufactured up to the point Windows 95 is shipped can be easily and automatically configured. Of course, your device comes with floppy disks containing the appropriate drivers, so if Windows 95 cannot configure itself for your particular device, you can follow the prompts for installing the device (as you'll see later in this chapter).

When you remove a device from your system, many times Windows 95 detects the change and automatically adjusts for it. This is particularly true with systems that are fully Plug-and-Play-compliant. With legacy systems, however, Windows 95 can't always be sure if a device was removed or if there is just a problem with the hardware. In these instances, the Device Manager can help you pinpoint the problem. For instance, say you remove a legacy network card from your system, and then you start up Windows 95. The operating system attempts to load the proper drivers for the card, and then initiate communication with it. Because it can't communicate with a nonexistent card, an error occurs.

Rather than make your entire system unusable, Windows 95 marks the device as defective and continues loading the operating system. When you open the Device Manager, the problem is highlighted. Figure 7.8 shows an example of how the Device Manager appears when a defective device has been detected.

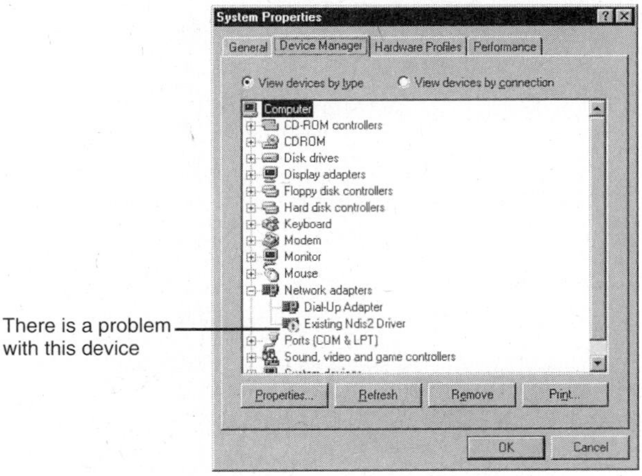

Fig. 7.8 The Device Manager informs you when there is a problem with a device in your system.

Notice that in the Network adapters group, the Existing Ndis 2 Driver device has an exclamation mark appearing over it. This mark tells you there is a problem with the device that Windows 95 cannot resolve. Had Windows 95 been able to determine that the card had been physically removed, it would have removed the device driver. Instead, it has marked the device, and you need to determine the cause of the problem. If you double-click on the device, you can get additional information in the Properties sheet, as shown in figure 7.9.

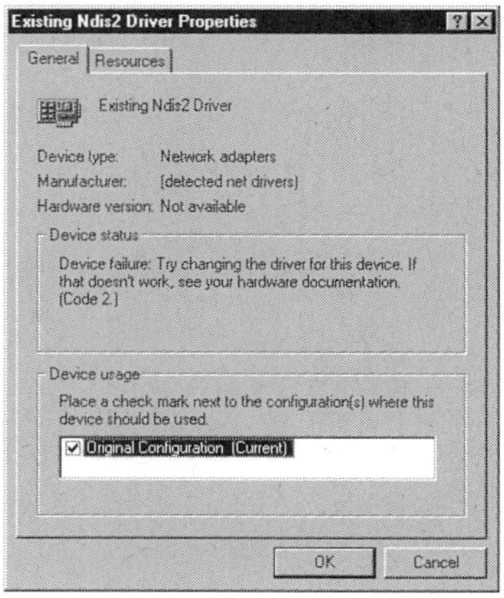

Fig. 7.9 The Properties sheet for a device can provide detailed information about the cause of an error.

In this case, where you know that you have physically removed the card, you have two choices. You can either leave the device driver intact or you can remove it. You would leave it in place if you had plans of adding the network card again at a later date. If you have no such plans, then you should remove the device from the Device Manager.

To remove a device from the Device Manager, highlight the device in the device list, and then click on the Remove button. You'll see a warning box asking you to confirm your action. When you click on OK, the device is removed. In most instances, you'll be prompted to restart your computer. Once this is done, the removal is complete.

Setting Up Hardware Profiles

There may be times when you might find it helpful to alternate between two or three different settings based on the hardware installed in your computer. For example, if you have a removable hard drive, an external tape drive that is moved between computers, or you have a laptop that uses a docking station, you can use different hardware configurations to instruct Windows 95 to load the appropriate drivers.

Once you "add" a new configuration, the next time you restart Windows 95, you'll be asked to select from a list of configurations. If your names are descriptive, you know immediately which configuration you need based on the changes you just made. When you select an option, Windows 95 will resume its startup with the chosen configuration.

Defining a Hardware Configuration

Windows 95 automatically has a hardware configuration created when you first install the operating system. The name of this configuration is Original Configuration. Defining another hardware configuration is easy. To start the process, follow these steps:

1. Right-click on the My Computer icon on your desktop.
2. From the context menu, choose the Properties option. The System Properties sheet appears.
3. Click on the Hardware Profiles tab. The System Properties sheet now appears, as shown in figure 7.10.

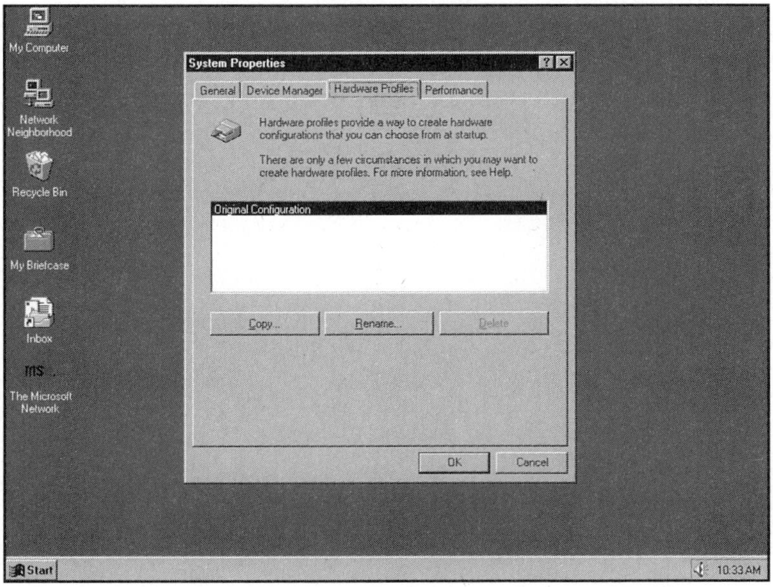

Fig. 7.10 The Hardware Profiles tab is used to manage the defined hardware profiles in your system.

4. Make sure the Original Configuration profile is selected, then click on the Copy button. You're asked for a name to use for the new profile.

5. Provide a new profile name descriptive of the way in which the profile will be used. Then click the OK button. This adds the new profile to the list of profiles in the dialog box.

At this point, you can click on the Device Manager tab and make changes to the profiles. This is done as was explained earlier in the section titled "Deactivating a Device." When you next restart your system, you'll see a text screen that indicates the available configuration options (see figure 7.11). Make your selection, and Windows 95 will use it when starting the system.

```
Windows cannot determine what configuration your
computer is in.
Select one of the following:
 1. Original Configuration
 2. Backup capable configuration
 3. None of the above
 Enter your choice:
```

Fig. 7.11 Windows allows you to pick a configuration when you boot your system.

> **Note:** If Windows 95 can make a configuration determination based on what it detects in your system, it will automatically make a profile choice without giving you the option. Typically, this happens with a portable computer with a docking station. You may have one configuration for the system out of the docking station, and another for when it is in the station. In such a case, Windows 95 can make an intelligent decision and will act accordingly.

Deleting a Hardware Configuration

To remove a hardware profile, follow these steps:

1. Right-click on the My Computer icon.
2. From the context menu, choose the Properties option. The System Properties sheet appears.
3. Click on the Hardware Profiles tab. The System Properties sheet appears, similar to what was shown earlier in figure 7.11.
4. Select the hardware profile you want to remove, making sure it is highlighted in the list of profiles.
5. Click on the Delete button. When asked to confirm your action, click on the Yes button.

The hardware profile is removed from the list of available profiles.

> **Note:** You cannot delete the original hardware profile created by Windows 95. When you choose the profile name (even if you rename it to something other than Original Configuration), the Delete button is no longer available.

Using the Add New Hardware Wizard

Integral to the Windows 95 operating system is the ability to quickly and painlessly install hardware. With several of its software products, Microsoft has introduced wizards to assist in creating or designing a spreadsheet, database, or letter. The idea is to make something that would normally be difficult, tedious, or time-consuming much faster. In this same vein, the Add New Hardware Wizard in Windows 95 helps you install hardware in your computer, basically by following the steps shown on-screen. If you have a Plug-and-Play system and you are adding a Plug-and-Play compatible device, this wizard is not necessary—devices are configured by the BIOS and operating system automatically. However, if you do not have such equipment, the Add New Hardware Wizard can be a great help.

> **Tip:** Any type of device, including a printer or mouse, can be installed from the Add New Hardware Wizard, even though you could install it also through another folder or program.

With the introduction of Plug and Play, hardware tends to take on a new classification depending on its construction. The devices that do not conform to the Plug-and-Play standard are called legacy devices, because they are (or soon will be) the older-style equipment, regardless of how easily they install. Chances are very good that you are using two types of legacy devices right now in your system—those with jumpers and those without. The hardware installation process you follow depends on which type of device you are installing.

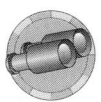

> **Note:** Keep in mind that most legacy cards function perfectly with Windows 95, but there are the occasional few that will behave erratically or won't function at all. These are typically identified, in advance, by Microsoft. Information on them is usually included on your installation disks or CD-ROM, as well as in Microsoft's electronic forums on various online services.

Legacy Devices with Jumpers

Jumpered devices can include any type of peripheral or add-on card, from sound to video to network cards. You set the jumpers manually to define which IRQ setting, DMA channel, and I/O address the card will use. To begin the installation process, you should follow the steps outlined earlier in this chapter in the section, "The Device Manager and

Adding New Hardware." Once you have followed those steps, you are ready to use the Add New Hardware Wizard. You can start the wizard in the following manner:

1. Choose the Settings option from the Start menu. The Settings menu appears.
2. From the Settings menu, choose the Control Panel option. The Control Panel window appears.
3. Double-click on the Add New Hardware applet. This starts the Add New Hardware Wizard, and you will shortly see the dialog box, as shown in figure 7.12.

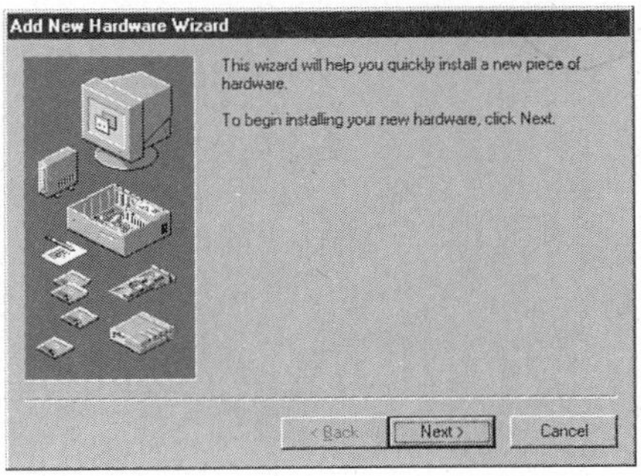

Fig. 7.12 The welcome dialog box is the start of the Add New Hardware Wizard.

Click the Next button to bypass the welcome screen. The next screen allows you to indicate whether you want Windows to automatically search for devices in your system. (See figure 7.13.) If you click on Yes, Windows assumes you've already installed the device inside your computer. It will attempt to identify the hardware, determine the driver to use, and what the device's default settings should be. Often with legacy devices this method produces conflicting settings that you can see by viewing the properties for the device in the Device Manager (as discussed earlier in the chapter).

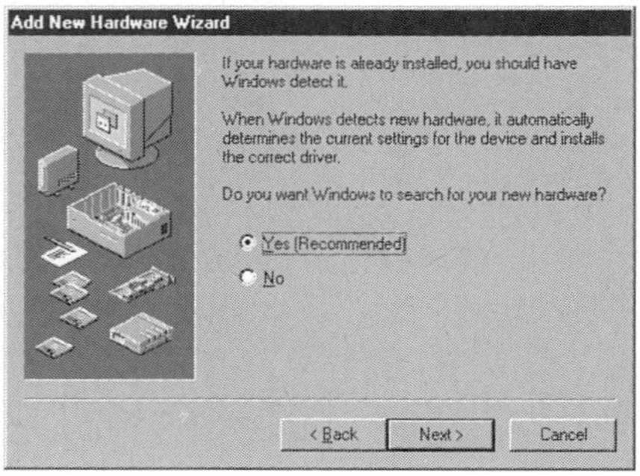

Fig. 7.13 The first step of the Add New Hardware Wizard is to select how you want the installation to proceed.

It is usually best to choose No at this point. When you do, you'll see a new dialog box that allows you to pick the type of hardware you want to install. Scroll through the list to identify the exact type of device you want to install. For example, if you want to install a sound card, you would scroll down until you find sound, video, and game controllers. Highlight the option and click on Next. The wizard then presents lists of the manufacturers and related models, as shown in figure 7.14.

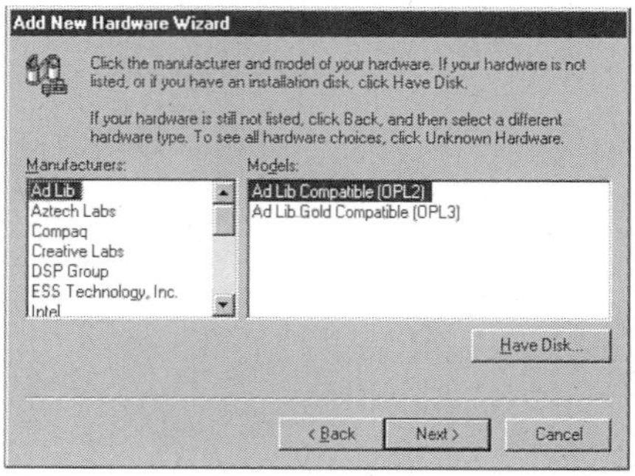

Fig. 7.14 Picking a manufacturer and model is essential to proper installation.

You should pick the manufacturer of your device (in this case, a sound card), and then the model of device. Make sure you pick the manufacturer first, as the choices in the model column will vary depending on

the manufacturer. If you don't see a choice that matches your hardware, click Have Disk to install the drivers from a manufacturer's disk. When you're through selecting your hardware make and model, click on the Next button.

If your manufacturer and product model is not listed in the wizard, and you don't have a Windows 95 driver disk from the manufacturer, you should choose a make and model that is compatible with your product. If this is not possible (if nothing listed is compatible), then you have no choice—you'll need to get a Windows 95 driver disk before you can use the device in Windows 95.

If you have a device driver disk, and you click on the Have Disk button, you're asked to specify the disk drive where you have inserted the disk. Indicate the disk drive (and folder, if necessary), and then click on OK. The wizard will then indicate the names of the drivers on the disk, and you can pick the one that is appropriate for your needs.

After you've picked a product make and model or have picked a device driver from disk, the next dialog box informs you of the resources that Windows 95 will assign to the new hardware device. If Windows 95 suspects a conflict with existing device settings, the Add New Hardware Wizard will notify you and offer suggestions for properly setting up your device. Otherwise, it prompts you to mark down (or click Print to send to printer) the settings. When you have done this and click on the Next button, the correct drivers are automatically loaded and you're prompted to click on Finish to complete the installation process.

Your changes will not take effect until you shut down and restart your system. Essentially, the Add New Hardware Wizard is designed to remove the guesswork on the installation process and simplify it by asking a few simple questions.

Legacy Devices Without Jumpers

Because jumperless devices are software configurable, it is understandable that Windows 95 can communicate and configure them properly. In fact, next to Plug and Play, this type of device is the easiest to install. To install such a device into your computer with the Add New Hardware Wizard, do the following:

1. Insert or attach the device to your computer.
2. Start your computer to load Windows 95.
3. Choose the Settings option from the Start menu. The Settings menu appears.
4. From the Settings menu, choose the Control Panel option. The Control Panel window appears.
5. Double-click on the Add New Hardware applet. This starts the Add New Hardware Wizard.
6. Click on Next at the welcome screen, make sure Yes is selected, and click on Next.

At this point the wizard explains that Windows will detect newly installed hardware and may take a few minutes. When you click on Next, the wizard attempts to determine what hardware is attached to your system. Depending on the speed of your computer, this can take anywhere from a minute to five minutes. After it's completed, you can see a list of detected devices by clicking on the Details button, as shown in figure 7.15.

If everything looks OK, then click on Finish. If you are then asked to verify that the device actually exists, click on OK.

If everything does not look OK, then you only have one real option. You should click on the Back button to return to the previous dialog box in the wizard. This is the screen that allows you to indicate that you want to manually specify the hardware to install. If you choose this route, see the instructions in the previous section.

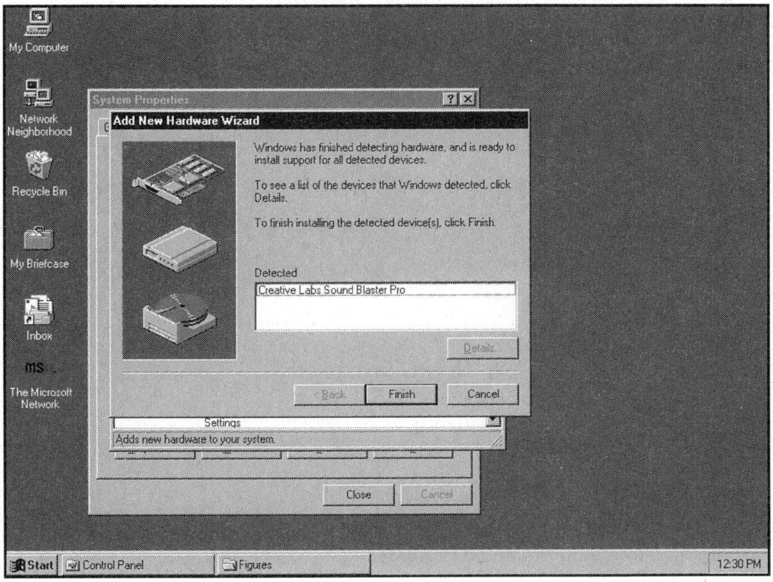

Fig. 7.15 With the Add New Hardware Wizard, Windows 95 automatically detects any new equipment you add.

KILLER WINDOWS 95

8

Examining the Hardware You Need for Windows 95

by Allen L. Wyatt

Windows 95 is a versatile operating system that demands far more of a computer system than any of its predecessors. The current low-end system for everyday use with Windows 95 is a 16MHz 386SX or better with 4M of RAM, a SuperVGA monitor and fast graphics adapter, and an 80M hard drive.

Evaluating Hard Drive Space

The more resources you can provide for Windows 95, the more satisfied you will be with its performance. If your system includes a small hard drive, the squeeze is on from the moment you install Windows 95. By itself, the operating system requires over 60M of hard drive space. The situation quickly gets out of hand as you add additional applications. For example, Word for Windows requires another 15M of disk space. The operating system and Word for Windows alone consume over 75M of space. If you have a smaller hard drive, you might be able to get by if you compress your disk drive, but the easiest solution is to run Windows 95 on a system with at least 150M.

Evaluating Graphics Capabilities

The need for a good monitor and a graphics accelerator board is equally compelling. When most programs were based on characters rather than graphics, users considered a .31 dot-pitch VGA monitor a luxury but made-do with EGA because that was all they really *needed.* Now, with the Windows 95 user interface and its bitmapped graphics, icons, menus, scroll bars, and What-You-See-Is-What-You-Get (WYSIWYG) display of documents, users need every bit of detail they can get. Furthermore, displays must be sharp if users are to work at monitors all day long and still be able to see well enough to drive home at night. A .28 dot-pitch monitor capable of 800×600 resolution and preferably 15 or 16 inches in size is rapidly becoming the minimum standard for a Windows 95 system.

Although Windows 95 is faster than earlier versions of Windows, it is much slower than older, character-based applications that ran under DOS, such as WordPerfect 5.1 and Lotus 1-2-3 version 2.2. You can run Windows 95 at speeds comparable to these applications, however, if you hook your monitor up to a graphics accelerator card capable of quickly displaying the huge amounts of graphics information presented by Windows 95.

Improving Hardware for Windows 95

Realistically, the high-end power system of yesterday is merely the adequate Windows 95 computer of today. If you're thinking about buying a new system, realistic low-end standards include a 66MHz 486 with 8M of RAM, a 300M 10-millisecond IDE hard drive, and a high-quality .28 dot-pitch 15- or 16-inch monitor with a graphics accelerator board. All the better if you can afford a faster CPU, more RAM, a larger hard drive, or a 17-inch monitor with a top-quality graphics accelerator.

The price difference between a 486SX/25 and a 486DX2/66 may be much less than you imagine, particularly if you buy from a top mail-order house like Gateway, Swan, Northgate, Dell, or Zeos. Given the consistent drop in computer prices, spurred by drastic price reductions in virtually every system component including CPU chips, computer RAM chips, hard drives, monitors, and graphics accelerator boards, even a 486DX2/66 is merely a mid-priced Windows 95 system.

Serious Windows 95 users benefit from their investment in good equipment. Windows 95's performance improves with every last bit of speed and capacity you can tweak from a system. Of particular benefit are a large, fast hard drive and a top-quality monitor with a graphics accelerator board.

This chapter covers the hardware essentials for running Windows 95 and, if necessary, for upgrading your system. It also tells you how to detect and correct incompatibilities between your system and Windows 95. The issues covered in this chapter include the following:

- Determining whether your computer is ready for Windows 95
- Checking system compatibility
- Looking at computers certified to run Windows 95
- Updating the BIOS

Consider the information in this chapter as a foundation for what is covered in Chapters 9 through 12 because this chapter provides an overview of the major parts of your computer system (CPU, hard drive, video system, and so on). In the following chapters you will learn the specifics of how you can improve the performance of each component of your Windows 95 system.

Getting Your Computer Ready for Windows 95

You can determine easily whether your computer is ready for Windows 95. If you have a 386 with a VGA monitor and card, only 4M of RAM, and a 40M hard drive, you really should buy a new system before you consider upgrading to Windows 95. Although it is possible to run Windows 95 on such systems, Microsoft acknowledges that it runs slowly and not very efficiently. The cost of trying to upgrade such a system to one capable of taking full advantage of Windows 95 is much greater than the cost of a new computer.

To evaluate whether your computer is up to the task of doing real work in Windows 95, remember this simple rule: a one-time hardware purchase is cheaper than the daily cost of you or your employees staring at a monitor in frustration as you wait for the computer to catch up. This rule is made particularly sound by the recent decline in the prices of computers, hard drives, RAM chips, and video subsystems.

Table 8.1 outlines the major system components that determine whether you can run Windows 95 on your 386SX or higher computer, or whether you need to upgrade some system components or purchase a new machine:

Table 8.1 Windows 95 Minimum Requirements

Component	Requires
RAM chips	Windows 95 can give users access to as much as 4G of RAM. Windows 95 and Windows 95 programs need a lot of RAM. The minimum for a 386SX or higher is 4M.
Hard drive	Windows 95 and its major applications each require many megabytes of hard drive space. The minimum reasonable requirement to run Windows 95 and more than one major Windows 95 application and to store their data files on-disk, is 300M of hard drive space. Even though you can run Windows 95 on a system with as little as 80M of space, the low cost of larger hard drives makes such a compromise unnecessary and unwise.
CD-ROM drive	While you don't absolutely need a CD-ROM drive to use Windows 95, it will come in handy. You can get a version of Windows 95 that installs from your CD-ROM drive, which makes installation and upgrading much faster and easier. (No diskettes to swap!) Any old CD-ROM will do, but if you can get one of the newer, faster models, so much the better. Investing in a triple- or quad-speed drive from a company like NEC or Mitsumi is well worth it.
Graphics accelerator card	Windows 95 is extremely slow unless you hook up your monitor to a graphics accelerator card designed to quickly display large amounts of video data. If you are purchasing a new system, make sure you get one with a PCI or VL-Bus; both will greatly speed up your graphics.
Monitor	With Windows 95, you need every bit of detail possible, displayed as sharply as possible. For Windows 95, the minimum recommended monitor is a .28 dot-pitch SuperVGA monitor capable of 800×600, preferably 15 or 16 inches in size. This resolution allows you the detail and clarity you need to be more productive.

If your system is at least a 386SX, but falls short in one or two of the preceding areas, you can consider upgrading your system hardware rather than buying a new computer. RAM chips currently sell for as little as $35 per megabyte from mail-order houses. Hard drive space now costs less than 50 cents per megabyte. Quality 15- or 16-inch monitors capable of non-interlaced resolutions up to 1024×768 range in price from $300 to $800, and 17-inch high-end monitors are available beginning at around $500. Top-rated graphics accelerator video cards with high resolution and color depth sell for as little as $250.

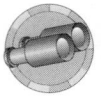

> **Note:** Any prices noted here are for information purposes only, and reflect prevailing prices when this book was written. If you talk to a computer supplier and get a price within these ranges, make sure you get a another quote. Because computer prices continue to drop, chances are good that you will be able to get even better prices by the time you read this.

Adding RAM

Most motherboard manuals detail whether users can add more RAM to their system board, as well as the process for doing so. Basically, on most 386SX or higher systems, you can add 8M or 16M of RAM quickly and easily. Many computers enable you to add as much as 64M of RAM to your motherboard; a few allow you to add much more.

On most systems sold today, memory is easily added by plugging SIMMs into the motherboard. Anywhere from one to eight SIMMs can be added, depending on the motherboard. If you have an older system, you may not be able to use SIMMs. Instead, you will need to plug individual RAM chips into the motherboard.

If you need help adding RAM, your system manufacturer might be willing to give you step-by-step instructions on how to do so. Additionally, several books on the market can help. (You may want to refer to *Upgrading and Repairing PCs,* published by Que Corporation.) If you don't feel comfortable installing the memory yourself, a computer store in your neighborhood may be willing to sell and install the chips for slightly more than the mail-order cost.

Replacing Your Hard Drive

If you can remove your computer's cover and find the major pieces that make up your PC, you can replace your hard drive with a larger and faster model. Mail-order houses such as Hard Drives International or DC Drives specialize in helping novices upgrade their hard drives, and several books offering help are on the market. You can pay significantly more when you have a new hard drive installed by a neighborhood computer store than you do when you purchase the hard drive through mail-order and install it yourself.

> **Caution:** Before attempting to change hard drives, you must do a full backup of your system, first to protect your programs and data, and second so that you can use the backup to restore these programs and data to the new hard drive. After you've installed a new hard drive, in most cases, you'll need to reinstall Windows 95. This reinstall will be necessary if your new hard drive is a different interface than the old one (for example, if you're replacing an ST506 drive with an IDE). Reinstallation is required because, in an effort to work with your system hardware, the Windows 95 Setup program detects the system's hard drive interface and bases Windows 95 configuration on it.

Types of Hard Drives

In general, Windows 95 works with the four hard drive types commonly used in the IBM-compatible personal computer market. These types are IDE, SCSI, ESDI, and ST506. The ST506 and ESDI drive interfaces are based on older technology and are rapidly being replaced by IDE and SCSI drives.

- *IDE* (Integrated Drive Electronics). IDE drives contain nearly all the electronics needed for operation, instead of major components being part of a separate controller card. In addition, IDE drives commonly are very fast and capable of storing large amounts of data. IDE hard drives capable of holding as much as 1G of data are easy to find, and even larger ones are making their way to the market. Because of the high degree of electronics integration and other refinements of hard drive technology, IDE drives can be small, which enables drives of large capacity to be installed in small computer systems. If you're considering a new hard drive for your system, consider an IDE drive.

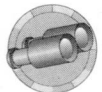

> **Note:** Many computer systems that advertise IDE drives are actually using the newer generation EIDE (enhanced IDE) interface. While this provides greater throughput speeds and hard drive capacity, for the end user it is effectively the same as an IDE system.

- *SCSI* (Small Computer System Interface). SCSI drives typically are very fast high-performance devices, and many are very large capacity. SCSI drives capable of storing more than 9G (9,100M) are available, and often are used on network servers. Most of the electronics for SCSI drives are integrated into the drive itself, rather than major components being part of a separate controller card, although this integration is not as complete as with IDE drives. An additional feature of SCSI electronics is that several SCSI devices, such as a hard drive, CD-ROM drive, tape backup drives, scanner, and other equipment can be added to a single interface card. But because of variations in how the SCSI standard is implemented, not all SCSI devices will work with all SCSI interface cards. For this reason, it is important before buying SCSI devices to ensure that they are compatible with one another (or what you already have) by consulting with a knowledgeable technician or actually testing the device on your system.

- *ESDI* (Enhanced Small Device Interface). The ESDI interface is an enhancement of the original ST506 interface used in early XT, AT, and IBM PS/2 computers. Although the ESDI interface doubles the throughput of ST506 drives, and stores twice as much data per track as ST506 drives, it requires a separate drive controller and is considered slower and less reliable than IDE and SCSI drives.
- *ST506*. The ST506 interface is the original drive interface used in early XT, AT and IBM PS/2 computers. The ST506 was the common drive interface used in IBM-compatible personal computers for many years. The ST506-interface uses two common encoding formats: Modified Frequency Modulation (MFM), and Run Length Limited (RLL). (ST506 interface drives often are referred to as MFM or RLL.) The ST506 technology, which requires a separate drive controller, has been all but replaced by faster and more reliable IDE and SCSI interface drives.

If you're considering a new hard drive, you should probably purchase an IDE drive because of several factors, including price, availability, reliability, and storage capacity.

Controller Cards

If you need a great deal of speed and data throughput, you should consider souping up your IDE or SCSI hard drive with a hardware caching controller card. A caching controller card can greatly improve the effective access time of a hard drive.

The prices of caching controllers have plunged in recent months. Such cards once cost thousands of dollars (when equipped with 2M of RAM); they now add as little as $200 to the price of a new hard drive, making such cards a solid option for someone interested in a fast Windows 95 computer system.

It is now possible to find controller cards that plug into a PCI or VL-Bus slot. These types of controllers are cutting-edge, and offer the best overall performance. These bus slots, originally intended primarily for video controllers, are covered in Chapter 11, "Video Cards, Drivers, and Monitors."

Adding a CD-ROM Drive

Adding a CD-ROM drive to your computer system is relatively easy. In fact, in some ways it is easier than adding a disk drive. All you need to do is connect it to the power supply and the controller card. Windows 95 takes care of the rest.

Many new computer systems these days are being sold with CD-ROM drives installed right off the bat. When you buy your computer, it is generally best to get the CD-ROM right away. Many software products and references are now available on CD-ROM, and you will want access to this wealth of information. In addition, a version of Windows 95 is available on CD-ROM. Thus, instead of installing from a series of floppy disks, you could install or update directly from a single CD-ROM. (A single CD-ROM can contain up to 660M of information, as compared to 1.44M for a high-density floppy disk.)

When looking for a CD-ROM, remember that they are not all the same. While a basic CD-ROM is acceptable for multimedia use, for a few dollars more you can greatly improve the performance of the drive. All you need to do is get a triple- or quad-speed drive. (Some companies are even starting to bring out faster 6X drives.) These drives spin the CD-ROM at three, four, or six times the speed of the original drives. This means the data on the CD-ROM can be accessed faster by your computer.

Installing Graphics Cards and Monitors

As a rule, installing a graphics accelerator card is relatively simple. Installation of the hardware entails nothing more than turning off your computer, opening its case, removing the old video card, plugging the new card into the slot vacated by the old one, and reconnecting the monitor cable. After the card is installed, Windows 95 may recognize it automatically (if it is a Plug-and-Play card), or you may need to instruct Windows 95 to check out the new card for you (if it is not a Plug-and-Play card), or at worst you will need to install video drivers from the manufacturer.

Note: Windows 95 requires that you use a VGA card. If you have an older system and are upgrading from an EGA to VGA, consult your system manual to determine how to reconfigure the system CMOS for the new card.

While the minimum requirements for Windows 95 only call for a VGA card, it is extremely slow unless you use a graphics accelerator card. These cards, which sell for as little as $250, are capable of running Windows 95 at speeds 25 times faster than traditional VGA cards. This entire area of picking a video adapter that takes advantage of graphics acceleration is discussed in depth in Chapter 11, "Video Cards, Drivers, and Monitors."

Installing a new monitor involves unplugging the old one from the computer and from the wall, and plugging in the new one. Remember, however, that the new monitor must be compatible with your video card.

Tip: Most mail-order houses gladly help with questions concerning the compatibility of a monitor and a video card. Furthermore, most of them have toll-free 800 numbers.

Checking System Compatibility

Windows, and in turn Windows 95, has driven the personal computer market to higher-powered hardware. The Windows family of operating systems has also spawned a curious change in terminology. Where computer manufacturers once claimed their systems were 100 percent "IBM-compatible," many now proclaim their systems "100 percent Windows-compatible."

> **Tip:** The best way to ensure Windows 95 compatibility for a new computer is to buy from a well-known computer manufacturer that offers a lengthy warranty and a liberal full-refund return policy.

In truth, the Microsoft beta test program for Windows 95 involved more users running more brands and types of computers than any other software product in history. When the test revealed a compatibility problem that affected even a small segment of existing computers, Microsoft worked hard to fix it.

With few exceptions, Windows 95 runs well on most computer systems sold today, partly because many of these systems were designed with an eye toward maximizing the use of Windows and, in particular, Windows 95. If you have problems running Windows 95, contact your manufacturer for help. The popularity of Windows has forced hardware manufacturers to work hard to iron out compatibility problems in the models they have sold in the past two or three years.

Microsoft has compiled a list of computers it considers "Windows 95 compatible." To learn whether your computer or a computer you are considering for purchase is on that list, consult the Hardware Compatibility list included with the Windows 95 documentation. This list is also available in the Windows 95 forum on CompuServe.

More than 1,000 computer makes and models are included on the list of Windows 95 compatible machines, so little chance exists that your system is incompatible. If your computer is incompatible, check with your manufacturer to see if a fix has been developed. It is just good business for manufacturers to help their customers with problems using Windows 95.

The Hardware Compatibility list included with the Windows 95 documentation also details hundreds of printers, networks, video display types, keyboards, pointing devices, and other Windows 95-compatible hardware. To determine whether your hardware (or hardware you are considering for purchase) is Windows 95-compatible, consult the Hardware Compatibility list.

Plug-and-Play Equipment

In Chapter 2, "Under-the-Hood Improvements," you learned how Windows 95 supports Plug-and-Play devices. The Plug-and-Play standard allows you to add devices to your system and have them be automatically configured for you. This is a big advantage for users, one you will readily acknowledge if you have ever had the headaches associated with configuring a system manually.

If you are in the market to upgrade your system (by adding devices or even purchasing a new computer), it would be well worth your time and effort to look for devices that are Plug-and-Play compatible. They may cost a few dollars more (particularly in 1995 and early 1996), but they could save you hours of sheer frustration.

If you are adding Plug-and-Play devices to your existing computer, you could also benefit by upgrading the BIOS on your system. A BIOS that supports Plug and Play can be easily added to an existing system by changing a few chips on the motherboard. For information on doing this, contact your computer dealer directly.

> **Caution:** Some computers have the BIOS chips soldered directly to the motherboard. If your system is one of these, it is impossible to upgrade the BIOS. Before you invest in new BIOS chips, make sure you look at your motherboard to make sure it will accept the upgrade.

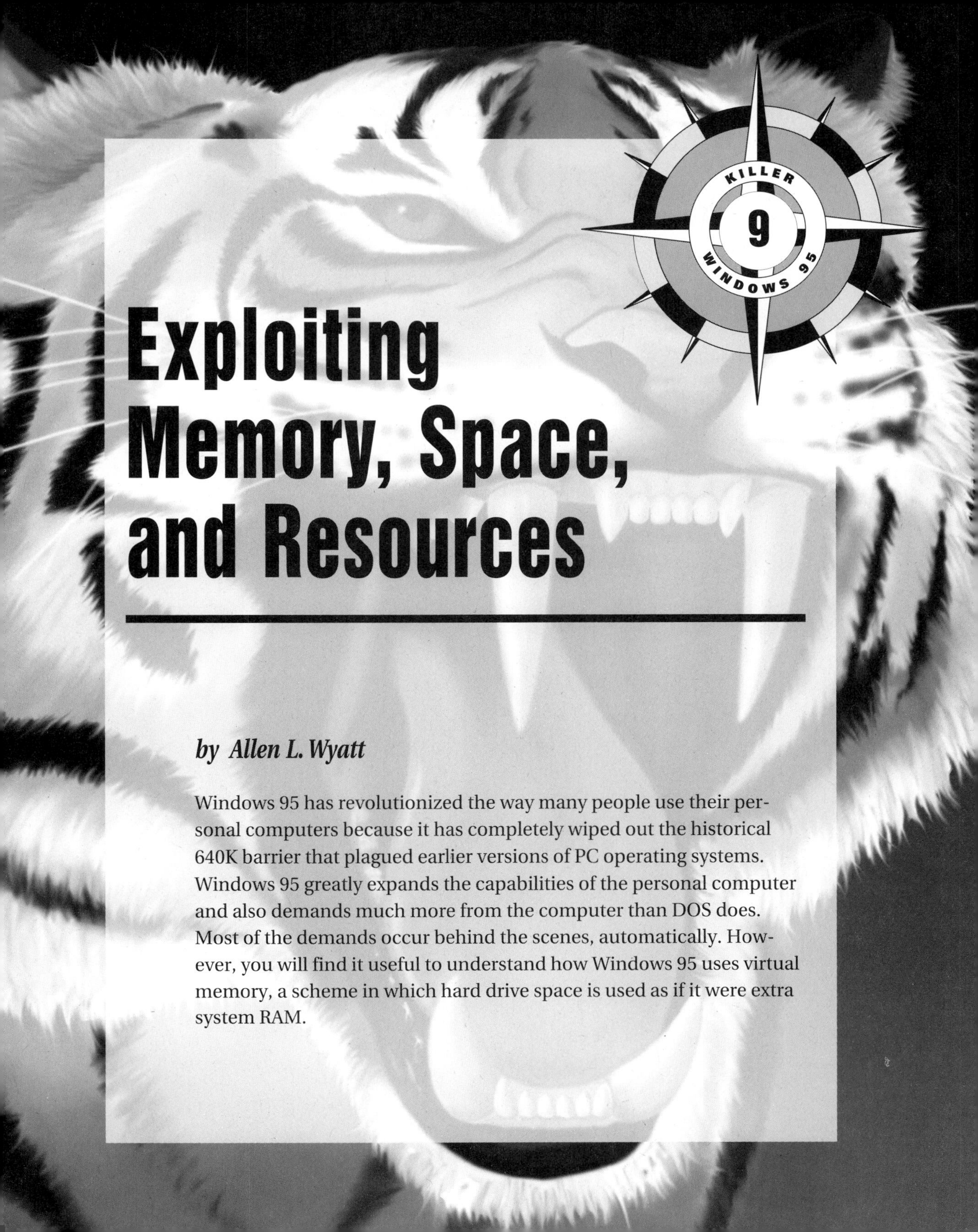

KILLER 9 WINDOWS 95

Exploiting Memory, Space, and Resources

by Allen L. Wyatt

Windows 95 has revolutionized the way many people use their personal computers because it has completely wiped out the historical 640K barrier that plagued earlier versions of PC operating systems. Windows 95 greatly expands the capabilities of the personal computer and also demands much more from the computer than DOS does. Most of the demands occur behind the scenes, automatically. However, you will find it useful to understand how Windows 95 uses virtual memory, a scheme in which hard drive space is used as if it were extra system RAM.

This chapter focuses on exploiting Windows 95 memory, disk space, and system resources. In this chapter, you learn how Windows 95 manages random-access and virtual memory.

This chapter discusses the following topics:

- How Windows 95 organizes system memory
- How Windows 95 manages virtual memory
- How you can change virtual memory settings
- How to determine when virtual memory settings should be changed
- How to control where Windows 95 stores temporary files

Understanding System Memory

To understand how Windows 95 uses memory on your system, you need to understand these terms related to memory:

- *Conventional memory* is system RAM below 640K.
- *Upper memory* is the area of memory above 640K and below 1M. This area is historically used by the system BIOS (basic input/output system), video BIOS, shadow RAM, and other system functions.
- *High memory* is the 64K area of memory immediately above the 1M mark.
- *Extended memory* is the area above high memory, up to the memory limit of the CPU.
- *Expanded memory* is memory above the 1M mark that conforms to the Lotus, Intel, Microsoft (LIM) specification. If your system contains expanded memory, you should reconfigure it as extended, using directions provided by the hardware manufacturer.
- *Virtual memory* is a scheme for using hard drive space as if it were system RAM.

In previous versions of Windows and under DOS, each of these memory areas played a critical role in the execution of programs under Windows. In Windows 95, several of these types of memory are no longer important. That is because of the way that Windows 95 views memory.

Under Windows 3.x, which operated in conjunction with DOS, memory was accessed by using a *segmented memory model.* (Sometimes referred to as 16-bit memory.) This meant that memory operations used two internal registers for addressing. One was the segment register, and the other an offset register. The combination of the segment and address register could be translated to a physical memory location within your system. The drawback to segmented memory is that you can only directly address 64K of memory—the largest number that can fit within the offset address register. After that, you need to change the segment register, recalculate a new offset register, and access memory again.

The use of segmented memory dates back to the earliest days of the PC. When the 8088/8086 CPU was introduced, it used segmented memory for a variety of reasons. The DOS operating system was based on the segmented model, which meant that DOS (and thus Windows) could only access memory in 64K blocks.

Windows 95 removes this barrier by using memory addressing capabilities that have been available in the CPU since the introduction of the 80386. This memory scheme views memory in a linear fashion, meaning that it is treated physically. To do this, Windows 95 uses a single 32-bit address register. Thus, Windows 95 uses 32-bit memory addressing, which allows 4G of memory to be addressed directly, without resorting to memory segments and offsets.

This change in memory models could be accomplished only by doing away with DOS, which historically has been the limiting factor. The benefit of this change is that programs written for Windows 95, using 32-bit addressing, can operate faster and more efficiently—there is less overhead in performing addressing manipulations.

Because memory is now treated in a linear fashion, historical constraints associated with conventional memory, upper memory, and high memory are done away with. Instead, you have only RAM and virtual memory; one is in your computer, and the other on your hard drive. The new memory manager in the Windows 95 kernel is charged with keeping things straight. It assigns memory areas to each procedure being executed, and the rest of memory is hidden from that procedure. This feature provides greater security and stability for both programs and the operating system itself.

> **Note:** Windows 95 uses the same memory addressing techniques employed in Windows NT. Thus, any 32-bit programs written for Windows NT will operate just fine under Windows 95, and vice-versa.

As mentioned earlier, with a 32-bit addressing register you can directly address up to 4G of memory. Of this memory, 2G is reserved for use by the operating system, and the other 2G for use by programs. Thus, the largest program that can be run under Windows 95 requires 2G of memory—more than enough for anything that may crop up for the next couple of years.

Understanding Conventional Memory

Historically, conventional memory has been the bane of operating systems and programmers. This memory—the first 640K of memory in your system—was considered "prime real estate." This area is where parts of DOS, device drivers, and the like were all installed. If too much conventional memory was occupied before Windows executed, then Windows would perform sluggishly, or not at all.

Windows 95 does away with the conventional memory problem. The only time this memory comes into play now is when you're working with an MS-DOS window within Windows 95. When you open an MS-DOS window, the Windows 95 memory manager creates a "virtual machine" that behaves just like an old DOS system. There is only one difference—memory management is more secure, because any program running in the virtual machine cannot access memory used by other Windows programs. As far as any DOS program is concerned, however, it has complete use of all the resources in the machine. The application is completely oblivious to the fact it is working in a contrived and controlled universe created by Windows 95.

Using Expanded Memory

Expanded memory is a hardware-related standard, devised in the 1980s by Lotus, Intel, and Microsoft. It allowed older computer systems to add memory and make it accessible to programs. If you have not done so already, you should configure any expanded memory in your system as extended memory. This typically involves making some changes to the jumpers on your memory card; you should refer to your hardware documentation for more information.

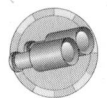

> **Note:** Some DOS programs require your system to have expanded memory to run properly. If you must run such a program, Windows 95 provides support for you. For more information, refer to Chapter 19, "Fine-Tuning Windows 95 for Your DOS Applications."

Understanding Virtual Memory

You have already learned that Windows 95 allows direct addressing of up to 4G of memory. Building a PC with this much RAM would be prohibitively expensive, so most systems come with 4M, 8M, or 16M of memory. At first, this small amount of memory might seem like a restraint of the operating system.

To get around the disparity between actual RAM space and the 4G memory space of the operating system, Windows 95 employs a

technique called *virtual memory*. This kind of memory is nothing new; virtual memory schemes have been around for years, and have been incorporated in previous versions of Windows.

Virtual memory uses hard drive space as if it were system RAM, temporarily storing information to free up system memory. This capability enables the computer to run more programs at the same time under Windows 95 than physical RAM alone would allow. Virtual memory functions are controlled by a virtual memory manager (VMM), a part of the Windows 95 kernel that handles swapping parts of memory to the disk and back again, as necessary. The area on disk into which memory chunks are stored is called a *swap file*.

Under previous versions of Windows, you had a large number of choices for managing your swap file. You could elect to use a temporary or permanent swap file, and you needed to determine the proper amount of memory to allocate to the file. This complexity is removed in Windows 95. There is no more decision to make about the type, location, or size of your swap file; Windows 95 can take care of all these matters automatically.

If you're familiar with the previous versions of Windows, you know that both temporary and permanent swap files had their advantages and drawbacks. Temporary swap files were dynamic, growing only as they were needed. Permanent swap files allowed faster access, because they were stored in a contiguous space on the disk. In Windows 95, there are no temporary or permanent swap files. Instead, a dynamic swap file is created and managed by the VMM, using 32-bit access. It could be said that the result is an optimized temporary swap file, with all the advantages of a permanent swap file.

Changing Virtual Memory Settings

Even though Windows 95 does an excellent job of managing virtual memory, there may be times you want to change the constraints under which it works. Windows 95 allows you to modify both the location and size of the virtual memory swap file. To do this, follow these steps:

1. Choose Settings from the Start menu. The Settings menu appears.
2. Choose Control Panel from the Settings menu. The Control Panel window appears.
3. Double-click on the System icon in the Control Panel. The System Properties dialog box appears.
4. Click on the Performance tab.
5. Click on the Virtual Memory button. The Virtual Memory dialog box appears, as shown in figure 9.1.

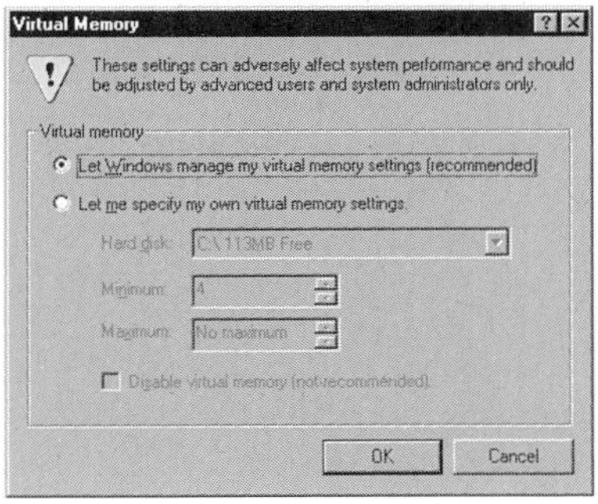

Fig. 9.1 The Virtual Memory dialog box allows you to control swap file settings.

6. Choose the virtual memory option that allows you to specify settings by clicking on the second radio button. The options in the middle of the dialog box then become available.
7. In the Hard disk drop-down list, select the hard drive where you want the swap file located.
8. In the Minimum area, indicate how small the swap file can be. (The smallest setting here is 4M.)
9. In the Maximum area, indicate how large the swap file can be. You can set any value, up to the current available space on your hard drive.
10. Click on OK.

At this point, when you exit from the System Properties dialog box, you'll be informed that you need to restart Windows in order for your changes to take effect. Once you do, the new virtual memory settings will be used.

Disabling Virtual Memory

If your hard drive space is at a premium, you can conserve disk space by preventing Windows 95 from swapping information to disk. To prevent Windows 95 from swapping, follow these steps:

1. Choose Settings from the Start menu. The Settings menu appears.
2. Choose Control Panel from the Settings menu. The Control Panel window appears.
3. Double-click on the System icon in the Control Panel. The System Properties dialog box appears.
4. Click on the Performance tab.
5. Click on the Virtual Memory button. The Virtual Memory dialog box appears, as shown earlier in figure 9.1.
6. Choose the virtual memory option that allows you to specify settings by clicking on the second radio button. The options in the middle of the dialog box then become available.
7. Click on the Disable virtual memory option.
8. Click on OK.

At this point, when you exit the System Properties dialog box, you will be informed you need to restart Windows in order for your changes to take effect. Once you do, the new virtual memory settings will be used.

> **Caution:** Turning off disk swapping can be detrimental to Windows—don't do it unless you absolutely have to. If you're running out of disk space, the better options are to delete files, compress your drive, or get a larger drive.

Optimizing Virtual Memory

Now that you know how to make changes to your virtual memory settings, you may wonder how you can determine whether you really should make a change. Windows 95 provides a diagnostic tool you can use to help make such a determination—System Monitor. If you installed the minimal system, System Monitor, along with many other options, is NOT automatically installed. However, you can install this program manually.

System Monitor is a program that allows you to analyze the performance of various parts of your computer system. Because the program is so comprehensive, full use of it is beyond the scope of this chapter. Portions of the program, however, can be used to determine the job your memory manager is performing.

To start the System Monitor, follow these steps:

1. Choose Programs from the Start menu. The Programs menu appears.
2. Choose Accessories from the Programs menu. The Accessories menu appears.
3. Choose System Tools from the Accessories menu. The System Tools menu appears.
4. Click on System Monitor. This starts the System Monitor program, as shown in figure 9.2.

The System Monitor features a menu, a toolbar, and a grid area. The grid area displays various performance statistics for your system. If you have not used the System Monitor before, the default area being monitored is the CPU usage on your system. The vertical axis on the grid shows the percentage of use, and the horizontal axis is time. Every few seconds, the usage of the CPU is calculated, and displayed on the graph. In figure 9.2, you can start to see some of the CPU usage being shown, at the lower-right corner of the grid. Over time, the percentage moves from right to left, and you can get an idea of your CPU use. Figure 9.3 shows an example of CPU usage after performing some

typical disk operations (such as formatting a floppy disk or running the ScanDisk program).

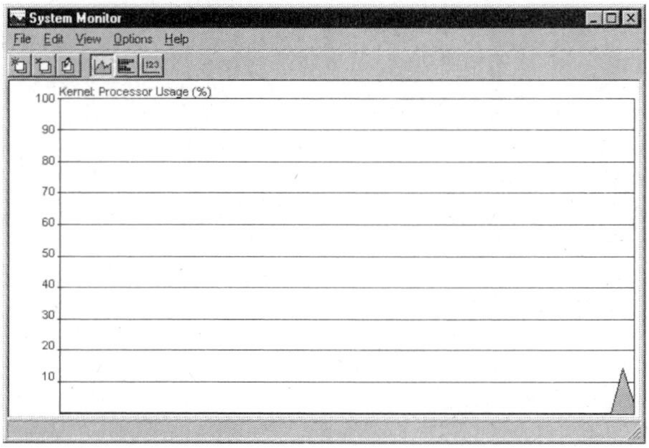

Fig. 9.2 The System Monitor is used to view the performance of your system components.

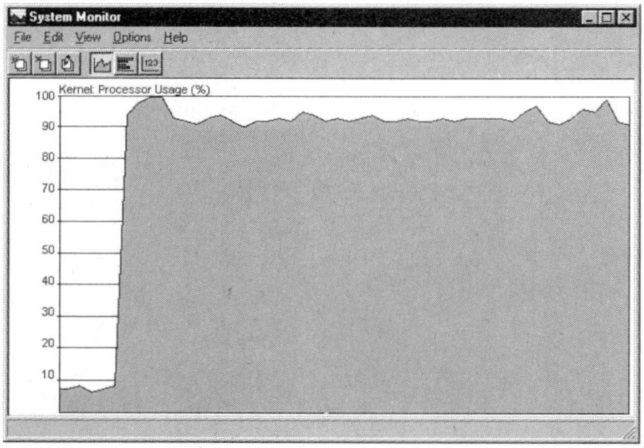

Fig. 9.3 After monitoring CPU usage for a few moments, you can get an idea of how your operations tax the CPU.

To change the performance area being monitored (which you need to do), choose Edit, Add Item. The Add Item dialog box appears, as shown in figure 9.4.

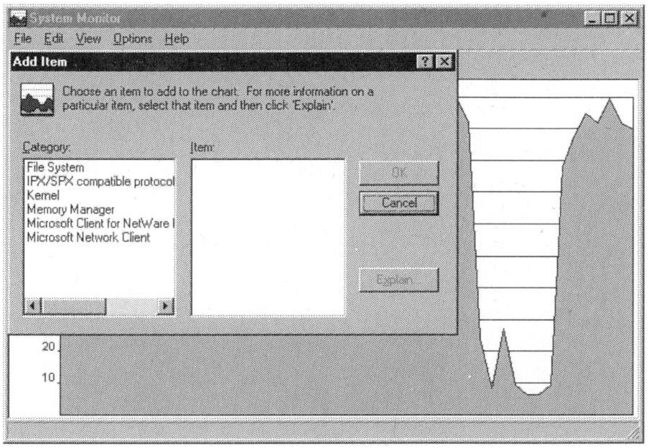

Fig. 9.4 The Add Item dialog box is used to select the performance areas you want to monitor.

This dialog box consists of two portions. The left side is where you select a category of performance items. Once you make a choice in this list, the items within that group will appear on the right side of the dialog box. To monitor items related to virtual memory, select the Memory Manager option in the Category list. The choices then displayed in the Item list are detailed in table 9.1.

> **Note:** The performance area categories listed in the Add Item dialog box will depend on the operating system components you have installed.

Table 9.1 Performance Items Related to Virtual Memory

Item	Meaning
Allocated memory	The amount of memory, in bytes, allocated by Windows to applications and operating system components.
Discards	Number of memory pages discarded per second.
Disk cache size	The size of the disk cache.

continues

Table 9.1 Continued

Item	Meaning
Free memory	The amount of physical memory currently available.
Instance faults	Number of instance faults per second.
Locked memory	The amount of memory allocated and locked either by applications or the operating system.
Maximum disk cache size	The maximum disk cache size.
Minimum disk cache size	The minimum disk cache size.
Other memory	Memory that has been allocated, but cannot be stored in the swap file.
Page faults	Number of page faults per second.
Page-ins	Number of transfers from the swap file to physical memory, per second.
Page-outs	Number of transfers from physical memory to the swap file, per second.
Swapfile defective	Swap file bytes determined to be defective. This indicates bad sectors on the disk drive.
Swapfile in use	The memory in the swap file, in bytes, currently being used.
Swapfile size	The size of the swap file, in bytes.
Swappable memory	Memory that has been allocated from the swap file, in bytes.

Obviously, not all of the performance items listed in Table 9.1 are going to be meaningful to the average user. However, you can use some of the items to get a clearer picture of the performance offered by your swap file. As an example, you can use the Swapfile size and Swapfile in use items to monitor the dynamic growth of your swap file, as well as what portion of the swap file is being used. If you monitor this while you have a memory-intensive program running, you can see what sort of job the manager is doing.

Tip: If you want to monitor how many times information is transferred to and from the swap file, you can use the Page-ins and Page-outs options.

Once you select the performance item you want to monitor, click on the OK button. The System Monitor screen is modified to display any existing performance items, in addition to the one you have chosen. Thus, if you choose the Swapfile size item, the System Monitor window would look similar to what is shown in figure 9.5.

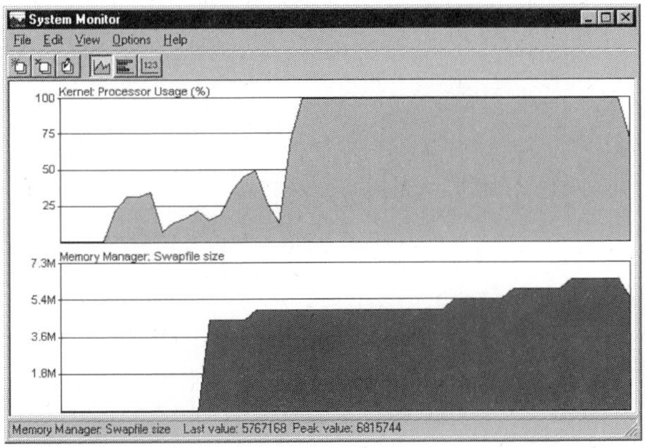

Fig. 9.5 Adding performance items modifies how the System Monitor grid area appears.

You can continue to add items to the monitor, or remove them, if desired. To remove an item, choose Edit, Remove Item, and then select the item to remove.

So how do you know when you should make changes? Simple. If you see that the swap file is maxing out the available space on the disk drive, then you may want to look at freeing up disk space. If you notice that the swaps are occurring slowly, you may want to get a faster hard drive, or change the swap file to another hard drive, which may be

faster. Selective and analytically using the System Monitor can help you tweak your virtual memory settings beyond what can be done automatically by Windows 95.

Understanding the TEMP Setting

Many programs use temporary files to store data while they're running. By swapping data to a disk in this manner, these programs are able to work more quickly and efficiently. By default, these temporary files are stored in the \WINDOWS\TEMP directory on your hard drive. This directory was created when you first installed Windows 95.

Notice that \WINDOWS\TEMP is a default directory for temporary files. You can change the location of the temporary files by modifying or creating your AUTOEXEC.BAT file, and setting the TEMP variable. This directory is read after Windows 95 is started, and temporary files are stored at the location you specify. For instance, adding the following line to your AUTOEXEC.BAT file instructs Windows 95 to store temporary files in the TEMP directory on the D drive:

```
SET TEMP=D:\TEMP
```

Some programs actually don't look for the TEMP variable. Instead, they look for a variable named TMP. This setting is particularly useful for DOS programs operating in an MS-DOS window. To set this variable, add a line such as the following to your AUTOEXEC.BAT file:

```
SET TMP=D:\TEMP
```

This command instructs the program to store the temporary files in the same location as you previously indicated for the TEMP variable.

Optimizing Your Disk Drives

by Allen L. Wyatt

In Chapter 8, "Examining the Hardware You Need for Windows 95," you learned that the absolute minimum system you need for Windows 95 is a 386SX with 4M of RAM and an 80M hard drive. If you're trying to run Windows 95 with a minimal system (one near the minimum requirements), this chapter presents valuable information about how you can get the most out of your system. In particular, this chapter focuses on maximizing performance of your disk drive systems.

This chapter discusses methods to access data more quickly, teaches you more about random-access memory (or RAM), and describes ways to increase the amount of data a small disk drive can hold. This chapter also provides housekeeping techniques that will help you keep your computer system streamlined, free up more disk space, allow you to install more programs, and give Windows 95 swap files more room to do their job.

If you try the suggestions in this chapter only to find that the improvement isn't enough, the last section of the chapter reviews what you can accomplish by upgrading your system. The review looks particularly at features that complement your system rather than conflict with it.

Whether you fine-tune or upgrade, many of the disk housekeeping suggestions in this chapter are necessary for maintaining optimum disk performance. This chapter presents many tips to simplify or automate disk cleaning.

Working with Caches

A cache is nothing more than a temporary storage area for information. In computer terms, a cache is a high-speed area used to store information until it can be processed by a slower device. Caches are used on computers to speed access to data stored on hard drives. As CPU speed continues to increase, the computer industry is relying more and more on caches to help data transmission by other components of the system keep pace with the CPU. Caches on the market today are of two basic types: RAM and disk. Each performs different—usually complementary—tasks, and this chapter reviews both. Although it may seem strange to be studying RAM in a chapter on disk drive performance, the best way to speed access to your drive is to move the data you're using to a faster location—that being RAM.

Examining RAM

The RAM installed in your computer is composed of dynamic RAM chips (DRAM), which are inexpensive but operate relatively slowly, at 130 to 200 ns (nanoseconds). This speed figure consists of access time (70 to 100 ns) plus the precharge time needed to refresh a RAM cell before data can be accessed again. The cycle of access and precharge time is improved by using a RAM design such as page mode or interleaved memory.

The RAM design used in a computer system is designed into the motherboard by engineers—you can't do anything to modify it. An understanding of how RAM can be designed can be beneficial if you're looking to upgrade or replace your system. The next two sections address two common methods of designing the RAM portion of your system.

Understanding Page Mode RAM Design

Page mode (and the similar static column access) design takes advantage of two aspects of computer design:

- Most of the time, computers read and write memory addresses that are clustered close together or sequentially.
- RAM chips are designed to store data in a matrix of rows and columns.

A page-mode DRAM chip includes a 2,048-bit buffer. When data is requested, the entire row of data represented by the first half of the address is read into the buffer. The second half of the address is then read, specifying the column where the bit of data is located. If the next request is for data located on the same row, the row is still in the buffer and the new bit can be accessed from the buffer. When the data is accessed from the buffer in this way, the precharge phase is unnecessary. This results in a page mode cycle, typically 40 to 60 ns, rather than a regular cycle of 130 to 200 ns.

Static column access design receives the second half of the address in a different but slightly more efficient manner. The advantage of both designs is that only a few additional RAM chips are required to implement them.

Understanding Interleaved RAM Design

Interleaved memory divides RAM into blocks (usually two or four). Memory addresses are assigned to the blocks sequentially, and data needed by the processor is written into each block of RAM in address order. Figure 10.1 shows a two-block arrangement of interleaved memory with address assignments appropriate for a 386 system with a 32-bit processor bus.

Address Lines	Block 0	Block 1
	16-19	20-23
	8-11	12-15
	0-3	4-7

Fig. 10.1 An interleaved memory layout featuring two blocks

When contiguous data is stored in RAM for use by the processor, that data is distributed in address order among the blocks of interleaved memory. If the processor needs this data again and the data is still stored in RAM, it's read from the blocks—alternately if using only two interleave blocks or sequentially if using four. Throughput is improved because data is accessed in one block while at least one other block is being precharged.

The more blocks of RAM used in an interleaved memory design, the less the chance of reading a block twice in a row. On the other hand, a drawback when upgrading interleaved memory is the need to add RAM to each block in equal amounts, often doubling or quadrupling the amount of RAM you must buy.

Effects of RAM Design

RAM design is incorporated into the motherboard of a system. A specific RAM design isn't a feature you can add as an easy upgrade. However, understanding how RAM design affects system performance gives you a starting point for evaluating ways to improve RAM access time as well as techniques that use RAM to speed access to disk data in Windows 95.

Consider how this information stacks up in relation to your present system. RAM access times range from 130 to 200 ns to a low in the neighborhood of 40 ns if one of the designs just discussed is implemented. A 33 MHz system has a clock cycle of 30 ns, and a 66 MHz system has a clock cycle of 15 ns. The specific CPU in a system affects the duration of the bus and instruction cycles of the system (which are linked to the clock cycles). In general, however, the bus cycles of the later chips (486 and Pentium) come closer to the actual clock cycles of the systems that use them. It's important to understand that it's possible for the effective speeds (throughput) of one generation of chips to overlap the throughput of the next generation of chips, depending on the clock speed. For instance, the performance of the fastest 486 systems (100 MHz) are just as great as the performance of the slower Pentium systems.

If the RAM design used in your system isn't tuned for optimal performance, it means that the CPU is automatically crippled. An efficient RAM design can deliver data at speeds equal to that of a fast processor. It's important to ensure that your system uses an efficient RAM design so that you can get the most performance possible from your system.

Processor performance isn't the only feature that depends on the manufacturer. The speed of the DRAM chips used in your system, for example, is an integral part of the system design. Refer to your operating manual or contact the motherboard manufacturer to see whether your system includes features such as adjustable wait-state settings or the capability to configure itself dynamically before you decide to buy and install faster DRAM chips.

Understanding RAM Caches

For speed faster than DRAM, static RAM (SRAM) chips are available. They boast access rates of 15 to 30 ns, with rates of less than 20 ns being most desirable. In addition to providing speed, static RAM doesn't need precharging or refreshing, as does dynamic RAM. This kind of speed is good enough to keep up with a fast CPU, but the memory chips are much more expensive (when compared to regular dynamic RAM). However, a small amount of SRAM (typically 16K to 256K) installed as a RAM cache can increase system performance substantially.

A RAM cache is managed by a cache controller circuit that acts as an intermediary between the CPU and regular RAM. It reads data from RAM that's requested by the processor, stores or tags the addresses of the data, places the information into the cache, and even prereads the next 8 to 16 bytes of data from RAM. The cache controller continues to intercept requests from the CPU, first checking its table of addresses to see whether the data is in the cache. If it is, the data is accessed at 20 ns speed or faster. If the data isn't in the cache, the cache controller reads the data from regular RAM, adds it to the cache, and then directs the processor to it. Most requests for data are channeled through the cache controller.

If the requested data is found in the cache, that bus cycle is referred to as a *cache hit*. If it's not found, the cycle is called a *cache miss*. Acceptable cache designs achieve a 95 percent hit rate, with 98 percent preferred, assuring that almost all data is delivered at the higher SRAM speeds.

A cache must be designed to read its address table and to discard old data efficiently. In a RAM cache, older data is discarded on a least recently used (LRU) algorithm. Efficient ways to read the address table is a more complex issue.

If you're shopping for a system with cache, you can choose from three designs used to organize the data in the cache:

- *Fully associative cache.* A fully associative cache allows data to be stored anywhere. The cache controller must then check the entire address table to find whether the data is in the cache. On many computers, the processor is giving the cache controller only 40 to 80 ns to do this, as well as to produce the data.

- *Direct-mapping cache.* A better design is a direct-mapping cache, where the cache is divided into address regions. This design allows the controller to check only a portion of the address table. The drawback is that a region can fill with continuous data while other regions remain empty.

- *Set-associative cache.* The most popular and efficient design is a set-associative cache. This system divides the cache into two to eight sets, or areas, and rotates the assignment of addresses among the sets in a fashion that somewhat resembles the way addresses are distributed in interleaved memory blocks (you may want to refer back to figure 10.1). All sets fill with data at a more balanced rate, which results in more hits, but the controller still must check two to eight entries in the address table. To avoid a slowdown at this step, the set-associative design also includes hardware that simultaneously checks all the addresses in a set.

None of these designs is inconsistent with the DRAM designs explained earlier in this chapter. Most cached systems use one of them, and their benefits are available whenever the cache needs to access RAM.

A larger cache doesn't necessarily mean faster performance, but it does mean a larger address table to read in the same amount of time. The efficiency of a system's cache controller and the system design can make a small cache outperform a large one. Similarly, an efficient, properly sized cache will show little performance increase if you add RAM to it. If you want to increase the size of a RAM cache, all you have to do is replace a set of chips on the motherboard and possibly change jumper settings. Manufacturers tend to increase cache size as processor speed is increased within a CPU family.

The 486 chip is designed with an 8K internal cache that uses a set-associative design with four sets. This cache is very efficient because it has a direct 128-bit data path to the chip's processing circuitry. Unfortunately, the size of the cache is small enough to reduce the hit rate to an unacceptable 90 percent. For this reason, a small on-board or external cache is usually included with 486 systems. For instance, a 486/33 system typically has a 64K cache.

The Pentium chip has two 8K internal caches, for a total of 16K of two-way set-associative caching. One cache is used for data and the other for code; both are software transparent to maintain compatibility with earlier CPU designs. Even though there's effectively twice the internal cache in the Pentium when compared with the 486, many system designs include a small external cache as well.

Understanding Disk Caches

Disk caches come in two types: software and disk drive. Although both cache the same data, notable differences exist between the two. In some instances, the differences are incompatible.

Whereas a RAM cache speeds the rate of accessing whatever's in memory, a disk cache speeds disk access by holding frequently requested data in memory (again, either in the drive electronics or in an area of computer RAM). This action substantially decreases the number of times that the hard disk must be read. Since RAM can be read faster than a hard drive can be accessed and read, the overall system performance is increased substantially by proper use of a disk cache.

Software Caches

Software caches occupy RAM, offering high-speed access to data usually stored on disks. A software cache operates in much the same way as a RAM cache—the major difference is the amount of data that can be read ahead to improve performance. Not only can the software cache hold recently read data on the assumption that you'll need it again soon, but also the next clusters of data are read on the assumption that this data is what you'll need next.

The following steps illustrate the operating sequence:

1. When you boot the system, caching software sets up a buffer area in extended or expanded RAM in the amount you specify in the software command line, usually somewhere between 512K and 2M.
2. When the processor requires data from a disk, it sends a request to the drive where the data is stored.

3. If you have a RAM cache, the cache controller intercepts the request, checks to see whether the data is in its cache, and, if not, forwards the request.
4. The software disk cache (located in RAM) receives the request and checks to see whether the data is in its cache.
5. If the data isn't in the software cache, the data is located on the appropriate disk drive.
6. The data is read into the software cache buffer, where it's accessed by the CPU. If a RAM cache is on the motherboard, the data is read into the RAM cache and the CPU is directed to it.
7. During times when the CPU is idle, the cache reads sectors next to those just read (read-ahead feature), thus anticipating that the processor needs that data next. This tendency of computers to read clustered data was pointed out in the review of RAM earlier in this chapter. When reading from disks, the effect of this technique depends on how fragmented your disk is.

Adjusting Caching Parameters

Windows 95 includes built-in caching software designed to make your disk drives operate as efficiently as possible. For most users, this caching operates behind the scenes, with no input or configuration necessary on their part. Windows, however, does allow you to control both read-ahead and write-behind caching. (The pros and cons of write-behind caching are discussed shortly.)

To change read-ahead caching for your hard drive, follow these steps:

1. Choose Start, Settings, Control Panel.
2. In the Control Panel window, double-click on the System icon. The System Properties sheet appears.
3. Click on the Performance tab.
4. Click on the File System button. The File System Properties sheet appears, with the Hard Disk tab selected, as shown in figure 10.2.

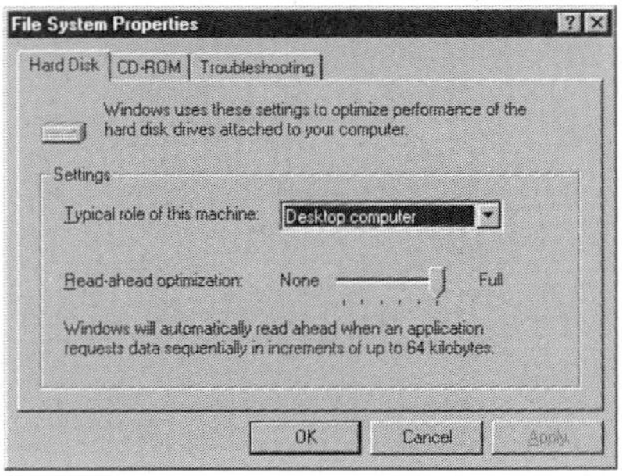

Fig. 10.2 Windows 95 allows you to modify how read-ahead caching is done on a hard drive.

There are two settings you can make in this sheet. The first is the pull-down list at the top of the Settings area. Here you can pick the typical use for your computer system, and then Windows will set the caching accordingly. There are three possible types of machines you can specify:

- **Desktop computer.** This setting is for an average system that is sitting on top of or beside your desk. Moderate-load caching is enabled when this machine type is selected.
- **Mobile or docking system.** You should select this as your machine type if you are running Windows 95 on a portable computer. Portable computers use their hard drives differently, and thus caching should be set accordingly. Windows does less read-ahead with this machine type so that there is not as much power drain (on the battery) through the hard drive.
- **Network server.** This type of machine typically has the highest disk performance requirements. The server basicly does nothing but access the disk to read and write information transmitted over the network. Because of this, the caching requirements are different than a single-user machine.

At the bottom of the Settings area is a slider control where you can indicate how big of read-ahead chunks you want Windows to use. Normally, at full read-ahead optimization, Windows will read up to the next 64K of information from the disk when your application is doing sequential data processing. You can set this cache amount to a lower value. Normally you should only do so if you have a very fast hard drive and your applications don't do much sequential processing of data.

Windows also allows you to set the same read-ahead caching parameters for your CD-ROM drives. To do this, follow these steps:

1. Choose Start, Settings, Control Panel.
2. In the Control Panel window, double-click on the System icon. The System Properties sheet appears.
3. Click on the Performance tab.
4. Click on the File System button, then on the CD-ROM tab. The File System Properties sheet appears, as shown in figure 10.3.

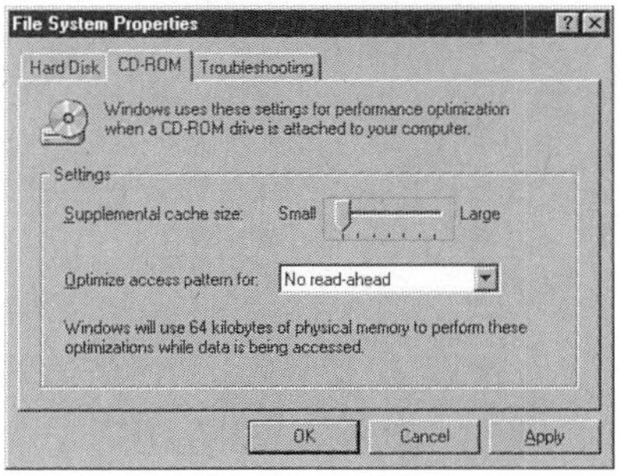

Fig. 10.3 Windows 95 allows you to modify how read-ahead caching is done on a CD-ROM drive.

Again, there are two settings you can make on this sheet. The first, at the top of the Settings area, is where you can set the supplemental read-ahead cache associated with the drive. Normally, this is set to the smallest setting possible. It is interesting to note that the smallest cache setting for the CD-ROM drive is the same value as the highest setting for the read-ahead cache on the hard drive—64K. This is because the CD-ROM is slower, and it is very conceivable you will want to set the cache to a larger value. If you find you do a lot of accessing of your CD-ROM drive, you can set the supplemental cache to a larger value by moving the slider control to the right.

At the bottom of the Settings area you can indicate how you want Windows to configure the read-ahead buffer for the CD-ROM. There are five possible settings accessed through the pull-down list:

- **No read-ahead.** This setting is the default, and means that Windows will do no read-ahead on the CD-ROM drive. Again, if you do a fair amount of processing from the drive, you'll want to choose one of the other optimization patterns.
- **Single-speed drives.** This setting is for conventional CD-ROM drives. With this pattern selected, you can specify a cache size (using the slider control) between 64K and 1,088K.
- **Double-speed drives.** This setting is for the popular double-speed drives. With this pattern selected, you can specify a cache size between 114K and 1138K.
- **Triple-speed drives.** Some systems come equipped with triple-speed drives. If so, you should select this pattern, which allows you to set a cache size between 164K and 1,188K.
- **Quad-speed or higher.** Most new high-performance systems sold today include a quad-speed CD-ROM drive, and some are coming equipped with a 6X drive. Selecting this option allows for cache sizes between 214K and 1,238K.

To change the write-behind cache used with disk drives (not CD-ROM drives, which are inherently read-only), follow these steps:

1. Choose Start, Settings, Control Panel.
2. In the Control Panel window, double-click on the System icon. The System Properties sheet appears.
3. Click on the Performance tab.
4. Click on the File System button and then the Troubleshooting tab. This displays the dialog box shown in figure 10.4.

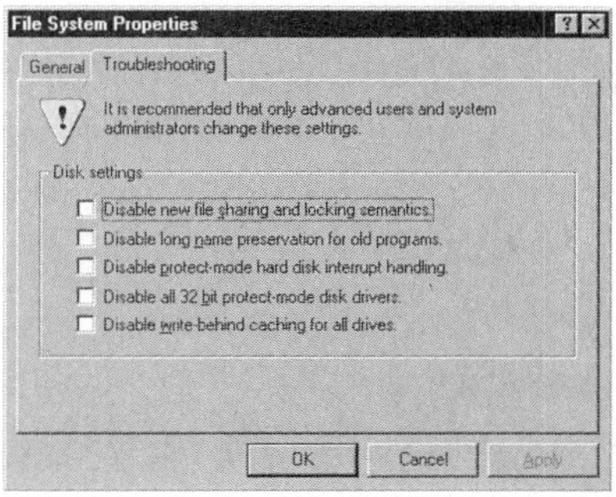

Fig. 10.4 Changing the file system properties is easy within Windows 95.

Notice that this dialog box has six check boxes. Each one allows you to control a different feature of the file system. The one you're interested in, however, is the final check box—Disable write-behind caching for all drives. If you select this check box, all information in Windows is written to the disk right away, rather than held in a software cache. While this provides for a greater degree of data integrity, it slows down your system a bit.

Using SmartDrive

In earlier versions of Windows that operated on top of the DOS operating system, it wasn't unusual to have a disk cache installed in the CONFIG.SYS file. These programs went by many different names, depending on the program vendor. One such program, provided with DOS and Windows, was SmartDrive. For many of the faster hard drives now available (particularly those with on-board caching), a software cache such as SmartDrive isn't necessary.

Many people think that Windows 95 has no need for the SmartDrive program. It's interesting, however, that a 32-bit version of SmartDrive is included with Windows 95. This new-and-improved caching program is loaded by Windows 95 if you had the older version of SmartDrive loaded in your CONFIG.SYS and/or AUTOEXEC.BAT files when you installed Windows 95. It's used primarily for DOS programs running under Windows 95.

> **Tip:** If you don't use DOS programs under Windows 95, remove the SmartDrive commands from your configuration files. SmartDrive isn't necessary for Windows programs, and you'll regain more memory for other programs.

The outward appearance of the Windows 95 version of SmartDrive is very similar to older versions of the program. Including the command line

```
C:\WINDOWS\SMARTDRV
```

in your AUTOEXEC.BAT file causes the following to happen:

- A disk cache is set up in extended memory. The size of the cache depends on the amount of extended memory on the system, as shown in the following table.

Extended Memory	InitCacheSize #	WinCacheSize #
Up to 4M	1M	512K
Up to 6M	2M	1M
6M or more	2M	2M

- All hard drives are read- and write-cached. Floppy drives and CD-ROM drives are read-cached only. Listing drive letters on the SmartDrive command line allows for the use of + and – to modify caching, as shown in the following list:

  d Read-ahead-caching only

  d+ Both read-and write-caching

  d- Don't cache

- The cache created will move 8,192 bytes at a time. You can specify 1,024, 2,048, and 4,096 by including **/e:ElementSize** after the driver letters on the command line.

➤ The read-ahead buffer is 16K but can be any multiple of ElementSize by adding **/b:BufferSize**.

> **Tip:** If your SCSI or ESDI disk controller uses bus mastering, you probably need to include the following line in your CONFIG.SYS file:
>
> DEVICE=C:\WINDOWS\SMARTDRV.EXE /DOUBLE_BUFFER
>
> Consult your disk controller manual, or type **SMARTDRV** at the DOS prompt and see a display of how SmartDrive is caching each drive. If `yes` appears under buffering in the line for your hard drive, you need double buffering.

The operation of SmartDrive allows caching of many drives such as Bernoullis, some hard cards, and many SCSI and WORM drives that require the use of device drivers. SmartDrive uses a FIFO (first in, first out) algorithm to determine what data to discard from the cache as new data is requested.

Write-Behind Caching

SmartDrive and the built-in Windows 95 caching software includes a write-behind feature that temporarily holds data to be written to disk in its cache. When a period of lower CPU activity occurs, the information held in the cache is written to the hard drive. The delay time isn't long—a maximum of 3 to 5 seconds. For some users, any write-behind delay time is unacceptable. For instance, you might want your changes committed to the disk immediately for security or data integrity reasons.

Earlier in this chapter you learned how you can turn off write-behind caching for Windows 95. SmartDrive also includes a way you can control write-behind caching. Unfortunately, the command syntax for SmartDrive is a bit vague. Here are some options:

Example: Set up only read-caching on all floppy drives and on hard drive C.

```
C:\WINDOWS\SMARTDRV c
```

Example: Set up read-caching on floppy drive A and the logical drive D.

```
C:\WINDOWS\SMARTDRV a d
```

Example: Disable caching your hard drive while defragmenting.

```
C:\WINDOWS\SMARTDRV c-
```

Testing Windows 95 with write-behind caching suggests that this feature is a major performance booster. If speed improvement is that important to you, look for other ways to protect your data from the write-behind feature. Delayed write caching provokes disagreement for some users. For users who might lose only a few numbers just entered on a spreadsheet or a few words in a document file, it's no big deal and might even be a help.

Power outages and freezing your system are examples of the disasters that loom when using the delayed write feature. You saved, the cache didn't. Some users complain about losses suffered when working with subroutines that write to multiple locations. Reconstructing that process may be impossible.

> **Tip:** When you exit from Windows 95 normally, all data stored in the SmartDrive buffers is written to disk; none is lost. If you're concerned about data loss from a power outage, invest in an uninterruptable power supply (UPS).

Hardware Caches

Most disks of 80M or larger with a built-in controller have a buffer of RAM on board. Also, internal and external disk caches, or hardware caches, are available. IDE and SCSI drives require a host adapter card for an external cache. ESDI drives have external controller cards.

At this point in the discussion, you'll benefit from knowing a few more definitions: A *buffer* is a holding tank for data read from the disk and awaiting transfer to the processor. A buffer can have read-ahead capability, reading neighboring data in case the system asks for the adjacent sectors. A variation of this is a full-track buffer, one that automatically reads the entire track containing the requested data. Although a buffer sounds like a cache, note that buffer activity doesn't require any logic to determine what is kept in the buffer and what is not. A cache may perform the same basic operations as a buffer, but algorithms are added to a cache to determine what data is replaced by incoming data.

Segmented caching technology is being adopted for internal caches, allowing greater speed and versatility. A segmented cache is divided into segments that store different types of data, and the size and contents of the segments can be automatically adjusted to match the way you work with your hard drive.

Hardware caches range in size from 256K to 64M, although caches of 1M or larger are disproportionately expensive compared to adding that much additional RAM to your motherboard. A large hardware cache can be advantageous on network servers, leaving system RAM free for multiuser applications. Possible software cache bottlenecks are thus eliminated, as are software conflicts.

Adding an external hardware cache if your drive has an internal cache isn't recommended. At some point, the housekeeping functions accumulate in various caches until they bog down. In fact, you may encounter similar problems with a software cache.

Using Compression Software

No matter how much you speed up your drive, if lack of space means you can't keep the applications and data files you need on your hard drive, all that speed won't do you any good. The idea of data compression started with the need to speed the process of downloading files from bulletin boards. Data compression has matured to become the easiest and least expensive way to increase space on your hard disk.

Archiving software has its roots in the DOS environment. These programs first appeared in 1985 in the form of ARC, created by System Enhancement Associates (SEA). Faster compression became available

with Phil Katz's PKARC and PKXARC, which, after some legal scuffles, became the familiar PKZIP and PKUNZIP. Although PKWare is the standard for file archiving and a necessity if you want to download from bulletin boards, improved packages such as LHARC are being used by major software producers to compress their large applications onto a manageable number of floppy disks. When you install those applications after purchase, the install or setup program uses the LHARC or similar decompression program when transferring the application to your hard drive.

Refinements have been added to data compression software in the time since it was introduced, such as the capability to add a special header to a compressed file that makes it executable, or self-extracting. Some compression programs work better with one kind of data file than another. However, file compression programs don't save much disk space unless you use them to encourage the removal of unnecessary files to floppy disks. The capability to compress multiple, related files into one file, add identifying comments to each, and view an index and the individual files while still compressed makes the process of backing up and then deleting old files and programs from your drive more tolerable than backup methods previously available.

It's a tempting idea, to be sure, to compress that 300K monthly audit report form and a few other rarely used space hogs, decompressing a copy as needed. If your need for space is this serious, put the compressed file on a floppy disk instead. Although retrieving from a floppy disk is slow, don't forget that you're retrieving a compressed—and therefore much smaller—file. Retrieving the file and then decompressing it in faster RAM isn't as time consuming as copying the uncompressed version from a floppy disk. So, in addition to helping you better organize data you delete from the hard drive, file compression speeds the process of retrieving it when needed.

As of this writing, all the major compression programs are still DOS-based. You can run them under Windows 95 in an MS-DOS window, but you should be aware of two things:

- Switching to a DOS window to run the compression software can be a headache, although some Windows-based shells are available (such as WINZIP). While these shells are convenient, they still rely on the presence of the DOS-based compression programs on your system.
- Compression programs don't co-exist peacefully with long file names in Windows 95. If you're compressing files, make sure that you rename them or copy them to a file that conforms to the familiar 8.3 file name length limitation.

With the advent of long file names for all Windows users, it's likely that it won't be long before native compression software is available that won't limit how you work in Windows 95.

Using Swap Files

Windows 95 uses swap files to implement the virtual memory management made possible by the demand-paging capabilities of today's computer hardware. As the number of concurrent applications in memory increases, code and data that must remain in memory are swapped to the hard drive to make the space necessary to meet new demands.

If a request for information is made to a memory address and the information isn't in physical memory, the Windows 95 Virtual Memory Manager (VMM) steps in and retrieves the information from the swap file, swapping out other data if required. This step makes it possible for the computer to run more applications in memory than would otherwise be possible.

Unless you specify otherwise, Windows 95 creates a swap file named WIN386.SWP in the directory where Windows is installed. This swap file is dynamic in nature—it can grow, shrink, or disappear as dictated by Windows' swap-file needs. In this respect, Windows 95 swap files are similar to temporary swap files in older versions of Windows. However, the drawbacks historically evidenced in using temporary swap files (such as slow access) have been "weeded out" of Windows 95 through improved programming and logic in the VMM.

Even though the logic used in the VMM has been improved, you may want to explicitly specify the swap file parameters to be used by Windows 95. For instance, if you have a slow hard drive, you may experience faster swap file access if you specify a permanent area on your hard drive for the swap file. To modify the virtual memory settings, follow these steps:

1. Choose Settings from the Start menu.
2. From the Settings menu, choose Control Panel.
3. Double-click on the System icon in the Control Panel window.
4. In the Properties for System dialog box, click on the Performance tab.
5. Click on the Virtual Memory button to display the Virtual Memory dialog box (see fig. 10.5).

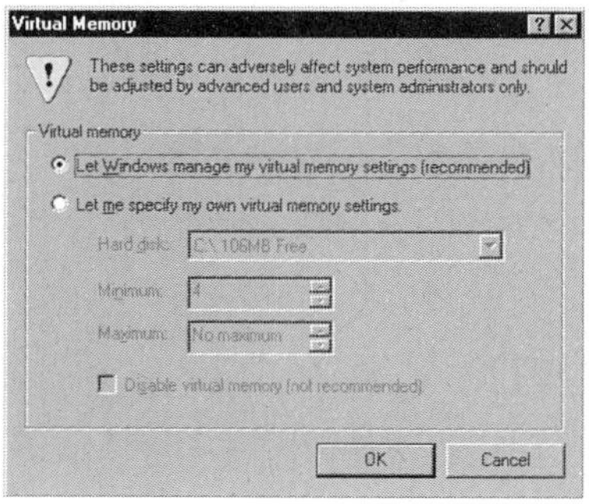

Fig. 10.5 The Virtual Memory dialog box allows you to specify how Windows 95 should manage its swap file.

Normally, the first option in the Virtual Memory dialog box is selected. This allows Windows to manage virtual memory (disk swapping) as it sees best. If you choose the second option, you either can specify disable virtual memory support (which would severely cripple the performance of Windows), or you can specify three parameters concerning the swap file:

- Where it should be located
- What the minimum swap file size should be
- What the maximum swap file size should be

If you make the minimum and maximum sizes the same, you effectively are setting up a permanent swap file on disk. Unless you calculate (or guess) correctly as to the swap file size, you could slow down Windows' performance. Make sure that you specify only manual swap file parameters if you learn, through experience, that such settings are best for your system. You should also make sure that your disk is defragmented before you make such a change.

Defragmenting Your Disk Drive

Windows 95 derives its disk organization heritage from DOS. (You learned a bit about this in Chapter 2, "Under-the-Hood Improvements.") This means that the same disk structure is effectively maintained in Windows 95 that existed in previous versions of Windows and DOS. The disk is divided into tracks, each of which is divided into 512-byte sectors. On large hard drives, these sectors can't be accessed individually because of limitations in the File Allocation System (FAT). For compatibility reasons, this limitation also exists in the VFAT file system used in Windows 95. Instead of information being accessible as sectors, information is instead processed in *clusters.* These clusters are composed of anywhere from 2 to 4 sectors. Thus, a cluster can consist of anywhere from 1K to 2K of data.

Note: Clusters represent the minimum storage unit that can be allocated to a file. Thus, a small file can have quite a bit of wasted space at the end of it. This is one of the attractions of using compressed disk drives, as discussed earlier in the chapter—they allow you to pack information tighter, thereby reclaiming the space typically lost when storing small files in a FAT environment.

As information is first stored to a disk drive, the disk drive fills up in an orderly manner. As existing data is erased, the FAT is changed to indicate which disk clusters are empty. Later, when additional data is written to the drive, Windows starts writing in the nearest empty cluster as determined by the FAT, and when that cluster fills, moves on to fill the next empty cluster, skipping any occupied clusters along the way. As you continue to retrieve, edit, and save again and again, you end up with pieces of many files scattered across the entire drive. This condition is called *file fragmentation*. When data needs to be read from a disk, moving the read/write heads all around the disk to collect scattered parts of a file can be very time-consuming.

Windows 95 includes a disk defragmentation utility that you can use to correct this problem. *Disk defragmenting* is the process of analyzing a disk's file structure and making sure that each file on the disk occupies a series of contiguous disk clusters. You should periodically run the defragmentation utility, depending on how much you use your system. If you use your system only lightly, you should defragment your drives monthly. If you use it heavily, you probably want to defragment on a weekly basis. Using the utility is quick and easy, so you don't need to block large amounts of time to perform this bit of housekeeping.

To start the defragmenting utility, follow these steps:

1. Choose Start, Programs, Accessories.
2. From the Accessories menu, choose System Tools.
3. From the System Tools menu, choose Disk Defragmenter. This starts the defragmenting utility.

Now you need to choose which disk drive you want to defragment. Windows 95 displays the dialog box shown in figure 10.6.

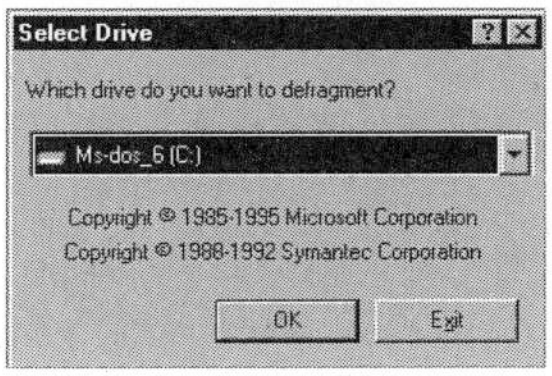

Fig. 10.6 Picking a disk drive is the first step in defragmenting.

You can pick any disk drive on your system, including floppy drives. (You can't, however, pick read-only drives such as a CD-ROM drive.) If you use the pull-down list in the dialog box, you can even pick the choice All Hard Drives, which runs the program on all the hard drives in your system. You should choose the disk drive (or drives) you want to defragment, and then click OK.

The program then checks to see how fragmented the disk already is. This is necessary so that the proper initialization areas can be set up. If the disk isn't very fragmented, you're advised of the fact, and you have the chance of forcing the defragmentation.

The amount of time necessary for defragmenting a drive depends on several factors, such as the size of your hard drive, how full it is, and how long it has been since you last defragmented. Defragmenting can take anywhere from several minutes to several hours to complete. As a result, you'll probably want to run the program when you know you'll have time to complete it. For example, run it as you are ready to quit work for the evening. That way, it can be done by the time you arrive at work the next morning.

When the program is done, you're given the opportunity to defragment another drive. You can select another one or close the program window.

Surviving with a Small Hard Drive

There are two major reasons to consider adopting the ideas presented in this section:

- You have an 80M or smaller drive with only 4M of memory and no data compression program.
- Your drive has reached its optimal speed, and you're ready to invest time to keep it that way.

There's no clear line dividing suggestions that increase speed and create extra space. You probably need to improve both because smaller drives are usually older drives using older technology that provide slow access times. Some of the following techniques have been discussed earlier in this chapter but are even more important for the small hard drive user to follow. Others are data management and housekeeping suggestions that help keep any disk in tip-top shape. All are designed to help you enhance the efficiency and effectiveness of your computer system.

Using Low-Level Formatting

Low-level formatting is a process that creates tracks and sectors on a disk. Many drives—such as those that use stepper motors—benefit from this process being repeated later in life. Low-level formatting addresses a frequent problem known as *alignment creep*. Alignment creep occurs as the stepper motor wears, which results in the sectors that pass under drive heads no longer being properly aligned with the heads. The low-level formatting process corrects this problem and also locates surface defects on the disks.

Many experts suggest that you low-level format your hard drive yearly. Most newer disk drives contain built-in utilities that allow you to perform a low-level format. Older drives may require a separate disk utility, which can be run from the floppy drive. All you need to do is boot to the floppy and run the formatting program.

Caution: Performing a low-level format too often can cause more harm than good. If you format more often than yearly, you run the risk of adding undue wear and tear on your drive.

Adjusting the Interleave

Older drives can't transfer disk data fast enough to be able to read the next sector before it's spun past the read/write head. To allow for this, sectors aren't numbered sequentially, but instead are numbered to skip every other one (2:1 interleave) or to skip 2 sectors (3:1 interleave), and so on. This allows time for the head to transfer data and be ready to read again. Older MFM and RLL drives were usually set with a 3:1 interleave, even though a 286 system could support a 2:1 interleaved drive.

Programs such as OPTune, SpinRite, Calibrate, and DiskFix can adjust the interleave without harming the data on your drive. When you're using Windows 95, these programs should be run after booting to a DOS diskette; you shouldn't run them from the Windows 95 command line.

Adjusting the disk interleave is a lengthy process, because each sector is renumbered and all data is transferred to new physical locations. The performance benefit of this one-time-only job is substantial.

Caution: Don't adjust the interleave on IDE or SCSI drives. Usually, optimizing software doesn't work on these drives, but some older IDE drives don't communicate their identity well. Refer to your owner's manual or obtain identifying data off the drive. Ask a dealer to look up the drive if you're unsure of the type of drive you have.

Cleaning Up Your Drive

All very small files waste space on your disk. This is because each file must occupy at least one cluster, even if the file isn't that large. For instance, a file that contains only 100 bytes of data still occupies an entire cluster of disk space; the rest of the cluster is simply wasted. If you can do without some of the smaller files, you should delete them. This has the potential of freeing up large amounts of disk space.

Also, many programs contain numerous files you don't need all the time. You can keep these files on floppy disks, which you can then use with your programs. For instance, programs such as Word for Windows allow you to specify the location of such files as clip art and templates. You can specify the new file location as the floppy drive. When it needs them, the program looks to the floppy drive. Database, desktop publishing, and some graphics programs might suffer an intolerable slowdown, but you won't notice a difference with other programs. If you need a directory display of a floppy disk often, set up a file manager window of the directory, and then switch back and forth as you need to view it.

Considering Hard Drive Upgrades

The final and most costly solution to the drive space crunch is to upgrade your hard drive. Many drives available feature access times of 10 milliseconds or less; you can easily find drives with access times of 8 ms. While small variations may not make much difference, jumping from a 16 ms drive to a 10 or 8 ms drive can make a large difference. Also, the faster your CPU, the faster access time you'll want for your disk drive.

Here are the questions you need to answer before selecting a specific drive (they aren't listed in any particular order):

- How much can you afford to pay? There's little difference in the price of drives of the same size.

- Does the price of the drive include everything, or do you need to buy a card or other items (such as a drive kit)?
- How much space do you need now and for the next two years? Windows 95 occupies about 60M. It's not uncommon for program sizes to double or triple from one major version to the next. Also, remember that as your expertise and ability increases, so does the number of programs you work with.
- What's compatible with your current system? What kind of drive is your system using now? Is the connector built into the motherboard?
- What peripherals are you using or wanting to buy?

The hard drives you need to consider for a Windows 95 system are those types large enough and fast enough to constitute a serious upgrade: a minimum size of 500M or larger at access speeds below 10 ms. As discussed in Chapter 8, "Examining the Hardware You Need for Windows 95," there are four types of hard drives: IDE, SCSI, ESDI, and ST506. However, IDE and SCSI are the only two generally available anymore due to the fact that ESDI and ST506 are older, slower, and less reliable technologies. Also, the older technology drives don't offer the speed and capacity of IDE and SCSI. There are pros and cons to both IDE and SCSI drives:

- IDE (Integrated Drive Electronics) drives range from 42M to more than 1G (1,000M). 230M and larger models consistently sport access times of 8 to 12 ms, with 10 and under readily available. Their transfer speeds have increased tremendously over the years.

  The name IDE comes from the fact that the controller electronics are built into the drive itself rather than on a separate card. Most of the systems being sold today feature an IDE drive for drives up to about 500M, and EIDE (an enhanced version of IDE) drives for larger capacities. Low-level formatting isn't needed, as the manufacturer precodes the drive's sector information.

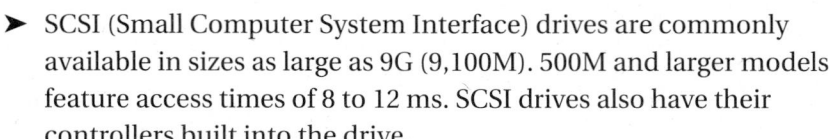

- SCSI (Small Computer System Interface) drives are commonly available in sizes as large as 9G (9,100M). 500M and larger models feature access times of 8 to 12 ms. SCSI drives also have their controllers built into the drive.

  The adapter card for the drive can support up to seven SCSI devices, such as tape backups and CD-ROM drives, and hard drives can be chained together to provide enormous amounts of storage. Because of this technology, SCSI drives are highly desirable for use with network servers. The large size, coupled with blazing transfer rates (40 to 80 megabits per second), can be combined with the more advanced system configurations found in network servers to give excellent performance.

> **Caution:** In the past, SCSI device drivers for host adapters suffered from chronic compatibility problems. To make your life easier, first find the other SCSI devices you want to use. Then ask what SCSI hard drives are compatible with them.

Hard drive technology is developing answers for more speed. One major area of change is in revolutions per minute. 3,600 rpm has long been the standard, and the ESDI interface is locked in to this speed. IDE and SCSI interfaces aren't, and 4,500 to 7,200 rpm drives are readily available. Another area of interest is in changing bus width from 8-bit to 16-bit or even 32-bit widths to increase data transfer rates.

> **Tip:** Most drives available today, including the drives discussed here, have a 1:1 interleave. You have one less thing to worry about while shopping, as they already will deliver maximum service.

Prices in the fall of 1994 were about $1 per megabyte for up to 150M, then dropping to $0.40 per megabyte for up to 1 gigabyte (1,000M), and as low as $0.35 per megabyte for the larger drives (those between 4G and 9G). That translates to about $175 for a 210M drive, $250 for the 340M that should keep many users happy for a few years, to $2,000 for 4 G (4,000M) for the power user. For drives over s4G, the cost ratio is somewhat lower.

Shopping for a hard drive can be a horrible experience. After you determine how much you can afford and how big a drive you want, figuring out what will really be compatible with your system can be a nightmare. Do your floppy drive cables plug into your present hard drive controller card? How much space do you have inside the box? What other peripherals are you using?

Get out your manual. Open the system and find all the numbers. Then sit down and start calling around. Hard Drives International at (800) 535-1506 is a reliable low-end price operation; Mega Haus at (800) 786-1185 is another good choice. Let them ask you questions and give you some options. Take a look at the Computer Shopper magazine for an extensive listing of equipment, best buys, and street pricing. Then call your local stores. If you've never installed a drive, you may want them to do it for you.

> **Tip:** If you're upgrading your entire computer system, make sure that you get one that has a PCI Bus or VL-Bus. These offer maximum performance, and you can even get hard drive controllers that use these faster buses.

11

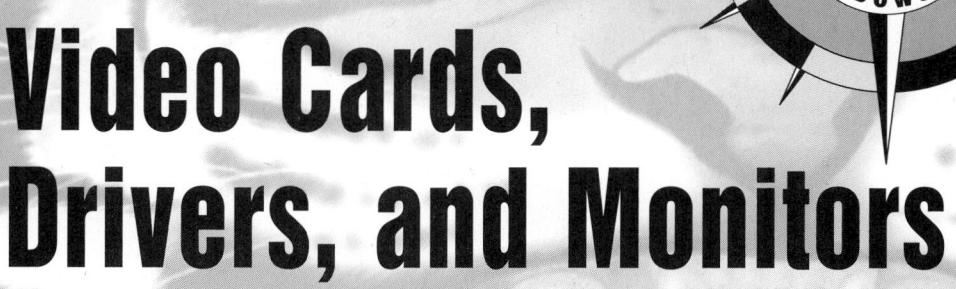

Video Cards, Drivers, and Monitors

by Allen L. Wyatt

The video subsystem of your computer contains two different elements: the video adapter card and the video monitor. These elements work together to provide you a "window" into what your PC is doing. Windows 95 uses video drivers to communicate with the video subsystem. By using the right video drivers with a high-quality video card and monitor, you can greatly improve your productivity and limit fatigue and eye-strain.

This chapter discusses the various video elements you'll find in your Windows 95 system. In this chapter, you'll learn about video cards, monitors, and drivers. You'll also learn what to look for in both video cards and monitors, as well as how to configure Windows 95 for your video hardware. Finally, you'll receive a crash course in what you can do to improve the video processing speed of your system.

Video Cards

The root of your video system is the video card, sometimes called a video adapter or video adapter card. This card is either built into your computer's motherboard or installed in an adapter slot in your PC. The video card serves as an intermediary between your CPU and the monitor. It is perhaps the single most critical part of your computer system, outside of the CPU itself.

Types of Video Cards

The marketplace fields a number of different video standards used to define how information is displayed on a video screen. Some of these standards, although historically significant, are not really suitable for use in a Windows system. For instance, the following video standards have uses in some application areas, but not with Windows:

- ***MDA.*** The monochrome display adapter used with the original IBM PCs and XTs.
- ***HGA.*** The Hercules graphics adapter, which made monochrome graphics popular in the early days of the PC.
- ***CGA.*** The first color graphics adapter marketed by IBM.
- ***EGA.*** The enhanced graphics adapter, which brought higher resolutions and more colors to the PC.
- ***MCGA.*** The multi-color graphics array, introduced as one of two successors to the EGA, but primarily for the low-end of the PS/2 line of computers.

In the video arena, you already know that the minimum system requirement for Windows 95 is a video card that meets VGA standards. The VGA (*video graphics array*) was introduced by IBM when it first introduced the PS/2 line of computers. IBM used the VGA primarily in its high-end systems for the line, but the standard has since been adopted by a variety of companies as a common video standard for stand-alone video cards. The VGA is the absolute, rock-bottom minimum for a video system.

The VGA is rapidly becoming a thing of the past. Any computer system sold within the past two years most likely will have some sort of SVGA card installed. SVGA is an acronym for *super video graphics array*. It was given this name because it offers a super-set of the capabilities designed into the VGA standard. The problem is that there is not just one SVGA standard. Instead, there are two or three chip sets used to implement SVGA. These chip sets add different capabilities to the VGA standard, and they supply the capabilities in different manners.

If you have an MCA-based computer (some of the IBM PS/2 computers used MCA busses), then you could have other types of video adapters, as well. For instance, the 8514/A was distributed for a time. It provided greater resolution, colors, and throughput than the VGA adapter, but not as great as many of the SVGA cards on the market right now. After a couple of years, IBM stopped using the 8514/A and adopted the XGA standard. IBM introduced the XGA (*extended graphics array*) in 1990 as a successor to VGA (and the 8514/A). However, because of XGA's primary use in MCA systems, it was viewed as a proprietary system and was therefore not adopted by many third-party card vendors. In 1992, IBM introduced the XGA/2, which added to the XGA many of the capabilities of a bare-bones SVGA card. Again, the use of the XGA/2 has been limited largely to systems based on the MCA bus.

Windows 95 will support the following types of video adapters:

- VGA
- SVGA
- 8514/A
- XGA
- XGA/2

Graphics Accelerators

As a rule, the greater the graphics needs of a program, the slower it will run. This speed is directly related to the amount of data that must be updated on the video screen. When a full-screen, 256-color display is changed, the computer must send 640 × 480 or 307,200 bytes of data to the video display card. The situation gets worse when you use the SVGA modes; 800 × 600 mode requires 480,000 bytes and a 1,024 × 768 display needs 786,432 bytes. If you increase the number of possible colors in the display, the amount of information to be processed is increased further still. For instance, if you use a video card that supports 65,535 colors, then you double the amount of graphics information to be processed, and a video card that handles 1.5M colors must handle three times the information. Table 11.1 shows how the amount of information to be processed can vary, depending on the card's operating mode.

Table 11.1 The amount of information a video card can process

Resolution	16 Colors	256 Colors	64K Colors	1.5M Colors
640 × 480	307,200	307,200	614,400	921,600
800 × 600	480,000	480,000	960,000	1,440,000
1,024 × 768	786,432	786,432	1,572,864	2,359,296

Processing huge amounts of video information puts quite a high demand on the CPU and on the system bus in your computer. It's not that your computer can't handle it—it can, given enough time. That's why complex video displays can take a while to display all the information they're asked to process.

The solution to this "video bottleneck" is to use a graphics accelerator. In fact, many SVGA cards are marketed as graphics accelerators because they provide specialized circuitry that allows them to process information much quicker than standard VGA cards. The effect of using these cards is simple—if you speed up the video, you speed up the entire computer system. This is because you don't need to wait as long on what is typically the slowest part of your computer system. Many graphics accelerators that have been fine-tuned for use with Windows boast speed increases of from 50 percent to 100 percent.

Understanding Busses

Getting a faster video card, in the form of a graphics accelerator, is only half the story, however. Regardless of how fast a video card you get, the I/O bus (which is used to interface the adapter cards with the CPU) is still relatively slow—around 8 or 10 MHz with a 16-bit data path. This situation makes the I/O bus the weakest link in most systems, particularly those with demanding graphics needs. While the CPU is trying to push graphics data through the slow I/O channel, it can't be doing much else. The need for the I/O bus to remain at a lower speed was due to the huge installed base of adapter cards that could operate only at the slower speeds. Figure 11.1 shows a conceptual block diagram of the busses in a computer system.

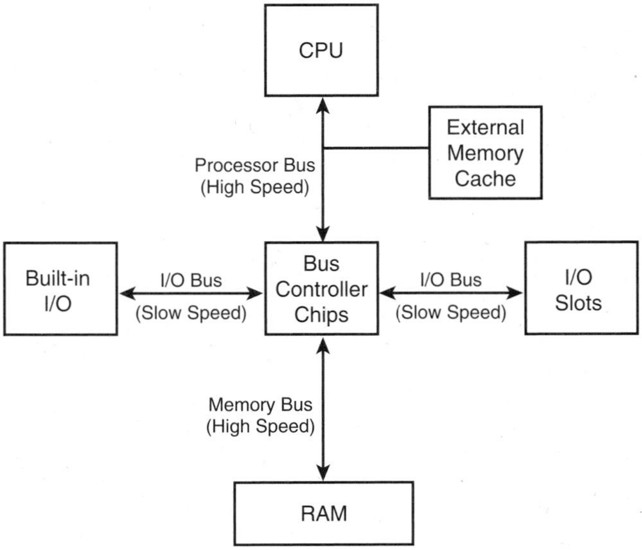

Fig. 11.1 The layout of a typical PC incorporates both high- and low-speed busses.

To overcome this bottleneck, local-bus systems were developed. This bus gets its name from putting one or two bus connectors (or direct devices) on the bus used by the CPU. This bus is local to the CPU, thus the term *local bus*. This bus arrangement is shown in figure 11.2.

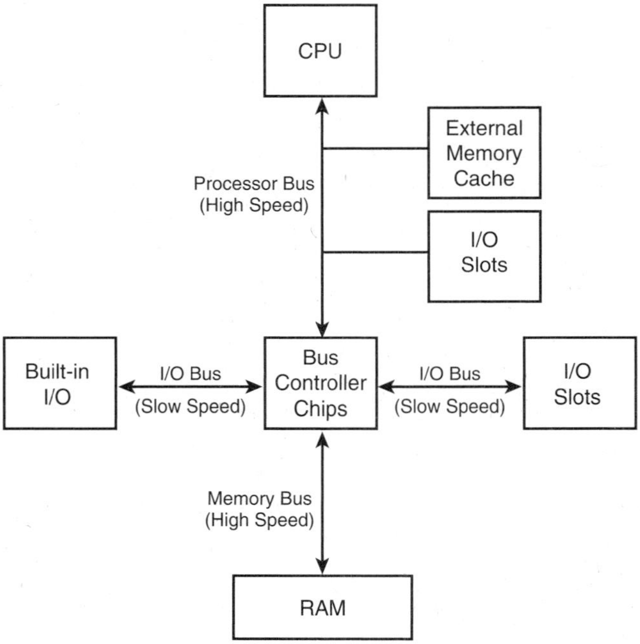

Fig. 11.2 A local-bus implementation includes I/O slots on both the normal I/O bus and the high-speed processor bus.

Note: It is important to note that local bus does not replace earlier bus standards, such as ISA or EISA. Instead, it complements them, which means that a system will typically be based on ISA or EISA, and have one or more local bus slots available as well. The result is that older adapter cards are still compatible with the system, but high-speed adapter cards can take advantage of the local-bus slots as well.

Primarily, the local bus is used for video subsystems and increasingly for disk drive controllers. To make your system as fast as it can be, you should look for a computer that implements one of the standard local busses. There are two such busses in wide use today—the VL-Bus and the PCI-bus. These are discussed in the next two sections.

VL-Bus

The initial implementations of local bus were designed to overcome video bottlenecks. The problem, however, is that there was no standard in these implementations. To overcome this oversight, the Video Electronics Standards Association (VESA) developed a standardized local-bus specification in 1992 and early 1993. This standardization became known as the *VESA Local Bus,* or simply as the *VL-Bus.* As with earlier local-bus implementations, the VL-Bus slot offers direct access to system memory at the speed of the processor itself. The VL-Bus can move data between the CPU and an adapter card 32 bits at a time—the full data width of the 486 chip. The maximum rated throughput of the VL-Bus is 128-132M/second. In other words, local bus went a long way toward removing the major bottlenecks existing in earlier bus configurations. The change made it possible to move enough data to refresh an entire 1,024 × 768 resolution screen, using 1.5M colors, many times per second.

Despite the benefits of the VL-Bus (and by extension, all local busses), there are a few drawbacks. These drawbacks are as follows:

- ***486 CPU dependent.*** The VL-Bus is inherently tied to the 486 processor bus. This bus is different from that used by the Pentium, and probably from those used by future CPUs. A VL-Bus that operates at the full rated speed of a Pentium has not been developed, although stop-gap measures (such as stepping down speed or developing bus bridges) are available.

- ***Speed limitations.*** The VL-Bus specification allows for speeds of up to 66 MHz on the bus, but the electrical characteristics of the VL-Bus connector limit an adapter card to no more than 50 MHz. If the main CPU uses a clock modifier (such as those that double clock speeds), then the VL-Bus uses the unmodified CPU clock speed as its bus speed.
- ***Electrical limitations.*** The processor bus has very tight timing rules, which may even vary from CPU to CPU. These timing rules were designed around only specialized circuitry being connected to the bus. As more circuitry is added (as with a VL-Bus), the electrical load on the bus is increased. If not implemented correctly, this increased load can lead to problems such as loss of data integrity and timing problems between the CPU and the VL-Bus adapter cards.
- ***Card limitations.*** Depending on the electrical loading of a system, the number of VL-Bus cards is limited. While the VL-Bus specification allows for as many as three cards, this can only be achieved at clock rates of up to 40 MHz with an otherwise low system-board load. As the system-board load increases and the clock rate increases, the number of cards supported decreases. Only one VL-Bus card can be supported at 50 MHz with a high system-board load.

These drawbacks should not dissuade you from investing in a VL-Bus system. Indeed, they provide an acceptable solution to the needs of high-speed computing. However, many critics complain that even though the VL-Bus is well suited to 486 systems, it is just that—a modified 486 system. They contend it is not adaptable or extensible, meaning it does not work well for non-video needs nor will it work well (without modification) for future generations of CPUs.

> **Note:** Several implementations of local-bus video with proprietary graphics adapter cards do not include a VESA feature connector. When the local-bus video is implemented on the motherboard, some manufacturers sacrifice VESA feature connectors to reduce manufacturing costs. If you are considering purchasing a computer with a local bus and at some time will want to take advantage of full-motion video or even video frame-grabbers, make sure a VESA feature connector is provided.
>
> Without the feature connector, you cannot add a conventional video-in-a-window card or an internal VGA-to-NTSC card to the system. In that case, to convert VGA output to NTSC television signals, you need an external scan converter. Scan converters with genlocking capability are considerably more expensive than their counterpart on an adapter card.

PCI Bus

In early 1992, an industry group (headed by Intel) was formed to overcome the bottlenecks imposed by earlier PC bus specifications. This group, the PCI Special Interest Group (PCI is an acronym for *peripheral component interconnect*), released its initial specification in June, 1992. The PCI bus redesigned the traditional PC bus by inserting another bus (referred to as a *bridge*) between the CPU and the native I/O bus. Rather than tap directly into the processor bus with its delicate electrical timing (as was done in the VL-Bus), a new set of controller chips was developed that extended the bus, as shown in figure 11.3.

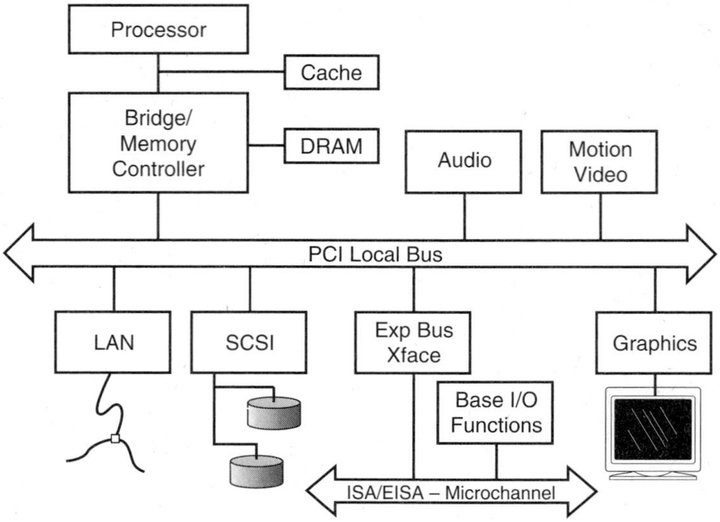

Fig. 11.3 The PCI bus adds another layer of busses to the traditional PC architecture.

PCI bypasses the standard I/O bus and uses the system bus to increase the bus clock speed and take full advantage of the CPU's data path. Systems integrating the PCI bus became available in mid-1993, and have since become the mainstay of high-end systems.

Information is transferred across the PCI bus at 33 MHz, at the full data width of the CPU. In addition, the PCI bus can operate concurrently with the processor bus; it does not supplant it. This means that the CPU can be processing data in an external cache while the PCI bus is busy transferring information between other parts of the system. This is a major design benefit of the PCI bus.

Monitors

The video monitor displays information sent to it by the video card. When examining a video subsystem, you don't want to spend all your time examining individual components without looking at the other components as well. In other words, you need to make sure that the

video monitor you use is well matched to the capabilities of the video card you get. If a good match does not exist, then you won't be satisfied with the results achieved. In fact, if there is enough of a mismatch, it is possible to physically damage a monitor by connecting it to some video cards.

How can damage occur? Primarily by trying to "drive" a monitor beyond its design specifications. For instance, if you have a video card that sustains a high refresh rate, and the monitor does not, then damage can result. Thus, the best course of action is to make sure that the monitor you get has capabilities either matching or exceeding those of your video card.

How do you know which features to look for in a video monitor? The number of possible features is limited. The features include the following elements:

- Screen size
- Dot pitch
- Screen curvature
- Refresh rate
- Interlacing

There is no real hierarchy among these features; each is as important as the other. They do, however, tend to have a cumulative effect, from the perspective of the user. You should look for the monitor that has the best characteristics within each feature area, and then make your buying decision accordingly. The following sections address each of the features you should consider.

Screen Size

You already know that video monitors come in different sizes. You can find some that are small, and others that come packaged on their own shipping pallet. How do you know which size is right for you?

Screen size is based on the size of the image. To get the correct screen size, just measure diagonally across the image. Thus, a 14-inch monitor can produce an image that is 14 inches from top-left corner to bottom-right corner. If you remember your geometry from high school, and remember that monitors always have a 4:3 size ratio (horizontal to vertical), you can calculate the image width, image height, and screen area of a monitor. Table 11.2 shows these figures for a range of screen sizes.

Table 11.2 Specifications for Various Screen Sizes.

Screen Size	Width	Height	Screen Area
12-in	9.6-in	7.2-in	69.12 sq in
13-in	10.4-in	7.8-in	81.12 sq in
14-in	11.2-in	8.4-in	94.08 sq in
15-in	12-in	9-in	108 sq in
16-in	12.8-in	9.6-in	122.88 sq in
17-in	13.6-in	10.2-in	138.72 sq in
18-in	14.4-in	10.8-in	155.52 sq in
19-in	15.2-in	11.4-in	173.28 sq in
20-in	16-in	12-in	192 sq in
21-in	16.8-in	12.6-in	211.68 sq in

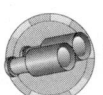

Note: Some monitor manufacturers have a tendency to exaggerate their monitor sizes. For instance, a 14-inch monitor may only produce a 13-inch (or less) image—cheaper video tubes tend to distort images near the corners of the image area. Manufacturers can get away with this exaggeration by quoting the unlimited image area instead of the actual image area, which should be the proper measure. Don't be afraid to take a ruler to the actual image area to determine the true image size. Use this measure for comparison.

In general, the screen size you use will depend on your personal preferences. If you work in a cramped area where space is scarce, then a larger screen is probably out of the question. However, if you do work in which higher screen resolutions are desirable or necessary, and work area is no problem, then you'll definitely want a larger screen.

On a desktop computer system, at 640 × 480 resolution, a 14-inch monitor generally suffices. Anything smaller, and you might find it difficult to read some smaller text or make out detail in some icons. At the opposite end of the spectrum, if you're working at 1,024 × 768, then you'll find the 21-inch screen most satisfactory.

> **Tip:** Before you purchase a monitor, if possible try out various sizes by using the software you work with most often. This way you can be sure you'll be happy with your monitor before you sign on the dotted line.

Dot Pitch

A video tube (CRT) used within a monitor is simple. It consists of three electron guns at the rear of the tube that shoot an electron stream at the front of the tube. This stream of electrons moves very rapidly across the screen. As it moves, it energizes a phosphor coating on the inside of the front of the tube. This illuminated phosphor is what creates the images you see on the monitor.

The phosphor is painted on the inside of the video tube in "groups." If you could get a powerful enough magnifying glass, you could actually see these groups on your screen. (This is why you can sometimes see color dots if there is a drop of water on your screen—the drop of water acts as a magnifying glass.) These groups consist of a red phosphor dot, a blue phosphor dot, and a green phosphor dot. The distance between these phosphor groups is termed *dot pitch.* The lower the dot pitch, the higher the picture quality that can be created on a monitor.

Dot pitch is provided in millimeters. Thus, a dot pitch of .30 means that there is .30 millimeters between phosphor groups on your. This translates to .011811 inches (1mm equals .03937 inches), or 84.67 dots per inch (approximately). If you look back at table 11.2, you'll see that a 14-inch monitor has an image that is 11.2 inches wide. This measurement means that there are approximately 948 phosphor groups across the width of the screen. Since each phosphor group can only be on or off at any given time, for the best picture, your horizontal resolution should not exceed the number of phosphor groups you have on a line.

You can also do the same calculations vertically, which for a 14-inch monitor would result in approximately 711 phosphor groups vertically. Thus, a 14-inch monitor would have 948 × 711 phosphor groups. For the best screen resolution, then, you should not exceed 800 × 600 resolution on a 14-inch monitor. If you use a higher resolution, you'll still be able to see an image, but not all the pixels will be displayed properly, and the picture might appear a bit fuzzy in places. Table 11.3 shows the approximate phosphor group configurations for the various monitor sizes at some popular dot pitches.

Table 11.3 Phosphor Group Configurations for Different Monitors

Screen Size	.31 Dot Pitch	.28 Dot Pitch	.25 Dot Pitch
12-in	787 × 590	871 × 653	975 × 732
13-in	852 × 639	943 × 708	1057 × 792
14-in	918 × 688	1016 × 762	1138 × 853
15-in	983 × 737	1089 × 816	1219 × 914
16-in	1049 × 787	1161 × 871	1300 × 975
17-in	1114 × 836	1234 × 925	1382 × 1036
18-in	1180 × 885	1306 × 980	1463 × 1097
19-in	1245 × 934	1379 × 1034	1544 × 1158
20-in	1311 × 983	1451 × 1089	1626 × 1219
21-in	1377 × 1032	1524 × 1143	1707 × 1280

When you look for a monitor, you should go for the lowest dot pitch you can find; the lower the dot pitch the sharper the image. Anything with a .28 dot pitch is considered a good monitor as of this writing. Higher dot pitches will not provide as good of an image as possible, and you should steer away from them.

> **Tip:** Even though you can show a crisp 800 × 600 image on a 14-inch monitor with a .30 dot pitch, that doesn't mean you'll be happy with the size of the display. The best advice is still to try before you buy.

Screen Curvature

Earlier you learned that some monitor vendors frequently exaggerate the size of their screens. This exaggeration is caused by the distortion that affects many screens at the corners. The reason for this distortion is because many video tubes are curved at the front—just like your television screen at home. This curvature leads to the distortion. To overcome this distortion, many vendors offer flat-screen monitors. While the name may be a bit of a misnomer (since flat-screen monitors are still a bit curved, although not nearly as much as normal video tubes), these monitors provide a better image because the distortion inherent in the curved-screen models is removed. The trade-off is that flat-screen monitors cost more to produce, and therefore the price tag is higher.

Refresh Rate

The refresh rate refers to the frequency at which the electron guns in your monitor actually redraw the image on your screen. The higher the refresh rate, the crisper the image on your screen.

Refresh rates are determined by the two scanning frequencies of a monitor. The horizontal scanning frequency refers to the time it takes

the electron gun to move all the way across the screen. The vertical scanning frequency refers to the time it takes to move the electron gun down the screen. Refresh rates are expressed in Hertz. A refresh rate of 60 Hz means that the image on the screen is redrawn 60 times a second. Likewise, a 72 Hz refresh rate means that the screen is redrawn 72 times a second.

It is important to match the refresh rates used by the monitor with the refresh rates produced by your video card. If the monitor expects a higher refresh rate than what the card produces, you won't see anything on the monitor. If the video card produces a higher refresh rate than the monitor can handle, then not only won't you see an image, but you can physically damage the monitor.

Interlacing

Interlacing refers to how the electron guns that "paint" the image on your screen actually do their job. You already know that the electron guns move back and forth, painting an image down the front of your video tube. In an interlaced monitor, the electron guns scan alternate lines. Thus, lines 1, 3, 5, 7, 9, and so on are scanned. When the bottom of the screen is reached, on the next pass the guns scan lines 2, 4, 6, 8, 10, and so on. This setup means that an interlaced monitor requires two complete vertical passes to create a complete image. A non-interlaced monitor does not do this. Instead, it scans lines consecutively, completing the screen in one pass.

Some users complain that interlaced monitors produce more flicker than non-interlaced, particularly at higher screen resolutions. Interlaced monitors typically cost less than non-interlaced models. Because they need to make two passes per screen, the refresh rates on interlaced monitors are also lower than on non-interlaced. If you spend a good deal of your time viewing high-resolution images, you'll definitely want a non-interlaced monitor.

Multisync Monitors

As you can imagine, the number of different video cards on the market means that there are a number of different specifications that a monitor must meet. This means that matching the proper monitor to the proper video card can be a time consuming and frustrating process.

Monitor vendors have a vested interest in making sure that their monitors will work with the widest variety of video cards. To address the many card specifications that exist, vendors have been (for the past few years) marketing multisync monitors. The primary feature of these monitors is that they can detect the frequencies used by your video card, and then adjust themselves to match. This feature makes matching up monitors to adapters much easier, and can prevent the damage possible if they should be mismatched.

Multisync monitors generally cost more than "monosync" monitors, but the investment is generally worth it. Why? Because there is a good chance that you'll upgrade your video card before you upgrade your monitor. If you don't have a multisync monitor, the chances are better that you'll need to change your monitor when you change the video card.

Video Drivers

You learned earlier that different video standards (such as VGA or XGA) have different specifications. You also learned that in the SVGA arena, different chip sets on the adapter cards accomplish video tasks in different ways. For Windows 95 to make the most use out of these video cards, it uses *video drivers.*

The use of video drivers is nothing new. Drivers have been used with different software (and Windows) for years. When you installed Windows 95, it attempted to determine what video card you have installed in your system. Most of the time, this testing is successful, and there is no problem. In some instances, however, the automatic testing could fail, in which case Windows 95 uses a generic driver for either the VGA, SVGA, or XGA cards.

In most instances, you (as a user) will never need to be concerned with which video driver is installed in your system. There are two instances where you need to be concerned, however:

- If your video card manufacturer provides an updated video driver specifically for Windows 95
- If you change the video card in your system

In this last instance, if you upgrade to a plug-and-play video card, you probably won't have any problem. If the card is not Plug-and-Play compatible, however, then you may need to manually change the driver. To change the video driver used by Windows 95, follow these steps:

1. Choose Settings from the Start menu. The Settings menu appears.
2. Choose Control Panel from the Settings menu. The Control Panel window appears.
3. Double-click on the Display icon in the Control Panel. The Display Properties sheet appears.
4. Click on the Settings tab.
5. Click on the Change Display Type button. The Change Display Type dialog box appears, as shown in figure 11.4.

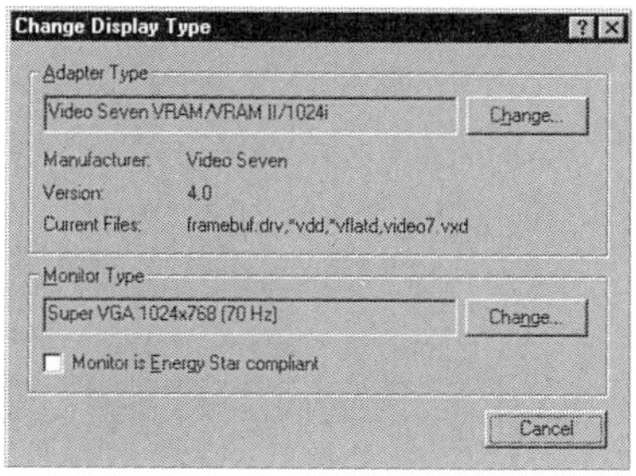

Fig. 11.4 The Change Display Type dialog box allows you to modify your video driver and monitor type.

You can change two settings from this dialog box. The first, at the top of the dialog box, is the type of video adapter card you have installed in your system. The second is covered in the next section. If the video adapter selected is incorrect, or if you have an updated video driver disk from the video card manufacturer, then click on the Change button. The Select Device dialog box appears, as shown in figure 11.5.

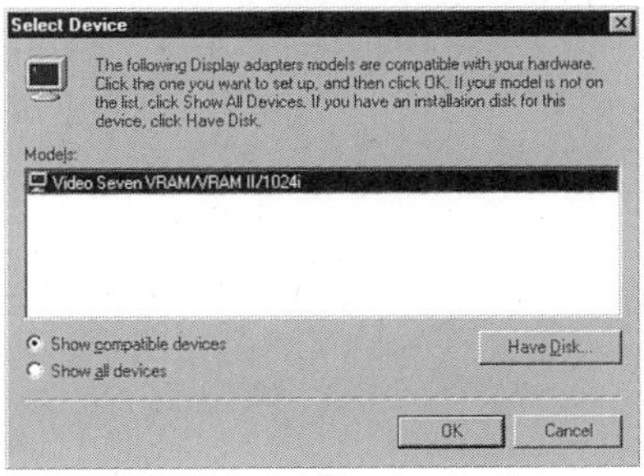

Fig. 11.5 The Select Device dialog box is used to select the video driver you want to use.

By default, Windows 95 lists in this dialog box only the video drivers it feels you can use. But what if you have an updated video driver disk? In this case (or if you want to try a different video driver), click on the Show all devices button at the bottom of the dialog box. Windows then lists all the video drivers that it knows about. You can select one of them, or click on the Have Disk button if you have a video driver disk from the manufacturer.

> **Caution:** You should only use the Have Disk button if you have a disk containing Windows 95 video drivers. Windows 3.1 drivers will not work properly with Windows 95.

When you're done specifying a video driver, click on the OK button. Your change is made either right away (if you choose a video driver compatible with your current driver), or you'll be prompted to restart Windows 95 before the change can occur.

Selecting a Monitor Type

Windows 95 also allows you to specify the type of monitor you have connected to your system. This setting acts as a modification to the video driver specification, and allows the video driver to interact properly with the monitor.

Unfortunately, Windows 95 cannot "reach out" and determine the type of monitor you have connected to your system. There is no interactive link between the video card and the monitor itself (all data travels one way—to the monitor). This means that you need to specify your monitor manually. To do this, follow these steps:

1. Choose Settings from the Start menu. The Settings menu appears.
2. Choose Control Panel from the Settings menu. The Control Panel window appears.
3. Double-click on the Display icon in the Control Panel. The Properties for Display dialog box appears.
4. Click on the Settings tab.
5. Click on the Change Display Type button. The Change Display Type dialog box appears, as shown earlier, in figure 11.4.

In the previous section you learned how to use the top portion of this dialog box, where you change your video driver. The bottom portion of this dialog box allows you to specify the monitor you have hooked up to your system. To change it, click on the Change button, and the Select Device dialog box appears, as shown in figure 11.6.

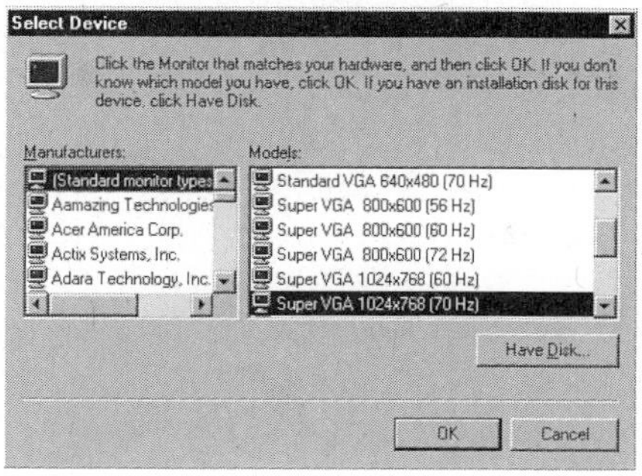

Fig. 11.6 The Select Device dialog box is used to select the monitor that is connected to your system.

You should pick a monitor vendor from the list at the left side of the dialog box. Your selection here controls what is then shown in the right side of the dialog box. Select a monitor model from the available list.

How do you determine the type of monitor you have? The easiest way is to look on the back of the monitor. Most monitors include some type of label that indicates the monitor manufacturer and model; this is the information you need. If such a label is not on your monitor, then you should refer to the documentation that came with the monitor or that came with your computer system. In some instances, you may even need to contact the vendor from which you purchased the monitor.

If you absolutely cannot determine the make and model of your monitor, you can select a generic monitor make and model. The first choice in the Manufacturers list is called Standard monitor types, as shown earlier in figure 11.6. You can select this manufacturer and then select the monitor resolution and refresh rate that works best for you. While this may take a bit of trial and error, going through the process of picking the monitor will provide the best display quality and least eye fatigue.

When you are through specifying a monitor, click on the OK button.

Changing Video Parameters

Earlier in this chapter you learned how different video cards support different types of displays. The video cards supported by Windows 95 can support a variety of display resolutions and colors. When you first install Windows 95, it sets your display parameters based on the following:

- If you updated from a previous version of Windows, then the same display parameters were used as you used in the previous version.
- If you installed Windows 95 on your machine without updating, then the display parameters are set to a default setting, namely 640 × 480 resolution and 16 colors.

You can change your display parameters to any values supported by your video card and monitor. To do this, follow these steps:

1. Choose Settings from the Start menu. The Settings menu appears.
2. Choose Control Panel from the Settings menu. The Control Panel window appears.
3. Double-click on the Display icon in the Control Panel. The Properties for Display dialog box appears.
4. Click on the Settings tab. The Properties for Display dialog box appears, as shown in figure 11.7.

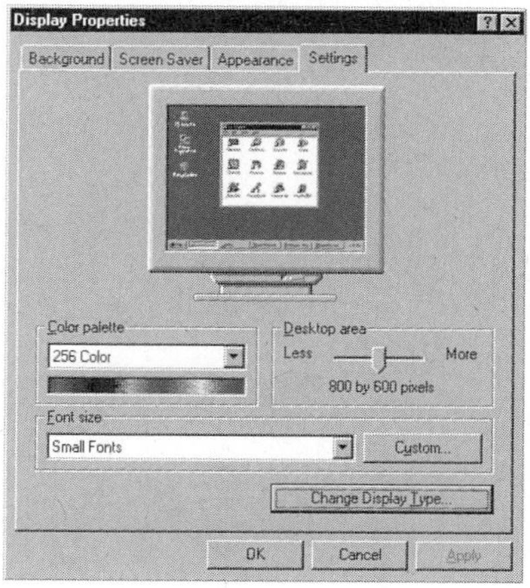

Fig. 11.7 The Properties for Display dialog box allows you to modify your video parameters.

The first setting many people like to change is the Desktop area setting, at the right side of the dialog box. This control contains a slider bar that specifies the screen resolution you want to use. The slider typically has three possible settings. The left-most setting is for 640 × 480 resolution, the middle one for 800 × 600, and the right-most for 1,024 × 768. Notice that as you make changes in the control, the sample display at the top of the dialog box also changes.

Now you can specify the number of screen colors you want to use. You do that in the Color palette area at the left side of the dialog box. If you display the pull-down list, you'll see the valid selections for your particular video card at the resolution you've specified.

Finally, at the bottom of the dialog box you can specify the Font size you want to use. This setting is a helpful one not necessarily related to your video card, but controls the size of font used by Windows to display information. Generally, the lower the resolution, the smaller the font you'll want to use. At higher resolutions you may want to use a larger font to make your displays more readable.

When you're done making changes to your display parameters, click on the OK button. Depending on your specifications, you may be asked to restart Windows in order for the changes to take effect, although this does not happen nearly as often as in earlier versions of Windows. Instead, you are informed that Windows 95 is about to make the changes, as shown in figure 11.8.

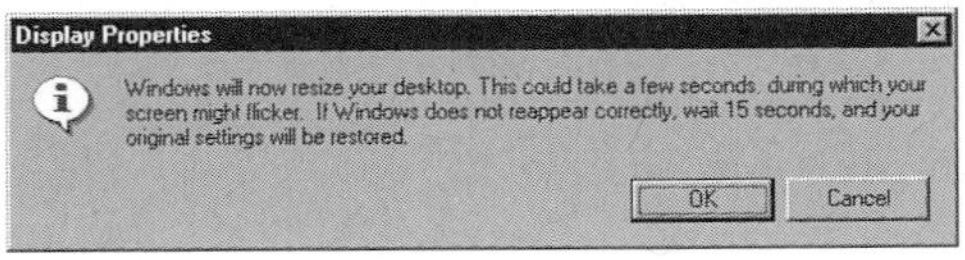

Fig. 11.8 Windows 95 allows you to change display properties on the fly.

When you click on the OK button, the display changes are made and you are asked to confirm the changes. If you don't confirm them within 15 seconds, your changes are abandoned, and you're returned to the Display Properties dialog box. This feature is a big improvement over earlier versions of Windows where it was possible to hang your system by choosing improper video settings.

Speeding Up Your Video

Now that you know the basics about video systems, you can turn your attention to speeding up your own system. If you want to increase the speed of your display, there are four primary methods you can use:

- Use fewer colors in your displays.
- Configure your software to place fewer demands on your video system.
- Install a graphics accelerator card.
- Buy a faster computer or motherboard, particularly one with high-speed local-bus video.

Using Fewer Display Colors

Perhaps the simplest way to increase your system speed is to change the number of colors you use in Windows 95. If you are currently using a 256-color or 65,535-color display, you can significantly increase the display refresh rate of Windows 95 by configuring Windows 95 so that you use only 16 colors. While you may not have as realistic a look to any exotic wallpaper or screen saver images you are using, the change won't hinder your use of most programs. In fact, most programs don't require more than 16 colors—unless you're using sophisticated graphics programs that rely on a high number of colors.

Many purchasers of SVGA cards use 256 colors (or more) because the card is capable of delivering the high number of colors, not because the extra colors are necessary. Computers purchased with Windows 95 preinstalled are almost invariably set up with the higher number of colors as the default. Sixteen colors are adequate for virtually all Windows 95 applications except those for image and video processing.

To change your display so it only uses 16 colors, take the following steps:

1. Choose Settings from the Start menu. The Settings menu appears.
2. Choose Control Panel from the Settings menu. The Control Panel window appears.
3. Double-click on the Display icon in the Control Panel. The Properties for Display dialog box appears.
4. Click on the Settings tab.
5. In the Color palette area of the dialog box, change the setting to 16 colors.
6. Click on the OK button.

Configuring Your Software

Another step you can take to improve your video performance is to configure your software so it does not perform as many graphics operations as it might otherwise. As an example, in Word for Windows you can turn on draft font and picture placeholders in the Options dialog box (on the View tab). This change will greatly improve the video performance of Word for Windows. Other Windows 95-based applications typically offer similar ways to speed up your video processing.

You can also use only standard fonts with your software. Processing will be fastest if you use one of the bit-mapped VGA-resident fonts supplied with Windows 95—MS Serif and MS Sans Serif—in one of their standard sizes (8, 10, 12, 14, 18, and 24 points) instead of TrueType or Adobe typefaces. VGA-resident fonts consist of individual bitmaps of the characters, so Windows doesn't need to convert the outline of a scaleable typeface to the size you specify. Even if the VGA-resident fonts do not appear in the list of fonts for your application, you can type their names (MS Serif or MS Sans Serif) into the text box of most applications' font selection combo boxes.

You can improve the graphics performance of some applications by allocating specific amounts of memory to store bitmaps. As an example, you can speed up the display of graphic images embedded in Word for Windows by making a change or two to the WINWORD6.INI file, which is located in your Word for Windows directory. You can add the line

```
BitMapMemory=nnn
```

to the `[Microsoft Word]` section of the file. The number you substitute for *nnn* specifies the amount of memory reserved in kilobytes, as shown in the following example:

```
[Microsoft Word]
BitMapMemory=512
CacheSize=128
```

This example allocates 512K of memory for bitmaps displayed in Word documents. Word normally allocates 1,024K (1M), so you free up half the memory normally reserved for this purpose. The second line, CacheSize=128, designates 128K of memory as a buffer area for storing documents. This is twice the default document cache size used by

Word. CacheSize is not related specifically to graphics, but usually improves the speed of paging through documents.

Only a few applications offer the ability to assign memory to store graphic images, and you might find it difficult to find the necessary instructions in the documentation. In some cases, the details are included in a README.TXT file on one of the distribution floppy disks and are not incorporated in the printed documentation.

The amount of memory (RAM) installed in your computer also plays an important role in graphics performance. If you use the preceding example to allocate blocks of memory to Word for Windows, the reserved memory will not be available to other applications while Word is running. Complex Windows applications, such as Microsoft Access, are resource-intensive; that is, the application consumes a substantial amount of memory when you launch it. Displaying large, bitmapped images adds to the amount of memory required. If you don't have enough RAM to store Windows itself, plus the application and the image, Windows uses the swap file on the disk as a substitute for RAM. If your disk activity light flashes constantly when you're using an application that involves graphics, you should consider adding 2M to 4M of RAM before investing in graphics hardware or software accelerators.

Installing Graphics Accelerator Cards

Earlier in this chapter, you learned about graphics accelerator cards, which can be plugged into local-bus slots in a computer. There is more to accelerator cards, however, than what has been presented so far.

Conventional VGA adapter cards are called *dumb frame buffers.* The cards store one display screen of data received from the computer's internal input/output (I/O) bus and convert the stored digital data to the RGB analog signals required by your monitor. (As you've already learned, the I/O bus runs at 8 MHz to 10 MHz, not at the speed of your computer's CPU chip.)

The amount of memory on the card determines the number of colors that can be displayed in the various operating modes supported by the card. Cards with 512K of memory can typically display 256 colors in 640 × 480 and 800 × 600 pixel modes but only 16 colors at 1,024 × 768 pixel resolution. You need 1M of memory to display 16 million colors at 640 × 480, 65,535 colors at 800 × 600, or 256 colors at 1024 × 768 mode.

Note: Some people think that more memory on a video card means that the card will operate faster. This is not true. Memory is directly related to the number of colors that can be displayed. Thus, unless you have a need for millions of colors as high resolutions, chances are good that you may be wasting money by purchasing a video card that has 2M or 4M of memory installed.

Graphics accelerator cards require the same amount of memory as a conventional VGA card to display the same number of colors. Most accelerator cards use video random-access memory (VRAM), a special type of memory chip that, unlike conventional RAM, can be written to and read from at the same time. This feature speeds up video processing immediately. Some early graphic accelerator cards substituted VRAM for conventional RAM and achieved a moderate speed-up. Most graphic accelerator cards currently available are designed specifically for Windows-based systems (including Windows 95) and perform two specific functions:

- By using a separate processor dedicated only to graphics, accelerator cards execute at a much faster rate than many of the graphics calculations that would normally be performed by the computer's CPU. The cards achieve this rate by using a special driver that works closely with the operating system to process graphics information as quickly as possible.
- The cards eliminate the bottleneck that stems from sending streams of bytes to the graphics adapter card over the computer's relatively slow I/O bus. (The I/O bus connects the adapter cards

to the CPU.) Because the graphics processor and the frame buffer memory are on the same card, the information does not have to travel over the computer's bus and can be stored in the VRAM at a faster rate.

Moderately priced Windows graphics accelerator cards (those priced around $200 or $300) provide a two- to five-fold improvement in overall system performance. The greatest benefit accrues in manipulating bitmapped images with a large number of colors at high resolutions, where you can realize improvements as great as 10-fold.

Under pressure to meet competitive prices, some manufacturers of Windows accelerator cards have chosen to omit the VESA feature adapter connector that is standard on virtually all conventional VGA and SVGA adapter cards. If the accelerator card you purchase does not have a feature adapter, you cannot connect it to most video-in-a-window and VGA-to-NTSC adapter cards used for displaying and generating standard NTSC video signals. Even if the accelerator card has a feature connector, its synchronization signal polarity and timing may not match that required by the video card you intend to attach to it. (Compatibility with video adapter cards is discussed in Chapter 28, "Understanding Full-Motion Video.")

Buying a Faster Computer

You can easily more than triple the speed of most Windows applications by replacing a 33 MHz 80386 system that has 4M of RAM with a 66 MHz 80486 DX2 computer with 8M of RAM, or with a Pentium system with the same amount of RAM. Many books are available that discusses what you should look for when buying a new computer. Also, it seems that every other month there is a feature article in computer magazines about the same topic. You should take your time and shop for the best system your budget will allow.

KILLER WINDOWS 95

12

Using Mice and Other Pointing Devices

by Allen L. Wyatt

Windows 95 is a Graphical User Interface (GUI) that combines menus, icons, scroll bars, and windows into an elegant and efficient working environment. The most efficient way to manipulate and control this environment is with a pointing device, such as a mouse. Indeed, the growth of the Windows environment (including Windows 95) over the past several years has made the mouse an integral part of a computer system.

This chapter discusses pointing devices, and specifically the mouse. In this chapter you learn the following:

- ➤ Why you need a pointing device
- ➤ How to choose a pointing device
- ➤ What pointing devices that serve the same functions of a mouse are available
- ➤ How to install a mouse or other pointing device
- ➤ How to fine-tune the performance of your mouse

Most people are familiar with the mouse as a pointing device. In addition to the mouse, a variety of other pointing devices that perform the same function are available. Devices include trackballs, pens, touch tablets, and digitizing tablets with a mouse emulation mode. Throughout this chapter, the generic term *mouse* means any pointing device that serves the same purpose as a mouse.

Using a Mouse

Almost all Windows 95 features are available by using the keyboard as well as by using a mouse, so why use a mouse? As already pointed out, a pointing device is the most efficient way to control the Windows 95 environment. In some Windows 95 applications, not using a mouse causes severe usability limitations. In desktop publishing and graphics programs, a mouse or other pointing device enables you to move and resize items on-screen quickly. With drawing or paint programs, working without a mouse is practically impossible.

A mouse also enables a new user to learn programs more quickly. More programs are providing graphical representations of functions on-screen rather than forcing users to learn function keys or memorize commands. With a mouse, you click to perform a function, whether the function is simple or complex.

Imagine the mouse as an extension of your hand. With the mouse, you can point at items on-screen, then use the mouse buttons to perform a

variety of actions. A mouse makes selecting these actions as natural as pushing a button with your finger.

All pointing devices enable you to move the pointer around the screen, pull down menus, select functions, and when used with a graphics program that supports it, do freehand drawing. However, the way each of the pointing devices operates and the added features they provide may differ quite a bit from the others. With the mouse, movement of the pointer occurs only when the mouse ball moves. Lifting the mouse and moving it (without the bottom of the mouse touching something) does not move the pointer.

Mice are manufactured in a variety of designs. Some have two buttons, some have three, and some have more. Also, mice can be connected to your computer in a variety of ways. Even infrared mice are available that allow the mouse to communicate with your computer without a wired connection.

Some functions can be performed faster with the keyboard; others faster with a mouse. You will be most efficient when you use a combination of the keyboard and mouse. With time, you'll know which functions you can do faster with the pointing device and which you can do faster with the keyboard. To select the proper pointing device, you must match what you do with your computer and the pointing technology available. What works best for you may not work best for someone else.

Understanding Mouse Sensitivity

In actual use, on a technical level, mice differ in one important point—*resolution.* Every time you move the pointing device, a series of pulses is sent to the computer. Resolution is the number of counts per inch (cpi) that a mouse can detect. The counts per inch are the number of those pulses sent by the pointing device to the computer in an inch of physical movement. The greater the resolution, the finer and more precise the movement the pointing device can sense. In addition to finer movement, the mouse pointer also appears to move more slowly across the screen, thereby providing greater control, particularly when working with detailed objects.

In many software setups for individual applications, you can adjust the mouse sensitivity for just that application. For instance, you can run WordPerfect for DOS from within Windows 95 and set WordPerfect's own mouse sensitivity without affecting Windows 95's mouse setting.

Using Mouse Shortcuts

In addition to standard mouse functions such as pointing, clicking, and dragging, most Windows 95 applications have shortcuts you can perform with a mouse that make the mouse even more useful. For example, double-clicking an item in a Windows 95 list box is usually the same as selecting the item and then choosing the default operation (often OK, Yes, or Select) for the dialog box. Selecting a figure in a graphics program normally is accomplished by clicking the item. After the item is selected, moving it is as easy as holding the mouse button while moving the mouse.

> **Caution:** Don't confuse the term *mouse shortcuts* with the new term making its debut in Windows 95—shortcuts. Shortcuts are described in detail in Chapter 3, "New Windows 95 Tools." Mouse shortcuts are those operations made faster by using a mouse rather than using the keyboard.

To show you how mouse shortcuts can help you use a Windows 95 application, Table 12.1 shows some of the mouse shortcuts used with WordPerfect for Windows. Many of the shortcuts also work with other Windows 95 applications.

Table 12.1 Typical Mouse Shortcuts in Windows 95 Applications

Action	Result
Click	Selects an object
Double-click	Selects and opens an object
Shift+click	Selects all items in a list from the previously selected item to the newly selected one
Ctrl+click	Selects an object in addition to all the other objects that may be selected
Click within a window	Makes that window active
Right-click	Displays a context menu for the object

Choosing a Pointing Device

After you decide to use a pointing device, you need to select the device that best meets your needs. Many newer systems come with a pointing device (such as a mouse), but you may want to replace it with one more suited to the work you do. With the variety of pointing devices available, plan on doing extensive research before you make your purchase—particularly if the purchase will cost a great deal of money. Each device may fit you differently or have different features that are important to you.

A large selection of alternative pointing devices is available. Trackballs have a ball held in a stationary holder that moves the on-screen pointer as you rotate the ball with your hand. Touch tablets enable you to run your fingers over a panel to move the pointer on-screen. A push on the panel sends the equivalent of the mouse click to the computer. You also have pointing devices that look like pens. The following section provides information to help you decide which type of device is best for you.

When choosing a pointing device, consider the following aspects:

- **Type.** The type of pointing device you select should reflect the type of work you plan to do. You can select a mouse or one of many alternative pointing devices. The most common types of pointing devices are the mouse, trackballs, touch tablets, light pens, joysticks, graphics tablets, and touch-screens.
- **Design.** The mouse and other pointing devices are manufactured in a variety of designs. Some devices have two buttons, and some have three or more. You also must consider how the design fits you physically and how comfortable you feel working with it. For instance, some mice are designed specifically for left-handed users.
- **Connection.** Make sure you know how the pointing device connects to your computer. The device may use a built-in connector, a serial port, or a special adapter card.
- **Compatibility.** Devices that are 100% compatible with a Microsoft mouse generally are easiest to install and run. Other devices may require their own drivers to work properly with your software. Make sure there is a Windows 95 device driver available before you commit to the device.
- **Resolution.** The resolution of a pointing device refers to how many times per second the device checks the position of the pointer or how small a movement the device can detect. The higher the resolution, the more precise operations you can perform with the pointing device.

To make sure the pointing device you select is best-suited for your needs, try to test the device before you make a final purchase. If possible, borrow a friend's pointing device and try it in your environment. You also can buy from a dealer who will allow you to return the pointing device if it doesn't meet your needs. Your pointing device must work well with your computer, your software, and you.

Getting Your Money's Worth

Nothing will sour you more quickly on using a pointing device than using one of poor quality. Poor devices hamper your efficiency, and you may find most functions faster with the keyboard. With a poor-quality mouse, fine movement may not be possible, the mouse may perform erratically, or the pointer may not move smoothly on-screen.

To help sell their products, some manufacturers frequently throw in a mouse for free or almost free. If the mouse provided is not good quality, you may be better off passing on the offer or purchasing a good-quality mouse and getting rid of the free one. A well-designed pointing device may cost a little more, but the investment pays dividends every time you use your system.

The Microsoft mouse is an example of a high-quality pointing device with good design. The device fits the hand comfortably. The ball, which records the movement of the mouse, is near the top of the mouse, by your fingers. This feature enables you to make very precise and accurate movements with the mouse. Other devices, like the IBM mouse, are high quality but fall short in design. The IBM mouse buttons are long and narrow and take quite a bit of pressure to click. The ball is farther away from the fingers. This condition can make fine movement more difficult than with the Microsoft mouse.

Understanding Connections

You can connect pointing devices to a computer through a dedicated mouse port, a serial port, or an adapter card plugged into the computer. Determine what type of connection your computer requires before you buy a pointing device. Some pointing devices come with the cables and electronics necessary to connect to a dedicated mouse port or a serial port. Other devices do not come with the necessary interface parts to work with all types of connections; you need to purchase these devices with the appropriate interface. After you have installed the mouse properly, the method of attachment makes no measurable difference in performance.

If your system has a dedicated mouse port, you may want to order a device that uses the port. This step saves you the expense of buying extra hardware or wasting a serial port or bus slot.

If your system doesn't have a dedicated mouse port, using a serial port probably is the least expensive way to proceed. Most systems have at least one serial port and often two. If one of your serial ports is available, then no additional hardware purchase (besides the mouse) is necessary. If you need to add a serial port, you generally can do so for under $25 through a mail-order company. (If you need assistance in this area, contact your local computer store.)

If your system does not have a mouse port and all the serial ports are in use, you may need to use a mouse with its own proprietary interface card that uses one of your computer's card slots. This device typically is called a *bus mouse.* It is also possible that some of the more exotic or esoteric pointing devices require their own special interface card. Because this type of pointing device comes with its own adapter card, it costs more than an equivalent pointing device that uses a built-in port or serial port. You also may have difficulty making the card work properly with the other equipment in your system. (For more information, see the section "Installing Your Pointing Device" later in this chapter.)

One last point about mouse ports. Some videoboards have mouse ports built into the board. If you want to utilize this special mouse port, make sure your mouse is compatible with such a port or that you can disable the port by some means. Otherwise, the port may not co-exist peacefully with the serial port mouse or bus mouse. Refer to the video board's manual or contact the video board's manufacturer for more details.

Examining Different Types of Mice

In general, there are three types of mice: the *mechanical mouse,* the *optical mouse,* and the *wireless mouse.*

The most common type of mouse is the mechanical mouse. It uses a hard rubber ball that rotates inside a compartment on the bottom of

the mouse. Two or three capstans inside the mouse roll against the rubber ball as you move the mouse. One of the capstans translates horizontal motion into electrical pulses, and the second capstan does the same for vertical motion. On some mice there is an optional third capstan that acts as a stabilizer so the ball doesn't wobble. The mouse sends these electrical pulses from the first two capstans to the computer and, ultimately, to the software.

One of the drawbacks of the mechanical mouse is that it can pick up dust, dirt, and other debris you may have on your work surface. This material gets inside the mouse and can make the rolling ball sticky. You must clean the mouse from time to time. Except in the most serious cases, you can clean the mouse with little effort and time. Most manufacturers include cleaning instructions in the mouse owner's manual. Several companies even sell mouse cleaning kits.

> **Tip:** You can limit the amount of dust and dirt picked up by your mouse by using a good quality, lint-free mouse pad. These are available at any computer or office-supply store.

An optical mouse operates by shining a beam of light through the bottom of the mouse onto a reflective surface. As you move the mouse, the light reflects back to a sensor in the mouse. This sensor translates reflective differences into electrical pulses and sends them to the computer, like the mechanical mouse does.

> **Tip:** If you operate an optical mouse in direct sunlight or in a very bright light, it is possible it will not act reliably. The sunlight can interfere with the brightness of the light beam that is reflected from the glass pad used by the optical mouse.

You can roll a mechanical mouse on any surface that provides enough friction to move the ball, but you must use an optical mouse on a special surface. Typically you use a small glass pad, the size of a normal mouse pad, which provides the reflective surface the mouse needs to operate properly. Because the optical mouse has no moving parts, it is less prone to picking up dirt and dust. The only cleaning an optical mouse requires is to periodically wipe off the glass pad and the sensor on the bottom of the mouse.

Finally, a wireless mouse is typically the same as a mechanical mouse, except no cable connects the mouse and the computer. Rather, the mouse transmits movement data to the computer through an infrared link or radio waves.

An infrared mouse works similarly to your television remote control. The mouse sends data by way of an infrared signal to a receiver connected to the computer. Reliable use of this kind of mouse depends on the positions of both the receiver and the mouse. If the mouse and the receiver have something between them (such as a stack of books), the mouse stops working. After you remove the obstruction and restore the line-of-sight positioning, the mouse starts working again.

The Logitech MouseMan Cordless mouse is a wireless mouse. Instead of using an infrared signal beamed at a receiver, the mouse functions by using radio signals to link the mouse to your computer. The MouseMan Cordless doesn't require line-of-sight positioning of the mouse and computer as does the infrared mouse. The computer even can be under a desk or located up to six feet away. The MouseMan Cordless can run on eight different frequencies, so you can use several mouse devices in close proximity without interference. The signals are also designed so they won't interfere with other devices that rely on radio signals.

Regardless of whether a mouse is mechanical, optical, or wireless, the number of buttons on the mouse is an open-ended issue. On the Macintosh computer, the mouse has only one button. Most mouse designs for the PC world have two or three buttons, although some designs have even more. Most PC applications utilize one or two buttons, although some packages (such as CAD programs) enable you to define additional buttons for your mouse.

Considering Mouse Alternatives

A mouse is not the only pointing device you can use in Windows 95. The variety of other devices includes trackballs, touch tablets, and pens. They all claim to make you more efficient. In the end, your comfort with the pointing device determines how efficient you are. The following information is provided to help you determine whether an alternative pointing device might work better for you than a mouse.

Trackballs

Compared with the surface area required to work with a mouse, trackballs require almost no desk space. Trackballs are very popular in any situation where space is at a premium. This feature makes trackballs the pointing device of choice for portable computers, laptops, or personal computers on a small desk.

One way to think of a trackball is it is an upside-down mechanical mouse. With a trackball, the case is stationary and a ball rests inside a compartment on top of the case. You move this ball with the palm of your hand, your fingers, or your thumb. Because the ball does not move around your desktop, it normally doesn't get dirty as fast as a mechanical mouse (unless you spill something on it).

Trackballs differ from one another in a number of ways, including the number of buttons, the arrangement of the buttons, the size of the ball, and the design of the case. The most common full-size trackballs have a billiard-size ball and two or three buttons.

As laptop computers become more popular, so do smaller trackballs. These trackballs normally clip to the right or left side of the keyboard and can be used easily in a very confined area. For more information about these smaller trackballs, read the section "Pointing Devices for Portable Computers" later in this chapter.

Pens

Today's market offers a number of pointing devices shaped like pens. Some of these devices are actually a mouse in a pen housing, and other devices are light pens.

One of the newer pointing devices on the market is the pointer pen or mouse pen. The mouse cable exits from the top of the pen; at the other end is a small ball. You hold the pointer pen like a regular pen and roll it around your desk as if you were writing with the pen. On the side of the pen are buttons used for performing the various mouse button functions.

Because the ball of the pen is so small, you can roll it on almost any surface, including a clipboard on your lap. These devices normally include some type of stand in which to rest the pen.

Light pens are fundamentally different from a mouse pen. You use a light pen to perform functions and move the cursor by pointing to your computer screen. Touch the screen with the pen, and the pen transmits the position to your software. Light pens typically are used with specialized software and CAD systems.

Touch Tablets

When referring to pointing devices, *tablet* normally refers to a digitizing tablet. You can think of these devices as electronic drawing boards. You use tablets most commonly with complex drawing programs and CAD packages. Digitizing tablets cost quite a bit more than mouse devices, trackballs, and pens, and tablets can be as small as a videotape or as large as a drafting table.

Rather than transmit movement information to the computer relative to where the on-screen pointer resides, tablets have a one-to-one correspondence to locations on your computer's screen. When you select a point on the digitizing tablet, the screen indicates the exact corresponding location. These tablets come with one of several types of pointing devices you use to change the location of the on-screen pointer. Some devices are plastic with buttons and a cross hair to enable you to select points on the tablet precisely (these devices are called *pucks*). Other tablet pointing devices are pens with one or more buttons. These tablets normally have a mouse mode that enables you to use them like a mouse.

Due to their cost and design, purchasing a tablet probably is not feasible unless you work with specialized applications that require a digitizing tablet. You probably would be more comfortable with one of the other pointing devices described in the preceding sections.

Another type of tablet is the touch tablet. Microtouch Systems, Inc., makes a touch tablet called the UnMouse. This tablet is very small, about three inches by five inches. With this touch tablet, you move the on-screen pointer by sliding your fingers over the glass panel. To click, you press on the glass. In the absolute mode, you can point to a location on the tablet, and the pointer instantly moves to the same place on-screen. By using a stylus (a pointer similar to a pen or pencil), you can use this device as a mini-graphics tablet.

A close relative to the touch tablet is the glidepoint. These devices are very small pads, with a surface area only a couple of inches wide and high. The pad on the glidepoint resembles the same shape as the video screen. You use the device by scooting your finger over the pad, which moves the pointer on-screen. There are buttons located in the housing of the glidepoint which perform the same function as mouse buttons.

Pointing Devices for Portable Computers

More and more computers are coming equipped with pointing devices already built in. For instance, the IBM ThinkPad includes what is called a Track Point, which is a small red-rubber button in the keypad. You can use your finger to wiggle the button in any direction, and the on-screen mouse pointer moves accordingly. While these built-in pointers conserve valuable space, they can be tricky to learn and master. Even

with the built-in devices, many people prefer to add an external pointing device since they are a bit more comfortable to use.

The most common pointing device used with portable computers is the mini-trackball. Many people use portable computers in locations where they cannot use a traditional mouse—places like an airplane, airport, or automobile. Mini-trackballs come in a wide variety of shapes and sizes. Some trackballs are built into the computer, some are separate, and some clip onto the computer keyboard.

With a clip-on trackball, look for a breakaway mechanical design to prevent accidental damage to the mouse or keyboard if the computer is bumped. You normally can mount the clip-on trackballs on the left or right side of the keyboard and at a variety of angles. Some trackballs include software that enables you to calibrate which way is up before you use the device. Then the trackball works properly with your software in a variety of mounted positions.

Most pointing devices for portable computers are designed for use with the serial port because most laptops have a limited number of slots available for adapter cards. You probably would not want to devote one of those scarce slots to a pointing device. With graphic applications becoming so popular and laptop computers becoming more powerful, many laptops now have a built-in PS/2-compatible mouse port, leaving the serial port free for a printer, modem, or other serial device.

The cables connected to portable pointing devices are typically shorter than cables on devices designed for desktop use. Often these cables are only a couple of feet long. This setup enables you to use the pointing device more easily in close quarters. Extension cables sometimes are included or are available at an additional cost.

Note: With most portable computers, the mouse pointer onscreen is difficult to see. Windows 95 has a solution for this problem, as described in the "Fine-Tuning Your Pointing Device" section later in this chapter.

Installing Your Pointing Device

After you have purchased a new pointing device, you need to install it. In most cases, the manufacturer provides detailed instructions for installing the pointing device.

Earlier you learned that there are several ways you can connect a mouse (or other pointing device) to your computer. The actual steps you follow when installing your pointing device depend, in large part, on the type of connection the device requires. Read the instructions provided with the device to learn how to successfully perform an installation.

If you are using an adapter card to install your pointing device, the card needs its own *interrupt* to communicate with your computer. No other hardware device may share this interrupt. If the pointing device is sharing an interrupt with another device, the pointing device may work erratically or not at all.

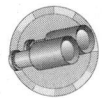

> **Note:** If your mouse and the adapter card support Plug and Play, then you do not need to worry about interrupt conflicts. These will be resolved automatically by your system.

Your pointing device and computer documentation can help you from the System Tools menu determine what interrupt your device is using and what alternatives are available. You can change most device interrupt settings by moving jumpers or switches on the device's adapter card. Try the default settings first; they work in the widest range of computers.

> **Tip:** If you plan to change any of the settings or switches in your system, make sure you write down the current settings before making any changes. This precaution enables you to easily change to the original settings if necessary.

Windows 95 includes utilities that provide a wealth of information about your system. For example, you can view information about your mouse and the hardware interrupts. To access this information, right-click the My Computer icon on your desktop. From the context menu, select the Properties option. You then will see the System Properties sheet. Click the Device Manager tab, and your screen will appear as shown in figure 12.1.

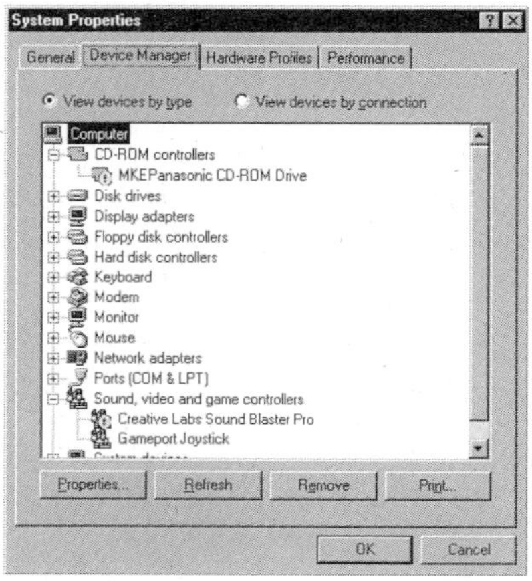

Fig. 12.1 The System Properties sheet, with the Device Manager tab selected, displays information about devices on your system.

This sheet shows all of the devices attached to your system, categorized by type. Notice that one of the devices listed, about two-thirds of the way down the list, is Mouse. Remember that this is a category of device; if you double-click it, you can find out what mice Windows 95 thinks are connected to your system. Double-clicking the mouse name itself displays a sheet similar to what is shown in figure 12.2.

This dialog box will differ based on the capabilities of your mouse and its driver. If you close the mouse properties dialog box and return to the System Properties sheet, you can explore other information that is pertinent to your pointing device. For instance, you can look at your

COM ports (if your pointing device is hooked up through a COM port), checking to see if there is a conflict.

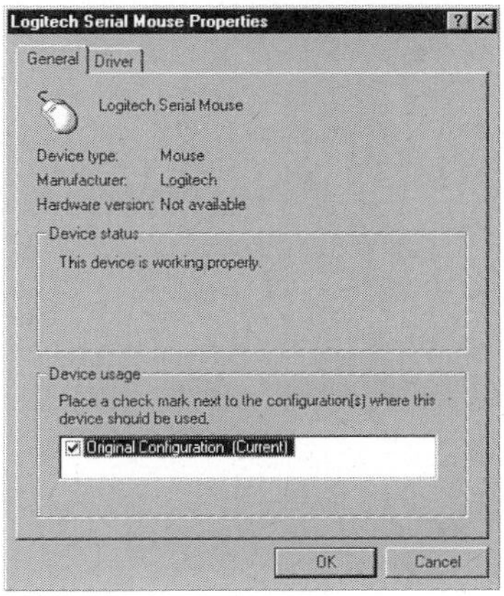

Fig. 12.2 Windows 95 provides a sheet that shows the properties associated with your mouse.

Likewise, you can check your system interrupts to see if there are conflicts. This is done by double-clicking the top-level Computer device in the System Properties sheet (refer to fig. 12.1; see the first item in the list). When you do this, a Computer Properties sheet appears, as shown in figure 12.3.

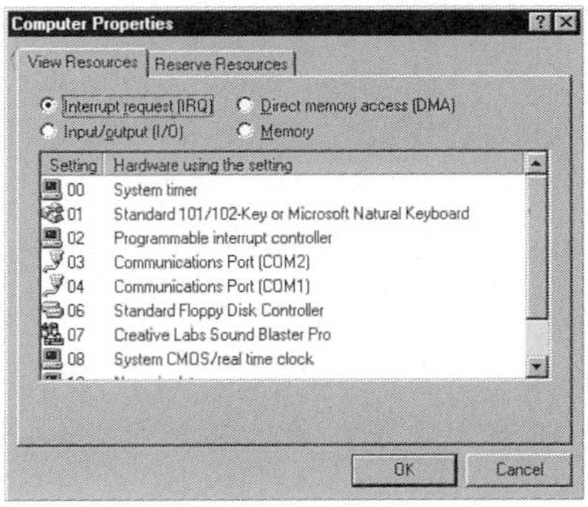

Fig. 12.3 The Computer Properties sheet, with the Interrupt request (IRQ) button selected, displays information about your system interrupts.

This sheet enables you to review the different resources in your system. At the top of the sheet are four buttons that enable you to choose which category of resources you want to view. When you first display the sheet, Interrupt request (IRQ) is selected by default. You can scroll through the list of interrupts, seeing exactly which interrupts are used which way. If there is a conflict that Windows 95 can pinpoint, then the conflict is shown in the list as well. If an interrupt conflict exists, you should correct it (at the hardware level) as quickly as possible so that both devices use different interrupts. This then allows them both to work properly.

Selecting the Correct Driver

When you first installed Windows 95, it went through a detection phase in which it attempted to identify all the hardware connected to your system. During this phase, it is highly possible that it detected your pointing device and installed the proper driver. The driver enables Windows 95 to communicate properly with the pointing device. If the wrong driver is installed, or if you change your hardware and don't change the driver, it is very possible that your pointing device will not work as intended.

To check which driver is installed for your pointing device, or to change the driver, follow these steps:

1. Choose Settings from the Start menu. The Settings menu appears.
2. Choose Control Panel from the Settings menu. The Control Panel window appears.
3. Double-click the Mouse icon in the Control Panel. The Mouse Properties sheet appears.
4. Click on the General tab.
5. Click on the Change button. The Select Device dialog box appears, as shown in figure 12.4.

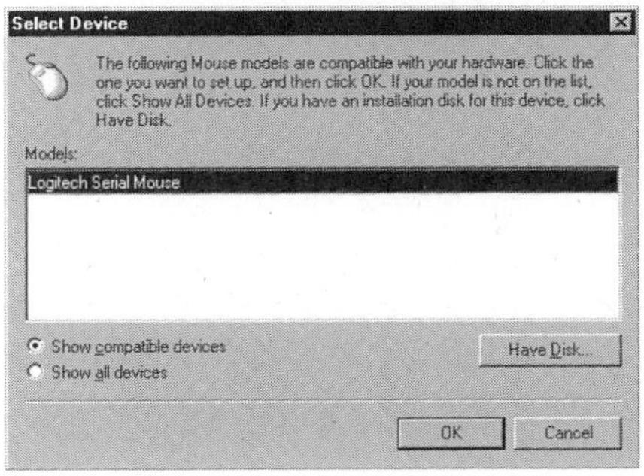

Fig. 12.4 This Select Device dialog box enables you to specify the mouse driver that Windows 95 should use.

At this point, the dialog box shows the different mouse models that Windows 95 feels are compatible with your hardware. If the information shown is not correct, you can click the Show all devices button at the bottom of the dialog box. The dialog box then changes so it displays two lists, as shown in figure 12.5.

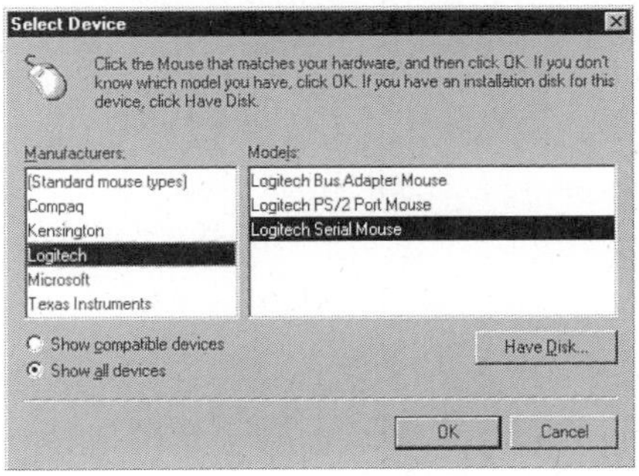

Fig. 12.5 In the Select Device dialog box you should pick both the vendor and the model of your mouse.

Your first task is to pick the manufacturer of your pointing device in the left-hand column. Based on the manufacturer, the information in the Models column changes. Pick the model of your pointing device, if it is shown. If it is not shown, and your vendor provided a Windows 95 driver disk, you can click the Have Disk button.

When you are done, click the OK button. This returns you to the Mouse Properties dialog box. At this point you can set other properties for your pointing device. This is done through the use of the other tabs in the dialog box. For instance, you can specify how the mouse buttons should be interpreted by clicking the Buttons tab. You also could change the way the mouse pointer looks and responds by choosing the Pointers tab. When you are finished, click the OK button to close the dialog box and effect your changes.

Troubleshooting Pointing Device Problems

If your mouse doesn't work, or if it operates erratically, you can take several steps to fix the problem. If the mouse won't work with Windows 95 applications, try the following things:

- If you can see a pointer on-screen but it won't move as you move your mouse, Windows 95 might have detected an unused mouse port and might be expecting it to have a mouse connected to it. If this is the case, contact the manufacturer of your computer or the device that has the unused mouse port to find out how to disable the extra mouse port.
- If you're using a serial mouse, make sure you've connected the pointing device to a properly configured serial port.
- Make sure the mouse cable is firmly connected to your PC. You may also want to make sure the connecting screws, if any, are tightened.
- Make sure the mouse driver being used by Windows 95 is the proper one for the pointing device being used.
- Determine which interrupt the mouse is using and make sure it is not sharing it with another hardware device.
- If the pointer moves erratically, the pointing device may need to be cleaned. See the documentation that came with the device for information about cleaning.

With a Microsoft mouse and most similar mouse devices, you can tell if the mouse is dirty or defective by removing the ball and moving the rollers with your finger. Watch the pointer on-screen. If the pointer is jumpy in one direction, the problem probably is a dirty or defective mouse. If the pointer is jumpy in two directions, the problem probably is the software. When you use your fingers to move the rollers in the cavity where the mouse ball goes, you may leave a fine coating of oil from your skin. After checking the mouse operation, clean the rollers with a soft, lint-free cloth and rubbing alcohol.

> **Tip:** If you suspect your mouse is dirty, carefully examine the rubber ball. Picking up dirt or something sticky from a work surface can cause the ball to get hung up and cause erratic pointer movement.

If these actions do not cure the problem, then there may be a problem with the mouse cord or the mouse itself. Connect the mouse to another computer system to determine if the mouse is defective.

Pointing for Physically Impaired Users

In previous versions of Windows, Microsoft had add-ons available that could be used by individuals with disabilities to make using Windows easier. In Windows 95, these add-ons have been incorporated into the Control Panel so they are always available. The Accessibility Options of the Control Panel enable you to modify Windows rather dramatically for those with disabilities. Most of these options are covered in Chapter 14, "Tailoring Windows 95 and the Registry," but one option is more appropriately discussed here.

Many people have a hard time with the manual dexterity necessary to use a mouse. One of the Accessibility Options available is called MouseKeys, which enables a person to use the keyboard to control the

mouse pointer. This feature makes the keys on your numeric keypad act like a built-in mouse. Each of the keys moves the mouse in a specific direction—just as if you were using a real mouse! The 5 key on the keypad serves as the primary mouse button (typically the left button); there is no secondary button.

To enable the MouseKeys option, follow these steps:

1. Choose Settings from the Start menu. The Settings menu appears.
2. Choose Control Panel from the Settings menu. The Control Panel window appears.
3. Double-click the Accessibility Options icon in the Control Panel. The Accessibility Properties sheet appears.
4. Click on the Mouse tab. The Accessibility Properties sheet appears, as shown in figure 12.6.

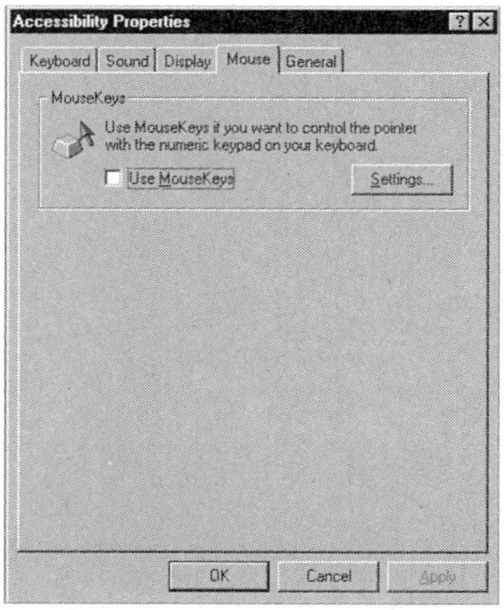

Fig. 12.6 The Accessibility Properties sheet, with the Mouse tab selected, enables you to enable or disable MouseKeys.

To turn on MouseKeys, select the check box next to the Use MouseKeys option. You also can click the Settings button to modify how MouseKeys functions.

With MouseKeys enabled, a small mouse icon appears on the status bar, near the right side. If you tap a mouse movement key (the arrow keys on the numeric keypad), the cursor moves one pixel in the specified direction. If you press and hold a movement key, the cursor moves continuously in the specified direction.

With MouseKeys turned on, you can use either the regular mouse or the keyboard as a mouse. The result is a system that is perhaps more accessible to those with disabilities.

How Windows 95 Interacts with Software

by Allen L. Wyatt

Any operating system provides a platform on which you can build and run applications. Windows 95 is no exception; it provides a robust and solid platform for a wide variety of applications. In this chapter you learn how Windows 95 interacts with software. Specifically, you learn the following:

- How the architecture of Windows 95 affects software
- What types of software can be installed on a Windows 95 system
- How to remove programs previously installed on your system

Understanding the Virtual Machine

To fully understand how Windows 95 interacts with software, you must understand a bit about the design of the operating system. Windows 95 includes a core service called *the Virtual Machine Manager*. The purpose of the VM Manager is to provide and manage the resources necessary to run both the operating system and the applications on your system. The environments created by the VM Manager are called *virtual machines.*

Think of a virtual machine as a logical computer within the physical computer. It is possible to have multiple virtual machines running within the same physical computer. From the perspective of an application program running within a VM, it is running within its own computer. It believes it has full access to the resources of the entire system, and that there are no other applications running within the system.

The resources (memory, disk space, I/O ports, and so on) needed by an application are made available to the application by the VM Manager. The VM where the operating system does its work is called the *System VM.* At any given time, there is only a single System VM in operation. In addition, you may have other DOS VMs also created within your system, as shown in figure 13.1. You'll learn more about the System and DOS VMs a little bit later in this chapter, in the section titled "Different Types of Software."

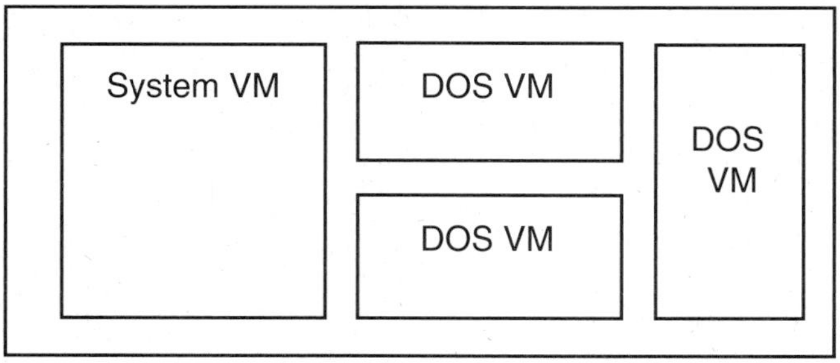

Fig. 13.1 Your Windows 95 system can have multiple virtual machines operating within it.

In administering your system, the VM Manager has three primary responsibilities:

- Process scheduling
- Memory paging
- MS-DOS Mode support

Each of these areas is discussed in the following sections.

Process Scheduling

A process is a task running on the computer. At any given time, you may have multiple tasks running on your system. A process can be either a portion of a program or the program as a whole.

The Process Scheduler is the portion of the VM Manager responsible for the following:

- Providing system resources to the processes running in the system
- Arbitrating between processes when they're competing for limited resources
- Scheduling which processes run in which order

System resources are provided to processes as they're requested. If there is a conflict (such as two applications that need to use the same resource), then whenever possible the resource is shared between the two processes. Some resources, such as memory or a disk drive, can be shared concurrently. Other resources, such as a printer, must be shared sequentially. Still other resources, such as a modem or an I/O port, must be shared exclusively. The Process Scheduler makes sure that processes do not "run over the top of each other" as they try to use resources that may be in short supply or in high demand.

The third responsibility of the Process Scheduler—scheduling—is the biggest responsibility of the three. This is why the Process Scheduler takes its name from this one aspect of its job. Scheduling concurrent

tasks involves a process known as multitasking—the ability to run more than one task at the same time. This scheduling revolves primarily around the use of the CPU, and two forms of multitasking are used: cooperative and preemptive.

Cooperative Multitasking

The first type of multitasking is known as *cooperative* multitasking. This is the type of multitasking used in previous versions of Windows. It is included in Windows 95 for compatibility with older Windows software.

Cooperative multitasking relies upon the different processes within the system to cooperate with each other. Windows 3.1 basically trusted applications to periodically check a message queue to see what other tasks were waiting within the system. If no tasks were waiting, then the application could continue using the system.

If the operating system needed the application to relinquish control so that another process could use the CPU, then it would place a message in the queue. The next time the application checked the queue, it would cooperate by relinquishing control to the operating system, which would in turn pass control to the needy process waiting in the wings.

The problem with cooperative multitasking is that different programs would check the queue at different times. For instance, one application might check it every few milliseconds. Another application, however, might check it every five or 10 seconds. The result was "CPU hogs" that tried to use a disproportionately large amount of CPU time. This caused some programs to run slowly and others to run quickly, but all of them to run in a jerky stop-and-start manner.

Preemptive Multitasking

Windows 95 also implements a form of multitasking known as *preemptive* multitasking. In this scheme, the operating system acts as a traffic cop—it times each application and either takes control after a certain amount of time, or grabs control if a higher-priority event needs to occur right away. Examples of high-priority events would be attending to an I/O port or refreshing the video display.

Windows 95 is not the first operating system to use preemptive multitasking. Windows NT has been using it since it came on the market, and it is also used in multitasking schemes for larger mini and mainframe computers.

There are many benefits to preemptive multitasking:

- The applications don't need to check a queue. This means there is less management code necessary within the application itself.
- There is more even distribution of processing time to the various applications in the system. This means that applications run smoother with less "start and stop."
- Applications can use threads to enhance their own performance.

This last benefit may need some explaining. A thread is nothing but a portion of an application, running as a process within the system. An application can have multiple threads running at the same time. For instance, a spreadsheet might implement the recalculation function as a thread. This would allow lengthy recalculations to occur in the background, while a user input thread was running in the foreground accepting user input. If threads are effectively used within a program, the application makes better use of the time it is allotted by the operating system. For instance, if the same spreadsheet program used only a single thread at a time, each time it received a chunk of time from the operating system, it would need to check for user input. If there was user input, then the program would need to wait while the user typed his or her entries. Because humans type notoriously slowly (in computer terms), the time between keystrokes is wasted time. If the spreadsheet used threads, that time could be used for other processes that need to be done, but are not dependent on a specific sequence. For instance, recalculating or printing or automatically saving to disk or sending information to another application—the possibilities are almost limitless. The result is that the user becomes more productive with the application.

Memory Paging

The second task of the VM Manager is *memory paging.* This involves swapping information from physical memory to logical memory, as necessary. This involves moving memory around in RAM and also paging it to disk (and back) as necessary.

Every virtual machine within your system is composed of *address spaces,* as shown in figure 13.2. Each process running within a VM is granted an address space 4G in size. Half of this space is used for system management, and the other half by the process itself. Thus, a single process can address up to 2G of memory—more than enough for today's most demanding applications.

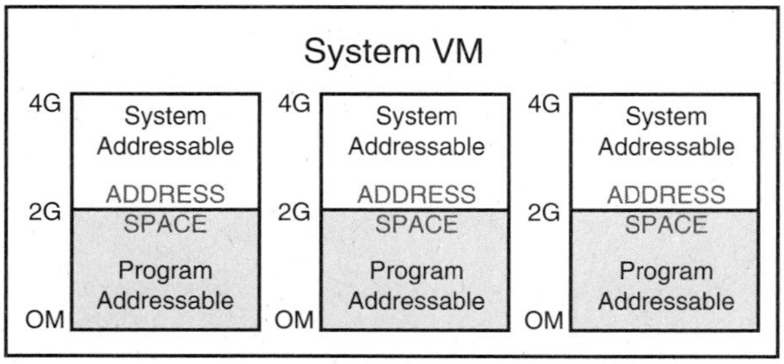

Fig. 13.2 A virtual machine is composed of processes running in address spaces.

It's pretty tough to find a machine that physically has 4G of memory installed (the RAM costs would be phenomenal, and the energy consumption huge). Thus, the address space is partly physical (the memory in the system) and partly virtual (what can be swapped to disk, as necessary). As far as the application running in the address space is concerned, the address space is *flat* and *linear.*

Flat and linear are characteristics of memory that mean it can be addressed with a single address register. This address register is 32-bits in size, which means it can hold an address between 0 and 4,294,967,295. (This is why there is a 4G address space assigned.)

Windows 95 uses a technique called *demand paging*. This refers to a method by which code and data are moved in pages from physical memory to a temporary paging file on disk. The Memory Pager portion of the VM Manager takes care of this process of moving memory pages within RAM and to and from the disk. As far as the application is concerned, however, the information (up to 2G) is available in RAM all the time.

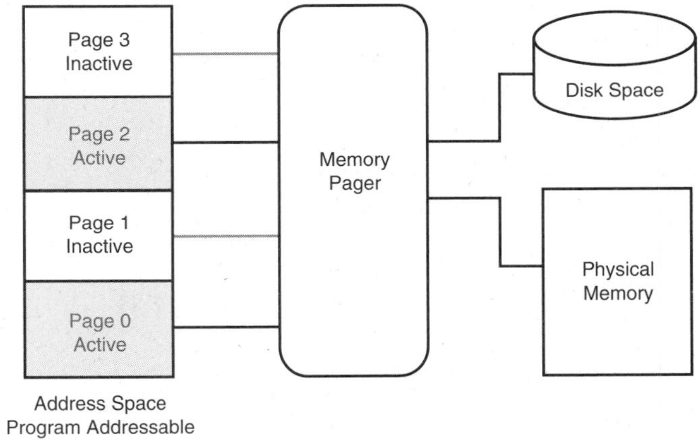

Fig. 13.3 The Memory Pager takes care of moving virtual memory to and from the disk.

The Memory Pager also takes care of mapping virtual addresses from the process's address space to physical pages in the computer's memory. In doing so, it hides the physical organization of memory from the application. This ensures that the application can access its memory as needed, but not the memory of other processes.

MS-DOS Mode

The final task of the VM Manager is to administer the system if it is required to operate in *MS-DOS mode*. This is a special mode of the operating system in which exclusive control of the entire machine and all its resources are given to a single MS-DOS task.

You should not confuse MS-DOS mode with opening an MS-DOS window on your system; they are not the same. MS-DOS mode is exclusive in nature, and an MS-DOS window can be used in a shared environment. MS-DOS mode is not required very often. In fact, most DOS programs can function quite well in the stable, isolated environment provided by an MS-DOS window in Windows 95. Some applications (very few, in reality) require the expanded and exclusive access to the system that can only be realized in MS-DOS mode.

When operating in MS-DOS mode, no other applications can be running in the system. Thus, the VM Manager takes care of shutting down all other processes when switching to MS-DOS mode. When the program running in this mode finishes running, the only way to exit from and reinitialize the system is to restart Windows.

Different Types of Software

Three general types of programs can be executed in Windows 95. Every program you run will fall into one of these categories:

- **Win32.** These are 32-bit Windows applications designed to take full advantage of the Windows 95 environment.
- **Win16.** These are traditional 13-bit Windows applications. They are carry-overs from earlier versions of Windows, but still operate satisfactorily in the Windows 95 environment.
- **MS-DOS.** These are programs designed to run in DOS, not in Windows. Windows 95 provides a suitable environment for running virtually any DOS program.

Both Win32 and Win16 programs occupy separate address spaces within the System VM, and each MS-DOS program runs concurrently within its own DOS VM. (This arrangement is shown in figure 13.4.) If a DOS program requires enough resources, then it is run in MS-DOS mode, where the DOS VM is the only VM defined in the machine.

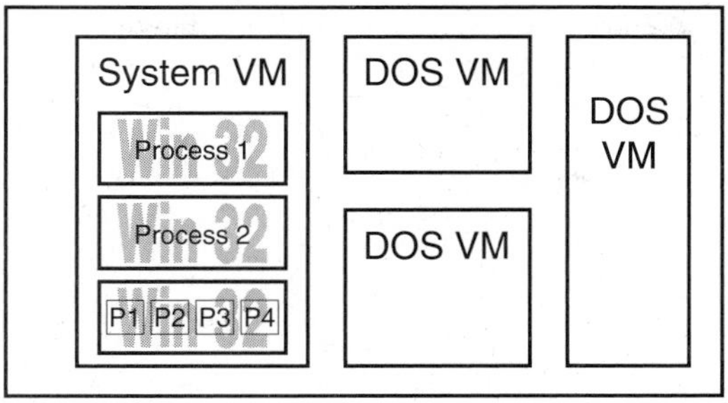

Fig. 13.4 Different program types reside in different VMs within your system.

Notice that each Win32 application occupies its own address space, while all Win16 applications share a joint address space. Every DOS application (every DOS window) occupies its own address space as well. In the case of DOS, however, the address space and the VM are the same.

If an application crashes for some reason, then the use of different memory areas protects the other applications (and the operating system) from being affected. The one possible exception is the Win16 programs. If one of these crashes, the crash may affect other Win16 applications because they're in the same address space. Improvements in Windows 95 resource management make such an occurrence less of a possibility than in earlier Windows versions.

If an application hangs, you can recover by pressing Ctrl+Alt+Del. This signals to Windows 95 that you want to end one of the applications—in effect recover either an address space or a VM (in the case of DOS). Windows displays a list of all applications in the system and asks which one you want to end. You can pick the offending application, and Windows 95 will close it after asking you to confirm your action.

Removing an Application

Later in Part III, "Software," you learn how to install programs in Windows 95. Chapter 16, "Installing Windows Applications," and Chapter 18, "Installing DOS Applications," walk you through the procedures necessary to add software to your system. This section covers how to remove software you have previously installed.

Exactly how you remove a program depends on which type of program you're removing. Because there are three types of programs that can run in the Windows 95 environment, there are three corresponding ways to remove your software.

Removing a Win32 Program

There are two types of Win32 programs you can install on your system—one designed for Windows 95 or one designed for Windows NT. In the future, as more and more programs are designed to work with both operating systems, such distinctions will become less clear, but for the short term it can make a big difference.

A Windows 95-aware program is one that not only includes 32-bit support, but also comes with programs designed to uninstall the software. These programs work with the Add/Remove Programs Wizard in the Control Panel to allow you to easily remove the software. A Windows NT 32-bit program does not include such removal capability, so you must remove it according to the tried-and-somewhat-true methods of traditional Windows software. This process is described in the next section.

To uninstall Windows 95 software, start by following these steps:

1. Make sure that the program you want to remove is not currently running. Close any windows used by the program.
2. Choose Settings from the Start menu. The Settings menu appears.
3. Choose Control Panel from the Settings menu. The Control Panel appears.

4. Double-click the Add/Remove Programs icon. The Add/Remove Programs Properties sheet appears, as shown in figure 13.5.

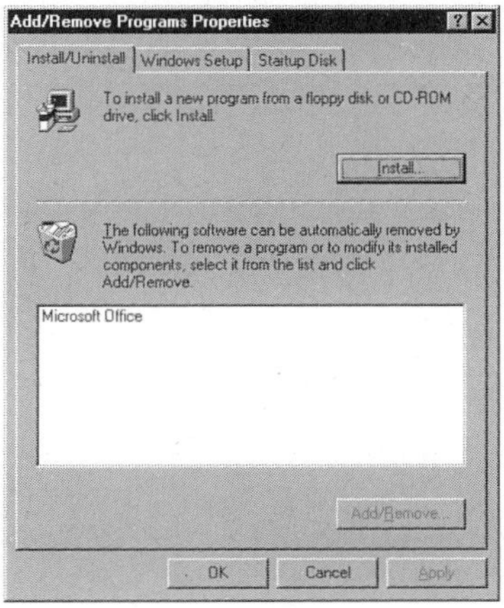

Fig. 13.5 The Add/Remove Programs Properties sheet is used to add or remove software from Windows 95.

5. At the bottom of the sheet is a list of installed software for your system. This is not all your software, just those programs designed to work with Windows 95. Click on the program you want to remove from your system.
6. Click on the Add/Remove button at the bottom of the sheet.

From this point, the software removal program for the application is actually running. Some programs include the removal as part of the setup program for the application, while others have a separate uninstall program. The steps you follow will vary based on how the setup or uninstall program was designed.

You should follow the instructions for the uninstall program for your application. You may need to refer to the documentation that came with your software for detailed instructions.

When the removal is complete, all elements of the application should have been removed. You may want to check to ensure that there are no shortcuts left over in places like the StartUp folder or in the Programs folder.

Removing a Win16 Program

People who have been around Windows for a while know that it can be difficult, at best, to remove Windows software. This is because the software almost becomes an extension of the operating system. It does not limit its effect to only a program folder, but instead may affect all of the following areas:

- DLL (dynamic link library) files may be copied into the Windows system folder
- INI files for the application are created in the Windows system folder
- Windows INI files (WIN.INI, SYSTEM.INI, and PROGMAN.INI)
- Program groups are modified to add program items for the software

Granted, not all of these are particularly germane under Windows 95. For instance, program groups no longer have applicability. However, the software you installed does not know that—it thinks it is still using the older Windows interface, and may have created program groups thinking they would be used by the operating system.

To remove Windows software, you should follow these steps:

1. Delete the folder(s) containing the application software.
2. Remove any shortcuts or menu items you had set up for the software.
3. Examine the INI files in the \WINDOWS folder to determine whether any of them belonged to the application. If you can clearly make such a determination, delete the file. Better yet, copy it to a floppy disk in case you're mistaken and need to restore the file.
4. Examine the WIN.INI and SYSTEM.INI files to see if there are any entries in them that clearly belonged to the application. If so, delete the entries.

5. Check the technical documentation for the program to see if it lists DLL files installed by the software. If so, you can remove the DLL files from either the \WINDOWS or \WINDOWS\SYSTEM folders.

This last step can be the trickiest. It is possible for more than one application to use a DLL file. If you remove a DLL file that you believe was used only by the application you are deleting, but it was instead needed by another piece of software, then the other piece of software will no longer function properly. If this occurs, the only option is to reinstall the software you still need so that the DLL files are restored.

When these steps are complete, you have probably deleted the program. No absolute can be given, however, because different programs have different impacts on a traditional Windows environment. There are, unfortunately, no absolutes with traditional Windows software. The Windows 95 improvement of clean uninstalls through effective use of the Registry is a long overdue change.

Removing an MS-DOS Program

Removing a DOS program is perhaps the simplest of all program removals in Windows 95. This is because DOS programs don't really manipulate the Windows environment like Windows applications do. They don't add DLL files or change the Registry or clutter the landscape with INI files.

To remove a DOS program, you need to follow these steps:

1. Delete the folder(s) containing the MS-DOS software.
2. Remove any Windows shortcuts you set up for your DOS programs.
3. Check to see if any residual commands were left in the CONFIG.SYS or AUTOEXEC.BAT files by the program.

This last step is the one that can potentially be the most confusing. It assumes you know what is in these files, and how the commands got there. Your MS-DOS program, not knowing or caring about Windows

95, could have added lines to the files to run programs like SHARE, to set BUFFERS and FILES to a certain level, or to include the SETVER program. None of these is necessary under Windows 95, so they can safely be removed.

KILLER 14 WINDOWS 95

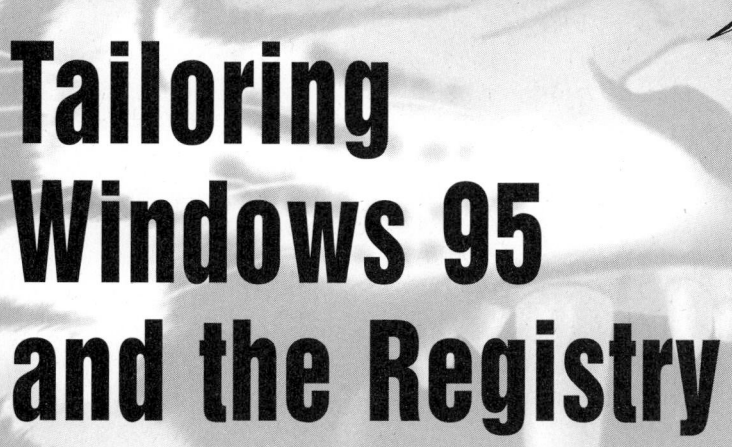

Tailoring Windows 95 and the Registry

by Clayton Walnum

As you've undoubtedly found out, the Windows 95 operating system is extremely powerful and flexible. It's not simply another revision of a tired, old program, but a completely new and robust operating system brimming with friendly and easy-to-use features. A long-time feature of the Windows GUI has been the option to modify its appearance to suit your taste and needs. Although Windows 3.X was customizable for your needs, Windows 95 offers even more flexibility in the way you configure and use it. You can now change and customize individual elements however you want. Much of Windows ability to cope with such flexibility stems from its use of

a centralized *Registry,* where virtually all pertinent information is stored about each component involved directly (and indirectly) with the operating system.

This chapter is designed for people who want to fine-tune Windows 95 for their needs. For those who want to become technically proficient with Windows, you can also learn to manage and troubleshoot most aspects of its daily operation. Unlike other Windows 95 books, this chapter is designed for people who are not yet Windows "experts."

Using This Chapter

If you're familiar with a previous version of Windows, you'll notice there are lots of changes. Some changes are subtle, while others are much different. For starters, the reliance on INI files has diminished greatly. In fact, Windows 95 hardly uses INI files, except where they are needed to maintain compatibility with previous versions of Windows and applications that just don't conform to the Windows 95 Registry structure.

This chapter addresses many aspects of configuring Windows for your specific needs. In addition, you'll learn about:

- The purpose of the Registry
- Editing the Registry
- Tuning Windows' Appearance
- Tuning Windows' Configuration

Several sections in this chapter have a short description of what you can expect to see in the Registry together with the location of the value in the Registry. For example, you might see:

```
Registry value: MouseTrails
Key location: MyComputer\HKEY_LOCAL_MACHINE\Config\0001
➥\Display\Settings
```

These show the Registry value and hierarchical location of that value. If you are viewing the Registry, simply navigate to the appropriate subfolder to view the current setting.

Understanding the Registry

One of the great improvements in Windows 95 from previous versions is the method in which it manages program and device information. This does not refer to the files you work with but the information that is automatically recorded by Windows 95 when you install or update a program or device. To understand the improvements that have been made, it is helpful to understand the way things used to be done in previous versions of Windows.

Until the advent of Windows 95, controlling information and parameters for the operating system were kept in a variety of INI files. These files controlled the look, behavior, and speed of Windows and the programs provided with Windows. Sure, you could quickly edit the files with any ASCII text editor, but just one typo or wrong deletion and you would spend more time than you intended just trying to fix it. In addition, information was spread all over the place (at least throughout different INI files) and became quite a nuisance if you wanted to "clean up" your system files.

Windows 95 has done away with this confusion, and has introduced the Registry. The Registry is a structured database describing information about your hardware, applications, and other Windows 95 settings. As you add or remove software and hardware, the Registry is dynamically updated so no "ghost" information lingers about recently removed applications or devices. If you run an application under Windows 95 that was designed to work with Windows 3.1, it continues to generate and maintain INI files, as if there had been no change. This is because 16-bit programs are not aware of the Registry, nor were they designed to take advantage of it. However, as new versions are released specifically for Windows 95, the reliance on INI files will be reduced drastically. Examine more closely how the Registry works.

How the Registry Works

The Registry's database approach to maintaining critical system and user information is very orderly and understandable compared to an

INI file. Technically speaking, the Registry consists of two files, *USER.DAT* and *SYSTEM.DAT*. Of course, both of these files are marked as hidden, so you won't see them (or inadvertently delete them) as you use the Explorer or work from the DOS prompt.

The file USER.DAT, which maintains information from the User Profiles, handles settings dealing with user preferences like screen type, size, file associations, network settings, and personal printer information. The information in USER.DAT varies, based on the users who are registered on the local machine.

The other file, SYSTEM.DAT, which tracks data from the Computer Profiles, maintains hardware settings including types of add-in cards, IRQ settings, and the like. SYSTEM.DAT maintains information that does not change based on who is using the machine.

Registry information is stored in separate files for a simple reason: You may want to store SYSTEM.DAT and USER.DAT in different places. The most common way to do this, in facilities that have large networks, is to keep the system-related information (SYSTEM.DAT) on the local system and the user-related information (USER.DAT) on a network server. This setup allows users to move from machine to machine and still have their preferences available wherever they work.

As you work with Windows 95 on a day-to-day basis, any changes you make to system settings are automatically recorded or updated in the Registry. It's easiest to imagine the Registry as a directory (or folder) structure, similar to the way Explorer displays the contents of your computer. The Registry consists of six keys, or groups, which comprise all aspects of the Windows operating system.

- **Hkey_Classes_Root.** OLE-related information, including shortcuts. This key is a pointer to the Key_Local_Machine\Software\Classes subkey. It is provided as a separate key for compatibility with older versions of the Windows registration database.
- **Hkey_Current_User.** User-specific settings, including preferences, color schemes, and so on. This key is nothing but a pointer

to a subkey within the Hkey_Users key, representing the user currently logged into the system.

- **Hkey_Local_Machine.** Machine-related specifics, such as installed hardware and swap file settings.
- **Hkey_Users.** Additional user-specific information geared more toward the default settings before data is changed in the Hkey_Current_User key.
- **Hkey_Current_Config.** Configuration information about the current hardware settings, such as notebooks that plug into a docking station. This key is nothing but a pointer to a subkey within the Hkey_Local_Machine\Config key.
- **Hkey_Dyn_Data.** System information for various devices, including Plug-and-Play devices, which is updated each time you restart Windows.

Notice that of the six keys, three are actually pointers to identical data stored in other keys. The Hkey_Dyn_Data key is not actually a file, but is a branch of the Registry maintained in RAM. This key is created every time you start your machine, and is maintained in RAM for fast access. The upshot of all this is that there are really only two keys in the entire Registry that are stored on disk: HKey_Local_Machine (which is SYSTEM.DAT) and HKey_Users (which is USERS.DAT).

Each key plays an important role in how Windows operates and how the user accesses the computer. To many users, this structure can be a bit intimidating. This means that most users stick to simply making changes from the Control Panel, rather than editing the Registry.

If you're familiar with the INI structures found in older versions of Windows, you know that each major section started with a heading surrounded by brackets, such as [Enhanced] or [Desktop]. These groupings are analogous to the keys used within the Registry. A major difference between the two is that there could be dozens or hundreds of groups within the various Windows INI files, while there are only six major groups within the Registry.

The Registry is organized in a hierarchical fashion. Each key can contain either values or subkeys. These subkeys can then contain either values or subkeys, and so on. Just as hard disk directories can contain files or subdirectories, the six major keys can contain values or subkeys. (This is not to say that Registry values are the same as files; they are not. It is only to point out that there is a strong parallel in the structure of the Registry and the structure of a disk drive.)

Values within a key contain data. This is nothing but the current setting for the value; in effect, the "value of the value." Data can be of three types: binary, DWORD, or string. Binary and DWORD values both contain numeric data, but the difference is that binary data can be of any length, while DWORD data is limited to a single 16-bit value. The exact type of data maintained for a value is determined by the purpose for which the value is used.

Changes to the Registry

On a system level, values within the Registry and the structure of the Registry itself are changed all the time. For example, you learned in Chapter 2, "Under-the-Hood Improvements," that Windows 95 is a Plug-and-Play operating system. This means that when starting up, the operating system reads information from the Plug-and-Play BIOS and later from devices installed in the system. That information is compared with information in the Registry and, if differences are detected, Windows modifies itself and loads the appropriate drivers and adapts accordingly.

On a user level, there are two ways you can change the values of the Registry or its structure. The first method (and by far the easiest) is to use Windows tools such as those within the Control Panel. As documented throughout the rest of this book (and even within this chapter), the Control Panel allows you to add hardware or software, change the appearance of your system, or perform any of a score of other operations. Each time you perform such a task, you're editing the Registry—it may not appear as such on the surface, but that is where your changes are stored.

The other way you can change the Registry is through the use of the Registry Editor. This method is much more direct because you're working with the database itself. Software developers, technicians, and network administrators who must alter the Registry's contents will typically be the only ones to benefit from editing the Registry directly. For end users (you and me), editing the Registry directly offers no clear advantage.

Of the two ways you can change the Registry, using the Windows tools is much easier and faster than using the Registry Editor. As an example, consider the process of enabling the screen saver. You can either pick a screen saver from the list in the Display Properties dialog box, or run the Registry editor, search for the screen saver entry (there can be well over 100,000 lines of entries to search through), change one of the Registry values to 0 or 1 (whichever is appropriate), assign a screen saver, then save and exit the Registry editor. Which seems easiest to you?

Manually Editing the Registry

To manually modify the Registry, you must use the Registry Editor, or *Regedit*, program. (The Registry can't be modified with a standard text editor as the INI files could be in previous versions of Windows.) Of course, Regedit is not initially available on any Windows menu—after all, it isn't meant to be used on a regular basis. Regedit should be used only in special circumstances, such as when you are directed what to do by a technical support technician. For instance, you might need to manually update an application's registration information after being directed to do so. In such a case, you must explicitly follow the technician's instructions on proper Registry editing.

To manually invoke the Registry editor, follow these steps:

1. Choose Run from the Start menu. The Run dialog box appears.
2. In the Open field, type **regedit**.
3. Click on the OK button or press Enter.
4. The Registry editor appears, as shown in figure 14.1.

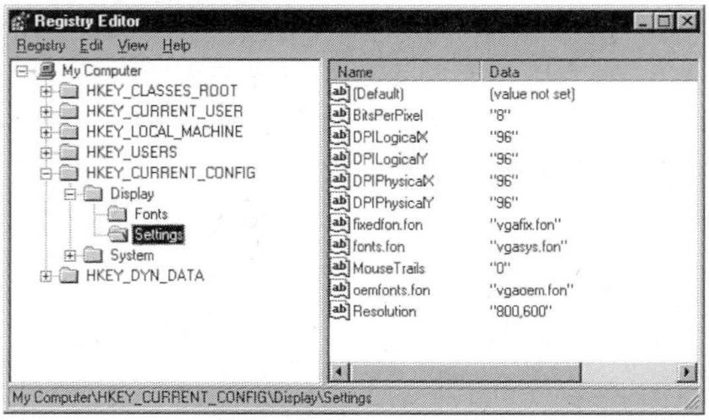

Fig. 14.1 The Registry editor shows keys in a hierarchical manner.

Notice the hierarchical structure of the Registry is similar to that in the Explorer. But beware—that's where the similarity ends. The Registry is divided into six major keys, as described in the previous section:

- Hkey_Classes_Root
- Hkey_Current_User
- Hkey_Local_Machine
- Hkey_Users
- Hkey_Current_Config
- Hkey_Dyn_Data

If you're familiar with modifying INI files in Windows 3.X, you won't see many similarities in editing the Registry. Again, the purpose of the Registry is to bring order to the chaos of Windows configuration and relieve users from endless tweaking to get Windows to act just the way they want.

Finding Information in the Registry

Editing the Registry requires knowing precisely what you want (or need) to edit. Typically, the advanced documentation or developer's kit for an application will document the area and value of the Registry entry should you need to modify a setting. There is no concise, comprehensive guide to Registry valid entries for Windows 95. The Registry was first used in Windows NT, and such a guide for NT did not become available for several years after it was introduced. When it did finally become available, it was several hundred pages long and was part of a larger documentation kit that cost around $150!

What can you do if you want to find something in the Registry and you don't have documentation or guidance available? Fortunately, the Registry Editor includes a search tool to find text anywhere within the database. Press Ctrl+F, or choose Edit, Find and enter the text for which you want to search (see fig. 14.2). For example, if you want to find where the entry for MouseTrails is located, enter that text and click on Find Next.

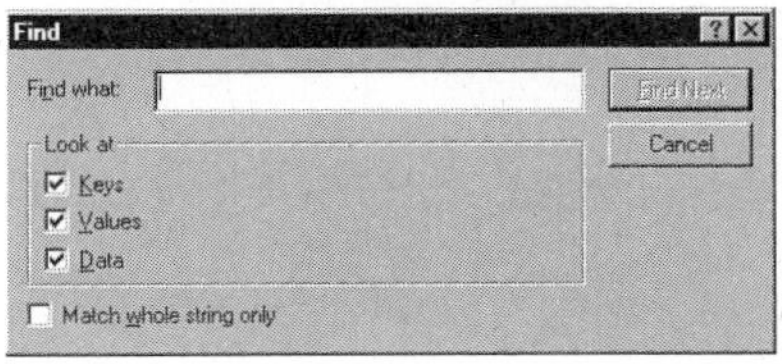

Fig. 14.2 You can use the Find dialog box to locate settings in the Registry.

If you use the search tool, it will locate any text matching the parameter you specify. This means the text may be in a key or subkey (displayed in the left pane of the Registry) or in Registry values (shown in the right pane).

Editing Value Data

Most editing tasks take place in the values shown in the right pane. To begin editing a value, either double-click on it or make sure it is highlighted and then press Enter. Depending on the specific value you are changing, a dialog box will appear that allows you to change the current value. Enter the appropriate value and click OK.

Caution: You should be forewarned that if you inappropriately change Registry values with the Registry Editor, your system may be rendered unstable or unusable. This is because the Registry Editor does no syntax or propriety checking—it blindly lets you do the editing and assumes you know what you are doing. Regedit will not stop you from shooting yourself in the foot.

As an example, say you wanted to edit the screen saver entry in the Registry—you know, the one that controls which screen saver is displayed. The first thing you need to do is open the Registry Editor and search for a term you think might be in the entry. If you search for Screen, you'll find a possible entry, as shown in figure 14.3.

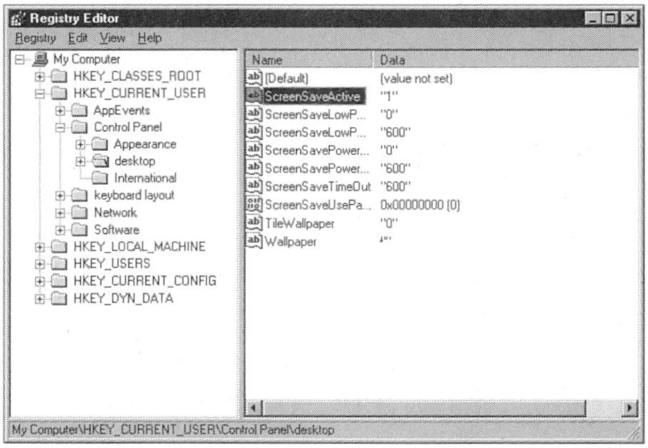

Fig. 14.3 The results of searching in the Registry Editor.

If you don't find such an entry, or if you find a different entry altogether, don't be concerned. About 10 entries in the Registry have the word *Screen* in them. Some of them deal with the screen saver; some do not. In fact, you might not find an entry related to the screen saver unless you've activated the screen saver in your system—this activation is what triggers Windows 95 to create the screen saver entries in the first place.

After you locate an entry, carefully examine it in the context of what you understand about the Registry structure, and then make an educated guess as to whether it's the key or value you want. For instance, from figure 14.3 you can see that the ScreenSaveActive value is within the HKEY_CURRENT_USER key (several subkeys down, but still there). Because the screen saver has to do with the appearance of the screen, and these types of settings are user-related, there is a very good chance that this is the value you are looking to change. The problem, however, is that you never are really sure unless you try things out. Thus, in many respects, working with the Registry Editor is a trial-and-error proposition unless you're given a detailed reference.

To change the value you've located, double-click on the ScreenSaveActive value. A dialog box appears, as shown in figure 14.4, prompting you for the new data to be stored in the value.

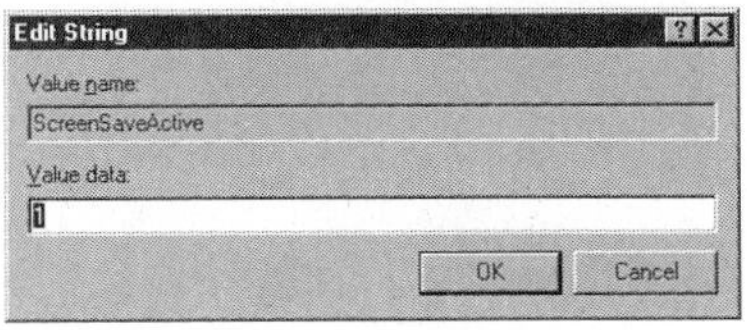

Fig. 14.4 When you change a value, Regedit prompts you for the new data.

The type of editing dialog box that appears depends on the type of value you're changing. If the value contains a string, then you see a dialog box like that shown in figure 14.4; other types of data require different types of dialog boxes. Regardless of the type, you can enter new data for the value, and then click on the OK button.

> **Caution:** Any changes you make to the Registry are instantly saved and permanent. There is no formal Save option or dialog box that asks whether you want to save or abandon changes. Neither is there an undo feature that lets you backtrack on your edits.

Adding Keys or Values

The Registry Editor allows you to add either new keys or values to existing keys. The worth of such additions will depend on whether the key or values will be used by software or the system. This presupposes that you know the proper syntax to make such an addition worthwhile; if you don't, then the software or Windows 95 itself will not know what to do with your entry.

To add a key, all you need to do is position and select, in the left pane, the key under which you want your new subkey to appear. For instance, if you want to add a subkey to the Hkey_Current_User\ControlPanel key, you expand the Hkey_Current_User key, and then select the ControlPanel key. Next, choose Edit, New, Key. The new key appears in the key tree, and you can change its name right away.

To add a value to an existing key, select the key to which you want to add the value, and then choose Edit, New. A submenu appears from which you can select the type of value you want to add: string, binary, or DWORD. You should make your selection based on the type of data you want the value to contain, as described earlier in this chapter. The new value then appears in the right-hand pane of the editor, and you can modify the name assigned to the value.

Deleting Keys or Values

The easiest way to delete a key or value is to select it in the Registry Editor, and then press the Delete key. You're asked if you really want to delete the object; if so, it is removed from the screen and from the Registry.

> **Caution:** There is no undo feature in the Registry Editor. Once you delete a key or value, it is gone for good. Remember, as well, that your deletions can make your system unusable, as can any edit to the Registry. Proceed with extreme caution.

Importing and Exporting the Registry

The data contained in the Registry can be imported or exported to text files. Why would you want or need to do this? In general, you may find it useful to move the entire Registry or parts of the Registry from one system to another. For example, say you've received 27 machines at your office for your employees. Instead of setting up each machine individually, you can configure one of them exactly the way you want. Then, in a stroke of time-saving genius, you can export the Registry to a text file on a floppy disk. Then, go to each of the other machines and import the Registry from the floppy disk. Viola—each of the other machines is a configured duplicate of the original machine.

> **Note:** If you copy the Registry to configure machines, make sure that you also copy supporting files to the other machines. This may include special drivers, screen savers, sound files, or wallpaper files. In short, whatever files you copied to the original machine should also be copied to the clone machines. Copying the Registry just precludes the need of going through the detailed configuration steps.

If you want a hard copy of the Registry, you can print it by choosing Print from the Registry menu. A hard copy lets you see the exact contents of a certain key or the entire database, depending on your print scope. The printed copy also provides a great way to see an "initial condition" of the Registry before you make any changes.

Emergency Registry Recovery

Despite all the warnings about how messing with the Registry can bring your system to its knees, you might still find yourself in that position some day. Fortunately, you can take one of several remedial actions to restore the Registry.

One action involves a backup copy of the Registry. If you have a recent copy of the Registry (one you created by exporting it), you can import the copy to reset everything back to its original state. This step presupposes, however, that you can at least get Windows 95 started. What happens if you cannot even get to that point?

Every time you start Windows 95, it creates a backup copy of both the SYSTEM.DAT and USER.DAT files. As you'll recall, these two files comprise the Registry. If you cannot successfully start Windows, you can follow these steps to restart your system:

1. Use a DOS disk or emergency boot disk to start your system.
2. Change to the directory in which Windows 95 is installed. Typically, this is the WINDOWS directory.
3. Use the following DOS commands to make the Registry files (and their backups) visible and to delete the original Registry files:

```
attrib -s -h -r system.da?
del system.dat
attrib -s -h -r user.da?
del user.dat
```

4. Use the following DOS commands to rename the backup Registry files:

```
ren system.da0 system.dat
ren user.da0 user.dat
```

5. Use the following DOS commands to set the newly renamed files to their proper condition:

```
attrib +s +h +r system.dat
attrib +s +h +r user.dat
```

6. Restart your system.

At this point, your system should restart properly. If it does not, you may have a more serious problem (such as a scrambled hard drive) for which more drastic measures would be necessary. At this point it would be best to consult a technician.

Accessing a Registry on a Remote System

People who administer large numbers of computers face a particularly tough job. One way to make that job easier is to access the Registry on a remote computer, over the network. This capability allows troubleshooting or checking to occur without having to be physically in front of the machine.

Accessing the Registry on a remote machine cannot be done unless the remote machine is first running the Microsoft Remote Registry service. Unfortunately, activating this on the remote machine requires that someone be at the remote machine. However, this service could be part of the normal setup of the machine before it is ever put into everyday use. To start this service, follow these steps:

1. Choose Start, Settings. The Settings menu appears.
2. Choose Settings, Control Panel. The Control Panel appears.
3. Double-click on the Network icon. The Network Properties sheet appears.

Tailoring Windows 95's Appearance

As you've learned already, the Registry is a complex and finely-tuned database maintained by the Windows 95 operating system. The majority of the time you'll never have need to poke around inside it via the Registry Editor. Indeed, there are less messy ways of getting Windows to look and act just the way you want.

Perhaps no other aspect of Windows 95 attracts as much attention as its appearance. The colors, combined with the attractive three-dimensional look of icons, buttons, and windows are enough to draw anyone away from a strictly DOS environment. To date, Windows lovers spend great amounts of time carefully changing colors, the screen saver, even the bitmap background graphics fondly referred to as "wallpaper." Interestingly enough, virtually all screen elements in Windows 95 can be changed by using the various tools in the Display Properties sheets. This section focuses on how to use the Control Panel to take full advantage of Windows 95's appearance.

Video Card and Monitor Settings

Changing the appearance of your Windows 95 system depends on the capabilities of both your video card and monitor. To a large degree, Windows can automatically detect the type of video card you have, and sometimes can discern your monitor. It cannot, however, determine the resolution at which you want to do your work, nor can it figure out which color palette you want to use.

The best thing to do is set these items by using the Control Panel. In most instances you should have to set them only once, unless you like to use different settings with different programs. To set the video card and monitor properties, click on the Settings tab of the Display Properties sheet. The sheet appears, as shown in figure 14.5.

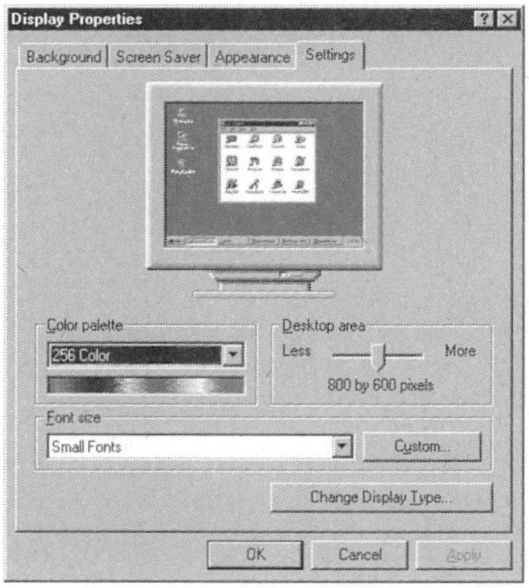

Fig. 14.5 Windows allows you to control how your video card and monitor are used.

You can make three settings on this page. The first, at the left side of the sheet, is the Color palette. Indicate the number of colors you want to use, from those available on your video card. At the right side of the sheet you can specify the resolution you want to use. Finally, at the bottom of the sheet you can pick the Font size you want to use. Each of these items is a matter of personal taste, and you should experiment to find the combination most pleasing and productive for you.

Also at the bottom of the sheet is a button, Change Display Type, which can be used to modify the type of monitor and video card installed in your system. If you click on the button, you will see the Change Display Type dialog box, as shown in figure 14.6.

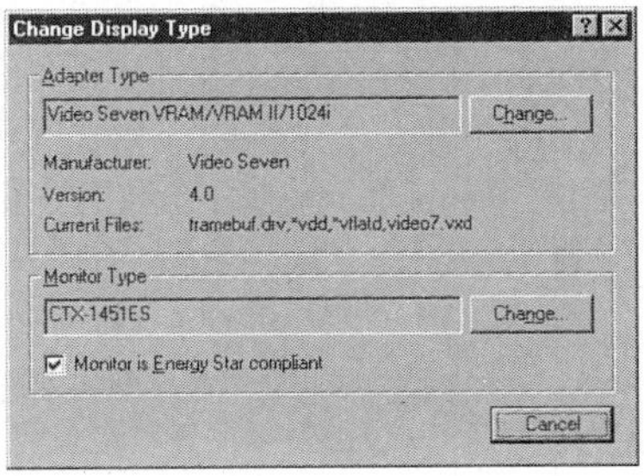

Fig. 14.6 The Change Display Type dialog box is used to specify both your video adapter and monitor.

Typically, you won't need to change your video card type; Windows 95 detects and sets this automatically. You should, however, set your monitor type by clicking on the Change button and then selecting a monitor make and model.

> **Note:** When you make changes in either the video adapter or the monitor, you should also make sure that your color palette and resolution are set the way you like them. These settings are sometimes made by Windows when you change the hardware on which they are based.

In the Registry, the video adapter and monitor information are considered part of the local machine key. As such, you can find the video adapter information in the first of the following two keys, and the monitor information in the second:

```
MyComputer\HKEY_LOCAL_MACHINE\System\CurrentControlSet\Services\
➥Class\Display\0000
MyComputer\HKEY_LOCAL_MACHINE\Enum\Monitor\Default_Monitor\0001
```

Modifying Your Background

Windows allows you to configure your desktop in virtually any manner you can imagine. One way you can do this is through the use of patterns and wallpaper. Both are available by using the Background page of the Display Properties sheet, as shown in figure 14.7.

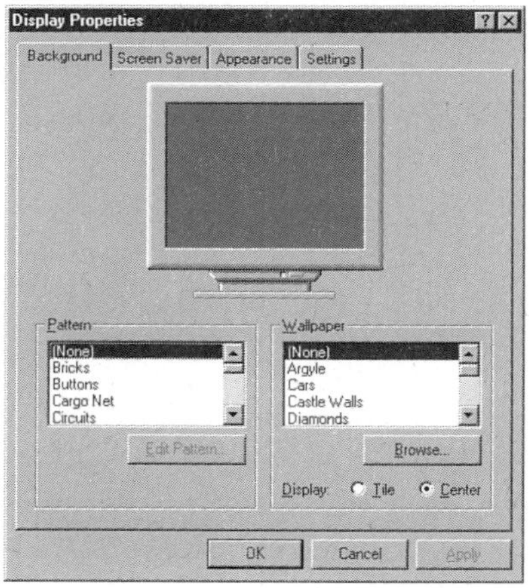

Fig. 14.7 You can change the appearance of your desktop by using the Background page of the Display Properties sheet.

Patterns refer to small bit-mapped images repeated over and over across your desktop; using patterns is similar to adding a texture to your desktop. The wallpaper setting controls the display of a graphic image on your desktop. This image can either be tiled (repeated to cover the entire desktop) or shown once (centered in the middle of the desktop).

> **Tip:** If you're short on system resources, don't use wallpaper. It can quickly consume precious resources and slow down the overall performance of your system.

In the Registry, the values concerning both patterns and wallpaper are in the following key:

```
MyComputer\HKEY_CURRENT_USER\ControlPanel\desktop
```

Changing Windows Colors and Styles

The easiest way to change colors in Windows 95 is to use the Display applet in the Control Panel. The applet lets you change the color of nearly any element of Windows 95, from the open background referred to as the *desktop*, to window borders, styles, and the fonts used in each window and title bar. As you make changes, you may notice that just a slight variation on the default is what you need to make Windows 95 even more pleasant. Color changes made in the Display applet also affect the colors used for Windows programs. Gone are the days of editing WIN.INI to get just the color scheme you want.

You can change the appearance of Windows 95 by using the Display Properties sheet. To display the proper sheet, follow these steps:

1. Choose Start, Settings. The Settings menu appears.
2. Choose Settings, Control Panel. The Control Panel appears.
3. Double-click on the Display icon. The Display Properties sheet appears.
4. Click on the Appearance tab. The Display Properties sheet appears, as shown in figure 14.8.

> **Tip:** A shortcut for accomplishing the first three steps is to right-click on a vacant area of the desktop and choose Properties from the context menu.

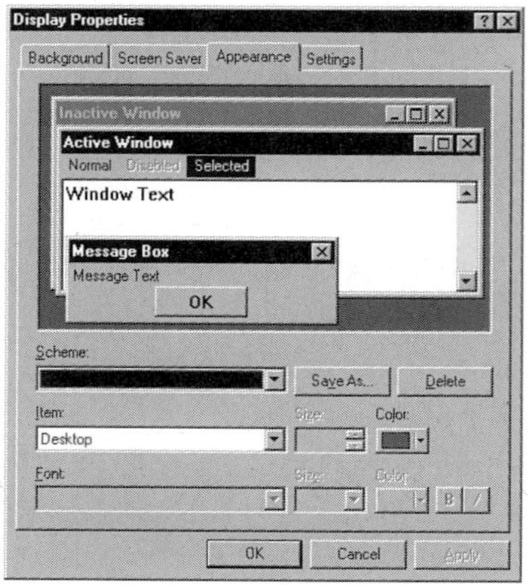

Fig. 14.8 The Appearance tab of the Display Properties sheet allows you to modify how Windows 95 looks.

Each of the following sections shows how to change specific items in the appearance of Windows 95.

Working with Schemes

Information about the appearance of Windows 95 is stored in schemes. These are nothing but named profiles that define specific colors and fonts for the objects used by Windows 95 to communicate information. You can pick an existing scheme by selecting it in the Scheme field—Windows 95 includes 27 different schemes, as follows:

- Brick
- Desert
- Eggplant
- Flat
- Flat (large)
- High Contrast Black
- High Contrast Black (large)
- High Contrast White
- High Contrast White (large)
- Lilac
- Lilac (large)
- Maple
- Marine (high color)
- Plum (high color)

- Pumpkin (large)
- Rainy Day
- Rose
- Rose (large)
- Slate
- Spruce
- Stars and Stripes (VGA)
- Storm (VGA)
- Teal (VGA)
- Wheat
- Windows Standard
- Windows Standard (extra large)
- Windows Standard (large)

As you pick a different scheme, the sample display at the top of the dialog box changes to show what the scheme will do to your desktop. If you don't like the way a scheme appears, you can modify it to your heart's content. (The next two sections discuss how to change elements of a scheme.)

Before modifying an existing scheme, save it under a new name, and then make changes to the copy. This method leaves the original intact in case you want to use it later. To save a scheme under a new name, click on the Save As button at the right of the scheme names. Windows asks you for the name of the new scheme, offering the current scheme name as a default. If you click on OK, the changes you have made overwrite the current scheme. If, however, you supply a new name, then it is saved as a new scheme and appears in the scheme list.

Schemes are stored in the Registry by using a single value for each scheme. These appear in the following Registry key:

```
MyComputer\HKEY_CURRENT_USER\ControlPanel\Appearance\Schemes
```

Figure 14.9 shows an example of what these schemes look like in the Registry. Notice that the data for the scheme values are stored in hexadecimal notation.

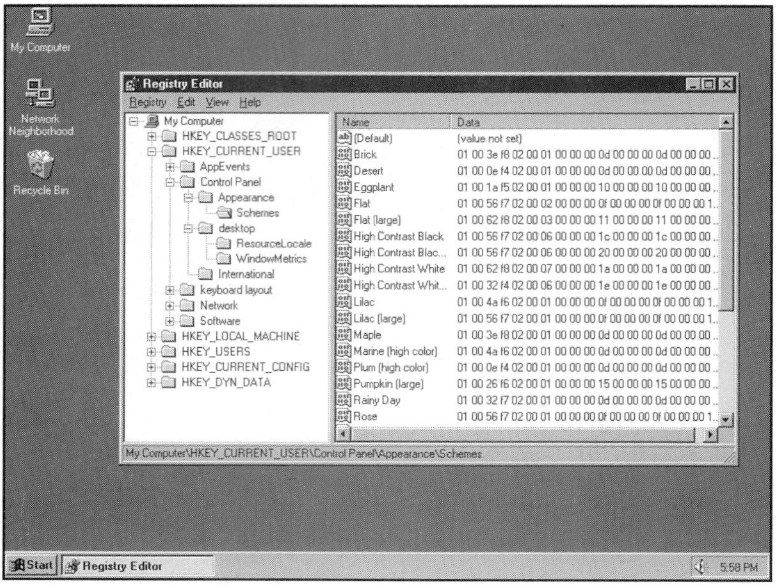

Fig. 14.9 Colors are stored under scheme names in the Registry.

Changing Item Color and Size

Part of the lure of Windows 95 is its ability to allow users to express their individuality. The next time you're near someone else's computer, take a look at the colors used in the color scheme. To you, the choice may be unappealing, but it suits the user just fine. Many users even modify their colors on a regular basis to liven things up. Windows 95 lets you use the Appearance tab in the Display Properties sheet (shown earlier, in fig. 14.5) to choose the precise color you want applied to various desktop items.

To change the colors associated with an object, you can take two approaches. First of all, you can select the item from the Item pull-down list, or you can simply use the mouse to click on the item in the sample desktop at the top of the sheet. Windows lets you modify the size and color of any of the screen elements listed in Table 14.1.

Table 14.1 Items Whose Size and Color Can Be Changed

Item	Size	Color
3D Objects		✔
Active Title Bar	✔	✔
Active Window Border	✔	✔
Application Background		✔
Caption Buttons	✔	
Desktop		✔
Icon	✔	
Icon Spacing (Horizontal)	✔	
Icon Spacing (Vertical)	✔	
Inactive Title Bar	✔	✔
Inactive Window Border	✔	✔
Menu	✔	✔
Palette Title	✔	
Scrollbar	✔	
Selected Items	✔	✔
ToolTip		✔
Window		✔

As you can see from Table 14.1, you cannot modify the size and color of all items. Once you have selected the object, you can modify the appropriate attribute—size or color. You modify the size by adjusting the Size value at the right side of the item name. Likewise, you modify the color by changing the Color field to the right of the item name.

The colors assigned to various elements of the desktop are stored in the following Registry path:

```
MyComputer\HKEY_CURRENT_USER\ControlPanel\Colors
```

Within this key are a large number of values that allow you to specify the colors of individual desktop items. The data assigned to each value consists of three numbers, separated by a space. The values of these individual numbers range from 0 to 255. These numbers represent the amount of red, green, and blue (the primary colors) which, when combined together, represent a color blend from a 256-color palette.

The size of desktop elements are stored in the values in the following Registry path:

```
MyComputer\HKEY_CURRENT_USER\ControlPanel\desktop
➥\WindowMetrics
```

Colors are also stored in the WIN.INI file, as in previous versions of Windows. They are in a section labeled [colors] with various entries which appear similar to:

```
[colors]
Scrollbar=192 192 192
Background=0 128 128
ActiveTitle=0 0 128
InactiveTitle=192 192 192
Menu=192 192 192
Window=255 255 255
WindowFrame=0 0 0
MenuText=0 0 0
WindowText=0 0 0
TitleText=255 255 255
ActiveBorder=192 192 192
InactiveBorder=192 192 192
AppWorkspace=128 128 128
Hilight=0 0 128
HilightText=255 255 255
ButtonFace=192 192 192
ButtonShadow=128 128 128
GrayText=128 128 128
ButtonText=0 0 0
InactiveTitleText=0 0 0
ButtonHilight=255 255 255
ButtonDkShadow=0 0 0
ButtonLight=192 192 192
InfoText=192 192 192
InfoWindow=0 0 0
```

Each entry in the [colors] section consists of a name representing a desktop element, followed by an equal sign and three numbers. These three numbers have the same purpose as the color numbers stored in the Registry. You can edit this file with a text editor, but doing so offers no benefit over making changes via the Control Panel.

You may ask yourself why these are included in both the Registry and WIN.INI. The purpose behind this, as well as other seemingly duplicated entries, is compatibility. Many 16-bit (Windows 3.X) applications aren't conversant with the Registry—they expect to retrieve and place information in the WIN.INI, among other INI files. Ultimately, this forms a compromise so that 16-bit programs can function normally in a 32-bit (Windows 95) environment.

Changing Font Color and Size

In your schemes you can change the font used quite a few items. Fonts can be any typeface installed on your system, whether ATM (Adobe) or TrueType. This flexibility enables you to make system fonts easier to read and to customize the look of the desktop to suit your style and needs. In addition to changing the font used for an item, you can also change the font size and apply attributes such as bold or italic. Table 14.2 shows the desktop items whose fonts, font sizes, and font colors you can change.

Table 14.2 Items Whose Font Size and Color Can Be Changed

Item	Size	Color
3D Objects		✔
Active Title Bar	✔	✔
Icon	✔	
Inactive Title Bar	✔	✔
Menu	✔	✔
Message Box	✔	✔
Palette Title	✔	
Selected Items	✔	✔
ToolTip	✔	✔
Window		✔

Notice that for some elements you can't change the color of the fonts because their colors are self-changing depending on the style of other items. For example, a lighter Desktop color changes the Icon color automatically to black text.

> **Note:** For the sake of aesthetics, use a simple sans serif font like MS Sans Serif—the default Windows 95 system font. Some fonts that appear nice in a heading or on paper take on a bizarre appearance when you have to stare at them on a screen.

As far as the Registry is concerned, information about the color and size of fonts used in the desktop is stored in a number of places. Text colors are stored in the first of the following keys, and sizes are stored in the second:

```
MyComputer\HKEY_CURRENT_USER\ControlPanel\Colors
MyComputer\HKEY_CURRENT_USER\ControlPanel\
desktop\WindowMetrics
```

Configuring the Screen Saver

The Windows screen saver fills the monitor screen when the computer has been free from any mouse or keyboard activity for a specified period of time. In the past, a continuous image left on a computer monitor would burn the image into the screen's phospors. Screen burn-in doesn't occur on today's VGA monitors mostly because of improvements in monitor technology. Screen savers are used mainly for amusement and, interestingly enough, security. The password protection feature of Windows 95 screen saver can protect your sensitive data from prying eyes. This section shows you how to configure the screen saver and use password protection.

The screen saver is controlled in the Display Properties sheet. To display the proper sheet, follow these steps:

1. Choose Start, Settings. The Settings menu appears.
2. Choose Settings, Control Panel. The Control Panel appears.

3. Double-click on the Display icon. The Display Properties sheet appears.
4. Click on the Screen Saver tab. The Display Properties sheet appears, as shown in figure 14.10.

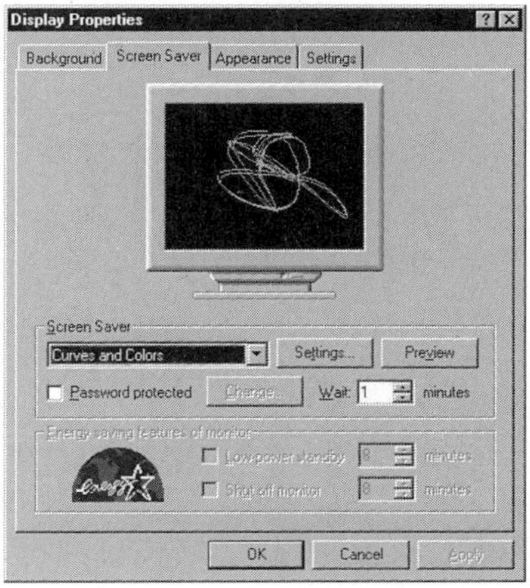

Fig. 14.10 The Screen Saver tab of the Display Properties sheet allows you to control the Windows 95 screen saver.

Tip: A shortcut for accomplishing the first three steps is to right-click on a vacant area of the desktop and choose Properties from the context menu.

Each of the following sections shows how to change specific items related to the screen saver.

Activating the Screen Saver

You activate the screen saver by specifying a screen saver in the Screen Saver field of the Screen Saver tab of the Display Properties sheet. (Whew! Who said these things were easy?) All you need to do is pick a screen saver from the drop-down list. As you pick a screen saver, you'll notice that it shows up in the preview monitor in the top part of the sheet.

Once you've decided on a screen saver, you can click on the Preview button to see how it will appear over your entire screen—not just the small preview monitor. Any keypress or movement of the mouse returns you to the dialog box. Click on OK when finished.

The screen saver is controlled by the ScreenSaveActive value in the following key in the Registry:

```
MyComputer\HKEY_CURRENT_USER\ControlPanel\Desktop
```

Setting the Screen Saver's Options

Windows 95 has a group of options you can set for every screen saver. These options include items such as how long before the system should be idle before the screen saver is invoked and a host of Energy Star options. These latter options are available only if both your video card and your monitor are Energy-Star compliant, meaning that they have incorporated the energy-saving guidelines published by the EPA.

Each screen saver included with Windows (except Blank Screen) also has configuration settings which you can modify. To change or view these settings after choosing a screen saver from the list, click on the Settings button. Because each screen saver is different, the settings for each will also vary. Figure 14.11 shows the settings for the screen saver module *Curves and Colors.*

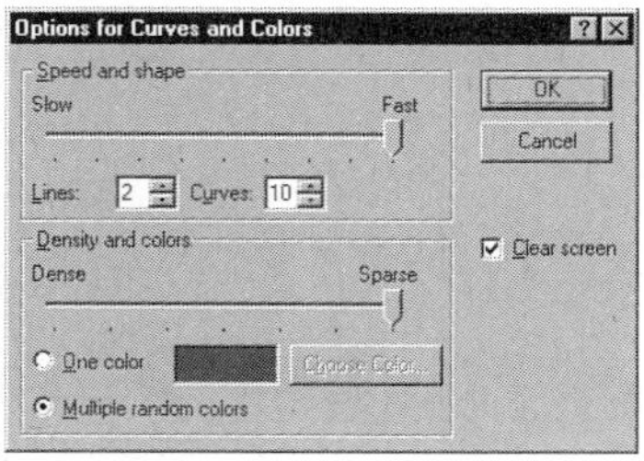

Fig. 14.11 The options for this screen saver offer a great deal of control over the image's shape, color, and speed.

A variety of values in the Registry control the screen saver. The values available will generally vary, depending on the type of screen saver you've selected. All of the values, however, are stored in the following key:

```
MyComputer\HKEY_CURRENT_USER\ControlPanel\Desktop
```

Some of the common values in this key, along with their meanings, are shown in Table 14.3.

Table 14.3 Common Screen Saver Registry Values

Registry Value	Meaning
ScreenSaveLowPowerActive	Determines whether low-power standby is enabled. This is an Energy-Star option.
ScreenSaveLowPowerTimeout	Specifies, in seconds, how long before the low-power standby signal is sent from the video card to the monitor. This is an Energy-Star option.
ScreenSavePowerOffActive	Determines whether shutting off the monitor is enabled. This is an Energy-Star option.
ScreenSavePowerOffTimeOut	Specifies, in seconds, how long after the monitor is in low-power mode that it should be turned off. This is an Energy-Star option.
ScreenSaveTimeOut	Specifies, in seconds, how long the system is idle before the screen saver is displayed.

Using Password Protection

The password protection option gives you the freedom to walk away from your computer without fear that someone will peek at your screen or access data from your computer. In fact, unless the correct password is entered, nobody can access the computer, including you.

In the Display Properties sheet, enable the Password protected check box and click on Change button to provide your password. Enter the password and, immediately below it enter it again to confirm, then click on OK. Your changes are enabled once you click OK in the Display Properties sheet. Now, if your computer is idle for the time you specified, any keypress or mouse movement will invoke the sheet shown in figure 14.12 requesting your password.

Fig. 14.12 To return to Windows you must enter the correct password and click on OK.

To remove password protection, remove the check from the Password protected check box and click on OK.

The Registry value ScreenSaveUsePassword controls the password. If you set the data for the value to 0, then the password is disabled, whereas setting it to 1 enables the password. The complete Registry path for this value is:

```
MyComputer\HKEY_CURRENT_USER\ControlPanel
➥\Desktop\ScreenSaveUsePassword
```

The password itself is also saved in the Registry, but it is encrypted. The exact encryption algorithm is unknown, but it appears that two bytes are stored for every single character of the password (this is consistent with the use of Unicode instead of ASCII in Windows 95). Rather than trying to change the password in the Registry, it is much more efficient to delete it and change the Registry values that control the use of the password. The following is the path of the Registry value used to store the screen saver password:

```
MyComputer\HKEY_CURRENT_USER\ControlPanel\Desktop\ScreenSave_Data
```

Tip: If you forget your screen saver password, you can get around it by turning off the computer and then turning it back on. After you log into Windows 95, edit the Registry to get rid of the screen saver password protection.

Setting the Date and Time

Your computer may not have the correct time and date. For a variety of reasons, many computers aren't set correctly. Perhaps the computer was purchased from a different part of the country, or maybe you just moved and haven't changed its clock, or perhaps you forgot to instruct Windows 95 to automatically adjust the clock for daylight savings time. It's important to make sure that your computer maintains the correct date and time because every file you create, update, or otherwise change gets "stamped" with whatever date and time are on your computer.

Windows 95 combines the date and time function into one convenient location. You can access this feature either by choosing Start, Settings, Control Panel, and selecting the Date/Time applet or by double-clicking on the clock on the taskbar. Choose the Date & Time tab and the Date/Time Properties sheet appears, as shown in figure 14.13.

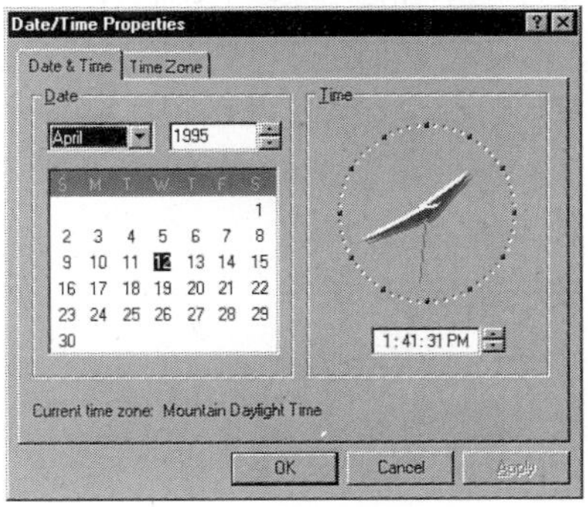

Fig. 14.13 You can adjust the date and time with a point and click.

The date is displayed in a calendar representation, so choosing the correct date is as simple as picking the date and year from the corresponding fields. You change the time somewhat differently by clicking in the hour, minute, second, or AM/PM designator and then changing the value with the buttons to the right of the time field.

If you inspect the Time Zone tab, you'll notice Windows 95 can automatically adjust for daylight savings time. This feature means that rather than manually setting your clock ahead or back by one hour for daylight savings time, Windows can handle this automatically. To use this feature, choose the Time Zone tab and check the box labeled `Automatically adjust clock for daylight saving changes`. Remember, if you ever relocate your computer to another part of the country (or the world), be sure to select the appropriate time zone by clicking directly on the map. This ensures that your computer clock is accurate year-round.

As with every other configuration option, the Registry maintains information related to system date and time. Information about various time zones is stored in a number of subkeys under the following Registry key:

```
MyComputer\HKEY_LOCAL_MACHINE\SOFTWARE\Microsoft\Windows
➥\CurrentVersion\TimeZones
```

Information about which time zone is applicable to your machine is stored in the following Registry key:

```
MyComputer\HKEY_LOCAL_MACHINE\System\CurrentControlSet
➥\control\TimeZoneInformation
```

Configuring the Mouse

Among the hardware items in your computer system, besides the computer itself, your mouse is the most important device. Without it, you could not productively access Windows. So, your mouse must be installed and configured properly to get the most out of Windows. This section takes a close look at the various mouse settings in Windows.

All mouse changes are done through the Mouse Properties sheet, accessed by choosing Start from the taskbar, Settings, Control Panel, and clicking on the Mouse applet. Figure 14.14 shows what this sheet looks like.

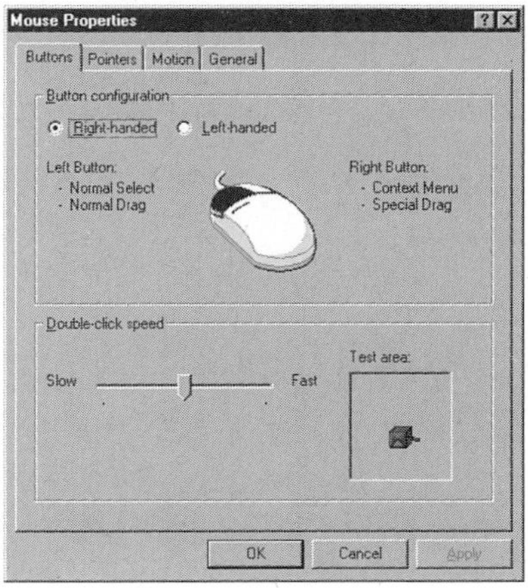

Fig. 14.14 Changing mouse settings is done in the Mouse Properties sheet.

Setting the Mouse Double-Click Speed

Double-clicking is the most common way to select items in Windows and Windows applications. A double-click occurs when you click a mouse button two times in quick succession. It's important to set the speed of the double-click properly, otherwise Windows will interpret your double-clicks inaccurately. Windows measures the time between each click and, if the value is less than the double-click setting, accepts it as a double-click.

To change the mouse double-click speed, select the Buttons tab in the Mouse Properties sheet and drag the slider control in the Double-click speed section either left (slower speed) or right (faster speed).

A slower setting increases the number of milliseconds you must wait between clicks while a faster setting requires you to double-click faster since there are fewer milliseconds between clicks. This setting has a value between 100 and 900 milliseconds.

In the Registry, the mouse double-click setting is stored in the following value:

```
MyComputer\HKEY_CURRENT_USER\ControlPanel\Mouse\DoubleClickSpeed
```

Enabling Pointer Trails

If you have a hard time spotting the mouse pointer or just watching it move across the screen, you can enable *pointer trails*. This option makes the pointer image remain on-screen as you move the mouse, giving the effect of a pointer trail. To enable this option, double-click on the Mouse applet in the Control Panel, select the Motion tab, and check the Show pointer trails box. If you want to adjust the length of trails displayed on-screen, move the slider control. Click on OK to close and accept your changes.

The Registry value that controls this setting is located as follows:

```
Registry value: MouseTrails
Key location:
MyComputer\HKEY_LOCAL_MACHINE\Config\0001\Display\Settings
```

Setting Mouse Acceleration

Mouse acceleration means how fast the pointer moves across the screen when you physically move the mouse. Depending on how you use your mouse and your current screen resolution, you may find that adjusting the acceleration can make using the mouse more comfortable.

At its most basic setting, the pointer moves across the screen as quickly as you move the mouse. Generally, this speed is fine for low resolutions such as 640 × 480, but as you increase the resolution, the distance the pointer must traverse the screen increases. This is due largely to the number of pixels visible at one time on your screen. For example, a resolution of 640 × 480 displays relatively few pixels, so a mouse appears to move more quickly. On the other hand, a resolution of 800 × 600 crams more pixels into the same screen area, so a mouse will appear to move a little slower. The higher resolution settings may cause you to move the mouse across the mouse pad several times before your pointer reaches a desired location on-screen.

To compensate for the screen resolution you are using, Windows lets you change the pointer speed. To do so, choose the Motion tab in the Mouse Properties sheet (see fig. 14.15). Click and drag the slider control to the desired setting and click Apply to test it. Basically, there are seven possible settings that determine how fast the pointer moves.

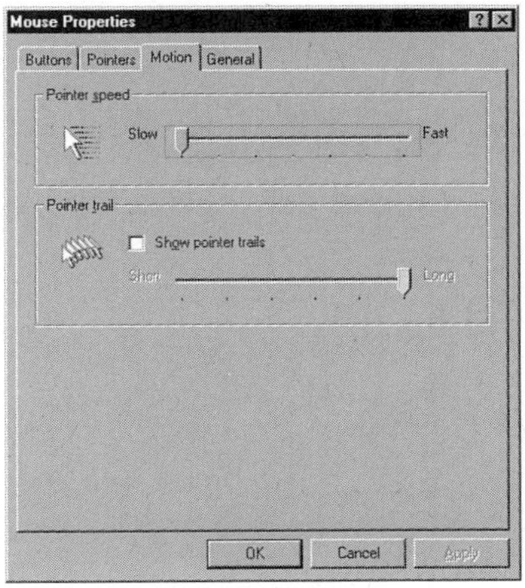

Fig. 14.15 Using the Mouse Properties sheet to adjust the speed of the pointer across the screen.

Technically speaking, mouse movement is based on specific settings: mouse speed and threshold. Windows sets these according to which of the seven settings you choose from the slider control. Table 14.4 shows the possible values placed into the Registry when you choose a pointer speed setting. The threshold values represent the number of pixels the pointer must traverse before acceleration kicks in. As you can see, when all parameters are set to zero, the mouse moves the slowest and does not accelerate as you move it. However, move the slider control to

the fastest setting and the pointer will double its speed as you exceed the Threshold1 value. If you also exceed the Threshold2 value, the pointer will quadruple its speed.

Table 14.4 Mouse Acceleration Settings

	Slower						Faster
Mouse Speed	0	1	1	1	2	2	2
Threshold1	0	10	7	4	4	4	4
Threshold2	0	0	0	0	12	9	6

The Registry value that controls this setting is located as follows:

```
Registry value: MouseSpeed, Mouse Threshold1, Mouse
Threshold2
Key location: MyComputer\HKEY_CURRENT_USER\ControlPanel\Mouse
```

Changing the Mouse Driver

When you install Windows 95, it automatically detects the kind of mouse you have and loads the appropriate driver. However, you may later upgrade your mouse driver or use a different pointing device altogether. To change the mouse type, perform the following steps:

1. Double-click the Mouse applet in the Control Panel folder.
2. Select the General tab and click on Change. The Select Device dialog box appears.
3. Choose the Show all device radio button and pick the corresponding manufacturer and model of your mouse or pointing device.
4. Click on OK.

If you have an unlisted mouse type, you can install your own mouse driver by placing a mouse driver disk in the floppy drive, clicking on Have Disk, and following the instructions.

The Registry value that controls this setting is located as follows:

```
Registry value:
Key location:
MyComputer\HKEY_LOCAL_MACHINE\System\CurrentControlSet\
Services\Class\Mouse\0000
```

Configuring Your Keyboard

Because the keyboard is one of the primary input devices for your system, you must be able to adjust its settings for maximum productivity. This section covers the various ways to change keyboard settings. In Windows 95, you change the keyboard settings by following these steps:

1. Choose Start, Settings. The Settings menu appears.
2. Choose Settings, Control Panel. The Control Panel appears.
3. Double-click on the Keyboard icon. The Keyboard Properties sheet appears, as shown in figure 14.16.

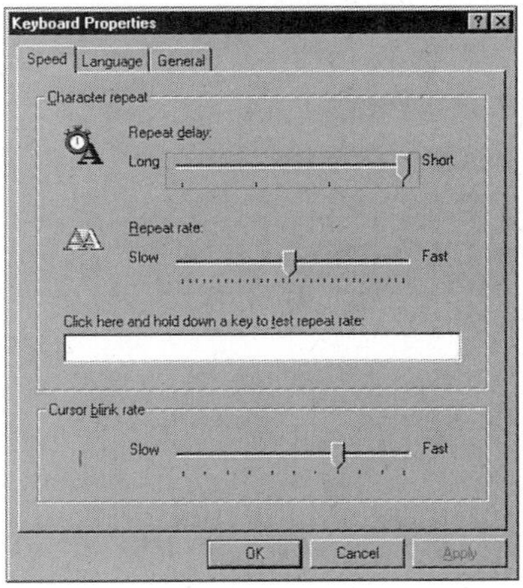

Fig. 14.16 Changing keyboard settings is done in the Keyboard Properties sheet.

Controlling the Cursor Blink Rate

Windows displays the cursor as a thin, black line that flashes nearly once each second. For some users, changing the cursor blink rate makes it easier to spot the cursor on-screen. To change the cursor's blink rate, move the slider control in the Keyboard Properties sheet to a slow or fast setting. Although the default cursor blink rate setting is 530 milliseconds, or one blink every 1/2 second, it can range from 100 (fast) to 1,200 (slow).

The Registry value is located as follows:

```
Registry value: CursorBlinkRate
Key location: MyComputer\HKEY_CURRENT_USER\Control
Panel\Desktop
```

Configuring the Keyboard Speed

Next to the actual quality of the keyboard itself, the keyboard's speed determines your productivity and comfort. By changing the keyboard's speed you can quickly enter or delete repetitive characters by holding down a key for a designated period of time. Also, you can move around in a document much faster—particularly when you use the directional keys. To change the keyboard's speed, make sure that the Speed tab is displayed in the Keyboard properties sheet (refer back to fig. 14.16). Then, modify the Repeat delay and Repeat rate settings as desired.

The Repeat delay specifies the length of time you must hold down a key before it begins repeating, and the Repeat rate controls how quickly the key repeats. Often, setting the keyboard to a short delay and a fast repeat rate is common. If a key repeats too soon after pressing it, move the Repeat delay slider one notch to the left. The default Repeat delay time is 2 milliseconds. The default Repeat rate is 31 milliseconds.

The Registry values for these two settings are located as followings:

```
MyComputer\HKEY_CURRENT_USER\ControlPanel
\Keyboard\KeyboardDelay
MyComputer\HKEY_CURRENT_USER\ControlPanel
\Keyboard\KeyboardSpeed
```

Picking a Type of Keyboard

You can use virtually any keyboard with Windows, so long as you choose the correct keyboard driver. When you first install Windows, the install process identifies your current keyboard. However, you might want to install a newer keyboard or resort to an old relic you found in your closet. To do so, follow these steps:

1. Double-click on the Keyboard applet in the Control Panel.
2. Choose the General tab in the Keyboard Properties sheet.
3. Click on the Change button and highlight the Show all devices button.
4. Select the appropriate keyboard and click on OK.

If your keyboard isn't listed, you can click on Have Disk and insert a disk containing the keyboard driver into the floppy drive.

In the Registry, the keyboard driver information is located in the following key:

```
MyComputer\HKEY_LOCAL_MACHINE\System\CurrentControlSet\Services\Class
\Keyboard\0000
```

Controlling Application Icons and Folders

As you learned earlier, part of the Registry is the USER.DAT file. If two users share the same computer at different times, one might prefer a blue background while the other enjoys a green background. Windows 95 accommodates both (or more) users by maintaining separate subkeys for each user in the Hkey_Users key of the Registry, which is stored in the USER.DAT file. When a user logs on to the system, the pointer responsible for the Hkey_Current_User key is updated to point to the proper subkey in Hkey_Users. Some of the adjustments and options unique to each user profile include the following:

- Location, size, and characteristics of the Taskbar
- Icon and applet size/arrangement

- Which programs launch automatically at startup
- Other user-related options such as screen saver, mouse settings, and sound events

Automatically Arranging Icons

Due to the nature of a graphical user interface like Windows, icons tend to become jumbled. Of course, trying to organize them manually is tedious. Fortunately, Windows can automatically arrange your icons for you. In fact, you can instruct Windows to arrange icons in a variety of ways.

To arrange a group of icons one time, right-click anywhere in the window and choose Arrange Icons from the context menu. Icons can be organized in one of four ways:

- **Name.** Arranged alphabetically in ascending order.
- **Type.** Arranged alphabetically by extension (file type).
- **Size.** Arranged by size in ascending order.
- **Date.** Arranged by date, most recent first.

To have Windows automatically arrange icons for a particular window, choose Auto Arrange from the context menu. Once enabled, any time you delete or add an icon, the icons are automatically arranged—no more jumbled icons. If you have a difficult time using the context menu, you can choose Arrange Icons from any window's View menu.

Controlling Program Applets

If you're familiar with a previous version of Windows, you'll recall how you could group applications within Program Groups. Now you have the option of maintaining your applications in any way you choose. For example, in Windows 95 you can place individual application icons (actually "shortcut" icons that act as pointers) anywhere—even on the desktop.

> **Note:** *Applet* is a term coined by Windows users to refer to small applications; not full-blown in their own right, but a smaller parts of the operating system.

When you install a program in Windows 95, it is stored in a single folder or folder structure. You can create any number of shortcut icons that "point" to the application, however. When you click on that specific icon, the program launches. For example, if you install an application like CorelDRAW!, the program files are stored in the folder Corel50, but the shortcuts for that application are kept in the \Windows\Start menu\Programs\Corel 5 folder. As such, you can put a shortcut on the desktop, in another folder, or virtually anywhere you like. You can even have shortcuts for the same application in multiple locations. So, instead of starting a program in the traditional way (navigating through the Start menus), place a shortcut on the desktop and double-click on it.

Tuning Windows Configuration

In addition to making changes to its appearance, you also need to understand the behind-the-scenes activity of Windows to gain maximum usefulness of the operating system. Indeed, Windows is installed according to the hardware it detects and other criteria you specify. However, there are a number of settings you can make based strictly on personal preference, including choosing startup preferences, reorganizing program groups, assigning sounds to certain events, and designating file associations.

Choosing Startup Preferences

Windows 95 allows you complete control over how you start the operating system. You can control not only how Windows 95 itself starts, but also which programs are run automatically after startup is complete. Settings related to these options are stored in the user information maintained by Windows 95.

You can find complete information on how the startup procedure can be modified in Chapter 15, "Taking Control of Windows 95 Startup."

Reorganizing Program Groups

You can easily change the location of programs in the Start menu. This feature lets you modify the default placement of program shortcuts and group them in a manner that suits your particular tastes. For example, one simple change might be to add a commonly accessed program directly to the Start menu (the menu that appears when you first click on the Start button). Or, you might have a number of the same categories of program, such as three word processors, three spreadsheets, two DTP programs, and so on. Rather than having each listed within the Programs menu, you can create submenus to contain them. This method would give you a Word Processor folder, a Spreadsheet folder, a DTP folder, and so on. Another situation might require that you rename a program group, such as when you want to maintain two versions of an application that install into the same folder. Also, you may want to rename a program name listed in the Start menu.

To add a program directly to the Start menu, you perform steps similar to adding a program to the Startup menu:

1. Choose Start from the Taskbar, Settings, Taskbar. The Taskbar Properties sheet appears.
2. Select the Start menu Programs tab and click on the Add button.
3. Type the program's executable file name (typically an EXE extension) in the Command line text box. If you're not sure where it is or what it's called, click on the Browse button instead to find the correct folder and file and click on Open to select it.
4. Click on Next, highlight the Start menu folder, and click on Next.
5. Provide a descriptive name for this program. Typically, Windows inserts the name of the executable file but you can retype it to display whatever you wish.

6. Click on Finish to complete the Start menu modification, then click on OK.

> **Tip:** If you've created a shortcut for a program, you can move it to the Start menu by dragging the icon for the shortcut and dropping it on the Start button.

Removing a program from the Start menu is just as easy. Open the Taskbar Properties sheet as mentioned previously, select the Start menu Programs tab, and click on Remove. Highlight the program and click on the Remove button, then click on Close.

To add new folders to the Start menu, take these steps:

1. Choose Start from the Taskbar, Settings, Taskbar. The Taskbar Properties sheet appears.
2. Select the Start menu Programs tab and click on the Advanced button.
3. Highlight the Programs folder, then choose File, New, Folder from the menu bar.
4. Give the new folder a descriptive name, such as Word Processors.

Now, click and drag the application folder, such as Winword, to the newly created Word Processors folder. Remember, the programs you see in the Winword folder are shortcuts, not the actual programs. These shortcuts are small files that point to the real location of the original application. Close the Explorer window and click on OK in the Taskbar Properties sheet.

You can rename a program group through the Explorer or through the Taskbar Properties sheet. From the Explorer or Taskbar Properties sheet, navigate to the appropriate folder (begin looking in the Windows\Start menu\Programs hierarchy). Right-click on the desired folder, choose Rename from the context menu, and enter a new name.

There are a few things you can't change about the Start menu and its program groups. First, the Start menu items themselves are unchangeable. There will always be the Programs, Documents, Settings, Find, Help, Run, and Shut Down options. Of course, as you just learned, you can add a number of programs—even new folders—above these defaults. Also, program groups and names within those groups are always displayed in alphabetical order.

Assigning Sounds to Windows Events

Windows lets you assign sounds to common events such as when you launch a program or exit from Windows. In fact, you can enable or disable sounds at your discretion so that, for example, the computer only makes a sound when an error occurs. All sounds are controlled from the Sounds Properties sheet. To assign sounds to events, open the Control Panel and double-click on the Sounds applet. This displays the Sounds Properties sheet, as shown in figure 14.17.

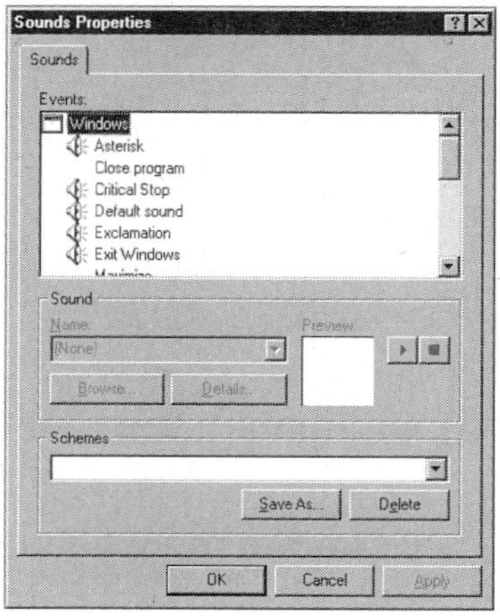

Fig. 14.17 Changing sound associations is done in the Sounds Properties sheet.

To change a sound event, all you need to do is highlight it in the list and choose a sound from the Name list. The Name list details all the sound files located in the Windows\Media folder.

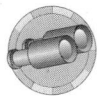

Note: If no sound card is present, Windows sounds a beep through the internal speaker.

The Sounds Properties sheet lists all applicable sound events on your system. Some events are applicable to Windows as a whole, and others are applicable to specific programs. Table 14.5 lists the sound events applicable to Windows as a whole, as well as what causes the events.

Table 14.5 Sound Events in Windows 95

Sound Event	How It Is Produced
Asterisk	Occurs when an informational message box appears
Close program	Occurs when an application is closed
Critical Stop	Occurs when a message box appears with a stop sign in it
Default sound	The default beep for system events
Exclamation	Occurs when a message box appears with an exclamation point in it
Exit from Windows	Occurs when you shut down your system
Maximize	Occurs when you maximize a window
Menu command	Occurs when you select a command from a menu
Menu popup	Occurs when a menu is displayed
Minimize	Occurs when you minimize a window
Open program	Occurs when you launch a program by double-clicking on it
Program error	Occurs when an application encounters a program error
Question	Occurs when an application needs information from the user, such as "Save changes to QUESTION.DOC?"

continues

Table 14.5 Continued

Sound Event	How It Is Produced
Restore Down	Occurs when restorint a window from its maximized state
Restore Up	Occurs when restoring a window from its minimized state
Start Windows	Occurs when Windows is first started
Empty Recycle Bin	Occurs when you empty the Recycle Bin

In addition to assigning sound events, Windows includes several *sound schemes* that contain numerous preassigned sound events. With these, you can pick a scheme and all sounds change accordingly. You can save various sound settings into your own sound scheme, too, by making the sound changes, clicking on Save As, and providing a name for the scheme.

Defining File Associations

Although the term seems unfriendly, *file association* is what helps make Windows user-friendly. Here's how it works. Most files on your system have some sort of extension that serves to classify the file. For example, files that have an extension such as EXE or BAT are considered in the category of executable files, and they are run automatically when you double-click on them in the Explorer. Typically, when you install an application, it automatically updates the Registry with pertinent file associations. For example, Windows associates the extension BMP with the Paint program, the extension TXT with Notepad, as well as the extension WAV with Sound Recorder. A double-click on any of these files automatically loads the associated program. A file extension such as XLS, which is an Excel file, is not native to Windows. However, when you install Excel, you update the Registry with certain file associations. From that moment on, if you double-click on a file with the extension XLS, Excel loads and displays the document.

To associate a file with a particular application, use the Explorer. Highlight the file, select Open With from the File menu, and choose the program with which you want to associate the file. Click on OK when you are finished.

You cannot have the same file extension associated with more than a single program. However, if you later want to change the association between file types, you can do so easily. Start at any browser or Explorer window and follow these steps:

1. Choose Options from the View menu. The Options dialog box appears.
2. Click on the File Types tab.
3. In the Registered file types list, highlight the type of file whose association you wish to change.
4. Click on the Edit button. The Edit File Type dialog box appears, as shown in figure 14.18.

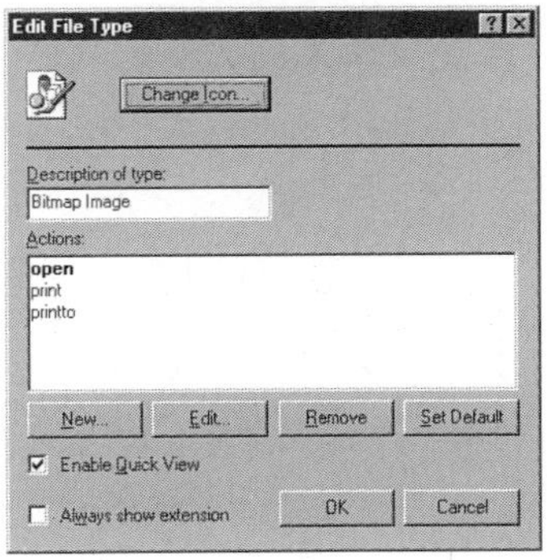

Fig. 14.18 The Edit File Type dialog box allows you to modify actions that can occur to a particular type of file.

5. In the middle of the dialog box is an Actions list. This list describes the actions that can be done with this file. Highlight the open action.
6. Click on the Edit button. A dialog box appears that allows you to change the application, which will be used to open the file type.

7. In the Application used to perform action field, specify the name of the program (along with its path) you want to use to open this type of file.
8. Click on OK.
9. Click on Close.
10. Click on Close again.

Changing the Name of the StartUp Folder

As you learned previously, you can automatically launch programs when you start Windows by placing application shortcuts in the StartUp folder. You can change this default startup folder by directly editing the Registry; Windows 95 does not provide a way to change it in a "user friendly" manner such as through the Control Panel.

The value controlling this part of your system is located in the Registry as follows:

```
Registry value: Start menu
Key location:
MyComputer\HKEY_USERS\Default\Software\Microsoft\Windows\
CurrentVersion\Explorer\ShellFolders
```

Most users have little reason to change the default Windows StartUp folder. Adding a program to the StartUp folder is a simple process as described earlier in this chapter, so this is not a recommended option.

Taking Control of Windows 95 Startup

by Allen L. Wyatt

Many people probably start Windows without even thinking about what is going on behind the scenes. In reality, there is quite a bit going on to get the operating system prepared to enable you to do your daily work.

If you're familiar with the DOS-based system, which may be rendered obsolete by Windows 95, you know that configuring your system can be a time-consuming process. When you configured your DOS system, it seemed you were subject to endless tweaking to get things "just right." Only the masochists at heart truly enjoyed going through this process. Windows 95 has eliminated much of the tweaking that used to be necessary. There is still tweaking that can be done, however, and much of that is covered in this chapter. Here you learn the following:

- How to control the startup process
- How to control the various system menus
- How to run programs when you start Windows 95

- How to make the most out of system resources

As stated earlier, DOS may be obsolete after Windows 95 is released. Although this is true to an extent, DOS still lurks in the background and under the new, fancy covers provided by Windows 95. Nowhere is this more apparent than during the startup process. As you read through this chapter, you'll find many references reminiscent of the days when DOS ruled the roost. Although these remnants hang on, belying the claim that DOS is dead, they are included primarily for compatibility with the DOS hand-me-down programs that still exist on many computer systems.

Controlling the Startup Process

In the "old days" of computers, systems went through a booting process. Windows 95 documentation no longer refers to booting, but to *startup* (as opposed to shutdown). It seems that the folks at Microsoft limit booting to what is done before their software takes over, which means that booting is limited to what the BIOS does. After control is passed to the operating system loaders and various components, then the startup has begun in earnest.

Many aspects of Windows 95 startup could be discussed, although many of the aspects would only have meaning to a systems programmer. There are facets, however, that are important for you, the user, to understand. In the following sections you learn what goes on in the startup and how you can exercise some degree of control over it.

Understanding the Startup

From a user's perspective, the startup process used by Windows 95 is remarkably similar to that used by previous versions of Windows. Whenever you boot your system, the following steps are followed.

1. If the system is a Plug-and-Play compatible system, then the BIOS performs its analysis of the various cards in the system, making

resource allocations as necessary. (See Chapter 2, "Under-the-Hood Improvements," for more information on Plug-and-Play systems.)

2. The system BIOS performs its power-on self test (POST). The POST is a preliminary check of the hardware, to make sure that the base system elements (keyboard, video adapter, and so forth) are responding properly.
3. The CONFIG.SYS file, if any, is processed. This file is provided for compatibility with older real-mode drivers that may not be supported directly by Windows 95.
4. The AUTOEXEC.BAT file, if any, is processed. Again, this file is provided for backward-compatibility purposes.
5. Protected-mode 32-bit drivers needed by Windows 95 are loaded, even though the system has not been switched to protected mode.
6. The CPU is switched to protected mode, in preparation for the final phases of booting.
7. Plug-and-Play device conflicts are resolved, using information gathered by the BIOS, if it is available.
8. Main protected-mode subsystems, such as the kernel, graphics interface, user interface, fonts, and so forth, are loaded.
9. You are prompted to log in, if network support has been installed.
10. The StartUp folder (described later in this chapter) is processed.

Considering the amount of work required during the startup, most Windows 95 computers are able to breeze through it fairly quickly. After all ten steps are completed, you're able to do your normal work with Windows 95.

Modifying the Startup

Normally when you start your computer, Windows 95 starts running right away, and the first opportunity you have to interact with Windows is when you are asked to log in (if you're connected to a network).

You can "grab control" of the booting process, however. This can be helpful for troubleshooting purposes, or if you want to load DOS without using Windows.

To grab control of the booting process, first reboot your machine. After the POST is completed (the hardware check), and before the first Windows screen appears, press the F8 key. You'll see the Startup menu, shown in figure 15.1.

```
Microsoft Windows 95 Startup Menu
=================================

   1. Normal
   2. Logged (\BOOTLOG.TXT)
   3. Safe mode
   4. Safe mode with network support
   5. Step-by-step confirmation
   6. Command prompt only
   7. Safe mode command prompt only
   8. Previous version of MS-DOS

Enter a choice: 1

F5=Safe mode  Shift+F5=Command prompt
Shift+F8=Step-by-step confirmation [N]
```

Fig. 15.1 The Startup menu for Windows 95.

The actual contents of the Startup menu will vary, depending on how certain startup options have been set and what is installed in your system. For instance, if you don't have network support in your system, then option 4 is not available, and all subsequent options are moved up one position in the menu.

Notice that this menu provides several different options. If you want a normal Windows 95 startup, you should choose option 1. Options 2 through 5 and 7 are used for troubleshooting the startup. Options 6 and 8 accomplish essentially the same tasks, but do it quite differently. In each case, you'll see the DOS command prompt after booting is complete. The difference is that option 5 uses the MS-DOS files provided with Windows 95. Thus, much of the Windows 95 code is

running in the background. Option 8 bypasses Windows 95 entirely and boots the version of DOS you had installed on your system when you first installed Windows 95.

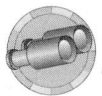

> **Note:** Your ability to begin DOS assumes that it was installed on your machine before you installed Windows 95. If it was not, you will not be able to run DOS unless it is within an MS-DOS window.

Startup Option Keys

In the previous section you learned that you can press F8 to display the Startup menu. The F8 key is only one of several startup option keys available in Windows 95. The following are the startup keys you can use after the POST is completed:

Key	Function
F4	Loads the previous version of DOS. Same as selecting the "Previous version of MS-DOS" option from the Startup menu.
F5	Starts Windows 95 in Safe mode. Same as selecting the "Safe mode" option from the Startup menu.
Shift+F5	Starts Windows 95 at the command prompt. Same as selecting the "Safe mode command prompt only" option from the Startup menu.
F6	Starts Windows 95 in Safe mode with network support. Same as selecting the "Safe mode with network support" option from the Startup menu.
F8	Displays the Startup menu.

In addition to these option keys, if you hold down the Shift key and press any function key (except F5), Windows 95 starts in Safe mode. This is the same effect as pressing the F5 key during startup.

Changing Startup Options

Internally, Windows 95 maintains options that modify how the startup process occurs. You can modify these options to affect the startup. These options are stored in a file called MSDOS.SYS, located in the root directory of the boot drive (typically C). The following is what the contents of this file may look like on your system:

```
[Options]
BootGUI=1

[Paths]
WinDir=C:\WINDOWS
WinBootDir=C:\WINDOWS
HostWinBootDrv=C
```

The organization of the MSDOS.SYS file is consistent with the organization structure used in most other INI files. The file is divided into sections, designated by section names in brackets. There are two possible sections in the MSDOS.SYS file. One of these is [Paths], which is used to maintain path information that Windows 95 needs to boot properly. If you change the settings in this section, it is highly possible you could stop Windows 95 from starting at all.

The other section, [Options], is used to set startup options. You can modify this section to contain any of 16 different options, as listed in Table 15.1. The options are entered as a keyword, followed by an equal sign, and then a value. Table 15.1 also lists the defaults for the options; these can be assumed to be in force unless you explicitly place a different option value in the [Options] section.

Table 15.1 MSDOS.SYS Option Keywords and Settings

Keyword	Default	Meaning
BootDelay	2	Number of seconds to delay before booting. This is the pause period after the POST but before the operating system loads. Longer delays allow the user a longer time in which to press a startup option key. This option has no meaning if BootKeys is disabled.

Keyword	Default	Meaning
BootFailSafe	1	Indicates that Fail-Safe Startup can be used. Set to 0 to disable.
BootGUI	1	Indicates that the normal Windows interface should be used. Set to 0 to start at the command prompt instead of Windows. Same as selecting the "Start only the command prompt" option from the Startup menu.
BootKeys	1	Controls whether startup option keys can be used. Set to 0 to disable.
BootMenu	0	If set to 1, then the Startup menu is displayed whenever the computer is booted. If set to 0, then the user must press F8 after the POST to see the Startup menu.
BootMenuDefault	1	The Startup menu option to use as a default.
BootMenuDelay	30	When displaying the Startup menu, indicates the number of seconds to delay before the default selection (BootMenuDefault) is automatically executed. Only has effect if BootMenu is set to 1.
BootMulti	1	Indicates whether dual booting capabilities are enabled. If set to 0, then user cannot use the F4 startup option key, and the "Start the version of MS-DOS previously installed on this computer" option on the Startup menu is not displayed.
BootWarn	1	Controls how the Fail-Safe mode is displayed by Windows. If set to 0, then Fail-Safe mode is disabled.
BootWin	1	Indicates the default operating system to use. If set to 1, Windows 95 is loaded. If set to 0, DOS is loaded. Similar to pressing the F4 startup option key or choosing the "Start the version of MS-DOS previously installed on this computer" option from the Startup menu.
DblSpace	1	Controls automatic loading of the DoubleSpace driver. If set to 0, driver is not loaded, even if needed.

continues

Table 15.1 Continued

Keyword	Default	Meaning
DoubleBuffer	0	Indicates whether a SCSI adapter in your system needs double buffering for caching. If set to 1, double buffering is enabled.
DrvSpace	1	Controls automatic loading of the DriveSpace driver. If set to 0, driver is not loaded, even if needed.
LoadTop	1	Indicates how COMMAND.COM or DRVSPACE.BIN should be loaded. If set to 1, they are loaded normally at the top of conventional memory. If set to 0, they are not. Some network operating systems may require setting this option to 0.
Logo	1	Controls display of the Windows 95 animated logo that is used when booting. If set to 0, logo is not displayed.
Network	0	Indicates whether network drivers are installed. If set to 1, then the "Start Windows, bypassing startup files, with network support" option is available on the Startup menu.

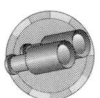

Note: MSDOS.SYS is stored as a hidden, read-only system file. If you want to change it, you need to change its read-only attribute first. Remember to change the attribute back after you have changed the file.

Controlling Menus

The Start menu is at the heart of Windows 95. Positioned at the left edge of the taskbar, the Start menu enables you to easily access programs, documents, and configuration settings for your entire system.

Windows 95 enables you to easily modify what appears on your Start menu. For instance, you could place the names of your favorite programs in the menu, or you could put them in the Programs menu, or you could put commonly accessed documents in the Documents menu. Each of the following sections explains how to accomplish these tasks.

Changing the Start Menu

You are already familiar with what the Start menu looks like. It contains commonly used programs and folders. You can modify the appearance of the Start menu any time you want. For instance, you might want to add your most-used programs (such as your spreadsheet or word processing programs) to the menu. This is easy to do if you follow these steps:

1. Right-click on the Start menu button. A context menu for the Start menu button appears.
2. From the context menu, choose the Open option. The Start Menu folder appears.
3. Create a shortcut for the program you want listed in the Start menu, placing the shortcut in the Start Menu folder window.
4. Close the Start Menu folder window.

If you now display the Start menu, you will notice that your shortcut is listed at the top of the menu. Figure 15.2 shows an example of a modified Start menu.

From these steps you might assume that the Start menu is nothing but a graphic representation of the structure of a folder on your disk drive. This is absolutely correct. Anything that appears within the Start Menu folder is shown on the Start menu; it is that simple.

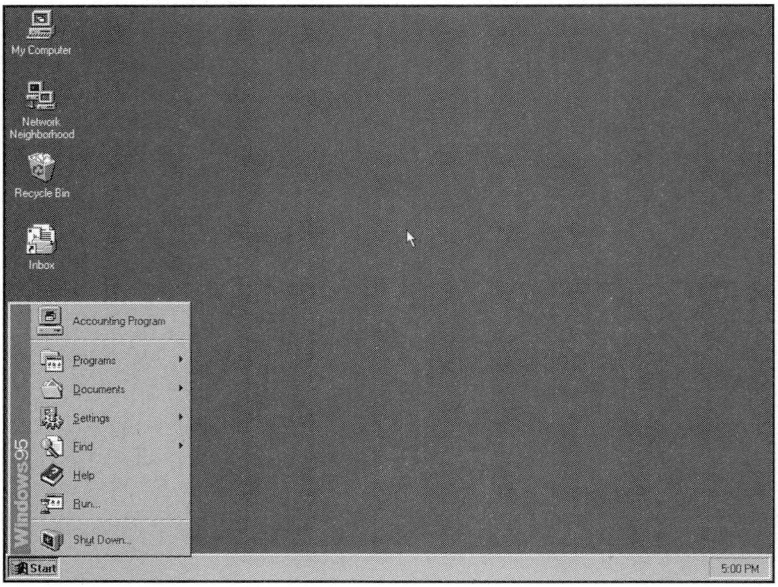

Fig. 15.2 Changing the Start menu is easy in Windows 95.

> **Note:** Even though you can install actual programs in the Start Menu folder and have them appear on the Start menu, this is not necessarily a good idea. If you do this, chances are good that your Start menu will quickly become cluttered with useless files. Instead, install the program in its own directory and place a shortcut to the program in the Start Menu folder. In this way you won't see all the ancillary files that are associated with an application; you will only see the icon for starting the application itself.

You also can add a new folder to the Start menu by following the same steps (just described), but creating a folder in the Start Menu folder instead. For instance, you might have several different but related programs you want grouped together. Placing them at the top of the Start menu would start to clutter the screen. Placing them in their own folder, however, makes more sense. Making the folder accessible from the Start menu makes sense, as well.

As an example, let's say you are working on the budget forecasts for your company. You spend a good part of each day working with them, using three different programs. You want the programs easily accessible, so you follow these steps to create a new folder in the Start menu:

1. Right-click on the Start menu button. A context menu for the Start menu button appears.
2. From the context menu, choose the Open option. The Start Menu folder appears.
3. In the Start Menu folder window, click File and then New. This displays a menu showing the types of objects you can create.
4. Choose Folder. A new folder appears in the Start Menu folder window.
5. Rename the folder to a descriptive name, such as Corporate Budget.
6. Close the Start Menu folder window.

Now the folder appears in the Start menu, as shown in figure 15.3. Whenever you select the folder from the Start menu, the contents of the folder are shown in menu form, as well. In this way, you quickly and easily can build your own menu structure for Windows 95.

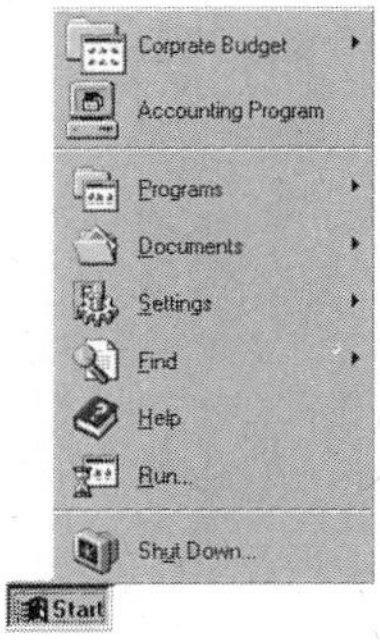

Fig. 15.3 Adding folders to the Start menu enables you to build your own menu structure.

> **Tip:** If you have an existing folder or shortcut you want added to the Start menu, you can do so by using the mouse to drag the object to the Start menu button. When you drop the item on the button, it appears in the Start menu.

Changing the Programs Menu

In the previous section you learned how you can add both programs (shortcuts to programs) and folders to the Start menu. You probably noticed that the icon for the Programs menu (visible on the Start menu) is a folder, as well. This would imply that, from a purely hierarchical perspective, the Programs menu is nothing more than a folder within the Start Menu folder. This implication is correct—in fact, adding programs to the Programs menu is as easy as copying them into the Programs folder. To accomplish this, follow these steps:

1. Right-click on the Start menu button. A context menu for the Start menu button appears.
2. From the context menu, choose the Open option. The Start Menu folder appears.
3. Double-click the Programs folder. This opens a window that shows the contents of the Programs folder, as shown in figure 15.4.

Fig. 15.4 The Programs folder window shows the contents of the Programs folder.

Notice that there are already six objects in the Programs folder window. These objects are the same choices you see when you select the Programs menu from the Start menu (see fig. 15.5).

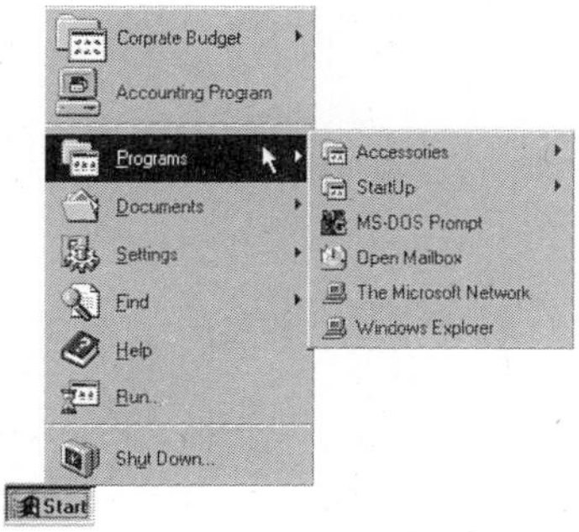

Fig. 15.5 The choices on the Programs menu are the same as the objects in the Programs folder.

You can modify the Programs menu by modifying the contents of the Programs folder. For instance, you could add your own shortcuts to programs or add additional folders. As you do, the Programs menu is automatically changed.

Changing the Documents Menu

The Documents menu is not as easily changed as the Start menu and Programs menu. In fact, many times the Documents menu seems to have a mind of its own.

In theory, the Documents menu is supposed to be the 15 most recently accessed documents—in other words, the 15 data files, spreadsheets, or word processing documents that you last accessed. The concept behind the Documents menu should be familiar to those who have been using Windows applications for some time. Many Windows applications include a list, at the bottom of the File menu, of the most recently used files. In this way, you easily and quickly can recall a file you recently worked on.

The Documents menu serves the same purpose. The 15 files it maintains are shown in alphabetical order; they are shortcuts to the documents themselves. If the menu contains 15 files, and you open a new file that is not already on the list, then the shortcut that has been on the menu the longest, without being accessed, is removed and replaced by the new file.

Exactly what mechanism is followed to determine what appears on the Documents menu is unclear. Files that you wouldn't assume to be "documents" often show up (like DLL files accessed through a file browser), while other files that could be assumed to be document files (such as the Registry accessed with the Registry Editor) don't show up.

You cannot explicitly force something onto the Documents menu without opening the document itself. Likewise, you cannot force something to stay on the Documents menu without periodically accessing it. You can, however, clear the entire Documents menu if (for some reason) you want to "start over." To clear the Documents menu, follow these steps:

1. Choose Settings from the Start menu. The Settings menu appears.
2. Choose Taskbar from the Settings menu. The contents of the Taskbar Properties sheet appear.
3. Click the Start Menu Programs tab. The sheet now appears as shown in figure 15.6.
4. Click the Clear button near the bottom of the sheet.
5. Click OK to close the sheet.

After following these steps, if you take another look at the Documents menu, you see that it is empty. It again starts to fill up as you access other documents.

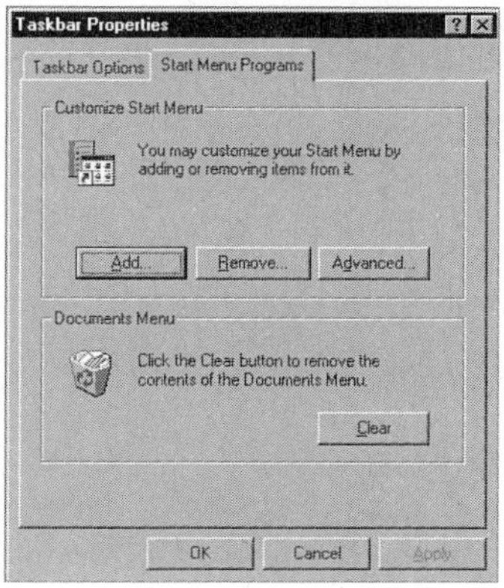

Fig. 15.6 The Clear button is used to delete all the Documents menu options.

Automatically Running Programs

If you are a long-time Windows user, you have probably already taken advantage of the StartUp program group. This powerful feature enables you to run programs whenever Windows is started. In previous versions of Windows, any program icon that was in the StartUp program group was automatically started whenever Windows was started.

Windows 95 also continues this feature. With Windows 95, you have complete control over what programs run whenever you boot your system. If you installed Windows 95 as an upgrade to an existing version of Windows, then the programs in your old StartUp group were automatically placed in the new version of the StartUp group. (It is not called a StartUp group any more; it is now called the StartUp folder.)

Since there is no real Program Manager in Windows 95, it may be a bit confusing to figure out where the StartUp folder is located. In reality, there are now two ways you can add or remove programs from your StartUp folder: either manually or through the use of a wizard.

Using a Wizard to Change the StartUp Folder

Perhaps the easiest way to add or remove things from the StartUp folder is by using a configuration wizard. To start the wizard, follow these steps:

1. Choose Settings from the Start menu. The Settings menu appears.
2. Choose Taskbar from the Settings menu. The Taskbar Properties sheet appears.

> **Tip:** A quick way to accomplish the first two steps is to right-click the taskbar and then choose Properties from the context menu.

3. Click the Start Menu Programs tab. The Taskbar Properties sheet should appear as shown earlier, in figure 15.6.
4. Click the Add button in the Customize Start Menu area. This starts the wizard, and you see the dialog box shown in figure 15.7.

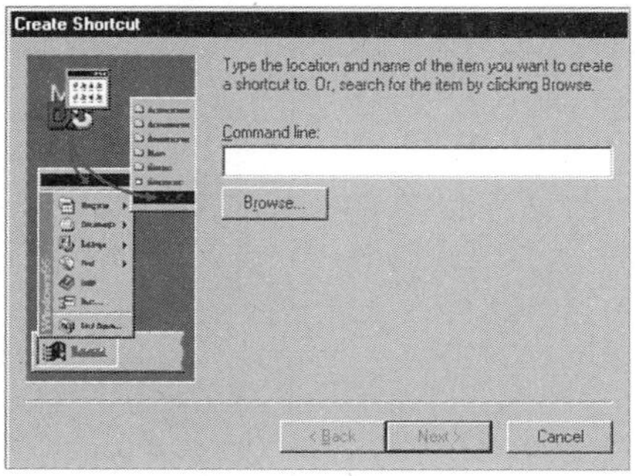

Fig. 15.7 The Create Shortcut Wizard can be used to add items to the StartUp Folder.

At this point, all you need to do is specify the program you want started when Windows starts. (You can click the Browse button, if desired, to help locate the program.) When you have provided the path and name of the program, click the Next button. You then see the dialog box shown in figure 15.8.

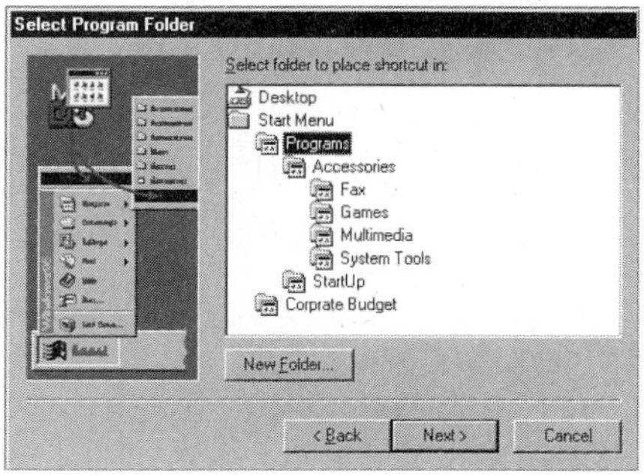

Fig. 15.8 The second step of the wizard is to specify where you want the shortcut stored.

The Select Program Folder dialog box is used to specify where the shortcut is to be placed. You should click the StartUp folder, shown at the bottom of the folder tree in the dialog box. Once you have highlighted the folder, you can click the Next button.

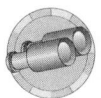

Note: If you select a folder other than the StartUp folder, the shortcut you are creating appears in the menu constructed from the folder you select. The concepts behind this were covered earlier in this chapter in the section titled "Controlling Menus."

You now should see the dialog box shown in figure 15.9. From this dialog box you specify the name of the shortcut you are creating. This can be any name you desire; it appears in both the StartUp folder listing and under the icon for the shortcut. When you have provided a name, click the Finish button.

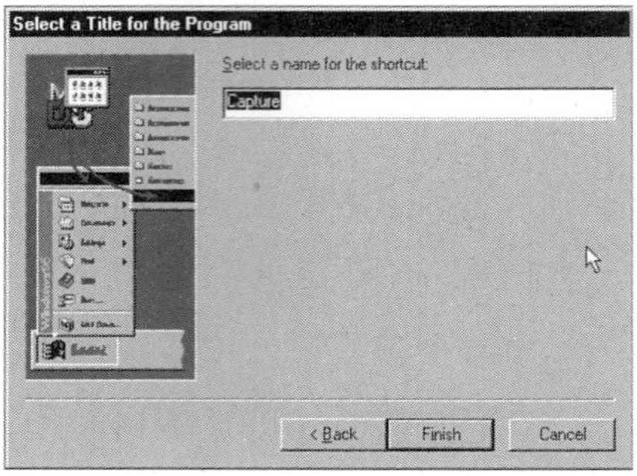

Fig. 15.9 The final step in the wizard is to specify a name for the new shortcut.

At this point, you are returned to the Taskbar Properties sheet, as shown earlier in figure 15.6. From here you can add more shortcuts to the StartUp folder, if you desire. When you are through, click OK to close the sheet. The next time you start Windows 95, the shortcuts in the StartUp folder are executed.

Manually Changing the StartUp Folder

Earlier in this chapter you learned how to change the Start menu and Programs menu by changing the contents of the proper folders. The same can be done with the StartUp folder. This manual process is closely related to how you managed the StartUp program group in older versions of Windows—you placed program items in the StartUp group.

To change the StartUp folder manually, follow these steps:

1. Right-click on the Start menu button. A context menu for the Start menu button appears.
2. From the context menu, choose the Open option. The Start Menu folder appears.

3. Double-click the Programs folder. This displays a window that shows the contents of the Programs folder.
4. Double-click the StartUp folder. This displays a window that shows the contents of the StartUp folder.
5. Create shortcuts for the programs you want run when Windows 95 starts. Place these shortcuts in the StartUp folder window.
6. Close the folder windows on your desktop.

The next time you start Windows 95, the shortcuts in the StartUp folder will be executed.

If you place a new folder in the StartUp Folder, that folder is opened and displayed when you start Windows 95. The contents of the folder are not executed; they are simply displayed. Only the following types of shortcuts are executed, and then only if they are located in the StartUp folder:

- Shortcuts to programs
- Shortcuts to documents associated with programs
- Actual program files

Conserving System Resources

Windows uses hard drive space as a general system resource. In addition to storing data files in hard drive space, Windows uses hard drive space as an extension of your RAM (random access memory) by means of the virtual memory management features discussed in Chapter 9, "Exploiting Memory, Space, and Resources." If you run short of hard drive space, you can delete nonessential Windows components (such as help files and dynamic-link libraries) from your system.

> **Caution:** Many Windows applications rely on dynamic-link library (DLL) files to operate properly. Before you delete such files willy-nilly, make sure you don't need them for your applications. You could also copy them to a floppy disk and make note of the original directories in which they belong. In this way you could later restore them if a problem arises.

Windows includes many different components, some of which you can remove from your system without disabling Windows. By deleting different components as you don't need them any more, you can free quite a bit of hard drive space. Windows 95 includes an easy way you can delete components from your system. To do so, follow these steps:

1. Choose Settings from the Start menu. The Settings menu appears.
2. Choose Control Panel from the Settings menu. The Control Panel window appears.
3. Double-click the Add/Remove Programs icon in the Control Panel. The Add/Remove Programs Properties sheet appears.
4. Click the Windows Setup tab. The sheet now appears as shown in figure 15.10.

In this sheet you can see the different Windows 95 components, as well as which ones are installed on your system. (Those that have a check mark in the box to the left of the component are installed.) To the right of the component is an indication of how much hard drive space is used by the component.

To delete a component from your system, simply clear the check box to the left of the component. When you are through, click the OK button, and Windows may ask you to confirm your action (depending on what you are removing). Once confirmed, the components are removed and you are returned to the desktop.

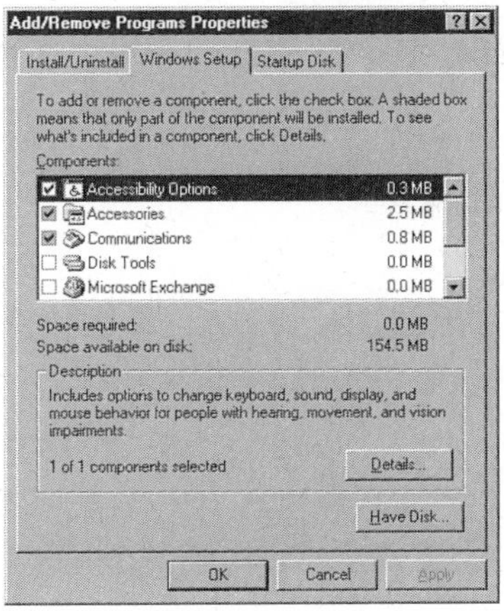

Fig. 15.10 Windows 95 enables you to easily add or delete different system components.

To later reinstall a component, repeat the steps previously listed. Instead of clearing a check box, however, you should select the check box. When you click the OK button, Windows prompts you for the Windows 95 program disks or CD-ROM. (This is necessary because you physically deleted the components from your disk drive.) When you have complied with the disk request, Windows copies the files to your hard drive.

KILLER 16 WINDOWS 95

Installing Windows Applications

by Allen L. Wyatt

Installing Windows applications is easier than ever with Windows 95. The operating system includes a new software installation wizard that can make adding software (or removing it later) as easy as clicking on a button. The following topics are covered in this chapter:

- How to install Windows applications by using the Add/Remove Software Wizard
- How to install Windows applications manually
- Differences between 16-bit and 32-bit Windows applications
- How to overcome compatibility issues for older 16-bit programs

In addition, you'll find tips explaining how to troubleshoot any glitches that may crop up as you install your applications.

Installing with a Wizard

Windows 95 includes a software installation wizard you can use to add software to your system. This wizard, located in the Control Panel, is the preferred method of adding software to Windows 95. As the wizard installs the software, it updates the Registry with the information related to the program. This step ensures that the system resources required by the software will be available.

If the application you're installing was created for Windows 95 (it has the Windows 95 logo on the software package), it will also update the Registry with additional information. For instance, the Registry will contain information about the following:

- Which components can be added to the software. For instance, you might have installed only a portion of the software package, and the Registry will contain information about what else is possible to install.
- Which parameters are needed by the application in order for it to run properly.
- Which files can be deleted from Windows 95 if the application is removed from the system.

Running the Installation Wizard

To run the software installation wizard, follow these steps:

1. Choose Settings from the Start menu. The Settings menu appears.
2. Choose Control Panel from the Settings menu. The Control Panel appears.
3. Double-click on the Add/Remove Programs icon. You'll see the Add/Remove Programs Properties sheet appear, as shown in figure 16.1.

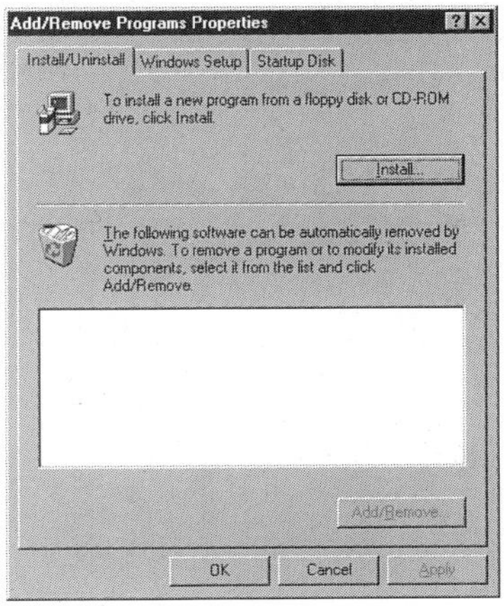

Fig. 16.1 The Add/Remove Programs Properties sheet is used to add or remove software from Windows 95.

4. Click on the Install button. This starts the wizard and displays the first screen, as shown in figure 16.2.

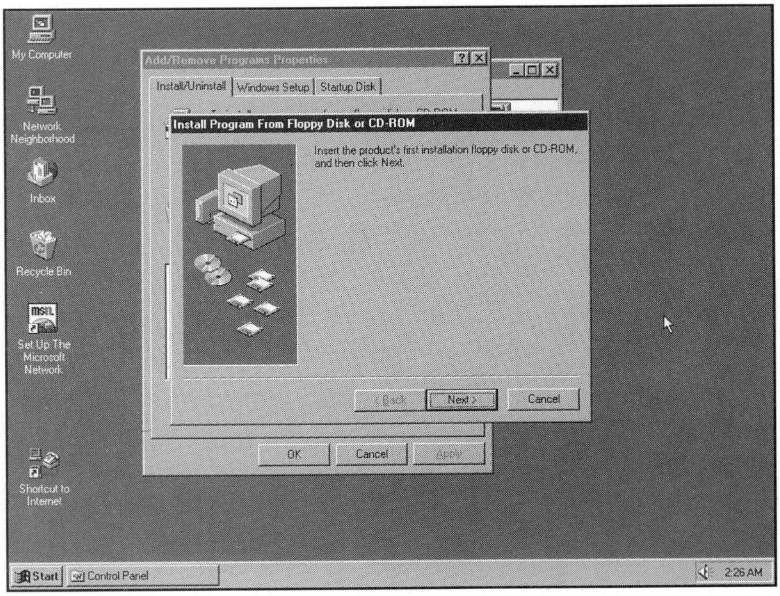

Fig. 16.2 Windows 95 includes a wizard that is used to install software from a floppy disk or CD-ROM.

Make sure that either the installation floppy disk for the software or the CD-ROM containing the installation files is inserted in a disk drive. When you're ready to proceed, click on the Next button. The wizard proceeds to look through your disk drives (and CD-ROM drives) to find a setup disk. It looks for program names, such as SETUP.EXE or INSTALL.EXE. When it finds a disk or CD-ROM that contains what it believes to be setup files, a new dialog box appears, which shows what was found.

The command line field in the middle of the sheet should reflect the command line necessary to install the software. You may want to check the command line against the command line indicated in the documentation for the software. If you need to, you can click on the Browse button to locate a different program to use in the installation routines.

When you're finished with the command line, click on the Finish button. This step ends the wizard and starts the setup program for your software. The steps you follow from this point depend on the software you're installing. Different applications have different setup programs that require different user input.

> **Tip:** If you're having trouble installing your software, refer to the manual that came with it. If that doesn't help, you may need to contact the vendor's technical support department.

Installation Wizard Problems

You probably will not encounter problems with the Add/Remove Programs wizard. If you have problems, but they occur after you click on the Finish button of the wizard, then the problem may lie with your program's ability to work with Windows 95. Later in this chapter, you'll learn what you can do in some of these instances.

The best solution if you have a problem is to contact the software vendor to see if the company has any other reported problems in using their

software with Windows 95. If they do, you can request a new version of the program or the steps to follow to install the software manually.

Installing Manually

Microsoft does not suggest that you install your software manually. By *manually* is meant two common ways of installing software:

- Directly running the installation program supplied with the software
- Copying the program files to a folder and running the program

In previous versions of Windows, there was very little problem in doing either of these actions. The problem under Windows 95 is related to the new Registry. If you are installing older 16-bit Windows applications, there is little chance that they are designed to recognize or take advantage of the Registry. Without using the Add/Remove Programs wizard, the Registry will not have a chance to be updated properly. This could lead to problems down the road when you want to remove the software or if you install other software that requires the application to be present.

There are a few cases when you can add software manually. You should be safe in directly running the installation program provided with your software if the program was created to be Windows 95 compatible. If it was, there is a good chance that it will update the Registry automatically during installation.

The other exception is if you have a very small program that doesn't require any special installation program. For instance, you may download a small utility program from a BBS system. This utility is designed to be run "as is." It doesn't have an installation program, and it doesn't really modify any INI files or the Registry. If this is the case, feel free to copy the file to a folder on your hard disk. You should remember the following when installing in this manner:

- If you install the program to a folder within the Start Menu folder (\Windows\Start Menu), then the program or folder will appear on the Start menu itself.
- If you install the program to a folder within the Programs folder (\Windows\Start Menu\Programs), then the program or folder will appear within the Programs option of the Start menu.

If you have problems with the application after you install it manually, remove it from your system and contact the program vendor. They may have an update or a setup disk available that will work properly with Windows 95.

32-Bit versus 16-Bit Windows Programs

There are two types of Windows applications you can install. The first type, sometimes called "legacy applications," are programs designed for older versions of Windows. These applications have been designed to work with 16-bit API (application program interface) functions. These programs will work just fine under Windows 95, but they're inherently less stable than their 32-bit counterparts.

The second type is a 32-bit application. These applications are called 32-bit because they use the Win32 API functions and are designed to run under a 32-bit operating system. These applications will work under both Windows NT and Windows 95, because both systems use the Win32 API.

> **Caution:** Windows NT applications, which take advantage of NT-specific API functions, will not work under Windows 95. These functions include security- and NTFS-related functions.

All things being equal, 16-bit applications will run as well (if not better) under Windows 95 as they would under Windows 3.1x. They run well because, as you learned in Chapter 2, "Under-the-Hood Improvements," significant parts of the operating system have been rewritten. The improved management algorithms and the 32-bit architecture ensures that while the operating system is running, it is running as efficiently as possible.

Windows 95 provides the same operating system resources to both 32-bit and 16-bit applications. However, 16-bit applications cannot use preemptive multitasking. They also use a shared memory pool and a common message queue, and their processes are scheduled cooperatively. 32-bit applications are designed to take full advantage of all of the Windows 95 performance enhancement features. These applications offer the following advantages when compared to 16-bit legacy applications:

- Preemptive multitasking
- Threaded operation
- Separate message queues
- Flat address space
- Memory protection
- Long file name support

Preemptive Multitasking

Under previous versions of Windows, control was passed from one application to another cooperatively. This meant that when one application gained control of the system, no other application could gain control until the running application became "cooperative" and relinquished control. At best, this situation led to sluggish performance in some applications.

Under Windows 95, preemptive multitasking is supported. This means that Windows 95 schedules the time allotted for running applications in the system. When the time allotted to an application is done, the operating system "preempts" the running application and passes

control on to the next scheduled task. This results in smoother concurrent processing and prevents any one application from using all system resources without permitting other tasks to run.

One of the reasons that 32-bit applications can run faster than 16-bit operations is that they don't need to have any scheduling routines built in to the application. For instance, 16-bit applications needed timers and the like to determine when it was appropriate to pass control back to the operating system. No such gymnastics are required of 32-bit applications because they rely on the operating system to take care of scheduling.

Threaded Operation

This feature is available to 32-bit applications, but not all of them may take advantage of it. Threaded operation means that different parts of the application can execute at the same time, resulting in better performance and use of resources. This feature is closely akin to multitasking.

Whereas multitasking generally means that multiple applications can be executing at the same time, threaded operation means that a single application creates multiple tasks, which are then simultaneously executed. It is a fine point, to be sure, but one that is not available to 16-bit applications.

Separate Message Queues

You've already learned thatWindows 95 uses preemptive multitasking for managing the affairs of applications running on the system. One feature implemented as part of this is that each 32-bit application on the system has its own "messaging queue." This queue is used to pass information between the application and the operating system or between the application and other tasks running on the system.

16-bit applications are written to take advantage of the old way that Windows used messaging queues. In previous versions of Windows, a single messaging queue was used for all applications running in the system. This worked fine, as long as the running application allowed other applications to check the queue. If this was not allowed (such as when the running application was ill-behaved or when it locked up), then the other applications locked up as well because they could not check the queue.

The result of independent message queues is that the operating environment is more stable than was previously possible. Each 32-bit application can check its own queue whenever deemed appropriate by the application, and is not affected by how other applications may check the queue.

Flat Address Space

Windows 95 looks at and manages memory differently than in earlier versions of the operating system. Instead of dealing with segmented memory, the operating system treats all of memory as a flat address space, meaning that larger memory operations can occur in a faster time frame.

32-bit applications are written to take advantage of APIs that use the flat memory space paradigm. The older 16-bit applications are written to an older API standard that relies on segmented memory access. The result is that 16-bit applications require additional code overhead and run slower than 32-bit applications.

Memory Protection

In previous versions of Windows, memory was allocated from a giant pool that could be used by all applications. The result, while very dynamic in nature, was not always very stable. People who have used Windows quite a bit are no doubt well acquainted with the dreaded GPF (general protection fault), which meant that some program mucked about in some other program's memory area. More often than not, the program being mucked with was Windows itself. The result was not only that the application that generated the error was shut down, but also that the resources used by the program were not always released back to the pool. This meant that the best way to handle a GPF was to exit from Windows and restart—a tiresome procedure, at best.

Under the 32-bit environment created by Windows 95, there are two categories of memory:

- 32-bit application protected memory
- 16-bit application pooled memory

32-bit programs—those designed to use Windows 95—pull their memory from the first category. Older 16-bit programs are lumped together in the second category.

The memory area used by 32-bit applications is sequestered from memory used by other applications. This means that the application cannot be interfered with by other applications, nor can it interfere with other applications (or the operating system itself). The result is a more stable program.

16-bit programs all share the same pooled memory space, as in previous versions of Windows. Thus, it is still possible to get a GPF if you are using an old application. The benefit under Windows 95, however, is that if the program crashes, it affects only the other 16-bit programs running at the time. The 32-bit applications and the operating system itself remain unaffected.

Long File Name Support

You learned in Chapter 2, "Under-the-Hood Improvements," how Windows 95 implements long file names. Applications written to the legacy 16-bit guidelines don't take advantage of long file names. On the other hand, 32-bit applications designed for Windows 95 can freely take advantage of long file names.

Note: 32-bit applications written for Windows NT do not necessarily recognize the long file names supported by Windows 95. The long file name algorithms used under Windows NT (for NTFS partitions) are different than the algorithms used to support long file names in a FAT partition (as is done in Windows 95).

16-Bit Application Problems

Some 16-bit applications may not run well under Windows 95 because they were designed with older operating systems in mind. For instance, a 16-bit application may take advantage of known quirks in previous versions of Windows, or it may count on the user interface appearing a certain way. The following sections address potential problem areas and how you can solve them.

Note: The best way to solve 16-bit application problems is to get an upgrade to your old program. You should use the workarounds described here only if you cannot get an upgrade.

User Interface Problems

Some 16-bit software is written to take great advantage of the older Windows user interface. For example, an application could use the title bar to add a special icon to a window, or it could place its own toolbar at the bottom of the desktop.

The problem with this is that Windows 95 has significantly changed the user interface. Now title bars are formatted differently, and the taskbar appears at the bottom of the desktop. These changes can cause information to appear "funny" when displayed under Windows 95. Information may be overwritten, or it may appear behind desktop objects.

These problems should not cause critical errors; you should still be able to use your software, although you may not be able to use the features not supported by the Windows 95 user interface. The only way to really cure this problem is to upgrade your software to a Windows 95 version.

Undocumented Features

A couple of years ago there were some books on the market that touted the discovery of "undocumented" features and functions (from a programmer's perspective) in Windows. Although these books caused quite a stir for a while, some programmers began to rely on the newly uncovered functions. Microsoft suggested they not do it, but some programmers persisted.

With the introduction of Windows 95, the old Windows is done away with; this is to be expected with the complete redesign of the operating system core. While Microsoft supports most of the long-established programming functions, it does not support all of the undocumented functions. Thus, if you have a 16-bit program that uses any of these undocumented functions, it will not work under Windows 95. The results of trying to run them will depend on the function calls being used. In some cases, certain program features may not work correctly or may not be available. In other cases the program could crash entirely, refusing to continue.

There is absolutely no way around this sort of problem short of getting a new version. Until you get a new version of your program, you should not run the old version because the results are so hard to predict.

Version Number Errors

Older applications can have two types of problems in regard to version numbers. Some applications may incorrectly check for the version number, and others may refuse to work if the Windows version number is not 3.1x.

If the application checks the version number incorrectly, it is usually because it "mixes up" the version information. For instance, the program may check the version number and see it as 10.3 instead of 3.10. Because most programs check for a minimum version number to ensure compatibility, Windows 95 always reports its version number as 3.95. In this way, if your application compares 3.95 to 3.10 (its base version requirement), it should conclude that it is OK to proceed. Even if the software reverses the version numbers, it is still comparing 95.3 to 10.3, and should still conclude that it is safe to continue.

Some applications check for the version number and refuse to proceed if the reported number is not exactly the same as what it expects. Thus, a program may falter if it does not believe it is running under Windows 3.1x. Windows 95 provides a way you can fool the older application into thinking it is running under Windows 3.1x. Believe it or not, this fix uses the WIN.INI file. (And you thought WIN.INI was a thing of the past.) All you need to do is edit the [Compatibility] section of the file by using a regular text editor, such as the Notepad accessory. The following is a portion of the contents of the [Compatibility] section on a newly installed version of Windows 95:

```
[Compatibility]
_3DPC=0x00400000
_BNOTES=0x224000
_LNOTES=0x00100000
ACAD=0x8000
ACT!=0x400004
ACROBAT=0x04000000
AD=0x10000000
ADW30=0x10000000
ALARMMGR=0x0040000
ALDSETUP=0x00400000
WPWIN60=0x00000400
WPWIN61=0x02000400
WSETUP=0x00200000
XPRESS=0x00000008
ZETA01=0x00400000
ZIFFBOOK=0x00200000
```

The left side of each entry in the [Compatibility] section contains information derived from the header of the executable program file; it is referred to as the compiled module name of the program. Most of the time you can find the compiled module name of an executable file by using the DOS TYPE command to view the contents of the file (the name will be in the first couple of lines of what you see on-screen).

> **Note:** If you cannot determine the compiled module name of the program by using the TYPE command, you should call the vendor and talk through the fix with them. They should be able to provide you with the name you need.

Create a new entry in this section for the application with which you're having version number problems. On the left side of the equal sign, place the compiled module name; on the right place the value 0x00200000. For example, if the compiled version name of the program was MYPROG, then the entry would look like this:

```
MYPROG=0x00200000
```

Save the file and restart Windows 95. This should fix the compatibility problem. If it does not, you'll need to contact the vendor agents to see if they have a fix for their program.

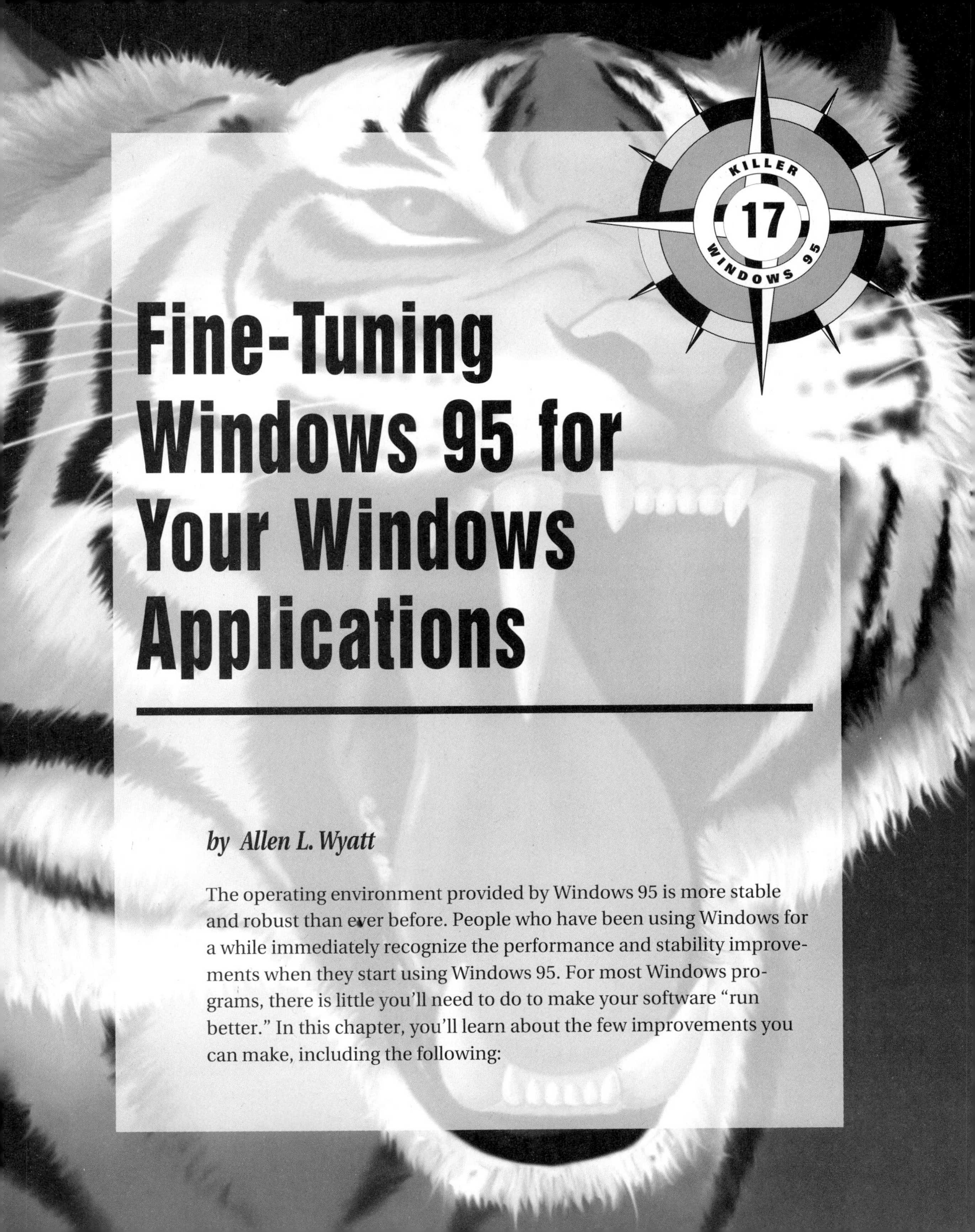

KILLER 17 WINDOWS 95

Fine-Tuning Windows 95 for Your Windows Applications

by Allen L. Wyatt

The operating environment provided by Windows 95 is more stable and robust than ever before. People who have been using Windows for a while immediately recognize the performance and stability improvements when they start using Windows 95. For most Windows programs, there is little you'll need to do to make your software "run better." In this chapter, you'll learn about the few improvements you can make, including the following:

- Changes you can make to your operating environment
- How you can set working folders in Windows 95
- What performance improvements can be made to 16-bit programs
- How the improved resource management in Windows 95 affects your programs

Changing Your Environment

If you've ever installed MS-DOS software under Windows 95, you know that there is quite a bit you can do to affect the operating environment of the software. (See Chapter 19, "Fine-Tuning Windows 95 for Your DOS Applications.") This is because, as you learned in Chapter 13, "How Windows 95 Interacts with Software," Windows 95 creates a Virtual Machine for each DOS program you run. When you change the environmental properties, you're modifying how that VM is created.

On the other hand, Windows programs (16-bit or 32-bit) operate within a single VM. There is little you can do to affect the environment created by Windows 95 for these applications. Instead, you can only adjust parameters that affect all Windows programs (these will be covered shortly).

Windows 95 does not allow you to individually change the operational environment of a Windows program. If you right-click on the program icon for a Windows program, and choose the Properties option from the context menu, you can modify the attributes of the file (read-only, hidden, and so on), but there are no environment-related properties to change as there are with DOS programs.

Improving Video Performance

To improve the performance of your video system, you may want to refer to Chapter 11, "Video Cards, Drivers, and Monitors." Windows 95 does a good job of optimizing the performance of your video system,

within certain constraints. It allows you to pick operational parameters for your video card that can affect the overall performance of your system.

If you notice that your system is giving sluggish performance, and you suspect that your video system is the culprit, follow these steps:

1. Choose Settings from the Start menu.
2. Choose Control Panel from the Settings menu.
3. Double-click on the Display icon. The Display Properties sheet appears.
4. Click on the Settings tab.
5. In the Color palette pull-down list, choose the 16 Color setting.
6. Move the Desktop area slider bar all the way to the left, so it is set to 640 by 480 pixels.
7. Click on OK.
8. Restart your computer, if necessary. (A dialog box may appear informing you that this is necessary.)

With these settings, your video system will operate as fast as possible (for the hardware). This is because the video settings have been placed at their least-demanding state. If this improves the speed of your software, then you're home free. Some software, however, doesn't work well at these low-level settings. For instance, some multimedia software is designed to work with at least 256 colors displayed on-screen. In such a case, you can try stepping up the number of colors used by your video card, but that may slow down your system a bit. If the speed reduction is not acceptable, the only solution you have is to upgrade your video card to a newer, faster model.

If the performance of your system does not improve, even with your video settings set as low as possible, then perhaps any perceived slowdown in your system is not due to the video system. You may want to reset the video settings back to their original values and see whether adjusting other performance factors affects your system more favorably.

Improving Disk Performance

Windows 95 works with a wide variety of disk drives, but not all disk drives have the same capabilities. As you learned in Chapter 10, "Optimizing Your Disk Drives," there is much more to the performance of a disk system than just the capacity of the hard drive.

If you're using software that uses the hard disk quite a bit, you can use the following tips to maximize the performance of your hard drives:

- Defragment your disk drives
- Adjust your disk cache size
- Disable DriveSpace or other disk compression

Detailed information on each of these steps is included in Chapter 10, but the quick information in the following sections may help you accomplish your goals in this area.

Defragmenting Your Drives

If your software uses the disk drives heavily, your drives may become fragmented quickly. You may even want to defragment your drives as often as once every other week. The defrag utility, included with Windows 95, is an excellent choice for performing this task. To start this utility, follow these steps:

1. Choose Programs from the Start menu.
2. Choose Accessories from the Programs menu.
3. Choose System Tools from the Accessories menu.
4. Choose Disk Defragmenter from the System Tools menu.
5. Select the disk drive you want to defragment, then click on OK.

Changing Your Disk Cache Size

The disk cache used by Windows 95 is geared toward normal disk-usage requirements. If you use software that relies heavily on the disk drive, you may want to adjust the cache size by following these steps:

1. Right-click on the My Computer icon on your desktop.
2. Choose Properties from the context menu.
3. Click on the Performance tab.
4. Click on the File System button at the bottom of the page.
5. In the pull-down list beside the Typical role of this machine field, select the setting Network server.
6. Make sure the slider for Read-ahead optimization is slid all the way to the right (toward Full).
7. Click on the OK button.
8. Click on the Close button.
9. Restart your computer, if necessary. (A dialog box may appear, informing you that this is necessary.)

Disabling Disk Compression

Any disk compression software, including the DriveSpace feature of Windows 95, adds overhead to your operating system. This overhead can introduce a slight performance penalty in accessing your drives. For your operating system to operate as quickly as possible in relation to your drive, you may want to remove the compression. To do this, follow these steps:

1. Choose Programs from the Start menu.
2. Choose Accessories from the Programs menu.
3. Choose System Tools from the Accessories menu.
4. Choose DriveSpace from the System Tools menu.
5. In the drive list, choose the disk drive you want to uncompress.
6. Choose Uncompress from the Drive menu.

This starts the uncompression portion of DriveSpace. You should follow the instructions as they appear on your screen as this process continues.

If you're using a different disk compression utility, you should refer to the instructions for your software to learn how to disable disk compression.

Improving CD-ROM Performance

More and more software is relying on the storage capacity and convenience of CD-ROM drives. If you use software that frequently accesses the CD-ROM drive, you can benefit by checking the performance settings of your CD-ROM. Do this by following these steps:

1. Right-click on the My Computer icon on your desktop.
2. Choose Properties from the context menu.
3. Click on the Performance tab.
4. Click on the File System button at the bottom of the page.
5. Click on the CD-ROM tab. The File System Properties sheet appears as shown in figure 17.1.

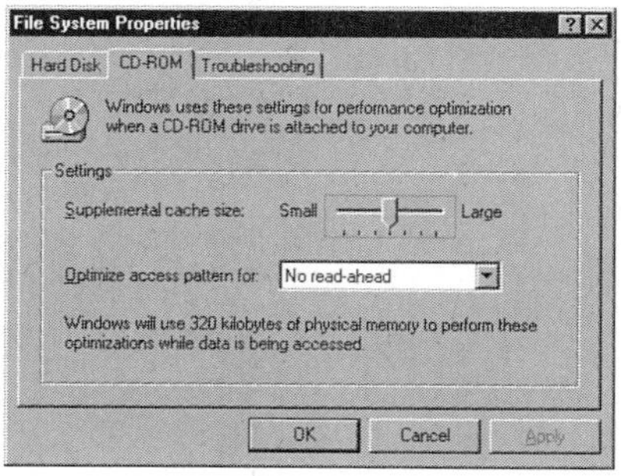

Fig. 17.1 The File System Properties sheet, with the CD-ROM tab selected, allows you to modify how Windows 95 uses the CD-ROM drive.

6. In the pull-down list beside the Optimize access pattern for field, select the setting that best matches the rated speed of your CD-ROM drive—single speed, double speed, and so on.

7. Move the slider for Supplemental cache size toward the right (toward Large).
8. Click on the OK button.
9. Click on the Close button.
10. Restart your computer, if necessary. (A dialog box may appear informing you that this is necessary.)

In general, the access pattern for your CD-ROM should be set to match the speed rating of your drive. If you use the CD-ROM a lot, then you should also increase the supplemental cache size until the performance of your system more closely matches your expectations.

Working Directories

If you're familiar with previous versions of Windows, you may remember that you were able to specify working folders for program items (these would be called working folders in Windows 95). This means that you could indicate the initial folder for a program to use when it first started. Unlike Windows 3.x, Windows 95 does not allow you to specify working folders for programs.

The stated reason for not permitting you to assign a working folder to a program is that there are links which Windows 95 sets up to the program, and these links expect very few changes to the program properties (which is where a working folder would be maintained). There is a way around this shortcoming, however—through the use of shortcuts.

In Chapter 2, "Under-the-Hood Improvements," you learned about shortcuts and how they're created in Windows 95. You can set working folders for shortcuts, even though you cannot for programs. While at first this may seem awkward, it is really more flexible. This means you can create shortcuts for different uses of the same program, and each shortcut can start the program by using a different working folder. For instance, you could have three shortcuts for your spreadsheet program:

➤ The first shortcut is labeled "Budget Figures" and uses the C:\BUDGET folder.

➤ The second shortcut is labeled "Tax Information" and uses the D:\FINANCE\TAXES folder.

➤ The third shortcut is labeled "Family Finances" and uses the C:\PERSONAL\FINANCES folder.

To set the working folder for a shortcut, follow these directions:

1. Right-click on the shortcut icon (the icon with a small arrow in the bottom left corner) you want to change.
2. Choose Properties from the context menu.
3. Click on the Shortcut tab. You'll see the Shortcut Properties sheet, similar to figure 17.2.

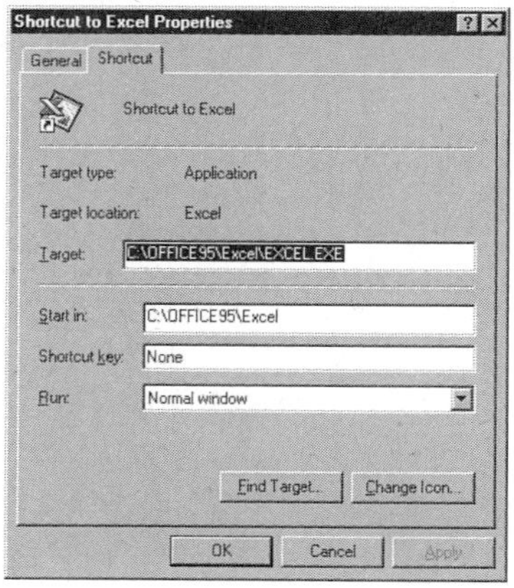

Fig. 17.2 The Shortcut Properties sheet allows you to modify how a shortcut starts a program.

4. In the Start in dialog box, indicate the working folder you want used when the program is started.
5. Click on the OK button.

The next time you use the shortcut to start the program, the folder you specified is used as the working folder.

16-Bit Program Performance

The best way to improve the performance of your 16-bit programs is to replace them with 32-bit versions, particularly if the 32-bit versions are optimized for Windows 95. If you do this, you'll be able to realize all the performance benefits covered in Chapter 16, "Installing Windows Applications." In addition, you'll be able to more easily remove the application if you ever need to.

If you must keep 16-bit applications on your system, remember the following pointers:

- 16-bit applications know nothing about the Windows 95 Registry. Thus, they still save their information in the various INI files for which Windows 3.x was famous. Windows 95 even includes abbreviated WIN.INI and SYSTEM.INI files for compatibility with older 16-bit programs. Do not delete INI files relied upon by your programs, including WIN.INI and SYSTEM.INI.
- Don't edit WIN.INI and SYSTEM.INI directly unless you absolutely have to. These files are updated automatically with some variables every time you modify the Registry. Thus, if you need to change a variable that affects your entire system (such as your display settings or the like), it is better to make the changes in the Registry (using the Control Panel) and let Windows take care of modifying the older WIN.INI and SYSTEM.INI files.
- Steer clear of 16-bit disk utilities designed for Windows. These rely on the outdated FAT file structure used in Windows 3.x. *Using such programs could wipe out any long file names you've used under Windows 95.*

System Resources

Under Windows 3.x, it was easy to crash your system. All you needed to do was have a program or two crash, and the resources in your system would be eaten up. All of a sudden, other programs were refusing to load or were running short on memory.

Under Windows 95, your 16-bit applications will automatically run better because the entire resource structure of Windows has been revamped. Now there are greater resources available to all programs, including 16-bit holdovers from Windows 3.x.

Under Windows 3.x, the operating system used 64K memory heaps for different system components. This memory area was used to store information about objects used in system function calls by both the operating system and the applications running in the system. When you looked at the percentage of system resources in the About box of the Help menu in any application, you were looking at how much of the 64K heap was left available. The closer this percentage got to zero, the closer you were to crashing your system.

To overcome this problem in Windows 95, many of the resources that used to quickly consume memory in the 64K heap have been reallocated to a new 32-bit heap. This means that there is much more room for tracking system objects and performing system function calls. The net result is that more resources are available, and programs are less likely to exhaust them.

For a comparison of the improvements, take a look at the information shown in Table 17.1. This shows the increases in limits on all aspects related to running 16-bit applications under Windows 95.

Table 17.1 Windows Resource Limits

System Resource	Windows 3.1 Limits	Windows 95 Limits
COM ports	4	Unlimited
Device contexts	Approx. 175	16,000
Edit control data	64K	Unlimited
Installed fonts	Approx. 250	1,000
Listbox data	64K	Unlimited
Listbox items	8K	32K
Logical fonts	64K local heap	Approx. 750
Logical objects	64K local heap	64K local heap

System Resource	Windows 3.1 Limits	Windows 95 Limits
LPT ports	4	Unlimited
Menu handles	Approx. 299	32K each
Physical objects	64K local heap	Unlimited
Regions	64K local heap	Unlimited
Timers	32	Unlimited

KILLER 18 WINDOWS 95

Installing DOS Applications

by Allen L. Wyatt

Microsoft has made more of a concerted effort to make Windows 95 compatible with MS-DOS programs than they have with any previous version of Windows. This is understandable, because you can't exit out of Windows and run your MS-DOS application, as you could previously. The result of this effort is a stable and robust environment for your MS-DOS programs. In this chapter you'll learn the following about installing your DOS applications:

- How to install a DOS program by using the Add/Remove Programs wizard
- How to manually install a DOS program
- What you should do after you've installed the software
- How Windows 95 uses the APPS.INF file to aid in running MS-DOS programs

Installing a Program

Most DOS programs know little about Windows. Some do, it is true, but by and large, they assume that you'll be running the program outside of Windows. Because of the stability of the Virtual Machine created for a DOS application, you can generally install directly from within Windows. There are two ways you can install your programs: by using the wizard supplied by Windows, or by manually installing. The following sections describe both approaches.

Using the Wizard

Windows 95 includes a software installation wizard you can use to add software to your system. This wizard, located in the Control Panel, is typically used to add Windows software, but it is also the preferred method of adding MS-DOS software. As the wizard installs the software, it checks in a special information file to determine whether there are any special configuration needs for the software. This special information file, APPS.INF, is fully described later in this chapter. If you don't use the wizard for installing, then the APPS.INF file is not consulted and the installation might not occur correctly.

To run the software installation wizard, follow these steps:

1. Choose Settings from the Start menu. The Settings menu appears.
2. Choose Control Panel from the Settings menu; the Control Panel appears.
3. Double-click on the Add/Remove Programs icon. You'll see the Add/Remove Programs Properties sheet appear, as shown in figure 18.1.
4. Click on the Install button. This starts the wizard and displays the first screen, as shown in figure 18.2.

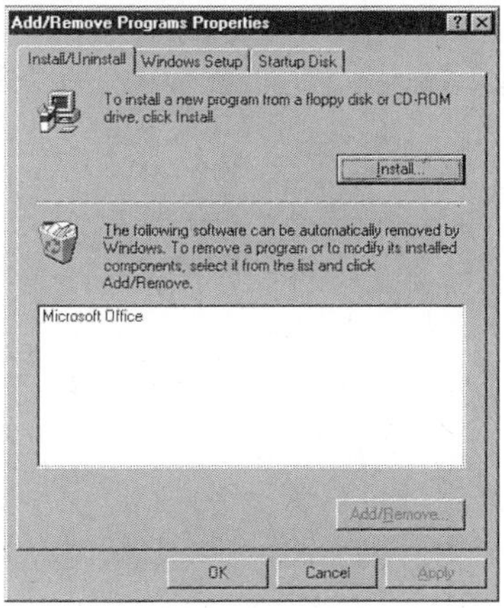

Fig. 18.1 The Add/Remove Programs Properties sheet is used to add or remove software from Windows 95.

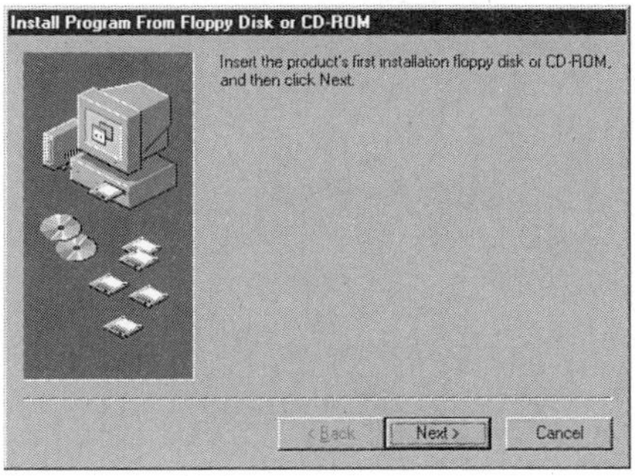

Fig. 18.2 Windows 95 includes a wizard used to install software from a floppy disk or CD-ROM.

Make sure that either the installation floppy disk for the software or the CD-ROM containing the installation files is inserted in a disk drive. When you're ready to proceed, click on the Next button. The wizard proceeds to look through your disk drives (and CD-ROM drives) to find a setup floppy disk. The wizard also looks for program names, such as SETUP.EXE or INSTALL.EXE. When it finds a disk or CD-ROM that contains what it believes to be setup files, a new dialog box appears that shows what was found (see figure 18.3).

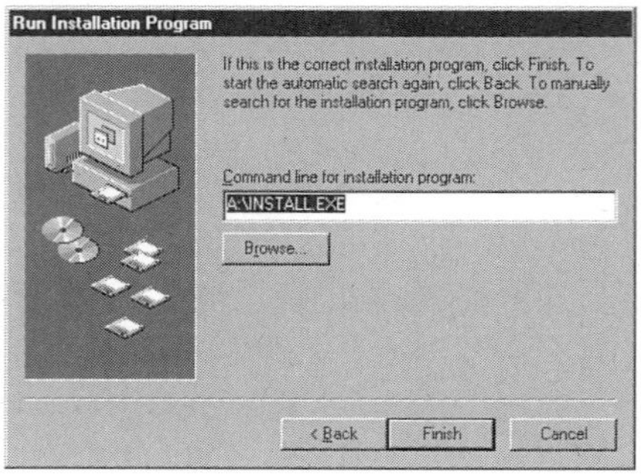

Fig. 18.3 When Windows 95 detects a setup disk, it displays information to let you know what it found.

The command line field in the middle of the dialog box should reflect the command line necessary to install the software. You may want to check the command line against the command line indicated in the documentation for the software. If you need to, you can click on the Browse button to locate a different program to use in the installation routines.

When you're finished with the command line, click on the Finish button. This ends the wizard and starts the setup program for your software. The steps you follow from this point depend on the software you're installing. Different applications have different setup programs that require different user input.

Manually Installing

Whenever possible, you should use the Add/Remove Programs wizard to install a DOS program. There may be times, however, when this is not feasible—for instance, if you get a shareware program from a friend or from a BBS, or you need to install a program you wrote. In most cases, you can directly run the setup or installation program, and Windows will configure an environment just fine. Although this may work in 90 percent of the installations you do, it is not necessarily the safest way to do the installation. In addition, your DOS application may be small enough that it doesn't even have an installation program.

In instances where you must install manually, it is a good idea if you follow these general steps:

1. Create a folder for the DOS program.
2. Copy the files from the floppy disk to the folder.
3. Determine which executable files are in the folder; write down their names on a piece of paper.
4. Right-click on the icon for an executable file.
5. Choose Properties from the context menu; the Properties sheet appears for the application.
6. Set the memory, screen, and other attributes particular to this executable file.
7. Click on the OK button.
8. Repeat steps 4 through 7 for every executable file in the folder, even the setup program and any batch files.

To complete step 6, you may need to refer to your program documentation for information about special needs of the program. Such information could be in the system requirements, technical notes, or troubleshooting sections of the manual. If you need help with setting the properties for the files, you can refer to Chapter 19, "Fine-Tuning Windows 95 for Your DOS Applications."

Once these steps are complete, you have a good chance of successfully running both the setup program (if there is one) and the application itself.

After Installation

After you're through installing your DOS software, and it has been copied to your disk drive, you're ready to use it. You may want to take the time to create a shortcut to access the program, however. Regardless of whether you install by using the wizard or do it manually, Windows 95 doesn't create shortcuts for DOS programs, nor does it make them available through the Start menu.

To make your DOS programs available through either shortcuts or the menu system, refer to Chapter 3, "New Windows 95 Tools," and Chapter 15, "Taking Control of Windows 95 Startup," for information on how to take advantage of these features.

The Application Information File

When you run an MS-DOS program for the first time, including any DOS setup programs, Windows checks the contents of a file called APPS.INF. This file, supplied with Windows 95, is located in the \WINDOWS\INF folder. It contains information on over 400 executable DOS programs, and supplies Windows with the environmental parameters that will allow the program to run the best.

The file is organized the same as any other Microsoft INF file. It contains sections, denoted by key words enclosed in brackets, and each section contains a series of individual entries. The file is divided into three groups of sections, and you can examine it with the WordPad accessory, if you desire. The groups of sections are:

- [PIF95]
- Applications
- [Strings]

Each of these is detailed in the following sections.

The [PIF95] Section

The first section, [PIF95], contains a master list of all the programs for which APPS.INF contains information—over 400 in all. For example, the following is the first part of the [PIF95] section:

```
[PIF95]
123.COM=%123.COM%,moricons.dll,50,,123.COM
123.EXE=%123.EXE.1%,moricons.dll,51,,123.EXE.1,WYSIWYG.APP
123.EXE=%123.EXE.2%,moricons.dll,51,,123.EXE.2,L123SMP3.RI
1942.EXE=%1942.EXE%,moricons.dll,1,,1942.EXE,MPSCOPY.EXE
1942.BAT=%1942.BAT%,moricons.dll,1,,1942.BAT,1942
```

```
ACAD.EXE=%ACAD.EXE%,moricons.dll,16,,ACAD.EXE,ACAD386.BAT
ACAD386.BAT=%ACAD386.BAT%,moricons.dll,16,,ACAD386.BAT,ACAD.EXE
ACCESS.COM=%ACCESS.COM.1%,moricons.dll,95,,ACCESS.COM.1,SYMPHONY.EXE
ACCESS.COM=%ACCESS.COM.2%,moricons.dll,101,,ACCESS.COM.2,ACCESS.MDM,1
ACROBAT.EXE=%ACROBAT.EXE%,moricons.dll,1,,ACROBAT.EXE,ACROMAIN.EXE
AEGIS.EXE=%AEGIS.EXE%,moricons.dll,1,,AEGIS.EXE,ARCTAN.TAB
AEGISV.EXE=%AEGISV.EXE%,moricons.dll,1,,AEGISV.EXE,ARCTAN.TAB
```

Notice that each entry in the section follows a specific format. To the left side of the equal sign is the executable file for the application, and to the right is information about that application. Notice, as well, that there can be more than one entry for a specific executable file. For instance, there are two entries for 123.EXE and for ACCESS.COM. The reason is that different DOS software packages can use the same executable file names for their products.

The information to the right of the equal sign can consist of up to seven fields. These fields, in order, are as follows:

- **Title key.** This is a string identifier that Windows uses to look up the wording that will appear in the title bar of the program's window. The title key is enclosed in percent signs, and ties to an entry in the [Strings] section, as described later.
- **Icon file.** The name of the file from which the icon for the program should be selected. More often than not, this is MORICONS.DLL, the catch-all icons file in Windows.
- **Icon index.** The number of the icon within the icon file. This is an offset within the file, starting at 0. Thus, a value of 51 means that the 52nd icon in the file is used for the program. The default value is 0. When the icon file is MORICONS.DLL, then the default setting appears to be 1 when a specific icon for the application is not available.
- **Working folder flag.** This is a flag that indicates whether Windows 95 can automatically set the working folder for the program. If set to 0 (the default), then setting is allowed; if set to 1, then the folder cannot be set automatically.

- **Section.** This is the name of the section (again, within brackets) of APPS.INF that contains detailed information about the application. The section name is often the same as the executable name that appears to the left of the equal sign, but not always. For instance, the section names for the two ACCESS.COM entries are ACCESS.COM.1 and ACCESS.COM.2. The individual application sections start immediately after the [PIF95] section, and will be discussed shortly.
- **Key file.** This is the name of a file within the program folder that identifies exactly which application this is. For instance, where the executable file can be duplicated (as with 123.EXE), the key file is checked. If a file of the same name is found in the folder, then Windows 95 knows that this is the correct entry for the application, because the two files match.
- **PIF flag.** This is a flag that indicates whether Windows 95 can create a PIF file for the application. If 0 (the default), then a PIF can be created; if 1, then it cannot be created.

The Applications Sections

Immediately following the [PIF95] section is the start of the applications sections. This part of the file consists of multiple sections, one for each application on which information is maintained. The section names are tied to the section field in individual entries within the [PIF95] section. Thus, if the section field within the [PIF95] section is LEARN.EXE.4, then the corresponding section within this part of the file will be [LEARN.EXE.4].

The section for each application contains three or four settings, all of which are optional. The purpose of the section is to indicate special environmental settings that need to be made in order for the program to run correctly under Windows 95. In addition, execution parameters can be indicated for the program.

Entries again consist of a key word, followed by an equal sign, and the settings related to that key word. For instance, the following is a small portion of the applications section:

```
[CCHELP.EXE]
LowMem=524
Enable=dos
Disable=win

[CHART.COM]
LowMem=256
Disable=win

[CKTEST.EXE]
LowMem=512
XMSMem=None
Enable=lml,rvm,dos,gmp
Disable=win,dit,hma,asp,aen

[CHECKIT.EXE]
LowMem=512
XMSMem=None
Enable=lml,rvm,dos,gmp
Disable=win,dit,hma,asp,aen

[CL.EXE.1]
Params="?"
LowMem=384
Enable=dos
Disable=win
```

The key words that can appear to the left of the equal sign can be any of the following:

- AppHack
- BatchFile
- Disable
- DPMIMem
- EMSMem
- Enable
- LowMem

- Params
- XMSMem

Not all key words need to be set for each application. Only those that vary from the default DOS window settings need to be noted. The following sections describe each of the key words.

AppHack

The exact purpose of this setting is not known. It is included in APPS.INF for only seven applications out of over 400. The apparent possible settings for the key word are the numeric values 4, 8, or 16.

BatchFile

This is the name of any batch file that must be run before the program is actually executed. In reality, this can be the name of a batch file or a DOS command that must be executed. There is only one application that has this key word used—for the program MenuWorks, as shown in the following application section:

```
[MW.EXE]
BatchFile="cls"
LowMem=512
Enable=cwe
Disable=win,hma
```

Microsoft indicates that the purpose of the batch file should not be to run the program, but instead to set up the environment in which the program will subsequently run. For instance, you may have a batch file that loads a TSR program necessary for the DOS program. If you were setting the batch file name manually, you would do so in the Properties sheet for the executable file, on the Program tab. The Batch file field on that tab should contain the same information as the BatchFile key word.

Disable

This key word defines attributes of the environment that must be disabled in order for the application to run. These are the same

attributes you can control manually in the Preferences dialog box for the application. (See Chapter 19, "Fine-Tuning Windows 95 for Your DOS Applications.") The attributes to be disabled are listed to the right of the equal sign, separated by commas and no spaces, as in the following application section for the Rules of Engagement 2 program:

```
[RULES2.COM]
LowMem=542
XMSMem=1024
Disable=win,hma
```

The possible attributes that can be used with the Disable key word are shown in Table 18.1. The other information shown in the table is the Property tab used to manually set the attribute, along with the setting on the tab.

Table 18.1 Attribute Meanings for the Disable Key Word

Attribute	Property Tab	Setting
aen	Misc	Alt+Enter
aes	Misc	Alt+Esc
afp	Misc	Fast pasting
aps	Misc	Alt+PrtSc
asp	Misc	Alt+Space
ata	Misc	Alt+Tab
bgd	Misc	Always suspend (Background)
ces	Misc	Ctrl+Esc
dit	Misc	Idle sensitivity
emt	Screen	Fast ROM emulation
hma	Memory	Uses HMA
psc	Misc	PrtSc
win	Screen	Full-screen / Window

DPMIMem

This is the setting for how much DPMI memory should be set aside for the program. It corresponds to the same setting on the Memory tab of the Properties sheet. If not specified, the value defaults to Auto; if set to -1, then the value corresponds to Auto.

EMSMem

This is the setting for how much EMS memory should be set aside for the program. This value can be manually changed on the Memory tab of the Properties sheet, provided there is EMS software installed for Windows 95. For more information, refer to Chapter 9, "Exploiting Memory, Space, and Resources."

Enable

This key word defines attributes of the environment, which must be enabled in order for the application to run; these are attributes that would otherwise be disabled. These are the same attributes you can control manually in the Preferences dialog box for the application. (See Chapter 19, "Fine-Tuning Windows 95 for Your DOS Applications.") The attributes to be enabled are listed to the right of the equal sign, separated by commas and no spaces, as in the following application section for the CheckIt! program:

```
[CHECKIT.EXE]
LowMem=512
XMSMem=None
Enable=lml,rvm,dos,gmp
Disable=win,dit,hma,asp,aen
```

The possible attributes that can be used with the Enable key word are shown in Table 18.2. The other information shown in the table is the Property tab used to manually set the attribute, along with the setting on the tab.

Table 18.2 Attribute Meanings for the Enable Key Word

Attribute	Property Tab	Setting / Meaning
cwe	Program	Close on exit
dos		Real mode
eml	Memory	EMS memory locked
gmp		Global memory protection
lie		
lml	Memory	Protected (conventional memory)
rvm	Screen	Dynamic memory allocation
uus		
xml	Memory	XMS memory locked

LowMem

An indication of how much conventional memory should be set aside for the program. This value can normally be set in the Memory tab of the Properties sheet. If not specified, the value defaults to Auto. The following is an example for BASICA, where the conventional memory is set to only 80 bytes. (BASICA is built in to the ROM on some systems.)

```
[BASICA.EXE]
LowMem=80
Disable=win
```

Params

This key word indicates any command-line parameters needed for the executable file. The parameters are enclosed in quote marks, as in the following example for the Folder Maintenance portion of PCTools:

```
[DM.EXE]
Params="/nf /ngm"
LowMem=330
Disable=win,afp,asp
```

If the parameter is a question mark, then Windows will ask for parameters when the program is run. The following is an example for QuickBASIC:

```
[QBASIC.EXE]
Params="?"
LowMem=330
EMSMem=None
XMSMem=None
Disable=win
```

XMSMem

This is the setting for how much extended (XMS) memory should be set aside for the program. It corresponds to the same setting on the Memory tab of the Properties sheet. If not specified, the value defaults to Auto; if set to -1 then the value corresponds to Auto.

The [Strings] Section

For the purposes of the APPS.INF file, the [Strings] section is used to define the wording that will appear in the title bar of a window. The section consists of a string identifier on the left side of the equal sign, and the actual string on the right side. The following is a small portion of the [Strings] section of the file:

```
[Strings]
123.COM="Lotus 1-2-3"
123.EXE.1="Lotus 1-2-3  2.3 WYSIWYG"
123.EXE.2="Lotus 1-2-3 version 3"
1942.EXE="1942: The Pacific Air War"
1942.BAT="1942: The Pacific Air War"
ACAD.EXE="Autocad"
ACAD386.BAT="Autocad"
ACCESS.COM.1="Symphony (Access)"
ACCESS.COM.2="MS Access for DOS"
ACROBAT.EXE="Adobe Acrobat"
AEGIS.EXE="Aegis: Guardian of the Fleet"
AEGISV.EXE="Aegis: Guardian of the Fleet"
AOD.EXE="Aces of the Deep"
AOD.BAT="Aces of the Deep CD"
ARCHON.EXE="Archon Ultra"
```

```
ARMADA.EXE="Wing Commander - Armada"
ADMIN.EXE="Microsoft Mail - Admin"
AFS.EXE="Chuck Yeager's FlightSim"
AFS.BAT="Chuck Yeager's Flight Simulat"
AFRAID.BAT="Are You Afraid of The Dark?"
AGENDA.EXE="Lotus Agenda"
ARCADE.BAT="Pinball Arcade"
```

Within APPS.INF, the string identifier is used in the [PIF95] section of the file. Each entry there has a title key, which is nothing but a string identifier. The title key points to a string identifier in the [Strings] section, and the corresponding string value is what is used in the title bar text for the application. As an example, the entry for RISE.EXE in the [PIF95] section has a title key of %RISE.EXE%. In the string section, the %RISE.EXE% string identifier corresponds to the text "Rise of the Robots." This is the text that will be used in the title bar.

KILLER 19 WINDOWS 95

Fine-Tuning Windows 95 for Your DOS Applications

by Allen L. Wyatt

When you install your DOS applications, Windows 95 creates an environment in which they can run. You can modify this environment rather easily through adjusting the attributes assigned to a program. This chapter covers the ways you can modify the environment in which your DOS programs are run. Here you will learn the following:

- What happened to the ever-present PIF files used in previous versions of Windows

- How you can change the way the DOS environment is initialized
- What you can do to modify the memory settings for a DOS program
- How the screen settings can be modified
- What tips you can use to avoid problems when running DOS programs

What About the PIF?

In previous versions of Windows, the PIF (program information file) was an integral part of making your DOS programs work correctly within Windows. It was used to define operational parameters for the DOS window created for the program.

The PIF file has not gone away; its maintenance has simply been "absorbed" into the mainstream Windows 95 interface. For instance, there is no longer a PIF Editor program in Windows. Instead, the functions of this program have been assumed by the PIFMGR.DLL, which is called when you choose to edit the properties of either a DOS window or an MS-DOS executable file.

The PIF file is created automatically when you first run a DOS program, and it is assumed to be in the same folder as the executable file. If the PIF file cannot be located, Windows creates one. When creating a PIF file, Windows first checks the APPS.INF file to see if information on the executable file is included there. (Detailed information on APPS.INF is included in Chapter 18, "Installing DOS Applications.") If it is, then the settings there are used for the PIF. If there is no information in APPS.INF on the executable file, then a default PIF is created, based on the file MS-DOS~1.PIF (MS-DOS Prompt.pif).

After the PIF file is created, you can modify it through either of these methods:

- Right-click the icon for the executable file, and then choose Properties from the context menu.

- While the DOS program is running, right-click the title bar for the program window, and then choose Properties from the context menu.

Either method displays the Properties sheet for the program. You can make any changes you want; they will be used the next time you run the program.

Program Initialization

When you open a DOS window, either manually or by running a DOS program, Windows 95 creates a complete environment for that window. You learned about this environment (referred to as a *Virtual Machine*) in Chapter 13, "How Windows 95 Interacts with Software."

While Windows 95 does an admirable job setting up a DOS environment, you can also take charge and configure the environment to your liking. The following sections describe how you can change the way a DOS program is initialized into its environment.

Changing the Environment Variables

Many programs require that environment variables be set in order to work properly. For instance, you may have a DOS program that requires the TEMP variable to be set to a specific location, or the LIB variable to be set to the folder where special library files are located. The easiest way to set environment variables is to follow these steps:

1. Create a batch file that contains the commands to set the necessary environment variables.
2. Open the Properties sheet for the DOS program icon. Make sure that the Program tab is selected, as shown in figure 19.1.
3. In the Batch file field, indicate the path and name of the batch file you created in step 1.
4. Click the OK button.

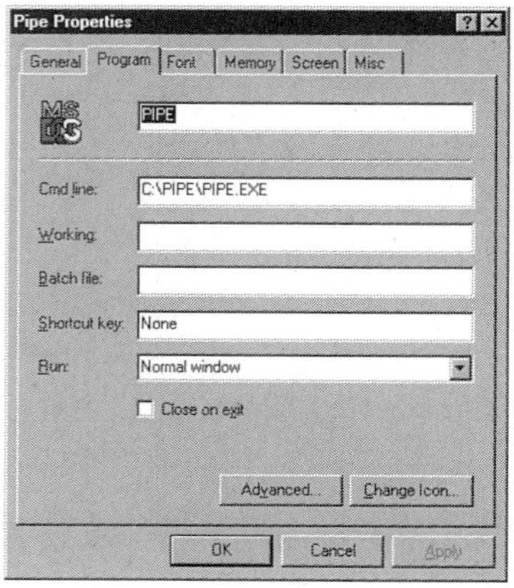

Fig. 19.1 Windows 95 enables you to run a batch file before executing a DOS program.

The next time you run the DOS program, the batch file you created will be run automatically, prior to running the program itself. When you close the DOS window, the environment variable values are discarded.

If you set too many environment variables, you might actually run out of environment space. This condition occurs when the number of DOS environment variables exceeds the amount of memory initially set aside for those variables. In older DOS-based systems, this was overcome with a change to the CONFIG.SYS file. In Windows 95, you can change it by following these steps:

1. Display the Properties sheet for the DOS program in which you want to increase the environment space.
2. Click the Memory tab. The dialog box will look similar to what you see in figure 19.2.
3. In the Initial environment field, use the pull-down list to select the number of bytes to allocate to the environment space. The minimum is 256 bytes; the maximum is 4,096 bytes. If you select Auto, then Windows 95 attempts to make an educated guess as to how much space to allocate.
4. Click the OK button.

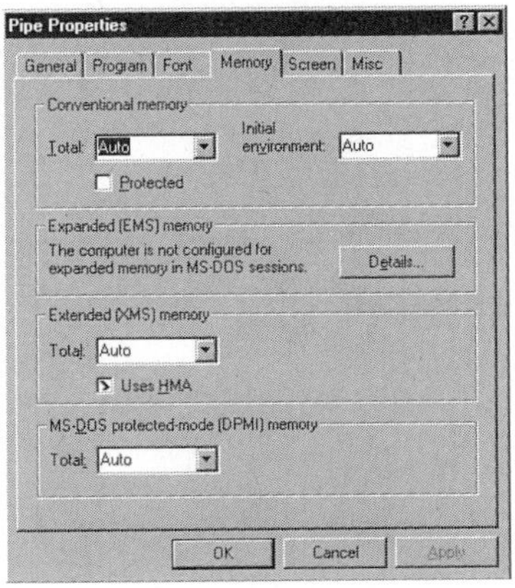

Fig. 19.2 You can use the Memory tab to change the amount of memory dedicated to the environment space in a DOS VM.

Setting the Path

There are two ways you can specify a DOS path. The first is to do it globally, and the other is to do it temporarily. The steps you follow for each of these are covered in the following sections.

Globally Setting the Path

The default path used by Windows 95, whenever you open the MS-DOS window or start a DOS program, is the following:

```
PATH=C:\WINDOWS;C:\WINDOWS\COMMAND
```

Obviously, if you installed Windows 95 in a folder other than C:\WINDOWS, that folder will instead appear in the path command. You can modify this default path by simply adding a path command to the AUTOEXEC.BAT file stored in your root folder. This file will be appended to the default path whenever you start Windows 95, and it becomes the default path for all DOS windows you open after that.

After you have changed the path, restart Windows 95. You can then open an MS-DOS window to make sure that the change has indeed occurred. For instance, I changed my AUTOEXEC.BAT file so that it contained a single line:

```
path=d:\
```

When I restarted Windows, opened an MS-DOS window, and issued the path command, the following was shown as the path:

```
PATH=C:\WINDOWS;C:\WINDOWS\COMMAND;D:\
```

Temporarily Setting the Path

You can temporarily set the path used with a particular program by setting it within a batch file that is run prior to running the program. To do this, follow the steps outlined earlier in this chapter, in the section "Changing the Environment Variables." The batch file you create should contain the proper path command to set the path as you need it.

After the batch file is in place and you have set the correct attribute in the Properties sheet, the batch file is executed by Windows 95 just before the corresponding DOS program is run. When the window is closed, the value to which you set the path is discarded.

Setting a Working Folder

Many programs enable you to work faster if you can start the program in a specific folder. For instance, if you are using a DOS word processor, you may want it to start in a folder where your files are located. Windows enables you to specify the folder where the DOS program should begin. To do this, simply display the Properties sheet for the program. Make sure that the Program tab is selected, as shown in figure 19.3.

The Working field is where you specify the path of the working folder you want to use. Simply enter the path of an existing folder, and then click the OK button. The next time you start the DOS program, it will start in the specified folder.

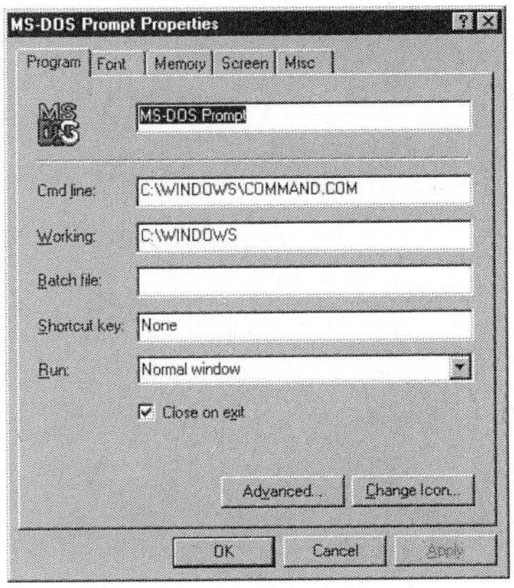

Fig. 19.3 Use the Program tab to indicate the working folder for a DOS program.

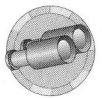

> **Note:** If the DOS program enables you to specify an initial folder within the program, that is where you should set the working folder. If the folder specified in the program is different from the one you specify in the Properties sheet, then the one in the program will be used.

Fine-Tuning Memory

Memory allocation and use for DOS programs can be confusing, to say the least. It is beyond the scope of this chapter to explain the different types of memory which DOS programs can use when running in real mode, but you can refer to Chapter 9, "Exploiting Memory, Space, and Resources," for additional information on the subject.

Windows 95 enables you to have complete control over the type and amount of memory you allocate to a DOS Virtual Machine. The next several sections explain how you can modify each type of memory.

Note: If the PIF file for your DOS program was set up automatically by Windows 95, there is probably very little you need to do to optimize memory. Memory settings are automatically configured when you first run the DOS program. For more information on how this happens, refer to Chapter 18, "Installing DOS Applications."

Conventional Memory

Conventional memory is where the majority of DOS programs actually execute. The reasons for this are long and involved, but suffice it to say that you can consider conventional memory to be "prime real estate" in the memory market.

Windows 95 enables you to allocate various amounts of conventional memory to your DOS applications quickly and easily. You can do this through the Memory tab of the Properties sheet for the application. You can set conventional memory to any multiple of 40K bytes, between 40K and 640K. You can also set the conventional memory to Auto, which means that Windows 95 makes the decision about what setting to use.

To change the conventional memory setting, follow these steps:

1. Display the Properties sheet for the DOS program in which you want to change conventional memory allocation.
2. Click the Memory tab. The dialog box will look similar to what you see in figure 19.4.
3. At the top of the dialog box, in the Total field, set the amount of conventional memory to use for the program. If you are in doubt, set it either to Auto or to 640.
4. Click on the OK button.

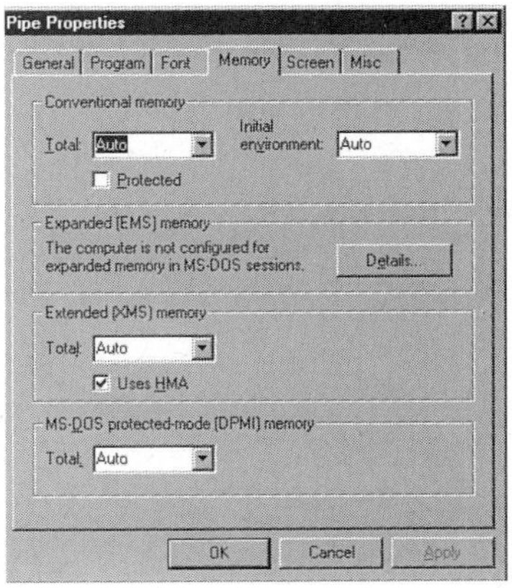

Fig. 19.4 Use the Memory tab to change the memory configuration for a DOS program.

Expanded Memory

Expanded memory (EMS) is a type of memory used by some older DOS programs. Typically it is used for large blocks of data that cannot fit into the 640K maximum of conventional memory. Special accessing functions were used to work with this memory, and special drivers or memory managers were required.

To use EMS memory with Windows 95, you must have a real-mode memory manager installed in the system. You must perform this installation according to the instructions of your memory manager software. It will involve changing or creating the CONFIG.SYS file and then restarting your system. After the memory manager is correctly installed, Windows will automatically make EMS memory available as your DOS programs need it.

Extended Memory

Extended memory (XMS) is a memory specification that came into popularity about two years after EMS. Most of the DOS programs in use today will utilize XMS memory in preference to EMS memory. The

XMS specification is more flexible in how it allows memory to be accessed, and to what uses the memory can be put.

To change the amount of XMS memory allocated to the DOS Virtual Machine by Windows 95, follow these steps:

1. Display the Properties sheet for the DOS program in which you want to change XMS memory allocation.
2. Click the Memory tab. The dialog box will look similar to what is shown earlier in figure 19.4.
3. Toward the bottom of the dialog box, in the Total field, set the XMS memory limit to impose on the program. You can pick any value between 1M (1024K) and 16M (16384K) in 1M increments. You can also set the value to None or Auto. If you choose the latter, then Windows 95 places no limit on the amount of XMS memory used by the program.
4. Select the Uses HMA check box if your program utilizes the high memory area just under the 1M memory boundary.
5. Click on the OK button.

If your program seems to be having problems working with extended memory, change the XMS setting to a value such as 8192 or lower. (Some programs have a hard time utilizing more than 8M of XMS.)

DPMI Memory

As hardware advances became more frequent, and memory more prolific in the advanced machines, a new memory specification emerged which allowed DOS to take advantage of protected mode operation. This specification was called DPMI, or DOS protected-mode interface. This specification was supported in Windows 3.x, as well as several commercial memory managers.

Some software on the market required the presence of DPMI functions in order to work. This is particularly true of high-end software such as CAD software. If your software requires such memory, then you should

try to leave the setting at Auto (the default). With this setting, Windows 95 makes up to 16M of DPMI memory available to a DOS program, as needed.

It is possible that your software will not work properly with an essentially unlimited supply of DPMI memory. If this is the case, you can change the DPMI setting by following these steps:

1. Display the Properties sheet for the DOS program in which you want to change DPMI memory allocation.
2. Click the Memory tab. The dialog box will look similar to what is shown earlier in figure 19.4.
3. Toward the bottom of the dialog box, in the Total: field, set the DPMI memory limit to impose on the program. You can pick any value between 1M (1024K) and 16M (16384K) in 1M increments.
4. Click on the OK button.

Video Memory Use

Your video system uses memory routinely to display graphics, text, and other information in the DOS window. You can modify the way your video system uses video memory by displaying the Properties sheet and then clicking the Screen tab. The dialog box should appear as shown in figure 19.5.

At the bottom of the dialog box, in the Performance area, are two check boxes. These settings come into play when you are not running the DOS program in full-screen mode; in other words, it is running in a window on your desktop. The first setting, Fast ROM Emulation, causes Windows 95 to move the ROM instructions into faster RAM memory. This utilizes a few more memory resources, but it also causes text and some graphics to be displayed faster; how you set the option is up to you.

The other setting, Dynamic Memory Allocation, controls how Windows allocates screen display memory. If the check box is selected, then Windows is free to use the screen memory area as necessary (and as appropriate) for the DOS program. If the check box is cleared, then the maximum amount of memory necessary for the screen display is always reserved for the program, and is therefore not available to other programs. Clearing this check box may speed up the DOS program running in the window, but it may also slow down any other programs you have running in Windows 95.

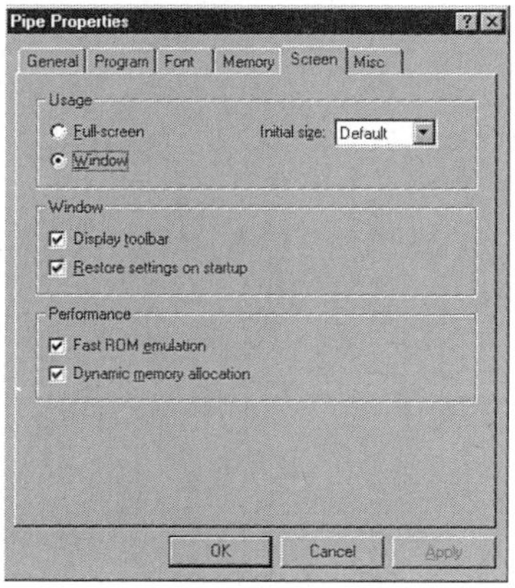

Fig. 19.5 The Performance area of the Screen tab enables you to control how Windows 95 uses video memory.

Fine-Tuning the Screen

One of the traditional areas where DOS programs have had problems in Windows is in displaying all text and graphics faithfully and without problem. Windows 95 has solved the traditional problems; you can now display virtually anything in a DOS window with no adverse side effects.

Windows 95 gives you a great deal of control over how the display screen is used in a DOS window. The following sections discuss how you can configure Windows 95 in order to get your DOS displays exactly the way you want them.

Changing Fonts

Windows includes fully scaleable windows for running DOS programs. This means that you can pick any size window you want; Windows will simply modify the size of the font to fit the requested information in the available space. Conversely, if you pick a different font size, then Windows adjusts the size of the DOS window so that all the information can be displayed.

The easiest way to change fonts in a DOS window is to simply select a font from the pull-down list on the toolbar. Both bitmapped system fonts and TrueType fonts are displayed. You can pick the one you want, and Windows makes the change right away. (For more information on how the font technology works, refer to Chapter 22, "Working with Fonts.")

You can also change fonts by using the Properties sheet. This dialog box enables you to indicate the default font (and subsequent window size) that should be used when you first start a DOS program. To change fonts in this manner, follow these steps:

1. Display the Properties sheet for the DOS program.
2. Click the Font tab. The dialog box will look similar to what you see in figure 19.6.

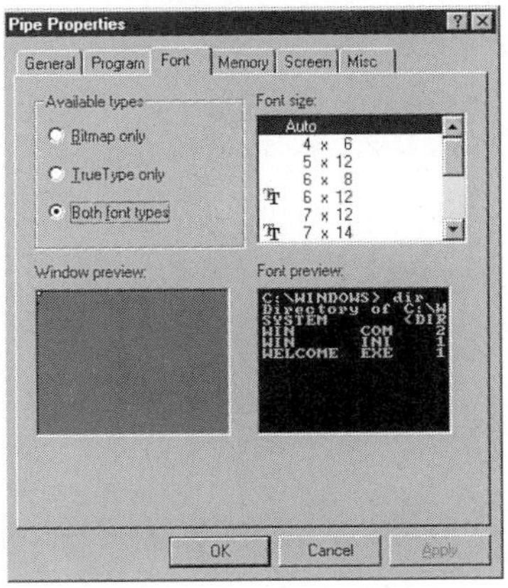

Fig. 19.6 Use the Font tab to specify the initial font used in a DOS window.

3. In the Available types area (upper-left corner of the dialog box), select the type of fonts that Windows should make available.
4. In the Font Size list, select the font size to use. The numbers indicate the number of pixels used to make each character. A TT symbol to the left of a particular font size indicates that the font is a TrueType font.

As you make changes, you can see at the bottom of the dialog box how text will appear within the DOS window. When you are satisfied with your changes, click the OK button.

Text-Mode Lines

Some text-based DOS software is designed to run best in a "nonstandard" screen size. The standard text screen is 80 characters wide by 25 lines deep; Windows 95 enables you to specify that a different line count should be used. You can pick from four settings:

- **Default.** Windows 95 will use whatever it detects as the value the program uses. Typically, this is the best choice to make.
- **25 lines.** The initial screen size is set to 25 lines deep. This is the normal size of a DOS text screen.
- **43 lines.** The initial screen size is set to 43 lines. This allows 72% more information in the DOS window at a time.
- **50 lines.** The initial screen size is set to 50 lines, which is 100% more information than normal.

To change the initial line count used by Windows 95, follow these steps:

1. Display the Properties sheet for the DOS program.
2. Click the Screen tab. The dialog box will look similar to what you see in figure 19.7.
3. Change the Initial Size field to reflect the number of lines you want Windows 95 to use in the DOS window.
4. Click the OK button.

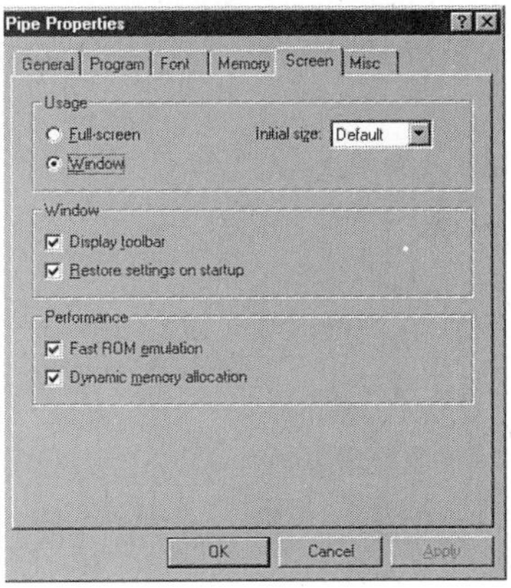

Fig. 19.7 Use the Screen tab to modify the initial screen settings for the DOS window.

When you are through changing the initial number of lines on the screen, you may want to change the font size. Different font sizes look different with various line counts.

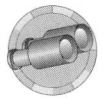

> **Note:** Understand that regardless of what you instruct Windows 95 to set as the initial line count, it is possible that your DOS software could reset the value to some other size.

Adjusting Screen Size

As you may already have surmised, Windows 95 provides you with complete control over the size of your DOS window. You can indicate an initial screen size in the Properties sheet, and then you can modify the screen size while you are using the program.

To set the initial screen size, open the Properties sheet for the program. Make sure that the Program dialog box is displayed, as shown in figure 19.8.

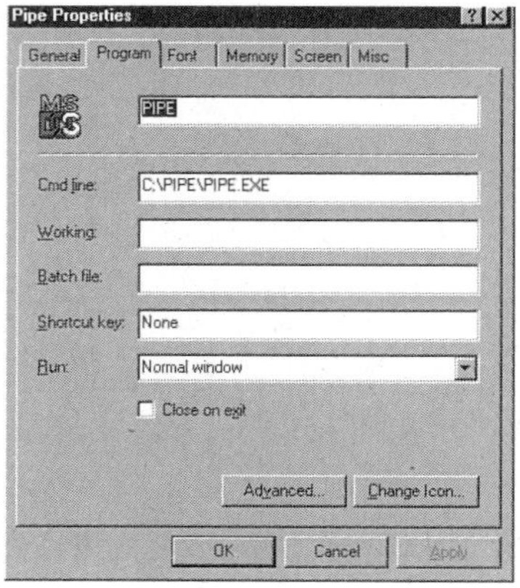

Fig. 19.8 The Program tab is where you indicate how the DOS program should initially run.

In the Run field, at the bottom of the dialog box, use the pull-down list to indicate how you want this DOS window to be opened. There are three choices:

- **Normal window**. The DOS window will simply be another window on the desktop.
- **Minimized**. The DOS window will be minimized to a button on the taskbar.
- **Maximized**. The DOS window will occupy the entire screen.

Notice that this is for the initial size of the screen; you can always change it after Windows 95 has created the DOS window. There are other settings, however, that enable you to indicate how the DOS program should use the DOS window. You can access this configuration area by clicking the Screen tab of the Properties sheet. (This tab was shown earlier in figure 19.7.)

At the top of the dialog box are two buttons in the Usage area; one is Full-screen, and the other is Window. These are mutually exclusive buttons—you can pick only one or the other. If you pick the Window button, then the DOS program can run in a window on the desktop, and the settings you made on the Program tab will be meaningful.

This setting is best for programs that use predominantly text screens. The other setting, Full-screen, is best for graphics programs, such as games. With this setting selected, the DOS window takes the entire screen, and you cannot reduce the window to take only part of the screen.

Finally, in the Window portion of the Screen tab you can indicate whether the DOS window toolbar is visible. If you clear the Display Toolbar check box, then the toolbar is not available. You may want to do this if you need the maximum window area for your program, or if you simply do not use the toolbar.

Other Fine-Tuning

The final group of DOS program settings is a hodgepodge of miscellaneous items. This is not to say that they are unimportant; on the contrary, these settings can greatly affect the use of your DOS programs. The following sections take a look at each of the other settings you can make to change your DOS window configuration.

Adjusting Multitasking

In the system architecture used by Windows 95, a DOS window normally receives as much attention as any other program window. You can modify how the operating system treats your DOS program, however. You do this from the Properties sheet for the program. Simply display the dialog box, and then click the Misc tab. The dialog box appears as shown in figure 19.9.

The first item you should pay attention to is the Always Suspend check box. Normally this check box is cleared, which means that when the window in which the DOS program is running is not in the foreground, it is treated like any other program window. If you select the check box, then whenever the program window is not in the foreground, the DOS program is suspended. In other words, this check box is a way to pause your DOS program whenever its window is not active.

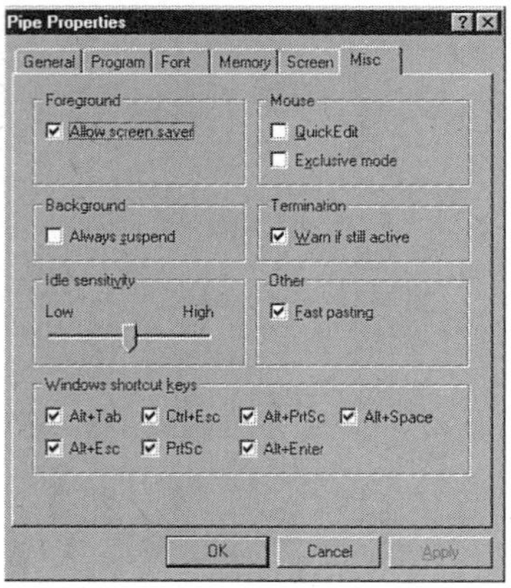

Fig. 19.9 You can use the Misc tab to control the multitasking attributes of a DOS program.

Also on this tab is the slider bar labeled Idle Sensitivity. This slider bar controls how Windows treats the DOS program when it is waiting for keyboard input. The lower the idle sensitivity, the longer the DOS program can run before Windows starts allocating resources to other tasks. Conversely, the higher the idle sensitivity, the shorter the time allowed before reallocation occurs.

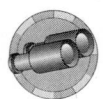

> **Note:** You should only adjust the idle sensitivity if you feel the program in the DOS window is not executing fast enough. When you move the slider toward the Low setting (meaning your DOS program holds on to resources longer when it is idle), your other Windows programs may run slower than otherwise.

The final setting that affects the multitasking rules which Windows applies to the DOS program is the Fast Pasting check box. This setting controls how Windows pastes information into the DOS window. If the check box is selected, then Windows pastes information into the DOS window just as fast as it does in any other program window. Most DOS programs can accept information at this rate, but some cannot. You

should clear this check box if you try pasting something into your DOS program and it does not paste properly.

Using a Mouse Under DOS

Normally, the mouse works just about the same in a DOS window as it does in any other window. I say "just about" because there are a few subtle differences that can affect how you work. The first involves using the mouse for editing.

In a Windows program, you can generally use the mouse to do editing tasks. Primarily, you can use the mouse to select text for a subsequent action (such as cutting or copying to the Clipboard). By default, you cannot use the mouse to select text in a DOS window. Instead, you must use the Mark command from the DOS window toolbar. The reason for this is that most DOS programs do not recognize the use of the mouse for this purpose. However, if you find yourself copying a lot of information within a DOS window or between a DOS window and another program, you can instruct Windows 95 to allow the mouse to be used for selecting text. To do this, follow these steps:

1. Display the Properties sheet for the DOS program in which you want this mouse capability enabled.
2. Click the Misc tab. The dialog box will look similar to what you see in figure 19.10.
3. Select the QuickEdit check box.

From this dialog box you can also modify whether the mouse should work only in the DOS window or whether it can be used in other windows, as well. If you select the Exclusive Mode check box, then the mouse will be available only in this program window, and in no others. This seems like an odd attribute because using Windows 95 without the mouse is even harder than in previous versions of Windows.

When you finish configuring your mouse, click the OK button to close the dialog box.

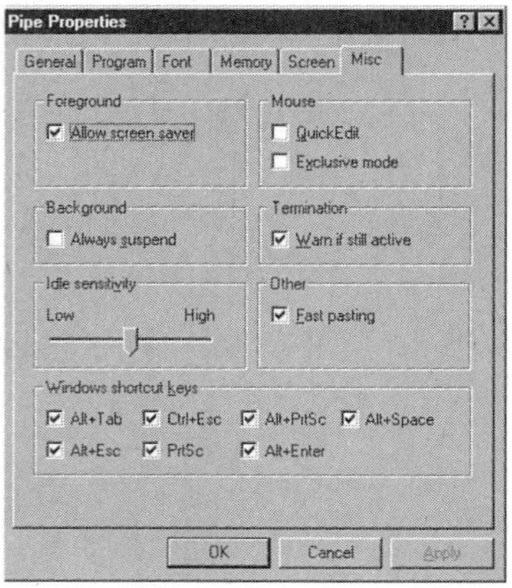

Fig. 19.10 Use the Misc tab to change the settings for how the mouse is used in a DOS window.

Shortcut Keys

Windows 95 uses a standard group of shortcut keys for system operations, which are used for moving between windows, controlling windows, and similar functions. These shortcut keys and their purposes are listed in Table 19.1.

Table 19.1 Windows 95 Shortcut Keys

Key	Purpose
Alt+Tab	Switch between Windows 95 tasks
Alt+Esc	Cycle through tasks in the order they were started
Ctrl+Esc	Display the Start menu
PrintScreen	Copy contents of the screen to the Clipboard (screen capture)
Alt+PrintScreen	Copy contents of the active window to the Clipboard
Alt+Enter	Switch between full screen and window operation
Alt+Spacebar	Display the window's System menu

While these shortcut keys work great in Windows programs, they can cause conflicts in some DOS programs. Normally, the purpose of the shortcut keys according to Windows takes precedence. However, you may want some of these keys to assume their designed purpose within the DOS program. To control how these keys work for your DOS program, follow these steps:

1. Display the Properties sheet for the DOS program in which you want to modify the shortcut keys.

2. Click the Misc tab. The dialog box will look similar to what you see in figure 19.11.

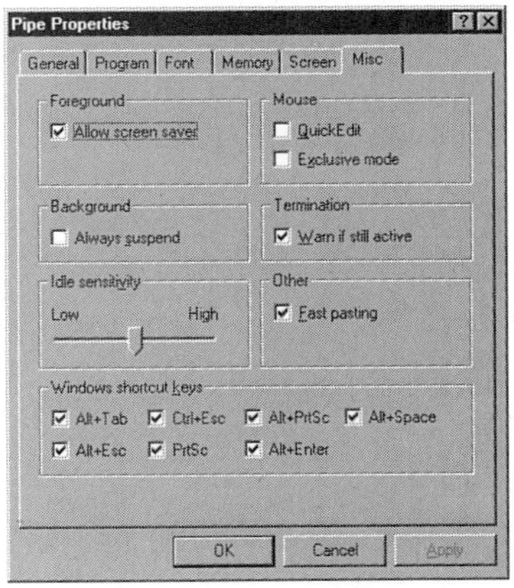

Fig. 19.11 You can use the Misc tab to modify how shortcut keys behave in a DOS window.

3. At the bottom of the screen is an area called Windows Shortcut Keys, which contains check boxes for seven keys. If a check box is selected, Windows rules take precedence; if it is cleared, then the DOS program's rules are in effect.

4. Change the settings for the shortcut keys as desired.

5. Click the OK button to close the dialog box.

MS-DOS Safety Tips

If you run MS-DOS programs under Windows 95, the relationship between the program and the operating system is strange and sometimes twisted. Granted, many of the quirks and work-arounds necessary in previous versions of Windows have been eliminated, but there are still some present. When you run MS-DOS programs, there are some pointers you will still want to keep in mind. The following sections address some potentially thorny issues.

The Registry

It is safe to say that DOS applications know nothing about the Windows 95 Registry. The Registry is so new that even "Windows aware" DOS programs have not had time to catch up. This may change in the future, but in the short term could cause a problem or two.

If you use a DOS program that was designed to work with a previous version of Windows, it may save some of its configuration information in the various INI files for which Windows 3.x was famous. Likewise, the program may count on finding some information in those files.

You should become familiar with how the DOS program interacts with Windows INI files. If DOS saves information in the INI files, you will not want to delete them, even though Windows 95 does not need them. To get around the problem of the program expecting to read information from the INI files, Windows 95 includes abbreviated WIN.INI and SYSTEM.INI files. These files contain only a limited amount of information, such as settings for the screen colors or the display resolution. If your program expects more information than this, chances are good that it will not work properly under Windows 95.

Disk Utilities

There are hundreds, if not thousands, of disk utilities that run under DOS. These do everything from defragmenting your disk to adding long file name capabilities. You should not run any such program under Windows 95. If you do, you run the risk of damaging the file system.

The biggest potential for corruption is with long file names. Windows 95 uses a new method of storing long file names, as described in Chapter 2, "Under-the-Hood Improvements." Your DOS program knows nothing about the changes necessary to implement the long file names. If you run the program, it may see the changes and assume that they are errors in the file structure. If the program "fixes" the perceived errors, then you will lose all your long file names.

Managing Your Printers

by Allen L. Wyatt and Bill Lawrence

Perhaps you are using Windows 95 in a single-user environment, where you are simply working with your computer in your home office. You have an inkjet printer, and you spend your day writing letters and preparing proposals. Or, perhaps you work in a large office, with your own printer and access to three other printers over a network. Either way, you need to be concerned with an important task—*managing your printers.*

Windows 95 makes it easy to manage printers. In fact, it is a much easier task than it used to be in previous versions of Windows. Now you can perform all your management chores from a single area, with only a few commands. This chapter will teach you the skills you need in order to manage your printers. Here you will learn the following:

- How to use the Printers folder
- How to add printers to Windows 95

- ➤ How to change printer properties
- ➤ How to remove a printer from Windows 95
- ➤ How to make your printer available over a network

Using the Printers Folder

Within Windows 95, all printer management occurs in the Printers folder. This folder is a special area that contains the printer drivers for your system. You can access the Printers folder by choosing Settings from the Start menu. This displays the Settings menu, from which you should choose the Printers option. You will then see the Printers folder window, similar to what is shown in figure 20.1.

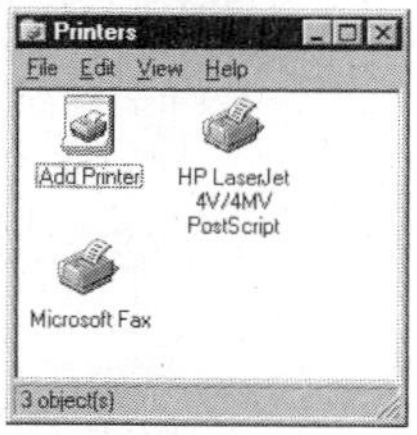

Fig. 20.1 The Printers folder is where you manage your printers.

Notice that the Printers folder contains icons. At a minimum, it will contain one icon—the one for Add Printer. The number and type of other icons it contains will depend on which printers you have installed for use with your system.

At the top of the Printers folder is a menu. Using the options in this menu, you can control how information within the folder appears. If you have used Windows for any length of time, many of these menus and their options should already be familiar:

- ➤ File. These options enable you to control a printer. You can delete or rename a printer, as well as change a printer's properties. This is the menu that is displayed as the context menu for a printer icon (when you right-click a printer icon).

- Edit. These options are basic editing options that apply to what you do within the Printers folder. The options deal with undoing an action, as well as cutting, copying, pasting, and selecting icons.
- View. The View options control how information is displayed within the Printers folder. You can change the size of icons, arrange them, turn the toolbar and status bar on and off, and access the properties for an icon.
- Help. The Help menu displays the various Help options for the folder.

Understanding Printer Drivers

Windows 95 actually prepares printer output using what is called a *printer driver.* Printer drivers contain the specifications and instructions necessary to communicate properly with a printer. These drivers essentially act as intermediaries between your applications, Windows 95, and the printer itself. They work to translate information from the format produced by the application into a format that the printer can understand.

Windows 95 provides direct, out-of-the-box support for over 700 different printers. For those printers that are not supported directly by Windows 95 (such as new printer models that have just entered the market), you can often get a printer driver from the printer manufacturer. Later in this chapter, you will learn how you can use such a disk when installing your printer.

Printer drivers are essential to the proper operation of Windows 95; without them, you could not use your printer with Windows at all. When you add or install a printer, you are actually adding or installing printer drivers. If you later delete a printer, you are deleting nothing but a printer driver. In the next several sections, you will learn how to perform these operations.

Adding a Printer

Adding a new printer in Windows 95 is quite easy. You accomplish this task by using the Add Printer Wizard, whose icon is located in the Printers folder. (In fact, on some systems it may be the only icon in the Printers folder.) To start the Add Printer Wizard, double-click the Add Printer icon.

> **Note:** The Printers folder is not the only place you can start the Add Printer Wizard; it is also indirectly available through the Control Panel. To do this, choose the Add New Hardware applet in the Control Panel, which starts the Add New Hardware Wizard. If you choose to add a printer from within this wizard, the Add Printer Wizard automatically starts.

After you start the Add Printer Wizard, you will see the dialog box shown in figure 20.2. If you were the person who installed Windows 95 on your system, this dialog box may look familiar. The Windows 95 Setup program uses the Add Printer Wizard so that you can specify a printer.

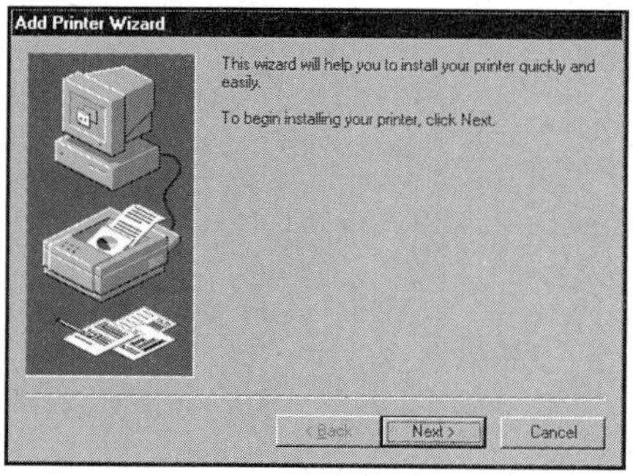

Fig. 20.2 You may already be familiar with the dialog boxes used in the Add Printer Wizard.

The first dialog box in the Add Printer Wizard is nothing more than a welcome screen. Read the information on the dialog box and click the

Next button. This displays the dialog box shown in figure 20.3, where you are asked to specify the type of printer you are adding.

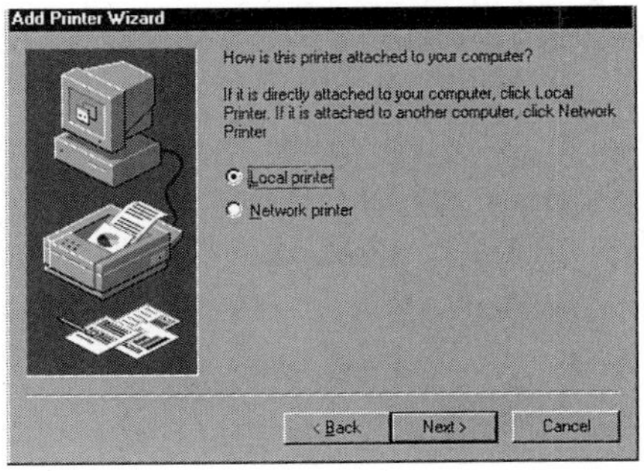

Fig. 20.3 If you're connected to a network, you can specify how your printer connection is made.

If your system is not connected to a network, or you do not have the networking capabilities installed on your system, then you will not see this dialog box. It is only shown if you are connected to a network. With Windows 95, you can print either to a local computer or to one you can access through a network. You should make your choice based on the type of printer you want to install:

- Choose Local Printer if the printer is physically connected to your computer via one of your parallel or serial ports, or if you will be printing to a disk file.
- Choose Network Printer if the printer is connected to a different computer that you can access through a network, or if the printer is connected directly to your network.

Note: The rest of this section assumes you are adding a local printer. If you are connecting to a network printer, you should skip the rest of this section and refer to the following section.

Picking a Type of Printer

After you have indicated whether your printer is connected locally or through a network, you can click the Next button to proceed to the next step. Shortly you will see a dialog box (shown in figure 20.4) that lists the types of printers directly supported by Windows 95.

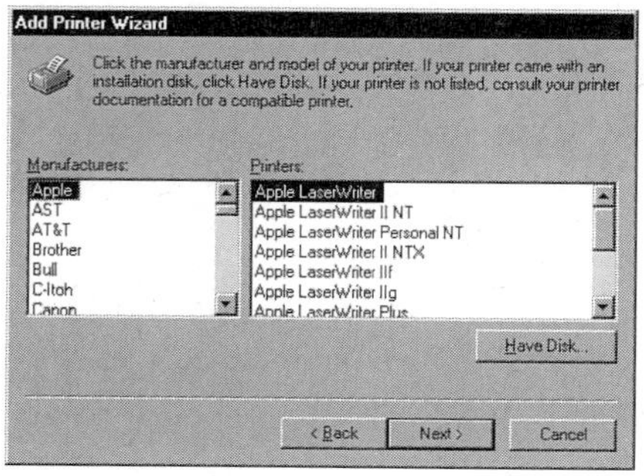

Fig. 20.4 Windows 95 directly supports a wide variety of printers.

In the Manufacturers list of this dialog box, select the manufacturer of your printer. In the Printers list, select the model of printer you want to install. Make sure that you select the manufacturer first, because the information in the Printers list of the dialog box changes whenever you pick a different manufacturer.

Windows 95 directly supports hundreds of different printers. It is possible, however, that you may have a new printer that just came on the market, or one that Windows 95 does not directly support. In this case, you should get a Windows 95 printer driver disk from the company that made your printer. With the disk, you can click the Have Disk button, which enables you to install a printer driver that Windows 95 does not have listed in the dialog box.

Go ahead and make your printer selection based on what is appropriate for your needs. For instance, if you are installing a Lexmark ValueWriter 600, you should choose IBM/Lexmarkin the Manufacturers list, and Lexmark ValueWriter 600 in the Printers list.

Picking a Printer Port

Now that you have specified the type of printer you want to install, click the Next button. The Add Printer Wizard then displays the dialog box shown in figure 20.5.

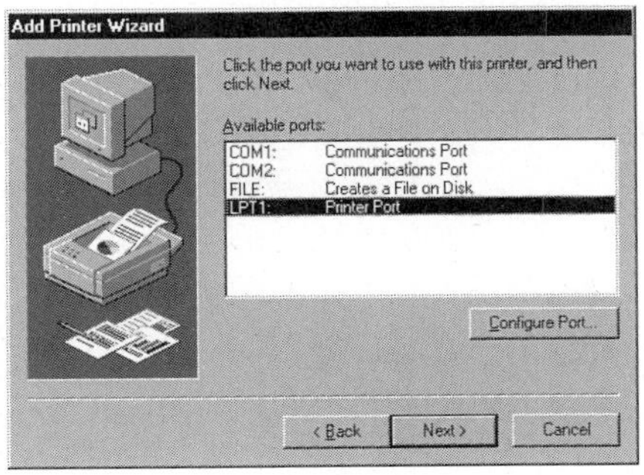

Fig. 20.5 You need to specify how your printer is connected to your system.

In this dialog box you are asked to specify how your printer is connected to your system. Although there are four possible connections listed in this example, your system may have other connections available. Typically, there will be connections for your serial ports (these begin with COM), connections for your parallel ports (these begin with LPT), and a choice for information to be sent to a disk file (FILE).

> **Caution:** Depending on how you have set up your system, you may also have the connections labeled FAX or PUB. These are visible if you have added the Microsoft Exchange portion of Windows 95. You should not choose either of these as your printer connection. Instead, let Microsoft Exchange manage these connections.

The choice you make at this dialog box depends on how your printer is connected to your system. If you are installing a printer that is physically connected to your computer, you should highlight the appropriate port name.

Configuring Your Printer Port

In most instances, you will not need to configure your printer port. The Add Printer Wizard enables you to either check or change the configuration by clicking the Configure Port button. For instance, figure 20.6 shows the dialog box displayed when you have selected LPT1 as your port and you click the button.

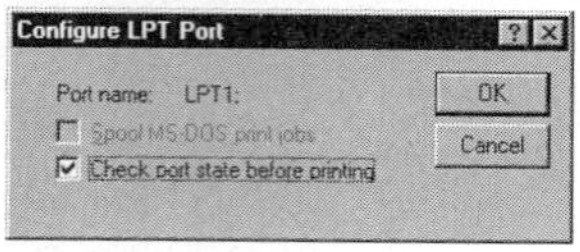

Fig. 20.6 There are not many configuration options available for a parallel port.

Here you can specify whether Windows 95 should use the spooler in managing this printer port when it is used from the MS-DOS window. With the Windows spooler, you can store information in a disk file until it is ready to be received by your printer. By storing information, you can "free up" the computer so that you can get back to using your applications quicker. (The spooler is covered in detail in Chapter 21, "Printing from Windows 95.") In most cases you will want to have the spooler active for DOS print jobs, so you should leave this option selected.

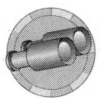

> **Note:** Remember that at this point in the Add Printer Wizard you are configuring the port, not the printer connection. If you make a change in a port's configuration, it is also changed for other printers using the same port. You should only make changes in the default port settings if you have a well-defined need to do so.

You can also specify whether Windows should check the status of the printer port before printing begins. With parallel ports, this is a good idea. For instance, if the printer is off-line, then by forcing Windows to check before printing, you are aware of this fact sooner (and can hopefully correct it).

If you instead are connecting your printer to a serial port, there are quite a few additional configuration options available. Figure 20.7 shows the dialog box displayed when you specify a serial port and click the Configure Port button.

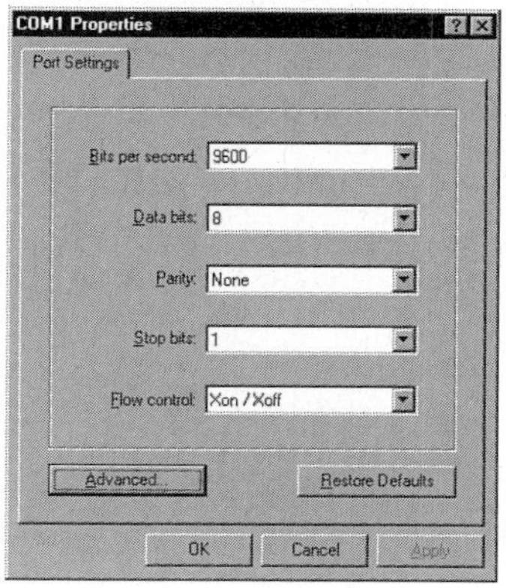

Fig. 20.7 When you connect to a serial port, you must specify how your printer expects communication to occur through the port.

The settings for configuring a serial port relate to how the communications channel should be maintained. In-depth information on serial ports is provided in Chapter 31, "Serial Communications Basics," but there are basically five settings you can control from this dialog box:

- **Bits per second.** This refers to how fast your printer can accept information. Most serial printers operate at 9600 bps, but you should check your printer manual to determine the data rate used by your printer model.
- **Data bits.** When information is sent over a serial connection, it is sent in packets. These packets contain a certain number of data bits, which convey the information to be printed. Normally, PC-based equipment uses eight data bits.
- **Parity.** Some serial connections use a parity bit to provide rudimentary error detection. Possible settings are Even (parity is based on whether there is an even number of data bits set to 1), Odd (opposite of Even), None (parity is not used), Mark (parity bit

is always set to 1), or Space (parity bit is always set to 0). The default is None, which is appropriate for most PC-based equipment.

- **Stop bits.** A communications packet also contains stop bits that mark the end of the packet. Some equipment uses 1.5 or 2 stop bits, but most use the default of 1.
- **Flow control.** This determines how the flow of information over the communications link is managed. The default of Xon/Xoff means that a software signal is used by the printer to indicate when it does not want to receive information, and another software signal to indicate when communication should resume. Hardware flow control means that dedicated wires in the serial cable are used for the same signals. Finally, if None is selected, then information is sent to the printer without pausing. You should check your printer manual to see which type of flow control the printer uses. (Xon/Xoff is the most universal, but Hardware is the most efficient.)

If you are using a serial printer, you should check with your printer manual to see which settings you should use. This is the easiest way, because the number of possible combinations of these five settings is quite high (2,925 possibilities, to be exact). If you do not have the information, then try the default settings (click Restore Defaults); these are the most common serial port settings.

If you click the Advanced button, you will see additional properties available for the serial port, as shown in figure 20.8. This dialog box only has meaning if your serial port uses an advanced UART chip that utilizes a FIFO (first in, first out) buffer. In most instances, you do not need to change these settings. More information on these settings is provided in Chapter 31, "Serial Communications Basics."

When you finish configuring your printer port, you can click the OK button to return to the Add Printer Wizard.

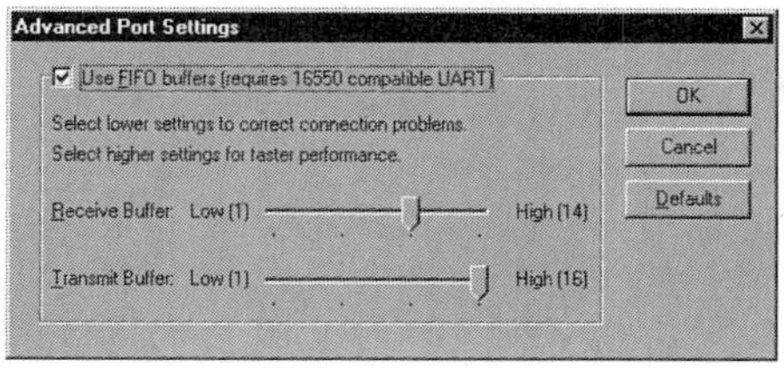

Fig. 20.8 The advanced serial properties control the features of the serial chip used for the port.

Finishing the Installation

When you finish specifying how the printer is connected to your system, click the Next button. The Add Printer Wizard asks you to provide a name for this printer (as shown in figure 20.9). This name can be anything you want, up to 31 characters in length.

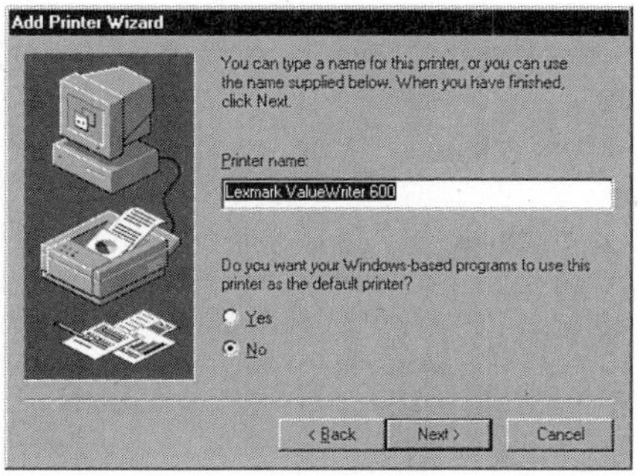

Fig. 20.9 You can specify any name you want for the printer you are adding.

After you have provided a name for your printer, click the Next button. This displays the final dialog box for the Add Printer Wizard, as shown in figure 20.10.

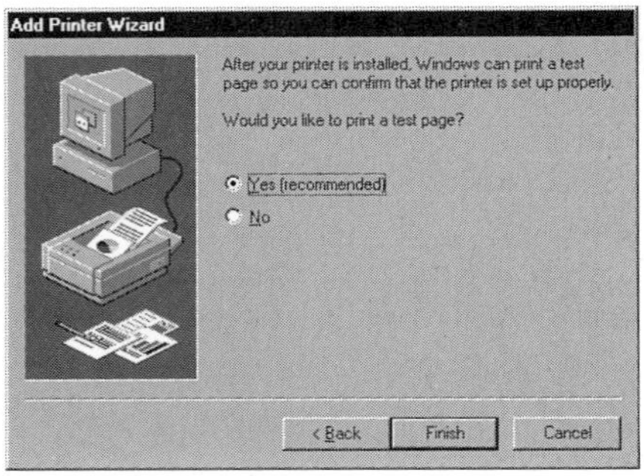

Fig. 20.10 Indicating whether Windows 95 should print a test page is the final step in adding a printer.

In this dialog box, you can indicate whether or not you want Windows to print a test page. If the printer you are installing is connected to a port on your system, you will probably want to click Yes. On the other hand, if your printer output is directed to a file, you will want to select No.

After you click the Finish button, the necessary printer driver is added to Windows 95. You may be asked at this point to supply the Windows 95 program diskettes or CD-ROM. When the driver installation is complete, the test page is generated, if you chose to print one.

When you have completed your printer installation, an icon appears in the Printers folder for your new printer. You can then use the icon to manage the printer, as described later in this chapter.

Adding a Network Printer

Earlier in this chapter, you learned how you can start to add a printer, using the Add Printer Wizard. The second step in the wizard enables you to indicate whether the printer is connected to your computer, or whether you will be accessing it through the network. If you selected the Network printer option, and clicked the Next button, you are ready to continue adding your printer. At this point, you will see the dialog box shown in figure 20.11.

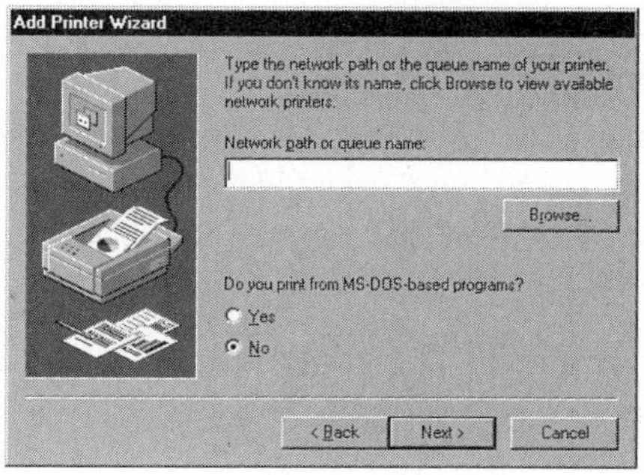

Fig. 20.11 If you are printing through a network, you need to indicate where the printer is located.

In this dialog box you should provide the name of the printer you will be using on the network. This network path is referred to as a *fully qualified network name.* It starts with two backslashes, and describes the route to follow to the printer. For instance, the following is a proper network path name for a printer:

```
\\Allen's Pentium\HPLJ_Net
```

If you do not know the exact path, you can click the Browse button, and choose the printer as you would choose a file in the Explorer.

> **Tip:** If you are still unsure about which printer you should use, check with your network administrator for help.

At the bottom of the dialog box is a place to indicate whether you want to print to this particular network printer from your DOS programs. Normally, DOS programs can only print to local printers—those connected to an LPT or COM port. If you do not use DOS programs, then you can accept the default of No. If you do use DOS programs, then you will want to change the setting to Yes. This causes Windows 95 to map the network printer to a local port. If you fail to do this, you will not be able to access the network printer from within an MS-DOS window.

When you finish providing a path for the printer, click the Next button. The wizard then checks to make sure that the printer you have specified can be selected. What happens next depends on whether the wizard can access the printer:

- If the wizard can access the printer, the wizard attempts to determine information about the printer, which it then uses in the setup steps that follow.
- If the wizard cannot access the printer right away, you are asked if you want to continue. Assuming you do, you are asked to specify the manufacturer and type of printer you are installing.

At this point, the installation procedure continues in a manner very similar to what you have already learned about local printers. When you finish installing the printer, it appears as an icon in your Printers folder. The only difference is that the icon has a network symbol over it, indicating that the printer is not attached to your local computer.

Understanding Printer Compatibility

If you do not have a printer driver available from your printer's manufacturer, and your printer is not directly supported by Windows 95, you may be able to select a different printer driver which is, in fact, compatible with your printer. For instance, many PostScript printers can use the generic PostScript printer driver provided with Windows 95. Likewise, many inkjet or dot-matrix printers provide compatibility with Epson printers.

> **Tip:** Your printer manufacturer, if it cannot provide a printer driver, should be able to direct you as to which compatible printer driver you can use.

Determining printer compatibility is a major source of frustration for many Windows users. For every printer recognized as a standard, you can have even more emulations from which to choose, complicating

the process of configuring and using printers. Novice and experienced users alike will eventually need help to properly install, configure, and troubleshoot a printer driver.

Hewlett-Packard LaserJet and compatible printers normally include Courier and Line Printer typefaces in portrait and landscape orientations. Printers emulating the LaserJet, however, may have not only those customary fonts and sizes, but also a selection of proportional typefaces and additional Courier and Line Printer type sizes.

Some printers even have additional fixed-pitch fonts (such as Prestige Elite and Letter Gothic) not found in standard LaserJet printers. And other laser printers may even emulate dot-matrix printers such as those from Epson or the IBM ProPrinter.

For dot-matrix printers, Epson's FX-86 printer or IBM's ProPrinter are the most common standards emulated by other printers. However, many dot-matrix printers can emulate more than one printer and offer enhanced features above and beyond the level offered by the printer being emulated.

When choosing a printer driver, if the Add Printer Wizard does not specifically list your printer, observe the following guidelines:

- ➤ If your laser printer is compatible with Hewlett-Packard's Printer Control Language (PCL) codes, choose the HP LaserJet+ driver.
- ➤ If your PostScript laser printer is compatible with the Apple LaserWriter (35-font PostScript Page Description Language or similar emulation built-in), choose the Apple LaserWriter or the Apple LaserWriter II driver.
- ➤ If your 9-pin dot-matrix printer is IBM-compatible, try using the IBM/Lexmark ProPrinter or Epson FX-80 drivers.
- ➤ If your 24-pin dot-matrix printer is IBM-compatible, try using the IBM/Lexmark ProPrinter X24 or the Epson LQ-1500 drivers.

➤ You can define your printer in Windows by using the Generic/ Text Only driver or the Unlisted Printer driver. Using these drivers provides plain text printing when you do not have a basic driver available to you for your printer. You can also use these generic drivers in Windows applications for draft printing so that you can quickly print a hard copy of your document or file.

When you are installing a printer driver, and if you are choosing a compatible printer, you may want to specify a printer name that lets you know you chose a compatible driver rather than a native one.

Understanding Printer Icons

After you add printer drivers to Windows 95, they appear as icons in the Printers folder. The appearance of these icons is a big clue to the connection used by the printer. Some of the icons may look familiar, but others may not. There are basically five ways an icon can look in the Printers folder:

 A local printer, connected to either a parallel (LPT) or serial (COM) port.

 A local printer, with output directed to a disk file (FILE).

 A local printer, connected to either a parallel (LPT) or serial (COM) port, that has been shared over the network.

 A printer that is accessed through the network, and is available.

 A printer that is accessed through the network, and is unavailable.

Setting Up Your Printer

After you have installed the printer driver for your printer, you may need to set the parameters by which the printer will operate. Typically, you will only need to set most parameters once, and then Windows will remember them from there on. Other parameters, however, may need to be set based on the type of information you will be printing in the next job.

To set printer properties, open the Printers folder and right-click the printer icon. This displays the context menu for the printer. From this list you can select the Properties option, after which the Properties sheet for the printer will be displayed. Exactly what is included in the dialog box depends on the printer. For instance, figure 20.12 shows an example of how the Properties sheet looks for an HP LaserJet 4V/4MV PostScript printer.

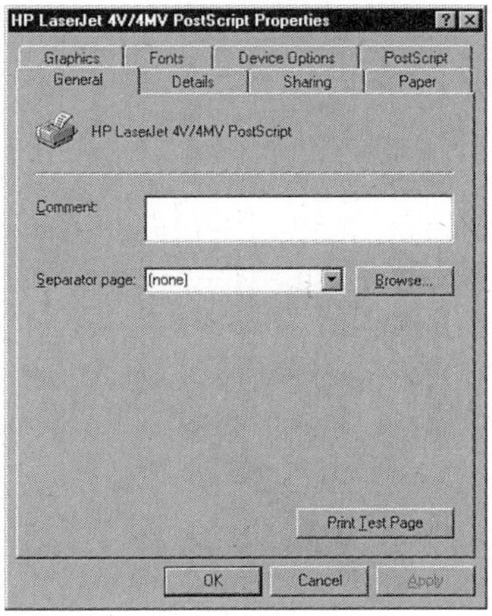

Fig. 20.12 The Properties sheet enables you to set configuration properties for a printer.

This Properties sheet may look rather complex (there are seven tabs for this printer), but remember that the properties displayed for your printer will probably vary. Figure 20.13 shows an example of the same dialog box, but for an IBM ProPrinter XL II.

In general, there are only a limited number of tabs that appear in printer Properties sheets. These tabs represent the general classifications of properties you can control. While the information on each tab may vary, the tabs themselves are fairly constant. (The tabs available may vary, based on your network environment, however.) The following sections cover some of the more common Properties tabs and what you use them for.

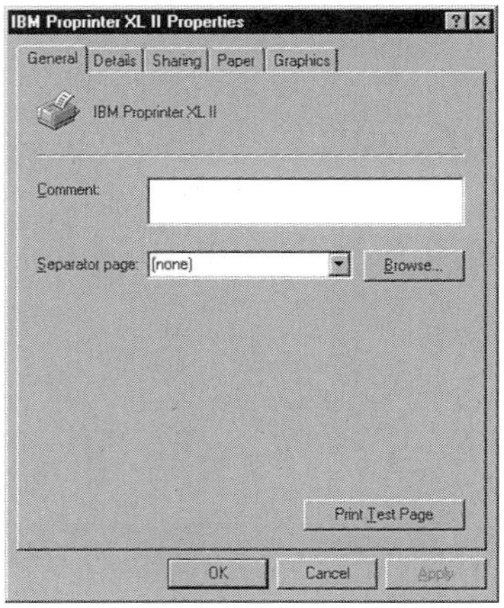

Fig. 20.13 The tabs displayed in the Properties sheet differ widely for different printers.

The General Tab

The General tab is visible when you first open the Properties sheet (as shown in figure 20.13). You use this tab to specify general printer information. For instance, you can indicate comments about your printer in the Comment field. These comments serve two purposes. First, they act as a memory jogger for you about the purpose or setup of a printer driver. Second, the printer comments are transferred over a network to a remote computer if the following conditions are met:

- The printer has been shared on the network.
- The remote user has set up the printer by using the Point and Print feature. (Point and Print is covered in Chapter 21, "Printing from Windows 95.")

This behavior is ideal, then, for supplying printer comments such as the rules under which the printer is available and who the remote user should contact for more information about the printer.

The other primary purpose of the General tab is to indicate whether you want to use a separator page. Separator pages are printed out at the start of each print job, and are used in busy environments to differentiate between jobs from different users. You can only specify this option for local printers attached to your computer. There are four options you can specify for this setting:

- **None.** No separator page is printed.
- **Simple.** A short and sweet separator page that consists of information such as the user's name, the date and time, and the application used to create the print job.
- **Full.** Same as the Simple selection, except more detail about the print job is provided. In addition, some graphic elements are added to the page.
- **Custom.** You can choose a custom separator page by clicking the Browse button and selecting a Windows metafile (.WMF extension) that contains the separator page information.

Clicking the Print Test Page button causes Windows 95 to print a test page to the printer. This test page is the same one you had the opportunity to print when you first installed the printer.

The Details Tab

The Details tab is the nuts and bolts of the printer definition. When you click this tab, the printer Properties sheet appears as shown in figure 20.14. This information in this tab consists of the specifications you made when you first installed the printer driver.

At the top of the dialog box, in the Print to the Following Port field, you can specify how this printer is connected to your system. Earlier in this chapter you learned about the various ports that you can specify for a printer; if you make a change here, you can easily modify the place where printer information is sent.

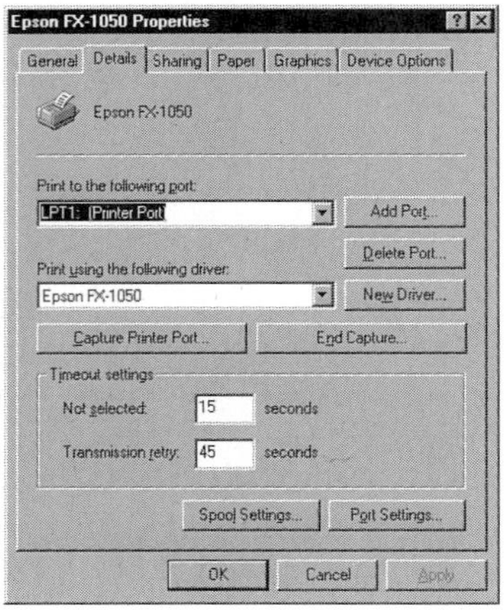

Fig. 20.14 The Details tab is the nuts and bolts of the printer definition.

Adding Ports

On most systems, the ports defined for the computer are fairly stable. Periodically you may add a new printer card or upgrade your serial ports. In such an instance, Windows 95 recognizes the change and modifies your system automatically. However, you may need to physically create a port, such as when you are printing over a network to a remote printer. For instance, suppose that you are working in a networked office environment, and you have been printing to a printer connected to your local printer port (LPT1). If this printer is taken from you and instead connected to a coworker's system down the hall, you need to change the printer port for your printer. To do this, you would click the Add Port button and then you would see the dialog box shown in figure 20.15.

Here, you simply need to click the Browse button and locate the remote printer. Alternatively, you could simply provide the path to the network printer in the field. When you click the OK button, the port is added to the list of available ports on your system.

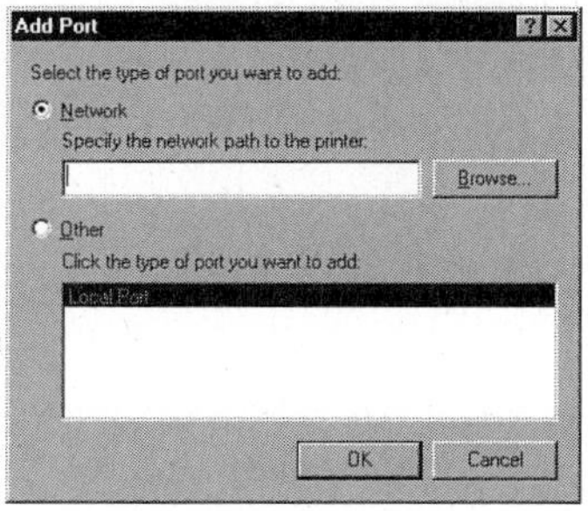

Fig. 20.15 Define a network port with the Add Port dialog box.

Picking a Printer Driver

The Details tab also enables you to indicate which printer driver is used for your printer. (The printer driver was specified when you first installed the printer and indicated a printer make and model.) You can either select from a driver already installed on your system, or click the New Driver button to select a printer make and model.

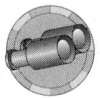

> **Note:** If you pick a different printer driver, the properties for the printer will change to reflect the characteristics of the new printer driver.

Mapping Ports

In the center of the Details tab are two buttons: Capture Printer Port and End Capture. These buttons control the mapping of individual ports to specific network printers. For instance, you can use the Capture Printer Port to capture information destined for LPT1 and redirect it to a remote network printer. When you click the button, you will see the dialog box shown in figure 20.16.

Select the parallel port you want to redirect, and then choose a network path at which the remote printer is located. You can redirect up to nine parallel ports (LPT1 through LPT9). If you do not click the Reconnect at logon check box, then the mapping you are creating is maintained only for your current computer session.

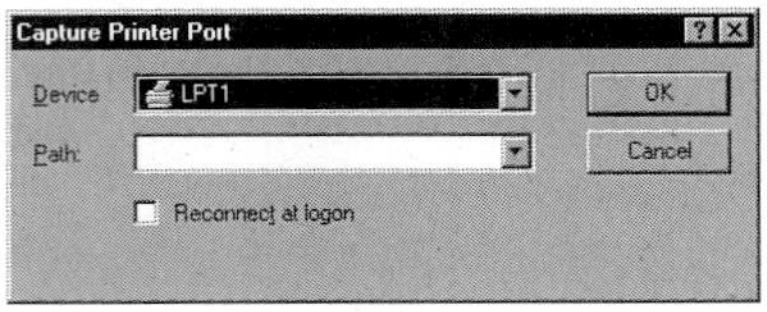

Fig. 20.16 You can redirect up to nine parallel ports in Windows 95.

For much of the software you use under Windows, you will never need to worry about capturing printer ports. Where this comes into play is with DOS programs that do not recognize network ports, but only recognize local ports such as LPT1 or LPT2. In this instance, you will need to redirect the printer information.

If you later want to disassociate a port with a network printer, you would click the Release Printer Port button and select the parallel port you want to disconnect.

Timeout Settings

If you are working with a local printer, you may want to modify the timeout settings at the bottom of the Details tab. There are two settings that indicate, in seconds, how long Windows should wait before it informs you something is wrong. The Not Selected timeout value is used when Windows detects that a printer is off-line. The default value is 45 seconds, which means that Windows will wait 45 seconds before letting you know that the printer is off-line. It is good to have some sort of time lag in here; otherwise Windows gives you no time at all to check and switch the printer status.

The second setting, Transmission Retry, is used to indicate how long Windows should wait before assuming that there is something wrong with the printer. The default, 260 seconds, means that Windows will wait 4 minutes and 20 seconds before determining that the printer is not working. If you know you have a fast printer, then you may want to set this value lower. However, if you get timeout errors periodically because your printer is taking too long to chunk away at a complex file, then you may want to increase the value in this field.

Spool Settings

If you click the Spool Settings button at the bottom of the Details tab, you can modify how this printer functions in relation to the Windows spooler. Detailed information about controlling the spooler is provided in Chapter 21, "Printing from Windows 95."

Port Settings

If you click the Port Settings button at the bottom of the Details tab, you can modify the configuration of your system ports. These are the same settings discussed earlier in the chapter, in the section entitled "Configuring Your Printer Port."

The Device Options Tab

Device options are those features of a printer that make it unique. This tab, more than any other, is intimately tied to the capabilities of the printer. Because of this, the contents of the tab can vary greatly from printer to printer. For instance, figure 20.17 shows an example of this tab for an HP LaserJet 4V/4MV PostScript printer.

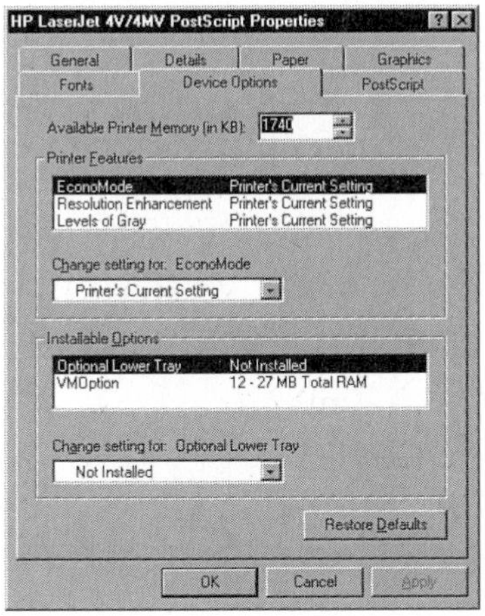

Fig. 20.17 The Device Options tab can vary greatly from printer to printer.

In this particular example, the Device Options tab enables you to indicate the amount of memory in the printer, how EconoMode, Resolution Enhancement, and Levels of Gray are implemented, and what options are installed in the printer. On a different printer, the information available will be different.

The best bet when working with the Device Options tab is to change the settings in it after you understand what your printer can really do. You should review your printer manual and make the changes based on how you want to take advantage of specific features and options.

The Fonts Tab

The purpose of the Fonts tab is to specify how you want TrueType fonts handled by the printer driver. The appearance of the tab will vary, depending on whether the printer is a graphics printer (such as a dot-matrix), a PCL printer (such as an HP), or a PostScript printer. Figure 20.18 shows how this tab appears for a Lexmark ValueWriter 600.

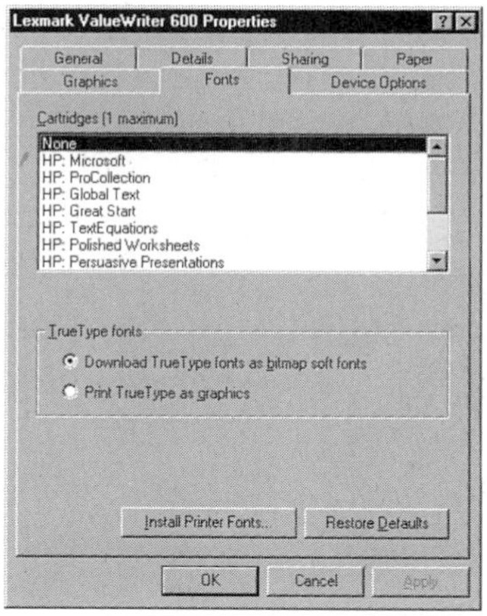

Fig. 20.18 The Fonts tab can differ based on the capabilities of your printer.

At the top of this dialog box you can indicate any font cartridges you have installed in your computer, in the middle you can specify how you want TrueType fonts handled by Windows, and at the bottom is a button that enables you to install printer fonts. Details on how to use the various settings in this tab are covered in Chapter 22, "Working with Fonts."

The Graphics Tab

If your printer is capable of generating graphics, the Graphics tab enables you to specify the quality of the graphics created. Because different printers differ in their graphics capabilities, the appearance of this tab also differs. For instance, figure 20.19 shows how this tab appears for an Epson FX-1050 printer.

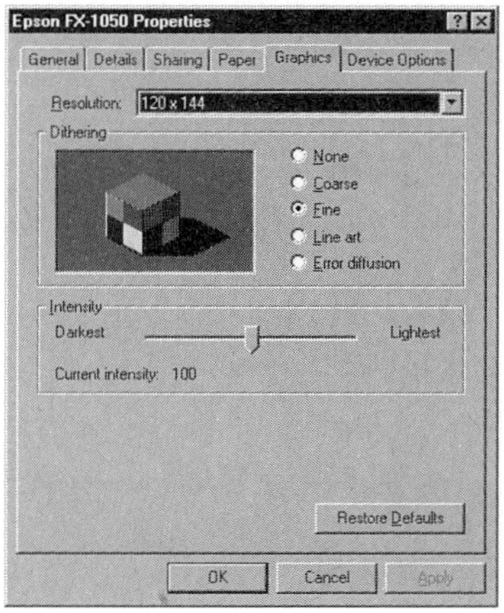

Fig. 20.19 Use the Graphics tab to control how graphics images are printed.

Notice that the graphics resolution indicated at the top of the tab is not real huge; this is a simple dot-matrix printer. In general, the tab enables you to indicate the resolution, dithering (color blending or shading), and the shade intensity for the printer. On PostScript printers, additional high-power settings such as lines per inch and half-tones are also provided. Graphics under Windows 95 is covered in detail in Chapter 23, "Handling Graphics."

The Paper Tab

You use the Paper tab to indicate the type and characteristics of paper used by the printer. For instance, figure 20.20 shows an example of the Paper tab for an HP LaserJet III Si, which is a high-powered network laser printer.

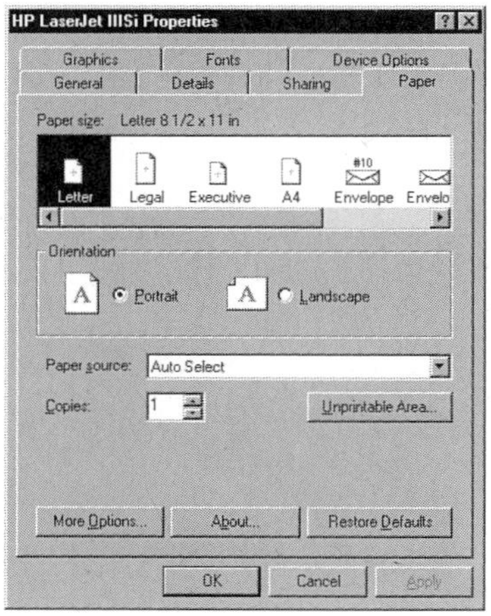

Fig. 20.20 Use the Paper tab to specify the type of paper used by a printer.

The appearance of this tab will vary widely, based on the printer you are using. For instance, some printers can handle 11×17 paper, while others can only handle letter size. Also, notice in figure 20.20 that there is a More Options button at the bottom of the dialog box. With this button, you can specify how options such as duplexing (two-sided printing) should be handled. Because these sorts of options are not available on all printers, they are likewise not available on the Paper tab on some printers.

Most of the settings on the Paper tab are handled automatically by your application software. For instance, if you are using Microsoft Word, it can automatically switch between landscape and portrait printing modes. Thus, there are only a few items that you might manually change on this tab.

One option you might want to change is displayed when you click the Unprintable Area button, as shown in figure 20.21.

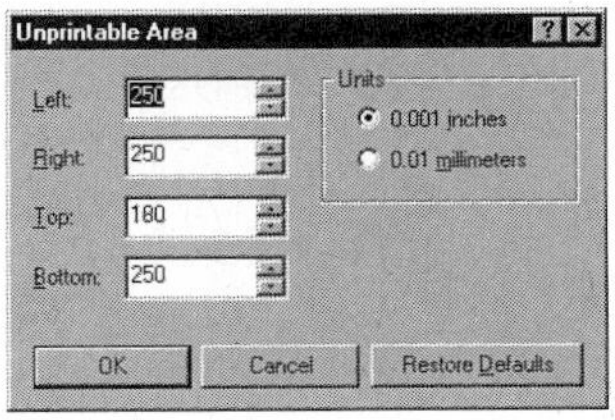

Fig. 20.21 Windows 95 printer drivers enable you to specify the unprintable margins for a piece of paper.

Most printers have an area around the outside of the paper where it is physically impossible for the printer to print. For instance, laser printers typically cannot print within 1/4-inch of the edge of the paper because this is where the printer's paper-handling mechanism grabs and transports the paper. For common printers, Windows 95 already knows what the unprintable area is, but you may need to modify the settings just a bit to get a better quality image. (This will take some trial and error on your part.)

The PostScript Tab

This tab appears only if the printer uses the PostScript language. When you select the tab, you will see the dialog box shown in figure 20.22.

The information on the PostScript tab is used to indicate how PostScript is to be generated for the particular printer, as well as how PostScript errors should be handled. There are several sections to this tab, as described in the following sections.

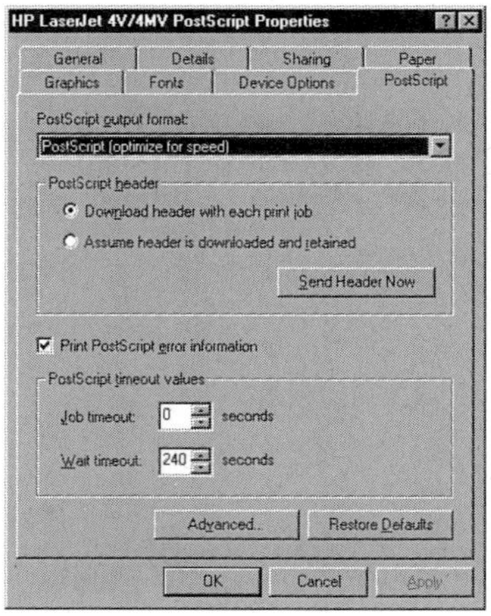

Fig. 20.22 The PostScript tab appears only for printers using the language.

PostScript Output Format

At the top of the tab you can indicate what output format should be used by the printer driver. There are four common formats you can specify in the PostScript Output Format field:

- **PostScript (Optimize for Speed).** This is the default setting, which is most appropriate for printing a document directly on a printer.
- **PostScript (Optimize for PortabilityADSC).** This option is intended for when you are printing to an output file instead of a printer. It utilizes the Adobe Document Structuring Conventions (ADSC), which means that the document is portable from one PostScript device to another. Each page in the output file is a self-contained object that can be processed independent of all others.
- **Encapsulated PostScript (EPS).** This option is intended for use when printing to a file, as well. The output file is in a format suitable for inclusion in other PostScript files; it is essentially a picture that you can use in other documents.

- **Archive Format.** This PostScript format is perhaps the most generic available. It utilizes none of the options of the local output device, so you can use it on differing PostScript equipment quite easily.

PostScript Header

Every PostScript job you print includes a header that has information about the page being printed. The header also includes information about the parameters of the job, the application that created the job, and the fonts being used. In most instances, you only need to download the header at the beginning of a print job; this is the safest way to print a PostScript document, because the information needed for the print job is included with the job.

Even though the default specifies that the header is downloaded for each job, you can indicate that you do not want it downloaded. For instance, you may have an application that sent specialized header commands with a previous print job, and you know they are still retained in the printer. In such a case, you can get faster printer performance by turning off header downloading.

There is also a button in this section of the tab (Send Header Now) that you can use to download the generic header information. It is a good idea to do this at the beginning of a series of similar print jobs, unless you are sure that the header was previously downloaded.

> **Tip:** If you are printing to a networked PostScript printer, you should download the header with each print job. Other people may print jobs in between your jobs, and that can play havoc with the secondary jobs. Downloading the header with the print job overcomes this potential problem.

PostScript Errors

PostScript is a page definition language that only works in full page increments. If you are printing a page, and an error occurs within the middle of the page (for instance, a command is used that your printer does not understand), the normal recourse is for the printer to flush the buffer and discard the page. In such a case, you will not see anything print out. To overcome this, some PostScript printers have the capability to print out the error messages when they occur. Windows 95 also includes such a capability, even if your printer does not.

By default, printer drivers will print error information. If you want, you can turn off the capability by clearing the check box entitled Print PostScript Error Information.

Just below this check box is an area where you can indicate timeout values. The Job Timeout value indicates how long the printer should wait for a print job to be completed before it assumes something is wrong and flushes the job. It is typically best to set this value to 0, which means the printer will wait indefinitely for a job (however long it takes).

The second timeout value is the Wait Timeout. This value specifies how long the printer should wait between pieces of a print job. For instance, if a part of the print job is sent, and then your computer pauses because it is busy doing something else, the idle time is what this timeout value measures. If you are printing complex print jobs, you should set the value fairly high. It is not a good idea, however, to set the Wait Timeout to 0. If you do, the printer will wait forever on a job, even if you have interrupted it (such as by unplugging the printer cable or turning off your computer).

> **Tip:** You should always set the PostScript timeout values lower than the timeout values specified in the Device Options tab.

Advanced Settings

You can access Advanced PostScript settings by clicking the Advanced button at the bottom of the PostScript tab. Doing so displays the Advanced PostScript Options dialog box, as shown in figure 20.23.

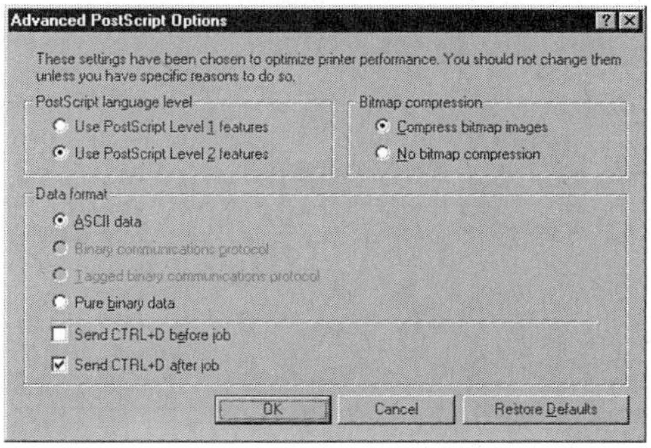

Fig. 20.23 The Advanced PostScript Options dialog box enables you to control low-level PostScript formatting.

In most instances, you should never have to change these options. They are set up for optimal use of your printer when you install the printer driver. When would you need to change them? A good time would be if you upgrade the firmware in your printer. For instance, you may have a printer that Windows 95 believes only understands PostScript Level 1. If you later upgrade your printer to PostScript Level 2, then you should change the language level in the Advanced PostScript Options dialog box. (Doing so will provide better compatibility and greater throughput.)

You may also want to change information when you have a need to create a peculiar PostScript file format. For instance, at the bottom of the dialog box you can indicate when the Ctrl+D character should be sent by the driver. This is the character that signals the end of a printer job, and most often in the PC environment it is sent at the end of the PostScript file. In the UNIX environment, however, the Ctrl+D is expected at the *beginning* of a job. Thus, if you are creating a file that will be used in such an environment, you will need to make the change here.

The Sharing Tab

If you are changing the properties of a local printer and you can share printers over your network, the Sharing tab is available. The tab appears as shown in figure 20.24.

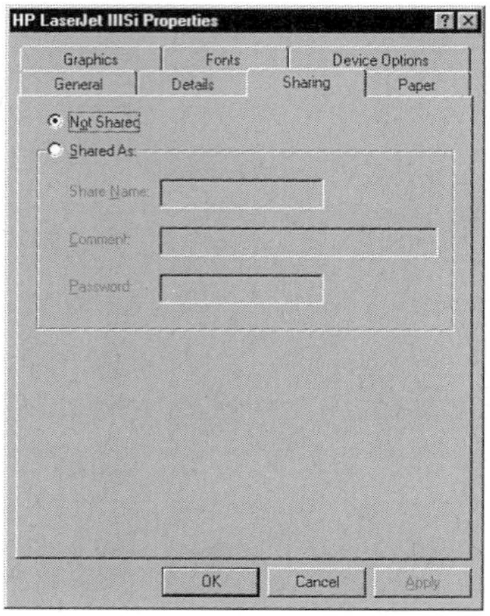

Fig. 20.24 Use the Sharing tab to set up rules for how you want your local printer shared over the network.

There are two primary options on this tab: You can specify that the printer is Not Shared (the default), or choose Shared As, which enables you to specify other sharing options. For instance, you can provide a name for your printer (such as Allen's Printer). This is the name that others will see when they are browsing the network. You can also specify a comment for the printer, which other people also see when browsing through the network. Finally, you can indicate a password that is needed to access the printer over the network.

Information about using a printer over the network is covered later in this chapter.

Deleting a Printer

From time to time you may have a need to delete a printer you previously installed. With Windows 95, deleting a printer is quite simple. All you need to do is follow these steps:

1. Open the Printers folder.
2. Select the icon for the printer you want to delete.
3. Press the Delete key, or choose File, Delete.

At this point, Windows asks you if you really want to delete the printer. If you choose Yes, you are asked another question, as shown in figure 20.25. Although the printer's availability is removed, Windows 95 can still keep the printer driver and related files on your hard disk. Click Yes to remove the driver and related files or No to keep them. Even though you may keep the files, you cannot print to that printer until you reinstall it.

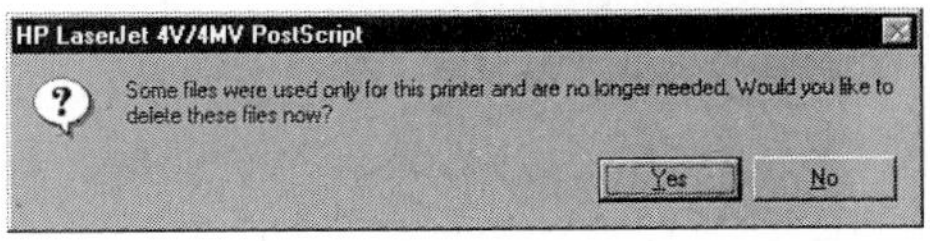

Fig. 20.25 Before actually deleting a printer, Windows asks you whether you want the driver file deleted.

Click Yes, and the files used for the printer driver are removed from your system.

> **Caution:** After you delete a printer, it is deleted for good. The only way to access the printer again is to reinstall it using the Add Printer Wizard, as described earlier in this chapter.

Special Network Considerations

If you have connected to a printer over a network, there are some extra steps and considerations that you may have. Before jumping into these, however, it should be pointed out that printing over a network is no different (from a program's perspective) than printing to a local printer.

The differences that come into play are because network printers are shared resources. This means that there may be a set of rules that govern the use of the resource. For instance, whoever is responsible for the printer may have placed usage restrictions on it. This means that the printer may only be available between certain hours of the day, or that you may need a password to access the printer. If you want a copy of the rules defined for a certain printer, you will need to get them from the person responsible for it.

> **Note:** The types of restrictions that can be placed on a printer depend entirely on the capabilities of the network operating system being used.

This brings us to another topic—what if *you* are the person responsible for a shared printer? How can you share your local printer, and how do you set up rules?

Sharing a Printer

The first step in making your printers available over the network is to make sure that you have installed your printer driver correctly. After installing, you should print a few documents to make sure that everything is working well on the printer.

When you are satisfied with the performance of your printer, you are ready to share it with others. You do this by first opening the Printers folder, and then right-clicking the icon for the printer you want to share. From the context menu, select the Sharing option. This displays the Sharing tab on the Properties sheet for the printer, as shown in figure 20.26.

> **Note:** If there is not a Sharing option on the context menu, or if there is no Sharing tab in the Properties sheet for your printer, then you cannot share printers. Either networking has not been enabled on your computer, or you have not chosen to be able to share printers over the network. For more information, refer to Chapter 37, "Using Windows 95 on a Network."

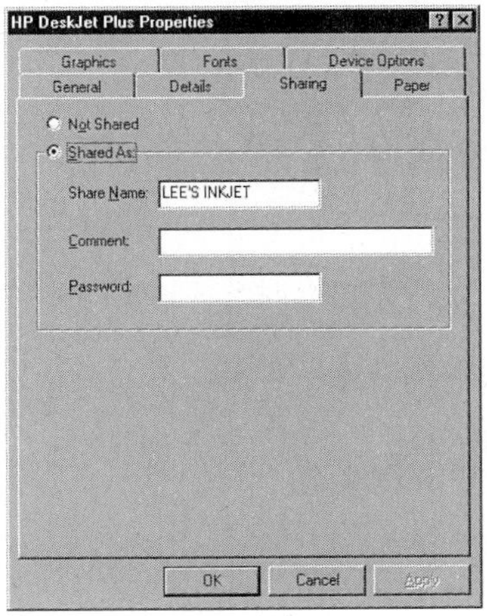

Fig. 20.26 Sharing a printer over the network is an easy task.

At this point, you only need to accomplish two steps. First, click the Shared As radio button. This enables the options in the middle of the dialog box. You can now provide a name, in the Shared Name field, that you want your printer known as on the network. When you finish, click the OK button. Your printer is now available on the network.

Network Printer Properties

After you have made your printer available to others on the network, you have complete control over who can access the printer. With Windows 95, you can specify a password that users must know before they can connect to your printer.

Access restriction is controlled from the Shared tab on the Properties sheet for the printer. Display this by right-clicking the printer icon, and then choosing Sharing from the context menu. Shortly, you will see the dialog box, similar to what is shown in figure 20.27.

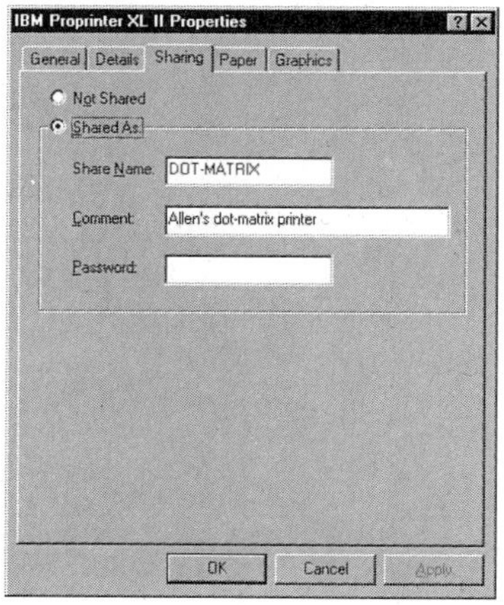

Fig. 20.27 Sharing a printer over the network is an easy task.

Notice that this printer has previously been shared on the network, but there is no password in the Password field. If you enter a password here, then users attempting to connect to the printer will be prompted for a password. If they do not know it, they cannot print to the printer.

Tuning Printing Performance with Shared Printers

When you send a print job to a shared printer, the print job makes a few stops before finally arriving at the printer. By default, the print job first goes to the print spooler on your Windows 95 workstation. The print spooler quickly captures your print job as a file on your hard disk so that your wait time is minimized while the job is printing. Next, the job travels over your network cable system to the print spooler on the workstation where the printer is attached. If you are printing to a dedicated server, this spooler is often called a *print queue.* In the print spooler or queue, the print job is again captured as a file. When the printer is available to print your job, the print job file in the spooler or queue is sent to the printer.

When to Bypass the Local Print Spooler

Windows 95 enables you to control these steps to customize printing performance. Open your printer Properties sheet and click the Details tab. Click the Spool Settings button to display the Spool Settings dialog box. If you want to bypass the local print spooler on your PC and print directly to the print spooler or queue on the PC or server connected to the shared printer, choose the Print Directly to the Printer option. This is a wise choice under two circumstances. When your network is fast and the print queue or spooler for the device connected to your shared printer is also fast and introduces minimal delays, printing directly to the printer will not noticeably slow down the time it takes for your print jobs to finish at your workstation and will result in jobs reaching the shared printer more quickly. The Print Directly to the Printer option also makes sense if most of the programs that you use to print have their own internal background printing feature (this is the case with most Windows-compatible word processors and spreadsheets).

When to Use the Local Print Spooler

If you need your print jobs to finish more quickly at your workstation and are less concerned about how quickly they reach the network shared printer, choose the Spool Print Jobs So Program Finishes Printing Faster setting. When you choose this setting, print jobs go first into the local spooler on your PC before going to the network printer. You can choose two options to customize the behavior of your local spooler. Select Start Printing After Last Page Is Spooled to specify that your spooler will wait until the print job is complete before releasing it to the network printer. Choose Start Printing After First Page Is Spooled to specify that the print job will be released to the network printer as soon as the first page is received. The former option is the safest—some types of graphical jobs may not print correctly if you do not choose this option.

Network Responsibilities

Sharing your printer on the network involves a bit more work than if you are the only one using the printer. If you have shared your printer, then you need to expect that others may use it from time to time. You should expect the following:

- **Delays.** There may be times when you cannot print for a while because someone else's print job is coming through your printer.
- **Interruptions.** If the printer is located in your office, then you will need to put up with people stopping by to pick up their print jobs.
- **Frustration.** There aren't many frustrations associated with having a printer all to yourself. You should expect that you will become frustrated periodically when someone leaves draft copies of documents laying around the printer, or a print job goes unclaimed for a few days. You will need to resist the urge to snap at other people because they do not treat your printer the same way you do.

- **Service needs.** Because there will be more print jobs going through your printer, it will need to be serviced more often. This includes adding paper and changing ribbons, toner, or ink more frequently.

Despite these points, you may still need to share your printer. Simple math lets you know that it is cheaper to share a printer (particularly an expensive or exotic printer) than it is to put that printer on all your co-workers' desks.

21

Printing from Windows 95

by Allen L. Wyatt

In the previous chapter you learned how you can set up printers in Windows 95. Setting up printers is only half the story, however. After setup, you must also learn how to use your printers (within Windows 95) on a daily basis. This chapter provides information you need in order to put your printers to work. Here you will learn the following:

- How the print spooler works to increase your productivity
- How you can create a print job in Windows 95
- How you can manage your print jobs after you create them
- The basics of printing to a network
- What the Point and Print feature of Windows 95 means to network users
- How improvements in Windows 95 benefit your DOS applications.

Using the Print Spooler

If you are familiar with older versions of Windows, you are already familiar with a print spooler—the Print Manager. In Windows 95, the printing process has been completely revamped and rewritten by using 32-bit code. This allows true behind-the-scenes print spooling, improved overall printing performance, and more intelligent management of print jobs.

From a user's perspective, there are many different components in the Windows 95 printing system besides a simple spooler. These components are illustrated in figure 21.1.

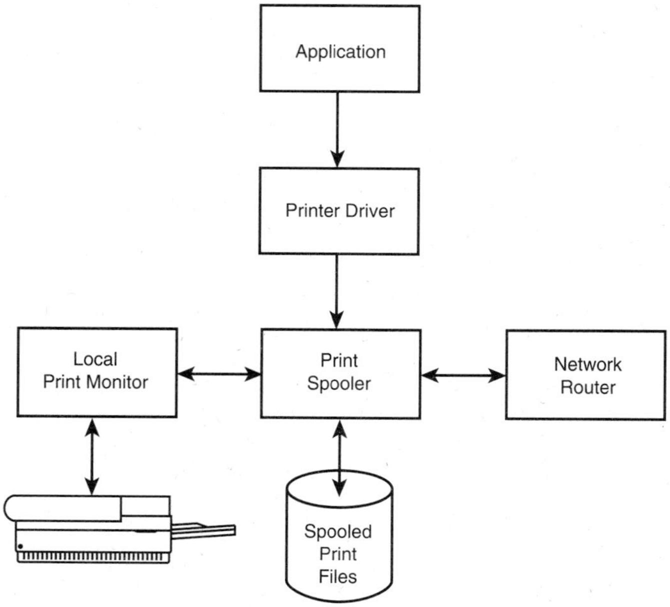

Fig. 21.1 The Windows 95 printing system consists of several major components besides a print spooler.

In effect, when you print from an application, the printer driver creates a print job (which you learned about in the last chapter). The printer driver then hands this print job to the print processor, which in turn works with the print request router to determine where the print job should be routed. If the print job is to be handled on a local printer, then it is routed to the local print spooler. If the print job is destined for a printer available through the network, then it is routed across the network to the appropriate destination where it is processed.

How the Print Spooler Works

Windows 95 uses a fully integrated 32-bit print spooler. The purpose of this spooler is to queue up print jobs destined for a particular printer. You are well aware that with the speed of today's computer systems, the printer is often much slower than the computer. The spooler acts as an intelligent buffer between your computer and a printer. In effect, when you print, you are printing to the spooler, not to the printer. The spooler can accept information as quickly as your software can send it. The information is then stored in print jobs and doled out to the printer as fast as the printer can handle it. All of this happens in the background, of course, in a manner that is completely transparent to the application you are using.

In older versions of Windows, the Print Manager was a spooler. With the Print Manager activated, you would print to it, and then the Print Manager would take care of sending your information to the printer. This enabled you to work on other tasks while information was being sent to your printer. Due to the way the Print Manager was implemented, Windows itself was often slowed down, and working on a different task while the Print Manager was busy was very disconcerting. Often, the process was jerky and disruptive, with the operating system being unresponsive while the Print Manager was doing its work.

In Windows 95, the Print Manager has been replaced with a more robust spooler that is a fully preemptive 32-bit application. This means you will no longer notice jerky responses while the spooler is working. Instead, printing is a true background process that will not interfere with whatever application you are using in the foreground.

Later in this chapter, you will learn how you can control both the printer and the print jobs that have been submitted to the spooler.

Controlling Print Spooling

Any print job you send to your printer under Windows is automatically spooled (placed in a queue) and printed in the background while you continue to work. For most users this is the most efficient way to print. Without a print spooler in place, Windows must wait until the printer has finished accepting the print job before it returns control of the computer back to you.

Spooling is printer-dependent, so if you have two (or more) printers defined in Windows, one printer might have spooling enabled while the other does not. To control how Windows 95 spools information to a printer, follow these steps:

1. Open the Printers folder by choosing Settings from the Start menu, and then choosing Printers.
2. Right-click the icon for the printer you want to change.
3. Choose Properties from the context menu. This opens the Properties sheet for that printer.
4. Select the Details tab.
5. Click the Spool Settings button. This displays the Spool Settings dialog box, as shown in figure 21.2.

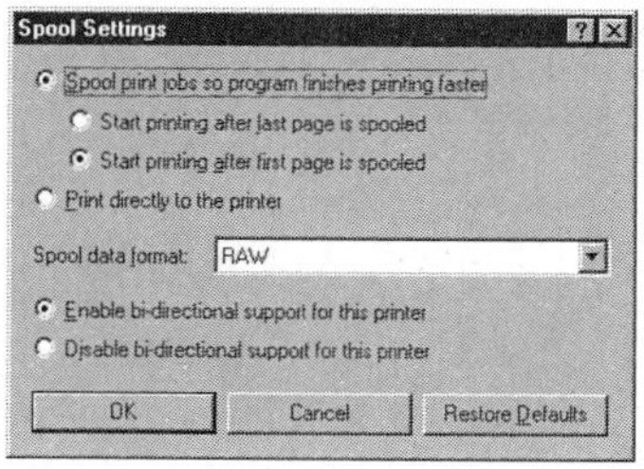

Fig. 21.2 The Spool Settings dialog box enables you to control spooling for a printer.

The Spool Settings dialog box presents you with several options, each of which affects how Windows 95 sends information to your printer. At the top of the dialog box there are two main options. The first (which is selected in figure 21.2) enables the print spooler. With this option selected, you have two ways that the spooling can occur. The first option, Start Printing After Last Page Is Spooled, causes the spooler to hold all information until it receives the entire print job from your application. Choosing this option can cause a disconcerting delay before you get the first page from your printer. The second option, Start Printing After First Page Is Spooled, causes information to be sent from the spooler to the printer as quickly as possible.

Because printing quickly is typically a good thing, why would you ever want to choose the first option? The biggest reason is if your printer is used by an application that "prints as it goes." For instance, suppose that you are creating a report from a database program, and after processing a record for a time, it prints a line or two of information. If it takes 15 seconds to process each record, then it could be 10 or 15 minutes before a completely printed page has been created—that's 10 or 15 minutes for each page of the report. If the spooler is set to start printing after the first page is ready to be printed, all other people wanting to use the printer will be waiting while the second and subsequent pages are assembled and printed by the database program. If you have an application similar to this, you will want the print spooler to hold the job until it is complete, and only then release it.

The second option at the top of the Spool Settings dialog box enables you to turn print spooling off. The Print Directly to the Printer option bypasses the spooler altogether, sending information to the printer in the old-fashioned way. This type of printing can be slow, because you are tied to the speed of the printer instead of the speed of your computer.

> **Tip:** If you have a printer that you have shared over the network, do not turn off print spooling for that printer. Because your printer will be handling jobs from many sources, print spooling is necessary.

In the middle of the dialog box is an option called Spool Data Format. This option enables you to specify how you want information stored in the spooler. RAW is the most likely format choice, which means that the information is stored in the format that is native to the printer. The other option, EMF, stores information in a metafile format (an intermediary format) that conserves on disk space.

Another advantage of EMF print files is faster apparent printing. The operative word here is "apparent." If you set the spooler to use EMF files, then much of the printer-dependent translation takes place in the background rather than as your document is printing. For instance, if your document requires a large rectangle to be printed, and you have EMF enabled, then the rectangle command is stored in the spool file and later translated to the printer-driver level. If you turn EMF off, then the rectangle is converted into a format the printer understands at print time. This process is more time-consuming (depending on the document), and can slow down the overall performance of Windows 95. The upshot is that you should choose the EMF format if at all possible.

> **Note:** Spool settings are printer dependent. If you are changing settings for a PostScript printer, the EMF format option is not available. The only option available to PostScript printers is RAW.

The two options at the bottom of the Spool Settings dialog box enable you to indicate how the spooler should expect to communicate with the printer. Both serial and parallel ports now support bidirectional communication, which can greatly increase the amount of information

you get back from your printer. For instance, over a bidirectional communications link, your printer can inform the operating system that it is out of paper, that the toner is low, or that there is a paper jam.

You seldom need to change the default setting for the printer, except in one situation. If you have an older system that does not have a bidirectional parallel port, then you should turn off the bidirectional feature. This choice will not necessarily slow down your printer, but it does inform Windows about the capabilities of the communication channel between your system and the printer.

When you are through changing the spooler settings, click the OK button. Your changes are saved and implemented immediately.

Creating a Print Job

In Windows 95, application programs create print jobs. For instance, you can create print jobs with your word processor or your spreadsheet program. The amount and type of programs that can create print jobs are almost innumerable.

Exactly how you print from an application will depend, in large part, on how the application was developed. While there are broad guidelines for how an application should appear and behave, the specifics of "how things look" are left up to the individual or company creating the software.

> **Tip:** Before you try to print with an application, you should make sure that you have installed the necessary printer drivers as described in Chapter 20, "Managing Your Printers."

Many Windows users do not install a single printer driver. This is particularly true in office environments, but may also apply to solitary users. Many applications send printer output to whatever you have set as the default printer. For instance, most of the accessories supplied

with Windows 95 send information to the default printer. Thus if you have installed more than one printer driver, make sure that you select the proper printer driver before you start to print.

There are two ways you can select the default printer. Some applications provide a way to do this, typically through the Print command, itself. You can always use the Printers folder to set the default printer, however. To do this, follow these steps:

1. Open the Printers folder by choosing Settings from the Start menu, and then choosing Printers.
2. Click the icon for the printer you want to use as the default printer. This highlights the printer icon.
3. Choose the Set as Default option from the File menu.

When you set the default printer, there is no change in the appearance of the Printers folder. Instead, Windows 95 knows where to send printer information, unless your application specifies a different printer. You can only tell which printer has been selected as the default by highlighting the printer and pulling down the File menu. If the highlighted printer is the default printer, a checkmark will appear next to the Set As Default option, as shown in figure 21.3.

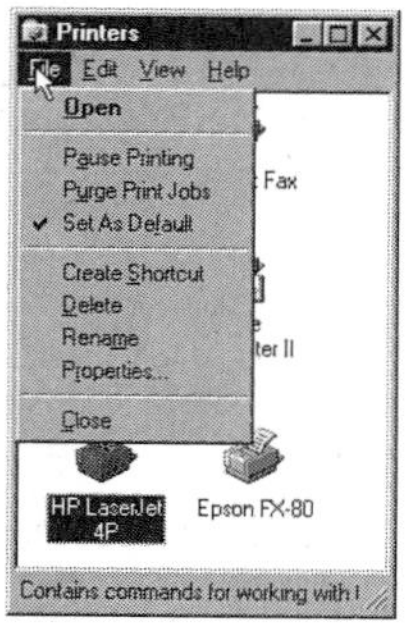

Fig. 21.3 A checkmark beside the Set As Default option indicates that the selected printer is the default.

When you are ready to create your print job, all you need to do is choose the Print command or follow the print procedure specific to your application. In general, if the program has a toolbar, you can find a print tool that will send your document to the printer. You can also typically find a Print option under the File menu for the application. For instance, figure 21.4 shows the dialog box that appears when you choose Print from the File menu in Microsoft Word for Windows.

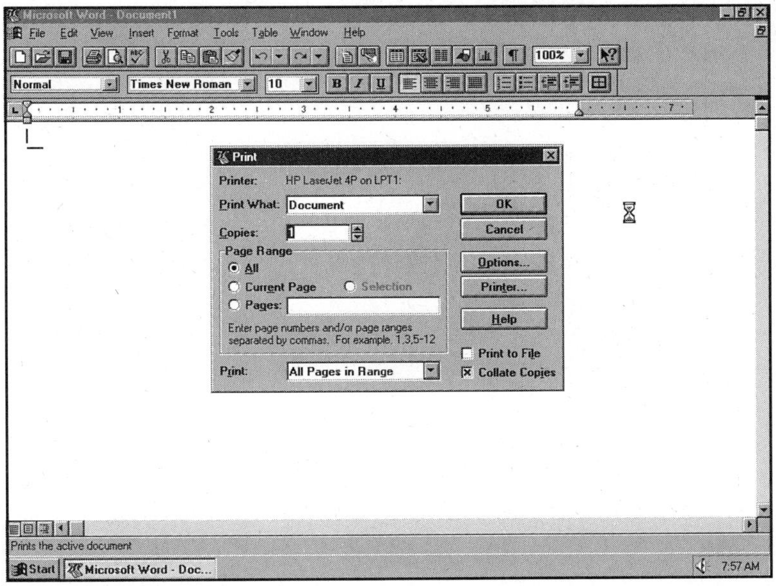

Fig. 21.4 Applications such as Word for Windows enable you to print from a toolbar or a menu option.

The Print dialog box is similar to the Print dialog boxes in many other applications. It enables you to specify what you want to print, as well as modify how it should be sent. Notice that the dialog box has information that indicates which printer driver will be used for this print job. In the case of figure 21.4, the printer is named HP LaserJet 4P on LPT1. If this is not the printer you want to use, click the appropriate button to change the printer. The exact button you use will vary from program to program; in the case of Word for Windows, it is the Printer button.

When the printer options are set correctly for your application, click the OK or Printer button. The application is instructed to compose the print job and send it to the printer driver. This information is then handed off to the spooling system, as described earlier in the chapter.

Managing Your Print Jobs

After you have created a print job and have sent it to the spooler, Windows 95 provides you with a great degree of flexibility in controlling the job. To manage the print job (as well as the printer), you use the printer icon in the Printers folder. To see how a printer is doing with the jobs it has to process, simply double-click the printer icon. You will see a window similar to the one shown in figure 21.5.

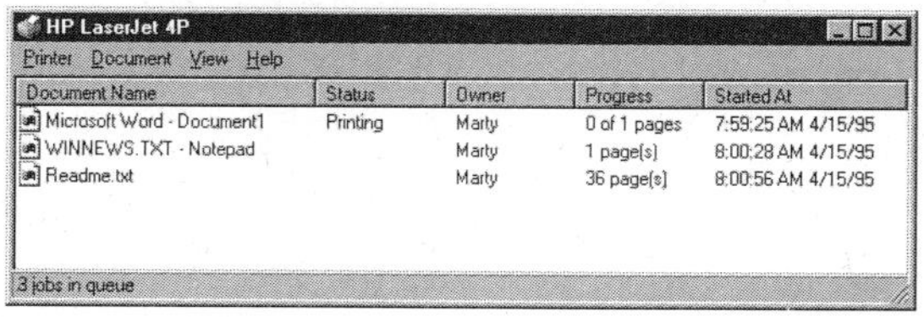

Fig. 21.5 Printer control windows enable you to manage both printers and print jobs.

> **Note:** If you are using a printer that sends information to a disk file, you cannot pull up a printer control window by double-clicking the printer icon. That is because the print job is sent to the output file immediately; there are no print jobs to manage.

The printer control window lists print jobs being worked on by the spooler. You can see information on the print job, as follows:

- **Document Name.** The name assigned to the print job by the application that created it. This may be the name of the document, the name of the application, or a combination of both.

- **Status.** The status of the printer in relation to this job. Typically, this is a single word, such as *Spooling, Printing,* or *Error.*
- **Owner.** The name of the user that sent the job to the printer. This is either the name of the person to whom Windows 95 is registered (in the case of a single-user system) or the name the person used when he or she logged on to the network.
- **Progress.** Information on either the size of the pending print job or the status of the print job being processed. Whenever possible, information is provided in terms of pages, although the veracity of this information may (at times) be questionable.
- **Started At.** The date and time the print job was created.

If there are quite a few print jobs in the queue (there could be if the printer is a heavily used network printer), you may want to sort the jobs in different ways. You do this by clicking the column header by which you want to sort. Thus, if you want to view the print jobs by who created them, just click the Owner column header. The print jobs are rearranged and shown in the order requested.

> **Tip:** If you want to display jobs in their original order, click the Started At column header. This displays jobs in the order in which they were submitted to the spooler.

Pausing Print Jobs

There are two ways you can pause print jobs, and the one you choose depends on the effect you want to have. If you want to pause all the print jobs at a printer, you pause the printer itself. If you want to pause a specific job, then you simply pause that individual print job.

To pause the entire printer, just choose Pause Printing from the Printer menu. As an alternative, you can also right-click anywhere in the printer control window (except on the name of a pending print job). This displays the context menu for the printer control window, which is the same as the Printer menu.

When you choose to pause a printer, all output to the printer is immediately halted. The print jobs are not deleted; they are simply suspended. The title bar for the window is also changed to indicate that the printer has been paused. Figure 21.6 shows an example of a paused printer.

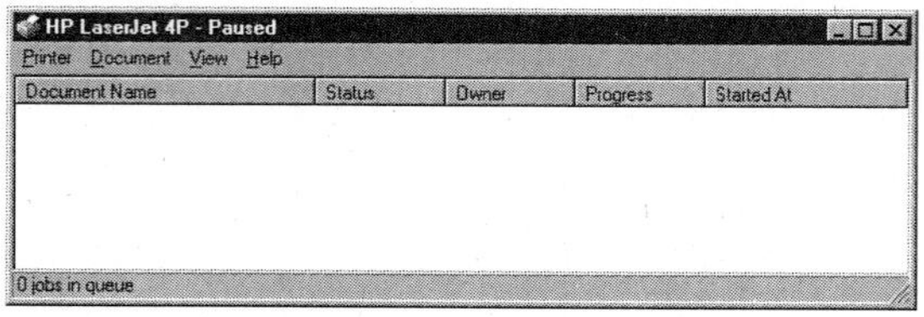

Fig. 21.6 The title bar tells you that the print jobs have been suspended.

If you want to individually pause a print job, follow these steps:

1. Display the printer control window containing the print job you want to pause.
2. Right-click the name of the print job to pause. This displays the context menu for the print job. (You could also select the print job and pull down the Document menu.)
3. Choose the Pause Printing option.

At this point, the spooler suspends the print job. If there are any other pending print jobs, they are sent to the printer normally; only the one single print job is affected. The paused job is indicated by the word `Paused` appearing in the Status column for the job (see figure 21.7).

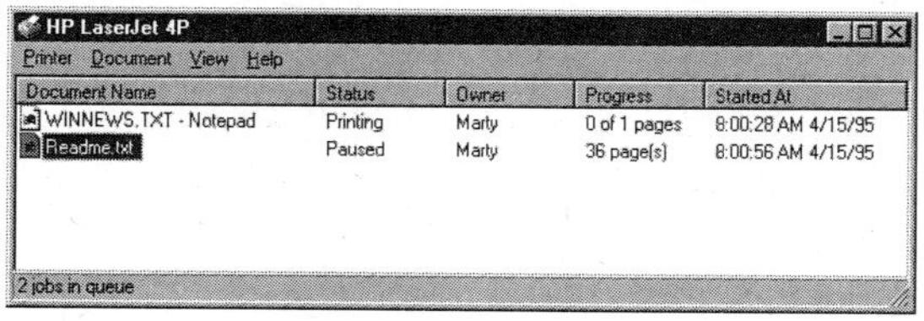

Fig. 21.7 Pausing a print job causes it to be suspended; all others are unaffected.

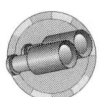

Note: Pausing a print job that is currently printing may have undesired effects. If you pause the job too long, your printer may timeout, which means what you have sent so far is flushed from the printer buffer. If this happens, you will need to delete the print job and start it again.

Resuming Print Jobs

If you know how to pause a print job, the chances are good that you also know how to resume one. Again, how you perform this task depends on whether you want to resume all print jobs (resume the printer) or resume individual print jobs.

To resume or unpause a printer, select the Pause Printing option from the Printer menu or from the context menu for the printer control window. The spooler immediately begins sending any pending information to the printer, and the title bar for the window is changed so the `Paused` notation no longer appears.

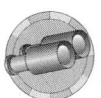

Note: Unpausing a printer has no effect on any individual print jobs that may be paused. If individual print jobs have been paused, you will need to individually unpause them.

To resume an individual print job, follow the same steps you used to initially pause the job:

1. Display the printer control window containing the print job you want to resume printing.
2. Right-click the name of a print job that was previously paused. This displays the context menu for the print job. You could also select the print job and pull down the Document menu.
3. Choose the Pause Printing option.

This releases the print job so it is processed normally by the spooler. The word `Paused` is removed from the Status column, and the job resumes its priority in the print queue based on the time the job was originally started.

Deleting Print Jobs

Windows 95 makes deleting an individual print job very easy. Just follow these steps:

1. Display the printer control window containing the print job you want to delete.
2. Click the name of the print job you want to delete. This highlights the print job.
3. Press the Delete key on your keyboard.

The print job is deleted, and its name removed from the printer control window.

> **Caution:** After a print job is deleted, you cannot resurrect it. Unlike deleted files (which are moved to the Recycle Bin), deleted print jobs are gone for good. The only option is to re-create the print job.

There are other ways to delete an individual print job, but pressing the Delete key is the easiest. For instance, you could right-click the name of the print job and choose Cancel Printing from the context menu, or you could choose the same option from the Document menu.

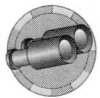

> **Note:** Deleting a print job that is in progress could have unwanted side effects. This is because even though you have deleted the job, your printer does not know this action has been taken—it can only tell that the data flow stopped. The result at your printer depends on the type and capabilities of your printer. In some rare instances, you may need to turn your printer off and back on or reset it.

If you want to delete all the print jobs queued up for a printer, you could delete them individually, but there is an easier way. Deleting all print jobs in a queue is called *purging*. You accomplish this by choosing Purge Print Jobs from the Printer menu or from the context menu for the printer control window. All print jobs for the printer are immediately deleted, regardless of their status.

Printing to a File

In Chapter 20, "Managing Your Printers," you learned that you can direct printer output to any number of devices. Normally, if you are using a local printer, you would print to either a parallel (LPT) or serial (COM) port.

Windows 95 also enables you to print to a file instead of a physical printer. This means the printer output is stored in a disk file, and you can later direct the file to the printer. The next section describes how to change the printer output to a file, and the following section teaches you what to do with the printer file once you have it.

Changing the Output Device

To print to a file, define the file as the destination of your printed output. You typically do this when you are preparing output for a printer make and model that you do not have physically connected to your system or available through your network. For instance, you might set up a printer definition for a printer you use at a service bureau. When the print files are created, the files can be taken to the service bureau for processing.

As an example, assume that you want to take advantage of the Linotronic 500 at the local print shop. All you need to do is install the printer driver for this printer, as described earlier in the chapter. When you are asked for the port used by the printer, choose the FILE option.

You can also change an existing printer driver so it is directed to a file, by following these steps:

1. Double-click the My Computer icon on your desktop.
2. Double-click the Printers icon. This displays the Printers folder.
3. Right-click the icon for the printer whose output you want directed to a file. This displays the context menu for the printer.
4. Choose the Properties option from the context menu. This displays the Properties sheet for the printer.
5. Click the Details tab.
6. In the Print To the Following Port field, choose the FILE option.
7. Click the OK button.

The icon for the printer is changed to indicate that the printer's output is directed to a file. Now, when you print by using this printer you are asked for a file name in which the output should be stored. When you supply the file name, the file is created and the print job is stored in the file.

Copying a Disk File to a Printer

When you have yourprinter output in a disk file, you are then faced with the problem of getting it to the target printer. This is most often a simple task of copying the file to a floppy disk, and then physically taking the disk to the computer connected to the target printer. For instance, if a service bureau operates the target printer, then you would take the disk file to the service bureau.

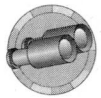

Note: A printer output file does not contain plain text. Instead, it contains the control codes and commands necessary for the printer to process the print job. This means that a printer output file is intrinsically different from the original document used to create the file. It is important to understand these differences when you send your output to a disk file.

The most efficient way to send the file to the target printer is to do it from a DOS prompt. How you get to the DOS prompt depends on the type of machine connected to the target printer.

- If the system is running DOS, then you are set; the DOS prompt should be visible on the screen.
- If the system is running an older version of Windows, then you will need to either exit Windows or choose MS-DOS prompt from the Main program group.
- If the system is running Windows 95, then you will need to select Programs from the Start menu, and then choose MS-DOS prompt.

When the DOS prompt is visible, you can follow these steps:

1. Insert the transfer disk (the one containing the print file) into a disk drive. Make a note of which disk drive it is (A: or B:).
2. Make a note of which printer port the target printer is connected to. Typically this is a port such as LPT1 or LPT2.
3. At the DOS prompt, enter the following command line, replacing *d:* with the disk drive in which your diskette is located, *file* with the printer file name, and *dest* with the printer port to which the target printer is connected.

```
copy d:\file dest
```

This copies the printer file to the target printer. Soon you should start to see your output appear on the device. If you do not, you will want to check the command line to make sure that you used the proper information: disk drive, file name, and destination printer port.

Printing on a Network

For all intents and purposes, printing to a network printer functions just the same as printing to a network printer. All you need to do is set up a printer driver for the network printer, and then send your print jobs to that printer. The printer driver for the network printer can be

set up either as described in Chapter 20, "Managing Your Printers," or by using the Point-and-Print feature, which is described later in this chapter.

> **Note:** For specific information on printing over networks, you can also refer to Chapter 37, "Using Windows 95 on a Network."

To gain maximum efficiency when printing to a network printer, implement these suggestions:

- Configure your printers to use direct network connections whenever possible. This provides fast throughput and flexible printer placement. It also removes the need for a dedicated printer server.
- If your printer does not have direct network connection capability, use a *parallel port* rather than a serial port. This avoids bottlenecks common to serial printers and networks.
- For slower laser printers designed primarily for text output, use the lowest print resolution, typically 75 or 150 dpi.
- Do not enable spooling for a network printer if you are using a separate spooling program provided with the network software.

You can perform each of these tasks from the Properties sheet for your printers. You can find information on the settings for the Properties sheet in Chapter 20, "Managing Your Printers."

Point-and-Print Capabilities

Windows 95 includes a new feature called *Point and Print.* This feature comes into play if you are connected to a network, and it allows simpler printing to a network printer.

In past networked versions of Windows, you needed to know quite a bit about a network printer before you could actually print to it. You needed to know what type of printer you were connecting to so that you could install the necessary printer drivers at your computer. This could cause problems, because it was not always easy to determine the characteristics of a remote printer.

In Windows 95, Point and Print removes this necessity. Now you need to know very little about the remote printer. Windows 95 will take care of determining what type of printer it is, and installing the proper printer driver on your computer. This driver is transferred across the network, so you do not need to worry about having the Windows 95 installations disks or CD-ROM at your computer.

> **Note:** The Point-and-Print feature of Windows 95 attempts to determine the type of remote printer you want to use. If it cannot discern the information it needs, you will still be asked for the printer manufacturer and model, as in previous versions of Windows. In such an event, you will actually need your Windows 95 diskettes or CD-ROM in order to install the proper printer driver.

The Point-and-Print feature functions by using the Registry. When you install a new printer driver on your system, the information about that printer is stored in the Registry. If you share the printer on the network, then others have access to the printer. When another network user attempts to print to your printer, his or her Windows 95 queries your Windows 95 about the printer. Your system then retrieves the information about the printer from the Registry, and sends it to the remote user's computer. If the remote system determines that it needs the printer driver, your system takes care of sending it over the network, where it is installed on the remote user's system and used to send information to your computer. All of this is done without intervention from either you or the remote user.

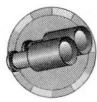

> **Note:** Point and Print will only function fully on Windows networks (Windows 95 and Windows NT) and on NetWare networks.

To enable Point and Print on your system, follow these steps:

1. Double-click the My Computer icon on your desktop. This opens a window showing the contents of your system.
2. In the My Computer window, double-click the C: drive icon (or whatever other drive contains your Windows folder). This opens a window for your disk drive.
3. In the disk drive window, double-click the Windows folder. This opens a window showing the contents of the Windows folder.
4. In the Windows folder window, right-click the System folder icon. This displays a context menu.
5. From the context menu, select the Sharing option. This displays the System Properties sheet with the Sharing tab selected.

In this dialog box, you set how you want others on the network to have access to your System folder. You do not need to fully share the folder, but you do need to give others read-only access to the folder. The only people that need to have access are those who you want to have Point-and-Print capabilities to your shared printers. Read-only access means they can read things from your System folder, but they cannot change them. They need to be able to read the folder in order to gain access to your printer drivers and the information in your Registry.

To use Point and Print, just browse through Network Neighborhood to find the printer you want to use. When you find it, simply drag the printer icon from the remote system, dropping it in your Printers folder window. The necessary printer driver information is transferred automatically, and the printer is set up. All you need to do is provide a name for the new printer driver on your system.

Printing from a DOS Application

If you have been using Windows for any length of time, you already know that printing from an MS-DOS window can be frustrating. This is because printing from an MS-DOS window went directly to the printer port, bypassing the Print Manager altogether. This could present problems, for instance, when you needed to print something from the Print Manager and from DOS at the same time.

Windows 95 has solved the historical problems in this area. All printing from the MS-DOS window is now routed through the print spooler, meaning that DOS printing jobs are handled the same as any other printing job.

One of the side benefits of this design change is the fact that you can now do work quicker in an MS-DOS window than you could in previous versions of Windows. This is because, previously, any MS-DOS printing went directly to the printer port. That meant that you needed to wait for the entire print job to be complete before returning to your application. With print jobs now routed through the regular print spooler, your application's output is accepted by the spooler instead of directly by the printer. The result is you are returned to the DOS application before your printed output is completed—the same benefit that has been inherent in Windows applications for some time.

KILLER 22 WINDOWS 95

Working with Fonts

by Allen L. Wyatt

You already know that Windows is a graphical user environment, based on the concept of WYSIWYG—what you see is what you get. That means that what you see on-screen should also represent what you see on printed output, or on a screen on a different system. While this is a great design concept, it unfortunately means that computer users must be concerned with details that users of less sophisticated systems don't need to pay attention to. Primarily, you need to be concerned with fonts.

This chapter discusses, in detail, how Windows 95 works with fonts. You learn not only what they are, but what types of fonts are available. You also learn how to install them in Windows and use them in your applications.

What Are Fonts?

A *font* is a collection of characters and symbols with a related design. The design itself is referred to as a *typeface.* A set of typefaces designed to be used together is a *typeface family.* For instance, common typeface families would be Times or Helvetica; these families can be found on many computer systems. Within these families, specific designs, or typefaces would be Times Roman or Times Italic (within the Times family) and Helvetica Narrow or Helvetica Bold (within the Helvetica family).

In effect, a font is a particular implementation of a typeface. These implementations vary from vendor to vendor. Thus, the Times Roman typeface from Adobe would be one font, while the Times Roman typeface from Bitstream would be another font.

In many instances (including within this chapter), the terms *typeface* and *font* are used interchangeably. This is not meant to cause confusion, it is just an indication of the reality that there is typically not much difference between implementations of the same typeface.

To understand fonts fully, you need to understand a few other key terms. It is not my intention to provide a complete tutorial on type design or layout, but a few key terms are appropriate to the discussion later in this chapter.

Type is composed of uppercase letters (ABC), lowercase letters (abc), numbers (123), and some symbols (such as punctuation marks). When type is placed on a page, there are three main parts to it. The x-height, or type body, is the height of a lowercase X, and it is also the height of the main part of every other letter. Ascenders are the parts of the letter that extend above the x-height, and descenders are those parts that fall below the x-height. Figure 22.1 shows an example of type, with the appropriate terms marked.

Fig. 22.1 There are three basic elements to a font.

The dividing line between the x-height area and the descender area is called the *base line*. This is the line on which the type is aligned vertically; it is the path your eye follows when you read text.

The size of a font is measured in points. A point is approximately 1/72 of an inch. Thus, a 10-point type is ten points high, and a 48-point type is 48 points high. This can be a bit misleading, however. Point sizes, as a scientific measurement, are a hold-over from the days when type was cast in lead and manually placed on a wooden rack. The point size of a font referred to the height of the lead block on which the actual letter was placed; it had nothing to do with the height of the actual letters in the font. Take a look at the different letters shown in figure 22.2.

Fig. 22.2 All these letters from different fonts are the same point size, but different actual sizes.

Every one of the letters in figure 22.2 is considered 30-point type. They appear different on the page, however, because the point size has no relevance to the height of the actual characters in the font. In general, you should use point sizes as a guide to the relative sizes of fonts, not to their absolute size.

Purposes for Fonts

Fonts are created for many different purposes. In the computer world, fonts are typically designed based on the output device on which they

will be used. In a Windows system, there are generally two font formats: printer fonts and display fonts. These two classifications are discussed in the following sections.

Printer Fonts

Fonts have been inextricably associated with printing since Gutenberg fired up his press. Fonts are the character applied to the content of what we read. In many cases they affect—either positively or negatively—our perception of what we are reading. Many times this effect is very subtle; we may not even be aware of it. Thus, fonts are very important to how we print and to what we print.

Printer fonts are used by a printer to control how text is formed on the printed page. They are stored in disk files on your computer, but if you use them in a document and then print the document, they are automatically downloaded to the printer so they can be used there. Downloaded printer fonts are often referred to as *soft fonts,* since they reside in software. When the printer is done using the fonts and your print job is complete, the fonts are erased from the printer's memory. They continue to reside on your computer, awaiting the next time they are needed by Windows to complete a print job.

Display (Screen) Fonts

The video display (along with the keyboard) is the primary interface device between you and the computer. On the display is where you do your work and view many of your results. Today's computer displays are more complex and capable than those of yesterday, and this trend will probably continue into the future.

Windows 95, being a graphical user interface, allows information to be displayed in virtually any way that program designers can create. One outgrowth of this is that the display of textual information has come very close to what we are used to seeing on the printed page. This

capability necessitates the use of *screen fonts,* which control how different typefaces appear on a video display.

When you install a font in Windows 95, typically you are thinking in terms of final printed output—how the font will appear when the document is printed. The installation process typically also installs display fonts which correspond to the printer fonts. This is done so that what you see on-screen corresponds to what is printed on the printer.

Types of Fonts

After a typeface has been designed, it must be stored in a disk file, in a format which can be understood by the computer. There are typically two ways in which fonts can be stored: as bitmaps or as outlines.

Bitmap Fonts

Bitmap fonts represent the oldest computer font technology. A *bitmap font* is nothing but a graphic representation of a series of characters. These are stored in a file in the same way that bitmapped graphics are—each bit in the definition represents a single dot on the output device. If a bit is on (set to 1), then a dot is printed; if a bit is off (set to 0), then a dot is not printed. As you might guess, the smaller the character, the fewer bits it takes to define it. Conversely, the larger the character, the more bits it takes. This means that the larger the point size of the font, the more space it can take to store the font both on disk and in a device such as a printer. Since the font takes more space, that also means that it takes longer to transfer and manipulate the font.

One drawback of bitmap fonts is that they cannot be displayed well at different resolutions. For instance, if you have a 10-point bitmapped font, and you enlarge it quite a bit, the quality of the font deteriorates. The most easily recognized deterioration is "jaggies," which appear around the edges of the characters. Outline fonts, described in the following section, do not have this limitation.

Outline Fonts

The other format for fonts is outlines. An outline font is nothing but a mathematical description of a series of characters. Since the outline is based on math, it easily can be manipulated mathematically. Also, regardless of the point size of the font, the outline description is consistent in space requirements. Thus, it takes the same amount of time to manipulate or transfer an outline font, regardless of its point size.

How can you tell the font types apart if you are using Windows? Later in this chapter you will learn about the Fonts window and how you can use it to manage the fonts on your system. If you look at the Fonts window (see figure 22.3), you see that there are two types of fonts displayed. Those that use an icon with the letter A in it are bitmap fonts; those that have the TT symbol are TrueType fonts, which are stored in an outline format.

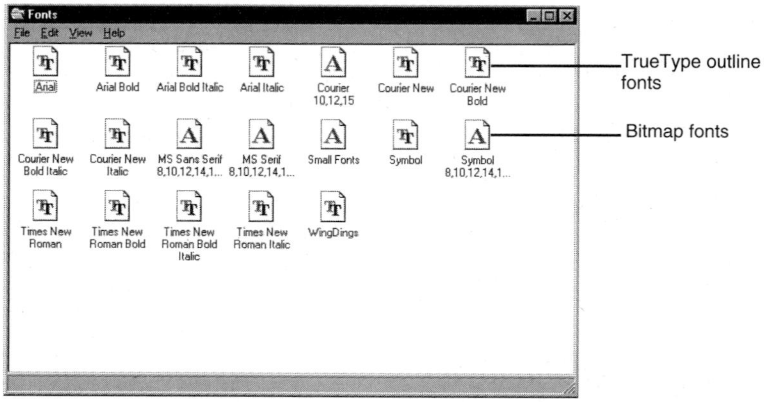

Fig. 22.3 There are two types of font file icons used in this Fonts folder window.

Notice, as well, that the names for the bitmap font files include numbers such as 8, 10, 12, 14, and so forth. These numbers represent the point sizes for each font within the file. If you use the font for a point size that is different from these, the font will be manipulated to that size, but it will not be as crisp or clear as if you used the bitmap font at one of the sizes it is designed for.

There are a variety of fonts available on the market. Each of these fonts come in any number of formats. The two most common types of fonts used in Windows systems are TrueType and PostScript fonts. These (as well as a few others) are discussed in the following sections.

TrueType Fonts

When you install Windows 95, several different fonts are automatically installed. These fonts are in the TrueType format, which was originally developed by Microsoft and several other vendors. In many ways, TrueType fonts are competitors to PostScript fonts, which are described in the following section.

Windows can scale TrueType fonts to any size. These fonts can be used with any graphic video adapter and any printer, provided that Windows 95 drivers exist for the devices. This capability alone is a boon to network users. In many environments, users may work from a variety of machines and use a variety of printers. Windows enables the same fonts to work anywhere.

The scaleable nature of the fonts makes them economical in their disk space requirements. Each TrueType font file occupies between 9K and 72K, and each typeface (bold, italic, condensed, and so on) requires a separate file. In contrast, bitmapped files would require separate files for each size of the same typeface, thereby occupying quite a bit more disk space.

> **Tip:** If you are running Windows 95 on a network, store your TrueType fonts in your master Windows directory on the server. This allows everyone to access the fonts and cuts down on redundant files on the network.

True Type Fonts Are Embedded into the File

TrueType fonts can be embedded in a document so that other users can print the document and still get the fonts printed properly, even if the original font is not on their system. TrueType fonts are encrypted when they are embedded into the document, which allows the font to be sent with the file, permitting the end-user recipient to view and print the file. The encrypting prevents the recipient from copying the font itself without licensing the font.

Font vendors have three levels of font embedding from which to choose. The most restrictive method doesn't permit the font to be embedded in a document. Instead, the document's recipient must substitute an available font for the original used to create the document. The second level only permits a recipient to view and print the document containing the font, but cannot affect the font itself. Recipients also cannot edit the document without deleting the font information first. The third type of embedding allows the recipient to edit and save the document without deleting the font information. This type of embedding permits the recipient to extract the font for personal use.

Printing TrueType Fonts

When printing a document containing TrueType fonts on a standard Hewlett-Packard compatible laser or ink-jet printer, Windows scans the first line printed and downloads only the characters needed. Then Windows scans the next line and downloads any additional characters needed for the next line. This process continues until the entire document is printed. This on-the-fly, download-if-needed strategy means that TrueType fonts print reasonably fast in spite of having several sizes and font styles in a document. Windows clears the printer's memory at the end of the print job and repeats the process afresh for new print jobs. To work in a networked environment, soft fonts need to be downloaded in this way. This method of downloading soft fonts is not a new idea. For years, soft fonts from SWFTE (Rockland, MD) have worked this way for DOS-based versions of Word and WordPerfect. For

Windows users, SWFTE has released its whole font series as TrueType fonts in a product called Typecase.

With PostScript laser printers, Windows converts TrueType fonts into Adobe Type 1 outline fonts or Adobe Type 3 bitmap fonts (both of these font types are discussed in the following section). If the point size you are printing is 8 points or smaller, you might find that printing them as Type 3 is faster because less data is required for a bitmap at this small size than is required for an outline font at this size. You can control the type of conversion you want to use for each printer installed on your system. How you do this is covered later in this chapter, in the section "Sending TrueType Fonts to a PostScript Printer."

On dot-matrix printers, TrueType fonts print as bitmapped graphics, and the quality is surprisingly good, even on the less sophisticated 9-pin printers.

PostScript Fonts

PostScript fonts have been around longer than TrueType fonts, and have many of the same benefits. They were originally developed by Adobe Systems, the developers of the PostScript language. Since they have been around longer, and since Adobe has done a wonderful marketing job, they are available in a wider array of high-quality printers and output devices.

There are two types of PostScript fonts on the market: bitmap and outline. Earlier in this chapter you learned the differences between these font formats. Bitmap fonts represent an older technology, and are often referred to as Adobe Type 1 fonts. Outline fonts, which are newer, are referred to as Adobe Type 3 fonts. All PostScript devices can handle Type 3 fonts, but some older PostScript devices cannot handle Type 1 fonts. This is because the older devices also use an older PostScript *interpreter,* which is the computing engine that processes the font information sent to it by the computer.

> **Note:** If you are creating a document that is ultimately intended for a high-quality output device, such as an imagesetter, check with the people that run the imagesetter to determine which types of fonts you should use. Typically, most imagesetters are intimately tied to PostScript fonts, and you should not use fonts in other formats (including TrueType). Using the wrong type of fonts can make your output job unsatisfactory or completely unusable.

Other Types of Fonts

Besides TrueType and PostScript fonts, there are a wide variety of other fonts available on the market. These fonts are available from vendors such as Bitstream, SWFTE, and others. Some of these font packages are available in TrueType format, some in Adobe Type 1, and still others in Adobe Type 3.

This does not mean that all fonts are in Type 1, Type 3, or TrueType formats. Indeed, there are other formats available, although they are not nearly as popular or pervasive as the font types already mentioned. Typically these font formats, such as Bitstream's QEM format, are a variation on the bitmap formatting already mentioned. These "other" types of fonts are typically not managed directly by Windows, but instead require a Windows font management program provided by the font vendor.

Installing Fonts

Installing a font in Windows 95 is quite easy. In Chapter 23, "Managing Your Printers," you learned how Windows 95 uses the Printers folder as a place to organize all your printer drivers. Likewise, the Fonts folder is used by Windows 95 as a place to hold all your fonts.

The first step in installing fonts is to display the Fonts folder window. To do this, follow these steps:

1. Choose Settings from the Start menu. The Settings menu appears.
2. Choose Control Panel from the Settings menu. The Control Panel window appears.
3. Double-click on the Fonts icon in the Control Panel. The Fonts folder window appears, as shown in figure 22.4.

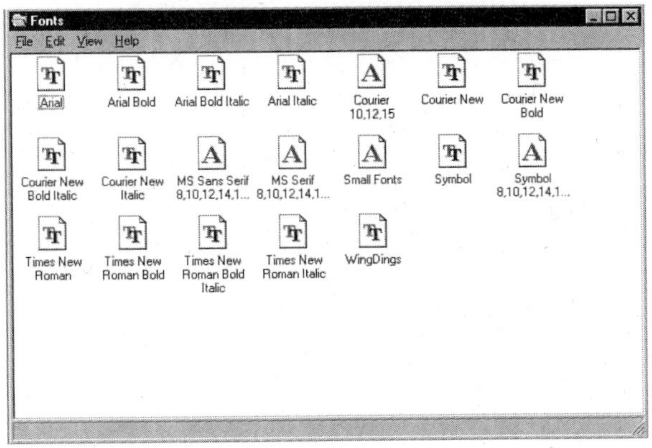

Fig. 22.4 The Fonts folder window shows all the fonts you have installed in your system.

Take another look at the Fonts icon in the Control Panel. Notice that this icon is actually a shortcut, as indicated by the arrow in the bottom- right corner of the icon. The Fonts folder physically resides in the Windows folder of your C: drive. If you browse through your system (possibly using the Explorer), you can open the Windows folder and then the Fonts folder. Regardless of whether you get to the Fonts folder window by browsing or through the Control Panel, you will see the same display and be able to take the same actions.

To install a font in your system, simply choose the Install New Font command from the File menu. This displays the Add Fonts dialog box, as shown in figure 22.5.

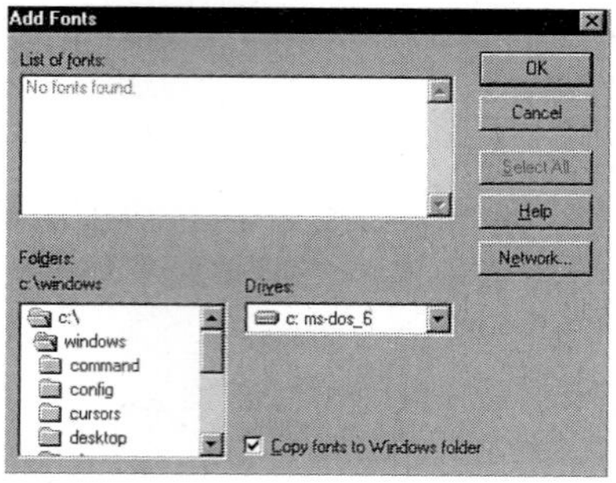

Fig. 22.5 The Add Fonts dialog box enables you to add fonts to Windows 95.

If you have been using Windows for any time, this dialog box should look somewhat familiar. It is similar to the dialog boxes used in previous versions of Windows to add fonts. All you need to do is select the drive and directory (folder) from where you are installing fonts. Typically, you will install fonts from either a floppy drive or a CD-ROM drive. When you specify where the fonts are located, the dialog box shows a list of the fonts available on the drive. For instance, figure 22.6 shows the fonts available on a CD-ROM that contains fonts.

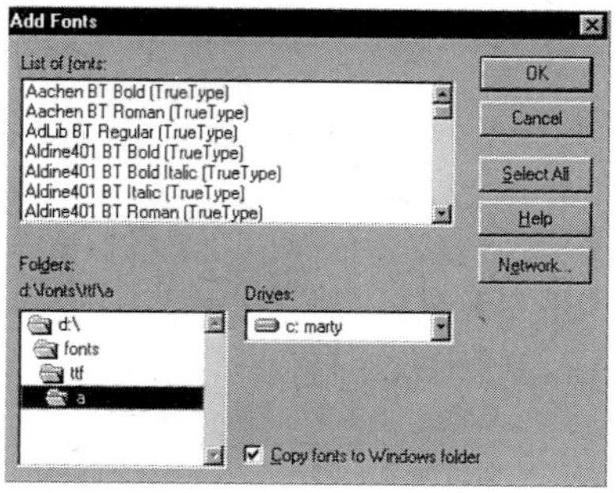

Fig. 22.6 When you have selected a drive and folder containing fonts, the fonts are listed in the Add Fonts dialog box.

To install one of the listed fonts, simply highlight the font name and click the OK button. You can select more than one font by using regular

Windows techniques: hold down the Shift key to select a consecutive series of fonts, or hold down the Ctrl key to select different, non-consecutive fonts.

> **Note:** There are literally thousands of fonts available on the market. Just because a font is available doesn't mean you should install it on your system. Too many fonts will slow down the performance of even the best Windows software, in addition to needlessly occupying disk space. Be selective and install only those fonts you need.

Once the fonts have been installed, an icon for the font appears in the Fonts folder window. These fonts will also appear the next time you start an application that uses fonts.

Controlling How TrueType Fonts Print

Earlier in this chapter you learned what TrueType fonts are. Depending on your printer type, Windows allows you quite a bit of control over how TrueType fonts are printed. If you have installed a dot-matrix printer, there is no real control over how TrueType fonts are printed—they are always printed as graphics characters. This allows the best reproduction of what you see when you use TrueType fonts on your screen.

If you have installed a printer that uses PCL (an acronym for Page Control Language, a page definition language used in HP and compatible printers) or one that uses PostScript, Windows allows you to send the fonts in different ways. Regardless of the printer type, you can specify how TrueType fonts are to be handled by displaying the Properties dialog box for the printer. To do this, follow these steps:

1. Double-click on the My Computer icon on your desktop.

2. Double-click on the Printers icon.
3. Right-click on the icon for the printer whose properties you want to change. The context menu for the printer appears.
4. Choose Properties from the context menu. The Properties dialog box for the printer appears.
5. Click on the Fonts tab. Figure 22.7 shows an example of the Properties dialog box for the HP LaserJet 4V, which is a PCL printer.

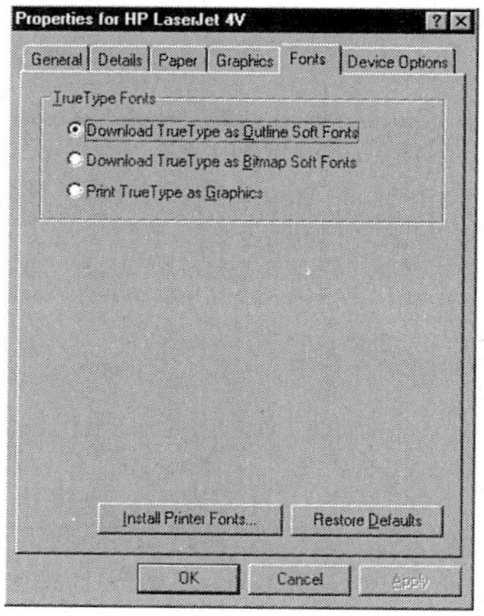

Fig. 22.7 The Fonts tab in the Properties for printer dialog box enables you to control how TrueType fonts are printed.

Notice that this dialog box provides three options for how TrueType fonts are printed. You can print them as an outline font, as a bitmap, or as graphics. Notice, also, that the default is the first option, to print them as outline fonts. This is because this choice typically provides the best quality output at a wide range of type sizes. Since different printers provide different quality output, you may want to experiment by selecting the other options here, as well.

If you have a PostScript printer installed, you have many of the same options in printing TrueType fonts. Figure 22.8 shows the Properties for HP LaserJet 4V/4MV PostScript dialog box, which represents a PostScript printer. Again, you have three options in this dialog box.

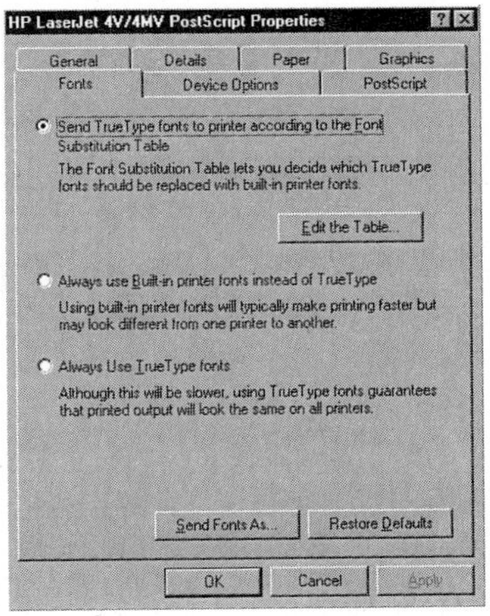

Fig. 22.8 The Fonts tab for a PostScript printer appears more complex than the same tab for a PCL printer.

TrueType Printer Options

The first option, which is the default, causes fonts to be sent according to what is called a font substitution table. This table is discussed in the next section.

The second option instructs Windows to always use built-in printer fonts rather than TrueType fonts. Printing with this option selected can be much faster than normal printing, since Windows does not need to download fonts with each print job. However, unless the printer contains fonts comparable to the TrueType fonts you are using, it will not produce satisfactory results every time. This is because the printer, if it cannot locate a requested font, substitutes its own fonts. If the printer cannot locate a font with the same name, the Courier font is often substituted. Thus, unless you know that all the fonts you will use are also available on the printer, you shouldn't choose this printing option.

The third option instructs Windows to always use TrueType fonts. This, in reality, is at the opposite end of the spectrum from the previous option. If you choose this, then your printing time can be increased tremendously, depending on how you use TrueType fonts in your document. This is because all the TrueType fonts must be downloaded every time they are used. The flip side of this, however, is that you will get the best match between what you see on your screen and what you see on your output. You can control how the fonts are sent by clicking the Send Fonts As button; using this feature is described later, in the section entitled "Sending TrueType Fonts to a PostScript Printer."

PostScript Font Substitution Table

If you have a PostScript printer, and you choose the first method of printing TrueType fonts (Send TrueType fonts to the printer according to the Font Substitution Table), then you may be interested in modifying the table itself. This allows you control over which fonts are substituted and which aren't. Depending on how many fonts are included with your PostScript printer, as well as how they are implemented, you may need to make extensive changes in the table.

To see the font substitution table, display the Properties for printer dialog box (refer to figure 22.8), and then click the Fonts tab. Finally, click the Edit the Table button. This displays the dialog box shown in figure 22.9.

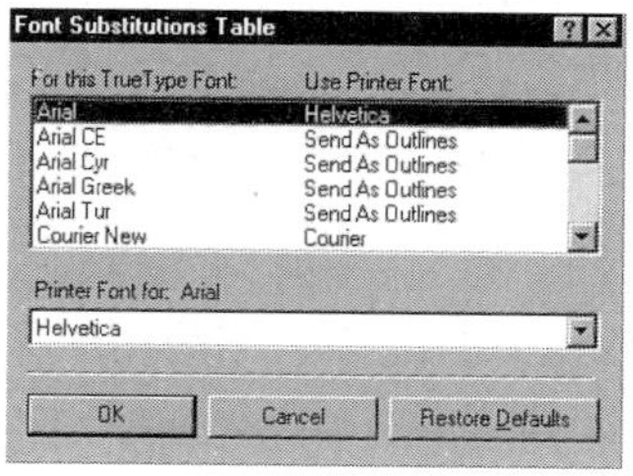

Fig. 22.9 The Font Substitutions Table dialog box enables you to control which PostScript fonts are substituted for which TrueType fonts.

There are two columns in the table. The left column shows all the TrueType fonts installed in your system. To the right of each font, in the right column, is the name of the PostScript font that will be substituted for the TrueType font. You can change the font to be substituted by following these steps:

1. Click the name of a TrueType font. This highlights in the table the row that you want to change.
2. In the drop-down list at the bottom of the dialog box, select a PostScript font to substitute. If you don't want the TrueType font sent without substitution, select the Send As Outlines option from the top of the list.

You can repeat these two steps for as many of the table entries as desired. When you are done making changes, click the OK button at the bottom of the dialog box. Your changes are saved, and are used the next time you print a document.

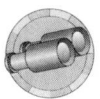

> **Note:** TrueType fonts won't show up in the Font Substitution Table until you have installed them in your system. Installing fonts is covered earlier in this chapter in the section titled "Installing Fonts."

Sending TrueType Fonts to a PostScript Printer

If you have a PostScript printer installed in your system, and you chose the third method of how TrueType fonts should be handled (Always Use TrueType fonts), you can control how Windows sends the fonts to the printer. This is done by displaying the Properties for printer dialog box, clicking the Fonts tab, and then clicking the Send Fonts As button at the bottom of the dialog box. This displays the dialog box shown in figure 22.10.

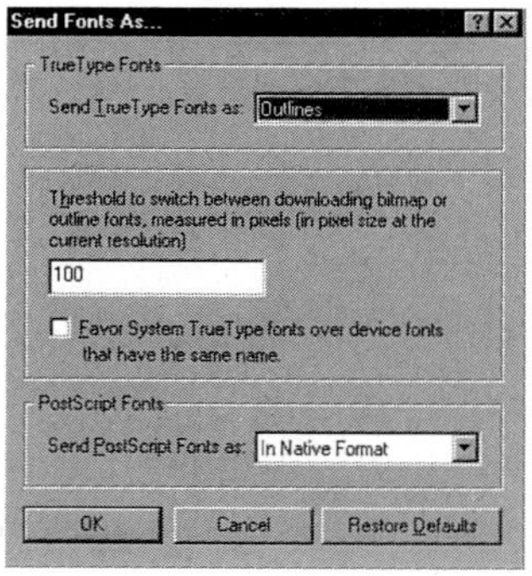

Fig. 22.10 The Send Fonts As dialog box controls how TrueType fonts are sent to a PostScript printer.

At the top of the dialog box, in the TrueType Fonts area, you can select how the fonts are to be sent. There are three possible selections in the drop-down list:

- ***Outlines.*** This option sends TrueType fonts as Adobe Type 1 font outlines. This font format is optimized for both speed (the fonts typically require less space than bitmaps) and scaleability (the outlines are easier to manipulate).
- ***Bitmaps.*** This option results in the TrueType fonts being converted to Adobe Type 3 fonts, which are scaled bitmaps. On some older PostScript printers this limitation may be required, since they might not understand Adobe Type 1 fonts.
- ***Don't Send.*** This option means that TrueType fonts are never sent to the printer. How the printer handles the font information is up to the printer, but typically a different font will be substituted by the printer itself.

You should select the option which is most appropriate to your printer. You also can adjust the parameters by which Windows makes a judgment between when Adobe Type 1 and Type 3 fonts are sent. For instance, you might select bitmaps as the way you typically want to send fonts to the printer, but then have Windows start sending outline fonts

when it makes more sense. This adjustment is made in the Threshold area, in the middle of the dialog box.

For example, in the Threshold area, you can specify a point size at which Windows will switch from bitmap to outline format. Why would you want to do this? Simply because outline fonts are fairly stable in their size requirements; after all, they are nothing but mathematical descriptions of the outline of a font. Bitmap fonts, on the other hand, can grow or shrink in size based on the point size of the typeface. Thus, a 6-point typeface takes less space than a 25-point typeface. It is very possible that the 6-point bitmap typeface will take less space than a 6-point outline typeface.

Exactly where the threshold should be set will vary, based on the resolution of your printer. This makes sense, since a 600 dpi printer requires four times the dots (vertical and horizontal) than a 300 dpi printer does to cover the same area. In general, there is an inverse relationship between the resolution of your printer and the threshold you should set. Thus, the higher the resolution of your printer, the lower the threshold should be. You will probably need to experiment with this setting to see if it offers noticeable results in your printing environment.

In the center, Threshold area of the dialog box, there also is a check box. This check box controls how Windows reacts when it determines that there is a font in your printer that has the same name as a TrueType font you are using. Normally, Windows will use the built-in printer font instead of downloading the TrueType font. If you select this check box, however, you force Windows to always download the TrueType font, regardless of what it detects on the printer.

Finally, at the bottom of the Send Fonts As dialog box is a control that indicates how native PostScript fonts should be handled. There are two settings here, the default being to send the PostScript fonts in their native format (this is the setting you will want most of the time). The other possible setting is Don't Send, which stops Windows from downloading PostScript fonts entirely.

Changing the Fonts Used by Windows

Windows 95 allows you a great deal of control over what fonts you use in the operating system itself. You can change fonts used in title bars, messages, status bars, and other desktop items. To make your own changes, follow these steps:

1. Choose Settings from the Start menu. The Settings menu appears.
2. Choose Control Panel from the Settings menu. The Control Panel window appears.
3. Double-click the Display icon in the Control Panel. The Properties for Display dialog box appears.
4. Click on the Appearance tab. The dialog box appears as shown in figure 22.11.

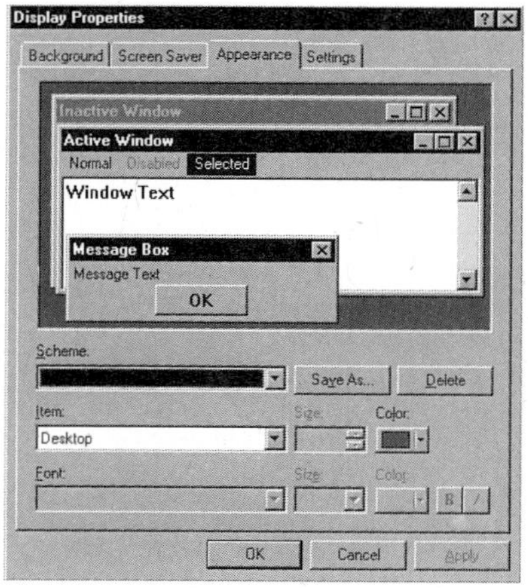

Fig. 22.11 With the Appearance tab selected in the Properties for Display dialog box, you are ready to change the fonts used by Windows.

This dialog box should look familiar if you have used Windows in the past. The dialog box enables you to change color schemes used when

displaying the desktop. However, Windows 95 also enables you to modify fonts used in the display. Notice at the bottom of the dialog box there is a selection labeled Font. To change a desktop item, just click it in the Appearance box example of the desktop. If the desktop object you have selected in the Item box uses text in any way, then the Font area is active and you can modify the font used. You also can change the font attributes, such as size, color, and style (bold, italic, or both).

Windows enables you to change fonts for the following objects:

- Active title bar
- Icon title
- Inactive title bar
- Menu
- Message box
- Palette title
- Selected items

After you select the item whose font you wish to change, you can select any TrueType or system (bitmap) font you desire. As you make changes in the display fonts used, notice that they are updated at the top of the dialog box. When you are satisfied with your changes, click the OK button and your changes are made system-wide.

Changing Fonts in Applications

Earlier in this chapter, you learned that when you install a font it is available for use in your applications. This is true for the next time you start the application. This means if the application is running when you install a font, the chances are good that the font will not be available until you close the application and restart it.

There is a problem with this, however. Application programs typically maintain a font list of their own, usually in some kind of INI file for the application. If the application is using the INI file at the time the fonts are being installed, it might not get updated properly during the font's installation process. Because of this, it is generally a good idea to close all your applications before you install a font. When you later start the application, the new font should be available in your font list.

How you actually use fonts in an application is beyond the scope of this chapter, since it can vary tremendously. You should refer to your application's manual or online help system to discover exactly how to put the new fonts to use.

23

Handling Graphics

by Ewan Grantham

In this chapter, you learn how to set up Windows 95 to make the most of the graphics you have, or are creating. If you're creating a business presentation, the right graphics can mean a more effective sales pitch, as well as making it easier to "sell your point." Regardless of what you use your system for, graphics can make it more entertaining, and even make it easier to get around.

Windows 95 incorporates a number of changes to take advantage of the improvement in video cards and displays. Whether you're a game designer working with WinG, or a casual user trying to set up a nice background, taking advantage of these changes can result in a more productive environment.

This chapter covers the following issues to help you get the most out of your Windows 95 graphics:

- How to associate your graphics applications in Explorer
- How to change your printer handles graphics
- How to identify and know when to use different graphics file types

- How to use the new Windows 95 features to adjust your system for its best graphics performance
- How to use Paint to create your own graphics

Properties for Graphics

One of the big changes in Windows 95 is the addition of the *Properties* setting to almost every object you can access. This means that you can adjust almost every part of your system to allow for greater customization, and make those adjustments without spending a lot of time changing device drivers or rebooting your computer. Graphics are no exception.

If you right-click on your desktop and select Properties, you get the Display Properties sheet, which has several tabs. The first tab that can affect your graphics is the Settings tab, which allows you to set your resolution and color depth as shown in figure 23.1.

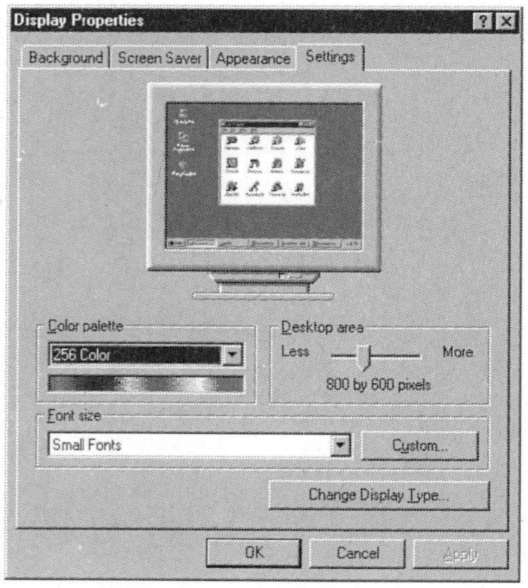

Fig. 23.1 The Display Properties Settings tab allows you to set your resolution and color depth.

With Windows 95, you can make most of these changes "on the fly" — in other words, without having to reboot your machine. This makes it easier to run in different resolutions and different color depths as your programs require.

Depending on what you're doing, you'll find that various settings have different effects. For example, if you're playing a digital video you'll discover that you want a resolution of 640 × 480 to make the image take up as much of your screen as possible, while your color depth will be either 256 colors (which plays back faster but doesn't look quite as good) or 16-bit color. On the other hand, if you're drawing a complex graphic, say of a gear assembly, you will probably want a resolution of 1024 × 768 to give you as much room on the screen as possible to work.

System Properties for Graphics

Just as you can change the screen settings, you can also change how graphics are treated at the system level. To do this, go to the Start menu, select Settings, Control Panel, and then double-click on the System icon. A window with four tabs appears. Select the Performance tab and you'll notice in the Advanced Settings box a button labeled Graphics. Click on the button and the window shown in figure 23.2 appears.

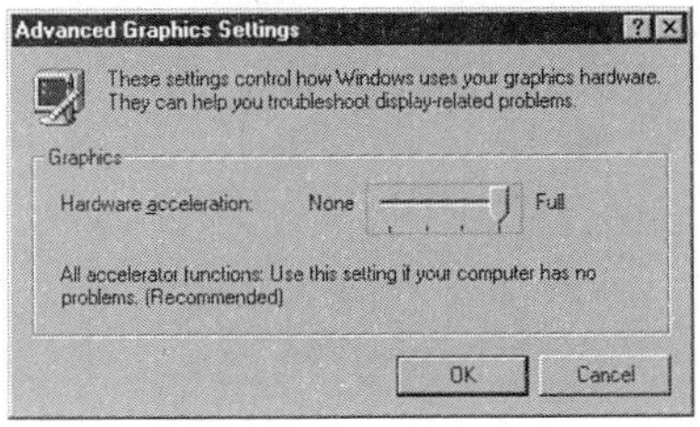

Fig. 23.2 The Graphics window set to its default values

The Graphics window shows you any problems the system has noticed with your graphics setup. It also has a default setting for the "acceleration" of graphics on your system based on the type of video card you have. In general, you want to leave the acceleration setting alone, as Windows has already tested your card when it did the hardware setup. Changing the values on this may speed your system up, but may also cause video problems to occur.

There are a few other places where working with the Windows 95 settings for graphics and graphics files can make using your system easier. To begin with, look at setting up associations for your graphics files.

Types of File Formats

When you work with graphics, you need to know the two basic graphics categories—*raster* and *vector*. You also need to know the various formats you might want to use, as well as their strengths and weaknesses.

Raster Graphics

Raster graphics (or *bit maps*) are graphics images composed of small dots (called *pixels*). The pixels can be simple *on-or-off bits* as in a black and white image, or represent various colors. Generally you will work with four levels of raster images: black and white (1 bit per pixel), 16-colors (4 bits per pixel), 256-colors (8 bits per pixel), or 16-million colors (24 bits per pixel, also called *Truecolor* mode). Raster graphics do not generally scale to larger sizes very well; the dots become squares or rectangles and the image appears grainy. Raster graphics also use lots of disk space and memory. However, they generally display faster than vector graphics and can show much more true-to-life detail than vector graphics. Examples of raster graphics are GIF files and BMP files. Following is a list of the major raster formats:

Extension	Type
BMP, DIB, RLE	**Windows bitmap files**. This is the standard bitmap format supported by Microsoft Windows in programs such as Paint. Unlike many other formats, BMPs and DIBs have no compression options, so even simple pictures can be quite large.
GIF	**CompuServe Graphics Interchange Format files**. The GIF format was developed by CompuServe to provide good file compression and relatively fast decompression speed— important criteria for pictures designed to be passed around electronically. The GIF format is a

Extension	Type
	very popular format for online services, but is limited to a maximum of 256 colors. Two standards have been developed: 87a and 89a.
JPG, JFI, JIF	**JPEG compressed files**. The JPEG format was developed to provide a high degree of compression for images. It is a "lossy" compression method, meaning that some color information from the original is lost. JPEG is generally appropriate for photographed and scanned images, and works best if the images originate from 24-bit sources. JPEG is generally inappropriate for any type of line-drawn art.
PCX	**ZSoft picture files**. PCX files are a fairly early PC graphics format, which has been extended over the years to support more and varied color depths. PCX files may or may not be compressed. For example, PCX is the standard used for submission of graphic files to be incorporated in Que books.
TIF	**Tagged Image Format files**. The Tagged Image Format was developed by several companies, including Aldus, to be the "be-all" and "end-all" of image file formats. Because of its scope and extensibility, it is an extremely complex format. It also is an example of a standard that has as many exceptions as it does requirements, thus making it a clear example of the danger of design by committee.

Vector Graphics

Vector graphics are graphics objects composed of the definition of drawn shapes and lines—rectangles, arcs, ellipses, curves, and so on. Because they are descriptions of shapes rather than a collection of individual dots (pixels), vector graphics may be scaled more readily and more accurately than raster graphics. This also means that they tend to be smaller. However, they often are slower to display than raster graphics because of the need to "calculate" the picture each time. The CGM and WPG files are examples of common vector graphics.

The vector formats you're most likely to work with are listed here:

Extension	Type
CDR, PAT, BMF	**CorelDRAW and CorelGALLERY**. These formats are used by Corel products and are a proprietary standard.
CGM	**Computer Graphics Metafile**. CGM files are vector graphic files that have been designed to be useful as clip art. They scale (grow larger or smaller) well and have the distinction of being the only ANSI standard graphic format. There are many flavors of CGM files as the original format was adopted, then "enhanced," by several different vendors. Although this is primarily a vector format, certain forms can also incorporate raster data.
EPS	**Encapsulated PostScript files**. EPS files are PostScript language files, created for PostScript printers. Many programs that understand PostScript (particularly from Adobe) will also use this format.
GEM, IMG	**GEM metafiles and GEM image format**. GEM metafiles are vector graphic files that include drawing commands for rendering pictures. They are similar to CGM files. GEM files originated on the Amiga, and have gone through several enhancement periods. The IMG format, on the other hand, was originally designed for the Atari computers, and then migrated to PCs for several GEM-based products, such as Ventura Publisher. IMG files may also be embedded in GEM metafiles.
WPG	**DrawPerfect graphics files**. WPG files are a vector format that WordPerfect Corporation developed for use with its word processing products. Like other formats, WPG has evolved over the years.

The particular image format you use depends on the tools you have available, what format any existing images you use come in, and what you're planning to use the images for.

> **Note:** One format not listed in the preceding table, but expected to become a major player soon, is the new graphics format that CompuServe has developed to replace the GIF standard. This new, enhanced 24-bit lossless (meaning that the image doesn't allow any bits of information to be lost to improve compression)

specification will offer the professional graphics community a significant enhancement to the earlier GIF 89a specification while also eliminating the proprietary LZW software, replacing it with compression technology compliant with the PNG (pronounced *ping*) specification. At this time it has not been announced whether this graphics format will be called PNG or will simply be referred to as a new version of GIF.

Setting Associations for Graphics Files

After you've had a computer for a while, you tend to have a number of graphics in different formats scattered around the system. Not only do you have the graphics that you have obtained or created, but also you have the graphics that various programs have loaded. One way to speed the process up is to set up associations in the Registry for various types of graphics files. This way, when you see a graphics file listed in the Explorer, you can double-click on it and have the appropriate graphics application display the file.

You can set up this association two ways. The first is to go into Explorer and right-click one of the graphics files you see listed. When the pop-up menu appears, choose Open With to bring up the Open With window. Type in the full path to the graphics application you want to use, or click on the Other button to bring up a File Open requestor for finding the graphics program you want.

A more direct way is to open an Explorer window and choose View, Options. From the two tabs that appear, select the File Types tab in which you can select a known program, or use a File Open requestor to specify what program will be used to view this type of image. An example is seen in figure 23.3.

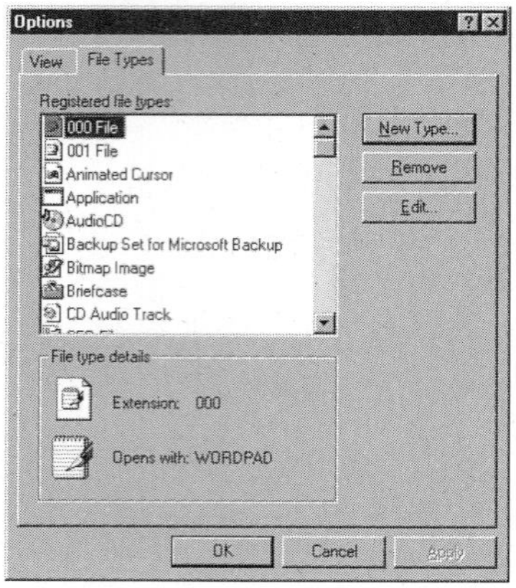

Fig. 23.3 Graphics extension assignment in Explorer using the File Types tab.

You can find more information about both of these methods in Chapter 3, "New Windows 95 Tools." With graphics files it is important to know these options because many graphics programs will try to change the association when they're installed. In other words, you may normally use a small viewer for your JPEG files, and then, after installing a graphics program, discover that it now gets loaded when you double-click on the graphics file. By using one of these methods, you can change things back to the way they were.

You can drag a graphics file from Explorer to the desktop for easy access. Double-clicking on the file will automatically start the application you "tied it to" in the Explorer association and then display the graphics file.

The Graphics Tab for Printing

Printers under Windows 95, as with Windows 3.11 before it, can use one of the Microsoft printer drivers, or a custom driver developed by the vendor. If your printer uses one of the Microsoft drivers, editing its properties will give you a screen with four tabs for controlling how it is used. The easiest way to get to these properties is to go to the Start menu and select Settings, Printers. Right-click the printer you want to edit, and the Properties sheet for that printer appears. Depending on the type of printer you have, the number of tabs available here will vary, but most printers will have a Graphics tab. Figure 23.4 shows what the Graphics tab looks like for the Fax printer in Windows 95.

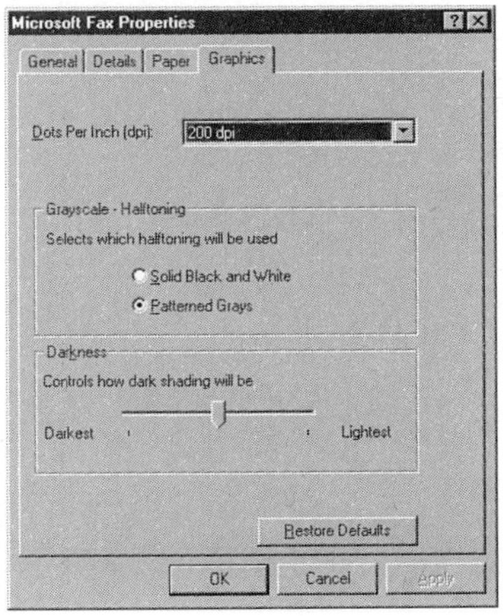

Fig. 23.4 Graphics tab showing settings for the Fax printer.

The setup for this is similar to what you would use for any dot-matrix or ink-jet printer that did not support color. DPI (dots per inch—how many bits will represent each inch of your image) should usually be adjusted to the highest number supported by the printer (in the case of a fax, it should be the highest number you think the fax on the *other* end will support). If you're working with graphics images, you almost never want to use the Solid Black and White option; however, if you're printing text only, it can save you a little speed. The Darkness option should be somewhere toward the middle of the scale unless your printer needs servicing. Otherwise your image will either look washed out (like an overexposed picture) or too dark (like an underexposed picture).

A color printer has many more options to consider, and almost always has a custom setup for this reason. For example, see figure 23.5, which shows the setup for an HP 560c (a color inkjet printer from Hewlett-Packard) in Windows 95.

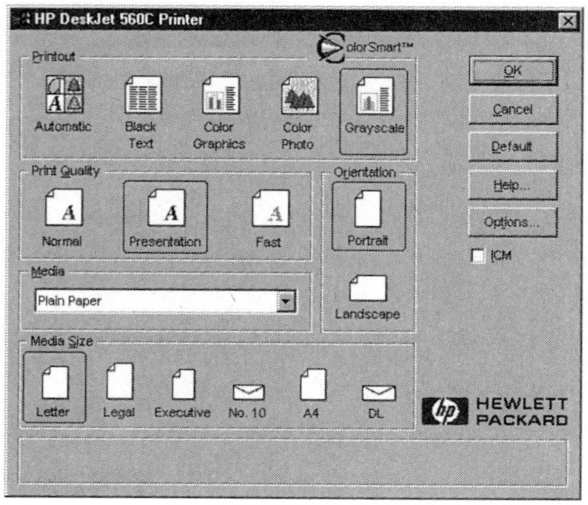

Fig. 23.5 Setup for an HP560c printer.

As you can see, you have many different options. These options give you the flexibility of having the best results for any type of graphic, whether a scanned photo or some black and white piece of clip art.

Using Windows 95 Paint

As you may know, Windows 3.1 came with a simple, yet useful graphics program called *Paintbrush.* Windows 95 comes with a graphics program called *Paint.* The big difference is the added functionality in the Windows 95 Paint program.

Figure 23.6 shows what many people think Paint is good for—drawing squiggly lines. Well, obviously you can do that, but at least you can draw them in several colors. Paint also prepares you for using the other tools.

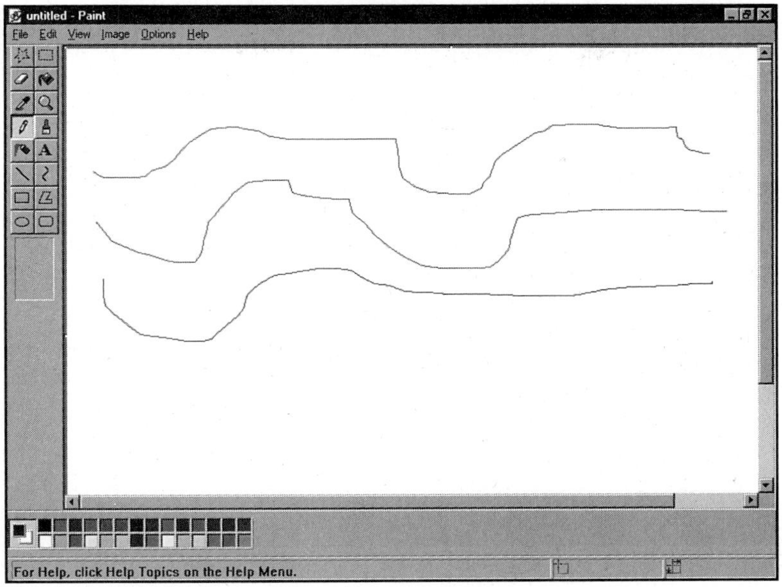

Fig. 23.6 Using Paint to draw squiggly lines.

Starting with the same line, you can use a different tool to create a very different effect. Figure 23.7 shows how you can use the Airbrush tool to create a squiggly line that has quite a bit of character. Notice how selecting each of the three different "dispersal" options affects the look of the lines. From a design aspect, also notice how using multiple lines in different weights gives a feeling of texture to a simple graphic.

Another useful tool is the Fill tool (which looks like a paint can). Normally you would think of using it to fill in a solid area (such as a square), but by using the lines you had earlier, you can get an abstract, *posterized* (also sometimes called solarized, referring to an image that looks like it was overexposed and then colored) effect by doing a fill of the background with a color. Look at figure 23.8, and you notice how certain areas remain unaffected, adding to the overall feel.

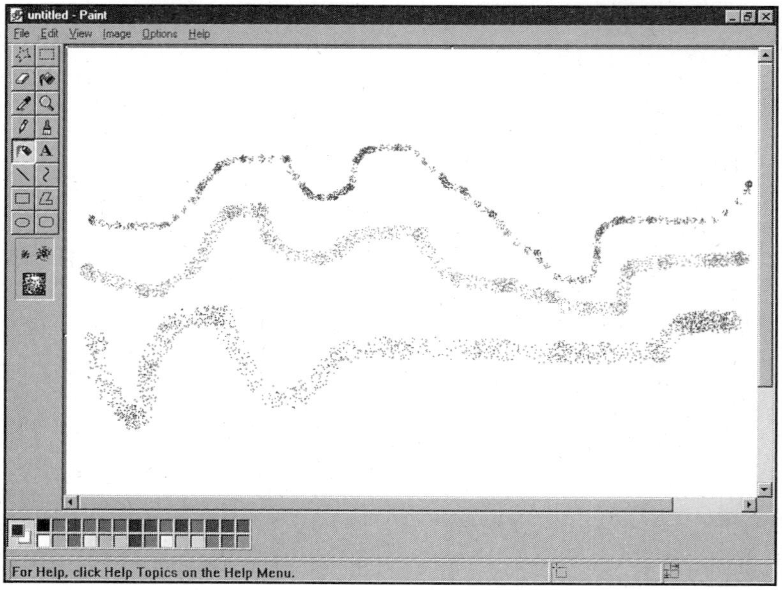

Fig. 23.7 Using the Airbrush tool to draw some lines in Windows 95 Paint.

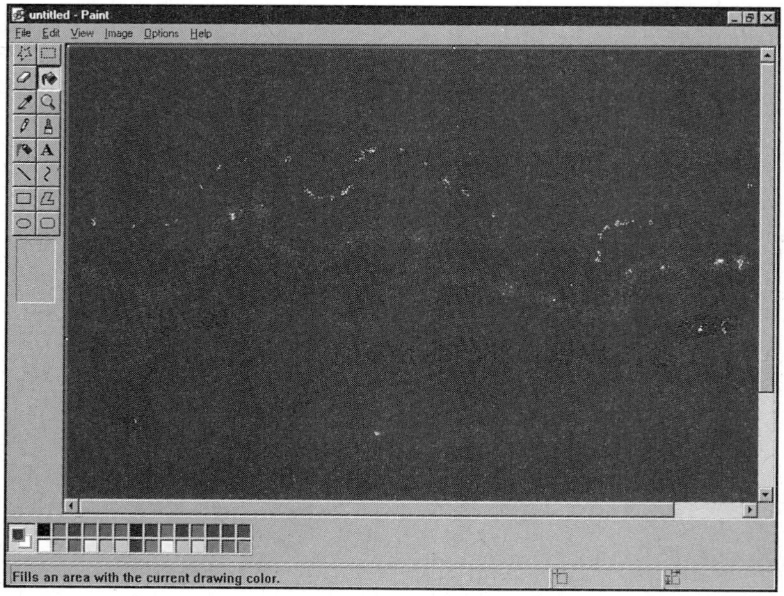

Fig. 23.8 An unusual use for the Fill tool.

While you drew a squiggly line earlier with the Pencil, going back and doing the same thing with the Paintbrush by using the various point options can give you many interesting variations. Figure 23.9 shows how the different strokes can give a variety of weights and textures to the end result.

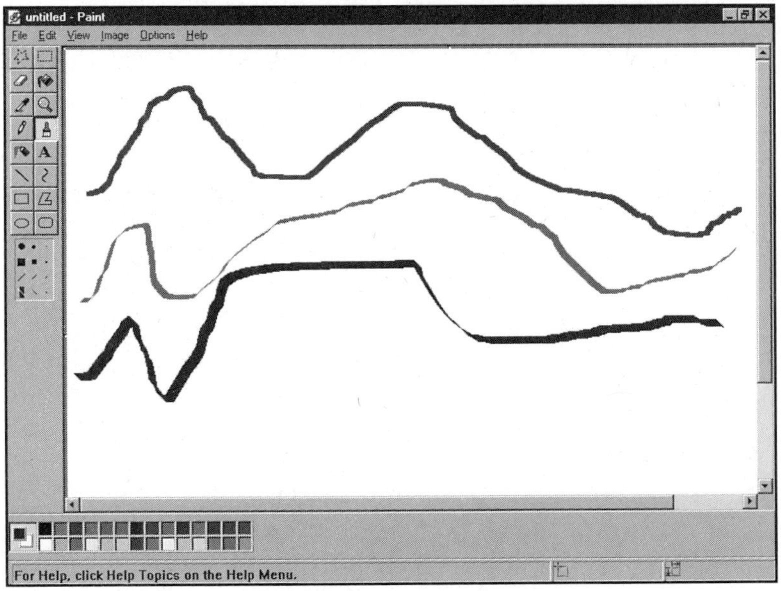

Fig. 23.9 Different types of lines drawn with Paint.

Finally, as an example of quickly building something attractive, look at figure 23.10, which is a sunset (sort of) that took under 10 minutes to create. In addition to the tools mentioned earlier, the Ellipse tool was used to create the sun and its companion.

One thing that many people do with the images they've created or modified is to use them as their desktop wallpaper. Formerly, you used Paintbrush (the Windows 3.x drawing applet) to create the image, and then used the Control Panel to set up your wallpaper. Because setting an image up as wallpaper is done so often, in Paint you can do this without leaving the program. If you look at the File menu, you will see two options for this, one called Set as Wallpaper (Tiled) and one called Set as Wallpaper (Centered). If you've already saved the loaded image, choose the appropriate menu selection. If you haven't saved the image yet, save it and then choose one of these wallpaper selections from the File menu.

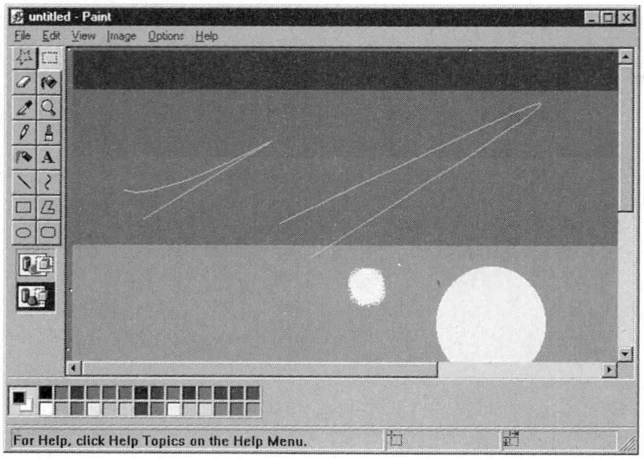

Fig. 23.10 Stylized sunset using several tools from Paint.

Looking at the Options menu, you can also work with what colors are available by using the Edit Colors option. This option gives you a color table with a slider that can be used to find the particular color you're interested in, and then add it to your palette.

Now that you've seen some of what Paint can do, you should think about using it the next time you need a quick, custom 2-D graphic.

KILLER WINDOWS 95

24

Getting the Most from Your Printer

by Allen L. Wyatt

Now that your printer is installed, you understand how the print spooler works, and your fonts are in place, you can use your printer with no problems, right? In most cases, the answer is yes. There are a few times, however, when things don't quite go as planned. The purpose of this chapter is to discuss ways you can get the most from your printer. Specifically, you will learn the following:

- How to speed up your printer
- What the solutions are to common printing problems
- How you can use the built-in Windows 95 Print Troubleshooter to help solve your printing problems

Speeding Up Your Printer

Printers come in a wide variety of shapes, sizes, and capabilities. This last attribute—capabilities—is the one that most affects your everyday use of the printer. Printing capabilities can dramatically affect the speed at which your print jobs are processed.

Regardless of the type of printer you use, you can put a multitude of tricks to work to improve the speed at which your printer operates. You can approach the issue from three directions: the Windows 95 side, the printer side, and the computer side.

The Windows 95 Side of the Fence

You can do a variety of things in Windows 95 to speed up your print jobs. The choices you make, however, often affect the quality of the output you receive. Before looking at those choices, however, look at what you can do without affecting quality.

If your computer has multiple hard drives, make sure Windows 95 is set so the swap files are stored on the fastest hard drive. This will improve performance when it comes to storing print jobs on the hard drive and later retrieving them. To change where the swap file is located, follow the directions in Chapter 9, "Exploiting Memory, Space, and Resources."

So there is no possibility of slowing down your print job, you can disable the print spooler altogether. This means your print job is sent directly to the printer, without an intermediate stop on your hard drive. Turning off print spooling is explained fully in Chapter 21, "Printing from Windows 95," but you can follow these steps as well:

1. Open the Printers folder and right-click on the icon for the printer you'll be using. This displays the context menu for the printer.

2. Choose the Properties option from the context menu. The Printer Properties sheet appears.
3. Make sure the Details tab is selected, and then click on the Spool Settings button. The Spool Settings dialog box appears.
4. At the top of the dialog box, select the Print directly to the printer option.

When you close the dialog boxes, any print job for that printer will bypass the print spooler entirely.

> **Note:** Although printing directly to the printer may make the print job go faster, it can decrease your productivity in the long run. While Windows 95 is waiting on your printer, you can't do any other work with the program that is printing. Make sure you temper your printing needs with the need to continue working on other projects.

To really speed up your print jobs, the trick is to make them as simple as possible. You can do a variety of things in Windows 95 to make the jobs simpler, but these also typically affect the quality of the print job. Try one or more of these suggestions:

- ***Turn off graphics output.*** Many programs allow you to control exactly what is sent to the printer. If you turn off graphics, the print jobs will be smaller. This is great for draft or intermediate printings of a document.
- ***Turn on draft quality.*** Some application programs allow you to enable a setting that turns on draft quality. This means the program uses fonts native to the printer, which decreases processing time. With some printers, you can change the printer properties to use a draft quality built in to the printer itself.

- ***Reduce resolution.*** Some printer drivers allow you to control the resolution at which graphics are printed. Printing at a lower resolution can speed processing time. This is covered in Chapter 23, "Handling Graphics."

- ***Turn off font downloading.*** If your printer has built-in fonts, you can use them instead of downloading TrueType fonts. You do this on the Fonts tab of the printer Properties sheet, as discussed in Chapter 22, "Working with Fonts." If you don't download fonts, the printer substitutes a font it has available, and processing of the print job takes less time.

The Printer Side of the Fence

With many printers, there is not much you can do to speed them up. This is particularly true with dot-matrix printers, which are limited by the speed at which the print head can travel across the page. There is one area you can check on your dot-matrix printer, however. Check to make sure that bidirectional printing is turned on. Many printers allow this to be controlled via a dip switch or a jumper setting. Bidirectional printing means that the print head can print as it moves in either direction on the page. Some printers come configured for only unidirectional printing, meaning that the print head wastes movement in one direction.

If you have an ink jet or laser printer, you typically have greater control over the performance of the unit. The first item to check is the amount of memory in the printer. If the printer understands some form of page description language (such as PCL or PostScript), then the entire page is constructed in the printer's memory before it is placed on the page. Thus, memory becomes particularly critical if you're printing large or complex print jobs—the printer needs more memory for these types of print jobs. Most printers come with a base amount of memory (such as a megabyte or two), but can be upgraded. Some printers can actually contain quite a bit of memory (24M or 32M). If you're working with complex print jobs, you should consider upgrading to 12M or more of printer memory.

Another area that can generally be improved on faster laser printers is the interface used for the printer. Some already come configured with two or three types of interfaces. Choosing the wrong interface can slow down your printer—in effect, the interface acts as a bottleneck. The laser printer could go faster, but it has to wait for information to arrive through the interface. When it comes to the interface, keep the following in mind:

- In most instances, the serial interface is the slowest you can choose. Only choose the serial interface when distance between the printer and your computer is excessive and speed is not an issue.
- The parallel interface is perhaps the most common interface used with printers. Make sure your computer and printer are using the highest-capability parallel settings possible. For instance, if your printer can handle bidirectional parallel communications, you should make sure your computer can as well. These types of parallel connections often have operational modes that are superior to the older IBM PC parallel interface.
- If you're printing over a network, consider getting a native interface for the network. For instance, if you have an Ethernet network, you can often get a 10BaseT interface that fits directly into the printer. This allows information to be transferred to the printer at the speed of your network—typically 10 Mbps or greater.

On most printers you can select the fonts or print mode that will be used by the printer. For instance, you can instruct the printer to use a draft font or a lower resolution when printing. While this may work for some jobs, other programs may override your settings by sending commands that change the font or resolution to higher settings.

Finally, some top-of-the-line laser printers have the capability of installing a hard drive. This disk is either contained within the printer itself, or sits externally, next to the printer. The hard drive is used to store printer fonts and predefined forms. Taking advantage of such a device can greatly increase the speed at which your print jobs are processed. The reason is quite simple—the font or form does not have to be downloaded from the computer with every print job. Instead, the command to use the font or form is downloaded, and the actual image is retrieved from the printer's hard drive. This can result in much faster performance of the printer.

Your Computer's Role

Believe it or not, your computer has a role in how quickly your printer can do its work. Many of today's printers are quite capable, and they can print pages very quickly. If your computer is not quite up to snuff, the printer could actually be waiting on your computer. The best way to make sure that your computer is not slowing down your printer is to check three areas: your CPU, RAM, and hard drive.

If your CPU is an older model (meaning 386), then it is very possible that your computer cannot perform all the tasks expected of it in an efficient manner. If you have print spooling turned on, your print job is in the spooler, and you're doing other work, then time is taken from your print spooler by a CPU that is not as quick at switching between tasks as it could be. If you print a lot of large print jobs, you may want to consider a faster CPU.

The amount of RAM in your computer determines how many things Windows 95 can do at once without resorting to the hard drive. Although print jobs are almost always spooled to the hard disk, there comes a time when they must be moved through memory to go to the printer. If memory is limited and you're running other programs, chances are good there is little free memory available for other operations. This means that virtual memory must be used, which slows down the overall speed of your system—including printing. This becomes particularly critical if you have only 4M of memory. In such an instance, consider upgrading to at least 8M, and possibly more.

Under Windows 95, your hard drive always gets a good workout. This is particularly true when using virtual memory or when printing large documents. Virtual memory results in RAM information being written to the swap file, on disk, for short periods of time. Print jobs, when they're spooled, are always stored on your hard disk. If the amount of space on your hard drive is limited, then the size of print jobs you can handle is also limited. If your hard drive is slow (14 ms or greater), then sending print jobs to and from the hard drive is slow, as well. If you routinely process large print jobs or a large quantity of small print jobs, consider upgrading to a newer, faster hard drive. You'll see an immediate improvement not only in your print speeds but also in your overall Windows performance.

Troubleshooting Common Problems

It never fails. Just when you thought you had everything under control, a new problem crops up. Printing is no exception. You are bound to run into glitches that will frustrate you until you discover the solutions. Your first step in determining where your problem lies is to find out if the printing problem is evidenced only in a particular application, or globally throughout Windows 95. The best way to discover this is to print a test page for the printer. To do this, follow these steps:

1. Display the Printers folder, and then right-click the printer you want to test. A context menu appears.
2. From the context menu, select Properties. The printer Properties sheet for the printer appears.
3. Click the Print Test Page button at the bottom of the sheet.

You should see a printout appear on your printer. If you do, and it appears properly, the printing problem probably lies with your application. If it does not print properly, you have a global problem you need to address within Windows 95. Many Windows 95 printing problems can be boiled down to a few common maladies. The following sections discuss common printing problems and what you can do to correct them.

Driver Problems

Printer drivers are at the heart of how Windows 95 uses printers. If you have the wrong printer driver installed, or you have the wrong printer driver settings, at best you won't be able to use your printer fully, and at worst you won't be able to use the printer at all.

Make sure the printer driver you have selected matches the printer actually connected to the printer port. If you can't find the proper printer driver, contact the vendor for a driver disk. Alternatively, you could select a compatible printer driver, but only if you're sure it can be used by the printer you have. Remember that if you choose a compatible printer driver (instead of one specifically for your printer), some printer options may not work from within Windows 95.

The Wrong Font Prints

If the fonts printed on paper don't match those you selected in your application, there could be several reasons. The first thing to check is to make sure you've installed the fonts correctly in your system. You should be able to select the desired fonts, and they should appear on-screen. For some types of fonts, you need to install both a screen and printer version. If you've installed the screen font, but not the printer font, this can lead to mismatches.

To install printer fonts, you have two options. You can use either the font installer program that was supplied with the fonts package, or Windows 95 capabilities. The latter can be accomplished if you're using a PCL printer that allows you to download soft fonts. To do this, follow these steps:

1. Display the Printers folder, and then right-click on the printer you want to use from DOS. A context menu appears.
2. From the context menu, select Properties. The printer Properties sheet for the printer appears.
3. Click on the Fonts tab, and then on the Install Printer Fonts button. The font installer dialog box appears, shown in figure 24.1.

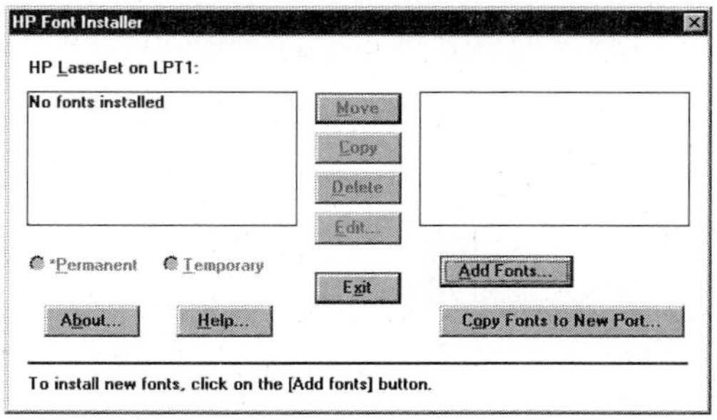

Fig. 24.1 The Fonts tab of the printer Properties sheet for a PCL printer allows you to install printer fonts.

4. Click on the Add Fonts button. You're asked where the fonts are located that you want to install.
5. Supply the drive and path to where the printer fonts are located. Typically this will be on a floppy disk provided with your printer or from the font provider. Once you have provided this information, click on OK.
6. In the right side of the font installer dialog box, select the fonts you want installed on the printer. Click the Move or Copy button to transfer the fonts.
7. Repeat steps 4 though 6 until you're satisfied with the fonts installed.
8. Click the Exit button when you're done.

Another item to check is that font downloading has not been disabled for the printer. Check the Fonts tab in the printer Properties sheet to make sure the fonts are being handled the way you expect.

Finally, check to make sure the printer driver you're using is the proper one for your printer. If you have substituted a different printer driver, then you can experience unexpected results. The printer driver, for instance, may believe the printer has a certain set of fonts. The printer, on the other hand, has a different set of fonts. Only those fonts indicated in the printer driver will show as available on the printer (even though they may not, in reality, be there).

TrueType Fonts Won't Print

You probably are using a printer that uses the PostScript page description language. You need to make sure you've enabled TrueType fonts

in the printer driver. If you have not, then other fonts will be substituted for the TrueType fonts, or you won't see any output at all.

To enable printing of TrueType fonts on a PostScript printer, follow these steps:

1. Display the Printers folder, and then right-click the printer you want to use from DOS. A context menu appears.
2. From the context menu, select Properties. The printer Properties sheet for the printer appears.
3. Click the Fonts tab. The dialog box shown in figure 24.2 appears.

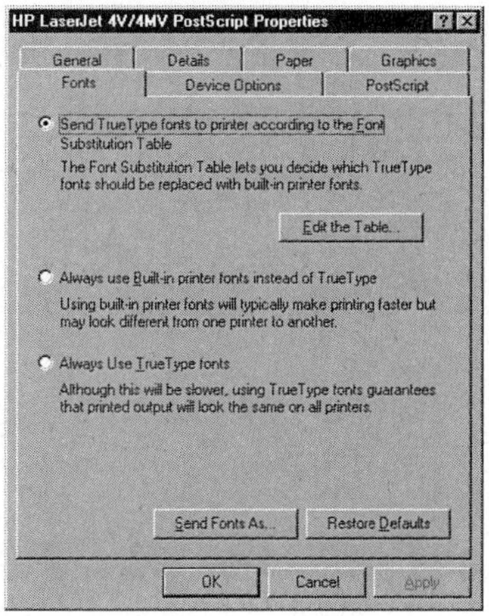

Fig. 24.2 The Fonts tab of the printer Properties sheet for a PostScript printer allows you to change how TrueType fonts are handled.

From this dialog box you can indicate how you want TrueType fonts to be handled by your printer. Make sure you're using settings consistent with both your desires and the capabilities of your printer. For a

complete discussion of how TrueType fonts are handled in various printers, refer to Chapter 22, "Working with Fonts."

Another possible cause of the problem is that your printer is incapable of printing TrueType fonts. Not all printers can print TrueType fonts. Older models of LaserJet printers, for example, cannot understand the PCL commands enabled in the LaserJet Series II and Series III printers, and other laser printers cannot accommodate downloadable fonts. Check your printer documentation to determine the capabilities of your individual printer.

You Can't Print in an MS-DOS Window

Printing in an MS-DOS window is a bit different than printing in Windows itself. Where Windows allows you to set up a wide variety of printers, DOS expects that you have only one or two printers connected to your system, and that they be connected to a parallel port. To use specific printers from DOS, you must map them to different ports. For instance, you might have five different printers defined within Windows, but you want to print to only one of them in a DOS window. So the print system knows which printer should be used, mapping the port is necessary. To map a printer to a port, follow these steps:

1. Display the Printers folder, and then right-click on the printer you want to use from DOS. A context menu appears.
2. From the context menu, select Properties. The printer Properties sheet for the printer appears.
3. Click on the Details tab, and then on the Port Settings button. The dialog box shown in figure 24.3 appears.
4. Make sure the Spool DOS Print Job check box is selected.

When you close the dialog boxes and open an MS-DOS window, you will be able to print to the port from your DOS programs.

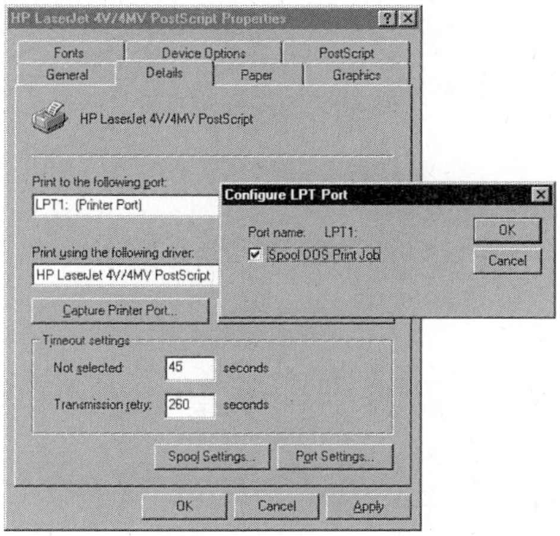

Fig. 24.3 The Configure LPT Port dialog box allows you to indicate if DOS printing is available from the port.

Your Print File Is Too Big

When trying to print a huge document, you might get an error indicating that your disk is full. What is happening is that the print spooler is trying to write the print job to the disk, and it cannot; it has run out of room. There are three solutions to this problem:

- ***Chop your printing job into smaller portions.*** Perhaps you can print only certain pages, or don't print the entire thing at once.
- ***Move your swap file so it is on a disk drive with more space.*** How you can do this is covered in Chapter 9, "Exploiting Memory, Space, and Resources."

- ***Print directly to your printer.*** Turn off the print spooler (as covered earlier in this chapter) so the job goes directly to the printer instead of being written to a disk file.

Incomplete Printing

If only part of a page is printed from your printer, chances are good it is because of the complexity of the page. Start by determining if the page had a lot of graphics or type fonts. If the answer is yes, then your printer may not have enough memory to handle the demands of the print job.

There are several ways you can work around the problem:

- ***Decrease the print resolution.*** If your printer allows you to select different print resolutions (for instance, 300 dpi vs. 600 dpi), try the lower setting. The quality of the output won't be as good, but you may be able to get the entire page out.

- ***Decrease the complexity of the job.*** Reduce the number of fonts or the size or quantity of graphics on the page. This, in turn, requires less printer memory, and you may be able to print the page.

- ***Print to another printer.*** You may know of another printer that has the resources to print your job. If you can reach the printer through your network, redirect the job. If the printer is located elsewhere and cannot be reached from your computer, print the job to a disk file. You can then take the disk file to the printer and output it there.

- ***Add memory to your printer.*** This is the best long-term solution, particularly if you'll be printing quite a few print jobs at this resolution or complexity. In order to do this, you'll need to refer to your printer documentation to determine what is possible and how to go about adding the memory.

Your Print Job Disappears

You've pressed the Print button in an application, and printing seems to go OK from your computer, but nothing comes out of the printer. Typically, this is the result of the printer being directed to the wrong printer port. Check to determine what printer port the printer is physically connected to. Then, open the Properties sheet for the printer and make sure (in the Details tab) that the printer is using the same port.

It may also be that your printer is "confused" for some reason. The easiest way to see whether this is the issue is to turn the printer off and back on. After the printer warms up and comes on-line (the on-line or ready light is illuminated), try printing your job again.

Printing Is Slower Than Normal

If you've been using your printer for some time, but lately it is printing a bit sluggishly, here are a few things you should try:

- Turn the printer off and back on. It may be that memory used in a previous print job was not released properly. Restarting the printer should clear the memory and make it all available again.
- In the Properties sheet for the printer, click on the Details tab and then on Spool Settings. Make sure the Spool data format is set to EMF. Enhanced Meta Files take less room and are faster to process than raw data files.
- Make sure that the printer driver you have loaded for the printer is the proper printer driver. Using a compatible printer driver

instead of the matching printer driver can slow down your print jobs.

- Run the Disk Defragmenter to clean up the hard disk that contains your swap file. It is possible that the disk is very fragmented, and thus slower when retrieving your print job.

Using the Print Troubleshooter

Windows 95 includes a new feature that can help you determine the best solution to your printing woes. This feature is called the Print Troubleshooter. It is part of the Help system built in to Windows. To use the Print Troubleshooter, follow these steps:

1. Choose Help from the Start menu. The Help Topics dialog box appears.
2. Click on the Index tab. The dialog box changes to what is shown in figure 24.4.

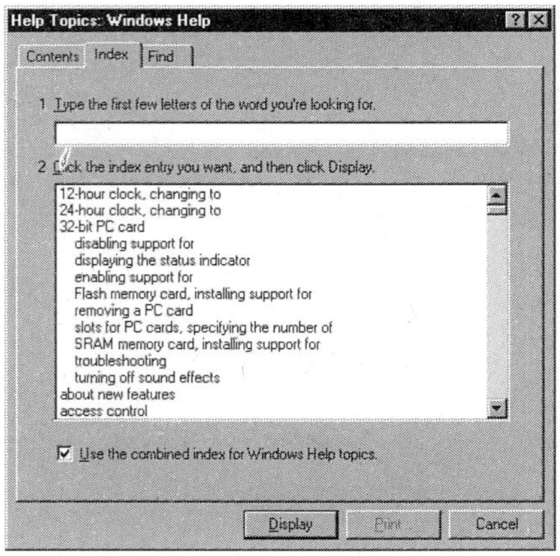

Fig. 24.4 The Help system Index tab allows you to search for topics of interest.

3. In the top portion of the dialog box, enter the word **Print**. The topics at the bottom portion of the dialog box will change accordingly.
4. In the bottom portion of the dialog box, click the print troubleshooting entry.
5. Click the Display button. The Print Troubleshooter dialog box appears, as shown in figure 24.5.

From this point, you can read the questions presented in the dialog box and make your choices from the options available. For instance, if you are having problems getting any output from your printer, the questions would lead you through printing a test page and determining where the problem lies.

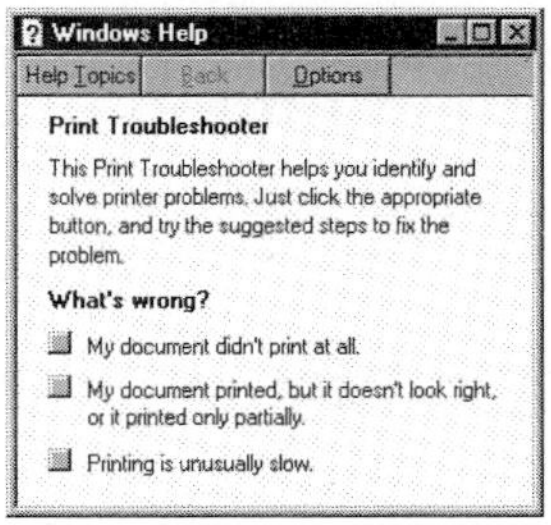

Fig. 24.5 The Print Troubleshooter is part of the Windows 95 Help system.

Adding Multimedia Capability to Your Computer

by Clayton Walnum

Perhaps no computing term has been thrown around more lately than "multimedia." A good portion of the software at your local computer store boasts multimedia features, and salespeople at computer stores use the term multimedia in much the same way snake-oil salesmen used the words "miracle cure." What exactly is multimedia? Is it really the big deal some people would like you to believe? Can multimedia make your computing experience more productive and gratifying?

How can you make your computer multimedia capable? In the discussions to follow, you'll get the answers to these questions (and many more!). In this chapter, you learn:

- What multimedia means
- How to interpret the multimedia standards
- The best systems for multimedia
- What to look for in a sound card
- How to install a sound card and CD-ROM drive

Understanding the Multimedia PC

There are almost as many definitions of the term *multimedia* as there are pages in this book. This is because multimedia is a general term, rather than something specific. Literally, multimedia means nothing more exotic than "many media." In other words, a multimedia application presents its information by using more than one type of media. For example, a slide show accompanied by a recorded voice is a multimedia presentation because it uses two types of media to present its information: slides and recorded tape.

Obviously, multimedia is nothing new. In fact, adding multimedia capabilities to a computer doesn't make the computer some sort of digital wonder of the future; it simply makes your computer able to do things that the rest of the world has been doing for decades. So much for all those Flash Gordon images that have been flitting through your head!

So, what's the big deal? In the early days of computing, computers presented information only as text on a screen. There's nothing wrong with text, of course. After all, the world's greatest thinkers presented their ideas to the brain-challenged masses in only text form. Pythagoras sure didn't have access to a CD-ROM player! Nowadays, though, computers use not only text, but also photographic-quality

images, digitized sound, and full-motion video to present information. And, in case you haven't guessed, such a computer is a multimedia computer.

The fact is that a multimedia PC is basically little more than a computer that's been equipped with a sound card and a CD-ROM drive. But, in order to acquire the coveted multimedia title, the computer has to perform to a specific set of standards created by some folks who know exactly what it takes to run today's (and tomorrow's) multimedia applications. You discover these standards in the next section.

Upgrading Your Hardware to MPC Standards

In order to be sure that the multimedia computer you buy performs well enough to run multimedia software, the Multimedia PC Marketing Council created the Multimedia PC (MPC) specifications. These specifications dictate minimum requirements for every component of your system that affects multimedia. Many older computers do not comply with these standards. If you can remember using your computer while watching first-run episodes of *Family Ties,* chances are good that you're due for a system upgrade! To help you decide how to best go about upgrading your computer, the MPC standards come in two levels.

The Level-1 Multimedia Standard

The Level-1 MPC standard is the absolute minimum requirements for a multimedia system. However, because the Level-1 requirements were determined way back in 1990, they are outdated. While you can run some types of multimedia software on a Level-1 MPC system, most of today's multimedia titles run too slowly, or not at all, on such a system. The Level-1 requirements are listed in Table 25.1.

Table 25.1 The Level-1 MPC Minimum Requirements

Device	Requirements
CPU	16-MHz 386SX
Operating system	Windows with Multimedia Extensions
Memory	2M
Hard disk	30M
Floppy disk	1.44M (high-density)
CD-ROM drive	Single speed with 150K transfer rate and one-second average seek time.
Sound card	8-bit digital sound, 11.025 KHz sampling rate, 8-note synthesizer, MIDI playback, microphone input, and speakers or headphones
Video	640x480 with 16 colors.
Ports	Joystick, MIDI I/O, serial, and parallel
Input	101-key keyboard and a two-button mouse

The Level-2 Multimedia Standard

As hinted at previously, the Level-1 MPC requirements are almost obsolete. If you're planning to upgrade your system for multimedia, you should shoot for at least the Level-2 requirements. This ensures that you'll be able to run most of the latest software. Of course, a Level-2 MPC system is more expensive to put together than a Level-1 system. Just remember the old saying: You get what you pay for! Table 25.2 lists the Level-2 MPC minimum requirements. These days, a Level-2 MPC system goes for about $1,000.

Table 25.2 The Level-2 MPC Minimum Requirements

Device	Requirements
CPU	25-MHz 486SX
Operating system	Windows 3.1 or later
Memory	4M

Device	Requirements
Hard disk	160M
Floppy disk	1.44M (high-density)
CD-ROM drive	Double-speed with 300K transfer rate and 400-ms average seek time.
Sound card	16-bit digital sound, 44.1 KHz sampling rate, stereo channels, 8-note synthesizer, and MIDI playback
Video	640 x 480 with 65,536 colors
Ports	Joystick, MIDI I/O, serial, and parallel
Input	101-key keyboard and a two-button mouse

Beyond Level-2

Keep in mind that although the Level-2 MPC requirements are the newest specifications, they represent only a minimum Level-2 MPC system. To get a truly worthwhile MPC system, you're going to have to boost some of the minimum requirements listed in the Level-2 standard. Table 25.3 shows the average MPC requirements for today's MPC systems. If you upgrade your system to meet Table 25.3's specifications, you'll be able to get satisfactory results with virtually any MPC software package on the market today.

Table 25.3 Recommended Average MPC Requirements

Device	Requirements
CPU	66-MHz 486
Operating system	Windows 95
Memory	8M
Hard disk	500M
Floppy disk	1.44M (high-density)

continues

Table 25.3 Continued

Device	Requirements
CD-ROM drive	Quad speed with 600K transfer rate and 250-ms average seek time
Sound card	16-bit digital sound, 44.1 KHz sampling rate, stereo channels, 8-note synthesizer, and MIDI playback
Video	640 x 480 with 65,536 colors
Ports	Joystick, MIDI I/O, serial, and parallel
Input	101-key keyboard and a two-button mouse

As you can see, the preceding recommended system requirements up the ante on the CPU, operating system, memory, CD-ROM drive, and hard disk. Many of today's multimedia software packages run sluggishly on anything less than a 60-MHz 486 with 8M of RAM. Also, because today's multimedia titles include so many audio and graphics files, they consume a great deal of hard disk space. A 500M hard disk drive is the minimum you should consider. Quad-speed CD-ROM drives are rapidly becoming the standard, so you shouldn't settle for less. Finally, Windows 95, which provides almost automatic configuration of multimedia devices, provides significantly better support for DOS programs as well. The system outlined in Table 25.3 goes for about $1,700.

Getting the Top of the Line

You say that you want a state-of-the-art system? How thick is your wallet? If you can pinch an inch or more of that folding green stuff, you might want to consider the powerhouse system recommendations listed in Table 25.4. Such a system not only runs today's multimedia software at blazing speeds, but also ensures that your system remains viable for a couple of years to come. Be prepared to pay around $3,500 or more for such an electronic marvel.

Table 25.4 State-of-the-Art MPC Recommendations

Device	Requirements
CPU	100-MHz Pentium
Operating system	Windows 95
Memory	16M
Hard disk	1G
Floppy disk	1.44M (high-density)
CD-ROM drive	Quad-speed with 600K transfer rate and 250-ms seek time
Sound card	16-bit digital sound, 44.1 KHz sampling rate, stereo channels, 32-note synthesizer, wavetable synthesis, and MIDI playback with General MIDI or Roland MT-32 sound sets
Video	800 x 600 with 16 million colors
Ports	Joystick, MIDI I/O, serial, and parallel
Input	101-key keyboard and a two-button mouse

The major differences in this system are the super-fast Pentium processor, an additional 8M of memory, and a 1G hard drive. If you really want the absolute, absolute best, you can substitute a 133 MHz Pentium and get a 6X CD-ROM rather than a 4X (quad speed). Now you're talking really big bucks!

Upgrading an Existing System

Of course, you don't necessarily have to run out and buy a new system in order to use today's multimedia software. You might be able to upgrade your existing system by adding and replacing components. In order to upgrade an existing system, though, it's highly recommended that you at least have a system that meets the CPU and video requirements you're shooting for. Replacing motherboards (the part of the system that holds the CPU) and matching up monitors and video cards can be a frustrating experience, one that is best left to a technician.

Moreover, when you add up the prices of several separate components, you may discover that it's actually wiser to buy a whole new system.

The bottom line is that the only components you should probably try to upgrade yourself is the CD-ROM drive and the sound card. The remaining sections of this chapter give you some general guidelines and instructions for accomplishing these relatively simple upgrade tasks. Keep in mind, though, that PCs are complex machines that come in an almost unlimited number of configurations. Often, even the easiest upgrades lead to complications that you must be prepared to handle. If the thought of opening up your system and poking around inside gives you dizzy spells and cold sweats, you should probably ask a qualified technician to do the upgrade for you.

How much will an upgrade cost? That depends on the number of components in your system that need to be replaced. The cheapest way to add (or replace) a CD-ROM drive and sound card is to purchase one of the many multimedia upgrade kits (figures 25.1 through 25.3) that are available at your local software store or by mail order. Such upgrades usually cost between $200 and $500, the price being based on the quality of the components and the extras that are included with the package.

A minimum multimedia upgrade kit includes a double-speed CD-ROM drive, a 16-bit sound card, and speakers. Most upgrade kits also come with a library of multimedia software to get you started.

You can also buy the CD-ROM drive, sound card, and speakers separately. However, because sound cards are often matched with a CD-ROM drive, you could run into configuration problems if you don't know exactly what you're doing. Moreover, you may end up having to buy both a sound card and a separate CD-ROM interface card, which adds to the cost. One of the big advantages of a complete multimedia upgrade kit is that the CD-ROM drive's interface is usually built in to the matching sound card, ensuring few configuration problems and eliminating the need to buy expensive interface cards that take up an extra slot in the back of your computer.

Fig. 25.1 A Sound Blaster multimedia upgrade kit from Creative Labs.

Learning About Sound Cards

Probably the most important multimedia component you can add to your system is a sound card. Virtually all modern software packages use sound extensively, for everything from digitized voices to explosions, gun shots, and roaring engines. Although you can sometimes get by without a CD-ROM drive (a lot of so-called multimedia software comes on floppy disks, as well as on CD-ROMs), you cannot get full value from your software purchases unless you have a quality sound card.

Unfortunately for the sound shopper, sound cards come in dozens of types, all the way from the very basic for about $70 to the fabulous for around $500 or more. No matter what price range you have in mind, though, there are some common specifications you should look for when choosing a sound card. These specifications are presented in the following sections.

Sound Blaster Compatibility

Over the years, the Sound Blaster sound card has become the industry standard. Virtually every piece of software supports Sound Blaster cards, so if you want to be able to run all software that requires a sound card, you should choose a Sound Blaster-compatible sound card.

A word of warning to folks who want to use their sound cards under DOS as well as under Windows 95: Many sound cards boast 100 percent Sound Blaster compatibility, but don't deliver it. Once you get the card home, you'll discover that some software simply won't work with the sound card. When you call for technical help, you'll get all kinds of technical excuses why the sound card doesn't work with certain software packages. Often, they'll blame the software, in spite of the fact that the software runs perfectly on a real Sound Blaster card.

How do they get away with claiming a sound card is 100 percent Sound Blaster compatible when it's really not? There is no way to really fully tell. But the reality is that supposedly 100 percent Sound Blaster-compatible cards are really only about 50 to 75 percent compatible. So, the fact is that the only way you can be 100 percent sure that your sound card will work with all software is to buy an actual Sound Blaster card.

The downside of this choice is that you may want sound features not available on a Sound Blaster-brand sound card. In this case, you'll just have to decide how much you want the additional features and balance that need against the possibility that some of your programs may have to run without sound.

Sound Cards and Windows

The preceding discussion about Sound Blaster compatibility is really only applicable to DOS software. If you're running your multimedia software under Windows, the Sound Blaster compatibility issue disappears, and you're free to choose any sound card that is Windows compatible. This is because every sound-card manufacturer who wants his product to work properly under Windows must supply a Windows sound driver. Because this sound driver is written by the manufacturer specifically for that one sound card, compatibility problems rarely crop up under Windows.

And, unless you've been living in a submarine for the last few years, you've noticed that DOS programs are starting to disappear, being slowly replaced with Windows versions. In fact, currently only game software is still clutching to the DOS era, due to the sluggishness of Windows graphics capabilities. Recently, however, Microsoft has gone to great lengths to make Windows a viable gaming operating system. Even such CPU-intensive games as the ever-popular DOOM are being ported to Windows. It won't be too long before DOS is a thing of the past.

What's my point? Thanks to Windows, the Sound Blaster standard is about to become a non-standard. Any sound card that comes with a Windows sound driver is a solid choice for your Windows system. Dropping the Sound Blaster compatibility issue opens up all kinds of new possibilities, because almost every sound card in existence includes drivers for Windows.

Sampling Quality

Currently, the most common sound cards provide 8-bit or 16-bit sampling. As you can see in the Level-2 MPC requirements back in Table 25.2, you should consider no less than a 16-bit sound card. The more bits used to sample sounds, the higher quality the result. Make sure that your 16-bit sound card provides 16-bit sound for both playback and recording. Sometimes, so-called 16-bit sound cards offer 16-bit sound only for playback, meaning that, if you want to record your own sounds, you'll have to live with reduced quality. Also, make sure that the sound card provides stereo sound in both playback and recording modes.

FM Synthesis versus Wavetable Synthesis

Sound cards produce instrument sounds in various ways, using an on-board synthesizer. The most common and least expensive synthesizer uses something called FM synthesis to produce sounds using formulas. The resulting sound has a kind of toy-like quality, often not sounding much like the instruments it's intended to mimic. On the plus side, a card that offers only FM synthesis is usually inexpensive. So, if you're not fussy about the music produced by your sound card, you can save some bucks by going with FM synthesis.

If you'd like your music to sound like the real thing, then you should look for wavetable synthesis in your sound card. (Such a sound card usually offers FM synthesis as well, so you don't have to give up anything to get wavetable synthesis.) The advantage of wavetable synthesis is that actual instrument sounds have been recorded and stored in the sound card's memory. The result is stunningly realistic music that sounds almost as if it were being played from a CD. Of course, wavetable cards are much more expensive, often twice as much as cards offering only FM synthesis.

General MIDI MPU-401

MIDI, which stands for Musical Instrument Digital Interface, is a way of transferring performance information between a musical instrument and computers. You don't have to know how to play a musical instrument to take advantage of MIDI on your computer. Often, your sound card acts as the musical instrument, playing back the music that's been stored in files for whatever program you're currently running. If you examine the files on your hard disk, you may find some with an MID extension. These are Windows MIDI files that you can play on a MIDI-capable sound card.

To be sure that all MIDI equipment is compatible, the General MIDI standard specifies the type of commands that can be sent between MIDI devices. It also specifies that a MIDI device must support 16 channels, each of which can play back a different instrument sound.

Because the General MIDI standard specifies 128 instrument sounds (or "patches," as they're called by the experts), a MIDI-capable sound card can reproduce just about any kind of music you can imagine, from Beethoven to Nirvana.

Besides the 16 channels and 128 patches, a MPC-compliant sound card must also be able to play at least three instrument sounds simultaneously with at least six simultaneous notes on each instrument. For good quality, however, you should look for a card that can play 16 instrument sounds simultaneously, with as many as 24 simultaneous notes on each instrument. Such a card is said to be 16-voice multitimbral and 24-note polyphonic.

For extra fun, you can pick up a MIDI-compatible keyboard, which you can plug into your sound card's MIDI ports. (You may need a MIDI adapter for your sound card in order to do this.) Then, you can play music directly into your computer and even record it by using a sequencer application (figure 25.2). Of course, if you can't play keyboards, you probably won't be doing yourself or anyone else any favors by trying to create your own music!

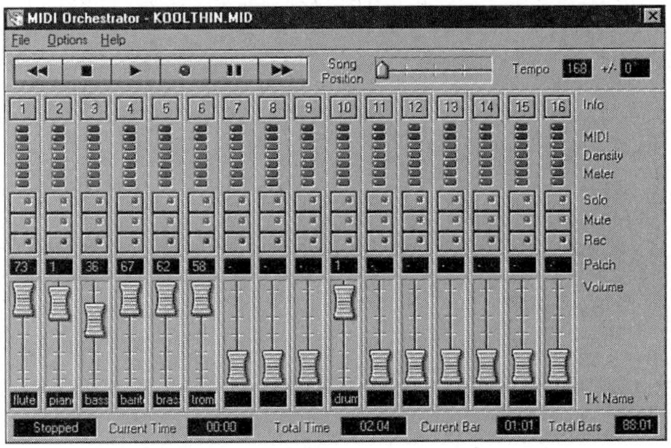

Fig. 25.2 A sequencer is an application that records and plays back MIDI information.

Adding a Sound Card to Your PC

Whether you buy a complete multimedia upgrade kit or buy your sound card separately, you must install the sound card into your computer. Although you should follow the installation instructions that come with your sound card, most sound-card installations require that you follow a basic set of procedures, which are:

- Configuring the sound card's IRQ, DMA, and I/O settings
- Inserting the card into your computer, by placing it into an empty expansion slot
- Attaching speakers, a CD-ROM drive, an amplifier, or headphones to the sound card
- Installing any software that came with the sound card
- Adding the new device to the Windows 95 system

Depending on what type of sound card you bought, the preceding steps can be easy or hard. The three main types of sound cards are as follows:

- Plug-and-Play sound card
- Sound card without jumpers
- Sound card with jumpers

Plug-and-Play Sound Cards

The Plug-and-Play type of sound card is the easiest to install, because Windows 95 can take care of all the configuration tasks for you. You insert the sound card into an expansion slot in the computer (figure 25.3), connect any external devices (figure 25.4), and reboot the computer. The operating system then senses that a new device has been installed and communicates with that device to ensure that it's configured properly. But in order to take full advantage of Plug-and-Play devices, your computer must also have a Plug-and-Play BIOS (Basic Input/Output System). Check your system's literature to see whether your system can accommodate such devices. Most newer systems can.

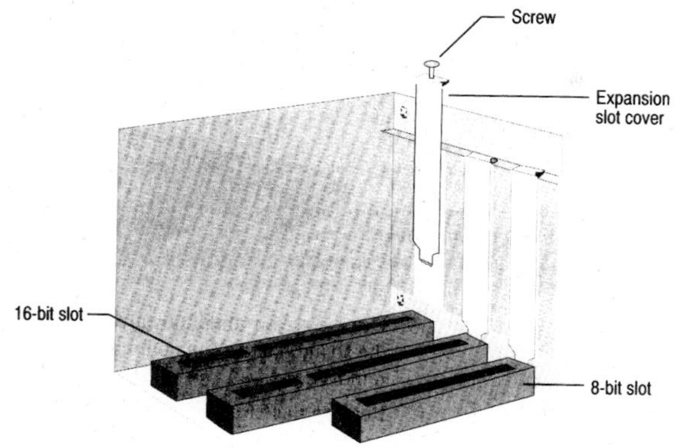

Fig. 25.3 You place a sound card into an empty expansion slot located at the back of your computer's system unit.

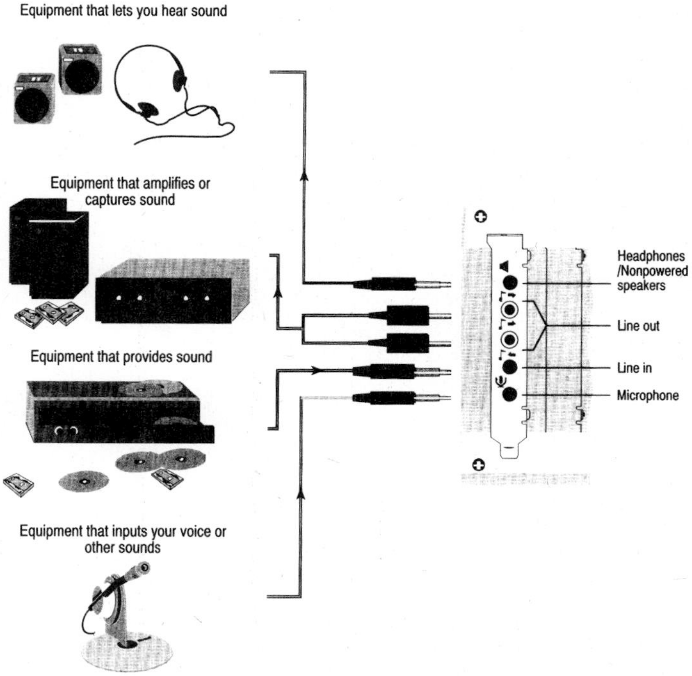

Fig. 25.4 You can connect many types of external devices to a sound card.

Jumperless Sound Cards

If you didn't get a Plug-and-Play sound card (there aren't too many of them around at this point), you can still get a lot of configuration help from Windows 95. The next easiest type of card to add to your system is the jumperless card. Because such a card can be configured by sending commands to the card, Windows 95 is likely able to set up the card for you, almost as if the card were Plug-and-Play.

As with the Plug-and-Play card, you first have to insert the card into one of your computer's expansion slots and then connect any external devices you need (speakers, CD-ROM, and so on). Then, close up the computer and turn it on. When Windows 95 appears on-screen, follow the instructions given in the next section, "Adding New Hardware."

Note that you can change the settings on a jumperless sound card, too, just as easily as Windows can. And you can change the settings without touching the card or even having to open your computer. Usually a jumperless device comes with a configuration program that, when started, enables you to change the device's settings right on the screen. This sure beats the old method of manually placing jumpers on the circuit board!

Sound Cards with Jumpers

The last type of sound card requires that you set the card's IRQ, DMA, and I/O settings right on the card itself. You do this by positioning jumpers on the appropriate jumper pins (figure 25.5). Which settings should you use? That's the hard part! You should first try the default settings, which should already be set when you buy the card. You can find these default settings listed in the sound card's manual.

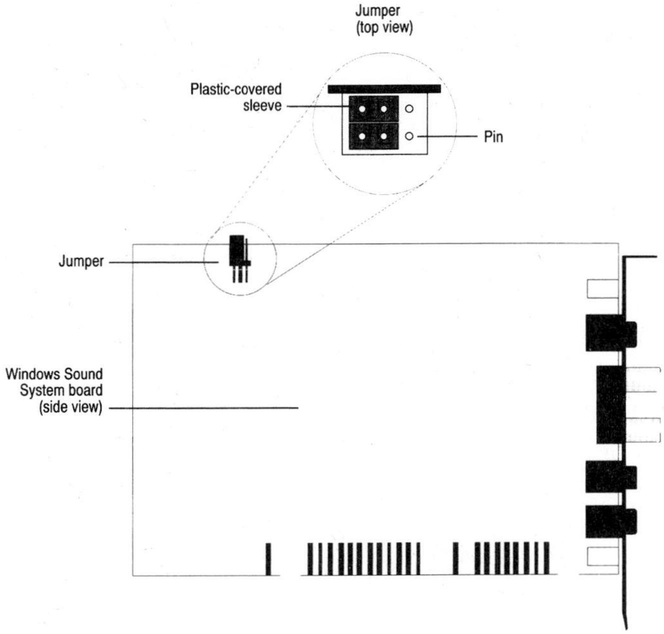

Fig. 25.5 Some sound cards require that you set jumpers on the circuit board.

Once you know what the default settings are, run Windows 95. Then, take the following steps:

1. Find Control Panel in the Settings section of the Start menu.
2. Run Control Panel by clicking on its entry in the Settings menu.
3. Click on the System icon to bring up the System Properties sheet. Make sure the Device Manager tab is selected (see figure 25.6).

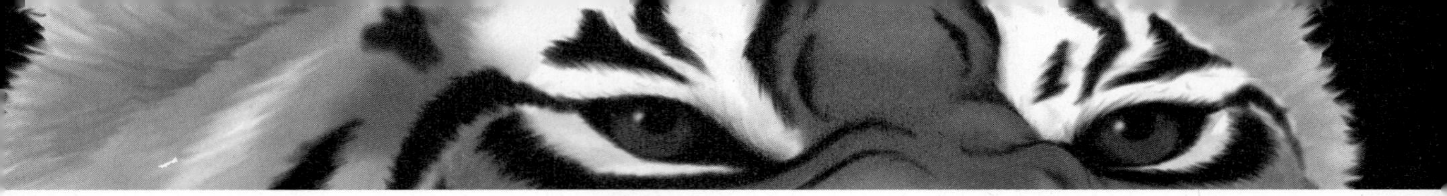

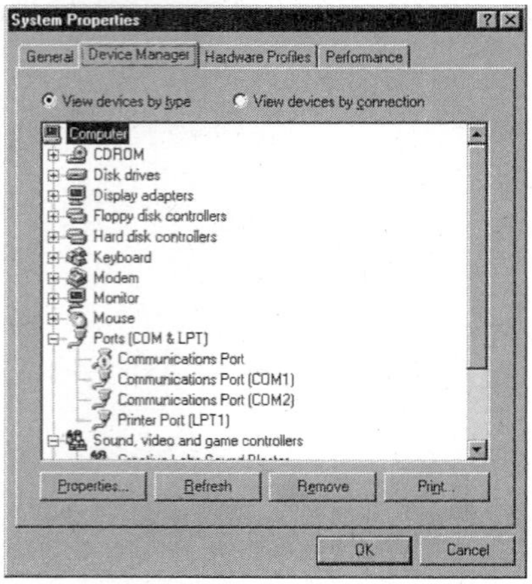

Fig. 25.6 The System Properties sheet with the Device Manager tab selected.

4. Click the Properties button, and then select the Interrupt Request (IRQ) option. You then see a list of interrupts currently being used by your system (figure 25.7).

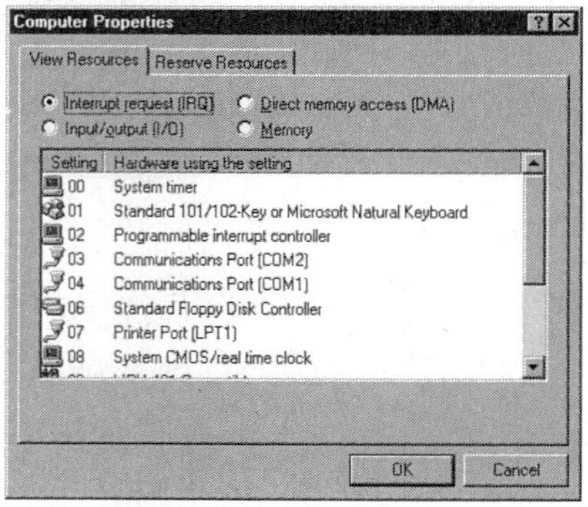

Fig. 25.7 The interrupt list in the Computer Properties sheet.

5. Make sure that the default IRQ on the sound card is not already being used. If the IRQ is in use, make note of an unused IRQ that's compatible with your card, and then change the card's jumper to the unused IRQ.

6. Follow the same procedure to set the card's DMA channel. Figure 25.8 shows the Computer Properties sheet with the Direct Memory Access (DMA) option selected.

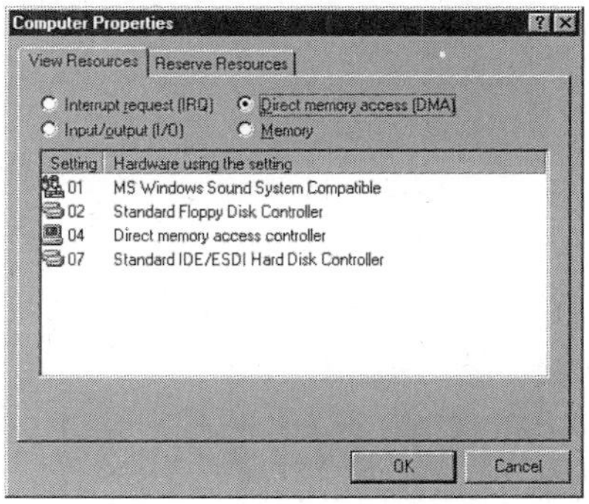

Fig. 25.8 The DMA list in the Computer Properties sheet.

Now that you have your sound card configured so that it doesn't conflict with other devices in the system, you can insert the card into one of the empty slots in your computer. (Turn off the computer first, of course.) If you made a mistake in the configuration process, and there is still a conflict in the system, Windows will not allow the device to operate, thus ensuring that the system doesn't lock up. You can solve your problem by using Windows 95's troubleshooting help. See this chapter's "Troubleshooting Your Sound Card" section for further information on this handy feature.

Adding New Hardware

Now that you have your sound card configured and installed in your computer, it's time to add the new hardware to Windows 95. You do this by using the Add New Hardware Wizard, as described in the following steps:

1. Restart Windows 95, run Control Panel, and select the Add New Hardware icon. When you do, you see the Add New Hardware Wizard, as shown in figure 25.9.

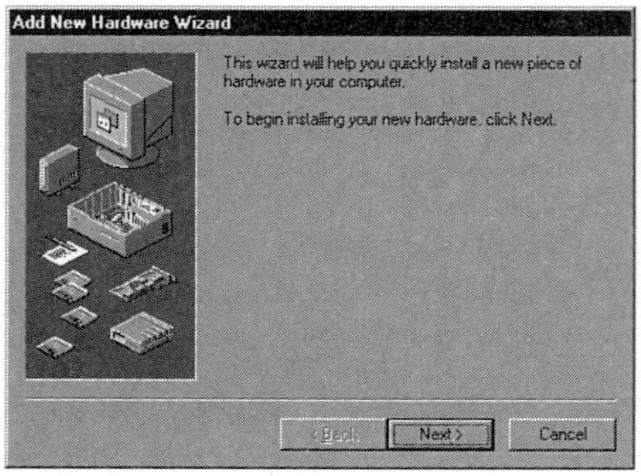

Fig. 25.9 The Add New Hardware Wizard helps you set up new devices.

2. Click on the Next button to start the wizard. When you do, you see the window shown in figure 25.10, which lists the various types of hardware you can add to your system.

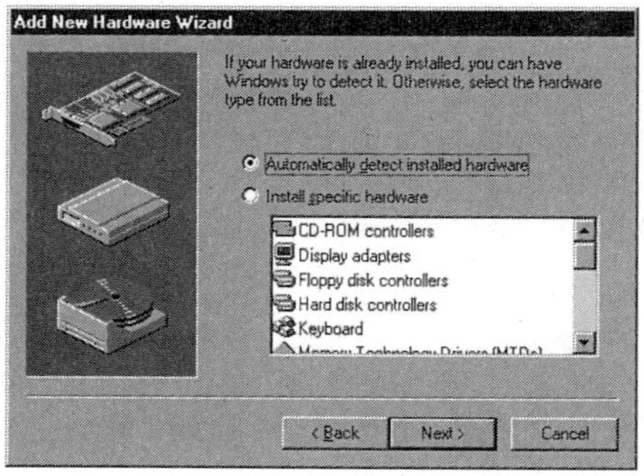

Fig. 25.10 The Add New Hardware Wizard's hardware list.

3. Click on the Install Specific Hardware button, and select Sound, video and game controllers in the hardware list (figure 25.11).

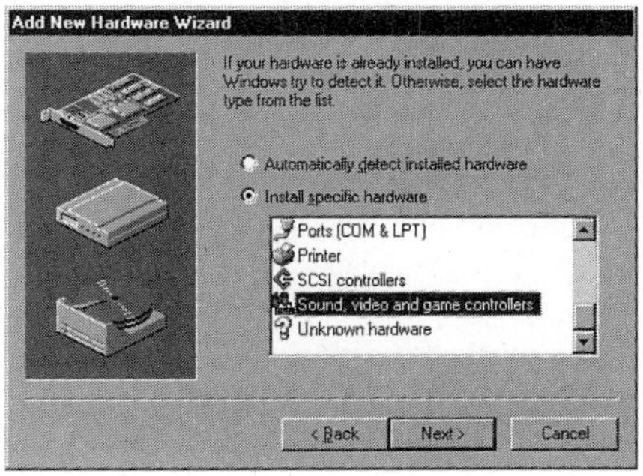

Fig. 25.11 Selecting the Sound hardware from the hardware list.

4. Click on the Next button to see a list of supported sound cards (figure 25.12).

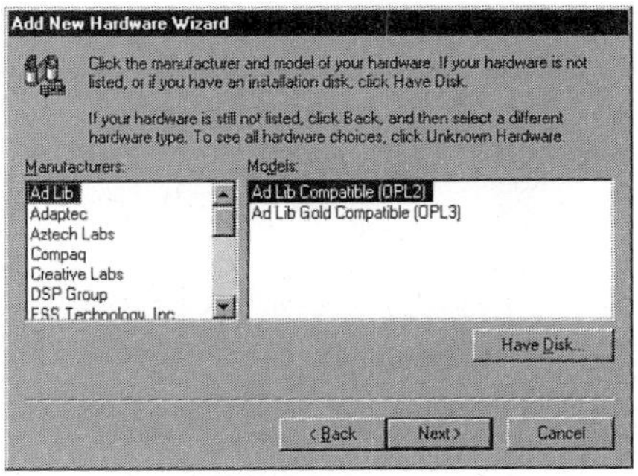

Fig. 25.12 The list of supported sound cards.

5. In the Manufacturers list, select the manufacturer of your sound card. In the Models list, select the sound card's model. Figure 25.13 shows the MediaVision sound cards selected. (If your sound card isn't listed, you need to have a driver disk from the manufacturer. Click the Have Disk button to load the drivers from the disk.)

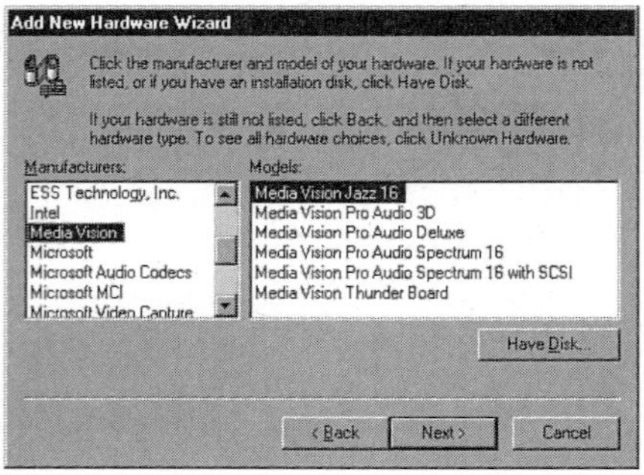

Fig. 25.13 Selecting the sound card's manufacturer and model.

6. Click on the Next button, and you see the window shown in figure 25.14. Click on the Finish button to install your new sound card into Windows 95.

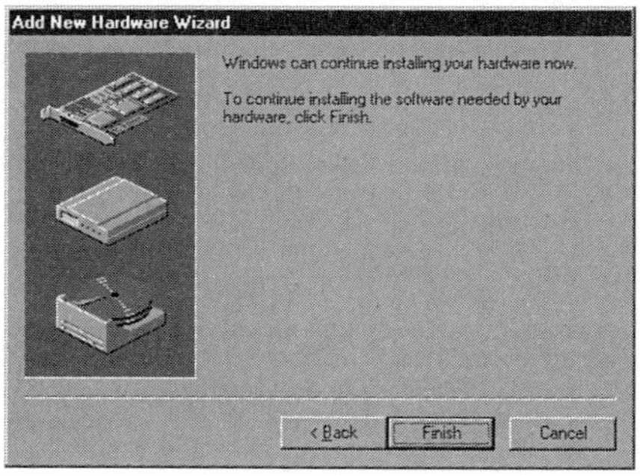

Fig. 25.14 Finishing the sound-card installation process.

Testing Your Sound Card

Once you have your sound card installed, it's time to see whether it's working properly. First, you want to be sure that it can play back both waveform files (digital sound effects) and MIDI files (MIDI music). To do this, select the Media Player entry from the Start/Programs/Accessories/Multimedia menu. When you do, you see the Media Player accessory, which looks like figure 25.15.

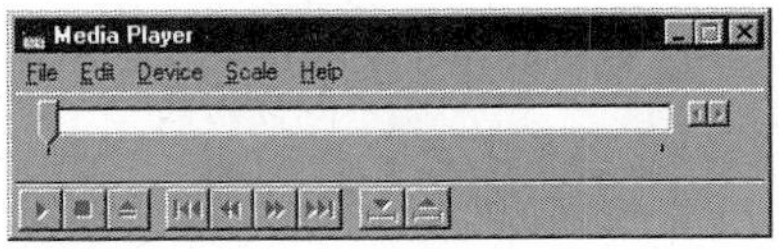

Fig. 25.15 Finishing the sound-card installation process.

Select the Open command from the File menu, and select a waveform Sound file. After loading the sound file, test the sound card by clicking on the Media Player's Play button (the first button at the bottom of the window). If you hear the sound effect, your sound card is playing Sound files properly.

Next, you want to be sure your sound card can handle MIDI files. Select the Open command from the File menu, and select a MIDI file. As you can see from figure 25.16, a MIDI file has an icon with two notes on it. (If you have Windows 95 set to display file extensions, you can also identify a MIDI file by its MID extension.) After loading the MIDI file, click on the Media Player's Play button. If you hear the song, your sound card is playing MIDI files properly.

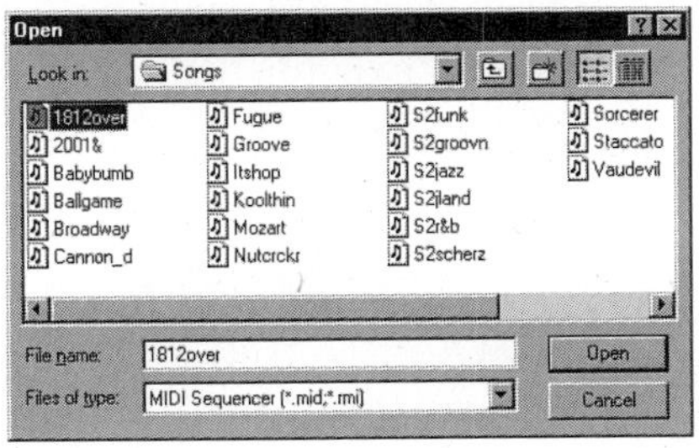

Fig. 25.16 Loading a MIDI file into Media Player.

Troubleshooting Your Sound Card

If you run into conflicts when trying to set up your sound card, you'll probably see a window like that shown in figure 25.17. Here, Windows warns that there is a conflict, but still allows you to proceed in order to troubleshoot the problem.

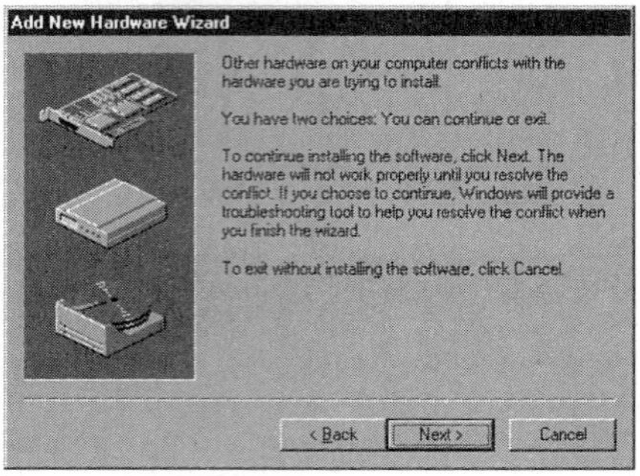

Fig. 25.17 Windows warns of conflicts in the system.

After installing the device drivers for the sound card you selected, Windows displays the dialog box shown in figure 25.18. When you click the Start Conflict Troubleshooter button, Windows guides you through the troubleshooting process, as shown in figure 25.19. Just follow the step-by-step instructions in each window.

Along the way, Windows has you check whether the device is installed twice, whether other devices are conflicting with the device you're trying to install, whether there are other settings you can use to get rid of any conflicts, and more. The detailed questions and answers guide you painlessly through the steps.

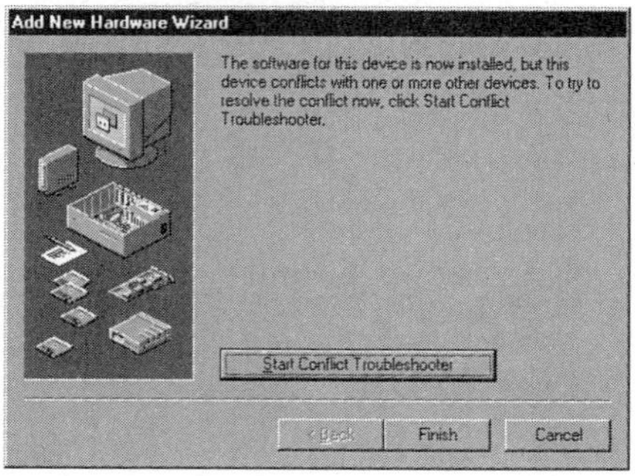

Fig. 25.18 This window gives you access to Windows device troubleshooter.

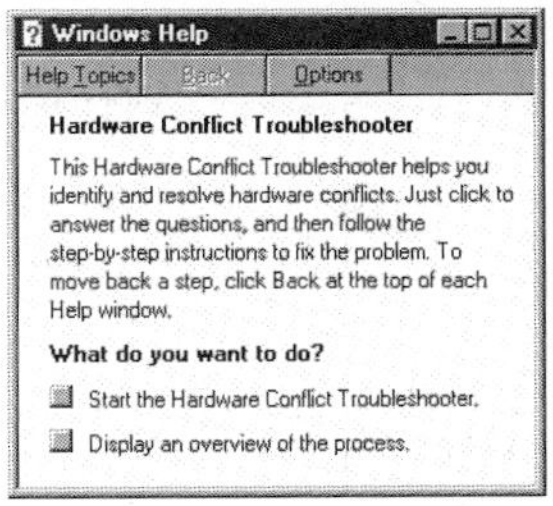

Fig. 25.19 The first troubleshooter window.

Installing a CD-ROM Drive

As mentioned previously, if you're going to add a CD-ROM drive to your system, your best bet is to get a multimedia upgrade package that includes both the CD-ROM player and the matching sound card. This ensures that the sound card includes the right interface for the CD-ROM drive. If you choose to buy a CD-ROM drive separately from a sound card, you must be sure that you also purchase the appropriate interface card.

While every CD-ROM drive comes with its own specific installation instructions, there are several basic steps that apply to all installations. Those steps are:

- Install the CD-ROM drive into an empty drive bay in your system unit.
- Install the CD-ROM drive's interface card. (This is often the sound card.)
- Connect the power, audio, and data cables.
- Use Control Panel's Add New Hardware option to install the new device into Windows 95.

The instructions that come with your specific CD-ROM drive or multimedia upgrade kit will provide detailed instructions for installing your CD-ROM drive into the computer. However, the instructions may not include detailed instructions for adding the device to Windows 95. Luckily, you already know most of what you need to know to get your CD-ROM to perform under Windows 95. Just refer back to this chapter's "Adding New Hardware" section. In step 3 of the instructions, however, you should select CD-ROM controllers instead of Sound, video and game controllers (figure 25.20).

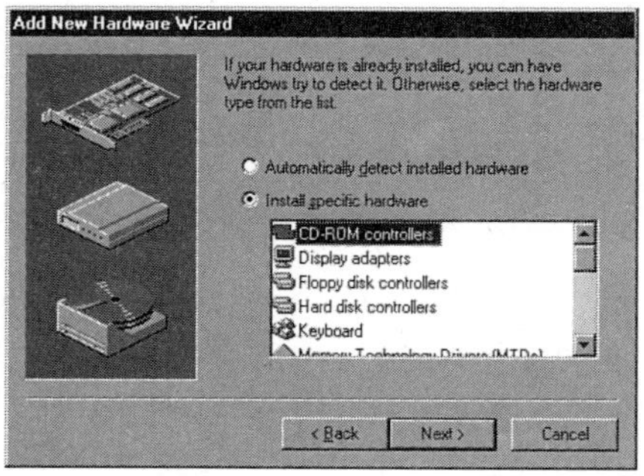

Fig. 25.20 Adding a CD-ROM drive to Windows 95.

Just as with a sound card, if you have trouble getting your CD-ROM to work under Windows 95, you can use Windows troubleshooting help to find the solution to your problem.

KILLER 26 WINDOWS 95

Using Multimedia on Your Computer

by Clayton Walnum

Now that your multimedia devices are installed and chugging along nicely, it's time to see a few things you can do with those devices under Windows 95. Keep in mind that this chapter only gets you started with multimedia. There are so many multimedia applications out there that it would take an entire book (or more!) to cover all the great stuff you can do with a multimedia system. But every journey begins with the first step. So, in this chapter, you learn the following:

- How to customize the sounds your computer makes
- How to create sound schemes
- How to play an audio CD with your CD-ROM drive and sound card
- How to personalize the CD Player application
- How to make Windows 95 remember the titles of CDs and songs from one session to the next

Assigning Sounds to Windows Events

If you're a Windows user, you've noticed how Windows plays sound effects whenever you do such things as click outside of a dialog box, bring up a system-alert message box, or exit from Windows. All of these sound effects are attached to the events by the Sounds Properties sheet. In this section, you learn how to use Sounds Properties to customize your Windows 95 sound.

Understanding the Sounds Properties Sheet

To view the Sounds Properties sheet, bring up the Control Panel, located in the Start/Settings menu. Then, double-click on the Sounds icon. When you do, you see the dialog box shown in figure 26.1.

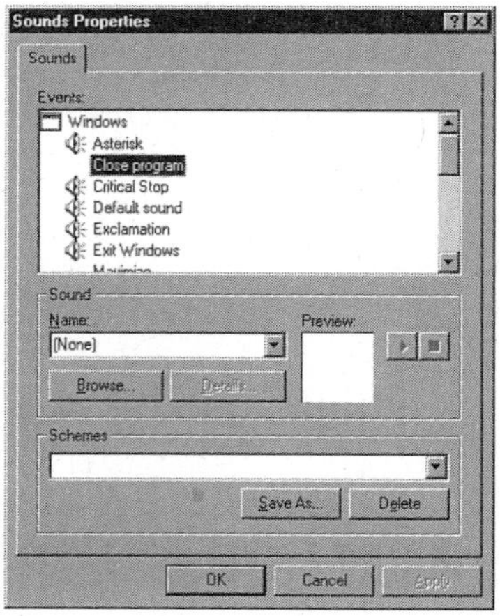

Fig. 26.1 The Sounds Properties sheet enables you to match sound effects to Windows events.

At the top of the dialog box, you see the list of Windows events to which you can attach sound effects. Some events are already associated with a sound, as you can tell by the speaker icon next to the entry.

Other events have no sounds attached to them. You can add whatever sounds you like to these events, as well as change the sounds associated with events that already have sounds. In the next section, you learn how to assign sounds to Windows events.

Viewing, Selecting, and Listening to Sounds

To see the sound that's already associated with an event, just click on the event in the window. When you do, the name of the sound file associated with the event appears in the Name list box.

To hear the selected sound effect, click on the play button just to the right of the Preview speaker icon. If you want to change the sound effect, you have a couple of choices. The easiest way to change the sound effect is to select one from the Name drop-down list box, as shown in figure 26.2. When you first bring up the Sounds Properties sheet, the sound effects shown in the drop-down list are found in your Windows\Media folder on your hard drive. If you change the current folder by using the Browse button (see the next paragraph), the drop-down list shows the sounds in the newly selected folder.

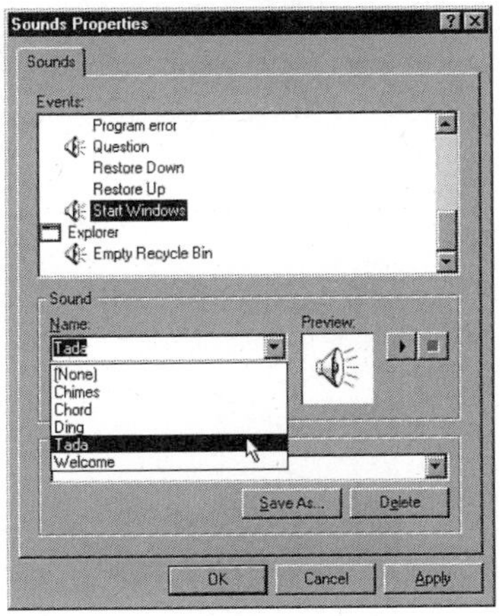

Fig. 26.2 You can select a new sound effect from the Name list box.

If you want to use a sound effect that's stored somewhere else on your hard disk, click on the Browse button. When you do, the Browse dialog box appears (figure 26.3), which enables you to search your entire system for the sound effect you want. Notice also that you can preview sound effects by selecting them in the window and then clicking the play button located near the bottom of the window, just to the right of the word "Preview."

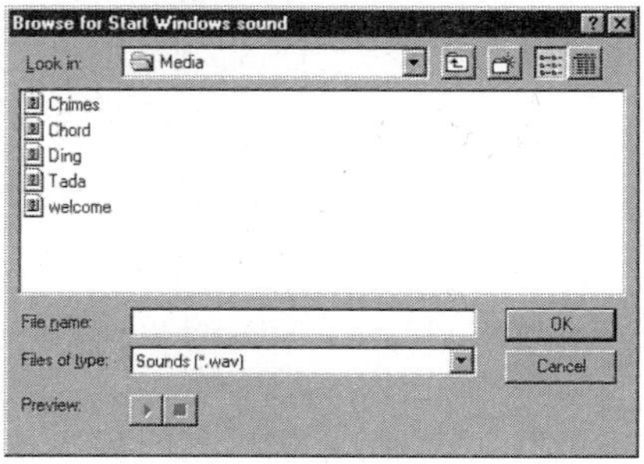

Fig. 26.3 You can use the Browse dialog box to find a sound effect.

Saving Sound Schemes

Once you have your sound effects set up the way you want them, you can save the "sound scheme" (as they call a collection of sounds) to disk along with the default sound schemes and any other sound schemes you may have created. To do this, click on the Save As button near the bottom of the Sounds Properties sheet. When you do, you see the Save Scheme As dialog box. Just type a name for your sound scheme and press Enter. Windows 95 then adds your sound scheme to the others listed in the Schemes list box (figure 26.4). The sound scheme you just saved will be active the next time you start Windows. (The new sounds won't take effect until then.)

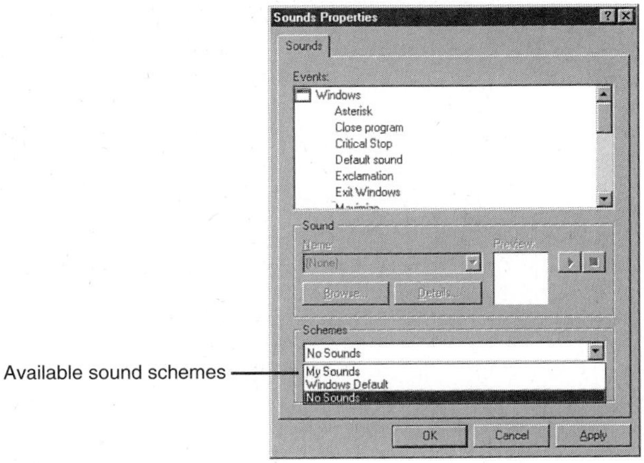

Fig. 26.4 The Schemes list box enables you to select whatever sound scheme you want.

Playing an Audio CD with CD Player

One of the coolest things you can do with your multimedia Windows 95 computer is play CDs while you work. In many cases, all you need to do is put an audio CD in your CD-ROM player, and Windows 95 automatically starts up the CD-ROM Player application. This little trick is accomplished by Windows' new AutoPlay function that'll also automatically start up games on CD-ROM. You can disable the AutoPlay feature, if you like, by following these steps:

1. Open Control Panel's System icon. The System Properties sheet appears.
2. Click on the Device Manager tab to display the Device Manager page.
3. Double-click on CD-ROM in the device list. Your CD-ROM driver appears in the list.
4. Click your CD-ROM driver to select it.
5. Click the Properties button to display the CD-ROM Properties sheet for your driver.

6. Click the Settings tab to display the Settings page.
7. Turn off the Auto Insert Notification option by clicking it with your mouse.

If you want to start CD Player "by hand," you can find this handy mini-application in the Start/Programs/Accessories/Multimedia folder. When you click on its entry in the menu, you see the window shown in figure 26.5. As you can see in the figure, CD Player has many of the same controls that a regular CD player has, and you use them in exactly the same way. For example, to start playing a CD, you click on the play button. When you want to pause the CD, click on the pause button. The other buttons also work just as you'd expect on a real CD player.

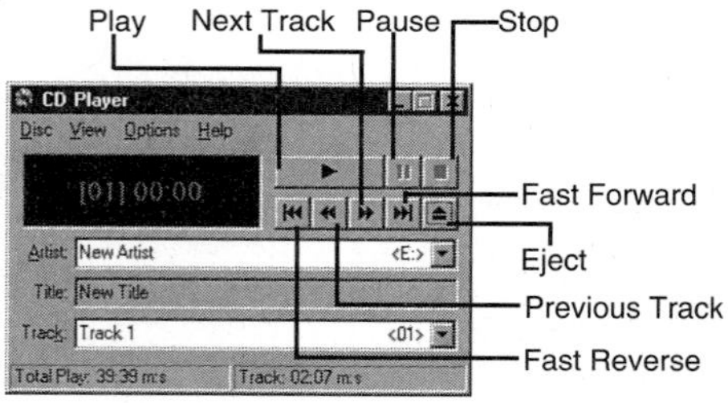

Fig. 26.5 CD Player has many of the same controls that a regular CD player has.

Creating a Play List

Although you can use CD Player just to play whatever CD happens to be in your computer's CD-ROM drive, you can do tons more. For example, look at the Artist, Title, and Track boxes in figure 26.6. You can edit the information shown in these boxes so that they show specific information about any CD. That is, you can have CD Player automatically recognize the CD in the drive and display the CD's artist and title, and the title for each track. How? Just follow these steps to create something called a play list:

1. Make sure that you have an audio CD in your CD-ROM drive, and then select the Edit Play List command from the Disc menu. When you do, you see the Disc Settings window as shown in figure 26.6.

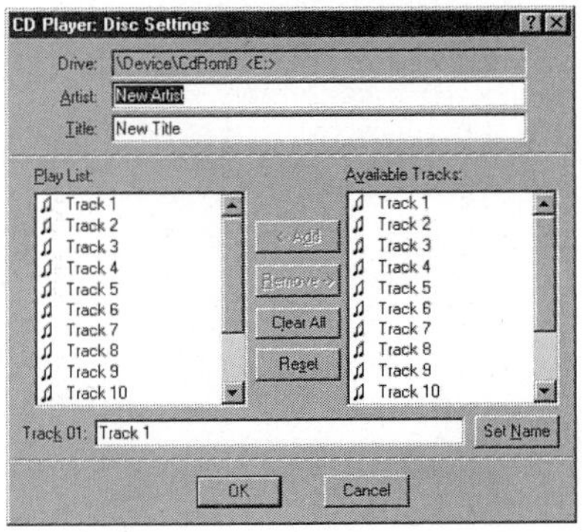

Fig. 26.6 The Disc Settings window.

2. Type the artist's name in the Artist box and the CD's title in the Title box.

3. Click on Track 1 in the Available Tracks list box, and then type the track's title into the Track text box, as shown in figure 26.7.

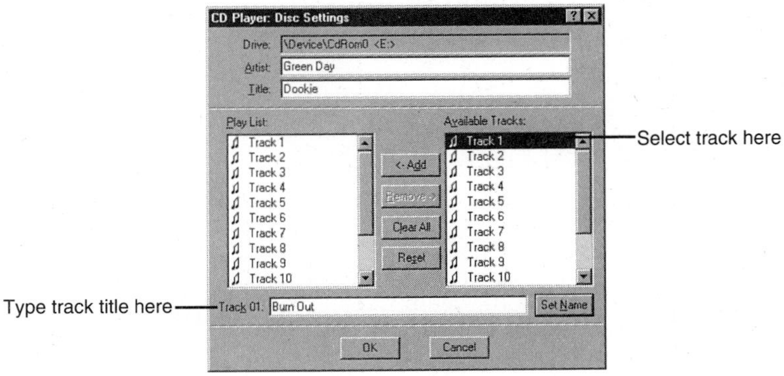

Fig. 26.7 Typing a title for track 1.

4. Press Enter, and CD Player adds the new track title to the Available Tracks list, as well as sets up track 2 for editing.
5. Repeat step 4 until you've entered all the CD's track titles, at which point the Disc Settings dialog box will look something like figure 26.8.

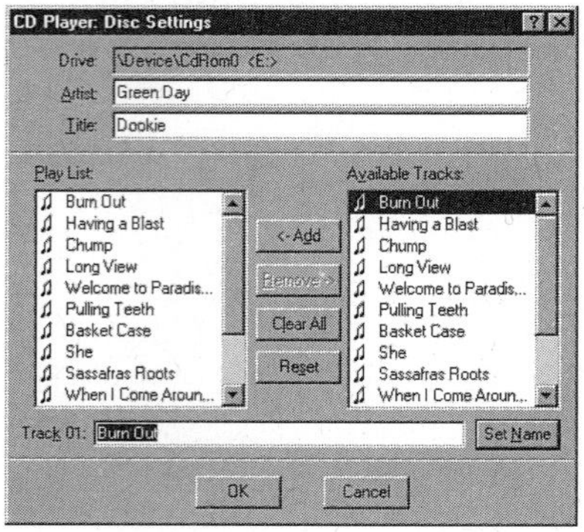

Fig. 26.8 The Disc Settings dialog box with all track titles entered.

6. Click on the OK button, and CD Player now shows the information for the new CD, as shown in figure 26.9.

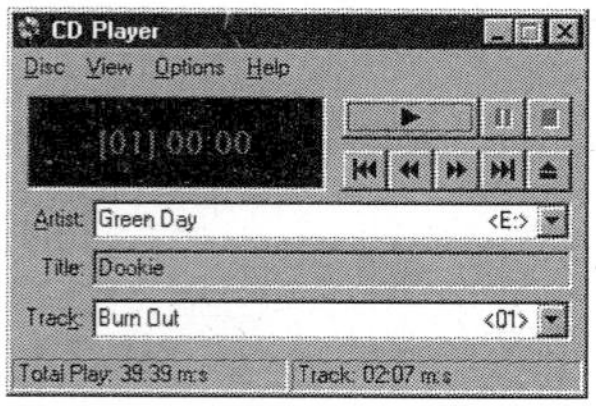

Fig. 26.9 CD Player with the new CD ready to play.

Notice that the Disc Settings dialog box has Add and Remove buttons that you can use to select exactly the tracks you want to play, as well as the order in which to play them. Don't like track 4? Just highlight the track in the Play List and click on the Remove button to zap it from the list. Conversely, the Add button enables you to move tracks from the Available Tracks list to the Play List.

After you complete the preceding steps, CD Player not only plays your CD but also displays the name of the artist, the title of the CD, and the title of the currently playing track. Best of all, CD Player saves all this information so that the next time you insert the CD, it will automatically find and display the correct information for the CD. Switch CDs, and *presto!*, CD Player finds and displays the new information (assuming, of course, that you previously entered the information).

If you click on the little arrow next to the Track list box, CD Player displays your play list (figure 26.10). You can instantly play any track in the list just by clicking on its name. Similarly, if you have a multi-disc CD-ROM drive (a special CD-ROM drive that can hold more than one disk), you can select different CDs by using the Artist list box.

Fig. 26.10 You can easily select songs from your play list.

Accessing CD Player's Toolbar

CD Player offers plenty of other options besides editing a play list. For example, if you select the View menu's Toolbar command, a toolbar appears in CD Player's window (figure 26.11). This toolbar provides quick access to most of the options available in CD Player's menus. Just click on a button to choose a command. If you want to see what a command button does before selecting it, just place your mouse pointer over the button for a second or two. When you do, a command tip appears.

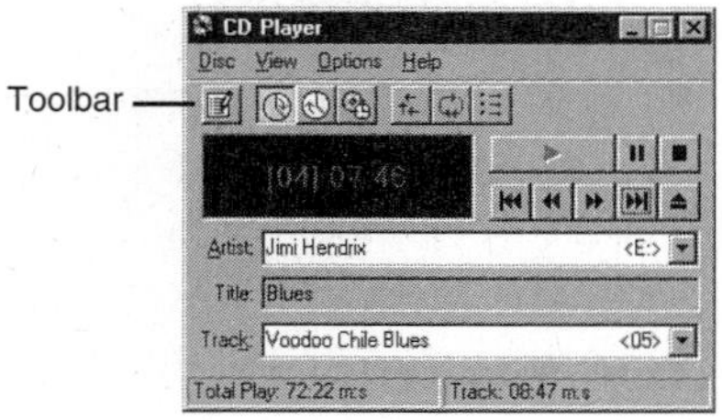

Fig. 26.11 The toolbar makes command selection as easy as a button click.

Setting CD Player's Options

Under the View menu, you'll also find commands for hiding and showing the track info and the status bar. In addition, you can set the time display to show elapsed track time, remaining track time, or remaining disc time. Finally, the View menu enables you to bring up Windows 95's volume control (figure 26.12), with which you can adjust the balance of the various sound devices operating on your system.

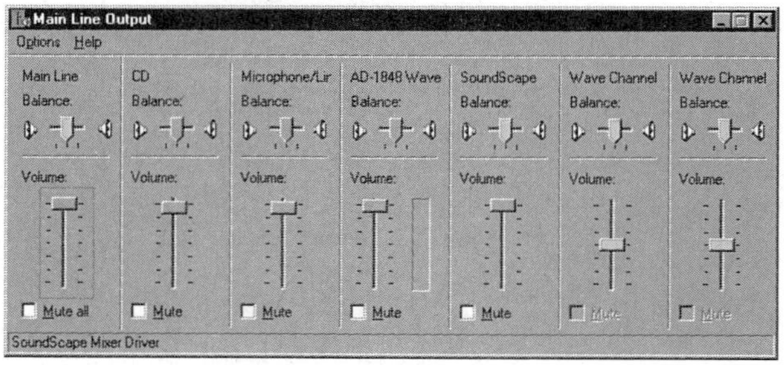

Fig. 26.12 The Volume Control accessory enables you to balance sound sources.

The Options menu, too, contains several handy commands. By selecting the Random Order command, you can have CD Player play the tracks on the CD in a random order. (This command is often called "shuffle" on real CD Players.) The Continuous Play command, on the other hand, causes the CD to play over and over, from beginning to end. Finally, when you select the Intro Play command, CD Player plays only the first few seconds of each song. When you find the song you want, just turn off the Intro Play command to hear the entire song.

Setting CD Player's Preferences

Finally, the View menu's Preferences command brings up the Preferences dialog box (figure 26.13), from which you can control several aspects of CD Player's operation. If the Stop CD Playing On Exit option is checked, the CD will stop playing when you exit from the program. If this option is not checked, you can close the CD Player application without stopping the CD; the CD continues to play in the background, although you no longer have control over it. (You can regain control just be restarting the CD Player application. When you do, CD Player determines the CD's current status and displays the appropriate information.)

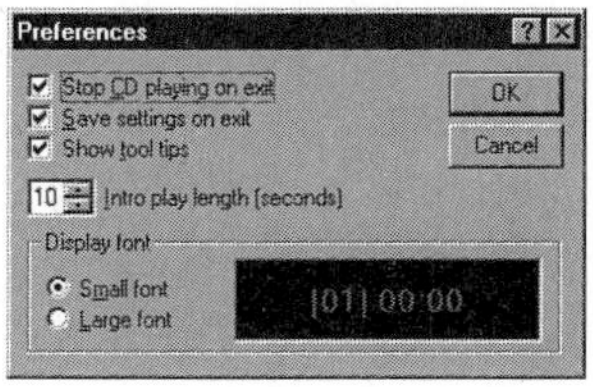

Fig. 26.13 Use the Preferences dialog box to set several aspects of CD Player's operation.

The Save Settings On Exit option ensures that CD Player remembers how you have it set up. The Show Tool Tips option controls whether tool tips (those tiny windows that tell you what buttons do) appear when you hold your mouse pointer over a button. If you like, you can change how much of a track the Intro Play command plays. To do this, just change the number of seconds displayed in the Intro Play Length box. Finally, you can change the size of the time display by selecting either the Small Font or Large Font option. The time display to the right of the options shows the selected font size.

27 Getting the Most out of Multimedia

by Clayton Walnum

Although Windows 95 makes using multimedia features as easy as possible (for example, by automatically playing an audio CD when you place it in your CD-ROM drive), there are many things you can do to customize your system's use of multimedia. By customizing how your system uses its multimedia features, you can make your system easier to use. In this chapter, then, you learn:

- Where to find your system's multimedia settings
- How to safely set the properties of audio and video devices
- How to add a MIDI keyboard to your system
- How to control and balance the volume of audio devices
- How to calibrate and test a joystick

Understanding the Multimedia Properties Sheet

As you now know, a multimedia computer contains many devices that work together to present information in many exciting ways. These devices include not only sound cards, but also video boards and CD-ROM players. Moreover, a couple of these devices do double duty. For example, a CD-ROM player can load a program from a CD-ROM or play music from an audio CD. In addition, a sound card can usually play back digital sound effects, as well as MIDI music files.

Each of your computer's multimedia features is controlled by a *driver*, which is a piece of software that matches Windows' multimedia system up with the specific devices you have on your computer. For example, a Sound Blaster sound card requires a different driver than a sound card from MediaVision. Similarly, different video cards and CD-ROM players also require specific drivers for the models you have installed on your system.

Luckily, when you installed Windows 95, Windows took care of matching up drivers with your devices. You probably didn't have to lift a finger to get everything working. (However, if you install new hardware that's not Plug-and-Play capable, you do need to inform Windows of the change. See the section "Adding New Hardware" in Chapter 25, "Adding Multimedia Capability to Your Computer," for more information on how to do this.)

Although different drivers control how your devices work with Windows, there are a number of device characteristics (or *properties*, as they're called in Windows 95) that you can set yourself. To do this, first click on Control Panel's entry in Windows' Start/Settings menu. When you do, the Control Panel appears on your screen. Next, double-click on the Multimedia icon to display the Multimedia Properties sheet (figure 27.1).

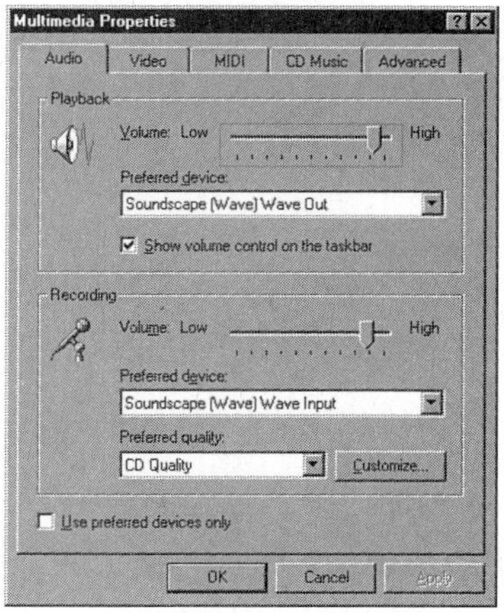

Fig. 27.1 The Multimedia Properties sheet enables you to fine-tune your multimedia devices.

As you can see by looking at the tabs across the top of the windows, the Multimedia Properties sheet provides pages for Audio, Video, MIDI, and CD Music devices, as well as a special Advanced page. Each page holds controls that you can use to fine-tune how a particular device works. To select a page, just click the appropriate tab. In the sections that follow, you learn how to use the various settings on each of the Multimedia Properties sheet's pages.

Setting Audio Properties

When the Multimedia Properties sheet first appears, the Audio tab is selected. The Audio page of the dialog box enables you to set several properties that determine how your system plays back and records sound. The upper part of the dialog box, labeled Playback, controls your system's playback properties, of course, whereas the Recording section controls recording properties.

Both sections enable you to set the volume for the device. In the playback section, the volume control determines how loudly your system plays sound effects, including the system effects that you hear when

you do things like start Windows, exit from Windows, or bring up a system alert box. (See the section "Assigning Sounds to Windows Events" in Chapter 26, "Using Multimedia on Your Computer," for more information on how to attach your own sound effects to Windows events.)

The Recording volume determines the level of input that Windows receives from your microphone or other input device. For example, if you have the recording volume set low, when you try to record a sound effect, it will come out very quietly. On the other hand, if you try to record a sound effect with the recording volume set all the way up, you'll probably end up with sound that's distorted. (See the section "Recording Sound" in Chapter 29, "Fine-Tuning Your Windows 95 Sound Card," for more information on how to create your own sound effects.)

Both the Playback and Recording sections of the Audio dialog box enable you to select the devices used to play back or record sound. You make this selection by using the Preferred Device list boxes. Normally, these list boxes should be set to your main sound card. In figure 27.2, you can see that the playback and recording devices are set to a Soundscape card.

In the Playback section, you can also find an option labeled Show volume control on the taskbar. When this option is checked, you'll have a small speaker icon in your Windows taskbar, as shown in figure 27.3. When you single-click on the speaker icon, the volume control window appears. You can use the slider in this window to set the volume of your sound card. If you click on the Mute option in the volume control, all sound is set to the minimum level until you uncheck the Mute option.

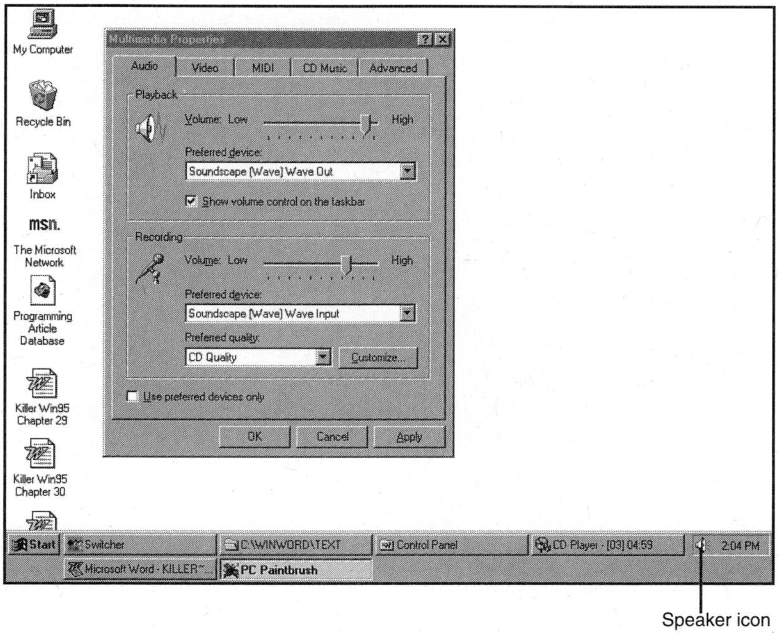

Fig. 27.2 The speaker icon on the taskbar gives you control over sound volume.

Finally, if you double-click on the speaker icon in the taskbar, you bring up the full volume-control accessory, which acts as a mixer for the various sound sources in your system. See the section "Using Volume Control" later in this chapter for more information on this handy accessory.

Getting back to the Audio page of the Multimedia Properties sheet, besides the other settings already discussed, the Recording section enables you to set the recording quality of sound. The easiest way to do this is to select a setting from the Preferred Quality list box, as shown in figure 27.4. CD Quality is the absolute best sound you can record, with Radio Quality yielding less quality, and Telephone Quality being the worst of all.

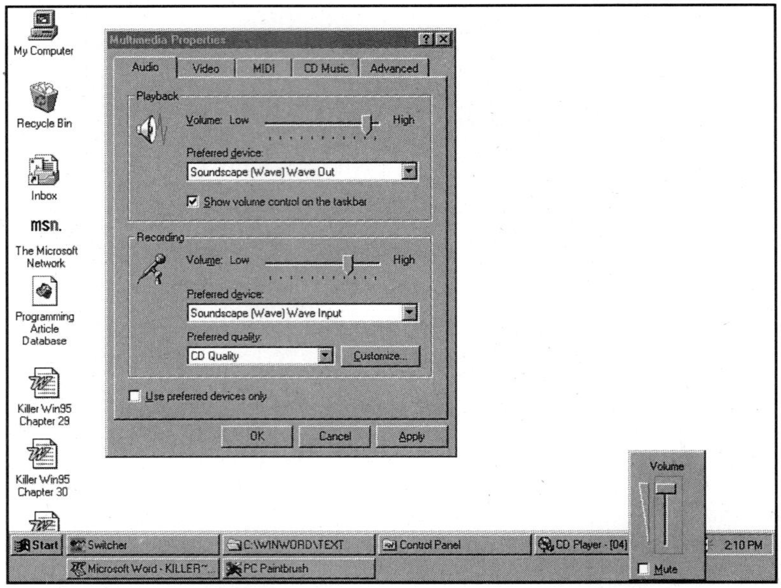

Fig. 27.3 The volume control enables you to set a volume level or mute sound.

If you want more control over the recording quality, click on the Customize button to display the Customize dialog box (figure 27.5). In this dialog box, the Name list box holds the names of the currently available quality settings. At first, this list box contains only the CD Quality, Radio Quality, and Telephone Quality entries. Using the Customize dialog box, you can add your own settings to the list. Please refer to the section "Setting Recording Quality" in Chapter 29 for more information on how to do this.

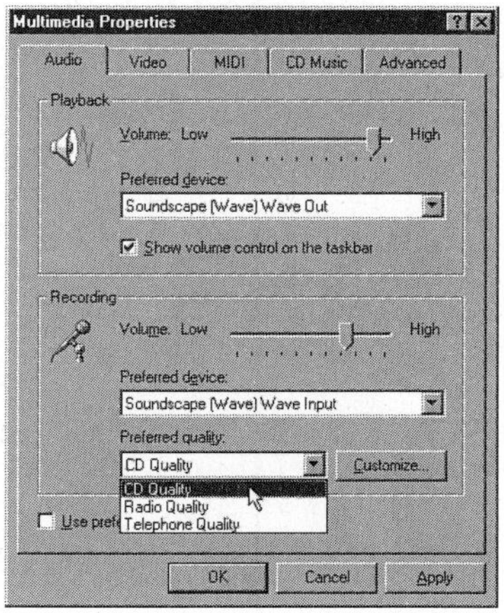

Fig. 27.4 Use the Preferred Quality list box to quickly set recording quality.

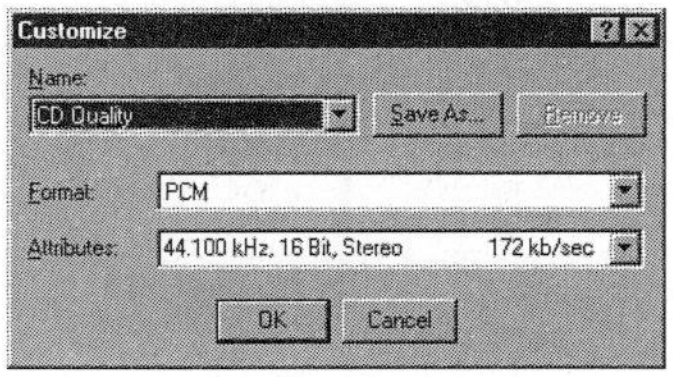

Fig. 27.5 Use the Customize dialog box to create your own record-quality settings.

Setting Video Properties

A multimedia computer is capable of displaying something called *full-motion video*, which is a lot like having a TV set right on your screen. Although full-motion video is a great way to present information, this multimedia feature is still in its infancy. If you run a video clip, for example, you'll see that the quality of the video isn't going to keep network executives up nights worrying about losing their market share to computers!

Still, full-motion video is an exciting multimedia feature of which you'll want to take full advantage. The Video page of the Multimedia Properties sheet (figure 27.6) lets you select the quality of the video presentation by controlling the size of the video image.

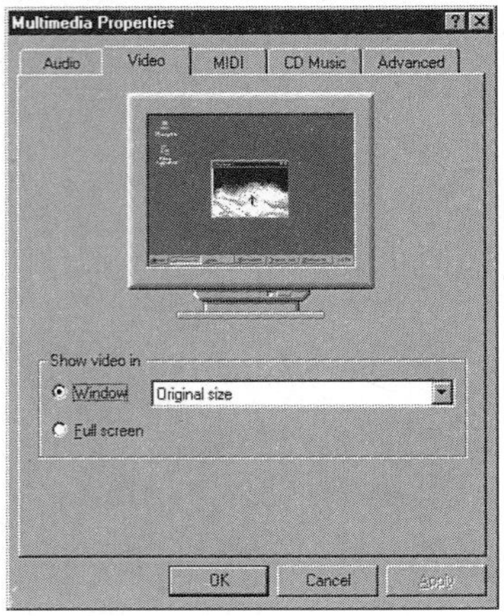

Fig. 27.6 The Video page of the Multimedia Properties sheet controls the size of the video image.

In most cases, you'll want to leave the video set to the Original Size setting, as shown in figure 27.7. This allows Windows to display the video at the same size with which it was created (figure 27.8). However, if you like, you can change the size of the video window. You do this by selecting a size from the list box (figure 27.9). As you can see, you have six different choices. If you don't want to have the video appear in a window at all, just click the Full Screen option. Then, the video will fill your entire screen. Keep in mind, though, that the bigger you make the video image, the slower it runs and the blockier the image looks.

Fig. 27.7 The Skiing video clip at its Original Size setting.

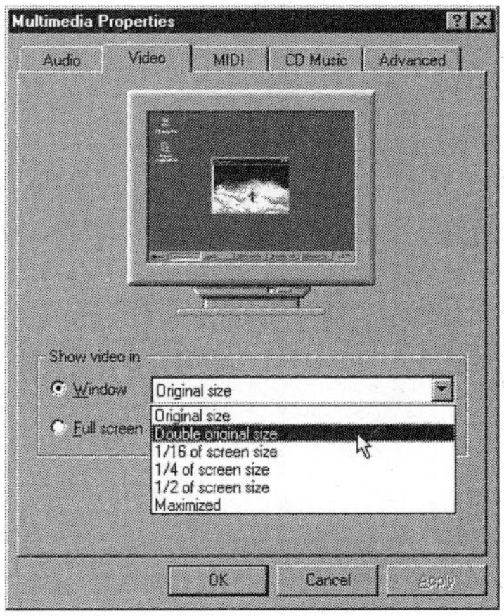

Fig. 27.8 Selecting a new video image size.

Setting MIDI Properties

Besides creating digitized sound effects and adding voice-overs to presentations, your sound card can play back MIDI files, which are files that contain commands that control MIDI synthesizers. The quality of the MIDI playback depends on the quality of your sound card (please see Chapter 29, "Fine-Tuning Your Windows 95 Sound Card," for more information about sound cards); but, in most cases, MIDI can provide the highest quality music of which your sound card is capable.

As you may have guessed, the MIDI page of the Multimedia Properties sheet (figure 27.9) provides controls for customizing how your system uses its MIDI features. The Single Instrument setting controls which instrument will receive MIDI commands when you play a MIDI file. In most cases, the MIDI "instrument" will be your sound card.

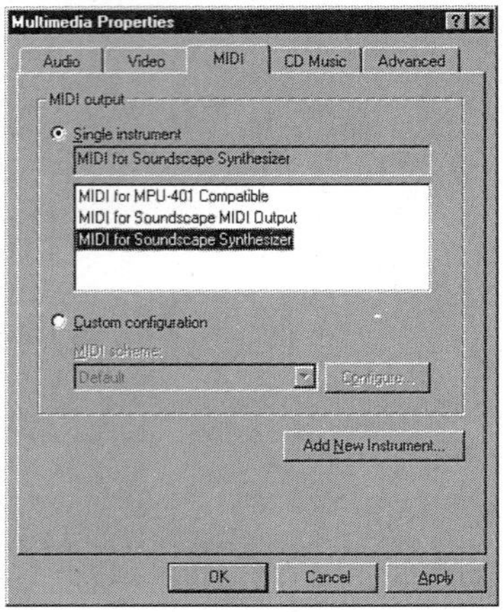

Fig. 27.9 The MIDI page of the Multimedia Properties sheet enables you to set your system's MIDI properties.

In figure 27.9, there are three instruments listed: MIDI for MPU-401 Compatible, MIDI for Soundscape MIDI Output, and MIDI for Soundscape Synthesizer. When you bring up the Multimedia Properties sheet on your system, you'll have a list of MIDI settings that match the sound card you've installed.

The MIDI for MPU-401 Compatible is a general MIDI standard that most sound cards support. This entry will probably appear for your sound card, too. You can have your MIDI for Soundscape MIDI Output setting send MIDI commands to your sound card's MIDI output port rather than to the sound card's on-board synthesizer. This will enable you to play MIDI files on a MIDI device, such as an electronic keyboard, attached to the sound card's MIDI output port.

Finally, the MIDI for Soundscape Synthesizer setting sends MIDI commands to the Soundscape sound card's on-board synthesizer. Again, your sound card may have a similar setting, although it may only have the MPU-401 Compatible setting. To select an instrument, just click on its entry in the list, and then click on the dialog box's OK button.

The MIDI page of the Multimedia Properties sheet also enables you to set up a custom configuration. To do this, click on the Custom Configuration option to enable the MIDI Scheme and Configure controls. The MIDI Scheme list box holds any configurations that you've created for your system. The first time you see this control, it'll probably only contain the Default entry. To create your own configuration, click on the Configure button. (For more information about creating a MIDI configuration, refer to the section "Creating a MIDI Configuration" in Chapter 29.)

The last thing you can do with the MIDI page is set up a new MIDI instrument that you've connected to your sound card's MIDI output port. This can be any MIDI-compatible instrument from a drum machine to a full-featured electronic keyboard and synthesizer. To add such an instrument to your system, you must first connect it to your sound card's MIDI port. To do this, you probably need special MIDI cables that are usually sold separately. Contact the company that made your sound card for more information.

Once you have the instrument physically connected to your sound card, you can use the MIDI page of the Multimedia Properties sheet to tell Windows 95 about the new instrument. To do this, click on the Add New Instrument button. You then see the first page of the MIDI Instrument Installation Wizard (figure 27.10).

This page enables you to select the MIDI port to which your instrument is attached. In figure 27.10, the Soundscape card's MIDI output port is selected. This is the port to which Windows 95 will direct MIDI commands when a MIDI file is played or some other sort of MIDI application is used, such as a sequencer program. (A sequencer program can do anything from play back MIDI files to let you compose music in an on-screen studio.)

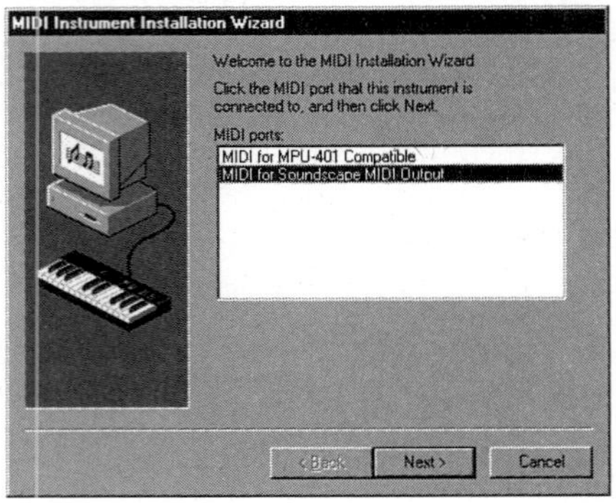

Fig. 27.10 Selecting a MIDI output port.

After selecting the MIDI port, click on the Next button to move to the next page (figure 27.11), where you can select the type of instrument you're installing. In most cases, the instrument will be a General MIDI Instrument, which is an instrument that conforms to the MIDI standard. Some special instruments—like drum machines, for example—may fit a different category. If you were installing a drum machine, you'd select the Percussion on Channel 16 option.

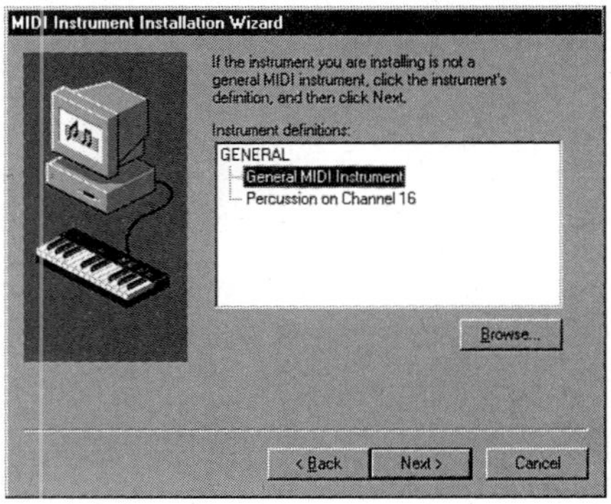

Fig. 27.11 Selecting the MIDI instrument type.

After selecting the instrument type, click on the Next button. The next page of the MIDI Instrument Installation Wizard (figure 27.12) gives you a chance to name the new instrument. You can type anything you

want into the Instrument Name box, or just stick with the default name. When you're finished typing, click on the Finish button. When you do, Windows 95 adds the new instrument to your MIDI configuration, as you can see in the Multimedia Properties sheet (figure 27.13).

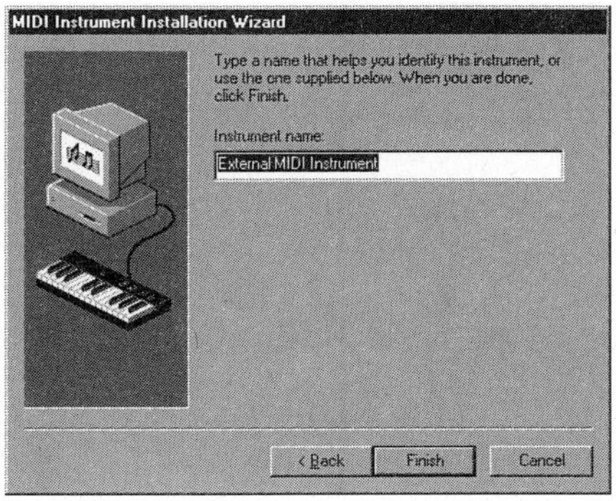

Fig. 27.12 Naming the new MIDI instrument.

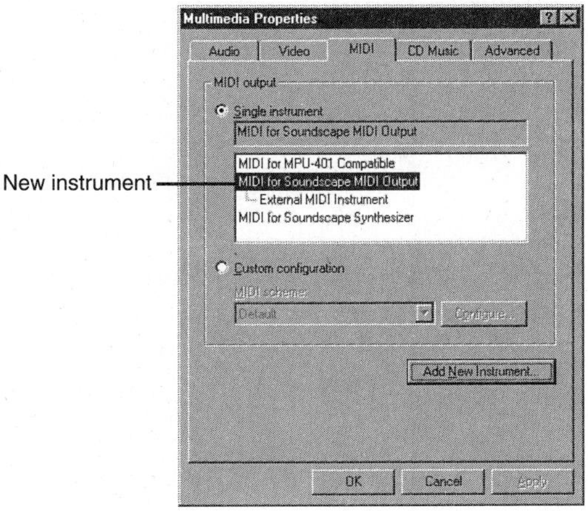

Fig. 27.13 The new MIDI instrument listed in the Multimedia Properties sheet.

You might expect that you can delete a MIDI instrument as easily as the wizard lets you install it. Unfortunately, to delete a MIDI instrument, you must access the Advanced page of the Multimedia

Properties sheet, as shown in figure 27.14. To get to this page, which lists all the multimedia devices in your system, click on the Advanced tab of the Multimedia Properties sheet.

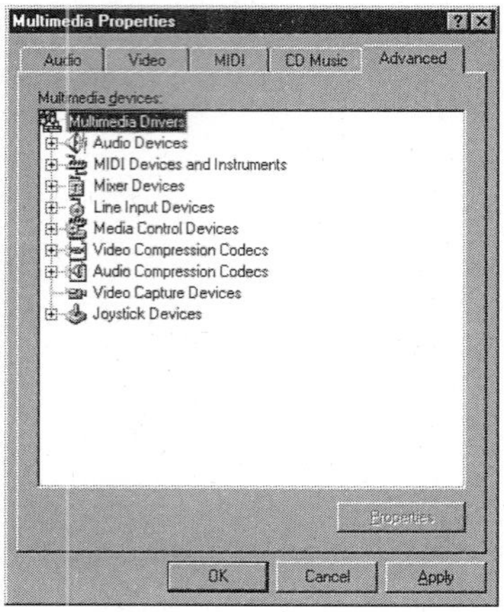

Fig. 27.14 The Advanced page of the Multimedia Properties sheet.

Once you have the Advanced page on-screen, click on the plus sign (+) next to the MIDI Devices and Instruments entry. You can then see the MIDI devices that are active on your system. To get to the instrument, click on the plus sign next to the MIDI device to which you added the instrument. Windows then displays the list of instruments for that device, as shown in figure 27.15.

To delete the instrument, click on its entry to highlight it. Then, click on the Properties button to display the External MIDI Instrument Properties sheet (figure 27.16). Click on the Remove button to remove the instrument from your system. When you do, the Advanced page of the Multimedia Properties sheet appears, this time with the deleted instrument removed from the instrument list.

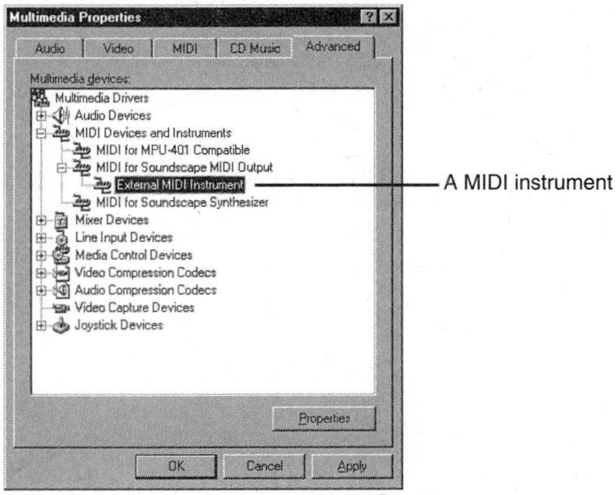

Fig. 27.15 Selecting an instrument in the Multimedia Properties sheet.

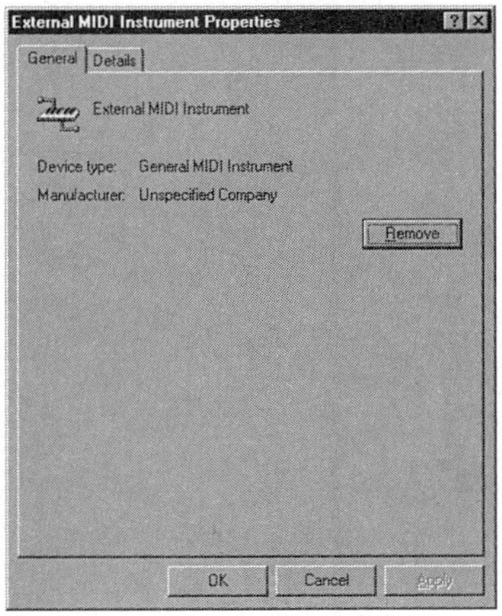

Fig. 27.16 The Remove button deletes a MIDI instrument from your system.

Setting CD Music Properties

The CD Player application enables you to play audio CDs with your CD-ROM drive. Most of the configuration tasks involved in using audio CDs are handled by that program. However, the Multimedia Properties sheet does have a page that lets you select a CD-ROM drive (if you happen to have more than one in your system) and adjust the volume control of the CD-ROM drive's headphone jack. To see the CD Music page (figure 27.17), just click on the CD Music tab in the Multimedia Properties sheet.

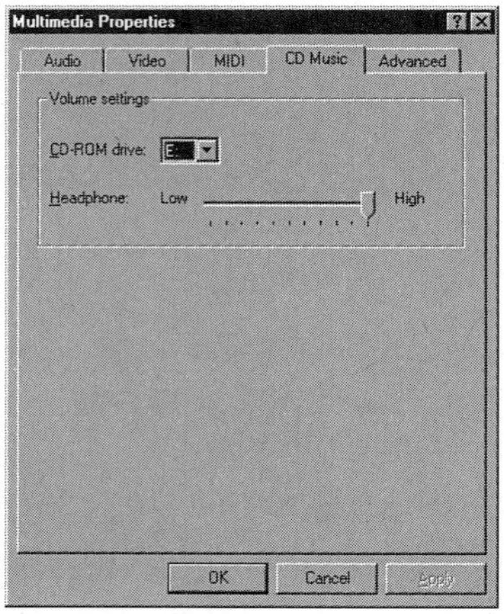

Fig. 27.17 The CD Music page of the Multimedia Properties sheet.

To change the volume of a CD-ROM drive's headphone jack, select the CD-ROM drive in the CD-ROM Drive list box. (Most people have only one drive listed.) Then, use your mouse to adjust the Headphone slider volume control. When you do this, you'll probably want to be playing an audio CD through your headphones so that you can hear the volume change.

Using the Advanced Page

The Multimedia Properties sheet has one final page called Advanced. As you may suspect, you shouldn't fiddle with the entries on this page unless you're sure you know what you're doing. Basically, this page enables you to view the properties of devices or to delete devices. While it's usually safe to view the properties of any device, you shouldn't delete any entries from the Advanced page unless you're positive you understand the results of the deletion.

To get to the Advanced page, click on the Advanced tab on the Multimedia Properties sheet. When you do, you see the window shown in figure 27.18. To view the properties of a device, first click on the plus mark next to the device category. Then select a device from the list that appears, and click on the Properties button. You then see a display that lists the properties of the selected device, as well as provides a Remove button for deleting the device from the list.

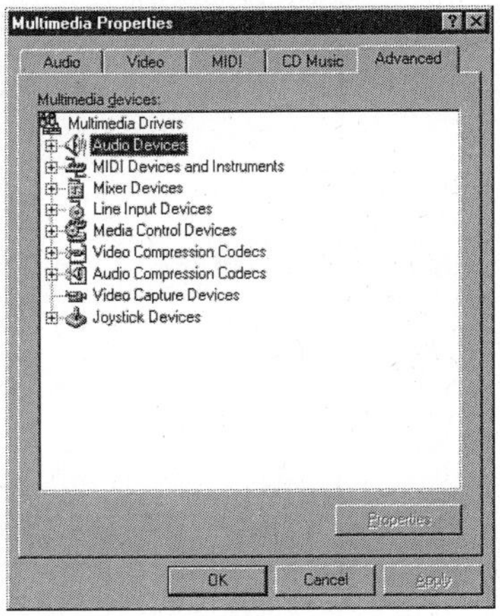

Fig. 27.18 The Advanced page of the Multimedia Properties sheet.

As you can see, the device's properties display provides option buttons to turn the device on or off. In addition, the device properties display may have enabled the Settings button, which lets you change the hardware settings for the device. When you click on this button, you see a window something like that shown in figure 27.19. Obviously, unless you understand I/O ports, interrupts, and DMA channels, you shouldn't change these settings. If you do change the settings, the device will probably stop working or even cause other devices to malfunction.

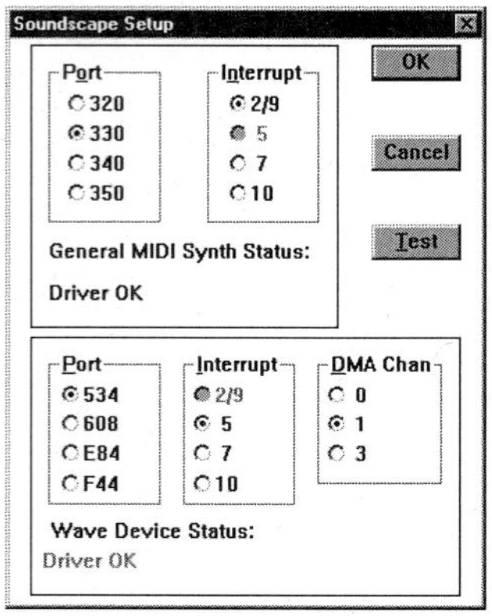

Fig. 27.19 Viewing a device's hardware settings.

Using Volume Control

Previously, in the "Setting Audio Properties" section, you learned about the volume-control accessory that you can access from the taskbar. To learn how to make the volume-control accessible from the taskbar, refer back to the "Setting Audio Properties" section. To bring up the volume-control accessory, double-click on the speaker icon found on the right side of the taskbar. You can also access the volume control from the Start/Programs/Accessories/Multimedia menu. When you run the volume-control accessory, you see a window something like that shown in figure 27.20.

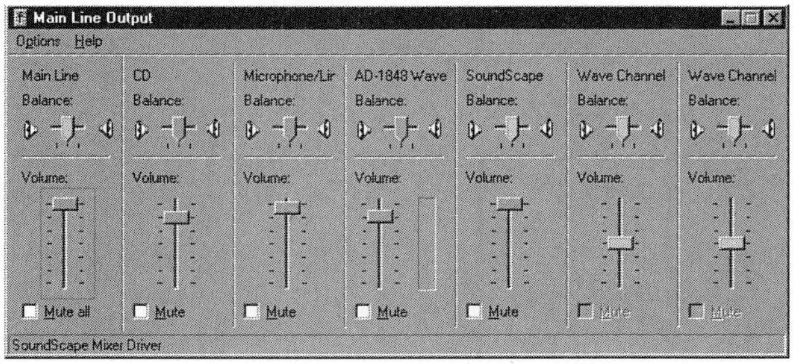

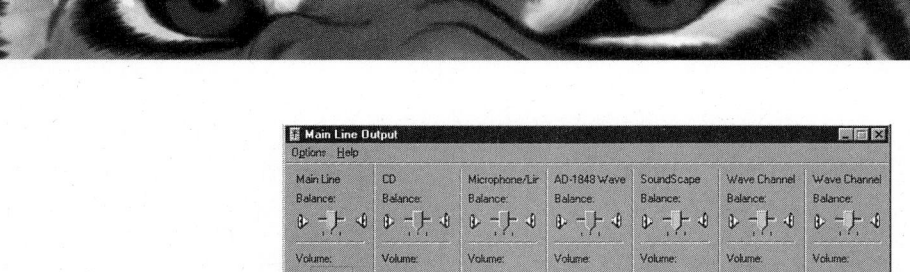

Fig. 27.20 The volume-control accessory is a sound mixer for balancing the volumes of various audio devices.

Exactly how the volume-control accessory looks depends on the devices attached to your computer and the program's options settings. As you can see, though, changing a device's volume is a simple matter of using your mouse to reposition the Volume slider for the device. For example, to lower the volume of your CD-ROM drive, slide the CD Volume control down. On the other hand, if you want to change the volume of digitized sound effects, you should use the Wave device's slider. To learn more about volume control and its many options, please refer to Chapter 29.

Configuring a Joystick

Many people use their multimedia computers for games. In fact, games were probably the first multimedia applications, using sound and animation long before the term *multimedia* was even coined. Most games these days can be controlled from your keyboard or by using your mouse. However, some games—especially arcade-type games—are easier to play by using a joystick.

Luckily, most sound cards include a port to which you can attach a joystick. However, because of the way joysticks work, they need to be calibrated before you use them in a game. Windows 95 probably already took care of this calibration, but to check your joystick or to

change its calibration, you can follow the instructions given in this section.

You calibrate a joystick by using the Joystick Properties sheet, which you can access from the Control Panel. First, bring up Control Panel, and then double-click on the Joystick icon. When you do, you see the Joystick Properties sheet.

Although most systems have only one joystick connected to them, Windows can handle up to 16. Before calibrating or testing a joystick, you must select the joystick in the Current Joystick list box. If you have only one joystick, the Current Joystick box should already be set properly.

Because joysticks come in many varieties, the Joystick Properties sheet enables you to select a type that matches your particular joystick device. You select the joystick type from the Joystick Selection list box (figure 27.21). This list box contains many types of joysticks, even many types with which you may not be familiar. Chances are you have a 2-axis, 2-button joystick. Other types of joysticks include gamepads, which look like the controllers that come with video-game consoles (Nintendo, Sega, and so forth), and light yokes, which look like airplane controls and are used mainly for flight simulators and racing games.

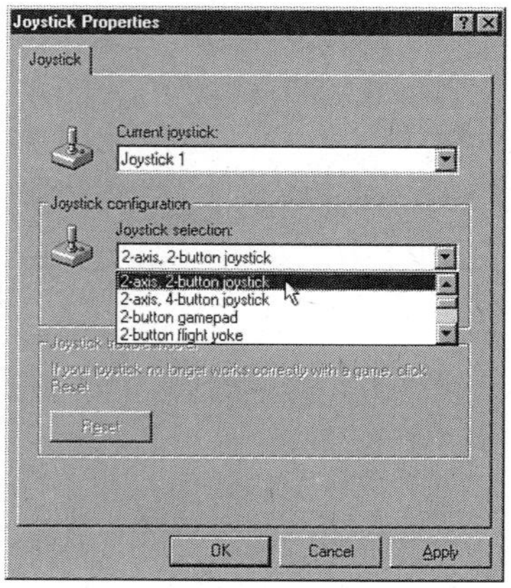

Fig. 27.21 Selecting the joystick type.

Once you have the joystick type set, click on the Calibrate button to bring up the first Joystick Calibration window, as shown in figure 27.22. Follow the instructions in the window. When you're done, you'll see a window that gives you a chance to test your joystick.

To test your joystick, click the Test button, which brings up the Joystick Test window, as shown in figure 27.23. Watch the small cross in the Position section while moving your joystick's handle. The cross should match the handle's movement. Finally, press the joystick's buttons to make sure that the appropriate button indicator in the Buttons section lights up. To complete the calibration, click on the Joystick Test dialog box's OK button, and then click on the Joystick Calibration dialog box's Finish button.

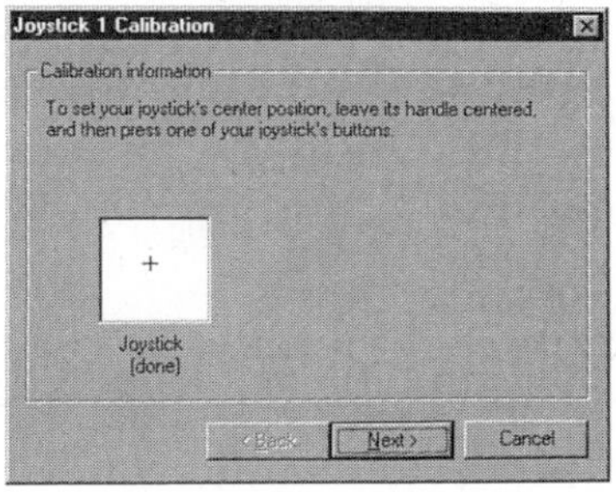

Fig. 27.22 The first step in calibrating a joystick.

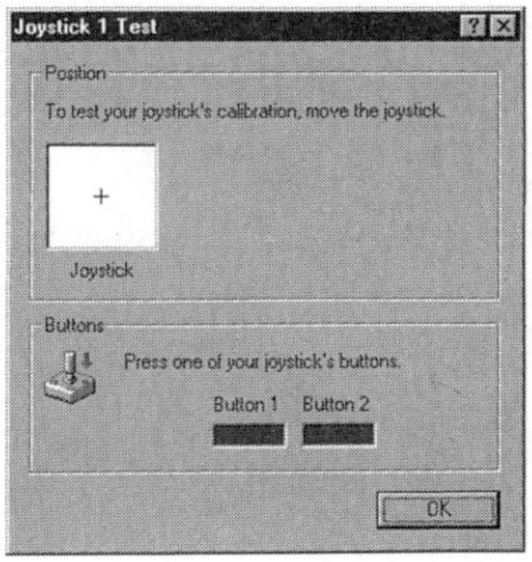

Fig. 27.23 The Joystick Text window gives you a chance to test your joystick's motion and buttons.

Checking CD-ROM Settings

When Windows 95 first configures your system, it does its best to identify and set up your hardware, including your CD-ROM drive. However, sometimes Windows 95 is unable to identify a CD-ROM drive and so uses less-efficient, default settings for that device. For this reason, you should check your CD-ROM settings to ensure that your CD-ROM is operating at peak efficiency.

Checking the CD-ROM's performance settings is easy. The trick is finding the settings in the first place, because they are deeply buried in the Windows system. Of course, discovering such hidden secrets is exactly why you bought this book, right? Follow these steps to find your CD-ROM's performance settings:

1. Right-click on the My Computer icon on your desktop, and select properties from the menu that pops up. The System Properties sheet appears.
2. Click on the Performance tab on the System Properties. The Performance page appears.
3. Click on the File System button. The File System Properties sheet appears.
4. Click on the CD-ROM tab. The CD-ROM page (figure 27.24), which contains your CD-ROM's performance properties, appears.

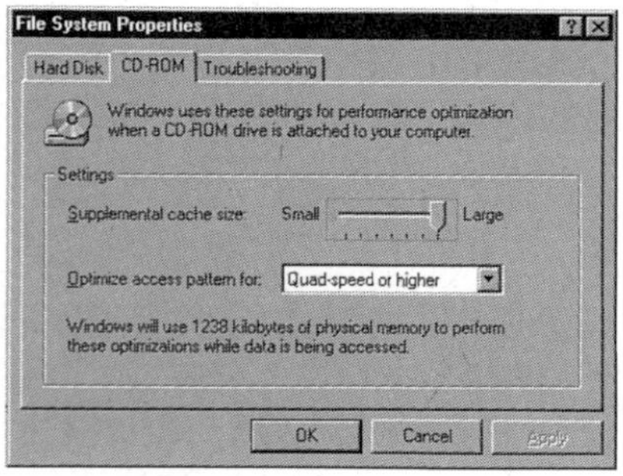

Fig. 27.24 The CD-ROM performance properties are well hidden in the Windows 95 system.

As you can see in figure 27.24, you can change two performance settings for your CD-ROM: the cache size and the access pattern. If you have 8M or more of memory in your computer, you should set the cache size to Large. With less memory, you'll have to experiment with the cache size to find the largest cache that doesn't adversely affect your system's performance.

The access pattern should be set to the type of CD-ROM drive you have. For example, if you have a quad-speed drive, you should set the access pattern setting to "Quad-speed or higher," whereas if you have a double-speed CD-ROM drive, the access pattern should be "Double-speed drives."

Understanding Full-Motion Video

by Robin Hohman

There are two kinds of video signals: analog and digital. Camcorders, VCRs, televisions, and laser discs transmit analog video, which is stored on videotape or videodisc. Digital video is made up of analog signals converted into bits and bytes that can be stored as a computer file.

The quality of analog video is higher than that of digital video, but the push is on to make digital video signals as seamless and color-rich as what you see on a TV screen.

In this chapter, you learn about the following:

- Video for Windows
- Hardware requirements for video
- Software requirements for video
- Video compression

- Video formats, such as MPEG and JPEG
- How to play video files

Video for Windows

Desktop digital video first debuted with QuickTime for the Macintosh, but didn't take off until Microsoft and Intel unveiled Video for Windows software in 1992.

QuickTime, and then Video for Windows (VfW), changed the way people thought about video production. As employed by TV stations and video houses, video production requires expensive tape and editing equipment. The standard method is to take video from one or more sources and copy it to a single videotape. The production has to be sequential, meaning you have to lay in shot A before shot B, and so forth. Each time you create a videotape from another tape, you lose quality. Each succeeding generation is subject to an increasing loss of quality.

The Video for Windows software converts the analog signal into a computer file, which is then stored on a hard disk, tape drive, floppy, or CD-ROM. That makes the video easily accessible for playback and editing. There is no generational loss of quality, because each time you view the video it comes from the original files. VfW also makes video a true hypermedia, because you can quickly retrieve the video shots in any sequence for any number of times.

Being hypermedia enables products that are created from digital video to be interactive, because the sequence of shots (and audio) is not limited to one person's design. For example, the popular CD-ROM Myst requires the user to choose different paths to follow during the course of the game. That's only possible with digital video. The game is programmed so that when the user makes a choice, the program searches the CD-ROM until that choice is found and presented on the screen. If the medium was videotape, you would have to go back and forth on the tape to access the desired sequence.

Most CD-ROM games don't employ *full-motion video.* Full-motion video is defined as stills displayed at 30 frames (still shots) per second (fps). At that rate, the human eye perceives the motion to be fluid and natural.

Digital video ranges from 10 to 30 fps, but it has two major drawbacks: it takes up huge amounts of storage space, and the quality and synchronization is dependent upon the speed and power of the computer. Uncompressed 30 fps video uses gigabytes of space per minute of video. It can also take up to 30M per second to transfer the data to display on a monitor.

Until huge hard drives and very fast computer chips became available, digital video remained a distant dream for most people. With the advent of the Pentium and other very fast chips, and the drop in prices and availability of 1+gigabyte hard drives, digital video came down to the masses.

Windows 95 makes video even more accessible because it includes VfW, which was formerly only available as an add-on development kit.

However, even with huge drives and faster computers, digital video must be compressed somehow to make PC video a realistic delivery tool for presentations, games, and even movies.

There are two ways to compress video for storage and playback: with video compression boards and with software. To capture video from an analog source, you must have a video capture board. To play video files, you can use a board or software that decompresses video files.

Video Hardware

Video capture boards grab raw analog video and convert it to digital data. The best rate for full-motion video is 30 fps, but not all cards can operate at that speed. Many capture 15 fps. The lower the fps, the less fluid the motion will seem. However, depending on what kind of video you're capturing and how you intend to distribute it, the lower fps may be suitable. The lower the fps, the less space needed to store it.

> **Tip:** Some video capture boards don't have the ability to display the incoming signals. If you want to display the data as it is captured, make sure the board supports that.

If you want to capture video, you must have a special board. If you only want to display and manipulate digital video, you have another choice: decompression software. Since there are many pitfalls inherent in adding internal hardware—it's expensive, time-consuming to install, and raises compatibility issues—software may be the better choice for people who don't need to capture their own video.

> **Caution:** Compatibility is the biggest problem with video capture boards. Before you buy and attempt to install a board, make certain it will be compatible with your system. Also make sure you can return it if it's not.

Video Software

Video software uses compression *codecs* (*co*mpression and *dec*ompression algorithms) that provide a shorthand for storing and playing the video. It's easier, cheaper, and more portable than hardware-assisted compression.

However, the same software used to compress the video must be used to decompress the video. That's where Video for Windows comes in.

Video for Windows

The single most important feature of VfW is the inclusion of a runtime engine, which allows people to play digital video on a PC without special hardware.

As of this writing, the VfW included with Windows 95 contains compression codecs for Cinepak, Indeo, YUV, RLE (Run Length Encoding),

and Video 1. These codecs allow you to play most files, but not MPEG (Moving Pictures Experts Group). The way people talk about it, MPEG is the most important development in desktop video since the Macintosh. Before you can understand what a big leap MPEG is, you have to first understand what came before it.

> **Tip:** The version of Cinepak that ships with Windows 95 (and Windows NT 3.5x) has an error in it that disables support for YUV. You can get the corrected software, version 1.10.0.6, from CompuServe's MS Win Multimedia forum in the Video for Windows library.

Compression Schemes

Video files would be unmanageable without compression. Remember, uncompressed 30 fps video uses more than a gigabyte of space per minute of video. Video files are compressed with so-called *lossy* compression. It means you will lose certain (perhaps unnoticeable) details in order to compress the file.

Compression works in one of two ways. Interframe works on the differences between similar frames. For example, a video of someone running along a beach would have many frames that are similar, with fewer that are different. Interframe compression captures key frames as whole frames, and only the differences in the delta frames.

Intraframe compression schemes work only within individual frames. Pixels are converted into mathematical formulas.

Lossy compression schemes sacrifice detail to compression ratio. That is, with lossy compression, you lose some of the original video frame, but fit more images in a smaller file.

The YUV compression scheme, for example, results in very high quality images, but the compression ratio is only 2:1. That is, two images in the original video are represented as one in the compressed video. You can

have compression ratios as high as 200:1, with a resulting loss in picture quality. Obviously, the lower the compression ratio, the bigger the file.

You can choose the amount of compression you're willing to put up with. Codec compression methods vary widely, and certain codecs might not be the best for particular tasks. For example, the RLE scheme only works with blocks of color, so you wouldn't want to use it for a close-up that demanded great detail.

The codecs vary in compression rate, compression ratio, file size, and quality. You can't determine the quality of the video by compression ratio alone. The quality of the video is highly dependent upon the types of images you're looking to compress.

The good news about Windows 95 is that, since several codecs are included, you can experiment without incurring additional expense.

Descriptions of the codecs included with the final beta release of Windows 95 follow.

Cinepak

Cinepak is an efficient, 24-bit codec designed to handle high compression rates without degrading the image quality. It uses an asymmetrical compression scheme, which means it compresses and decompresses images at different speeds, and takes a relatively long time to compress.

Intel Indeo R3.1 and R3.2

Intel's Indeo is slower than Cinepak, and it depends heavily upon the speed of the CPU running the software. However, Indeo has a somewhat better color quality than Cinepak, and you can enhance the speed with hardware-assisted compression/decompression.

> **Note:** Both Cinepak and Indeo will be available in 32-bit versions, which will considerably speed up the compression/decompression process. They're slated to ship with Windows 95.

YUV9

This is the encoding standard used by the broadcast industry. Many capture cards employ the YUV standard. YUV, which is also called component video, splits a video signal into two chroma signals and one brightness signal. The quality is very high, but the compression ratio is only 2:1.

RLE

RLE is a simple but not dazzling compression scheme. It uses *banding* techniques to encode the video; that is, rows of pixels are grouped together to portray the image. It's mainly used for animation.

Video 1

Video 1 was created by Microsoft and distributed with the Video for Windows Developer's Kit, so it automatically had a chance to be among the most popular schemes. Now that Microsoft is distributing other codecs as well, which codec you choose might just come down to personal preference. One thing that might limit the appeal of Video 1 is that it works as software only; that is, you can't enhance its performance with a video board as you can with Indeo.

MPEG-1

MPEG-1 is undoubtedly the way to squeeze full-screen, high-quality audio and video for wide distribution. MPEG-1, and its subset JPEG (Joint Photographic Experts Group), compress and decompress digital video in a new, more manageable way. Both are high-quality standards for compressing video signals.

MPEG-1 uses a technique called *transform coding*. That means it transforms all the time-based information for frequency components and looks for redundancies in the frequency domain to compress the video. It has a lower *compression ratio* than earlier codecs (50:1) because it treats every frame as a key frame. MPEG-1 compression is done in two phases: in the spatial direction and also in the conception of motion.

Earlier techniques such as Indeo and Cinepak use *vector quantization*, which is like sending a secret code from one place to another. If you know the code, you can decipher the content.

With Indeo and Cinepak, the information is coded into a *codebook*, and the codebook itself is transmitted. On the decompression side, the codebook is used to create the decoded (decompressed) video signals.

MPEG files are popping up everywhere, most visibly on World Wide Web pages on the Internet. University home pages in particular, but other pages as well, increasingly include hypertext links to nearly real-time full-motion videos.

Until recently, MPEG-1 was a hardware-dependent codec, which meant that you had to have an MPEG compression/decompression board to play MPEG files. Now there are codecs that allow you to play MPEG without special hardware.

There is one major advantage to hardware compression/decompression over software-only routines: you will get full-motion video at 30 fps regardless of the speed or power of your computer.

Software fps scales directly with CPU performance. In fact, a leading company marketing MPEG-1 software recommends no less than a 486DX2-66 for playing MPEG files. Even with that CPU, the computer won't be able to reach the maximum of 24 fps, but will hover around 10 fps—not enough speed to look like full-motion video.

> **Note:** Standard broadcast video is shown at 30 fps; movies are shown at 24 fps and codecs range from 15-30 fps.

Several companies are now marketing MPEG software, but one company has become the front-runner due to a deal with Microsoft. In early June 1995, Microsoft signed a deal with Santa Clara, Ca.-based Mediamatics, a three-year-old software company, to include its MPEG Arcade Player software with future releases of Windows 95 and Windows NT. The deal was struck too late for inclusion in the premiere August release of Windows 95, but will be included in the add-on developer's kit.

MPEG Arcade Player allows you to display MPEG files without any special hardware. The software is now included with some graphics cards, such as Western Digital, Diamond Multimedia, and Brooktree cards. But if you use Windows 95, you can use any graphics card. Depending on your needs, however, a high-end graphics card may still be the way to go.

However, all is not rosy in the MPEG video world. Software-only MPEG video won't run on less than a 90MHz Pentium, and at that all you'll get is 24 fps.

MPEG-2

The latest entry into digital video is MPEG-2, which can yield a 200:1 *compression ratio.* MPEG-1's best ratio is 6:1. As with all compression techniques, the actual ratio depends on the playback quality and content.

Another advantage MPEG-2 offers over MPEG-1 and other codecs is the *screen resolution rate.* Screen resolution describes the amount of detail within a shot. Without scaling, MPEG-1 offers a resolution of 352 by 240 pixels. MPEG-2 offers a resolution of 720 by 480 pixels at 30 fps, with high-quality audio.

MPEG-2, however, takes a great deal of time to compress even one second of video—sometimes at rates of hundreds of seconds to compress each second of video. New fast encoding chips will bring that time down considerably.

MPEG-3

There was an MPEG-3 designed to handle *HDTV (High Definition Television)*, but it's been dropped in favor of the MPEG-2 codec.

MPEG-4

MPEG-4 isn't scheduled to debut until 1998. It will use video synthesis, fractal geometry, and artificial intelligence to encode and decode video. As the technology improves, MPEG-4 will undoubtedly provide higher-quality video at perhaps higher compression ratios. The initial cost, however, may be a drawback.

Windows 95 Codecs

The codec you want to use must be installed in Windows 95. To view the codecs included with Windows 95, do the following:

> **Tip:** You can also take advantage of Windows 95's interactive help to find and configure most options. To use help, click on Start, Help, Index. Type in the word you're looking for and click on the entry. An interactive help screen will guide you to the right place to change settings.

If you have no programs open, click on My Computer, Control Panel to get the Multimedia Properties window.

If you have one or more open programs, click on Start, Settings and Control Panel.

Double-click on the Multimedia icon to display the Multimedia Properties window. Click on the Advanced tab to display the Multimedia devices list shown in figure 28.1.

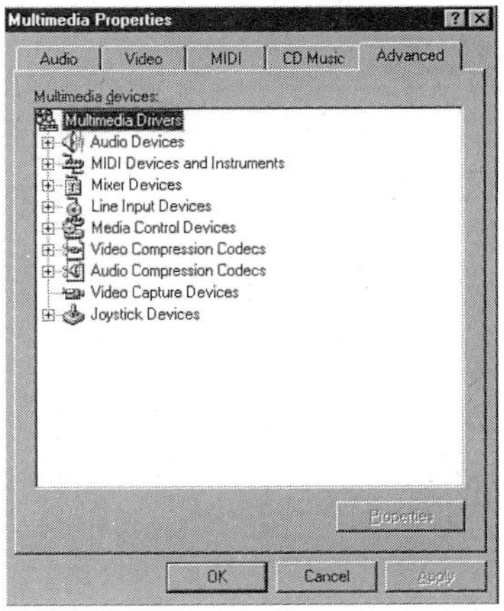

Fig. 28.1 The Advanced tab under the Multimedia Properties window lets you choose a codec for compressing/decompressing video.

Click on the + to the left of the Video Compression Codecs for a full listing of available schemes (see figure 28.2).

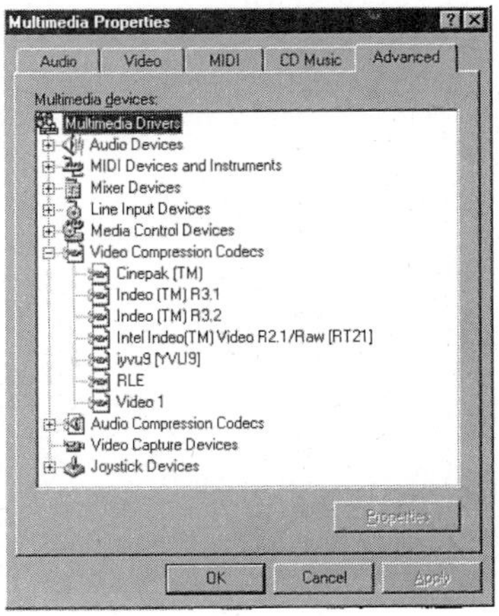

Fig. 28.2 Windows 95 ships with various codecs for working with video.

Click on any of the codecs (Cinepak, Indeo, Video 1, etc.) to make the Properties option available. Click on the Properties button to display the tab for that coding (figure 28.3).

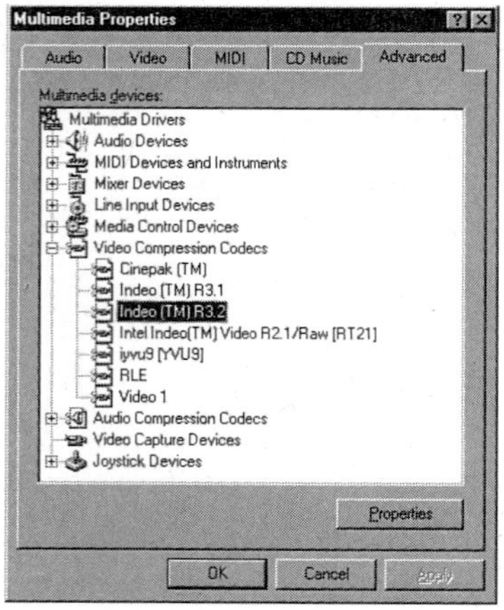

Fig. 28.3 Each codec has its own settings tab to customize it for your needs.

Click Settings to customize it for your use. To save space or to install an updated codec, click on Remove to delete a codec from your computer.

Viewing AVI Files

Audio Video Interleaved (AVI) files contain synchronized video and sound. Windows 95 supports AVI, MIDI (Musical Instrument Digital Interface), and audio waveform (WAV) files. See Chapter 25, "Adding Multimedia Capability to Your Computer," and Chapter 26, "Using Multimedia on Your Computer."

Windows 95 comes ready with AVI files and the codecs needed to play them. All you need is a sound card (although a CD-ROM drive and speakers or headphones are nearly a must as well).

Media Player

You can use the Media Player (figure 28.4) to play AVI files by doing the following:

Click on Start, Programs, Accessories, Multimedia, Media Player to display the Media Player.

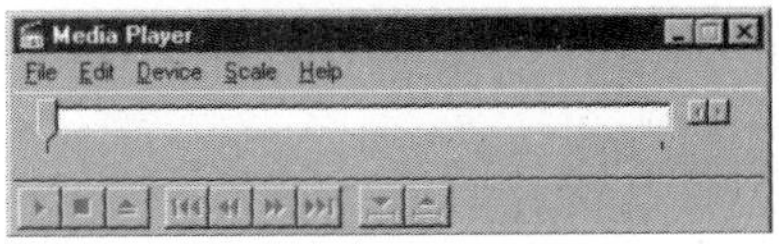

Fig. 28.4 The Media Player comes ready-made to play digital video.

To play AVI files, do the following:

1. With the Media Player open, click Device.
2. Click 1, Video for Windows.
3. Enter a File name or browse through the folders for the file you want to play.
4. Click on the file.
5. Click Open. You'll get the screen shown in figure 28.5.

> **Tip:** Look in the Media folder in the Windows folder to find multimedia files that come with Windows 95.

The Media Player will become active with an audio-tape-like panel on-screen, as in figure 28.5.

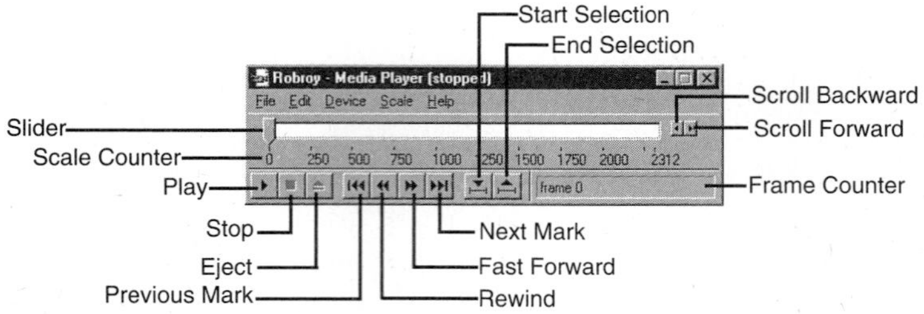

Fig. 28.5 Once enabled, Media Player displays control buttons.

6. Click the play button to play the video.

Scale: Frames

You can set the scale that is displayed; you have a choice between *frames* and *time*. That is, you can track the video frame by frame, with each frame counting as one, or you can count how long the video takes to run (see figure 28.6). To set the scale to frames, click on Scale, Frames.

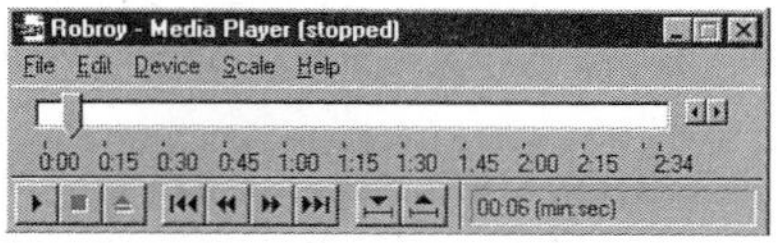

Fig. 28.6 You can view the video by frame or by second.

When the scale is set to frames, you can move ahead frame by frame by clicking on the Scroll Forward and Scroll Backward buttons. The frame number will appear in the frames box.

If you click the Fast Forward or Rewind buttons, the video will move by 12-frame increments.

Scale: Time

There may be times when you want to work with seconds instead of frames. Set the scale to time by clicking on Scale, Time.

When you click the Fast Forward or Rewind buttons, the video display moves in increments of roughly .70 of a second.

Playing the File

Click and hold on the slider to move the video forward or backward. You can click the Play button at any time to start the video. It will begin at the slider point. You can click on the Stop or Pause buttons at any time.

> **Tip:** The Pause button replaces the Play button whenever Play is activated.

Selection Points

When you're working with video, you often have to use a small bit of the file to edit it or to synchronize the audio. You can choose selection points to make it easier to find or to skip over specified areas in the video. There are two ways to set the selection points:

> **Note:** You can only create one set of selection points at a time. You can expand or decrease the selection, but the first set will disappear if you create a second set.

1. Move the slide control to the point you want to mark, and click on the Start Selection button. A small caret appears at that point on the scale line.
2. Drag the slide control to the point where you want to end the selection. A blue bar appears on the viewing line, and a small caret appears at that point on the scale line.
3. You can now use the Previous Mark and Next Mark to navigate back and forth in the video.

> **Note:** The selection doesn't carry over from time to frames or vice versa.

You can also set the selection points in a more precise way by using the Set Selection dialog box.

To use the Set Selection dialog box, do the following:

1. Choose frame or time mode.
2. Select Edit, Selection to get the screen shown in figure 28.7.

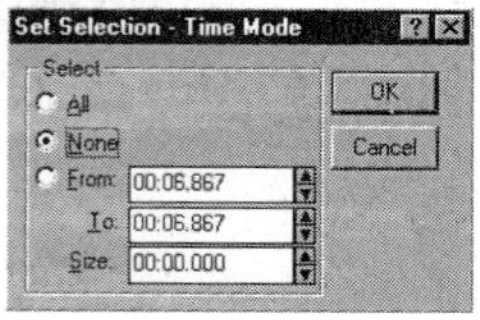

Fig. 28.7 The Set Selection Frame Mode lets you group a block of frames.

3. Select All, None, or From. To specify a sequence of frames (or time), either click the scroll buttons to get to the desired numbers, or type in the numbers.
4. You can instead choose a size (frames or seconds) by using the scroll button in the Size box or by typing in a number.
5. Click OK to mark the selection.

Properties

Setting the Properties is the most important parameter for the quality of the playback video. Properties allows you to choose what size the video plays back.

Select Device, Properties, and the Video tab to get the screen shown in figure 28.8.

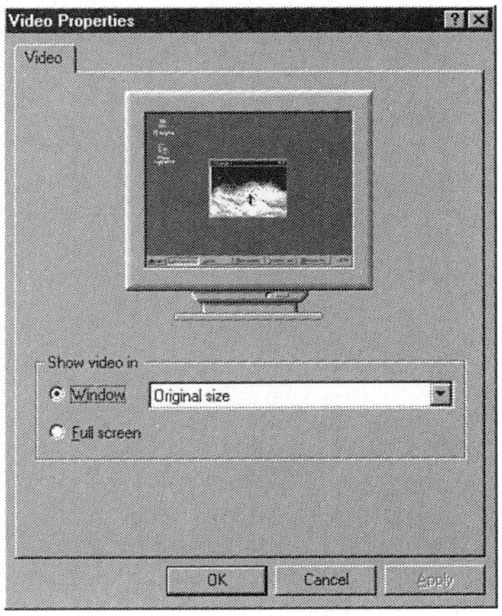

Fig. 28.8 You can select a playback size in the Video Properties sheet.

Take a look at the different ways you can play an image. Figure 28.9 shows a sample avi file.

Fig. 28.9 Using Windows 95's Media Player, the CBT_demo.avi file included with Asymmetrix Multimedia Toolbook authoring software.

The default window size is quite small but offers the least distortion of color or image. The screen can be resized by dragging on its borders. Notice what happens when the screen is resized to roughly twice its original size, as in figure 28.10.

Fig. 28.10 An AVI file increased to about double its size loses a lot of quality.

The quality is far more grainy than the original size, and it's plagued by the blockiness that results from reducing frames to color blocks in a run through the codec.

The default size is the original size. You have the following options:

- Original size
- Double original size
- 1/16 of screen size
- 1/4 of screen size
- 1/2 of screen size
- Maximized

The following five figures illustrate the difference in size and quality:

Fig. 28.11 Original size.

Fig. 28.12 Double original size.

Fig. 28.13 1/16 of screen size.

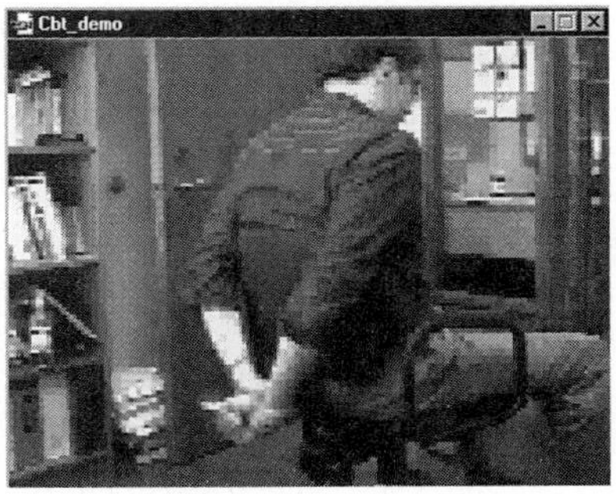

Fig. 28.14 1/4 of screen size.

Fig. 28.15 1/2 of screen size.

A maximized, or full-screen, size is about twice the size of figure 28.15, but looks considerably more distorted.

OLE

Perhaps the most outstanding result of the video capabilities of Windows 95 is that you can easily use OLE (object linking and embedding) to drop video clips into presentations, word processing documents, spreadsheets, and many other Windows programs.

The instructions are similar for most Windows programs. I'm going to drop a video clip into Microsoft Word for Windows:

1. Open a Word document and position the cursor where you want the clip to go.
2. Select Insert, Object to get the Object dialog box.
3. Click the Create New tab.
4. Highlight and click Media Clip.
5. Click OK. In the document, you'll get the Media Clip placeholder as shown in figure 28.16. You'll also get a modified form of the Media Player box.

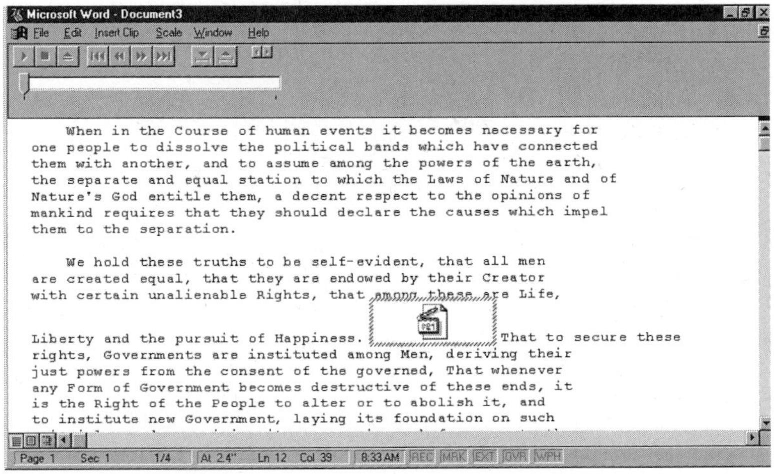

Fig. 28.16 The Media Clip placeholder points the way to the OLE clip.

6. Select Insert Clip.

> **Tip:** If you go to another task and lose the modified version of the Media Player, double-click on the placeholder shown in figure 28.17 to get it back.

7. Select 1, Video for Windows.
8. Choose a folder and a file name.
9. Click Open. The file will open within the document, as in figure 28.17.

Fig. 28.17 The media clip appears where the placeholder was inserted.

10. Select Insert Clip, Properties and set a size.
11. Click OK.
12. If you only want a portion of the clip to play, select Edit, Selection.
13. Specify a range.
14. Click OK.
15. If you want to control the volume, select Insert Clip, Volume Control and set the volume.

    Click Options, Exit.

> **Tip:** Play the clip before you close it to verify that you've chosen the right one.

16. Click anywhere else in the document to close the play panel.

> **Tip:** To move the clip within the document, click once on it to define it, and then drag and drop it to the desired place.

To play the clip, double-click on it.

Options

There are seven different options you can set for the clip. To see the options, select Edit, Options to get the screen shown in figure 28.18.

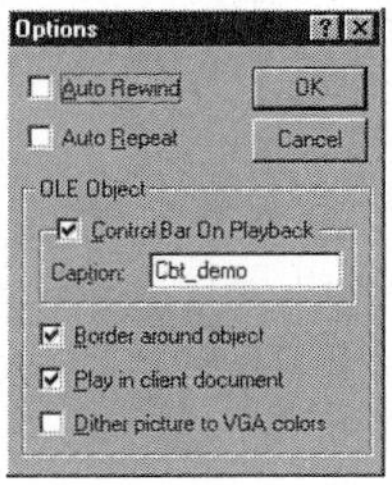

Fig. 28.18 You can set different options for the media clip.

You can choose to have the clip Auto Rewind or Auto Repeat after it plays.

If you're linking and embedding the clip in another Windows application, you can choose to display the control bar on playback. You can also designate a caption or choose not to have one. The default caption is the clip's file name.

DCI

In mid 1994, Microsoft released the *Display Control Interface* (DCI) display driver development kit, which was developed along with Intel. DCI enables Windows to implement advanced hardware features to speed up the way games and digital video read and write to disc. DCI allows the following features:

- Overlay
- Color-space conversion
- Double buffering
- Chroma key
- Asynchronous drawing
- Stretching

Note: You need a high-quality graphics adapter card to make these features work.

As of this writing (early summer 1995), Microsoft planned to drop support for DCI for the first release of Windows 95. It will be included in later versions.

Just how much that would affect developers and end users is disputed. Microsoft anticipates no problems, but some companies expressed concerns about compatibility with multimedia software. Mostly, it will affect packages that need software MPEG, Apple QuickTime for Windows, and hardware enhancement to run.

Killer Windows 95 — 29

Fine-Tuning Your Windows 95 Sound Card

by Clayton Walnum

At this point, you've got your multimedia system all set up and ready to go. All your devices are installed and configured, and you've even had some time to experiment a bit, playing audio CDs or MIDI files, or maybe even watching full-motion video clips. Although you've had a chance to use many of your multimedia devices, you've yet to learn how to really control your sound card. Because a sound card is probably the most complicated device in your new multimedia system, it gets an entire chapter of its own!

In this chapter, you learn the following:

- ➤ How to mix sounds with the Volume Control accessory
- ➤ How to set recording levels

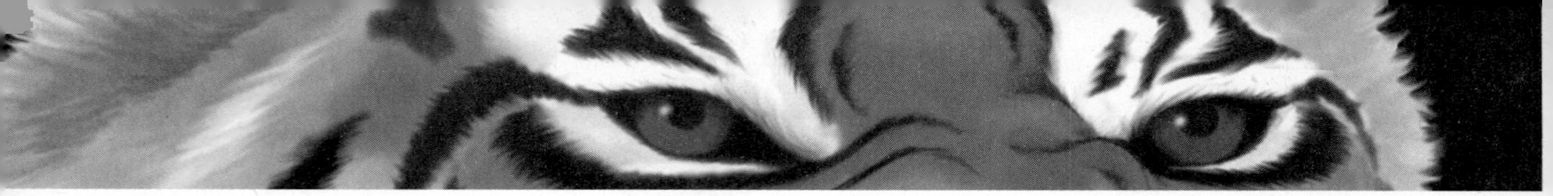

- How to add or remove the volume control from the taskbar
- How to set your sound card's recording quality
- How to record sound effects for use with Windows
- How to assign sound cards and instruments to different MIDI channels

Using Volume Control

Back in Chapter 27, you used the Multimedia Properties sheet to customize how some of your multimedia devices work. However, much of the details of dealing with a sound card were left to this chapter. One of the topics that got skipped over was the Volume Control accessory. In this section, you make up for that lack, by learning the details of using Volume Control with your sound card.

To start Volume Control, you can select it from the Start/Programs/Accessories/Multimedia menu. When you do, Volume Control's main window appears on-screen, as shown in figure 29.1. As you can see, this window contains various controls for mixing the sound sources installed in your system.

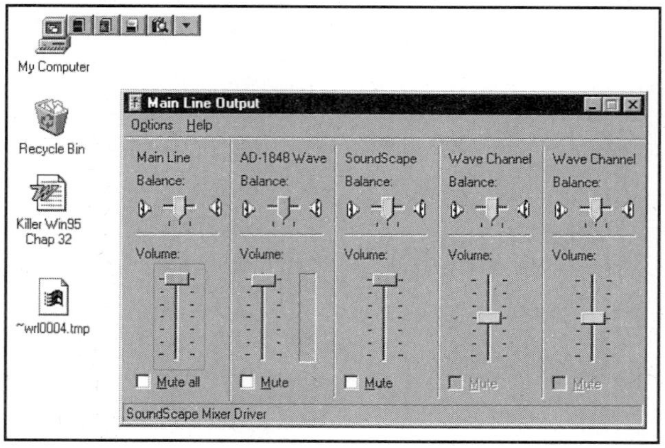

Fig. 29.1 Volume Control's main window looks like a studio-style mixer.

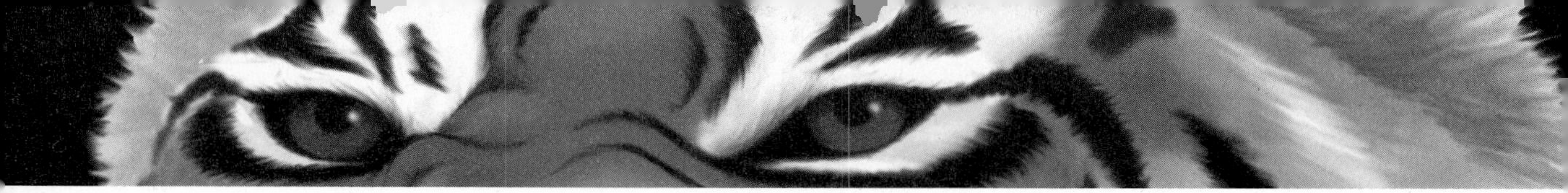

Choosing Which Channels to Display

When you first run Volume Control, you may notice that not all your audio devices are represented by a channel on the mixer. You can remedy this situation by selecting the Properties command from the Options menu. When you do, you see the Properties sheet (figure 29.2).

At the bottom of the dialog box is a list of available devices. To expand the Volume Control window so that it provides a channel for each device, just make sure there's a check mark in each box in the list. To remove a channel from the main window, remove its check mark from the list. In this way, you can display channels for only those devices you need. Figure 29.3 shows a typical Volume Control, with a channel displayed for every device.

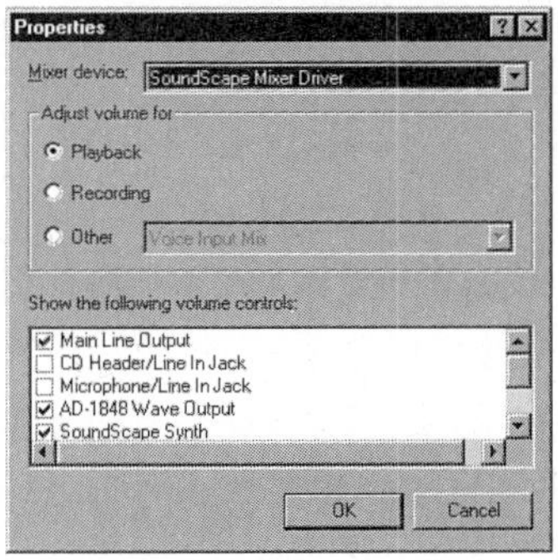

Fig. 29.2 The Properties sheet enables you to customize the Volume Control accessory.

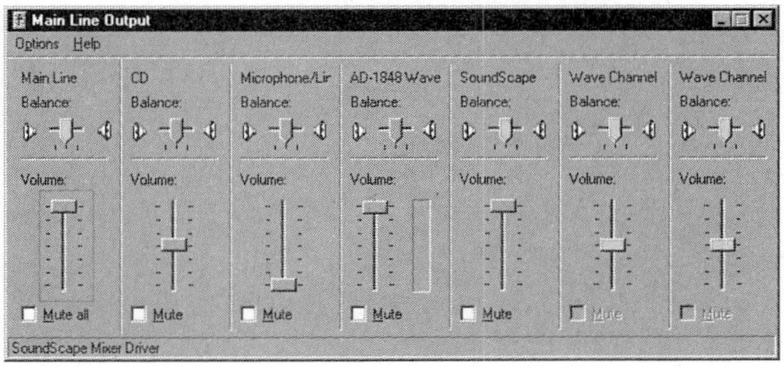

Fig. 29.3 You can display as many or as few channels as you like.

Mixing Sound

How do you control sound with Volume Control? A good question! Notice that the first channel in the mixer is called Main Line. (Your version of Volume Control may look different, depending on the type and capabilities of your sound card.) Like all the other channels, the Main Line channel has a balance control, a volume slider, and a mute box. Unlike the other channels, however, the Main Line channel controls the sound of every device simultaneously. That is, the Main Line controls are the master controls.

To reduce the volume of every sound device, drag the Main Line volume slider down. To increase the volume of every channel, you would, of course, drag the slider back up. Dragging the Balance slider left or right changes the amount of sound that comes from the left or right speakers. When the slider is all the way to the left, only the left speaker produces sound. Similarly, when the slider is all the way to the right, only the right speaker produces sound. In most cases, you'll want the Balance slider exactly in the center, so your speaker can produce the best stereo effect.

Finally, you can instantly bring every channel down to its minimum volume by clicking the Mute all box. When you do, a check mark appears in the box, which indicates that every channel is at its minimum level. To turn all channels back on, click on the Mute all box again to remove the check mark.

Each of the other device channels works similarly to the Main Line channel, except they control only the specific devices that are marked at the top of the channel. For example, to change the volume of the CD device, you would adjust the volume slider in the CD channel. Likewise, the Balance and Mute controls in the CD channel only affect the CD device.

By setting the channels in various ways, you can achieve some interesting results. You can, for example, set the Wave channel's balance control all the way to the left and the Microphone channel balance all the way to the right. Then, digitized sound effects will come from the left

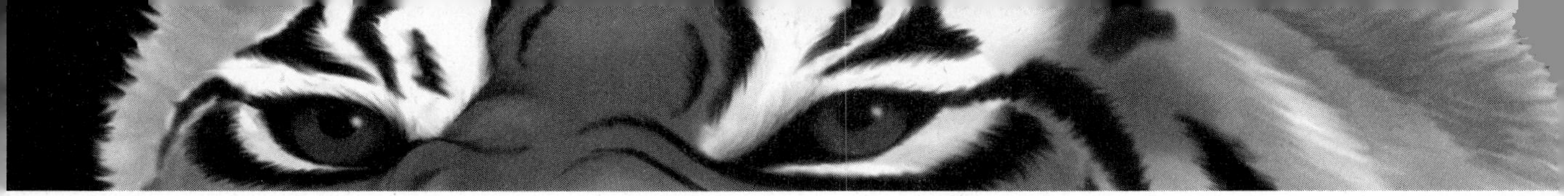

speaker, while at the same time, someone speaking into the microphone will be heard in the right speaker. You can, of course, shut off any individual channel by clicking its Mute box.

Notice that the Main Line controls always affect all the other channels. For example, the setting of the Main Line volume slider sets the maximum sound level attainable by any other channel. If you have the Main Line volume slider set at its halfway point, all the other volume sliders must work within the set range. That is, if you drag a device's volume slider to its maximum position, the volume of the device will be the Main Line's volume setting, with lower device volume settings representing a volume level somewhere between off and the Main Line's volume setting.

Setting Record Levels

In the previous section, you used Volume Control's Properties sheet to determine which devices have channels displayed in the mixer. What you may not have realized at the time was that you were controlling which playback channels were to be displayed. *Playback channels* control sound being played back by a sound device. For example, when you play an audio CD or listen to a digitized sound effect (a wave file), you're using a playback channel. The opposite of playback is record, and Volume Control also has a set of *record channels*, which control the sound being recorded. (When you record sound, you're storing it for later playback. You learn to record sounds later in this chapter, in the section titled, "Recording Sound.")

If you have a cassette deck in your home, you know that you can change the volume of a tape by turning up the volume on your stereo. This is the equivalent of manipulating Volume Control's playback channels. You probably also know that you can capture a radio broadcast to tape by recording the radio with your cassette deck. You control the volume of the recording by turning up your cassette deck's record level. This is the equivalent of manipulating Volume Control's recording channels.

To access the recording channels, you must first display the Properties sheet, which you do by selecting the Properties command in the Options menu. As you saw back in figure 29.3, the Properties sheet contains a section with three option buttons labeled Playback, Recording, and Other. When the dialog box first appears, the Playback option is selected, which means that you're setting the properties for the playback channels. To change to the recording channels, click the Recording option button.

When you click the recording option button, the devices listed at the bottom of the dialog box change to show the recording devices. Use this list to select the devices for which you want a channel in the mixer. To select a device, place a check mark in its box, by clicking on the box. To deselect a device, remove its check mark, by clicking on the box again. When you're finished selecting recording devices, click on the dialog box's OK button. You'll then see that Volume Control now displays the recording channels you selected (figure 29.4). You can tell that you're now dealing with recording channels because the window is labeled "Record Input Mix."

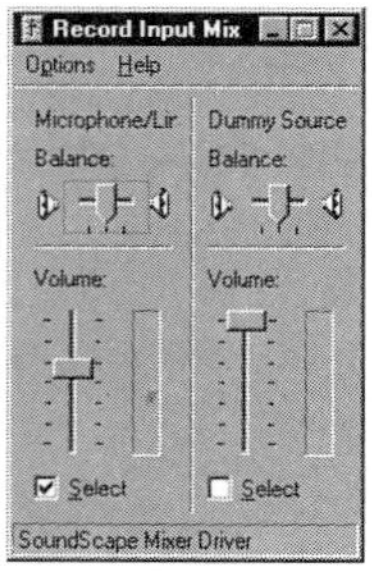

Fig. 29.4 Volume Control can also display recording channels.

Just as the playback controls affect how sounds are played, the controls on the recording channels change how sound is recorded. The Balance control determines how much of the sound is recorded for the left and right speakers. The volume slider determines how loudly the sound is recorded. Finally, the Select option determines which channel is the source of the sound to record.

If you look in the Options menu, you may find that the Advanced Controls command is enabled. If it is, you can click on it to display the Advanced button in the Volume Control window, as shown in figure 29.5. Clicking on this button displays the Advanced Controls dialog box for the channel (figure 29.6). The controls in this dialog box enable you to modify such settings as tone (treble and bass) for sound devices that support such functions. Because every sound card is different, you should check your sound card's manual to determine what the advanced controls do for your sound card.

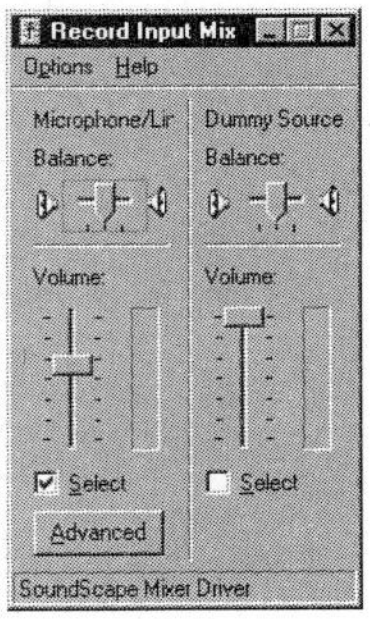

Fig. 29.5 The Advanced button provides access to advanced controls for a specific device's channel.

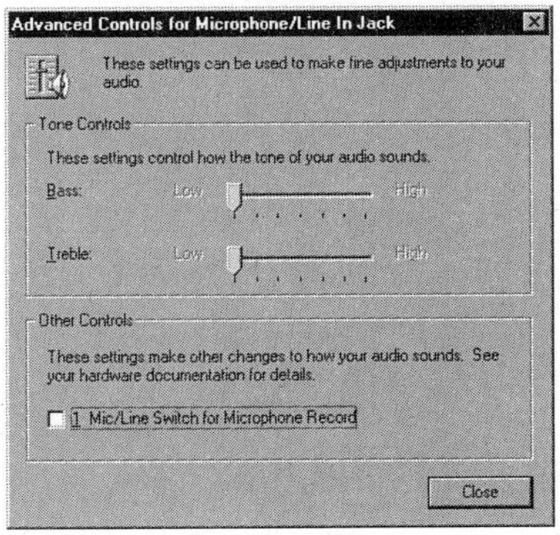

Fig. 29.6 The Advanced Controls dialog box contains extra controls that may be supported by a sound device.

Accessing Volume Control from the Taskbar

In its default state, the taskbar displays a speaker icon that represents the Volume Control accessory. As you learned in Chapter 27, "Getting the Most out of Multimedia," if you single-click on the speaker icon, a small volume control appears (figure 29.7). This miniature version of the Volume Control accessory determines the volume for all sound channels in your system. In that way, it acts just like the Main Line volume slider in the full-featured version of the Volume Control accessory. (If the speaker icon does not appear on your taskbar, refer to the next paragraph to learn how to enable and disable this option.)

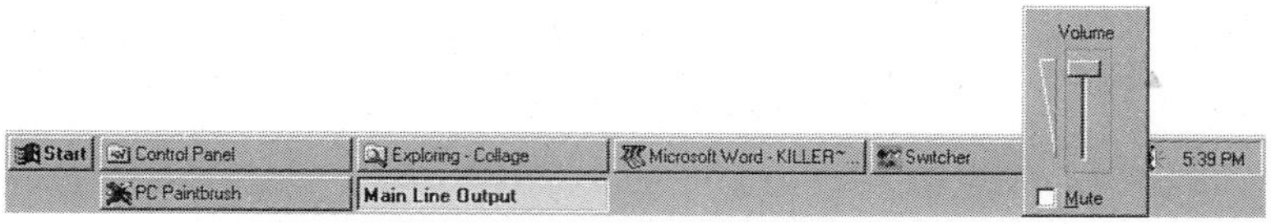

Fig. 29.7 The miniature version of Volume Control sets the volume for every sound channel simultaneously.

If you double-click on the speaker icon, Windows displays the full version of the Volume Control accessory, which you can use as described earlier in this section. If you'd rather that the speaker icon not appear in the taskbar, you can remove it with the Multimedia Properties sheet. (You can also add the speaker icon to the taskbar with the Multimedia Properties sheet.) To display this dialog box, double-click on the Multimedia icon in the Control Panel window. When you do, Windows displays the Multimedia Properties sheet, as shown in figure 29.8. To remove the Volume Control icon from the taskbar, remove the check mark from the Show Volume Control on the taskbar option. Another way to access the Show Volume Control option is to right-click the speaker icon in the taskbar and select the Adjust Audio Properties option in the pop-up menu.

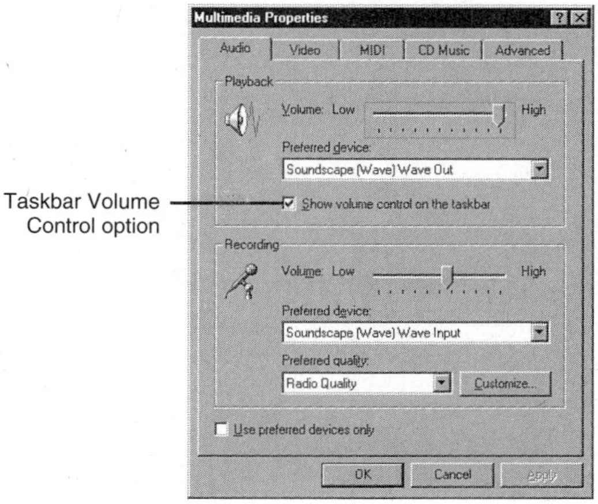

Fig. 29.8 The Multimedia Properties sheet enables you to add or remove Volume Control from the taskbar.

Setting Recording Quality

The Multimedia Properties sheet also enables you to set the recording quality of your sound device. As you learned back in Chapter 27, "Getting the Most out of Multimedia," the easiest way to set the recording quality is to select a setting from the Preferred Quality list box, as shown in figure 29.9. However, if you want more control over the recording quality, click on the Customize button to display the Customize dialog box.

In the Customize dialog box, the Name list box holds the names of the currently available quality settings. At first, this list box contains only the default CD Quality, Radio Quality, and Telephone Quality entries. Using the Customize dialog box, you can add your own settings to the list.

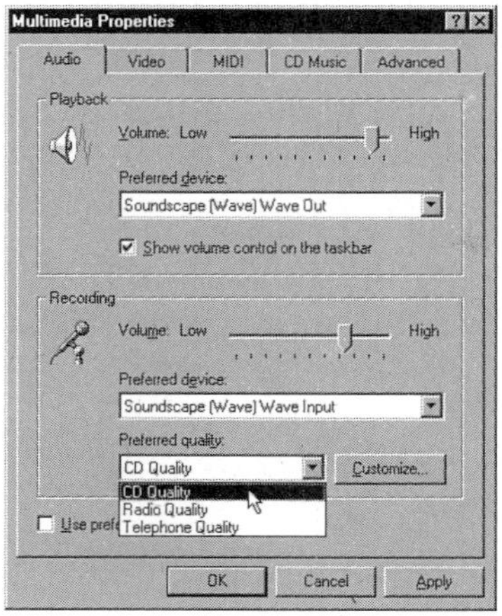

Fig. 29.9 The Preferred Quality list box enables you to set recording quality quickly and easily.

Unless you really know what you're doing, you should probably leave the Format box set just as it is. You can safely experiment with the Attributes list box, though, which displays the various sound-quality settings you can use, as shown in figure 29.10. The four values displayed in each list entry contribute to the quality of the recording; the higher the number, the better the quality.

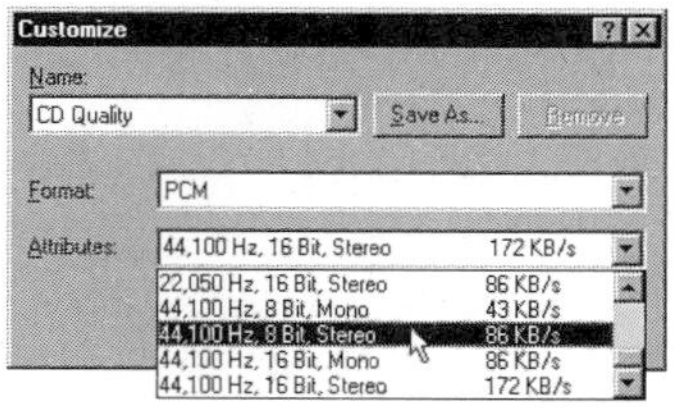

Fig. 29.10 Use the Customize dialog box to create your own recording-quality settings.

The first number (for example, 44,100 Hz) is the sampling rate, the second is the sampling size (for example, 16 bits), the third setting selects between mono and stereo sound, and the last setting (for example, 172 kb/sec) shows how much memory or disk space is required for each second of sound. Notice that the higher the sound quality, the more memory and disk space required to store the sound.

When you select a new sound setting from the Attributes list box, the Name list box shows the name [untitled]. To make use of your new setting, you should give the setting a name and then save it to disk. You do this by clicking on the Save As button, entering a name into the dialog box that appears, and then clicking on the dialog's OK button. When you finish the Save As procedure, your new sound setting appears in the Name list box, where it will be whenever you display the Audio page of the Multimedia Properties sheet.

Figure 29.11 shows a new sound format, My Sound Format, in the Name list box. Notice that, when a custom sound format is displayed in the Name box, Windows enables the Remove button. This is so you can remove from the Name list any custom sound formats that you've created. To remove the format, first make sure that the sound format you want to remove is displayed in the Name box; then, just click the Remove button.

Recording Sound

If you've never recorded sound effects under Windows before, you're in for a treat. Not only is the job easy, but it's also fun. Besides Sound Recorder, which comes with Windows, most sound cards also come with the software you need to create sound effects for any application that can handle wave files. Moreover, many of these sound-recording programs can edit sounds in various ways, from clipping unwanted noise to adding echo or even reversing a sound effect.

On some systems, for example, you can have an Ensoniq Soundscape Wavetable sound card. It comes with a sound recording, editing, and playback program called Audiostation (figure 29.11). This program can do everything from record WAV files to play your favorite CD.

Fig. 29.11 The Audiostation sound application not only looks cool, but works great, too.

If you have a Sound Blaster 16 sound card, you might have a program called WaveStudio, which, although not as elaborate as Audiostation, provides all the basic editing features you need to create sound effects for use under Windows. Other types of sound cards come with similar sound-editing programs.

No matter what sound card you have and what software you'll be using to record and edit sound effects, the first step is to plug a microphone into the sound card. Then, whatever sounds the microphone picks up are transmitted to the sound card and on to whatever sound-editing program you're running. In this book, you learn about the Sound Recorder accessory that comes with Windows, but most of what is discussed here, you can apply to any sound-recording application.

Once you have the microphone plugged in, start Sound Recorder by clicking on its entry in the Start/Programs/Accessories/Multimedia menu. When you do, you see the window shown in figure 29.12. To start recording, just click on the Record button. When you do, the time in the Position box starts counting upward and any sound picked up by your microphone is stored in the computer's memory.

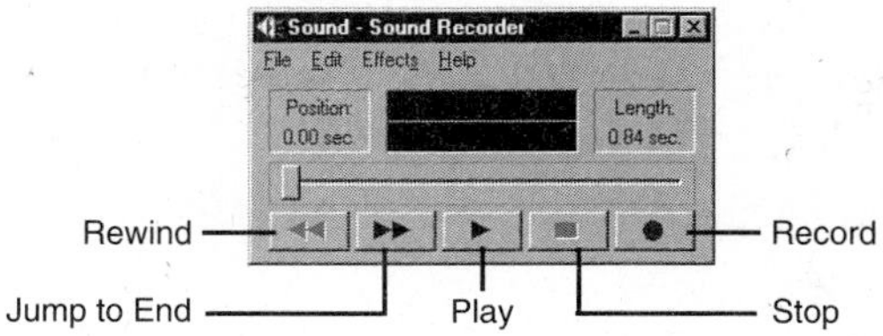

Fig. 29.12 The Windows Sound Recorder records sound effects.

For example, suppose that you want to record the words *Welcome, Master*, to be used as a greeting when you start Windows (replacing the famous *tada*). After plugging in your microphone, starting Sound Recorder, and clicking the Record button, just speak into the microphone. When you're done speaking, click on the Stop button. To hear what you've just recorded, click on the Play button. The rewind and jump-to-end buttons bring you to the very beginning or end of the sound effect, respectively. (If you like, you can drag the slider control to position yourself at any point in the sound effect you want.)

When you have your sound effect recorded just the way you want it (it'll probably take a few tries unless you're a professional announcer), you must save it to disk so that other programs can use it. To do this, click on the File menu's Save As command, enter a name for the file into the Save As dialog box, and click on the dialog box's Save button. Notice that you don't need to add the WAV extension (normally used for sound files) to the sound name. Sound Recorder does this for you.

Now, your sound effect is safely stored on disk, and you can use it with any application that can play wave files. If you want to attach your sound effects to Windows events (such as replacing that aforementioned *tada* sound), use the Sounds Properties sheet. For more information on the Sounds Properties sheet, see Chapter 26, "Using Multimedia on Your Computer."

A final note: If your sound effects don't seem to be recording as loudly as they should be, remember that you can use the Volume Control accessory to change the recording volume. Refer to this chapter's "Setting Record Levels" section for more information.

Editing Sounds

Once you have a sound effect recorded, you'll almost always need to edit it somehow. Different sound programs have different editing features, but most of them let you delete various portions of the sound, as well as change the volume of the sound.

One piece of editing you'll almost certainly have to do is delete part of the beginning and end of the sound. This is because you're going to have a second or two of silence before the actual sound wave you want. Why? It takes a second or two for you to go from turning on the sound program's record function to actually creating the sound you want to record. Similarly, you may not get to the stop button as quickly as you'd like.

As you can see from figure 29.13, Sound Recorder's Edit menu contains a number of commands that you can use to clean up your sound recordings. To delete the beginning portion of a sound effect, drag the slider control to the end of the area that you'd like to delete, and then select the Edit menu's Delete Before Current Position command. Similarly, to delete an ending portion from the sound effect, drag the slider to the start of the area that you want to delete, and then select the Delete After Current Position command. (You can also position the slider by playing the sound effect and then clicking the stop button at the appropriate point.)

Fig. 29.13 Use Sound Recorder's Edit menu to clean up your sound effects.

Another thing you may have to do is increase the volume of the sound effects. For some reason, they never seem to record loud enough. In Sound Recorder, you can increase the volume of the sound effects by selecting the Effects menu's Increase Volume command (figure 29.14). If you need to reduce the sound effects' volume, select the Effects menu's Decrease Volume command.

Fig. 29.14 Sound Recorder's Effects menu offers interesting ways to modify a sound effect.

Notice that these commands do not change the volume of your playback or record channels. Instead, they increase the amplitude of the sound itself. *Amplitude* is the height of a sound wave. The higher a sound effect's amplitude, the higher its volume. Figure 29.15 shows a sound effect's waveform before the volume has been increased. Figure 29.16 shows the same waveform after the volume has been increased. Notice how the waveform is higher.

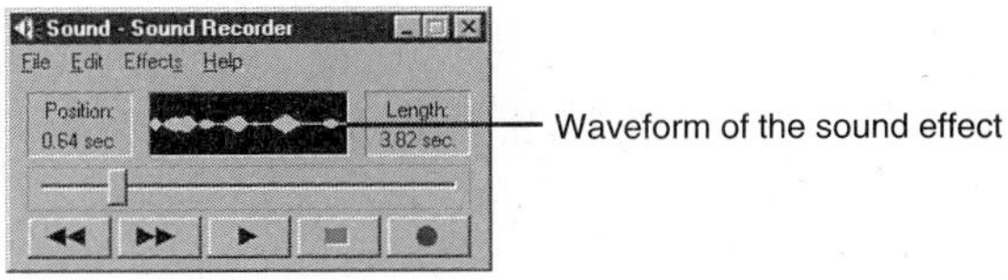

Fig. 29.15 The waveform in this window is shown at its normal amplitude.

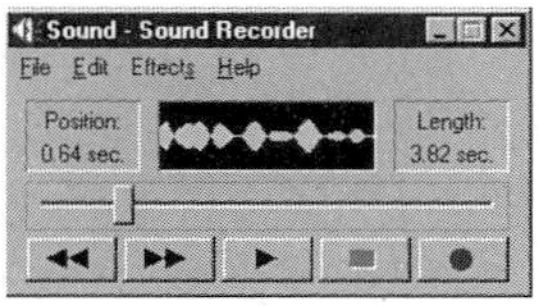

Fig. 29.16 This is the same waveform, but with its amplitude increased.

Other commands on the Effects menu let you increase or decrease the sound effect's speed (which has the effect of speeding or slowing a tape), add echo to the sound, or even reverse the sound so that it plays backward! With all these tools at your command, you should be able to come up with some strange and interesting effects.

Creating a MIDI Configuration

In Chapter 27, "Getting the Most out of Multimedia," you learned to add MIDI instruments to your system. As you discovered, these instruments can be anything from electronic keyboards to drum machines and any other type of sound module that responds to MIDI commands. What you didn't know then was that MIDI commands can be sent on any of 16 different channels. This means that you can route MIDI commands to as many as 16 different instruments just by assigning each instrument to its own MIDI channel.

The MIDI page of the Multimedia Properties sheet enables you to assign instruments to channels by setting up a custom MIDI configuration. To do this, first display the Multimedia Properties sheet by clicking on Control Panel's Multimedia icon. Then, select the dialog box's MIDI tab to display the MIDI page, as shown in figure 29.17.

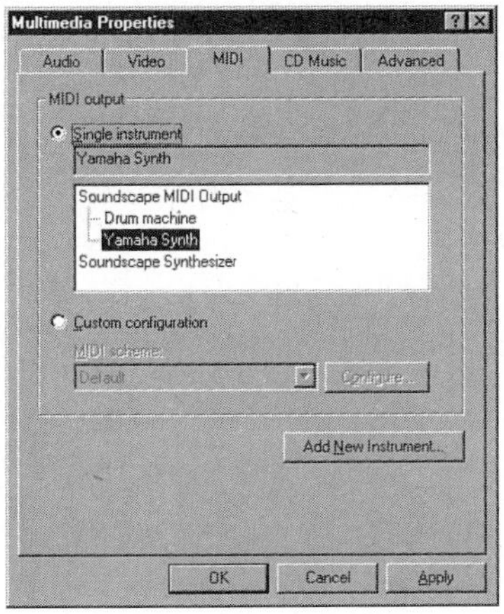

Fig. 29.17 Use the MIDI page of the Multimedia Properties sheet to set up a custom MIDI configuration for your sound card.

As you can see, the list box on the MIDI page shows the instruments installed on your system. You can select any single instrument to receive MIDI commands by clicking on the instrument in the box. But, if you'd like to have different instruments on different channels and thus use many instruments simultaneously, click on the Custom Configuration option to enable the MIDI Scheme and Configure controls. Then, click on the Configure button, which displays the MIDI Configuration dialog box (figure 29.18).

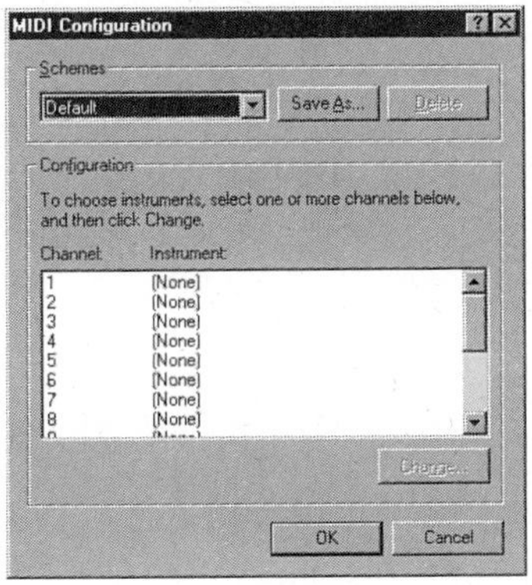

Fig. 29.18 The MIDI Configuration dialog box assigns MIDI channels to specific instruments.

In the MIDI Configuration dialog box, the Schemes list box holds any configurations that you've created for your system. The first time you see this control, it'll probably only contain the Default entry. Your task now is to add your own custom MIDI configuration to the list. To do this, first click on the channel with which you want to associate one of your MIDI instruments. Then, click the Changebutton to bring up the Change MIDI Instrument dialog box (figure 29.19).

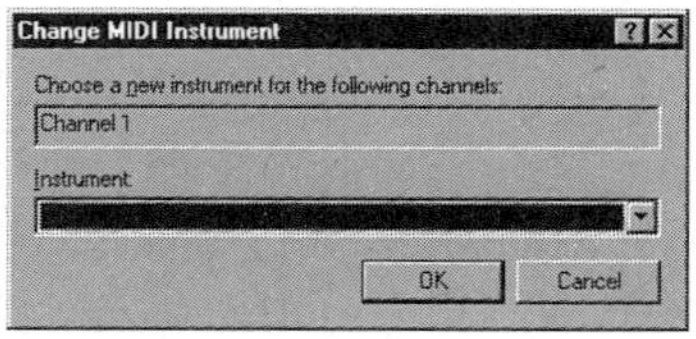

Fig. 29.19 The Change MIDI Instrument dialog box lets you associate an instrument with the selected MIDI channel.

The upper box in the dialog shows the channel that you're currently assigning. The list box in the lower part of the dialog box holds all the MIDI instruments attached to your system. Just select an instrument from the list and *presto!* that instrument is assigned to the selected channel. If, for example, you assign MIDI channel 1 to an electronic keyboard and MIDI channel 2 to your sound card, any MIDI commands targets for channel 1 go to the keyboard and commands on channel 2 go to the sound card.

After you've set up your MIDI configuration, you'll want to save it for future use. To do this, click on the Save As button, enter a name for the configuration into the dialog that appears, and then click on the dialog's OK button. You can delete any custom MIDI configurations you add to the list by selecting the configuration in the Schemes list box and then clicking on the MIDI Configuration dialog box's Delete button.

30

Using OLE to Communicate with Other Applications

by Allen L. Wyatt

Through your computer experience, you've learned that you generally perform a specialized type of work with a given application. For example, for word processing, you use a word processing application. For spreadsheets, you switch to a spreadsheet application, and so on. But the programming wizards at Microsoft have visualized a completely different way to use computers.

In tomorrow's computers (and to a degree, in Windows 95), the emphasis on individual applications will slip into the background, and instead the focus will be on documents. You'll use more than one application to create a single document, and as you do, a variety of application tools will be instantly available for your work. You'll draw on

word processing tools to create text, presentation graphics tools to create a chart, and font-design tools to create an attractive document title. Moreover, data entered into one document will be automatically and dynamically linked with similar data in another document so that changes made to the source document are automatically and instantly reflected in all the copies. When you receive notice that a correspondent's address has changed, for example, you'll type it once, and the computer will take care of updating every last copy you've made of that address, regardless of the application in which the address is used.

Sound futuristic? Tomorrow isn't all that far off, as you will find out by working with Windows 95. The foundation for this new way of using computers was laid with Windows 3.1, and has been strengthened and enhanced with the introduction of Windows 95. Incorporated into the operating system are two sets of standards that permit *interprocess communication,* which is the sending of messages from one application to another.

The first (and earliest) of these standards is *dynamic data exchange* (DDE). This standard establishes the basis for linking, in which the changes you make to a source document are automatically updated in copies you've made of this document and inserted in other documents, even those of other applications. Linking closely resembles Clipboard copying, except that the copy is dynamically updated when the original changes. With many applications, you can display and edit the source data just by double-clicking any of the copies you've made of this data.

Windows has included DDE capabilities since version 2.0; however, before Windows version 3.1, DDE was hard to use: you had to write complicated commands to create DDE links. For example, Word for Windows and Microsoft Excel have both, for some time, allowed you to type external reference commands that create DDE links.

Because DDE command syntax is difficult to master, few Windows users (or programmers) took advantage of DDE. Interprocess communication started to take off, however, with the introduction of a new standard called *object linking and embedding* (OLE) in Windows 3.1. OLE (pronounced *olay*) has been strengthened with the release of OLE 2.0, and it has been fully integrated into Windows 95.

In brief, OLE provides easy-to-use menu commands so anyone can create links just by choosing options from menus. OLE also makes possible a new kind of application integration called *embedding*. With embedding, you can create a compound document in which the various parts are created by different applications. Such a document could contain text created by Ami Pro for Windows, a beautiful title created by Microsoft WordArt, a presentation-quality graphic created by Microsoft Excel, and a spreadsheet table created by Quattro Pro for Windows. To edit such a document, you just place the cursor in the portion you want to edit, and Windows starts the application that created the object.

Linking and embedding may sound futuristic, but you can put it to work right now. If you spend a little time learning how to create links and embed objects, you'll ensure that every copy you make of authoritative source data, such as a price list, is always up to date and correct. And what's more, you'll find it much easier to locate and edit this source data, should changes become necessary. With Windows 95 and OLE-capable applications, the source document—and the application that created it—is no more than a double-click away.

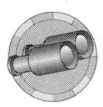

Note: OLE makes enormous demands on your computer system's microprocessor. Although you can link and embed with any system on which you can run Windows 95, some operations may take a few seconds to a minute or more. If you plan to use interprocess communication extensively, you should plan to upgrade to an 80486DX-based computer running at 33 MHz or better, and preferably with at least 16M of memory.

Understanding OLE

OLE is sufficiently unfamiliar that some introduction and terminology will prove helpful. In this section, you learn the difference between linking and embedding, and you learn when to choose one over the other. In any discussion of OLE, however, you will find a knowledge of some basic terms useful. The following terms have special meaning in relation to OLE:

- An *object* is a whole document or part of a document, such as part of an Excel spreadsheet or Paintbrush drawing, produced by a particular application. For OLE and DDE purposes, then, you'll encounter references to Excel objects, Ami Pro objects, and the like. Here, *objects* just means "documents" or "selected portions of documents."

- A *server application* is a Windows application capable of creating an object that can be used by other Windows applications. For example, Ami Pro objects are created by Ami Pro, which is the server application. Not all Windows applications are capable of performing as a server application.

- A *client application* is a Windows application capable of using an object created by a server application. As an example, Word for Windows can incorporate objects created by server application. In this instance, Word for Windows is the client application. Not all Windows applications are capable of performing as client applications. Some applications, however, can function as both servers and clients.

- The *source document* is the document from which you copy an object. You create a source document with a server application. For example, if you create a chart with Excel that you intend to incorporate into a document created with a client application, then the chart is the source document.

- The *destination document* is a document into which you paste or embed an object. You create a destination document with a client application. Continuing the example, if you create a document with Word for Windows and link the source document created by Excel (the chart mentioned in the previous definition), then the Word for Windows document is the destination document.
- An *OLE-capable application* is one that can function as a server application, as a client application, or as both. All of the applications mentioned in each of the foregoing definitions refer to OLE-capable applications.

Understanding Linking

When you link one document with another, you copy a document or part of a document by using the Clipboard. The only difference between ordinary Clipboard copying and linking is what happens when you paste.

With linking, you choose a special Edit menu command. Applications vary in the name they use for this command; examples are Link, Paste Link, or Paste Special. But they all share the same function: they paste the Clipboard object into your document, and they create the dynamic link between the server and client applications. The result is a *hot link,* which means that the link between client and server is active and dynamic—it is automatically and instantly updated when you make changes to the source document.

To illustrate linking, consider the Excel worksheet shown in figure 30.1. This worksheet calculates the monthly principal plus interest (P&I) payment needed to amortize a mortgage.

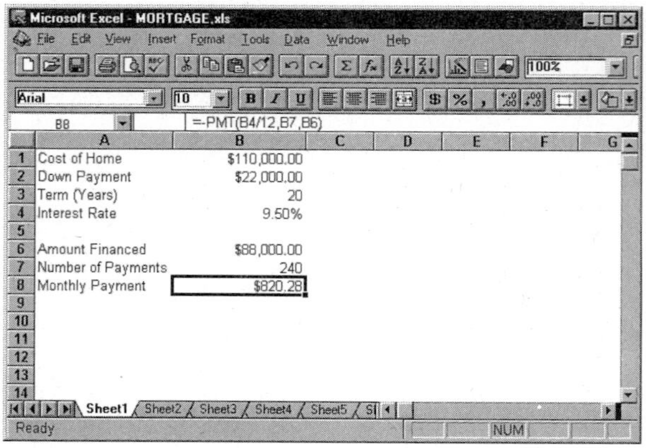

Fig. 30.1 A spreadsheet can be used to calculate a mortgage payment.

Say you wanted to create a link between this spreadsheet and a letter that will contain the figures created in the spreadsheet. To do this, follow these steps:

1. In the Excel spreadsheet, select the cells you want included in the letter.
2. Copy the cells to the Clipboard, using the Copy command from the Edit menu, or by pressing Ctrl+C.
3. Open the Word for Windows document in which you want to place the figures.
4. Within the document, position the cursor at the point where you want the figures placed.
5. Choose the Paste Special command from the Edit menu in Word for Windows. The Paste Special dialog box appears, shown in figure 30.2.

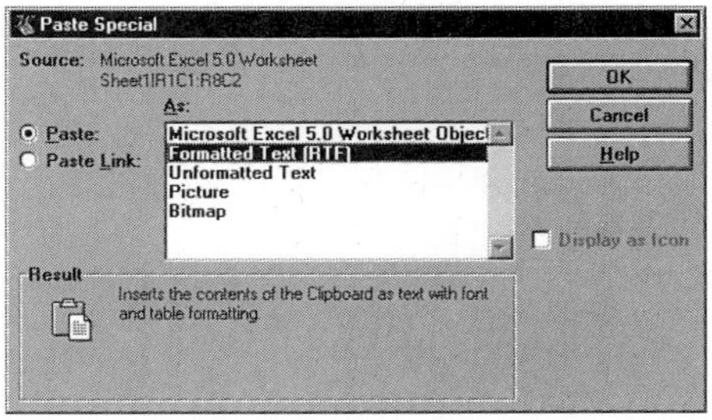

Fig. 30.2 The Paste Special dialog box allows you to perform different types of pasting in a document.

6. Choose the Paste Link button at the left side of the dialog box.
7. In the As list, choose the first option, Microsoft Excel 5.0 Worksheet Object.
8. Click on OK. Word inserts the object at the cursor's location.

After pasting the object into Word, it appears just as it would if you had performed the paste by using ordinary Clipboard techniques (see figure 30.3), but there's a big difference. If you make a change to the source document (the Excel worksheet), Windows automatically updates the object you've placed in the Word document. In figure 30.4, the home's cost has been changed to $99,500, causing the down payment, amount financed, and monthly payment to change accordingly. When you switch to Word, you will see that the altered figures have been immediately and automatically posted to your Word document (see figure 30.5).

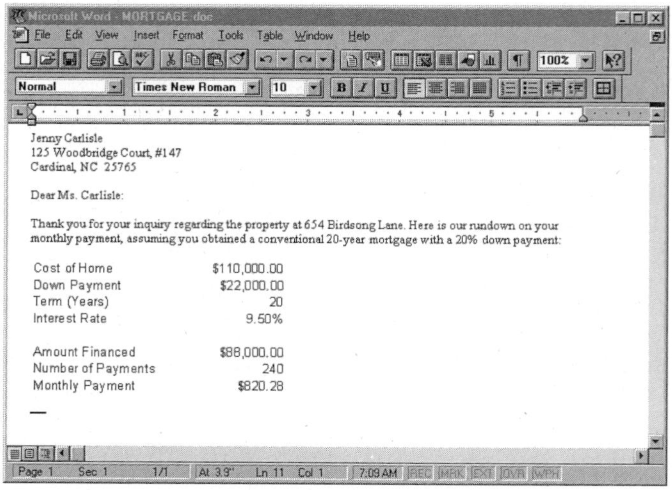

Fig. 30.3 After pasting and establishing a link, the information appears in the document as if you had pasted it normally.

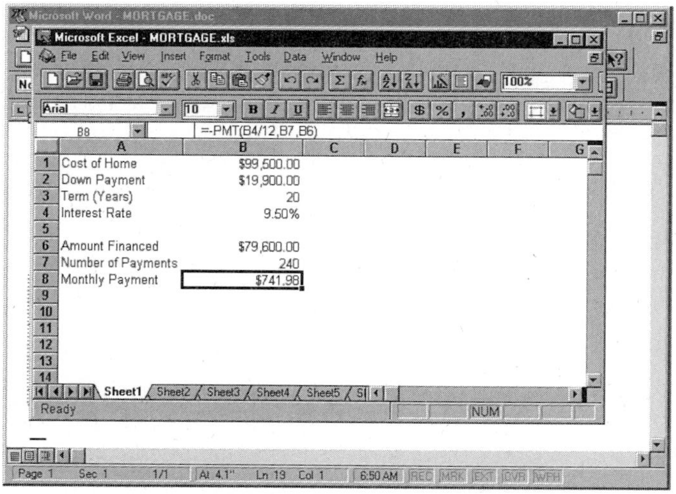

Fig. 30.4 Changes can easily be made to the original spreadsheet in Excel.

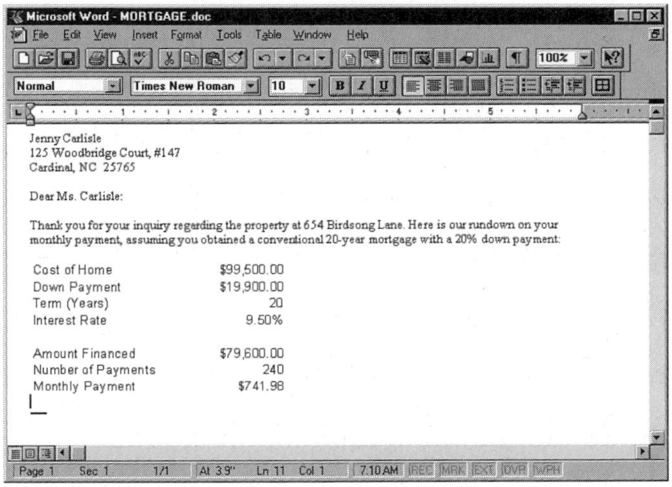

Fig. 30.5 After changing the original spreadsheet, the linked information in the Word for Windows document is automatically updated.

In a real estate office, the letter shown in figures 30.3 and 30.5 could be saved as a template document, which contains the body text, but not the address. To create a version of the letter quickly, open the template, add the name and address, switch to Excel, type in the required data (cost of home, and so forth), switch back to Word, and print.

You can automate this process even more by using a Word for Windows macro. When you open the template, the macro will display a dialog box that prompts you to supply the name and address of the correspondent, the cost of the home, the down payment, the interest rate, and the payment period. After you choose OK, the macro inserts the name and address in the letter. Then it automatically opens Excel, displays the Mortgage worksheet, inserts the altered variables in the correct cells, and prints the updated letter.

If linking seems like magic, you're wrong—it's just good technology. Knowing more about how linking works will help you work with it more successfully. When you use a linking command, (such as Link, Paste Link, or Paste Special) to paste the object in your document,

Windows stores hidden information about the source of the file. This information includes the name and location of the source document. If you make changes to the source document, the client application detects these changes and recopies the information. In short, linking really is an automated version of Clipboard copying. The only real difference between Clipboard copying and linking is that the client application can automatically detect a change in the source document. When it does, it recopies the information automatically.

After you create a link, often you can edit the linked object directly. But it doesn't make much sense to do so. After all, when the client application (in this case, Word for Windows) detects a change in the source document (the Excel spreadsheet), the client application will recopy the object, thus wiping out all your changes. Notice, though, that some client applications will retain the formatting you do to the linked object. Word for Windows, for example, preserves fonts, font sizes, type styles such as bold or italic, and other formats, even if the linked data are repeatedly updated.

To edit the linked object, the best course of action is to edit the source document directly. In applications that do a good job of implementing OLE, you can quickly access the source document from the destination document. You just double-click on the linked object, and the source document appears on-screen. After you make and save changes to the source document, these changes are automatically reflected in the destination document.

You can create links that involve more than two documents, if you want. For example, an Excel worksheet containing quarterly sales report figures could be linked to a memo, a report, and a letter. In addition, you can include as many links as you want within a destination document, subject to the limitations of your computer's memory and processing prowess. These links can involve more than one server application.

In summary, linking provides one of the pathways toward Microsoft's vision of future computing. Within your destination document, you can place objects that were created by different applications. To edit

these objects, you just double-click on the object, and the server application appears on-screen, with the source document displayed. You use the server application's tools to edit the source data. When you switch back to the client application, you see that your changes appear there, too. Soon, you stop thinking, "I'm working with a word processing program—I can write, but I really can't do anything else." You start focusing on your document, and on all the varied types of data you can include—databases, spreadsheets, graphics, and more.

> **Caution:** After you start linking information in your OLE-aware programs, don't delete your source documents or move them to different directories. Client applications record links with hidden information about the source document's location. If you erase the source document or move it out of its original directory, the client application won't be able to locate it, and you'll see an error message. You'll learn subsequently how to fix this problem, but the best practice is to leave your documents where they are.

Understanding Embedding

When you link an object, you establish links between the source document and the linked object (or objects, if you made more than one copy). The linked object is just an on-screen simulation of the information in the source document. It doesn't contain the programming code necessary to alter the source document. For this reason, the copied object isn't really editable. It just seems to be, because when you double-click on the object, Windows starts the server application, displays the source document, and allows you to edit the source document. When you switch back to the destination document, you find that the client application has deleted the old object, overwriting it with the new, updated version.

Embedding is different. When you embed an object, Windows actually physically includes, within the destination document's file, all the information that the server application requires to let you edit the object—not just a link to the source document. The result is a *compound document,* a document that contains supporting information for more than one application. For example, suppose you embed a Microsoft Graph column chart into a Word for Windows document. (Microsoft Graph is a business graphics package included with Word for Windows) The result is a compound document (see figure 30.6) that contains some parts created by Microsoft Graph, and other parts by Word for Windows.

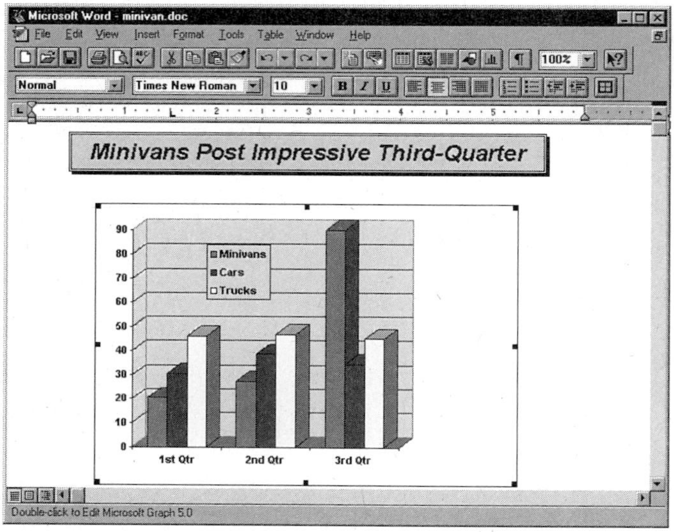

Fig. 30.6 Word for Windows also allows you to embed objects in a document.

Now suppose you want to edit the embedded object. You double-click the object, and Windows starts the server application—Microsoft Graph, in this case. You see the object in the application's workspace, with the tools applicable to that application enabled, as shown in figure 30.7. The embedded object contains all the hidden information required by the server application. When you double-click on the embedded object to edit it, Windows starts the server application, and you actually edit the embedded object, not the source document.

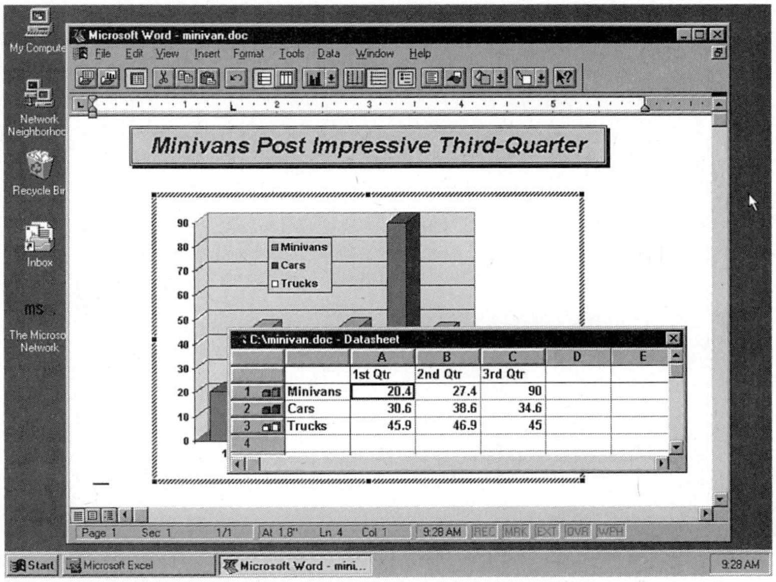

Fig. 30.7 Double-clicking on an embedded object allows you to edit the object by using all the tools appropriate to the object.

The major difference is that, with embedding, no link is created between the source document and the destination document—the embedded object stands on its own. When you make changes to the embedded object, the changes do not affect the source document.

If you do not create a link between the source document and the destination document, why bother with embedding? Why not just use the regular Clipboard methods? Embedding creates a fully editable copy of the original document; you can modify this copy as much as you like without worrying about modifying the original. And as you modify the embedded object, you have available to you all the tools and resources of the application that created it. Suppose that you've created a fantastic graphic with Paintbrush and you want to keep the graphic just the way it is. But you're creating a Write document that calls for a slight modification to the graphic. After embedding the object in the Write document, you can modify the embedded graphic without affecting the original.

In summary, embedding gives you a way of adding a fully editable but unlinked copy of an object to your destination document. You can change the object as you please without affecting the original.

> **Note:** Compound documents take much more disk space than documents that contain linked objects. When you embed rather than link, Windows places into the destination document all the hidden information needed to let you edit the object. This information takes up much more disk space than a simple link.

Choosing Between Linking and Embedding

Both linking and embedding facilitate the editing and updating of copied information placed in a destination document. With either technique, you just double-click on the object to have Windows start the server application, display the object, and give you all the tools you need to make the needed change.

Both techniques increase the amount of application computing power available to you as you work with documents. You can bring all the tools of two, three, or more applications to bear on the work you're doing in a single document. When you need text processing power, you have a word processing program. When you need number-crunching power, you have a spreadsheet. And when you need graphics capabilities, you have graphics programs. With linking and embedding, you can use all these tools, and more, to create a single document. The programs themselves seem to recede into the background; what counts is your document, not the applications used to create those documents. To shape your document just as you like, you have a wide range of tools readily available. Many users find that this sensation of power is thrilling and satisfying—and, once experienced, it is close to impossible to go back to less technologically advanced systems.

The difference between linking and embedding is simple. With linking, you can create two or more dynamically linked copies of the source object. A change to any one of them is reflected automatically in all the others. With embedding, editing is convenient, but the changes affect only the embedded object.

Linking is useful when you want to maintain one authoritative version of an object, which you might want to copy many times. This object could be an entire document, a portion of a document, or just a tiny little cell that happens to contain the bottom line result of a huge worksheet. Here's an example of when keeping an authoritative version of a file would be useful: Suppose that you keep your firm's price list in an Excel worksheet. You often copy all or part of this price list to Word documents, such as reports or proposals. You always want a change in the Excel worksheet to be reflected automatically in all the copies you have placed in Word documents. After all, you wouldn't want to quote the wrong price. In such a case, you would choose linking.

Embedding is useful when you want to place just one copy of an object in a file, and you don't want the changes you make to this object to be reflected in the original or in any other copies. For example, suppose you embed your firm's price list in a proposal. Just for this one client, and this one only, you want to cut all your prices by 10 percent. You don't want this change to be reflected in the original Excel worksheet, do you? You choose embedding. After embedding the object, you double-click on it. Windows starts Excel and displays the embedded object, not the source object. You can use all of Excel's number-crunching prowess to cut the prices by the requisite 10 percent, without affecting the original Excel worksheet. Here, embedding is the best choice.

Understanding Packaging

Windows includes a feature called Object Packager that adds a new wrinkle to linking and embedding. With Object Packager, you can insert a linked or embedded object from virtually any other application that has OLE capabilities. In many respects, the Object Packager provides another way to add objects to your documents.

Packaging is useful if you're inserting or embedding a very lengthy object, or one so complex that it takes a long time for your computer to scroll through it. While you're editing the document, you can package all the objects, displaying them as icons, which speeds scrolling considerably. Then you can unpack them when you're ready to print.

Another nifty way to use packaged objects is in a document that your correspondent can read on-screen, with the same application that created it. For example, suppose that your friend Robin has Word and Excel. You can send her a Word document with an Excel object packaged in it, as shown in figure 30.8. When (and if) Robin wants to examine or work with the original document, all she has to do is double-click on the object icon, and the Excel object is "unpackaged" on her machine.

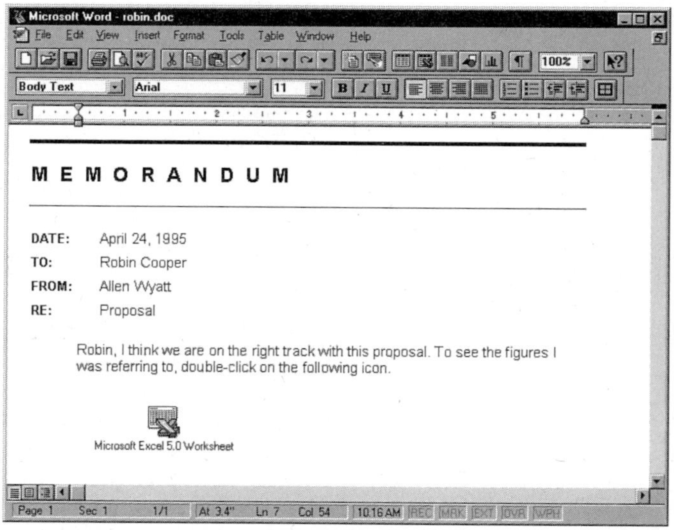

Fig. 30.8 Packaged objects appear only as icons in an OLE-capable application, which allows the destination document to be quickly displayed and scrolled.

Creating and Managing Links

Earlier in this chapter you learned how to paste information into a document so it is linked to the original document, created by a different application. Linking is almost as easy as copying with the Clipboard. The underlying differences between ordinary Clipboard copying and linking aren't apparent to the user—until you see that the copied data is dynamically updated.

Links are easy to create. As in all outstanding technology, the user need not learn the technical details—and, for the most part, isn't even aware of them. With linking, though, you must manage the links, after you've created them. That's where some of the following complexities creep in:

- Links aren't always automatically updated. In some cases, you may have to update the links manually. In Word for Windows, links between Word documents must be manually updated—automatic updating is available only for links with external documents (documents created by another OLE-compatible application).
- You may need to choose the appropriate data type (such as Rich Text Format [RTF] or unformatted text) for the paste operation. In some applications, linking is available only when you choose the correct data type. (The term *data type* refers to the format, such as RTF, Picture, or Bitmap, used to transfer the data via the Clipboard.)
- Applications vary in the linking features they provide. Some do not implement linking completely, and a few provide no linking capabilities at all.
- After creating the link, you must learn special procedures for redirecting the link, repairing broken links, and breaking existing links.
- When working with a document containing links, you may encounter error messages informing you that Windows couldn't find the server application or the source document.

In short, there's plenty to learn about linking. This section demonstrates the procedures you'll use to create links, edit linked documents, open documents that contain links, control existing links, and troubleshoot linking problems.

> **Note:** Linking procedures vary among applications. There are, as yet, no hard-and-fast rules about how linking commands should be located on menus—it's true even for applications created by the same software publisher. Despite such variations, the underlying concepts of linking are the same for all OLE-capable Windows applications, and the general procedures apply well enough that you can learn all the fundamentals of linking. The information in this chapter provides a good understanding of what's involved in creating links and keeping them operating smoothly.

Creating Links Between Windows Applications

The most common use of linking is to link one application's source document with another application's destination document. In this section, you learn how to create a dynamic link between two applications.

When establishing any link, one application acts as a server, and the other as a client. The server is the application that created the source document, and the client is the one used for the destination document. To create a dynamic link between two applications, follow these general steps:

1. Start the server application, and display or create the source document.
2. Save the source document in a disk file, using the steps customary for the server application. For example, if the server application was Excel, you would choose File Save and provide a name for the document (workbook) you were saving.

3. Open the client application and display or create the destination document.
4. Switch to the server application, and select the data you want to link into the destination document.
5. Copy the data to the Clipboard. This is done in different ways from different applications. For example, you might need to choose Copy from the Edit menu, or press Ctrl+C.
6. Switch to the client application, and position the cursor at the point where you want the information placed and the link established.
7. How you proceed from this point can vary widely by application. Generally, some sort of special pasting feature should be available on the Edit menu. Look for options such as Paste Link, Paste Special, or Links. Choose the option appropriate for the application you are using.

The client application inserts the information into your document and creates the link.

Editing Linked Documents

If properly implemented, a client application's linking capabilities should enable you to edit the source document with ease. (That's not always the case with all client applications.) Ideally, you should be able to edit the linked object without having to leave the client application. If your application is capable of editing linked objects, you can correct the linked data.

Follow these steps to edit the linked object:

1. In the client application, double-click on the linked object.
2. In the server application, make the needed change to the source document.
3. Save the source document. (If you don't save the document, Windows can't update the destination document.)

4. Close the server application. The destination document will reflect the change you've made.

As an example, say you have a Microsoft Word document that contains a business proposal. Besides text explaining a new service your company is offering, it also contains charts and figures showing sales forecasts. These figures and charts are from different Excel workbooks, but are linked into the Word document. When you want to update the sales figures while you're using Word, all you need to do is double-click on the figures. Excel appears (Windows even starts the application, if necessary), and you can make your changes. When you're done in Excel, save your changes and exit from the program. That's it; your changes have been made in both the source and destination documents.

> **Note:** If you see an alert box that informs you that the server isn't available, don't panic; the server application might be busy performing some task. Wait a few moments, and try again. If you still get this message, switch to the server application and close all open dialog boxes or text response fields. You might also have to wait until it completes the operation that's consuming its attention, such as printing or recalculating.

Opening Documents that Contain Links

How a client application behaves when you open a document containing links depends on the application. In some applications, the links might be updated without any intervention necessary on your part. In some applications, you may be asked if you want to update links.

In general, if you see a dialog box asking whether you want to update links, you should choose Yes if you want the links updated, or No if you don't need to update at the moment. (For instance, you might not be ready to print yet, and so the updated information is not relevant yet.)

As the client application goes through the process of updating links, you may see additional dialog boxes. Read each one carefully, and make your choices based on your needs at the time.

Editing Multiple Links

One advantage of linking is that you can create multiple links. In a multiple link, one source document is linked to two or more destination documents. In a multiple link, as in an ordinary (single) link, any changes you make to the copied objects do not affect the source (or any other copies). If you want the changes to be made consistently to all copies of the source object, switch to the source document and make the change.

Controlling Update Frequency

Most client applications let you choose between automatic updating (the default) and manual updating. If you want to change the update type, you must usually do so after you've created the link. You use an Edit menu command (typically Edit Link or Link) that displays a list of all the links in your document, together with their current settings. Figure 30.9 shows Word for Windows link list (produced by choosing Links from the Edit menu).

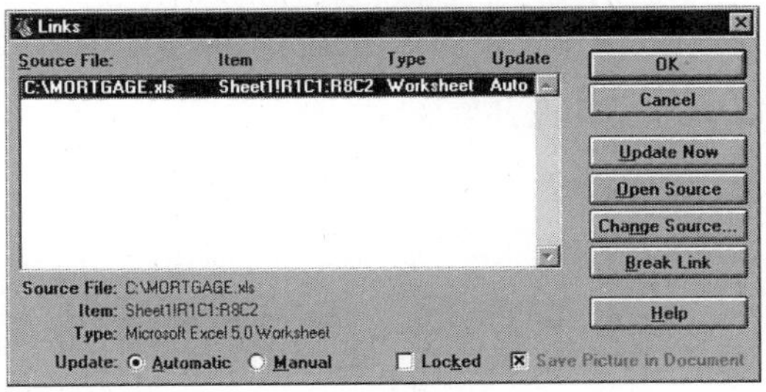

Fig. 30.9 The Links dialog box in Word for Windows allows you to modify properties associated with individual links.

Why choose manual updating, when the whole point of linking is to create dynamic links between the source and destination documents? After you've edited a document with many links in it, you'll understand why. Automatic links make heavy demands on your computer's microprocessor, which is constantly comparing the two documents to see whether they're the same. If you're editing a destination document that has many links, switch them to manual until you're finished editing, and then switch back to automatic. Your application will display and scroll the document more quickly.

Choosing Manual Updating

To choose manual updating, follow these steps:

1. In the destination document, choose the command that lets you edit the links in the document. This command is usually found in the Edit menu and is called Links or Edit Links. After you choose this command, you see the link list (see figure 30.9). The link list dialog box indicates the source of the link and whether the link is set to automatic or manual.
2. Select the link you want to change.
3. Choose Manual. This will be some type of control, such as a button, radio button, or check box.
4. Click on the OK button.

To switch back to automatic updating, repeat the steps just given, but in step 3 choose Automatic instead.

Updating Manual Links

If you've chosen manual updating for any of the links in your destination document, the client application will not automatically update this document when you change the source document. To update the destination document, you must choose an update command. In most Windows applications, the update command is available as an option in the link list.

To update the manual links in a document, follow these steps:

1. In the destination document, choose the command that lets you edit the links in the document. This command is usually found in the Edit menu and is called Links or Edit Links. This displays the link list (see figure 30.9). The link list dialog box indicates the source of the link and whether the link is set to automatic or manual.

2. In the link list, highlight the manual link you want to update.
3. Click on the Update or Update Now button.
4. Click on the OK button.

Breaking the Link

If a dynamic link no longer serves any need, you can break the link. Doing so does not erase the object that you've pasted into your document; it just erases the hidden information that specifies the source file's location.

To break a link, follow these steps:

1. In the destination document, choose the command (such as Edit Link, Edit Link Options, or Edit Link Delete) that displays the document's link list so that you can break a link.
2. In the link list, highlight the link you want to break.
3. Choose the button that cancels the link. This button is variously called Cancel Link, Delete, or Break Link.
4. Choose OK to confirm the deletion.

Some applications display an alert box warning you that you are about to sever a link. If you're certain you've broken the correct link, choose OK. To cancel the break, choose Cancel.

After you break the link, you still see the formerly linked information in your document. However, the client application will not update this information if you make changes to the source document.

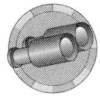

> **Note:** Some applications, such as Word for Windows, let you lock linked objects. If you lock an object, Windows cannot update the link, even if it is set to automatic linking. However, you can still modify the linked object within the destination application, and the destination will retain all the link information. Locking is preferable to breaking the link because, should you change your mind and wish to restore dynamic linking, you can do so easily.

Restoring a Broken Link

You can break a link in two ways: deliberately (as just described), or accidentally. Accidental breaks result when you move the source document after creating the link. After the move, Windows can't find the source document, so you see an alert dialog box informing you that the source document is missing or, worse, corrupted.

Follow these steps to restore the broken link:

1. Choose the command that displays the link list (such as Edit Link, Edit Link Options, Edit Link Edit, or File Links). You see the link list in a dialog box.
2. Choose the option that lets you change the link. In Word for Windows, for example, you click the Change Source button.
3. In the dialog box that appears, carefully change the part of the link command that lists the source document's location.
4. Click on the OK button.

Embedding Objects

Embedding differs from linking in two very important ways.

- When you embed an object, you actually put into the destination document all the information that the application requires for you to edit the object. The result is a compound document, a document that contains supporting information for more than one application.
- Embedding creates no links, dynamic or otherwise. You can embed an object by copying data from one document to another, as you learned earlier in this chapter, but Windows will not update the copy if you make changes to the original.

What follows from these two differences is simple: use embedding when ease of object editing is your chief concern and you don't care about automatic updating. Figure 30.10 provides an example of an embedded object that wouldn't need updating (but might need

different formatting): the company name that has been incorporated into a Word for Windows document. (Why doesn't this object need updating? Company names don't change very often.) The handsome type was created in Microsoft WordArt, an OLE-capable application packaged with Word for Windows.

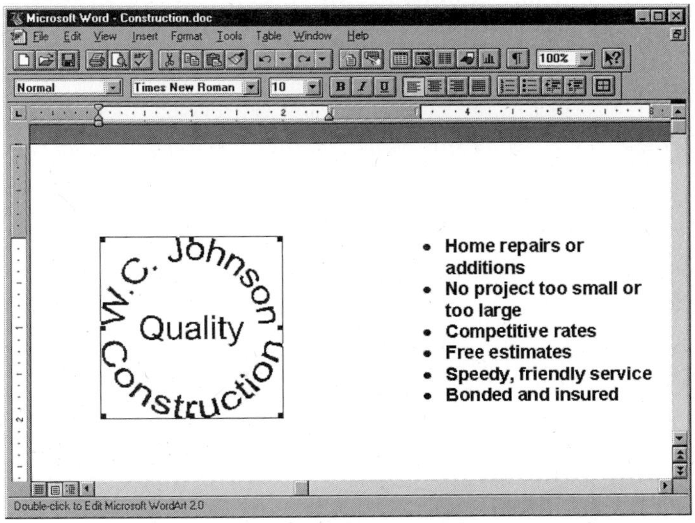

Fig. 30.10 An embedded object, created with WordArt, probably wouldn't need updating that often—at least not as a source document.

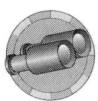

> **Note:** Embedding creates fewer editing problems than linking. You can run into problems editing a linked object because Windows must locate the source document as well as the server application, starting from the client application. With embedding, editing is faster, easier, and less prone to error. If you want to include an object in your document and don't care about dynamic updating, embedding is an excellent choice.

After you have embedded an object into your document, you have a compound document, a document created by more than one application.

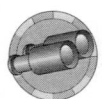

> **Note:** Compound documents are longer than normal documents. They must contain all the information for editing needed by the applications that contributed the objects. If you're short on disk space, you might want to link instead of embed. Linking requires much less disk space because when Windows links, you see only a picture of your data (or unformatted text) in the destination document.

Properly implemented, an application with embedding capabilities seems to have an endless set of alternative command menus, serving to expand its functionality to an amazing degree. With Word for Windows, for example, you can switch almost instantly to applications that create graphs, drawings, artistic typography effects, and mathematical equations.

Choosing the Correct Embedding Procedure

You can embed an object in two ways. The first way is to create the object (such as a chart or drawing) in the server application, and then copy the object to the destination document by using the Clipboard. So far, this procedure is identical with linking. However, you insert the object by displaying the link list and choosing the Object data type instead of the usual linking data type options (Formatted Text, Picture, and so on). When you choose the Object data type, the Paste Link button grays, informing you that linking has become unavailable. The client application inserts the object, but no link is created.

The second way to embed an object is to start from the client application. You choose a command (named Insert Object or Insert New Object) that displays a list of OLE-capable applications (see figure 30.11).

You choose an application, and Windows starts it, displaying a blank workspace with all the server application's commands available. You can open an existing document or create a new one. To exit, you choose Update from the File menu; the server application quits, and you see the object in the destination document.

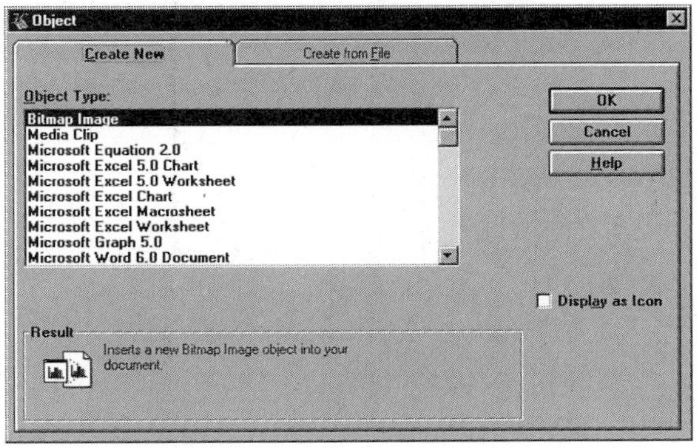

Fig. 30.11 Creating an embedded object can be done from within the client application.

Creating an Embedded Object

As you've just learned, you can use two methods to embed objects in an OLE-capable client application. You can start from the server application, which is the best technique to use when you want to embed part of a document you have already created and saved with the server application. You can also start from the client application. This technique is the best to use when you want to create the object from scratch. The following sections detail both techniques.

Starting from the Server Application

This technique, which closely resembles linking by using the Clipboard, is best used when you want to embed some information from a server application document you've already created. For example, you would use this technique when you want to embed into a Word for

Windows document a portion of an Excel worksheet you have already created and saved.

To embed an object from the server application, follow these steps:

1. Open the server application and the document that contains the information you want to embed.
2. Select the information you want to embed.
3. Choose Copy from the Edit menu.
4. Switch to the client application, and place the cursor where you want the object to appear.
5. Choose the Edit menu command that lets you choose the data type as you paste (typically, this command is called Paste Special). This should display a dialog box.
6. Select the object type (such as ObjectLink, Embedded OLE, Native, or Paste), which ensures that the data will be imported as an embedded object.
7. Choose Paste or OK.
8. Save the destination document.
9. Switch back to the server application, and save or discard the source document.

Yes, you read that correctly. Discarding the source document is indeed an option. When you inserted the object into the client application, you created a compound document. This document contains all the information the server application needs to open the object and allow you to edit it. When you saved the destination document in step 8, you saved all your work, including the work you did to create the object.

> **Tip:** After you insert the object, you can size and scale it by dragging the handles that appear when it is selected. However, it's best to edit the object in its server application, as described later in this chapter. The next time you update the object by editing it with the server application, you may lose the changes you made directly to the object.

Starting from the Client Application

The preceding technique employs the familiar Clipboard method of copying and uses Edit menu commands. When you create an embedded object starting from the client application, however, a new command (called Object or Insert Object) comes into play. In both Word and Excel, you find this command on the Insert menu.

This technique is best used when you need to create the embedded object from scratch. When Windows switches to the server application, you see a new, blank workspace. You create the new object there.

Follow these steps to embed an object starting from the client application:

1. Choose Object from the Insert menu. (If such a menu choice is not available in your application, look for one called Insert Object, or for an object-related command under the File or Edit menus.)
2. Choose the server application you want to use, and click on OK. You will see the server application.
3. Create the object.
4. Choose Update from the File menu. (This command appears only when you are using the server application to create an embedded object.)
5. Close the server application. This step isn't necessary in some applications; the application closes automatically after you choose Update from the File menu.
6. Save the destination document.

> **Tip:** If you decide that you don't want to embed the object after creating it, choose Close in the server application's File menu. You'll see a dialog box asking whether you want to update the destination document. Choose No.

Editing Embedded Objects

Editing an embedded object is simplicity itself. You don't need to worry about whether the source document has moved; the source document is part of the document that contains the object!

To edit an embedded object, follow these steps:

1. Double-click on the embedded object, or choose the object editing command from the Edit menu.
2. Edit the object within the workspace.
3. Choose Update from the File menu.
4. Close the server application. (This step isn't necessary in some applications; the application closes automatically after you choose Update from the File menu.)

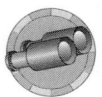

> **Note:** Some embedded objects are designed to perform actions when you double-click on them. For example, Sound Recorder objects produce a sound when double-clicked. For these objects, you must choose the Object command from the Edit menu to initiate editing.

Deleting an Embedded Object

To delete an embedded object, select it and choose Cut or Clear from the Edit menu, or press the Delete key. Before doing so, bear in mind that there may not be any other copy of the object on disk. The following procedure shows you how to save an embedded object in a separate file before you delete the object from the source document.

To save an embedded object in a separate file follow these steps:

1. In the destination document, double-click on the embedded object or choose Object from the Edit menu.
2. In the server application's workspace, choose Save As or Save Copy As from the File menu and save the object.

3. Choose Exit from the File menu. When you're prompted to update the destination document, choose No.

Canceling Embedding Without Deleting the Object

In a compound document, embedded objects take up lots of space. If you want to cut down on the amount of space a file consumes, you can convert objects into pictures or unformatted text. After you've done so, the object becomes a static object rather than a dynamic one. You can't edit the object, and double-clicking on it won't start the server application. But it will take up much less room, and with most applications, it still looks exactly the same.

The procedure you follow to cancel embedding without deleting the object varies widely from application to application. For example, in Word for Windows you highlight the embedded object, and then press the Unlink Field key (Ctrl+Shift+F9). You can also choose WordArt Object from the Edit menu, and then choose Convert. To discover the steps to follow in your application, you will need to consult your applications on-line help or documentation.

Serial Communications Basics

by Allen L. Wyatt

Serial communications can be both a rewarding and frustrating experience. As a computer without a printer is nothing more than a fancy game machine, a computer without a modem keeps its user in a prison of only his or her ideas. More than one user likely has given up on using a modem because of problems encountered while trying to "make it work."

There are many factors that, when done properly, combine to make data communications work. In this chapter you'll learn the basics of data communications. Here you will learn the following:

- What serial communications is and how it works
- What modems do, how they do it, and what their capabilities are

- How serial ports relate to modems, and what makes for the best serial port
- What place communications software has in data communications
- How you can set up Windows 95 to use a modem

Understanding Serial Communications

Data communications, through a modem, is often referred to as *serial communications.* The word serial is used because the data sent through your communications port to your modem is sent in a serial, or bit-by-bit, format. Data inside your computer is moved around in a parallel format using 16, 32, or 64 bits at a time. Serial ports are typically used for modems (although there are parallel modems) because you need only one wire to send the actual data. Parallel ports require one wire per data bit, and normally have eight data bits per port. Besides the wires used to transmit data, both serial and parallel connections have additional wires that are used for tasks such as handshaking signals. (*Handshaking* refers to an agreed-upon method of synchronizing the two ends of a connection.)

All IBM-compatible serial ports use the RS-232 standard, which allows serial signals to go much further than is possible in a standard parallel connection. Your computer uses a UART (universal asynchronous receiver/transmitter—discussed later in this chapter) to convert the internal parallel data used by your computer to a serial format that can be used by the modem. One UART will exist on both the sending and receiving ends of a serial connection. Using a serial port connected to a modem has become the standard way to communicate.

You may understand serial communications better if you first step back and look at the big picture. For example, consider the following three elements:

1. You must have a computer system with a properly configured serial port.
2. You need a modem of sufficient speed to perform the required tasks. This modem is connected to your serial port (if it is an external modem) or includes the serial port (if it is an internal modem).
3. You need a software communications program capable of managing your modem. This marriage of hardware and software permits you to communicate within your local area and beyond.

Understanding Modems

You probably already know how to use your PC for word processing, spreadsheets, and information management. Certainly, you are familiar with telephones. Learning to use a PC to communicate over telephone lines would seem a logical next step. The problem, however, is that telephones are designed to transmit sound, and computers use different types of signals based on digital technology. Much of the complexity of telecommunications comes down to this dichotomy.

Analog and Digital Signals

Understanding a little bit about how telephones transmit sound signals can help you comprehend how computer data is sent. When you use your voice, your vocal chords cause the air to vibrate in a wave-like motion. The vibrating air, called a *sound wave,* causes a listener's eardrum to vibrate, enabling the listener to hear the sound you make. The frequency of the sound wave (the number of wave cycles in a given period of time) is heard as pitch. The amplitude (size) of the wave is heard as volume.

When you speak into your telephone, the telephone electronically converts the sound wave into an electromagnetic wave that can be transmitted over telephone lines. The frequency and amplitude of this electromagnetic wave correlate directly to the frequency and amplitude of the sound wave—your voice. As the sound wave's frequency varies up or down, the electromagnetic wave's frequency varies up or down in the same proportion. As the sound wave's amplitude varies, so does the electromagnetic wave's amplitude. In other words, the electromagnetic wave is an analog representation of the sound wave. The signal your telephone sends over the telephone lines often is referred to as an analog signal (see figure 31.1). When this signal reaches the other end of the line, the phone at that end converts the signal back into a sound wave.

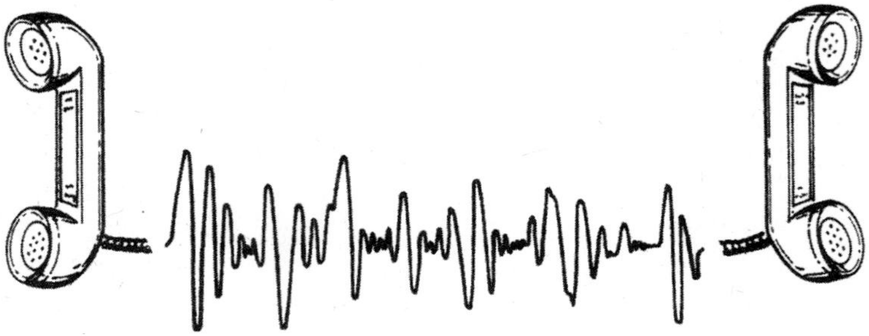

Fig. 31.1 The signal transmitted by telephones is analog in nature.

Computers do not, however, communicate by sound waves. They use discrete electrical pulses that represent numbers. All data is encoded as a stream of 1s and 0s called *bits*. A bit (short for *binary digit*) is the most basic form in which a PC stores information. To transmit a bit with a value of 1, for example, the computer may set the line voltage to –12 volts (direct current) for a set length of time. This set length of time determines the transmission speed. The computer may transmit a bit with a value of 0 by setting the voltage to +12 volts for a set length of time. A typical transmission speed is 1,200 bits per second. At that speed, each voltage pulse is 1/1,200th of a second in duration. Some PCs and compatibles can send as many as 115,200 bits per second with each pulse lasting only 1/115,200th of a second.

When one of the communicating computers needs to send the code 01001011, for example, the computer sets the voltage to +12 volts for one unit of time, –12 volts for one unit of time, +12 volts for two units of time, and so on. (The unit of time can be any set length of time agreed on by the two computers.)

The square-shaped waves shown in figure 31.2 show the voltage pulses that the computer uses to transmit this code. Because a signal of this sort is transmitting bits, it usually is called a digital signal.

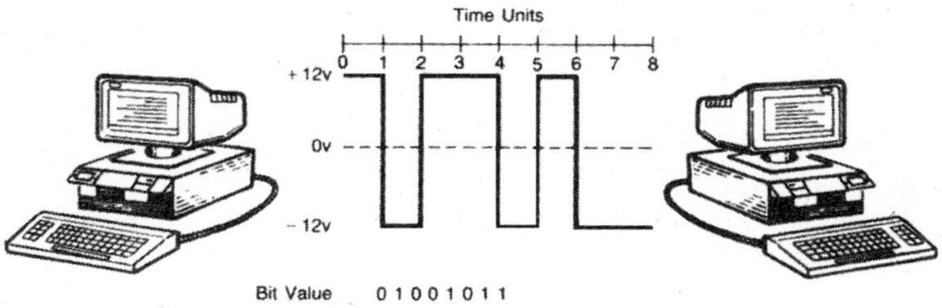

Fig. 31.2 Signals are transmitted directly between and within computers in a digital form.

In some areas of the country, Integrated Services Digital Networks (ISDNs) are available, and should be available most everywhere before the end of the century. These networks are slowly replacing the traditional analog phone networks, and are able to carry simultaneously voice, data, and image transmissions. Until ISDNs are more widely available, however, you must convert your PC's digital signal to an analog signal—a process known as *modulation*—in order to be sent over the phone lines. The analog signal then must be converted back to a digital signal—known as *demodulation*—before your PC can communicate with another computer at the other end. The piece of hardware that accomplishes both modulation and demodulation is the modem, short for modulator-demodulator (see figure 31.3). Without a modem at each end of the phone line, the two computers cannot communicate.

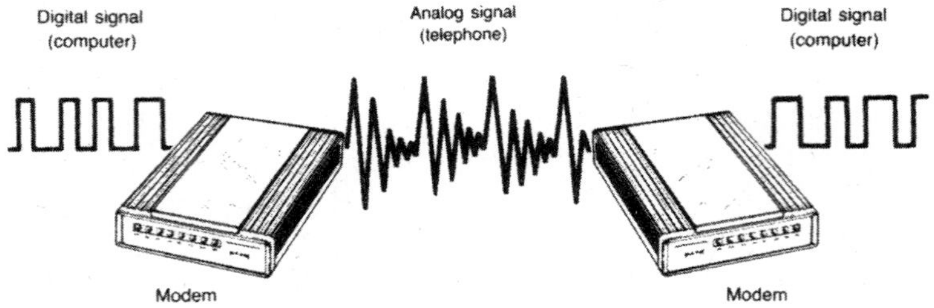

Fig. 31.3 Modems convert digital signals into analog signals, and vice-versa.

Modem Speed

Although all modems modulate and demodulate transmitted signals, all modems are not equal. The most important difference among the various types of modems is the maximum speed at which they can transmit data.

Only a few years ago, communications programs used modems that sent data at a maximum rate of 300 bits per second (bps). To put this transmission rate into perspective, consider the number of bits required to represent meaningful information. All information stored and used in your PC is represented by combining eight bits—called a *byte*—at a time.

When you are transmitting text or typing at your keyboard on-line (connected to another computer), each character sent to the other computer is represented in ASCII (American Standard Code for Information Interchange). The IBM version of ASCII uses a single byte to represent each character.

At eight bits per character and 300 bits per second, you may think the modem can transfer 37.5 characters per second, or 375 five-letter words per minute. PCs, however, normally add to each byte two extra bits, called start and stop bits (see "Understanding Serial Ports" later in this chapter). Consequently, a single character requires 10 bits of data when transmitted through a modem. Thus, a speed of 300 bps results in a data-transmission speed of approximately 30 characters per second, or about 300 five-letter words per minute. In comparison, a fast typist usually averages less than 80 words per minute.

This 80-word rate is fast enough when you want to type an instruction to a remote computer or chat (type messages back and forth) on-line with another user. This rate is not adequate, however, when you are sending a large document you already have typed. At about 1,000 words per page, sending a 10-page document can take nearly 30 minutes. If you send the document over long-distance lines, use of a 300-bps modem can translate into expensive telephone bills.

In recent years, modem speeds have increased and prices have decreased. Soon after IBM introduced the PC in August 1981, the Smartmodem 300 and Smartmodem 1,200 by Hayes Microcomputer Products became the standard modems for business use. More recently, a growing number of users are using 14,400 bps and 28,800 bps modems. Technological advances in the manufacture of integrated circuits and fierce competition have brought the prices of modems down so far that you have little, if any, reason to buy a less capable modem.

You sometimes may hear the term *baud* used synonymously with bits per second, but they are not the same. Although 300-bps modems also are referred to as 300-baud modems, 1200-bps modems do not operate at 1,200 baud; they usually operate at 600 baud.

Baud is a technical term that means the number of symbols per second sent over a communication line. (The term is named after J.M.E. Baudot, a French telegraphy expert.) Each symbol may be represented by a certain voltage, a certain combination of frequencies (tones), or a certain wave phase (angle). Each symbol may be able to represent more than one bit. In 2,400-bps modems, for example, each symbol represents four bits. Although the modem transmits only 600 symbols per second (600 baud), data is transmitted at 2,400 bits per second.

The term baud is misused so often that its technical meaning largely is ignored. You, therefore, can assume that the salesperson who wants to sell you a 9,600-baud modem means a 9,600-bps modem (and that he should be selling you a faster modem).

Modem speed can have a great impact on productivity (how much work can be done in a given period of time). For example, say you need to transmit a document across the country, and the file containing the document occupies 20,000 bytes on your disk. Table 31.1 shows how long it would take to transmit the file at various modem speeds, assuming there are no errors during transmission. Notice how much time is spent at the slower speeds—time that could productively be spent doing other work.

Table 34.1 Modem Speed Comparison When Transmitting 20,000 Characters

Speed	Time to Transmit
300 bps	11 minutes, 7 seconds
1,200 bps	2 minutes, 47 seconds
2,400 bps	1 minute, 23 seconds
9,600 bps	21 seconds
14,400 bps	14 seconds
28,800 bps	7 seconds

Modulation Standards for Modems

The speed at which modems communicate is one of several attributes that must be consistent between two modems in order for them to be able to send and receive data reliably. These attributes are referred to collectively as *modulation standards.*

Bell 103 is the U.S. and Canadian modulation standard used by 300-bps modem connections. This standard uses Frequency Shift Keying (FSK) modulating at 300 baud and sends one bit per baud. Even though this speed is the slowest, most modems work at 300 baud.

Frequency shift keying toggles between two different audio tones in response to the data being sent. The transitions between these two tones are used to represent the data. Differential Phase Shift Keying changes the phase of an audio signal in relation to reference audio

signal. The toggling in phase (0–180 degrees) between the signal and its reference is used to represent the data.

Bell 212A is the U.S. and Canadian standard for 1200 bps transmissions. This standard uses Differential Phase Shift Keying (DPSK) working at 600 baud and sends out two bits per baud.

The CCITT (Consultative Committee on International Telephone and Telegraph) is an international communications standards organization and an agency of the United Nations. CCITT V.22bis is the data transmission standard used by 2,400 bps modems in the United States. V.22bis is an improved standard of V.22 that is used outside the United States. V.22 was never used much in the United States. CCITT V.22bis is an international standard for 2,400 bps communications. V.22bis operates by using quadrature amplitude modulation, known as QAM. It works at 600 bps and can transmit four bits per baud. Four bits times 600 produces the 2,400 bps rating.

CCITT V.32 is the standard for full duplex communications at 9600 bps. CCITT V.32 includes full forward error-correction and echo cancellation. Using 9,600 bps connections often works when 2,400 bps does not. Recent advances in modem chip sets make this a relatively inexpensive modem speed to use. The actual transmission uses Trellis Coded Quadrature Amplitude Modulation (TCQAM) working at 2,400 baud to send 4 bits per second. Four times 2,400 gives the effective 9,600 bps.

CCITT V.32bis is an improvement over V.32 and can send data at a full duplex rate of 14,400 bits per second. CCITT V.32bis modems also use TCQAM, working at 2,400 baud, to send six bits per second. The effective rate is six times 2,400 or 14,400 bits per second. This protocol defines a method to fall back to CCITT V.32 if the phone line is impaired. According to many experts in the industry, this modulation standard is the best you can buy for standard phone line modems that meet international standards.

V.34 is the newest modulation standard to be approved. It is an extension of V.32 and V.32bis and offers a higher transmission speed of 28,800 bits per second. This standard is widely recognized as the fastest

and most advanced that data communications can get over regular analog phone lines. V.34 is probably the last analog-based transmission scheme, since most telephone systems will be converted to digital (ISDN) in the not-too-distant future.

While all this talk of modulation standards may sound confusing, most of the details can be safely ignored. You should recognize what the current standards are, however, and look for modems that support them. Thus, you should now look for modems that comply with the V.34 standard. In this way, you will be able to communicate at the fastest speeds possible (provided the modem at the other end is also capable of communicating at V.34 speeds).

Hayes-Compatible Modems

The series of software commands that activate the Hayes Smartmodem's smart features usually begin with the letters AT (short for attention). This command set therefore has come to be known as the *AT command set.* To dial a telephone number by using touch-tone signals, for example, communications software typically sends the modem the command sequence ATDT, followed by the telephone number.

The prefix of ATDT instructs the modem what to do with the phone number that follows. The AT part gets the modem's attention, and then the DT instructs it to dial a number using tone signals. The phone number is sent out after the ATDT and ends with a carriage return (CR).

There are a wide variety of commands in the AT command set, and most of them are now set up and used automatically by your communications software. The majority of modems on the market today follow this same command set. Virtually every modem manufacturer has adopted the AT command set as the de facto standard command language for modems intended for use with PCs. Modems that recognize this command set often are called *Hayes-compatible modems.* Not all so-called Hayes-compatible modems, however, implement the entire command set. In this sense, some modems are more compatible than others.

When Hayes introduced the Smartmodem 2400, the company also introduced new commands to the AT command set. Other manufacturers have implemented this *extended AT command set* to varying degrees. You can use most Windows communication software effectively, regardless of whether your modem supports the extended AT command set. Using a modem that supports the AT command set, however, is the most convenient.

Error-Control

To be effective, computer data must be transmitted error-free. The detection and elimination of errors in computer data transmissions usually is called *error-checking,* or *error-control.* Although a telephone line doesn't have to be perfectly clear of static or interference for effective voice transmission, a slight variation or interruption of a computer signal can change completely the meaning of the data the signal carries.

Many communications programs can run checks on incoming data to determine whether any errors were introduced into the data during transmission. The techniques used to perform this error-checking are called *error-checking protocols.* (A *protocol* is a set of agreed-on rules.)

Instead of requiring that the communications software perform error-control, most modem manufacturers now produce modems that do this chore automatically. When compared to the results of software error-checking, error-detection and the overall speed of transmission improve when the modem handles error-control. For this feature to work, however, the modems on both ends of the connection must be using the same error-control protocol.

Two types of error-control protocols have developed a significant following. Fortunately, an industry standard has emerged that incorporates the following two competing error-control schemes:

- Hayes Microcomputer Products produces a line of modems called the Hayes V-series modems. At the low end of this line is a 2400-bps modem that performs error-control by using a method called Link-Access Procedure for Modems (LAPM).

- Nearly all other PC modem manufacturers produce modems that support a different set of error-control protocols—the Microcom Networking Protocol (MNP) Classes 1 through 4, developed by Microcom, Inc. The MNP protocols are progressive. A modem can support Class 1, Classes 1 and 2, Classes 1 through 3, or Classes 1 through 4. The higher the class, the faster the transmission. These protocols are not compatible with LAPM.

Two 2,400-bps modems using the two different standards can still communicate, but only as 2,400-bps modems without modem-based error-control. (In this case, your software must take care of error detection to ensure that line impairment during transmission doesn't corrupt the transmitted data.)

In 1989, the CCITT established an error-control standard called V.42. This standard includes the protocol used by Hayes V-series (LAPM) as well as MNP Classes 1 through 4 error-control protocols, with a bias toward LAPM. When connected to another modem, a V.42-compliant modem attempts to use the LAPM protocol. If this approach fails, the V.42 modem then attempts to use the MNP protocols. If the other modem supports neither of these error-control protocols, the V.42 modem acts like a standard modem, without error control.

When using a V.42 compliant modem, using software error-correction increases overhead, and therefore slows down transmission. Selecting a file transfer protocol that does not use error correction increases overall throughput. This step leaves error-correction to the two connecting modems.

Data Compression

Many modems that provide built-in error-control also compress the data as it is sent. A compatible modem on the other end decompresses the data. Compressing data is similar to sitting on a loaf of bread; you squeeze out the air but leave the nourishment.

A modem compresses data by matching long strings (sequential patterns) of characters in the data with entries in a dictionary of known strings. Each entry in the dictionary has an index value, or code. The sending modem finds a code for each string of characters in the data and transmits only the codes. The receiving modem in turn converts these codes back into the original data.

By reducing the number of characters the modem has to send, this process often can more than double the effective transmission speed. In other words, a 4,800-bps modem using data compression sometimes can send as much information in the same length of time as a 9600-bps modem not using data compression.

As with error-control methods, two data-compression standards have developed in the PC modem market. This time, however, a CCITT standard replaces them both (it does not incorporate them). Hayes Microcomputer Products V-series modems perform data compression by using a proprietary algorithm. Many other PC-modem manufacturers follow Microcom's lead and use the MNP Class 5 data-compression algorithm. Again, these two competing data-compression methods are not compatible.

In September 1989, the CCITT ratified the V.42bis standard, which adds data compression to the existing V.42 error-control standard. The data-compression scheme included in this new standard is neither the Hayes algorithm nor the MNP algorithm. The CCITT V.42bis proposes, instead, the use of an algorithm known as the British Telecom Lempel-Ziv (BTLZ) compression algorithm.

The V.42bis standard does not include MNP data compression (MNP Class 5). Many manufacturers, however, produce modems that support V.42bis data compression as well as MNP data compression. Hayes has upgraded its V-series modems to include V.42bis and MNP Class 5.

External Versus Internal Modems

In addition to modems capable of transmitting data at different speeds, manufacturers often produce modems in external and internal versions. Each type offers several advantages.

An external modem typically is a metal or plastic box about 10 inches by 6 inches by 2 inches, with a panel of LED (light emitting diodes) on the front. The modem is connected to your PC by a serial cable and powered by an AC adapter. The external modem has at least one telephone jack for connecting the modem to the telephone line and often a second jack for connecting a telephone.

Many vendors also produce a small external modem that can be called a pocket modem. These are small enough to fit in your pocket and can run on batteries. These types of modems typically plug directly into a serial port on your computer and are particularly handy for laptop computer users who don't have the newer PCMCIA slots on their systems.

An external modem has the following advantages:

- You can move it easily from one computer to another.
- You can use it with nearly any type or brand of computer that has an asynchronous serial port (see "Understanding Serial Ports," later in this chapter).
- It can be shared by several computers through a serial switch box, but, only one computer at a time can use the modem.
- You often can stash it under your desk telephone or on top of your PC.
- If it's a pocket-sized modem you usually can plug it directly into a serial port, taking up no room on your desk.
- It usually has a panel of LEDs (light-emitting diodes) that enable you to monitor continuously the state of certain modem parameters.

Table 31.2 lists the meanings of the LEDs on the front panel of external Hayes modems and many external Hayes-compatible modems.

Table 31.2 Hayes Smartmodem LEDs

LED	Meaning
HS	High Speed
AA	Auto-Answer
CD	Carrier Detect
OH	On Hook
RD	Receive Data
SD	Send Data
TR	Terminal Ready
MR	Modem Ready

On the negative side, an external modem usually is a little more expensive than an internal modem with otherwise identical features from the same manufacturer. An external modem also requires your computer to have an available serial port and a serial cable.

Each internal modem is built on a circuit board that plugs into an empty expansion slot inside your PC, and thus takes up no room on your desk. Some internal modems are long enough to fill up a long expansion slot; others need only a half-size slot.

Because an internal modem is designed to work only with a PC, internal modems usually are bundled and sold with PC communications software. This setup is an advantage, unless you don't like the software.

The major disadvantage of an internal modem is that it is inconvenient to use with several different computers. If you need to move a modem among several computers or want to share a modem, an external modem is the better choice. For some users, the lack of status LEDs also is an annoyance.

Telephone Line Requirements

Both external and internal modems must be connected to a working telephone line. The modems, however, do not require a special type of telephone line; a voice-quality line is sufficient. You can use touch-tone or pulse dial service because nearly all auto-dial modems can dial either type of signal.

> **Caution:** One type of special telephone feature can cause problems for modem transmission. The feature, usually known as *call waiting,* is available from most telephone companies. Call waiting uses an audible click or beep to alert you to an incoming call while you are talking on the line. If your modem is on the line, this call-waiting signal may disrupt and even disconnect your transmission. If you have this type of service and plan to use your modem during periods when you might receive incoming calls, consider removing the service. In some areas, you can disable the feature temporarily by entering a special code on your telephone keypad or by transmitting the code in a software dial command. Check with your local telephone company to determine whether such a code is available and how to use it.

Understanding Serial Ports

Before your modem can transmit data, your PC must send the data from your keyboard or disk to the modem. The computer sends data to the modem through a serial port in your PC. A serial port, or COM port, is an outlet through which your computer can send data as a stream of bits, one bit at a time (that is, in serial). Data normally moves around the computer eight bits at a time—referred to as in parallel.

You can think of the internal modem as having its serial port built in. When you use an internal modem, you don't connect the modem to a serial port. A special chip on the modem, called the UART (universal asynchronous receiver/transmitter), performs the same function as a serial port; it converts the parallel signal into a serial signal. When you install the modem, you must configure it as one of your computer's COM ports.

Most PCs come with one or two serial ports already installed. The single most common device to use a serial port is a mouse. The modem comes in second, and possibly a serial-driven printer third. You can identify serial ports because they use the logical device names of COM1, COM2, COM3, and COM4.

Every serial port has a UART, and it is one of the following four types, or a clone of one of these:

- The 8250 was the original IBM PC and XT UART. Although most software works with the 8250 UART, the 8250 is not recommended for high-speed serial communications.
- The 16450 is the UART the IBM PC/AT computer system uses and is what you find on almost all computers using the Intel 80286 CPU or better. It is more suited to high-speed serial communications than the 8250, but it looks almost the same as an 8250 to your software.
- The 16550 was the first UART used in the IBM PS/2 computers. The 16550 was the first UART to include a 16-byte FIFO (first in first out) buffer. However, the FIFO buffer in this chip is defective and you cannot use it reliably. Because the FIFO buffer is defective in this chip, do not enable it or attempt to use it; loss of data is the result.
- The 16550A UART was released by National Semiconductor as a replacement for the 16550 and includes a working FIFO buffer. With the FIFO buffer, very high baud rates can be supported without losing characters. This feature is very important in multitasking environments like Windows 3.1. Some software may not work correctly if the FIFO buffer is turned on and your software expects only an 8250 or 16450 to be present.

The easiest way to identify the type of serial ports in your system is to use the MSD program, which is distributed with Windows 95. If you have been using DOS or Windows for some time, you're probably already familiar with this program. If not, you can follow these steps to start it:

1. Choose Programs from the Start menu. The Programs menu appears.
2. Choose MS-DOS Prompt from the Programs menu. This choice opens an MS-DOS window on the desktop.
3. At the command line, type **MSD** and press Enter. This step starts the Microsoft Diagnostics program.
4. Choose the COM Ports option from the menu.

At this point, you'll see a display about the serial ports installed in your system. At the bottom of the display you can see the types of chips installed in your PC. When you are done, you can exit the program and close the DOS window.

Adding a 16550A UART

To add a 16550A UART to your system, you typically need to purchase a new serial card. When you get ready to purchase, you will need to examine the card or ask the salesperson whether it features a 16550A UART. If the salesperson cannot answer your question, don't make any assumptions—find a vendor who can answer the question.

The 16550A UART provides an extra margin of safety in Windows multitasking environment; it makes sure that no characters are lost because of high baud rates or switching between various applications. Losing data is still always possible, but the 16550A provides a way to reduce that chance.

The Serial Connector

On IBM PC, PC/XT, and PS/2 computers, as well as on most compatibles, each serial port is a D-shaped connector that has 25 protruding metal pins and is located on the back of the computer. This type of connector is called a DB-25 M (male) connector. The connector on the serial cable that attaches the modem to this serial port has 25 holes to match the male connector's 25 pins. This connector is called a DB-25 F (female) connector.

The serial ports on IBM PC AT computers and most compatibles use D-shaped connectors with nine protruding pins, called DB-9 M connectors. To connect a serial cable to such a port, the cable must end in a DB-9 F connector.

Depending on the brand of computer, each port may be marked with the label COM, Serial, or RS-232. (RS-232 is a published communications hardware standard with which PC serial ports comply.)

Asynchronous and Synchronous Transmissions

Data sent through a serial port comes out as a stream of bits in single file, but each bit means nothing by itself. Because a PC stores information in eight-bit bytes, the receiving computer must be able to reconstruct the bytes of data from the stream of bits. Computers use two ways to identify clearly each byte of data sent through a serial port: *synchronous transmission* and *asynchronous transmission.*

When computers use the synchronous method of transmitting data, bytes of data are sent at precisely timed intervals. Both the sending and receiving modems must be synchronized perfectly for this method to work properly.

PCs typically use the asynchronous method to send data through a serial port. The sending PC marks with a start bit the beginning of each byte that is to be transmitted. This start bit informs the receiving computer that a byte of data follows. To mark the end of the byte, the PC sends one or two stop bits (the number of stop bits is a user option). The stop bits inform the receiving computer that it has just received the entire byte. Timing is not critical with this procedure.

When you set up PC communications software to communicate with another computer, you need to specify whether to use one or two stop bits. The number of stop bits used on your end must match the number used by the computer on the other end. When in doubt, use one stop bit. You seldom, if ever, find two stop bits used by another computer.

Because a PC uses the asynchronous method to send data through its serial port, a protocol converter is required for a PC to communicate with a computer using the synchronous method. The protocol converter converts the signal from asynchronous to synchronous. Many mainframe computers communicate only in synchronous mode, but they often have an asynchronous dial-in port with a built-in protocol converter. This design enables PCs and other computers to connect by using an asynchronous signal.

Synchronous transmission can achieve higher transmission rates, but it requires higher-quality telephone lines. Telephone lines used for synchronous transmission often are specially prepared and used exclusively for that purpose. These lines usually must be leased from the telephone company, making synchronous transmission extremely expensive for use in everyday PC communications.

Data Bits

As mentioned previously, the PC uses eight bits to represent a byte of data. Because exactly 256 ways are available to arrange eight 1s and 0s (2 to the 8th power), eight bits are needed to represent each of the 256 characters in IBM's extended ASCII character set. Many other types of computers—including mainframes used by on-line services—use only seven data bits per byte. The ASCII character set used by these computers includes only the first 128 characters of the IBM extended ASCII character set (2 to the 7th power). These 128 characters include all the numbers and letters (uppercase and lowercase), punctuation marks, and some extra control characters. Special characters, such as foreign letters and box-drawing characters, require all eight bits.

When you set up PC communications software to communicate with another computer, you need to specify whether data occupies the first seven bits or all eight bits of each byte. Some software calls this specification the number of data bits. Other programs may use the term *word length* or *character length* for the same specification. You sometimes may use your PC to communicate with another PC that needs eight data bits per byte. At other times, you may communicate with a type of

computer that can use only seven data bits per byte. The only way to know for sure which setting you need is to ask the operator of the other computer.

A simple rule of thumb is to use eight data bits for PC-to-PC or PC-to-BBS connections. All PCs need eight-bit bytes to represent the full IBM character set and to transmit program files. When calling an on-line service, such as CompuServe, or another mainframe-based system, use seven data bits. Most such systems are run on computers that can handle only seven data bits per byte. CompuServe defaults to 7 data bits and even parity. You can change the default to 8 data bits and no parity if you like. File transfer requires using 8 data bits. If your software does not support auto switching of the data bit configuration from 7 data bits to 8 data bits during a file download, you need to use 8 data bits at all times.

Parity Checking

An error in transmission of even a single bit can change completely the meaning of the byte that includes that bit. To help detect these errors as they occur, some computers use the eighth bit of each byte as a *parity bit.* The parity of an integer (whole number) is whether it is odd or even. You can use a parity bit in two ways. Both methods add the other seven digits in each byte and check whether the sum is an even or odd number.

When using the *even parity method,* the computer sets the value of the parity bit (either 1 or 0) so that the total of all eight bits is even. If the sum of the first seven bits is odd, such as 0000001, the parity bit becomes a 1. The eight-bit byte transmitted is therefore 00000011. If the sum of the first seven bits is even, such as 0010001, the parity bit becomes 0, and the eight-bit transmitted byte is 00100010. In both cases, adding all eight bits results in an even number—2 in both examples. The receiving computer then adds the digits of each byte when it receives them. If the sum is odd, an error must have been introduced during transmission, so the computer software asks that the byte be sent again.

Similarly, the *odd parity method* assigns the value of the parity bit so that the sum of all digits in each byte always is an odd number.

One parity bit method, known as *mark parity,* always sets the parity bit to the value 1. Another method, known as *space parity,* always sets the parity bit to the value 0.

> **Note:** Parity-checking provides rather minimal error-checking when compared to the many other more sophisticated error-checking methods now available in software (see the "Transferring Files" section of this chapter) and hardware (see "Error Control," earlier in this chapter).

For PC-to-PC communication, including transmission to bulletin boards, use the None (no parity) setting. When connecting to an on-line service, you usually have to use Even parity. If you are connected to an on-line service and are receiving nothing but strange-looking characters, you probably have parity set to None. Try changing the parity to Even.

Interrupt Request Lines

Before any computer can operate a COM port at high speed or in a multitasking environment, it must make use of one of the hardware interrupt request lines (IRQs). By using an IRQ, the computer CPU is free to do other things until new data is received that must be processed. The interrupt triggers an interrupt handler in the PC that gets the data from the port and places that data in the correct location for the communications program to process when ready. The CPU then resets the interrupt and continues about its other business until another interrupt comes in.

A possible 17 interrupt request lines are available, numbered from 0 to 15 and one called Non-Mask Able Interrupt (NMI). The NMI is the only interrupt the CPU can never ignore or turn off. All other IRQs can be turned on or off depending on what the computer is doing. Table 31.3 shows the normal assignments.

Table 31.3 Standard IRQ Assignments in ISA and EISA Bus Systems

Interrupt Request Line Number	Normal Assignment
NMI	Memory Parity Errors
0	Internal Timer
1	Keyboard
2	Cascade to second 8259, IRQs 8 to 15
3	COM2,COM3 (also COM4 on MCA BUS PS/2s)
4	COM1,COM4 (no COM4 if on a MCA PS/2)
5	LPT2
6	Floppy disk controller
7	LPT1
8	Clock/Calendar (CMOS RTC)
9	Redirected IRQ2, used by many Network cards
10	Reserved (may be available)
11	Reserved (may be available)
12	PS/2 Mouse (may be available on ISA BUS)
13	Math Co-Processor
14	Hard disk controller
15	Reserved (may be available)

Windows uses the standard default IRQs for ISA, EISA, and MCA bus computers. The default IRQ settings for ISA and EISA computers are as follows:

Port	Interrupt Request Line (IRQ)
COM1	4
COM2	3
COM3	4
COM4	3

On an MCA computer, COM1 and COM2 use the same interrupts as ISA and EISA computers. COM3 and COM4, however, use IRQ3. In an MCA computer, default COM port IRQ settings are as follows:

Port	Interrupt Request Line (IRQ)
COM1	4
COM2	3
COM3	3
COM4	3

ISA computers support no more than two COM ports operating simultaneously by using the two default interrupt request lines. EISA and MCA computers, however, can support more than one port using the same hardware interrupt by permitting the ports to share the interrupt. If you own an EISA or MCA bus computer, Windows, by default, enables interrupts to be shared. Windows disables interrupt sharing for ISA machines.

To change Windows assignment of serial port IRQ settings, follow these steps:

1. Right-click on the My Computer icon on the desktop. The context menu for the object appears.
2. Choose Properties from the context menu. The System Properties sheet appears.
3. Click on the Device Manager tab. The System Properties sheet now appears, as shown in figure 34.4.
4. Double-click on the Ports (COM & LPT) in the lower portion of the device list. This expands the device list, showing all your serial and parallel ports.
5. Double-click on the serial port you want to change. The Communication Port Properties sheet appears.
6. Click on the Resources tab. The Communication Port Properties sheet appears as shown in figure 31.5.

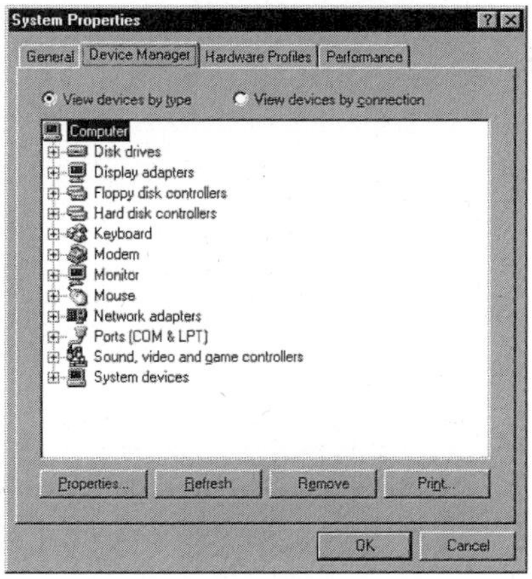

Fig. 31.4 The Device Manager tab in the System Properties sheet allows you to identify components in your system.

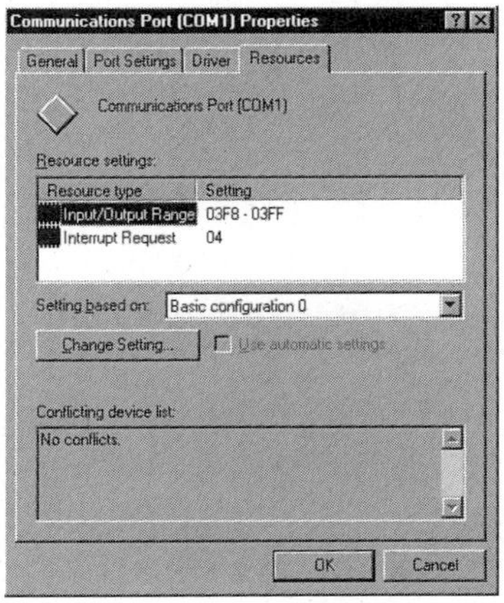

Fig. 31.5 The Communication Port Properties sheet allows you to configure your serial ports.

To use more than two COM ports on an ISA bus system, change the Interrupt Request setting to one of the other possible interrupt request lines. If your computer does not have an LPT2 (second printer) port, you can use IRQ5 for either COM3 or COM4 (assuming your serial card provides a method of selecting one of these interrupt request lines—

refer to your adapter card's documentation to find out the possible settings). IRQ5 is sometimes used by a BUS mouse and, therefore, may not be available. IRQ2 is also a possibility, but it serves as the cascade to interrupt lines 8 through 15. Sometimes trying to use IRQ2 can cause a problem, but it may be worth a try.

If only IRQ3 and IRQ4 are available for assignment to a serial port, make the assignments in only one of the following combinations.

COM1 (IRQ4) with COM2 (IRQ3)

COM1 (IRQ4) with COM4 (IRQ3)

COM2 (IRQ3) with COM3 (IRQ4)

COM3 (IRQ4) with COM4 (IRQ3)

Any combination of ports that puts two devices, being used at the same time, on the same IRQ almost certainly leads to problems.

Base Addresses

One other parameter of your serial ports that must be identified to Windows is the base address. This is a memory address used to transfer information between the CPU and the UART that comprises the serial port. In Windows 95, this base address is actually referred to as an input/output range. In most instances, this range is automatically identified by Windows 95 and will not need to be changed.

In an ISA system, there are four base addresses generally recognized as belonging to COM1 through COM4. These are:

Port	Base Address
COM1	3F8H
COM2	2F8h
COM3	2E8h
COM4	2E0h

Most PCs store COM port addresses in a table in the BIOS at memory address 40:00 hex; it is placed there during the boot process. Windows accesses this information, if it exists, to establish the base addresses used by the system. If your computer doesn't store COM port addresses in a BIOS table, you may need to manually adjust the input/output ranges within Windows 95. To do this, display the Communications Port Properties dialog box, as described in the previous section. The base addresses (input/output ranges) used by the serial ports are resources you can modify as you see fit.

Understanding Communications Software

To use a modem effectively, you need some sort of communications software. The purpose of the software is to facilitate routine communications and file transfer with a remote system, using your modem as the go-between.

In Chapter 32, "Communicating with a Modem," you'll learn how you can use specific software to communicate. Before jumping into that, however, there are some basics that apply to communications software, regardless of who makes it.

Understanding Terminal Emulation

Terminal emulation performs a function similar to that of a United Nations translator. If you've ever seen or read about the United Nations General Assembly, you probably know that an army of translators is always at work so that representatives of all nations can understand what is being said, regardless of the language spoken. All the representatives can listen with ear phones to a simultaneous translation of the proceedings into their native language.

When a communications program is emulating a particular type of terminal, the program is performing a simultaneous translation between different languages. However, the program translates in two directions at once. Each time you press a key on your keyboard, the program converts the keystroke into the code that would be generated by a real terminal; this code is the language the host minicomputer or mainframe computer expects to receive. This conversion of outgoing keystrokes is referred to as keyboard mapping. At the same time, the host computer is sending to your computer codes intended to control the screen and printer of a real terminal; these codes are in a language the terminal understands. The communications program also translates these incoming codes into codes your PC understands.

Just as the United Nations needs translators for more than one pair of spoken languages, your communications software also needs to emulate more than one type of terminal. Terminals from different manufacturers often don't speak exactly the same language, and not all host computers are designed to work with the same type of terminal. Unless your software emulates a terminal that speaks and understands the language spoken and understood by the host computer to which your computer is connected, effective communication cannot take place. Your communications program, therefore, typically gives you several terminal emulations from which to choose, in an effort to provide at least one emulation that each host computer can understand.

Each emulation maps your PC's keyboard in a different way and expects a different set of screen (and sometimes printer) control signals from the host computer. Standard typewriter keys—A through Z and 0 through 9—are understood universally by other computers, regardless of the type of terminal your software is emulating. This understanding is possible because all terminals emulated by your software send the generic ASCII character codes for these keys. The remaining, so-called special keys on the keyboard, however, are the crux of the issue. You can use these keys—alone, or with another key (Shift, Ctrl, or Shift-Ctrl)—to program (or map) so that you can send a different code to the remote computer for each different type of terminal emulation.

Your communications software maps your keyboard to act like the keyboard of a real terminal. Each time you press a mapped key, the software sends the code that would be sent by pressing a corresponding key on a real terminal's keyboard. Each terminal emulation uses a particular keyboard mapping specially designed to match the codes generated by a real terminal.

Always keep in mind that terminal emulation is never 100 percent effective. Just as all PCs are not alike, each type of terminal has its own special features and capabilities. Although the power and flexibility of your PC enables programmers to make it act like many different types of terminals, your PC cannot always perform every special function of every type of terminal.

Transferring Files

File transfer is a two-way street. Communications software enables you to send and receive computer files to and from the remote computer. The steps you take to send a file are similar to but not exactly the same as the steps necessary to receive a file.

Transferring files can be broken into several sections. You first need to know the basics of transferring files. To understand transferring files, you must be familiar with several of the *file-transfer protocols,* which define how the file is physically sent between two systems. Understanding file-transfer protocols is the key to successfully moving files to and from your system by modem.

Sending or Receiving a File

In most communications programs, the phrases *send a file, upload a file,* and *transmit a file* mean the same. They refer to the act of transferring a computer file from your computer to a remote computer. Sometimes new users are confused by the term upload. You may think, for example, that it refers to uploading a file to your computer, which is receiving the file. When used in most programs, however, the phrase upload a file means to send a file to another computer. This usage is easiest to understand in the context of sending files to a host computer, such as a bulletin board. When you send a file to the bulletin board, you are uploading the file to the host. Receiving a file from the host is called *downloading* a file.

Before you can use a Windows communications program to send or receive a file, you must be connected to the remote computer. If the remote computer is a PC that is not operating a bulletin board, you must inform the remote computer's operator that you are about to upload a file. For file transfer to occur, the remote operator must begin the appropriate download procedure soon after you execute your upload procedure.

When you're connected to a host system (an on-line service such as CompuServe, for example, or a PC bulletin board), you inform the host program that you intend to upload (send) or download (receive) a file by selecting an appropriate menu option or command. (The exact command depends on the host program with which you are communicating.) You usually have to type the name of the file (or select a file name from a file list) you're going to upload to the host or download from the host and indicate a file-transfer protocol.

A *file-transfer protocol* is an agreed upon set of rules that controls the flow of data between two computers. The agreed upon rules often screen transmitted data for errors introduced by the transmission process. As you learned earlier in the chapter, this error-screening process usually is referred to as *error checking* or *error control.* Using a file-transfer protocol that performs error checking ensures that the data received by the remote computer is the same as the data your computer sends. Like most other communication parameters, the file-transfer protocol you choose must match that used by the remote computer.

Tip: If both your modem and the remote modem support error-correcting protocols at a modem level, it is redundant to choose a file-transfer protocol that includes error correction.

When the host (remote computer) instructs you to begin your transfer, you begin the upload or download procedure for your software.

Understanding File-Transfer Protocols

When you type a message to someone who is sitting at the keyboard of a remote computer, your communications software sends ASCII characters to the screen of the remote computer. The operator of the remote

computer can detect transmission errors by reading the characters on-screen. If characters look like hieroglyphics, that condition reflects a transmission error. Most computer files, however, are not stored entirely as ASCII characters. Computer programs, most word processing files, spreadsheet files, database files, and other types of computer files contain data that cannot be displayed on-screen as transmitted. These non-ASCII files typically are referred to as *binary files*. To send binary files, you must use a file-transfer protocol that can send data without displaying it to the screen, and you must take steps through software or hardware to detect data errors that may be caused by degradation of the telephone signal.

Each time you begin uploading or downloading files by using your Windows communications software, you typically can choose among several file-transfer protocols. The following guidelines can help you decide which protocol to use:

- ***Use matching file-transfer protocols.*** The same file-transfer protocol must be used on the sending and receiving ends of the file-transfer process. This requirement limits the number of protocols available to you during any particular communication session to the protocols that your communications software and the remote program have in common.

- ***Use the ASCII protocol only for ASCII files.*** When sending or receiving a file that contains only printable ASCII characters, you have the option of choosing the ASCII protocol. This protocol sends data character by character, just as when you type a message at the keyboard.

- ***Send and receive the largest blocks of data possible.*** For maximum transmission speed when sending binary files, use the file-transfer protocol that sends blocks of the largest size. YMODEM, COMPUSERVE B+, YMODEM (Batch), and ZMODEM protocols can send blocks of 1,024 bytes.

  However, if you're having a great number of data transfer errors, you might want to select a file-transfer protocol that uses a smaller block size. The smaller block size may allow you to sneak more blocks through between errors. This step can reduce the amount of data you must resend and avoid an ultimate file-transfer termination because of the total error count.

- ***Send and receive multiple files.*** Some file-transfer protocols enable you to send or receive multiple files with one command. This type of transfer often is called a *batch transfer*. Protocols that can send or receive multiple files include COMPUSERVE B+, KERMIT, YMODEM (Batch), YMODEM G (Batch), and ZMODEM.

- ***Send and receive file characteristics.*** Several file-transfer protocols also send with the file such file characteristics as file name, file size, and the date and time the file was last changed. When you are downloading a file, this information enables your communications software to display information about the progress of the file transmission. The protocols that transmit at least one of these file characteristics include YMODEM, YMODEM (Batch), COMPUSERVE B+, KERMIT, and ZMODEM.

- ***Use sliding windows on PDNs and over long-distance lines.*** When you connect to a host computer over a *public data network* (PDN), such as Tymnet and Telenet (or any other packet-switching network), or over long-distance telephone lines that may go through satellite relays, most file-transfer protocols can be slowed significantly. PDNs and satellite relays often cause an appreciable increase in the time needed for the receiving computer to reply to each block sent. The sending computer can spend a great deal of time just waiting. The KERMIT, ZMODEM, and CompuServe B+ protocols, however, take advantage of the full-duplex nature of your modem. Instead of waiting for a reply before sending another block, the protocols send blocks and simultaneously watch for the reply to previous blocks. These protocols send several blocks before requiring any reply. ZMODEM and CompuServe B+ probably are the best choices for use on public data networks.

- ***Use appropriate protocols with error-control modems.*** If you are using a modem that performs error control in hardware, such as a modem that supports MNP Classes 1 through 4 or CCITT V.42, use a protocol that sends data without doing any error checking in software. Two protocols in this group are YMODEM and YMODEM (Batch).

Some file-transfer protocols have the ability to restart a terminated file-transfer. Two such file-transfer protocols are ZMODEM and CompuServe B+. The ability to restart where the transfer was terminated could save considerable time depending on the size of the file.

Understanding XMODEM

The most widely available PC-based file-transfer protocol is XMODEM. Like so many other communications terms, XMODEM can mean different things to different people, so you need to understand a little about the background of this protocol.

As most broadly used, the term XMODEM refers to a file-transfer protocol included in the program MODEM2, written by Ward Christensen and introduced in 1979. This file-transfer protocol originally was called the MODEM protocol and was intended to transfer files between computers running the CP/M operating system. Over the years since 1979, however, the MODEM file-transfer protocol has become known as XMODEM and has been implemented in countless communications programs for use in transferring files between computers running many different operating systems. Virtually all popular communications programs for PCs include an implementation of XMODEM. Since its introduction, several new and improved versions of the protocol have appeared under various names.

The original XMODEM used the checksum error-checking scheme. This method of detecting errors is adequate for low-speed data transmission (300 bps or less) but can miss errors that are more likely to occur when you're sending data at higher transmission speeds (or over noisy phone lines). One popular variation of XMODEM adds the CCITT CRC-16 error-checking scheme, which is much more reliable than the checksum method at the higher transmission rates.

The CRC-16 version of XMODEM often is called XMODEM/CRC, but many programs refer to the protocol simply as XMODEM. Use of the

name in this manner leads to no problems, however, because the CRC-16 version of XMODEM is backward compatible with the checksum version. In other words, you can use the CRC-16 version of XMODEM to send or receive a file to or from a computer that is using the original checksum version of XMODEM or the newer CRC-16 version.

Several other modified versions of XMODEM seem to have overtaken XMODEM in popularity. To varying degrees, these other protocols overcome XMODEM's recognized weaknesses: 128-byte blocks, no multiple file transfers, no file characteristics transferred, and no sliding windows. The 1K-XMODEM version of XMODEM is a CRC XMODEM with a 1,024-byte (1K) packet rather than the 128-byte packet. The 1K-XMODEM-G version of XMODEM is the same as the 1K-XMODEM but provides no software error detection and relies on the modem error-correction hardware to provide that function.

Other protocols that have evolved directly or indirectly from the original XMODEM protocol are SEALINK, TELINK, WXMODEM, YMODEM, and ZMODEM.

Understanding YMODEM

The YMODEM protocol was introduced in 1985 by Chuck Forsberg of Omen Technology, Inc., as an extension of Ward Christensen's XMODEM protocol. As implemented originally, Forsberg's YMODEM protocol includes CRC-16 error checking; 1,024-byte blocks; multiple file transfer; and transmission of file name, file size, and the date and time each file was last modified. Forsberg's YMODEM also includes an option called the G option, which enables you to take full advantage of modems that perform error control.

Understanding ZMODEM

The ZMODEM protocol also was developed by Chuck Forsberg of Omen Technology for the public domain under a Telenet contract in 1986. This protocol has rapidly become a favorite among many users.

ZMODEM was designed to eliminate many of the problems or limitations associated with older protocols such as XMODEM and YMODEM

while taking advantage of new technologies in modem hardware. According to Forsberg, "The ZMODEM file-transfer protocol provides reliable file and command transfers with complete end-to-end data integrity between application programs. ZMODEM's 32-bit CRC catches errors that continue to sneak into even the most advanced networks."

Because ZMODEM has buffering and windowing modes, it can work efficiently on a number of data networks. ZMODEM provides faster transfers than other protocols—particularly with error-correcting modems—on timesharing systems (such as CompuServe), satellite relays, and any other kinds of packet-switched networks. The sophisticated error-correction capabilities make ZMODEM useful if you are transferring information over noisy telephone lines.

ZMODEM's benefits are not just limited to its technological advances. ZMODEM also is easy to use. Its Auto Download feature enables you to skip some of the steps necessary with other protocols. After you specify a download, for example, the ZMODEM transfer begins without you having to initiate the protocol (by clicking the Receive File Action icon) or having to type the file name again. Unlike many other protocols, ZMODEM can preserve a file's date and time stamp as well as the file's exact size during transmission, which eliminates the annoying problem of having unneeded characters at the end of a file—a common problem with some other protocols.

The Crash Recovery feature in ZMODEM is also impressive. If a download is interrupted before completion and is restarted, ZMODEM can pick up where the download left off, saving you valuable connect time. ZMODEM also has multiple-file capability, which means that you can specify file transfers by using global characters (such as *.DOC).

Of the many file-transfer protocols available in most Windows communications programs, ZMODEM probably is the best to use when transferring files to and from PC bulletin boards or on public data networks. The protocol's 1,024-byte block size, coupled with multiple-file-transfer capability, automatic transfer, and sliding windows, makes ZMODEM a fast protocol that also is easy to use.

Understanding KERMIT

KERMIT is the name of a program, a file-transfer protocol, and a famous frog. In fact, the program and protocol are named after the Jim Henson muppet, Kermit the Frog. Unless specifically noted otherwise, this section discusses the file-transfer protocol KERMIT rather than the KERMIT program.

KERMIT was developed in 1981 at Columbia University by Frank da Cruz and Bill Catchings and released into the public domain. In contrast to XMODEM, which requires eight data bits to operate, KERMIT can be used on computers that can handle only seven data bits (many mainframe computers, for example) and still can manage to transmit files that contain bytes made up of eight bits per byte. Since 1981, KERMIT has been implemented on countless brands and models of computers, from mainframes to microcomputers. Since its introduction, KERMIT has enjoyed numerous enhancements.

Transferring Files on CompuServe

Use the CompuServe B, B+, or QuickB file-transfer protocols when sending and receiving files over the CompuServe on-line service. The primary difference between the CompuServe B and CompuServe Quick B protocols is that Quick B has sliding windows. As implied by the name, CompuServe Quick B transfers files faster than CompuServe B. The B+ protocol introduces some new enhancements to the Quick B protocol, which gives CompuServe B+ some of the advantages of the ZMODEM protocol.

Setting Up Your Modem in Windows 95

Adding a modem in Windows 95 is much easier than in previous versions of Windows. In most instances, it is simply a matter of selecting your modem type from the list maintained by Windows.

Specifying the type of modem installed in your system allows Windows to automatically configure it for any communications needs you may have. To specify a modem, display the Control Panel, and then double-click on the Modems icon. You'll shortly see the sheet shown in figure 31.6.

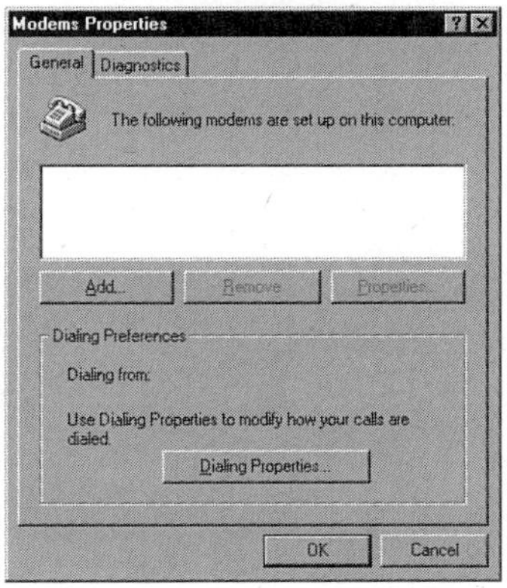

Fig. 31.6 The Modems Properties sheet allows you to configure your modem.

Selecting a Modem

The General tab within the Modems Properties sheet is where you specify the types of modems you use in your system. You can have Windows 95 configured for more than one modem, if desired. For instance, if you use external modems, you may want to switch between different modems from time to time, depending on what's available at the time.

To add a modem, click on the Add button. This action starts the Install New Modem Wizard, as shown in figure 31.7.

By default, the Wizard attempts to automatically determine the type of modem in your system. It does this by analyzing all your serial ports to see whether there are any devices attached. If so, and the device appears to be a modem, the Wizard sends commands to the modem to see if it can identify itself. (Most modems now marketed provide

information that can help an operating system or communications software identify the modem.)

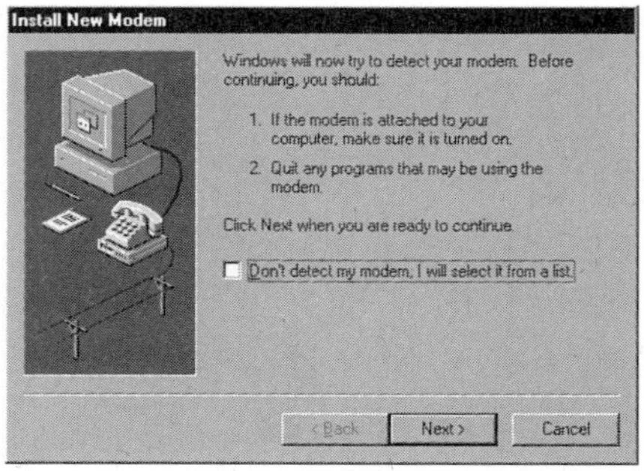

Fig. 31.7 Windows 95 provides a Wizard to help with the installation of a new modem.

At this first Wizard dialog box, you can indicate whether you want Windows to automatically try to detect the modem. In most instances, you should allow automatic identification. If you would rather specify the modem yourself, then you can click on the Don't detect check box.

At this point, you should click on the Next button. If you're allowing the Wizard to automatically identify the modem, there will be a delay as the identification is attempted. If you want to pick the modem yourself, or if the Wizard can't determine which modem you have installed, you'll see the dialog box in figure 31.8.

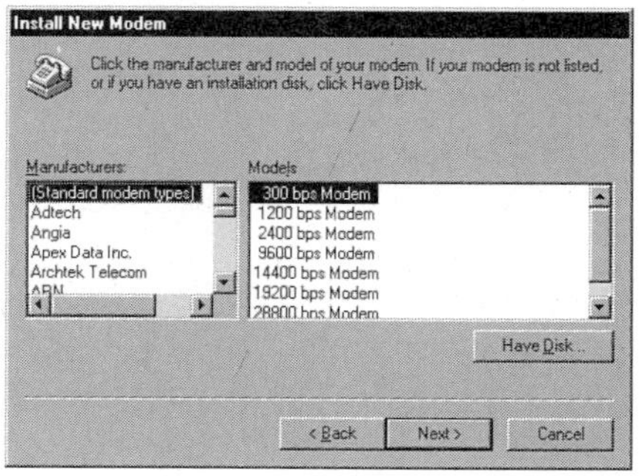

Fig. 31.8 Picking a modem type is similar to installing other types of devices in Windows 95.

From the list of manufacturers and models, you should select the modem installed in your system. Make sure you pick the manufacturer first, as the available models will vary by manufacturer. When you're done, click on the Next button, and you'll see the dialog box in figure 31.9.

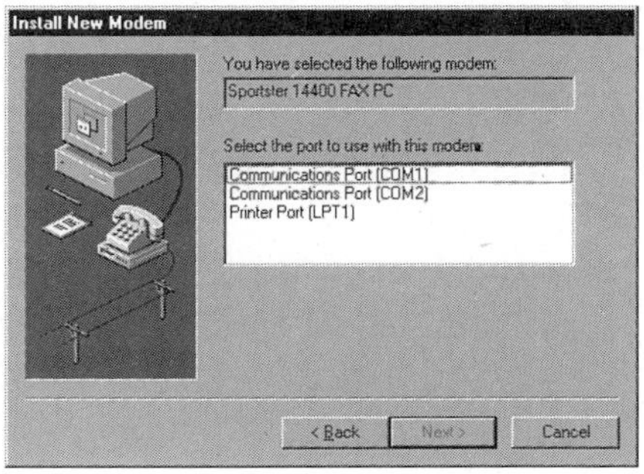

Fig. 31.9 After picking a modem type, you need to specify where it is connected within your system.

At this dialog box, you can pick how the modem is connected to your system. If your modem was automatically detected, this step is taken care of automatically. Pick the port to which the modem is connected, and then click on the Next button. The proper settings for your modem are then recorded in the Registry, and you'll shortly see the dialog box shown in figure 31.10.

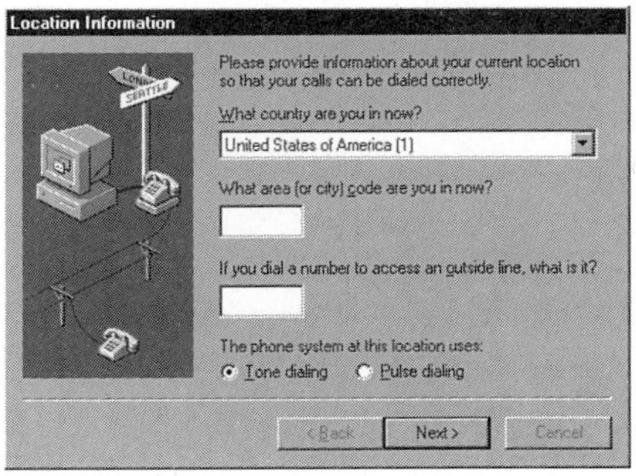

Fig. 31.10 Windows 95 keeps track of where you live in order to make calls on the modem correctly.

There are four settings you can make on this dialog box. The first is the country in which you are using the modem. (If you use the pull-down list, over 230 different countries are available.) The second setting is where you indicate the area (or city) code in which you are located. For instance, if you were making your calls from Wyoming, you would enter a 307 area code.

The third setting is used if you must dial a number to get an outside line. Typically, this setting is used only in offices, where it is common to dial 9 or some other number to get an outside line.

> **Tip:** You may want to put a comma after the access number (such as 9,). This action causes your modem to wait two seconds after dialing the access number before it dials the rest of the phone number.

The final setting is used to indicate whether your phone uses tone or pulse dialing. If you work in an office, and you must dial 9 to get an outside line, it is a virtual certainty that you use tone dialing. On other phones, you can tell if you use tone dialing by listening to the sounds your phone makes as you dial a number. If you hear "beeps," then you use tones. If you hear any "clicks," then you use pulses. (In a pulse-dial system, you hear a click for every number being dialed. For instance, if you dial the number 5, you will hear five clicks.)

When you have completed making your choices, click on the Next button. This displays the final dialog box in the Wizard, which informs you that the installation is completed. At this point, click on the Finish button.

Configuring Your Modem

Once your modem is set up, you can make changes to its configuration any time you desire. You do this by double-clicking on the Modems icon in the Control Panel. The Modems Properties sheet appears, as shown in figure 31.11.

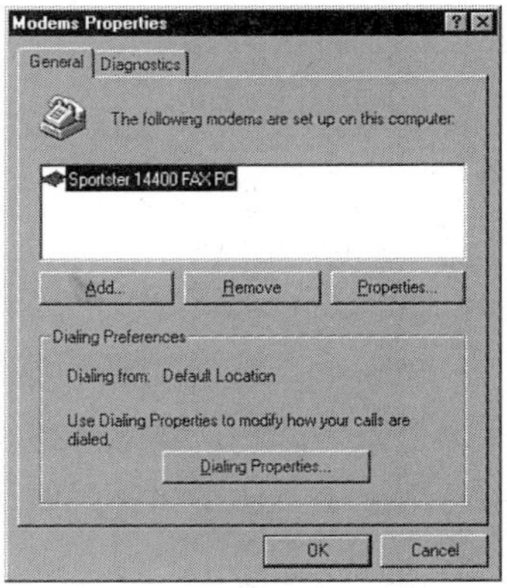

Fig. 31.11 To change modem configuration, you start at the Modems Properties sheet.

On your system, the Modems Properties sheet may show more than one modem installed. If this is the case, you should select the modem whose properties you want to change. Then click on the Properties button. You will shortly see the dialog box shown in figure 31.12.

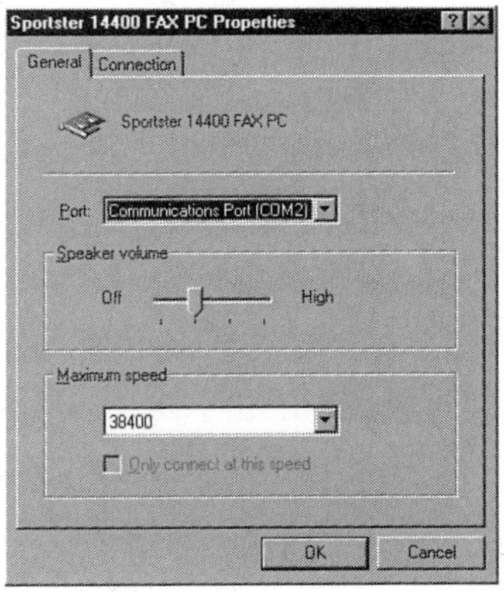

Fig. 31.12 A properties dialog box for individual modems allows you to change their configuration.

The exact appearance of this Properties sheet may differ from modem to modem, depending on the capabilities of the modem. In this

instance, for this modem, there are two tabs in the dialog box. The first tab, General, allows you to change the port assignment for the modem, the speaker volume, and the speed at which the modem communicates.

The Connection tab is a bit more complicated. This is where you specify the default communications parameters for the modem. Figure 31.13 shows an example of the sheet with the Connection tab selected.

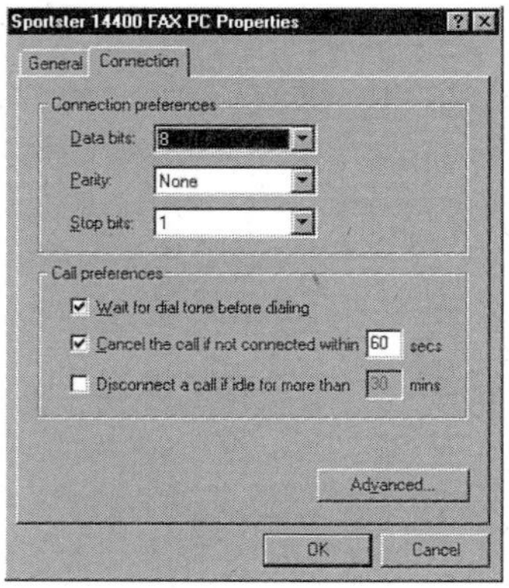

Fig. 34.13 The Connection tab is used to modify default communications parameters.

In the Connection Preferences area at the top of the sheet, you can set parameters you learned about earlier in the chapter. Here you set the default data bits, parity, and stop bits. Remember that these are default values, and can be overridden by whatever communication software you're using.

The next area of the dialog box allows you to indicate, in general, how a call should be handled. You can indicate whether the modem should wait for a dial tone before dialing (typically a good idea), and how long the modem should wait (in seconds) before giving up on making a connection. Notice that there is also an option (not selected by default) which allows you to specify how long a connection should be held if there is no activity. If you do quite a bit of unattended modem work, you may want to select this option and choose an inactivity time, in minutes.

> **Note:** If you're using a modem to directly connect your PC to another PC (not going through the phone system), then you should turn off the Wait for dial tone option. In this instance, waiting for a dial tone would stop you from ever establishing a connection.

Notice that there is an Advanced button at the bottom of the dialog box. If you click on this button, you'll see the dialog box shown in figure 31.14.

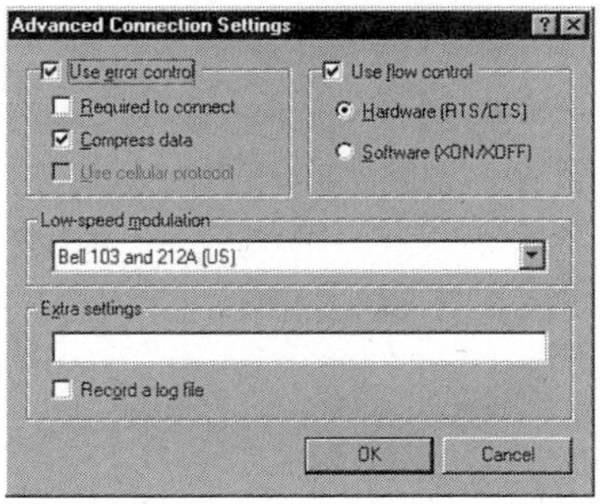

Fig. 31.14 Advanced modem settings are used to control behind-the-scenes aspects of a connection.

When you display this dialog box, it may not appear exactly the same as what is shown in figure 31.14. The settings available on this dialog box depend on the capabilities of your modem, and can vary accordingly. The upper-left corner is where you indicate whether your modem should use error-control and data compression. You learned about these two topics earlier in the chapter. If your modem supports these capabilities, by default Windows 95 will use them. You can turn off support for these features in this area. (You can also indicate whether such capabilities are required by both modems before a connection can be established.)

> **Note:** The error-control area of the dialog box also allows you to indicate whether your modem should use cellular protocols. Only certain modems have these capabilities—typically if the modems are used in mobile computing. If your modem does have these capabilities, and you will be using it for an extended time over regular phone lines, you may want to disable this feature. It will help improve connection time and possibly data speed.

In the upper-right corner of the dialog box you can indicate how you want to handle the data flow between your computer and the modem. You need flow control any time the modem sends or receives data faster than the modem or the computer can deal with it. When a data buffer becomes full, for either the modem or the computer, some method must be present to tell the other end to stop sending data.

Windows 95 supports two types of flow control, or you can turn flow control off altogether.

- If you turn off the Use flow control option, then none is done, and data is sent or received without regulation.
- Hardware (RTS/CTS) is the most common choice when using the serial port to communicate with a modem. You must use hardware flow control when you are using a high-speed error-checking modem to get optimum throughput.
- Software (XON/XOFF) works best when you are connecting your computer to dumb text-based systems by modem, typically at lower speeds.

In the middle of the dialog box is the Low-speed modulation specification. Here you indicate how you want the modem to communicate when working at 300- and 1200-bps connections. Typically, this will not be an issue; most modem connections these days are handled at rates of 9,600 bps or greater. The default setting (Bell 103 and 212A)

should generally be left undisturbed, but you can change it to another communications standard if there is a compelling need. The only times this should be necessary is if you are communicating with computers outside the U.S.

At the bottom of the dialog box is a field called Extra settings. This field is used to send special initialization strings to the modem after the initialization information from Windows 95 has been sent. You create these initialization commands with commands from the AT command set described earlier in the chapter. If you need to enter any such commands, you should refer to the user's guide that came with your modem for information on proper command syntax.

Finally, at the very bottom of the dialog box is a check box labeled Record a log file. If this check box is selected, Windows 95 will keep a record of all modem commands and responses. This is helpful if you're trying to trouble-shoot what is happening with a modem. The log file is named MODEMLOG.TXT, and is stored in the Windows directory. When you are done troubleshooting your modem, don't forget to turn the log file off, as it can quickly become very large.

Configuring Dialing Properties

Dialing properties refer to the parameters that govern how Windows 95 will actually dial a phone call. These properties are related to the modem, but only indirectly. In reality they are influenced more by the location from where you are making your call.

To specify your dialing parameters, again display the Modem Properties sheet, as shown earlier in figure 31.11. Click on the Dialing Properties button at the bottom of the sheet. You will then see the Dialing Properties sheet, as shown in figure 31.15.

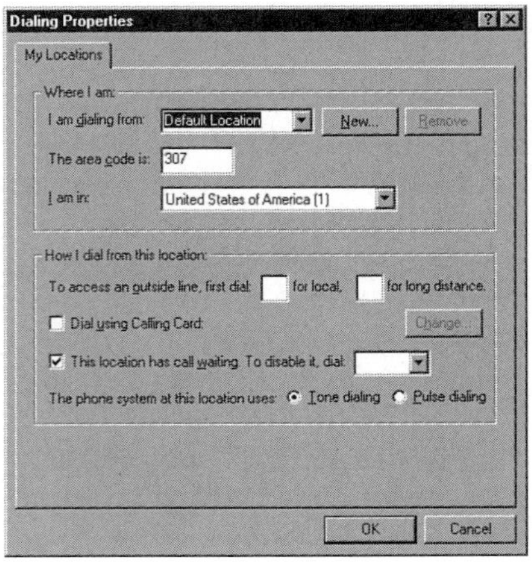

Fig. 31.15 The Dialing Properties sheet allows you to specify how your outgoing calls should be placed.

Dialing Locations

At the top of the Dialing Properties sheet you can specify originating locations for your calls. The first field, titled I am dialing from, is where you specify a location. For most people who use a computer in the same location every day, you can leave this set to the Default Location setting. If you're using Windows 95 on the road, however, you can set up dialing profiles for each location from which you might place calls. The exception to this is if you have different ways to place calls from the same location. For instance, if you're using a computer at work, you might want to define a location that reflects parameters for your work-related calls and another location with parameters for personal calls.

If you want to add a new location, click on the New button to the right of the location name. You're asked what you want the location called, after which the name is added to the location list.

Pick the location for which you want to define properties from the list of available locations. You then need to supply an area code and country for this location. If you're setting up dialing properties for outside the United States, you should use the city code in place of the area code.

If you have defined multiple locations, at some time you may want to remove a location profile. This is done by choosing the location name at the top of the Dialing Properties sheet, and then clicking on the Remove button. You are asked to confirm your action, after which the profile is erased. Windows 95 will not allow you to remove the Default Location profile.

How Calls Should Be Placed

At the bottom of the Dialing Properties sheet, you can specify how the call is to be made. The first two fields are used to indicate prefacing numbers you may need dialed in order to get an outside line for both local and long distance calls. For instance, in some offices, you may need to dial 9 before you get an outside dial tone. In some hotels, you may need to dial 9 for a local call or 8 for a long-distance call.

> **Tip:** It's a good idea to place a comma after the outside line number. This forces your modem to wait two seconds before dialing the rest of the phone number. This pause should accommodate any delays introduced by the office or hotel switching system.

The next option has to do with calling cards. Windows 95 allows you to dial the modem by using calling card information, as well as direct dialing. Most often, calling card information will come in handy for those traveling on the road. Calling cards are covered in detail in the next section.

The third option allows you to specify what Windows 95 should do about call waiting. Earlier in the chapter you learned that call waiting can disconnect a modem call (which can be quite frustrating). If you click the check box in the call waiting area, you can indicate the proper numbers to use to disable it. Windows 95 includes three different codes in the pull-down list for this option: *70, 70#, and 1170. You can also define custom sequences that disable call waiting simply by typing them into the field. Each sequence can be up to five characters long.

> **Tip:** The exact sequence to disable call waiting varies from phone system to phone system. Check with the local phone company for the location you're defining to determine the proper sequence you should use.

The final option on the Dialing Properties sheet refers to the type of phone service you have. There are two different phone service types: tone and pulse dialing. With tone dialing, the phone equipment generates "beep tones," which are understood by the phone company's switching equipment. Older systems, still used in many parts of the country, do not use tone dialing. Instead, they use pulse dialing which relies on a series of clicks for each number dialed—when you dial 3, the equipment generates three clicks, for 7 there are seven clicks generated, and so on.

You can find out which type of service you have by listening on your phone as you dial a number. If you hear tones only, then you have a tone dialing system. If you hear any clicks at all (with or without tones), then you have a pulse dialing system. You should set this property according to your needs at the location whose properties you are defining.

Using Calling Cards

Calling cards have become a way of life, especially for travelers. Windows 95 supports the use of calling cards when placing a modem call. To specify that calls made from a specific location should use a calling card, enable the Dial using Calling Card option on the Dialing Properties sheet. You should then see the Change Calling Card page appear, as shown in figure 31.16. (If it does not appear, click on the Change button to the right of the Calling Card option.)

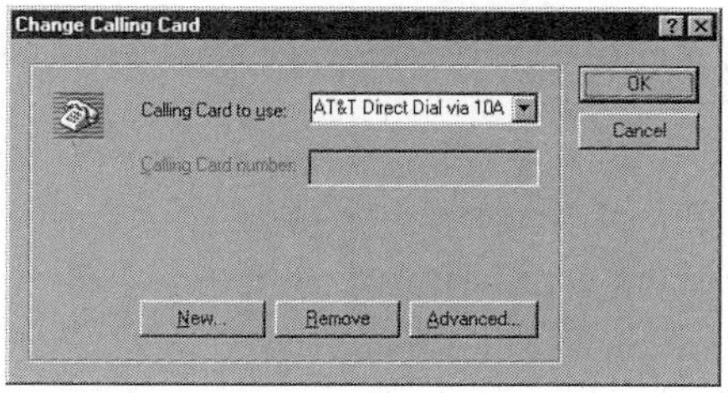

Fig. 31.16 The Change Calling Card page is where you pick the type of calling card to use from a given location.

At the top of the dialog box you can specify which calling card you want to use. Windows 95 already includes definitions for 22 of the most common calling cards:

- AT&T Direct Dial via 10ATT1
- AT&T via 1-800-321-0280
- AT&T via 10ATT0
- British Telecom (UK)
- Calling Card via 0
- Carte France Telecom
- CLEAR Communications (New Zealand)
- Global Card (Taiwan to USA)
- MCI Direct Dial via 102221
- MCI via 1-800-674-0700
- MCI via 1-800-674-7000
- MCI via 1-800-950-1022
- MCI via 102220
- Mercury (UK)
- Optus (Australia) via 008551812

- Optus (Australia) via 1812
- Telecom Australia via 1818 (fax)
- Telecom Australia via 1818 (voice)
- Telecom New Zealand
- US Sprint Direct Dial via 103331
- US Sprint via 1-800-877-8000
- US Sprint via 103330

To use one of these pre-defined cards, select the card, enter the calling card number in the approprite field on the dialog box, and then click on OK—Windows 95 will take care of the rest. There may be a specialized calling card you want to use, however. If this is the case, you can click on the New button at the bottom of the dialog box. You are then asked for the name of the calling card. (You can provide a descriptive name, as the preceding list shows.) Once provided, the descriptive name is added to the list, and then you can click on the Advanced button to change the rules by which the calling card operates. The Dialing Rules dialog box appears, as shown in figure 31.17.

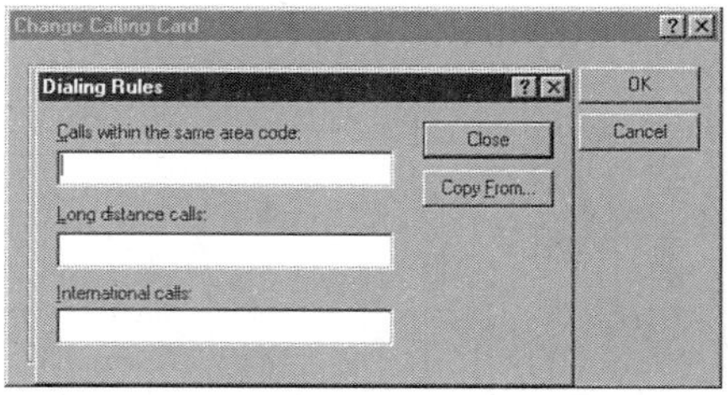

Fig. 31.17 The Dialing Rules dialog box allows you to specify exactly how your calling card should be used.

This dialog box contains three fields, each of which can contain a dialing rule. The first field is for long-distance calls within the current area code (or city code), the second is for domestic long-distance, and the third for international long-distance. You can fill each of these fields with a character sequence that describes how the calling card is to be

used. Don't confuse this sequence with the modem commands you can use in your modem properties. While there are similarities, those are based on the Hayes AT command set, whereas dialing rules are constructed from characters that have different meanings. Table 31.4 shows the characters you can include in a dialing rule, along with what they mean.

Table 31.4 Dialing Rule Characters and Their Meanings

Character	Meaning
!	Generate hook-flash
#	Pound key
$	Wait for calling card prompt tone
*	Star key
,	Pause for two seconds
?	Pause for user input during dialing sequence
@	Wait for ringback followed by five seconds of silence
0-9	The digit is dialed
E	Country code
F	Area or city code
G	Local number
H	Calling card number
P	Switches to pulse dialing
T	Switches to tone dialing
W	Wait for second dial tone

As an example, if you entered a rule such as 0FG$TH, then Windows would perform the following steps when placing the call:

1. Dial 0 (zero).
2. Dial area or city code.
3. Dial the phone number.

4. Wait for the calling card prompt tone (that strange "bong" sound you hear when dialing with a 0).
5. Switch to tone dialing (in case pulse dialing was used so far).
6. Dial the calling card number.

As you can see, dialing rules can be powerful. In fact, they can be used for other specialized dialing needs instead of just calling cards. Using the characters in Table 31.4, you can create any type of calling sequence you desire.

Checking Out Your Modem

If you ever suspect that your modem is not working properly with Windows 95, you can get information about how the modem is working by starting at the Control Panel and double-clicking on the Modems icon. The Modems Properties sheet appears, where you should click on the Diagnostics tab. The sheet will then appear similar to what is shown in figure 34.18.

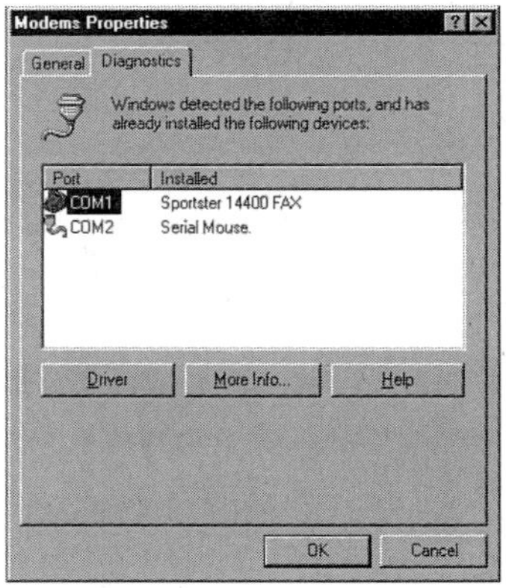

Fig. 31.18 The Diagnostics tab of the Modems Properties sheet allows you to check the connection to your modem.

Here you should highlight the port to which your modem is attached—in this instance, COM1—and then click on the More Info button.

Windows 95 then attempts to interrogate the modem, to see what information it can determine. After a few moments you will see a dialog box similar to what is shown in figure 31.19.

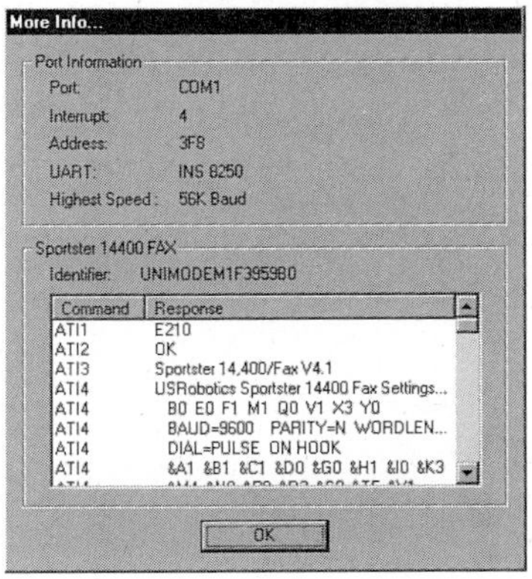

Fig. 31.19 Windows 95 can determine quite a bit of information about a modem.

The amount of information derived by Windows 95 depends solely on the capabilities of the modem. This information not only tells you about the modem and the connection, but also lets you know that Windows 95 can, in fact, communicate with the modem. Thus, if you continue to have problems establishing a communications link with a remote system, the chances are good that it is not because of your system or modem.

KILLER 32 WINDOWS 95

Communicating with a Modem

by Yvonne Johnson

The previous chapter, "Serial Communications Basics," explained the ins-and-outs of communications hardware and software settings. In this chapter, the rubber meets the road, so to speak. All the hardware and software specifications and setup are put into action with the features discussed here.

Several features in Windows 95 use the modem as the hardware vehicle, including the Phone Dialer, HyperTerminal, Dial-Up Networking, Microsoft Network, and Microsoft Exchange. The dialing properties used by the communications features are all organized in one central location: the Dialing Properties sheet.

The Basis of Communications in Windows 95

Windows 95 provides extensive and consistent support for telecommunications based on the Telephony API (TAPI), a standard by which communications programs can control transmission of data, fax, and voice calls. TAPI manages all the signaling between a computer and a telephone network, and it arbitrates among the communications programs that want to share communications ports and devices. TAPI manages the basic functions of establishing, answering, and terminating a call, as well as supplementary functions, such as hold, transfer, conference, and call park. In addition, TAPI also accommodates features that are specific to certain service providers. TAPI's built-in extensibility will accommodate future telephony features and telephone networks as they become available.

TAPI's arbitration among communications programs allows the computer to simultaneously run several communications programs (that is, it eliminates the need to perform only one telecommunications task at a time). For example, you can send a fax at the same time that Dial-Up Networking waits for an incoming call. There is no need to terminate Dial-Up Networking to send the fax, because TAPI allows programs to share the same device in a cooperative manner.

Setting Dialing Properties

Dialing properties govern the way outgoing calls are made. You can access the Dialing Properties sheet from the Control Panel, but because dialing properties are used by all the communications features of Windows 95, you also can access the Dialing Properties sheet from any of the features.

The following steps show you how to access the Dialing Properties sheet from the Control Panel:

1. Click Start, point to Settings, and click Control Panel.

2. Double-click the Modems object to display the Modems Properties sheet (figure 32.1).

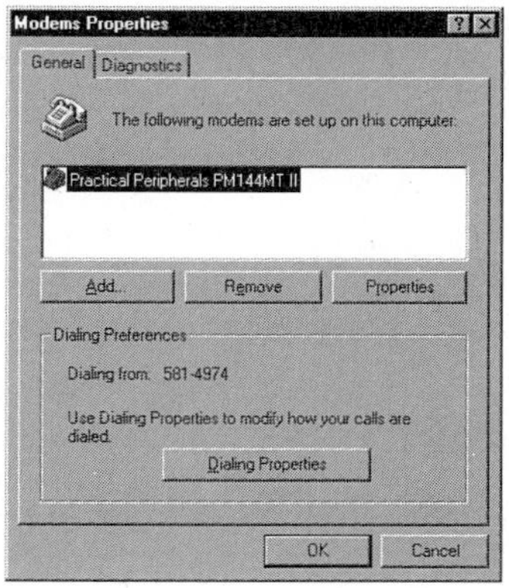

Fig. 32.1 The Modems Properties sheet is one place that you can access the Dialing Properties.

3. If there is more than one modem listed, select the one you want to configure and then click the Dialing Properties button. The Dialing Properties sheet appears (figure 32.2).

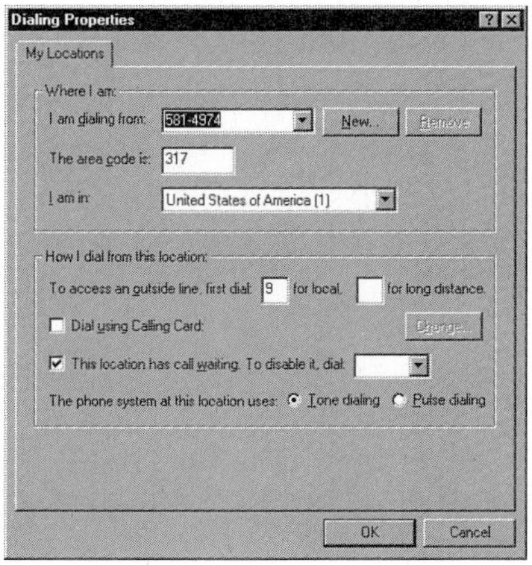

Fig. 32.2 The Dialing Properties sheet has settings for two broad categories: where you are and how you want to make the call.

4. Select the correct location from the drop-down list. If you want to create a new location name, click New, type a new name, and click OK. (Notice that you can also delete a location by selecting the location, clicking Remove, and choosing Yes.)

5. Enter the correct area code if the correct area code is not displayed by default. (Some settings in the Dialing Properties sheet—location, area code, and country code—are obtained by Windows 95 when you set up the modem initially.)

6. Verify that the I am in location is correct, or select a location from the drop-down list. The location that you select determines the international country code used for dialing international calls.

7. In the How I dial from this location section of the dialog box, specify the numbers you have to dial (if any) to get an outside line for local or long-distance calls (usually 9 for local calls and 8 for long distance).

8. If you want to dial using a Calling Card number, select Dial using Calling Card. The Change Calling Card dialog box opens as shown in figure 32.3. Choose a calling card from the drop-down list, or click New, enter your Calling Card number, and click OK. Then click OK to close the Change Calling Card dialog box. (If Dial using Calling Card is already selected, you can display the Change Calling Card dialog box by clicking Change.)

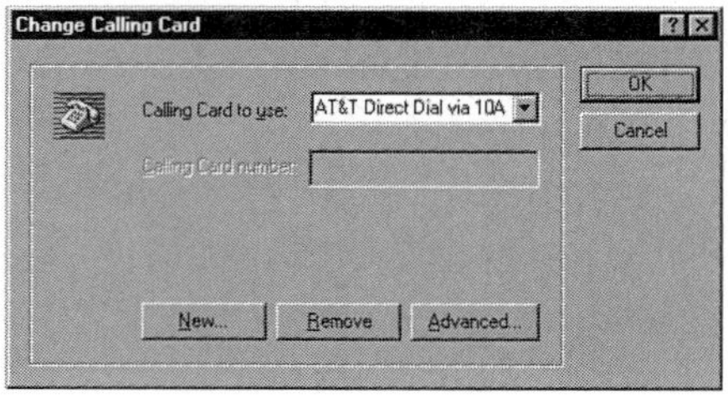

Fig. 32.3 You can add or remove Calling Card numbers in the Change Calling Card dialog box.

9. If you have call waiting, you certainly want to disable it because receiving a call waiting signal during a fax or modem transmission will break the connection. Choose This location has call waiting, and then enter the number that suspends call waiting.

> **Note:** Different areas of the country have different numbers that you dial before making a call to suspend the call waiting feature. The feature is only suspended during the next call that is made. As soon as the call is disconnected, call waiting is automatically reactivated. To obtain the number, look in the information pages of your local telephone book, or check with your local phone company.

10. Select the type of dialing system you have: Tone dialing for Touch-Tone or Pulse dialing for rotary dial.
11. Click OK to close the Dialing Properties sheet. Click OK to close the Modems Properties sheet.

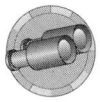

> **Note:** The Dialing Properties that you set are stored in the TELEPHON.INI file instead of the Registry to ensure backward compatibility with Windows 16-bit communications applications.

Defining Dialing Rules. To be more specific about how a number is dialed, you can define dialing rules. The dialing rules tell the modem exactly what to dial based on the criteria you specify.

To define dialing rules, follow these steps:

1. Display the Dialing Properties sheet. Display the Change Calling Card dialog box and click the Advanced button. The Dialing Rules dialog box displays as shown in figure 32.4.

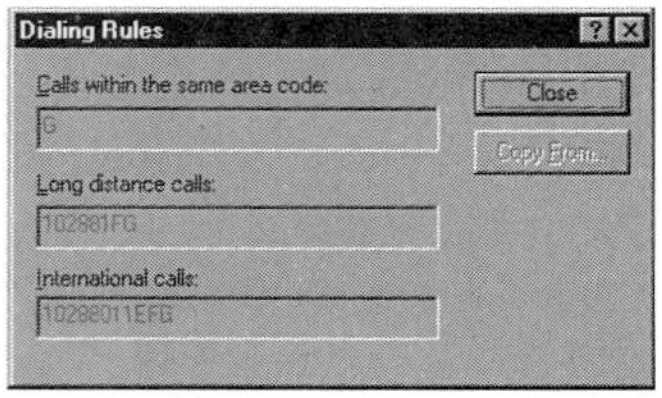

Fig. 32.4 By specifying dialing rules, you can specify the exact numbers that should or should not be dialed.

2. Fill in each box with the appropriate codes and numbers. To see a list of the codes, click the What's This button, and then click one of the text boxes. The codes are listed in Table 32.1.
3. When finished, click Close.

Table 32.1 Codes Used for Dialing Rules

Code	Description
0 - 9	Dialable digits
ABCD	Dialable digits
E	Country code
F	Area code
G	Local number
H	Calling Card number
*, #	Dialable digits
T	The following digits are tone
P	The following digits are pulse
,	Pause for a specified period of time
!	Hookflash (used, for example, to answer a call if you have the call waiting feature
W	Wait for second dial tone
@	Wait for ringback followed by five seconds of silence
$	Wait for Calling Card prompt tone
?	Ask for input before dialing continues

In the following example, which might be used on a PBX system, the modem would dial only the local number for calls in the same area, only the area code and local number for long distance (the mandatory 1 would not be dialed because the PBX takes care of it), and 011 plus the country code, area code, and local number for international calls.

Calls within the same area	G
Long-distance calls	FG
International calls	011EFG

Using Phone Dialer

The Phone Dialer is an accessory that dials phone numbers for voice telephone calls. It is used in conjunction with a telephone that is plugged into the phone jack (not the telecom jack) of the modem card. The Phone Dialer includes a telephone dial pad, user-programmable speed dialing, and a call log that tracks both incoming and outgoing calls.

Opening the Phone Dialer

These steps open the Phone Dialer:

1. Click Start, point to Programs, and click Accessories.
2. Click Phone Dialer. The Phone Dialer opens as shown in figure 32.5.

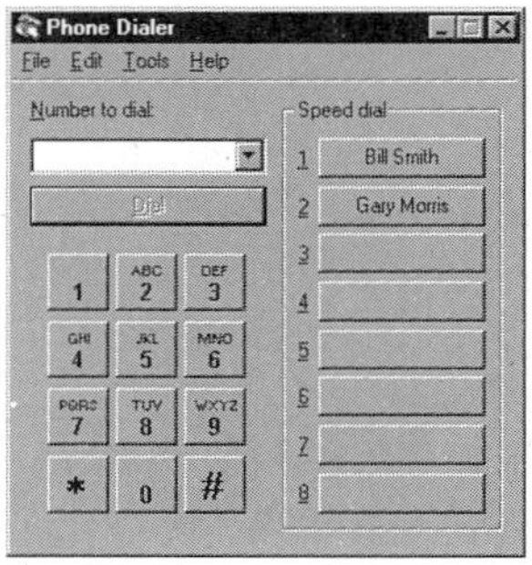

Fig. 32.5 The Phone Dialer makes outgoing voice calls and logs both outgoing and incoming calls.

Dialing a Number

With Phone Dialer, you can use several different methods to dial a number, including:

- Clicking a speed-dial button.
- Typing the phone number and clicking Dial.
- Clicking the numbers on the Phone Dialer numeric pad and clicking Dial.
- Selecting a number from the drop-down list, which contains the most recently used numbers.

After you dial the number, lift the receiver and click Talk. (The party that answers will not be able to hear you until you click Talk even though you have lifted the receiver.) If desired, type a name to place in the call log that is kept automatically by Phone Dialer. When finished with the call, replace the receiver in the cradle and click Hang Up.

Storing a Number on a Speed Dial Button

To store a number on a speed dial button, click an empty speed dial button and type a name. Type the number and click Save. The name appears on the speed dial button.

Note: You can type as many as 40 characters in the number text box, so you have plenty of room to type even an international phone number. All non-numeric characters that you type in the number are ignored except the plus sign (+) if it is typed at the beginning of the number. International format for a number begins with a plus sign and requires parentheses around the area code, for example: +1 (206) 555-8080.

Editing Speed Dial Buttons

To change the name or number associated with a speed dial button, choose Edit, Speed Dial. The Edit Speed Dial dialog box displays as shown in figure 32.6. Select a button and enter a new name or number. Edit as many buttons as necessary, and then click Save.

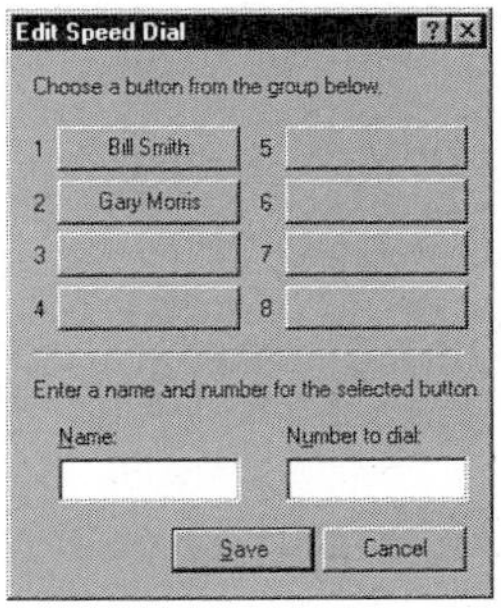

Fig. 32.6 In the Edit Speed Dial dialog box, you can modify speed dial buttons that you have previously defined, and you can define empty speed dial buttons.

Using the Call Log

Phone Dialer keeps a log of the calls that are made using Phone Dialer as well as the calls received on a telephone that is connected through the computer. By default, it logs both incoming and outgoing calls. To view the log of calls, choose Tools, Show Log. The log displays in the Call Log window as shown in figure 32.7.

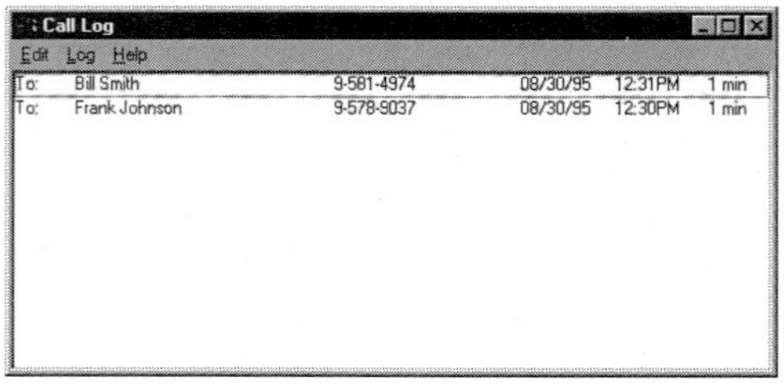

Fig. 32.7 The calling log can be set up to show incoming calls, outgoing calls, both types of calls, or no calls.

Both incoming and outgoing calls can be kept in the log. To specify the types of calls, choose Log, Options in the Call Log window. Choose the type of calls you want to log and click OK.

> **Tip:** To call a number that is listed in the log, simply double-click the number in the log.

To delete entries in the log, first select the entries by dragging the mouse over them if the entries you want to select are listed contiguously, or by pointing to an individual entry and pressing Ctrl while you click. Then choose Edit from the menu bar and choose either Cut or Delete.

Although there is no option to print the log, you can easily do so with some quick maneuvering. First select the entries in the log and choose Edit, Copy. Then open a text editor, such as WordPad or your favorite word processing program, and choose Edit, Paste. Then print the document.

Using HyperTerminal

The HyperTerminal accessory is a telecommunications program that connects you with a remote computer via a modem. Once connected, you can type messages back and forth or send and receive files. You

can save the communication settings that you use in a session so you can use them again. HyperTerminal is a 32-bit application that replaces the 16-bit application, Terminal, which was provided in Windows 3.x.

HyperTerminal is not installed by default. If it is not installed on your system, open the Add/Remove Programs object in the Control Panel and go to the Windows Setup page. HyperTerminal is listed in the Communications category.

Starting the HyperTerminal Program

To start the HyperTerminal program, click Start, point to Programs, point to Accessories, and click HyperTerminal. The HyperTerminal folder opens in a window. Double-click the icon for Hypertrm.exe. The HyperTerminal program starts and displays the Connection Description dialog box as shown in figure 32.8.

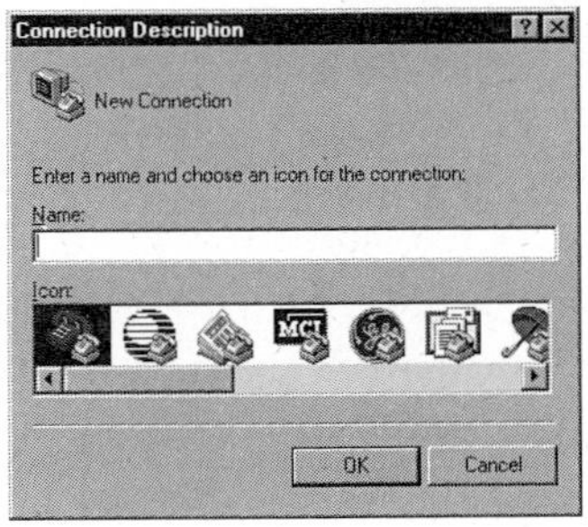

Fig. 32.8 The Connection Description dialog box gathers information about the communications session that will be retained if the session is saved.

Making a Connection with a Remote Computer

After starting HyperTerminal, follow these steps to make a connection with a remote computer:

1. In the Connection Description dialog box, type a name for the connection. The name should describe the location or type of connection in some way, such as *Sales Office, ABC Company,* or *Monthly Upload.*
2. Select an icon to represent the connection.
3. Click OK. The Phone Number dialog box displays as shown in figure 32.9.

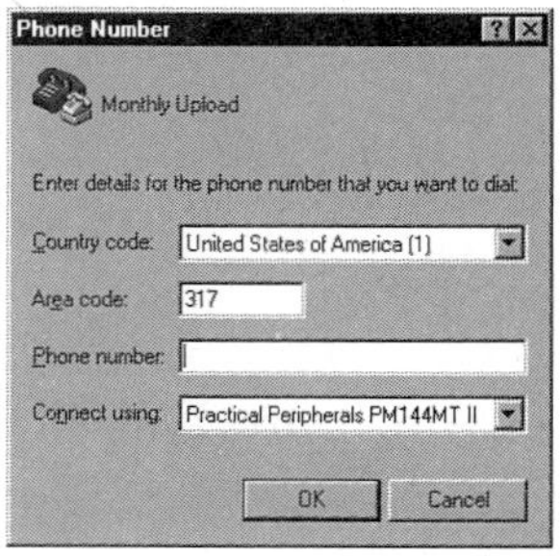

Fig. 32.9 The Phone Number dialog box collects information about the remote PC's telephone number and the modem that you are using.

4. Select the appropriate Country code from the drop-down list.
5. Enter an area code in the Area code text box.
6. Enter the phone number in the Phone number text box.
7. Select the modem you will use from the drop-down list.
8. Click OK and the Connect dialog box displays (figure 32.10).

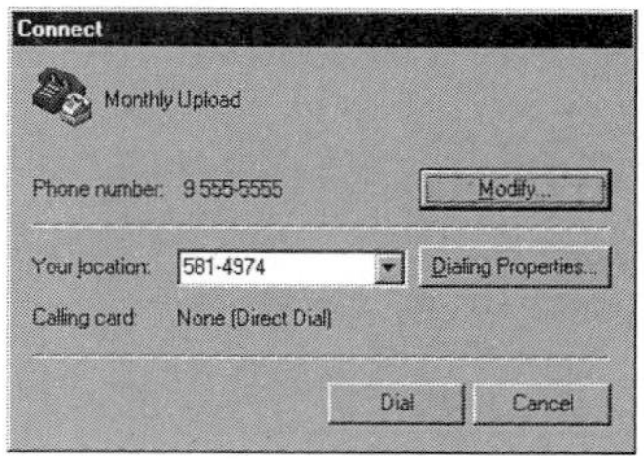

Fig. 32.10 The Connect dialog box contains the information about the number from which you are calling and the way in which you want to make the call.

9. At this point, it is a good idea to check the dialing properties. Although you probably will use the same dialing properties all the time, you may need to change some of the properties for a particular connection. For example, you might need to use a special Calling Card that you are only allowed to use when you make this connection. Enter the appropriate information and make the appropriate selections to describe the way you will make this call. Then click OK. (See "Setting Dialing Properties" earlier in this chapter.)

> **Caution:** If you change the dialing properties, the changes will stay in effect for all other communications, so you may need to change them back to the way they were after you make the connection.

10. Click Dial. The modem dials the number. If a connection is made, connection information is displayed in the HyperTerminal window. If there is no answer or the line is busy, the dialog box displays the word Busy and changes the Dial button to Dial Now.

> **Tip:** If you plan to connect with the same computer repeatedly, save the session so you can use it each time you want to connect.

Disconnecting and Saving a Session

To disconnect, choose Call, Disconnect, or simply click the Disconnect button in the toolbar. HyperTerminal asks if you want to save the session. Click Yes, and the icon will be placed in the HyperTerminal folder automatically. If you want to save the session before you actually make the connection, choose File from the menu bar and choose Save.

Making a Connection with a Saved Session

Use these steps to connect with a remote computer using a saved session.

1. Click Start, point to Programs, point to Accessories, and click HyperTerminal. The HyperTerminal folder opens. Double-click the icon for the session you want to start. The HyperTerminal program starts and displays the Connection dialog box for the selected session.
2. Click Dial. The modem dials the number. If a connection is made, connection information is displayed in the HyperTerminal window. If there is no answer or the line is busy, the dialog box displays the word Busy and changes the Dial button to Dial Now.

Chatting

Once you are connected with another user at a remote PC, you can engage in a real-time conversation (*chatting*) by typing messages back and forth to each other. To send a message to the remote, type the text and press Enter. (The text that you type appears on your screen.) Wait for a response. When the remote user types text and presses Enter, the text will appear on your screen.

Saving or Printing the Text of a Session

Sometimes it is helpful to save the text that appears on your screen during a telecommunications session. For example, if you connect with an unfamiliar bulletin board, you can save both the text that you see and that you type while exploring it. Later you can review the file so that you will be able to maneuver more quickly the next time you connect with the bulletin board. You also can send the text to the printer instead of saving it as a file.

To save the text of a session, choose Transfer from the menu bar. Choose Capture text, type the location and name of a file, and click Start. To print the text, choose Transfer, Capture to Printer. (This option is a toggle and should be turned off when you no longer want to use it.)

Sending a File

Before you can send a file to a remote computer, the remote must prepare for receiving the file. If the remote PC is using Windows 95 HyperTerminal, the remote user prepares to receive the file as described in the next topic. If the remote is using bulletin board software or some other type of telecommunications software, it will have its own routine for preparing to receive a file. Usually, when you upload to a bulletin board, you must select the Upload task from a menu, and then the bulletin board responds by telling you when it is ready.

These steps send a file to the remote computer after a connection has been made.

1. Choose Transfer from the menu bar.
2. Choose Send File.
3. Type the path and name of the file.
4. Select a protocol from the drop-down list. (For information about protocols, refer to Chapter 31, "Serial Communications Basics.")

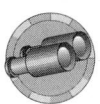

> **Note:** Both computers must use the same protocol.

5. Click Send.

Receiving a File

In order to receive a file from a remote PC, the user of the receiving PC must perform these steps:

1. Choose Transfer from the menu bar.
2. Choose Receive File.
3. Specify the location where the file will be stored.
4. Select a protocol from the drop-down list. (As when sending a file, both computers must use the same protocol when receiving a file.)
5. Click Receive.

Using Terminal Emulation

To communicate with some remote systems, you must have a specific type of terminal because the keys are mapped differently on the terminal than the way the keys are mapped on a PC. HyperTerminal can emulate several different types of terminals including ANSI, Viewdata (for the United Kingdom), Minitel (for France), DEC VT 100, Auto Detect, VT 52, and TTY.

Before starting a telecommunications session that requires a different type of terminal, you can choose the terminal you want HyperTerminal to emulate by choosing File, Properties. Click the tab for the Settings page, and choose an emulation from the drop-down list (see figure 32.11).

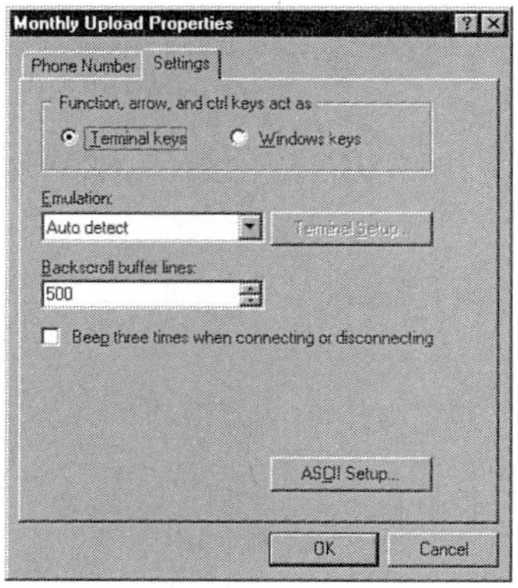

Fig. 32.11 On the Settings page of the Properties sheet, you can choose a different kind of terminal to emulate.

Once a terminal type is selected, click Terminal Setup and choose the appropriate options to set up the terminal. Each terminal uses different options. Options for the VT100, a common terminal, are shown in figure 32.12. The options for the VT100 terminal determine the appearance of the cursor and the way the keypad keys and cursor keys are used, divide the screen into 132 columns instead of 80, and specify the character set that will be used.

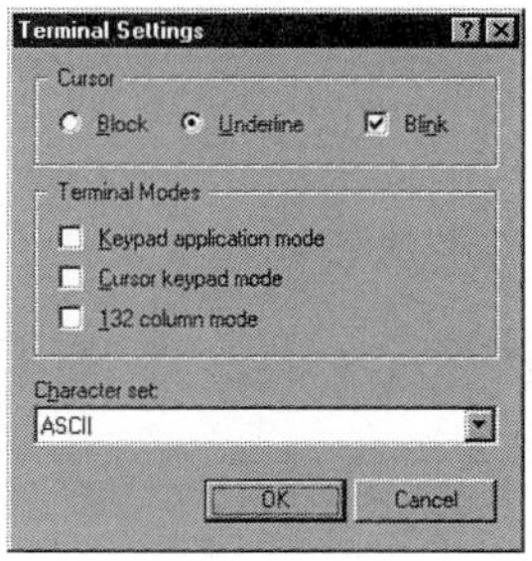

Fig. 32.12 The options for the VT100 terminal direct how your PC should function when emulating a VT100.

Additional options on the Settings page include the following:

- Terminal keys. Uses the terminal functions for the function, arrow, and Control keys.
- Windows key. Uses Windows functions for the function, arrow, and Control keys.
- Backscroll buffer lines. Determines the number of lines that you can scroll to with the PgUp key.
- Beep three times when connecting or disconnecting. Causes your computer to beep three times when it receives a bell signal from the remote.

If you click the ASCII Setup button, the dialog box shown in figure 32.13 displays. Options in this dialog box include:

- Send line ends with line feeds. Sends a carriage return to the remote each time you complete a line by pressing Enter.

- Echo typed characters locally. Displays commands on your computer as you type them.
- Line delay. Specifies the number of milliseconds that a line is delayed before being sent to the remote. (This is an Xon/Xoff-type of control.)
- Character delay. Specifies the number of milliseconds that characters will be delayed before being sent to the remote. (This is another type of Xon/Xoff-type of control.)
- Append line feeds to incoming line ends. Inserts a carriage return at the end of every line that you receive from the remote.
- Force incoming data to 7-bit ASCII. Forces 8-bit ASCII to be translated to 7-bit ASCII.
- Wrap lines that exceed terminal width. Wraps text to the next line if it will not fit in the width used by your PC.

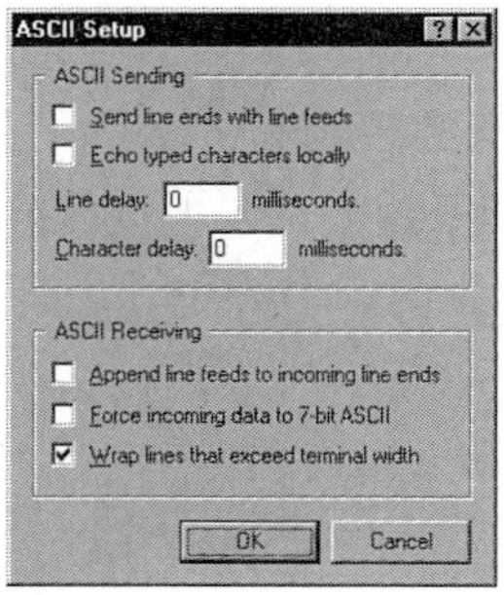

Fig. 32.13 The ASCII Setup dialog box determines how ASCII text is sent and received.

> **Note:** Another way to change the emulation setting is to point to the icon for the session in the HyperTerminal folder, and click the secondary mouse button. Choose Properties, click the tab for the Settings page, and then select the emulation type from the drop-down list.

Using Third-Party Communications Software

Many third-party communications software packages are available for use with modems and fax/modems. Many of these programs do little more than HyperTerminal, while other programs are more sophisticated. Some allow you to set up telecommunication scripts to automate telecommunication sessions by making connections, sending and receiving files, etc., without the intervention of the user.

Any telecommunications software that works with Windows 3.1 should work with Windows 95; however, you can expect to see 32-bit upgrades made to work specifically with Windows 95 to take advantage of preemptive multitasking, as well as other features. Preemptive multitasking is particularly important in the realm of telecommunications, where uploading and downloading files tie up the system.

Understanding Online Services

"Online services," "surfing the information highway," and "cyberspace"—terms that crop up in TV commercials and are casually bandied about by many computer users—still hold a mysterious meaning for many people. These terms are all associated with the new "electronic frontier," in which every home will be wired to online services that let you make bank transfers, purchase groceries, reserve airline tickets, rent movies, video-conference, get sports scores, buy and sell stock, etc., etc. The system that will magically provide all these services will somehow be bound up with a television, a computer, the phone lines, and some other microcombobulator that is not in production yet, but undoubtedly is already in the mind of Bill Gates or one of his cronies.

Many online-service providers are already in place and doing well. The five major commercial services (listed in alphabetical order) are America Online, CompuServe Information Service, Dow Jones News/Retrieval, GEnie, and Prodigy.

Then there's the prodigious Internet, which is not a commercial service at all, but a worldwide network of millions of computers located at universities, government offices, research institutions, and corporations. (For more information about the Internet, see Chapter 35, "Internet Communications.")

A newcomer (but sure to be well-known and popular in a hurry) to online services is Microsoft Network (MSN). The Microsoft Network provides or has plans to provide all the services currently being provided by the established services, and its front-end software is include in Windows 95. (For more information about the MSN, see Chapter 33, "The Microsoft Network.")

If you are a true "killer" computer user, you already know that the online services offer e-mail, downloadable information and software, information forums, chat rooms for real-time conversations, and other miscellaneous services, such as online shopping. In fact, you probably subscribe to several of these services and surf the Internet on a regular basis. For those readers who aspire to the killer-computer-user status, it is mandatory that you get connected. Prodigy, America Online, GEnie, and CompuServe are all favorites of home users.

Most of the online services have several different pricing structures based on the amount of usage and sometimes the speed of the modem. Other costs that may be incurred when using an online service include long distance charges (if you are in an area where a local number cannot be provided) and the cost of front-end software to navigate the service.

> **Note:** Many times, if you buy the front-end program that is sold by the online system, the cost of the software is credited back to you in free connect time.

All of the 16-bit front-end software currently designed to connect with online services works with Windows 95. Soon you can expect to see new 32-bit programs designed to work with Windows 95. You also can expect the online services to provide MAPI drivers to allow them to interact with Microsoft Exchange (i.e., store messages in the Microsoft Exchange universal Inbox). CompuServe already has such a driver, which is included in Windows 95.

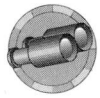

> **Note:** Almost all online services have forums on Windows 95. It is a great place to get information and get help with problems.

Using Microsoft Exchange

Microsoft Exchange is a new network feature of Windows 95. It sends and retrieves messages for members of a Windows workgroup and connects them with many kinds of information services, including Microsoft Mail, Microsoft Fax, and the Microsoft Network. Microsoft Exchange provides one location for all user mail and provides efficient ways to organize and store mail.

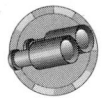

> **Note:** If you install Windows 95 over Windows or Windows for Workgroups, Microsoft Exchange automatically replaces Microsoft Mail or Windows for Workgroups Mail, but it retains your old post office and converts all mail to the new Microsoft Exchange format.

Two important components of Microsoft Exchange are the *Personal Address Book* (PAB) and the *Personal Information Store* (PST). Individual users can set up and maintain their own Personal Address Book, which contains names, phone and fax numbers, mailing addresses, personal contact information, and multiple electronic mail addresses (for different services). Through MAPI interfaces, a PAB can be used by a wide variety of applications.

The Personal Information Store is a database that stores messages, forms, documents, and other information in folders. It functions as the user's local mailbox and organizes and sorts messages.

Starting Microsoft Exchange

There are several ways to start Microsoft Exchange. You can double-click the Inbox on the Windows 95 desktop, select Microsoft Exchange from the Programs menu, or double-click the envelope icon that appears on the Windows 95 taskbar when you get a message. The Microsoft Exchange is shown in figure 32.14.

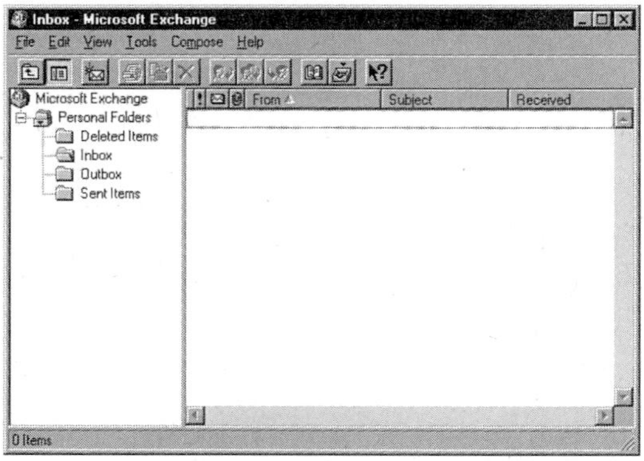

Fig. 32.14 The Microsoft Exchange window is very similar in design to Windows Explorer.

Reading Mail

To read a message that has been sent to Microsoft Exchange, open Microsoft Exchange, click the Inbox in the left pane, and double-click the message that you want to read in the right pane.

Composing and Sending Mail

To compose a new message and send it, follow these steps:

1. Choose Compose, New Message from the menu bar, or click the New Message icon in the toolbar. A screen like the one in figure 32.15 displays. Type the name of the recipient, or click the To button and choose the address name from a list. Click OK.

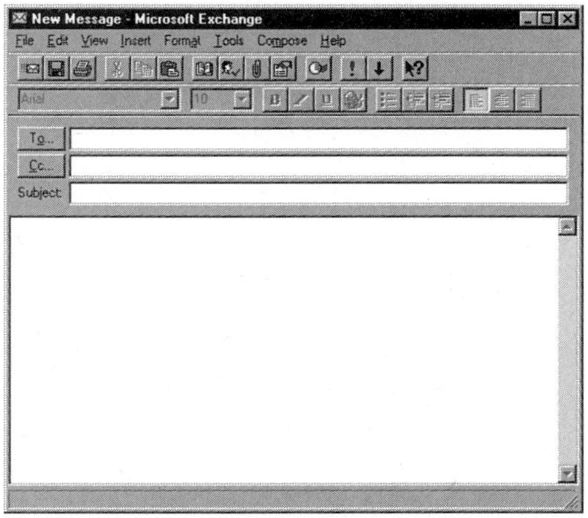

Fig. 32.15 The message screen contains areas for addressing the message, and sending "carbon copies," a subject, and the text of the message.

2. To send copies of the message, type the address names of the recipients, or click the Cc button and select the names from a list. Click OK.

3. Type the subject.

4. Type the message.
5. Choose File, Send from the menu, or click the Send button in the toolbar.

KILLER 33 WINDOWS 95

The Microsoft Network

by Yvonne Johnson

The Microsoft Network (MSN) is the newest entrant in the international electronic information service market. Although it is a new service, it breaks on the scene full-blown. As with CompuServe, Prodigy, and America Online, it has e-mail, product forums, special interest groups, bulletin boards, chat rooms, file libraries, and online shopping, and, of course, it is the single best place to get information and support for Microsoft products. You can also connect with information services that provide news, sports, weather reports, stock information, and so on.

In May of 1995 Microsoft and NBC announced a broad multimedia alliance. As part of the alliance, the announcement said that NBC would build new online services for MSN encompassing all NBC content areas, including NBC Entertainment, NBC Sports, NBC Productions, CNBC, America's Talking, NBC's international ventures, and NBC-owned stations. Additionally, NBC's advertisers and its more

than 200 affiliates would be invited to participate in NBC's service on MSN. The prospects of what the MSN will eventually become are overwhelming.

Before the May 1995 announcement, Microsoft already had an impressive list of companies committed to offering content and services on the MSN. The list is too long to enumerate, but it's filled with names you would recognize immediately, such as American Greetings; Borland International, Inc.; C-SPAN; Corel Systems Corporation; Epson America Inc.; Gateway 2000 Inc.; Hayes Microcomputer Products Inc.; Hewlett-Packard Company; Lotus Development Corporation (now a part of IBM); New York Times Sports Leisure Magazines; Toshiba America Information Systems, Inc.; US News & World Report; and Ziff-Davis Interactive, to name only a few.

Connecting to and Disconnecting from MSN

Before you can connect to MSN, you must install the software. If you did not install MSN in the initial installation, you can do so by using the Windows Setup tab of Add/Remove Programs in the Control Panel dialog box. Of course, you must also have a modem to connect with MSN.

Becoming a Member of MSN

The first time you connect with MSN you'll have the opportunity to become a member. Follow these steps to sign on to MSN and become a member:

1. Double-click on the MSN icon on the desktop. The screen shown in figure 33.1 appears. Click on OK to continue.
2. Enter the area code (if it is not displayed) and the first three digits of the telephone number used by your modem and click on OK. The screen shown in figure 33.2 shows the local access number you'll use to call MSN.

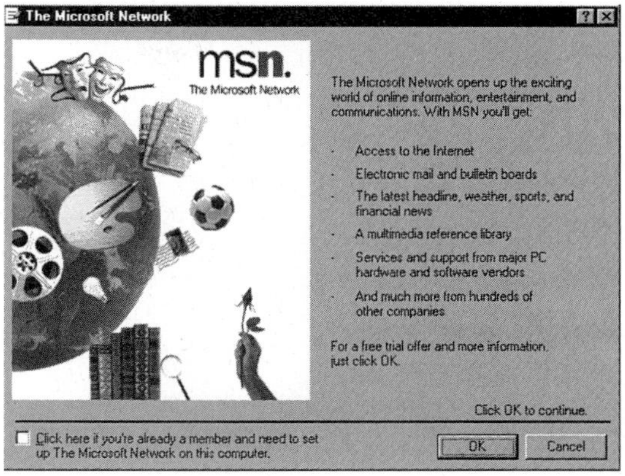

Fig. 33.1 This screen appears the first time you attempt to log on to MSN.

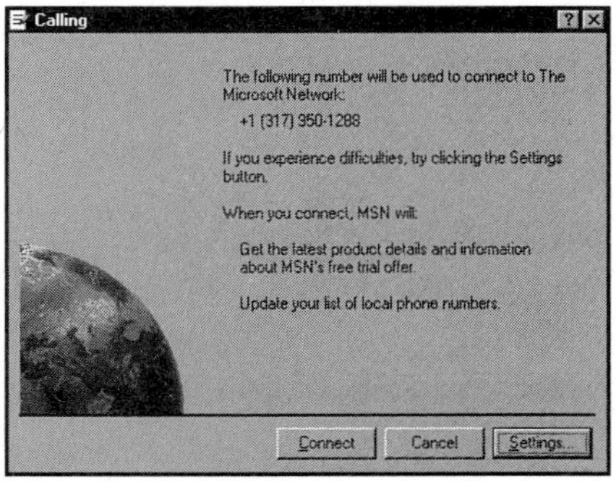

Fig. 33.2 After you have entered your area code and the first three digits of your phone number, you're given an access number.

3. Click on Settings to verify your access numbers, dialing properties, and modem settings as shown in figure 33.3.

   Click on Access Numbers to see the primary and backup numbers that Windows 95 will use to connect you with MSN. If you want to change either the primary or backup number, click on the Change button for either number. Choose the country, state/region, and the access number from the appropriate lists. Click on OK twice.

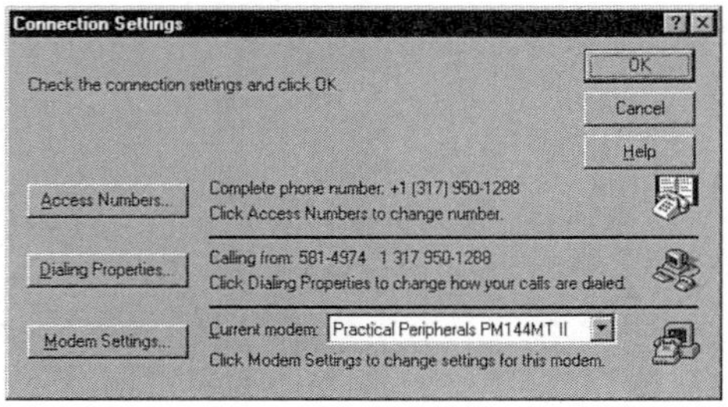

Fig. 33.3 Before logging on, you can change or verify the settings for the access number, dialing properties, and the modem.

Click on Dialing Properties to display the Dialing Properties sheet. Make any changes that you want on this sheet; but remember, these dialing properties are used for all programs that use the modem, including the Phone Dialer, Hyperterminal, third-party software, and so on. When finished, click on OK.

To use a different modem, select a modem from the Current modem drop-down list. Then click on Modem Settings to verify or change the modem configuration. If you make changes to the modem configuration, remember that these settings will be used by any telecommunications program that uses the modem. When finished, click on OK.

Click on OK to return to the Calling window.

4. Click on Connect. Before you start the process, click on the Details button and read the information there about what the MSN contains. Click on Close and then click on Price. Read the pricing information. When finished, click on Close.

   Click Tell for your name and address. Fill in the appropriate information about yourself, click the box in the bottom-left corner if you don't want to receive special promotions from Microsoft, and click on OK.

Click on Next, select a way to pay. Select a credit card from the list, fill in the card number, expiration date, and name on the card, and click on OK.

Click on Then. Read the rules and click on I Agree if you want to continue.

5. Click on Join Now; then click on OK; and finally, click on Connect.

> **Note:** If more than one person uses the PC, you can apply for multiple memberships and each member will be billed as a separate account. To sign up more than one member on one computer, open the Program Files folder, double-click on the Microsoft Network folder, and double-click on the MSN Signup icon. Follow the directions and provide the information about the new member.

Connecting to MSN

You connect to MSN by double-clicking on either the MSN icon on your desktop or on a shortcut to an area of the MSN (see "Getting There the Fastest Way," later in this chapter). The Sign In dialog box appears as shown in figure 33.4. If you have previously signed on to MSN and entered your member ID and password, your member ID appears by default. If Remember my password is marked, the password (represented by asterisks) is also displayed by default. If Remember my password is not selected, you must enter your password each time you log on to MSN. (If other people use your computer, you may not want to select Remember my password.) Click on Connect. The screen called MSN Central appears, as shown in figure 33.5.

Note: Your password must be at least eight but no more than 16 characters long. Passwords may use only the following characters: A through Z (upper- or lowercase), 0 through 9, and a hyphen (-).

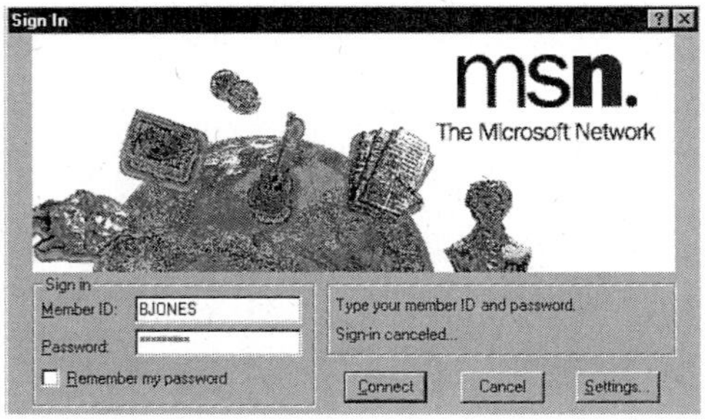

Fig. 33.4 The Sign In dialog box lists the password (with asterisks) by default because Remember my password is checked.

When you dial into MSN, you're actually dialing the number of a network provider. Network providers have local nodes all over the world that allow users to connect to MSN by making a local phone call. After you're connected to the network provider, the provider further connects you to the MSN Data Center by using a high-speed network that is much faster than phone lines. The MSN Data Center is where the actual exchange of information between your computer and the network takes place.

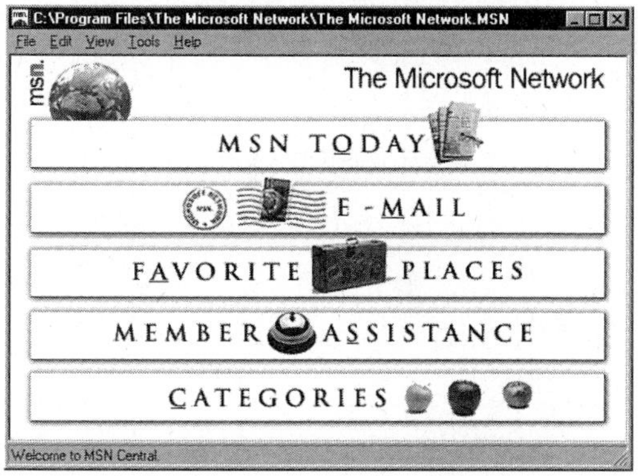

Fig. 33.5 The MSN Central screen displays when you connect with MSN.

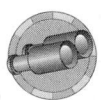

> **Note:** From time to time, Microsoft will upgrade the MSN software. When you log on to MSN, the system checks your network software version in the Registry to see whether it's the latest version. If it isn't, you're prompted to upgrade. You must accept the upgrade, or you won't be able to log on to MSN. After you click on Yes, the files download and you must restart the PC to complete the upgrade.

Changing Your Password

To change your password, log on to MSN and choose Tools, Password. Type your current password, type your new password, type your new password again, and then click on OK.

Disconnecting from MSN

There are several ways to initiate disconnecting from the network:

- Click on the Sign Out button in the toolbar.
- Choose File, Sign Out from the menu bar.
- Point to the Connection Indicator (MSN) in the status bar (next to the time) and click the secondary mouse button. Choose Sign Out.
- Close all windows.

If you choose any of the preceding methods, MSN displays a prompt asking if you want to disconnect from the network. Select Yes.

Exploring MSN Central

The MSN Central screen has a menu bar, five categories, and a toolbar. The categories include MSN Today, E-Mail, Favorite Places, Member Assistance, and Categories. Each category is covered in the following sections.

MSN Today

MSN Today is an information screen that changes from day to day. It usually has an inviting tidbit about something you can access on the network and a shortcut that will take you right to it. MSN Today may have daily highlights, tips, links to other MSN services, and previews of upcoming services. To see what's scheduled on MSN for the week, click on Calendar of Events. The calendar shows dates, times, and places for scheduled events. Examples include Bi-weekly Moderated Comedy Chats in LuLu's Lounge, OS/2 Chat in the OS/2 chat room, and Recovery Chat: Getting Free of Nicotine in the Recovery chat room.

E-Mail

E-Mail starts Microsoft Exchange, which enables you to send or receive e-mail messages to and from MSN members or anyone with a mailbox on the Internet (if you have the Plus Pak). Although Microsoft Exchange also provides other services, such as faxing, you would not want to use valuable time online to do anything with Microsoft Exchange except exchange e-mail. For more information about the capabilities of Microsoft Exchange, see Chapter 34, "Using Microsoft Exchange."

Favorite Places

Favorite Places is empty when you first sign on to MSN. It is a location where you can store shortcuts to your favorite places on the network.

Member Assistance

Member Assistance has topics to help you get started using the MSN. It has a user's guide, billing information, frequently asked questions (FAQs), and so on. Member Assistance is a good place to start if you're unfamiliar with online services or you have a particular question about using the service.

Categories

Categories is a list of the broad general categories of services and information on the network. Another name used for a broad general category is *forum*. Each category has several subcategories, which may also have several subcategories, and so on. The structure of the network is just like the hierarchical structure of a hard disk. In fact, if you use the explore mode, as explained later in this chapter, the structure of MSN is represented by folders.

The Menu Bar

The menu bar has five options: File, Edit, View, Tools, and Help. The options in these drop-down menus vary depending on where you are in MSN.

The Toolbar

The toolbar found on the MSN Central screen has the following drop-down list and buttons: Go to a different folder (drop-down list), Up One Level, Go to MSN Central, Go to Favorite Places, and Sign Out. Table 33.1 shows the buttons and what they do.

Table 33.1 Buttons on the Toolbar

Icon	Name	Description
	Go to a different folder	Displays the hierarchy of folders on MSN.
	Up One Level	Move up one level in the hierarchy. (MSN Central is as high as you go in the hierarchy, so this button has no use on the MSN Central screen unless you are using the Windows Explorer mode.)
	Go to MSN Central	Takes you back to the MSN Central screen.
	Go to Favorite Places	Opens Favorite Places.
	Sign Out	Logs off the network.

Navigating the Network by Using My Computer

Microsoft provides two interfaces for the Microsoft Network. One is similar to My Computer—this is the default—and the other is similar to Windows Explorer. Because both interfaces should be familiar to Windows 95 users, navigating the Microsoft Network is relatively easy.

When you connect to MSN by double-clicking on the MSN icon on the desktop, the MSN Central screen appears. This is the My Computer mode. To open any of the five areas on the MSN Central screen, click anywhere inside the rectangle that borders the title. For example, to open Categories, click inside the rectangle at the bottom of the screen. A window (like My Computer) opens that contains icons for the various forums offered. (An icon that leads to other topics is represented by a folder. An icon that opens a service has an appropriate symbol, like an "i" in a blue circle for information kiosk.)

You'll notice that a forum window also has a toolbar with the same buttons found on the MSN Central screen plus these additional buttons: Properties, Add to favorite places, Large icons, Small icons, List, and Details.

Graphic	Name	Description
	Properties	Displays the Properties sheet.
	Add to Favorite Places	Adds a shortcut for the selected item in the Favorite Places area.
	Large icons	Changes the icons to large icons.
	Small icons	Changes the icons to small icons.
	List	Changes the icons to a list.
	Details	Changes the icons to a list with details.

To show how easy it is to navigate the network, click on Categories on the MSN Central screen. The Categories window opens, as shown in figure 33.6. Double-click on Business & Finance and a window appears as shown in figure 33.7. Double-click on Small Office/Home Office and a window appears as shown in figure 33.8. Double-click on SOHO Advisors and a window appears as shown in figure 33.9. Double-click on Janet Attard Business Know-How and a window appears as shown in figure 33.10. Double-click on Business Know-How Reports BBS, and the topics posted on the bulletin board appear as shown in figure 33.11. You can move back up a level in the hierarchy at any time by clicking the Up One Level button, or you can return to MSN Central by clicking the Go to MSN Central button.

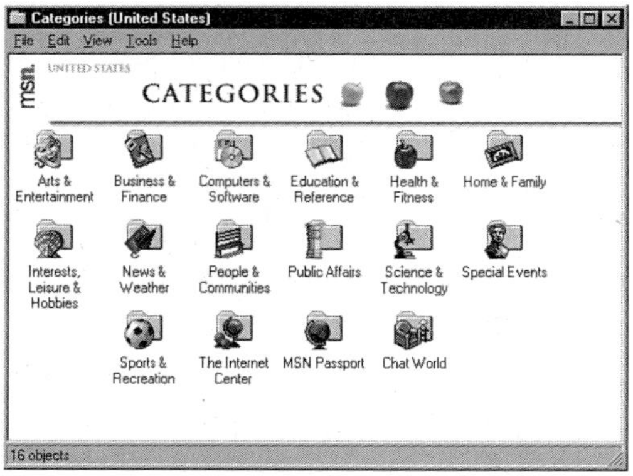

Fig. 33.6 The Categories window shows the broad, general topics on MSN.

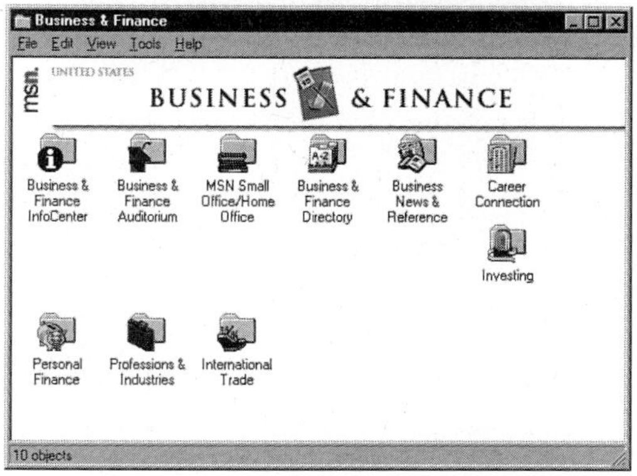

Fig. 33.7 The Business and Finance window shows a variety of topics.

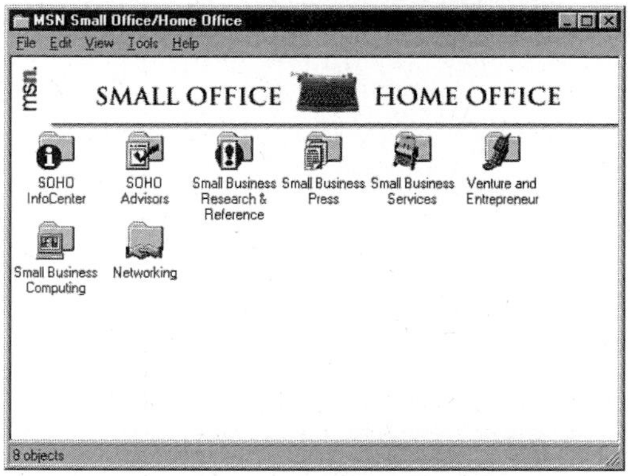

Fig. 33.8 The Small Office/Home Office window has topics specific to starting a new business, business services, education, and so on.

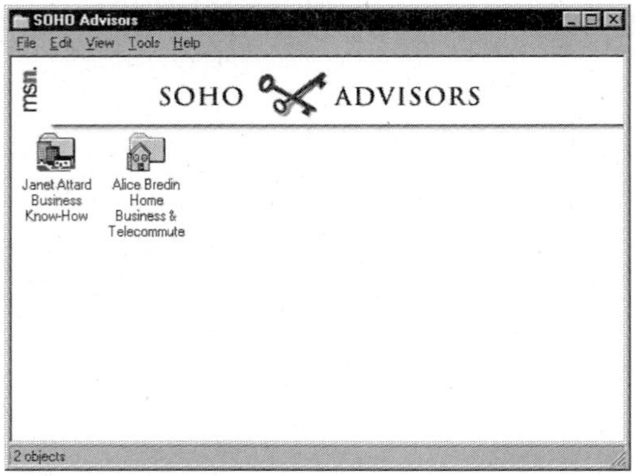

Fig. 33.9 The SOHO Advisors window lists two sources of information for small offices and home offices.

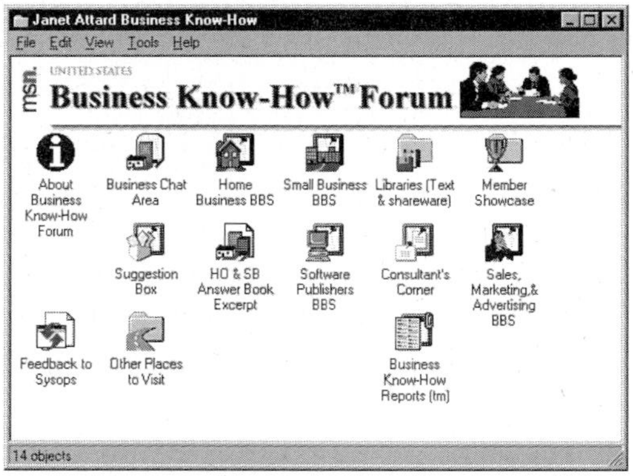

Fig. 33.10 The Janet Attard Business Know-How window lists the topics covered by the author, Janet Attard, in her Business Know-How forum.

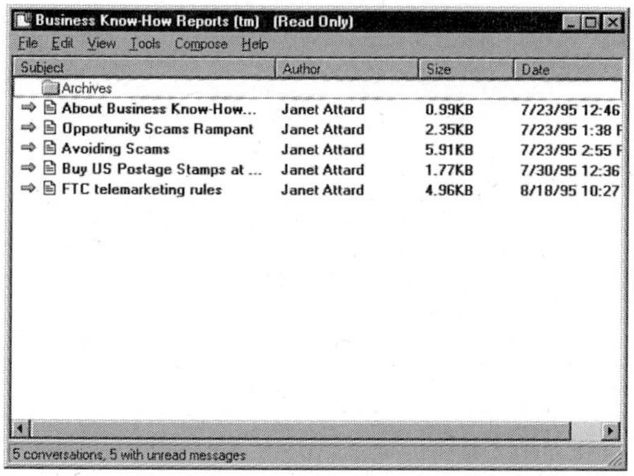

Fig. 33.11 The messages on the Business Know-How Reports bulletin board are listed in order by date.

Navigating the Network by Using the Explorer

To start MSN in the Windows Explorer mode, point to the MSN icon on the desktop and click the right mouse button. Choose Explore. When the Sign In screen appears, enter your password if necessary and then click on Connect. The MSN Central screen looks like figure 33.12. Now, take the same route through the hierarchy to get to the Home Business by using the left pane of the window. First, click on the plus sign (+) beside Categories in the left pane. Then click on the plus sign (+) beside Business and Finance. Click on the plus sign beside Small Office/ Home Office. Click on the plus sign beside SOHO Advisors. At this point, you might want to make the left pane wider so you can see all the text. Click on the plus sign beside Janet Attard Business Know-How. Click Home Business BBS. The messages posted on the bulletin board appear in the right pane as shown in figure 33.13.

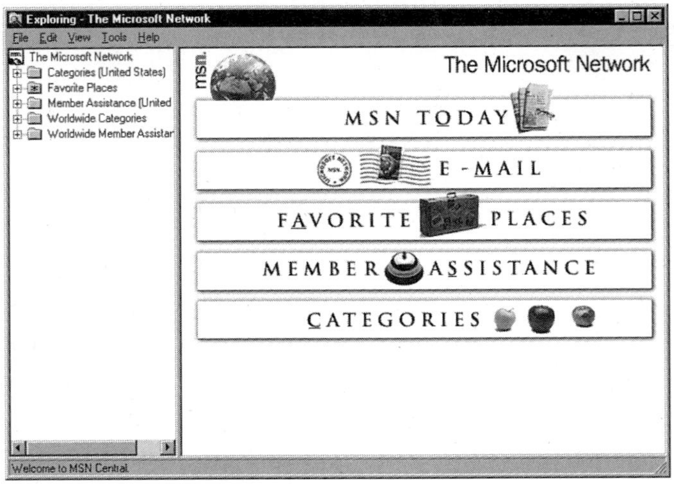

Fig. 33.12 The Windows Explorer mode for MSN uses the familiar two-pane view.

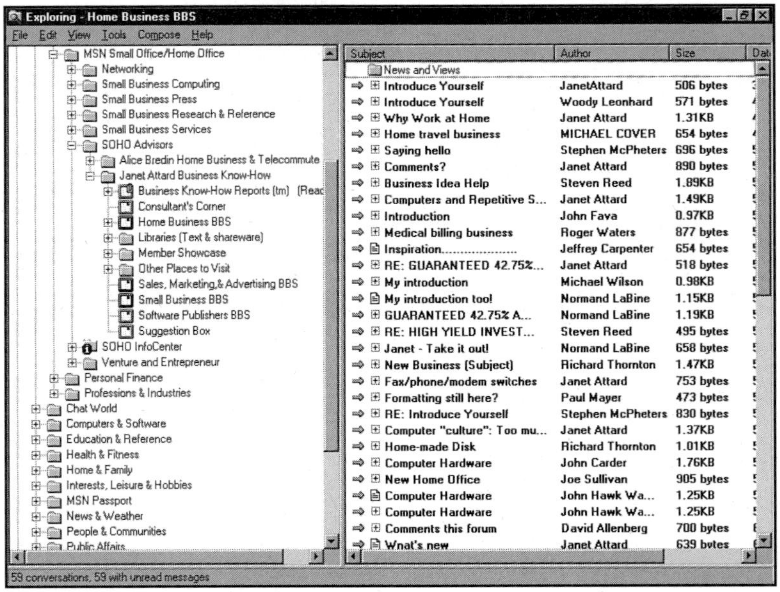

Fig. 33.13 Messages in the Home Business bulletin board appear in the right pane.

Getting General Information about Forums and Services

Because Windows 95 now uses long file names, the names of forums and services are usually very explanatory. However, if the name does not give you a good clue to the content of the folder or service, you can look at the Properties sheet. To view the Properties sheet, right-click on the icon for the folder or service and click on the Properties button in the pop-up menu. Figure 33.14 shows the Properties sheet for the Science and Technology category. It lists the scope of the forum as math, science, biology, engineering, and so on.

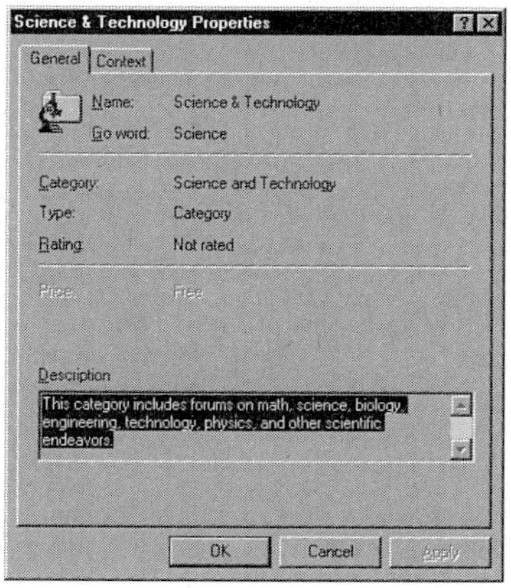

Fig. 33.14 The Properties sheet for the Science and Technology category describes the scope of the category.

Getting There the Fastest Way

Whenever you find a place or a program that you want to return to frequently, you'll want some way to get there quickly. You can do so by choosing one of three methods: adding the folder or service to Favorite Places, creating a shortcut, or using a Go word.

Adding to Favorite Places

It's simple to add an area to Favorite Places; just select the icon and click on the Add to Favorite Places button in the toolbar. The next time you return to the MSN Central screen and click on Favorite Places, you'll see an icon for the favorite place you added. When you double-click on the icon in Favorite Places, the folder or service opens. When the folder or service is open, you can click on the Up One Level button in the toolbar, to return to Favorite Places, not to the parent folder of the folder or service.

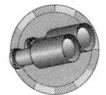

> **Note:** If you want to delete one of your favorite places, select the icon and choose File, Delete. The original icon from which the favorite place came is NOT deleted—only the favorite place icon is removed.

Creating a Shortcut

To create a shortcut, select the folder or service and choose File, Create Shortcut. A verification message appears telling you that a shortcut has been successfully created and placed on your desktop. Click on OK. Alternatively, you can just drag the icon for the MSN folder or service to the desktop.

Double-clicking the shortcut displays the MSN sign on-screen. When you click on Connect, the folder or service opens immediately, bypassing the MSN Central screen.

> **Note:** To delete a shortcut on the desktop, use one of these three methods: point to the shortcut, click the right mouse button, choose Delete, and then click on Yes; click on the shortcut to select it, and press Delete; drag the shortcut icon to the Recycle Bin icon.

Using a Go Word

A Go word takes you directly to a folder or service on the network. Go words are listed on the folder or services' Properties sheet. To see the properties sheet, select the folder or service, and click on the Properties button in the toolbar.

To use a Go word, choose Edit, Goto, Other Location. Type the Go word and click on OK.

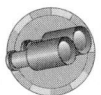

> **Note:** When you first go to an area in MSN, the icons used in that area download to a file in Program Files\The Microsoft Network\Cache. The next time you go to that area, the service will be faster because it accesses the files in the cache.

Setting Up MSN

You have only a few options for setting up the Microsoft Network. To locate these options, choose View, Options from the menu bar. The Options dialog box displays with the General tab selected as shown in figure 33.15.

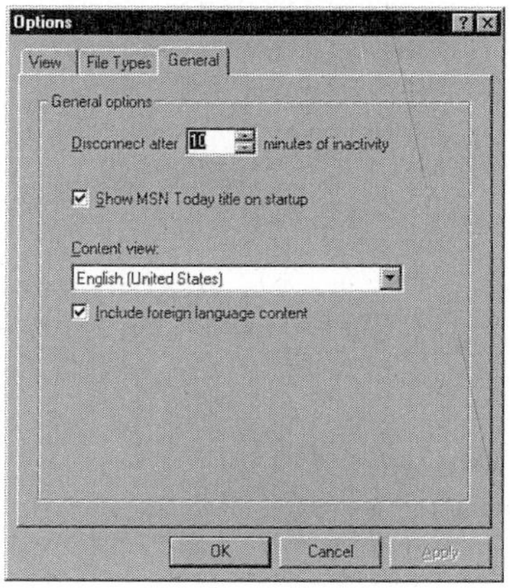

Fig. 33.15 Set the idle time in the Microsoft Network Options dialog box so that you are prompted at a reasonable time before MSN automatically disconnects.

Notice that the options include the amount of time that MSN can be inactive before you're prompted to disconnect, whether you want to see the MSN Today screen when you start MSN, what language to use for the content, and whether or not you want to include foreign language in messages, chat rooms, and so on.

Other pages in the Options sheet include View, File Types, and Folder. These properties sheets should be familiar to you because they are the same ones used by My Computer and Windows Explorer. Figure 33.16 shows the View page.

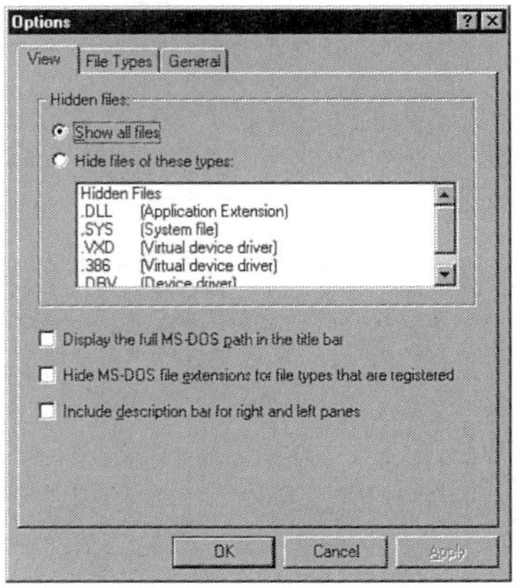

Fig. 33.16 The View page of the Options Properties sheet is just the same in MSN as it is on the Windows 95 desktop.

Exploring Kiosks

A *kiosk* is a read-only file that has information about a particular area. The file may include a summary of what is in the category, information about updates, what's new, and so on. The file is always represented by a blue circle with a white letter "i" icon. For example, the Albion Channel kiosk explains what the Albion Channel is, who is hosting the online service, and what its goals are. The Albion Channel is hosted by Albion Books, a San Francisco-based publisher of computer networking books and related online services. When you open a kiosk, it opens a document in WordPad or, if Microsoft Word is installed, in Word.

Exploring Bulletin Boards

In addition to its own bulletin boards, MSN also provides access to the Internet bulletin boards (called newsgroups). MSN carries two kinds of bulletin boards:

- Read-only boards that do not allow you to post messages or replies.
- Read-write boards that allow you to post messages and replies. Most MSN bulletin boards fall into this category.

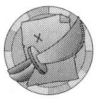

> **Tip:** You can recognize an Internet bulletin board by its name. The name (always lowercase) has a period in it, as in misc.biz.

A file library is a special kind of bulletin board that has files, such as useful software programs, that you can download. There may be a fee for copying some files. Be sure to check the file's properties before downloading to see if there is a charge.

Every MSN bulletin board has a manager who monitors and maintains the board. If you need to discuss an issue about the way a bulletin board is being run, you can send messages directly to the manager. If the bulletin boards are Internet bulletin boards, they may or may not have a manager.

Reading Messages

By default, messages are listed on a bulletin board in ascending order by date, but you can sort on any column (subject, author, size, or date) by clicking on the column heading. Click on the column heading again to sort in the other direction. Also by default, the bulletin board window shows only the messages that have accumulated since the most recently read message. If you want to see all the messages, choose Tools, Show All Messages. The number of messages displays in the status bar.

Messages with a plus sign (+) beside them have replies. This is called a conversation or a thread. To see all the replies in a conversation, press Shift and click on the plus sign to expand the message. To expand all messages, choose View, Expand All Conversations.

To open a message on a bulletin board, double-click on the message. (You may have to scroll through the list of messages if it is long.) Figure 33.17 shows an open message. Notice that message screens have their own toolbar. See Table 33.2 for an explanation of the buttons in the toolbar.

> **Tip**: Press Home to go to the first message in the list and End to go to the last message.

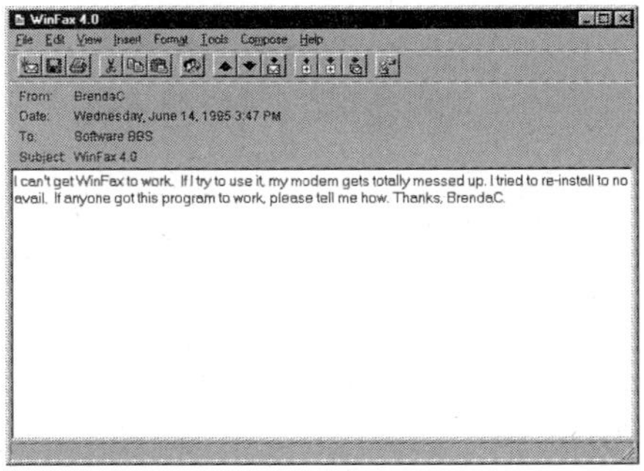

Fig. 33.17 This message is a request for help in a software forum.

Table 33.2 Buttons on Message Screens

Graphic	Name	Description
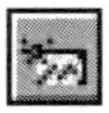	New Message	Opens a screen for creating a new message

Graphic	Name	Description
	Save	Save the current message as a file
	Print	Prints the current message
	Cut	Cuts the selected text to the Clipboard
	Copy	Copies the selected text to the Clipboard
	Paste	Pastes the contents of the Clipboard at the cursor location
	Reply to BBS	Opens a screen for creating a reply to the current message
	Previous	Displays the previous message
	Next	Displays the next message
	Next Unread Message	Displays the next unread message
	Previous Conversation	Displays the previous conversation
	Next Conversation	Displays the next conversation
	Next Unread Message	Displays the next unread message
	File Transfer Status	Displays the status of a file transfer

Tip: To find out more about the sender of a message, open the message and choose Tools, Member Properties. Or just double-click on the sender's name.

Replying to a Message

You can post a reply to a message on the bulletin board, or you can send the reply directly to the author of the message by e-mail. To send a reply to the bulletin board, open the message and click on the Reply button in the toolbar (or choose Compose, Reply to BBS). Type the reply in the space provided and then click on the Post button.

To send a reply by e-mail, open the message and click on Compose, Reply by E-mail. Type the reply and click on the Send button.

To forward a message to someone else, open the message and click on Compose, Forward by E-Mail. Type the recipient's name and click the Send button.

Posting a New Message

When you want to post a new message on a bulletin board, open the board and click on the New Message button. Type the message in the space provided and click on the Send button. You may not see your message posted immediately—posting sometimes takes a few minutes.

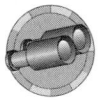

> **Note:** The Microsoft Network does not notify you when you receive a reply to a message you've posted. You must physically check the bulletin board for a reply. If you've left several messages at different times on the same bulletin board, you can sort the messages by author so that all your messages are listed together.

Downloading Files

To download a file from a bulletin board message, follow these steps:

1. Open the message that contains the file you want to download.
2. Click on the file's icon. Choose Edit, File Object, Properties to see how large the file is, how long it will take to copy, and whether there is a fee for copying the file.

3. Click on the Download File button. The File Transfer Status dialog box appears. This dialog box has a progress bar that shows how much of the file has been downloaded and tells approximately how much time remains until the remainder of the file is downloaded.

> **Tip:** You also can copy a file by dragging the file icon in a message to your desktop or to a window or folder on your desktop.

Setting Options for Downloading

By default, files are downloaded to \Programs Files\The Microsoft Network\Transferred Files. You can specify the path for downloaded files and other options for downloading files by choosing Tools, File Transfer Status. Choose Tools again and then choose Options. The download options include:

- Pause files as they are queued. If this option is selected, you must select each file in the queue and click Pause to start the download. If this option is not selected, files in the queue are downloaded automatically.
- Delete compressed file after decompressing. Deletes zipped files after they are downloaded and decompressed.
- Automatically decompress files. Decompresses zipped files automatically when they are downloaded.

If you click on Browse, you can select a different folder for the default download folder.

Exploring Chat Rooms

A chat room (see figure 33.18) is an area where a "live" conversation takes place on a particular subject. However, because chat rooms are live conversations, they are just as likely to stray into other subjects as a conversation at a party. If a chat room is monitored, it has a host. The host, if there is one, is indicated in the list on the right side with a gavel icon, and he or she can designate members as participants or spectators. If there is no host, all members who join a chat room are participants. Their names are also listed on the right.

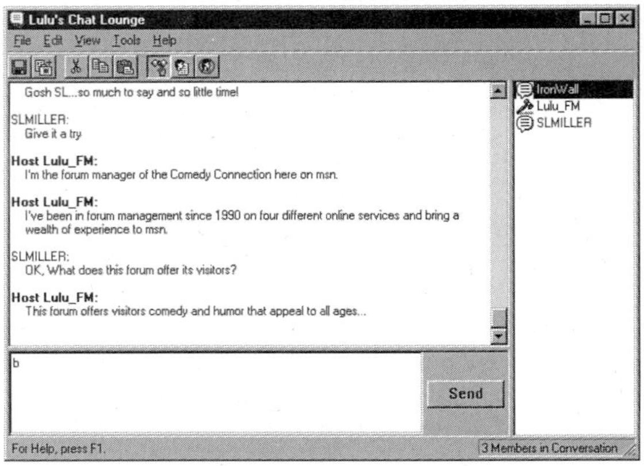

Fig. 33.18 This chat room is called LuLu's Lounge and currently has several participants as well as a host.

When you join a chat room, people who are already in the chat room see your name on the list. If a member of the chat has set the option to be notified when someone joins the chat, the member will see a message on the screen that says you've joined the conversation. To find out more about people in the chat room, you can view the person's properties. Double-click on the person's name in the list (or select the name in the list and then click on the Member Properties button).

To send a message, type the message in the lower pane and click on Send (or press Enter). If you type a message that exceeds the maximum number of characters, the computer will beep.

If a chat member sends you a message filled with question marks, the chat member is using a language (like Kanji, for example) that uses the

Double Byte Character Set (DBCS). English-speaking chat rooms use the Single Byte Character Set (SBCS). When a DBCS text string is sent into an SBCS chat session, MSN converts all the characters to question marks.

> **Note:** The DBCS was introduced to handle languages that have too many characters to be defined by the standard ASCII and ANSI character sets.

Setting Chat Options

To set the options for a chat room, choose Tools, Options. The Options dialog box has the following settings:

- Join the chat. Displays a message when a person joins the chat.
- Leave the chat. Displays a message when a person leaves the chat.
- Save chat history before clearing or exiting. Prompts you to save the chat if you try to clear or exit without saving.
- Insert blank line between messages. Inserts a blank line between the messages.

Saving a Chat

If you're involved in a particularly interesting chat or a chat with a famous person, you may want to save the chat. To save a chat, choose File, Save History. Type a name for the file and click on Save. You can start saving a chat at any point during the chat.

To make sure that you don't forget to save a chat, choose Tools, Options, and make sure that Save chat history before clearing or exiting is checked. Then if you try to exit without saving, you will be reminded to save with a prompt.

Scheduled Chats with Famous People

Quite often chats will be scheduled with well-known people, including authors, actors, O.J. Simpson's attorneys, Microsoft moguls, and so forth. Look for these chats in the Calendar of Events on MSN Today as well as in the forum most closely associated with the subject. If you can't participate in the chat because it's scheduled at a bad time for you, you usually can get a transcript of the chat by downloading a file that is posted in a given area.

Sending E-Mail

To send an e-mail message, click on E-Mail on MSN Central. The Microsoft Exchange opens. Compose and send the message as you normally would. (See Chapter 34, "Using Microsoft Exchange.")

Finding Topics of Interest

The Find command, located in the Tools menu of MSN or on the Start menu, helps you locate topics of interest on the MSN. Figure 33.19 shows the Find: All MSN services dialog box. In Containing, type a keyword for the topic you want to find, such as "communications." Select one or all of the In options (Name; Topic, place and people; or Description). To select a type of service, click on the Of type drop-down list. When you've specified the search criteria, click on Find Now. The results of the search appear in the pane at the bottom of the window. To go to a location listed in the pane, double-click on the pane.

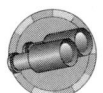

> **Note:** If you use the Find command when MSN is not open, the Sign In screen appears and you'll have to log on to MSN before the search can be started.

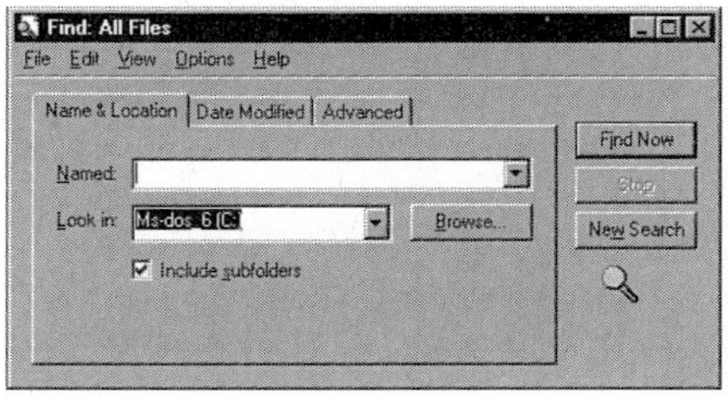

Fig. 33.19: The Find: All MSN services dialog box allows you to specify a keyword to search for on the network.

Problems You Might Encounter

If you boot Windows 95 in the Safe mode, you won't be able to connect to the MSN because the path to the MSN is not set up. The message `Modem is busy or cannot be found` will appear. To solve the problem, reboot Windows 95.

If you connect to another computer in a LAN that has MSN, you won't be able to run MSN from that computer. MSN components don't support being shared across LANs. You must run MSN locally.

Finally, don't drag the MSN icon from the desktop to the Start menu. If you do, MSN will not start, and you'll have to reinstall it.

Checking Your Bill

To see the charges on your bill, choose Tools, Billing, and Summary of Charges. Click on the Get Details button. Select the billing period and click on OK. When you're finished looking at your charges, click on the Close button.

To change the billing information, choose Tools, Billing, Payment method. Click on Name and address. Make changes as needed to your name, address, and phone number and click OK.

To change the billing method, choose Tools, Billing, Payment method. Click on Payment method. Choose the credit card you want to use from the drop-down list. Fill in the card information (card number, expiration date, and name on the card) and click on OK.

Using Microsoft Exchange

by Yvonne Johnson

Microsoft Exchange is a new network feature of Windows 95 that replaces Windows for Workgroups Mail and Microsoft Mail. It has been dubbed "the universal inbox" because you can communicate (send and receive messages) with members of a Windows workgroup as well as with many kinds of information services, including Microsoft Mail, Microsoft Fax, Internet Mail, and the Microsoft Network (MSN). In addition, Microsoft Exchange is able to communicate with other online services like CompuServe if they have MAPI (Messaging API) drivers. A MAPI driver, like a gateway, specifies all the connection and addressing settings needed to communicate with a network on one end and with Windows 95 on the other end. The MAPI drivers must be obtained from the online services; they are not provided by Microsoft.

Microsoft Exchange takes the place of third-party software that accesses, schedules, routes, and organizes e-mail. Microsoft Exchange does it all. You can send messages to anyone with an online address,

schedule logons to services like CompuServe, route your mail with address books, and view various information about incoming mail.

If you install Windows 95 in the former Windows or Windows for Workgroups folder, Microsoft Exchange automatically replaces Windows for Workgroups Mail or Microsoft Mail 3.2, and all MMF files are automatically converted to the Microsoft Exchange format (PST). Additionally, if you install Windows 95 over Windows for Workgroups, the workgroup postoffice is retained for use with Microsoft Exchange.

When you install Microsoft Exchange, either during the initial installation or as an add-on later, the Microsoft Exchange Setup Wizard guides you in configuring Microsoft Exchange and setting up a profile.

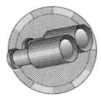

> **Note:** If you install Microsoft Exchange during the initial installation of Windows 95, the Microsoft Exchange Setup Wizard appears at the end of Setup. Unless you already have a postoffice created from Windows for Workgroups, you will not have had an opportunity to create a postoffice, and when you're prompted to enter the path for the postoffice, you'll have to cancel the wizard. When you cancel, the wizard tells you that you can set up the postoffice and then configure Microsoft Exchange any time by double-clicking on the Inbox icon on the desktop.

Setting Up the Microsoft Exchange Postoffice

The Microsoft Workgroup Postoffice Admin Wizard helps you configure the postoffice; but before you start the Wizard, you should decide where the postoffice will be stored. It can reside on any computer in the workgroup, but the computer should have at least 2M of storage space and more than 4M of memory. The disk space available on the postoffice PC should be expandable because more space will be needed as the number of users and messages increases.

Tip: If you have more than 20 users, consider using a dedicated PC for the Postoffice. If you have more than 100 users, you should upgrade to the full Microsoft Mail Server.

Creating the Postoffice

To set up a postoffice, follow these steps:

1. Open the Control Panel and double-click on the Microsoft Mail Postoffice icon. The Microsoft Workgroup Postoffice Admin Wizard appears.
2. In the Microsoft Workgroup Postoffice Admin dialog box, click on Create A New Workgroup Postoffice and then click on Next.
3. Specify where you want the workgroup postoffice to be located and click on Next.
4. The wizard displays the path and asks you to verify the path. Accept or change the path (as needed) and click on Next. The Enter Your Administrator Account Details dialog box appears.
5. Type information about the postoffice administrator, including name and mailbox name, and a password to restrict administration of the postoffice to the administrator. Click on OK to finish creating the postoffice. A message appears that advises you to make sure the folder that contains the postoffice is a shared folder. Click on OK.

Caution: If you create more than one postoffice for your workgroup, the users will not be able to send mail to each other.

Sharing the Folder That Contains the Postoffice

1. Open Windows Explorer or My Computer, point to the folder for the workgroup postoffice, and click on the right mouse button. Choose Sharing. The Sharing page of the Properties sheet appears. It looks like figure 34.1 if access control is set on user-level.

> **Note:** If no Sharing option appears on the shortcut menu, you have not enabled the network property of file sharing. Open the Control Panel, double-click on Network, click on the File and Print Sharing button, and mark I want to be able to give others access to my files.

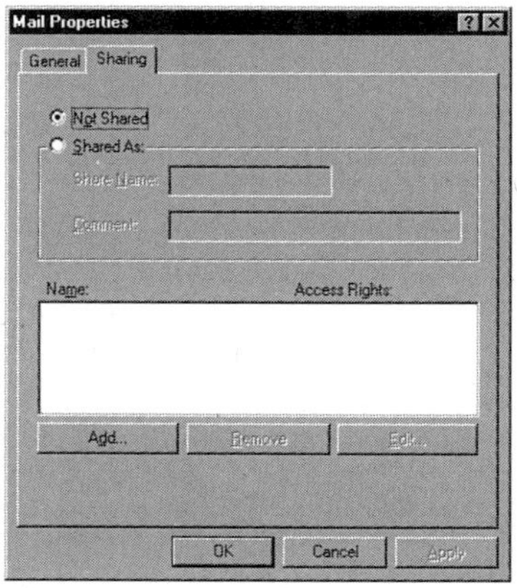

Fig. 34.1 The Sharing page of the postoffice folder Properties sheet allows you to specify the names of users if access control is set on user-level.

2. In the Sharing folder, click on Shared As and verify the name of the postoffice in the Share Name field. You can also add a comment in the Comment field. The comment shows when you open

Network Neighborhood and look at a list of computers on the network (if you're using the Detail view).

3. If access control is set on share-level, choose the Access Type that you prefer.

   ➤ **Read Only**—Allows users to read and copy files.

   ➤ **Full-Access—**Allows users to read, copy, change, add, and remove files.

   ➤ **Depends on Password**—Allows you to specify different types of access for different users.

   Type the passwords that you require in the Read-Only Password field and/or the Full-Access Password field. Click OK.

   If access control is set on user-level, click on the Add button to add people to the access list.

4. Click on OK.

> **Note:** Although Microsoft Exchange can send and receive messages in the same postoffice, it cannot communicate between postoffices; that is, it cannot communicate with another workgroup. The full Microsoft Mail Server is required for this.

Setting Up Profiles for Users

Before you can use Microsoft Exchange, you must have a profile, and every person who uses the PC should have a unique profile. The profile includes the location of a user's postoffice, Personal Address Book, and Personal Information Store, and the types of services available to the user, such as Microsoft Mail, the Microsoft Network, faxing, and so on. When Microsoft Exchange is set up initially, the Setup Wizard creates a profile at the end of the setup routine; however, it is necessary to set up another profile if there is another user on the machine.

To create another profile, follow these steps:

1. Open the Control Panel and double-click on the Mail and FAX icon. The MS Exchange Settings Properties sheet appears showing the Services page, which lists the services for the default profile.
2. Click on Show Profiles. The Microsoft Exchange Profiles dialog box appears with a list of all the profiles defined on the computer. (You can see what a profile includes by selecting a profile and clicking on Properties.)
3. Click on Add. The Microsoft Exchange Setup Wizard starts.
4. Make selections as prompted and click on Next to advance to the next screen. The prompts vary depending on which information services you add to the profile, but they'll include user name, mailbox name, user password, and the locations of the Personal Address Book and the Personal Information Store. (The properties of all services are discussed later in this chapter if you have any questions about what settings you should make for a service.)

After the profile is created it is listed on the General page of the Microsoft Exchange Profiles dialog box. You should select the profile and click on Properties to configure the services included in the profile. To configure a service, select the service and then click on the Properties button.

Specifying Internet Mail Properties

Internet Mail is offered as a service only if you've installed the Internet Jumpstart Kit in Microsoft Plus! When you install the Internet Jumpstart Kit, a wizard helps you configure it at that time. To reconfigure the Internet Mail Properties after the installation, choose the service in the desired profile and click on the Properties button. The Properties sheet for Internet Mail has two pages: General and Connection.

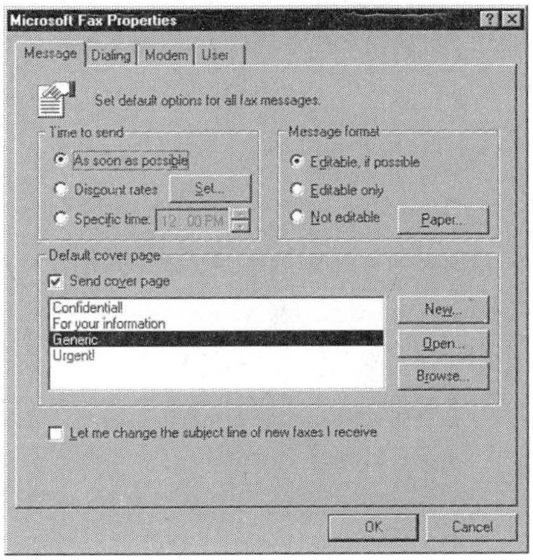

Fig. 34.2 The Message page of the Microsoft Fax Properties sheet has options for the time the message is sent, the format of the message, and the cover page.

The Paper button on the Message page displays the Message Format dialog box, which has options for the paper size, the image quality (in terms of dpi or resolution), and orientation.

The Dialing Page

The Dialing page (see figure 34.3) includes a Dialing Properties button, a Toll Prefixes button, the Number of retries (defaults to three), and the Time between retries (defaults to two minutes). If you've set up a modem for any other purpose, the Dialing Properties are already set up for you.

If you want to change any of the dialing properties, click on the Dialing Properties button, make the desired changes, and then click on OK. The Dialing Properties sheet includes these options that describe your dialing location:

- **I am dialing from**—Describes your location, like "Office."
- **The area code is**—Displays the area code of your calling area.

- **I am in**—Specifies your country so Windows 95 can determine the international code.

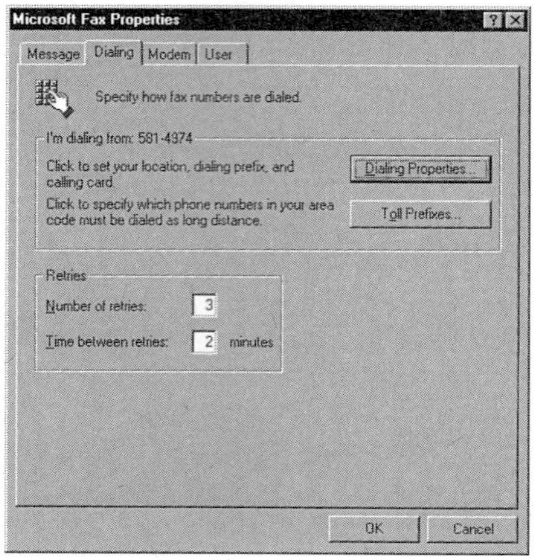

Fig. 34.3 The Dialing page gives information about your location and dialing properties as well as how many times to retry the fax and how often.

The following options describe how you dial:

- **To access an outside line first dial**—Specifies the number to dial for local and long distance.
- **Dial using Calling Card**—Specifies whether you want to use a Calling Card or not. If you select this option, the Change Calling Card dialog box appears and you can specify the Calling Card to use and the Calling Card number. (To make a change to the Calling Card information, click on the Change button to display the Change Calling Card dialog box.
- **This location has call waiting**—Allows you to specify the number that you can dial before making a call to disable call waiting (which can break a telecommunication connection).
- **The phone system at this location uses**—Provides an option for Tone dialing or Pulse dialing.

To specify the prefixes that require long-distance dialing in your area, click on Toll Prefixes button. A list of local phone numbers appears in a list box on the left (see figure 34.4). Select a local phone number that requires you to dial 1 + the area code and then click on the Add button. Add each local number that requires long-distance dialing and then click on OK.

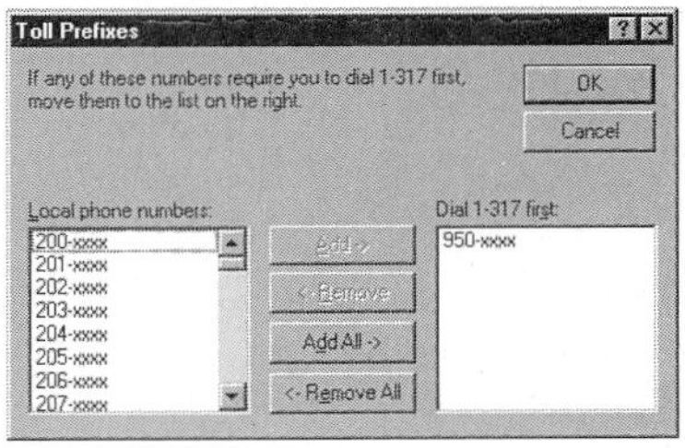

Fig. 34.4 The Toll Prefixes dialog box allows you to specify which area codes must be dialed.

The Modem Page

The Modem page (see figure 34.5) lists the available modems and allows you to select one as the active fax modem. You also can choose to let other people share your modem.

To configure a modem, select the modem in the Available fax modems list and click on the Properties button. The Fax Modem Properties sheet appears (see figure 34.6). You can set the answer mode for the fax to answer after three rings, wait until you answer it manually, or not answer at all. (You would disable answering if you were using a program that used the same COM port as the fax modem.) A slider bar allows you to set the volume of the speaker, and the Turn off after connected option turns the speaker off after a connection is made if it is selected. Call preferences include Wait for dial tone before dialing and Hang up if busy tone. Additionally, you can specify the number of seconds to wait for an answer after dialing.

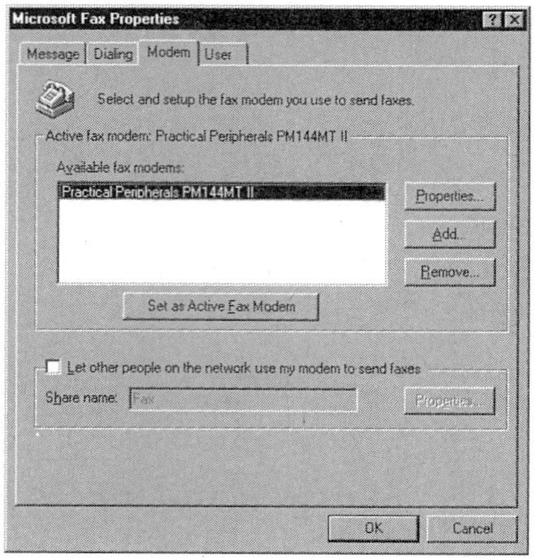

Fig. 34.5 The Modem page specifies the modem and how it is used.

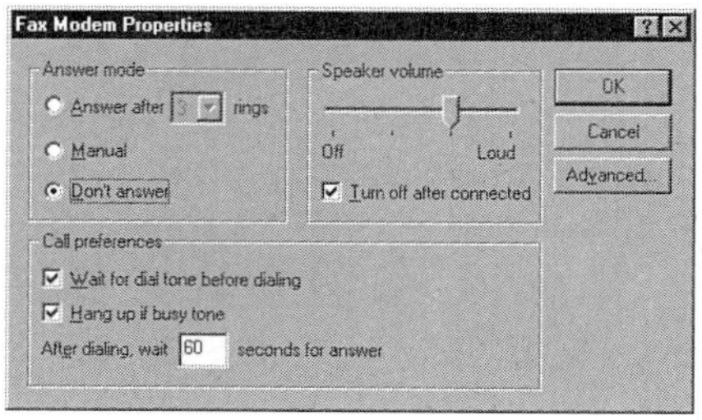

Fig. 34.6 The Fax Modem Properties sheet allows you to configure the modem.

If you click on the Advanced button, you can set these additional options:

- **Disable high speed transmission**—Disables transfers at speeds higher than 9600 baud. This option is selected only if your fax modem is unreliable at high speeds.
- **Disable error correction mode**—Disables error correction when you're sending uneditable file formats (bitmaps).
- **Enable MR compression**—Compresses fax files when they're sent. This option makes fax transmission faster, but a compressed file is more susceptible to line noise.

- **Use Class 2 if available**—Specifies the modem as a Class 2 device. You cannot send or receive editable faxes or use error correction if this option is selected.
- **Reject pages received with errors**—Will not accept pages with too many errors. The error tolerance is set in the Tolerance list box. Tolerances include high, medium, low, and very low.

If you select the option on the Modem page to let other people share your modem to send faxes, you can set the properties of sharing by clicking on the Properties button. The NetFax Properties sheet displays the same options that you see for sharing a printer or a folder. The options are determined by the type of access control that is enabled for the network (share-level or user-level).

The User Page

The User page (figure 34.7) includes information about you that you can use on the fax cover sheet. (The default cover sheets do not use every field of information on the User page, but you can add any of these fields to the default cover sheets). Additionally, you can create your own cover sheet that uses any of the fields from the User page.

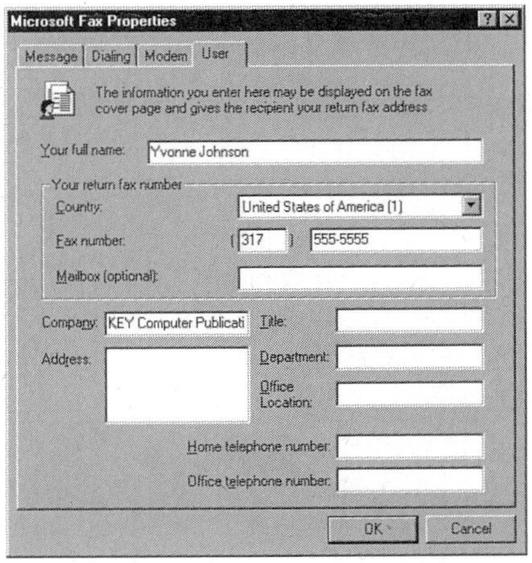

Fig. 34.7 The User page gives information about the user that may appear on the cover page of the fax.

Specifying Microsoft Mail Properties for Local Use

To configure the Microsoft Mail Properties, choose the service in the desired profile (on the General page) and click on the Properties button. The Properties sheet for Microsoft Mail has five pages for local properties: Connection, Logon, Delivery, LAN Configuration, and Log. Additionally, there are three pages for remote properties.

The Connection Page

The Connection page (figure 34.8) includes the following options:

- **Enter the path to your postoffice**—Specifies the network location of your postoffice.
- **Select how this service should connect at startup**—Specifies the way you're connected to your postoffice. If you select Automatically sense LAN or Remote, Windows 95 senses whether your computer is connected to your postoffice by a LAN connection or a modem. If your postoffice cannot detect a connection type, Microsoft Mail prompts you for one. If you select Local Area Network, you're connected via the LAN. If you choose Remote using a modem and Dial-Up Networking, you're connected via a modem, and you can store mail in your Outgoing folder and then send and receive mail when you connect to your postoffice. If you select Offline, you're not connected to the postoffice, and you cannot send or receive mail, but you can compose mail and store it in the Outbox folder.

The Logon Page

The Logon page (figure 34.9) has the following options:

- **Enter the name of your mailbox**—Specifies the name of your mailbox.

- **Enter your mailbox password**—Specifies the password. (The password does not appear, but is represented by asterisks.)
- **When logging on, automatically enter password**—Enters your password for you so you don't have to type it each time you log on. If you use this option, anyone can log on to your mailbox from your PC if you have logged on to the system already.

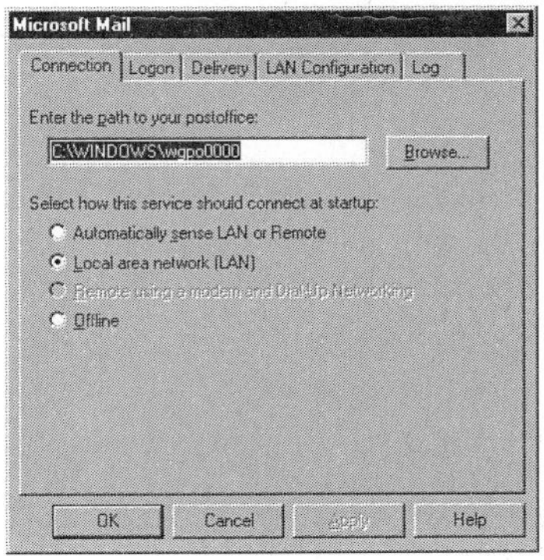

Fig. 34.8 The Connection page specifies how you're connected to Microsoft Mail.

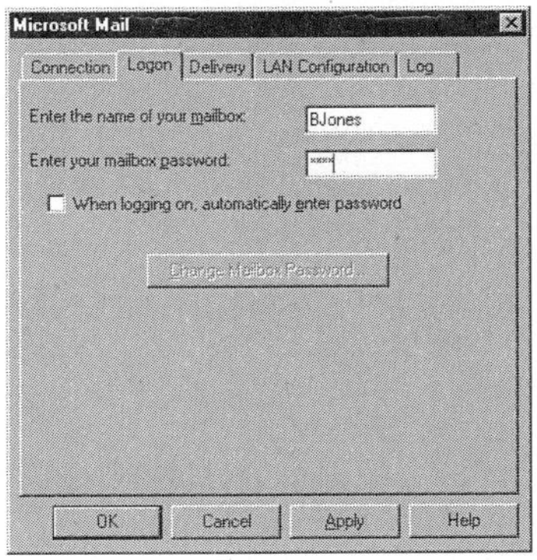

Fig. 34.9 The Logon page specifies how you log on to Microsoft Mail.

To change the mailbox password, click on the Change Mailbox Password button. The Change Mailbox Password dialog box appears. By entering your old password and then a new password and verifying the new password, you can change your mailbox password.

The Delivery Page

The Delivery page (figure 34.10) includes these options:

- **Enable incoming mail delivery**—Delivers mail from the postoffice to your inbox.
- **Enable outgoing mail delivery**—Sends mail to your postoffice.
- **Address types**—Clicking the Address types button displays a list of mail types that you can select. Types that are not selected cannot be delivered.
- **Check for new mail every *n* minutes**—Sets the interval (in minutes) for mail delivery.
- **Immediate notification**—Notifies you of the arrival of mail and notifies the recipient of your mail's arrival (if this option is marked). This option requires NetBIOS.
- **Display Global Address List only**—Displays only the global address list, reducing the size of the name list.

The LAN Configuration Page

The LAN Configuration page (figure 34.11) has only these three options:

- **Use Remote Mail**—Displays mail headers instead of downloading mail.
- **Use local copy**—Uses the Address Book stored on your computer instead of the Address Book for your postoffice.
- **Use external delivery agent**—Uses an external delivery mail program to deliver mail.

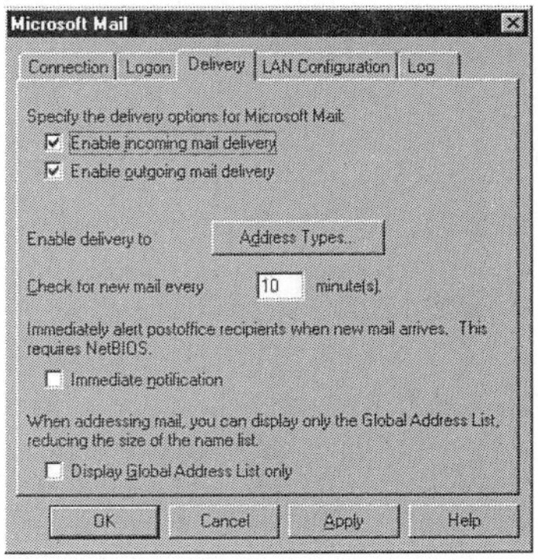

Fig. 34.10 The Delivery page specifies how mail is sent and received.

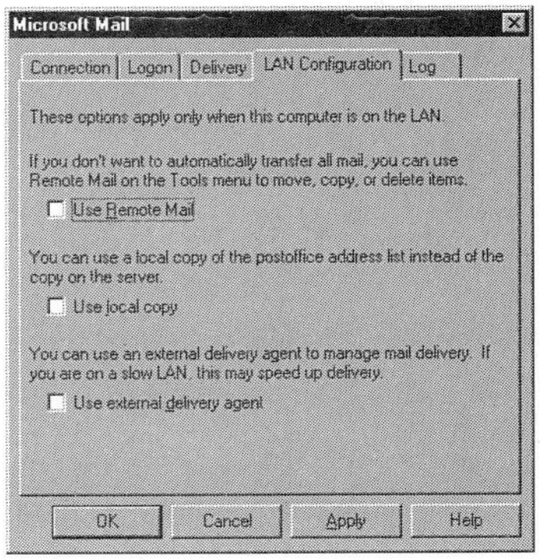

Fig. 34.11 The LAN Configuration page specifies how you use the LAN.

The Log Page

The Log page (figure 34.12) includes the name of your mailbox and your password. The option, When logging on, automatically enter password eliminates the need for you to enter your password each time you open Microsoft Exchange. The Change Mailbox Password button allows you to change your password.

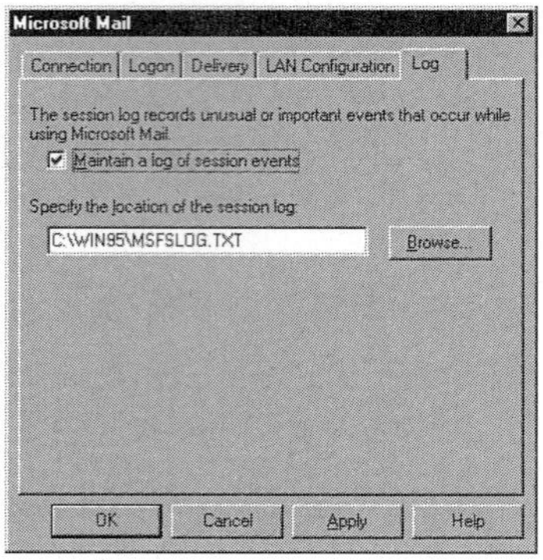

Fig. 34.12 The Log page contains settings that you use to log on.

Specifying Personal Address Book Properties

The Personal Address Book properties specify the name and path of the address book and how to display names, by first name first or by last name first. A Notes page allows you to enter any comments you may have about the address book.

Specifying Personal Information Store Properties

The properties of the Personal Information Store include the path and name of the store and the type of encryption selected when the store was created. The Properties sheet also allows you to change the password used with the store, compact the store so it takes up less disk space, and enter comments about the store.

Specifying Microsoft Network Online Service Properties

If you want to use the Microsoft Network Online Service (MSN) to exchange mail, you must establish an account with MSN. The Microsoft Network Properties sheet (figure 34.13) has two pages: the Transport page and the Address Book page. The Transport page has the following options:

- **Download mail when e-mail starts up from MSN**—Copies your e-mail to your mailbox as soon as you start Microsoft Network (MSN).
- **Disconnect after Updating Headers from Remote Mail**—Copies the subject lines of your e-mail to your Inbox and disconnects from MSN. You can screen your e-mail this way and use Remote Mail to copy only the messages you want and delete the others.
- **Disconnect after Transferring Mail from Remote Mail**—Copies your e-mail to your mailbox and disconnects. This saves you connect time because you can read your e-mail off line.

The Address Book page has only one option: Connect to MSN to check names. If you do not select this option, you can compose mail messages offline. If you select this option, when you address an e-mail message, you'll be connected with MSN so that the address can be verified (if you're using an MSN address).

Configuring the Options of Microsoft Exchange

The Microsoft Exchange has many options that control the way the program works. Options are divided among the General, Read, Send, Spelling, Services, Delivery, and Addressing pages. To see these pages, start Microsoft Exchange and choose Tools, Options.

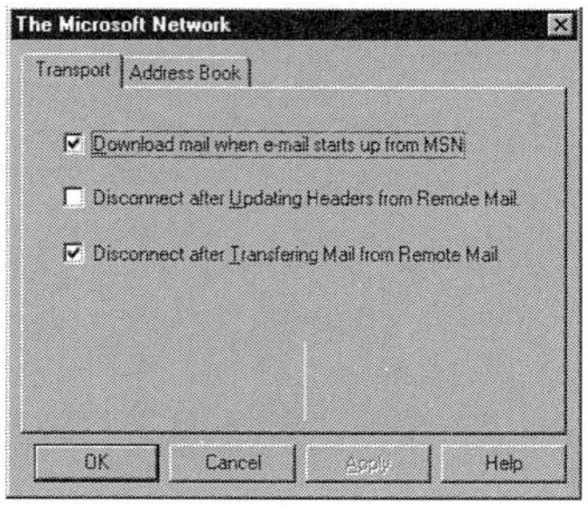

Fig. 34.13 The Transport page specifies how mail will be received from Microsoft Network.

The General Page

The General page (see figure 34.14) contains options for the general operation of Microsoft Exchange, such as what to do when new mail arrives, what to do with deleted items, what profile to use, and so on.

When new mail arrives, you can specify that the system do any or all of the following: play a sound (specified by the New Mail Notification setting in Control Panel), briefly change the pointer to the shape of an envelope, or display a notification message.

When deleting an item, you can have the system warn you before permanently deleting the item and have the Deleted Items folder emptied automatically when you exit from Microsoft Exchange.

When starting Microsoft Exchange, you can use a default profile or have the system prompt you for the profile you want to use. If several people use the same PC, you should choose Prompt for a profile to be used so that each person can use his or her own profile. You cannot switch between profiles while you're running Microsoft Exchange. You must exit and choose a different profile.

Additional options on the General page include Show ToolTips on toolbars and When Selecting, Automatically Select Entire Word (which selects an entire word when you drag the pointer).

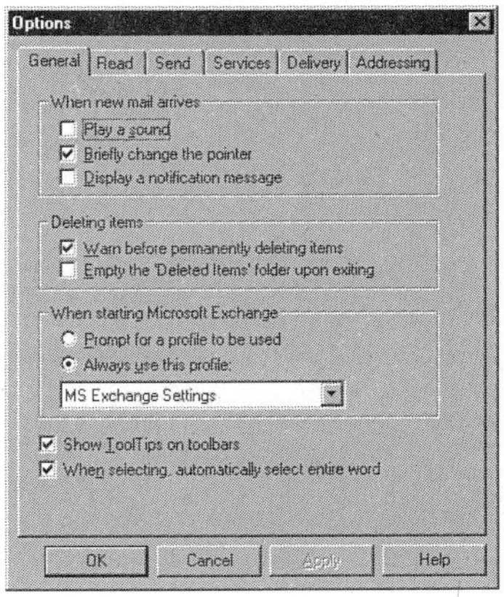

Fig. 34.14 On the General page, you can set options to control what happens when mail arrives.

Note: Some users have experienced problems and degradation of speed when using a profile with two or more dial-up services. If you run into a similar situation, try creating a separate profile for each dial-up service. Then choose the Prompt for a profile to be used option on the General page so you can choose the profile you want to use.

The Read Page

The Read page (figure 34.15) sets options for reading messages and formatting replies and forwards.

The category After Moving Or Deleting An Open Item includes these options:

- **Open the item above it**—Opens the previous item in the folder.
- **Open the item below it**—Opens the next item in the folder.
- **Return To Microsoft Exchange**—Returns to the Inbox window.

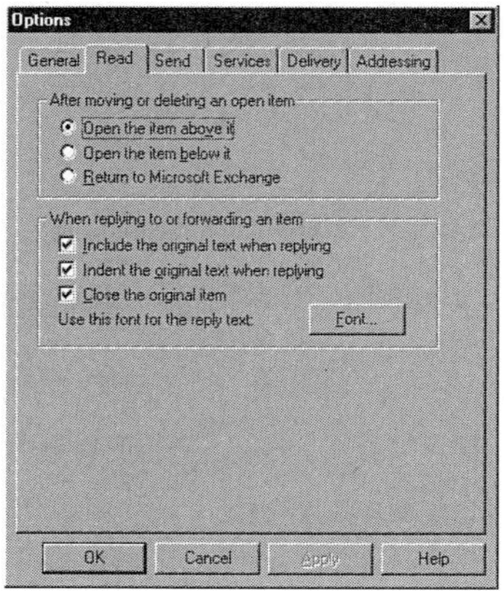

Fig. 34.15 The Read page has options that control what happens next when you are reading mail and decide to delete or move the message to a different folder.

The category When Replying To Or Forwarding An Item includes these options:

- **Include the original text when replying**—Includes the text of the original message below the text of your reply.
- **Indent the original text when replying**—Includes the text of the original message and indents it below the text of your reply.
- **Close the original item**—Closes the item you're replying to or forwarding.

The Font button displays the Font dialog box in which you can select the default font, size, color, and so on, for the text used in replies and forwards.

The Send Page

The Send page (figure 34.16) sets options for sending and formatting new messages.

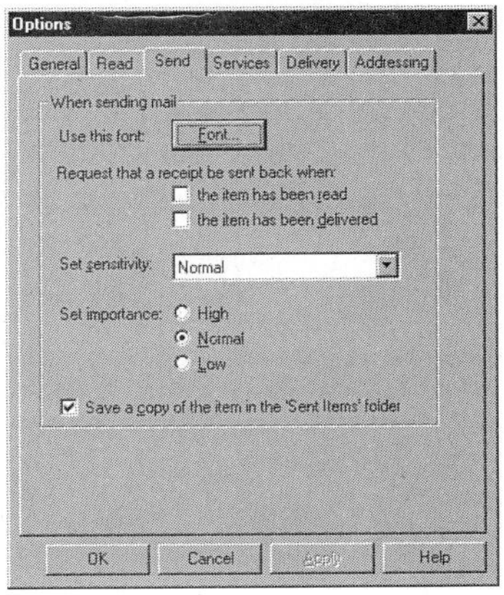

Fig. 34.16 Options on the Send page determine the appearance of messages that you sent.

The Font button displays the Font dialog box in which you can select the default font, size, color, and so on, for the text used in new messages.

You can request that a receipt be sent back to you when the item has been opened or delivered. This option provides assurance as well as documentation that your message has been received or read.

The Set sensitivity option assigns one of these sensitivity levels to outgoing mail: Normal, Personal, Private (prohibits the recipient from modifying your original message when it is replied to or forwarded), and Confidential. The sensitivity level appears in the Sensitivity column, if this column is used. The Sensitivity column will be blank for an item if the item has a normal sensitivity level.

You can set a default importance level for all outgoing mail by selecting High, Normal, or Low. If the Importance column is used, a message with a high importance level shows an exclamation point (!), and a message with a low level of importance shows a down arrow.

If you choose Save a copy of the item in the Sent Items folder, Microsoft Exchange saves a copy of every message that you send and stores it in the Sent Items folder.

The Spelling Page

The Spelling page specifies options for checking spelling. This page is not available unless you have a 32-bit Microsoft application installed that contains a spell checking feature.

The General options include Always suggest replacements for misspelled words, and Always check spelling before sending.

When checking spelling, you can instruct Microsoft Exchange always to ignore words in UPPERCASE, words with numbers, and the original text in a reply or forward.

The Services Page

The Services page (figure 34.17) allows you to add and remove services to and from a profile. The services listed on the Services page depend on the services that you have installed. For example, they may include CompuServe Mail (if you have installed it with the CompuServe program that can be downloaded from the WINNEWS forum), Internet Mail (if you have installed it with Microsoft Plus!), Microsoft Fax, Microsoft Mail, Personal Address Book, Personal Information Store, and the Microsoft Network Online Service. It also allows you to copy a service in the existing profile to another profile, and it shows the properties of the services.

To add a service, click on the Add button. Choose the service you want to add and click on OK. To remove a service, select the service in the list and click on the Remove button.

The About button displays the About Information Service dialog box, which lists the DLL files used by a service and gives other details about the service such as the description, company, version, language, creation date, and size.

The Delivery Page

The Delivery page (figure 34.18) sets the location where your incoming mail is delivered and the order in which your outgoing mail is sent.

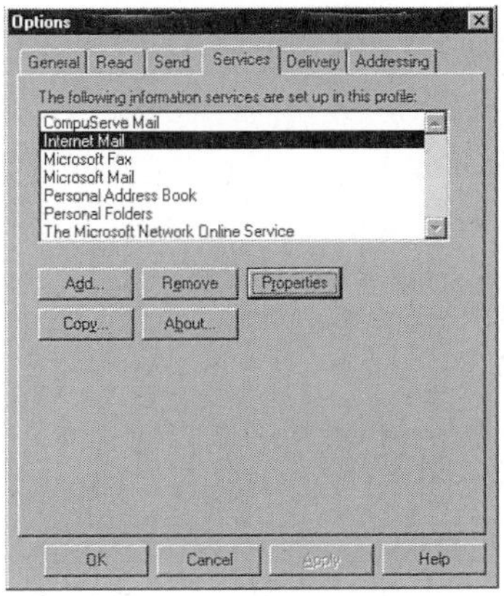

Fig. 34.17 The Services page lists all the services available to include in a profile.

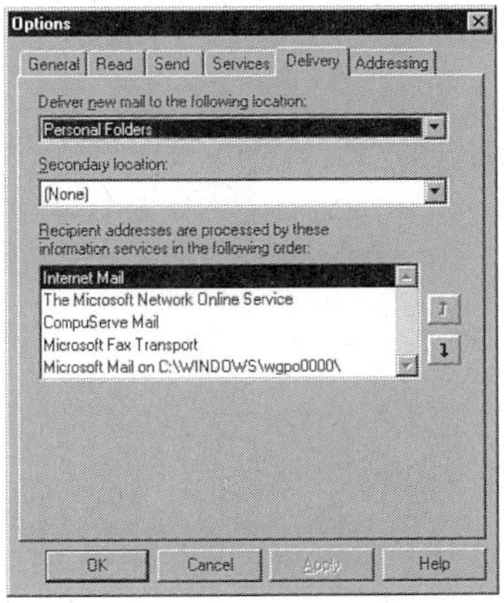

Fig. 34.18 Specify the default delivery location for mail on the Delivery page.

To specify the default location where new mail will be delivered, choose Deliver new mail to the following location and specify the location. Personal Information Store is selected by default. This location is created for you when you set up Microsoft Exchange. You can create your own Personal Information Stores, using different names, and they'll be listed in the drop-down list.

To specify an alternate location for mail delivery, choose Secondary location and specify the location.

The option, Recipient addresses are processed by these information services in the following order, lists the services in the profile in a particular order. You can change the order by clicking on the up or down arrow beside the list box.

The Addressing Page

The Addressing page (figure 34.19) sets options for using the Address Book.

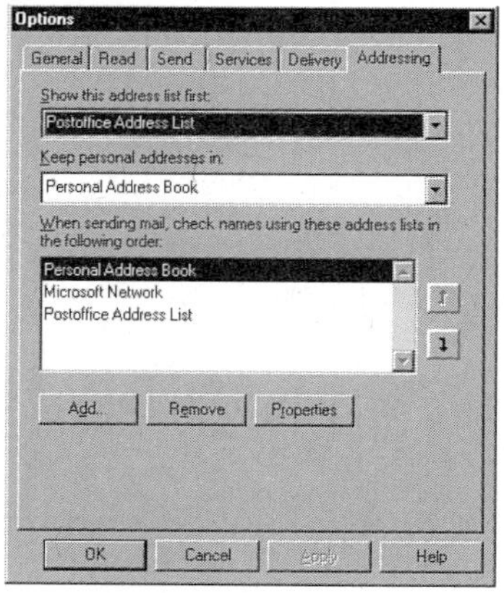

Fig. 34.19 To set defaults for your address lists, use the Addressing page.

To specify a default address list, choose a list from the Show this address list first drop-down list. To specify which address list to keep personal addresses in, choose an address book from the Keep Personal Addresses In drop-down list.

The Addressing page determines the order of the address lists in which Microsoft Exchange will check names when sending mail. To change the order, use the up or down arrow keys next to the list box. The Add button adds an address list to the list box and the Remove button removes an address list from the list. The Properties button displays the properties of a list.

Using Microsoft Exchange More Efficiently

In Chapter 32, "Communicating with a Modem," you learned to use Microsoft Exchange to send and receive messages. In this chapter you'll explore two features of Microsoft Exchange that will help you use Microsoft Exchange more efficiently: the Personal Address Book and the Personal Information Store.

Using a Personal Address Book

The Personal Address Book (PAB) is an important component of Microsoft Exchange that is used when addressing mail messages. When you create the first profile, Microsoft Exchange automatically creates a Personal Address Book, which is maintained by the user, and a Postoffice Address List, which is maintained by the postoffice administrator. An address book contains names, phone and fax numbers, mailing addresses, personal contact information, and multiple electronic mail addresses (for different services). When you address a message, you can select the recipient from the address book to ensure that the message goes to the right place.

> **Note:** Users can copy addresses from the postoffice address book to their own PAB.

Selecting a Name from a PAB

When you compose a new message, you can type the name of the person you want the message to go to, but using the PAB to supply the name ensures that the message is addressed correctly. To select a name from the PAB, follow these steps:

1. Start a new message in Microsoft Exchange (Compose, New Message).

2. Click on the Address Book button on the toolbar. The Address Book dialog box appears as shown in figure 34.20.

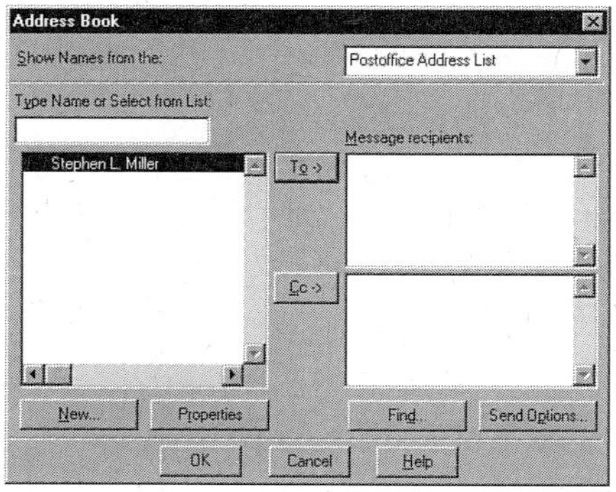

Fig. 34.20 The Address Book dialog box shows the names in the specified address list.

3. Select the address list you want from the drop-down list.

4. Click on the name you want, and then click on To or Cc. Click OK. The name appears in the To line (or Cc line) of the message.

Adding a Name to a PAB

You can add names to your PAB by using the Address dialog box, or you can add names to the PAB "on the fly" when you're creating a message. To add names to the PAB by using the Address Book dialog box, follow these steps:

1. Open Microsoft Exchange. Choose Tools, Address Book or click on the Address Book button in the toolbar.

2. Choose File, New Entry or click on the New Entry button in the toolbar. The New Entry dialog box appears (figure 34.21).

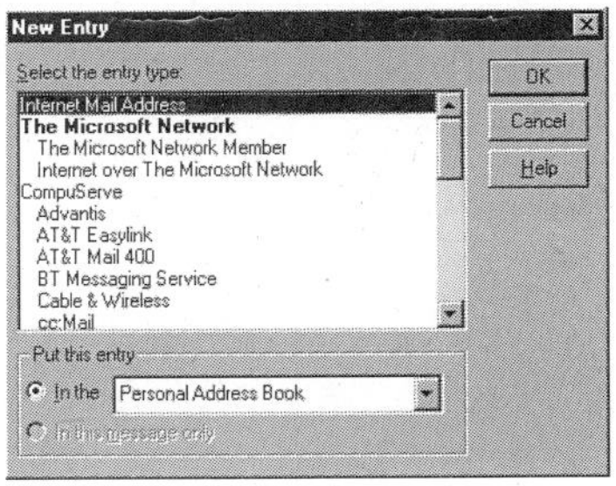

Fig. 34.21 The New Entry dialog box allows you to add new entries in an address list.

3. Choose the type of entry and the place where you want to put the entry and click on OK. An appropriate dialog box appears. For example, if you select Other Address, the dialog box shown in figure 34.22 appears.

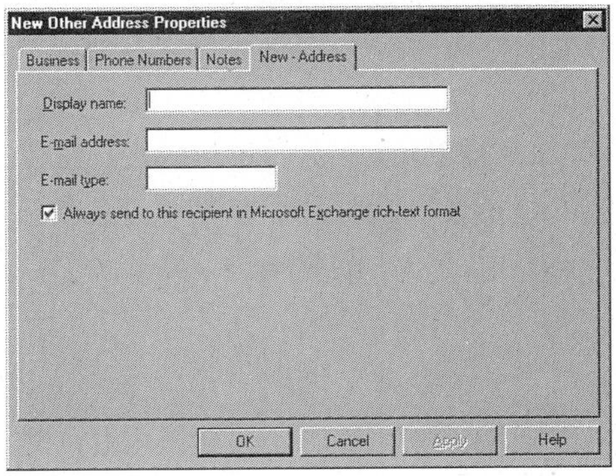

Fig. 34.22 The Other Address dialog box has the same pages as all the address lists' dialog boxes, but the first page of each dialog box has options specific to the type of address book.

4. Fill in the appropriate information on each page of the dialog box and click on OK.

To add a new address when you're composing a message, follow these steps:

1. On the new message screen, click on the To button or the Cc button. The Address Book dialog box appears.
2. Select the address book you want to add the new name to and click on New. The New Entry dialog box appears.
3. Choose the type of entry and the place where you want to put the entry, and click on OK. An appropriate dialog box appears. Fill in the information (there may be more than one page) and click on OK.

> **Tip:** If you have an e-mail message open, you can add an address to the PAB directly from the message header by double-clicking the From name, clicking on Personal Address Book, and clicking on OK.

Keeping the PAB Up-to-Date

It is a fact of life that people leave an organization, new people are hired, and people change their phone numbers and e-mail addresses. To keep the PAB updated, follow these steps:

1. Display the Address Book dialog box in Microsoft Exchange. Double-click on the name that you need to update.
2. Make the appropriate changes and click on OK.

Using the Personal Information Stores

A Personal Information Store (PST) is a database that stores mail messages, forms, documents, and other information in these specific folders: Deleted Items, Inbox, Outbox, and Sent Items. These folders are visible in the left pane of Microsoft Exchange as shown in figure 34.23. The Personal Information Store stores messages for all the information services you're connected to through Microsoft Exchange. It functions as the user's local mailbox and organizes, sorts, and filters messages.

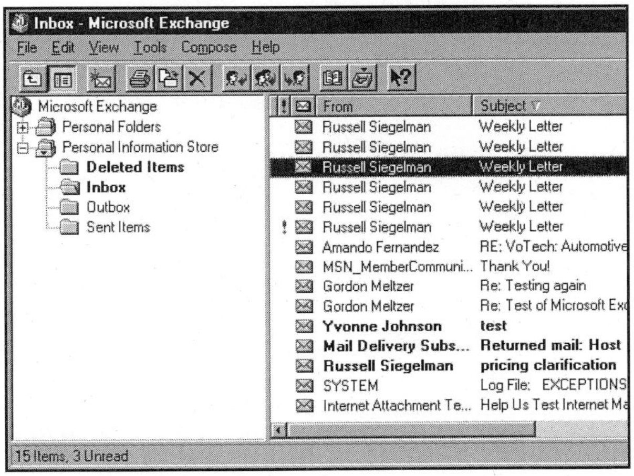

Fig. 34.23 The Microsoft Exchange displays the Personal Information Store in the left pane.

Adding Personal Folders

In addition to the PST, you can have personal folders. For example, you may want to add personal folders to hold old messages or messages from different services. To add a personal folder, follow these steps:

1. Open Microsoft Exchange and choose Tools, Services.
2. Click on the Add button. The Add Service to Profile dialog box appears.
3. Select Personal Folders and click on OK. The Create/Open Personal Folders File dialog box appears.
4. Type a name for the file and click on Open. The Create Microsoft Personal Folders dialog box appears (see figure 34.24).

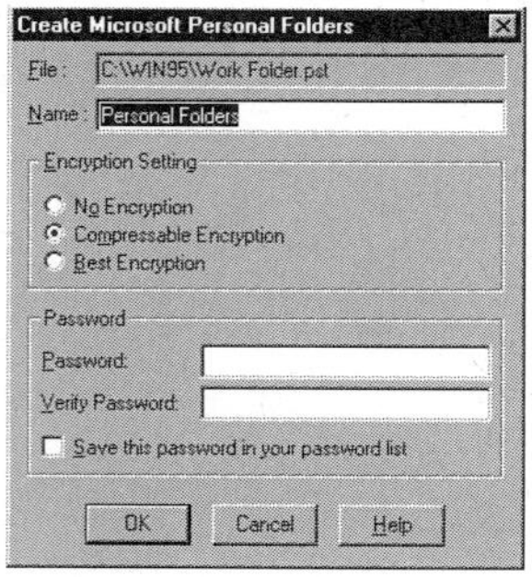

Fig. 34.24 Set the encryption method and password in the Create Microsoft Personal Information dialog box.

5. Type a name for the set of personal folders. This name will appear in the Services list and in the left pane of the Inbox.
6. Select an encryption setting. Because a personal folder file can be opened and read in other programs (even if it is password-protected) you should secure the file by encrypting the information. If you select Compressible Encryption, your files are encrypted as well as compressed. If you choose Best Encryption, your files are encrypted in an uncompressible format. This option provides the greatest degree of protection, but the files occupy more room on the disk.
7. Enter a password in the Password text box. Enter the same password in the Verify Password text box. If you want, choose Save this password in your password list. Click OK.

The new Personal Information Store appears in the left pane of Microsoft Exchange.

Arranging and Finding Messages

By default, certain categories of information are displayed for each message in the Microsoft Exchange window, and messages are arranged in order by the date received. You can choose the columns of information you want to display about messages, sort messages by the column of your choice, and find messages based on specific criteria.

Selecting the Columns of Information That Are Viewed

If you're using the default settings for Microsoft Exchange, the right pane of the Microsoft Exchange displays the following columns of information about messages: Importance, Item Type, Attachment, From, Subject, Received (date), and Size. Other columns such as Application Name, Category, Keywords, and Number of Words, also are available.

To add or remove columns from the display, choose View, Columns. The Columns dialog box appears as shown in figure 34.25. To add a column, select a column you want from the list on the left and click on Add. To remove a column, select a column from the list on the right and click on Remove. To arrange the columns in the list on the right, select the column and click on Move Up or Move Down. To set the width of each column, select the column in the list on the right and specify the number of pixels in the Width text box. If you want to return the display to the default settings, click on Reset. When you have the columns selected and arranged the way you want them, click on OK.

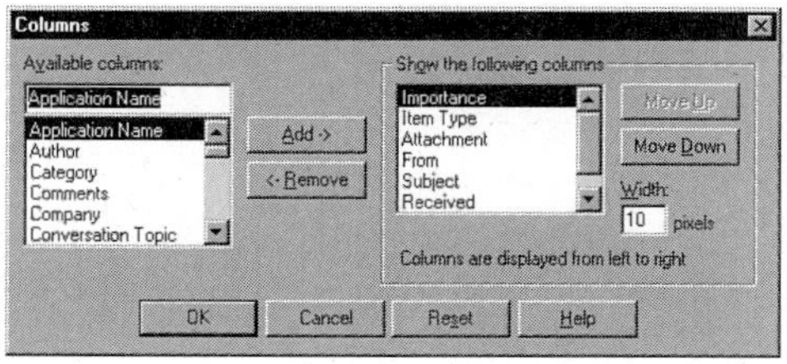

Fig. 34.25 The Columns dialog box lists the available columns on the left and the columns that you want to display on the right.

Sorting the Information

To sort messages by a particular column, click on the heading for the column. That column will display a triangle that points up (if the sort is ascending) or down (if the sort is descending). To change the order of the sort, point to the column heading, click on the right mouse button, and choose the sort that you want.

Finding Messages

The Find dialog box finds messages based on criteria that you specify. To find a particular message, follow these steps:

1. In the Microsoft Exchange window, choose Tools, Find. The Find dialog box appears (see figure 34.26).
2. Click Folder to specify a different location for Look in.
3. Specify the criteria necessary to find the messages including From, Sent To, Sent directly to me, Copied (Cc) to me, Subject, and Message body.
4. Click on Advanced to specify additional criteria such as size, date, importance, sensitivity, unread items, items with attachments, and items that do not match the criteria. Click on OK to close the Advanced dialog box.
5. Click Find Now to activate the search.

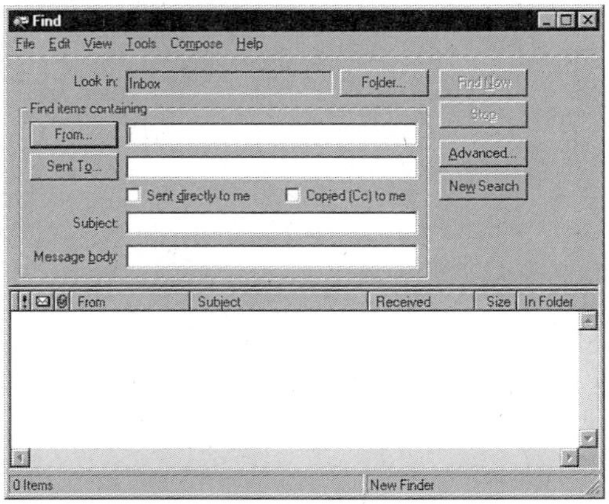

Fig. 34.26 The Find dialog box can find messages based on many different criteria.

Messages that meet the criteria appear in the bottom pane of the dialog box. You can open a message displayed in this pane by double-clicking on it.

Attaching Files, Messages, and Objects to Messages

A common practice among users is to send files to each other. Attaching a file to a message is one way to send a file; however, if most of the messages sent on a network have files attached to them, large amounts of disk space will be used. To conserve disk space, it is better to link a file to a message. A link is a pointer to the file that works like a shortcut. The user can double-click on the pointer to open the file. In addition to attaching files, you can attach other messages as well as objects to messages.

To attach a file to a message, by simple attachment or by link, follow these steps:

1. In the message screen, choose Insert, File. The Insert File dialog box appears. (See figure 34.27.)

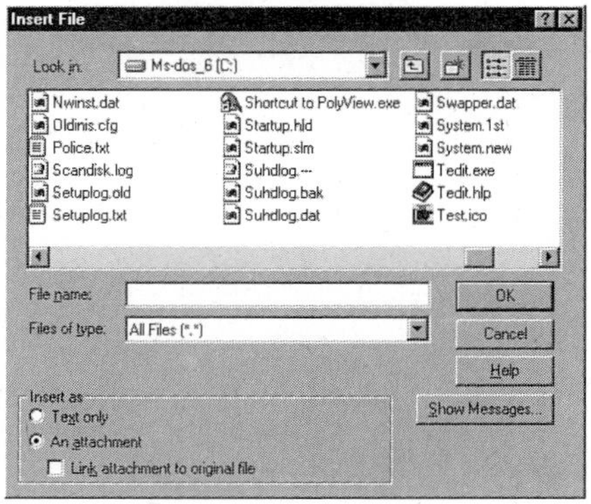

Fig. 34.27 The Insert File dialog box allows you to attach or link a file to a message.

2. Double-click on the folder that contains the file, and then click on the file you want to attach.
3. Click An attachment if you want to attach the file.

   If you want to link the file, click on An attachment and Link attachment.

> **Note:** To attach a message link to a file, the file must be in a shared folder on a computer that is part of the network.

4. Click on OK. An icon appears in the body area of the message.

> **Note:** You also can attach a file to a message by dragging the file to the message, if the file supports OLE.

To attach an existing message to a new message, follow these steps:

1. In the message screen, choose Insert, Message. The Insert Message dialog box appears. (See figure 34.28.)
2. Double-click on the folder that contains the message you want to attach, and then click on the message you want to attach.

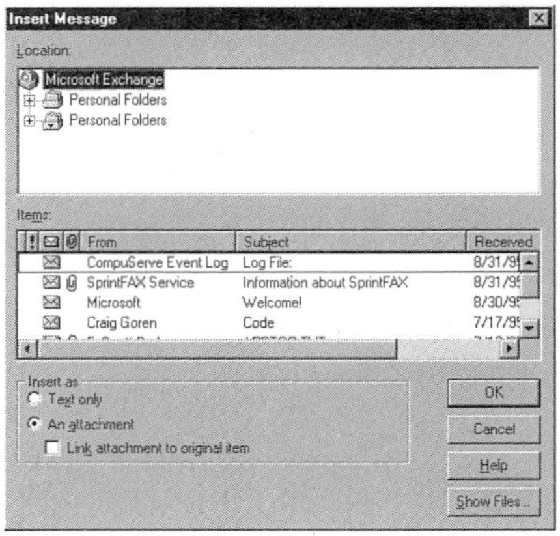

Fig. 34.28 The Insert Message dialog box allows you to attach or link existing messages.

3. Click on An attachment if you want to attach the message.

   If you want to link the message, click on An attachment and Link attachment.

4. Click on OK. An envelope icon appears in the body area of the message.

To insert an object in a message, follow these steps:

1. In the message screen, choose Insert, Object. The Insert Object dialog box appears. (See fig. 34.29.)

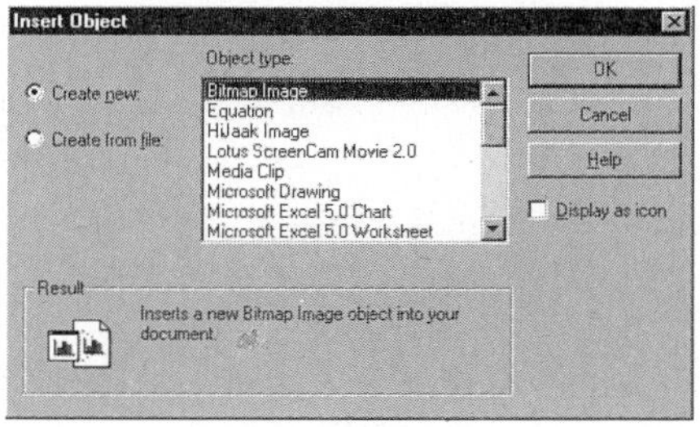

Fig. 34.29 The Insert Object dialog box allows you to embed or link an OLE object.

2. Choose Create new, select an object type from the list, and click on OK. The program that creates the object opens. Create the object and choose File, Exit & Return to Mail Message.

   Or choose Create from file. Specify the file and, if desired, choose Link. Click on OK.

Internet Communications

by Yvonne Johnson

The Internet is undoubtedly the most famous network in the world today. It has tens of thousands of computers connected to each other using a common protocol called TCP/IP (Transmission Control Protocol/Internetwork Protocol). Some estimates say that over 30 million users have e-mail addresses on the Internet. The fact that the Internet has evolved to its current state without central planning or a controlling body is truly mind boggling.

What Can You Do on the Internet?

You can find every imaginable kind of information on the Internet, from cookie recipes to the North American Free Trade Agreement. You can even contact Rush Limbaugh, but rumor has it he never reads mail from an Internet address. (I sent him a message on CompuServe, but he didn't answer that either.) The problem is, how do you access all the information you desire on the Internet?

The information flows across the Internet as e-mail, in newsgroups and mailing lists, in World Wide Web documents, in FTP files, and via Telnet. First we'll examine each of these methods of acquiring information. Later in the chapter, you will learn exactly how Windows 95 fits into the picture.

E-Mail

E-mail is the most popular activity on the Internet. To send and receive mail on the Internet, you must have an Internet e-mail address.

E-mail addresses use the Domain Name System (DNS). A typical e-mail address from another country might look like this:

mhampton@hum.rhodes.edu.uk

The address begins with the user's or organization's name (mhampton). The at sign (@) connects the name of the user with the identification of his location. This particular address has two descriptors and two extensions. The descriptors are *hum* (humanities department) and *rhodes* (Rhodes College); the second descriptor (rhodes) is the domain. The two extensions are *edu* (educational institution) and *uk* which denotes the country (United Kingdom). E-mail addresses in the United States usually omit the country extension. Table 35.1 lists several of the most commonly used extensions and their descriptions.

Table 35.1 Commonly Used Extensions

Extension	Meaning
ca	Canadian domain
com	commercial organization
edu	educational institution
fr	French domain
gov	U.S. government network or organization
int	international organization
mil	U.S. Department of Defense network or organization

Extension	Meaning
net	network or organization running a network on the Internet
org	research or non-profit organization
uk	United Kingdom domain
us	United States domain

Note: Don't send unsolicited e-mail messages. Many Internet users must pay a fee for each piece of e-mail they receive.

An e-mail address, also known as a DNS address, is really an alias for a numeric string that is used to connect to the Internet. DNS numbers are kept in databases, and DNS servers translate a DNS address into the numeric string called an IP address. An IP address might look like this:

198.79.88.20

Newsgroups and Mailing Lists

Newsgroups, collectively referred to as *USENET*, are similar to Microsoft Network bulletin boards. The USENET newsgroups are all loosely organized around seven topics: comp (computer), misc (miscellaneous), news (news), rec (recreation), sci (science), soc (social), and talk (talk). These seven hierarchies follow a specified set of rules, and you should not start posting to these newsgroups until you become familiar with their rules.

In addition to USENET newsgroups, there are other newsgroups (the most notable of which is the alt group) that follow very different rules from each other and from USENET newsgroups.

Newsgroup messages can include attachments, which are binary files, but the attachments must be encoded when they are sent and decoded when they are received. Two popular programs used for encoding and decoding attachments are UUencode and UUdecode. Both of these files can be downloaded from various sites on the Internet as well as from MSN.

Mailing lists are managed by list servers. When a member of the mailing list sends an e-mail message, the list server sends the e-mail message to every member on the mailing list. To join a mailing list, you must send an e-mail that includes your Internet e-mail address. The exact syntax of the message varies with the list server. When your message has been successfully accepted, you'll receive a reply that confirms your acceptance and contains valuable information about how to *unsubscribe* to the list. Be sure to keep this information on file for future reference. You may tire of the list or find that you have subscribed to a list that does not have the content you want.

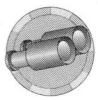

> **Note:** Mailing list members can receive hundreds of e-mail messages a day.

World Wide Web

The World Wide Web (WWW) is a network of servers that provide multimedia "publications" that use hypertext links to jump from file to file. You can be in a file located on a server in the United States, click a hypertext link (which might be an underlined word, an icon, a graphic, and so on), and jump to another file located on a server in a country that is on the other side of the globe.

WWW servers use HTML (Hypertext Markup Language) documents that are very similar to Windows help files in the way they work. For example, when you click on an underlined word or phrase in a help file, you jump to the help topic that explains that word or phrase. The underlined word is the hypertext link.

WWW was started by CERN European Particle Physics Laboratory, and their Web pages are a great source of information about the WWW itself (http:www.cern.ch). *PC Magazine* is another example of a WWW server on the Internet (http:www.pcmag.ziff.com/~pcmag).

To use the WWW you have to have a tool called a *web browser*. Mosaic, one of the first Web browsers that is still widely used, was developed by the National Center for Supercomputing Applications at the University of Illinois at Champaign-Urbana. This program has probably done more to popularize the Internet than any other program. Mosaic accesses WWW as well as other services on the Internet. It is free and can be downloaded from many sites on the Internet as well as MSN. Many commercial programs, like Internet in a Box, include enhanced versions of Mosaic.

Another popular Web browser, Netscape, is also available for downloading from many sites. This Web browser offers more features than the original Mosaic and has become widely used.

Web sites have a home page that is displayed when you connect with the site. Each WWW home page has a unique Uniform Resource Locator (URL) that serves as its address. For example, the URL for the Macmillan home page is http://www.mcp.com.

Gopher

The Gopher system was developed by the University of Minnesota. A Gopher is a hierarchical menu system that tunnels deeper and deeper into the Internet. The top level Gopher at the University of Minnesota is gopher.micro.mnu.edu. Many Gopher servers have joined the ranks of the university, including the InterNIC gopher (gopher.internic.net), the official source of information about the Internet.

Windows 95 does not provide Gopher software, but you can download many different Gophers from various places. The University of Minnesota is a good place to find Gopher software.

Veronica (Very Easy Rodent-Oriented Netwide Index to Computerized Archives) is a utility program that searches Gopher sites. A Veronica search produces a menu of Gopher items, each of which is a direct pointer to a Gopher data source. Because Veronica is accessed through a Gopher client, it is easy to use, and gives access to all types of data supported by the Gopher protocol.

The following is a list of Gopher sites accessible to the public at large (these addresses are subject to change or termination):

Hostname	IP Address	Area
consultant.micro.umn.edu	134.84.132.4	North America
ux1.cso.uiuc.edu	128.174.5.59	North America
panda.uiowa.edu	128.255.40.201	North America
gopher.msu.edu	35.8.2.61	North America
gopher.ebone.net	192.36.125.2	Europe
gopher.sunet.se	192.36.125.10	Sweden
info.anu.edu.au	150.203.84.20	Australia
tolten.puc.cl	146.155.1.16	South America
ecnet.ec	157.100.45.2	South America
gan.ncc.go.jp	160.190.10.1	Japan

FTP Sites

FTP (File Transfer Protocol) refers to a protocol as well as to a program that uses the protocol to transfer files. The Internet has thousands of anonymous servers with a variety of files available for downloading. The servers are called anonymous because the user is allowed to log on as “anonymous” and use his or her e-mail address as a password.

Caution: Lots of freeware and shareware is downloadable from FTP sites, but many are not checked for viruses, so be careful.

To use FTP sites effectively, you must have an FTP program (one is supplied by Windows 95). The commands used by the FTP program are very similar to UNIX commands. If you're not familiar with UNIX commands, you can display the list of commands that FTP uses once you have started FTP. (See "Using FTP" later in this chapter for more information about FTP commands.)

Unless you know something about the FTP site and the files that exist there, it helps to use a tool, such as Archie, that searches for the information you want. FTP sites are indexed by title and keyword on a regular basis, sometimes every day. Archie searches these indexes for the files you want based on the title or key word that you specify.

Here are some FTP sites you might want to explore:

Microsoft: ftp.microsoft.com

University of Illinois: ftp.ncsa.uiuc.edu

Indiana University: ftp.cica.indiana,edu

Project Gutenberg: ftp.mrcnet.cso.uiuc.edu

InterNIC: ftp.internic.net

Telnet

Telnet is probably the least exciting feature of the Internet. This service allows you to log on to a remote network using terminal emulation (most commonly VT100 and VT320). Once logged on, you can perform any task that the network can perform.

WAIS

WAIS (Wide-Area Information Server) is a server system used for searching databases (referred to as sources) that contain mostly text, but may also contain sound, pictures, or video. You can find WAIS servers listed on many Gopher menus. The WAIS databases may be organized in different ways, using various query languages and syntax, but using a WAIS client, the user can type natural language queries to find relevant documents.

Connecting to the Internet

Before examining the way Windows 95 connects to the Internet, let's look at the traditional ways of connecting to the network. There are three possibilities; you can connect via:

- a network
- a SLIP/PPP connection
- an online service

Network Connection

A network is the fastest and most complete type of connection to the Internet. It is also the most expensive. For a dedicated 56 Kbps line, prices start at about $2,000 per month. (Prices vary by bandwidth, or speed, of connection.) LAN-based connections also require routers at the local site.

With a network connection, your network is connected directly to the Internet using TCP/IP. Your computer must be connected to your network with a network adapter card and be running either ODI (Open Data-link Interface) or NDIS (Network Driver Interface Specification) packet drivers. (Both drivers allow multiple transport protocols to run on one network card simultaneously.) If you are running any version of Windows, you need Winsock support. Winsock is an API that allows Windows applications to run over a TCP/IP network.

With a network you have access to everything the Internet has to offer.

SLIP/PPP Connection

With a SLIP (Serial Line Interface Protocol) or PPP (Point-to-Point Protocol) connection, you must connect with a service provider that lets you dial into a SLIP or PPP server. Service providers generally include service for networks as well as stand-alone PCs. Prices are based on bandwidth and the hours of usage.

For a stand-alone PC using Dial-Up Networking, the fee for using a service provider will range from about $10 to $150 a month (based on the number of hours of usage and the locality). The bandwidth for this kind of service is typically 14.4K to 56K. If you have an ISDN adapter, you can connect at a bandwidth of 64K, and you might pay $50 to $300 a month depending on the number of hours of usage and the locality.

For a network connection the prices may range from $200 a month to $2000. Most network connections are full-time—that is, not based on hours of usage—and the bandwidth may range from 64K to 128K to a T-1 connection, which is 25 times faster than 64K.

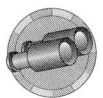

> **Note:** Microsoft plans to provide PPP connection through the Microsoft Network, but rates and speeds are unknown at this writing.

With a SLIP or PPP connection you are a full peer on the Internet and have access to everything the Internet has to offer. The only drawback is speed. A direct connection is much faster than a SLIP or PPP connection. Modems below the speed of 14.4 Kbps are too slow to use on the Internet.

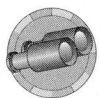

> **Note:** SLIP and PPP providers are easy to find in magazines about the Internet. You can also download a list of service providers called PDIAL from many Internet sites. Of course, if you can't get on the Internet, you can't download the list, so have a friend do it for you or see if your online service has it.

Online Connection

If you connect to the Internet with an online service, all you need is a modem and an account with an online service. All the major online services—America Online, CompuServe, Delphi, GEnie, Prodigy, and so on—give you access to the Internet. It varies with the online service, but many give you access to WWW, e-mail, FTP, Telnet, and Gopher. Charges for these services also vary.

Connecting to the Internet with Windows 95

Now that you know the three ways to connect to the Internet, all you have to know is that Windows 95 uses all three types of connections. You can install TCP/IP (it's supplied with Windows 95) and a network adapter, connect to a network that is connected to the Internet, and you're off and running. Secondly, you can install TCP/IP, SLIP or PPP software (supplied by Windows 95), and Dial-Up Networking (also supplied by Windows 95), subscribe to a SLIP or PPP service provider, and you're off and running again. Finally, if you are connected to the Microsoft Network, you don't have to do anything special to connect with the Internet, but you are limited to e-mail and newsgroup services (at this time). Microsoft plans to add other Internet services in the future.

Installing and Configuring TCP/IP

Installing TCP/IP is the first step you must take toward setting up a connection with the Internet, regardless of whether you'll be connecting through your network or though Dial-Up Networking on a stand-alone PC. Windows 95 provides TCP/IP, so there is nothing extra you have to purchase. To install TCP/IP, follow these steps:

1. Open the Control Panel and double-click the Network icon. Then click the Add button. The Select Network Component Type dialog box displays. (See figure 35.1.)

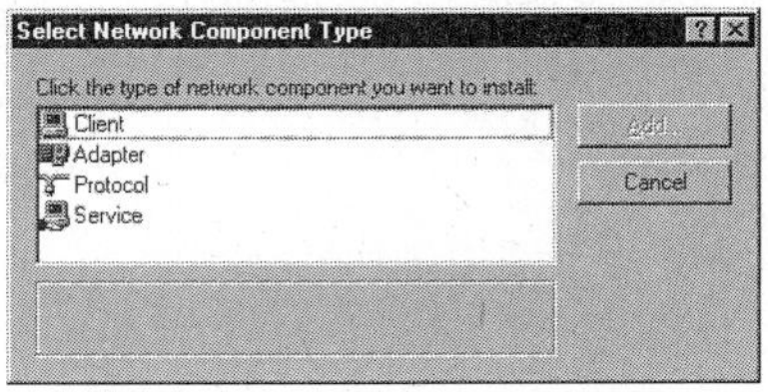

Fig. 35.1 The Select Network Component Type lists the network components.

2. Double-click Protocol. The Select Network Protocol dialog box displays as shown in figure 35.2.

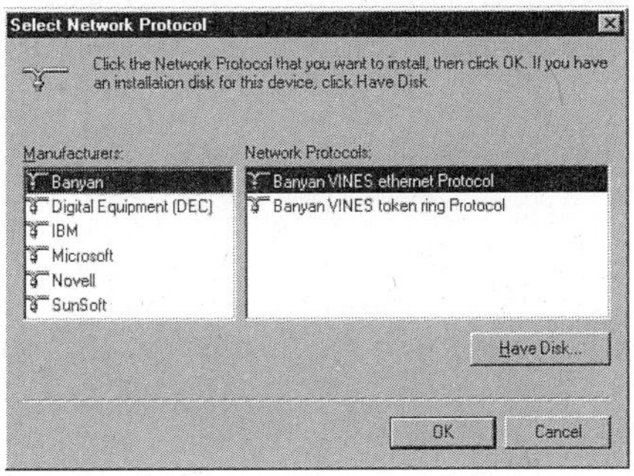

Fig. 35.2 The Select Network Protocol dialog box lists the network protocols that Windows supports.

3. In the Manufacturers box, click Microsoft, and click TCP/IP in the Network Protocols list. Click OK.

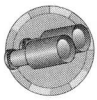

Note: Make sure that the TCP/IP protocol is bound to the dial-up adapter or network card by checking the Binding page of the adapter's Properties sheet.

Understanding the Properties of TCP/IP

If installing the TCP/IP were all you had to do to connect to the Internet, life would be so good. Unfortunately, you also have to configure TCP/IP. This is where things might begin to get a little complicated, so dig in. Before going through the steps to configure the properties of TCP/IP, you must know what information you need for proper configuration.

To configure TCP/IP you have to configure a DNS server, and possibly an IP address, a subnet mask IP address, and a gateway IP address. You will need an IP address, subnet mask IP, and a gateway IP only if your provider does not have Dynamic Host Configuration Protocol (DHCP). With DHCP, the provider can dynamically assign you these three addresses each time you connect to the Internet. Regardless of whether or not the addresses are assigned dynamically, the TCP/IP protocol relies on the IP address, subnet mask IP, and gateway IP to receive and deliver data packets between hosts (nodes on the same network).

IP Addresses

Every node on a TCP/IP network has a unique IP address. Earlier you learned that an e-mail address is really an alias for a numeric string which is the IP address. An IP address is a 32-bit address. The four 8-bit bytes are represented in dotted decimal notation like this:

    102.54.94.97

Each octet (byte) of the address is represented by its decimal value and separated from the other octets with a period. The IP address contains two pieces of information: the network ID and the host ID. Here network is defined as a group of computers and other devices that are all located on the same logical network (which may be interconnected by routers). Host is defined as any device attached to the network that uses TCP/IP. A unique network ID must be obtained from the InterNIC. The unique host IDs are assigned by the network administrator.

The first octet in the IP address always refers to the network ID. The remaining octets may refer to the network ID or the host ID as explained in Table 35.2.

The first octet in the IP address identifies the class of the network as defined by the InterNIC. See Table 35.2. Class A, the class that contains the largest networks, has only 126 IDs reserved by the InterNIC. IBM and Hewlett-Packard both have addresses in this "elite neighborhood." Each network in a class A network can have 16,777,214 hosts per network. Class B has 16,384 available network addresses, with 65,534 hosts available per network. Class C has 2,097,151 network addresses available, with 254 hosts per network.

Table 35.2 IP Addresses

Class	Values of 1st Octet	NetworkID	Host ID
A	1-126	First octet	Remaining 3 octets
B	128-191	First 2 octets	Remaining 2 octets
C	192-223	First 3 octets	Remaining 1 octet

DNS Server

You also learned earlier that e-mail addresses are translated into numbers by DNS servers. The DNS server itself has a DNS address. For example, the server named rex.isdn.net has the numeric address of 198.79.88.10. When you configure the DNS server in the TCP/IP Properties sheet, you need to know both the server name and the numeric character string for the DNS server.

Subnet Mask IP

A subnet mask distinguishes the network ID portion of an IP address from the host ID portion so that recipients of IP packets can recognize a node on the same system. Subnet masks are also used to split network addresses into subnetwork addresses so you do not have to apply for additional network IDs. For example, if the logical network is composed of 12 LANs, you can apply for one network ID and then subdivide the network ID with subnets to provide 11 more addresses.

Gateway IP

A gateway is a connection between two networks that would otherwise be incompatible, such as between a LAN and a WAN. The gateway IP is just like the IP address in that it is a 32-bit address that uses dotted decimal notation.

Configuring TCP/IP

Regardless of whether you're connecting to the Internet via a network or a dial-up connection, you must configure TCP/IP. Before setting the properties of TCP/IP, make sure you know the following information:

- What is the name and IP address of the DNS server?
- Does the DNS server use DHCP?
- If the DNS server does not use DHCP, what is the IP address, the subnet address, and the gateway address?

Additionally, if you'll be connecting to the Internet via Dial-Up Networking, you need to obtain the following information from your service provider:

- access phone number
- logon name
- logon password

Configuring DNS

To configure DNS, open the Network Properties sheet and display the properties for TCP/IP. Click the DNS Configuration tab to display the properties page and follow these steps:

1. Choose Enable DNS unless you are on a network that uses a WINS (Windows Internet Naming Service). If your network uses a WINS, choose Disable DNS and click OK. Then click the WINS Configuration tab and see "Configuring the WINS" later in this section.
2. Type the name for the Host (the name of your computer) and the name for the Domain (the name of the DNS server).
3. Type the address of the DNS server and click Add. The address appears in the list box. See figure 35.3.
4. If additional server addresses are available, type each one, clicking Add for each. (Server addresses should be entered in the same order in which you want the servers to be searched.)
5. If you have a domain suffix, type it and click Add. (A domain suffix is used in conjunction with your host name to further identify your computer.)

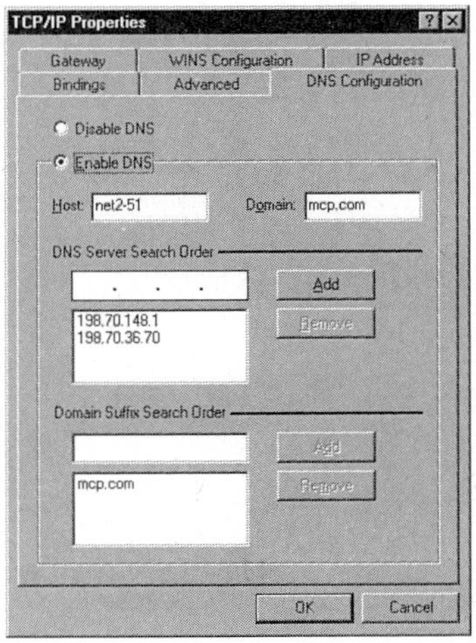

Fig. 35.3 The DNS configuration shows that the host name is "yvonne" and the domain name is "isdn.net."

Configuring the IP Address

The IP address is specified on the IP address page of the TCP/IP Properties sheet. Display the page (see figure 35.4) and follow these steps if you are connected to a server that does *not* use the DHCP protocol:

1. Choose Specify an IP Address.
2. Type the IP Address (given to you by your service provider).
3. Type the Subnet Mask (given to you by your service provider).

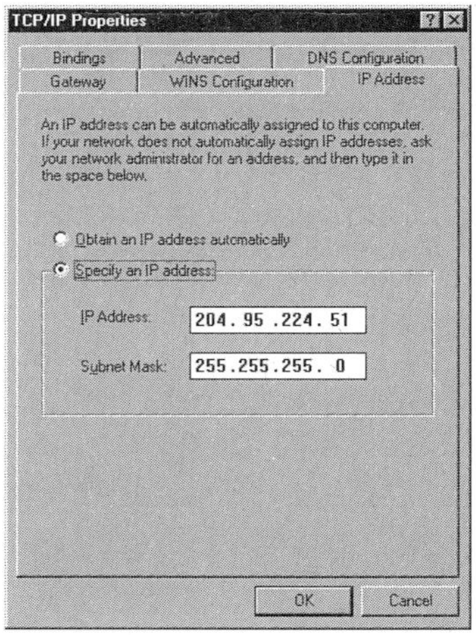

Fig. 35.4 The IP Address page allows you to specify the IP address and the subnet mask.

If you use a server that dynamically assigns IP addresses and subnet masks, choose Obtain an IP address automatically on the IP page.

Additional TCP/IP Settings for a Network

If you're connecting to the Internet via a network, you may also have to configure the Gateway and the WINS (Windows Internet Naming Service). If you are using Dial-Up Networking, you do not need to be concerned with a gateway or WINS.

Configuring the Gateway

You need to configure the gateway **only** if you are using a server that does not have DHCP. Click the gateway page of the TCP/IP Properties sheet, type the gateway address, and click Add. Since this is the last setting you have to make in the TCP/IP Properties sheet, click OK to close the TCP/IP Properties sheet and then click OK again to close the Network Properties sheet.

Configuring the WINS

You need to configure the WINS **only** if your network uses WINS, which is similar to a DNS server. WINS requires that one or more Windows NT servers be configured as WINS servers, and that they contain a dynamic database for mapping computer names to IP addresses. DNS servers are generally used for Internet communications rather than WINS servers, but you can use either.

Click the WINS Configuration tab and choose Enable WINS Resolution or Use DHCP for WINS Resolution if you have this protocol to supply the WINS configuration dynamically. If you choose Enable WINS Resolution, then enter the address of the primary and secondary WINS servers. Enter the Scope ID, if there is one. A scope ID identifies a group of computers on the network that recognize a registered NetBIOS name. These computers can "hear" each others' messages. When finished, click on OK.

Installing and Setting Up Dial-Up Networking

If you're using a network, no other configuration is needed. You're ready to use the Internet with whatever tools you have installed on your system. However, if you are using Dial-Up Networking, you have more configuration to do. Your next step in connecting with the Internet is configuring Dial-Up Networking.

Installing Dial-Up Networking

If you have not installed Dial-Up Networking, follow these steps to do so:

1. Open the Control Panel and double-click Add/Remove Programs.
2. Click the Windows Setup tab.
3. Click Communications and then click Details.
4. Click Dial-Up Networking and click OK. Click OK again. If prompted, insert the Windows installation disk or CD.

Creating a Connection

Once Dial-Up Networking is installed, follow these steps to create a new connection for the Internet:

1. Double-click My Computer and then double-click the Dial-Up Networking icon.
2. Double-click Make New Connection. The Make New Connection Wizard starts (see figure 35.5).

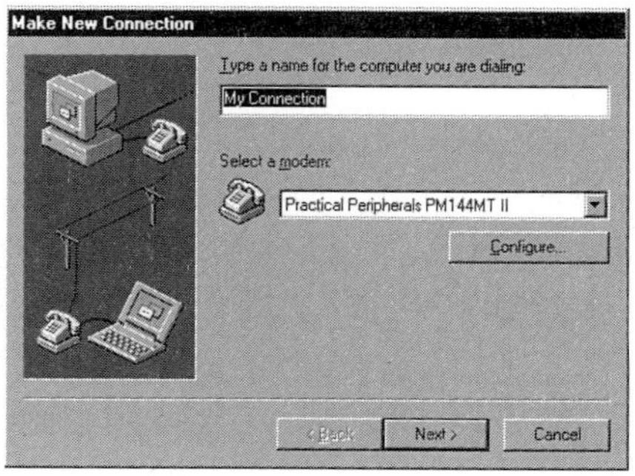

Fig. 35.5 The Make New Connection Wizard displays the modem that is installed.

3. Type a name for the connection (like Internet) and click Next.
4. Type the area code (if not a local number) and the phone number given to you by the service provider.
5. Choose the correct country and click Next.

6. Click Finish. The new connection displays an icon in the Dial-Up Networking window.

This may be all you need to do to configure Dial-Up Networking, but if your service provider requires encrypted passwords, you will have to do some further configuration.

Configuring Encrypted Passwords

Encrypted passwords are required by servers that do not support the Password Authentication Protocol (PAP) or the Challenge-Handshake Authentication Protocol (CHAP). To enable encrypted passwords, right-click the dial-up icon for the Internet and choose Properties. Click the Server Type button to display the screen shown in figure 35.6. Choose Require encrypted password and click OK to close the Server Types dialog box. Then click OK to close the Properties sheet.

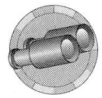

Note: If you are using a PPP provider, you will notice on the Server Type dialog box that the option Enable software compression is selected by default. This option specifies that your computer will try to compress information before sending it, but compression will occur only if the computer you are connecting to is using a compatible compression program. Compressing data improves the throughput and transfer times because it reduces the amount of information that needs to be transmitted over the modem.

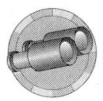

Note: If you need to enter commands to control your modem, either before or after you dial your service provider, you must specify that a terminal window display. To do this, right-click the dial-up icon for the Internet, choose Properties, and click the Configure button. Click the Options tab (see figure 35.7). Choose Bring up terminal window before dialing or Bring up terminal window after dialing and click OK. Refer to the modem manual for the commands that you type to control the modem.

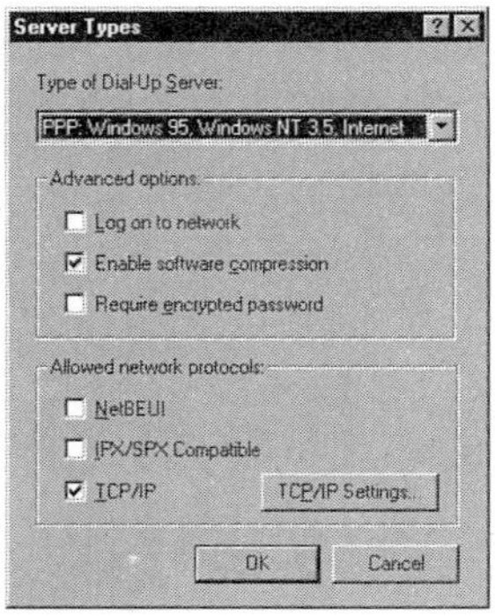

Fig. 35.6 Server types may be selected from the drop-down list at the top of the dialog box.

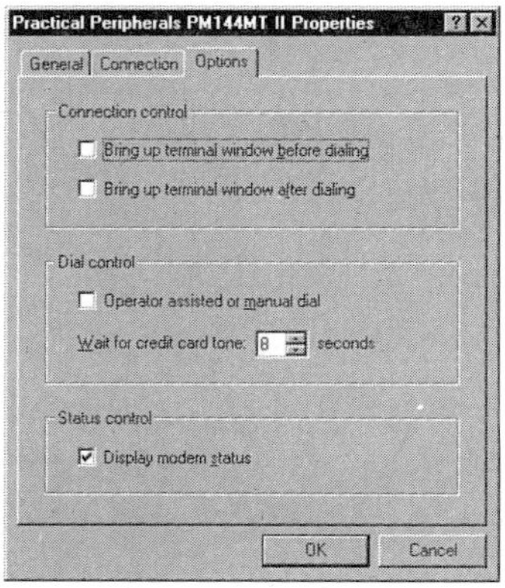

Fig. 35.7 You can display a terminal window for entering commands directly to the modem either before or after dialing the service provider.

Connecting to the Internet through PPP

You're getting close now! If you have a PPP provider, all you have to do to connect to the Internet is use your new dial-up connection. If you have a SLIP provider, this section does not apply to you. Skip to the next section, "Configuring and Using SLIP."

To connect, follow these steps:

1. Double-click My Computer and then double-click Dial-Up Networking.
2. Double-click the icon that represents your Internet connection. A Connect To dialog box displays as shown in figure 35.8

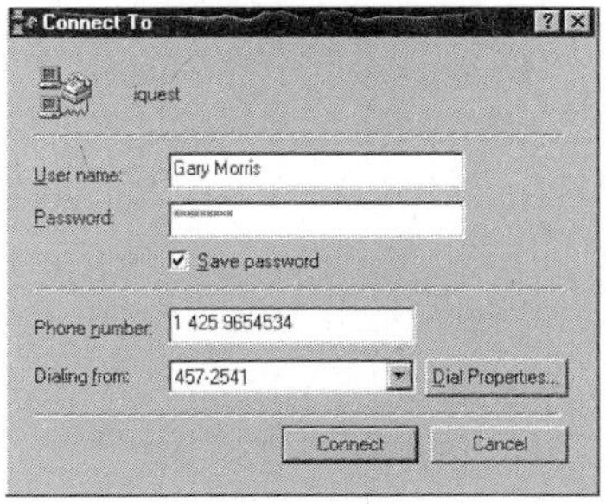

Fig. 35.8 Your user name will display in the Connect To dialog box by default after you have entered it the first time.

3. Type your user name and password. If desired, choose Save Password.
4. And now for the big moment—connecting to the Internet. Click the Connect button. The Connect To dialog box displays to show you the status. (See figure 35.9.) First the dialog box says it's dialing. (The anticipation is mounting.) Then it says it is verifying the user name and password. (You're bursting with anticipation now.) And finally the dialog box says that you are connected . Nothing else changes on the screen. You begin to wonder when something will happen. The duration field is ticking off the seconds and still nothing happens. You begin to say to yourself, "Is this all there is? This is the big Internet that everyone is so worked up over? Where's all the e-mail? Where are the newsgroups?" The pent up excitement turns to disappointment, and finally, in desperation, you click the Disconnect button.

> **Note:** If you are experiencing this disappointment right now, see immediately "What to Do Once You Get Connected," later in this chapter.

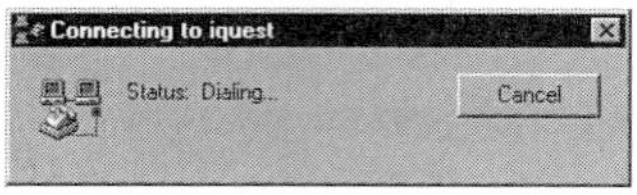

Fig. 35.9 The connect dialog box shows what is happening while your modem tries to connect to the service provider.

Configuring and Using SLIP

SLIP is an older, less robust protocol than PPP and is used by some service providers if they have older UNIX servers. Only about one in a hundred service provider accounts is set up as a SLIP account. If you have a choice, you should always choose PPP over SLIP. If you have a PPP provider, skip this section; it does not apply to you.

Windows supports SLIP, but does not install it automatically. SLIP must be installed as a new program (using the Add/Remove Programs object in the Control Panel), and it is located on the CD in the ADMIN\APPTOOLS\DSCRIPT folder.

Once SLIP is installed, you must configure the dial-up connection so it displays a terminal logon after dialing. Additionally you will have to select SLIP as the type of server.

Specifying a Terminal Window after Dialing

To specify that a terminal window display after dialing your service provider, right-click the Internet connection icon in Dial-Up Networking. Choose Properties and click the Options tab. Choose Bring up terminal window after dialing and click OK to return to the General page of the Connection Properties sheet.

Specifying the Server Type

To specify SLIP as the server type, click Server Type (on the General page of the Connection Properties sheet). Choose SLIP from the Type of Dial-Up Server drop-down list. Click OK twice to close the Server Types dialog box and then the connection dialog box.

Connecting to the Internet through SLIP

To connect with a SLIP service provider, double-click the dial-up connection icon and enter your password. Click Connect. The terminal window displays. When you receive the TCP/IP address, press F7 to continue. The terminal window closes. Type the assigned address and click OK. You are connected to the Internet, but as you will see, nothing exciting happens. After waiting for a frustrating period of time for something (anything) to happen, you may eventually give up and click the Disconnect button.

What to Do Once You Get Connected

Now if you had just read a little further in this book, dear reader, you wouldn't have had such a disappointing first experience. After you get connected to the Internet, one of the first things you'll want to do is download a Web browser.

Probably the easiest way to download a Web browser is to connect to your own service provider's site. Ask your service provider the name of the file and the name of the folder that contains the file. Then use FTP to download the file.

Using FTP

Once connected to the Internet, open an MS-DOS Prompt window, change to the folder where FTP is stored (usually \Windows) and enter this command:

ftp

The prompt changes to ftp>.

Now suppose that the service provider's site is an anonymous server with this address: rex.isdn.net. Enter this command to connect to it:

open rex.isdn.net

When prompted, enter the user name *anonymous.* Then enter your Internet address as the password. If you are successfully connected, you can begin to enter commands to move around on the site and eventually download files.

To see a list of commands used by FTP, type **help** and press Enter. To get information on a particular command, type **help** followed by the command word and press Enter.

Common Commands

Look at the commands you might want to enter. To see the organization of folders at the site, enter this command:

dir

Figure 35.10 shows the output of this command.

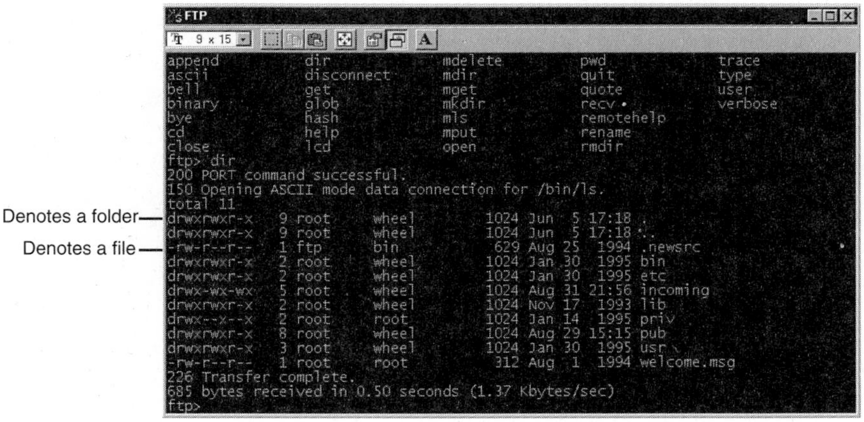

Fig. 35.10 The listing of a folder at an FTP site uses "d" in the first column to designate a folder and an "r" to designate a file.

To change to a different folder, enter this command:

cd *foldername*

To see the files in the folder, enter the **dir** command again. When you see a file you want to download, change the folder on your computer so the file will be downloaded to the proper folder. Enter this command:

lcd *foldername*

If the file that you want to download is a binary file, enter this command to set the download mode to binary (as opposed to ASCII):

binary

To download the file, enter this command:

get *filename*

Tip: Most folders have "readme" files that you can download to get more information about the site, how it is organized, what's in the particular folder, and so on.

Disconnecting and Exiting FTP

When you want to disconnect from the FTP site, type the command **disconnect**. If you want to disconnect and exit FTP, type **bye** or **quit**. Be aware that disconnecting from the site does not disconnect you from the service provider. To disconnect from the service provider, return to the desktop and click Disconnect in the Connected to dialog box.

Using a Web Browser

Suppose that you download the 32-bit version of Netscape 1.1 to use as a Web browser. The file may be a self extracting file (with an EXE extension) or a zipped file (with a ZIP extension). Extract the file or unzip it and then install the file as you would any Windows program. The next time you dial up your service provider and connect to the Internet, start Netscape from the Programs menu. Then you will truly be impressed. This is what you were expecting! Figure 35.11 shows the home page of Netscape.

Notice the Netsite prompt at the top. If you know a location that you want to go to directly, you can type it in this prompt and Netscape will take you there. For example, to go to the home page of Macmillan Publishing, enter this URL in the Netsite text box:

http://www.mcp.com

Fig. 35.12 shows the Macmillan home page at this URL.

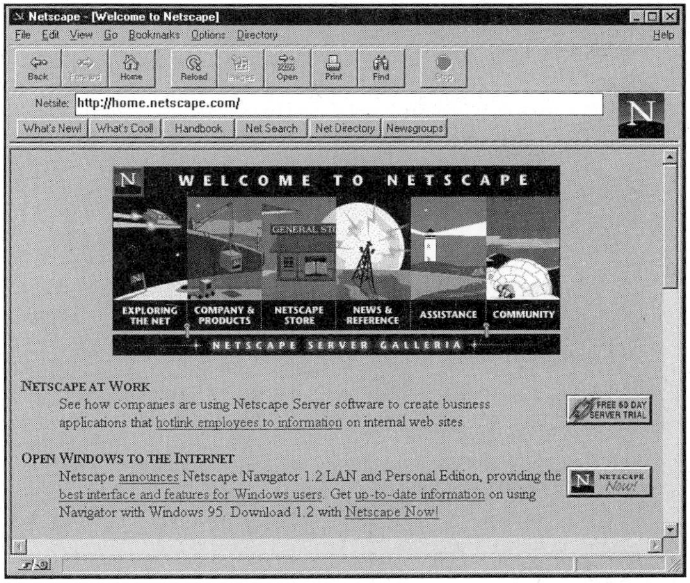

Fig. 35.11 The home page of Netscape shows many of the features that Netscape provides.

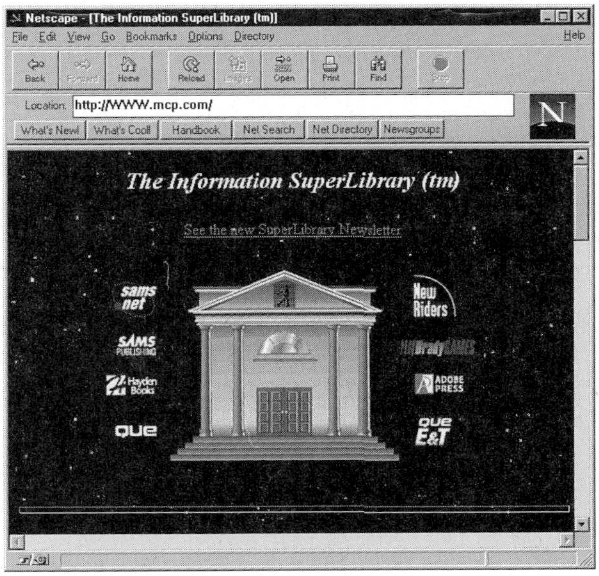

Fig. 35.12 The home page of the Macmillan site lists the publishing divisions you can go to by clicking on the name of the division.

Using a Windows Gopher

As mentioned previously, Windows 95 does not supply a Gopher. One of the best locations to download a Gopher is http://uts.cc.utexas.edu/~neuroses/cwa.html. This site contains one of the most complete lists of Winsock applications. The applications are listed by category (one category is Gophers) and each application is rated so you will have some idea of how good it is.

If you have downloaded a Gopher program, you can start it after making connection with the Internet. Figure 35.13 shows the gopher WSGOPHER.EXE and its main menu at the University of Illinois. A different Gopher program, BCGOPHER.EXE, connects to Boston College as shown in figure 35.14.

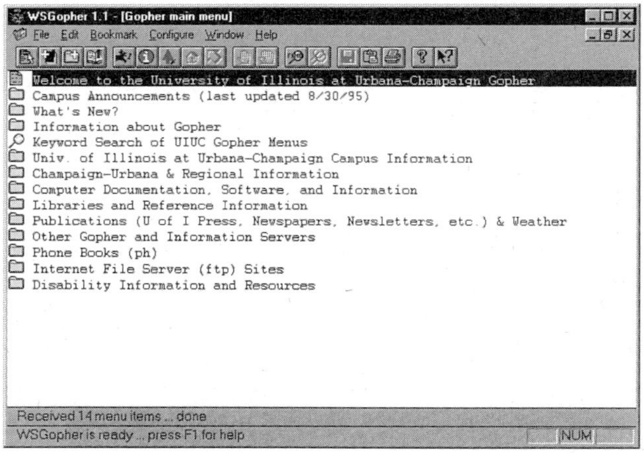

Fig. 35.13 The menu of the University of Illinois Gopher lists categories that pertain to the University.

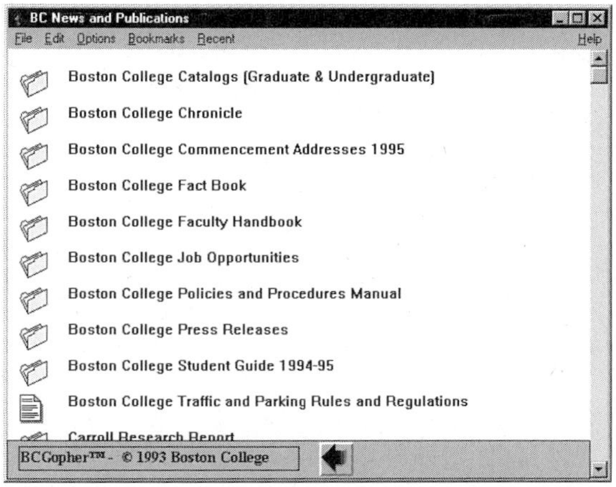

Fig. 35.14 The Boston College Gopher menu looks quite different from the University of Illinois Gopher, and, of course, the menu options are different.

Using Telnet

Windows 95 provides Telnet software. It should be stored in the Windows folder. To connect with Telnet, open an MS-DOS Prompt window, change to the folder that contains Telnet.exe, and enter the **Telnet** command. When Telnet opens, choose Connect, Remote System. Enter the name of the host, the port, and the terminal type and click Connect. Once connected, perform commands that you would if you were a node on the network.

> **Note:** You can enter the Telnet command and the connection address in one command from the DOS prompt.

If you would like to practice with Telnet and Gopher at the same time, change to the folder that contains Telnet and enter the following command at the DOS prompt:

telnet consultant.micro.umn.edu

When prompted, logon as **gopher**.

> **Tip:** Maximize the Telnet window. Some logons display data at the bottom of the screen, and the data is not visible if the window is not maximized; therefore, you think nothing is happening.

Figure 35.15 shows the Telnet connection. To exit Telnet, choose Connect, Exit or close the Telnet window.

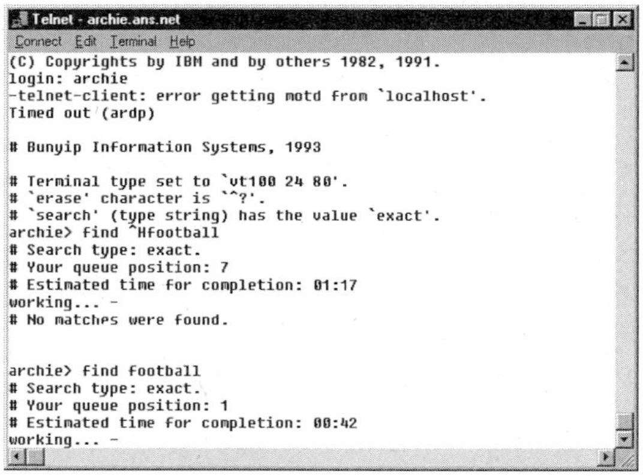

Fig. 35.15 This Telnet connection is logged on to the University of Minnesota Gopher.

Using Archie

Archie, as you may or may not recall (depending on how frazzled your brain is with all these acronyms), searches the indexes of FTP sites for files that match a title or key word that you specify. Figure 35.16 shows a Telnet connection with Archie at archie.ans.net. (The login is "archie.") The results of the command *find football* are shown on the screen.

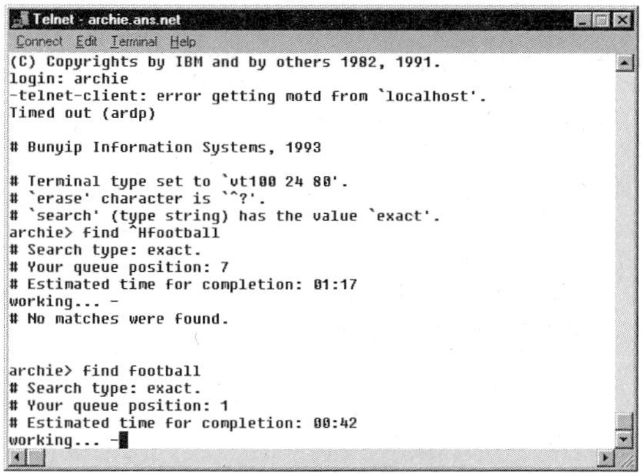

Fig. 35.16 This Archie search lists the sites that contain information about football.

Tip: It is wise to choose Terminal, Start Logging before performing a search. This command creates a telnet.log file that contains the results of the search.

Archie is also found on many Gopher menus. Figure 35.17 shows the screen that displays when you initiate an Archie search from the WSGOPHER menu at the University of Illinois.

Using WAIS

WAIS client software is not provided with Windows 95, but you can download free WAIS programs from various locations. If you would like to practice with WAIS in an emulation mode, you can use Telnet and connect to sunsite.unc.edu, logging in as **swais**. Figure 35.18 shows what the WAIS looks like at this site. Notice the directions at the bottom of the screen that tell you how to select a database, how to enter a key word, and how to search.

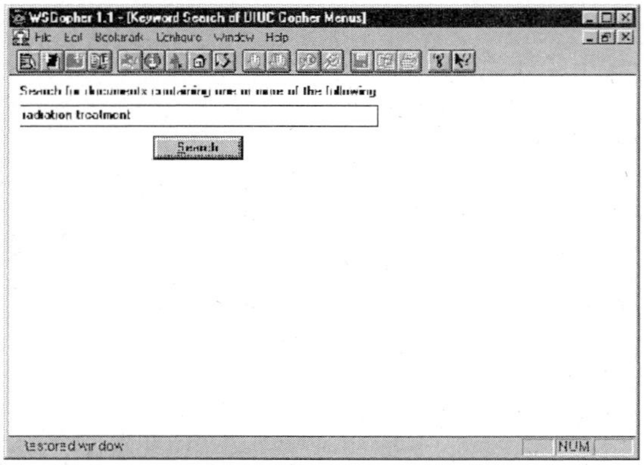

Fig. 35.17 The WSGOPHER menu displays a prompt for the key words to be used in an Archie search.

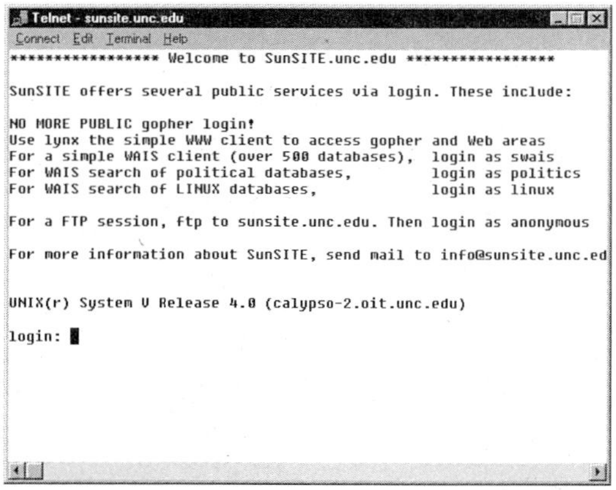

Fig. 35.18 This WAIS emulation is performed in the text mode because it originates in the Telnet window.

When you perform a WAIS search, you select a set of databases to be searched and then formulate a query consisting of key words. When the query is run, WAIS asks for information from each selected database. Headlines of documents satisfying the query are displayed, and the selected documents are ranked according to the number of matches.

To retrieve a document, you simply select it from the resulting list. The WAIS client retrieves the document and displays its contents on the screen.

36

Communicating with a Network

by Allen L. Wyatt and Bill Lawrence

Windows 95 has been written with networks in mind from the ground up. Throughout this book you have seen references to how you can use network resources as easily and conveniently as your local resources. You also know that Windows 95 provides much more network support than previous versions of Windows.

In this chapter you will learn more about how the network interfaces function. By learning this information you will be better able to understand what is going on "behind the scenes" and to make network-related adjustments to your system. In this chapter you will learn the following:

- How Windows 95 uses network components
- How you can change your network configuration
- How network identification and access control work

- How to configure your system for a Microsoft network
- How to configure your system for a NetWare network
- What the purpose of the PROTOCOL.INI file is

There is much, much more that could be written about networking. In fact, entire books have been written on this very subject. The information presented here provides a good user-oriented approach to the topic. When you combine this information with that in Chapter 37, "Using Windows 95 on a Network," you will be able to use your network connections like an expert.

Understanding Network Components

There are four types of components which combine to provide networking support to Windows 95. Think of these components as drivers, each providing a different layer of networking support. The types of components are:

- **Adapters.** These components enable you to communicate with the actual network interface card in your computer.
- **Protocols.** These components define the different communication methods that will be used over your network. These communication methods are comparable to languages, and the protocols provide the set of definitions necessary to use the languages.
- **Clients.** These components enable you to use devices available over the network. For instance, without clients you could not use disk drives or printers shared by other computers.
- **Services.** These components enable you to provide or use different services over the network. For instance, one service enables you to share files and printers, while another enables you to do automatic network backups.

To work with a network, at a minimum you need an adapter, a protocol, and a client; services are optional. In Windows 95 you can typically specify each of these components for use with your network. There are exceptions, however. If you have a Plug-and-Play system, and you use a Plug-and-Play network adapter, Windows 95 will detect the new network adapter right after you add it to your system. When you first boot, the new adapter components for that network card will be added, automatically, to the operating system.

To manually make changes to your network connection type, you simply add, remove, or make changes to the different components. You can do this from the Network dialog box. To access this dialog box, follow these steps:

1. Choose Settings from the Start menu.
2. Choose Control Panel from the Settings menu.
3. Double-click the Network icon in the Control Panel.

At this point you will see the Network dialog box, as shown in figure 36.1.

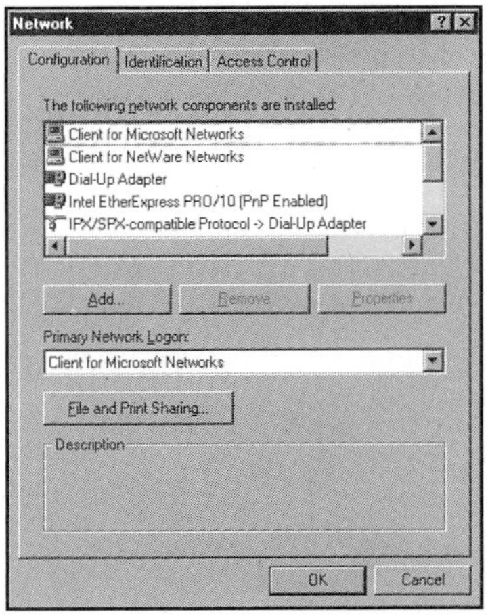

Fig. 36.1 Use the Network dialog box to control the configuration of your network.

With the Configuration tab selected, you can see the different components installed for your network at the top of the dialog box, in the list area. Each component has an icon to the left of it which identifies the type of component category to which it belongs.

- Adapters 
- Protocols 
- Clients 
- Services 

You can select different components by scrolling through the list and clicking the component you want. Later in this chapter you will learn how to use the Network dialog box to modify the configuration of your network.

Your Initial Network Configuration

When you first install Windows 95, it attempts to determine your network setup. In reality, the extent of the attempts is limited to determining the type of network adapter you have installed in your system. Although Windows 95 does pretty well at determining hardware, the "automatic nature" of the operating system comes to a dead end. Windows cannot automatically determine the type of network you are using, nor can it determine which protocols you should install for your network.

> **Note:** If you are upgrading to Windows 95 from a previous version of Windows or DOS that has networking enabled, Windows 95 can set up the proper network clients and protocols for your system. It does this by detecting the type of network that is currently configured on your system. The assumption is then made that you want to use the same network configuration under Windows 95.

After Windows 95 initially determines the type of network adapter installed in your system, and if you do not have networking installed with a previous version of Windows or DOS, it has to make a few assumptions. The safest assumption about your network is that you are using one of the two most popular networks on the market (Novell NetWare or a Microsoft network). It then loads the following two clients automatically:

- **Client for Microsoft Networks.** This client enables you to communicate with a Windows NT (client/server), LAN Manager (client/server), or Windows for Workgroups (peer-to-peer) network. If you are not using these types of networks, you can safely remove the client.

- **Client for NetWare Networks.** This client enables you to communicate with a NetWare 3.x or 4.x (client/server) network. If you are not using this type of network, you can safely remove the client.

Furthermore, Windows automatically assumes that you are using one of the network protocols most common to these two types of networks. The components for these protocols are automatically added to your system:

- **IPX/SPX-compatible Protocol.** This is the protocol used predominantly in NetWare environments. If you are not using this type of network, you can safely remove the protocol.

- **NetBEUI.** This term is a contraction for NetBIOS Extended User Interface. IBM introduced NetBEUI in 1985, and it has since been adopted by Microsoft for use in its networks. If you are not using a Microsoft network, you can safely remove the protocol.

The Purpose of Bindings

Bindings is just a fancy word to describe the links that exist between network adapters and network protocols. The bindings inform the operating system (Windows 95) which protocols should be used with which network adapters.

You can look at the listed network components in the Network dialog box to see which bindings are in effect. If you look at the protocol lines, you will see the name of the protocol followed by a right-pointing arrow and the name of an adapter, as shown in figure 36.2. These indicate the bindings in effect between a protocol and an adapter.

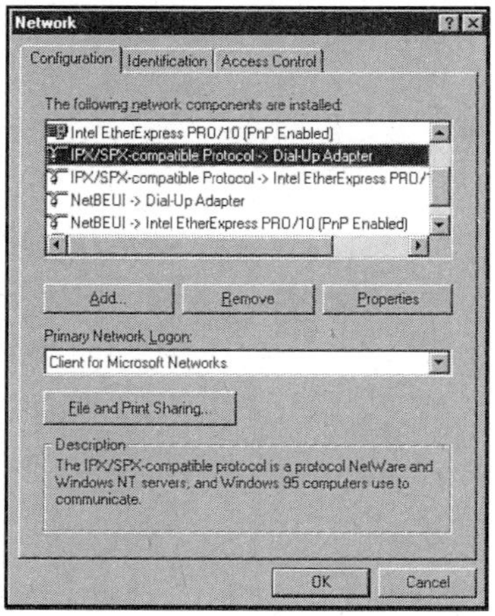

Fig. 36.2 Bindings are indicated in the list of network components on the Network dialog box.

If you have only one adapter card in your system, and you have only one or two protocols loaded, then each of the protocols will be bound to the adapter card you have installed. Later in this chapter you will learn how you can change bindings for your system.

Changing Your Network Configuration

You can change an existing network configuration from the Network dialog box. This is the same dialog box you accessed earlier in this chapter. To display the dialog box, follow these steps:

1. Choose Settings from the Start menu.
2. Choose Control Panel from the Settings menu.
3. Double-click the Network icon in the Control Panel.

> **Tip:** To quickly access the Network dialog box, you can right-click the Network Neighborhood icon on your desktop, and then choose Properties from the context menu.

At this point you will see the Network dialog box, as shown in figure 36.1 earlier in the chapter.

Now you can select different network components in the list at the top of the dialog box, and then you can use the other controls in the dialog box to change your configuration. The following sections describe the different actions you can take.

Adding Network Components

To add a component to your network, click the Add button in the Network dialog box. This displays the Select Network Component Type dialog box, as shown in figure 36.3.

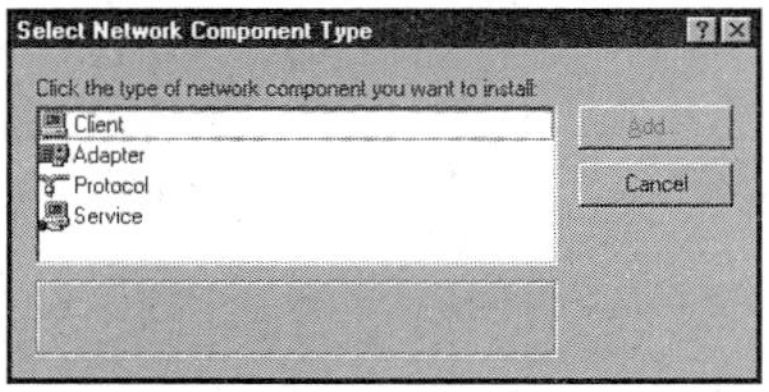

Fig. 36.3 The first step in adding a network component is to identify the type of component you want to add.

The four different network components are listed in this dialog box, and you can select the one you want to add. After you select the component type, simply click the Add button. The following sections describe the different aspects of adding each type of component.

Adding Clients

When you choose to add a network client, you are shown the Select Network Client dialog box which lists the different manufacturers and models of clients you can add (see figure 36.4). Select the make and model of your network.

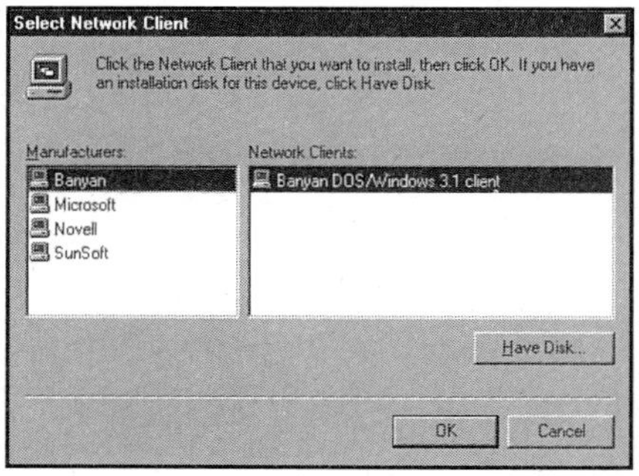

Fig. 36.4 Windows 95 enables you to specify a wide variety of network clients.

Windows 95 supports over six different network clients from four different manufacturers:

- **Banyan.** There is only one client available for this vendor. The Banyan DOS/Windows 3.1 client supports the Banyan Vines network configuration.
- **Microsoft.** There are two different Microsoft clients provided. These two clients, for Microsoft networks and for Novell NetWare, are the clients described earlier in the chapter as the default clients loaded by Windows 95.
- **Novell.** The Novell-specific clients are used if you are using real-mode network device drivers. One client interfaces with the Novell 3.x workstation shell, and the other with the 4.x shell. Microsoft suggests that you do not use these clients, as the real-mode drivers offer inferior performance when compared to the 32-bit support offered by the Microsoft client for Novell.
- **SunSoft.** A single SunSoft client is provided: SunSoft PC-NFS (version 5.0). This network client provides connectivity to SunSoft networks.

In addition, if you have an updated or different client from a network manufacturer, you can click the Have Disk button in order to install your client from a disk.

Adding Adapters

When you choose to add an adapter, you will see the Select Network Adapter dialog box, which enables you to select the vendor and adapter model used in your system (see figure 36.5).

When you specify a vendor in the Manufacturers list, the choices available in the Network Adapters list change to reflect the products from that vendor. Windows 95 supports over 248 cards from 50 different vendors, so the chances are quite good that you can find the adapter card applicable to your network.

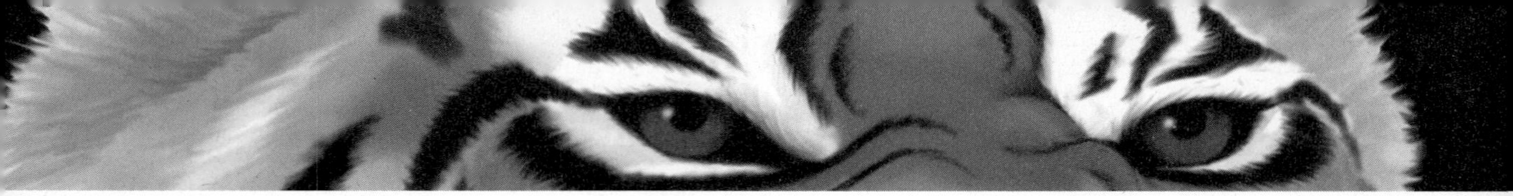

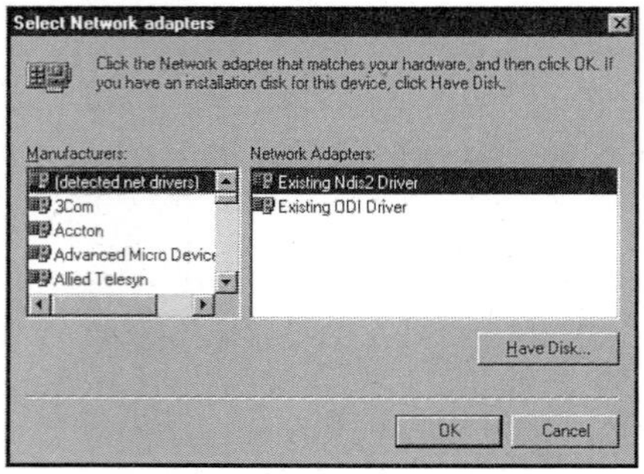

Fig. 36.5 Picking a network adapter is a simple matter of selecting a vendor and a card type.

> **Tip:** If you cannot determine what type of adapter you have, you should refer to the documentation for the card or contact your network administrator. If you do not have a network administrator, then contact the person that sold you the card or installed it.

If, for some reason, you cannot find your particular adapter in the list of those available, you can use the Have Disk button to load an adapter driver from disk.

Adding Protocols

When you choose to add a network protocol, you will see the Select Network Protocol dialog box, as shown in figure 36.6. Network protocols are closely related to the type of network client you have specified. All you need to do is pick a vendor (from the Manufacturers list) and then a protocol applicable to that vendor.

Windows 95 provides support for 14 protocols from 6 different vendors. In most cases you should select the same manufacturer as you did when you specified a network client. Then pick the protocol you want to use in your network. If you are connecting to an already established network, check with your network administrator to see what protocol is used on the network.

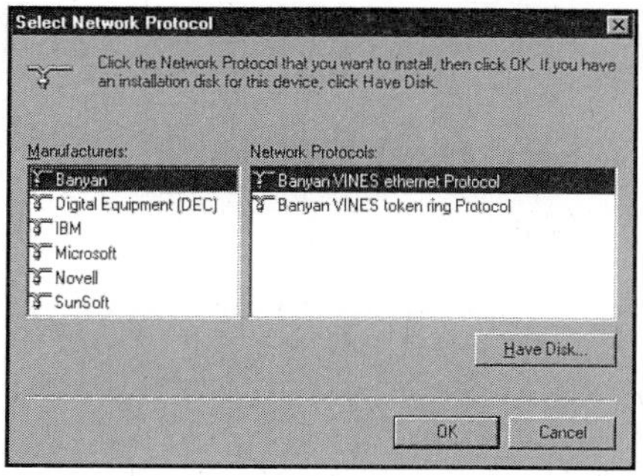

Fig. 36.6 You use network protocols to define communication procedures over the network.

> **Caution:** If you do not pick a compatible protocol when connecting to an existing network, you will not be able to communicate with other computers on the network. Furthermore, you may also stop other computers on the network from communicating properly.

If your network protocol is not available from the list, you can click the Have Disk button to add a protocol provided by your vendor.

Adding Services

Network services are used to provide well-defined features that other computers on the network can access. The two most common examples of network services are file sharing and printer sharing. The network service is the operating system component that enables a feature. For instance, if you don't load the printer sharing network service, you won't be able to share your printers on the network.

When you choose to add a service, you will see the Select Network Service dialog box shown in figure 36.7.

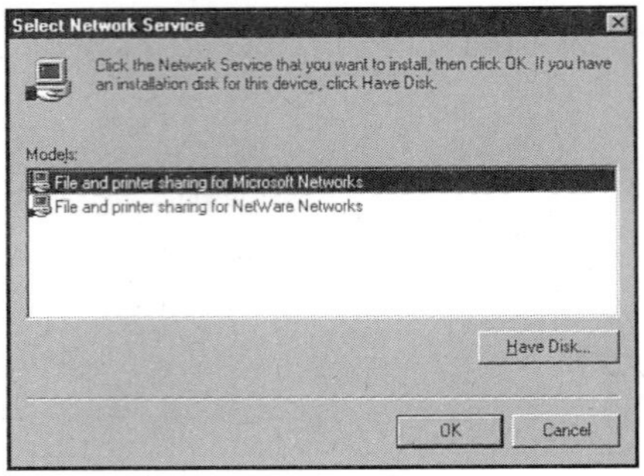

Fig. 36.7 Adding services allows you to offer resources to the network.

The Select Network Service dialog box is where you will most likely use the Have Disk button. For instance, you may purchase a network archival system that enables you to back up your entire network. The vendor may have supplied a Windows 95 disk that includes the service driver necessary to utilize its hardware.

Removing Network Components

To remove a network component, all you need to do is highlight it in the Network dialog box, and then click the Remove button. The component is immediately removed, without asking for confirmation. After it is removed, the only way to undo your action is to again add the component to your system.

Changing Bindings

You will remember from the discussion earlier in this chapter that bindings are the linking of a protocol with an adapter. If you have only one adapter card in your system, and you have only one or two protocols loaded, chances are good that you will never need to change bindings. If you have multiple adapter cards connected to dissimilar networks, then you may need to change bindings. For instance, if you have an adapter card used to connect to a Microsoft network and another loaded to connect with a NetWare network, then you will need to bind the proper protocols to the proper adapter cards for each type of network.

To change bindings, you can start with either the protocol or the adapter. If you want to change bindings from the aspect of the adapter, start with the Network dialog box displayed. Then, follow these steps:

1. In the list of network components, highlight the adapter for which you want the bindings changed.
2. Click the Properties button. You will see the Properties sheet for the adapter.
3. Click the Bindings tab. The dialog box now appears, as shown in figure 36.8.

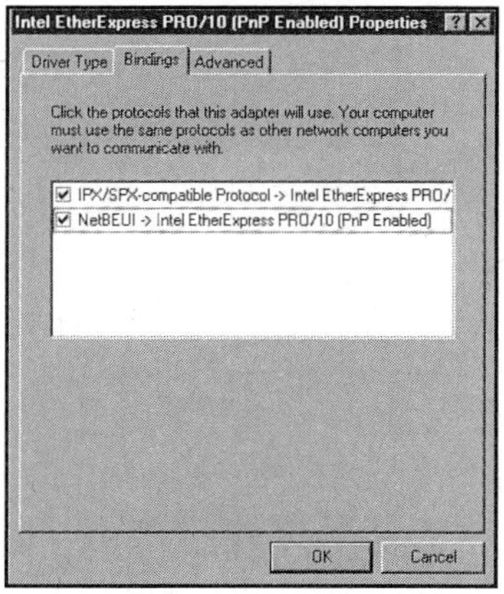

Fig. 36.8 Windows 95 enables you to easily change the bindings to an adapter.

The dialog box lists all the protocols that are loaded for your system. In the check box to the left of each protocol you can see whether it is bound to the adapter whose properties you are changing. To break the binding, simply clear the check box; to establish the binding, select the check box. When you are done, click the OK button.

You can also change bindings by starting with the protocol instead of the adapter. To do this, display the Network dialog box, and then follow these steps:

1. In the list of network components, highlight the protocol for which you want the bindings changed.
2. Click the Properties button. You will see the Properties sheet for the protocol.
3. Click the Bindings tab. The dialog box now appears, as shown in figure 36.9.

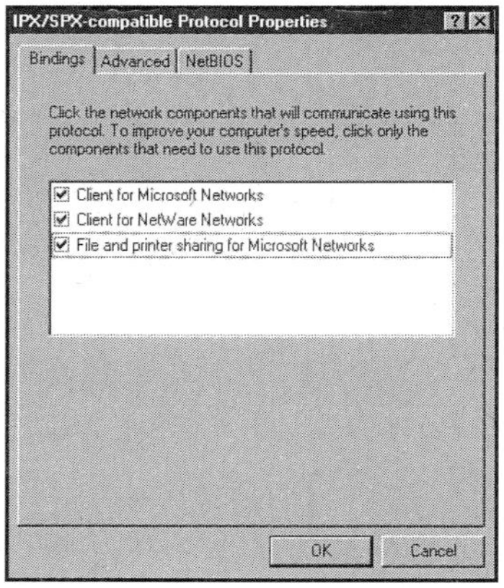

Fig. 36.9 Windows 95 enables you to easily change the bindings for a protocol.

Notice that the list in this dialog box is a bit different from the earlier list. Here you see a list of all the network components (clients and services) that can communicate using the protocol you have selected. By default, the protocol is bound to every component that can possibly use it.

Tip: To improve the performance of your system, disable the binding between the protocol and a component that you know will never use that protocol. To break the binding, simply clear the check box; to establish the binding, select the check box.

Remember that you should only have the network components loaded that you will actually be using in your network. To have extraneous components loaded can slow down the performance of your system in relation to the network. Therefore, delete the components you absolutely do not need, and then check your bindings to ensure they reflect the logical links appropriate for your network.

File and Print Sharing

Earlier in this chapter you learned that network services enable you to share both files and printers over the network. You can either add this service as you would any other network component (as described earlier in the section "Adding Network Components"), or you can simply use the shortcut that Windows 95 provides for this feature. At the bottom of the Network dialog box, first shown in figure 36.1, is a button labeled File and Print Sharing. If you click this button, you will see the dialog box shown in figure 36.10.

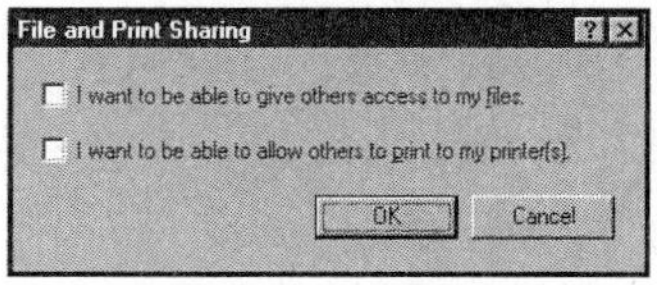

Fig. 36.10 The File and Print Sharing dialog box is a quick way to indicate what resources you want to share.

From this dialog box you can select the type of file and printer sharing you want done. Simply select the check box to the left of the option (or options) that expresses what you want to do. When you finish, click the OK button. If the File and Printer Sharing for Microsoft Networks service is not already installed on your system, it is added to fulfill your request.

> **Note:** If you are using a Microsoft network under Windows 95, file sharing is actually a misnomer. In reality, you share folders, which in turn contain files. Thus, you cannot make an individual file available on the network, unless that file is the only one within a folder you have shared.

Your Primary Network Logon

Near the middle of the Network dialog box (shown in figure 36.1), you may have noticed a pull-down list entitled Primary Network Logon. This list enables you to specify the network definition to which you want to log on whenever you start Windows. The choices in this list are defined by which clients you have installed. For instance, if you are using a Microsoft network, and you have the client for Microsoft networks installed, this is one of the choices in the pull-down list.

The client you choose in this list defines how your logon process occurs. It is a safe bet that every network client requires that you provide a user ID and a password, but from the type of network you are connecting to these network clients will dictate what steps will occur. For instance, some clients may require you to identify a workgroup, domain, or server to use for your initial connection.

Regardless of the clients you have installed, there is one other choice always available in the pull-down list—Windows Logon. This option is used to log you on to Windows 95, but no network authentication is performed. Thus, if you type the wrong user ID or password, you can still receive access to Windows 95. Choosing this logon process (as opposed to a specific network logon) should only be used if your computer is physically disconnected from a network for a time.

For instance, you may be using a portable system that keeps getting network connection errors whenever you are on the road. To solve this problem, simply select Windows Logon as your logon process.

Network Identification

Regardless of the type of network you have installed, Windows 95 requires you to specify information that identifies your machine to your network. At the highest level, you can do this by using the Identification tab in the Network dialog box. To change your identification settings, follow these steps:

1. Choose Settings from the Start menu.
2. Choose Control Panel from the Settings menu.
3. Double-click the Network icon in the Control Panel.
4. Click the Identification tab. The Network dialog box appears, as shown in figure 36.11.

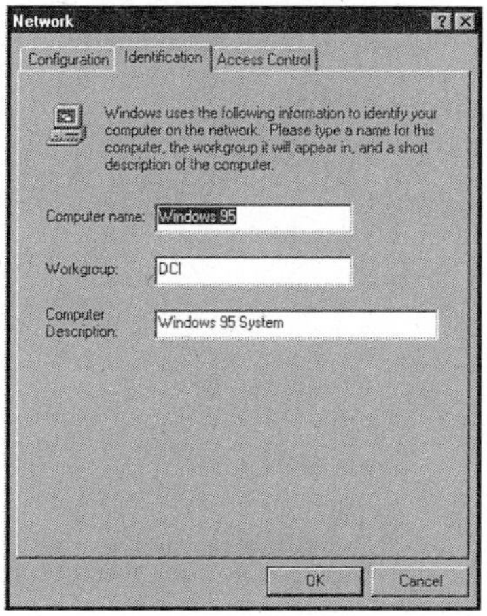

Fig. 36.11 Identification information is used to identify your machine on the network.

Depending on your network configuration, you can use the three pieces of information in this dialog box in different ways. For instance, if your network client and protocol require the use of domains or workgroups, then use the Workgroup setting in this dialog box to identify which one you belong to. If you enter the name of an existing workgroup, then you are grouped with that workgroup. If you enter the name of a new workgroup (even if it is by misspelling an existing name), then a new workgroup is created with you as the only member.

Regardless of your network type, the contents of the Computer name and Computer Description fields are used whenever you browse through the Network Neighborhood. The fields in this dialog box have the following constraints:

- **Computer name.** Any name used to identify your system. The name is required and can contain up to 15 characters. The name cannot contain any of the characters listed in Table 36.1.
- **Workgroup.** Any name that uniquely identifies the workgroup or domain to which you belong. The name is required and can be up to 15 characters long; it cannot contain any of the characters listed in Table 36.1.
- **Computer Description.** Any comment about your computer that you want displayed to other network members. This is an optional field, and can be as long as you want.

Table 36.1 Illegal Characters for Computer and Workgroup Names

Character	Name
!	Exclamation point
#	Pound sign
$	Dollar sign
%	Percent sign
&	Ampersand
'	Apostrophe

Character	Name
()	Parentheses
-	Minus sign/dash
.	Period
@	At sign
^	Caret
_	Underscore
{}	Braces
~	Tilde
	Space

It is very possible that your company already has some sort of identification system set up for computers on the network. You will want to check with your system administrator to see if you should include specific information in the identification fields. For instance, the rules of your network may require that a phone number, department name, or office number be included in the Computer Description field.

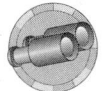

Note: If you are using the TCP/IP protocol on your network, you will also be required to specify additional identification settings for your computer. You do this through the Properties sheet for the TCP/IP protocol. The exact details of TCP/IP settings are described in detail in Chapter 35, "Internet Communications."

Access Control

Access control refers to how other computers on the network can access resources attached to your computer, such as printers or files. Windows 95 enables you to specify the rules by which you want access to occur. To change the access control settings, follow these steps:

1. Choose Settings from the Start menu.
2. Choose Control Panel from the Settings menu.
3. Double-click the Network icon in the Control Panel.
4. Click the Access Control tab. The Network dialog box appears as shown in figure 36.12.

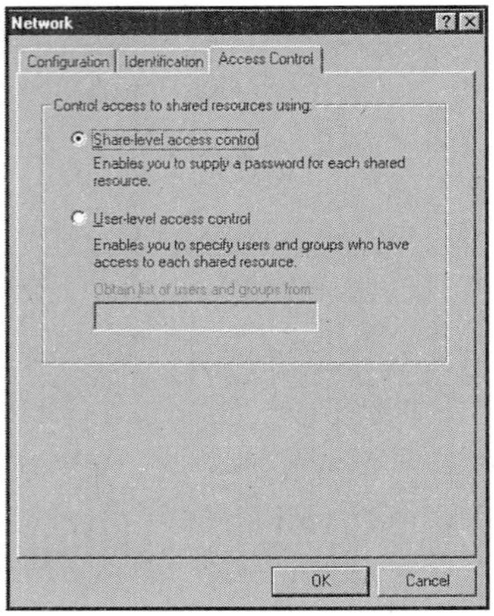

Fig. 36.12 You use access control information to control how your system resources are tapped.

You can pick either of two settings in this dialog box. The first setting (Share-level access control) is the default. With this option chosen, access is controlled on a printer-by-printer or file-by-file basis. When you share the printer or file, you have the opportunity to specify a password which is required for others to use the resource.

If you choose the second access option (User-level access control), then users or groups of users will always have access to your shared printers or files. A user who is not the one you specified (or, if you specified a group, in the group you specified), cannot access your resources. With this option selected, you must specify a server or domain where the list of authorized users is stored. You should note that

User-level Access Control is available only if you are using a client/server networking environment running under Windows NT (thus, the domain name requirement) or NetWare (the server name requirement).

> **Note:** You can set the access control rules anytime you want, but they only have meaning if you have chosen to share files or printers for your system.

Configuring Your System for a Microsoft Network

After you have set up your Microsoft network for the first time, you will need to be concerned with how Windows 95 is configured to use the network. You do this by accomplishing the following three tasks:

- Specifying whether Microsoft network is the primary client for logging on your system.
- Specifying whether your system is part of a Windows NT domain.
- Specifying how network drives should be treated in relation to your system.

The order in which you perform these tasks is not important. Each task is covered in the following sections.

Setting the Primary Network

Specifying a primary network logon has already been touched on earlier in the chapter. To specify Microsoft network as your logon choice, follow these steps:

1. Choose Settings from the Start menu.
2. Choose Control Panel from the Settings menu.

3. Double-click the Network icon in the Control Panel. This displays the Network dialog box.
4. Click the pull-down control at the right side of the Primary Network Logon field. This displays a list of available network clients.
5. Select the Client for Microsoft Networks option.

If there is no Client for Microsoft Networks option in the pull-down list, then you have not installed the client. Refer to the section on adding a client, earlier in this chapter, for information on how to do this.

Specifying Domain and Network Drive Information

You can accomplish two of the steps in setting up a Microsoft network by changing the properties associated with the Microsoft networks client. To display this dialog box, follow these steps:

1. Choose Settings from the Start menu.
2. Choose Control Panel from the Settings menu.
3. Double-click the Network icon in the Control Panel.
4. In the list of network components at the top of the dialog box, choose Client for Microsoft Networks.
5. Click the Properties button. You should see the Properties sheet appear, as shown in figure 36.13.

To change the domain information, modify the information in the Logon validation area of the dialog box. If you select the check box, then anytime you log on to your system, you also automatically log on to your Windows NT network. The domain name you specify is checked for your user ID and password. If they are found, you are given the appropriate level of access to the network. (Your access level is determined and managed by the network administrator.) If either your user ID or password is incorrect, then you will not see any errors, but you will not have full access to the network.

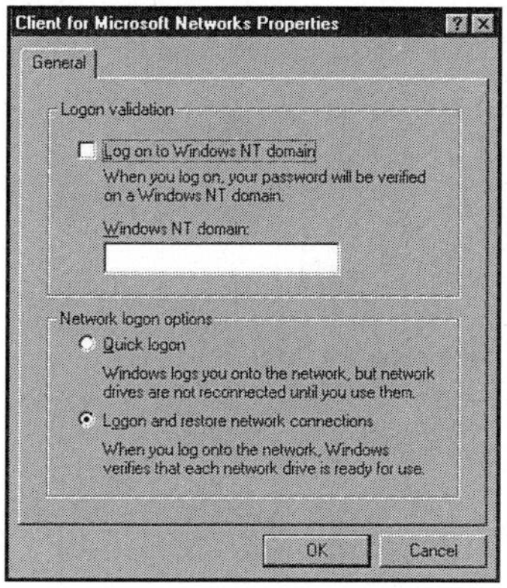

Fig. 36.13 You can modify the properties of the Microsoft network client.

If you are not part of a Windows NT network, but instead are using a peer-to-peer network consisting of Windows 95, Windows for Workgroups, or Windows NT workstation systems, then you should make sure that the Log on to Windows NT Domain option is not selected. Because a peer-to-peer network does not have a server used for centralized administration, checking the server is not necessary.

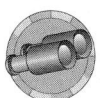

> **Note:** If you instruct Windows 95 to verify your account with a Windows NT server, but do not supply a domain name, then you will be asked for a domain name whenever you log in to the system.

At the bottom of the dialog box, in the Network Logon Options section, you can specify how you want your network drives treated during the logon process. If you select the first option, Quick Logon, then the validity of network drives is not checked during the logon process. Instead, network drives are only checked when you first attempt to use one. The other option, Logon and Restore Network Connections, causes a delay in logging on, but you are sure that the network drives are available right away.

Most users should select the Quick Logon option. In many networks you could have drives coming on and off line all the time. Thus, even though the validity of a drive connection is checked when you first log on, it may change by the time you access the drive.

Running Windows 95 on a Novell Network

If you are running Windows 95 on a network where most or all of the servers are running Novell NetWare, you need to make some important choices. For starters, you have the choice of two network clients—Microsoft's NetWare client or the client that comes with Novell's workstation requester. Each client has its pros and cons, which you learn about later in this section. Your choice of clients also influences which tools you use to log in to servers, map drive letters, and connect to print queues.

Besides exploring the differences between the Novell and Microsoft NetWare clients, you also learn how to install the Novell client and how to configure the NetWare settings in Windows 95.

Choosing the Right NetWare Client

How do you choose between Microsoft's built-in NetWare client and the client that comes with Novell's DOS and Windows requester? It depends on what is important to you. Microsoft's client is a true 32-bit protected mode client and thereby holds an edge in terms of performance and tight integration with Windows 95. It is the client to choose if you never want to see the DOS prompt and you do not mind trading some compatibility for the privilege. Novell's client boasts complete compatibility with all NetWare versions and features, but requires that you use Novell's real-mode DOS-compatible network drivers.

As you weigh the pluses and minuses of each client, consider these factors:

- Do you need the client to be compatible with NetWare Folder Services (which comes with NetWare version 4.x)?
- Do you need or prefer to use the NetWare Windows utilities NWADMIN and NWUSER?
- Do you need to run protocols besides NetWare's IPX/SPX? Do you need to run the TCP/IP protocol, for example, to access the Internet?
- Is all the NetWare-aware software that you need to run compatible with the client you are choosing?

The Microsoft NetWare Client

You learned previously in this chapter how to install Microsoft's built-in NetWare client. Microsoft's Windows 95 NetWare client offers the following strengths:

- High performance and no DOS memory consumption because the client is a protected mode 32-bit application.
- Almost complete compatibility with NetWare 3.x and software that uses Novell's IPX/SPX protocol.
- Windows-based login including the ability to execute NetWare 3.x login scripts.

You will encounter the following drawbacks if you decide to use the Microsoft NetWare client:

- No compatibility with NetWare 4.x's NetWare Folder Services (NDS). NDS provides a global name and resource folder for a network comprised of NetWare 4.x servers.
- NetWare Windows utilities such as NWUSER and NWADMIN are not compatible with the Microsoft NetWare client.

The Microsoft client for NetWare is worth a try if you want the highest performance and do not need NetWare 4.x or NetWare Folder Services compatibility. If you discover any serious compatibility issues with other software that you need to use, you can easily switch to Novell's Windows client.

Novell's NetWare Client

Windows 95 is fully compatible with Novell's DOS and Windows client (which is included as part of the NetWare DOS requester that comes with NetWare 3.12 and NetWare 4.x). Novell's client offers the following benefits:

- Complete compatibility with all NetWare versions and features and a long track record of compatibility and stability.
- All software that requires the IPX/SPX protocol should be compatible with the Novell NetWare client.
- NetWare's Windows utilities (NWADMIN and NWUSER) are fully supported.
- Novell's client can coreside with the Windows 95 client for Microsoft networks, so you can connect to both NetWare and Windows NT servers and also use Windows 95's peer-to-peer network features.

The Novell client is weak in the following areas:

- Because it uses real-mode DOS network card drivers, protocols, and a DOS requester (VLM.EXE), the Novell client consumes DOS memory and is not as fast as the Microsoft NetWare client.
- For best results and to execute your login scripts, you will need to log in from DOS before the Windows 95 graphical interface starts.

Table 36.2 details the differences between the Novell and Microsoft clients for Windows 95.

Table 36.2 Novell and Microsoft Client Feature Comparison

Feature	Microsoft Client	Novell Client
Real or protected mode?	Protected mode	Real mode
NetWare version	NetWare 3.x only	NetWare 3.x and 4.x compatibility
Logging in	Log in from Windows	Log in from DOS
Combined login and password with Windows and Microsoft networks?	Yes	No
Login scripts	Partial NetWare 3.x compatibility	Full NetWare 3.x and 4.x compatibility
Compatible with NWUSER and NWADMIN?	No	Yes
Can coreside with other protocols and other Windows 95 network clients?	Yes	Yes
Compatible with all built-in Windows 95 drive mapping and printer connection tools?	Yes	Yes

Installing Novell's client for NetWare is fairly simple but not quite as automatic as installing Microsoft's client for NetWare (a process that you learned about previously in this chapter). You need to start the Network dialog box (which you can open by right-clicking the desktop's Network Neighborhood icon and choosing Properties or by starting the Control Panel and clicking the Network icon). When the Network dialog box appears, choose the Configuration tab and click the Add button. Choose Client from the Select Network Component dialog box that appears, and then choose Novell from the client manufacturers that are listed.

When you select Novell from the list of client manufacturers, you can choose the version of the Novell client that matches the workstation

requester or shell that you are using. After you have made your selection, click OK. Windows 95 prompts you to take the following steps:

1. Restart your computer (Windows 95 has modified your AUTOEXEC.BAT file so that your PC starts in DOS mode and displays special prompt messages about the following steps).
2. Run the NetWare DOS Requester installation program. This places the adapter drivers, protocol drivers, and NetWare requester files (DOS and Windows) on your PC.
3. Modify your AUTOEXEC.BAT to automatically load the network card and protocol drivers and requester files. Also modify your AUTOEXEC.BAT to execute NetWare's LOGIN command, which prompts you to log in. While you are modifying AUTOEXEC.BAT, remove the prompt messages referred to in step 1.
4. Restart your computer and log in. Then start Windows 95 by typing **WIN**.
5. Start the Control Panel and click the Network icon, or right-click the Network Neighborhood icon and choose Properties. Windows 95 automatically updates your network configuration as required, and prompts you to restart your computer once more.

After you perform these steps, Windows 95 is configured to run Novell's client for NetWare.

Configuration Options for the Microsoft Client for NetWare

If you opt to use the Microsoft Client for NetWare, there are three options that you can configure after you install and activate the client. To set these options, start the Control Panel and click the Network icon or right-click the Network Neighborhood icon on the desktop and choose Properties. The Network dialog box opens. Double-click the NetWare client listing in this box, and a dialog box appears that enables you to configure three options: your preferred server, the first network drive, and whether or not to process login scripts when you log in.

In the box labeled Preferred Server, enter the name of the NetWare server to which you want the NetWare client to connect at startup. In the First Network Drive box, choose the drive letter that should be assigned to the SYS volume on that server when you activate the NetWare client. Place a check mark in the Process Login Script box to execute your NetWare login script when you log in using the Microsoft client for NetWare. Click OK when you finish setting these options.

Understanding the PROTOCOL.INI File

Windows 95 includes a file called PROTOCOL.INI in the folder in which Windows is installed. You use this file for two purposes:

- As a configuration guide if you are using real-mode device drivers for your networking.
- If you ever boot your system in safe mode with networking support (as discussed in Chapter 6, "Troubleshooting Windows 95 Installation and Startup").

> **Caution:** Use extreme care in modifying PROTOCOL.INI. Incorrect information in the file can cause unpredictable errors in running Windows 95, or can damage other Windows 95 configuration files. Always make a backup copy of the file before you make any changes.

The contents of PROTOCOL.INI are established by the Setup program when you first install Windows 95. Thereafter, the contents are modified as necessary by changes you make in the Network section of the Control Panel. It is possible that you may need to directly modify the information in PROTOCOL.INI if you are using real-mode network drivers and your system has a resource conflict for which Windows 95 cannot automatically compensate. As an example, if you have a network card that uses real-mode drivers, and the card conflicts with the

IRQs or I/O addresses used by your video card, then you may need to make changes in PROTOCOL.INI.

The following is an example of a PROTOCOL.INI file:

```
[protman$]
priority=ndishlp$
DriverName=protman$

[ndishlp$]
DriverName=ndishlp$
Bindings=EPRO$

[data]
version=v4.00.490
netcards=EPRO$,*INT1030

[nwlink$]
Frame_Type=4
cachesize=0
Bindings=EPRO$
DriverName=nwlink$

[NETBEUI$]
sessions=10
ncbs=12
Bindings=EPRO$
DriverName=NETBEUI$
Lanabase=1

[EPRO$]
INTERRUPT=11
ioaddress=0x240
DriverName=EPRO$
```

Notice that the file follows the traditional construction of an INI file. The file is a plain ASCII text file, major sections defined by a section name surrounded by brackets. Thus, [EPRO$] is a section within the PROTOCOL.INI file. The order of the sections within the file is not critical, but the composition of each section can be critical.

Individual sections are composed of entries that define settings. Each entry is composed of a setting name, an equal sign, and a value. The setting name is on the left side of the equal sign, and the setting value is on the right side. The major sections in PROTOCOL.INI are described in detail in the following sections.

In addition to major sections, there will also be other sections in the file that relate to each of the drivers' references in the major sections. For instance, in the listing of PROTOCOL.INI just provided, the first section, [protman$], is a major section. Within this section there is a reference to ndishlp$. Another section within the file actually defines the parameters of this driver.

The [protman$] Section

This section is used to provide settings for the protocol manager. There are two entries typically in this section, and their order does not matter. One entry, DriverName, is used to specify the device driver used for the protocol manager. The other entry is priority, which is used to specify the order in which incoming data frames are processed by the protocol manager.

The [NETBEUI$] Section

This particular section is named after the network protocol installed on the system—NETBEUI. There will be a corresponding protocol section in the file for each network protocol you have installed. Each protocol section will have, at minimum, the following types of entries:

- **Bindings.** This entry defines the network adapter cards to which the protocol is bound. In other words, if the protocol is used to communicate through the card, the card name is used in this entry. The card name is the same as the name of a card section defined elsewhere within PROTOCOL.INI. In the example file listed previously, the card cited in the entry is EPRO$, which is also the name of another section in the file. Because a protocol can be bound to multiple cards, you can include more than one card name for the Bindings setting. To do this, simply separate the card names with commas.
- **Lanabase.** This number is determined by the Setup program and specifies the binding between the network protocol and the network adapter.

Other settings within the protocol section can vary, depending on the protocol. For instance, the NETBEUI$ protocol section contains information on the number of sessions and ncbs for the driver.

The [nwlink$] Section

This is another protocol section, except this time it is related to the Client for NetWare Networks. The entries within the section define the parameters used by the NetWare protocol. The same comments made in the last section, in relation to NETBEUI, refer to this section of the file as well.

The [EPRO$] Section

The [EPRO$] section will not be available, by this name, in all PROTOCOL.INI files. Instead, a name will be used for this section that represents the actual card installed in the system. This particular PROTOCOL.INI file is from a system that has an Intel EtherPro PnP card. Other cards will have different names, but each card in a system will have a corresponding section within PROTOCOL.INI.

The entries within the card section define the various settings for the card. Because each network card varies, the contents of the section can vary as well. In the example file listed earlier, the settings define the IRQ used by the card (INTERRUPT=11), the I/O address used by the card (ioaddress=0x240), and the device driver used by the card (DriverName=EPRO$). In virtually all instances, if you compare the contents of this card section with what you know about the card from reading its manual, you can figure out what the entries represent.

37

Using Windows 95 on a Network

by Allen L. Wyatt

Networks can greatly increase your productivity, or they can present one more layer of complexity, thereby hindering productivity. The difference is in how the network is designed, administered, and used by all concerned. In this chapter, you will learn how you can use the network-specific features of Windows 95. Here you will learn the following:

- How you can share information on your system with others on the network
- How you can access information on other people's systems by mapping network drives

- Special network features when printing over a network
- How you can manage your network

Sharing Information

One of the primary purposes of a network is to facilitate the communal sharing of information. Windows 95 enables you to share information on your system and to access information that is on other people's systems. The next several sections describe how to both give and receive information.

Sharing Folders

When you are working in a networked environment, you may want to share information on your computer with another user on the network. This is easy to do using Windows 95 by simply sharing your folders. Shared folders and their contents are visible to other network users as they browse through the Net.

For example, let's assume that you are working with other people in your workgroup on a project. Your task is to come up with figures for a product manual being developed by your company. To keep the figures in a logical place, you have created a folder named FIGURES on your C: drive. To make this folder available to other network users, you would follow these steps:

1. Double-click the My Computer icon on the desktop. This displays the drives available on your system.
2. Double-click the C disk drive. This displays all the files and folders in your C drive, as shown in figure 37.1.

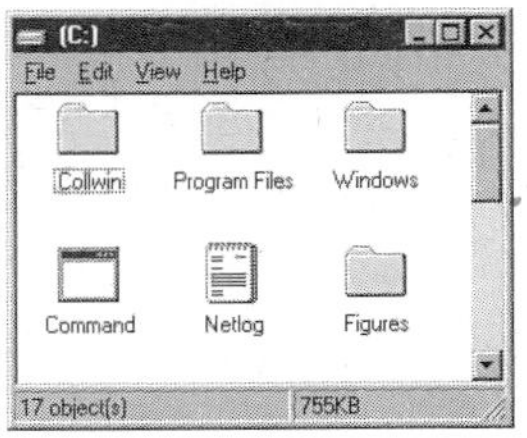

Fig. 37.1 The Figures folder is visible in the window that shows the contents of the C drive.

3. Right-click the Figures folder icon. This displays the context menu for the folder.
4. From the context menu, choose the Sharing option. This displays the Properties sheet for the folder, with the Sharing tab selected, as shown in figure 37.2.

> **Note:** If the Sharing option is not available from the context menu, then you need to set up file sharing as described in Chapter 36, "Communicating with a Network."

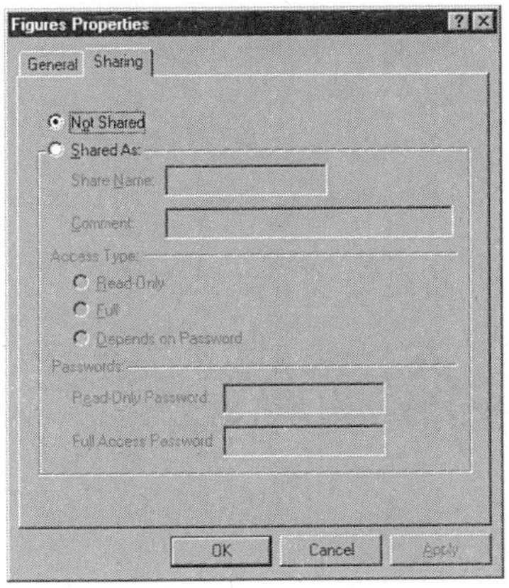

Fig. 37.2 The Sharing tab enables you to specify how a folder should be shared.

At this point you can specify that you want to share the folder by simply clicking the Shared As option. You can then specify the name by which the folder should be shared, and the type of access you want to provide.

Naming a Shared Folder

After you have clicked the Shared As option, the Share Name field becomes active. In the Share Name field you can indicate the name you want to use for this folder when it is shared over the network. Windows 95 provides the actual name of the folder (Figures) as a default, but you can change it to any name you want.

Underneath the shared name for the folder is a field where you can include a comment. This comment has no value other than as a piece of information for whoever is browsing through the network. When the browser is looking through the detail for your computer, the comment appears to the right of the folder name.

Setting Access Rights

When you are sharing a folder, you can grant other people either read-only privileges (which means they cannot alter the files or the folder) or full privileges (which means they can do anything they want with the folder). To offer read-only privileges, click the Read-Only button; to offer full privileges, click the Full button.

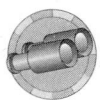

> **Note:** The access rights that you can grant to other people depends on the type of network client you are using. For instance, with NetWare you have a much finer level of control over access rights than with Microsoft networks.

There is a third access right available—Depends on Password. With this access right selected, what remote users can do to your folder depends on whether they know the proper password. Passwords are entered at the bottom of the Sharing tab. There are two passwords available—read-only and full. All you need to do is enter the passwords that you want associated with your folder.

> **Tip:** If you are not concerned over the contents of your folder and who has access to it, simply leave the password fields blank. Without a password, anyone can access your system at the access level that you specify.

Determining Who Can Do What

By creatively mixing the settings of the access type and the passwords, you gain quite a bit of control over who can do what with your system. Table 37.1 shows how you can mix the settings to provide different types of access.

Table 37.1 Determining Types of Access

Type of Access	Access Type	Read-Only Password	Full-Access Password
Anyone can read	Read-only	Don't set	
Anyone can change	Full	Don't set	
Some people can read	Read-only	Set	
Some people can change	Full	Set	
Some people can read and change	Depends on password	Set	Set

Changing What Is Shared

After a folder on your system is shared on the network, you can modify the way in which it is shared at any time. To do this, simply select a folder you previously shared. You can tell which folders you have shared by the fact that they appear with a small hand holding them when you view the folder's icon (see figure 37.3).

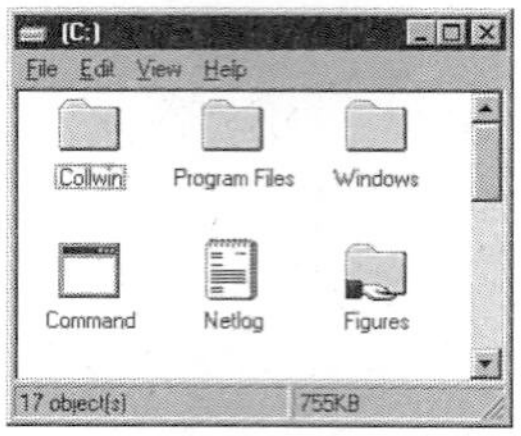

Fig. 37.3 A shared folder has a small hand under the folder icon.

Just right-click the shared folder and choose Sharing from the context menu. The Properties sheet for the folder appears, with the Sharing tab selected. At this point, you can change any aspect of the sharing you want. If you want to stop sharing the folder all together, simply click the Not Shared option.

Accessing Other People's Data

The process of accessing data on other people's systems is called *mapping a drive*. This simply means that you create a drive letter on your system which is really a pointer to a folder on another system. This is the same process that other network users go through when they want to access information on your computer.

To map a drive to another person's system, you must first know the other system's UNC path.

Mapping a Drive

To map a drive on your system, follow these steps:

1. Right-click either the My Computer or the Network Neighborhood icons on your desktop. This displays a context menu for the object.
2. Select the Map Network Drive option from the context menu. This displays the Map Network Drive dialog box, as shown in figure 37.4.

Fig. 37.4 You map a network drive by picking a drive letter and specifying a path to the remote folder.

3. In the Drive field, select a drive letter to use on your system when referring to the network drive. You can see the drive letters currently in use by clicking the arrow at the right side of the field.
4. In the Path field supply the full UNC path to the shared folder you want to access.
5. Select the Reconnect at logon check box if you want this network drive to be available every time you use Windows 95.
6. Click the OK button.

At this point, you can access the network drive as if it were a local drive on your system. Your ability to map a network drive depends on several points:

- The folder you want to access on a different system must have been shared by whoever controls that system.
- The remote system must be available on the network.
- You must know the passwords necessary to access the folder (if any) before mapping is complete.

While the mapping process just described is quick and easy, it assumes you know the system and folder name that you want to map. If you refer to figure 37.4, you will notice that there is no browse button on the Map Network Drive dialog box. There is one other way you can map a network drive. This method involves using either the browser or the Windows Explorer.

To illustrate, let's assume that you want to access a folder on a remote system that is used for budget data. You could double-click the

Network Neighborhood icon on your desktop, and then simply start looking through the different computers in the network. You only need to double-click a computer, and you will see the folders that have been shared on that system. When you find the folder you want, right-click the folder and choose Map Network Drive from the context menu. Figure 37.5 shows the results of going through this process.

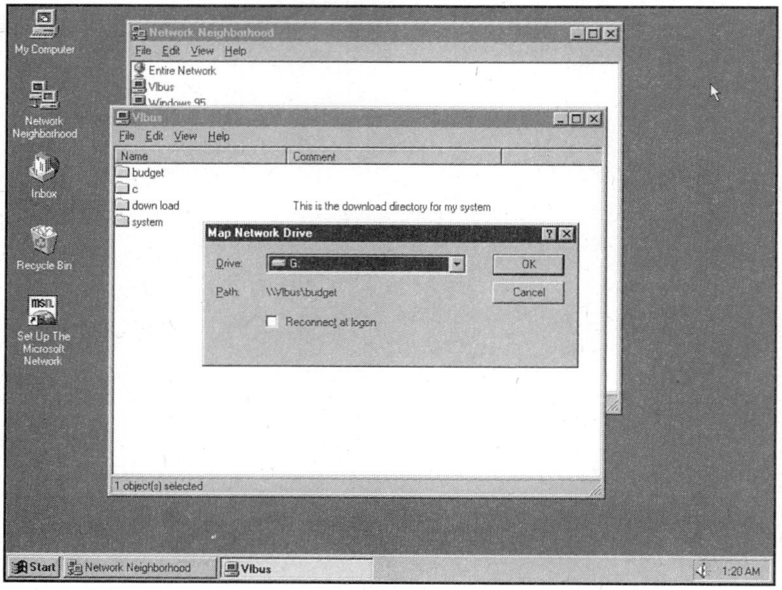

Fig. 37.5 Mapping a network drive is easy as you are browsing through the Net.

The Map Network Drive dialog box looks the same as shown earlier, except the Path field is filled in for you. All you need to do is confirm that the drive letter you want is selected, set the Reconnect at logon check box as desired, and then click OK.

Regardless of how you map a network drive, the drive shows up whenever you browse through My Computer, as shown in figure 37.6. You may wonder why the drives show up here rather than in the Network Neighborhood portion of your system. The answer is that the network drives are now assigned to local drive letters on your system, and disk resources on your system show up under the My Computer icon.

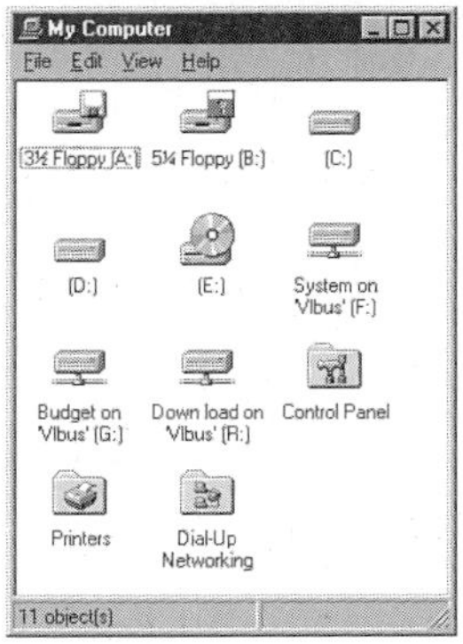

Fig. 37.6 Mapped drives show up in the My Computer window on your system.

Disconnecting a Network Drive

The point at which network drives are disconnected depends on their *persistence.* Persistence is a property that you set when you check or clear the Reconnect at logon check box when originally mapping the drive. If you check the box, then the only way that the drive is disconnected is if you manually do it; if the check box is clear, then whenever you restart your system, the connection with the remote folder is broken.

To manually disconnect a previously mapped drive, follow these steps:

1. Double-click the My Computer icon on the desktop.
2. Right-click the icon for the drive you want to disconnect. This displays the context menu for the drive.
3. Choose Disconnect from the context menu.

At this point, the drive is disconnected, and you will no longer see the icon in the My Computer folder. If you later want to access the drive, simply go through the process of mapping the drive again.

Printing in a Networked Environment

In Chapter 20, "Managing Your Printers," and Chapter 21, "Printing from Windows 95," you learned the basics of using printers. Those basics are applicable to using printers whether you are printing to a local printer or through a network. There are a few other printing topics that are unique to the network environment which are addressed in the following sections.

Adding Separator Pages

Windows 95 enables you to add separator pages between print jobs you send to a printer. Separator pages print out between print jobs, making it easier in a shared-printer environment to determine to whom the printout should be sent. Although you can specify separator pages for a local printer, it does not make much sense because you are aware of everything you print on your own printer.

To instruct Windows 95 to use a separator page, follow these steps:

1. Choose Settings from the Start menu.
2. Choose Printers from the Settings menu.
3. Right-click the icon for the printer that needs a separator page. This displays the context menu for the printer.
4. Choose Properties from the context menu. This displays the Properties sheet for the printer.
5. Select the General tab. The dialog box should appear as shown in figure 37.7.

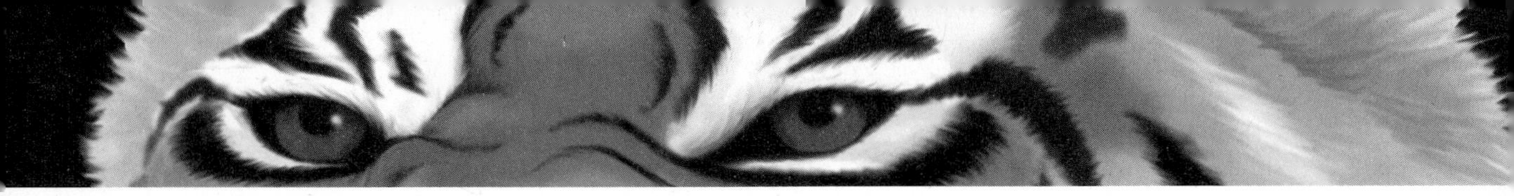

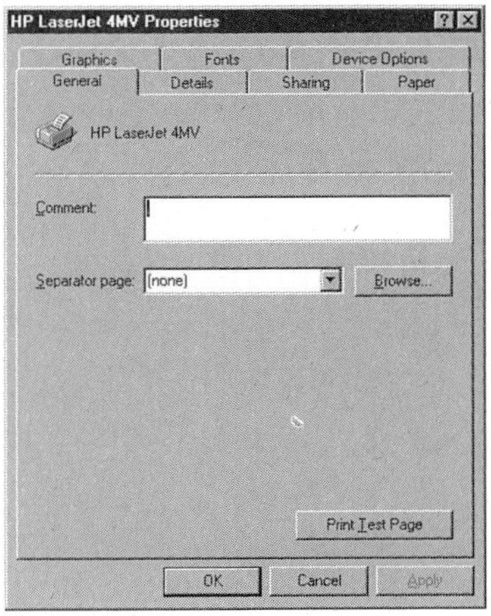

Fig. 37.7 You can specify a separator page for a printer using the General tab of the Properties sheet.

As you might surmise, the Separator page field controls the printing of a separator page. In this field you have three choices:

- **None.** No separator page is printed between print jobs. This is the default setting for each printer.
- **Full.** Prints a fancy page that includes graphics. Takes longer to process and print than a simple separator page.
- **Simple.** Prints a page that consists of text only. Prints faster than a full separator page.

In addition to the three basic choices, you can also pick a custom separator page to print. Windows 95 enables you to use any Windows metafile as a separator page. You can create these types of files with many types of graphics programs, such as the Paint accessory.

Customizing Separator Pages for NetWare Printers

If the network printer you are configuring is serviced via a NetWare server, you have some additional options that you can customize when you set up the separator page. When you display the dialog box for a NetWare shared printer, click the Capture Settings tab. You can set NetWare-specific settings such as the form name or number, the timeout value, the name that appears on the separator page, and the number of copies of each print job that should be printed.

Using Fonts

One of the challenges that face network users is the issue of fonts. In Chapter 22, "Working with Fonts," you learned how you can use fonts effectively. While the instructions and guidance contained in that chapter are appropriate for a locally connected printer, there are some nuances that are applicable when printing in a networked environment.

The problem for network users is how to guarantee that the needed font is available and how you can downloaded it to the printer. This is particularly true when you are trying to print the documents you loaded from a network drive. If the fonts used in the document are also available on your local machine, you have no problem. This is not always the case, however.

One solution is to download fonts directly to the printer so that they are available there. In that instance, you would not need to worry about where the fonts resided; they would always be available on the printer. The danger in downloading fonts to the printer is that they are lost if someone shuts off the printer to clear a problem such as a paper jam. Some printers overcome this problem by adding a hard disk to the printer, on which you can store fonts until you need them. The number of printers with hard drives actually installed is rather low, however.

For a network, an obvious (and satisfactory) solution is to load your fonts onto a shared network drive. With Windows 95 you can treat the fonts as if they are loaded on your local system, even though they are actually on a remote system. To do this, the network administrator will need to install the fonts to the network drive. Do not use the Fonts folder in Windows 95 to do this; that is only helpful for loading fonts to your local computer. Instead, either use the font loader provided with the font collection, or simply copy the TTF (TrueType) font files to the shared network folder.

When you are ready to access the fonts from your local machine, follow these steps:

1. Choose Settings from the Start menu.
2. Choose Control Panel from the Settings menu.
3. Double-click the Fonts icon in the Control Panel. This displays the Fonts folder window.
4. Choose the Install New Font option from the File menu. This displays the Add Fonts dialog box.
5. Select the drive and folder for the network drive that contains the TTF files.
6. Clear the Copy fonts to Fonts folder check box at the bottom of the dialog box.
7. Select the fonts you want to use on your local system.
8. Click the OK button.

At this point, the Registry is updated so that it contains the pointers to the font files on the network drive, but the font files themselves have not been copied to your hard drive. When you look at the Fonts folder window, you can tell which fonts are not on your local system by the presence of a shortcut arrow on the font icon. This is illustrated with the Algerian font, in figure 37.8.

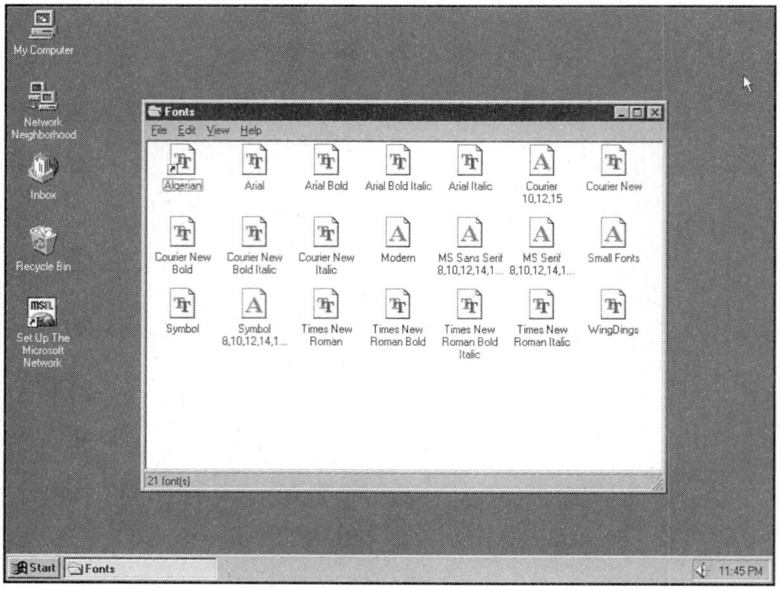

Fig. 37.8 Fonts not loaded on the local system are displayed with a shortcut arrow on the font icon in the Fonts folder.

Managing the Network

The amount of management done on a network depends on the type of network you are using. If you have a small peer-to-peer network (perhaps a couple of computers in your office), then there is not much management required. If you have a larger network (perhaps several hundred computers in a client/server network), then your network management tasks become much more complex and time-consuming.

In larger networks, the job of managing the network typically is the responsibility of a single person called the *network administrator.* In smaller or mid-size networks, the job of administering the network may be just one hat worn by a technician or a "power user" in the office. Regardless of the type of network you are using, there is always some sort of network management that must take place. The following sections describe some guidelines for managing your network.

Managing a Peer-to-Peer Network

Peer-to-peer networks are very simple in concept, and are intended for small offices and workgroups. They are characterized by the lack of a centralized file server and often lack a formal network administrator.

Peer-to-peer networking is built directly in to Windows 95. Managing such a network generally consists of the following tasks:

- Determining the location of network printers.
- Determining the location of centralized files.
- Setting workgroup standards.

Each of these topics is addressed in the following sections.

Network Printers

Adding printers to your network is a fairly easy task. You learned in Chapter 20, "Managing Your Printers," exactly how to add printers and make them available over the network. Many times the hard part is determining where network printers will be located. Wherever they are located, you know that there will be pretty high traffic to and from the printer. With this in mind, you could use the following guidelines in picking a location:

- Pick a location that is centrally located to the bulk of the printer users. This does not necessarily mean that the printer should be right in the middle of all the users. Instead, you should think through who will be using the printer the most, and then locate the printer in the middle of those people.
- Do not use network printers for sensitive data. It is not always a good idea for management or finance people to use the network printers. They are often printing sensitive information that is best not shared around the water cooler. For people who work with sensitive data, you may want to get local printers or special network printers that require passwords to use.

- If possible, place the printer near someone that will accept responsibility for it. Printers often need to be fed, and adding paper to a network printer can be frustrating if you need to walk to the other end of the building to do it. Instead, find someone near the printer who can watch it and change paper, toner, or ribbons if necessary.

Centralized Files

Because networks are designed to primarily share information, it is not unusual for even the smallest network to have files that are shared on a regular basis. These files might be something as simple as a common document repository, or as complex as the business accounting files.

Where you place common files has quite a bit to do with the productivity derived from your network. The following guidelines will help you make a sound decision in this area:

- Pick a computer system that has a large hard drive. Larger hard drives can accommodate more rapid growth in the quantity or size of shared files. In addition, the larger hard drives tend to have faster access rates, which can significantly boost throughput on network data.

- Pick a computer system that does not belong to a computer neophyte. There is less chance of accidentally deleting shared files or damaging them in some other way if the computer user is more comfortable with computers.

- Pick a system that has a fast CPU. If the system that has the shared files has a slow CPU, the user might notice a slowdown in the system as data is being accessed for users on the network. Faster CPU speeds mean less slowdown and less chance for developing bottlenecks.

- Pick a system that has at least 12M of memory. Actually, the more memory in the computer that has the shared files, the better. More memory means there is less disk swapping at the computer, and thus critical disk requests (such as those to send data over the network) can be processed faster.

- Pick a system that will not be turned off. Many people have a tendency to just flip their machines off at the end of the day. If you are dealing with files to be shared across the network, this can cause havoc. Make sure that the system with the files will be left on and available all the time.

Workgroup Standards

Workgroups (and the networks they use) have a tendency to grow over time. It seems that everyone on the network has a different way of doing things, as well. While this is acceptable for individual machines, it can quickly devolve into management anarchy when dealing with shared resources.

Early in the development of your network, you should develop a set of standards to which people on the network should adhere. For instance, you might develop the following:

- A shared folder structure. You should decide where common files will be placed on the network. For instance, you might place accounting data on one person's system and budget files on another person's system. Make sure that everyone maps the shared drives to the same letter.

- A common file-naming convention. When dealing with common documents, you should use a common naming standard that everyone can learn. With this system, you can recognize any file by its name. For instance, you might specify that any final documents begin with the word FINAL, or that spreadsheet names include both the responsible department and the quarter the spreadsheet represents.

- A standard device-naming method. As you share printers and folders on the network, you might want to require that the comments field include information that nails down the source of the resource. For instance, the field could contain a person's name, phone extension, or office number.

There are probably dozens of other ways you can think of to develop standards for your network. The whole idea behind developing workgroup standards is to increase productivity. If each computer on the network is set up to do the same tasks in a different way, then any given person will be completely lost if they switch to another workstation on the network.

As you develop standards, you should write them down and share them with others on the network. These could even become part of the employee manual or the information presented to the employee during training sessions.

Managing a Client/Server Network

Client/server networks differ from peer-to-peer networks primarily in one way: On a client/server network, dedicated servers provide shared disk space, processing capability, and printer management (unlike peer-to-peer networks where workstations double as disk and printer sharing devices). Dedicated servers are generally designed to provide high performance as well as near full-time availability. The most common server operating system for these dedicated servers is Novell NetWare, but Microsoft Windows NT and Banyan Vines are also popular operating system options.

The issues involved in managing shared resources in a client/server environment are similar to those with a peer-to-peer network, except that management responsibilities are often handled by a central group of network administrators. As with a peer-to-peer network, it is important that common and readily understandable naming conventions be used, and it is also important that shared resources such as servers and printers offer high performance and are available whenever users need them.

Client/server operating systems such as NetWare, Windows NT, and Vines offer greater capabilities in the areas of fine-tuning user access and managing shared printing.

Setting Up User Privileges

Your options for controlling user access levels are much broader when you work with a full featured client/server network operating system such as NetWare or Windows NT. With Windows 95's file and print sharing, you can grant others read-only or full-access, and you can optionally require users to enter a password to access a shared disk or folder. With a dedicated network operating system, you can grant and withhold a variety of user rights to fine-tune user access levels. Novell NetWare, for example, enables you to give or withhold the following eight rights to folders and files:

READ

WRITE

CREATE

ERASE

FILE SCAN

ACCESS CONTROL

MODIFY

SUPERVISOR

If you want users to be able to read from and write to a shared database file, but you want to be sure that those same users cannot accidentally or intentionally delete the file, you can grant the rights READ and WRITE but withhold the right ERASE.

Managing User Accounts

Full-featured network operating systems, such as NetWare and Windows NT, also enable you to provide users with individual accounts. When a user receives an account on a server, he or she has a unique login name. You can also require that each user have a password, and you can specify that those users change those passwords regularly. Because users have individual accounts, you can customize each user's access levels as required by granting each user an individual set of

rights. If you want to provide each user with a private personal folder on a server, for example, you can do so by assigning to each user's account the rights that he or she needs to access his or her personal folder. For all other users, rights are withheld from that personal folder.

Using Resources on a NetWare Server

When you map drive letters to disks and folders or connect to shared printers on a server running NetWare, you must know how to translate the names that NetWare uses into the Universal Naming Convention (UNC) scheme used by Windows 95. With NetWare, a subdirectory on a server disk has been traditionally identified by the following name:

SERVER/VOLUME:FOLDER\SUBDIRECTORY

The folder structure \WPWIN\DOC on the SYS volume on the SERV1 server, for example, would be named SERV1\SYS:WPWIN\DOC. Using the UNC system, folders and subdirectories are named using this method:

\\SERVER\VOLUME\FOLDER\SUBDIRECTORY

The \WPWIN\DOC folder in the previous example would be named as

\\SERV1\SYS\WPWIN\DOC

using the UNC scheme.

NetWare print queues are named using this method:

\\SERVER\QUEUE

A queue named MRKTING-LJ on a server named SERV3 would be identified as

\\SERV3\MRKTING-LJ

38

Setting Up Remote Computing

by Gregory J. Root

Remote computing is becoming more and more a part of doing business today. As laptop computers are becoming more powerful, Windows 95 helps to further increase their power and to make connectivity easier than ever before.

Remote computing used to mean configuring IRQs and I/O ports, setting up cables, running arcane MS-DOS programs, and wasting altogether too much time transferring and updating files. Windows 95 running on your laptop will allow you to connect to your office without all these headaches. Almost any function you do on your desktop computer can be done on a remote computer with Windows 95.

With the advent of PC Cards (formerly known as PCMCIA cards), Plug-and-Play technology, and Windows 95, working away from your desk has never been easier. As you work, you can send faxes, print documents, or send electronic mail. You'll be able to quickly reconnect to your desktop workstation without reloading network drivers or

restarting your computer. Once reconnected, Windows 95 will fax, print, and send everything you've done since you last connected.

In this chapter, you'll learn how to do the following:

- Extend your laptop's battery life
- Install the tools you need to remote compute
- Defer printing, faxing, and e-mail

Advanced Power Management (APM)

Keeping your laptop up and running while you're on the road is an important aspect of remote computing. Advanced Power Management (APM) lets you maximize the battery life of your laptop by suspending power usage of key components after a specified time period. As part of managing the remaining battery power, APM will stop your hard drive from spinning when you aren't accessing it. By doing this, APM puts a major source of battery drain in a state of suspended animation. The same is true for your display: APM will turn it off after a period of inactivity to save battery time. On some laptops, APM can even slow down your CPU to save a large amount of battery life. When you need to perform calculations, access the hard drive, or use the display, APM will quickly turn on the suspended devices for you.

Eventually, when your battery does become too low, APM intervenes. For example, if applications are running, APM automatically saves open files.

Most laptop manufacturers provide a program or keyboard combination to change the setup of the time-outs. These changes must usually be made from a DOS mode (see your laptop's manual for more details). By turning on APM, Windows 95 uses the values you specified when you configured your laptop's BIOS for APM.

To use APM, do the following steps. If you aren't sure if your laptop supports APM, try this procedure anyway; you'll be able to tell in the first few steps.

1. Right-click the My Computer icon on your desktop and choose Properties at the bottom of the menu. The System Properties sheet appears.
2. Click on the Device Manager tab.
3. Click on the + to the left of System devices.
4. Double-click on the Advanced Power Management support System device.

> **Tip:** If there is no listing for Advanced Power Management Support, your computer doesn't support it.

5. Click on the Settings tab in the Advanced Power Management dialog box, as shown in figure 38.1.
6. If it's not selected, click on the box next to Enable power management support.

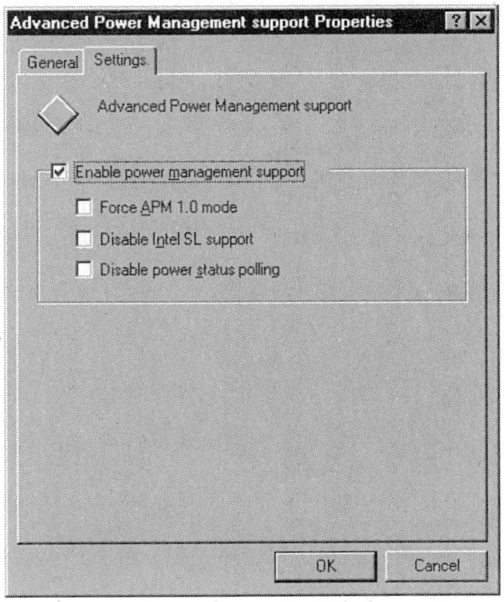

Fig. 38.1 You can enable Advanced Power Management by choosing Enable power management support.

If you want to force APM to use the mode compatible with Windows 3.1, place a check mark next to Force APM 1.0 mode. Microsoft and Intel originally developed the power management interface in your computer's BIOS for use under Windows 3.1. Since that time, advances have been made in BIOS technology. However, not all BIOS correctly handle the new features in APM 1.1. If you experience problems with your computer automatically moving into suspend mode, selecting this option may clear up those problems.

If your computer does not come out of suspend mode, try selecting Disable Intel SL support. This may allow your laptop to return from suspend mode without locking up.

If your computer spontaneously shuts down without your interacting with it, this may be caused by Windows 95 communicating with APM much more frequently than Windows 3.x would. If you have this problem, select Disable power status polling, which will disable the battery meter on the taskbar.

7. Click on OK to save your changes.
8. Click on OK to close the System Properties sheet. When asked if you want to restart your computer, click Yes. If you want to wait until later to restart your computer, click No. Be aware that APM won't become active until you restart.

Read the next section if you would like to learn how to add a status display that tells you how much battery power remains.

Showing the Battery Meter

When you use your computer away from an AC power source, battery life becomes an important factor in determining how much work you can accomplish. Windows 95 can assist you by displaying a battery meter, which can be displayed on the taskbar, so you're always aware of the status of your battery.

To display the battery meter on the taskbar, do the following:

1. From the taskbar, click Start, Settings, Control Panel.
2. Double-click the Power control panel icon in the Control Panel dialog box.
3. Click Enable battery meter on the taskbar if it's not already selected (see figure 38.2).

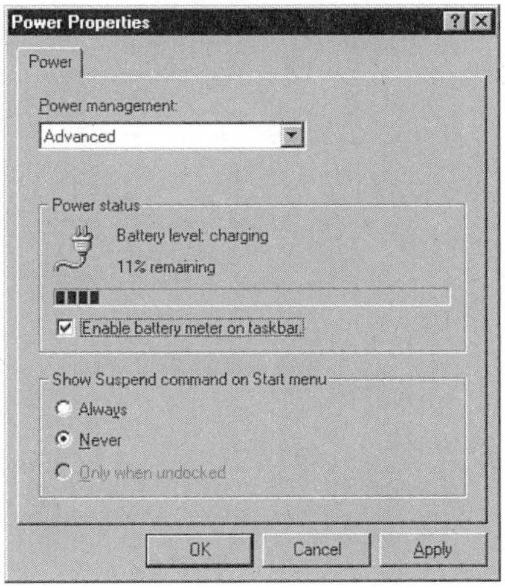

Fig. 38.2 You can choose to display the battery meter on the taskbar, so you're always aware of battery life.

4. Click OK at the bottom of the Power dialog box to save your change.

Now to check your battery supply, move the cursor over the battery symbol on the taskbar. As shown in figure 38.3, a box will pop up indicating the amount of power left. When the laptop is plugged into an AC adapter, a plug icon will display on the taskbar instead of the battery symbol, as shown in the second screen in figure 38.3.

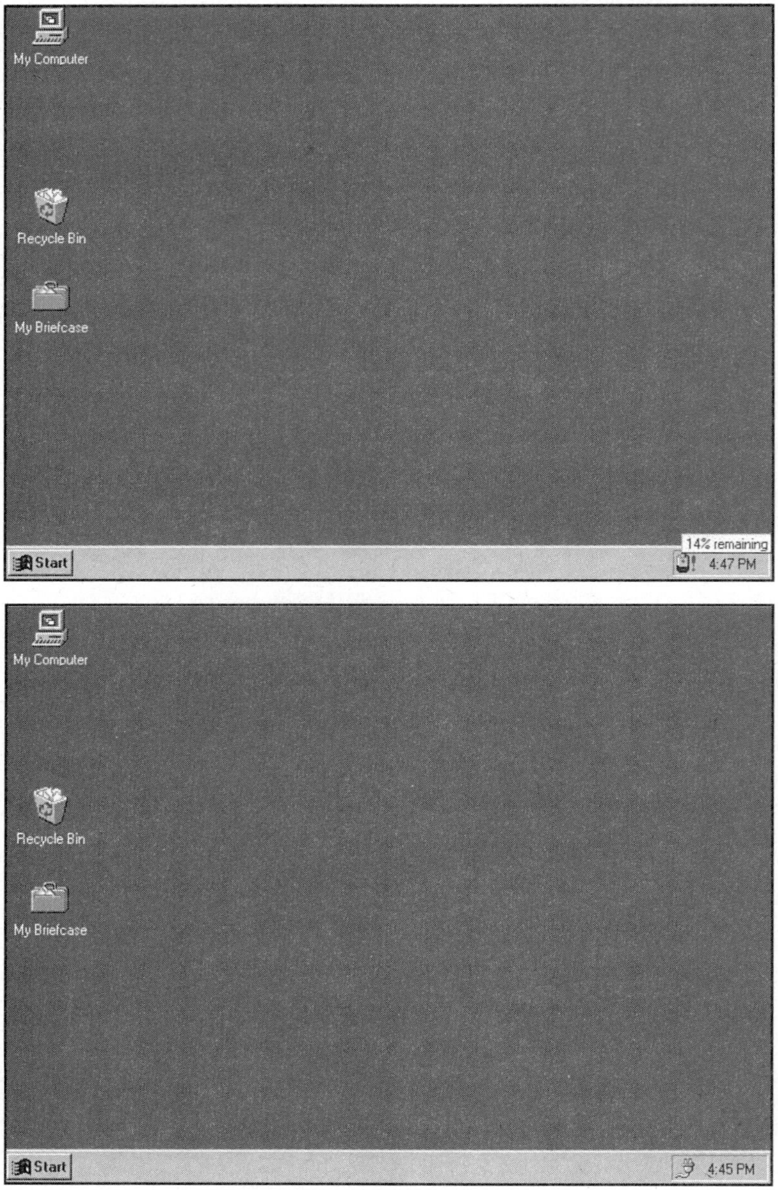

Fig. 38.3 The battery icon in the tray on the taskbar shows how much battery remains when you move your mouse over it. If the battery is being charged, a power plug appears instead.

Tip: If the battery meter shows that you're almost out of power, just plug in the AC adapter while the computer is running. The battery meter will show the plug icon to indicate that your battery is being recharged.

Finally, if you want to be notified that the battery is running out of power, you can turn on the low battery warning by following these steps:

1. Double-click the battery or power plug icon, as shown in figure 38.4. The Battery Meter dialog box appears.

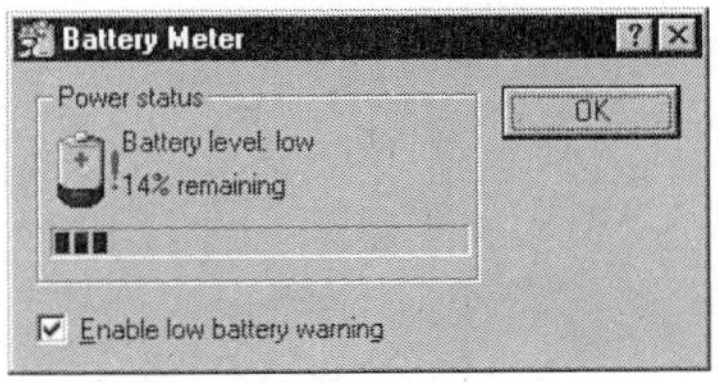

Fig. 38.4 The Battery Meter dialog box allows you to turn on a warning that notifies you when the battery supply is running low.

2. Select the Enable low battery warning check box.
3. Click OK to save your change.

Enabling Suspend Mode

When using your laptop away from an AC power source, every minute of battery power is valuable. As discussed earlier, Advanced Power Management will automatically suspend different functions of your computer based on your preferences. For example, you may have configured your laptop to go into complete suspend mode after 15 minutes. But if you know you're going to leave your laptop for a longer period, you can invoke suspend mode manually. This way, you won't have to shut all your programs down and then wait for Windows 95 to restart when you're ready to work.

When you manually activate the suspend mode, the current state of all your open programs and files is remembered, and your laptop will be placed in a mode that uses much less power. When you want to use the computer again, all your files and programs will be as you left them.

To immediately enable the suspend mode, do the following:

1. From the taskbar, click Start, Settings, Control Panel.
2. Double-click on the Power control panel icon in the Control Panel dialog box.
3. As shown in figure 38.5, choose Always under the Show Suspend command on the Start menu to have Suspend show on your Start menu every time.

   Choose Only when undocked to show the Suspend menu when you've taken your laptop out of the docking station.

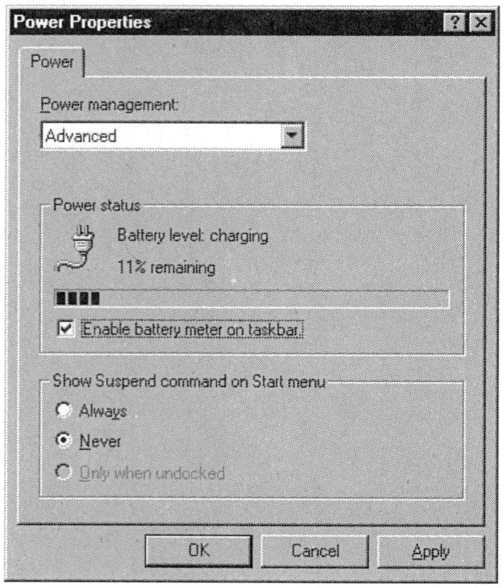

Fig. 38.5 You have to enable suspend mode to be able to access Suspend on the Start menu.

Note: If the Only when undocked option is disabled, this means that your laptop is unable to dock. Your best option, in this case, is to show the Suspend menu item Always.

4. Once you've made the appropriate choice, click on OK to save your changes.

Now when you click Start, depending on your choice, you'll have access to Suspend, as shown in figure 38.6.

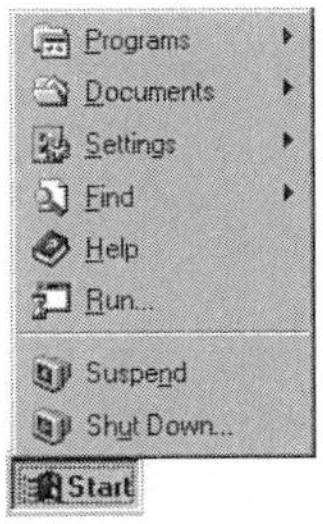

Fig. 38.6 Choosing Suspend on the Start menu immediately places your laptop in a state of low power usage.

To restore your computer, turn the power on. (Check with your laptop's documentation if that doesn't work. You may have to do something else.) All programs and files will be as they were before you initiated the suspend mode.

Note: Your network connections may not be restored when the laptop comes out of suspend mode. Therefore, it's a good idea to save any documents that you have open from the network *before* you choose the Suspend mode.

Preparing to Connect a Laptop to a Desktop

With Windows 95, you can hook your laptop up to a desktop computer to print your documents, send your e-mail or faxes, or update your master files with the changes that you made while you were on the road. In the next section, you'll learn how to perform those specific tasks. Before you can go on the road, you may need to set up your laptop and desktop computer. The kind of setup depends on your hardware.

If your laptop normally docks at a docking station, uses PC Cards (PCMCIA cards), or communicates through standard ports on the back to access network, printer, and telephone services, you won't have to configure anything. Windows 95 automatically detects when your network, printing, and electronic mail services are available. In the case of a docking station, Windows 95 senses your docking state. If you use a 32-bit PC Card to access network services, Windows 95 automatically enables it without shutting down. Additionally, as you connect your local printer, Windows begins to send your documents when it comes online.

However, you'll need to install some additional Windows 95 components to store files and send electronic mail if you don't have a place to attach your laptop to a network. You'll also need these components if the printer you normally access is on the network and you don't have an extra connection to the network in your work area.

Installing Remote Networking

Windows 95 ships with two programs that allow your laptop to talk to other computers without a network between them: (1) Dial-Up Networking allows you to connect your laptop to other computers via a modem; (2) Direct Cable Connection allows you to connect your laptop to another computer through a parallel or serial port. These components give your laptop access to all the resources your desktop computer has. In other words, if your desktop computer has access to network servers, printers, and electronic mail, your laptop will too. In fact, the manner in which your laptop will access these resources is no different from using your desktop computer.

When you installed Windows 95 on your laptop by using the Portable installation type, the Direct Cable Connection and Dial-Up Networking components should have been installed for you. However, if you plan to connect to your desktop computer via a serial or parallel cable, you'll need to install the Direct Cable Connection on your desktop computer. If you aren't sure if everything is set up correctly, use these steps to install the required components for your laptop and desktop computers.

1. Insert the Windows 95 CD-ROM into your CD-ROM drive.
   If you're using a protected-mode CD-ROM driver, Windows 95 automatically displays the Windows 95 main installation menu window. Close the window for now.
2. From the taskbar, click Start, Settings, Control Panel.
3. Double-click on the Add/Remove Programs icon in the Control Panel dialog box to begin the installation.
4. As figure 38.7 shows, click on the Windows Setup tab to access the optional components of Windows 95.
5. Click on Communications. Notice that under Description, you're told two of four components are already installed (That's the default; it will be different if you've added others.)
6. Click on Details. The Communications dialog box appears (see figure 38.8).

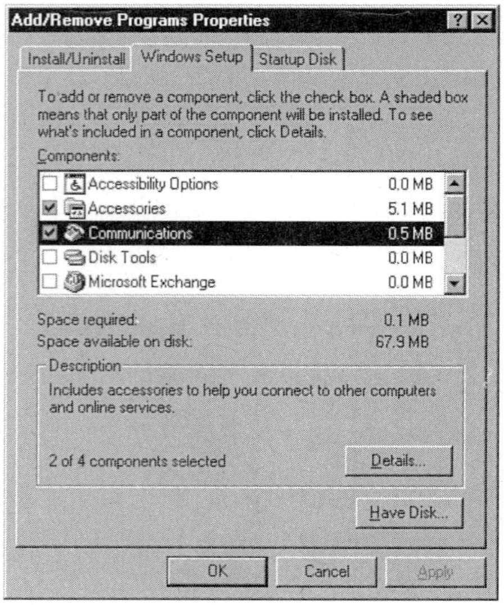

Fig. 38.7 Select the Communications component to access the Direct Cable Connection and Dial-Up Networking components.

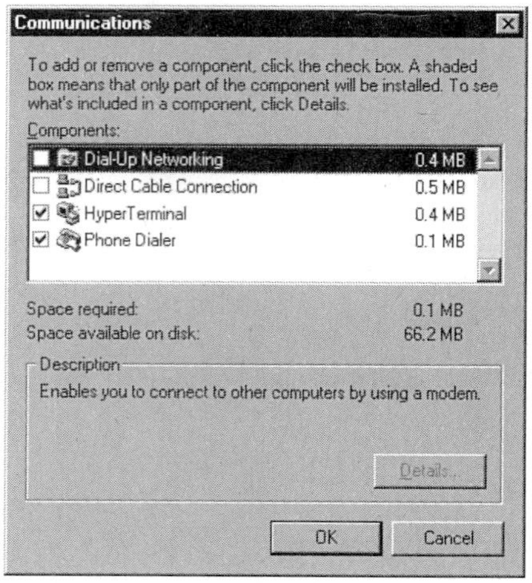

Fig. 38.8 To connect your computer to other computers, select the Dial-Up Networking and Direct Cable Connection components.

7. Select Dial-Up Networking and Direct Cable Connection by clicking on the box next to the options.
8. Click on OK to save your modifications. You'll be returned to the Add/Remove Programs Properties sheet.
9. Click on OK to finalize your changes. Windows 95 will now install the additional components from the CD-ROM.
10. A prompt tells you to enter the computer and workgroup name that will identify your computer. The computer name lets other people on the network find your computer. The workgroup identifies the group of computers to which you want to belong. Common examples of workgroups are departments or floors of a building. Click OK when you've entered them.

> **Note:** The computer name and workgroup name can't be the same.

> **Caution:** If you receive the following message, proceed with caution: A file being copied is older than the file currently on your computer. It is recommended that you keep your existing file. When in doubt, leave the existing version, especially if it's a DLL file.

A message appears stating that the system settings have been reconfigured.

You'll also briefly see a message that the system is updating shortcuts. The Dial-Up Networking and Direct Cable Connection options are being placed on the Start menu under Accessories.

11. Click on OK to restart your computer for the changes to take effect.

Note: The next time you turn on your computer, you will be prompted to enter a user name and password. If you are normally connected to a network, use your regular user ID and password, and click OK. To ignore it, click Cancel.

Caution: In order for the two computers to communicate, they must both have a common network protocol installed. Additionally, only shared resources using IPX/SPX and NetBEUI protocols are accessible to the laptop computer (the guest to the desktop). Even if TCP/IP is configured correctly on the desktop, the TCP/IP services are not passed on to the laptop.

Your computers are now ready to begin transferring information. To learn how to defer printing documents, sending faxes and electronic mail, and updating files, read the next few sections.

To learn how to actually transfer your work in progress between your laptop and the desktop computer, Chapter 39, "Seamless Remote Computing," instructs you for every type of connection.

Serial and Parallel Connections

You can connect your laptop to a stand-alone desktop or a workstation with a serial or parallel cable. Parallel cables are generally faster than serial cables. Additionally, if the two computers have ECP parallel ports, the speed is approximately four times that of a serial port connection.

Beware: Direct Cable Connection will *not* work with a plain parallel or serial cable. To run a parallel connection, the cable has to be a standard or basic 4-bit cable (also known as a Laplink or an Interlink parallel cable, or an ECP or UCM cable). To run a serial connection, you need a serial, null-modem RS-232 cable. It's not easy to get. You usually have to get it from a big computer dealer or a parts supplier, or by

mail. Retail office-supply stores usually don't carry that item. In an emergency, you can buy a program—such as LapLink or FastMove!—that comes with the right parallel cables and is available at most software stores. It's an expensive option, though.

Installing Microsoft Briefcase

Windows 95 comes with a feature called Briefcase that synchronizes your laptop and desktop files. If your computer uses a docking station, a PC Card (PCMCIA), or Dial-Up Networking, Windows 95 will automatically begin synchronizing your files as soon as the connection is made to the network. If you connect to your desktop computer by a Direct Cable Connection, you manually initiate the synchronization process. If the program that created the files supports merging two revisions of a file (such as Microsoft Word for Windows), Windows 95 will try to use those features to update the files. However, not many applications provide this functionality yet. Instead, Briefcase will compare the dates of the files and keep the newest one.

You install Briefcase only on the computer that will modify the files. Therefore, you need to install Briefcase only on your laptop computer. You won't have to install it on your desktop computer.

To make sure Briefcase is installed on your laptop computer, right-click on a blank portion of the desktop and select New from the context menu. If Briefcase appears on the submenu, Briefcase is ready to go. If it doesn't appear, install Briefcase by following these steps:

1. Insert the Windows 95 CD-ROM in your CD-ROM drive. Windows 95 may automatically load the CD and bring up the main Windows 95 installation menu window. Close the window for now.
2. From the taskbar, click Start, Settings, Control Panel.
3. Double-click on the Add/Remove Programs icon in the Control Panel dialog box to begin the installation.
4. As figure 38.9 shows, click on the Windows Setup tab to access the optional components of Windows 95.

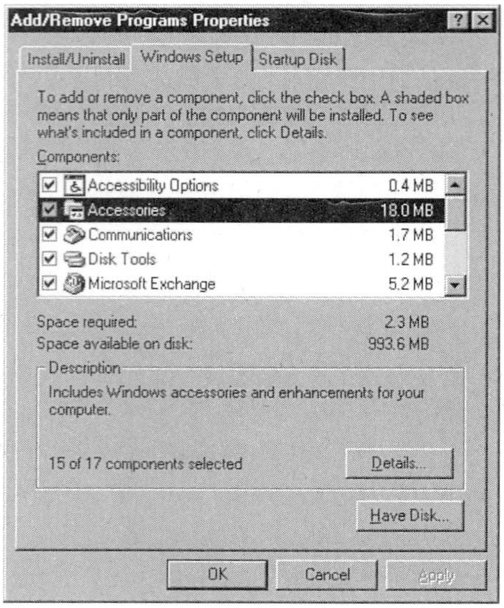

Fig. 38.9 Select the Accessories component to access the Direct Cable Connection and Dial-Up Networking components.

5. Click on Accessories. Notice that under Description, you're told 2 of 4 components are already installed (That's the default; it will be different if you've added others.)
6. Click Details. The Accessories dialog box appears (see figure 38.10).
7. Select Briefcase by clicking on the box next to the options.

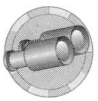

> **Note:** If Briefcase isn't listed in the components, it's already installed, and your computer is already set to use Briefcase.

8. Click on OK to save your modifications. You'll be returned to the Add/Remove Programs Properties sheet.
9. Click on OK to finalize your changes. Windows 95 will now install the additional components from the CD-ROM.

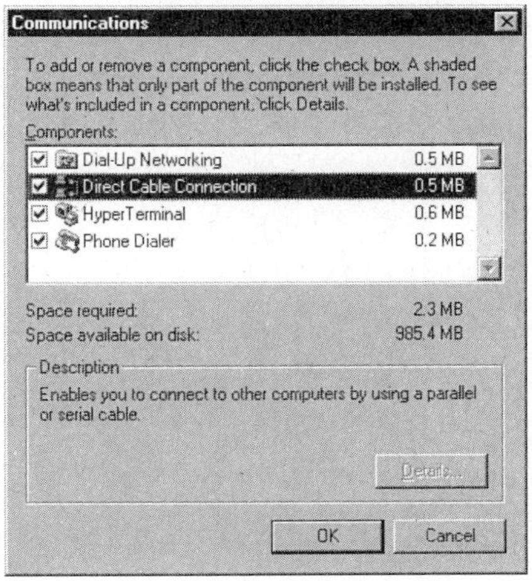

Fig. 38.10 To connect your computer to other computers, select the Dial-Up Networking and Direct Cable Connection components.

Caution: If you receive the following message, proceed with caution: A file being copied is older than the file currently on your computer. It is recommended that you keep your existing file. When in doubt, leave the existing version, especially if it's a DLL file.

A message appears stating that the system settings have been reconfigured.

10. Click OK to restart your computer so that the changes take effect.

Deferring Communications on a Portable Computer

When you work at your desktop computer, printing is as easy as clicking on the Print button. When you worked remotely before Windows 95, you had to remember to print every file after hooking up your laptop. Or maybe you solved the problem by transferring your laptop files onto a floppy disk and then using the floppy in your desktop computer. Not only were those methods time-consuming, they were annoying. Furthermore, it wasn't possible to create electronic mail or faxes and store them until later. Previous versions of Windows required immediate access to a network to create these types of communications.

With the deferred communications features, Windows 95 keeps track of your outbound printing, mail, and faxes. Windows 95 automatically prints whenever the remote computer is hooked up to the network or direct cable connection. It also sends electronic mail and faxes when the connection is reestablished to the postoffice and a peer fax server.

Deferred Printing

You might want to use deferred printing on a laptop that doesn't have a printer installed. In that case, you'll have to install the same printer that's available on the computer to which you'll be connecting. To install the printer, follow the steps in Chapter 20, "Managing Your Printers."

Once you have your printer installed, you're ready to use deferred printing. You can defer your print jobs by doing the following:

1. Open the Printers folder by clicking on Start, Settings, Printers or double-clicking on My Computer on the desktop and double-clicking the Printers folder. Either way, the Printers window will be displayed similarly to figure 38.11.
2. Right-click the icon for your printer and check Work Offline. If your printer was originally defined as a local printer, Work Offline is replaced on the menu by Pause Printing. In our example above, this is a local printer that can be directly attached to the laptop computer.

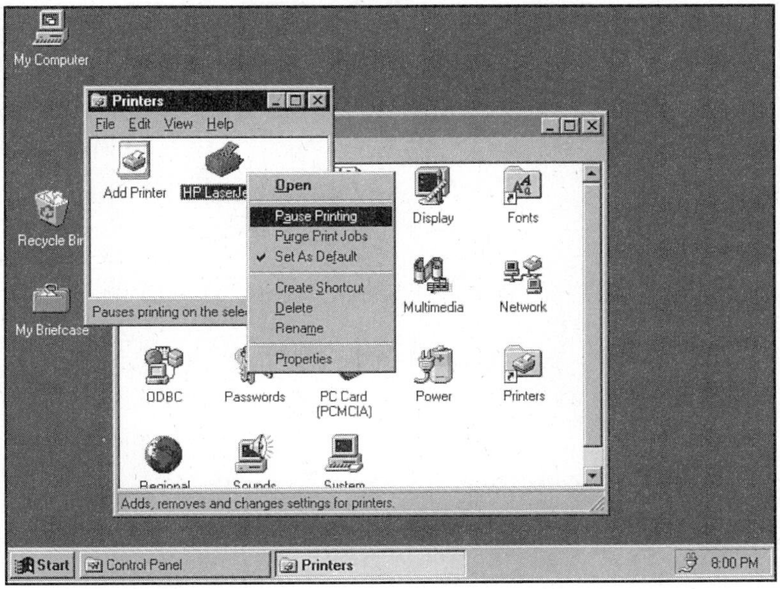

Fig. 38.11 The Printers window can be accessed via the Start menu or the My Computer dialog box.

That's all there is to it. Whenever you send a job to the printer, it will spool (store) instead of print.

As soon as your laptop is connected to the network containing the printer, Windows 95 will begin to print your jobs automatically. If you plan to use a Direct Cable Connection when you get back to your desktop, you'll need to uncheck manually Work Offline on the printer's context menu to begin printing (see figure 38.11).

Deferred Electronic Mail

If you want to create electronic mail to send when you get back to your office or send a fax, you'll need to have the Microsoft Exchange component installed on your laptop. If it's already installed, read through this section to verify that all the options are set correctly for remote computing.

To install Microsoft Exchange as part of remote computing, follow these steps:

1. Connect your laptop to the network. The Microsoft Exchange client must be able to communicate directly with the postoffice to complete the installation.
2. From the taskbar click on Start, Settings, Control Panel.
3. Once the Control Panel dialog box appears, double-click the Add/ Remove Programs icon.
4. Click on the Windows Setup tab to access the optional components of Windows 95.
5. In the Components list box, place a check mark in the box next to Microsoft Exchange, as shown in figure 38.12. Click OK at the bottom of the dialog box to begin the installation.

   During this time, Windows displays the progress of installation and updating of the shortcuts. Once complete, you will be returned to the Control Panel dialog box.

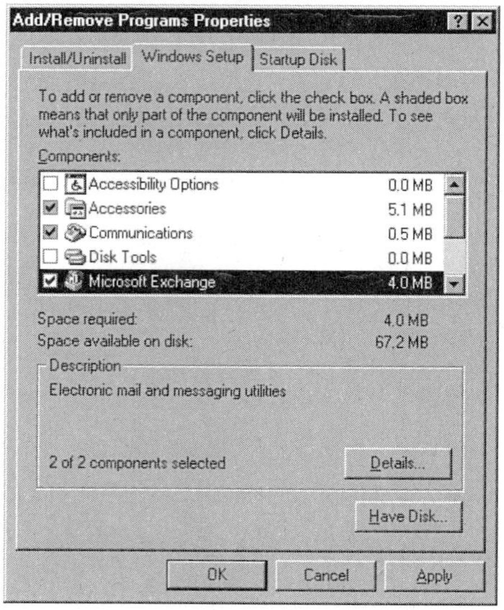

Fig. 38.12 Microsoft Exchange is added via the Windows Setup tab of the Add/Remove Programs Control Panel.

6. Once the Exchange client is installed, you need to modify its properties for remote computing. To do this in the Control Panel, double-click on the Mail and Fax icon. This will display the MS Exchange Settings Properties sheet, as shown in figure 38.13.

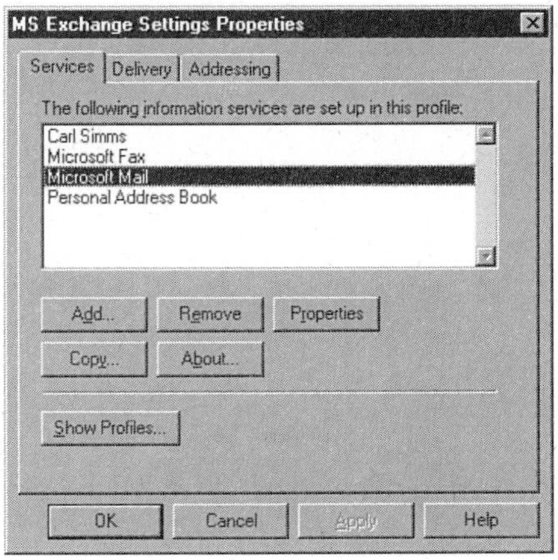

Fig. 38.13 Select the appropriate service for remote computing.

7. From the Services tab, double-click the information service to be used for remote computing on the laptop. The service configuration dialog box will appear (see figure 38.14).

8. Enter the location of the postoffice in the text box at the top of the dialog box. If you aren't sure where it is, click the Browse button to search for it.

9. Choose Automatically sense LAN or Remote option under Select to see how this service should connect at startup. Since you'll probably set up this information service only once, choosing this option will give you the most flexibility in the long term. In any case, if Windows 95 can't figure out which mode you're in, it will present you with a choice.

   When you choose Automatically sense LAN or Remote, Windows 95 will use its capability to sense the correct choice of the three other options.

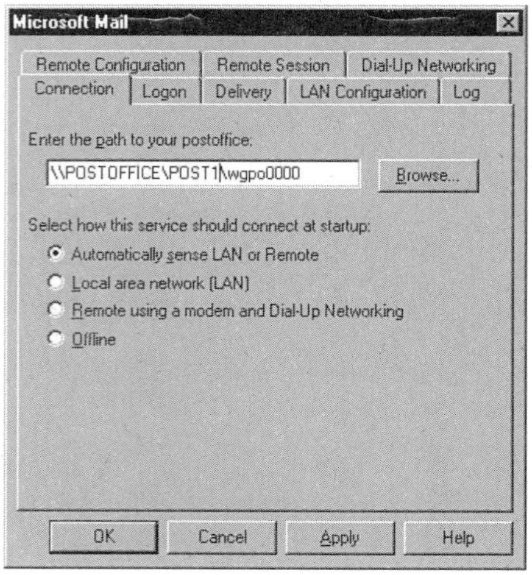

Fig. 38.14 The selected information service will display its Connection properties.

Selecting the Local area network option will cause Exchange to expect to find the postoffice using a network card or the Direct Cable Connection. It will also include the configuration choices you make on the LAN Configuration tab in this dialog box.

Clicking Remote using a modem and Dial-Up Networking will cause Exchange to look for the database over the dial-up connection. It will also use the configuration choices in Remote Configuration, Remote Session, and Dial-Up Networking tabs.

However, if you know the laptop will never directly connect to a local area network, then choose Remote using a modem and Dial-Up Networking.

10. On the Remote Configuration tab (see figure 38.15), make sure to select Use Remote Mail and Use local copy. Use Remote Mail will allow you to store your mail until you're ready to send it. Use local copy allows you to download a complete copy of the main Postoffice Address List to your computer. You'll need this list to address your messages while you're on the road.

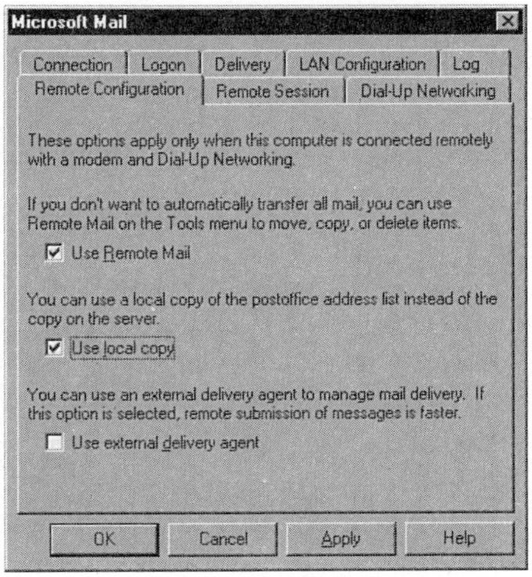

Fig. 38.15 Selecting Use local copy allows you to download a copy of the main Postoffice Address list.

11. Click on OK to save your changes. Click on OK in the MS Exchange Settings Properties to finalize your settings.
12. From the Inbox dialog box, choose Tools, Microsoft Mail Tools, Download Address Lists. This will place a copy of the main Postoffice Address list on your computer.

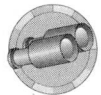

> **Note:** If you plan to send faxes as well, Microsoft Fax uses either the same address list as your electronic mail or a phone number you specify when you create the fax.

13. Click OK to save your changes.

If you want to send faxes while on the road, you must either have a fax modem in your laptop or set up your laptop to use a network fax modem. Chapter 34, "Using Microsoft Exchange," tells you how to configure Exchange to access the network fax. Once the network fax modem is configured, Microsoft Exchange takes care of the rest for you automatically. Exchange places the outbound fax in your Outbox.

Now you're ready to go on the road. Chapter 39, "Seamless Remote Computing," will show you how to seamlessly transfer your work from your laptop to your desktop in a remote computing environment.

KILLER 39 WINDOWS 95

Seamless Remote Computing

by Gregory J. Root

In the days before Windows 95, connecting to a host network or desktop computer was complicated and very technical. If you used MS-DOS 6.x, you were able to transfer files with Interlink but couldn't easily access printers and electronic mail. Windows 95 overcomes those obstacles by giving you full access to a network whether you're at home or on the road. What's more, your network doesn't have to run Windows 95; only your laptop does. Your access to the network is only limited by the privileges given to you. You can share files, print to the network printer, transfer documents, and send and receive e-mail. If you don't have a network, you can still access the same types of resources on a stand-alone computer.

The features added to Windows 95 make connections happen behind the scenes. With some minor setup dialog boxes, those connections allow you to interact with servers, printers, and other resources just as if they were actually connected to your laptop. A *host* provides the connection to those resources. With Windows 95 on your laptop, you can connect to many different types of hosts. You can connect to hosts using TCP/IP, IPX/SPX, and NetBEUI network protocols. To connect to a host, you can use any one of the connection protocols, such as PPP, RAS, SLIP, and NetWare Connect. The wide range of protocol support allows you to remotely connect to Windows NT, Novell NetWare, Banyan VINES, UNIX, DEC PATHWORKS, and SunSelect PC-NFS networks. If you have the Windows 95 Plus! Pack, you can even connect to your own desktop computer.

This chapter will show you the procedures to seamlessly connect your remote computer to your desktop or network. You will learn how to do the following:

- Establish a remote connection
- Keep your files in sync
- Transfer your deferred communications tasks

Establishing the Remote Connection

The connection from your laptop to the host is the most important part of remote computing. Therefore, understanding the capabilities and limitations of the network protocols, communication protocols, and connection types will help you correctly configure your remote access computing.

By default, Windows 95 installs several networking components when you install Dial-Up Networking and Direct Cable Connections. These are shown in figure 39.1.

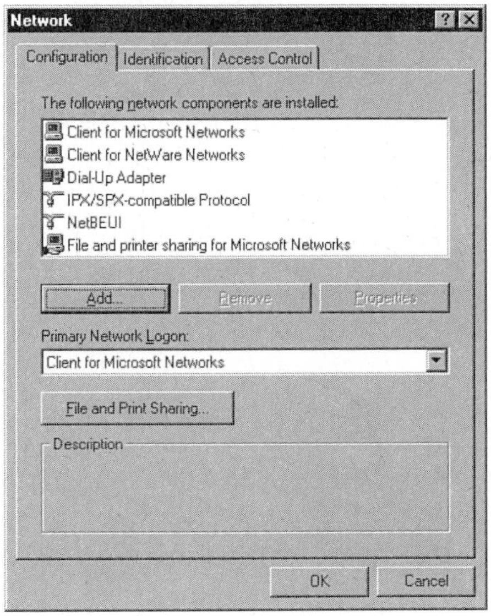

Fig. 39.1 The Network control panel shows the network components installed for Dial-Up Networking and Direct Cable Connection.

The following items are other useful components that may appear in your list, such as network cards or special services:

- **Clients.** Client software allows you to use files and printers shared by other computers on many different types of networks. Windows 95 ships with the clients for Microsoft networks and NetWare networks.

- **Adapter.** The adapter is the hardware that physically connects your computer to a network. The Dial-Up Adapter that comes with Windows 95 allows you to connect to PPP, RAS, NetWare Connect, and SLIP dial-up servers. You can connect by modem or directly with cables.

- **Protocol.** The protocol is the network protocol used to format the data being sent out through the adapter. By default, Windows 95 installs IPX/SPX-compatible Protocol and NetBEUI.

Choosing the Right Protocols

Windows 95 installs the protocols you'll most likely need to connect your remote computer to the host. However, you may have removed a network protocol or you'll need to add one based on the host with which you'll connect. A common protocol between your laptop and the host is necessary. Before you can decide which protocols to use, let's take a look at the important difference between network and communications protocols.

What's a Protocol?

A protocol is a set of formal rules to transmit data. The structure of the packets of information containing the data being transferred between two computers is called a network protocol. Some familiar network protocols include IPX/SPX, TCP/IP, NetBEUI, and NetBIOS. The methods and rules by which two computers pass the packets are called a communications protocol. NetWare Connect, PPP, RAS, SLIP, and CSLIP are well-known communications protocols.

As you can imagine, many combinations of network and communications protocols can exist. In the past, communications and network protocols were tightly integrated by the companies offering remote-networking solutions. Today, the combinations are becoming blurred with new advances in technology. Network administrators now want to select the best performing protocols for their network. Therefore, the companies that used almost-standard protocols have based their products on the true network and communication protocols. This allows network administrators to pick and choose the network and communications protocols best suited to the network users' needs for performance and functionality.

Remote Access Configurations

Windows 95 supports many different combinations of network and communication protocols. However, certain host types cannot understand specific network or communication protocols. To simplify what could be a complicated description. Table 39.1 shows the relationship between host type and the supported communications and network protocols.

Table 39.1 Supported Combinations of Host Types, Communication Protocols, and Network Protocols for a Remote Computer

Host Type	Communication Protocols	Network Protocol(s)	Remote Computer Can Share Its Own Resources
Internet, PPP server, Windows 95, Windows NT 3.x, Shiva LanRover, NetWare	PPP	IPX, NetBEUI, TCP/IP	Yes
Internet, UNIX, SLIP	SLIP, CSLIP	TCP/IP	No
Windows 95, Windows NT 3.x, Windows for Workgroups 3.11, LAN Manager	RAS	NetBEUI	Yes
NetWare Connect	NetWare Connect	IPX	No
Direct Cable Connection	Serial, Parallel	PPP	No

If you plan to use Dial-Up Networking, you should contact the administrator of the remote access host for the communication and network protocols used. These two pieces of information determine which remote computing component you'll use. Alternately, if you're using a direct-cable connection, you'll need to use a serial or parallel connection.

For example, say you have a Windows 95 computer at home and you want to connect to your Novell NetWare server at work to access files. The dial-up server at work is a Windows NT 3.5 Server running Remote Access Services. The preceding table shows that you'll need to use a PPP communications protocol with an IPX network protocol to access the NetWare server.

> **Note:** If you use the Microsoft Plus! pack to configure your Windows 95 desktop computer as a dial-in server, it will not pass data using TCP/IP to the remote computer.

Installing a Protocol

Windows 95 normally installs IPX/SPX and NetBEUI protocols for remote computing, which should be adequate for most needs. However, if you reviewed Table 39.1 in the previous section and discovered that you need to install a network protocol on your laptop or remote computer, follow these steps:

1. Open the Network components dialog box by right-clicking the Network Neighborhood and choosing Properties from the context menu.

2. Add a new network component by clicking Add under the list of network components. The Select Network Component Type dialog box is displayed, as shown in figure 39.2.

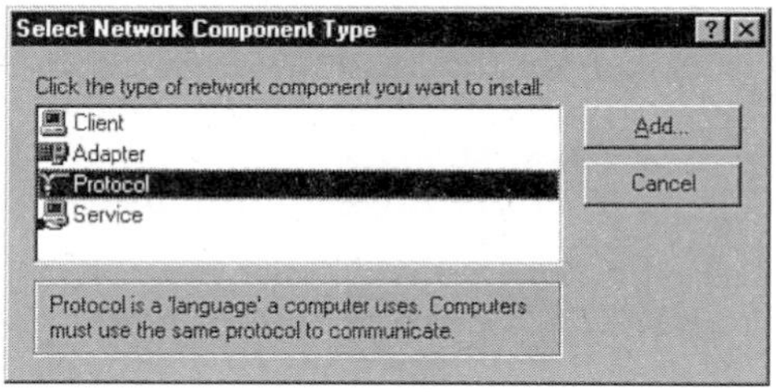

Fig. 39.2 Choose Protocol from the list of network component types.

3. Choose Protocol from the list of possible components types and then click Add… to select the protocol.
4. As shown in figure 39.3, select the appropriate network protocol from Manufacturers and the list of Network Protocols. You'll be able to add only one new protocol at a time.

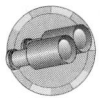

> **Note:** IPX/SPX, NetBEUI, and TCP/IP (the most common protocols) are available under Microsoft.

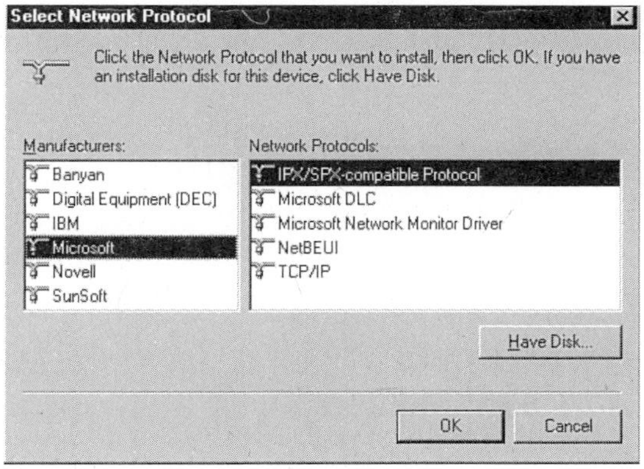

Fig. 39.3 Choose the manufacturer and then a protocol to install.

When ready, click OK to add the protocol to the network component list.

5. Click OK on the Network dialog box to begin installing the software for the new protocol. You will need your Windows 95 installation disks, CD-ROM, or a disk from the protocol manufacturer.

> **Note:** If you've chosen to install TCP/IP, it's very important that you contact your network administrator. He or she will tell you the exact configuration you'll need to set. For example, your network could use a *Dynamic Host Configuration Protocol* (DHCP) server instead of using a specific TCP/IP address.

6. When prompted, choose Restart to make the change take effect. Until you restart your computer, it will not know how to communicate using the new protocol.

From here, you'll want to establish the connection for your laptop to communicate via a Dial-Up Connection or a Direct Cable Connection. When you complete the connection, you'll be able to transfer files and access shared resources.

Dial-Up Networking

Once you've chosen the proper network and communication protocols, you have to configure the client software on your remote computer to access the host (server). To configure your computer to access resources on a dial-up connection, you'll need to perform some basic steps. Depending upon the type of host, specific tips will be identified as you progress.

> **Caution:** Using Dial-Up Networking requires that you have first configured a modem under Windows 95. To learn how to install one, see Chapter 32, "Communicating with a Modem," before you proceed.

Access the Dial-Up Networking folder from the Start menu. Click Start, Programs, Accessories, Dial-Up Networking. The Dial-Up Networking folder is just like any other folder. The menus are the same as other folders:

- **File**. These options allow you to control the set of dial-up connections. You can create a shortcut to a connection and delete, rename, or modify the properties of a connection.
- **Edit**. These options are normally used to cut, copy, and paste objects. However, dial-up connections are a special type of object and cannot be manipulated in this manner.

- **View**. These options control how connections are displayed within the Dial-Up Networking folder. You can change the size or arrangement of icons, and turn the toolbar or status bar on and off.

- **Connections**. These options allow you to perform the same tasks to initiate a connection or create a new connection by double-clicking on the icons in the folder. Additionally, you can configure settings for all your connections. As figure 39.4 shows, you can specify the number of times to redial and the amount of time between each attempt. When establishing a network connection, you can request Windows 95 to prompt you before beginning the process. Further, if you've installed the Windows 95 Dial-Up Server from the Microsoft Plus! pack, the server configuration can be modified from the Connections menu. Details on configuring this server can be found at the end of this section.

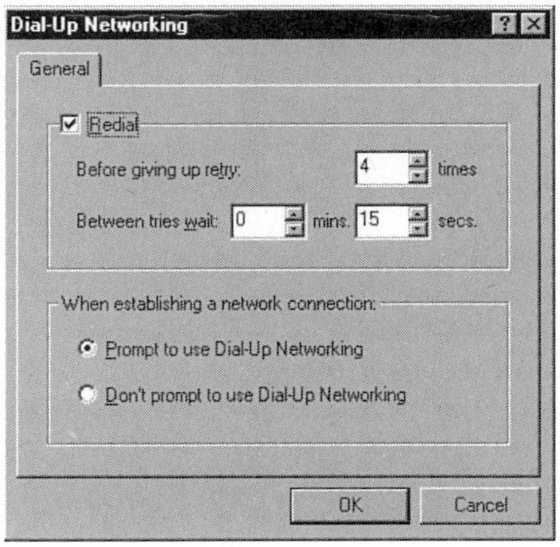

Fig. 39.4 Specify the Dial-Up Networking settings that are common to all connections from the Connection, Settings menu.

- **Help**. The Help menu displays the various help options for Dial-Up Networking.

Creating the Connection

To begin creating a new dial-up connection, double-click the Make New Connection icon in the Dial-Up Networking window as shown in figure 39.5.

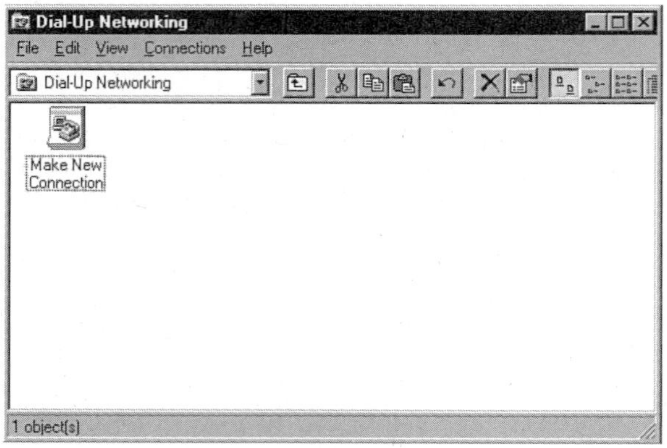

Fig. 39.5 Selecting Make New Connection will begin creating the connection to the host.

Tip: If you haven't already installed the remote computing components, see Chapter 38, "Setting Up Remote Computing."

As seen in the next dialog box of the Make New Connection Wizard, Type a name for the computer that you are dialing. Then, click on Select a modem. Only those modems you've previously configured on this computer will be listed. Select Configure to check or modify the properties of the selected modem. If you do select Configure, you'll see the same Modem Properties sheet that appeared when you installed the modem. When you're ready to move to the next step, select Next.

To identify where your host can be reached, enter the Area code, Telephone number, and Country code, as shown in figure 39.6. Windows 95 uses the area code and country code to create the correct dialing

string. Click Next to display the final dialog box for the Make New Connection Wizard. To complete the first phase of your configuration, click Finish.

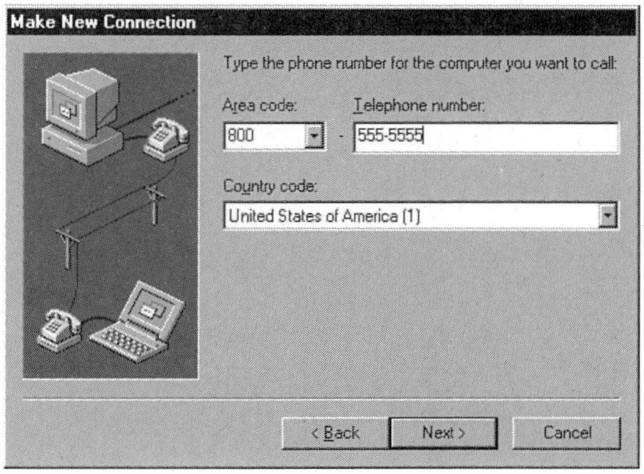

Fig. 39.6 Enter only the area code, telephone number, and country code of the dial-up network connection.

> **Tip:** When you enter these values, don't try to take into account your location by entering long-distance and outside line codes, credit card numbers, or area codes. You defined these local settings when you installed the modem.

Specifying a Server Type

You have to specify the type of server to which you're going to connect. Windows 95 needs to know the correct protocols to send and receive information. Review Table 39.1 in the previous section to determine the choice of server type.

To choose a server, open the properties of the connection you want to configure. To do this, access the Dial-Up Networking folder by clicking Start, Programs, Accessories, Dial-Up Networking. Then right-click the desired connection name and select Properties from the context menu.

From the Connection Properties sheet, you'll want to select the Server Type to specify the specific server type for this connection. The Server Types dialog box appears, as shown in figure 39.7.

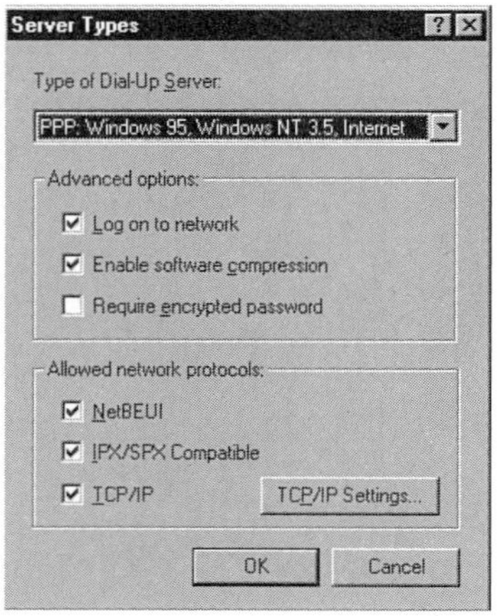

Fig. 39.7 You can choose the type of server to which you're going to connect.

From the Server Types dialog box, choose the Type of Dial-Up Server to which you're going to connect by clicking and holding the scrollable arrow. You have the following options:

- NRN NetWare Connect
- PPP: Windows 95, Windows NT 3.5, Internet
- Windows for Workgroups and Windows NT 3.1

Note that the options and allowed network protocols will change with each server type. For example, using NRN NetWare Connect, your only advanced option is Log on to network. The only network protocol allowed is IPX/SPX Compatible. For Advanced options, Windows will allow certain activities for the selected connection:

- Log on to network. When the connection is made to the host, Windows 95 will attempt to log onto the network that you are calling with the user name and password you used when you started your computer.

➤ Enable software compression. If both sides of the connection support compression, the data will be compressed before being sent over the connection to increase the transmission speed.

➤ Require encrypted password. If both sides of the connection support encryption, Windows 95 will encrypt the password you use for increased security against intrusion.

Windows 95 also permits you to limit the network protocols transmitted over the connection. You can set the connection to use or restrict NetBEUI, IPX/SPX, or TCP/IP protocols. If the host supports TCP/IP, you can specify additional settings for dynamic or manual TCP/IP configuration. As shown in figure 39.8, you can manually configure or allow the host to

➤ Assign an IP address

➤ Assign a name server address

➤ Use IP header compression to speed up the connection

➤ Use the default gateway on the remote network

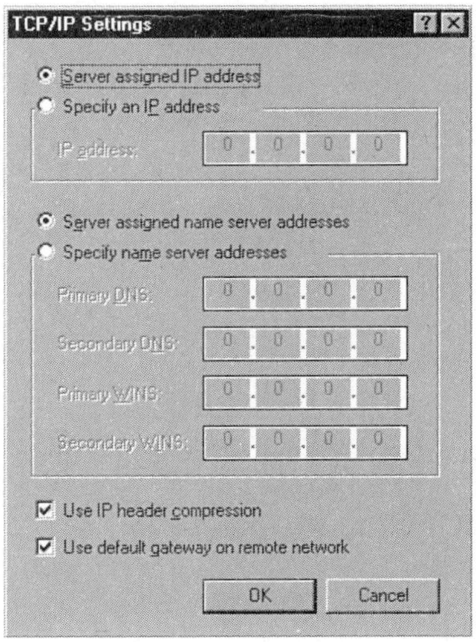

Fig. 39.8 If the host supports TCP/IP, additional configuration options can be specified.

> **Note:** Not all hosts support all the options. Unless these settings are correct, your connection may not work. Be sure to contact the administrator of the host for the correct values for all fields.

Once you've modified the settings to your liking, save your changes by selecting OK on each dialog box until you return to the Dial-Up Networking folder.

Establishing the Connection

Now that you've selected the right protocols and defined the server type, it's time to make the connection. To connect to the host, open the Dial-Up Networking folder if it isn't already open. Double-click on the name of the desired connection you wish to make.

As seen in figure 39.9, you'll be prompted to enter the User name and Password on the host. You can optionally Save the password in an encrypted format for the next time you connect to this particular host. Based upon where you are Dialing from, the Phone number contains area codes, credit card numbers, outside access line codes, or call waiting cancel codes. When you've verified all the information, select the Connect button to initiate the connection to the host.

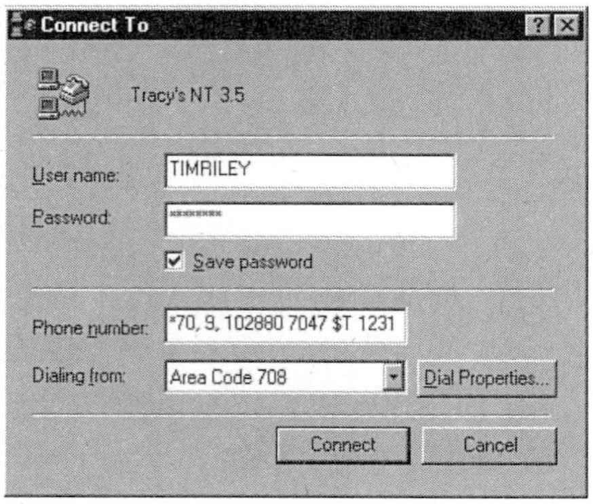

Fig. 39.9 Enter the user name and password, and select your location.

Tip: If you want to modify the Dialing from properties for the current location, select Dial Properties to edit these codes. For more details, see Chapter 32, "Communicating with a Modem," describing how to configure your modem.

You will see a series of messages, on a progress dialog box, similar to those at the left-hand side of figure 39.10. When the connection is ready for you to use, the dialog box changes, as shown at the right side of figure 39.10.

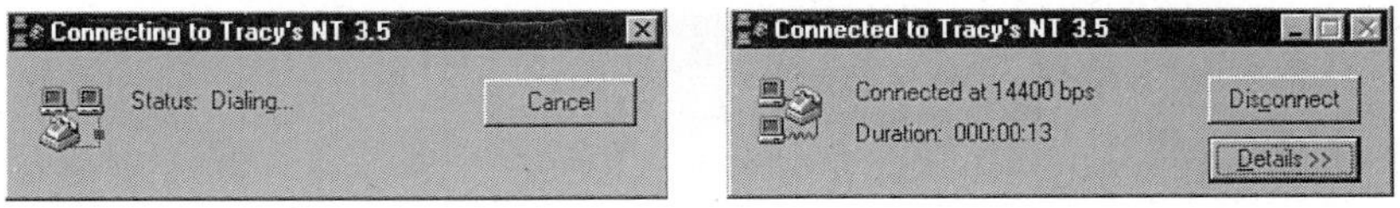

Fig. 39.10 Windows 95 shows you the progression and completion of the network connection.

Now that the connection is made, you have complete access to all the resources on the remote network. Additionally, your host may support the capability for your remote computer to share its resources with other network workstations. Table 39.1 in the previous section identifies which hosts support this.

Transferring Your Deferred Communications

If you deferred printing documents, sending faxes, or sending electronic mail, Windows 95 can begin the process of sending your communications once the network connection is made. If you've deferred printing, Windows 95 automatically detects when the printer is available and begins to send the print jobs to their destinations. If you've deferred faxes, just double-click on the Inbox icon on your desktop. Windows 95 detects when the network fax server is available and begins sending the stored faxes.

If you've deferred electronic mail because you specified the use of the Remote Mail tools for your mail service (as described in Chapter 38, "Setting Up Remote Computing"), you can selectively manipulate messages from the postoffice. However, here is an overview of the Tools menu, as shown in figure 39.11:

- Connect, Disconnect. You can selectively connect and disconnect from the postoffice. This allows you to determine when to receive and send mail.
- Update Headers. To check for new mail without being forced to receive its entire contents, select this option to preview the author, subject, priority, and other types of information about the messages.
- Transfer Mail. This option performs the actions specified for each message based upon how it was marked using the Edit menu.

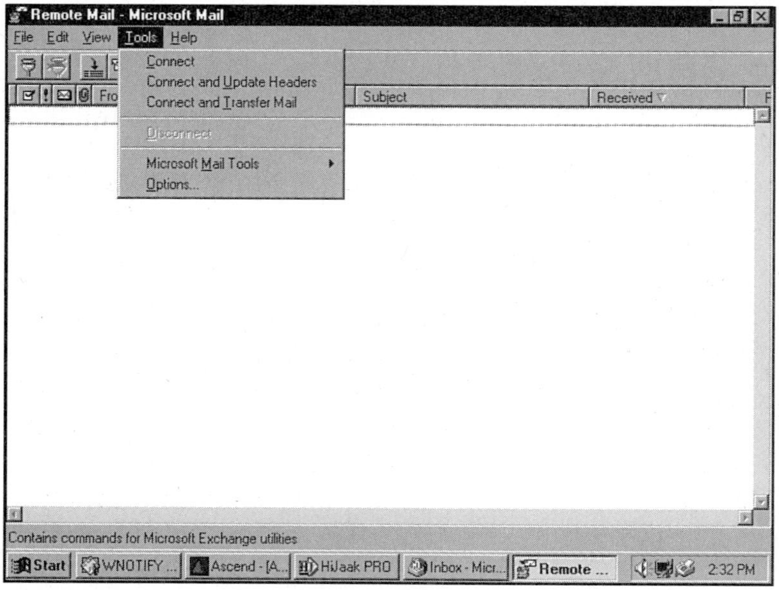

Fig. 39.11 The Remote Mail tool allows to you selectively transfer messages from the remote postoffice.

The Edit menu of the Remote Mail tool allows you to mark each message with an action to be performed. These actions include:

- Mark to Retrieve. By marking a message with this action, you will copy the message to your personal folders and then remove the copy on the postoffice. A return receipt will be generated at this time if the incoming message was marked as such.
- Mark to Retrieve a Copy. Marking a message with this action will copy the message to your personal folder without deleting it from the postoffice. A return receipt will be generated at this time.
- Mark to Delete. This action will delete the specified message from the postoffice when you select Transfer Mail from the Tools menu.

To establish a Remote Mail connection, choose Tools, Remote Mail from the Inbox dialog. From the Remote Mail dialog, choose Tools, Connect. Enter your user ID and password. By selecting Tools, Update Headers, choose one or more options to Send mail waiting to be distributed, Receive marked items from the list in the Remote Mail dialog, Update view of mail headers to show new mail in the Remote Mail dialog, Download address lists to show new potential recipients, or Disconnect after actions are completed. Once you've read your mail, created new messages, or deleted old ones, be sure to Update Headers one last time. You don't want to accidentally leave a message in your local mail file. When complete, select Tools, Disconnect from the Remote Mail dialog to finish your session.

Direct Cable Connections

Using a direct-cable connection allows you to transfer files and access resources on a desktop computer from a second computer with only a serial or parallel cable connecting them. In addition, if the desktop computer has access to network resources using IPX/SPX or NetBEUI, the second computer will too!

Once connected, no special programs (such as InterLink) are required to transfer files. You can perform almost any task on your laptop—just as if it were at your desktop machine. However, the link between your desktop and laptop computers is a one-way connection. Your laptop computer cannot share its resources with the desktop computer or other network workstations.

To establish a direct-cable connection, you should first install the Direct Cable Connection component and obtain the proper cable. Chapter 38, "Setting Up Remote Computing," shows you how to perform these tasks. Once completed, you're ready to set up the host and remote computers.

Setting Up the Host Computer

You have to designate one computer as the *guest* and one computer as the *host*. The guest computer is able to access the resources available to the host computer. The host computer cannot access the guest computer. For example, if I want to transfer files from my desktop to my laptop, I would designate my laptop as the guest and the desktop as the host.

To set up a host computer, you'll need to share a folder that the guest can access. By using the Windows Explorer or double-clicking on My Computer on the desktop, locate the folder you wish to share. Right-click the folder and select Sharing from the context menu.

> **Tip:** If the Sharing option does not appear on the context menu, you have not yet enabled file sharing. See Chapter 36, "Communicating with a Network," to use file sharing to its fullest.

The selected folder's Properties sheet shows the Sharing tab. If you enabled Share-level security in the Network Control Panel, the dialog box will look like the one on the left-hand side of figure 39.12. If you enabled User-level security, the dialog box will look like the one on the right.

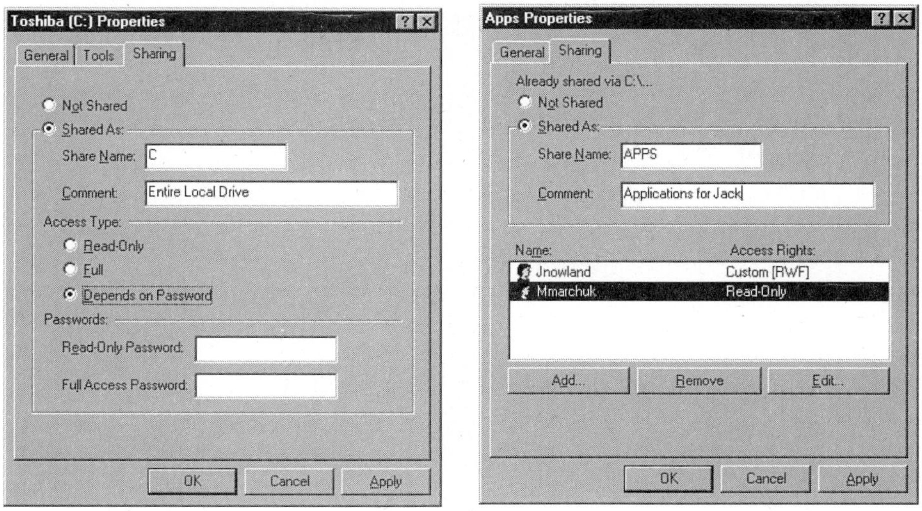

Fig. 39.12 You have to share at least one folder on the host computer for Direct Cable Connection to work.

Click Shared As and provide a Share Name. If you'd like, you may also enter a short Comment about the share. Since other network users don't know what you are sharing, placing a description of what can be found inside the folder is a good use for the comment field.

If you are using Share-level security, define what Access Type other users will have. There are three types of security:

- Read-Only. This allows other users to view the contents and make copies of any file or folder in the drive or folder being shared. Other users will not be able to delete or rename files and folders.
- Full. This allows other users to view the contents and make copies of any file or folder in the share. Additionally, other users will be able to delete or rename files and folders.
- Depends on Password. When users connect to your share, they will be granted either read-only or full access, depending upon which password they give. As you can see at the bottom of figure 39.12, you can enter passwords for both types when the Depends on Password option is selected.

If you chose to set up your computer to use User-level access control, you'll need to add user or group names to the Name list. With the existing list of Names, you can perform three actions:

- Add. Allows you to specify a user name or group defined by the server you specified in the Access Control tab of the Network Control Panel. For each one, you can allow full access, read-only access, or a custom set of access privileges. A custom set can include one or more of the following privileges: Read Files, Write to Files, Create Files and Folders, Delete Files, Change File Attributes, List Files, and Change Access Control.
- Remove. For the selected name in the list, you can remove the access you've previously granted. Once you select the OK or Apply buttons, the change is permanent.
- Edit. For the selected name in the list, you can modify the current access privileges just as if you were adding the name for the first time.

> **Tip:** Notice in figure 39.12 the words "Already shared via C:\..." immediately under the Sharing tab. Windows 95 is telling you the folder has already been shared. If you specified User-level security, the names listed are those who already have access to this folder. For just this share, you may add, remove, or edit their access privileges.

Now that you've provided a share for the guest to access, initiate the connection on the host. On that computer, click Start, Programs, Accessories, Direct Cable Connection. If you haven't already set the computer to be a host, figure 39.13 shows the first step.

Select the Host option and click Next. Windows 95 will indicate that it's configuring ports. When prompted, select the port to which you've connected the cable. Figure 39.14 shows the selection of a parallel port. Click Next to accept your port selection.

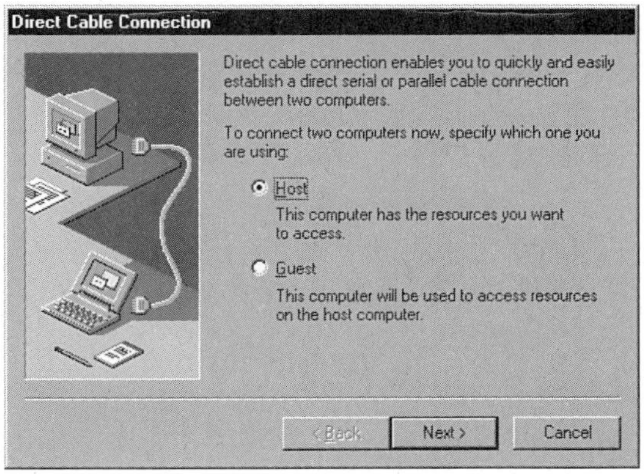

Fig. 39.13 You can access Direct Cable Connection through Accessories.

> **Tip:** The fastest type is a parallel *Extended Capabilities Port* (ECP) using a *Universal Cable Module* (UCM) cable. The BIOS in your computer defines the type of parallel port. Your local hardware dealer should be able to provide a UCM cable.

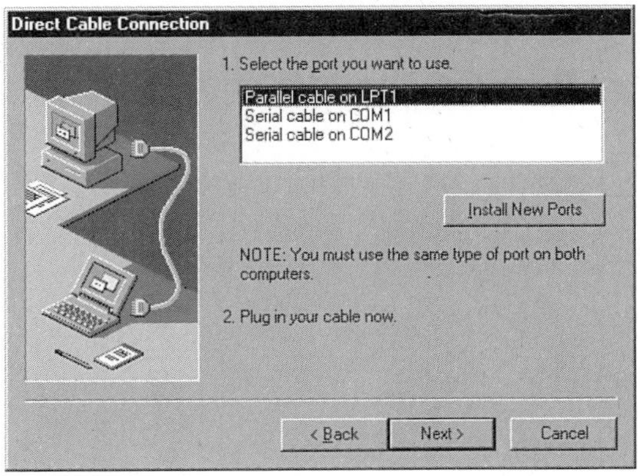

Fig. 39.14 Parallel ports run three- to four-times faster than serial cables.

If you'd like to require the guest to enter a password when it connects to the host, click Use password protection and enter a password. In either case, click Finish to begin waiting for the guest to connect. If the guest computer isn't configured yet, see the following section, "Setting Up the Guest Computer." While you do this, the host will continue to wait for a guest connection.

Setting Up the Guest Computer

To access a host computer, you'll need to set up the guest computer in the Direct Cable Connection dialog box. On the computer you wish to designate as the guest, click Start, Programs, Accessories, Direct Cable Connection. Figure 39.14 is then displayed.

Select the Guest option and click Next. Windows 95 will indicate that it's configuring ports. When prompted, select the port to which you've connected the cable. Figure 39.15 shows the selection of a parallel port. Click Next to accept your port selection.

> **Tip:** The fastest type is a parallel *Extended Capabilities Port* (ECP) using a *Universal Cable Module* (UCM) cable. The BIOS in your computer defines the type of parallel port. Your local hardware dealer should be able to provide a UCM cable.

If the host computer requires a password to complete the connection, you'll be asked for it at this point. Enter it to complete the connection.

Using Direct Cable Connection

When you've installed Direct Cable Connection and established a connection, the guest computer has access to the shared resources on the host computer. If the host is connected to a network, the guest also has access to those resources (excluding those using TCP/IP protocol).

When the connection is established, Windows 95 will immediately open a folder on the guest computer. This folder (see figure 39.15) contains all the resources shared on the host computer, including shared folders and shared printers. Notice that it is just like any other folder on your desktop. If the host computer has access to other network resources, the Network Neighborhood will show those same resources on the guest computer.

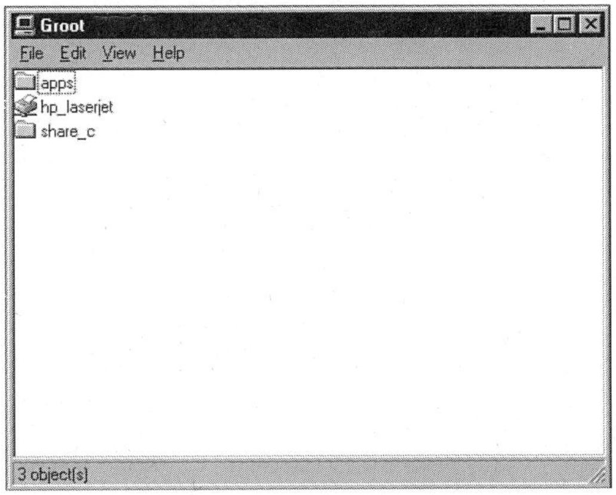

Fig. 39.15 The guest computer displays the folders and printers you have access to on the host computer.

> **Tip:** If you share a new folder from the host while you're connected, you have to refresh the guest computer. To do so, click View, Refresh.

If you shared access to individual folders within a drive, they'll be indicated separately. To view the contents of a folder, you can then double-click on it to open it.

To browse the entire network, double-click the Network Neighborhood icon on your desktop. If you don't have access to the whole network, you'll get an error message saying so.

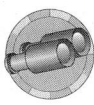

> **Note:** The guest computer still has access to its own folders.

Using Quick View you can access many files even if you don't have the program on the guest machine. Although you can run programs on the guest computer that are resident on the host, this procedure is very slow. As a rule of thumb, your guest computer should contain all the applications needed to do your work.

To disconnect, click on the Direct Cable Connection icon on the taskbar and click Close on each machine.

To transfer updated files in a Briefcase, see "Keeping Your Files in Sync," later in this chapter.

Changing from Guest to Host

If at any time you want to reverse the access capabilities between the guest and host, it's just a button click away. On each computer, click Start, Programs, Accessories, Direct Cable Connection. You'll get the Direct Cable Connection screen shown in figure 39.16. Select the Change button. By doing this, you restart (from scratch) the configuration of the computer as part of a Direct Cable Connection. If you want to configure the computer as a host, read the earlier section, "Setting Up the Host Computer." If you want to configure the computer as a Guest, "Setting Up the Guest Computer" will teach you.

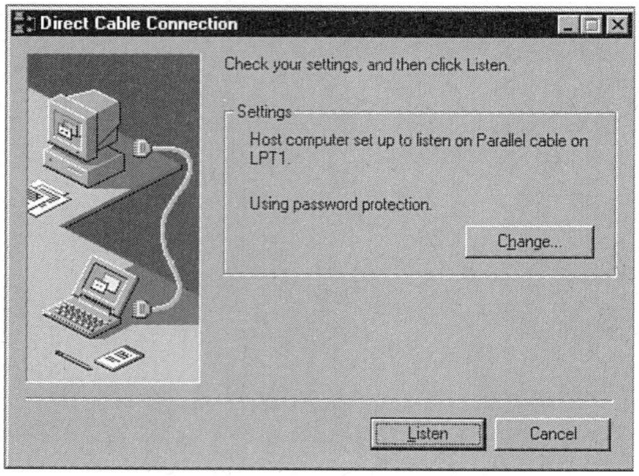

Fig. 39.16 You can change from host to guest or guest to host.

Troubleshooting a Direct Cable Connection

Here are some basic items to check if you are having problems establishing a Direct Cable Connection. Make sure you have

- Run Direct Cable Connection on both computers
- Set up one computer as the guest and one computer as the host
- Used the correct cable
- Secured the cable on both computers
- Given each computer a unique name
- Enabled sharing on the host computer

If these suggestions don't solve the problem, Windows 95's online help has an excellent interactive troubleshooting section for Direct Cable Connection. To access it, click Start, Help and type **Direct Cable Connection.** Choose the Troubleshooting option and click Display.

Hot-Docking

Because the three widely used protocols (IPX/SPX, TCP/IP, and NetBEUI) are Plug-and-Play enabled, the Windows 95 system runs even if the network becomes unavailable. That allows *hot-docking* for docking stations that support the Plug-and-Play BIOS. Without turning off the computer, the network is automatically enabled when it becomes docked. Windows 95 also notifies print, fax, and mail queues that the network resources are available to begin transferring deferred communications. When the computer becomes undocked, Windows 95 reconfigures the laptop's resources to conserve memory and power usage.

Note: If you use any real-mode network components, you will not be able to use hot-docking. Windows 95 only supports hot-docking with protected mode adapter cards, network clients, and protocols.

Caution: Be sure you confirm that your docking station is Plug-and-Play BIOS compliant. If not, it is possible to corrupt your open files. Without the application being notified that the network is no longer available, it may attempt to save the file and become confused. If your docking station isn't Plug-and-Play compliant, be sure to save and close your work before ejecting the computer.

Using Briefcase

When you work remotely, whether it's on a laptop away from home or on a desktop away from work, you often have to juggle multiple copies of the same file. With just a moment of carelessness, you can accidentally replace an updated file with an earlier version. Without a doubt, you're destined to print the wrong version at least once.

With the new Briefcase feature, you don't have to worry about any of that. Briefcase makes updating files a snap. If the program you used to create two versions of the same file supports merging file revisions (such as Microsoft Word for Windows), Briefcase will try to use the features provided by the program to merge the two versions together. However, not many applications provide this functionality yet. Briefcase will then compare the dates of the files and keep the newest one. You can use Briefcase with Dial-Up Networking and Direct Cable Connection, or move it to a floppy.

Briefcase prompts you to update files that have been changed since you copied them into the Briefcase. That way, you won't forget to transfer the latest version.

The Briefcase icon resides on your desktop. If it's not there, you need to create it. To create the Briefcase icon, do the following:

1. On the desktop, click the right mouse button.
2. Click on New.
3. Click on Briefcase. The Briefcase icon appears.

> **Tip:** If you share a Briefcase, you won't be able to synchronize any files that you drag-and-drop there while sharing is enabled. That means every document will display an *orphan status* and won't be updated.

To copy a file to Briefcase, do the following:

1. In the Windows Explorer, locate and click the icon for the file you want to update. (The file has to be closed.) This file can be located on any drive, folder, or shared resource to which your computer has access.
2. Reduce the size of the Explorer window so you can see the Briefcase icon.
3. Drag-and-drop the icon for the file you want to take with you into the Briefcase icon.

> **Tip:** If you know the name of the document but not the path, click Start, Find, Files or Folders. Type in the name of the file you want to find. You can then drag-and-drop the icon right from the Find window.

The file will be copied into Briefcase. When you double-click on Briefcase, you'll get a window showing the large icons of all items copied inside. To view file details, click View, Details. You'll get a screen similar to the one shown in figure 39.17.

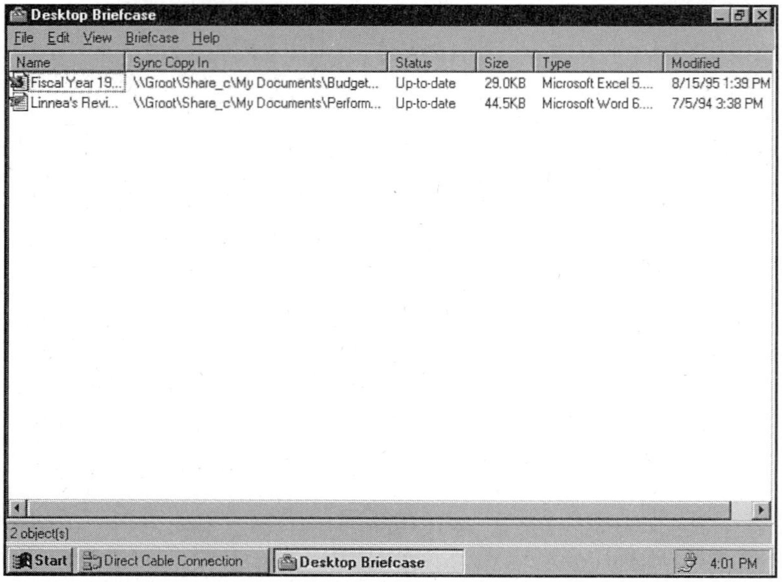

Fig. 39.17 A list view of Briefcase after two files have been copied into it.

> **Caution:** You can change the name of the file in Briefcase, but if you do, you'll sever the link to the original file. Then Briefcase won't keep track of which file has changed.

Another way to copy a file into Briefcase is to click on the file's icon (the file has to be closed), and then click File, Send to, My Briefcase.

When you first copy a file into Briefcase, the status will indicate that it's Up-to-date. Whenever you save changes to the original file, the status will change to Needs updating.

Note: If the Briefcase window is open when you save the original file, the status won't reflect the change until you close the window and open it again.

To update the Briefcase version of a file, do the following:

1. Double-click on the Briefcase icon to open the window.
2. Click on the icon of the file you wish to update.
3. Click Briefcase, Update Selection. You'll get a screen similar to the one shown in figure 39.18.

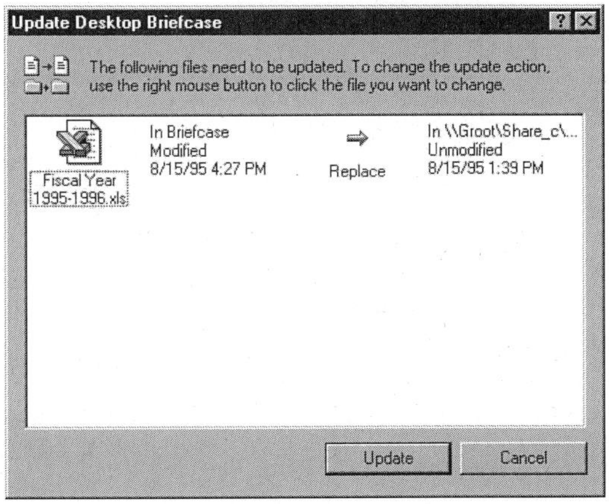

Fig. 39.18 Briefcase shows you the location of each file, and the date and time each file was modified, before it updates files.

4. Click Update.

The direction of the green arrow indicates which version of the file will be replaced. In this case, the file on the right, the one located in \\GROOT\Share_C, will replace the file on the left, which is an earlier version located in Briefcase.

If you want the earlier version of the file to replace the later version, do the following:

Caution: Replacing the latest version with an earlier version this way will backdate your original file. You will lose all revisions made since the Briefcase version. Make absolutely certain this is what you want to do before you do it. It cannot be reversed.

1. In the Update My Briefcase window, select the file you want to update (see the preceding instructions).
2. Move the cursor to the word Replace and right-click. You'll get the screen shown in figure 39.19.

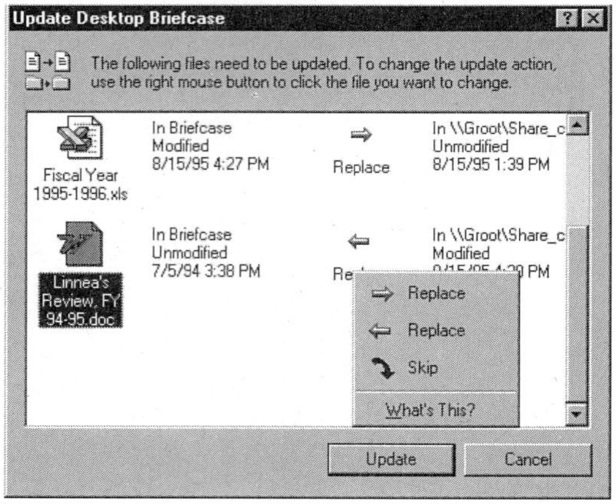

Fig. 39.19 You have the options to replace the latest version with the earlier version or to skip replacement altogether.

3. Click the green arrow to indicate the way you want the files updated.
4. Click Update.

If you aren't sure where the original file came from, Briefcase helps you find the original file. It also shows you all kinds of statistics about the versions.

To find the original file, do the following:

1. In the Briefcase window, click on the icon for the file you want to find out about.
2. Click File, Properties. You'll get the screen shown in figure 39.20.

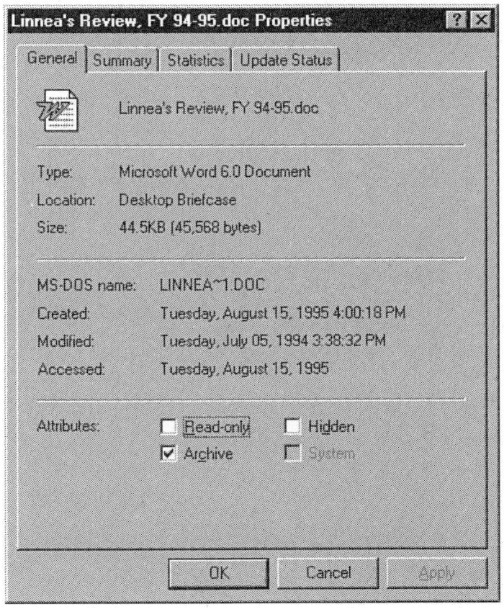

Fig. 39.20 The General Properties tab in Briefcase indicates the date the file was created, modified, and accessed. The accessed date tells you when Briefcase was opened.

3. Click the Update Status tab. You'll get the screen shown in figure 39.21.
4. Click Find Original to find the file. Briefcase will open the folder window.
5. Double-click on the file if you want to open it.

The easiest way to use Briefcase to synchronize files from one computer to another is to drag-and-drop the Briefcase to a floppy and take it with you. Then, when you get to your other computer, drag-and-drop the Briefcase onto the desktop and follow the preceding instructions for updating files.

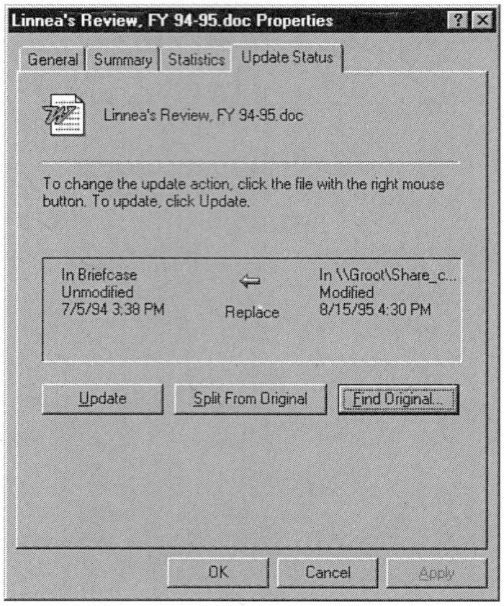

Fig. 39.21 Briefcase lets you find and access the original file.

You can use Briefcase to synchronize files with Direct Cable Connection or Dial-Up Networking, both described earlier in this chapter.

To use Briefcase to synchronize files on computers that are directly cabled or connected via a Dial-Up Connection, do the following:

1. Share the Briefcase from the computer with the updated files. (Click the Briefcase icon, click the right mouse button, click Sharing, click the Sharing tab, and click Shared As.)

> **Caution:** Remember to take sharing off the Briefcase icon after you've transferred it. Otherwise, you won't be able to save linked files and all files will be orphaned.

2. Connect the computers with a Direct Cable Connection or Dial-Up Networking. You'll get a screen similar to the one shown in figure 39.22.

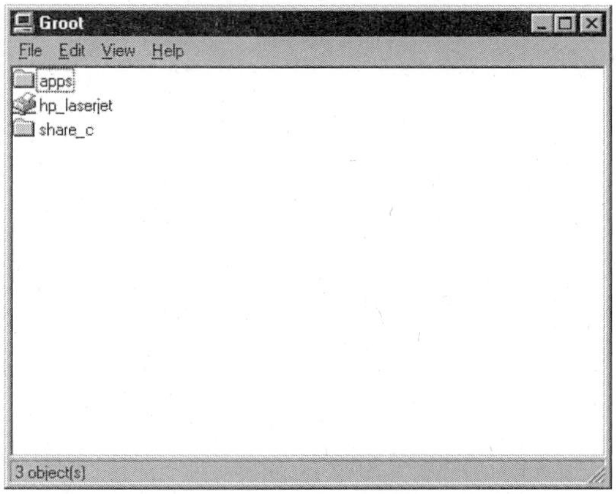

Fig. 39.22 The remote computer displays all of the shared folders from the host computer.

3. Double-click on My Briefcase from the host computer. You'll get a screen showing you the files.
4. Drag-and-drop the file you want to update from the host to the remote. (Or you can click on the file you want to copy, and click File, Properties, Send To My Briefcase.)
5. Click Yes.

To make sure you've copied the right file, double-click on My Briefcase on the remote computer. Click View, Details. Notice that under Sync Copy In there will be something similar to \\Robin\My Briefcase. That indicates the updated file came from a Briefcase folder on another computer.

If you don't want to bother connecting computers, you can simply copy the Briefcase to a floppy. Of course you can drag-and-drop the file, but there's an easier way to do it.

To copy a file from Briefcase to a floppy, do the following:

1. Open the Briefcase window and click on the file you want to copy.
2. Click File, Send to, 3 1/2-inch Floppy (A).
3. Make sure you put the Briefcase back on your other computer.

You can also send files this way to a fax recipient or a mail recipient.

Operating in Windows 95 DOS

by Allen L. Wyatt

You have learned long ago that Windows 95 signals a change in the fundamental relationship between DOS and Windows. In previous versions of Windows, DOS was required because Windows ran as an adjunct to DOS. Now, DOS runs as an adjunct to Windows. Although DOS is still available, it is more “behind the scenes” than it has been historically.

This chapter covers information you need to know about using the MS-DOS command line. Here you will find the following:

- The historical DOS commands removed from Windows 95
- The new commands added to Windows 95
- How to use the command line interface
- How to change the properties of an MS-DOS window

This chapter does not present a complete list of commands available in the DOS window. Indeed, an effective discussion would take an entire book by itself. Instead, you should find a good DOS reference and use it as your basis for what you do in the DOS window. The information in this chapter will help you with the commands that have been deleted and added to Windows 95.

DOS Commands No Longer Available

If you have been using computers for a while, chances are good that you are already familiar with many DOS commands. The release of Windows 95 has meant a change in the way that DOS is both perceived and used. The DOS that you can use in Windows 95 does not include all of the commands you could previously use in DOS. Some commands have been replaced by integrated Windows utilities, but others are simply not needed anymore.

The DOS commands no longer available under Windows 95 are divided into several categories: disk commands, device drivers, file commands, memory management, printer management, and miscellaneous. Each of these categories is covered in the following sections.

Disk Commands

As you learned in Chapter 2, "Under-the-Hood Improvements," the disk access routines used by Windows 95 have been completely rewritten. In the process, a whopping 14 DOS commands were deleted from Windows 95. The following disk-related commands were deleted:

- **APPEND**. The APPEND command was used to link together different folders on a disk. Now that you can easily browse through your system (and other systems on the network), it is obsolete.
- **ASSIGN.** The ASSIGN command enabled you to create alias drive letters to refer to other drives. The same functionality is built in to the drive mapping capabilities of Windows 95.

- **BACKUP.** This DOS-based backup program has been replaced by the Windows 95 Backup utility.
- **FASTOPEN.** The FASTOPEN command provided for faster opening of disk files by keeping the disk folder in memory. The same functionality has been built directly in to the Windows 95 file routines.
- **INTERLNK.** The INTERLNK command was used to facilitate network communications in the DOS environment. Because Windows 95 has been built from the ground up with networking in mind, the INTERLNK command is obsolete.
- **INTERSVR.** The INTERSVR command was designed to work with the INTERLNK command to provide some networking capabilities. It has been rendered obsolete by Windows 95.
- **JOIN.** The JOIN command was used to provide an alias for different drives on your system. Originally provided as a work-around for software that could not easily access hard drives, the command is no longer needed. Some of the functionality of JOIN is provided by the drive mapping capabilities of Windows 95.
- **MIRROR.** The MIRROR command was used in conjunction with the UNFORMAT command. Because the UNFORMAT command has been deleted, MIRROR has been deleted as well.
- **MSBACKUP.** This is the DOS-based backup command. The capabilities of the MSBACKUP command have been replaced by the Backup utility.
- **MWBACKUP.** This is the Windows-based backup command included with previous versions of DOS. The capabilities of the MWBACKUP command have been replaced by the Backup utility.
- **RECOVER.** The RECOVER command was used to salvage data from a badly damaged disk. It is no longer necessary because of the improved filing system used in Windows 95. In addition, some of the remedial actions provided by RECOVER are now provided by the ScanDisk utility.

- **RESTORE.** The RESTORE command was used to restore information saved with the BACKUP command. It has been absorbed into the Windows 95 Backup utility.
- **SMARTMON.** The SMARTMON command was deleted because Windows 95 enables you to control disk caching and virtual memory settings directly from the Control Panel.
- **UNFORMAT.** It was easy in earlier versions of DOS to inadvertently format a disk by typing in the wrong drive letter; the UNFORMAT command helped undo such an error. With Windows 95, you can format disks from two places: from within Windows and from the MS-DOS command prompt. You can format floppies only from within Windows. If you issue the format command from the command prompt, you are asked to verify your action before it is executed. This double-checking makes it less likely you will need the UNFORMAT command.

File Commands

The improved file management capabilities of Windows 95 mean that some of the commands originally provided in DOS for this purpose are no longer necessary. The following file-related DOS commands were deleted in Windows 95:

- **COMP.** The COMP command was actually deleted in DOS 6.0, but it was still available on the Supplemental Disk. The COMP command is not available at all with Windows 95 because the FC command (available from the command line) provides a superset of COMP's capabilities.
- **MWUNDEL.** This Windows-based program enabled you to undelete files. With the introduction of the Recycle Bin, the MWUNDEL command was no longer necessary.
- **REPLACE.** The REPLACE command enabled you to selectively update files on a disk. Now you can update files through the Explorer.

- **SHARE.** The SHARE command was used to allow multiple programs to share information in the same file. The integrated networking capabilities of Windows 95 make SHARE obsolete.
- **TREE.** The TREE command enabled you to see a tree-type depiction of your folder structure. Such a command is redundant with the browsing capabilities of Windows 95, as well as the Explorer.
- **UNDELETE.** This DOS-based program was used for undeleting files. The same function is now provided through the use of the Recycle Bin on the Windows 95 desktop.
- **VSAFE.** The VSAFE program was used to ensure that data was written to disk immediately. The improved caching routines built in to Windows 95 make such a command unnecessary.

Memory Management

When you last saw DOS, the memory management capabilities could best be described as "tenuous." Management was effected through a collection of arcane commands and switches. After your memory configuration was set, you were often afraid to "mess with it" for fear it would cause your system to become unstable (or more unstable).

Windows 95 provides huge improvements in memory management. Most aspects of memory management are taken care of behind the scenes, without any human intervention. The biggest improvement of all was the removal of the 640K conventional memory barrier that was intrinsic to DOS. Now Windows 95 does virtually everything in protected mode or in *virtual real mode* in the case of DOS windows.

Because Windows 96 now handles memory management, the DOS MEMMAKER command was deleted. There is no longer a need for the program, which was used to automatically check various memory configurations and determine which was best for your system.

It is interesting to note that some commands which were related to DOS memory management are still available in Windows 95. Most notable is the LH or LOADHIGH command, which you use to load device drivers into upper memory. Because you may need to use some real-mode device drivers on your system, this command is still supported under Windows 95.

Printer Management

As you learned in Chapter 20, "Managing Your Printers," and Chapter 21, "Printing from Windows 95," the entire print spooler and printer management portions of Windows 95 have been rewritten. The new 32-bit subsystems now operate much more smoothly than in previous versions of Windows. The other big advantage is that printing from the DOS command line is routed through the Windows printer management subsystem. This feature allows for a more consistent approach to printer management, and fewer headaches reconciling Windows with DOS.

Due to the improved printer management, the following printer-related commands have been deleted from Windows 95:

- **GRAPHICS.** The GRAPHICS command was used so that the Print Screen key could be used to print the contents of screens displayed in graphics modes. With the printer drivers supplied with Windows 95, you can print graphics just as well as text, so the command is no longer needed.
- **PRINT.** The PRINT command implemented a print spooler for background printing. This task is now handled by the Windows 95 print spooler.

Device Drivers

Several device drivers have been deleted from Windows 95; they have been largely absorbed into the operating system itself. The following drivers used to be distributed with DOS, but are not distributed with Windows 95:

- **EGA.SYS.** The EGA.SYS driver was used in conjunction with the DOS Shell to correct problems that occurred when task switching on a system that used an EGA monitor. Because the DOS Shell is no longer necessary, and EGA cards will not work with Windows 95, the driver is not needed.
- **MONOUMB.386.** The MONOUMB.386 driver was used in previous versions of Windows to indicate when the DOS memory management functions had used the monochrome display region at B000h to B7FFh as upper memory. This is no longer necessary under Windows 95.
- **PRINTER.SYS.** The PRINTER.SYS driver provided international code page support for some IBM printers. The same capabilities are built-in as part of Windows 95.
- **RAMDRIVE.SYS.** The RAMDRIVE.SYS driver was used to create a RAM drive in memory. It is no longer supported under Windows 95.
- **VFINTD.386.** The VFINTD.386 driver allowed the Windows-based backup program (MWBACKUP.EXE) to access the floppy drives properly. Because this backup program has been deleted from Windows 95, the driver is no longer necessary.
- **WINA20.386.** The WINA20.386 driver was used to support some enhanced-mode device drivers in earlier versions of Windows. The functions it provided have been rendered obsolete by the newer sections of Windows 95.

As you can tell, most drivers have been deleted because they are simply no longer needed under Windows 95. The one surprise on the list may be the RAMDRIVE.SYS driver. The upshot of this is that you can no longer create a RAM drive after Windows 95 is installed on your system. Although this may seem to be a potential disadvantage, a look at the historical reasons for RAM drives may put this change in perspective.

When RAM drives were first introduced on PCs, there were two main reasons for their acceptance. First, RAM prices were much cheaper

than hard drive prices, and second, RAM was much faster than hard drives. The former reason is no longer a big issue since the prices of hard drives have fallen through the floor. You can now find 1G drives for under $400. This means that the price is under 40 cents per megabyte—much cheaper than RAM prices.

The latter reason (speed) is also less of a concern. With the smart disk caching and fast disk speeds and transfer rates on today's disk drives, the speed differential is less of an issue than it used to be.

The final issue related to RAM drives is that whenever you use part of your memory for a dedicated purpose—such as a RAM drive—you cannot use it for something that may be more critical. In particular, the more memory you take for a RAM drive, the less memory Windows has to work with and the more likely it will need to swap memory to the hard drive. Thus, the use of a RAM drive could mean a slowdown in the performance of your system.

Miscellaneous Commands

A few DOS commands that have been deleted in Windows 95 do not readily fit into the other command categories. The following ten miscellaneous commands have been deleted from Windows 95:

- **DOSSHELL.** This is the graphical DOS Shell supplied with some versions of DOS. It would not make much sense to run the DOS Shell within a DOS window, so it was deleted.
- **EDLIN.** This is the venerable (and ancient) text editor available since the first version of DOS. It has been replaced by the EDIT command, which is still available from the DOS command line.
- **FASTHELP.** This method of getting help has been removed from DOS. Instead, you can use the /? switch on any command, or you can attempt to find DOS commands in the online help (the pickings are pretty sparse).

- **GRAFTABL.** The GRAFTABL command was used to support extended graphics characters on CGA graphics adapters. Because the CGA is not supported in Windows 95 (a VGA card is the minimum requirement), the command is no longer necessary.
- **HELP.** This was the full-blown help system available under DOS. It has been removed in favor of the command-oriented /? switch. You can also try to use the online help to find a few DOS commands.
- **MSAV.** The MSAV program was the DOS-based version of the Microsoft antivirus program. This feature has been deleted, with no explanation, from Windows 95.
- **MWAV.** The MWAV program was the Windows-based version of the Microsoft antivirus program. Like the MSAV program, it was deleted with no explanation.
- **MWAVTSR.** This was a TSR (terminate and stay resident) program that worked with the Windows-based version of the antivirus program. Because the antivirus program was deleted, there was no need for the TSR support.
- **POWER.** The POWER command provided support for the APM (advanced power management) specification in laptop computers. The functionality of this command has been built in to the Windows 95 Control Panel.
- **QBASIC.** This text-based version of BASIC apparently does not have a place in the fancy world of Windows-oriented graphics. It has been deleted, and wanna-be programmers will need to use a program such as Visual Basic to do their tinkering.

New Commands

The added capabilities of Windows 95 have meant that a few extra command-line commands have been introduced. This is understandable because there needs to be a way to access new features from the command line. The new commands fall into two categories: network commands and TCP/IP commands. Another major addition to the command line is the START command. Each of these areas is discussed in the following sections.

Network Commands

By this point in the book you have already learned that Windows 95 is a networking environment. This means that network resources are easily accessed both from within Windows 95 and from the DOS command line. Most operations enable you to utilize resources transparently. For instance, if you have mapped a network drive, calling it drive H:, you can simply use DOS commands at the command line to access drive H:. Windows 95 takes care of the rest, behind the scenes, to make sure that your commands are carried out as you intend.

To facilitate the use of the network, Windows 95 has included quite a few different network commands that you can use from the command line. These commands all consist of two keywords, and start with the word *NET*. The following are the different network commands:

- NET CONFIG
- NET DIAG
- NET HELP
- NET INIT
- NET LOGOFF
- NET LOGON
- NET PASSWORD
- NET PRINT
- NET START
- NET STOP
- NET TIME
- NET USE

- NET VER
- NET VIEW

These commands are intended to help you manage your network connections and network resources from the command line. In addition, there are two other network commands provided with Windows 95. The NETSTAT command (notice that it is one word, not two) is used to discover information about your network workstation and the network connections you have made. If you are using a network based on NetBIOS protocols (such as Novell), then you can use the NBTSTAT command, which provides much the same information, but procures it through NetBIOS functions.

The following sections detail the purpose and composition of each of the new DOS commands.

NET CONFIG

The NET CONFIG command displays information about your local workstation. You will see information about your computer name, user name, workgroup, root folder, and operating system version information, as shown in figure 40.1.

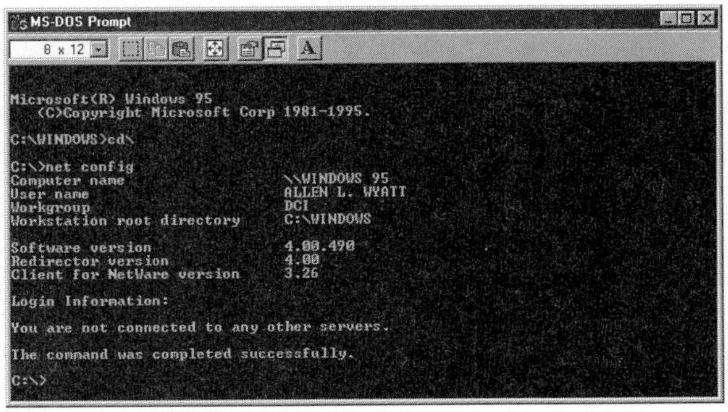

Fig. 40.1 The NET CONFIG command returns information about your network connection.

You can run the NET CONFIG command from the DOS command line in an MS-DOS window.

NET DIAG

The NET DIAG command is used to troubleshoot the connection between two computers on your network. This command presupposes that there are at least two computers using the same command. When you first use it, it will search for another computer using the same program, and establish the link with it. If it cannot find another system using NET DIAG, then it will start to act as a diagnostics server, awaiting some other system on the network to run the same program.

When you have two computers running NET DIAG, you can view the statistics reported by the program. These statistics can help you diagnose where you may be having problems with the net.

NET HELP

The NET HELP command is used to get a short bit of information about the various network commands provided with Windows 95. For instance, figure 40.2 shows an example of the help information returned by the program for the NET PRINT command.

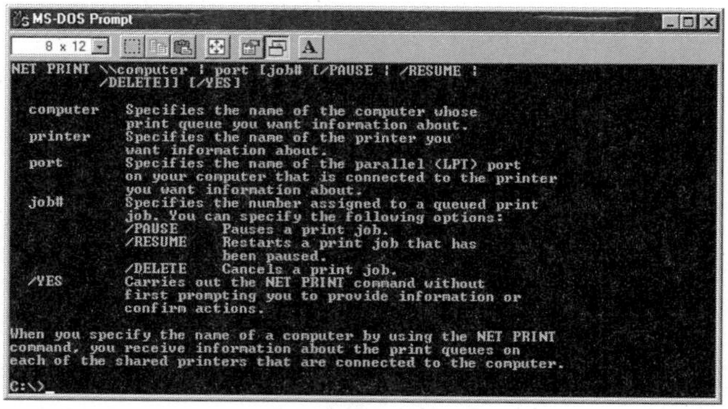

Fig. 40.2 The help information returned for the NET PRINT command.

> **Tip:** You can also get help on a network command by entering the command as you normally would, and then using a /? switch after the command.

In addition, you can use the NET HELP command to provide information about errors which may occur when using network commands. To use the command in this way, simply append the number of the error to the command.

NET INIT

The NET INIT command is used to load network drivers without binding them to the Protocol Manager. Typically, this command is used with third-party network drivers. You can use NET INIT in real-mode operation only. This means that you cannot use it in an MS-DOS window. Instead, you must restart your system at the command prompt. Afterwards, you can use it with no problem.

After using NET INIT, you can use the NET START NETBIND command to bind the drivers to the Protocol Manager. If you experience problems with some third-party networks, you might try using NET INIT with the /dynamic switch. This loads the drivers dynamically and may cure the problem.

NET LOGOFF

You can use the NET LOGOFF command in real-mode operation only. This means that you cannot use it in an MS-DOS window. Instead, you must restart your system at the command prompt. Afterwards, you can use NET LOGOFF.

The purpose of NET LOGOFF is to provide the same function in real mode that you would normally do within Windows 95. Using the command logs you off the network immediately, without any confirmation. You can use the NET LOGON command to again gain access to the network.

NET LOGON

The NET LOGON command is the opposite of NET LOGOFF. You can use NET LOGON in real-mode operation only, which means you cannot use it in an MS-DOS window. Instead, you must restart your system at the command prompt. Afterwards, you can use NET LOGON.

Normally, if you are using the Windows 95 graphical interface, you gain access to the network by logging on the system when you first start Windows. Similarly, you can use the features in the Control Panel to log on and off. In real mode you obviously do not have access to these features, so you must use the NET LOGON command to connect your system to the network.

When you use the command, you should follow it with your user ID, your password, an optional domain name, and an indication of whether you want the password saved. The syntax for the command is as follows:

```
NET LOGON user password /DOMAIN:name /yes /SAVEPW:NO
```

The /yes switch between the domain name and the save password flag is used if you want to carry out the logon process without asking for confirmation.

NET PASSWORD

There are three different forms of the NET PASSWORD command. Each of them is designed to help change your network password, but each is used in a different situation.

If you want to change your password on the current system, you can only do so from real mode. This means that you cannot have the Windows 95 graphical interface running. The best way to get rid of it is to restart the system at the command prompt. Then, when you are connected to the network, you can use the command as follows:

```
NET PASSWORD oldpw newpw
```

All you need to do is replace *oldpw* and *newpw* with your old and new passwords, respectively. The second form of the command enables you to change your password on another server. You can do this from the command line of an MS-DOS window. To use this form of the command, use the following syntax:

```
NET PASSWORD \\server user oldpw newpw
```

Notice that you must now include both the server address and your user ID. Similarly, you can use the third form of NET PASSWORD to change your password on a particular domain:

```
NET PASSWORD /DOMAIN:domain user oldpw newpw
```

Here you have replaced the server name with the /DOMAIN: key word and the name of the domain. You can also use this version of the command in an MS-DOS window.

NET PRINT

The NET PRINT command is used to control print jobs over the network or on your own system. In effect, the command provides a way to control a printer queue from the command line rather than using the Printers folder. Available options enable you to view the queue, as well as to pause, resume, and delete individual jobs.

The normal way you use the command is to first view the queue. This is done using the following command at the DOS command line:

```
NET PRINT location /yes
```

The location parameter is a port number (such as LPT1 or LPT2) or a UNC path for a network printer. The command returns a list of the print jobs currently in the queue. Associated with each print job is a job number. This number can then be used in a NET PRINT command that affects the individual job. For instance, if you want to delete print job 14, you would use the following command:

```
NET PRINT location 14 /DELETE /yes
```

Again, the location is the name of the printer whose queue you are modifying. NET PRINT recognizes two other commands as well—/PAUSE and /RESUME. You can use these commands on the command line in place of the /DELETE command.

Even though the NET PRINT command works just fine, it is much easier to use the Printers folder to manage individual printer queues. NET PRINT is provided primarily for the development of batch files that automatically manage the print queue.

NET START

The NET START command is used to start different network services. You use this command after you have used NET INIT. You can use NET START in real-mode operation only, which means that you cannot use it in an MS-DOS window. Instead, you must restart your system at the command prompt.

To start a service, you use the following syntax:

```
NET START service /yes /verbose /nondis
```

The last three parameters are optional. The /yes parameter carries out the startup process without asking for confirmation. The /verbose parameter indicates that you want detailed information about device drivers and services as they are loaded. The /nondis parameter starts the network redirector without loading any device drivers.

The *service* parameter is used to indicate the type of network service you want to start. Table 40.1 lists the different services you can specify on the command line.

Table 40.1 Network Services Used with the NET START Command

Service	Meaning
BASIC	Basic network redirector
NWREDIR	Microsoft Client for NetWare
WORKSTATION	The default redirector
NETBIND	Binds protocols and drivers
NETBEUI	Extended NetBIOS interface
NWLINK	IPX/SPX interface

If you want to list the active services on the workstation, you can use the following command:

```
NET START /LIST
```

NET STOP

The NET STOP command is the opposite of the NET START command. It is used to halt network services, and can be used in real-mode operation only. This means that you cannot use it in an MS-DOS window. Instead, you must restart your system at the command prompt.

> **Tip:** It is a good idea to list the different active network services before you use NET STOP. You do this by using the NET START /LIST command.

To use the NET STOP command, all you need to do is append the name of the service you want to stop. You can use the service names detailed earlier in Table 40.1.

NET TIME

The NET TIME command is used to view the time on another computer in your workgroup or domain; it will work only on a Windows network. This remote computer is called a *time server*. You can also use the command to synchronize the time on your workstation with the time on the remote system.

To view the time on another system, use the following command:

```
NET TIME location /yes
```

The *location* parameter indicates the name of the computer or workgroup you want to check. If you are checking a specific computer, a fully qualified UNC name must be provided. If you are checking the time on a workgroup, then the format is /WORKGROUP:*name*, where *name* is the name of the workgroup. You can only check the time of a workgroup if the workgroup has a defined time server for the group.

To set your system time based on the time on another system, use the following command:

```
NET TIME location /set /yes
```

The only change from the command to view the time is the inclusion of the /set switch, which tells NET TIME you want to set your local computer time.

NET USE

The NET USE command is used to manage your network connections with remote resources such as disks or printers. This command is similar in purpose to the network mapping functions of Windows 95. You can also use NET USE to display information about existing connections. You can see the currently defined network connections by entering the following command at the MS-DOS command prompt:

```
NET USE
```

To connect to a remote resource, you simply need to provide the name of the local device to which you want the resource mapped, and then provide the path to the network resource. For instance, if you wanted to map the printer at //Accounting/laser to your system, you would use the following command:

```
NET USE lpt2: //Accounting/laser Dollars /SAVEPW:NO
```

This example assumes that the password for the printer (if necessary) is *Dollars,* and that you do not care if the password is saved in the password file. You can also append a /yes or /no switch which is used to indicate how you want to answer any dialog boxes that may pop up. After this command is successfully completed, anything you print to LPT2 is automatically sent to the accounting department's laser printer.

Likewise, you can map a local drive letter to a network drive by using the same sort of command line (here the password is *Fiscal*):

```
NET USE G: //Accounting/Budget/New Fiscal /SAVEPW:NO
```

> **Tip:** If you use an asterisk (*) instead of a drive letter when mapping a network drive, the next available drive letter is automatically used.

To later disconnect the mapped resource, you would simply provide the local name you used for the mapping, and then use the /DELETE switch. For instance, if you wanted to delete the association between LPT2 and the accounting laser printer, you would use the following command line:

```
NET USE lpt2: /DELETE
```

NET VER

NET VER is a very simple command that displays the version number of your network redirector. If you are ever wondering what network redirector version is running on your workstation, type **NET VER** at the DOS command line; figure 40.3 shows an example of the output produced by the command.

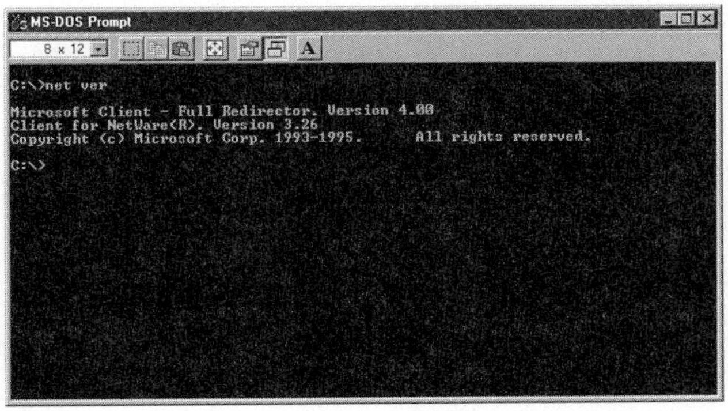

Fig. 40.3 The NET VER command indicates the version of your network redirector.

The NET VER command is typically used for diagnostic purposes. For instance, your network administrator may need to know your redirector version number to make sure that you are using the proper drivers.

NET VIEW

The NET VIEW command is used to determine which computers are available in a workgroup, or which resources are being shared by a specific computer on the network. To see a list of the computers in your workgroup, use the following at the DOS command prompt:

```
NET VIEW
```

To see a list of computers in a specific workgroup on a Microsoft network, just append the name of the workgroup as follows:

```
NET VIEW /WORKGROUP:name /yes
```

You must, of course, substitute the name of the workgroup for the *name* parameter. You can also use the NET VIEW command to see a list of the resources used by a specific workstation. You do this by including the UNC path to the workstation on the command line. For instance, if you wanted to see the resources on the production department's system (in the Acme domain), you would enter the following command:

```
NET VIEW \\Acme\production /yes
```

NETSTAT

The NETSTAT command displays information and statistics about your current TCP/IP network connections. In many ways it is similar to the NBTSTAT command, described in the next section. Information displayed by NETSTAT includes the IP address and port number of a network connection, the IP address of your local system, the protocol used by a connection, and the status of a connection.

The format and exact content of the information displayed by NETSTAT can be modified by using command-line switches. Table 40.2 lists the different switches and their purposes.

Table 40.2 Command-line Switches for the NETSTAT Command

Switch	Meaning
-a	Shows all network connections.
-e	Shows only Ethernet statistics.
-n	Displays information in numerical form, as opposed to displaying name equivalencies.
-s	Displays statistics by protocol.
-p *protocol*	Indicates the protocols for which statistics should be displayed. Valid values for *protocol* without using the -s switch are tcp and udp. If you use the -s switch, valid values for *protocol* are tcp, udp, icmp, or ip.
-r	Shows the contents of the network routing table.
interval	Indicates the interval, in seconds, at which the requested statistics should be updated and redisplayed. Using this parameter places NETSTAT in a continuous updating mode; you can break the cycle by pressing Ctrl+C.

NBTSTAT

The NBTSTAT command displays network information, in table form, using NetBIOS protocols instead of TCP/IP protocols. This command is diagnostic in nature, and can be used to resolve network difficulties. Because it is a diagnostic tool, it is much more likely to be used by network administrators than by regular users.

You can enter the NBTSTAT command at the DOS command line. The switches for the command are listed in Table 40.3.

Table 40.3 Command-line Switches for the NBTSTAT Command

Switch	Meaning
-a *host*	Uses the name table from the specified host computer.
-A *address*	Uses the name table at the specified IP address.
-c	Lists the contents of the NetBIOS name cache.
-n	Lists local NetBIOS names.
-R	Purges the NetBIOS name cache and then reloads the LMHOSTS file.
-r	Lists name resolution information for Windows networking.
-S	Displays both workstation and server sessions, using IP addresses for remote hosts.
-s	Displays both workstation and server sessions, using host names for remote hosts wherever possible.
interval	Indicates the interval, in seconds, at which the requested statistics should be updated and redisplayed. Using this parameter places NBTSTAT in a continuous updating mode; you can stop the command by pressing Ctrl+C.

The NBTSTAT command relies on NetBIOS protocols to derive its statistics. This implies that you can only use the command with a network that uses NetBIOS (such as Novell).

TCP/IP Commands

When you configure Windows 95 for your network, you can install the TCP/IP client protocols. (Adding network protocols is discussed in Chapter 36, "Communicating with a Network.") If you do add TCP/IP, a group of network-related commands becomes available to you:

- ARP
- FTP

- PING
- ROUTE
- TELNET
- TRACERT

If you have worked on a UNIX system connected to the Internet before, some of these commands may look familiar. They should; they have been freely borrowed from the UNIX world. For instance, the FTP command starts the FTP utility program. Each of these commands is described in the following sections.

ARP

ARP is an acronym for *address resolution protocol.* This command enables you to modify the IP-to-Ethernet or Token Ring address translation tables used by the network services of Windows 95. You use the ARP command from the command line in an MS-DOS window. The switches you can use with ARP are detailed in Table 40.4.

Table 40.4 Command-line Switches for the ARP Program

Switch	Meaning
-a *address* -N *netaddr*	Displays information from the ARP table. If *address* is provided, then only information on that IP address is returned. If the -N option is used, then the ARP table from the server at the IP address *netaddr* is used.
-d *address netaddr*	Deletes the ARP table entry specified by the IP *address* provided. If *netaddr* is included, then the action is taken on the ARP table at that address.
-s *address physical netaddr*	Adds an ARP table entry. The IP *address* is associated with the physical Ethernet address specified by *physical.* If *netaddr* is included, then the entry is added to the ARP table at that IP address.

FTP

FTP is an acronym for *file transfer protocol,* and it is a command-line program for transferring files across TCP/IP networks. This utility started in the UNIX environment, but has migrated to other environments connected to the Internet. It is now available in Windows 95.

To start FTP, simply enter the command at a command prompt in an MS-DOS window. The FTP command can use any of the command-line switches listed in Table 40.5.

Table 40.5 Command-line Switches for the FTP Program

Switch	Meaning
host	Indicates the host name or IP address of the system to which you want to connect.
-d	Turns on debugging displays, which results in all FTP commands between your computer and the remote system being displayed, even if they would otherwise have been suppressed.
-g	Turns off ability to use wildcard characters in file name specifications.
-I	Turns off interactive prompts when transferring multiple files.
-n	Turns off auto-login when initially connected to a remote system.
-s: *filename*	Indicates the name of a text file from which FTP commands should be executed, rather than allowing command input from the keyboard.
-v	Turns off the display of the remote system's responses.

After you have used FTP to connect to a remote system, you are presented with the FTP command prompt. At this point there are many different commands that you can use with FTP. These commands, along with their meanings, are listed in Table 40.6.

Table 40.6 FTP Commands and Their Meanings

Command	Meaning
! *command*	Runs *command* on the local computer.
?	Displays a list of, or descriptions for, FTP commands. Identical to the help command.
append	Appends a local file to a file on the remote computer, using the current file type setting.
ascii	Sets the file transfer type to ASCII (the default).
bell	Toggles the bell setting. If the bell is on, a bell rings after each file transfer is completed; if off (the default), no bell is used.
binary	Sets the file transfer type to binary.
bye	Breaks the connection with the remote system and exits the FTP program. Identical to the quit command.
cd *folder*	On the remote computer, changes the working folder to *folder.*
close	Breaks the connection with the remote system and remains in the FTP program. Identical to the disconnect command.
debug	Toggles the debug setting. If on, messages between you and the remote system are displayed; if off (the default), messages are suppressed.
delete *filename*	Deletes the specified files on the remote system.
dir	Displays a folder on the remote system.
disconnect	Breaks the connection with the remote system and remains in the FTP program. Identical to the close command.
get *filename*	Copies *filename* from the remote system to your computer by using the current file transfer type. Identical to the recv command.
glob	Toggles the "globbing" setting. If on (the default), wildcard characters can be used in file names; if off, wildcard characters cannot be used.

continues

Table 40.6 Continued

Command	Meaning
hash	Toggles hash setting. If on, a pound sign (#) is printed for each 2K bytes of data transferred with get or put; if off (the default), hash marks are not displayed.
help	Displays a list of, or descriptions for, FTP commands. Identical to the ? command.
lcd *folder*	On your system, changes the working folder to *folder.*
ls	Displays an abbreviated folder on the remote system.
mdelete *filelist*	Deletes multiple files on the remote system.
mdir *filelist*	Same as dir command, but allows multiple files or folders to be specified.
mget *filelist*	Copies the files in *filelist* from the remote system to the working folder on your computer by using the current file transfer type.
mkdir *folder*	Creates a folder on the remote system.
mls *filelist*	Same as ls command, but allows multiple files or folders to be specified.
mput *filelist*	Copies the files in *filelist* from your computer to the remote system by using the current file transfer type.
open *host*	Establishes a connection with the remote system whose host name or IP address is specified by *host.*
prompt	Toggles prompting setting. If on (the default), you are prompted during multiple file transfers about your desire to transfer each file; if off, no prompting occurs.
put *filename*	Copies *filename* from your computer to the remote system by using the current file transfer type. Identical to the send command.
pwd	Displays the name of the current folder on the remote system.
quit	Breaks the connection with the remote system and exits the FTP program. Identical to the bye command.

Command	Meaning
recv *filename*	Copies *filename* from the remote system to your computer by using the current file transfer type. Identical to the get command.
rename *file1 file2*	On the remote system, renames *file1* to *file2*.
rmdir *folder*	Deletes the specified *folder* on the remote system.
send *filename*	Copies *filename* from your computer to the remote system by using the current file transfer type. Identical to the put command.
status	Displays the current status of the connection with the remote system, as well as the settings of any toggles.
trace	Toggles the packet tracing setting. If on, the route of each data packet is displayed (between your system and the remote system); if off (the default), then routing is not displayed.
type *xfertype*	Sets or displays the file transfer type. Type binary is identical to the binary command; type ascii is identical to the ascii command. Without the *xfertype* parameter, the current transfer type setting is displayed.
verbose	Toggles verbose setting. If on (the default), all commands from your system or from the remote system are displayed; if off, no commands are displayed.

While the list of commands that you can use in FTP looks rather long, you will probably only use a couple of them. For instance, the most common commands are get (which transfers a file to your system) and bye (which disconnects you from the remote system).

Notice, as well, that many of the commands are simply synonyms for other commands. For instance, the get and recv commands do the same thing, as do the bye and quit commands. If the synonyms were removed, there would be approximately a third fewer FTP commands.

PING

The PING command verifies an active connection with a remote computer by sending ECHO packets across the network. The remote computer, when receiving the packets, sends them back to your computer. This allows a response time to be calculated and displayed.

The PING command is used at the command prompt in an MS-DOS window. You can use the command-line switches shown in Table 40.7.

Table 40.7 Command-line Switches for the PING Command

Switch	Meaning
list	The list of host names or IP addresses to ping.
-a	Disables host name IP address resolution. Results in IP addresses being displayed rather than host names.
-f	Causes packets sent to the remote system to be unfragmented by intermediate gateways.
-i *ttl*	Indicates the value to use for the Time To Live field in the PING packets. Effectively limits the number of reroutings that the packets can make.
-j *list*	Indicates the route to be used as the PING packets are transmitted. The *list* consists of up to nine host names or IP addresses separated by spaces. The host list indicates that those hosts must be included in the routing, although additional intermediate hosts can also be used where necessary.
-k *list*	Same as the -j switch, except that no intermediate hosts can be used.
-l *length*	Indicates the amount of data (in bytes) to be included in each ECHO packet. The default length is 64, but you can specify any value between 1 and 8192.
-n *count*	Indicates how many ECHO packets to send in each PING. If omitted, the default count of 4 packets is used.
-v *tos*	Indicates the value to use for the Type of Service field in the PING packets.

Switch	Meaning
-r *count*	Indicates how many hosts should be recorded during the round-trip taken by the ECHO packets. You may specify a *count* between 1 and 9.
-t	Continuously pings the specified host until interrupted, by pressing Ctrl+C.
-w *timeout*	Indicates the timeout interval, in milliseconds.

When you are using PING, you can combine command-line switches as long as the switch does not require a value. For instance, either of the following would be a legal use of the PING command:

```
ping -a -f
ping -af
```

PING is generally viewed as a diagnostic command, used to make sure that a remote system really can be reached from your system. If you try PING with a DNS host name (such as foo.bar.net) and the PING does not work, try it using the IP address for the host (such as 147.192.40.2). If the IP address works, and you did not misspell the host name, then you have a problem with the DNS server you are using.

ROUTE

The ROUTE command is actually four commands in one. When used as the initial part of the command, it enables you to manage the routing table used by the networking services of Windows 95. The different forms of the command are:

- **ROUTE ADD.** Adds an entry to the routing table.
- **ROUTE CHANGE.** Changes an entry in the routing table.
- **ROUTE PRINT.** Prints the routing table.
- **ROUTE DELETE.** Deletes an entry from the routing table.

To add a gateway entry to the routing table, you would follow the command by the host name, the mask name, and the gateway to use, as in the following:

```
ROUTE ADD host MASK mask gateway
```

In this example, *host, mask,* and *gateway* should be replaced with their respective IP addresses. The syntax is the same if you are changing, printing, or deleting—the only change in the command is the second word.

You can also use the ROUTE command, with only the -f switch, to clear the entire routing table. You would enter this command as follows:

```
ROUTE -f
```

If you use the -f switch in a command line with any other ROUTE command, the clearing takes place before the other portion of the command line (add, change, print, or delete) is completed.

> **Caution:** Make sure that you have a printout of the routing table before you delete it using the -f switch. After it is deleted, you cannot undo your action without manually rebuilding the table.

TELNET

You can use the TELNET program to connect your computer to remote computer so that your computer can act as if it were a terminal for the remote system. This command originated in the UNIX environment, where all TELNET operations took place on the command line. The Windows 95 implementation of the program is quite different, however. If you enter the TELNET command at the DOS command line, a new window appears, containing a Windows-based version of the TELNET program (see figure 40.4).

With the menu choices in the TELNET window, you can connect to a TELNET server elsewhere on a network (such as the Internet) and behave as a terminal to that system. The Connect menu is used to control the connection with the remote system. This menu includes the following choices:

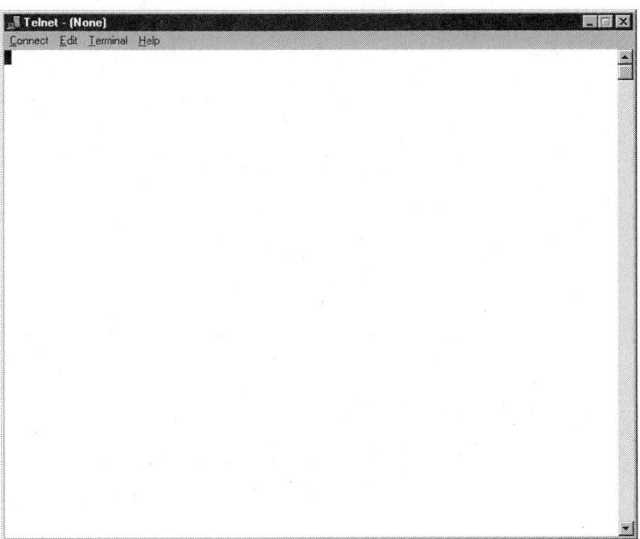

Fig. 40.4 The TELNET window is the result of running the TELNET command.

- **Remote System.** Used to specify the remote system with which you want a connection established. You can indicate the host name (or IP address), the port, and the terminal type to use.
- **Disconnect.** Used to break an established connection with a remote system.
- **Exit.** Used to exit the TELNET program.

The Edit menu serves much the same purpose as similar menus in other Windows programs. The choices on this menu are as follows:

- **Copy.** Used to copy the selected text into the Clipboard.
- **Paste.** Used to copy the contents of the Clipboard to the location of the cursor.
- **Select All.** Used to select all the text on the screen. (Provides a fast way to select everything before you use the Copy command.)

The Terminal menu is used to change the attributes of the TELNET window or the TELNET session. This menu also contains three choices:

- **Preferences.** Enables you to change the attributes of the TELNET window. Attributes include items such as terminal emulation, terminal options, background color, font, and buffer size.
- **Start Logging.** Saves the current TELNET session into a text file.
- **Stop Logging.** Stops saving information in a log file.

The final menu, Help, is used to get assistance in how to run TELNET.

TRACERT

TRACERT is a diagnostic utility that enables you to determine the network route between your system and a remote system. It does this by using much the same process as the PING command—sending out an ECHO packet to the remote host. The difference is that the ttl (Time To Live) field is manipulated by the TRACERT program to determine the route of the packet.

The first packet sent out has the ttl field set to 1, meaning that it will only go to the first gateway and then be returned. TRACERT then increases the ttl field by 1 (to 2) and sends out the packet again. This incremental approach is continued until the destination host is reached. At that point, the ttl field indicates how many steps the packet had to travel to reach the destination.

The TRACERT command is used from the MS-DOS command line. The switches you can use with the command are shown in Table 40.8.

Table 40.8 Command-line Switches for the TRACERT Command

Switch	Meaning
host	The host name or IP address of the ultimate target of the command.
-d	Disables host name IP address resolution. Results in IP addresses being displayed rather than host names.
-h *steps*	Indicates the maximum number of steps that the command should use before giving up.

Switch	Meaning
-j *list*	Indicates the route to be used as the ECHO packets are transmitted. The *list* consists of up to nine host names or IP addresses separated by spaces. The host list indicates that those hosts must be included in the routing, although additional intermediate hosts can also be used where necessary.
-w *timeout*	Indicates the timeout interval in milliseconds.

The route returned by the TRACERT command should not be considered an absolute. Routes may change over time, and the results of the TRACERT command depend on how well intermediate hosts follow accepted procedure. If a host does not return an indication of where a packet expired, then TRACERT has no way of reporting that host as an intermediate step on the route.

The Start Command

Perhaps the biggest addition to Windows 95 is the START command. This command, when entered at the command line, gives you a new way to execute a program.

Normally, all you need to do to run a program is simply enter the program name at the DOS command line. For instance, to run your favorite game, you might enter a command such as PLAY at the command line. This would search for a file such as PLAY.COM, PLAY.EXE, or PLAY.BAT, and then execute that file. You can still run programs this way at the Windows 95 command line. If you enter the program name, the program is run in the current window, and when you exit the program, you are returned to the command line. There is now another way, however.

If you preface the program name with the START command, the program will be run in a new DOS window. For instance, if you wanted to run your favorite game, you might enter the START PLAY command. Windows 95 then opens a DOS window for the program, and executes

PLAY within that window. When you exit the game program, the window opened for that program is automatically closed. All the while your original DOS window (the one in which you executed the START command) is still available for other purposes.

Using the Command Line

There are two main ways you can access the DOS command line in Windows 95. One involves working within Windows itself, and the other involves bypassing a normal Windows startup.

Using a DOS Window

To open a DOS window, follow these two steps:

1. Choose Programs from the Start menu.
2. Choose MS-DOS Prompt from the Programs menu.

Shortly you will see a DOS window appear, similar to what is shown in figure 40.5.

If you are familiar with using a DOS window under previous versions of Windows, you should feel right at home with using the Windows 95 DOS window. When you are at the command line you can go about business as usual and run the programs or other commands you want to use.

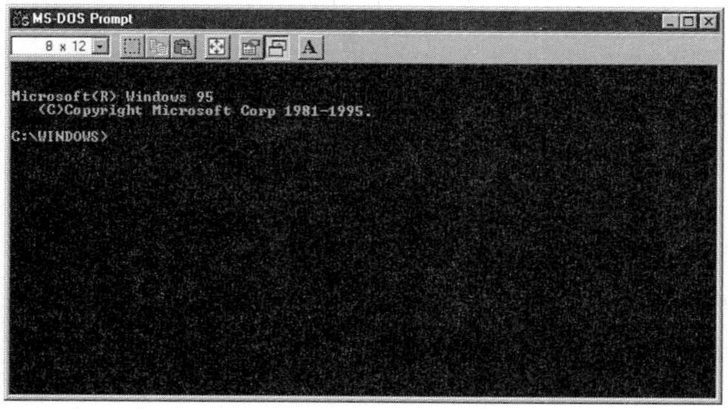

Fig. 40.5 The DOS window uses a command-line interface.

How DOS Windows Work Under Windows 95

You already know that Windows is a multitasking operating system. Depending on the amount of memory you have installed in your system, Windows 95 enables you to have many applications running at the same time—even multiple DOS applications.

When you open a DOS window under Windows 95, the operating system creates what is termed a *virtual machine,* or VM. A VM is maintained by Windows 95 in such a way that any application you run within a DOS window thinks it is actually running in DOS, without Windows or any other application being present. The side effect of using a VM arrangement is that your system is more stable—applications running in one DOS window cannot interfere with applications in another window, even if one of them crashes.

In Windows 95 you can have any number of DOS windows running concurrently, giving you the ability to multitask DOS applications. This is a huge improvement over previous versions of Windows. Again, this arrangement is enabled by the shift in the relationship between DOS and Windows. (Whereas Windows used to run under DOS, DOS now runs under Windows.)

Controlling the Appearance of the DOS Window

Notice that when you first open a DOS window, it does not occupy the entire screen. Depending on the size of your video monitor and the resolution of your video card, this may make the text in the window barely readable. You can increase the size of the window to occupy the entire screen by pressing Alt+Enter, or by clicking the maximize button in the upper-right window corner.

If you are working with a DOS window that does not occupy the entire screen, you will notice a toolbar at the top of the window. The addition of a toolbar to DOS windows is a departure from previous versions of Windows. The toolbar enables you to modify the appearance of what you see in the DOS window. You can modify the font and point size of text, copy and paste directly from the DOS window to a Windows 95 application, resize the window, and modify other performance settings of the DOS session.

Tip: If the DOS toolbar is not visible, you can activate it by right-clicking the title bar of the DOS window and choosing Toolbar.

The controls on the DOS toolbar, from left to right, are as follows:

- **Font list.** This control shows the various fonts you can use to display text in the DOS window. You should pick the font that is best for your display environment. Both bitmapped screen fonts and TrueType fonts are included in the Font list. (See Chapter 22, "Working with Fonts," for more information on fonts.)
- **Mark.** This button enables you to mark text in the DOS window on which you want to take a subsequent action. After the text is marked, you can delete it by pressing the Delete key, or you can copy it to the Clipboard by clicking the Copy button.
- **Copy.** You use this button after using the Mark button to mark a block of text. Whatever you copy is placed in the Clipboard, where it can be used in other Windows applications.
- **Paste.** After you have copied or cut text within the DOS window (or from another window), you can paste it at the current cursor position by clicking this button.
- **Full screen.** This is the same as clicking the maximize button. The DOS window expands to fill the entire screen. To later reduce the window size, press Alt+Enter.
- **Properties.** Clicking here enables you to change the attributes used in this DOS window. The various properties are discussed later in the section entitled "DOS Window Properties."
- **Exclusive.** Clicking this button suspends operation of other Windows programs, turning full attention of the CPU over to the DOS program running in this window.
- **Background.** This button turns off exclusive mode. It allows the program in the DOS window to run in conjunction with other

programs you are running. This is the normal operational mode for DOS windows.

- **Font properties.** Clicking here enables you to change other font properties, in addition to the font type (which can be changed from the Font list).

To close the DOS window, use the EXIT command at the command line. This closes the window and returns you to your Windows 95 desktop. If the command line is visible, you can also click the close icon in the upper-right corner of the DOS window.

Jumping to the Command Line

For some programs, operating within a DOS window simply will not do. You may have a DOS program that has exceptional memory requirements, or that needs tight control of other computer resources. In this case, you have two options. First, you can use a tried-and-true brute-force method of booting to a floppy disk and then running your software from there. A better solution, however, is to simply not load the Windows graphical interface. Windows 95 enables you to start the system and use only the command-line interface instead of the familiar graphical interface. To do this, follow these steps:

1. Shut down and restart your system.
2. After the initial system testing is complete, you will see a single-line message that says `Starting Windows 95`.
3. Press the F8 key. This displays the boot menu shown in figure 40.6.
4. Choose option 6, "Command prompt only."

This displays a screen that looks like a full-screen DOS window. The graphical Windows interface is not running, and you can work in this screen the same as you would have in regular DOS.

To run Windows from the command line, simply enter the WIN command. This starts Windows 95, the same as if you restarted your system.

```
Microsoft Windows 95 Startup Menu
==================================

   1. Normal
   2. Logged (\BOOTLOG.TXT)
   3. Safe mode
   4. Safe mode with network support
   5. Step-by-step confirmation
   6. Command prompt only
   7. Safe mode command prompt only
   8. Previous version of MS-DOS

Enter a choice: 1

F5=Safe mode  Shift+F5=Command prompt
Shift+F8=Stype-by-step confirmation [N]
```

Fig. 40.6 You can use the Startup menu for Windows 95 to access the command line.

DOS Window Properties

Earlier in this chapter you learned how you can access the properties of a DOS window—by clicking the Properties tool on the toolbar. Windows 95 enables you to modify quite a few properties of a DOS window. When you first display the MS-DOS Prompt Properties sheet, it looks similar to what is shown in figure 40.7.

There are five different tabs in the Properties sheet: Program, Font, Memory, Screen, and Misc. Each of these is covered in detail in the following sections.

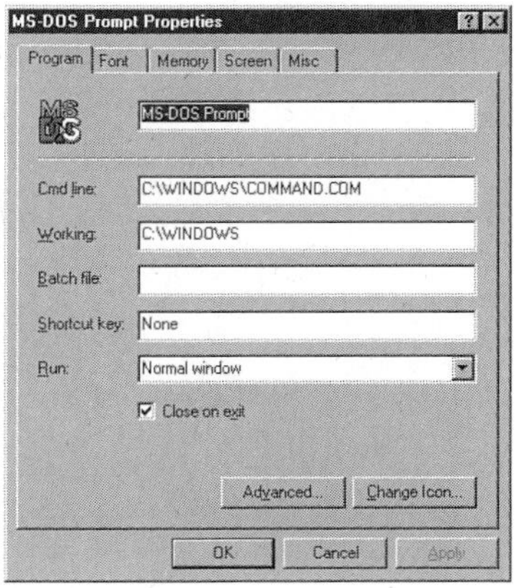

Fig. 40.7 The MS-DOS Prompt Properties sheet enables you to modify how your DOS sessions are managed by Windows 95.

The Program Tab

The Program tab is the default tab displayed when you first open the MS-DOS Prompt Properties sheet (see figure 40.7). This tab enables you to change different aspects of how Windows 95 behaves when it opens the DOS window. At the top of the dialog box is a field where you can change the title bar wording for the DOS window. This effectively is the name of the program, and probably should not be changed for a generic MS-DOS window. You would normally change the title for windows used to run DOS-based programs.

You use the Cmd Line field to specify the command line used to run the program contained within the DOS window. Notice that the command line for the generic DOS window is the command interpreter (COMMAND.COM). If you were running a different program, then the name of the program's executable file would be in this field.

The Working field enables you to specify the working folder associated with this program. The default folder is C:\WINDOWS, or whatever folder it was in which you installed Windows 95.

You use the Batch File field to specify the name of a batch file that should be run when the window is opened. For instance, you may need to run a batch file to run several programs in a row or to run some configuration programs before you run your DOS program.

You use the Shortcut key field to define a keyboard shortcut that you can use to switch to the window. The shortcut must consist of the Ctrl key (and optionally the Alt key) in addition to another key. For instance, you could define Ctrl+J or Ctrl+Alt+B to switch to the DOS window.

> **Caution:** You cannot use the Esc, Enter, Tab, Spacebar, Print Screen, or Backspace keys as shortcut keys for DOS windows. If the shortcut key is the same as something used in a Windows-based program, your shortcut key always takes precedence. In other words, the shortcut key in the Windows-based program will not work.

You use the Run field to indicate how the DOS window should be first run. If set to Normal window, then the window does not open in a full-screen mode, but instead opens on your desktop. If set to Minimized, then the window opens as a task on the taskbar (in a minimized condition). If set to Maximized, then the program starts in full-screen mode.

> **Tip:** To get out of full-screen mode, press Ctrl+Enter.

Finally, you use the Close on Exit check box to indicate how Windows 95 should treat the window when the program it is running is completed. Most of the time you will want to select Close on Exit, so that the window is eliminated when the program is over. If you clear the check box, then the window stays open even when the program is done; you are returned to the DOS command prompt.

If you click the Change Icon button, you can change the icon associated with the MS-DOS window. Normally this icon is automatically determined by Windows 95, based on the program you are running in the window.

If you click the Advanced button, you will see the Advanced Program Settings dialog box, as shown in figure 40.8.

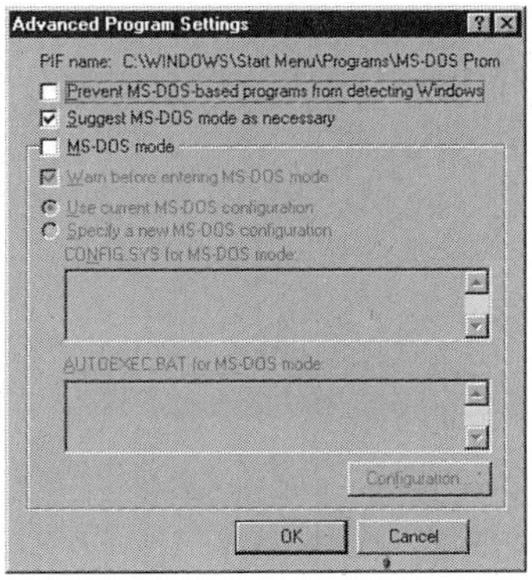

Fig. 40.8 The Advanced Program Settings dialog box enables you to configure the environment used by the DOS window.

You use the settings in this dialog box to determine the environment offered by the DOS window. In older versions of Windows, this type of information was contained within a PIF file (program information file). Windows 95 enables you to change the settings in a dialog box, instead.

Most of the time you will not need to change the settings in the Advanced Program Settings dialog box. Some programs, however, may benefit by tweaking some of the settings here.

Realistically, the first setting is the one you are most likely to change. It controls whether the DOS program can even detect the presence of Windows. Some older DOS programs refuse to run unless Windows is not running. If this is the case, selecting this check box can hide the presence of Windows completely.

The next two check boxes determine the operating mode of the MS-DOS program you are defining. Microsoft suggests that you leave the first option, Suggest MS-DOS mode as necessary, selected. MS-DOS mode simply means that the program running in the DOS window displaces any other program running in your system. Some DOS programs work so closely to the hardware or require so many resources that it is impossible for Windows to effectively run. If you select the first option, and Windows detects that the DOS program would work best in MS-DOS mode, then it takes care of the transition for you.

If you select the other MS-DOS mode option, then the program you are defining will automatically kick your machine into MS-DOS mode. In this mode, all other Windows-based programs are closed, all DOS windows are closed, and the system starts in MS-DOS mode. The benefit to your DOS programs is that they are the exclusive program running on the system. The downside is that no other programs can run concurrently, and when the program is done, the system needs to be restarted to again use Windows 95.

If you choose MS-DOS mode, then you can also specify how the DOS-mode environment is configured. The first check box, Warn Before Entering MS-DOS mode, controls whether you will have a chance to back out of the DOS-mode switch. If the check box is selected (the default), then you are prompted before a switch is made. If the check box is clear, then the switch to DOS mode is done without any warning. Because this could play havoc with some other programs running on your system, you will probably always want to be warned.

Finally, you can specify whether Windows 95 should use the default DOS environment, or whether you want to define a special environment. If you choose the latter, you can indicate the contents of the CONFIG.SYS and AUTOEXEC.BAT files right in this dialog box. (You should consult a good DOS reference manual for information on putting together these special configuration files.)

The Font Tab

When you click the Font tab, the MS-DOS Prompt Properties sheet looks like what you see in figure 40.9.

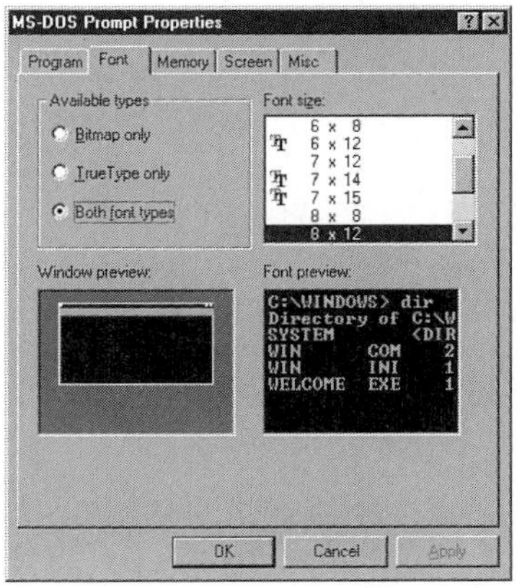

Fig. 40.9 The MS-DOS Prompt Properties sheet, with the Font tab selected, enables you to pick the display font for the DOS window.

This dialog box enables you to pick the font used to display information in the DOS window. At the upper-left corner you can specify the different types of fonts from which you can choose. (Fonts are covered in detail in Chapter 22, “Working with Fonts.”)

At the upper-right corner you can pick the size of the font you want displayed. The font you choose will also result in a size change for the window, and can greatly affect the readability of the screen. You may need to play with different font sizes to find the one that is right for you. (I personally like the 8×12 font; it is crisp, clear, and easy to read.) Font sizes are indicated in pixels, so the smaller the numbers, the smaller the size of the characters on the screen.

As you modify the fonts and pick different font sizes, the preview screens (at the bottom of the dialog box) indicate the approximate appearance of your DOS window.

The Memory Tab

Clicking the Memory tab of the MS-DOS Prompt Properties sheet results in a window that looks like figure 40.10.

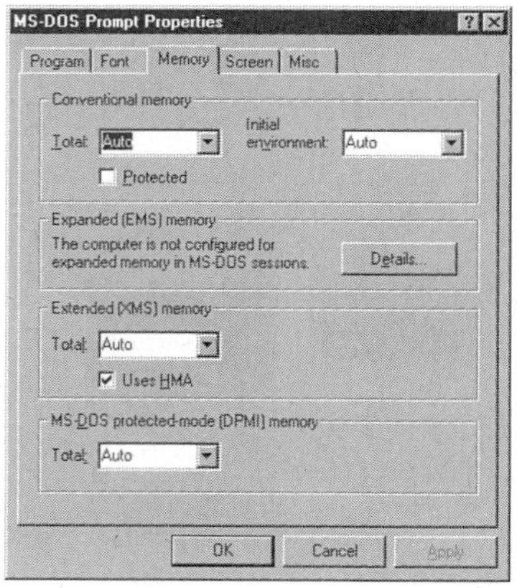

Fig. 40.10 The MS-DOS Prompt Properties sheet, with the Memory tab selected, enables you to configure the memory settings for the DOS session.

Even though Windows 95 does the vast majority of its work in protected mode, treating memory as a large contiguous block, older DOS programs have been written to a different standard. These programs may need special amounts of conventional, expanded, and extended memory. The settings in the Memory tab enable you to modify the memory portion of the DOS environment to suit the special needs of your programs.

Caution: In most instances you should never need to change the memory settings in this dialog box. Do not make changes without being sure that you need the changes for a specific program. In other words, do not make the changes unless you are sure that your program will not work with the default Windows settings.

To make the settings in this dialog box properly, you should refer to your advanced documentation for your DOS program. In addition, you may want to read Chapter 9, “Exploiting Memory, Space, and Resources,” for more information about memory settings.

The Screen Tab

With the Screen tab of the MS-DOS Prompt Properties sheet selected, you are ready to modify aspects of the DOS window’s appearance. With the tab selected, the dialog box should appear as shown in figure 40.11.

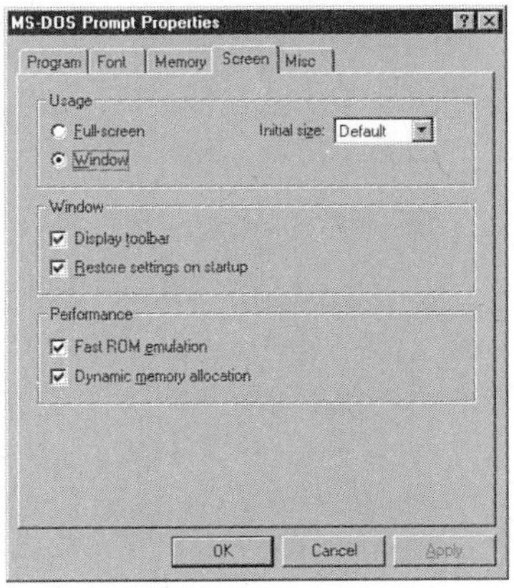

Fig. 40.11 The MS-DOS Prompt Properties sheet, with the Screen tab selected, is used to set aspects of the window appearance.

There are three sections to this tab. At the top of the dialog box you can indicate how you want the DOS window to appear when it is first opened. The Initial Size setting is the most important item here; it is used to indicate how many lines of text you want to appear in the DOS window. If you set it to Default, then the program running in the window controls the screen size. There are three possible settings in this pull-down list (besides Default): 25 lines, 40 lines, and 50 lines. The selection you make here affects the size of the DOS window, and if you make a change you will probably want to change the font selection as well.

At the left side of the Usage area is a place where you can select whether the DOS window should be functioning as a desktop Window or as a Full-screen application. Do not confuse this with the window size setting in the Program tab (discussed earlier); that setting refers to the initial condition of the DOS window, whereas this setting refers to the current condition.

In the middle of the dialog box you can specify the attributes of the DOS window. If Display Toolbar is selected, then the toolbar is shown at the top of the DOS window. If the Restore settings on startup check box is selected, then Windows 95 does not remember the DOS window appearance settings from one session to the next. For instance, the location of the DOS window will always revert to a standard position when this check box is selected. Clear the check box if you want Windows 95 to remember the settings.

Finally, at the bottom of the dialog box are two check boxes that control the performance of the DOS program when it is running within a window (less than full screen). The first setting, Fast ROM Emulation, causes Windows 95 to move the ROM instructions into faster RAM memory. This causes text and some graphics to be displayed faster. The other setting, Dynamic Memory Allocation, controls how Windows allocates screen display memory. If the check box is selected, then Windows is free to use the screen memory area as necessary (and as appropriate). If the check box is cleared, then the maximum amount of memory necessary for the screen display is always reserved for the program, and is therefore not available to other programs. Clearing this check box may speed up the DOS program running in the window, but it may also slow down any other programs you have running in Windows 95.

The Misc Tab

When you select the Misc tab, the MS-DOS Prompt Properties sheet appears, as shown in figure 40.12.

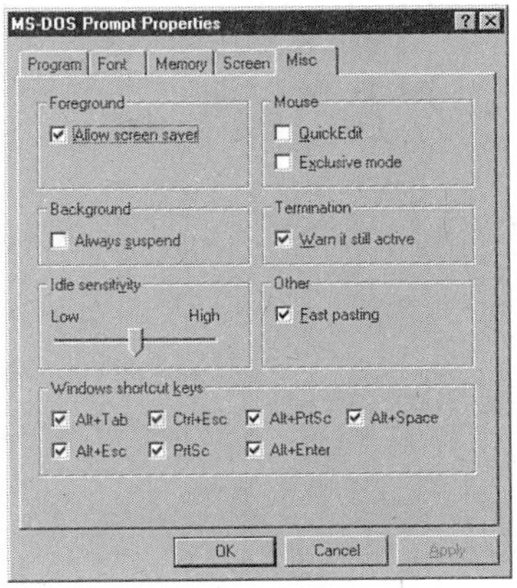

Fig. 40.12 The MS-DOS Prompt Properties sheet, with the Misc tab selected, is used to set various DOS window properties.

The Misc tab contains quite a few settings, evidently placed here because they are not readily categorized with the subjects of the other tabs. Each area is explained in the following sections.

Foreground. The Foreground area of the Misc tab contains only one setting, which controls how the Windows screen saver functions. If you clear this check box, then the Windows screen saver cannot start up when the DOS window is visible. Normally, you would only want to clear this if you are operating the window in full-screen mode.

If you select the check box, then the screen saver can work as required. You should note that this setting does not control whether the screen saver is enabled; that is controlled in the Display area of the Control Panel. You can find more information on the screen saver in Chapter 14, "Tailoring Windows 95 and the Registry."

Mouse. There are two check boxes in this area of the Misc tab. The first check box controls whether the mouse can be used for the QuickEdit feature. This feature is applicable only in DOS windows; it refers to the ability to use the mouse to mark text for subsequent editing. Without the check box selected, you must use the Mark tool on the toolbar in order to mark text.

Exclusive mode has to do with how the mouse behaves in relation to the DOS program. If selected, then the mouse will only work in this DOS window; it will not work in any other program under Windows 95. (Because Windows 95 is so difficult to use without the mouse, I can't think of a really good reason to enable this option.)

Background. Windows 95 usually shares system resources among all active programs as necessary. Each program, even though it is not currently active, continues to run in the background to complete whatever tasks are necessary. If you select the Always Suspend check box, then when the DOS window is in the background, the program within it will not run. You should select this option only if you want the program to run while you watch it.

Termination. When you try to close a DOS window with an active program still running, Windows warns you that you are ending the program abnormally. The check box in this area controls this warning feature. If the Warn If Still Active check box is cleared, then no warning is given and the program in the DOS window is terminated. You should only clear this check box if you are certain that the program running in the window will not be adversely affected by closing abnormally. For instance, some programs write configuration information to disk when you exit the program. It would not be a good idea for this type of program to be abnormally terminated.

Idle Sensitivity. This slider controls how much attention the DOS window receives from Windows 95. There is an inverse relationship between the amount of attention received and the slider setting. Thus, if the slider is moved toward the Low setting, then the program in the window receives more resources for a longer period of time. Conversely, if the slider is moved toward the High setting, then system resources are freed up more quickly and allocated to other programs.

You should only adjust this setting if you feel the program in the DOS window is not executing fast enough. When you do move the slider toward the Low setting, your other Windows programs may run more slowly than otherwise.

Other. The Fast Pasting check box controls how Windows pastes information into the DOS window. Most programs can accept information at the rate achieved with Fast Pasting enabled, but some programs cannot. You should clear this check box if you try pasting something into your DOS program and it does not paste properly.

Windows Shortcut Keys. Windows 95 uses a standard group of shortcut keys for system operations. The seven shortcut keys listed in this portion of the dialog box are those standard keys. If the check box beside the shortcut key is enabled, then the shortcut key will work as it should in Windows 95. You should only clear the check box associated with a shortcut key if that key combination is used by the DOS program for a different purpose. In that case, clearing the check box will disable the Windows use of the keys and allow the DOS program to use them.

> **Caution:** If you disable the Alt+Tab, Alt+Esc, and Alt+Enter shortcuts, and then switch the DOS window to full screen, there is no way to switch between the screen and the Windows programs running in the background. The only way around this problem is to exit the DOS program and thereby close the DOS window.

Monitoring Your Windows 95 Vital Files

by Ewan Grantham

When you're trying to determine what files to back up and maintain in your system, you want to start with files that affect the configuration and operation of your computer because, without them, your system will not run. These files are what constitute your system's vital files. For Windows 95, vital files include a group of files that control how the system is booted and operates. The files can be from previous versions of DOS and Windows that may still be important and INI files that affect your applications' configuration.

Knowing about these files can also help in determining what went wrong when a new application is installed and your system starts "acting funny." Being aware of these files and their role in your

system's overall operation can also help you avoid doing anything to them yourself (such as deleting them) that will affect your computer's performance. In this chapter, you see what these files are and learn some ways to back up and maintain them.

In this chapter, you learn about the following:

- Important boot files
- Registry files
- DOS and Windows 3.x files still vital to Windows 95

Windows 95 Vital Files

Files that are vital to the configuration and performance of Windows 95 can be divided into two general categories:

- Files that affect how your system boots up after being turned on or rebooted. These files are referred to as *Boot files.*
- Files that affect how the system runs after Windows 95 has been started. These files are associated with the Registry.

In the following sections, you learn about both types of files and how to work with them.

Boot Files

With Windows 3.x, your computer relied upon five DOS files to manage booting after the computer was turned on or rebooted. Two of these files, IO.SYS and MSDOS.SYS, are hidden system files that told your system BIOS how to boot the operating system (OS) and work with the boot disk (either floppy disk or hard drive). Another file, COMMAND.COM, was used to support basic OS commands. The last two files, AUTOEXEC.BAT and CONFIG.SYS, loaded any special device drivers, configured the OS environment with commands such as FILES and COMSPEC, and specified any other programs or information the system needed to boot.

So, for example, your CONFIG.SYS might include lines such as:

```
device=c:\dos\ansi.sys
```

to make sure your screen display was compatible with programs that used ANSI escape sequences, while your AUTOEXEC.BAT almost certainly had the line:

```
PATH=c:\dos;c:\windows
```

to set the path that programs would use when searching for files.

In Windows 95, your computer needs only two files to boot, though you may need to add a version of your old AUTOEXEC.BAT and your CONFIG.SYS to get full functionality. The first file, IO.SYS, replaces the functionality of the old IO.SYS, most of the old MSDOS.SYS, and the old COMMAND.COM, but it is still a hidden system file. The second file, MSDOS.SYS, now contains information about where things are on your computer and some information about various boot options (see figure 41.1). This file is located in your root folder—C:\ (in most cases). In this way, the MSDOS.SYS file takes some of the functionality of the old CONFIG.SYS and AUTOEXEC.BAT files.

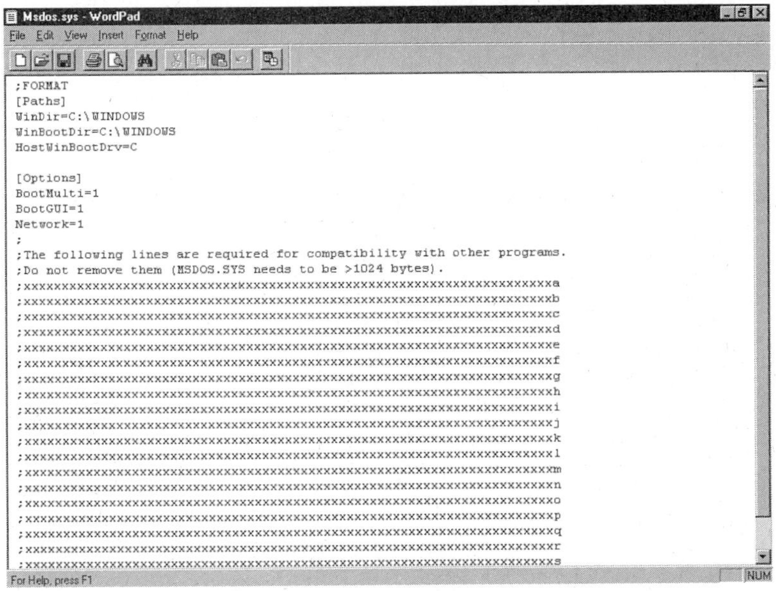

Fig. 41.1 What the MSDOS.SYS file contains.

Common MSDOS.SYS Elements

Although your MSDOS.SYS file may look different from the one shown in figure 41.1, this file usually contains several common entries on any system running Windows 95. The following is a list of these entries and what they do:

- **WinDir** This entry specifies the folder or subdirectory where Windows is located on the system.
- **WinBootDir** This entry controls where files that are needed for specifying how to bring up Windows 95 are located (almost always the same as WinDir).
- **HostWinBootDrv** This tells Windows which drive contains the essential boot files.
- **BootGUI** This is used to specify whether to boot into the Windows 95 interface (by using a 1 here), or into the command prompt interface (by using a 0).
- **Network** This entry is used to specify whether or not the computer is attached to a network. Even if all you use is Dial-Up Networking, your computer is considered part of a network. If you aren't part of ANY network, then this value should be a 0.
- **BootMulti** Used to specify whether or not to support booting into multiple operating systems (including old versions of Windows). Generally this won't be in the file unless you've specified to keep the old version of DOS/Windows when you installed Windows 95.
- **BootMenu** Specifies that a menu should be presented to users to allow them to select which OS they want to boot into, or which option for booting Windows 95 they want (similar to BootGUI). If this is a 1 they get a menu, if it's a 0 then they don't.

- **BootMenuDefault** Says which menu option is the default selection. Use 7 for your old version of DOS, and 1 for Windows 95.
- **BootMenuDelay** This specifies how many seconds the menu should be shown before the default value in BootMenuDefault is automatically selected.

Finally, it's important that when you modify the MSDOS.SYS file that you DON'T remove any of the x's from the lines in the bottom of the file. These HAVE to be there to ensure that MSDOS.SYS is at least 1,024 bytes long to remain compatible with previous versions of DOS.

Needing Your CONFIG.SYS and AUTOEXEC.BAT Files

Certain things may still require you to have a CONFIG.SYS and an AUTOEXEC.BAT file. The most common reason you still need CONFIG.SYS is to load a device driver for a piece of hardware that doesn't provide a version of its driver for Windows 95. You may still want an AUTOEXEC.BAT to set the PATH or have functions such as DOSKEY loaded and ready for your virtual DOS sessions.

Although you can back up these files, you usually need to have them available to help reload your system to start your backup program. In other words, having a backup made with either the backup applet or a third-party program will be no help for these files because you can't boot Windows 95 without them being present. The first two files (IO.SYS and MSDOS.SYS) are saved to the Emergency floppy created when you installed Windows 95. However, if you've made manual changes to your MSDOS.SYS since then, you lose those changes.

For this reason, it's often a good idea to go to a DOS session (either by booting to the command line, or by opening a DOS command line in Windows 95), and copy the MSDOS.SYS, CONFIG.SYS, and

AUTOEXEC.BAT files to a floppy disk. When you format the floppy it probably is a good idea to make it bootable by using the /s switch. So if your disk is in the A drive, you enter

```
FORMAT A: /S
```

It's also a good idea to copy other files to this floppy that you might need in an emergency, such as EDIT, FDISK, and XCOPY. Having all this on a floppy gives you added flexibility in case your hard drive breaks down or a virus infects your computer. A good way of doing this is to take the emergency disk that Windows 95 Setup creates for you, add your AUTOEXEC.BAT and CONFIG.SYS files to it with different extensions so that they aren't automatically loaded, and make sure that FDISK and XCOPY are on it. With this group of files, you can work around almost any software problem.

Setup Information in INF Files

In addition to these specific files, the group of files located in the C:\WINDOWS\INF folder contains setup information on any cards you may have. When doing a backup, you want to make sure you get the information that is in here as well.

While you will find INF files scattered throughout your system (they are information files created in a specific format for use by Windows 95 in setting up programs and peripherals), only the ones in the \WINDOWS\INF file are "vital." Losing the rest would be a nuisance, but not a major one.

The Registry Files

With your boot files safely stored, it's time to take a look at the files that make up the Registry. Most of the information is stored in two files: SYSTEM.DAT and USER.DAT. In addition, every time these files are updated, the old versions are saved as SYSTEM.DAO and USER.DAO.

All four of these files are located in your main Windows directory. These files are hidden and read-only, so they won't normally show up under the Explorer. To make them show up, go into Explorer, select the View menu, then the Options choice. Next, select the View tab, and click on "Show all files."

You can use the Backup applet in Windows 95 to back up these files, but if they are damaged or corrupted, you may be unable to run Backup to restore them. The backup applet is located off the Start menu at Start>>Programs>>Accessories>>System Tools>>Backup. Because you may not be able to run a restore, there are a number of techniques you should be aware of for saving and restoring this vital information.

Using REGEDIT to Copy the Registry to a Text File

An option that can help you to better understand your system, as well as protect it, is to export the Registry to a text file. This gives you the opportunity to have a hard copy of the information by printing out the text file. You can also copy the text file to a floppy and then import it back into your system if it's needed.

To do this, you first need to start a program called REGEDIT located in your C:\WINDOWS folder (or wherever you have installed your Windows 95 files). REGEDIT (also known as the Registry Editor) is a program designed to make viewing and working with your Registry files easier—and safer. Figure 41.2 shows you what REGEDIT looks like when it has been started.

From here, you can export the Registry to a text file by following these steps:

1. From the REGEDIT menu bar, choose Registry, Export Registry File.
2. The Export Registry File dialog box appears (see figure 41.3).

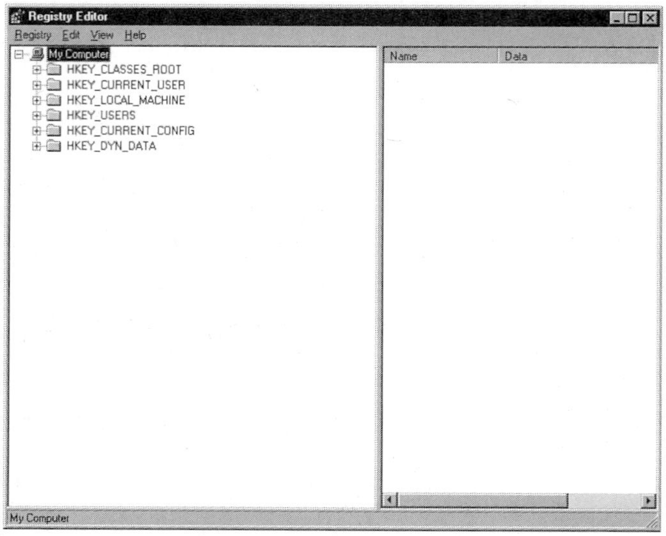

Fig. 41.2 The REGEDIT opening screen.

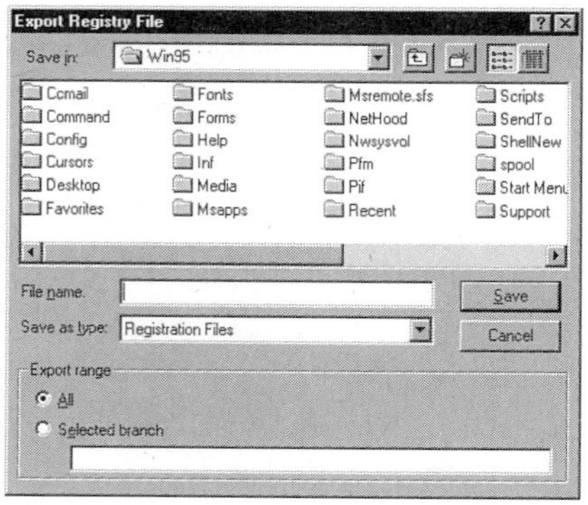

Fig. 41.3 The Export Registry File dialog box.

3. In the Export Range section choose All to back up the entire Registry or choose Selected Branch to back up only a particular branch of the Registry tree. If you're going to use Selected Branch, click on the folder at the level of the branch you want to start with.

Looking at figure 41.2 may lead you to think that there isn't much in the Registry. But if you look at figure 41.4 when you begin getting below the surface, you see that a lot of information is stored here. You'll also notice that values are not what come to mind if someone asks you for the settings of your system's audio.

To get to this point in the file, you start by double-clicking on HKEY_CURRENT_USER, then double-clicking on Software, then double-clicking on Microsoft, then double-clicking on Multimedia, and finally double-clicking on Audio. Not necessarily intuitive, but somewhat understandable. If you have a sound card on your system, try this and compare the values.

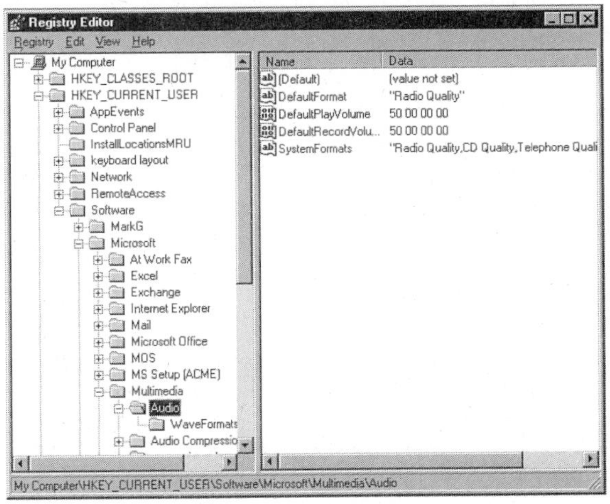

Fig. 41.4 Registry Editor values for Multimedia Audiox

You should note that the REG files created by doing this export can be edited by any text editor. The default place for placing the exported file is in your C:\WINDOWS folder, but you may want to have the file stored directly to a floppy disk instead. If you decide to store it to a floppy disk, make sure there is nothing else on the disk because these files can run as large as a megabyte each.

If you want just a printed record of the Registry, you can use the following:

1. If you want to print only part of the Registry, click on the icon for the folder of the area you want to print.
2. Choose Registry, Print. If you want to print the entire Registry, select All here.

You want to be very careful about selecting All here. The standard Registry can take up to 200 pages and something with a lot of customization can go far beyond that.

Restoring the Registry

Somewhere down the line you might want to or have to restore the Registry settings using the information you exported. To do that, choose Registry, Import Registry File. The Import dialog box appears. Choose the file you want to import.

You may make a change in a value some day and then discover that Windows is behaving unusually or that something has stopped working. If you've backed up the Registry files, you have some options for repairing this. But there is also a fallback option. The most recent version before your change was saved with the DAO extension.

To restore the previous version of the Registry, follow these steps:

1. Shut down Windows by choosing the "Restart the computer in MS-DOS mode" option.
2. Once your machine returns with a DOS prompt, change to your C:\WINDOWS folder. For example, if your Windows folder is C:\WINDOWS, you enter

```
CD C:\WINDOWS
```

3. Enter each of the following:

`ATTRIB -H -R -S SYSTEM.DAT`	Makes the System.DAT file visible (-H), editable (-R), and no longer having the system file attribute (-S). This is the same for the files below.
`ATTRIB -H -R -S SYSTEM.DA0`	
`COPY SYSTEM.DA0 SYSTEM.DAT`	Copies the old (good) System file over the new (bad) one.
`ATTRIB -H -R -S USER.DAT`	
`ATTRIB -H -R -S USER.DA0`	
`COPY USER.DA0 USER.DAT`	Copies the old (good) User file over the new (bad) one.

4. Reboot your computer.

Still Needed DOS and Windows 3.x Files

Although Windows 95 replaces much of what you used in DOS and Windows 3.x, some of your applications still rely on files that came with these earlier versions of Windows. This is particularly true of applications that don't currently have a Windows 95 version. For this reason, you probably want to use the Backup applet to back up these files or copy them to a floppy disk.

DOS files you want to keep an eye on are as follows:

- **Device drivers** The most common cards not supported directly by Windows 95 are scanner interface cards.
- **CONFIG.SYS** If this file is present, it's probably because you have a device driver that isn't supported or because a program you installed automatically wrote to this file.

- **AUTOEXEC.BAT** You may have put this file in yourself to set the PATH environmental variable or to load other DOS utilities (such as DOSKEY) for your DOS sessions.

Windows 3.x files you want to keep an eye on are as follows:

- **WIN.INI** This file contains setup information for older Windows programs that you may have on your system. Some Windows 3.x programs also store registration information. Generally, if the file exists, something is using it, and it should be backed up.
- **SYSTEM.INI** and **PROGMAN.INI** These files are maintained for compatibility with older Windows programs that expect to be able to access them. You can remove them if you use only Windows 95 applications, but it is generally better to keep them for backward compatibility reasons.

It's hard to put any value in these three files that affect the running of Windows 95 directly, although it's always possible to confuse and crash an application.

Application INI File Considerations

Even though Windows 95 applications should be using the Registry to store setup information, old habits die hard, and many applications still create their own INI file that is placed in either the application's folder or the C:\WINDOWS folder. You generally don't have to worry about the contents of these files, unless you move the application. In that case you want to edit the file by using Notepad or WordPad to reflect the new location of files.

You do want to make sure that these files are safeguarded, however, because losing the file can often mean that you have to reinstall the application.

KILLER WINDOWS 95

42

Dealing with Viruses and Security

by Glenn Fincher

The title of this book, *Killer Windows 95* takes on a more sinister meaning in terms of security. That there are "killers" out there waiting to invade your computer and ravage your data is certainly true when it comes to computer viruses. That there are likewise more personal "killers" wishing to gain unauthorized access to your data is also true. Many of the key features of Windows 95 are designed with security in mind even as they actually seem to offer new avenues for this security to be overcome.

The built-in peer-to-peer networking, Internet connectivity, Dial-Up Networking—both outbound and inbound—increases the potential for unauthorized access to your computer data. And though Windows 95 has built-in tools and features to assist you in protecting the integrity of your data, these tools will not help you defend your computer unless you know about them and know how to use these tools or features.

In this chapter, you'll learn about the following:

- Dealing with viruses and security
- Understanding the computer virus and Trojan horse
- Using effective antivirus strategies
- "Designed for Windows 95"—an antivirus example
- Backing up your system
- Using backup Agents

Windows 95 Virus Software

At the time of this writing, many antivirus software developers had announced that Windows 95-specific versions of their products were currently scheduled and would ship coincident with the release date or within 60 days of that date. Windows 95-specific versions of McAfee's ViruScan, Symantec's Norton Anti-Virus, and Datafellows F-Prot Professional will be available shortly after Windows 95 ships or possibly by the time this book is available. One example of what to expect of these "Designed for Windows 95" releases is shown in the following sections as you look at a pre-release version of VirusScan 95 by McAfee Associates.

> **Caution:** Previous versions of MS-DOS shipped with an antivirus utility named Microsoft Anti-Virus or MSAV. Microsoft does not ship a Windows 95 version of this utility. Additionally, the previous versions should not be used with Windows 95 because attempting to remove a virus may result in either Windows 95 disallowing the process, not working, or actually causing damage to the VFAT file system.

Why do you need a Windows 95-specific version? In short, the main reason is that Windows 95 is a 32-bit operating system, and the existing antivirus products are either 16-bit DOS or 16-bit Windows programs.

Written for DOS, these programs expect to have unlimited access directly to the hard drive using INT 13h or INT 21h. These programs depend on the ability to directly access the boot sector of the hard drive to disinfect certain types of viruses. Also, these programs may have a TSR component that expects to have access to all processes so that the processes can be examined for virus activity. Though not as robust as similar protection in Windows NT, Windows 95 virtualizes access to the hard drive, thus disallowing INT 13H and INT 21H, and will not allow programs direct access to processes as required to directly manipulate data on disk as antivirus programs are designed to do.

At best, the program may be able to identify a virus infection but will be incapable of removing the virus. In worse cases, the software may actually lock up your computer or cause file system damage if it tries to deal with the new long file name (LFN) feature of Windows 95. You may think that booting to DOS from a DOS floppy disk will do the trick, but even this may result in damage to a file or folder using an LFN. If you have installed Windows 95 into its own folder rather than in a preexisting Windows 3.x folder, you will be able to boot to the DOS, and run your older 16-bit application. Be aware though that if the application attempts repairs that result in the file allocation table being changed that you may damage any long file or folder names. The best and really the last time you should use an older DOS or Windows 3.x antivirus program is before you install Window 95 for the first time. This should be one of the preparatory steps taken before installation, but remember that these programs cannot be depended on in Windows 95.

Dealing with Viruses and Security

Like its biological namesake, the computer virus is a plague of the computer age. Every user of a computer in today's environment has to pay at least cursory attention to the possibility of getting a virus infection. Because of the wide proliferation of viruses, it is likely that either you or someone you know will be hit with a virus attack. Though the avenues of attack are well known, it is the very nature of the computing

world of the '90s that assist their proliferation. Computer users work in an increasingly network-connected environment. Whether it's the connectivity offered by a LAN, the Internet, online networks, or Bulletin Board Systems (BBS), there are more opportunities for viral infection than in the not so distant past. According to some experts in the field, there are around 5,000 known viruses including the miscellaneous virus strains or families. There are also more viruses being written and subsequently discovered in a seemingly endless cycle. Some have suggested that the virus writer and the antivirus software developer are in sort of a deadly symbiotic relationship with each depending on the other for existence. In this scenario, the user is the one in the middle, the unwilling victim of this quasi-biological menace.

A virus's ability to destroy your data is just one of the security problems you face with a virus infection. Even if the particular virus you encounter is one of the relatively docile ones, an infection will at the very minimum cause your system to slow down or use up an increasing amount of disk space. Though many of the reported 5,000 viruses are relatively docile. They may do no malicious damage like formatting your hard drive or rewriting your boot files, but the time you'll spend with a regular scan of your hard drive is time well spent to eliminate the possibility of an infection.

Understanding the Computer Virus

According to Dr. Fred B. Cohen's book, *A Short Course on Computer Viruses*, a computer virus is "a computer program that can infect other computer programs by modifying them in such a way as to include a (possibly evolved) copy of itself."

By this definition, a program doesn't actually have to do any damage at all to be considered a virus. If a program can replicate itself and infect other programs, you have a virus. And, even if it is a docile virus, if that docile virus interrupts a computer from its normal operation and that computer happens to be in use in a critical role, that docile virus suddenly becomes one of the killers. Any unsolicited invasion of your computer data by such a program is exactly that—an invasion—and it should be treated with no less concern than if it was an intruder in your home. It is the action you need to take to eliminate these killers that you learn about in this chapter.

Computer viruses take several recognizable forms. They may be the type of program commonly called a *worm*—a program with the ability to propagate itself across networks beyond the confines of the computer that it first attacks. The Trojan horse is so named because of its apparently useful facade, hiding the potentially malicious code within. Generally, viruses are categorized by their method of transmission. The most destructive are usually the *boot-sector viruses,* while others are called *file* or *program viruses.* The former attacks the boot sector of a hard or floppy drive, while the latter attacks individual files. There is also a *multipartite virus* that may be both a boot-sector and file virus. For the sake of precision, some may further define these into *parasitic, stealth,* or *polymorphic* viruses because of the peculiar propensity of some viruses to either directly attack specific types of files or the ability to mask their true nature to avoid detection.

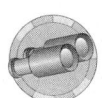

Note: Having more than one antivirus product in your antivirus suite is generally advised. One product may be particularly good at detecting certain strains of boot-sector viruses but not as good with other types of viruses. Another product may be particularly good at detecting previously unidentified viruses.

As mentioned earlier, the boot-sector virus is probably the most destructive because it replaces the existing Master Boot Record (MBR) or boot-sector of a hard disk or floppy disk with its own code and usually arbitrarily moves the original boot-sector to a fixed location. This relocation sometimes results in destroyed data because the original boot-sector is dropped over the file allocation table (FAT) or another file.

A drive's MBR is actually a special program executed when the computer's BIOS boots the system. This program is responsible for locating an active partition with the operating system (OS) files and then passing control to the OS files. A boot-sector virus usually does the following:

- Checks whether it has already infected the disk
- Relocates the original boot sector
- Copies its own boot-sector replacement to the MBR or DOS boot sector
- Installs its memory resident portion
- Loads the original boot sector to continue the normal boot process
- Monitors floppy-disk access to infect the boot sector of additional floppy disks

For a boot-sector virus to infect an uninfected hard disk, an infected floppy disk's boot sector must be accessed. Note, however, that this floppy disk does not have to be a bootable floppy disk. When the BIOS searches for a bootable partition, the act of accessing the boot sector of an otherwise unbootable floppy disk can infect a hard disk with the virus. Thus an easy way to protect yourself from this type of virus is to avoid booting from a floppy disk of unknown origin. Also, many newer system BIOSs have an antivirus boot-sector setting that prohibits any direct writes to the MBR. Since this is a BIOS setting and the BIOS code executes before a disk is accessed, if your computer BIOS has this setting, this can be an added bit of security to prevent a virus infection.

> **Caution:** Be extremely careful when making changes in your computer BIOS. Make only those changes suggested or that you are absolutely sure of the effect. You can inadvertently disable your computer if you change the wrong setting.

The BIOS settings of your computer are commonly referred to as the CMOS, named so after the type of memory device originally used for this storage. Other CMOS or BIOS settings that may assist in preventing an infection are as follows:

- Disabling access to drive A at boot time
- Changing the normal boot sequence to boot from drive C before booting from drive A

> **Note:** If you enable the antivirus feature that prevents direct writes to the MBR before loading Windows 95, Windows 95's setup fails when attempting to write the Windows 95 boot sector. Setup will complain that your computer is running virus protection software. You must disable this setting for Windows 95 Setup to succeed. Setup will also generate the same error if you're running an older antivirus product when you attempt to install Windows 95. You may need to disable the software by remarking or commenting the lines in either your CONFIG.SYS or AUTOEXEC.BAT files to enable Windows 95 to complete its installation.

Understanding the Windows 95 Boot Sequence

You need to learn about the typical boot sequence of a PC to see exactly how a virus can gain such a vital hold on your computer. The Windows 95 boot sequence proceeds almost exactly as the DOS sequence with the important differences being the Windows 95 boot files, the addition of Plug and Play, and the necessary differences added by multiple hardware profiles, and so on. But the basic boot sequence that a virus exploits is the same. Look at the sequence to see the points that a virus can interject itself to infect your system.

When you first turn on your computer, it goes through a set sequence of steps. The first of these is the *Power On Self Test* (POST). This set of instructions is a step-by-step sequence that briefly checks each hardware subsystem for basic functionality. If you are fortunate enough to have a newer computer with Plug-and-Play BIOS, this sequence is considerably more involved than that found on older computers, but the

results regarding the boot sequence are the same. The POST is followed by an initialization sequence, which involves setting up the different subsystems of the computer to default states. This initialization sequence may include setting registers, loading parameters, or establishing a more detailed list of the equipment present. After this BIOS initialization, any remaining BIOS routines, such as found on adapter cards, execute. At the end of the initialization sequence, the BIOS accesses the drives as it attempts to locate a valid bootable partition to continue booting the computer. Depending on the previously mentioned settings regarding the order of disk access, the BIOS attempts to locate a special kind of program called a *boot record*. This program is actually a small bit of executable code that further details the location of a valid operating system's boot files. When located, the initialization sequence passes control to this program and the boot process continues with this program now in control.

The initialization sequence locates and reads the contents of the first 512-byte sector of either a floppy disk or the first hard drive. This 512-byte sector is the MBR and contains program code to continue the remaining boot sequence. On a hard disk, the first 466 bytes of this sector is actually the program code, while the remaining bytes contain a two-byte header and four 16-byte entries defining up to four partitions. By definition, these partitions can be either four primary partitions or three primary partitions and one extended partition with logical drives. This *partition table* is used to locate an active partition to continue loading the OS. The first 512 bytes of the first primary partition that is marked "active" in the MBR is then loaded, and like the MBR itself, the executable code contained in these 512 bytes runs to complete loading the OS. This 512-byte sector is called the DOS boot record or simply the boot sector since you are no longer dealing with a necessarily MS-DOS structure. It is this boot sector that actually loads the OS boot files; thus until this step, a virus can interject itself and control what follows.

You can see why a virus attacking either of these boot sectors is potentially disastrous. This is why many of the most destructive viruses infect the MBR. The virus is loaded in memory before the OS loads, giving the virus an upper hand in either continuing to infect other programs or floppy disks when they are accessed and even resisting attempts to check for the presence of the virus in memory by redirecting such attempts. These programs can be killers indeed.

Boot-Sector Viruses

There are several viruses that have become well known because of their destructive potential. Probably the most well known of these is the virus that has been named Michelangelo. It is so named because the virus basically sits dormant until March 6, Michelangelo's birthday, and then activates and overwrites part of the hard disk with random information from memory, thus destroying any data that it overwrites. While it is dormant, it silently replicates itself to every floppy disk that is accessed, potentially spreading to other infected machines as these floppies are passed from one user to another. The Michelangelo virus remains a frequently reported virus, probably because it does no apparent damage unless you happen to boot up on March 6.

> **Tip:** One of the best defenses you have against a virus infection is frequent scanning of your hard drive. If you haven't already done so, create a Windows 95 boot disk by choosing the Add/Remove Programs applet in the Control Panel. Choose the Startup Disk tab. Copy your virus scanning software to the disk and then enable the write-protect tab on this diskette to protect it from infection. Clearly label this disk as an antivirus boot disk and keep it handy for a reassuring once a week scan.

Many of the boot sector viruses can be easily removed from your hard disk without using an antivirus product at all. Since MS-DOS 5.0, the FDISK program has had a command-line switch to rewrite the MBR. This feature of FDISK can be used to remove Michelangelo from your hard disk, as well as the 20 or so strains or *variants* of the Stoned virus. You cannot use this method to remove the virus from floppy disks because FDISK is only for fixed nonremovable media. To use this /mbr switch, follow these steps:

1. Use Start/Shut Down to shut down your computer before powering off. This step is required to ensure that the virus is not resident in memory.
2. Boot the computer from a write-protected floppy disk. The Windows 95 Startup boot disk you created when you installed Windows 95 has FDISK.EXE on the disk.
3. At the command prompt enter **FDISK /MBR**. This step will rewrite the Master Boot Record.
4. Turn off your computer and remove the floppy disk.
5. When you turn the computer back on, the virus should have been removed.
6. Use your antivirus software to scan and clean any suspect floppy disks that may have been used while the computer was infected.

Caution: The primary use of FDISK is to initially prepare a hard disk by creating partition(s) prior to a "high-level" format. If used without the above /MBR switch, FDISK will present a menu that allows you to perform these functions. There should be no need to change the partition information on your hard drive unless you are initially preparing your drive. *Any changes made when running FDISK in it's interactive mode may render your hard drive unaccessible and unreadable.*

Once your computer is infected with the Monkey virus, direct detection is almost impossible. It is called a stealth virus because it hides itself from detection by redirecting INT 12, which is used to determine the amount of free contigous memory, so that attempts to detect the virus in memory are turned away. It will also redirect attempts to read the MBR directly by presenting the "real" MBR to programs attempting to detect the virus. The MBR is encrypted so that unless the Monkey virus is resident in memory, the data is unreadable. There are a couple of clues that you may have a Monkey virus infection though. Either of the following may indicate a Monkey virus infection:

- If after you boot from a floppy disk, attempts to change to the hard drive give you the error, Invalid drive specification, this may indicate a Monkey infection.
- When the Monkey virus is resident in memory, the MEM or CHKDSK command shows a decrease of 1,024 bytes in total available system memory.

Understanding Trojan Horses

The Trojan horse is another destructive virus that takes the particularly nasty form of a popular utility that may actually do something useful while it wreaks its hidden havoc. One of the common targets of Trojan horse writers is popular antivirus programs themselves. If the creator of a Trojan horse can successfully hide a destructive virus as a well-known antivirus program and advertise it as an important upgrade or patch release, many unsuspecting users can be tricked into attempting to use the program. Many writers of antivirus software refuse to classify Trojan horses as viruses. The argument is that since a virus is by definition a program that modifies another program and replicates itself; the typical Trojan horse does not fit this definition. Hence, some discussions of viruses do not mention Trojan horses at all. But since Trojan horses can actually be written to fit the strict definition of a virus, I mention them here.

A Trojan horse can be as simple as a program that is advertised for one purpose—say a calculator. But when the program is run, it may display offensive language or pictures on your screen. This type of program is not considered by most to be a virus. If this same program not only displays the offensive language but also seeks out other EXE or COM programs and infects these with the same code that caused the offensive display, this program is rightly called a virus. Recently an example

of a Trojan horse was mentioned in the computer press and online forums. This Trojan horse, a bogus version of PKWARE's PKZIP product parading as version 3.00, was actually uploaded to PKWARE's own BBS as a file named PKZ300B.EXE or PKZ300B.ZIP. If either the PKZ300B.EXE file or the EXE contained inside the ZIP file is run, this Trojan horse formats your hard drive. Encountering this particular virus will be deadly. Preventing an attack by a virus or Trojan horse becomes a matter of following a few simple rules. Later on you'll look at effective antivirus strategies, but first look at a few examples of "File" viruses.

Understanding File Viruses

The type of virus that primarily infects other files is as equally dangerous as the ones already discussed. These viruses are the real parasites of the software world. They maliciously attach themselves to other program executables and wait for an opportunity to infect another program. A file virus may be as simple as the famous Lehigh virus that only infected COMMAND.COM but had the side effect of trashing the FAT after only four replications. Or a file virus may be one like the multipartite Natas virus that not only attacks files but also infects disk boot sectors.

You may first encounter a virus like Natas in an infected file, but once your computer is infected, your hard disk and any floppy disk accessed from the computer is also be infected. Natas also seeks out and infects all EXE and COM files by attaching itself to the file. Unfortunately, Natas also hides the subsequent size change in the folder. Thus when it's in memory, a folder listing shows no change in file sizes. While Natas is resident in memory, it decreases total system memory by 6K. A MEM check reveals 634K total memory. Natas contains a destructive routine that, when semirandomly activated, overwrites most of the first hard disk that it locates. If Natas is found on your system, you must make a thorough check of any floppy disks that you have used, as well as any files that you have shared with others by network.

Using Effective Antivirus Strategies

What kind of things do you need to do to ensure that your computer will not be the next victim of a virus? How can you protect your data from infection? The following simple guidelines are a start:

- Frequently scan your computer using a combination of at least two antivirus products preferably employing both scanners and an inoculator or integrity checker.
- Scan any floppy disk before installing any floppy-based software.
- Use BIOS settings to disable boot-sector writes.
- Use BIOS to disable booting from a floppy disk.
- Scan any downloaded software before use.
- Maintain a good backup strategy.

The preceding steps may cause you to ask a few additional questions. What do I mean by a *scanner* or *inoculator*? Do you have to scan each file separately; isn't there something to automate the process?

Current Virus Technology

The current level of virus activity worldwide is growing. By most people's estimation, the overall level of sophistication of virus developers is increasing. Because of the proliferation of tools like the "virus toolkit," virtually anyone with access to the Internet or a modem can actually download all the necessary tools to create a virus with only a nominal knowledge of the programming. The virus toolkit was created by the writer who calls himself the Dark Avenger, the notorious creator of one of the first *polymorphic viruses*. His creation has the ability to change its appearance with each subsequent infection, thus making it harder for antivirus software to detect the virus. His toolkit assists in the creation of whole new strains of virus all with polymorphic characteristics.

The stealth virus was mentioned earlier in this chapter. This type of virus technology has the capability of hiding from detection. A stealth

virus may redirect DOS interrupts to avoid detection or a combination of both stealth and polymorphic technology to hide from antivirus software. Another common technique of a stealth virus is to alter folder listings to mask its change of an infected file.

Encryption is another technique commonly used by a virus developer. An encrypted virus encrypts its code while dormant. But to execute, it must decrypt itself; thus, these viruses are vulnerable to detection. The encrypted virus is particularly hard to detect while in memory or when it has infected a file or other portion of the data on a disk. Only when the virus activates can it usually be seen. Unfortunately, this may be too late.

Viruses may use events to trigger their activity—for example, the Michelangelo virus waiting for March 6. They may also wait for a number of keystrokes or invocations of a certain program before waging their havoc or wait for a combination of events to trigger, all the while silently infecting files or floppy disks as they are accessed. Because of all these different virus techniques, antivirus software must be increasingly updated to stay ahead of the virus. And antivirus software must use several techniques to defeat the different types of virus.

Current Antivirus Technology

To detect the many types of viruses, antivirus software typically uses a combination of methods. The methods used can help in categorizing the software, and most antivirus software packages employ several methods rather than depending on any one technique. The methods most commonly employed are as follows:

- Scanning and disinfecting
- Generic monitoring
- Inoculation
- Heuristics

Antivirus Scanning

Perhaps the most common method of the antivirus tool is the scanner. This tool is the one you use to check for the existence of a virus and may also be used to disinfect or remove a found virus. This tool is represented by VirusScan by the McAfee Corporation or F-Prot by Data Fellows, Incorporated. Typically you boot and run the software from a floppy disk and search for existing virus infections. If an infection is found, the scanner usually has a companion tool to remove the infection. It is this tool that requires frequent updates from the manufacturer. Most scanners work by containing data with actual binary strings of data identifying known viruses. These strings or *signatures* are used to identify suspected virus infections and thus require that whenever a new virus is discovered "in the wild," a new version of the scanning software must be released. Most commercial scanning software companies offer a subscription service for these updates or make updates available on a BBS or other online locations.

Monitoring Antivirus

Generic monitoring may be used in addition to a scanner or used as stand-alone program. Generic monitoring represents a logical addition to your antivirus arsenal. Most antivirus software developers have recognized the importance of this tool and include monitoring software as part of a total antivirus solution. Monitoring is usually accomplished by the use of a device driver in your CONFIG.SYS or AUTOEXEC.BAT file that loads every time you boot your computer. This software remains resident in memory and monitors every program loaded using scanning technology; the memory resident program also monitors potential "viral" activity; i.e., attempts to directly write to areas of the hard drive's boot sector or FAT or to write to other executable files. A monitor program may also look at every program's attempt to go resident in memory, giving you a chance to catch a program that is doing something that you do not expect. Most scanning software also has to include some mechanism for you to identify programs that routinely use any of these functions in their normal operation so that you don't have to always approve their use. One weakness of the monitoring

program is that because it loads in one of your startup files, it cannot protect against a boot-sector virus that loads before these files are accessed. Another is that because a mechanism exists to bypass its checking function, many users may become lax and simply approve most or all of the program's prompts.

Inoculation or Integrity Method

Inoculation or integrity checking may be employed by a scanning program, used by monitoring programs, or simply used by itself. This technique is typically used in combination with other methods to improve the ability of detecting file infections. This usually is implemented as some type of CRC or CHECKSUM that is either kept in a database, separate files on the hard drive, or even attached to the file that is being inoculated. Once this CHECKSUM is computed, anytime the inoculated file is scanned or otherwise checked, any changes in the file are easily detected. Some of the more sophisticated inoculators actually store enough information about the file that a complete recovery of the file may be possible if the file is infected. One problem with an integrity checker is that some files are self-modifying, thus making them subject to change naturally. Like the monitor programs, inoculators usually have some facility to identify such programs so that false alarms won't be generated every time you run the program.

Rule-Based Antivirus Checking

Finally, a relatively modern advance in antivirus technology is the use of heuristics or rule-based detection of a virus. Heuristic technology relies on the fact that viruses of a specific type act the same or contain code that perform the same type of functions. Thus, heuristic searches can assist in determining whether a suspect program may be a virus. Heuristics may actually generate more false positives but are still quite useful in your antivirus arsenal.

The best defensive tool might employ several or even all of the above methods. It's not uncommon for a suite of tools to include a scanner, inoculator, and monitor utility and use heuristics in at least one of

these tools. Your best bet to defeat a virus is to use a combination of these tools. When you do encounter an infection, it's usually wise to use a second product, possibly from another vendor, to verify and even increase the odds of locating a virus the first package may have missed. Even antivirus software can have blind spots that may miss an infection.

Controlling the Portals of Entry to Your Computer

One sure way to avoid a virus infection altogether is to control the ways a virus may enter your computer. The methods of entry are actually few: by floppy disk or network, whether the network is a BBS, a LAN, or other online resource. Another method of receipt may be an unsolicited attachment in a mail message. Like any other files or programs you receive, it is up to you to be sure that the software you are going to load to your computer does not contain a virus. Only you can guarantee that.

Watching Out for Dangerous Floppy Disks

Probably the single most common method of virus infection is by an infected floppy disk. It's not usually a malicious attack but rather an unsuspecting associate whose computer has already been infected who passes a virus along with the data that you are really expecting. This may even be a floppy disk that was formatted long before the actual infection was even suspected. It has also been a too frequent occurrence that commercial software has been inadvertently infected at some point in the manufacturing process, thus unknowingly infecting all the recipients of the software. Pirated software can be a source of a floppy infection as well. If a co-worker offers a copy of a program that you know to be a pirated version of software, "Just say No!" A pirate may not be anymore reticent to pass on a virus as to pass on a pirated piece of software.

Protecting Your Network from Viruses

In today's heterogeneous network environment, it may be harder to protect your computer network from a virus infection. Many antivirus companies have special network versions of their software to enable LAN-wide or even WAN-wide protection. This software may also employ one or more of the above techniques to offer real-time protection of individual computers or check each file that is written to a network drive for virus infections. In general, though, by using the same type of protection on a network that is used on the local computer, you'll not be likely to pick up an infection.

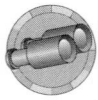

> **Note:** This section frequently mentions the Dial-Up Server, which is the Remote Network Access Server component delivered with Microsoft Plus! It is not delivered with the base Windows 95 product. Its inclusion here is to present the access control features of Windows 95 regarding dial-in access to your computer.

Another area of potential concern is when you have enabled either Windows NT Remote Access Services' (RAS) or Windows 95's own Dial-Up Server to allow remote computers access to your network. If you intend to allow remote access, be careful that you only allow specific users access to the network. Though the likelihood of someone accidentally gaining access from a remote node is limited, use the built-in security of the Dial-Up Server or RAS to define user access.

With Windows 95, the type of access restrictions you can set for the Dial-Up Server is the same access that you have set for the overall computer. Windows 95 allows you to use share-level or user-level access. Share-level access allows a per-share password, while user-level requires the pass-through validation of users from an NT Domain or NetWare Server. To check or configure your access control, open the Control Panel's Network applet. In the Network dialog box, choose the Access Control tab (see figure 42.1).

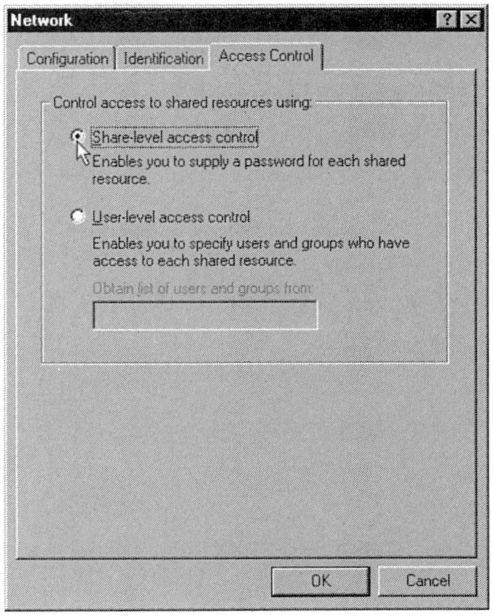

Fig. 42.1 The Access Control tab showing the selection of Share-level access control.

If you selected Share-level access control, when you configured the Dial-Up Server, you were allowed to set only a single password (see figure 42.2).

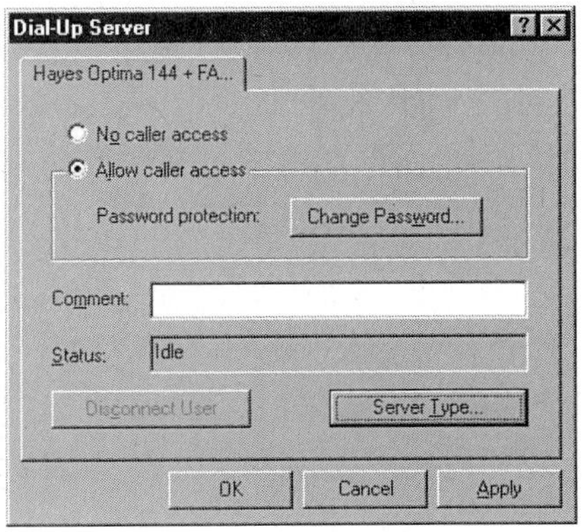

Fig. 42.2 This is how the Dial-Up Server dialog box appears when networking is configured for share-level access.

Note that this dialog box allows you to set a password for access and that this access is for anyone dialing in to the server. When you select the Change Password button, the Dial-Up Networking Password dialog box allows you to set the access password (see figure 42.3).

Fig. 42.3 The Dial-Up Server Networking Password dialog box allows setting or changing the server access password.

User-level access provides more security than share-level access because this method uses the advanced security of Windows NT or NetWare user account data. User-level access is only available when connected to a Windows NT or NetWare server. The Dial-Up Server approves or denies the request for access based on the "pass-through" account validation from the Windows NT or NetWare server. As previously mentioned, you configure the default access control using the Network applet in Control Panel. Figure 42.4 shows the User-level access control selected.

> **Note:** User-level access control requires a Windows NT or Novell NetWare Server for user authentication and that you define a valid domain controller or server in the Access Control dialog.

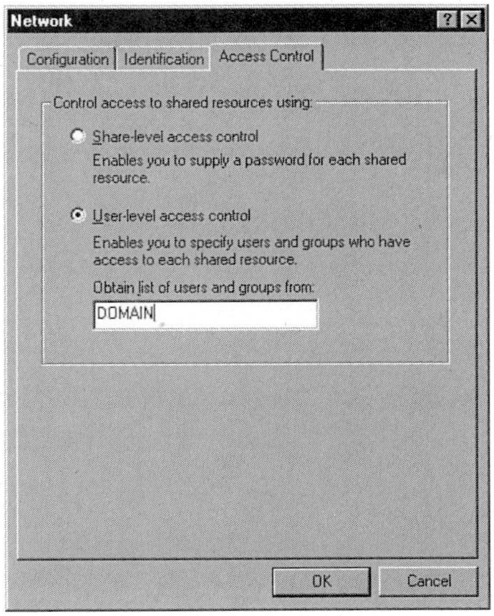

Fig. 42.4 The Access Control tab showing the selection of User-level access control.

Once you have set up user-level access control, you can configure the Dial-Up Server by selecting the Dial-Up Server from the Dial-Up Networking window (see figure 42.5).

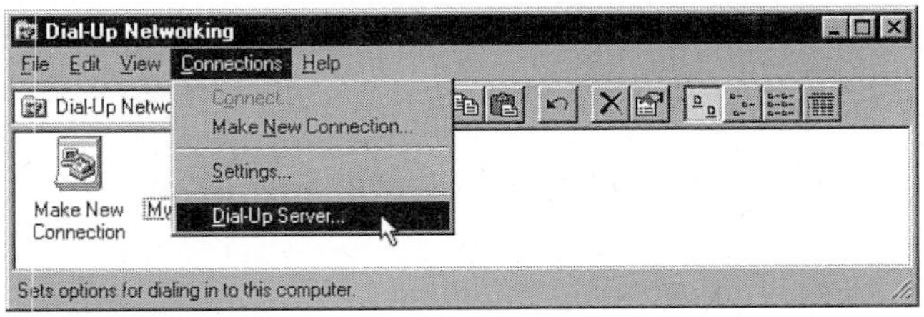

Fig. 42.5 Selection and configuration of the Dial-Up Server is done by using the Connections, Dial-Up Server selection in the Dial-Up Networking dialog box.

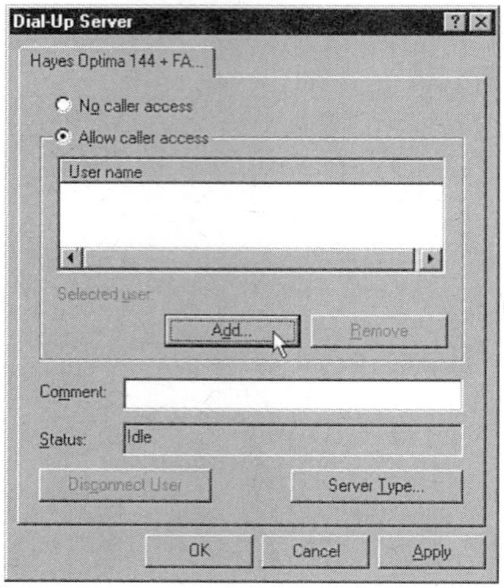

Fig. 42.6 The Dial-Up Server dialog box as it appears when configured for user-level access.

Now you can set up access using the advanced authentication of user-level access. Note that in figure 42.6, the Dial-Up Server dialog box looks different because it is user-based; when you click the Add button, you are allowed to choose users from the domain or server you selected in the Network dialog box (see figure 42.7).

With this type of access you have the added security of knowing exactly who is given access because the odds of someone gaining access to a specific user's name and password is less likely. With this method, you don't have to give access to everyone, but you do have the ability to assign access individually. With share-level access, anyone with the single password can gain access to your network.

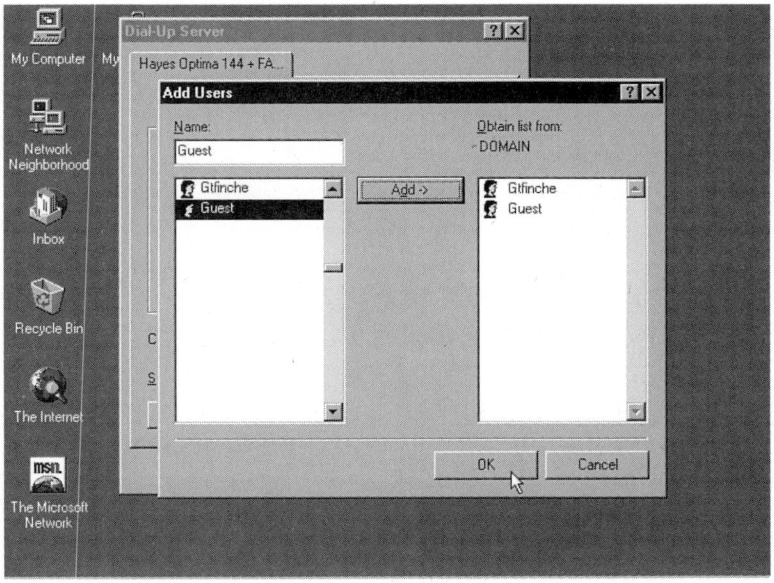

Fig. 42.7 The Dial-Up Server dialog box showing the Add Users access dialog box.

An additional item to consider is that Windows 95 will offer to save any password required in a dialog box which uses a password. These passwords are encrypted and saved in a PWL (password list) file named for the currently logged in user. If you elect to save these passwords and someone else uses your computer, that person can log on to your remote connections without having to enter a password (see figure 42.8). Unless you are very sure of the security of your computer, it is wise not to save these passwords.

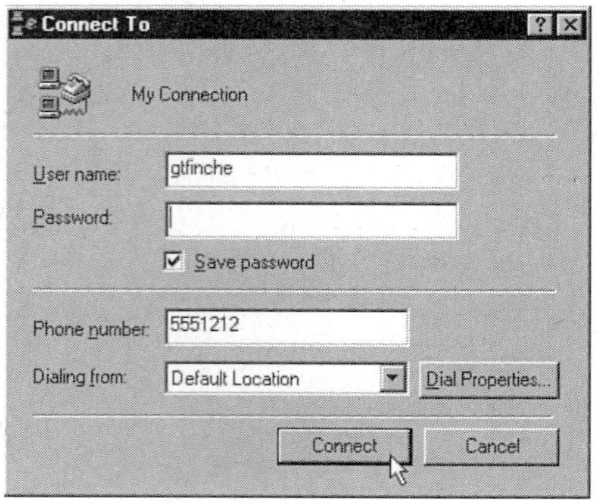

Fig. 42.8 This Dial-up Networking Connect To dialog box showing the Save Password selection enabled.

Knowing the Risks of Downloaded Software

There are risks involved in using downloaded software from any online source. It has been fashionable to routinely blame the BBS as the largest potential risk, but this simply is not the case. The majority of the operators of BBSs use a variety of techniques to assure their users that they are not going to download a virus. Most use a protected upload area where recent uploaded programs are "quarantined" until they have been verified. Also, popular shareware authors usually use one or more methods to ensure the validity of the archives that are commonly used for online distribution. Many shareware or commercial developers maintain dedicated BBS, FTP, or WWW locations for legitimate versions of their products. If you're downloading software, use either the author's own online point of distribution or another equally legitimate source like some of the larger BBSs or online collections available on the Internet. And always scan any downloads before using. It's your data you're protecting.

Online Sources for Antivirus Information

Probably the best defenses you can set up is increased awareness and knowledge of the changing virus landscape. There are a multitude of resources available to you, many of which are available on the Internet or by e-mail. Most vendors of antivirus software maintain BBSs, Wide World Web or FTP sites, or other electronic forums such as those on CompuServe, America Online, Prodigy, or the Microsoft Network. These can all be excellent sources of updated data. Whether your are looking for generic information about viruses, antivirus programs, or updates to a program, it is likely to be available online. Table 42.1 lists some of the sources that you may find helpful. Note that by listing these resources we're not endorsing any specific vendor or the sufficiency of the tools that may be listed nor have all the vendors announced Windows 95 versions of their software products.

Table 42.1 Online Antivirus Resources

Location	Identification
http://www.brs.ibm.com/ibmav.html	IBM Computer Virus Home Page
http://www.symantec.com/virus/virus.html	Symantec Anti-virus Reference Center
http://csrc.ncsl.nist.gov/virus/virusl/	VIRUS-L Forum
http://www.mcafee.com	McAfee software WWW page
http://www.sands.com/	Dr. Solomon's software
http://www.datafellows.fi/index.html	Data Fellows F-Prot software
http://www.icubed.com/ic.html	Sophos Intercheck software
http://www.nha.com/	NH&A software
http://www.thenet.ch/metro/av-links.html	MetroNet BBS—Anti-virus resources
http://ciac.llnl.gov/ciac/	Computer Incident Advisory Capability

Designed for Windows 95—An AntiVirus Example

As mentioned earlier, most if not all developers of antivirus software for the PC platform have announced that Windows 95 versions of their products will be available soon after the initial release of Windows 95. Each of these developers will take a slightly different approach to the task, and each program will certainly have its merits. Though you'll take a quick peek at one such program, McAfee Associates' VirusScan 95, you'll make no attempt here to gauge the relative performance of this or any other antivirus program. The preceding locations have a wealth of data, including performance comparisons that may help you in determining which program best suits your situation.

Shortly before this book went to print in September 1995, McAfee Associates released the first "External Test" Beta version of VirusScan 95 (first called "SCAN 95") to the McAfee FTP site and BBS. This release was one of the first glimpses of what a "Designed for Windows 95" antivirus product might be expected to look like. McAfee soon released a second version as a "Release Candidate" for a final scheduled release coincident with Windows 95's August 24, 1995 worldwide rollout. At this writing there is every indication that McAfee Associates intends to continue to offer this product as shareware, with evaluation versions available online at either of McAfee's WWW, FTP, or BBS locations. To locate the file on the McAfee Associate FTP site, you would look in either the /pub/antivirus or /pub/beta folder for a file called VS95.EXE or something similar. This file contains the complete program in a convenient self-extracting, self-installing format. You can install the program by running the executable directly or by using the Add/Remove Programs applet in Control Panel. As expected, once the program is installed, you can also remove the program by using the same Add/Remove Programs dialog box.

Once installed, VirusScan 95 is tightly integrated with Windows 95. The program will install the VSHEILD.EXE TSR in your AUTOEXEC.BAT file, and the VSHLDWIN.EXE program in the Start Menu/Startup folder; thus enabling the detection portion of VirusScan 95. This detection portion will attempt to prevent a virus from infecting your computer by preventing such activity as detailed in the preceding section. The main VirusScan 95 program is installed in the \Windows\McAfee folder or any other folder of your choice, and a corresponding McAfee VirusScan 95 shortcut menu is added as well. You can execute the program directly by using the VirusScan 95 icon in this group, but the best way to exectute the program is by using a file's context menu in Explorer. Figure 42.9 shows the Scan for Viruses selection that VirusScan 95 adds to this menu.

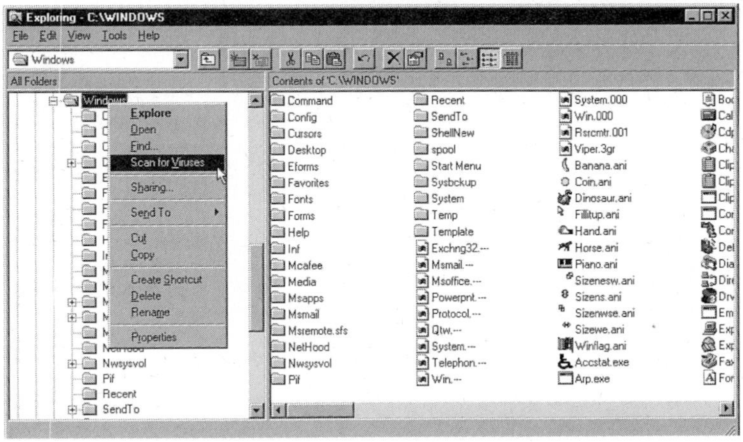

Fig. 42.9 The Explorer showing the addition of Scan for Viruses that VirusScan 95 adds to the context menu.

When you make this selection, the main VirusScan 95 dialog box opens (figure 42.10), which looks much like the Windows 95 Find Files dialog box (figure 42.11).

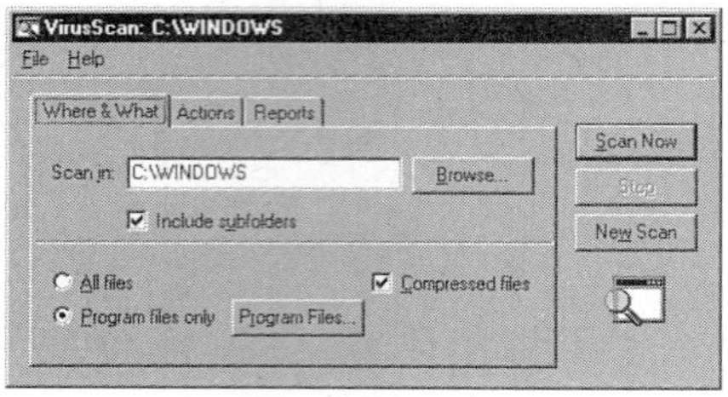

Fig. 42.10 The main VirusScan 95 dialog looks very much like the Windows 95 Find Files dialog box.

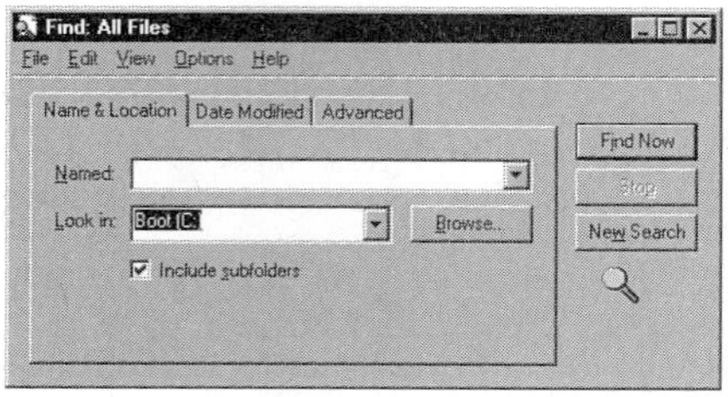

Fig. 42.11 The Windows 95 Find Files dialog box shown for comparison.

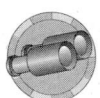

Note: Notice that you can have either VirusScan 95 scan All files or Program files only or even scan inside compressed executable files. Also be aware that the New Scan button restores the programs defaults for a new scan selection.

If you want to immediately scan the selected file, folder, or drive, you click on Scan Now to begin the scan process. Because VirusScan is a 32-bit program, it can run in the background while you continue to work in another program. If a suspected virus is found, VirusScan will take whatever steps you have specified in the Actions tab (figure 42.12).

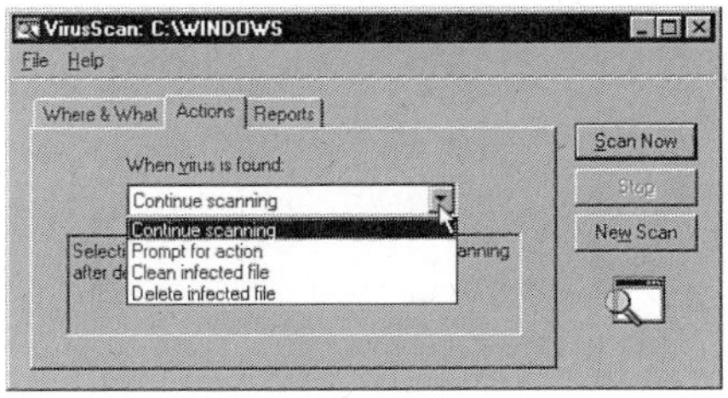

Fig. 42.12 The main VirusScan 95 dialog Action tab showing the possible actions that can be configured.

You use the Reports tab (figure 42.13) to display a message or sound an alert when a virus is found, or to log any results to a file.

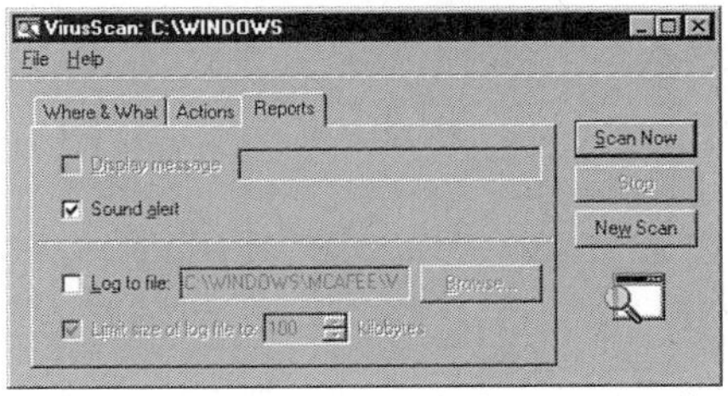

Fig. 42.13 The main VirusScan 95 dialog box Reports tab showing report functions that can be configured.

This has been a quick look at one developer's approach to Windows 95 antivirus protection. Fortunately, VirusScan 95 didn't find any virus' on your system. Following the recommendations you learned about earlier and those that follow should help you have similar results! Now, turn your attention again to backup—the best way *back* from an antivirus attack.

Backing Up Your System

Anytime the potential destruction or loss of data is mentioned, the issue of having a recent backup needs to be considered. Probably one of the most frequent mistakes of most PC users is that no backup plan is in place. Restoring lost data after a catastrophic occurrence like a virus infection may be the only way to recover from an infection like that caused by the Monkey virus. And other viruses equally destructive may result in significant loss of irreplaceable data. Many companies suffer financial damage when data is lost to a virus attack or to other catastrophic damage when no recent backup exists.

Windows 95 ships with several backup options. Microsoft Backup is used to back up to a local floppy, tape, or network drive. This application was developed by Colorado Memory Systems for Windows 95 and supports many well-known tape drives. The following tape drives are compatible with Microsoft Backup:

QIC 40, 80, and 3010 tape drives made by the following companies, and connected to the primary floppy-disk controller:

- Colorado Memory Systems
- Conner
- Iomega
- Wangtek (only in hardware phantom mode)
- Colorado Memory Systems QIC 40, 80, and 3010 tape drives connected through a parallel port

Windows 95 Microsoft Backup is very easy to use. It's so easy that if you have access to a local tape drive, I strongly recommend you use it. Figure 42.9 shows the main Microsoft Backup window.

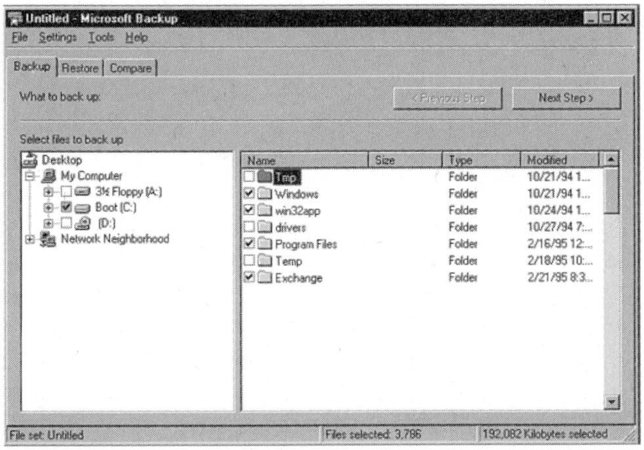

Fig. 42.14 The main Microsoft Backup dialog showing the selection of backup sources.

Selecting files to back up is a simple point-and-click operation. Once you have made your backup choices, you simply select Next Step to proceed with your backup. Figure 42.15 shows the destination window that you use to select a floppy disk, or tape drive, or a local or network drive for a backup destination.

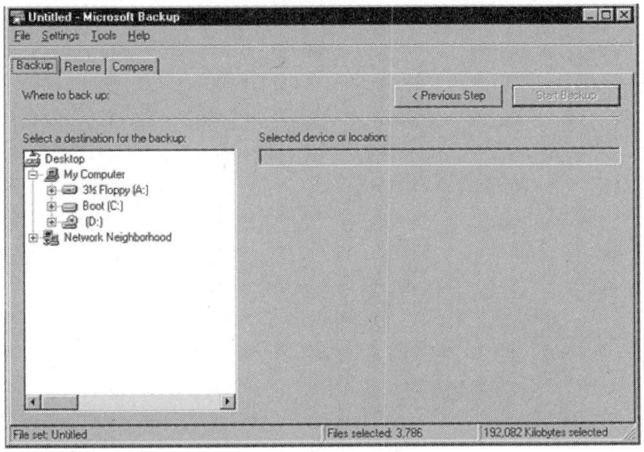

Fig. 42.15 The main Microsoft Backup dialog showing the selection of a backup destination.

You use the Microsoft Backup Settings, Options menu to modify your backup settings. You also use this dialog box to modify Restore options. Figures 42.16 and 42.17 illustrate the options for Backup and Restore.

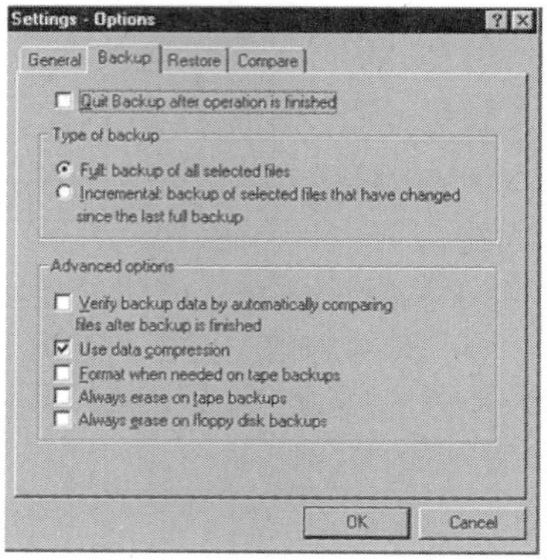

Fig. 42.16 The Microsoft Backup Settings,Options dialog box showing the Backup options page.

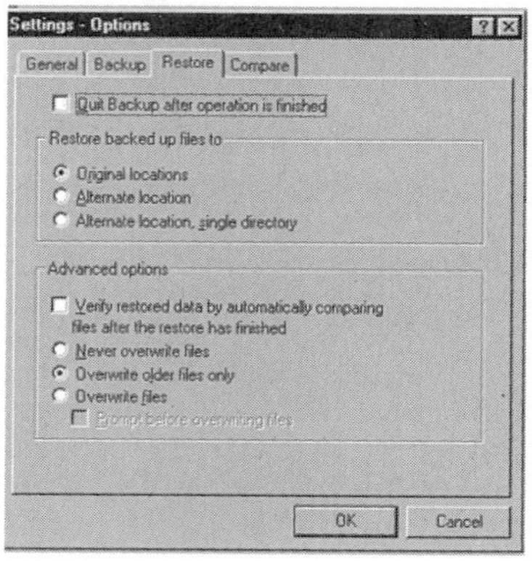

Fig. 42.17 The Microsoft Backup Settings, Options dialog showing the Restore options page.

Windows also includes Backup Agents to assist in remote backup of a Windows system to a network tape drive. These agents from Arcada (Backup Exec Agent) and Cheyenne Software (ARCserve Agent) assist in unattended backup to the corresponding network tape drive. Armed with the appropriate agent, an administrator can be sure that important data is regularly backed up to the network tape drive. The Arcada and Cheyenne backup agents require the corresponding server-based network backup software from either Arcada or Cheyenne. The server components are available for either Novell NetWare or Windows NT Servers.

Because these agents require network connections to a server, you use the Network dialog box to install the related software (see figure 42.13 and 42.14). Microsoft lists these as a service, so you choose Add and double-click Service to open the Select Network Service dialog box. You then install the appropriate manufacturer's service and configure it for your backup server.

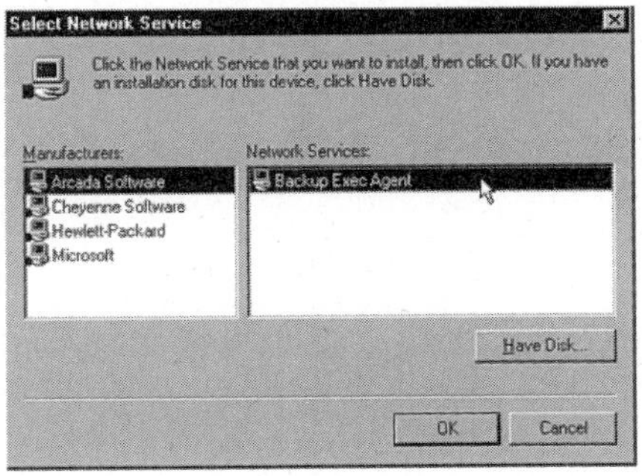

Fig. 42.18 The Select Network Service dialog box showing the selection of the Arcada Backup Exec Agent.

You'll step through a typical setup of Arcada's Backup Exec Agent to show the steps to take to enable a network backup. Remember, without one of these backup servers, you won't be able to use the agents.

The Arcada Backup Exec Agent delivered with Windows requires Arcada Backup Exec for NetWare, Enterprise Edition or Single Server Edition, version 5.01, or Arcada Backup Exec 6.0 for Windows NT. If your NetWare or Windows NT Server is running the appropriate Arcada products, you can use the Arcada Backup Exec Agent to regularly archive important data from your workstation. Installing the Backup Exec Agent is easy. Once you have located the service, you only need to click OK to install the software (refer figure 42.18). Then you have to configure the software by either double-clicking on Backup Exec Agent in the Network dialog box and then clicking on Properties to see the Backup Exec Agent Properties sheet for the agent (see figure 42.19).

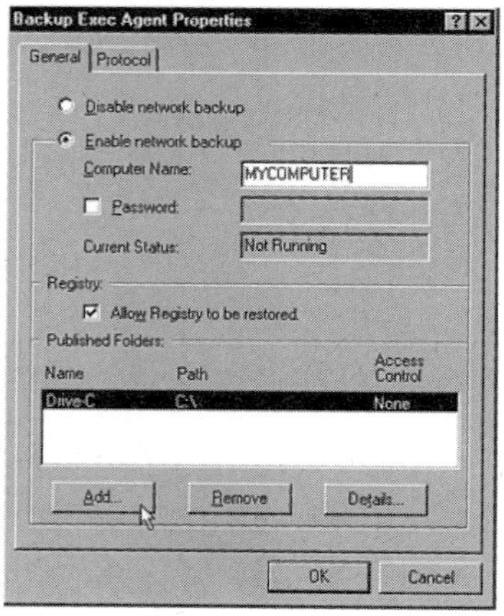

Fig. 42.19 The Backup Exec Agent Properties sheet showing the General page.

> **Note:** When you first install your software, Current Status indicates Not Running. After you install and configure the agent this status changes to Running.

When you enable the software, the NetWare or Windows NT Server software sees the Windows 95 computer as a backup source. The information that you need to pay careful attention to in this Properties sheet is as follows:

- You must enable the agent
- If needed, you must set a password

- Determine if you want the Registry to be restored
- Determine which folders need to be backed up using the Add, Remove, and Details dialog boxes

> **Caution:** If you mark the Allow Registry To Be Restored check box, changes to the Registry you may have made explicitly or any that a program may have made since the last backup will be overwritten.

If you only want to back up your main Documents folder and your electronic mail Exchange folder, you use the Add dialog box, which opens the Select Folder to Publish dialog box (see figure 42.20) to select the folder you want backed up and then the Remove dialog box to remove any you don't want to back up.

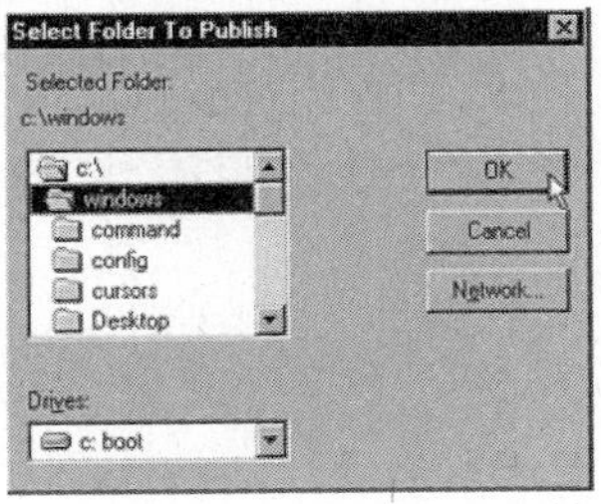

Fig. 42.20 The Backup Exec Agent's Select Folder To Publish dialog box showing the currently selected folders.

Click on the folders you want to add to the backup, click OK to bring up the Folders Details dialog where you can set any required passwords (see figure 42.21).

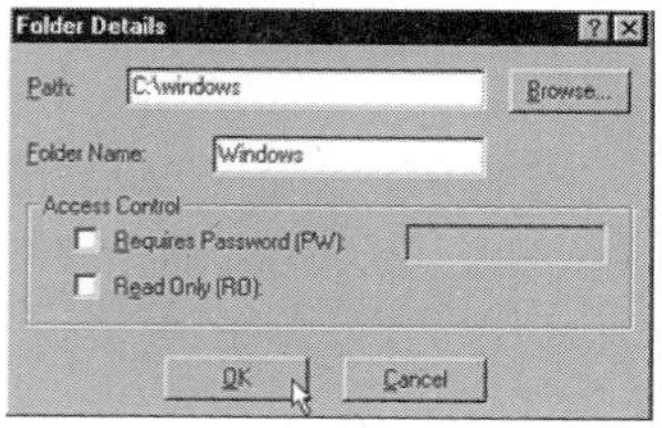

Fig. 42.21 The Folder Details dialog box allows you to assign appropriate access control.

Add any folders that you want to back up, and then check to see if you have set up the access control correctly. In this case, Read-Only access on the Windows folder was set up (see figure 42.22).

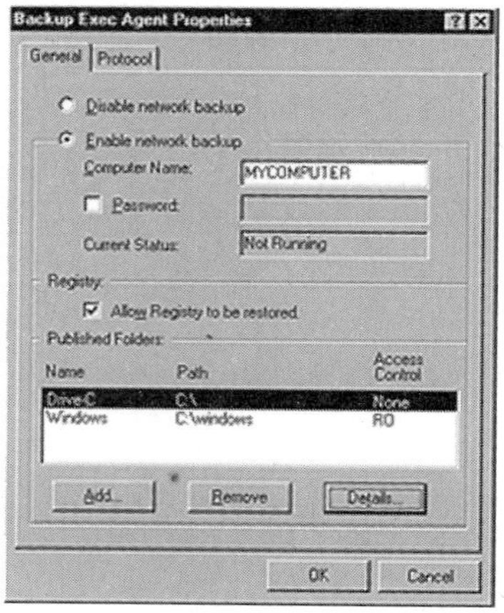

Fig. 42.22 The Backup Exec Agent General properties sheet showing the currently assigned access control.

You now need to set the appropriate protocol for the server. On the Protocol page, you find that you can use either the SPX/IPX or TCP/IP protocols (see figure 42.23). Also, if you select TCP/IP, you need to use either the correct TCP/IP address or server name. To add information, the Add button allows you to input the correct information. When you have made all the changes necessary, simply click the OK button to leave the Backup Exec Agent Properties sheet and click OK again to

save the information. When you exit the Network dialog box, you are prompted to reboot the computer to accept the changes. Click the Yes button. When your computer is rebooted, you can visit these dialog boxes to see that the Backup Exec Agent is indeed running.

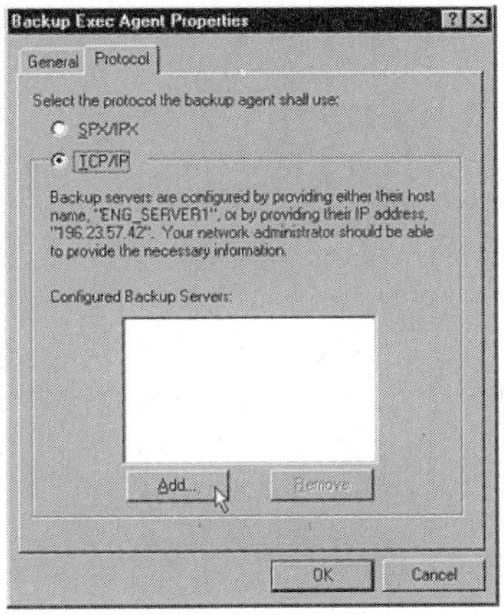

Fig. 42.23 The Backup Exec Agent Protocol Properties sheet showing the selection for the TCP/IP protocol.

If your server is running Cheyenne's backup software, you need to install the ARCserve backup agent which involves a similar set of steps.

43

System Agent

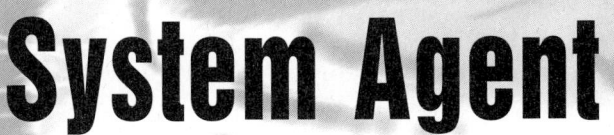

by Gordon Meltzer

The System Agent that is part of Microsoft Plus! is a powerful tool for scheduling applications and utilities. With System Agent, you can run other programs automatically, at certain preprogrammed times, in the background.

You can choose when to run the programs you schedule, and under what conditions they will start.

In this chapter, you learn about the following:

- How to use System Agent to schedule disk utilities
- The different kinds of programs you can launch with System Agent
- How to work with System Agent's optional settings
- How System Agent works with battery-operated computers

The programs that Microsoft pre-installs into System Agent are disk maintenance tools that, for now, seem to be the most useful types of programs to run in scheduled mode. They perform work that you should do regularly, but may often neglect. It's no surprise that these are the only pre-installed tools because, as you'll see, programs need to have settings configured to run properly in unattended mode. They also need settings that can alter the course of program execution, depending on the state of the computer at the time of scheduled execution.

Some programs that can benefit from scheduling, such as third-party backup solutions and third-party communications programs, already have scheduling built in. It would have been easy for Microsoft to build scheduling into Disk Defragmenter and the other applets, too.

Why then, did the system designers choose to put System Agent into the operating system itself?

The answer is simple. The answer builds on the premise established by Windows 1.0 back in 1985. The idea is to build uniform functionality for all programs into the operating system itself.

The first Windows was revolutionary, because it put printer drivers and display drivers into the operating system, and removed the need for these drivers to be part of Windows applications. Finally, video and printer drivers presented a universal interface to all programs. All Windows programs, for example, that used a printer used similar printer selection and setup dialog boxes, because the dialog box was really a part of the operating system.

In the same way, Microsoft designers decided to present a universal scheduling interface that would be available for designers of all programs to implement. No longer will the user have to remember a different set of scheduling commands for each program that can run unattended. The user interface and API in System Agent will be available to all program designers and coders.

This will make life easier for the user who wants to run a program in scheduled mode. Users can expect to see a large number of Windows 95 programs written to work with and take advantage of the power that is available in System Agent.

Exploring System Agent's Files

System Agent is a background scheduling application. It is implemented with several executables and a 32-bit virtual device, with a help system attached. The 10 files that collectively make up System Agent are as follows:

1. SAGE.EXE
2. SAGE.DLL
3. SAGE.VXD
4. SAGE.DEF
5. SAGE.DAT
6. SAGELOG.TXT
7. SYSAGENT.EXE
8. SYSAGENT.HLP
9. SYSAGENT.CNT
10. SYSAGENT.GID

System Agent starts when Windows 95 is loaded. It indicates that it is running by putting its icon in the system tray, next to the clock. It indicates its state by changing the properties of that icon.

Automatic Startup

The mechanism for automatically starting System Agent when Windows starts is new for Windows 95. You're used to seeing programs start automatically if they're listed on the RUN= or LOAD= lines of the WIN.INI file. You also know programs start automatically if they're in the STARTUP group on the Start button.

System Agent starts in a different way. System Agent makes use of the new Registry automatic startup service. The Registry setting that provides the automatic startup service for System Agent is buried deeply at the following Registry location, which can be viewed or edited with REGEDIT.EXE:

> HKEY_LOCAL_MACHINE, SOFTWARE, Microsoft, Windows, CurrentVersion, Run.

System Agent is designed by Microsoft to run programs in the background at certain times. In its default as-shipped configuration, System Agent is set to run the common disk utilities shown in figure 43.1. But it is capable of much more than this simple set of tasks.

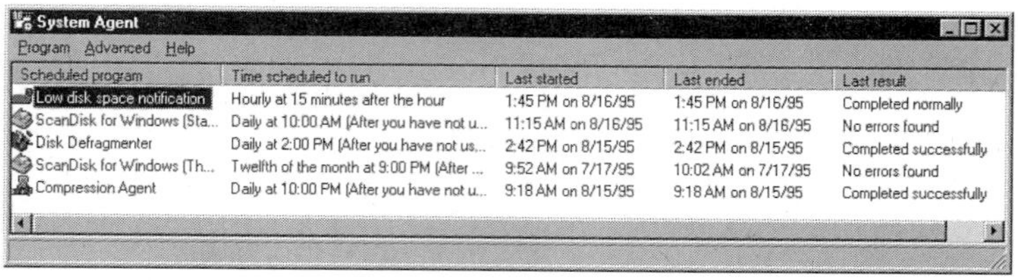

Fig. 43.1 Default System Agent configuration.

Understanding the System Agent File Functions

In the following sections, you take a look at how the 10 System Agent files work together, and examine the function of each.

The SAGE.XXX Files

SAGE.EXE is the background scheduler program engine. This program actually runs all the time in the background after you choose to install System Agent from PLUS! setup. SAGE.DLL is the library file for the scheduler engine. SAGE.DEF and SAGE.DAT are the data files containing the configuration of the System Agent. The DEF file is the default as-shipped configuration, and the DAT file is your user-modified System Agent configuration.

The SAGE.VXD is the virtual device driver that System Agent uses to take control of the system when it's time to run a scheduled program. This multitasking VXD will ensure that the scheduled program runs only if its tasking state conditions are met.

The SYSAGENT.XXX Files

These files are the front-end interface system for System Agent. When you use the interface to schedule a program, you're running SYSAGENT.EXE. This file also contains the icon image that you see in the system tray whenever you start a Windows 95 system that has Plus! installed.

SYSAGENT.EXE allows you to do the following:

- Schedule a new program
- Change a program's schedule
- Examine the properties of a scheduled program
- Run a scheduled program immediately
- Disable a scheduled program so it will not run on a schedule
- Remove a program from the list of scheduled programs

You'll also be using SYSAGENT.EXE if you want to do the following:

- Suspend the entire System Agent system

or

- De-install System Agent entirely

This program is also your interface to view the System Agent log file named SAGELOG.TXT.

The front end also includes the help system. SYSAGENT.HLP is the main help file, and SYSAGENT.CNT is the table of contents index for System Agent help. Finally, SYSAGENT.GID is the Windows 95 word index database file.

Working with System Agent's Defaults

By default, System Agent comes configured to run Low Disk Space Notification, ScanDisk for Windows, and Disk Defragmenter.

Look at the options System Agent gives you when working with these programs. You'll be able to schedule the programs and set some useful conditions for running them. These tasking state conditions can be modified by you to create an environment that works best for you. In determining how to set up System Agent, you'll want to consider whether your computer is left on all the time or only for a few hours a day. Your work schedule will also be important in determining how best to use the feature set.

Working with Low Disk Space Notification

System Agent calls DISKALM.EXE to run the Low Disk Space Notification. The default setting is to run this program once each hour, at 15 minutes past the hour, on local hard disk C, and notify you if disk space falls below 20M free.

You can alter the following settings for DISKALM.EXE:

- Change the schedule of activation
- Change the threshold of available disk space for notification
- Change the drives on which the program acts

Changing the Schedule

Figure 43.2 shows the basic options for running DISKALM.EXE. These settings apply also to any program that System Agent schedules. You have the option to change Run frequency, Start at time, and state dependence from this screen. Notice that the Start at option in the figure is tied to the Run Hourly selection in the same dialog box.

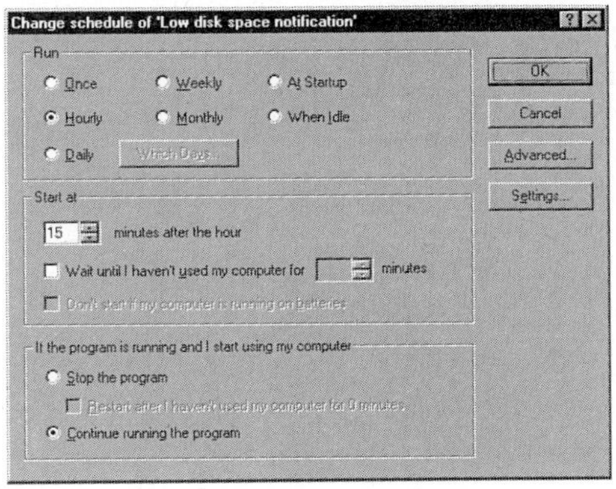

Fig. 43.2 System Agent's Change Schedule option.

The Change Schedule screen changes, depending on which Run frequency option you select. The Run frequency options to run the scheduled program are as follows:

- Once
- At Startup
- When Idle
- Hourly
- Daily
- Weekly
- Monthly

Click on one of the preceding options and then the Advanced button to configure when the low disk notification is to check whether one of

your disks is low on available disk space. If you click on Advanced with Hourly selected, for example, the Advanced Options dialog box appears, as shown in figure 43.3. This dialog box gives you several options to configure the time intervals to check for low disk space. The first group of settings is called Deadline. Deadline settings let you tell the computer what to do if the computer is busy at the time low disk space notification is supposed to run. In the example shown in figure 43.3, System Agent will keep trying to start the program until 15 minutes after the hour. This 15 minutes past the hour setting is the deadline.

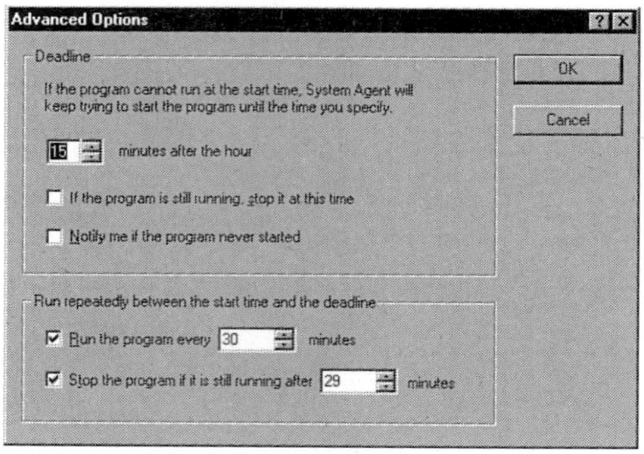

Fig. 43.3 The different Hourly Advanced options are shown here.

The idea in each case is the same. System Agent lets you choose when to start the program. If the program cannot start running in the background because your computer is in use, you choose a deadline time. This step creates a time window. The time window starts at the start time and ends at the deadline time. During this time, System Agent will try to run the program, and optionally notify you if it can't.

> **Note:** Programs scheduled to run At Startup or When Idle have no deadline options because they are not dependent on a set start time.

Changing the Settings

Although the Change Schedule dialog boxes and options are the same for any program scheduled by System Agent, the Settings dialog box shown in the preceding figures is tied tightly to the program being scheduled.

Keep working with the low disk space alarm. From the main System Agent screen, choose Program, Change Schedule, then choose Settings to display the Settings options shown in figure 43.4.

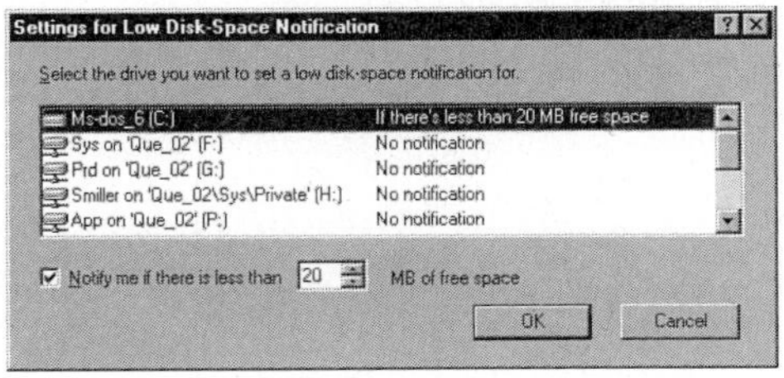

Fig. 43.4 System Agent's settings for low disk space notification.

The computer in use here has three disks eligible for examination by DISKALM.EXE. The local hard disk, drive C, is being examined, and the local CD-ROM, drive F, the compressed drive D, and host drive H are not. You can choose the amount of free disk space to set as a notification threshold in this dialog box.

Tip: Set the low disk space notification threshold to no lower than 10 percent of total capacity on each monitored drive, or twice the amount of RAM, whichever is greater. This step will avoid virtual memory errors.

Changing the Low Disk Space Notification

You have access to the Properties sheet from the System Agent main screen. Highlight Low disk space notification, and right-click. Next, choose Properties.

The Low disk space notification Properties sheet will appear. You'll be able to make some major changes here, but be careful because you can change the executable associated with the description Low disk space notification. You can also change the description itself if you wish. In this dialog box you can also choose to log the results of DISKALM.EXE to disk. If you do this, you'll find the results in the SAGELOG.TXT file in the C:\Program Files\Plus! folder. You'll want to log the results of DISKALM.EXE if you're having intermittent problems with low disk space on a computer that is often unattended. When you look at the log, you'll know when disk space became low, and this can serve as a clue to solving the problem.

From this dialog box, you also have access to the Change Schedule and Settings dialog boxes covered in the earlier sections. Figure 43.5 shows how it looks on-screen.

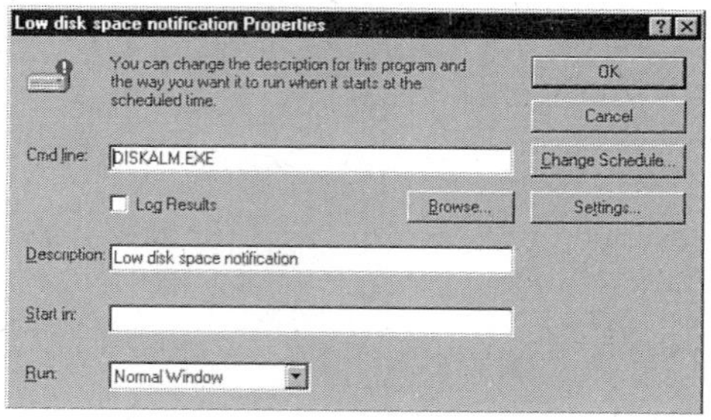

Fig. 43.5 Low disk space notification Properties.

Low Disk Space Notification Output

System Agent will run DISKALM.EXE in accordance with all the scheduling options and settings you've chosen. If disk space on the monitored drives is above the amount of free disk space you specify, no output will be written to the screen. The log file will be updated if you have *logging* enabled.

If disk space falls below your threshold setting, you'll see an alarm on-screen like the one shown in figure 43.6.

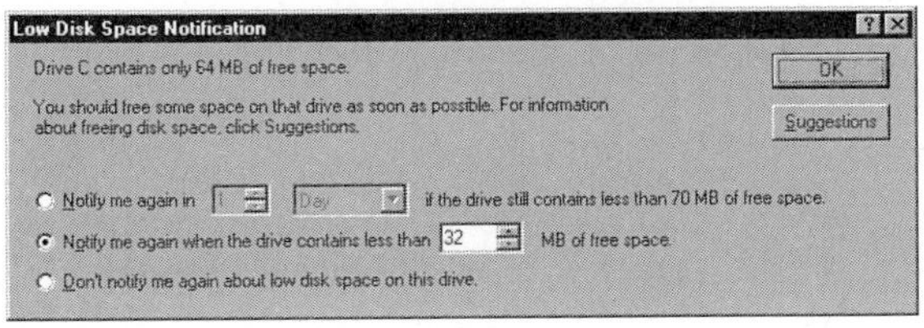

Fig. 43.6 The Low Disk Space Notification program alarm.

When disk space falls to a low level and the alarm is shown on-screen, you have five options to close the alarm dialog box. Figure 43.6 shows these options:

- Choose OK, which will not change DISKALM.EXE settings.
- Choose Notify me again in x days, which will change the scheduling options in System Agent.
- Choose Notify me again when the drive contains less, which will also change the scheduling options in System Agent.
- Choose Don't notify me again, which will disable the DISKALM.EXE program within System Agent.
- Choose Suggestions, which will open the Help Troubleshooter dialog box in figure 43.7.

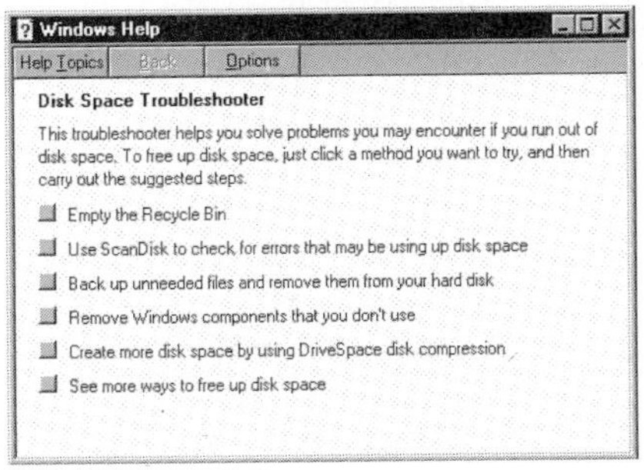

Fig. 43.7 Disk Space Troubleshooter.

Working with ScanDisk for Windows

ScanDisk is a perfect candidate for scheduled operation. This tool can alert you to problems forming on the disk before they become critical.

ScanDisk can be configured around two types of operation:

- Standard test
- Thorough test

ScanDisk in Standard Configuration

The Standard test checks only for logical disk problems. First it verifies VFAT integrity and then looks at folders. It checks folders for common disk errors such as lost file fragments, crosslinking, and invalid file names, dates, and times. These errors can occur if a program crashes, or if you turn off your computer without going through the proper shutdown process.

ScanDisk in Thorough Configuration

The Thorough ScanDisk test adds a physical test of the disk surface to the Standard test, and takes much longer to perform. In the physical test, ScanDisk checks each sector of the disk to verify that good data can be read from each sector. This check is also called a surface test.

Physical errors are usually caused by defects in the surface of the disk platter. All disks have some physical surface defects when they come from the factory. During the low-level format of the disk, these bad spots are identified and marked *bad*. When a spot on the disk surface is marked *bad*, the sector or sectors located on that spot are locked out of the file allocation table by the operating system. No data can be written to those bad sectors.

Some physical surface defects don't exist when the drive comes from the factory, but are created later. These are called grown defects. Physical defects can grow on your disk if the drive head touches the spinning platter while the disk is running. The contact between the head and spinning disk can damage the disk surface and cause a grown defect.

The Thorough ScanDisk will find these physical defects and mark the sectors involved as bad, so no data can be written to them. If there is data in the damaged sector, ScanDisk will attempt to move the data to an undamaged area of the disk; but, since the source area is damaged, you can expect data loss.

Because it takes so much longer to do a Thorough ScanDisk test, System Agent by default schedules the Thorough test to run at night, after the computer has been idle for almost an hour. System Agent expects the computer to continue being idle under those conditions long enough to complete the surface test.

> **Tip:** Whichever ScanDisk option you select, make sure you check the Automatically fix errors option shown in figure 43.8 or System Agent will not be able to operate unattended. Do this through the Change Schedule or Settings dialog boxes, or on ScanDisk's main screen.

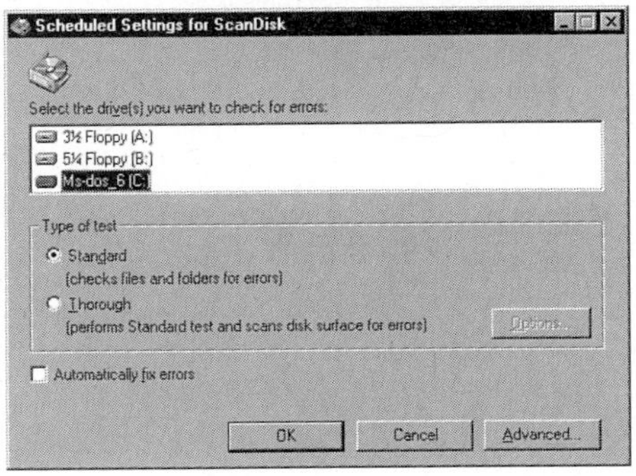

Fig. 43.8 The Scheduled Setting for ScanDisk for Windows dialog box.

Advanced ScanDisk Options

Chapter 10, "Optimizing Your Disk Drives," covers ScanDisk for Windows in a normal, stand-alone, unscheduled environment. With System Agent in control, it is important to remember that the system needs to be idle when ScanDisk executes. If there is other disk activity while ScanDisk is running it will have to start over again, which it will do automatically up to 10 times. After 10 restarts, ScanDisk will halt, which means that ScanDisk can't complete automatically as it is intended to under System Agent's scheduled operation.

It's important then, that no other processes (like the screen saver or defrag) are scheduled at the same time ScanDisk wants to run. There are advanced settings you can use to tell ScanDisk what to do when it comes across disk errors.

You can reach the ScanDisk Advanced Options from the main System Agent screen. Highlight ScanDisk for Windows, double-click to display Scheduled Settings for ScanDisk, choose Settings, and then, choose Advanced. Figure 43.9 shows you the choices you can make.

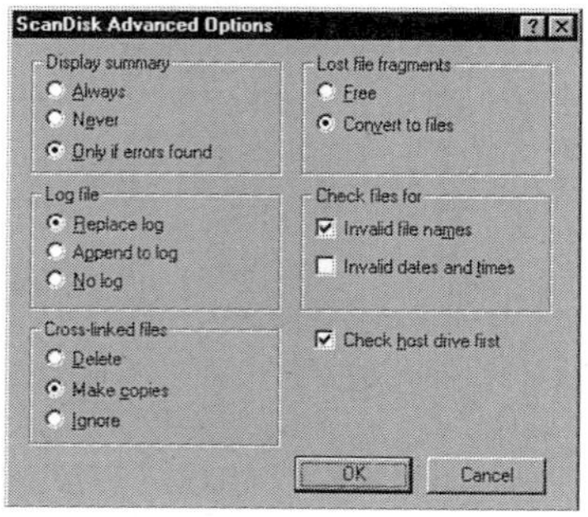

Fig. 43.9 The ScanDisk Advanced Options dialog box.

It's important to know that none of the advanced options will prevent ScanDisk from completing unattended, as long as you've chosen Automatically fix errors.

The advanced choices you make will affect how your disk looks after ScanDisk encounters errors, so you should know what they mean and what they do.

There are six groups of advanced options for ScanDisk.

- **Display summary.** The choices here are Always, Never, and Only if errors are found. Because System Agent is running ScanDisk in unattended mode, you'll probably want to select Never, so you won't have to manually close the summary display dialog box.

- **Log file.** You can choose to Replace log, Append to log, or No log. Choose Replace if you only want to keep results of the latest ScanDisk session in a file. Choose Append, and your log file will grow each time ScanDisk writes its results to the end of the log file. No log means that ScanDisk will not write a log of results. If you set enable logging in Advanced Options, ScanDisk will write a file in the root folder of your boot disk when it's finished running. The file name is SCANDISK.LOG. Figure 43.10 shows an example of this file.

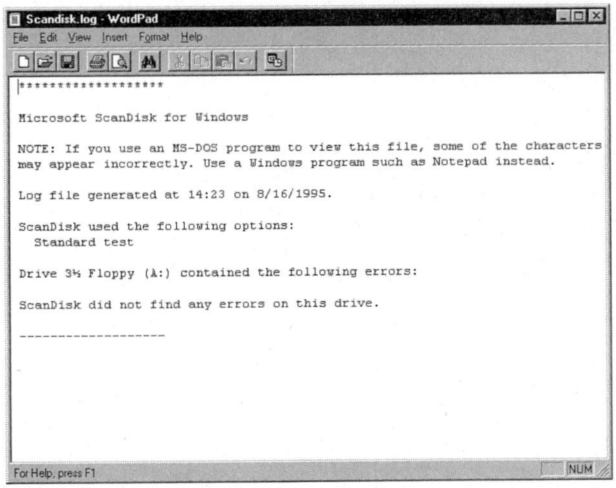

Fig. 43.10 An example of a typical ScanDisk log.

- **Cross-linked files.** If, due to an error, the operating system writes a file allocation table that says two or more different files occupy the same spot on the drive, the two or more files are said to be cross-linked. Cross-linked files cause problems for Windows, and constitute disk corruption. You can choose to Make copies of all

the cross-linked files and have ScanDisk store the copies in proper, separate locations. You can choose to have ScanDisk delete all the cross-linked files. Delete is a good bet, because files that are cross-linked are usually damaged. The Make copies option will probably make copies of damaged files that will do you no good. The only time you can benefit from Make copies is when the files cross-linked are text files. Then, you can recover some of the text. If the cross-linked files are binaries, or program files, any small error will make the file useless. That's why Delete is recommended. You should ignore the Ignore option, since leaving cross-linked files on your drive will lead to bigger disk problems.

- **Lost file fragments.** These are harmless errors. See the section "ScanDisk in Standard Configuration" for more information on lost file fragments. The best choice is to Free the disk space taken up by these lost fragments.
- You can, and should, check files for Invalid file names and Invalid dates and times. Letting ScanDisk correct any of these errors will help keep your disk tuned and in top shape.
- If your disk is compressed, you should Check host drive first. If there are errors on the compressed drive's host drive, they should be fixed on the host drive first. Fixing errors on the host may automatically correct errors on the compressed drive.

Working with Disk Defragmenter

The program described as Disk Defragmenter in System Agent is set by default to be DEFRAG.EXE. You can change the description as well as the program to be executed in the Program, Properties sheet in the main System Agent screen.

Continue looking at the default settings, and see how System Agent plans to schedule and run Disk Defragmenter.

Settings and Thresholds

Disk Defragmenter will run in different ways depending on its settings and threshold levels of fragmentation. You have the option, in standalone Defrag's settings dialog box, to choose from three modes of operation:

- Full defragmentation of both files and free space
- Defragment files only
- Consolidate free space only

The first option combines the functions of the second two. Choosing Defragment files only will ensure that all the files on the disk are contiguous but will leave small gaps of free space in between disk areas containing files. Choosing Consolidate free space only will close the gaps, making all the free space appear in one big section at the end of the drive, but will leave all files on this disk in whatever state of fragmentation they were previously. The Full option takes much longer to run than either of the other two.

When Disk Defragmenter runs in scheduled mode under the control of System Agent, another important option is added to Settings. You can choose the level of disk fragmentation necessary to cause Disk Defragmenter to run at all when scheduled. (See figure 43.11.)

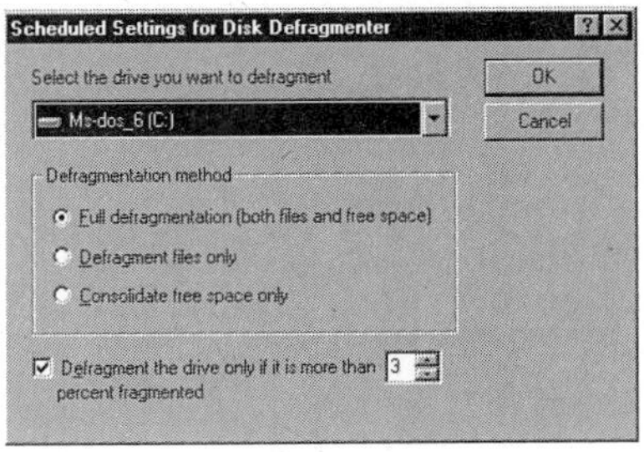

Fig. 43.11 The fragmentation threshold settings.

System Agent sets the fragmentation threshold to 3 percent by default. You'll want to adjust this percent depending on the type of work you do and the type and size of files you work with.

> **Tip:** If you commonly work with large files greater than 1M, set your fragmentation threshold to a lower level than the default, such as example 1 percent. This setting applies if you're installing and deinstalling large Windows applications, too.

The way Disk Defragmenter reads the level of fragmentation on a disk doesn't take into consideration the gaps between file areas. There can be many small free gaps in an otherwise defragmented disk. In this case, Disk Defragmenter will report that the disk is not fragmented and that Disk Defragmenter doesn't need to run. But this type of situation is a guarantee that future files written to the disk will in fact be fragmented, because Windows will try to write them in the small gaps, and will have to bridge those gaps with files larger than the gaps, writing the files into two or more nonsequential areas. This lack of intelligence is a limitation of the VFAT file system used in Windows 95.

This is exactly why you'll want to consider lowering the level of disk fragmentation needed to kick Disk Defragmenter into action.

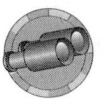

> **Note:** Running Disk Defragmenter in any mode other than Full defragmentation is really counterproductive. Although the other settings will complete faster, they leave gaps or fragmented files on the disk and thus are not useful. Running in those modes also guarantees that a full defragment will be needed more often than if you only run in Full mode.

Scheduling Options

All the standard System Agent scheduling options are active when scheduling Disk Defragmenter. The default setting is to run once daily after your computer has been idle for at least 10 minutes. You should pick a time when your computer will be on, but idle, for an extended time, to make Disk Defragmenter most useful. With modern hard drives of between 500M and 1G, allow at least 20 minutes for Disk Defragmenter to do a full defragmentation.

Interruptions and Restarts

Disk Defragmenter is very sensitive to other disk activity, just like ScanDisk for Windows. And like ScanDisk, if the disk state changes during operation, it will have to start over from the beginning. With all the things that can happen in the background affecting the disk, it's almost amazing that these types of programs can ever complete successfully. Everything from cache flushing to an incoming e-mail or fax can cause a running Disk Defragmenter session to have to restart.

This is taken into consideration in the scheduling dialog box. You should always schedule Disk Defragmenter to Continue running the program if the computer is used during its operation. Unlike ScanDisk, which will halt with a warning dialog after 10 restarts, Disk Defragmenter will start over an unlimited number of times until it is complete, while running in the background. This behavior ensures compatibility with a scheduler like System Agent.

Output and Logging

Unlike ScanDisk and Low Disk Space Notification, Disk Defragmenter creates no output, and writes no log. It doesn't even write to the SAGELOG.TXT file that the other programs record in.

The only way to see what Disk Defragmenter has done is to look in the main System Agent screen. You'll be able to see information on only the last run of the program. You'll see the last start time, the last end time, and whether the program completed successfully.

Working with System Agent Options

Until now you've looked at System Agent defaults, and worked with the default program installations. However, there are other options in the scheduling engine that you haven't worked with. These other options, which you'll cover in the next sections, are as follows:

- Running a scheduled program now
- Disabling a scheduled program
- Removing a scheduled program
- Suspending System Agent
- Stopping System Agent
- Scheduling a new program

Running a Scheduled Program Now

You can run any of the scheduled programs immediately. You might do this to get a quick handle on disk fragmentation levels or a quick look at free disk space on a local or network drive. To run the programs, select Program, Run Now from System Agent's main screen.

> **Caution:** Of the three default scheduled programs, only Low Disk Space Notification will operate on network drives. System Agent cannot ScanDisk or defragment a network drive.

Disabling a Scheduled Program

You can stop a scheduled program from running without shutting down all scheduled programs. To do so, highlight a program in System Agent, and choose Program, Disable. A check mark will appear in the drop-down menu next to Disable, and Disabled will appear in the Time Scheduled to Run column for that program. Figure 43.12 shows you what you can expect to see on-screen when you've disabled a scheduled program.

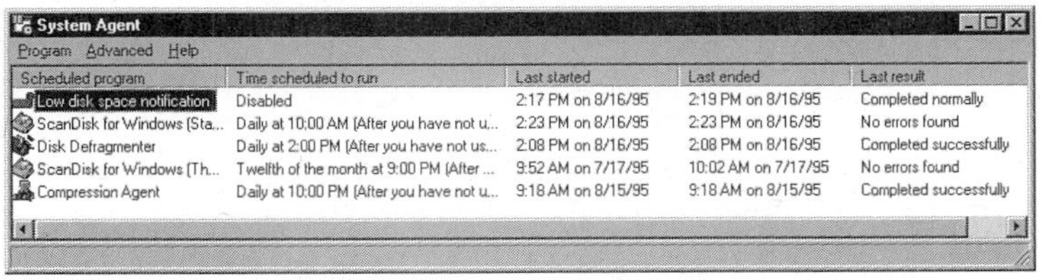

Fig. 43.12 The Disabled program display.

If you want to work with a scheduled program's settings, and if it is set to start running almost immediately, you can use Disable while you're adjusting the settings to prevent the program from running with the old parameters.

You'll notice that when a program is disabled, the Run Now option in the Program menu is grayed out.

Notice, though, that Disabled programs are reinstated with their last active settings, when you restart Windows.

Removing a Scheduled Program

Use the Remove a scheduled program option if you no longer want to schedule a certain program under System Agent control. To use this option from System Agent's main screen, highlight the program to be removed permanently, and choose Program, Remove. After a confirmation dialog box appears, choose Yes to delete the highlighted program from the list of scheduled programs. Of course, you can always add it back later as a new program.

Suspending System Agent

What if you temporarily want to stop all System Agent programs from running? You won't want to disable them individually because it's easier to suspend System Agent entirely for the amount of time you choose. This length of time is not programmable; it's handled by you manually.

Because the System Agent icon in the system tray is not active when right-clicked, you'll have to take this step, too. To do so, access System Agent's main screen, and choose Advanced, Suspend System Agent.

None of your scheduled programs will run at its scheduled time.

The System Agent icon in the system tray will appear with a large red X through it, indicating that it is disabled. However, the SAGE.EXE engine will remain loaded in memory.

Stopping System Agent

Stopping System Agent prevents the SAGE.EXE engine from loading when you start Windows 95. Of course, none of your scheduled programs will run. In fact, you won't have any scheduled programs any more.

Although stopping System Agent may have some minimal effect on the system performance by freeing up monitoring clock cycles, its effect on memory and system resources is negligible.

Scheduling a New Program

This option is found through System Agent's main screen, under Program, Schedule a new program. This is the way you'll schedule a program to run automatically under control of System Agent. The real question is what kind of programs are useful when run in scheduled mode, beside the three default programs that are pre-installed?

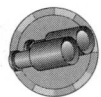

> **Note:** Compression Agent, which is covered in Chapter 44, is also installed by default into System Agent when you choose to install DriveSpace 3 disk compression.

Backup Programs

Besides disk analysis and defragmenting, the function that most benefits from automatic scheduling is tape backup. You know that only certain types of programs really lend themselves to scheduling. These programs, such as ScanDisk for Windows, Low Disk Space Notification, and Disk Defragmenter, have hooks to settings that can be controlled by System Agent. These settings make it possible to have the programs' complete operation completely unattended.

Microsoft Backup comes bundled with Windows 95. Although Backup is not designed to run completely unattended, it can be scheduled by System Agent and you may find it useful, if your tape capacity is as large as your disk capacity. Of course, floppy backup will not be useful in unattended mode without a robotic floppy swapper, which is not bundled with the operating system.

Communications Programs

You may have a communications program that logs on to an online service and downloads information for you. Many such programs have built-in automatic scheduling features. Some, however, do not, and may be suitable for scheduling with System Agent.

System Agent and Portable Computers

System Agent operates differently when it's installed onto a computer that can be battery powered. Because any program running unattended can deplete batteries quickly, and disk intensive programs like Disk Defragmenter and ScanDisk for Windows especially so, System Agent includes an option named Don't start if my computer is running on batteries.

If you're using a desktop machine, or running your portable computer on AC power, that option will be grayed out as it is in figure 43.13.

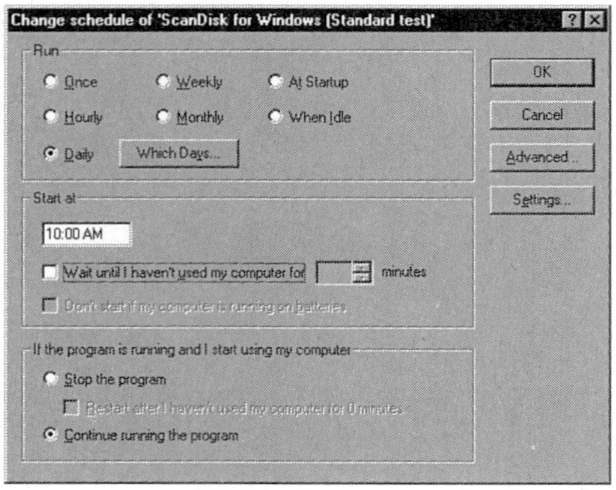

Fig. 43.13 The portable computer option.

You'll have this option for any scheduled program in System Agent on a computer that can sometimes be powered by batteries.

Chapter 44

DriveSpace 3 and Compression Agent

by Gordon Meltzer

Compression Agent acts as an intelligent assistant to help you with compressed disk drives. Microsoft Plus! includes a new type of drive-compression program, DriveSpace 3. Once you've installed DriveSpace 3 and used it to compress your hard drive, Compression Agent works in the background to ensure that your compressed drive is always in its most efficient state of compression. This way, Compression Agent makes sure that you can fit as much information as possible on your drive. You won't have to perform analyses of your compression ratios and make adjustments to optimize your drive's compression. Compression Agent does it automatically for you in the background.

In this chapter, you learn how to

- Install DriveSpace 3 and Compression Agent

- Compress your disk drives to gain more free space
- Configure Compression Agent to keep your compressed drive in optimum condition

Understanding Drive Compression Compromises

Disk-drive compression technologies have been in use for several years. Several software publishers have tried their hand at writing useful disk-compression software. Microsoft includes a simple form of drive compression in Windows, called DriveSpace. In the past, disk compression always involved compromises. One compromise involved system speed, when using disk compression. As free disk space was gained by compressing data into a smaller space on the drive, system speed decreased because the CPU spent time compressing and decompressing data, instead of spending time running applications. Another compromise involved inefficient use of free space on the disk. In previous disk-compression technologies, if you wanted to compress a cluster that was larger than the available contiguous sectors, the cluster could not be compressed. Finally, earlier forms of disk compression limited a compressed disk to 512M.

DriveSpace 3, included in Microsoft Plus!, remedies some of the performance compromises earlier types of disk compression required.

Features of DriveSpace 3

DriveSpace 3 works in a multistep process. First, DriveSpace 3 creates a host disk drive that is, by default, mnemonically called drive H. (If drive H is already in use on your system, Windows will choose the next available drive letter, after H).Then DriveSpace 3 compresses all the data on your hard-disk drive C into one large compressed file on the host drive. Next, DriveSpace 3 swaps and interprets the large compressed file into uncompressed files as needed, and they appear as regular uncompressed files on drive C. When a file that has been uncompressed from the host drive for use as a regular file on drive C is no longer needed by an application program, it's stored in compressed form again. See Chapter 10, "Optimizing Your Disk Drives," for more information on drive compression software.

> **Note:** *Host drive* is a term used in connection with drive compression software. A host drive is an uncompressed disk drive that contains a compressed volume file (CVF). This large file appears to the user as a compressed drive. In fact, it is a single file on the host drive.

You can select whether the host drive should be visible or hidden during the DriveSpace 3 setup process. Typically, if there will be usable space left on the host drive after disk compression takes place, you'd choose to keep the host drive visible. If all free space on the host drive is used up during compression, you'd want to make the host drive invisible. You can also choose to hide or unhide the host drive at any time, as you'll see in the following sections.

DriveSpace 3 works with floppy drives, too.

The following section discusses how DriveSpace 3 has features that make drive compression work quickly and efficiently. It also explains some of the features that make it easier for you to work with your compressed drives.

DriveSpace 3 Performance Features

When you use DriveSpace 3 compression, your data is stored on your drive, compressed, with the following properties and features:

- Data can be stored in noncontiguous sectors with DriveSpace 3. This is an improvement over DriveSpace. DriveSpace requires a compressed cluster to be stored in contiguous sectors. If the drive is fragmented, there may not be enough contiguous sectors to hold a cluster. With the older DriveSpace, a cluster can take 16 sectors. With DriveSpace 3 however, a cluster can be split into whatever free sectors are available, and DriveSpace 3 keeps a list of where the data is stored. This list operates like a mini file allocation table and is responsible for DriveSpace 3's ability to store more data on the disk than its predecessor.

Note: A sector in Windows is always 512 bytes. Clusters vary in size depending on the drive's size. The larger the drive, the larger the cluster size. In uncompressed drives 512M or over, the cluster size is 8K. This means any file, even a one-byte file, takes 8K on the disk, leading to wasted slack space. DriveSpace 3 uses the slack space to store files, increasing efficiency.

- DriveSpace 3 stores data on your drive in 32K blocks. The earlier form of DriveSpace used only 8K blocks. 32K blocks are more efficiently stored on your drive, and mean higher compression ratios, and higher compression ratios mean that more data can be compressed into the same disk space.
- DriveSpace 3 uses two new different compression formats. This means that data can be compressed to two different levels of compression, at your option. The two levels are called HiPack and UltraPack. You'll learn more about both of these compression formats and how to work with them in "Working with Compression Agent" later in this chapter.
- DriveSpace 3 can create compressed drives up to 2G in size. This is a fourfold improvement over previous versions of DriveSpace.
- DriveSpace 3 runs faster than earlier versions of DriveSpace on computers with a Pentium processor. DriveSpace 3 is one of the first Pentium-optimized programs available to computer users. Microsoft claims speed gains of up to 20% for DriveSpace 3 compared to standard Windows 95 DriveSpace on Pentium machines.

DriveSpace 3 Convenience Features

When you want to work with your compressed drives, DriveSpace 3 makes it easy with the following features:

- Each drive's Properties sheet includes compression statistics.
- When you've installed DriveSpace 3, you can compress uncompressed drives directly from their Property sheets.
- You have the option of working with an individual drive with its Property sheet or with all drives on the system using the DriveSpace 3 program.

Installing DriveSpace 3

To get started with DriveSpace 3 and Compression Agent, insert the Microsoft Plus! CD-ROM or installation disk. Then run the Setup program on the Microsoft Plus! CD-ROM or disk.

> **Caution:** If you are using Banyan Vines 5.5x or earlier as your network software, do not install DriveSpace 3. DriveSpace 3 and Vines both need large amounts of memory below 640K and cannot coexist. Contact Banyan for an updated Vines version that is compatible with DriveSpace 3.

You can choose either a Typical or Custom installation of Microsoft Plus! If you choose the Typical installation, DriveSpace 3 and Compression Agent are installed for you. If you choose the Custom installation, you'll have to make sure that DriveSpace 3 is checked in the Custom dialog box (see figure 44.1).

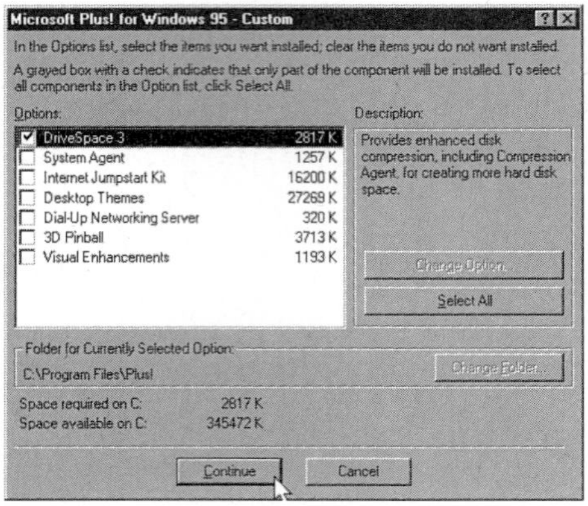

Fig. 44.1 Microsoft Plus! custom installation must include DriveSpace 3 to compress drives and work with Compression Agent.

After you've checked the DriveSpace 3 box in your custom installation, choose Continue. When Microsoft Plus! Setup has installed DriveSpace 3, Compression Agent will automatically be installed for you. Then Setup needs to restart your computer. When your computer restarts, Setup is finished, and you are ready to compress your drives. Setup will update the Start menu and add shortcuts to help you work with the compressed drives, as you'll see next.

Configuring DriveSpace 3

To get started working with compressed drives, choose a drive to compress. Or if you already have a drive that has been compressed with DriveSpace, choose a drive to compress with DriveSpace 3.

Running DriveSpace 3 on an Uncompressed Drive

To start Drivespace 3, follow these steps:

1. Open the Start menu and choose Programs, Accessories, System Tools, DriveSpace.
2. Choose a drive to compress by clicking on it in the DriveSpace 3 dialog box. The click will highlight the drive (see figure 44.2).
3. Choose Drive, Compress.
4. The Compress a Drive dialog box appears showing the amount free space and used space before and after compression (see figure 44.3). Choose Start.
5. The Are You Sure? dialog box gives you a chance to Cancel, Back Up Files using Microsoft Backup, or Compress Now (see figure 44.4). Choose Compress Now to continue. Before you do, you should perform the backup offered as a choice, for safety's sake. The tool you will be given to perform the backup is the Windows 95 accessory, Microsoft Backup.
6. The Compression Options dialog box appears to confirm the compression procedure. Choose Yes to proceed with DriveSpace 3 compression. Compression may take a very long time. You may measure the time in tens of hours, if you have a large drive and a slow system.

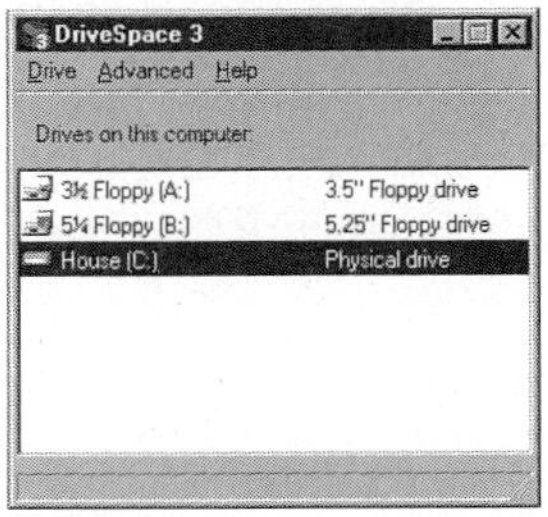

Fig. 44.2 The main DriveSpace 3 window where compression operations can be performed.

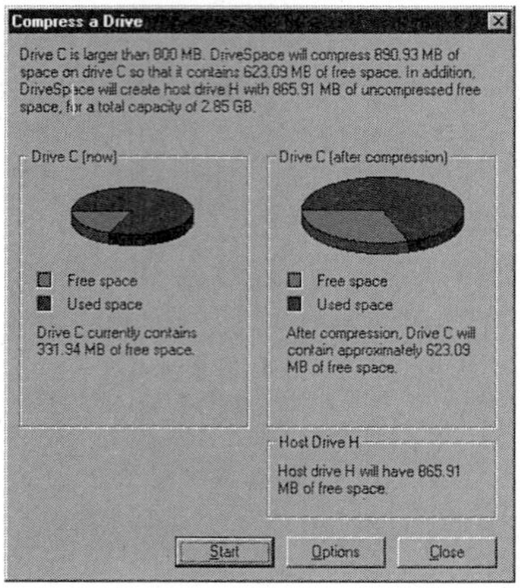

Fig. 44.3 The Compress a Drive dialog box shows before and after space estimates for your drive.

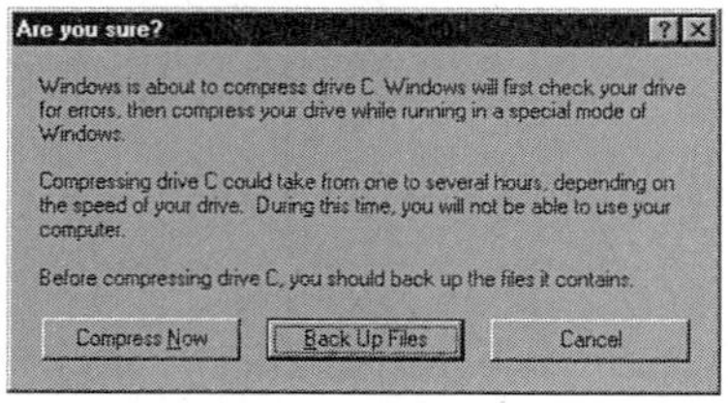

Fig. 44.4 The Are you sure? dialog box offers you a chance to back up your drive before compression.

When working with a disk drive under 800M, there are only 2M of uncompressed space left on drive H. In that case, you'll probably want to use the Compression Options dialog box in step 4 to Hide drive H. Hiding the nearly unusable 2M host drive H makes for simpler, cleaner displays for browsing in Explorer, My Computer, any dialog box, and any window. The 2M disk space is unusable because it is too small. If you use it, you will likely run out of space in the middle of a disk operation and lose data.

After DriveSpace 3 has finished compressing your hard drive, you will have to reboot your system. When your system reboots, the compression operation is finished, and you can examine the space gained by compressing your drive.

DriveSpace 3 Compression Information Screens

After DriveSpace 3 is implemented, it is easy to find out how much free space was gained. This information is gathered the same way for any drive you compress. For the rest of this chapter, you examine a system's C drive. Start My Computer, right-click on the icon for your C drive, and choose Properties. The C drive's Properties sheet appears. Choose the Compression tab (see figure 44.5).

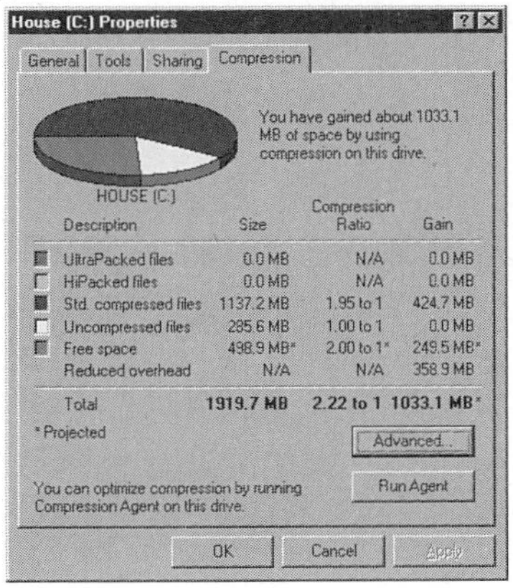

Fig. 44.5 The Compression page shows the results of DriveSpace 3 compression.

The pie chart in figure 44.5 shows how much free space you have on your drive after compression. In drive C, there were 332M free before compression. Now there are 498.9M free on drive C. There were 1137.2M of files on drive C before compression. These files have been compressed and now use only 424.7M of space, which is a compression ratio of 1.95 to 1.

In this page there is a Total row, and the text claims that you gained 1033.1M by compressing the drive. However, there are only 498.9M free on drive C, a gain of only about 150M from the starting free space of 332M. How does DriveSpace 3 claim a projected gain of 1033.1M?

To understand this, you have to look at drive C and the newly created host drive H. When you examine both drives together, the answer is clear. Right-click drive H's icon and choose Properties. Choose the Compression tab (see figure 44.6).

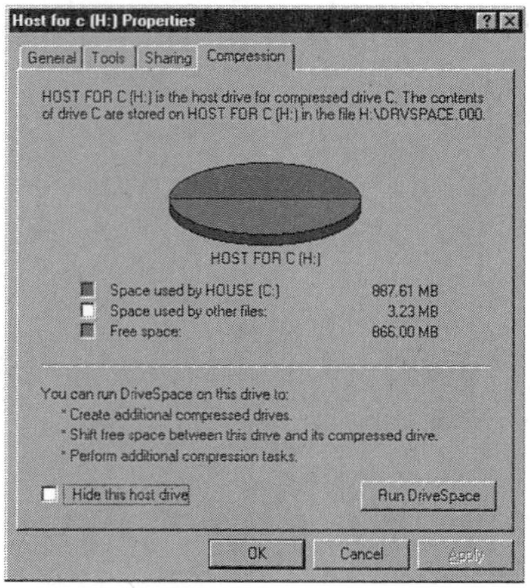

Fig. 44.6 Adding free space on drive C and on drive H shows the true free space on the physical disk drive that has just been compressed.

Figure 44.6 gives you very good information. Look at the information presented next to understand how DriveSpace 3 chooses projected space gain numbers.

- The contents of drive C are stored on the drive H, in a compressed file called DRVSPACE.000.
- Drive C uses only 887.61M of space.
- The free space on drive H is 866M. This space is not compressed and is fully available for your use.

When you look at the whole picture of drives C and H, the following facts show the value of DriveSpace 3.

The physical disk in question is 1800M.

Before compression, there were 1,137M of files. There were 332M free. Those figures only add up to 1,469M. The drive holds 1,800M. What happened to the other 331M that you'd expect the drive to hold? The answer is that the 331M is lost as slack space in the area holding files. That means there were 331M of wasted, slack space because of the use of 8K clusters in disks over 512M in size.

After compression, there are 500M free on drive C and 886M free on drive H. The total free space is now 1366M—hence, the explanation of the 1033M gain of free space.

Now that you've seen basic DriveSpace 3 compression at work on a real-world disk drive, you learn how DriveSpace 3 can get even more usable space from your drive using HiPack and UltraPack file formats. You also learn how Compression Agent squeezes more free room from your drive.

Notice the legend for the pie chart in figure 44.6 includes UltraPacked and HiPacked files, but no files of these types appear in the chart itself. This is because so far, DriveSpace 3 has only created Standard compressed files. DriveSpace 3 and Compression Agent can further optimize the drive, as you see in "Working with DriveSpace 3" and "Working with Compression Agent" later in this chapter.

Running DriveSpace 3 on a Drive Compressed with DriveSpace

When you run DriveSpace 3 on a drive that has already been compressed with an earlier version of DriveSpace, you perform an upgrade installation of DriveSpace 3.

To perform the upgrade, open the Start menu and Programs, Accessories, System Tools, DriveSpace 3. When the program starts, highlight the drive you want to compress with DriveSpace 3. Then choose Drive, Upgrade.

From here, the installation proceeds as if you were compressing an uncompressed drive in the previous section.

Adjusting DriveSpace 3's Settings

When you have created a compressed drive, you can manually make the following adjustments to its configuration:

- The amount of free space—balancing the available free space between your C and H drives.
- The estimated compression ratio.
- The compression method—using HiPack compression to generate more free disk space. (This method is only recommended for Pentium computers because on 386 and 486 computers HiPack compression is too slow to be useful.)

Adjusting Free Space

Compressing a disk drive certainly complicates the way drive statistics are presented to you. After compression, there are two drives where formerly one existed. You have to deal with free space on both of them. You should understand the relationship between the free space on both drives C and H.

The free space on drive H can be used for three purposes:

- File storage
- To create another empty compressed drive
- To allow drive C to grow and have more free space

The unused, free space on drive H can be used to resize drive C and make more free space available on drive C. Windows provides a set of graphical tools that make it easy to divide the free space between drives H and C.

From the main DriveSpace 3 program window, highlight compressed drive C, then choose Drive, Adjust Free Space. You see the Adjust Free Space dialog box (see figure 44.7).

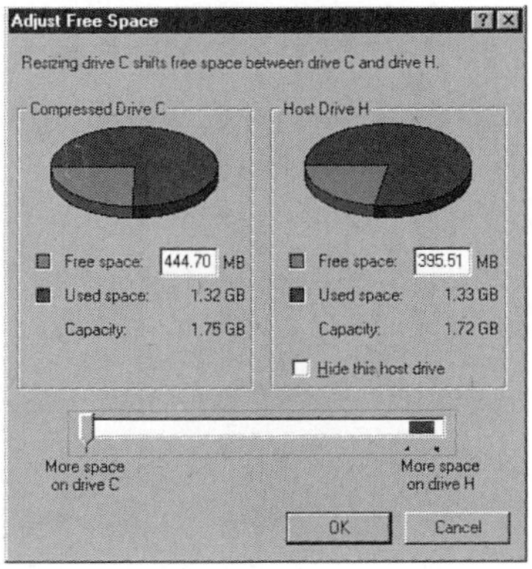

Fig. 44.7 Use the Adjust Free Space dialog box to divide the free space on your disk between drives H and C.

The settings shown in figure 44.7 are only one possible choice. Using the slider, you can divide the free space on your disk. At the left end of the slider, you can create the most free space possible on drive C. At the right end of the slider, you can give all the free space to drive H (see figure 44.8).

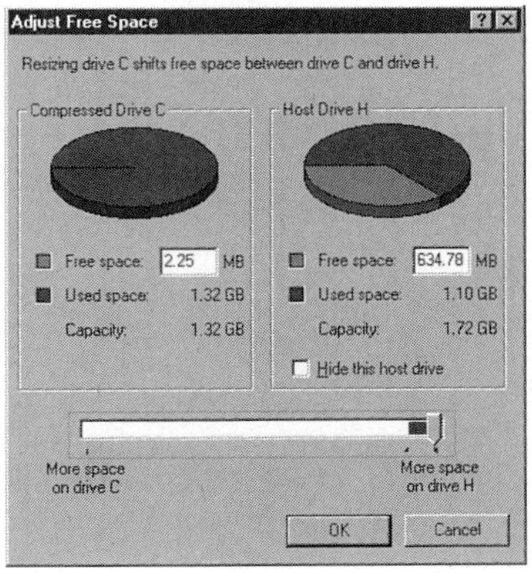

Fig. 44.8 All the free space has been given to drive H.

Notice with all free space given to drive H there is almost no space available on compressed drive C. This setting may not be very useful, so you may want to choose a balanced setting by dragging the slider to somewhere near the middle of the two drives.

A balanced setting allows drive C to continue operating normally, with enough free space to fill your immediate needs. With the slider set near the middle, you have more than 400M available on drive H. What can be done with those free megabytes? Before answering that question, choose OK to adjust the free space to the balanced setting somewhere near the middle.

Creating an Empty Compressed Drive

If you have space on your host drive left over after compression, you can compress this left-over space to form a new, empty, compressed drive that will hold much more than the left-over space would hold.

I said earlier that the free space on drive H can be used to create an empty, compressed drive. When you do this, you turn the more than 400M in the example drive into much more free space.

From the DriveSpace 3 window, highlight the drive H. Then choose Advanced, Create Empty.

You can take 485M of free space from drive H and create a new compressed drive D (pick any free drive letter). Based on the average, default compression ratio of 2:1 used for estimates by DriveSpace 3, the new, empty, compressed drive D contains 969M of free space.

Figure 44.9 shows the Create a New Compressed Drive dialog box. In this dialog box, you can choose the name for the new drive using the Create a New Drive Named drop-down list to choose any available drive letter.

You can also choose how much of the free space on the host drive to use for your new, empty, compressed drive by changing the space shown in the Using text box.

Tip: Don't use so much space on the host drive it runs out of space entirely.

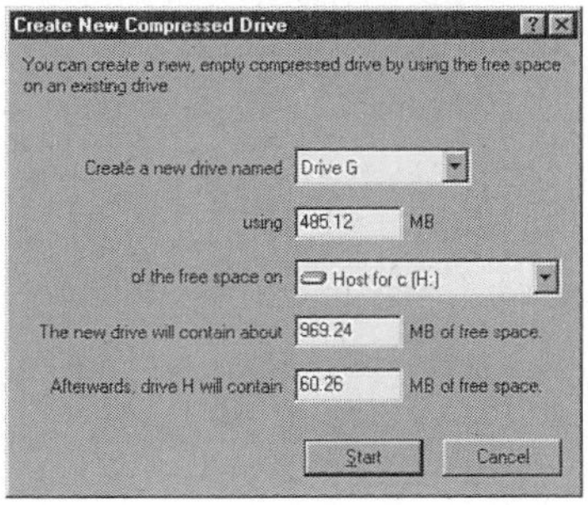

Fig. 44.9 You can create a new compressed drive from the free space on the drive H.

When you're ready to create a new, empty, compressed drive, choose Start. The host drive is checked for errors, and if any are found they will be fixed automatically if possible. Then the new compressed drive is created.

After the drive is created, double-click it in the DriveSpace 3 window, and you see your new drive's Properties sheet (see figure 44.10).

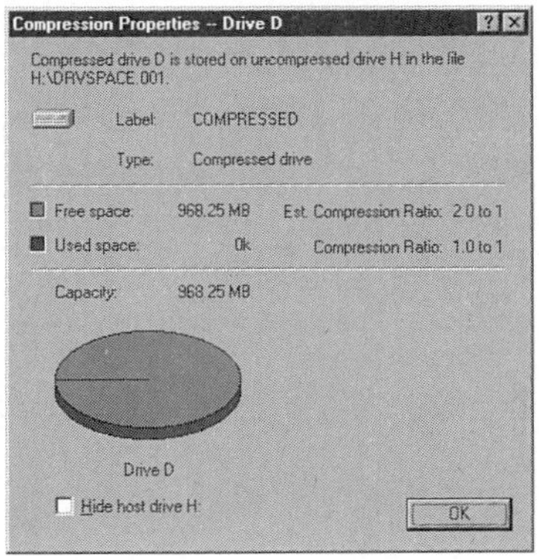

Fig. 44.10 You can see the compression properties of your new, empty, compressed drive.

Drive D, like drive C , is stored on drive H, and all the drive D files are compressed into the DRVSPACE.001 file.

Choosing the Type of Compression

When DriveSpace 3 created your compressed drive C, it used the Standard compression file format. DriveSpace 3 can instead compress your files using the HiPack format. HiPack compression improves the speed at which your files are compressed and decompressed by using an improved lookup algorithm.

From the DriveSpace 3 window, choose Advanced, Settings. The Disk Compression Settings dialog box tells you that your files are compressed in the Standard format. If you have a Pentium microprocessor, you may want to use the Pentium-optimized code used for HiPack compression. To compress your files with HiPack, choose HiPack compression and then choose OK.

Working with Compression Agent

Compression Agent works in the background to ensure that your compressed drive is always in its most efficient state of compression. You won't have to perform analyses of your compression ratios and make adjustments to optimize your drive's compression.

Now that you have DriveSpace 3 installed and configured, you can use Compression Agent to gain more free space and make the files on your drives compress more efficiently. Using Compression Agent speeds up uncompressing files for use by applications.

To start Compression Agent, open the Start menu and choose Programs, Accessories, System Tools, Compression Agent.

When Compression Agent first starts, it asks you which compressed drive you want to work with. In this example, we'll continue with drive C. Next, you'll see the Compression Agent dialog box, and you'll have to make some choices before Compression Agent goes to work (see figure 44.11).

Choose the Settings button in the Compression Agent dialog box. Compression Agent lets you UltraPack your files. The UltraPack format gives the best compression, but your system accesses UltraPacked files more slowly than Standard compressed files.

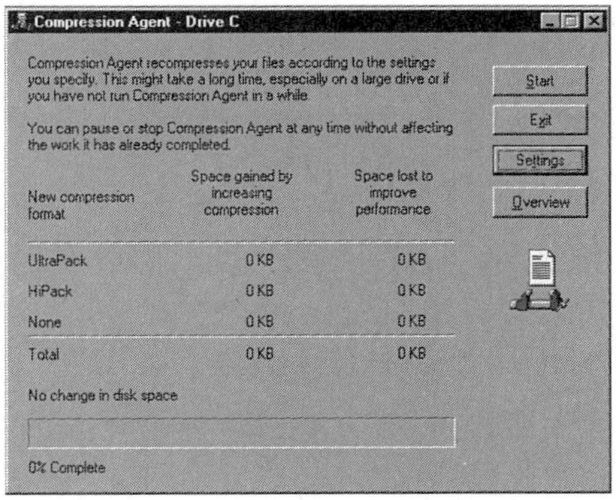

Fig. 44.11 Compression Agent is ready to run for the first time.

You can choose to UltraPack none or all of your files, or you can choose the default, which uses UltraPack on all files not accessed within the last 30 days. If you choose the default method, you can change the threshold value, from 1 to 999 days.

To choose the default, mark the UltraPack Only Files Not Used Within the Last 30 Days check box. To choose not to use UltraPack at all, mark the Do Not UltraPack Any Files check box. To UltraPack everything, mark the UltraPack All Files check box.

If you choose not to UltraPack anything or to UltraPack files based on date of last use, you have to decide how and if to compress the rest of your files that are not set to be UltraPacked.

You can choose to HiPack the rest of your files or leave them uncompressed. To HiPack the rest of your files, mark the Yes check box. To leave the rest of your files uncompressed, mark the No, Store Them Uncompressed check box.

> **Note:** When you use Compression Agent on your compressed disk, the Standard compression format is no longer used. You can choose no compression, HiPack compression, or UltraPack compression.
>
> Remember, HiPack compression works best on Pentium computers.

Compression Agent Exceptions

In working with the Compression Agent Settings in the last section, you chose what compression method to use for certain groups of files. You can also choose how to compress particular files, folders, or types of files. The files and folders handled outside the rules set by Compression Agent Settings are called exceptions. To begin working with exceptions, choose the Exceptions button on the Compression Agent dialog box. Then on the Exceptions dialog box, choose Add. You'll see the Add Exceptions dialog box (see figure 44.12).

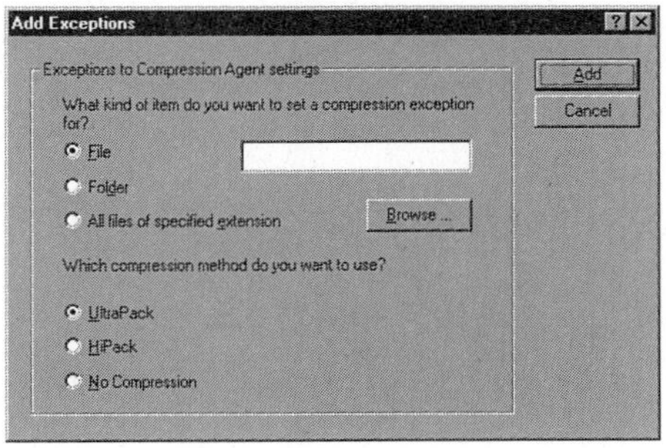

Fig. 44.12 Use the Add Exceptions dialog box to choose files to compress with special rules.

To choose a file as a compression exception, mark the File option button and enter the file name in the text box. You can also browse for the file you want with the Browse button. Next, choose how you want to compress the file. You can choose from UltraPack, HiPack, or No Compression. When you've chosen the file name and compression method, choose Add.

1. Choose either a file, folder, or file extension to compress. You can browse for a file name using the Browse button.
2. Choose the type of compression you want: UltraPack, HiPack, or No Compression.
3. Choose Add. Continue adding as many exceptions as you want. When you are finished adding exceptions, choose OK.

> **Tip:** To maximize system speed, choose all EXE and DLL files as exceptions and specify No Compression for them.

Advanced Compression Agent Settings

You may have told Compression Agent to use settings that reduce the free space on your drive. When you started Compression Agent for the first time, all your files were compressed using the Standard format. If you told Compression Agent that you didn't want to HiPack the rest of your files in "Working with Compression Agent," they were stored uncompressed. To do this, they are uncompressed by Compression Agent. This reduces the space available on drive C. To make sure you don't run out of disk space on drive C because you told Compression Agent to uncompress some files, choose the Advanced button from the Compression Agent Settings dialog box, which displays the Advanced Settings dialog box (see figure 44.13).

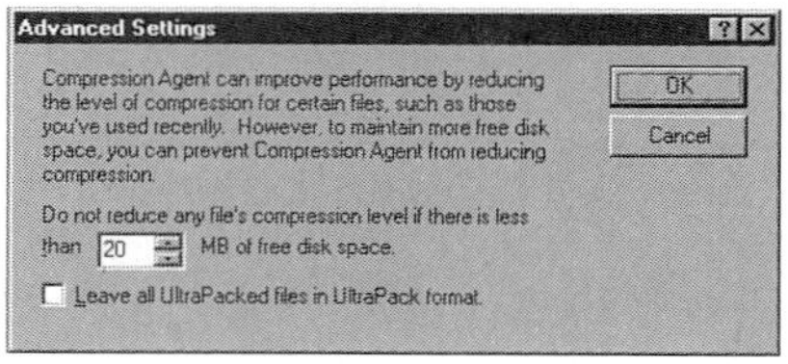

Fig. 44.13 The Advanced Settings dialog box prevents you from running out of space.

In its default, Advanced Settings does not uncompress any files if there are less than 20M free on the drive. You can change this value by entering the threshold megabyte size in the scroll box. Then, choose OK. If you want to leave all UltraPack files in UltraPack format regardless of how long it has been since they were accessed, check the Leave All UltraPacked Files in UltraPack Format check box.

When you've finished working with Compression Agent Settings, choose OK.

Running Compression Agent for the First Time

When you've configured Compression Agent settings, you'll be back at the Compression Agent dialog box seen in figure 44.11. Now, choose Start to have Compression Agent recompress your drive to match the settings you've chosen.

The recompression may take a long time. You may stop Compression Agent anytime. When you restart it, Compression Agent picks up right where it left off. No work is lost by stopping or pausing Compression Agent.

When Compression Agent has finished running, you see a report telling you how much space was gained through HiPack and UltraPack and how much space was lost because of the files you expanded.

Scheduling Compression Agent

The most useful way to use Compression Agent is to run it at a time you're not using your computer. To do this, you use System Agent and schedule Compression Agent to run at a time that is most convenient. The most convenient time may be at your lunch or late at night. System Agent gives you the flexibility to choose when, and how often, to run Compression Agent. The more frequently you run Compression Agent, the less time it takes to do its job. To learn how to schedule Compression Agent with System Agent, see Chapter 43, "System Agent."

Understanding DriveSpace 3's Memory Requirements

DriveSpace 3 uses about 150K of memory below 640K. The 150K is used by the DriveSpace 3 device driver and once you install DriveSpace 3 there is no way to eliminate this memory use. While this is not a problem for Windows applications and should not be a problem for

DOS applications running in a window or full-screen under Windows 95, it can be a problem when you run programs in MS-DOS mode. For information on MS-DOS mode, see Chapter 19, "Fine-Tuning Windows 95 for Your DOS Applications."

If you are running DOS applications or games that need over 500K of memory, and you are running them in MS-DOS mode, you may have a problem using DriveSpace 3. To work around this, set up your CONFIG.SYS file using HIMEM.SYS and EMM386.SYS. Also, set DOS=UMB and DOS=HIGH. Then use MEMMAKER.EXE to load as many of your startup files into the UMB area as possible. This may free up enough conventional memory so that your DOS application or game runs. Optimizing memory with MEMMAKER.EXE does not affect system performance under Windows 95.

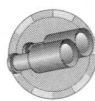

Note: If you installed Windows 95 as a stand-alone product rather than an upgrade to DOS and Windows 3.x, your system might lack a copy of MEMMAKER.EXE. If so, you must manually load the DriveSpace 3 compression driver in high memory. You do so in your CONFIG.SYS file, which is in the root directory of your boot disk.

```
Insert the following three lines in your
CONFIG.SYS file:

DEVICE=C: \WINDOWS\HIMEM.SYS

DEVICE=C:\WINDOWS\EMM386.EXE RAM NOEMS

DEVICEHIGH=C:\WINDOWS\COMMAND\DRVSPACE>SYS /MOVE

When you reboot your system, you'll be loading 113K
compression driver into high memory, which will allow DOS
programs that are memory hungry to run properly.
```

Desktop Additions

by Gordon Meltzer

Microsoft Plus! is a collection of utility groups. Not all the programs in Microsoft Plus! are productivity oriented. Some are just for fun, and to make using your computer a more relaxed experience. The Desktop Additions group of utilities contains programs to make Windows more fun to use by making it more visually attractive, and it also contains a great game, 3D Pinball. This game, besides being fun to play, is a programming tour-de-force. If Windows 95 is the family car, Desktop Additions make it look like the newest creation from the Ferrari factory.

The Desktop Additions group of utilities consists of separate programs in three groups: Desktop themes, 3D Pinball Game, and Visual Enhancements.

In this chapter, you cover the following:

- Visual enhancements Microsoft Plus! gives your system's desktop
- Various desktop themes in Microsoft Plus!
- Microsoft Plus! 3D Pinball

Installing Desktop Additions

To get started working with the desktop additions, install Microsoft Plus!. To do this, insert your Microsoft Plus! CD-ROM or setup disk, and run the Setup program for Plus!. Choose Custom Setup when prompted, and you will see a dialog box with an options list similar to the one shown in figure 45.1. Place check marks beside the boxes titled Desktop Themes, 3D Pinball, and Visual Enhancements. Then choose Continue.

After Setup checks for enough free disk space to install the options you have chosen, Desktop Additions will be installed. Finally, Setup will ask you to restart your computer. When you restart, installation of Desktop Additions will be complete.

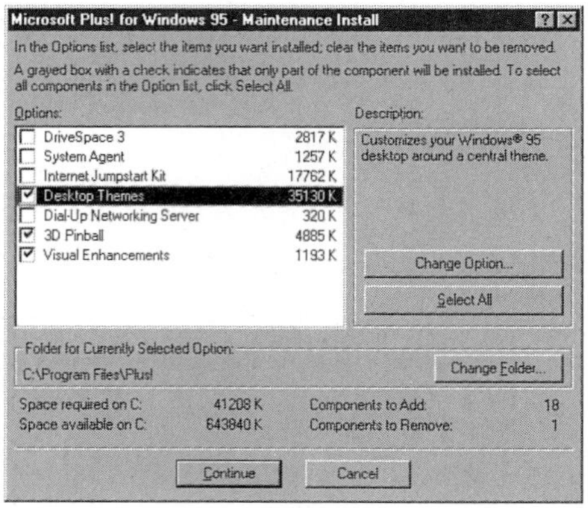

Fig. 45.1 Check these three items in Plus! custom setup to install Desktop Additions.

The disk space requirements for Desktop Additions are pretty extensive. Desktop Themes, if all themes are installed, uses 35M of disk space. 3D Pinball uses 4.5M, and the Visual Enhancements, if all are installed, uses about 1M.

The best approach to take in determining which of these modules to install is to install them all, if you have the space. Then, read the sections that follow, explaining Themes and Visual Enhancements. Get

an understanding of what each theme does, and learn whether you can use each theme on your system. Next, experiment on your system. Try the Themes and Enhancements. It is easy to delete the ones you do not want, to reclaim lots of disk space.

If you decide to delete one of the Plus! modules, use the Control Panel. Then, choose Add/Remove Programs. Highlight Microsoft Plus! in the list of installed programs, and choose Add/Remove. When the Plus! setup dialog appears, choose Add/Remove. Put a check next to any modules you want to remove, and choose OK.

Visual Enhancements

The first thing you will notice after the installation of Desktop Additions is complete is the Visual Enhancements. As you begin to use your computer, your desktop and windows operate a bit differently and you will have access to new features that you will learn about in the next sections.

Full-Window Drag

Normally, when you move a window on your screen to a new position, the process works like this:

1. You choose a window to which you want to relocate.
2. You click the title bar of the chosen window and move your mouse toward the destination location for the window.
3. At the moment the window starts to move, the contents of the window disappear, and all that you see moving across your screen is an outline of the window.
4. When the outline of the window is in the destination location onscreen, you release the mouse button. The window contents reappear, inside the outline.

With Full-Window Drag enabled, the outline of the windows is not all you see, as you start to move the window across the screen. Instead, the entire window (with contents) moves as directed by your pointing device. This simple enhancement is very versatile. It is especially useful when the position of a window is critical. Seeing the contents of the window as it moves across the screen enables much more accurate window placement than working with the window outline alone.

Full-Window Drag is the kind of enhancement that you will appreciate every time you use your computer, because it seems to eliminate eyestrain. Moving a window complete with its contents across the screen is a natural mode of operation, and you will immediately see what a mediocre mode of operation outline dragging was.

The enhanced functionality of Full-Window Drag is not free. Like all the enhancements in the Microsoft Plus! product, there is a cost in processor cycles, which translates to a performance hit. With Full-Window Drag, the performance hit is minimal if your video card uses an accelerator chip. Using an accelerator on the card (such as an ATI Mach chip, or any of the S3 or Weitek video chips and others) transfers much of the processing burden required to move the image across the screen from the system CPU to the accelerator on the video card. If, however, your video card is not an accelerator, but simply a frame buffer, you will see a noticeable system slowdown when you are doing a Full-Screen Drag. Examples of the nonaccelerated, or minimally accelerated, video chips are the popular Tseng Labs ET4000 and the early Cirrus Logic chips.

Font Smoothing

Since Windows made the graphical user interface popular, users have been confronted with the *jaggies*. This well-known phenomenon shows up by making jagged edges on large fonts on-screen. You won't see jagged edges in the small fonts of menu bars and dialog boxes, but if you work with type sizes more than 24 points in your word processor, or in a page layout program, you've seen the jaggies.

In the past, users just had to put up with the jaggies. One video card maker, ATI, incorporated a proprietary technology in its Windows video drivers to reduce the jagged edges of screen fonts. This technology, which proved incompatible with many leading application programs, was called *Crystal Fonts.*

Microsoft has taken a font smoothing utility and integrated it into the Windows 95 operating system. This system-level integration of the smoothing feature ensures the smoothing technology is compatible with all Windows applications.

To put font smoothing to work, you must have a video card and monitor that can run in *High Color mode.* High Color mode is sometimes called *16-bit Color mode,* and sometimes called *64,000 Color mode.*

You must set your system to display in High Color mode to use Font Smoothing. To set up High Color display mode, follow these steps:

1. Right-click on an empty space on your desktop. A pop-up menu will appear.
2. Choose Properties from the list of choices.
3. Choose the Settings tab from the Display Properties sheet.
4. In the scroll list under Color palette, choose High Color.
5. Click OK to exit the dialog box.

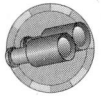

Note: Font Smoothing requires at least High Color mode. It will also work in display modes with more color than High Color. In fact, Font Smoothing works best at 24-bit and 32-bit True Color modes.

Your system will now be in High Color mode. Before you enable Font Smoothing, look at some large text on-screen. The example shown in figure 45.2 is 132-point text. You can see the jagged edges on the fonts anywhere there is a curve in the shape of a letter. With Font Smoothing enabled, however, the jaggies are gone!

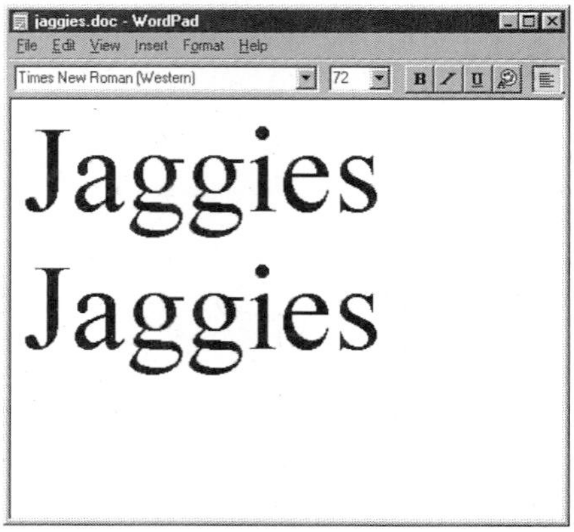

Fig. 45.2 Before Font Smoothing, text looked jagged, like this.

To turn on Font Smoothing and make on-screen text look clean and sharp, follow these steps:

1. Right-click on an empty place on your desktop. A dialog box will appear.
2. Choose Properties from the list of choices.
3. Choose the Plus! page.
4. Put a check in the box called Smooth Edges of Screen Fonts.
5. Click OK to enable Font Smoothing. You will not have to restart your computer for smoothing to take effect.

The Plus! page dialog box for steps 4 and 5 is shown in figure 45.3.

How Font Smoothing Works

Font Smoothing looks like magic on-screen, but it uses a simple science to operate. Suppose that, as is usually true, your text is black and your background is white. The text is formed of black pixels which are square-like dots of a certain size. Because the letters are formed of these rather square-like dots, lining them up in a curve, as seen in all the letters with curves, results in a jagged collection of black dots, not a smooth line.

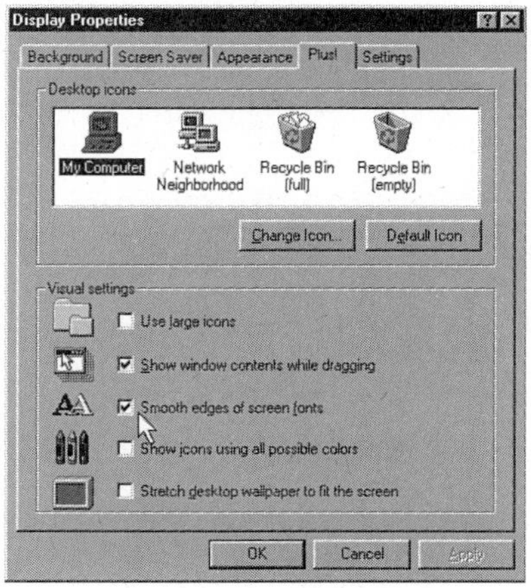

Fig. 45.3 Use the Display Properties Plus! page to enable Font Smoothing.

Because your monitor can have only about 72 of these dots per inch of screen space, the effect is amplified.

Font Smoothing fills in the white spaces, located between the jagged black squares, with barely visible intermediate shades of gray. These shades of gray are also made of square-like dots, but because they are halfway between paper-white and text-black, they blend in to make it seem as if the fonts are smooth. Font Smoothing is really an optical illusion, because if you look at the smoothed fonts on-screen really closely, or with a magnifying glass, you can see the gray dots all along the curved edges of the letters. The closer you look at the letters, the fuzzier the gray dots make the text look. At normal viewing distance, the letters look really sharp and clean, especially when you are used to looking at the jaggies.

Font Smoothing uses memory to calculate and display its dots. If your system is low on memory, you may want to turn off Font Smoothing. Try it, and see if it works for you as well as the Microsoft Plus! designers intended.

Enhanced MS-DOS Font

When you run a DOS window under Windows 95, you have a choice of fonts to use within the window. Windows 95 offers a selection of choices from both single size bitmapped fonts and scaleable True Type fonts.

There are eight bitmapped fonts supplied for use at the DOS prompt with Windows, and a single True Type font, which is available in an eight scale size.

While the bitmapped fonts are clear and easy to read, the True Type font supplied for the DOS box is thin and not very legible at any size.

Microsoft Plus! fixes that problem by including a special True Type font, called *Lucida*, and installing Lucida for use at the command prompt. When you have installed Desktop Additions, True Type Lucida becomes available for your use in DOS boxes.

Lucida is a clearer font than the standard Windows 95 DOS font, and you can scale it to a larger size. When you have installed Lucida (the enhanced MS-DOS font), you will have a choice of 16 different sizes. Figure 45.4 shows how clear Lucida appears in a DOS box under Windows 95, with Microsoft Plus! installed.

Animated Pointers

Windows 95 comes with a selection of mouse pointers, in addition to the standard arrow pointer, hourglass, and insertion bar that were included with Windows 3.x. Windows 95 supplies some dual purpose pointers that were inherited from Windows NT. Windows 95 comes with a Working in the Background pointer, which is half pointer arrow and half hourglass. Windows 95 also introduces a new type of mouse pointer, the animated pointer. Windows 95 comes with only one type of animated pointer, an animated hourglass that drops grains of sand, and spins, as you wait for Windows to finish a task.

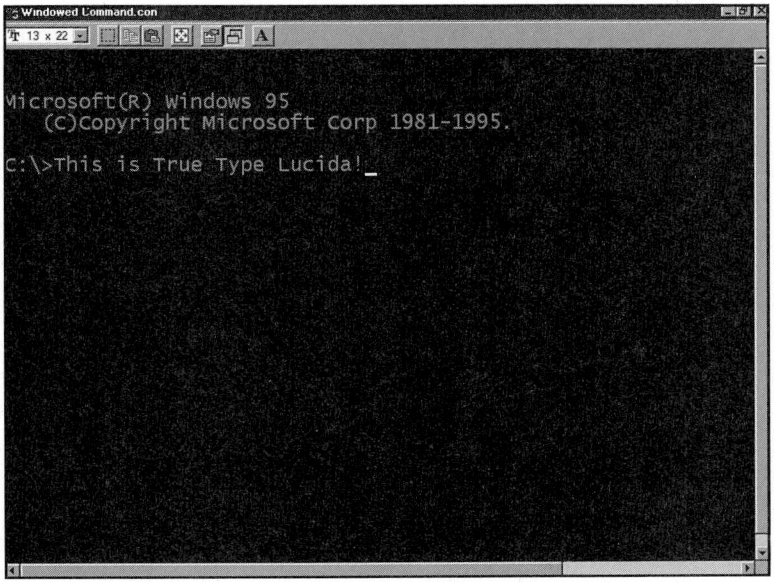

Fig. 45.4 Desktop Additions includes Lucida, the Enhanced MS-DOS Font.

You can see the animated hourglass by using Control Panel, Mouse, and choosing the Pointers page. Then, in the Scheme scroll box, scroll down and select Animated Hourglasses, as shown in figure 45.5. When you highlight the Busy pointer, the hourglass will perform its movements in a demonstration of the Animated Pointers feature.

The little spinning hourglass pales in comparison to the animated pointers included with Microsoft Plus!. You will learn about those animations in Desktop Themes, later in this chapter.

You can install an animated cursor without installing an entire desktop theme. To do this, follow these steps:

1. Use Control Panel, then double-click on Mouse.
2. Choose the Pointers page.
3. Highlight the cursor you want to replace with an animated cursor. Then, choose Browse.

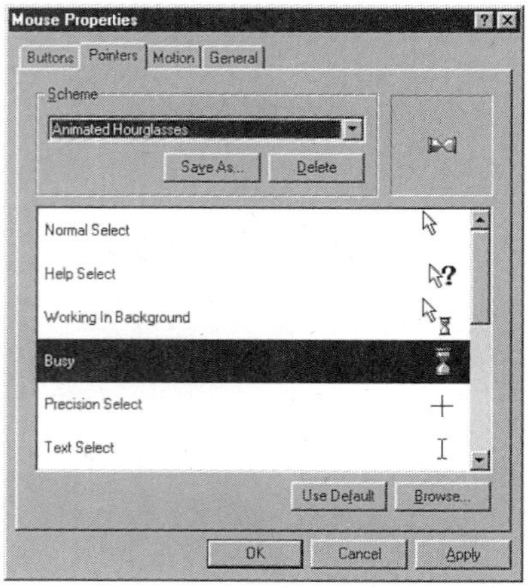

Fig. 45.5 Animated Pointers is a fun feature of Windows 95.

4. Using the browse tools, display the folder called C:\Program Files\Plus!\Themes. You'll see a large number of animated cursors displayed.

5. Highlight a cursor you'd like to use. When you highlight the cursor, you'll see an animated preview.

6. If you want to use the cursor you're previewing, choose Open, then choose OK.

If your animated pointers do not animate, check the following situations. Each of these situations is a potential cause for animated pointers that just do not move:

- If you have Windows 3.x remote control software installed, such as PC Anywhere or Laplink for Windows, you will lose your animated pointers.

- If you are using a video driver set to less than 256 colors, you will lose your animated pointers. Set the driver to at least 256 colors to make the animated pointers work.

- If you are using an ATI Mach 8 Ultra, a Diamond Viper, or a VGA or Microsoft Super VGA video driver, your animated pointers will not animate.
- Finally, make sure that you are using 32-bit protected mode disk drivers. To check, use Control Panel, System, and choose the Performance tab. Then, choose File System, Troubleshooting. Make sure that Disable All 32 Bit Protect-mode Disk Drivers is NOT checked.

High Color Icons

The normal icons that Windows 95 scatters all over your desktop are VGA compatible, 16-color icons. They look the same on the lowliest 16-color VGA system as they do on a high-end true color graphics workstation. These default Windows 95 icons are all stored in two files called SHELL32.DLL and EXPLORER.EXE, which are found in your \WINDOWS\SYSTEM folder.

Microsoft Plus! Desktop Additions aims to eliminate the 16-color doldrums by supplying a collection of High Color icons you can use to replace the default set. The Microsoft programmers tell what they think of High Color icons by the name they gave the file that holds the High Color icons. It's called COOL.DLL, and you can also find it in the \WINDOWS\SYSTEM folder.

To use High Color icons, you first need to have a display card and monitor that is capable of displaying High Color, which is 64,000 on-screen colors at a time. High Color is also called 16-bit color. If your system is so equipped, use Control Panel, Display, and then click the Plus! page. Put a check in the box called Show Icons Using All Possible Colors. Then, click OK. You will have to restart your computer for the High Color icons to appear. The change is subtle, but it is a building block that adds to the overall polished effect of Desktop Additions.

While you are working with High Color icons, you can use the COOL.DLL file to change the default icons used for:

- My Computer
- Network Neighborhood
- Recycle Bin (full)
- Recycle Bin (empty)

To change these icons, use Control Panel, Display, and choose the Plus! page, shown earlier in the chapter in figure 45.4. Highlight one of the four default icons shown in the preceding list. Highlight whichever icon you want to change first. Then, choose Change Icon, Browse. You can choose icons from EXPLORER.EXE, SHELL32.DLL, or COOL.DLL, by browsing for those file names, highlighting the file name, and choosing Open. Next, you will see a dialog box called Change Icon, similar to the one shown in figure 45.6. In this dialog box, you can choose an icon to replace one of the four in the preceding list.

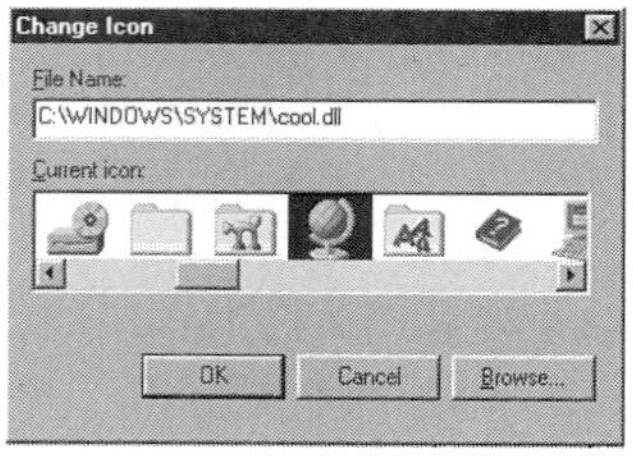

Fig. 45.6 Use the Change Icon dialog box to replace one of the major desktop icons.

Large Icons

Microsoft Plus! Desktop Additions contains a set of large icons you can use to replace the standard desktop icons. This set will be useful if you are running your screen at a very high resolution, 1024 × 768 pixel or higher. At those high resolutions, the normal icons supplied with Windows 95 are very small, and can be hard to interpret.

Another use for the large icons supplied with the Plus! product is to help a visually challenged user see the screen more clearly.

To enable large icons, use Control Panel, Display, and choose the Plus! page. Then, put a check in the box called Use Large Icons. Next, click OK. The icons on your desktop, and all through your system, will become twice as large as they were.

Figure 45.7 shows Control Panel with standard icons, and figure 45.8 shows Control Panel with the large icons that come with Desktop Additions.

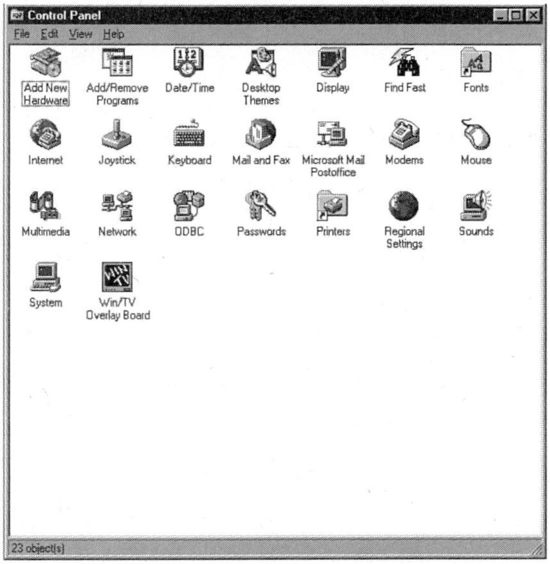

Fig. 45.7 Control Panel shown with Windows 95 default icons.

If you have installed Large Icons, some of the icons on your desktop may look very jagged and unclear. These icons come from programs whose maker has not supplied Windows 95 with compatible large icons. You can either contact the program's publisher for an update or stop using large icons.

Fig. 45.8 Control Panel shown with large icons from Microsoft Plus!.

Taskbar Auto Hide

Desktop Additions includes two other minor enhancements. The first of these has no name, and is not even documented, but it adds polish to the operating system. If you set your taskbar to Auto Hide (Start button, Settings, Taskbar, Auto Hide), the taskbar will be hidden until you pass your mouse pointer over it; then, it will pop into visible position.

After you install Desktop Additions, the behavior of the taskbar is altered. When you pass your mouse pointer over the hidden taskbar, it will not pop into place, instead, it will gently glide into place. And when you move your pointer off the taskbar, it will gracefully retract into its hidden state. This little enhancement adds polish to the operating environment.

To enable this enhancement, use the Start button, then choose Settings, Taskbar. Check the Auto hide box, and choose OK.

Wallpaper Stretching

The last Visual Enhancement provided by Plus! is wallpaper stretching. Before the Plus! product, your options were to display desktop wallpaper bitmap files at original size, or tiled to fill the screen with repetitive displays. Plus! adds the option to stretch a single bitmap image to fill the entire screen.

To enable desktop wallpaper stretching, use Control Panel, Display, Plus!, and put a check in the box called Stretch Desktop Wallpaper to Fit the Screen. The Plus! dialog box for this operation is shown in figure 45.3, earlier in this chapter.

Desktop Themes

Desktop Themes is the heart of Desktop Additions. Themes are collections of screen elements, all installed together, based around a central theme.

The screen elements that are linked together to form themes are:

- Screen saver
- Sound events
- Mouse pointers
- Desktop wallpaper
- Icons
- Colors of fonts, menu bars, and all other screen elements
- Font names and styles
- Font and window sizes

When you install a Desktop Theme, every visual and sound element of your environment will change, to match the feeling of the theme.

Microsoft Plus! ships with the following themes:

- Dangerous Creatures

- Inside Your Computer (High Color)
- Leonardo da Vinci
- More Windows (High Color)
- Mystery (High Color)
- Nature (High Color)
- Science
- Sports
- The 60's USA
- The Golden Era (High Color)
- Travel (High Color)
- Windows 95

Each theme is only a starting point for you to customize the look, feel, and sound of your system. You can install a theme, then choose to change settings for any or all of the screen elements. You can mix and match elements of any theme with elements of another. For example, if you install the Travel theme, you may want to remove the mouse pointers that are part of Travel, and replace them with the nifty set of pointers from the Science theme. It is easy to get started with Desktop Themes. Each theme is a radical departure from the standard Windows blue-gray-white look and feel.

Starting with Themes

To install your first desktop theme, use Control Panel, Desktop Themes. You will see a screen similar to the one shown in figure 45.9.

In the scroll bar called Themes, choose a theme that appeals to you, and that is compatible with your video display.

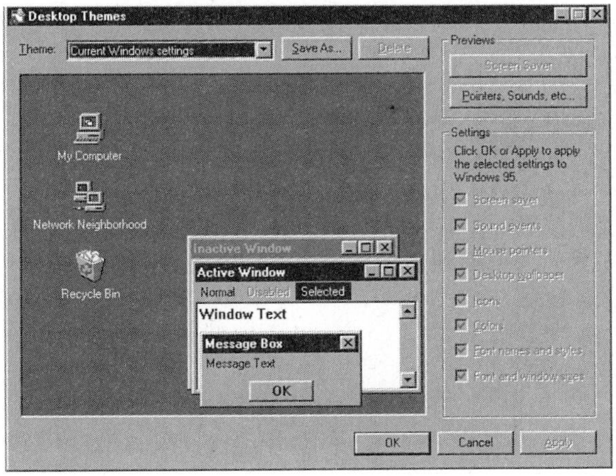

Fig. 45.9 Use the Desktop Themes dialog box to choose and customize a theme.

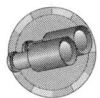

Note: To use Desktop Themes, you must have your display driver set to use 256 or more colors. Some of the themes will not even work at 256 colors, and some will require (at minimum) a High Color driver to properly display. The themes that require a High Color display driver are listed in the preceding section followed by "(High Color)."

When you have highlighted the theme you want to try, click OK. For this example, choose the Dangerous Creatures theme. When you have highlighted the theme you want, in the Theme scroll box, the Desktop Themes dialog box changes to display the elements of your selected theme. This preview display, shown in figure 45.10, enables you to examine some of the properties of the theme you have selected, without actually installing it in your system.

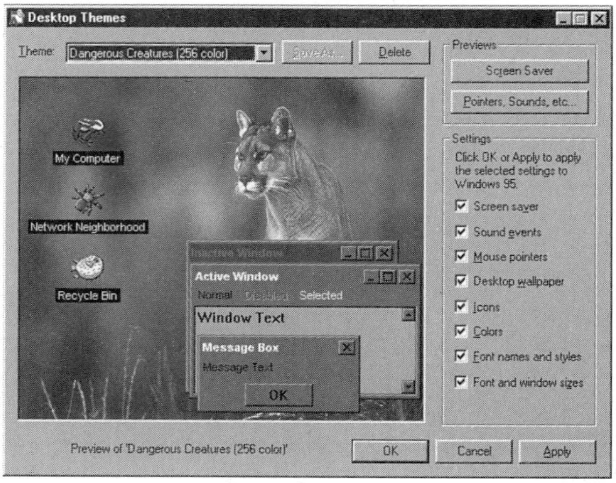

Fig. 45.10 The Desktop Themes dialog box shows the elements of the Dangerous Creatures theme.

Previewing Theme Elements

You can see the desktop wallpaper, some new icons, and some dialog box fonts and styles in figure 45.11. You cannot see the screen saver that belongs to the theme, and you cannot see the animated pointers and sound events that belong to the theme. But the Desktop Themes dialog box provides gateways to preview the screen saver and the pointers and sounds.

To see the screen saver associated with the Dangerous Creatures theme, choose the Screen Saver button in the Desktop Themes dialog box. When you choose the button, your entire screen turns into a preview of the screen saver that is part of the Dangerous Creatures theme. This screen saver for Dangerous Creatures consists of swimming sting rays, floating bubbles, and gurgling sounds from an associated WAV file.

You can preview the mouse pointers associated with your selected theme, and preview the theme's sound events by choosing Pointers, Sounds, and so on, from the Desktop Themes dialog box. Then, the

Preview Dangerous Creatures dialog box will appear. Choose the Pointers page to see all the mouse pointers associated with the Dangerous Creatures theme.

In each Desktop Theme, some of the mouse pointers are going to be animated, and these are cleverly done. In Dangerous Creatures, the Working in Background pointer, normally represented by Windows' familiar arrow/hourglass icon, has changed to a color animation of a bee flying, complete with red wings and a yellow, striped body.

To hear a preview of the sounds associated with system events, choose the Sounds page, in the Preview Dangerous Creatures dialog box. The sounds chosen for this theme range from lions roaring (exit Windows) to a rattlesnake's rattle (program error). The programming of sounds is, at the least, creative.

When you have finished exploring the previews, click Close.

Running the Theme

When you have satisfied yourself that you do, in fact, want to inundate your desktop with a Desktop Theme, click OK from the Desktop Themes dialog box. In just a few seconds, you will be living amongst the Dangerous Creatures.

Screen Saver Hot Spots

Third-party screen savers have had hot spots for years. When you put your mouse pointer on a hot spot, the saver will either activate immediately, or not activate at all, depending on what kind of hot spot you have chosen. Now, Windows 95 has hot spots in screen savers.

In an example of Plus! components working together, you can only use hot spots if you have installed System Agent. This hot spot function relies on part of the SAGE.EXE scheduler for its engine. See Chapter 43, "System Agent," for more on SAGE.EXE.

To activate hot spots on your Plus! screen saver, use Control Panel, Display, Screen Saver. Then, choose Settings. In the Screen Saver Properties sheet, shown in figure 45.11, you can place a check mark in a corner of the screen. The check mark makes the corner act as a hot spot to activate the screen saver immediately. If you put a dot in a corner of the screen, the screen saver will never display, as long as your mouse pointer rests on that hot spot on-screen.

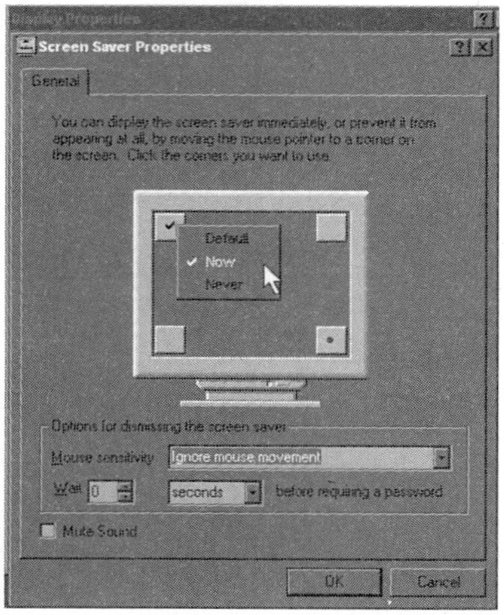

Fig. 45.11 You can select which corner to place your screen saver hot spot.

3D Pinball

When you have thoroughly explored all the Desktop Themes that come with Microsoft Plus!, it is time for a refreshing graphics game. Before Windows 95, you played PC action games in DOS. The game programmers needed the free-for-all DOS environment for their programming. They needed to interact directly with the video hardware in your computer, in order to make their games seem realistically fast and action packed.

Windows was never a good environment for game programmers. Windows graphics were too slow, and programmers working in Windows could not interact directly with the hardware. What games there were for Windows could never be described as action-packed.

Some time in 1994, Microsoft released a set of DLL and related files designed to make it possible for game programmers to work in Windows and still achieve acceptably fast graphics. Few have risen to the challenge up to this point. In fact, the Hover game that Microsoft wrote and shipped with Windows 95 has been the fastest game available for Windows. Then came 3D Pinball.

The programmers at Maxis wrote 3D Pinball for Microsoft. Only you can decide whether Hover, or Pinball, is the current Windows game champ. 3D Pinball is a very realistic simulation game. The programmers have achieved, in virtual form, an amazing degree of similarity to the functioning of a real pinball machine.

While the 3D in the game's name may come from the elevated ramps on the game's playing board, the three dimensionality is not the source of the game's most chilling realism.

The programmers have managed to duplicate, in code, the exact behavior of a metal pinball, as it hits thumper-bumpers and is sent flying; as the ball caroms off stretched rubber loops propelled by solenoid powered strikers, and as it sits, bouncing ever so slightly on rubber loop covered flippers, waiting to be sent back to the top of the board.

The degree of realism, in terms of ball behavior, in this simulation is totally uncanny. The sound effects are also pretty realistic. If you have ever played a real, mechanical pinball machine, you will be amazed. And, you may not go back to work for a long time.

Figure 45.12 shows the Pinball game table, but cannot begin to do justice to this awesome toy.

Fig. 45.12 3D Pinball is a very realistic pinball machine game included in Microsoft Plus!.

The sophisticated sound effects in Pinball have trouble with some Soundblaster clone sound cards. If you are having sound problems with 3D Pinball, run the program WMCONFIG.EXE. It is in the \Program Files\Plus!\Pinball folder.

When WMCONFIG is running, choose your sound card from the list shown in the scroll box. If your card is not shown by name, choose Generic Option One, and then choose Test. If the sounds are still not the way you want them, choose Generic Option Two, and so on, until you like the way that Pinball sounds.

KILLER 46 WINDOWS 95

Internet Explorer and Jumpstart Kit

by Benjamin F. Miller

The simplest way to connect to the Internet is by using the Internet Explorer. The Internet Explorer is a Web Browser that is part of Microsoft Plus! and is based on Spry's groundbreaking Mosaic Web Browser. Spry's Mosaic was the first Web Browser to catapult the world onto the Web, and set the standard for Internet browsers to come. The Internet Explorer makes it easy to get onto and surf the World Wide Web. Because the Explorer is designed as a Windows 95 application from the ground up, it takes full advantage of the advanced file management utilities and usability features of Windows 95.

In this chapter, you'll learn how to do the following:

- Use the Internet Setup Wizard
- Connect to the Internet with Internet Explorer
- Change Internet Explorer properties

- Use Internet Explorer with the Microsoft Network
- Use Internet Explorer to take full advantage of Windows 95. 2

Using the Internet Setup Wizard

When you install Microsoft Plus!, one of your options is Internet tools. When Microsoft Plus! has finished installing, it will place an Internet Tools folder inside your Accessories folder. To get to that folder, open Start menu, choose Accessories, and then Internet Tools. From there you'll have the option of either accessing the Internet Startup Wizard or Internet Explorer. Choose Internet Startup Wizard to begin configuring Internet Explorer. (See figure 46.1.) To get on the Internet by using the Internet Explorer, you need to do one of three things: establish an Internet Service provider, obtain a Microsoft Network account, or establish a LAN-based TCP/IP connection. Once that's done, you'll have the connectivity in place to get on the Web.

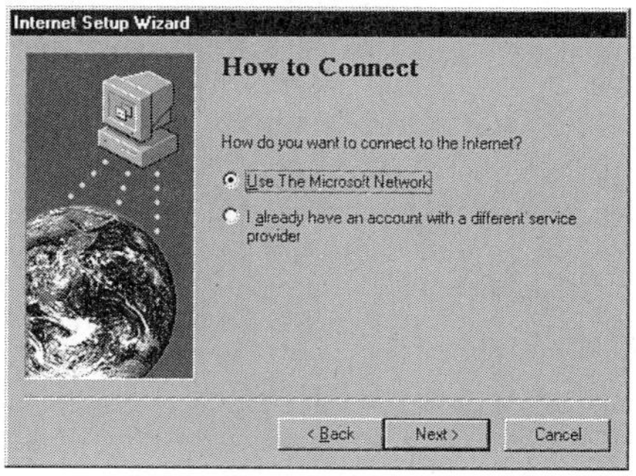

Fig. 46.1 The Internet Setup Wizard sets up your PC for the Internet.

The Setup Wizard is used to configure your dial-up Internet connection. The first question you're asked is whether you want to use the Microsoft Network as your Internet service provider or another service provider of your choice. The Internet Explorer will work with any Post

Office Protocol 3 (POP3) compliant Internet Service Provider. The Internet Setup Wizard will help you with whatever method you need in your particular setup. In the following section, you'll learn about the three different ways to access the Internet: via Microsoft Network, by using another Internet Service Provider, or through a local area network.

Connecting to the Internet Through Microsoft Network

If you choose the Microsoft Network as your service provider, you're asked if you're already a member of Microsoft Network. Whether or not you're a member, you see the Microsoft Network opening page. The opening page lets you know that the Internet Startup Wizard can identify Microsoft Network on your PC. Click on the connect button to log on. Microsoft Network is not required to use Internet Explorer to access the Web, but Microsoft has made it very easy to use Microsoft Network—setup requires only a few mouse clicks and you never have to worry about configuring TCP/IP networking.

Next, you'll see a dialog box that provides details on the Microsoft Network. After you click OK on the bottom of this dialog box, you'll see another dialog box that prompts you for your local area code.

Armed with your area code, the Internet Startup Wizard dials an 800 number that connects to a database that the Wizard searches for a local phone number you can connect to. Microsoft has set up local dial-up servers around the world so you don't have to call long distance to connect to either the Internet or the Microsoft Network. Once this has been done, Microsoft Exchange will be configured to call your local service number. Next, you'll see the Microsoft Network sign-on dialog box. If you're already a member, type in your name and password and press Connect. If you're using a different Internet Service Provider, you won't see any dialog box at all.

If you're the sole user of your computer, click on the box marked `Remember My Password`—it saves you the trouble of having to remember it. When Microsoft Network is finished researching your local access number, it automatically disconnects and displays a dialog box that offers you a choice of the best primary and backup phone numbers for your use. The backup number is used when you can't connect to the primary number.

There are a couple of telephone number access issues to keep in mind when using the Microsoft Network or any Internet Service provider to connect to the Internet:

- Access numbers change over time. If you use Microsoft Network regularly, the online service will notify you of phone number changes and even download the new numbers for you and automatically update your local database.
- The phone numbers you see listed will offer connection speeds from 9,600 to 28,800 bps. If the higher speed is offered in your area, take advantage of that phone number. If you upgrade your modem, you'll be able to take advantage of your faster modem without having to reconfigure your Internet connection. You will, however, have to make some changes to the Windows 95 modem control panel to take optimum advantage of your new modem. If you install one of the newer Plug-and-Play modems, Windows 95 will recognize the change in modems and make the configuration changes for you. Also, even with a slower modem, you'll be able to take advantage of the better data compression and error correction provided by those faster modems.

Now that your Internet connection has been configured, double-click on the Internet Explorer on your Windows 95 desktop and you'll be connected to the Internet. You can also drag the Internet Explorer icon onto the Start menu. This creates a shortcut to Internet Explorer on your Start menu so you can easily start it no matter what application you're in or where you are in Windows 95.

Connecting to the Internet Through a Service Provider

If you already have an Internet Service Provider and don't want to use the Microsoft network to connect to the Internet, click on the button `I already have an account with a different service provider` and then click on the Next button.

Later in the sign-up process you'll be asked questions about your service that you'll be able to answer only after you've contracted with that service. To connect to your service provider, you need to tell the Internet Setup Wizard the following:

- The name of your service provider
- IP address (if your service provider doesn't automatically assign it for you)
- The DNS address of your service provider
- Your Internet Service Provider's e-mail server [name]

If you are subscribing to a provider for the first time, don't use the Internet Setup Wizard to sign up.

Next, enter your Internet account name and password. If this is your first time using the Internet service, leave the password blank in case your Internet Service Provider assigns you a different password. This step will save you the trouble of having to change it later. Click on Next to continue.

The next dialog box, showing IP address, is very important. Depending on how your service provider configures itself, you may get an IP address you need to enter yourself. If this is the case, click on Always Use the Following and then enter the IP address in the IP Address box. If your service provider assigns an IP address each time you sign on, choose My Internet Service Provider Automatically Assigns Me One (see figure 46.2). This information will be given to you by your service provider when you first get an account. Most commercial Internet Service Providers use the latter method. Once you've entered the IP information, click on Next.

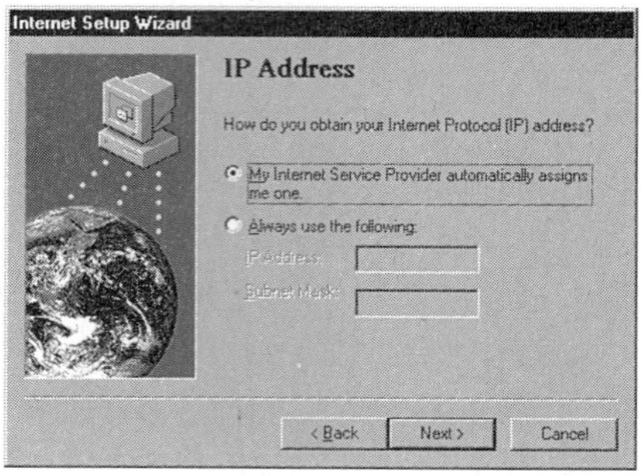

Fig. 46.2 Most Internet service providers automatically assign IP addresses.

You must also enter a DNS address for your service provider, which you need to obtain from your Internet Service Provider in advance. A standard DNS address comes in this format: 111.222.333.444 (see figure 46.3). Enter your DNS address and click on Next.

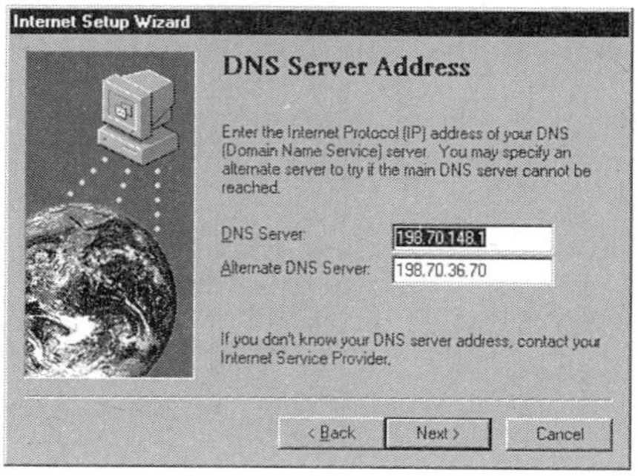

Fig. 46.3 Enter the DNS address in IP format.

The capability of sending and receiving e-mail is one of the most compelling reasons for getting on the Internet. Before you can send or receive e-mail, however, you must first enter the e-mail address assigned to you. You must also enter the name of your Internet Service Provider's e-mail server (see figure 46.4). If your provider assigns IP addresses dynamically, you may have to specifically request this information. Enter your service provider's e-mail address and the name of your Internet mail server and click on Next.

Fig. 46.4 You may have to specifically ask for the name of your Internet Service Provider's e-mail server.

You won't see anything about e-mail in the Internet Explorer; that will be handled by Exchange, Windows 95's universal inbox. The Internet Setup Wizard is just that, a place to configure Windows 95 to connect to the Internet. Although you're just going through the steps here to learn how to use the Internet Explorer, the Setup Wizard is a global routine for all the applications Windows 95 may use to communicate with the Internet.

Here are two tips to keep in mind when using your Internet e-mail:

- If you want to make any changes to your e-mail service later, choose Services (see figure 46.5) from the Exchange Tools menu, select the Internet Mail service, and click on the Properties button. You can use the Alt-T,V key combination to access your e-mail services.
- If you're using Microsoft Network as your Internet Service Provider, Microsoft Network Mail and Internet mail will be one and the same.

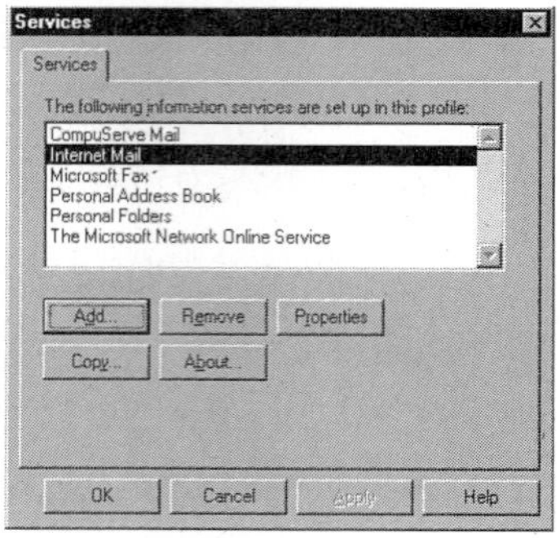

Fig. 46.5 Use Microsoft Exchange to send and configure your Internet mail.

The Internet Mail dialog box asks you to create an Exchange profile for your Internet mail. To create the profile, follow these instructions:

- Internet Mail is really useful only if you're attached to the Internet via a LAN or through an Internet Service Provider other than the Microsoft Network. The first filetab asks you for the name of your Internet server; that name usually looks something like "Microsoft.Com" and your user name and password. All of this information can be obtained from your network administrator or from your Internet Service Provider.
- The Connection tab configures your method for connecting to your Internet server, whether through modem or LAN.
- By clicking on the Schedule button on the bottom of this file tab, you can ask Exchange to look for your Internet mail at specified times. Perhaps even more helpful is the option to work off-line and use remote mail. Checking this box allows you to dial into your Internet server, see if there is mail waiting and, if so, determine the subject lines of your mail. You can then choose to

download any or all of your messages. This feature can save you time and money if your Internet Service provider charges by the hour or if you're dialing long distance.

- Once you've set your Internet Mail settings, click on OK to close the Services dialog box. Then quit Microsoft Exchange so that your new mail service can take effect.

> **Caution:** If you have any other mail services to set up, create a new profile by clicking on the New button. Otherwise, your default settings will be overwritten to contain your new mail settings; any older mail configurations you have will be lost.

Connecting to the Internet Through a Network

You don't need the Internet Setup Wizard if you have a direct, network-based connection to the Internet. A direct connection means that an Ethernet or Token-Ring LAN is physically connected to the Internet. This connection can be through physical cabling or in some cases over a dial-up connection. If this is the case, the only thing you need to configure is your TCP/IP setting in your Network control panel. To do this, have your network administrator assign you an IP address, then configure your TCP/IP control panel as follows. Double-click on your network Control Panel. If you don't have TCP/IP installed, click on the Add button, double-click on Protocol, and then double-click on Microsoft. Choose TCP/IP and click on the Enter button. TCP/IP will appear in the main Network Control Panel window. Select and it and click on Properties to configure it. (See figure 46.6.)

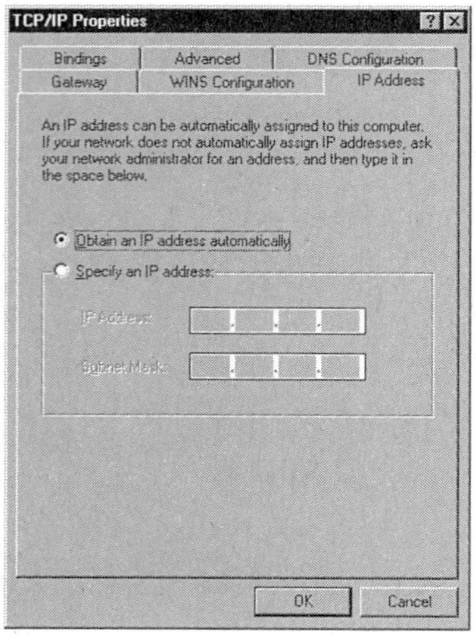

Fig. 46.6 IP addresses are needed for direct LAN Internet access.

Click on the IP address filetab to enter your IP address and your Subnet Mask. A Subnet Mask is a filter that distinguishes the network ID portion of an IP address from its host ID address.

If you're connecting to the Internet via Microsoft Network or another service provider, after you've set up your dial-in properties as outlined here, you're ready to surf the Net.

Working with the Internet Explorer

The Internet Explorer icon is on your desktop by default. Just double-click on the icon to start your connection to the Internet. The first screen you see after you double-click will vary depending on which of the following methods you use to access the Internet:

- **Microsoft Network as your service provider**—When you first launch the Internet Explorer, you see the Microsoft Network startup screen. Click on the Connect button and Microsoft Network connects you to an Internet dial-up server.
- **Your own service provider**—You see only a dialog box that tells you the modem is dialing.

- **Connected to the Internet via your LAN**—You won't see any new screens, just your home page as Internet Explorer loads it.

After the connection is established, you see the Microsoft homepage. Later, you'll see how to change your homepage so you don't have to start this way. After your homepage of choice is up and running, the World Wide Web is yours to explore. The following section provides several useful tips that will make using Internet Explorer a worthwhile experience.

Tips on Using the Internet Explorer

Text will always load onto the page you're downloading before graphics, which always takes much longer. As soon as the hyperlinked text is finished loading, you can click on your next destination and be speeding toward it long before the original page finishes materializing on-screen. This feature reduces your on-line charges and helps you avoid frustration while you're waiting to surf to the next page.

The Internet Explorer does an excellent job of giving messages about where you are and where you're going on the Internet. On the View menu, make sure that status bar is checked. The status bar is the strip at the bottom of the page that lets you know your status as you hop from one page to the next. Messages such as `opening`, `connecting`, and `accessing` tell you how close you are to arriving at a new Web page.

Once you're on the page, each time you move your cursor over an object you can connect to, the address or name of that object appears on the status bar. Anytime you download something, you see a progression of blue squares on the bottom right of the status bar. The farther the squares progress to the right, the closer you are to finishing your download.

Although the file menu in Internet Explorer may be what you would expect from a Windows 95 application, this file menu has the following subtle differences that add to the power of Internet Explorer:

- You can type any URL location in the address line or look at the pull-down list of recently accessed sites and choose a location from the list. Notice also the check box that says Open in New Window. This feature allows you to continue to download an image or information from one page while you access another. Only system resources and bandwidth limitations will stop you from opening successive windows.

- Internet Explorer also lets you open any file type supported by Internet Explorer such as JPEG, GIF, AU, WAV—in fact, any file type found in the Windows 95 Registry. If the application linked to a particular file type is located on your PC (Microsoft Word, for example), Internet Explorer will open the program as well as the file.

- Use the View menu to directly configure your Internet Explorer environment. The toolbar contains the typical Windows commands such as Cut and Paste. It also contains specific commands for going to a homepage, such as moving backward and forward. Finally, it has two buttons for accessing your Favorites folder and the Options dialog box.

- The Favorites menu makes it easy for you to create and use a hotlist of your favorite Web sites (more on Favorites later) as shown in figure 46.7.

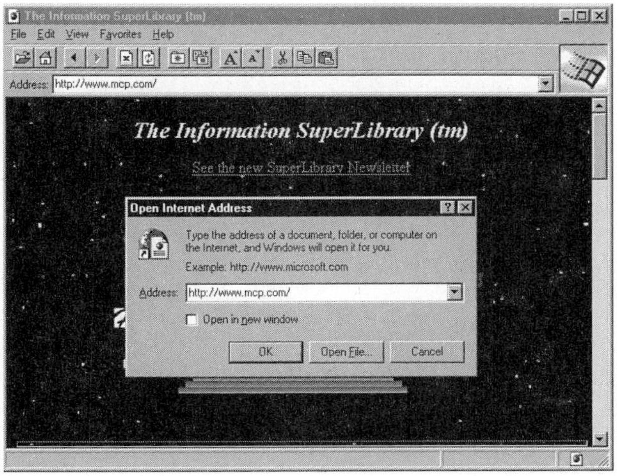

Fig. 46.7 You can open URL addresses or any other Internet file directly from Internet Explorer.

Setting Options

Use the Options selection in the View menu to configure the essential elements of Internet Explorer, such as Internet Explorer's appearance and where your Start page is located, so you can work in the most comfortable fashion for you.

The Appearance filetab of the Options dialog box (see figure 46.8) allows you to alter the way that text and graphics are displayed by Internet Explorer. You can toggle pictures on and off (displaying text without graphics makes things go much faster). Enabling custom colors allows you to change the colors of the text and background as Internet Explorer displays them. Another useful feature is the ability to change the colors of hypertext links that you either have or have not traveled to. This will make it very easy to remember where you've been on the World Wide Web—if you see a hyperlink on a Web page that is colored differently, you'll know you've been there.

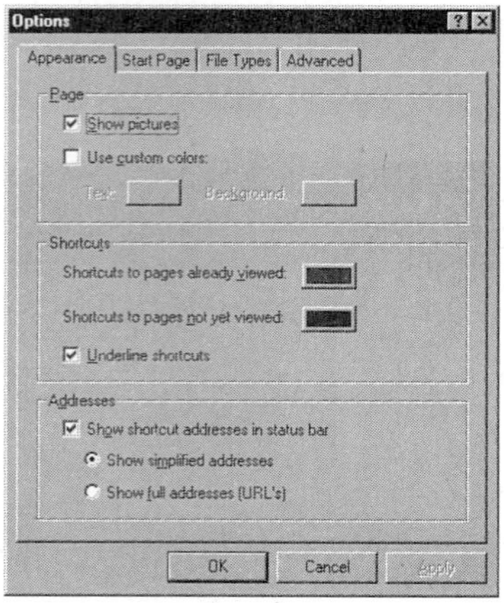

Fig. 46.8 You can easily change your startup home page.

The second filetab, Start Page, is very helpful if you don't want to log on to the Microsoft page every time you launch Internet Explorer. The trick here is that you have to be connected to the site you want as a homepage in order to set it that way. This can be helpful, though, if you frequently change your homepage whenever you find a new site that interests you.

The File Types filetab (see figure 46.9) allows you to associate different file types with the Internet Explorer. By associating files, you allow Windows 95 to recognize different files you may encounter on the Internet, and use them with different applications on your hard drive. There are a few exceptions to this, most notably AU files, which are UNIX sound files. Windows 95 Media Player doesn't understand the UNIX format, but Internet Explorer can play AU files for you upon downloading.

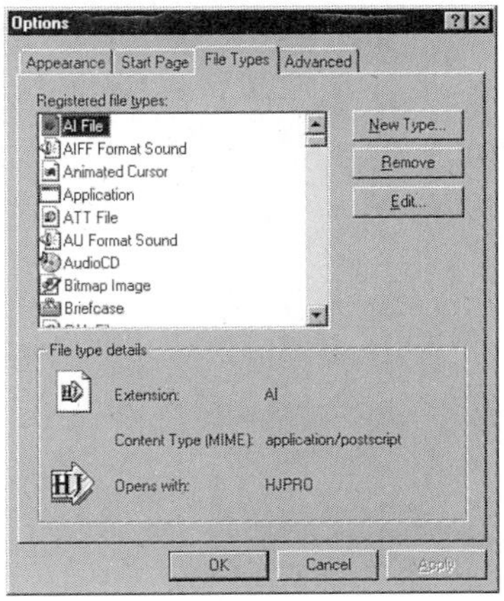

Fig. 46.9 By associating file types, you make it easier for Internet Explorer to work with Windows 95.

By associating file types, you enable Internet Explorer to instantly recognize files and either open them directly or call another application—for example, Microsoft Word—to open them. Associating a file means creating a link between Internet Explorer and a particular file extension (the three letters following the dot on a PC file name). To associate a new file type, click on the View menu and choose Options, then click on the File Type tab. Click on the New Type button and enter the required information. For example, on Description of type, enter a few words to remind yourself what this particular file type is used for. This has no bearing on the file association. In the Associated extension line, enter the three-letter file extension you want to associate (for example, MDF). The next line, Content_Type(MIME), is the Internet's way of determining what a particular file does (text, graphics, sound, and so on). Scroll down through the list menu provided and determine which description best matches your file type. To assign an application to the file type, click on the new button. This step opens a mini-Explorer. Navigate through the mini-Explorer until you find that application you want to associate and click on Enter. If you scroll down the list of associated programs, you should see your new association listed.

The Advanced filetab (see figure 46.10) is critical if you value your disk space. Internet Explorer increases its performance by caching recently accessed Web sites onto the hard drive in folders called History and Cache. Because you can visit Web sites differently, it makes sense to keep them stored in these two separate folders. But, if you keep too many sites on your hard drive, your hard drive space will erode away before you know it. Here are some pointers to help you preserve your disk space:

- The default number of sites visited and kept in History is 300. Unless you're a true Web wizard, this number is probably far more than you'll ever need. Try reducing it to no more than 150 sites. That number will free up disk space and enable you to continue surfing the Web quickly. There is also a button marked Empty, which works like a Delete button. Use this button regularly. In addition to saving you disk storage space, it will also weed out any repetitious Web sites that you may have stored.

- If you have a site in History that you want to keep, copy it out of the History folder before you use the Clear option. After your house cleaning is done, you can move the site back into History.

- In the Cache portion of the filetab, you can set the amount of hard disk you want to use to store Internet history. Again, unless you're an information hog, you probably don't need more than 10 percent of your hard drive set aside for caching. Use the Empty button as frequently as you can to keep a "clean house."

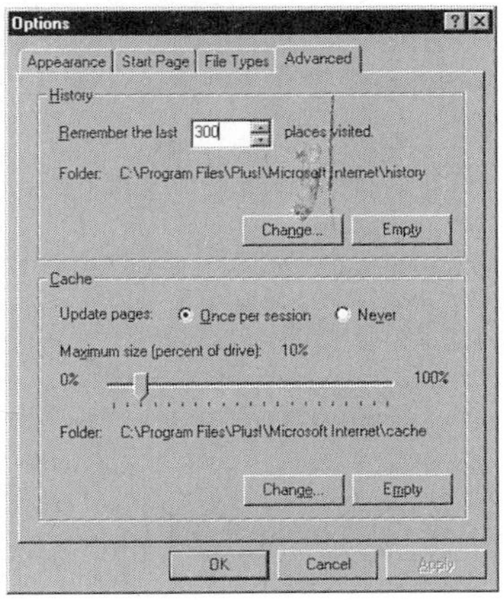

Fig. 46.10 Pay close attention to your cache settings, especially if you have limited hard drive space.

Favorites and Shortcuts

Internet Explorer borrows from a concept called Favorites, which is used by both Microsoft Network and Microsoft Office 95. But the Explorer takes the concept one step further. A Favorite can be any file, folder, or shortcut that you access frequently. Technically, a Favorite is any file, folder, or shortcut present in the Favorites folder, regardless of which application you use to open it. The idea behind this is that you should only be concerned with the task you want to accomplish, not the application you use to accomplish that task.

In the Favorites folder (see figure 46.11), notice that the shortcuts to Web sites share the folder with Word documents, an Access database, and even other folders. This sharing allows you to administer all of your favorite documents, whether they are Web shortcuts or otherwise.

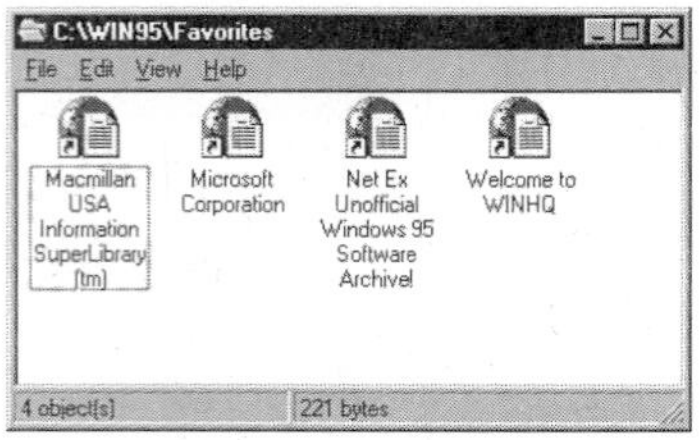

Fig. 46.11 Internet Explorer shares the Favorites folder with the rest of Windows 95.

Why shortcuts to Web sites and not actual files like the other members of the Favorites folder? Although Web sites exist on the Web, they may not be available the next time you try to connect to them. So, capitalizing on the shortcut technology used so well throughout Windows 95, Microsoft decided to implement shortcuts here as well. Like any other shortcut in Windows 95, there is a host of things you can do with your Internet Explorer shortcuts:

- **Put them anywhere you like.** For example, if you have a favorite Web site you visit every day, drag the shortcut to the desktop. Once there, just double-click on it. Internet Explorer will launch and take you straight to your favorite site.
- **Send them to a friend.** Using Microsoft Exchange as an e-mail client, you can drag the shortcut to an e-mail message and send it to a friend or co-worker. If your friends or co-workers also are using Windows 95 and Exchange, all they have to do is double-click on the shortcut when they open the message and they'll be led right to that Web site (see figure 46.12).

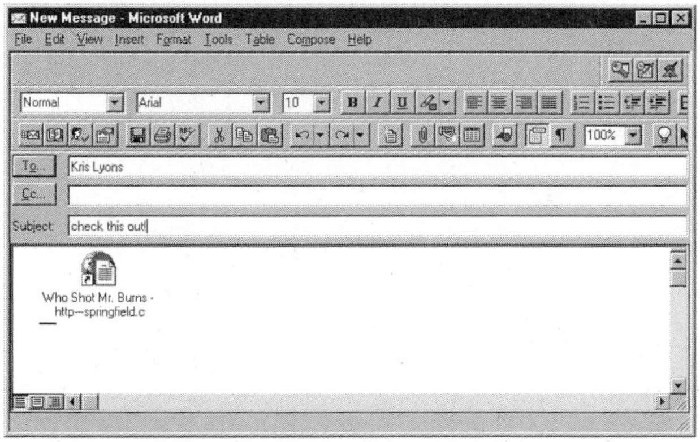

Fig. 46.12 E-mail Web site shortcuts to your friends and associates.

Internet Explorer and Microsoft Network

Neither Internet Explorer nor Microsoft Network offers everything a user needs. However, both programs working in tandem offer a complete set of online services and tools, as shown in the following:

- The Internet Explorer does not provide mail services. Any e-mail you want to send has to be sent through Microsoft Exchange, Microsoft Network, or through any other e-mail package.

- Newsgroups. Internet Explorer does not include a mail reader. Microsoft Network, however, does provide access to countless Internet newsgroups. If you have a Microsoft Network account and are using Internet Explorer on a dial-up connection, type **News:*newsgroup*** in the URL line (see figure 46.13) and Microsoft Network will launch and open a window containing that newsgroup.

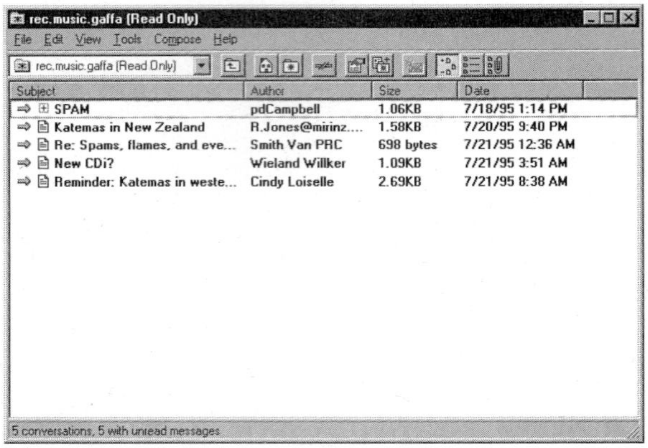

Fig. 46.13 Microsoft Network will bring your newsgroups right to you.

➤ Web pages on Microsoft Network. In several places on the Microsoft Network, you'll find Web pages (see figure 46.14). Although you can't read them on Microsoft Network, you can double-click on them and they'll instantly launch Internet Explorer and take you straight to that site.

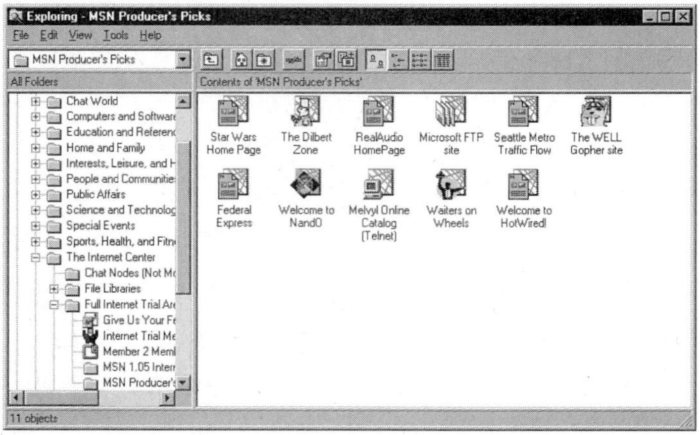

Fig. 46.14 Double-clicking on a Web page immediately starts Internet Explorer.

Internet Explorer and the Right Mouse Button

As with the rest of Windows 95, you can accomplish a lot with the right mouse button.

- You can cut, copy, and paste by using the right mouse button. This feature makes it easy to copy URL addresses from any other source and paste them directly into the address line. You'll never fuss with messy URLs again. Also, remember that you never have to type **http://** because Internet Explorer will add that for you.
- Any graphic you find can be saved as your Windows wallpaper (see figure 46.15). When you find a photo or graphic on the Web you think would make a nifty wallpaper for your PC, right-click on the graphic and choose Set As Desktop Wallpaper. Open the Display Control Panel and among the standard wallpaper files is one called Internet Explorer Wallpaper. You can center or tile it and treat it as you would any other wallpaper (BMP) file. Just remember that if you want to save the file, you'll have to rename it, because Internet Explorer will overwrite it the next time it grabs wallpaper off the Web.

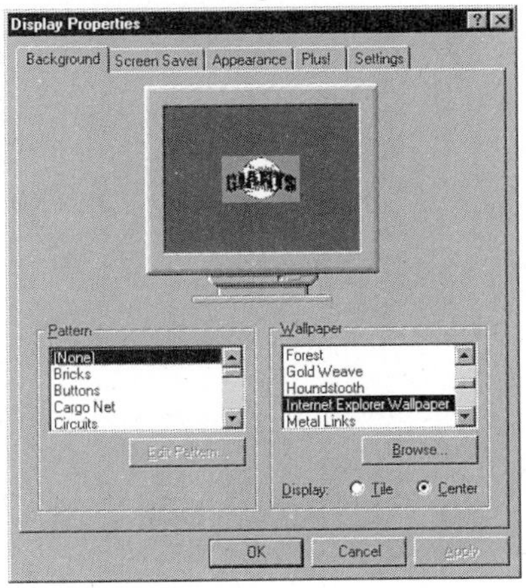

Fig. 46.15 With one click, you can change your Windows wallpaper to something new and exciting.

- Using the right mouse button, you can also copy images directly from a Web page onto your hard drive. Right-click and choose Save Picture As. A Windows 95 File Save dialog box will appear so you can choose a name for your file and pick a place on your hard disk where you want to store it. This is no different from managing a word processor or spreadsheet document.

Some Things to Remember While Surfing the Web

To put it poetically, the World Wide Web is a vast ocean of information, and, like the ocean, is constantly changing. Web sites spring into existence only to mysteriously vanish forever. Surfing the Web is really just what it sounds like, a journey over eddies and currents that may never take you to the same place twice, which is discussed further in the following:

- **Just because you accessed a Web site an hour ago doesn't mean that it will still be there an hour from now.**

  A number of variables affect Internet availability, and speed as well. For example, Web servers are constantly going up and down, and when more people log on to a server than it can handle, it won't answer. Watch the status bar on the bottom of Internet Explorer. If the bar shows "opening" for a long time, cancel your trip to that page and try again later. This delay in responding usually means that your host server is having trouble negotiating a connection to the remote Web site, which further means that you could be waiting there a while only to get the inevitable `Sorry, this Web page doesn't exist` message. This tip is extremely useful if your Internet Service Provider charges by the hour.

- **Web Page locations vary wildly.**

  Because anyone can create a Web page on the Internet, the information highway is saturated with thousands of Web pages. If you don't know the exact location of the Web page you want, be prepared to spend a lot of time searching for it. Several guides are available to help you search for Web sites. One of the first places to use as a guide should be WWW.Yahoo.Com. The folks at Yahoo do a tremendous job of listing and indexing Web sites by subject, category, and subcategory. This site is updated daily.

- **Your PC configuration can make a substantial performance difference in Internet Explorer and Microsoft Network.**

  To effectively run any of the Plus! components, Microsoft suggests that your PC be a 486/50 with at least 8M of RAM. Even if your PC meets these requirements, if you run Internet Explorer and Microsoft Network together, be prepared to wait as you switch between the two applications. Particularly if you use large cache settings for Internet Explorer, a significant amount of file swapping takes place on the hard drive between these two applications. Unless you like the sound of your disk grinding away, the more memory you can throw at Internet Explorer, the faster it will run. This may be a truism for any software package, but it bears repeating.

Adding and Removing Windows 95 Components

by Allen L. Wyatt

When you first set up Windows, various accessories and components are installed along with it. These optional elements lend to the operating system's usefulness and contribute in varying degrees to your productivity. Components such as Disk Defragmenter and ScanDisk let you monitor your hard disk's health while the WordPad program gives you a simple, yet powerful, word processor.

This appendix shows you how to install and remove these optional components. In addition, you learn how to remove Windows 95 completely from your computer.

Understanding the Windows 95 Components

In an attempt to make Windows 95 more useful for everyone, Microsoft has included many accessories and utilities with the operating system. Now you can choose from a full array of options. These options can be logically separated into several categories as shown in Table A.1.

Table A.1 Windows 95 Components

Category	Component	Disk Space
Accessibility Options	Accessibility Options	300K
Accessories	Calculator	200K
	Clipboard Viewer	100K
	Desktop Wallpaper	600K
	Document Templates	100K
	Games	600K
	Paint	1.1M
	Screen Savers	100K
	System Resource Meter	100K
	Windows 95 Tour	2.5M
	WinPopup	100K
	WordPad	1.2M
Communications	Dial-Up Networking	400K
	Direct Cable Connection	500K
	HyperTerminal	400K
	Phone Dialer	100K
Disk Tools	Backup	1.0M
Microsoft Exchange	Microsoft Exchange	3.5M
	Microsoft Mail Services	600K
Microsoft Fax	Microsoft Fax Services	1.7M
	Microsoft Fax Viewer	300K
Multimedia	Audio Compression	200K
	Video Compression	400K
	Media Player	200K
	Sound Recorder	200K
	Volume Control	100K
The Microsoft Network	The Microsoft Network	2.0M

> **Note:** The Windows 95 components that are available to you depend on whether you purchased the floppy disk or CD-ROM version. If you have the CD-ROM version, additional components are available that are not listed in Table A.1.

Depending on how Windows was installed on your computer, it's possible that not all available options were installed. For example, when you select Typical setup during the installation, only the most typical options are installed. But you might not be so typical—you might want more! This is no problem. Windows 95 gives you the ability to add or remove individual components at will. In fact, some users might have already squeezed Windows 95 onto their hard disk. In such a case, removing unwanted components is certainly desirable. On the other hand, the Portable setup installs only the options common to notebook and laptop users. What if you want the game Hearts, which isn't installed by default with Portable setup? Simply add it. The next section explains how to go about adding and removing Windows 95 components.

Adding and Removing Components

When you add components to Windows 95, the application or utility is installed and the menu is updated with the new icon(s). Conversely, removing a component deletes the programs or files and removes the icons from the menu. To add or remove a component, follow these steps:

1. Click on Start, Settings, then choose Control Panel
2. Double-click on the Add/Remove Programs applet.
3. Select the Windows Setup tab in the Properties sheet. This displays all possible components that you can add or remove (see figure A.1).

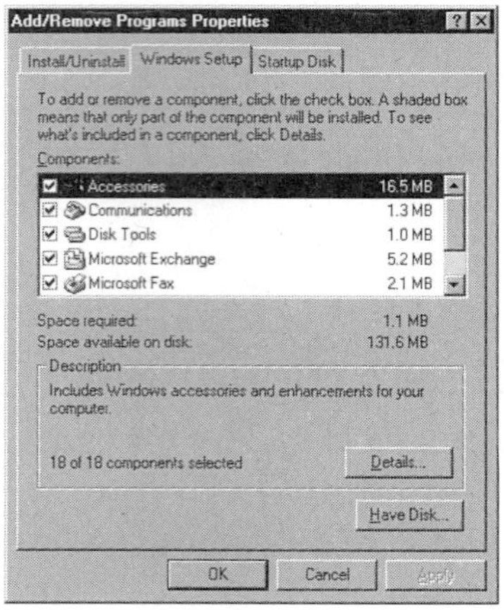

Fig. A.1 The Add/Remove Program Properties sheet shows which items are installed and those that aren't.

4. To add the item, highlight an unchecked component and click the check box beside it. Notice the size in megabytes to the right of the component—this is how much more disk space will be consumed. To remove the item, highlight a checked component and click on the check box to remove the check mark.
5. If you only want certain components added or removed from a group (such as Accessories), highlight the item and click on Details. A dialog box appears that lists individual components for that group (see figure A.2).
6. Choose the components you want to add or remove and click on OK.
7. Once you've selected all the components you want to add or remove, click on OK.

As soon as you choose OK, those components you selected will be installed and/or removed. In most cases, Windows will alert you to shut down and restart the computer.

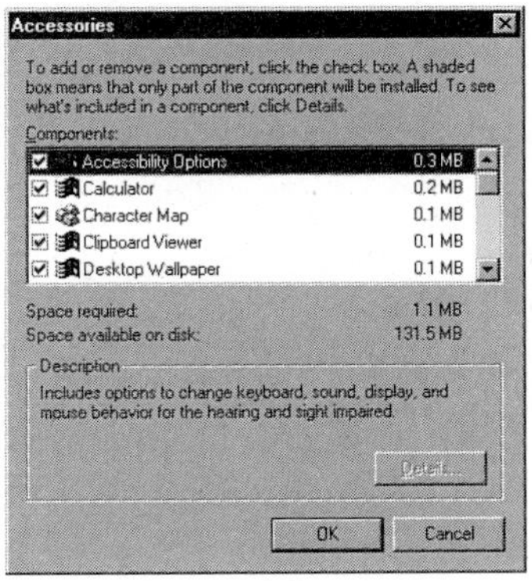

Fig. A.2 Choose Details to select individual components from a group.

Depending on which components you already have installed, some items may not be selected in the Add/Remove Programs Properties sheet. (The check mark beside the component indicates it is installed.) Windows 95 components are grouped into eight categories (refer to Table A.1). Within these groups you can add or remove specific components. This allows you to pick only the options and accessories you'll really use. Remember these rules for adding and removing components:

- If you place a check mark beside an option, it will be installed.
- If you remove the check mark from an item, it will be removed.

Removing Windows 95 from Your Computer

When you install Windows 95, several transformations take place. Though many DOS files are deleted, some are replaced by newer versions adapted to Windows 95 and reside in the Windows\Command directory. The system files IO.SYS and MSDOS.SYS in your root directory are converted into Windows 95 system files. A few new directories are created including a hidden Recycled directory. Even a variety of hidden files are placed in the root directory. Indeed, removing Windows 95 from your computer can be fairly complex, but as long as you know what to expect, it's not too difficult.

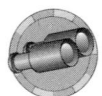

> **Note:** Windows 95 includes an "uninstall" feature that can be used to restore a previous version of Windows or Windows for Workgroups. While this feature is nice, it assumes several things. First, that you made a backup of your old system as you installed Windows 95 (most people do not for some reason). Second, that you want to return to a previous version of Windows (many people prefer to start from scratch at a DOS level).

If you want to delete Windows 95—that is, completely remove it and return your system to its previous state—there are several items to consider *before* you set out to wipe it from the hard disk.

- **Backup.** You should back up your data before proceeding. Also, if you still have your backup before installing Windows 95, you're one step ahead in restoring your system exactly as it was before Windows 95 was installed.
- **Bootable floppy.** Make sure you always have a floppy disk with your MS-DOS system files on it. This means the files IO.SYS, MSDOS.SYS, DRVSPACE.BIN, and COMMAND.COM. The file SYS.COM is required for transferring these system files after you delete Windows 95. Of course, copies of your AUTOEXEC.BAT and CONFIG.SYS are a plus.
- **MS-DOS floppy disks.** You'll want to reinstall DOS after erasing Windows 95 because many of the files in your DOS directory will have been erased. This is why it's a good idea to copy the contents of your DOS directory to another unassuming location, such as a directory named C:\FRESHDOS.

Each of these items is necessary to smoothly and quickly remove Windows 95 from your computer. If you don't have them, you might be in for a frustrating experience. However, I'll assume you've done everything by the book and you now have each of these in front of you.

There are five basic steps in deleting Windows 95.

1. Boot to DOS.
2. Delete the directories associated with Windows 95.
3. Remove system files from the root directory.
4. If available, copy files to the DOS directory from a backup location.
5. Restart computer and transfer system files.

The following sections discuss each of these steps in greater detail.

Boot to DOS

You can't delete Windows 95 until you exit from its graphical interface. Hacking and cutting from the Explorer just won't suffice (although you can try it and really hang your system). You must boot to MS-DOS or the Windows 95 command prompt. It doesn't matter which you choose because the real MS-DOS system files aren't in the root directory.

For the quickest response time, make sure you have SmartDrive enabled. To do this, type **SMARTDRV** at the DOS prompt. With disk caching enabled, erasing complex directory structures such as the Windows 95 hierarchy will complete in 1/10 the time. Otherwise, you can expect to wait for five minutes while erasing files. Also, this is beneficial if you copy files to the DOS directory from another backup location.

Delete All Directories Associated with Windows 95

To delete a directory and its subdirectories in one fell swoop, use the DELTREE command. From the C:\> prompt, type the following:

```
DELTREE WINDOWS
```

> **Caution:** If your version of Windows 95 is installed in a directory other than WINDOWS, make sure you use the proper directory name with the DELTREE command. You want to delete the Windows 95 directory; nothing else.

This command removes the WINDOWS directory, and all subdirectories for WINDOWS. Windows 95 also creates several other root-level directories that you'll need to remove. You should look for each of the following on your system, and remove them if necessary:

- WINDOWS
- PROGRA~1 (known as Program Files in Windows 95)
- MYDOCU~1 (known as My Documents in Windows 95)
- RECYCLED (this is a hidden directory)
- EXCHANGE
- WININST0.400 (this is the Setup directory and is only available if you aborted a Windows 95 installation)

It's possible that one or more of these folders does not exist. For instance, if you haven't put any files in the Recycle Bin, the directory RECYCLED won't be there. Also, don't forget to delete Windows applications installed under the Windows 95 operating system. Leaving them is a waste of space because they won't work until you reinstall them under Windows 3.1.

Remove System Files

In the root directory are a number of hidden and visible files placed there by Windows 95. If you fail to remove these files, your computer will always boot to the Windows 95 command prompt instead of the MS-DOS prompt. So, to successfully delete all Windows 95 files, you must use the ATTRIB command to strip all attributes of these files.

Table A.2 lists the files added to your root directory or updated at one time or another when Windows 95 is installed. The attribute is shown to the right of the file name.

Table A.2 Root Directory Files

File Name	File Attributes
AUTOEXEC.BAT	
AUTOEXEC.DOS	
BOOTLOG.PRV	
BOOTLOG.TXT	Hidden
COMMAND.COM	
COMMAND.DOS	
CONFIG.DOS	
CONFIG.SYS	
DBLSPACE.BIN	System, Hidden, Read-only
DETLOG.OLD	
DETLOG.TXT	
DRVSPACE.BIN	System, Hidden, Read-only
IO.DOS	
IO.SYS	System, Hidden, Read-only
MSDOS.---	Hidden
MSDOS.BAK	System, Hidden, Read-only
MSDOS.DOS	
MSDOS.SYS	System, Hidden, Read-only
NETLOG.TXT	
SCANDISK.LOG	
SETUPLOG.OLD	Hidden
SETUPLOG.TXT	Hidden
SUHDLOG.---	Hidden, Read-only
SUHDLOG.DAT	Hidden, Read-only
SYSTEM.1ST	System, Hidden, Read-only

To change the files so they can be deleted, type the following at the command prompt:

```
ATTRIB -R -S -H *.*
```

This command will change the attributes of all the files in the root directory. If you want to change the attribute of an individual file instead, type the following:

```
ATTRIB -R -S -H IO.SYS
```

where *IO.SYS* is the name of the file.

> **Tip:** You may want to copy the few essential files such as AUTOEXEC.DOS and CONFIG.DOS to a floppy disk, remove the attributes of all files in the root directory, delete all the files, and then copy the files from the floppy disk. This saves time over erasing each individual Windows 95 file.

Whatever your method of removing these files, be sure to copy the AUTOEXEC.DOS and CONFIG.DOS files to the root directory after deleting all system files. When you install Windows 95, these two files are renamed with a DOS extension. You should then rename them to their proper file names AUTOEXEC.BAT and CONFIG.SYS, respectively.

Copy MS-DOS Files to DOS Directory

If you have another location where you copied the contents of your DOS directory before installing Windows 95, you should now go to the DOS directory and summon those files. For instance, you may want to keep a copy of the DOS files in a directory called FRESHDOS. These files represent DOS before it is modified by Windows 95. To copy the files from this directory to the DOS directory, enter the following at the DOS prompt:

```
COPY \FRESHDOS\*.*
```

You'll then be asked whether you want to overwrite files, to which you should type **A,** meaning you want to overwrite all files in the directory. This saves a great deal of time over installing DOS from scratch.

Transfer System Files

Finally, all files related to Windows 95 are now gone from your computer. But now you have no operating system files in the root directory. The quick fix for this dilemma is to insert your bootable MS-DOS floppy disk in the floppy drive and restart the computer. After your computer boots to the floppy disk, type the following at the DOS prompt:

```
SYS C:
```

This transfers the system files to your C drive. When the transfer is complete, you can restart your system. Thereafter, you should have a pristine DOS system just the way it was before you installed Windows 95.

KILLER B WINDOWS 95

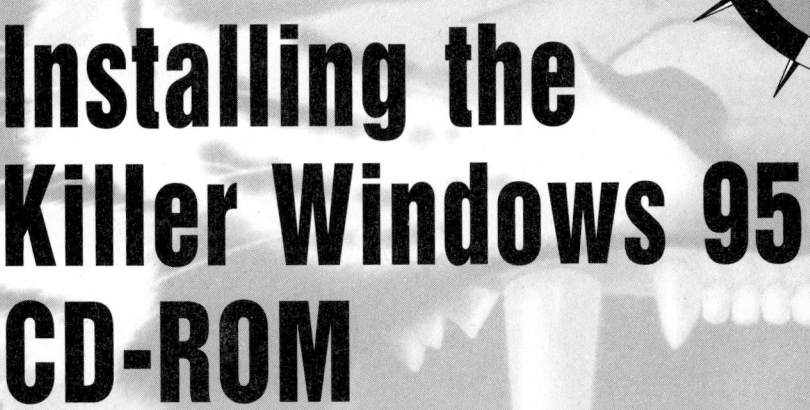

Installing the Killer Windows 95 CD-ROM

by Stephen L. Miller

Before you can use the programs on the CD-ROM that comes with this book, you must first install the CD-ROM. This appendix helps you make that installation.

The Killer Windows 95 CD-ROM contains over 40 programs and games that represent some of the best shareware programs currently available for Windows 95.

Many of the applications are 32-bit, multithreaded, and use the Windows 95 interface, taking full advantage of the new power Windows 95 has to offer.

In this appendix, you learn how to do the following:

- Start the Killer CD-ROM Setup Program
- Find the programs you want to install
- Install the individual programs
- Exit from the Killer CD-ROM Setup Program

Starting the Killer 95 CD-ROM Setup Program

The Killer CD-ROM Setup Program (see figure B.1) makes selecting and installing the various shareware programs easy. You can start the setup program two ways. The following sections discuss both alternatives.

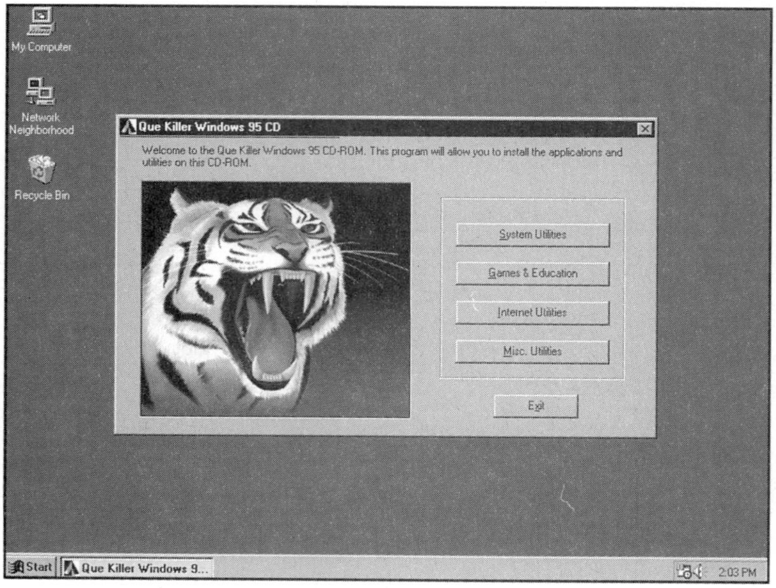

Fig. B.1 The Main Killer Windows 95 CD Setup Screen.

Starting the Killer CD-ROM with AutoPlay

The Killer CD-ROM takes advantage of Windows 95's AutoPlay feature. The AutoPlay feature starts the CD-ROM as soon as the disc is inserted in the CD-ROM drive. No command, such as D:\INSTALL.EXE, is required.

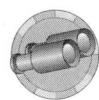

Note: AutoPlay is a Windows 95 feature that can be turned on or off at any time, but the setting is a little hard to find. Here's how to set AutoPlay the way you want it on your system:

1. Right-click on My Computer, then select Properties.
2. Click on the Device Manager tab, then double-click on CD-ROM.
3. Click on your CD-ROM drive's description, then on the Properties button.
4. Click on the Settings tab.

   If the "Auto insert notification" box has a check in it, AutoPlay is active on your system. If you want to turn AutoPlay off, click on the box and the check mark disappears, which turns off Autoplay.
5. Click on OK and the Properties sheet disappears.
6. Click OK on the Systems Properties sheet.
7. A page appears that tells you to restart your system in order for the new settings to take effect.
8. Click on OK. Your system reboots and the new AutoPlay setting is in effect.

Starting the Killer CD-ROM Manually

If you have AutoPlay turned off, the Killer CD will not start automatically. However, you can start the setup program manually, as you would any other program you need to start in Windows 95.

Here's how to manually start the Killer CD Setup Program:

1. Click on Start, then Run.
2. Type the letter of your CD-ROM drive, then type **:\INSTALL.EXE**. If your CD-ROM drive is D, for example, you type **D:\INSTALL.EXE**.
3. Click on OK.
4. The Killer CD Setup Program starts (see figure B.1).

The Different Killer Program Categories

Before you can start installing the programs, you need to know how to find them in the setup program. To make that task easier, the programs are divided into the following four categories:

- System Utilities
- Games & Education
- Internet Utilities
- Misc. Utilities

You'll use these categories in the next section to help you install the individual programs.

Installing the Individual Killer Programs

Now that you know how to start the setup program and find the programs you want to install, you may find it helpful to practice an example installation. (If you don't want to install a program at this time, click on the Exit button to end the setup program.) For instance, say you want to install a program from the Internet Utilities, such as Web Wizard: The Duke of URL.

To install this Internet program to your hard drive, follow these steps:

1. Start the Killer CD and click on the Internet Utilities button (see figure B.1). The Killer Windows 95 Internet Utilities dialog box appears.

> **Tip:** Double-clicking on the program's name also starts the install routine. This shortcut works for all installation types.

2. Click on Install Web Wizard: The Duke of URL (see figure B.2).

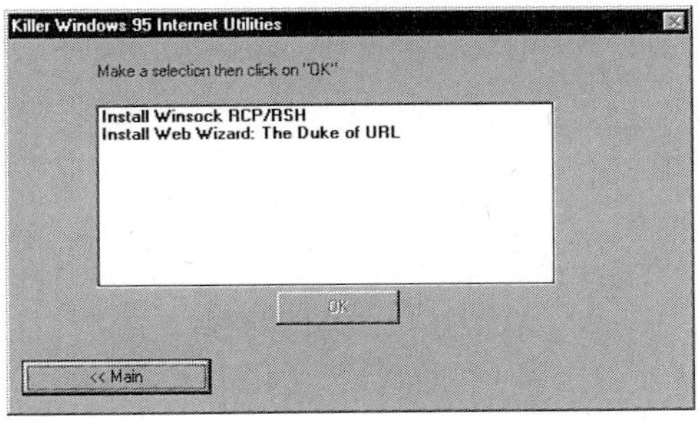

Fig. B.2 Select the program you want to install and click on OK.

3. Click on OK. A Welcome! dialog box appears, which tells you this is the install program for the Web Wizard.
4. Click on OK. The Select Destination Directory dialog box appears and asks you in which directory you want to install the Web Wizard (see figure B.3).
5. Click on OK to accept the default directory or type the directory of your choice and click on OK. The Make a Backup? dialog box asks whether you want to replace backups of the files you replace (see figure B.4).

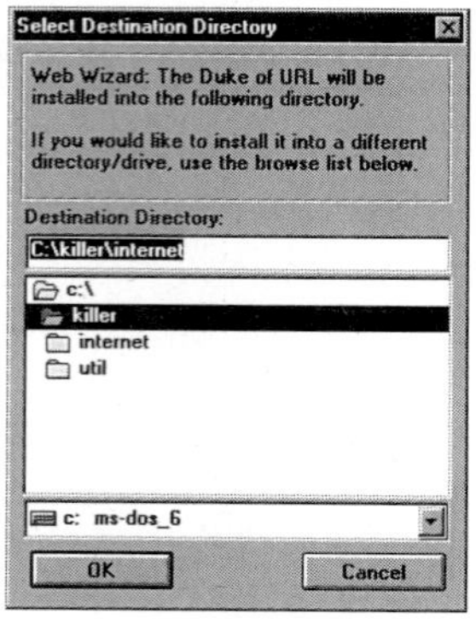

Fig. B.3 You can tell the setup program where to install the program files.

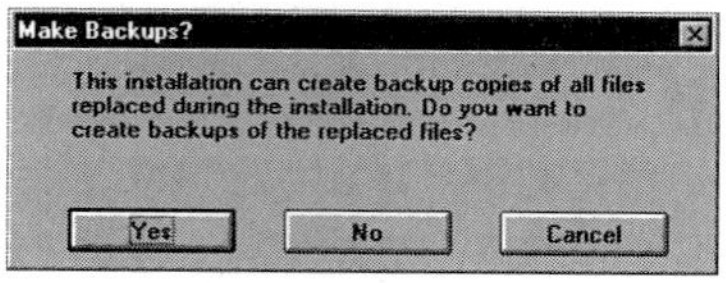

Fig. B.4 The setup program lets you back up any files your installation replaces.

6. If you need to save the original files, click on Yes. If you don't need to save the files being replaced with this installation, click on No.

The files are copied to your system's hard drive and the Killer Windows 95 Internet Utilities dialog box is available to install the next application or exit from the Killer setup program. Exiting from the setup program is covered in the next section.

Some of the programs on the Killer CD come with their own installation routines. This means that after you select the program to be installed and click on OK, the program automatically goes through whatever steps are necessary to complete its install routine. When the installation routine is complete, you're returned to the Killer CD Setup Program dialog box.

Quitting the Killer CD Setup Program

When you're done installing the various programs, you'll probably want to exit from the Killer CD Setup Program. If you practiced the example installation, then you're still in the Internet Utilities dialog box.

To quit the Killer CD Setup program, follow these steps:

1. Click on the << Main button in the Internet Utilities dialog box. This returns you to the setup program's main menu.
2. Click on Exit.

The program ends. You can now remove the Killer CD from your CD-ROM drive.

Index

Symbols

A

B

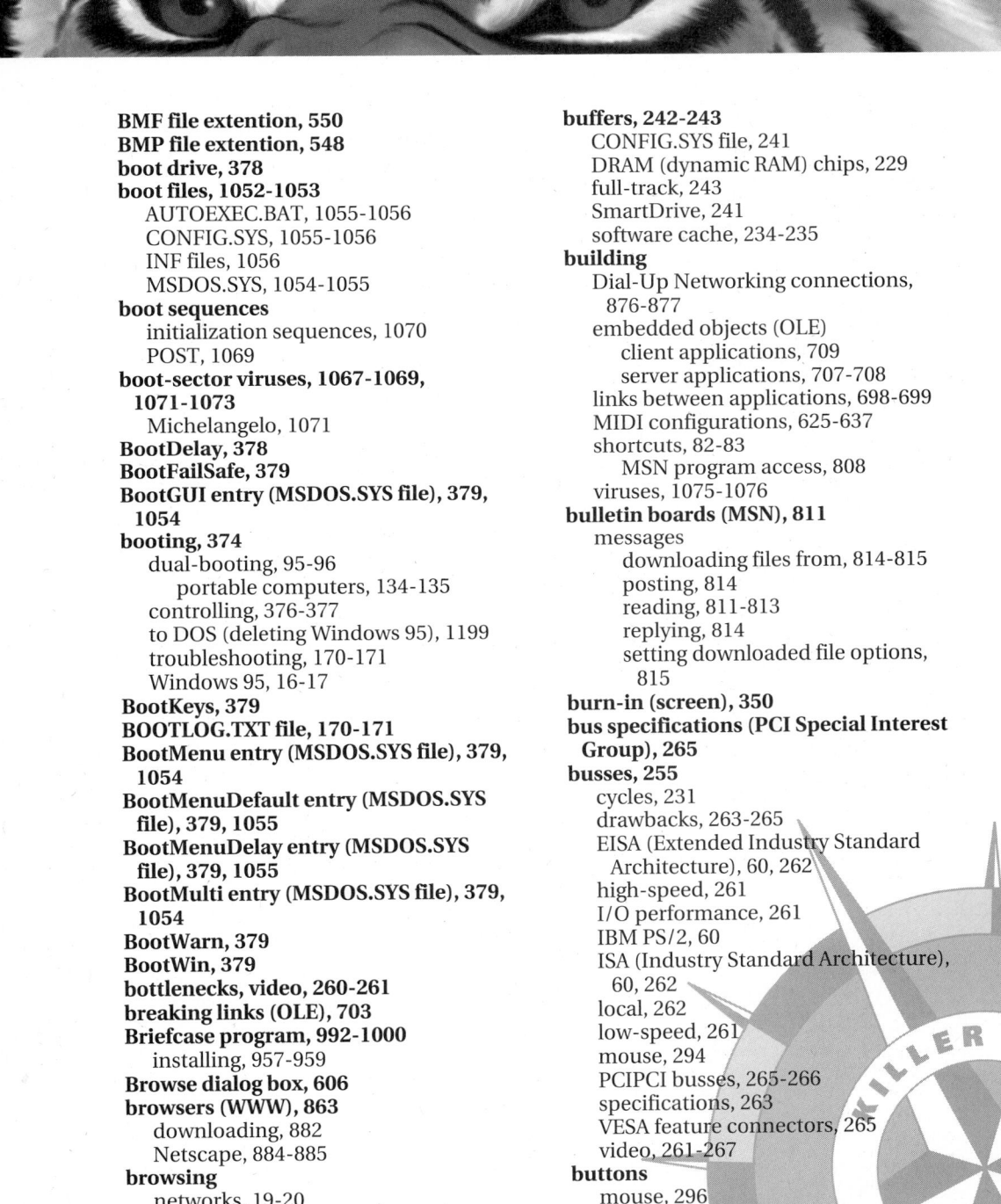

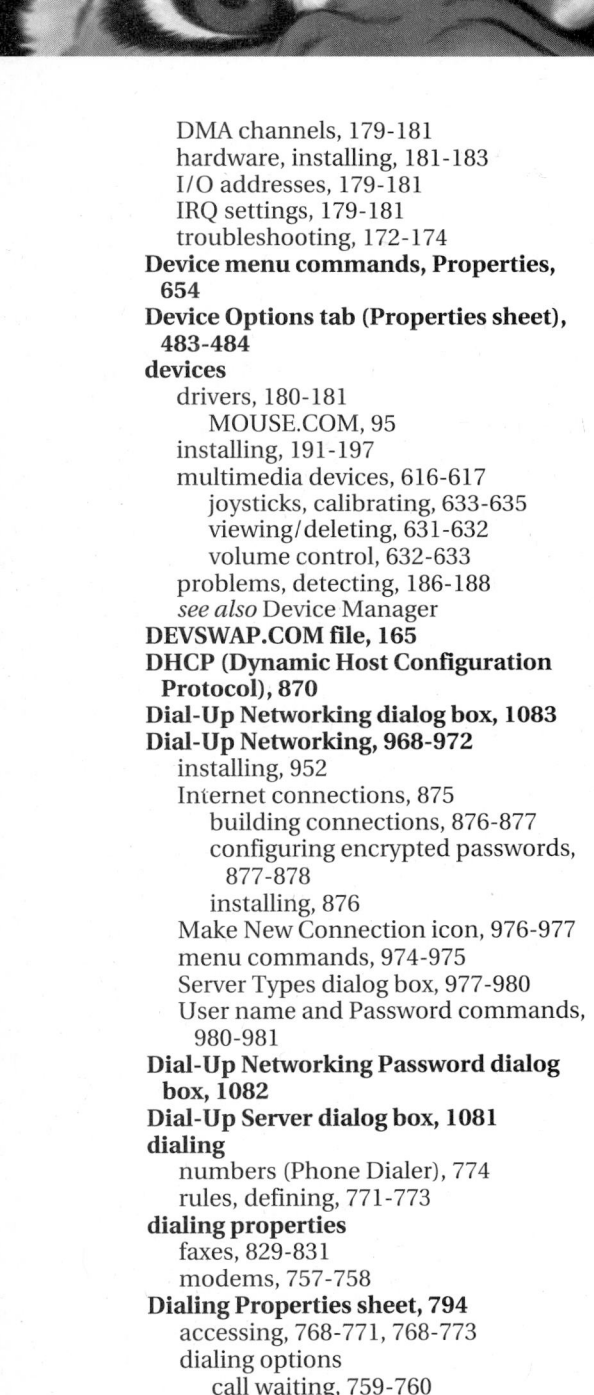

E

F

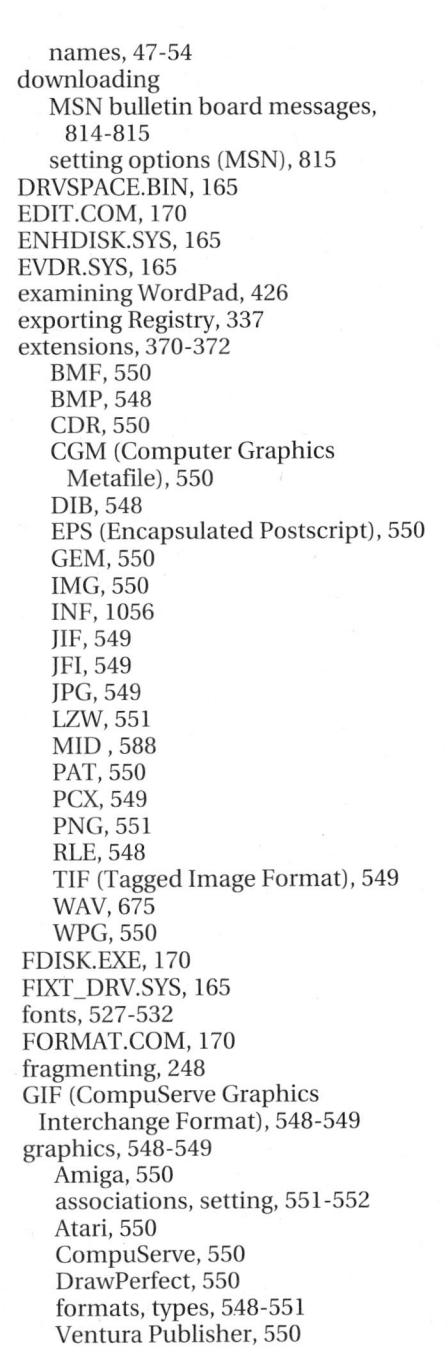

G

H

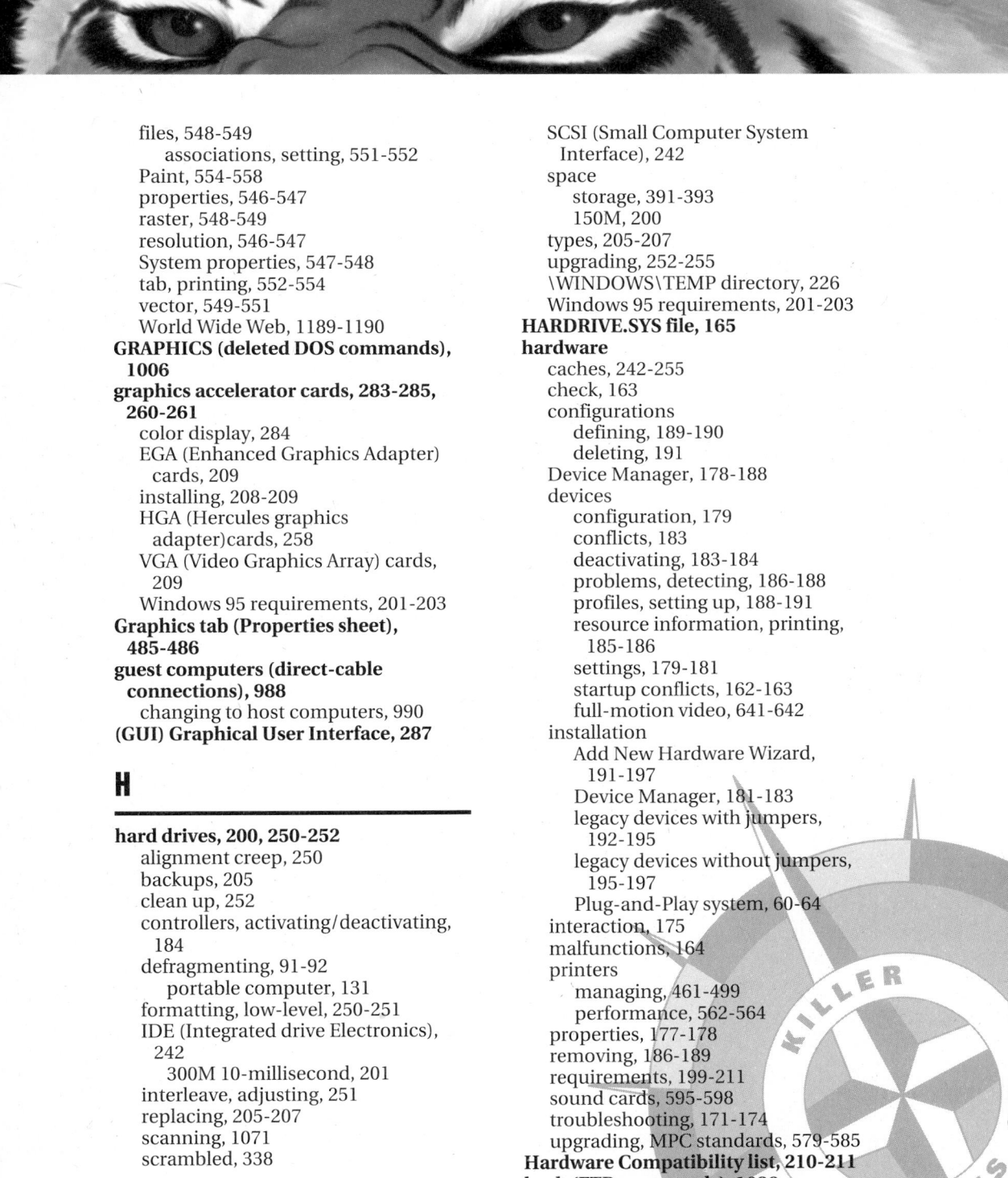

I

J

K

L

M

N

P

Q

R

S

T

U

V

W

X

Y

Z

User-Friendly References for All Your Computing Needs

Using Windows 95
0-7897-0092-1, $19.99 USA
Publication Date: 8/95

Using The Microsoft Network
0-7897-0398-X, $19.99 USA
Publication Date: 9/95

Using PowerPoint for Windows 95
0-7897-0365-3, $19.99 USA
Publication Date: 11/95

Using Excel for Windows 95
0-7897-0111-1, $19.99 USA
Publication Date: 9/95

The new *Using* series gives readers just the information they need to perform specific tasks quickly and move on to other things. *Using* books provide bite-sized information for quick and easy reference, along with real-world analogies and examples to explain new concepts.

QUE® For more information on these and other Que products, visit your local book retailer or call 1-800-772-0477.

Source code ISBN: 0-7897-0085-9

Complete and Return this Card for a *FREE* Computer Book Catalog

Thank you for purchasing this book! You have purchased a superior computer book written expressly for your needs. To continue to provide the kind of up-to-date, pertinent coverage you've come to expect from us, we need to hear from you. Please take a minute to complete and return this self-addressed, postage-paid form. In return, we'll send you a free catalog of all our computer books on topics ranging from word processing to programming and the internet.

Mr. ☐ Mrs. ☐ Ms. ☐ Dr. ☐

Name (first) ______ (M.I.) ☐ (last) ______

Address ______

______

City ______ State ______ Zip ______ ______

Phone ______ ______ ______ Fax ______ ______ ______

Company Name ______

E-mail address ______

1. Please check at least (3) influencing factors for purchasing this book.

- Front or back cover information on book ☐
- Special approach to the content ☐
- Completeness of content ☐
- Author's reputation ☐
- Publisher's reputation ☐
- Book cover design or layout ☐
- Index or table of contents of book ☐
- Price of book ☐
- Special effects, graphics, illustrations ☐
- Other (Please specify): ______ ☐

2. How did you first learn about this book?

- Saw in Macmillan Computer Publishing catalog ☐
- Recommended by store personnel ☐
- Saw the book on bookshelf at store ☐
- Recommended by a friend ☐
- Received advertisement in the mail ☐
- Saw an advertisement in: ______ ☐
- Read book review in: ______ ☐
- Other (Please specify): ______ ☐

3. How many computer books have you purchased in the last six months?

- This book only ☐
- 2 books ☐
- 3 to 5 books ☐
- More than 5 ☐

4. Where did you purchase this book?

- Bookstore ☐
- Computer Store ☐
- Consumer Electronics Store ☐
- Department Store ☐
- Office Club ☐
- Warehouse Club ☐
- Mail Order ☐
- Direct from Publisher ☐
- Internet site ☐
- Other (Please specify): ______ ☐

5. How long have you been using a computer?

- ☐ Less than 6 months
- ☐ 6 months to a year
- ☐ 1 to 3 years
- ☐ More than 3 years

6. What is your level of experience with personal computers and with the subject of this book?

	With PCs	With subject of book
New	☐	☐
Casual	☐	☐
Accomplished	☐	☐
Expert	☐	☐

Source Code ISBN: 0-7897-0001-8

7. Which of the following best describes your job title?

Administrative Assistant ☐
Coordinator ☐
Manager/Supervisor ☐
Director ☐
Vice President ☐
President/CEO/COO ☐
Lawyer/Doctor/Medical Professional ☐
Teacher/Educator/Trainer ☐
Engineer/Technician ☐
Consultant ☐
Not employed/Student/Retired ☐
Other (Please specify): ______________ ☐

8. Which of the following best describes the area of the company your job title falls under?

Accounting ☐
Engineering ☐
Manufacturing ☐
Operations ☐
Marketing ☐
Sales ☐
Other (Please specify): ______________ ☐

9. What is your age?

Under 20 ☐
21-29 ☐
30-39 ☐
40-49 ☐
50-59 ☐
60-over ☐

10. Are you:

Male ☐
Female ☐

11. Which computer publications do you read regularly? (Please list)

____
____
____
____
____
____
____
____
____

Comments: ______________________________
____
____

Fold here and scotch-tape to mail.

NO POSTAGE NECESSARY IF MAILED IN THE UNITED STATES

BUSINESS REPLY MAIL
FIRST-CLASS MAIL PERMIT NO. 9918 INDIANAPOLIS IN

POSTAGE WILL BE PAID BY THE ADDRESSEE

ATTN MARKETING
MACMILLAN COMPUTER PUBLISHING
MACMILLAN PUBLISHING USA
201 W 103RD ST
INDIANAPOLIS IN 46209-9042